The NUMERICAL DISCOURSES *of the* BUDDHA

THE TEACHINGS OF THE BUDDHA SERIES

The Suttanipāta:
An Ancient Collection of the Buddha's Discourses
Together with Its Commentaries

The Buddha's Teachings on Social and Communal Harmony:
An Anthology of Discourses from the Pāli Canon

The Connected Discourses of the Buddha:
A Translation of the Saṃyutta Nikāya

Great Disciples of the Buddha:
Their Lives, Their Works, Their Legacy

In the Buddha's Words:
An Anthology of Discourses from the Pāli Canon

The Long Discourses of the Buddha:
A Translation of the Dīgha Nikāya

The Middle Length Discourses of the Buddha:
A Translation of the Majjhima Nikāya

THE TEACHINGS OF THE BUDDHA

The Numerical Discourses *of the* Buddha

A Translation of the

Aṅguttara Nikāya

Translated from the Pāli

by

Bhikkhu Bodhi

Wisdom

Wisdom Publications
199 Elm Street
Somerville MA 02144 USA
wisdompubs.org

Library of Congress Cataloging-in-Publication Data

Tipiṭaka. Suttapiṭaka. Aṅguttaranikāya. English.
The numerical discourses of the Buddha : a translation of the Aṅguttara Nikāya / translated from the Pāli by Bhikkhu Bodhi.
pages cm — (The teachings of the Buddha)
The present work offers a complete translation of the Aṅguttara Nikāya, the fourth major collection in the Sutta Piṭaka, or Basket of Discourses, belonging to the Pāli Canon.
Includes bibliographical references and indexes.
ISBN 1-61429-040-7 (hardback : alk. paper)
I. Bodhi, Bhikkhu, translator. II. Title.
BQ1342.E5B63 2012
294.3'823—dc23
2012007302

ISBN 978-1-61429-040-7 eBook ISBN 978-1-61429-044-5

21 20 19 18
6 5 4 3

Cover and interior design by Gopa&Ted2. Set in Palladio 10/12.4.

Wisdom Publications' books are printed on acid-free paper and meet the guidelines for permanence and durability of the Production Guidelines for Book Longevity of the Council on Library Resources.

Printed in the United States of America.

Contents

Indexes

Preface

The present work offers a complete translation of the Aṅguttara Nikāya, the fourth major collection in the Sutta Piṭaka, or "Basket of Discourses," belonging to the Pāli Canon. An English translation of the Aṅguttara Nikāya published by the Pali Text Society has long been in print under the title *The Book of the Gradual Sayings*. It was issued in five volumes, I, II, and V translated by F. L. Woodward, and III and IV by E. M. Hare. First published between 1932 and 1936, this translation is now dated both in style and technical terminology, and thus a fresh English rendering of the entire work has long been a pressing need. In the late 1990s I collected Nyanaponika Thera's four-part series of Wheel booklets, *An Aṅguttara Nikāya Anthology*, into a single volume for the International Sacred Literature Trust. I added sixty suttas to the original anthology, and the resulting volume was published as *Numerical Discourses of the Buddha: An Anthology of Suttas from the Aṅguttara Nikāya* (Walnut Creek, CA: AltaMira Press 1999). This compilation, with a total of 208 suttas, contained perhaps an eighth of the full Aṅguttara Nikāya. Translations of many individual Aṅguttara suttas have also been available over the internet, but a selection, however valuable, cannot do service for a translation of the complete work.

This translation, like my previous renderings from the Pāli Canon and commentaries, aims to fulfill two ideals that are to some degree in tension with one another: first, to be faithful to the meaning of the original; and second, to express this meaning in clear contemporary English. My translation is based on three different editions of the Pāli text. I used the Sinhala-script Buddha Jayanti edition as my root text, and I am grateful to Ven. Dhammajīva Thera of Mitirigala Nissaraṇa Vanaya for presenting me with a full set of these volumes. I compared this edition with the Vipassana Research Institute's electronic version of the Burmese-script Chaṭṭha Saṅgāyana (Sixth Council) edition and with the PTS's Roman-script edition. I also consulted the variants noted in the PTS edition, which occasionally, in my view, had a better reading than the printed editions. In defense of this "eclectic" approach I appeal to Professor E. Hardy's words in his preface to part V of his PTS edition of the Aṅguttara Nikāya: "It may be open to dispute, whether our Sinhalese Mss. [manuscripts] of the Aṅguttara are the more reliable, or our Burmese. . . . As a rule, there is no Ms. nor any set of Mss. which can be relied on indiscriminately" (p. v).

The contents of the Aṅguttara Nikāya (AN) prove especially challenging to modern readers because there is virtually no "rhyme or reason" to their order apart from their conformity to the numerical scheme that governs each book. To help the reader make sense of the work, I prepared a thematic study guide to AN, which follows the introduction (see pp. 75–84). The guide lays out the principal themes of this collection in a meaningful sequence, which is similar to the one I used in my anthology *In the Buddha's Words*. On this basis I then classified the suttas (the great majority, though not all) according to the way they exemplify the scheme. I suggest that readers new to AN consider reading the work twice. First, read the suttas in the order in which they fit into the thematic guide; then read the entire Nikāya again in the original order, from the Ones through the Elevens. The first reading will enable readers to grasp the main contours of the Buddha's teachings as they are represented by AN; the second will enable them to follow the work in its original arrangement. My long introduction is primarily intended to explain AN using the thematic guide as a framework for making sense of the mountain of material found in this collection.

In the course of preparing this translation, I have had the generous help of several people whose contributions have been invaluable. First and foremost is John Kelly, who offered his help even before I actually embarked on the project and unfailingly assisted me through the six years it has taken to bring the work to completion. A keen student of Pāli since 2003, John read the translation alongside the Pāli text at several stages, offering useful comments and suggestions and occasionally catching lines of text that I had overlooked. He maintained the electronic files, entered the page numbers of the PTS edition into the files, compiled the two appendixes and index of proper names, and checked page proofs. His article, "The Buddha's Teachings to Lay People," which I cite several times in the introduction, is a bountiful source of information that helps us better understand the place of the Aṅguttara Nikāya in the corpus of Buddhist canonical literature. Occasionally John's wife Lynn also offered suggestions.

Another major helper was Bhikkhu Brahmāli of Bodhinyana Monastery in Serpentine, Australia. Ven. Brahmāli read the translation alongside the Pāli text in two stages, offering incisive comments. Often his comments necessitated revisions in the draft or required me to add explanatory notes to clarify the reasons behind my rendering. On a few occasions I have quoted Ven. Brahmāli's comments in my notes.

Ven. Vanarata Ānanda Thera, a senior bhikkhu in Sri Lanka, checked my translations of the verse portions of AN. He wrote extremely helpful comments into a printout of the manuscript, which Bhikkhu Nyanatusita kindly photographed and sent to me by email. I have occasionally included Ven. Vanarata's remarks in the notes.

Bhikkhu Pāsādiko, William Pruitt, and Bhikkhu Khemaratana read various versions of the translation and offered useful suggestions and comments. Pamela Kirby reviewed the proofs with sharp eyes for minor typographical and stylistic flaws. My student Pohui Chang helped review the indexes and checked my Chinese renderings in the notes.

I must also thank Tim McNeill and the team at Wisdom Publications for such a fine job of production, consistent with their treatment of the earlier volumes in this series. I reserve a special word of thanks to David Kittelstrom, Megan Anderson, and Laura Cunningham for their work on the present volume.

I am grateful to all these helpers for their selfless assistance, offered entirely from their love of the Dhamma. May they share in any merits that might arise from the publication of this work. I myself, of course, take responsibility for any errors or faults that remain.

Bhikkhu Bodhi
Chuang Yen Monastery
Carmel, New York

[illegible] presented the page numbers [illegible] Ven. [illegible] compiled the [illegible] lists and index of proper names and the [illegible] page [illegible] The Buddha's [illegible] several [illegible] introduction is a helpful source of information that helps us better understand the place of the Aṅguttara Nikāya [illegible] of Buddhist [illegible] literature [illegible] suggestions.

Another [illegible] Bhikkhu Brahmāli of Bodhinyana Monastery in Perth, Australia. Ven. Brahmāli read the translation [illegible] offering [illegible] comments [illegible] revisions of the draft [illegible] to add explanatory notes [illegible] I have [illegible] Ven. Brahmāli's comments in the notes.

Ven. [illegible] checked my translations of the verse portions of the Nikāya [illegible] helpful comments [illegible] manuscript [illegible] kindly photographed and sent [illegible] I have occasionally included Ven. [illegible] remarks in the notes.

[illegible] read various versions of the translation and offered [illegible] suggestions and comments. [illegible] reviewed the proofs with [illegible] typographical and [illegible] Chinese [illegible] in the notes.

I [illegible] also thank [illegible] for [illegible] publications [illegible] consistent with their [illegible] the earlier volumes in this series [illegible] thanks to David Kittelstrom, [illegible] Anderson, and [illegible] Cunningham for their work on the present volume.

I am grateful to [illegible] for [illegible] assistance [illegible] Chuang Yen Monastery [illegible] the publication of this work. I am, of course, [illegible] responsible for any errors [illegible] inaccuracies.

Bhikkhu Bodhi
Chuang Yen Monastery
Carmel, New York

Key to the Pronunciation of Pāli

The Pāli Alphabet

Vowels:
a, ā, i, ī, u, ū, e, o

Consonants:

Gutturals	k, kh, g, gh, ṅ
Palatals	c, ch, j, jh, ñ
Retroflexes (or Cerebrals)	ṭ, ṭh, ḍ, ḍh, ṇ
Dentals	t, th, d, dh, n
Labials	p, ph, b, bh, m
Semivowels	y, r, ḷ, l, v,
Sibilant	s
Aspirate	h
Niggahīta	ṃ

Pronunciation

a as in "cut"
ā as in "ah"
i as in "king"
ī as in "keen"
u as in "put"
ū as in "rule"
e as in "way"
o as in "home"

Of the vowels, *e* and *o* are long before a single consonant and short before a double consonant. Among the consonants, *g* is always pronounced as in "good," *c* as in "church," *ñ* as in "onion." The retroflexes (or cerebrals) are spoken with the tongue on the roof of the mouth; the dentals with the tongue behind the upper teeth. The aspirates—*kh, gh, ch, jh, ṭh, ḍh, th, dh, ph, bh*—are single consonants pronounced with slightly more force than the non-aspirates, thus *th* as in "Thomas" (not as in "thin"); *ph* as in "puff" (not as in "phone"). Double consonants are always enunciated separately, thus *dd* as in "mad dog," *gg* as in "big gun." The *niggahīta,* the pure nasal *ṃ,* is pronounced like the *ng* in "song." An *o* and an *e* always carry a stress; otherwise the stress falls on a long vowel—*ā, ī, ū,* or on a double consonant, or on *ṃ.*

Abbreviations

I. Primary Texts

AN	Aṅguttara Nikāya
Be	Burmese-script ed. of AN (Chaṭṭha Saṅgāyana Tipiṭaka 4.0 electronic version)
Ee	Roman-script ed. of AN (Pali Text Society ed.)
Ce	Sinhala-script ed. of AN (Buddha Jayanti Tripitaka Series, printed ed.)
Mp	Manorathapūraṇī (Aṅguttara Nikāya-aṭṭhakathā)
Mp-ṭ	Manorathapūraṇī-ṭīkā (Sāratthamañjūsā IV-ṭikā)

When Be and Ce are used to designate versions of Mp, they refer respectively to the Chaṭṭha Saṅgāyana Tipiṭaka 4.0 electronic version (based on the Burmese-script edition and issued by the Vipassana Research Institute of Igatpuri, India) and the Sinhala-script Simon Hewavitarne Bequest edition (1923–31). If neither abbreviation is used relative to Mp, I am relying on the Chaṭṭha Saṅgāyana electronic version.

II. Other Pāli Texts

Ap	Apadāna
As	Atthasālinī (Dhammasaṅgaṇī-aṭṭhakathā)
Dhp	Dhammapada
Dhs	Dhammasaṅgaṇī
DN	Dīgha Nikāya
It	Itivuttaka
It-a	Itivuttaka-aṭṭhakathā
Mil	Milindapañha
MN	Majjhima Nikāya

Nett	Nettippakaraṇa
Nidd I	Mahāniddesa
Nidd II	Cūḷaniddesa
Paṭis	Paṭisambhidāmagga
Paṭis-a	Paṭisambhidāmagga-aṭṭhakathā
Pp	Puggalapaññatti
Pp-a	Puggalapaññatti-aṭṭhakathā
Ps	Papañcasūdanī (Majjhima Nikāya-aṭṭhakathā)
SN	Saṃyutta Nikāya
Sn	Suttanipāta
Sp	Samantapāsādikā (Vinaya-aṭṭhakathā)
Spk	Sāratthappakāsinī (Saṃyutta Nikāya-aṭṭhakathā)
Spk-pṭ	Sāratthappakāsinī-purāṇa-ṭīkā (Saṃyutta Nikāya-purāṇa-ṭīkā)
Sv	Sumaṅgalavilāsinī (Dīgha Nikāya-aṭṭhakathā)
Th	Theragāthā
Th-a	Theragāthā-aṭṭhakathā
Thī	Therīgāthā
Ud	Udāna
Ud-a	Udāna-aṭṭhakathā
Vibh	Vibhaṅga
Vibh-a	Vibhaṅga-aṭṭhakathā (Sammohavinodanī)
Vin	Vinaya
Vism	Visuddhimagga
Vism-mhṭ	Visuddhimagga-mahāṭīkā (Paramatthamañjūsā)

References to Pāli texts, unless specified otherwise, are to volume and page number of the PTS edition, with relevant line numbers in reduced type. References to DN and MN usually give first the sutta and section number in LDB and MLDB, respectively, followed by the source from the PTS edition. References to individual words or phrases, however, usually give only the source from the PTS edition. References to SN give first the sutta number in CDB followed by the volume and page number of the PTS edition; those to Udāna and Itivuttaka give the sutta number followed by the page number of the PTS edition. Page references to Vism are to the PTS edition, followed by the chapter and paragraph number in Ppn (see below).

III. Works in Chinese

DĀ	Dīrghāgama (長阿含經)
EĀ	Ekottarikāgama (增壹阿含經)
MĀ	Madhyamāgama (中阿含經)
SĀ	Saṃyuktāgama (雜阿含經)
SĀ[2]	Saṃyuktāgama (another translation; incomplete) (別譯雜阿含經)
T	Taisho edition

All references are to the Taisho edition transcribed in the CBETA Chinese Electronic Tripiṭaka Collection.

IV. Abbreviations of Other Works

CDB	*The Connected Discourses of the Buddha* (translation of SN; see Bodhi 2000)
CMA	*A Comprehensive Manual of Abhidhamma* (see Bodhi 1993)
LDB	*The Long Discourses of the Buddha* (translation of DN; see Walshe 1995)
MLDB	*The Middle Length Discourses of the Buddha* (translation of MN; see Ñāṇamoli 1995)
Ppn	*The Path of Purification* (translation of Vism; see Ñāṇamoli 1956)

V. Reference Works
(see under editor's name in bibliography)

BHSD	*Buddhist Hybrid Sanskrit Dictionary* (see Edgerton 1953)
DOP	*A Dictionary of Pāli*, Part I (see Cone 2001)
DPPN	*Dictionary of Pāli Proper Names* (see Malalasekera 1937–38)
SED	*Sanskrit-English Dictionary* (see Monier-Williams 1899)
PED	*Pāli-English Dictionary* (see Rhys Davids and Stede 1921–25)

VI. Other Abbreviations

BHS	Buddhist Hybrid Sanskrit
PTS	Pali Text Society
Skt	Sanskrit
VRI	Vipassana Research Institute (Igatpuri, India)
n., nn.	note, notes
p., pp.	page, pages
*	before title: title is hypothetical reconstruction; before word: word not listed in dictionary

In the introduction and notes, textual references in bold are to suttas within this translation (e.g., **6:10**).

Introduction

The Aṅguttara Nikāya as a Collection

The Aṅguttara Nikāya is the fourth of the four major Nikāyas making up the Sutta Piṭaka of the Pāli Canon, the collection of texts that Theravāda Buddhists regard as *buddhavacana* or "word of the Buddha." The work is arranged according to a pedagogical technique often employed by the Buddha, namely, the use of a numerical scheme as the underpinning of a discourse. In a period in Indian history when writing might not have been known,[1] or in any case was not used to record spiritual teachings, memorization and preservation of the teachings required that they could be easily retained in mind. The use of numbers served this purpose well. Anyone who has regularly given lectures knows how helpful it is to draw up an outline that organizes the theme of the lecture into a numerical list. Precisely this is the principle that lies behind the *suttas*, or discourses, of the Aṅguttara Nikāya.

The word *aṅguttara* is a compound that might be rendered "increasing-by-a-factor." The compilation is occasionally referred to in the commentaries as the Ekuttaranikāya, "the collection increasing by one," and also as the Aṅguttarāgama. This suggests that in the age of the commentators, several ways of designating the work were still in circulation. The corresponding work in the Northern Buddhist tradition is known as the Ekottarāgama or Ekottarikāgama, *āgama* ("heritage") being the word used in the Northern tradition in place of *nikāya* to designate the compilations of discourses. One full version of the Ekottarāgama in Chinese translation is included in the Chinese Tripiṭaka. The occasional use of the word *āgama* in the Pāli commentaries to designate the discourse collections indicates that the Northern Buddhists had no monopoly on this word.

The name Aṅguttara is given to this collection because it is arranged according to a scheme in which the number of items in the suttas of each successive part increases incrementally over those of the preceding part. The collection contains eleven *nipātas* or "books" named simply after their numerical basis: the *Ekakanipāta*, the Book of the Ones; the *Dukanipāta*, the Book of the Twos; and so forth up to the *Ekādasakanipāta*, the Book of the Elevens. From the Book of the Sixes upward we occasionally find that the number of items needed for a sutta to fit into the scheme is obtained by combining smaller sets.

The summary verse (*uddāna*) at the end of the last volume states that the Aṅguttara Nikāya contains 9,557 suttas. An exact figure is hard to arrive at because it is uncertain whether particular suttas are to be counted separately or as composite wholes. The large figure probably results from counting separately all the suttas generated by the "Lust and So Forth Repetition Series" found at the end of each *nipāta* after the first (see below, pp. 62–63). According to my numbering scheme, AN contains a total of 8,122 suttas, of which 4,250 belong to the "Lust and So Forth Repetition Series." This means that there are only 3,872 suttas independent of that series. Many of these, however, occur in repetition sequences of their own, so even this figure is misleading if it is taken to imply that the contents of the suttas are autonomous. For example, the total number of suttas in the Fives, the Sevens, and the Elevens is greatly inflated by the inclusion in each of entire series of suttas derived from permutations. If these are bracketed, the number of independent suttas would be much reduced. The following table shows the total number of suttas in each *nipāta* and in the "Lust and So Forth Repetition Series."

In each *nipāta*, the suttas are gathered into *vaggas*, which may be called "chapters." The vaggas are constructed according to an ideal plan according to which they would each contain ten suttas, but—given that ideals are seldom realized in our world, even in Buddhist scriptures—in individual cases the actual number may vary from as many as 262 down to a minimum of seven. On occasion all, or most, of the suttas in a single vagga may relate to a single topic, indicated by the vagga's title, but this is rare. It is much more common for merely two or three suttas—and often only one—to bear a clear relation to the title.

Nipāta	*Total Number of Suttas*	*Lust etc. Repetition Suttas*	*Independent Suttas*
Ones	627	—	627
Twos	479	170	309
Threes	352	170	182
Fours	783	510	273
Fives	1152	850	302
Sixes	649	510	139
Sevens	1124	510	614
Eights	627	510	117
Nines	432	340	92
Tens	746	510	236
Elevens	1,151	170	981
Total	8,122	4,250	3,872

TABLE 1. TOTAL NUMBER OF SUTTAS

There is no apparent significance in the sequence of vaggas, though we might suppose that the redactors included in the first few vaggas of any book suttas they considered especially weighty. Although on a first reading the apparently haphazard organization of AN may be disconcerting, over time this becomes one of the most enjoyable features of the collection, exposing the knowledgeable reader to a constantly shifting succession of topics and ideas without allowing preconceptions to determine what will come next. All the reader can know for certain is that the successive suttas will conform to the numerical plan that governs the individual book (but sometimes even this is hard to detect).

The suttas of the Aṅguttara Nikāya, it seems, were not originally given titles as we understand the word. Modern editions, such as the Sri Lankan Buddha Jayanti and Burmese Chaṭṭha Saṅgāyana versions, do title them, but these titles are the work of recent editors. The typical procedure was to include, at the end of each vagga, an *uddāna* or summary verse, which labels each sutta by a key word related to its subject matter. I have drawn my sutta titles from the *uddānas*, and they are therefore very short. Some vaggas do not have summary verses, and thus their suttas are untitled. This is especially the case with those that are extremely short, such as the suttas of the Ones and the Twos.

While the four main Nikāyas of the Sutta Piṭaka are each highly variegated, close examination of their contents suggests that each has a dominant purpose in conveying a particular aspect of the Buddha's message. This concern, I should stress, is by no means evident in every sutta in the respective collection but only pertains to the collection when viewed as a whole. The Dīgha Nikāya is largely governed by the aim of propagating Buddhism within its cultural milieu. Its suttas attempt to establish the supremacy of the Buddha and his Dhamma over their competitors on the Indian religious and social scene. Thus the first sutta of DN surveys the philosophical views that the Buddha flatly rejected, the second repudiates the teachings of six contemporary teachers, while many of the following texts pit the Buddha in debate against brahmins and members of other sects; other suttas serve the purpose of glorifying the Buddha and demonstrating his superiority to the gods, the nature spirits, and the ascetics and contemplatives who traveled over the Ganges plain. The Majjhima Nikāya, on the other hand, turns its spotlight inward on the Buddhist community. Many of the suttas deal with the fundamentals of the doctrine and with meditation and other aspects of Buddhist practice. This makes it particularly well suited for the instruction of monks who need to be integrated into the community.

The Saṃyutta Nikāya and Aṅguttara Nikāya consist mostly of short suttas and thus lack the scenarios and dramatic confrontations that make the two longer collections so fascinating. The Saṃyutta is governed by a thematic principle and contains many short suttas disclosing the Buddha's radical insights and the topography of the path. This collection would have served the needs of two types of specialists in the monastic order. One were those monks and nuns who were capable of grasping the deeper ramifications of Buddhist wisdom and were therefore charged with clarifying these for others. The other were those who had already fulfilled the preliminary stages of meditative training and were intent on developing insight and realizing the goal.

With the move from the Saṃyutta to the Aṅguttara Nikāya, a shift in emphasis takes place from comprehension to personal edification. Because the short suttas that explain the philosophical "theory" and the main methods of training found their way into the Majjhima and the Saṃyutta, what remained to be incorporated into the Aṅguttara were short suttas whose primary concern is practical. To some extent, in its practical orientation, the Aṅguttara partly overlaps the last book of the Saṃyutta, which contains chapters devoted to the seven groups that make up the thirty-seven "aids to enlightenment" (*bodhipakkhiyā dhammā*). To avoid unnecessary duplication, the redactors of the canon did not include these suttas again in the Aṅguttara under their numerical headings. The topics do appear in the repetition series at the end of each *nipāta,* but here their role is stereotyped and secondary. The Aṅguttara focuses instead on aspects of practical training that are not comprised in the standard sets, thereby helping us understand the Buddhist training from new angles. Perhaps we might say that if the last part of the Saṃyutta gives us an anatomy of the Buddhist path, the Aṅguttara takes a physiological slant on the path, viewing it by way of its dynamic unfolding rather than by way of its constituents.

It would be unrealistic, however, to insist that a single criterion has governed the compilation of the Aṅguttara Nikāya, which includes material from the Vinaya, lists of eminent disciples, cosmological ideas, and odd registers of terms that defy easy categorization. What can be said with confidence is that a broad survey of its contents would show a preponderance of texts dealing with Buddhist practice. Their subjects range from the basic ethical observances recommended to the busy layperson, through the pillars of mind training, to the highest meditative state, the *samādhi* or concentration of the arahant.

Approaching the Aṅguttara

Because the suttas of AN constantly shift from one topic to another with little to connect them apart from the exemplification of a particular numerical scheme, readers of this Nikāya often come away bewildered. While they may profit from individual suttas, they can discern no way to fit them together into an intelligible whole. The text itself is not particularly helpful in this respect, for it does not articulate a comprehensive framework that reveals the contours of its teachings.

The Dīgha Nikāya and the Majjhima Nikāya, of course, are also arranged in an apparently haphazard manner, with little more than a simple theme governing each vagga or chapter. But because these collections are composed of suttas that are either long or of middle length—as their respective titles indicate—their contents are substantial enough to engage the reader with material for reflection and contemplation. The major discourses in these Nikāyas also show a sufficient degree of internal organization to reveal the chief categories into which the Buddha's discourses are cast: the courses of wholesome and unwholesome kamma, the graduated training, dependent origination, the four establishments of mindfulness, the four noble truths, and so forth. Though the Saṃyutta Nikāya contains mostly short suttas, the method of grouping connected texts dealing with a single theme makes fewer demands on the reader's patience than a collection with no intelligible organizational principle.

When it comes to AN, however, a neophyte reader may feel as if he or she has been dropped off in a boat far out at sea, with no land in sight and without a compass or map. I pick a chapter at random—the sixth vagga of the Book of the Fives—and I find the following: two suttas on the five hindrances (one embellished with a simile, the other little more than an enumeration); a sutta on the five factors of striving, followed by another on the five wrong and right occasions for striving; a sutta about the perils that separate mother and son; next, one on the training of a monk; a discourse on five themes for reflection; next, one on the proper uses of wealth; and finally two brief suttas on the hardships of those who enter monastic life in old age. With such apparently arbitrary organization, one cannot but wonder what the compilers had in mind when they assembled the chapter.

To assist the reader, I have developed a thematic guide to the Aṅguttara Nikāya that organizes the contents of the collection in accordance with a systematic pattern. The scheme, which follows the introduction on pages 75–84, is similar to the one I used as the scaffolding for my anthology *In the Buddha's Words*. I do not assign every sutta in AN to a niche in this guide. Some suttas resist classification, while others are too short or insubstantial for inclusion. Rather than try to be all-inclusive, I have proposed a framework, with divisions and subdivisions, and included enough discourses under each heading to enable the reader to see how the texts of AN can be fit together into a meaningful pattern.

Inevitably, the attempt to assign particular suttas to specific categories involved abstraction and painful decision-making. Many suttas in AN can be viewed from different points of view, any of which could have resulted in a sutta being placed in different categories. For instance, the suttas often explain practices or qualities by way of the persons who exemplify them, or alternatively, they explain persons by way of their practices and qualities. Thus I had to decide whether the sutta should be classified in terms of practices and qualities or in terms of persons. In some cases a given sutta covers a range of topics and thus fits comfortably into several categories. I did not want my guide to turn into an index, which would lack the degree of specificity needed to help the reader fit the sutta into the ground plan of the whole. Thus, while my ideal was "one sutta, one category," I often had to assign a single sutta to two categories and sometimes to three. However, I do not think I have exceeded three places for a single sutta.

The broadest categories that I used for the scheme are the "Three Jewels": the Buddha, the Dhamma, and the Saṅgha. I begin with the section on the Buddha, honoring him as the founder of the Buddhist heritage and the ultimate source of all the teachings comprised in the Aṅguttara Nikāya. Section II, titled "The Dhamma and Discipline," deals with the Buddha's teaching as a body of instructions that can be summarized, applied, and realized, and also as a corpus of texts that need to be preserved and transmitted to posterity. Following this section come eight sections devoted to the teachings themselves. This portion of the outline is intended to cover the Dhamma in its full range as we find it in AN. It begins with a survey of the Buddha's worldview (section III), covering the cosmological background to the Buddhist liberation project, the problematic nature of human experience, and the determinants of human destiny. I then proceed in stages through the different forms of Buddhist practice, beginning with life in the world: family relations, livelihood, wealth, community, and state (section IV). These spheres of human activity are often neglected by writers on Buddhism, who succumb to the error of assuming that monastic practice represents the Dhamma in its entirety. The Aṅguttara is a treasury of inspiring and informative discourses on righteous living in the confines of the world, and these texts are essential to arriving at an adequate picture of early Buddhism.

While the Buddha stressed the virtues conducive to domestic harmony, his teaching does not stop there but leads on to the training for a higher rebirth and ultimate liberation. Though the former of these two trainings was directed toward lay disciples and the latter toward the bhikkhus and bhikkhunīs, the two share many values. These values constitute a common platform of spiritual cultivation for both lay disciples and monastics. Under this theme, I have gathered into section V a variety of texts that concentrate on the practices of the devoted lay disciple who is not content merely to observe an ethical life but also seeks to advance along the path to liberation. The Aṅguttara Nikāya is a rich source of guidance for earnest lay followers, and this section attempts to do justice to such texts.

To inspire in his followers an aspiration for the final goal, the Buddha highlights the defects and dangers of mundane existence, which illustrate the noble truth of suffering. Section VI therefore groups together a number of topics and texts devoted to the task of "dispelling the world's enchantment." What binds us to conditioned existence, with its round of repeated birth and death and the danger of descent to lower realms of rebirth, are the defilements of the mind. Suttas dealing with this topic play a very prominent role in AN, and these have been gathered into section VII. The next division, section VIII, groups together suttas on the monastic training, which flows out from the spirit of renunciation and aims at the attainment of nibbāna. The heart of the monastic training is the practice of meditation, which is given a section of its own, section IX. Here I have allocated suttas that emphasize the practices that lead to the higher states of concentration (*samādhi*). Section X takes us into the next phase of the higher training, the development of wisdom (*paññā*), culminating in liberation and the realization of nibbāna, the final goal of the teaching.

The next portion of the outline represents the third Jewel of Buddhism, the Saṅgha. It deals with both the institutional Saṅgha, the order of ordained monks and nuns (bhikkhus and bhikkhunīs), and the *ariyasaṅgha*, the community of noble ones, those who have attained the paths and fruits of enlightenment.

The last major section of the ground plan deals with types of persons. This is an area where the Aṅguttara differs significantly from the Saṃyutta. The major chapters of the Saṃyutta focus on the main philosophical themes of the teaching, the principles and categories that the Buddha proposed as templates for contemplation and insight. Thus we find in the Saṃyutta huge chapters on dependent origination, the elements, the five aggregates, the six sense bases, and the path factors, often explained in bare phenomenological terms with only minimal references to actual persons. The Aṅguttara, in contrast, abounds in different ways of classifying people—both monastics and laypeople, noble ones and ordinary people—and it gives primacy to their qualities, their struggles for happiness and meaning, their aspirations and attainments. The Aṅguttara thus became the inspiration and a major source for one of the books of the Abhidhamma Piṭaka, the Puggalapaññatti or "Descriptions of Persons," the one treatise in the collection that departs from the strict Abhidhamma method of phenomenological reduction in order to survey types of persons as they relate to the values and goals of the Dhamma.

The Buddha in the Aṅguttara Nikāya

In what follows I will explore the contents of AN through the major categories of the Thematic Guide, highlighting prominent themes that emerge in this Nikāya and citing suttas that exemplify them. At the risk of being repetitive, I have to assert once again that the assignment of individual suttas to particular categories is largely done for the sake of expediency and risks nullifying the complexity in the contents of particular texts.

In a work that focuses largely on persons, it is fitting that we find a substantial number of suttas devoted to the Buddha himself, not merely as the teacher and expounder of the Dhamma, but as a person with his own life story and achievements. I have distinguished the suttas that deal with the Buddha into three classes: those that refer to his life and thus constitute the building blocks of a biography; those that extol his spiritual qualities and attainments; and, as a distinct category, those that speak of the Buddha not so much as a unique individual but as an archetype, the exemplar of the fully enlightened teacher who embodies his message in his person. This last heading comprises those suttas in which the Buddha speaks of himself as "the Tathāgata."

The Nikāyas never sought to construct a continuous biography of the Buddha. The suttas that refer to events in his life are widely spread out in the different collections and seldom provide the clues that would be needed to connect these into a single coherent sequence. The Mahāparinibbāna Sutta (DN 16) gives us a connected account of the Buddha's last days, culminating in his death and cremation. But beyond this, the biographical material has to be ferreted out from widely scattered texts, and we must rely on speculation, imagination, and hints in the texts themselves (such as settings and occasional references to related incidents) to assign these to specific phases of the Buddha's life.

Nevertheless, AN does allude to the incidents familiar to us from the connected accounts of his life that were composed later. We can see these perhaps as the raw material that the poets and hagiographers would draw upon to construct the glorious Buddha biography. Thus **4:127** speaks about the wonders that accompanied his conception in the womb, his physical birth, his enlightenment, and his setting in motion the wheel of the Dhamma. In **3:39** he speaks about his delicate and luxurious upbringing, and he recounts the reflections on old age, illness, and death that roused him from his intoxication with youth, health, and life. He discusses his efforts to master the various stages of meditation during his struggle for enlightenment in **8:64** and **9:40**, two accounts that are not included in the familiar Buddha biography. Sutta **5:196** tells of the five dreams that he had while still a bodhisatta, foretokens of his awakening, and **8:11** relates the traditional account of the enlightenment as proceeding through the four jhānas and the three higher knowledges to the destruction of the taints. In **4:21** he tells of his reflections after his enlightenment and of his decision to honor only the Dhamma. In **8:70** he claims that if he so wished, he could live out the eon, and he decides to "relinquish his life force" because Ānanda failed to request him to extend his life. This incident is familiar to us from the Mahāparinibbāna Sutta.

While texts offering biographical information on the Buddha are relatively sparse, those that extol his virtues and attainments are plentiful. He is praised as the "one person who arises in the world . . . out of compassion for the world, for the good, welfare, and happiness of devas and human beings" (**1:170**). His bodily form is endowed with such extraordinary marks that an inquisitive brahmin cannot believe he is a mere human being (**4:36**). He has perfected noble virtue, concentration, wisdom, and liberation (**4:1**). He possesses the qualities expected of a fully accomplished spiritual teacher (**5:100**). He is praised by the monk Udāyī in verses of great beauty (**6:43**) and extolled by his lay disciple King Pasenadi (**10:30**). He dwells in the world detached from the world, with all defilements gone, free from birth, old age, and death, like a lotus flower that is "born in the water and grown up in the water, but rises up above the water and stands unsoiled by the water" (**4:36, 10:81**).

The suttas in which the Buddha speaks of himself as the "Tathāgata" are sufficiently impressive to warrant being assigned to a class of their own. In these suttas I see the Buddha referring to himself not simply as a unique individual but as the latest representative of the "dynasty" of Buddhas, those extraordinary beings who appear at rare intervals in the cosmic process to rediscover the lost path to nibbāna and teach it to the world. In AN, we find explicit references to only two of the six Buddhas of the past that we know from other Nikāyas. Sikhī, the fifth back, is referred to at **3:80**, and Kassapa, Gotama's predecessor, at **5:180**. But there are a fair number of references to Tathāgatas in the plural, which indicates that the idea of a succession of Buddhas was already known to the compilers.

From the perspective of the Nikāyas, all the Tathāgatas partake of the same essential attributes that qualify them to serve as world teachers. The Tathāgata is declared to be "without a peer, without counterpart, incomparable, matchless, unrivaled, unequaled, without equal, the foremost of bipeds" (**1:174**). He is the foremost of beings, and those who have confidence in him have confidence in the best (**4:34**). His arising is "the manifestation of great vision, light, and radiance" (**1:175–77**). He has fully awakened to "whatever is seen, heard, sensed, cognized, reached, sought after, and examined by the mind," and therefore whatever he teaches "is just so and not otherwise" (**4:23**). He is endowed with the "ten Tathāgata powers" and the "four kinds of self-confidence" on the basis of which "he claims the place of the chief bull, roars his lion's roar in the assemblies, and sets in motion the brahma wheel" (**4:8, 10:22**; see too **6:64**). His "lion's roar" on impermanence is so powerful that it even causes the long-lived deities to quake and tremble (**4:33**).

The Dhamma and the Discipline

Although the Buddha is the supreme person in the spiritual realm, he still revered something superior to himself: the Dhamma. After his enlightenment, seeking in vain for someone to honor, he decided: "Let me honor, respect, and dwell in dependence only on this Dhamma to which I have become fully enlightened" (**4:22**). When he teaches others, he does so "relying just on the Dhamma, honoring, respecting, and venerating the Dhamma, taking the Dhamma as his standard, banner, and authority" (**3:14, 5:133**). Whomever he teaches, he teaches respectfully, "because the Tathāgata has respect for the Dhamma, reverence for the Dhamma" (**5:99**).

The Dhamma in this sense is not so much the verbally expressed doctrine as the corpus of spiritual principles that makes possible spiritual growth and liberation. Its ultimate referents are the noble eightfold path, the foremost of all conditioned phenomena, and nibbāna, the foremost of all things conditioned and unconditioned (**4:34**). The Buddha summed up the essence of the Dhamma in various ways that all flow out of the same body of principles. In one place, he says that the unlimited expressions of the Dhamma converge on four things: understanding what is unwholesome and abandoning it, and understanding what is wholesome and developing it (**4:188**). He taught Mahāpajāpatī, his foster mother, eight criteria of the true Dhamma (**8:53**), and more concisely he told the bhikkhu Upāli that the teaching could be found in "those things that lead exclusively to disenchantment, to dispassion, to cessation, to peace, to direct knowledge, to enlightenment, to nibbāna" (**7:83**).

Contrary to many of his contemporaries, the Buddha refused to indulge in speculative views about matters irrelevant to the quest for release from suffering. He particularly refused to make pronouncements about the fate of the liberated one after death or to answer the ten idle speculative questions (see **7:54**). Instead, he stressed that he taught the Dhamma "for the purification of beings, for the overcoming of sorrow and lamentation, for the passing away of pain and dejection, for the achievement of the method, for the realization of nibbāna" (**9:20**). Yet, though he maintained a kind of "metaphysical reticence," he did not hesitate to criticize those views he considered detrimental to the spiritual life. The texts sometimes mention three that he expressly repudiated: past-action determinism, deterministic theism, and denial of causality (**3:61**). He decidedly rejects as a wrong view the thesis that "there is no fruit or result of good and bad actions," which disavows the principle of kamma (**10:176**, **10:211**, etc.). He also strongly criticized the "hard determinist" view that our decisions are irrevocably caused by factors and forces outside ourselves. Against the determinist position that "there is no kamma, no deed, no energy," he says that all the perfectly enlightened Buddhas teach "a doctrine of kamma, a doctrine of deeds, a doctrine of energy" (**3:137**). He insisted that there are such things as instigation, initiative, choice, and exertion, by reason of which people are responsible for their own destiny (**6:38**).

The Buddha claimed that his Dhamma was "directly visible" (*sandiṭṭhika*), a word that became one of its epithets. When questioned how this was to be confirmed, he explained in ways that directed the inquirers back to their own immediate experience. When a person is overwhelmed by lust, hatred, and delusion, he said, he acts for his own harm, the harm of others, and the harm of both, and he experiences suffering and dejection; but when lust, hatred, and delusion are abandoned, he is free to act for the well-being of all and no longer experiences suffering and grief (see **3:53–54**). The destruction of lust, hatred, and delusion is nibbāna, and in this respect nibbāna too is directly visible (**3:55**).

In AN, the Dhamma is viewed not merely as the path of practice and the goal of realization but also as the collection of verbal discourses that the Buddha gave during his teaching career. Thus the suttas occasionally refer to the nine types of teaching into which the discourses were classified in the earliest period, before they were compiled into Nikāyas (**4:102**, **4:107**, **5:73–74**, etc.). Because the Buddha's teachings, which disclose the path to enlightenment and liberation, were collected into a body of scriptures, the vigor, purity, and longevity of the Dhamma depend on the proper preservation and transmission of the texts. Among the four Nikāyas, AN is the one that insists most often on the need to properly preserve the Dhamma and thereby protect it from decay and disappearance.

Suttas that dwell on this theme are found throughout the work. A series of short texts in the Ones delineates the factors that cause the good Dhamma to vanish and, conversely, the factors that sustain its vitality (**1:30–69**). The latter can be summed up as not confusing what is the Dhamma with what is not the Dhamma; not confusing the discipline with what is contrary to the discipline; quoting the Buddha accurately, describing his conduct correctly, and not confounding different categories of disciplinary rules. In one sutta, the Buddha gives instructions to the monks on the criteria for determining whether teachings reported after his passing are authentic or spurious (**4:180**). Another sutta says that the good Dhamma degenerates when the monks do not preserve the teachings properly, misinterpret their meaning, fail to teach others, and backslide in the practice. But when, to the contrary, they preserve the teachings properly, interpret them correctly, teach others, and strive in the practice, the teaching lasts long (**4:160**).

The Shifting Kaleidoscope of Experience

Given the importance of preserving the teaching and ensuring its longevity, what exactly is the content of the Dhamma that the Buddha discovered, and why is it so special? Before answering this question, it is useful to briefly review the Buddha's picture of the universe in order to see the background setting for the quest for liberation. The Nikāyas envision a universe of inconceivably vast dimensions undergoing alternating phases of development and decline. The basic unit of cosmic time is the eon (*kappa*). Those who acquire the power of recalling their past lives, the texts say, can recollect "many eons of world-dissolution, many eons of world-evolution, many eons of world-dissolution and world-evolution" (**3:58**, **3:101**, etc.). The eon is divided into four phases: dissolving, prolonged dissolution, evolving, and completed evolution. Each of these is beyond calculation in hundreds of thousands of years (**4:156**). A world system has not only vast temporal duration but is also stratified by way of various realms of existence, ranging from the dismal hell realms, worlds of intense suffering, through the animal realm, to the sphere of afflicted spirits (sometimes called "hungry ghosts"); then on to the human realm, and upward through an ascending series of celestial realms inhabited by the *devas* and *brahmās*, the deities and divine beings. There are six sensual heavenly realms: the heaven of the four divine kings, the Tāvatiṃsa devas, the Yāma devas, the Tusita devas, the devas who delight in creation, and the devas who control what is created by others (**3:70**, **6:10**, **8:36**, etc.). Above these are the brahmā world and still higher realms, spheres of rebirth for those who have mastered the meditative attainments.

Despite their many differences, there is one thing that unites all sentient beings from the lowest to the highest: they all seek freedom from suffering and the achievement of true happiness. This inherent urge of a sentient being is precisely what the Buddha makes the commanding theme of his teaching, the linchpin holding all the doctrines and practices together. But rather than take our common assumptions for granted, the Buddha embarks on a critical inquiry into the question of what constitutes suffering and what offers the prospect for indissoluble happiness. Our preconceptions about what will make us happy are often deceptive, stemming from a fixation on immediate sensation that excludes recognition of the deeper repercussions and long-term consequences of our behavior.

Experience is ever changing, always shifting its shape without regard for our wishes and expectations. Despite our hopes, we cannot avoid old age, illness, and death, the decay of our possessions, the loss of those who are dear. The foolish worldling and the wise disciple both share this fate. They differ in that the worldling does not reflect on the universality of this law, and therefore, when his fate catches up with him, "he sorrows, languishes, laments, weeps beating his breast, and becomes confused." The wise disciple, in contrast, realizes that old age, illness, and death, destruction and loss, are our universal destiny; he thus draws out "the poisonous dart of sorrow" and dwells happily, free of darts (**5:48**). Again, both worldling and disciple are subject to the "eight worldly conditions": gain and loss, disrepute and fame, blame and praise, and pleasure and pain. The worldling, attracted to one and repelled by the other, "is not freed from birth, from old age and death, from sorrow, lamentation, pain, dejection, and anguish." But the noble disciple, recognizing that all these unstable conditions are impermanent and subject to change, discards attraction and repulsion and achieves inner freedom (**8:6**).

What the Buddha emphasizes as a starting point in the quest for true happiness is the close correlation between the ethical quality of our conduct and the felt tone of our experience. Bodily deeds, speech, and thoughts can be distinguished ethically into two broad classes, the unwholesome (*akusala*) and the wholesome (*kusala*). The Buddha noted that the unwholesome is a source of misery, the wholesome a source of blessedness. Greed, hatred, and delusion lead to harm and suffering, while their removal brings well-being and happiness (**3:65–66**). His constant injunction to his disciples, therefore, was to make a determined effort to abandon the unwholesome and to develop the wholesome (**2:19**). Wholesome endeavor brings a far greater, richer, and more enduring happiness than the indulgence of craving. A series of very short suttas contrasts different kinds of happiness and assesses their relative worth: the happiness of monastic life is superior to that of lay life; the happiness of renunciation superior to sensual happiness; the happiness without acquisitions superior to the happiness arisen from acquisitions; the happiness without taints superior to that with taints; and spiritual happiness superior to worldly happiness (**2:64–68**).

According to the Buddha, the "ever-shifting kaleidoscope" of suffering and happiness does not change its configurations only in a single life on earth; it changes even more radically as we travel onward in the round of rebirths known as *saṃsāra*, "the wandering." The governing factor in this process, which makes the entire course of rebirth a lawful one, is a force called *kamma* (Skt: *karma*). The word *kamma* literally means "action," but the Buddha uses it to refer specifically to volitional or intentional action: "It is volition, bhikkhus, that I call *kamma*; for having willed, one acts by body, speech, or mind" (**6:63 §5**). Kamma thus denotes deeds that originate from volition, which may remain purely mental, creating kamma through our thoughts, plans, and desires; or it may come to expression in bodily and verbal deeds. Kamma also denotes the moral force created by our deeds. All our morally determinate deeds create a potential to bring forth results (*vipāka*) that correspond to their ethical quality. Our deeds generate kamma, and when suitable conditions come together, the kamma ripens and produces the appropriate fruits, bringing misery or happiness in dependence on the moral quality of the original action. The kamma we create may ripen in this very life, in the next rebirth, or on some subsequent occasion (**3:34**, **10:217**). The one thing that is certain is that as long as we travel on in the cycle of rebirths, our stockpile of kamma is capable of ripening and yielding its due results. Thus the Buddha teaches, again and again, that "beings are the owners of their kamma, the heirs of their kamma; they have kamma as their origin, kamma as their relative, kamma as their resort; whatever kamma they do, good or bad, they are its heirs" (**10:216**; see too **5:57**, **10:48**).

The differences in kamma account for the wide diversity in the fortunes of people, who are constantly revolving in the cycle of existence, rising and falling, sometimes heading from darkness to light, sometimes from light to darkness (**4:85**). Kamma is the principal determinant of rebirth. Unwholesome kamma conduces to an unfortunate rebirth and painful results, wholesome kamma to a fortunate rebirth and pleasant results (**2:16–17**, **3:111**, **10:217–18**). Rebirth is not confined to the human realm, for kamma varies in its quality and potency and thus may produce rebirth in any of the five *gatis* or destinations: hell, the animal realm, the realm of afflicted spirits, the human world, or the deva world (**6:63 §5**). Beings are constantly migrating from realm to realm, but relatively few are reborn in the human or deva worlds compared to the much greater number who are reborn in the hells, the animal realm, and the spirit realms, collectively called the plane of misery, the bad destinations, or the lower world (**1:348–77**). Modernists who propose interpreting these realms as psychological states that we experience in our human existence would have a hard time finding support for their position in the Nikāyas. In AN we read again and again, in almost every *nipāta*, of how beings are reborn in hell or in heaven "with the breakup of the body, after death" (*kāyassa bhedā paraṃmaraṇā*). The expression is one of the main leitmotifs of the Nikāyas, and there are no indications that it is intended metaphorically.

The criterion for judging the volition responsible for an action to be unwholesome or wholesome is its accompanying motives or "roots." Three roots are unwholesome: greed, hatred, and delusion. From these such secondary defilements as anger, hostility, envy, miserliness, conceit, and arrogance arise, and from the roots and secondary defilements arise defiled actions with their potential to produce rebirth in the plane of misery (**6:39**). Wholesome kamma, on the other hand, is action that originates from the three wholesome roots: non-greed, non-hatred, and non-delusion, which may be expressed more positively as generosity, loving-kindness, and wisdom. Whereas actions springing from the unwholesome roots are necessarily tied to the round of repeated birth and death, actions born from the wholesome roots are of two kinds, mundane and world-transcending. Mundane wholesome actions have the potential to produce a fortunate rebirth in the higher realms (**6:39**). The world-transcending or supramundane (*lokuttara*) wholesome actions—namely, the kamma generated by practicing the noble eightfold path and the seven factors of enlightenment—dismantles the entire process of karmic causation and thereby leads to liberation from the round of rebirths (**3:34**, **4:233**, **4:237–38**).

The texts do not leave us guessing what kinds of deeds create wholesome and unwholesome kamma but provide precise maps over the terrain of right and wrong conduct. The standard list contains ten kinds of unwholesome action—three of body, four of speech, and three of mind—and ten corresponding types of wholesome kamma (**10:167–233**; see **10:176** for a detailed analysis). All these actions, however, ultimately spring from the mind. Thus mind is revealed as the underlying source of good and evil and, through the actions that flow from it, the fundamental cause of suffering and happiness.

By tracing the roots of suffering and happiness back to our intentions, the Buddha demonstrates that the key to happiness is the training and mastery of the mind. In a series of paired suttas, he says that he sees nothing that leads to such harm and suffering as the mind that is undeveloped, uncultivated, untamed, unguarded, unprotected, and unrestrained; while nothing leads to such great good and happiness as the mind that is developed, cultivated, tamed, guarded, protected, and restrained (**1:23–40**). Thus the core of the Buddha's teaching is the development and cultivation of the mind, which, as a result of such cultivation, will unfold its intrinsic luminosity and ultimately arrive at the bliss of liberation.

Maintaining a Harmonious Household

Although early Buddhism prescribes a path of self-cultivation leading to the extinction of suffering, the Buddha realized that spiritual development does not occur in a social vacuum but rests upon a healthy and harmonious social order that exemplifies the kinds of virtues that nurture the spiritual life. Spiritual influences begin at the top of the social hierarchy and gradually spread downward, affecting the whole society and even the biological and physical domains (**4:70**). Thus the Buddha devotes considerable effort to instilling in his followers the lifestyle and sense of social responsibility that conduces to a harmonious society in which people act in accordance with the civic virtues. Among the four Nikāyas, the Aṅguttara—along with the Sīgalaka Sutta (DN 31)—is probably the richest source of such teachings. John Kelly notes that this Nikāya has the largest number of suttas concerned with laypeople, either directly, by being addressed to them, or indirectly, by being spoken to the monks about the practices proper for a lay disciple. (See table 2.)

From the number of discourses on family relationships, it is evident that the Buddha regarded the family as the primary agent of acculturation. Since the head of the family has a particularly powerful impact on his household, the Buddha tried to promote the positive transformation of society by offering

	Dīgha	*Majjhima*	*Saṃyutta*	*Aṅguttara*	*Khuddaka*
Total Suttas in the *Nikāya*[2]	34	152	2,904	8,122	601[3]
Directly to Laypeople	14	47	121	125	30
Indirectly to Laypeople	1	3	7	36	6
Total	15	50	128	161	36

TABLE 2. SUTTAS TO LAYPEOPLE BY NIKĀYA
(Source: Kelly 2011: 8)

householders guidelines to righteous living. He set up a pragmatic but inspiring ideal for the laity, that of the *sappurisa* or "good person," who lives "for the good, welfare, and happiness of many people," his parents, his wife and children, the domestic help, his friends, and contemplative renouncers (**5:42**). When the head of the family sets a good example, those who depend on him grow in all that is worthy: in faith, virtue, learning, generosity, and wisdom (**3:48, 5:40**).

In offering guidance to the family, the Buddha lays down the duties of children toward their parents (**2:33, 3:31**), advises husbands and wives how to live together (**4:53**), and even instructs a loving couple how they can be assured of reuniting in future lives (**4:55**). He distinguishes between wrong livelihood and right livelihood, defines the proper ways of acquiring and utilizing wealth, and prescribes the appropriate means for sustaining cordial relationships: giving, endearing speech, beneficent conduct, and impartiality (**4:32**). He not only instructed individuals and families, but he also advised states and rulers. He taught the people of the Vajji confederacy, who maintained a republican form of government, "seven principles of non-decline" (**7:21**). For kings he set up the ideal of the "wheel-turning monarch" (*rājā cakkavati*), the righteous king who rules by the Dhamma and provides righteous protection for all in his realm, including the animals and the birds (**3:14, 5:133**).

The Way Leading Upward

While early Buddhism sees a righteous society as providing the optimal conditions for collective well-being and happiness, its focus is not on social stability as such but on the spiritual development and liberation of the individual. The most congenial conditions for the unhindered pursuit of the final goal are provided by the lifestyle of a renunciant monk or nun, who is free from the constraints and liabilities of household life. But, almost unprecedented for his time, the Buddha also held that householders earning their living by "the sweat of their arms" and supporting a family could also advance spiritually and reach three of the four stages of awakening (see pp. 55–56 below). He thus laid down guideposts to spiritual cultivation for his lay followers that would be compatible with their time-consuming schedules of work and family responsibilities. These would enable the lay disciple to win a higher rebirth and even reach the plane of the noble ones, where final liberation is assured.

Many of the factors that enter into the foundational stage of spiritual development are common to the renunciant and the householder. Thus, though the suttas often describe these qualities in terms of a bhikkhu, they can be understood to pertain to lay disciples as well. The seed of spiritual development is a triad of qualities consisting of faith (*saddhā*), confidence (*pasāda*), and reverence (*gārava*). Faith is a faculty and a power, and as such is defined as belief in the enlightenment of the Buddha (**5:2**, **5:14**). It is a deep trust in his wisdom and a readiness to comply with his advice. From faith arise the other four powers that inspire and direct the training: moral shame, moral dread, energy, and wisdom. Closely connected with faith is confidence, a feeling of serenity and mental clarity that arises from faith. The disciple has confidence that the Buddha is the best of beings, the Dhamma the best of teachings, and the Saṅgha of noble ones the best of spiritual communities (**4:34**). Along with faith and confidence comes reverence, a sense of respect and esteem directed toward the Three Jewels and the training (**6:32–33**).

For a disciple endowed with faith, spiritual growth is furthered by associating with good friends, people who can give guidance and serve as inspiring models. The Buddha's statement to Ānanda (SN 45:2) that good friendship is the whole of the spiritual life finds powerful analogues in AN. We read that there is "no single thing that so causes unarisen wholesome qualities to arise and arisen unwholesome qualities to decline as good friendship" (**1:71**). A pair of suttas beautifully enumerates the traits to be sought for in a good friend (**7:36–37**), and a discourse to a householder advises him to befriend other householders accomplished in faith, virtuous behavior, generosity, and wisdom (**8:54 §3**).

A large part of the practice for a householder involves engaging in meritorious deeds, activities that generate wholesome kamma conducive to a happy rebirth, good fortune, and spiritual progress. The Buddha even urges the bhikkhus, "Do not be afraid of merit," and he details the benefits he reaped in a previous life by cultivating a mind of loving-kindness (**7:62**). The texts enumerate three "bases of meritorious activity": giving, virtuous behavior, and meditative development (**8:36**). They also mention four "streams of merit" for a noble disciple: unwavering confidence in the Three Jewels together with virtuous behavior (**4:52**). The list is expanded to eight streams of merit by combining the Three Refuges with the five precepts (**8:39**).

Many short texts in AN are concerned with the etiquette of giving and generosity, with the emphasis on providing material support to monks and nuns as well as other ascetics who live in dependence on the lay community. Though the Buddha encouraged his disciples to support renunciants of all convictions, even his rivals (**8:12**), he also taught that the merit gained by giving is proportional to the spiritual qualities of the recipients, and thus the noble persons, especially arahants, serve as the most fertile field of merit (**3:57**). Virtuous behavior begins by observing the five training rules: abstinence from taking life, stealing, sexual misconduct, false speech, and use of intoxicants. The code of good conduct can be expanded into the ten courses of wholesome action, which cover not only bodily and verbal behavior but wholesome dispositions and correct views (**10:176**). A number of texts give specific directives on right speech. I already referred to right livelihood in the previous section.

Of particular value for the earnest lay devotee intent on merit is the *uposatha* observance adopted on new-moon and full-moon days. On these occasions devout lay followers undertake eight precepts that emulate the precepts of a novice monk (**3:70, 8:41–45**). They may spend the day practicing meditation, and one text recommends loving-kindness as especially suitable for the uposatha (**9:18**). Another text recommends five recollections, called means of cleansing the defiled mind (**3:70**).[4] The Buddha explains that observing the uposatha complete in its eight factors is more beneficial than sovereignty over the continent, for the merit acquired can lead to rebirth in the heavenly worlds.

In an interesting table reproduced here, Kelly has calculated the prevailing aims across Nikāyas in the discourses addressed to laypeople. He distinguishes between aims concerned with mundane welfare—in this life and a heavenly rebirth—and those connected with the attainment of liberation:[5]

Goal	*Dīgha*	*Majjhima*	*Saṃyutta*	*Aṅguttara*	*Khuddaka*	*All*
This Life / Next Life	6 (33%)	16 (32%)	44 (34%)	97 (60%)	21 (58%)	184 (47%)
Liberation	9 (50%)	24 (48%)	58 (45%)	34 (21%)	13 (36%)	138 (35%)
Unspecified	3 (17%)	10 (20%)	26 (20%)	30 (19%)	2 (6%)	71 (18%)
Total	18 (100%)	50 (100%)	128 (100%)	161 (100%)	36 (100%)	393 (100%)

TABLE 3. GOALS FOR LAYPEOPLE PER NIKĀYA
(Source: Kelly 2011: 19)

Kelly notes that AN has a much stronger emphasis than the other Nikāyas on the two mundane goals as against the attainment of stream-entry or higher stages on the path. However, even in AN the practice for a lay follower is not exhausted by merit. In several suttas the Buddha mentions four qualities that lead to the superior welfare of a lay follower. The first three are faith, virtue, and generosity, the constituents of merit. But the fourth is wisdom, specifically "the wisdom that discerns arising and passing away, which is noble and penetrative and leads to the complete destruction of suffering" (**8:54, 8:76**). This is the wisdom of insight into impermanence, which leads beyond all spheres of rebirth to the final goal of the Dhamma, the realization of nibbāna and release from the round of rebirths.

Dispelling the World's Enchantment

To steer his disciples away from their attachment to transient objects of clinging, the Buddha employs an arsenal of techniques intended to uncover the abyss that lies just beneath the apparently innocent joys of a virtuous life. These techniques are intended to instill in the aspirant a quality called *saṃvega*, a word without a precise English equivalent. To convey the sense it is necessary to resort to a makeshift phrase like "a sense of urgency." *Saṃvega* might be described as the inner commotion or shock we experience when we are jolted out of our usual complacency by a stark encounter with truths whose full gravity we normally refuse to face. *Saṃvega* arises from the recognition that our self-assumed security is illusory, that we are perpetually treading on thin ice, which at any moment may crack beneath our feet.

The chief catalyst in inducing this sense of urgency is our confrontation with our inevitable mortality as revealed by old age, illness, and death. This encounter shakes us out of our habituation to mundane comforts and sets us in quest of unshakable peace and freedom. The future Buddha himself had to undergo this "shock of recognition" before he could embark on his own quest for enlightenment. His deep reflections on old age, illness, and death shattered his infatuation with youth, health, and vitality and drove him from his palace out into the forest seeking the unaging, illness-free, and deathless nibbāna (**3:39**).

In many suttas, the Buddha employs a template involving three standpoints designed to induce the sense of urgency. These three standpoints are gratification (*assāda*), danger (*ādīnava*), and escape (*nissaraṇa*).[6] We begin with what is immediately obvious: that our experience in the world provides some degree of *gratification* or enjoyment, which consists in the pleasure and joy that arise with the fulfillment of our desires. It is because people experience gratification that they become attached to the things that give them pleasure. When, however, we look more deeply, we can see that just beneath the glittering surface of joy there is a dark underbelly of pain and distress. This is their *danger*, stemming from their impermanence (*anicca*), liability to suffering (*dukkha*), and nature to change and decay (*vipariṇāmadhamma*). The third step, *escape*, shows us the release from danger. When we see that our craving for pleasure binds us to what is inherently flawed, we can drop the craving. Thus the escape lies in "the removal and abandoning of desire and lust."

It is for the purpose of provoking a sense of urgency that the Buddha stresses aspects of experience that we typically try to conceal from ourselves. These points of emphasis give the teaching a "pessimistic" flavor, but it is a pessimism that does not lead to the blind alley of nihilism but to the open fields of liberation, the end of suffering. In accordance with this strategy, the Buddha teaches his disciples, whether monastics or laypeople, to often reflect on the fact that they are subject to old age, illness, and death; that they must be parted from everyone and everything they love; and that they are the heirs of their own kamma (**5:57**). He underscores the misery in sensual pleasures, calling them perilous, suffering, a disease, a boil, a tie, and a swamp (**6:23**; see too **8:56**). He declares that even a trifling amount of conditioned existence, "even for a mere finger snap," is like a lump of feces (**1:328**). He calls attention to the foulness of the body, which contains thirty-one unattractive constituents, is prey to a host of diseases, and resembles a boil with nine orifices (**10:60 §§3–4**; **9:15**). He stresses the transience of human life, which is short, limited, and fleeting, beset by suffering and misery (**7:74**). He points out that at some point in the future even this great earth with its mighty mountains will burn up and vanish (**7:66**). Even more, he says, the entire world system will dissolve along with its powerful deities. Understanding this, the wise disciple "becomes disenchanted and dispassionate toward the foremost, not to speak of what is inferior" (**10:29 §§2–3**).

The Defilements of the Mind

Once we clearly recognize the defects in sensual pleasures and the futility of meandering from life to life in the realms of conditioned existence, the urge arises to break free from bondage and reach the end of repeated becoming, which is also the end of suffering. To fulfill this urge, we have to investigate the cause of our bondage, for it is only by removing the cause that we can eliminate the result. The Buddha locates the cause of suffering in the bonds of our own minds. Hence the stress in the teaching on honest self-assessment (**10:51**). As part of a diagnosis of the origin of suffering, the Nikāyas are replete with catalogues of the various defilements to which the mind is prey. In AN we find many such groups, which are usually given metaphorical names to indicate how they affect us: taints, hindrances, floods, fetters, and so forth.

When reading the Nikāyas, we are likely to be awed by the wide range of the defilements that are listed, and also to be confused about the distinctive roles played by the different groupings. To make sense of these lists, I have sorted them into three categories. The categories are of my own devising and are not mentioned as such either in the canonical texts or the commentaries. However, though the groups should not be thought of as rigidly exclusive, the classification seems to stand up to examination.

(1) The first class are the defilements responsible for *flawed behavior*. These are the underlying motives of misconduct and unwholesome kamma. The most important of such groups are the three unwholesome roots: greed (or lust), hatred, and delusion, referred to above in the discussion of kamma. They are often mentioned as the causes of bodily, verbal, and mental misconduct, and they are also explicitly aligned with the ten courses of unwholesome action (**10:174**). The three roots are sometimes expanded to "four wrong courses" (**4:17–20**)—desire, hatred, delusion, and fear—when motives for biased decisions are taken up for consideration.

Sexual desire is a defilement of crucial concern to monastics, who are committed to a life of celibacy and thus need to curb and master their sexual urges. The Buddha often speaks about the dangers in sensual pleasures and cautions the monks about forming close bonds with members of the opposite sex (**5:225–26**). In a monastic community that brings together people with sharply differing personalities and strong opinions, anger and resentment can also have a corrosive effect on group dynamics, and thus the Buddha and his chief disciples prescribe methods to dispel these disruptive emotions (**5:161–62**; **9:29–30**;

10:79–80). Anger and hostility jointly form the first of six "roots of dispute," which the Buddha saw as a danger to the harmony of the Saṅgha (**6:36**). Since monastics are in principle taught to share their gains—whether material things, lay supporters, or knowledge—the Buddha enumerated five kinds of miserliness that must be uprooted to ensure that everyone in the community gets to fulfill their potential (**5:115**, **5:224**). Laypeople, too, are instructed to dwell at home "with a mind devoid of the stain of miserliness, freely generous, openhanded, delighting in relinquishment, devoted to charity, delighting in giving and sharing" (**6:10**).

(2) The second class of defilements in this threefold scheme are those that *impede the success of meditation*. The most elementary in this group is the simplest: sheer laziness, resistance to the work of "arousing energy for the attainment of the as-yet-unattained, for the achievement of the as-yet-unachieved, for the realization of the as-yet-unrealized" (**8:80**). Once a meditator overcomes laziness and makes the endeavor to meditate, the defilements he or she is likely to encounter fall into a set known as the five hindrances, so called because they are "obstructions, hindrances, encumbrances of the mind, states that weaken wisdom." They even prevent one from knowing one's own good and the good of others (**5:51**). The Buddha condemns them as "a complete heap of the unwholesome" (**5:52**) and compares them to corruptions of gold (**5:23**) and impurities in a bowl of water (**5:193**). A series of suttas at the beginning of AN explains the principal triggers for each of the five hindrances and the most effective contemplative techniques for subduing them (**1:11–20**).

The Aṅguttara mentions other sets of defilements that obstruct meditation practice. These include the three kinds of unwholesome thoughts (**4:11**), the five kinds of mental barrenness (**5:205**), and the five mental bondages (**5:206**). These can more or less be correlated with the five hindrances. All these defilements are overcome, tentatively, through the successful practice of serenity meditation, which reaches fulfillment in *samādhi*, mental collectedness or concentration.

(3) The defilements of the third type are the deepest and the most obstinate. These are the defilements lodged at the base of the stream of consciousness that *maintain bondage to the cycle of*

rebirths. Such defilements lie dormant in the mind even when the meditator achieves exalted states of concentration. They can be removed only by the development of wisdom, by insight that penetrates deep into the truth of the Dhamma. In the language of the Pāli commentaries, they are totally eradicated only by the "supramundane" or world-transcending paths (*lokuttaramagga*), states of consciousness that break through the barriers of conditioned reality and penetrate the unconditioned nibbāna.

The most primordial of these fundamental defilements are called the *āsavas*, inadequately translated as "taints." These consist of craving for sensual pleasures, craving for continued existence, and ignorance (**6:63 §4**). They are fully eradicated only with the attainment of arahantship, and thus the fruit of arahantship is described as "the taintless liberation of mind, liberation by wisdom achieved with the destruction of the taints." Other groups of fundamental defilements include the four bonds (**4:10**), identical in content with the three *āsavas* but augmented by the bond of views;[7] the seven underlying tendencies (**7:11–12**); and the ten fetters, whose eradication in clusters marks the attainment of the successive stages of awakening (**10:13**). The three unwholesome roots—lust, hatred, and delusion—also operate at this level and thus must be uprooted to gain liberation. All these defilements fall under the dominion of ignorance and craving for existence, which drive the process of saṃsāra forward from one existence to the next (**3:76–77**). Final liberation therefore ultimately depends on eliminating ignorance and craving, which occurs through the world-transcendent wisdom that deeply discerns the four noble truths.

The Path of Renunciation

Although the Buddha taught the Dhamma openly and broadly to both renunciants and laypeople, he gave special attention to those who followed him from the household life into homelessness to pursue the goal that he himself had realized. Thus the full range of Dhamma practice is incorporated into the systematic training of the bhikkhu or bhikkhunī. The graduated course of monastic training is treated in greatest detail in the Dīgha and Majjhima Nikāyas, but the same sequence also appears once in AN (**4:198**).

The precondition for the training is the arising of the Tathāgata and his proclamation of the Dhamma. Having heard the teaching, the student acquires faith and goes forth into the homeless life. Now a bhikkhu, he undertakes the ethical discipline of a renunciant, which requires a life of harmlessness and purity in bodily and verbal action. He should be content with the simplest requisites, yet without priding himself on his austerity (**4:28**). To facilitate the passage to concentration, he practices restraint of the sense faculties and exercises mindfulness and clear comprehension in all activities. Other texts on the monastic training mention two other measures that fit into this phase: moderation in eating and wakefulness (**3:16, 4:37**). The bhikkhu resorts to a secluded dwelling place, cleanses his mind of the five hindrances, and masters the four jhānas, the stages of deep concentration. He then directs the concentrated mind toward the three kinds of higher knowledge: the recollection of past lives, perception of the passing away and rebirth of beings, and the penetration of the four noble truths. This process reaches consummation in the liberation of the mind from the *āsavas*.

Another sutta, **10:99**, begins with the same series of preparatory steps, but from the attainment of the four jhānas it proceeds to the four formless meditative attainments: the base of the infinity of space, the base of the infinity of consciousness, the base of nothingness, and the base of neither-perception-nor-non-perception. From there the meditator continues to the "cessation of perception and feeling"—also known as the attainment of cessation—on emerging from which he "sees with wisdom" and attains the destruction of the *āsavas*. In this version of the training, the first two higher knowledges are not mentioned, and the process of mental development is continued through all nine meditative attainments. Yet, despite this difference, both conclude with the destruction of the *āsavas*.

Though AN shares this comprehensive description of the monastic training with other Nikāyas, it includes formulations that seem to be specific, if not entirely unique, to itself. One such is the threefold training: the higher virtuous behavior, the higher mind (of concentration), and the higher wisdom (**3:81–90**). Of particular interest in this series of texts is a pair of suttas stating that a monk can fall into offenses regarding the lesser and minor training rules, undergo rehabilitation, and attain the four stages of awakening (**3:86–87**). What he upholds firmly are "those training rules that are fundamental to the spiritual life, in conformity with the spiritual life." These two suttas also correlate the threefold training with the four stages of awakening: the stream-enterer and once-returner fulfill virtuous behavior but not the other two trainings, the non-returner fulfills virtue and concentration but not wisdom, and the arahant fulfills all three trainings.

Another perspective on the sequential course of practice is offered by a series of "expanded parallels" that begins in the Fives (with **5:24**) and continues with augmentation into later *nipātas* as far as the Elevens. This series can be stratified in terms of the threefold training and its culmination in liberation, but it exhibits the finer transitional stages that lie between the main stages. Thus in the most complete version (**11:3**), it proceeds from virtuous behavior to non-regret, thence in steps to joy, rapture, tranquility, pleasure, concentration, knowledge and vision of things as they really are, disenchantment, dispassion, and the knowledge and vision of liberation. Presumably, liberation itself should be wedged in after dispassion, but this would require a Book of Twelves.

The monastic quest does not always culminate in the nirvanic realization that inspired the monk to embark on the life of renunciation. The Nikāyas show a keen awareness of human weakness and thus ring precautionary alarms. One sutta mentions four "perils" that face a clansman who has "gone forth out of faith from the household life into homelessness": anger at being instructed by younger monks, craving for food that is frustrated by the regulations governing meals, attraction to the five kinds of sensual pleasure, and the encounter with seductive women (**4:122**). Another discourse says that any bhikkhu or bhikkhunī who gives up the training and reverts to lay life does so because of insufficient faith, moral shame, moral dread, energy, and wisdom (**5:5**). And two long discourses compare the bhikkhu who is deflected from the training to a warrior defeated in battle. In one case the cause is "a woman or a girl who is beautiful, attractive, graceful, possessing supreme beauty of complexion" (**5:75**). In the other it is the passion that arises from seeing women on alms round "with their dress in disarray and loosely attired" (**5:76**). The Aṅguttara shows that while the Buddha had deep trust in the capacity of human beings to triumph over all bonds and fetters, he was not oblivious to the difficulty of the endeavor or to the strength and cunning of the defilements that have to be confronted and vanquished.

Meditation

The heart of the monastic life is the practice of what we call *meditation*, the methodical effort to tame and master the mind and to develop its capacity for calm and insight. The training begins with the undeveloped mind, clouded and unruly, beset by passions and defilements. It ends in the liberated mind, tranquil, tamed, bright and luminous, freed from defilements and bondage to repeated existence.

Methods of mental cultivation fall into two categories, serenity (*samatha*) and insight (*vipassanā*); the former is considered the means to develop concentration, the latter the means to develop wisdom. Serenity brings the tentative abandoning of lust and results in liberation of mind. Insight brings the abandoning of ignorance and results in liberation by wisdom (**2:31**). Jointly, "liberation of mind" and "liberation by wisdom" constitute arahantship, the final goal.

Although the usual sequence of meditative training proceeds from concentration to wisdom, several suttas in AN show that meditators can choose various routes to reach the world-transcending path. The disciple Ānanda states that all those who attain arahantship do so in one of four ways: either by developing serenity first and then insight (the standard sequence), by developing insight first and then serenity, by developing the two in conjunction, and by emerging from "restlessness about the Dhamma" and achieving a unified mind (**4:170**). Another sutta advises one who gains either serenity or insight (but not the other) to seek out a teacher who can give instructions on obtaining the missing factor; one who gains neither should seek instructions on gaining both; while one who gains both should develop them to capacity to reach the destruction of the *āsavas* (**4:94**).

The subjects of meditation mentioned in AN are many and diverse. Like the other Nikāyas, AN does not give detailed instructions on the technology of meditation, but it introduces a wide variety of meditation subjects. Apparently these had to be diverse to accommodate the different dispositions of the people who came to the Buddha for instruction. The Book of the Ones includes a virtual "catalogue" of themes and attainments pertaining to meditation practice, all set forth in connection with what makes a bhikkhu worthy to receive almsfood (**1:394–575**). The same *nipāta* concludes with an extended paean to mindfulness of the body (**1:575–627**), declared to be the key to realizing the deathless.

Suttas in AN describe many of the familiar meditation subjects that receive more detailed treatment in such works as the *Visuddhimagga*. We find here mindfulness of breathing (**10:60 §10**), the six devotional recollections (**6:10, 6:25**), loving-kindness (**8:1, 11:15**) along with all four immeasurables or "divine abodes" (**3:65, 8:63**), and mindfulness of death (**6:19–20, 8:73–74**). Walking meditation is praised for bringing five benefits (**5:29**). Of particular interest is the emphasis AN places on the "perceptions" (*saññā*), meditation subjects that initially involve a fair amount of reflection rather than bare mindful observation. AN **7:49**, for instance, mentions seven perceptions, which are said to "culminate in the deathless, to have the deathless as their consummation." The seven are the perception of unattractiveness, the perception of death, the perception of the repulsiveness of food, the perception of non-delight in the entire world, the perception of impermanence, the perception of suffering in the impermanent, and the perception of non-self in what is suffering. Each of these perceptions is then connected to a specific distorted perception or inclination that it counteracts. Thus the perception of unattractiveness eliminates desire for sexual intercourse, the perception of death counters attachment to life, the perception of the repulsiveness of food causes the mind to shrink away from craving for tastes. The popular Girimānanda Sutta describes ten perceptions, which the Buddha instructs Ānanda to recite in order to restore the health of the bhikkhu Girimānanda, who was afflicted with a grave illness (**10:60**).

Some of the meditation subjects mentioned in AN pertain, in traditional Theravāda exegesis, to the development of serenity, others to the development of insight. What is interesting in AN, however, is that while serenity and insight are treated as distinct domains of meditation with their own points of emphasis and fruits, a hard and fast line is not drawn between meditation subjects as pertaining to the one or the other. It is quite conceivable that in the Buddha's own view of meditation, serenity and insight represent not two separate categories of meditation objects but two complementary subjective orientations that can be developed on the basis of the same set of meditation objects.

In AN the higher states of consciousness achieved through meditation are often mentioned. The most frequent, of course, are the four jhānas. In addition we also come across such sets as the eight bases of overcoming (**8:65**), the eight emancipations (**8:66**), and the nine progressive abidings (**9:31–61**). Success in meditation is sometimes shown to culminate in the three true knowledges, the *tevijjā* (**3:58–59**), which the Buddha himself attained on the night of his enlightenment (**8:11**). Elsewhere meditation brings attainment of the six kinds of superior knowledge later known as the *abhiññās* (**3:101–2, 5:23, 6:2**). Five of these involve psychic powers, while the sixth is the world-transcending knowledge of the destruction of the *āsavas*.

Wisdom

When pursued as an end in itself, deep concentration is accompanied by exalted joy, bliss, calm, and equanimity. These experiences can convince the unwary meditator that he has reached the final goal and discovered "the nirvanic peace within." Such lofty states, however, are achieved simply through the intensification of consciousness, not through the deep insight that cuts off the bonds of repeated existence. The superior states of concentration generate powerful wholesome kamma, which can lead to rebirth in the form or formless realm—the realms of super-divine stature—depending on the attainments reached during the meditator's human existence. Without the deep discernment of wisdom, this kamma will eventually be exhausted, and the divine being will pass away and take rebirth elsewhere, perhaps even in the bad destinations (**3:116, 4:123–26**). For the path to reach completion and culminate in the deathless, it must eventually bring forth wisdom. Thus the Buddha praises wisdom as the foremost splendor, radiance, light, luster, and luminary (**4:141–45**).

Despite the analogy with light, however, wisdom does not flare up suddenly and spontaneously through pious good wishes; rather, it is gradually begotten by following a prescribed course of training. One sutta enumerates eight conditions for acquiring and maturing the wisdom that pertains to the spiritual life (**8:2**). These include relying on a teacher, asking questions to clear away one's doubts, observing the rules of discipline, learning and reflection, and contemplating the arising and vanishing of the five aggregates. Another supporting factor for the growth of wisdom is right view. The Buddha assigned right view to the first place among the factors of the noble eightfold path and the ten kinds of rightness (**10:103**). From right view originate the other nine factors, ending in right knowledge and right liberation (**10:105**).

Learning and investigating the Dhamma also contribute to the growth of wisdom. Among the four Nikāyas, it is perhaps AN that places the greatest emphasis on learning. Learning is described as one of the five kinds of wealth (**5:47**) and as a quality that makes a bhikkhu respected and esteemed by his fellow monks (**5:87**). Of course, a disciple who has learned just a little but puts what he or she has learned into practice is superior to one who learns much without applying it (**4:6**). But learning does possess intrinsic value, and those who excel in learning and also obtain the four jhānas and the three true knowledges are regarded as especially worthy of respect (**10:97**). Mastery over the Dhamma qualifies one to teach, so that one can not only expedite one's own progress but also promote the good of others (**8:62**).

The suttas of AN do not merely praise learning but provide concrete instructions on *how* to learn and teach the Dhamma. Since the Dhamma was always conveyed orally, not in written documents, the texts emphasize the need for both attentive listening and retention. One who does not attend closely is like an inverted bowl, which cannot hold water; one who attends but does not retain what has been learned is like a man who upsets the contents of his lap; while the one who both attends to discourses and retains what has been learned preserves it for a long time, just as an upright bowl long retains water (**3:30**). Ānanda, the most learned of the bhikkhus, mentions six factors conducive to mastery of the Dhamma, among them learning many discourses, teaching others, and visiting elders to clear up points one does not fully understand (**6:51**).

Listening to the Dhamma can serve as an occasion for entering the irreversible path to final liberation, but to gain this benefit one has to listen properly. This means that one has to listen with a respectful and open mind, not with a mind intent on finding faults and disparaging the discourse and the speaker (**5:151–53**). Listening and teaching can even precipitate the attainment of liberation. While listening to the Dhamma, teaching it, reciting it, or examining its meaning, one may gain inspiration, experience joy, and set in motion a process that ends in full liberation from the *āsavas* (**5:28**). Learning, however, should be accompanied by practice. Thus the Buddha urges the monks not to spend all their time on study, teaching, recitation, and reflection but to go apart and devote themselves to the development of internal serenity and experiential wisdom (**5:73–74**).

Learning and teaching play a vital role in ensuring the longevity of the Dhamma. The Dhamma declines and disappears, says one sutta, when the bhikkhus do not respectfully listen to it, learn it, retain it in mind, examine the meaning, and put it into practice; it continues without degeneration when the bhikkhus are devoted to learning, reflection, and practice (**5:154**). Other suttas stress the importance of teaching and making others recite the texts (**5:155**). When teaching, one has to select the appropriate topic, assessing the interests and expectations of the audience, and then give a talk that matches their inclinations (**5:157**). The Buddha prescribes five guidelines for a teacher of the Dhamma: he should give a talk that follows a progressive sequence; he should provide reasons to support his assertions; he should have empathy with his audience; he should not be intent on material gain; and he should not say anything harmful to himself or others (**5:159**).

Penetrative wisdom is not a matter of merely mastering a body of texts or a system of ideas but of seeing into the true nature of phenomena. The principles to be seen with wisdom are the "three characteristics" of impermanence, suffering, and non-self. We are told that whether Tathāgatas arise in the world or not, this fixed law remains: that all conditioned phenomena are impermanent; that all conditioned phenomena are suffering; and that all phenomena whatsoever are non-self (**3:136**).

To see the true nature of phenomena thus means to see them as impermanent, suffering, and non-self. Normally, our minds are subject to perceptual and conceptual distortion, so that we construe things as being permanent, pleasurable, and self. However obvious these notions seem to us, the texts describe them as an inversion of perception and as forms of cognitive derangement (**4:49**). The task of insight is to correct this distortion by contemplating things "as they really are," that is, as impermanent, suffering, and non-self (**7:16–18**). Interestingly, several suttas in AN add a fourth theme of contemplation: contemplating nibbāna as happiness (**6:101**, **7:19**).

Contemplation of conditioned phenomena as impermanent and suffering, contemplation of all phenomena as non-self, and contemplation of nibbāna as happiness enable the disciple to acquire "a conviction in conformity" with the Dhamma (*anulomikā khanti*). This prepares the mind for still deeper insight, and when that insight becomes aligned with the Dhamma itself, it induces entry upon "the fixed course of rightness" (*sammattaniyāma*), the world-transcending path that leads unfailingly to the four stages of awakening (**6:98–101**).

The Buddha insisted that the ultimate goal of his teaching was the extinction of suffering in this very life, and for this reason he constantly urged the bhikkhus not to remain satisfied with any partial achievement but to press on toward the final goal. He enjoined them to resolve: "I will not relax my energy so long as I have not attained what can be attained by manly strength, energy, and exertion" (**2:5**). Two suttas in AN give us an inside glimpse of the contemplative process by which the disciple realizes the final goal. One discourse explains that a bhikkhu enters any of the four jhānas or lower three formless attainments and contemplates its constituents—the five aggregates comprised in the attainment (four aggregates in the formless attainments)—as impermanent, suffering, an illness, a boil, a dart, misery, affliction, alien, disintegrating, empty, and non-self. At a certain point he turns his mind away from those phenomena and directs it to the deathless element, nibbāna. On this basis he attains either the destruction of the *āsavas*, that is, arahantship, or if he cannot complete the work, the stage of non-returner (**9:36**). The other sutta is spoken by Ānanda to a lay devotee who has asked how a bhikkhu reaches the destruction of the taints. Ānanda explains that the bhikkhu enters any of the four jhānas, the four immeasurables (loving-kindness, compassion, altruistic joy, and equanimity), or the three lower formless attainments. He then reviews the attainment as "constructed and produced by volition," and observes: "Whatever is constructed and produced by volition is impermanent, subject to cessation." In this case, too, he attains either arahantship or non-returning (**11:16**).

The Saṅgha

According to traditional exegesis, the word *saṅgha* is used in two senses: as a designation for the monastic order consisting of bhikkhus and bhikkhunīs, sometimes called the "institutional Saṅgha" or "conventional Saṅgha" (*sammutisaṅgha*), and as a designation for the "community of noble ones" (*ariyasaṅgha*), which consists of the eight types of noble persons, the four pairs of those who have attained the world-transcending paths and fruits. On the basis of this distinction it is then said that the conventional Saṅgha consists only of monastics, whether noble ones or ordinary people, while the noble Saṅgha is said to include laypeople who have attained the paths and fruits as well as monastics. In AN a distinction between these two kinds of Saṅgha is discernible, but the boundaries between them are not as clear-cut as tradition makes them out to be. First, whenever new converts to the Dhamma declare that they go for refuge, they state the third object of refuge to be the "Saṅgha of bhikkhus" (presumably also including bhikkhunīs). This shows that they (or, more likely, the compilers of the texts) understood the monastic community to be the third refuge. Second, the formula for the noble Saṅgha describes it in terms that apply more readily to renunciants than to householders: it is "worthy of gifts, worthy of hospitality, worthy of offerings, worthy of reverential salutation." Such an encomium again establishes a connection between the monastic Saṅgha and the noble Saṅgha.

However, one sutta speaks of "four kinds of persons who adorn the Saṅgha." These are well-disciplined and learned bhikkhus, bhikkhunīs, male lay followers, and female lay followers (**4:7**; see too **4:211**). This suggests that the word *saṅgha* even in the conventional sense can include laypeople, unless one understands the statement to mean that bhikkhus and bhikkhunīs adorn the Saṅgha as its members while laypeople adorn it as its supporters. In any case, almost everywhere else when the texts speak about the Saṅgha without specific reference to the noble ones, the monastic order (or subgroups within it) is intended.

Several AN suttas show that the monastic Saṅgha did not always measure up to the criteria the Buddha had set for it. In **2:42–51** a series of contrasts is drawn between pairs of assemblies, one censurable, the other laudable. The two assemblies are specifically described in terms of bhikkhus. The censurable arm of each pair includes the shallow assembly, in which the bhikkhus are "restless, puffed up, and vain"; the inferior assembly, in which they are luxurious and lax; the dregs of an assembly, in which they enter a wrong course on account of desire, hatred, delusion, or fear; and the assembly that values worldly things, not the good Dhamma. Heedlessness and worldliness were not the only problems that the Buddha had to deal with in the monastic order. Scattered throughout AN are references to quarrels and disputes among the bhikkhus. Thus we read about situations when the bhikkhus had taken to "arguing and quarreling and fell into a dispute, stabbing each other with piercing words" (**10:50**; see too **2:43**, **3:124**). On some occasions the threat of schism cast its shadow. To forestall this danger, the Buddha proposed six guidelines to promote cordial relationships among the bhikkhus (**6:12**), and he urged them to assemble often and conduct the affairs of the Saṅgha in harmony (**7:23**). He also cautioned them about six roots of disputes that had to be extirpated whenever they arose (**6:36**). Yet despite the faults of its members, the Buddha had high regard for the monastic Saṅgha. He praised the Saṅgha of diligent bhikkhus as an unsurpassed field of merit worth traveling many miles to see (**4:190**), and he was pleased when he saw monks living "in concord, harmoniously, without disputes, blending like milk and water, viewing each other with eyes of affection" (**10:50**).

The monastic Saṅgha not only provided optimal conditions for those intent on leading the spiritual life in full earnestness, but it also served as a field of blessings and a channel for spreading the Buddha's teachings to the lay community.

Bhikkhus and bhikkhunīs offered laypeople the opportunity to gain merit by supporting them with robes, almsfood, dwellings, and medicine. The monastics also used their encounters with laypeople as opportunities to teach the Dhamma to the people in the homes, villages, and towns that they visited. Hence the Buddha laid strong emphasis on the need for both partners in this symbiotic relationship to fulfill their respective duties. The monastics are obliged to provide an inspiring model of disciplined conduct to the laity, behaving in such a way that "those without confidence gain confidence and those with confidence increase in their confidence" (**8:54**; see too **4:245 §1**). The lay community is responsible for seeing to the material needs of the monastics. In doing so, they are expected to act with proper etiquette, saluting the monastic disciples respectfully, offering them a seat, giving generously, and showing solicitude for their well-being (**7:13**). The lay devotees should also sit close by to listen to the Dhamma and savor the flavor of the words (**9:17**).

The noble Saṅgha consists of eight types of noble persons, who are joined into four pairs in relation to the four stages of awakening. The two members of each pair are the one who has attained the stage itself and the one who has entered the path leading irreversibly toward that stage. They are stated concisely thus: "The stream-enterer, the one practicing for realization of the fruit of stream-entry; the once-returner, the one practicing for realization of the fruit of once-returning; the non-returner, the one practicing for realization of the fruit of non-returning; the arahant, the one practicing for realization of the fruit of arahantship" (**8:59**). In one sutta another term is added to the list of eight, the *gotrabhū* or "clan member" (**9:10**; see too **10:16**). Strangely, the relationship of this figure to the others is not explained in the Nikāyas. The commentaries interpret this term through the lens of the later Theravādin exegetical system, according to which *gotrabhū* refers to the single mind-moment that makes the transition from the peak of insight to the world-transcending path. But this explanation presupposes the development of technical schemes not discernible in the Nikāyas, and it is therefore unlikely to represent the term's original meaning.

The four main stages are distinguished by the fetters that they eliminate and the number of rebirths that remain for those who attain them (see **3:86**, **4:210**). With the destruction of the three lower fetters (see **10:13**), the disciple becomes a stream-enterer (*sotāpanna*), no longer subject to rebirth in the three lower realms and bound to reach liberation in a maximum of seven more lives, passed either in the human realm or in the deva world. With the destruction of three fetters and the additional diminishing of greed, hatred, and delusion, one becomes a once-returner (*sakadāgāmī*), who comes back to this world one more time and then makes an end of suffering. With the destruction of all five lower fetters, the disciple becomes a non-returner (*anāgāmī*), who takes spontaneous rebirth in the form realm (usually in a special region called the *pure abodes*) and attains final nibbāna there without returning from that world. And with the complete destruction of the taints, the disciple becomes an arahant, a fully liberated one.[8]

Though the explanations in the texts are often phrased in terms of bhikkhus, laypeople are also able to attain the first three fruits and even the fourth. In the last case, however, tradition says that they either attain arahantship on the verge of death or almost at once leave the household life for homelessness. We find in AN the testimony of several lay non-returners. Thus the laywoman Nandamātā insinuates that she is a non-returner (at **7:53**), as do Ugga of Vesālī and Ugga of Hatthigāma (at **8:21** and **8:22**, respectively). The Sixes (**6:119–39**) mention a large number of male lay followers who have "reached certainty about the Tathāgata and become seers of the deathless," a phrase that implies that they are noble disciples (but not arahants). Many female lay followers are elsewhere confirmed as winners of the noble fruits.

Another method of distinguishing the noble ones into seven types is mentioned at **7:14**, where they are simply listed without explanation; explanations are found in MN 70. The seven are the one liberated in both respects, the one liberated by wisdom, the body witness, the one attained to view, the one liberated by faith, the Dhamma follower, and the faith follower. The first two are arahants, who are distinguished in that the former can also attain the "peaceful formless emancipations" (the formless meditations and the attainment of cessation) while the latter cannot. The middle three are types of *sekhas*, disciples in higher training, who are distinguished according to their dominant faculty. The first excels in concentration, the second in wisdom, the third in faith. As **3:21** points out, these three cannot be ranked against one another in terms of superiority, since each can comprise anyone ranging from a stream-enterer to a person on the path to arahantship. The Dhamma follower and the faith follower are two types who have entered the path to stream-entry but have not yet attained the fruit. They are distinguished respectively by whether their dominant faculty is wisdom or faith. At the end of **7:56**, the Buddha mentions another "seventh person" in place of the faith follower. This type is called "one who dwells in the markless" (*animittavihārī*), a term unexplained in the sutta itself and never taken up for elaboration in the post-canonical Buddhist tradition. The commentary simply identifies this figure with the faith follower, but that may be an attempt to fit unusual ideas into the slots of an established system.

The ideal spiritual figure of AN, as of the Nikāyas as a whole, is the arahant, who is called "the best among devas and humans: one who has reached the ultimate conclusion, won ultimate security from bondage, lived the ultimate spiritual life, and gained the ultimate consummation" (**3:143, 11:10**). The arahants "have destroyed the taints, lived the spiritual life, done what had to be done, laid down the burden, reached their own goal, utterly destroyed the fetters of existence, and are completely liberated through final knowledge" (**6:49, 9:7**). They are "devoid of lust through the destruction of lust; devoid of hatred through the destruction of hatred; devoid of delusion through the destruction of delusion" (**6:55**). They are no longer subject to return to any realm of existence, whether sense-sphere existence, form-sphere existence, or formless-sphere existence (**9:25**). They enter and dwell in the taintless liberation of mind, the liberation by wisdom, and on their passing away attain final nibbāna.

Though all arahants are alike in their eradication of all defilements and their liberation from saṃsāra, AN introduces an interesting distinction between two kinds of arahants. One, the "white-lotus ascetic" (*puṇḍarīkasamaṇa*), does not attain the eight emancipations, while the other, the "red-lotus ascetic" (*padumasamaṇa*), does so. The commentary interprets the first type as one who attains none of the eight emancipations, and thus as a dry-insight arahant (*sukkhavipassaka*), who attains arahantship without attainment of the jhānas. This figure is not explicitly found in the Nikāyas, and thus questions may be raised whether the commentary is not reading into the text an idea arisen from a later period. An interpretation that accords better with such suttas as MN 70 would regard the white-lotus ascetic as the arahant "liberated by wisdom" (*paññāvimutta*), who can attain the four jhānas but not the formless emancipations, while the red-lotus ascetic would be the arahant "liberated in both respects" (*ubhatobhāgavimutta*). In addition to the jhānas and the formless emancipations, some arahants attain the "three true knowledges": knowledge of past lives, knowledge of the passing away and rebirth of beings, and knowledge of the destruction of the *āsavas* (**3:58**). Still others attain six superior knowledges, which include, in addition to the three just mentioned, the psychic powers, the divine ear, and the knowledge of the minds of others (**6:2**).

Types of Persons

The Aṅguttara is distinguished among the four Nikāyas by its interest in defining and describing types of persons. These classifications are not proposed from the standpoint of objective psychological analysis but in order to relate different types of persons to the values and goals of the Dhamma. Most, but not all, of the distinctions are drawn among monastics and are put forward as pairs or groups with three or more types.

We thus find distinctions drawn between such personality types as the fool and the wise person, the bad person and the good person, the blameworthy monk and the esteemed monk. This last pair is sometimes painted in finer detail by describing more fully the characteristics of the monk who is incorrigibly evil and the monk held up as an exemplar. Similar distinctions are drawn between laypersons, so that we have laypeople of bad intent and those who serve as examples for the lay community.

One distinction drawn among persons should dispel a misconception about early Buddhism that in recent years has receded but may not be completely extinct: namely, that in its stress on personal responsibility it was narrowly individualistic. In later times, this misconception (which might have been fostered by attitudes that prevailed in certain sections of the Saṅgha) led to the designation Hīnayāna, or "Little Vehicle," being ascribed to the schools that adhered to the ancient scriptures. A series of suttas, **4:95–99**, distinguishes persons into four types ranked by way of ascending excellence: (1) one who is practicing neither for his own welfare nor for the welfare of others; (2) one who is practicing for the welfare of others but not for his own welfare; (3) one who is practicing for his own welfare but not for the welfare of others; and (4) one who is practicing both for his own welfare and for the welfare of others. The text not only rates the fourth as best but commends it in superlatives as "the foremost, the best, the preeminent, the supreme, and the finest of these four persons." Another series of suttas, **5:17–20**, explains how a bhikkhu can practice for his own welfare and the welfare of others. And still another sutta broadens the altruistic motivation further, concluding that a person of great wisdom "thinks only of his own welfare, the welfare of others, the welfare of both, and the welfare of the whole world" (**4:186**).

Bhikkhunīs and Women in the Aṅguttara Nikāya

Although most of the suttas in AN are addressed to bhikkhus and describe their subjects as such, they occasionally feature bhikkhunīs, fully ordained nuns, as their protagonists or subjects. We find in AN the story of the origins of the Bhikkhunī Saṅgha (**8:51**) as preserved also in the Cūḷavagga of the Vinaya. The story is controversial: first, because of the Buddha's initial reluctance to allow women to enter the homeless life; and second, because, after giving them permission to go forth, he declares that the ordination of women will have a corrosive effect on the teaching, shortening its life span from a thousand years to five hundred years. Whether such an account is historically trustworthy has been questioned by modern-day scholars, for it contains anachronisms hard to reconcile with other chronological information in the canon and commentaries. But the sutta has been responsible for a distrustful attitude toward bhikkhunīs in Theravāda countries and may explain why conservative elders have resisted the revival of the Bhikkhunī Saṅgha currently taking place in such countries as Sri Lanka and Thailand.

AN includes, in the sequence on foremost disciples, a section on outstanding bhikkhunīs. But whereas the section on bhikkhus consists of four vaggas containing forty-seven categories (several occupied by the same person), that on bhikkhunīs contains only one vagga with thirteen names. Perhaps this was because the number of bhikkhunīs was much smaller than the number of bhikkhus, but it may also reflect the biases of the age and perhaps attitudes that prevailed in the school that preserved the Pāli Canon. It seems that the Ekottarāgama of the Chinese Tripiṭaka, stemming from another early school, includes many more bhikkhunīs among the eminent disciples.

At **7:56** the Buddha reports that two deities informed him that a number of bhikkhunīs have been "well liberated without residue remaining." In **8:53**, he explains to the bhikkhunī Mahāpajāpati Gotamī the eight qualities distinctive of the proper Dhamma and discipline. In **10:28** a "bhikkhunī from Kajaṅgalā" responds to ten numerical questions. When her answers are related to the Buddha, he says: "The bhikkhunī of Kajaṅgalā is wise, of great wisdom. If you had asked me about this matter, I would have answered exactly as she has done."

But it is not only in favorable terms that AN speaks about bhikkhunīs. A series of six suttas, **5:115–20**, explains various causes for bhikkhunīs to be reborn in hell. She is miserly, she criticizes and praises others indiscriminately, she squanders gifts given out of faith, she is envious, holds wrong views, speaks and acts wrongly, and so on. It is puzzling that the text should single out bhikkhunīs for such stern remarks, but perhaps they were seen as necessary precautions. In any case, at **5:236–40** the same statements are made about bhikkhus.

Among the four Nikāyas, AN has the largest number of suttas addressed to women,[9] but a small number of discourses in the collection testify to a misogynistic attitude that strikes us as discordant, distasteful, and simply unjustified. These texts depict women as driven by powerful passions that impair their abilities and undermine their morals. At **2:61**, the Buddha declares that women are never satiated in two things: sexual intercourse and giving birth. When Ānanda asks why women do not sit on councils, engage in business, or travel to distant regions, the Buddha answers that this is because they are full of anger, envious, miserly, and devoid of wisdom (**4:80**). Two suttas compare women to a black snake (**5:229–30**) in that they are "wrathful, hostile, of deadly venom, double-tongued, and betray friends." Their venom is their strong lust, their double tongue is their proclivity to slander, and they betray friends in that "for the most part women are adulterous." In **5:55** we read about a mother and son who were ordained as bhikkhunī and bhikkhu. They continued to keep close company, fell in love, and indulged in sexual relations with one another. When this was reported to the Buddha, he is shown laying the blame on women: "If one could rightly say of anything that it is entirely a snare of Māra, it is precisely of women that one might say this."

Whether these statements should really be attributed to the Buddha or regarded as interpolations by monastic editors is a question that may not be possible to settle with complete certainty. Such statements, however, are surely contrary to the more liberal spirit displayed elsewhere in the Nikāyas. Moreover, in a text like AN, with its many short suttas, it would have been relatively easy for monks, apprehensive about their own sexuality or the spiritual potentials of women, to insert such passages into the canon. These suttas do not have counterparts in the Chinese Āgamas, but that fact on its own is inconclusive; for many suttas in the Pāli Aṅguttara Nikāya are without counterparts in the Chinese canon. Other suttas in AN that deal with sexuality show a more symmetrical approach, such as **1:1–10**, **7:51**, and **8:17–18**, where the sexual attractions of men toward women and of women toward men are precisely balanced.

Quite in contrast to the suttas with a misogynistic tone are others that show the Buddha acting cordially toward women and generously bestowing his teaching upon them. He teaches the lay devotee Visākhā how the uposatha observance can be of great fruit and benefit (**3:70, 8:43**). He teaches Suppavāsā the merits of giving food (**4:57**). He explains to Queen Mallikā, the wife of King Pasenadi, the karmic causes through which women can achieve beauty, wealth, and influence (**4:197**). He answers the questions of the princess Cundī on the best kinds of confidence and virtuous behavior (**5:32**). He instructs a group of girls about to be married on how to behave when they go to live with their husbands (**5:33**), and he instructs a boisterous wife about the seven kinds of wives (**7:63**). He explains to Visākhā how a woman is heading to victory both in this world and the next (**8:49**). He extols the bhikkhunīs Khemā and Uppalavaṇṇā as models for his bhikkhunī followers and the female lay devotees Khujjuttarā and Veḷukaṇṭakī Nandamātā as models for his female lay disciples (**4:176**). It is hard to reconcile such texts, which display a friendly and empathetic attitude toward women, with the passages that categorically denigrate their capacities.

The Repetition Series

Each of the *nipātas* from the Twos to the Elevens concludes with a "Lust and So Forth Repetition Series" (*rāgādipeyyāla*).[10] This is created by establishing permutations among three sequences of terms. One is a list of seventeen defilements: lust, hatred, delusion, anger, hostility, denigration, insolence, envy, miserliness, deceitfulness, craftiness, obstinacy, vehemence, conceit, arrogance, intoxication, and heedlessness. The second is a series of ten terms showing the tasks that are to be fulfilled in relation to these seventeen defilements: direct knowledge, full understanding, utter destruction, abandoning, destruction, vanishing, fading away, cessation, giving up, and relinquishment. The first two are complementary cognitive operations; the other eight are synonyms for eradication by world-transcending wisdom. Taken in combination, we obtain an initial total of 170 operations.

The third sequence of terms consists of sets of practices that fall under the numerical rubric of the *nipāta*. These may be as few as one or as many as five. Each set of practices is applied to each of the 170 operations, generating a sutta for each possibility. The Twos and Threes each have only one set of practices: the pair of serenity and insight in the Twos and the three kinds of concentration in the Threes. Thus in each of these two *nipātas* only 170 suttas are generated. But the Fours have three practice sets: the four establishments of mindfulness, the four right strivings, and the four bases of psychic potency. So this *nipāta* generates 510 suttas. The Fives have five practice sets, which generates the maximum number of repetition suttas: 850. Several nipātas have three sets, generating 510 suttas each. On account of the repetition series, the number of suttas in AN more than doubles beyond the number constituted by the independent suttas.

Other Formal Features of the Aṅguttara Nikāya

Apart from the "Lust and So Forth Repetition Series," AN exhibits a number of other formal features that deserve brief comment. One is what I call "expanded parallels." An expanded parallel is a sutta that is modeled on an earlier sutta and includes its contents (or most of its contents) but then introduces another item that elevates it to a higher *nipāta*. I mention these in the notes, but it is useful to look at them collectively. To assist with this, I have included a list of expanded parallels as appendix 1. Most expanded parallels extend over only two *nipātas*, which may follow in immediate succession or be more widely separated. The most extensive expanded parallelism in AN is a series of terms on the successive steps culminating in "the knowledge and vision of liberation." It occurs in six *nipātas*. The sequence first appears in **5:24**, and then reappears, enlarged by the addition of factors, in **6:50**, **7:65**, **8:81**, **10:3**, and **11:3**. The next fullest set of expanded parallels is a group of perceptions said to "culminate in the deathless" that occurs four times. This set first appears in **5:61** and reappears in **7:48**, **9:16**, and **10:56**. In the third most prominent set, the bhikkhu Kimbila asks the Buddha why the Dhamma does not endure long after the passing away of a Tathāgata. The set occurs three times, at **5:201**, **6:40**, and **7:59**. The others that I have discovered all extend only over two *nipātas*. Their topics range from reverence for mother and father, to the ways an evil monk resembles a master thief, to the special *samādhi* that a bhikkhu enters to perceive nibbāna.

A second formal feature is what I call "composite numerical suttas." These are discourses that acquire the number of items characteristic of a particular *nipāta* by combining smaller sets of terms. These composites are listed in appendix 2. For example, a series of suttas at **6:105–16** arrives at six items by combining sets of three defilements with three counteractive measures per sutta. Another sutta, **7:58**, falls into the Sevens by combining four things that the Tathāgata need not hide with three ways he is irreproachable. At **8:49**, the Buddha teaches Visākhā four ways a woman is heading for victory in this world and four ways she is heading for victory in the next world. In **9:3**, he explains to his attendant Meghiya five things that mature the mind for liberation and then teaches him four meditation subjects. Occasionally multiple sets are combined. Thus **11:10** enumerates three groups of three qualities, and one pair of qualities, that make a bhikkhu "best among devas and humans." In this way the sutta fits into the Elevens.

The number of suttas in AN is increased by several techniques that amplify the amount of material without adding much significantly new to the content. Some suttas share a common mold and multiply themselves by using a few nearly synonymous terms to make the same point. An example is **3:6–8**, which describe the distinction between the fool and the wise person simply by using different descriptive words. An alternative method of establishing a variation is to use a different image to convey the point. Thus **3:51** and **3:52** are virtually identical in content, but one uses the image of a flood sweeping over the world, the other the image of a fire. Toward the end of the Threes, seven suttas, **3:156–62**, are created from the same mold simply by changing the group of "aids to enlightenment" taken to represent the middle way. In some suttas the subject remains the same but the content used to define the subject differs. An example is **4:201–6**, where the subject is constant, namely, the bad person and the good person, but the qualities that pertain to each type differ from one sutta to the next.

Another recurrent formal technique in AN is to include in close proximity two or more suttas on the same topic, the first simply enunciating a set of factors and the second giving formal definitions of them. Examples of this are fairly numerous. Thus **4:161** enumerates the four modes of practice without explanation, while **4:162–63** elaborate on them. Sutta **4:232** enumerates the four kinds of kamma, while **4:233–38** define them and explore them from several angles. Suttas **5:1–2** provide back-to-back enumerations and definitions of the five trainee's powers; **5:13–14** do the same for the five powers; **7:3–4** treat seven powers in this way; and **7:5–6** declare and define the seven kinds of noble wealth. Again, **8:5–6** applies this treatment to the eight worldly conditions, and **10:19–20** do the same for the ten abodes of the noble ones. Occasionally a large gap separates the brief and the detailed treatment; for instance, **6:9** enumerates the six things unsurpassed, but their elaboration comes only at **6:30**. This raises the question how such gaps could have entered, but it is difficult to give a cogent explanation.

Still another interesting feature of AN (noticeable, too, in the Saṃyutta Nikāya) is the use of what I call "auditor-setting variants." With this technique, a discourse having the exact same content is given to several people. Thus in **8:25** and **8:26** the Buddha answers the same questions on the qualities of a lay disciple raised respectively by Mahānāma and Jīvaka. In **8:43** and **8:45** he gives the same discourse on the uposatha to Visākhā and Bojjhā, and in **8:91–117** (much abridged) to twenty-seven other women, if we are to trust the commentary. Often the Buddha will deliver a discourse to an individual and then, in another sutta, say the same thing to the monks. Thus in **4:53** he speaks about different kinds of marriage to a group of householders and then teaches the same thing to the monks in **4:54**. He teaches Anāthapiṇḍika how a noble disciple might declare himself a stream-enterer in **8:28** and in **8:29** repeats the same explanation to the monks.

There is variation not only in the auditor but in the speaker. One of the monks, usually Sāriputta, gives a discourse that repeats exactly what the Buddha said earlier. We see examples of this in **5:163–64**, which mirror **5:65–66**; in **8:77–78**, which mirror **8:61–62**; and in **10:4** and **10:5**, where Sāriputta and Ānanda give the same discourse that the Buddha gave in **10:3**. It is a puzzle why such suttas were included in the Nikāya when there is no difference in their contents from those given by the Buddha himself.

There are several instances of two suttas that appear to be "expanded parallels" but in which the content is so different that the parallelism is dubious. Moreover, the framework of these paired suttas is such that it is virtually impossible for both to have been historically authentic. Thus the Buddha gives discourses on the visible benefits of giving to the general Sīha at **5:34** and **7:57**. Yet the content differs so much that one may well doubt that the Buddha really spoke both to Sīha. The case is even stronger with regard to **6:44** and **10:75**, where on two different occasions a laywoman named Migasālā makes the same complaint about statements the Buddha issued concerning the rebirth of her father and her uncle. The Buddha's responses to the criticism differ prominently on each occasion, and it thus seems improbable that both are reproducing actual statements made within the same narrative framework.

In the Tens, we meet two large blocks of text that state the same thing across forty or fifty suttas, using two different doctrinal lists to provide content. In **10:113–66** the subject is the tenfold rightness, and in **10:167–210** it is the ten courses of unwholesome and wholesome kamma. The number of short suttas in AN is increased still more by the use of permutations to generate a large number of texts from a few simple doctrinal sets. I explained above how this was done in the "Lust and So Forth Repetition Series." A similar process is used in **7:95–622** to generate 520 suttas by combining modes of contemplation with different objects. Again, at the end of the Elevens, 960 suttas are created by a similar process of combination and permutation.

The Aṅguttara Nikāya Commentary

To assist the reader in understanding the suttas, I have provided a copious set of notes. The notes serve at least four purposes: (1) to provide background information to the sutta; (2) to explain obscure words or phrases in the original; (3) to bring out the doctrinal implications of a statement; (4) and to make explicit the reading I have adopted among competing alternatives. As noted above, my translation relies on the Sri Lankan, Burmese, and PTS editions of AN, which occasionally differ in their readings. I have used the Sri Lankan Buddha Jayanti edition as my primary text, but I sometimes prefer readings from one of the other versions or from a manuscript referred to in the notes to these editions. For the benefit of those with access to the Pāli text, I feel obliged to state which reading I have chosen, to record plausible variants, and sometimes to explain why I made the choice I did over and against the alternatives.

In the notes (as in this introduction) references to AN suttas have been set in bold. When a textual source is followed by volume, page, and (sometimes) line numbers, these refer to the PTS editions. Many of the notes are drawn from the authorized Pāli commentary on AN, the *Aṅguttara Nikāya-aṭṭhakathā*, also known by its proper name, the *Manorathapūraṇī* (Mp), "The Fulfiller of Wishes." This is ascribed to the great Buddhist commentator Ācariya Buddhaghosa, who came from South India to Sri Lanka in the fifth century C.E. and compiled the commentaries to the canonical texts on the basis of the ancient Sinhala commentaries (no longer extant) that had been kept at the Mahāvihāra in Anurādhapura. Buddhaghosa occasionally refers to the "Great Commentary" (*Mahā Aṭṭhakathā*) as the source of his own commentary. In the colophon to the *Manorathapūraṇī* he says that he completed it "by taking the essence of the Great Commentary" (*sā hi mahāaṭṭhakathāya sāramādāya niṭṭhitā esā*). Whereas the canonical texts had been preserved in Pāli, the Great Commentary had been transmitted in the old Sinhala language, intelligible only to the residents of the island (and perhaps by Buddhaghosa's time only to the most erudite among them). Buddhaghosa translated this material into lucid and elegant Pāli, thereby making it accessible to the bhikkhus in India and perhaps in the outlying regions to which Buddhism had spread. In his colophon to the work, Buddhaghosa explains why he gave his commentary its title, using the word Āgamas instead of the more familiar Nikāyas to designate the four main sutta collections:

> Because this work fulfilled my wish to comment on all the Āgamas,
> it has been given the name "The Fulfiller of Wishes."[11]

The other exegetical work to which I occasionally refer is the subcommentary, the *Aṅguttara Nikāya-ṭīkā*, also known as the *Manorathapūraṇī-ṭīkā* (Mp-ṭ) and under its proper name, the *Sāratthamañjūsā IV-ṭīkā*, "The Casket of the Essential Meaning, Part IV." This subcommentary does not belong to the set of "old subcommentaries" (*purāṇaṭīkā*), known as the *Līnatthappakāsinī* and ascribed to Ācariya Dhammapāla, the (seventh-century?) South Indian author of the subcommentaries to the other three Nikāyas.[12] It is ascribed, rather, to the great Sri Lankan elder Sāriputta, who worked during the reign of King Parakramabāhu I (1153–86) at the capital Polonnaruwa. Since the sutta and commentary are usually sufficiently clear on their own, I have not had to refer to the *ṭīkā* as often as I did to the *Saṃyutta Nikāya-purāṇaṭīkā* in my notes to the *Connected Discourses of the Buddha*. Words in bold in Pāli citations from the commentary and *ṭīkā* represent the *lemma*, the word or phrase being commented upon.

I should state, as a precaution, that as useful as they are, the commentaries explain the suttas as they were understood sometime around the first century C.E., when the old commentaries drawn upon by Buddhaghosa were closed to further additions. The commentaries view the suttas through the lens of the complex exegetical method that had evolved within the Theravāda school, built up from the interpretations of the ancient teachers and welded to a framework constructed largely from the principles of the Abhidhamma system. This exegetical method does not necessarily correspond to the way the teachings were understood in the earliest period of Buddhist history, but it seems likely that its nucleus goes back to the first generation of monks who had gathered around the Buddha and were entrusted with the task of giving detailed systematic explanations of his discourses. The fact that I cite the commentaries so often in the notes does not necessarily mean that I always agree with them, though where I interpret a passage differently I generally say so.

I want to briefly mention two tenets, central to the commentarial method, that seem to be in tension with the texts themselves. Both must have emerged when the early teachings were being recast into the more rigorous and analytically precise system that underlies the Theravāda Abhidhamma. The stages by which the doctrinal evolution from suttas to Abhidhamma occurred, and the specific maneuvers involved, are still barely understood in detail and thus constitute a wide-open field for scholarly investigation.

The first tenet distinctive of the commentaries concerns the meaning of the terms *path* and *fruit*. In the Abhidhamma, the four stages of awakening are regarded as temporal events, each consisting of two phases joined in immediate succession. First comes a single mind-moment known as the *path* (*magga),* which is followed at once by its corresponding *fruition* (*phala*). Thus there are the paths of stream-entry, once-returning, nonreturning, and arahantship, each followed in immediate succession respectively by the fruit of stream-entry and so forth. The path is sometimes called the "world-transcending path" (*lokuttaramagga*), to distinguish it from the preliminary or preparatory practice (*pubbabhāgapaṭipadā*), the course of training leading up to the world-transcending path. The commentaries take up this scheme from the Abhidhamma and apply it as a tool of exegesis, reading it back into the early suttas as if it had already been intended by the original texts. I mentioned above (pp. 55–56) that in the Nikāyas, the noble Saṅgha is said to consist of eight types of noble persons, who are joined into four pairs in relation to the four stages of awakening: the person practicing for realization of a particular fruit and the person who has attained that fruit. The commentaries identify the person practicing for the attainment with the path-attainer of the Abhidhamma, and the one who has attained the corresponding fruit with the one who has undergone the fruition experience.

In the Nikāyas, no such tenet is discernible, at least not in this form. The Nikāyas call the crucial awakening experience the "breakthrough to the Dhamma" (*dhammābhisamaya*) or the "gaining of the Dhamma eye" (*dhammacakkhupaṭilābha*). The experience appears to be sudden, but it is not identified with the path as such nor is it said to last only a single mind-moment. Several suttas suggest, to the contrary, that the path is a temporally extended course of practice that becomes irreversible when the disciple enters "the fixed course of rightness" (*okkanto sammattaniyāmaṃ*). At that point the practitioner transcends the level of a worldling or ordinary person (*puthujjana*) and becomes either a Dhamma follower (*dhammānusārī*) or a faith follower (*saddhānusārī*). While reaching the path guarantees realization of the fruit, the fruit does not necessarily arise a moment after entering the path. All that the texts say is that those who have entered the fixed course of rightness *cannot pass away* without realizing the fruit of stream-entry (see SN 25:1; III 224). This implies that further practice, perhaps over days or weeks, may be needed to realize the fruit.

Once the path has arisen, the practitioner then "pursues this path, develops it, and cultivates it," as a result of which "the fetters are abandoned and the underlying tendencies are uprooted" (**4:170**). These expressions suggest that the path is an extended process of cultivation rather than an instantaneous event. Though the course of practice will be punctuated by sudden breakthrough attainments, the word "path" itself refers to the whole process of development rather than a momentary event, and the fruit seems to be simply the attainment of the relevant stage of awakening, not a special contemplative experience.

Further support in AN for the extended nature of the path is at **8:22**. Here the householder Ugga declares that when he is serving the Saṅgha with a meal, though deities inform him of the monks' spiritual attainments, he still serves them equally, without being biased on the basis of their spiritual status. Among those who receive his offerings are faith followers and Dhamma followers. If these persons existed as such only for the duration of a momentary breakthrough experience, it is hard to see how they could be spoken of as recipients of a meal offering. It certainly takes more than one mind-moment to receive and eat a meal.

The second point over which some degree of tension surfaces between the Nikāyas and the commentaries concerns the question whether rebirth occurs immediately after death or after an interval of time. During the age of Sectarian Buddhism, when different schools branched off from the originally unified Saṅgha and doctrinal differences began to emerge, the Pāli school adopted the tenet that rebirth occurs in the very moment following death, with no interval separating the moments of death and rebirth (or reconception). It seems that this position, articulated in the commentaries, is based on a particular reading of certain passages in the final book of the Abhidhamma Piṭaka, the *Paṭṭhāna*. Yet there are suttas that can be read as contradicting this doctrinal position.

The Aṅguttara offers one of the strongest counterweights against the hypothesis of instantaneous rebirth. The Nikāyas often analyze the person at the third stage of realization, the *anāgāmī* or non-returner, into five subtypes. The first among them, the one with the sharpest faculties, is called *antarāparinibbāyī*, which I render "an attainer of nibbāna in the interval." The commentaries explain this figure as one who attains nibbāna in the first half of the life span; they then go on to interpret the other four types in a way that accords with this explanation. However, **7:55** distinguishes three subtypes of *antarāparinibbāyī*, each of which it illustrates with a simile. The similes—of a blazing metal chip going out at different points before hitting the ground—suggest that the *antarāparinibbāyī* attains nibbāna *before taking rebirth*, thus supporting the hypothesis of an intermediate stage separating death and rebirth, at least for certain non-returners (but surely capable of a broader generalization). This was the position advocated by some of the rival schools with which the Theravāda competed on Indian soil, most notably the Sarvāstivādins.

Similes are not always a reliable basis for drawing doctrinal conclusions, and the question whether rebirth is instantaneous or follows an interval seems to have minimal practical importance. But a commitment to instantaneous rebirth is fundamental to the Theravāda commentaries. The tone of certain arguments in the commentaries suggests that among the early Indian Buddhist schools, the issue generated a degree of heat that hardly seems warranted by its practical bearings. Perhaps underlying the conflict was apprehension that acknowledgment of an intermediate state could be taken to imply a self or soul that migrates from life to life. But other schools felt comfortable enough accepting the intermediate state without seeing it as threatening the doctrine of non-self.

The Chinese Parallels

In my notes I have also occasionally compared the Pāli versions of suttas in AN with their parallels preserved in Chinese translation, primarily in the Chinese Āgamas and occasionally in independent translations. I mentioned above (p. 17) that there is a counterpart to AN that had been translated into Chinese, the Ekottarāgama or Ekottarikāgama. It would be a mistake, however, to suppose that the Pāli Aṅguttara Nikāya and the Ekottarāgama are close parallels.

While the four Pāli Nikāyas all belonged to one school, known today as the Theravāda, the four Āgamas in Chinese translation derived from several schools that arose during the period of Sectarian Buddhism, none identical with the progenitor of the Theravāda. The Dīrghāgama (counterpart of the Dīgha Nikāya) was translated from a version belonging to the Dharmaguptaka school, which flourished in Gandhāra. The Madhyamāgama (counterpart of the Majjhima Nikāya) is believed to have descended from a branch of the Sarvāstivāda. According to Enomoto, its affiliation was most likely with the Kashmirian Sarvāstivādins.[13] Enomoto finds reasons for ascribing the Chinese Saṃyuktāgama (counterpart of the Saṃyutta Nikāya) to the Mūlasarvāstivadins, who had their headquarters in Mathurā.[14] The school affiliation of the Ekottarāgama is problematic. Anesaki wrote over a century ago that "there are strong reasons to believe that the version was made from a text handed down by a school which had a very different tradition from the Theravāda, possibly by one of the Mahāsāṃghika sections."[15] Its affiliation with the Mahāsāṃghikas became a widespread supposition, often stated as a matter of fact. However, more recently, Enomoto writes that questions concerning the school, place of formation, and language of the original text of this work "have yet to be solved."[16]

Because the Āgamas descend from different schools, the arrangement of their contents differs. While the different schools all apparently distributed their suttas into four main collections with the same names, they made different choices in their allocation of the material. Thus the parallels of many shorter suttas that the Pāli tradition assigned to AN are to be found, in the Chinese Āgamas, in the Saṃyuktāgama (for example, the parallels of **3:81–90** all occur in SĀ, the parallel of **4:111** is SĀ 923, the parallel of **5:167** is SĀ 497, etc.). Often the parallels of longer AN suttas occur in the Chinese Madhyamāgama (for example, **6:43** occurs as MĀ 118, **7:55** as MĀ 6, **10:51** as MĀ 110, etc.). Since the school affiliations were different, it is not unusual for an AN sutta to have two or more parallels in the Āgamas, as well as one or more independent translations. To take but one example, **6:55**, the Buddha's advice to the bhikkhu Soṇa, occurs as MĀ 123, SĀ 254, EĀ 23.3, and as two independent translations. There are also many AN suttas that are without Āgama parallels.

Comparisons between the Pāli and Āgama versions proved helpful in a number of respects. Sometimes a simpler Chinese translation helped to clarify the intention of a phrase that seemed unnecessarily convoluted in Pāli. For example, the plea that somebody makes to the Buddha when he wants to avoid misrepresenting him (see **3:57**) is so complex that it even misled the commentator into giving an implausible explanation. The Chinese treatment of the same phrase (see p. 1646, note 416) supports the simpler explanation borne out by another occurrence of the Pāli expression in a different context at **5:5**. Sometimes, when there was a discrepancy between readings of a Pāli expression, the Chinese version, by agreeing with one as against the other, supported its claim to antiquity. For example, a verse in **4:40** describes the Buddhas as *yaññassa kovidā*, "skilled in sacrifice," in the Be version, but in the Ce and Ee versions the phrase is read *puññassa kovidā*, "skilled in merit." Two Chinese parallels render the phrase in a way that indicates its translators were working from an original that said the Buddhas were skilled in sacrifice, thereby supporting Be. Again, there is a verse spoken by the bhikkhu Udāyī in **6:43** in which all three printed editions of AN read the third line as *saṅkhāresūpasantesu*, meaning "when all conditioned things have become still," but a Burmese variant (referred to in the notes of Be and Ee) and the version in the Theragāthā read it as *aṅgāresu ca santesu*, meaning "when the coals have gone out." The Chinese parallel, though not exactly identical, still supports the Burmese variant against the three printed editions of AN (see p. 1758, note 1326).

Another interesting example is at **10:26** (see p. 1838, note 2000) where in Ce and Ee we find a triad *ādi, ādīnava, nissaraṇa* instead of the usual *assāda, ādīnava, nissaraṇa*. The editors of Be obviously assumed an error had occurred here and replaced *ādi* with *assāda*. But the Chinese parallel has 本, which corresponds to *ādi*, not to *assāda*, and thereby confirms the antiquity of the Ce and Ee reading. A sutta near the end of the Tens, **10:219**, "The Deed-Born Body," contains no set of ten items to explain its inclusion in the Tens, but the text uses a demonstrative pronoun to refer to a subject who was not previously introduced; so it seems as if a passage had been elided in the course of transmission. The Chinese parallel, MĀ 15, begins with the Buddha enumerating the ten types of unwholesome kamma. It then asserts that a noble disciple discards those ten kinds of kamma, and following this comes a passage referring to that disciple with a demonstrative pronoun. Thus this version shows that a passage with ten items had in fact been elided from the AN sutta.

An intriguing divergence between the two traditions occurs in a discourse widely known as the Kālāma Sutta, which records the Buddha's advice to the people of Kesaputta. In contemporary Buddhist circles it has become almost *de rigueur* to regard the Kālāma Sutta as *the* essential Buddhist text, almost equal in importance to the discourse on the four noble truths. The sutta is held up as proof that the Buddha anticipated Western empiricism, free inquiry, and the scientific method, that he endorsed the personal determination of truth. Though until the late nineteenth century this sutta was just one small hill in the mountain range of the Nikāyas, since the start of the twentieth century it has become one of the most commonly quoted Buddhist texts, offered as the key to convince those with modernist leanings that the Buddha was their forerunner. However, the Chinese parallel to the Kālāma Sutta, MĀ 16 (at T I 438b13–439c22), is quite different. Here the Buddha does not ask the Kālāmas to resolve their doubts by judging matters for themselves. Instead, he advises them not to give rise to doubt and perplexity and he tells them point blank: "You yourselves do not have pure wisdom with which to know whether there is an afterlife or not. You yourselves do not have pure wisdom to know which deeds are transgressions and which are not transgressions." He then explains to them the three unwholesome roots of kamma, how they lead to moral transgressions, and the ten courses of wholesome kamma.

In other instances, the Pāli and Chinese versions of a sutta offer such different perspectives one can only conclude that the original in one tradition was inverted, but we cannot say for sure *which one* underwent inversion. A case in point is **2:36**, in which Sāriputta speaks about "the person fettered internally" and "the person fettered externally." In the Pāli version Sāriputta explains the former as "a returner, one who returns to this state of being" (that is, to the sense sphere) and the latter as "a non-returner, one who does not return to this state of being." But the Chinese parallel inverts this explanation: "The person with an internal fetter is the non-returner, who does not come back to this world. And the person with an external fetter is one who is not a non-returner but who comes back to this world." In a case like this it is virtually impossible to mediate between the two versions, and there is little to fall back on to support one reading as against the other.

A Thematic Guide to the Aṅguttara Nikāya

I. The Buddha

1. Biographical 3:39, 4:21, 4:118, 4:127, 5:196, 8:11, 8:64, 8:69, 8:70, 9:41
2. Qualities and attainments 1:277, 2:37, 3:35, 3:63, 3:64, 4:1, 4:24, 4:35–36, 4:87, 5:100, 5:104, 6:43, 8:12, 10:30
3. The Tathāgata 1:170–86, 2:22–25, 2:52–56, 3:14, 3:80; 4:8, 4:15, 4:23, 4:33, 5:11, 5:99, 5:131, 5:133, 6:64, 7:58, 8:85, 10:21–22, 10:81

II. The Dhamma and Discipline

1. The Dhamma in brief 4:25, 4:29–30, 4:188, 7:83, 8:19–20, 8:30, 8:53
2. The rejection of views 3:61, 3:137, 4:77, 4:173–74, 6:38, 6:95, 7:54, 9:38, 10:20, 10:93, 10:95–96
3. A directly visible Dhamma 3:53–54, 3:65–66, 4:193, 4:195, 6:47–48, 9:46
4. The ninefold textual Dhamma 4:102, 4:107, 5:73–74, 5:155, 6:51, 7:68
5. Preserving the Dhamma 1:130–69, 2:20, 2:41, 4:160, 4:180, 5:79–80, 5:154–56, 5:201, 6:40, 7:59

III. The Shifting Kaleidoscope of Experience

1. Cosmological background 3:70, 3:80, 4:45–46, 4:156, 7:44, 7:66, 8:42, 8:70, 9:24, 10:29, 10:89
2. Happiness and sorrow 1:29–30, 1:324–27, 2:19, 2:64–76, 2:250–69, 3:65–66, 4:51–52, 4:62, 4:193, 5:3, 5:45, 5:48–50, 5:128, 5:170, 6:45, 6:75, 6:78, 7:19, 7:62, 8:6, 8:38–39, 8:42, 8:44, 8:54, 8:61, 9:34, 10:46, 10:65–66
3. Mind is the key 1:21–52, 1:56–57, 3:109–10, 4:186
4. Kamma and its results 3:23, 3:34, 3:36, 3:74, 3:100, 3:111–

12, 4:85, 4:134, 4:171, 4:195, 4:232–38, 6:39, 6:57, 6:63 §5, 8:40, 9:13, 10:47, 10:167–233
5. The round of rebirths 1:348–77, 10:177, 10:216–218
6. Heaven and hell 1:290–95, 2:16–18, 2:26–29, 2:210–29, 3:10, 3:36, 3:113, 3:117–18, 3:129, 3:146–49, 3:163–82, 4:64, 4:81–84, 4:212–220, 4:239–40, 4:264–73, 5:4, 5:115–20, 5:129–30, 5:145, 5:236–40, 5:286–302, 6:62, 6:81–82, 7:72, 10:211–214, 10:220–24, 10:229–32

IV. Maintaining a Harmonious Household
1. The family
   (1) General 3:48, 4:258, 5:42
   (2) Parents and children 2:33, 3:31, 4:63, 5:39,
   (3) Husbands and wives 4:53–56, 5:33, 7:63, 8:46, 8:49
2. Present welfare, future welfare 4:61–62, 5:58, 8:49, 8:54, 8:76, 10:73
3. Wrong and right livelihood 4:79, 5:177, 6:18, 8:54, 10:91
4. Wealth 4:61–62, 5:41, 5:47, 5:58, 5:227, 6:45, 7:5–7
5. Sustaining favorable relationships 4:32, 4:256, 8:24, 9:5
6. The state and the community 4:70, 7:21–22
7. The wheel-turning monarch 1:278, 1:280, 2:52–55, 3:14, 4:130, 5:131–33, 7:62, 7:66

V. The Way Leading Upward
1. Faith, confidence, and reverence 3:42, 3:48, 3:75, 4:21, 4:34, 4:52, 4:65, 4:118, 5:21–22, 5:32, 5:38, 5:40, 5:179, 5:250, 6:30, 6:32–33, 6:69, 7:32–35, 7:57, 7:70, 9:27, 11:14
2. Spiritual friendship 1:70–71, 1:110–111, 1:126–27, 3:24, 3:26–27, 3:135, 4:242, 5:146, 6:67, 7:36–37, 8:54, 9:1, 9:3, 9:6, 10:61–62, 10:155–66, 10:199–210
3. Merit 3:41, 3:45–46, 4:34, 4:51–52, 5:43, 5:45, 5:199, 6:37, 7:62, 8:36, 8:39, 9:20
4. Giving and generosity 2:35, 2:141–52, 3:41–42, 3:57, 4:39–40, 4:51, 4:57–60, 4:78–79, 4:197, 5:31, 5:34–37, 5:44–45, 5:141, 5:147–48, 6:37, 6:59, 7:52, 7:57, 8:31–35, 8:37, 9:20, 10:177
5. Moral discipline
   (1) Moral shame and dread 2:9, 10:76
   (2) Bad conduct and good conduct 1:284–95, 2:1, 2:3–4, 2:11–12, 2:17–19, 2:34, 3:2, 3:6–8, 3:14–15, 3:17–18, 3:28,

3:120–22, 3:146–55, 4:111, 4:121, 5:213, 5:241–48, 6:57, 10:23
- (3) The five training rules 4:99, 4:201, 5:145, 5:171–74, 5:178–79, 5:286–302, 8:39, 9:27, 9:63, 10:92
- (4) Wrong speech and right speech 3:28, 4:3, 4:22, 4:73, 4:82–83, 4:100, 4:148–49, 4:183, 4:221, 4:250–53, 5:116–20, 5:198, 5:214, 5:236–38, 8:67–68, 10:69–70
- (5) The uposatha observance 3:70, 8:41–45, 9:18, 10:46

6. Decline and progress [of lay followers] 7:29–31

VI. Dispelling the World's Enchantment

1. Acquiring a sense of urgency 1:328–47, 4:113, 5:77–78, 8:29
2. Old age, illness, and death 3:36, 3:39, 3:51–52, 3:62, 4:113, 4:119, 4:182, 4:184, 5:48–50, 5:57, 6:14–16, 7:74
3. Gratification, danger, and escape 3:103–6, 10:91
4. The pitfalls in sensual pleasures 3:108, 4:122, 5:7, 5:139, 6:23, 6:63 §1, 6:45, 7:72, 8:56, 9:65
5. Disenchantment with the body 9:15, 10:49
6. Universal impermanence 3:47, 4:33, 7:66, 7:74, 10:29

VII. The Defilements of the Mind

1. The springs of bad conduct
   - (1) Greed, hate, delusion 2:123–24, 3:34–35, 3:53–55, 3:65–66, 3:68–69, 3:71–72, 3:111, 4:117, 4:158, 4:193, 6:47–48, 6:107, 10:174
   - (2) Wrong courses (four) 4:17–20
   - (3) Sexuality 1:1–10, 3:108, 4:159, 5:55, 5:75–76, 5:225–26, 7:50–51, 8:17–18
   - (4) Affection and hatred 4:200
   - (5) Anger and resentment 3:25, 3:27, 3:132, 4:43–44, 4:84, 4:108, 4:110, 4:122, 4:197, 5:161–62, 5:215–16, 7:64, 7:73, 9:11, 9:29–30, 10:79–80
   - (6) Miserliness (fivefold) 5:115, 5:224, 5:239–40, 5:254–71, 9:69
   - (7) Roots of dispute (six) 6:36
   - (8) Defilements of ascetics (four) 4:50
2. Obstacles to meditation
   - (1) Laziness 6:17, 8:80
   - (2) Unwholesome thoughts and their removal 3:40, 3:101, 4:11, 4:14, 5:200, 6:13, 10:51

(3) Hindrances (five) 1:11–20, 4:61, 5:23, 5:51–52, 5:193, 6:27–28
(4) Mental barrenness (five) 5:205, 9:71, 10:14
(5) Bondages of the mind (five) 5:206, 9:72, 10:14
(6) Drowsiness 7:61

3. Bondage to saṃsāra
(1) Craving and ignorance 3:76–77, 4:9, 4:199, 4:257, 6:61–62, 6:106, 9:23, 10:61–62
(2) Taints 2:108–17, 4:36, 4:195, 6:58, 6:63 §4
(3) Inversions (four) 4:49
(4) Bonds (four) 4:10
(5) Fetters (four) 4:131; (five) 9:67, 9:70; (seven) 7:8–10; (ten) 10:13
(6) Underlying tendencies (seven) 7:11–12

VIII. The Path of Renunciation

1. Going forth into homelessness 2:2, 3:12, 3:60, 4:122, 5:59–60, 5:75–76, 7:69, 10:48, 10:59
2. Wrong practice and right practice 1:58–75, 3:156–62, 3:78, 3:156, 4:196, 4:198, 5:181–90, 10:103–166
3. The training of the monk (general) 3:16, 3:19–20, 3:40, 3:49, 3:91, 3:128, 3:130, 4:27–28, 4:37, 4:71–72, 4:157, 4:245, 5:56, 5:114, 7:20, 7:42–43, 7:67, 7:71, 8:30, 9:1, 9:3, 10:17–18, 10:48, 10:101
4. Monastic discipline 2:15, 2:127–29, 2:280–309, 4:12, 4:244, 5:251–53, 5:272–85, 7:75–82, 10:31–36, 10:44, 10:71
5. Reproving others 5:167, 10:44
6. Aids to the training
(1) Heedfulness 1:58–59, 1:98–99, 1:114–15, 4:116–17, 6:53, 10:15
(2) Careful attention 1:20, 1:66–67, 1:74–75, 1:106–7, 1:122–23
(3) Seclusion 2:30, 4:138, 4:262, 5:110, 5:127, 5:176, 6:42, 8:86
(4) Health 5:29, 5:123–26, 5:207–8
(5) Trainee's powers 5:1–12, 7:15
(6) Factors of striving (five) 5:53–54, 5:135–36, 10:11
(7) Aids to self-confidence (five) 5:101
7. The sequential course of practice
(1) Virtue, concentration, wisdom 3:73, 3:81–90, 3:92, 4:2, 4:136–37, 6:105, 9:12

(2) Proximate causes 5:24, 6:50, 7:65, 8:81, 10:1–3, 11:1–3
(3) Modes of practice 4:161–70
(4) Four purifications 4:194
(5) From faith to liberation 4:198, 10:99
(6) From right association to liberation 10:61–62
(7) Ending birth and death 10:76

8. Decline and progress [of monks] 2:200–9, 4:158, 5:8–10, 5:89–90, 5:149–50, 6:21–22, 6:31–33, 6:62, 6:68–69, 7:23–28, 7:32–35, 8:79, 9:6, 10:53–55, 10:67–68, 10:82, 10:84–86, 11:17
9. Giving up the training 3:39, 4:122, 5:5, 5:75–76, 6:60, 8:14

IX. Meditation

1. Serenity and insight 2:31, 4:92–94, 4:170, 5:73–74, 9:4, 10:54
2. Aids to meditation
   (1) Establishments of mindfulness (four) 3:156, 6:117–18, 9:63–72
   (2) Right striving (four) and right effort 2:5, 3:157, 4:13–14, 4:69, 6:55, 8:80, 9:73–82
   (3) Bases of psychic potency (four) 5:67–68, 9:83–92
   (4) Faculties (four) 4:151; (five) 6:3
   (5) Powers (two) 2:11–13; (four) 4:152–55, 4:261, 9:5; (five) 5:13–16, 6:4; (seven) 7:3–4
   (6) Factors of enlightenment (seven) 1:74–75, 4:14, 4:238, 10:102
3. Subjects of meditation
   (1) Overview 1:394–574
   (2) Mindfulness of the body 1:575–627, 9:11
   (3) Mindfulness of breathing 5:96–98, 10:60
   (4) Walking meditation 5:29
   (5) Perceptions and contemplations 5:30, 5:57, 5:61–62, 5:69–72, 5:121–22, 5:144, 6:35, 6:102–4, 7:16–19, 7:48–49, 7:55, 9:1, 9:3, 9:16, 10:56–57, 10:59–60, 10:101
   (6) Mindfulness of death 6:19–20, 8:73–74
   (7) Recollections 1:296–305, 3:70, 6:9–10, 6:25–26, 11:11–13
   (8) Loving-kindness and the four immeasurables 1:53–55, 3:63, 3:65, 4:67, 4:125–26, 4:190, 6:13, 7:62, 8:1, 8:63, 9:18, 10:219, 11:15–16
   (9) *Kasiṇas* (ten) 10:25–26, 10:29

4. Concentration 3:32, 3:101–2, 4:41, 5:27–28, 5:113, 6:24, 6:70, 6:72–74, 7:40–41, 7:45, 7:67, 8:63, 9:37, 10:6–7, 11:7–9, 11:16
5. The stages of meditative development 5:28
   (1) Jhānas 3:58, 3:63, 4:123–24, 4:190, 5:28, 6:60, 6:73–74, 11:16
   (2) Eight bases of overcoming 8:65, 10:29
   (3) Eight emancipations 8:66
   (4) Nine progressive attainments 9:31–61
6. Meditative attainments and rebirth 3:116, 4:123–26
7. Three true knowledges 3:58–59
8. Six direct knowledges 3:101–2, 5:23, 5:28, 5:67–68, 6:2, 6:70, 9:35

X. Wisdom

1. Praise of wisdom 4:141–45
2. Aids to the growth of wisdom 4:248, 8:2
3. Right view (and wrong view) 1:268–76, 1:306–18, 2:125–26, 5:25, 6:98–101, 10:93
4. Learning the Dhamma 3:20, 3:30, 3:67, 3:127, 4:6, 4:102, 4:107, 4:191, 5:26, 5:65–66, 5:73–74, 5:151–53, 5:165, 5:169, 5:194, 5:202, 6:51, 6:56, 6:86–88, 8:82, 9:4
5. Teaching the Dhamma 1:320–27, 2:14, 3:14, 3:22, 3:43–44, 3:125, 3:131, 4:42, 4:48, 4:111, 4:128, 4:139–40, 5:26, 5:99, 5:131–33, 5:157, 5:159, 9:4, 10:83
6. The domain of wisdom
   (1) Dependent origination 3:61, 10:92
   (2) The five aggregates 4:41, 4:90, 9:66
   (3) The three characteristics (collectively) 3:136, 4:49, 6:98–100, 6:102–4, 7:16–18, 10:93
   (4) Non-self 3:32–33, 4:177
   (5) Four noble truths 3:58, 3:61, 4:186, 4:190, 9:13
   (6) Questions and answers 6:63, 8:83, 9:14, 10:27–28, 10:58
7. The fruits of wisdom
   (1) The fixed course of rightness 3:22, 5:151–53, 6:86–88, 6:98–101
   (2) Analytical knowledges 4:172, 5:86, 5:95, 7:38–39
   (3) Liberation 2:31, 2:87, 3:101–2, 4:178, 5:25–26, 5:71–72, 5:134, 5:170, 7:55, 9:36, 10:95, 11:16

7. One's own welfare and others' welfare 4:95–99, 4:186, 5:17–20, 7:68, 8:25, 8:62
8. Laypersons, good and bad 2:132–33, 3:79, 4:60, 4:176, 5:42, 5:47, 5:58, 5:63–64, 5:171–75, 6:16, 7:53, 8:21–24, 8:25, 8:38, 10:74, 11:11–13
9. Bhikkhunīs 1:235–47, 4:159, 5:115–20, 7:56, 8:51–52, 10:28
10. Women 1:279–83, 2:61, 3:129, 4:80, 4:197, 5:55, 5:229–30, 7:63, 8:46, 8:49, 8:51, 10:213–15

XIV. Closing Repetition Series

Twos
Serenity and insight

Threes
Emptiness concentration, markless concentration, wishless concentration

Fours
(1) Four establishments of mindfulness
(2) Four right strivings
(3) Four bases of psychic potency

Fives
(1) Five perceptions: of unattractiveness, of death, of danger, of the repulsiveness of food, and of non-delight in the entire world
(2) Five perceptions: of impermanence, of non-self, of death, of the repulsiveness of food, and of non-delight in the entire world
(3) Five perceptions: of impermanence, of suffering in what is impermanent, of non-self in what is suffering, of abandoning, and of dispassion
(4) Five faculties
(5) Five powers

Sixes
(1) Six unsurpassed things: the unsurpassed sight, hearing, gain, training, service, and recollection
(2) Six recollections: recollection of the Buddha, of the

Dhamma, of the Saṅgha, of virtuous behavior, of generosity, and of the deities

(3) Six perceptions: of impermanence, of suffering in what is impermanent, of non-self in what is suffering, of abandoning, of dispassion, and of cessation

Sevens

(1) Seven factors of enlightenment

(2) Seven perceptions: of impermanence, of non-self, of unattractiveness, of danger, of abandoning, of dispassion, and of cessation

(3) Seven perceptions: of unattractiveness, of death, of the repulsiveness of food, of non-delight in the entire world, of impermanence, of suffering in the impermanent, and of non-self in what is suffering

Eights

(1) Eight noble path factors

(2) Eight bases of overcoming

(3) Eight emancipations

Nines

(1) Nine perceptions: of unattractiveness, of death, of the repulsiveness of food, of non-delight in the entire world, of impermanence, of suffering in the impermanent, of non-self in what is suffering, of abandoning, and of dispassion

(2) Nine progressive dwellings

Tens

(1) Ten perceptions: of unattractiveness, of death, of the repulsiveness of food, of non-delight in the entire world, of impermanence, of suffering in the impermanent, of non-self in what is suffering, of abandoning, of dispassion, and of cessation

(2) Ten perceptions: of impermanence, of non-self, of the repulsiveness of food, of non-delight in the entire world, of a skeleton, of a worm-infested corpse, of a livid corpse, of a festering corpse, of a fissured corpse, and of a bloated corpse

(3) Right view, right intention, right speech, right action, right livelihood, right effort, right mindfulness, right concentration, right knowledge, and right liberation

Elevens

The four jhānas; the liberation of the mind by loving-kindness, compassion, altruistic joy, and equanimity; the base of the infinity of space, the base of the infinity of consciousness, and the base of nothingness

THE BOOK OF THE ONES

(*Ekakanipāta*)

The Book of the Ones

[1] # The Book of the Ones

Homage to the Blessed One, the Arahant,
the Perfectly Enlightened One

I. Obsession of the Mind

1 (1)

Thus have I heard. On one occasion the Blessed One was dwelling at Sāvatthī in Jeta's Grove, Anāthapiṇḍika's Park. There the Blessed One addressed the bhikkhus: "Bhikkhus!"

"Venerable sir!" those bhikkhus replied. The Blessed One said this:

"Bhikkhus, I do not see even one other form that so obsesses the mind[17] of a man as the form of a woman. The form of a woman obsesses the mind of a man."

2 (2)

"Bhikkhus, I do not see even one other sound that so obsesses the mind of a man as the sound of a woman. The sound of a woman obsesses the mind of a man."

3 (3)

"Bhikkhus, I do not see even one other odor that so obsesses the mind of a man as the odor of a woman. The odor of a woman obsesses the mind of a man."[18] [2]

4 (4)

"Bhikkhus, I do not see even one other taste that so obsesses the mind of a man as the taste of a woman. The taste of a woman obsesses the mind of a man."[19]

5 (5)
"Bhikkhus, I do not see even one other touch that so obsesses the mind of a man as the touch of a woman. The touch of a woman obsesses the mind of a man."[20]

6 (6)[21]
"Bhikkhus, I do not see even one other form that so obsesses the mind of a woman as the form of a man. The form of a man obsesses the mind of a woman."

7 (7)
"Bhikkhus, I do not see even one other sound that so obsesses the mind of a woman as the sound of a man. The sound of a man obsesses the mind of a woman."

8 (8)
"Bhikkhus, I do not see even one other odor that so obsesses the mind of a woman as the odor of a man. The odor of a man obsesses the mind of a woman."

9 (9)
"Bhikkhus, I do not see even one other taste that so obsesses the mind of a woman as the taste of a man. The taste of a man obsesses the mind of a woman."

10 (10)
"Bhikkhus, I do not see even one other touch that so obsesses the mind of a woman as the touch of a man. The touch of a man obsesses the mind of a woman." [3]

II. Abandoning the Hindrances[22]

11 (1)
"Bhikkhus, I do not see even one other thing on account of which unarisen sensual desire arises and arisen sensual desire increases and expands so much as the mark of the attractive.[23] For one who attends carelessly to the mark of the attractive, unarisen sensual desire arises and arisen sensual desire increases and expands."

12 (2)

"Bhikkhus, I do not see even one other thing on account of which unarisen ill will arises and arisen ill will increases and expands so much as the mark of the repulsive.[24] For one who attends carelessly to the mark of the repulsive, unarisen ill will arises and arisen ill will increases and expands."

13 (3)

"Bhikkhus, I do not see even one other thing on account of which unarisen dullness and drowsiness arise and arisen dullness and drowsiness increase and expand so much as discontent, lethargy, lazy stretching, drowsiness after meals, and sluggishness of mind.[25] For one with a sluggish mind, unarisen dullness and drowsiness arise and arisen dullness and drowsiness increase and expand."

14 (4)

"Bhikkhus, I do not see even one other thing on account of which unarisen restlessness and remorse arise and arisen restlessness and remorse increase and expand so much as an unsettled mind.[26] For one with an unsettled mind, unarisen restlessness and remorse arise and arisen restlessness and remorse increase and expand." [4]

15 (5)

"Bhikkhus, I do not see even one other thing on account of which unarisen doubt arises and arisen doubt increases and expands so much as careless attention.[27] For one who attends carelessly, unarisen doubt arises and arisen doubt increases and expands."

16 (6)[28]

"Bhikkhus, I do not see even one other thing on account of which unarisen sensual desire does not arise and arisen sensual desire is abandoned so much as the mark of the unattractive.[29] For one who attends carefully to the mark of the unattractive, unarisen sensual desire does not arise and arisen sensual desire is abandoned."[30]

17 (7)

"Bhikkhus, I do not see even one other thing on account of which unarisen ill will does not arise and arisen ill will is abandoned so much as the liberation of the mind by loving-kindness.[31] For one who attends carefully to the liberation of the mind by loving-kindness, unarisen ill will does not arise and arisen ill will is abandoned."[32]

18 (8)

"Bhikkhus, I do not see even one other thing on account of which unarisen dullness and drowsiness do not arise and arisen dullness and drowsiness are abandoned so much as the element of instigation, the element of persistence, the element of exertion.[33] For one who has aroused energy, unarisen dullness and drowsiness do not arise and arisen dullness and drowsiness are abandoned."[34]

19 (9)

"Bhikkhus, I do not see even one other thing on account of which unarisen restlessness and remorse do not arise and arisen restlessness and remorse are abandoned so much as pacification of the mind.[35] For one with a pacified mind, unarisen restlessness and remorse do not arise and arisen restlessness and remorse are abandoned."[36]

20 (10)

"Bhikkhus, I do not see even one other thing [5] on account of which unarisen doubt does not arise and arisen doubt is abandoned so much as careful attention.[37] For one who attends carefully, unarisen doubt does not arise and arisen doubt is abandoned."[38]

III. Unwieldy

21 (1)

"Bhikkhus, I do not see even one other thing that when undeveloped is so unwieldy as the mind. An undeveloped mind is unwieldy."

22 (2)
"Bhikkhus, I do not see even one other thing that when developed is so wieldy as the mind. A developed mind is wieldy."

23 (3)
"Bhikkhus, I do not see even one other thing that when undeveloped leads to such great harm as the mind. An undeveloped mind leads to great harm."

24 (4)
"Bhikkhus, I do not see even one other thing that when developed leads to such great good as the mind. A developed mind leads to great good."

25 (5)
"Bhikkhus, I do not see even one other thing that, when undeveloped and unmanifested,[39] leads to such great harm as the mind. The mind, when undeveloped and unmanifested, leads to great harm."

26 (6)
"Bhikkhus, I do not see even one other thing [6] that, when developed and manifested, leads to such great good as the mind. The mind, when developed and manifested, leads to great good."

27 (7)
"Bhikkhus, I do not see even one other thing that, when undeveloped and uncultivated, leads to such great harm as the mind. The mind, when undeveloped and uncultivated, leads to great harm."

28 (8)
"Bhikkhus, I do not see even one other thing that, when developed and cultivated, leads to such great good as the mind. The mind, when developed and cultivated, leads to great good."

29 (9)
"Bhikkhus, I do not see even one other thing that, when undeveloped and uncultivated, brings such suffering as the

mind. The mind, when undeveloped and uncultivated, brings suffering."

30 (10)
"Bhikkhus, I do not see even one other thing that, when developed and cultivated, brings such happiness as the mind. The mind, when developed and cultivated, brings happiness."

IV. Untamed

31 (1)
"Bhikkhus, I do not see even one other thing that when untamed leads to such great harm as the mind. An untamed mind leads to great harm."

32 (2)
"Bhikkhus, I do not see even one other thing that when tamed leads to such great good as the mind. A tamed mind leads to great good."

33 (3)
"Bhikkhus, I do not see even one other thing [7] that when unguarded leads to such great harm as the mind. An unguarded mind leads to great harm."

34 (4)
"Bhikkhus, I do not see even one other thing that when guarded leads to such great good as the mind. A guarded mind leads to great good."

35 (5)
"Bhikkhus, I do not see even one other thing that when unprotected leads to such great harm as the mind. An unprotected mind leads to great harm."

36 (6)
"Bhikkhus, I do not see even one other thing that when protected leads to such great good as the mind. A protected mind leads to great good."

37 (7)

"Bhikkhus, I do not see even one other thing that when unrestrained leads to such great harm as the mind. An unrestrained mind leads to great harm."

38 (8)

"Bhikkhus, I do not see even one other thing that when restrained leads to such great good as the mind. A restrained mind leads to great good."

39 (9)

"Bhikkhus, I do not see even one other thing that, when untamed, unguarded, unprotected, and unrestrained, leads to such great harm as the mind. The mind, when untamed, unguarded, unprotected, and unrestrained, leads to great harm."

40 (10)

"Bhikkhus, I do not see even one other thing that, when tamed, guarded, protected, and restrained, leads to such great good as the mind. The mind, when tamed, guarded, protected, and restrained, leads to great good." [8]

V. A Spike

41 (1)

"Bhikkhus, suppose a misdirected spike of hill rice or barley were pressed by the hand or foot. It is impossible that it would pierce the hand or the foot and draw blood. For what reason? Because the spike is misdirected. So too, it is impossible that a bhikkhu with a misdirected mind would pierce ignorance, arouse true knowledge, and realize nibbāna. For what reason? Because the mind is misdirected."

42 (2)

"Bhikkhus, suppose a well-directed spike of hill rice or barley were pressed by the hand or foot. It is possible that it would pierce the hand or the foot and draw blood. For what reason? Because the spike is well directed. So too, it is possible that a bhikkhu with a well-directed mind would pierce ignorance, arouse true knowledge, and realize nibbāna. For what reason? Because the mind is well directed."

43 (3)

"Here, bhikkhus, having encompassed a mentally corrupted person's mind with my own mind, I understand that if this person were to die at this time, he would be deposited in hell as if brought there.[40] For what reason? Because his mind is corrupted.[41] It is because of mental corruption that with the breakup of the body, after death, some beings here are reborn in the plane of misery, in a bad destination, in the lower world, in hell."

44 (4)

"Here, bhikkhus, having encompassed a mentally placid person's mind with my own mind, I understand that if [9] this person were to die at this time, he would be deposited in heaven as if brought there. For what reason? Because his mind is placid.[42] It is because of mental placidity that with the breakup of the body, after death, some beings here are reborn in a good destination, in a heavenly world."

45 (5)

"Bhikkhus, suppose there were a pool of water that was cloudy, turbid, and muddy. Then a man with good sight standing on the bank could not see shells, gravel and pebbles, and shoals of fish swimming about and resting. For what reason? Because the water is cloudy. So too, it is impossible for a bhikkhu with a cloudy mind to know his own good, the good of others, or the good of both, or to realize a superhuman distinction in knowledge and vision worthy of the noble ones. For what reason? Because his mind is cloudy."[43]

46 (6)

"Bhikkhus, suppose there were a pool of water that was clear, serene, and limpid. Then a man with good sight standing on the bank could see shells, gravel and pebbles, and shoals of fish swimming about and resting. For what reason? Because the water is limpid. So too, it is possible for a bhikkhu with a limpid mind to know his own good, the good of others, and the good of both, and to realize a superhuman distinction in knowledge and vision worthy of the noble ones.[44] For what reason? Because his mind is limpid."

47 (7)

"Bhikkhus, just as sandalwood is declared to be the best of trees with respect to malleability and wieldiness, so too I do not see even one other thing that, when developed and cultivated, is so malleable and wieldy as the mind. A developed and cultivated mind is malleable and wieldy." [10]

48 (8)

"Bhikkhus, I do not see even one other thing that changes so quickly as the mind.[45] It is not easy to give a simile for how quickly the mind changes."

49 (9)

"Luminous, bhikkhus, is this mind, but it is defiled by adventitious defilements."[46]

50 (10)

"Luminous, bhikkhus, is this mind, and it is freed from adventitious defilements."

VI. Luminous

51 (1)

"Luminous, bhikkhus, is this mind, but it is defiled by adventitious defilements. The uninstructed worldling does not understand this as it really is; therefore I say that for the uninstructed worldling there is no development of the mind."[47]

52 (2)

"Luminous, bhikkhus, is this mind, and it is freed from adventitious defilements. The instructed noble disciple understands this as it really is; therefore I say that for the instructed noble disciple there is development of the mind."[48]

53 (3)

"Bhikkhus, if for just the time of a finger snap a bhikkhu pursues a mind of loving-kindness, he is called a bhikkhu who is not devoid of jhāna, who acts upon the teaching of the Teacher, who responds to his advice, and who does not eat the country's almsfood in vain.[49] How much more, then, those who cultivate it!"

54 (4)

"Bhikkhus, if for just the time of a finger snap a bhikkhu develops a mind of loving-kindness, he is called a bhikkhu who is not devoid of jhāna, who acts upon the teaching of the Teacher, who responds to his advice, and who does not eat the country's almsfood in vain. How much more, then, those who cultivate it!" [11]

55 (5)

"Bhikkhus, if for just the time of a finger snap a bhikkhu attends to a mind of loving-kindness, he is called a bhikkhu who is not devoid of jhāna, who acts upon the teaching of the Teacher, who responds to his advice, and who does not eat the country's almsfood in vain. How much more, then, those who cultivate it!"

56 (6)

"Bhikkhus, whatever qualities are unwholesome, partake of the unwholesome, and pertain to the unwholesome, all have the mind as their forerunner.[50] Mind arises first followed by the unwholesome qualities."

57 (7)

"Bhikkhus, whatever qualities are wholesome, partake of the wholesome, and pertain to the wholesome, all have the mind as their forerunner. Mind arises first followed by the wholesome qualities."

58 (8)

"Bhikkhus, I do not see a single thing that so causes unarisen unwholesome qualities to arise and arisen wholesome qualities to decline as heedlessness.[51] For one who is heedless, unarisen unwholesome qualities arise and arisen wholesome qualities decline."

59 (9)

"Bhikkhus, I do not see a single thing that so causes unarisen wholesome qualities to arise and arisen unwholesome qualities to decline as heedfulness. For one who is heedful, unarisen wholesome qualities arise and arisen unwholesome qualities decline."

60 (10)

"Bhikkhus, I do not see a single thing that so causes unarisen unwholesome qualities to arise and arisen wholesome qualities to decline as laziness. For one who is lazy, unarisen unwholesome qualities arise and arisen wholesome qualities decline." [12]

VII. Arousal of Energy

61 (1)

"Bhikkhus, I do not see even a single thing that so causes unarisen wholesome qualities to arise and arisen unwholesome qualities to decline as arousal of energy. For one who has aroused energy, unarisen wholesome qualities arise and arisen unwholesome qualities decline."

62 (2)

"Bhikkhus, I do not see even a single thing that so causes unarisen unwholesome qualities to arise and arisen wholesome qualities to decline as strong desire.[52] For one with strong desire, unarisen unwholesome qualities arise and arisen wholesome qualities decline."

63 (3)

"Bhikkhus, I do not see even a single thing that so causes unarisen wholesome qualities to arise and arisen unwholesome qualities to decline as fewness of desires.[53] For one with few desires, unarisen wholesome qualities arise and arisen unwholesome qualities decline."

64 (4)
"Bhikkhus, I do not see even a single thing that so causes unarisen unwholesome qualities to arise and arisen wholesome qualities to decline as non-contentment.[54] For one who is not content, unarisen unwholesome qualities arise and arisen wholesome qualities decline."

65 (5)
"Bhikkhus, I do not see even a single thing that so causes unarisen wholesome qualities to arise and arisen unwholesome qualities to decline as contentment.[55] For one who is content, unarisen wholesome qualities arise and arisen unwholesome qualities decline." [13]

66 (6)
"Bhikkhus, I do not see even a single thing that so causes unarisen unwholesome qualities to arise and arisen wholesome qualities to decline as careless attention. For one who attends carelessly, unarisen unwholesome qualities arise and arisen wholesome qualities decline."

67 (7)
"Bhikkhus, I do not see even a single thing that so causes unarisen wholesome qualities to arise and arisen unwholesome qualities to decline as careful attention. For one who attends carefully, unarisen wholesome qualities arise and arisen unwholesome qualities decline."

68 (8)
"Bhikkhus, I do not see even a single thing that so causes unarisen unwholesome qualities to arise and arisen wholesome qualities to decline as lack of clear comprehension. For one who does not clearly comprehend, unarisen unwholesome qualities arise and arisen wholesome qualities decline."

69 (9)
"Bhikkhus, I do not see even a single thing that so causes unarisen wholesome qualities to arise and arisen unwholesome qualities to decline as clear comprehension.[56] For one who clearly comprehends, unarisen wholesome qualities arise and arisen unwholesome qualities decline."

70 (10)

"Bhikkhus, I do not see even a single thing that so causes unarisen unwholesome qualities to arise and arisen wholesome qualities to decline as bad friendship. For one with bad friends, unarisen unwholesome qualities arise and arisen wholesome qualities decline." [14]

VIII. Good Friendship

71 (1)

"Bhikkhus, I do not see even a single thing that so causes unarisen wholesome qualities to arise and arisen unwholesome qualities to decline as good friendship. For one with good friends, unarisen wholesome qualities arise and arisen unwholesome qualities decline."[57]

72 (2)

"Bhikkhus, I do not see even a single thing that so causes unarisen unwholesome qualities to arise and arisen wholesome qualities to decline as the pursuit of unwholesome qualities and the non-pursuit of wholesome qualities. Through the pursuit of unwholesome qualities and the non-pursuit of wholesome qualities, unarisen unwholesome qualities arise and arisen wholesome qualities decline."

73 (3)

"Bhikkhus, I do not see even a single thing that so causes unarisen wholesome qualities to arise and arisen unwholesome qualities to decline as the pursuit of wholesome qualities and the non-pursuit of unwholesome qualities. Through the pursuit of wholesome qualities and the non-pursuit of unwholesome qualities, unarisen wholesome qualities arise and arisen unwholesome qualities decline."

74 (4)

"Bhikkhus, I do not see even a single thing that so causes unarisen factors of enlightenment not to arise and arisen factors of enlightenment not to reach fulfillment by development as careless attention. For one who attends carelessly, unarisen factors of enlightenment do not arise and arisen factors of enlightenment do not reach fulfillment by development."

75 (5)
"Bhikkhus, I do not see even a single thing that so causes unarisen factors of enlightenment to arise and arisen factors of enlightenment to reach fulfillment by development as careful attention. [15] For one who attends carefully, unarisen factors of enlightenment arise and arisen factors of enlightenment reach fulfillment by development."

76 (6)
"Insignificant, bhikkhus, is the loss of relatives. The worst thing to lose is wisdom."

77 (7)
"Insignificant, bhikkhus, is the increase of relatives. The best thing in which to increase is wisdom. Therefore, bhikkhus, you should train yourselves thus: 'We will increase in wisdom.' It is in such a way that you should train yourselves."

78 (8)
"Insignificant, bhikkhus, is the loss of wealth. The worst thing to lose is wisdom."

79 (9)
"Insignificant, bhikkhus, is the increase of wealth. The best thing in which to increase is wisdom. Therefore, bhikkhus, you should train yourselves thus: 'We will increase in wisdom.' It is in such a way that you should train yourselves."

80 (10)
"Insignificant, bhikkhus, is the loss of fame. The worst thing to lose is wisdom."

81 (11)[58]
"Insignificant, bhikkhus, is the increase of fame. The best thing in which to increase is wisdom. Therefore, bhikkhus, you should train yourselves thus: 'We will increase in wisdom.' It is in such a way that you should train yourselves." [16]

IX. Heedlessness

82 (1)

"Bhikkhus, I do not see even a single thing that leads to such great harm as heedlessness. Heedlessness leads to great harm."

83 (2)

"Bhikkhus, I do not see even a single thing that leads to such great good as heedfulness. Heedfulness leads to great good."

84 (3)–97 (16)

(84) "Bhikkhus, I do not see even a single thing that leads to such great harm as laziness ... (85) ... that leads to such great good as arousal of energy ..."

(86) "... strong desire ... (87) ... fewness of desires ..."

(88) "... non-contentment ... (89) ... contentment ..."

(90) "... careless attention ... (91) ... careful attention ..."

(92) "... lack of clear comprehension ... (93) ... clear comprehension ..."

(94) "... bad friendship ... (95) ... good friendship ..."

(96) "... the pursuit of unwholesome qualities and the non-pursuit of wholesome qualities ... (97) ... the pursuit of wholesome qualities and the non-pursuit of unwholesome qualities. The pursuit of wholesome qualities and the non-pursuit of unwholesome qualities leads to great good."

X. Internal[59]

98 (1)

"Among internal factors, bhikkhus, I do not see even a single factor that leads to such great harm as heedlessness. Heedlessness leads to great harm."

99 (2)

"Among internal factors, bhikkhus, I do not see even a single factor that leads to such great good as heedfulness. [17] Heedfulness leads to great good."

100 (3)–113 (16)

(100) "Among internal factors, bhikkhus, I do not see even a single factor that leads to such great harm as laziness . . . (101) . . . that leads to such great good as arousal of energy . . ."[60]

(102) ". . . strong desire . . . (103) . . . fewness of desires . . ."

(104) ". . . non-contentment . . . (105) . . . contentment . . ."

(106) ". . . careless attention . . . (107) . . . careful attention . . ."

(108) ". . . lack of clear comprehension . . . (109) . . . clear comprehension . . ."

(110) "Among external factors, bhikkhus, I do not see even a single factor that leads to such great harm as bad friendship. . . ."

(111) "Among external factors, bhikkhus, I do not see even a single factor that leads to such great good as good friendship. . . ."

(112) "Among internal factors, bhikkhus, I do not see even a single factor that leads to such great harm as the pursuit of unwholesome qualities and the non-pursuit of wholesome qualities . . . (113) . . . that leads to such great good as the pursuit of wholesome qualities and the non-pursuit of unwholesome qualities. The pursuit of wholesome qualities and the non-pursuit of unwholesome qualities leads to great good."

114 (17)

"Bhikkhus, I do not see even a single thing that so leads to the decline and disappearance of the good Dhamma as heedlessness. Heedlessness leads to the decline and disappearance of the good Dhamma."

115 (18)

"Bhikkhus, I do not see even a single thing that so leads to the continuation, non-decline, and non-disappearance of the good Dhamma as heedfulness. [18] Heedfulness leads to the continuation, non-decline, and non-disappearance of the good Dhamma."

116 (19)–129 (32)

(116) "Bhikkhus, I do not see even a single thing that so leads to the decline and disappearance of the good Dhamma as laziness . . . (117) . . . that so leads to the continuation, non-decline,

and non-disappearance of the good Dhamma as arousal of energy..."

(118) "...strong desire...(119)...fewness of desires..."

(120) "...non-contentment...(121)...contentment..."

(122) "...careless attention...(123)...careful attention..."

(124) "...lack of clear comprehension...(125)...clear comprehension..."

(126) "...bad friendship...(127)...good friendship..."

(128) "...the pursuit of unwholesome qualities and the non-pursuit of wholesome qualities...(129)...the pursuit of wholesome qualities and the non-pursuit of unwholesome qualities. The pursuit of wholesome qualities and the non-pursuit of unwholesome qualities leads to the continuation, non-decline, and non-disappearance of the good Dhamma."

130 (33)

"Bhikkhus, those bhikkhus who explain non-Dhamma as Dhamma are acting for the harm of many people, the unhappiness of many people, for the ruin, harm, and suffering of many people, of devas and human beings.[61] These bhikkhus generate much demerit and cause this good Dhamma to disappear."

131 (34)–139 (42)

(131) "Bhikkhus, those bhikkhus who explain Dhamma as non-Dhamma...(132)...non-discipline as discipline[62]...(133)...discipline as non-discipline...(134)...what has not been stated and uttered by the Tathāgata as having been stated and uttered by him...[19] (135)...what has been stated and uttered by the Tathāgata as not having been stated and uttered by him...(136)...what has not been practiced by the Tathāgata as having been practiced by him...(137)...what has been practiced by the Tathāgata as not having been practiced by him...(138)...what has not been prescribed by the Tathāgata as having been prescribed by him...(139)...what has been prescribed by the Tathāgata as not having been prescribed by him are acting for the harm of many people, for the unhappiness of many people, for the ruin, harm, and suffering of many people, of devas and human beings. These bhikkhus generate much demerit and cause this good Dhamma to disappear."[63]

XI. Non-Dhamma[64]

140 (1)

"Bhikkhus, those bhikkhus who explain non-Dhamma as non-Dhamma are acting for the welfare of many people, for the happiness of many people, for the good, welfare, and happiness of many people, of devas and human beings. These bhikkhus generate much merit and sustain this good Dhamma."

141 (2)–149 (10)

(141) "Bhikkhus, those bhikkhus who explain Dhamma as Dhamma . . . (142) . . . non-discipline as non-discipline . . . (143) . . . discipline as discipline . . . (144) . . . what has not been stated and uttered by the Tathāgata as not having been stated and uttered by him . . . (145) . . . what has been stated and uttered by the Tathāgata as having been stated and uttered by him. . . [20] (146) . . . what has not been practiced by the Tathāgata as not having been practiced by him . . . (147) . . . what has been practiced by the Tathāgata as having been practiced by him . . . (148) . . . what has not been prescribed by the Tathāgata as not having been prescribed by him . . . (149) . . . what has been prescribed by the Tathāgata as having been prescribed by him are acting for the welfare of many people, for the happiness of many people, for the good, welfare, and happiness of many people, of devas and human beings. These bhikkhus generate much merit and sustain this good Dhamma."

XII. Not an Offense[65]

150 (1)

"Bhikkhus, those bhikkhus who explain what is not an offense as an offense are acting for the harm of many people, for the unhappiness of many people, for the ruin, harm, and suffering of many people, of devas and human beings. These bhikkhus generate much demerit and cause this good Dhamma to disappear."

151 (2)–159 (10)

(151) "Bhikkhus, those bhikkhus who explain what is an offense as no offense ... (152) ... a light offense as a grave offense ... (153) ... a grave offense as a light offense ... (154) ... a coarse offense as not a coarse offense ... (155) ... an offense that is not coarse as a coarse offense ... (156) ... a remediable offense as an irremediable offense ... [21] (157) ... an irremediable offense as a remediable offense ... (158) ... an offense with redress as an offense without redress ... (159) ... an offense without redress as an offense with redress are acting for the harm of many people, for the unhappiness of many people, for the ruin, harm, and suffering of many people, of devas and human beings.[66] These bhikkhus generate much demerit and cause this good Dhamma to disappear."

160 (11)

"Bhikkhus, those bhikkhus who explain what is no offense as no offense are acting for the welfare of many people, for the happiness of many people, for the good, welfare, and happiness of many people, of devas and humans. These bhikkhus generate much merit and sustain this good Dhamma."

161 (12)–169 (20)

(161) "Bhikkhus, those bhikkhus who explain an offense as an offense ... (162) ... a light offense as a light offense ... (163) ... a grave offense as a grave offense ... (164) ... a coarse offense as a coarse offense ... (165) ... an offense that is not coarse as not a coarse offense ... (166) ... a remediable offense as a remediable offense ... (167) ... an irremediable offense as an irremediable offense ... (168) ... an offense with redress as an offense with redress ... (169) ... an offense without redress as an offense without redress are acting for the welfare of many people, for the happiness of many people, for the good, welfare, and happiness of many people, of devas and humans. These bhikkhus generate much merit and sustain this good Dhamma." [22]

XIII. One Person

170 (1)

"Bhikkhus, there is one person who arises in the world for the welfare of many people, for the happiness of many people, out of compassion for the world, for the good, welfare, and happiness of devas and human beings.[67] Who is that one person? The Tathāgata, the Arahant, the Perfectly Enlightened One. This is that one person who arises in the world ... for the good, welfare, and happiness of devas and human beings."

171 (2)–174 (5)

(171) "Bhikkhus, the manifestation of one person is rare in the world ... (172) ... there is one person arising in the world who is extraordinary ... (173) ... the death of one person is lamented by many people ... (174)[68] ... there is one person arising in the world who is unique, without a peer, without counterpart, incomparable, matchless, unrivaled, unequaled, without equal,[69] the foremost of bipeds.[70] Who is that one person? The Tathāgata, the Arahant, the Perfectly Enlightened One. This is that one person arising in the world who is ... the foremost of bipeds."

175 (6)–186 (17)[71]

"Bhikkhus, the manifestation of one person is the (175) manifestation of great vision ... (176) ... the manifestation of great light ... (177) ... the manifestation of great radiance ... (178) ... the manifestation of the six things unsurpassed ... (179) ... the realization of the four analytical knowledges ... (180) ... the penetration of numerous elements ... (181) ... the penetration of the diversity of elements ... (182) ... the realization of the fruit of true knowledge and liberation [23] ... (183) ... the realization of the fruit of stream-entry ... (184) ... the realization of the fruit of once-returning ... (185) ... the realization of the fruit of non-returning ... (186) ... the realization of the fruit of arahantship. Who is that one person? The Tathāgata, the Arahant, the Perfectly Enlightened One. This is that one person whose manifestation is the manifestation of great vision ... the realization of the fruit of arahantship."[72]

187 (18)

"Bhikkhus, I do not see even a single person who properly continues to keep in motion the unsurpassed wheel of the Dhamma set in motion by the Tathāgata as does Sāriputta. Sāriputta properly continues to keep in motion the unsurpassed wheel of the Dhamma set in motion by the Tathāgata."

XIV. Foremost[73]

i. First Subchapter

188 (1)–197 (10)

(188) "Bhikkhus, the foremost of my bhikkhu disciples in seniority is Aññākoṇḍañña."[74]

(189) "... among those with great wisdom is Sāriputta."[75]

(190) "... among those with psychic potency is Mahāmoggallāna."[76]

(191) "... among those who expound the ascetic practices is Mahākassapa."[77]

(192) "... among those with the divine eye is Anuruddha."[78]

(193) "... among those from eminent families is Bhaddiya Kāḷigodhāyaputta."[79]

(194) "... among those with a sweet voice is Lakuṇṭaka Bhaddiya."[80]

(195) "... among those with the lion's roar is Piṇḍola Bhāradvāja."[81]

(196) "... among those who speak on the Dhamma is Puṇṇa Mantāṇiputta."[82]

(197) "... among those who explain in detail the meaning of what has been stated in brief is Mahākaccāna." [24]

ii. Second Subchapter

198 (1)–208 (11)

(198) "Bhikkhus, the foremost of my bhikkhu disciples among those who create a mind-made body is Cullapanthaka."[83]

(199) "... among those skilled in mental transformation is Cullapanthaka."

(200) "... among those skilled in the transformation of perception is Mahāpanthaka."[84]

(201) "... among those who dwell without conflict is Subhūti."[85]

(202) "... among those worthy of gifts is Subhūti."

(203) "... among forest dwellers is Revata Khadiravaniya."[86]

(204) "... among meditators is Kaṅkhārevata."[87]

(205) "... among those who arouse energy is Soṇa Koḷivīsa."[88]

(206) "... among those who are excellent speakers is Soṇa Kuṭikaṇṇa."[89]

(207) "... among those who make gains is Sīvalī."[90]

(208) "... among those resolved through faith is Vakkalī."[91]

iii. Third Subchapter

209 (1)–218 (10)

(209) "Bhikkhus, the foremost of my bhikkhu disciples among those who desire the training is Rāhula."[92]

(210) "... among those who have gone forth out of faith is Raṭṭhapāla."[93]

(211) "... among those who are first to take meal tickets is Kuṇḍadhāna."[94]

(212) "... among those who compose inspired verse is Vaṅgīsa."[95]

(213) "... among those who inspire confidence in all respects is Upasena Vaṅgantaputta."[96]

(214) "... among those who assign lodgings is Dabba Mallaputta."[97]

(215) "... among those pleasing and agreeable to the deities is Piḷindavaccha."[98]

(216) "... among those who quickly attain direct knowledge is Bāhiya Dārucīriya."[99]

(217) "... among those with variegated speech is Kumārakassapa."[100]

(218) "... among those who have attained the analytical knowledges is Mahākoṭṭhita."[101]

iv. Fourth Subchapter

219 (1)–234 (16)

(219) "Bhikkhus, the foremost of my bhikkhu disciples among those who are learned is Ānanda."[102]

(220) "... among those with good memory is Ānanda." [25]

(221) "... among those with a quick grasp is Ānanda."[103]

(222) "... among those who are resolute is Ānanda."[104]

(223) "... among personal attendants is Ānanda."

(224) "... among those with a large retinue is Uruvelakassapa."[105]

(225) "... among those who inspire confidence in families is Kāludāyi."[106]

(226) "... among those with good health is Bakkula."[107]

(227) "... among those who recollect past lives is Sobhita."[108]

(228) "... among the upholders of the discipline is Upāli."[109]

(229) "... among those who exhort bhikkhunīs is Nandaka."[110]

(230) "... among those who guard the doors of the sense faculties is Nanda."[111]

(231) "... among those who exhort bhikkhus is Mahākappina."[112]

(232) "... among those with skill with the fire element is Sāgata."[113]

(233) "... among those who receive eloquent discourses is Rādha."[114]

(234) "... among those who wear coarse robes is Mogharājā."[115]

v. Fifth Subchapter

235 (1)–247 (13)

(235) "Bhikkhus, the foremost of my bhikkhunī disciples in seniority is Mahāpajāpatī Gotamī."[116]

(236) "... among those with great wisdom is Khemā."[117]

(237) "... among those with psychic potency is Uppalavaṇṇā."[118]

(238) "... among those who uphold the discipline is Paṭācārā."[119]

(239) "... among speakers on the Dhamma is Dhammadinnā."[120]

(240) "... among meditators is Nandā."[121]

(241) "... among those who arouse energy is Soṇā."[122]

(242) "... among those with the divine eye is Sakulā."[123]

(243) "... among those who quickly attain direct knowledge is Bhaddā Kuṇḍalakesā."[124]

(244) "... among those who recollect past lives is Bhaddā Kāpilānī."[125]

(245) "... among those who attain great direct knowledge is Bhaddā Kaccānā."[126]

(246) "... among those who wear coarse robes is Kisāgotamī."[127]

(247) "... among those resolved through faith is Sigālamātā."[128]

vi. Sixth Subchapter

248 (1)–257 (10)

(248) "Bhikkhus, the foremost of my male lay followers in being the first to go for refuge [26] are the merchants Tapussa and Bhallika."[129]

(249) "... among donors is the householder Sudatta Anāthapiṇḍika."[130]

(250) "... among speakers on the Dhamma is the householder Citta of Macchikāsaṇḍa."[131]

(251) "... among those who make use of the four means of attracting and sustaining others is Hatthaka of Āḷavī."[132]

(252) "... among those who give what is excellent is Mahānāma the Sakyan."[133]

(253) "... among those who give what is agreeable is the householder Ugga of Vesālī."[134]

(254) "... among attendants of the Saṅgha is the householder Uggata."[135]

(255) "... among those with unwavering confidence is Sūra Ambaṭṭha."[136]

(256) "... among those with confidence in persons is Jīvaka Komārabhacca."[137]

(257) "... among those who have trust is the householder Nakulapitā."[138]

vii. Seventh Subchapter

258 (1)–267 (10)

(258) "Bhikkhus, the foremost of my female lay followers in being the first to go for refuge is Sujātā, daughter of Senānī."[139]

(259) "... among donors is Visākhā Migāramātā."[140]

(260) "... among those who are learned is Khujjuttarā."[141]

(261) "... among those who dwell in loving-kindness is Sāmāvatī."[142]

(262) "... among meditators is Uttarā Nandamātā."[143]

(263) "... among those who give what is excellent is Suppavāsā the Koliyan daughter."[144]

(264) "... among those who attend on the sick is the female lay follower Suppiyā."[145]

(265) "... among those with unwavering confidence is Kātiyānī."[146]

(266) "...among those who are intimate is the housewife Nakulamātā."[147]

(267) "...among those whose confidence is based on hearsay is the female lay follower Kāḷī of Kuraraghara."[148]

XV. Impossible[149]

268 (1)

"It is impossible and inconceivable, bhikkhus, that a person accomplished in view could consider any conditioned phenomenon as permanent; there is no such possibility. But it is possible [27] that a worldling might consider some conditioned phenomenon as permanent; there is such a possibility."[150]

269 (2)

"It is impossible and inconceivable, bhikkhus, that a person accomplished in view could consider any conditioned phenomenon as pleasurable; there is no such possibility. But it is possible that a worldling might consider some conditioned phenomenon as pleasurable; there is such a possibility."[151]

270 (3)

"It is impossible and inconceivable, bhikkhus, that a person accomplished in view could consider anything as a self; there is no such possibility. But it is possible that a worldling might consider something as a self; there is such a possibility."[152]

271 (4)–276 (9)

(271) "It is impossible and inconceivable, bhikkhus, that a person accomplished in view could deprive his mother of life...(272) that a person accomplished in view could deprive his father of life...(273) that a person accomplished in view could deprive an arahant of life...(274) that a person accomplished in view could, with a mind of hatred, shed the blood of the Tathāgatha...(275) that a person accomplished in view could create a schism in the Saṅgha...(276) that a person accomplished in view could acknowledge someone other [than the Buddha] as teacher; there is no such possibility. But it is possible that a worldling could acknowledge someone other [than the Buddha] as teacher; there is such a possibility."[153]

277 (10)

"It is impossible and inconceivable, bhikkhus, that two arahants who are perfectly enlightened Buddhas[154] [28] could arise contemporaneously in one world system; there is no such possibility. But it is possible that one arahant who is a perfectly enlightened Buddha might arise in one world system; there is such a possibility."[155]

278 (11)

"It is impossible and inconceivable, bhikkhus, that two wheel-turning monarchs could arise contemporaneously in one world system; there is no such possibility.[156] But it is possible that one wheel-turning monarch might arise in one world system; there is such a possibility."

279 (12)–283 (16)

(279) "It is impossible and inconceivable, bhikkhus, that a woman could be an arahant who is a perfectly enlightened Buddha . . . (280) . . . that a woman could be a wheel-turning monarch . . . (281) . . . that a woman could occupy the position of Sakka . . . (282) . . . that a woman could occupy the position of Māra . . . (283) . . . that a woman could occupy the position of Brahmā; there is no such possibility. But it is possible that a man could occupy the position of Brahmā; there is such a possibility."[157]

284 (17)–286 (19)

(284) "It is impossible and inconceivable, bhikkhus, that a wished for, desired, agreeable result could be produced from bodily misconduct . . . (285) . . . that a wished for, desired, agreeable result could be produced from verbal misconduct . . . (286) . . . that a wished for, desired, agreeable result could be produced from mental misconduct; there is no such possibility. But it is possible that an unwished for, undesired, disagreeable result might be produced [from bodily misconduct . . . from verbal misconduct . . .] from mental misconduct; there is such a possibility."

287 (20)–289 (22)

(287) "It is impossible and inconceivable, bhikkhus, that an unwished for, undesired, disagreeable result could be produced from bodily good conduct [29] . . . (288) . . . that an unwished for,

undesired, disagreeable result could be produced from verbal good conduct...(289)...that an unwished for, undesired, disagreeable result could be produced from mental good conduct; there is no such possibility. But it is possible that a wished for, desired, agreeable result could be produced [from bodily good conduct...from verbal good conduct...] from mental good conduct; there is such a possibility."[158]

290 (23)–292 (25)

(290) "It is impossible and inconceivable, bhikkhus, that a person engaging in bodily misconduct could on that account, for that reason, with the breakup of the body, after death, be reborn in a good destination, in a heavenly world...(291)...that a person engaging in verbal misconduct could on that account, for that reason, with the breakup of the body, after death, be reborn in a good destination, in a heavenly world...(292)...that a person engaging in mental misconduct could on that account, for that reason, with the breakup of the body, after death, be reborn in a good destination, in a heavenly world; there is no such possibility. But it is possible that a person engaging [in bodily misconduct...in verbal misconduct...] in mental misconduct could on that account, for that reason, with the breakup of the body, after death, be reborn in the plane of misery, in a bad destination, in the lower world, in hell; there is such a possibility."

293 (26)–295 (28)

(293) "It is impossible and inconceivable, bhikkhus, that a person engaging in bodily good conduct could on that account, for that reason, with the breakup of the body, after death, be reborn in the plane of misery, in a bad destination, in the lower world, in hell...(294)...that a person engaging in verbal good conduct could on that account, for that reason, with the breakup of the body, after death, be reborn in the plane of misery, in a bad destination, in the lower world, in hell...(295)...that a person engaging in mental good conduct could on that account, for that reason, with the breakup of the body, after death, be reborn in the plane of misery, in a bad destination, in the lower world, in hell; there is no such possibility. But it is possible [30] that a person engaging [in bodily good conduct...in verbal

good conduct...] in mental good conduct could on that account, for that reason, with the breakup of the body, after death, be reborn in a good destination, in a heavenly world; there is such a possibility."

XVI. One Thing[159]

i. First Subchapter

296 (1)

"Bhikkhus, there is one thing that, when developed and cultivated, leads exclusively to disenchantment, to dispassion, to cessation, to peace, to direct knowledge, to enlightenment, to nibbāna.[160] What is that one thing? Recollection of the Buddha.[161] This is that one thing that, when developed and cultivated, leads exclusively to disenchantment... to nibbāna."

297 (2)–305 (10)[162]

(297) "Bhikkhus, there is one thing that, when developed and cultivated, leads exclusively to disenchantment, to dispassion, to cessation, to peace, to direct knowledge, to enlightenment, to nibbāna. What is that one thing? Recollection of the Dhamma.... (298) Recollection of the Saṅgha.... (299) Recollection of virtuous behavior.... (300) Recollection of generosity.... (301) Recollection of the devas.... (302) Mindfulness of breathing.... (303) Mindfulness of death.... (304) Mindfulness directed to the body.... (305) Recollection of peace.[163] This is that one thing that, when developed and cultivated, leads exclusively to disenchantment... to nibbāna."

ii. Second Subchapter[164]

306 (1)

"Bhikkhus, I do not see even a single thing on account of which unarisen unwholesome qualities arise and arisen unwholesome qualities increase and expand so much as wrong view. For one of wrong view, unarisen unwholesome qualities arise and arisen unwholesome qualities increase and expand."

307 (2)

"Bhikkhus, I do not see even a single thing on account of which unarisen wholesome qualities arise and arisen wholesome qualities increase and expand so much as right view. [31] For one of right view, unarisen wholesome qualities arise and arisen wholesome qualities increase and expand."

308 (3)

"Bhikkhus, I do not see even a single thing on account of which unarisen wholesome qualities do not arise and arisen wholesome qualities decline so much as wrong view.[165] For one of wrong view, unarisen wholesome qualities do not arise and arisen wholesome qualities decline."

309 (4)

"Bhikkhus, I do not see even a single thing on account of which unarisen unwholesome qualities do not arise and arisen unwholesome qualities decline so much as right view.[166] For one of right view, unarisen unwholesome qualities do not arise and arisen unwholesome qualities decline."

310 (5)

"Bhikkhus, I do not see even a single thing on account of which unarisen wrong view arises and arisen wrong view increases so much as careless attention. For one of careless attention, unarisen wrong view arises and arisen wrong view increases."[167]

311 (6)

"Bhikkhus, I do not see even a single thing on account of which unarisen right view arises and arisen right view increases so much as careful attention. For one of careful attention, unarisen right view arises and arisen right view increases."[168]

312 (7)

"Bhikkhus, I do not see even a single thing on account of which, with the breakup of the body, after death, beings are reborn in the plane of misery, in a bad destination, in the lower world, in hell, so much as wrong view. Possessing wrong view, with the breakup of the body, after death, beings are reborn in the plane of misery, in a bad destination, in the lower world, in hell."

313 (8)

"Bhikkhus, I do not see even a single thing [32] on account of which, with the breakup of the body, after death, beings are reborn in a good destination, in a heavenly world, so much as right view. Possessing right view, with the breakup of the body, after death, beings are reborn in a good destination, in a heavenly world."

314 (9)[169]

"Bhikkhus, for a person of wrong view, whatever bodily kamma, verbal kamma, and mental kamma he instigates and undertakes in accordance with that view, and whatever his volition, yearning, inclination, and volitional activities, all lead to what is unwished for, undesired, and disagreeable, to harm and suffering. For what reason? Because the view is bad.

"Suppose, bhikkhus, a seed of neem, bitter cucumber, or bitter gourd[170] were planted in moist soil. Whatever nutrients it takes up from the soil and from the water would all lead to its bitter, pungent, and disagreeable flavor. For what reason? Because the seed is bad. So too, for a person of wrong view ... all lead to what is unwished for, undesired, and disagreeable, to harm and suffering. For what reason? Because the view is bad."

315 (10)

"Bhikkhus, for a person of right view, whatever bodily kamma, verbal kamma, and mental kamma he instigates and undertakes in accordance with that view, and whatever his volition, yearning, inclination, and volitional activities, all lead to what is wished for, desired, and agreeable, to well-being and happiness. For what reason? Because the view is good.

"Suppose, bhikkhus, a seed of sugar cane, hill rice, or grape were planted in moist soil. Whatever nutrients it takes up from the soil and from the water would all lead to its sweet, agreeable, and delectable flavor.[171] For what reason? Because the seed is good. So too, for a person of right view ... all lead to what is wished for, desired, and agreeable, to welfare and happiness. For what reason? Because the view is good." [33]

iii. Third Subchapter[172]

316 (1)

"Bhikkhus, there is one person who arises in the world for the harm of many people, for the unhappiness of many people, for the ruin, harm, and suffering of many people, of devas and human beings. Who is that one person? It is one who holds wrong view and has an incorrect perspective. He draws many people away from the good Dhamma and establishes them in a bad Dhamma. This is that one person who arises in the world for the harm of many people, the unhappiness of many people, for the ruin, harm, and suffering of many people, of devas and human beings."[173]

317 (2)

"Bhikkhus, there is one person who arises in the world for the welfare of many people, for the happiness of many people, for the good, welfare, and happiness of many people, of devas and human beings. Who is that one person? It is one who holds right view and has a correct perspective. He draws many people away from a bad Dhamma and establishes them in the good Dhamma. This is that one person who arises in the world for the welfare of many people, for the happiness of many people, for the good, welfare, and happiness of many people, of devas and human beings."[174]

318 (3)

"Bhikkhus, I do not see even a single thing so blameworthy as wrong view. Wrong view is the worst of things that are blameworthy."

319 (4)

"Bhikkhus, I do not see even a single person who is acting so much for the harm of many people, the unhappiness of many people, for the ruin, harm, and suffering of many people, of devas and human beings, as the hollow man Makkhali.[175] Just as a trap set at the mouth of a river would bring about harm, suffering, calamity, and disaster for many fish, so too, the hollow man Makkhali is, as it were, a 'trap for people'[176] who has arisen in the world for the harm, suffering, calamity, and disaster of many beings." [34]

320 (5)

"Bhikkhus, one who encourages [others] in a badly expounded Dhamma and discipline, and the one whom he encourages, and the one who, thus encouraged, practices in accordance with it, all generate much demerit. For what reason? Because that Dhamma is badly expounded."

321 (6)

"Bhikkhus, one who encourages [others] in a well-expounded Dhamma and discipline, and the one whom he encourages, and the one who, thus encouraged, practices in accordance with it, all generate much merit. For what reason? Because that Dhamma is well expounded."

322 (7)

"Bhikkhus, with a badly expounded Dhamma and discipline, moderation should be known by the giver [of a gift], not by the recipient.[177] For what reason? Because that Dhamma is badly expounded."

323 (8)

"Bhikkhus, with a well-expounded Dhamma and discipline, moderation should be known by the recipient [of a gift], not by the giver.[178] For what reason? Because that Dhamma is well expounded."

324 (9)

"Bhikkhus, whoever arouses energy in a badly expounded Dhamma and discipline dwells in suffering. For what reason? Because that Dhamma is badly expounded."

325 (10)

"Bhikkhus, whoever is lazy in a well-expounded Dhamma and discipline dwells in suffering. For what reason? Because that Dhamma is well expounded."

326 (11)

"Bhikkhus, whoever is lazy in a badly expounded Dhamma and discipline dwells in happiness. For what reason? Because that Dhamma is badly expounded."

327 (12)

"Bhikkhus, whoever arouses energy in a well-expounded Dhamma and discipline dwells in happiness. For what reason? Because that Dhamma is well expounded."

328 (13)

"Bhikkhus, just as even a trifling amount of feces is foul smelling, so too I do not praise even a trifling amount of existence, even for a mere finger snap."[179]

329 (14)–332 (17)[180]

(329) "Bhikkhus, just as even a trifling amount of urine is foul smelling... (330) a trifling amount of saliva is foul smelling... (331) a trifling amount of pus is foul smelling... [35]... (332) a trifling amount of blood is foul smelling, so too I do not praise even a trifling amount of existence, even for a mere finger snap."

iv. Jambudīpa Repetition Series [Fourth Subchapter][181]

333 (1)–347 (15)[182]

(333) "Just as, bhikkhus, in this Jambudīpa,[183] delightful parks, groves, landscapes, and lotus ponds are few, while more numerous are the hills and slopes, rivers that are hard to cross, places with stumps and thorns, and rugged mountains, so too those beings are few who are born on dry ground; more numerous are those beings who are born in water."

(334) "... so too those beings are few who are reborn among human beings; more numerous are those beings who have been reborn elsewhere than among human beings."

(335) "... so too those beings are few who are reborn in the middle provinces; more numerous are those who have been reborn in the outlying provinces among the uncouth foreigners."[184]

(336) "... so too those beings are few who are wise, intelligent, astute, able to understand the meaning of what has been well stated and badly stated; more numerous are those who are

unwise, stupid, obtuse, unable to understand the meaning of what has been well stated and badly stated."

(337) "...so too those beings are few who are endowed with the noble eye of wisdom; more numerous are those beings who are confused and immersed in ignorance."[185]

(338) "...so too those beings are few who get to see the Tathāgata; more numerous are those beings who do not get to see him."

(339) "...so too those beings are few who get to hear the Dhamma and discipline expounded by the Tathāgata; [36] more numerous are those who do not get to hear it."

(340) "...so too those beings are few who, having heard the Dhamma, retain it in mind; more numerous are those who, having heard the Dhamma, do not retain it in mind."

(341) "...so too those beings are few who examine the meaning of the teachings that have been retained in mind; more numerous are those who do not examine the meaning of the teachings that have been retained in mind."

(342) "...so too those beings are few who understand the meaning and the Dhamma and then practice in accordance with the Dhamma; more numerous are those who do not understand the meaning and the Dhamma and do not practice in accordance with the Dhamma."[186]

(343) "...so too those beings are few who acquire a sense of urgency about things inspiring urgency; more numerous are those who do not acquire a sense of urgency about things inspiring urgency."[187]

(344) "...so too those beings are few who, when inspired with a sense of urgency, strive carefully; more numerous are those who, when inspired with a sense of urgency, do not strive carefully."

(345) "...so too those beings are few who gain concentration, one-pointedness of mind, based on release; more numerous are those who do not gain concentration, one-pointedness of mind, based on release."[188]

(346) "...so too those beings are few who obtain the exquisite taste of delicious food; more numerous are those who do not gain such food but subsist on scraps brought in a bowl."

(347) "...so too those beings are few who obtain the taste of the meaning, the taste of the Dhamma, the taste of liberation; more

numerous are those who do not obtain the taste of the meaning, the taste of the Dhamma, the taste of liberation.[189] Therefore, bhikkhus, you should train yourselves thus: 'We will obtain the taste of the meaning, the taste of the Dhamma, the taste of liberation.' It is in such a way that you should train yourselves." [37]

348 (16)–377 (45)[190]

(348)–(350) "Just as, bhikkhus, in this Jambudīpa delightful parks, groves, landscapes, and lotus ponds are few, while more numerous are the hills and slopes, rivers that are hard to cross, places with stumps and thorns, and rugged mountains, so too those beings are few who, when they pass away as human beings, are reborn among human beings. More numerous are those who, when they pass away as human beings, are reborn in hell ... in the animal realm ... in the sphere of afflicted spirits."[191]

(351)–(353) "... so too those beings are few who, when they pass away as human beings, are reborn among the devas. More numerous are those who, when they pass away as human beings, are reborn in hell ... in the animal realm ... in the sphere of afflicted spirits."

(354)–(356) "... so too those beings are few who, when they pass away as devas, are reborn among the devas. More numerous are those who, when they pass away as devas, are reborn in hell ... in the animal realm ... in the sphere of afflicted spirits."

(357)–(359) "... so too those beings are few who, when they pass away as devas, are reborn among human beings. More numerous are those who, when they pass away as devas, are reborn in hell ... in the animal realm ... in the sphere of afflicted spirits."

(360)–(362) "... so too those beings are few who, when they pass away from hell, are reborn among human beings. More numerous are those who, when they pass away from hell, are reborn in hell ... in the animal realm ... in the sphere of afflicted spirits."

(363)–(365) "... so too those beings are few who, when they pass away from hell, are reborn among the devas. More numerous are those who, when they pass away from hell, are reborn in hell ... in the animal realm ... in the sphere of afflicted spirits."

(366)–(368) "... so too those beings are few who, when they pass away from the animal realm, are reborn among human beings. More numerous are those who, when they pass away from the animal realm, are reborn in hell . . . in the animal realm . . . in the sphere of afflicted spirits."

(369)–(371) ". . . so too those beings are few who, when they pass away from the animal realm, are reborn among the devas. More numerous are those [38] who, when they pass away from the animal realm, are reborn in hell . . . in the animal realm . . . in the sphere of afflicted spirits."

(372)–(374) ". . . so too those beings are few who, when they pass away from the sphere of afflicted spirits, are reborn among human beings. More numerous are those who, when they pass away from the sphere of afflicted spirits, are reborn in hell . . . in the animal realm . . . in the sphere of afflicted spirits."

(375)–(377) ". . . so too those beings are few who, when they pass away from the sphere of afflicted spirits, are reborn among the devas. More numerous are those who, when they pass away from the sphere of afflicted spirits, are reborn in hell . . . in the animal realm . . . in the sphere of afflicted spirits."

XVII. Qualities Engendering Confidence

378 (1)–393 (16)[192]

"Bhikkhus, this is certainly a type of gain, namely, (378) being a forest-dweller, (379) being one who lives on food acquired on alms round, (380) being a wearer of rag robes, (381) having just three robes,[193] (382) being a speaker on the Dhamma, (383) being an upholder of the discipline, (384) great learning, (385) long-standing, (386) having proper deportment, (387) the acquisition of a retinue, (388) having a large retinue, (389) coming from a good family, (390) being handsome, (391) being an excellent speaker, (392) having few desires, (393) having good health."

XVIII. Finger Snap[194]

394 (1)

"Bhikkhus, if for just the time of a finger snap a bhikkhu develops the first jhāna, he is called a bhikkhu who is not devoid of jhāna, who acts upon the teaching of the Teacher, who responds to his advice, and who does not eat the country's almsfood in vain. How much more, then, those who cultivate it!"

395 (2)–401 (8)

"Bhikkhus, if for just the time of a finger snap a bhikkhu develops (395) the second jhāna... (396) the third jhāna... (397) the fourth jhāna... (398) the liberation of the mind by loving-kindness... (399) the liberation of the mind by compassion... [39] (400) the liberation of the mind by altruistic joy... (401) the liberation of the mind by equanimity,[195] he is called a bhikkhu who is not devoid of jhāna, who acts upon the teaching of the Teacher, who responds to his advice, and who does not eat the country's almsfood in vain. How much more, then, those who cultivate it!"

402 (9)–405 (12)[196]

"... (402) dwells contemplating the body in the body,[197] ardent, clearly comprehending, mindful, having removed longing and dejection in regard to the world... (403) dwells contemplating feelings in feelings... (404) dwells contemplating mind in mind... (405) dwells contemplating phenomena in phenomena, ardent, clearly comprehending, mindful, having removed longing and dejection in regard to the world..."

406 (13)–409 (16)

"... (406) generates desire for the non-arising of unarisen bad unwholesome qualities; makes an effort, arouses energy, applies his mind, and strives... (407) generates desire for the abandoning of arisen bad unwholesome qualities; makes an effort, arouses energy, applies his mind, and strives... (408) generates desire for the arising of unarisen wholesome qualities; makes an effort, arouses energy, applies his mind, and strives... (409) generates desire for the maintenance of arisen wholesome qualities, for their non-decline, increase, expansion, and fulfillment by development; makes an effort, arouses energy, applies his mind, and strives..."

410 (17)–413 (20)

"... (410) develops the basis for psychic potency that possesses concentration due to desire and activities of striving... (411) develops the basis for psychic potency that possesses concentration due to energy and activities of striving... (412) develops the basis for psychic potency that possesses concentration due to mind and activities of striving ... (413) develops the basis for psychic potency that possesses concentration due to investigation and activities of striving ..."

414 (21)–423 (30)

"... (414) develops the faculty of faith ... (415) develops the faculty of energy ... (416) develops the faculty of mindfulness ... (417) develops the faculty of concentration ... (418) develops the faculty of wisdom ... (419) develops the power of faith ... (420) develops the power of energy ... (421) develops the power of mindfulness ... (422) develops the power of concentration ... (423) develops the power of wisdom ..."

424 (31)–430 (37)

"... (424) develops the enlightenment factor of mindfulness ... (425) develops the enlightenment factor of discrimination of phenomena ... (426) develops the enlightenment factor of energy [40] ... (427) develops the enlightenment factor of rapture ... (428) develops the enlightenment factor of tranquility ... (429) develops the enlightenment factor of concentration ... (430) develops the enlightenment factor of equanimity ..."

431 (38)–438 (45)

"... (431) develops right view ... (432) develops right intention ... (433) develops right speech ... (434) develops right action ... (435) develops right livelihood ... (436) develops right effort ... (437) develops right mindfulness ... (438) develops right concentration ..."

439 (46)–446 (53)[198]

"... (439) percipient of forms internally, sees forms externally, limited, beautiful or ugly, and having overcome them, is percipient thus: 'I know, I see' ... (440) percipient of forms internally, sees forms externally, measureless, beautiful or ugly, and having overcome them, is percipient thus: 'I know, I see' ... (441) not percipient of forms internally, sees forms externally, limited, beautiful or ugly, and having overcome them, is percipient thus: 'I know, I see' ... (442) not percipient of forms internally, sees forms externally, measureless, beautiful or ugly, and having overcome them, is percipient thus: 'I know, I see'...(443) not percipient of forms internally, sees forms externally, blue ones, blue in color, with a blue hue, with a blue tint, and having overcome them, he is percipient thus: 'I know, I see'...(444) not percipient of forms internally, sees forms externally, yellow ones, yellow in color, with a yellow hue, with a yellow tint, and having overcome them, he is percipient thus: 'I know, I see'...(445) not percipient of forms internally, sees forms externally, red ones, red in color, with a red hue, with a red tint, and having overcome them, he is percipient thus: 'I know, I see'...(446) not percipient of forms internally, sees forms externally, white ones, white in color, with a white hue, with a white tint, and having overcome them, he is percipient thus: 'I know, I see'..."

447 (54)–454 (61)[199]

"...(447) possessing form sees forms...[41] (448) not percipient of forms internally sees forms externally...(449) is focused only on 'beautiful'...(450) with the complete surmounting of perceptions of forms, with the passing away of perceptions of sensory impingement, with non-attention to perceptions of diversity, [perceiving] 'space is infinite,' enters and dwells in the base of the infinity of space...(451) by completely surmounting the base of the infinity of space, [perceiving] 'consciousness is infinite,' enters and dwells in the base of the infinity of consciousness...(452) by completely surmounting the base of the infinity of consciousness, [perceiving] 'there is nothing,' enters and dwells in the base of nothingness...(453) by completely surmounting the base of nothingness, enters and dwells in the base of neither-perception-nor-non-perception...(454) by completely surmounting the base of neither-perception-nor-non-perception, he enters and dwells in the cessation of perception and feeling..."

455 (62)–464 (71)

"...(455) develops the earth *kasiṇa*...[200] (456) develops the water *kasiṇa*...(457) develops the fire *kasiṇa*...(458) develops the air *kasiṇa*...(459) develops the blue *kasiṇa*...(460) develops the yellow *kasiṇa*...(461) develops the red *kasiṇa*...(462) develops the white *kasiṇa* . . . (463) develops the space *kasiṇa* . . . (464) develops the consciousness *kasiṇa* . . ."

465 (72)–474 (81)

". . . (465) develops the perception of unattractiveness . . . (466) develops the perception of death . . . (467) develops the perception of the repulsiveness of food . . . (468) develops the perception of non-delight in the entire world . . . (469) develops the perception of impermanence . . . (470) develops the perception of suffering in the impermanent . . . (471) develops the perception of non-self in what is suffering . . . (472) develops the perception of abandoning . . . (473) develops the perception of dispassion . . . (474) develops the perception of cessation . . ."

475 (82)–484 (91)

". . . (475) develops the perception of impermanence . . . (476) develops the perception of non-self . . . [42] (477) develops the perception of death . . . (478) develops the perception of the repulsiveness of food . . . (479) develops the perception of non-delight in the entire world. . . (480) develops the perception of a skeleton . . . (481) develops the perception of a worm-infested corpse . . . (482) develops the perception of a livid corpse . . . (483) develops the perception of a fissured corpse . . . (484) develops the perception of a bloated corpse . . ."[201]

485 (92)–494 (101)

". . . (485) develops recollection of the Buddha . . . (486) develops recollection of the Dhamma . . . (487) develops recollection of the Saṅgha . . . (488) develops recollection of virtuous behavior . . . (489) develops recollection of generosity . . . (490) develops recollection of the deities . . . (491) develops mindfulness of breathing . . . (492) develops mindfulness of death . . . (493) develops mindfulness directed to the body . . . (494) develops recollection of peace . . ."

495 (102)–534 (141)

". . . (495) develops the faculty of faith accompanied by the first jhāna . . . (496) develops the faculty of energy . . . (497) develops the faculty of mindfulness . . . (498) develops the faculty of concentration . . . (499) develops the faculty of wisdom . . . (500) develops the power of faith . . . (501) develops the power of energy . . . (502) develops the power of mindfulness . . . (503) develops the power of concentration . . . (504) develops the power of wisdom accompanied by the first jhāna . . ."

". . . (505)–(514) develops the faculty of faith . . . the power of wisdom accompanied by the second jhāna . . . (515)–(524) develops the faculty of faith . . . the power of wisdom accompanied by the third jhāna . . . (525)–(534) develops the faculty of faith . . . the power of wisdom accompanied by the fourth jhāna . . ."[202]

535 (142)–574 (181)

". . . (535) develops the faculty of faith accompanied by loving-kindness . . . (536) develops the faculty of energy . . . (537) develops the faculty of mindfulness . . . (538) develops the faculty of concentration . . . (539) develops the faculty of wisdom . . . (540) develops the power of faith . . . (541) develops the power of energy . . . (542) develops the power of mindfulness . . . (543) develops the power of concentration . . . (544) develops the power of wisdom accompanied by loving-kindness . . ."

". . . (545)–(554) develops the faculty of faith . . . develops the power of wisdom accompanied by compassion . . . (555)–(564) develops the faculty of faith . . . the power of wisdom accompanied by altruistic joy . . . (565)–(574) develops the faculty of faith . . . the power of wisdom accompanied by equanimity[203] . . . [43] . . . he is called a bhikkhu who is not devoid of jhāna, who acts upon the teaching of the Teacher, who responds to his advice, and who does not eat the country's almsfood in vain. How much more, then, those who cultivate it!"

XIX. Mindfulness Directed to the Body[204]

575 (1)

"Bhikkhus, even as one who encompasses with his mind the great ocean includes thereby all the streams that run into the ocean, just so, whoever develops and cultivates mindfulness directed to the body includes all wholesome qualities that pertain to true knowledge."[205]

576 (2)–582 (8)

Bhikkhus, one thing, when developed and cultivated, (576) leads to a strong sense of urgency[206] . . . (577) leads to great good . . . (578) leads to great security from bondage . . . (579) leads to mindfulness and clear comprehension . . . (580) leads to the attainment of knowledge and vision . . . (581) leads to a pleasant dwelling in this very life . . . (582) leads to realization of the fruit of knowledge and liberation. What is that one thing? Mindfulness directed to the body. This is the one thing that, when developed and cultivated, leads to realization of the fruit of knowledge and liberation."

583 (9)[207]

"Bhikkhus, when one thing is developed and cultivated, the body becomes tranquil, the mind becomes tranquil, thought and examination subside, and all wholesome qualities that pertain to true knowledge reach fulfillment by development. What is that one thing? Mindfulness directed to the body. [44] When this one thing is developed and cultivated, the body becomes tranquil . . . and all wholesome qualities that pertain to true knowledge reach fulfillment by development."

584 (10)[208]

"Bhikkhus, when one thing is developed and cultivated, unarisen unwholesome qualities do not arise and arisen unwholesome qualities are abandoned. What is that one thing? Mindfulness directed to the body. When this one thing is developed and cultivated, unarisen unwholesome qualities do not arise and arisen unwholesome qualities are abandoned."

585 (11)[209]

"Bhikkhus, when one thing is developed and cultivated, unarisen wholesome qualities arise and arisen wholesome qualities increase and expand. What is that one thing? Mindfulness directed to the body. When this one thing is developed and cultivated, unarisen wholesome qualities arise and arisen wholesome qualities increase and expand."

586 (12)–590 (16)[210]

"Bhikkhus, when one thing is developed and cultivated, (586) ignorance is abandoned . . . (587) true knowledge arises . . . (588) the conceit 'I am' is abandoned . . . (589) the underlying tendencies are uprooted . . . (590) the fetters are abandoned. What is that one thing? Mindfulness directed to the body. When this one thing is developed and cultivated, ignorance is abandoned ... true knowledge arises ... the conceit 'I am' is abandoned ... the underlying tendencies are uprooted ... the fetters are abandoned."

591 (17)–592 (18)

"Bhikkhus, one thing, when developed and cultivated, (591) leads to differentiation by wisdom ... (592) leads to nibbāna through non-clinging.[211] What is that one thing? Mindfulness directed to the body. This is the one thing that, when developed and cultivated, leads to differentiation by wisdom ... leads to nibbāna through non-clinging."

593 (19)–595 (21)

"Bhikkhus, when one thing is developed and cultivated, (593) penetration of numerous elements occurs ... (594) penetration of the diversity of elements occurs ... (595) analytical knowledge of numerous elements occurs.[212] What is that one thing? It is mindfulness directed to the body. When this one thing is developed and cultivated, penetration of the various elements occurs ... penetration of the diversity of elements occurs ... analytical knowledge of the various elements occurs."

596 (22)–599 (25)

"Bhikkhus, one thing, when developed and cultivated, leads (596) to realization of the fruit of stream-entry ... (597) to realization of the fruit of once-returning ... (598) to realization of the fruit of non-returning [45] ... (599) to realization of the fruit of arahantship. What is that one thing? It is mindfulness directed to the body. This is the one thing that, when developed and cultivated, leads to realization of the fruit of stream-entry ... to realization of the fruit of once-returning ... to realization of the fruit of non-returning ... to realization of the fruit of arahantship."

600 (26)–615 (41)

"Bhikkhus, one thing, when developed and cultivated, leads (600) to the obtaining of wisdom ... (601) to the growth of wisdom ... (602) to the expansion of wisdom ... (603) to greatness of wisdom ... (604) to diversity of wisdom ... (605) to vastness of wisdom ... (606) to depth of wisdom ... (607) to a state of unsurpassed wisdom ... (608) to breadth of wisdom ... (609) to abundance of wisdom ... (610) to rapidity of wisdom ... (611) to buoyancy of wisdom ... (612) to joyousness of wisdom ... (613) to swiftness of wisdom ... (614) to keenness of wisdom ... (615) to penetrativeness of wisdom.[213] What is that one thing? Mindfulness directed to the body. This is the one thing that, when developed and cultivated, leads to penetrativeness of wisdom."

XX. The Deathless[214]

616 (1)[215]

"Bhikkhus, they do not partake of the deathless who do not partake of mindfulness directed to the body. They partake of the deathless who partake of mindfulness directed to the body."

617 (2)

"Bhikkhus, the deathless has not been partaken of by those who have not partaken of mindfulness directed to the body. The deathless has been partaken of by those who have partaken of mindfulness directed to the body."

618 (3)

"Bhikkhus, they have fallen away from the deathless who have fallen away from mindfulness directed to the body. They have not fallen away from the deathless who have not fallen away from mindfulness directed to the body."

619 (4)

"Bhikkhus, they have neglected the deathless who have neglected mindfulness directed to the body. [46] They have undertaken the deathless who have undertaken mindfulness directed to the body."

620 (5)

"Bhikkhus, they are heedless about the deathless who are heedless about mindfulness directed to the body. They are not heedless about the deathless who are not heedless about mindfulness directed to the body."

621 (6)

"Bhikkhus, they have forgotten the deathless who have forgotten mindfulness directed to the body. They have not forgotten the deathless who have not forgotten mindfulness directed to the body."

622 (7)

"Bhikkhus, they have not pursued the deathless who have not pursued mindfulness directed to the body. They have pursued the deathless who have pursued mindfulness directed to the body."

623 (8)

"Bhikkhus, they have not developed the deathless who have not developed mindfulness directed to the body. They have developed the deathless who have developed mindfulness directed to the body."

624 (9)

"Bhikkhus, they have not cultivated the deathless who have not cultivated mindfulness directed to the body. They have cultivated the deathless who have cultivated mindfulness directed to the body."

625 (10)

"Bhikkhus, they have not directly known the deathless who have not directly known mindfulness directed to the body. They have directly known the deathless who have directly known mindfulness directed to the body."

626 (11)

"Bhikkhus, they have not fully understood the deathless who have not fully understood mindfulness directed to the body. They have fully understood the deathless who have fully understood mindfulness directed to the body."

627 (12)

"Bhikkhus, they have not realized the deathless who have not realized mindfulness directed to the body. They have realized the deathless who have realized mindfulness directed to the body."

The Book of the Ones is finished.

The Book of the Twos
(*Dukanipāta*)

The Book of the Twos

[47] # The Book of the Twos

Homage to the Blessed One, the Arahant,
the Perfectly Enlightened One

I. Entering upon the Rains

1 (1) Faults

Thus have I heard. On one occasion the Blessed One was dwelling at Sāvatthī in Jeta's Grove, Anāthapiṇḍika's Park. There the Blessed One addressed the bhikkhus: "Bhikkhus!"

"Venerable sir!" those bhikkhus replied. The Blessed One said this:

"Bhikkhus, there are these two faults. What two? The fault pertaining to the present life and the fault pertaining to the future life.

"And what is the fault pertaining to the present life? Here, someone sees that when kings arrest a robber, a criminal, they subject him to various punishments: they have him flogged with whips, beaten with canes, beaten with clubs; they have his hands cut off, his feet cut off, his hands and feet cut off; his ears cut off, his nose cut off, his ears and nose cut off; they have him subjected to the 'porridge pot,' to the 'polished-shell shave,' to the 'Rāhu's mouth,' to the 'fiery wreath,' to the 'flaming hand,' to the 'blades of grass,' [48] to the 'bark dress,' to the 'antelope,' to the 'meat hooks,' to the 'coins,' to the 'lye pickling,' to the 'pivoting pin,' to the 'rolled-up palliasse'; and they have him splashed with boiling oil, and they have him devoured by dogs, and they have him impaled alive on stakes, and they have his head cut off with a sword.[216]

"It occurs to him: 'When kings have arrested a robber, a criminal, they subject him to various punishments because of his bad deeds: they have him flogged with whips . . . they have his head cut off with a sword. Now if I were to commit such a bad deed, and if kings were to arrest me, they would subject me to the same punishments. They would have me flogged with whips . . . they would have my head cut off with a sword.' Afraid of the fault pertaining to the present life, he does not plunder the belongings of others.[217] This is called the fault pertaining to the present life.

"And what is the fault pertaining to the future life? Here, someone reflects thus: 'Bodily misconduct has a bad, painful result[218] in the future life; verbal misconduct has a bad, painful result in the future life; mental misconduct has a bad, painful result in the future life. Now if I were to engage in misconduct by body, speech, and mind, then, with the breakup of the body, after death, I would be reborn in the plane of misery, in a bad destination, in the lower world, in hell!' [49] Afraid of the fault pertaining to the future life, he abandons bodily misconduct and develops bodily good conduct; he abandons verbal misconduct and develops verbal good conduct; he abandons mental misconduct and develops mental good conduct; he maintains himself in purity. This is called the fault pertaining to the future life.

"These, bhikkhus, are the two faults. Therefore, bhikkhus, you should train yourselves thus: 'We will fear the fault pertaining to the present life; we will fear the fault pertaining to the future life. We will be fearful of faults and see peril in faults.' It is in such a way that you should train yourselves. It is to be expected that one who is fearful of faults and sees peril in faults will be freed from all faults."

2 (2) *Striving*

"Bhikkhus, there are these two strivings that are hard to achieve in the world. What two? The striving of laypeople who dwell at home for the purpose of presenting [monastics with] robes, almsfood, lodgings, and medicines and provisions for the sick, and the striving of those who have gone forth from the household life into homelessness for the relinquishment of all acquisitions. These are the two strivings that are hard to achieve in the world.

"Of these two strivings, bhikkhus, the foremost is the striving for the relinquishment of all acquisitions.[219] Therefore, bhikkhus, you should train yourselves thus: 'We will strive for the relinquishment of all acquisitions.' It is in such a way that you should train yourselves."

3 (3) Causing Torment

"Bhikkhus, there are these two things that cause torment. What two? Here, someone has engaged in bodily misconduct but failed to engage in bodily good conduct; engaged in verbal misconduct but failed to engage in verbal good conduct; engaged in mental misconduct but failed to engage in mental good conduct. He is tormented, [thinking]: 'I have engaged in bodily misconduct'; he is tormented, [thinking]: 'I have failed to engage in bodily good conduct'; he is tormented, [thinking]: 'I have engaged in verbal misconduct'; he is tormented, [thinking]: 'I have failed to engage in verbal good conduct'; he is tormented, [thinking]: 'I have engaged in mental misconduct'; he is tormented, [thinking]: 'I have failed to engage in mental good conduct.' These, bhikkhus, are the two things that cause torment."[220]

4 (4) Not Causing Torment

"Bhikkhus, there are these two things that do not cause torment. [50] What two? Here, someone has engaged in bodily good conduct and avoided engaging in bodily misconduct; engaged in verbal good conduct and avoided engaging in verbal misconduct; engaged in mental good conduct and avoided engaging in mental misconduct. He is not tormented, [knowing]: 'I have engaged in bodily good conduct'; he is not tormented, [knowing]: 'I have avoided engaging in bodily misconduct'; he is not tormented, [knowing]: 'I have engaged in verbal good conduct'; he is not tormented, [knowing]: 'I have avoided engaging in verbal misconduct'; he is not tormented, [knowing]: 'I have engaged in mental good conduct'; he is not tormented, [knowing]: 'I have avoided engaging in mental misconduct.' These, bhikkhus, are the two things that do not cause torment."

5 (5) Known

"Bhikkhus, I have personally known two things: non-contentment in regard to wholesome qualities and indefatigability in striving.[221] I strove indefatigably, [resolved]: 'Willingly, let only my skin, sinews, and bones remain, and let the flesh and blood dry up in my body, but I will not relax my energy so long as I have not attained what can be attained by manly strength, energy, and exertion.'[222] It was by heedfulness that I achieved enlightenment, bhikkhus; it was by heedfulness that I achieved the unsurpassed security from bondage.[223]

"If, bhikkhus, you too would strive indefatigably, [resolved]: 'Willingly, let only my skin, sinews, and bones remain, and let the flesh and blood dry up in my body, but I will not relax my energy so long as I have not attained what can be attained by manly strength, energy, and exertion,' you too will, in no long time, realize for yourselves with direct knowledge, in this very life, that unsurpassed consummation of the spiritual life for the sake of which clansmen rightly go forth from the household life into homelessness, and having entered upon it, you will dwell in it. Therefore, bhikkhus, you should train yourselves thus: 'We will strive indefatigably, [resolved]: "Willingly, let only my skin, sinews, and bones remain, and let the flesh and blood dry up in my body, but I will not relax my energy so long as I have not attained what can be attained by manly strength, energy, and exertion."' It is in such a way that you should train yourselves."

6 (6) Fetter

"Bhikkhus, there are these two things. What two? Contemplation of gratification in things that can fetter and contemplation of disenchantment in things that can fetter.[224] One who dwells contemplating gratification in things that can fetter does [51] not abandon lust, hatred, and delusion. Not having abandoned lust, hatred, and delusion, one is not freed from birth, from old age and death, from sorrow, lamentation, pain, dejection, and anguish; one is not freed from suffering, I say. One who dwells contemplating disenchantment in things that can fetter abandons lust, hatred, and delusion. Having abandoned lust, hatred, and delusion, one is freed from birth, from old age and death, from sorrow, lamentation, pain, dejection, and anguish; one is freed from suffering, I say. These, bhikkhus, are the two things."

7 (7) Dark

"Bhikkhus, there are these two dark qualities. What two? Moral shamelessness and moral recklessness. These are the two dark qualities."

8 (8) Bright

"Bhikkhus, there are these two bright qualities. What two? Moral shame and moral dread.[225] These are the two bright qualities."

9 (9) Behavior

"Bhikkhus, these two bright qualities protect the world. What two? Moral shame and moral dread. If these two bright qualities did not protect the world, there would not be seen here [any restraint regarding] one's mother, aunts, or the wives of one's teachers and [other] respected people.[226] The world would become promiscuous, like goats and sheep, chickens and pigs, dogs and jackals. But because these two bright qualities protect the world, there is seen here [restraint regarding] one's mother, aunts, or the wives of one's teachers and [other] respected people."

10 (10) Entering upon the Rains

"Bhikkhus, there are these two [occasions for] entering upon the rains.[227] What two? The earlier and the later. These are the two [occasions for] entering upon the rains." [52]

II. Disciplinary Issues

11 (1)

"Bhikkhus, there are these two powers. What two? The power of reflection and the power of development.

"And what is the power of reflection? Here, someone reflects thus: 'Bodily misconduct has a bad result[228] in the present life and in the future life; verbal misconduct has a bad result in the present life and in the future life; mental misconduct has a bad result in the present life and in the future life.' Having reflected thus, he abandons bodily misconduct and develops bodily good conduct; he abandons verbal misconduct and develops verbal good conduct; he abandons mental misconduct and develops mental good conduct; he maintains himself in purity. This is called the power of reflection.

"And what is the power of development? The power of development is the power of trainees.[229] For relying on the power of a trainee, one abandons lust, hatred, and delusion. Having abandoned lust, hatred, and delusion, one does not do anything unwholesome; one does not pursue anything bad. This is called the power of development.

"These, bhikkhus, are the two powers."

12 (2)

"Bhikkhus, there are these two powers. What two? The power of reflection and the power of development.

"And what is the power of reflection? Here, someone reflects thus: 'Bodily misconduct has a bad result in the present life and in the future life; verbal misconduct has a bad result in the present life and in the future life; mental misconduct has a bad result in the present life and in the future life.' Having reflected thus, he abandons bodily misconduct and develops bodily good conduct; he abandons verbal misconduct and develops verbal good conduct; he abandons mental misconduct and develops mental good conduct; he maintains himself in purity. This is called the power of reflection.

"And what is the power of development? Here, [53] a bhikkhu develops the enlightenment factor of mindfulness that is based upon seclusion, dispassion, and cessation, maturing in release. He develops the enlightenment factor of discrimination of phenomena . . . the enlightenment factor of energy . . . the enlightenment factor of rapture . . . the enlightenment factor of tranquility . . . the enlightenment factor of concentration . . . the enlightenment factor of equanimity that is based upon seclusion, dispassion, and cessation, maturing in release. This is called the power of development.

"These, bhikkhus, are the two powers."

13 (3)

"Bhikkhus, there are these two powers. What two? The power of reflection and the power of development.

"And what is the power of reflection? Here, someone reflects thus: 'Bodily misconduct has a bad result in the present life and in the future life; verbal misconduct has a bad result in the present life and in the future life; mental misconduct has a bad result in the present life and in the future life.' Having reflected thus, he abandons bodily misconduct and develops bodily good conduct; he abandons verbal misconduct and develops verbal good conduct; he abandons mental misconduct and develops mental good conduct; he maintains himself in purity. This is called the power of reflection.

"And what is the power of development? Here, secluded from sensual pleasures, secluded from unwholesome states, a bhikkhu enters and dwells in the first jhāna, which consists of rapture and pleasure born of seclusion, accompanied by thought and examination. With the subsiding of thought and examination, he enters and dwells in the second jhāna, which has internal placidity and unification of mind and consists of rapture and pleasure born of concentration, without thought and examination. With the fading away as well of rapture, he dwells equanimous and, mindful and clearly comprehending, he experiences pleasure with the body; he enters and dwells in the third jhāna of which the noble ones declare: 'He is equanimous, mindful, one who dwells happily.' With the abandoning of pleasure and pain, and with the previous passing away of joy and dejection, he enters and dwells in the fourth jhāna, neither painful nor pleasant, which has purification of mindfulness by equanimity. This is called the power of development.

"These, bhikkhus, are the two powers."

14 (4)

"Bhikkhus, the Tathāgata has these two kinds of Dhamma teaching. What two? In brief and in detail.[230] The Tathāgata has these two kinds of Dhamma teaching."

15 (5)

"Bhikkhus, if, in regard to a particular disciplinary issue,[231] the bhikkhu who has committed an offense and the bhikkhu who reproves him do not each thoroughly reflect upon themselves, it can be expected that this disciplinary issue [54] will lead to acrimony and animosity for a long time and the bhikkhus will not dwell at ease. But if the bhikkhu who has committed an offense and the bhikkhu who reproves him each thoroughly reflect upon themselves, it can be expected that this disciplinary issue will not lead to acrimony and animosity for a long time and the bhikkhus will dwell at ease.

"And how does the bhikkhu who has committed an offense thoroughly reflect upon himself? Here, the bhikkhu who has committed an offense reflects thus: 'I have committed a particular unwholesome misdeed with the body.[232] That bhikkhu saw me doing so. If I had not committed a particular unwholesome misdeed with the body, he would not have seen me doing so. But because I committed a particular unwholesome misdeed with the body, he saw me doing so. When he saw me committing a particular unwholesome misdeed with the body, he became displeased. Being displeased, he expressed his displeasure to me. Because he expressed his displeasure to me, I became displeased. Being displeased, I informed others. Thus in this case I was the one who incurred a transgression, just as a traveler does when he evades the customs duty on his goods.'[233] It is in this way that the bhikkhu who has committed an offense thoroughly reflects upon himself.

"And how does the reproving bhikkhu thoroughly reflect upon himself? Here, the reproving bhikkhu reflects thus: 'This bhikkhu has committed a particular unwholesome misdeed with the body. I saw him doing so. If this bhikkhu had not committed a particular unwholesome misdeed with the body, I would not have seen him doing so. [55] But because he committed a particular unwholesome misdeed with the body, I saw him doing so. When I saw him committing a particular unwholesome misdeed with the body, I became displeased. Being displeased, I expressed my displeasure to him.[234] Because I expressed my displeasure to him, he became displeased. Being displeased, he informed others. Thus in this case I was the one who incurred a transgression, just as a traveler does when he evades the customs duty on his goods.' It is in this way that the reproving bhikkhu thoroughly reflects upon himself.

"If, bhikkhus, in regard to a particular disciplinary issue, the bhikkhu who has committed an offense and the bhikkhu who reproves him do not thoroughly reflect upon themselves, it can be expected that this disciplinary issue will lead to acrimony and animosity for a long time and the bhikkhus will not dwell at ease. But if the bhikkhu who has committed an offense and the bhikkhu who reproves him thoroughly reflect upon themselves, it can be expected that this disciplinary issue will not lead to acrimony and animosity for a long time and the bhikkhus will dwell at ease."

16 (6)

Then a certain brahmin approached the Blessed One and exchanged greetings with him. When they had concluded their greetings and cordial talk, he sat down to one side and said to the Blessed One: "Why is it, Master Gotama, that some beings here, with the breakup of the body, after death, are reborn in the plane of misery, in a bad destination, in the lower world, in hell?"

"It is, brahmin, because of conduct contrary to the Dhamma, unrighteous conduct, that some beings here, with the breakup of the body, after death, are reborn in the plane of misery, in a bad destination, in the lower world, in hell."[235]

"But why is it, Master Gotama, that some beings here with the breakup of the body, after death, are reborn in a good destination, in a heavenly world?"

"It is, brahmin, because of conduct in accordance with the Dhamma, righteous conduct, [56] that some beings here, with the breakup of the body, after death, are reborn in a good destination, in a heavenly world."

"Excellent, Master Gotama! Excellent, Master Gotama! Master Gotama has made the Dhamma clear in many ways, as though he were turning upright what had been overthrown, revealing what was hidden, showing the way to one who was lost, or holding up a lamp in the darkness so those with good eyesight can see forms. I now go for refuge to Master Gotama, to the Dhamma, and to the Saṅgha of bhikkhus. Let Master Gotama consider me a lay follower who from today has gone for refuge for life."

17 (7)

Then the brahmin Jāṇussoṇī approached the Blessed One and exchanged greetings with him. When they had concluded their greetings and cordial talk, he sat down to one side and said to the Blessed One: "Why is it, Master Gotama, that some beings here, with the breakup of the body, after death, are reborn in the plane of misery, in a bad destination, in the lower world, in hell?"

"It is, brahmin, because of what has been done and what has not been done that some beings here, with the breakup of the body, after death, are reborn in the plane of misery, in a bad destination, in the lower world, in hell."

"Why is it, Master Gotama, that some beings here, with the breakup of the body, after death, are reborn in a good destination, in a heavenly world?"

"It is, brahmin, because of what has been done and what has not been done that some beings here, with the breakup of the body, after death, are reborn in a good destination, in a heavenly world."[236]

"I do not understand in detail the meaning of this statement that Master Gotama has spoken in brief without analyzing the meaning in detail. It would be good if Master Gotama would teach me the Dhamma so that I would understand in detail the meaning of this statement."

"Well then, brahmin, listen and attend closely. I will speak." [57]

"Yes, sir," the brahmin Jāṇussoṇī replied. The Blessed One said this:

"Here, brahmin, someone has done deeds of bodily misconduct, not deeds of bodily good conduct; he has done deeds of verbal misconduct, not deeds of verbal good conduct; he has done deeds of mental misconduct, not deeds of mental good conduct. Thus it is because of what has been done and what has not been done that some beings here, with the breakup of the body, after death, are reborn in the plane of misery, in a bad destination, in the lower world, in hell. But someone here has done deeds of bodily good conduct, not deeds of bodily misconduct; he has done deeds of verbal good conduct, not deeds of verbal misconduct; he has done deeds of mental good conduct, not deeds of mental misconduct. Thus it is because of what has been done and what has not been done that some beings here, with the breakup of the body, after death, are reborn in a good destination, in a heavenly world."

"Excellent, Master Gotama! . . . [as in 2:16] . . . Let Master Gotama consider me a lay follower who from today has gone for refuge for life."

18 (8)

Then the Venerable Ānanda approached the Blessed One, paid homage to him, and sat down to one side. The Blessed One then said to him:

"I say definitively, Ānanda, that deeds of bodily misconduct, verbal misconduct, and mental misconduct are not to be done."

"Since, Bhante, the Blessed One has declared definitively that deeds of bodily misconduct, verbal misconduct, and mental misconduct are not to be done, what danger is to be expected in acting thus?"

"Ānanda, I have declared definitively that deeds of bodily misconduct, verbal misconduct, and mental misconduct are not to be done because in acting thus this danger is to be expected: one blames oneself; the wise, having investigated, censure one; a bad report circulates about one; one dies confused; and with the breakup of the body, after death, one is reborn in the plane of misery, in a bad destination, in the lower world, in hell. I have declared definitively that deeds of bodily misconduct, verbal misconduct, and mental misconduct are not to be done because in acting thus this danger is to be expected.

"I say definitively, Ānanda, [58] that deeds of bodily good conduct, verbal good conduct, and mental good conduct are to be done."

"Since, Bhante, the Blessed One has declared definitively that deeds of bodily good conduct, verbal good conduct, and mental good conduct are to be done, what benefit is to be expected in acting thus?"

"Ānanda, I have declared definitively that deeds of bodily good conduct, verbal good conduct, and mental good conduct are to be done because in acting thus this benefit is to be expected: one does not blame oneself; the wise, having investigated, praise one; one acquires a good reputation; one dies unconfused; and with the breakup of the body, after death, one is reborn in a good destination, in a heavenly world. I have declared definitively that deeds of bodily good conduct, verbal good conduct, and mental good conduct are to be done because in acting thus this benefit is to be expected."

19 (9)

"Bhikkhus, abandon the unwholesome! It is possible to abandon the unwholesome. If it were not possible to abandon the unwholesome, I would not say: 'Bhikkhus, abandon the unwholesome!' But because it is possible to abandon the unwholesome, I say: 'Bhikkhus, abandon the unwholesome!' If this abandoning of the unwholesome led to harm and suffering, I would not tell you to abandon it. But because the abandoning of the unwholesome leads to welfare and happiness, I say: 'Bhikkhus, abandon the unwholesome!'

"Bhikkhus, develop the wholesome! It is possible to develop the wholesome. If it were not possible to develop the wholesome, I would not say: 'Bhikkhus, develop the wholesome!' But because it is possible to develop the wholesome, I say: 'Bhikkhus, develop the wholesome!' If this developing of the wholesome led to harm and suffering, I would not tell you to develop it. But because the developing of the wholesome leads to welfare and happiness, I say: 'Bhikkhus, develop the wholesome!'"

20 (10)[237]

"Bhikkhus, there are these two things that lead to the decline and disappearance of the good Dhamma. What two? [59] Badly set down words and phrases and badly interpreted meaning.[238] When the words and phrases are badly set down, the meaning is badly interpreted. These are the two things that lead to the decline and disappearance of the good Dhamma.

"Bhikkhus, there are these two things that lead to the continuation, non-decline, and non-disappearance of the good Dhamma. What two? Well-set down words and phrases and well-interpreted meaning.[239] When the words and phrases are well set down, the meaning is well interpreted. These are the two things that lead to the continuation, non-decline, and non-disappearance of the good Dhamma."

III. Fools

21 (1)

"Bhikkhus, there are these two kinds of fools. What two? One who does not see his transgression as a transgression and one who does not, in accordance with the Dhamma, accept the transgression of one who is confessing. These are the two kinds of fools.[240]

"Bhikkhus, there are these two kinds of wise people. What two? One who sees his transgression as a transgression and one who, in accordance with the Dhamma, accepts the transgression of one who is confessing. These are the two kinds of wise people."

22 (2)

"Bhikkhus, these two misrepresent the Tathāgata. Which two? One full of hate who harbors hatred and one endowed with faith because of his misunderstanding. These two misrepresent the Tathāgata."[241]

23 (3)[242]

"Bhikkhus, these two misrepresent the Tathāgata. Which two? [60] One who explains what has not been stated and uttered by the Tathāgata as having been stated and uttered by him, and one who explains what has been stated and uttered by the Tathāgata as not having been stated and uttered by him. These two misrepresent the Tathāgata.

"Bhikkhus, these two do not misrepresent the Tathāgata. Which two? One who explains what has not been stated and uttered by the Tathāgata as not having been stated and uttered by him, and one who explains what has been stated and uttered by the Tathāgata as having been stated and uttered by him. These two do not misrepresent the Tathāgata."

24 (4)

"Bhikkhus, these two misrepresent the Tathāgata. Which two? One who explains a discourse whose meaning requires interpretation as a discourse whose meaning is explicit, and one who explains a discourse whose meaning is explicit as a discourse whose meaning requires interpretation. These two misrepresent the Tathāgata."[243]

25 (5)

"Bhikkhus, these two do not misrepresent the Tathāgata. Which two? One who explains a discourse whose meaning requires interpretation as a discourse whose meaning requires interpretation, and one who explains a discourse whose meaning is explicit as a discourse whose meaning is explicit. These two do not misrepresent the Tathāgata."

26 (6)

"Bhikkhus, for one with concealed actions one of two destinations is to be expected: hell or the animal realm.[244]

"For one with unconcealed actions one of two destinations is to be expected: the deva realm or the human realm."

27 (7)[245]

"Bhikkhus, for one who holds wrong view one of two destinations is to be expected: hell or the animal realm."

28 (8)

"Bhikkhus, for one who holds right view one of two destinations is to be expected: the deva realm or the human realm."

29 (9)

"Bhikkhus, for an immoral person there are two receptacles:[246] hell or the animal realm. For a virtuous person, there are two receptacles: the deva realm or the human realm."

30 (10)

"Bhikkhus, seeing two advantages, I resort to remote lodgings in forests and jungle groves.[247] What two? For myself I see a pleasant dwelling in this very life [61] and I have compassion for later generations.[248] Seeing these two advantages, I resort to remote lodgings in forests and jungle groves."

31 (11)

"Bhikkhus, these two things pertain to true knowledge.[249] What two? Serenity and insight. When serenity is developed, what benefit does one experience? The mind is developed. When the mind is developed, what benefit does one experience? Lust is abandoned. When insight is developed, what benefit does one experience? Wisdom is developed. When wisdom is developed, what benefit does one experience? Ignorance is abandoned.[250]

"A mind defiled by lust is not liberated, and wisdom defiled by ignorance is not developed. Thus, bhikkhus, through the fading away of lust there is liberation of mind, and through the fading away of ignorance there is liberation by wisdom."[251]

IV. Same-Minded

32 (1)

"Bhikkhus, I will teach you the plane of the bad person and the plane of the good person. Listen and attend closely. I will speak."

"Yes, Bhante," those bhikkhus replied. The Blessed One said this:

"And what is the plane of the bad person? A bad person is ungrateful and unthankful. For ingratitude and unthankfulness are extolled by the bad. Ingratitude and unthankfulness belong entirely to the plane of the bad person.

"And what is the plane of the good person? A good person is grateful and thankful. For gratitude and thankfulness are extolled by the good. Gratitude and thankfulness belong entirely to the plane of the good person."

33 (2)

"Bhikkhus, there are two persons that cannot easily be repaid. What two? One's mother and father.

"Even if one should carry about one's mother on one shoulder [62] and one's father on the other, and [while doing so] should have a life span of a hundred years, live for a hundred years; and if one should attend to them by anointing them with balms, by massaging, bathing, and rubbing their limbs, and they even void their urine and excrement there, one still would not have done enough for one's parents, nor would one have repaid them. Even if one were to establish one's parents as the supreme lords and rulers over this great earth abounding in the seven treasures, one still would not have done enough for one's parents, nor would one have repaid them. For what reason? Parents are of great help to their children; they bring them up, feed them, and show them the world.

"But, bhikkhus, if, when one's parents lack faith, one encourages, settles, and establishes them in faith; if, when one's parents are immoral, one encourages, settles, and establishes them in virtuous behavior; if, when one's parents are miserly, one encourages, settles, and establishes them in generosity; if, when one's parents are unwise, one encourages, settles, and establishes them in wisdom: in such a way, one has done enough for one's parents, repaid them, and done more than enough for them."[252]

34 (3)

Then a certain brahmin approached the Blessed One and exchanged greetings with him. When they had concluded their greetings and cordial talk, he sat down to one side and said to the Blessed One: "What does Master Gotama assert, what does he declare?"

"Brahmin, I assert a doctrine of deeds and a doctrine of non-doing."[253]

"But in what way does Master Gotama assert a doctrine of deeds and a doctrine of non-doing?"

"I assert non-doing with regard to bodily, verbal, and mental misconduct; I assert non-doing with regard to the numerous kinds of bad unwholesome qualities. I assert doing with regard to good bodily, verbal, and mental conduct; I assert doing with regard to the numerous kinds of wholesome qualities. It is in this way, brahmin, that I assert a doctrine of deeds and a doctrine of non-doing."

"Excellent, Master Gotama! Excellent, Master Gotama! Master Gotama has made the Dhamma clear in many ways, as though he were turning upright what had been overthrown, revealing what was hidden, showing the way to one who was lost, or holding up a lamp in the darkness so those with good eyesight can see forms. I now go for refuge to Master Gotama, to the Dhamma, and to the Saṅgha of bhikkhus. Let Master Gotama consider me a lay follower who from today has gone for refuge for life."

35 (4)

Then the householder Anāthapiṇḍika approached the Blessed One, [63] paid homage to him, sat down to one side, and said to him:

"Who in the world, Bhante, is worthy of offerings, and where is a gift to be given?"

"There are, householder, two in the world worthy of offerings: the trainee and the one beyond training.[254] These are the two in the world worthy of offerings and a gift is to be given to them."

This is what the Blessed One said. Having said this, the Fortunate One, the Teacher, further said this:

> "In this world the trainee and one beyond training
> are worthy of the gifts of those practicing charity;
> upright in body, speech, and mind,
> they are the field for those practicing charity;
> what is given to them brings great fruit."

36 (5)

Thus have I heard. On one occasion the Blessed One was dwelling at Sāvatthī in Jeta's Grove, Anāthapiṇḍika's Park. Now on that occasion the Venerable Sāriputta was dwelling at Sāvatthī in Migāramātā's Mansion in the Eastern Park. There the Venerable Sāriputta addressed the bhikkhus: "Friends, bhikkhus!"[255]

"Friend!" those bhikkhus replied. The Venerable Sāriputta said this:

"Friends, I will teach you about the person fettered internally and the person fettered externally.[256] Listen and attend closely. I will speak."

"Yes, friend," those bhikkhus replied. The Venerable Sāriputta said this:

"And who, friends, is the person fettered internally? Here, a bhikkhu is virtuous; he dwells restrained by the Pātimokkha, possessed of good conduct and resort, seeing danger in minute faults. Having undertaken the training rules, he trains in them. With the breakup of the body, after death, he is reborn in a certain order of devas. Passing away from there, he is a returner, one who returns to this state of being. This is called the person fettered internally, who is a returner, one who returns to this state of being.[257] [64]

"And who, friends, is the person fettered externally? Here, a bhikkhu is virtuous; he dwells restrained by the Pātimokkha, possessed of good conduct and resort, seeing danger in minute faults. Having undertaken the training rules, he trains in them. Having entered upon a certain peaceful liberation of mind, he dwells in it.[258] With the breakup of the body, after death, he is reborn in a certain order of devas. Passing away from there, he is a non-returner, one who does not return to this state of being. This is called the person fettered externally, who is a non-returner, one who does not return to this state of being.[259]

"Again, friends, a bhikkhu is virtuous. . . . Having undertaken the training rules, he trains in them. He is practicing for disenchantment with sensual pleasures, dispassion toward them, and for their cessation.[260] He is practicing for disenchantment with states of existence, for dispassion toward them, and for their cessation.[261] He is practicing for the destruction of craving. He is practicing for the destruction of greed.[262] With the breakup of the body, after death, he is reborn in a certain order of devas. Passing away from there, he is a non-returner, one who does not return to this state of being. This is called a person fettered externally, who is a non-returner, one who does not return to this state of being."[263]

Then a number of same-minded deities[264] approached the Blessed One, paid homage to him, stood to one side, and said to him: "Bhante, at Migāramātā's Mansion in the Eastern Park, Venerable Sāriputta is teaching the bhikkhus about the person fettered internally and the person fettered externally. The assembly is thrilled. It would be good, Bhante, if the Blessed One would approach the Venerable Sāriputta out of compassion."[265] The Blessed One consented by silence.

Then, just as a strong man might extend his drawn-in arm or draw in his extended arm, the Blessed One disappeared from Jeta's Grove and reappeared at Migāramātā's Mansion in the Eastern Park in the presence of the Venerable Sāriputta. He sat down in the seat that was prepared. The Venerable Sāriputta [65] paid homage to the Blessed One and sat down to one side. The Blessed One then said to the Venerable Sāriputta:

"Here, Sāriputta, a number of same-minded deities approached me, paid homage to me, stood to one side, and said: 'Bhante, at Migāramātā's Mansion in the Eastern Park, Venerable Sāriputta is teaching the bhikkhus about the person fettered internally and the person fettered externally. The assembly is thrilled. It would be good, Bhante, if the Blessed One would approach the Venerable Sāriputta out of compassion.'

"Those deities—ten, twenty, thirty, forty, fifty, and even sixty in number—stand in an area even as small as the tip of an awl yet do not encroach upon one another. It may be, Sāriputta, that you think: 'Surely, it was there that those deities developed their minds in such a way that ten . . . and even sixty in number stand in an area even as small as the tip of an awl yet do not encroach upon one another.' But this should not be regarded in such a way. Rather, it was right here that those deities developed their minds in such a way that ten . . . and even sixty in number stand in an area even as small as the tip of an awl yet do not encroach upon one another.[266]

"Therefore, Sāriputta, you should train yourselves thus: 'We will have peaceful sense faculties and peaceful minds.'[267] It is in such a way that you should train yourselves. When you have peaceful sense faculties and peaceful minds, your bodily action will be peaceful, your verbal action will be peaceful, and your mental action will be peaceful. [Thinking:] 'We will offer only peaceful service to our fellow monks,' it is in such a way, Sāriputta, that you should train yourselves. Sāriputta, those wanderers of other sects are lost who did not get to hear this exposition of the Dhamma."

37 (6)

Thus have I heard. On one occasion the Venerable Mahākaccāna was dwelling at Varaṇā on a bank of the Kaddama Lake. [66] Then the brahmin Ārāmadaṇḍa approached the Venerable Mahākaccāna and exchanged greetings with him. When they had concluded their greetings and cordial talk, he sat down to one side and said to him: "Why is it, Master Kaccāna, that khattiyas fight with khattiyas, brahmins with brahmins, and householders with householders?"

"It is, brahmin, because of adherence to lust for sensual pleasures, bondage [to it], fixation [on it], obsession [by it], holding firmly [to it],[268] that khattiyas fight with khattiyas, brahmins with brahmins, and householders with householders."

"Why is it, Master Kaccāna, that ascetics fight with ascetics?"

"It is, brahmin, because of adherence to lust for views, bondage [to it], fixation [on it], obsession [by it], holding firmly [to it], that ascetics fight with ascetics."

"Is there then anyone in the world who has overcome this adherence to lust for sensual pleasures . . . holding firmly [to it], and this adherence to lust for views . . . holding firmly [to it]?"

"There is."

"And who is that?"

"There is, brahmin, a town to the east called Sāvatthī. There the Blessed One, the Arahant, the Perfectly Enlightened One is now dwelling. The Blessed One has overcome this adherence to lust for sensual pleasures, bondage [to it], fixation [on it], obsession [by it], holding firmly [to it], [67] and he has overcome this adherence to lust for views, bondage [to it], fixation [on it], obsession [by it], holding firmly [to it]."

When this was said, the brahmin Ārāmadaṇḍa rose from his seat, arranged his upper robe over one shoulder, lowered his right knee to the ground, reverently saluted in the direction of the Blessed One, and uttered this inspired utterance three times: "Homage to the Blessed One, the Arahant, the Perfectly Enlightened One. Homage to the Blessed One, the Arahant, the Perfectly Enlightened One. Homage to the Blessed One, the Arahant, the Perfectly Enlightened One. Indeed, that Blessed One has overcome this adherence to lust for sensual pleasures, bondage [to it], fixation [on it], obsession [by it], holding firmly [to it], and he has overcome this adherence to lust for views, bondage [to it], fixation [on it], obsession [by it], holding firmly [to it].

"Excellent, Master Kaccāna! Excellent, Master Kaccāna! Master Kaccāna has made the Dhamma clear in many ways, as though he were turning upright what had been overthrown, revealing what was hidden, showing the way to one who was lost, or holding up a lamp in the darkness so those with good eyesight can see forms. Master Kaccāna, I now go for refuge to Master Gotama, to the Dhamma, and to the Saṅgha of bhikkhus. Let Master Kaccāna consider me a lay follower who from today has gone for refuge for life."

38 (7)

On one occasion the Venerable Mahākaccāna was dwelling at Madhurā in Gundā's Grove. Then the brahmin Kaṇḍarāyana approached the Venerable Mahākaccāna and exchanged greetings with him. When they had concluded their greetings and cordial talk, he sat down to one side and said to him:

"I have heard, Master Kaccāna: 'The ascetic Kaccāna does

not pay homage to brahmins who are old, aged, burdened with years, advanced in life, come to the last stage; nor does he stand up for them or offer them a seat.' This is indeed true, for Master Kaccāna does not pay homage to brahmins who are old, aged, burdened with years, advanced in life, come to the last stage; nor does he stand up for them or offer them a seat. This is not proper, Master Kaccāna."[269]

"Brahmin, the Blessed One, the Arahant, [68] the Perfectly Enlightened One, knowing and seeing, has proclaimed the stage of an elder and the stage of a youth. Even though someone is old—eighty, ninety, or a hundred years from birth—if he enjoys sensual pleasures, dwells in sensual pleasures,[270] burns with a fever for sensual pleasures, is consumed with thoughts of sensual pleasures, is eager in the quest for sensual pleasures, then he is reckoned as a foolish [childish] elder. But even though someone is young, a youth with dark black hair, endowed with the blessing of youth, in the prime of life, if he does not enjoy sensual pleasures, does not dwell in sensual pleasures, does not burn with a fever for sensual pleasures, is not consumed with thoughts of sensual pleasures, is not eager in the quest for sensual pleasures, then he is reckoned as a wise elder."

When this was said, the brahmin Kaṇḍarāyana rose from his seat, arranged his upper robe over one shoulder, and bowed down with his head at the feet of the young bhikkhus, [saying]: "You elders stand at the stage of an elder; we youths stand at the stage of a youth.

"Excellent, Master Kaccāna! . . . [as in 2:37] . . . Let Master Kaccāna consider me a lay follower who from today has gone for refuge for life."

39 (8)

"Bhikkhus, when robbers are strong, kings are weak. At that time the king is not at ease when re-entering [his capital], or when going out, or when touring the outlying provinces. At that time brahmins and householders, too, are not at ease when re-entering [their towns and villages], or when going out, or when attending to work outside.

"So too, when evil bhikkhus are strong, well-behaved bhikkhus are weak. At that time the well-behaved bhikkhus sit silently in the midst of the Saṅgha[271] or they resort to[272] the outlying provinces. This is for the harm of many people, for the unhappiness of many people, for the ruin, harm, and suffering of many people, of devas and human beings. [69]

"Bhikkhus, when kings are strong, robbers are weak. At that time the king is at ease when re-entering [his capital], and when going out, and when touring the outlying provinces. At that time brahmins and householders, too, are at ease when re-entering [their towns and villages], and when going out, and when attending to work outside.

"So too, when well-behaved bhikkhus are strong, evil bhikkhus are weak. At that time the evil bhikkhus sit silently in the midst of the Saṅgha or they depart for other regions.[273] This is for the welfare of many people, for the happiness of many people, for the good, welfare, and happiness of many people, of devas and human beings."

40 (9)[274]

"Bhikkhus, I do not praise the wrong practice of two [kinds of people]: a layperson and one gone forth [into homelessness]. Whether it is a layperson or one gone forth who is practicing wrongly, because of wrong practice, they do not attain the true way, the Dhamma that is wholesome.[275]

"Bhikkhus, I praise the right practice of two [kinds of people]: a layperson and one gone forth. Whether it is a layperson or one gone forth who is practicing rightly, because of right practice, they attain the true way, the Dhamma that is wholesome."

41 (10)

"Bhikkhus, those bhikkhus who exclude the meaning and the Dhamma by means of badly acquired discourses whose phrasing is a semblance [of the correct phrasing][276] are acting for the harm of many people, for the unhappiness of many people, for the ruin, harm, and suffering of many people, of devas and human beings. These bhikkhus generate much demerit and cause the good Dhamma to disappear.

"Bhikkhus, those bhikkhus who conform to the meaning and the Dhamma with well-acquired discourses whose phrasing is not [mere] semblance[277] are acting for the welfare of many people, for the happiness of many people, for the good, welfare, and happiness of many people, of devas and human beings.

These bhikkhus generate much merit and sustain the good Dhamma." [70]

V. Assemblies

42 (1)

"Bhikkhus, there are these two kinds of assemblies. What two? The shallow assembly and the deep assembly.

"And what is the shallow assembly? The assembly in which the bhikkhus are restless, puffed up, vain, talkative, rambling in their talk, with muddled mindfulness, lacking in clear comprehension, unconcentrated, with wandering minds, with loose sense faculties, is called the shallow assembly.

"And what is the deep assembly? The assembly in which the bhikkhus are not restless, puffed up, vain, talkative, and rambling in their talk but have established mindfulness, clearly comprehend, are concentrated, with one-pointed minds and restrained sense faculties, is called the deep assembly.

"These, bhikkhus, are the two kinds of assemblies. Of these two kinds of assemblies, the deep assembly is foremost."[278]

43 (2)

"Bhikkhus, there are these two kinds of assemblies. What two? The divided assembly and the harmonious assembly.

"And what is the divided assembly? The assembly in which the bhikkhus take to arguing and quarreling and fall into disputes, stabbing each other with piercing words, is called the divided assembly.[279]

"And what is the harmonious assembly? The assembly in which the bhikkhus dwell in concord, harmoniously, without disputes, blending like milk and water, viewing each other with eyes of affection, is called the harmonious assembly.

"These, bhikkhus, are the two kinds of assemblies. Of these two kinds of assemblies, the harmonious assembly is foremost."

44 (3)

"Bhikkhus, there are these two kinds of assemblies. What two? The assembly of the inferior and the assembly of the foremost. [71]

"And what is the assembly of the inferior? Here, in this kind of assembly the elder bhikkhus are luxurious and lax, leaders in backsliding, discarding the duty of solitude; they do not arouse energy for the attainment of the as-yet-unattained, for the achievement of the as-yet-unachieved, for the realization of the as-yet-unrealized. [Those in] the next generation follow their example.[280] They too become luxurious and lax, leaders in backsliding, discarding the duty of solitude; they too do not arouse energy for the attainment of the as-yet-unattained, for the achievement of the as-yet-unachieved, for the realization of the as-yet-unrealized. This is called the assembly of the inferior.

"And what is the assembly of the foremost? Here, in this kind of assembly the elder bhikkhus are not luxurious and lax but discard backsliding and take the lead in solitude; they arouse energy for the attainment of the as-yet-unattained, for the achievement of the as-yet-unachieved, for the realization of the as-yet-unrealized. [Those in] the next generation follow their example. They too do not become luxurious and lax but discard backsliding and take the lead in solitude; they too arouse energy for the attainment of the as-yet-unattained, for the achievement of the as-yet-unachieved, for the realization of the as-yet-unrealized. This is called the assembly of the foremost.

"These, bhikkhus, are the two kinds of assemblies. Of these two kinds of assemblies, the assembly of the foremost is foremost."[281]

45 (4)

"Bhikkhus, there are these two kinds of assemblies. What two? The assembly of the noble and the assembly of the ignoble.

"And what is the assembly of the ignoble? The assembly in which the bhikkhus do not understand as it really is: 'This is suffering'; do not understand as it really is: 'This is the origin of suffering'; do not understand as it really is: 'This is the cessation of suffering'; do not understand as it really is: 'This is the way leading to the cessation of suffering' is called the assembly of the ignoble.

"And what is the assembly of the noble? The assembly in which the bhikkhus understand as it really is: 'This is suffering'; understand as it really is: 'This is the origin of suffering'; [72]

understand as it really is: 'This is the cessation of suffering'; understand as it really is: 'This is the way leading to the cessation of suffering' is called the assembly of the noble.[282]

"These, bhikkhus, are the two kinds of assemblies. Of these two kinds of assemblies, the assembly of the noble is foremost."

46 (5)

"Bhikkhus, there are these two kinds of assemblies. What two? The dregs of an assembly and the cream of an assembly.

"And what is the dregs of an assembly? The assembly in which the bhikkhus enter upon a wrong course on account of desire, hatred, delusion, or fear is called the dregs of an assembly.[283]

"And what is the cream of an assembly? The assembly in which the bhikkhus do not enter upon a wrong course on account of desire, hatred, delusion, or fear is called the cream of an assembly.

"These, bhikkhus, are the two kinds of assemblies. Of these two kinds of assemblies, the cream of an assembly is foremost."

47 (6)

"Bhikkhus, there are these two kinds of assemblies. What two? The assembly trained in vain talk, not in interrogation, and the assembly trained in interrogation, not in vain talk.[284]

"And what is the assembly trained in vain talk, not in interrogation? Here, in this kind of assembly, when those discourses spoken by the Tathāgata are being recited that are deep, deep in meaning, world-transcending, connected with emptiness, the bhikkhus do not want to listen to them, do not lend an ear to them, or apply their minds to understand them; they do not think those teachings should be studied and learned. But when those discourses are being recited that are mere poetry composed by poets, beautiful in words and phrases, created by outsiders, spoken by disciples, they want to listen to them, lend an ear to them, and apply their minds to understand them; they think those teachings should be studied and learned.[285] And having learned those teachings, they do not interrogate each other about them or examine them thoroughly, [73] [asking]: 'How is this? What is the meaning of this?' They do not disclose [to others] what is obscure and elucidate what is unclear, or dispel their perplexity about numerous perplexing points. This is called the assembly trained in vain talk, not in interrogation.

"And what is the assembly trained in interrogation, not in vain talk? Here, in this kind of assembly, when those discourses are being recited that are mere poetry composed by poets, beautiful in words and phrases, created by outsiders, spoken by disciples, the bhikkhus do not want to listen to them, do not lend an ear to them, or apply their minds to understand them; they do not think those teachings should be studied and learned. But when those discourses spoken by the Tathāgata are being recited that are deep, deep in meaning, world-transcending, connected with emptiness, the bhikkhus want to listen to them, lend an ear to them, and apply their minds to understand them; they think those teachings should be studied and learned. And having learned those teachings, they interrogate each other about them and examine them thoroughly, [asking]: 'How is this? What is the meaning of this?' [They] disclose to [others] what is obscure and elucidate what is unclear, and dispel their perplexity about numerous perplexing points. This is called the assembly trained in interrogation, not in vain talk.

"These, bhikkhus, are the two kinds of assemblies. Of these two kinds of assemblies, the assembly trained in interrogation, not in vain talk, is foremost."

48 (7)

"Bhikkhus, there are these two kinds of assemblies. What two? The assembly that values worldly things, not the good Dhamma, and the assembly that values the good Dhamma, not worldly things.[286]

"And what is the assembly that values worldly things, not the good Dhamma? Here, in this kind of assembly the bhikkhus speak one another's praises in the presence of householders clad in white, saying: 'The bhikkhu so-and-so is one liberated in both respects; so-and-so is one liberated by wisdom; [74] so-and-so is a body witness; so-and-so is one attained to view; so-and-so is one liberated by faith; so-and-so is a Dhamma follower; so-and-so is a faith follower; so-and-so is virtuous and of good character; so-and-so is immoral and of bad character.'[287] They thereby receive gains, which they use while being tied to them, infatuated with them, blindly absorbed in them, not seeing the danger in them, not understanding the escape. This is called the assembly that values worldly things, not the good Dhamma.

"And what is the assembly that values the good Dhamma, not worldly things? Here, in this kind of assembly the bhikkhus do not speak one another's praises in the presence of householders clad in white, saying: 'The bhikkhu so-and-so is one liberated in both respects . . . so-and-so is immoral and of bad character.' They thereby receive gains, which they use without being tied to them, uninfatuated with them, not blindly absorbed in them, seeing the danger in them, understanding the escape. This is called the assembly that values the good Dhamma, not worldly things.

"These, bhikkhus, are the two kinds of assemblies. Of these two kinds of assemblies, the assembly that values the good Dhamma, not worldly things, is foremost."

49 (8)

"Bhikkhus, there are these two kinds of assemblies. What two? The unrighteous assembly and the righteous assembly.

"And what is the unrighteous assembly? Here, in this assembly disciplinary acts contrary to the Dhamma are enacted and disciplinary acts in accordance with the Dhamma are not enacted; disciplinary acts contrary to the discipline are enacted and disciplinary acts in accordance with the discipline are not enacted. Disciplinary acts contrary to the Dhamma are explained and disciplinary acts in accordance with the Dhamma are not explained; disciplinary acts contrary to the discipline are explained and disciplinary acts in accordance with the discipline are not explained. This, bhikkhus, is called the unrighteous assembly. It is because it is unrighteous that in this assembly disciplinary acts contrary to the Dhamma are enacted . . . [75] . . . and disciplinary acts in accordance with the discipline are not explained.[288]

"And what is the righteous assembly? Here, in this assembly disciplinary acts that accord with the Dhamma are enacted and disciplinary acts contrary to the Dhamma are not enacted; disciplinary acts that accord with the discipline are enacted and disciplinary acts contrary to the discipline are not enacted.

Disciplinary acts that accord with the Dhamma are explained and disciplinary acts contrary to the Dhamma are not explained; disciplinary acts that accord with the discipline are explained and disciplinary acts contrary to the discipline are not explained. This, bhikkhus, is called the righteous assembly. It is because it is righteous that in this assembly disciplinary acts that accord with the Dhamma are enacted . . . and disciplinary acts contrary to the discipline are not explained.

"These, bhikkhus, are the two kinds of assemblies. Of these two kinds of assemblies, the righteous assembly is foremost."

50 (9)

"Bhikkhus, there are these two kinds of assemblies. What two? The assembly that acts contrary to the Dhamma and the assembly that acts in accordance with the Dhamma. . . . [as in 2:49] . . .

"These, bhikkhus, are the two kinds of assemblies. Of these two kinds of assemblies, the assembly that acts in accordance with the Dhamma is foremost."

51 (10)

"Bhikkhus, there are these two kinds of assemblies. What two? The assembly that speaks non-Dhamma and the assembly that speaks Dhamma.

"And what is the assembly that speaks non-Dhamma? Here, in this kind of assembly the bhikkhus take up a disciplinary issue,[289] one that may accord with the Dhamma or be contrary to the Dhamma. Having taken up the issue, they do not persuade one another and do not allow themselves to be persuaded; they do not deliberate and do not welcome deliberation. Lacking the power of persuasion and the power of deliberation, [76] unwilling to relinquish their opinion, they wrongly grasp that disciplinary issue even more tightly, and adhering to their position, they declare: 'This alone is true; anything else is wrong.' This is called the assembly that speaks non-Dhamma.

"And what is the assembly that speaks Dhamma? Here, in this kind of assembly the bhikkhus take up a disciplinary issue, one that may accord with the Dhamma or be contrary to the Dhamma. Having taken up the issue, they persuade one another and allow themselves to be persuaded; they deliberate and welcome deliberation. Possessing the power of persuasion and the power of deliberation, willing to relinquish their opinion, they do not wrongly grasp that disciplinary issue even more tightly, nor, adhering to their position, do they declare: 'This alone is true; anything else is wrong.' This is called the assembly that speaks Dhamma.

"These, bhikkhus, are the two kinds of assemblies. Of these two kinds of assemblies, the assembly that speaks Dhamma is foremost."

VI. People

52 (1)

"Bhikkhus, there are these two people who arise in the world for the welfare of many people, for the happiness of many people, for the good, welfare, and happiness of devas and humans. What two? The Tathāgata, the Arahant, the Perfectly Enlightened One and the wheel-turning monarch. These are the two people who arise in the world for the welfare of many people, for the happiness of many people, for the good, welfare, and happiness of devas and humans."[290]

53 (2)

"Bhikkhus, there are these two people arising in the world who are extraordinary humans. [77] What two? The Tathāgata, the Arahant, the Perfectly Enlightened One and the wheel-turning monarch. These are the two people arising in the world who are extraordinary humans."

54 (3)

"Bhikkhus, there are these two people whose passing away is mourned by many people. What two? The Tathāgata, the Arahant, the Perfectly Enlightened One and the wheel-turning monarch. These are the two people whose passing away is mourned by many people."

55 (4)

"Bhikkhus, there are these two who are worthy of a stupa.[291] What two? The Tathāgata, the Arahant, the Perfectly Enlightened One and the wheel-turning monarch. These are the two who are worthy of a stupa."

56 (5)
"Bhikkhus, there are these two enlightened ones. What two? The Tathāgata, the Arahant, the Perfectly Enlightened One and the paccekabuddha.[292] These are the two enlightened ones."

57 (6)
"Bhikkhus, there are these two that are not terrified by a bursting thunderbolt. What two? A bhikkhu whose taints are destroyed and a thoroughbred elephant. These are the two that are not terrified by a bursting thunderbolt."[293]

58 (7)
"Bhikkhus, there are these two that are not terrified by a bursting thunderbolt. What two? A bhikkhu whose taints are destroyed and a thoroughbred horse. These are the two that are not terrified by a bursting thunderbolt."

59 (8)
"Bhikkhus, there are these two that are not terrified by a bursting thunderbolt. What two? A bhikkhu whose taints are destroyed and a lion, king of the beasts. These are the two that are not terrified by a bursting thunderbolt."

60 (9)
"Bhikkhus, for two reasons fauns do not utter human speech.[294] What two? [Thinking:] 'May we not speak falsely, and may we not misrepresent another with what is contrary to fact.' For these two reasons fauns do not utter human speech." [78]

61 (10)
"Bhikkhus, women die unsatisfied and discontent in two things. What two? Sexual intercourse and giving birth. Women die unsatisfied and discontent in these two things."

62 (11)
"Bhikkhus, I will teach you about co-residency among the bad and about co-residency among the good. Listen and attend closely. I will speak."

"Yes, Bhante," those bhikkhus replied. The Blessed One said this:

"And how is there co-residency among the bad, and how do the bad live together? Here, it occurs to an elder bhikkhu: 'An elder [bhikkhu]—or one of middle standing or a junior [bhikkhu]—should not correct me.[295] I should not correct an elder [bhikkhu], or one of middle standing or a junior [bhikkhu]. If an elder [bhikkhu] corrects me, he might do so without sympathy, not sympathetically. I would then say "No!" to him and would trouble him,[296] and even seeing [my offense] I would not make amends for it. If [a bhikkhu] of middle standing corrects me . . . If a junior [bhikkhu] corrects me, he might do so without sympathy, not sympathetically. I would then say "No!" to him and would trouble him, and even seeing [my offense] I would not make amends for it.'

"It occurs, too, to [a bhikkhu] of middle standing . . . to a junior [bhikkhu]: 'An elder [bhikkhu]—or one of middle standing or a junior [bhikkhu]—should not correct me. I should not correct an elder [bhikkhu] . . . [79] . . . and even seeing [my offense] I would not make amends for it.' It is in this way that there is co-residency among the bad, and it is in this way that the bad live together.

"And how, bhikkhus, is there co-residency among the good, and how do the good live together? Here, it occurs to an elder bhikkhu: 'An elder [bhikkhu]—and one of middle standing and a junior [bhikkhu]—should correct me. I should correct an elder [bhikkhu], one of middle standing, and a junior [bhikkhu]. If an elder [bhikkhu] corrects me, he might do so sympathetically, not without sympathy. I would then say "Good!" to him and would not trouble him, and seeing [my offense] I would make amends for it. If [a bhikkhu] of middle standing speaks to me . . . If a junior [bhikkhu] corrects me, he might do so sympathetically, not without sympathy, I would then say "Good!" to him and would not trouble him, and seeing [my offense] I would make amends for it.'

"It occurs, too, to [a bhikkhu] of middle standing . . . to a junior [bhikkhu]: 'An elder [bhikkhu]—and one of middle standing and a junior [bhikkhu]—should correct me. I should correct an elder [bhikkhu] . . . and seeing [my offense] I would make amends for it.' It is in this way that there is co-residency among the good, and it is in this way that the good live together."

63 (12)

"Bhikkhus, when, in regard to a disciplinary issue, the exchange of words between both parties,[297] the insolence about views, and the resentment, bitterness, and exasperation [80] are not settled internally,[298] it can be expected that this disciplinary issue will lead to acrimony and animosity for a long time, and the bhikkhus will not dwell at ease.

"Bhikkhus, when, in regard to a disciplinary issue, the exchange of words between both parties, the insolence about views, and the resentment, bitterness, and exasperation are well settled internally, it can be expected that this disciplinary issue will not lead to acrimony and animosity for a long time, and the bhikkhus will dwell at ease."[299]

VII. Happiness

64 (1)

"Bhikkhus, there are these two kinds of happiness. What two? The happiness of a layperson and the happiness of one who has gone forth [into homelessness].[300] These are the two kinds of happiness. Of these two kinds of happiness, the happiness of one who has gone forth is foremost."

65 (2)

"Bhikkhus, there are these two kinds of happiness. What two? Sensual happiness and the happiness of renunciation. These are the two kinds of happiness. Of these two kinds of happiness, the happiness of renunciation is foremost."

66 (3)

"Bhikkhus, there are these two kinds of happiness. What two? The happiness bound up with acquisitions and the happiness without acquisitions. These are the two kinds of happiness. Of these two kinds of happiness, the happiness without acquisitions is foremost."[301]

67 (4)

"Bhikkhus, there are these two kinds of happiness. What two? [81] The happiness with taints and the happiness without taints. These are the two kinds of happiness. Of these two kinds of happiness, the happiness without taints is foremost."

68 (5)

"Bhikkhus, there are these two kinds of happiness. What two? Worldly happiness and spiritual happiness.[302] These are the two kinds of happiness. Of these two kinds of happiness, spiritual happiness is foremost."

69 (6)

"Bhikkhus, there are these two kinds of happiness. What two? Noble happiness and ignoble happiness. These are the two kinds of happiness. Of these two kinds of happiness, noble happiness is foremost."

70 (7)

"Bhikkhus, there are these two kinds of happiness. What two? Bodily happiness and mental happiness. These are the two kinds of happiness. Of these two kinds of happiness, mental happiness is foremost."

71 (8)

"Bhikkhus, there are these two kinds of happiness. What two? The happiness accompanied by rapture and the happiness without rapture. These are the two kinds of happiness. Of these two kinds of happiness, the happiness without rapture is foremost."[303]

72 (9)

"Bhikkhus, there are these two kinds of happiness. What two? Pleasurable happiness and the happiness of equanimity. These are the two kinds of happiness. Of these two kinds of happiness, the happiness of equanimity is foremost."[304]

73 (10)

"Bhikkhus, there are these two kinds of happiness. What two? The happiness of concentration and the happiness without concentration. These are the two kinds of happiness. Of these two kinds of happiness, the happiness of concentration is foremost."

74 (11)

"Bhikkhus, there are these two kinds of happiness. What two? The happiness based on the presence of rapture and the happiness based on the absence of rapture. [82] These are the two kinds of happiness. Of these two kinds of happiness, the happiness based on the absence of rapture is foremost."[305]

75 (12)

"Bhikkhus, there are these two kinds of happiness. What two? The happiness based on pleasure and the happiness based on equanimity. These are the two kinds of happiness. Of these two kinds of happiness, the happiness based on equanimity is foremost."

76 (13)

"Bhikkhus, there are these two kinds of happiness. What two? The happiness based on form and the happiness based on the formless. These are the two kinds of happiness. Of these two kinds of happiness, the happiness based on the formless is foremost."[306]

VIII. With a Basis

77 (1)

"Bhikkhus, bad unwholesome qualities arise with a basis, not without a basis. With the abandoning of this basis, these bad unwholesome qualities do not occur."[307]

78 (2)

"Bhikkhus, bad unwholesome qualities arise through a source, not without a source. With the abandoning of this source, these bad unwholesome qualities do not occur."

79 (3)

"Bhikkhus, bad unwholesome qualities arise through a cause, not without a cause. With the abandoning of this cause, these bad unwholesome qualities do not occur."

80 (4)

"Bhikkhus, bad unwholesome qualities arise through causal activities, not without causal activities. With the abandoning of these causal activities, these bad unwholesome qualities do not occur."[308]

81 (5)
"Bhikkhus, bad unwholesome qualities arise with a condition, not without a condition. With the abandoning of this condition, these bad unwholesome qualities do not occur." [83]

82 (6)
"Bhikkhus, bad unwholesome qualities arise along with form, not without form. With the abandoning of this form, these bad unwholesome qualities do not occur."

83 (7)
"Bhikkhus, bad unwholesome qualities arise along with feeling, not without feeling. With the abandoning of this feeling, these bad unwholesome qualities do not occur."

84 (8)
"Bhikkhus, bad unwholesome qualities arise along with perception, not without perception. With the abandoning of this perception, these bad unwholesome qualities do not occur."

85 (9)
"Bhikkhus, bad unwholesome qualities arise along with consciousness, not without consciousness. With the abandoning of this consciousness, these bad unwholesome qualities do not occur."

86 (10)
"Bhikkhus, bad unwholesome qualities arise based on the conditioned, not without a basis in the conditioned. With the abandoning of the conditioned, these bad unwholesome qualities do not occur."

IX. Dhamma

87 (1)
"Bhikkhus, there are these two things. What two? Liberation of mind and liberation by wisdom. These are the two things."[309]

88 (2)–97 (11)
"Bhikkhus, there are these two things. What two? (88) Exertion and non-distraction... (89) Name and form... (90) True

knowledge and liberation ... (91) The view of existence and the view of extermination ... (92) Moral shamelessness and moral recklessness ... (93) Moral shame and moral dread ... (94) Being difficult to correct and bad friendship ... (95) Being easy to correct and good friendship ... (96) Skillfulness in the elements and skillfulness in attention ... [84] ... (97) Skillfulness in regard to offenses and skillfulness in rehabilitation from offenses. These are the two things."

X. Fools

98 (1)
"Bhikkhus, there are these two kinds of fools. What two? One who takes responsibility for what does not befall him and one who does not take responsibility for what befalls him. These are the two kinds of fools."

99 (2)
"Bhikkhus, there are these two kinds of wise people. What two? One who takes responsibility for what befalls him and one who does not take responsibility for what does not befall him.[310] These are the two kinds of wise people."

100 (3)
"Bhikkhus, there are these two kinds of fools. What two? One who perceives what is unallowable as allowable and one who perceives what is allowable as unallowable.[311] These are the two kinds of fools."

101 (4)
"Bhikkhus, there are these two kinds of wise people. What two? One who perceives what is unallowable as unallowable and one who perceives what is allowable as allowable. These are the two kinds of wise people."

102 (5)
"Bhikkhus, there are these two kinds of fools. What two? One who perceives what is not an offense as an offense and one who perceives what is an offense as no offense. These are the two kinds of fools."

103 (6)

"Bhikkhus, there are these two kinds of wise people. What two? One who perceives what is not an offense as no offense and one who perceives what is an offense as an offense. These are the two kinds of wise people." [85]

104 (7)

"Bhikkhus, there are these two kinds of fools. What two? One who perceives what is non-Dhamma as Dhamma and one who perceives what is Dhamma as non-Dhamma. These are the two kinds of fools."

105 (8)

"Bhikkhus, there are these two kinds of wise people. What two? One who perceives what is non-Dhamma as non-Dhamma and one who perceives what is Dhamma as Dhamma. These are the two kinds of wise people."

106 (9)

"Bhikkhus, there are these two kinds of fools. What two? One who perceives what is non-discipline as discipline and one who perceives what is discipline as non-discipline. These are the two kinds of fools."

107 (10)

"Bhikkhus, there are these two kinds of wise people. What two? One who perceives what is non-discipline as non-discipline and one who perceives what is discipline as discipline. These are the two kinds of wise people."

108 (11)

"Bhikkhus, the taints increase for two [kinds of persons]. What two? One who feels remorse about a matter over which one need not feel remorse and one who does not feel remorse about a matter over which one should feel remorse. The taints increase for these two [kinds of persons]."

109 (12)

"Bhikkhus, the taints do not increase for two [kinds of persons]. What two? One who does not feel remorse for a matter over which one need not feel remorse and one who feels remorse for a matter over which one should feel remorse. The taints do not increase for these two [kinds of persons]."

110 (13)

"Bhikkhus, the taints increase for two [kinds of persons]. What two? One who perceives what is unallowable as allowable and one who perceives what is allowable as unallowable. The taints increase for these two [kinds of persons]."

111 (14)

"Bhikkhus, the taints do not increase for two [kinds of persons]. What two? One who perceives what is unallowable as unallowable and one who perceives what is allowable as allowable. The taints do not increase for these two [kinds of persons]."

112 (15)

"Bhikkhus, the taints increase for two [kinds of persons]. What two? [86] One who perceives what is not an offense as an offense and one who perceives what is an offense as no offense.[312] The taints increase for these two [kinds of persons]."

113 (16)

"Bhikkhus, the taints do not increase for two [kinds of persons]. What two? One who perceives what is not an offense as no offense and one who perceives what is an offense as an offense.[313] The taints do not increase for these two [kinds of persons]."

114 (17)

"Bhikkhus, the taints increase for two [kinds of persons]. What two? One who perceives what is non-Dhamma as Dhamma and one who perceives what is Dhamma as non-Dhamma. The taints increase for these two [kinds of persons]."

115 (18)

"Bhikkhus, the taints do not increase for two [kinds of persons]. What two? One who perceives what is non-Dhamma as non-Dhamma and one who perceives what is Dhamma as Dhamma.[314] The taints do not increase for these two [kinds of persons]."

116 (19)

"Bhikkhus, the taints increase for two [kinds of persons]. What two? One who perceives what is non-discipline as discipline and one who perceives what is discipline as non-discipline. The taints increase for these two [kinds of persons]."

117 (20)

"Bhikkhus, the taints do not increase for two [kinds of persons]. What two? One who perceives what is non-discipline as non-discipline and one who perceives what is discipline as discipline. The taints do not increase for these two [kinds of persons]."

XI. Desires

118 (1)

"Bhikkhus, these two desires are hard to abandon. What two? The desire for gain and the desire for life. These two desires are hard to abandon."[315] [87]

119 (2)

"Bhikkhus, these two kinds of persons are rare in the world. What two? One who takes the initiative in helping others and one who is grateful and thankful. These two kinds of persons are rare in the world."

120 (3)

"Bhikkhus, these two kinds of persons are rare in the world. What two? One who is satisfied and one who provides satisfaction. These two kinds of persons are rare in the world."

121 (4)

"Bhikkhus, these two kinds of persons are hard to satisfy. What two? One who amasses what he gains and one who squanders what he gains.[316] These two kinds of persons are hard to satisfy."

122 (5)

"Bhikkhus, these two kinds of persons are easy to satisfy. What two? One who does not amass what he gains and one who does not squander what he gains. These two kinds of persons are easy to satisfy."

123 (6)

"Bhikkhus, there are these two conditions for the arising of greed. What two? The mark of the attractive and careless attention. These are the two conditions for the arising of greed."[317]

124 (7)

"Bhikkhus, there are these two conditions for the arising of hatred. What two? The mark of the repulsive and careless attention. These are the two conditions for the arising of hatred."

125 (8)

"Bhikkhus, there are these two conditions for the arising of wrong view. What two? The utterance of another [person] and careless attention. These are the two conditions for the arising of wrong view."

126 (9)

"Bhikkhus, there are these two conditions for the arising of right view. What two? The utterance of another [person] and careful attention. These are the two conditions for the arising of right view."

127 (10)

"Bhikkhus, there are these two kinds of offenses. What two? [88] A light offense and a grave offense. These are the two kinds of offenses."[318]

128 (11)

"Bhikkhus, there are these two kinds of offenses. What two? A coarse offense and an offense that is not coarse. These are the two kinds of offenses."

129 (12)

"Bhikkhus, there are these two kinds of offenses. What two? A remediable offense and an irremediable offense. These are the two kinds of offenses."

XII. Aspiring

130 (1)

"Bhikkhus, a bhikkhu endowed with faith, rightly aspiring, should aspire thus: 'May I become like Sāriputta and Moggallāna!' This is the standard and criterion[319] for my bhikkhu disciples, that is, Sāriputta and Moggallāna."

131 (2)

"Bhikkhus, a bhikkhunī endowed with faith, rightly aspiring, should aspire thus: 'May I become like the bhikkhunīs Khemā and Uppalavaṇṇā!' This is the standard and criterion for my bhikkhunī disciples, that is, the bhikkhunīs Khemā and Uppalavaṇṇā."[320]

132 (3)

"Bhikkhus, a male lay follower endowed with faith, rightly aspiring, should aspire thus: 'May I become like Citta the householder and Hatthaka of Āḷavī!' This is the standard and criterion for my male lay disciples, that is, Citta the householder and Hatthaka of Āḷavī."[321]

133 (4)

"Bhikkhus, a female lay follower endowed with faith, rightly aspiring, should aspire thus: 'May I become like the female lay followers Khujjuttarā and Veḷukaṇṭakī Nandamātā!' [89] This is the standard and criterion for my female lay disciples, that is, the female lay followers Khujjuttarā and Veḷukaṇṭakī Nandamātā."[322]

134 (5)[323]

"Bhikkhus, possessing two qualities, the foolish, incompetent, bad person maintains himself in a maimed and injured condition; he is blameworthy and subject to reproach by the wise; and he generates much demerit. What two? Without investigating and scrutinizing, he speaks praise of one who deserves dispraise. Without investigating and scrutinizing, he speaks dispraise of one who deserves praise. Possessing these two qualities, the foolish, incompetent, bad person maintains himself in a maimed and injured condition; he is blameworthy and subject to reproach by the wise; and he generates much demerit.

"Bhikkhus, possessing two qualities, the wise, competent, good person preserves himself unmaimed and uninjured; he is blameless and beyond reproach by the wise; and he generates much merit. What two? Having investigated and scrutinized, he speaks dispraise of one who deserves dispraise. Having investigated and scrutinized, he speaks praise of one who deserves praise. Possessing these two qualities, the wise, competent, good person preserves himself unmaimed and uninjured; he is blameless and beyond reproach by the wise; and he generates much merit."

135 (6)[324]

"Bhikkhus, possessing two qualities, the foolish, incompetent, bad person maintains himself in a maimed and injured condition; he is blameworthy and subject to reproach by the wise; and he generates much demerit. What two? Without investigating and scrutinizing, he believes a matter that merits suspicion. Without investigating and scrutinizing, he is suspicious about a matter that merits belief. Possessing these two qualities, the foolish, incompetent, bad person maintains himself in a maimed and injured condition; he is blameworthy and subject to reproach by the wise; and he generates much demerit. [90]

"Bhikkhus, possessing two qualities, the wise, competent, good person preserves himself unmaimed and uninjured; he is blameless and beyond reproach by the wise; and he generates much merit. What two? Having investigated and scrutinized, he is suspicious about a matter that merits suspicion. Having investigated and scrutinized, he believes a matter that merits belief. Possessing these two qualities, the wise, competent, good person preserves himself unmaimed and uninjured; he is blameless and beyond reproach by the wise; and he generates much merit."

136 (7)

"Bhikkhus, behaving wrongly toward two persons, the foolish, incompetent, bad person maintains himself in a maimed and injured condition; he is blameworthy and subject to reproach by the wise; and he generates much demerit. What two? His mother and his father. Behaving wrongly toward these two persons, the foolish, incompetent, bad person maintains himself in a maimed and injured condition; he is blameworthy and subject to reproach by the wise; and he generates much demerit.

"Bhikkhus, behaving rightly toward two persons, the wise, competent, good person preserves himself unmaimed and uninjured; he is blameless and beyond reproach among the wise; and he generates much merit. What two? His mother and his father. Behaving rightly toward these two persons, the wise, competent, good person preserves himself unmaimed and uninjured; he is blameless and beyond reproach by the wise; and he generates much merit."

137 (8)

"Bhikkhus, behaving wrongly toward two persons, the foolish, incompetent, bad person maintains himself in a maimed and injured condition; he is blameworthy and subject to reproach by the wise; and he generates much demerit. What two? The Tathāgata and a disciple of the Tathāgata.[325] Behaving wrongly toward these two persons, the foolish, incompetent, bad person maintains himself in a maimed and injured condition; he is blameworthy and subject to reproach by the wise; and he generates much demerit. [91]

"Bhikkhus, behaving rightly toward two persons, the wise, competent, good person preserves himself unmaimed and uninjured; he is blameless and beyond reproach among the wise; and he generates much merit. What two? The Tathāgata and a disciple of the Tathāgata. Behaving rightly toward these two persons, the wise, competent, good person preserves himself unmaimed and uninjured; he is blameless and beyond reproach by the wise; and he generates much merit."

138 (9)

"Bhikkhus, there are these two things. What two? Cleansing one's own mind and one does not cling to anything in the world.[326] These are the two things."

139 (10)

"Bhikkhus, there are these two things. What two? Anger and hostility. These are the two things."

140 (11)
"Bhikkhus, there are these two things. What two? The removal of anger and the removal of hostility. These are the two things."

XIII. Gifts

141 (1)
"Bhikkhus, there are these two kinds of gifts. What two? The gift of material goods and the gift of the Dhamma. These are the two kinds of gifts. Of these two kinds of gifts, the gift of the Dhamma is foremost."

142 (2)
"Bhikkhus, there are these two kinds of offerings. What two? The offering of material goods and the offering of the Dhamma. These are the two kinds of offerings. Of these two kinds of offerings, the offering of the Dhamma is foremost." [92]

143 (3)
"Bhikkhus, there are these two kinds of generosity. What two? Generosity with material goods and generosity with the Dhamma. These are the two kinds of generosity. Of these two kinds of generosity, generosity with the Dhamma is foremost."

144 (4)
"Bhikkhus, there are these two kinds of relinquishment. What two? The relinquishment of material goods and relinquishment [by giving] the Dhamma. These are the two kinds of relinquishment. Of these two kinds of relinquishment, relinquishment [by giving] the Dhamma is foremost."

145 (5)
"Bhikkhus, there are these two kinds of wealth. What two? Material wealth and the wealth of the Dhamma. These are the two kinds of wealth. Of these two kinds of wealth, the wealth of the Dhamma is foremost."

146 (6)
"Bhikkhus, there are these two kinds of enjoyment. What two? The enjoyment of material goods and the enjoyment of

the Dhamma. These are the two kinds of enjoyment. Of these two kinds of enjoyment, the enjoyment of the Dhamma is foremost."

147 (7)

"Bhikkhus, there are these two kinds of sharing. What two? Sharing material goods and sharing the Dhamma. These are the two kinds of sharing. Of these two kinds of sharing, sharing the Dhamma is foremost."

148 (8)

"Bhikkhus, there are these two ways of sustaining a favorable relationship.[327] What two? Sustaining a favorable relationship with material goods and doing so with the Dhamma. These are the two ways of sustaining a favorable relationship. Of these two ways, sustaining a favorable relationship with the Dhamma is foremost."

149 (9)

"Bhikkhus, there are these two kinds of assistance. What two? Assistance with material goods and assistance with the Dhamma. These are the two kinds of assistance. Of these two kinds of assistance, assistance with the Dhamma is foremost."

150 (10)

"Bhikkhus, there are these two kinds of compassion.[328] What two? Compassion shown with material goods and compassion shown with the Dhamma. These are the two kinds of compassion. Of these two kinds of compassion, compassion shown with the Dhamma is foremost." [93]

XIV. Munificence

151 (1)

"Bhikkhus, there are these two kinds of munificence.[329] What two? Munificence with material goods and munificence with the Dhamma. These are the two kinds of munificence. Of these two kinds of munificence, munificence with the Dhamma is foremost."

152 (2)
"Bhikkhus, there are these two kinds of hospitality. What two? Hospitality with material goods and hospitality with the Dhamma. These are the two kinds of hospitality. Of these two kinds of hospitality, hospitality with the Dhamma is foremost."

153 (3)
"Bhikkhus, there are these two kinds of search. What two? The search for material goods and the search for the Dhamma. These are the two kinds of search. Of these two kinds of search, the search for the Dhamma is foremost."

154 (4)
"Bhikkhus, there are these two kinds of quests. What two? The quest for material goods and the quest for the Dhamma. These are the two kinds of quest. Of these two kinds of quest, the quest for the Dhamma is foremost."

155 (5)
"Bhikkhus, there are these two kinds of seeking. What two? Seeking for material goods and seeking for the Dhamma. These are the two kinds of seeking. Of these two kinds of seeking, seeking for the Dhamma is foremost."

156 (6)
"Bhikkhus, there are these two kinds of veneration. What two? Veneration with material goods and veneration with the Dhamma. These are the two kinds of veneration. Of these two kinds of veneration, veneration with the Dhamma is foremost."

157 (7)
"Bhikkhus, there are these two kinds of gifts to present to a guest.[330] What two? The gift of material goods and the gift of the Dhamma. These are the two kinds of gifts to present to a guest. Of these two kinds of gifts to present to a guest, the gift of the Dhamma is foremost."

158 (8)

"Bhikkhus, there are these two kinds of success. What two? Success relating to material goods and success relating to the Dhamma. These are the two kinds of success. Of these two kinds of success, success relating to the Dhamma is foremost." [94]

159 (9)

"Bhikkhus, there are these two kinds of growth. What two? Growth in material goods and growth in the Dhamma. These are the two kinds of growth. Of these two kinds of growth, growth in the Dhamma is foremost."

160 (10)

"Bhikkhus, there are these two kinds of gems. What two? A material gem and the gem of the Dhamma. These are the two kinds of gems. Of these two kinds of gems, the gem of the Dhamma is foremost."

161 (11)

"Bhikkhus, there are these two kinds of accumulation. What two? The accumulation of material goods and the accumulation of the Dhamma. These are the two kinds of accumulation. Of these two kinds of accumulation, the accumulation of the Dhamma is foremost."

162 (12)

"Bhikkhus, there are these two kinds of expansion. What two? Expansion in material goods and expansion in the Dhamma. These are the two kinds of expansion. Of these two kinds of expansion, expansion in the Dhamma is foremost."

XV. Meditative Attainment

163 (1)

"Bhikkhus, there are these two qualities. What two? Skillfulness in [entering] a meditative attainment and skillfulness in emerging from a meditative attainment. These are the two qualities."[331]

164 (2)–179 (17)
"Bhikkhus, there are these two qualities. What two? (164) Rectitude and gentleness... (165) Patience and mildness... (166) Softness of speech and hospitality... (167) Harmlessness and purity... (168) Not guarding the doors of the sense faculties and immoderation in eating... (169) Guarding the doors of the sense faculties and moderation in eating... (170) The power of reflection and the power of development... (171) The power of mindfulness and the power of concentration... [95]... (172) Serenity and insight... (173) Failure in virtuous behavior and failure in view... (174) Accomplishment of virtuous behavior and accomplishment of view... (175) Purity of virtuous behavior and purity of view... (176) Purity of view and striving in accordance with one's view... (177) Non-contentment in regard to wholesome qualities and indefatigability in striving... (178) Muddle-mindedness and lack of clear comprehension... (179) Mindfulness and clear comprehension. These are the two qualities."

XVI. Anger

180 (1)–184 (5)[332]
"Bhikkhus, there are these two qualities. What two? (180) Anger and hostility... (181) Denigration and insolence... (182) Envy and miserliness... (183) Deceitfulness and craftiness... (184) Moral shamelessness and moral recklessness. These are the two qualities."

185 (6)–189 (10)
"Bhikkhus, there are these two qualities. What two? (185) Non-anger and non-hostility... (186) Non-denigration and non-insolence... (187) Non-envy and non-miserliness... (188) Non-deceitfulness and non-craftiness... (189) Moral shame and moral dread. These are the two qualities."

190 (11)–194 (15)
"Bhikkhus, possessing two qualities, one dwells in suffering. What two? (190) Anger and hostility... (191) Denigration and insolence... (192) Envy and miserliness... (193) Deceitfulness and craftiness... (194) Moral shamelessness and moral reck-

lessness. [96] Possessing these two qualities, one dwells in suffering."

195 (16)–199 (20)

"Bhikkhus, possessing two qualities, one dwells happily. What two? (195) Non-anger and non-hostility . . . (196) Non-denigration and non-insolence . . . (197) Non-envy and non-miserliness . . . (198) Non-deceitfulness and non-craftiness . . . (199) Moral shame and moral dread. Possessing these two qualities, one dwells happily."

200 (21)–204 (25)

"Bhikkhus, these two qualities lead to the decline of a bhikkhu who is a trainee. What two? (200) Anger and hostility . . . (201) Denigration and insolence . . . (202) Envy and miserliness . . . (203) Deceitfulness and craftiness . . . (204) Moral shamelessness and moral recklessness. These two qualities lead to the decline of a bhikkhu who is a trainee."

205 (26)–209 (30)

"Bhikkhus, these two qualities lead to the non-decline of a bhikkhu who is a trainee. What two? (205) Non-anger and non-hostility . . . (206) Non-denigration and non-insolence . . . (207) Non-envy and non-miserliness . . . (208) Non-deceitfulness and non-craftiness . . . (209) Moral shame and moral dread. These two qualities lead to the non-decline of a bhikkhu who is a trainee."

210 (31)–214 (35)

"Bhikkhus, possessing two qualities, one is deposited in hell as if brought there. What two? (210) Anger and hostility . . . (211) Denigration and insolence . . . (212) Envy and miserliness . . . (213) Deceitfulness and craftiness . . . (214) Moral shamelessness and moral recklessness. Possessing these two qualities, one is deposited in hell as if brought there." [97]

215 (36)–219 (40)

"Bhikkhus, possessing two qualities, one is deposited in heaven as if brought there. What two? (215) Non-anger and non-hostility . . . (216) Non-denigration and non-insolence . . . (217)

Non-envy and non-miserliness... (218) Non-deceitfulness and non-craftiness... (219) Moral shame and moral dread. Possessing these two qualities, one is deposited in heaven as if brought there."

220 (41)–224 (45)

"Bhikkhus, possessing two qualities, with the breakup of the body, after death, someone here is reborn in the plane of misery, in a bad destination, in the lower world, in hell. What two? (220) Anger and hostility... (221) Denigration and insolence... (222) Envy and miserliness... (223) Deceitfulness and craftiness... (224) Moral shamelessness and moral recklessness. Possessing these two qualities, with the breakup of the body, after death, someone here is reborn in the plane of misery, in a bad destination, in the lower world, in hell."

225 (46)–229 (50)

"Bhikkhus, possessing two qualities, with the breakup of the body, after death, someone here is reborn in a good destination, in a heavenly world. What two? (225) Non-anger and non-hostility... (226) Non-denigration and non-insolence... (227) Non-envy and non-miserliness... (228) Non-deceitfulness and non-craftiness... (229) Moral shame and moral dread. Possessing these two qualities, with the breakup of the body, after death, someone here is reborn in a good destination, in a heavenly world."

XVII. Unwholesome Repetition Series[333]

230 (1)–234 (5)[334]

"Bhikkhus, there are these two unwholesome qualities. What two? (230) Anger and hostility... (231) Denigration and insolence... (232) Envy and miserliness... (233) Deceitfulness and craftiness... (234) Moral shamelessness and moral recklessness. These are the two unwholesome qualities."

235 (6)–239 (10)

"Bhikkhus, there are these two wholesome qualities. What two? (235) Non-anger and non-hostility... (236) Non-denigration and non-insolence... (237) Non-envy and non-miserliness... (238)

Non-deceitfulness and non-craftiness... (239) Moral shame and moral dread. These are the two wholesome qualities."

240 (11)–244 (15)

"Bhikkhus, there are these two blameworthy qualities. What two? (240) Anger and hostility... (241) Denigration and insolence... (242) Envy and miserliness... (243) Deceitfulness and craftiness... (244) Moral shamelessness and moral recklessness. These are the two blameworthy qualities."

245 (16)–249 (20)

"Bhikkhus, there are these two blameless qualities. What two? (245) Non-anger and non-hostility... (246) Non-denigration and non-insolence... (247) Non-envy and non-miserliness... (248) Non-deceitfulness and non-craftiness... (249) Moral shame and moral dread. These are the two blameless qualities."

250 (21)–254 (25)

"Bhikkhus, there are these two qualities that have suffering as their outcome. What two? (250) Anger and hostility... (251) Denigration and insolence... (252) Envy and miserliness... (253) Deceitfulness and craftiness... (254) Moral shamelessness and moral recklessness. These are the two qualities that have suffering as their outcome."

255 (26)–259 (30)

"Bhikkhus, there are these two qualities that have happiness as their outcome. What two? (255) Non-anger and non-hostility... (256) Non-denigration and non-insolence... (257) Non-envy and non-miserliness... (258) Non-deceitfulness and non-craftiness... (259) Moral shame and moral dread. These are the two qualities that have happiness as their outcome."

260 (31)–264 (35)

"Bhikkhus, there are these two qualities that result in suffering. What two? (260) Anger and hostility... (261) Denigration and insolence... (262) Envy and miserliness... (263) Deceitfulness and craftiness... (264) Moral shamelessness and moral recklessness. These are the two qualities that result in suffering." [98]

265 (36)–269 (40)
"Bhikkhus, there are these two qualities that result in happiness. What two? (265) Non-anger and non-hostility...(266) Non-denigration and non-insolence...(267) Non-envy and non-miserliness... (268) Non-deceitfulness and non-craftiness... (269) Moral shame and moral dread. These are the two qualities that result in happiness."

270 (41)–274 (45)
"Bhikkhus, there are these two afflictive qualities. What two? (270) Anger and hostility...(271) Denigration and insolence...(272) Envy and miserliness...(273) Deceitfulness and craftiness...(274) Moral shamelessness and moral recklessness. These are the two afflictive qualities."

275 (46)–279 (50)
"Bhikkhus, there are these two non-afflictive qualities. What two? (275) Non-anger and non-hostility... (276) Non-denigration and non-insolence... (277) Non-envy and non-miserliness... (278) Non-deceitfulness and non-craftiness... (279) Moral shame and moral dread. These are the two non-afflictive qualities."

XVIII. Discipline Repetition Series[335]

280 (1)[336]
"Bhikkhus, it is for these two reasons that the Tathāgata has prescribed the training rules for his disciples. What two? For the well-being of the Saṅgha and for the ease of the Saṅgha...For keeping recalcitrant persons in check and so that well-behaved bhikkhus can dwell at ease...For the restraint of taints pertaining to this present life and for the dispelling of taints pertaining to future lives...For the restraint of enmities pertaining to this present life and for the dispelling of enmities pertaining to future lives...For the restraint of faults pertaining to this present life and for the dispelling of faults pertaining to future lives...For the restraint of perils pertaining to this present life and for the dispelling of perils pertaining to future lives...For the restraint of unwholesome qualities pertaining to this present life and for the dispelling of unwholesome qualities pertaining to future

lives ... Out of compassion for laypeople and to stop the faction of those with evil desires ... So that those without confidence might gain confidence and for increasing [the confidence] of those with confidence ... For the continuation of the good Dhamma and for promoting the discipline. It is for these two reasons that the Tathāgata has prescribed the training rules for his disciples."

281 (2)–309 (30)

"Bhikkhus, it is for these two reasons that the Tathāgata (281) has prescribed the Pātimokkha for his disciples ... [this sutta and those to follow should be elaborated as above] ...[337]

(282) "... has prescribed the recitation of the Pātimokkha ..." [99]

(283) "... has prescribed the suspension of the Pātimokkha ..."

(284) "... has prescribed the invitation ceremony ..."

(285) "... has prescribed the suspension of the invitation ceremony ..."

(286) "... has prescribed the legal act of censure ..."

(287) "... has prescribed the legal act of [placing under] dependence ..."

(288) "... has prescribed the legal act of banishment ..."

(289) "... has prescribed the legal act of reconciliation ..."

(290) "... has prescribed the legal act of suspension ..."

(291) "... has prescribed the imposition of probation ..."

(292) "... has prescribed sending back to the beginning ..."

(293) "... has prescribed the imposition of penance ..."

(294) "... has prescribed rehabilitation ..."

(295) "... has prescribed reinstatement ..."

(296) "... has prescribed removal ..."

(297) "... has prescribed full ordination ..."

(298) "... has prescribed a legal act that consists in a motion ..."

(299) "... has prescribed a legal act that includes a motion as the second [factor] ..."

(300) "... has prescribed a legal act that includes a motion as the fourth [factor] ..."

(301) "... has prescribed [a training rule] when none had been prescribed before ..."

(302) "... has added an amendment [to a training rule already] prescribed ..."

(303) "... has prescribed removal by presence ..."

(304) "...has prescribed removal on account of recollection..."

(305) "...has prescribed removal on account of [past] insanity..."

(306) "...has prescribed the acknowledgment [of an offense]..."

(307) "...has prescribed [the opinion of] the majority..."

(308) "...has prescribed [the pronouncement of] aggravated misconduct..."

(309) "...has prescribed covering over with grass. What two? For the well-being of the Saṅgha and for the ease of the Saṅgha...[100]...For the continuation of the good Dhamma and for promoting the discipline. It is for these two reasons that the Tathāgata has prescribed the covering over with grass."

XIX. Lust and So Forth Repetition Series[338]

310 (1)

"Bhikkhus, for direct knowledge of lust, two things are to be developed. What two? Serenity and insight. For direct knowledge of lust, these two things are to be developed."

311 (2)–319 (10)

"Bhikkhus, for full understanding of lust...for the utter destruction of lust...for the abandoning of lust...for the destruction of lust...for the vanishing of lust...for the fading away of lust...for the cessation of lust...for the giving up of lust...for the relinquishment of lust, these two things are to be developed. What two? Serenity and insight. For the relinquishment of lust, these two things are to be developed."

320 (11)–479 (170)

"Bhikkhus, for direct knowledge...for full understanding...for the utter destruction...for the abandoning...for the destruction...for the vanishing...for the fading away...for the cessation...for the giving up...for the relinquishment of hatred...of delusion...of anger...of hostility...of denigration...of insolence...of envy...of miserliness...of deceitfulness...of craftiness...of obstinacy...of vehemence...of conceit...of arrogance...of intoxication...of heedlessness, these two things are to be developed. What two? Serenity and insight. For the relinquishment of heedlessness, these two things are to be developed."

The Book of the Twos is finished.

The Book of the Threes
(*Tikanipāta*)

The Book of the Threes

The First Fifty

The Second Fifty

The Third Fifty

[101] # The Book of the Threes

Homage to the Blessed One, the Arahant,
the Perfectly Enlightened One

The First Fifty

I. The Fool

1 (1) Peril

Thus have I heard. On one occasion the Blessed One was dwelling at Sāvatthī in Jeta's Grove, Anāthapiṇḍika's Park. There the Blessed One addressed the bhikkhus: "Bhikkhus!"

"Venerable sir!" those bhikkhus replied. The Blessed One said this:

"Bhikkhus, whatever perils arise all arise on account of the fool, not on account of the wise person. Whatever calamities arise all arise on account of the fool, not on account of the wise person. Whatever misfortunes arise all arise on account of the fool, not on account of the wise person. Just as a fire that starts in a house made of reeds or grass burns down even a house with a peaked roof, plastered inside and out, draft-free, with bolts fastened and shutters closed; so too, whatever perils arise . . . all arise on account of the fool, not on account of the wise person. (1) Thus, bhikkhus, the fool brings peril, the wise person brings no peril; (2) the fool brings calamity, the wise person brings no calamity; (3) the fool brings misfortune, the wise person brings no misfortune. There is no peril from the wise person; there is no calamity from the wise person; there is no misfortune from the wise person.

"Therefore, bhikkhus, you should train yourselves thus: 'We will avoid the three qualities possessing which one is known as a fool, and we will undertake and practice the three qualities possessing which one is known as a wise person.' It is in this way that you should train yourselves." [102]

2 (2) Characteristics

"Bhikkhus, the fool is characterized by his actions; the wise person is characterized by his actions. Wisdom shines in its manifestation.[339]

"Bhikkhus, one who possesses three qualities should be known as a fool. What three? Bodily misconduct, verbal misconduct, and mental misconduct. One who possesses these three qualities should be known as a fool. One who possesses three qualities should be known as a wise person. What three? Bodily good conduct, verbal good conduct, and mental good conduct. One who possesses these three qualities should be known as a wise person.

"Therefore, bhikkhus, you should train yourselves thus: 'We will avoid the three qualities possessing which one is known as a fool, and we will undertake and observe the three qualities possessing which one is known as a wise person.' It is in this way that you should train yourselves."

3 (3) Thinking

"Bhikkhus, the fool has these three characteristics of a fool, marks of a fool, manifestations of a fool.[340] What three? Here, a fool thinks badly, speaks badly, and acts badly. If the fool did not think badly, speak badly, and act badly, how would wise people know of him: 'This fellow is a fool, a bad person'? But because the fool thinks badly, speaks badly, and acts badly, wise people know of him: 'This fellow is a fool, a bad person.' These are the fool's three characteristics of a fool, marks of a fool, manifestations of a fool.

"The wise person has these three characteristics of a wise person, marks of a wise person, manifestations of a wise person. What three? Here, a wise person thinks well, speaks well, and acts well. If the wise person did not think well, speak well, and act well, how would wise people know of him: 'This fellow is wise, a good person'? [103] But because the wise person thinks well, speaks well, and acts well, wise people know of him: 'This fellow is wise, a good person.' These are the wise person's three characteristics of a wise person, marks of a wise person, manifestations of a wise person.

"Therefore... [as in 3:2]... It is in this way that you should train yourselves."[341]

4 (4) Transgression

"Bhikkhus, one who possesses three qualities should be known as a fool. What three? (1) He does not see his transgression as a transgression. (2) When he sees his transgression as a transgression, he does not make amends for it in accordance with the Dhamma. (3) When another person confesses a transgression to him, he does not accept it in accordance with the Dhamma. One who possesses these three qualities should be known as a fool.

"One who possesses three qualities should be known as a wise person. What three? (1) He sees a transgression as a transgression. (2) When he sees a transgression as a transgression, he makes amends for it in accordance with the Dhamma. (3) When another person confesses a transgression to him, he accepts it in accordance with the Dhamma. One who possesses these three qualities should be known as a wise person.

"Therefore... It is in this way that you should train yourselves."

5 (5) Carelessly

"Bhikkhus, one who possesses three qualities should be known as a fool. What three? (1) He formulates a question carelessly; (2) he replies to a question carelessly; (3) when another person replies to a question carefully, with well-rounded and coherent words and phrases, he does not approve of it. One who possesses these three qualities should be known as a fool.

"One who possesses three qualities should be known as a wise person. What three? (1) He formulates a question carefully; (2) he replies to a question carefully; (3) when another person replies to a question carefully, with well-rounded and coherent words and phrases, he approves of it. One who possesses these three qualities should be known as a wise person.

"Therefore... It is in this way that you should train yourselves."

6 (6) Unwholesome

"Bhikkhus, one who possesses three qualities should be known as a fool. What three? [104] Unwholesome bodily action, unwholesome verbal action, and unwholesome mental action. One who possesses these three qualities should be known as a fool.

"One who possesses three qualities should be known as a wise person. What three? Wholesome bodily action, wholesome verbal action, and wholesome mental action. One who possesses these three qualities should be known as a wise person.

"Therefore... It is in this way that you should train yourselves."

7 (7) Blameworthy

"Bhikkhus, one who possesses three qualities should be known as a fool. What three? Blameworthy bodily action, blameworthy verbal action, and blameworthy mental action. One who possesses these three qualities should be known as a fool.

"One who possesses three qualities should be known as a wise person. What three? Blameless bodily action, blameless verbal action, and blameless mental action. One who possesses these three qualities should be known as a wise person.

"Therefore... It is in this way that you should train yourselves."

8 (8) Afflictive

"Bhikkhus, one who possesses three qualities should be known as a fool. What three? Afflictive bodily action, afflictive verbal action, and afflictive mental action. One who possesses these three qualities should be known as a fool.

"One who possesses three qualities should be known as a wise person. What three? Unafflictive bodily action, unafflictive verbal action, and unafflictive mental action. One who possesses these three qualities should be known as a wise person.

"Therefore, bhikkhus, you should train yourselves thus: 'We will avoid the three qualities possessing which one is known as a fool, and we will undertake and observe the three qualities possessing which one is known as a wise person.' It is in this way that you should train yourselves." [105]

9 (9) Maimed

"Bhikkhus, possessing three qualities, the foolish, incompetent, bad person maintains himself in a maimed and injured condition; he is blameworthy and subject to reproach by the wise; and he generates much demerit. What three? Bodily misconduct, verbal misconduct, and mental misconduct. Possessing these three qualities, the foolish, incompetent, bad person maintains himself in a maimed and injured condition; he is blameworthy and subject to reproach by the wise; and he generates much demerit.

"Bhikkhus, possessing three qualities, the wise, competent, good person preserves himself unmaimed and uninjured; he is blameless and beyond reproach by the wise; and he generates much merit. What three? Bodily good conduct, verbal good conduct, and mental good conduct. Possessing these three qualities, the wise, competent, good person preserves himself unmaimed and uninjured; he is blameless and beyond reproach by the wise; and he generates much merit."

10 (10) Stains

"Bhikkhus, possessing three qualities and without having abandoned three stains, one is deposited in hell as if brought there. What three? (1) One is immoral and has not abandoned the stain of immorality. (2) One is envious and has not abandoned the stain of envy. (3) One is miserly and has not abandoned the stain of miserliness. Possessing these three qualities and without having abandoned these three stains, one is deposited in hell as if brought there.

"Bhikkhus, possessing three qualities and having abandoned three stains, one is deposited in heaven as if brought there. What three? (1) One is virtuous and has abandoned the stain of immorality. (2) One is not envious and has abandoned the stain of envy. (3) One is not miserly and has abandoned the stain of miserliness. Possessing these three qualities and having abandoned these three stains, one is deposited in heaven as if brought there." [106]

II. The Cart Maker

11 (1) Well Known

"Bhikkhus, possessing three qualities, a well-known bhikkhu is acting for the harm of many people, for the unhappiness of many people, for the ruin, harm, and suffering of many people, of devas and human beings. What three? He encourages them in discordant bodily action, discordant verbal action, and discordant [mental] qualities.[342] Possessing these three qualities, a well-known bhikkhu is acting for the harm of many people, for the unhappiness of many people, for the ruin, harm, and suffering of many people, of devas and human beings.

"Bhikkhus, possessing three qualities, a well-known bhikkhu is acting for the welfare of many people, for the happiness of many people, for the good, welfare, and happiness of many people, of devas and human beings. What three? He encourages them in concordant bodily action, concordant verbal action, and concordant [mental] qualities. Possessing these three qualities, a well-known bhikkhu is acting for the welfare of many people, for the happiness of many people, for the good, welfare, and happiness of many people, of devas and human beings."

12 (2) To Be Remembered

"Bhikkhus, there are these three [places] that a head-anointed khattiya king should remember all his life. What three? (1) The first is the place where he was born. (2) The second is the place where he was head-anointed a khattiya king. (3) And the third is the place where, having triumphed in battle, he emerged victorious and settled at the head of the battlefield. These are the three [places] that a head-anointed khattiya king should remember all his life. [107]

"So too, bhikkhus, there are these three [places] that a bhikkhu should remember all his life. What three? (1) The first is the place where he shaved off his hair and beard, put on ochre robes, and went forth from the household life into homelessness. (2) The second is the place where he understood as it really is: 'This is suffering,' and 'This is the origin of suffering,' and 'This is the cessation of suffering,' and 'This is the way leading to the cessation of suffering.' (3) And the third is the place where, with the destruction of the taints, he realized for himself with direct knowledge, in this very life, the taintless liberation of mind, liberation by wisdom, and having entered upon it, dwelled in it.[343] These are the three [places] that a bhikkhu should remember all his life."

13 (3) A Bhikkhu

"Bhikkhus, there are these three kinds of persons found existing in the world. What three? The one without expectation, the one full of expectation, and the one who has overcome expectation.

(1) "And what, bhikkhus, is the person without expectation? Here, a person has been reborn in a low family—a family of caṇḍālas, bamboo workers, hunters, cart makers, or flower scavengers[344]—one that is poor, with little food and drink, that subsists with difficulty, where food and clothing are obtained with difficulty; and he is ugly, unsightly, dwarfish, with much illness: blind, crippled, lame, or paralyzed. He does not obtain food, drink, clothing, and vehicles; garlands, scents, and unguents; bedding, housing, and lighting. He hears: 'The khattiyas have anointed such and such a khattiya.' It does not occur to him: 'When will the khattiyas anoint me too?' This is called the person without expectation.

(2) "And what is the person full of expectation? [108] Here, the eldest son of a head-anointed khattiya king, one due to be anointed but not yet anointed, has attained the unshaken.[345] He hears: 'The khattiyas have anointed such and such a khattiya.' It occurs to him: 'When will the khattiyas anoint me too?' This is called the person full of expectation.

(3) "And what is the person who has overcome expectation? Here, a head-anointed khattiya king hears: 'Such and such a khattiya has been anointed by the khattiyas.' It does not occur to him: 'When will the khattiyas anoint me too?' For what reason? Because his past expectation of anointment subsided when he was anointed. This is called the person who has overcome expectation.

"These are the three kinds of persons found existing in the world.

"So too, bhikkhus, there are three kinds of persons found existing among the bhikkhus. What three? The one without expectation, the one full of expectation, and the one who has overcome expectation.

(1) "And what, bhikkhus, is the person without expectation? Here, some person is immoral, of bad character, of impure and suspect behavior, secretive in his actions, not an ascetic though

claiming to be one, not a celibate though claiming to be one, inwardly rotten, corrupt, depraved. He hears: 'Such and such a bhikkhu, with the destruction of the taints, has realized for himself with direct knowledge, in this very life, the taintless liberation of mind, liberation by wisdom, and having entered upon it, he dwells in it.' It does not occur to him: 'When will I, too, with the destruction of the taints, realize for myself with direct knowledge, in this very life, the taintless liberation of mind, liberation by wisdom, and having entered upon it, dwell in it?' This is called the person without expectation.

(2) "And what is the person full of expectation? Here, a bhikkhu is virtuous, of good character. He [109] hears: 'Such and such a bhikkhu, with the destruction of the taints, has realized for himself with direct knowledge, in this very life, the taintless liberation of mind, liberation by wisdom, and having entered upon it, he dwells in it.' It occurs to him: 'When will I, too, with the destruction of the taints, realize for myself with direct knowledge, in this very life, the taintless liberation of mind, liberation by wisdom, and having entered upon it, dwell in it?' This is called the person full of expectation.

(3) "And what is the person who has overcome expectation? Here, a bhikkhu is an arahant, one whose taints are destroyed. He hears: 'Such and such a bhikkhu, with the destruction of the taints, has realized for himself with direct knowledge, in this very life, the taintless liberation of mind, liberation by wisdom, and having entered upon it, he dwells in it.' It does not occur to him: 'When will I, too, with the destruction of the taints, realize for myself with direct knowledge, in this very life, the taintless liberation of mind, liberation by wisdom, and having entered upon it, dwell in it?' For what reason? Because his past expectation of liberation subsided when he was liberated. This is called the person who has overcome expectation.

"These, bhikkhus, are the three kinds of persons found existing among the bhikkhus."

14 (4) Wheel-Turning

"Bhikkhus, even a wheel-turning monarch, a righteous king who rules by the Dhamma, does not turn the wheel without a king above him."

When this was said, a certain bhikkhu said to the Blessed One: "But, Bhante, who is the king above a wheel-turning monarch, a righteous king who rules by the Dhamma?"

"It is the Dhamma, bhikkhu," the Blessed One said.[346] "Here, bhikkhu, a wheel-turning monarch, a righteous king who rules by the Dhamma, relying just on the Dhamma, honoring, respecting, and venerating the Dhamma, taking the Dhamma as his standard, banner, and authority, provides righteous protection, shelter, and guard for the people in his court. Again, a wheel-turning monarch, a righteous king who rules by the Dhamma, relying just on the Dhamma, honoring, respecting, and venerating the Dhamma, taking the Dhamma as his standard, banner, and authority, provides righteous protection, shelter, and guard for his khattiya vassals, his army, [110] brahmins and householders, the people of town and countryside, ascetics and brahmins, and the animals and birds. Having provided such righteous protection, shelter, and guard for all these beings, that wheel-turning monarch, a righteous king who rules by the Dhamma, turns the wheel solely through the Dhamma,[347] a wheel that cannot be turned back by any hostile human being.[348]

(1) "So too, bhikkhu, the Tathāgata, the Arahant, the Perfectly Enlightened One, the righteous king of the Dhamma, relying just on the Dhamma, honoring, respecting, and venerating the Dhamma, taking the Dhamma as his standard, banner, and authority, provides righteous protection, shelter, and guard in regard to bodily action, saying: 'Such bodily action should be cultivated; such bodily action should not be cultivated.'

(2) "Again, the Tathāgata, the Arahant, the Perfectly Enlightened One, the righteous king of the Dhamma, relying just on the Dhamma, honoring, respecting, and venerating the Dhamma, taking the Dhamma as his standard, banner, and authority, provides righteous protection, shelter, and guard in regard to verbal action, saying: 'Such verbal action should be cultivated; such verbal action should not be cultivated.'

(3) "Again, the Tathāgata, the Arahant, the Perfectly Enlightened One, the righteous king of the Dhamma, relying just on the Dhamma, honoring, respecting, and venerating the Dhamma, taking the Dhamma as his standard, banner, and authority,

provides righteous protection, shelter, and guard in regard to mental action, saying: 'Such mental action should be cultivated; such mental action should not be cultivated.'

"Having provided such righteous protection, shelter, and guard in regard to bodily action, verbal action, and mental action, the Tathāgata, the Arahant, the Perfectly Enlightened One, the righteous king of the Dhamma, sets in motion the unsurpassed wheel of the Dhamma solely through the Dhamma, a wheel that cannot be turned back by any ascetic, brahmin, deva, Māra, or Brahmā, or by anyone in the world."

15 (5) Pacetana[349]

On one occasion the Blessed One was dwelling at Bārāṇasī in the deer park at Isipatana. There the Blessed One addressed the bhikkhus: "Bhikkhus!" [111]

"Venerable sir!" those bhikkhus replied. The Blessed One said this:

"Bhikkhus, in the past there was a king named Pacetana. Then King Pacetana addressed a chariotmaker: 'Friend chariotmaker, six months from now there will be a battle. Can you make me a new pair of wheels?' – 'I can, lord,' the chariotmaker replied. After six months less six days the chariotmaker had finished one wheel. King Pacetana then addressed the chariotmaker: 'Six days from now there will be a battle. Is the new pair of wheels finished?' [The chariotmaker replied:] 'In the past six months less six days, lord, I have finished one wheel.' – 'But, friend chariotmaker, can you finish a second wheel for me in the next six days?' – 'I can, lord,' the chariotmaker replied. Then, over the next six days, the chariotmaker finished the second wheel. He brought the new pair of wheels to King Pacetana and said: 'This is the new pair of wheels that I have made for you, lord.' – 'What is the difference, friend chariotmaker, between the wheel that took six months less six days to complete and the one that took six days to complete? I do not see any difference between them.' – 'There is a difference, lord. Observe the difference.'

"Then the chariotmaker rolled the wheel that took six days to finish. It rolled as far as the impetus carried it,[350] and then it wobbled and fell to the ground. But the wheel that took six months [112] less six days to finish rolled as far as the impetus carried it and then stood still as if fixed on an axle.[351]

"[The king asked:] 'Why is it, friend chariotmaker, that the wheel that took six days to finish rolled as far as the impetus carried it, and then wobbled and fell to the ground, while the wheel that took six months less six days to finish rolled as far as the impetus carried it and then stood still as if fixed on an axle?'

"[The chariotmaker replied:] 'The wheel that took six days to finish, lord, has a rim that is crooked, faulty, and defective; spokes that are crooked, faulty, and defective; and a nave that is crooked, faulty, and defective. For this reason, it rolled as far as the impetus carried it and then it wobbled and fell to the ground. But the wheel that took six months less six days to finish has a rim without crookedness, faults, and defects; it has spokes without crookedness, faults, and defects; and it has a nave that is without crookedness, faults, and defects. For this reason, it rolled as far as the impetus carried it and then stood still as if fixed on an axle.'

"It may be, bhikkhus, that you think: 'On that occasion the chariotmaker was someone else.' But you should not think in such a way. On that occasion, I myself was the chariotmaker. Then I was skilled in crookedness, faults, and defects in wood. But now I am the Arahant, the Perfectly Enlightened One, (1) skilled in crookedness, faults, and defects of the body; (2) skilled in crookedness, faults, and defects of speech; and (3) skilled in crookedness, faults, and defects of mind.

"Any bhikkhu or bhikkhunī who has not abandoned crookedness, faults, and defects of the body, speech, and mind [113] has fallen down from this Dhamma and discipline, just as the wheel that was finished in six days [fell to the ground].

"Any bhikkhu or bhikkhunī who has abandoned crookedness, faults, and defects of the body, speech, and mind is established in this Dhamma and discipline, just as the wheel that was finished in six months less six days [remained standing].

"Therefore, bhikkhus, you should train yourselves thus: 'We will abandon crookedness, faults, and defects of the body; we will abandon crookedness, faults, and defects of speech; we will abandon crookedness, faults, and defects of the mind.' It is in this way that you should train yourselves."

16 (6) The Unmistaken

"Bhikkhus, possessing three qualities, a bhikkhu is practicing the unmistaken way and has laid the groundwork for the destruction of the taints.[352] What three? Here, a bhikkhu guards the doors of the sense faculties, observes moderation in eating, and is intent on wakefulness.[353]

(1) "And how, bhikkhus, does a bhikkhu guard the doors of the sense faculties? Here, having seen a form with the eye, a bhikkhu does not grasp its marks and features. Since, if he left the eye faculty unrestrained, bad unwholesome states of longing and dejection might invade him, he practices restraint over it; he guards the eye faculty, he undertakes the restraint of the eye faculty. Having heard a sound with the ear... Having smelled an odor with the nose... Having tasted a taste with the tongue... Having felt a tactile object with the body... Having cognized a mental phenomenon with the mind, a bhikkhu does not grasp its marks and features. Since, if he left the mind faculty unrestrained, bad unwholesome states of longing and dejection might invade him, he practices restraint over it; he guards the mind faculty, he undertakes the restraint of the mind faculty. It is in this way that a bhikkhu guards the doors of the sense faculties. [114]

(2) "And how does a bhikkhu observe moderation in eating? Here, reflecting carefully, a bhikkhu consumes food neither for amusement nor for intoxication nor for the sake of physical beauty and attractiveness, but only for the support and maintenance of this body, for avoiding harm, and for assisting the spiritual life, considering: 'Thus I shall terminate the old feeling and not arouse a new feeling, and I shall be healthy and blameless and dwell at ease.' It is in this way that a bhikkhu observes moderation in eating.

(3) "And how is a bhikkhu intent on wakefulness? Here, during the day, while walking back and forth and sitting, a bhikkhu purifies his mind of obstructive qualities. In the first watch of the night, while walking back and forth and sitting, he purifies his mind of obstructive qualities. In the middle watch of the night he lies down on the right side in the lion's posture, with one foot overlapping the other, mindful and clearly comprehending, after noting in his mind the idea of rising. After rising, in the last watch of the night, while walking back and forth and sitting, he purifies his mind of obstructive qualities. It is in this way that a bhikkhu is intent on wakefulness.

"A bhikkhu who possesses these three qualities is practicing the unmistaken way and has laid the groundwork for the destruction of the taints."

17 (7) Oneself

"Bhikkhus, these three qualities lead to one's own affliction, the affliction of others, and the affliction of both. What three? Bodily misconduct, verbal misconduct, and mental misconduct. These three qualities lead to one's own affliction, the affliction of others, and the affliction of both.

"These three [other] qualities do not lead to one's own affliction, the affliction of others, and the affliction of both. What three? Bodily good conduct, verbal good conduct, and mental good conduct. These three qualities do not lead to one's own affliction, the affliction of others, and the affliction of both." [115]

18 (8) Deva

"Bhikkhus, if wanderers of other sects were to ask you thus: 'Friends, do you lead the spiritual life under the ascetic Gotama for the sake of rebirth in the deva world?' wouldn't you be repelled, humiliated, and disgusted?"

"Yes, Bhante."

"Thus, bhikkhus, since you are repelled, humiliated, and disgusted with a celestial life span, celestial beauty, celestial happiness, celestial glory, and celestial authority, so much more then should you be repelled, humiliated, and disgusted with bodily misconduct, verbal misconduct, and mental misconduct."

19 (9) Shopkeeper (1)

"Bhikkhus, possessing three factors, a shopkeeper is incapable of acquiring wealth not yet acquired or of increasing wealth already acquired. What three? Here, a shopkeeper does not diligently apply himself to his work in the morning, in the middle of the day, or in the evening. Possessing these three factors, a shopkeeper is incapable of acquiring wealth not yet acquired or of increasing wealth already acquired.

"So too, possessing three factors, a bhikkhu is incapable of achieving a wholesome state not yet attained or of increasing a wholesome state already attained. What three? Here, a bhikkhu does not diligently apply himself to an object of concentration in the morning, in the middle of the day, or in the evening. Possessing these three factors, a bhikkhu is incapable of achieving a wholesome state not yet attained or of increasing a wholesome state already attained. [116]

"Bhikkhus, possessing three factors, a shopkeeper is capable of acquiring wealth not yet acquired and of increasing wealth already acquired. What three? Here, a shopkeeper diligently applies himself to his work in the morning, in the middle of the day, and in the evening. Possessing these three factors, a shopkeeper is capable of acquiring wealth not yet acquired and of increasing wealth already acquired.

"So too, possessing three factors, a bhikkhu is capable of achieving a wholesome state not yet attained and of increasing a wholesome state already attained. What three? Here, a bhikkhu diligently applies himself to an object of concentration in the morning, in the middle of the day, and in the evening. Possessing these three factors, a bhikkhu is capable of achieving a wholesome state not yet attained and of increasing a wholesome state already attained."

20 (10) Shopkeeper (2)

"Bhikkhus, possessing three factors, a shopkeeper soon attains vast and abundant wealth. What three? Here, a shopkeeper has keen eyes, is responsible, and has benefactors.

(1) "And how, bhikkhus, does a shopkeeper have keen eyes? Here, a shopkeeper knows of an item: 'If this item is bought at such a price and sold at such a price, it will require this much capital and bring this much profit.' It is in this way that a shopkeeper has keen eyes.

(2) "And how is a shopkeeper responsible? Here, a shopkeeper is skilled in buying and selling goods. It is in this way that a shopkeeper is responsible.

(3) "And how does a shopkeeper have benefactors? [117] Here, rich, wealthy, affluent householders and householders' sons know him thus: 'This good shopkeeper has keen eyes and is responsible; he is able to support his wife and children and pay us back from time to time.' So they deposit wealth with him, saying: 'Having earned wealth with this, friend shopkeeper, support your wife and children and pay us back from time to time.' It is in this way that a shopkeeper has benefactors.

"Possessing these three factors, a shopkeeper soon attains vast and abundant wealth.

"So too, bhikkhus, possessing three qualities, a bhikkhu soon attains vast and abundant wholesome qualities. What three? Here, a bhikkhu has keen eyes, is responsible, and has benefactors.

(1) "And how, bhikkhus, does a bhikkhu have keen eyes? Here, a bhikkhu understands as it really is: 'This is suffering'... 'This is the way leading to the cessation of suffering.' It is in this way that a bhikkhu has keen eyes.

(2) "And how is a bhikkhu responsible? Here, a bhikkhu has aroused energy for abandoning unwholesome qualities and acquiring wholesome qualities; he is strong, firm in exertion, not casting off the duty of cultivating wholesome qualities. It is in this way that a bhikkhu is responsible.

(3) "And how does a bhikkhu have benefactors? Here, from time to time a bhikkhu approaches those bhikkhus who are learned, heirs to the heritage, experts on the Dhamma, experts on the discipline, experts on the outlines,[354] and inquires: 'How is this, Bhante? What is the meaning of this?' Those venerable ones then disclose to him what has not been disclosed, clear up what is obscure, and dispel his perplexity about numerous perplexing points. It is in this way that a bhikkhu has benefactors. [118]

"Possessing these three qualities, a bhikkhu soon attains vast and abundant wholesome qualities."

III. Persons

21 (1) Saviṭṭha

Thus have I heard. On one occasion the Blessed One was dwelling at Sāvatthī in Jeta's Grove, Anāthapiṇḍika's Park. Then the Venerable Saviṭṭha and the Venerable Mahākoṭṭhita approached the Venerable Sāriputta and exchanged greetings with him. When they had concluded their greetings and cordial talk, they sat down to one side. The Venerable Sāriputta then said to the Venerable Saviṭṭha:

"Friend Saviṭṭha, there are these three kinds of persons found existing in the world. What three? The body witness, the one attained to view, and the one liberated by faith.[355] These are the three kinds of persons found existing in the world. Which of these three kinds of persons do you consider the most excellent and sublime?"

"Friend Sāriputta, of those three kinds of persons, I consider the one liberated by faith to be the most excellent and sublime.[356] For what reason? Because this person's faculty of faith is predominant."

Then the Venerable Sāriputta said to the Venerable Mahākoṭṭhita: "Friend Koṭṭhita, there are these three kinds of persons found existing in the world.... [119] Which of these three kinds of persons do you consider the most excellent and sublime?"

"Friend Sāriputta, of those three kinds of persons, I consider the body witness to be the most excellent and sublime. For what reason? Because this person's faculty of concentration is predominant."

Then the Venerable Mahākoṭṭhita said to the Venerable Sāriputta: "Friend Sāriputta, there are these three kinds of persons found existing in the world.... Which of these three kinds of persons do you consider the most excellent and sublime?"

"Friend Koṭṭhita, of those three kinds of persons, I consider the one attained to view to be the most excellent and sublime. For what reason? Because this person's faculty of wisdom is predominant."

Then the Venerable Sāriputta said to the Venerable Saviṭṭha and the Venerable Mahākoṭṭhita: "Friends, we have each explained according to our own ideal. Come, let's approach the Blessed One and report this matter to him. We will retain it in mind as he explains it to us."

"Yes, friend," the Venerable Saviṭṭha and the Venerable Mahākoṭṭhita replied. Then the Venerable Sāriputta, the Venerable Saviṭṭha, and the Venerable Mahākoṭṭhita approached the Blessed One, paid homage to him, and sat down to one side. [120] The Venerable Sāriputta then reported to him the entire conversation that had taken place.

[The Blessed One said:] "It isn't easy, Sāriputta, to make a definitive declaration about this matter and say: 'Of these three kinds of persons, this one is the most excellent and sublime.'

(1) "For it is possible that a person liberated by faith is practicing for arahantship, while a body witness and one

attained to view are once-returners or non-returners. It isn't easy, Sāriputta, to make a definitive declaration about this matter and say: 'Of these three kinds of persons, this one is the most excellent and sublime.'

(2) "It is possible that a person who is a body witness is practicing for arahantship, while one liberated by faith and one attained to view are once-returners or non-returners. It isn't easy, Sāriputta, to make a definitive declaration about this matter and say: 'Of these three kinds of persons, this one is the most excellent and sublime.'

(3) "It is possible that a person attained to view is practicing for arahantship,[357] while one liberated by faith and a body witness are once-returners or non-returners. It isn't easy, Sāriputta, to make a definitive declaration about this matter and say: 'Of these three kinds of persons, this one is the most excellent and sublime.'"

22 (2) Patients

"Bhikkhus, there are these three kinds of patients found existing in the world. What three? (1) Here, one patient will not recover from his illness whether or not he gets suitable food, suitable medicine, [121] and a competent attendant. (2) Another patient will recover from his illness whether or not he gets suitable food, suitable medicine, and a competent attendant. (3) Still another patient will recover from his illness only if he gets suitable food, not if he fails to get it; only if he gets suitable medicine, not if he fails to get it; and only if he gets a competent attendant, not if he fails to get one.

"Food and medicine and a competent attendant are prescribed particularly for the sake of the patient who will recover from his illness only if he gets suitable food, not if he fails to get it; only if he gets suitable medicine, not if he fails to get it; and only if he gets a competent attendant, not if he fails to get one. But because of this patient, the other patients should also be served. These are the three kinds of patients found existing in the world.

"So too, bhikkhus, there are these three kinds of persons similar to patients found existing in the world. What three? (1) Here, some person will not enter upon the fixed course [consisting in] rightness in wholesome qualities whether or not he gets to see the Tathāgata and whether or not he gets to hear the Dhamma and discipline proclaimed by the Tathāgata.[358] (2) Then another person will enter upon the fixed course [consisting in] rightness in wholesome qualities whether or not he gets to see the Tathāgata and whether or not he gets to hear the Dhamma and discipline proclaimed by the Tathāgata. (3) And still another person will enter upon the fixed course [consisting in] rightness in wholesome qualities only if he gets to see the Tathāgata, not if he fails to see him; only if he gets to hear the Dhamma and discipline proclaimed by the Tathāgata, not if he fails to hear it. [122]

"The teaching of the Dhamma is prescribed particularly for the sake of the person who will enter upon the fixed course [consisting in] rightness in wholesome qualities only if he gets to see the Tathāgata, not if he fails to see him; only if he gets to hear the Dhamma and discipline proclaimed by the Tathāgata, not if he fails to hear it. But because of this person, the Dhamma should also be taught to the others. These are the three kinds of persons similar to patients found existing in the world."

23 (3) Volitional Activities

"Bhikkhus, there are three kinds of persons found existing in the world. What three?

(1) "Here, bhikkhus, some person generates afflictive bodily activities, afflictive verbal activities, and afflictive mental activities.[359] In consequence, he is reborn in an afflictive world. When he is reborn in an afflictive world, afflictive contacts touch him. Being touched by afflictive contacts, he feels afflictive feelings, exclusively painful, as in the case of hell-beings.

(2) "Someone else generates unafflictive bodily activities, unafflictive verbal activities, and unafflictive mental activities. In consequence, he is reborn in an unafflictive world. When he is reborn in an unafflictive world, unafflictive contacts touch him. Being touched by unafflictive contacts, he feels unafflictive feelings, exclusively pleasant, as in the case of the devas of refulgent glory.[360]

(3) "Still another generates bodily activities that are both afflictive and unafflictive, verbal activities that are both afflictive and unafflictive, and mental activities that are both afflictive and unafflictive. In consequence, [123] he is reborn in a world that is both afflictive and unafflictive. When he is reborn

in a world that is both afflictive and unafflictive, both afflictive and unafflictive contacts touch him. Being touched by both afflictive and unafflictive contacts, he feels both afflictive and unafflictive feelings, mingled pleasure and pain, as in the case of human beings, some devas, and some beings in the lower worlds.[361]

"These, bhikkhus, are the three kinds of persons found existing in the world."

24 (4) Helpful

"Bhikkhus, these three persons are helpful to another person. What three?

(1) "The person through whom another has gone for refuge to the Buddha, the Dhamma, and the Saṅgha. This person is helpful to the other person.

(2) "Again, the person through whom another comes to understand as it really is: 'This is suffering,' and 'This is the origin of suffering,' and 'This is the cessation of suffering,' and 'This is the way leading to the cessation of suffering.' This person is helpful to the other person.[362]

(3) "Again, the person through whom, with the destruction of the taints, another realizes for himself with direct knowledge, in this very life, the taintless liberation of mind, liberation by wisdom, and having entered upon it, dwells in it. This person is helpful to the other person.

"These three persons are helpful to another person.

"I say, bhikkhus, that there is no one more helpful to another person than these three persons. I say, too, that it is not easy to repay these three persons by paying homage to them, by rising up for them, by reverential salutation, by proper conduct, and by presenting them with robes, almsfood, lodging, and medicines and provisions for the sick."

25 (5) Diamond

"Bhikkhus, there are these three kinds of persons found existing in the world. [124] What three? One whose mind is like an open sore, one whose mind is like lightning, and one whose mind is like a diamond.

(1) "And what, bhikkhus, is the person whose mind is like an open sore? Here, some person is prone to anger and easily

exasperated. Even if he is criticized slightly he loses his temper and becomes irritated, hostile, and stubborn; he displays irritation, hatred, and bitterness. Just as a festering sore, if struck by a stick or a shard, will discharge even more matter, so too some person here is prone to anger . . . and displays irritation, hatred, and bitterness. This person is said to have a mind like an open sore.

(2) "And what is the person whose mind is like lightning? Here, some person understands as it really is: 'This is suffering,' and 'This is the origin of suffering,' and 'This is the cessation of suffering,' and 'This is the way leading to the cessation of suffering.' Just as, in the dense darkness of night, a man with good sight can see forms by a flash of lightning, so too some person here understands as it really is: 'This is suffering' . . . 'This is the way leading to the cessation of suffering.' This person is said to have a mind like lightning.

(3) "And what is the person whose mind is like a diamond? Here, with the destruction of the taints, some person realizes for himself with direct knowledge, in this very life, the taintless liberation of mind, liberation by wisdom, and having entered upon it, dwells in it. Just as there is nothing that a diamond cannot cut, whether gem or stone, so too, with the destruction of the taints, some person realizes for himself with direct knowledge . . . the taintless liberation of mind, liberation by wisdom, and . . . dwells in it. This person is said to have a mind like a diamond.

"These, bhikkhus, are the three kinds of persons found existing in the world."

26 (6) To Be Associated With

"Bhikkhus, there are these three kinds of persons found existing in the world. What three? (1) There is a person who is not to be associated with, followed, and served; (2) a person who is to be associated with, followed, and served; and (3) [125] a person who is to be associated with, followed, and served with honor and respect.

(1) "And what kind of person, bhikkhus, is not to be associated with, followed, and served? Here, some person is inferior [to oneself] in virtuous behavior, concentration, and wisdom. Such a person is not to be associated with, followed, and served except out of sympathy and compassion.

(2) "And what kind of person is to be associated with, followed, and served? Here, some person is similar [to oneself] in virtuous behavior, concentration, and wisdom. Such a person is to be associated with, followed, and served. For what reason? [Because one considers:] 'Since we are similar with regard to virtuous behavior, we will have a discussion on virtuous behavior, and it will flow on smoothly between us, and we will feel at ease. Since we are similar with regard to concentration, we will have a discussion on concentration, and it will flow on smoothly between us, and we will feel at ease. Since we are similar with regard to wisdom, we will have a discussion on wisdom, and it will flow on smoothly between us, and we will feel at ease.' Therefore such a person is to be associated with, followed, and served.

(3) "And what kind of person is to be associated with, followed, and served with honor and respect? Here, some person is superior [to oneself] in virtuous behavior, concentration, and wisdom. Such a person is to be associated with, followed, and served with honor and respect. For what reason? [Because one considers:] 'In such a way I will fulfill the aggregate of virtuous behavior that I have not yet fulfilled or assist with wisdom in various respects the aggregate of virtuous behavior that I have fulfilled. I will fulfill the aggregate of concentration that I have not yet fulfilled or assist with wisdom in various respects the aggregate of concentration that I have fulfilled. I will fulfill the aggregate of wisdom that I have not yet fulfilled or assist with wisdom in various respects the aggregate of wisdom that I have fulfilled.'[363] Therefore such a person is to be associated with, followed, and served with honor and respect.

"These, bhikkhus, are the three kinds of persons found existing in the world." [126]

> One who associates with an inferior person declines;
> one who associates with an equal does not decline;
> attending on a superior person one develops quickly;
> therefore you should follow one superior to yourself.

27 (7) Disgust

"Bhikkhus, there are these three kinds of persons found existing in the world. What three? (1) There is a person who is to be looked upon with disgust, not to be associated with, followed, and served; (2) a person who is to be looked upon with equanimity, not to be associated with, followed, and served; and (3) a person who is to be associated with, followed, and served.

(1) "And what kind of person, bhikkhus, is to be looked upon with disgust, not to be associated with, followed, and served? Here, some person is immoral, of bad character, impure, of suspect behavior, secretive in his actions, not an ascetic though claiming to be one, not a celibate though claiming to be one, inwardly rotten, corrupt, depraved. Such a person is to be looked upon with disgust, not to be associated with, followed, and served. For what reason? Even though one does not follow the example of such a person, a bad report still circulates about oneself: 'He has bad friends, bad companions, bad comrades.' Just as a snake that has passed through feces, though it does not bite one, would smear one, so too, though one does not follow the example of such a person, a bad report still circulates about oneself: 'He has bad friends, bad companions, bad comrades.' Therefore such a person is to be looked upon with disgust, not to be associated with, followed, and served.

(2) "And what kind of person is to be looked upon with equanimity, not to be associated with, followed, and served? Here, some person is prone to anger [127] and easily exasperated. Even if he is criticized slightly he loses his temper and becomes irritated, hostile, and stubborn; he displays irritation, hatred, and bitterness. Just as a festering sore, if struck by a stick or a shard, will discharge even more matter, so too... Just as a firebrand of the *tinduka* tree, if struck by a stick or shard, will sizzle and crackle even more, so too... Just as a pit of feces, if struck by a stick or a shard, becomes even more foul-smelling, so too some person here is prone to anger and... displays irritation, hatred, and bitterness. Such a person is to be looked upon with equanimity, not to be associated with, followed, and served. For what reason? [With the thought:] 'He might insult me, revile me, and do me harm.' Therefore such a person is to be looked upon with equanimity, not to be associated with, followed, and served.

(3) "And what kind of person is to be associated with, followed, and served? Here, some person is virtuous and of good character. Such a person is to be associated with, followed, and served. For what reason? Even though one does not follow

the example of such a person, a good report still circulates about oneself: 'He has good friends, good companions, good comrades.' Therefore such a person is to be associated with, followed, and served.

"These, bhikkhus, are the three kinds of persons found existing in the world."

[A verse is attached identical with that in 3:26.]

28 (8) Speech Like Dung

"Bhikkhus, there are these three kinds of persons found existing in the world. [128] What three? The one whose speech is like dung, the one whose speech is like flowers, and the one whose speech is like honey.

(1) "And what, bhikkhus, is the person whose speech is like dung? Here, if he is summoned to a council, to an assembly, to his relatives' presence, to his guild, or to the court, and questioned as a witness thus: 'So, good man, tell what you know,' then, not knowing, this person says, 'I know,' or knowing, he says, 'I do not know'; not seeing, he says, 'I see,' or seeing, he says, 'I do not see.' Thus he consciously speaks falsehood for his own ends, or for another's ends, or for some trifling worldly end.[364] This is called the person whose speech is like dung.

(2) "And what is the person whose speech is like flowers? Here, if he is summoned to a council, to an assembly, to his relatives' presence, to his guild, or to the court, and questioned as a witness thus: 'So, good man, tell what you know,' then, not knowing, this person says, 'I do not know,' or knowing, he says, 'I know'; not seeing, he says, 'I do not see,' or seeing, he says, 'I see'; he does not consciously speak falsehood for his own ends, or for another's ends, or for some trifling worldly end. This is called the person whose speech is like flowers.

(3) "And what is the person whose speech is like honey? Here, some person, having abandoned harsh speech, abstains from harsh speech. He speaks such words as are gentle, pleasing to the ear, and lovable, as go to the heart, are courteous, desired by many, and agreeable to many. This is the person whose speech is like honey.

"These, bhikkhus, are the three kinds of persons found existing in the world."

29 (9) Blind

"Bhikkhus, there are these three kinds of persons found existing in the world. What three? The blind person, the one-eyed person, and the two-eyed person.

(1) "And what, bhikkhus, is the blind person? Here, some person lacks the kind of eye [129] with which one can acquire wealth not yet acquired and increase wealth already acquired, and he also lacks the kind of eye with which one can know wholesome and unwholesome qualities, blameworthy and blameless qualities, inferior and superior qualities, dark and bright qualities with their counterparts. This is called the blind person.

(2) "And what is the one-eyed person? Here, some person has the kind of eye with which one can acquire wealth not yet acquired and increase wealth already acquired, but he lacks the kind of eye with which one can know wholesome and unwholesome qualities, blameworthy and blameless qualities, inferior and superior qualities, dark and bright qualities with their counterparts. This is called the one-eyed person.

(3) "And what is the two-eyed person? Here, some person has the kind of eye with which one can acquire wealth not yet acquired and increase wealth already acquired, and he also has the kind of eye with which one can know wholesome and unwholesome qualities, blameworthy and blameless qualities, inferior and superior qualities, dark and bright qualities with their counterparts. This is called the two-eyed person.

"These, bhikkhus, are the three kinds of persons found existing in the world."

He does not possess such wealth,
nor does he do deeds of merit;
the blind man destitute of eyes
casts an unlucky throw in both respects.

The person described as one-eyed
is a hypocrite who seeks wealth,
[sometimes] righteously
[and sometimes] unrighteously.

Both by thievish cheatful acts
and by means of false speech

the man indulging in sensual pleasures
is skilled in amassing wealth.
Having gone from here to hell,
the one-eyed person is tormented.

One with two eyes is said to be
the best kind of person.
His wealth[365] is acquired by his own exertion,
with goods righteously gained. [130]

With best intentions he then gives,
this person with an undivided mind.
He goes to [rebirth in] an excellent state
where, having gone, one does not sorrow.

One should avoid from afar
the blind one and the one-eyed person,
but should befriend the one with two eyes,
the best kind of person.

30 (10) Inverted

"Bhikkhus, there are these three kinds of persons found existing in the world. What three? The person with inverted wisdom, the person with lap-like wisdom, and the person with wide wisdom.

(1) "And what, bhikkhus, is the person with inverted wisdom? Here, some person often goes to the monastery to listen to the Dhamma from the bhikkhus. The bhikkhus teach him the Dhamma that is good in the beginning, good in the middle, and good in the end, with the right meaning and phrasing; they reveal the perfectly complete and pure spiritual life. While he is sitting in his seat, he does not attend to that talk at the beginning, in the middle, or at the end. After he has risen from his seat, he still does not attend to that talk at the beginning, in the middle, or at the end. Just as, when a pot is turned upside down, the water that had been poured into it runs off and does not remain there, so too, some person often goes to the monastery to listen to the Dhamma from the bhikkhus.... After he has risen from his seat, he still does not attend to that talk at the beginning, in the middle, or at the end. This is called the person with inverted wisdom.

(2) "And what is the person with lap-like wisdom? Here, some person often goes to the monastery to listen to the Dhamma from the bhikkhus. The bhikkhus teach him the Dhamma that is good in the beginning, good in the middle, and good in the end, with the right meaning and phrasing; they reveal the perfectly complete and pure spiritual life. While he is sitting in his seat, he attends to that talk at the beginning, in the middle, and at the end. But after he has risen from his seat, he does not attend to that talk at the beginning, in the middle, or at the end. Just as, when a person has various food stuffs strewn over his lap—sesamum seeds, rice grains, cakes, and jujubes—if he loses his mindfulness when rising from that seat, [131] he would scatter them all over, so too, some person often goes to the monastery to listen to the Dhamma from the bhikkhus.... But after he has risen from his seat, he does not attend to that talk at the beginning, in the middle, or at the end. This is called the person with lap-like wisdom.

(3) "And what is the person with wide wisdom? Here, some person often goes to the monastery to listen to the Dhamma from the bhikkhus. The bhikkhus teach him the Dhamma that is good in the beginning, good in the middle, and good in the end, with the right meaning and phrasing; they reveal the perfectly complete and pure spiritual life. While he is sitting in his seat, he attends to that talk at the beginning, in the middle, and at the end. After he has risen from his seat, again he attends to that talk at the beginning, in the middle, and at the end. Just as, when a pot is kept upright, the water that had been poured into it stays there and does not run off, so too, some person often goes to the monastery to listen to the Dhamma from the bhikkhus.... After he has risen from his seat, again he attends to that talk at the beginning, in the middle, and at the end. This is called the person with wide wisdom.

"These, bhikkhus, are the three kinds of persons found existing in the world."

The person with inverted wisdom,
stupid and undiscerning,
often goes to visit bhikkhus
[to hear them teach the Dhamma].

Yet this person cannot grasp
anything from the talk,
at its beginning, middle, and end,
for he utterly lacks wisdom.

The person with lap-like wisdom
is said to be better than the former.
He too often goes to visit bhikkhus
[to hear them teach the Dhamma].

While sitting in his seat,
he grasps the phrasing of the talk,
at its beginning, middle, and end.
But after rising, he no longer understands,
but forgets what he had learned.

The person with wide wisdom
is said to be the best of these.
He too often goes to visit bhikkhus
[to hear them teach the Dhamma].

While sitting in his seat,
he comprehends the phrasing,
at the beginning, middle, and end
of the talk [given by the bhikkhu].

This person of the best intentions,
his mind undivided, retains [what he hears].
Practicing in accordance with the Dhamma,
he can make an end of suffering. [132]

IV. Divine Messengers

31 (1) Brahmā

(1) "Bhikkhus, those families dwell with Brahmā where at home the mother and father are revered by their children. (2) Those families dwell with the first teachers where at home the mother and father are revered by their children. (3) Those families dwell with the gift-worthy where at home the mother and father are revered by their children.

"'Brahmā,' bhikkhus, is a designation for mother and father. 'First teachers' is a designation for mother and father. 'Gift-worthy' is a designation for mother and father. For what reason? Mother and father are helpful to their children: they raise them, nurture them, and show them the world."

Mother and father are called "Brahmā"
and also "first teachers."
They are worthy of gifts from their children,
for they have compassion for their offspring.

Therefore a wise person should revere them,
and show them due honor,
serve them with food and drink,
with clothes and bedding,
by massaging and bathing them,
and by washing their feet.

Because of this service
to mother and father,
the wise praise one in this world
and after death one rejoices in heaven.

32 (2) Ānanda

Then the Venerable Ānanda approached the Blessed One, paid homage to him, sat down to one side, and said to him:

"Bhante, could a bhikkhu obtain such a state of concentration that (1) he would have no I-making, mine-making, and underlying tendency to conceit in regard to this conscious body; (2) he would have no I-making, mine-making, and underlying tendency to conceit in regard to all external objects; and (3) he would enter and dwell in that liberation of mind, liberation by wisdom, through which there is no more I-making, mine-making, and underlying tendency to conceit for one who enters and dwells in it?"[366]

"He could, Ānanda."

"But how, Bhante, could he obtain such a state of concentration?" [133]

"Here, Ānanda, a bhikkhu thinks thus: 'This is peaceful, this is sublime, that is, the stilling of all activities, the relinquishing of all acquisitions, the destruction of craving, dispassion, cessation, nibbāna.' In this way, Ānanda, a bhikkhu could obtain such a state of concentration that he would have no I-making, mine-making, and underlying tendency to conceit in regard to this conscious body; he would have no I-making, mine-making, and underlying tendency to conceit in regard to all external objects; and he would enter and dwell in that liberation of mind, liberation by wisdom, through which there is no more I-making, mine-making, and underlying tendency to conceit for one who enters and dwells in it. And it was with reference to this that I said in the Pārāyana, in 'The Questions of Puṇṇaka':[367]

> "Having comprehended the highs and lows in the world,
> he is not perturbed by anything in the world.
> Peaceful, fumeless, untroubled, wishless,
> he has, I say, crossed over birth and old age."

33 (3) Sāriputta[368]

Then the Venerable Sāriputta approached the Blessed One, paid homage to him, and sat down to one side. The Blessed One then said to him:

"Sāriputta, I can teach the Dhamma briefly; I can teach the Dhamma in detail; I can teach the Dhamma both briefly and in detail. It is those who can understand that are rare."

"It is the time for this, Blessed One. It is the time for this, Fortunate One. The Blessed One should teach the Dhamma briefly; he should teach the Dhamma in detail; he should teach the Dhamma both briefly and in detail. There will be those who can understand the Dhamma."

"Therefore, Sāriputta, you should train yourselves thus: (1) 'There will be no I-making, mine-making, and underlying tendency to conceit in regard to this conscious body; (2) there will be no I-making, mine-making, and underlying tendency to conceit in regard to all external objects; and (3) we will enter and dwell in that liberation of mind, liberation by wisdom, through which there is no more I-making, mine-making, and underlying tendency to conceit for one who enters and dwells in it.' It is in this way, Sāriputta, that you should train yourselves.

"When, Sāriputta, a bhikkhu [134] has no I-making, mine-making, and underlying tendency to conceit in regard to this conscious body; when he has no I-making, mine-making, and underlying tendency to conceit in regard to all external objects; and when he enters and dwells in that liberation of mind, liberation by wisdom, through which there is no more I-making, mine-making, and underlying tendency to conceit for one who enters and dwells in it, he is called a bhikkhu who has cut off craving, stripped off the fetter, and, by completely breaking through conceit, has made an end of suffering. And it was with reference to this that I said in the Pārāyana, in 'The Questions of Udaya':[369]

> "The abandoning of both
> sensual perceptions and dejection;
> the dispelling of dullness,
> the warding off of remorse;[370]
>
> "purified equanimity and mindfulness
> preceded by reflection on the Dhamma:
> this, I say, is emancipation by final knowledge,
> the breaking up of ignorance."[371]

34 (4) Causes

"Bhikkhus, there are these three causes for the origination of kamma. What three? Greed is a cause for the origination of kamma; hatred is a cause for the origination of kamma; delusion is a cause for the origination of kamma.

(1) "Any kamma, bhikkhus, fashioned through greed, born of greed, caused by greed, originated by greed, ripens wherever the individual is reborn. Wherever that kamma ripens, it is there that one experiences its result, either in this very life, or in the [next] rebirth, or on some subsequent occasion.[372]

(2) "Any kamma fashioned through hatred, born of hatred, caused by hatred, originated by hatred, ripens wherever the individual is reborn. Wherever that kamma ripens, it is there that one experiences its result, either in this very life, or in the [next] rebirth, or on some subsequent occasion.

(3) "Any kamma fashioned through delusion, born of delusion, caused by delusion, originated by delusion, ripens wherever the individual is reborn. Wherever that kamma ripens, [135] it is there that one experiences its result, either in this very life, or in the [next] rebirth, or on some subsequent occasion.

"Suppose, bhikkhus, seeds that are intact, unspoiled, not damaged by wind and the sun's heat, fecund, well preserved, were deposited in well-prepared ground in a good field and receive proper rainfall: in this way, those seeds would grow, increase, and mature. So too, any kamma that is fashioned through greed... hatred... delusion, born of delusion, caused by delusion, originated by delusion, ripens wherever the individual is reborn. Wherever that kamma ripens, it is there that one experiences its result, either in this very life, or in the [next] rebirth, or on some subsequent occasion.

"These are the three causes for the origination of kamma.

"Bhikkhus, there are these three [other] causes for the origination of kamma. What three? Non-greed is a cause for the origination of kamma; non-hatred is a cause for the origination of kamma; non-delusion is a cause for the origination of kamma.

(1) "Any kamma, bhikkhus, fashioned through non-greed, born of non-greed, caused by non-greed, originated by non-greed, is abandoned when greed has vanished; it is cut off at the root, made like a palm stump, obliterated so that it is no more subject to future arising.[373]

(2) "Any kamma fashioned through non-hatred, born of non-hatred, caused by non-hatred, originated by non-hatred, is abandoned when hatred has vanished; it is cut off at the root, made like a palm stump, obliterated so that it is no more subject to future arising.

(3) "Any kamma fashioned through non-delusion, born of non-delusion, caused by non-delusion, originated by non-delusion, is abandoned when delusion has vanished; it is cut off at the root, made like a palm stump, obliterated so that it is no more subject to future arising.

"Suppose, bhikkhus, there are seeds that are intact, unspoiled, [136] not damaged by wind and the sun's heat, fecund, well preserved. Then a man would burn them in a fire, reduce them to ashes, and winnow the ashes in a strong wind or let them be carried away by the swift current of a river. In this way, those seeds would be cut off at the root, made like a palm stump, obliterated so that they are no more subject to future arising. So too, any kamma that is fashioned through non-greed... non-hatred... non-delusion, born of non-delusion, caused by non-delusion, originated by non-delusion, is abandoned when delusion has vanished; it is cut off at the root, made like a palm stump, obliterated so that it is no more subject to future arising."

"These, bhikkhus, are the three causes for the origination of kamma."

Whatever kamma an ignorant person [has done]
born of greed, hatred, and delusion,
whether what was fashioned by him be little or much,
it is to be experienced right here:
there exists no other site [for it].[374]

Therefore a wise person should abandon
[any deed] born of greed, hatred, and delusion.
A bhikkhu, giving rise to knowledge,
should abandon all bad destinations.[375]

35 (5) Hatthaka

On one occasion the Blessed One was dwelling at Āḷavī on a heap of leaves spread out on a cow track in a siṃsapā grove. Then Hatthaka of Āḷavī,[376] while walking and wandering for exercise, saw the Blessed One sitting there. He then approached the Blessed One, paid homage to him, sat down to one side, and said to the Blessed One:

"Bhante, did the Blessed One sleep well?"

"Yes, prince, I slept well. I am one of those in the world who sleep well."

"But, Bhante, the winter nights are cold. It is the eight-day interval, the time when snow falls.[377] The ground trampled by the hooves of cattle is rough, the spread of leaves is thin, [137] the leaves on the tree are sparse, the ochre robes leave one cold, and the gale wind blows cold. Yet the Blessed One says thus: 'Yes, prince, I slept well. I am one of those in the world who sleep well.'"

"Well then, prince, I will question you about this matter. You should answer as you see fit. What do you think, prince? A householder or a householder's son might have a house with a peaked roof, plastered inside and out, draft-free, with bolts fastened and shutters closed. There he might have a couch spread with rugs, blankets, and covers, with an excellent covering of antelope hide, with a canopy above and red bolsters at both ends. An oil lamp would be burning and his four wives would serve him in extremely agreeable ways. What do you think, would he sleep well or not, or what do you think about this?"

"He would sleep well, Bhante. He would be one of those in the world who sleep well."

(1) "What do you think, prince? Might there arise in that householder or householder's son bodily and mental fevers born of lust, which would torment him so that he would sleep badly?"

"Yes, Bhante."

"There might arise in that householder or householder's son bodily and mental fevers born of lust, which would torment him so that he would sleep badly; but the Tathāgata has abandoned such lust, cut it off at the root, made it like a palm stump, obliterated it so that it is no more subject to future arising. Therefore I have slept well.

(2) "What do you think, prince? Might there arise in that householder or householder's son bodily and mental fevers born of hatred . . . (3) . . . bodily and mental fevers born of delusion, which would torment him so that he would sleep badly?"

"Yes, Bhante."

"There might arise in that householder or householder's son bodily and mental fevers born of delusion, which would torment him so that he would sleep badly; but the Tathāgata has abandoned such delusion, cut it off at the root, made it like a palm stump, [138] obliterated it so that it is no more subject to future arising. Therefore I have slept well."

He always sleeps well,
the brahmin who has attained nibbāna,
cooled off, without acquisitions,
not tainted by sensual pleasures.

Having cut off all attachments,
having removed anguish in the heart,
the peaceful one sleeps well,
having attained peace of mind.[378]

36 (6) Messengers[379]

"Bhikkhus, there are these three divine messengers.[380] What three?

"Here, bhikkhus, someone engages in misconduct by body,

speech, and mind. In consequence, with the breakup of the body, after death, he is reborn in the plane of misery, in a bad destination, in the lower world, in hell. There the wardens of hell grab him by both arms and show him to King Yama,[381] [saying]: 'This person, your majesty, did not behave properly toward his mother and father; he did not behave properly toward ascetics and brahmins; and he did not honor the elders of the family. May your majesty inflict due punishment on him!'

(1) "Then King Yama questions, interrogates, and cross-examines him about the first divine messenger: 'Good man, didn't you see the first divine messenger that appeared among human beings?' And he replies: 'No, lord, I didn't see him.'

"Then King Yama says to him: 'But, good man, didn't you ever see among human beings a man or a woman, eighty, ninety or a hundred years of age, frail, bent like a roof bracket, crooked, wobbling as they go along leaning on a stick, ailing, youth gone, with broken teeth, with grey and scanty hair or bald, with wrinkled skin and blotched limbs?' And the man replies: 'Yes, lord, I have seen this.'

"Then King Yama says to him: 'Good man, didn't it occur to you, an intelligent and mature person: "I too am subject to old age, I am not exempt from old age. Let me now do good by body, speech, and mind"?' [139] – 'No, lord, I could not. I was heedless.'

"Then King Yama says: 'Through heedlessness, good man, you failed to do good by body, speech, or mind. Surely, they will treat you in a way that fits your heedlessness. That bad kamma of yours was not done by your mother or father, nor by your brother or sister, nor by your friends and companions, nor by your relatives and family members, nor by the deities, nor by ascetics and brahmins. Rather, you were the one who did that bad kamma, and you yourself will have to experience its result.'

(2) "When King Yama has questioned, interrogated, and cross-examined him about the first divine messenger, he again questions, interrogates, and cross-examines him about the second divine messenger: 'Good man, didn't you see the second divine messenger that appeared among human beings?' And he replies: 'No, lord, I didn't see him.'

"Then King Yama says to him: 'But, good man, didn't you

ever see among human beings a man or a woman, sick, afflicted, gravely ill, lying in his own urine and excrement, having to be lifted up by some and put down by others?' And he replies: 'Yes, lord, I have seen this.'

"Then King Yama says to him: 'Good man, didn't it occur to you, an intelligent and mature person: "I too am subject to illness, I am not exempt from illness. Let me now do good by body, speech, and mind"?' – 'No, lord, I could not. I was heedless.'

"Then King Yama says: [140] 'Through heedlessness, good man, you failed to do good by body, speech, or mind. Surely, they will treat you in a way that fits your heedlessness. That bad kamma of yours was not done by your mother or father, nor by your brother or sister, nor by your friends and companions, nor by your relatives and family members, nor by the deities, nor by ascetics and brahmins. Rather, you were the one who did that bad kamma, and you yourself will have to experience its result.'

(3) "When King Yama has questioned, interrogated, and cross-examined him about the second divine messenger, he again questions, interrogates, and cross-examines him about the third divine messenger: 'Good man, didn't you see the third divine messenger that appeared among human beings?' And he replies: 'No, lord, I didn't see him.'

"Then King Yama says to him: 'But, good man, didn't you ever see among human beings a man or a woman, one, two, or three days dead, the corpse bloated, livid, and festering?' And he replies: 'Yes, lord, I have seen this.'

"Then King Yama says to him: 'Good man, didn't it occur to you, an intelligent and mature person: "I too am subject to death, I am not exempt from death. Let me now do good by body, speech, and mind"?' – 'No, lord, I could not. I was heedless.'

"Then King Yama says: 'Through heedlessness, good man, you failed to do good by body, speech, or mind. Surely, they will treat you in a way that fits your heedlessness. That bad kamma of yours was not done by your mother or father, nor by your brother or sister, nor by your friends and companions, nor by your relatives and family members, nor by the deities, nor by ascetics and brahmins. Rather, you were the one who did that bad kamma, and you yourself will have to experience its result.'

"When, bhikkhus, King Yama has questioned, interrogated, and cross-examined him about the third divine messenger, he falls silent. [141] Then the wardens of hell torture him with the fivefold transfixing. They drive a red-hot iron stake through one hand and another red-hot iron stake through the other hand; they drive a red-hot iron stake through one foot and another red-hot iron stake through the other foot; they drive a red-hot iron stake through the middle of his chest. There he feels painful, racking, piercing feelings,[382] yet he does not die so long as that bad kamma is not exhausted.

"Next the wardens of hell throw him down and pare him with axes. There he feels painful, racking, piercing feelings, yet he does not die so long as that bad kamma is not exhausted. Next the wardens of hell turn him upside down and pare him with adzes.... Next the wardens of hell harness him to a chariot and drive him back and forth across ground that is burning, blazing, and glowing.... Next the wardens of hell make him climb up and down a great mound of coals that are burning, blazing, and glowing.... Next the wardens of hell turn him upside down and plunge him into a red-hot copper cauldron that is burning, blazing, and glowing. He is cooked there in a swirl of foam. And as he is being cooked there in a swirl of foam, he is swept now up, now down, and now across. There he feels painful, racking, piercing feelings, yet he does not die so long as that bad kamma is not exhausted.

"Next the wardens of hell throw him into the great hell. Now, bhikkhus, as to that great hell:

"It has four corners and four doors
and is divided into separate compartments;
it is surrounded by iron ramparts
and shut in with an iron roof. [142]

"Its floor as well is made of iron
and heated till it glows with fire.
The range is a full hundred *yojanas*
which it ever covers pervasively.

"Once, bhikkhus, in the past King Yama thought: 'Those in the world who do evil deeds are punished with such diverse tortures. Oh, that I might attain the human state! That a Tathāgata, Arahant, Perfectly Enlightened One might arise in the world! That I might attend upon that Blessed One! That the Blessed One might teach me the Dhamma, and that I might come to understand his Dhamma!'

"Bhikkhus, I am not repeating something that I heard from another ascetic or brahmin, but rather I am speaking about a matter that I have actually known, seen, and understood myself."

Though warned by the divine messengers,
those people who remain heedless
sorrow for a long time,
having fared on to a lower realm.

But those good people here who,
when warned by the divine messengers,
never become heedless
in regard to the noble Dhamma;
who, having seen the peril in clinging
as the origin of birth and death,
are liberated by non-clinging
in the extinction of birth and death:
those happy ones have attained security;[383]
they have reached nibbāna in this very life.
Having overcome all enmity and peril,
they have transcended all suffering.

37 (7) Kings (1)

"Bhikkhus, (1) on the eighth of the fortnight, the ministers and assembly members of the four great kings wander over this world,[384] [thinking]: 'We hope there are many people who behave properly toward their mother and father, behave properly toward ascetics and brahmins, honor the elders of the family, observe the uposatha, keep the extra observance days, and do meritorious deeds.'[385] (2) On the fourteenth of the fortnight, the sons of the four great kings wander over this world, [thinking]: 'We hope there are many people who behave properly toward their mother and father . . . [143] . . . and do meritorious deeds.' (3) On the fifteenth, the uposatha day, the four great kings themselves wander over this world, [thinking]: 'We hope there are many people who behave properly toward their mother and father . . . and do meritorious deeds.'

"If, bhikkhus, there are few people who behave properly toward their mother and father . . . and do meritorious deeds, the four great kings report this to the Tāvatiṃsa devas when they meet and are sitting together in the Sudhamma council hall: 'Revered sirs, there are few people who behave properly toward their mother and father . . . and do meritorious deeds.' Then, because of this, the Tāvatiṃsa devas become displeased, [saying]: 'Alas, the celestial company will decline and the company of asuras will flourish!'

"But if there are many people who behave properly toward their mother and father . . . and do meritorious deeds, the four great kings report this to the Tāvatiṃsa devas when they meet and are sitting together in the Sudhamma council hall: 'Revered sirs, there are many people who behave properly toward their mother and father, behave properly toward ascetics and brahmins, honor the elders of the family, observe the uposatha, keep the extra observance days, and do meritorious deeds.' Then, because of this, the Tāvatiṃsa devas become elated, [saying]: 'Indeed, the celestial company will flourish and the company of asuras will decline!'"

"Bhikkhus, once in the past, when Sakka, ruler of the devas, was guiding the Tāvatiṃsa devas, he recited this verse:[386] [144]

"'The person who would be like me
should observe the uposatha
complete in the eight factors,
on the fourteenth, fifteenth,
and eighth of the fortnight,
and during special fortnights.'[387]

"This verse, bhikkhus, was badly recited by Sakka, ruler of the devas, not well recited. It was badly stated, not well stated. For what reason? Because Sakka, ruler of the devas, is not devoid of lust, hatred, and delusion. But in the case of a bhikkhu who is an arahant—one whose taints are destroyed, who has lived the spiritual life, done what had to be done, laid down the burden, reached his own goal, utterly destroyed the fetters of existence, one completely liberated through final knowledge—it is fitting for him to say:

> "'The person who would be like me . . .
> and during special fortnights.'

"For what reason? Because that bhikkhu is devoid of lust, hatred, and delusion."

38 (8) Kings (2)

"Bhikkhus, once in the past, when Sakka, ruler of the devas, was guiding the Tāvatiṃsa devas, on that occasion he recited this verse:[388]

> "'The person who would be like me . . .
> and during special fortnights.'

"This verse, bhikkhus, was badly recited by Sakka, ruler of the devas, not well recited. It was badly stated, not well stated. For what reason? Because Sakka, ruler of the devas, is not free from birth, old age and death, from sorrow, lamentation, pain, dejection, and anguish; he is not free from suffering, I say. But in the case of a bhikkhu who is an arahant—one whose taints are destroyed . . . one completely liberated through final knowledge—it is fitting for him to say:

> "'The person who would be like me . . .
> and during special fortnights.' [145]

"For what reason? Because that bhikkhu is free from birth, old age and death, from sorrow, lamentation, pain, dejection, and anguish; he is free from suffering, I say."

39 (9) Delicate

"Bhikkhus, I was delicately nurtured, most delicately nurtured, extremely delicately nurtured. At my father's residence lotus ponds were made just for my enjoyment: in one of them blue lotuses bloomed, in another red lotuses, and in a third white lotuses.[389] I used no sandalwood unless it came from Kāsi and my headdress, jacket, lower garment, and upper garment were made of cloth from Kāsi.[390] By day and by night a white canopy was held over me so that cold and heat, dust, grass, and dew would not settle on me.

"I had three mansions: one for the winter, one for the summer, and one for the rainy season.[391] I spent the four months of the rains in the rainy-season mansion, being entertained by musicians, none of whom were male,[392] and I did not leave the mansion. While in other people's homes slaves, workers, and servants are given broken rice together with sour gruel for their meals, in my father's residence they were given choice hill rice, meat, and boiled rice.

(1) "Amid such splendor and a delicate life, it occurred to me: 'An uninstructed worldling, though himself subject to old age, not exempt from old age, feels repelled, humiliated, and disgusted when he sees another who is old, overlooking his own situation.[393] Now I too am subject to old age and am not exempt from old age. Such being the case, if I were to feel repelled, humiliated, [146] and disgusted when seeing another who is old, that would not be proper for me.' When I reflected thus, my intoxication with youth was completely abandoned.

(2) "[Again, it occurred to me:] 'An uninstructed worldling, though himself subject to illness, not exempt from illness, feels repelled, humiliated, and disgusted when he sees another who is ill, overlooking his own situation. Now I too am subject to illness and am not exempt from illness. Such being the case, if I were to feel repelled, humiliated, and disgusted when seeing another who is ill, that would not be proper for me.' When I reflected thus, my intoxication with health was completely abandoned.

(3) "[Again, it occurred to me:] 'An uninstructed worldling, though himself subject to death, not exempt from death, feels repelled, humiliated, and disgusted when he sees another who has died, overlooking his own situation. Now I too am subject to death and am not exempt from death. Such being the case, if I were to feel repelled, humiliated, and disgusted when seeing another who has died, that would not be proper for me.' When I reflected thus, my intoxication with life was completely abandoned.

"There are, bhikkhus, these three kinds of intoxication.[394] What three? Intoxication with youth, intoxication with health, and intoxication with life. (1) An uninstructed worldling, intoxicated with youth, engages in misconduct by body, speech, and mind. With the breakup of the body, after death, he is reborn in the plane of misery, in a bad destination, in the lower world, in hell. (2) An uninstructed worldling, intoxicated with health, engages in misconduct by body, speech, and mind. With the breakup of the body, after death, he is reborn in the plane of misery, in a bad destination, in the lower world, in hell. (3) An uninstructed worldling, intoxicated with life, engages in misconduct by body, [147] speech, and mind. With the breakup of the body, after death, he is reborn in the plane of misery, in a bad destination, in the lower world, in hell.

"Intoxicated with youth, a bhikkhu gives up the training and reverts to the lower life; or intoxicated with health, he gives up the training and reverts to the lower life; or intoxicated with life, he gives up the training and reverts to the lower life.

"Worldlings subject to illness,
old age, and death, are disgusted
[by other people] who exist
in accordance with their nature.[395]

"If I were to become disgusted
with beings who have such a nature,
that would not be proper for me
since I too have the same nature.

"While I was dwelling thus,
having known the state without acquisitions,
I overcame all intoxications—
intoxication with health,
with youth, and with life—
having seen security in renunciation.[396]

"Zeal then arose in me
as I clearly saw nibbāna.
Now I am incapable
of indulging in sensual pleasures.

Relying on the spiritual life,
never will I turn back."[397]

40 (10) Authorities

"Bhikkhus, there are these three authorities. What three? Oneself as one's authority, the world as one's authority, and the Dhamma as one's authority.[398]

(1) "And what, bhikkhus, is oneself as one's authority? Here, having gone to the forest, to the foot of a tree, or to an empty hut, a bhikkhu reflects thus: 'I did not go forth from the household life into homelessness for the sake of a robe, almsfood, or lodging, or for the sake of becoming this or that,[399] but rather [with the thought]: "I am immersed in birth, old age, and death; in sorrow, lamentation, pain, dejection, and anguish. I am immersed in suffering, afflicted by suffering. Perhaps an ending of this entire mass of suffering can be discerned." [148] As one who has gone forth from the household life into homelessness, it would not be proper for me to seek out sensual pleasures similar to or worse than those that I have discarded.' He then reflects thus: 'Energy will be aroused in me without slackening; mindfulness will be established without confusion; my body will be tranquil without disturbance; my mind will be concentrated and one-pointed.' Having taken himself as his authority, he abandons the unwholesome and develops the wholesome; he abandons what is blameworthy and develops what is blameless; he maintains himself in purity. This is called oneself as one's authority.

(2) "And what, bhikkhus, is the world as one's authority? Here, having gone to the forest, to the foot of a tree, or to an empty hut, a bhikkhu reflects thus: 'I did not go forth from the household life into homelessness for the sake of a robe... but rather [with the thought]: "I am immersed in birth, old age, and death... Perhaps an ending of this entire mass of suffering can be discerned." As one who has gone forth from the household life into homelessness, I might think sensual thoughts, thoughts of ill will, or thoughts of harming. But the abode of the world is vast. In the vast abode of the world there are ascetics and brahmins with psychic potency and the divine eye who know the minds of others. They see things from a distance but they are not themselves seen even when they're close; they know the

minds [of others] with their own mind. They would know me thus: "Look at this clansman: though he has gone forth from the household life into homelessness out of faith, he is tarnished by bad unwholesome states." There are deities, too, with psychic potency and the divine eye who know the minds of others. They see even from a distance but are not seen themselves even when close; they too know the minds [of others] with their own mind. They too would know me thus: "Look at this clansman: though he has gone forth from the household life into homelessness out of faith, he is tarnished by bad unwholesome states."' He then reflects thus: 'Energy will be aroused in me [149] without slackening; mindfulness will be established without confusion; my body will be tranquil without disturbance; my mind will be concentrated and one-pointed.' Having taken the world as his authority, he abandons the unwholesome and develops the wholesome; he abandons what is blameworthy and develops what is blameless; he maintains himself in purity. This is called the world as one's authority.

(3) "And what, bhikkhus, is the Dhamma as one's authority? Here, having gone to the forest, to the foot of a tree, or to an empty hut, a bhikkhu reflects thus: 'I did not go forth from the household life into homelessness for the sake of a robe...but rather [with the thought]: "I am immersed in birth, old age, and death...Perhaps an ending of this entire mass of suffering can be discerned." The Dhamma is well expounded by the Blessed One, directly visible, immediate, inviting one to come and see, applicable, to be personally experienced by the wise. There are fellow monks of mine who know and see. As one who has gone forth from the household life into homelessness in this well-expounded Dhamma and discipline, it would be improper for me to be lazy and heedless.' He then reflects thus: 'Energy will be aroused in me without slackening; mindfulness will be established without confusion; my body will be tranquil without disturbance; my mind will be concentrated and one-pointed.' Having taken the Dhamma as his authority, he abandons the unwholesome and develops the wholesome; he abandons what is blameworthy and develops what is blameless; he maintains himself in purity. This is called the Dhamma as one's authority.

"These, bhikkhus, are the three authorities."

For one performing an evil deed
there is no place in the world called "hidden."
The self within you knows, O person,
whether it is true or false.[400]

Indeed, sir, you the witness
despise your good self;
you conceal the evil self
existing within yourself.[401] [150]

The devas and Tathāgatas see the fool
acting unrighteously in the world.
Therefore one should fare mindfully,
taking oneself as authority;
alert and meditative, taking the world as authority;
and fare in accordance with the Dhamma,
taking the Dhamma as authority.
Truly exerting himself, a sage does not decline.

Having vanquished Māra
and overcome the end-maker,
the striver has finished with birth.
Such a sage, wise, a world-knower,
identifies with nothing at all.[402]

V. The Minor Chapter

41 (1) Present

"Bhikkhus, when three things are present, a clansman endowed with faith generates much merit. What three? (1) When faith is present, a clansman endowed with faith generates much merit. (2) When an object to be given is present, a clansman endowed with faith generates much merit. (3) When those worthy of offerings are present, a clansman endowed with faith generates much merit. When these three things are present, a clansman endowed with faith generates much merit."

42 (2) Cases

"Bhikkhus, in three cases one may be understood to have faith and confidence. What three? When one desires to see those of virtuous behavior; when one desires to hear the good Dhamma; and when one dwells at home with a mind devoid of the stain of miserliness, freely generous, openhanded, delighting in relinquishment, devoted to charity, delighting in giving and sharing. In these three cases, one may be understood to have faith and confidence."

> One who desires to see the virtuous ones,
> who wishes to hear the good Dhamma,
> who has removed the stain of miserliness,
> is called a person endowed with faith. [151]

43 (3) Advantages

"Bhikkhus, when one sees three advantages, it is enough to teach others the Dhamma. What three? (1) The one who teaches the Dhamma experiences the meaning and the Dhamma.[403] (2) The one who hears the Dhamma experiences the meaning and the Dhamma. (3) Both the one who teaches the Dhamma and the one who hears the Dhamma experience the meaning and the Dhamma. Seeing these three advantages, it is enough to teach others the Dhamma."

44 (4) Smooth Flow

"Bhikkhus, in three cases talk flows smoothly. What three? (1) When the one who teaches the Dhamma experiences the meaning and the Dhamma. (2) When the one who hears the Dhamma experiences the meaning and the Dhamma. (3) When both the one who teaches the Dhamma and the one who hears the Dhamma experience the meaning and the Dhamma. In these three cases talk flows smoothly."

45 (5) The Wise

"Bhikkhus, there are these three things prescribed by the wise, prescribed by good people. What three? (1) Giving is prescribed by the wise, prescribed by good people. (2) The going forth is prescribed by the wise, prescribed by good people. (3) Attending upon one's mother and father is prescribed by the wise, prescribed by good people. These three things are prescribed by the wise, prescribed by good people."

> Good people prescribe giving,
> harmlessness, self-control, and self-taming,
> service to one's mother and father
> and to the peaceful followers of the spiritual life.[404]
>
> These are the deeds of the good
> which the wise person should pursue.
> The noble one possessed of vision
> goes to an auspicious world.

46 (6) Virtuous

"Bhikkhus, when virtuous renunciants dwell in dependence on a village or a town, the people there generate much merit in three ways. What three? [152] By body, speech, and mind. When virtuous renunciants dwell in dependence on a village or a town, the people there generate much merit in these three ways."

47 (7) Conditioned

"Bhikkhus, there are these three characteristics that define the conditioned.[405] What three? An arising is seen, a vanishing is seen, and its alteration while it persists is seen. These are the three characteristics that define the conditioned.

"Bhikkhus, there are these three characteristics that define the unconditioned.[406] What three? No arising is seen, no vanishing is seen, and no alteration while it persists is seen. These are the three characteristics that define the unconditioned."

48 (8) Mountains

"Bhikkhus, based on the Himalayas, the king of mountains, great sal trees grow in three ways. What three? (1) They grow in branches, leaves, and foliage; (2) they grow in bark and shoots; and (3) they grow in softwood and heartwood. Based on the Himalayas, the king of mountains, great sal trees grow in these three ways.

"So too, when the head of a family is endowed with faith, the people in the family who depend on him grow in three ways. What three? (1) They grow in faith; (2) they grow in virtuous behavior; and (3) they grow in wisdom. When the head of a family is endowed with faith, the people in the family who depend on him grow in these three ways."

Just as the trees that grow
in dependence on a rocky mountain
in a vast forest wilderness
might become great "woodland lords,"
so, when the head of a family here
possesses faith and virtue,
his wife, children, and relatives
all grow in dependence upon him;
so too his friends, his family circle,
and those dependent on him. [153]

Those possessed of discernment,
seeing that virtuous man's good conduct,
his generosity and good deeds,
emulate his example.

Having lived here in accord with Dhamma,
the path leading to a good destination,
those who desire sensual pleasures rejoice,
delighting in the deva world.

49 (9) Ardor

"Bhikkhus, in three cases ardor should be exercised. What three? (1) Ardor should be exercised for the non-arising of unarisen bad unwholesome qualities. (2) Ardor should be exercised for the arising of unarisen wholesome qualities. (3) Ardor should be exercised for enduring arisen bodily feelings that are painful, racking, sharp, piercing, harrowing, disagreeable, sapping one's vitality. In these three cases ardor should be exercised.

"When a bhikkhu exercises ardor for the non-arising of unarisen bad unwholesome qualities, for the arising of unarisen wholesome qualities, and for enduring arisen bodily feelings that are painful, racking, sharp, piercing, harrowing, disagreeable, sapping one's vitality, he is called a bhikkhu who is ardent, alert, and mindful in order to make a complete end of suffering."

50 (10) A Master Thief

"Bhikkhus, possessing three factors, a master thief breaks into houses, plunders wealth, commits banditry, and ambushes highways. What three? Here, a master thief depends on the uneven, on thickets, and on powerful people.

(1) "And how does a master thief depend on the uneven? Here, a master thief depends on rivers that are hard to cross and rugged mountains. It is in this way that a master thief depends on the uneven.

(2) "And how does a master thief depend on thickets? Here, a master thief depends on a thicket of cane, [154] a thicket of trees, a coppice,[407] or a large dense jungle. It is in this way that a master thief depends on thickets.

(3) "And how does a master thief depend on powerful people? Here, a master thief depends on kings or royal ministers. He thinks: 'If anyone accuses me of anything, these kings or royal ministers will dismiss the case.' If anyone accuses him of anything, those kings or royal ministers dismiss the case. It is in this way that a master thief depends on powerful people.

"It is by possessing these three factors that a master thief breaks into houses, plunders wealth, commits banditry, and ambushes highways.

"So too, bhikkhus, possessing three qualities, an evil bhikkhu maintains himself in a maimed and injured condition, is blameworthy and subject to reproach by the wise, and generates much demerit. What three? Here, an evil bhikkhu depends on the uneven, on thickets, and on powerful people.

(1) "And how does an evil bhikkhu depend on the uneven? Here, an evil bhikkhu engages in unrighteous bodily, verbal, and mental action. It is in this way that an evil bhikkhu depends on the uneven.

(2) "And how does an evil bhikkhu depend on thickets? Here, an evil bhikkhu holds wrong view, adopts an extremist view. It is in this way that an evil bhikkhu depends on thickets.

(3) "And how does an evil bhikkhu depend on powerful people? Here, an evil bhikkhu depends on kings or royal ministers. He thinks: 'If anyone accuses me of anything, these kings or royal ministers will dismiss the case.' If anyone accuses him of anything, those kings or royal ministers dismiss the case. It is in this way that an evil bhikkhu depends on the powerful. [155]

"It is by possessing these three qualities that an evil bhikkhu maintains himself in a maimed and injured condition, is blameworthy and subject to reproach by the wise, and generates much demerit."

The Second Fifty

I. Brahmins

51 (1) Two Brahmins (1)

Then two brahmins who were old, aged, burdened with years, advanced in life, come to the last stage, a hundred and twenty years of age, approached the Blessed One and exchanged greetings with him. When they had concluded their greetings and cordial talk, they sat down to one side and said to the Blessed One:

"We are brahmins, Master Gotama, old, aged . . . a hundred and twenty years of age. But we have not done anything good and wholesome, nor have we made a shelter for ourselves. Let Master Gotama exhort us and instruct us in a way that will lead to our welfare and happiness for a long time!"

"Truly, brahmins, you are old, aged, burdened with years, advanced in life, come to the last stage, a hundred and twenty years of age, but you have not done anything good and wholesome, nor have you made a shelter for yourselves. Indeed, this world is swept away by old age, illness, and death. But though the world is swept away by old age, illness, and death, when one has departed, bodily, verbal, and mental self-control will provide a shelter, a harbor, an island, a refuge, and a support."

Life is swept along, short is the life span,
no shelters exist for one who has grown old.
Seeing clearly this peril in death,
one should do deeds of merit that bring happiness.[408]

When one departs [this life],
self-control over body, speech, and mind,
and the deeds of merit one did while living,
lead to one's happiness. [156]

52 (2) Two Brahmins (2)

Then two brahmins who were old, aged, burdened with years, advanced in life, come to the last stage, a hundred and twenty years of age, approached the Blessed One... and said to him:

"We are brahmins, Master Gotama, old, aged... a hundred and twenty years of age. But we have not done anything good and wholesome, nor have we made a shelter for ourselves. Let Master Gotama exhort us and instruct us in a way that will lead to our welfare and happiness for a long time!"

"Truly, brahmins, you are old, aged, burdened with years, advanced in life, come to the last stage, a hundred and twenty years of age, but you have not done anything good and wholesome, nor have you made a shelter for yourselves. Indeed, this world is burning with old age, illness, and death. But though the world is burning with old age, illness, and death, when one has departed, bodily, verbal, and mental self-control will provide a shelter, a harbor, an island, a refuge, and a support."

When one's house is ablaze
the vessel taken out
is the one that will be useful to you,
not the one that is burnt inside.

So since the world is ablaze
with old age and death,
one should take out by giving:
what is given is well taken out.[409]

When one departs [this life],
self-control over body, speech, and mind,
and the deeds of merit one did while alive,
lead to one's happiness.

53 (3) A Certain Brahmin

Then a certain brahmin approached the Blessed One... and said to him:

"Master Gotama, it is said: 'A directly visible Dhamma, a directly visible Dhamma.'[410] In what way is the Dhamma directly visible, immediate, inviting one to come and see, applicable, to be personally experienced by the wise?"

(1) "Brahmin, one excited by lust, overcome by lust, with mind obsessed by it, [157] intends for his own affliction, for the affliction of others, and for the affliction of both, and he experiences mental suffering and dejection. But when lust is abandoned, he does not intend for his own affliction, for the affliction of others, or for the affliction of both, and he does not experience mental suffering and dejection. It is in this way that the Dhamma is directly visible....

(2) "One full of hate, overcome by hatred, with mind obsessed by it, intends for his own affliction, for the affliction of others, and for the affliction of both, and he experiences mental suffering and dejection. But when hatred is abandoned, he does not intend for his own affliction, for the affliction of others, or for the affliction of both, and he does not experience mental suffering and dejection. It is in this way, too, that the Dhamma is directly visible....

(3) "One who is deluded, overcome by delusion, with mind obsessed by it, intends for his own affliction, for the affliction of others, and for the affliction of both, and he experiences mental suffering and dejection. But when delusion is abandoned, he does not intend for his own affliction, for the affliction of others, or for the affliction of both, and he does not experience mental suffering and dejection. It is in this way, too, that the Dhamma is directly visible, immediate, inviting one to come and see, applicable, to be personally experienced by the wise."

"Excellent, Master Gotama! Excellent, Master Gotama! Master Gotama has made the Dhamma clear in many ways, as though he were turning upright what had been overthrown, revealing what was hidden, showing the way to one who was lost, or holding up a lamp in the darkness so those with good eyesight can see forms. I now go for refuge to Master Gotama, to the Dhamma, and to the Saṅgha of bhikkhus. Let Master Gotama consider me a lay follower who from today has gone for refuge for life."

54 (4) A Wanderer

Then a certain brahmin wanderer approached the Blessed One... and said to him:

"Master Gotama, it is said: 'A directly visible Dhamma, a directly visible Dhamma.' In what way is the Dhamma directly visible, immediate, inviting one to come and see, applicable, to be personally experienced by the wise?"

(1) "Brahmin, one excited by lust, overcome by lust, with mind obsessed by it, intends for his own affliction, for the affliction of others, or for the affliction of both, and he experiences mental suffering and dejection. But when lust is abandoned, he does not intend for his own affliction, for the affliction of others, or for the affliction of both, and he does not experience mental suffering and dejection. [158] One excited by lust, overcome by lust, with mind obsessed by it, engages in misconduct by body, speech, and mind. But when lust is abandoned, he does not engage in misconduct by body, speech, and mind. One excited by lust, overcome by lust, with mind obsessed by it, does not understand as it really is his own good, the good of others, or the good of both. But when lust is abandoned, he understands as it really is his own good, the good of others, and the good of both. It is in this way, brahmin, that the Dhamma is directly visible... to be personally experienced by the wise.

(2) "One full of hate, overcome by hatred...

(3) "One who is deluded, overcome by delusion, with mind obsessed by it, intends for his own affliction, for the affliction of others, or for the affliction of both, and he experiences mental suffering and dejection. But when delusion is abandoned, he does not intend for his own affliction, for the affliction of others, or for the affliction of both, and he does not experience mental suffering and dejection. One who is deluded, overcome by delusion, with mind obsessed by it, engages in misconduct by body, speech, and mind. But when delusion is abandoned, he does not engage in misconduct by body, speech, and mind. One who is deluded, overcome by delusion, with mind obsessed by it, does not understand as it really is his own good, the good of others, or the good of both. But when delusion is abandoned, he understands as it really is his own good, the good of others, and the good of both. It is in this way, too, that the Dhamma is directly visible, immediate, inviting one to come and see, applicable, to be personally experienced by the wise."

"Excellent, Master Gotama!... Let Master Gotama consider me a lay follower who from today has gone for refuge for life."

55 (5) Nibbāna

Then the brahmin Jāṇussoṇī approached the Blessed One . . . and said to him:

"Master Gotama, it is said: 'Directly visible nibbāna, directly visible nibbāna.' In what way is nibbāna directly visible, immediate, inviting one to come and see, applicable, to be personally experienced by the wise?" [159]

(1) "Brahmin, one excited by lust, overcome by lust, with mind obsessed by it, intends for his own affliction, for the affliction of others, or for the affliction of both, and he experiences mental suffering and dejection. But when lust is abandoned, he does not intend for his own affliction, for the affliction of others, or for the affliction of both, and he does not experience mental suffering and dejection. It is in this way that nibbāna is directly visible.

(2) "One full of hate, overcome by hatred . . .

(3) "One who is deluded, overcome by delusion, with mind obsessed by it, intends for his own affliction, for the affliction of others, or for the affliction of both, and he experiences mental suffering and dejection. But when delusion is abandoned, he does not intend for his own affliction, for the affliction of others, or for the affliction of both, and he does not experience mental suffering and dejection. It is in this way, too, that nibbāna is directly visible.

"When, brahmin, one experiences the remainderless destruction of lust, the remainderless destruction of hatred, and the remainderless destruction of delusion, it is in this way, too, that nibbāna is directly visible, immediate, inviting one to come and see, applicable, to be personally experienced by the wise."

"Excellent, Master Gotama! . . . Let Master Gotama consider me a lay follower who from today has gone for refuge for life."

56 (6) Depopulation

Then a certain affluent brahmin approached the Blessed One . . . and said to him:

"Master Gotama, I have heard older brahmins who are aged, burdened with years, teachers of teachers, saying: 'In the past this world was so thickly populated one would think there was no space between people. The villages, towns, and capital cities were so close that cocks could fly between them.'[411] Why is it, Master Gotama, that at present the number of people has declined, depopulation is seen,[412] and villages, [160] towns, cities, and districts have vanished?"[413]

(1) "At present, brahmin, people are excited by illicit lust, overcome by unrighteous greed, afflicted by wrong Dhamma.[414] As a result, they take up weapons and slay one another. Hence many people die. This is a reason why at present the number of people has declined, depopulation is seen, and villages, towns, cities, and districts have vanished.

(2) "Again, at present people are excited by illicit lust, overcome by unrighteous greed, afflicted by wrong Dhamma. When this happens, sufficient rain does not fall. As a result, there is a famine, a scarcity of grain; the crops become blighted and turn to straw. Hence many people die. This is another reason why at present the number of people has declined, depopulation is seen, and villages, towns, cities, and districts have vanished.

(3) "Again, at present people are excited by illicit lust, overcome by unrighteous greed, afflicted by wrong Dhamma. When this happens, the yakkhas release wild spirits.[415] Hence many people die. This is yet another reason why at present the number of people has declined, depopulation is seen, and villages, towns, cities, and districts have vanished."

"Excellent, Master Gotama!... Let Master Gotama consider me a lay follower who from today has gone for refuge for life."

57 (7) Vaccha

Then the wanderer Vacchagotta approached the Blessed One ... and said to him:

"Master Gotama, I have heard: 'The ascetic Gotama says: "Alms should be given only to me, [161] not to others; alms should be given only to my disciples, not to the disciples of others. Only what is given to me is very fruitful, not what is given to others; only what is given to my disciples is very fruitful, not what is given to the disciples of others."' Do those who speak thus state what has been said by Master Gotama and not misrepresent him with what is contrary to fact? Do they explain in accordance with the Dhamma so that they would not incur any reasonable criticism or ground for censure?[416] For we do not want to misrepresent Master Gotama."

"Those, Vaccha, who say: 'The ascetic Gotama says: "Alms should be given only to me . . . only what is given to my disciples is very fruitful, not what is given to the disciples of others,"' do not state what has been said by me but misrepresent me with what is untrue and contrary to fact. One who prevents another from giving alms creates an obstruction and stumbling block for three people. What three? He creates an obstruction to the donor's acquiring merit, to the recipients' gaining a gift, and already he has maimed and injured himself. One who prevents another from giving alms creates an obstruction and stumbling block for these three people.

"But, Vaccha, I say that one acquires merit even if one throws away dishwashing water in a refuse dump or cesspit with the thought: 'May the living beings here sustain themselves with this!' How much more, then, [does one acquire merit] when one gives to human beings! However, I say that what is given to one of virtuous behavior is more fruitful than [what is given] to an immoral person. And [the most worthy recipient] is one who has abandoned five factors and possesses five factors.

"What five factors has he abandoned? Sensual desire, ill will, dullness [162] and drowsiness, restlessness and remorse, and doubt. These are the five factors that he has abandoned.

"And what five factors does he possess? The virtuous behavior, concentration, wisdom, liberation, and knowledge and vision of liberation of one beyond training. These are the five factors that he possesses.

"It is in such a way, I say, that what is given to one who has abandoned five factors and possesses five factors is very fruitful."

Among cattle of any sort,
whether black, white, red, or golden,
mottled, uniform, or pigeon-colored,
the tamed bull is born,
the one that can bear the load,
possessing strength, advancing with good speed.
They yoke the burden just to him;
they are not concerned about his color.

So too, among human beings
it is in any kind of birth—
among khattiyas, brahmins, vessas,
suddas, caṇḍālas, or scavengers—
among people of any sort
that the tamed person of good manners is born:
one firm in Dhamma, virtuous in conduct,
truthful in speech, endowed with moral shame;
one who has abandoned birth and death,
consummate in the spiritual life,
with the burden dropped, detached,
who has done his task, free of taints;
who has gone beyond all things [of the world]
and by non-clinging has reached nibbāna:
an offering is truly vast
when planted in that spotless field.

Fools devoid of understanding,
dull-witted, unlearned,
do not attend on the holy ones[417]
but give their gifts to those outside.
Those, however, who attend on the holy ones,
on the wise ones esteemed as sagely,[418]
and those whose faith in the Fortunate One
is deeply rooted and well established,
go to the world of the devas
or are born here in a good family.
Advancing in successive steps,
those wise ones attain nibbāna. [163]

58 (8) Tikaṇṇa

Then the brahmin Tikaṇṇa approached the Blessed One and exchanged greetings with him.... Then, sitting to one side, the brahmin Tikaṇṇa, in the presence of the Blessed One, spoke praise of the brahmins who had mastered the threefold knowledge: "Such are the brahmins who are masters of the threefold knowledge; thus are the brahmins who are masters of the threefold knowledge."

[The Blessed One said:] "But how, brahmin, do the brahmins describe a brahmin who is a master of the threefold knowledge?"

"Here, Master Gotama, a brahmin is well born on both his maternal and paternal sides, of pure descent, unassailable and impeccable with respect to birth as far back as the seventh paternal generation. He is a reciter and preserver of the hymns, a master of the three Vedas with their vocabularies, ritual, phonology, and etymology, and the histories as a fifth; skilled in philology and grammar, he is fully versed in natural philosophy and in the marks of a great man. It is in this way that the brahmins describe a brahmin who is a master of the threefold knowledge."

"Brahmin, a master of the threefold knowledge in the Noble One's discipline is quite different from a brahmin who is a master of the threefold knowledge as the brahmins describe him."

"But in what way, Master Gotama, is one a master of the threefold knowledge in the Noble One's discipline? It would be good if Master Gotama would teach me the Dhamma in such a way as to make clear how one is a master of the threefold knowledge in the Noble One's discipline."

"Well then, brahmin, listen and attend closely. I will speak."

"Yes, sir," the brahmin Tikaṇṇa replied. The Blessed One said this:

"Here, brahmin, secluded from sensual pleasures, secluded from unwholesome states, a bhikkhu enters and dwells in the first jhāna, which consists of rapture and pleasure born of seclusion, accompanied by thought and examination. With the subsiding of thought and examination, he enters and dwells in the second jhāna, which has internal placidity and unification of mind and consists of rapture and pleasure born of concentration, without thought and examination. With the fading away as well of rapture, he dwells equanimous and, mindful and clearly comprehending, he experiences pleasure with the body; he enters and dwells in the third jhāna of which the noble ones declare: 'He is equanimous, mindful, one who dwells happily.' With the abandoning of pleasure and pain, and with the previous passing away of joy and dejection, [164] he enters and dwells in the fourth jhāna, neither painful nor pleasant, which has purification of mindfulness by equanimity.

(1) "When his mind is thus concentrated, purified, cleansed, unblemished, rid of defilement, malleable, wieldy, steady, and

attained to imperturbability, he directs it to the knowledge of the recollection of past abodes. He recollects his manifold past abodes, that is, one birth, two births, three births, four births, five births, ten births, twenty births, thirty births, forty births, fifty births, a hundred births, a thousand births, a hundred thousand births, many eons of world-dissolution, many eons of world-evolution, many eons of world-dissolution and world-evolution, thus: 'There I was so named, of such a clan, with such an appearance, such was my food, such my experience of pleasure and pain, such my life span; passing away from there, I was reborn elsewhere, and there too I was so named, of such a clan, with such an appearance, such was my food, such my experience of pleasure and pain, such my life span; passing away from there, I was reborn here.' Thus he recollects his manifold past abodes with their aspects and details.

"This is the first true knowledge attained by him. Ignorance is dispelled, true knowledge has arisen; darkness is dispelled, light has arisen, as happens when one dwells heedful, ardent, and resolute.

(2) "When his mind is thus concentrated, purified, cleansed, unblemished, rid of defilement, malleable, wieldy, steady, and attained to imperturbability, he directs it to the knowledge of the passing away and rebirth of beings. With the divine eye, which is purified and surpasses the human, he sees beings passing away and being reborn, inferior and superior, beautiful and ugly, fortunate and unfortunate, and he understands how beings fare in accordance with their kamma thus: 'These beings who engaged in misconduct by body, speech, and mind, who reviled the noble ones, held wrong view, and undertook kamma based on wrong view, with the breakup of the body, after death, have been reborn in the plane of misery, in a bad destination, in the lower world, in hell; but these beings who engaged in good conduct by body, speech, and mind, who did not revile the noble ones, who held right [165] view, and undertook kamma based on right view, with the breakup of the body, after death, have been reborn in a good destination, in a heavenly world.' Thus with the divine eye, which is purified and surpasses the human, he sees beings passing away and being reborn, inferior and superior, beautiful and ugly, fortunate and unfortunate, and he understands how beings fare in accordance with their kamma.

"This is the second true knowledge attained by him. Ignorance is dispelled, true knowledge has arisen; darkness is dispelled, light has arisen, as happens when one dwells heedful, ardent, and resolute.

(3) "When his mind is thus concentrated, purified, cleansed, unblemished, rid of defilement, malleable, wieldy, steady, and attained to imperturbability, he directs it to the knowledge of the destruction of the taints. He understands as it really is: 'This is suffering'; he understands as it really is: 'This is the origin of suffering'; he understands as it really is: 'This is the cessation of suffering'; he understands as it really is: 'This is the way leading to the cessation of suffering.' He understands as it really is: 'These are the taints'; he understands as it really is: 'This is the origin of the taints'; he understands as it really is: 'This is the cessation of the taints'; he understands as it really is: 'This is the way leading to the cessation of the taints.'

"When he knows and sees thus, his mind is liberated from the taint of sensuality, from the taint of existence, and from the taint of ignorance. When it is liberated there comes the knowledge: '[It's] liberated.' He understands: 'Destroyed is birth, the spiritual life has been lived, what had to be done has been done, there is no more coming back to any state of being.'

"This is the third true knowledge attained by him. Ignorance is dispelled, true knowledge has arisen; darkness is dispelled, light has arisen, as happens when one dwells heedful, ardent, and resolute.

"He whose virtue has no vacillation,
who is alert and meditative,
whose mind has been mastered,
one-pointed, well concentrated;

"the wise one, dispeller of darkness,
the triple-knowledge bearer, victor over death;
the one they call an abandoner of all,
benefactor of devas and humans;

"the one possessing the three knowledges,
who dwells without delusion;
they worship him, the Buddha
Gotama, bearing his final body.

"One who knows his past abodes,
who sees heaven and the plane of misery,
and has reached the destruction of birth
is a sage consummate in direct knowledge.[419]

"Through these three kinds of knowledge
one is a triple-knowledge brahmin.
I call him a triple-knowledge master,
not the other who utters incantations. [166]

"It is in this way, brahmin, that one is a master of the threefold knowledge in the Noble One's discipline."

"Master Gotama, a master of the threefold knowledge in the Noble One's discipline is quite different from a master of the threefold knowledge according to the brahmins. And a master of the threefold knowledge according to the brahmins is not worth a sixteenth part of a master of the threefold knowledge in the Noble One's discipline.

"Excellent, Master Gotama! . . . Let Master Gotama consider me a lay follower who from today has gone for refuge for life."

59 (9) Jāṇussoṇī

Then the brahmin Jāṇussoṇī approached the Blessed One . . . and said to him:

"Master Gotama, whoever has a sacrifice, a memorial meal, an offering dish, or something to be given should give the gift to brahmins who are masters of the threefold knowledge."[420]

[The Blessed One said:] "But how, brahmin, do the brahmins describe a brahmin who is a master of the threefold knowledge?"

"Here, Master Gotama, a brahmin is well born on both sides . . . [as in 3:58] . . . and [skilled] in the marks of a great man. It is in this way that the brahmins describe a master of the threefold knowledge."

"Brahmin, a master of the threefold knowledge in the Noble One's discipline is quite different from the one that the brahmins describe."

"But in what way, Master Gotama, is one a master of the threefold knowledge in the Noble One's discipline? It would be good if Master Gotama would teach me the Dhamma in such a way as to make clear how one is a master of the threefold knowledge in the Noble One's discipline."

"Well then, brahmin, listen and attend closely. I will speak."

"Yes, sir," the brahmin Jāṇussoṇī replied. The Blessed One said this:

"Here, brahmin, secluded from sensual pleasures... [all as in 3:58, down to:] [167]... This is the third true knowledge attained by him. Ignorance is dispelled, true knowledge has arisen; darkness is dispelled, light has arisen, as happens when one dwells heedful, ardent, and resolute.

"One consummate in virtue and observances,
who is resolute and composed,
whose mind has been mastered,
one-pointed and well concentrated;

"one who knows his past abodes,
who sees heaven and the plane of misery,
and has reached the destruction of birth
is a sage consummate in direct knowledge. [168]

"Through these three kinds of knowledge
one is a triple-knowledge brahmin.
I call him a triple-knowledge master,
not the other who utters incantations.

"It is in this way, brahmin, that one is a master of the threefold knowledge in the Noble One's discipline."

"A master of the threefold knowledge in the Noble One's discipline, Master Gotama, is quite different from a master of the threefold knowledge according to the brahmins. And a master of the threefold knowledge according to the brahmins is not worth a sixteenth part of a master of the threefold knowledge in the Noble One's discipline.

"Excellent, Master Gotama!... Let Master Gotama consider me a lay follower who from today has gone for refuge for life."

60 (10) Saṅgārava

Then the brahmin Saṅgārava approached the Blessed One and exchanged greetings with him.... Then, sitting to one side, the brahmin Saṅgārava said this to the Blessed One:

"Master Gotama, we brahmins sacrifice and enjoin others to offer sacrifices. Now both one who himself sacrifices and one who enjoins others to offer sacrifices engage in a meritorious practice that extends to many people, that is, one based on sacrifice. But one who leaves his family and goes forth from the household life into homelessness tames only himself, calms only himself, and leads to nibbāna only himself. In such a case, he engages in a meritorious practice that extends to only one person, that is, one based on going forth."

"Well then, brahmin, I will question you about this matter. You should answer as you see fit. What do you think, brahmin? Here, a Tathāgata arises in the world, an arahant, perfectly enlightened, accomplished in true knowledge and conduct, fortunate, knower of the world, unsurpassed trainer of persons to be tamed, teacher of devas and humans, an Enlightened One, a Blessed One. He says thus: 'Come, this is the path, this is the way. Practicing in accordance with it, I have realized for myself with direct knowledge the unsurpassed culmination of the spiritual life[421] and make it known to others. Come, you too practice thus. Practicing in accordance with it, you too will realize for yourselves with direct knowledge the unsurpassed culmination of the spiritual life and dwell in it.' Thus the teacher teaches this Dhamma and others [169] practice accordingly. There are many hundreds, many thousands, many hundreds of thousands who do so. What do you think? When this is the case, is that act of going forth a meritorious practice that extends to one person or to many people?"

"When that is the case, Master Gotama, this is a meritorious practice that extends to many people, that is, one based on going forth."

When this was said, the Venerable Ānanda said to the brahmin Saṅgārava: "Of these two practices, brahmin, which appeals to you more as being simpler and less harmful, and as being more fruitful and beneficial?"

Thereupon the brahmin Saṅgārava said to the Venerable Ānanda: "I consider Master Gotama and Master Ānanda worthy of veneration and praise."[422]

A second time the Venerable Ānanda said to the brahmin: "Brahmin, I am not asking you whom you consider worthy of veneration and praise. I am asking you which of those two practices appeals to you as being simpler and less harmful, and also as more fruitful and beneficial?"

But a second time the brahmin Saṅgārava replied: "I consider Master Gotama and Master Ānanda worthy of veneration and praise."

A third time the Venerable Ānanda said to the brahmin: "Brahmin, I am not asking you whom you consider worthy of veneration and praise. I am asking you which of those two practices appeals to you as being simpler and less harmful, and also as more fruitful and beneficial?"

But a third time the brahmin Saṅgārava replied: "I consider Master Gotama and Master Ānanda worthy of veneration and praise." [170]

Then the Blessed One thought: "Even for a third time the brahmin Saṅgārava, on being asked a legitimate question by Ānanda, falters and does not answer. Let me release him." Then the Blessed One said to the brahmin Saṅgārava: "What conversation, brahmin, arose today among the king's retinue when they assembled and were sitting in the royal palace?"

"The conversation was this, Master Gotama: 'Formerly there were fewer bhikkhus, but more who displayed superhuman wonders of psychic potency. But now there are more bhikkhus, but fewer who display superhuman wonders of psychic potency.' This was the conversation that arose today among the king's retinue."

"There are, brahmin, these three kinds of wonders. What three? The wonder of psychic potency, the wonder of mind-reading, and the wonder of instruction.[423]

(1) "And what, brahmin, is the wonder of psychic potency? Here, a bhikkhu wields the various kinds of psychic potency: having been one, he becomes many; having been many, he becomes one; he appears and vanishes; he goes unhindered through a wall, through a rampart, through a mountain as though through space; he dives in and out of the earth as though it were water; he walks on water without sinking as though it were earth; seated cross-legged, he travels in space like a bird; with his hand he touches and strokes the moon and sun so powerful and mighty; he exercises mastery with the body as far as the brahmā world. This is called the wonder of psychic potency.

(2) "And what, brahmin, is the wonder of mind-reading?

There is one who, by means of some clue,[424] declares: 'Your thought is thus, such is what you are thinking, your mind is in such and such a state.' And even if he makes many declarations, they are exactly so and not otherwise.

"Again, someone does not declare [the state of mind] on the basis of a clue, [171] but he hears the sound of people, spirits, or deities [speaking] and then declares: 'Your thought is thus, such is what you are thinking, your mind is in such and such a state.' And even if he makes many declarations, they are exactly so and not otherwise.

"Again, someone does not declare [the state of mind] on the basis of a mark, or by hearing the sound of people, spirits, or deities [speaking], but he hears the sound of the diffusion of thought[425] as one is thinking and examining [some matter] and then declares: 'Your thought is thus, such is what you are thinking, your mind is in such and such a state.' And even if he makes many declarations, they are exactly so and not otherwise.

"Again, someone does not declare [the state of mind] on the basis of a mark, or by hearing the sound of people, spirits, or deities [speaking], or by hearing the sound of the diffusion of thought as one is thinking and examining [some matter], but with his own mind he encompasses the mind of one who has attained concentration without thought and examination and he understands: 'This person's mental activities are so disposed that immediately afterward he will think this thought.'[426] And even if he makes many declarations, they are exactly so and not otherwise. This is called the wonder of mind-reading.

(3) "And what, brahmin, is the wonder of instruction? Here, someone instructs [others] thus: 'Think in this way and not in that way! Attend to this and not to that! Abandon this and enter and dwell in that!' This is called the wonder of instruction.[427]

"These, brahmin, are the three kinds of wonders. Of these three wonders, which appeals to you as the most excellent and sublime?"

"Among these, Master Gotama, when someone performs this wonder by which he wields the various kinds of psychic potency . . . exercises mastery with the body as far as the brahmā world, only the one who performs this wonder experiences it and it occurs only to him. This wonder seems to me like a magical trick.

"Again, Master Gotama, when someone performs this wonder by which he declares another's state of mind on the basis of a clue...by hearing the sound of people, spirits, or deities...by hearing the sound of the diffusion of thought while he is thinking and examining [some matter]...by encompassing with his own mind the mind of one who has attained concentration that is without thought and examination such that he understands: [172] 'This person's mental activities are so disposed that immediately afterward he will think this thought,' and, even if he makes many declarations, they are exactly so and not otherwise—again, only the one who performs this wonder experiences it and it occurs only to him. This wonder, too, seems to me like a magical trick.

"But, Master Gotama, when someone performs this wonder by which he instructs [others] thus: 'Think in this way and not in that way! Attend to this and not to that! Abandon this and enter and dwell in that!'—this wonder appeals to me as the most excellent and sublime of those three wonders.

"It is astounding and amazing, Master Gotama, how well this has been stated by Master Gotama! We consider Master Gotama to be one who can perform these three wonders. For Master Gotama wields the various kinds of psychic potency...exercises mastery with the body as far as the brahmā world. Master Gotama encompasses with his own mind the mind of one who has attained concentration that is without thought and examination such that he understands: 'This person's mental activities are so disposed that immediately afterward he will think this thought.' And Master Gotama instructs [others] thus: 'Think in this way and not in that way! Attend to this and not to that! Abandon this and enter and dwell in that!'"

"Surely, brahmin, your words are prying and intrusive.[428] Nevertheless, I will answer you. I do wield the various kinds of psychic potency...exercise mastery with the body as far as the brahmā world. I do encompass with my own mind the mind of one who has attained a state of concentration that is without thought and examination such that I understand: 'This person's mental activities are so disposed that immediately afterward he will think this thought.' And I do instruct [others] thus: 'Think in this way and not in that way! Attend to this and not to that! Abandon this and enter and dwell in that!'"

"But, Master Gotama, is there even one other bhikkhu apart from Master Gotama who can perform these three wonders?"

"There is not just one hundred, two hundred, three hundred, four hundred, or five hundred bhikkhus, but even more who can perform these three wonders."

"But where are those bhikkhus presently dwelling?" [173]

"Right here, brahmin, in this Saṅgha of bhikkhus."

"Excellent, Master Gotama! . . . Let Master Gotama consider me a lay follower who from today has gone for refuge for life."

II. The Great Chapter

61 (1) Sectarian

"Bhikkhus, there are these three sectarian tenets[429] which, when questioned, interrogated, and cross-examined by the wise, and taken to their conclusion, will eventuate in non-doing.[430] What are the three?

(1) "There are, bhikkhus, some ascetics and brahmins who hold such a doctrine and view as this: 'Whatever this person experiences—whether pleasure, pain, or neither-pain-nor-pleasure—all that is caused by what was done in the past.' (2) There are other ascetics and brahmins who hold such a doctrine and view as this: 'Whatever this person experiences—whether pleasure, pain, or neither-pain-nor-pleasure—all that is caused by God's creative activity.' (3) And there are still other ascetics and brahmins who hold such a doctrine and view as this: 'Whatever this person experiences—whether pleasure, pain, or neither-pain-nor-pleasure—all that occurs without a cause or condition.'[431]

(1) "Bhikkhus, I approached those ascetics and brahmins who hold such a doctrine and view as this: 'Whatever this person experiences—whether pleasure, pain, or neither-pain-nor-pleasure—all that is caused by past deeds,'[432] and I said to them: 'Is it true that you venerable ones hold such a doctrine and view?' When I ask them this, they affirm it. [174] Then I say to them: 'In such a case, it is due to past deeds that you might destroy life, take what is not given, indulge in sexual activity, speak falsehood, utter divisive speech, speak harshly, indulge in idle chatter; that you might be full of longing, have a mind of ill will, and hold wrong view.'[433]

"Those who fall back on past deeds as the essential truth have no desire [to do] what should be done and [to avoid doing] what should not be done, nor do they make an effort in this respect. Since they do not apprehend as true and valid anything that should be done or should not be done, they are muddle-minded, they do not guard themselves, and even the personal designation 'ascetic' could not be legitimately applied to them. This was my first legitimate refutation of those ascetics and brahmins who hold such a doctrine and view.

(2) "Then, bhikkhus, I approached those ascetics and brahmins who hold such a doctrine and view as this: 'Whatever this person experiences—whether pleasure, pain, or neither-pain-nor-pleasure—all that is caused by God's creative activity,' and I said to them: 'Is it true that you venerable ones hold such a doctrine and view?' When I ask them this, they affirm it. Then I say to them: 'In such a case, it is due to God's creative activity that you might destroy life...and hold wrong view.'

"Those who fall back on God's creative activity as the essential truth have no desire [to do] what should be done and [to avoid doing] what should not be done, nor do they make an effort in this respect. Since they do not apprehend as true and valid anything that should be done or should not be done, they are muddle-minded, they do not guard themselves, and even the personal designation 'ascetic' could not be legitimately applied to them. This was my second legitimate refutation of those ascetics and brahmins who hold such a doctrine and view. [175]

(3) "Then, bhikkhus, I approached those ascetics and brahmins who hold such a doctrine and view as this: 'Whatever this person experiences—whether pleasure, pain, or neither-pain-nor-pleasure—all that occurs without a cause or condition,' and I said to them: 'Is it true that you venerable ones hold such a doctrine and view?' When I ask them this, they affirm it. Then I say to them: 'In such a case, it is without a cause or condition that you might destroy life...and hold wrong view.'

"Those who fall back on absence of cause and condition as the essential truth have no desire [to do] what should be done and [to avoid doing] what should not be done, nor do they make an effort in this respect. Since they do not apprehend as true and valid anything that should be done or should not be done, they are muddle-minded, they do not guard themselves, and even the personal designation 'ascetic' could not be legitimately applied to them. This was my third legitimate refutation of those ascetics and brahmins who hold such a doctrine and view.

"These, bhikkhus, are the three sectarian tenets which, when questioned, interrogated, and cross-examined by the wise, and taken to their conclusion, will eventuate in non-doing.

"But, bhikkhus, this Dhamma taught by me is unrefuted, undefiled, irreproachable, and uncensured by wise ascetics and brahmins.[434] And what is the Dhamma taught by me that is unrefuted, undefiled, irreproachable, and uncensured by wise ascetics and brahmins?

"'These are the six elements': this, bhikkhus, is the Dhamma taught by me that is unrefuted . . . uncensured by wise ascetics and brahmins. 'These are the six bases for contact' . . . 'These are the eighteen mental examinations' . . . 'These are the four noble truths': this, bhikkhus, is the Dhamma taught by me that is unrefuted, undefiled, irreproachable, and uncensured by wise ascetics and brahmins.

"When it was said: '"These are the six elements": this, bhikkhus, is the Dhamma taught by me that is unrefuted . . . uncensured by wise ascetics and brahmins,' for what reason was this said? There are [176] these six elements: the earth element, the water element, the fire element, the air element, the space element, and the consciousness element.[435] When it was said: '"These are the six elements": this, bhikkhus, is the Dhamma taught by me that is unrefuted . . . uncensured by wise ascetics and brahmins,' it is because of this that this was said.

"When it was said: '"These are the six bases for contact": this, bhikkhus, is the Dhamma taught by me that is unrefuted . . . uncensured by wise ascetics and brahmins,' for what reason was this said? There are these six bases for contact: the eye as a base for contact, the ear as a base for contact, the nose as a base for contact, the tongue as a base for contact, the body as a base for contact, and the mind as a base for contact. When it was said: '"These are the six bases for contact": this, bhikkhus, is the Dhamma taught by me that is unrefuted . . . uncensured by wise ascetics and brahmins,' it is because of this that this was said.

"When it was said: '"These are the eighteen mental examinations": this, bhikkhus, is the Dhamma taught by me that is unrefuted...uncensured by wise ascetics and brahmins,' for what reason was this said?[436] Having seen a form with the eye, one examines a form that is a basis for joy; one examines a form that is a basis for dejection; one examines a form that is a basis for equanimity. Having heard a sound with the ear...Having smelled an odor with the nose...Having tasted a taste with the tongue...Having felt a tactile object with the body...Having cognized a mental phenomenon with the mind, one examines a mental phenomenon that is a basis for joy; one examines a mental phenomenon that is a basis for dejection; one examines a mental phenomenon that is a basis for equanimity. When it was said: '"These are the eighteen mental examinations": this, bhikkhus, is the Dhamma taught by me that is unrefuted...uncensured by wise ascetics and brahmins,' it is because of this that this was said.

"When it was said: '"These are the four noble truths": this, bhikkhus, is the Dhamma taught by me that is unrefuted...uncensured by wise ascetics and brahmins,' for what reason was this said? In dependence on the six elements the descent of a [future] embryo occurs.[437] When the descent takes place, there is name-and-form; with name-and-form as condition, there are the six sense bases; with the six sense bases as condition, there is contact; with contact as condition, there is feeling. Now it is for one who feels that I proclaim: 'This is suffering,' and 'This is the origin of suffering,' and 'This is the cessation of suffering,' and 'This is the way leading to the cessation of suffering.'

"And what, bhikkhus, is the noble truth of suffering? Birth is suffering, old age is suffering, illness is suffering, death [177] is suffering; sorrow, lamentation, pain, dejection, and anguish are suffering; not to get what one wants is suffering; in brief, the five aggregates subject to clinging are suffering. This is called the noble truth of suffering.

"And what, bhikkhus, is the noble truth of the origin of suffering? With ignorance as condition, volitional activities [come to be]; with volitional activities as condition, consciousness; with consciousness as condition, name-and-form; with name-and-form as condition, the six sense bases; with the six sense bases as condition, contact; with contact as condition, feeling; with feeling as condition, craving; with craving as condition, clinging; with clinging as condition, existence; with existence as condition, birth; with birth as condition, old age and death, sorrow, lamentation, pain, dejection, and anguish come to be. Such is the origin of this whole mass of suffering. This is called the noble truth of the origin of suffering.[438]

"And what, bhikkhus, is the noble truth of the cessation of suffering? With the remainderless fading away and cessation of ignorance comes cessation of volitional activities; with the cessation of volitional activities, cessation of consciousness; with the cessation of consciousness, cessation of name-and-form; with the cessation of name-and-form, cessation of the six sense bases; with the cessation of the six sense bases, cessation of contact; with the cessation of contact, cessation of feeling; with the cessation of feeling, cessation of craving; with the cessation of craving, cessation of clinging; with the cessation of clinging, cessation of existence; with the cessation of existence, cessation of birth; with the cessation of birth, old age and death, sorrow, lamentation, pain, dejection, and anguish cease. Such is the cessation of this whole mass of suffering. This is called the noble truth of the cessation of suffering.

"And what, bhikkhus, is the noble truth of the way leading to the cessation of suffering? It is just this noble eightfold path; that is, right view, right intention, right speech, right action, right livelihood, right effort, right mindfulness, and right concentration. This is called the noble truth of the way leading to the cessation of suffering.

"When it was said: '"These are the four noble truths": this, bhikkhus, is the Dhamma taught by me that is unrefuted, undefiled, irreproachable, and uncensured by wise ascetics and brahmins,' it is because of this that this was said." [178]

62 (2) Perils

"Bhikkhus, the uninstructed worldling speaks of these three perils that separate mother and son.[439] What three?

(1) "There comes a time when a great conflagration arises. When the great conflagration has arisen, it burns up villages, towns, and cities. When villages, towns, and cities are burning up, the mother does not find her son and the son does not find his mother. This is the first peril that separates mother and son of which the uninstructed worldling speaks.

(2) "Again, there comes a time when a great rain cloud arises. When the great rain cloud has arisen, a great deluge takes place. When the great deluge takes place, villages, towns, and cities are swept away. When villages, towns, and cities are being swept away, the mother does not find her son and the son does not find his mother. This is the second peril that separates mother and son of which the uninstructed worldling speaks.

(3) "Again, there comes a time of perilous turbulence in the wilderness, when the people of the countryside, mounted on their vehicles, flee on all sides. When there is perilous turbulence in the wilderness, and the people of the countryside, mounted on their vehicles, are fleeing on all sides, the mother does not find her son and the son does not find his mother. This is the third peril that separates mother and son of which the uninstructed worldling speaks.

"These are the three perils that separate mother and son of which the uninstructed worldling speaks.

"There are, bhikkhus, these three perils when mother and son reconnect that the uninstructed worldling speaks of as perils that separate mother and son.[440] What three?

(1) "There comes a time when a great conflagration arises. When the great conflagration has arisen, it burns up villages, towns, and cities. When villages, towns, and cities are burning up, there is sometimes an occasion when the mother [179] finds her son and the son finds his mother. This is the first peril when mother and son reconnect that the uninstructed worldling speaks of as a peril that separates mother and son.

(2) "Again, there comes a time when a great rain cloud arises. When the great rain cloud has arisen, a great deluge takes place. When the great deluge takes place, villages, towns, and cities are swept away. When villages, towns, and cities are being swept away, there is sometimes an occasion when the mother finds her son and the son finds his mother. This is the second peril when mother and son reconnect that the uninstructed worldling speaks of as a peril that separates mother and son.

(3) "Again, there comes a time of perilous turbulence in the wilderness, when the people of the countryside, mounted on their vehicles, flee on all sides. When there is perilous turbulence in the wilderness, and the people of the countryside, mounted on their vehicles, are fleeing on all sides, there is sometimes an occasion when the mother finds her son and the

son finds his mother. This is the third peril when mother and son reconnect that the uninstructed worldling speaks of as a peril that separates mother and son.

"These are the three perils when mother and son reconnect that the uninstructed worldling speak of as perils that separate mother and son.

"There are, bhikkhus, these three perils that separate mother and son.[441] What three? The peril of old age, the peril of illness, and the peril of death.

(1) "When the son is growing old, the mother cannot fulfill her wish: 'Let me grow old, but may my son not grow old!' And when the mother is growing old, the son cannot fulfill his wish: 'Let me grow old, but may my mother not grow old!'

(2) "When the son has fallen ill, the mother cannot fulfill her wish: 'Let me fall ill, but may my son not fall ill!' And when the mother has fallen ill, the son cannot fulfill his wish: 'Let me fall ill, but may my mother not fall ill!'

(3) "When the son is dying, the mother cannot fulfill her wish: 'Let me die, but may my son not die!' And when the mother is dying, the son cannot fulfill his wish: 'Let me die, but may my mother not die!'

"These are the three perils that separate mother and son. [180]

"There is a path, bhikkhus, there is a way that leads to the abandoning and overcoming of these three perils when mother and son reconnect and of these three perils that separate mother and son. And what is the path and way? It is just this noble eightfold path; that is, right view, right intention, right speech, right action, right livelihood, right effort, right mindfulness, and right concentration. This is the path and way that leads to the abandoning and overcoming of these three perils when mother and son reconnect and of these three perils that separate mother and son."

63 (3) Venāga

On one occasion the Blessed One was wandering on tour among the Kosalans together with a large Saṅgha of bhikkhus when he reached the Kosalan brahmin village named Venāgapura. The brahmin householders of Venāgapura heard: "It is said that the ascetic Gotama, the son of the Sakyans who went forth from a

Sakyan family, has arrived at Venāgapura. Now a good report about that Master Gotama has circulated thus: 'That Blessed One is an arahant, perfectly enlightened, accomplished in true knowledge and conduct, fortunate, knower of the world, unsurpassed leader of persons to be tamed, teacher of devas and humans, the Enlightened One, the Blessed One. Having realized by his own direct knowledge this world with its devas, Māra, and Brahmā, this population with its ascetics and brahmins, its devas and humans, he makes it known to others. He teaches a Dhamma that is good in the beginning, good in the middle, and good in the end, with the right meaning and phrasing; he reveals a spiritual life that is perfectly complete and pure.' Now it is good to see such arahants."

Then the brahmin householders of Venāgapura approached the Blessed One. Some paid homage to the Blessed One and sat down to one side; some exchanged greetings with him [181] and, when they had concluded their greetings and cordial talk, sat down to one side; some reverentially saluted him and sat down to one side; some pronounced their name and clan and sat down to one side; some kept silent and sat down to one side. The brahmin Vacchagotta of Venāgapura then said to the Blessed One:

"It is astounding and amazing, Master Gotama, how Master Gotama's faculties are tranquil and the color of his skin is pure and bright. Just as a yellow jujube fruit in the autumn is pure and bright, so Master Gotama's faculties are tranquil and the color of his skin is pure and bright. Just as a palm fruit that has just been removed from its stalk is pure and bright, so Master Gotama's faculties are tranquil and the color of his skin is pure and bright. Just as an ornament of finest gold, well prepared by a skilled goldsmith and very skillfully wrought in the furnace, placed on red brocade, shines and beams and radiates, so Master Gotama's faculties are tranquil and the color of his skin is pure and bright.

"Whatever high and luxurious kinds of bedding there are—that is, a sofa, a divan, a long-haired coverlet, a coverlet of diverse colors, a white coverlet, a woolen coverlet with floral designs, a quilt of cotton wool, a woolen coverlet ornamented with animal figures, a woolen coverlet with double borders, a woolen coverlet with a single border, a silken sheet studded with gems, a sheet made with silk threads and studded with gems, a dancer's rug, an elephant rug, a horse rug, a chariot rug, a rug of antelope hide, a spread made of the hide of the *kadali*-deer, [a bed] with a canopy above and red bolsters at both ends—Master Gotama surely gains them at will, without trouble or difficulty."[442]

"Brahmin, those high and luxurious kinds of bedding are rarely obtained by those who have gone forth, and if they are obtained, they are not allowed.

"But, brahmin, there are three kinds of high and luxurious beds that at present I gain at will, without trouble or difficulty. What three? [182] The celestial high and luxurious bed, the divine high and luxurious bed, and the noble high and luxurious bed.[443] These are the three kinds of high and luxurious beds that at present I gain at will, without trouble or difficulty."

(1) "But, Master Gotama, what is the celestial high and luxurious bed that at present you gain at will, without trouble or difficulty?"

"Here, brahmin, when I am dwelling in dependence on a village or town, in the morning I dress, take my bowl and robe, and enter that village or town for alms. After the meal, when I have returned from the alms round, I enter a grove. I collect some grass or leaves that I find there into a pile and then sit down. Having folded my legs crosswise and straightened my body, I establish mindfulness in front of me. Then, secluded from sensual pleasures, secluded from unwholesome states, I enter and dwell in the first jhāna, which consists of rapture and pleasure born of seclusion, accompanied by thought and examination. With the subsiding of thought and examination, I enter and dwell in the second jhāna, which has internal placidity and unification of mind and consists of rapture and pleasure born of concentration, without thought and examination. With the fading away as well of rapture, I dwell equanimous and, mindful and clearly comprehending, I experience pleasure with the body; I enter and dwell in the third jhāna of which the noble ones declare: 'He is equanimous, mindful, one who dwells happily.' With the abandoning of pleasure and pain, and with the previous passing away of joy and dejection, I enter and dwell in the fourth jhāna, neither painful nor pleasant, which has purification of mindfulness by equanimity.

"Then, brahmin, when I am in such a state, if I walk back and forth, on that occasion my walking back and forth is celestial.[444] If I am standing, on that occasion my standing is celestial. If I am sitting, on that occasion my sitting is celestial. If I lie down, on that occasion this is my celestial high and luxurious bed. This is that [183] celestial high and luxurious bed that at present I can gain at will, without trouble or difficulty."

"It is astounding and amazing, Master Gotama! Who else, apart from Master Gotama, can gain at will, without trouble or difficulty, such a celestial high and luxurious bed?

(2) "But, Master Gotama, what is the divine high and luxurious bed that at present you gain at will, without trouble or difficulty?"

"Here, brahmin, when I am dwelling in dependence on a village or town, in the morning I dress, take my bowl and robe, and enter that village or town for alms. After the meal, when I have returned from the alms round, I enter a grove. I collect some grass or leaves that I find there into a pile and then sit down. Having folded my legs crosswise and straightened my body, I establish mindfulness in front of me. Then I dwell pervading one quarter with a mind imbued with loving-kindness, likewise the second quarter, the third quarter, and the fourth quarter. Thus above, below, across, and everywhere, and to all as to myself, I dwell pervading the entire world with a mind imbued with loving-kindness, vast, exalted, measureless, without enmity, without ill will. I dwell pervading one quarter with a mind imbued with compassion... with a mind imbued with altruistic joy... with a mind imbued with equanimity, likewise the second quarter, the third quarter, and the fourth quarter. Thus above, below, across, and everywhere, and to all as to myself, I dwell pervading the entire world with a mind imbued with equanimity, vast, exalted, measureless, without enmity, without ill will.

"Then, brahmin, when I am in such a state, if I walk back and forth, on that occasion my walking back and forth is divine. If I am standing, on that occasion my standing is divine. If I am sitting, on that occasion my sitting is divine. If I lie down, on that occasion this is my divine high and luxurious bed. This is that divine high and luxurious bed that at present I can gain at will, without trouble or difficulty." [184]

"It is astounding and amazing, Master Gotama! Who else, apart from Master Gotama, can gain at will, without trouble or difficulty, such a high and luxurious bed?

(3) "But, Master Gotama, what is the noble high and luxurious bed that at present you gain at will, without trouble or difficulty?"

"Here, brahmin, when I am dwelling in dependence on a village or town, in the morning I dress, take my bowl and robe, and enter that village or town for alms. After the meal, when I have returned from the alms round, I enter a grove. I collect some grass or leaves that I find there into a pile and then sit down. Having folded my legs crosswise and straightened my body, I establish mindfulness in front of me. Then I understand thus: 'I have abandoned greed, cut it off at the root, made it like a palm stump, obliterated it so that it is no more subject to future arising. I have abandoned hatred, cut it off at the root, made it like a palm stump, obliterated it so that it is no more subject to future arising. I have abandoned delusion, cut it off at the root, made it like a palm stump, obliterated it so that it is no more subject to future arising.'[445]

"Then, brahmin, when I am in such a state, if I walk back and forth, on that occasion my walking back and forth is noble. If I am standing, on that occasion my standing is noble. If I am sitting, on that occasion my sitting is noble. If I lie down, on that occasion this is my noble high and luxurious bed. This is that noble high and luxurious bed that at present I can gain at will, without trouble or difficulty."

"It is astounding and amazing, Master Gotama! Who else, apart from Master Gotama, can gain at will, without trouble or difficulty, such a noble high and luxurious bed?

"Excellent, Master Gotama! Excellent, Master Gotama! Master Gotama has made the Dhamma clear in many ways, as though he were turning upright what had been overthrown, revealing what was hidden, showing the way to one who was lost, or holding up a lamp in the darkness so those with good eyesight can see forms. We now go for refuge to Master Gotama, [185] to the Dhamma, and to the Saṅgha of bhikkhus. Let Master Gotama consider us lay followers who from today have gone for refuge for life."

64 (4) Sarabha

On one occasion the Blessed One was dwelling at Rājagaha on Mount Vulture Peak. Now on that occasion a wanderer named Sarabha had recently left this Dhamma and discipline.[446] He had been telling an assembly in Rājagaha: "I have learned the Dhamma of the ascetics who follow the Sakyan son. After I learned their Dhamma, I left that Dhamma and discipline."

Then, one morning, a number of bhikkhus dressed, took their bowls and robes, and entered Rājagaha for alms. They then heard the wanderer Sarabha making such a statement to an assembly in Rājagaha. When those bhikkhus had walked for alms in Rājagaha, after their meal, when they returned from their alms round, they approached the Blessed One, paid homage to him, sat down to one side, and said to him:

"Bhante, the wanderer Sarabha, who recently left this Dhamma and discipline, has been telling an assembly in Rājagaha: 'I have learned the Dhamma of the ascetics who follow the Sakyan son. After I learned their Dhamma, I left that Dhamma and discipline.' It would be good, Bhante, if the Blessed One would go to the wanderers' park on the bank of the Sappinikā [river] and, out of compassion, approach the wanderer Sarabha." The Blessed One consented by silence.

Then, in the evening, the Blessed One emerged from seclusion and went to the wanderers' park on the bank of the Sappinikā [river]. He approached the wanderer Sarabha, sat down on the seat that was prepared [186] for him, and said to him: "Is it true, Sarabha, that you have been saying: 'I have learned the Dhamma of the ascetics who follow the Sakyan son. After I learned their Dhamma, I left that Dhamma and discipline'?" When this was said, the wanderer Sarabha was silent.

A second time the Blessed One said to the wanderer Sarabha: "Tell me, Sarabha, how have you learned the Dhamma of the ascetics who follow the Sakyan son? If you have not learned it completely, I will complete it. But if you have learned it completely, I will rejoice." But a second time the wanderer Sarabha was silent.

A third time the Blessed One said to the wanderer Sarabha:[447] "Tell me, Sarabha, how have you learned the Dhamma of the ascetics who follow the Sakyan son? If you have not learned it completely, I will complete it. But if you have learned it completely, I will rejoice." But a third time the wanderer Sarabha was silent.[448]

Then those wanderers said to the wanderer Sarabha: "The ascetic Gotama has offered to give you whatever you might ask him for, friend Sarabha. Speak, friend Sarabha! How have you learned the Dhamma of the ascetics who follow the Sakyan son? If you have not learned it completely, the ascetic Gotama will complete it for you. But if you have learned it completely, he will rejoice." When this was said, the wanderer Sarabha sat silenced, disconcerted, hunched over, downcast, glum, and speechless.

Then the Blessed One, having understood that the wanderer Sarabha [sat] silenced, disconcerted, hunched over, downcast, glum, and speechless, said to those wanderers:

(1) "Wanderers, if anyone should say about me: 'Though you claim to be perfectly enlightened, you are not fully enlightened about these things,' [187] I might question him closely about this matter, interrogate him, and cross-examine him.[449] When he is being closely questioned by me, interrogated, and cross-examined, it is impossible and inconceivable that he would not incur one or another of three consequences: he would either answer evasively and divert the discussion to an irrelevant subject; [or] display anger, hatred, and bitterness; or would sit silenced, disconcerted, hunched over, downcast, glum, and speechless, just like the wanderer Sarabha.[450]

(2) "If, wanderers, anyone should say about me: 'Though you claim to be one whose taints are destroyed, you have not fully destroyed these taints,' I might question him closely about this matter, interrogate him, and cross-examine him. When he is being closely questioned by me, interrogated, and cross-examined, it is impossible and inconceivable that he would not incur one or another of three consequences: he would either answer evasively and divert the discussion to an irrelevant subject; [or] display anger, hatred, and bitterness; or would sit silenced, disconcerted, hunched over, downcast, glum, and speechless, just like the wanderer Sarabha.

(3) "If, wanderers, anyone should say about me: 'The Dhamma does not lead one who practices it to the complete destruction of suffering, the goal for the sake of which you teach it,'[451] I might question him closely about this matter, interrogate him,

and cross-examine him. When he is being closely questioned by me, interrogated, and cross-examined, it is impossible and inconceivable that he would not incur one or another of three consequences: he would either answer evasively and divert the discussion to an irrelevant subject, [or] display anger, hatred, and bitterness, or would sit silenced, disconcerted, hunched over, downcast, glum, and speechless, just like the wanderer Sarabha."

Then the Blessed One, having roared his lion's roar three times in the wanderers' park on the bank of the Sappinikā [river], rose up into the air and departed.[452]

Then, soon after the Blessed One had left, those wanderers gave the wanderer Sarabha a thorough verbal lashing,[453] [saying:] "Just as an old jackal in a huge forest might think: 'I will roar a lion's roar,' and yet would only howl and yelp like a jackal, so, friend Sarabha, claiming in the absence of the ascetic Gotama: 'I will roar a lion's roar,' [188] you only howled and yelped like a jackal. Just as, friend Sarabha, a chick might think: 'I will sing like a cock,' and yet would only sing like a chick, so, friend Sarabha, claiming in the absence of the ascetic Gotama: 'I will sing like a cock,' you only sang like a chick.[454] Just as, friend Sarabha, a bull might think to bellow deeply in an empty cow shed, so, friend Sarabha, in the absence of the ascetic Gotama you thought you could bellow deeply." [In this way] those wanderers gave the wanderer Sarabha a thorough verbal lashing.

65 (5) Kesaputtiya[455]

On one occasion the Blessed One was wandering on tour among the Kosalans together with a large Saṅgha of monks when he reached the town of the Kālāmas named Kesaputta. The Kālāmas of Kesaputta heard: "It is said that the ascetic Gotama, the son of the Sakyans who went forth from a Sakyan family, has arrived at Kesaputta. Now a good report about that Master Gotama has circulated thus: 'That Blessed One is an arahant, perfectly enlightened . . . [as at 3:63] . . . [and] reveals a spiritual life that is perfectly complete and pure.' Now it is good to see such arahants."

Then the Kālāmas of Kesaputta approached the Blessed One. Some paid homage to the Blessed One and sat down to one side... [as at 3:63]... some kept silent and sat down to one side. Sitting to one side, the Kālāmas said to the Blessed One:

"Bhante, there are some ascetics and brahmins who come to Kesaputta. They explain and elucidate their own doctrines, but disparage, denigrate, deride, and denounce the doctrines of others. But then some other ascetics and brahmins come to Kesaputta, [189] and they too explain and elucidate their own doctrines, but disparage, denigrate, deride, and denounce the doctrines of others. We are perplexed and in doubt, Bhante, as to which of these good ascetics speak truth and which speak falsehood."

"It is fitting for you to be perplexed, Kālāmas, fitting for you to be in doubt. Doubt has arisen in you about a perplexing matter.[456] Come, Kālāmas, do not go by oral tradition, by lineage of teaching, by hearsay, by a collection of scriptures, by logical reasoning, by inferential reasoning, by reasoned cogitation, by the acceptance of a view after pondering it, by the seeming competence [of a speaker], or because you think: 'The ascetic is our guru.'[457] But when, Kālāmas, you know for yourselves: 'These things are unwholesome; these things are blameworthy; these things are censured by the wise; these things, if accepted and undertaken, lead to harm and suffering,' then you should abandon them.

(1) "What do you think, Kālāmas? When greed arises in a person, is it for his welfare or for his harm?"[458]

"For his harm, Bhante."

"Kālāmas, a greedy person, overcome by greed, with mind obsessed by it, destroys life, takes what is not given, transgresses with another's wife, and speaks falsehood; and he encourages others to do likewise. Will that lead to his harm and suffering for a long time?"

"Yes, Bhante."

(2) "What do you think, Kālāmas? When hatred arises in a person, is it for his welfare or for his harm?"

"For his harm, Bhante."

"Kālāmas, a person who is full of hate, overcome by hatred, with mind obsessed by it, destroys life... and he encourages others to do likewise. Will that lead to his harm and suffering for a long time?"

"Yes, Bhante."

(3) "What do you think, Kālāmas? When delusion arises in a person, is it for his welfare or for his harm?"

"For his harm, Bhante." [190]

"Kālāmas, a person who is deluded, overcome by delusion, with mind obsessed by it, destroys life... and he encourages others to do likewise. Will that lead to his harm and suffering for a long time?"

"Yes, Bhante."

"What do you think, Kālāmas? Are these things wholesome or unwholesome?" – "Unwholesome, Bhante." – "Blameworthy or blameless?" – "Blameworthy, Bhante." – "Censured or praised by the wise?" – "Censured by the wise, Bhante." – "Accepted and undertaken, do they lead to harm and suffering or not, or how do you take it?" – "Accepted and undertaken, these things lead to harm and suffering. So we take it."

"Thus, Kālāmas, when we said: 'Come, Kālāmas, do not go by oral tradition... But when you know for yourselves: "These things are unwholesome; these things are blameworthy; these things are censured by the wise; these things, if undertaken and practiced, lead to harm and suffering," then you should abandon them,' it is because of this that this was said.

"Come, Kālāmas, do not go by oral tradition, by lineage of teaching, by hearsay, by a collection of scriptures, by logical reasoning, by inferential reasoning, by reasoned cogitation, by the acceptance of a view after pondering it, by the seeming competence [of a speaker], or because you think: 'The ascetic is our guru.' But when you know for yourselves: 'These things are wholesome; these things are blameless; these things are praised by the wise; these things, if accepted and undertaken, lead to welfare and happiness,' then you should live in accordance with them.

(1) "What do you think, Kālāmas? When non-greed arises in a person, is it for his welfare or for his harm?"

"For his welfare, Bhante."

"Kālāmas, a person without greed, not overcome by greed, his mind not obsessed by it, does not destroy life, take what is not given, transgress with another's wife, or speak falsehood; nor does he encourage others to do likewise. [191] Will that lead to his welfare and happiness for a long time?"

"Yes, Bhante."

(2) "What do you think, Kālāmas? When non-hatred arises in a person, is it for his welfare or for his harm?"

"For his welfare, Bhante."

"Kālāmas, a person who is without hate, not overcome by hatred, his mind not obsessed by it, does not destroy life . . . nor does he encourage others to do likewise. Will that lead to his welfare and happiness for a long time?"

"Yes, Bhante."

(3) "What do you think, Kālāmas? When non-delusion arises in a person, is it for his welfare or for his harm?"

"For his welfare, Bhante."

"Kālāmas, a person who is undeluded, not overcome by delusion, his mind not obsessed by it, does not destroy life . . . nor does he encourage others to do likewise. Will that lead to his welfare and happiness for a long time?"

"Yes, Bhante."

"What do you think, Kālāmas? Are these things wholesome or unwholesome?" – "Wholesome, Bhante." – "Blameworthy or blameless?" – "Blameless, Bhante." – "Censured or praised by the wise?" – "Praised by the wise, Bhante." – "Accepted and undertaken, do they lead to welfare and happiness or not, or how do you take it?" – "Accepted and undertaken, these things lead to welfare and happiness. So we take it."

"Thus, Kālāmas, when we said: 'Come, Kālāmas, do not go by oral tradition . . . But when you know for yourselves: "These things are wholesome; these things are blameless; these things are praised by the wise; these things, if accepted and undertaken, lead to welfare and happiness," then you should [192] live in accordance with them,' it is because of this that this was said.

"Then, Kālāmas, that noble disciple, who is thus devoid of longing, devoid of ill will, unconfused, clearly comprehending, ever mindful, dwells pervading one quarter with a mind imbued with loving-kindness . . . with a mind imbued with compassion . . . with a mind imbued with altruistic joy . . . with a mind imbued with equanimity, likewise the second quarter, the third quarter, and the fourth quarter. Thus above, below, across, and everywhere, and to all as to himself, he dwells pervading the entire world with a mind imbued with equanimity, vast, exalted, measureless, without enmity, without ill will.

"This noble disciple, Kālāmas, whose mind is in this way without enmity, without ill will, undefiled, and pure, has won four assurances in this very life.

"The first assurance he has won is this: 'If there is another world, and if there is the fruit and result of good and bad deeds, it is possible that with the breakup of the body, after death, I will be reborn in a good destination, in a heavenly world.'

"The second assurance he has won is this: 'If there is no other world, and there is no fruit and result of good and bad deeds, still right here, in this very life, I maintain myself in happiness, without enmity and ill will, free of trouble.

"The third assurance he has won is this: 'Suppose evil comes to one who does evil. Then, when I have no evil intentions toward anyone, how can suffering afflict me, since I do no evil deed?'[459]

"The fourth assurance he has won is this: 'Suppose evil does not come to one who does evil. Then right here I see myself purified in both respects.'[460]

"This noble disciple, Kālāmas, whose mind is in this way without enmity, without ill will, undefiled, and pure, has won these four assurances in this very life."[461]

"So it is, Blessed One! So it is, Fortunate One! This noble disciple whose mind is in this way without enmity, without ill will, undefiled, and pure, [193] has won four assurances in this very life.

"The first assurance he has won ... [as above, down to:] ... The fourth assurance he has won is this: 'Suppose evil does not befall the evil-doer. Then right here I see myself purified in both respects.'

"This noble disciple, Bhante, whose mind is in this way without enmity, without ill will, undefiled, and pure, has won these four assurances in this very life.

"Excellent, Bhante! ... We go for refuge to the Blessed One, to the Dhamma, and to the Saṅgha of bhikkhus. Let the Blessed One consider us lay followers who from today have gone for refuge for life."

66 (6) Sāḷha

Thus have I heard. On one occasion the Venerable Nandaka was dwelling at Sāvatthī in Migāramātā's Mansion in the Eastern

Park. Then Sāḷha, Migāra's grandson, and Rohaṇa, Pekhuniya's grandson, approached the Venerable Nandaka, paid homage to him, and sat down to one side. The Venerable Nandaka then said to Sāḷha:

"Come, Sāḷha, do not go by oral tradition, by lineage of teaching, by hearsay, by a collection of scriptures, by logical reasoning, by inferential reasoning, by reasoned cogitation, by the acceptance of a view after pondering it, by the seeming competence [of a speaker], or because you think: 'The ascetic is our guru.' But when you [194] know for yourselves: 'These things are unwholesome; these things are blameworthy; these things are censured by the wise; these things, if accepted and undertaken, lead to harm and suffering,' then you should abandon them.

(1) "What do you think, Sāḷha, is there greed?"

"Yes, Bhante."

"I say this means longing. A greedy person, full of longing, destroys life, takes what is not given, transgresses with another's wife, and speaks falsehood; and he encourages others to do likewise. Will that lead to his harm and suffering for a long time?"

"Yes, Bhante."

(2) "What do you think, Sāḷha, is there hatred?"

"Yes, Bhante."

"I say this means ill will. A person full of hate, with a mind of ill will, destroys life . . . and he encourages others to do likewise. Will that lead to his harm and suffering for a long time?"

"Yes, Bhante."

(3) "What do you think, Sāḷha, is there delusion?"

"Yes, Bhante."

"I say this means ignorance. A deluded person, immersed in ignorance, destroys life . . . and he encourages others to do likewise. Will that lead to his harm and suffering for a long time?"

"Yes, Bhante."

"What do you think, Sāḷha? Are these things wholesome or unwholesome?" – "Unwholesome, Bhante." – "Blameworthy or blameless?" – "Blameworthy, Bhante." – "Censured or praised by the wise?" – "Censured by the wise, Bhante." – "Accepted and undertaken, do they lead to harm and suffering or not, or how do you take it?" [195] – "Accepted and undertaken, these things lead to harm and suffering. So we take it."

"Thus, Sāḷha, when we said: 'Come, Sāḷha, do not go by oral tradition…But when you know for yourselves: "These things are unwholesome; these things are blameworthy; these things are censured by the wise; these things, if undertaken and practiced, lead to harm and suffering," then you should abandon them,' it is because of this that this was said.

"Come, Sāḷha, do not go by oral tradition, by lineage of teaching, by hearsay, by a collection of scriptures, by logical reasoning, by inferential reasoning, by reasoned cogitation, by the acceptance of a view after pondering it, by the seeming competence [of a speaker], or because you think: 'The ascetic is our guru.' But when you know for yourselves: 'These things are wholesome; these things are blameless; these things are praised by the wise; these things, if accepted and undertaken, lead to welfare and happiness,' then you should live in accordance with them.

(1) "What do you think, Sāḷha, is there non-greed?"

"Yes, Bhante."

"I say this means absence of longing. A person without greed, without longing, does not destroy life, take what is not given, transgress with another's wife, or speak falsehood; nor does he encourage others to do likewise. Will that lead to his welfare and happiness for a long time?"

"Yes, Bhante."

(2) "What do you think, Sāḷha, is there non-hatred?"

"Yes, Bhante."

"I say this means good will. A person without hate, with a mind of good will, does not destroy life…nor does he encourage others to do likewise. Will that lead to his welfare and happiness for a long time?"

"Yes, Bhante."

(3) "What do you think, Sāḷha, is there non-delusion?"

"Yes, Bhante."

"I say this means true knowledge. An undeluded person, [196] who has arrived at true knowledge, does not destroy life…nor does he encourage others to do likewise. Will that lead to his welfare and happiness for a long time?"

"Yes, Bhante."

"What do you think, Sāḷha? Are these things wholesome or unwholesome?" – "Wholesome, Bhante." – "Blameworthy or blameless?" – "Blameless, Bhante." – "Censured or praised by the wise?" – "Praised by the wise, Bhante." – "Accepted and undertaken, do they lead to welfare and happiness or not, or how do you take it?" – "Accepted and undertaken, these things lead to welfare and happiness. So we take it."

"Thus, Sāḷha, when we said: 'Come, Sāḷha, do not go by oral tradition ... But when you know for yourselves: "These things are wholesome; these things are blameless; these things are praised by the wise; these things, if accepted and undertaken, lead to welfare and happiness," then you should live in accordance with them,' it is because of this that this was said.

"Then, Sāḷha, that noble disciple, who is thus devoid of longing, devoid of ill will, unconfused, clearly comprehending, ever mindful, dwells pervading one quarter with a mind imbued with loving-kindness ... with a mind imbued with compassion ... with a mind imbued with altruistic joy ... with a mind imbued with equanimity, likewise the second quarter, the third quarter, and the fourth quarter. Thus above, below, across, and everywhere, and to all as to himself, he dwells pervading the entire world with a mind imbued with equanimity, vast, exalted, measureless, without enmity, without ill will.

"He then understands thus: 'There is this; there is the inferior; there is the superior; there is a further escape from whatever is involved with perception.'[462] When he knows and sees thus, his mind is liberated from the taint of sensuality, from the taint of existence, and from the taint of ignorance. [197] When it is liberated there comes the knowledge: '[It's] liberated.' He understands: 'Destroyed is birth, the spiritual life has been lived, what had to be done has been done, there is no more coming back to any state of being.'

"He understands thus: 'Formerly, there was greed; that was unwholesome. Now there is none; thus this is wholesome. Formerly, there was hatred; that was unwholesome. Now there is none; thus this is wholesome. Formerly, there was delusion; that was unwholesome. Now there is none; thus this is wholesome.'

"Thus in this very life he dwells hungerless, quenched and cooled, experiencing bliss, having himself become divine."[463]

67 (7) Bases of Talk

"Bhikkhus, there are these three bases of talk. What three? (1) Referring to the past, one would say: 'So it was in the past.' (2) Referring to the future, one would say: 'So it will be in the future.' (3) Referring to the present, one would say: 'So it is now, at present.'

"It is in relation to talk, bhikkhus, that a person may be understood as either fit to talk or unfit to talk. If this person is asked a question that should be answered categorically and he does not answer it categorically; [if he is asked] a question that should be answered after making a distinction and he answers it without making a distinction; [if he is asked] a question that should be answered with a counter-question and he answers it without asking a counter-question; [if he is asked] a question that should be set aside and he does not set it aside, in such a case this person is unfit to talk.[464]

"But if this person is asked a question that should be answered categorically and he answers it categorically; [if he is asked] a question that should be answered after making a distinction and he answers it after making a distinction; [if he is asked] a question that should be answered with a counter-question and he answers it with a counter-question; [if he is asked] a question that should be set aside and he sets it aside, in such a case this person is fit to talk.

"It is in relation to talk, bhikkhus, that a person should be understood as either fit to talk or unfit to talk. If this person is asked a question and he does not stand firm in regard to his position and the opposing position; if he does not stand firm in his stratagem; if he does not [198] stand firm in an assertion about what is known; if he does not stand firm in the procedure, in such a case this person is unfit to talk.[465]

"But if this person is asked a question and he stands firm in regard to his position and the opposing position; if he stands firm in his stratagem; if he stands firm in an assertion about what is known; if he stands firm in the procedure, in such a case this person is fit to talk.

"It is in relation to talk, bhikkhus, that a person should be understood as either fit to talk or unfit to talk. If this person is asked a question and he answers evasively, diverts the discussion to an irrelevant subject, and displays anger, hatred, and bitterness, in such a case this person is unfit to talk.

"But if this person is asked a question and he does not answer evasively, divert the discussion to an irrelevant subject, or display anger, hatred, and bitterness, in such a case this person is fit to talk.

"It is in relation to talk, bhikkhus, that a person should be understood as either fit to talk or unfit to talk. If this person is asked a question and he overwhelms [the questioner], crushes him, ridicules him, and seizes upon a slight error,[466] in such a case this person is unfit to talk.

"But if this person is asked a question and he does not overwhelm [the questioner], or crush him, or ridicule him, or seize upon a slight error, in such a case this person is fit to talk.

"It is in relation to talk, bhikkhus, that a person should be understood as either having a supporting condition or not having a supporting condition. One who does not lend an ear does not have a supporting condition; one who lends an ear has a supporting condition. One who has a supporting condition directly knows one thing, fully understands one thing, abandons one thing, and realizes one thing. Directly knowing one thing, fully understanding one thing, abandoning one thing, and realizing one thing, he reaches right liberation.[467]

"This, bhikkhus, is the goal of talk, the goal of discussion, the goal of a supporting condition, the goal of lending an ear, that is, the emancipation of the mind through non-clinging." [199]

Those who speak with quarrelsome intent,
settled in their opinions, swollen with pride,
ignoble, having assailed virtues,[468]
look for openings [to attack] one another.

They mutually delight when their opponent
speaks badly and makes a mistake,
[they rejoice] in his bewilderment and defeat;
but noble ones don't engage in such talk.

If a wise person wants to talk,
having known the time is right,
without quarrelsomeness or pride,

the sagely person should utter
the speech that the noble ones practice,
which is connected with the Dhamma and meaning.[469]

Not being insolent or aggressive,
with a mind not elated,[470]
he speaks free from envy
on the basis of right knowledge.
He should approve of what is well expressed
but should not attack what is badly stated.

He should not train in faultfinding
nor seize on the other's mistakes;
he should not overwhelm and crush his opponent,
nor speak mendacious words.
Truly, a discussion among the good
is for the sake of knowledge and confidence.

Such is the way the noble discuss things;
this is the discussion of the noble ones.
Having understood this, the wise person
should not swell up but should discuss things.

68 (8) Other Sects

"Bhikkhus, wanderers of other sects may ask you: 'Friends, there are these three things. What three? Greed, hatred, and delusion. These are the three. What, friends, is the distinction, the disparity, the difference between them?' If you are asked this, how would you answer?"

"Bhante, our teachings are rooted in the Blessed One, guided by the Blessed One, take recourse in the Blessed One. It would be good if the Blessed One would clear up the meaning of this statement. Having heard it from him, the bhikkhus will retain it in mind."

"Then listen, bhikkhus, and attend closely. I will speak."

"Yes, Bhante," those bhikkhus replied. The Blessed One said this:

"Bhikkhus, if wanderers of other sects should ask you such a question, [200] you should answer them as follows: 'Lust, friends, is slightly blameworthy but slow to fade away; hatred is very blameworthy but quick to fade away; delusion is very blameworthy and slow to fade away.'[471]

(1) "[Suppose they ask:] 'But, friends, what is the reason unarisen lust arises and arisen lust increases and expands?' You should answer: 'An attractive object. For one who attends carelessly to an attractive object, unarisen lust arises and arisen lust increases and expands. This, friends, is the reason unarisen lust arises and arisen lust increases and expands.'

(2) "[Suppose they ask:] 'But what, friends, is the reason unarisen hatred arises and arisen hatred increases and expands?' You should answer: 'A repulsive object. For one who attends carelessly to a repulsive object, unarisen hatred arises and arisen hatred increases and expands. This, friends, is the reason unarisen hatred arises and arisen hatred increases and expands.'

(3) "[Suppose they ask:] 'But what, friends, is the reason unarisen delusion arises and arisen delusion increases and expands?' You should answer: 'Careless attention. For one who attends carelessly, unarisen delusion arises and arisen delusion increases and expands. This, friends, is the reason unarisen delusion arises and arisen delusion increases and expands.'

(1) "[Suppose they ask:] 'But what, friends, is the reason unarisen lust does not arise and arisen lust is abandoned?' You should answer: 'An unattractive object. For one who attends carefully to an unattractive object, unarisen lust does not arise [201] and arisen lust is abandoned. This, friends, is the reason unarisen lust does not arise and arisen lust is abandoned.'

(2) "[Suppose they ask:] 'But what, friends, is the reason unarisen hatred does not arise and arisen hatred is abandoned?' You should answer: 'The liberation of the mind by loving-kindness. For one who attends carefully to the liberation of the mind by loving-kindness, unarisen hatred does not arise and arisen hatred is abandoned. This, friends, is the reason unarisen hatred does not arise and arisen hatred is abandoned.'

(3) "[Suppose they ask:] 'But what, friends, is the reason unarisen delusion does not arise and arisen delusion is abandoned?' You should answer: 'Careful attention. For one who attends carefully, unarisen delusion does not arise and arisen delusion is abandoned. This, friends, is the reason unarisen delusion does not arise and arisen delusion is abandoned.'"

69 (9) Roots

"Bhikkhus, there are these three unwholesome roots. What three? The unwholesome root, greed; the unwholesome root, hatred; and the unwholesome root, delusion.

(1) "Whatever greed occurs, bhikkhus, is unwholesome. Whatever [deed] a greedy person performs by body, speech, and mind is also unwholesome. When a greedy person, overcome by greed, with mind obsessed by it, inflicts suffering upon another under a false pretext[472]—by killing, imprisonment, confiscation, censure, or banishment—[thinking]: 'I am powerful, I want power,' that too is unwholesome. Thus numerous bad unwholesome qualities originate in him born of greed, caused by greed, arisen from greed, conditioned by greed.

(2) "Whatever hatred occurs is unwholesome. Whatever [deed] a person full of hate performs by body, speech, and mind is also unwholesome. When a person full of hate, overcome by hatred, with mind obsessed by it, inflicts suffering upon another under a false pretext... [thinking]: 'I am powerful, [202] I want power,' that too is unwholesome. Thus numerous bad unwholesome qualities originate in him born of hatred, caused by hatred, arisen from hatred, conditioned by hatred.

(3) "Whatever delusion occurs is unwholesome. Whatever [deed] a deluded person performs by body, speech, and mind is also unwholesome. When a deluded person, overcome by delusion, with mind obsessed by it, inflicts suffering upon another under a false pretext... [thinking]: 'I am powerful, I want power,' that too is unwholesome. Thus numerous bad unwholesome qualities originate in him born of delusion, caused by delusion, arisen from delusion, conditioned by delusion.

"Such a person, bhikkhus, is called one who speaks at an improper time, who speaks falsely, who speaks what is unbeneficial, who speaks non-Dhamma, who speaks non-discipline. And why is such a person called one who speaks at an improper time... who speaks non-discipline? This person inflicts suffering upon another under a false pretext—by killing, imprisonment, confiscation, censure, or banishment—thinking: 'I am powerful, I want power.' Thus when spoken to in accordance with fact, he despises [the one who reproaches him]; he does not admit [his faults]. When spoken to contrary to fact, he does not make an effort to unravel what is said to him:

'For such and such a reason this is untrue; for such and such a reason this is contrary to fact.' Therefore such a person is called one who speaks at an improper time, who speaks falsely, who speaks what is unbeneficial, who speaks non-Dhamma, who speaks non-discipline.

"Such a person, overcome by bad unwholesome qualities born of greed ... born of hatred ... born of delusion, with his mind obsessed by them, dwells in suffering in this very life, with distress, anguish, and fever, and with the breakup of the body, after death, a bad destination can be expected for him.

"Suppose a tree[473] was choked and enveloped by three *māluvā* creepers. It would meet with calamity, with disaster, with calamity and disaster. So too, such a person overcome by bad unwholesome qualities born of greed [203] ... born of hatred ... born of delusion, with his mind obsessed by them, dwells in suffering in this very life, with distress, anguish, and fever, and with the breakup of the body, after death, a bad destination can be expected for him. These are the three unwholesome roots.

"There are, bhikkhus, these three wholesome roots. What three? The wholesome root, non-greed; the wholesome root, non-hatred; and the wholesome root, non-delusion.

(1) "Whatever non-greed occurs, bhikkhus, is wholesome. Whatever [deed] one without greed performs by body, speech, and mind is also wholesome. When one without greed, not overcome by greed, with mind not obsessed by it, does not inflict suffering upon another under a false pretext—by killing, imprisonment, confiscation, censure, or banishment—thinking: 'I am powerful, I want power,' that too is wholesome. Thus numerous wholesome qualities originate in him born of non-greed, caused by non-greed, arisen from non-greed, conditioned by non-greed.

(2) "Whatever non-hatred occurs is wholesome. Whatever [deed] one without hate performs by body, speech, and mind is also wholesome. When one without hate, not overcome by hatred, with mind not obsessed by it, does not inflict suffering upon another under a false pretext ... that too is wholesome. Thus numerous wholesome qualities originate in him born of non-hatred, caused by non-hatred, arisen from non-hatred, conditioned by non-hatred.

(3) "Whatever non-delusion occurs is wholesome. Whatever [deed] one who is undeluded performs by body, speech, and mind is also wholesome. When one who is undeluded, not overcome by delusion, with mind not obsessed by it, does not inflict suffering upon another under a false pretext... that too is wholesome. Thus [204] numerous wholesome qualities originate in him born of non-delusion, caused by non-delusion, arisen from non-delusion, conditioned by non-delusion.

"Such a person, bhikkhus, is called one who speaks at the proper time, who speaks in accordance with fact, who speaks what is beneficial, who speaks Dhamma, who speaks discipline. And why is such a person called one who speaks at the proper time... who speaks discipline? This person does not inflict suffering upon another under a false pretext—by killing, imprisonment, confiscation, censure, or banishment—thinking: 'I am powerful, I want power.' Thus when spoken to in accordance with fact, he admits [his faults]; he does not despise [the one who reproaches him]. When spoken to contrary to fact, he makes an effort to unravel what is said to him: 'For such and such a reason this is untrue; for such and such a reason this is contrary to fact.' Therefore such a person is called one who speaks at the proper time, who speaks in accordance with fact, who speaks what is beneficial, who speaks Dhamma, who speaks discipline.

"Such a person has abandoned the bad unwholesome qualities born of greed... born of hatred... born of delusion, cut them off at the root, made them like a palm stump, obliterated them so that they are no more subject to future arising. He dwells happily in this very life, without distress, anguish, or fever, and in this very life he attains nibbāna.

"Suppose a tree was choked and enveloped by three *māluvā* creepers. Then a man would come along bringing a shovel and a basket. He would cut down the creepers at their roots, dig them up, and pull out the roots, even the fine rootlets and root-fiber. He would cut the creepers into pieces, split the pieces, and reduce them to slivers. Then he would dry the slivers in the wind and sun, burn them in a fire, [205] reduce them to ashes, and winnow the ashes in a strong wind or let them be carried away by the swift current of a river. In this way, those *māluvā* creepers would be cut off at the root, made like a palm stump, obliterated so that they are no more subject to future arising.

"So too, bhikkhus, such a person has abandoned the bad unwholesome qualities born of greed...born of hatred...born of delusion, cut them off at the root, made them like a palm stump, obliterated them so that they are no more subject to future arising. He dwells happily in this very life, without distress, anguish, or fever, and in this very life he attains nibbāna. These are the three wholesome roots."

70 (10) Uposatha

Thus have I heard. On one occasion the Blessed One was dwelling at Sāvatthī in Migāramātā's Mansion in the Eastern Park. Then Visākhā Migāramātā, on the day of the uposatha, approached the Blessed One, paid homage to him, and sat down to one side. The Blessed One then said to her:

"Why, Visākhā, have you come in the middle of the day?"

"Today, Bhante, I am observing the uposatha."

"There are, Visākhā, three kinds of uposathas. What three? The cowherds' uposatha, the Nigaṇṭhas' uposatha,[474] and the noble ones' uposatha.

(1) "And how, Visākhā, is the cowherds' uposatha observed? Suppose, Visākhā, in the evening a cowherd returns the cows to their owners. He reflects thus: 'Today the cows grazed in such and such a place and drank water in such and such a place. Tomorrow the cows will graze in such and such a place and drink water in such and such a place.' So too, someone here observing the uposatha reflects thus: 'Today I ate this and that food; today I ate a meal of this and that kind. [206] Tomorrow I will eat this and that food; tomorrow I will eat a meal of this and that kind.' He thereby passes the day with greed and longing in his mind. It is in such a way that the cowherds' uposatha is observed. The cowherds' uposatha, thus observed, is not of great fruit and benefit, nor is it extraordinarily brilliant and pervasive.

(2) "And how, Visākhā, is the Nigaṇṭhas' uposatha observed? There are, Visākhā, ascetics called Nigaṇṭhas. They enjoin their disciples thus: 'Come, good man, lay down the rod toward living beings dwelling more than a hundred *yojanas'* distance in the eastern quarter.[475] Lay down the rod toward living beings

dwelling more than a hundred *yojanas'* distance in the western quarter. Lay down the rod toward living beings dwelling more than a hundred *yojanas'* distance in the northern quarter. Lay down the rod toward living beings dwelling more than a hundred *yojanas'* distance in the southern quarter.' Thus they enjoin them to be sympathetic and compassionate toward some living beings, but not to others. On the uposatha day, they enjoin their disciples thus: 'Come, good man, having laid aside all clothes, recite: 'I am not anywhere the belonging of anyone, nor is there anywhere anything in any place that is mine.'[476] However, his parents know: 'This is our son.' And he knows: 'These are my parents.' His wife and children know: 'He is our supporter.' And he knows: 'These are my wife and children.' His slaves, workers, and servants know: 'He is our master.' And he knows: 'These are my slaves, workers, and servants.' Thus on an occasion when they should be enjoined in truthfulness, [the Nigaṇṭhas] enjoin them in false speech. This, I say, is false speech. When that night has passed, he makes use of possessions that have not been given. This, I say, is taking what has not been given. It is in such a way that the Nigaṇṭhas' uposatha is observed. When one has observed the uposatha in the way of the Nigaṇṭhas, the uposatha is not of great fruit and benefit, nor is it extraordinarily brilliant and pervasive.

(3) "And how, Visākhā, is the noble ones' uposatha observed? [207] The defiled mind is cleansed by exertion.[477] And how is the defiled mind cleansed by exertion? Here, Visākhā, a noble disciple recollects the Tathāgata thus: 'The Blessed One is an arahant, perfectly enlightened, accomplished in true knowledge and conduct, fortunate, knower of the world, unsurpassed trainer of persons to be tamed, teacher of devas and humans, the Enlightened One, the Blessed One.' When a noble disciple recollects the Tathāgata, his mind becomes placid, joy arises, and the defilements of the mind are abandoned in the same way that one's head, when dirty, is cleansed by exertion.

"And how, Visākhā, does one cleanse a dirty head by exertion? By means of cleansing paste, clay, water, and the appropriate effort by the person. It is in such a way that one's head, when dirty, is cleansed by exertion. So too, the defiled mind is cleansed by exertion. And how is the defiled mind cleansed by exertion? Here, Visākhā, a noble disciple recollects the Tathāgata thus: 'The Blessed One is... teacher of devas and humans, the Enlightened One, the Blessed One.' When a noble disciple recollects the Tathāgata, his mind becomes placid, joy arises, and the defilements of the mind are abandoned. This is called a noble disciple who observes the uposatha of Brahmā, who dwells together with Brahmā, and it is by considering Brahmā that his mind becomes placid, joy arises, and the defilements of the mind are abandoned.[478] It is in this way that the defiled mind is cleansed by exertion.

"The defiled mind, Visākhā, is cleansed by exertion. And how is the defiled mind cleansed by exertion? Here, Visākhā, a noble disciple recollects the Dhamma thus: 'The Dhamma is well expounded by the Blessed One, directly visible, immediate, inviting one to come and see, applicable, to be personally experienced by the wise.' When a noble disciple recollects the Dhamma, his mind becomes placid, joy arises, and the defilements of the mind [208] are abandoned in the same way that one's body, when dirty, is cleansed by exertion.

"And how, Visākhā, does one cleanse a dirty body by exertion? By means of a bathing brush, lime powder, water, and the appropriate effort by the person. It is in such a way that one's body, when dirty, is cleansed by exertion. So too, the defiled mind is cleansed by exertion. And how is the defiled mind cleansed by exertion? Here, Visākhā, a noble disciple recollects the Dhamma thus: 'The Dhamma is well expounded by the Blessed One... to be personally experienced by the wise.' When a noble disciple recollects the Dhamma, his mind becomes placid, joy arises, and the defilements of the mind are abandoned. This is called a noble disciple who observes the uposatha of the Dhamma, who dwells together with the Dhamma, and it is by considering the Dhamma that his mind becomes placid, joy arises, and the defilements of the mind are abandoned. It is in this way that the defiled mind is cleansed by exertion.

"The defiled mind, Visākhā, is cleansed by exertion. And how is the defiled mind cleansed by exertion? Here, Visākhā, a noble disciple recollects the Saṅgha thus: 'The Saṅgha of the Blessed One's disciples is practicing the good way, practicing the straight way, practicing the true way, practicing the proper way; that is, the four pairs of persons, the eight types of individuals—this

Saṅgha of the Blessed One's disciples is worthy of gifts, worthy of hospitality, worthy of offerings, worthy of reverential salutation, the unsurpassed field of merit for the world.' When a noble disciple recollects the Saṅgha, his mind becomes placid, joy arises, and the defilements of the mind are abandoned in the same way that a dirty cloth is cleansed by exertion.

"And how, Visākhā, does one cleanse a dirty cloth by exertion? [209] By means of heat, lye, cow dung, water, and the appropriate effort by the person. It is in such a way that a dirty cloth is cleansed by exertion. So too, the defiled mind is cleansed by exertion. And how is the defiled mind cleansed by exertion? Here, Visākhā, a noble disciple recollects the Saṅgha thus: 'The Saṅgha of the Blessed One's disciples is practicing the good way... the unsurpassed field of merit for the world.' When a noble disciple recollects the Saṅgha, his mind becomes placid, joy arises, and the defilements of the mind are abandoned. This is called a noble disciple who observes the uposatha of the Saṅgha, who dwells together with the Saṅgha, and it is by considering the Saṅgha that his mind becomes placid, joy arises, and the defilements of the mind are abandoned. It is in this way that the defiled mind is cleansed by exertion.

"The defiled mind, Visākhā, is cleansed by exertion. And how is the defiled mind cleansed by exertion? Here, Visākhā, a noble disciple recollects his own virtuous behavior as unbroken, flawless, unblemished, unblotched, freeing, praised by the wise, ungrasped, leading to concentration. When a noble disciple recollects his virtuous behavior, his mind becomes placid, joy arises, and the defilements of the mind are abandoned in the same way that a dirty mirror is cleansed by exertion.

"And how, Visākhā, is a dirty mirror cleansed by exertion? By means of oil, ashes, a roll of cloth, and the appropriate effort by the person. It is in such a way that a dirty mirror is cleansed by exertion. So too, the defiled mind is cleansed by exertion. And how is the defiled mind cleansed by exertion? [210] Here, Visākhā, a noble disciple recollects his own virtuous behavior as unbroken... leading to concentration. When a noble disciple recollects his virtuous behavior, his mind becomes placid, joy arises, and the defilements of the mind are abandoned. This is called a noble disciple who observes the uposatha of virtuous behavior, who dwells together with virtuous behavior, and it is by considering virtuous behavior that his mind becomes placid, joy arises, and the defilements of the mind are abandoned. It is in this way that the defiled mind is cleansed by exertion.

"The defiled mind, Visākhā, is cleansed by exertion. And how is the defiled mind cleansed by exertion? Here, Visākhā, a noble disciple recollects the deities thus: 'There are devas [ruled by] the four great kings, Tāvatiṃsa devas, Yāma devas, Tusita devas, devas who delight in creation, devas who control what is created by others, devas of Brahmā's company, and devas still higher than these.[479] I too have such faith as those deities possessed because of which, when they passed away here, they were reborn there; I too have such virtuous behavior ... such learning ... such generosity ... such wisdom as those deities possessed because of which, when they passed away here, they were reborn there.' When a noble disciple recollects the faith, virtuous behavior, learning, generosity, and wisdom in himself and in those deities, his mind becomes placid, joy arises, and the defilements of the mind are abandoned in the same way that impure gold is cleansed by exertion.

"And how, Visākhā, is impure gold cleansed by exertion? By means of a furnace, salt, red chalk, a blow-pipe and tongs, and the appropriate effort by the person. It is in such a way that impure gold is cleansed by exertion. So too, the defiled mind is cleansed by exertion. [211] And how is the defiled mind cleansed by exertion? Here, Visākhā, a noble disciple recollects the deities thus: 'There are devas [ruled by] the four great kings ... and devas still higher than these. I too have such faith ... such wisdom as those deities possessed because of which, when they passed away here, they were reborn there.' When a noble disciple recollects the faith, virtuous behavior, learning, generosity, and wisdom in himself and in those deities, his mind becomes placid, joy arises, and the defilements of the mind are abandoned. This is called a noble disciple who observes the uposatha of the deities, who dwells together with the deities, and it is by considering the deities that his mind becomes placid, joy arises, and the defilements of the mind are abandoned. It is in this way that the defiled mind is cleansed by exertion.

(i) "This noble disciple, Visākhā, reflects thus:[480] 'As long as they live the arahants abandon and abstain from the destruction of life; with the rod and weapon laid aside, conscientious and kindly, they dwell compassionate toward all living beings. Today, for this night and day, I too shall abandon and abstain from the destruction of life; with the rod and weapon laid aside, conscientious and kindly, I too shall dwell compassionate toward all living beings. I shall imitate the arahants in this respect and the uposatha will be observed by me.

(ii) "'As long as they live the arahants abandon and abstain from taking what is not given; they take only what is given, expect only what is given, and are honest at heart, devoid of theft. Today, for this night and day, I too shall abandon and abstain from taking what is not given; I shall accept only what is given, expect only what is given, and be honest at heart, devoid of theft. I shall imitate the arahants in this respect and the uposatha will be observed by me.

(iii) "'As long as they live the arahants abandon sexual activity and observe celibacy, living apart, abstaining from sexual intercourse, the common person's practice. Today, for this night and day, I too shall abandon sexual activity and observe celibacy, living apart, abstaining from sexual intercourse, the common person's practice. I shall imitate the arahants in this respect and the uposatha will be observed by me. [212]

(iv) "'As long as they live the arahants abandon and abstain from false speech; they speak truth, adhere to truth; they are trustworthy and reliable, no deceivers of the world. Today, for this night and day, I too shall abandon and abstain from false speech; I shall be a speaker of truth, an adherent of truth, trustworthy and reliable, no deceiver of the world. I shall imitate the arahants in this respect and the uposatha will be observed by me.

(v) "'As long as they live the arahants abandon and abstain from liquor, wine, and intoxicants, the basis for heedlessness. Today, for this night and day, I too shall abandon and abstain from liquor, wine, and intoxicants, the basis for heedlessness. I shall imitate the arahants in this respect and the uposatha will be observed by me.

(vi) "'As long as they live the arahants eat once a day,[481] abstaining from eating at night and from food outside the proper time. Today, for this night and day, I too shall eat once a day, abstaining from eating at night and from food outside the proper time. I shall imitate the arahants in this respect and the uposatha will be observed by me.

(vii) "'As long as they live the arahants abstain from dancing, singing, instrumental music, and unsuitable shows, and from adorning and beautifying themselves by wearing garlands and applying scents and unguents. Today, for this night and day, I too shall abstain from dancing, singing, instrumental music, and unsuitable shows, and from adorning and beautifying myself by wearing garlands and applying scents and unguents. I shall imitate the arahants in this respect and the uposatha will be observed by me.

(viii) "'As long as they live the arahants abandon and abstain from the use of high and luxurious beds; they lie down on a low resting place, either a small bed or a straw mat. Today, for this night and day, I too shall abandon and abstain from the use of high and luxurious beds; I shall lie down on a low resting place, either a small bed or a straw mat. I shall imitate the arahants in this respect and the uposatha will be observed by me.'

"It is in this way, Visākhā, that the noble ones' uposatha is observed. When one has observed the uposatha in the way of the noble ones it is of great fruit and benefit, extraordinarily brilliant and pervasive.

"To what extent is it of great fruit and benefit? To what extent is it extraordinarily brilliant and pervasive? Suppose, Visākhā, one were to exercise sovereignty and kingship over these sixteen great countries abounding in the seven precious substances,[482] [213] that is, [the countries of] the Aṅgans, the Magadhans, the Kāsis, the Kosalans, the Vajjis, the Mallas, the Cetis, the Vaṅgas, the Kurus, the Pañcālas, the Macchas, the Sūrasenas, the Assakas, the Avantis, the Gandhārans, and the Kambojans:[483] this would not be worth a sixteenth part of the uposatha observance complete in those eight factors. For what reason? Because human kingship is poor compared to celestial happiness.

"For the devas [ruled by] the four great kings,[484] a single night and day is equivalent to fifty human years; thirty such days make up a month, and twelve such months make up a year. The life span of the devas [ruled by] the four great kings is five hundred such celestial years. It is possible, Visākhā, that a woman or man here who observes the uposatha complete in these eight factors will, with the breakup of the body, after death, be reborn in companionship with the devas [ruled by] the four great kings. It was with reference to this that I said human kingship is poor compared to celestial happiness.

"For the Tāvatiṃsa devas a single night and day is equivalent to a hundred human years; thirty such days make up a month, and twelve such months make up a year. The life span of the Tāvatiṃsa devas is a thousand such celestial years. It is possible, Visākhā, that a woman or man here who observes the uposatha complete in these eight factors will, with the breakup of the body, after death, be reborn in companionship with the Tāvatiṃsa devas. It was with reference to this that I said human kingship is poor compared to celestial happiness.

"For the Yāma devas a single night and day is equivalent to two hundred human years; thirty such days make up a month, and twelve such months make up a year. The life span of the Yāma devas is two thousand such celestial years. It is possible, Visākhā, that a woman or man here who observes the uposatha complete in these eight factors will, with the breakup of the body, after death, be reborn in companionship with the Yāma devas. It was with reference to this [214] that I said human kingship is poor compared to celestial happiness.

"For the Tusita devas, a single night and day is equivalent to four hundred human years; thirty such days make up a month, and twelve such months make up a year. The life span of the Tusita devas is four thousand such celestial years. It is possible, Visākhā, that a woman or man here who observes the uposatha complete in these eight factors will, with the breakup of the body, after death, be reborn in companionship with the Tusita devas. It was with reference to this that I said human kingship is poor compared to celestial happiness.

"For the devas who delight in creation, a single night and day is equivalent to eight hundred human years; thirty such days make up a month, and twelve such months make up a year. The life span of the devas who delight in creation is eight thousand such celestial years. It is possible, Visākhā, that a woman or man here who observes the uposatha complete in these eight factors will, with the breakup of the body, after death, be reborn in companionship with the devas who delight in creation. It was with reference to this that I said human kingship is poor compared to celestial happiness.

"For the devas who control what is created by others, a single night and day is equivalent to sixteen hundred human years; thirty such days make up a month, and twelve such months make up a year. The life span of the devas who control what is created by others is sixteen thousand such celestial years. It is possible, Visākhā, that a woman or man here who observes the uposatha complete in these eight factors will, with the breakup of the body, after death, be reborn in companionship with the devas who control what is created by others. It was with reference to this that I said human kingship is poor compared to celestial happiness."

One should not kill living beings or take what is not given;
one should not speak falsehood or drink intoxicants; [215]
one should refrain from sexual activity, from unchastity;
one should not eat at night or at an improper time.

One should not wear garlands or apply scents;
one should sleep on a [low] bed or a mat on the ground;
this, they say, is the eight-factored uposatha
proclaimed by the Buddha,
who reached the end of suffering.

As far as the sun and moon revolve,
shedding light, so beautiful to gaze upon,
dispellers of darkness, moving through the firmament,
they shine in the sky,[485] brightening up the quarters.

Whatever wealth exists in this sphere—
pearls, gems, and excellent beryl,[486]
horn gold and mountain gold,
and the natural gold called *haṭaka*—[487]

those are not worth a sixteenth part
of an uposatha complete in the eight factors,
just as all the hosts of stars
[do not match] the moon's radiance.[488]

Therefore a virtuous woman or man,
having observed the uposatha complete in eight factors,

and having made merit productive of happiness,
goes blameless to a heavenly state.

III. Ānanda

71 (1) Channa

Then the wanderer Channa approached the Venerable Ānanda and exchanged greetings with him. When they had concluded their greetings and cordial talk, he sat down to one side and said to the Venerable Ānanda:

"Friend Ānanda, do you prescribe the abandoning of lust, hatred, and delusion?"[489]

"We do, friend." [216]

"But what is the danger that you have seen on account of which you prescribe the abandoning of lust, hatred, and delusion?"

(1) "One excited by lust, friend, overcome by lust, with mind obsessed by it, intends for his own affliction, for the affliction of others, and for the affliction of both, and he experiences mental suffering and dejection. But when lust is abandoned, he does not intend for his own affliction, for the affliction of others, or for the affliction of both, and he does not experience mental suffering and dejection.

"One excited by lust, overcome by lust, with mind obsessed by it, engages in misconduct by body, speech, and mind. But when lust is abandoned, one does not engage in misconduct by body, speech, and mind. One excited by lust, overcome by lust, with mind obsessed by it, does not understand as it really is his own good, the good of others, and the good of both. But when lust is abandoned, one understands as it really is one's own good, the good of others, and the good of both. Lust leads to blindness, loss of vision, and lack of knowledge; it is obstructive to wisdom, aligned with distress, and does not lead to nibbāna.

(2) "One full of hate, overcome by hatred...

(3) "One deluded, overcome by delusion, with mind obsessed by it, intends for his own affliction, for the affliction of others, and for the affliction of both, and he experiences mental suffering and dejection. But when delusion is abandoned, he does not intend for his own affliction, for the affliction of others, or for the affliction of both, and he does not experience mental suffering and dejection.

"One deluded, overcome by delusion, with mind obsessed by it, engages in misconduct by body, speech, and mind. But when delusion is abandoned, he does not engage in misconduct by body, speech, and mind. One deluded, overcome by delusion, with mind obsessed by it, does not understand as it really is his own good, the good of others, and the good of both. But when delusion [217] is abandoned, one understands as it really is one's own good, the good of others, and the good of both. Delusion leads to blindness, loss of vision, and lack of knowledge; it is obstructive to wisdom, aligned with distress, and does not lead to nibbāna.

"Having seen these dangers in lust, hatred, and delusion, we prescribe their abandoning."

"But is there a path, friend, is there a way to the abandoning of lust, hatred, and delusion?"

"There is a path, friend, there is a way to the abandoning of lust, hatred, and delusion."

"But what is the path, what is the way to the abandoning of lust, hatred, and delusion?"

"It is just this noble eightfold path, that is, right view ... right concentration. This is the path, the way to the abandoning of lust, hatred, and delusion."

"Excellent, friend, is the path, excellent the way to the abandoning of lust, hatred, and delusion. It is enough, friend Ānanda, to be heedful."

72 (2) Ājīvaka

On one occasion the Venerable Ānanda was dwelling at Kosambī in Ghosita's Park. Then a certain householder, a disciple of the Ājīvakas,[490] approached the Venerable Ānanda, paid homage to him, sat down to one side, and said to him:

(1) "Bhante Ānanda, whose Dhamma is well expounded? (2) Who in the world are practicing the good way? (3) Who in the world are the fortunate ones?"[491]

"Well then, householder, I will question you about this matter. You should answer as you see fit.

(1) "What do you think, householder? Is the Dhamma of those who teach the abandoning of lust, hatred, and delusion well expounded or not, or how do you take it?" [218]

"The Dhamma of those who teach the abandoning of lust, hatred, and delusion is well expounded. So I take it."

(2) "What do you think, householder? Are those practicing for the abandoning of lust, hatred, and delusion practicing the good way in the world or not, or how do you take it?"

"Those practicing for the abandoning of lust, hatred, and delusion are practicing the good way in the world. So I take it."

(3) "What do you think, householder? Are those who have abandoned lust, hatred, and delusion, cut them off at the root, made them like a palm stump, obliterated them so that they are no more subject to future arising fortunate ones in the world or not, or how do you take it?"

"Those who have abandoned lust, hatred, and delusion, cut them off at the root, made them like a palm stump, obliterated them so that they are no more subject to future arising are fortunate ones in the world. So I take it."

"Thus, householder, you have declared: 'The Dhamma of those who teach the abandoning of lust, hatred, and delusion is well expounded.' You have declared: 'Those practicing for the abandoning of lust, hatred, and delusion are practicing the good way in the world.' And you have declared: 'Those who have abandoned lust, hatred, and delusion, cut them off at the root, made them like a palm stump, obliterated them so that they are no more subject to future arising are fortunate ones in the world.'"

"It is astounding and amazing, Bhante, that there is no extolling of one's own Dhamma nor any denigration of the Dhamma of others, but just the teaching of the Dhamma in its own sphere. The meaning is stated, but one does not bring oneself into the picture.[492]

"Bhante Ānanda, you teach the Dhamma for the abandoning of lust, hatred, and delusion, [219] so your Dhamma is well expounded. You are practicing for the abandoning of lust, hatred, and delusion, so you are practicing the good way in the world. You have abandoned lust, hatred, and delusion, cut them off at the root, made them like a palm stump, obliterated them so that they are no more subject to future arising, so you are the fortunate ones in the world.

"Excellent, Bhante! Excellent, Bhante! The noble Ānanda has made the Dhamma clear in many ways, as though he were turning upright what had been overthrown, revealing what was hidden, showing the way to one who was lost, or holding up a lamp in the darkness so those with good eyesight can see forms. Bhante Ānanda, I now go for refuge to the Blessed One, to the Dhamma, and to the Saṅgha of bhikkhus. Let the Noble Ānanda consider me a lay follower who from today has gone for refuge for life."

73 (3) The Sakyan

On one occasion the Blessed One was dwelling among the Sakyans at Kapilavatthu in the Banyan Tree Park. Now on that occasion the Blessed One had just recently recovered from illness. Then the Sakyan Mahānāma approached the Blessed One, paid homage to him, sat down to one side, and said to him:

"For a long time, Bhante, I have understood the Dhamma taught by the Blessed One thus: 'Knowledge occurs for one who is concentrated, not for one who lacks concentration.' Does concentration precede knowledge, Bhante, or does knowledge precede concentration?"

Then it occurred to the Venerable Ānanda: "The Blessed One has just recently recovered from his illness, yet this Mahānāma the Sakyan asks him a very deep question. Let me lead Mahānāma the Sakyan off to one side and teach him the Dhamma."

Then the Venerable Ānanda took Mahānāma the Sakyan by the arm, led him off to one side, and said to him: "The Blessed One has spoken about the virtuous behavior of a trainee and the virtuous behavior of one beyond training, the concentration of a trainee [220] and the concentration of one beyond training, the wisdom of a trainee and the wisdom of one beyond training.

(1) "And what, Mahānāma, is the virtuous behavior of a trainee? Here, a bhikkhu is virtuous; he dwells restrained by the Pātimokkha, possessed of good conduct and resort, seeing danger in minute faults. Having undertaken the training rules, he trains in them. This is called the virtuous behavior of a trainee.

(2) "And what is the concentration of a trainee?[493] Here, secluded from sensual pleasures, secluded from unwholesome states, a bhikkhu enters and dwells in the first jhāna ... [as at 3:58] ... the fourth jhāna.... This is called the concentration of a trainee.

(3) "And what is the wisdom of a trainee? Here, a bhikkhu understands as it really is: 'This is suffering' ... [as in 3:12] ... 'This

is the way leading to the cessation of suffering.' This is called the wisdom of a trainee.

"When this noble disciple is thus accomplished in virtuous behavior, concentration, and wisdom, with the destruction of the taints, he realizes for himself with direct knowledge, in this very life, the taintless liberation of mind, liberation by wisdom, and having entered upon it, he dwells in it.[494]

"It is in this way, Mahānāma, that the Blessed One has spoken about the virtuous behavior of a trainee and the virtuous behavior of one beyond training; about the concentration of a trainee and the concentration of one beyond training; about the wisdom of a trainee and the wisdom of one beyond training."

74 (4) The Nigaṇṭha

On one occasion the Venerable Ānanda was dwelling at Vesālī in the hall with the peaked roof in the Great Wood. Then the Licchavi Abhaya and the Licchavi Paṇḍitakumāra approached the Venerable Ānanda, paid homage to him, and sat down to one side.[495] The Licchavi Abhaya then said to the Venerable Ānanda:

"Bhante, the Nigaṇṭha Nātaputta claims to be all-knowing and all-seeing and to have all-embracing knowledge and vision, [saying]: 'When I am walking, standing, sleeping, and awake, knowledge and vision are constantly and continuously present to me.'[496] He prescribes the termination of old kammas by means of austerity and the demolition of the bridge by not creating any new kamma.[497] [221] Thus, through the destruction of kamma, suffering is destroyed. Through the destruction of suffering, feeling is destroyed. Through the destruction of feeling, all suffering will be worn away. In this way, the overcoming [of suffering] takes place through this directly visible purification by wearing away.[498] What does the Blessed One say about this?"

"Abhaya, these three kinds of wearing-away purification have been properly expounded by the Blessed One, the Arahant, the Perfectly Enlightened One who knows and sees, for the purification of beings, for the overcoming of sorrow and lamentation, for the passing away of pain and dejection, for the achievement of the method, for the realization of nibbāna. What three?

(1) "Here, Abhaya, a bhikkhu is virtuous ... [as in 3:73] ... Having undertaken the training rules, he trains in them. He does not

create any new kamma and he terminates the old kamma having contacted it again and again.[499] The wearing away is directly visible, immediate, inviting one to come and see, applicable, to be personally experienced by the wise.

(2) "When, Abhaya, this bhikkhu is thus accomplished in virtuous behavior, secluded from sensual pleasures, secluded from unwholesome states, he enters and dwells in the first jhāna . . . [as in 3:58] . . . the fourth jhāna. . . . He does not create any new kamma and he terminates the old kamma having contacted it again and again. The wearing away is directly visible, immediate, inviting one to come and see, applicable, to be personally experienced by the wise.

(3) "When, Abhaya, this bhikkhu is thus accomplished in virtuous behavior and concentration, then, with the destruction of the taints, he realizes for himself with direct knowledge, in this very life, the taintless liberation of mind, liberation by wisdom, and having entered upon it, he dwells in it. He does not create any new kamma and he terminates the old kamma having contacted it again and again. The wearing away is directly visible, immediate, inviting one to come and see, applicable, to be personally experienced by the wise.[500]

"These, Abhaya, are the three kinds of wearing-away purification that have been properly expounded by the Blessed One, the Arahant, the Perfectly Enlightened One who knows and sees, for the purification of beings, for the overcoming of sorrow and lamentation, for the passing away of pain and dejection, for the achievement of the method, for the realization of nibbāna."

When this was said, the Licchavi Paṇḍitakumāra said to the Licchavi Abhaya: "Why, friend Abhaya, don't you thank[501] the Venerable Ānanda for his well-stated words?"

"How, friend, could I not thank the Venerable Ānanda for his well-stated words? [222] If one were not to thank the Venerable Ānanda for his well-stated words, one's head would split apart!"

75 (5) Should Be Encouraged

Then the Venerable Ānanda approached the Blessed One, paid homage to him, and sat down to one side. The Blessed One then said to him:

"Ānanda, those for whom you have compassion and who

think you should be heeded, whether friends or companions, relatives or family members, should be encouraged, settled, and established by you in three things. What three?

(1) "They should be encouraged, settled, and established in unwavering confidence[502] in the Buddha thus: 'The Blessed One is...[as in 3:70]...teacher of devas and humans, the Enlightened One, the Blessed One.'

(2) "They should be encouraged, settled, and established in unwavering confidence in the Dhamma thus: 'The Dhamma is well expounded by the Blessed One, directly visible...[as in 3:70]...to be personally experienced by the wise.'

(3) "They should be encouraged, settled, and established in unwavering confidence in the Saṅgha thus: 'The Saṅgha of the Blessed One's disciples is practicing the good way...[as in 3:70]...the unsurpassed field of merit for the world.'

"There might be, Ānanda, alteration in the four great elements—the earth element, the water element, the fire element, and the air element—but there cannot be alteration in a noble disciple who possesses unwavering confidence in the Buddha. In this context, this is alteration: that this noble disciple who possesses unwavering confidence in the Buddha could be reborn in hell, in the animal realm, or in the sphere of afflicted spirits. Such a thing is impossible. [223]

"There might be, Ānanda, alteration in the four great elements—the earth element, the water element, the fire element, and the air element—but there cannot be alteration in a noble disciple who possesses unwavering confidence in the Dhamma...in the Saṅgha. In this context, this is alteration: that this noble disciple who possesses unwavering confidence in the Saṅgha could be reborn in hell, in the animal realm, or in the sphere of afflicted spirits. Such a thing is impossible.

"Ānanda, those for whom you have compassion and who think you should be heeded, whether friends or companions, relatives or family members, should be encouraged, settled, and established by you in these three things."

76 (6) Existence

Then the Venerable Ānanda approached the Blessed One, paid homage to him, sat down to one side, and said to him:

"Bhante, it is said: 'existence, existence.' In what way, Bhante, is there existence?"[503]

(1) "If, Ānanda, there were no kamma ripening in the sensory realm, would sense-sphere existence be discerned?"

"No, Bhante."

"Thus, Ānanda, for beings hindered by ignorance and fettered by craving, kamma is the field, consciousness the seed, and craving the moisture for their consciousness to be established in an inferior realm. In this way there is the production of renewed existence in the future.[504]

(2) "If, Ānanda, there were no kamma ripening in the form realm, would form-sphere existence be discerned?"

"No, Bhante."

"Thus, Ānanda, for beings hindered by ignorance and fettered by craving, kamma is the field, consciousness the seed, and craving the moisture for their consciousness to be established in a middling realm. In this way there is the production of renewed existence in the future.

(3) "If, Ānanda, there were no kamma ripening in the formless realm, would formless-sphere existence be discerned?" [224]

"No, Bhante."

"Thus, Ānanda, for beings hindered by ignorance and fettered by craving, kamma is the field, consciousness the seed, and craving the moisture for their consciousness to be established in a superior realm. In this way there is the production of renewed existence in the future.

"It is in this way, Ānanda, that there is existence."

77 (7) Volition and Aspiration

Then the Venerable Ānanda approached the Blessed One . . . and said to him:

"Bhante, it is said: 'existence, existence.' In what way, Bhante, is there existence?"

(1) "If, Ānanda, there were no kamma ripening in the sensory realm, would sense-sphere existence be discerned?"

"No, Bhante."

"Thus, Ānanda, for beings hindered by ignorance and fettered by craving, kamma is the field, consciousness the seed, and craving the moisture for their volition and aspiration[505] to be established in an inferior realm. In this way there is the production of renewed existence in the future.

(2) "If, Ānanda, there were no kamma ripening in the form realm, would form-sphere existence be discerned?"

"No, Bhante."

"Thus, Ānanda, for beings hindered by ignorance and fettered by craving, kamma is the field, consciousness the seed, and craving the moisture for their volition and aspiration to be established in a middling realm. In this way there is the production of renewed existence in the future.

(3) "If, Ānanda, there were no kamma ripening in the formless realm, would formless-sphere existence be discerned?"

"No, Bhante."

"Thus, Ānanda, for beings hindered by ignorance and fettered by craving, kamma is the field, consciousness the seed, and craving the moisture for their volition and aspiration to be established in a superior realm. In this way there is the production of renewed existence in the future.

"It is in this way, Ānanda, that there is existence." [225]

78 (8) Setting Up

Then the Venerable Ānanda approached the Blessed One.... The Blessed One then said to him:

"Ānanda, are all behavior and observances, [austere] lifestyles, and spiritual life fruitful when set up as the essence?"[506]

"Not exclusively so, Bhante."

"Well then, Ānanda, distinguish [them]."

"Bhante, suppose one cultivates behavior and observances, an [austere] lifestyle, and a spiritual life, setting them up as if they were the essence. If unwholesome qualities then increase and wholesome qualities decline, such behavior and observances, [austere] lifestyle, and spiritual life, set up as the essence, are fruitless. But if unwholesome qualities decline and wholesome qualities increase, then such behavior and observances, [austere] lifestyle, and spiritual life, set up as the essence, are fruitful."

This is what the Venerable Ānanda said. The Teacher agreed. Then the Venerable Ānanda, thinking, "The Teacher has agreed," paid homage to the Blessed One, circumambulated him keeping the right side toward him, and left.

Then, not long after the Venerable Ānanda had left, the Blessed One addressed the bhikkhus: "Bhikkhus, Ānanda is a trainee, but it is not easy to find one equal to him in wisdom."

79 (9) Fragrance

Then the Venerable Ānanda approached the Blessed One . . . and said to him:

"Bhante, there are these three fragrances that spread with the wind but not against the wind. What three? The fragrance of roots, the fragrance of heartwood, and the fragrance of flowers. These three fragrances spread with the wind but not against the wind. Is there any fragrance that spreads with the wind, against the wind, and both with and against the wind?"

"There is, Ānanda, a fragrance that spreads with the wind, [226] against the wind, and both with and against the wind."

"But, Bhante, what is that fragrance?"

"Here, Ānanda, in whatever village or town a man or a woman has gone for refuge to the Buddha, the Dhamma, and the Saṅgha; he or she is virtuous and of good character, abstaining from the destruction of life, taking what is not given, sexual misconduct, false speech, and liquor, wine, and intoxicants, the basis for heedlessness; and he or she dwells at home with a heart devoid of the stain of miserliness, freely generous, openhanded, delighting in relinquishment, devoted to charity, delighting in giving and sharing—in such a case, ascetics and brahmins in [all] quarters speak praise, saying: 'In such and such a village or town a man or a woman has gone for refuge to the Buddha, the Dhamma, and the Saṅgha . . . delighting in giving and sharing.'

"The deities and the spirits,[507] too, speak praise, saying: 'In such and such a village or town a man or a woman has gone for refuge to the Buddha, the Dhamma, and the Saṅgha . . . is virtuous and of good character . . . delighting in giving and sharing.'

"This, Ānanda, is the fragrance that spreads with the wind, against the wind, and both with and against the wind."

The fragrance of flowers does not spread against the
 wind,
nor the fragrance of sandal, *tagara*,[508] or jasmine.
But the fragrance of good people spreads against the
 wind:
the good person's fragrance pervades all quarters.[509]

80 (10) Abhibhū

Then the Venerable Ānanda approached the Blessed One ... [227] ... and said to him:

"Bhante, in the presence of the Blessed One I heard this; in his presence I learned this: 'Abhibhū, a disciple of the Blessed One Sikhī, while staying in the brahmā world, conveyed his voice throughout a thousandfold world system.'[510] How far, Bhante, can the Blessed One, the Arahant, the Perfectly Enlightened One convey his voice?"

"He was a disciple, Ānanda. The Tathāgatas are immeasurable."[511]

A second time the Venerable Ānanda said to the Blessed One: "Bhante, in the presence of the Blessed One I heard this.... How far, Bhante, can the Blessed One, the Arahant, the Perfectly Enlightened One convey his voice?"

"He was a disciple, Ānanda. The Tathāgatas are immeasurable."

A third time the Venerable Ānanda said to the Blessed One: "Bhante, in the presence of the Blessed One I heard this.... How far, Bhante, can the Blessed One, the Arahant, the Perfectly Enlightened One convey his voice?"

"Have you heard, Ānanda, about a thousandfold minor world system?"

"It is the time for this, Blessed One. It is the time for this, Fortunate One. The Blessed One should speak. Having heard this from the Blessed One, the bhikkhus will retain it in mind."

"Well then, Ānanda, listen and attend closely. I will speak."

"Yes, Bhante," the Venerable Ānanda replied. The Blessed One said this:

(1) "A thousand times the world in which the sun and moon revolve and light up the quarters with their brightness is called a thousandfold minor world system.[512] In that thousandfold world system there are a thousand moons, a thousand suns, a thousand Sinerus king of mountains, a thousand Jambudīpas, a thousand Aparagoyānas, a thousand Uttarakurus, a thousand Pubbavidehas,[513] and a thousand four great oceans; a thousand four great kings, a thousand [heavens] of devas [ruled by] the four great kings, a thousand Tāvatiṃsa [heavens], a thousand [228] Yāma [heavens], a thousand Tusita [heavens], a thousand

[heavens] of devas who delight in creation, a thousand [heavens] of devas who control what is created by others, a thousand brahmā worlds.

(2) "A world that is a thousand times a thousandfold minor world system is called a thousand-to-the-second-power middling world system.[514] (3) A world that is a thousand times a thousand-to-the-second-power middling world system is called a thousand-to-the-third-power great world system. Ānanda, the Tathāgata can convey his voice as far as he wants in a thousand-to-the-third-power great world system."

"But in what way, Bhante, can the Tathāgata convey his voice as far as he wants in a thousand-to-the-third-power great world system?"

"Here, Ānanda, the Tathāgata suffuses with his radiance a thousand-to-the-third-power great world system. When those beings perceive that light, then the Tathāgata projects his voice and makes them hear its sound. It is in such a way, Ānanda, that the Tathāgata can convey his voice as far as he wants in a thousand-to-the-third-power great world system."[515]

When this was said, the Venerable Ānanda said to the Blessed One: "It is my good fortune! I am very fortunate that my Teacher is so powerful and mighty."

When this was said, the Venerable Udāyī said to the Venerable Ānanda: "What is it to you, friend Ānanda, that your Teacher is so powerful and mighty?"[516]

When this was said, the Blessed One said to the Venerable Udāyī: "Do not say so, Udāyī! Do not say so, Udāyī![517] Udāyī, if Ānanda were to die without being free of lust, then because of his confidence he would exercise celestial kingship among the devas seven times and great kingship in this Jambudīpa seven times. However, in this very life Ānanda will attain final nibbāna." [229]

IV. Ascetics

81 (1) Ascetics

"Bhikkhus, there are these three ascetic tasks to be practiced by an ascetic. What three? (1) The undertaking of the training in the higher virtuous behavior, (2) the undertaking of the training in the higher mind, and (3) the undertaking of the training in the higher wisdom. These are the three ascetic tasks to be practiced by an ascetic.

"Therefore, bhikkhus, you should train yourselves thus: 'We will have a keen desire to undertake the training in the higher virtuous behavior; we will have a keen desire to undertake the training in the higher mind; we will have a keen desire to undertake the training in the higher wisdom.' It is in this way that you should train yourselves."

82 (2) The Donkey[518]

"Bhikkhus, suppose a donkey was following right behind a herd of cattle, [thinking]: 'I'm a cow too, I'm a cow too.'[519] (1) But his appearance would not be like that of the cows, (2) his braying would not be like that of the cows, and (3) his footprint would not be like that of the cows. Yet he follows right behind a herd of cattle, [thinking]: 'I'm a cow too, I'm a cow too.'

"So too, a bhikkhu might be following right behind the Saṅgha of bhikkhus, [thinking]: 'I'm a bhikkhu too, I'm a bhikkhu too.' (1) But his desire to undertake the training in the higher virtuous behavior is not like that of the other bhikkhus; (2) his desire to undertake the training in the higher mind is not like that of the other bhikkhus; (3) his desire to undertake the training in the higher wisdom is not like that of the other bhikkhus. Yet he follows right behind the Saṅgha of bhikkhus, [thinking]: 'I'm a bhikkhu too, I'm a bhikkhu too.'

"Therefore, bhikkhus, you should train yourselves thus: 'We will have a keen desire to undertake the training in the higher virtuous behavior; we will have a keen desire to undertake the training in the higher mind; we will have a keen desire to undertake the training in the higher wisdom.' It is in this way that you should train yourselves."

83 (3) The Field

"Bhikkhus, there are these three preliminary tasks of a farmer. What three? (1) Here, the farmer first of all thoroughly plows and harrows the field. (2) Next, he sows seeds at the proper time. (3) And then he occasionally irrigates [230] and drains the field. These are the three preliminary tasks of a farmer.

"So too, bhikkhus, there are these three preliminary tasks of a bhikkhu. What three? (1) The undertaking of the training in the higher virtuous behavior, (2) the undertaking of the training in the higher mind, and (3) the undertaking of the training in the higher wisdom. These are the three preliminary tasks of a bhikkhu.

"Therefore, bhikkhus, you should train yourselves thus: 'We will have a keen desire to undertake the training in the higher virtuous behavior . . . the training in the higher mind . . . the training in the higher wisdom.' It is in this way that you should train yourselves."

84 (4) The Young Vajji

Thus have I heard. On one occasion the Blessed One was dwelling at Vesālī in the hall with the peaked roof in the Great Wood. Then a certain Vajji bhikkhu approached the Blessed One, paid homage to him, and said to him:

"Bhante, every half-month more than a hundred and fifty training rules come up for recitation. I cannot train in them."

"Can you train in the three trainings, bhikkhu: the training in the higher virtuous behavior, the training in the higher mind, and the training in the higher wisdom?"

"I can, Bhante."

"Therefore, bhikkhu, train in the three trainings: the training in the higher virtuous behavior, the training in the higher mind, and the training in the higher wisdom. As you train in them, you will abandon lust, hatred, and delusion. With the abandoning of lust, hatred, and delusion, you will do nothing unwholesome or resort to anything bad."

Then, sometime later, that bhikkhu trained in the higher virtuous behavior, the higher mind, and the higher wisdom. As he [231] trained in them, he abandoned lust, hatred, and delusion. With the abandoning of lust, hatred, and delusion, he did nothing unwholesome and did not resort to anything bad.

85 (5) A Trainee

Then a certain bhikkhu approached the Blessed One . . . and said to him: "Bhante, it is said: 'A trainee, a trainee.' In what way is one a trainee?"

"He trains, bhikkhu, therefore he is called a trainee. And in what does he train? He trains in the higher virtuous behavior; he trains in the higher mind; he trains in the higher wisdom. He trains, bhikkhu, therefore he is called a trainee."

As the trainee trains
along the straight path,
the knowledge of destruction arises first
immediately followed by final knowledge.[520]

Thereafter, when the fetters of existence are destroyed,
for one liberated by final knowledge,
the knowledge arises:
"My liberation is unshakable."[521]

86 (6) The Process of Training (1)

"Bhikkhus, every half-month more than a hundred and fifty training rules come up for recitation; clansmen who desire their own good train in these. These are all comprised within these three trainings. What three? The training in the higher virtuous behavior, the training in the higher mind, and the training in the higher wisdom. These are the three trainings in which all this is comprised.

"Here, bhikkhus, a bhikkhu fulfills virtuous behavior, but cultivates concentration and wisdom only to a moderate extent. He falls into offenses in regard to the lesser and minor training rules and rehabilitates himself.[522] For what reason? Because I have not said that he is incapable of this.[523] But in regard to those training rules that are fundamental to the spiritual life, in conformity with the spiritual life,[524] his behavior is constant and steadfast. Having undertaken the training rules, he trains in them. With the utter destruction of three fetters, [232] he is a stream-enterer, no longer subject to [rebirth in] the lower world, fixed in destiny, with enlightenment as his destination.

"Another bhikkhu fulfills virtuous behavior, but cultivates concentration and wisdom only to a moderate extent. He falls into offenses in regard to the lesser and minor training rules and rehabilitates himself. For what reason? Because I have not said that he is incapable of this. But in regard to those training rules that are fundamental to the spiritual life, in conformity with the spiritual life, his behavior is constant and steadfast. Having undertaken the training rules, he trains in them. With the utter destruction of three fetters and with the diminishing of greed, hatred, and delusion, he is a once-returner who, after coming back to this world only one more time, will make an end of suffering.

"Another bhikkhu fulfills virtuous behavior and concentration, but cultivates wisdom only to a moderate extent. He falls into offenses in regard to the lesser and minor training rules and rehabilitates himself. For what reason? Because I have not said that he is incapable of this. But in regard to those training rules that are fundamental to the spiritual life, in conformity with the spiritual life, his behavior is constant and steadfast. Having undertaken the training rules, he trains in them. With the utter destruction of the five lower fetters, he is one of spontaneous birth, due to attain final nibbāna there without returning from that world.

"Another bhikkhu fulfills virtuous behavior, concentration, and wisdom. He falls into offenses in regard to the lesser and minor training rules and rehabilitates himself. For what reason? Because I have not said that he is incapable of this. But in regard to those training rules that are fundamental to the spiritual life, in conformity with the spiritual life, his behavior is constant and steadfast. Having undertaken the training rules, he trains in them. With the destruction of the taints, he realizes for himself with direct knowledge, in this very life, the taintless liberation of mind, liberation by wisdom, and having entered upon it, he dwells in it.

"Thus, bhikkhus, one who cultivates in part succeeds in part; one who cultivates fully reaches fulfillment. These training rules, I say, are not barren."

87 (7) The Process of Training (2)

"Bhikkhus, every half-month more than a hundred and fifty training rules come up for recitation; clansmen who desire their own good [233] train in these. These are all comprised within these three trainings. What three? The training in the higher virtuous behavior, the training in the higher mind, and the training in the higher wisdom. These are the three trainings in which all this is comprised.

"Here, bhikkhus, a bhikkhu fulfills virtuous behavior, but cultivates concentration and wisdom only to a moderate extent. He falls into offenses in regard to the lesser and minor training rules and rehabilitates himself. For what reason? Because I have not said that he is incapable of this. But in regard to those training rules that are fundamental to the spiritual life, in conformity with the spiritual life, his behavior is constant and steadfast. Having undertaken the training rules, he trains in them. With the utter destruction of three fetters, he is a seven-times-at-most attainer who, after roaming and wandering on among devas and humans seven times at most, makes an end of suffering.[525] With the utter destruction of three fetters, he is a family-to-family attainer who, after roaming and wandering on among good families two or three times, makes an end of suffering. With the utter destruction of three fetters, he is a one-seed attainer who, after being reborn once more in human existence, makes an end of suffering. With the utter destruction of three fetters and with the diminishing of greed, hatred, and delusion, he is a once-returner who, after coming back to this world only one more time, makes an end of suffering.

"Another bhikkhu fulfills virtuous behavior and concentration, but cultivates wisdom only to a moderate extent. He falls into offenses in regard to the lesser and minor training rules and rehabilitates himself. For what reason? Because I have not said that he is incapable of this. But in regard to those training rules that are fundamental to the spiritual life, in conformity with the spiritual life, his behavior is constant and steadfast. Having undertaken the training rules, he trains in them. With the utter destruction of the five lower fetters, he is one bound upstream, heading toward the Akaniṭṭha realm . . . an attainer of nibbāna through exertion . . . an attainer of nibbāna without exertion . . . an attainer of nibbāna upon landing . . . an attainer of nibbāna in the interval.[526]

"Another bhikkhu fulfills virtuous behavior, concentration, and wisdom. He [234] falls into offenses in regard to the lesser and minor training rules and rehabilitates himself. For what reason? Because I have not said that he is incapable of this. But in regard to those training rules that are fundamental to the spiritual life, in conformity with the spiritual life, his behavior is constant and steadfast. Having undertaken the training rules, he trains in them. With the destruction of the taints, he realizes for himself with direct knowledge, in this very life, the taintless liberation of mind, liberation by wisdom, and having entered upon it, he dwells in it.

"Thus, bhikkhus, one who cultivates in part succeeds in part; one who cultivates fully reaches fulfillment. These training rules, I say, are not barren."

88 (8) The Process of Training (3)

"Bhikkhus, every half-month more than a hundred and fifty training rules come up for recitation; clansmen who desire their own good train in these. These are all comprised within these three trainings. What three? The training in the higher virtuous behavior, the training in the higher mind, and the training in the higher wisdom. These are the three trainings in which all this is comprised.

"Here, bhikkhus, a bhikkhu fulfills virtuous behavior, concentration, and wisdom. He falls into offenses in regard to the lesser and minor training rules and rehabilitates himself. For what reason? Because I have not said that he is incapable of this. But in regard to those training rules that are fundamental to the spiritual life, in conformity with the spiritual life, his behavior is constant and steadfast. Having undertaken the training rules, he trains in them. With the destruction of the taints, he realizes for himself with direct knowledge, in this very life, the taintless liberation of mind, liberation by wisdom, and having entered upon it, he dwells in it.

"If he does not attain and penetrate this,[527] with the utter destruction of the five lower fetters, he is an attainer of nibbāna in the interval. If he does not attain and penetrate this, with the utter destruction of the five lower fetters, he is an attainer of nibbāna upon landing . . . an attainer of nibbāna without exertion . . . an attainer of nibbāna through exertion . . . one bound upstream, heading toward the Akaniṭṭha realm.

"If he does not attain and penetrate this, with the utter destruction of three fetters and with the diminishing of greed, hatred, and delusion, he is a once-returner who, after coming back to this [235] world only one more time, makes an end of suffering. If he does not attain and penetrate this, with the utter destruction of three fetters, he is a one-seed attainer who, after being reborn once more in human existence, makes an end of suffering. If he does not attain and penetrate this, with the utter destruction of three fetters, he is a family-to-family attainer who, after roaming and wandering on among good families two or three times, makes an end of suffering. If he does not attain and penetrate this, with the utter destruction of three fetters, he is a seven-times-at-most attainer who, after roaming and wandering on among devas and humans seven times at most, makes an end of suffering.

"Thus, bhikkhus, one who cultivates fully reaches fulfillment; one who cultivates in part succeeds in part. These training rules, I say, are not barren."

89 (9) The Trainings (1)

"Bhikkhus, there are these three trainings. What three? The training in the higher virtuous behavior, the training in the higher mind, and the training in the higher wisdom.

"And what, bhikkhus, is the training in the higher virtuous behavior? Here, a bhikkhu is virtuous.... Having undertaken the training rules, he trains in them. This is called the training in the higher virtuous behavior.

"And what, bhikkhus, is the training in the higher mind? Here, secluded from sensual pleasures, secluded from unwholesome states, a bhikkhu enters and dwells in the first jhāna ... the fourth jhāna.... This is called the training in the higher mind.

"And what, bhikkhus, is the training in the higher wisdom? Here, a bhikkhu understands as it really is: 'This is suffering' ... 'This is the way leading to the cessation of suffering.' This is called the training in the higher wisdom.

"These, bhikkhus, are the three trainings."

90 (10) The Trainings (2)

"Bhikkhus, there are these three trainings. What three? The training in the higher virtuous behavior, the training in the higher mind, and the training in the higher wisdom.

"And what, bhikkhus, is the training in the higher virtuous behavior? Here, a bhikkhu is virtuous.... Having undertaken the training rules, he trains in them. This is called the training in the higher virtuous behavior.

"And what, bhikkhus, is the training in the higher mind? Here, secluded from sensual pleasures, secluded from unwholesome states, a bhikkhu enters and dwells in the first jhāna ... [236] the fourth jhāna.... This is called the training in the higher mind.

"And what, bhikkhus, is the training in the higher wisdom? Here, with the destruction of the taints, a bhikkhu realizes for himself with direct knowledge, in this very life, the taintless liberation of mind, liberation by wisdom, and having entered upon it, he dwells in it.

"These, bhikkhus, are the three trainings."

Energetic, strong, and resolute,
meditative, mindful, the faculties guarded,
one should practice the higher virtue,
the higher mind, and the higher wisdom.

As before, so after;
as after, so before;
as below, so above;
as above, so below;

as by day, so at night;
as at night, so by day,
having overcome all quarters,
with measureless concentration.[528]

They call him a trainee on the path,
whose conduct has been well purified.
They call him enlightened in the world,
a wise one who has fulfilled the practice.[529]

For one freed by craving's destruction,
with the cessation of consciousness
the emancipation of the mind
is like the extinguishing of a lamp.[530]

91 (11) Paṅkadhā

On one occasion the Blessed One was wandering on tour among the Kosalans together with a large Saṅgha of bhikkhus when he reached the Kosalan town of Paṅkadhā. He then dwelled near Paṅkadhā.

Now on that occasion the bhikkhu Kassapagotta was resident at Paṅkadhā. There the Blessed One instructed, encouraged, inspired, and gladdened the bhikkhus with a Dhamma talk connected with the training rules. Then, while the Blessed One was instructing . . . and gladdening the bhikkhus with a talk on the Dhamma connected with the training rules, the bhikkhu Kassapagotta became impatient and bitter, [thinking]: "This ascetic is too stringent."[531]

Then, having dwelled at Paṅkadhā as long as he wanted,

the Blessed One set out on tour toward Rājagaha. Wandering on tour, the Blessed One eventually arrived at Rājagaha. [237] There, at Rājagaha, the Blessed One dwelled on Mount Vulture Peak. Then, not long after the Blessed One had left, the bhikkhu Kassapagotta was filled with remorse and regret, [thinking]: "It is my misfortune and loss that when the Blessed One was instructing, encouraging, inspiring, and gladdening the bhikkhus with a Dhamma talk connected with the training rules, I became impatient and bitter, [thinking]: 'This ascetic is too stringent.' Let me now go to the Blessed One and confess my transgression to him."

Then the bhikkhu Kassapagotta cleaned up his lodging, took his bowl and robe, and set out for Rājagaha. Eventually he arrived at Rājagaha and went to Mount Vulture Peak. He approached the Blessed One, paid homage to him, sat down to one side, and said:

"Bhante, on one occasion the Blessed One was dwelling at the Kosalan town of Paṅkadhā. There the Blessed One instructed, encouraged, inspired, and gladdened the bhikkhus with a Dhamma talk connected with the training rules. While he was instructing . . . and gladdening them, I became impatient and bitter, thinking: 'This ascetic is too stringent.' Then, having dwelled at Paṅkadhā as long as he wanted, the Blessed One set out on tour for Rājagaha. Not long after he left, I was filled with remorse and regret, thinking: 'It is my misfortune and loss that when the Blessed One was instructing . . . and gladdening the bhikkhus with a Dhamma talk connected with the training rules, I became impatient and bitter, thinking: "This ascetic is too stringent." Let me now go to the Blessed One and confess my transgression to him.'

"Bhante, I have committed a transgression [238] in that, when the Blessed One was instructing, encouraging, inspiring, and gladdening the bhikkhus with a Dhamma talk connected with the training rules, I so foolishly, stupidly, and unskillfully became impatient and bitter, thinking: 'This ascetic is too stringent.' Bhante, may the Blessed One accept my transgression seen as a transgression for the sake of future restraint."

"Surely, Kassapa, you have committed a transgression in that, when I was instructing, encouraging, inspiring, and gladdening the bhikkhus with a talk on the Dhamma connected with the training rules, you so foolishly, stupidly, and unskillfully became impatient and bitter, thinking: 'This ascetic is too stringent.' But since you see your transgression as a transgression and make amends for it in accordance with the Dhamma, we accept it. For it is growth in the Noble One's discipline that one sees one's transgression as a transgression, makes amends for it in accordance with the Dhamma, and undertakes future restraint.

(1) "If, Kassapa, an elder bhikkhu[532] does not desire to train and does not speak praise of undertaking the training; if he does not encourage in the training other bhikkhus who do not desire to train; and if he does not speak genuine, real, and timely praise of those bhikkhus who desire to train, I do not speak praise of such an elder bhikkhu. For what reason? Because other bhikkhus, [hearing]: 'The Teacher speaks praise of him,' might associate with him, and those who associate with him might follow his example. If they follow his example, this would lead to their harm and suffering for a long time. Therefore I do not speak praise of such an elder bhikkhu.

(2) "If, Kassapa, a bhikkhu of middle standing . . . (3) If a junior bhikkhu does not desire to train and does not speak praise of undertaking the training; if he does not encourage in the training other bhikkhus who do not desire to train; and if he does not speak genuine, real, and timely praise of those bhikkhus who desire to train, I do not speak praise of such a junior bhikkhu. For what reason? Because other bhikkhus, [hearing]: 'The Teacher speaks praise of him,' might associate with him, and those who associate with him [239] might follow his example. If they follow his example, this would lead to their harm and suffering for a long time. Therefore I do not speak praise of such a junior bhikkhu.

(1) "If, Kassapa, an elder bhikkhu desires to train and speaks praise of undertaking the training; if he encourages in the training other bhikkhus who do not desire to train; and if he speaks genuine, real, and timely praise of those bhikkhus who desire to train, I speak praise of such an elder bhikkhu. For what reason? Because other bhikkhus, [hearing]: 'The Teacher speaks praise of him,' might associate with him, and those who associate with him might follow his example. If they follow his example, this would lead to their welfare and happiness for a long time. Therefore I speak praise of such an elder bhikkhu.

(2) "If, Kassapa, a bhikkhu of middle standing . . . (3) If a junior bhikkhu desires to train and speaks praise of undertaking the training; if he encourages in the training other bhikkhus who do not desire to train; and if he speaks genuine, real, and timely praise of those bhikkhus who desire to train, I speak praise of such a junior bhikkhu. For what reason? Because other bhikkhus, [hearing]: 'The Teacher speaks praise of him,' might associate with him, and those who associate with him might follow his example. If they follow his example, this would lead to their welfare and happiness for a long time. Therefore I speak praise of such a junior bhikkhu."

V. A Lump of Salt[533]

92 (1) Urgent

"Bhikkhus, there are these three urgent tasks of a farmer.[534] What three? (1) First, the farmer swiftly yet thoroughly plows the field and swiftly yet thoroughly harrows it. (2) Next, he swiftly sows seeds. (3) And then he swiftly [240] irrigates and drains the field. These are the three urgent tasks of a farmer.

"This farmer has no psychic potency or spiritual might [by which he could command]: 'Let my crops start growing today! Let them mature tomorrow! Let them bear grain the day after tomorrow!' But, with the change of seasons, there comes a time when the crops grow, mature, and bear grain.

"So too, bhikkhus, there are these three urgent tasks of a bhikkhu. What three? (1) The undertaking of the training in the higher virtuous behavior, (2) the undertaking of the training in the higher mind, and (3) the undertaking of the training in the higher wisdom. These are the three urgent tasks of a bhikkhu.

"This bhikkhu has no psychic potency or spiritual might [by which he could command]: 'Let my mind be liberated from the taints by non-clinging today, or tomorrow, or the day after tomorrow!' Rather, as this bhikkhu trains in the higher virtuous behavior, the higher mind, and the higher wisdom, there comes an occasion when his mind is liberated from the taints by non-clinging.

"Therefore, bhikkhus, you should train yourselves thus: 'We will have a keen desire to undertake the training in the higher virtuous behavior, the training in the higher mind, and the training in the higher wisdom.' It is in this way that you should train yourselves."

93 (2) Solitude

"Bhikkhus, wanderers of other sects prescribe these three kinds of solitude. What three? Solitude with respect to robes, solitude with respect to almsfood, and solitude with respect to lodgings.[535]

"This, bhikkhus, is what wanderers of other sects prescribe as solitude with respect to robes: they wear hemp robes, robes of hemp-mixed cloth, shroud robes, rag-robes; robes made from tree bark, antelope hides, strips of antelope hide; robes of *kusa* grass, bark fabric, or wood-shavings fabric; a blanket made of head hair or of animal wool, [241] a covering made of owls' wings. That is what wanderers of other sects prescribe as solitude with respect to robes.

"This is what wanderers of other sects prescribe as solitude with respect to almsfood: they eat greens, millet, forest rice, hide-parings, moss, rice bran, the scum of rice, sesamum flour, grass, or cow dung. They subsist on forest roots and fruits; they feed on fallen fruits. That is what wanderers of other sects prescribe as solitude with respect to almsfood.

"This is what wanderers of other sects prescribe as solitude with respect to lodgings: a forest, the foot of a tree, a charnel ground, remote lodgings in forests and jungle groves, the open air, a heap of straw, a chaff-house. That is what wanderers of other sects prescribe as solitude with respect to lodgings.

"These are the three kinds of solitude that wanderers of other sects prescribe.

"In this Dhamma and discipline, bhikkhus, there are these three kinds of solitude for a bhikkhu. What three?

"Here, (1) a bhikkhu is virtuous; he has abandoned immorality and remains secluded from it. (2) He holds right view; he has abandoned wrong view and remains secluded from it.[536] (3) He is one whose taints are destroyed; he has abandoned the taints and remains secluded from them.

"When a bhikkhu is virtuous, one who has abandoned immorality and remains secluded from it; when he is one of right view, who has abandoned wrong view and remains secluded from it; when he is one whose taints are destroyed, who has abandoned the taints and remains secluded from them, he is then called a bhikkhu who has attained the foremost, attained the core, one who is pure and established in the core.

"Suppose, bhikkhus, there is a farmer whose field of hill rice has ripened. The farmer would swiftly have the plants cut. Then he would swiftly have the plants collected. Then he would swiftly [242] have them transported [to the threshing place]. Then he would swiftly pile them up, have them threshed, get the straw removed, get the chaff removed, and winnow it. Then he would swiftly have it brought over, get it pounded, and get the husks removed. In this way, the farmer's grains of rice would be foremost, attained the core, pure, and established in the core.

"So too, bhikkhus, when a bhikkhu is virtuous . . . one of right view . . . one who has abandoned the taints and remains secluded from them, he is then called a bhikkhu who is foremost, attained the core, pure, and established in the core."

94 (3) Autumn[537]

"Bhikkhus, just as, in the autumn, when the sky is clear and cloudless, the sun, ascending in the sky, dispels all darkness from space as it shines and beams and radiates, so too, when the dust-free, stainless Dhamma-eye arises in the noble disciple, then, together with the arising of vision, the noble disciple abandons three fetters: personal-existence view, doubt, and wrong grasp of behavior and observances.[538]

"Afterward, when he departs from two states, longing and ill will, then, secluded from sensual pleasures, secluded from unwholesome states, he enters and dwells in the first jhāna, which consists of rapture and pleasure born of seclusion, accompanied by thought and examination. If, bhikkhus, the noble disciple should pass away on that occasion, there is no fetter bound by which he might return to this world."[539]

95 (4) Assemblies

"Bhikkhus, there are these three kinds of assemblies.[540] What three? The assembly of the foremost, the divided assembly, and the harmonious assembly. [243]

(1) "And what, bhikkhus, is the assembly of the foremost?

Here, in this kind of assembly the elder bhikkhus do not become luxurious and lax, but discard backsliding and take the lead in solitude; they arouse energy for the attainment of the as-yet-unattained, for the achievement of the as-yet-unachieved, for the realization of the as-yet-unrealized. [Those in] the next generation follow their example. They too do not become luxurious and lax, but discard backsliding and take the lead in solitude; they too arouse energy for the attainment of the as-yet-unattained, for the achievement of the as-yet-unachieved, for the realization of the as-yet-unrealized. This is called the assembly of the foremost.

(2) "And what is the divided assembly? Here, the assembly in which the bhikkhus take to arguing and quarreling and fall into disputes, stabbing each other with piercing words, is called the divided assembly.

(3) "And what is the harmonious assembly? Here, the assembly in which the bhikkhus dwell in concord, harmoniously, without disputes, blending like milk and water, viewing each other with eyes of affection, is called the harmonious assembly.

"When the bhikkhus dwell in concord, harmoniously, without disputes, blending like milk and water, viewing each other with eyes of affection, on that occasion they generate much merit. On that occasion the bhikkhus dwell in a divine abode, that is, in the liberation of mind through altruistic joy. When one is joyful, rapture arises. For one with a rapturous mind, the body becomes tranquil. One tranquil in body feels pleasure. For one feeling pleasure, the mind becomes concentrated.

"Just as, when it is raining and the rain pours down in thick droplets on a mountain top, the water flows down along the slope and fills the clefts, gullies, and creeks; these, becoming full, fill up the pools; these, becoming full, fill up the lakes; these, becoming full, fill up the streams; these, becoming full, fill up the rivers; and these, becoming full, fill up the ocean; so too, when the bhikkhus dwell in concord, harmoniously, without disputes, blending like milk and water, viewing each other [244] with eyes of affection, on that occasion they generate much merit. On that occasion the bhikkhus dwell in a divine abode, that is, in the liberation of mind through altruistic joy. When one is joyful, rapture arises. For one with a rapturous mind, the body becomes tranquil. One tranquil in body feels pleasure. For one feeling pleasure, the mind becomes concentrated.

"These, bhikkhus, are the three kinds of assemblies."

96 (5) Thoroughbred (1)

"Bhikkhus, possessing three factors a king's excellent thoroughbred horse is worthy of a king, an accessory of a king, and reckoned as a factor of kingship. What three? Here, a king's excellent thoroughbred horse possesses beauty, strength, and speed. Possessing these three factors, a king's excellent thoroughbred horse is . . . reckoned as a factor of kingship.

"So too, possessing three qualities, a bhikkhu is worthy of gifts, worthy of hospitality, worthy of offerings, worthy of reverential salutation, an unsurpassed field of merit for the world. What three? Here, a bhikkhu possesses beauty, strength, and speed.

(1) "And how does a bhikkhu possess beauty? Here, a bhikkhu is virtuous; he dwells restrained by the Pātimokkha, possessed of good conduct and resort, seeing danger in minute faults. Having undertaken the training rules, he trains in them. It is in this way that a bhikkhu possesses beauty.

(2) "And how does a bhikkhu possess strength? Here, a bhikkhu arouses energy for abandoning unwholesome qualities and acquiring wholesome qualities; he is strong, firm in exertion, not casting off the duty of cultivating wholesome qualities. It is in this way that a bhikkhu possesses strength.

(3) "And how does a bhikkhu possess speed? Here, a bhikkhu understands as it really is: 'This is suffering,' and 'This is the origin of suffering, [245] and 'This is the cessation of suffering,' and 'This is the way leading to the cessation of suffering.' It is in this way that a bhikkhu possesses speed.

"Possessing these three qualities, a bhikkhu is worthy of gifts, worthy of hospitality, worthy of offerings, worthy of reverential salutation, an unsurpassed field of merit for the world."

97 (6) Thoroughbred (2)

[All as in 3:96, with only the following difference in factor (3):]

"And how does a bhikkhu possess speed? Here, with the utter destruction of the five lower fetters, a bhikkhu is one of spontaneous birth, due to attain final nibbāna there without ever returning from that world. It is in this way that a bhikkhu possesses speed.

"Possessing these three qualities, a bhikkhu is . . . an unsurpassed field of merit for the world."

98 (7) Thoroughbred (3)

[All as in 3:96, with only the following difference in factor (3):] [246]

"And how does a bhikkhu possess speed? Here, with the destruction of the taints, a bhikkhu has realized for himself with direct knowledge, in this very life, the taintless liberation of mind, liberation by wisdom, and having entered upon it, he dwells in it. It is in this way that a bhikkhu possesses speed.

"Possessing these three qualities, a bhikkhu is . . . an unsurpassed field of merit for the world."

99 (8) Bark Fabric

"Bhikkhus, when it is new, cloth made of bark fabric[541] is ugly, uncomfortable, and of little value. When it has been worn,[542] cloth made of bark fabric is ugly, uncomfortable, and of little value. When it is old, cloth made of bark fabric is still ugly, uncomfortable, and of little value. They use old cloth made of bark fabric for cleaning pots or they discard it on a rubbish heap.

(1) (i)[543] "So too, bhikkhus, if a junior bhikkhu is immoral, of bad character, this, I say, counts as his ugliness. [247] Just as cloth made of bark fabric is ugly, so, I say, this person is similar.

(ii) "For those who associate with him, resort to him, attend on him, and follow his example, this leads to their harm and suffering for a long time. This, I say, counts as his uncomfortableness. Just as cloth made of bark fabric is uncomfortable, so, I say, this person is similar.

(iii) "When he accepts a robe, almsfood, lodging, and medicines and provisions for the sick, this [acceptance] is not of great fruit and benefit for those [who offer such things]. This, I say, counts as his being of little value. Just as cloth made of bark fabric is of little value, so, I say, this person is similar.

(2) "If a bhikkhu of middle standing . . .

(3) "If an elder bhikkhu is immoral, of bad character, this, I say, counts as his ugliness. . . . [all as above] . . . Just as cloth made of bark fabric is of little value, so, I say, this person is similar.

"If such an elder bhikkhu speaks in the midst of the Saṅgha, the bhikkhus say to him: 'What gives you, an incompetent fool, the right to speak? Do you think you too are entitled to speak?' He then becomes angry and displeased and utters speech on account of which the Saṅgha expels him, as if [discarding] the clothing made of bark fabric on the rubbish heap.[544]

"When it is new, bhikkhus, cloth from Kāsi is beautiful, comfortable, and of great value. When it has been worn, [248] cloth from Kāsi is beautiful, comfortable, and of great value. When it is old, cloth from Kāsi is beautiful, comfortable, and of great value. They use old cloth from Kāsi as a wrapping for gems or they deposit it in a fragrant casket.

(1) (i) "So too, if a junior bhikkhu is virtuous, of good character, this, I say, counts as his beauty. Just as cloth from Kāsi is beautiful, so, I say, this person is similar.

(ii) "For those who associate with him, resort to him, attend on him, and follow his example, this leads to their welfare and happiness for a long time. This, I say, counts as his comfortableness. Just as cloth from Kāsi is comfortable, so, I say, this person is similar.

(iii) "When he accepts a robe, almsfood, lodging, and medicines and provisions for the sick, this [acceptance] is of great fruit and benefit for those [who offer such things]. This, I say, counts as his being of great value. Just as cloth from Kāsi is of great value, so, I say, this person is similar.

(2) "If a bhikkhu of middle standing . . .

(3) "If an elder bhikkhu is virtuous, of good character, this, I say, counts as his beauty. . . . [all as above] . . . Just as cloth from Kāsi is of great value, so, I say, this person is similar.

"If such an elder bhikkhu speaks in the midst of the Saṅgha, [249] the bhikkhus say: 'Please let the venerable ones be quiet. An elder bhikkhu is speaking on the Dhamma and the discipline.' Those words of his should be preserved, just as they deposit a cloth from Kāsi in a fragrant casket.[545]

"Therefore, bhikkhus, you should train yourselves thus: 'We will be like cloth from Kāsi, not like cloth made of bark fabric.' It is in such a way that you should train yourselves."

100 (9) A Lump of Salt

"Bhikkhus, if one were to say thus: 'A person experiences kamma in precisely the same way that he created it,' in such a case there could be no living of the spiritual life and no opportunity would be seen for completely making an end of suffering.[546] But if one were to say thus: 'When a person creates kamma that is to be experienced in a particular way, he experiences its result precisely in that way,' in such a case the living of the spiritual life is possible and an opportunity is seen for completely making an end of suffering.[547]

"Here, bhikkhus, some person has created trifling bad kamma yet it leads him to hell, while some other person here has created exactly the same trifling kamma yet it is to be experienced in this very life, without even a slight [residue] being seen, much less abundant [residue].

"What kind of person creates trifling bad kamma that leads him to hell? Here, some person is undeveloped in body, virtuous behavior, mind, and wisdom; he is limited and has a mean character,[548] and he dwells in suffering.[549] When such a person creates trifling bad kamma, it leads him to hell.

"What kind of person creates exactly the same trifling bad kamma and yet it is to be experienced in this very life, without even a slight [residue] being seen, much less abundant [residue]? Here, some person is developed in body, virtuous behavior, mind, and wisdom. He is unlimited and has a lofty character, and he dwells without measure.[550] When such a person creates exactly the same trifling bad kamma, it is to be experienced in this very life, without even a slight [residue] being seen, much less abundant [residue].[551] [250]

(1) "Suppose a man would drop a lump of salt into a small bowl of water. What do you think, bhikkhus? Would that lump of salt make the small quantity of water in the bowl[552] salty and undrinkable?"

"Yes, Bhante. For what reason? Because the water in the bowl is limited, thus that lump of salt would make it salty and undrinkable."

"But suppose a man would drop a lump of salt into the river Ganges. What do you think, bhikkhus? Would that lump of salt make the river Ganges become salty and undrinkable?"

"No, Bhante. For what reason? Because the river Ganges contains a large volume of water, thus that lump of salt would not make it salty and undrinkable."

"So too, bhikkhus, some person here has created trifling bad kamma yet it leads him to hell, while some other person here has created exactly the same trifling kamma yet it is to be experienced in this very life, without even a slight [residue] being seen, much less abundant [residue].

"What kind of person creates trifling bad kamma that leads him to hell? Here, some person is undeveloped in body, virtuous behavior, mind, and wisdom. When such a person creates a trifling bad kamma, it leads him to hell.

"What kind of person creates exactly the same trifling bad kamma and yet it is to be experienced in this very life, without even a slight [residue] being seen, much less an abundant [residue]? Here, some person is developed in body, virtuous behavior, mind, and wisdom. When such a person has created exactly the same trifling bad kamma, it is to be experienced in this very life, without even a slight [residue] being seen, much less abundant [residue].

(2) "Here, bhikkhus, someone is imprisoned for [stealing] half a *kahāpaṇa*, a *kahāpaṇa*, [251] or a hundred *kahāpaṇas*,[553] while someone else is not imprisoned for [stealing] the same amount of money.

"What kind of person is imprisoned for [stealing] half a *kahāpaṇa*, a *kahāpaṇa*, or a hundred *kahāpaṇas*? Here, someone is poor, with little property and wealth. Such a person is imprisoned for [stealing] half a *kahāpaṇa*, a *kahāpaṇa*, or a hundred *kahāpaṇas*.

"What kind of person is not imprisoned for [stealing] half a *kahāpaṇa*, a *kahāpaṇa*, or a hundred *kahāpaṇas*? Here, someone is rich, with much money and wealth. Such a person is not imprisoned for [stealing] half a *kahāpaṇa*, a *kahāpaṇa*, or a hundred *kahāpaṇas*.

"So too, bhikkhus, some person has created trifling bad kamma yet it leads him to hell, while some other person here has created exactly the same trifling kamma yet it is to be experienced in this very life, without even a slight [residue] being seen, much less abundant [residue].

"What kind of person creates trifling bad kamma that leads him to hell? Here, some person is undeveloped in body . . . and wisdom. When such a person has created trifling bad kamma, it leads him to hell.

"What kind of person creates exactly the same trifling bad kamma and yet it is to be experienced in this very life, without even a slight [residue] being seen, much less an abundant [residue]? Here, some person is developed in body, virtuous behavior, mind, and wisdom. When such a person has created exactly the same trifling bad kamma, it is to be experienced in this very life, without even a slight [residue] being seen, much less abundant [residue].

(3) "Bhikkhus, take the case of a sheep merchant or butcher, [252] who can execute, imprison, fine, or otherwise penalize someone who has stolen one of his sheep but can't do so to someone else who has stolen his sheep.

"What kind of person[554] can the sheep merchant or butcher execute, imprison, fine, or otherwise penalize for stealing a sheep? One who is poor, with little property and wealth. The sheep merchant or butcher can execute, imprison, fine, or otherwise penalize such a person for stealing a sheep.

"What kind of person can't the sheep merchant or butcher execute, imprison, fine, or otherwise penalize for stealing a sheep? One who is rich, with a lot of money and wealth, a king or royal minister. The sheep merchant or butcher can't execute, imprison, fine, or otherwise penalize such a person for stealing a sheep; he can only plead with him: 'Sir, return my sheep or pay me for it.'

"So too, bhikkhus, some person has created trifling bad kamma yet it leads him to hell, while some other person here has created exactly the same trifling kamma yet it is to be experienced in this very life, without even a slight [residue] being seen, much less abundant [residue].

"What kind of person creates trifling bad kamma that leads him to hell? Here, some person is undeveloped in body, virtuous behavior, mind, and wisdom; he is limited and has a mean character, and he dwells in suffering. When such kind of [253] person has created a trifling bad kamma, it leads him to hell.

"What kind of person creates exactly the same trifling bad kamma and yet it is to be experienced in this very life, without even a slight [residue] being seen, much less an abundant [residue]? Here, some person is developed in body, virtuous behavior, mind, and wisdom. He is unlimited and has a lofty character, and he dwells without measure. When such a person has created exactly the same trifling bad kamma, it is to be experienced in this very life, without even a slight [residue] being seen, much less abundant [residue].

"If, bhikkhus, one were to say thus: 'A person experiences kamma in precisely the same way that he created it,' in such a case there could be no living of the spiritual life and no opportunity would be seen for completely making an end of suffering. But if one were to say thus: 'When a person creates kamma that is to be experienced in a particular way, he experiences its result precisely in that way,' in such a case the living of the spiritual life is possible and an opportunity is seen for completely making an end of suffering."

101 (10) The Soil Remover

"Bhikkhus, there are gross defilements of gold: soil, grit, and gravel. Now the soil remover or his apprentice first pours the gold into a trough and washes, rinses, and cleans it. When that has been removed and eliminated, there still remain middle-size defilements in the gold: fine grit and coarse sand. The soil remover or his apprentice washes, rinses, and cleans it again. When that has been removed and eliminated, there still remain subtle defilements in the gold: fine sand and black dust. So the soil remover or his apprentice washes, rinses, and cleans it again. When that has been removed and eliminated, only grains of gold remain.

"The goldsmith or his apprentice now pours the gold into a melting pot, and fans it, melts it, [254] and smelts it. But even when this has been done, the gold is not yet settled and the dross has not yet been entirely removed.[555] The gold is not yet malleable, wieldy, and luminous, but still brittle and not properly fit for work.

"But as the goldsmith or his apprentice continues to fan, melt, and smelt the gold, a time comes when the gold is settled and the dross has been entirely removed, so that the gold becomes malleable, wieldy, and luminous, pliant and properly fit for work. Then whatever kind of ornament the goldsmith wishes to make from it—whether a bracelet, earrings, a necklace, or a golden garland—he can achieve his purpose.

"So too, bhikkhus, when a bhikkhu is devoted to the higher mind, (1) there are in him gross defilements: bodily, verbal, and mental misconduct. An earnest, capable bhikkhu abandons, dispels, terminates, and obliterates them. When this has been done, (2) there remain in him middling defilements: sensual thoughts, thoughts of ill will, and thoughts of harming. An earnest, capable bhikkhu abandons, dispels, terminates, and obliterates them. When this has been done, (3) there remain in him subtle defilements: thoughts about his relations,[556] thoughts about his country, and thoughts about his reputation.[557] An earnest, capable bhikkhu abandons, dispels, terminates, and obliterates them. When this has been done, then there remain thoughts connected with the Dhamma.[558] That concentration is not peaceful and sublime, not gained by full tranquilization,[559] not attained to unification, but is reined in and checked by forcefully suppressing [the defilements].[560]

"But, bhikkhus, there comes a time when his mind becomes internally steady, composed, unified, and concentrated. That concentration is peaceful and sublime, gained by full tranquilization, and attained to unification; it is not reined in and checked by forcefully suppressing [the defilements].[561] Then, there being a suitable basis, he is capable of realizing any state realizable by direct knowledge toward which he might incline his mind.[562] [255]

"If he wishes:[563] 'May I wield the various kinds of psychic potency: having been one, may I become many; having been many, may I become one; may I appear and vanish; may I go unhindered through a wall, through a rampart, through a mountain as though through space; may I dive in and out of the earth as though it were water; may I walk on water without sinking as though it were earth; seated cross-legged, may I travel in space like a bird; with my hand may I touch and stroke the moon and sun so powerful and mighty; may I exercise mastery with the body as far as the brahmā world,' he is capable of realizing it, there being a suitable basis.

"If he wishes: 'May I, with the divine ear element, which is purified and surpasses the human, hear both kinds of sounds, the divine and human, those that are far as well as near,' he is capable of realizing it, there being a suitable basis.

"If he wishes: 'May I understand the minds of other beings and persons, having encompassed them with my own mind. May I understand a mind with lust as a mind with lust and a mind without lust as a mind without lust; a mind with hatred as a mind with hatred and a mind without hatred as a mind without hatred; a mind with delusion as a mind with delusion and a mind without delusion as a mind without delusion; a contracted mind as contracted and a distracted mind as distracted;

an exalted mind as exalted and an unexalted mind as unexalted; a surpassable mind as surpassable and an unsurpassable mind as unsurpassable; a concentrated mind as concentrated and an unconcentrated mind as unconcentrated; a liberated mind as liberated and an unliberated mind as unliberated,'[564] he is capable of realizing it, there being a suitable basis.

"If he wishes: 'May I recollect my manifold past abodes, that is, one birth, two births, three births, four births, five births, ten births, twenty births, thirty births, forty births, fifty births, a hundred births, a thousand births, a hundred thousand births, many eons of world-dissolution, many eons of world-evolution, many eons of world-dissolution and world-evolution thus: "There [256] I was so named, of such a clan, with such an appearance, such was my food, such my experience of pleasure and pain, such my life span; passing away from there, I was reborn elsewhere, and there too I was so named, of such a clan, with such an appearance, such was my food, such my experience of pleasure and pain, such my life span; passing away from there, I was reborn here"—may I thus recollect my manifold past abodes with their aspects and details,' he is capable of realizing it, there being a suitable basis.

"If he wishes: 'May I, with the divine eye, which is purified and surpasses the human, see beings passing away and being reborn, inferior and superior, beautiful and ugly, fortunate and unfortunate, and understand how beings fare in accordance with their kamma thus: "These beings who engaged in misconduct by body, speech, and mind, who reviled the noble ones, held wrong view, and undertook kamma based on wrong view, with the breakup of the body, after death, have been reborn in the plane of misery, in a bad destination, in the lower world, in hell; but these beings who engaged in good conduct by body, speech, and mind, who did not revile the noble ones, who held right view, and undertook kamma based on right view, with the breakup of the body, after death, have been reborn in a good destination, in the heavenly world"—thus with the divine eye, which is purified and surpasses the human, may I see beings passing away and being reborn, inferior and superior, beautiful and ugly, fortunate and unfortunate, and understand how beings fare in accordance with their kamma,' he is capable of realizing it, there being a suitable basis.

"If he wishes: 'May I, with the destruction of the taints, in this very life realize for myself with direct knowledge the taintless liberation of mind, liberation by wisdom, and having entered upon it, may I dwell in it,' he is capable of realizing it, there being a suitable basis."

102 (11) A Goldsmith[565]

"Bhikkhus, when a bhikkhu is devoted to the higher mind, from time to time he should give attention to three marks.[566] (1) From time to time he should give attention to the mark of concentration, (2) from time to time to the mark of exertion, and (3) from time to time to the mark of equanimity.

"If a bhikkhu devoted to the higher mind attends exclusively to the mark of concentration, it is possible that his mind will veer toward laziness. If he attends exclusively to the mark of exertion, it is possible that his mind will veer toward restlessness. If [257] he attends exclusively to the mark of equanimity, it is possible that his mind will not be properly concentrated for the destruction of the taints. But when a bhikkhu devoted to the higher mind from time to time gives attention to the mark of concentration, from time to time to the mark of exertion, and from time to time to the mark of equanimity, his mind becomes malleable, wieldy, and luminous, pliant and properly concentrated for the destruction of the taints.

"Suppose, bhikkhus, a goldsmith or his apprentice would prepare a furnace, heat up the crucible, take some gold with tongs, and put it into the crucible. Then from time to time he would blow on it, from time to time sprinkle water over it, and from time to time just look on. If the goldsmith or his apprentice were to exclusively blow on the gold, it is possible that the gold would just burn up. If he were to exclusively sprinkle water on the gold, it is possible the gold would cool down. If he were exclusively to just look on, it is possible the gold would not reach the right consistency. But if the goldsmith or his apprentice from time to time blows on it, from time to time sprinkles water over it, and from time to time just looks on, the gold would become malleable, wieldy, and luminous, pliant and properly fit for work. Then whatever kind of ornament the goldsmith wishes to make from it—whether a bracelet, earrings, a necklace, or a golden garland—he can achieve his purpose.

"So too, when a bhikkhu is devoted to the higher mind, from time to time he should give attention to three marks. From time to time he should give attention to the mark of concentration, from time to time to the mark of exertion, and from time to time to the mark of equanimity.

"If a bhikkhu devoted to the higher mind attends exclusively to the mark of concentration, [258] it is possible that his mind will veer toward laziness. If he attends exclusively to the mark of exertion, it is possible that his mind will veer toward restlessness. If he attends exclusively to the mark of equanimity, it is possible that his mind will not be properly concentrated for the destruction of the taints. But when from time to time he gives attention to the mark of concentration, from time to time to the mark of exertion, and from time to time to the mark of equanimity, his mind becomes malleable, wieldy, and luminous, not brittle but properly concentrated for the destruction of the taints. Then, there being a suitable basis, he is capable of realizing any state realizable by direct knowledge toward which he might incline his mind.

"If he wishes: 'May I wield the various kinds of psychic potency' . . . [all as in 3:101, down to:] . . . If he wishes: 'May I, with the destruction of the taints, in this very life realize for myself with direct knowledge the taintless liberation of mind, liberation by wisdom, and having entered upon it, may I dwell in it,' he is capable of realizing it, there being a suitable basis."

The Third Fifty

I. Enlightenment

103 (1) Before

"Bhikkhus, before my enlightenment, while I was just a bodhisatta, not yet fully enlightened, it occurred to me: (1) 'What is the gratification in the world? (2) What is the danger in it? (3) What is the escape from it?'[567]

"Then, bhikkhus, it occurred to me: 'The pleasure and joy that arise in dependence on the world: this is the gratification in the world. That the world is impermanent, suffering, and subject to change: this is the danger in the world. The removal and abandonment of desire and lust for the world: this is the escape from the world.'

"So long, bhikkhus, as I did not directly know as they really are the gratification in the world [259] as gratification, the danger as danger, and the escape from it as escape, I did not claim to have awakened to the unsurpassed perfect enlightenment in this world with its devas, Māra, and Brahmā, in this population with its ascetics and brahmins, its devas and humans. But when I directly knew as it really is the gratification in the world as gratification, the danger as danger, and the escape from it as escape, then I claimed to have awakened to the unsurpassed perfect enlightenment in this world with . . . its devas and humans.

"The knowledge and vision arose in me: 'Unshakable is my liberation of mind; this is my last birth; now there is no more renewed existence.'"

104 (2) Gratification (1)[568]

(1) "Bhikkhus, I set out seeking the gratification in the world. Whatever gratification there is in the world—that I found. I have clearly seen with wisdom just how far the gratification in the world extends.

(2) "I set out seeking the danger in the world. Whatever danger there is in the world—that I found. I have clearly seen with wisdom just how far the danger in the world extends.

(3) "I set out seeking the escape from the world. Whatever escape there is from the world—that I found. I have clearly seen with wisdom just how far the escape from the world extends.

"So long, bhikkhus, as I did not directly know as they really are the gratification in the world as gratification, the danger as danger, and the escape from it as the escape, I did not claim to have awakened to the unsurpassed perfect enlightenment in this world with its devas, Māra, and Brahmā, in this generation with its ascetics and brahmins, its devas and humans. But when I directly knew as it really is the gratification in the world as gratification, the danger as danger, and the escape from it as escape, then I claimed to have awakened to the unsurpassed perfect enlightenment in this world with . . . its devas and humans.

"The knowledge and vision arose in me: 'Unshakable is my liberation of mind; this is my last birth; now there is no more renewed existence.'" [260]

105 (3) Gratification (2)

"Bhikkhus, (1) if there were no gratification in the world, beings would not become enamored of it; but because there is gratification in the world, beings become enamored of it. (2) If there were no danger in the world, beings would not become disenchanted with it; but because there is danger in the world, beings become disenchanted with it. (3) If there were no escape from the world, beings would not escape from it; but because there is an escape from the world, beings escape from it.

"So long, bhikkhus, as beings have not directly known as they really are the gratification in the world as gratification, the danger as danger, and the escape from it as escape, they have not escaped from this world with its devas, Māra, and Brahmā, from this population with its ascetics and brahmins, its devas and humans; they have not become detached from it, released from it, nor do they dwell with a mind rid of barriers. But when beings have directly known as it really is the gratification in the world as gratification, the danger as danger, and the escape from it as escape, then they have escaped from this world with . . . its devas and humans; they have become detached from it, released from it, and they dwell with a mind rid of barriers."

106 (4) Ascetics[569]

"Bhikkhus, those ascetics or brahmins who do not understand as it really is (1) the gratification in the world as gratification, (2) the danger as danger, and (3) the escape from it as escape: these I do not consider to be ascetics among ascetics or brahmins among brahmins, and these venerable ones do not, by realizing it for themselves with direct knowledge, in this very life enter and dwell in the goal of asceticism or the goal of brahminhood.

"But those ascetics and brahmins who understand as it really is the gratification in the world as gratification, the danger as danger, and the escape from it as escape: these I consider to be ascetics among ascetics and brahmins among brahmins, and these venerable ones, by realizing it for themselves with direct knowledge, in this very life enter and dwell in the goal of asceticism and the goal of brahminhood." [261]

107 (5) Wailing

"Bhikkhus, (1) in the Noble One's discipline, singing is wailing. (2) In the Noble One's discipline, dancing is madness. (3) In the Noble One's discipline, to laugh excessively, displaying one's teeth, is childishness. Therefore, bhikkhus, in regard to singing and dancing [let there be] the demolition of the bridge. When you smile rejoicing in the Dhamma, you may simply show a smile."[570]

108 (6) No Satiation

"Bhikkhus, there are three things that give no satiation by indulging in them. What three? (1) There is no satiation by indulging in sleep. (2) There is no satiation by indulging in liquor and wine. (3) There is no satiation by indulging in sexual intercourse. These are the three things that give no satiation by indulging in them."

109 (7) Peaked Roof (1)

Then the householder Anāthapiṇḍika approached the Blessed One, paid homage to him, and sat down to one side. The Blessed One then said to him:

"Householder, when the mind is unprotected, bodily, verbal, and mental actions are unprotected.

"For one whose bodily, verbal, and mental deeds are unprotected, bodily, verbal, and mental actions become tainted.[571] For one whose bodily, verbal, and mental deeds become tainted, bodily, verbal, and mental actions become rotten. One whose bodily, verbal, and mental deeds become rotten will not have a good death.[572]

"Suppose a house with a peaked roof is badly thatched: then the roof peak, the rafters, and the walls are unprotected; the roof peak, the rafters, and the walls become tainted; the roof peak, the rafters, and the walls become rotten.

"So too, householder, [262] when the mind is unprotected, bodily, verbal, and mental actions are unprotected.... One whose bodily, verbal, and mental deeds are rotten will not have a good death.

"When, householder, the mind is protected, bodily, verbal, and mental actions are protected.

"For one whose bodily, verbal, and mental deeds are protected, bodily, verbal, and mental actions do not become tainted.

For one whose bodily, verbal, and mental deeds do not become tainted, bodily, verbal, and mental actions do not become rotten. One whose bodily, verbal, and mental deeds do not become rotten will have a good death.

"Suppose a house with a peaked roof is well thatched: then the roof peak, the rafters, and the walls are protected; the roof peak, the rafters, and the walls do not become tainted; the roof peak, the rafters, and the walls do not become rotten.

"So too, householder, when the mind is protected, bodily, verbal, and mental actions are protected.... One whose bodily, verbal, and mental deeds do not become rotten will have a good death."

110 (8) Peaked Roof (2)

The Blessed One then said to the householder Anāthapiṇḍika:

"Householder, when the mind has failed, bodily, verbal, and mental actions fail. One whose bodily, verbal, and mental deeds fail will not have a good death.

"Suppose a house with a peaked roof is badly thatched: then the roof peak, the rafters, and the walls fail. So too, when the mind has failed, bodily, verbal, and mental actions fail. One whose bodily, verbal, and mental deeds have failed will not have a good death.

"Householder, when the mind has not failed, bodily, verbal, and mental actions do not fail. One whose deeds of body, speech, and mind do not fail will have a good death.

"Suppose a house with a peaked roof is well thatched: then the roof peak, [263] the rafters, and the walls do not fail. So too, when the mind has not failed, bodily, verbal, and mental actions do not fail. One whose deeds of body, speech, and mind do not fail will have a good death."

111 (9) Causes (1)

"Bhikkhus, there are these three causes for the origination of kamma. What three? Greed is a cause for the origination of kamma; hatred is a cause for the origination of kamma; delusion is a cause for the origination of kamma.

(1) "Any kamma fashioned by greed, born of greed, caused by greed, originating from greed, is unwholesome and blameworthy and results in suffering. That kamma leads to the origination of kamma, not to the cessation of kamma.[573]

(2) "Any kamma fashioned by hatred ... (3) Any kamma fashioned by delusion, born of delusion, caused by delusion, originating from delusion, is unwholesome and blameworthy and results in suffering. That kamma leads to the origination of kamma, not to the cessation of kamma.

"These are the three causes for the origination of kamma.[574]

"There are, bhikkhus, these three [other] causes for the origination of kamma.[575] What three? Non-greed is a cause for the origination of kamma; non-hatred is a cause for the origination of kamma; non-delusion is a cause for the origination of kamma.

(1) "Any kamma fashioned by non-greed, born of non-greed, caused by non-greed, originating from non-greed, is wholesome and blameless and results in happiness. That kamma leads to the cessation of kamma, not to the origination of kamma.

(2) "Any kamma fashioned by non-hatred ... (3) Any kamma fashioned by non-delusion, born of non-delusion, caused by non-delusion, originating from non-delusion, is wholesome and blameless and results in happiness. That kamma leads to the cessation of kamma, not to the origination of kamma.

"These are the three [other] causes for the origination of kamma." [264]

112 (10) Causes (2)

"Bhikkhus, there are these three causes for the origination of kamma. What three? (1) Desire arises with reference to things in the past that are the basis for desire and lust. (2) Desire arises with reference to things in the future that are the basis for desire and lust. (3) Desire arises with reference to things presently existing that are the basis for desire and lust.

(1) "And how, bhikkhus, does desire arise with reference to things in the past that are the basis for desire and lust? One thinks about and mentally examines things in the past that are the basis for desire and lust. As one does so, desire arises. When desire springs up, one is fettered by those things. The mental infatuation is what I call the fetter. It is in this way that desire arises with reference to things in the past that are the basis for desire and lust.

(2) "And how does desire arise with reference to things in the future that are the basis for desire and lust? One thinks

about and mentally examines things in the future that are the basis for desire and lust. As one does so, desire arises. When desire springs up, one is fettered by those things. The mental infatuation is what I call the fetter. It is in this way that desire arises with reference to things in the future that are the basis for desire and lust.

(3) "And how does desire arise with reference to things presently existing that are the basis for desire and lust? One thinks about and mentally examines things presently existing that are the basis for desire and lust. As one does so, desire arises. When desire springs up, one is fettered by those things. The mental infatuation is what I call the fetter. It is in this way that desire arises with reference to things presently existing that are the basis for desire and lust.

"These are the three causes for the origination of kamma.[576] [265]

"There are, bhikkhus, these three [other] causes for the origination of kamma. What three? Desire does not arise with reference to things in the past that are the basis for desire and lust. Desire does not arise with reference to things in the future that are the basis for desire and lust. Desire does not arise with reference to things presently existing that are the basis for desire and lust.

(1) "And how, bhikkhus, does desire not arise with reference to things in the past that are the basis for desire and lust? One understands the future result of things in the past that are the basis for desire and lust. Having understood the future result, one avoids it.[577] Having avoided it, one becomes dispassionate in mind, and having pierced through with wisdom, one sees.[578] It is in this way that desire does not arise with reference to things in the past that are the basis for desire and lust.

(2) "And how, bhikkhus, does desire not arise with reference to things in the future that are the basis for desire and lust? One understands the future result of things in the future that are the basis for desire and lust. Having understood the future result, one avoids it. Having avoided it, one becomes dispassionate in mind and, having pierced through with wisdom, one sees. It is in this way that desire does not arise with reference to things in the future that are the basis for desire and lust.

(3) "And how, bhikkhus, does desire not arise with reference

to things presently existing that are the basis for desire and lust? One understands the future result of things presently existing that are the basis for desire and lust. Having understood the future result, one avoids it. Having avoided it, one becomes dispassionate in mind and, having pierced through with wisdom, one sees. It is in this way that desire does not arise with reference to things presently existing that are the basis for desire and lust.

"These are the three [other] causes for the origination of kamma."

II. Bound for the Plane of Misery

113 (1) Bound for the Plane of Misery

"Bhikkhus, there are three who, if they do not abandon this [fault of theirs], are bound for the plane of misery, bound for hell. Which three? [266] (1) One who, though not celibate, claims to be celibate; (2) one who slanders a pure celibate leading a pure celibate life with a groundless charge of non-celibacy; and (3) one who holds such a doctrine and view as this: 'There is no fault in sensual pleasures,' and then falls into indulgence in sensual pleasures.[579] These are the three who, if they do not abandon this [fault of theirs], are bound for the plane of misery, bound for hell."

114 (2) Rare

"Bhikkhus, the manifestation of three [persons] is rare in the world. What three? (1) The manifestation of a Tathāgata, an Arahant, a Perfectly Enlightened One is rare in the world. (2) A person who teaches the Dhamma and discipline proclaimed by the Tathāgata is rare in the world. (3) A grateful and thankful person is rare in the world. The manifestation of these three [persons] is rare in the world."

115 (3) Immeasurable

"Bhikkhus, there are these three kinds of persons found existing in the world. What three? The one who is easily measured, the one who is hard to measure, and the immeasurable one.

(1) "And what, bhikkhus, is the person who is easily measured? Here, some person is restless, puffed up, personally

vain, talkative, rambling in his talk, muddle-minded, without clear comprehension, unconcentrated, with a wandering mind, with loose sense faculties. This is called the person who is easily measured.

(2) "And what is the person who is hard to measure? Here, some person is not restless, puffed up, and personally vain; he is not talkative and rambling in his talk; he has mindfulness established and clearly comprehends, is concentrated, with a one-pointed mind, with restrained sense faculties. This is called the person who is hard to measure.

(3) "And what is the person who is immeasurable? Here, a bhikkhu is an arahant, one whose taints have been destroyed. This is called the person who is immeasurable.

"These are the three kinds of persons found existing in the world." [267]

116 (4) Imperturbable

"Bhikkhus, there are these three kinds of persons found existing in the world. What three?

(1) "Here, bhikkhus, with the complete surmounting of perceptions of forms, with the passing away of perceptions of sensory impingement, with non-attention to perceptions of diversity, [perceiving] 'space is infinite,' some person enters and dwells in the base of the infinity of space. He relishes it, desires it, and finds satisfaction in it. If he is firm in it, focused on it, often dwells in it, and has not lost it when he dies, he is reborn in companionship with the devas of the base of the infinity of space. The life span of the devas of the base of the infinity of space is 20,000 eons. The worldling remains there all his life, and when he has completed the entire life span of those devas, he goes to hell, to the animal realm, or to the sphere of afflicted spirits.[580] But the Blessed One's disciple remains there all his life, and when he has completed the entire life span of those devas, he attains final nibbāna in that very same state of existence. This is the distinction, the disparity, the difference between the instructed noble disciple and the uninstructed worldling, that is, when there is future destination and rebirth.[581]

(2) "Again, by completely surmounting the base of the infinity of space, [perceiving] 'consciousness is infinite,' someone here enters and dwells in the base of the infinity of consciousness.

He relishes it, desires it, and finds satisfaction in it. If he is firm in it, focused on it, often dwells in it, and has not lost it when he dies, he is reborn in companionship with the devas of the base of the infinity of consciousness. The life span of the devas of the base of the infinity of consciousness is 40,000 eons. The worldling remains there all his life, and when he has completed the entire life span of those devas, he goes to hell, to the animal realm, or to the sphere of afflicted spirits. But the Blessed One's disciple remains there all his life, and when he has completed the entire life span of those devas, he attains final nibbāna in that very same state of existence. This is the distinction, the disparity, the difference [268] between the instructed noble disciple and the uninstructed worldling, that is, when there is future destination and rebirth.

(3) "Again, bhikkhus, by completely surmounting the base of the infinity of consciousness [perceiving] 'there is nothing,' some person here enters and dwells in the base of nothingness. He relishes it, desires it, and finds satisfaction in it. If he is firm in it, focused on it, often dwells in it, and has not lost it when he dies, he is reborn in companionship with the devas of the base of nothingness. The life span of the devas of the base of nothingness is 60,000 eons. The worldling remains there all his life, and when he has completed the entire life span of those devas, he goes to hell, to the animal realm, or to the sphere of afflicted spirits. But the Blessed One's disciple remains there all his life, and when he has completed the entire life span of those devas, he attains final nibbāna in that very same state of existence. This is the distinction, the disparity, the difference between the instructed noble disciple and the uninstructed worldling, that is, when there is future destination and rebirth.

"These, bhikkhus, are the three kinds of persons found existing in the world."

117 (5) Failures and Accomplishments

"Bhikkhus, there are these three failures. What three? Failure in virtuous behavior, failure in mind, and failure in view.

(1) "And what is failure in virtuous behavior? Here, someone destroys life, takes what is not given, engages in sexual misconduct, speaks falsehood, speaks divisively, speaks harshly, and indulges in idle chatter. This is called failure in virtuous behavior.

(2) "And what is failure in mind? Here, someone is full of longing and has a mind of ill will. This is called failure in mind.

(3) "And what is failure in view? Here, someone holds wrong view and has an incorrect perspective thus: 'There is nothing given, nothing sacrificed, nothing offered; there is no [269] fruit or result of good and bad actions; there is no this world, no other world; there is no mother, no father; there are no beings spontaneously reborn; there are in the world no ascetics and brahmins of right conduct and right practice who, having realized this world and the other world for themselves by direct knowledge, make them known to others.' This is called failure in view.

"Because of failure in virtuous behavior, with the breakup of the body, after death, beings are reborn in the plane of misery, in a bad destination, in the lower world, in hell. Because of failure in mind . . . Because of failure in view, with the breakup of the body, after death, beings are reborn in the plane of misery, in a bad destination, in the lower world, in hell.

"These, bhikkhus, are the three failures.

"There are, bhikkhus, these three accomplishments. What three? Accomplishment in virtuous behavior, accomplishment in mind, and accomplishment in view.

(1) "And what is accomplishment in virtuous behavior? Here, someone abstains from the destruction of life, from taking what is not given, from sexual misconduct, from false speech, from divisive speech, from harsh speech, and from idle chatter. This is called accomplishment in virtuous behavior.

(2) "And what is accomplishment in mind? Here, someone is without longing and has a mind free of ill will. This is called accomplishment in mind.

(3) "And what is accomplishment in view? Here, someone holds right view and has a correct perspective thus: 'There is what is given, sacrificed, and offered; there is fruit and result of good and bad actions; there is this world and the other world; there is mother and father; there are beings spontaneously reborn; there are in the world ascetics and brahmins of right conduct and right practice who, having realized this world and the other world for themselves by direct knowledge, make them known to others.' This is called accomplishment in view. [270]

"Because of accomplishment in virtuous behavior, with the breakup of the body, after death, beings are reborn in a good destination, in a heavenly world. Because of accomplishment in mind . . . Because of accomplishment in view, with the breakup of the body, after death, beings are reborn in a good destination, in a heavenly world.

"These, bhikkhus, are the three accomplishments."

118 (6) Dice

"Bhikkhus, there are these three failures. What three? Failure in virtuous behavior, failure in mind, and failure in view.

"And what is failure in virtuous behavior? Here, someone destroys life . . . [as in 3:117] . . . This is called failure in view.

"Because of failure in virtuous behavior, with the breakup of the body, after death, beings are reborn in the plane of misery, in a bad destination, in the lower world, in hell. Because of failure in mind . . . Because of failure in view, with the breakup of the body, after death, beings are reborn in the plane of misery, in a bad destination, in the lower world, in hell.

"Just as dice,[582] when thrown upward, will rest firmly wherever they fall, so too, because of failure in virtuous behavior . . . failure in mind . . . failure in view, with the breakup of the body, after death, beings are reborn in the plane of misery, in a bad destination, in the lower world, in hell.

"These, bhikkhus, are the three failures.

"There are, bhikkhus, these three accomplishments. What three? Accomplishment in virtuous behavior, accomplishment in mind, and accomplishment in view.

"And what, bhikkhus, is accomplishment in virtuous behavior? Here, someone abstains from the destruction of life . . . [as in 3:117] . . . This is called accomplishment in view.

"Because of accomplishment in virtuous behavior, with the breakup of the body, after death, beings are reborn in a good destination, in a heavenly world. Because of accomplishment in mind . . . Because of accomplishment in view, with the breakup of the body, after death, beings are reborn in a good destination, in a heavenly world.

"Just as dice, when thrown upward, will rest firmly wherever they fall, so too, because of accomplishment in virtuous behavior . . . accomplishment in mind . . . accomplishment in view, with the breakup of the body, after death, beings are reborn in a good destination, in a heavenly world.

"These, bhikkhus, are the three accomplishments."

119 (7) Activity

"Bhikkhus, there are these three failures. What three? Failure in activity, failure in livelihood, and failure in view.

(1) "And what is failure in activity? Here, someone destroys life . . . and indulges in idle chatter. This is called failure in activity.

(2) "And what is failure in livelihood? Here, someone is of wrong livelihood and earns a living by a wrong type of livelihood. This is called failure in livelihood.

(3) "And what is failure in view? [271] Here, someone holds wrong view and has an incorrect perspective thus: 'There is nothing given . . . there are in the world no ascetics and brahmins of right conduct and right practice who, having realized this world and the other world for themselves by direct knowledge, make them known to others.' This is called failure in view.

"These are the three failures.

"There are, bhikkhus, these three accomplishments. What three? Accomplishment in activity, accomplishment in livelihood, and accomplishment in view.

(1) "And what is accomplishment in activity? Here, someone abstains from the destruction of life . . . and from idle chatter. This is called accomplishment in activity.

(2) "And what is accomplishment in livelihood? Here, someone is of right livelihood and earns a living by a right type of livelihood. This is called accomplishment in livelihood.

(3) "And what is accomplishment in view? Here, someone holds right view and has a correct perspective thus: 'There is what is given . . . there are in the world ascetics and brahmins of right conduct and right practice who, having realized this world and the other world for themselves by direct knowledge, make them known to others.' This is called accomplishment in view.

"These, bhikkhus, are the three accomplishments."

120 (8) Purity (1)

"Bhikkhus, there are these three purities. What three? Bodily purity, verbal purity, and mental purity.

(1) "And what is bodily purity? Here, someone abstains from

the destruction of life, from taking what is not given, and from sexual misconduct. This is called bodily purity.

(2) "And what is verbal purity? Here, someone abstains from false speech, from divisive speech, from harsh speech, and from idle chatter. This is called verbal purity.

(3) "And what is mental purity? Here, someone is without longing, without ill will, [272] and holds right view. This is called mental purity.

"These, bhikkhus, are the three purities."

121 (9) Purity (2)

"Bhikkhus, there are these three purities. What three? Bodily purity, verbal purity, and mental purity.

(1) "And what is bodily purity? Here, a bhikkhu abstains from the destruction of life, from taking what is not given, and from sexual activity. This is called bodily purity.

(2) "And what is verbal purity? Here, a bhikkhu abstains from false speech, from divisive speech, from harsh speech, and from idle chatter. This is called verbal purity.

(3) "And what is mental purity?[583] Here, when there is sensual desire in him, a bhikkhu understands: 'There is sensual desire in me'; or when there is no sensual desire in him, he understands: 'There is no sensual desire in me'; and he also understands how unarisen sensual desire arises, how arisen sensual desire is abandoned, and how abandoned sensual desire does not arise again in the future.

"When there is ill will in him . . . When there is dullness and drowsiness in him . . . When there is restlessness and remorse in him . . . [273] . . . When there is doubt in him, he understands: 'There is doubt in me'; or when there is no doubt in him, he understands: 'There is no doubt in me'; and he also understands how unarisen doubt arises, how arisen doubt is abandoned, and how abandoned doubt does not arise again in the future. This is called mental purity.

"These, bhikkhus, are the three purities."

Pure in body, pure in speech,
pure in mind, without taints:
they call the pure one, accomplished in purity,
"one who has washed away evil."

122 (10) Sagacity

"Bhikkhus, there are these three kinds of sagacity. What three? Bodily sagacity, verbal sagacity, and mental sagacity.

(1) "And what is bodily sagacity? Here, someone abstains from the destruction of life, from taking what is not given, and from sexual activity. This is called bodily sagacity.

(2) "And what is verbal sagacity? Here, someone abstains from false speech, from divisive speech, from harsh speech, and from idle chatter. This is called verbal sagacity.

(3) "And what is mental sagacity? Here, with the destruction of the taints, a bhikkhu has realized for himself with direct knowledge, in this very life, the taintless liberation of mind, liberation by wisdom, and having entered upon it, he dwells in it. This is called mental sagacity.

"These, bhikkhus, are the three kinds of sagacity."

> A sage by body, a sage in speech,
> a sage in mind, without taints:
> they call the sage, accomplished in sagacity,
> "one who has abandoned all." [274]

III. Bharaṇḍu[584]

123 (1) Kusinārā

On one occasion the Blessed One was dwelling at Kusinārā, in the Baliharaṇa forest thicket. There the Blessed One addressed the bhikkhus . . .

"Here, bhikkhus, a bhikkhu dwells in dependence on a certain village or town. A householder or a householder's son approaches him and invites him for the next day's meal. If he wishes, the bhikkhu accepts. When the night has passed, in the morning the bhikkhu dresses, takes his bowl and robe, and goes to the residence of that householder or householder's son. He sits down in the seat that has been prepared and that householder or householder's son, with his own hand, serves and satisfies him with various kinds of delicious food. (1) It occurs to him: 'How good, indeed, that this householder or householder's son, with his own hand, serves and satisfies me with various kinds of delicious food!' (2) It also occurs to him: 'Oh, in the future too may this householder or householder's son, with his own hand, serve and satisfy me with a similar variety of delicious food!' (3) He uses that food while being tied to it, infatuated with it, blindly absorbed in it, not seeing the danger in it and understanding the escape from it. He thinks sensual thoughts in relation to it; he thinks thoughts of ill will; he thinks thoughts of harming. What is given to such a bhikkhu, I say, is not of great fruit. For what reason? Because the bhikkhu is heedless.

"Here, a bhikkhu dwells in dependence on a certain village or town. A householder or a householder's son approaches him and invites him for the next day's meal. If he wishes, the bhikkhu accepts. When the night has passed, in the morning the bhikkhu dresses, takes his bowl and robe, and goes to the residence of that householder or householder's son. He sits down in the seat that has been prepared and that householder or householder's son, with his own hand, serves and satisfies him with various kinds of delicious food. (1) It does not occur to him: 'How good, indeed, that this householder [275] or householder's son, with his own hand, serves and satisfies me with various kinds of delicious food!' (2) It also does not occur to him: 'Oh, in the future too may this householder or householder's son, with his own hand, serve and satisfy me with a similar variety of delicious food!' (3) He uses that food without being tied to it, infatuated with it, and blindly absorbed in it, but seeing the danger in it and understanding the escape from it. He thinks thoughts of renunciation in relation to it; he thinks thoughts of good will; he thinks thoughts of non-harming. What is given to such a bhikkhu, I say, is of great fruit. For what reason? Because the bhikkhu is heedful."

124 (2) Arguments

"Bhikkhus, wherever bhikkhus take to arguing and quarreling and fall into a dispute, stabbing each other with piercing words, I am uneasy even about directing my attention there, let alone about going there. I conclude about them: 'Surely, those venerable ones have abandoned three things and cultivated three [other] things.'

"What are the three things they have abandoned? Thoughts of renunciation, thoughts of good will, and thoughts of non-harming. These are the three things they have abandoned.

"What are the three things they have cultivated? Sensual

thoughts, thoughts of ill will, and thoughts of harming. These are the three things they have cultivated.

"Wherever bhikkhus take to arguing and quarreling and fall into a dispute . . . I conclude: 'Surely, those venerable ones have abandoned these three things and cultivated these three [other] things.'

"Bhikkhus, wherever bhikkhus are dwelling in concord, harmoniously, without disputes, blending like milk and water, viewing each other with eyes of affection, I am at ease about going there, let alone about directing my attention there. I conclude: 'Surely, those venerable ones have abandoned three things and cultivated three [other] things.'

"What are the three things they have abandoned? [276] Sensual thoughts, thoughts of ill will, and thoughts of harming. These are the three things they have abandoned.

"What are the three things they have cultivated? Thoughts of renunciation, thoughts of good will, and thoughts of non-harming. These are the three things they have cultivated.

"Wherever bhikkhus are dwelling in concord . . . I conclude: 'Surely, those venerable ones have abandoned these three things and cultivated these three [other] things.'"

125 (3) Gotamaka

On one occasion the Blessed One was dwelling at Vesālī at the Gotamaka Shrine.[585] There the Blessed One addressed the bhikkhus . . .

"Bhikkhus, (1) I teach the Dhamma through direct knowledge, not without direct knowledge. (2) I teach the Dhamma with a basis, not without a basis. (3) I teach the Dhamma that is antidotal, not one without antidotes.[586] Since I teach the Dhamma through direct knowledge, not without direct knowledge; since I teach the Dhamma with a basis, not without a basis; since I teach the Dhamma that is antidotal, not one without antidotes, my exhortation should be acted upon, my instructions should be acted upon. It is enough for you to rejoice, enough for you to be elated, enough for you to be joyful: 'The Blessed One is perfectly enlightened! The Dhamma is well expounded by the Blessed One! The Saṅgha is practicing the good path!'"

This is what the Blessed One said. Elated, those bhikkhus delighted in the Blessed One's statement. And while this discourse was being spoken, the thousandfold world system shook.

126 (4) Bharaṇḍu

On one occasion the Blessed One was wandering on tour among the Kosalans when he reached Kapilavatthu. Mahānāma the Sakyan heard: "The Blessed One has arrived at Kapilavatthu." Then Mahānāma the Sakyan approached the Blessed One, paid homage to him, and stood to one side. The Blessed One then said to him:

"Go, Mahānāma, and find a suitable rest house in Kapilavatthu where we might stay for the night." [277]

"Yes, Bhante," Mahānāma replied. He then entered Kapilavatthu and searched the entire city but did not see a suitable rest house where the Blessed One could stay for the night. So he returned to the Blessed One and told him: "Bhante, there is no suitable rest house in Kapilavatthu where the Blessed One might stay for the night. But Bharaṇḍu the Kālāma, formerly the Blessed One's fellow monk, [is here].[587] Let the Blessed One spend the night at his hermitage."

"Go, Mahānāma, and prepare a mat for me."

"Yes, Bhante," Mahānāma replied. Then he went to Bharaṇḍu's hermitage, prepared a mat, set out water for washing the feet, returned to the Blessed One, and said:

"I have spread a mat, Bhante, and set out water for washing the feet. The Blessed One may go at his own convenience."

Then the Blessed One went to Bharaṇḍu's hermitage, sat down on the seat that was prepared for him, and washed his feet. It then occurred to Mahānāma: "This is not a proper time for staying with the Blessed One, for he is tired. I will visit him tomorrow." Then he paid homage to the Blessed One, circumambulated him keeping the right side toward him, and departed.

Then, when the night had passed, Mahānāma approached the Blessed One, paid homage to him, and sat down to one side. The Blessed One then said to him:

"There are, Mahānāma, these three kinds of teachers found existing in the world. What three?

(1) "Here, Mahānāma, some teacher prescribes the full understanding of sensual pleasures, but not of forms or feelings. (2) Another teacher prescribes the full understanding of sensual

pleasures and forms, but not [278] of feelings. (3) Still another teacher prescribes the full understanding of sensual pleasures, forms, and feelings. These are the three kinds of teachers found existing in the world. Is the goal of these three kinds of teachers the same or different?"

When this was said, Bharaṇḍu the Kālāma said to Mahānāma: "Say the same, Mahānāma." But the Blessed One said to Mahānāma: "Say different, Mahānāma."

A second time . . . A third time Bharaṇḍu the Kālāma said to Mahānāma: "Say the same, Mahānāma." But the Blessed One said to Mahānāma: "Say different, Mahānāma."

Then it occurred to Bharaṇḍu: "The ascetic Gotama has contradicted me three times in front of the influential Mahānāma the Sakyan. I had better leave Kapilavatthu."

Then Bharaṇḍu the Kālāma left Kapilavatthu. When he left Kapilavatthu, he left for good and never returned.

127 (5) Hatthaka

On one occasion the Blessed One was dwelling at Sāvatthī in Jeta's Grove, Anāthapiṇḍika's Park. Then, when the night had advanced, the young deva Hatthaka,[588] illuminating the entire Jeta's Grove, approached the Blessed One. Having approached, [while thinking:] "I will stand in front of the Blessed One," he sank down, descended, and could not remain in place. Just as ghee or oil, when poured on sand, sinks down, descends, and does not remain in place, so the young deva Hatthaka, [while thinking:] "I will stand in front of the Blessed One," sank down, descended, and could not remain in place. [279]

Then the Blessed One said to Hatthaka: "Create a gross body, Hatthaka."

"Yes, Bhante," Hatthaka replied. Then he created a gross body, paid homage to the Blessed One, and stood to one side. The Blessed One then said to him:

"Hatthaka, do those teachings that you could recall in the past, when you were a human being, come back to you now?"[589]

"Bhante, those teachings that I could recall in the past, when I was a human being, come back to me now; and those teachings that I could not recall in the past, when I was a human being, come back to me now.[590] Just as the Blessed One is now hemmed in by bhikkhus, bhikkhunīs, male and female lay followers, kings and royal ministers, sectarian teachers and their disciples, so I am hemmed in by other young devas. Young devas come to me even from a distance, [thinking]: 'We will hear the Dhamma from the young deva Hatthaka.'

"I died, Bhante, insatiable and unquenchable in three things. What three? (1) I died insatiable and unquenchable in seeing the Blessed One. (2) I died insatiable and unquenchable in hearing the good Dhamma. (3) I died insatiable and unquenchable in attending upon the Saṅgha. I died insatiable and unquenchable in these three things.

"I could never get enough of
seeing the Blessed One,
hearing the good Dhamma,
and attending on the Saṅgha.

"Training in the higher virtuous behavior,
I rejoiced in hearing the good Dhamma.
Hatthaka has gone to [rebirth in] Aviha[591]
not having gotten enough of these three things."

128 (6) Pollution

On one occasion the Blessed One was dwelling in Bārāṇasī at the deer park in Isipatana. Then, in the morning, the Blessed One dressed, took his bowl and robe, and entered Bārāṇasī for alms. [280] While walking for alms near the cattle-yoking fig tree,[592] the Blessed One saw a dissatisfied bhikkhu, [seeking] gratification outwardly,[593] muddle-minded, without clear comprehension, unconcentrated, with a wandering mind and loose sense faculties. Having seen him, he said to that bhikkhu:

"Bhikkhu, bhikkhu! Do not pollute yourself.[594] It is inevitable, bhikkhu, that flies will pursue and attack one who has polluted himself and been tainted by a stench."[595]

Then, being exhorted thus by the Blessed One, that bhikkhu acquired a sense of urgency.[596]

When the Blessed One had walked for alms in Bārāṇasī, after his meal, when he had returned from his alms round, he addressed the bhikkhus:

"Bhikkhus, this morning I dressed, took my bowl and robe, and entered Bārāṇasī for alms. While walking for alms near the cattle-yoking fig tree, I saw a dissatisfied bhikkhu [seeking] gratification outwardly, muddle-minded, without clear comprehension, unconcentrated, with a wandering mind and loose sense faculties. Having seen him, I said to that bhikkhu: 'Bhikkhu, bhikkhu! Do not pollute yourself. It is inevitable, bhikkhu, that flies will pursue and attack one who has polluted himself and been tainted by a stench.' Then, being exhorted thus by me, that bhikkhu acquired a sense of urgency."

When this was said, a certain bhikkhu asked the Blessed One: "What, Bhante, is meant by 'pollution'? What is the 'stench'? And what are the 'flies'?"

(1) "Longing, bhikkhu, is what is meant by 'pollution.' (2) Ill will is the 'stench.' (3) Bad unwholesome thoughts are the 'flies.' It is inevitable that flies will pursue and attack one who has polluted himself and been tainted by a stench." [281]

The flies—thoughts based on lust—
will run in pursuit of one
unrestrained in the sense faculties,
unguarded in the eye and ear.

A bhikkhu who is polluted,
tainted by a stench,
is far from nibbāna
and reaps only distress.

Whether in the village or the forest,
the unwise foolish person,
not having gained peace for himself,
goes around followed by flies.[597]

But those accomplished in virtuous behavior
who delight in wisdom and peace,
those peaceful ones live happily,
having destroyed the flies.[598]

129 (7) Anuruddha (1)

Then the Venerable Anuruddha approached the Blessed One, paid homage to him, sat down to one side, and said: "Now, Bhante, with the divine eye, which is purified and surpasses the human, I see that women, with the breakup of the body, after death, are mostly reborn in the plane of misery, in a bad destination, in the lower world, in hell. What qualities does a woman possess on account of which, with the breakup of the body, after death, she is reborn in the plane of misery, in a bad destination, in the lower world, in hell?"

"When she possesses three qualities, Anuruddha, with the breakup of the body, after death, a woman is reborn in the plane of misery, in a bad destination, in the lower world, in hell. What three?

(1) "Here, Anuruddha, in the morning a woman dwells at home with a mind obsessed by the stain of miserliness. (2) At midday she dwells at home with a mind obsessed by envy. (3) And in the evening she dwells at home with a mind obsessed by sensual lust. When she possesses these three qualities, with the breakup of the body, after death, a woman is reborn in the plane of misery, in a bad destination, in the lower world, in hell."

130 (8) Anuruddha (2)

Then the Venerable Anuruddha approached the Venerable Sāriputta and exchanged greetings with him. When they had concluded their greetings and cordial talk, [282] he sat down to one side and said to the Venerable Sāriputta:

"Here, friend Sāriputta, with the divine eye, which is purified and surpasses the human, I survey a thousandfold world system. Energy is aroused in me without slackening; my mindfulness is established without confusion; my body is tranquil without disturbance; my mind is concentrated and one-pointed. Yet my mind is still not liberated from the taints through non-clinging."

[The Venerable Sāriputta said:] (1) "Friend Anuruddha, when you think: 'With the divine eye, which is purified and surpasses the human, I survey a thousandfold world system,' this is your conceit.

(2) "And when you think: 'Energy is aroused in me without slackening; my mindfulness is established without confusion; my body is tranquil without disturbance; my mind is concentrated and one-pointed,' this is your restlessness.

(3) "And when you think: 'Yet my mind is still not liberated from the taints through non-clinging,' this is your remorse.

"It would be good if you would abandon these three qualities and stop attending to them. Instead, direct your mind to the deathless element."

Some time later the Venerable Anuruddha abandoned those three qualities and stopped attending to them. Instead, he directed his mind to the deathless element. Then, dwelling alone, withdrawn, heedful, ardent, and resolute, in no long time the Venerable Anuruddha realized for himself with direct knowledge, in this very life, that unsurpassed consummation of the spiritual life for the sake of which clansmen rightly go forth from the household life into homelessness, and having entered upon it, he dwelled in it. He directly knew: "Destroyed is birth, the spiritual life has been lived, what had to be done has been done, there is no more coming back to any state of being." And the Venerable Anuruddha became one of the arahants.

131 (9) Concealed

"Bhikkhus, there are these three things that flourish when concealed, not when exposed. What three? (1) Women flourish when concealed, not when exposed.[599] (2) The hymns of the brahmins flourish when concealed, not [283] when exposed. (3) And wrong views flourish when concealed, not when exposed. These are the three things that flourish when concealed, not when exposed.

"Bhikkhus, there are these three things that shine when exposed, not when concealed. What three? (1) The moon shines when exposed, not when concealed. (2) The sun shines when exposed, not when concealed. (3) The Dhamma and discipline proclaimed by the Tathāgata shines when exposed, not when concealed. These are the three things that shine when exposed, not when concealed."

132 (10) Line Etched in Stone

"Bhikkhus, there are these three kinds of persons found existing in the world. What three? The person who is like a line etched in stone, the person who is like a line etched in the ground, and the person who is like a line etched in water.

(1) "And what kind of person is like a line etched in stone? Here, some person often gets angry, and his anger persists for a long time. Just as a line etched in stone is not quickly erased

by the wind and water but persists for a long time, so too, some person often gets angry, and his anger persists for a long time. This is called the person who is like a line etched in stone.

(2) "And what kind of person is like a line etched in the ground? Here, some person often gets angry, but his anger does not persist for a long time. Just as a line etched in the ground is quickly erased by the wind and water and does not persist for a long time, so too, some person often gets angry, but his anger does not persist for a long time. This is called the person who is like a line etched in the ground.

(3) "And what kind of person is like a line etched in water? Here, some person, even when spoken to roughly [284] and harshly, in disagreeable ways, remains on friendly terms [with his antagonist], mingles [with him], and greets [him]. Just as a line etched in water quickly disappears and does not persist for a long time, so too, some person, even when spoken to roughly and harshly, in disagreeable ways, remains on friendly terms [with his antagonist], mingles [with him], and greets [him]. This is called the person who is like a line etched in water.

"These, bhikkhus, are the three kinds of persons found existing in the world."

IV. A Warrior

133 (1) A Warrior

"Bhikkhus, possessing three factors, a warrior is worthy of a king, an accessory of a king, and reckoned a factor of kingship. What three? Here, a warrior is a long-distance shooter, a sharp-shooter, and one who splits a great body. Possessing these three factors, a warrior is worthy of a king, an accessory of a king, and reckoned a factor of kingship. So too, possessing three factors, a bhikkhu is worthy of gifts, worthy of hospitality, worthy of offerings, worthy of reverential salutation, an unsurpassed field of merit for the world. What three? Here, a bhikkhu is a long-distance shooter, a sharp-shooter, and one who splits a great body.

(1) "And how is a bhikkhu a long-distance shooter? Here, any kind of form whatsoever—whether past, future, or present, internal or external, gross or subtle, inferior or superior, far or near—a bhikkhu sees all form as it really is with correct

wisdom thus: 'This is not mine, this I am not, this is not my self.' Any kind of feeling whatsoever... [285]... Any kind of perception whatsoever... Any kind of volitional activities whatsoever... Any kind of consciousness whatsoever—whether past, future, or present, internal or external, gross or subtle, inferior or superior, far or near—a bhikkhu sees all consciousness as it really is with correct wisdom thus: 'This is not mine, this I am not, this is not my self.' It is in this way that a bhikkhu is a long-distance shooter.

(2) "And how is a bhikkhu a sharp-shooter? Here, a bhikkhu understands as it really is: 'This is suffering.' He understands as it really is: 'This is the origin of suffering.' He understands as it really is: 'This is the cessation of suffering.' He understands as it really is: 'This is the way leading to the cessation of suffering.' It is in this way that a bhikkhu is a sharp-shooter.

(3) "And how is a bhikkhu one who splits a great body? Here, a bhikkhu splits the great mass of ignorance. It is in this way that a bhikkhu is one who splits a great body.

"Possessing these three qualities, a bhikkhu is worthy of gifts, worthy of hospitality, worthy of offerings, worthy of reverential salutation, an unsurpassed field of merit for the world."

134 (2) Assemblies

"Bhikkhus, there are these three kinds of assemblies. What three? The assembly trained in vain talk, the assembly trained in interrogation, and the assembly trained to the limits. These are the three kinds of assemblies."[600] [286]

135 (3) A Friend

"Bhikkhus, one should associate with a friend who possesses three factors. What three? (1) Here, a bhikkhu gives what is hard to give. (2) He does what is hard to do. (3) He patiently endures what is hard to endure. One should associate with a friend who possesses these three factors."

136 (4) Arising

(1) "Bhikkhus, whether Tathāgatas arise or not, there persists that law, that stableness of the Dhamma, that fixed course of the Dhamma:[601] 'All conditioned phenomena are impermanent.' A Tathāgata awakens to this and breaks through to it, and then

he explains it, teaches it, proclaims it, establishes it, discloses it, analyzes it, and elucidates it thus: 'All conditioned phenomena are impermanent.'[602]

(2) "Bhikkhus, whether Tathāgatas arise or not, there persists that law, that stableness of the Dhamma, that fixed course of the Dhamma: 'All conditioned phenomena are suffering.' A Tathāgata awakens to this and breaks through to it, and then he explains it, teaches it, proclaims it, establishes it, discloses it, analyzes it, and elucidates it thus: 'All conditioned phenomena are suffering.'

(3) "Bhikkhus, whether Tathāgatas arise or not, there persists that law, that stableness of the Dhamma, that fixed course of the Dhamma: 'All phenomena are non-self.' A Tathāgata awakens to this and breaks through to it, and then he explains it, teaches it, proclaims it, establishes it, discloses it, analyzes it, and elucidates it thus: 'All phenomena are non-self.'"

137 (5) A Hair Blanket

"Bhikkhus, a hair blanket is declared to be the worst kind of woven garment.[603] A hair blanket is cold in cold weather, hot in hot weather, ugly, foul-smelling, and uncomfortable. So too, the doctrine of Makkhali is declared the worst among the doctrines of the various ascetics.[604] The hollow man Makkhali teaches the doctrine and view: 'There is no kamma, no deed, no energy.' [287]

(1) "Bhikkhus, the Blessed Ones, Arahants, Perfectly Enlightened Ones of the past taught a doctrine of kamma, a doctrine of deeds, a doctrine of energy. Yet the hollow man Makkhali contradicts them [with his claim]: 'There is no kamma, no deed, no energy.'

(2) "The Blessed Ones, Arahants, Perfectly Enlightened Ones of the future will also teach a doctrine of kamma, a doctrine of deeds, a doctrine of energy. Yet the hollow man Makkhali contradicts them [with his claim]: 'There is no kamma, no deed, no energy.'

(3) "At present I am the Arahant, the Perfectly Enlightened One, and I teach a doctrine of kamma, a doctrine of deeds, a doctrine of energy. Yet the hollow man Makkhali contradicts me [with his claim]: 'There is no kamma, no deed, no energy.'

"Just as a trap set at the mouth of a river would bring about harm, suffering, calamity, and disaster to many fish, so too, the hollow man Makkhali is, as it were, a 'trap for people' who has arisen in the world for the harm, suffering, calamity, and disaster of many beings."

138 (6) Accomplishment

"Bhikkhus, there are these three accomplishments. What three? Accomplishment of faith, accomplishment of virtuous behavior, and accomplishment of wisdom. These are the three accomplishments."

139 (7) Growth[605]

"Bhikkhus, there are these three kinds of growth. What three? Growth in faith, growth in virtuous behavior, and growth in wisdom. These are the three kinds of growth."

140 (8) Horses (1)

"Bhikkhus, I will teach you the three kinds of wild colts and the three kinds of persons who are like wild colts. Listen and attend closely. I will speak."

"Yes, Bhante," those bhikkhus replied. The Blessed One said this:

"And what, bhikkhus, are the three kinds of wild colts? [288] (1) Here, one kind of wild colt possesses speed but not beauty or the right proportions. (2) Another kind of wild colt possesses speed and beauty but not the right proportions. (3) And still another kind of wild colt possesses speed, beauty, and the right proportions. These are the three kinds of wild colts.

"And what, bhikkhus, are the three kinds of persons who are like wild colts? (1) Here, one kind of person who is like a wild colt possesses speed but not beauty or the right proportions. (2) Another kind of person who is like a wild colt possesses speed and beauty but not the right proportions. (3) And still another kind of person who is like a wild colt possesses speed, beauty, and the right proportions.

(1) "And how does a person who is like a wild colt possess speed but not beauty or the right proportions? Here, a bhikkhu understands as it really is: 'This is suffering,' and 'This is the origin of suffering,' and 'This is the cessation of suffering,' and 'This is the way leading to the cessation of suffering.' This, I say, is his speed. But when asked a question pertaining to the Dhamma or the discipline, he falters and does not answer.

This, I say, is his lack of beauty. And he does not gain robes, almsfood, lodgings, and medicines and provisions for the sick. This, I say, is his lack of the right proportions. In this way a person who is like a wild colt possesses speed but not beauty or the right proportions.

(2) "And how does a person who is like a wild colt possess speed and beauty but not the right proportions? Here, a bhikkhu understands as it really is: 'This is suffering' ... 'This is the way leading to the cessation of suffering.' This, I say, is his speed. And when asked a question pertaining to the Dhamma or the discipline, he answers and does not falter. This, I say, is his beauty. But he does not gain robes ... and provisions for the sick. This, I say, is his lack of the right proportions. In this way [289] a person who is like a wild colt possesses speed and beauty but not the right proportions.

(3) "And how does a person who is like a wild colt possess speed, beauty, and the right proportions? Here, a bhikkhu understands as it really is: 'This is suffering,' and 'This is the origin of suffering,' and 'This is the cessation of suffering,' and 'This is the way leading to the cessation of suffering.' This, I say, is his speed. And when asked a question pertaining to the Dhamma or the discipline, he answers and does not falter. This, I say, is his beauty. And he gains robes ... and provisions for the sick. This, I say, is his right proportions. In this way a person who is like a wild colt possesses speed, beauty, and the right proportions.

"These, bhikkhus, are the three kinds of persons who are like wild colts."

141 (9) Horses (2)

"Bhikkhus, I will teach you the three kinds of good horses and the three kinds of persons who are like good horses.[606] Listen ...

"And what, bhikkhus, are the three kinds of good horses? (1) Here, one kind of good horse possesses speed but not beauty or the right proportions. (2) Another kind of good horse possesses speed and beauty but not the right proportions. (3) Still another kind of good horse possesses speed, beauty, and the right proportions. These are the three kinds of good horses.

"And what, bhikkhus, are the three kinds of persons who are

like good horses? (1) Here, one kind of person who is like a good horse possesses speed but not beauty or the right proportions. (2) Another kind of person who is like a good horse possesses speed and beauty but not the right proportions. (3) Still another kind of person who is like a good horse possesses speed, beauty, and the right proportions. [290]

(1) "And how does a person who is like a good horse possess speed but not beauty or the right proportions? Here, with the utter destruction of the five lower fetters, a bhikkhu becomes one of spontaneous birth, due to attain final nibbāna there without ever returning from that world. This, I say, is his speed. But when asked a question pertaining to the Dhamma or the discipline, he falters and does not answer. This, I say, is his lack of beauty. And he does not gain robes, almsfood, lodgings, and medicines and provisions for the sick. This, I say, is his lack of the right proportions. In this way a person who is like a good horse possesses speed but not beauty or the right proportions.

(2) "And how does a person who is like a good horse possess speed and beauty but not the right proportions? Here, with the utter destruction of the five lower fetters, a bhikkhu becomes one of spontaneous birth, due to attain final nibbāna there without ever returning from that world. This, I say, is his speed. And when asked a question pertaining to the Dhamma or the discipline, he answers and does not falter. This, I say, is his beauty. But he does not gain robes . . . and provisions for the sick. This, I say, is his lack of the right proportions. In this way a person who is like a good horse possesses speed and beauty but not the right proportions.

(3) "And how does a person who is like a good horse possess speed, beauty, and the right proportions? Here, with the utter destruction of the five lower fetters, a bhikkhu becomes one of spontaneous birth, due to attain final nibbāna there without ever returning from that world. This, I say, is his speed. And when asked a question pertaining to the Dhamma or the discipline, he answers and does not falter. This, I say, is his beauty. And he gains robes . . . and provisions for the sick. This, I say, is his right proportions. In this way a person who is like a good horse possesses speed, beauty, and the right proportions.

"These, bhikkhus, are the three kinds of persons who are like good horses."

142 (10) Horses (3)

"Bhikkhus, I will teach you the three kinds of excellent thoroughbred horses and the three kinds of excellent thoroughbred persons. Listen . . . [291]

"And what, bhikkhus, are the three kinds of excellent thoroughbred horses? Here, one kind of excellent thoroughbred horse . . . possesses speed, beauty, and the right proportions. These are the three kinds of excellent thoroughbred horses.

"And what, bhikkhus, are the three kinds of excellent thoroughbred persons? Here, one kind of person . . . possesses speed, beauty, and the right proportions.

"And how does an excellent thoroughbred person . . . possess speed, beauty, and the right proportions? Here, with the destruction of the taints, a bhikkhu has realized for himself with direct knowledge, in this very life, the taintless liberation of mind, liberation by wisdom, and having entered upon it, he dwells in it. This, I say, is his speed. And when asked a question pertaining to the Dhamma or the discipline, he answers and does not falter. This, I say, is his beauty. And he gains robes . . . and provisions for the sick. This, I say, is his right proportions. In this way an excellent thoroughbred person possesses speed, beauty, and the right proportions.

"These, bhikkhus, are the three kinds of excellent thoroughbred persons."

143 (11) The Peacock Sanctuary (1)[607]

On one occasion the Blessed One was dwelling at Rājagaha at the wanderers' park, the peacock sanctuary. There the Blessed One addressed the bhikkhus: . . .

"Bhikkhus, possessing three qualities, a bhikkhu is best among devas and humans: one who has reached the ultimate conclusion, won ultimate security from bondage, lived the ultimate spiritual life, and gained the ultimate consummation. What three? (1) The aggregate of virtuous behavior of one beyond training, (2) the aggregate of concentration of one beyond training, and (3) the aggregate of wisdom of one beyond training.[608] Possessing these three qualities, a bhikkhu is best among devas and humans . . . and gained the ultimate consummation."

144 (12) The Peacock Sanctuary (2)

"Bhikkhus, possessing three qualities, a bhikkhu is best among devas and humans: one who has reached the ultimate conclusion, won ultimate security from bondage, lived the ultimate spiritual life, and gained the ultimate consummation. What three? [292] (1) The wonder of psychic potency, (2) the wonder of mind-reading, and (3) the wonder of instruction. Possessing these three qualities, a bhikkhu is best among devas and humans . . . and gained the ultimate consummation."

145 (13) The Peacock Sanctuary (3)

"Bhikkhus, possessing three qualities, a bhikkhu is best among devas and humans: one who has reached the ultimate conclusion, won ultimate security from bondage, lived the ultimate spiritual life, and gained the ultimate consummation. What three? (1) Right view, (2) right knowledge, and (3) right liberation. Possessing these three qualities, a bhikkhu is best among devas and humans . . . and gained the ultimate consummation."

V. Auspicious

146 (1) Unwholesome

"Bhikkhus, possessing three qualities, one is deposited in hell as if brought there. What three? Unwholesome bodily action, unwholesome verbal action, and unwholesome mental action. Possessing these three qualities, one is deposited in hell as if brought there.

"Possessing three qualities, one is deposited in heaven as if brought there. What three? Wholesome bodily action, wholesome verbal action, and wholesome mental action. Possessing these three qualities, one is deposited in heaven as if brought there."

147 (2) Blameworthy

"Bhikkhus, possessing three qualities, one is deposited in hell as if brought there. What three? Blameworthy bodily action, blameworthy verbal action, and blameworthy mental action. Possessing these three qualities, one is deposited in hell as if brought there.

"Possessing three qualities, one is deposited in heaven as if brought there. What three? Blameless bodily action, blameless verbal action, and blameless mental action. Possessing these three qualities, one is deposited in heaven as if brought there." [293]

148 (3) Unrighteous

"Bhikkhus, possessing three qualities, one is deposited in hell as if brought there. What three? Unrighteous bodily action, unrighteous verbal action, and unrighteous mental action. Possessing these three qualities, one is deposited in hell as if brought there.

"Possessing three qualities, one is deposited in heaven as if brought there. What three? Righteous bodily action, righteous verbal action, and righteous mental action. Possessing these three qualities, one is deposited in heaven as if brought there."

149 (4) Impure

"Bhikkhus, possessing three qualities, one is deposited in hell as if brought there. What three? Impure bodily action, impure verbal action, and impure mental action. Possessing these three qualities, one is deposited in hell as if brought there.

"Possessing three qualities, one is deposited in heaven as if brought there. What three? Pure bodily action, pure verbal action, and pure mental action. Possessing these three qualities, one is deposited in heaven as if brought there."

150 (5) Maimed (1)

"Bhikkhus, possessing three qualities, the foolish, incompetent, bad person maintains himself in a maimed and injured condition; he is blameworthy and subject to reproach by the wise; and he generates much demerit. What three? Unwholesome bodily action, unwholesome verbal action, and unwholesome mental action. Possessing these three qualities . . . he generates much demerit.

"Possessing three qualities, the wise, competent, good person preserves himself unmaimed and uninjured; he is blameless and beyond reproach by the wise; and he generates much merit. What three? Wholesome bodily action, wholesome verbal action, and wholesome mental action. Possessing these three qualities . . . he generates much merit."

151 (6) Maimed (2)

"Bhikkhus, possessing three qualities . . . Blameworthy bodily action, blameworthy verbal action, and blameworthy mental action. . . .

"Possessing three qualities . . . Blameless bodily action, blameless verbal action, and blameless mental action. . . ."

152 (7) Maimed (3)

"Bhikkhus, possessing three qualities . . . Unrighteous bodily action, unrighteous verbal action, and unrighteous mental action. . . . [294]

"Bhikkhus, possessing three qualities . . . Righteous bodily action, righteous verbal action, and righteous mental action. . . ."

153 (8) Maimed (4)

"Bhikkhus, possessing three qualities . . . Impure bodily action, impure verbal action, and impure mental action. . . .

"Bhikkhus, possessing three qualities . . . Pure bodily action, pure verbal action, and pure mental action. Possessing these three qualities, the wise, competent, good person preserves himself unmaimed and uninjured; he is blameless and beyond reproach by the wise; and he generates much merit."

154 (9) Homage

"Bhikkhus, there are these three kinds of homage. What three? By body, by speech, and by mind. These are the three kinds of homage."

155 (10) A Good Morning

"Bhikkhus, those beings who engage in good conduct by body, speech, and mind in the morning have a good morning. Those beings who engage in good conduct by body, speech, and mind in the afternoon have a good afternoon. And those beings who engage in good conduct by body, speech, and mind in the evening have a good evening."

Truly propitious and auspicious,
a happy daybreak and a joyful rising,
a precious moment and a blissful hour
will come for those who offer alms

to those leading the spiritual life.
Upright acts of body and speech,
upright thoughts and aspirations:
when one does what is upright
one gains upright benefits.
Those happy ones who have gained such benefits
come to growth in the Buddha's teaching.
May you and all your relatives
be healthy and happy! [295]

VI. Ways of Practice[609]

156 (1) [Establishments of Mindfulness][610]

"Bhikkhus, there are these three ways of practice. What three? The coarse way of practice, the blistering way of practice, and the middle way of practice.[611]

(1) "And what, bhikkhus, is the coarse way of practice? Here, someone holds such a doctrine and view as this: 'There is no fault in sensual pleasures,' and then indulges in sensual pleasures. This is called the coarse way of practice.

(2) "And what is the blistering way of practice?[612] Here, someone goes naked, rejecting conventions, licking his hands, not coming when asked, not stopping when asked; he does not accept food brought or food specially made or an invitation to a meal; he receives nothing from a pot, from a bowl, across a threshold, across a stick, across a pestle, from two eating together, from a pregnant woman, from a woman nursing a child, from a woman being kept by a man, from where food is advertised to be distributed, from where a dog is waiting, from where flies are buzzing; he accepts no fish or meat; he drinks no liquor, wine, or fermented brew.

"He keeps to one house [on alms round], to one morsel of food; he keeps to two houses, to two morsels . . . he keeps to seven houses, to seven morsels. He lives on one saucer a day, on two saucers a day . . . on seven saucers a day. He takes food once a day, once every two days . . . once every seven days; thus even up to once every fortnight, he dwells pursuing the practice of taking food at stated intervals.

"He is an eater of greens or millet or forest rice or hide-parings or moss or rice bran or rice scum or sesame flour or grass or cow dung. He subsists on forest roots and fruits; he feeds on fallen fruits.

"He wears hemp robes, robes of hemp-mixed cloth, shroud robes, rag-robes; robes made from tree bark, antelope hides, strips of antelope hide; robes of *kusa* grass, bark fabric, or wood-shavings fabric; a mantle made of head hair [296] or of animal wool; a covering made of owls' wings.

"He is one who pulls out hair and beard, pursuing the practice of pulling out hair and beard. He is one who stands continuously, rejecting seats. He is one who squats continuously, devoted to maintaining the squatting position. He is one who uses a mattress of thorns; he makes a mattress of thorns his bed. He dwells pursuing the practice of bathing in water three times daily including the evening. Thus in such a variety of ways he dwells pursuing the practice of tormenting and mortifying the body. This is called the blistering way of practice.

(3) "And what is the middle way of practice? Here, a bhikkhu dwells contemplating the body in the body, ardent, clearly comprehending, mindful, having removed longing and dejection in regard to the world. He dwells contemplating feelings in feelings . . . mind in mind . . . phenomena in phenomena, ardent, clearly comprehending, mindful, having removed longing and dejection in regard to the world. This is called the middle way of practice.

"These, bhikkhus, are the three ways of practice."

157 (2)–162 (7) [Right Strivings, Etc.][613]

(157) "Bhikkhus, there are these three ways of practice. What three? The coarse way of practice, the blistering way of practice, and the middle way of practice.

(1) "And what, bhikkhus, is the coarse way of practice? . . . [as in 3:156] . . . This is called the coarse way of practice.

(2) "And what is the blistering way of practice? . . . [as in 3:156] . . . This is called the blistering way of practice.

(3) "And what is the middle way of practice? Here, a bhikkhu generates desire for the non-arising of unarisen bad unwholesome states; he makes an effort, arouses energy, applies his mind, and strives. He generates desire for the abandoning of arisen bad unwholesome states . . . for the arising of unarisen wholesome states . . . for the maintenance of arisen wholesome

states, for their non-decline, increase, expansion, and fulfillment by development; [297] he makes an effort, arouses energy, applies his mind, and strives. . . ."

(158) ". . . he develops the basis for psychic potency that possesses concentration due to desire and activities of striving. He develops the basis for psychic potency that possesses concentration due to energy and activities of striving . . . that possesses concentration due to mind and activities of striving . . . that possesses concentration due to investigation and activities of striving. . . ."

(159) ". . . he develops the faculty of faith, the faculty of energy, the faculty of mindfulness, the faculty of concentration, the faculty of wisdom. . . ."

(160) ". . . he develops the power of faith, the power of energy, the power of mindfulness, the power of concentration, the power of wisdom. . . ."

(161) ". . . he develops the enlightenment factor of mindfulness, the enlightenment factor of discrimination of phenomena, the enlightenment factor of energy, the enlightenment factor of rapture, the enlightenment factor of tranquility, the enlightenment factor of concentration, the enlightenment factor of equanimity. . . ."

(162) ". . . he develops right view, right intention, right speech, right action, right livelihood, right effort, right mindfulness, right concentration. This is called the middle way of practice.

"These, bhikkhus, are the three ways of practice."

VII. Courses of Kamma Repetition Series

163 (1)–182 (20)[614]

(163) "Bhikkhus, one possessing three qualities is deposited in hell as if brought there. What three? (1) One destroys life oneself, (2) encourages others to destroy life, and (3) approves of the destruction of life. One possessing these three qualities is deposited in hell as if brought there."

(164) "Bhikkhus, one possessing three qualities is deposited in heaven as if brought there. What three? (1) One abstains from the destruction of life oneself, (2) encourages others to abstain from the destruction of life, and (3) approves of abstaining from

the destruction of life. One possessing these three qualities is deposited in heaven as if brought there."

(165) "... (1) One takes what is not given oneself, (2) encourages others to take what is not given, and (3) approves of taking what is not given...."

(166) "... (1) One abstains from taking what is not given oneself, (2) encourages others to abstain from taking what is not given, and (3) approves of abstaining from taking what is not given...."

(167) "... (1) One engages in sexual misconduct oneself, (2) encourages others [298] to engage in sexual misconduct, and (3) approves of engaging in sexual misconduct...."

(168) "... (1) One abstains from sexual misconduct oneself, (2) encourages others to abstain from sexual misconduct, and (3) approves of abstaining from sexual misconduct...."

(169) "... (1) One speaks falsely oneself, (2) encourages others to speak falsely, and (3) approves of false speech...."

(170) "... (1) One abstains from false speech oneself, (2) encourages others to abstain from false speech, and (3) approves of abstaining from false speech...."

(171) "... (1) One speaks divisively oneself, (2) encourages others to speak divisively, and (3) approves of divisive speech...."

(172) "... (1) One abstains from divisive speech oneself, (2) encourages others to abstain from divisive speech, and (3) approves of abstaining from divisive speech...."

(173) "... (1) One speaks harshly oneself, (2) encourages others to speak harshly, and (3) approves of harsh speech...."

(174) "... (1) One abstains from harsh speech oneself, (2) encourages others to abstain from harsh speech, and (3) approves of abstaining from harsh speech...."

(175) "... (1) One indulges in idle chatter oneself, (2) encourages others to indulge in idle chatter, and (3) approves of indulging in idle chatter...."

(176) "... (1) One abstains from idle chatter oneself, (2) encourages others to abstain from idle chatter, and (3) approves of abstaining from idle chatter...."

(177) "... (1) One is full of longing oneself, (2) encourages others in longing, and (3) approves of longing...."

(178) "... (1) One is without longing oneself, (2) encourages

others to be without longing, and (3) approves of being without longing. . . ." [299]

(179) ". . . (1) One has ill will oneself, (2) encourages others in ill will, and (3) approves of ill will. . . ."

(180) ". . . (1) One is without ill will oneself, (2) encourages others to be without ill will, and (3) approves of being without ill will. . . ."

(181) ". . . (1) One holds wrong view oneself, (2) encourages others in wrong view, and (3) approves of wrong view. . . ."

(182) ". . . (1) One holds right view oneself, (2) encourages others in right view, and (3) approves of right view. One possessing these three qualities is deposited in heaven as if brought there."

VIII. Lust and So Forth Repetition Series[615]

183 (1)

"Bhikkhus, for direct knowledge of lust, three things[616] are to be developed. What three? Emptiness concentration, markless concentration, and wishless concentration.[617] For direct knowledge of lust, these three things are to be developed."

184 (2)–352 (170)

"Bhikkhus, for full understanding of lust . . . for the utter destruction . . . for the abandoning . . . for the destruction . . . for the vanishing . . . for the fading away . . . for the cessation . . . for the giving up . . . For the relinquishment of lust, these three things are to be developed.

"Bhikkhus, for direct knowledge . . . for full understanding . . . for the utter destruction . . . for the abandoning . . . for the destruction . . . for the vanishing . . . for the fading away . . . for the cessation . . . for the giving up . . . for the relinquishment of hatred . . . delusion . . . anger . . . hostility . . . denigration . . . insolence . . . envy . . . miserliness . . . deceitfulness . . . craftiness . . . obstinacy . . . vehemence . . . conceit . . . arrogance . . . intoxication . . . heedlessness, three things are to be developed. What three? Emptiness concentration, markless concentration, and wishless concentration. For the relinquishment of heedlessness, these three things are to be developed."

This is what the Blessed One said. Elated, those bhikkhus delighted in the Blessed One's statement.

The Book of the Threes is finished.

The Book of the Fours
(*Catukkanipāta*)

The Book of the Fours

The First Fifty

The Second Fifty

The Third Fifty

The Fourth Fifty

The Fifth Fifty

[1]

The Book of the Fours

Homage to the Blessed One, the Arahant,
the Perfectly Enlightened One

The First Fifty

I. Bhaṇḍagāma

1 (1) Understood

Thus have I heard. On one occasion the Blessed One was dwelling among the Vajjis at Bhaṇḍagāma. There the Blessed One addressed the bhikkhus: "Bhikkhus!"

"Venerable sir!" those bhikkhus replied. The Blessed One said this:[618] "Bhikkhus, it is because of not understanding and penetrating four things that you and I have roamed and wandered for such a long stretch of time.[619] What four?

"It is, bhikkhus, because of not understanding and penetrating noble virtuous behavior, noble concentration, noble wisdom, and noble liberation that you and I have roamed and wandered for such a long stretch of time.

"Noble virtuous behavior has been understood and penetrated. Noble concentration has been understood and penetrated. Noble wisdom has been understood and penetrated. Noble liberation has been understood and penetrated. Craving for existence has been cut off; the conduit to existence has been destroyed;[620] now there is no more renewed existence."

This is what the Blessed One said. Having said this, the Fortunate One, the Teacher, further said this: [2]

"Virtuous behavior, concentration, wisdom,
and unsurpassed liberation:

these things the illustrious Gotama
understood by himself.

"Having directly known these things,
the Buddha taught the Dhamma to the bhikkhus.
The Teacher, the end-maker of suffering,
the One with Vision, has attained nibbāna."[621]

2 (2) Fallen

At Sāvatthī. "Bhikkhus, one who does not possess four things is said to have fallen from this Dhamma and discipline. What four? (1) One who does not possess noble virtuous behavior is said to have fallen from this Dhamma and discipline. (2) One who does not possess noble concentration . . . (3) One who does not possess noble wisdom . . . (4) One who does not possess noble liberation is said to have fallen from this Dhamma and discipline. One who does not possess these four things is said to have fallen from this Dhamma and discipline.

"But, bhikkhus, one who possesses four things is said to be secure[622] in this Dhamma and discipline. What four? (1) One who possesses noble virtuous behavior is said to be secure in this Dhamma and discipline. (2) One who possesses noble concentration . . . (3) One who possesses noble wisdom . . . (4) One who possesses noble liberation is said to be secure in this Dhamma and discipline. One who possesses these four things is said to be secure in this Dhamma and discipline."

Collapsed and fallen, they fall away;
the greedy ones come back again.
Done is the task, the delightful is delighted in;
happiness is reached by happiness.[623]

3 (3) Maimed (1)

"Bhikkhus, possessing four qualities, the foolish, incompetent, bad person maintains himself in a maimed and injured condition; he is blameworthy [3] and subject to reproach by the wise; and he generates much demerit. What four?

(1) "Without investigating and scrutinizing, he speaks praise of one who deserves dispraise. (2) Without investigating and scrutinizing, he speaks dispraise of one who deserves praise.

(3) Without investigating and scrutinizing, he believes a matter that merits suspicion. (4) Without investigating and scrutinizing, he is suspicious about a matter that merits belief. Possessing these four qualities, the foolish, incompetent, bad person maintains himself in a maimed and injured condition; he is blameworthy and subject to reproach by the wise; and he generates much demerit.

"Bhikkhus, possessing four qualities, the wise, competent, good person preserves himself unmaimed and uninjured; he is blameless and beyond reproach by the wise; and he generates much merit. What four?

(1) "Having investigated and scrutinized, he speaks dispraise of one who deserves dispraise. (2) Having investigated and scrutinized, he speaks praise of one who deserves praise. (3) Having investigated and scrutinized, he is suspicious about a matter that merits suspicion. (4) Having investigated and scrutinized, he believes a matter that merits belief. Possessing these four qualities, the wise, competent, good person preserves himself unmaimed and uninjured; he is blameless and beyond reproach by the wise; and he generates much merit."

He who praises one deserving blame,
or blames one deserving praise,
casts with his mouth an unlucky throw
by which he finds no happiness.[624]

Slight is the unlucky throw at dice
that results in the loss of one's wealth,
[the loss] of all, oneself included;
much worse is this unlucky throw
of harboring hate against the fortunate ones.[625]

For a hundred thousand and thirty-six
nirabbudas, plus five *abbudas*, [4]
the slanderer of noble ones goes to hell,
having defamed them with evil speech and mind.[626]

4 (4) Maimed (2)

"Bhikkhus, behaving wrongly toward four persons, the foolish, incompetent, bad person maintains himself in a maimed and injured condition; he is blameworthy and subject to reproach by the wise; and he generates much demerit. What four? (1) Behaving wrongly toward his mother, the foolish, incompetent, bad person maintains himself in a maimed and injured condition; he is blameworthy and subject to reproach by the wise; and he generates much demerit. (2) Behaving wrongly toward his father . . . (3) Behaving wrongly toward the Tathāgata . . . (4) Behaving wrongly toward a disciple of the Tathāgata . . . Behaving wrongly toward these four persons, the foolish, incompetent, bad person maintains himself in a maimed and injured condition; he is blameworthy and subject to reproach by the wise; and he generates much demerit.

"Bhikkhus, behaving rightly toward four persons, the wise, competent, good person preserves himself unmaimed and uninjured; he is blameless and beyond reproach by the wise; and he generates much merit. What four? (1) Behaving rightly toward his mother, the wise, competent, good person preserves himself unmaimed and uninjured; he is blameless and beyond reproach by the wise; and he generates much merit. (2) Behaving rightly toward his father . . . (3) Behaving rightly toward the Tathāgata. . . (4) Behaving rightly toward a disciple of the Tathāgata. . . Behaving rightly toward these four persons, the wise, competent, good person preserves himself unmaimed and uninjured; he is blameless and beyond reproach by the wise; and he generates much merit."

A person who behaves wrongly
toward his mother and father,
toward the enlightened Tathāgata,
or toward his disciple, [5]
generates much demerit.

Because of that unrighteous conduct
toward mother and father,
the wise criticize one here in this world
and after death one goes to the plane of misery.

A person who behaves rightly
toward his mother and father,
toward the enlightened Tathāgata,

or toward his disciple,
generates much merit.

Because of that righteous conduct
toward mother and father,
the wise praise one in this world
and after death one rejoices in heaven.[627]

5 (5) Along with the Stream

"Bhikkhus, there are these four kinds of persons found existing in the world. What four? The person who goes along with the stream; the one who goes against the stream; the one who is inwardly firm; and the one who has crossed over and gone beyond, the brahmin who stands on high ground.[628]

(1) "And what is the person who goes along with the stream? Here, someone indulges in sensual pleasures and performs bad deeds. This is called the person who goes along with the stream.

(2) "And what is the person who goes against the stream? Here, someone does not indulge in sensual pleasures or perform bad deeds. Even with pain and dejection, weeping with a tearful face, he lives the complete and purified spiritual life. This is called the person who goes against the stream.

(3) "And what is the person who is inwardly firm? Here, with the utter destruction of the five lower fetters, some person is of spontaneous birth, due to attain final nibbāna there without ever returning from that world. This is called the person who is inwardly firm.

(4) "And what is the one who has crossed over and gone beyond, the brahmin who stands on high ground? [6] Here, with the destruction of the taints, some person has realized for himself with direct knowledge, in this very life, the taintless liberation of mind, liberation by wisdom, and having entered upon it, he dwells in it. This is called the person who has crossed over and gone beyond, the brahmin who stands on high ground.

"These, bhikkhus, are the four kinds of persons found existing in the world."

Those people who are uncontrolled in sense pleasures,
not rid of lust, enjoying sense pleasures here,

repeatedly coming back to[629] birth and old age,
immersed in craving, are "the ones who go along with
the stream."

Therefore a wise person with mindfulness established,
not resorting to sense pleasures and bad deeds,
should give up sense pleasures even if it's painful:
they call this person "one who goes against the stream."

One who has abandoned five defilements,
a fulfilled trainee,[630] unable to retrogress,
attained to mind's mastery, his faculties composed:
this person is called "one inwardly firm."

One who has comprehended things high and low,
burnt them up, so they're gone and exist no more:
that sage who has lived the spiritual life,
reached the world's end, is called
"one who has gone beyond."

6 (6) One of Little Learning

"Bhikkhus, there are these four kinds of persons found existing in the world. What four? One of little learning who is not intent on what he has learned; one of little learning who is intent on what he has learned; one of much learning who is not intent on what he has learned; and one of much learning who is intent on what he has learned.

(1) "And how is a person one of little learning who is not intent on what he has learned? [7] Here, someone has learned little—that is, of the discourses, mixed prose and verse, expositions, verses, inspired utterances, quotations, birth stories, amazing accounts, and questions-and-answers[631]—but he does not understand the meaning of what he has learned; he does not understand the Dhamma; and he does not practice in accordance with the Dhamma. In such a way, a person is one of little learning who is not intent on what he has learned.

(2) "And how is a person one of little learning who is intent on what he has learned? Here, someone has learned little—that is, of the discourses . . . questions-and-answers—but having understood the meaning of what he has learned, and having

understood the Dhamma, he practices in accordance with the Dhamma. In such a way, a person is one of little learning who is intent on what he has learned.

(3) "And how is a person one of much learning who is not intent on what he has learned? Here, someone has learned much—that is, of the discourses . . . questions-and-answers—but he does not understand the meaning of what he has learned; he does not understand the Dhamma; and he does not practice in accordance with the Dhamma. In such a way, a person is one of much learning who is not intent on what he has learned.

(4) "And how is a person one of much learning who is intent on what he has learned? Here, someone has learned much—that is, of the discourses . . . questions-and-answers—and having understood the meaning of what he has learned, and having understood the Dhamma, he practices in accordance with the Dhamma. In such a way, a person is one of much learning who is intent on what he has learned.

"These, bhikkhus, are the four kinds of persons found existing in the world."

If one has little learning
and is not settled in the virtues,
they criticize him on both counts,
virtuous behavior and learning.

If one has little learning
but is well settled in the virtues,
they praise him for his virtuous behavior;
his learning has succeeded.[632]

If one is highly learned
but is not settled in the virtues,
they criticize him for his lack of virtue;
his learning has not succeeded. [8]

If one is highly learned
and is settled in the virtues,
they praise him on both counts,
virtuous behavior and learning.

When a disciple of the Buddha is highly learned,
an expert on the Dhamma, endowed with wisdom,
like a coin of refined mountain gold,
who is fit to blame him?
Even the devas praise such a one;
by Brahmā too he is praised.

7 (7) They Adorn

"Bhikkhus, these four kinds of persons who are competent, disciplined, self-confident, learned, experts on the Dhamma, practicing in accordance with the Dhamma, adorn the Saṅgha. What four?

(1) "A bhikkhu who is competent, disciplined, self-confident, learned, an expert on the Dhamma, practicing in accordance with the Dhamma, adorns the Saṅgha. (2) A bhikkhunī who is competent... (3) A male lay follower who is competent... (4) A female lay follower who is competent, disciplined, self-confident, learned, an expert on the Dhamma, practicing in accordance with the Dhamma, adorns the Saṅgha.

"Bhikkhus, these four kinds of persons who are competent, disciplined, self-confident, learned, upholders of the Dhamma, practicing in accordance with the Dhamma, adorn the Saṅgha."

One who is competent and self-confident,
learned, an expert on the Dhamma,
practicing in accord with the Dhamma,
is called an adornment of the Saṅgha.

A bhikkhu accomplished in virtue,
a learned bhikkhunī,
a male lay follower endowed with faith,
a female lay follower endowed with faith:
these are the ones that adorn the Saṅgha;
these are the Saṅgha's adornments.

8 (8) Self-Confidence

"Bhikkhus, there are these four kinds of self-confidence that the Tathāgata has, possessing which he claims the place of the chief bull, [9] roars his lion's roar in the assemblies, and sets in motion the brahma wheel.[633] What four?

(1) "I do not see any ground on the basis of which an ascetic or brahmin or deva or Māra or Brahmā or anyone in the world might reasonably reprove me, saying: 'Though you claim to be perfectly enlightened, you are not fully enlightened about these things.' Since I do not see any such ground, I dwell secure, fearless, and self-confident.

(2) "I do not see any ground on the basis of which an ascetic or brahmin or deva or Māra or Brahmā or anyone in the world might reasonably reprove me, saying: 'Though you claim to be one whose taints are destroyed, you have not fully destroyed these taints.' Since I do not see any such ground, I dwell secure, fearless, and self-confident.

(3) "I do not see any ground on the basis of which an ascetic or brahmin or deva or Māra or Brahmā or anyone in the world might reasonably reprove me, saying: 'These things that you have said to be obstructive are not able to obstruct one who engages in them.' Since I do not see any such ground, I dwell secure, fearless, and self-confident.

(4) "I do not see any ground on the basis of which an ascetic or brahmin or deva or Māra or Brahmā or anyone in the world might reasonably reprove me, saying: 'The Dhamma does not lead one who practices it to the complete destruction of suffering, the goal for the sake of which you teach it.'[634] Since I do not see any such ground, I dwell secure, fearless, and self-confident.

"These, bhikkhus, are the four kinds of self-confidence that the Tathāgata has, possessing which he claims the place of the chief bull, roars his lion's roar in the assemblies, and sets in motion the wheel of Brahmā."

These pathways of doctrine,
formulated in diverse ways,
relied upon by ascetics and brahmins,
do not reach the Tathāgata,
the self-confident one who has passed
beyond the pathways of doctrine.[635]

Consummate, having overcome [everything],
he set in motion the wheel of Dhamma
out of compassion for all beings.
Beings pay homage to such a one,

the best among devas and humans,
who has gone beyond existence. [10]

9 (9) Craving

"Bhikkhus, there are these four ways in which craving arises in a bhikkhu. What four? Craving arises in a bhikkhu because of robes, almsfood, lodgings, or for the sake of life here or elsewhere.[636] These are the four ways in which craving arises in a bhikkhu."

With craving as companion
a person wanders during this long time.
Going from one state to another,
he does not overcome saṃsāra.

Having known this danger—
that craving is the origin of suffering—
free from craving, devoid of grasping,
a bhikkhu should wander mindfully.

10 (10) Bonds

"Bhikkhus, there are these four bonds. What four? The bond of sensuality, the bond of existence, the bond of views, and the bond of ignorance.

(1) "And what, bhikkhus, is the bond of sensuality? Here, someone does not understand as they really are the origin and the passing away, the gratification, the danger, and the escape in regard to sensual pleasures. When one does not understand these things as they really are, then sensual lust, sensual delight, sensual affection, sensual infatuation, sensual thirst, sensual passion, sensual attachment, and sensual craving lie deep within one in regard to sensual pleasures. This is called the bond of sensuality.

(2) "Such is the bond of sensuality. And how is there the bond of existence? Here, someone does not understand as they really are the origin and the passing away, the gratification, the danger, and the escape in regard to states of existence.[637] When one does not understand these things as they really are, then lust for existence, delight in existence, affection for existence, infatuation with existence, thirst for existence, passion for

existence, attachment to existence, and craving for existence lie deep within one in regard to states of existence. This is called the bond of existence.

(3) "Such are the bond of sensuality and the bond of existence. And how is there the bond of views? Here, someone does not understand as they really are the origin and the passing away, the gratification, the danger, and the escape in regard to views. When one does not understand these things as they really are, [11] then lust for views, delight in views, affection for views, infatuation with views, thirst for views, passion for views, attachment to views, and craving for views lie deep within one in regard to views. This is called the bond of views.

(4) "Such are the bond of sensuality, the bond of existence, and the bond of views. And how is there the bond of ignorance? Here, someone does not understand as they really are the origin and the passing away, the gratification, the danger, and the escape in regard to the six bases for contact. When one does not understand these things as they really are, then, ignorance and unknowing lie deep within one in regard to the six bases for contact. This is called the bond of ignorance. Such are the bond of sensuality, the bond of existence, the bond of views, and the bond of ignorance.

"One is fettered by bad unwholesome states that are defiling, conducive to renewed existence, troublesome, ripening in suffering, leading to future birth, old age, and death; therefore one is said to be 'not secure from bondage.' These are the four bonds.

"There are, bhikkhus, these four severances of bonds. What four? The severance of the bond of sensuality, the severance of the bond of existence, the severance of the bond of views, and the severance of the bond of ignorance.

(1) "And what, bhikkhus, is the severance of the bond of sensuality? Here, someone understands as they really are the origin and the passing away, the gratification, the danger, and the escape in regard to sensual pleasures. When one understands these things as they really are, then sensual lust, sensual delight, sensual affection, sensual infatuation, sensual thirst, sensual passion, sensual attachment, and sensual craving do not lie within one in regard to sensual pleasures. This is called the severance of the bond of sensuality.

(2) "Such is the severance of the bond of sensuality. And how is there the severance of the bond of existence? Here, someone understands as they really are the origin and the passing away, the gratification, the danger, and the escape in regard to states of existence. When one understands these things as they really are, then lust for existence, delight in existence, affection for existence, infatuation with existence, thirst for existence, passion for existence, attachment to existence, and craving for existence do not lie within one in regard to states of existence. This is called the severance of the bond of existence.

(3) "Such are the severance of the bond of sensuality and the severance of the bond of existence. And how is there the severance of the bond of views? Here, someone understands as they really are the origin and the passing away, the gratification, the danger, and [12] the escape in regard to views. When one understands these things as they really are, then lust for views, delight in views, affection for views, infatuation with views, thirst for views, passion for views, attachment to views, and craving for views do not lie within one in regard to views. This is called the severance of the bond of views.

(4) "Such are the severance of the bond of sensuality, the severance of the bond of existence, and the severance of the bond of views. And how is there the severance of the bond of ignorance? Here, someone understands as they really are the origin and the passing away, the gratification, the danger, and the escape in regard to the six bases for contact. When one understands these things as they really are, then ignorance and unknowing do not lie within one in regard to the six bases for contact. This is called the severance of the bond of ignorance. Such are the severance of the bond of sensuality, the severance of the bond of existence, the severance of the bond of views, and the severance of the bond of ignorance.

"One is detached from bad unwholesome states that are defiling, conducive to renewed existence, troublesome, ripening in suffering, leading to future birth, old age, and death; therefore one is said to be 'secure from bondage.' These are the four severances of bonds."

Fettered by the bond of sensuality
and the bond of existence,

fettered by the bond of views,
preceded by ignorance,
beings go on in saṃsāra,
led on in birth and death.

But having entirely understood
sense pleasures and the bond of existence,
having uprooted the bond of views
and dissolved ignorance,
the sages have severed all bonds;
they have gone beyond bondage.[638] [13]

II. Walking

11 (1) Walking[639]

(1) "Bhikkhus, if a sensual thought, a thought of ill will, or a thought of harming arises in a bhikkhu while walking, and he tolerates it, does not abandon it, dispel it, terminate it, and obliterate it, then that bhikkhu is said to be devoid of ardor and moral dread; he is constantly and continuously lazy and lacking in energy while walking.

(2) "If a sensual thought . . . arises in a bhikkhu while standing . . . (3) If a sensual thought . . . arises in a bhikkhu while sitting . . . (4) If a sensual thought, a thought of ill will, or a thought of harming arises in a bhikkhu while wakefully lying down, and he tolerates it, does not abandon it, dispel it, terminate it, and obliterate it, then that bhikkhu is said to be devoid of ardor and moral dread; he is constantly and continuously lazy and lacking in energy while wakefully lying down.

(1) "But, bhikkhus, if a sensual thought, a thought of ill will, or a thought of harming arises in a bhikkhu while walking, and he does not tolerate it but abandons it, dispels it, terminates it, and obliterates it, then that bhikkhu is said to be ardent and to dread wrongdoing; he is constantly and continuously energetic and resolute while walking.

(2) "If a sensual thought . . . arises in a bhikkhu while standing . . . (3) If a sensual thought . . . arises in a bhikkhu while sitting . . . (4) If a sensual thought, a thought of ill will, or a thought of harming arises in a bhikkhu while wakefully lying down,

and he does not tolerate it but abandons it, dispels it, terminates it, [14] and obliterates it, then that bhikkhu is said to be ardent and to dread wrongdoing; he is constantly and continuously energetic and resolute while walking."

Whether walking or standing,
sitting or lying down,
one who thinks bad thoughts
connected with the household life
has entered upon a dire path,
infatuated by delusive things:
such a bhikkhu cannot reach
the highest enlightenment.

But one who, whether walking,
standing, sitting, or lying down,
has calmed his thoughts
and delights in the stilling of thought:
a bhikkhu such as this can reach
the highest enlightenment.

12 (2) Virtuous Behavior

"Bhikkhus, dwell observant of virtuous behavior, observant of the Pātimokkha. Dwell restrained by the Pātimokkha, possessed of good conduct and resort, seeing danger in minute faults. Having undertaken them, train in the training rules. When you have done so, what further should be done?

(1) "Bhikkhus, if a bhikkhu has gotten rid of longing and ill will while walking; if he has abandoned dullness and drowsiness, restlessness and remorse, and doubt;[640] if his energy is aroused without slackening; if his mindfulness is established and unmuddled; if his body is tranquil and undisturbed; if his mind is concentrated and one-pointed, then that bhikkhu is said to be ardent and to dread wrongdoing; he is constantly and continuously energetic and resolute while walking.

(2) "If a bhikkhu has gotten rid of longing and ill will while standing . . . (3) If a bhikkhu has gotten rid of longing and ill will while sitting . . . [15] . . . (4) If a bhikkhu has gotten rid of longing and ill will while wakefully lying down; if he has abandoned dullness and drowsiness, restlessness and remorse, and

doubt; if his energy is aroused without slackening; if his mindfulness is established and unmuddled; if his body is tranquil and undisturbed; if his mind is concentrated and one-pointed, then that bhikkhu is said to be ardent and to dread wrongdoing; he is constantly and continuously energetic and resolute while wakefully lying down."

Controlled in walking, controlled in standing,
controlled in sitting and in lying down;
controlled, a bhikkhu draws in the limbs,
and controlled, he stretches them out.

Above, across, and below,
as far as the world extends,
he is one who scrutinizes the arising and vanishing
of such phenomena as the aggregates.

Training in what is conducive
to serenity of mind, always mindful,
they call such a bhikkhu
one constantly resolute.

13 (3) Striving

"Bhikkhus, there are these four right strivings. What four? (1) Here, a bhikkhu generates desire for the non-arising of unarisen bad unwholesome states; he makes an effort, arouses energy, applies his mind, and strives. (2) He generates desire for the abandoning of arisen bad unwholesome states; he makes an effort, arouses energy, applies his mind, and strives. (3) He generates desire for the arising of unarisen wholesome states; he makes an effort, arouses energy, applies his mind, and strives. (4) He generates desire for the persistence of arisen wholesome states, for their non-decline, increase, expansion, and fulfillment by development; he makes an effort, arouses energy, applies his mind, and strives. These are the four right strivings."

Those who strive rightly
overcome the realm of Māra;
they are unattached,
gone beyond fear of birth and death.

They are contented and unstirred,
having conquered Māra and his mount;
those happy ones have overcome
all Namuci's armies.[641] [16]

14 (4) Restraint

"Bhikkhus, there are these four strivings. What four? Striving by restraint, striving by abandonment, striving by development, and striving by protection.

(1) "And what, bhikkhus, is striving by restraint? Here, having seen a form with the eye, a bhikkhu does not grasp its marks and features. Since, if he left the eye faculty unrestrained, bad unwholesome states of longing and dejection might invade him, he practices restraint over it, he guards the eye faculty, he undertakes the restraint of the eye faculty. Having heard a sound with the ear . . . Having smelled an odor with the nose . . . Having tasted a taste with the tongue . . . Having felt a tactile object with the body . . . Having cognized a mental phenomenon with the mind, a bhikkhu does not grasp its marks and features. Since, if he left the mind faculty unrestrained, bad unwholesome states of longing and dejection might invade him, he practices restraint over it, he guards the mind faculty, he undertakes the restraint of the mind faculty. This is called striving by restraint.

(2) "And what is striving by abandonment? Here, a bhikkhu does not tolerate an arisen sensual thought; he abandons it, dispels it, terminates it, and obliterates it. He does not tolerate an arisen thought of ill will . . . an arisen thought of harming . . . bad unwholesome states whenever they arise; he abandons them, dispels them, terminates them, and obliterates them. This is called striving by abandonment.

(3) "And what is striving by development? Here, a bhikkhu develops the enlightenment factor of mindfulness, which is based upon seclusion, dispassion, and cessation, maturing in release. He develops the enlightenment factor of discrimination of phenomena . . . the enlightenment factor of energy . . . the enlightenment factor of rapture . . . the enlightenment factor of tranquility . . . the enlightenment factor of concentration . . . the enlightenment factor of equanimity, which is based upon seclusion, dispassion, and cessation, maturing in release. This is called striving by development. [17]

(4) "And what is striving by protection? Here, a bhikkhu protects an arisen excellent object of concentration:[642] the perception of a skeleton, the perception of a worm-infested corpse, the perception of a livid corpse, the perception of a festering corpse, the perception of a fissured corpse, the perception of a bloated corpse. This is called striving by protection.

"These, bhikkhus, are the four kinds of striving."

> Restraint and abandonment,
> development and protection:
> these four strivings were taught
> by the Kinsman of the Sun.
> By these means an ardent bhikkhu here
> can attain the destruction of suffering.

15 (5) Proclamations

"Bhikkhus, there are these four proclamations of the foremost. What four?

(1) "The foremost of those with bodies is Rāhu, lord of the asuras.[643] (2) The foremost of those who enjoy sensual pleasures is King Mandhātā.[644] (3) The foremost of those who exercise authority is Māra the Evil One. (4) In this world with its devas, Māra, and Brahmā, among this population with its ascetics and brahmins, its devas and humans, the Tathāgata, the Arahant, the Perfectly Enlightened One is declared foremost. These are the four proclamations of those who are foremost."

> Rāhu is the foremost of those with bodies,
> Mandhātā, of those enjoying sense pleasures;
> Māra is the foremost of rulers,
> blazing with power and glory.
>
> In this world together with its devas
> above, across, and below,
> as far as the world extends,
> the Buddha is declared foremost.

16 (6) Exquisiteness

"Bhikkhus, there are these four kinds of exquisiteness.[645] What four? (1) Here, a bhikkhu possesses supreme exquisiteness of form. He does not perceive any other exquisiteness of form more excellent or sublime than that one; he does not yearn for any other exquisiteness of form more excellent or sublime than that one. (2) He possesses supreme exquisiteness of feeling [18] . . . (3) . . . supreme exquisiteness of perception . . . (4) . . . supreme exquisiteness of volitional activities. He does not perceive any other exquisiteness of volitional activities more excellent or sublime than that one; he does not yearn for any other exquisiteness of volitional activities more excellent or sublime than that one.

"These are the four kinds of exquisiteness."

> Having known the exquisiteness of form,
> the origination of feelings,
> how perception arises,
> and where it disappears;
> having known volitional activities
> as alien, as suffering, and not as self,
> truly that bhikkhu who sees rightly,[646]
> peaceful, delights in the peaceful state.
> He bears his final body,
> having conquered Māra and his mount.

17 (7) Wrong Courses (1)

"Bhikkhus, there are these four ways of taking a wrong course. What four? One takes a wrong course because of desire, because of hatred, because of delusion, or because of fear. These are the four ways of taking a wrong course."

> If through desire, hate, fear, or delusion
> one transgresses against the Dhamma,
> one's fame diminishes like the moon
> in the dark fortnight.

18 (8) Wrong Courses (2)

"Bhikkhus, there are these four ways of not taking a wrong course. What four? One does not take a wrong course because of desire, because of hatred, because of delusion, or because of fear. These are the four ways of not taking a wrong course."

If one does not transgress the Dhamma
through desire, hate, fear, or delusion,
one's fame becomes full like the moon
in the bright fortnight.

19 (9) Wrong Courses (3)

"Bhikkhus, there are these four ways of taking a wrong course. What four? [19] One takes a wrong course because of desire . . . [as in 4:17] . . . These are the four ways of taking a wrong course.

"Bhikkhus, there are these four ways of not taking a wrong course. What four? One does not take a wrong course because of desire . . . [as in 4:18] . . . These are the four ways of taking a wrong course."

If through desire, hate, fear, or delusion
one transgresses against the Dhamma,
one's fame diminishes like the moon
in the dark fortnight.

If one does not transgress the Dhamma
through desire, hate, fear, or delusion,
one's fame becomes full like the moon
in the bright fortnight.

20 (10) An Assigner of Meals

"Bhikkhus, if an assigner of meals[647] possesses four qualities, he is deposited in hell as if brought there. What four? He takes a wrong course because of desire, because of hatred, because of delusion, or because of fear. If an assigner of meals possesses these four qualities, he is deposited in hell as if brought there.

"Bhikkhus, if an assigner of meals possesses four qualities, he is deposited in heaven as if brought there. What four? He does not take a wrong course because of desire, because of hatred, because of delusion, or because of fear. If an assigner of meals possesses these four qualities, he is deposited in heaven as if brought there."

Those people uncontrolled in sensual pleasures,
who are unrighteous, not revering the Dhamma,
gone [astray] through desire, hate, and fear[648]

are called a stained assembly.
Such is said by the Ascetic who knows.

Therefore those good persons who are praiseworthy,
firm in the Dhamma, who do nothing bad,
unswayed by desire, hate, and fear,
are called an elite assembly.
Such is said by the Ascetic who knows. [20]

III. Uruvelā

21 (1) Uruvelā (1)[649]

Thus have I heard. On one occasion the Blessed One was dwelling at Sāvatthī in Jeta's Grove, Anāthapiṇḍika's Park. There the Blessed One addressed the bhikkhus: "Bhikkhus!"

"Venerable sir!" those bhikkhus replied. The Blessed One said this:

"Bhikkhus, on one occasion I was dwelling at Uruvelā, by the goatherds' banyan tree on the bank of the Neranjarā River, just after I had attained full enlightenment. Then, while I was alone in seclusion, a course of thought arose in my mind thus: 'It is painful to dwell without reverence and deference. Now what ascetic or brahmin can I honor, respect, and dwell in dependence on?'

"Then it occurred to me: (1) 'If my aggregate of virtuous behavior were incomplete, for the sake of completing it I would honor, respect, and dwell in dependence on another ascetic or brahmin. However, in this world with its devas, Māra, and Brahmā, among this population with its ascetics and brahmins, its devas and humans, I do not see another ascetic or brahmin more accomplished in virtuous behavior than myself whom I could honor, respect, and dwell in dependence on.

(2) "'If my aggregate of concentration were incomplete, for the sake of completing it I would honor, respect, and dwell in dependence on another ascetic or brahmin. However . . . I do not see another ascetic or brahmin more accomplished in concentration than myself. . . .

(3) "'If my aggregate of wisdom were incomplete, for the sake of completing it I would honor, respect, and dwell in dependence on another ascetic or brahmin. However . . . I do not see

another ascetic or brahmin more accomplished in wisdom than myself. . . .

(4) "'If my aggregate of liberation were incomplete, for the sake of completing it I would honor, respect, and dwell in dependence on another ascetic or brahmin. However, in this world with its devas, Māra, and Brahmā, among this population with its ascetics and brahmins, its devas and humans, I do not see another ascetic or brahmin more accomplished in liberation than myself whom I could honor, respect, and dwell in dependence on.

"It occurred to me: 'Let me then honor, respect, and dwell in dependence only on this Dhamma to which I have become fully enlightened.'

"Then Brahmā Sahampati, [21] having known with his own mind the reflection in my mind, disappeared from the brahmā world and reappeared before me just as a strong man might extend his drawn-in arm or draw in his extended arm. He arranged his upper robe over one shoulder, bent down with his right knee on the ground, reverently saluted me, and said: 'So it is, Blessed One! So it is, Fortunate One! Bhante, those who were the Arahants, the Perfectly Enlightened Ones in the past—those Blessed Ones, too, honored, respected, and dwelled in dependence only on the Dhamma. Those who will be the Arahants, the Perfectly Enlightened Ones in the future—those Blessed Ones, too, will honor, respect, and dwell in dependence only on the Dhamma. Let the Blessed One, too, who is at present the Arahant, the Perfectly Enlightened One, honor, respect, and dwell in dependence only on the Dhamma.'

"This is what Brahmā Sahampati said. Having said this, he further said this:

"'The perfect Buddhas of the past,
the Buddhas of the future,
and the present Buddha
who removes the sorrow of many:
all those dwelled, now dwell,
and [in the future] will dwell
revering the good Dhamma.
This is the nature of the Buddhas.

"'Therefore one desiring the good,[650]
aspiring for greatness,
should revere the good Dhamma,
recollecting the Buddhas' teaching.'

"This was what Brahmā Sahampati said. He then paid homage to me, and keeping me on his right, he disappeared right there. Then, having acknowledged Brahmā's request and what was proper for myself, I honored, respected, and dwelled in dependence only on the Dhamma to which I had become fully enlightened. And now that the Saṅgha has acquired greatness, I have respect for the Saṅgha, too." [22]

22 (2) Uruvelā (2)

"Bhikkhus, on one occasion I was dwelling at Uruvelā, by the goatherds' banyan tree on the bank of the Neranjarā River, just after I had attained full enlightenment. Then a number of brahmins, old, aged, burdened with years, advanced in life, come to the last stage, approached me and exchanged greetings with me. When they had concluded their greetings and cordial talk, they sat down to one side and said to me:

"'We have heard, Master Gotama: "The ascetic Gotama does not pay homage to brahmins who are old, aged, burdened with years, advanced in life, come to the last stage; nor does he stand up for them or offer them a seat." This is indeed true, for Master Gotama does not pay homage to brahmins who are old, aged, burdened with years, advanced in life, come to the last stage; nor does he stand up for them or offer them a seat. This is not proper, Master Gotama.'[651]

"It then occurred to me: These venerable ones do not know what an elder is or what the qualities that make one an elder are. Even though someone is old—eighty, ninety, or a hundred years from birth—if he speaks at an improper time, speaks falsely, speaks what is unbeneficial, speaks contrary to the Dhamma and the discipline, if at an improper time he speaks words that are worthless, unreasonable, rambling, and unbeneficial, then he is reckoned as a foolish [childish] elder.

"But even though someone is young, a youth with black hair, endowed with the blessing of youth, in the prime of life, if he speaks at a proper time, speaks what is truthful, speaks what is beneficial, speaks on the Dhamma and the discipline, and if at a proper time he speaks words that are worth recording, reasonable, succinct, and beneficial, then he is reckoned as a wise elder.

"There are, bhikkhus, these four qualities that make one an elder. What four?

(1) "Here, a bhikkhu is virtuous; he dwells restrained by the Pātimokkha, possessed of good conduct and resort, seeing danger in minute faults. Having undertaken the training rules, he trains in them.

(2) "He has learned much, [23] remembers what he has learned, and accumulates what he has learned. Those teachings that are good in the beginning, good in the middle, and good in the end, with the right meaning and phrasing, which proclaim the perfectly complete and pure spiritual life—such teachings as these he has learned much of, retained in mind, recited verbally, investigated with the mind, and penetrated well by view.

(3) "He is one who gains at will, without trouble or difficulty, the four jhānas that constitute the higher mind and are pleasant dwellings in this very life.

(4) "With the destruction of the taints, he has realized for himself with direct knowledge, in this very life, the taintless liberation of mind, liberation by wisdom, and having entered upon it, he dwells in it.

"These are the four qualities that make one an elder."

The dullard with a restless mind[652]
who speaks much chatter,
his thoughts unsettled,
delighting in a bad teaching,
holding bad views, disrespectful,
is far from an elder's stature.

But one accomplished in virtue,
learned and discerning,
self-controlled in the factors of firmness,
who clearly sees the meaning with wisdom;
gone beyond all phenomena,
not barren, discerning;[653]

who has abandoned birth and death,
consummate in the spiritual life,
in whom there are no taints—
he is the one I call an elder.
With the destruction of the taints
a bhikkhu is called an elder.

23 (3) The World[654]

"Bhikkhus, the Tathāgata has fully awakened to the world;[655] the Tathāgata is detached from the world. The Tathāgata has fully awakened to the origin of the world; the Tathāgata has abandoned the origin of the world. The Tathāgata has fully awakened to the cessation of the world; the Tathāgata has realized the cessation of the world. The Tathāgata has fully awakened to the way leading to the cessation of the world; the Tathāgata has developed the way leading to the cessation of the world.

(1) "Bhikkhus, in this world with its devas, Māra, and Brahmā, among this population with its ascetics and brahmins, its devas and humans, whatever is seen, heard, sensed, cognized, reached, sought after, [24] examined by the mind—all that the Tathāgata has fully awakened to; therefore he is called the Tathāgata.[656]

(2) "Bhikkhus, whatever the Tathāgata speaks, utters, or expounds in the interval between the night when he awakens to the unsurpassed perfect enlightenment and the night when he attains final nibbāna,[657] all that is just so and not otherwise; therefore he is called the Tathāgata.[658]

(3) "Bhikkhus, as the Tathāgata speaks, so he does; as he does, so he speaks. Since he does as he speaks and speaks as he does, therefore he is called the Tathāgata.[659]

(4) "Bhikkhus, in this world with its devas, Māra, and Brahmā, among this population with its ascetics and brahmins, its devas and humans, the Tathāgata is the vanquisher, the unvanquished, the universal seer, the wielder of mastery; therefore he is called the Tathāgata."

Having directly known all the world—
all in the world just as it is—
he is detached from all the world,
disengaged from all the world.

He is the vanquisher of all,
the wise one who has untied all knots.
He has reached the supreme peace,
nibbāna, inaccessible to fear.

He is the Buddha, his taints destroyed,
untroubled, all doubts cut off;
having reached the destruction of all kamma,
he is liberated in the extinction of acquisitions.

He is the Blessed One, the Buddha,
he is the lion unsurpassed;
in this world with its devas,
he set in motion the wheel of Brahmā.

Thus those devas and human beings
who have gone for refuge to the Buddha
assemble and pay homage to him,
the great one free from diffidence:

"Tamed, he is the best of tamers;
peaceful, he is the seer among peace-bringers;
freed, he is the chief of liberators;
crossed over, he is the best of guides across."

Thus indeed they pay him homage,
the great one free from diffidence.
In this world together with its devas,
there is no one who can rival you.

24 (4) Kāḷaka

[Thus have I heard.][660] On one occasion the Blessed One was dwelling at Sāketa, at Kāḷaka's Park.[661] There the Blessed One addressed the bhikkhus: "Bhikkhus!"

"Venerable sir!" those bhikkhus replied. The Blessed One said this: [25]

"Bhikkhus, in this world with its devas, Māra, and Brahmā, among this population with its ascetics and brahmins, its devas and humans, whatever is seen, heard, sensed, cognized, reached, sought after, examined by the mind—that I know.

"Bhikkhus, in this world with its devas, Māra, and Brahmā,

among this population with its ascetics and brahmins, its devas and humans, whatever is seen, heard, sensed, cognized, reached, sought after, examined by the mind—that I have directly known. It has been known by the Tathāgata,[662] but the Tathāgata did not become subservient to it.[663]

"Bhikkhus, if I were to say, 'In this world with its devas . . . whatever is seen, heard, sensed, cognized, reached, sought after, examined by the mind—that I do not know,' that would be a falsehood on my part.

"Bhikkhus, if I were to say, 'In this world with its devas . . . whatever is seen, heard, sensed, cognized, reached, sought after, examined by the mind—that I both know and do not know,' that too would be just the same.[664]

"Bhikkhus, if I were to say, 'In this world with its devas . . . whatever is seen, heard, sensed, cognized, reached, sought after, examined by the mind—that I neither know nor do not know,' that would be a fault on my part.[665]

(1) "So, having seen what can be seen, the Tathāgata does not misconceive the seen, does not misconceive the unseen, does not misconceive what can be seen, does not misconceive one who sees.[666] (2) Having heard what can be heard, he does not misconceive the heard, does not misconceive the unheard, does not misconceive what can be heard, does not misconceive one who hears. (3) Having sensed what can be sensed, he does not misconceive the sensed, does not misconceive the unsensed, does not misconceive what can be sensed, does not misconceive one who senses. (4) Having cognized what can be cognized, he does not misconceive the cognized, does not misconceive the uncognized, does not misconceive what can be cognized, does not misconceive one who cognizes.

"Thus, bhikkhus, being ever stable among things seen, heard, sensed, and cognized, the Tathāgata is a stable one.[667] And, I say, there is no stable one more excellent or sublime than that stable one."

> Amid those who are self-constrained, the Stable One
> would not posit as categorically true or false
> anything seen, heard, or sensed,
> clung to and considered truth by others.[668]

Since they have already seen this dart[669]
to which people cling and adhere, [26]
[saying] "I know, I see, it is just so,"
the Tathāgatas cling to nothing.

25 (5) The Spiritual Life

"Bhikkhus, this spiritual life is not lived for the sake of deceiving people and cajoling them; nor for the benefit of gain, honor, and praise; nor for the benefit of winning in debates; nor with the thought: 'Let the people know me thus.' But rather, this spiritual life is lived for the sake of restraint, abandoning, dispassion, and cessation."[670]

The Blessed One taught the spiritual life,
not based on tradition, culminating in nibbāna,
lived for the sake of
restraint and abandoning.[671]

This is the path of the great beings,[672]
the path followed by the great seers.
Those who practice it
as taught by the Buddha,
acting upon the Teacher's guidance,
will make an end of suffering.

26 (6) Deceivers[673]

(1) "Bhikkhus, those bhikkhus who are deceivers, stubborn, talkers, imposters, haughty, and unconcentrated are not bhikkhus of mine.[674] (2) They have strayed from this Dhamma and discipline, and they do not achieve growth, progress, and maturity in this Dhamma and discipline. (3) But those bhikkhus who are honest, sincere, steadfast, compliant, and well concentrated are bhikkhus of mine. (4) They have not strayed from this Dhamma and discipline, and they achieve growth, progress, and maturity in this Dhamma and discipline."

Those who are deceivers, stubborn, talkers,
imposters, haughty, unconcentrated,
do not make progress in the Dhamma
that the Perfectly Enlightened One has taught.

But those who are honest and sincere,
steadfast, compliant, and well concentrated,
make progress in the Dhamma
that the Perfectly Enlightened One has taught.

27 (7) Contentment

"Bhikkhus, there are these four trifles, easily gained and blameless. What four?

(1) "A rag-robe is a trifle among robes, easily gained [27] and blameless. (2) A lump of almsfood is a trifle among meals, easily gained and blameless. (3) The foot of a tree is a trifle among lodgings, easily gained and blameless. (4) Putrid urine is a trifle among medicines, easily gained and blameless.[675]

"These are the four trifles, easily gained and blameless. When a bhikkhu is satisfied with what is trifling and easily gained, I say that he has one of the factors of the ascetic life."

When one is content with what is blameless,
trifling and easily gained;
when one's mind is not distressed
because of a lodging,
robe, drink, and food,
one is not hindered anywhere.[676]

These qualities, rightly said
to conform to the ascetic life,
are acquired by a bhikkhu[677]
who is content and heedful.

28 (8) Noble Lineages[678]

"Bhikkhus, there are these four noble lineages, primal, of long standing, traditional, ancient, unadulterated and never before adulterated, which are not being adulterated and will not be adulterated, which are not repudiated by wise ascetics and brahmins. What four?

(1) "Here, a bhikkhu is content with any kind of robe, and he speaks in praise of contentment with any kind of robe, and he does not engage in a wrong search, in what is improper, for the sake of a robe.[679] If he does not get a robe he is not agitated, and if he gets one he uses it without being tied to it, infatuated

with it, and blindly absorbed in it, seeing the danger in it and understanding the escape from it. Yet he does not extol himself or disparage others because of this. Any bhikkhu who is skillful in this, diligent, clearly comprehending and ever mindful, is said to be standing in an ancient, primal noble lineage.

(2) "Again, a bhikkhu is content with any kind of almsfood, and he speaks in praise of contentment with any kind of almsfood, and he does not engage in a wrong search, in what is improper, for the sake of almsfood. If he does not get almsfood he is not agitated, and if he gets some he uses it without being tied to it, infatuated with it, and blindly absorbed in it, seeing the danger in it and understanding the escape from it. [28] Yet he does not extol himself or disparage others because of this. Any bhikkhu who is skillful in this, diligent, clearly comprehending and ever mindful, is said to be standing in an ancient, primal noble lineage.

(3) "Again, a bhikkhu is content with any kind of lodging, and he speaks in praise of contentment with any kind of lodging, and he does not engage in a wrong search, in what is improper, for the sake of lodging. If he does not get lodging he is not agitated, and if he gets it he uses it without being tied to it, infatuated with it, and blindly absorbed in it, seeing the danger in it and understanding the escape from it. Yet he does not extol himself or disparage others because of this. Any bhikkhu who is skillful in this, diligent, clearly comprehending and ever mindful, is said to be standing in an ancient, primal noble lineage.

(4) "Again, a bhikkhu finds delight in development, is delighted with development, finds delight in abandoning, is delighted with abandoning.[680] Yet he does not extol himself or disparage others because of this. Any bhikkhu who is skillful in this, diligent, clearly comprehending and ever mindful, is said to be standing in an ancient, primal noble lineage.

"These, bhikkhus, are the four noble lineages, primal, of long standing, traditional, ancient, unadulterated and never before adulterated, which are not being adulterated and will not be adulterated, which are not repudiated by wise ascetics and brahmins.

"Bhikkhus, when a bhikkhu possesses these four noble lineages, if he dwells in the east he vanquishes discontent,

discontent does not vanquish him; if he dwells in the west he vanquishes discontent, discontent does not vanquish him; if he dwells in the north he vanquishes discontent, discontent does not vanquish him; if he dwells in the south he vanquishes discontent, discontent does not vanquish him. For what reason? Because he is a steadfast one who vanquishes discontent and delight."

Discontent does not vanquish the steadfast one,[681]
[for] the steadfast one is not vanquished by discontent.[682]
The steadfast one vanquishes discontent,
for the steadfast one is a vanquisher of discontent. [29]

Who can obstruct the dispeller
who has discarded all kamma?
Who is fit to blame one who is like
a coin of refined gold?
Even the devas praise such a one;
by Brahmā too he is praised.

29 (9) Dhamma Factors

"Bhikkhus, there are these four Dhamma factors,[683] primal, of long standing, traditional, ancient, unadulterated and never before adulterated, which are not being adulterated and will not be adulterated, which are not repudiated by wise ascetics and brahmins. What four?

(1) "Non-longing is a Dhamma factor, primal, of long standing, traditional, ancient, unadulterated and never before adulterated, which is not being adulterated and will not be adulterated, which is not repudiated by wise ascetics and brahmins. (2) Good will is a Dhamma factor, primal, of long standing . . . (3) Right mindfulness is a Dhamma factor, primal, of long standing . . . (4) Right concentration is a Dhamma factor, primal, of long standing . . . not repudiated by wise ascetics and brahmins.

"These are the four Dhamma factors, primal, of long standing, traditional, ancient, unadulterated and never before adulterated, which are not being adulterated and will not be adulterated, which are not repudiated by wise ascetics and brahmins."

One should dwell free from longing
with a heart of good will.
One should be mindful and one-pointed in mind,
internally well concentrated.

30 (10) Wanderers

On one occasion the Blessed One was dwelling at Rājagaha on Mount Vulture Peak. Now on that occasion a number of very well-known wanderers were residing at the wanderers' park on the bank of the river Sappinī, namely, Annabhāra, Varadhara, Sakuludāyī the wanderer, and other very well-known wanderers.

Then, in the evening, the Blessed One emerged from seclusion and went to the wanderers' park on the bank of the Sappinī. He sat down on a seat that was prepared and said to those wanderers: "Wanderers, there are these four Dhamma factors that are primal, [30] of long standing, traditional, ancient, unadulterated and never before adulterated, which are not being adulterated and will not be adulterated, which are not repudiated by wise ascetics and brahmins. What four?

(1) "Non-longing is a Dhamma factor that is primal, of long standing, traditional, ancient, unadulterated and never before adulterated, which is not being adulterated and will not be adulterated, which is not repudiated by wise ascetics and brahmins. (2) Good will is a Dhamma factor that is primal, of long standing . . . (3) Right mindfulness is a Dhamma factor that is primal, of long standing . . . (4) Right concentration is a Dhamma factor that is primal, of long standing . . . not repudiated by wise ascetics and brahmins.

"These are the four Dhamma factors that are primal, of long standing, traditional, ancient, unadulterated and never before adulterated, which are not being adulterated and will not be adulterated, which are not repudiated by wise ascetics and brahmins.

(1) "If, wanderers, anyone should say: 'I will reject this Dhamma factor of non-longing and point out a [real] ascetic or brahmin who is full of longing, deeply passionate about sensual pleasures,' I would respond to him thus: 'Let him come, speak, and converse. Let me see how mighty he is!' Indeed, it would be impossible for him to reject non-longing as a Dhamma factor

and to point out a [real] ascetic or brahmin who is full of longing, deeply passionate about sensual pleasures.

(2) "If anyone should say: 'I will reject this Dhamma factor of good will and point out a [real] ascetic or brahmin who has a mind of ill will and intentions of hate,' I would respond to him thus: 'Let him come, speak, and converse. Let me see how mighty he is!' Indeed, it would be impossible for him to reject good will as a Dhamma factor and to point out a [real] ascetic or brahmin who has a mind of ill will and intentions of hate.

(3) "If anyone should say: 'I will reject this Dhamma factor of right mindfulness and point out a [real] ascetic or brahmin who is muddled in mind and lacks clear comprehension,' I would respond to him thus: 'Let him come, speak, and converse. Let me see how mighty he is!' Indeed, it would be impossible for him to reject right mindfulness as a Dhamma factor and to point out a [real] ascetic or brahmin who is muddled in mind and lacks clear comprehension.

(4) "If anyone should say: 'I will reject this Dhamma factor of right concentration and point out a [real] ascetic or brahmin who is unconcentrated, with a wandering mind,' I would respond to him thus: 'Let him come, speak, [31] and converse. Let me see how mighty he is!' Indeed, it would be impossible for him to reject right concentration as a Dhamma factor and to point out a [real] ascetic or brahmin who is unconcentrated, with a wandering mind.

"If, wanderers, anyone thinks these four Dhamma factors should be censured and repudiated, then, in this very life, he incurs four reasonable criticisms and grounds for censure.[684] What four?

"'If you censure and repudiate this Dhamma factor of non-longing, then you must regard as worthy of worship and praise those ascetics and brahmins who are full of longing and deeply passionate about sensual pleasures. If you censure and repudiate this Dhamma factor of good will, then you must regard as worthy of worship and praise those ascetics and brahmins who have minds of ill will and intentions of hate. If you censure and repudiate this Dhamma factor of right mindfulness, then you must regard as worthy of worship and praise those ascetics and brahmins who are muddle-minded and lack clear comprehension. If you censure and repudiate this Dhamma factor of right concentration, then you must regard as worthy of worship and praise those ascetics and brahmins who are unconcentrated, with wandering minds.'

"If, wanderers, anyone thinks these four Dhamma factors should be censured and repudiated, then, in this very life, he incurs these four reasonable criticisms and grounds for censure. Even those wanderers Vassa and Bhañña of Ukkalā, who were proponents of non-causality, inactivity, and nihilism, did not think that these four Dhamma factors should be censured and repudiated. For what reason? From fear of blame, attack, and refutation."[685]

One of good will, ever mindful,
inwardly well concentrated,
training to remove longing,
is said to be heedful. [32]

IV. The Wheel

31 (1) The Wheel

"Bhikkhus, there are these four wheels. When these four wheels turn, those devas and humans who possess them soon attain greatness and abundance of wealth. What four? Dwelling in a suitable locality, relying on good persons, right resolution, and merits done in the past.[686] These are the four wheels. When these four wheels turn, those devas and humans who possess them soon attain greatness and abundance of wealth."

When a person dwells in a suitable locality
and makes friends with the noble ones,
when he has formed right resolutions,
and done deeds of merit in the past,
grain, riches, fame, and reputation,
along with happiness accrue to him.

32 (2) Sustaining

"Bhikkhus, there are these four means of sustaining a favorable relationship. What four? Giving, endearing speech, beneficent conduct, and impartiality.[687] These are the four means of sustaining a favorable relationship."

Giving, endearing speech,
beneficent conduct, and impartiality
under diverse worldly conditions,
as is suitable to fit each case: these means
of sustaining a favorable relationship
are like the linchpin of a rolling chariot.

If there were no such means
of sustaining a favorable relationship,
neither mother nor father
would be able to obtain esteem
and veneration from their children.

But since there exist these means
of sustaining a favorable relationship,
wise people respect them;
thus they attain to greatness
and are highly praised. [33]

33 (3) The Lion

"Bhikkhus, in the evening the lion, the king of beasts, comes out from his lair, stretches his body, surveys the four quarters all around, and roars his lion's roar three times. Then he sets out in search of game.

"Whatever animals hear the lion roaring for the most part are filled with fear, a sense of urgency, and terror. Those who live in holes enter their holes; those who live in the water enter the water; those who live in the woods enter the woods; and the birds resort to the sky. Even those royal bull elephants, bound by strong thongs in the villages, towns, and capital cities, burst and break their bonds asunder; frightened, they urinate and defecate and flee here and there. So powerful among the animals is the lion, the king of beasts, so majestic and mighty.

"So too, bhikkhus, when the Tathāgata arises in the world, an arahant, perfectly enlightened, accomplished in true knowledge and conduct, fortunate, knower of the world, unsurpassed trainer of persons to be tamed, teacher of devas and humans, the Enlightened One, the Blessed One, he teaches the Dhamma thus: '(1) Such is personal existence, (2) such the origin of personal existence, (3) such the cessation of personal existence, (4) such the way to the cessation of personal existence.'[688]

"When those devas who are long-lived, beautiful, abounding in happiness, dwelling for a long time in lofty palaces, hear the Tathāgata's teaching of the Dhamma, for the most part they are filled with fear, a sense of urgency, and terror thus:[689] 'It seems that we are actually impermanent, though we thought ourselves permanent; it seems that we are actually transient, though we thought ourselves everlasting; it seems that we are actually non-eternal, though we thought ourselves eternal. It seems that we are impermanent, transient, non-eternal, included in personal existence.'[690] So powerful is the Tathāgata, so majestic and mighty is he in this world together with its devas." [34]

When, through direct knowledge,
the Buddha, the teacher, the peerless person
in this world with its devas,
sets in motion the wheel of Dhamma,
[he teaches] personal existence, its cessation,
the origin of personal existence,
and the noble eightfold path
that leads to the calming down of suffering.

Then even those devas with long life spans—
beautiful, ablaze with glory—
become fearful and filled with terror,
like beasts who hear the lion's roar.
"It seems that we are impermanent,
not beyond personal existence," [they say],
when they hear the word of the Arahant,
the Stable One who is fully freed.

34 (4) Confidence

"Bhikkhus, there are these four foremost kinds of confidence. What four?

(1) "To whatever extent there are beings, whether footless or with two feet, four feet, or many feet, whether having form or formless, whether percipient or non-percipient, or neither percipient nor non-percipient, the Tathāgata, the Arahant, the Perfectly Enlightened One is declared the foremost among them. Those who have confidence in the Buddha have confidence in the foremost, and for those who have confidence in the foremost, the result is foremost.

(2) "To whatever extent there are phenomena that are conditioned, the noble eightfold path is declared the foremost among them. Those who have confidence in the noble eightfold path have confidence in the foremost, and for those who have confidence in the foremost, the result is foremost.

(3) "To whatever extent there are phenomena conditioned or unconditioned,[691] dispassion is declared the foremost among them, that is, the crushing of pride, the removal of thirst, the uprooting of attachment, the termination of the round, the destruction of craving, dispassion, cessation, nibbāna. Those who have confidence in the Dhamma have confidence in the foremost, and for those who have confidence in the foremost, the result is foremost.

(4) "To whatever extent there are Saṅghas or groups, the Saṅgha of the Tathāgata's disciples is declared the foremost among them, that is, the four pairs of persons, the eight types of individuals—this Saṅgha of the Blessed One's disciples is worthy of gifts, worthy of hospitality, worthy of offerings, worthy of reverential salutation, the unsurpassed field of merit for the world. [35] Those who have confidence in the Saṅgha have confidence in the foremost, and for those who have confidence in the foremost, the result is foremost.

"These are the four foremost kinds of confidence."

For those confident in regard to the foremost,
knowing the foremost Dhamma,
confident in the Buddha—the foremost—
unsurpassed, worthy of offerings;

for those confident in the foremost Dhamma,
in the blissful peace of dispassion;
for those confident in the foremost Saṅgha,
the unsurpassed field of merit;

for those giving gifts to the foremost,
the foremost kind of merit increases:
the foremost life span, beauty, and glory,
good reputation, happiness, and strength.

The wise one who gives to the foremost,[692]
concentrated upon the foremost Dhamma,

having become a deva or a human being,
rejoices, having attained the foremost.

35 (5) Vassakāra

On one occasion the Blessed One was dwelling at Rājagaha in the Bamboo Grove, the squirrel sanctuary. Then the brahmin Vassakāra, the chief minister of Magadha, approached the Blessed One and exchanged greetings with him. When they had concluded their greetings and cordial talk, he sat down to one side and said to the Blessed One:

"Master Gotama, we describe someone who possesses four qualities as a great man with great wisdom. What four? (1) Here, someone is highly learned in the various fields of learning. (2) He understands the meaning of various statements, so that he can say: 'This is the meaning of this statement; this is the meaning of that one.' (3) He has a good memory; he remembers and recollects what was done and said long ago. (4) He is skillful and diligent in attending to the diverse chores of a householder; he possesses sound judgment about them in order to carry out and arrange them properly. We describe someone who possesses these four qualities as a great man with great wisdom. If Master Gotama thinks what I say should be approved, let him approve it. If he thinks what I say should be rejected, let him reject it."

"I neither approve of your [statement], brahmin, nor do I reject it. [36] Rather, I describe one who possesses four [other] qualities as a great man with great wisdom. What four? (1) Here, he is practicing for the welfare and happiness of many people; he is one who has established many people in the noble method, that is, in the goodness of the Dhamma, in the wholesomeness of the Dhamma.[693] (2) He thinks whatever he wants to think and does not think what he does not want to think; he intends whatever he wants to intend and does not intend what he does not want to intend; thus he has attained to mental mastery over the ways of thought. (3) He gains at will, without trouble or difficulty, the four jhānas that constitute the higher mind and are pleasant dwellings in this very life. (4) With the destruction of the taints, he has realized for himself with direct knowledge, in this very life, the taintless liberation of mind, liberation by wisdom, and having entered upon it, he dwells in it.

"I neither approve of your [statement], brahmin, nor do I

reject it. But I describe someone who possesses these four qualities as a great man with great wisdom."

"It is astounding and amazing, Master Gotama, how well this has been stated by Master Gotama. And we consider Master Gotama as one who possesses these four qualities. (1) For he is practicing for the welfare and happiness of many people; he is one who has established many people in the noble method, that is, in the goodness of the Dhamma, in the wholesomeness of the Dhamma. (2) He thinks whatever he wants to think and does not think what he does not want to think; he intends whatever he wants to intend and does not intend what he does not want to intend; thus he has attained to mental mastery over the ways of thought. (3) He gains at will, without trouble or difficulty, the four jhānas that constitute the higher mind and are pleasant dwellings in this very life. (4) With the destruction of the taints, he has realized for himself with direct knowledge, in this very life, the taintless liberation of mind, liberation by wisdom, and having entered upon it, he dwells in it." [37]

"Surely, brahmin, your words are prying and intrusive.[694] Nevertheless, I will answer you. (1) Indeed, I am practicing for the welfare and happiness of many people; I have established many people in the noble method, that is, in the goodness of the Dhamma, in the wholesomeness of the Dhamma. (2) I think what I want to think and do not think what I do not want to think; I intend what I want to intend and do not intend what I do not want to intend; thus I have attained to mental mastery over the ways of thought. (3) I gain at will, without trouble or difficulty, the four jhānas that constitute the higher mind and are pleasant dwellings in this very life. (4) With the destruction of the taints, I have realized for myself with direct knowledge, in this very life, the taintless liberation of mind, liberation by wisdom, and having entered upon it, I dwell in it."

> He who found for the sake of all beings
> release from the snare of death;
> who revealed the Dhamma, the method,
> for the benefit of devas and humans;
> he in whom many people gain confidence
> when they see and listen to him;
> the one skilled in the path and what is not the path,

the taintless one who accomplished his task;
the Enlightened One bearing his final body
is called "a great man of great wisdom."

36 (6) Doṇa

On one occasion the Blessed One was traveling along the highway between Ukkaṭṭhā and Setavya. The brahmin Doṇa was also traveling along the highway between Ukkaṭṭhā and Setavya. The brahmin Doṇa then saw the thousand-spoked wheels of the Blessed One's footprints, with their rims and hubs, complete in all respects,[695] and thought: "It is astounding and amazing! These surely could not be the footprints of a human being!" [38]

Then the Blessed One left the highway and sat down at the foot of a tree, folding his legs crosswise, straightening his body, and establishing mindfulness in front of him. Tracking the Blessed One's footprints, the brahmin Doṇa saw the Blessed One sitting at the foot of the tree—graceful, inspiring confidence, with peaceful faculties and peaceful mind, one who had attained to the highest taming and serenity, [like] a tamed and guarded bull elephant with controlled faculties. He then approached the Blessed One and said to him:

(1) "Could you be a deva, sir?"[696]

"I will not be a deva, brahmin."

(2) "Could you be a gandhabba, sir?"[697]

"I will not be a gandhabba, brahmin."

(3) "Could you be a yakkha, sir?"

"I will not be a yakkha, brahmin."

(4) "Could you be a human being, sir?"

"I will not be a human being, brahmin."

"When you are asked: 'Could you be a deva, sir?' you say: 'I will not be a deva, brahmin.' When you are asked: 'Could you be a gandhabba, sir?' you say: 'I will not be a gandhabba, brahmin.' When you are asked: 'Could you be a yakkha, sir?' you say: 'I will not be a yakkha, brahmin.' When you are asked: 'Could you be a human being, sir?' you say: 'I will not be a human being, brahmin.' What, then, could you be, sir?"

(1) "Brahmin, I have abandoned those taints because of which I might have become a deva; I have cut them off at the root, made them like palm stumps, obliterated them so that they

are no longer subject to future arising. (2) I have abandoned those taints because of which I might have become a gandhabba . . . (3) . . . might have become a yakkha . . . (4) . . . might have become a human being; I have cut them off at the root, made them like palm stumps, obliterated them so that they are no longer subject to future arising. Just as a blue, red, or white lotus flower, though born in the water and grown up in the water, rises above the water and stands [39] unsoiled by the water, even so, though born in the world and grown up in the world, I have overcome the world and dwell unsoiled by the world. Remember me, brahmin, as a Buddha.

"I have destroyed those taints by which
I might have been reborn as a deva
or as a gandhabba that travels through the sky;
by which I might have reached the state of a yakkha,
or arrived back at the human state:[698]
I have dispelled and cut down these taints.

"As a lovely white lotus
is not soiled by the water,
I am not soiled by the world:
therefore, O brahmin, I am a Buddha."[699]

37 (7) Non-Decline

"Bhikkhus, a bhikkhu who possesses four qualities is incapable of decline and is in the vicinity of nibbāna. What four? Here, a bhikkhu is accomplished in virtuous behavior, guards the doors of the sense faculties, observes moderation in eating, and is intent on wakefulness.

(1) "And how is a bhikkhu accomplished in virtuous behavior? Here, a bhikkhu is virtuous; he dwells restrained by the Pātimokkha, possessed of good conduct and resort, seeing danger in minute faults. Having undertaken the training rules, he trains in them. It is in this way that a bhikkhu is accomplished in virtuous behavior.

(2) "And how does a bhikkhu guard the doors of the sense faculties? Here, having seen a form with the eye, a bhikkhu does not grasp its marks and features. Since, if he left the eye faculty unrestrained, bad unwholesome states of longing and dejection might invade him, he practices restraint over it; he guards the

eye faculty, he undertakes the restraint of the eye faculty. Having heard a sound with the ear . . . Having smelled an odor with the nose . . . Having tasted a taste with the tongue . . . Having felt a tactile object with the body . . . Having cognized a mental phenomenon with the mind, a bhikkhu does not grasp its marks and features. Since, if he left the mind faculty unrestrained, bad unwholesome states of longing and dejection [40] might invade him, he practices restraint over it; he guards the mind faculty, he undertakes the restraint of the mind faculty. It is in this way that a bhikkhu guards the doors of the sense faculties.

(3) "And how does a bhikkhu observe moderation in eating? Here, reflecting carefully, a bhikkhu consumes food neither for amusement nor for intoxication nor for the sake of physical beauty and attractiveness, but only for the support and maintenance of this body, for avoiding harm, and for assisting the spiritual life, considering: 'Thus I shall terminate the old feeling and not arouse a new feeling,[700] and I shall be healthy and blameless and dwell at ease.' It is in this way that a bhikkhu observes moderation in eating.

(4) "And how is a bhikkhu intent on wakefulness? Here, during the day, while walking back and forth and sitting, a bhikkhu purifies his mind of obstructive qualities. In the first watch of the night, while walking back and forth and sitting, he purifies his mind of obstructive qualities. In the middle watch of the night he lies down on the right side in the lion's posture, with one foot overlapping the other, mindful and clearly comprehending, after noting in his mind the idea of rising. After rising, in the last watch of the night, while walking back and forth and sitting, he purifies his mind of obstructive qualities. It is in this way that a bhikkhu is intent on wakefulness.

"A bhikkhu who possesses these four qualities is incapable of decline and is in the vicinity of nibbāna."

Established in virtuous behavior,
restrained in the sense faculties,
moderate in eating,
intent on wakefulness:

a bhikkhu dwells thus ardently,
unwearying by day and night,

developing wholesome qualities[701]
to attain security from bondage.

A bhikkhu who delights in heedfulness,
seeing the danger in heedlessness,
is incapable of decline:
he is close to nibbāna.[702] [41]

38 (8) Drawn Back

"Bhikkhus, a bhikkhu who has dispelled personal truths, totally renounced seeking, and tranquilized bodily activity is said to have drawn back.[703]

(1) "And how, bhikkhus, has a bhikkhu dispelled personal truths?[704] Here, whatever ordinary personal truths may be held by ordinary ascetics and brahmins—that is, 'The world is eternal' or 'The world is not eternal'; 'The world is finite' or 'The world is infinite'; 'The soul and the body are the same' or 'The soul is one thing, the body another'; 'The Tathāgata exists after death,' or 'The Tathāgata does not exist after death,' or 'The Tathāgata both exists and does not exist after death,' or 'The Tathāgata neither exists nor does not exist after death'—a bhikkhu has discarded and dispelled them all, given them up, rejected them, let go of them, abandoned and relinquished them.[705] It is in this way that a bhikkhu has dispelled personal truths.

(2) "And how has a bhikkhu totally renounced seeking? Here, a bhikkhu has abandoned the search for sensual pleasures and the search for existence and has allayed the search for a spiritual life.[706] It is in this way that a bhikkhu has totally renounced seeking.

(3) "And how has a bhikkhu tranquilized bodily activity? Here, with the abandoning of pleasure and pain, and with the previous passing away of joy and dejection, a bhikkhu enters and dwells in the fourth jhāna, neither painful nor pleasant, which has purification of mindfulness by equanimity. It is in this way that a bhikkhu has tranquilized bodily activity.[707]

(4) "And how has a bhikkhu drawn back? Here, a bhikkhu has abandoned the conceit 'I am,' cut it off at the root, made it like a palm stump, obliterated it so that it is no longer subject to future arising. It is in this way that a bhikkhu has drawn back.

"Bhikkhus, a bhikkhu who has dispelled personal truths,

totally renounced seeking, and tranquilized bodily activity is said to have drawn back." [42]

Seeking for sense pleasures,
seeking for existence,
seeking for a spiritual life;
the tight grasp "Such is the truth,"
viewpoints [that are] swellings:[708]

for one entirely detached from lust,
liberated by the destruction of craving,
such seeking has been relinquished,
and viewpoints are uprooted.

That peaceful, mindful bhikkhu,
tranquil, undefeated, enlightened
by breaking through conceit,
is called "one who has drawn back."

39 (9) Ujjaya

Then the brahmin Ujjaya approached the Blessed One and exchanged greetings with him. When they had concluded their greetings and cordial talk, he sat down to one side and said to the Blessed One:

"Does Master Gotama praise sacrifice?"

"I do not praise all sacrifice, brahmin, nor do I withhold praise from all sacrifice. (1) I do not praise a violent sacrifice at which cattle, goats, rams, chickens, and pigs are slain, at which various creatures are led to slaughter. (2) For what reason? Because arahants and those who have entered the path to arahantship do not attend a violent sacrifice.

(3) "But I praise a nonviolent sacrifice at which cattle, goats, rams, chickens, and pigs are not slain, where various creatures are not slaughtered, that is, a regular giving, a sacrifice offered by family custom.[709] (4) For what reason? Because arahants and those who have entered the path to arahantship attend a nonviolent sacrifice."[710]

The horse sacrifice, human sacrifice,
sammāpāsa, *vājapeyya*, [43] *niraggaḷa*:[711]

these grand sacrifices, fraught with violence,[712]
do not bring great fruit.

The great seers of right conduct
do not attend a sacrifice
where goats, rams, cattle,
and various creatures are slain.

But when they regularly offer by family custom
sacrifices free from violence,
no goats, sheep, and cattle
or various creatures are slain.

That is the sacrifice the great seers
of right conduct attend.
The wise person should offer this;
this sacrifice is very fruitful.

For one who makes such sacrifice
it is indeed better, never worse.
Such a sacrifice is truly vast
and the deities too are pleased.

40 (10) Udāyī

Then the brahmin Udāyī approached the Blessed One . . . and said to him:

[The prose portion is identical with that of 4:39.]

When a sacrifice is timely and allowable,
well prepared and nonviolent, [44]
the self-controlled followers of the spiritual life
attend such a sacrifice as this.

Those in the world who have removed the coverings,[713]
transcenders of time and destination,[714]
the Buddhas who are proficient in sacrifice,[715]
praise this kind of sacrifice.

Having prepared an appropriate gift,
whether of the ordinary kind or in memory of the dead,

one makes the sacrifice with a confident mind
to a fertile field, to followers of the spiritual life.

When what has been properly obtained
is properly offered, properly sacrificed,
to those worthy of offerings,
the sacrifice is vast and the deities are pleased.

The wise person endowed with faith,
having sacrificed thus with a generous mind,
is reborn in a happy world,
in [a realm] without affliction.

V. Rohitassa

41 (1) Concentration

"Bhikkhus, there are these four developments of concentration. What four? (1) There is a development of concentration that leads to dwelling happily in this very life.[716] (2) There is a development of concentration that leads to obtaining knowledge and vision. (3) There is a development of concentration that leads to mindfulness and clear comprehension. (4) There is a development of concentration that leads to the destruction of the taints. [45]

(1) "And what, bhikkhus, is the development of concentration that leads to dwelling happily in this very life? Here, secluded from sensual pleasures, secluded from unwholesome states, a bhikkhu enters and dwells in the first jhāna, which consists of rapture and pleasure born of seclusion, accompanied by thought and examination. With the subsiding of thought and examination, he enters and dwells in the second jhāna, which has internal placidity and unification of mind and consists of rapture and pleasure born of concentration, without thought and examination. With the fading away as well of rapture, he dwells equanimous and, mindful and clearly comprehending, he experiences pleasure with the body; he enters and dwells in the third jhāna of which the noble ones declare: 'He is equanimous, mindful, one who dwells happily.' With the abandoning of pleasure and pain, and with the previous passing away of joy and dejection, he enters and dwells in the fourth jhāna, neither

painful nor pleasant, which has purification of mindfulness by equanimity. This is called the development of concentration that leads to dwelling happily in this very life.[717]

(2) "And what is the development of concentration that leads to obtaining knowledge and vision?[718] Here, a bhikkhu attends to the perception of light; he focuses on the perception of day thus: 'As by day, so at night; as at night, so by day.'[719] Thus, with a mind that is open and uncovered, he develops a mind imbued with luminosity. This is the development of concentration that leads to obtaining knowledge and vision.

(3) "And what is the development of concentration that leads to mindfulness and clear comprehension? Here, a bhikkhu knows feelings as they arise, as they remain present, as they disappear; he knows perceptions as they arise, as they remain present, as they disappear; he knows thoughts as they arise, as they remain present, as they disappear.[720] This is the development of concentration that leads to mindfulness and clear comprehension.

(4) "And what is the development of concentration that leads to the destruction of the taints? Here, a bhikkhu dwells contemplating arising and vanishing in the five aggregates subject to clinging: 'Such is form, such its origin, such its passing away; such is feeling . . . such is perception . . . such are volitional activities . . . such is consciousness, such its origin, such its passing away.' This is the development of concentration that leads to the destruction of the taints.

"These are the four developments of concentration. And it was with reference to this that I said in the Pārāyana, in 'The Questions of Puṇṇaka':

> "Having comprehended the world's highs and lows,
> he is not perturbed by anything in the world. [46]
> Peaceful, fumeless, untroubled, wishless,
> he has, I say, crossed over birth and old age."[721]

42 (2) Questions

"Bhikkhus, there are these four ways of answering questions.[722] What four? (1) There is a question to be answered categorically; (2) there is a question to be answered after making a distinction; (3) there is a question to be answered with a counter-question;

and (4) there is a question to be set aside. These are the four ways of answering questions."

One kind is given a categorical answer,
another is answered after making a distinction;
to the third, one should raise a counter-question,
but the fourth should be set aside.

When a bhikkhu knows how to answer
each type in the appropriate way,
they say that he is skilled
in the four kinds of questions.

He is hard to attack, hard to defeat,
deep, hard to assault;
he is proficient in both
what is beneficial and harmful.

The wise person avoids what is harmful,
and takes up what is beneficial.
By arriving at what is beneficial,
the steadfast one is said to be wise.

43 (3) Anger (1)

"Bhikkhus, there are these four kinds of persons found existing in the world. What four? (1) One who values anger, not the good Dhamma; (2) one who values denigration, not the good Dhamma; (3) one who values gain, not the good Dhamma; and (4) one who values honor, not the good Dhamma. These are the four kinds of persons found existing in the world.

"There are, bhikkhus, these four [other] kinds of persons found existing in the world. What four? (1) One who values the good Dhamma, not anger; (2) one who values the good Dhamma, not denigration; (3) one who values the good Dhamma, not gain; (4) one who values the good Dhamma, not honor. [47] These are the [other] four kinds of persons found existing in the world."

Bhikkhus who value anger and denigration,
who value gain and honor,

do not grow in the good Dhamma
taught by the Perfectly Enlightened One.

But those who value the good Dhamma,
who dwelled thus in the past and dwell thus now,
truly grow in the Dhamma
taught by the Perfectly Enlightened One.

44 (4) Anger (2)

"Bhikkhus, there are these four things contrary to the good Dhamma. What four? (1) Valuing anger, not the good Dhamma; (2) valuing denigration, not the good Dhamma; (3) valuing gain, not the good Dhamma; and (4) valuing honor, not the good Dhamma. These are four things contrary to the good Dhamma.

"There are, bhikkhus, these four [other] things in accord with the good Dhamma. What four? (1) Valuing the good Dhamma, not anger; (2) valuing the good Dhamma, not denigration; (3) valuing the good Dhamma, not gain; and (4) valuing the good Dhamma, not honor. These are the four [other] things in accord with the good Dhamma."

Bhikkhus who value anger and denigration,
who value gain and honor,
are like rotten seeds in a fertile field:
they do not grow in the good Dhamma.

But those who value the good Dhamma,
who dwelled thus in the past and dwell thus now,
are like moistened medicinal plants:
they grow in the Dhamma.

45 (5) Rohitassa (1)[723]

On one occasion the Blessed One was dwelling at Sāvatthī in Jeta's Grove, Anāthapiṇḍika's Park. Then, when the night had advanced, the young deva Rohitassa, of stunning beauty, illuminating the entire Jeta's Grove, approached the Blessed One. He paid homage to the Blessed One, stood to one side, and said:

"Is it possible, Bhante, by traveling to know, see, or reach the end of the world, where one is not born, does not grow old and die, [48] does not pass away and get reborn?"

"I say, friend, that by traveling one cannot know, see, or reach that end of the world where one is not born, does not grow old and die, does not pass away and get reborn."

"It is astounding and amazing, Bhante, how well this was stated by the Blessed One: 'I say, friend, that by traveling one cannot know, see, or reach that end of the world where one is not born, does not grow old and die, does not pass away and get reborn.'

"In the past, Bhante, I was a seer named Rohitassa, son of Bhoja, one possessing psychic potency, able to travel through the sky. My speed was like that of a light arrow easily shot by a firm-bowed[724] archer—one trained, skillful, and experienced[725]—across the shadow of a palmyra tree. My stride was such that it could reach from the eastern ocean to the western ocean. Then, while I possessed such speed and such a stride, the wish arose in me: 'I will reach the end of the world by traveling.' Having a life span of a hundred years, living for a hundred years, I traveled for a hundred years without pausing except to eat, drink, chew, and taste, to defecate and urinate, and to dispel fatigue with sleep; yet I died along the way without having reached the end of the world.

"It is astounding and amazing, Bhante, how well this was stated by the Blessed One: 'I say, friend, that by traveling one cannot know, see, or reach that end of the world where one is not born, does not grow old and die, does not pass away and get reborn.'"

"I say, friend, that by traveling one cannot know, see, or reach that end of the world where one is not born, does not grow old and die, does not pass away and get reborn. Yet I say that without having reached the end of the world there is no making an end of suffering. It is in this fathom-long body endowed with perception and mind that I proclaim (1) the world, (2) the origin of the world, (3) the cessation of the world, and (4) the way leading to the cessation of the world." [49]

The end of the world can never be reached
by means of traveling [across the world];
yet without reaching the world's end
there is no release from suffering.

Hence the wise one, the world-knower,
who has reached the world's end and lived the spiritual
life,
having known the world's end, at peace,
does not desire this world or another.

46 (6) Rohitassa (2)

Then when that night had passed, the Blessed One addressed the bhikkhus: "Bhikkhus, last night, when the night had advanced, the young deva Rohitassa, of stunning beauty, illuminating the entire Jeta's Grove, approached me, paid homage to me, stood to one side, and said:

"'Is it possible, Bhante, by traveling to know, see, or reach the end of the world, where one is not born, does not grow old and die, does not pass away and get reborn?'"

[What follows is identical with 4:45, including the verses, but spoken in the first-person narrative voice.] [50]

47 (7) Far Apart

"Bhikkhus, there are these four pairs of things extremely far apart. What four? (1) The sky and the earth. (2) The near and the far shores of the ocean. (3) The place where the sun rises and the place where it sets. (4) The teaching of the good and the teaching of the bad. These are the four pairs of things extremely far apart." [51]

The sky and the earth are far apart,
the ocean's far shore is said to be far,
and so the place where the sun rises
from the place where it sets.

But even farther apart, they say,
are the teachings of the good and the bad.[726]
The company of the good is constant;
so long as it endures, it is just the same.
But the company of the bad is fickle;
thus the teaching of the good
is far from the bad.

48 (8) Visākha[727]

On one occasion the Blessed One was dwelling at Sāvatthī in Jeta's Grove, Anāthapiṇḍika's Park. Now on that occasion the Venerable Visākha Pañcāliputta was instructing, exhorting, inspiring, and gladdening the bhikkhus in the assembly hall with a Dhamma talk, [spoken] with speech that was polished, clear, articulate, expressive of the meaning, comprehensive, and unhindered.

Then, in the evening, the Blessed One emerged from seclusion and approached the assembly hall. He sat down on the appointed seat and addressed the bhikkhus: "Bhikkhus, who has been instructing, exhorting, inspiring, and gladdening the bhikkhus in the assembly hall with a Dhamma talk, [spoken] with speech that is polished, clear, articulate, expressive of the meaning, comprehensive, and unhindered?"

"It was Venerable Visākha Pañcāliputta, Bhante."

Then the Blessed One said to the Venerable Visākha Pañcāliputta: "Good, good, Visākha! It is good that you instruct, exhort, inspire, and gladden the bhikkhus in the assembly hall with a Dhamma talk, [spoken] with speech that is polished, clear, articulate, expressive of the meaning, comprehensive, and unhindered."

> When the wise man is in the midst of fools,
> they do not know him if he does not speak.[728]
> But they know him when he speaks,
> teaching the deathless state.
>
> He should speak and illustrate the Dhamma;
> he should lift high the seers' banner.
> Well-spoken words are the seers' banner:
> for the Dhamma is the banner of seers. [52]

49 (9) Inversions

"Bhikkhus, there are these four inversions of perception, inversions of mind, and inversions of view.[729] What four? (1) The inversion of perception, mind, and view that takes the impermanent to be permanent; (2) the inversion of perception, mind, and view that takes what is suffering to be pleasurable;[730] (3) the inversion of perception, mind, and view that takes what is non-self to be self; (4) the inversion of perception, mind, and view that takes what is unattractive to be attractive. These are the four inversions of perception, mind, and view.

"There are, bhikkhus, these four non-inversions of perception, non-inversions of mind, and non-inversions of view. What four? (1) The non-inversion of perception, mind, and view that takes the impermanent to be impermanent; (2) the non-inversion of perception, mind, and view that takes what is suffering to be suffering; (3) the non-inversion of perception, mind, and view that takes what is non-self to be non-self; (4) the non-inversion of perception, mind, and view that takes what is unattractive to be unattractive. These are the four non-inversions of perception, mind, and view."

Perceiving permanence in the impermanent,
perceiving pleasure in what is suffering,
perceiving a self in what is non-self,
and perceiving attractiveness in what is unattractive,
beings resort to wrong views,[731]
their minds deranged, their perception twisted.

Such people are bound by the yoke of Māra,
and do not reach security from bondage.
Beings continue in saṃsāra,
going to birth and death.

But when the Buddhas arise in the world,
sending forth a brilliant light,
they reveal this Dhamma that leads
to the stilling of suffering.

Having heard it, wise people
have regained their sanity.
They have seen the impermanent as impermanent
and what is suffering as suffering.

They have seen what is non-self as non-self
and the unattractive as unattractive.
By the acquisition of right view,
they have overcome all suffering. [53]

50 (10) Defilements

"Bhikkhus, there are these four defilements of the sun and moon because of which the sun and moon do not shine, blaze, and radiate. What four? Clouds are a defilement of the sun and moon because of which the sun and moon do not shine, blaze, and radiate; fog is a defilement of the sun and moon[732] . . . smoke and dust is a defilement of the sun and moon . . . and Rāhu, lord of the asuras, is a defilement of the sun and moon because of which the sun and moon do not shine, blaze, and radiate. These are the four defilements of the sun and moon because of which the sun and moon do not shine, blaze, and radiate.

"So too, bhikkhus, there are four defilements of ascetics and brahmins because of which some ascetics and brahmins do not shine, blaze, and radiate. What four?

(1) "There are some ascetics and brahmins who drink liquor and wine and do not refrain from drinking liquor and wine. This is the first defilement of ascetics and brahmins because of which some ascetics and brahmins do not shine, blaze, and radiate.

(2) "There are some ascetics and brahmins who indulge in sexual intercourse and do not refrain from sexual intercourse. This is the second defilement of ascetics and brahmins because of which some ascetics and brahmins do not shine, blaze, and radiate.

(3) "There are some ascetics and brahmins who accept gold and silver and do not refrain from receiving gold and silver. This is the third defilement of ascetics and brahmins because of which some ascetics and brahmins do not shine, blaze, and radiate.

(4) "There are some ascetics and brahmins who earn their living by wrong livelihood and do not refrain from wrong livelihood. This is the fourth defilement of ascetics and brahmins because of which some ascetics and brahmins do not shine, blaze, and radiate.

"These are the four defilements of ascetics and brahmins [54] because of which some ascetics and brahmins do not shine, blaze, and radiate."[733]

Some ascetics and brahmins
are dragged around by lust and hatred;

men hindered by ignorance
seek delight in pleasant things.

They drink liquor and wines,
indulge in sexual activity;
the ignorant accept
silver and gold.

Some ascetics and brahmins
live by wrong livelihood.
These are the defilements that the Buddha,
Kinsman of the Sun, described.

Defiled by these,
some ascetics and brahmins—
impure, dusty creatures—[734]
do not shine and blaze.

Shrouded in darkness,
slaves of craving, led along,
they take renewed existence
and fill the terrible charnel ground.

The Second Fifty

I. Streams of Merit

51 (1) Streams of Merit (1)

"Bhikkhus, there are these four streams of merit, streams of the wholesome, nutriments of happiness—heavenly, ripening in happiness, conducive to heaven—that lead to what is wished for, desired, and agreeable, to one's welfare and happiness. What four?[735]

"(1) When a bhikkhu enters and dwells in a measureless concentration of mind[736] while using a robe [that one has given him], one acquires a measureless stream of merit, stream of the wholesome, a nutriment of happiness . . . that leads . . . to one's welfare and happiness. (2) When a bhikkhu enters and dwells in a measureless concentration of mind while using almsfood [that one has given him], one acquires a measureless stream of merit, stream of the wholesome, a nutriment of happiness . . . that leads . . . to one's welfare and happiness. [55] (3) When a bhikkhu enters and dwells in a measureless concentration of mind while using a lodging [that one has given him], one acquires a measureless stream of merit, stream of the wholesome, a nutriment of happiness . . . that leads . . . to one's welfare and happiness. (4) When a bhikkhu enters and dwells in a measureless concentration of mind while using medicines and provisions for the sick [that one has given him], one acquires a measureless stream of merit, stream of the wholesome, a nutriment of happiness . . . that leads to one's welfare and happiness.

"These are the four streams of merit, streams of the wholesome, nutriments of happiness—heavenly, ripening in happiness, conducive to heaven—that lead to what is wished for, desired, and agreeable, to one's welfare and happiness.

"When, bhikkhus, a noble disciple possesses these four streams of merit, streams of the wholesome, it is not easy to measure his merit thus: 'Just so much is his stream of merit, stream of the wholesome, nutriment of happiness . . . that leads to . . . one's welfare and happiness'; rather, it is reckoned simply as an incalculable, immeasurable, great mass of merit.

"Bhikkhus, just as it is not easy to measure the water in the great ocean thus: 'There are so many gallons of water,' or 'There are so many hundreds of gallons of water,' or 'There are so many thousands of gallons of water,' or 'There are so many hundreds of thousands of gallons of water,' but rather it is reckoned simply as an incalculable, immeasurable, great mass of water; so too, when a noble disciple possesses these four streams of merit . . . it is reckoned simply as an incalculable, immeasurable, great mass of merit."

Just as the many rivers used by the hosts of people,
flowing downstream, reach the ocean,
the great mass of water, the boundless sea,
the fearsome receptacle of heaps of gems; [56]
so the streams of merit reach the wise man
who is a giver of food, drink, and cloth;
[they reach] the donor of beds, seats, and covers
like rivers carrying their waters to the sea.

52 (2) Streams of Merit (2)[737]

"Bhikkhus, there are these four streams of merit, streams of the wholesome, nutriments of happiness—heavenly, ripening in happiness, conducive to heaven—that lead to what is wished for, desired, and agreeable, to one's welfare and happiness. What four?

(1) "Here, a noble disciple possesses unwavering confidence in the Buddha thus: 'The Blessed One is an arahant, perfectly enlightened, accomplished in true knowledge and conduct, fortunate, knower of the world, unsurpassed trainer of persons to be tamed, teacher of devas and humans, the Enlightened One, the Blessed One.' This is the first stream of merit....

(2) "Again, a noble disciple possesses unwavering confidence in the Dhamma thus: 'The Dhamma is well expounded by the Blessed One, directly visible, immediate, inviting one to come and see, applicable, to be personally experienced by the wise.' This is the second stream of merit....

(3) "Again, a noble disciple possesses unwavering confidence in the Saṅgha thus: 'The Saṅgha of the Blessed One's disciples is practicing the good way, practicing the straight way, practicing the true way, practicing the proper way; that is, the four pairs of persons, the eight types of individuals—this Saṅgha of the Blessed One's disciples is worthy of gifts, worthy of hospitality, worthy of offerings, worthy of reverential salutation, the unsurpassed field of merit for the world.' This is the third stream of merit....

(4) "Again, a noble disciple possesses the virtuous behavior loved by the noble ones, unbroken, flawless, unblemished, [57] unblotched, freeing, praised by the wise, ungrasped, leading to concentration. This is the fourth stream of merit....

"These are the four streams of merit, streams of the wholesome, nutriments of happiness—heavenly, ripening in happiness, conducive to heaven—that lead to what is wished for, desired, and agreeable, to one's welfare and happiness."

When one has faith in the Tathāgata,
unshakable and well established,
and virtuous behavior that is good,
loved by the noble ones and praised;
when one has confidence in the Saṅgha

and one's view has been straightened out,
they say that one is not poor,
that one's life is not lived in vain.

Therefore an intelligent person,
remembering the Buddhas' teaching,
should be intent on faith and virtuous behavior,
confidence and vision of the Dhamma.[738]

53 (3) Living Together (1)

On one occasion the Blessed One was traveling along the highway between Madhurā and Verañjā. A number of male and female householders were also traveling along the same highway. Then the Blessed One left the highway and sat down at the foot of a tree. The male and female householders saw the Blessed One sitting there and approached him, paid homage to him, and sat down to one side. The Blessed One then said to them:

"Householders, there are these four ways of living together. What four? A wretch lives together with a wretch;[739] a wretch lives together with a female deva; a deva lives together with a wretch; a deva lives together with a female deva.

(1) "And how, householders, does a wretch live together with a wretch? [58] Here, the husband is one who destroys life, takes what is not given, engages in sexual misconduct, speaks falsely, and indulges in liquor, wine, and intoxicants, the basis for heedlessness; he is immoral, of bad character; he dwells at home with a heart obsessed by the stain of miserliness; he insults and reviles ascetics and brahmins. And his wife is also one who destroys life . . . she insults and reviles ascetics and brahmins. It is in such a way that a wretch lives together with a wretch.

(2) "And how does a wretch live together with a female deva? Here, the husband is one who destroys life . . . he insults and reviles ascetics and brahmins. But his wife is one who abstains from the destruction of life, from taking what is not given, from sexual misconduct, from false speech, and from liquor, wine, and intoxicants, the basis for heedlessness; she is virtuous, of good character; she dwells at home with a heart free from the stain of miserliness; she does not insult or revile ascetics and

brahmins. It is in such a way that a wretch lives together with a female deva.

(3) "And how does a deva live together with a wretch? Here, the husband is one who abstains from the destruction of life . . . he does not insult or revile ascetics and brahmins. But his wife is one who destroys life . . . she insults and reviles ascetics and brahmins. It is in such a way that a deva lives together with a wretch.

(4) "And how does a deva live together with a female deva? Here, the husband is one who abstains from the destruction of life . . . he does not insult or revile ascetics and brahmins. And his wife is also one who abstains from the destruction of life . . . she does not insult or revile ascetics and brahmins. It is in such a way that a deva lives together with a female deva. [59]

"These are the four ways of living together."

When both are immoral,
miserly and abusive,
husband and wife
live together as wretches.

The husband is immoral,
miserly and abusive,
but his wife is virtuous,
charitable, generous.
She is a female deva living
with a wretched husband.

The husband is virtuous,
charitable, generous,
but his wife is immoral,
miserly and abusive.
She is a wretch living
with a deva husband.

Both husband and wife are endowed with faith,
charitable and self-controlled,
living their lives righteously,
addressing each other with pleasant words.

Then many benefits accrue to them
and they dwell at ease.
Their enemies are saddened
when both are the same in virtue.

Having practiced the Dhamma here,
the same in virtuous behavior and observances,
delighting [after death] in a deva world,
they rejoice, enjoying sensual pleasures.

54 (4) Living Together (2)

"Bhikkhus, there are these four ways of living together. What four? A wretch lives together with a wretch; a wretch lives together with a female deva; a deva lives together with a wretch; a deva lives together with a female deva.

[The rest, including the verses, is identical with 4:53 but addressed to the bhikkhus.] [60–61]

55 (5) The Same in Living (1)

On one occasion the Blessed One was dwelling among the Bhaggas in Suṃsumāragira in the deer park at Bhesakalā Grove. Then, in the morning, the Blessed One dressed, took his bowl and robe, and went to the residence of the householder Nakulapitā, where he sat down in the prepared seat. Then the householder Nakulapitā and the housewife Nakulamātā approached the Blessed One, paid homage to him, and sat down to one side.[740] The householder Nakulapitā then said to the Blessed One:

"Bhante, since I was young, when the young girl Nakulamātā was given to me in marriage, I do not recall ever transgressing against her even in thought, much less by deed. We wish, Bhante, to see one another not only in this present life but also in future lives."

The housewife Nakulamātā in turn said to the Blessed One: "Bhante, since I was a young girl given to the young householder Nakulapitā in marriage, I do not recall ever transgressing against him even in thought, much less by deed. We wish, Bhante, to see one another not only in this present life but also in future lives." [62]

"Householders, if both husband and wife wish to see one

another not only in this present life but also in future lives, they should have the same faith, the same virtuous behavior, the same generosity, and the same wisdom. Then they will see one another not only in this present life but also in future lives."

Both husband and wife are endowed with faith,
charitable and self-controlled,
living their lives righteously,
addressing each other with pleasant words,

Then many benefits accrue to them
and they dwell at ease.
Their enemies are saddened
when both are the same in virtue.

Having practiced the Dhamma here,
the same in virtuous behavior and observances,
delighting [after death] in a deva world,
they rejoice, enjoying sensual pleasures.

56 (6) The Same in Living (2)

"Bhikkhus, if both husband and wife wish to behold one another not only in this present life but also in future lives, they should have the same faith, the same virtuous behavior, the same generosity, and the same wisdom. Then they will behold one another not only in this present life but also in future lives."

[The verses are identical with those of 4:55.]

57 (7) Suppavāsā

On one occasion the Blessed One was dwelling among the Koliyans near the Koliyan town named Sajjanela. Then, in the morning, the Blessed One dressed, took his bowl and robe, and went to the residence of the Koliyan daughter Suppavāsā, where he sat down in the prepared seat.[741] Then the Koliyan daughter Suppavāsā, [63] with her own hand, served and satisfied the Blessed One with various kinds of delicious food. When the Blessed One had finished eating and had put away his bowl, the Koliyan daughter Suppavāsā sat down to one side. The Blessed One then said to her:

"Suppavāsā, a female noble disciple who gives food gives the recipients four things. What four? She gives life, beauty, happiness, and strength. (1) Having given life, she partakes of life, whether celestial or human. (2) Having given beauty, she partakes of beauty, whether celestial or human. (3) Having given happiness, she partakes of happiness, whether celestial or human. (4) Having given strength, she partakes of strength, whether celestial or human. Suppavāsā, a female noble disciple who gives food gives the recipients these four things."

When one gives well-prepared food,
pure, delicious, and flavorful,
to the upright ones who are
exalted and of excellent conduct,
that offering, which links merit with merit,
is praised as very fruitful
by the world-knowers.[742]

Those recollecting such generosity
dwell in the world inspired by joy.
Having removed the stain of miserliness and its root,
blameless, they go to the heavenly abode.

58 (8) Sudatta

Then the householder Anāthapiṇḍika approached the Blessed One. . . . The Blessed One then said to him:

"Householder, a noble disciple who gives food gives the recipients four things. What four? [64] He gives life, beauty, happiness, and strength. (1) Having given life, he partakes of life, whether celestial or human. (2) Having given beauty, he partakes of beauty, whether celestial or human. (3) Having given happiness, he partakes of happiness, whether celestial or human. (4) Having given strength, he partakes of strength, whether celestial or human. Householder, a noble disciple who gives food gives the recipients these four things."

One who respectfully gives timely food
to those self-controlled ones who eat what others give,
provides them with four things:
life, beauty, happiness, and strength.

The man who gives life and beauty,
who gives happiness and strength,
will obtain long life and fame
wherever he is reborn.

59 (9) Food

"Bhikkhus, when a donor gives food, he gives the recipients four things. What four? . . . [as in preceding sutta] . . . Bhikkhus, when a donor gives food, he gives the recipients these four things."

[The verses are identical with those of 4:58.] [65]

60 (10) The Layperson's Proper Practice

Then the householder Anāthapiṇḍika approached the Blessed One. . . . The Blessed One said to him:

"Householder, a noble disciple who possesses four qualities is practicing the way proper to the layperson, a way that brings the attainment of fame and leads to heaven. What four?

"Here, householder, a noble disciple serves the Saṅgha of bhikkhus with robes; he serves the Saṅgha of bhikkhus with almsfood; he serves the Saṅgha of bhikkhus with lodgings; he serves the Saṅgha of bhikkhus with medicines and provisions for the sick.[743]

"Householder, a noble disciple who possesses these four qualities is practicing the way proper to the layperson, a way that brings the attainment of fame and leads to heaven."

When the wise practice the way
proper for the layperson, they serve
the virtuous monks of upright conduct
with robes, almsfood, lodgings, and medicines:

for them both by day and night
merit always increases;
having done excellent deeds,
they pass on to a heavenly state.

II. Worthy Deeds

61 (1) Worthy Deeds

Then the householder Anāthapiṇḍika approached the Blessed One. . . . The Blessed One said to him: [66]

"Householder, there are these four things that are wished for, desired, agreeable, and rarely gained in the world. What four?

(1) "One thinks: 'May wealth come to me righteously!' This is the first thing in the world that is wished for . . . and rarely gained in the world.

(2) "Having gained wealth righteously, one thinks: 'May fame come to me and to my relatives and preceptors!'[744] This is the second thing . . . rarely gained in the world.

(3) "Having gained wealth righteously and having gained fame for oneself and for one's relatives and preceptors, one thinks: 'May I live long and enjoy a long life span!' This is the third thing . . . rarely gained in the world.

(4) "Having gained wealth righteously, having gained fame for oneself and for one's relatives and preceptors, living long and enjoying a long life span, one thinks: 'With the breakup of the body, after death, may I be reborn in a good destination, in a heavenly world!' This is the fourth thing . . . rarely gained in the world.

"These are the four things that are wished for, desired, agreeable, and rarely gained in the world.

"There are, householder, four [other] things that lead to obtaining those four things. What four? Accomplishment in faith, accomplishment in virtuous behavior, accomplishment in generosity, and accomplishment in wisdom.

(1) "And what, householder, is accomplishment in faith? Here, a noble disciple is endowed with faith; he places faith in the enlightenment of the Tathāgata thus: 'The Blessed One is an arahant, perfectly enlightened, accomplished in true knowledge and conduct, fortunate, knower of the world, unsurpassed trainer of persons to be tamed, teacher of devas and humans, the Enlightened One, the Blessed One.' This is called accomplishment in faith.

(2) "And what is accomplishment in virtuous behavior? Here, a noble disciple abstains from the destruction of life . . . abstains

from liquor, wine, and intoxicants, the basis for heedlessness. This is called accomplishment in virtuous behavior.

(3) "And what is accomplishment in generosity? Here, a noble disciple dwells at home with a mind free from the stain of miserliness, freely generous, openhanded, delighting in relinquishment, devoted to charity, delighting in giving and sharing. This is called accomplishment in generosity.

(4) "And what is accomplishment in wisdom? [67] If one dwells with a heart overcome by longing and unrighteous greed, one does what should be avoided and neglects one's duty, so that one's fame and happiness are spoiled. If one dwells with a heart overcome by ill will . . . by dullness and drowsiness . . . by restlessness and remorse . . . by doubt, one does what should be avoided and neglects one's duty, so that one's fame and happiness are spoiled.

"When, householder, a noble disciple has understood thus: 'Longing and unrighteous greed are a defilement of the mind,' he abandons them. When he has understood thus: 'Ill will is a defilement of the mind,' he abandons it. When he has understood thus: 'Dullness and drowsiness are a defilement of the mind,' he abandons them. When he has understood thus: 'Restlessness and remorse are a defilement of the mind,' he abandons them. When he has understood thus: 'Doubt is a defilement of the mind,' he abandons it.

"When, householder, a noble disciple has understood thus: 'Longing and unrighteous greed are a defilement of the mind' and has abandoned them; when he has understood thus: 'Ill will . . . Dullness and drowsiness . . . Restlessness and remorse . . . Doubt is a defilement of the mind,' and has abandoned it, he is then called a noble disciple of great wisdom, of wide wisdom, one who sees the range,[745] one accomplished in wisdom. This is called accomplishment in wisdom.

"These are the four [other] things that lead to obtaining the four things that are wished for, desired, agreeable, and rarely gained in the world.

"With wealth acquired by energetic striving, amassed by the strength of his arms, earned by the sweat of his brow, righteous wealth righteously gained, the noble disciple undertakes four worthy deeds. What four?

(1) "Here, householder, with wealth acquired by energetic

striving . . . righteously gained, the noble disciple makes himself happy and pleased and properly maintains himself in happiness; he makes his parents happy and pleased and properly maintains them in happiness; he makes his wife and children, his slaves, workers, and servants happy and pleased and properly maintains them in happiness; he makes his friends and companions happy and pleased and properly maintains them in happiness. This is the first case of wealth that has gone to good use, that has been properly utilized and used for a worthy cause. [68]

(2) "Again, with wealth acquired by energetic striving . . . righteously gained, the noble disciple makes provisions against the losses that might arise from fire, floods, kings, thieves, or displeasing heirs; he makes himself secure against them. This is the second case of wealth that has gone to good use . . . for a worthy cause.

(3) "Again, with wealth acquired by energetic striving . . . righteously gained, the noble disciple makes the five oblations: to relatives, guests, ancestors, the king, and the deities. This is the third case of wealth that has gone to good use . . . for a worthy cause.

(4) "Again, with wealth acquired by energetic striving . . . righteously gained, the noble disciple establishes an uplifting offering of alms—an offering that is heavenly,[746] resulting in happiness, conducive to heaven—to those ascetics and brahmins who refrain from intoxication and heedlessness, who are settled in patience and mildness, who tame themselves, calm themselves, and train themselves for nibbāna. This is the fourth case of wealth that has gone to good use, that has been properly employed and used for a worthy cause.

"These, householder, are the four worthy deeds that the noble disciple undertakes with wealth acquired by energetic striving, amassed by the strength of his arms, earned by the sweat of his brow, righteous wealth righteously gained. When anyone exhausts wealth on anything apart from these four worthy deeds, that wealth is said to have gone to waste, to have been squandered, to have been used frivolously. But when anyone exhausts wealth on these four worthy deeds, that wealth is said to have gone to good use, to have been properly used, to have been utilized for a worthy cause."

"I've enjoyed wealth,
supported my dependents,
and overcome adversities.
I have given an uplifting offering
and performed the five oblations.
I have served the virtuous monks,
the self-controlled celibate ones.[747]

"I have achieved whatever purpose
a wise person, dwelling at home, [69]
might have in desiring wealth;
what I have done brings me no regret."

Recollecting this, a mortal
remains firm in the noble Dhamma.
They praise him here in this life,
and after death he rejoices in heaven.

62 (2) Freedom from Debt

Then the householder Anāthapiṇḍika approached the Blessed One.... The Blessed One said to him:

"Householder, there are these four kinds of happiness that may be achieved by a layperson who enjoys sensual pleasures, depending on time and occasion. What four? The happiness of ownership, the happiness of enjoyment, the happiness of freedom from debt, and the happiness of blamelessness.[748]

(1) "And what, householder, is the happiness of ownership? Here, a clansman has acquired wealth by energetic striving, amassed by the strength of his arms, earned by the sweat of his brow, righteous wealth righteously gained. When he thinks, 'I have acquired wealth by energetic striving... righteously gained,' he experiences happiness and joy. This is called the happiness of ownership.

(2) "And what is the happiness of enjoyment? Here, with wealth acquired by energetic striving, amassed by the strength of his arms, earned by the sweat of his brow, righteous wealth righteously gained, a clansman enjoys his wealth and does meritorious deeds. When he thinks, 'With wealth acquired by energetic striving... righteously gained, I enjoy my wealth and do meritorious deeds,' he experiences happiness and joy. This is called the happiness of enjoyment.

(3) "And what is the happiness of freedom from debt? Here, a clansman has no debts to anyone, whether large or small. When he thinks, 'I have no debts to anyone, whether large or small,' he experiences happiness and joy. This is called the happiness of freedom from debt.

(4) "And what is the happiness of blamelessness? Here, householder, a noble disciple is endowed with blameless bodily, verbal, and mental action. [70] When he thinks, 'I am endowed with blameless bodily, verbal, and mental action,' he experiences happiness and joy. This is called the happiness of blamelessness.

"These are the four kinds of happiness that a layperson who enjoys sensual pleasures may achieve, depending on time and occasion."

> Having known the happiness of freedom from debt,
> one should recall[749] the happiness of ownership.
> Enjoying the happiness of enjoyment,
> a mortal then sees things clearly with wisdom.
>
> While seeing things clearly, the wise one
> knows both kinds[750] of happiness.
> The other is not worth a sixteenth part
> of the bliss of blamelessness.[751]

63 (3) With Brahmā[752]

(1) "Bhikkhus, those families dwell with Brahmā where at home the mother and father are revered by their children. (2) Those families dwell with the first teachers where at home the mother and father are revered by their children. (3) Those families dwell with the first deities where at home the mother and father are revered by their children. (4) Those families dwell with the gift-worthy where at home the mother and father are revered by their children.

"'Brahmā,' bhikkhus, is a designation for mother and father. 'First teachers' is a designation for mother and father. 'First deities' is a designation for mother and father. 'Gift-worthy' is a designation for mother and father. And why? Mother and father are very helpful to their children: they raise them, nurture them, and show them the world."

Mother and father are called "Brahmā,"
and also "first teachers."
They are worthy of gifts from their children,
for they have compassion for their offspring.
Therefore a wise person should revere them
and treat them with honor.

One should serve them with food and drink,
with clothes and bedding,
by massaging and bathing them,
and by washing their feet.

Because of that service
to mother and father,
the wise praise one in this world
and after death one rejoices in heaven. [71]

64 (4) Hell[753]

"Bhikkhus, one who possesses four qualities is cast into hell as if brought there. What four? He destroys life, takes what is not given, engages in sexual misconduct, and speaks falsely. One who possesses these four qualities is cast into hell as if brought there."

The destruction of life, taking what is not given,
the uttering of false speech,
and consorting with others' wives:
the wise do not praise such deeds.

65 (5) Form

"Bhikkhus, there are these four kinds of persons found existing in the world. What four? (1) One who judges on the basis of form, whose confidence is based on form. (2) One who judges on the basis of speech, whose confidence is based on speech. (3) One who judges on the basis of austerity, whose confidence is based on austerity. (4) One who judges on the basis of the Dhamma, whose confidence is based on the Dhamma. These are the four kinds of persons found existing in the world."[754]

Those who judge on the basis of form
and those who follow because of speech
have come under the control of desire and lust;
those people do not understand.[755]

One who does not know the inside
and does not see the outside,
a fool obstructed on all sides,
is carried away by speech.

One who does not know the inside
yet who clearly sees the outside,
seeing the fruit externally,
is also carried away by speech.

But one who understands the inside
and who clearly sees the outside,
seeing without hindrances,
is not carried away by speech.

66 (6) Lustful

"Bhikkhus, there are these four kinds of persons found existing in the world. What four? The lustful, the hating, the deluded, and the conceited. These are the four kinds of persons found existing in the world." [72]

Beings enamored of tantalizing things,
seeking delight in whatever is pleasing,
low beings bound by delusion,[756]
increase their bondage.

The ignorant go about
creating unwholesome kamma
born of lust, hatred, and delusion:
distressful deeds productive of suffering.

People hindered by ignorance,
blind, lacking eyes to see,
in accordance with their own nature,
do not think of it in such a way.[757]

67 (7) Snakes

On one occasion the Blessed One was dwelling at Sāvatthī in Jeta's Grove, Anāthapiṇḍika's Park. Now on that occasion, in Sāvatthī, a certain bhikkhu had been bitten by a snake and had died.[758] Then a number of bhikkhus approached the Blessed One, paid homage to him, sat down to one side, and said: "Bhante, a certain bhikkhu here in Sāvatthī was bitten by a snake and died."

[The Blessed One said:] "Surely, bhikkhus, that bhikkhu did not pervade the four royal families of snakes[759] with a mind of loving-kindness. For if he had done so, he would not have been bitten by a snake and died. What are the four? The *virūpakkha* royal family of snakes, the *erāpatha* royal family of snakes, the *chabyāputta* royal family of snakes, and the black *gotamaka* royal family of snakes. Surely, that bhikkhu did not pervade these four royal families of snakes with a mind of loving-kindness. For if he had done so, he would not have been bitten by a snake and died.

"I enjoin you, bhikkhus, to pervade these four royal families of snakes with a mind of loving-kindness, for your own security, safety, and protection."

I have loving-kindness for the *virūpakkha* snakes;
for the *erāpatha* snakes I have loving-kindness.
I have loving-kindness for the *chabyāputta* snakes;
for the black *gotamakas* I have loving-kindness.

I have loving-kindness for footless creatures;
for those with two feet I have loving-kindness. [73]
I have loving-kindness for those with four feet;
for those with many feet I have loving-kindness.

May footless beings not harm me;
may no harm come to me from those with two feet;
may four-footed beings not harm me;
may no harm come to me from those with many feet.

May all beings, all living things,
all creatures, every one,
meet with good fortune;
may nothing bad come to anyone.

The Buddha is measureless, the Dhamma is measureless, the Saṅgha is measureless; creeping things, snakes, scorpions, centipedes, spiders, lizards, and rats are finite. I have made a safeguard, I have made protection. Let the creatures retreat. I pay homage to the Blessed One, homage to the seven Perfectly Enlightened Ones.[760]

68 (8) Devadatta

On one occasion the Blessed One was dwelling at Rājagaha on Mount Vulture Peak soon after Devadatta had left.[761] There the Blessed One, with reference to Devadatta, addressed the bhikkhus: "Bhikkhus, Devadatta's gain, honor, and praise led to his own ruin and destruction. (1) Just as a plantain tree yields fruit to its own ruin and destruction, so Devadatta's gain, honor, and praise led to his own ruin and destruction. (2) Just as a bamboo yields fruit to its own ruin and destruction, so Devadatta's gain, honor, and praise led to his own ruin and destruction. (3) Just as a reed yields fruit to its own ruin and destruction, so Devadatta's gain, honor, and praise led to his own ruin and destruction. (4) Just as a mule becomes pregnant to its own ruin and destruction, so Devadatta's gain, honor, and praise led to his own ruin and destruction."

> As its own fruit destroys the plantain,
> as its fruit destroys the bamboo and reed,
> as its embryo destroys the mule,
> so does honor destroy the vile man. [74]

69 (9) Striving

"Bhikkhus, there are these four strivings. What four? Striving by restraint, striving by abandonment, striving by development, and striving by protection.

(1) "And what, bhikkhus, is striving by restraint? Here, a bhikkhu generates desire for the non-arising of unarisen bad unwholesome qualities; he makes an effort, arouses energy, applies his mind, and strives. This is called striving by restraint.

(2) "And what is striving by abandonment? Here, a bhikkhu generates desire for the abandoning of arisen bad unwholesome qualities; he makes an effort, arouses energy, applies his mind, and strives. This is called striving by abandonment.

(3) "And what is striving by development? Here, a bhikkhu generates desire for the arising of unarisen wholesome qualities; he makes an effort, arouses energy, applies his mind, and strives. This is called striving by development.

(4) "And what is striving by protection? Here, a bhikkhu generates desire for the maintenance of arisen wholesome qualities, for their non-decline, increase, expansion, and fulfillment by development; he makes an effort, arouses energy, applies his mind, and strives. This is called striving by protection.

"These are the four strivings."

> Restraint and abandonment,
> development and protection:
> by means of these four strivings
> taught by the Kinsman of the Sun
> a bhikkhu who is ardent here
> can attain the destruction of suffering.

70 (10) Unrighteous[762]

"Bhikkhus, when kings are unrighteous,[763] the royal vassals become unrighteous. When the royal vassals are unrighteous, brahmins and householders become unrighteous.[764] When brahmins and householders are unrighteous, the people of the towns and countryside become unrighteous. When the people of the towns and countryside are unrighteous, the sun and moon [75] proceed off course. When the sun and moon proceed off course, the constellations and the stars proceed off course. When the constellations and the stars proceed off course, day and night proceed off course . . . the months and fortnights proceed off course . . . the seasons and years proceed off course. When the seasons and years proceed off course, the winds blow off course and at random. When the winds blow off course and at random, the deities become upset. When the deities are upset, sufficient rain does not fall. When sufficient rain does not fall, the crops ripen irregularly. When people eat crops that ripen irregularly, they become short-lived, ugly, weak, and sickly.[765]

"Bhikkhus, when kings are righteous, the royal vassals become righteous. When the royal vassals are righteous, brahmins and householders become righteous. When brahmins and householders are righteous, the people of the towns and countryside become righteous. When the people of the towns and countryside are righteous, the sun and moon proceed on course. When the sun and moon proceed on course, the constellations and the stars proceed on course. When the constellations and the stars proceed on course, day and night proceed on course . . . the months and fortnights proceed on course . . . the seasons and years proceed on course. When the seasons and years proceed on course, the winds blow on course and dependably. When the winds blow on course and dependably, the deities do not become upset. When the deities are not upset, sufficient rain falls. When sufficient rain falls, the crops ripen in season. When people eat crops that ripen in season, they become long-lived, beautiful, strong, and healthy."

When cattle are crossing [a ford],
if the chief bull goes crookedly,
all the others go crookedly
because their leader has gone crookedly.

So too, among human beings,
when the one considered the chief
behaves unrighteously,
other people do so as well. [76]
The entire kingdom is dejected
if the king is unrighteous.

When cattle are crossing [a ford]
if the chief bull goes straight across,
all the others go straight across
because their leader has gone straight.

So too, among human beings,
when the one considered the chief
conducts himself righteously,
other people do so as well.
The entire kingdom rejoices
if the king is righteous.

III. Unmistakable

71 (1) Striving

"Bhikkhus, a bhikkhu who possesses four qualities is practicing the unmistakable way and has laid the groundwork for the destruction of the taints.[766] What four? Here, a bhikkhu is virtuous, learned, energetic, and wise. A bhikkhu who possesses these four qualities is practicing the unmistakable way and has laid the groundwork for the destruction of the taints."

72 (2) View

"Bhikkhus, a bhikkhu who possesses four qualities is practicing the unmistakable way and has laid the groundwork for the destruction of the taints. What four? The thought of renunciation, the thought of good will, the thought of non-harming, and right view.[767] A bhikkhu who possesses these four qualities [77] is practicing the unmistakable way and has laid the groundwork for the destruction of the taints."

73 (3) The Bad Person: The Bride

"Bhikkhus, one who possesses four qualities can be understood to be a bad person. What four?

(1) "Here, bhikkhus, a bad person discloses the faults of others even when not asked about them, how much more then when asked. But when he is asked about them, then, led on by questions, he speaks about the faults of others without gaps or omissions, fully and in detail. It can be understood: 'This fellow is a bad person.'

(2) "Again, a bad person does not disclose the virtues of others even when asked about them, how much less then when not asked. But when he is asked about them, then, though led on by questions, he speaks about the virtues of others with gaps and omissions, not fully or in detail. It can be understood: 'This fellow is a bad person.'

(3) "Again, a bad person does not disclose his own faults even when asked about them, how much less then when not asked. But when he is asked about them, then, though led on by questions, he speaks about his own faults with gaps and omissions, not fully or in detail. It can be understood: 'This fellow is a bad person.'

(4) "Again, a bad person discloses his own virtues even when

not asked about them, how much more then when asked. But when he is asked about them, then, led on by questions, he speaks about his own virtues without gaps and omissions, fully and in detail. It can be understood: 'This fellow is a bad person.'

"One who possesses these four qualities can be understood to be a bad person.

"Bhikkhus, one who possesses [another] four qualities can be understood to be a good person. What four?

(1) "Here, bhikkhus, a good person does not disclose the faults of others even when asked about them, how much less then when not asked. But when he is asked about them, then, though led on by questions, he speaks about the faults of others with gaps and omissions, [78] not fully or in detail. It can be understood: 'This fellow is a good person.'

(2) "Again, a good person discloses the virtues of others even when not asked about them, how much more then when asked. But when he is asked about them, then, led on by questions, he speaks about the virtues of others without gaps and omissions, fully and in detail. It can be understood: 'This fellow is a good person.'

(3) "Again, a good person discloses his own faults even when not asked about them, how much more then when asked. But when he is asked about them, then, led on by questions, he speaks about his own faults without gaps and omissions, fully and in detail. It can be understood: 'This fellow is a good person.'

(4) "Again, a good person does not disclose his own virtues even when asked about them, how much less then when not asked. But when he is asked about them, then, led on by questions, he speaks about his own virtues with gaps and omissions, not fully or in detail. It can be understood: 'This fellow is a good person.'

"One who possesses these four qualities can be understood as a good person.

"Bhikkhus,[768] when a bride is first brought into the home, whether at night or during the day, at first she sets up a keen sense of moral shame and moral dread toward her mother-in-law, her father-in-law, her husband, and even the slaves, workers, and servants. But after some time, as a result of living together and intimacy with them, she says to her mother-in-law, her father-in-law, and her husband: 'Go away! What do you know?'

"So too, when some bhikkhu here has gone forth from the household life into homelessness, whether by night or during the day, at first he sets up a keen sense of moral shame and moral dread toward the bhikkhus, the bhikkhunīs, the male lay followers, the female lay followers, and even toward the monastery workers and novices. But after some time, as a result of living together and intimacy with them, he says even to his teacher and his preceptor: 'Go away! What do you know?'

"Therefore, bhikkhus, you should train yourselves thus: 'We will dwell with a mind like that of a newly arrived bride.' It is in such a way that you should train yourselves." [79]

74 (4) Foremost (1)

"Bhikkhus, there are these four things that are foremost. What four? The foremost kind of virtuous behavior, the foremost kind of concentration, the foremost kind of wisdom, and the foremost kind of liberation. These are the four things that are foremost."

75 (5) Foremost (2)

"Bhikkhus, there are these four things that are foremost. What four? The foremost of forms, the foremost of feelings, the foremost of perceptions, and the foremost among states of existence. These are the four things that are foremost."[769]

76 (6) Kusinārā

On one occasion the Blessed One was dwelling at Kusinārā between the twin sal trees in the sal-tree grove of the Mallas at Upavattana, on the occasion of his final nibbāna. There the Blessed One addressed the bhikkhus: "Bhikkhus!"

"Venerable sir!" those bhikkhus replied. The Blessed One said this:

"Bhikkhus, it may be that even a single bhikkhu has some doubt or uncertainty about the Buddha, the Dhamma, or the Saṅgha, about the path or the practice.[770] Then ask, bhikkhus. Do not be remorseful later, thinking: 'Our teacher was present before us, yet we could not bring ourselves to question the Blessed One when we were in his presence.'

When this was said, the bhikkhus were silent. A second time ... A third time the Blessed One addressed the bhikkhus ... And a third time the bhikkhus were silent.

Then the Blessed One addressed the bhikkhus: "It may be the case, bhikkhus, that you do not ask out of respect for the teacher. Then report your questions to a friend." When this was said, the bhikkhus were still silent. [80]

Then the Venerable Ānanda said to the Blessed One: "It is astounding and amazing, Bhante! I am confident that there is not a single bhikkhu in this Saṅgha who has any doubt or uncertainty about the Buddha, the Dhamma, or the Saṅgha, about the path or the practice."

"You speak out of confidence, Ānanda, but the Tathāgata knows this for a fact. For among these five hundred bhikkhus, even the least is a stream-enterer, no longer subject to [rebirth in] the lower world, fixed in destiny, heading for enlightenment."

77 (7) Inconceivable Matters

"Bhikkhus, there are these four inconceivable matters[771] that one should not try to conceive; one who tries to conceive them would reap either madness or frustration. What four? (1) The domain of the Buddhas is an inconceivable matter that one should not try to conceive; one who tries to conceive it would reap either madness or frustration. (2) The domain of one in jhāna is an inconceivable matter ... (3) The result of kamma is an inconceivable matter ... (4) Speculation about the world is an inconceivable matter that one should not try to conceive; one who tries to conceive it would reap either madness or frustration.[772] These are the four inconceivable matters that one should not try to conceive; one who tries to conceive them would reap either madness or frustration."

78 (8) Offerings

"Bhikkhus, there are these four purifications of offerings.[773] What four? (1) There is an offering that is purified through the donor but not through the recipients; (2) there is an offering that is purified through the recipients but not through the donor; (3) there is an offering that is not purified through either the donor or the recipients; (4) there is an offering that is purified through both the donor and the recipients. [81]

(1) "And how, bhikkhus, is an offering purified through the donor but not through the recipients? Here, the donor is virtuous and of good character, but the recipients are immoral and of bad character. It is in this way that an offering is purified through the donor but not through the recipients.

(2) "And how is an offering purified through the recipients but not through the donor? Here, the donor is immoral and of bad character, but the recipients are virtuous and of good character. It is in this way that an offering is purified through the recipients but not through the donor.

(3) "And how is an offering not purified through either the donor or the recipients? Here, the donor is immoral and of bad character, and the recipients too are immoral and of bad character. It is in this way that an offering is not purified through either the donor or the recipients.

(4) "And how is an offering purified through both the donor and the recipients? Here, the donor is virtuous and of good character, and the recipients too are virtuous and of good character. It is in this way that an offering is purified through both the donor and the recipients.

"These are the four purifications of offerings."

79 (9) Business

Then the Venerable Sāriputta approached the Blessed One, paid homage to him, sat down to one side, and said: "Bhante, (1) why is it that for one person here, the business he undertakes ends in failure? (2) Why is it that for another the same kind of business does not fulfill his expectations? (3) Why is it that for still another the same kind of business fulfills his expectations? (4) And why is it that for still another the same kind of business surpasses his expectations?"

(1) "Here, Sāriputta, someone approaches an ascetic or a brahmin and invites him to ask for what he needs, [82] but does not give him what was requested. When he passes away from there, if he comes back to this world, whatever business he undertakes ends in failure.

(2) "Someone else approaches an ascetic or a brahmin and invites him to ask for what he needs. He gives it to him but does not fulfill his expectations. When he passes away from there, if he comes back to this world, whatever business he undertakes does not fulfill his expectations.

(3) "Someone else approaches an ascetic or a brahmin and invites him to ask for what he needs. He gives it to him and fulfills his expectations. When he passes away from there, if he comes back to this world, whatever business he undertakes fulfills his expectations.

(4) "Someone else approaches an ascetic or a brahmin and invites him to ask for what he needs. He gives it to him and surpasses his expectations. When he passes away from there, if he comes back to this world, whatever business he undertakes surpasses his expectations.

"This, Sāriputta, is the reason why for one person here the business he undertakes ends in failure, for another the same kind of business does not fulfill his expectations, for still another the same kind of business fulfills his expectations, and for still another the same kind of business surpasses his expectations."

80 (10) Kamboja

On one occasion the Blessed One was dwelling at Kosambī in Ghosita's Park. Then the Venerable Ānanda approached the Blessed One, paid homage to him, sat down to one side, and said:

"Bhante, why is it that women do not sit in council, or engage in business, or go to Kamboja?"[774]

"Ānanda, women are prone to anger; women are envious; [83] women are miserly; women are unwise. This is why women do not sit in council, engage in business, or go to Kamboja."

IV. Unshakable

81 (1) The Destruction of Life

"Bhikkhus, one possessing four qualities is deposited in hell as if brought there. What four? One destroys life, takes what is not given, engages in sexual misconduct, and speaks falsely. One possessing these four qualities is deposited in hell as if brought there.

"Bhikkhus, one possessing four [other] qualities is deposited in heaven as if brought there. What four? One abstains from the destruction of life, from taking what is not given, from sexual misconduct, and from false speech. One possessing these four qualities is deposited in heaven as if brought there."

82 (2) False Speech

"Bhikkhus, one possessing four qualities is deposited in hell as if brought there. What four? One speaks falsely, speaks divisively, speaks harshly, and indulges in idle chatter. One possessing these four qualities is deposited in hell as if brought there. [84]

"Bhikkhus, one possessing four [other] qualities is deposited in heaven as if brought there. What four? One abstains from false speech, from divisive speech, from harsh speech, and from idle chatter. One possessing these four qualities is deposited in heaven as if brought there."

83 (3) Dispraise

"Bhikkhus, one possessing four qualities is deposited in hell as if brought there. What four? (1) Without investigating and scrutinizing, one speaks praise of one who deserves dispraise. (2) Without investigating and scrutinizing, one speaks dispraise of one who deserves praise. (3) Without investigating and scrutinizing, one believes a matter that merits suspicion. (4) Without investigating and scrutinizing, one is suspicious about a matter that merits belief. Possessing these four qualities one is deposited in hell as if brought there.

"Bhikkhus, one possessing four [other] qualities is deposited in heaven as if brought there. What four? (1) Having investigated and scrutinized, one speaks dispraise of one who deserves dispraise. (2) Having investigated and scrutinized, one speaks praise of one who deserves praise. (3) Having investigated and scrutinized, one is suspicious about a matter that merits suspicion. (4) Having investigated and scrutinized, one believes a matter that merits belief. Possessing these four qualities one is deposited in heaven as if brought there."

84 (4) Anger

"Bhikkhus, one possessing four qualities is deposited in hell as if brought there. What four? One values anger, not the good Dhamma; one values denigration, not the good Dhamma; one values gain, not the good Dhamma; one values honor, not the good Dhamma. One possessing these four qualities is deposited in hell as if brought there. [85]

"Bhikkhus, one possessing four [other] qualities is deposited in heaven as if brought there. What four? One values the good Dhamma, not anger; one values the good Dhamma, not denigration; one values the good Dhamma, not gain; one values the good Dhamma, not honor. One possessing these four qualities is deposited in heaven as if brought there."

85 (5) Darkness[775]

"Bhikkhus, there are these four kinds of persons found existing in the world. What four? The one heading from darkness to darkness, the one heading from darkness to light, the one heading from light to darkness, and the one heading from light to light.

(1) "And how, bhikkhus, is a person heading from darkness to darkness? Here, some person has been reborn in a low family—a family of caṇḍālas, bamboo workers, hunters, cart makers, or flower scavengers[776]—one that is poor, with little food and drink, that subsists with difficulty, where food and clothing are obtained with difficulty; and he is ugly, unsightly, dwarfish, with much illness—blind, crippled, lame, or paralyzed. He does not obtain food, drink, clothing, and vehicles; garlands, scents, and unguents; bedding, housing, and lighting. He engages in misconduct by body, speech, and mind. In consequence, with the breakup of the body, after death, he is reborn in the plane of misery, in a bad destination, in the lower world, in hell. It is in this way that a person is heading from darkness to darkness.

(2) "And how is a person heading from darkness to light? Here, some person has been reborn in a low family . . . where food and clothing are obtained with difficulty; and he is ugly . . . or paralyzed. He does not obtain food . . . and lighting. He engages in good conduct by body, speech, and mind. In consequence, with the breakup of the body, after death, he is reborn in a good destination, in a heavenly world. It is in this way that a person is heading from darkness to light.

(3) "And how is a person heading from light to darkness? [86] Here, some person has been reborn in a high family—an affluent khattiya family, an affluent brahmin family, or an affluent householder family—one that is rich, with great wealth and property, with abundant gold and silver, with abundant treasures and belongings, with abundant wealth and grain; and he is handsome, attractive, graceful, possessing supreme beauty

of complexion. He obtains food, drink, clothing, and vehicles; garlands, scents, and unguents; bedding, housing, and lighting. He engages in misconduct by body, speech, and mind. In consequence, with the breakup of the body, after death, he is reborn in the plane of misery, in a bad destination, in the lower world, in hell. It is in this way that a person is heading from light to darkness.

(4) "And how is a person heading from light to light? Here, some person has been reborn in a high family . . . with abundant wealth and grain; and he is handsome . . . possessing supreme beauty of complexion. He obtains food . . . and lighting. He engages in good conduct by body, speech, and mind. In consequence, with the breakup of the body, after death, he is reborn in a good destination, in a heavenly world. It is in this way that a person is heading from light to light.

"These, bhikkhus, are the four kinds of persons found existing in the world."

86 (6) Bent Down

"Bhikkhus, there are these four kinds of persons found existing in the world. What four? The one bent down who bends lower, the one bent down who rises, the one risen who bends down, and the one risen who rises higher.[777]

"These are the four kinds of persons found existing in the world."

87 (7) The Son

"Bhikkhus, there are these four kinds of persons found existing in the world. What four? The ascetic unshaken, the red-lotus ascetic, the white-lotus ascetic, and the delicate ascetic among ascetics.[778]

(1) "And how, bhikkhus, is a person an ascetic unshaken? Here, a bhikkhu is a trainee practicing the way who dwells aspiring for the unsurpassed security from bondage. Just as [87] the eldest son of a head-anointed khattiya king—one due to be anointed but not yet anointed—would have attained the unshaken,[779] so too a bhikkhu is a trainee practicing the way who dwells aspiring for the unsurpassed security from bondage.[780] It is in this way that a person is an ascetic unshaken.

(2) "And how is a person a white-lotus ascetic? Here, with

the destruction of the taints, a bhikkhu has realized for himself with direct knowledge, in this very life, the taintless liberation of mind, liberation by wisdom, and having entered upon it, he dwells in it; yet he does not dwell having contacted with the body the eight emancipations. It is in this way that a person is a white-lotus ascetic.[781]

(3) "And how is a person a red-lotus ascetic? Here, with the destruction of the taints, a bhikkhu has realized for himself with direct knowledge, in this very life, the taintless liberation of mind, liberation by wisdom, and having entered upon it, he dwells in it; and he dwells having contacted with the body the eight emancipations. It is in this way that a person is a red-lotus ascetic.[782]

(4) "And how is a person a delicate ascetic among ascetics? Here, a bhikkhu usually uses a robe that has been specifically offered to him, seldom one that has not been specifically offered to him;[783] he usually eats almsfood that has been specifically offered to him, seldom almsfood that has not been specifically offered to him; he usually uses a lodging that has been specifically offered to him, seldom one that has not been specifically offered to him; he usually uses medicines and provisions for the sick that have been specifically offered to him, seldom those that have not been specifically offered to him. His fellow monks, those with whom he dwells, usually behave toward him in agreeable ways by body, speech, and mind, seldom in disagreeable ways. They usually present him what is agreeable, seldom what is disagreeable. Discomfort originating from bile, phlegm, wind, or their combination;[784] discomfort produced by change of climate; discomfort produced by careless behavior; discomfort produced by assault; or discomfort produced as the result of kamma—these do not often arise in him.[785] He is seldom ill. He gains at will, without trouble or difficulty, the four jhānas that constitute the higher mind and are pleasant dwellings in this very life. With the destruction of the taints, he has realized for himself with direct knowledge, in this very life, the taintless liberation of mind, [88] liberation by wisdom, and having entered upon it, he dwells in it. It is in this way that a person is a delicate ascetic among ascetics.

"If, bhikkhus, one could rightly say of anyone: 'He is a delicate ascetic among ascetics,' it is precisely of me that one might say this. For I usually use a robe that has been specifically offered to me, seldom one that has not been specifically offered to me; I usually eat almsfood that has been specifically offered to me, seldom almsfood that has not been specifically offered to me; I usually use a lodging that has been specifically offered to me, seldom one that has not been specifically offered to me; I usually use medicines and provisions for the sick that have been specifically offered to me, seldom those that have not been specifically offered to me. Those bhikkhus with whom I dwell usually behave toward me in agreeable ways by body, speech, and mind, seldom in disagreeable ways. They usually present me what is agreeable, seldom what is disagreeable. Discomfort originating from bile, phlegm, wind, or their combination; discomfort produced by change of climate; discomfort produced by careless behavior; discomfort produced by assault; or discomfort produced as the result of kamma—these do not often arise in me. I am seldom ill. I gain at will, without trouble or difficulty, the four jhānas that constitute the higher mind and are pleasant dwellings in this very life. With the destruction of the taints, I have realized for myself with direct knowledge, in this very life, the taintless liberation of mind, liberation by wisdom, and having entered upon it, I dwell in it. If one could rightly say of anyone: 'He is a delicate ascetic among ascetics,' it is precisely of me that one might say this.

"These, bhikkhus, are the four kinds of persons found existing in the world."

88 (8) Fetters

"Bhikkhus, there are these four kinds of persons found existing in the world. What four? The ascetic unshaken, the white-lotus ascetic, the red-lotus ascetic, and the delicate ascetic among ascetics.

(1) "And how, bhikkhus, is a person an ascetic unshaken? Here, with the utter destruction of three fetters, [89] a bhikkhu is a stream-enterer, no longer subject to [rebirth in] the lower world, fixed in destiny, heading for enlightenment. It is in this way that a person is an ascetic unshaken.

(2) "And how is a person a white-lotus ascetic? Here, with the utter destruction of three fetters and with the diminishing of greed, hatred, and delusion, a bhikkhu is a once-returner

who, after coming back to this world only one more time, will make an end of suffering. It is in this way that a person is a white-lotus ascetic.

(3) "And how is a person a red-lotus ascetic? Here, with the utter destruction of the five lower fetters, a bhikkhu is one of spontaneous birth, due to attain final nibbāna there without returning from that world. It is in this way that a person is a red-lotus ascetic.

(4) "And how is a person a delicate ascetic among ascetics? Here, with the destruction of the taints, a bhikkhu has realized for himself with direct knowledge, in this very life, the taintless liberation of mind, liberation by wisdom, and having entered upon it, he dwells in it. It is in this way that a person is a delicate ascetic among ascetics.

"These, bhikkhus, are the four kinds of persons found existing in the world."

89 (9) View

"Bhikkhus, there are these four kinds of persons found existing in the world. What four? The ascetic unshaken, the white-lotus ascetic, the red-lotus ascetic, and the delicate ascetic among ascetics.

(1) "And how, bhikkhus, is a person an ascetic unshaken? Here, a bhikkhu is one of right view, right intention, right speech, right action, right livelihood, right effort, right mindfulness, and right concentration. It is in this way that a person is an ascetic unshaken.

(2) "And how is a person a white-lotus ascetic? Here, a bhikkhu is one of right view, right intention, right speech, right action, right livelihood, right effort, right mindfulness, right concentration, right knowledge, and right liberation; yet he does not dwell having contacted with the body the eight emancipations. [90] It is in this way that a person is a white-lotus ascetic.

(3) "And how is a person a red-lotus ascetic? Here, a bhikkhu is one of right view, right intention, right speech, right action, right livelihood, right effort, right mindfulness, right concentration, right knowledge, and right liberation; and he dwells having contacted with the body the eight emancipations. It is in this way that a person is a red-lotus ascetic.

(4) "And how is a person a delicate ascetic among ascetics? Here, a bhikkhu usually uses a robe that has been specifically offered to him, seldom one that has not been specifically offered to him . . . [as in 4:87] . . . If one could rightly say of anyone: 'He is a delicate ascetic among ascetics,' it is precisely of me that one might say this.

"These, bhikkhus, are the four kinds of persons found existing in the world."[786]

90 (10) Aggregates

"Bhikkhus, there are these four kinds of persons found existing in the world. What four? The ascetic unshaken, the white-lotus ascetic, the red-lotus ascetic, and the delicate ascetic among ascetics.

(1) "And how, bhikkhus, is a person an ascetic unshaken? Here, a bhikkhu is a trainee who has not attained his mind's ideal, one who dwells aspiring for the unsurpassed security from bondage. It is in this way that a person is an ascetic unshaken.

(2) "And how is a person a white-lotus ascetic? Here, a bhikkhu dwells contemplating arising and vanishing in the five aggregates subject to clinging: 'Such is form, such its origin, such its passing away; such is feeling, such its origin, such its passing away; such is perception, such its origin, such its passing away; such are volitional activities, such their origin, such their passing away; such is consciousness, such its origin, such its passing away'; yet he does not dwell having contacted with the body the eight emancipations. It is in this way that a person is a white-lotus ascetic.

(3) "And how is a person a red-lotus ascetic? Here, a bhikkhu dwells contemplating arising and vanishing in the five aggregates subject to clinging: 'Such is form, such its origin, such its passing away; such is feeling . . . such is perception . . . such are volitional activities . . . such is consciousness, such its origin, [91] such its passing away'; and he dwells having contacted with the body the eight emancipations. It is in this way that a person is a red-lotus ascetic.

(4) "And how is a person a delicate ascetic among ascetics? Here, a bhikkhu usually uses a robe that has been specifically offered to him, seldom one that has not been specifically offered

to him . . . [as in 4:87] . . . If one could rightly say of anyone: 'He is a delicate ascetic among ascetics,' it is precisely of me that one might say this.

"These, bhikkhus, are the four kinds of persons found existing in the world."

V. Asuras

91 (1) Asuras

"Bhikkhus, there are these four kinds of persons found existing in the world. What four? The asura with a retinue of asuras, the asura with a retinue of devas, the deva with a retinue of asuras, and the deva with a retinue of devas.

(1) "And how, bhikkhus, is a person an asura with a retinue of asuras? Here, someone is immoral, of bad character, and his retinue is immoral, of bad character. It is in this way that someone is an asura with a retinue of asuras.

(2) "And how is a person an asura with a retinue of devas? Here, someone is immoral, of bad character, but his retinue is virtuous, of good character. It is in this way that someone is an asura with a retinue of devas.

(3) "And how is a person a deva with a retinue of asuras? [92] Here, someone is virtuous, of good character, but his retinue is immoral, of bad character. It is in this way that someone is a deva with a retinue of asuras.

(4) "And how is a person a deva with a retinue of devas? Here, someone is virtuous, of good character, and his retinue is virtuous, of good character. It is in this way that someone is a deva with a retinue of devas.

"These, bhikkhus, are the four kinds of persons found existing in the world."

92 (2) Concentration (1)

"Bhikkhus, there are these four kinds of persons found existing in the world. What four? (1) Here, some person gains internal serenity of mind but not the higher wisdom of insight into phenomena.[787] (2) Some other person gains the higher wisdom of insight into phenomena but not internal serenity of mind. (3) Still another gains neither internal serenity of mind nor the higher wisdom of insight into phenomena. (4) And still another gains both internal serenity of mind and the higher wisdom of insight into phenomena. These are the four kinds of persons found existing in the world."

93 (3) Concentration (2)

"Bhikkhus, there are these four kinds of persons found existing in the world. What four? (1) Here, some person gains internal serenity of mind but not the higher wisdom of insight into phenomena. (2) Some other person gains the higher wisdom of insight into phenomena but not internal serenity of mind. (3) Still another gains neither internal serenity of mind nor the higher wisdom of insight into phenomena. (4) And still another gains both internal serenity of mind and the higher wisdom of insight into phenomena.

(1) "Bhikkhus, the person among these who gains internal [93] serenity of mind but not the higher wisdom of insight into phenomena should base himself on internal serenity of mind and make an effort to gain the higher wisdom of insight into phenomena. Then, some time later, he gains both internal serenity of mind and the higher wisdom of insight into phenomena.

(2) "The person who gains the higher wisdom of insight into phenomena but not internal serenity of mind should base himself on the higher wisdom of insight into phenomena and make an effort to gain internal serenity of mind. Then, some time later, he gains both the higher wisdom of insight into phenomena and internal serenity of mind.

(3) "The person who gains neither internal serenity of mind nor the higher wisdom of insight into phenomena should put forth extraordinary desire, effort, zeal, enthusiasm, indefatigability, mindfulness, and clear comprehension to obtain both those wholesome qualities. Just as one whose clothes or head had caught fire would put forth extraordinary desire, effort, zeal, enthusiasm, indefatigability, mindfulness, and clear comprehension to extinguish [the fire on] his clothes or head, so that person should put forth extraordinary desire, effort, zeal, enthusiasm, indefatigability, mindfulness, and clear comprehension to obtain both those wholesome qualities. Then, some time later, he gains both internal serenity of mind and the higher wisdom of insight into phenomena.

(4) "The person who gains both internal serenity of mind

and the higher wisdom of insight into phenomena should base himself on those same wholesome qualities and make a further effort to reach the destruction of the taints.

"These, bhikkhus, are the four kinds of persons found existing in the world."

94 (4) Concentration (3)

"Bhikkhus, there are these four kinds of persons found existing in the world. What four? (1) Here, bhikkhus, some person gains internal serenity of mind but not the higher wisdom of insight into phenomena. [94] (2) Some other person gains the higher wisdom of insight into phenomena but not internal serenity of mind. (3) Still another gains neither internal serenity of mind nor the higher wisdom of insight into phenomena. (4) And still another gains both internal serenity of mind and the higher wisdom of insight into phenomena.

(1) "Bhikkhus, the person among these who gains internal serenity of mind but not the higher wisdom of insight into phenomena should approach one who gains the higher wisdom of insight into phenomena and inquire of him: 'How, friend, should conditioned phenomena be seen? How should conditioned phenomena be explored? How should conditioned phenomena be discerned by insight?' The other then answers him as he has seen and understood the matter thus: 'Conditioned phenomena should be seen in such a way, explored in such a way, discerned by insight in such a way.'[788] Then, some time later, he gains both internal serenity of mind and the higher wisdom of insight into phenomena.

(2) "The person who gains the higher wisdom of insight into phenomena but not internal serenity of mind should approach one who gains internal serenity of mind and inquire of him: 'How, friend, should the mind be steadied? How should the mind be composed? How should the mind be unified? How should the mind be concentrated?' The other then answers him as he has seen and understood the matter thus: 'The mind should be steadied in such a way, composed in such a way, unified in such a way, concentrated in such a way.'[789] Then, some time later, he gains both the higher wisdom of insight into phenomena and internal serenity of mind.

(3) "The person who gains neither internal serenity of mind

nor the higher wisdom of insight into phenomena should approach one who gains both and inquire of him: 'How, friend, should the mind be steadied? How should the mind be composed? How should the mind be unified? How should the mind be concentrated? How should conditioned phenomena be seen? How should conditioned phenomena be explored? How should conditioned phenomena be discerned by insight?' The other then answers him as he has seen and understood the matter thus: 'The mind should be steadied in such a way, composed in such a way, unified in such a way, concentrated in such a way. Conditioned phenomena should be seen in such a way, explored in such a way, discerned by insight in such a way.' Then, some time later, [95] he gains both internal serenity of mind and the higher wisdom of insight into phenomena.

(4) "The person who gains both internal serenity of mind and the higher wisdom of insight into phenomena should base himself on those same wholesome qualities and make a further effort for the destruction of the taints.

"These, bhikkhus, are the four kinds of persons found existing in the world."

95 (5) Cremation Brand

"Bhikkhus, there are these four kinds of persons found existing in the world. What four? (1) One who is practicing neither for his own welfare nor for the welfare of others; (2) one who is practicing for the welfare of others but not for his own welfare; (3) one who is practicing for his own welfare but not for the welfare of others; and (4) one who is practicing both for his own welfare and for the welfare of others.

(1) "Suppose, bhikkhus, a cremation brand was blazing at both ends and smeared with dung in the middle: it could not be used as timber either in the village or in the forest. Just like this, I say, is the person who is practicing neither for his own welfare nor for the welfare of others.

(2) "Bhikkhus, the person among these who is practicing for the welfare of others but not for his own welfare is the more excellent and sublime of the [first] two persons. (3) The person practicing for his own welfare but not for the welfare of others is the more excellent and sublime of the [first] three persons. (4) The person practicing both for his own welfare and for the

welfare of others is the foremost, the best, the preeminent, the supreme, and the finest of these four persons. Just as from a cow comes milk, from milk curd, from curd butter, from butter ghee, and from ghee cream-of-ghee, which is reckoned the foremost of all these, so the person practicing both for his own welfare and for the welfare of others is the foremost, the best, the preeminent, the supreme, and the finest of these four persons. [96]

"These, bhikkhus, are the four kinds of persons found existing in the world."

96 (6) Lust

"Bhikkhus, there are these four kinds of persons found existing in the world. What four? (1) One who is practicing for his own welfare but not for the welfare of others; (2) one who is practicing for the welfare of others but not for his own welfare; (3) one who is practicing neither for his own welfare nor for the welfare of others; and (4) one who is practicing both for his own welfare and for the welfare of others.

(1) "And how, bhikkhus, is a person practicing for his own welfare but not for the welfare of others? Here, some person practices to remove his own lust, hatred, and delusion but does not encourage others to remove their lust, hatred, and delusion. It is in this way that a person is practicing for his own welfare but not for the welfare of others.

(2) "And how is a person practicing for the welfare of others but not for his own welfare? Here, some person encourages others to remove their lust, hatred, and delusion, but does not practice to remove his own lust, hatred, and delusion. It is in this way that a person is practicing for the welfare of others but not for his own welfare.

(3) "And how is a person practicing neither for his own welfare nor for the welfare of others? Here, some person does not practice to remove his own lust, hatred, and delusion, nor does he encourage others to remove their lust, hatred, and delusion. It is in this way that a person is practicing neither for his own welfare nor for the welfare of others.

(4) "And how is a person practicing both for his own welfare and for the welfare of others? Here, some person practices to remove his own lust, hatred, and delusion, and he encourages

others to remove their lust, hatred, and delusion. [97] It is in this way that a person is practicing both for his own welfare and for the welfare of others.

"These, bhikkhus, are the four kinds of persons found existing in the world."

97 (7) Quick-Witted

"Bhikkhus, there are these four kinds of persons found existing in the world. What four? (1) One who is practicing for his own welfare but not for the welfare of others; (2) one who is practicing for the welfare of others but not for his own welfare; (3) one who is practicing neither for his own welfare nor for the welfare of others; and (4) one who is practicing both for his own welfare and for the welfare of others.

(1) "And how, bhikkhus, is a person practicing for his own welfare but not for the welfare of others? Here, some person is quick in attending to wholesome teachings, is able to retain in mind the teachings he has heard, and examines the meaning of the teachings he has retained. Having understood the meaning and the Dhamma, he practices in accordance with the Dhamma. However, he is not a good speaker with a good delivery; he is not gifted with speech that is polished, clear, articulate, expressive of the meaning; and he does not instruct, encourage, inspire, and gladden his fellow monks. It is in this way that a person is practicing for his own welfare but not for the welfare of others.

(2) "And how is a person practicing for the welfare of others but not for his own welfare? Here, some person is not quick in attending to wholesome teachings, is unable to retain in mind the teachings he has heard, and does not examine the meaning of the teachings he has retained. Having no understanding of the meaning and the Dhamma, he does not practice in accordance with the Dhamma. However, he is a good speaker with a good delivery; he is gifted with speech that is polished, clear, articulate, expressive of the meaning; and he instructs, encourages, inspires, and gladdens his fellow monks. It is in this way that a person is practicing for the welfare of others but not for his own welfare. [98]

(3) "And how is a person practicing neither for his own welfare nor for the welfare of others? Here, some person is not

quick in attending to wholesome teachings . . . he does not practice in accordance with the Dhamma. Moreover, he is not a good speaker with a good delivery . . . and he does not instruct, encourage, inspire, and gladden his fellow monks. It is in this way that a person is practicing neither for his own welfare nor for the welfare of others.

(4) "And how is a person practicing both for his own welfare and for the welfare of others? Here, some person is quick in attending to wholesome teachings . . . he practices in accordance with the Dhamma. Moreover, he is a good speaker with a good delivery . . . and he instructs, encourages, inspires, and gladdens his fellow monks. It is in this way that a person is practicing both for his own welfare and for the welfare of others.

"These, bhikkhus, are the four kinds of persons found existing in the world."

98 (8) One's Own Welfare

"Bhikkhus, there are these four kinds of persons found existing in the world. What four? (1) One who is practicing for his own welfare but not for the welfare of others; (2) one who is practicing for the welfare of others but not for his own welfare; (3) one who is practicing neither for his own welfare nor for the welfare of others; and (4) one who is practicing both for his own welfare and for the welfare of others. These are the four kinds of persons found existing in the world."

99 (9) Training Rules

"Bhikkhus, there are these four kinds of persons found existing in the world. What four? (1) One who is practicing for his own welfare [99] but not for the welfare of others; (2) one who is practicing for the welfare of others but not for his own welfare; (3) one who is practicing neither for his own welfare nor for the welfare of others; and (4) one who is practicing both for his own welfare and for the welfare of others.

(1) "And how, bhikkhus, is a person practicing for his own welfare but not for the welfare of others? Here, some person himself abstains from the destruction of life but does not encourage others to abstain from the destruction of life. He himself abstains from taking what is not given but does not encourage others to abstain from taking what is not given. He himself

abstains from sexual misconduct but does not encourage others to abstain from sexual misconduct. He himself abstains from false speech but does not encourage others to abstain from false speech. He himself abstains from liquor, wine, and intoxicants, the basis for heedlessness, but does not encourage others to abstain from them. It is in this way that a person is practicing for his own welfare but not for the welfare of others.

(2) "And how is a person practicing for the welfare of others but not for his own welfare? Here, some person does not himself abstain from the destruction of life but he encourages others to abstain from the destruction of life.... He does not himself abstain from liquor, wine, and intoxicants, the basis for heedlessness, but he encourages others to abstain from them. It is in this way that a person is practicing for the welfare of others but not for his own welfare.

(3) "And how is a person practicing neither for his own welfare nor for the welfare of others? Here, some person does not himself abstain from the destruction of life and does not encourage others to abstain from the destruction of life.... He does not himself abstain from liquor, wine, and intoxicants, the basis for heedlessness, and does not encourage others to abstain from them. It is in this way that a person is practicing neither for his own welfare nor for the welfare of others.

(4) "And how is a person practicing both for his own welfare and for the welfare of others? Here, some person himself abstains from the destruction of life and encourages others to abstain from the destruction of life.... He himself abstains from liquor, wine, and intoxicants, the basis for heedlessness, and encourages others to abstain from them. It is in this way that he is practicing both for his own welfare and for the welfare of others.

"These, bhikkhus, are the four kinds of persons found existing in the world." [100]

100 (10) Potaliya

Then the wanderer Potaliya approached the Blessed One and exchanged greetings with him. When they had exchanged greetings and cordial talk, the wanderer Potaliya sat down to one side, and the Blessed One then said to him:

"Potaliya, there are these four kinds of persons found existing in the world. What four? (1) Here, some person speaks dispraise of someone who deserves dispraise, and the dispraise is accurate, truthful, and timely; but he does not speak praise of someone who deserves praise, though the praise would be accurate, truthful, and timely. (2) Some other person speaks praise of someone who deserves praise, and the praise is accurate, truthful, and timely; but he does not speak dispraise of someone who deserves dispraise, though the dispraise would be accurate, truthful, and timely. (3) Still another person does not speak dispraise of someone who deserves dispraise, though the dispraise would be accurate, truthful, and timely; and he does not speak praise of someone who deserves praise, though the praise would be accurate, truthful, and timely. (4) And still another person speaks dispraise of someone who deserves dispraise, and the dispraise is accurate, truthful, and timely; and he also speaks praise of someone who deserves praise, and the praise is accurate, truthful, and timely. These are the four kinds of persons found existing in the world. Now, Potaliya, which among these four kinds of persons seems to you the most excellent and sublime?"

"There are, Master Gotama, those four kinds of persons found existing in the world.[790] [101] Of those four, the one that seems to me the most excellent and sublime is the one who does not speak dispraise of someone who deserves dispraise, though the dispraise would be accurate, truthful, and timely; and who does not speak praise of someone who deserves praise, though the praise would be accurate, truthful, and timely. For what reason? Because what excels, Master Gotama, is equanimity."

"There are, Potaliya, those four kinds of persons found existing in the world. Of those four, the one that is the most excellent and sublime is the one who speaks dispraise of someone who deserves dispraise, and the dispraise is accurate, truthful, and timely; and who also speaks praise of someone who deserves praise, and the praise is accurate, truthful, and timely. For what reason? Because what excels, Potaliya, is knowledge of the proper time to speak in any particular case."[791]

"There are, Master Gotama, those four kinds of persons found existing in the world. Of those four, the one that seems to me the most excellent and sublime is the one who speaks dispraise of someone who deserves dispraise, and the dispraise is accurate, truthful, and timely; and who also speaks praise of someone who deserves praise, and the praise is accurate, truthful, and timely. For what reason? Because what excels, Master Gotama, is knowledge of the proper time to speak in any particular case.

"Excellent, Master Gotama! Excellent, Master Gotama! Master Gotama has made the Dhamma clear in many ways, as though he were turning upright what had been overthrown, revealing what was hidden, showing the way to one who was lost, or holding up a lamp in the darkness so those with good eyesight can see forms. I now go for refuge to Master Gotama, to the Dhamma, and to the Saṅgha of bhikkhus. Let Master Gotama consider me a lay follower who from today has gone for refuge for life." [102]

The Third Fifty

I. Clouds

101 (1) Clouds (1)

On one occasion the Blessed One was dwelling at Sāvatthī in Jeta's Grove, Anāthapiṇḍika's Park. There the Blessed One addressed the bhikkhus: "Bhikkhus!"

"Venerable sir!" those bhikkhus replied. The Blessed One said this:

"Bhikkhus, there are these four kinds of clouds. What four? The one that thunders but does not rain; the one that rains but does not thunder; the one that neither thunders nor rains; and the one that both thunders and rains. These are the four kinds of clouds. So too, there are these four kinds of persons similar to clouds found existing in the world. What four? The one who thunders but does not rain; the one who rains but does not thunder; the one who neither thunders nor rains; and the one who both thunders and rains.

(1) "And how, bhikkhus, is a person one who thunders but does not rain? Here, someone is a talker, not a doer. It is in this way that a person is one who thunders but does not rain. So, I say, this person is just like a cloud that thunders but does not rain.

(2) "And how is a person one who rains but does not thunder? Here, someone is a doer, not a talker. It is in this way that a person is one who rains but does not thunder. So, I say, this person is just like a cloud that rains but does not thunder.

(3) "And how is a person one who neither thunders nor rains? Here, someone is neither a talker nor a doer. It is in this way that a person is one who neither thunders nor rains. So, I say, this person is just like a cloud that neither thunders nor rains.

(4) "And how is a person one who both thunders and rains? Here, someone is both a talker and a doer. It is in this way that a person is one who both thunders and rains. So, I say, this person is just like a cloud that both thunders and rains.

"These, bhikkhus, are the four kinds of persons similar to clouds found existing in the world." [103]

102 (2) Clouds (2)

"Bhikkhus, there are these four kinds of clouds. What four? . . . [as above] . . .

(1) "And how, bhikkhus, is a person one who thunders but does not rain? Here, someone masters the Dhamma—the discourses, mixed prose and verse, expositions, verses, inspired utterances, quotations, birth stories, amazing accounts, and questions-and-answers[792]—but he does not understand as it really is: 'This is suffering,' and 'This is the origin of suffering,' and 'This is the cessation of suffering,' and 'This is the way leading to the cessation of suffering.' It is in this way that a person is one who thunders but does not rain. So, I say, this person is just like a cloud that thunders but does not rain.

(2) "And how is a person one who rains but does not thunder? Here, someone does not master the Dhamma—the discourses . . . questions-and-answers—but he understands as it really is: 'This is suffering' . . . 'This is the way leading to the cessation of suffering.' It is in this way that a person is one who rains but does not thunder. So, I say, this person is just like a cloud that rains but does not thunder.

(3) "And how is a person one who neither thunders nor rains? Here, someone does not master the Dhamma—the discourses . . . questions-and-answers—and he does not understand as it really is: 'This is suffering' . . . 'This is the way leading to the cessation of suffering.' It is in this way that a person is

one who neither thunders nor rains. So, I say, this person is just like a cloud that neither thunders nor rains.

(4) "And how is a person one who both thunders and rains? Here, someone masters the Dhamma—the discourses, mixed prose and verse, expositions, verses, inspired utterances, quotations, birth stories, amazing accounts, and questions-and-answers—and he understands as it really is: 'This is suffering,' and 'This is the origin of suffering,' and 'This is the cessation of suffering,' and 'This is the way leading to the cessation of suffering.' It is in this way that a person is one who both thunders and rains. So, I say, this person is just like a cloud that both thunders and rains. [104]

"These, bhikkhus, are the four kinds of persons similar to clouds found existing in the world."

103 (3) Pots

"Bhikkhus, there are these four kinds of pots. What four? The one that is empty and covered; the one that is full and open; the one that is empty and open; and the one that is full and covered. These are the four kinds of pots. So too, there are these four kinds of persons similar to pots found existing in the world. What four? The one who is empty and covered; the one who is full and open; the one who is empty and open; and the one who is full and covered.

(1) "And how, bhikkhus, is a person empty and covered? Here, someone inspires confidence by his manner of going forward and returning, looking ahead and looking aside, drawing in and extending the limbs, wearing his robes and carrying his outer robe and bowl; but he does not understand as it really is: 'This is suffering,' and 'This is the origin of suffering,' and 'This is the cessation of suffering,' and 'This is the way leading to the cessation of suffering.' It is in this way that a person is empty and covered. So, I say, this person is just like a pot that is empty and covered.

(2) "And how is a person full and open? Here, someone does not inspire confidence by his manner of going forward and returning . . . and carrying his outer robe and bowl; but he understands as it really is: 'This is suffering' . . . 'This is the way leading to the cessation of suffering.' It is in this way that a person is full and open. So, I say, this person is just like a pot that is full and open.

(3) "And how is a person empty and open? Here, someone does not inspire confidence by his manner of going forward and returning . . . and carrying his outer robe and bowl; and he does not understand as it really is: 'This is suffering' . . . 'This is the way leading to the cessation of suffering.' It is in this way that a person is empty and open. So, I say, this person is just like a pot that is empty and open.

(4) "And how is a person full and covered? Here, someone inspires confidence by his manner of going forward and returning, looking ahead and looking aside, drawing in and extending the limbs, wearing his robes and carrying his outer robe and bowl; [105] and he understands as it really is: 'This is suffering,' and 'This is the origin of suffering,' and 'This is the cessation of suffering,' and 'This is the way leading to the cessation of suffering.' It is in this way that a person is full and covered. So, I say, this person is just like a pot that is full and covered.

"These, bhikkhus, are the four kinds of persons similar to pots found existing in the world."

104 (4) Pools of Water

"Bhikkhus, there are these four kinds of pools of water. What four? The one that is shallow but appears to be deep; the one that is deep but appears to be shallow; the one that is shallow and appears to be shallow; and the one that is deep and appears to be deep. These are the four kinds of pools of water.[793] So too, there are these four kinds of persons similar to pools of water found existing in the world. What four? The one who is shallow but appears to be deep; the one who is deep but appears to be shallow; the one who is shallow and appears to be shallow; and the one who is deep and appears to be deep.

(1) "And how, bhikkhus, is a person one who is shallow but appears to be deep? Here, someone inspires confidence by his manner of going forward and returning, looking ahead and looking aside, drawing in and extending the limbs, wearing his robes and carrying his outer robe and bowl; but he does not understand as it really is: 'This is suffering,' and 'This is the origin of suffering,' and 'This is the cessation of suffering,' and 'This is the way leading to the cessation of suffering.' It is in this way that a person is shallow but appears to be deep. So, I say, this person is just like a pool of water that is shallow but appears to be deep. [106]

(2) "And how is a person one who is deep but appears to be shallow? Here, someone does not inspire confidence by his manner of going forward and returning . . . and carrying his outer robe and bowl; but he understands as it really is: 'This is suffering' . . . 'This is the way leading to the cessation of suffering.' It is in this way that a person is deep but appears to be shallow. So, I say, this person is just like a pool of water that is deep but appears to be shallow.

(3) "And how is a person one who is shallow and appears to be shallow? Here, someone does not inspire confidence by his manner of going forward and returning . . . and carrying his outer robe and bowl; and he does not understand as it really is: 'This is suffering' . . . 'This is the way leading to the cessation of suffering.' It is in this way that a person is shallow and appears to be shallow. So, I say, this person is just like a pool of water that is shallow and appears to be shallow.

(4) "And how is a person one who is deep and appears to be deep? Here, someone inspires confidence by his manner of going forward and returning, looking ahead and looking aside, drawing in and extending the limbs, wearing his robes and carrying his outer robe and bowl; and he understands as it really is: 'This is suffering,' and 'This is the origin of suffering,' and 'This is the cessation of suffering,' and 'This is the way leading to the cessation of suffering.' It is in this way that a person is deep and appears to be deep. So, I say, this person is just like a pool of water that is deep and appears to be deep.

"These, bhikkhus, are the four kinds of persons similar to pools of water found existing in the world."

105 (5) Mangoes

"Bhikkhus, there are these four kinds of mangoes. What four? The one that is unripe but appears ripe; the one that is ripe but appears unripe; the one that is unripe and appears unripe; and the one that is ripe and appears ripe. These are the four kinds of mangoes. So too, there are these four kinds of persons similar to mangoes found existing in the world. What four? The one who is unripe but appears ripe; the one who is ripe but appears unripe; the one who is unripe and appears unripe; and the one who is ripe and appears ripe.

(1) "And how, bhikkhus, is a person one who is unripe but appears to be ripe? [107] Here, someone inspires confidence by his manner of going forward and returning, looking ahead and looking aside, drawing in and extending the limbs, wearing his robes and carrying his outer robe and bowl; but he does not understand as it really is: 'This is suffering,' and 'This is the origin of suffering,' and 'This is the cessation of suffering,' and 'This is the way leading to the cessation of suffering.' It is in this way that a person is unripe but appears to be ripe. So, I say, this person is just like a mango that is unripe but appears to be ripe.

(2) "And how is a person one who is ripe but appears to be unripe? Here, someone does not inspire confidence by his manner of going forward and returning . . . and carrying his outer robe and bowl; but he understands as it really is: 'This is suffering' . . . 'This is the way leading to the cessation of suffering.' It is in this way that a person is ripe but appears to be unripe. So, I say, this person is just like a mango that is ripe but appears to be unripe.

(3) "And how is a person one who is unripe and appears to be unripe? Here, someone does not inspire confidence by his manner of going forward and returning . . . and carrying his outer robe and bowl; and he does not understand as it really is: 'This is suffering' . . . 'This is the way leading to the cessation of suffering.' It is in this way that a person is unripe and appears to be unripe. So, I say, this person is just like a mango that is unripe and appears to be unripe.

(4) "And how is a person one who is ripe and appears to be ripe? Here, someone inspires confidence by his manner of going forward and returning, looking ahead and looking aside, drawing in and extending the limbs, wearing his robes and carrying his outer robe and bowl; and he understands as it really is: 'This is suffering,' and 'This is the origin of suffering,' and 'This is the cessation of suffering,' and 'This is the way leading to the cessation of suffering.' It is in this way that a person is ripe and appears to be ripe. So, I say, this person is just like a mango that is ripe and appears to be ripe.

"These, bhikkhus, are the four kinds of persons similar to mangoes found existing in the world."

106 (6) [Mangoes]

[No text of this sutta occurs in any edition. The *uddāna* verse at the end of the vagga says: *dve honti ambāni*, "there are two [on] mangoes," which is apparently why Be assigns the title. Mp says only, "The sixth is clear." Both Ce and Be, referring to this comment, have a note: "The commentary says, 'The sixth is clear,' but it is not found in the canonical text."]

107 (7) Mice

"Bhikkhus, there are these four kinds of mice. What four? The one that makes a hole but does not live in it; the one that lives in a hole but does not make one; the one that neither makes a hole nor lives in one; and the one that both makes a hole and lives in it. These are the four kinds of mice. So too, there are these four kinds of persons similar to mice found existing in the world. What four? The one who makes a hole but does not live in it; the one who lives in a hole but does not make one; the one who neither makes a hole nor lives in one; and the one who both makes a hole and lives in it. [108]

(1) "And how, bhikkhus, is a person one who makes a hole but does not live in it? Here, someone masters the Dhamma—the discourses, mixed prose and verse, expositions, verses, inspired utterances, quotations, birth stories, amazing accounts, and questions-and-answers—but he does not understand as it really is: 'This is suffering,' and 'This is the origin of suffering,' and 'This is the cessation of suffering,' and 'This is the way leading to the cessation of suffering.' It is in this way that a person is one who makes a hole but does not live in it. So, I say, this person is just like a mouse that makes a hole but does not live in it.

(2) "And how is a person one who lives in a hole but does not make one? Here, someone does not master the Dhamma—the discourses . . . questions-and-answers—but he understands as it really is: 'This is suffering' . . . 'This is the way leading to the cessation of suffering.' It is in this way that a person is one who lives in a hole but does not make one. So, I say, this person is just like a mouse that lives in a hole but does not make one.

(3) "And how is a person one who neither makes a hole nor lives in one? Here, someone does not master the Dhamma—the discourses . . . questions-and-answers—and he does not

understand as it really is: 'This is suffering' . . . 'This is the way leading to the cessation of suffering.' It is in this way that a person is one who neither makes a hole nor lives in one. So, I say, this person is just like a mouse that neither makes a hole nor lives in one.

(4) "And how is a person one who both makes a hole and lives in it? Here, someone masters the Dhamma—the discourses, mixed prose and verse, expositions, verses, inspired utterances, quotations, birth stories, amazing accounts, and questions-and-answers—and he understands as it really is: 'This is suffering,' and 'This is the origin of suffering,' and 'This is the cessation of suffering,' and 'This is the way leading to the cessation of suffering.' It is in this way that a person is one who both makes a hole and lives in it. So, I say, this person is just like a mouse that both makes a hole and lives in it.

"These, bhikkhus, are the four kinds of persons similar to mice found existing in the world."

108 (8) Bulls

"Bhikkhus, there are these four kinds of bulls. What four? [109] The one wrathful toward its own cattle, not toward the cattle of others; the one wrathful toward the cattle of others, not toward its own cattle; the one wrathful both toward its own cattle and toward the cattle of others; and the one wrathful neither toward its own cattle nor toward the cattle of others. These are the four kinds of bulls. So too, there are these four kinds of persons similar to bulls found existing in the world. What four? The one wrathful toward his own cattle, not toward the cattle of others; the one wrathful toward the cattle of others, not toward his own cattle; the one wrathful both toward his own cattle and toward the cattle of others; and the one wrathful neither toward his own cattle nor toward the cattle of others.

(1) "And how, bhikkhus, is a person wrathful toward his own cattle, not toward the cattle of others? Here, someone intimidates his own retinue but not the retinues of others. It is in this way that a person is wrathful toward his own cattle, not toward the cattle of others. So, I say, this person is just like a bull wrathful toward its own cattle, not toward the cattle of others.

(2) "And how is a person wrathful toward the cattle of others, not toward his own cattle? Here, someone intimidates

the retinues of others but not his own retinue. It is in this way that a person is wrathful toward the cattle of others, not toward his own cattle. So, I say, this person is just like a bull wrathful toward the cattle of others, not toward his own cattle.

(3) "And how is a person wrathful both toward his own cattle and toward the cattle of others? Here, someone intimidates both the retinues of others and also his own retinue. It is in this way that a person is wrathful both toward his own cattle and toward the cattle of others. So, I say, this person is just like a bull wrathful both toward his own cattle and toward the cattle of others.

(4) "And how is a person wrathful neither toward his own cattle nor toward the cattle of others? Here, someone does not intimidate his own retinue or the retinues of others. It is in this way that a person is wrathful neither toward his own cattle nor toward the cattle of others. So, I say, this person is just like a bull wrathful neither toward his own cattle nor toward the cattle of others.

"These, bhikkhus, are the four kinds of persons similar to bulls found existing in the world."

109 (9) Trees

"Bhikkhus, there are these four kinds of trees. What four? [110] The one made of softwood that is surrounded by softwood [trees]; the one made of softwood that is surrounded by hardwood [trees]; the one made of hardwood that is surrounded by softwood [trees]; and the one made of hardwood that is surrounded by hardwood [trees]. These are the four kinds of trees. So too, there are these four kinds of persons similar to trees found existing in the world. What four? The one made of softwood who is surrounded by softwood [trees]; the one made of softwood who is surrounded by hardwood [trees]; the one made of hardwood who is surrounded by softwood [trees]; and the one made of hardwood who is surrounded by hardwood [trees].

(1) "And how, bhikkhus, is a person made of softwood and surrounded by softwood [trees]? Here, someone is immoral, of bad character, and his retinue is also immoral, of bad character. It is in this way that a person is made of softwood and surrounded by softwood [trees]. So, I say, this person is just like a tree made of softwood and surrounded by softwood [trees].

(2) "And how is a person made of softwood but surrounded by hardwood [trees]? Here, someone is immoral, of bad character, but his retinue is virtuous, of good character. It is in this way that a person is made of softwood but surrounded by hardwood [trees]. So, I say, this person is just like a tree made of softwood but surrounded by hardwood [trees].

(3) "And how is a person made of hardwood but surrounded by softwood [trees]? Here, someone is virtuous, of good character, but his retinue is immoral, of bad character. It is in this way that a person is made of hardwood but surrounded by softwood [trees]. So, I say, this person is just like a tree made of hardwood but surrounded by softwood [trees].

(4) "And how is a person made of hardwood and surrounded by hardwood [trees]? Here, someone is virtuous, of good character, and his retinue is also virtuous, of good character. It is in this way that a person is made of hardwood and surrounded by hardwood [trees]. So, I say, this person is just like a tree made of hardwood and surrounded by hardwood [trees].

"These, bhikkhus, are the four kinds of persons similar to trees found existing in the world."

110 (10) Vipers

"Bhikkhus, there are these four kinds of vipers. What four? The one whose venom is quick to come up but not virulent; the one whose venom is virulent but not quick to come up; the one whose venom is both quick to come up and virulent; and the one whose venom is neither quick to come up nor virulent. These are the four kinds of vipers. [111] So too, there are these four kinds of persons similar to vipers found existing in the world. What four? The one whose venom is quick to come up but not virulent; the one whose venom is virulent but not quick to come up; the one whose venom is both quick to come up and virulent; and the one whose venom is neither quick to come up nor virulent.

(1) "And how, bhikkhus, is a person one whose venom is quick to come up but not virulent? Here, someone often becomes angry, but his anger does not linger for a long time. It is in this way that a person is one whose venom is quick to come up but not virulent. So, I say, this person is just like a viper whose venom is quick to come up but not virulent.

(2) "And how is a person one whose venom is virulent but not quick to come up? Here, someone does not often become angry, but his anger lingers for a long time. It is in this way that a person is one whose venom is virulent but not quick to come up. So, I say, this person is just like a viper whose venom is virulent but not quick to come up.

(3) "And how is a person one whose venom is both quick to come up and virulent? Here, someone often becomes angry, and his anger lingers for a long time. It is in this way that a person is one whose venom is both quick to come up and virulent. So, I say, this person is just like a viper whose venom is both quick to come up and virulent.

(4) "And how is a person one whose venom is neither quick to come up nor virulent? Here, someone does not often become angry, and his anger does not linger for a long time. It is in this way that a person is one whose venom is neither quick to come up nor virulent. So, I say, this person is just like a viper whose venom is neither quick to come up nor virulent.

"These, bhikkhus, are the four kinds of persons similar to vipers found existing in the world." [112]

II. Kesi

111 (1) Kesi

Then Kesi the horse trainer approached the Blessed One, paid homage to him, and sat down to one side. The Blessed One then said to him:

"Kesi, you are reputed to be a horse trainer. Just how do you discipline a horse to be tamed?"

"Bhante, I discipline one kind of horse gently, another kind sternly, and still another kind both gently and sternly."

"But, Kesi, if a horse to be tamed by you won't submit to discipline by any of these methods, how do you deal with him?"

"Bhante, if a horse to be tamed by me won't submit to discipline by any of these methods, then I kill him. For what reason? So that there will be no disgrace to my teacher's guild. But, Bhante, the Blessed One is the unsurpassed trainer of persons to be tamed. Just how does the Blessed One discipline a person to be tamed?"

"I discipline one kind of person gently, another kind sternly, and still another kind both gently and sternly. (1) This, Kesi, is the gentle method: 'Such is bodily good conduct, such the result of bodily good conduct; such is verbal good conduct, such the result of verbal good conduct; such is mental good conduct, such the result of mental good conduct; such are the devas, such are human beings.' (2) This is the stern method: 'Such is bodily misconduct, such the result of bodily misconduct; such is verbal misconduct, such the result of verbal misconduct; such is mental misconduct, such the result of mental misconduct; such is hell, such the animal realm, such the sphere of afflicted spirits.' (3) This is the gentle and stern method: 'Such is bodily good conduct, such the result of bodily good conduct; such is bodily misconduct, such the result of bodily misconduct. Such is verbal good conduct, such the result of verbal good conduct; such is verbal misconduct, such the result of verbal misconduct. Such is mental good conduct, such the result of mental good conduct; such is mental misconduct, such the result of mental misconduct. Such are the devas, such are human beings; such is hell, such the animal realm, such the sphere of afflicted spirits.'"

"But, Bhante, if a person to be tamed by you won't submit to discipline by any of these methods, [113] how does the Blessed One deal with him?"

(4) "If a person to be tamed by me won't submit to discipline by any of these methods, then I kill him."

"But, Bhante, it isn't allowable for the Blessed One to destroy life. Yet he says, 'Then I kill him.'"

"It is true, Kesi, that it isn't allowable for the Tathāgata to destroy life. However, when a person to be tamed won't submit to discipline by the gentle method, the stern method, or the method that is both gentle and stern, then the Tathāgata thinks he should not be spoken to and instructed, and his wise fellow monks, too, think he should not be spoken to and instructed. For this, Kesi, is 'killing' in the Noble One's discipline: the Tathāgata thinks one should not be spoken to and instructed, and one's wise fellow monks, too, think one should not be spoken to and instructed."

"He is indeed well slain, Bhante, when the Tathāgata thinks he should not be spoken to and instructed, and his wise fellow monks, too, think he should not be spoken to and instructed.

"Excellent, Bhante! Excellent, Bhante! The Blessed One has made the Dhamma clear in many ways, as though he were turning upright what had been overthrown, revealing what was hidden, showing the way to one who was lost, or holding up a lamp in the darkness so those with good eyesight can see forms. I now go for refuge to the Blessed One, to the Dhamma, and to the Saṅgha of bhikkhus. Let the Blessed One consider me a lay follower who from today has gone for refuge for life."

112 (2) Speed

"Bhikkhus, possessing four factors a king's excellent thoroughbred horse is worthy of a king, an accessory of a king, and reckoned as a factor of kingship. What four? Rectitude, speed, patience, and mildness. Possessing these four factors, a king's excellent thoroughbred horse is . . . reckoned as a factor of kingship.

"So too, bhikkhus, possessing four qualities a bhikkhu is worthy of gifts, worthy of hospitality, worthy of offerings, worthy of reverential salutation, an unsurpassed field of merit for the world. What four? Rectitude, speed, patience, and mildness. Possessing these four factors, [114] a bhikkhu is worthy of gifts, worthy of hospitality, worthy of offerings, worthy of reverential salutation, an unsurpassed field of merit for the world."

113 (3) Goad

"Bhikkhus, there are these four kinds of excellent thoroughbred horses found existing in the world. What four?

(1) "Here, bhikkhus, one kind of excellent thoroughbred horse is stirred and acquires a sense of urgency as soon as it sees the shadow of the goad, thinking: 'What[794] task will my trainer set for me today? What can I do to satisfy him?' Such is one kind of excellent thoroughbred horse here. This is the first kind of excellent thoroughbred horse found existing in the world.

(2) "Again, one kind of excellent thoroughbred horse is not stirred nor does it acquire a sense of urgency as soon as it sees the shadow of the goad, but it is stirred and acquires a sense of urgency when its hairs are struck by the goad, thinking: 'What task will my trainer set for me today? What can I do to satisfy him?' Such is one kind of excellent thoroughbred horse. This is the second kind of excellent thoroughbred horse found existing in the world.

(3) "Again, one kind of excellent thoroughbred horse is not stirred nor does it acquire a sense of urgency as soon as it sees the shadow of the goad, nor when its hairs are struck by the goad, but it is stirred and acquires a sense of urgency when its hide is struck by the goad, thinking: 'What task now will my trainer set for me today? What can I do to satisfy him?' Such is one kind of excellent thoroughbred horse. This is the third kind of excellent thoroughbred horse found existing in the world.

(4) "Again, one kind of excellent thoroughbred horse is not stirred nor does it acquire a sense of urgency as soon as it sees the shadow of the goad, nor when its hairs are struck by the goad, nor when its hide is struck by the goad, but it is stirred and acquires a sense of urgency when its bone is struck by the goad, thinking: [115] 'What task now will my trainer set for me today? What can I do to satisfy him?' Such is one kind of excellent thoroughbred horse. This is the fourth kind of excellent thoroughbred horse found existing in the world.

"These are the four kinds of excellent thoroughbred horses found existing in the world.

"So too, bhikkhus, there are these four kinds of excellent thoroughbred persons found existing in the world. What four?

(1) "Here, bhikkhus, one kind of excellent thoroughbred person hears: 'In such and such a village or town some woman or man has fallen ill or died.' He is stirred by this and acquires a sense of urgency. Stirred, he strives carefully. Resolute, he realizes the supreme truth with the body and, having pierced it through with wisdom, he sees it.[795] I say that this excellent thoroughbred person is similar to the excellent thoroughbred horse that is stirred and acquires a sense of urgency as soon as it sees the shadow of the goad. Such is one kind of excellent thoroughbred person. This is the first kind of excellent thoroughbred person found existing in the world.

(2) "Again, one kind of excellent thoroughbred person does not hear: 'In such and such a village or town some woman or man has fallen ill or died.' Rather, he himself sees a woman or a man who has fallen ill or died. He is stirred by this and acquires a sense of urgency. Stirred, he strives carefully. Resolute, he realizes the supreme truth with the body and, having pierced it through with wisdom, he sees it. I say that this excellent thoroughbred person is similar to the excellent thoroughbred horse that is stirred and acquires a sense of urgency when

its hairs are struck by the goad. Such is one kind of excellent thoroughbred person. This is the second kind of excellent thoroughbred person found existing in the world.

(3) "Again, one kind of excellent thoroughbred person does not hear: 'In such and such a village or town some woman or man has fallen ill or died,' nor does he himself see a woman or a man who has fallen ill or died. Rather, a relative or family member of his has fallen ill or died. He is stirred by this and acquires a sense of urgency. [116] Stirred, he strives carefully. Resolute, he realizes the supreme truth with the body and, having pierced it through with wisdom, he sees it. I say that this excellent thoroughbred person is similar to the excellent thoroughbred horse that is stirred and acquires a sense of urgency when its hide is struck by the goad. Such is one kind of excellent thoroughbred person. This is the third kind of excellent thoroughbred person found existing in the world.

(4) "Again, one kind of excellent thoroughbred person does not hear: 'In such and such a village or town some woman or man has fallen ill or died,' nor does he himself see a woman or a man who has fallen ill or died, nor has a relative or family member of his fallen ill or died. Rather, he himself is stricken by bodily feelings that are painful, racking, sharp, piercing, harrowing, disagreeable, sapping one's vitality. He is stirred by this and acquires a sense of urgency. Stirred, he strives carefully. Resolute, he realizes the supreme truth with the body and, having pierced it through with wisdom, he sees it. I say that this excellent thoroughbred person is similar to the excellent thoroughbred horse that is stirred and acquires a sense of urgency when its bone is struck by the goad. Such is one kind of excellent thoroughbred person. This is the fourth kind of excellent thoroughbred person found existing in the world.

"These, bhikkhus, are the four kinds of excellent thoroughbred persons found existing in the world."

114 (4) Bull Elephant

"Bhikkhus, possessing four factors a king's bull elephant is worthy of a king, an accessory of a king, and reckoned as a factor of kingship. What four? Here, a king's bull elephant is one who listens, who destroys, who patiently endures, and who goes.

(1) "And how, bhikkhus, is a king's bull elephant one who

listens? Here, whatever task the elephant trainer sets for it, whether or not it has ever done it before, the king's bull elephant heeds it, attends to it, directs his whole mind to it, and listens with eager ears. It is in this way that a king's bull elephant is one who listens.

(2) "And how is a king's bull elephant one who destroys? Here, when a king's bull elephant has entered the battle, it destroys elephants and elephant riders; it destroys horses and cavalry; [117] it destroys chariots and charioteers; it destroys infantry. It is in this way that a king's bull elephant is one who destroys.

(3) "And how is a king's bull elephant one who patiently endures? Here, when a king's bull elephant has entered the battle, it patiently endures being struck by spears, swords, arrows, and axes; it endures the thundering of drums, kettle-drums, conches, and tom-toms. It is in this way that a king's bull elephant is one who patiently endures.

(4) "And how is a king's bull elephant one who goes? Here, the king's bull elephant quickly goes to whatever region the elephant trainer sends it, whether or not it has ever gone there before. It is in this way that a king's bull elephant is one who goes.

"Possessing these four factors, a king's bull elephant is worthy of a king, an accessory of a king, and reckoned as a factor of kingship.

"So too, bhikkhus, possessing four qualities, a bhikkhu is worthy of gifts, worthy of hospitality, worthy of offerings, worthy of reverential salutation, an unsurpassed field of merit for the world. What four? Here, a bhikkhu is one who listens, who destroys, who patiently endures, and who goes.

(1) "And how, bhikkhus, is a bhikkhu one who listens? Here, when the Dhamma and discipline proclaimed by the Tathāgata is being taught, a bhikkhu heeds it, attends to it, directs his whole mind to it, and listens with eager ears. It is in this way that a bhikkhu is one who listens.

(2) "And how is a bhikkhu one who destroys? Here, a bhikkhu does not tolerate an arisen sensual thought, but abandons it, dispels it, terminates it, and obliterates it. He does not tolerate an arisen thought of ill will... an arisen thought of harming... any other bad unwholesome states that arise from time

to time, but abandons them, dispels them, terminates them, and obliterates them. It is in this way that a bhikkhu is one who destroys.

(3) "And how is a bhikkhu one who patiently endures? Here, a bhikkhu patiently endures cold and heat; hunger and thirst; contact with flies, mosquitoes, wind, the burning sun, and serpents; rude and offensive ways of speech; [118] he is able to bear up with arisen bodily feelings that are painful, racking, sharp, piercing, harrowing, disagreeable, sapping one's vitality. It is this way that a bhikkhu is one who patiently endures.

(4) "And how is a bhikkhu one who goes? Here, a bhikkhu quickly goes to that region where he has never before gone in this long stretch of time, that is, to the stilling of all activities, the relinquishment of all acquisitions, the destruction of craving, dispassion, cessation, nibbāna. It is in this way that a bhikkhu is one who goes.

"Possessing these four qualities, a bhikkhu is worthy of gifts . . . an unsurpassed field of merit for the world."

115 (5) Deeds

"Bhikkhus, there are these four cases of deeds.[796] What four? (1) There is a deed that is disagreeable to do which will prove harmful. (2) There is a deed that is disagreeable to do which will prove beneficial. (3) There is a deed that is agreeable to do which will prove harmful. (4) There is a deed that is agreeable to do which will prove beneficial.

(1) "Bhikkhus, take first the case of the deed that is disagreeable to do which will prove harmful. One considers that this deed should not be done on both grounds: because it is disagreeable to do and because it will prove harmful. One considers that this deed should not be done on both grounds.

(2) "Next, take the case of the deed that is disagreeable to do which will prove beneficial. It is in this case that one can understand who is a fool and who is a wise person in regard to manly strength, manly energy, and manly exertion. The fool does not reflect thus: 'Although this deed is disagreeable to do, still [119] it will prove beneficial.' So he does not do that deed, and his refraining from it proves harmful. But the wise person does reflect thus: 'Although this deed is disagreeable to do, still it will prove beneficial.' So he does that deed, and it proves beneficial.

(3) "Next, take the case of the deed that is agreeable to do which will prove harmful. It is in this case, too, that one can understand who is a fool and who is a wise person in regard to manly strength, manly energy, and manly exertion. The fool does not reflect thus: 'Although this deed is agreeable to do, still it will prove harmful.' So he does that deed, and it proves harmful. But the wise person does reflect thus: 'Although this deed is agreeable to do, still it will prove harmful.' So he does not do that deed, and his refraining from it proves beneficial.

(4) "Next, take the case of the deed that is agreeable to do which will prove beneficial. This deed is considered one that should be done on both grounds: because it is agreeable to do and because it proves beneficial. This deed is considered one that should be done on both grounds.

"These, bhikkhus, are the four cases of deeds."

116 (6) Heedfulness

"Bhikkhus, there are four occasions when heedfulness should be practiced. What four?

(1) "Abandon bodily misconduct and develop bodily good conduct; do not be heedless in this. (2) Abandon verbal misconduct and develop verbal good conduct; do not be heedless in this. (3) Abandon mental misconduct and develop mental good conduct; do not be heedless in this. (4) Abandon wrong view and develop right view; do not be heedless in this. [120]

"Bhikkhus, when a bhikkhu has abandoned bodily misconduct and developed bodily good conduct; when he has abandoned verbal misconduct and developed verbal good conduct; when he has abandoned mental misconduct and developed mental good conduct; when he has abandoned wrong view and developed right view, then he need not fear death in the future."[797]

117 (7) Guarding

"Bhikkhus, one bent on his own welfare[798] should practice heedfulness, mindfulness, and guarding of the mind in four instances. What four?

(1) "'May my mind not become excited by things that provoke lust!' One bent on his own welfare should practice heedfulness, mindfulness, and guarding of the mind thus.

(2) "'May my mind not be full of hate toward things that

provoke hatred!' One bent on his own welfare should practice heedfulness, mindfulness, and guarding of the mind thus.

(3) "'May my mind not be deluded by things that cause delusion!' One bent on his own welfare should practice heedfulness, mindfulness, and guarding of the mind thus.

(4) "'May my mind not be intoxicated by things that intoxicate!'[799] One bent on his own welfare should practice heedfulness, mindfulness, and guarding of the mind thus.

"Bhikkhus, when a bhikkhu's mind is not excited by things that provoke lust because he has gotten rid of lust; when his mind is not full of hate toward things that provoke hatred because he has gotten rid of hatred; when his mind is not deluded by things that cause delusion because he has gotten rid of delusion; when his mind is not intoxicated by things that intoxicate because he has gotten rid of intoxication, then he does not cower, does not shake, does not tremble or become terrified, nor is he swayed by the words of [other] ascetics."[800]

118 (8) Inspiring[801]

"Bhikkhus, these four inspiring places should be seen by a clansman endowed with faith. What four? (1) The place where the Tathāgata was born is an inspiring place that should be seen by a clansman endowed with faith. (2) The place where the Tathāgata awakened to the unsurpassed perfect enlightenment is an inspiring place that should be seen by a clansman endowed with faith. (3) The place where the Tathāgata set in motion the unsurpassed wheel of the Dhamma is an inspiring place that should be seen by a clansman endowed with faith. (4) The place where the Tathāgata attained final nibbāna by the nibbāna element without residue remaining is an inspiring place that should be seen by a clansman endowed with faith. [121] These, bhikkhus, are the four inspiring places that should be seen by a clansman endowed with faith."[802]

119 (9) Perils (1)

"Bhikkhus, there are these four perils. What four? The peril of birth, the peril of old age, the peril of illness, and the peril of death. These are the four perils."

120 (10) Perils (2)

"Bhikkhus, there are these four perils. What four? The peril of fire, the peril of floods, the peril of kings, and the peril of bandits. These are the four perils."

III. Perils

121 (1) Self-Reproach

"Bhikkhus, there are these four perils. What four? The peril of self-reproach, the peril of reproach by others, the peril of punishment, and the peril of a bad destination.

(1) "And what, bhikkhus, is the peril of self-reproach? Here, someone reflects thus: 'If I were to engage in bodily, verbal, or mental misconduct, wouldn't I reprove myself because of my behavior?' Afraid of the peril of self-reproach, he abandons bodily misconduct and develops bodily good conduct; he abandons verbal misconduct and develops verbal good conduct; he abandons mental misconduct and develops mental good conduct; he maintains himself in purity. This is called the peril of self-reproach.

(2) "And what is the peril of reproach by others? [122] Here, someone reflects thus: 'If I were to engage in bodily, verbal, or mental misconduct, wouldn't others reprove me because of my behavior?' Afraid of the peril of reproach by others, he abandons bodily misconduct and develops bodily good conduct; he abandons verbal misconduct and develops verbal good conduct; he abandons mental misconduct and develops mental good conduct; he maintains himself in purity. This is called the peril of reproach by others.

(3) "And what is the peril of punishment?[803] Here, someone sees that when kings arrest a thief who has committed a crime, they subject him to various punishments: they have him flogged with whips, beaten with canes, beaten with clubs; they have his hands cut off, his feet cut off, his hands and feet cut off; his ears cut off, his nose cut off, his ears and nose cut off; they have him subjected to the 'porridge pot,' to the 'polished-shell shave,' to the 'Rāhu's mouth,' to the 'fiery wreath,' to the 'flaming hand,' to the 'blades of grass,' to the 'bark dress,' to the 'antelope,' to the 'meat hooks,' to the 'coins,' to the 'lye pickling,' to the 'pivoting pin,' to the 'rolled-up palliasse'; and they have him

splashed with boiling oil, and they have him devoured by dogs, and they have him impaled alive on a stake, and they have his head cut off with a sword.

"It occurs to him: 'When kings have arrested a thief who has committed a crime, they subject him to various punishments because of such bad deeds: they have him flogged with whips . . . they have his head cut off with a sword. Now if I were to commit such an evil deed, and if kings were to arrest me, they would subject me to the same punishments. They would have me flogged with whips . . . they would have my head cut off with a sword.' Afraid of the peril of punishment, he does not go about plundering the belongings of others. This is called the peril of punishment. [123]

(4) "And what is the peril of a bad destination? Here, someone reflects thus: 'Bodily misconduct has bad results[804] in future lives; verbal misconduct has bad results in future lives; mental misconduct has bad results in future lives. Now if I were to engage in misconduct with body, speech, and mind, then with the breakup of the body, after death, I would be reborn in the plane of misery, in a bad destination, in the lower world, in hell.' Afraid of the peril of a bad destination, he abandons bodily misconduct and develops bodily good conduct; he abandons verbal misconduct and develops verbal good conduct; he abandons mental misconduct and develops mental good conduct; he maintains himself in purity. This is called the peril of a bad destination.

"These, bhikkhus, are the four perils."[805]

122 (2) Waves[806]

"Bhikkhus, there are these four perils to be expected for one who enters the water. What four? The peril of waves, the peril of crocodiles, the peril of whirlpools, and the peril of fierce fish. These are the four perils to be expected for one who enters the water. So too, there are these four perils to be expected for a clansman who has gone forth out of faith from the household life into homelessness in this Dhamma and discipline. What four? The peril of waves, the peril of crocodiles, the peril of whirlpools, and the peril of fierce fish.

(1) "And what, bhikkhus, is the peril of waves? Here, a clansman has gone forth out of faith from the household life into

homelessness with the thought: 'I am immersed in birth, old age, and death; in sorrow, lamentation, pain, dejection, and anguish. I am immersed in suffering, afflicted by suffering. Perhaps an ending of this entire mass of suffering can be attained.' Then, after he has thus gone forth, his fellow monks exhort and instruct him: 'You should go forward in this way, return in this way; [124] look ahead in this way, look aside in this way; draw in your limbs in this way, extend them in this way; you should wear your robes and carry your outer robe and bowl in this way.' He thinks: 'Formerly, when I was a layman, I exhorted and instructed others. But now these [monks], who are young enough to be my sons or grandsons, presume to exhort and instruct me.' Being angry and displeased, he gives up the training and reverts to the lower life. This is called a bhikkhu who has given up the training and reverted to the lower life because of the peril of waves. 'The peril of waves' is a designation for anger and irritation. This is called the peril of waves.

(2) "And what is the peril of crocodiles? Here, a clansman has gone forth out of faith from the household life into homelessness with the thought: 'I am immersed in birth, old age, and death; in sorrow, lamentation, pain, dejection, and anguish. I am immersed in suffering, afflicted by suffering. Perhaps an ending of this entire mass of suffering can be attained.' Then, after he has thus gone forth, his fellow monks exhort and instruct him: 'You may consume this but not that; you may eat this but not that;[807] you may taste this but not that; you may drink this but not that. You can consume, eat, taste, and drink what is allowable, not what is unallowable. You may consume, eat, taste, and drink within the proper time, not outside the proper time.' He thinks: 'Formerly, when I was a layman, I consumed whatever I wanted to consume and did not consume anything I did not wish to consume. I ate whatever I wanted to eat and did not eat anything I did not wish to eat. I tasted whatever I wanted to taste and did not taste anything I did not wish to taste. I drank whatever I wanted to drink and did not drink anything I did not wish to drink. I consumed, ate, tasted, and drank both what was allowable and what was not allowable. I consumed, ate, tasted, and drank both within the proper time and outside the proper time. [125] But now when faithful householders give us delicious things to consume and

eat during the day outside the proper time, these [monks] seem to put a gag over our mouths.' Being angry and displeased, he gives up the training and reverts to the lower life. This is called a bhikkhu who has given up the training and reverted to the lower life because of the peril of crocodiles. 'The peril of crocodiles' is a designation for gluttony. This is called the peril of crocodiles.

(3) "And what is the peril of whirlpools? Here, a clansman has gone forth out of faith from the household life into homelessness with the thought: 'I am immersed in birth, old age, and death; in sorrow, lamentation, pain, dejection, and anguish. I am immersed in suffering, afflicted by suffering. Perhaps an ending of this entire mass of suffering can be attained.' Then, after he has thus gone forth, in the morning he dresses, takes his bowl and robe, and enters a village or town for alms, with body, speech, and mind unguarded, without having established mindfulness, his sense faculties unrestrained. He sees a householder or a householder's son there enjoying himself, furnished and endowed with the five objects of sensual pleasure. It occurs to him: 'Formerly, when I was a layman, I enjoyed myself, furnished and endowed with the five objects of sensual pleasure. My family has wealth. I can both enjoy that wealth and do meritorious deeds. Let me now give up the training and revert to the lower life so that I can both enjoy that wealth and do meritorious deeds.' So he gives up the training and reverts to the lower life. This is called a bhikkhu who has given up the training and reverted to the lower life because of the peril of whirlpools. 'The peril of whirlpools' is a designation for the five objects of sensual pleasure. This is called the peril of whirlpools.

(4) "And what is the peril of fierce fish? Here, a clansman has gone forth out of faith from the household life into homelessness with the thought: 'I am immersed in birth, old age, and death; in sorrow, lamentation, pain, dejection, and anguish. I am immersed in suffering, afflicted by suffering. Perhaps an ending of this entire mass of suffering can be attained.' Then, after he has thus gone forth, in the morning he dresses, takes his bowl and robe, and enters a village or town for alms, [126] with body, speech, and mind unguarded, without having established mindfulness, his sense faculties unrestrained. There he sees

women with their dress in disarray and loosely attired. When he sees them, lust invades his mind. With his mind invaded by lust, he gives up the training and reverts to the lower life. This is called a bhikkhu who has given up the training and reverted to the lower life because of the peril of fierce fish. 'The peril of fierce fish' is a designation for women. This is called the peril of fierce fish.

"These, bhikkhus, are the four perils to be expected for a clansman who has gone forth out of faith from the household life into homelessness in this Dhamma and discipline."

123 (3) Difference (1)

"Bhikkhus, there are these four kinds of persons found existing in the world. What four?

(1) "Here, bhikkhus, secluded from sensual pleasures, secluded from unwholesome states, some person enters and dwells in the first jhāna, which consists of rapture and pleasure born of seclusion, accompanied by thought and examination. He relishes it, desires it, and finds satisfaction in it. If he is firm in it, focused on it, often dwells in it, and has not lost it when he dies, he is reborn in companionship with the devas of Brahmā's company. The life span of the devas of Brahmā's company is an eon.[808] The worldling remains there all his life, and when he has completed the entire life span of those devas, he goes to hell, to the animal realm, or to the sphere of afflicted spirits.[809] But the Blessed One's disciple remains there all his life, and when he has completed the entire life span of those devas, he attains final nibbāna in that very same state of existence.[810] This is the distinction, the disparity, the difference between the instructed noble disciple and the uninstructed worldling, that is, when there is future destination and rebirth.[811] [127]

(2) "Again, some person, with the subsiding of thought and examination, enters and dwells in the second jhāna, which has internal placidity and unification of mind and consists of rapture and pleasure born of concentration, without thought and examination. He relishes it, desires it, and finds satisfaction in it. If he is firm in it, focused on it, often dwells in it, and has not lost it when he dies, he is reborn in companionship with the devas of streaming radiance. The life span of the devas of streaming radiance is two eons.[812] The worldling remains there all his life,

and when he has completed the entire life span of those devas, he goes to hell, to the animal realm, or to the sphere of afflicted spirits. But the Blessed One's disciple remains there all his life, and when he has completed the entire life span of those devas, he attains final nibbāna in that very same state of existence. This is the distinction, the disparity, the difference between the instructed noble disciple and the uninstructed worldling, that is, when there is future destination and rebirth.

(3) "Again, some person, with the fading away as well of rapture, dwells equanimous and, mindful and clearly comprehending, he experiences pleasure with the body; he enters and dwells in the third jhāna of which the noble ones declare: 'He is equanimous, mindful, one who dwells happily.' He relishes it, desires it, and finds satisfaction in it. If he is firm in it, focused on it, often dwells in it, and has not lost it when he dies, he is reborn in companionship with the devas of refulgent glory. The life span of the devas of refulgent glory is four eons.[813] The worldling remains there all his life, and when he has completed the entire life span of those devas, he goes to hell, to the animal realm, or to the sphere of afflicted spirits. But the Blessed One's disciple remains there all his life, and when he has completed the entire life span of those devas, he attains final nibbāna in that very same state of existence. This is the distinction, the disparity, the difference between the instructed noble disciple and the uninstructed worldling, that is, when there is future destination and rebirth.

(4) "Again, some person, with the abandoning of pleasure and pain, and with the previous passing away of joy and dejection, enters and dwells in the fourth jhāna, neither painful nor pleasant, which has purification of mindfulness by equanimity. He relishes it, desires it, and finds satisfaction in it. [128] If he is firm in it, focused on it, often dwells in it, and has not lost it when he dies, he is reborn in companionship with the devas of great fruit. The life span of the devas of great fruit is five hundred eons.[814] The worldling remains there all his life, and when he has completed the entire life span of those devas, he goes to hell, to the animal realm, or to the sphere of afflicted spirits. But the Blessed One's disciple remains there all his life, and when he has completed the entire life span of those devas, he attains final nibbāna in that very same state of existence.

This is the distinction, the disparity, the difference between the instructed noble disciple and the uninstructed worldling, that is, when there is future destination and rebirth.

"These, bhikkhus, are the four kinds of persons found existing in the world."

124 (4) Difference (2)

"Bhikkhus, there are these four kinds of persons found existing in the world. What four?

(1) "Here, bhikkhus, secluded from sensual pleasures... some person enters and dwells in the first jhāna.... He contemplates whatever phenomena there pertain to form, feeling, perception, volitional activities, and consciousness as impermanent, as suffering, as a disease, as a boil, as a dart, as misery, as an affliction, as alien, as disintegrating, as empty, as non-self.[815] With the breakup of the body, after death, he is reborn in companionship with the devas of the pure abodes.[816] This is a rebirth not shared with worldlings.

(2) "Again, some person, with the subsiding of thought and examination, enters and dwells in the second jhāna.... (3) With the fading away as well of rapture... he enters and dwells in the third jhāna.... (4) With the abandoning of pleasure and pain, and with the previous passing away of joy and dejection, he enters and dwells in the fourth jhāna, neither painful nor pleasant, which has purification of mindfulness by equanimity. He contemplates whatever phenomena there pertain to form, feeling, perception, volitional activities, and consciousness as impermanent, as suffering, as a disease, as a boil, as a dart, as misery, as an affliction, as alien, as disintegrating, as empty, as non-self. With the breakup of the body, after death, he is reborn in companionship with the devas of the pure abodes. This is a rebirth not shared with worldlings.

"These, bhikkhus, are the four kinds of persons found existing in the world."

125 (5) Loving-Kindness (1)

"Bhikkhus, there are these four kinds of persons found existing in the world. What four?

(1) "Here, bhikkhus, some person dwells pervading one quarter with a mind imbued with loving-kindness, [129] likewise the

second quarter, the third quarter, and the fourth quarter. Thus above, below, across, and everywhere, and to all as to himself, he dwells pervading the entire world with a mind imbued with loving-kindness, vast, exalted, measureless, without enmity, without ill will. He relishes it, desires it, and finds satisfaction in it. If he is firm in it, focused on it, often dwells in it, and has not lost it when he dies, he is reborn in companionship with the devas of Brahmā's company.[817] The life span of the devas of Brahmā's company is an eon. The worldling remains there all his life, and when he has completed the entire life span of those devas, he goes to hell, to the animal realm, or to the sphere of afflicted spirits. But the Blessed One's disciple remains there all his life, and when he has completed the entire life span of those devas, he attains final nibbāna in that very same state of existence. This is the distinction, the disparity, the difference between the instructed noble disciple and the uninstructed worldling, that is, when there is future destination and rebirth.

(2) "Again, some person dwells pervading one quarter with a mind imbued with compassion, likewise the second quarter, the third quarter, and the fourth quarter. Thus above, below, across, and everywhere, and to all as to himself, he dwells pervading the entire world with a mind imbued with compassion, vast, exalted, measureless, without enmity, without ill will. He relishes it, desires it, and finds satisfaction in it. If he is firm in it, focused on it, often dwells in it, and has not lost it when he dies, he is reborn in companionship with the devas of streaming radiance. The life span of the devas of streaming radiance is two eons. The worldling remains there all his life, and when he has completed the entire life span of those devas, he goes to hell, to the animal realm, or to the sphere of afflicted spirits. But the Blessed One's disciple remains there all his life, and when he has completed the entire life span of those devas, he attains final nibbāna in that very same state of existence. This is the distinction, the disparity, the difference between the instructed noble disciple and the uninstructed worldling, that is, when there is future destination and rebirth.

(3) "Again, some person dwells pervading one quarter with a mind imbued with altruistic joy, likewise the second quarter, the third quarter, and the fourth quarter. Thus above, below, across, and everywhere, and to all as to himself, he dwells per-

vading the entire world with a mind imbued with altruistic joy, vast, exalted, measureless, without enmity, without ill will. He relishes it, desires it, and finds satisfaction in it. If he is firm in it, focused on it, often dwells in it, and has not lost it when he dies, he is reborn in companionship with the devas of refulgent glory. The life span of the devas of refulgent glory is four eons. The worldling remains there all his life, and when he has completed the entire life span of those devas, he goes to hell, to the animal realm, or to the sphere of afflicted spirits. But the Blessed One's disciple remains there all his life, and when he has completed the entire life span of those devas, he attains final nibbāna in that very same state of existence. This is the distinction, the disparity, the difference between the instructed noble disciple and the uninstructed worldling, that is, when there is future destination and rebirth.

(4) "Again, some person here dwells pervading one quarter with a mind imbued with equanimity, likewise the second quarter, the third quarter, and the fourth quarter. Thus above, below, across, and everywhere, and to all as to himself, he dwells pervading the entire world with a mind imbued with equanimity, vast, exalted, measureless, without enmity, without ill will. He relishes it, desires it, and finds satisfaction in it. If he is firm in it, focused on it, often dwells in it, and has not lost it when he dies, he is reborn in companionship with the devas of great fruit. The life span of the devas of great fruit is five hundred eons. The worldling remains there all his life, and when he has completed the entire life span of those devas, he goes to hell, to the animal realm, or to the sphere of afflicted spirits. But the Blessed One's disciple remains there all his life, and when he has completed the entire life span of those devas, he attains final nibbāna in that very same state of existence. This is the distinction, the disparity, the difference between the instructed noble disciple and the uninstructed worldling, that is, when there is future destination and rebirth.

"These, bhikkhus, are the four kinds of persons found existing in the world." [130]

126 (6) Loving-Kindness (2)

"Bhikkhus, there are these four kinds of persons found existing in the world. What four?

(1) "Here, bhikkhus, some person dwells pervading one

quarter with a mind imbued with loving-kindness, likewise the second quarter, the third quarter, and the fourth quarter. Thus above, below, across, and everywhere, and to all as to himself, he dwells pervading the entire world with a mind imbued with loving-kindness, vast, exalted, measureless, without enmity, without ill will. He contemplates whatever phenomena there pertain to form, feeling, perception, volitional activities, and consciousness as impermanent, as suffering, as a disease, as a boil, as a dart, as misery, as an affliction, as alien, as disintegrating, as empty, as non-self. With the breakup of the body, after death, he is reborn in companionship with the devas of the pure abodes. This is a rebirth not shared with worldlings.

(2) "Again, some person dwells pervading one quarter with a mind imbued with compassion . . . (3) . . . altruistic joy . . . (4) . . . equanimity, likewise the second quarter, the third quarter, and the fourth quarter. Thus above, below, across, and everywhere, and to all as to himself, he dwells pervading the entire world with a mind imbued with equanimity, vast, exalted, measureless, without enmity, without ill will. He contemplates whatever phenomena there pertain to form, feeling, perception, volitional activities, and consciousness as impermanent, as suffering, as a disease, as a boil, as a dart, as misery, as an affliction, as alien, as disintegrating, as empty, as non-self. With the breakup of the body, after death, he is reborn in companionship with the devas of the pure abodes. This is a rebirth not shared with worldlings.

"These, bhikkhus, are the four kinds of persons found existing in the world."

127 (7) Astounding (1)

"Bhikkhus, with the manifestation of a Tathāgata, an Arahant, a Perfectly Enlightened One, four astounding and amazing things become manifest.[818] What four?

(1) "When, bhikkhus, a bodhisatta passes away from the Tusita heaven and mindfully and with clear comprehension enters his mother's womb, then in this world with its devas, Māra, and Brahmā, in this population with its ascetics and brahmins, its devas and humans, a measureless glorious radiance becomes manifest, surpassing the divine majesty of the devas. Even in those world intervals, vacant and abysmal, regions of

gloom and impenetrable darkness where the light of the sun and moon, so powerful and mighty, does not reach,[819] there too a measureless glorious radiance becomes manifest, surpassing the divine majesty of the devas. Those beings who have been reborn there perceive one another by this radiance and say: 'Indeed, it seems there are other beings who have been reborn here.'[820] [131] This is the first astounding and amazing thing that becomes manifest with the manifestation of a Tathāgata, an Arahant, a Perfectly Enlightened One.

(2) "Again, when a bodhisatta mindfully and with clear comprehension emerges from his mother's womb, then in this world with its devas, Māra, and Brahmā, in this population with its ascetics and brahmins, its devas and humans, a measureless glorious radiance becomes manifest, surpassing the divine majesty of the devas. Even in those world intervals . . . [beings] say: 'Indeed, it seems there are other beings who have been reborn here.' This is the second astounding and amazing thing that becomes manifest with the manifestation of a Tathāgata, an Arahant, a Perfectly Enlightened One.

(3) "Again, when a Tathāgata awakens to the unsurpassed perfect enlightenment, then in this world with its devas, Māra, and Brahmā, in this population with its ascetics and brahmins, its devas and humans, a measureless glorious radiance becomes manifest, surpassing the divine majesty of the devas. Even in those world intervals . . . [beings] say: 'Indeed, it seems there are other beings who have been reborn here.' This is the third astounding and amazing thing that becomes manifest with the manifestation of a Tathāgata, an Arahant, a Perfectly Enlightened One.

(4) "Again, when a Tathāgata sets in motion the unsurpassed wheel of the Dhamma, then in this world with its devas, Māra, and Brahmā, in this population with its ascetics and brahmins, its devas and humans, a measureless glorious radiance becomes manifest, surpassing the divine majesty of the devas. Even in those world intervals, vacant and abysmal, regions of gloom and impenetrable darkness where the light of the sun and moon, so powerful and mighty, does not reach, there too a measureless glorious radiance becomes manifest, surpassing the divine majesty of the devas. Those beings who have been reborn there perceive one another by this radiance and say:

'Indeed, it seems there are other beings who have been reborn here.' This is the fourth astounding and amazing thing that becomes manifest with the manifestation of a Tathāgata, an Arahant, a Perfectly Enlightened One.

"These, bhikkhus, are the four astounding and amazing things that become manifest with the manifestation of a Tathāgata, an Arahant, a Perfectly Enlightened One."

128 (8) Astounding (2)

"Bhikkhus, with the manifestation of a Tathāgata, an Arahant, a Perfectly Enlightened One, four astounding and amazing things become manifest. What four?

(1) "People delight in attachment,[821] take delight in attachment, rejoice in attachment. But when a Tathāgata is teaching the Dhamma about non-attachment,[822] people wish to listen, and they lend an ear and set their minds on understanding it. This is the first astounding and amazing thing that becomes manifest with the manifestation of a Tathāgata, an Arahant, a Perfectly Enlightened One.

(2) "People delight in conceit, take delight in conceit, rejoice in conceit. [132] But when a Tathāgata is teaching the Dhamma for the removal of conceit, people wish to listen, and they lend an ear and set their minds on understanding it. This is the second astounding and amazing thing that becomes manifest with the manifestation of a Tathāgata, an Arahant, a Perfectly Enlightened One.

(3) "People delight in excitement,[823] take delight in excitement, rejoice in excitement. But when a Tathāgata is teaching the Dhamma that leads to peace, people wish to listen, and they lend an ear and set their minds on understanding it. This is the third astounding and amazing thing that becomes manifest with the manifestation of a Tathāgata, an Arahant, a Perfectly Enlightened One.

(4) "People are immersed in ignorance, become like an egg, completely enveloped.[824] But when a Tathāgata is teaching the Dhamma for the removal of ignorance, people wish to listen, and they lend an ear and set their minds on understanding it. This is the fourth astounding and amazing thing that becomes manifest with the manifestation of a Tathāgata, an Arahant, a Perfectly Enlightened One.

"These, bhikkhus, are the four astounding and amazing things that become manifest with the manifestation of a Tathāgata, an Arahant, a Perfectly Enlightened One."

129 (9) Astounding (3)[825]

"Bhikkhus, there are these four astounding and amazing things about Ānanda. What four?

(1) "If an assembly of bhikkhus comes to see Ānanda, they are elated when they see him. If Ānanda speaks to them on the Dhamma, they are also elated by his speech, and that assembly of bhikkhus is still unsated when Ānanda falls silent.

(2) "If an assembly of bhikkhunīs comes to see Ānanda, they are elated when they see him. If Ānanda speaks to them on the Dhamma, they are also elated by his speech, and that assembly of bhikkhunīs is still unsated when Ānanda falls silent.

(3) "If an assembly of male lay followers comes to see Ānanda, they are elated when they see him. If Ānanda speaks to them on the Dhamma, they are also elated by his speech, and that assembly of male lay followers is still unsated when Ānanda falls silent.

(4) "If an assembly of female lay followers comes to see Ānanda, they are elated when they see him. If Ānanda speaks to them on the Dhamma, they are also elated by his speech, and that assembly of female lay followers is still unsated when Ānanda falls silent.

"These, bhikkhus, are the four astounding and amazing things about Ānanda." [133]

130 (10) Astounding (4)

"Bhikkhus, there are these four astounding and amazing things about a wheel-turning monarch. What four?

(1) "If an assembly of khattiyas comes to see a wheel-turning monarch, they are elated when they see him. If the wheel-turning monarch speaks to them, they are also elated by his speech, and that assembly of khattiyas is still unsated when the wheel-turning monarch falls silent.

(2) "If an assembly of brahmins comes to see a wheel-turning monarch, they are elated when they see him. If the wheel-turning monarch speaks to them, they are also elated by his speech, and that assembly of brahmins is still unsated when the wheel-turning monarch falls silent.

(3) "If an assembly of householders comes to see a wheel-

turning monarch, they are elated when they see him. If the wheel-turning monarch speaks to them, they are also elated by his speech, and that assembly of householders is still unsated when the wheel-turning monarch falls silent.

(4) "If an assembly of ascetics comes to see a wheel-turning monarch, they are elated when they see him. If the wheel-turning monarch speaks to them, they are also elated by his speech, and that assembly of ascetics is still unsated when the wheel-turning monarch falls silent.

"These, bhikkhus, are the four astounding and amazing things about a wheel-turning monarch.

"So too, bhikkhus, there are these four astounding and amazing things about Ānanda. What four? . . . [complete as in 4:129] . . .

"These, bhikkhus, are the four astounding and amazing things about Ānanda."

IV. Persons

131 (1) Fetters

"Bhikkhus, there are these four kinds of persons found existing in the world. What four?

"(1) Here, bhikkhus, some person has not abandoned the lower fetters, the fetters for obtaining rebirth, or the fetters for obtaining existence.[826] [134] (2) Some other person has abandoned the lower fetters, but not the fetters for obtaining rebirth or the fetters for obtaining existence. (3) Still another person has abandoned the lower fetters and the fetters for obtaining rebirth, but not the fetters for obtaining existence. (4) And still another person has abandoned the lower fetters, the fetters for obtaining rebirth, and the fetters for obtaining existence.

(1) "What kind of person has not abandoned the lower fetters, the fetters for obtaining rebirth, or the fetters for obtaining existence? The once-returner.[827] This person has not abandoned the lower fetters, the fetters for obtaining rebirth, or the fetters for obtaining existence.

(2) "What kind of person has abandoned the lower fetters, but not the fetters for obtaining rebirth or the fetters for obtaining existence? The one bound upstream, heading toward the Akaniṭṭha realm.[828] This person has abandoned the lower fetters

but not the fetters for obtaining rebirth or the fetters for obtaining existence.

(3) "What kind of person has abandoned the lower fetters and the fetters for obtaining rebirth but not the fetters for obtaining existence? The one who attains final nibbāna in the interval.[829] This person has abandoned the lower fetters and the fetters for obtaining rebirth but not the fetters for obtaining existence.

(4) "What kind of person has abandoned the lower fetters, the fetters for obtaining rebirth, and the fetters for obtaining existence? The arahant. For this person has abandoned the lower fetters, the fetters for obtaining rebirth, and the fetters for obtaining existence.

"These, bhikkhus, are the four kinds of persons found existing in the world." [135]

132 (2) Discernment

"Bhikkhus, there are these four kinds of persons found existing in the world. What four? One whose discernment is incisive but not free-flowing;[830] one whose discernment is free-flowing but not incisive; one whose discernment is both incisive and free-flowing; and one whose discernment is neither incisive nor free-flowing. These are the four kinds of persons found existing in the world."

133 (3) Of Quick Understanding

"Bhikkhus, there are these four kinds of persons found existing in the world. What four? One who understands quickly; one who understands through elaboration; one who needs to be guided; and one for whom the word is the maximum. These are the four kinds of persons found existing in the world."[831]

134 (4) Effort

"Bhikkhus, there are these four kinds of persons found existing in the world. What four? One who lives off the fruit of his effort but not off the fruit of his kamma; one who lives off the fruit of his kamma but not off the fruit of his effort; one who lives off the fruit of both his effort and his kamma; and one who lives off the fruit of neither his effort nor his kamma. These are the four kinds of persons found existing in the world."[832]

135 (5) Blameworthy

"Bhikkhus, there are these four kinds of persons found existing in the world. What four? The blameworthy, the mostly blameworthy, the slightly blameworthy, and the blameless.

(1) "And how, bhikkhus, is a person blameworthy? Here, a person engages in blameworthy bodily action, blameworthy verbal action, and blameworthy mental action. It is in this way that a person is blameworthy. [136]

(2) "And how is a person mostly blameworthy? Here, a person engages in bodily action that is mostly blameworthy, verbal action that is mostly blameworthy, and mental action that is mostly blameworthy. It is in this way that a person is mostly blameworthy.

(3) "And how is a person slightly blameworthy? Here, a person engages in bodily action that is mostly blameless, verbal action that is mostly blameless, and mental action that is mostly blameless. It is in this way that a person is slightly blameworthy.

(4) "And how is a person blameless? Here, a person engages in blameless bodily action, blameless verbal action, and blameless mental action. It is in this way that a person is blameless.

"These are the four kinds of persons found existing in the world."[833]

136 (6) Virtuous Behavior (1)

"Bhikkhus, there are these four kinds of persons found existing in the world. What four? (1) Here, bhikkhus, some person does not fulfill virtuous behavior, concentration, and wisdom. (2) Another person fulfills virtuous behavior but does not fulfill concentration and wisdom. (3) Still another person fulfills virtuous behavior and concentration but does not fulfill wisdom. (4) And still another person fulfills virtuous behavior, concentration, and wisdom. These are the four kinds of persons found existing in the world."[834]

137 (7) Virtuous Behavior (2)

"Bhikkhus, there are these four kinds of persons found existing in the world. What four? [137]

(1) "Here, bhikkhus, some person does not value virtuous behavior or take virtuous behavior as an authority, does not

value concentration or take concentration as an authority, and does not value wisdom or take wisdom as an authority.

(2) "Another person values virtuous behavior and takes virtuous behavior as an authority, but does not value concentration or take concentration as an authority, and does not value wisdom or take wisdom as an authority.

(3) "Still another person values virtuous behavior and takes virtuous behavior as an authority, values concentration and takes concentration as an authority, but does not value wisdom or take wisdom as an authority.

(4) "And still another person values virtuous behavior and takes virtuous behavior as an authority, values concentration and takes concentration as an authority, and values wisdom and takes wisdom as an authority.

"These are the four kinds of persons found existing in the world."

138 (8) Retreat

"Bhikkhus, there are these four kinds of persons found existing in the world. What four? One who has gone on retreat by body but not gone on retreat by mind; one who has not gone on retreat by body but has gone on retreat by mind; one who has not gone on retreat either by body or by mind; and one who has gone on retreat both by body and by mind.

(1) "And how, bhikkhus, has a person gone on retreat by body but not gone on retreat by mind? Here, some person resorts to remote lodgings in forests and jungle groves, but there he thinks sensual thoughts, thoughts of ill will, and thoughts of harming. It is in this way that a person has gone on retreat by body but has not gone on retreat by mind.

(2) "And how has a person not gone on retreat by body but gone on retreat by mind? Here, some person does not resort to remote lodgings in forests and jungle groves, but he thinks thoughts of renunciation, thoughts of good will, and thoughts of harmlessness. It is in this way that a person has not gone on retreat by body but gone on retreat by mind.

(3) "And how has a person gone on retreat neither by body nor by mind? Here, some person does not resort to remote lodgings in forests and jungle groves, [138] and he thinks sensual thoughts, thoughts of ill will, and thoughts of harming. It is in

this way that a person has gone on retreat neither by body nor by mind.

(4) "And how has a person gone on retreat both by body and by mind? Here, some person resorts to remote lodgings in forests and jungle groves, and there he thinks thoughts of renunciation, thoughts of good will, and thoughts of harmlessness. It is in this way that a person has gone on retreat both by body and by mind.

"These, bhikkhus, are the four kinds of persons found existing in the world."

139 (9) Dhamma Speakers

"Bhikkhus, there are these four kinds of Dhamma speakers. What four?

(1) "Here, bhikkhus, some Dhamma speaker speaks little and [his speech is] pointless, and his assembly is not skilled in distinguishing what is meaningful from what is pointless. Such a Dhamma speaker is reckoned as a Dhamma speaker by such an assembly.

(2) "Another Dhamma speaker speaks little but [his speech is] meaningful, and his assembly is skilled in distinguishing what is meaningful from what is pointless. Such a Dhamma speaker is reckoned as a Dhamma speaker by such an assembly.

(3) "Still another Dhamma speaker speaks much but [his speech is] pointless, and his assembly is not skilled in distinguishing what is meaningful from what is pointless. Such a Dhamma speaker is reckoned as a Dhamma speaker by such an assembly.

(4) "And still another Dhamma speaker speaks much and [his speech is] meaningful, and his assembly is skilled in distinguishing what is meaningful from what is pointless. Such a Dhamma speaker is reckoned as a Dhamma speaker by such an assembly.

"These, bhikkhus, are the four kinds of Dhamma speakers."

140 (10) Speakers

"Bhikkhus, there are these four speakers. What four? [139] (1) There is the speaker who exhausts the meaning but not the phrasing. (2) There is the speaker who exhausts the phrasing but not the meaning. (3) There is the speaker who exhausts both the meaning and the phrasing. (4) And there is the speaker who does not exhaust either the meaning or the phrasing. These are the four speakers. It is impossible and inconceivable that one who possesses the four analytical knowledges will exhaust either the meaning or the phrasing."[835]

V. Splendors

141 (1) Splendors

"Bhikkhus, there are these four splendors. What four? The splendor of the moon, the splendor of the sun, the splendor of fire, and the splendor of wisdom. These are the four splendors. Of these four splendors, the splendor of wisdom is foremost."

142 (2) Radiances

"Bhikkhus, there are these four radiances. What four? The radiance of the moon, the radiance of the sun, the radiance of fire, and the radiance of wisdom. These are the four radiances. Of these four radiances, the radiance of wisdom is foremost."

143 (3) Lights

"Bhikkhus, there are these four lights. What four? The light of the moon, the light of the sun, the light of fire, and the light of wisdom. These are the four lights. Of these four lights, the light of wisdom is foremost."

144 (4) Lusters

"Bhikkhus, there are these four lusters. What four? The luster of the moon, the luster of the sun, the luster of fire, and the luster of wisdom. [140] These are the four lusters. Of these four lusters, the luster of wisdom is foremost."

145 (5) Luminaries

"Bhikkhus, there are these four luminaries. What four? The moon is a luminary, the sun is a luminary, fire is a luminary, and wisdom is a luminary. These are the four luminaries. Of these four luminaries, wisdom is foremost."

146 (6) Times (1)

"There are, bhikkhus, these four times. What four? The time for listening to the Dhamma, the time for discussing the Dhamma, the time for serenity,[836] and the time for insight. These are the four times."

147 (7) Times (2)

"Bhikkhus, these four times, rightly developed and coordinated, gradually culminate in the destruction of the taints. What four? The time for listening to the Dhamma, the time for discussing the Dhamma, the time for serenity, and the time for insight. These four times, rightly developed and coordinated, gradually culminate in the destruction of the taints.

"Just as, when it is raining and the rain pours down in thick droplets on a mountain top, the water flows down along the slope and fills the clefts, gullies, and creeks; these, becoming full, fill up the pools; these, becoming full, fill up the lakes; these, becoming full, fill up the streams; these, becoming full, fill up the rivers; and these, becoming full, fill up the great ocean; so too, these four times, rightly developed and coordinated, gradually culminate in the destruction of the taints." [141]

148 (8) Conduct (1)

"Bhikkhus, there are these four kinds of verbal misconduct. What four? False speech, divisive speech, harsh speech, and idle chatter. These are the four kinds of verbal misconduct."

149 (9) Conduct (2)

"Bhikkhus, there are these four kinds of verbal good conduct. What four? Truthful speech, non-divisive speech, gentle speech, and judicious speech. These are the four kinds of verbal good conduct."

150 (10) Cores

"Bhikkhus, there are these four cores. What four? The core of virtuous behavior, the core of concentration, the core of wisdom, and the core of liberation. These are the four cores."

The Fourth Fifty

I. Faculties

151 (1) Faculties

"Bhikkhus, there are these four faculties. What four? The faculty of faith, the faculty of energy, the faculty of mindfulness, and the faculty of concentration. These are the four faculties."[837]

152 (2) Faith

"Bhikkhus, there are these four powers. What four? The power of faith, the power of energy, the power of mindfulness, and the power of concentration. These are the four powers." [142]

153 (3) Wisdom

"Bhikkhus, there are these four powers. What four? The power of wisdom, the power of energy, the power of blamelessness, and the power of sustaining a favorable relationship. These are the four powers."

154 (4) Mindfulness

"Bhikkhus, there are these four powers. What four? The power of mindfulness, the power of concentration, the power of blamelessness, and the power of sustaining a favorable relationship. These are the four powers."

155 (5) Reflection

"Bhikkhus, there are these four powers. What four? The power of reflection, the power of development, the power of blamelessness, and the power of sustaining a favorable relationship. These are the four powers."

156 (6) Eon

"Bhikkhus, there are these four incalculable divisions of an eon.[838] What four?

(1) "The time during which an eon dissolves, which cannot easily be calculated as 'so many years' or 'so many hundreds of years' or 'so many thousands of years' or 'so many hundreds of thousands of years.'[839]

(2) "The time during which an eon remains in a state of dis-

solution, which cannot easily be calculated as 'so many years' or 'so many hundreds of years' or 'so many thousands of years' or 'so many hundreds of thousands of years.'

(3) "The time during which an eon evolves, which cannot easily be calculated as 'so many years' or 'so many hundreds of years' or 'so many thousands of years' or 'so many hundreds of thousands of years.'

(4) "The time during which an eon remains in a state of evolution, which cannot easily be calculated as 'so many years' or 'so many hundreds of years' or 'so many thousands of years' or 'so many hundreds of thousands of years.'

"These, bhikkhus, are the four incalculable divisions of an eon."

157 (7) Illness

"Bhikkhus, there are these two kinds of illness. Which two? [143] Bodily illness and mental illness. People are found who can claim to enjoy bodily health for one, two, three, four, and five years; for ten, twenty, thirty, forty, and fifty years; and even for a hundred years and more. But apart from those whose taints have been destroyed, it is hard to find people in the world who can claim to enjoy mental health even for a moment.

"There are, bhikkhus, these four illnesses incurred by a monk. What four? (1) Here, a bhikkhu has strong desires, undergoes distress, and is not content with any kind of robe, almsfood, lodging, or medicines and provisions for the sick.[840] (2) Because he has strong desires, undergoes distress, and is not content with any kind of robe, almsfood, lodging, and medicines and provisions for the sick, he submits to evil desire for recognition and for gain, honor, and praise. (3) He arouses himself, strives, and makes an effort to obtain recognition and gain, honor, and praise. (4) He cunningly approaches families, cunningly sits down, cunningly speaks on the Dhamma, and cunningly holds in his excrement and urine.[841] These are the four illnesses incurred by a monk.

"Therefore, bhikkhus, you should train yourselves thus: 'We will not have strong desires or undergo distress, and we will not be discontent with any kind of robe, almsfood, lodging, and medicines and provisions for the sick. We will not submit to evil desires for recognition and for gain, honor, and praise. We will not arouse ourselves, strive, and make an effort to obtain recognition and gain, honor, and praise. We will patiently endure cold and heat, hunger and thirst; contact with flies, mosquitoes, wind, the burning sun, and serpents; rude and offensive ways of speech; we will bear up with arisen bodily feelings that are painful, racking, sharp, piercing, harrowing, disagreeable, sapping one's vitality.' It is in this way, bhikkhus, that you should train yourselves."

158 (8) Decline

There the Venerable Sāriputta addressed the bhikkhus: "Friends, [144] bhikkhus!"

"Friend!" those bhikkhus replied. The Venerable Sāriputta said this:

"Friends, any bhikkhu or bhikkhunī who observes four things inwardly can come to the conclusion: 'I am declining in wholesome qualities. This is called decline by the Blessed One.' What four? An abundance of lust, an abundance of hatred, an abundance of delusion, and his wisdom eye does not tread in the deep matters of what is possible and impossible.[842] Any bhikkhu or bhikkhunī who observes these four things inwardly can come to the conclusion: 'I am declining in wholesome qualities. This is called decline by the Blessed One.'

"Friends, any bhikkhu or bhikkhunī who observes four things inwardly can come to the conclusion: 'I am not declining in wholesome qualities. This is called non-decline by the Blessed One.' What four? The diminishing of lust, the diminishing of hatred, the diminishing of delusion, and his wisdom eye treads in the deep matters of what is possible and impossible. Any bhikkhu or bhikkhunī who observes these four things inwardly can come to the conclusion: 'I am not declining in wholesome qualities. This is called non-decline by the Blessed One.'"

159 (9) The Bhikkhunī

On one occasion the Venerable Ānanda was dwelling at Kosambī in Ghosita's Park. Then a certain bhikkhunī addressed a man thus: 'Come, good man, approach Master Ānanda and pay homage to him in my name with your head at his feet. Then say: 'Bhante, the bhikkhunī so-and-so is sick, afflicted, gravely ill. She pays homage to Master Ānanda with her head at his feet.' Then say: 'It would be good, Bhante, if, out of compassion, Master Ānanda would come to visit that bhikkhunī in the bhikkhunīs' quarters.'"

"Yes, noble lady," that man replied. He then approached the Venerable Ānanda, [145] paid homage to him, sat down to one side, and delivered his message. The Venerable Ānanda consented by silence.

Then the Venerable Ānanda dressed, took his bowl and robe, and went to the bhikkhunīs' quarters. When that bhikkhunī saw the Venerable Ānanda coming in the distance, she covered herself from the head down and lay down on her bed.[843] Then the Venerable Ānanda approached that bhikkhunī, sat down in the appointed seat, and said to her:

"Sister, this body has originated from nutriment; in dependence on nutriment, nutriment is to be abandoned. This body has originated from craving; in dependence on craving, craving is to be abandoned. This body has originated from conceit; in dependence on conceit, conceit is to be abandoned. This body has originated from sexual intercourse, but in regard to sexual intercourse the Blessed One has declared the demolition of the bridge.[844]

(1) "When it was said: 'This body, sister, has originated from nutriment; in dependence on nutriment, nutriment is to be abandoned,' for what reason was this said? Here, sister, reflecting carefully, a bhikkhu consumes food neither for amusement nor for intoxication nor for the sake of physical beauty and attractiveness, but only for the support and maintenance of this body, for avoiding harm, and for assisting the spiritual life, considering: 'Thus I shall terminate the old feeling and not arouse a new feeling, and I shall be healthy and blameless and dwell at ease.' Some time later, in dependence upon nutriment, he abandons nutriment.[845] When it was said: 'This body, sister, has originated from nutriment; in dependence on nutriment, nutriment is to be abandoned,' it is because of this that this was said.

(2) "When it was said: 'This body has originated from craving; in dependence on craving, craving is to be abandoned,' for what [146] reason was this said? Here, sister, a bhikkhu hears: 'The bhikkhu named so-and-so, with the destruction of the taints, has realized for himself with direct knowledge, in this very life, the taintless liberation of mind, liberation by wisdom,

and having entered upon it, he dwells in it.' He thinks: 'When will I, with the destruction of the taints, realize for myself with direct knowledge, in this very life, the taintless liberation of mind, liberation by wisdom, and having entered upon it, dwell in it?' Some time later, in dependence upon craving, he abandons craving. When it was said: 'This body has originated from craving; in dependence on craving, craving is to be abandoned,' it was because of this that this was said.

(3) "When it was said: 'This body has originated from conceit; in dependence on conceit, conceit is to be abandoned.' With reference to what was this said? Here, sister, a bhikkhu hears: 'The bhikkhu named so-and-so, with the destruction of the taints, has realized for himself with direct knowledge, in this very life, the taintless liberation of mind, liberation by wisdom, and having entered upon it, he dwells in it.' He thinks: 'That venerable one, with the destruction of the taints, has realized for himself with direct knowledge, in this very life, the taintless liberation of mind, liberation by wisdom, and having entered upon it, he dwells in it. Why, so can I!' Some time later, in dependence upon conceit, he abandons conceit. When it was said: 'This body has originated from conceit; in dependence on conceit, conceit is to be abandoned,' it was because of this that this was said.

(4) "This body, sister, has originated from sexual intercourse, but in regard to sexual intercourse the Blessed One has declared the demolition of the bridge."[846]

Then that bhikkhunī got up from her bed, arranged her upper robe over one shoulder, and having prostrated herself with her head at the Venerable Ānanda's feet, she said to the Venerable Ānanda: "Bhante, I have committed a transgression in that I so foolishly, stupidly, and unskillfully behaved as I did. Bhante, may Master Ānanda accept my transgression seen as a transgression for the sake of future restraint."

"Surely, sister, you have committed a transgression in that you so foolishly, stupidly, and unskillfully behaved as you did. But since you see your transgression as a transgression and make amends for it in accordance with the Dhamma, we accept it. For it is growth in the Noble One's discipline that one sees one's transgression as a transgression, makes amends for it in accordance with the Dhamma, and undertakes future restraint." [147]

160 (10) A Fortunate One[847]

"Bhikkhus, while the Fortunate One or the Fortunate One's discipline remains in the world, this is for the welfare of many people, for the happiness of many people, out of compassion for the world, for the good, welfare, and happiness of devas and humans.

"And who, bhikkhus, is the Fortunate One? Here, the Tathāgata arises in the world, an arahant, perfectly enlightened, accomplished in true knowledge and conduct, fortunate, knower of the world, unsurpassed trainer of persons to be tamed, teacher of devas and humans, the Enlightened One, the Blessed One. This is the Fortunate One.

"And what is the Fortunate One's discipline? He teaches the Dhamma that is good in the beginning, good in the middle, and good in the end, with the right meaning and phrasing; he reveals the perfectly complete and pure spiritual life. This is the Fortunate One's discipline. Thus while the Fortunate One or the Fortunate One's discipline remains in the world, this is for the welfare of many people, for the happiness of many people, out of compassion for the world, for the good, welfare, and happiness of devas and humans.

"There are, bhikkhus, these four things that lead to the decline and disappearance of the good Dhamma. What four?

(1) "Here, the bhikkhus learn discourses that have been badly acquired, with badly set down words and phrases.[848] When the words and phrases are badly set down, the meaning is badly interpreted. This is the first thing that leads to the decline and disappearance of the good Dhamma.

(2) "Again, the bhikkhus are difficult to correct and possess qualities that make them difficult to correct. They are impatient and do not accept instruction respectfully. This is the second thing that leads to the decline and disappearance of the good Dhamma.

(3) "Again, those bhikkhus who are learned, heirs to the heritage, experts on the Dhamma, experts on the discipline, experts on the outlines, do not respectfully teach the discourses to others. When they have passed away, the discourses are cut off at the root, left without anyone to preserve them. This is the third thing that leads to the decline and disappearance of the good Dhamma.

(4) "Again, the elder bhikkhus are luxurious [148] and lax, leaders in backsliding, discarding the duty of solitude; they do not arouse energy for the attainment of the as-yet-unattained, for the achievement of the as-yet-unachieved, for the realization of the as-yet-unrealized. [Those in] the next generation follow their example. They, too, become luxurious and lax, leaders in backsliding, discarding the duty of solitude; they, too, do not arouse energy for the attainment of the as-yet-unattained, for the achievement of the as-yet-unachieved, for the realization of the as-yet-unrealized. This is the fourth thing that leads to the decline and disappearance of the good Dhamma.

"These are the four things that lead to the decline and disappearance of the good Dhamma.

"There are, bhikkhus, these four [other] things that lead to the continuation, non-decline, and non-disappearance of the good Dhamma. What four?

(1) "Here, the bhikkhus learn discourses that have been well acquired, with well set down words and phrases. When the words and phrases are well set down, the meaning is well interpreted. This is the first thing that leads to the continuation, non-decline, and non-disappearance of the good Dhamma.

(2) "Again, the bhikkhus are easy to correct and possess qualities that make them easy to correct. They are patient and accept instruction respectfully. This is the second thing that leads to the continuation, non-decline, and non-disappearance of the good Dhamma.

(3) "Again, those bhikkhus who are learned, heirs to the heritage, experts on the Dhamma, experts on the discipline, experts on the outlines, respectfully teach the discourses to others. When they have passed away, the discourses are not cut off at the root for there are those who preserve them. This is the third thing that leads to the continuation, non-decline, and non-disappearance of the good Dhamma.

(4) "Again, the elder bhikkhus are not luxurious and lax, but they discard backsliding and take the lead in solitude; they arouse energy for the attainment of the as-yet-unattained, for the achievement of the as-yet-unachieved, for the realization of the as-yet-unrealized. [Those in] the next generation follow their example. They, too, do not become luxurious and lax, but they discard backsliding and take the lead in solitude; they, too,

arouse energy for the attainment of the as-yet-unattained, for the achievement of the as-yet-unachieved, for the realization of the as-yet-unrealized. This is the fourth thing that leads to the continuation, non-decline, and non-disappearance of the good Dhamma. [149]

"These, bhikkhus, are the four things that lead to the continuation, non-decline, and non-disappearance of the good Dhamma."

II. Modes of Practice

161 (1) In Brief[849]

"Bhikkhus, there are these four modes of practice. What four? (1) Practice that is painful with sluggish direct knowledge; (2) practice that is painful with quick direct knowledge; (3) practice that is pleasant with sluggish direct knowledge; and (4) practice that is pleasant with quick direct knowledge.[850] These are the four modes of practice."

162 (2) In Detail

"Bhikkhus, there are these four modes of practice. What four? (1) Practice that is painful with sluggish direct knowledge; (2) practice that is painful with quick direct knowledge; (3) practice that is pleasant with sluggish direct knowledge; and (4) practice that is pleasant with quick direct knowledge.

(1) "And what, bhikkhus, is the practice that is painful with sluggish direct knowledge? Here, someone is by nature strongly prone to lust and often experiences pain and dejection born of lust. By nature he is strongly prone to hatred and often experiences pain and dejection born of hatred. By nature he is strongly prone to delusion and often experiences pain and dejection born of delusion. These five faculties arise in him feebly: the faculty of faith, the faculty of energy, the faculty of mindfulness, the faculty of concentration, and the faculty of wisdom. Because these five faculties are feeble in him, he sluggishly attains the immediacy condition for the destruction of the taints.[851] This is called practice that is painful with sluggish direct knowledge.

(2) "And what is practice that is painful with quick direct knowledge? Here, someone is by nature strongly prone to lust . . . hatred . . . delusion and often experiences pain and

dejection born of delusion. These five faculties arise in him prominently: [150] the faculty of faith . . . the faculty of wisdom. Because these five faculties are prominent in him, he quickly attains the immediacy condition for the destruction of the taints. This is called practice that is painful with quick direct knowledge.

(3) "And what is practice that is pleasant with sluggish direct knowledge? Here, someone by nature is not strongly prone to lust and does not often experience pain and dejection born of lust. By nature he is not strongly prone to hatred and does not often experience pain and dejection born of hatred. By nature he is not strongly prone to delusion and does not often experience pain and dejection born of delusion. These five faculties arise in him feebly: the faculty of faith . . . the faculty of wisdom. Because these five faculties are feeble in him, he sluggishly attains the immediacy condition for the destruction of the taints. This is called practice that is pleasant with sluggish direct knowledge.

(4) "And what is practice that is pleasant with quick direct knowledge? Here, someone by nature is not strongly prone to lust . . . hatred . . . delusion and does not often experience pain and dejection born of delusion. These five faculties arise in him prominently: the faculty of faith . . . the faculty of wisdom. Because these five faculties are prominent in him, he quickly attains the immediacy condition for the destruction of the taints. This is called practice that is pleasant with quick direct knowledge.

"These, bhikkhus, are the four modes of practice."

163 (3) Unattractiveness

[Opening paragraph as above.]

(1) "And what, bhikkhus, is practice that is painful with sluggish direct knowledge? Here, a bhikkhu dwells contemplating the unattractiveness of the body, perceiving the repulsiveness of food, perceiving non-delight in the entire world, contemplating impermanence in all conditioned phenomena; and he has the perception of death well established internally. He dwells depending upon these five trainee powers: the power of faith, the power of moral shame, the power of moral dread, [151] the power of energy, and the power of wisdom.[852] These five

faculties arise in him feebly: the faculty of faith, the faculty of energy, the faculty of mindfulness, the faculty of concentration, and the faculty of wisdom. Because these five faculties are feeble, he sluggishly attains the immediacy condition for the destruction of the taints. This is called practice that is painful with sluggish direct knowledge.

(2) "And what is practice that is painful with quick direct knowledge? Here, a bhikkhu dwells contemplating the unattractiveness of the body . . . and he has the perception of death well established internally. He dwells depending upon these five trainee powers: the power of faith . . . the power of wisdom. These five faculties arise in him prominently: the faculty of faith . . . the faculty of wisdom. Because these five faculties are prominent, he quickly attains the immediacy condition for the destruction of the taints. This is called practice that is painful with quick direct knowledge.

(3) "And what is practice that is pleasant with sluggish direct knowledge? Here, secluded from sensual pleasures, secluded from unwholesome states, a bhikkhu enters and dwells in the first jhāna, which consists of rapture and pleasure born of seclusion, accompanied by thought and examination. With the subsiding of thought and examination, he enters and dwells in the second jhāna, which has internal placidity and unification of mind and consists of rapture and pleasure born of concentration, without thought and examination. With the fading away as well of rapture, he dwells equanimous and, mindful and clearly comprehending, he experiences pleasure with the body; he enters and dwells in the third jhāna of which the noble ones declare: 'He is equanimous, mindful, one who dwells happily.' With the abandoning of pleasure and pain, and with the previous passing away of joy and dejection, he enters and dwells in the fourth jhāna, neither painful nor pleasant, which has purification of mindfulness by equanimity. He dwells depending upon these five trainee powers: the power of faith . . . the power of wisdom. These five faculties arise in him feebly: the faculty of faith . . . the faculty of wisdom. Because these five faculties are feeble, he sluggishly attains the immediacy condition for the destruction of the taints. This is called practice that is pleasant with sluggish direct knowledge.

(4) "And what is practice that is pleasant with quick direct

knowledge? Here, secluded from sensual pleasures, secluded from unwholesome states, a bhikkhu enters and dwells in the first jhāna . . . the second jhāna . . . the third jhāna . . . [152] the fourth jhāna. He dwells depending upon these five trainee powers: the power of faith . . . the power of wisdom. These five faculties arise in him prominently: the faculty of faith . . . the faculty of wisdom. Because these five faculties are prominent, he quickly attains the immediacy condition for the destruction of the taints. This is called practice that is pleasant with quick direct knowledge.

"These, bhikkhus, are the four modes of practice."

164 (4) Patient (1)

"Bhikkhus, there are these four modes of practice. What four? The impatient practice, the patient practice, the taming practice, and the calming practice.

(1) "And what, bhikkhus, is the impatient practice? Here, someone insults one who insults him, scolds one who scolds him, and argues with one who picks an argument with him. This is called the impatient practice.

(2) "And what is the patient practice? Here, someone does not insult one who insults him, does not scold one who scolds him, and does not argue with one who picks an argument with him. This is called the patient practice.

(3) "And what is the taming practice? Here, having seen a form with the eye, a bhikkhu does not grasp its marks and features. Since, if he left the eye faculty unrestrained, bad unwholesome states of longing and dejection might invade him, he practices restraint over it; he guards the eye faculty, he undertakes the restraint of the eye faculty. Having heard a sound with the ear . . . Having smelled an odor with the nose . . . Having tasted a taste with the tongue . . . Having felt a tactile object with the body . . . Having cognized a mental phenomenon with the mind, a bhikkhu does not grasp its marks and features. Since, if he left the mind faculty unrestrained, bad unwholesome states of longing and dejection might invade him, he practices restraint over it; [153] he guards the mind faculty, he undertakes the restraint of the mind faculty. This is called the taming practice.

(4) "And what is the calming practice? Here, a bhikkhu does not tolerate an arisen sensual thought; he abandons it, dispels

it, calms it down, terminates it, and obliterates it.[853] He does not tolerate an arisen thought of ill will . . . an arisen thought of harming . . . bad unwholesome states whenever they arise; he abandons them, dispels them, calms them down, terminates them, and obliterates them. This is called the calming practice.

"These, bhikkhus, are the four modes of practice."

165 (5) Patient (2)

"Bhikkhus, there are these four modes of practice. What four? The impatient practice, the patient practice, the taming practice, and the calming practice.

(1) "And what, bhikkhus, is the impatient practice? Here, someone does not patiently endure cold and heat; hunger and thirst; contact with flies, mosquitoes, wind, the burning sun, and serpents; rude and offensive ways of speech; he is unable to bear up with arisen bodily feelings that are painful, racking, sharp, piercing, harrowing, disagreeable, sapping one's vitality. This is called the impatient practice.

(2) "And what is the patient practice? Here, someone patiently endures cold and heat . . . rude and offensive ways of speech; he is able to bear up with arisen bodily feelings that are painful, racking, sharp, piercing, harrowing, disagreeable, sapping one's vitality. This is called the patient practice.

(3) "And what, bhikkhus, is the taming practice? . . . [as in 4:164] . . .

(4) "And what, bhikkhus, is the calming practice? . . . [as in 4:164] . . .

"These, bhikkhus, are the four modes of practice." [154]

166 (6) Both

"Bhikkhus, there are these four modes of practice. What four? (1) Practice that is painful with sluggish direct knowledge; (2) practice that is painful with quick direct knowledge; (3) practice that is pleasant with sluggish direct knowledge; and (4) practice that is pleasant with quick direct knowledge.

(1) "The mode of practice that is painful with sluggish direct knowledge is declared to be inferior for both reasons: because it is painful and because direct knowledge is sluggish. This mode of practice is declared to be inferior for both reasons.

(2) "The mode of practice that is painful with quick di-

rect knowledge is declared to be inferior because of its painfulness.

(3) "The mode of practice that is pleasant with sluggish direct knowledge is declared to be inferior because of its sluggishness.

(4) "The mode of practice that is pleasant with quick direct knowledge is declared to be superior for both reasons: because practice is pleasant and because direct knowledge is quick. This mode of practice is declared to be superior for both reasons.

"These, bhikkhus, are the four modes of practice."

167 (7) Moggallāna

Then the Venerable Sāriputta approached the Venerable Mahāmoggallāna and exchanged greetings with him. When they had concluded their greetings and cordial talk, he sat down to one side and said to the Venerable Mahāmoggallāna:

"Friend Moggallāna, there are these four modes of practice. What four? (1) Practice that is painful with sluggish direct knowledge; (2) practice that is painful with quick direct knowledge; (3) practice that is pleasant with sluggish direct knowledge; and (4) practice that is pleasant with quick direct knowledge. Through which of these four modes of practice was your mind liberated from the taints by non-clinging?" [155]

"Of these four modes of practice, friend Sāriputta, it was through the mode that is painful with quick direct knowledge that my mind was liberated from the taints by non-clinging."[854]

168 (8) Sāriputta

Then the Venerable Mahāmoggallāna approached the Venerable Sāriputta ... and said to him:

"Friend Sāriputta, there are these four modes of practice.... Through which of these four modes of practice was your mind liberated from the taints by non-clinging?"

"Of these four modes of practice, friend Moggallāna, it was through the mode that is pleasant with quick direct knowledge that my mind was liberated from the taints by non-clinging."

169 (9) Through Exertion

"Bhikkhus, there are these four kinds of persons found existing in the world. What four?

(1) "Here, some person attains nibbāna through exertion in this very life. (2) Another person attains nibbāna through exertion with the breakup of the body.[855] (3) Still another person attains nibbāna without exertion in this very life. (4) And still another person attains nibbāna without exertion with the breakup of the body.[856]

(1) "And how, bhikkhus, does a person attain nibbāna through exertion in this very life? Here, a bhikkhu dwells contemplating the unattractiveness of the body, perceiving the repulsiveness of food, perceiving non-delight in the entire world, contemplating impermanence in all conditioned phenomena; and he has the perception of death [156] well established internally. He dwells depending upon these five trainee powers: the power of faith, the power of moral shame, the power of moral dread, the power of energy, and the power of wisdom. These five faculties arise in him prominently: the faculties of faith, energy, mindfulness, concentration, and wisdom. Because these five faculties are prominent, he attains nibbāna through exertion in this very life. This is how a person attains nibbāna through exertion in this very life.

(2) "And how does a person attain nibbāna through exertion with the breakup of the body? Here, a bhikkhu dwells contemplating the unattractiveness of the body . . . and he has the perception of death well established internally. He dwells depending upon these five trainee powers: the powers of faith . . . and wisdom. These five faculties arise in him feebly: the faculties of faith . . . and wisdom. Because these five faculties are feeble, he attains nibbāna through exertion with the breakup of the body. This is how a person attains nibbāna through exertion with the breakup of the body.

(3) "And how does a person attain nibbāna without exertion in this very life? Here, secluded from sensual pleasures, secluded from unwholesome states, a bhikkhu enters and dwells in the first jhāna . . . the fourth jhāna. He dwells depending upon these five trainee powers: the powers of faith . . . and wisdom. These five faculties arise in him prominently: the faculties of faith . . . and wisdom. Because these five faculties are prominent, he attains nibbāna without exertion in this very life. This is how a person attains nibbāna without exertion in this very life.

(4) "And how does a person attain nibbāna without exertion

with the breakup of the body? Here, secluded from sensual pleasures, secluded from unwholesome states, a bhikkhu enters and dwells in the first jhāna . . . the fourth jhāna. He dwells depending upon these five trainee powers: the powers of faith . . . and wisdom. These five faculties arise in him feebly: the faculties of faith . . . and wisdom. Because these five faculties are feeble, he attains nibbāna without exertion with the breakup of the body. This is how a person attains nibbāna without exertion with the breakup of the body.

"These, bhikkhus, are the four kinds of persons found existing in the world."

170 (10) In Conjunction

On one occasion the Venerable Ānanda was dwelling at Kosambī in Ghosita's Park. There the Venerable Ānanda addressed the bhikkhus:

"Friends, bhikkhus!"

"Friend," those bhikkhus replied. The Venerable Ānanda said this: [157]

"Friends, whatever bhikkhu or bhikkhunī has declared the attainment of arahantship in my presence has done so by these four paths[857] or by a certain one among them. What four?

(1) "Here, a bhikkhu develops insight preceded by serenity. As he is developing insight preceded by serenity, the path is generated.[858] He pursues this path, develops it, and cultivates it. As he is pursuing, developing, and cultivating this path, the fetters are abandoned and the underlying tendencies are uprooted.[859]

(2) "Again, a bhikkhu develops serenity preceded by insight.[860] As he is developing serenity preceded by insight, the path is generated. He pursues this path, develops it, and cultivates it. As he is pursuing, developing, and cultivating this path, the fetters are abandoned and the underlying tendencies are uprooted.

(3) "Again, a bhikkhu develops serenity and insight in conjunction.[861] As he is developing serenity and insight in conjunction, the path is generated. He pursues this path, develops it, and cultivates it. As he is pursuing, developing, and cultivating this path, the fetters are abandoned and the underlying tendencies are uprooted.

(4) "Again, a bhikkhu's mind is seized by restlessness about

the Dhamma.[862] But there comes an occasion when his mind becomes internally steady, composed, unified, and concentrated. Then the path is generated in him. He pursues this path, develops it, and cultivates it. As he is pursuing, developing, and cultivating this path, the fetters are abandoned and the underlying tendencies are uprooted.

"Whatever bhikkhu or bhikkhunī, friends, has declared the attainment of arahantship in my presence has done so by these four paths or by a certain one among them."

III. Volitional

171 (1) Volition[863]

"Bhikkhus, when there is the body, then because of bodily volition [158] pleasure and pain arise internally; when there is speech, then because of verbal volition pleasure and pain arise internally; when there is the mind, then because of mental volition pleasure and pain arise internally—with ignorance itself as condition.[864]

"Either on one's own, bhikkhus, one performs that bodily volitional activity conditioned by which pleasure and pain arise in one internally, or others make one generate that bodily volitional activity conditioned by which pleasure and pain arise in one internally. Either with clear comprehension one performs that bodily volitional activity conditioned by which pleasure and pain arise in one internally, or without clear comprehension one performs that bodily volitional activity conditioned by which pleasure and pain arise in one internally.[865]

"Either on one's own, bhikkhus, one performs that verbal volitional activity conditioned by which pleasure and pain arise in one internally, or others make one perform that verbal volitional activity conditioned by which pleasure and pain arise in one internally. Either with clear comprehension one performs that verbal volitional activity conditioned by which pleasure and pain arise in one internally, or without clear comprehension one performs that verbal volitional activity conditioned by which pleasure and pain arise in one internally.

"Either on one's own, bhikkhus, one performs that mental volitional activity conditioned by which pleasure and pain arise in one internally, or others make one perform that mental volitional activity conditioned by which pleasure and pain arise in one internally. Either with clear comprehension one performs that mental volitional activity conditioned by which pleasure and pain arise in one internally, or without clear comprehension one performs that mental volitional activity conditioned by which pleasure and pain arise in one internally.

"Ignorance is comprised within these states.[866] But with the remainderless fading away and cessation of ignorance that body does not exist conditioned by which that pleasure and pain arise in one internally; that speech does not exist conditioned by which that pleasure and pain arise in one internally; that mind does not exist conditioned by which that pleasure and pain arise in one internally.[867] That field does not exist, that site [159] does not exist, that base does not exist, that location does not exist conditioned by which that pleasure and pain arise in one internally.[868]

* * *

"Bhikkhus, there are these four acquisitions of individuality.[869] What four? (1) There is an acquisition of individuality in which one's own volition operates, not the volition of others. (2) There is an acquisition of individuality in which the volition of others operates, not one's own volition. (3) There is an acquisition of individuality in which both one's own volition and the volition of others operate. (4) And there is an acquisition of individuality in which neither one's own volition nor the volition of others operates. These are the four acquisitions of individuality."

When this was said, the Venerable Sāriputta said to the Blessed One: "Bhante, I understand in detail the meaning of this statement that the Blessed One has spoken in brief to be as follows. (1) In that acquisition of individuality in which one's own volition operates but not the volition of others, it is by reason of their own volition that beings pass away from that group.[870] (2) In that acquisition of individuality in which the volition of others operates but not one's own volition, it is by reason of the volition of others that beings pass away from that group.[871] (3) In that acquisition of individuality in which both one's own volition and the volition of others operate, it is by reason of both one's own volition and the volition of others that beings pass away from that group.[872] (4) But, Bhante, what kind of devas should be understood as the acquisition of individuality in which neither one's own volition nor the volition of others operates?"[873]

"They are, Sāriputta, the devas of the base of neither-perception-nor-non-perception."

"Why is it, Bhante, that some beings who pass away from that group are returners, who come back to this state of being, while [160] others are non-returners, who do not come back to this state of being?"[874]

"Here, Sāriputta, some person has not abandoned the lower fetters. In this very life he enters and dwells in the base of neither-perception-nor-non-perception. He relishes it, desires it, and finds satisfaction in it. If he is firm in it, focused on it, often dwells in it, and has not lost it when he dies, he is reborn in companionship with the devas in the base of neither-perception-nor-non-perception. When he passes away from there he is a returner who comes back to this state of being.

"But some [other] person here has abandoned the lower fetters. In this very life he enters and dwells in the base of neither-perception-nor-non-perception. He relishes it, desires it, and finds satisfaction in it. If he is firm in it, focused on it, often dwells in it, and has not lost it when he dies, he is reborn in companionship with the devas in the base of neither-perception-nor-non-perception. When he passes away from there he is a non-returner who does not come back to this state of being.

"This, Sāriputta, is the reason some beings here who pass away from that group are returners, who come back to this state of being, while others are non-returners, who do not come back to this state of being."

172 (2) Analysis

There the Venerable Sāriputta addressed the bhikkhus: "Friends, bhikkhus!"

"Friend!" those bhikkhus replied. The Venerable Sāriputta said this:

(1) "A half-month, friends, after my full ordination I realized the analytical knowledge of meaning by way of its divisions and formulation.[875] In many ways I explain it, teach it, proclaim it, establish it, disclose it, analyze it, and elucidate it.[876] [Let] anyone who is perplexed or uncertain [approach] me with a

question; I [will satisfy him] with my answer.[877] Our teacher, who is highly skilled in our teachings, is present.[878]

(2) "A half-month after my full ordination I realized the analytical knowledge of the Dhamma by way of its divisions and formulation. In many ways I explain it, teach it, proclaim it, establish it, disclose it, analyze it, and elucidate it. [Let] anyone who is perplexed or uncertain [approach] me with a question; I [will satisfy him] with my answer. Our teacher, who is highly skilled in our teachings, is present.

(3) "A half-month after my full ordination I realized the analytical knowledge of language by way of its divisions and formulation. In many ways I explain it, teach it, proclaim it, establish it, disclose it, analyze it, and elucidate it. [Let] anyone who is perplexed or uncertain [approach] me with a question; I [will satisfy him] with my answer. Our teacher, who is highly skilled in our teachings, is present.

(4) "A half-month after my full ordination I realized the analytical knowledge of discernment by way of its divisions and formulation. In many ways I explain it, teach it, proclaim it, establish it, disclose it, analyze it, and elucidate it. [Let] anyone who is perplexed or uncertain [approach] me with a question; I [will satisfy him] with my answer. Our teacher, who is highly skilled in our teachings, is present." [161]

173 (3) Koṭṭhita

Then the Venerable Mahākoṭṭhita approached the Venerable Sāriputta and exchanged greetings with him. When they had concluded their greetings and cordial talk, he sat down to one side and asked the Venerable Sāriputta:

(1) "Friend, with the remainderless fading away and cessation of the six bases for contact, is there anything else?"[879]

"Do not say so, friend."

(2) "With the remainderless fading away and cessation of the six bases for contact, is there nothing else?"

"Do not say so, friend."

(3) "With the remainderless fading away and cessation of the six bases for contact, is there both something else and nothing else?"

"Do not say so, friend."

(4) "With the remainderless fading away and cessation of

the six bases for contact, is there neither something else nor nothing else?"

"Do not say so, friend."[880]

"Friend, when you are asked: 'With the remainderless fading away and cessation of the six bases for contact, is there something else?' you say: 'Do not say so, friend.' And when you are asked: 'With the remainderless fading away and cessation of the six bases for contact, is there nothing else? . . . Is there both something else and nothing else? . . . Is there neither something else nor nothing else?' [in each case] you say: 'Do not say so, friend.' In what way should the meaning of this statement be understood?"

(1) "Friend, if one says: 'With the remainderless fading away and cessation of the six bases for contact, there is something else,' one proliferates that which is not to be proliferated.[881] (2) If one says: 'Friend, with the remainderless fading away and cessation of the six bases for contact, there is nothing else,' one proliferates that which is not to be proliferated. (3) If one says: 'Friend, with the remainderless fading away and cessation of the six bases for contact, there is both something else and nothing else,' one proliferates that which is not to be proliferated. (4) If one says: 'Friend, with the remainderless fading away and cessation of the six bases for contact, there is neither something else nor nothing else,' one proliferates that which is not to be proliferated.

"Friend, as far as the range of the six bases for contact extends, just so far extends the range of proliferation.[882] As far as the range of proliferation extends, [162] just so far extends the range of the six bases for contact. With the remainderless fading away and cessation of the six bases for contact there is the cessation of proliferation, the subsiding of proliferation."

174 (4) Ānanda

Then the Venerable Ānanda approached the Venerable Mahākoṭṭhita and exchanged greetings with him.

[This sutta is exactly the same as 4:173 except that here Ānanda asks the questions and Mahākoṭṭhita responds.][883] [163]

175 (5) Upavāṇa

Then the Venerable Upavāṇa approached the Venerable Sāriputta . . . and said to him:

(1) "Friend Sāriputta, does one become an end-maker by means of knowledge?"[884]

"This is not the case, friend."

(2) "Then does one become an end-maker by means of conduct?"

"This is not the case, friend."

(3) "Then does one become an end-maker by means of knowledge and conduct?"

"This is not the case, friend."

(4) "Then does one become an end-maker otherwise than by means of knowledge and conduct?"

"This is not the case, friend."

"When you are asked: 'Friend Sāriputta, does one become an end-maker by means of knowledge?' you say: 'This is not the case, friend.' When you are asked: 'Then does one become an end-maker by means of conduct?... by means of knowledge and conduct?... otherwise than by means of knowledge and conduct?' [in each case] you say: 'This is not the case, friend.' Then in what way does one become an end-maker?"

(1) "If, friend, one were to become an end-maker by means of knowledge, even one who still has clinging would become an end-maker. (2) If one were to become an end-maker by means of conduct, even one who still has clinging would become an end-maker. (3) If one were to become an end-maker by means of knowledge and conduct, even one who still has clinging would become an end-maker. (4) If one were to become an end-maker otherwise than by means of knowledge and conduct, then a worldling would be an end-maker; for a worldling is destitute of knowledge and conduct.

"Friend, one deficient in conduct does not know and see things as they are. One accomplished in conduct [164] knows and sees things as they are. Knowing and seeing things as they are, one becomes an end-maker."[885]

176 (6) Aspiring[886]

(1) "Bhikkhus, a bhikkhu endowed with faith, rightly aspiring, should aspire thus: 'May I become like Sāriputta and Moggallāna!' This is the standard and criterion for my bhikkhu disciples, that is, Sāriputta and Moggallāna.

(2) "Bhikkhus, a bhikkhunī endowed with faith, rightly aspiring, should aspire thus: 'May I become like the bhikkhunīs

Khemā and Uppalavaṇṇā!' This is the standard and criterion for my bhikkhunī disciples, that is, the bhikkhunīs Khemā and Uppalavaṇṇā.

(3) "Bhikkhus, a male lay follower endowed with faith, rightly aspiring, should aspire thus: 'May I become like Citta the householder and Hatthaka of Āḷavī!' This is the standard and criterion for my male lay disciples, that is, Citta the householder and Hatthaka of Āḷavī.

(4) "Bhikkhus, a female lay follower endowed with faith, rightly aspiring, should aspire thus: 'May I become like the female lay follower Khujjuttarā and Veḷukaṇṭakī Nandamātā!' This is the standard and criterion for my female lay disciples, that is, the female lay follower Khujjuttarā and Veḷukaṇṭakī Nandamātā."

177 (7) Rāhula

Then the Venerable Rāhula approached the Blessed One, paid homage to him, and sat down to one side. The Blessed One then said to him:[887]

(1) "Rāhula, the internal earth element and the external earth element are just the earth element. This should be seen as it really is with correct wisdom thus: 'This is not mine, this I am not, this is not my self.' Having seen this thus as it really is with correct wisdom, one becomes disenchanted with the earth element; one detaches the mind from the earth element.[888]

(2) "Rāhula, the internal water element and the external water element [165] are just the water element. This should be seen as it really is with correct wisdom thus: 'This is not mine, this I am not, this is not my self.' Having seen this thus as it really is with correct wisdom, one becomes disenchanted with the water element; one detaches the mind from the water element.

(3) "Rāhula, the internal fire element and the external fire element are just the fire element. This should be seen as it really is with correct wisdom thus: 'This is not mine, this I am not, this is not my self.' Having seen this thus as it really is with correct wisdom, one becomes disenchanted with the fire element; one detaches the mind from the fire element.

(4) "Rāhula, the internal air element and the external air element are just the air element. This should be seen as it really is with correct wisdom thus: 'This is not mine, this I am not, this

is not my self.' Having seen this thus as it really is with correct wisdom, one becomes disenchanted with the air element; one detaches the mind from the air element.

"When, Rāhula, a bhikkhu does not recognize a self or the belongings of a self in these four elements, he is called a bhikkhu who has cut off craving, stripped off the fetter, and by completely breaking through conceit, has made an end of suffering."

178 (8) The Reservoir

"Bhikkhus, there are these four kinds of persons found existing in the world. What four?

(1) "Here, a bhikkhu enters and dwells in a certain peaceful liberation of mind. He attends to the cessation of personal existence.[889] As he is doing so, his mind does not launch out toward it, acquire confidence, become steady, and focus on it. This bhikkhu cannot be expected to attain the cessation of personal existence. Suppose a man were to grab hold of a branch with his hand smeared with gum. His hand would stick to it, adhere to it, and be fastened to it. So too, a bhikkhu enters and dwells in a certain peaceful liberation of mind. . . . This bhikkhu cannot be expected to attain the cessation of personal existence.

(2) "Here, a bhikkhu enters and dwells in a certain peaceful liberation of mind. [166] He attends to the cessation of personal existence. As he is doing so, his mind launches out toward it, acquires confidence, becomes steady, and focuses on it. This bhikkhu can be expected to attain the cessation of personal existence. Suppose a man were to grab hold of a branch with a clean hand. His hand would not stick to it, adhere to it, or be fastened to it. So too, a bhikkhu enters and dwells in a certain peaceful liberation of mind. . . . This bhikkhu can be expected to attain the cessation of personal existence.

(3) "Here, a bhikkhu enters and dwells in a certain peaceful liberation of mind. He attends to the breaking up of ignorance. As he is doing so, his mind does not launch out toward it, acquire confidence, become steady, and focus on it. This bhikkhu cannot be expected to attain the breaking up of ignorance. Suppose there were a reservoir many years old. A man would close off its inlets and open up its outlets, and sufficient rain would not

fall. In such a case, it could not be expected that this reservoir's embankment would break. So too, a bhikkhu enters and dwells in a certain peaceful liberation of mind. . . . This bhikkhu cannot be expected to attain the breaking up of ignorance.

(4) "Here, a bhikkhu enters and dwells in a certain peaceful liberation of mind. He attends to the breaking up of ignorance. As he is doing so, his mind launches out toward it, acquires confidence, becomes steady, and focuses on it. This bhikkhu can be expected to attain the breaking up of ignorance. Suppose there were a reservoir many years old. A man would open up its inlets and close off its outlets, and sufficient rain would fall. In such a case, it could be expected that this reservoir's embankment would break. So too, a bhikkhu enters and dwells in a certain peaceful liberation of mind. He attends to the breaking up of ignorance. [167] As he is doing so, his mind launches out toward it, acquires confidence, becomes steady, and focuses on it. This bhikkhu can be expected to attain the breaking up of ignorance.

"These, bhikkhus, are the four kinds of persons found existing in the world."

179 (9) Nibbāna

Then the Venerable Ānanda approached the Venerable Sāriputta . . . and said to him:

"Why is it, friend Sāriputta, that some beings do not attain nibbāna in this very life?"

"Here, friend Ānanda, [some] beings do not understand as it really is: 'These perceptions pertain to deterioration; these perceptions pertain to stabilization; these perceptions pertain to distinction; these perceptions pertain to penetration.' This is why some beings here do not attain nibbāna in this very life.

"Why is it, friend Sāriputta, that some beings here attain nibbāna in this very life?"

"Here, friend Ānanda, [some] beings understand as it really is: 'These perceptions pertain to deterioration; these perceptions pertain to stabilization; these perceptions pertain to distinction; these perceptions pertain to penetration.' This is why some beings here attain nibbāna in this very life."[890]

180 (10) The Great References[891]

On one occasion the Blessed One was dwelling at Bhoganagara near the Ānanda Shrine. There the Blessed One addressed the bhikkhus: "Bhikkhus!"

"Venerable sir!" those bhikkhus replied. The Blessed One said this:

"Bhikkhus, I will teach you these four great references.[892] [168] Listen and attend closely; I will speak."

"Yes, Bhante," those bhikkhus replied. The Blessed One said this:

"What, bhikkhus, are the four great references?

(1) "Here, bhikkhus, a bhikkhu might say: 'In the presence of the Blessed One I heard this; in his presence I learned this: "This is the Dhamma; this is the discipline; this is the Teacher's teaching!"' That bhikkhu's statement should neither be approved nor rejected. Without approving or rejecting it, you should thoroughly learn those words and phrases and then check for them in the discourses and seek them in the discipline.[893] If, when you check for them in the discourses and seek them in the discipline, [you find that] they are not included among the discourses and are not to be seen in the discipline, you should draw the conclusion: 'Surely, this is not the word of the Blessed One, the Arahant, the Perfectly Enlightened One. It has been badly learned by this bhikkhu.' Thus you should discard it.

"But a bhikkhu might say: 'In the presence of the Blessed One I heard this; in his presence I learned this: "This is the Dhamma; this is the discipline; this is the Teacher's teaching!"' That bhikkhu's statement should neither be approved nor rejected. Without approving or rejecting it, you should thoroughly learn those words and phrases and then check for them in the discourses and seek them in the discipline. If, when you check for them in the discourses and seek them in the discipline, [you find that] they are included among the discourses and are to be seen in the discipline, you should draw the conclusion: 'Surely, this is the word of the Blessed One, the Arahant, the Perfectly Enlightened One. It has been learned well by this bhikkhu.' You should remember this first great reference.

(2) "Then a bhikkhu might say: 'In such and such a residence a Saṅgha is dwelling with elders and prominent monks. In the presence of that Saṅgha I heard this; in its presence I learned this:

"This is the Dhamma; this is the discipline; this is the Teacher's teaching."' That bhikkhu's statement should neither be approved nor rejected. Without approving or rejecting it, you should thoroughly learn those words and phrases and then check for them in the discourses and seek them in the discipline. If, when you check for them in the discourses and seek them in the discipline, [you find that] they are not included among the discourses and are not to be seen in the discipline, you should draw the conclusion: 'Surely, this is not the word of the Blessed One, the Arahant, the Perfectly Enlightened One. [169] It has been badly learned by that Saṅgha.' Thus you should discard it.

"But . . . if, when you check for them in the discourses and seek them in the discipline, [you find that] they are included among the discourses and are to be seen in the discipline, you should draw the conclusion: 'Surely, this is the word of the Blessed One, the Arahant, the Perfectly Enlightened One. It has been learned well by that Saṅgha.' You should remember this second great reference.

(3) "Then a bhikkhu might say: 'In such and such a residence several elder bhikkhus are dwelling who are learned, heirs to the heritage, experts on the Dhamma, experts on the discipline, experts on the outlines. In the presence of those elders I heard this; in their presence I learned this: "This is the Dhamma; this is the discipline; this is the Teacher's teaching!"' That bhikkhu's statement should neither be approved nor rejected. Without approving or rejecting it, you should thoroughly learn those words and phrases and then check for them in the discourses and seek them in the discipline. If, when you check for them in the discourses and seek them in the discipline, [you find that] they are not included among the discourses and are not to be seen in the discipline, you should draw the conclusion: 'Surely, this is not the word of the Blessed One, the Arahant, the Perfectly Enlightened One. It has been badly learned by those elders.' Thus you should discard it.

"But . . . if, when you check for them in the discourses and seek them in the discipline, [you find that] they are included among the discourses and are to be seen in the discipline, you should draw the conclusion: 'Surely, this is the word of the Blessed One, the Arahant, the Perfectly Enlightened One. It has been learned well by those elders.' You should remember this third great reference.

(4) "Then a bhikkhu might say: 'In such and such a residence one elder bhikkhu is dwelling [170] who is learned, an heir to the heritage, an expert on the Dhamma, an expert on the discipline, an expert on the outlines. In the presence of that elder I heard this; in his presence I learned this: "This is the Dhamma; this is the discipline; this is the Teacher's teaching!"' That bhikkhu's statement should neither be approved nor rejected. Without approving or rejecting it, you should thoroughly learn those words and phrases and then check for them in the discourses and seek them in the discipline. If, when you check for them in the discourses and seek them in the discipline, [you find that] they are not included among the discourses and are not to be seen in the discipline, you should draw the conclusion: 'Surely, this is not the word of the Blessed One, the Arahant, the Perfectly Enlightened One. It has been badly learned by that elder.' Thus you should discard it.

"But a bhikkhu might say: 'In such and such a residence one elder bhikkhu is dwelling who is learned, an heir to the heritage, an expert on the Dhamma, an expert on the discipline, an expert on the outlines. In the presence of that elder I heard this; in his presence I learned this: "This is the Dhamma; this is the discipline; this is the Teacher's teaching!"' That bhikkhu's statement should neither be approved nor rejected. Without approving or rejecting it, you should thoroughly learn those words and phrases and then check for them in the discourses and seek them in the discipline. If, when you check for them in the discourses and seek them in the discipline, [you find that] they are included among the discourses and are to be seen in the discipline, you should draw the conclusion: 'Surely, this is the word of the Blessed One, the Arahant, the Perfectly Enlightened One. It has been learned well by that elder.' You should remember this fourth great reference.

"These, bhikkhus, are the four great references."[894]

IV. Brahmins

181 (1) Warrior

"Bhikkhus, possessing four factors, a warrior is worthy of a king, an accessory of a king, and reckoned a factor of kingship. What four? Here, a warrior is skilled in places, a long-distance shooter, a sharp-shooter, and one who splits a great body.

Possessing these four factors, a warrior is worthy of a king, an accessory of a king, and reckoned a factor of kingship. [171] So too, possessing four factors, a bhikkhu is worthy of gifts, worthy of hospitality, worthy of offerings, worthy of reverential salutation, an unsurpassed field of merit for the world. What four? Here, a bhikkhu is skilled in places, a long-distance shooter, a sharp-shooter, and one who splits a great body.

(1) "And how, bhikkhus, is a bhikkhu skilled in places? Here, a bhikkhu is virtuous; he dwells restrained by the Pātimokkha, possessed of good conduct and resort, seeing danger in minute faults. Having undertaken the training rules, he trains in them. It is in this way that a bhikkhu is skilled in places.

(2) "And how is a bhikkhu a long-distance shooter? Here, any kind of form whatsoever—whether past, future, or present, internal or external, gross or subtle, inferior or superior, far or near—a bhikkhu sees all form as it really is with correct wisdom thus: 'This is not mine, this I am not, this is not my self.' Any kind of feeling whatsoever . . . Any kind of perception whatsoever . . . Any kind of volitional activities whatsoever . . . Any kind of consciousness whatsoever—whether past, future, or present, internal or external, gross or subtle, inferior or superior, far or near—a bhikkhu sees all consciousness as it really is with correct wisdom thus: 'This is not mine, this I am not, this is not my self.' It is in this way that a bhikkhu is a long-distance shooter.

(3) "And how is a bhikkhu a sharp-shooter? Here, a bhikkhu understands as it really is: 'This is suffering.' He understands as it really is: 'This is the origin of suffering.' He understands as it really is: 'This is the cessation of suffering.' He understands as it really is: 'This is the way leading to the cessation of suffering.' It is in this way that a bhikkhu is a sharp-shooter.

(4) "And how is a bhikkhu one who splits a great body? Here, a bhikkhu splits the great mass of ignorance. It is in this way that a bhikkhu is one who splits a great body.

"Possessing these four qualities, a bhikkhu is worthy of gifts, worthy of hospitality, worthy of offerings, worthy of reverential salutation, an unsurpassed field of merit for the world." [172]

182 (2) Guarantor

"Bhikkhus, against four things there can be no guarantor, neither an ascetic, a brahmin, a deva, Māra, Brahmā, nor anyone in the world. What four?

(1) "There can be no guarantor, neither an ascetic . . . nor anyone in the world, that what is subject to old age will not grow old.

(2) "There can be no guarantor, neither an ascetic . . . nor anyone in the world, that what is subject to illness will not fall ill.

(3) "There can be no guarantor, neither an ascetic . . . nor anyone in the world, that what is subject to death will not die.

(4) "There can be no guarantor, neither an ascetic . . . nor anyone in the world, that bad kamma—defiled, conducive to renewed existence, troublesome, ripening in suffering, leading to future birth, old age, and death—will not produce its result.

"Against these four things, bhikkhus, there can be no guarantor, neither an ascetic, a brahmin, a deva, Māra, Brahmā, nor anyone in the world."

183 (3) Heard

On one occasion the Blessed One was dwelling at Rājagaha in the Bamboo Grove, the squirrel sanctuary. Then the brahmin Vassakāra, the chief minister of Magadha, approached the Blessed One and exchanged greetings with him. . . . Then, sitting to one side, he said to the Blessed One:

"Master Gotama, I hold the thesis and view that there is no fault when one speaks about the seen, saying: 'Such was seen by me'; no fault when one speaks about the heard, saying: 'Such was heard by me'; no fault when one speaks about the sensed, saying: 'Such was sensed by me'; no fault when one speaks about the cognized, saying: 'Such was cognized by me.'"

(1) "I do not say, brahmin, that everything seen should be spoken about, nor do I say that nothing seen should be spoken about. (2) I do not say that everything heard should be spoken about, nor do I say that nothing heard [173] should be spoken about. (3) I do not say that everything sensed should be spoken about, nor do I say that nothing sensed should be spoken about. (4) I do not say that everything cognized should be spoken about, nor do I say that nothing cognized should be spoken about.

(1) "For, brahmin, if, when one speaks about what one has seen, unwholesome qualities increase and wholesome qualities decline, I say that one should not speak about what one has seen. But if, when one speaks about what one has seen, unwholesome

qualities decline and wholesome qualities increase, I say that one should speak about what one has seen.[895]

(2) "If, when one speaks about what one has heard, unwholesome qualities increase and wholesome qualities decline, I say that one should not speak about what one has heard. But if, when one speaks about what one has heard, unwholesome qualities decline and wholesome qualities increase, I say that one should speak about what one has heard.

(3) "If, when one speaks about what one has sensed, unwholesome qualities increase and wholesome qualities decline, I say that one should not speak about what one has sensed. But if, when one speaks about what one has sensed, unwholesome qualities decline and wholesome qualities increase, I say that one should speak about what one has sensed.

(4) "If, when one speaks about what one has cognized, unwholesome qualities increase and wholesome qualities decline, I say that one should not speak about what one has cognized. But if, when one speaks about what one has cognized, unwholesome qualities decline and wholesome qualities increase, I say that one should speak about what one has cognized."

Then the brahmin Vassakāra, the chief minister of Magadha, having delighted and rejoiced in the Blessed One's statement, rose from his seat and departed.

184 (4) Fearless

Then the brahmin Jāṇussoṇī approached the Blessed One and exchanged greetings with him.... Then, sitting to one side, he said to the Blessed One:

"Master Gotama, I hold the thesis and view that there is no one subject to death who is not frightened and terrified of death."

"Brahmin, there are those subject to death that are frightened and terrified of death, but there are also those subject to death that are not frightened and terrified of death.

"And, brahmin, who are those subject to death that are frightened and terrified of death?

(1) "Here, someone is not devoid of lust, desire, [174] affection, thirst, passion, and craving for sensual pleasures. When he incurs a severe and debilitating illness, he thinks: 'Alas, the sen-

sual pleasures dear to me will leave me, and I will have to leave those sensual pleasures.' He sorrows, languishes, and laments; he weeps beating his breast and becomes confused. This is one subject to death who is frightened and terrified of death.

(2) "Again, someone is not devoid of lust, desire, affection, thirst, passion, and craving for the body. When he incurs a severe and debilitating illness, he thinks: 'Alas, this body dear to me will leave me, and I will have to leave this body.' He sorrows, languishes, and laments; he weeps beating his breast and becomes confused. This, too, is one subject to death who is frightened and terrified of death.

(3) "Again, someone has not done what is good and wholesome or made a shelter for himself, but he has done what is evil, cruel, and defiled. When he incurs a severe and debilitating illness, he thinks: 'Alas, I have not done anything good and wholesome, nor have I made a shelter for myself, but I have done what is evil, cruel, and defiled. When I pass on, I will meet the appropriate fate.' He sorrows, languishes, and laments; he weeps beating his breast and becomes confused. This, too, is one subject to death who is frightened and terrified of death.

(4) "Again, someone here is perplexed, doubtful, and undecided about the good Dhamma. When he incurs a severe and debilitating illness, he thinks: 'Alas, I am perplexed, doubtful, and undecided about the good Dhamma.' He sorrows, languishes, and laments; he weeps beating his breast and becomes confused. This, too, is one subject to death who is frightened and terrified of death.

"These are four subject to death that are frightened and terrified of death. [175]

"And, brahmin, who are those subject to death that are not frightened and terrified of death?

(1) "Here, someone is devoid of lust, desire, affection, thirst, passion, and craving for sensual pleasures. When he incurs a severe and debilitating illness, he does not think: 'Alas, the sensual pleasures dear to me will leave me, and I will have to leave those sensual pleasures.' He does not sorrow, languish, and lament; he does not weep beating his breast and become confused. This is one subject to death who is not frightened and terrified of death.

(2) "Again, someone is devoid of lust, desire, affection, thirst,

passion, and craving for the body. When he incurs a severe and debilitating illness, he does not think: 'Alas, this body dear to me will leave me, and I will have to leave this body.' He does not sorrow, languish, and lament; he does not weep beating his breast and become confused. This, too, is one subject to death who is not frightened and terrified of death.

(3) "Again, someone has not done what is evil, cruel, and defiled, but has done what is good and wholesome and made a shelter for himself. When he incurs a severe and debilitating illness, he thinks: 'Indeed, I have not done anything evil, cruel, and defiled, but I have done what is good and wholesome and made a shelter for myself. When I pass on, I will meet the appropriate fate.' He does not sorrow, languish, and lament; he does not weep beating his breast and become confused. This, too, is one subject to death who is not frightened and terrified of death.

(4) "Again, someone is unperplexed, doubt-free, and decided about the good Dhamma. When he incurs a severe and debilitating illness, he thinks: 'I am unperplexed, doubt-free, and decided about the good Dhamma.' He does not sorrow, languish, and lament; he does not weep beating his breast and become confused. [176] This, too, is one subject to death who is not frightened and terrified of death.

"These, brahmin, are four subject to death that are not frightened and terrified of death."

"Excellent, Master Gotama! . . . [as at 4:100] . . . Let Master Gotama consider me a lay follower who from today has gone for refuge for life."

185 (5) Brahmin Truths

On one occasion the Blessed One was dwelling at Rājagaha on Mount Vulture Peak. Now on that occasion a number of very well-known wanderers were residing at the wanderers' park on the bank of the river Sappinī, that is, Annabhāra, Varadhara, Sakuludāyī, and other very well-known wanderers. Then, in the evening, the Blessed One emerged from seclusion and went to the wanderers' park on the bank of the river Sappinī. Now on that occasion the wanderers of other sects had assembled and were sitting together when this conversation arose: "Such are the brahmin truths, such are the brahmin truths."

Then the Blessed One approached those wanderers, sat down

on a seat that was prepared, and asked them: "Wanderers, what discussion were you engaged in just now? What was the conversation that was underway?"

"Here, Master Gotama, we had assembled and were sitting together when this conversation arose: 'Such are the brahmin truths, such are the brahmin truths.'"

"Wanderers, there are these four brahmin truths that I have proclaimed, having realized them for myself with direct knowledge. What four?

(1) "Here, wanderers, a brahmin says thus: 'All living beings are to be spared.' Speaking thus, a brahmin speaks truth, not falsehood. He does not, on that account, misconceive himself as 'an ascetic' or as 'a brahmin.' He does not misconceive: 'I am better' or 'I am equal' or 'I am worse.' Rather, having directly known the truth in that, he is practicing simply out of sympathy and compassion for living beings.

(2) "Again, a brahmin says thus: [177] 'All sensual pleasures are impermanent, suffering, and subject to change.' Speaking thus, a brahmin speaks truth, not falsehood. He does not, on that account, misconceive himself as 'an ascetic' or as 'a brahmin.' He does not misconceive: 'I am better' or 'I am equal' or 'I am worse.' Rather, having directly known the truth in that, he is practicing simply for disenchantment with sensual pleasures, for their fading away and cessation.

(3) "Again, a brahmin says thus: 'All states of existence are impermanent, suffering, and subject to change.' Speaking thus, a brahmin speaks truth, not falsehood. He does not, on that account, misconceive himself as 'an ascetic' or as 'a brahmin.' He does not misconceive: 'I am better' or 'I am equal' or 'I am worse.' Rather, having directly known the truth in that, he is practicing simply for disenchantment with states of existence, for their fading away and cessation.

(4) "Again, wanderers, a brahmin says thus: 'I am not anywhere the belonging of anyone, nor is there anywhere anything in any place that is mine.'[896] Speaking thus, a brahmin speaks truth, not falsehood. He does not, on that account, misconceive himself as 'an ascetic' or as 'a brahmin.' He does not misconceive: 'I am better' or 'I am equal' or 'I am worse.' Rather, having directly known the truth in that, he is practicing the path of nothingness.[897]

"These, wanderers, are the four brahmin truths that I have

proclaimed, having realized them for myself with direct knowledge."

186 (6) Acumen

Then a certain bhikkhu approached the Blessed One . . . and said to him:

(1) "Bhante, by what is the world led? By what is the world dragged around? When what has arisen does [the world] go under its control?"[898]

"Good, good, bhikkhu! Your acumen is excellent. Your discernment is excellent.[899] Your inquiry is a good one. For you have asked thus: 'Bhante, by what is the world led? By what is the world dragged around? When what has arisen does [the world] go under its control?'"

"Yes, Bhante."

"The world, bhikkhu, is led by the mind; it is dragged around by the mind; when the mind has arisen, [the world] goes under its control." [178]

Saying, "Good, Bhante," that bhikkhu delighted and rejoiced in the Blessed One's statement. Then he asked the Blessed One a further question:

(2) "It is said, Bhante, 'a learned expert on the Dhamma, a learned expert on the Dhamma.' In what way is one a learned expert on the Dhamma?"

"Good, good, bhikkhu! Your acumen is excellent. Your discernment is excellent. Your inquiry is a good one. For you have asked thus: 'It is said, Bhante, "a learned expert on the Dhamma, a learned expert on the Dhamma." In what way is one a learned expert on the Dhamma?'"

"Yes, Bhante."

"I have taught many teachings, bhikkhu: discourses, mixed prose and verse, expositions, verses, inspired utterances, quotations, birth stories, amazing accounts, and questions-and-answers. If, after learning the meaning and Dhamma of even a four-line verse, one practices in accordance with the Dhamma, that is enough for one to be called 'a learned expert on the Dhamma.'"

Saying, "Good, Bhante," that bhikkhu delighted and rejoiced in the Blessed One's statement. Then he asked the Blessed One a further question:

(3) "It is said, Bhante, 'learned, of penetrative wisdom;

learned, of penetrative wisdom.' In what way is one learned, of penetrative wisdom?"

"Good, good, bhikkhu! Your acumen is excellent. Your discernment is excellent. Your inquiry is a good one. For you have asked thus: 'It is said, Bhante, "learned, of penetrative wisdom; learned, of penetrative wisdom." In what way is one learned, of penetrative wisdom?'"

"Yes, Bhante."

"Here, bhikkhu, a bhikkhu has heard: 'This is suffering,' and he sees the meaning of this, having pierced through it with wisdom. He has heard: 'This is the origin of suffering,' and he sees the meaning of this, having pierced through it with wisdom. He has heard: 'This is the cessation of suffering,' and he sees the meaning of this, having pierced through it with wisdom. He has heard: 'This is the way leading to the cessation of suffering,' and he sees the meaning of this, having pierced through it with wisdom. It is in this way that one is learned, of penetrative wisdom."

Saying, "Good, Bhante," that bhikkhu delighted and rejoiced in the Blessed One's statement. Then he asked the Blessed One a further question:

(4) "It is said, Bhante, 'a wise person of great wisdom, a wise person of great wisdom.' In what way is one a wise person of great wisdom?" [179]

"Good, good, bhikkhu! Your acumen is excellent. Your discernment is excellent. Your inquiry is a good one. For you have asked thus: 'It is said, Bhante, "a wise person of great wisdom, a wise person of great wisdom." In what way is one a wise person of great wisdom?'"

"Yes, Bhante."

"Here, bhikkhu, a wise person of great wisdom does not intend for his own affliction, or for the affliction of others, or for the affliction of both. Rather, when he thinks, he thinks only of his own welfare, the welfare of others, the welfare of both, and the welfare of the whole world.[900] It is in this way that one is a wise person of great wisdom."

187 (7) Vassakāra

On one occasion the Blessed One was dwelling at Rājagaha in the Bamboo Grove, the squirrel sanctuary. Then the brahmin Vassakāra, the chief minister of Magadha, approached the

Blessed One and exchanged greetings with him. . . . Then, sitting to one side, he said to the Blessed One:

(1) "Master Gotama, can a bad person know of a bad person: 'This fellow is a bad person'?"

"It is, brahmin, impossible and inconceivable that a bad person can know of a bad person: 'This fellow is a bad person.'"

(2) "Then can a bad person know of a good person: 'This fellow is a good person'?"

"It is also impossible and inconceivable that a bad person can know of a good person: 'This fellow is a good person.'"

(3) "Then can a good person know of a good person: 'This fellow is a good person'?"

"It is possible that a good person can know of a good person: 'This fellow is a good person.'"

(4) "Then can a good person know of a bad person: 'This fellow is a bad person'?"

"It is also possible that a good person can know of a bad person: 'This fellow is a bad person.'"

"It is astounding and amazing, Master Gotama, how [180] well this has been stated by Master Gotama: 'It is, brahmin, impossible and inconceivable that a bad person can know of a bad person . . . [all as above] . . . It is also possible that a good person can know of a bad person: "This fellow is a bad person."'

"On one occasion, Master Gotama, the members of the brahmin Todeyya's assembly were carping against others, [saying]: 'This King Eḷeyya is a fool, for he has complete confidence in the ascetic Rāmaputta and shows him supreme honor by paying homage to him, rising up for him, reverentially saluting him, and observing proper etiquette toward him.[901] These vassals of King Eḷeyya—Yamaka, Moggalla, Ugga, Nāvindakī, Gandhabba, and Aggivessa—are fools as well, for they, too, have complete confidence in the ascetic Rāmaputta and show him supreme honor by paying homage to him, rising up for him, reverentially saluting him, and observing proper etiquette toward him.' Thereupon the brahmin Todeyya led them around by this method: 'What do you think, sirs, in matters pertaining to tasks and administrative duties, to edicts and proclamations, isn't King Eḷeyya wise and more astute even than those who are very astute?'

"[They replied:] 'Yes, sir, in matters pertaining to tasks and administrative duties, to edicts and proclamations, King Eḷeyya is wise and more astute even than those who are very astute.'

"'But, sirs,' [he said,] 'it is because the ascetic Rāmaputta is wiser than the wise King Eḷeyya, more astute than this astute [king] in matters pertaining to tasks and administrative duties, to edicts and proclamations, that King Eḷeyya has complete confidence in him and shows him supreme honor by paying homage to him, rising up for him, reverentially saluting him, and observing proper etiquette toward him.

"'What do you think, sirs, in matters pertaining to tasks and administrative duties, to edicts and proclamations, are King Eḷeyya's vassals—Yamaka, Moggalla, [181] Ugga, Nāvindakī, Gandhabba, Aggivessa—wise and more astute even than those who are very astute?'

"'Yes, sir, in matters pertaining to tasks and administrative duties, to edicts and proclamations, King Eḷeyya's vassals—Yamaka . . . Aggivessa—are wise and more astute even than those who are very astute.'

"'But, sirs, it is because the ascetic Rāmaputta is wiser than King Eḷeyya's vassals, more astute than those astute [vassals] in matters pertaining to tasks and administrative duties, to edicts and proclamations, that King Eḷeyya's vassals have complete confidence in him and show him supreme honor by paying homage to him, rising up for him, reverentially saluting him, and observing proper etiquette toward him.'"[902]

"It is astounding and amazing, Master Gotama, how well this has been stated by Master Gotama: 'It is impossible and inconceivable that a bad person can know of a bad person: "This fellow is a bad person." It is also impossible and inconceivable that a bad person can know of a good person: "This fellow is a good person." It is possible that a good person can know of a good person: "This fellow is a good person." It is also possible that a good person can know of a bad person: "This fellow is a bad person."' And now, Master Gotama, we must be going. We are busy and have much to do."

"You may go, brahmin, at your own convenience."

Then the brahmin Vassakāra, the chief minister of Magadha, having delighted and rejoiced in the Blessed One's statement, rose from his seat and departed.

188 (8) Upaka

On one occasion the Blessed One was dwelling at Rājagaha on Mount Vulture Peak. Then Upaka Maṇḍikāputta approached the Blessed One, paid homage to him, sat down to one side, and said:

"Bhante, I hold such a thesis and view as this: If anyone carps against others and does not at all substantiate it, he is blameworthy and at fault."

"If, Upaka, anyone carping against others does not substantiate it, [182] he is blameworthy and at fault. But you carp against others and do not substantiate it, so you are blameworthy and at fault."

"Bhante, just as one might catch [a fish] emerging [from the water] with a large snare, just so, when I emerged, the Blessed One caught me with a large snare in debate."

(1) "Upaka, I have proclaimed: 'This is unwholesome.' The Tathāgata has unlimited Dhamma teachings about this, with unlimited words and phrases, [declaring]: 'For such and such reasons, this is unwholesome.'

(2) "Upaka, I have proclaimed: 'That which is unwholesome should be abandoned.' The Tathāgata has unlimited Dhamma teachings about this, with unlimited words and phrases, [declaring]: 'For such and such reasons, that which is unwholesome should be abandoned.'

(3) "Upaka, I have proclaimed: 'This is wholesome.' The Tathāgata has unlimited Dhamma teachings about this, with unlimited words and phrases, [declaring]: 'For such and such reasons, this is wholesome.'

(4) "Upaka, I have proclaimed: 'That which is wholesome should be developed.' The Tathāgata has unlimited Dhamma teachings about this, with unlimited words and phrases, [declaring]: 'For such and such reasons, that which is wholesome should be developed.'"

Then Upaka Maṇḍikāputta, having delighted and rejoiced in the Blessed One's statement, rose from his seat, paid homage to the Blessed One, and circumambulated him keeping the right side toward him. He then went to King Ajātasattu Vedehiputta of Magadha and reported to the king his entire conversation with the Blessed One.

When he had spoken, King Ajātasattu became angry and displeased and said to Upaka Maṇḍikāputta: "How bold indeed is this salt-maker's boy! How rude, how impudent, in that he thinks he can attack the Blessed One, the Arahant, the Perfectly Enlightened One. Go away, Upaka, be gone! Get out of my sight!"

189 (9) Realization

"Bhikkhus, there are these four things to be realized. What four? [183]

"There are things to be realized by the body; there are things to be realized by memory; there are things to be realized by the eye; there are things to be realized by wisdom.

(1) "And what, bhikkhus, are the things to be realized by the body? The eight emancipations, bhikkhus, are to be realized by the body. (2) And what are the things to be realized by memory? One's past abodes are to be realized by memory. (3) And what are the things to be realized by the eye? The passing away and rebirth of beings are to be realized by the eye. (4) And what are the things to be realized by wisdom? The destruction of the taints is to be realized by wisdom.

"These, bhikkhus, are the four things to be realized."

190 (10) Uposatha

On one occasion the Blessed One was dwelling at Sāvatthī in Migāramātā's Mansion in the Eastern Park. Now on that occasion, on the day of the uposatha, the Blessed One was sitting surrounded by the Saṅgha of bhikkhus. Then, having surveyed the utterly silent Saṅgha of bhikkhus, the Blessed One addressed the bhikkhus:

"Bhikkhus, this assembly is free from prattle; this assembly is without prattle, pure, established in the core. Such a Saṅgha of bhikkhus, such an assembly, is rarely seen in the world. Such a Saṅgha of bhikkhus, such an assembly, is worthy of gifts, worthy of hospitality, worthy of offerings, worthy of reverential salutation, an unsurpassed field of merit for the world. Even a little given to such a Saṅgha of bhikkhus, to such an assembly, becomes plentiful, while much given to it becomes even more plentiful. Such a Saṅgha of bhikkhus, such an assembly, is worth traveling many *yojanas* to see, even with a shoulder bag. Such is this Saṅgha of bhikkhus. [184]

"There are bhikkhus in this Saṅgha who dwell having attained the state of devas. There are bhikkhus in this Saṅgha who dwell having attained the state of brahmās. There are bhikkhus in this Saṅgha who dwell having attained the imperturbable. There are bhikkhus in this Saṅgha who dwell having attained the state of noble ones.

(1) "And how has a bhikkhu attained the state of a deva? Here, secluded from sensual pleasures, secluded from unwholesome states, a bhikkhu enters and dwells in the first jhāna, which consists of rapture and pleasure born of seclusion, accompanied by thought and examination. With the subsiding of thought and examination, he enters and dwells in the second jhāna, which has internal placidity and unification of mind and consists of rapture and pleasure born of concentration, without thought and examination. With the fading away as well of rapture, he dwells equanimous and, mindful and clearly comprehending, he experiences pleasure with the body; he enters and dwells in the third jhāna of which the noble ones declare: 'He is equanimous, mindful, one who dwells happily.' With the abandoning of pleasure and pain, and with the previous passing away of joy and dejection, he enters and dwells in the fourth jhāna, neither painful nor pleasant, which has purification of mindfulness by equanimity. It is in this way that a bhikkhu has attained the state of a deva.

(2) "And how has a bhikkhu attained the state of a brahmā? Here, a bhikkhu dwells pervading one quarter with a mind imbued with loving-kindness, likewise the second quarter, the third quarter, and the fourth quarter. Thus above, below, across, and everywhere, and to all as to himself, he dwells pervading the entire world with a mind imbued with loving-kindness, vast, exalted, measureless, without enmity, without ill will. He dwells pervading one quarter with a mind imbued with compassion . . . with a mind imbued with altruistic joy . . . with a mind imbued with equanimity, likewise the second quarter, the third quarter, and the fourth quarter. Thus above, below, across, and everywhere, and to all as to himself, he dwells pervading the entire world with a mind imbued with equanimity, vast, exalted, measureless, without enmity, without ill will. It is in this way that a bhikkhu has attained the state of a brahmā.

(3) "And how has a bhikkhu attained the imperturbable?

Here, with the complete surmounting of perceptions of forms, with the passing away of perceptions of sensory impingement, with non-attention to perceptions of diversity, [perceiving] 'space is infinite,' a bhikkhu enters and dwells in the base of the infinity of space. By completely surmounting the base of the infinity of space, [perceiving] 'consciousness is infinite,' he enters and dwells in the base of the infinity of consciousness. By completely surmounting the base of the infinity of consciousness, [perceiving] 'there is nothing,' he enters and dwells in the base of nothingness. By completely surmounting the base of nothingness, he enters and dwells in the base of neither-perception-nor-non-perception. It is in this way that a bhikkhu has attained the imperturbable.

(4) "And how has a bhikkhu attained the state of a noble one? Here, a bhikkhu understands as it really is: 'This is suffering.' He understands as it really is: 'This is the origin of suffering.' He understands as it really is: 'This is the cessation of suffering.' He understands as it really is: 'This is the way leading to the cessation of suffering.' It is in this way that a bhikkhu has attained the state of a noble one." [185]

V. The Great Chapter

191 (1) Followed by Ear

"Bhikkhus, when one has followed the teachings by ear,[903] recited them verbally, examined them with the mind, and penetrated them well by view, four benefits are to be expected. What four?

(1) "Here, a bhikkhu masters the Dhamma: discourses, mixed prose and verse, expositions, verses, inspired utterances, quotations, birth stories, amazing accounts, and questions-and-answers. He has followed those teachings by ear, recited them verbally, examined them with the mind, and penetrated them well by view. He passes away muddled in mind and is reborn into a certain group of devas. There, the happy ones recite passages of the Dhamma to him.[904] The arising of his memory is sluggish, but then that being quickly reaches distinction. This is the first benefit to be expected when one has followed the teachings by ear, recited them verbally, examined them with the mind, and penetrated them well by view.

(2) "Again, a bhikkhu masters the Dhamma: discourses . . . and questions-and-answers. He has followed those teachings by ear, recited them verbally, examined them with the mind, and penetrated them well by view. He passes away muddled in mind and is reborn into a certain group of devas. There, the happy ones do not recite passages of the Dhamma to him, but a bhikkhu with psychic potency who has attained mastery of mind teaches the Dhamma to an assembly of devas. It occurs to him: 'This is the Dhamma and discipline in which I formerly lived the spiritual life.' The arising of his memory is sluggish, but then that being quickly reaches distinction. Suppose a man were skilled in the sound of a kettledrum. While traveling along a highway he might hear the sound of a kettledrum and would not be at all perplexed or uncertain about the sound; rather, he would conclude: 'That is the sound of a kettledrum.' So too, a bhikkhu masters the Dhamma [186] . . . The arising of his memory is sluggish, but then that being quickly reaches distinction. This is the second benefit to be expected when one has followed the teachings by ear, recited them verbally, examined them with the mind, and penetrated them well by view.

(3) "Again, a bhikkhu masters the Dhamma: discourses . . . and questions-and-answers. He has followed those teachings by ear, recited them verbally, examined them with the mind, and penetrated them well by view. He passes away muddled in mind and is reborn into a certain group of devas. There, the happy ones do not recite passages of the Dhamma to him, nor does a bhikkhu with psychic potency who has attained mastery of mind teach the Dhamma to an assembly of devas. However, a young deva teaches the Dhamma to an assembly of devas. It occurs to him: 'This is the Dhamma and discipline in which I formerly lived the spiritual life.' The arising of his memory is sluggish, but then that being quickly reaches distinction. Suppose a man were skilled in the sound of a conch. While traveling along a highway he might hear the sound of a conch and he would not be at all perplexed or uncertain about the sound; rather, he would conclude: 'That is the sound of a conch.' So too, a bhikkhu masters the Dhamma . . . The arising of his memory is sluggish, but then that being quickly reaches distinction. This is the third benefit to be expected when one has followed the teachings by ear, recited them verbally, examined them with the mind, and penetrated them well by view.

(4) "Again, a bhikkhu masters the Dhamma: discourses . . . and questions-and-answers. He has followed those teachings by ear, recited them verbally, examined them with the mind, and penetrated them well by view. He passes away muddled in mind and is reborn into a certain group of devas. There, the happy ones do not recite passages of the Dhamma to him, nor does a bhikkhu with psychic potency who has attained mastery of mind teach the Dhamma to an assembly of devas, nor does a young deva teach the Dhamma to an assembly of devas. However, one being who has been spontaneously reborn reminds another who has been spontaneously reborn: 'Do you remember, dear sir? Do you remember where we formerly lived the spiritual life?' The other says: 'I remember, dear sir. I remember.' The arising of his memory is sluggish, but then that being quickly reaches distinction. Suppose there were two friends who had played together in the mud. By chance they would meet one another later in life. Then one friend would say to the other: 'Do you remember this, friend? Do you remember that, friend?' And the other would say: [187] 'I remember, friend. I remember.' So too, a bhikkhu masters the Dhamma . . . The arising of his memory is sluggish, but then that being quickly reaches distinction. This is the fourth benefit to be expected when one has followed the teachings by ear, recited them verbally, examined them with the mind, and penetrated them well by view.

"These are the four benefits to be expected when one has followed the teachings by ear, recited them verbally, examined them with the mind, and penetrated them well by view."

192 (2) Facts

"Bhikkhus, four facts [about people] can be known from four [other] facts. What four?

(1) "By dwelling together their virtuous behavior can be known, and this only after a long time, not casually; by one who is attentive, not by one who is inattentive; and by one who is wise, not by one who is unwise.

(2) "By dealing [with them] their integrity can be known, and this only after a long time, not casually; by one who is attentive, not by one who is inattentive; and by one who is wise, not by one who is unwise.

(3) "In misfortune their fortitude can be known, and this only

after a long time, not casually; by one who is attentive, not by one who is inattentive; and by one who is wise, not by one who is unwise.

(4) "By conversation their wisdom can be known, and this only after a long time, not casually; by one who is attentive, not by one who is inattentive; and by one who is wise, not by one who is unwise.

(1) "It was said: 'By dwelling together their virtuous behavior can be known, and this only after a long time, not casually; by one who is attentive, not by one who is inattentive; and by one who is wise, not by one who is unwise.' On account of what was this said?

"Here, bhikkhus, by dwelling together with another person, one comes to know him thus: 'For a long time this venerable one's conduct has been broken, flawed, blemished, and blotched, and he does not consistently observe and follow virtuous behavior. This venerable one is immoral, not virtuous.'

"But in another case, by dwelling together with another person, one comes to know him thus: 'For a long time this venerable one's conduct has been unbroken, flawless, unblemished, and unblotched, [188] and he consistently observes and follows virtuous behavior. This venerable one is virtuous, not immoral.'

"It was on account of this that it was said: 'By dwelling together their virtuous behavior can be known, and this only after a long time, not casually; by one who is attentive, not by one who is inattentive; and by one who is wise, not by one who is unwise.'

(2) "Further it was said: 'By dealing [with them] their integrity can be known, and this only after a long time, not casually; by one who is attentive, not by one who is inattentive; and by one who is wise, not by one who is unwise.' On account of what was this said?

"Here, bhikkhus, when dealing with a person, one comes to know him thus: 'This venerable one deals with one person in one way, in another way if he deals with two, in still another way if he deals with three, and in still another way if he deals with many. His dealings in one case deviate from his dealings in another.[905] This venerable one is impure in his dealings with others, not pure in such dealings.'

"But in another case, when dealing with a person, one comes to know him thus: 'In the same way as he deals with one, he deals with two, three, or many. His dealings in one case do not deviate from his dealings in another. This venerable one is pure in his dealings with others, not impure in such dealings.'

"It was on account of this that it was said: 'By dealing [with them] their integrity can be known, and this only after a long time, not casually; by one who is attentive, not by one who is inattentive; and by one who is wise, not by one who is unwise.'

(3) "Further it was said: 'In misfortune their fortitude can be known, and this only after a long time, not casually; by one who is attentive, not by one who is inattentive; and by one who is wise, not by one who is unwise.' On account of what was this said?

"Here, bhikkhus, someone is afflicted with the loss of relatives, wealth, or health, but he does not reflect thus: 'Human life in the world is of such a nature[906] that the eight worldly conditions revolve around the world, and the world revolves around these eight worldly conditions, namely, gain and loss, disrepute and fame, blame and praise, and pleasure and pain.' Thus when afflicted with loss of relatives, wealth, or health, he sorrows, languishes, and laments; he weeps beating his breast and becomes confused.

"But in another case, someone is afflicted with the loss of relatives, [189] wealth, or health, but he does reflect thus: 'Human life in the world is such that the eight worldly conditions revolve around the world, and the world revolves around these eight worldly conditions, namely, gain and loss, disrepute and fame, blame and praise, and pleasure and pain.' Thus when afflicted with the loss of relatives, wealth, or health, he does not sorrow, languish, and lament; he does not weep beating his breast and become confused.

"It was on account of this that it was said: 'In misfortune their fortitude can be known, and this only after a long time, not casually; by one who is attentive, not by one who is inattentive; and by one who is wise, not by one who is unwise.'

(4) "Further it was said: 'By conversation their wisdom can be known, and this only after a long time, not casually; by one who is attentive, not by one who is inattentive; and by one

who is wise, not by one who is unwise.' On account of what was this said?

"Here, bhikkhus, when conversing with someone, one comes to know: 'Judging from the way this venerable one initiates, formulates, and poses a question, he is unwise, not wise. For what reason? This venerable one does not speak about matters that are deep, peaceful, sublime, beyond the sphere of reasoning, subtle, comprehensible to the wise. When this venerable one speaks on the Dhamma, he is not able to explain, teach, describe, establish, reveal, analyze, and explicate its meaning either briefly or in detail. This venerable one is unwise, not wise.' Just as if a man with good sight, standing on the bank of a pond, were to see a small fish emerging, he would think: 'Judging from the way this fish emerges, from the ripples it makes, and from its force, this is a small fish, not a big one,' so too, when conversing with a person, one comes to know: 'Judging from the way this venerable one initiates, formulates, and poses a question, he is unwise, not wise.'

"But in another case, when conversing with someone, one comes to know: 'Judging from the way this venerable one initiates, formulates, and poses a question, he is wise, not unwise. For what reason? This venerable one speaks about matters that are deep, peaceful, sublime, beyond the sphere of reasoning, subtle, comprehensible to the wise. When this venerable one speaks on the Dhamma, he is able to explain, teach, describe, establish, reveal, analyze, and explicate its meaning both briefly and in detail. This venerable one is wise, not unwise.' Just as if a man with good sight, standing on the bank of a pond, were to see a big fish emerging, [190] he would think: 'Judging from the way this fish emerges, from the ripples it makes, and from its force, this is a big fish, not a small one,' so too, when conversing with someone, one comes to know: 'Judging from the way this venerable one initiates, formulates, and poses a question, he is wise, not unwise.'

"It was on account of this that it was said: 'By conversation their wisdom can be known, and this only after a long time, not casually; by one who is attentive, not by one who is inattentive; and by one who is wise, not by one who is unwise.'

"These, bhikkhus, are the four facts [about people] that can be known from four [other] facts."

193 (3) Bhaddiya

On one occasion the Blessed One was dwelling at Vesālī in the hall with the peaked roof in the Great Wood. Then Bhaddiya the Licchavi approached the Blessed One, paid homage to him, sat down to one side, and said to him:

"Bhante, I have heard this: 'The ascetic Gotama is a magician who knows a converting magic by which he converts the disciples of teachers of other sects.' Do those who speak thus state what has been said by the Blessed One and not misrepresent him with what is contrary to fact? Do they explain in accordance with the Dhamma so that they do not incur any reasonable criticism or ground for censure? For we do not want to misrepresent the Blessed One."[907] [191]

"Come, Bhaddiya, do not go by oral tradition, by lineage of teaching, by hearsay, by a collection of scriptures, by logical reasoning, by inferential reasoning, by reasoned cogitation, by the acceptance of a view after pondering it, by the seeming competence [of a speaker], or because you think: 'The ascetic is our guru.' But when you know for yourself: 'These things are unwholesome; these things are blameworthy; these things are censured by the wise; these things, if accepted and undertaken, lead to harm and suffering,' then you should abandon them.[908]

(1) "What do you think, Bhaddiya? When greed arises in a person, is it for his welfare or for his harm?"

"For his harm, Bhante."

"Bhaddiya, a greedy person, overcome by greed, with mind obsessed by it, destroys life, takes what is not given, transgresses with another's wife, and speaks falsehood; and he encourages others to do likewise. Will that lead to his harm and suffering for a long time?"

"Yes, Bhante."

(2) "What do you think, Bhaddiya? When hatred . . . (3) . . . delusion . . . (4) . . . vehemence arises in a person, is it for his welfare or for his harm?"[909]

"For his harm, Bhante."

"Bhaddiya, a vehement person, overcome and with mind obsessed by vehemence, destroys life . . . and he encourages others to do likewise. Will that lead to his harm and suffering for a long time?"

"Yes, Bhante."

"What do you think, Bhaddiya? Are these things wholesome or unwholesome?" – "Unwholesome, Bhante." – "Blameworthy or blameless?" – "Blameworthy, Bhante." – "Censured or praised by the wise?" – "Censured by the wise, Bhante." – "Accepted and undertaken, do they lead to harm and suffering or not, or how do you take it?" – "Accepted and undertaken, these things lead to harm and suffering. So we take it."

"Thus, Bhaddiya, when we said: 'Come, Bhaddiya, do not go by oral tradition . . . [192] . . . But when you know for yourself: "These things are unwholesome; these things are blameworthy; these things are censured by the wise; these things, if undertaken and practiced, lead to harm and suffering," then you should abandon them,' it is because of this that this was said.

"Come, Bhaddiya, do not go by oral tradition, by lineage of teaching, by hearsay, by a collection of texts, by logical reasoning, by inferential reasoning, by reasoned cogitation, by the acceptance of a view after pondering it, by the seeming competence [of a speaker], or because you think: 'The ascetic is our guru.' But when you know for yourself: 'These things are wholesome; these things are blameless; these things are praised by the wise; these things, if accepted and undertaken, lead to welfare and happiness,' then you should live in accordance with them.

(1) "What do you think, Bhaddiya? When non-greed arises in a person, is it for his welfare or for his harm?"

"For his welfare, Bhante."

"Bhaddiya, a person without greed, not overcome by greed, his mind not obsessed by it, does not destroy life, take what is not given, transgress with another's wife, or speak falsehood; nor does he encourage others to do likewise. Will that lead to his welfare and happiness for a long time?"

"Yes, Bhante."

(2) "What do you think, Bhaddiya? When non-hatred . . . (3) . . . non-delusion . . . (4) . . . non-vehemence arises in a person, is it for his welfare or his harm?"

"For his welfare, Bhante."

"Bhaddiya, a non-vehement person, not overcome by vehemence, his mind not obsessed by it, does not destroy life . . . nor does he encourage others to do likewise. Will that lead to his welfare and happiness for a long time?"

"Yes, Bhante."

"What do you think, Bhaddiya? Are these things wholesome or unwholesome?" – "Wholesome, Bhante." – "Blameworthy or blameless?" – "Blameless, Bhante." – "Censured or praised by the wise?" – "Praised by the wise, Bhante." [193] – "Accepted and undertaken, do they lead to welfare and happiness or not, or how do you take it?" – "Accepted and undertaken, these things lead to welfare and happiness. So we take it."

"Thus, Bhaddiya, when we said: 'Come, Bhaddiya, do not go by oral tradition . . . But when you know for yourself: "These things are wholesome; these things are blameless; these things are praised by the wise; these things, if accepted and undertaken, lead to welfare and happiness," then you should live in accordance with them,' it is because of this that this was said.

"Bhaddiya, the good persons in the world encourage their disciples thus: 'Come, good man, you should constantly remove greed.[910] When you constantly remove greed, you will not do any action born of greed, whether by body, speech, or mind. You should constantly remove hatred. When you constantly remove hatred, you will not do any action born of hatred, whether by body, speech, or mind. You should constantly remove delusion. When you constantly remove delusion, you will not do any action born of delusion, whether by body, speech, or mind. You should constantly remove vehemence. When you constantly remove vehemence, you will not do any action born of vehemence, whether by body, speech, or mind.'"

When this was said, Bhaddiya the Licchavi said to the Blessed One: "Excellent, Bhante! . . . [as at 4:111] . . . Let the Blessed One consider me a lay follower who from today has gone for refuge for life."

"Now, Bhaddiya, did I say to you: 'Come, Bhaddiya, be my disciple and I will be your teacher?'"

"Surely not, Bhante."

"But, Bhaddiya, though I speak thus and declare [my teaching] in such a way, some ascetics and brahmins untruthfully, baselessly, falsely, and wrongly misrepresent me when they say: 'The ascetic Gotama is a magician who knows a converting magic by which he converts the disciples of teachers of other sects.'" [194]

"Excellent is that converting magic, Bhante! Good is that converting magic! If my beloved relatives and family members would be converted by this conversion, that would lead to their welfare and happiness for a long time. If all khattiyas would be converted by this conversion, that would lead to their welfare and happiness for a long time. If all brahmins . . . vessas . . . suddas would be converted by this conversion, that would lead to their welfare and happiness for a long time."[911]

"So it is, Bhaddiya, so it is! If all khattiyas would be converted by this conversion toward the abandoning of unwholesome qualities and the acquisition of wholesome qualities, that would lead to their welfare and happiness for a long time. If all brahmins . . . vessas . . . suddas would be converted by this conversion toward the abandoning of unwholesome qualities and the acquisition of wholesome qualities, that would lead to their welfare and happiness for a long time. If the world with its devas, Māra, and Brahmā, this population with its ascetics and brahmins, its devas and humans, would be converted by this conversion toward the abandoning of unwholesome qualities and the acquisition of wholesome qualities, that would lead to the welfare and happiness of the world for a long time. If these great sal trees would be converted by this conversion toward the abandoning of unwholesome qualities and the acquisition of wholesome qualities, that would lead to the welfare and happiness even of these great sal trees for a long time, if they could choose.[912] How much more then for a human being!"

194 (4) Sāpūga

On one occasion the Venerable Ānanda was dwelling among the Koliyans near the Koliyan town named Sāpūga. Then a number of young Koliyans from Sāpūga approached the Venerable Ānanda, paid homage to him, and sat down to one side. The Venerable Ānanda then said to them:

"Byagghapajjas, there are these four factors of striving for purity[913] that the Blessed One, the Arahant, the Perfectly Enlightened One, knowing and seeing, [195] has rightly expounded for the purification of beings, for the overcoming of sorrow and lamentation, for the passing away of pain and dejection, for the achievement of the method, for the realization of nibbāna. What four? The factor of striving for purity of virtuous behavior, the factor of striving for purity of mind, the factor of striving for purity of view, and the factor of striving for purity of liberation.[914]

(1) "And what, Byagghapajjas, is the factor of striving for purity of virtuous behavior? Here, a bhikkhu is virtuous . . . [as at 4:181] . . . he trains in them. This is called purity of virtuous behavior. The desire, effort, zeal, enthusiasm, indefatigability, mindfulness, and clear comprehension [applied with the intention]: 'In just such a way I will fulfill purity of virtuous behavior that I have not yet fulfilled or assist with wisdom in various respects purity of virtuous behavior that I have fulfilled'[915]—this is called the factor of striving for purity of virtuous behavior.

(2) "And what, Byagghapajjas, is the factor of striving for purity of mind? Here, secluded from sensual pleasures . . . a bhikkhu enters and dwells in the fourth jhāna. This is called purity of mind. The desire, effort, zeal, enthusiasm, indefatigability, mindfulness, and clear comprehension [applied with the intention]: 'In just such a way I will fulfill purity of mind that I have not yet fulfilled or assist with wisdom in various respects purity of mind that I have fulfilled'—this is called the factor of striving for purity of mind.

(3) "And what, Byagghapajjas, is the factor of striving for purity of view? Here, a bhikkhu understands as it really is: 'This is suffering' . . . 'This is the way leading to the cessation of suffering.' This is called purity of view.[916] The desire, effort, zeal, enthusiasm, indefatigability, mindfulness, and clear comprehension [applied with the intention]: 'In just such a way I will fulfill purity of view that I have not yet fulfilled or assist with wisdom in various respects purity of view that I have fulfilled'—this is called the factor of striving for purity of view.

(4) "And what, Byagghapajjas, is the factor of striving for purity of liberation? That same noble disciple, possessing this factor of striving for purity of virtuous behavior, [196] this factor of striving for purity of mind, and this factor of striving for purity of view, detaches his mind from the things that cause attachment and emancipates his mind through the things that bring emancipation. He thereby reaches right liberation. This is called purity of liberation.[917] The desire, effort, zeal, enthusiasm, indefatigability, mindfulness, and clear comprehension [applied with the intention]: 'In just such a way I will fulfill purity of liberation that I have not yet fulfilled or assist with wisdom in various respects purity of liberation that I have fulfilled'—this is called the factor of striving for purity of liberation.

"These, Byagghapajjas, are the four factors of striving for

purity that the Blessed One, the Arahant, the Perfectly Enlightened One, knowing and seeing, has rightly expounded for the purification of beings, for the overcoming of sorrow and lamentation, for the passing away of pain and dejection, for the achievement of the method, for the realization of nibbāna."

195 (5) Vappa

On one occasion the Blessed One was dwelling among the Sakyans at Kapilavatthu in the Banyan Tree Park. Then Vappa the Sakyan, a disciple of the Nigaṇṭhas, approached the Venerable Mahāmoggallāna, paid homage to him, and sat down to one side. The Venerable Mahāmoggallāna then said to him:

"Here, Vappa, if one is restrained by body, speech, and mind, then, with the fading away of ignorance and the arising of true knowledge, do you see anything on account of which taints productive of painful feeling might flow in upon such a person in future lives?"

"I do see such a possibility, Bhante. In the past one did an evil deed whose result has not yet ripened. On that account taints productive of painful feeling might flow in upon a person in some future life."[918]

While this conversation between the Venerable Mahāmoggallāna and Vappa the Sakyan was underway, in the evening the Blessed One emerged from seclusion [197] and went to the attendance hall. He sat down on the appointed seat and said to the Venerable Mahāmoggallāna: "What, Moggallāna, was the discussion that you were engaged in just now? And what was the conversation of yours that was underway?"

[The Venerable Mahāmoggallāna here relates his entire conversation with Vappa the Sakyan, concluding:]

"This, Bhante, was the conversation I was having with Vappa the Sakyan when the Blessed One arrived."

Then the Blessed One said to Vappa the Sakyan: "If, Vappa, you would admit what should be admitted and reject what should be rejected; and if, when you do not understand the meaning of my words, you would question me about them further, saying: 'How is this, Bhante? What is the meaning of this?'; then we might discuss this."

"Bhante, I will admit to the Blessed One what should be admitted and reject what should be rejected; and when I do not understand the meaning of his words, I will question him about them further, saying: 'How is this, Bhante? What is the meaning of this?' So let's discuss this."

(1) "What do you think, Vappa? Those taints, distressing and feverish, that might arise because of bodily undertakings do not occur when one refrains from them. He does not create any new kamma and he terminates the old kamma having contacted it again and again.[919] [198] The wearing away is directly visible, immediate, inviting one to come and see, applicable, to be personally experienced by the wise. Do you see, Vappa, anything on account of which taints productive of painful feeling might flow in upon such a person in future lives?"

"No, Bhante."

(2) "What do you think, Vappa? Those taints, distressing and feverish, that might arise because of verbal undertakings do not occur when one refrains from them. He does not create any new kamma and he terminates the old kamma having contacted it again and again. The wearing away is directly visible, immediate, inviting one to come and see, applicable, to be personally experienced by the wise. Do you see, Vappa, anything on account of which taints productive of painful feeling might flow in upon such a person in future lives?"

"No, Bhante."

(3) "What do you think, Vappa? Those taints, distressing and feverish, that might arise because of mental undertakings do not occur when one refrains from them. He does not create any new kamma and he terminates the old kamma having contacted it again and again. The wearing away is directly visible, immediate, inviting one to come and see, applicable, to be personally experienced by the wise. Do you see, Vappa, anything on account of which taints productive of painful feeling might flow in upon such a person in future lives?"

"No, Bhante."

(4) "What do you think, Vappa? With the fading away of ignorance and the arising of true knowledge, those taints, distressing and feverish, that arise with ignorance as condition no longer occur. He does not create any new kamma and he terminates the old kamma having contacted it again and again. The wearing away is directly visible, immediate, inviting one to come and see, applicable, to be personally experienced by the

wise. Do you see, Vappa, anything on account of which taints productive of painful feeling might flow in upon such a person in future lives?"

"No, Bhante."

"A bhikkhu thus perfectly liberated in mind, Vappa, achieves six constant dwellings. Having seen a form with the eye, he is neither joyful nor saddened, but dwells equanimous, mindful and clearly comprehending.[920] Having heard a sound with the ear . . . Having smelled an odor with the nose . . . Having experienced a taste with the tongue . . . Having felt a tactile object with the body . . . Having cognized a mental phenomenon with the mind, he is neither joyful nor saddened, but dwells equanimous, mindful and clearly comprehending.

"When he feels a feeling terminating with the body, he understands: 'I feel a feeling terminating with the body.' When he feels a feeling terminating with life, he understands: 'I feel a feeling terminating with life.' He understands: 'With the breakup of the body, following the exhaustion of life, all that is felt, not being delighted in, will become cool right here.'[921]

"Suppose, Vappa, a shadow is seen on account of a stump. Then [199] a man would come along bringing a shovel and a basket. He would cut down the stump at its foot, dig it up, and pull out the roots, even the fine rootlets and root-fibers. He would cut the stump into pieces, split the pieces, and reduce them to slivers. Then he would dry the slivers in the wind and sun, burn them in a fire, and reduce them to ashes. Having done so, he would winnow the ashes in a strong wind or let them be carried away by the swift current of a river. Thus the shadow that depended on that stump would be cut off at the root, made like a palm stump, obliterated so that it is no more subject to future arising.[922]

"So too, Vappa, a bhikkhu thus perfectly liberated in mind achieves six constant dwellings. Having seen a form with the eye . . . Having cognized a mental phenomenon with the mind, he is neither joyful nor saddened, but dwells equanimous, mindful and clearly comprehending. When he feels a feeling terminating with the body, he understands . . . 'With the breakup of the body, following the exhaustion of life, all that is felt, not being delighted in, will become cool right here.'"

When this was said, Vappa the Sakyan, a disciple of the

Nigaṇṭhas, said to the Blessed One: "Suppose, Bhante, there was a man in quest of profit who raised horses for sale, but he would not gain a profit and instead would only reap weariness and distress. Just so, in quest of profit, I attended upon the foolish Nigaṇṭhas, but I did not gain a profit and instead only reaped weariness and distress. Starting today, whatever confidence I had in the foolish Nigaṇṭhas, I winnow in a strong wind or let it be carried away by the current of a river.

"Excellent, Bhante! . . . [200] . . . Let the Blessed One consider me as a lay follower who from today has gone for refuge for life."

196 (6) Sāḷha

On one occasion the Blessed One was dwelling at Vesālī in the hall with the peaked roof in the Great Wood. Then Sāḷha the Licchavi and Abhaya the Licchavi approached the Blessed One, paid homage to him, and sat down to one side. Sāḷha the Licchavi then said to the Blessed One:

"Bhante, there are some ascetics and brahmins who proclaim the crossing of the flood through two things: by means of purification of virtuous behavior and by means of austerity and disgust.[923] What does the Blessed One say about this?"

"I say, Sāḷha, that purification of virtuous behavior is one of the factors of asceticism. But those ascetics and brahmins who advocate austerity and disgust, who regard austerity and disgust as the essence, and who adhere to austerity and disgust are incapable of crossing the flood.[924] Also, those ascetics and brahmins whose bodily, verbal, and mental behavior are impure, and whose livelihood is impure, are incapable of knowledge and vision, of unsurpassed enlightenment.

"Suppose, Sāḷha, a man desiring to cross a river were to take a sharp axe and enter a grove. There he would see a large sal sapling, straight, fresh, without a fruit-bud core. He would cut it down at its root, cut off the top, completely strip off the branches and foliage, trim it with axes, trim it further with hatchets, scrape it with a scraping tool, polish it with a stone ball, and set out to cross the river. What do you think, Sāḷha? Could that man cross the river?"

"No, Bhante. For what reason? Because although that sal sapling has been thoroughly prepared externally, [201] it has not been purified within. It can be expected that the sal sapling will sink and the man will meet with calamity and disaster."

"So too, Sāḷha, those ascetics and brahmins who advocate austerity and disgust, who regard austerity and disgust as the essence, and who adhere to austerity and disgust are incapable of crossing the flood. Also, those ascetics and brahmins whose bodily, verbal, and mental behavior are impure, and whose livelihood is impure, are incapable of knowledge and vision, of unsurpassed enlightenment.

"But, Sāḷha, those ascetics and brahmins who do not advocate austerity and disgust, who do not regard austerity and disgust as the essence, and who do not adhere to austerity and disgust are capable of crossing the flood. Also, those ascetics and brahmins whose bodily, verbal, and mental behavior are pure, and whose livelihood is pure, are capable of knowledge and vision, of unsurpassed enlightenment.

"Suppose, Sāḷha, a man desiring to cross a river were to take a sharp axe and enter a grove. There he would see a large sal sapling, straight, fresh, without a fruit-bud core. He would cut it down at its root, cut off the top, completely strip off the branches and foliage, trim it with axes, trim it further with hatchets, take a chisel and thoroughly cleanse it within, scrape it with a scraping tool, polish it with a stone ball, and make it into a boat. Then he would equip it with oars and a rudder and set out to cross the river. What do you think, Sāḷha? Could that man cross the river?"

"Yes, Bhante. For what reason? Because that sal sapling has been thoroughly prepared externally, well purified within, made into a boat, and equipped with oars and a rudder. It can be expected that the sal sapling will not sink and the man will safely reach the other shore."

(1) "So too, Sāḷha, those ascetics and brahmins who do not advocate austerity and disgust, who do not regard austerity and disgust as the essence, and who do not adhere to austerity and disgust are capable of crossing the flood. Also, those ascetics and brahmins [202] whose bodily, verbal, and mental behavior are pure, and whose livelihood is pure, are capable of knowledge and vision, of unsurpassed enlightenment.

"Even though a warrior knows many different feats that can be done with arrows, it is only if he possesses three qualities that he is worthy of a king, an accessory of a king, and reckoned a factor of kingship. What three? He is a long-distance shooter, a sharp-shooter, and one who splits a great body.

(2) "Just as the warrior is a long-distance shooter, so too the noble disciple has right concentration. Whatever kind of form there is—whether past, future, or present, internal or external, gross or subtle, inferior or superior, far or near—a noble disciple with right concentration sees all form as it really is with correct wisdom thus: 'This is not mine, this I am not, this is not my self.' Whatever kind of feeling there is . . . Whatever kind of perception there is . . . Whatever kind of volitional activities there are . . . Whatever kind of consciousness there is—whether past, future, or present, internal or external, gross or subtle, inferior or superior, far or near—a noble disciple with right concentration sees all consciousness as it really is with correct wisdom thus: 'This is not mine, this I am not, this is not my self.'

(3) "Just as the warrior is a sharp-shooter, so too the noble disciple has right view. The noble disciple with right view understands as it really is: 'This is suffering.' He understands as it really is: 'This is the origin of suffering.' He understands as it really is: 'This is the cessation of suffering.' He understands as it really is: 'This is the way leading to the cessation of suffering.'

(4) "Just as the warrior splits a great body, so too the noble disciple has right liberation. The noble disciple with right liberation has split the great mass of ignorance."[925]

197 (7) Mallikā

On one occasion the Blessed One was dwelling at Sāvatthī, in Jeta's Grove, Anāthapiṇḍika's Park. Then Queen Mallikā approached the Blessed One, paid homage to him, sat down to one side, and said to him:[926] [203]

(1) "Bhante, why is it that some women here are (i) ugly, ill formed, and unsightly; (ii) poor, destitute, and indigent; and (iii) lacking in influence? (2) And why is it that some are (i) ugly, ill formed, and unsightly; but (ii) rich, with great wealth and property; and (iii) influential? (3) And why is it that some women here are (i) beautiful, attractive, and graceful, possessing supreme beauty of complexion; but (ii) poor, destitute, and indigent; and (iii) lacking in influence? (4) And why is it that some are (i) beautiful, attractive, and graceful, possessing

supreme beauty of complexion; (ii) rich, with great wealth and property; and (iii) influential?"

(1) "Here, Mallikā, (i) some woman is prone to anger and easily exasperated. Even if she is criticized slightly she loses her temper and becomes irritated, hostile, and stubborn; she displays anger, hatred, and bitterness. (ii) She does not give things to ascetics or brahmins: food and drink; clothing and vehicles; garlands, scents, and unguents; bedding, dwellings, and lighting. (iii) And she is envious, one who envies, resents, and begrudges the gain, honor, respect, esteem, homage, and worship given to others. When she passes away from that state, if she comes back to this world, wherever she is reborn (i) she is ugly, ill formed, and unsightly; (ii) poor, destitute, and indigent; and (iii) lacking in influence.

(2) "Another woman is (i) prone to anger and easily exasperated.... (ii) But she gives things to ascetics or brahmins.... (iii) And she is without envy, one who does not envy, resent, or begrudge the gain, honor, respect, esteem, homage, and worship given to others. When she passes away from that state, if she comes back to this world, wherever [204] she is reborn (i) she is ugly, ill formed, and unsightly; (ii) but she is rich, with great wealth and property; and (iii) influential.

(3) "Still another woman is (i) not prone to anger or often exasperated. Even if she is criticized a lot she does not lose her temper and become irritated, hostile, and stubborn; she does not display anger, hatred, and bitterness. (ii) But she does not give things to ascetics or brahmins.... (iii) And she is envious, one who envies, resents, and begrudges the gain, honor, respect, esteem, homage, and worship given to others. When she passes away from that state, if she comes back to this world, wherever she is reborn (i) she is beautiful, attractive, and graceful, possessing supreme beauty of complexion; (ii) but she is poor, destitute, with little wealth; (iii) and lacking in influence.

(4) "And still another woman is (i) not prone to anger or often exasperated.... (ii) And she gives things to ascetics or brahmins.... (iii) And she is without envy, one who does not envy, resent, or begrudge the gain, honor, respect, esteem, homage, and worship given to others. When she passes away from that state, if she comes back to this world, wherever she is reborn (i) she is beautiful, attractive, and graceful, possessing supreme

beauty of complexion; (ii) rich, with great wealth and property; and (iii) influential.

"This, Mallikā, is why some women here are (i) ugly, ill formed, and unsightly; (ii) poor, destitute, and indigent; and (iii) lacking in influence. This is why some are (i) ugly, ill formed, and unsightly; but (ii) rich, with great wealth and property; and (iii) influential. This is why some women here are (i) beautiful, attractive, and graceful, possessing supreme beauty of complexion; but (ii) poor, destitute, and indigent; and (iii) lacking in influence. This is why some are (i) beautiful, attractive, and graceful, possessing supreme beauty of complexion; (ii) rich, with great wealth and property; and (iii) influential."

When this was said, Queen Mallikā said to the Blessed One: "I suppose, Bhante, (i) that in some earlier life I was prone to anger and often exasperated; that even when I was criticized slightly I lost my temper and became irritated, [205] hostile, and stubborn, and displayed anger, hatred, and bitterness. Therefore I am now ugly, ill formed, and unsightly. (ii) But I suppose that in some earlier life I gave things to ascetics or brahmins ... bedding, dwellings, and lighting. Therefore I am now rich, with great wealth and property. (iii) And I suppose that in some earlier life I was without envy, not one who envied, resented, and begrudged the gain, honor, respect, esteem, homage, and worship given to others. Therefore I am now influential. In this court there are girls of khattiya, brahmin, and householder families over whom I exercise command.

"From today, Bhante, (i) I will not be prone to anger and often exasperated. Even when I am criticized a lot I will not lose my temper and become irritated, hostile, and stubborn; I will not display anger, hatred, and bitterness. (ii) And I will give things to ascetics or brahmins: food and drink; clothing and vehicles; garlands, scents, and unguents; bedding, dwellings, and lighting. (iii) And I will not be envious, one who envies, resents, and begrudges the gain, honor, respect, esteem, homage, and worship given to others.

"Excellent, Bhante! ... [as at 4:111] ... Let the Blessed One consider me a lay follower who from today has gone for refuge for life."

198 (8) Self-Torment[927]

"Bhikkhus, there are these four kinds of persons found existing in the world. What four? (1) Here, a certain kind of person torments himself and pursues the practice of torturing himself. (2) But another kind of person torments others and pursues the practice of torturing others. (3) Still another kind of person torments himself and pursues the practice of torturing himself, and also torments others and pursues the practice of torturing others. (4) And still another kind of person does not torment himself or pursue the practice of torturing himself, [206] and does not torment others or pursue the practice of torturing others. Since he torments neither himself nor others, in this very life he dwells hungerless, quenched and cooled, experiencing bliss, having himself become divine.[928]

(1) "And how, bhikkhus, is a person one who torments himself and pursues the practice of torturing himself?[929] Here, a certain person goes naked, rejecting conventions, licking his hands, not coming when asked, not stopping when asked; he does not accept food brought or food specially made or an invitation to a meal; he receives nothing from a pot, from a bowl, across a threshold, across a stick, across a pestle, from two eating together, from a pregnant woman, from a woman nursing a child, from a woman being kept by a man, from where food is advertised to be distributed, from where a dog is waiting, from where flies are buzzing; he accepts no fish or meat, he drinks no liquor, wine, or fermented brew. He keeps to one house [on alms round], to one morsel of food; he keeps to two houses, to two morsels . . . he keeps to seven houses, to seven morsels. He lives on one saucer a day, on two saucers a day . . . on seven saucers a day. He takes food once a day, once every two days . . . once every seven days; thus even up to once every fortnight, he dwells pursuing the practice of taking food at stated intervals.

"He is an eater of greens or millet or forest rice or hide-parings or moss or rice bran or rice scum or sesame flour or grass or cow dung. He subsists on forest roots and fruits; he feeds on fallen fruits.

"He wears hemp robes, robes of hemp-mixed cloth, robes made from shrouds, rag-robes, tree bark, antelope hides, strips of antelope hide, robes of *kusa* grass, bark fabric, or wood-shavings fabric; a mantle made of head hair or of animal wool, a covering made of owls' wings.

"He is one who pulls out hair and beard, pursuing the practice of pulling out hair and beard. He is one who stands continuously, rejecting seats. He is one who squats continuously, devoted to maintaining the squatting position. He is one who uses a mattress of thorns; he makes a mattress of thorns his bed. He dwells pursuing the practice of bathing in water three times daily including the evening. [207] Thus in such a variety of ways he dwells pursuing the practice of tormenting and mortifying the body. It is in this way that a person torments himself and pursues the practice of torturing himself.

(2) "And how is a person one who torments others and pursues the practice of torturing others? Here, a certain person is a butcher of sheep, a butcher of pigs, a fowler, a trapper of wild beasts, a hunter, a fisherman, a thief, an executioner,[930] a prison warden, or one who follows any other such bloody occupation. It is in this way that a person is one who torments others and pursues the practice of torturing others.

(3) "And how is a person one who torments himself and pursues the practice of torturing himself and also torments others and pursues the practice of torturing others? Here, some person is a head-anointed khattiya king or an affluent brahmin. Having had a new sacrificial temple built to the east of the city, and having shaved off his hair and beard, dressed himself in rough antelope hide, and greased his body with ghee and oil, scratching his back with a deer's horn, he enters the sacrificial temple together with his chief queen and his brahmin high priest. There he lies down on the bare ground strewn with grass. The king lives on the milk in the first teat of a cow with a calf of the same color while the chief queen lives on the milk in the second teat and the brahmin high priest lives on the milk in the third teat; the milk in the fourth teat they pour onto the fire, and the calf lives on what is left. He says: 'Let so many bulls be slaughtered for sacrifice, let so many bullocks be slaughtered for sacrifice, let so many heifers be slaughtered for sacrifice, let so many goats be slaughtered for sacrifice, let so many sheep be slaughtered for sacrifice, let so many trees be felled for the sacrificial posts, let so much grass be cut for the sacrificial grass.' [208] And then his slaves, messengers, and servants make preparations,

weeping with tearful faces, being spurred on by threats of punishment and by fear. It is in this way that a person is one who torments himself and pursues the practice of torturing himself and who also torments others and pursues the practice of torturing others.

(4) "And how is a person one who does not torment himself or pursue the practice of torturing himself and does not torment others or pursue the practice of torturing others—the one who, since he torments neither himself nor others, in this very life dwells hungerless, quenched and cooled, experiencing bliss, having himself become divine?

"Here, bhikkhus, the Tathāgata arises in the world, an arahant, perfectly enlightened, accomplished in true knowledge and conduct, fortunate, knower of the world, unsurpassed trainer of persons to be tamed, teacher of devas and humans, the Enlightened One, the Blessed One. Having realized with his own direct knowledge this world with its devas, Māra, and Brahmā, this population with its ascetics and brahmins, with its devas and humans, he makes it known to others. He teaches the Dhamma that is good in the beginning, good in the middle, and good in the end, with the right meaning and phrasing; he reveals the perfectly complete and pure spiritual life.

"A householder or householder's son or one born in some other clan hears this Dhamma. He then acquires faith in the Tathāgata and considers thus: 'Household life is crowded and dusty; life gone forth is wide open. It is not easy, while living at home, to lead the spiritual life that is utterly perfect and pure as a polished conch shell. Suppose I shave off my hair and beard, put on ochre robes, and go forth from the household life into homelessness.' On a later occasion, having abandoned a small or a large fortune, having abandoned a small or a large circle of relatives, he shaves off his hair and beard, puts on ochre robes, and goes forth from the household life into homelessness.

"Having thus gone forth and possessing the bhikkhus' training and way of life, having abandoned the destruction of life, he abstains from the destruction of life; with the rod and weapon laid aside, conscientious and kindly, he dwells compassionate toward all living beings. Having abandoned the taking of what is not given, he abstains from taking what is not given; [209] he takes only what is given, expects only what is given, and dwells honestly without thoughts of theft. Having abandoned sexual activity, he observes celibacy, living apart, abstaining from sexual intercourse, the common person's practice.

"Having abandoned false speech, he abstains from false speech; he speaks truth, adheres to truth; he is trustworthy and reliable, no deceiver of the world. Having abandoned divisive speech, he abstains from divisive speech; he does not repeat elsewhere what he has heard here in order to divide [those people] from these, nor does he repeat to these what he has heard elsewhere in order to divide [these people] from those; thus he is one who reunites those who are divided, a promoter of unity, who enjoys concord, rejoices in concord, delights in concord, a speaker of words that promote concord. Having abandoned harsh speech, he abstains from harsh speech; he speaks words that are gentle, pleasing to the ear, lovable, words that go to the heart, courteous words that are desired by many people and agreeable to many people. Having abandoned idle chatter, he abstains from idle chatter; he speaks at a proper time, speaks what is truthful, speaks what is beneficial, speaks on the Dhamma and the discipline; at the proper time he speaks such words as are worth recording, reasonable, succinct, and beneficial.

"He abstains from injuring seeds and plants. He eats once a day,[931] abstaining from eating at night and outside the proper time. He abstains from dancing, singing, instrumental music, and unsuitable shows. He abstains from adorning and beautifying himself by wearing garlands and applying scents and unguents. He abstains from high and large beds. He abstains from accepting gold and silver, raw grain, raw meat, women and girls, men and women slaves, goats and sheep, fowl and pigs, elephants, cattle, horses, and mares, fields and land. He abstains from going on errands and running messages; from buying and selling; from cheating with weights, metals, and measures; from accepting bribes, deceiving, defrauding, and trickery. He abstains from wounding, murdering, binding, brigandage, plunder, and violence.

"He is content with robes to protect his body and almsfood to maintain his stomach, and wherever he goes he sets out taking only these with him. Just as a bird, wherever it goes, [210] flies with its wings as its only burden, so too, a bhikkhu is content with robes to protect his body and almsfood to maintain his stomach, and wherever he goes he sets out taking only these with him. Possessing this aggregate of noble virtuous behavior, he experiences blameless bliss within himself.

"Having seen a form with the eye, he does not grasp at its marks and features. Since, if he left the eye faculty unrestrained, bad unwholesome states of longing and dejection might invade him, he practices restraint over it; he guards the eye faculty, he undertakes the restraint of the eye faculty. Having heard a sound with the ear . . . Having smelled an odor with the nose . . . Having tasted a taste with the tongue . . . Having felt a tactile object with the body . . . Having cognized a mental phenomenon with the mind, he does not grasp at its marks and features. Since, if he left the mind faculty unrestrained, bad unwholesome states of longing and dejection might invade him, he practices restraint over it; he guards the mind faculty, he undertakes the restraint of the mind faculty. Possessing this noble restraint of the faculties, he experiences unsullied bliss within himself.

"He acts with clear comprehension when going forward and returning; he acts with clear comprehension when looking ahead and looking away; he acts with clear comprehension when bending and stretching his limbs; he acts with clear comprehension when wearing his robes and carrying his outer robe and bowl; he acts with clear comprehension when eating, drinking, consuming food, and tasting; he acts with clear comprehension when defecating and urinating; he acts with clear comprehension when walking, standing, sitting, falling asleep, waking up, talking, and keeping silent.

"Possessing this aggregate of noble virtuous behavior, and this noble restraint of the faculties, and this noble mindfulness and clear comprehension, he resorts to a secluded lodging: the forest, the root of a tree, a mountain, a ravine, a hillside cave, a charnel ground, a jungle thicket, an open space, a heap of straw.

"After his meal, on returning from his alms round, he sits down, folding his legs crosswise, straightening his body, and establishing mindfulness in front of him. Having abandoned longing for the world, he dwells with a mind free from longing; he purifies his mind from longing. Having abandoned ill will and hatred, he dwells with a mind free from ill will, compassionate toward all living beings; he purifies his mind from ill will and hatred. Having abandoned dullness and drowsiness,

[211] he dwells free from dullness and drowsiness, percipient of light, mindful and clearly comprehending; he purifies his mind from dullness and drowsiness. Having abandoned restlessness and remorse, he dwells without agitation, with a mind inwardly peaceful; he purifies his mind from restlessness and remorse. Having abandoned doubt, he dwells having gone beyond doubt, unperplexed about wholesome qualities; he purifies his mind from doubt.

"Having thus abandoned these five hindrances, defilements of the mind, qualities that weaken wisdom, secluded from sensual pleasures, secluded from unwholesome states, he enters and dwells in the first jhāna, which consists of rapture and pleasure born of seclusion, accompanied by thought and examination. With the subsiding of thought and examination, he enters and dwells in the second jhāna, which has internal placidity and unification of mind and consists of rapture and pleasure born of concentration, without thought and examination. With the fading away as well of rapture, he dwells equanimous and, mindful and clearly comprehending, he experiences pleasure with the body; he enters and dwells in the third jhāna of which the noble ones declare: 'He is equanimous, mindful, one who dwells happily.' With the abandoning of pleasure and pain, and with the previous passing away of joy and dejection, he enters and dwells in the fourth jhāna, neither painful nor pleasant, which has purification of mindfulness by equanimity.

"When his mind has been concentrated in this way, purified, cleansed, unblemished, rid of defilement, malleable, wieldy, steady, and attained to imperturbability, he directs it to the knowledge of the recollection of past abodes . . . [as in 3:58 §1] . . . to the knowledge of the passing away and rebirth of beings . . . [as in 3:58 §2] . . . to the knowledge of the destruction of the taints. He understands as it really is: 'This is suffering'; he understands as it really is: 'This is the origin of suffering'; he understands as it really is: 'This is the cessation of suffering'; he understands as it really is: 'This is the way leading to the cessation of suffering.' He understands as it really is: 'These are the taints'; he understands as it really is: 'This is the origin of the taints'; he understands as it really is: 'This is the cessation of the taints'; he understands as it really is: 'This is the way leading to the cessation of the taints.'

"When he knows and sees thus, his mind is liberated from

the taint of sensuality, from the taint of existence, and from the taint of ignorance. When it is liberated there comes the knowledge: '[It's] liberated.' He understands: 'Destroyed is birth, the spiritual life has been lived, what had to be done has been done, there is no more coming back to any state of being.'

"It is in this way that a person is one who does not torment himself or pursue the practice of torturing himself and who does not torment others or pursue the practice of torturing others—one who, since he torments neither himself nor others, in this very life dwells hungerless, quenched and cooled, experiencing bliss, having himself become divine.

"These, bhikkhus, are the four kinds of persons found existing in the world."

199 (9) Craving

"Bhikkhus, I will teach you about craving—the ensnarer, streaming, widespread, and sticky[932]—by which this world has been smothered and enveloped, and by which it has become a tangled skein, a knotted ball of thread, a mass of reeds and rushes, [212] so that it does not pass beyond the plane of misery, the bad destination, the lower world, saṃsāra. Listen and attend closely; I will speak."

"Yes, Bhante," those bhikkhus replied. The Blessed One said this:

"And what, bhikkhus, is craving—the ensnarer, streaming, widespread, and sticky—by which this world has been smothered and enveloped, and by which it has become a tangled skein, a knotted ball of thread, a mass of reeds and rushes, so that it does not pass beyond the plane of misery, the bad destination, the lower world, saṃsāra?

"There are, bhikkhus, these eighteen currents of craving related to the internal and eighteen currents of craving related to the external.

"And what are the eighteen currents of craving related to the internal? When there is [the notion] 'I am,' there are [the notions] 'I am thus,' 'I am just so,' 'I am otherwise,' 'I am lasting,' 'I am evanescent,' 'I may be,' 'I may be thus,' 'I may be just so,' 'I may be otherwise,' 'May I be,' 'May I be thus,' 'May I be just so,' 'May I be otherwise,' 'I shall be,' 'I shall be thus,' 'I shall be just so,' 'I shall be otherwise.' These are the eighteen currents of craving related to the internal.[933]

"And what are the eighteen currents of craving related to the external?[934] When there is [the notion], 'I am because of this,'[935] there are [the notions]: 'I am thus because of this,' 'I am just so because of this,' 'I am otherwise because of this,' 'I am lasting because of this,' 'I am evanescent because of this,' 'I may be because of this,' 'I may be thus because of this,' 'I may be just so because of this,' 'I may be otherwise because of this,' 'May I be because of this,' 'May I be thus because of this,' 'May I be just so because of this,' 'May I be otherwise because of this,' 'I shall be because of this,' 'I shall be thus because of this,' 'I shall be just so because of this,' 'I shall be otherwise because of this.' These are the eighteen currents of craving related to the external.

"Thus there are eighteen currents of craving related to the internal, and eighteen currents of craving related to the external. These are called the thirty-six currents of craving. There are thirty-six such currents of craving pertaining to the past, thirty-six pertaining to the future, [213] and thirty-six pertaining to the present. So there are one hundred and eight currents of craving.

"This, bhikkhus, is that craving—the ensnarer, streaming, widespread, and sticky—by which this world has been smothered and enveloped, and by which it has become a tangled skein, a knotted ball of thread, a mass of reeds and rushes, so that it does not pass beyond the plane of misery, the bad destination, the lower world, saṃsāra."[936]

200 (10) Affection

"Bhikkhus, there are these four things that are born. What four? Affection is born from affection; hatred is born from affection; affection is born from hatred; and hatred is born from hatred.

(1) "And how, bhikkhus, is affection born from affection? Here, one person is desirable, lovable, and agreeable to another. Others treat that person in a way that is desirable, lovable, and agreeable. It occurs to the latter: 'Others treat that person who is desirable, lovable, and agreeable to me in a way that is desirable, lovable, and agreeable.' He thus feels affection for them. It is in this way that affection is born from affection.

(2) "And how is hatred born from affection? Here, one person is desirable, lovable, and agreeable to another. Others treat that person in a way that is undesirable, unlovable, and disagreeable.

It occurs to the latter: 'Others treat that person who is desirable, lovable, and agreeable to me in a way that is undesirable, unlovable, and disagreeable.' He thus feels hatred for them. It is in this way that hatred is born from affection.

(3) "And how is affection born from hatred? Here, one person is undesirable, unlovable, and disagreeable to another. Others treat that person in a way that is undesirable, unlovable, and disagreeable. It occurs to the latter: 'Others treat that person who is undesirable, unlovable, and disagreeable to me in a way that is undesirable, unlovable, and disagreeable.' He thus feels affection for them. It is in this way that affection is born from hatred.

(4) "And how is hatred born from hatred? Here, one person is undesirable, unlovable, [214] and disagreeable to another. Others treat that person in a way that is desirable, lovable, and agreeable. It occurs to the latter: 'Others treat that person who is undesirable, unlovable, and disagreeable to me in a way that is desirable, lovable, and agreeable.' He thus feels hatred for them. It is in this way that hatred is born from hatred.

"These are the four things that are born.

"When, secluded from sensual pleasures . . . a bhikkhu enters and dwells in the first jhāna, on that occasion affection born from affection does not exist in him, hatred born from affection does not exist in him, affection born from hatred does not exist in him, and hatred born from hatred does not exist in him.

"When, with the subsiding of thought and examination, a bhikkhu enters and dwells in the second jhāna . . . the third jhāna . . . the fourth jhāna, on that occasion affection born from affection does not exist in him, hatred born from affection does not exist in him, affection born from hatred does not exist in him, and hatred born from hatred does not exist in him.

"When, with the destruction of the taints, a bhikkhu has realized for himself with direct knowledge, in this very life, the taintless liberation of mind, liberation by wisdom, and having entered upon it, he dwells in it, then he has abandoned affection born from affection, cut it off at the root, made it like a palm stump, obliterated it so that it is no more subject to future arising; he has abandoned hatred born from affection, cut it off at the root, made it like a palm stump, obliterated it so that it is no more subject to future arising; he has abandoned affection born from hatred, cut it off at the root, made it like a palm stump, obliterated it so that it is no more subject to future arising; and he has abandoned hatred born from hatred, cut it off at the root, made it like a palm stump, obliterated it so that it is no more subject to future arising.

"This is called a bhikkhu who neither picks up nor pushes away, who does not fume, does not blaze, and does not ruminate.

"And how does a bhikkhu pick up?[937] Here, a bhikkhu regards form as self, or self as possessing form, or form as in self, or self as in form. He regards feeling as self . . . [215] . . . perception as self . . . volitional activities as self . . . consciousness as self, or self as possessing consciousness, or consciousness as in self, or self as in consciousness. It is in this way that a bhikkhu picks up.

"And how does a bhikkhu not pick up? Here, a bhikkhu does not regard form as self, or self as possessing form, or form as in self, or self as in form. He does not regard feeling as self . . . perception as self . . . volitional activities as self . . . consciousness as self, or self as possessing consciousness, or consciousness as in self, or self as in consciousness. It is in this way that a bhikkhu does not pick up.

"And how does a bhikkhu push away? Here, a bhikkhu insults one who insults him, scolds one who scolds him, and argues with one who picks an argument with him. It is in this way that a bhikkhu pushes away.

"And how does a bhikkhu not push away? Here, a bhikkhu does not insult one who insults him, does not scold one who scolds him, and does not argue with one who picks an argument with him. It is in this way that a bhikkhu does not push away.

"And how does a bhikkhu fume? When there is [the notion] 'I am,' there are [the notions] 'I am thus,' 'I am just so,' 'I am otherwise,' 'I am lasting,' 'I am evanescent,' 'I may be,' 'I may be thus,' 'I may be just so,' 'I may be otherwise,' 'May I be,' 'May I be thus,' 'May I be just so,' 'May I be otherwise,' 'I shall be,' 'I shall be thus,' 'I shall be just so,' 'I shall be otherwise.' It is in this way that a bhikkhu fumes.

"And how does a bhikkhu not fume? When there is no [notion] 'I am,' there are no [notions] 'I am thus' . . . [216] . . . 'I shall be otherwise.' It is in this way that a bhikkhu does not fume.

"And how does a bhikkhu blaze? When there is [the notion],

'I am because of this,' there are [the notions]: 'I am thus because of this,' 'I am just so because of this,' 'I am otherwise because of this,' 'I am lasting because of this,' 'I am evanescent because of this,' 'I may be because of this,' 'I may be thus because of this,' 'I may be just so because of this,' 'I may be otherwise because of this,' 'May I be because of this,' 'May I be thus because of this,' 'May I be just so because of this,' 'May I be otherwise because of this,' 'I shall be because of this,' 'I shall be thus because of this,' 'I shall be just so because of this,' 'I shall be otherwise because of this.' It is in this way that a bhikkhu blazes.

"And how does a bhikkhu not blaze? When there is no [notion], 'I am because of this,' there are no [notions]: 'I am thus because of this' . . . 'I shall be otherwise because of this.' It is in this way that a bhikkhu does not blaze.

"And how does a bhikkhu ruminate?[938] Here, a bhikkhu has not abandoned the conceit 'I am,' cut it off at the root, made it like a palm stump, obliterated it so that it is no more subject to future arising. It is in this way that a bhikkhu ruminates.

"And how does a bhikkhu not ruminate? Here, a bhikkhu has abandoned the conceit 'I am,' cut it off at the root, made it like a palm stump, obliterated it so that it is no more subject to future arising. It is in this way that a bhikkhu does not ruminate." [217]

The Fifth Fifty

I. The Good Person

201 (1) Training Rules

"Bhikkhus, I will teach you about the bad person and the person inferior to the bad person; about the good person and the person superior to the good person. Listen and attend closely; I will speak."

"Yes, Bhante," those bhikkhus replied. The Blessed One said this:

(1) "And who, bhikkhus, is the bad person? Here, someone destroys life, takes what is not given, engages in sexual misconduct, speaks falsely, and indulges in liquor, wine, and intoxicants, the basis for heedlessness. This is called the bad person.

(2) "And who is the person inferior to the bad person? Here, someone himself destroys life and encourages others to destroy life; he himself takes what is not given and encourages others to take what is not given; he himself engages in sexual misconduct and encourages others to engage in sexual misconduct; he himself speaks falsely and encourages others to speak falsely; he himself indulges in liquor, wine, and intoxicants, the basis for heedlessness, and encourages others to indulge in liquor, wine, and intoxicants, the basis for heedlessness. This is the person inferior to the bad person.

(3) "And who is the good person? Here, someone abstains from the destruction of life, abstains from taking what is not given, abstains from sexual misconduct, abstains from false speech, and abstains from liquor, wine, and intoxicants, the basis for heedlessness. This is called the good person.

(4) "And who is the person superior to the good person? Here, someone himself abstains from the destruction of life and encourages others to abstain from the destruction of life; he himself abstains from taking what is not given and encourages others to abstain from taking what is not given; he himself abstains from sexual misconduct and encourages others to abstain from sexual misconduct; he himself abstains from false speech and encourages others to abstain from false speech; he himself abstains from liquor, wine, and intoxicants, the basis for heedlessness, and encourages others to abstain from liquor, wine, and intoxicants, the basis for heedlessness. This is called the person superior to the good person." [218]

202 (2) Devoid of Faith

[Opening as in 4:201.]

(1) "And who, bhikkhus, is the bad person? Here, someone is devoid of faith, morally shameless, morally reckless, deficient in learning, lazy, muddle-minded, and unwise. This is called the bad person.

(2) "And who is the person inferior to the bad person? Here, someone is himself devoid of faith and encourages others to be devoid of faith; he is himself morally shameless and encourages others to be morally shameless; he is himself morally reckless and encourages others to be morally reckless; he is himself deficient in learning and encourages others to be deficient in

learning; he is himself lazy and encourages others in laziness; he is himself muddle-minded and encourages others in being muddle-minded; he is himself unwise and encourages others in lack of wisdom. This is called the person inferior to the bad person.

(3) "And who is the good person? Here, someone is endowed with faith, has a sense of moral shame and moral dread, and is learned, energetic, mindful, and wise. This is called the good person.

(4) "And who is the person superior to the good person? Here, someone is himself accomplished in faith and encourages others to be accomplished in faith; he himself has a sense of moral shame and encourages others in moral shame; he himself has moral dread and encourages others in moral dread; he is himself learned and encourages others in learning; he is himself energetic and encourages others to arouse energy; he is himself mindful and encourages others to establish mindfulness; he is himself wise and encourages others to be accomplished in wisdom. This is called the person superior to the good person."

203 (3) Seven Actions

[Opening as in 4:201.] [219]

(1) "And who, bhikkhus, is the bad person? Here, someone destroys life, takes what is not given, engages in sexual misconduct, speaks falsehood, speaks divisively, speaks harshly, and indulges in idle chatter.

(2) "And who is the person inferior to the bad person? Here, someone himself destroys life and encourages others to destroy life . . . he himself indulges in idle chatter and encourages others to indulge in idle chatter. This is called the person inferior to the bad person.

(3) "And who is the good person? Here, someone abstains from the destruction of life . . . abstains from idle chatter. This is called the good person.

(4) "And who is the person superior to the good person? Here, someone himself abstains from the destruction of life and encourages others to abstain from the destruction of life . . . he himself abstains from idle chatter and encourages others to

abstain from idle chatter. This is called the person superior to the good person."

204 (4) Ten Actions

[Opening as in 4:201.] [220]

(1) "And who, bhikkhus, is the bad person? Here, someone destroys life . . . indulges in idle chatter; he is full of longing, bears ill will, and holds wrong view. This is called the bad person.

(2) "And who is the person inferior to the bad person? Here, someone himself destroys life and encourages others to destroy life . . . he himself holds wrong view and encourages others in wrong view. This is called the person inferior to the bad person.

(3) "And who is the good person? Here, someone abstains from the destruction of life . . . abstains from idle chatter; he is without longing, of good will, and holds right view. This is called the good person.

(4) "And who is the person superior to the good person? Here, someone himself abstains from the destruction of life and encourages others to abstain from the destruction of life . . . he is himself without longing and encourages others in non-longing; he is himself of good will and encourages others in good will; he himself holds right view and encourages others in right view. This is called the person superior to the good person."

205 (5) Eightfold

[Opening as in 4:201.]

(1) "And who, bhikkhus, is the bad person? Here, someone is of wrong view, wrong intention, wrong speech, wrong action, wrong livelihood, wrong effort, wrong mindfulness, and wrong concentration. [221] This is called the bad person.

(2) "And who is the person inferior to the bad person? Here, someone is himself of wrong view and encourages others in wrong view . . . he is himself of wrong concentration and encourages others in wrong concentration. This is called the person inferior to the bad person.

(3) "And who is the good person? Here, someone is of right view, right intention, right speech, right action, right livelihood, right effort, right mindfulness, and right concentration. This is called the good person.

(4) "And who is the person superior to the good person? Here, someone is himself of right view and encourages others in right view . . . he is himself of right concentration and encourages others in right concentration. This is called the person superior to the good person."

206 (6) Tenfold Path

[Opening as in 4:201.]

(1) "And who, bhikkhus, is the bad person? [222] Here, someone is of wrong view . . . wrong concentration, wrong knowledge, and wrong liberation. This is called the bad person.

(2) "And who is the person inferior to the bad person? Here, someone is himself of wrong view and encourages others in wrong view . . . he is himself of wrong liberation and encourages others in wrong liberation. This is called the person inferior to the bad person.

(3) "And who is the good person? Here, someone is of right view . . . right concentration, right knowledge, and right liberation. This is called the good person.

(4) "And who is the person superior to the good person? Here, someone is himself of right view and encourages others in right view . . . he is himself of right liberation and encourages others in right liberation. This is called the person superior to the good person."

207 (7) Bad Character (1)

"Bhikkhus, I will teach you what is bad and what is worse than that bad. And I will teach you what is good and what is better than that good. Listen. . . .

(1) "And what, bhikkhus, is bad? Here, someone destroys life . . . and holds wrong view. This is called bad.

(2) "And what is worse than that bad? Here, someone himself destroys life and encourages others to destroy life . . . he himself holds wrong view and encourages others in wrong view. This is called what is worse than that bad.

(3) "And what is good? Here, someone abstains from the destruction of life . . . and holds right view. [223] This is called good.

(4) "And what is better than that good? Here, someone himself abstains from the destruction of life and encourages others

to abstain from the destruction of life . . . he himself holds right view and encourages others in right view. This is called what is better than that good."

208 (8) Bad Character (2)

[Opening as in 4:207.]

(1) "And what, bhikkhus, is bad? Here, someone is of wrong view . . . wrong liberation. This is called bad.

(2) "And what is worse than that bad? Here, someone is himself of wrong view and encourages others in wrong view . . . he is himself of wrong liberation and encourages others in wrong liberation. This is called what is worse than that bad.

(3) "And what is good? Here, someone is of right view . . . of right liberation. This is called good.

(4) "And what is better than that good? Here, someone is himself of right view and encourages others in right view . . . he is himself of right liberation and encourages others in right liberation. This is called what is better than that good."

209 (9) Bad Character (3)

"Bhikkhus, I will teach you about one of bad character [224] and about one of still worse character. I will teach you about one of good character and about one of still better character. Listen. . . .

(1) "And who, bhikkhus, is of bad character? Here, someone destroys life . . . and holds wrong view. This is called one of bad character.

(2) "And who is one of still worse character? Here, someone himself destroys life and encourages others to destroy life . . . he holds wrong view himself and encourages others in wrong view. This is called one of still worse character.

(3) "And what is one of good character? Here, someone abstains from the destruction of life . . . and holds right view. This is called one of good character.

(4) "And what is one of still better character? Here, someone himself abstains from the destruction of life and encourages others to abstain from the destruction of life . . . he himself holds right view and encourages others in right view. This is called one of still better character."

210 (10) Bad Character (4)

[Opening as in 4:209.]

(1) "And what, bhikkhus, is one of bad character? Here, someone is of wrong view ... of wrong liberation. This is called one of bad character.

(2) "And what is one of still worse character? Here, someone is himself of wrong view [225] and encourages others in wrong view ... he is himself of wrong liberation and encourages others in wrong liberation. This is called one of still worse character.

(3) "And what is one of good character? Here, someone is of right view ... of right liberation. This is called one of good character.

(4) "And what is one of still better character? Here, someone is himself of right view and encourages others in right view ... he is himself of right liberation and encourages others in right liberation. This is called one of still better character."

II. Adornments of the Assembly

211 (1) Assembly

"Bhikkhus, these four are blemishes of an assembly. What four? A bhikkhu who is immoral, of bad character; a bhikkhunī who is immoral, of bad character; a male lay follower who is immoral, of bad character; and a female lay follower who is immoral, of bad character. These four are blemishes of an assembly.

"Bhikkhus, these four are adornments of an assembly. What four? A bhikkhu who is virtuous, of good character; [226] a bhikkhunī who is virtuous, of good character; a male lay follower who is virtuous, of good character; and a female lay follower who is virtuous, of good character. These four are adornments of an assembly."

212 (2) View

"Bhikkhus, one possessing four qualities is deposited in hell as if brought there. What four? Bodily misconduct, verbal misconduct, mental misconduct, and wrong view. One possessing these four qualities is deposited in hell as if brought there.

"Bhikkhus, one possessing four qualities is deposited in heaven as if brought there. What four? Bodily good conduct, verbal good conduct, mental good conduct, and right view.

One possessing these four qualities is deposited in heaven as if brought there."

213 (3) Ingratitude

"Bhikkhus, one possessing four qualities is deposited in hell as if brought there. What four? Bodily misconduct, verbal misconduct, mental misconduct, and ingratitude or non-thankfulness. One possessing these four qualities is deposited in hell as if brought there.

"Bhikkhus, one possessing four qualities is deposited in heaven as if brought there. What four? Bodily good conduct, verbal good conduct, mental good conduct, and gratitude or thankfulness. One possessing these four qualities is deposited in heaven as if brought there."

214 (4) Destruction of Life

[4:214–19 follow the same pattern as 4:213, with the following qualities respectively responsible for rebirth in hell and heaven.]

"... One destroys life, takes what is not given, engages in sexual misconduct, and speaks falsely....

"... One abstains from the destruction of life, from taking what is not given, from sexual misconduct, and from false speech...." [227]

215 (5) Path (1)

"... One is of wrong view, wrong intention, wrong speech, and wrong action....

"... One is of right view, right intention, right speech, and right action...."

216 (6) Path (2)

"... One is of wrong livelihood, wrong effort, wrong mindfulness, and wrong concentration....

"... One is of right livelihood, right effort, right mindfulness, and right concentration...."

217 (7) Courses of Expression (1)

"... One says that one has seen what one has not seen; one says that one has heard what one has not heard; one says that one has sensed what one has not sensed; one says that one has cognized what one has not cognized....[939]

"...One says that one has not seen what one has not seen; one says that one has not heard what one has not heard; one says that one has not sensed what one has not sensed; one says that one has not cognized what one has not cognized...."

218 (8) Courses of Expression (2)

"...One says that one has not seen what one has seen; one says that one has not heard what one has heard; one says that one has not sensed what one has sensed; one says that one has not cognized what one has cognized....

"...One says that one has seen what one has seen; one says that one has heard what one has heard; one says that one has sensed what one has sensed; one says that one has cognized what one has cognized...."

219 (9) Morally Shameless

"...One is devoid of faith, immoral, morally shameless, and morally reckless....

"...One is endowed with faith, virtuous, and has a sense of moral shame and moral dread...."

220 (10) Unwise

"Bhikkhus, one possessing four qualities is deposited in hell as if brought there. What four? One is devoid of faith, immoral, lazy, and unwise. One possessing these four qualities is deposited in hell as if brought there.

"Bhikkhus, one possessing four [other] qualities is deposited in heaven as if brought there. What four? [228] One is endowed with faith, virtuous, energetic, and wise. One possessing these four qualities is deposited in heaven as if brought there."

III. Good Conduct

221 (1) Misconduct

"Bhikkhus, there are these four kinds of verbal misconduct. What four? False speech, divisive speech, harsh speech, and idle chatter. These are the four kinds of verbal misconduct.

"Bhikkhus, there are these four kinds of verbal good conduct. What four? Truthful speech, non-divisive speech, gentle speech, and judicious speech. These are the four kinds of verbal good conduct."

222 (2) View

"Bhikkhus, possessing four qualities, the foolish, incompetent, bad person maintains himself in a maimed and injured condition; he is blameworthy and subject to reproach by the wise; and he generates much demerit. What four? Bodily misconduct, verbal misconduct, mental misconduct, and wrong view. Possessing these four qualities . . . he generates much demerit.

"Bhikkhus, possessing four [other] qualities, the wise, competent, good person preserves himself unmaimed and uninjured; he is blameless and beyond reproach by the wise; and he generates much merit. What four? Bodily good conduct, verbal good conduct, mental good conduct, and right view. Possessing these four qualities . . . he generates much merit." [229]

223 (3) Ingratitude

"Bhikkhus, possessing four qualities, the foolish, incompetent, bad person maintains himself in a maimed and injured condition; he is blameworthy and subject to reproach by the wise; and he generates much demerit. What four? Bodily misconduct, verbal misconduct, mental misconduct, and ingratitude or nonthankfulness. Possessing these four qualities . . . he generates much demerit.

"Bhikkhus, possessing four [other] qualities, the wise, competent, good person preserves himself unmaimed and uninjured; he is blameless and beyond reproach by the wise; and he generates much merit. What four? Bodily good conduct, verbal good conduct, mental good conduct, and gratitude or thankfulness. Possessing these four qualities . . . he generates much merit."

224 (4) Destruction of Life

". . . He destroys life, takes what is not given, engages in sexual misconduct, and speaks falsely. . . .

". . . He abstains from the destruction of life, abstains from taking what is not given, abstains from sexual misconduct, and abstains from false speech. . . ."

225 (5) Path (1)

"...He is of wrong view, wrong intention, wrong speech, and wrong action....

"...He is of right view, right intention, right speech, and right action...."

226 (6) Path (2)

"...He is of wrong livelihood, wrong effort, wrong mindfulness, and wrong concentration....

"...He is of right livelihood, right effort, right mindfulness, and right concentration...."

227 (7) Courses of Expression (1)

"...He says that he has seen what he has not seen; he says that he has heard what he has not heard; he says that he has sensed what he has not sensed; he says that he has cognized what he has not cognized....

"...He says that he has not seen what he has not seen; he says that he has not heard what he has not heard; he says that he has not sensed what he has not sensed; he says that he has not cognized what he has not cognized...."

228 (8) Courses of Expression (2)

"...He says that he has not seen what he has seen; he says that he has not heard what he has heard; he says that he has not sensed what he has sensed; he says that he has not cognized what he has cognized....

"...He says that he has seen what he has seen; he says that he has heard what he has heard; he says that he has sensed what he has sensed; he says that he has cognized what he has cognized...."

229 (9) Morally Shameless

"...He is devoid of faith, immoral, morally shameless, and morally reckless....

"...He is endowed with faith, virtuous, and has a sense of moral shame and moral dread...." [230]

230 (10) Unwise

"Bhikkhus, possessing four qualities, the foolish, incompetent, bad person maintains himself in a maimed and injured condition; he is blameworthy and subject to reproach by the wise; and he generates much demerit. What four? He is devoid of faith, immoral, lazy, and unwise. Possessing these four qualities . . . he generates much demerit.

"Bhikkhus, possessing four [other] qualities, the wise, competent, good person preserves himself unmaimed and uninjured; he is blameless and beyond reproach by the wise; and he generates much merit. What four? He is endowed with faith, is virtuous, energetic, and wise. Possessing these four qualities . . . he generates much merit."

231 (11) Poets

"Bhikkhus, there are these four kinds of poets. What four? The reflective poet, the narrative poet, the didactic poet, and the inspirational poet.[940] These are the four kinds of poets."

IV. Kamma

232 (1) In Brief

"Bhikkhus, there are these four kinds of kamma proclaimed by me after I realized them for myself with direct knowledge. What four? There is dark kamma with dark result; there is bright kamma with bright result; there is dark-and-bright kamma with dark-and-bright result; and there is kamma that is neither dark nor bright with neither-dark-nor-bright result, kamma that leads to the destruction of kamma. These are the four kinds of kamma proclaimed by me after I realized them for myself with direct knowledge."

233 (2) In Detail[941]

"Bhikkhus, there are these four kinds of kamma proclaimed by me after I realized them for myself with direct knowledge. What four? There is dark kamma with dark result; there is bright kamma with bright result; there is [231] dark-and-bright kamma with dark-and-bright result; and there is kamma that is neither dark nor bright with neither-dark-nor-bright result, kamma that leads to the destruction of kamma.

(1) "And what, bhikkhus, is dark kamma with dark result? Here, someone performs an afflictive bodily volitional activity, an afflictive verbal volitional activity, an afflictive mental volitional activity.[942] As a consequence, he is reborn in an afflictive world. When he is reborn in such a world, afflictive contacts

touch him. Being touched by afflictive contacts, he feels afflictive feelings, exclusively painful, as in the case of hell beings. This is called dark kamma with dark result.

(2) "And what is bright kamma with bright result? Here, someone performs a non-afflictive bodily volitional activity, a non-afflictive verbal volitional activity, a non-afflictive mental volitional activity.[943] As a consequence he is reborn in a non-afflictive world.[944] When he is reborn in such a world, non-afflictive contacts touch him. Being touched by non-afflictive contacts, he feels non-afflictive feelings, exclusively pleasant, as in the case of the devas of refulgent glory.[945] This is called bright kamma with bright result.

(3) "And what is dark-and-bright kamma with dark-and-bright result? Here, someone performs a bodily volitional activity that is both afflictive and non-afflictive, a verbal volitional activity that is both afflictive and non-afflictive, a mental volitional activity that is both afflictive and non-afflictive. As a consequence he is reborn in a world that is both afflictive and non-afflictive. When he is reborn in such a world, [232] contacts that are both afflictive and non-afflictive touch him. Being touched by contacts that are both afflictive and non-afflictive, he feels feelings that are both afflictive and non-afflictive, mingled pleasure and pain, as in the case of human beings and some devas and some beings in the lower worlds. This is called dark-and-bright kamma with dark-and-bright result.

(4) "And what is kamma that is neither dark nor bright with neither-dark-nor-bright result, kamma that leads to the destruction of kamma? The volition for abandoning the kind of kamma that is dark with dark result, the volition for abandoning the kind of kamma that is bright with bright result, and the volition for abandoning the kind of kamma that is dark and bright with dark-and-bright result: this is called kamma that is neither dark nor bright with neither-dark-nor-bright result, kamma that leads to the destruction of kamma.[946]

"These, bhikkhus, are the four kinds of kamma proclaimed by me after I realized them for myself with direct knowledge."

234 (3) Soṇakāyana

Then the brahmin Sikhāmoggallāna approached the Blessed One and exchanged greetings with him. . . . Then, sitting to one side, he said to the Blessed One:

"In earlier days, Master Gotama, a long time ago, the brahmin student Soṇakāyana approached me and said: 'The ascetic Gotama prescribes the desistance from all kamma. But by prescribing the desistance from all kamma, he advocates the annihilation of the world. This world, sir, which has kamma as its substance, continues through the undertaking of kamma.'"

[The Blessed One:] "I do not recall even seeing the brahmin student Soṇakāyana, brahmin. How then could there have been such a discussion? There are, brahmin, these four kinds of kamma proclaimed by me after I realized them for myself with direct knowledge. What four?"

[The rest of the sutta is identical with 4:233.] [233]

235 (4) Training Rules (1)

[Opening as in 4:233.] [234]

(1) "And what, bhikkhus, is dark kamma with dark result? Here, someone destroys life, takes what is not given, engages in sexual misconduct, speaks falsely, and indulges in liquor, wine, and intoxicants, the basis for heedlessness. This is called dark kamma with dark result.

(2) "And what is bright kamma with bright result? Here, someone abstains from the destruction of life, abstains from taking what is not given, abstains from sexual misconduct, abstains from false speech, and abstains from liquor, wine, and intoxicants, the basis for heedlessness. This is called bright kamma with bright result.

(3) "And what is dark-and-bright kamma with dark-and-bright result? Here, someone performs a bodily volitional activity that is both afflictive and non-afflictive, a verbal volitional activity that is both afflictive and non-afflictive, a mental volitional activity that is both afflictive and non-afflictive. As a consequence, he is reborn in a world that is both afflictive and non-afflictive. When he is reborn in such a world, contacts that are both afflictive and non-afflictive touch him. Being touched by contacts that are both afflictive and non-afflictive, he feels feelings that are both afflictive and non-afflictive, mingled pleasure and pain, as in the case of human beings and some devas and some beings in the lower worlds. This is called dark-and-bright kamma with dark-and-bright result.

(4) "And what is kamma that is neither dark nor bright with

neither-dark-nor-bright result, kamma that leads to the destruction of kamma? The volition for abandoning the kind of kamma that is dark with dark result, the volition for abandoning the kind of kamma that is bright with bright result, and the volition for abandoning the kind of kamma that is dark and bright with dark-and-bright result: this is called kamma that is neither dark nor bright with neither-dark-nor-bright result, kamma that leads to the destruction of kamma.

"These, bhikkhus, are the four kinds of kamma proclaimed by me after I realized them for myself with direct knowledge."

236 (5) Training Rules (2)

[Opening as in 4:233.]

(1) "And what, bhikkhus, is dark kamma with dark result? Here, someone takes his mother's life, takes his father's life, takes an arahant's life, with a mind of hatred sheds the Tathāgata's blood, or creates a schism in the Saṅgha. [235] This is called dark kamma with dark result.

(2) "And what is bright kamma with bright result? Here, someone abstains from the destruction of life, abstains from taking what is not given, abstains from sexual misconduct, abstains from false speech, abstains from divisive speech, abstains from harsh speech, and abstains from idle chatter; he is without longing, of good will, and holds right view. This is called bright kamma with bright result.

(3) "And what is dark-and-bright kamma with dark-and-bright result? . . . [as in 4:235] . . . This is called dark-and-bright kamma with dark-and-bright result.

(4) "And what is kamma that is neither dark nor bright with neither-dark-nor-bright result, kamma that leads to the destruction of kamma? . . . [as in 4:235] . . . this is called kamma that is neither dark nor bright with neither-dark-nor-bright result, kamma that leads to the destruction of kamma.

"These, bhikkhus, are the four kinds of kamma proclaimed by me after I realized them for myself with direct knowledge."

237 (6) Noble Path

"Bhikkhus, there are these four kinds of kamma proclaimed by me after I realized them for myself with direct knowledge. What four?

[All as in 4:233 down to:] [236]

"And what is kamma that is neither dark nor bright with neither-dark-nor-bright result, kamma that leads to the destruction of kamma? Right view, right intention, right speech, right action, right livelihood, right effort, right mindfulness, and right concentration: this is called kamma that is neither dark nor bright with neither-dark-nor-bright result, kamma that leads to the destruction of kamma.

"These, bhikkhus, are the four kinds of kamma proclaimed by me after I realized them for myself with direct knowledge."

238 (7) Enlightenment Factors

"Bhikkhus, there are these four kinds of kamma proclaimed by me after I realized them for myself with direct knowledge. What four?

[All as in 4:233 down to:] [237]

"And what is kamma that is neither dark nor bright with neither-dark-nor-bright result, kamma that leads to the destruction of kamma? The enlightenment factor of mindfulness, the enlightenment factor of discrimination of phenomena, the enlightenment factor of energy, the enlightenment factor of rapture, the enlightenment factor of tranquility, the enlightenment factor of concentration, and the enlightenment factor of equanimity: this is called kamma that is neither dark nor bright with neither-dark-nor-bright result, kamma that leads to the destruction of kamma.

"These, bhikkhus, are the four kinds of kamma proclaimed by me after I realized them for myself with direct knowledge."

239 (8) Blameworthy

"Bhikkhus, one possessing four qualities is deposited in hell as if brought there. What four? Blameworthy bodily action, blameworthy verbal action, blameworthy mental action, and blameworthy view. One possessing these four qualities is deposited in hell as if brought there.

"Bhikkhus, one possessing four qualities is deposited in heaven as if brought there. What four? Blameless bodily action, blameless verbal action, blameless mental action, and blameless view. One possessing these four qualities is deposited in heaven as if brought there."

240 (9) Non-Afflictive

"Bhikkhus, one possessing four qualities is deposited in hell as if brought there. What four? Afflictive bodily action, afflictive verbal action, afflictive mental action, and afflictive view. One possessing these four qualities is deposited in hell as if brought there. [238]

"Bhikkhus, one possessing four qualities is deposited in heaven as if brought there. What four? Non-afflictive bodily action, non-afflictive verbal action, non-afflictive mental action, and non-afflictive view. One possessing these four qualities is deposited in heaven as if brought there."

241 (10) Ascetics

"Bhikkhus, 'only here is there an ascetic, a second ascetic, a third ascetic, and a fourth ascetic. The other sects are empty of ascetics.'[947] It is in such a way that you should rightly roar your lion's roar.

(1) "And what, bhikkhus, is the first ascetic? Here, with the utter destruction of three fetters, a bhikkhu is a stream-enterer, no longer subject to [rebirth in] the lower world, fixed in destiny, heading for enlightenment. This is the first ascetic.

(2) "And what is the second ascetic? Here, with the utter destruction of three fetters and with the diminishing of greed, hatred, and delusion, a bhikkhu is a once-returner who, after coming back to this world only one more time, will make an end of suffering. This is the second ascetic.

(3) "And what is the third ascetic? Here, with the utter destruction of the five lower fetters, a bhikkhu is of spontaneous birth, due to attain final nibbāna there without returning from that world. This is the third ascetic.

(4) "And what is the fourth ascetic? Here, with the destruction of the taints, a bhikkhu has realized for himself with direct knowledge, in this very life, the taintless liberation of mind, liberation by wisdom, and having entered upon it, he dwells in it. This is the fourth ascetic.

"Bhikkhus, 'only here is there an ascetic, a second ascetic, a third ascetic, and a fourth ascetic. The other sects are empty of ascetics.' It is in such a way that you should rightly roar your lion's roar." [239]

242 (11) Benefits of a Good Person

"Bhikkhus, by relying on a good person, four benefits are to be expected. What four? One grows in noble virtuous behavior; one grows in noble concentration; one grows in noble wisdom; and one grows in noble liberation. By relying on a good person, these four benefits are to be expected."

V. Perils of Offenses

243 (1) Schism

On one occasion the Blessed One was dwelling at Kosambī in Ghosita's Park. Then the Venerable Ānanda approached the Blessed One, paid homage to him, and sat down to one side. The Blessed One then said to him:

"Has that disciplinary issue been settled yet, Ānanda?"[948]

"How could that disciplinary issue be settled, Bhante? The Venerable Anuruddha's pupil Bāhiya is still fully intent on creating a schism in the Saṅgha, but the Venerable Anuruddha doesn't think of saying even a single word about it."

"But, Ānanda, when has Anuruddha ever concerned himself with disciplinary issues in the midst of the Saṅgha? Shouldn't you, and Sāriputta and Moggallāna, settle any disciplinary issues that arise?

"Seeing these four advantages, Ānanda, an evil bhikkhu delights in a schism in the Saṅgha. What four?

(1) "Here, an evil bhikkhu is immoral, of bad character, impure, of suspect behavior, secretive in his actions, not an ascetic though claiming to be one, not a celibate though claiming to be one, [240] inwardly rotten, corrupt, depraved. It occurs to him: 'If the bhikkhus find out that I am immoral . . . depraved, and they are united, they will expel me, but if they are divided into factions they won't expel me.' Seeing this first advantage, an evil bhikkhu delights in a schism in the Saṅgha.

(2) "Again, an evil bhikkhu holds wrong view; he resorts to an extremist view. It occurs to him: 'If the bhikkhus find out that I hold wrong view, that I resort to an extremist view, and they are united, they will expel me, but if they are divided into factions they won't expel me.' Seeing this second advantage, an evil bhikkhu delights in a schism in the Saṅgha.

(3) "Again, an evil bhikkhu is of wrong livelihood; he earns

his living by wrong livelihood. It occurs to him: 'If the bhikkhus find out that I am of wrong livelihood and earn my living by wrong livelihood, and they are united, they will expel me, but if they are divided into factions they won't expel me.' Seeing this third advantage, an evil bhikkhu delights in a schism in the Saṅgha.

(4) "Again, an evil bhikkhu is desirous of gain, honor, and admiration. It occurs to him: 'If the bhikkhus find out that I am desirous of gain, honor, and admiration, and they are united, they will not honor, respect, esteem, and venerate me; but if they are divided into factions they will honor, respect, esteem, and venerate me.' Seeing this fourth advantage, an evil bhikkhu delights in a schism in the Saṅgha.

"Seeing these four advantages, Ānanda, an evil bhikkhu delights in a schism in the Saṅgha."

244 (2) Offenses

"Bhikkhus, there are these four perils of offenses. What four?

(1) "Suppose, bhikkhus, they were to arrest a thief, a criminal, and show him to the king, saying: 'Your majesty, this is a thief, a criminal. Let your majesty impose a penalty on him.' The king would say to them: [241] 'Go, sirs, and tie this man's arms tightly behind his back with a strong rope, shave his head, and lead him around from street to street, from square to square, to the ominous beating of a drum. Then take him out through the south gate and behead him south of the city.' The king's men would do as instructed and behead that man south of the city. A man standing on the sidelines might think: 'Truly, this man must have committed an evil deed, reprehensible, punishable by beheading, insofar as the king's men tied his arms tightly behind his back with a strong rope . . . and beheaded him south of the city. Indeed, I should never do such an evil deed, reprehensible, punishable by beheading.'

"So too, when a bhikkhu or bhikkhunī has set up such a keen perception of peril in regard to the *pārājika* offenses, it can be expected that one who has never yet committed a *pārājika* offense will not commit one; and one who has committed such an offense will make amends for it in accordance with the Dhamma.[949]

(2) "Suppose, bhikkhus, a man were to wrap himself in a black cloth, loosen his hair, put a club on his shoulder, and tell a

large crowd of people: 'Worthy sirs,[950] I have committed an evil deed, reprehensible, punishable by clubbing. Let me do whatever will make you pleased with me.' A man standing on the sidelines might think: 'Truly, this man must have committed an evil deed, reprehensible, punishable by clubbing, insofar as he has wrapped himself in a black cloth, loosened his hair, put a club on his shoulder, and tells a large crowd of people: "Worthy sirs, I have committed an evil deed, reprehensible, deserving a clubbing. Let me do whatever will make you pleased with me." [242] Indeed, I should never do such an evil deed, reprehensible, punishable by clubbing.'

"So too, when a bhikkhu or bhikkhunī has set up such a keen perception of peril in regard to the *saṅghādisesa* offenses, it can be expected that one who has never yet committed a *saṅghādisesa* offense will not commit one, and one who has committed such an offense will make amends for it in accordance with the Dhamma.[951]

(3) "Suppose, bhikkhus, a man were to wrap himself in a black cloth, loosen his hair, put a sack of ashes on his shoulder, and tell a large crowd of people: 'Worthy sirs, I have committed an evil deed, reprehensible, punishable by a sack of ashes.[952] Let me do whatever will make you pleased with me.' A man standing on the sidelines might think: 'Truly, this man must have committed an evil deed, reprehensible, punishable by a sack of ashes, insofar as he has wrapped himself in a black cloth, loosened his hair, put a sack of ashes on his shoulder, and tells a large crowd of people: "Worthy sirs, I have committed an evil deed, reprehensible, punishable by a sack of ashes. Let me do whatever will make you pleased with me." Indeed, I should never do such an evil deed, reprehensible, [to be punished with] a sack of ashes.'

"So too, when a bhikkhu or bhikkhunī has set up such a keen perception of peril in regard to the *pācittiya* offenses, it can be expected that one who has never yet committed a *pācittiya* offense will not commit one, and one who has committed such an offense will make amends for it in accordance with the Dhamma.[953]

(4) "Suppose, bhikkhus, a man were to wrap himself in a black cloth, loosen his hair, and tell a large crowd of people: 'Worthy sirs, I have committed an evil deed, reprehensible, censurable. Let me do whatever will make you pleased with me.'

A man standing on the sidelines might think: 'Truly, this man must have committed an evil deed, reprehensible, censurable, insofar as he has wrapped himself in a black cloth, loosened his hair, and tells a large crowd of people: [243] "Worthy sirs, I have committed an evil deed, reprehensible, censurable. Let me do whatever will make you pleased with me." Indeed, I should never do such an evil deed, reprehensible, censurable.'

"So too, when a bhikkhu or bhikkhunī has set up such a keen perception of peril in regard to the *pāṭidesanīya* offenses, it can be expected that one who has never yet committed a *pāṭidesanīya* offense will not commit one, and one who has committed such an offense will make amends for it in accordance with the Dhamma.[954]

"These, bhikkhus, are the four perils of offenses."

245 (3) Training

"Bhikkhus, this spiritual life is lived with the training as its benefit, with wisdom as its supervisor, with liberation as its core, and with mindfulness as its authority.[955]

(1) "And how, bhikkhus, is training its benefit? Here, the training pertaining to proper conduct[956] has been prescribed by me to my disciples so that those without confidence gain confidence and those with confidence increase [in their confidence]. One takes up this training pertaining to proper conduct in just the way that I have prescribed it to my disciples, keeping it unbroken, flawless, unblemished, and unblotched, so that those without confidence gain confidence and those with confidence increase [in their confidence]. Having undertaken them, one trains in the training rules.

"Again, the training fundamental to the spiritual life[957] has been prescribed by me to my disciples for the utterly complete destruction of suffering. One takes up this training fundamental to the spiritual life in just the way that I have prescribed it to my disciples for the utterly complete destruction of suffering, keeping it unbroken, flawless, unblemished, and unblotched. Having undertaken them, one trains in the training rules. It is in this way that the training is its benefit.

(2) "And how is wisdom its supervisor? Here, the teachings have been taught by me to my disciples for the utterly complete destruction of suffering. One scrutinizes those teachings with

wisdom in just the way that I have taught them to my disciples for the utterly complete destruction of suffering. It is in this way that wisdom is its supervisor.[958] [244]

(3) "And how is liberation its core? Here, the teachings have been taught by me to my disciples for the utterly complete destruction of suffering. Through liberation one experiences those teachings in just the way that I have taught them to my disciples for the utterly complete destruction of suffering. It is in this way that liberation is its core.[959]

(4) "And how is mindfulness its authority? One's mindfulness is well established internally thus: 'In just such a way I will fulfill the training pertaining to good conduct that I have not yet fulfilled or assist with wisdom in various respects the training pertaining to good conduct that I have fulfilled.'[960] And one's mindfulness is well established internally thus: 'In just such a way I will fulfill the training pertaining to the fundamentals of the spiritual life that I have not yet fulfilled or assist with wisdom in various respects the training pertaining to the fundamentals of the spiritual life that I have fulfilled.' And one's mindfulness is well established internally thus: 'In just such a way I will scrutinize with wisdom the teachings that I have not yet scrutinized or assist with wisdom in various respects the teachings that I have scrutinized.' And one's mindfulness is well established internally thus: 'In just such a way I will experience through liberation the Dhamma that I have not yet experienced or assist with wisdom in various respects the Dhamma that I have experienced.' It is in this way that mindfulness is its authority.

"Thus when it was said: 'Bhikkhus, this spiritual life is lived with the training as its benefit, with wisdom as its supervisor, with liberation as its core, and with mindfulness as its authority,' it is because of this that this was said."

246 (4) Lying Down

"Bhikkhus, there are these four postures for lying down. What four? The corpse's posture, the sensualist's posture, the lion's posture, and the Tathāgata's posture.

(1) "And what is the corpse's posture? Corpses usually lie flat on their backs. This is called the corpse's posture.

(2) "And what is the sensualist's posture? The sensualist

usually lies on his left side. This is called the sensualist's posture.

(3) "And what is the lion's posture? [245] The lion, the king of beasts, lies down on his right side, having covered one foot with the other and tucked his tail in between his thighs. When he awakens, he raises his front quarters and looks back at his hind quarters. If the lion sees any disorderliness or distension of his body, he is displeased. If he does not see any disorderliness or distension of his body, he is pleased. This is called the lion's posture.

(4) "And what is the Tathāgata's posture? Here, secluded from sensual pleasures, secluded from unwholesome states, the Tathāgata enters and dwells in the first jhāna . . . the fourth jhāna. This is called the Tathāgata's posture.

"These are the four postures."

247 (5) Worthy of a Stūpa

"Bhikkhus, these four are worthy of a stupa. What four? The Tathāgata, the Arahant, the Perfectly Enlightened One; a paccekabuddha; a Tathāgata's disciple; and a universal monarch. These four are worthy of a stupa."[961]

248 (6) The Growth of Wisdom

"Bhikkhus, these four things lead to the growth of wisdom. What four? Association with good persons, hearing the good Dhamma, careful attention, and practice in accordance with the Dhamma. These four things lead to the growth of wisdom."[962]

249 (7) Helpful[963]

"Bhikkhus, these four things are helpful to a human being. What four? Association with good persons, hearing the good Dhamma, careful attention, and practice in accordance with the Dhamma. [246] These four things are helpful to a human being."

250 (8) Declarations (1)

"Bhikkhus, there are these four ignoble declarations. What four? Saying that one has seen what one has not seen, saying that one has heard what one has not heard, saying that one has sensed what one has not sensed, saying that one has cognized what one has not cognized. There are these four ignoble declarations."

251 (9) Declarations (2)

"Bhikkhus, there are these four noble declarations. What four? Saying that one has not seen what one has not seen, saying that one has not heard what one has not heard, saying that one has not sensed what one has not sensed, saying that one has not cognized what one has not cognized. There are these four noble declarations."

252 (10) Declarations (3)

"Bhikkhus, there are these four ignoble declarations. What four? Saying that one has not seen what one has seen, saying that one has not heard what one has heard, saying that one has not sensed what one has sensed, saying that one has not cognized what one has cognized. There are these four ignoble declarations."

253 (11) Declarations (4)

"Bhikkhus, there are these four noble declarations. What four? Saying that one has seen what one has seen, saying that one has heard what one has heard, saying that one has sensed what one has sensed, saying that one has cognized what one has cognized. There are these four noble declarations."

VI. Direct Knowledge

254 (1) Direct Knowledge

"Bhikkhus, there are these four things. What four? (1) There are things to be fully understood by direct knowledge. (2) There are [247] things to be abandoned by direct knowledge. (3) There are things to be developed by direct knowledge. (4) There are things to be realized by direct knowledge.[964]

(1) "And what, bhikkhus, are the things to be fully understood by direct knowledge? The five aggregates subject to clinging. These are called the things to be fully understood by direct knowledge.

(2) "And what are the things to be abandoned by direct knowledge? Ignorance and craving for existence. These are called the things to be abandoned by direct knowledge.

(3) "And what are the things to be developed by direct knowledge? Serenity and insight. These are called the things to be developed by direct knowledge.

(4) "And what are the things to be realized by direct knowledge? True knowledge and liberation. These are called the things to be realized by direct knowledge.

"These, bhikkhus, are the four things."

255 (2) Quests

"Bhikkhus, there are these four ignoble quests.[965] What four? (1) Here, someone who is himself subject to old age seeks only what is subject to old age; (2) who is himself subject to illness seeks only what is subject to illness; (3) who is himself subject to death seeks only what is subject to death; and (4) who is himself subject to defilement seeks only what is subject to defilement. These are the four ignoble quests.

"There are, bhikkhus, these four noble quests. What four? (1) Here, someone who is himself subject to old age, having understood the danger in what is subject to old age, seeks the unaging, unsurpassed security from bondage, nibbāna; (2) who is himself subject to illness, having understood the danger in what is subject to illness, seeks the illness-free, unsurpassed security from bondage, nibbāna; (3) who is himself subject to death, having understood the danger in what is subject to death, seeks the deathless, unsurpassed security from bondage, nibbāna; (4) who is himself subject to defilement, having understood the danger in what is subject to defilement, [248] seeks the undefiled, unsurpassed security from bondage, nibbāna. These are the four noble quests."

256 (3) Sustaining

"Bhikkhus, there are these four means of sustaining a favorable relationship. What four? Giving, endearing speech, beneficent conduct, and impartiality. These are the four means of sustaining a favorable relationship."[966]

257 (4) Māluṅkyāputta

Then the Venerable Māluṅkyāputta approached the Blessed One, paid homage to him, sat down to one side, and said:[967]

"Bhante, it would be good if the Blessed One would teach me the Dhamma in brief, so that, having heard the Dhamma from the Blessed One, I might dwell alone, withdrawn, heedful, ardent, and resolute."

"Here now, Māluṅkyāputta, what should we say to the young bhikkhus when an old man like you, decrepit and advanced in years, asks for a brief exhortation from the Tathāgata?"

"Bhante, let the Blessed One teach me the Dhamma in brief! Let the Fortunate One teach me the Dhamma in brief! Perhaps I can understand the meaning of the Blessed One's statement; perhaps I can become an heir of the Blessed One's statement."

"There are, Māluṅkyāputta, these four sources of craving for a bhikkhu. What four? Craving arises in a bhikkhu because of robes, almsfood, lodgings, or for the sake of life here or elsewhere.[968] These are the four sources of craving for a bhikkhu. [249] When, Māluṅkyāputta, a bhikkhu has abandoned craving, cut it off at the root, made it like a palm stump, obliterated it so that it is no more subject to future arising, he is called a bhikkhu who has cut off craving, stripped off the fetter, and by completely breaking through conceit, has made an end of suffering."

Then the Venerable Māluṅkyāputta, exhorted in this way by the Blessed One, rose from his seat, paid homage to the Blessed One, circumambulated him keeping the right side toward him, and departed.

Then, dwelling alone, withdrawn, heedful, ardent, and resolute, in no long time the Venerable Māluṅkyāputta realized for himself with direct knowledge, in this very life, that unsurpassed consummation of the spiritual life for the sake of which clansmen rightly go forth from the household life into homelessness, and having entered upon it, he dwelled in it. He directly knew: "Destroyed is birth, the spiritual life has been lived, what had to be done has been done, there is no more coming back to any state of being." And the Venerable Māluṅkyāputta became one of the arahants.

258 (5) Families

"Bhikkhus, whatever families do not last long after attaining abundance of wealth, all do not last long for four reasons, or a particular one among them. What four? (1) They do not seek what has been lost; (2) they do not repair what has become decrepit; (3) they overindulge in eating and drinking; or (4) they appoint an immoral woman or man to be their chief. Whatever families do not last long after attaining abundance of wealth, all do not last long for these four reasons, or a particular one among them.[969]

"Bhikkhus, whatever families last long after attaining abundance of wealth, all last long for four reasons, or a particular one among them. What four? (1) They seek what has been lost; (2) they repair what has become decrepit; (3) they are moderate in eating and drinking; and (4) they appoint a virtuous woman or man to be their chief. Whatever families last long after attaining abundance of wealth, all last long for these four reasons, or a particular one among them." [250]

259 (6) Thoroughbred (1)

"Bhikkhus, possessing four factors a king's excellent thoroughbred horse is worthy of a king, an accessory of a king, and reckoned as a factor of kingship.[970] What four? Here, a king's excellent thoroughbred horse possesses beauty, strength, speed, and the right proportions. Possessing these four factors, a king's excellent thoroughbred horse is . . . reckoned as a factor of kingship.

"So too, bhikkhus, possessing four qualities, a bhikkhu is worthy of gifts, worthy of hospitality, worthy of offerings, worthy of reverential salutation, an unsurpassed field of merit for the world. What four? Here, a bhikkhu possesses beauty, strength, speed, and the right proportions.

(1) "And how does a bhikkhu possess beauty? Here, a bhikkhu is virtuous; he dwells restrained by the Pātimokkha, possessed of good conduct and resort, seeing danger in minute faults. Having undertaken the training rules, he trains in them. It is in this way that a bhikkhu possesses beauty.

(2) "And how does a bhikkhu possess strength? Here, a bhikkhu has aroused energy for abandoning unwholesome qualities and acquiring wholesome qualities; he is strong, firm in exertion, not casting off the duty of cultivating wholesome qualities. It is in this way that a bhikkhu possesses strength.

(3) "And how does a bhikkhu possess speed? Here, a bhikkhu understands as it really is: 'This is suffering'; he understands as it really is: 'This is the origin of suffering'; he understands as it really is: 'This is the cessation of suffering'; he understands as it really is: 'This is the way leading to the cessation of suffering.' It is in this way that a bhikkhu possesses speed.

(4) "And how does a bhikkhu possess the right proportions? Here, a bhikkhu is one who gains robes, almsfood, lodgings, and medicines and provisions for the sick. It is in this way that a bhikkhu possesses the right proportions. [251]

"Possessing these four qualities, a bhikkhu is worthy of gifts, worthy of hospitality, worthy of offerings, worthy of reverential salutation, an unsurpassed field of merit for the world."

260 (7) Thoroughbred (2)

[All as in 4:259, with only the following difference:][971]

(3) "And how does a bhikkhu possess speed? Here, with the destruction of the taints, a bhikkhu has realized for himself with direct knowledge, in this very life, the taintless liberation of mind, liberation by wisdom, and having entered upon it, he dwells in it. It is in this way that a bhikkhu possesses speed." [252]

261 (8) Powers

"Bhikkhus, there are these four powers. What four? The power of energy, the power of mindfulness, the power of concentration, and the power of wisdom. These are the four powers."

262 (9) Forest

"Bhikkhus, possessing four qualities a bhikkhu is not fit to resort to remote lodgings in forests and jungle groves. What four? [He thinks] (1) sensual thoughts, (2) thoughts of ill will, and (3) thoughts of harming; and (4) he is unwise, stupid, dull. Possessing these four qualities a bhikkhu is not fit to resort to remote lodgings in forests and jungle groves.

"Possessing four [other] qualities a bhikkhu is fit to resort to remote lodgings in forests and jungle groves. What four? [He thinks] (1) thoughts of renunciation, (2) good will, and (3) harmlessness; and (4) he is wise, not stupid or dull. Possessing these four qualities a bhikkhu is fit to resort to remote lodgings in forests and jungle groves."

263 (10) Action

"Bhikkhus, possessing four qualities, the foolish, incompetent, bad person maintains himself in a maimed and injured condition; he is blameworthy and subject to reproach by the wise;

and he generates much demerit. What four? Blameworthy bodily action, blameworthy verbal action, blameworthy mental action, and blameworthy view. [253] Possessing these four qualities . . . he generates much demerit.

"Bhikkhus, possessing four [other] qualities, the wise, competent, good person preserves himself unmaimed and uninjured; he is blameless and beyond reproach by the wise; and he generates much merit. What four? Blameless bodily action, blameless verbal action, blameless mental action, and blameless view. Possessing these four qualities . . . he generates much merit."

VII. Courses of Kamma

264 (1) The Destruction of Life

"Bhikkhus, one possessing four qualities is deposited in hell as if brought there. What four? He himself destroys life; he encourages others to destroy life; he approves of the destruction of life; and he speaks in praise of the destruction of life. One possessing these four qualities is deposited in hell as if brought there.

"Bhikkhus, one possessing four [other] qualities is deposited in heaven as if brought there. What four? He himself abstains from the destruction of life; he encourages others to abstain from the destruction of life; he approves of abstaining from the destruction of life; and he speaks in praise of abstaining from the destruction of life. One possessing these four qualities is deposited in heaven as if brought there."

265 (2)–273 (10) Taking What Is Not Given, Etc.

"Bhikkhus, one possessing four qualities is deposited in hell as if brought there. What four?[972] (1) He himself takes what is not given . . . [254] . . . engages in sexual misconduct . . . speaks falsely . . . speaks divisively . . . speaks harshly . . . [255] . . . indulges in idle chatter . . . is full of longing . . . bears ill will . . . holds wrong view; (2) he encourages others in wrong view; (3) he approves of wrong view; and (4) he speaks in praise of wrong view. One possessing these four qualities is deposited in hell as if brought there.

"Bhikkhus, one possessing four [other] qualities is deposited in heaven as if brought there. What four? (1) He himself abstains from taking what is not given . . . holds right view; (2) he encourages others in right view; (3) he approves of right view; and (4) he speaks in praise of right view. [256] One possessing these four qualities is deposited in heaven as if brought there."

VIII. Lust and So Forth Repetition Series

274 (1) Four Establishments of Mindfulness

"Bhikkhus, for direct knowledge of lust, four things are to be developed. What four? (1) Here, a bhikkhu dwells contemplating the body in the body, ardent, clearly comprehending, mindful, having removed longing and dejection in regard to the world. (2) He dwells contemplating feelings in feelings . . . (3) . . . mind in mind . . . (4) . . . phenomena in phenomena, ardent, clearly comprehending, mindful, having removed longing and dejection in regard to the world. For direct knowledge of lust, these four things are to be developed."

275 (2) Four Right Strivings

"Bhikkhus, for direct knowledge of lust, four things are to be developed. What four? (1) Here, a bhikkhu generates desire for the non-arising of unarisen bad unwholesome states; he makes an effort, arouses energy, applies his mind, and strives. (2) He generates desire for the abandoning of arisen bad unwholesome states . . . (3) . . . for the arising of unarisen wholesome states . . . (4) . . . for the maintenance of arisen wholesome states, for their non-decline, increase, expansion, and fulfillment by development; he makes an effort, arouses energy, applies his mind, and strives. For direct knowledge of lust, these four things are to be developed."

276 (3) Four Bases for Psychic Potency

"Bhikkhus, for direct knowledge of lust, four things are to be developed. What four? (1) Here, a bhikkhu develops the basis for psychic potency that possesses concentration due to desire and activities of striving. (2) He develops the basis for psychic potency that possesses concentration due to energy . . . (3) . . . that possesses concentration due to mind . . . (4) . . . that possesses concentration due to investigation and activities of striving. For direct knowledge of lust, these four things are to be developed."

277 (4)–303 (30)

"Bhikkhus, for full understanding of lust . . . for the utter destruction . . . for the abandoning . . . [257] . . . for the destruction . . . for the vanishing . . . for the fading away . . . for the cessation . . . for the giving up . . . For the relinquishment of lust, these four things are to be developed."[973]

304 (31)–783 (510)

"Bhikkhus, for direct knowledge . . . for full understanding . . . for the utter destruction . . . for the abandoning . . . for the destruction . . . for the vanishing . . . for the fading away . . . for the cessation . . . for the giving up . . . for the relinquishment of hatred . . . of delusion . . . of anger . . . of hostility . . . of denigration . . . of insolence . . . of envy . . . of miserliness . . . of deceitfulness . . . of craftiness . . . of obstinacy . . . of vehemence . . . of conceit . . . of arrogance . . . of intoxication . . . of heedlessness, these four things are to be developed. What four? (1) Here, a bhikkhu dwells contemplating the body in the body . . . (2) . . . feelings in feelings . . . (3) . . . mind in mind . . . (4) . . . phenomena in phenomena, ardent, clearly comprehending, mindful, having removed longing and dejection in regard to the world. (1) Here, a bhikkhu generates desire for the non-arising of unarisen bad unwholesome states . . . (2) . . . for the abandoning of arisen bad unwholesome states . . . (3) . . . for the arising of unarisen wholesome states . . . (4) . . . for the maintenance of arisen wholesome states, for their non-decline, increase, expansion, and fulfillment by development; he makes an effort, arouses energy, applies his mind, and strives. (1) Here, a bhikkhu develops the basis for psychic potency that possesses concentration due to desire . . . (2) . . . that possesses concentration due to energy . . . (3) . . . that possesses concentration due to mind . . . (4) . . . that possesses concentration due to investigation and activities of striving. For the relinquishment of heedlessness, these four things are to be developed."

This is what the Blessed One said. Elated, those bhikkhus delighted in the Blessed One's statement.

The Book of the Fours is finished.

The Book of the Fives
(*Pañcakanipāta*)

The Book of the Fives

The First Fifty

The Second Fifty

The Third Fifty

The Fourth Fifty

The Fifth Fifty

The Sixth Fifty

Discourses Extra to the Chapter

[1] # The Book of the Fives

Homage to the Blessed One, the Arahant,
the Perfectly Enlightened One

The First Fifty

I. The Trainee's Powers

1 (1) In Brief

Thus have I heard. On one occasion the Blessed One was dwelling at Sāvatthī in Jeta's Grove, Anāthapiṇḍika's Park. There the Blessed One addressed the bhikkhus: "Bhikkhus!"

"Venerable sir!" those bhikkhus replied. The Blessed One said this:

"Bhikkhus, there are these five trainee's powers.[974] What five? The power of faith, the power of moral shame, the power of moral dread, the power of energy, and the power of wisdom. These are the five trainee's powers. Therefore, bhikkhus, you should train yourselves thus: 'We will possess the power of faith, a trainee's power; we will possess the power of moral shame, a trainee's power; we will possess the power of moral dread, a trainee's power; we will possess the power of energy, a trainee's power; we will possess the power of wisdom, a trainee's power.' Thus, bhikkhus, should you train yourselves." [This is what the Blessed One said. Elated, those bhikkhus delighted in the Blessed One's statement.][975] [2]

2 (2) In Detail

At Sāvatthī. "Bhikkhus, there are these five trainee's powers. What five? The power of faith, the power of moral shame, the power of moral dread, the power of energy, and the power of wisdom.

(1) "And what, bhikkhus, is the power of faith? Here, a noble disciple is endowed with faith. He places faith in the enlightenment of the Tathāgata thus: 'The Blessed One is an arahant, perfectly enlightened, accomplished in true knowledge and conduct, fortunate, knower of the world, unsurpassed trainer of persons to be tamed, teacher of devas and humans, the Enlightened One, the Blessed One.' This is called the power of faith.

(2) "And what is the power of moral shame? Here, a noble disciple has a sense of moral shame; he is ashamed of bodily, verbal, and mental misconduct; he is ashamed of acquiring evil, unwholesome qualities. This is called the power of moral shame.

(3) "And what is the power of moral dread? Here, a noble disciple dreads wrongdoing; he dreads bodily, verbal, and mental misconduct; he dreads acquiring evil, unwholesome qualities. This is called the power of moral dread.[976]

(4) "And what is the power of energy? Here, a noble disciple has aroused energy for abandoning unwholesome qualities and acquiring wholesome qualities; he is strong, firm in exertion, not casting off the duty of cultivating wholesome qualities. This is called the power of energy.

(5) "And what is the power of wisdom? Here, a noble disciple is wise; he possesses the wisdom that discerns arising and passing away, which is noble and penetrative and leads to the complete destruction of suffering.[977] This is called the power of wisdom.

"These are the five trainee's powers. Therefore, bhikkhus, you should train yourselves thus: 'We will possess the power of faith, a trainee's power; we will possess the power of moral shame, a trainee's power; we will possess the power of moral dread, [3] a trainee's power; we will possess the power of energy, a trainee's power; we will possess the power of wisdom, a trainee's power.' Thus, bhikkhus, should you train yourselves."

3 (3) Suffering

"Bhikkhus, possessing five qualities, a bhikkhu dwells in suffering in this very life—with distress, anguish, and fever—and with the breakup of the body, after death, a bad destination can be expected for him. What five? Here, a bhikkhu is devoid of faith, morally shameless, morally reckless, lazy, and unwise. Possessing these five qualities, a bhikkhu dwells in suffering in this very life—with distress, anguish, and fever—and with the breakup of the body, after death, he can expect a bad destination.

"Bhikkhus, possessing five [other] qualities, a bhikkhu dwells happily in this very life—without distress, anguish, and fever—and with the breakup of the body, after death, a good destination can be expected for him. What five? Here, a bhikkhu is endowed with faith, has a sense of moral shame, has moral dread, and is energetic and wise. Possessing these five qualities, a bhikkhu dwells happily in this very life—without distress, anguish, and fever—and with the breakup of the body, after death, a good destination can be expected for him."

4 (4) As If Brought There

"Bhikkhus, possessing five qualities, a bhikkhu is deposited in hell as if brought there. What five? Here, a bhikkhu is devoid of faith, morally shameless, morally reckless, lazy, and unwise. Possessing these five qualities, a bhikkhu is deposited in hell as if brought there. [4]

"Bhikkhus, possessing five [other] qualities, a bhikkhu is deposited in heaven as if brought there. What five? Here, a bhikkhu is endowed with faith, has a sense of moral shame, has moral dread, and is energetic and wise. Possessing these five qualities, a bhikkhu is deposited in heaven as if brought there."

5 (5) Training

"Bhikkhus, any bhikkhu or bhikkhunī who gives up the training and reverts to the lower life incurs five reasonable criticisms and grounds for censure in this very life. What five? (1) 'You did not have faith in [cultivating] wholesome qualities. (2) You did not have a sense of moral shame in [cultivating] wholesome qualities. (3) You did not have moral dread in [cultivating] wholesome qualities. (4) You did not have energy in [cultivating] wholesome qualities. (5) You did not have wisdom in [cultivating] wholesome qualities.' Any bhikkhu or bhikkhunī who gives up the training and reverts to the lower life incurs these five reasonable criticisms and grounds for censure in this very life.

"Bhikkhus, any bhikkhu or bhikkhunī who lives the complete and pure spiritual life, even with pain and dejection, weeping with a tearful face, gains five reasonable grounds for praise in this very life. What five? (1) 'You have had faith in [cultivating] wholesome qualities. (2) You have had a sense of moral shame in [cultivating] wholesome qualities. (3) You have had moral dread in [cultivating] wholesome qualities. (4) You have had energy in [cultivating] wholesome qualities. (5) You have had wisdom in [cultivating] wholesome qualities.' Any bhikkhu or bhikkhunī who lives the complete and pure spiritual life, even with pain and dejection, weeping with a tearful face, [5] gains these five reasonable grounds for praise in this very life."

6 (6) Entering

(1) "Bhikkhus, there is no entering upon the unwholesome so long as faith is securely settled in [cultivating] wholesome qualities. But when faith has disappeared and lack of faith obsesses one, then there is the entering upon the unwholesome.

(2) "There is no entering upon the unwholesome so long as a sense of moral shame is securely settled in [cultivating] wholesome qualities. But when a sense of moral shame has disappeared and moral shamelessness obsesses one, then there is the entering upon the unwholesome.

(3) "There is no entering upon the unwholesome so long as moral dread is securely settled in [cultivating] wholesome qualities. But when moral dread has disappeared and lack of moral dread obsesses one, then there is the entering upon the unwholesome.

(4) "There is no entering upon the unwholesome so long as energy is securely settled in [cultivating] wholesome qualities. But when energy has disappeared and laziness obsesses one, then there is the entering upon the unwholesome.

(5) "There is no entering upon the unwholesome so long as wisdom is securely settled in [cultivating] wholesome qualities. But when wisdom has disappeared and lack of wisdom obsesses one, then there is the entering upon the unwholesome."

7 (7) Sensual Pleasures

"Bhikkhus, beings for the most part are captivated by sensual pleasures. When a clansman has forsaken the sickle and carrying-pole and gone forth from the household life into homelessness, he can be described as a clansman who has gone forth out of faith. For what reason? Sensual pleasures, whether of this or that kind, can be obtained by a youth. Inferior sensual pleasures, middling sensual pleasures, and superior sensual pleasures are all reckoned simply as sensual pleasures. [6]

"Suppose a young infant boy, ignorant, lying on his back, were to put a stick or pebble in his mouth because of his nurse's heedlessness. His nurse would quickly attend to him and try to take it out. If she could not quickly take it out, she would brace the boy's head with her left hand and, hooking a finger of her right hand, she would take it out even if she had to draw blood. For what reason? There would be some distress for the boy—this I don't deny—but the nurse has to do so for his good and welfare, out of compassion for him. However, when the boy has grown up and has enough sense, the nurse would be unconcerned about him, thinking: 'The boy can now look after himself. He won't be heedless.'

"So too, so long as a bhikkhu is still not accomplished in faith in [cultivating] wholesome qualities, in a sense of shame in [cultivating] wholesome qualities, in moral dread in [cultivating] wholesome qualities, in energy in [cultivating] wholesome qualities, and in wisdom in [cultivating] wholesome qualities, I must still look after him. But when that bhikkhu is accomplished in faith in [cultivating] wholesome qualities . . . accomplished in wisdom in [cultivating] wholesome qualities, then I am unconcerned about him, thinking: 'The bhikkhu can now look after himself. He won't be heedless.'"[978]

8 (8) Falling Away (1)

"Bhikkhus, possessing five qualities a bhikkhu falls away and is not established in the good Dhamma. What five? (1) A bhikkhu devoid of faith falls away and is not established [7] in the good Dhamma. (2) A morally shameless bhikkhu . . . (3) A morally reckless bhikkhu . . . (4) A lazy bhikkhu . . . (5) An unwise bhikkhu falls away and is not established in the good Dhamma.

Possessing these five qualities, a bhikkhu falls away and is not established in the good Dhamma.

"Bhikkhus, possessing five [other] qualities a bhikkhu does not fall away but is established in the good Dhamma. What five? (1) A bhikkhu endowed with faith does not fall away but is established in the good Dhamma. (2) A bhikkhu who has a sense of moral shame ... (3) A bhikkhu who has moral dread ... (4) An energetic bhikkhu ... (5) A wise bhikkhu does not fall away but is established in the good Dhamma. Possessing these five qualities, a bhikkhu does not fall away but is established in the good Dhamma."

9 (9) Falling Away (2)

"Bhikkhus, possessing five qualities, an irreverent and undeferential bhikkhu falls away and is not established in the good Dhamma. What five? (1) An irreverent and undeferential bhikkhu devoid of faith falls away and is not established in the good Dhamma. (2) An irreverent and undeferential morally shameless bhikkhu ... (3) An irreverent and undeferential morally reckless bhikkhu ... (4) An irreverent and undeferential lazy bhikkhu ... (5) An irreverent and undeferential unwise bhikkhu falls away and is not established in the good Dhamma. Possessing these five qualities, an irreverent and undeferential bhikkhu is not established in the good Dhamma. [8]

"Bhikkhus, possessing five [other] qualities, a reverential and deferential bhikkhu does not fall away but is established in the good Dhamma. What five? (1) A reverential and deferential bhikkhu endowed with faith does not fall away but is established in the good Dhamma. (2) A reverential and deferential bhikkhu who has a sense of moral shame ... (3) A reverential and deferential bhikkhu who has moral dread ... (4) A reverential and deferential bhikkhu who is energetic ... (5) A reverential and deferential bhikkhu who is wise does not fall away but is established in the good Dhamma. Possessing these five qualities, a reverential and deferential bhikkhu does not fall away but is established in the good Dhamma."

10 (10) Irreverent

"Bhikkhus, possessing five qualities, an irreverent and undeferential bhikkhu is not capable of achieving growth, progress, and maturity in this Dhamma and discipline. What five? (1) An irreverent and undeferential bhikkhu devoid of faith is not capable of achieving growth, progress, and maturity in this Dhamma and discipline. (2) An irreverent and undeferential bhikkhu who is morally shameless... (3) An irreverent and undeferential bhikkhu who is morally reckless... (4) An irreverent and undeferential bhikkhu who is lazy... (5) An irreverent and undeferential bhikkhu who is unwise is not capable of achieving growth, progress, and maturity in this Dhamma and discipline. Possessing these five qualities, an irreverent and undeferential bhikkhu is not capable of achieving growth, progress, and maturity in this Dhamma and discipline.

"Bhikkhus, possessing five [other] qualities, a reverential and deferential bhikkhu is capable of achieving growth, progress, and maturity in this Dhamma and discipline. What five? (1) A reverential and deferential bhikkhu who is endowed with faith is capable of achieving growth, progress, and maturity in this Dhamma and discipline. (2) A reverential and deferential bhikkhu who has a sense of moral shame... (3) A reverential and deferential bhikkhu who has moral dread... [9]... (4) A reverential and deferential bhikkhu who is energetic... (5) A reverential and deferential bhikkhu who is wise is capable of achieving growth, progress, and maturity in this Dhamma and discipline. Possessing these five qualities, a reverential and deferential bhikkhu is capable of achieving growth, progress, and maturity in this Dhamma and discipline."

II. Powers

11 (1) Not Heard Before

"Bhikkhus, I claim to have attained the consummation and perfection of direct knowledge regarding things not heard before.[979]

"There are these five Tathāgata's powers that the Tathāgata has, possessing which he claims the place of the chief bull, roars his lion's roar in the assemblies, and sets in motion the brahma wheel.[980] What five? The power of faith, the power of moral shame, the power of moral dread, the power of energy, and the power of wisdom. These are the five Tathāgata's powers that the Tathāgata has, possessing which he claims the place of the chief bull, roars his lion's roar in the assemblies, and sets in motion the brahma wheel." [10]

12 (2) Peak (1)

"Bhikkhus, there are these five trainee's powers. What five? The power of faith, the power of moral shame, the power of moral dread, the power of energy, and the power of wisdom. These are the five trainee's powers. Among these five trainee's powers, the power of wisdom is foremost, the one that holds all the others in place, the one that unifies them. Just as the peak is the chief part of a peaked-roof house, the part that holds all the others in place, that unifies them, so among these five trainee powers, the power of wisdom is foremost, the one that holds all the others in place, the one that unifies them.

"Therefore, bhikkhus, you should train yourselves thus: (1) 'We will possess the power of faith, a trainee's power; (2) the power of moral shame, a trainee's power; (3) the power of moral dread, a trainee's power; (4) the power of energy, a trainee's power; (5) the power of wisdom, a trainee's power.' Thus, bhikkhus, should you train yourselves."

13 (3) In Brief

"Bhikkhus, there are these five powers. What five? The power of faith, the power of energy, the power of mindfulness, the power of concentration, and the power of wisdom. These are the five powers."[981]

14 (4) In Detail

"Bhikkhus, there are these five powers. What five? The power of faith, the power of energy, the power of mindfulness, the power of concentration, and the power of wisdom.

(1) "And what, bhikkhus, is the power of faith? Here, a noble disciple is endowed with faith. He places faith in the enlightenment of the Tathāgata thus: 'The Blessed One is an arahant, perfectly enlightened... [as in 5:2] . . . the Enlightened One, the Blessed One.' [11] This is called the power of faith.

(2) "And what is the power of energy? Here, a noble disciple has aroused energy for abandoning unwholesome qualities and acquiring wholesome qualities; he is strong, firm in exertion, not casting off the duty of cultivating wholesome qualities. This is called the power of energy.

(3) "And what is the power of mindfulness? Here, the noble disciple is mindful, possessing supreme mindfulness and alertness, one who remembers and recollects what was done and said long ago. This is called the power of mindfulness.

(4) "And what is the power of concentration? Here, secluded from sensual pleasures, secluded from unwholesome states, a bhikkhu enters and dwells in the first jhāna, which consists of rapture and pleasure born of seclusion, accompanied by thought and examination. With the subsiding of thought and examination, he enters and dwells in the second jhāna, which has internal placidity and unification of mind and consists of rapture and pleasure born of concentration, without thought and examination. With the fading away as well of rapture, he dwells equanimous and, mindful and clearly comprehending, he experiences pleasure with the body; he enters and dwells in the third jhāna of which the noble ones declare: 'He is equanimous, mindful, one who dwells happily.' With the abandoning of pleasure and pain, and with the previous passing away of joy and dejection, he enters and dwells in the fourth jhāna, neither painful nor pleasant, which has purification of mindfulness by equanimity. This is called the power of concentration.

(5) "And what is the power of wisdom? Here, a noble disciple is wise; he possesses the wisdom that discerns arising and passing away, which is noble and penetrative and leads to the complete destruction of suffering. This is called the power of wisdom.

"These, bhikkhus, are the five powers."

15 (5) To Be Seen

"Bhikkhus, there are these five powers. What five? The power of faith, the power of energy, the power of mindfulness, the power of concentration, [12] and the power of wisdom.

(1) "And where, bhikkhus, is the power of faith to be seen? The power of faith is to be seen in the four factors of stream-entry.[982] (2) And where is the power of energy to be seen? The power of energy is to be seen in the four right strivings. (3) And where is the power of mindfulness to be seen? The power of mindfulness is to be seen in the four establishments of mindfulness. (4) And where is the power of concentration to be seen? The power of concentration is to be seen in the four jhānas. (5)

And where is the power of wisdom to be seen? The power of wisdom is to be seen in the four noble truths.

"These, bhikkhus, are the five powers."

16 (6) Peak (2)

"Bhikkhus, there are these five powers. What five? The power of faith, the power of energy, the power of mindfulness, the power of concentration, and the power of wisdom. These are the five powers. Among these five powers, the power of wisdom is foremost, the one that holds all in place, the one that unifies them. Just as the peak is the chief part of a peaked-roof house, the part that that holds all in place, that unifies them, so among these five powers, the power of wisdom is foremost, the one that holds all in place, the one that unifies them."

17 (7) Welfare (1)

"Bhikkhus, possessing five qualities, a bhikkhu is practicing for his own welfare but not for the welfare of others. What five? (1) Here, a bhikkhu is himself accomplished in virtuous behavior but does not encourage others to become accomplished in virtuous behavior; (2) he is himself accomplished in concentration but does not encourage others to become accomplished in concentration; (3) he is himself accomplished in wisdom but does not encourage others to become accomplished in wisdom; (4) he is himself accomplished in liberation but does not encourage others to become accomplished in liberation; (5) he is himself accomplished in the knowledge and vision of liberation but does not encourage others to become accomplished in the knowledge and vision of liberation. [13] Possessing these five qualities, a bhikkhu is practicing for his own welfare but not for the welfare of others."

18 (8) Welfare (2)

"Bhikkhus, possessing five qualities, a bhikkhu is practicing for the welfare of others but not for his own welfare. What five? (1) Here, a bhikkhu is not accomplished in virtuous behavior himself but he encourages others to become accomplished in virtuous behavior; (2) he is not accomplished in concentration himself but he encourages others to become accomplished in concentration; (3) he is not accomplished in wisdom himself but he encourages others to become accomplished in wisdom; (4) he is not accomplished in liberation himself but he encourages others to become accomplished in liberation; (5) he is not accomplished in the knowledge and vision of liberation himself but he encourages others to become accomplished in the knowledge and vision of liberation. Possessing these five qualities, a bhikkhu is practicing for the welfare of others but not for his own welfare."

19 (9) Welfare (3)

"Bhikkhus, possessing five qualities, a bhikkhu is practicing neither for his own welfare nor for the welfare of others. What five? (1) Here, a bhikkhu is not accomplished in virtuous behavior himself and does not encourage others to become accomplished in virtuous behavior; (2) he is not accomplished in concentration himself and does not encourage others to become accomplished in concentration; (3) he is not accomplished in wisdom himself and does not encourage others to become accomplished in wisdom; (4) he is not accomplished in liberation himself and does not encourage others to become accomplished in liberation; (5) he is not accomplished in the knowledge and vision of liberation himself and does not encourage others to become accomplished in the knowledge and vision of liberation. [14] Possessing these five qualities, a bhikkhu is practicing neither for his own welfare nor for the welfare of others."

20 (10) Welfare (4)

"Bhikkhus, possessing five qualities, a bhikkhu is practicing both for his own welfare and for the welfare of others. What five? (1) Here, a bhikkhu is himself accomplished in virtuous behavior and encourages others to become accomplished in virtuous behavior; (2) he is himself accomplished in concentration and encourages others to become accomplished in concentration; (3) he is himself accomplished in wisdom and encourages others to become accomplished in wisdom; (4) he is himself accomplished in liberation and encourages others to become accomplished in liberation; (5) he is himself accomplished in the knowledge and vision of liberation and encourages others to become accomplished in the knowledge and vision of liberation. Possessing these five qualities, a bhikkhu is practicing both for his own welfare and for the welfare of others."

III. Five Factored

21 (1) Irreverent (1)

"(1) Bhikkhus, when a bhikkhu is irreverent and undeferential, and his behavior is uncongenial to his fellow monks, it is impossible for him to fulfill the factor of proper conduct. [15] (2) Without fulfilling the factor of proper conduct, it is impossible for him to fulfill the factor of a trainee. (3) Without fulfilling the factor of a trainee, it is impossible for him to fulfill virtuous behavior. (4) Without fulfilling virtuous behavior, it is impossible for him to fulfill right view. (5) Without fulfilling right view, it is impossible for him to fulfill right concentration.[983]

"(1) But, bhikkhus, when a bhikkhu is reverential and deferential, and his behavior is congenial to his fellow monks, it is possible for him to fulfill the duty of proper conduct. (2) Having fulfilled the duty of proper conduct, it is possible for him to fulfill the duty of a trainee. (3) Having fulfilled the duty of a trainee, it is possible for him to fulfill virtuous behavior. (4) Having fulfilled virtuous behavior, it is possible for him to fulfill right view. (5) Having fulfilled right view, it is possible for him to fulfill right concentration."

22 (2) Irreverent (2)

"(1) Bhikkhus, when a bhikkhu is irreverent and undeferential, and his behavior is uncongenial to his fellow monks, it is impossible for him to fulfill the factor of proper conduct. (2) Without fulfilling the factor of proper conduct, it is impossible for him to fulfill the factor of a trainee. (3) Without fulfilling the factor of a trainee, it is impossible for him to fulfill the aggregate of virtuous behavior. (4) Without fulfilling the aggregate of virtuous behavior, it is impossible for him to fulfill the aggregate of concentration. (5) Without fulfilling the aggregate of concentration, it is impossible for him to fulfill the aggregate of wisdom.

"(1) But, bhikkhus, when a bhikkhu is reverential and deferential, and his behavior is congenial to his fellow monks, it is possible for him to fulfill the factor of proper conduct. (2)

Having fulfilled the factor of proper conduct, it is possible for him to fulfill the factor of a trainee. (3) Having fulfilled the factor of a trainee, it is possible for him to fulfill the aggregate of virtuous behavior. (4) Having fulfilled the aggregate of virtuous behavior, it is possible for him to fulfill the aggregate of concentration. [16] (5) Having fulfilled the aggregate of concentration, it is possible for him to fulfill the aggregate of wisdom."

23 (3) Defilements

"Bhikkhus,[984] there are these five defilements of gold, defiled by which gold is not malleable, wieldy, and luminous, but brittle and not properly fit for work. What five? Iron, copper, tin, lead, and silver. These are the five defilements of gold, defiled by which gold is not malleable, wieldy, and luminous, but brittle and not properly fit for work. But when gold is freed from these five defilements, it is malleable, wieldy, and luminous, pliant and properly fit for work. Then whatever kind of ornament one wishes to make from it—whether a bracelet, earrings, a necklace, or a golden garland—one can achieve one's purpose.[985]

"So too, bhikkhus, there are these five defilements of the mind, defiled by which the mind is not malleable, wieldy, and luminous, but brittle and not properly concentrated for the destruction of the taints. What five? Sensual desire, ill will, dullness and drowsiness, restlessness and remorse, and doubt. These are the five defilements of the mind, defiled by which the mind is not malleable, wieldy, and luminous, but brittle and not properly concentrated for the destruction of the taints. But when the mind is freed from these five defilements, it becomes malleable, wieldy, [17] and luminous, pliant and properly concentrated for the destruction of the taints. Then, there being a suitable basis, one is capable of realizing any state realizable by direct knowledge toward which one might incline the mind.[986]

"If one wishes: 'May I wield the various kinds of psychic potency: having been one, may I become many; having been many, may I become one; may I appear and vanish; may I go unhindered through a wall, through a rampart, through a mountain as though through space; may I dive in and out of the earth as though it were water; may I walk on water without sinking as though it were earth; seated cross-legged, may I travel in space like a bird; with my hand may I touch and stroke the moon and sun so powerful and mighty; may I exercise mastery with the body as far as the brahmā world,' one is capable of realizing it, there being a suitable basis.

"If one wishes: 'May I, with the divine ear element, which is purified and surpasses the human, hear both kinds of sounds, the divine and human, those that are far as well as near,' one is capable of realizing it, there being a suitable basis.

"If one wishes: 'May I understand the minds of other beings and persons, having encompassed them with my own mind. May I understand a mind with lust as a mind with lust, and a mind without lust as a mind without lust; [18] a mind with hatred as a mind with hatred, and a mind without hatred as a mind without hatred; a mind with delusion as a mind with delusion, and a mind without delusion as a mind without delusion; a contracted mind as contracted and a distracted mind as distracted; an exalted mind as exalted and an unexalted mind as unexalted; a surpassable mind as surpassable and an unsurpassable mind as unsurpassable; a concentrated mind as concentrated and an unconcentrated mind as unconcentrated; a liberated mind as liberated and an unliberated mind as unliberated,' one is capable of realizing it, there being a suitable basis.

"If one wishes: 'May I recollect my manifold past abodes, that is, one birth, two births, three births, four births, five births, ten births, twenty births, thirty births, forty births, fifty births, a hundred births, a thousand births, a hundred thousand births, many eons of world-dissolution, many eons of world-evolution, many eons of world-dissolution and world-evolution thus: "There I was so named, of such a clan, with such an appearance, such was my food, such my experience of pleasure and pain, such my life span; passing away from there, I was reborn elsewhere, and there too I was so named, of such a clan, with such an appearance, such was my food, such my experience of pleasure and pain, such my life span; passing away from there, I was reborn here"—may I thus recollect my manifold past abodes with their aspects and details,' one is capable of realizing it, there being a suitable basis. [19]

"If one wishes: 'May I, with the divine eye, which is purified and surpasses the human, see beings passing away and being reborn, inferior and superior, beautiful and ugly, fortunate and unfortunate, and understand how beings fare in accordance with their kamma thus: "These beings who engaged in misconduct by body, speech, and mind, who reviled the noble ones, held wrong view, and undertook kamma based on wrong view, with the breakup of the body, after death, have been reborn in the plane of misery, in a bad destination, in the lower world, in hell; but these beings who engaged in good conduct by body, speech, and mind, who did not revile the noble ones, who held right view, and undertook kamma based on right view, with the breakup of the body, after death, have been reborn in a good destination, in a heavenly world"—thus with the divine eye, which is purified and surpasses the human, may I see beings passing away and being reborn, inferior and superior, beautiful and ugly, fortunate and unfortunate, and understand how beings fare in accordance with their kamma,' one is capable of realizing it, there being a suitable basis.

"If one wishes: 'May I, with the destruction of the taints, in this very life realize for myself with direct knowledge the taintless liberation of mind, liberation by wisdom, and having entered upon it, may I dwell in it,' one is capable of realizing it, there being a suitable basis."

24 (4) Immoral

"Bhikkhus, (1) for an immoral person, for one deficient in virtuous behavior, (2) right concentration lacks its proximate cause. When there is no right concentration, for one deficient in right concentration, (3) the knowledge and vision of things as they really are lacks its proximate cause. When there is no knowledge and vision of things as they really are, for one deficient in the knowledge and vision of things as they really are, (4) disenchantment and dispassion lack their proximate cause. When there is no disenchantment and dispassion, for one deficient in disenchantment and dispassion, (5) the knowledge and vision of liberation lacks its proximate cause.[987]

"Suppose there is a tree deficient in branches and foliage. Then its shoots do not grow to fullness; also its bark, [20] softwood, and heartwood do not grow to fullness. So too, for an immoral person, one deficient in virtuous behavior, right concentration lacks its proximate cause. When there is no right concentration . . . the knowledge and vision of liberation lacks its proximate cause.

"Bhikkhus, (1) for a virtuous person, for one whose behavior is virtuous, (2) right concentration possesses its proximate cause. When there is right concentration, for one possessing right concentration, (3) the knowledge and vision of things as they really are possesses its proximate cause. When there is the knowledge and vision of things as they really are, for one possessing the knowledge and vision of things as they really are, (4) disenchantment and dispassion possess their proximate cause. When there is disenchantment and dispassion, for one possessing disenchantment and dispassion, (5) the knowledge and vision of liberation possesses its proximate cause.

"Suppose there is a tree possessing branches and foliage. Then its shoots grow to fullness; also its bark, softwood, and heartwood grow to fullness. So too, for a virtuous person, one whose behavior is virtuous, right concentration possesses its proximate cause. When there is right concentration . . . the knowledge and vision of liberation possesses its proximate cause."

25 (5) Assisted

"Bhikkhus, when right view is assisted by five factors, it has liberation of mind as its fruit, liberation of mind as its fruit and benefit; it has liberation by wisdom as its fruit, liberation by wisdom as its fruit and benefit.[988] What five? [21] Here, right view is assisted by virtuous behavior, learning, discussion, calm, and insight. When right view is assisted by these five factors, it has liberation of mind as its fruit, liberation of mind as its fruit and benefit; it has liberation by wisdom as its fruit, liberation by wisdom as its fruit and benefit."

26 (6) Liberation

"Bhikkhus, there are these five bases of liberation[989] by means of which, if a bhikkhu dwells heedful, ardent, and resolute, his unliberated mind is liberated, his undestroyed taints are utterly destroyed, and he reaches the as-yet-unreached unsurpassed security from bondage. What five?

(1) "Here, bhikkhus, the Teacher or a fellow monk in the position of a teacher teaches the Dhamma to a bhikkhu. In whatever way the Teacher or that fellow monk in the position of a teacher teaches the Dhamma to the bhikkhu, in just that way he experiences inspiration in the meaning and inspiration in

the Dhamma.[990] As he does so, joy arises in him. When he is joyful, rapture arises. For one with a rapturous mind, the body becomes tranquil. One tranquil in body feels pleasure. For one feeling pleasure, the mind becomes concentrated.[991] This is the first basis of liberation, by means of which, if a bhikkhu dwells heedful, ardent, and resolute, his unliberated mind is liberated, his undestroyed taints are utterly destroyed, and he reaches the as-yet-unreached unsurpassed security from bondage.

(2) "Again, neither the Teacher nor a fellow monk in the position of a teacher teaches the Dhamma to a bhikkhu, but he himself teaches the Dhamma to others in detail as he has heard it and learned it. In whatever way the bhikkhu [22] teaches the Dhamma to others in detail as he has heard it and learned it, in just that way, in relation to that Dhamma, he experiences inspiration in the meaning and inspiration in the Dhamma. As he does so, joy arises in him. When he is joyful, rapture arises. For one with a rapturous mind, the body becomes tranquil. One tranquil in body feels pleasure. For one feeling pleasure, the mind becomes concentrated. This is the second basis of liberation, by means of which, if a bhikkhu dwells heedful, ardent, and resolute, his unliberated mind is liberated, his undestroyed taints are utterly destroyed, and he reaches the as-yet-unreached unsurpassed security from bondage.

(3) "Again, neither the Teacher nor a fellow monk in the position of a teacher teaches the Dhamma to a bhikkhu, nor does he himself teach the Dhamma to others in detail as he has heard it and learned it, but he recites the Dhamma in detail as he has heard it and learned it. In whatever way the bhikkhu recites the Dhamma in detail as he has heard it and learned it, in just that way, in relation to that Dhamma, he experiences inspiration in the meaning and inspiration in the Dhamma. As he does so, joy arises in him. When he is joyful, rapture arises. For one with a rapturous mind, the body becomes tranquil. One tranquil in body feels pleasure. For one feeling pleasure, the mind becomes concentrated. This is the third basis of liberation, by means of which, if a bhikkhu dwells heedful, ardent, and resolute, his unliberated mind is liberated, his undestroyed taints are utterly destroyed, and he reaches the as-yet-unreached unsurpassed security from bondage.

(4) "Again, neither the Teacher nor a fellow monk in the

position of a teacher teaches the Dhamma to a bhikkhu, nor does he teach the Dhamma to others in detail as he has heard it and learned it, nor does he recite the Dhamma in detail as he has heard it and learned it, but he ponders, [23] examines, and mentally inspects the Dhamma as he has heard it and learned it. In whatever way the bhikkhu ponders, examines, and mentally inspects the Dhamma as he has heard it and learned it, in just that way, in relation to that Dhamma, he experiences inspiration in the meaning and inspiration in the Dhamma. As he does so, joy arises in him. When he is joyful, rapture arises. For one with a rapturous mind, the body becomes tranquil. One tranquil in body feels pleasure. For one feeling pleasure, the mind becomes concentrated. This is the fourth basis of liberation, by means of which, if a bhikkhu dwells heedful, ardent, and resolute, his unliberated mind is liberated, his undestroyed taints are utterly destroyed, and he reaches the as-yet-unreached unsurpassed security from bondage.

(5) "Again, neither the Teacher nor a fellow monk in the position of a teacher teaches the Dhamma to a bhikkhu, nor does he teach the Dhamma to others in detail as he has heard it and learned it, nor does he recite the Dhamma in detail as he has heard it and learned it, nor does he ponder, examine, and mentally inspect the Dhamma as he has heard it and learned it, but he has grasped well a certain object of concentration, attended to it well, sustained it well, and penetrated it well with wisdom. In whatever way the bhikkhu has grasped well a certain object of concentration, attended to it well, sustained it well, and penetrated it well with wisdom, in just that way, in relation to that Dhamma, he experiences inspiration in the meaning and inspiration in the Dhamma. As he does so, joy arises in him. When he is joyful, rapture arises. For one with a rapturous mind, the body becomes tranquil. One tranquil in body feels pleasure. For one feeling pleasure, the mind becomes concentrated. This is the fifth basis of liberation, by means of which, if a bhikkhu dwells heedful, ardent, and resolute, [24] his unliberated mind is liberated, his undestroyed taints are utterly destroyed, and he reaches the as-yet-unreached unsurpassed security from bondage.

"These, bhikkhus, are the five bases of liberation, by means of which, if a bhikkhu dwells heedful, ardent, and resolute, his unliberated mind is liberated, his undestroyed taints are utterly destroyed, and he reaches the as-yet-unreached unsurpassed security from bondage."

27 (7) Concentration

"Bhikkhus, being alert and mindful, develop concentration that is measureless.[992] When, alert and mindful, you develop concentration that is measureless, five kinds of knowledge arise that are personally yours. What five? (1) The knowledge arises that is personally yours: 'This concentration is presently pleasant and in the future has a pleasant result.' (2) The knowledge arises that is personally yours: 'This concentration is noble and spiritual.' (3) The knowledge arises that is personally yours: 'This concentration is not practiced by low persons.' (4) The knowledge arises that is personally yours: 'This concentration is peaceful and sublime, gained by full tranquilization, and attained to unification; it is not reined in and checked by forcefully suppressing [the defilements].'[993] (5) The knowledge arises that is personally yours: 'I enter this concentration[994] mindfully and I emerge from it mindfully.' Bhikkhus, being alert and continuously mindful, develop concentration that is measureless. When you are alert and mindful, developing concentration that is measureless, these five kinds of knowledge arise that are personally yours." [25]

28 (8) Five-Factored

"Bhikkhus, I will teach you the development of noble five-factored right concentration.[995] Listen and attend closely. I will speak."

"Yes, Bhante," those bhikkhus replied. The Blessed One said this:

"And what, bhikkhus, is the development of noble five-factored right concentration?

(1) "Here, secluded from sensual pleasures, secluded from unwholesome states, a bhikkhu enters and dwells in the first jhāna, which consists of rapture and pleasure born of seclusion, accompanied by thought and examination. He makes the rapture and happiness born of seclusion drench, steep, fill, and pervade this body, so that there is no part of his whole body that is not pervaded by the rapture and happiness born of seclusion.

Just as a skillful bath man or a bath man's apprentice might heap bath powder in a metal basin and, sprinkling it gradually with water, would knead it until the moisture wets his ball of bath powder, soaks it, and pervades it inside and out, yet the ball itself does not ooze; so too, the bhikkhu makes the rapture and happiness born of seclusion drench, steep, fill, and pervade this body, so that there is no part of his whole body that is not pervaded by the rapture and happiness born of seclusion. This is the first development of noble five-factored right concentration.

(2) "Again, with the subsiding of thought and examination, a bhikkhu enters and dwells in the second jhāna, which has internal placidity and unification of mind and consists of rapture and pleasure born of concentration, without thought and examination. He makes the rapture and happiness born of concentration drench, steep, fill, and pervade this body, so that there is no part of his whole body that is not pervaded by the rapture and happiness born of concentration. Just as there might be a lake whose waters welled up from below with no inflow from east, west, north, [26] or south, and the lake would not be replenished from time to time by showers of rain, then the cool fount of water welling up in the lake would make the cool water drench, steep, fill, and pervade the lake, so that there would be no part of the whole lake that is not pervaded by cool water; so too, the bhikkhu makes the rapture and happiness born of concentration drench, steep, fill, and pervade this body, so that there is no part of his whole body that is not pervaded by the rapture and happiness born of concentration. This is the second development of noble five-factored right concentration.

(3) "Again, with the fading away as well of rapture, a bhikkhu dwells equanimous and, mindful and clearly comprehending, he experiences pleasure with the body; he enters and dwells in the third jhāna of which the noble ones declare: 'He is equanimous, mindful, one who dwells happily.' He makes the happiness divested of rapture drench, steep, fill, and pervade this body, so that there is no part of his whole body that is not pervaded by the happiness divested of rapture. Just as, in a pond of blue or red or white lotuses, some lotuses that are born and grow in the water might thrive immersed in the water without rising out of it, and cool water would drench, steep, fill, and

pervade them to their tips and their roots, so that there would be no part of those lotuses that would not be pervaded by cool water; so too, the bhikkhu makes the happiness divested of rapture drench, steep, fill, and pervade this body, so that there is no part of his whole body that is not pervaded by the happiness divested of rapture. This is the third development of noble five-factored right concentration.

(4) "Again, with the abandoning of pleasure [27] and pain, and with the previous passing away of joy and dejection, a bhikkhu enters and dwells in the fourth jhāna, neither painful nor pleasant, which has purification of mindfulness by equanimity. He sits pervading this body with a pure bright mind, so that there is no part of his whole body that is not pervaded by the pure bright mind. Just as a man might be sitting covered from the head down with a white cloth, so that there would be no part of his whole body that is not pervaded by the white cloth; so too, the bhikkhu sits pervading this body with a pure bright mind, so that there is no part of his whole body that is not pervaded by the pure bright mind. This is the fourth development of noble five-factored right concentration.

(5) "Again, a bhikkhu has grasped well the object of reviewing,[996] attended to it well, sustained it well, and penetrated it well with wisdom. Just as one person might look upon another—as one standing might look upon one sitting down, or one sitting down might look upon one lying down—so too, a bhikkhu has grasped well the object of reviewing, attended to it well, sustained it well, and penetrated it well with wisdom. This is the fifth development of noble five-factored right concentration.

"When, bhikkhus, noble five-factored right concentration has been developed and cultivated in this way, then, there being a suitable basis, he is capable of realizing any state realizable by direct knowledge toward which he might incline his mind.[997]

"Suppose a water jug full of water has been set out on a stand, the jug being full of water right up to the brim so that crows could drink from it. If a strong man would tip it in any direction, would water come out?"

"Yes, [28] Bhante."

"So too, bhikkhus, when noble five-factored right concentration has been developed and cultivated in this way, then, there being a suitable basis, he is capable of realizing any state realizable by direct knowledge toward which he might incline his mind.

"Suppose on level ground there was a four-sided pond, contained by an embankment, full of water right up to the brim so that crows could drink from it. If a strong man were to remove the embankment on any side, would water come out?"

"Yes, Bhante."

"So too, bhikkhus, when noble five-factored right concentration has been developed and cultivated in this way, then, there being a suitable basis, he is capable of realizing any state realizable by direct knowledge toward which he might incline his mind.

"Suppose on even ground at a crossroads a chariot was standing harnessed to thoroughbreds, with a goad ready at hand, so that a skillful trainer, the charioteer, could mount it, and taking the reins in his left hand and the goad in his right, might drive out and return wherever and whenever he likes. So too, bhikkhus, when noble five-factored right concentration has been developed and cultivated in this way, then, there being a suitable basis, he is capable of realizing any state realizable by direct knowledge toward which he might incline his mind.

"If he wishes: 'May I wield the various kinds of psychic potency: [29] having been one, may I become many . . . [here and below as in 5:23] . . . may I exercise mastery with the body as far as the brahmā world,' he is capable of realizing it, there being a suitable basis.

"If he wishes: 'May I, with the divine ear element, which is purified and surpasses the human, hear both kinds of sounds, the divine and human, those that are far as well as near,' he is capable of realizing it, there being a suitable basis.

"If he wishes: 'May I understand the minds of other beings and persons, having encompassed them with my own mind. May I understand . . . an unliberated mind as unliberated,' he is capable of realizing it, there being a suitable basis.

"If he wishes: 'May I recollect my manifold past abodes . . . with their aspects and details,' he is capable of realizing it, there being a suitable basis.

"If he wishes: 'May I, with the divine eye, which is purified and surpasses the human, see beings passing away and being reborn . . . and understand how beings fare in accordance with their kamma,' he is capable of realizing it, there being a suitable basis.

"If he wishes: 'May I, with the destruction of the taints, in this very life realize for myself with direct knowledge the taintless liberation of mind, liberation by wisdom, and having entered upon it, may I dwell in it,' he is capable of realizing it, there being a suitable basis."

29 (9) Walking Meditation

"Bhikkhus, there are these five benefits of walking meditation. What five? [30] One becomes capable of journeys; one becomes capable of striving; one becomes healthy; what one has eaten, drunk, consumed, and tasted is properly digested; the concentration attained through walking meditation is long lasting.[998] These are the five benefits of walking meditation."

30 (10) Nāgita

Thus have I heard. On one occasion the Blessed One was wandering on tour among the Kosalans together with a large Saṅgha of bhikkhus when he reached the Kosalan brahmin village named Icchānaṅgala. There the Blessed One dwelled in the Icchānaṅgala woodland thicket. The brahmin householders of Icchānaṅgala heard: "It is said that the ascetic Gotama, the son of the Sakyans who went forth from a Sakyan family, has arrived at Icchānaṅgala and is now dwelling in the Icchānaṅgala woodland thicket. Now a good report about that Master Gotama has circulated thus: 'That Blessed One is an arahant, perfectly enlightened, accomplished in true knowledge and conduct, fortunate, knower of the world, unsurpassed leader of persons to be tamed, teacher of devas and humans, the Enlightened One, the Blessed One. Having realized by his own direct knowledge this world with its devas, Māra, and Brahmā, this population with its ascetics and brahmins, its devas and humans, he makes it known to others. He teaches a Dhamma that is good in the beginning, good in the middle, and good in the end, with the right meaning and phrasing; he reveals a spiritual life that is perfectly complete and pure.' Now it is good to see such arahants."

Then, when the night had passed, the brahmin householders of Icchānaṅgala took abundant food of various kinds and went to the Icchānaṅgala woodland thicket. They stood outside the entrance making an uproar and a racket. [31] Now on that occasion the Venerable Nāgita was the Blessed One's attendant. The Blessed One addressed the Venerable Nāgita: "Who is making such an uproar and a racket, Nāgita? One would think it was fishermen at a haul of fish."

"Bhante, these are the brahmin householders of Icchānaṅgala who have brought abundant food of various kinds. They are standing outside the entrance, [wishing to offer it] to the Blessed One and the Saṅgha of bhikkhus."

"Let me never come upon fame, Nāgita, and may fame never catch up with me. One who does not gain at will, without trouble or difficulty, this bliss of renunciation, bliss of solitude, bliss of peace, bliss of enlightenment that I gain at will, without trouble or difficulty, might accept that vile pleasure, that slothful pleasure, the pleasure of gain, honor, and praise."

"Let the Blessed One now consent, Bhante, let the Fortunate One consent. This is now the time for the Blessed One to consent. Wherever the Blessed One will go now, the brahmin householders of town and countryside will incline in the same direction. Just as, when thick drops of rain are pouring down, the water flows down along the slope, so too, wherever the Blessed One will go now, the brahmin householders of town and country will incline in the same direction. For what reason? Because of the Blessed One's virtuous behavior and wisdom."

"Let me never come upon fame, Nāgita, and may fame never catch up with me. One who does not gain at will, without trouble or difficulty, this bliss of renunciation . . . might accept that vile pleasure, that slothful pleasure, the pleasure of gain, honor, and praise. [32]

(1) "Nāgita, what is eaten, drunk, consumed, and tasted winds up as feces and urine: this is its outcome. (2) From the change and alteration of things that are dear arise sorrow, lamentation, pain, dejection, and anguish: this is its outcome. (3) For one devoted to practicing meditation on the mark of unattractiveness, revulsion toward the mark of the beautiful becomes established: this is its outcome. (4) For one who dwells contemplating impermanence in the six bases for contact, revulsion toward contact becomes established: this is its outcome. (5) For one who dwells contemplating arising and vanishing in the

five aggregates subject to clinging, revulsion toward clinging becomes established: this is its outcome."[999]

IV. Sumanā

31 (1) Sumanā

On one occasion the Blessed One was dwelling at Sāvatthī in Jeta's Grove, Anāthapiṇḍika's Park. Then Princess Sumanā,[1000] accompanied by five hundred chariots and five hundred court girls, approached the Blessed One, paid homage to him, and sat down to one side. Princess Sumanā then said to the Blessed One:

"Here, Bhante, there might be two disciples of the Blessed One equal in faith, virtuous behavior, and wisdom, but one is generous while the other is not. With the breakup of the body, [33] after death, they would both be reborn in a good destination, in a heavenly world. When they have become devas, would there be any distinction or difference between them?"

"There would be, Sumanā," the Blessed One said. "The generous one, having become a deva, would surpass the other in five ways: in celestial life span, celestial beauty, celestial happiness, celestial glory, and celestial authority. The generous one, having become a deva, would surpass the other in these five ways."

"But, Bhante, if these two pass away from there and again become human beings, would there still be some distinction or difference between them?"

"There would be, Sumanā," the Blessed One said. "When they again become human beings, the generous one would surpass the other in five ways: in human life span, human beauty, human happiness, human fame, and human authority. When they again become human beings, the generous one would surpass the other in these five ways."

"But, Bhante, if these two should go forth from the household life into homelessness, would there still be some distinction or difference between them?"

"There would be, Sumanā," the Blessed One said. "The generous one, having gone forth, would surpass the other in five ways.[1001] (1) He would usually use a robe that has been specifically offered to him, seldom one that had not been specifically offered to him. (2) He would usually eat almsfood that has been specifically offered to him, seldom almsfood that had not been specifically offered to him. (3) He would usually use a lodging that had been specifically offered to him, seldom one that had not been specifically offered to him. (4) He would usually use medicines and provisions for the sick that had been specifically offered to him, seldom those that had not been specifically offered to him. (5) His fellow monastics, those with whom he dwells, would usually behave toward him in agreeable ways by bodily, verbal, and mental action, seldom in disagreeable ways. They would usually present him what is agreeable, seldom [34] what is disagreeable. The generous one, having gone forth, would surpass the other in these five ways."

"But, Bhante, if both attain arahantship, would there still be some distinction or difference between them after they have attained arahantship?"

"In this case, Sumanā, I declare, there would be no difference between the liberation [of one] and the liberation [of the other]."

"It's astounding and amazing, Bhante! Truly, one has good reason to give alms and do meritorious deeds, since they will be helpful if one becomes a deva, [again] becomes a human being, or goes forth."

"So it is, Sumanā! So it is, Sumanā! Truly, one has good reason to give alms and do meritorious deeds, since they will be helpful if one becomes a deva, [again] becomes a human being, or goes forth."

This is what the Blessed One said. Having said this, the Fortunate One, the Teacher, further said this:

"As the stainless moon
moving through the sphere of space
outshines with its radiance
all the stars in the world,
so one accomplished in virtuous behavior,
a person endowed with faith,
outshines by generosity
all the misers in the world.

"As the hundred-peaked rain cloud,
thundering, wreathed in lightning,
pours down rain upon the earth,
inundating the plains and lowlands,
so the Perfectly Enlightened One's disciple,
the wise one accomplished in vision,
surpasses the miserly person
in five specific respects:
life span and glory,
beauty and happiness.[1002]
Possessed of wealth, after death
he rejoices in heaven." [35]

32 (2) Cundī[1003]

On one occasion the Blessed One was dwelling at Rājagaha in the Bamboo Grove, the squirrel sanctuary. Then Princess Cundī,[1004] accompanied by five hundred chariots and five hundred court girls, approached the Blessed One, paid homage to him, and sat down to one side. Princess Cundī then said to the Blessed One:

"Bhante, my brother is Prince Cunda. He says thus: 'Whenever a man or a woman has gone for refuge to the Buddha, the Dhamma, and the Saṅgha, and abstains from the destruction of life, from taking what is not given, from sexual misconduct, from false speech, and from indulging in liquor, wine, and intoxicants, the basis for heedlessness, with the breakup of the body, after death, he is reborn only in a good destination, not in a bad destination.' I ask the Blessed One: 'What kind of teacher, Bhante, should one have confidence in, so that, with the breakup of the body, after death, one is reborn only in a good destination, not in a bad destination? What kind of Dhamma should one have confidence in, so that, with the breakup of the body, after death, one is reborn only in a good destination, not in a bad destination? What kind of Saṅgha should one have confidence in, so that, with the breakup of the body, after death, one is reborn only in a good destination, not in a bad destination? What kind of virtuous behavior should one fulfill so that, with the breakup of the body, after death, one is reborn only in a good destination, not in a bad destination?"

(1) "Cundī, to whatever extent there are beings, whether footless or with two feet, four feet, or many feet, whether having form or formless, whether percipient, non-percipient, or neither percipient nor non-percipient, the Tathāgata, the Arahant, the Perfectly Enlightened One is declared the foremost among them. Those who have confidence in the Buddha have confidence in the foremost, and for those who have confidence in the foremost, the result is foremost.

(2) "To whatever extent, Cundī, there are phenomena that are conditioned, the noble eightfold path is declared the foremost among them. Those who have confidence in the noble eightfold path have confidence in the foremost, and for those who have confidence in the foremost, the result is foremost.[1005]

(3) "To whatever extent, Cundī, there are phenomena whether conditioned or unconditioned, dispassion is declared the foremost among them, that is, the crushing of pride, the removal of thirst, the uprooting of attachment, the termination of the round, the destruction of craving, dispassion, cessation, nibbāna. Those who [36] have confidence in the Dhamma, in dispassion,[1006] have confidence in the foremost, and for those who have confidence in the foremost, the result is foremost.

(4) "To whatever extent, Cundī, there are Saṅghas or groups, the Saṅgha of the Tathāgata's disciples is declared the foremost among them, that is, the four pairs of persons, the eight types of individuals—this Saṅgha of the Blessed One's disciples is worthy of gifts, worthy of hospitality, worthy of offerings, worthy of reverential salutation, the unsurpassed field of merit for the world. Those who have confidence in the Saṅgha have confidence in the foremost, and for those who have confidence in the foremost, the result is foremost.

(5) "To whatever extent, Cundī, there is virtuous behavior, the virtuous behavior loved by the noble ones is declared the foremost among them, that is, when it is unbroken, flawless, unblemished, unblotched, freeing, praised by the wise, ungrasped, leading to concentration. Those who fulfill the virtuous behavior loved by the noble ones fulfill the foremost, and for those who fulfill the foremost, the result is foremost."

For those confident in regard to the foremost,[1007]
knowing the foremost Dhamma,

confident in the Buddha—the foremost—
unsurpassed, worthy of offerings;

for those confident in the foremost Dhamma,
in the blissful peace of dispassion;
for those confident in the foremost Saṅgha,
the unsurpassed field of merit;

for those giving gifts to the foremost,
the foremost kind of merit increases:
the foremost life span, beauty, and glory,
good reputation, happiness, and strength.

The wise one who gives to the foremost,
concentrated upon the foremost Dhamma,
having become a deva or human being,
rejoices having attained the foremost.

33 (3) Uggaha

On one occasion the Blessed One was dwelling at Bhaddiya in the Jātiyā Grove. Then Uggaha, Meṇḍaka's grandson, approached the Blessed One, paid homage to him, sat down to one side, and said to the Blessed One:

"Bhante, let the Blessed One together with three other monks[1008] consent to accept tomorrow's [37] meal from me."

The Blessed One consented by silence. Then Uggaha, having understood that the Blessed One had consented, rose from his seat, paid homage to the Blessed One, circumambulated him keeping the right side toward him, and departed.

Then, when the night had passed, in the morning the Blessed One dressed, took his bowl and robe, and went to Uggaha's residence, where he sat down on the appointed seat. Then, with his own hands, Uggaha, Meṇḍaka's grandson, served and satisfied the Blessed One with various kinds of delicious food.

When the Blessed One had finished eating and had put away his bowl, Uggaha sat down to one side and said to the Blessed One: "Bhante, these girls of mine will be going to their husbands' families. Let the Blessed One exhort them and instruct them in a way that will lead to their welfare and happiness for a long time."

The Blessed One then said to those girls:

(1) "So then, girls, you should train yourselves thus: 'To whichever husband our parents give us—doing so out of a desire for our good, seeking our welfare, taking compassion on us, acting out of compassion for us—we will rise before him and retire after him, undertaking whatever needs to be done, agreeable in our conduct and pleasing in our speech.' Thus should you train yourselves.

(2) "And you should train yourselves thus: 'We will honor, respect, esteem, and venerate those whom our husband respects—his mother and father, ascetics and brahmins—and when they arrive we will offer them a seat and water.' Thus should you train yourselves.

(3) "And you should train yourselves thus: 'We will be skillful and diligent in attending to our husband's domestic chores, whether knitting or weaving; we will possess sound judgment about them in order to carry out and arrange them properly.' Thus should you train yourselves.

(4) "And you should train yourselves thus: 'We will find out what our husband's domestic helpers—whether slaves, messengers, or [38] workers—have done and left undone; we will find out the condition of those who are ill; and we will distribute to each an appropriate portion of food.' Thus should you train yourselves.

(5) "And you should train yourselves thus: 'We will guard and protect whatever income our husband brings home—whether money or grain, silver or gold—and we will not be spendthrifts, thieves, wastrels, or squanderers of his earnings.' Thus should you train yourselves.

"When, girls, a woman possesses these five qualities, with the breakup of the body, after death, she is reborn in companionship with the agreeable-bodied devas."[1009]

She does not despise her husband,
the man who constantly supports her,
who ardently and eagerly
always brings her whatever she wants.

Nor does a good woman scold her husband
with speech caused by jealousy;[1010]

the wise woman shows veneration
to all those whom her husband reveres.

She rises early, works diligently,
manages the domestic help;
she treats her husband in agreeable ways
and safeguards the wealth he earns.

The woman who fulfills her duties thus,
following her husband's will and wishes,
is reborn among the devas
called "the agreeable ones."

34 (4) Sīha

On one occasion the Blessed One was dwelling at Vesālī in the hall with the peaked roof in the Great Wood. Then Sīha the general approached [39] the Blessed One, paid homage to him, sat down to one side, and said:[1011]

"Is it possible, Bhante, to point out a directly visible fruit of giving?"[1012]

"It is, Sīha," the Blessed One said.

(1) "A donor, Sīha, a munificent giver, is dear and agreeable to many people. This is a directly visible fruit of giving.

(2) "Again, good persons resort to a donor, a munificent giver. This, too, is a directly visible fruit of giving.

(3) "Again, a donor, a munificent giver, acquires a good reputation. This, too, is a directly visible fruit of giving.

(4) "Again, whatever assembly a donor, a munificent giver, approaches—whether of khattiyas, brahmins, householders, or ascetics—he approaches it confidently and composed.[1013] This too is a directly visible fruit of giving.

(5) "Again, with the breakup of the body, after death, a donor, a munificent giver, is reborn in a good destination, in a heavenly world. This is a fruit of giving pertaining to future lives."[1014]

When this was said, Sīha the general said to the Blessed One: "Bhante, I do not go by faith in the Blessed One concerning those four directly visible fruits of giving declared by him. I know them, too. For I am a donor, a munificent giver, and I am dear and agreeable to many people. I am a donor, a munificent giver, and many good persons resort to me. I am a donor, a munificent giver, and I have acquired a good reputation as a donor, sponsor, and supporter of the Saṅgha. I [40] am a donor, a munificent giver, and whatever assembly I approach—whether of khattiyas, brahmins, householders, or ascetics—I approach it confidently and composed. I do not go by faith in the Blessed One concerning these four directly visible fruits of giving declared by him. I know them, too. But when the Blessed One tells me: 'Sīha, with the breakup of the body, after death, a donor, a munificent giver, is reborn in a good destination, in a heavenly world,' I do not know this, and here I go by faith in the Blessed One."

"So it is, Sīha, so it is! With the breakup of the body, after death, a donor, a munificent giver, is reborn in a good destination, in a heavenly world."

By giving, he becomes dear and many resort to him.
He attains a good reputation and his fame increases.
The generous man is composed
and confidently enters the assembly.

Therefore, seeking happiness,
wise persons give gifts,
having removed the stain of miserliness.
When they are settled in the triple heaven,
for a long time they delight
in companionship with the devas.

Having taken the opportunity to do wholesome deeds,
passing from here, self-luminous, they roam in
Nandana,[1015]
where they delight, rejoice, and enjoy themselves,
furnished with the five objects of sensual pleasure.
Having fulfilled the word of the unattached Stable One,
the Fortunate One's disciples rejoice in heaven. [41]

35 (5) The Benefits of Giving

"Bhikkhus, there are these five benefits of giving. What five? (1) One is dear and agreeable to many people. (2) Good persons resort to one. (3) One acquires a good reputation. (4) One is not deficient in the layperson's duties. (5) With the breakup of the body, after death, one is reborn in a good destination, in a heavenly world. These are the five benefits in giving."

By giving, one becomes dear,
one follows the duty of the good;
the good self-controlled monks
always resort to one.

They teach one the Dhamma
that dispels all suffering,
having understood which
the taintless one here attains nibbāna.

36 (6) Timely

"Bhikkhus, there are these five timely gifts. What five? (1) One gives a gift to a visitor. (2) One gives a gift to one setting out on a journey. (3) One gives a gift to a patient. (4) One gives a gift during a famine. (5) One first presents the newly harvested crops and fruits to the virtuous ones. These are the five timely gifts."

At the proper time, those wise,
charitable, and generous folk
give a timely gift to the noble ones,
who are stable and upright;
given with a clear mind,
one's offering is vast.

Those who rejoice in such deeds
or who provide [other] service
do not miss out on the offering;
they too partake of the merit.

Therefore, with a non-regressing mind,
one should give a gift where it yields great fruit.
Merits are the support of living beings
[when they arise] in the other world. [42]

37 (7) Food

"Bhikkhus, a donor who gives food gives the recipients five things. What five? One gives life, beauty, happiness, strength, and discernment.[1016] (1) Having given life, one partakes of life, whether celestial or human. (2) Having given beauty, one partakes of beauty, whether celestial or human. (3) Having given happiness, one partakes of happiness, whether celestial or human. (4) Having given strength, one partakes of strength, whether celestial or human. (5) Having given discernment, one partakes of discernment, whether celestial or human. A donor who gives food gives the recipients these five things."

> The wise one is a giver of life,
> strength, beauty, and discernment.
> The intelligent one is a donor of happiness
> and in turn acquires happiness.
>
> Having given life, strength, beauty,
> happiness, and discernment,
> one is long-lived and famous
> wherever one is reborn.

38 (8) Faith

"Bhikkhus, these five benefits come to a clansman endowed with faith. What five? (1) When the good persons in the world show compassion,[1017] they first show compassion to the person with faith, not so to the person without faith. (2) When they approach anyone, they first approach the person with faith, not so the person without faith. (3) When they receive alms, they first receive alms from the person with faith, not so from the person without faith. (4) When they teach the Dhamma, they first teach the Dhamma to the person with faith, not so to the person without faith. (5) With the breakup of the body, after death, a person with faith is reborn in a good destination, in a heavenly world. These are the five benefits that come to a clansman who has faith.

"Just as at a crossroads on level ground, a great banyan tree becomes the resort for birds all around, so [43] the clansman endowed with faith becomes the resort for many people:

for bhikkhus, bhikkhunīs, male lay followers, and female lay followers."

A large tree with a mighty trunk,
branches, leaves, and fruit,
firm roots, and bearing fruit,
is a support for many birds.
Having flown across the sky,
the birds resort to this delightful base:
those in need of shade partake of its shade;
those needing fruit enjoy its fruit.

Just so, when a person is virtuous,
endowed with faith,
of humble manner, compliant,
gentle, welcoming, soft,
those in the world who are fields of merit—
devoid of lust and hatred,
devoid of delusion, taintless—
resort to such a person.

They teach him the Dhamma
that dispels all suffering,
having understood which
the taintless one here attains nibbāna.

39 (9) Son

"Bhikkhus, considering five prospects, mother and father wish for a son to be born in their family. What five? (1) 'Having been supported by us, he will support us. (2) Or he will do work for us. (3) Our family lineage will be extended. (4) He will manage the inheritance, (5) or else, when we have passed on, he will give an offering on our behalf.' Considering these five prospects, mother and father wish for a son to be born in their family."

Considering the five prospects,
wise people wish for a son.
"Supported by us, he will support us,
or he will do work for us.

The family lineage will be extended,
he will manage the inheritance,
or else, when we have passed on,
he will make an offering on our behalf."

Considering these prospects,
wise people wish for a son.
Therefore good persons,
grateful and appreciative,
support their mother and father,
recalling how they helped one in the past; [44]
they do what is necessary for them
as they did for oneself in the past.

Following their advice,
nurturing those who brought him up,
continuing the family lineage,
endowed with faith, virtuous:
this son is worthy of praise.

40 (10) Sal Trees[1018]

"Bhikkhus, based on the Himalayas, the king of mountains, great sal trees grow in five ways. What five? (1) They grow in branches, leaves, and foliage; (2) they grow in bark; (3) they grow in shoots; (4) they grow in softwood; and (5) they grow in heartwood. Based on the Himalayas, the king of mountains, great sal trees grow in these five ways.

"So too, when the head of the family[1019] is endowed with faith, the people in the family who depend on him grow in five ways. What five? (1) They grow in faith; (2) they grow in virtuous behavior; (3) they grow in learning; (4) they grow in generosity; and (5) they grow in wisdom. When the head of a family is endowed with faith, the people in the family who depend on him grow in these five ways."

Just as the trees that grow
in dependence on a rocky mountain
in a vast forest wilderness
might become great 'woodland lords,'

so, when the head of a family here
possesses faith and virtue,
his wife, children, and relatives
all grow in dependence on him;
so too his companions, his family circle,
and those dependent on him.

Those possessed of discernment,
seeing that virtuous man's good conduct,
his generosity and good deeds,
emulate his example.

Having lived here in accord with Dhamma,
the path leading to a good destination,
those who desire sensual pleasures rejoice,
delighting in the deva world. [45]

V. Muṇḍa the King

41 (1) Utilization

On one occasion the Blessed One was dwelling at Sāvatthī in Jeta's Grove, Anāthapiṇḍika's Park. Then the householder Anāthapiṇḍika approached the Blessed One, paid homage to him, and sat down to one side. The Blessed One then said to him:

"Householder, there are these five utilizations of wealth. What five?[1020]

(1) "Here, householder, with wealth acquired by energetic striving, amassed by the strength of his arms, earned by the sweat of his brow, righteous wealth righteously gained, the noble disciple makes himself happy and pleased and properly maintains himself in happiness; he makes his parents happy and pleased and properly maintains them in happiness; he makes his wife and children, his slaves, workers, and servants happy and pleased and properly maintains them in happiness. This is the first utilization of wealth.

(2) "Again, with wealth acquired by energetic striving . . . righteously gained, the noble disciple makes his friends and companions happy and pleased and properly maintains them in happiness. This is the second utilization of wealth.

(3) "Again, with wealth acquired by energetic striving . . . righteously gained, the noble disciple makes provisions with his wealth against the losses that might arise because of fire or floods, kings or bandits or unloved heirs; he makes himself secure against them. This is the third utilization of wealth.

(4) "Again, with wealth acquired by energetic striving . . . righteously gained, the noble disciple makes the five oblations: to relatives, guests, ancestors, the king, and the deities. This is the fourth utilization of wealth.

(5) "Again, with wealth acquired by energetic striving . . . [46] . . . righteously gained, the noble disciple establishes an uplifting offering of alms—an offering that is heavenly, resulting in happiness, conducive to heaven—to those ascetics and brahmins who refrain from intoxication and heedlessness, who are settled in patience and mildness, who tame themselves, calm themselves, and train themselves for nibbāna. This is the fifth utilization of wealth.

"These, householder, are the five utilizations of wealth. Householder, if a noble disciple's wealth is exhausted when he has utilized it in these five ways, he thinks: 'I have utilized wealth in these five ways and my wealth is exhausted.' Thus he has no regret. But if a noble disciple's wealth increases when he has utilized it in these five ways, he thinks: 'I have utilized wealth in these five ways and my wealth has increased.' Thus, either way, he has no regret."

"I've enjoyed wealth,
supported my dependents,
and overcome adversities.
I have given an uplifting offering,
and performed the five oblations.
I have served the virtuous monks,
the self-controlled celibate ones.

"I have achieved whatever purpose
a wise person, dwelling at home,
might have in desiring wealth;
what I have done brings me no regret."

Recollecting this, a mortal
remains firm in the noble Dhamma.
They praise him here in this life,
and after death he rejoices in heaven.

42 (2) The Good Person

"Bhikkhus, when a good person is born in a family, it is for the good, welfare, and happiness of many people. It is for the good, welfare, and happiness of (1) his mother and father, (2) his wife and children, (3) his slaves, workers, and servants, (4) his friends and companions, and (5) ascetics and brahmins. Just as a great rain cloud, nurturing all the crops, appears for the good, welfare, and happiness of many people, so too, [47] when a good person is born in a family, it is for the good, welfare, and happiness of many people. It is for the good, welfare, and happiness of his mother and father . . . ascetics and brahmins."

The deities protect one guarded by the Dhamma,[1021]
who has managed his wealth for the welfare of many.
Fame does not forsake one steadfast in the Dhamma,
who is learned and of virtuous behavior and
observances.

Who is fit to blame him,
standing in Dhamma,
accomplished in virtuous behavior,
a speaker of truth,
possessing a sense of shame,
[pure] like a coin of refined gold?
Even the devas praise him;
by Brahmā, too, he is praised.

43 (3) Wished For

Then the householder Anāthapiṇḍika approached the Blessed One, paid homage to him, and sat down to one side. The Blessed One then said to him:

"Householder, there are these five things that are wished for, desired, agreeable, and rarely gained in the world. What five? Long life, householder, is wished for, desired, agreeable, and rarely gained in the world. Beauty . . . Happiness . . . Fame . . . The heavens are wished for, desired, agreeable, and rarely gained in the world. These are the five things that are wished for, desired, agreeable, and rarely gained in the world.[1022]

"These five things, householder, that are wished for, desired, agreeable, and rarely gained in the world, I say, are not obtained by means of prayers or aspirations. If these five things that are wished for, desired, agreeable, and rarely gained in the world could be obtained by means of prayers [48] or aspirations, who here would be lacking in anything?

(1) "Householder, the noble disciple who desires long life ought not to pray for long life or delight in it or [passively] yearn for it.[1023] A noble disciple who desires long life should practice the way conducive to long life.[1024] For when he practices the way conducive to long life, it leads to obtaining long life, and he gains long life either celestial or human.

(2) "Householder, the noble disciple who desires beauty . . . (3) . . . who desires happiness . . . (4) . . . who desires fame ought not to pray for fame or delight in it or [passively] yearn for it. A noble disciple who desires fame should practice the way conducive to fame. For when he practices the way conducive to fame, it leads to obtaining fame, and he gains fame either celestial or human.

(5) "Householder, the noble disciple who desires the heavens ought not to pray for the heavens or delight in them or [passively] yearn for them. A noble disciple who desires the heavens should practice the way conducive to heaven. For when he practices the way conducive to heaven, it leads to obtaining the heavens, and he gains the heavens."[1025]

For one desiring long life, beauty, fame,[1026]
acclaim, heaven, high families,
and lofty delights
following in succession,
the wise praise heedfulness
in doing deeds of merit. [49]

Being heedful, the wise person
secures both kinds of good:
the good in this life,

and the good of the future life.
By attaining the good,[1027] the steadfast one
is called one of wisdom.

44 (4) The Giver of the Agreeable

On one occasion the Blessed One was dwelling at Vesālī in the hall with the peaked roof in the Great Wood. Then, in the morning, the Blessed One dressed, took his bowl and robe, and went to the residence of the householder Ugga of Vesālī, where he sat down in the appointed seat. Then the householder Ugga of Vesālī approached the Blessed One, paid homage to him, sat down to one side, and said to the Blessed One:

"Bhante, in the presence of the Blessed One I heard and learned this: 'The giver of what is agreeable gains what is agreeable.' Bhante, my sal flower porridge is agreeable.[1028] Let the Blessed One accept it from me, out of compassion." The Blessed One accepted, out of compassion.

"Bhante, in the presence of the Blessed One I heard and learned this: 'The giver of what is agreeable gains what is agreeable.' Bhante, my pork embellished with jujubes is agreeable.[1029] Let the Blessed One accept it from me, out of compassion." The Blessed One accepted, out of compassion.

"Bhante, in the presence of the Blessed One I heard and learned this: 'The giver of what is agreeable gains what is agreeable.' Bhante, my fried vegetable stalks are agreeable.[1030] Let the Blessed One accept them from me, out of compassion." The Blessed One accepted, out of compassion.

"Bhante, in the presence of the Blessed One I heard and learned this: 'The giver of what is agreeable gains what is agreeable.' Bhante, my boiled hill rice cleared of dark grains, accompanied by various sauces and condiments, is agreeable. Let the Blessed One accept it from me, out of compassion." The Blessed One accepted, out of compassion. [50]

"Bhante, in the presence of the Blessed One I heard and learned this: 'The giver of what is agreeable gains what is agreeable.' Bhante, my cloths from Kāsi are agreeable. Let the Blessed One accept them from me, out of compassion." The Blessed One accepted, out of compassion.

"Bhante, in the presence of the Blessed One I heard and learned this: 'The giver of what is agreeable gains what is agreeable.'

Bhante, my couch spread with rugs, blankets, and covers, with an excellent covering of antelope hide, with a canopy above and red bolsters at both ends, is agreeable. Although I know this is not allowable for the Blessed One, this sandalwood plank of mine is worth over a thousand.[1031] Let the Blessed One accept it from me, out of compassion." The Blessed One accepted, out of compassion.

Then the Blessed One expressed his appreciation to the householder Ugga of Vesālī thus:

"The giver of the agreeable gains the agreeable,
when he gives willingly to the upright ones
clothing, bedding, food, and drink,
and various kinds of requisites.

"Having known the arahants to be like a field
for what is relinquished and offered, not held back,[1032]
the good person gives what is hard to give:
the giver of agreeable things gains what is agreeable."

Then, after expressing his appreciation to the householder Ugga of Vesālī, the Blessed One rose from his seat and left. Then, some time later, the householder Ugga of Vesālī passed away. After his death, the householder Ugga of Vesālī was reborn among a certain group of mind-made [deities].[1033] On that occasion the Blessed One was dwelling at Sāvatthī in Jeta's Grove, Anāthapiṇḍika's Park. Then, when the night had advanced, the young deva Ugga, of stunning beauty, illuminating the entire [51] Jeta's Grove, approached the Blessed One, paid homage to him, and stood to one side. The Blessed One then said to him: "I hope, Ugga, that it is as you would have wished."

"Surely, Bhante, it is as I had wished."

Then the Blessed One addressed the young deva Ugga with verses:

"The giver of the agreeable gains the agreeable;
the giver of the foremost again gains the foremost;
the giver of the excellent gains the excellent;
the giver of the best reaches the best state.

"The person who gives the best,
the giver of the foremost,
the giver of the excellent,
is long-lived and famous
wherever he is reborn."[1034]

45 (5) Streams[1035]

"Bhikkhus, there are these five streams of merit, streams of the wholesome, nutriments of happiness—heavenly, ripening in happiness, conducive to heaven—that lead to what is wished for, desired, and agreeable, to one's welfare and happiness. What five?

"(1) When a bhikkhu enters and dwells in a measureless concentration of mind while using a robe [that one has given him], one acquires a measureless stream of merit, stream of the wholesome, a nutriment of happiness . . . that leads . . . to one's welfare and happiness. (2) When a bhikkhu enters and dwells in a measureless concentration of mind while using almsfood [that one has given him], one acquires a measureless stream of merit, stream of the wholesome, a nutriment of happiness . . . that leads . . . to one's welfare and happiness. (3) When a bhikkhu enters and dwells in a measureless concentration of mind while using a dwelling [that one has given him], one acquires a measureless stream of merit, stream of the wholesome, a nutriment of happiness . . . that leads . . . to one's welfare and happiness. (4) When a bhikkhu enters and dwells in a measureless concentration of mind while using a bed and chair [that one has given him], one acquires a measureless stream of merit, stream of the wholesome, a nutriment of happiness . . . that leads . . . to one's welfare and happiness. (5) When a bhikkhu enters and dwells in a measureless concentration of mind while using medicines and provisions for the sick [that one has given him], [52] one acquires a measureless stream of merit, stream of the wholesome, a nutriment of happiness . . . that leads to one's welfare and happiness.

"These are the five streams of merit, streams of the wholesome, nutriments of happiness—heavenly, ripening in happiness, conducive to heaven—that lead to what is wished for, desired, and agreeable, to one's welfare and happiness.

"When, bhikkhus, a noble disciple possesses these five streams of merit, streams of the wholesome, it is not easy to measure his merit thus: 'Just so much is his stream of merit, stream of the wholesome, nutriment of happiness—heavenly . . . that leads to . . . one's welfare and happiness'; rather, it is reckoned simply as an incalculable, immeasurable, great mass of merit.

"Bhikkhus, just as it is not easy to measure the water in the great ocean thus: 'There are so many gallons of water,' or 'There are so many hundreds of gallons of water,' or 'There are so many thousands of gallons of water,'[1036] or 'There are so many hundreds of thousands of gallons of water,' but rather it is reckoned simply as an incalculable, immeasurable, great mass of water; so too, when a noble disciple possesses these five streams of merit . . . it is reckoned simply as an incalculable, immeasurable, great mass of merit."

Just as the many rivers used by the hosts of people,
flowing downstream, reach the ocean,
the great mass of water, the boundless sea,
the fearsome receptacle of heaps of gems; [53]
so the streams of merit reach the wise man
who is a giver of food, drink, and cloth;
[they reach] the donor of beds, seats, and covers
like rivers carrying their waters to the sea.

46 (6) Accomplishments

"Bhikkhus, there are these five accomplishments. What five? Accomplishment in faith, accomplishment in virtuous behavior, accomplishment in learning, accomplishment in generosity, and accomplishment in wisdom. These are the five accomplishments."

47 (7) Wealth

"Bhikkhus, there are these five kinds of wealth. What five? The wealth of faith, the wealth of virtuous behavior, the wealth of learning, the wealth of generosity, and the wealth of wisdom.

(1) "And what, bhikkhus, is the wealth of faith? Here, a noble disciple is endowed with faith. He places faith in the enlight-

enment of the Tathāgata thus: 'The Blessed One is an arahant, perfectly enlightened, accomplished in true knowledge and conduct, fortunate, knower of the world, unsurpassed trainer of persons to be tamed, teacher of devas and humans, the Enlightened One, the Blessed One.' This is called the wealth of faith.

(2) "And what is the wealth of virtuous behavior? Here, a noble disciple abstains from the destruction of life, abstains from taking what is not given, abstains from sexual misconduct, abstains from false speech, abstains from liquor, wine, and intoxicants, the basis for heedlessness. This is called the wealth of virtuous behavior.

(3) "And what is the wealth of learning? Here, a noble disciple has learned much, remembers what he has learned, and accumulates what he has learned. Those teachings that are good in the beginning, good in the middle, and good in the end, with the right meaning and phrasing, which proclaim the perfectly complete and pure spiritual life—such teachings as these he has learned much of, retained in mind, recited verbally, mentally investigated, and penetrated well by view.[1037]

(4) "And what is the wealth of generosity? Here, a noble disciple dwells at home with a heart devoid of the stain of miserliness, freely generous, openhanded, delighting in relinquishment, devoted to charity, delighting in giving and sharing. This is called the wealth of generosity.

(5) "And what is the wealth of wisdom? Here, a noble disciple is wise; he possesses the wisdom that discerns arising and passing away, which is noble and penetrative and leads to the complete destruction of suffering. This is called the wealth of wisdom.

"These, bhikkhus, are the five kinds of wealth." [54]

When one has faith in the Tathāgata,[1038]
unshakable and well established,
and virtuous behavior that is good,
loved and praised by the noble ones;
when one has confidence in the Saṅgha
and one's view has been straightened out,
they say that one is not poor,
that one's life is not lived in vain.

Therefore an intelligent person,
remembering the Buddhas' teaching,
should be intent on faith and virtuous behavior,
confidence and vision of the Dhamma.

48 (8) Situations

"Bhikkhus, there are these five situations that are unobtainable by an ascetic or a brahmin, by a deva, Māra, or Brahmā, or by anyone in the world. What five? (1) 'May what is subject to old age not grow old!': this is a situation that is unobtainable by an ascetic or a brahmin, by a deva, Māra, or Brahmā, or by anyone in the world. (2) 'May what is subject to illness not fall ill!': this is a situation that is unobtainable by an ascetic . . . or by anyone in the world. (3) 'May what is subject to death not die!': this is a situation that is unobtainable by an ascetic . . . or by anyone in the world. (4) 'May what is subject to destruction not be destroyed!': this is a situation that is unobtainable by an ascetic . . . or by anyone in the world. (5) 'May what is subject to loss not be lost!': this is a situation that is unobtainable by an ascetic or a brahmin, by a deva, Māra, or Brahmā, or by anyone in the world.

(1) "Bhikkhus, for the uninstructed worldling, what is subject to old age grows old. When this happens, he does not reflect thus: 'I am not the only one for whom what is subject to old age grows old. For all beings that come and go, that pass away and undergo rebirth, what is subject to old age grows old. If I were to sorrow, languish, lament, weep beating my breast, and become confused when what is subject to old age grows old, I would lose my appetite and my features would become ugly. I would not be able to do my work, my enemies would be elated, and my friends would become saddened.' Thus, when what is subject to old age grows old, he sorrows, languishes, laments, weeps beating his breast, and becomes confused. This is called an uninstructed worldling pierced by the poisonous dart of sorrow who only torments himself.

(2) "Again, for the uninstructed worldling, [55] what is subject to illness falls ill . . . (3) . . . what is subject to death dies . . . (4) . . . what is subject to destruction is destroyed . . . (5) . . . what is subject to loss is lost. When this happens, he does not reflect thus: 'I am not the only one for whom what is subject to loss

is lost. For all beings who come and go, who pass away and undergo rebirth, what is subject to loss is lost. If I were to sorrow, languish, lament, weep beating my breast, and become confused when what is subject to loss is lost, I would lose my appetite and my features would become ugly. I would not be able to do my work, my enemies would be elated, and my friends would become saddened.' Thus, when what is subject to loss is lost, he sorrows, languishes, laments, weeps beating his breast, and becomes confused. This is called an uninstructed worldling pierced by the poisonous dart of sorrow who only torments himself.

(1) "Bhikkhus, for the instructed noble disciple, what is subject to old age grows old. When this happens, he reflects thus: 'I am not the only one for whom what is subject to old age grows old. For all beings that come and go, that pass away and undergo rebirth, what is subject to old age grows old. If I were to sorrow, languish, lament, weep beating my breast, and become confused when what is subject to old age grows old, I would lose my appetite and my features would become ugly. I would not be able to do my work, my enemies would be elated, and my friends would become saddened.' Thus, when what is subject to old age grows old, he does not sorrow, languish, lament, weep beating his breast, and become confused. This is called an instructed noble disciple who has drawn out the poisonous dart of sorrow pierced by which the uninstructed worldling only torments himself. Sorrowless, without darts, the noble disciple realizes nibbāna.[1039]

(2) "Again, for the instructed noble disciple, what is subject to illness falls ill . . . (3) . . . what is subject to death dies . . . (4) . . . what is subject to destruction is destroyed . . . (5) . . . what is subject to loss is lost. When this happens, he reflects thus: 'I am not the only one for whom what is subject to loss is lost. For all beings that come and go, that pass away and undergo rebirth, what is subject to loss [56] is lost. If I were to sorrow, languish, lament, weep beating my breast, and become confused when what is subject to loss is lost, I would lose my appetite and my features would become ugly. I would not be able to do my work, my enemies would be elated, and my friends would become saddened.' Thus, when what is subject to loss is lost, he does not sorrow, languish, lament, weep beating his breast, and become

confused. This is called an instructed noble disciple who has drawn out the poisonous dart of sorrow pierced by which the uninstructed worldling only torments himself. Sorrowless, without darts, the noble disciple realizes nibbāna.

"These, bhikkhus, are the five situations that are unobtainable by an ascetic or a brahmin, by a deva, Māra, or Brahmā, or by anyone in the world.

"It is not by sorrowing and lamenting
that even the least good here can be gained.[1040]
Knowing that one is sorrowful and sad,
one's enemies are elated.

"When the wise person does not shake in adversities,
knowing how to determine what is good,
his enemies are saddened, having seen
that his former facial expression does not change.

"Wherever one might gain one's good,
in whatever way—by chanting, mantras,
maxims, gifts, or tradition[1041]—there
one should exert oneself in just that way.

"But if one should understand: 'This good
cannot be obtained by me or anyone else,'
one should accept the situation without sorrowing,
thinking: 'The kamma is strong; what can I do now?'" [57]

49 (9) Kosala

On one occasion the Blessed One was dwelling at Sāvatthī in Jeta's Grove, Anāthapiṇḍika's Park. Then King Pasenadi of Kosala approached the Blessed One, paid homage to him, and sat down to one side. [Now on that occasion Queen Mallikā had just died.][1042] Then a man approached King Pasendi and whispered in his ear: "Sire, Queen Mallikā has just died." When this was said, King Pasenadi was pained and saddened, and he sat there with slumping shoulders, facing downward, glum, and speechless.

Then the Blessed One, having known the king's condition, said to him:

"Great king, there are these five situations that are unobtainable by an ascetic or a brahmin, by a deva, Māra, or Brahmā, or by anyone in the world."

[The rest of this sutta is identical with 5:48, including the verses.]

50 (10) Nārada

On one occasion the Venerable Nārada was dwelling at Pāṭaliputta at the Cock's Park. Now on that occasion King Muṇḍa's [wife] Queen Bhaddā, who had been dear and beloved to him, had died. Since her death, he did not bathe, anoint himself, eat his meals, or undertake his work. Day and night, he remained brooding over Queen Bhaddā's body. Then King Muṇḍa addressed his treasurer, Piyaka: "Well then, friend Piyaka, [58] immerse Queen Bhaddā's body in an iron vat filled with oil and enclose it in another iron vat so that we can see Queen Bhaddā's body still longer."

"Yes, sire," the treasurer Piyaka replied. Then he immersed Queen Bhaddā's body in an iron vat filled with oil and enclosed it in another iron vat.

Then it occurred to the treasurer Piyaka: "King Muṇḍa's [wife] Queen Bhaddā has died, and she was dear and beloved to him. Since her death, he does not bathe, anoint himself, eat his meals, or undertake his work. Day and night, he remains brooding over the queen's body. What ascetic or brahmin can King Muṇḍa visit, so that, having heard his Dhamma, he might abandon the dart of sorrow?"

Then it occurred to Piyaka: "The Venerable Nārada is dwelling at Pāṭaliputta, in the Cock's Park. Now a good report about this Venerable Nārada has circulated thus: 'He is wise, competent, intelligent, learned, an artful speaker, eloquent, mature, and an arahant.' Suppose King Muṇḍa would visit the Venerable Nārada: perhaps if he hears the Venerable Nārada's Dhamma, he would abandon the dart of sorrow."

Then the treasurer Piyaka approached King Muṇḍa and said to him: "Sire, the Venerable Nārada is dwelling at Pāṭaliputta, in the Cock's Park. Now a good report about this Venerable Nārada has circulated thus: 'He is wise . . . and an arahant.' Your majesty should visit the Venerable Nārada. Perhaps, when you hear the Venerable Nārada's Dhamma, you would abandon the dart of sorrow." [The king said:] "Well then, friend Piyaka, [59] inform the Venerable Nārada. For how can one like me think of approaching an ascetic or brahmin living in his realm without first informing him?"

"Yes, sire," Piyaka replied. Then he went to the Venerable Nārada, paid homage to him, sat down to one side, and said: "Bhante, King Muṇḍa's [wife] Queen Bhaddā, who was dear and beloved to him, has died. Since the queen's death, he does not bathe, anoint himself, eat his meals, or undertake his work. Day and night, he remains brooding over the queen's body. It would be good, Bhante, if the Venerable Nārada would teach the Dhamma to King Muṇḍa in such a way that he can abandon the dart of sorrow."

"Then let King Muṇḍa come at his own convenience."

Then the treasurer Piyaka rose from his seat, paid homage to the Venerable Nārada, circumambulated him keeping the right side toward him, and went to King Muṇḍa. He told the king: "Sire, the Venerable Nārada has given his consent. You may go at your own convenience."

"Well then, friend Piyaka, get the finest carriages harnessed!"

"Yes, sire," Piyaka replied, and after he had gotten the finest carriages harnessed he told King Muṇḍa: "Sire, the finest carriages have been harnessed. You may go at your own convenience."

Then King Muṇḍa mounted a fine carriage, and along with the other carriages he set out in full royal splendor for the Cock's Park to see the Venerable Nārada. He went by carriage as far as the ground was suitable for a carriage, and then he dismounted from his carriage and entered the park on foot. He approached the Venerable Nārada, paid homage to him, and sat down to one side. [60] The Venerable Nārada then said to him:

"Great king, there are these five situations that are unobtainable by an ascetic or a brahmin, by a deva, Māra, or Brahmā, or by anyone in the world. What five? (1) 'May what is subject to old age not grow old!': this is a situation that is unobtainable by an ascetic or a brahmin, by a deva, Māra, or Brahmā, or by anyone in the world. (2) 'May what is subject to illness not fall ill!': this is a situation that is unobtainable by an ascetic . . . or by anyone in the world. (3) 'May what is subject to death not die!': this is a situation that is unobtainable by an ascetic . . . or by anyone in the world. (4) 'May what is subject to destruction not be destroyed!': this is a situation that is unobtainable by an ascetic... or by anyone in the world. (5) 'May what is subject to loss not be lost!': this is a situation that is unobtainable by an ascetic or a brahmin, by a deva, Māra, or Brahmā, or by anyone in the world....

[The sequel is identical to 5:48, including the verses.] [61–62]

When this was said, King Muṇḍa asked the Venerable Nārada: "Bhante, what is the name of this exposition of the Dhamma?"

"Great king, this exposition of the Dhamma is named the extraction of the dart of sorrow."[1043]

"Surely, Bhante, it is the extraction of the dart of sorrow! Surely, it is the extraction of the dart of sorrow! For having heard this exposition of the Dhamma, I have abandoned the dart of sorrow."

Then King Muṇḍa said to the treasurer Piyaka: "Well then, friend Piyaka, have Queen Bhaddā's body cremated and build a memorial mound for her. From today on, I will bathe and anoint myself and eat my meals and undertake my work." [63]

The Second Fifty

I. Hindrances

51 (1) Obstructions

Thus have I heard. On one occasion the Blessed One was dwelling at Sāvatthī in Jeta's Grove, Anāthapiṇḍika's Park. There the Blessed One addressed the bhikkhus: "Bhikkhus!"

"Venerable sir!" those bhikkhus replied. The Blessed One said this:

"Bhikkhus, there are these five obstructions, hindrances, encumbrances of the mind, states that weaken wisdom. What five? (1) Sensual desire is an obstruction, a hindrance, an encumbrance of the mind, a state that weakens wisdom. (2) Ill will... (3) Dullness and drowsiness... (4) Restlessness and remorse... (5) Doubt is an obstruction, a hindrance, an encumbrance of the mind, a state that weakens wisdom. These are the five obstructions, hindrances, encumbrances of the mind, states that weaken wisdom.

"Bhikkhus, without having abandoned these five obstructions, hindrances, encumbrances of the mind, states that weaken wisdom, it is impossible that a bhikkhu, with his powerless and feeble wisdom, might know his own good, the good of others, [64] or the good of both, or realize a superhuman distinction in knowledge and vision worthy of the noble ones. Suppose a river were flowing down from a mountain, traveling a long distance, with a swift current, carrying along much flotsam. Then, on both of its banks, a man would open irrigation channels.[1044] In such a case, the current in the middle of the river would be dispersed, spread out, and divided, so that the river would no longer travel a long distance, with a swift current, carrying along much flotsam. So too, without having abandoned these five obstructions . . . it is impossible that a bhikkhu . . . might realize a superhuman distinction in knowledge and vision worthy of the noble ones.

"But, bhikkhus, having abandoned these five obstructions, hindrances, encumbrances of the mind, states that weaken wisdom, it is possible that a bhikkhu, with his powerful wisdom, might know his own good, the good of others, and the good of both, and realize a superhuman distinction in knowledge and vision worthy of the noble ones. Suppose a river were flowing down from a mountain, traveling a long distance, with a swift current, carrying along much flotsam. Then a man would close up the irrigation channels on both of its banks. In such a case, the current in the middle of the river would not be dispersed, spread out, and divided, so that the river could travel a long distance, with a swift current, carrying along much flotsam. So too, having abandoned these five obstructions . . . it is possible that a bhikkhu . . . might realize a superhuman distinction in knowledge and vision worthy of the noble ones." [65]

52 (2) A Heap

"Bhikkhus, saying 'a heap of the unwholesome,' it is about the five hindrances that one could rightly say this.[1045] For the five hindrances are a complete heap of the unwholesome. What five? The hindrance of sensual desire, the hindrance of ill will, the hindrance of dullness and drowsiness, the hindrance of restlessness and remorse, and the hindrance of doubt. Bhikkhus, saying 'a heap of the unwholesome,' it is about these five hindrances that one could rightly say this. For these five hindrances are a complete heap of the unwholesome."

53 (3) Factors

"Bhikkhus, there are these five factors that assist striving. What five?

(1) "Here, a bhikkhu is endowed with faith. He places faith in the enlightenment of the Tathāgata thus: 'The Blessed One is an arahant, perfectly enlightened, accomplished in true knowledge and conduct, fortunate, knower of the world, unsurpassed trainer of persons to be tamed, teacher of devas and humans, the Enlightened One, the Blessed One.'

(2) "He is seldom ill or afflicted, possessing an even digestion that is neither too cool nor too hot but moderate and suitable for striving.

(3) "He is honest and open, one who reveals himself as he really is to the Teacher and his wise fellow monks.

(4) "He has aroused energy for abandoning unwholesome qualities and acquiring wholesome qualities; he is strong, firm in exertion, not casting off the duty of cultivating wholesome qualities.

(5) "He is wise; he possesses the wisdom that discerns arising and passing away, which is noble and penetrative and leads to the complete destruction of suffering.

"These, bhikkhus, are the five factors that assist striving."

54 (4) Occasions

"Bhikkhus, there are these five unfavorable occasions for striving. What five? [66]

(1) "Here, a bhikkhu is old, overcome by old age. This is the first unfavorable occasion for striving.

(2) "Again, a bhikkhu is ill, overcome by illness. This is the second unfavorable occasion for striving.

(3) "Again, there is a famine, a poor harvest, a time when almsfood is difficult to obtain and it is not easy to subsist by means of gleaning.[1046] This is the third unfavorable occasion for striving.

(4) "Again, there is peril, turbulence in the wilderness, and the people of the countryside, mounted on their vehicles, flee on all sides. This is the fourth unfavorable occasion for striving.

(5) "Again, there is a schism in the Saṅgha, and when there is a schism in the Saṅgha there are mutual insults, mutual reviling, mutual disparagement, and mutual rejection.[1047] Then those without confidence do not gain confidence, while some of those with confidence change their minds. This is the fifth unfavorable occasion for striving.

"These are the five unfavorable occasions for striving.

"There are, bhikkhus, these five favorable occasions for striving. What five?

(1) "Here, a bhikkhu is young, a black-haired young man endowed with the blessing of youth, in the prime of life. This is the first favorable occasion for striving.

(2) "Again, a bhikkhu is seldom ill or afflicted, possessing an even digestion that is neither too cool nor too hot but moderate and suitable for striving. This is the second favorable occasion for striving.

(3) "Again, food is plentiful; there has been a good harvest [67] and almsfood is abundant, so that one can easily sustain oneself by means of gleaning. This is the third favorable occasion for striving.

(4) "Again, people are dwelling in concord, harmoniously, without disputes, blending like milk and water, viewing each other with eyes of affection. This is the fourth favorable occasion for striving.

(5) "Again, the Saṅgha is dwelling at ease—in concord, harmoniously, without disputes, with a single recitation. When the Saṅgha is in concord, there are no mutual insults, no mutual reviling, no mutual disparagement, and no mutual rejection. Then those without confidence gain confidence and those with confidence increase [in their confidence].[1048] This is the fifth favorable occasion for striving.

"These are the five favorable occasions for striving."

55 (5) Mother and Son

On one occasion the Blessed One was dwelling at Sāvatthī in Jeta's Grove, Anāthapiṇḍika's Park. Now on that occasion a mother and a son, being respectively a bhikkhunī and a bhikkhu, had entered the rains residence at Sāvatthī. They often wanted to see one another, the mother often wanting to see her son, and the son his mother. Because they often saw one another, a bond was formed; because a bond formed, intimacy arose; because there was intimacy, lust found an opening.[1049] With their minds in the grip of lust, without having given up the training and declared their weakness, they engaged in sexual intercourse.[1050]

Then a number of bhikkhus approached the Blessed One, paid homage to him, sat down to one side, and reported what had happened. [68] [The Blessed One said:]

"Bhikkhus, did that foolish man think: 'A mother does not fall in love with her son, or a son with his mother'? (1) Bhikkhus, I do not see even one other form that is as tantalizing, sensuous, intoxicating, captivating, infatuating, and as much of an obstacle to achieving the unsurpassed security from bondage as the form of a woman. Beings who are lustful for the form of a woman—ravenous, tied to it, infatuated, and blindly absorbed in it[1051]—sorrow for a long time under the control of a woman's form. (2) I do not see even one other sound . . . (3) . . . even one other odor . . . (4) . . . even one other taste . . . (5) . . . even one other touch that is as tantalizing, sensuous, intoxicating, captivating, infatuating, and as much of an obstacle to achieving the unsurpassed security from bondage as the touch of a woman. Beings who are lustful for the touch of a woman—ravenous, tied to it, infatuated, and blindly absorbed in it—sorrow for a long time under the control of a woman's touch.

"Bhikkhus, while walking, a woman obsesses the mind of a man; while standing . . . while sitting . . . while lying down . . . while laughing . . . while speaking . . . while singing . . . while crying a woman obsesses the mind of a man. When swollen,[1052] too, a woman obsesses the mind of a man. Even when dead, a woman obsesses the mind of a man. If, bhikkhus, one could rightly say of anything: 'Entirely a snare of Māra,' it is precisely of women that one could say this."[1053] [69]

One might talk with a murderous foe,
one might talk with an evil spirit,
one might even approach a viper
whose bite means certain death;
but with a woman, one to one,
one should never talk.

They bind one whose mind is muddled
with a glance and a smile,
with their dress in disarray,
and with gentle speech.
It is not safe to approach[1054] such a person
though she is swollen and dead.

These five objects of sensual pleasure
are seen in a woman's body:
forms, sounds, tastes, and odors,
and also delightful touches.

Those swept up by the flood of sensuality,
who do not fully understand sense pleasures,
are plunged headlong into saṃsāra, [into] time,
destination, and existence upon existence.[1055]

But those who have fully understood sense pleasures
live without fear from any quarter.
Having attained the destruction of the taints,
while in the world, they have gone beyond.

56 (6) Preceptor

Then a certain bhikkhu approached his own preceptor and said to him: "Bhante, my body now seems as if it has been drugged, I have become disoriented, and the teachings are no longer clear to me. Dullness and drowsiness obsess my mind. I live the spiritual life dissatisfied and have doubt about the teachings."[1056]

Then the preceptor took his pupil to the Blessed One. He paid homage to the Blessed One, sat down to one side, and told the Blessed One what his pupil had said. [70] [The Blessed One said:]

"So it is, bhikkhu! (1) When one is unguarded in the doors of the sense faculties, (2) immoderate in eating, (3) and not intent on wakefulness; (4) when one lacks insight into wholesome qualities (5) and does not dwell intent on the endeavor to develop the aids to enlightenment in the earlier and later phases of the night, one's body seems as if it had been drugged, one becomes disoriented, and the teachings are no longer clear to one. Dullness and drowsiness obsess one's mind. One lives the spiritual life dissatisfied and has doubt about the teachings.

"Therefore, bhikkhu, you should train yourself thus: (1) 'I will be guarded in the doors of the sense faculties, (2) moderate in eating, (3) and intent on wakefulness; (4) I will have insight into wholesome qualities (5) and will dwell intent on the endeavor to develop the aids to enlightenment in the earlier and later phases of the night.' It is in such a way, bhikkhu, that you should train yourself."

Then, having received such an exhortation from the Blessed One, that bhikkhu rose from his seat, paid homage to the Blessed One, circumambulated him keeping the right side toward him, and departed. Then, dwelling alone, withdrawn, heedful, ardent, and resolute, in no long time that bhikkhu realized for himself with direct knowledge, in this very life, that unsurpassed consummation of the spiritual life for the sake of which clansmen rightly go forth from the household life into homelessness, and having entered upon it, he dwelled in it. He directly knew: "Destroyed is birth, the spiritual life has been lived, what had to be done has been done, there is no more coming back to any state of being." And that bhikkhu became one of the arahants.

Then, after attaining arahantship, that bhikkhu approached his preceptor and said to him: "Bhante, my body now no longer seems as if it had been drugged, I have become well oriented, and the teachings are clear to me. Dullness and drowsiness do not obsess my mind. I live the spiritual life joyfully and have no doubt about the teachings."

Then the preceptor took his pupil to the Blessed One. [71] He paid homage to the Blessed One, sat down to one side, and told the Blessed One what his pupil had said. [The Blessed One said:]

"So it is, bhikkhu! When one is guarded in the doors of the sense faculties, moderate in eating, and intent on wakefulness; when one has insight into wholesome qualities and dwells intent on the endeavor to develop the aids to enlightenment in the earlier and later phases of the night, one's body does not seem as if it had been drugged, one becomes well oriented, and the teachings are clear to one. Dullness and drowsiness do not obsess one's mind. One lives the spiritual life joyfully and has no doubt about the teachings.

"Therefore, bhikkhus,[1057] you should train yourselves thus: (1) 'We will be guarded in the doors of the sense faculties, (2) moderate in eating, and (3) intent on wakefulness; (4) we will have insight into wholesome qualities (5) and will dwell intent on the endeavor to develop the aids to enlightenment in the earlier and later phases of the night.' It is in such a way, bhikkhus, that you should train yourselves."

57 (7) Themes

"Bhikkhus, there are these five themes that should often be reflected upon by a woman or a man, by a householder or one gone forth.[1058] What five? (1) A woman or a man, a householder or one gone forth, should often reflect thus: 'I am subject to old age; I am not exempt from old age.' (2) A woman or a man, a householder or one gone forth, should often reflect thus: 'I am subject to illness; I am not exempt from illness.' (3) A woman or a man, a householder or one gone forth, should often reflect thus: 'I am subject to death; I am not exempt from death.' (4) A woman or a man, a householder or one gone forth, should often reflect [72] thus: 'I must be parted and separated from everyone and everything dear and agreeable to me.'[1059] (5) A woman or a man, a householder or one gone forth, should often reflect thus: 'I am the owner of my kamma, the heir of my kamma; I have kamma as my origin, kamma as my relative, kamma as my resort; I will be the heir of whatever kamma, good or bad, that I do.'

(1) "For the sake of what benefit should a woman or a man, a householder or one gone forth, often reflect thus: 'I am subject to old age; I am not exempt from old age'? In their youth beings are intoxicated with their youth, and when they are intoxicated with their youth they engage in misconduct by body, speech, and mind. But when one often reflects upon this theme, the intoxication with youth is either completely abandoned or diminished. It is for the sake of this benefit that a woman or a man, a householder or one gone forth, should often reflect thus: 'I am subject to old age; I am not exempt from old age.'

(2) "And for the sake of what benefit should a woman or a man, a householder or one gone forth, often reflect thus: 'I am subject to illness; I am not exempt from illness'? In a state of

health beings are intoxicated with their health, and when they are intoxicated with their health they engage in misconduct by body, speech, and mind. But when one often reflects upon this theme, the intoxication with health is either completely abandoned or diminished. It is for the sake of this benefit that a woman or a man, a householder or one gone forth, should often reflect thus: 'I am subject to illness; I am not exempt from illness.'

(3) "And for the sake of what benefit should a woman or a man, a householder or one gone forth, often reflect thus: 'I am subject to death; I am not exempt from death'? During their lives beings are intoxicated with life, and when they are intoxicated with life they engage in misconduct by body, speech, [73] and mind. But when one often reflects upon this theme, the intoxication with life is either completely abandoned or diminished. It is for the sake of this benefit that a woman or a man, a householder or one gone forth, should often reflect thus: 'I am subject to death; I am not exempt from death.'

(4) "And for the sake of what benefit should a woman or a man, a householder or one gone forth, often reflect thus: 'I must be parted and separated from everyone and everything dear and agreeable to me'? Beings have desire and lust in regard to those people and things that are dear and agreeable, and excited by this lust, they engage in misconduct by body, speech, and mind. But when one often reflects upon this theme, the desire and lust in regard to everyone and everything dear and agreeable is either completely abandoned or diminished. It is for the sake of this benefit that a woman or a man, a householder or one gone forth, should often reflect thus: 'I must be parted and separated from everyone and everything dear and agreeable to me.'

(5) "And for the sake of what benefit should a woman or a man, a householder or one gone forth, often reflect thus: 'I am the owner of my kamma, the heir of my kamma; I have kamma as my origin, kamma as my relative, kamma as my resort; I will be the heir of whatever kamma, good or bad, that I do'? People engage in misconduct by body, speech, and mind. But when one often reflects upon this theme, such misconduct is either completely abandoned or diminished. It is for the sake of this benefit that a woman or a man, a householder or one gone

forth, should often reflect thus: 'I am the owner of my kamma, the heir of my kamma; I have kamma as my origin, kamma as my relative, kamma as my resort; I will be the heir of whatever kamma, good or bad, that I do.'

(1) "This noble disciple reflects thus: [74] 'I am not the only one who is subject to old age, not exempt from old age. All beings that come and go, that pass away and undergo rebirth, are subject to old age; none are exempt from old age.' As he often reflects on this theme, the path is generated. He pursues this path, develops it, and cultivates it. As he does so, the fetters are entirely abandoned and the underlying tendencies are uprooted.[1060]

(2) "This noble disciple reflects thus: 'I am not the only one who is subject to illness, not exempt from illness. All beings that come and go, that pass away and undergo rebirth, are subject to illness; none are exempt from illness.' As he often reflects on this theme, the path is generated. He pursues this path, develops it, and cultivates it. As he does so, the fetters are entirely abandoned and the underlying tendencies are uprooted.

(3) "This noble disciple reflects thus: 'I am not the only one who is subject to death, not exempt from death. All beings that come and go, that pass away and undergo rebirth, are subject to death; none are exempt from death.' As he often reflects on this theme, the path is generated. He pursues this path, develops it, and cultivates it. As he does so, the fetters are entirely abandoned and the underlying tendencies are uprooted.

(4) "This noble disciple reflects thus: 'I am not the only one who must be parted and separated from everyone and everything dear and agreeable. All beings that come and go, that pass away and undergo rebirth, must be parted and separated from everyone and everything dear and agreeable.' As he often reflects on this theme, the path is generated. He pursues this path, develops it, and cultivates it. As he does so, the fetters are entirely abandoned and the underlying tendencies are uprooted.

(5) "This noble disciple reflects thus: 'I am not the only one who is the owner of one's kamma, the heir of one's kamma; who has kamma as one's origin, kamma as one's relative, kamma as one's resort; who will be the heir of whatever kamma, good or bad, that one does. All beings that come and go, that pass

away and undergo rebirth, are owners of their kamma, heirs of their kamma; all have kamma as their origin, kamma as their relative, kamma as their resort; all will be heirs of whatever kamma, good or bad, that they do.' [75] As he often reflects on this theme, the path is generated. He pursues this path, develops it, and cultivates it. As he does so, the fetters are entirely abandoned and the underlying tendencies are uprooted.

"Worldlings subject to illness,[1061]
old age, and death are disgusted
[by other people] who exist
in accordance with their nature.

"If I were to become disgusted
with beings who have such a nature,
that would not be proper for me
since I too have the same nature.

"While I was dwelling thus,
having known the state without acquisitions,
I overcame all intoxications—
intoxication with health,
with youth, and with life—
having seen security in renunciation.[1062]

"Zeal then arose in me
as I clearly saw nibbāna.
Now I am incapable
of indulging in sensual pleasures.
Relying on the spiritual life,
never will I turn back."

58 (8) Licchavi Youths

On one occasion the Blessed One was dwelling at Vesālī in the hall with the peaked roof in the Great Wood. Then, in the morning, the Blessed One dressed, took his bowl and robe, and entered Vesālī for alms. Having walked for alms in Vesālī, after the meal, when he had returned from his alms round, he entered the Great Wood and sat down at the foot of a tree to dwell for the day.

Now on that occasion a number of Licchavi youths had taken their strung bows and were walking and wandering in the Great Wood, accompanied by a pack of dogs, when they saw the Blessed One seated at the foot of a tree to dwell for the day. When they saw him, they put down their strung bows, sent the dogs off to one side, and approached him. They paid homage to the Blessed One [76] and silently stood in attendance upon him with their hands joined in reverential salutation.

Now on that occasion the Licchavi youth Mahānāma was walking and wandering for exercise in the Great Wood when he saw the Licchavi youths silently standing in attendance upon the Blessed One with their hands joined in reverential salutation. He then approached the Blessed One, paid homage to him, sat down to one side, and uttered this inspired utterance: "They will be Vajjis! They will be Vajjis!"

[The Blessed One said:] "But why, Mahānāma, do you say: 'They will be Vajjis! They will be Vajjis!'?"

"These Licchavi youths, Bhante, are violent, rough, and brash. They are always plundering any sweets that are left as gifts among families, whether sugar cane, jujube fruits, cakes, pies, or sugarballs, and then they devour them. They give women and girls of respectable families blows on their backs.[1063] Now they are standing silently in attendance upon the Blessed One with their hands joined in reverential salutation."

"Mahānāma, in whatever clansman five qualities are found—whether he is a consecrated khattiya king, a country gentleman, the general of an army, a village headman, a guildmaster, or one of those who exercise private rulership over various clans—only growth is to be expected, not decline. What five?

(1) "Here, Mahānāma, with wealth acquired by energetic striving, amassed by the strength of his arms, earned by the sweat of his brow, righteous wealth righteously gained, a clansman honors, respects, esteems, [77] and venerates his parents. His parents, being honored, respected, esteemed, and venerated, have compassion on him with a good heart, thinking: 'May you live long and maintain a long life span.' When a clansman's parents have compassion for him, only growth is to be expected for him, not decline.

(2) "Again, Mahānāma, with wealth acquired by energetic striving, amassed by the strength of his arms, earned by the

sweat of his brow, righteous wealth righteously gained, a clansman honors, respects, esteems, and venerates his wife and children, his slaves, workers, and servants. Being honored, respected, esteemed, and venerated, they have compassion on him with a good heart, thinking: 'May you live long!' When a clansman's wife and children, slaves, workers, and servants have compassion for him, only growth is to be expected for him, not decline.

(3) "Again, Mahānāma, with wealth acquired by energetic striving, amassed by the strength of his arms, earned by the sweat of his brow, righteous wealth righteously gained, a clansman honors, respects, esteems, and venerates the owners of the neighboring fields and those with whom he does business.[1064] Being honored, respected, esteemed, and venerated, they have compassion on him with a good heart, thinking: 'May you live long!' When the owners of the neighboring fields and those with whom he does business have compassion for a clansman, only growth is to be expected for him, not decline.

(4) "Again, Mahānāma, with wealth acquired by energetic striving, amassed by the strength of his arms, earned by the sweat of his brow, righteous wealth righteously gained, a clansman honors, respects, esteems, and venerates the oblational deities.[1065] Being honored, respected, esteemed, and venerated, they have compassion on him with a good heart, thinking: 'May you live long!' When the oblational deities have compassion for a clansman, only growth is to be expected for him, not decline.

(5) "Again, Mahānāma, with wealth acquired by energetic striving, amassed by the strength of his arms, earned by the sweat of his brow, righteously gained, a clansman honors, respects, esteems, and venerates ascetics and brahmins. Being honored, respected, esteemed, and venerated, they have compassion on him with a good heart, thinking: 'May you live long!' When ascetics and brahmins have compassion [78] for a clansman, only growth is to be expected for him, not decline.

"Mahānāma, in whatever clansman these five qualities are found—whether he is a consecrated khattiya king, a country gentleman, the general of an army, a village headman, a guildmaster, or one of those who exercise private rulership over various clans—only growth is to be expected, not decline."

He always does his duty toward his parents;
he promotes the welfare of his wife and children.
He takes care of the people in his home
and those who live in dependence on him.

The wise person, charitable and virtuous,
acts for the good of both kinds of relatives,
those who have passed away
and those still living in this world.

[He benefits] ascetics and brahmins,
and [also] the deities;
he is one who gives rise to joy
while living a righteous life at home.

Having done what is good,
he is worthy of veneration and praise.
They praise him here in this world
and after death he rejoices in heaven.

59 (9) Gone Forth in Old Age (1)

"Bhikkhus, it is rare to find one gone forth in old age who possesses five qualities. What five? It is rare to find one gone forth in old age (1) who is astute; (2) who has the proper manner; (3) who is learned; (4) who can speak on the Dhamma; and (5) who is an expert on the discipline. It is rare to find one gone forth in old age who possesses these five qualities."

60 (10) Gone Forth in Old Age (2)

"Bhikkhus, it is rare to find one gone forth in old age who possesses five qualities. What five? It is rare to find one gone forth in old age (1) who is easy to correct; [79] (2) who firmly retains in mind what he has learned; (3) who accepts instruction respectfully; (4) who can speak on the Dhamma; and (5) who is an expert on the discipline. It is rare to find one gone forth in old age who possesses these five qualities."

II. Perceptions

61 (1) Perceptions (1)

"Bhikkhus, these five perceptions, when developed and cultivated, are of great fruit and benefit, culminating in the deathless, having the deathless as their consummation. What five? The perception of unattractiveness, the perception of death, the perception of danger, the perception of the repulsiveness of food, and the perception of non-delight in the entire world.[1066] These five perceptions, when developed and cultivated, are of great fruit and benefit, culminating in the deathless, having the deathless as their consummation."

62 (2) Perceptions (2)

"Bhikkhus, these five perceptions, when developed and cultivated, are of great fruit and benefit, culminating in the deathless, having the deathless as their consummation. What five? The perception of impermanence, the perception of non-self, the perception of death, the perception of the repulsiveness of food, and the perception of non-delight in the entire world.[1067] [80] These five perceptions, when developed and cultivated, are of great fruit and benefit, culminating in the deathless, having the deathless as their consummation."

63 (3) Growth (1)

"Bhikkhus, growing in five ways, a male noble disciple grows by a noble growth, and he absorbs the essence and the best of this life. What five? He grows in faith, virtuous behavior, learning, generosity, and wisdom. Growing in these five ways, a male noble disciple grows by a noble growth, and he absorbs the essence and the best of this life."

> He who grows in faith and virtuous behavior,
> in wisdom, generosity, and learning—
> such a discerning superior man
> absorbs for himself the essence of this life.

64 (4) Growth (2)

"Bhikkhus, growing in five ways, a female noble disciple grows by a noble growth, and she absorbs the essence and the best of this life. What five? She grows in faith, virtuous behavior, learning, generosity, and wisdom. Growing in these five ways, a female noble disciple grows by a noble growth, and she absorbs the essence and the best of this life."

> She who grows in faith and virtuous behavior,
> in wisdom, generosity, and learning—
> such a virtuous female lay follower
> absorbs for herself the essence of this life. [81]

65 (5) Discussion

"Bhikkhus, when a bhikkhu possesses five qualities, it is fitting for his fellow monks to hold a discussion with him. What five? (1) Here, a bhikkhu is himself accomplished in virtuous behavior, and he answers questions that come up in a discussion on accomplishment in virtuous behavior. (2) He is himself accomplished in concentration, and he answers questions that come up in a discussion on accomplishment in concentration. (3) He is himself accomplished in wisdom, and he answers questions that come up in a discussion on accomplishment in wisdom. (4) He is himself accomplished in liberation, and he answers questions that come up in a discussion on accomplishment in liberation. (5) He is himself accomplished in the knowledge and vision of liberation, and he answers questions that come up in a discussion on accomplishment in the knowledge and vision of liberation. When a bhikkhu possesses these five qualities, it is fitting for his fellow monks to hold a discussion with him."

66 (6) Way of Life

"Bhikkhus, when a bhikkhu possesses five qualities, it is fitting for his fellow monks to live together with him.[1068] What five? (1) Here, a bhikkhu is himself accomplished in virtuous behavior, and he answers questions posed during a discussion on accomplishment in virtuous behavior. (2) He is himself accomplished in concentration, and he answers questions posed during a discussion on accomplishment in concentration. (3) He is himself accomplished in wisdom, and he answers questions posed during a discussion on accomplishment in wisdom. (4) He is himself accomplished in liberation, and he answers questions posed during a discussion on accomplishment in liberation. (5) He is himself accomplished in the knowledge and vision of liberation, and he answers questions posed during a discussion on accomplishment in the knowledge and vision of liberation. When a bhikkhu possesses these five qualities, it is fitting for his fellow monks to live together with him."

67 (7) Bases for Psychic Potency (1)

"Bhikkhus, when any bhikkhu or bhikkhunī develops and cultivates five things, one of two fruits is to be expected: [82] either final knowledge in this very life or, if there is a residue remaining, the state of non-returning. What five?

"(1) Here, a bhikkhu develops the basis for psychic potency that possesses concentration due to desire and activities of striving. (2) He develops the basis for psychic potency that possesses concentration due to energy and activities of striving. (3) He develops the basis for psychic potency that possesses concentration due to mind and activities of striving. (4) He develops the basis for psychic potency that possesses concentration due to investigation and activities of striving.[1069] (5) Enthusiasm itself is the fifth.[1070]

"When, bhikkhus, any bhikkhu or bhikkhunī develops and cultivates these five things, one of two fruits is to be expected: either final knowledge in this very life or, if there is a residue remaining, the state of non-returning."

68 (8) Bases for Psychic Potency (2)

"Bhikkhus, before my enlightenment, while I was just a bodhisatta, not yet fully enlightened, I developed and cultivated five things. What five?

"(1) I developed the basis for psychic potency that possesses concentration due to desire and activities of striving. (2) I developed the basis for psychic potency that possesses concentration due to energy and activities of striving. (3) I developed the basis for psychic potency that possesses concentration due to mind and activities of striving. (4) I developed the basis for psychic potency that possesses concentration due to investigation and activities of striving. (5) Enthusiasm itself was the fifth.

"Because I had developed and cultivated these things with enthusiasm as the fifth, there being a suitable basis, I was capable of realizing any state realizable by direct knowledge toward which I inclined my mind.

"If I wished: 'May I wield the various kinds of psychic potency:

having been one, may I become many . . . [as in 5:23] . . . may I exercise mastery with the body as far as the brahmā world,' I was capable of realizing it, there being a suitable basis . . . [as in 5:23] . . .

"If I wished: [83] 'May I, with the destruction of the taints, in this very life realize for myself with direct knowledge the taintless liberation of mind, liberation by wisdom, and having entered upon it, may I dwell in it,' I was capable of realizing it, there being a suitable basis."

69 (9) Disenchantment

"Bhikkhus, these five things, when developed and cultivated, lead exclusively to disenchantment, to dispassion, to cessation, to peace, to direct knowledge, to enlightenment, to nibbāna. What five? Here, a bhikkhu dwells contemplating the unattractiveness of the body, perceiving the repulsiveness of food, perceiving non-delight in the entire world, contemplating impermanence in all conditioned phenomena; and he has the perception of death well established internally. These five things, when developed and cultivated, lead exclusively to disenchantment, to dispassion, to cessation, to peace, to direct knowledge, to enlightenment, to nibbāna."

70 (10) Destruction of the Taints

"Bhikkhus, these five things, when developed and cultivated, lead to the destruction of the taints. What five? Here, a bhikkhu dwells contemplating the unattractiveness of the body, perceiving the repulsiveness of food, perceiving non-delight in the entire world, contemplating impermanence in all conditioned phenomena; and he has the perception of death well established internally. These five things, when developed and cultivated, lead to the destruction of the taints." [84]

III. Future Perils

71 (1) Liberation of Mind (1)

"Bhikkhus, these five things, when developed and cultivated, have liberation of mind as their fruit, liberation of mind as their fruit and benefit; they have liberation by wisdom as their fruit, liberation by wisdom as their fruit and benefit.[1071] What five?

Here, a bhikkhu dwells contemplating the unattractiveness of the body, perceiving the repulsiveness of food, perceiving non-delight in the entire world, contemplating impermanence in all conditioned phenomena; and he has the perception of death well established internally. These five things, when developed and cultivated, have liberation of mind as their fruit, liberation of mind as their fruit and benefit; they have liberation by wisdom as their fruit, liberation by wisdom as their fruit and benefit.

"When a bhikkhu is liberated in mind and liberated by wisdom, he is called a bhikkhu who has removed the crossbar, filled in the moat, pulled out the pillar, a boltless one, a noble one with banner lowered, with burden dropped, detached.[1072]

"And how has a bhikkhu removed the crossbar? Here, a bhikkhu has abandoned ignorance, cut it off at the root, made it like a palm stump, obliterated it so that it is no more subject to future arising. It is in this way that a bhikkhu has removed the crossbar.

"And how has a bhikkhu filled in the moat? Here, a bhikkhu has abandoned the wandering on in birth that brings renewed existence; he has cut it off at the root, made it like a palm stump, obliterated it so that it is no more subject to future arising. It is in this way that a bhikkhu has filled in the moat.

"And how has a bhikkhu pulled out the pillar? [85] Here, a bhikkhu has abandoned craving, cut it off at the root, made it like a palm stump, obliterated it so that it is no more subject to future arising. It is in this way that a bhikkhu has pulled out the pillar.

"And how is a bhikkhu a boltless one? Here, a bhikkhu has abandoned the five lower fetters, cut them off at the root, made them like a palm stump, obliterated them so that they are no more subject to future arising. It is in this way that a bhikkhu is a boltless one.

"And how is a bhikkhu a noble one with banner lowered, with burden dropped, detached? Here, a bhikkhu has abandoned the conceit 'I am,' cut it off at the root, made it like a palm stump, obliterated it so that it is no more subject to future arising. It is in this way that a bhikkhu is a noble one with banner lowered, with burden dropped, detached."

72 (2) Liberation of Mind (2)

"Bhikkhus, these five things, when developed and cultivated, have liberation of mind as their fruit, liberation of mind as their fruit and benefit; they have liberation by wisdom as their fruit, liberation by wisdom as their fruit and benefit. What five? The perception of impermanence, the perception of suffering in the impermanent, the perception of non-self in what is suffering, the perception of abandoning, the perception of dispassion.[1073] These five things, when developed and cultivated, have liberation of mind as their fruit, liberation of mind as their fruit and benefit; they have liberation by wisdom as their fruit, liberation by wisdom as their fruit and benefit.

"When a bhikkhu is liberated in mind and liberated by wisdom, he is called a bhikkhu who has removed the crossbar, filled in the moat, pulled out the pillar, a boltless one, a noble one with banner lowered, with burden dropped, detached.

"And how is a bhikkhu one who has removed the crossbar? . . . [all as in 5:71, down:] [86] . . . It is in this way that a bhikkhu is a noble one with banner lowered, with burden dropped, detached."

73 (3) One Who Dwells in the Dhamma (1)

Then a certain bhikkhu approached the Blessed One, paid homage to him, sat down to one side, and said:

"It is said, Bhante, 'one who dwells in the Dhamma, one who dwells in the Dhamma.'[1074] In what way is a bhikkhu one who dwells in the Dhamma?"

(1) "Here, bhikkhu, a bhikkhu learns the Dhamma: the discourses, mixed prose and verse, expositions, verses, inspired utterances, quotations, birth stories, amazing accounts, and questions-and-answers. He passes the day in learning the Dhamma but neglects seclusion and does not devote himself to internal serenity of mind. This is called a bhikkhu who is absorbed in learning, not one who dwells in the Dhamma. [87]

(2) "Again, a bhikkhu teaches the Dhamma to others in detail as he has heard and learned it. He passes the day communicating the Dhamma[1075] but neglects seclusion and does not devote himself to internal serenity of mind. This is called a bhikkhu who is absorbed in communication, not one who dwells in the Dhamma.

(3) "Again, a bhikkhu recites the Dhamma in detail as he

has heard it and learned it. He passes the day in recitation but neglects seclusion and does not devote himself to internal serenity of mind. This is called a bhikkhu who is absorbed in recitation, not one who dwells in the Dhamma.

(4) "Again, a bhikkhu ponders, examines, and mentally inspects the Dhamma as he has heard it and learned it. He passes the day in thinking about the Dhamma but neglects seclusion and does not devote himself to internal serenity of mind. This is called a bhikkhu who is absorbed in thought, not one who dwells in the Dhamma.

(5) "Here, a bhikkhu learns the Dhamma—the discourses, mixed prose and verse, expositions, verses, inspired utterances, quotations, birth stories, amazing accounts, and questions-and-answers—but he does not pass the day [solely] in learning the Dhamma. He does not neglect seclusion but devotes himself to internal serenity of mind.[1076] It is in this way that a bhikkhu is one who dwells in the Dhamma.

"Thus, bhikkhu, I have taught the one absorbed in learning, the one absorbed in communication, the one absorbed in recitation, the one absorbed in thought, and the one who dwells in the Dhamma. Whatever should be done by a compassionate teacher out of compassion for his disciples, seeking their welfare, that I have done for you. These are the feet of trees, these are empty huts. Meditate, bhikkhu, do not be heedless. Do not have cause to regret it later. This is our instruction to you." [88]

74 (4) One Who Dwells in the Dhamma (2)

Then a certain bhikkhu approached the Blessed One, paid homage to him, sat down to one side, and said:

"It is said, Bhante, 'one who dwells in the Dhamma, one who dwells in the Dhamma.' In what way is a bhikkhu one who dwells in the Dhamma?"

(1) "Here, bhikkhu, a bhikkhu learns the Dhamma—the discourses, mixed prose and verse, expositions, verses, inspired utterances, quotations, birth stories, amazing accounts, and questions-and-answers—but he does not go further and understand its meaning with wisdom.[1077] This is called a bhikkhu who is absorbed in learning, not one who dwells in the Dhamma.

(2) "Again, a bhikkhu teaches the Dhamma to others in detail as he has heard and learned it, but he does not go further and understand its meaning with wisdom. This is called a bhikkhu

who is absorbed in communication, not one who dwells in the Dhamma.

(3) "Again, a bhikkhu recites the Dhamma in detail as he has heard it and learned it, but he does not go further and understand its meaning with wisdom. This is called a bhikkhu who is absorbed in recitation, not one who dwells in the Dhamma.

(4) "Again, a bhikkhu ponders, examines, and mentally inspects the Dhamma as he has heard it and learned it, but he does not go further and understand its meaning with wisdom. This is called a bhikkhu who is absorbed in thought, not one who dwells in the Dhamma.

(5) "Here, a bhikkhu learns the Dhamma—the discourses, mixed prose and verse, expositions, verses, inspired utterances, quotations, birth stories, amazing accounts, and questions-and-answers—but he goes further and understands its meaning with wisdom. It is in this way that a bhikkhu is one who dwells in the Dhamma.

"Thus, bhikkhu, I have taught the one absorbed in learning, [89] the one absorbed in communication, the one absorbed in recitation, the one absorbed in thought, and the one who dwells in the Dhamma. Whatever should be done by a compassionate teacher out of compassion for his disciples, seeking their welfare, that I have done for you. These are the feet of trees, these are empty huts. Meditate, bhikkhu, do not be heedless. Do not have cause to regret it later. This is our instruction to you."

75 (5) Warriors (1)

"Bhikkhus, there are these five kinds of warriors found in the world. What five?

(1) "Here, some warrior, when he sees the cloud of dust,[1078] sinks, founders, does not brace himself, and cannot enter the battle. There is, bhikkhus, such a warrior here. This is the first kind of warrior found in the world.

(2) "Again, some warrior can endure the cloud of dust, but when he sees the crests of the standards, he sinks, founders, does not brace himself, and cannot enter the battle. There is, bhikkhus, such a warrior here. This is the second kind of warrior found in the world.

(3) "Again, some warrior can endure the cloud of dust and the crests of the standards, but when he hears the uproar, he

sinks, founders, does not brace himself, and cannot enter the battle. There is, bhikkhus, such a warrior here. This is the third kind of warrior found in the world.

(4) "Again, some warrior can endure the cloud of dust, the crests of the standards, and the uproar, but he is struck down and wounded by blows. There is, bhikkhus, such a warrior here. This is the fourth kind of warrior found in the world.

(5) "Again, some warrior can endure the cloud of dust, the crests of the standards, the uproar, [90] and the blows. Having triumphed in that battle, he emerges victorious and settles at the head of the battlefield. There is, bhikkhus, such a warrior here. This is the fifth kind of warrior found in the world.

"These are the five kinds of warriors found in the world.

"So too, there are these five kinds of persons similar to warriors found among the bhikkhus. What five?

(1) "Here, some bhikkhu, when he sees the cloud of dust, sinks, founders, does not brace himself, and cannot maintain the spiritual life. He discloses his weakness in the training, gives up the training, and reverts to the lower life.[1079] What is the cloud of dust in his case? The bhikkhu hears: 'In such and such a village or town the women or girls are beautiful, attractive, graceful, possessing supreme beauty of complexion.' Having heard this, he sinks, founders, does not brace himself, and cannot maintain the spiritual life. He discloses his weakness in the training, gives up the training, and reverts to the lower life. This is the cloud of dust in his case. I say that this person is just like the warrior who, when he sees the cloud of dust, sinks, founders, does not brace himself, and cannot enter the battle. There is, bhikkhus, such a person here. This is the first kind of person similar to a warrior found among the bhikkhus.

(2) "Again, some bhikkhu can endure the cloud of dust, but when he sees the crests of the standards, he sinks, founders, does not brace himself, and cannot maintain the spiritual life. He discloses his weakness in the training, gives up the training, and reverts to the lower life. What are the crests of the standards in his case? The bhikkhu does not hear: 'In such and such a village or town the women or girls are beautiful, attractive, graceful, possessing supreme beauty of complexion,' but he himself sees a woman or a girl who is beautiful, attractive, graceful, possessing supreme beauty of complexion. Having

seen her, he sinks, founders, does not brace himself, and [91] cannot maintain the spiritual life. He discloses his weakness in the training, gives up the training, and reverts to the lower life. These are the crests of the standards in his case. I say that this person is just like the warrior who can endure the cloud of dust, but when he sees the crests of the standards, he sinks, founders, does not brace himself, and cannot enter the battle. There is, bhikkhus, such a person here. This is the second kind of person similar to a warrior found among the bhikkhus.

(3) "Again, some bhikkhu can endure the cloud of dust and the crests of the standards, but when he hears the uproar, he sinks, founders, does not brace himself, and cannot maintain the spiritual life. He discloses his weakness in the training, gives up the training, and reverts to the lower life. What is the uproar in his case? When the bhikkhu has gone to the forest, to the foot of a tree, or to an empty hut, a woman approaches him, smiles at him, chats with him, laughs at him, and teases him. As the woman is smiling at him, chatting with him, laughing at him, and teasing him, he sinks, founders, does not brace himself, and cannot maintain the spiritual life. He discloses his weakness in the training, gives up the training, and reverts to the lower life. This is the uproar in his case. I say that this person is just like the warrior who can endure the cloud of dust and the crests of the standards, but when he hears the uproar, he sinks, founders, does not brace himself, and cannot enter the battle. There is, bhikkhus, such a person here. This is the third kind of person similar to a warrior found among the bhikkhus.

(4) "Again, some bhikkhu can endure the cloud of dust, the crests of the standards, and the uproar, but he is struck down and wounded by a blow. What is the blow in his case? When the bhikkhu has gone to the forest, to the foot of a tree, [92] or to an empty hut, a woman approaches him, sits down or lies down next to him, and embraces him. When she does so, he has sexual intercourse with her without having given up the training and disclosed his weakness. This is the blow in his case. I say that this person is just like the warrior who can endure the cloud of dust, the crests of the standards, and the uproar, but who is struck down and wounded by a blow. There is, bhikkhus, such a person here. This is the fourth kind of person similar to a warrior found among the bhikkhus.

(5) "Again, some bhikkhu can endure the clouds of dust, the crests of the standards, the uproar, and a blow. Having triumphed in that battle, he emerges victorious and settles at the head of the battlefield. What is the victory in his case? When the bhikkhu has gone to the forest, to the foot of a tree, or to an empty hut, a woman approaches him, sits down or lies down next to him, and embraces him. But he disentangles himself, frees himself, and goes off wherever he wants.

"He resorts to a secluded lodging: the forest, the foot of a tree, a mountain, a ravine, a hillside cave, a charnel ground, a jungle highland, the open air, a heap of straw. Gone to the forest, to the foot of a tree, or to an empty hut, he sits down, folding his legs crosswise, straightening his body, and establishing mindfulness in front of him. Having abandoned longing for the world, he dwells with a mind free from longing; he purifies his mind from longing. Having abandoned ill will and hatred, he dwells with a mind free from ill will, compassionate toward all living beings; he purifies his mind from ill will and hatred. Having abandoned dullness and drowsiness, he dwells free from dullness and drowsiness, percipient of light, mindful and clearly comprehending; he purifies his mind from dullness and drowsiness. Having abandoned restlessness and remorse, he dwells without agitation, with a mind inwardly peaceful; he purifies his mind from restlessness and remorse. Having abandoned doubt, he dwells having gone beyond doubt, [93] unperplexed about wholesome qualities; he purifies his mind from doubt.

"Having abandoned these five hindrances, defilements of the mind that weaken wisdom, secluded from sensual pleasures, secluded from unwholesome states, he enters and dwells in the first jhāna . . . the fourth jhāna, neither painful nor pleasant, which has purification of mindfulness by equanimity.

"When his mind is thus concentrated, purified, cleansed, unblemished, rid of defilement, malleable, wieldy, steady, and attained to imperturbability, he directs it to the knowledge of the destruction of the taints.[1080] He understands as it really is: 'This is suffering.' He understands as it really is: 'This is the origin of suffering.' He understands as it really is: 'This is the cessation of suffering.' He understands as it really is: 'This is the way leading to the cessation of suffering.' He understands as it really is: 'These are the taints.' He understands as it really is: 'This is the origin of the taints.' He understands as it really is: 'This is the cessation of the taints.' He understands as it really is: 'This is the way leading to the cessation of the taints.' When he knows and sees thus, his mind is liberated from the taint of sensual desire, from the taint of existence, and from the taint of ignorance. When it is liberated, there comes the knowledge: '[It's] liberated.' He understands: 'Destroyed is birth, the spiritual life has been lived, what had to be done has been done, there is no more coming back to any state of being.' This is his victory in battle.

"Bhikkhus, I say that this person is like the warrior who can endure the cloud of dust, the crests of the standards, the uproar, and the blow, and who, having triumphed in that battle, emerges victorious and settles at the head of the battlefield. There is, bhikkhus, such a person here. This is the fifth kind of person similar to a warrior found among the bhikkhus.

"These are the five kinds of persons similar to warriors found among the bhikkhus."

76 (6) Warriors (2)

"Bhikkhus, there are these five kinds of warriors found in the world. What five?

(1) "Here, some warrior takes up a sword and shield, [94] arms himself with a bow and quiver, and enters the fray of battle. He strives and exerts himself in the battle, but his foes slay him and finish him off. There is, bhikkhus, such a warrior here. This is the first kind of warrior found in the world.

(2) "Again, some warrior takes up a sword and shield, arms himself with a bow and quiver, and enters the fray of battle. He strives and exerts himself in the battle, but his foes wound him. [His comrades] carry him off and bring him to his relatives. While he is being brought to his relatives, he dies along the way even before he arrives. There is, bhikkhus, such a warrior here. This is the second kind of warrior found in the world.

(3) "Again, some warrior takes up a sword and shield, arms himself with a bow and quiver, and enters the fray of battle. He strives and exerts himself in the battle, but his foes wound him. [His comrades] carry him off and bring him to his relatives. His relatives nurse him and look after him, but while they are doing

so he dies from that injury. There is, bhikkhus, such a warrior here. This is the third kind of warrior found in the world.

(4) "Again, some warrior takes up a sword and shield, arms himself with a bow and quiver, and enters the fray of battle. He strives and exerts himself in the battle, but his foes wound him. [His comrades] carry him off and bring him to his relatives. His relatives nurse him and look after him, and as a result he recovers from that injury. There is, bhikkhus, such a warrior here. This is the fourth kind of warrior found in the world.

(5) "Again, some warrior takes up a sword and shield, arms himself with a bow and quiver, and enters the fray of battle. Having triumphed in that battle, he emerges victorious [95] and settles at the head of the battlefield. There is, bhikkhus, such a warrior here. This is the fifth kind of warrior found in the world.

"These are the five kinds of warriors found in the world.

"So too, there are these five kinds of persons similar to warriors found among the bhikkhus. What five?

(1) "Here, some bhikkhu dwells in dependence upon a certain village or town. In the morning, he dresses, takes his robe and bowl, and enters that village or town for alms, with body, speech, and mind unguarded, without having established mindfulness, his sense faculties unrestrained. There he sees women with their dress in disarray and loosely attired. When he sees them, lust invades his mind. With his mind invaded by lust, he has sexual intercourse without having disclosed his weakness and given up the training. This person, I say, is just like the warrior who takes up a sword and shield, arms himself with a bow and quiver, and enters the fray of battle, and whose foes slay him and finish him off while he is striving and exerting himself in battle. There is, bhikkhus, such a person here. This is the first kind of person similar to a warrior found among the bhikkhus.

(2) "Again, some bhikkhu dwells in dependence upon a certain village or town. In the morning, he dresses, takes his robe and bowl, and enters that village or town for alms . . . [and] lust invades his mind. With his mind invaded by lust, he burns bodily and mentally [with the fever of lust]. He thinks: 'Let me return to the monastery [96] and inform the bhikkhus: "Friends, I am obsessed by lust, oppressed by lust. I cannot maintain the

spiritual life. Having disclosed my weakness in the training, I will give up the training and revert to the lower life."' While he is returning to the monastery, even before he arrives, he discloses his weakness in the training, gives up the training, and reverts to the lower life along the way. This person, I say, is just like the warrior who takes up a sword and shield, arms himself with a bow and quiver, enters the fray of battle, is wounded by his foes while he strives and exerts himself in the battle, and is then carried off and brought to his relatives but dies along the way even before he arrives. There is, bhikkhus, such a person here. This is the second kind of person similar to a warrior found among the bhikkhus.

(3) "Again, some bhikkhu dwells in dependence upon a certain village or town. In the morning, he dresses, takes his robe and bowl, and enters that village or town for alms . . . [and] lust invades his mind. With his mind invaded by lust, he burns bodily and mentally [with the fever of lust]. He thinks: 'Let me return to the monastery and inform the bhikkhus: "Friends, I am obsessed by lust, oppressed by lust. I cannot maintain the spiritual life. Having disclosed my weakness in the training, I will give up the training and revert to the lower life."' He returns to the monastery and informs the bhikkhus: 'Friends, I am obsessed by lust, oppressed by lust. I cannot maintain the spiritual life. Having disclosed my weakness in the training, I will give up the training and revert to the lower life.' His fellow monks then exhort and instruct him: [97] 'Friend, the Blessed One has stated that sensual pleasures provide little gratification, much suffering and anguish, and that the danger in them is more.[1081] With the simile of the skeleton the Blessed One has stated that sensual pleasures provide little gratification, much suffering and anguish, and that the danger in them is more. With the simile of the piece of meat . . . with the simile of the grass torch . . . with the simile of the charcoal pit . . . with the simile of the dream . . . with the simile of the borrowed goods . . . with the simile of fruits on a tree . . . with the simile of the butcher's knife and block . . . with the simile of the sword stake . . . with the simile of the snake's head, the Blessed One has stated that sensual pleasures provide little gratification, much suffering and anguish, and that the danger in them is more. Enjoy the spiritual life. Do not think you are unable to follow the training, give it

up, and revert to the lower life.' While he is being exhorted and instructed by his fellow monks in this way, he protests: 'Friends, although the Blessed One has stated that sensual pleasures provide little gratification, much suffering and anguish, and that the danger in them is more, still, I am unable to maintain the spiritual life. Having disclosed my weakness in the training, I will give up the training and revert to the lower life.' Having disclosed his weakness in the training, he gives up the training and reverts to the lower life. This person, I say, is just like the warrior who takes up a sword and shield, arms himself with a bow and quiver, enters the fray of battle, is wounded by his foes while he strives and exerts himself in the battle, and is then carried off [98] and brought to his relatives, who nurse him and look after him, but who dies from that injury. There is, bhikkhus, such a person here. This is the third kind of person similar to a warrior found among the bhikkhus.

(4) "Again, some bhikkhu dwells in dependence upon a certain village or town. In the morning, he dresses, takes his robe and bowl, and enters that village or town for alms . . . lust invades his mind. With his mind invaded by lust, he burns bodily and mentally [with the fever of lust]. He thinks: 'Let me return to the monastery and inform the bhikkhus: "Friends, I am obsessed by lust, oppressed by lust. I cannot maintain the spiritual life. Having disclosed my weakness in the training, I will give up the training and revert to the lower life."' He returns to the monastery and informs the bhikkhus: 'Friends, I am obsessed by lust, oppressed by lust. I cannot maintain the spiritual life. Having disclosed my weakness in the training, I will give up the training and revert to the lower life.' His fellow monks then exhort and instruct him: 'Friend, the Blessed One has stated that sensual pleasures provide little gratification, much suffering and anguish, and that the danger in them is more. With the simile of the skeleton . . . [99] . . .with the simile of the snake's head, the Blessed One has stated that sensual pleasures provide little gratification, much suffering and anguish, and that the danger in them is more. Enjoy the spiritual life. Do not think you are unable to follow the training, give it up, and revert to the lower life.' While he is being exhorted and instructed by his fellow monks in this way, he says: 'I will try, friends, I will carry on, I will enjoy it. I won't think I am unable

to follow the training, give it up, and revert to the lower life.' This person, I say, is just like the warrior who takes up a sword and shield, arms himself with a bow and quiver, and enters the fray of battle, who is wounded by his foes while he strives and exerts himself in the battle, and is then carried off and brought to his relatives, who nurse him and look after him, and who then recovers from that injury. There is, bhikkhus, such a person here. This is the fourth kind of person similar to a warrior found among the bhikkhus.

(5) "Again, some bhikkhu dwells in dependence upon a certain village or town. In the morning, he dresses, takes his robe and bowl, and enters that village or town for alms with body, speech, and mind guarded, mindfulness established, and sense faculties restrained. Having seen a form with the eye, he does not grasp its marks and features. Since, if he left the eye faculty unrestrained, bad unwholesome states of longing and dejection might invade him, he practices restraint over it; he guards the eye faculty, he undertakes the restraint of the eye faculty. Having heard a sound with the ear . . . Having smelled an odor with the nose . . . Having tasted a taste with the tongue . . . [100] . . . Having felt a tactile object with the body . . . Having cognized a mental phenomenon with the mind, he does not grasp its marks and features. Since, if he left the mind faculty unrestrained, bad unwholesome states of longing and dejection might invade him, he practices restraint over it; he guards the mind faculty, he undertakes the restraint of the mind faculty. After his meal, on returning from his alms round, he resorts to a secluded lodging: the forest, the foot of a tree, a mountain, a ravine, a hillside cave, a charnel ground, a jungle highland, the open air, a heap of straw. Gone to the forest, to the foot of a tree, or to an empty hut, he sits down, folding his legs crosswise, straightening his body, and establishing mindfulness in front of him. Having abandoned longing for the world . . . [as in 5:75] . . . he purifies his mind from doubt.

"Having abandoned these five hindrances, defilements of the mind that weaken wisdom, secluded from sensual pleasures, secluded from unwholesome states, he enters and dwells in the first jhāna . . . the second jhāna . . . the third jhāna . . . the fourth jhāna, neither painful nor pleasant, which has purification of mindfulness by equanimity.

"When his mind is thus concentrated, purified, cleansed, unblemished, rid of defilement, malleable, wieldy, steady, and attained to imperturbability, he directs it to the knowledge of the destruction of the taints. He understands as it really is: 'This is suffering' . . . 'Destroyed is birth, the spiritual life has been lived, what had to be done has been done, there is no more coming back to any state of being.' This person, I say, is just like the warrior who takes up a sword and shield, arms himself with a bow and quiver, enters the fray of battle, and having triumphed in that battle, emerges victorious and settles at the head of the battlefield. There is, bhikkhus, such a person here. This is the fifth kind of person similar to a warrior found among the bhikkhus.

"These are the five kinds of persons similar to warriors found among the bhikkhus."

77 (7) Future Perils (1)

"Bhikkhus, when a forest bhikkhu considers five future perils, it is enough for him to dwell heedful, ardent, [101] and resolute for the attainment of the as-yet-unattained, for the achievement of the as-yet-unachieved, for the realization of the as-yet-unrealized. What five?

(1) "Here, a forest bhikkhu reflects thus: 'I am now dwelling all alone in the forest. But while I am living here, a snake might bite me, a scorpion might sting me, or a centipede might sting me. Because of that I might die, which would be an obstacle for me. Let me now arouse energy for the attainment of the as-yet-unattained, for the achievement of the as-yet-unachieved, for the realization of the as-yet-unrealized.' This is the first future peril considering which it is enough for a forest bhikkhu to dwell heedful, ardent, and resolute . . . for the realization of the as-yet-unrealized.

(2) "Again, a forest bhikkhu reflects thus: 'I am now dwelling all alone in the forest. But while I am living here, I might trip and fall down, or the food that I have eaten might harm me, or my bile or phlegm or sharp winds might become agitated in me. Because of that I might die, which would be an obstacle for me. Let me now arouse energy for the attainment of the as-yet-unattained, for the achievement of the as-yet-unachieved, for the realization of the as-yet-unrealized.' This is the second

future peril considering which it is enough for a forest bhikkhu to dwell heedful, ardent, and resolute . . . for the realization of the as-yet-unrealized.

(3) "Again, a forest bhikkhu reflects thus: 'I am now dwelling all alone in the forest. But while I am living here, I might encounter wild beasts, such as a lion, a tiger, a leopard, a bear, or a hyena, and they might take my life. Because of that I would die, [102] which would be an obstacle for me. Let me now arouse energy for the attainment of the as-yet-unattained, for the achievement of the as-yet-unachieved, for the realization of the as-yet-unrealized.' This is the third future peril considering which it is enough for a forest bhikkhu to dwell heedful, ardent, and resolute . . . for the realization of the as-yet-unrealized.

(4) "Again, a forest bhikkhu reflects thus: 'I am now dwelling all alone in the forest. But while I am living here, I might encounter hoodlums escaping a crime or planning one and they might take my life. Because of that I would die, which would be an obstacle for me. Let me now arouse energy for the attainment of the as-yet-unattained, for the achievement of the as-yet-unachieved, for the realization of the as-yet-unrealized.' This is the fourth future peril considering which it is enough for a forest bhikkhu to dwell heedful, ardent, and resolute . . . for the realization of the as-yet-unrealized.

(5) "Again, a forest bhikkhu reflects thus: 'I am now dwelling all alone in the forest. But in the forest there are wild spirits,[1082] and they might take my life. Because of that I would die, which would be an obstacle for me. Let me now arouse energy for the attainment of the as-yet-unattained, for the achievement of the as-yet-unachieved, for the realization of the as-yet-unrealized.' This is the fifth future peril considering which it is enough for a forest bhikkhu to dwell heedful, ardent, and resolute . . . for the realization of the as-yet-unrealized.

"These, bhikkhus, are the five future perils considering which it is enough for a forest bhikkhu to dwell heedful, ardent, and resolute for the attainment of the as-yet-unattained, for the achievement of the as-yet-unachieved, for the realization of the as-yet-unrealized." [103]

78 (8) Future Perils (2)

"Bhikkhus, when a forest bhikkhu considers five future perils, it is enough for him to dwell heedful, ardent, and resolute for the attainment of the as-yet-unattained, for the achievement of the as-yet-unachieved, for the realization of the as-yet-unrealized. What five?

(1) "Here, a bhikkhu reflects thus: 'I am now young, a black-haired young man endowed with the blessing of youth, in the prime of life. But there will come a time when old age assails this body. Now when one is old, overcome by old age, it is not easy to attend to the Buddhas' teaching; it is not easy to resort to remote lodgings in forests and jungle groves. Before that unwished for, undesirable, disagreeable condition comes upon me, let me in advance arouse energy for the attainment of the as-yet-unattained, for the achievement of the as-yet-unachieved, for the realization of the as-yet-unrealized. Thus when I am in that condition, I will dwell at ease even though I am old.' This is the first future peril considering which it is enough for a bhikkhu to dwell heedful, ardent, and resolute . . . for the realization of the as-yet-unrealized.

(2) "Again, a bhikkhu reflects thus: 'I am now seldom ill or afflicted; I possess an even digestion that is neither too cool nor too hot but moderate and suitable for striving. But there will come a time when illness assails this body. Now when one is ill, overcome by illness, it is not easy to attend to the Buddhas' teaching; it is not easy to resort to remote lodgings in forests and jungle groves. Before that unwished for, undesirable, disagreeable condition comes upon me, let me in advance arouse energy for the attainment of the as-yet-unattained, for the achievement of the as-yet-unachieved, for the realization of the as-yet-unrealized. [104] Thus when I am in that condition, I will dwell at ease even though I am ill.' This is the second future peril considering which it is enough for a bhikkhu to dwell heedful, ardent, and resolute . . . for the realization of the as-yet-unrealized.

(3) "Again, a bhikkhu reflects thus: 'Food is now plentiful; there has been a good harvest and almsfood is abundant, so that one can easily subsist by means of gleaning. But there will come a time of famine, a poor harvest, when almsfood is hard to obtain and one cannot easily subsist by means of gleaning. In a time of famine, people migrate to places where food is plentiful and living conditions there are congested and crowded. Now when living conditions are congested and crowded, it is not easy to attend to the Buddhas' teaching; it is not easy to resort

to remote lodgings in forests and jungle groves. Before that unwished for, undesirable, disagreeable condition comes upon me, let me in advance arouse energy for the attainment of the as-yet-unattained, for the achievement of the as-yet-unachieved, for the realization of the as-yet-unrealized. Thus when I am in that condition, I will dwell at ease even in a famine.' This is the third future peril considering which it is enough for a bhikkhu to dwell heedful, ardent, and resolute . . . for the realization of the as-yet-unrealized.

(4) "Again, a bhikkhu reflects thus: 'People are now dwelling in concord, harmoniously, without disputes, blending like milk and water, viewing each other with eyes of affection. But there will come a time of peril, of turbulence in the wilderness, when the people of the countryside, mounted on their vehicles, flee on all sides. In a time of peril, people migrate to places where there is safety and living conditions there are congested and crowded. [105] Now when living conditions are congested and crowded, it is not easy to attend to the Buddhas' teaching; it is not easy to resort to remote lodgings in forests and jungle groves. Before that unwished for, undesirable, disagreeable condition comes upon me, let me in advance arouse energy for the attainment of the as-yet-unattained, for the achievement of the as-yet-unachieved, for the realization of the as-yet-unrealized. Thus when I am in that condition, I will dwell at ease even in time of peril.' This is the fourth future peril considering which it is enough for a bhikkhu to dwell heedful, ardent, and resolute . . . for the realization of the as-yet-unrealized.

(5) "Again, a bhikkhu reflects thus: 'The Saṅgha is now dwelling at ease—in concord, harmoniously, without disputes, with a single recitation. But there will come a time when there will be a schism in the Saṅgha. Now when there is a schism in the Saṅgha, it is not easy to attend to the Buddhas' teaching; it is not easy to resort to remote lodgings in forests and jungle groves. Before that unwished for, undesirable, disagreeable condition comes upon me, let me in advance arouse energy for the attainment of the as-yet-unattained, for the achievement of the as-yet-unachieved, for the realization of the as-yet-unrealized. Thus when I am in that condition, I will dwell at ease even though there is a schism in the Saṅgha.' This is the fifth future peril considering which it is enough for a bhikkhu

to dwell heedful, ardent, and resolute . . . for the realization of the as-yet-unrealized.

"These, bhikkhus, are the five future perils considering which it is enough for a bhikkhu to dwell heedful, ardent, and resolute for the attainment of the as-yet-unattained, for the achievement of the as-yet-unachieved, for the realization of the as-yet-unrealized."

79 (9) Future Perils (3)

"Bhikkhus, there are these five future perils as yet unarisen that will arise in the future. You should recognize them [106] and make an effort to abandon them. What five?

(1) "In the future, there will be bhikkhus who are undeveloped in body, virtuous behavior, mind, and wisdom.[1083] They will give full ordination to others but will not be able to discipline them in the higher virtuous behavior, the higher mind, and the higher wisdom. These [pupils] too will be undeveloped in body, virtuous behavior, mind, and wisdom. They in turn will give full ordination to others but will not be able to discipline them in the higher virtuous behavior, the higher mind, and the higher wisdom. These [pupils] too will be undeveloped in body, virtuous behavior, mind, and wisdom. Thus, bhikkhus, through corruption of the Dhamma comes corruption of the discipline, and from corruption of the discipline comes corruption of the Dhamma.[1084] This is the first future peril as yet unarisen that will arise in the future. You should recognize it and make an effort to abandon it.

(2) "Again, in the future there will be bhikkhus who are undeveloped in body, virtuous behavior, mind, and wisdom. They will give dependence[1085] to others but will not be able to discipline them in the higher virtuous behavior, the higher mind, and the higher wisdom. These [pupils] too will be undeveloped in body, virtuous behavior, mind, and wisdom. They in turn will give dependence to others but will not be able to discipline them in the higher virtuous behavior, the higher mind, and the higher wisdom. These [pupils] too will be undeveloped in body, virtuous behavior, mind, and wisdom. Thus, bhikkhus, through corruption of the Dhamma comes corruption of the discipline, and from corruption of the discipline comes corruption of the Dhamma. This is the second future peril as yet unarisen

that will arise in the future. You should recognize it and make an effort to abandon it. [107]

(3) "Again, in the future there will be bhikkhus who are undeveloped in body, virtuous behavior, mind, and wisdom. While engaged in talk pertaining to the Dhamma, in questions-and-answers,[1086] they will slide down into a dark Dhamma but will not recognize it. Thus, bhikkhus, through corruption of the Dhamma comes corruption of the discipline, and from corruption of the discipline comes corruption of the Dhamma. This is the third future peril as yet unarisen that will arise in the future. You should recognize it and make an effort to abandon it.

(4) "Again, in the future there will be bhikkhus who are undeveloped in body, virtuous behavior, mind, and wisdom. When those discourses spoken by the Tathāgata are being recited that are deep, deep in meaning, world-transcending, connected with emptiness, they will not want to listen to them, will not lend an ear to them, or apply their minds to understand them; they will not think those teachings should be studied and learned.[1087] But when those discourses are being recited that are mere poetry composed by poets, beautiful in words and phrases, created by outsiders, spoken by disciples, they will want to listen to them, lend an ear to them, and apply their minds to understand them; they will think those teachings should be studied and learned. Thus, bhikkhus, through corruption of the Dhamma comes corruption of the discipline, and from corruption of the discipline comes corruption of the Dhamma. This is the fourth future peril as yet unarisen that will arise in the future. You should recognize it and make an effort to abandon it.

(5) "Again, in the future there will be bhikkhus who are undeveloped in body, virtuous behavior, mind, [108] and wisdom. The elder bhikkhus—being undeveloped in body, virtuous behavior, mind, and wisdom—will be luxurious and lax, leaders in backsliding, discarding the duty of solitude; they will not arouse energy for the attainment of the as-yet-unattained, for the achievement of the as-yet-unachieved, for the realization of the as-yet-unrealized. Those in the next generation will follow their example. They, too, will be luxurious and lax, leaders in backsliding, discarding the duty of solitude; they, too, will not arouse energy for the attainment of the as-yet-unattained, for the achievement of the as-yet-unachieved, for the realization

of the as-yet-unrealized. Thus, bhikkhus, through corruption of the Dhamma comes corruption of the discipline, and from corruption of the discipline comes corruption of the Dhamma. This is the fifth future peril as yet unarisen that will arise in the future. You should recognize it and make an effort to abandon it.

"These, bhikkhus, are the five future perils as yet unarisen that will arise in the future. You should recognize them and make an effort to abandon them."

80 (10) Future Perils (4)

"Bhikkhus, there are these five future perils as yet unarisen that will arise in the future. You should recognize them and make an effort to abandon them. What five?

(1) "In the future, there will be bhikkhus who desire fine robes. They will give up the use of rag robes, give up remote lodgings in forests and jungle groves, and having converged upon the villages, towns, and capital cities, will take up their residence there; and they will engage in many kinds of wrong and improper searches for the sake of a robe. This is the first future peril as yet unarisen that will arise in the future. You should recognize it and make an effort to abandon it. [109]

(2) "Again, in the future there will be bhikkhus who desire fine almsfood. They will give up going on alms round, give up remote lodgings in forests and jungle groves, and having converged upon the villages, towns, and capital cities, will take up their residence there, seeking the finest delicacies with the tips of their tongues; and they will engage in many kinds of wrong and improper searches for the sake of almsfood. This is the second future peril as yet unarisen that will arise in the future. You should recognize it and make an effort to abandon it.

(3) "Again, in the future there will be bhikkhus who desire fine lodgings. They will give up dwelling at the foot of a tree, will give up remote lodgings in forests and jungle groves, and having converged upon the villages, towns, and capital cities, will take up their residence there; and they will engage in many kinds of wrong and improper searches for the sake of lodgings. This is the third future peril as yet unarisen that will arise in the future. You should recognize it and make an effort to abandon it.

(4) "Again, in the future there will be bhikkhus who bond closely with bhikkhunīs, female probationers, and novices.[1088] When they form such close bonds, it can be expected that they will live the spiritual life dissatisfied, commit a certain defiled offense,[1089] or give up the training and revert to the lower life. This is the fourth future peril as yet unarisen that will arise in the future. You should recognize it and make an effort to abandon it.

(5) "Again, in the future there will be bhikkhus who bond closely with monastery workers and novices. When they form such close bonds, it can be expected that they will engage in the use of various kinds of stored-up goods [110] and give gross hints in regard to the ground and vegetation.[1090] This is the fifth future peril as yet unarisen that will arise in the future. You should recognize it and make an effort to abandon it.

"These, bhikkhus, are the five future perils as yet unarisen that will arise in the future. You should recognize them and make an effort to abandon them."

IV. Elders

81 (1) Provoking Lust

"Bhikkhus, possessing five qualities, an elder bhikkhu is displeasing and disagreeable to his fellow monks and is neither respected nor esteemed by them. What five? (1) He is filled with lust toward that which provokes lust; (2) he is filled with hatred toward that which provokes hatred; (3) he is deluded by that which deludes; (4) he is agitated by that which agitates; (5) and he is intoxicated by that which intoxicates. Possessing these five qualities, an elder bhikkhu is displeasing and disagreeable to his fellow monks and is neither respected nor esteemed by them.

"Bhikkhus, possessing five [other] qualities, an elder bhikkhu is pleasing and agreeable to his fellow monks and is respected and esteemed by them. What five? [111] (1) He is not filled with lust toward that which provokes lust; (2) he is not filled with hatred toward that which provokes hatred; (3) he is not deluded by that which deludes; (4) he is not agitated by that which agitates; (5) and he is not intoxicated by that which intoxicates. Possessing these five qualities, an elder bhikkhu is pleasing and agreeable to his fellow monks and is respected and esteemed by them."

82 (2) Devoid of Lust

"Bhikkhus, possessing five qualities, an elder bhikkhu is displeasing and disagreeable to his fellow monks and is neither respected nor esteemed by them. What five? He is not devoid of lust; he is not devoid of hatred; he is not devoid of delusion; he is denigrating; and he is insolent. Possessing these five qualities . . . nor esteemed by them.

"Bhikkhus, possessing five [other] qualities an elder bhikkhu is pleasing and agreeable to his fellow monks and is respected and esteemed by them. What five? He is devoid of lust; he is devoid of hatred; he is devoid of delusion; he is not denigrating; and he is not insolent. Possessing these five qualities . . . and esteemed by them."

83 (3) A Schemer

"Bhikkhus, possessing five qualities, an elder bhikkhu is displeasing and disagreeable to his fellow monks and is neither respected nor esteemed by them. What five? He is a schemer, a flatterer, a hinter, a belittler, and one who pursues gain with gain.[1091] Possessing these five qualities . . . nor esteemed by them. [112]

"Bhikkhus, possessing five [other] qualities, an elder bhikkhu is pleasing and agreeable to his fellow monks and is respected and esteemed by them. What five? He is not a schemer, a flatterer, a hinter, a belittler, or one who pursues gain with gain. Possessing these five qualities . . . and esteemed by them."

84 (4) Devoid of Faith

"Bhikkhus, possessing five qualities, an elder bhikkhu is displeasing and disagreeable to his fellow monks and is neither respected nor esteemed by them. What five? He is devoid of faith, morally shameless, morally reckless, lazy, and unwise. Possessing these five qualities . . . nor esteemed by them.

"Bhikkhus, possessing five [other] qualities, an elder bhikkhu is pleasing and agreeable to his fellow monks and is respected and esteemed by them. What five? He is endowed with faith, has a sense of moral shame, has moral dread, and is energetic and wise. Possessing these five qualities . . . and esteemed by them."

85 (5) Cannot Patiently Endure

"Bhikkhus, possessing five qualities, an elder bhikkhu is displeasing and disagreeable to his fellow monks and is neither respected nor esteemed by them. What five? He cannot patiently endure forms, sounds, odors, tastes, and tactile objects. [113] Possessing these five qualities . . . nor esteemed by them.

"Bhikkhus, possessing five [other] qualities, an elder bhikkhu is pleasing and agreeable to his fellow monks and is respected and esteemed by them. What five? He can patiently endure forms, sounds, odors, tastes, and tactile objects. Possessing these five qualities . . . and esteemed by them."

86 (6) Analytical Knowledges

"Bhikkhus, possessing five qualities, an elder bhikkhu is pleasing and agreeable to his fellow monks and is respected and esteemed by them. What five? He has attained the analytical knowledge of meaning, the analytical knowledge of the Dhamma, the analytical knowledge of language, the analytical knowledge of discernment,[1092] and he is skillful and diligent in attending to the diverse chores that are to be done for his fellow monks; he possesses sound judgment about them in order to carry out and arrange them properly. Possessing these five qualities . . . and esteemed by them."

87 (7) Virtuous

"Bhikkhus, possessing five qualities, an elder bhikkhu is pleasing and agreeable to his fellow monks and is respected and esteemed by them. What five?

(1) "He is virtuous; he dwells restrained by the Pātimokkha, possessed of good conduct and resort, seeing danger in minute faults. Having undertaken the training rules, he trains in them.

(2) "He has learned much, remembers what he has learned, and accumulates what he has learned. Those teachings that are good in the beginning, good in the middle, [114] and good in the end, with the right meaning and phrasing,[1093] which proclaim the perfectly complete and pure spiritual life—such teachings

as these he has learned much of, retained in mind, recited verbally, mentally investigated, and penetrated well by view.

(3) "He is a good speaker with a good delivery; he is gifted with speech that is polished, clear, articulate, expressive of the meaning.

(4) "He gains at will, without trouble or difficulty, the four jhānas that constitute the higher mind and are pleasant dwellings in this very life.

(5) "With the destruction of the taints, he has realized for himself with direct knowledge, in this very life, the taintless liberation of mind, liberation by wisdom, and having entered upon it, he dwells in it.

"Possessing these five qualities, bhikkhus, an elder bhikkhu is pleasing and agreeable to his fellow monks and is respected and esteemed by them."

88 (8) An Elder

"Bhikkhus, possessing five qualities, an elder bhikkhu is acting for the harm of many people, for the unhappiness of many people, for the ruin, harm, and suffering of many people, of devas and humans. What five?

"(1) An elder is of long standing and has long gone forth. (2) He is well known and famous and has a retinue of many people, including householders and monastics. (3) He gains robes, almsfood, lodgings, and medicines and provisions for the sick. (4) He has learned much, remembers what he has learned, and accumulates what he has learned. Those teachings that are good in the beginning, good in the middle, and good in the end, with the right meaning and phrasing, which proclaim the perfectly complete and pure spiritual life—such teachings as these he has learned much of, retained in mind, recited verbally, mentally investigated, and penetrated well by view.[1094] (5) He holds wrong view and has a distorted perspective.

"He draws many people away from the good Dhamma and establishes them in a bad Dhamma. Thinking, 'The elder bhikkhu is of long standing and has long gone forth,' [115] they follow his example. Thinking, 'The elder bhikkhu is well known and famous and has a retinue of many people, including householders and monastics,' they follow his example. Thinking, 'The elder bhikkhu gains robes, almsfood, lodgings, and medicines and provisions for the sick,' they follow his example. Thinking, 'The elder bhikkhu has learned much, remembers what he has learned, and accumulates what he has learned,' they follow his example.

"Possessing these five qualities, an elder bhikkhu is acting for the harm of many people, for the unhappiness of many people, for the ruin, harm, and suffering of many people, of devas and humans.

"Bhikkhus, possessing five [other] qualities, an elder bhikkhu is acting for the welfare of many people, for the happiness of many people, for the good, welfare, and happiness of many people, of devas and human beings. What five?

"(1) An elder is of long standing and has long gone forth. (2) He is well known and famous and has a retinue of many people, including householders and monastics. (3) He gains robes, almsfood, lodgings, and medicines and provisions for the sick. (4) He has learned much, remembers what he has learned, and accumulates what he has learned. Those teachings that are good in the beginning . . . he has penetrated well by view. (5) He holds right view and has a correct perspective.

"He draws many people away from a bad Dhamma and establishes them in the good Dhamma. Thinking, 'The elder bhikkhu is of long standing and has long gone forth,' they follow his example. Thinking, 'The elder bhikkhu is well known and famous and has a retinue of many people, including householders and monastics,' they follow his example. Thinking, 'The elder bhikkhu gains robes, almsfood, lodgings, and medicines and provisions for the sick,' they follow his example. Thinking, 'The elder bhikkhu has learned much, remembers what he has learned, and accumulates what he has learned,' they follow his example.

"Possessing these five qualities, an elder bhikkhu is acting for the welfare of many people, for the happiness of many people, [116] for the good, welfare, and happiness of many people, of devas and humans."

89 (9) A Trainee (1)

"Bhikkhus, these five qualities lead to the decline of a bhikkhu who is a trainee. What five? Delight in work, delight in talk, delight in sleep, and delight in company; and he does not review the extent to which his mind is liberated.[1095] These five qualities lead to the decline of a bhikkhu who is a trainee.

"Bhikkhus, these five qualities lead to the non-decline of a bhikkhu who is a trainee. What five? Not delighting in work, not delighting in talk, not delighting in sleep, not delighting in company; and he reviews the extent to which his mind is liberated. These five qualities lead to the non-decline of a bhikkhu who is a trainee."[1096]

90 (10) A Trainee (2)

"Bhikkhus, these five things lead to the decline of a bhikkhu who is a trainee. What five?

(1) "Here, a bhikkhu who is a trainee has many tasks and duties and is competent in various chores that must be done, so he neglects seclusion and does not devote himself to internal serenity of mind. This is the first thing that leads to the decline of a bhikkhu who is a trainee.

(2) "Again, a bhikkhu who is a trainee spends the day on some trifling work, so he neglects seclusion and does not devote himself to internal [117] serenity of mind. This is the second thing that leads to the decline of a bhikkhu who is a trainee.

(3) "Again, a bhikkhu who is a trainee bonds closely with householders and monastics, socializing in an unfitting manner typical of laypeople,[1097] so he neglects seclusion and does not devote himself to internal serenity of mind. This is the third thing that leads to the decline of a bhikkhu who is a trainee.

(4) "Again, a bhikkhu who is a trainee enters a village too early and returns too late in the day, so he neglects seclusion and does not devote himself to internal serenity of mind. This is the fourth thing that leads to the decline of a bhikkhu who is a trainee.

(5) "Again, a bhikkhu who is a trainee does not get to hear at will, without trouble or difficulty, talk concerned with the austere life that is conducive to opening up the heart, that is, talk on fewness of desires, on contentment, on solitude, on not getting bound up [with others], on arousing energy, on virtuous behavior, on concentration, on wisdom, on liberation, on the knowledge and vision of liberation; so he neglects seclusion and does not devote himself to internal serenity of mind. This is the fifth thing that leads to the decline of a bhikkhu who is a trainee.

"These five things lead to the decline of a bhikkhu who is a trainee.

"Bhikkhus, these five things lead to the non-decline of a bhikkhu who is a trainee. What five?

(1) "Here, a bhikkhu who is a trainee does not have many tasks and duties; though he is competent in the various chores that must be done, he does not neglect seclusion but devotes himself to internal serenity of mind. This is the first thing that leads to the non-decline of a bhikkhu who is a trainee.

(2) "Again, a bhikkhu who is a trainee does not spend the day on some trifling work, so he does not neglect seclusion but devotes himself to internal serenity of mind. This is the second thing that leads to the non-decline of a bhikkhu who is a trainee.

(3) "Again, a bhikkhu who is a trainee does not bond closely with householders and monastics, socializing in an unfitting manner typical of laypeople, so he does not neglect seclusion but devotes himself to internal serenity of mind. [118] This is the third thing that leads to the non-decline of a bhikkhu who is a trainee.

(4) "Again, a bhikkhu who is a trainee does not enter a village too early or return too late in the day, so he does not neglect seclusion but devotes himself to internal serenity of mind. This is the fourth thing that leads to the non-decline of a bhikkhu who is a trainee.

(5) "Again, a bhikkhu who is a trainee gets to hear at will, without trouble or difficulty, talk concerned with the austere life that is conducive to opening up the heart, that is, talk on fewness of desires . . . on the knowledge and vision of liberation; so he does not neglect seclusion but devotes himself to internal serenity of mind. This is the fifth thing that leads to the non-decline of a bhikkhu who is a trainee.

"These five things lead to the non-decline of a bhikkhu who is a trainee."

V. Kakudha

91 (1) Accomplishments (1)

"Bhikkhus, there are these five accomplishments. What five? Accomplishment in faith, accomplishment in virtuous behavior, accomplishment in learning, accomplishment in generosity, and accomplishment in wisdom. These are the five accomplishments." [119]

92 (2) Accomplishments (2)

"Bhikkhus, there are these five accomplishments. What five? Accomplishment in virtuous behavior, accomplishment in concentration, accomplishment in wisdom, accomplishment in liberation, and accomplishment in the knowledge and vision of liberation. These are the five accomplishments."

93 (3) Declarations

"Bhikkhus, there are these five declarations of final knowledge.[1098] What five? (1) One declares final knowledge because of one's dullness and stupidity; (2) one declares final knowledge because one has evil desires and is motivated by desire; (3) one declares final knowledge because one is mad and mentally deranged; (4) one declares final knowledge because one overrates oneself; and (5) one correctly declares final knowledge. These are the five declarations of final knowledge."

94 (4) Dwelling at Ease

"Bhikkhus, there are these five kinds of dwelling at ease. What five? (1) Here, secluded from sensual pleasures, secluded from unwholesome states, a bhikkhu enters and dwells in the first jhāna . . . (2) . . . the second jhāna . . . (3) . . . the third jhāna . . . (4) . . . the fourth jhāna. (5) With the destruction of the taints, he has realized for himself with direct knowledge, in this very life, the taintless liberation of mind, liberation by wisdom, and having entered upon it, he dwells in it. These are the five kinds of dwelling at ease."

95 (5) The Unshakable

"Bhikkhus, possessing five things, a bhikkhu in no long time penetrates to the unshakable.[1099] What five? [120] Here, a bhikkhu has attained the analytical knowledge of meaning, the analytical knowledge of the Dhamma, the analytical knowledge of language, and the analytical knowledge of discernment; and he reviews the extent to which his mind is liberated. Possessing these five things, a bhikkhu in no long time penetrates to the unshakable."

96 (6) What One Has Learned

"Bhikkhus, possessing five things, a bhikkhu pursuing mindfulness of breathing in no long time penetrates to the unshakable. What five? (1) Here, a bhikkhu has few undertakings, few tasks, is easy to support, and is easily contented with the requisites of life. (2) He eats little and is intent on abstemiousness regarding food. (3) He is seldom drowsy and is intent on vigilance. (4) He has learned much, remembers what he has learned, and accumulates what he has learned. Those teachings that are good in the beginning, good in the middle, and good in the end, with the right meaning and phrasing, which proclaim the perfectly complete and pure spiritual life—such teachings as these he has learned much of, retained in mind, recited verbally, mentally investigated, and penetrated well by view. (5) He reviews the extent to which his mind is liberated. Possessing these five things, a bhikkhu pursuing mindfulness of breathing in no long time penetrates to the unshakable."

97 (7) Talk

"Bhikkhus, possessing five things, a bhikkhu developing mindfulness of breathing in no long time penetrates to the unshakable. What five? (1) Here, a bhikkhu has few undertakings . . . (2) He eats little . . . (3) He is seldom drowsy . . . [121] (4) He gets to hear at will, without trouble or difficulty, talk concerned with the austere life that is conducive to opening up the heart, that is, talk on fewness of desires, on contentment, on solitude, on not getting bound up [with others], on arousing energy, on virtuous behavior, on concentration, on wisdom, on liberation, on the knowledge and vision of liberation. (5) He reviews the extent to which his mind is liberated. Possessing these five things, a bhikkhu developing mindfulness of breathing in no long time penetrates to the unshakable."

98 (8) A Forest Dweller

"Bhikkhus, possessing five things, a bhikkhu cultivating mindfulness of breathing in no long time penetrates to the unshakable. What five? (1) Here, a bhikkhu has few undertakings . . . (2) He eats little . . . (3) He is seldom drowsy. . . (4) He is a forest dweller who resorts to remote lodgings. (5) He reviews the extent to which his mind is liberated. Possessing these five things, a bhikkhu cultivating mindfulness of breathing in no long time penetrates to the unshakable."

99 (9) The Lion

"Bhikkhus, in the evening the lion, the king of beasts, comes out from his lair, stretches his body, surveys the four quarters all around, and roars his lion's roar three times. Then he sets out in search of game.

(1) "If he gives a blow to an elephant, he always gives the blow respectfully, not disrespectfully.[1100] (2) If he gives a blow to a buffalo . . . (3) . . . to a cow . . . (4) . . . to a leopard . . . (5) If he gives a blow [122] to any smaller animals, even a hare or a cat, he gives the blow respectfully, not disrespectfully. For what reason? [Thinking:] 'Let my training not be lost.'

"The lion, bhikkhus, is a designation for the Tathāgata, the Arahant, the Perfectly Enlightened One. When the Tathāgata teaches the Dhamma to an assembly, this is his lion's roar. (1) If the Tathāgata teaches the Dhamma to bhikkhus, he teaches it respectfully, not disrespectfully. (2) If the Tathāgata teaches the Dhamma to bhikkhunīs . . . (3) . . . to male lay followers . . . (4) . . . to female lay followers, he teaches it respectfully, not disrespectfully. (5) If the Tathāgata teaches the Dhamma to worldlings, even to food-carriers and hunters,[1101] he teaches it respectfully, not disrespectfully. For what reason? Because the Tathāgata has respect for the Dhamma, reverence for the Dhamma."

100 (10) Kakudha

Thus have I heard.[1102] On one occasion the Blessed One was dwelling at Kosambī in Ghosita's Park. Now on that occasion Kakudha the Koliyan son, the Venerable Mahāmoggallāna's attendant, had recently died and been reborn among a certain group of mind-made [deities].[1103] His body was two or three times the size of the fields of a Magadhan village, but he did not obstruct either himself or others with that body.[1104]

Then the young deva Kakudha approached the Venerable Mahāmoggallāna, paid homage to him, stood to one side, and [123] said to him: "Bhante, such a desire arose in Devadatta: 'I will take charge of the Saṅgha of bhikkhus.' And together with the arising of this thought, Devadatta lost that psychic potency."[1105] This is what the young deva Kakudha said. He then paid homage to the Venerable Mahāmoggallāna, circumambulated him keeping the right side toward him, and disappeared right there.

Then the Venerable Mahāmoggallāna approached the Blessed One, paid homage to him, sat down to one side, and reported all that had happened. [The Blessed One said:] "But, Moggallāna, have you encompassed his mind with your mind and understood of the young deva Kakudha: 'Whatever the young deva Kakudha says is all true and not otherwise'?"

"Yes, Bhante."

"Take note of this statement, Moggallāna! Now that foolish man will, of his own accord, expose himself.

"There are, Moggallāna, these five kinds of teachers found in the world. What five? [124]

(1) "Here, some teacher whose behavior is unpurified claims: 'I am one whose behavior is purified. My behavior is purified, cleansed, undefiled.' His disciples know him thus: 'This honorable teacher, though of unpurified behavior, claims: "I am one whose behavior is purified. My behavior is purified, cleansed, undefiled." Now he would not like it if we were to report this to the laypeople. How can we treat him in a way that he would not like? Further, he is honored with robes, almsfood, lodgings, and medicines and provisions for the sick. A person will be known by what he himself does.'[1106] His disciples cover up such a teacher with respect to his behavior, and such a teacher expects to be covered up by his disciples with respect to his behavior.

(2) "Again, some teacher whose livelihood is unpurified claims: 'I am one whose livelihood is purified. My livelihood is purified, cleansed, undefiled.' His disciples know him thus: 'This honorable teacher, though of unpurified livelihood, claims: "I am one whose livelihood is purified. My livelihood is purified, cleansed, undefiled." Now he would not like it if we were to report this to the laypeople. How can we treat him in a way that he would not like? Further, he is honored with robes, almsfood, lodgings, and medicines and provisions for the sick. A person will be known by what he himself does.' His disciples cover up such a teacher with respect to his livelihood, and such a teacher expects to be covered up by his disciples with respect to his livelihood.

(3) "Again, some teacher whose Dhamma teaching is unpurified claims: 'I am one whose Dhamma teaching is purified. My Dhamma teaching is purified, cleansed, undefiled.' His disciples know him thus: 'This honorable teacher, though of unpurified Dhamma teaching, [125] claims: "I am one whose Dhamma teaching is purified. My Dhamma teaching is purified, cleansed, undefiled." Now he would not like it if we were to report this to the laypeople. How can we treat him in a way that he would not like? Further, he is honored with robes, almsfood, lodgings, and medicines and provisions for the sick. A person will be known by what he himself does.' His disciples cover up such a teacher with respect to his Dhamma teaching, and such a teacher expects to be covered up by his disciples with respect to his Dhamma teaching.

(4) "Again, some teacher whose explanations are unpurified[1107] claims: 'I am one whose explanations are purified. My explanations are purified, cleansed, undefiled.' His disciples know him thus: 'This honorable teacher, though giving unpurified explanations, claims: "I am one whose explanations are purified. My explanations are purified, cleansed, undefiled." Now he would not like it if we were to report this to the laypeople. How can we treat him in a way that he would not like? Further, he is honored with robes, almsfood, lodgings, and medicines and provisions for the sick. A person will be known by what he himself does.' His disciples cover up such a teacher with respect to his explanations, and such a teacher expects to be covered up by his disciples with respect to his explanations.

(5) "Again, some teacher whose knowledge and vision are unpurified claims: 'I am one whose knowledge and vision are purified. My knowledge and vision are purified, cleansed, undefiled.' His disciples know him thus: 'This honorable teacher, though of unpurified knowledge and vision, claims: "I am one whose knowledge and vision are purified. My knowledge and vision are purified, cleansed, undefiled." Now he would not like it if we were to report this to the laypeople. How can we treat him in a way that he would not like? [126] Further, he is honored with robes, almsfood, lodgings, and medicines and provisions for the sick. A person will be known by what he himself does.' His disciples cover up such a teacher with respect to his knowledge and vision, and such a teacher expects to be

covered up by his disciples with respect to his knowledge and vision.

"These are five kinds of teachers found in the world.

(1) "But, Moggallāna, I am one whose behavior is purified and I claim: 'I am one whose behavior is purified. My behavior is purified, cleansed, undefiled.' My disciples do not cover me up with respect to my behavior, and I do not expect to be covered up by my disciples with respect to my behavior. (2) I am one whose livelihood is purified and I claim: 'I am one whose livelihood is purified. My livelihood is purified, cleansed, undefiled.' My disciples do not cover me up with respect to my livelihood, and I do not expect to be covered up by my disciples with respect to my livelihood. (3) I am one whose Dhamma teaching is purified and I claim: 'I am one whose Dhamma teaching is purified. My Dhamma teaching is purified, cleansed, undefiled.' My disciples do not cover me up with respect to my Dhamma teaching, and I do not expect to be covered up by my disciples with respect to my Dhamma teaching. (4) I am one whose explanations are purified and I claim: 'I am one whose explanations are purified. My explanations are purified, cleansed, undefiled.' My disciples do not cover me up with respect to my explanations, and I do not expect to be covered up by my disciples with respect to my explanations. (5) I am one whose knowledge and vision are purified and I claim: 'I am one whose knowledge and vision are purified. My knowledge and vision are purified, cleansed, undefiled.' My disciples do not cover me up with respect to my knowledge and vision, and I do not expect to be covered up by my disciples with respect to my knowledge and vision." [127]

The Third Fifty

I. Dwelling at Ease

101 (1) Timidity

"Bhikkhus, there are these five qualities that make for self-confidence in a trainee.[1108] What five? Here, a bhikkhu is endowed with faith and is virtuous, learned, energetic, and wise. (1) Whatever timidity[1109] there is in one without faith does not exist in one endowed with faith; therefore this quality makes for self-confidence in a trainee. (2) Whatever timidity there is in one who is immoral does not exist in one who is virtuous; therefore this quality makes for self-confidence in a trainee. (3) Whatever timidity there is in one who is unlearned does not exist in one who is learned; therefore this quality makes for self-confidence in a trainee. (4) Whatever timidity there is in one who is lazy does not exist in one who is energetic; therefore this quality makes for self-confidence in a trainee. (5) Whatever timidity there is in one who is unwise does not exist in one who is wise; therefore this quality makes for self-confidence in a trainee. These are the five qualities that make for self-confidence in a trainee." [128]

102 (2) Suspected

"Bhikkhus, on five grounds a bhikkhu is suspected and distrusted as 'an evil bhikkhu' though he be of unshakable character.[1110] What five? Here, a bhikkhu often visits prostitutes, widows, unmarried women, eunuchs, or bhikkhunīs.[1111] On these five grounds a bhikkhu is suspected and distrusted as 'an evil bhikkhu' though he be of unshakable character."

103 (3) A Thief[1112]

"Bhikkhus, possessing five factors, a master thief breaks into houses, plunders wealth, commits banditry, and ambushes highways. What five? Here, a master thief (1) depends upon the uneven, (2) on thickets, and (3) on powerful people; (4) he offers bribes, and (5) he moves alone.

(1) "And how does a master thief depend on the uneven? Here, a master thief depends on rivers that are hard to cross and rugged mountains. It is in this way that a master thief depends on the uneven.

(2) "And how does a master thief depend on thickets? Here, a master thief depends on a thicket of cane, a thicket of trees, a coppice, or a large dense jungle. It is in this way that a master thief depends on thickets.

(3) "And how does a master thief depend on powerful people? Here, a master thief depends on kings or royal ministers. He thinks: 'If anyone [129] accuses me of anything, these kings or royal ministers will dismiss the case.' If anyone accuses

him of anything, those kings or royal ministers dismiss the case. It is in this way that a master thief depends on powerful people.

(4) "And how does a master thief offer bribes? Here, a master thief is rich, with great wealth and property. He thinks: 'If anyone should accuse me of anything, I'll placate him with a bribe.' If anyone accuses him of anything, he placates him with a bribe. It is in this way that a master thief offers bribes.

(5) "And how does a master thief move alone? Here, a master thief executes his raids[1113] all alone. For what reason? [With the thought:] 'My secret deliberations[1114] shouldn't spread to others!' It is in this way that a master thief moves alone.

"It is by possessing these five factors that a master thief breaks into houses, plunders wealth, commits banditry, and ambushes highways.

"So too, bhikkhus, possessing five qualities, an evil bhikkhu maintains himself in a maimed and injured condition, is blameworthy and subject to reproach by the wise, and generates much demerit. What five? Here, an evil bhikkhu (1) depends on the uneven, (2) depends on thickets, and (3) depends on powerful people; (4) he offers bribes and (5) moves alone.

(1) "And how does an evil bhikkhu depend on the uneven? Here, an evil bhikkhu engages in unrighteous bodily, verbal, and mental action. It is in this way that an evil bhikkhu depends on the uneven.

(2) "And how does an evil bhikkhu depend on thickets? [130] Here, an evil bhikkhu holds wrong view; he has adopted an extremist view.[1115] It is in this way that an evil bhikkhu depends upon thickets.

(3) "And how does an evil bhikkhu depend on powerful people? Here, an evil bhikkhu depends on kings or royal ministers. He thinks: 'If anyone should accuse me of anything, these kings or royal ministers will dismiss the case.' If anyone accuses him of anything, those kings or royal ministers dismiss the case. It is in this way that an evil bhikkhu depends on the powerful people.

(4) "And how does an evil bhikkhu offer bribes? Here, an evil bhikkhu gains robes, almsfood, lodgings, and medicines and provisions for the sick. He thinks: 'If anyone should accuse me of anything, I'll placate him with one of these gains.' If anyone

accuses him of anything, he placates him with one of his gains. It is in this way that an evil bhikkhu offers bribes.

(5) "And how does an evil bhikkhu move alone? Here, an evil bhikkhu sets up a solitary residence for himself in the borderlands. Approaching families there, he obtains gains. It is in this way that an evil bhikkhu moves alone.

"It is by possessing these five qualities that an evil bhikkhu maintains himself in a maimed and injured condition, is blameworthy and subject to reproach by the wise, and generates much demerit."

104 (4) Delicate[1116]

"Bhikkhus, possessing five qualities, a bhikkhu is a delicate ascetic among ascetics. What five? (1) He usually uses a robe that has been specifically offered to him, seldom one that has not been specifically offered to him; he usually eats almsfood that has been specifically offered to him, seldom almsfood that has not been specifically offered to him; he usually uses a lodging that has been specifically offered to him, seldom one that has not been specifically offered to him; he usually uses medicines and provisions for the sick that have been specifically offered to him, seldom those that have not been specifically offered to him. [131] (2) His fellow monks, those with whom he dwells, usually behave toward him in agreeable ways by body, speech, and mind, seldom in disagreeable ways. They usually present him what is agreeable, seldom what is disagreeable. (3) Discomfort originating from bile, phlegm, wind, or their combination; discomfort produced by change of climate; discomfort produced by careless behavior; discomfort produced by assault; or discomfort produced as the result of kamma—these do not often arise in him. He is seldom ill. (4) He gains at will, without trouble or difficulty, the four jhānas that constitute the higher mind and are pleasant dwellings in this very life. (5) With the destruction of the taints, he has realized for himself with direct knowledge, in this very life, the taintless liberation of mind, liberation by wisdom, and having entered upon it, he dwells in it. It is by possessing these five qualities that a bhikkhu is a delicate ascetic among ascetics.

"If, bhikkhus, one could rightly say of anyone: 'He is a

delicate ascetic among ascetics,' it is precisely of me that one might say this. (1) For I usually use a robe that has been specifically offered to me, seldom one that has not been specifically offered to me; I usually eat almsfood that has been specifically offered to me, seldom almsfood that has not been specifically offered to me; I usually use a lodging that has been specifically offered to me, seldom one that has not been specifically offered to me; I usually use medicines and provisions for the sick that have been specifically offered to me, seldom those that have not been specifically offered to me. (2) Those bhikkhus with whom I dwell usually behave toward me in agreeable ways by body, speech, and mind, seldom in disagreeable ways. They usually present me what is agreeable, seldom what is disagreeable. (3) Discomfort originating from bile, phlegm, wind, or their combination; discomfort produced by change of climate; discomfort produced by careless behavior; discomfort produced by assault; or discomfort produced as the result of kamma—these [132] do not often arise in me. I am seldom ill. (4) I gain at will, without trouble or difficulty, the four jhānas that constitute the higher mind and are pleasant dwellings in this very life. (5) With the destruction of the taints, I have realized for myself with direct knowledge, in this very life, the taintless liberation of mind, liberation by wisdom, and having entered upon it, I dwell in it. If, bhikkhus, one could rightly say of anyone: 'He is a delicate ascetic among ascetics,' it is precisely of me that one might say this."

105 (5) At Ease

"Bhikkhus, there are these five means of dwelling at ease.[1117] What five? (1) Here, a bhikkhu maintains bodily acts of loving-kindness toward his fellow monks, both openly and privately. (2) He maintains verbal acts of loving-kindness toward his fellow monks, both openly and privately. (3) He maintains mental acts of loving-kindness toward his fellow monks, both openly and privately. (4) He dwells both openly and privately possessing in common with his fellow monks virtuous behavior that is unbroken, flawless, unblemished, unblotched, freeing, praised by the wise, ungrasped, leading to concentration. (5) He dwells both openly and privately possessing in common with his fellow monks the view that is noble and emancipating, which leads one who acts upon it to the complete destruction of suffering. These, bhikkhus, are the five means of dwelling at ease."

106 (6) Ānanda

On one occasion the Blessed One was dwelling at Kosambī in Ghosita's Park. Then the Venerable Ānanda approached the Blessed One, paid homage to him, sat down to one side, and said:

"(1) Bhante, in what way can a bhikkhu dwell at ease while living in the Saṅgha?"

"When, Ānanda, [133] a bhikkhu is himself accomplished in virtuous behavior but does not exhort others in regard to virtuous behavior,[1118] to this extent he can dwell at ease while living in the Saṅgha."

(2) "But, Bhante, might there be another way by which a bhikkhu can dwell at ease while living in the Saṅgha?"

"There can be, Ānanda. When a bhikkhu is himself accomplished in virtuous behavior but does not exhort others in regard to virtuous behavior, and he examines himself but does not examine others, to this extent he can dwell at ease while living in the Saṅgha."

(3) "But, Bhante, might there be another way by which a bhikkhu can dwell at ease while living in the Saṅgha?"

"There can be, Ānanda. When a bhikkhu is himself accomplished in virtuous behavior but does not exhort others in regard to virtuous behavior, and he examines himself but does not examine others, and he is not well known but is not agitated by lack of renown, to this extent he can dwell at ease while living in the Saṅgha."

(4) "But, Bhante, might there be another way by which a bhikkhu can dwell at ease while living in the Saṅgha?"

"There can be, Ānanda. When a bhikkhu is himself accomplished in virtuous behavior but does not exhort others in regard to virtuous behavior; and he examines himself but does not examine others; and he is not well known but is not agitated by lack of renown; and he gains at will, without trouble or difficulty, the four jhānas that constitute the higher mind and are pleasant dwellings in this very life, to this extent he can dwell at ease while living in the Saṅgha."

(5) "But, Bhante, might there be another way by which a bhikkhu can dwell at ease while living in the Saṅgha?"

"There can be, Ānanda. When a bhikkhu is himself accomplished in virtuous behavior but does not exhort others in regard to virtuous behavior; and he examines himself but does not examine others; [134] and he is not well known but is not agitated by lack of renown; and he gains at will, without trouble or difficulty, the four jhānas that constitute the higher mind and are pleasant dwellings in this very life; and, with the destruction of the taints, he has realized for himself with direct knowledge, in this very life, the taintless liberation of mind, liberation by wisdom, and having entered upon it, he dwells in it, to this extent he can dwell at ease while living in the Saṅgha. And, Ānanda, I say there is no other way of dwelling at ease more excellent or sublime than this."

107 (7) Virtuous Behavior

"Bhikkhus, possessing five qualities, a bhikkhu is worthy of gifts, worthy of hospitality, worthy of offerings, worthy of reverential salutation, an unsurpassed field of merit for the world. What five? Here, a bhikkhu is accomplished in virtuous behavior, accomplished in concentration, accomplished in wisdom, accomplished in liberation, and accomplished in the knowledge and vision of liberation. Possessing these five qualities, a bhikkhu is worthy of gifts, worthy of hospitality, worthy of offerings, worthy of reverential salutation, an unsurpassed field of merit for the world."

108 (8) One Beyond Training

"Bhikkhus, possessing five qualities, a bhikkhu is worthy of gifts . . . an unsurpassed field of merit for the world. What five? Here, a bhikkhu possesses the aggregate of virtuous behavior of one beyond training, the aggregate of concentration of one beyond training, the aggregate of wisdom of one beyond training, the aggregate of liberation of one beyond training, the aggregate of the knowledge and vision of liberation of one beyond training. Possessing these five qualities, a bhikkhu is worthy of gifts . . . an unsurpassed field of merit for the world." [135]

109 (9) At Home in the Four Quarters

"Bhikkhus, possessing five qualities, a bhikkhu is at home in the four quarters.[1119] What five? (1) Here, a bhikkhu is virtuous; he dwells restrained by the Pātimokkha, possessed of good conduct and resort, seeing danger in minute faults. Having undertaken the training rules, he trains in them. (2) He has learned much, remembers what he has learned, and accumulates what he has learned. Those teachings that are good in the beginning, good in the middle, and good in the end, with the right meaning and phrasing, which proclaim the perfectly complete and pure spiritual life—such teachings as these he has learned much of, retained in mind, recited verbally, mentally investigated, and penetrated well by view. (3) He is content with any kind of robes, almsfood, lodgings, and medicines and provisions for the sick. (4) He gains at will, without trouble or difficulty, the four jhānas that constitute the higher mind and are pleasant dwellings in this very life. (5) With the destruction of the taints, he has realized for himself with direct knowledge, in this very life, the taintless liberation of mind, liberation by wisdom, and having entered upon it, he dwells in it. Possessing these five qualities, a bhikkhu is at home in the four quarters."

110 (10) Forest

"Bhikkhus, possessing five qualities, a bhikkhu is fit to resort to remote lodgings in forests and jungle groves. What five? (1) Here, a bhikkhu is virtuous . . . he trains in them. (2) He has learned much . . . and penetrated well by view. (3) He has aroused energy for abandoning unwholesome qualities and acquiring wholesome qualities; he is strong, firm in exertion, not casting off the duty of cultivating wholesome qualities. (4) He gains at will, without trouble or difficulty, the four jhānas that constitute the higher mind and are pleasant dwellings in this very life. (5) With the destruction of the taints, he has realized for himself with direct knowledge, in this very life, the taintless liberation of mind, [136] liberation by wisdom, and having entered upon it, he dwells in it. Possessing these five qualities, a bhikkhu is fit to resort to remote lodgings in forests and jungle groves."

II. Andhakavinda[1120]

111 (1) A Visitor of Families

"Bhikkhus, possessing five qualities, a bhikkhu who is a visitor of families is displeasing and disagreeable to them and is neither respected nor esteemed by them. What five? (1) He presumes intimacy upon mere acquaintance; (2) he distributes things that he does not own; (3) he consorts with those who are divided;[1121] (4) he whispers in the ear; and (5) he makes excessive requests. Possessing these five qualities, a bhikkhu who is a visitor of families is displeasing and disagreeable to them and is neither respected nor esteemed by them.

"Bhikkhus, possessing five [other] qualities, a bhikkhu who is a visitor of families is pleasing and agreeable to them and is respected and esteemed by them. What five? (1) He does not presume intimacy upon mere acquaintance; (2) he does not distribute things that he does not own; (3) he does not consort with those who are divided; (4) he does not whisper in the ear; and (5) he does not make excessive requests. [137] Possessing these five qualities, a bhikkhu who is a visitor of families is pleasing and agreeable to them and is respected and esteemed by them."

112 (2) An Attendant Monk

"Bhikkhus, possessing five qualities, someone should not be taken along as an attendant monk. What five? (1) He walks too far behind or too close; (2) he does not take your bowl when it is full; (3) he does not restrain you when your speech is bordering on an offense; (4) he keeps on interrupting you while you are speaking; and (5) he is unwise, stupid, obtuse. Possessing these five qualities, someone should not be taken along as an attendant monk.

"Bhikkhus, possessing five [other] qualities, someone may be taken along as an attendant monk. What five? (1) He does not walk too far behind or too close; (2) he takes your bowl when it is full; (3) he restrains you when your speech is bordering on an offense; (4) he does not keep on interrupting you while you are speaking; and (5) he is wise, intelligent, astute. Possessing these five qualities, someone may be taken along as an attendant monk."

113 (3) Concentration

"Bhikkhus, possessing five qualities, a bhikkhu is incapable of entering and dwelling in right concentration. What five? Here, a bhikkhu cannot patiently endure forms, sounds, odors, tastes, and tactile objects. Possessing these five qualities, a bhikkhu is incapable of entering and dwelling in right concentration.

"Bhikkhus, possessing five [other] qualities, a bhikkhu is capable of entering and dwelling in right concentration. What five? [138] Here, a bhikkhu can patiently endure forms, sounds, odors, tastes, and tactile objects. Possessing these five qualities, a bhikkhu is capable of entering and dwelling in right concentration."

114 (4) Andhakavinda

On one occasion the Blessed One was dwelling among the Magadhans at Andhakavinda. Then the Venerable Ānanda approached the Blessed One, paid homage to him, and sat down to one side. The Blessed One then said to him:

"Ānanda, those bhikkhus who are newcomers, who have recently gone forth, who have just come to this Dhamma and discipline, should be encouraged, settled, and established by you in five things. What five?

(1) "They should be encouraged, settled, and established in the restraint of the Pātimokkha thus: 'Come, friends, be virtuous; dwell restrained by the Pātimokkha, possessed of good conduct and resort, seeing danger in minute faults. Having undertaken the training rules, train in them.'

(2) "They should be encouraged, settled, and established in the restraint of the sense faculties thus: 'Come, friends, guard the doors of the sense faculties; take mindfulness as protector; be mindful and alert, possessing a protected mind, a mind under the protection of mindfulness.'

(3) "They should be encouraged, settled, and established in limiting their speech thus: 'Come, friends, do not talk much. Put limits on your speech.'

(4) "They should be encouraged, settled, and established in bodily seclusion thus: 'Come, friends, be forest dwellers. Resort to remote lodgings in forests and jungle groves.'

(5) "They should be encouraged, settled, and established in a correct perspective thus: 'Come, friends, hold right view and have a correct perspective.'[1122] [139]

"Ānanda, those bhikkhus who are newcomers, who have recently gone forth, who have just come to this Dhamma and discipline, should be encouraged, settled, and established by you in these five things."

115 (5) Miserly

"Bhikkhus, possessing five qualities, a bhikkhunī is deposited in hell as if brought there. What five? She is miserly with dwellings, families, gains, praise, and the Dhamma.[1123] Possessing these five qualities, a bhikkhunī is deposited in hell as if brought there.

"Bhikkhus, possessing five [other] qualities, a bhikkhunī is deposited in heaven as if brought there. What five? She is not miserly with dwellings, families, gains, praise, and the Dhamma. Possessing these five qualities, a bhikkhunī is deposited in heaven as if brought there."

116 (6) Praise

"Bhikkhus, possessing five qualities, a bhikkhunī is deposited in hell as if brought there. What five? (1) Without investigating and scrutinizing, she speaks praise of one who deserves dispraise. (2) Without investigating and scrutinizing, she speaks dispraise of one who deserves praise. (3) Without investigating and scrutinizing, she believes a matter that merits suspicion. (4) Without investigating and scrutinizing, she is suspicious about a matter that merits belief. (5) She squanders gifts given out of faith.[1124] Possessing these five qualities, a bhikkhunī is deposited in hell as if brought there.

"Bhikkhus, possessing five [other] qualities, a bhikkhunī is deposited in heaven as if brought there. What five? (1) Having investigated and scrutinized, she speaks dispraise of one who deserves dispraise. (2) Having investigated and scrutinized, she speaks praise of one who deserves praise. [140] (3) Having investigated and scrutinized, she is suspicious about a matter that merits suspicion. (4) Having investigated and scrutinized, she believes a matter that merits belief. (5) She does not squander gifts given out of faith. Possessing these five qualities, a bhikkhunī is deposited in heaven as if brought there."

117 (7) Envious

"Bhikkhus, possessing five qualities, a bhikkhunī is deposited in hell as if brought there. What five? (1) Without investigating and scrutinizing, she speaks praise of one who deserves dispraise. (2) Without investigating and scrutinizing, she speaks dispraise of one who deserves praise. (3) She is envious (4) and miserly. (5) She squanders gifts given out of faith. Possessing these five qualities, a bhikkhunī is deposited in hell as if brought there.

"Bhikkhus, possessing five [other] qualities, a bhikkhunī is deposited in heaven as if brought there. (1) Having investigated and scrutinized, she speaks dispraise of one who deserves dispraise. (2) Having investigated and scrutinized, she speaks praise of one who deserves praise. (3) She is free from envy (4) and from miserliness. (5) She does not squander gifts given out of faith. Possessing these five qualities, a bhikkhunī is deposited in heaven as if brought there."

118 (8) View

"Bhikkhus, possessing five qualities, a bhikkhunī is deposited in hell as if brought there. What five? (1) Without investigating and scrutinizing, she speaks praise of one who deserves dispraise. (2) Without investigating and scrutinizing, she speaks dispraise of one who deserves praise. (3) She holds wrong view (4) and has wrong intentions. (5) She squanders gifts given out of faith. Possessing these five qualities, a bhikkhunī is deposited in hell as if brought there. [141]

"Bhikkhus, possessing five [other] qualities, a bhikkhunī is deposited in heaven as if brought there. What five? (1) Having investigated and scrutinized, she speaks dispraise of one who deserves dispraise. (2) Having investigated and scrutinized, she speaks praise of one who deserves praise. (3) She holds right view (4) and has right intentions. (5) She does not squander gifts given out of faith. Possessing these five qualities, a bhikkhunī is deposited in heaven as if brought there."

119 (9) Speech

[As in 5:118, but replace the third and fourth qualities leading to hell and heaven respectively with the following:]

"... (3) She is of wrong speech and (4) wrong action...."

"... (3) She is of right speech and (4) right action...."

120 (10) Effort

[As in 5:118, but replace the third and fourth qualities leading to hell and heaven respectively with the following:]

"... (3) She is of wrong effort and (4) wrong mindfulness.... [142]

"... (3) She is of right effort and (4) right mindfulness...."

III. Sick

121 (1) Sick

On one occasion the Blessed One was dwelling at Vesālī in the hall with the peaked roof in the Great Wood. Then, in the evening, the Blessed One emerged from seclusion and approached the infirmary, where he saw a certain bhikkhu who was frail and sick. He then sat down in the prepared seat and addressed the bhikkhus:

"Bhikkhus, if five things do not slip away from a frail and sick bhikkhu, it can be expected of him: 'In no long time, with the destruction of the taints, he will realize for himself with direct knowledge, in this very life, the taintless liberation of mind, liberation by wisdom, and having entered upon it, he will dwell in it.' What five? Here, a bhikkhu dwells contemplating the unattractiveness of the body, perceiving the repulsiveness of food, perceiving non-delight in the entire world, [143] contemplating impermanence in all conditioned phenomena; and he has the perception of death well established internally. If these five things do not slip away from a frail and sick bhikkhu, it can be expected of him: 'In no long time, with the destruction of the taints, he will realize for himself with direct knowledge, in this very life, the taintless liberation of mind, liberation by wisdom, and having entered upon it, he will dwell in it.'"

122 (2) Establishment of Mindfulness

"Bhikkhus, if any bhikkhu or bhikkhunī develops and cultivates five things, one of two fruits is to be expected: either final knowledge in this very life or, if there is a residue remaining, the state of non-returning. What are the five? Here, a bhikkhu has mindfulness well established internally for [gaining] the wisdom that discerns the arising and passing away of phenomena;[1125] he dwells contemplating the unattractiveness of the body, perceiving the repulsiveness of food, perceiving non-delight in the entire world, and contemplating impermanence in all conditioned phenomena. If any bhikkhu or bhikkhunī develops and cultivates these five things, one of two fruits is to be expected: either final knowledge in this very life or, if there is a residue remaining, the state of non-returning."

123 (3) An Attendant (1)

"Bhikkhus, possessing five qualities, a patient is difficult to take care of. What five? (1) He does what is harmful. (2) He does not observe moderation in what is beneficial. (3) He does not take his medicine. (4) He does not accurately disclose his symptoms to his kindhearted attendant; he does not report, as fits the case, that his condition is getting worse, or getting better, or remaining the same. (5) He cannot patiently endure arisen bodily feelings that are painful, racking, sharp, piercing, harrowing, disagreeable, sapping one's vitality. [144] Possessing these five qualities, a patient is difficult to take care of.

"Bhikkhus, possessing five [other] qualities, a patient is easy to take care of. What five? (1) He does what is beneficial. (2) He observes moderation in what is beneficial. (3) He takes his medicine. (4) He accurately discloses his symptoms to his kindhearted attendant; he reports, as fits the case, that his condition is getting worse, or getting better, or remaining the same. (5) He can patiently endure arisen bodily feelings that are painful, racking, sharp, piercing, harrowing, disagreeable, sapping one's vitality. Possessing these five qualities, a patient is easy to take care of."

124 (4) An Attendant (2)

"Bhikkhus, possessing five qualities, an attendant is not qualified to take care of a patient. What five? (1) He is unable to prepare medicine. (2) He does not know what is beneficial and harmful, so he offers what is harmful and withholds what is beneficial. (3) He takes care of the patient for the sake of material rewards, not with a mind of loving-kindness. (4) He is disgusted at having to remove feces, urine, vomit, or spittle. (5)

He is unable from time to time to instruct, encourage, inspire, and gladden the patient with a Dhamma talk. Possessing these five qualities, an attendant is not qualified to take care of a patient.

"Bhikkhus, possessing five [other] qualities, an attendant is qualified to take care of a patient. What five? (1) He is able to prepare medicine. (2) He knows what is beneficial and harmful, so that he withholds what is harmful and offers what is beneficial. (3) He takes care of the patient with a mind of loving-kindness, not for the sake of material rewards. (4) He is not disgusted at having to remove feces, urine, vomit, or spittle. (5) He is able from time to time to instruct, encourage, inspire, and gladden the patient with a Dhamma talk. [145] Possessing these five qualities, an attendant is qualified to take care of a patient."

125 (5) Vitality (1)

"Bhikkhus, there are these five things that reduce vitality. What five? One does what is harmful; one does not observe moderation in what is beneficial; one has poor digestion; one walks [for alms] at an improper time;[1126] one is not celibate. These are the five things that reduce vitality.

"Bhikkhus, there are these five things that increase vitality. What five? One does what is beneficial; one observes moderation in what is beneficial; one has good digestion; one walks [for alms] at the proper time; one is celibate. These are the five things that increase vitality."

126 (6) Vitality (2)

"Bhikkhus, there are these five things that reduce vitality. What five? One does what is harmful; one does not observe moderation in what is beneficial; one has poor digestion; one is immoral; one has bad friends. These are the five things that reduce vitality.

"Bhikkhus, there are these five things that increase vitality. What five? One does what is beneficial; one observes moderation in what is beneficial; one has good digestion; one is virtuous; one has good friends. These are the five things that increase vitality."

127 (7) Living Apart

"Bhikkhus, possessing five qualities, a bhikkhu is not fit to live apart from the Saṅgha. What five? He is not content with any kind of robe; he is not content with any kind of almsfood; he is not content with any kind of lodging; he is not content with any kind of medicines and provisions for the sick; and he dwells engrossed in thoughts of sensuality. Possessing these five qualities, a bhikkhu is not fit to live apart from the Saṅgha.

"Bhikkhus, possessing five [other] qualities, a bhikkhu is fit to live apart from the Saṅgha. What five? [146] He is content with any kind of robe; he is content with any kind of almsfood; he is content with any kind of lodging; he is content with any kind of medicines and provisions for the sick;[1127] and he dwells engrossed in thoughts of renunciation. Possessing these five qualities, a bhikkhu is fit to live apart from the Saṅgha."

128 (8) An Ascetic's Happiness

"Bhikkhus, there are these five kinds of suffering for an ascetic. What five? Here, a bhikkhu is not content with any kind of robe; he is not content with any kind of almsfood; he is not content with any kind of lodging; he is not content with any kind of medicines and provisions for the sick; and he lives the spiritual life dissatisfied. These are the five kinds of suffering for an ascetic.

"Bhikkhus, there are these five kinds of happiness for an ascetic. What five? Here, a bhikkhu is content with any kind of robe; he is content with any kind of almsfood; he is content with any kind of lodging; he is content with any kind of medicines and provisions for the sick; and he lives the spiritual life with satisfaction. These are the five kinds of happiness for an ascetic."

129 (9) Lesions

"Bhikkhus, there are these five incurable lesions[1128] that lead to the plane of misery, that lead to hell. What five? One deprives one's mother of life; one deprives one's father of life; one deprives an arahant of life; with a mind of hatred one sheds the Tathāgata's blood; one creates a schism in the Saṅgha. These are the five incurable lesions that lead to the plane of misery, that lead to hell." [147]

130 (10) Accomplishments

"Bhikkhus, there are these five disasters. What five? Disaster due to [loss of] relatives, disaster due to [loss of] wealth, disaster due to illness, disaster regarding virtuous behavior, and disaster regarding view.[1129] It is not because of a disaster due to [loss of] relatives, or a disaster due to [loss of] wealth, or a disaster due to illness that with the breakup of the body, after death, beings are reborn in the plane of misery, in a bad destination, in the lower world, in hell. It is because of a disaster regarding virtuous behavior and a disaster regarding view that with the breakup of the body, after death, beings are reborn in the plane of misery, in a bad destination, in the lower world, in hell. These are the five disasters.

"Bhikkhus, there are these five accomplishments. What five? Accomplishment in relatives, accomplishment in wealth, accomplishment in health, accomplishment in virtuous behavior, and accomplishment in view. It is not because of accomplishment in relatives, accomplishment in wealth, or accomplishment in health that with the breakup of the body, after death, beings are reborn in a good destination, in a heavenly world. It is because of accomplishment in virtuous behavior and accomplishment in view that with the breakup of the body, after death, beings are reborn in a good destination, in a heavenly world. These are the five accomplishments."

IV. Kings

131 (1) Continuing to Turn the Wheel (1)

"Bhikkhus, possessing five factors, a wheel-turning monarch sets the wheel in motion solely through the Dhamma,[1130] a wheel that [148] cannot be turned back by any hostile creature in human form. What five? Here, a wheel-turning monarch is one who knows what is good, who knows the Dhamma, who knows the right measure, who knows the proper time, and who knows the assembly. Possessing these five factors, a wheel-turning monarch sets the wheel in motion solely through the Dhamma, a wheel that cannot be turned back by any hostile creature in human form.

"So too, bhikkhus, possessing five qualities, the Tathāgata, the Arahant, the Perfectly Enlightened One sets in motion the unsurpassed wheel of the Dhamma solely through the Dhamma, a wheel that cannot be turned back by any ascetic, brahmin, deva, Māra, or Brahmā, or by anyone in the world. What five? Here, the Tathāgata, the Arahant, the Perfectly Enlightened One is one who knows what is good, who knows the Dhamma, who knows the right measure, who knows the proper time, and who knows the assembly.[1131] Possessing these five qualities, the Tathāgata . . . sets in motion the unsurpassed wheel of the Dhamma solely through the Dhamma, a wheel that cannot be turned back . . . by anyone in the world."

132 (2) Continuing to Turn the Wheel (2)

"Bhikkhus, possessing five factors, the eldest son of a wheel-turning monarch continues, solely through the Dhamma, to turn the wheel set in motion by his father, a wheel that cannot be turned back by any hostile creature in human form. What five? Here, the eldest son of a wheel-turning monarch is one who knows what is good, who knows the Dhamma, who knows the right measure, who knows the proper time, and who knows the assembly. Possessing these five factors, the eldest son of a wheel-turning monarch continues, solely through the Dhamma, to turn the wheel set in motion by his father, a wheel that cannot be turned back by any hostile creature in human form. [149]

"So too, bhikkhus, possessing five qualities, Sāriputta continues, solely through the Dhamma, to turn the unsurpassed wheel of the Dhamma set in motion by the Tathāgata, a wheel that cannot be turned back by any ascetic, brahmin, deva, Māra, or Brahmā, or by anyone in the world.[1132] What five? Here, Sāriputta is one who knows what is good, who knows the Dhamma, who knows the right measure, who knows the proper time, and who knows the assembly. Possessing these five qualities, Sāriputta continues, solely through the Dhamma, to turn the unsurpassed wheel of the Dhamma set in motion by the Tathāgata, a wheel that cannot be turned back by any ascetic, brahmin, deva, Māra, or Brahmā, or by anyone in the world."

133 (3) The King[1133]

"Bhikkhus, even a wheel-turning monarch, a righteous king who rules by the Dhamma, does not turn the wheel without a king above him."

When this was said, a certain bhikkhu said to the Blessed One: "But, Bhante, who could be the king above a wheel-turning monarch, a righteous king who rules by the Dhamma?"

"It is the Dhamma, bhikkhu," the Blessed One said. "Here, a wheel-turning monarch, a righteous king who rules by the Dhamma, relying just on the Dhamma, honoring, respecting, and venerating the Dhamma, taking the Dhamma as his standard, banner, and authority, provides righteous protection, shelter, and guard for the people in his court. Again, a wheel-turning monarch, a righteous king who rules by the Dhamma . . . provides righteous protection, shelter, and guard for his khattiya vassals; for his army; for brahmins and householders; for the people of town and countryside; for ascetics and brahmins; for the animals and birds. [150] Having provided such righteous protection, shelter, and guard, that wheel-turning monarch, a righteous king who rules by the Dhamma, turns the wheel solely through the Dhamma, a wheel that cannot be turned back by any hostile creature in human form.

"So too, bhikkhu, the Tathāgata, the Arahant, the Perfectly Enlightened One, the righteous king of the Dhamma, relying just on the Dhamma, honoring, respecting, and venerating the Dhamma, taking the Dhamma as his standard, banner, and authority, provides righteous protection, shelter, and guard for the bhikkhus, saying: (1) 'Such bodily action should be cultivated; such bodily action should not be cultivated. (2) Such verbal action should be cultivated; such verbal action should not be cultivated. (3) Such mental action should be cultivated; such mental action should not be cultivated. (4) Such livelihood should be cultivated; such livelihood should not be cultivated. (5) Such a village or town should be resorted to; such a village or town should not be resorted to.'

"Again, the Tathāgata, the Arahant, the Perfectly Enlightened One, the righteous king of the Dhamma, relying just on the Dhamma, honoring, respecting, and venerating the Dhamma, taking the Dhamma as his standard, banner, and authority, provides righteous protection, shelter, and guard for the bhikkhunīs . . . for the male lay followers . . . for the female lay followers, saying: 'Such bodily action should be cultivated. . . . Such verbal action should be cultivated. . . . Such mental action should be cultivated. . . . Such livelihood should be cultivated; such livelihood should not be cultivated. Such a village or town should be resorted to; such a village or town should not be resorted to.'

"Having provided such righteous protection, shelter, and guard, the Tathāgata, the Arahant, the Perfectly Enlightened One, [151] the righteous king of the Dhamma, sets in motion the unsurpassed wheel of the Dhamma solely through the Dhamma, a wheel that cannot be turned back by any ascetic, brahmin, deva, Māra, or Brahmā, or by anyone in the world."

134 (4) In Whatever Quarter

"Bhikkhus, in whatever quarter he might dwell, a head-anointed khattiya king who possesses five factors dwells in his own realm. What five?

"(1) Here, a head-anointed khattiya king is well born on both his maternal and paternal sides, of pure descent, unassailable and impeccable with respect to birth as far back as the seventh paternal generation.[1134] (2) He is rich, with great wealth and property, with full treasuries and storerooms. (3) He is powerful, possessing an army of four divisions that is obedient and compliant to his commands. (4) His counselor is wise, competent, and intelligent, able to consider benefits pertaining to the past, future, and present.[1135] (5) These four qualities of his promote his fame. Possessing these five qualities inclusive of fame, he dwells in his own realm in whatever quarter he might dwell. For what reason? Because this is how it is for the victorious ones.

"So too, bhikkhus, in whatever quarter he might dwell, a bhikkhu who possesses five qualities dwells liberated in mind. What five?

"(1) Here, a bhikkhu is virtuous; he dwells restrained by the Pātimokkha, possessed of good conduct and resort, seeing danger in minute faults. Having undertaken the training rules, he trains in them. [152] This is like the head-anointed khattiya king's being well born. (2) He has learned much, remembers what he has learned, and accumulates what he has learned.

Those teachings that are good in the beginning, good in the middle, and good in the end, with the right meaning and phrasing, which proclaim the perfectly complete and pure spiritual life—such teachings as these he has learned much of, retained in mind, recited verbally, mentally investigated, and penetrated well by view. This is like the head-anointed khattiya king's being rich, with great wealth and property, with full treasuries and storerooms. (3) He has aroused energy for abandoning unwholesome qualities and acquiring wholesome qualities; he is strong, firm in exertion, not casting off the duty of cultivating wholesome qualities. This is like the head-anointed khattiya king's being powerful. (4) He is wise; he possesses the wisdom that discerns arising and passing away, which is noble and penetrative and leads to the complete destruction of suffering. This is like the head-anointed khattiya king's having a good counselor. (5) These four qualities of his promote his liberation. Possessing these five qualities inclusive of liberation, in whatever quarter he might dwell, he dwells liberated in mind. For what reason? Because this is how it is for those who are liberated in mind."

135 (5) Yearning

"Bhikkhus, possessing five factors, the eldest son of a head-anointed khattiya king yearns for kingship. What five? (1) Here, the eldest son of a head-anointed khattiya king is well born on both his maternal and paternal sides, of pure descent, unassailable and impeccable with respect to birth as far back as the seventh paternal generation. (2) He is handsome, attractive, graceful, possessing supreme beauty of complexion. (3) He is pleasing and agreeable to his parents. (4) He is pleasing and agreeable to the people of the towns and countryside. (5) He is trained and proficient in the arts of head-anointed khattiya kings, whether elephant riding, horsemanship, driving a chariot, archery, or swordsmanship. [153]

"It occurs to him: (1) 'I am well born on both sides . . . impeccable with respect to birth, so why shouldn't I yearn for kingship? (2) I am handsome, attractive, graceful, possessing supreme beauty of complexion, so why shouldn't I yearn for kingship? (3) I am pleasing and agreeable to my parents, so why shouldn't I yearn for kingship? (4) I am pleasing and agreeable to the people of the towns and countryside, so why shouldn't I yearn for kingship? (5) I am trained and proficient in the arts of head-anointed khattiya kings, whether elephant riding, horsemanship, driving a chariot, archery, or swordsmanship, so why shouldn't I yearn for kingship?' Possessing these five factors, the eldest son of a head-anointed khattiya king yearns for kingship.

"So too, bhikkhus, possessing five qualities, a bhikkhu yearns for the destruction of the taints. What five? (1) Here, a bhikkhu is endowed with faith. He places faith in the enlightenment of the Tathāgata thus: 'The Blessed One is an arahant, perfectly enlightened . . . teacher of devas and humans, the Enlightened One, the Blessed One.' (2) He is seldom ill or afflicted, possessing an even digestion that is neither too cool nor too hot but moderate and suitable for striving. (3) He is honest and open, one who reveals himself as he really is to the Teacher and his wise fellow monks. (4) He has aroused energy for abandoning unwholesome qualities and acquiring wholesome qualities; he is strong, firm in exertion, not casting off the duty of cultivating wholesome qualities. (5) He is wise; he possesses the wisdom that discerns arising and passing away, which is noble and penetrative and leads to the complete destruction of suffering.

"It occurs to him: (1) 'I am endowed with faith; I place faith in the enlightenment of the Tathāgata thus: "The Blessed One is an arahant, perfectly enlightened . . . teacher of devas and humans, the Enlightened One, the Blessed One," so why shouldn't I [154] yearn for the destruction of the taints? (2) I am seldom ill or afflicted, possessing an even digestion that is neither too cool nor too hot but moderate and suitable for striving, so why shouldn't I yearn for the destruction of the taints? (3) I am honest and open; I reveal myself as I really am to the Teacher and my wise fellow monks, so why shouldn't I yearn for the destruction of the taints? (4) I have aroused energy for the abandoning of unwholesome qualities . . . not casting off the duty of cultivating wholesome qualities, so why shouldn't I yearn for the destruction of the taints? (5) I am wise; I possess the wisdom . . . [that] leads to the complete destruction of suffering, so why shouldn't I yearn for the destruction of the taints?'

"Possessing these five qualities, a bhikkhu yearns for the destruction of the taints."

136 (6) Yearning (2)

"Bhikkhus, possessing five factors, the eldest son of a head-anointed khattiya king yearns to be the viceroy. What five? (1) Here, the eldest son of a head-anointed khattiya king is well born . . . as far back as the seventh paternal generation. (2) He is handsome, attractive, graceful, possessing supreme beauty of complexion. (3) He is pleasing and agreeable to his parents. (4) He is pleasing and agreeable to the armed forces. (5) He is wise, competent, and intelligent, able to consider benefits pertaining to the past, future, and present.

"It occurs to him: (1) 'I am well born . . . as far back as the seventh paternal generation, so why shouldn't I yearn to be the viceroy? (2) I am handsome, attractive, graceful, possessing supreme beauty of complexion, so why shouldn't I yearn to be the viceroy? (3) I am pleasing and agreeable to my parents, so why shouldn't I yearn to be the viceroy? [155] (4) I am pleasing and agreeable to the armed forces, so why shouldn't I yearn to be the viceroy? (5) I am wise, competent, and intelligent, able to consider benefits pertaining to the past, future, and present, so why shouldn't I yearn to be the viceroy?' Possessing these five factors, the eldest son of a head-anointed khattiya king yearns to be the viceroy.

"So too, bhikkhus, possessing five qualities, a bhikkhu yearns for the destruction of the taints. What five? (1) Here, a bhikkhu is virtuous . . . he trains in them. (2) He has learned much . . . and penetrated well by view. (3) He is one whose mind is well established in the four establishments of mindfulness. (4) He has aroused energy . . . not casting off the duty of cultivating wholesome qualities. (5) He is wise; he possesses the wisdom . . . [that] leads to the complete destruction of suffering.

"It occurs to him: (1) 'I am virtuous . . . I train in them, so why shouldn't I yearn for the destruction of the taints? (2) I have learned much . . . and penetrated well by view, so why shouldn't I yearn for the destruction of the taints? (3) I am one whose mind is well established in the four establishments of mindfulness, so why shouldn't I yearn for the destruction of the taints? (4) I have aroused energy for the abandoning of unwholesome qualities . . . not casting off the duty of cultivating wholesome qualities, so why shouldn't I yearn for the destruction of the taints? (5) I am wise; I possess the wisdom . . . [156]

[that] leads to the complete destruction of suffering, so why shouldn't I yearn for the destruction of the taints?'

"Possessing these five qualities, a bhikkhu yearns for the destruction of the taints."

137 (7) Little Sleep

"Bhikkhus, these five sleep little at night but mostly keep awake. What five? A woman intent on a man, a man intent on a woman, a thief intent on theft, a king engaged with his royal duties, and a bhikkhu intent on severing the bonds. These five sleep little at night but mostly keep awake."

138 (8) A Consumer of Food

"Bhikkhus, possessing five factors, a king's bull elephant is a consumer of food, an occupant of space, a discharger of dung, a ticket-taker,[1136] and yet still is reckoned as a king's bull elephant. What five? It cannot patiently endure forms, cannot patiently endure sounds, cannot patiently endure odors, cannot patiently endure tastes, and cannot patiently endure tactile objects. Possessing these five factors, a king's bull elephant is a consumer of food . . . yet still is reckoned as a king's bull elephant.

"So too, bhikkhus, possessing five qualities, a bhikkhu is a consumer of food, an occupant of space, a crusher of chairs,[1137] a ticket-taker,[1138] and yet still is reckoned as a bhikkhu. What five? [157] Here, a bhikkhu cannot patiently endure forms, cannot patiently endure sounds, cannot patiently endure odors, cannot patiently endure tastes, and cannot patiently endure tactile objects. Possessing these five factors, a bhikkhu is a consumer of food, an occupant of space . . . yet still is reckoned as a bhikkhu."

139 (9) Cannot Patiently Endure

"Bhikkhus, possessing five factors, a king's bull elephant is not worthy of a king, not an accessory of a king, and not reckoned as a factor of kingship. What five? It cannot patiently endure forms, cannot patiently endure sounds, cannot patiently endure odors, cannot patiently endure tastes, and cannot patiently endure tactile objects.

(1) "And how is it that a king's bull elephant cannot patiently endure forms? Here, when a king's bull elephant has gone to

battle, on seeing the elephant troops, the cavalry, the charioteers, or the infantry, it sinks, founders, does not brace itself, and cannot enter the battle. It is in this way that a king's bull elephant cannot patiently endure forms.

(2) "And how is it that a king's bull elephant cannot patiently endure sounds? Here, when a king's bull elephant has gone to battle, on hearing the sounds of elephants, horses, chariots, or infantrymen, or the sounds of drums, kettledrums, conches, and tom-toms, it sinks, founders, does not brace itself, and cannot enter the battle. It is in this way that a king's bull elephant cannot patiently endure sounds.

(3) "And how is it that a king's bull elephant cannot patiently endure odors? [158] Here, when a king's bull elephant has gone to battle, on smelling the odor of the urine and feces of the royal bull elephants that are of pedigree stock and accustomed to battle, it sinks, founders, does not brace itself, and cannot enter the battle. It is in this way that a king's bull elephant cannot patiently endure odors.

(4) "And how is it that a king's bull elephant cannot patiently endure tastes? Here, when a king's bull elephant has gone to battle, if it is deprived of one portion of grass and water, or two, three, four, or five portions, it sinks, founders, does not brace itself, and cannot enter the battle. It is in this way that a king's bull elephant cannot patiently endure tastes.

(5) "And how is it that a king's bull elephant cannot patiently endure tactile objects? Here, when a king's bull elephant has gone to battle, if it is pierced by one volley of arrows, or by two, three, four, or five volleys, it sinks, founders, does not brace itself, and cannot enter the battle. It is in this way that a king's bull elephant cannot patiently endure tactile objects.

"Possessing these five factors, a king's bull elephant is not worthy of a king, not an accessory of a king, and not reckoned as a factor of kingship.

"So too, bhikkhus, possessing five qualities,[1139] a bhikkhu is not worthy of gifts, worthy of hospitality, worthy of offerings, worthy of reverential salutation, an unsurpassed field of merit for the world. What five? He cannot patiently endure forms, cannot patiently endure sounds, cannot patiently endure odors, cannot patiently endure tastes, and cannot patiently endure tactile objects.

(1) "And how is it that a bhikkhu cannot patiently endure forms? Here, when a bhikkhu sees a form with the eye, he becomes enamored of a tantalizing form and cannot concentrate his mind. It is in this way that a bhikkhu cannot patiently endure forms.

(2) "And how is it that a bhikkhu cannot patiently endure sounds? [159] Here, when a bhikkhu hears a sound with the ear, he becomes enamored of a tantalizing sound and cannot concentrate his mind. It is in this way that a bhikkhu cannot patiently endure sounds.

(3) "And how is it that a bhikkhu cannot patiently endure odors? Here, when a bhikkhu smells an odor with the nose, he becomes enamored of a tantalizing odor and cannot concentrate his mind. It is in this way that a bhikkhu cannot patiently endure odors.

(4) "And how is it that a bhikkhu cannot patiently endure tastes? Here, when a bhikkhu experiences a taste with the tongue, he becomes enamored of a tantalizing taste and cannot concentrate his mind. It is in this way that a bhikkhu cannot patiently endure tastes.

(5) "And how is it that a bhikkhu cannot patiently endure tactile objects? Here, when a bhikkhu feels a tactile object with the body, he becomes enamored of a tantalizing tactile object and cannot concentrate his mind. It is in this way that a bhikkhu cannot patiently endure tactile objects.

"Possessing these five qualities, a bhikkhu is not worthy of gifts, worthy of hospitality, worthy of offerings, worthy of reverential salutation, an unsurpassed field of merit for the world.

"Bhikkhus, possessing five factors, a king's bull elephant is worthy of a king, an accessory of a king, and reckoned as a factor of kingship. What five? It patiently endures forms, patiently endures sounds, patiently endures odors, patiently endures tastes, and patiently endures tactile objects.

(1) "And how is it that a king's bull elephant patiently endures forms? Here, when a king's bull elephant has gone to battle, on seeing the elephant troops, the cavalry, the charioteers, or the infantry, it does not sink and founder, but braces itself and can enter the battle. It is in this way that a king's bull elephant patiently endures forms.

(2) "And how is it that a king's bull elephant patiently endures sounds? [160] Here, when a king's bull elephant has gone to battle, on hearing the sounds of elephants, horses, chariots, or infantrymen, or the sounds of drums, kettledrums, conches, and tom-toms, it does not sink and founder but braces itself and can enter the battle. It is in this way that a king's bull elephant patiently endures sounds.

(3) "And how is it that a king's bull elephant patiently endures odors? Here, when a king's bull elephant has gone to battle, on smelling the odor of the urine and feces of royal bull elephants that are of pedigree stock and accustomed to battle, it does not sink and founder but braces itself and can enter the battle. It is in this way that a king's bull elephant patiently endures odors.

(4) "And how is it that a king's bull elephant patiently endures tastes? Here, when a king's bull elephant has gone to battle, though it is deprived of one portion of grass and water, or of two, three, four, or five portions, it does not sink and founder but braces itself and can enter the battle. It is in this way that a king's bull elephant patiently endures tastes.

(5) "And how is it that a king's bull elephant patiently endures tactile objects? Here, when a king's bull elephant has gone to battle, though it is pierced by one volley of arrows, or by two, three, four, or five volleys, it does not sink and founder but braces itself and can enter the battle. It is in this way that a king's bull elephant patiently endures tactile objects.

"Possessing these five factors, a king's bull elephant is worthy of a king, an accessory of a king, and reckoned as a factor of kingship.

"So too, bhikkhus, possessing five qualities, a bhikkhu is worthy of gifts, worthy of hospitality, worthy of offerings, worthy of reverential salutation, an unsurpassed field of merit for the world. What five? He patiently endures forms, patiently endures sounds, patiently endures odors, patiently endures tastes, and patiently endures [161] tactile objects.

(1) "And how is it that a bhikkhu patiently endures forms? Here, when a bhikkhu sees a form with the eye, he does not become enamored of a tantalizing form and can concentrate his mind. It is in this way that a bhikkhu patiently endures forms.

(2) "And how is it that a bhikkhu patiently endures sounds? Here, when a bhikkhu hears a sound with the ear, he does not

become enamored of a tantalizing sound and can concentrate his mind. It is in this way that a bhikkhu patiently endures sounds.

(3) "And how is it that a bhikkhu patiently endures odors? Here, when a bhikkhu smells an odor with the nose, he does not become enamored of a tantalizing odor and can concentrate his mind. It is in this way that a bhikkhu patiently endures odors.

(4) "And how is it that a bhikkhu patiently endures tastes? Here, when a bhikkhu experiences a taste with the tongue, he does not become enamored of a tantalizing taste and can concentrate his mind. It is in this way that a bhikkhu patiently endures tastes.

(5) "And how is it that a bhikkhu patiently endures tactile objects? Here, when a bhikkhu feels a tactile object with the body, he does not become enamored of a tantalizing tactile object and can concentrate his mind. It is in this way that a bhikkhu patiently endures tactile objects.

"Possessing these five qualities, a bhikkhu is worthy of gifts, worthy of hospitality, worthy of offerings, worthy of reverential salutation, an unsurpassed field of merit for the world."

140 (10) One Who Listens

"Bhikkhus, possessing five factors, a king's bull elephant is worthy of a king, an accessory of a king, and reckoned as a factor of kingship. What five? Here, a king's bull elephant is one who listens, who destroys, who guards, who patiently endures, and who goes.

(1) "And how is a king's bull elephant one who listens? Here, whatever task the elephant trainer sets for it, whether or not [162] it has ever done it before, the king's bull elephant heeds it, attends to it, directs its whole mind to it, and listens with eager ears. It is in this way that a king's bull elephant is one who listens.

(2) "And how is a king's bull elephant one who destroys? Here, when a king's bull elephant has entered the battle, it destroys elephants and elephant riders, horses and cavalry, chariots and charioteers, and infantry. It is in this way that a king's bull elephant is one who destroys.

(3) "And how is a king's bull elephant one who guards? Here, when the king's bull elephant has entered a battle, it guards its

front quarters, its back quarters, its front feet, its back feet, its head, its ears, its tusks, its trunk, its tail, and its rider. It is in this way that a king's bull elephant is one who guards.

(4) "And how is a king's bull elephant one who patiently endures? Here, when a king's bull elephant has entered the battle, it patiently endures being struck by spears, swords, arrows, and axes; it endures the sounds of drums, kettledrums, conches, and tom-toms. It is in this way that a king's bull elephant is one who patiently endures.

(5) "And how is a king's bull elephant one who goes? Here, the king's bull elephant quickly goes to whatever region the elephant trainer sends it, whether or not it has ever gone there before. It is in this way that a king's bull elephant is one who goes.

"Possessing these five factors, a king's bull elephant is worthy of a king, an accessory of a king, and reckoned as a factor of kingship.

"So too, bhikkhus, possessing five qualities, a bhikkhu is worthy of gifts, worthy of hospitality, worthy of offerings, worthy of reverential salutation, an unsurpassed field of merit for the world. What five? Here, a bhikkhu is one who listens, who destroys, [163] who guards, who patiently endures, and who goes.

(1) "And how is a bhikkhu one who listens? Here, when the Dhamma and discipline proclaimed by the Tathāgata is being taught, a bhikkhu heeds it, attends to it, directs his whole mind to it, and listens to the Dhamma with eager ears. It is in this way that a bhikkhu is one who listens.

(2) "And how is a bhikkhu one who destroys? Here, a bhikkhu does not tolerate an arisen sensual thought, but abandons it, dispels it, terminates it, and obliterates it. He does not tolerate an arisen thought of ill will . . . an arisen thought of harming . . . any other bad unwholesome states that arise from time to time, but abandons them, dispels them, terminates them, and obliterates them. It is in this way that a bhikkhu is one who destroys.

(3) "And how is a bhikkhu one who guards? Here, having seen a form with the eye, a bhikkhu does not grasp its marks and features. Since, if he left the eye faculty unrestrained, bad unwholesome states of longing and dejection might invade

him, he practices restraint over it; he guards the eye faculty, he undertakes the restraint of the eye faculty. Having heard a sound with the ear . . . Having smelled an odor with the nose . . . Having tasted a taste with the tongue . . . Having felt a tactile object with the body . . . Having cognized a mental phenomenon with the mind . . . he guards the mind faculty, he undertakes the restraint of the mind faculty. It is in this way that a bhikkhu is one who guards.

(4) "And how is a bhikkhu one who patiently endures? Here, a bhikkhu patiently endures cold and heat; hunger and thirst; contact with flies, mosquitoes, wind, the burning sun, and serpents; rude and offensive ways of speech; he is able to bear up with arisen bodily feelings that are painful, racking, sharp, piercing, harrowing, disagreeable, sapping one's vitality. It is in this way that a bhikkhu is one who patiently endures.

(5) "And how is a bhikkhu one who goes? [164] Here, a bhikkhu is one who quickly goes to that region where he has never before gone in this long time, that is, to the stilling of all activities, the relinquishment of all acquisitions, the destruction of craving, dispassion, cessation, nibbāna. It is in this way that a bhikkhu is one who goes.

"Possessing these five qualities, a bhikkhu is worthy of gifts, worthy of hospitality, worthy of offerings, worthy of reverential salutation, an unsurpassed field of merit for the world."

V. Tikaṇḍakī

141 (1) Having Given, One Despises

"Bhikkhus, there are these five kinds of persons found in the world. What five? The one who gives and then despises; the one who despises as a result of living together; the one gullible for gossip; the capricious one; and the one who is dull and stupid.

(1) "And how is a person one who gives and then despises? Here, one person gives another a robe, almsfood, lodging, and medicines and provisions for the sick. It occurs to him: 'I give; he receives.' Having given to him, he despises him. It is in this way that a person is one who gives and then despises.

(2) "And how does a person despise as a result of living

together? [165] Here, one person lives together with another for two or three years. He then despises the other because they have lived together. It is in this way that a person despises as a result of living together.

(3) "And how is a person gullible for gossip? Here, when praise or dispraise is being spoken about another person, he readily believes it. It is in this way that a person is gullible for gossip.

(4) "And how is a person capricious? Here, a person's faith, devotion, affection, and confidence are fickle. It is in this way that a person is capricious.

(5) "And how is a person dull and stupid? Here, a person does not know which qualities are wholesome and which unwholesome, which qualities are blameworthy and which blameless, which qualities are inferior and which superior; he does not know dark and bright qualities along with their counterparts. It is in this way that a person is dull and stupid.

"These, bhikkhus, are the five kinds of persons found in the world."

142 (2) One Violates

"Bhikkhus, there are these five kinds of persons found in the world. What five?

(1) "Here, one person violates and then becomes remorseful, and does not understand as it really is the liberation of mind, liberation by wisdom, where these arisen bad unwholesome states of his cease without remainder.[1140]

(2) "Here, one person violates and does not become remorseful,[1141] and does not understand as it really is the liberation of mind, liberation by wisdom, where these arisen bad unwholesome states of his cease without remainder.

(3) "Here, one person does not violate [166] and yet becomes remorseful,[1142] and does not understand as it really is the liberation of mind, liberation by wisdom, where these arisen bad unwholesome states of his cease without remainder.

(4) "Here, one person does not violate and does not become remorseful, and does not understand as it really is the liberation of mind, liberation by wisdom, where these arisen bad unwholesome states of his cease without remainder.

(5) "Here, one person does not violate and does not become

remorseful, and understands as it really is the liberation of mind, liberation by wisdom, where these arisen bad unwholesome states of his cease without remainder.

(1) "Bhikkhus, the person among these who violates and then becomes remorseful, and does not understand as it really is the liberation of mind, liberation by wisdom, where these arisen bad unwholesome states of his cease without remainder, should be told: 'Taints born of violation are found in you, and taints born of remorse increase. Please abandon the taints born of violation and dispel the taints born of remorse; then develop your mind and wisdom.[1143] In this way you will be exactly the same as the fifth type of person.'

(2) "The person among these who violates and does not become remorseful, and does not understand as it really is the liberation of mind, liberation by wisdom, where these arisen bad unwholesome states of his cease without remainder, should be told: 'Taints born of violation are found in you, but taints born of remorse do not increase. Please abandon the taints born of violation, and then develop your mind and wisdom. In this way you will be exactly the same as the fifth type of person.'

(3) "The person among these who does not violate and yet becomes remorseful, and does not understand as it really is the liberation of mind, liberation by wisdom, where these arisen bad unwholesome states of his cease without remainder, should be told: [167] 'Taints born of violation are not found in you, yet taints born of remorse increase. Please dispel the taints born of remorse, and then develop your mind and wisdom. In this way you will be exactly the same as the fifth type of person.'

(4) "The person among these who does not violate and does not become remorseful, and does not understand as it really is the liberation of mind, liberation by wisdom, where these arisen bad unwholesome states of his cease without remainder, should be told: 'Taints born of violation are not found in you, and taints born of remorse do not increase. Please develop your mind and wisdom. In this way you will be exactly the same as the fifth type of person.'

(5) "Thus, bhikkhus, when persons of these four types are exhorted and instructed by the example of the fifth type of person, they gradually attain the destruction of the taints."

143 (3) Sārandada

On one occasion the Blessed One was dwelling at Vesālī in the hall with the peaked roof in the Great Wood. Then, in the morning, the Blessed One dressed, took his bowl and robe, and entered Vesālī for alms. Now on that occasion five hundred Licchavis had assembled at the Sārandada Shrine and were sitting together when this conversation arose: "The manifestation of five gems is rare in the world. What five? The elephant-gem, the horse-gem, the jewel-gem, the woman-gem, and the steward-gem. The manifestation of these five gems is rare in the world." [168]

Then the Licchavis stationed a man on the road and told him: "Good man, when you see the Blessed One coming, you should inform us." The man saw the Blessed One coming in the distance, went to the Licchavis, and told them: "Sirs, this Blessed One, the Arahant, the Perfectly Enlightened One is coming. You may go at your own convenience."

Then the Licchavis approached the Blessed One, paid homage to him, and stood to one side. Standing there, they said to him: "Please, Bhante, let the Blessed One go to the Sārandada Shrine out of compassion." The Blessed One silently consented. He went to the Sārandada Shrine, sat down on a seat that was prepared, and said to the Licchavis:

"What discussion were you engaged in just now as you were sitting together here? What was the conversation that was underway?"

"Here, Bhante, when we had assembled and were sitting together, this conversation arose . . . [He here repeats the entire conversation above.] . . . 'The manifestation of these five gems is rare in the world.'"

"Intent on sensual pleasures, the Licchavis were engaged in a conversation about sensual pleasures! Licchavis, the manifestation of five gems is rare in the world. What five? (1) The manifestation of a Tathāgata, an Arahant, a Perfectly Enlightened One is rare in the world. (2) A person who teaches the Dhamma and discipline proclaimed by a Tathāgata [169] is rare in the world. (3) When the Dhamma and discipline proclaimed by a Tathāgata has been taught, a person who understands it is rare in the world. (4) When the Dhamma and discipline proclaimed by a Tathāgata has been taught and understood, a person who practices in accordance with the Dhamma is rare in the world. (5) A grateful and thankful person is rare in the world. Licchavis, the manifestation of these five gems is rare in the world."

144 (4) Tikaṇḍakī

On one occasion the Blessed One was dwelling at Sāketa in the Tikaṇḍakī Grove. There the Blessed One addressed the bhikkhus: "Bhikkhus!"

"Venerable sir," those bhikkhus replied. The Blessed One said this:

"(1) Bhikkhus, it is good for a bhikkhu from time to time to dwell perceiving the repulsive in the unrepulsive. (2) It is good for a bhikkhu from time to time to dwell perceiving the unrepulsive in the repulsive. (3) It is good for a bhikkhu from time to time to dwell perceiving the repulsive in both the unrepulsive and the repulsive. (4) It is good for a bhikkhu from time to time to dwell perceiving the unrepulsive in both the repulsive and the unrepulsive. (5) It is good for a bhikkhu from time to time to dwell equanimous, mindful and clearly comprehending, having turned away from both the repulsive and the unrepulsive.[1144]

(1) "And for the sake of what benefit should a bhikkhu dwell perceiving the repulsive in the unrepulsive? 'Let no lust arise in me toward things provocative of lust!': for the sake of this benefit a bhikkhu should dwell perceiving the repulsive in the unrepulsive.

(2) "And for the sake of what benefit should a bhikkhu dwell perceiving the unrepulsive in the repulsive? 'Let no hatred arise in me toward things provocative of hatred!': for the sake of this benefit a bhikkhu should dwell perceiving the unrepulsive in the repulsive.

(3) "And for the sake of what [170] benefit should a bhikkhu dwell perceiving the repulsive in both the unrepulsive and the repulsive? 'Let no lust arise in me toward things provocative of lust, and no hatred toward things provocative of hatred!': for the sake of this benefit a bhikkhu should dwell perceiving the repulsive in both the unrepulsive and the repulsive.

(4) "And for the sake of what benefit should a bhikkhu dwell perceiving the unrepulsive in both the repulsive and the

unrepulsive? 'Let no hatred arise in me toward things provocative of hatred, and no lust toward things provocative of lust!': for the sake of this benefit a bhikkhu should dwell perceiving the unrepulsive in both the repulsive and the unrepulsive.

(5) "And for the sake of what benefit should a bhikkhu dwell equanimous, mindful and clearly comprehending, having turned away from both the repulsive and the unrepulsive? 'Let no lust at all arise in me anywhere in any way regarding things provocative of lust! Let no hatred at all arise in me anywhere in any way regarding things provocative of hatred! May no delusion at all arise in me anywhere in any way regarding things that breed delusion!':[1145] for the sake of this benefit a bhikkhu should dwell equanimous, mindful and clearly comprehending, having turned away from both the repulsive and the unrepulsive."

145 (5) Hell

"Bhikkhus, one possessing five qualities is deposited in hell as if brought there. What five? One destroys life, takes what is not given, engages in sexual misconduct, speaks falsely, and indulges in liquor, wine, and intoxicants, the basis for heedlessness. One possessing these five qualities is deposited in hell as if brought there. [171]

"Bhikkhus, one possessing five [other] qualities is deposited in heaven as if brought there. What five? One abstains from the destruction of life, abstains from taking what is not given, abstains from sexual misconduct, abstains from false speech, abstains from liquor, wine, and intoxicants, the basis for heedlessness. One possessing these five qualities is deposited in heaven as if brought there."

146 (6) Friend

"Bhikkhus, one should not take as a friend a bhikkhu who possesses five qualities. What five? He instigates work projects; he takes up disciplinary issues; he is hostile toward eminent bhikkhus; he is intent on lengthy and unsettled wandering; he is unable to instruct, encourage, inspire, and gladden one from time to time with a Dhamma talk. One should not take as a friend a bhikkhu who possesses these five qualities.

"Bhikkhus, one should take as a friend a bhikkhu who

possesses five [other] qualities. What five? He does not instigate work projects; he does not take up disciplinary issues; he is not hostile toward eminent bhikkhus; he is not intent on lengthy and unsettled wandering; he is able to instruct, encourage, inspire, and gladden one from time to time with a Dhamma talk. One should take as a friend a bhikkhu who possesses these five qualities."

147 (7) A Bad Person

"Bhikkhus, there are these five gifts of a bad person. What five? He gives casually; he gives without reverence; he does not give with his own hand; he gives what would be discarded; he gives without a view about the returns of giving.[1146] These are the five gifts of a bad person. [172]

"Bhikkhus, there are these five gifts of a good person. What five? He gives respectfully; he gives with reverence; he gives with his own hand; he gives what would not be discarded; he gives with a view about the returns of giving.[1147] These are the five gifts of a good person."

148 (8) A Good Person

"Bhikkhus, there are these five gifts of a good person. What five? He gives a gift out of faith; he gives a gift respectfully; he gives a timely gift; he gives a gift unreservedly; he gives a gift without injuring himself or others.

"(1) Because he has given a gift out of faith, wherever the result of that gift is produced, he becomes rich, with great wealth and property, and he is handsome, attractive, graceful, possessing supreme beauty of complexion. (2) Because he has given a gift respectfully, wherever the result of that gift is produced, he becomes rich, with great wealth and property, and his sons and wives, slaves, servants, and workers are obedient, lend an ear, and apply their minds to understand. (3) Because he has given a timely gift, wherever the result of that gift is produced, he becomes rich, with great wealth and property, and timely benefits come to him in abundance. (4) Because he has given a gift unreservedly, wherever the result of that gift is produced, he becomes rich, with great wealth and property, and his mind inclines to the enjoyment of the five kinds of fine sensual pleasures. [173] (5) Because he has given a gift without injuring himself or others, wherever the result of that gift is produced, he becomes rich, with great wealth and property, and no damage comes to his property from any source, whether from fire, floods, kings, thieves, or displeasing heirs. These are the five gifts of a good person."

149 (9) Temporarily Liberated (1)

"Bhikkhus, these five things lead to the decline of a temporarily liberated bhikkhu.[1148] What five? Delight in work, delight in talk, delight in sleep, delight in company; and he does not review the extent to which the mind is liberated. These five things lead to the decline of a temporarily liberated bhikkhu.

"Bhikkhus, these five things lead to the non-decline of a temporarily liberated bhikkhu. What five? There is no delight in work, no delight in talk, no delight in sleep, no delight in company; and he reviews the extent to which the mind is liberated. These five things lead to the non-decline of a temporarily liberated bhikkhu."

150 (10) Temporarily Liberated (2)

"Bhikkhus, these five things lead to the decline of a temporarily liberated bhikkhu. What five? Delight in work, delight in talk, delight in sleep, not guarding the doors of the sense faculties, and lack of moderation in eating. These five things lead to the decline of a temporarily liberated bhikkhu.

"Bhikkhus, these five things lead to the non-decline of a temporarily liberated bhikkhu. What five? There is no delight in work, no delight in talk, no delight in sleep, guarding the doors of the sense faculties, and moderation in eating. [174] These five things lead to the non-decline of a temporarily liberated bhikkhu."

The Fourth Fifty

I. The Good Dhamma

151 (1) The Fixed Course of Rightness[1149] (1)

"Bhikkhus, possessing five qualities, even while listening to the good Dhamma one is incapable of entering upon the fixed course [consisting in] rightness in wholesome qualities.[1150] What five? One disparages the talk; one disparages the speaker; one disparages oneself; one listens to the Dhamma with a distracted and scattered mind; one attends to it carelessly. Possessing these five qualities, even while listening to the good Dhamma one is incapable of entering upon the fixed course [consisting in] rightness in wholesome qualities.

"Bhikkhus, possessing five qualities, while listening to [175] the good Dhamma one is capable of entering upon the fixed course [consisting in] rightness in wholesome qualities. What five? One does not disparage the talk; one does not disparage the speaker; one does not disparage oneself; one listens to the Dhamma with an undistracted and one-pointed mind; one attends to it carefully. Possessing these five qualities, while listening to the good Dhamma one is capable of entering upon the fixed course [consisting in] rightness in wholesome qualities."

152 (2) The Fixed Course of Rightness (2)

"Bhikkhus, possessing five qualities, even while listening to the good Dhamma one is incapable of entering upon the fixed course [consisting in] rightness in wholesome qualities. What five? One disparages the talk; one disparages the speaker; one disparages oneself; one is unwise, stupid, obtuse; one imagines that one has understood what one has not understood. Possessing these five qualities, even while listening to the good Dhamma one is incapable of entering upon the fixed course [consisting in] rightness in wholesome qualities.

"Bhikkhus, possessing five qualities, while listening to the good Dhamma one is capable of entering upon the fixed course [consisting in] rightness in wholesome qualities. What five? One does not disparage the talk; one does not disparage the speaker; one does not disparage oneself; one is wise, intelligent, astute; one does not imagine that one has understood what one has not understood. Possessing these five qualities, while listening to the good Dhamma one is capable of entering upon the fixed course [consisting in] rightness in wholesome qualities."

153 (3) The Fixed Course of Rightness (3)

"Bhikkhus, possessing five qualities, even while listening to the good Dhamma one is incapable of entering upon the fixed course [consisting in] rightness in wholesome qualities. What five? (1) One listens to the Dhamma as a denigrator obsessed with denigration; (2) one listens to the Dhamma with the intention of criticizing it, seeking faults; [176] (3) one is ill disposed toward the teacher, intent on attacking him; (4) one is unwise, stupid, obtuse; (5) one imagines that one has understood what one has not understood. Possessing these five qualities, even while listening to the good Dhamma one is incapable of entering upon the fixed course [consisting in] rightness in wholesome qualities.

"Bhikkhus, possessing five qualities, while listening to the good Dhamma one is capable of entering upon the fixed course [consisting in] rightness in wholesome qualities. What five? (1) One does not listen to the Dhamma as a denigrator obsessed with denigration; (2) one listens to the Dhamma without any intention of criticizing it, not as one who seeks faults; (3) one is not ill disposed toward the teacher and intent on attacking him; (4) one is wise, intelligent, astute; (5) one does not imagine that one has understood what one has not understood. Possessing these five qualities, while listening to the good Dhamma one is capable of entering upon the fixed course [consisting in] rightness in wholesome qualities."

154 (4) Decline of the Good Dhamma (1)

"Bhikkhus, there are these five things that lead to the decline and disappearance of the good Dhamma. What five? (1) Here, the bhikkhus do not respectfully listen to the Dhamma; (2) they do not respectfully learn the Dhamma; (3) they do not respectfully retain the Dhamma in mind; (4) they do not respectfully examine the meaning of the teachings they have retained in mind; (5) they do not respectfully understand the meaning and the Dhamma and then practice in accordance with the Dhamma. These five things lead to the decline and disappearance of the good Dhamma.

"Bhikkhus, there are these five [other] things that lead to the continuation, non-decline, and non-disappearance of the good Dhamma. What five? (1) Here, the bhikkhus respectfully listen to the Dhamma; (2) they respectfully learn the Dhamma; (3) they respectfully retain the Dhamma in mind; (4) they respectfully examine the meaning of the teachings they have retained in mind; (5) they respectfully understand the meaning and the

Dhamma and then practice in accordance with the Dhamma. [177] These five things lead to the continuation, non-decline, and non-disappearance of the good Dhamma."

155 (5) Decline of the Good Dhamma (2)

"Bhikkhus, there are these five things that lead to the decline and disappearance of the good Dhamma. What five?

(1) "Here, the bhikkhus do not learn the Dhamma: discourses, mixed prose and verse, expositions, verses, inspired utterances, quotations, birth stories, amazing accounts, and questions-and-answers. This is the first thing that leads to the decline and disappearance of the good Dhamma.

(2) "Again, the bhikkhus do not teach the Dhamma to others in detail as they have heard it and learned it. This is the second thing that leads to the decline and disappearance of the good Dhamma.

(3) "Again, the bhikkhus do not make others repeat the Dhamma in detail as they have heard it and learned it. This is the third thing that leads to the decline and disappearance of the good Dhamma.

(4) "Again, the bhikkhus do not recite the Dhamma in detail as they have heard it and learned it. This is the fourth thing that leads to the decline and disappearance of the good Dhamma.

(5) "Again, the bhikkhus do not ponder, examine, and mentally inspect the Dhamma as they have heard it and learned it. This is the fifth thing that leads to the decline and disappearance of the good Dhamma.

"These are the five things that lead to the decline and disappearance of the good Dhamma.

"Bhikkhus, there are these five [other] things that lead to the continuation, non-decline, and non-disappearance of the good Dhamma. What five?

(1) "Here, the bhikkhus learn the Dhamma: discourses . . . and questions-and-answers. This is [178] the first thing that leads to the continuation, non-decline, and non-disappearance of the good Dhamma.

(2) "Again, the bhikkhus teach the Dhamma to others in detail as they have heard it and learned it. This is the second thing that leads to the continuation, non-decline, and non-disappearance of the good Dhamma.

(3) "Again, the bhikkhus make others repeat the Dhamma in detail as they have heard it and learned it. This is the third thing that leads to the continuation, non-decline, and non-disappearance of the good Dhamma.

(4) "Again, the bhikkhus recite the Dhamma in detail as they have heard it and learned it. This is the fourth thing that leads to the continuation, non-decline, and non-disappearance of the good Dhamma.

(5) "Again, the bhikkhus ponder, examine, and mentally inspect the Dhamma as they have heard it and learned it. This is the fifth thing that leads to the continuation, non-decline, and non-disappearance of the good Dhamma.

"These are the five things that lead to the continuation, non-decline, and non-disappearance of the good Dhamma."

156 (6) Decline of the Good Dhamma (3)

"Bhikkhus, there are these five things that lead to the decline and disappearance of the good Dhamma. What five?[1151]

(1) "Here, the bhikkhus learn discourses that have been badly acquired, with badly set down words and phrases. When the words and phrases are badly set down, the meaning is badly interpreted. This is the first thing that leads to the decline and disappearance of the good Dhamma.

(2) "Again, the bhikkhus are difficult to correct and possess qualities that make them difficult to correct. They are impatient and do not accept instruction respectfully. This is the second thing that leads to the decline and disappearance of the good Dhamma. [179]

(3) "Again, those bhikkhus who are learned, heirs to the heritage, experts on the Dhamma, experts on the discipline, experts on the outlines, do not respectfully teach the discourses to others. When they have passed away, the discourses are cut off at the root, left without anyone to preserve them. This is the third thing that leads to the decline and disappearance of the good Dhamma.

(4) "Again, the elder bhikkhus are luxurious and lax, leaders in backsliding, discarding the duty of solitude; they do not arouse energy for the attainment of the as-yet-unattained, for the achievement of the as-yet-unachieved, for the realization of the as-yet-unrealized. [Those in] the next generation follow their example. They, too, become luxurious and lax, leaders in

backsliding, discarding the duty of solitude; they, too, do not arouse energy for the attainment of the as-yet-unattained, for the achievement of the as-yet-unachieved, for the realization of the as-yet-unrealized. This is the fourth thing that leads to the decline and disappearance of the good Dhamma.

(5) "Again, there is a schism in the Saṅgha, and when there is a schism in the Saṅgha there are mutual insults, mutual reviling, mutual disparagement, and mutual rejection. Then those without confidence do not gain confidence, while some of those with confidence change their minds.[1152] This is the fifth thing that leads to the decline and disappearance of the good Dhamma.

"These are the five things that lead to the decline and disappearance of the good Dhamma.

"There are, bhikkhus, these five [other] things that lead to the continuation, non-decline, and non-disappearance of the good Dhamma. What five?

(1) "Here, the bhikkhus learn discourses that have been well acquired, with well set-down words and phrases. When the words and phrases are well set down, the meaning is well interpreted. This is the first thing that leads to the continuation, non-decline, and non-disappearance of the good Dhamma. [180]

(2) "Again, the bhikkhus are easy to correct and possess qualities that make them easy to correct. They are patient and accept instruction respectfully. This is the second thing that leads to the continuation, non-decline, and non-disappearance of the good Dhamma.

(3) "Again, those bhikkhus who are learned, experts on the Dhamma, experts on the discipline, experts on the outlines, respectfully teach the discourses to others. When they have passed away, the discourses are not cut off at the root, for there are those who preserve them. This is the third thing that leads to the continuation, non-decline, and non-disappearance of the good Dhamma.

(4) "Again, the elder bhikkhus are not luxurious and lax, but discard backsliding and take the lead in solitude; they arouse energy for the attainment of the as-yet-unattained, for the achievement of the as-yet-unachieved, for the realization of the as-yet-unrealized. [Those in] the next generation follow their example. They, too, do not become luxurious and lax, but discard backsliding and take the lead in solitude; they, too, arouse energy for the attainment of the as-yet-unattained, for

the achievement of the as-yet-unachieved, for the realization of the as-yet-unrealized. This is the fourth thing that leads to the continuation, non-decline, and non-disappearance of the good Dhamma.

(5) "Again, the Saṅgha is dwelling at ease—in concord, harmoniously, without disputes, with a single recitation. When the Saṅgha is in concord, there are no mutual insults, no mutual reviling, no mutual disparagement, and no mutual rejection. Then those without confidence gain confidence and those with confidence increase [in their confidence]. This is the fifth thing that leads to the continuation, non-decline, and non-disappearance of the good Dhamma.

"These, bhikkhus, are the five things that lead to the continuation, non-decline, and non-disappearance of the good Dhamma." [181]

157 (7) Wrongly Addressed Talk

"Bhikkhus, a talk is wrongly addressed when, having weighed one type of person against another, it is addressed to these five [inappropriate] types of persons. What five? A talk on faith is wrongly addressed to one devoid of faith; a talk on virtuous behavior is wrongly addressed to an immoral person; a talk on learning is wrongly addressed to one of little learning; a talk on generosity is wrongly addressed to a miser; a talk on wisdom is wrongly addressed to an unwise person.

(1) "And why, bhikkhus, is a talk on faith wrongly addressed to one devoid of faith? When a talk on faith is being given, a person devoid of faith loses his temper and becomes irritated, hostile, and stubborn; he displays anger, hatred, and bitterness. For what reason? Because he does not perceive that faith in himself and obtain rapture and joy based upon it. Therefore a talk on faith is wrongly addressed to a person devoid of faith.

(2) "And why is a talk on virtuous behavior wrongly addressed to an immoral person? When a talk on virtuous behavior is being given, an immoral person loses his temper and becomes irritated, hostile, and stubborn; he displays anger, hatred, and bitterness. For what reason? Because he does not perceive that virtuous behavior in himself and obtain rapture and joy based upon it. Therefore a talk on virtuous behavior is wrongly addressed to an immoral person.

(3) "And why is a talk on learning wrongly addressed to

a person of little learning? When a talk on learning is being given, a person of little learning loses his temper and becomes irritated, hostile, and stubborn; he displays anger, hatred, and bitterness. For what reason? Because he does not perceive that learning in himself and obtain rapture and joy based upon it. Therefore a talk on learning is wrongly addressed to a person of little learning.

(4) "And why is a talk on generosity wrongly addressed to a miser? When a talk on generosity is being given, a miser loses his temper and becomes irritated, hostile, and stubborn; he displays anger, hatred, and bitterness. For what reason? Because he does not perceive that generosity in himself and [182] obtain rapture and joy based upon it. Therefore a talk on generosity is wrongly addressed to a miser.

(5) "And why is a talk on wisdom wrongly addressed to an unwise person? When a talk on wisdom is being given, an unwise person loses his temper and becomes irritated, hostile, and stubborn; he displays anger, hatred, and bitterness. For what reason? Because he does not perceive that wisdom in himself and obtain rapture and joy based upon it. Therefore a talk on wisdom is wrongly addressed to an unwise person.

"A talk is wrongly addressed when, having weighed one type of person against another, it is addressed to these five [inappropriate] types of persons.

"Bhikkhus, a talk is properly addressed when, having weighed one type of person against another, it is addressed to these five [appropriate] types of persons. What five? A talk on faith is properly addressed to one endowed with faith; a talk on virtuous behavior is properly addressed to a virtuous person; a talk on learning is properly addressed to a learned person; a talk on generosity is properly addressed to a generous person; a talk on wisdom is properly addressed to a wise person.

(1) "And why, bhikkhus, is a talk on faith properly addressed to one endowed with faith? When a talk on faith is being given, a person endowed with faith does not lose his temper and become irritated, hostile, and stubborn; he does not display anger, hatred, and bitterness. For what reason? Because he perceives that faith in himself and obtains rapture and joy based upon it. Therefore a talk on faith is properly addressed to a person endowed with faith.

(2) "And why is a talk on virtuous behavior properly

addressed to a virtuous person? When a talk on virtuous behavior is being given, a virtuous person does not lose his temper and become irritated, hostile, and stubborn; he does not display anger, hatred, and bitterness. For what reason? Because he perceives that virtuous behavior in himself and obtains rapture and joy based upon it. Therefore a talk on virtuous behavior is properly addressed to a virtuous person.

(3) "And why is a talk on learning properly addressed to a learned person? When a talk on learning is being given, a learned person does not lose his temper and become irritated, hostile, and [183] stubborn; he does not display anger, hatred, and bitterness. For what reason? Because he perceives that learning in himself and obtains rapture and joy based upon it. Therefore a talk on learning is properly addressed to a learned person.

(4) "And why is a talk on generosity properly addressed to a generous person? When a talk on generosity is being given, a generous person does not lose his temper and become irritated, hostile, and stubborn; he does not display anger, hatred, and bitterness. For what reason? Because he perceives that generosity in himself and obtains rapture and joy based upon it. Therefore a talk on generosity is properly addressed to a generous person.

(5) "And why is a talk on wisdom properly addressed to a wise person? When a talk on wisdom is being given, a wise person does not lose his temper and become irritated, hostile, and stubborn; he does not display anger, hatred, and bitterness. For what reason? Because he perceives that wisdom in himself and obtains rapture and joy based upon it. Therefore a talk on wisdom is properly addressed to a wise person.

"Bhikkhus, a talk is properly addressed when, having weighed one type of person against another, it is addressed to these five [appropriate] types of persons."

158 (8) Timidity[1153]

"Bhikkhus, possessing five qualities, a bhikkhu is overcome by timidity. What five? Here, a bhikkhu is devoid of faith, immoral, unlearned, lazy, and unwise. Possessing these five qualities, a bhikkhu is overcome by timidity.

"Bhikkhus, possessing five [other] qualities, a bhikkhu is self-confident. What five? Here, a bhikkhu is endowed with faith, virtuous, learned, energetic, and wise. [184] Possessing these five qualities, a bhikkhu is self-confident."

159 (9) Udāyī

Thus have I heard. On one occasion the Blessed One was dwelling at Kosambī in Ghosita's Park. Now on that occasion the Venerable Udāyī, surrounded by a large assembly of laypeople, was sitting teaching the Dhamma.[1154] The Venerable Ānanda saw this and approached the Blessed One, paid homage to him, sat down to one side, and said: "Bhante, the Venerable Udāyī, surrounded by a large assembly of laypeople, is teaching the Dhamma."

"It isn't easy, Ānanda, to teach the Dhamma to others. One who teaches the Dhamma to others should first set up five qualities internally. What five? (1) [Having determined:] 'I will give a progressive talk,' one should teach the Dhamma to others.[1155] (2) [Having determined:] 'I will give a talk that shows reasons,' one should teach the Dhamma to others.[1156] (3) [Having determined:] 'I will give a talk out of sympathy,' one should teach the Dhamma to others. (4) [Having determined:] 'I will not give a talk while intent on material gain,' one should teach the Dhamma to others. (5) [Having determined:] 'I will give a talk without harming myself or others,' one should teach the Dhamma to others. It isn't easy, Ānanda, to teach the Dhamma to others. One who teaches the Dhamma to others should first set up these five qualities internally."

160 (10) Hard to Dispel

"Bhikkhus, these five things, once arisen, are hard to dispel. What five? [185] Lust, once arisen, is hard to dispel. Hatred... Delusion... Discernment... The urge to travel, once arisen, is hard to dispel. These five things, once arisen, are hard to dispel."

II. Resentment

161 (1) Removing Resentment (1)

"Bhikkhus, there are these five ways of removing resentment by which a bhikkhu should entirely remove resentment when it has arisen toward anyone.[1157] What five? (1) One should develop loving-kindness for the person one resents; in this way one should remove the resentment toward that person. (2) One should develop compassion for the person one resents; in this way one should remove the resentment toward that person. (3) One should develop equanimity toward the person one resents; in this way one should remove the resentment toward that person. [186] (4) One should disregard the person one resents and pay no attention to him; in this way one should remove the resentment toward that person. (5) One should apply the idea of the ownership of kamma to the person one resents, thus: 'This venerable one is the owner of his kamma, the heir of his kamma; he has kamma as his origin, kamma as his relative, kamma as his resort; he will be the heir of any kamma he does, good or bad.' In this way one should remove the resentment toward that person. These are the five ways of removing resentment by which a bhikkhu should entirely remove resentment when it has arisen toward anyone."

162 (2) Removing Resentment (2)

There the Venerable Sāriputta addressed the bhikkhus: "Friends, bhikkhus!"

"Friend," those bhikkhus replied. The Venerable Sāriputta said this:

"Friends, there are these five ways of removing resentment by which a bhikkhu should entirely remove resentment when it has arisen toward anyone. What five? (1) Here, a person's bodily behavior is impure, but his verbal behavior is pure; one should remove resentment toward such a person. (2) A person's verbal behavior is impure, but his bodily behavior is pure; one should also remove resentment toward such a person. (3) A person's bodily behavior and verbal behavior are impure, but from time to time he gains an opening of the mind, placidity of mind;[1158] one should also remove resentment toward such a person. (4) A person's bodily behavior and verbal behavior are impure, and he does not gain [187] an opening of the mind, placidity of mind from time to time; one should also remove resentment toward such a person. (5) A person's bodily behavior and verbal behavior are pure, and from time to time he gains an opening of the mind, placidity of mind; one should also remove resentment toward such a person.

(1) "How, friends, should resentment be removed toward the person whose bodily behavior is impure but whose verbal behavior is pure? Suppose a rag-robed bhikkhu sees a rag by the roadside. He would press it down with his left foot, spread it out with his right foot, tear off an intact section, and take it away with him; so too, when a person's bodily behavior is impure but his verbal behavior is pure, on that occasion one should not attend to the impurity of his bodily behavior but should instead attend to the purity of his verbal behavior. In this way resentment toward that person should be removed.

(2) "How, friends, should resentment be removed toward the person whose verbal behavior is impure but whose bodily behavior is pure? Suppose there is a pond covered with algae and water plants. A man might arrive, afflicted and oppressed by the heat, weary, thirsty, and parched. He would plunge into the pond, sweep away the algae and water plants with his hands, drink from his cupped hands, and then leave; so too, [188] when a person's verbal behavior is impure but his bodily behavior is pure, on that occasion one should not attend to the impurity of his verbal behavior but should instead attend to the purity of his bodily behavior. In this way resentment toward that person should be removed.

(3) "How, friends, should resentment be removed toward the person whose bodily behavior and verbal behavior are impure but who from time to time gains an opening of the mind, placidity of mind? Suppose there is a little water in a puddle. Then a person might arrive, afflicted and oppressed by the heat, weary, thirsty, and parched. He would think: 'This little bit of water is in the puddle. If I try to drink it with my cupped hands or a vessel, I will stir it up, disturb it, and make it undrinkable. Let me get down on all fours, suck it up like a cow, and depart.' He then gets down on all fours, sucks the water up like a cow, and departs. So too, when a person's bodily behavior and verbal behavior are impure but from time to time he gains an opening of the mind, placidity of mind, on that occasion one should not attend to the impurity of his bodily and verbal behavior, but should instead attend [189] to the opening of the mind, the placidity of mind, he gains from time to time. In this way resentment toward that person should be removed.

(4) "How, friends, should resentment be removed toward the

person whose bodily and verbal behavior are impure and who does not gain an opening of the mind, placidity of mind, from time to time? Suppose a sick, afflicted, gravely ill person was traveling along a highway, and the last village behind him and the next village ahead of him were both far away. He would not obtain suitable food and medicine or a qualified attendant; he would not get [to meet] the leader of the village district. Another man traveling along the highway might see him and arouse sheer compassion, sympathy, and tender concern for him, thinking: 'Oh, may this man obtain suitable food, suitable medicine, and a qualified attendant! May he get [to meet] the leader of the village district! For what reason? So that this man does not encounter calamity and disaster right here.' So too, when a person's bodily and verbal behavior are impure and he does not gain from time to time an opening of the mind, placidity of mind, on that occasion one should arouse sheer compassion, sympathy, and tender concern for him, thinking, 'Oh, may this venerable one abandon bodily misbehavior and develop good bodily behavior; may he abandon verbal misbehavior and develop good verbal behavior; may he abandon mental misbehavior and develop good mental behavior! For what reason? So that, with the breakup of the body, after death, he will not be reborn in the plane of misery, in a bad destination, in the lower world, in hell.' In this way resentment toward that person should be removed. [190]

(5) "How, friends, should resentment be removed toward the person whose bodily and verbal behavior are pure and who from time to time gains an opening of the mind, placidity of mind? Suppose there were a pond with clear, sweet, cool water, clean, with smooth banks, a delightful place shaded by various trees. Then a man might arrive, afflicted and oppressed by the heat, weary, thirsty, and parched. Having plunged into the pond, he would bathe and drink, and then, after coming out, he would sit or lie down in the shade of a tree right there. So too, when a person's bodily and verbal behavior are pure and from time to time he gains an opening of the mind, placidity of mind, on that occasion one should attend to his pure bodily behavior, to his pure verbal behavior, and to the opening of the mind, the placidity of mind, that he gains from time to time. In this way resentment toward that person should be removed. Friends, by

means of a person who inspires confidence in every way, the mind gains confidence.[1159]

"These, friends, are the five ways of removing resentment by means of which a bhikkhu can entirely remove resentment toward whomever it has arisen."

163 (3) Discussions

[This sutta is identical with 5:65, except that it is spoken by Sāriputta to the bhikkhus.] [191]

164 (4) Way of Life

[This sutta is identical with 5:66, except that it is spoken by Sāriputta to the bhikkhus.]

165 (5) Asking Questions

There the Venerable Sāriputta . . . said this:

"Friends, whoever asks another person a question does so for five reasons or for a particular one among them. What five? (1) One asks another person a question because of one's dullness and stupidity; (2) one with evil desires, motivated by desire, asks another person a question; [192] (3) one asks another person a question as a way of reviling [the other person]; (4) one asks another person a question because one wishes to learn; (5) or one asks another person a question with the thought: 'If, when he is asked a question by me, he answers correctly, that is good; but if he does not answer correctly, I will give him a correct explanation.' Friends, whoever asks another person a question does so for these five reasons or for a particular one among them. Friends, I ask another person a question with the thought: 'If, when he is asked a question by me, he answers correctly, that is good; but if he does not answer correctly, I will give him a correct explanation.'"

166 (6) Cessation

There the Venerable Sāriputta . . . said this:

"Here, friends, a bhikkhu accomplished in virtuous behavior, concentration, and wisdom might enter and emerge from the cessation of perception and feeling. There is this possibility. But if he does not reach final knowledge in this very life, having been reborn among a certain group of mind-made [deities] that transcend the company of devas that subsist on edible food, he might [again] enter and emerge from the cessation of perception and feeling.[1160] There is this possibility."

When this was said, the Venerable Udāyī said to the Venerable Sāriputta: "This is impossible, friend Sāriputta, it cannot happen that a bhikkhu, having been reborn among a certain group of mind-made [deities] that transcend the company of devas that subsist on edible food, might [again] enter and emerge from the cessation of perception and feeling. There is no such possibility."

A second time . . . A third time, [193] the Venerable Sāriputta said: "Here, friends, it is possible that a bhikkhu accomplished in virtuous behavior . . . having been reborn among a certain group of mind-made [deities] . . . might [again] enter and emerge from the cessation of perception and feeling. There is this possibility." A third time, the Venerable Udāyī said to the Venerable Sāriputta: "This is impossible, friend Sāriputta, it cannot happen that a bhikkhu, having been reborn among a certain group of mind-made [deities] . . . might [again] enter and emerge from the cessation of perception and feeling. There is no such possibility."

Then it occurred to the Venerable Sāriputta: "The Venerable Udāyī has rejected me up to the third time, and not a single bhikkhu expresses agreement with me. Let me approach the Blessed One." Then the Venerable Sāriputta approached the Blessed One, paid homage to him, sat down to one side, and addressed the bhikkhus: "Here, friends, a bhikkhu accomplished in virtuous behavior, concentration, and wisdom might [again] enter and emerge from the cessation of perception and feeling. There is this possibility. If he does not reach final knowledge in this very life, having been reborn among a certain group of mind-made [deities] that transcend the company of devas that subsist on edible food, he might [again] enter and emerge from the cessation of perception and feeling. There is this possibility."

When this was said, the Venerable Udāyī said to the Venerable Sāriputta: "This is impossible, friend Sāriputta, it cannot happen that a bhikkhu, having been reborn among a certain group of mind-made [deities] transcending the company of devas that subsist on edible food, might [again] enter and emerge from the cessation of perception and feeling. There is no such possibility."

A second time . . . A third time, the Venerable Sāriputta addressed the bhikkhus: "Here, friends, a bhikkhu accomplished in virtuous behavior . . . [194] . . . having been reborn among a certain group of mind-made [deities] . . . might [again] enter and emerge from the cessation of perception and feeling. There is this possibility." A third time, the Venerable Udāyī said to the Venerable Sāriputta: "This is impossible, friend Sāriputta, it cannot happen that a bhikkhu . . . reborn among a certain group of mind-made [deities] . . . might [again] enter and emerge from the cessation of perception and feeling. There is no such possibility."

Then it occurred to the Venerable Sāriputta: "Even when I am in the presence of the Blessed One, the Venerable Udāyī rejects me up to the third time, and not a single bhikkhu expresses agreement with me. Let me just keep silent." Then the Venerable Sāriputta fell silent.

Then the Blessed One addressed the Venerable Udāyī: "Udāyī, just what do you understand by a mind-made group?"

"Bhante, it is those devas that are formless, perception-made."[1161]

"What are you saying, Udāyī, you foolish and incompetent fellow? Yet you think you have to speak up!"

Then the Blessed One addressed the Venerable Ānanda: "Ānanda, do you just look on passively as an elder bhikkhu is being harassed? Don't you have any compassion toward an elder bhikkhu when he's being harassed?"

Then the Blessed One addressed the bhikkhus: "Here, bhikkhus, a bhikkhu accomplished in virtuous behavior, concentration, and wisdom might enter and emerge from the cessation of perception and feeling. If he does not reach final knowledge in this very life, then, having been reborn among a certain group of mind-made [deities] that transcend the company of devas that subsist on edible food, he might [again] enter and emerge from the cessation of perception and feeling. There is this possibility." This is what the Blessed One said. Having said this, the Fortunate One got up from his seat and entered his dwelling. [195]

Then, not long after the Blessed One had left, the Venerable Ānanda approached the Venerable Upavāṇa and said to him: "Here, friend Upavāṇa, they were harassing other elder bhikkhus, but we didn't question them.[1162] It would not be surprising if this evening, when he emerges from seclusion, the Blessed One makes a pronouncement about this matter, and he might call upon the Venerable Upavāṇa himself [to give an account].[1163] Just now I feel timid."

Then, in the evening, the Blessed One emerged from seclusion and went to the meeting hall. He sat down in the appointed seat and said to the Venerable Upavāṇa:

"Upavāṇa, how many qualities should an elder bhikkhu possess to be pleasing and agreeable to his fellow monks and to be respected and esteemed by them?"

"Possessing five qualities, Bhante, an elder bhikkhu is pleasing and agreeable to his fellow monks and is respected and esteemed by them. What five? (1) He is virtuous; he dwells restrained by the Pātimokkha . . . [as in 5:134] . . . he trains in them. (2) He has learned much . . . [as in 5:134] . . . he has penetrated well by view. (3) He is a good speaker with a good delivery; he is gifted with speech that is polished, clear, articulate, expressive of the meaning. (4) He gains at will, without trouble or difficulty, the four jhānas that constitute the higher mind and are pleasant dwellings in this very life. (5) With the destruction of the taints, he has realized for himself with direct knowledge, in this very life, the taintless liberation of mind, liberation by wisdom, and having entered upon it, he dwells in it. Possessing these five qualities, an elder is pleasing and agreeable to his fellow monks and is respected and esteemed by them." [196]

"Good, good, Upavāṇa! Possessing those five qualities, an elder is pleasing and agreeable to his fellow monks and is respected and esteemed by them. But if these five qualities are not found in an elder bhikkhu, why should his fellow monks honor, respect, esteem, and venerate him?[1164] On account of his broken teeth, grey hair, and wrinkled skin? But because these five qualities are found in an elder bhikkhu, his fellow monks honor, respect, esteem, and venerate him."

167 (7) Reproving

There the Venerable Sāriputta addressed the bhikkhus thus: . . .

"Friends, a bhikkhu who wishes to reprove another should first establish five things in himself. What five? (1) [He should consider:] 'I will speak at a proper time, not at an improper time;

(2) I will speak truthfully, not falsely; (3) I will speak gently, not harshly; (4) I will speak in a beneficial way, not in a harmful way; (5) I will speak with a mind of loving-kindness, not while harboring hatred.' A bhikkhu who wishes to reprove another should first establish these five things in himself.

"Here, friends, I see some person being reproved at an improper time, not disturbed[1165] at a proper time; being reproved about what is false, not disturbed about what is true; being reproved harshly, not disturbed gently; being reproved in a harmful way, not disturbed in a beneficial way; being reproved by one who harbors hatred, not disturbed by one with a mind of loving-kindness.

"Friends, when a bhikkhu is reproved in a way contrary to the Dhamma, non-remorse should be induced in him in five ways: (1) 'Friend, you were reproved at an improper time, not [197] at a proper time; that is sufficient for you to be without remorse. (2) You were reproved falsely, not truthfully; that is sufficient for you to be without remorse. (3) You were reproved harshly, not gently; that is sufficient for you to be without remorse. (4) You were reproved in a harmful way, not in a beneficial way; that is sufficient for you to be without remorse. (5) You were reproved by one harboring hatred, not by one with a mind of loving-kindness; that is sufficient for you to be without remorse.' When a bhikkhu is reproved in a way contrary to the Dhamma, non-remorse should be induced in him in these five ways.

"Friends, when a bhikkhu reproves in a way contrary to the Dhamma, remorse should be induced in him in five ways: (1) 'Friend, you reproved him at an improper time, not at a proper time; that is sufficient for you to feel remorse. (2) You reproved him falsely, not truthfully; that is sufficient for you to feel remorse. (3) You reproved him harshly, not gently; that is sufficient for you to feel remorse. (4) You reproved him in a harmful way, not in a beneficial way; that is sufficient for you to feel remorse. (5) You reproved him while harboring hatred, not with a mind of loving-kindness; that is sufficient for you to feel remorse.' When a bhikkhu reproves in a way contrary to the Dhamma, remorse should be induced in him in these five ways. For what reason? So that another bhikkhu would not think of reproving falsely.

"Here, friends, I see some person being reproved at a proper time, not disturbed at an improper time; being reproved truthfully, not disturbed falsely; being reproved gently, not disturbed harshly; being reproved in a beneficial way, not disturbed in a harmful way; being reproved by one with a mind of loving-kindness, not disturbed by one who harbors hatred.

"Friends, when a bhikkhu is reproved in accordance with the Dhamma, remorse should be induced in him in five ways: (1) 'Friend, you were reproved at a proper time, not at an improper time; that is sufficient for you to feel remorse. (2) You were reproved truthfully, not falsely; that is sufficient for you to feel remorse. (3) You were reproved gently, not harshly; that is sufficient for you to feel remorse. (4) You were reproved in a beneficial way, not in a harmful way; that is sufficient for you to feel remorse. (5) You were reproved by one with a mind of loving-kindness, not by one harboring hatred; that is sufficient for you to feel remorse.' [198] When a bhikkhu is reproved in accordance with the Dhamma, remorse should be induced in him in these five ways.

"Friends, when a bhikkhu reproves in accordance with the Dhamma, non-remorse should be induced in him in five ways: (1) 'Friend, you reproved him at a proper time, not at an improper time; that is sufficient for you to be without remorse. (2) You reproved him truthfully, not falsely; that is sufficient for you to be without remorse. (3) You reproved him gently, not harshly; that is sufficient for you to be without remorse. (4) You reproved him in a beneficial way, not in a harmful way; that is sufficient for you to be without remorse. (5) You reproved him with a mind of loving-kindness, not while harboring hatred; that is sufficient for you to be without remorse.' When a bhikkhu reproves in accordance with the Dhamma, non-remorse should be induced in him in these five ways. For what reason? So that another bhikkhu would think of reproving about what is true.

"Friends, a person who is reproved should be established in two things: in truth and non-anger. If others should reprove me—whether at a proper time or at an improper time; whether about what is true or about what is false; whether gently or harshly; whether in a beneficial way or in a harmful way; whether with a mind of loving-kindness or while harboring hatred—I should still be established in two things: in truth and non-anger.

"If I know: 'There is such a quality in me,' I tell him: 'It exists. This quality is found in me.' If I know: 'There is no such quality in me,' I tell him: 'It doesn't exist. This quality isn't found in me.'

[The Blessed One said:] "Sariputta, even when you are speaking to them in such a way, some foolish men here do not respectfully accept what you say."

"There are, Bhante, persons devoid of faith who have gone forth from the household life into homelessness, not [199] out of faith but intent on earning a living; they are crafty, hypocritical, deceptive, restless, puffed up, vain, talkative, rambling in their talk, unguarded over the doors of the senses, immoderate in eating, not intent on wakefulness, indifferent to the ascetic life, not keenly respectful of the training, luxurious and lax, leaders in backsliding, discarding the duty of solitude, lazy, devoid of energy, muddle-minded, lacking in clear comprehension, unconcentrated, with wandering minds, unwise, stupid. When I speak to them in such a way, they do not respectfully accept what I say.

"But, Bhante, there are clansmen who have gone forth from the household life into homelessness out of faith, who are not crafty, hypocritical, deceptive, restless, puffed up, vain, talkative, and rambling in their talk; who keep guard over the doors of the senses; who are moderate in eating, intent on wakefulness, intent upon the ascetic life, keenly respectful of the training; who are not luxurious and lax; who discard backsliding and take the lead in solitude; who are energetic, resolute, mindful, clearly comprehending, concentrated, with one-pointed minds, wise, intelligent. When I speak to them in such a way, they respectfully accept what I say."

"Sāriputta, leave alone those people who are devoid of faith and have gone forth from the household life into homelessness, not out of faith but intent on earning a living; who are crafty . . . unwise, stupid. But, Sariputta, you should speak to those clansmen who have gone forth from the household life into homelessness out of faith, who are not crafty . . . who are wise, intelligent. [200] Exhort your fellow monks, Sāriputta! Instruct your fellow monks, Sāriputta, [thinking:] 'I will cause my fellow monks to emerge from what is contrary to the good Dhamma and will establish them in the good Dhamma.' Thus, Sāriputta, should you train yourself."

168 (8) Virtuous Behavior

[This sutta is identical with 5:24, except that it is spoken by Sāriputta to the bhikkhus.] [201]

169 (9) Of Quick Apprehension

Then the Venerable Ānanda approached the Venerable Sāriputta and exchanged greetings with him. When they had concluded their greetings and cordial talk, he sat down to one side and said: "In what way, friend Sāriputta, is a bhikkhu one of quick apprehension concerning wholesome teachings, one who grasps well what he has learned, learns abundantly, and does not forget what he has learned?"

"The Venerable Ānanda is learned, so let him clear this up himself."

"Then listen, friend Sāriputta, and attend closely. I will speak."

"Yes, friend," the Venerable Sāriputta replied. The Venerable Ānanda said this:

"Here, friend Sāriputta, a bhikkhu is skilled in meaning, skilled in the Dhamma, skilled in language, skilled in phrasing, and skilled in sequence.[1166] In this way, friend Sāriputta, a bhikkhu is one of quick apprehension concerning wholesome teachings, one who grasps well what he has learned, learns abundantly, and does not forget what he has learned."

"It's astounding and amazing, friend, how well this has been stated by the Venerable Ānanda! We consider the Venerable Ānanda to be one who possesses these five qualities: 'The Venerable Ānanda is skilled in meaning, skilled in Dhamma, skilled in language, skilled in phrasing, and skilled in sequence.'" [202]

170 (10) Bhaddaji

On one occasion the Venerable Ānanda was dwelling at Kosambī in Ghosita's Park. Then the Venerable Bhaddaji approached the Venerable Ānanda and exchanged greetings with him. When they had concluded their greetings and cordial talk, he sat down to one side. The Venerable Ānanda then said to him:

"Friend Bhaddaji, what is the foremost of sights? What is the foremost kind of hearing? What is the foremost happiness? What is the foremost perception? What is the foremost among states of existence?"

"(1) There is, friend, Brahmā, the vanquisher, the unvanquished, the universal seer, the wielder of power. Getting to see Brahmā is the foremost sight. (2) There are the devas of streaming radiance who are suffused and inundated with happiness. They sometimes utter the inspired utterance: 'Oh, what happiness! Oh, what happiness!' Getting to hear that sound is the foremost kind of hearing. (3) There are the devas of refulgent glory. Being happy, they experience very peaceful happiness:[1167] this is the foremost happiness. (4) There are the devas of the base of nothingness: this is the foremost perception. (5) There are the devas of the base of neither-perception-nor-nonperception: this is the foremost state of existence."

"Then does the Venerable Bhaddaji agree with the multitude about this?"[1168]

"The Venerable Ānanda is learned, so let him clear this up himself."

"Then listen, friend Bhaddaji, and attend closely. I will speak."

"Yes, friend," the Venerable Bhaddaji replied. The Venerable Ānanda said this:

"(1) In whatever way, friend, one sees such that immediately afterward the destruction of the taints occurs:[1169] this is the foremost sight. (2) In whatever way one hears such that immediately afterward the destruction of the taints occurs: this is the foremost kind of hearing. (3) In whatever way one is happy such that immediately afterward the destruction of the taints occurs: this is the foremost happiness. (4) In whatever way one perceives such that immediately afterward the destruction of the taints occurs: this is the foremost perception. (5) In whatever way one exists such that immediately afterward the destruction of the taints occurs: this is the foremost state of existence." [203]

III. The Lay Follower

171 (1) Timidity

On one occasion the Blessed One was dwelling at Sāvatthī in Jeta's Grove, Anāthapiṇḍika's Park. There the Blessed One addressed the bhikkhus: "Bhikkhus!"

"Venerable sir!" those bhikkhus replied. The Blessed One said this:

"Bhikkhus, possessing five qualities, a lay follower is overcome by timidity. What five? He destroys life, takes what is not given, engages in sexual misconduct, speaks falsely, and indulges in liquor, wine, and intoxicants, the basis for heedlessness. Possessing these five qualities, a lay follower is overcome by timidity.

"Bhikkhus, possessing five qualities, a lay follower is self-confident. What five? He abstains from the destruction of life, abstains from taking what is not given, abstains from sexual misconduct, abstains from false speech, abstains from liquor, wine, and intoxicants, the basis for heedlessness. Possessing these five qualities, a lay follower is self-confident."

172 (2) Self-Confidence

"Bhikkhus, possessing five qualities, a lay follower dwells without self-confidence at home. What five? [204] He destroys life, takes what is not given, engages in sexual misconduct, speaks falsely, and indulges in liquor, wine, and intoxicants, the basis for heedlessness. Possessing these five qualities, a lay follower dwells without self-confidence at home.

"Bhikkhus, possessing five qualities, a lay follower dwells self-confident at home. What five? He abstains from the destruction of life, abstains from taking what is not given, abstains from sexual misconduct, abstains from false speech, abstains from liquor, wine, and intoxicants, the basis for heedlessness. Possessing these five qualities, a lay follower dwells self-confident at home."

173 (3) Hell

"Bhikkhus, possessing five qualities, a lay follower is deposited in hell as if brought there. What five? He destroys life, takes what is not given, engages in sexual misconduct, speaks falsely, and indulges in liquor, wine, and intoxicants, the basis for heedlessness. Possessing these five qualities, a lay follower is deposited in hell as if brought there.

"Bhikkhus, possessing five qualities, a lay follower is deposited in heaven as if brought there. What five? He abstains from the destruction of life, abstains from taking what is not given, abstains from sexual misconduct, abstains from false speech, abstains from liquor, wine, and intoxicants, the basis for heedlessness. Possessing these five qualities, a lay follower is deposited in heaven as if brought there."

174 (4) Enmities

Then the householder Anāthapiṇḍika approached the Blessed One, paid homage to him, and sat down to one side. The Blessed One then said to him:

"Householder, without having abandoned five perils and enmities, one is called immoral and is reborn in hell. What five? The destruction of life, taking what is not given, sexual misconduct, false speech, and [indulging in] liquor, wine, and intoxicants, the basis for heedlessness. [205] Without having abandoned these five perils and enmities, one is called immoral and is reborn in hell.

"Householder, having abandoned five perils and enmities, one is called virtuous and is reborn in heaven. What five? The destruction of life . . . and [indulging in] liquor, wine, and intoxicants, the basis for heedlessness. Having abandoned these five perils and enmities, one is called virtuous and is reborn in heaven.

(1) "Householder, one who destroys life thereby engenders peril and enmity pertaining to the present life and the future life, and also experiences mental pain and dejection. One who abstains from the destruction of life does not engender peril and enmity pertaining to the present life and the future life, nor does he experience mental pain and dejection. For one who abstains from the destruction of life, that peril and enmity has thus subsided.

(2) "Householder, one who takes what is not given . . . (3) . . . engages in sexual misconduct . . . (4) . . . speaks falsely . . . (5) . . . indulges in liquor, wine, and intoxicants, the basis for heedlessness, thereby engenders peril and enmity pertaining to

the present life and the future life, and also experiences mental pain and dejection. One who abstains from liquor, wine, and intoxicants, the basis for heedlessness, does not engender peril and enmity pertaining to the present life and the future life, nor does he experience mental pain and dejection. For one who abstains from liquor, wine, and intoxicants, the basis for heedlessness, that peril and enmity has thus subsided."

There's a man in the world who destroys life,
speaks falsely, and takes what is not given,
who goes to the wives of others,
and indulges in liquor and wine.

Harboring within the five enmities,
he is called immoral.
With the breakup of the body,
that unwise person is reborn in hell.

But there is a man in the world
who does not destroy life,
speak falsely, take what is not given,
go to the wives of others, [206]
or indulge in liquor and wine.

Having abandoned the five enmities,
he is called virtuous.
With the breakup of the body,
that wise person is reborn in heaven.

175 (5) Caṇḍāla

"Bhikkhus, possessing five qualities, a lay follower is a caṇḍāla of a lay follower, a stain of a lay follower, the last among lay followers.[1170] What five? (1) He is devoid of faith; (2) he is immoral; (3) he is superstitious and believes in auspicious signs, not in kamma; (4) he seeks outside here for a person worthy of offerings;[1171] and (5) he first does [meritorious] deeds there. Possessing these five qualities, a lay follower is a caṇḍāla of a lay follower, a stain of a lay follower, the last among lay followers.

"Bhikkhus, possessing five qualities, a lay follower is a gem of a lay follower, a red lotus of a lay follower, a white lotus of a lay follower.[1172] What five? (1) He is endowed with faith; (2) he is virtuous; (3) he is not superstitious and believes in kamma, not in auspicious signs; (4) he does not seek outside here for a person worthy of offerings; and he first does [meritorious] deeds here. Possessing these five qualities, a lay follower is a gem of a lay follower, a red lotus of a lay follower, a white lotus of a lay follower."

176 (6) Rapture

Then the householder Anāthapiṇḍika, accompanied by five hundred lay followers, approached the Blessed One, paid homage to him, and sat down to one side. The Blessed One then said to the householder Anāthapiṇḍika [and his retinue]:

"Householders, you have presented robes, almsfood, lodgings, and medicines and provisions for the sick to the Saṅgha of bhikkhus. You should not be content merely with this much, [thinking]: 'We have presented robes, almsfood, lodgings, and medicines and provisions for the sick to the Saṅgha of bhikkhus.' Therefore, householders, you should train yourselves thus: [207] 'How can we from time to time enter and dwell in the rapture of solitude?'[1173] It is in such a way that you should train yourselves."

When this was said, the Venerable Sāriputta said to the Blessed One: "It's astounding and amazing, Bhante, how well that was said by the Blessed One. Bhante, whenever a noble disciple enters and dwells in the rapture of solitude, on that occasion five things do not occur in him. (1) Pain and dejection connected with sensuality do not occur in him. (2) Pleasure and joy connected with sensuality do not occur in him. (3) Pain and dejection connected with the unwholesome do not occur in him. (4) Pleasure and joy connected with the unwholesome do not occur in him. (5) Pain and dejection connected with the wholesome do not occur in him. Bhante, whenever a noble disciple enters and dwells in the rapture of solitude, on that occasion these five things do not occur in him."

"Good, good, Sāriputta! Sāriputta, whenever [208] a noble disciple enters and dwells in the rapture of solitude... [The Buddha repeats in full the entire statement of the Venerable Sāriputta, down to:]... on that occasion these five things do not occur in him."

177 (7) Trades

"Bhikkhus, a lay follower should not engage in these five trades. What five? Trading in weapons, trading in living beings, trading in meat, trading in intoxicants, and trading in poisons. A lay follower should not engage in these five trades."

178 (8) Kings

(1) "Bhikkhus, what do you think? Have you ever seen or heard that when a person abandons and abstains from the destruction of life, kings have him arrested on the charge of so abstaining and then execute him, imprison him, banish him, or do with him as the occasion demands?"

"Surely not, Bhante."

"Good, bhikkhus! I too have not seen or heard of such a thing. But rather [209] it is when they inform kings of his evil deed, saying: 'This person has taken the life of a woman or a man,' that kings have him arrested on the charge of taking life and then execute him, imprison him, banish him, or do with him as the occasion demands. Have you ever seen or heard of such a case?"

"We have seen this, Bhante, and we have heard of it, and we will hear of it [in time to come]."

(2) "Bhikkhus, what do you think? Have you ever seen or heard that when a person abandons and abstains from taking what is not given, kings have him arrested on the charge of so abstaining and then execute him, imprison him, banish him, or do with him as the occasion demands?"

"Surely not, Bhante."

"Good, bhikkhus! I too have not seen or heard of such a thing. But rather it is when they inform kings of his evil deed, saying: 'This person has stolen something from the village or forest,' that kings have him arrested on the charge of stealing and then execute him, imprison him, banish him, or do with him as the occasion demands. Have you ever seen or heard of such a case?"

"We have seen this, Bhante, and we have heard of it, and we will hear of it [in time to come]."

(3) "Bhikkhus, what do you think? Have you ever seen or heard that when a person abandons and abstains from sexual misconduct, kings have him arrested on the charge of so

abstaining and then execute him, imprison him, banish him, or do with him as the occasion demands?"

"Surely not, Bhante."

"Good, bhikkhus! I too have not seen or heard of such a thing. [210] But rather it is when they inform kings of his evil deed, saying: 'This man has committed misconduct with someone else's women and girls,' that kings have him arrested on the charge of sexual misconduct and then execute him, imprison him, banish him, or do with him as the occasion demands. Have you ever seen or heard of such a case?"

"We have seen this, Bhante, and we have heard of it, and we will hear of it [in time to come]."

(4) "Bhikkhus, what do you think? Have you ever seen or heard that when a person abandons and abstains from false speech, kings have him arrested on the charge of so abstaining and then execute him, imprison him, banish him, or do with him as the occasion demands?"

"Surely not, Bhante."

"Good, bhikkhus! I too have not seen or heard of such a thing. But rather it is when they inform kings of his evil deed, saying: 'This person has ruined a householder or a householder's son with false speech,' that kings have him arrested on the charge of false speech and then execute him, imprison him, banish him, or do with him as the occasion demands. Have you ever seen or heard of such a case?"

"We have seen this, Bhante, and we have heard of it, and we will hear of it [in time to come]."

(5) "Bhikkhus, what do you think? Have you ever seen or heard that when a person abandons and abstains from liquor, wine, and intoxicants, the basis for heedlessness, kings have him arrested on the charge of so abstaining and then execute him, imprison him, banish him, or do with him as the occasion demands?"

"Surely not, Bhante."

"Good, bhikkhus! I too have not seen or heard of such a thing. [211] But rather it is when they inform kings of his evil deed, saying: 'This person, under the influence of liquor, wine, and intoxicants, has taken the life of a woman or a man; or he has stolen something from a village or a forest; or he has committed misconduct with someone else's women and girls; or he has ruined a householder or a householder's son with false speech,' that kings have him arrested on the charge of using liquor, wine, and intoxicants, the basis for heedlessness, and then execute him, imprison him, banish him, or do with him as the occasion demands. Have you ever seen or heard of such a case?"

"We have seen this, Bhante, and we have heard of it, and we will hear of it [in time to come]."

179 (9) A Layman

Then the householder Anāthapiṇḍika, accompanied by five hundred lay followers, approached the Blessed One, paid homage to him, and sat down to one side. The Blessed One then addressed the Venerable Sāriputta: "You should know, Sāriputta, that any white-robed householder whose actions are restrained by five training rules and who gains at will, without trouble or difficulty, four pleasant visible dwellings that pertain to the higher mind, might, if he so wished, declare of himself: 'I am finished with hell, the animal realm, and the sphere of afflicted spirits; I am finished with the plane of misery, the bad destination, the lower world; I am a stream-enterer, no longer subject to [rebirth in] the lower world, fixed in destiny, heading for enlightenment.'

(1) "What are the five training rules by which his actions are restrained? [212] Here, Sāriputta, a noble disciple abstains from the destruction of life, from taking what is not given, from sexual misconduct, from false speech, and from liquor, wine, and intoxicants, the basis for heedlessness. His actions are restrained by these five training rules.

"What are the four pleasant visible dwellings that pertain to the higher mind, which he gains at will, without trouble or difficulty?

(2) "Here, the noble disciple possesses unwavering confidence in the Buddha thus: 'The Blessed One is an arahant, perfectly enlightened, accomplished in true knowledge and conduct, fortunate, knower of the world, unsurpassed trainer of persons to be tamed, teacher of devas and humans, the Enlightened One, the Blessed One.' This is the first pleasant visible dwelling that pertains to the higher mind, which he has achieved for the purification of the impure mind, for the cleansing of the unclean mind.

(3) "Again, the noble disciple possesses unwavering confidence in the Dhamma thus: 'The Dhamma is well expounded by the Blessed One, directly visible, immediate, inviting one to come and see, applicable, to be personally experienced by the wise.' This is the second pleasant visible dwelling that pertains to the higher mind, which he has achieved for the purification of the impure mind, for the cleansing of the unclean mind.

(4) "Again, the noble disciple possesses unwavering confidence in the Saṅgha thus: 'The Saṅgha of the Blessed One's disciples is practicing the good way, practicing the straight way, practicing the true way, practicing the proper way; that is, the four pairs of persons, the eight types of individual—this Saṅgha of the Blessed One's disciples is worthy of gifts, worthy of hospitality, worthy of offerings, worthy of reverential salutation, the unsurpassed field of merit for the world.' This is the third pleasant visible dwelling that pertains to the higher mind, which he has achieved [213] for the purification of the impure mind, for the cleansing of the unclean mind.

(5) "Again, the noble disciple possesses the virtuous behavior loved by the noble ones, unbroken, flawless, unblemished, unblotched, freeing, praised by the wise, ungrasped, leading to concentration. This is the fourth pleasant visible dwelling that pertains to the higher mind, which he has achieved for the purification of the impure mind, for the cleansing of the unclean mind.

"These are the four pleasant visible dwellings that pertain to the higher mind, which he gains at will, without trouble or difficulty.

"You should know, Sāriputta, that any white-robed householder whose actions are restrained by these five training rules and who gains at will, without trouble or difficulty, these four pleasant visible dwellings that pertain to the higher mind, might, if he so wished, declare of himself: 'I am finished with hell, the animal realm, and the sphere of afflicted spirits; I am finished with the plane of misery, the bad destination, the lower world; I am a stream-enterer, no longer subject to [rebirth in] the lower world, fixed in destiny, heading for enlightenment.'"

Having seen the peril in the hells,
one should avoid evil deeds;

having undertaken the noble Dhamma,
the wise one should avoid them.

To the utmost of one's ability,
one should not injure living beings;
one should not knowingly speak falsely;
one should not take what is not given.

One should be content with one's own wives,[1174]
and should refrain from the wives of others.[1175]
A person should not drink wine and liquor,
which cause mental confusion.

One should recollect the Buddha
and ponder on the Dhamma.
One should develop a benevolent mind,
which leads to the world of the devas.

When things to be given are available,
for one needing and wanting merit[1176]
an offering becomes vast
if first given to the holy ones.

I will describe the holy ones,
Sāriputta, listen to me.[1177] [214]
Among cattle of any sort,
whether black, white, red, or golden,
mottled, uniform, or pigeon-colored,
the tamed bull is born,
the one that can bear the load,
possessing strength, advancing with good speed.
They yoke the burden just to him;
they are not concerned about his color.
So too, among human beings
it is in any kind of birth—
among khattiyas, brahmins, vessas,
suddas, caṇḍālas, or scavengers—
among people of any sort
that the tamed person of good manners is born:
one firm in Dhamma, virtuous in conduct,
truthful in speech, endowed with moral shame;

one who has abandoned birth and death,
consummate in the spiritual life,
with the burden dropped, detached,
who has done his task, free of taints;
who has gone beyond all things [of the world]
and by non-clinging has reached nibbāna:
an offering is truly vast
when planted in that spotless field.

Fools devoid of understanding,
dull-witted, unlearned,
do not attend on the holy ones
but give their gifts to those outside.
Those, however, who attend on the holy ones,
on the wise ones esteemed as sagely,
and those whose faith in the Fortunate One
is deeply rooted and well established,
go to the world of the devas
or are born here in a good family.
Advancing in successive steps,
those wise ones attain nibbāna.

180 (10) Gavesī

On one occasion the Blessed One was wandering on tour among the Kosalans together with a large Saṅgha of bhikkhus. Then, while traveling along the highway, the Blessed One saw a large sal-tree grove in a certain place. He left the highway, entered the sal-tree grove, and smiled when he reached a certain place.

Then it occurred to the Venerable Ānanda: "Why did the Blessed One smile? Tathāgatas do not smile without a reason." Then the Venerable Ānanda [215] said to the Blessed One: "Why, Bhante, did the Blessed One smile? Tathāgatas do not smile without a reason."

"In the past, Ānanda, in this place there was an affluent, prosperous, well-populated city, one teeming with people. Now the Blessed One, the Arahant, the Perfectly Enlightened One Kassapa lived in dependence on that city. The Blessed One Kassapa had a lay follower named Gavesī who had not fulfilled virtuous behavior. And Gavesī taught and guided five hundred lay followers who had not fulfilled virtuous behavior.

(1) "Then, Ānanda, it occurred to Gavesī: 'I am the benefactor,

the leader, and the guide of these five hundred lay followers, yet neither I myself nor these five hundred lay followers have fulfilled virtuous behavior. Thus we are on the same level, and I am not the least bit better. Let me surpass them.'

"Then Gavesī approached the five hundred lay followers and said to them: 'From today on, you should consider me to be one fulfilling virtuous behavior.' Then it occurred to those five hundred lay followers: 'Master Gavesī is our benefactor, leader, and guide. Now Master Gavesī will fulfill virtuous behavior. Why shouldn't we do so too?'

"Then those five hundred lay followers approached Gavesī and said to him: 'From today onward let Master Gavesī consider us to be fulfilling virtuous behavior.'

(2) "Then, Ānanda, it occurred to the lay follower Gavesī: 'I am the benefactor, leader, and guide of these five hundred lay followers. Now I am fulfilling virtuous behavior, and so too are these five hundred lay followers. [216] Thus we are on the same level, and I am not the least bit better. Let me surpass them.'

"Then Gavesī approached the five hundred lay followers and said to them: 'From today on, you should consider me to be celibate, living apart, abstaining from sexual intercourse, the common person's practice.' Then it occurred to those five hundred lay followers: 'Master Gavesī is our benefactor, leader, and guide. Now Master Gavesī will be celibate, living apart, abstaining from sexual intercourse, the common person's practice. Why shouldn't we do so too?'

"Then those five hundred lay followers approached Gavesī and said to him: 'From today onward let Master Gavesī consider us to be celibate, living apart, abstaining from sexual intercourse, the common person's practice.'

(3) "Then, Ānanda, it occurred to the lay follower Gavesī: 'I am the benefactor, leader, and guide of these five hundred lay followers. Now I am fulfilling virtuous behavior, and so too are these five hundred lay followers. I am celibate, living apart, abstaining from sexual intercourse, the common person's practice, and so too are these five hundred lay followers. Thus we are on the same level, and I am not the least bit better. Let me surpass them.'

"Then Gavesī approached the five hundred lay followers and said to them: 'From today on, you should consider me to be eating once a day, refraining from a night meal, abstaining from eating outside the proper time.' Then it occurred to those five hundred lay followers: 'Master Gavesī is our benefactor, leader, and guide. Now Master Gavesī eats once a day, refraining from a night meal, abstaining from eating outside the proper time. Why shouldn't we do so too?'

"Then those five hundred lay followers approached Gavesī and [217] said to him: 'From today onward let Master Gavesī consider us to be eating once a day, refraining from a night meal, abstaining from eating outside the proper time.'

(4) "Then, Ānanda, it occurred to the lay follower Gavesī: 'I am the benefactor, leader, and guide of these five hundred lay followers. Now I am fulfilling virtuous behavior, and so too are these five hundred lay followers. I am celibate, living apart, abstaining from sexual intercourse, the common person's practice, and so too are these five hundred lay followers. I eat once a day, refraining from a night meal, abstaining from eating outside the proper time, and so too do these five hundred lay followers. Thus we are on the same level, and I am not the least bit better. Let me surpass them.'

"Then Gavesī approached the Blessed One, the Arahant, the Perfectly Enlightened One Kassapa, and said to him: 'Bhante, may I obtain the going forth and full ordination under the Blessed One?' The lay follower Gavesī obtained the going forth and full ordination under the Blessed One, the Arahant, the Perfectly Enlightened One Kassapa. Soon after his full ordination, dwelling alone, withdrawn, heedful, ardent, and resolute, the bhikkhu Gavesī realized for himself with direct knowledge, in this very life, that unsurpassed consummation of the spiritual life for the sake of which clansmen rightly go forth from the household life into homelessness, and having entered upon it, he dwelled in it. He directly knew: 'Destroyed is birth, the spiritual life has been lived, what had to be done has been done, there is no more coming back to any state of being.' And the bhikkhu Gavesī became one of the arahants.

"Then, Ānanda, it occurred to those five hundred lay followers: 'Master Gavesī is our benefactor, leader, and guide. Now Master Gavesī, having shaved off his hair and beard and put on ochre robes, has gone forth from the household life into homelessness. Why shouldn't we do so too?'

"Then those five hundred lay followers approached the Blessed One, the Arahant, the Perfectly Enlightened One Kassapa, [218] and said to him: 'Bhante, may we obtain the going forth and full ordination under the Blessed One?' Then those five hundred lay followers obtained the going forth and full ordination under the Blessed One, the Arahant, the Perfectly Enlightened One Kassapa.

(5) "Then, Ānanda, it occurred to the bhikkhu Gavesī: 'I obtain at will, without trouble or difficulty, the unsurpassed bliss of liberation. Oh, that these five hundred bhikkhus could obtain at will, without trouble or difficulty, the unsurpassed bliss of liberation!' Then, Ānanda, dwelling each alone, withdrawn, heedful, ardent, and resolute, in no long time those five hundred bhikkhus realized for themselves with direct knowledge, in this very life, that unsurpassed consummation of the spiritual life for the sake of which clansmen rightly go forth from the household life into homelessness, and having entered upon it, they dwelled in it. They directly knew: 'Destroyed is birth, the spiritual life has been lived, what had to be done has been done, there is no more coming back to any state of being.'

"Thus, Ānanda, those five hundred bhikkhus headed by Gavesī, striving in successively higher and more sublime ways, realized the unsurpassed bliss of liberation.[1178] Therefore, Ānanda, you should train yourselves thus: 'Striving in successively higher and more sublime ways, we will realize the unsurpassed bliss of liberation.' Thus, Ānanda, should you train yourselves." [219]

IV. Forest Dwellers

181 (1) Forest Dwellers

"Bhikkhus, there are these five kinds of forest dwellers. What five? (1) One who becomes a forest dweller because of his dullness and stupidity; (2) one who becomes a forest dweller because he has evil desires, because he is driven by desire;[1179] (3) one who becomes a forest dweller because he is mad and mentally deranged; (4) one who becomes a forest dweller, [thinking]: 'It is praised by the Buddhas and the Buddhas' disciples'; (5) and one who becomes a forest dweller for the sake of fewness of desires, for the sake of contentment, for the sake of eliminating [defilements], for the sake of solitude, for the sake of simplicity. These are the five kinds of forest dwellers. One who becomes a forest dweller for the sake of fewness of desires, for the sake of contentment, for the sake of eliminating [defilements], for the sake of solitude, for the sake of simplicity, is the foremost, the best, the preeminent, the supreme, and the finest of these five kinds of forest dwellers.

"Just as, bhikkhus, from a cow comes milk, from milk comes curd, from curd comes butter, from butter comes ghee, and from ghee comes cream-of-ghee, which is reckoned the foremost of all these, so one who becomes a forest dweller for the sake of fewness of desires . . . for the sake of simplicity, is the foremost, the best, the preeminent, the supreme, and the finest of these five kinds of forest dwellers."

182 (2)–190 (10) Wearers of Rag-Robes, Etc.

"Bhikkhus, there are these five kinds of wearers of rag-robes[1180] . . . these five who dwell at the foot of a tree . . . [220] . . . these five who dwell in a charnel ground . . . these five who dwell in the open air . . . these five who observe the sitter's practice . . . these five who observe the any-bed-user's practice . . . these five who observe the one-session practice . . . these five who observe the later-food-refuser's practice . . . these five who observe the practice of eating only food in the almsbowl. What five? (1) One who observes the practice of eating only food in the almsbowl because of his dullness and stupidity; (2) one who observes the practice of eating only food in the almsbowl because he has evil desires, because he is driven by desire; (3) one who observes the practice of eating only food in the almsbowl because he is mad and mentally deranged; (4) one who observes the practice of eating only food in the almsbowl, [thinking]: 'It is praised by the Buddhas and Buddhas' disciples'; (5) and one who observes the practice of eating only food in the almsbowl for the sake of fewness of desires, for the sake of contentment, for the sake of eliminating [defilements], for the sake of solitude, for the sake of simplicity. These are the five who observe the practice of eating only food in the almsbowl. One who observes the practice of eating only food in the almsbowl for the sake of fewness of desires . . . for the sake of simplicity, is the foremost, the best, the preeminent, the supreme, and the finest of these five who observe the practice of eating only food in the almsbowl.

"Just as, bhikkhus, from a cow comes milk, from milk comes curd, from curd comes butter, from butter comes ghee, and from ghee comes cream-of-ghee, which is reckoned the foremost of all these, so this one who observes the practice of eating only food in the almsbowl [221] for the sake of fewness of desires . . . for the sake of simplicity, is the foremost, the best, the preeminent, the supreme, and the finest of these five who observe the practice of eating only food in the almsbowl."

V. Dogs

191 (1) Dogs

"Bhikkhus, there are these five ancient brahmin practices that are now seen among dogs but not among brahmins. What five?

(1) "In the past, brahmins coupled only with brahmin women, not with non-brahmin women. But now brahmins couple with both brahmin women and non-brahmin women. Dogs, however, still couple only with female dogs, not with other female animals. This is the first ancient brahmin practice that is now seen among dogs but not among brahmins.

(2) "In the past, brahmins coupled with brahmin women only when they were in season, not out of season. But now [222] brahmins couple with brahmin women both when they are in season and out of season. Dogs, however, still couple with female dogs only when they are in season, not out of season. This is the second ancient brahmin practice that is now seen among dogs but not among brahmins.

(3) "In the past, brahmins did not buy and sell brahmin women, and they would initiate cohabitation only through mutual affection, doing so for the sake of family continuity.[1181] But now brahmins buy and sell brahmin women, and they initiate cohabitation both through mutual affection and without mutual affection, doing so for the sake of family continuity.[1182] Dogs, however, still do not buy and sell female dogs, and they initiate cohabitation only through mutual affection, doing so for the sake of family continuity. This is the third ancient brahmin practice that is now seen among dogs but not among brahmins.

(4) "In the past, brahmins did not store up wealth, grain, silver, and gold. But now brahmins store up wealth, grain, silver, and gold. Dogs, however, still do not store up wealth, grain, silver, and gold. This is the fourth ancient brahmin practice that is now seen among dogs but not among brahmins.

(5) "In the past, brahmins went seeking almsfood in the evening for their evening meal and in the morning for their morning meal. But now brahmins eat as much as they want until their bellies are full, and then leave taking the leftovers away. Dogs, however, still go seeking food in the evening for their evening meal and in the morning for their morning meal. This is the fifth ancient brahmin practice that is now seen among dogs but not among brahmins.

"These, bhikkhus, are the five ancient brahmin practices that are now seen among dogs but not among brahmins." [223]

192 (2) Doṇa

Then the brahmin Doṇa approached the Blessed One and exchanged greetings with him. When he had concluded his greetings and cordial talk, he sat down to one side and said to the Blessed One: "I have heard, Master Gotama: 'The ascetic Gotama does not pay homage to brahmins who are old, aged, burdened with years, advanced in life, come to the last stage; nor does he stand up for them or offer them a seat.'[1183] This is indeed true, for Master Gotama does not pay homage to brahmins who are old, aged, burdened with years, advanced in life, come to the last stage; nor does he stand up for them or offer them a seat. This is not proper, Master Gotama."

"Do you too claim to be a brahmin, Doṇa?"

"Master Gotama, if one could rightly say of anyone: 'He is a brahmin well born on both his maternal and paternal sides, of pure descent, unassailable and impeccable with respect to birth as far back as the seventh paternal generation; he is a reciter and preserver of the hymns, a master of the three Vedas with their vocabularies, ritual, phonology, and etymology, and the histories as a fifth; skilled in philology and grammar, he is fully versed in natural philosophy and in the marks of a great man'—it is precisely of me that one might say this. For I, Master Gotama, am a brahmin well born on both his maternal and paternal sides, of pure descent, unassailable and impeccable with respect to birth as far back as the seventh paternal generation. I am a reciter and preserver of the hymns, a master of the three Vedas with their vocabularies, ritual, phonology, and etymology, and the histories as a fifth; skilled in philology and grammar, I am fully versed in natural philosophy and in the marks of a great man."

"Doṇa, the ancient [224] seers among the brahmins—that is, Aṭṭhaka, Vāmaka, Vāmadeva, Vessāmitta, Yamataggi, Aṅgīrasa, Bhāradvāja, Vāseṭṭha, Kassapa, and Bhagu—were the creators of the hymns and the composers of the hymns, and it is their ancient hymns, formerly chanted, declared, and compiled, that the brahmins nowadays still chant and repeat, repeating what was spoken, reciting what was recited, and teaching what was taught. Those ancient seers described these five kinds of brahmins: the one similar to Brahmā, the one similar to a deva, the one who remains within the boundary, the one who has crossed the boundary, and the caṇḍāḷa of a brahmin as the fifth. Which of these are you, Doṇa?"

"We do not know these five kinds of brahmins, Master Gotama. All we know is [the word] 'brahmins.' Please, let Master Gotama teach me the Dhamma in such a way that I might know these five kinds of brahmins."

"Then listen, brahmin, and attend closely. I will speak."

"Yes, sir," the brahmin Doṇa replied. The Blessed One said this:

(1) "And how, Doṇa, is a brahmin similar to Brahmā? Here, a brahmin is well born on both his maternal and paternal sides, of pure descent, unassailable and impeccable with respect to birth as far back as the seventh paternal generation. He lives the spiritual life of virginal celibacy[1184] for forty-eight years, studying the hymns. He then seeks a teacher's fee for his teacher solely in accordance with the Dhamma, not contrary to the Dhamma. And what, Doṇa, is the Dhamma in that case? [225] Not by agriculture, not by trade, not by raising cattle, not by archery, not by service to the king, not by a particular craft, but solely by wandering for alms without scorning the alms bowl. Having offered the teacher's fee to his teacher, he shaves off his hair and beard, puts on ochre robes, and goes forth from the household life into homelessness.[1185] When he has gone forth, he dwells pervading one quarter with a mind imbued with loving-kindness, likewise the second quarter, the third quarter, and the

fourth quarter. Thus above, below, across, and everywhere, and to all as to himself, he dwells pervading the entire world with a mind imbued with loving-kindness, vast, exalted, measureless, without enmity, without ill will. He dwells pervading one quarter with a mind imbued with compassion . . . with a mind imbued with altruistic joy . . . with a mind imbued with equanimity, likewise the second quarter, the third quarter, and the fourth quarter. Thus above, below, across, and everywhere, and to all as to himself, he dwells pervading the entire world with a mind imbued with equanimity, vast, exalted, measureless, without enmity, without ill will. Having developed these four divine abodes,[1186] with the breakup of the body, after death, he is reborn in a good destination, in the brahmā world. In this way a brahmin is similar to Brahmā.

(2) "And how, Doṇa, is a brahmin similar to a deva? Here, a brahmin is well born on both his maternal and paternal sides, of pure descent, unassailable and impeccable with respect to birth as far back as the seventh paternal generation. He lives the spiritual life of virginal celibacy for forty-eight years, studying the hymns. He then seeks a teacher's fee for his teacher solely in accordance with the Dhamma, not contrary to the Dhamma. And what, Doṇa, is the Dhamma in that case? Not by agriculture, not by trade, not by raising cattle, not by archery, not by service to the king, not by a particular craft, but solely by wandering for alms [226] without scorning the alms bowl. Having offered the teacher's fee to his teacher, he seeks a wife solely in accordance with the Dhamma, not contrary to the Dhamma. And what, Doṇa, is the Dhamma in that case? Not by buying and selling, [he takes] only a brahmin woman given to him by the pouring of water. He couples only with a brahmin woman, not with a khattiya woman, a vessa woman, a sudda woman, or a caṇḍāla woman, nor with a woman from a family of hunters, bamboo workers, chariot makers, or flower scavengers. He does not couple with a pregnant woman, nor with a woman who is nursing, nor with a woman out of season.

"And why, Doṇa, doesn't the brahmin couple with a pregnant woman? Because, if he were to couple with a pregnant woman, the little boy or girl would be born in excessive filth; therefore he does not couple with a pregnant woman. And why doesn't he couple with a woman who is nursing? Because, if he were to couple with a woman who is nursing, the little boy or girl would drink back the foul substance;[1187] therefore he does not couple with a woman who is nursing. Why doesn't he couple with a woman out of season? Because his brahmin wife does not serve for sensual pleasure, amusement, and sensual delight, but only for procreation.[1188] When he has engaged in sexual activity, he shaves off his hair and beard, puts on ochre robes, and goes forth from the household life into homelessness. When he has gone forth, secluded from sensual pleasures, secluded from unwholesome states . . . he enters and dwells in the first jhāna . . . [as in 5:14] . . . the fourth jhāna. Having developed these four jhānas, [227] with the breakup of the body, after death, he is reborn in a good destination, in a heavenly world. In this way a brahmin is similar to a deva.

(3) "And how, Doṇa, is a brahmin one who remains within the boundary? Here, a brahmin is well born on both his maternal and paternal sides, of pure descent, unassailable and impeccable with respect to birth as far back as the seventh paternal generation. He lives the spiritual life of virginal celibacy for forty-eight years. . . . [all as above down to] . . . Because his brahmin wife does not serve for sensual pleasure, amusement, or sensual delight, but only for procreation. When he has engaged in sexual activity, out of attachment to his sons he remains settled on his property and does not go forth from the household life into homelessness. He stops at the boundary of the ancient brahmins but does not violate it. Since he stops at the boundary of the ancient brahmins but does not violate it, he is called a brahmin who remains within the boundary. It is in this way that a brahmin is one who remains within the boundary.

(4) "And how, Doṇa, is a brahmin one who has crossed the boundary? [228] Here, a brahmin is well born on both his maternal and paternal sides, of pure descent, unassailable and impeccable with respect to birth as far back as the seventh paternal generation. He lives the spiritual life of virginal celibacy for forty-eight years, studying the hymns. He then seeks a teacher's fee for his teacher solely in accordance with the Dhamma, not contrary to the Dhamma. And what, Doṇa, is the Dhamma in that case? Not by agriculture, not by trade, not by raising cattle, not by archery, not by service to the king, not by a particular

craft, but solely by wandering for alms without scorning the alms bowl. Having offered the teacher's fee to his teacher, he seeks a wife both in accordance with the Dhamma and contrary to the Dhamma. [He takes a wife] by buying and selling as well as a brahmin woman given to him by the pouring of water. He couples with a brahmin woman, a khattiya woman, a vessa woman, a sudda woman, and a caṇḍāla woman, and a woman from a family of hunters, bamboo workers, chariot makers, or flower scavengers. He couples with a pregnant woman, a woman who is nursing, a woman in season, and a woman out of season. His brahmin wife serves for sensual pleasure, amusement, and sensual delight, as well as for procreation.[1189] He does not stop at the boundary of the ancient brahmins but violates it. Since he does not stop at the boundary of the ancient brahmins but violates it, he is called a brahmin who has crossed the boundary. It is in this way that a brahmin is one who has crossed the boundary.

(5) "And how, Doṇa, is a brahmin a caṇḍāla of a brahmin? Here, a brahmin is well born on both his maternal and paternal sides, of pure descent, unassailable and impeccable with respect to birth as far back as the seventh paternal generation. He [229] lives the spiritual life of virginal celibacy for forty-eight years, studying the hymns. He then seeks a teacher's fee for his teacher both in accordance with the Dhamma and contrary to the Dhamma—by agriculture, by trade, by raising cattle, by archery, by service to the king, by a particular craft, and not only[1190] by wandering for alms without scorning the alms bowl. Having offered the teacher's fee to his teacher, he seeks a wife both in accordance with the Dhamma and contrary to the Dhamma. [He takes a wife] by buying and selling as well as a brahmin woman given to him by the pouring of water. He couples with a brahmin woman, a khattiya woman, a vessa woman, a sudda woman, and a caṇḍāla woman, and a woman from a family of hunters, bamboo workers, chariot makers, or flower scavengers. He couples with a pregnant woman, a woman who is nursing, a woman in season, and a woman out of season. His brahmin wife serves for sensual pleasure, amusement, and sensual delight, as well as for procreation. He earns his living by all kinds of work. Brahmins say to him: 'Why, sir, while claiming to be a brahmin, do you earn your living by all kinds

of work?' He answers them: 'Just as fire burns pure things and impure things yet is not thereby defiled, so too, sirs, if a brahmin earns his living by all kinds of work, he is not thereby defiled.' Since he earns his living by all kinds of work, this brahmin is called a caṇḍāla of a brahmin. It is in this way that a brahmin is a caṇḍāla of a brahmin.

"Doṇa, the ancient seers among the brahmins—that is, Aṭṭhaka, Vāmaka, Vāmadeva, Vessāmitta, Yamataggi, Aṅgīrasa, Bhāradvāja, [230] Vāseṭṭha, Kassapa, and Bhagu—were the creators of the hymns and the composers of the hymns, and it is their ancient hymns, formerly chanted, declared, and compiled, that the brahmins nowadays still chant and repeat, repeating what was spoken, reciting what was recited, and teaching what was taught. Those ancient seers described these five kinds of brahmins: the one similar to Brahmā, the one similar to a deva, the one who remains within the boundary, the one who has crossed the boundary, and the caṇḍāḷa of a brahmin as the fifth. Which of these are you, Doṇa?"

"Such being the case, Master Gotama, we do not even measure up to the caṇḍāla of a brahmin. Excellent, Master Gotama! Excellent, Master Gotama! Master Gotama has made the Dhamma clear in many ways, as though he were turning upright what had been overthrown, revealing what was hidden, showing the way to one who was lost, or holding up a lamp in the darkness so those with good eyesight can see forms. I now go for refuge to Master Gotama, to the Dhamma, and to the Saṅgha of bhikkhus. Let Master Gotama consider me a lay follower who from today has gone for refuge for life."

193 (3) Saṅgārava[1191]

Then the brahmin Saṅgārava approached the Blessed One and exchanged greetings with him. When they had concluded their greetings and cordial talk, he sat down to one side and said to the Blessed One:

"Master Gotama, why is it that sometimes even those hymns that have been recited over a long period do not recur to the mind, let alone those that have not been so recited? Why is it that sometimes even those hymns that have not been recited over a long period recur to the mind, let alone those that have been so recited?"

[Why the hymns are not remembered]

(1) "Brahmin, when one dwells with a mind obsessed and oppressed by sensual lust, and one does not understand as it really is the escape from arisen sensual lust,[1192] on that occasion one does not know and see as it really is one's own good, the good of others, and the good of both.[1193] Then even those hymns that have been recited over a long period do not recur to the mind, let alone those that have not been so recited. Suppose there were a bowl of water mixed with lac, turmeric, blue dye, or crimson dye. If a man with good sight [231] were to examine his own facial reflection in it, he would not know and see it as it really is. So too, when one dwells with a mind obsessed and oppressed by sensual lust . . . let alone those that have not been so recited.

(2) "Again, when one dwells with a mind obsessed and oppressed by ill will, and one does not understand as it really is the escape from arisen ill will, on that occasion one does not know and see as it really is one's own good, the good of others, and the good of both. Then even those hymns that have been recited over a long period do not recur to the mind, let alone those that have not been so recited. Suppose there were a bowl of water being heated over a fire, bubbling and boiling. If a man with good sight were to examine his own facial reflection in it, he would not know and see it as it really is. So too, when one dwells with a mind obsessed and oppressed by ill will . . . let alone those that have not been so recited.

(3) "Again, when one dwells with a mind obsessed and oppressed by dullness and drowsiness, and one does not understand as it really is the escape from arisen dullness and drowsiness, on that occasion one does not know and see as it really is one's own good, the good of others, and the good of both. [232] Then even those hymns that have been recited over a long period do not recur to the mind, let alone those that have not been so recited. Suppose there were a bowl of water covered over with algae and water plants. If a man with good sight were to examine his own facial reflection in it, he would not know and see it as it really is. So too, when one dwells with a mind obsessed and oppressed by dullness and drowsiness . . . let alone those that have not been so recited.

(4) "Again, when one dwells with a mind obsessed and

oppressed by restlessness and remorse, and one does not understand as it really is the escape from arisen restlessness and remorse, on that occasion one does not know and see as it really is one's own good, the good of others, and the good of both. Then even those hymns that have been recited over a long period do not recur to the mind, let alone those that have not been so recited. Suppose there were a bowl of water stirred by the wind, rippling, swirling, churned into wavelets. If a man with good sight were to examine his own facial reflection in it, he would not know and see it as it really is. So too, when one dwells with a mind obsessed and oppressed by restlessness and worry . . . [233] . . . let alone those that have not been so recited.

(5) "Again, when one dwells with a mind obsessed and oppressed by doubt, and one does not understand as it really is the escape from arisen doubt, on that occasion one does not know and see as it really is one's own good, the good of others, and the good of both. Then even those hymns that have been recited over a long period do not recur to the mind, let alone those that have not been so recited. Suppose there were a bowl of water that is cloudy, turbid, and muddy, placed in the dark. If a man with good sight were to examine his own facial reflection in it, he would not know and see it as it really is. So too, when one dwells with a mind obsessed and oppressed by doubt, and one does not understand as it really is the escape from arisen doubt, on that occasion one does not know and see as it really is one's own good, the good of others, and the good of both. Then even those hymns that have been recited over a long period do not recur to the mind, let alone those that have not been so recited.

[Why the hymns are remembered]

(1) "Brahmin, when one dwells with a mind that is not obsessed and oppressed by sensual lust, and one understands as it really is the escape from arisen sensual lust, on that occasion one knows and sees as it really is one's own good, the good of others, and the good of both. Then even those hymns that have not been recited over a long period recur to the mind, let alone those that have been so recited. Suppose there were a bowl of water not mixed with lac, turmeric, blue dye, [234] or crimson dye. If a man with good sight were to examine his own facial reflection in it, he would know and see it as it really is. So too, when

one dwells with a mind that is not obsessed and oppressed by sensual lust ... let alone those that have been so recited.

(2) "Again, when one dwells with a mind that is not obsessed and oppressed by ill will, and one understands as it really is the escape from arisen ill will, on that occasion one knows and sees as it really is one's own good, the good of others, and the good of both. Then even those hymns that have not been recited over a long period recur to the mind, let alone those that have been so recited. Suppose there were a bowl of water not heated over a fire, not bubbling and boiling. If a man with good sight were to examine his own facial reflection in it, he would know and see it as it really is. So too, when one dwells with a mind that is not obsessed and oppressed by ill will ... let alone those that have been so recited.

(3) "Again, when one dwells with a mind that is not obsessed and oppressed by dullness and drowsiness, and one understands as it really is the escape from arisen dullness and drowsiness, on that occasion one knows and sees as it really is one's own good, the good of others, and the good of both. Then even those hymns that have not been recited over a long period recur to the mind, [235] let alone those that have been so recited. Suppose there were a bowl of water not covered over with algae and water plants. If a man with good sight were to examine his own facial reflection in it, he would know and see it as it really is. So too, when one dwells with a mind that is not obsessed and oppressed by dullness and drowsiness ... let alone those that have been so recited.

(4) "Again, when one dwells with a mind that is not obsessed and oppressed by restlessness and remorse, and one understands as it really is the escape from arisen restlessness and remorse, on that occasion one knows and sees as it really is one's own good, the good of others, and the good of both. Then even those hymns that have not been recited over a long period recur to the mind, let alone those that have been so recited. Suppose there were a bowl of water not stirred by the wind, without ripples, without swirls, not churned into wavelets. If a man with good sight were to examine his own facial reflection in it, he would know and see it as it really is. So too, when one dwells with a mind that is not obsessed and oppressed by restlessness and remorse ... let alone those that have been so recited.

(5) "Again, when one dwells with a mind that is not obsessed

and oppressed by doubt, and one understands as it really is the escape from arisen doubt, [236] on that occasion one knows and sees as it really is one's own good, the good of others, and the good of both. Then even those hymns that have not been recited over a long period recur to the mind, let alone those that have been so recited. Suppose there were a bowl of water that is clear, serene, and limpid, placed in the light. If a man with good sight were to examine his own facial reflection in it, he would know and see it as it really is. So too, when one dwells with a mind that is not obsessed and oppressed by doubt, and one understands as it really is the escape from arisen doubt, on that occasion one knows and sees as it really is one's own good, the good of others, and the good of both. Then even those hymns that have not been recited over a long period recur to the mind, let alone those that have been so recited.

"This, brahmin, is the reason why sometimes even those hymns that have been recited over a long period do not recur to the mind, let alone those that have not been so recited. This is the reason why sometimes even those hymns that have not been recited over a long period recur to the mind, let alone those that have been so recited."

"Excellent, Master Gotama! . . . Let Master Gotama consider me a lay follower who from today has gone for refuge for life."

194 (4) Kāraṇapālī

On one occasion the Blessed One was dwelling at Vesālī in the hall with the peaked roof in the Great Wood. Now on that occasion the brahmin Kāraṇapālī was getting some work done for the Licchavis.[1194] The brahmin Kāraṇapālī saw the brahmin Piṅgiyānī [237] coming in the distance and said to him:

"Where is Master Piṅgiyānī coming from in the middle of the day?"

"I am coming, sir, from the presence of the ascetic Gotama."[1195]

"What do you think of the ascetic Gotama's competence in wisdom? Do you consider him wise?"

"Who am I, sir, that I could know the ascetic Gotama's competence in wisdom? Certainly, only one like him could know his competence in wisdom!"

"You praise the ascetic Gotama with lofty praise, indeed."

"Who am I, sir, that I could praise the ascetic Gotama? Praised by those who are praised, Master Gotama is best among devas and humans!"

"What grounds do you see, Master Piṅgiyānī, for placing such full confidence in the ascetic Gotama?"

(1) "Just as a man who has found satisfaction in the best of tastes will no longer desire tastes of an inferior kind; so too, sir, whatever one hears of Master Gotama's Dhamma—be it discourses, mixed prose and verse, expositions, or amazing accounts—one will no longer yearn for the doctrines of ordinary ascetics and brahmins.[1196]

(2) "Just as a man oppressed by hunger and weakness who receives a honey cake will enjoy a sweet, delicious taste wherever he eats of it; so too, sir, whatever one hears of Master Gotama's Dhamma—discourses, mixed prose and verse, expositions, or amazing accounts—one will obtain satisfaction and placidity of mind.

(3) "Just as a man who comes upon a piece of sandalwood, whether yellow sandalwood or red sandalwood, will enjoy a pure, fragrant scent wherever he smells it, be it at the bottom, the middle, or the top [238]; so too, sir, whatever one hears of Master Gotama's Dhamma—discourses, mixed prose and verse, expositions, or amazing accounts—one will derive elation and joy.

(4) "Just as a capable physician might instantly cure one who is afflicted, sick, and gravely ill; so too, sir, whatever one hears of Master Gotama's Dhamma—discourses, mixed prose and verse, expositions, or amazing accounts—one's sorrow, lamentation, pain, dejection, and anguish will vanish.

(5) "Just as there might be a delightful pond with pleasant banks, its water clear, agreeable, cool, and limpid, and a man oppressed and exhausted by the heat, fatigued, parched, and thirsty, might come by, enter the pond, and bathe and drink; thus all his affliction, fatigue, and feverish burning would subside. So too, sir, whatever one hears of Master Gotama's Dhamma—discourses, mixed prose and verse, expositions, or amazing accounts—all one's affliction, fatigue, and feverish burning subside."

When this was said, the brahmin Kāraṇapālī rose from his

seat, arranged his upper robe over one shoulder, and placing his right knee on the ground, he reverently saluted the Blessed One and uttered three times these inspired words:

"Homage to the Blessed One, the Arahant, the Perfectly Enlightened One! Homage to the Blessed One, the Arahant, the Perfectly Enlightened One! Homage to the Blessed One, the Arahant, the Perfectly Enlightened One!

"Excellent, Master Piṅgiyānī! Excellent, Master Piṅgiyānī! Master Piṅgiyānī has made the Dhamma clear in many ways, as though he were turning upright what had been overthrown, revealing what was hidden, showing the way to one who was lost, [239] or holding up a lamp in the darkness so those with good sight can see forms. Master Piṅgiyānī, I now go for refuge to Master Gotama, to the Dhamma, and to the Saṅgha of bhikkhus. Let Master Piṅgiyānī consider me a lay follower who from today has gone for refuge for life."

195 (5) Piṅgiyānī

On one occasion the Blessed One was dwelling at Vesālī in the hall with the peaked roof in the Great Wood. Now on that occasion five hundred Licchavis were visiting the Blessed One. Some Licchavis were blue, with a blue complexion, clothed in blue, wearing blue ornaments. Some Licchavis were yellow, with a yellow complexion, clothed in yellow, wearing yellow ornaments. Some Licchavis were red, with a red complexion, clothed in red, wearing red ornaments. Some Licchavis were white, with a white complexion, clothed in white, wearing white ornaments. Yet the Blessed One outshone them all with his beauty and glory.

Then the brahmin Piṅgiyānī rose from his seat, arranged his upper robe over one shoulder, and having reverently saluted the Blessed One, he said: "An inspiration has come to me, Blessed One! An inspiration has come to me, Fortunate One!"

"Then express your inspiration, Piṅgiyānī," the Blessed One said.[1197] Then, in the presence of the Blessed One, the brahmin Piṅgiyānī extolled him with an appropriate verse:[1198]

> "As the fragrant red *kokanada* lotus
> blooms in the morning, its fragrance unspent,
> behold Aṅgīrasa radiant
> like the sun beaming in the sky."

Then those Licchavis presented the brahmin Piṅgiyānī with five hundred upper robes. The brahmin Piṅgiyānī presented those five hundred upper robes to the Blessed One. [240] The Blessed One then said to those Licchavis:

"Licchavis, the manifestation of five gems is rare in the world.[1199] What five? (1) The manifestation of a Tathāgata, an Arahant, a Perfectly Enlightened One is rare in the world. (2) A person who can teach the Dhamma and discipline proclaimed by a Tathāgata is rare in the world. (3) When the Dhamma and discipline proclaimed by a Tathāgata has been taught, a person who can understand it is rare in the world. (4) When the Dhamma and discipline proclaimed by a Tathāgata has been taught, a person who can understand it and practice in accordance with the Dhamma is rare in the world. (5) A grateful and thankful person is rare in the world. Licchavis, the manifestation of these five gems is rare in the world."

196 (6) Dreams

"Bhikkhus, before his enlightenment, while he was just a bodhisatta, not fully enlightened, five great dreams appeared to the Tathāgata, the Arahant, the Perfectly Enlightened One. What five?

(1) "Before his enlightenment, while he was just a bodhisatta, not fully enlightened, the Tathāgata, the Arahant, the Perfectly Enlightened One [dreamt] that this mighty earth was his bedstead; the Himālaya, king of mountains, was his pillow; his left hand rested on the eastern sea, his right hand on the western sea, and his two feet on the southern sea. This was the first great dream that appeared to the Tathāgata, the Arahant, the Perfectly Enlightened One before his enlightenment, while he was just a bodhisatta, not fully enlightened.

(2) "Again, before his enlightenment . . . the Tathāgata, the Arahant, the Perfectly Enlightened One [dreamt] that a kind of grass called *tiriyā* rose up from his navel and stood touching the sky. [241] This was the second great dream that appeared to the Tathāgata . . . while he was just a bodhisatta, not fully enlightened.

(3) "Again, before his enlightenment . . . the Tathāgata, the Arahant, the Perfectly Enlightened One [dreamt] that white worms with black heads crawled from his feet up to his knees and covered them. This was the third great dream that appeared

to the Tathāgata . . . while he was just a bodhisatta, not fully enlightened.

(4) "Again, before his enlightenment . . . the Tathāgata, the Arahant, the Perfectly Enlightened One [dreamt] that four birds of different colors came from the four quarters, fell at his feet, and turned all white. This was the fourth great dream that appeared to the Tathāgata . . . while he was just a bodhisatta, not fully enlightened.

(5) "Again, before his enlightenment . . . the Tathāgata, the Arahant, the Perfectly Enlightened One [dreamt] that he climbed up a huge mountain of dung without being soiled by it. This was the fifth great dream that appeared to the Tathāgata . . . while he was just a bodhisatta, not fully enlightened.

(1) "Now, bhikkhus, when the Tathāgata, the Arahant, the Perfectly Enlightened One—before his enlightenment, while just a bodhisatta, not fully enlightened—[dreamt] that this mighty earth was his bedstead and the Himālaya, king of mountains, his pillow; that his left hand rested on the eastern sea, his right hand on the western sea, and his two feet on the southern sea, [this was a foretoken] that he would awaken to the unsurpassed, perfect enlightenment.[1200] This first great dream appeared to him [as a sign] that his awakening [was imminent].[1201] [242]

(2) "When the Tathāgata, the Arahant, the Perfectly Enlightened One . . . [dreamt] that *tiriyā* grass rose up from his navel and stood touching the sky, [this was a foretoken] that he would awaken to the noble eightfold path and would proclaim it well among devas and humans. This second great dream appeared to him [as a sign] that his awakening [was imminent].

(3) "When the Tathāgata, the Arahant, the Perfectly Enlightened One . . . [dreamt] that white worms with black heads crawled from his feet up to his knees and covered them, [this was a foretoken] that many white-robed householders would go for lifelong refuge to the Tathāgata. This third great dream appeared to him [as a sign] that his awakening [was imminent].

(4) "When the Tathāgata, the Arahant, the Perfectly Enlightened One . . . [dreamt] that four birds of different colors came from the four quarters, fell at his feet, and turned all white, [this was a foretoken] that members of the four classes—khattiyas,

brahmins, vessas, and suddas—would go forth from the household life into homelessness in the Dhamma and discipline proclaimed by the Tathāgata and realize unsurpassed liberation. This fourth great dream appeared to him [as a sign] that his awakening [was imminent].

(5) "When the Tathāgata, the Arahant, the Perfectly Enlightened One . . . [dreamt] that he climbed up a huge mountain of dung without being soiled by it, [this was a foretoken] that he would receive robes, almsfood, dwellings, and medicines and provisions for the sick, and he would use them without being tied to them, infatuated with them, and blindly absorbed in them, seeing the danger and knowing the escape. This fifth great dream appeared to him [as a sign] that his awakening [was imminent].

"These, bhikkhus, were the five great dreams that appeared to the Tathāgata, the Arahant, the Perfectly Enlightened One, before his enlightenment, while he was just a bodhisatta, not fully enlightened." [243]

197 (7) Rain

"Bhikkhus, there are these five obstacles to rain that the forecasters do not know about, where their eyes do not tread.[1202] What five?

(1) "Bhikkhus, the heat element in the upper regions of the sky becomes disturbed. Because of this, the clouds that have arisen are scattered. This is the first obstacle to rain that the forecasters do not know about, where their eyes do not tread.

(2) "Again, the air element in the upper regions of the sky becomes disturbed. Because of this, the clouds that have arisen are scattered. This is the second obstacle to rain. . . .

(3) "Again, Rāhu the asura king receives the water with his hand and discards it into the ocean. This is the third obstacle to rain. . . .

(4) "Again, the rain-cloud devas become heedless. This is the fourth obstacle to rain. . . .

(5) "Again, human beings become unrighteous. This is the fifth obstacle to rain. . . .

"These are the five obstacles to rain that the forecasters do not know about, where their eyes do not tread."

198 (8) Speech

"Bhikkhus, possessing five factors, speech is well spoken, not badly spoken; it is blameless and beyond reproach by the wise. What five? [244] It is spoken at the proper time; what is said is true; it is spoken gently; what is said is beneficial; it is spoken with a mind of loving-kindness. Possessing these five factors, speech is well spoken, not badly spoken; it is blameless and beyond reproach by the wise."

199 (9) Families

"Bhikkhus, whenever virtuous monastics[1203] come to a home, the people there generate much merit on five grounds. What five? (1) When people see virtuous monastics come to their home and they arouse hearts of confidence [toward them], on that occasion that family is practicing the way conducive to heaven. (2) When people rise, pay homage, and offer a seat to virtuous monastics who come to their home, on that occasion that family is practicing the way conducive to birth in high families. (3) When people remove the stain of miserliness toward virtuous monastics who come to their home, on that occasion that family is practicing the way conducive to great influence. (4) When, according to their means, people share what they have with virtuous monastics who come to their home, on that occasion that family is practicing the way conducive to great wealth. (5) When people question virtuous monastics who come to their home, make inquiries about the teachings, and listen to the Dhamma, on that occasion that family is practicing the way conducive to great wisdom. [245] Bhikkhus, whenever virtuous monastics come to a home, the people there generate much merit on these five grounds."

200 (10) Escape

"Bhikkhus, there are these five elements of escape.[1204] What five?

(1) "Here, when a bhikkhu is attending to sensual pleasures,[1205] his mind does not launch out upon them, and become placid, settled, and focused on them.[1206] But when he is attending to renunciation, his mind launches out upon it and becomes placid, settled, and focused on it. His mind is well departed,[1207] well developed, well emerged, well liberated, and well detached from sensual pleasures. And he is freed from those taints, dis-

tressful and feverish, that arise with sensual pleasures as condition. He does not feel that kind of feeling.[1208] This is declared to be the escape from sensual pleasures.

(2) "Again, when a bhikkhu is attending to ill will, his mind does not launch out upon it, and become placid, settled, and focused on it. But when he is attending to good will, his mind launches out upon it and becomes placid, settled, and focused on it. His mind is well departed, well developed, well emerged, well liberated, and well detached from ill will. And he is freed from those taints, distressful and feverish, that arise with ill will as condition. He does not feel that kind of feeling. This is declared to be the escape from ill will.

(3) "Again, when a bhikkhu is attending to harming, his mind does not launch out upon it and become placid, settled, and focused on it. But when he is attending to non-harming, his mind launches out upon it and becomes placid, settled, and focused on it. His mind is well departed, well developed, well emerged, well liberated, and well detached from harming. And he is freed from those taints, distressful and feverish, that arise with harming as condition. He does not feel that kind of feeling. This is declared to be the escape from harming. [246]

(4) "Again, when a bhikkhu is attending to form, his mind does not launch out upon it and become placid, settled, and focused on it. But when he is attending to the formless, his mind launches out upon it and becomes placid, settled, and focused on it. His mind is well departed, well developed, well emerged, well liberated, and well detached from form. And he is freed from those taints, distressful and feverish, that arise with form as condition. He does not feel that kind of feeling. This is declared to be the escape from form.

(5) "Again, when a bhikkhu is attending to personal existence, his mind does not launch out upon it and become placid, settled, and focused on it. But when he is attending to the cessation of personal existence, his mind launches out upon it and becomes placid, settled, and focused on it. His mind is well departed, well developed, well emerged, well liberated, and well detached from personal existence. And he is freed from those taints, distressful and feverish, that arise with personal existence as condition. He does not feel that feeling. This is declared to be the escape from personal existence.

"Delight in sensual pleasures does not lie within him; delight in ill will does not lie within him; delight in harming does not lie within him; delight in form does not lie within him; delight in personal existence does not lie within him. Because he is without the underlying tendencies toward delight in sensual pleasures, delight in ill will, delight in harming, delight in form, and delight in personal existence, he is called a bhikkhu devoid of underlying tendencies. He has cut off craving, stripped off the fetter, and by completely breaking through conceit, he has made an end of suffering. These, bhikkhus, are the five elements of escape." [247]

The Fifth Fifty

I. Kimbila

201 (1) Kimbila

On one occasion the Blessed One was dwelling at Kimbilā in a *nicula* grove.[1209] Then the Venerable Kimbila approached the Blessed One, paid homage to him, sat down to one side, and said:

"What is the cause and reason why, Bhante, the good Dhamma does not continue long after a Tathāgata has attained final nibbāna?"[1210]

"(1) Here, Kimbila, after a Tathāgata has attained final nibbāna, the bhikkhus, bhikkhunīs, male lay followers, and female lay followers dwell without reverence and deference toward the Teacher. (2) They dwell without reverence and deference toward the Dhamma. (3) They dwell without reverence and deference toward the Saṅgha. (4) They dwell without reverence and deference toward the training. (5) They dwell without reverence and deference toward each other. This is the cause and reason why the good Dhamma does not continue long after a Tathāgata has attained final nibbāna.

"What is the cause and reason why, Bhante, the good Dhamma continues long after a Tathāgata has attained final nibbāna?"

"(1) Here, Kimbila, after a Tathāgata has attained final nibbāna, the bhikkhus, bhikkhunīs, male lay followers, and female lay followers dwell with reverence and deference toward the Teacher. (2) They dwell with reverence and deference toward the Dhamma. (3) They dwell with reverence and deference toward the Saṅgha. (4) They dwell with reverence and deference toward the training. (5) They dwell with reverence and deference toward each other. This is the cause and reason why the good Dhamma continues long after a Tathāgata has attained final nibbāna." [248]

202 (2) Listening to the Dhamma

"Bhikkhus, there are these five benefits in listening to the Dhamma. What five? One hears what one has not heard; one clarifies what has been heard; one emerges from perplexity; one straightens out one's view; one's mind becomes placid. These are the five benefits in listening to the Dhamma."

203 (3) Thoroughbred[1211]

"Bhikkhus, possessing five factors, a king's excellent thoroughbred horse is worthy of a king, an accessory of a king, and reckoned as a factor of kingship. What five? Rectitude, speed, gentleness, patience, and mildness. Possessing these five factors, a king's excellent thoroughbred horse is . . . reckoned as a factor of kingship.

"So too, possessing five qualities, a bhikkhu is worthy of gifts, worthy of hospitality, worthy of offerings, worthy of reverential salutation, an unsurpassed field of merit for the world. What five? Rectitude, speed, gentleness, patience, and mildness. Possessing these five qualities, a bhikkhu is worthy of gifts, worthy of hospitality, worthy of offerings, worthy of reverential salutation, an unsurpassed field of merit for the world."

204 (4) Powers

"Bhikkhus, there are these five powers. What five? The power of faith, the power of moral shame, the power of moral dread, the power of energy, and the power of wisdom. These are the five powers."

205 (5) Barrenness[1212]

"Bhikkhus, there are these five kinds of mental barrenness.[1213] What five?

(1) "Here, a bhikkhu is perplexed about the Teacher, doubts him, [249] is not convinced about him, and does not place

confidence in him. When a bhikkhu is perplexed about the Teacher, doubts him, is not convinced about him, and does not place confidence in him, his mind does not incline to ardor, effort, perseverance, and striving. Since his mind does not incline to ardor . . . and striving, this is the first kind of mental barrenness.

(2) "Again, a bhikkhu is perplexed about the Dhamma, doubts it, is not convinced about it and does not place confidence in it. When a bhikkhu is perplexed about the Dhamma, doubts it, is not convinced about it and does not place confidence in it, his mind does not incline to ardor, effort, perseverance, and striving. Since his mind does not incline to ardor . . . and striving, this is the second kind of mental barrenness.

(3) "Again, a bhikkhu is perplexed about the Saṅgha, doubts it, is not convinced about it, and does not place confidence in it. When a bhikkhu is perplexed about the Saṅgha, doubts it, is not convinced about it and does not place confidence in it, his mind does not incline to ardor, effort, perseverance, and striving. Since his mind does not incline to ardor . . . and striving, this is the third kind of mental barrenness.

(4) "Again, a bhikkhu is perplexed about the training, doubts it, is not convinced about it, and does not place confidence in it. When a bhikkhu is perplexed about the training, doubts it, is not convinced about it, and does not place confidence in it, his mind does not incline to ardor, effort, perseverance, and striving. Since his mind does not incline to ardor . . . and striving, this is the fourth kind of mental barrenness.

(5) "Again, a bhikkhu is irritated by his fellow monks, displeased with them, resentful toward them, ill disposed toward them. When a bhikkhu is irritated by his fellow monks, displeased with them, resentful toward them, ill disposed toward them, his mind does not incline to ardor, effort, perseverance, and striving. Since his mind does not incline to ardor . . . and striving, this is the fifth kind of mental barrenness.

"These, bhikkhus, are the five kinds of mental barrenness."

206 (6) Bondages[1214]

"Bhikkhus, there are these five bondages of the mind.[1215] What five?

(1) "Here, a bhikkhu is not devoid of lust for sensual plea-

sures, not devoid of desire, affection, thirst, passion, and craving for them. When a bhikkhu is not devoid of lust for sensual pleasures, not devoid of desire, affection, thirst, passion, and craving for them, his mind does not incline to ardor, effort, perseverance, and striving. Since his mind does not incline to ardor . . . and striving, this is the first bondage of the mind.

(2) "Again, a bhikkhu is not devoid of lust for the body, not devoid of desire, affection, thirst, passion, and craving for it. When a bhikkhu is not devoid of lust for the body, not devoid of desire, affection, thirst, passion, and craving for it, his mind does not incline to ardor, effort, perseverance, and striving. Since his mind does not incline to ardor . . . and striving, this is the second bondage of the mind.

(3) "Again, a bhikkhu is not devoid of lust for form, not devoid of desire, affection, thirst, passion, and craving for it. When a bhikkhu is not devoid of lust for form, not devoid of desire, affection, thirst, passion, and craving for it, his mind does not incline to ardor, effort, perseverance, and striving. Since his mind does not incline to ardor . . . and striving, this is the third bondage of the mind.

(4) "Again, having eaten as much as he wants until his belly is full, a bhikkhu yields to the pleasure of rest, the pleasure of sloth, the pleasure of sleep. When a bhikkhu . . . yields to the pleasure of rest, the pleasure of sloth, the pleasure of sleep, his mind does not incline to ardor, effort, perseverance, and striving. Since his mind does not incline to ardor . . . and striving, this is the fourth bondage of the mind.

(5) "Again, a bhikkhu lives the spiritual life aspiring for [rebirth in] a certain order of devas, [250] thinking: 'By this virtuous behavior, observance, austerity, or spiritual life I will be a deva or one [in the retinue] of the devas.' When he lives the spiritual life aspiring for [rebirth in] a certain order of devas . . . his mind does not incline to ardor, effort, perseverance, and striving. Since his mind does not incline to ardor . . . and striving, this is the fifth bondage of the mind.

"These, bhikkhus, are the five bondages of the mind."

207 (7) Rice Porridge

"Bhikkhus, there are these five benefits in rice porridge. What five? It stills hunger, dispels thirst, settles wind, cleans out the bladder, and promotes the digestion of the remnants of undigested food. These are the five benefits in rice porridge."

208 (8) Brushing

"Bhikkhus, there are these five dangers in not brushing one's teeth.[1216] What five? It is bad for one's eyes; one's breath stinks; one's taste buds are not purified; bile and phlegm envelop one's food; and one's food does not agree with one. These are the five dangers in not brushing one's teeth.

"Bhikkhus, there are these five benefits in brushing one's teeth. What five? It is good for one's eyes; one's breath does not stink; one's taste buds are purified; bile and phlegm do not envelop one's food; and one's food agrees with one. These are the five benefits in brushing one's teeth." [251]

209 (9) Intonation

"Bhikkhus, there are these five dangers in reciting the Dhamma with a drawn-out, song-like intonation.[1217] What five? (1) One becomes infatuated with one's own intonation. (2) Others become infatuated with one's intonation. (3) Householders complain: 'Just as we sing, so, too, do these ascetics who follow the son of the Sakyans.' (4) There is a disruption of concentration for one wanting to refine the intonation. (5) [Those in] the next generation follow one's example. These are the five dangers in reciting the Dhamma with a drawn-out, song-like intonation."

210 (10) With a Muddled Mind

"Bhikkhus, there are these five dangers for one who falls asleep with a muddled mind, lacking clear comprehension.[1218] What five? He sleeps badly; he awakens miserably; he has bad dreams; the deities do not protect him; and semen is emitted. These are the five dangers for one who falls asleep with a muddled mind, lacking clear comprehension.

"Bhikkhus, there are these five benefits for one who falls asleep mindfully and with clear comprehension. What five? He sleeps well; he awakens happily; he does not have bad dreams; deities protect him; and semen is not emitted. These are the five benefits for one who falls asleep mindfully and with clear comprehension." [252]

II. One Who Insults

211 (1) One Who Insults

"Bhikkhus, when a bhikkhu is one who insults and disparages his fellow monks, a reviler of the noble ones, five dangers can be expected for him. What five? (1) He either commits a *pārājika* and cuts off the outlet,[1219] or (2) commits a certain defiled offense,[1220] or (3) contracts a severe illness. (4) He dies confused. (5) With the breakup of the body, after death, he is reborn in the plane of misery, in a bad destination, in the lower world, in hell. When a bhikkhu is one who insults and disparages his fellow monks, a reviler of the noble ones, these five dangers can be expected for him."

212 (2) Arguments

"Bhikkhus, when a bhikkhu is a maker of arguments, quarrels, disputes, contentious talk, and disciplinary issues in the Saṅgha, five dangers can be expected for him. What five? (1) He does not achieve what he has not yet achieved; (2) he falls away from what he has achieved; (3) a bad report circulates about him; (4) he dies confused; and (5) with the breakup of the body, after death, he is reborn in the plane of misery, in a bad destination, in the lower world, in hell. When a bhikkhu is a maker of arguments, quarrels, disputes, contentious talk, and disciplinary issues in the Saṅgha, these five dangers can be expected for him."

213 (3) Virtuous Behavior

"Bhikkhus, there are these five dangers for an immoral person because of his deficiency in virtuous behavior. What five?

(1) "Here, an immoral person deficient in virtuous behavior loses much wealth because of heedlessness. This is the first danger for an immoral person because of his deficiency in virtuous behavior.

(2) "Again, a bad report circulates about an immoral person deficient in virtuous behavior. This is the second danger.... [253]

(3) "Again, whatever assembly an immoral person deficient in virtuous behavior approaches—whether of khattiyas, brahmins, householders, or ascetics—he approaches it timid and disconcerted. This is the third danger...."

(4) "Again, an immoral person deficient in virtuous behavior dies confused. This is the fourth danger. . . .

(5) "Again, with the breakup of the body, after death, an immoral person deficient in virtuous behavior is reborn in the plane of misery, in a bad destination, in the lower world, in hell. This is the fifth danger. . . .

"These are the five dangers for an immoral person because of his deficiency in virtuous behavior.

"Bhikkhus, there are these five benefits for a virtuous person because of his accomplishment in virtuous behavior. What five?

(1) "Here, a virtuous person accomplished in virtuous behavior accumulates much wealth because of heedfulness. This is the first benefit for a virtuous person because of his accomplishment in virtuous behavior.

(2) "Again, a virtuous person accomplished in virtuous behavior acquires a good reputation. This is the second benefit. . . .

(3) "Again, whatever assembly a virtuous person accomplished in virtuous behavior approaches—whether of khattiyas, brahmins, householders, or ascetics—he approaches it confidently and composed. This is the third benefit. . . .

(4) "Again, a virtuous person accomplished in virtuous behavior dies unconfused. This is the fourth benefit. . . .

(5) "Again, with the breakup of the body, after death, a virtuous person accomplished in virtuous behavior is reborn in a good destination, in a heavenly world. This is the fifth benefit. . . . [254]

"These are the five benefits for a virtuous person because of his accomplishment in virtuous behavior."

214 (4) Speaking Much

"Bhikkhus, there are these five dangers for a person who speaks much. What five? He speaks falsely; he speaks divisively; he speaks harshly; he speaks idle chatter; with the breakup of the body, after death, he is reborn in the plane of misery, in a bad destination, in the lower world, in hell. These are the five dangers for a person who speaks much.

"Bhikkhus, there are these five benefits for a person of judicious speech. What five? He does not speak falsely; he does not speak divisively; he does not speak harshly; he does not speak idle chatter; with the breakup of the body, after death, he is reborn in a good destination, in a heavenly world. These are the five benefits for a person of judicious speech."

215 (5) Impatience (1)

"Bhikkhus, there are these five dangers in impatience. What five? One is displeasing and disagreeable to many people; one has an abundance of enmity;[1221] one has an abundance of faults; one dies confused; with the breakup of the body, after death, one is reborn in the plane of misery, in a bad destination, in the lower world, in hell. These are the five dangers in impatience.

"Bhikkhus, there are these five benefits in patience. What five? One is pleasing and agreeable to many people; one does not have an abundance of enmity; one does not have an abundance of faults; one dies unconfused; with the breakup of the body, after death, one is reborn in a good destination, in a heavenly world. These are the five benefits in patience." [255]

216 (6) Impatience (2)

"Bhikkhus, there are these five dangers in impatience. What five? One is displeasing and disagreeable to many people; one is violent; one is remorseful; one dies confused; with the breakup of the body, after death, one is reborn in the plane of misery, in a bad destination, in the lower world, in hell. These are the five dangers in impatience.

"Bhikkhus, there are these five benefits in patience. What five? One is pleasing and agreeable to many people; one is not violent; one is without remorse; one dies unconfused; with the breakup of the body, after death, one is reborn in a good destination, in a heavenly world. These are the five benefits in patience."

217 (7) Not Inspiring Confidence (1)

"Bhikkhus, there are these five dangers in conduct that does not inspire confidence. What five? One blames oneself; the wise, having investigated, censure one; one acquires a bad reputation; one dies confused; with the breakup of the body, after death, one is reborn in the plane of misery, in a bad destination, in the lower world, in hell. These are the five dangers in conduct that does not inspire confidence.

"Bhikkhus, there are these five benefits in conduct that inspires confidence. What five? One does not blame oneself; the wise, having investigated, praise one; one acquires a good reputation; one dies unconfused; with the breakup of the body, after death, one is reborn in a good destination, in a heavenly world. These are the five benefits in conduct that inspires confidence."

218 (8) Not Inspiring Confidence (2)

"Bhikkhus, there are these five dangers in conduct that does not inspire confidence. What five? [256] Those without confidence do not gain confidence; some of those with confidence change their minds; the teaching of the Teacher is not carried out; [those in] the next generation follow one's example; and one's own mind does not become placid.[1222] These are the five dangers in conduct that does not inspire confidence.

"Bhikkhus, there are these five benefits in conduct that inspires confidence. What five? Those without confidence gain confidence; those with confidence increase [in their confidence]; the teaching of the Teacher is carried out; [those in] the next generation follow one's example; and one's own mind becomes placid. These are the five benefits in conduct that inspires confidence."

219 (9) Fire

"Bhikkhus, there are these five dangers in fire. What five? It is not good for the eyes; it causes a bad complexion; it causes weakness; it promotes fondness of company; and it conduces to pointless talk. These are the five dangers in fire."

220 (10) Madhurā

"Bhikkhus, there are these five dangers in Madhurā.[1223] What five? It is uneven; it is dusty; its dogs are fierce; it has wild spirits; and it is difficult to gain almsfood there. These are the five dangers in Madhurā." [257]

III. Lengthy Wandering

221 (1) Lengthy Wandering (1)

"Bhikkhus, there are these five dangers for one who engages in lengthy and unsettled wandering.[1224] What five? One does not hear what one has not heard; one does not clarify what one has heard; one is not confident about the portion that one has heard; one contracts a severe illness; and one has no friends. These are the five dangers for one who engages in lengthy and unsettled wandering.

"Bhikkhus, there are these five benefits in periodic wandering. What five? One gets to hear what one has not heard; one clarifies what one has heard; one is confident about some things one has heard; one does not contract a severe illness; and one has friends. These are the five benefits in periodic wandering."

222 (2) Lengthy Wandering (2)

"Bhikkhus, there are these five dangers for one who engages in lengthy and unsettled wandering. What five? One does not achieve what one has not yet achieved; one falls away from what one has already achieved; one is timid about some things one has achieved; one contracts a severe illness; and one has no friends. These are the five dangers for one who engages in lengthy and unsettled wandering.

"Bhikkhus, there are these five benefits in periodic wandering. What five? One achieves what one has not yet achieved; one does not fall away from what one has already achieved; one is confident about the portion that one has achieved; one does not contract a severe illness; and one has friends. These are the five benefits in periodic wandering." [258]

223 (3) Residing Too Long

"Bhikkhus, there are these five dangers in residing too long [in the same place]. What five? (1) One comes to own and accumulate many goods; (2) one comes to own and accumulate many medicines; (3) one takes on many tasks and duties and becomes competent in the various things to be done; (4) one forms bonds with householders and monastics in an unsuitable way typical of laypeople; and (5) when one departs from that monastery, one departs full of concern. These are the five dangers in residing too long [in the same place].

"Bhikkhus, there are these five benefits in residing for a balanced period [in the same place]. What five? (1) One does not come to own and accumulate many goods; (2) one does not come to own and accumulate many medicines; (3) one does not take on many tasks and duties and become competent in the various things to be done; (4) one does not form bonds with householders and monastics in an unsuitable way typical of laypeople; and (5) when one departs from that monastery, one departs without concern. These are the five benefits in residing for a balanced period [in the same place]."

224 (4) Miserly

"Bhikkhus, there are these five dangers in residing too long [in the same place]. What five? One becomes miserly with dwelling places, miserly with families, miserly with gains, miserly with praise, and miserly with the Dhamma. These are the five dangers in residing too long [in the same place].

"Bhikkhus, there are these five benefits in residing for a balanced period [in the same place]. What five? One does not become miserly with dwelling places, miserly with families, miserly with gains, miserly with praise, and miserly with the Dhamma. These are the five benefits in residing for a balanced period [in the same place]."

225 (5) One Who Visits Families (1)

"Bhikkhus, there are these five dangers for one who visits families. What five? [259] (1) One commits the offense of going to visit [families] without taking leave [of another bhikkhu]. (2) One commits the offense of sitting privately [with a woman]. (3) One commits the offense of sitting on a concealed seat [with a woman]. (4) One commits the offense of teaching the Dhamma to a woman in more than five or six sentences. (5) One is infested by sensual thoughts. These are the five dangers for one who visits families."[1225]

226 (6) One Who Visits Families (2)

"Bhikkhus, there are these five dangers when a bhikkhu who visits families bonds too closely with them. What five? (1) He often gets to see women. (2) When he often gets to see them, he bonds with them. (3) When he bonds with them, they become intimate. (4) When they become intimate, lust finds an opening. (5) When his mind is in the grip of lust, it can be expected that he will lead the spiritual life dissatisfied, commit a certain defiled offense, or give up the training and return to the lower life.[1226] These are the five dangers when a bhikkhu who visits families bonds too closely with them."

227 (7) Wealth

"Bhikkhus, there are these five dangers in wealth. What five? It is shared by fire, water, kings, thieves, and displeasing heirs. These are the five dangers in wealth.

"Bhikkhus, there are these five benefits in wealth. What five? By means of wealth, (1) one makes oneself happy and pleased and properly maintains oneself in happiness; (2) one makes one's parents happy and pleased and properly maintains them in happiness; (3) one makes one's wife and children, slaves, workers, and servants happy and pleased and properly maintains them in happiness; (4) one makes one's friends and companions happy and pleased and properly maintains them in happiness; (5) one establishes for ascetics and brahmins an uplifting offering of alms that is heavenly, resulting in happiness, and conducive to heaven. These are the five benefits in wealth." [260]

228 (8) A Meal

"Bhikkhus, there are these five dangers for a family that prepares their meal late in the day.[1227] What five? (1) Guests who are visiting are not served on time. (2) The deities that receive oblations are not served on time. (3) Ascetics and brahmins who eat once a day and refrain from eating at night, abstaining from meals outside the proper time, are not served on time. (4) Slaves, workers, and servants grimace when they do their work. (5) Much of a poorly timed meal is not nutritious. These are the five dangers for a family that prepares their meal late in the day.

"Bhikkhus, there are these five benefits for a family that prepares their meal at the proper time.[1228] What five? (1) Guests who are visiting are served on time. (2) The deities that receive oblations are served on time. (3) Ascetics and brahmins who eat once a day and refrain from eating at night, abstaining from meals outside the proper time, are served on time. (4) Slaves, workers, and servants do their work without grimacing. (5) Much of a properly timed meal is nutritious. These are the five benefits for a family that prepares their meal at the proper time."

229 (9) Snake (1)

"Bhikkhus, there are these five dangers in a black snake. What five? It is impure, foul-smelling, frightening, dangerous, and it betrays friends. These are the five dangers in a black snake. So too, there are these five dangers in women. What five? They are impure, foul-smelling, frightening, dangerous, and they betray friends. These are the five dangers in women."[1229]

230 (10) Snake (2)

"Bhikkhus, there are these five dangers in a black snake. What five? It is wrathful, hostile, of virulent venom, double-tongued, and it betrays friends. [261] These are the five dangers in a black snake. So too, there are these five dangers in women. What five? They are wrathful, hostile, of virulent venom, double-tongued, and they betray friends.

"Bhikkhus, this is how women are of virulent venom: for the most part they have strong lust. This is how women are double-tongued: for the most part they utter divisive speech. This is how women betray friends: for the most part they are adulterous. These are the five dangers in women."[1230]

IV. Resident

231 (1) Not to Be Esteemed

"Bhikkhus, possessing five qualities, a resident bhikkhu is not to be esteemed. What five? (1) He is not accomplished in manners and duties; (2) he is not learned or an expert in learning; (3) he is not given to effacement nor is he one who delights in seclusion; (4) he is not a good speaker and he lacks a good delivery; (5) he is unwise, stupid, and obtuse. Possessing these five qualities, a resident bhikkhu is not to be esteemed.

"Bhikkhus, possessing five qualities, a resident bhikkhu is to be esteemed. What five? [262] (1) He is accomplished in manners and duties; (2) he is learned and an expert in learning; (3) he is given to effacement and delights in seclusion; (4) he is a good speaker with a good delivery; (5) he is wise, intelligent, and astute. Possessing these five qualities, a resident bhikkhu is to be esteemed."

232 (2) Pleasing

"Bhikkhus, possessing five qualities, a resident bhikkhu is pleasing and agreeable to his fellow monks and is respected and esteemed by them. What five? (1) He is virtuous; he dwells restrained by the Pātimokkha, possessed of good conduct and resort, seeing danger in minute faults. Having undertaken the training rules, he trains in them. (2) He has learned much, remembers what he has learned, and accumulates what he has learned. Those teachings that are good in the beginning, good in the middle, and good in the end, with the right meaning and phrasing, which proclaim the perfectly complete and pure spiritual life—such teachings as these he has learned much of, retained in mind, recited verbally, mentally investigated, and penetrated well by view. (3) He is a good speaker with a good delivery; he is gifted with speech that is polished, clear, articulate, expressive of the meaning. (4) He gains at will, without trouble or difficulty, the four jhānas that constitute the higher mind and are pleasant dwellings in this very life. (5) With the destruction of the taints, he has realized for himself with direct knowledge, in this very life, the taintless liberation of mind, liberation by wisdom, and having entered upon it, he dwells in it. Possessing these five qualities, a resident bhikkhu is pleasing and agreeable to his fellow monks and is respected and esteemed by them."

233 (3) Beautifying

"Bhikkhus, possessing five qualities, a resident bhikkhu beautifies a monastery. What five? [263] (1) He is virtuous; he dwells restrained by the Pātimokkha . . . he trains in them. (2) He has learned much . . . and penetrated well by view. (3) He is a good speaker with a good delivery; he is gifted with speech that is polished, clear, articulate, expressive of the meaning. (4) He is able to instruct, encourage, inspire, and gladden with a Dhamma talk those who approach him. (5) He gains at will, without trouble or difficulty, the four jhānas that constitute the higher mind and are pleasant dwellings in this very life. Possessing these five qualities, a resident bhikkhu beautifies a monastery."

234 (4) Very Helpful

"Bhikkhus, possessing five qualities, a resident bhikkhu is very helpful to a monastery. What five? (1) He is virtuous; he dwells restrained by the Pātimokkha . . . he trains in them. (2) He has learned much . . . and penetrated well by view. (3) He repairs what is broken and split. (4) When a large Saṅgha of bhikkhus has arrived including bhikkhus from various states, he approaches laypeople and informs them: 'Friends, a large Saṅgha of bhikkhus has arrived including bhikkhus from various states. Make merit. It is an occasion to make merit.' (5) He gains at will, without trouble or difficulty, the four jhānas that constitute the higher mind and are pleasant dwellings in this very life. Possessing these five qualities, a resident bhikkhu is very helpful to a monastery."

235 (5) Compassionate

"Bhikkhus, possessing five qualities, a resident bhikkhu shows compassion to laypeople. What five? (1) He encourages them in regard to virtuous behavior. (2) He settles them in the vision of the Dhamma.[1231] (3) When they are ill he approaches them and arouses mindfulness in them, saying: [264] 'Let the honorable ones establish mindfulness on that which is worthy.'[1232] (4) When a large Saṅgha of bhikkhus has arrived, including bhikkhus from various states, he approaches laypeople and informs them: 'Friends, a large Saṅgha of bhikkhus has arrived including bhikkhus from various states. Make merit. It is an occasion to make merit.' (5) He himself eats whatever food they give him, whether coarse or excellent; he does not squander what has been given out of faith. Possessing these five qualities, a resident bhikkhu shows compassion to laypeople."

236 (6) One Who Deserves Dispraise (1)

"Bhikkhus, possessing five qualities, a resident bhikkhu is deposited in hell as if brought there. What five? (1) Without investigating and scrutinizing, he speaks praise of one who deserves dispraise. (2) Without investigating and scrutinizing, he speaks dispraise of one who deserves praise. (3) Without investigating and scrutinizing, he believes a matter that merits suspicion. (4) Without investigating and scrutinizing, he is suspicious about a matter that merits belief. (5) He squanders what has been given out of faith. Possessing these five qualities, a resident bhikkhu is deposited in hell as if brought there.

"Bhikkhus, possessing five qualities, a resident bhikkhu is deposited in heaven as if brought there. What five? (1) Having investigated and scrutinized, he speaks dispraise of one who deserves dispraise. (2) Having investigated and scrutinized, he speaks praise of one who deserves praise. (3) Having investigated and scrutinized, he is suspicious about a matter that merits suspicion. (4) Having investigated and scrutinized, he believes a matter that merits belief. (5) He does not squander what has been given out of faith. Possessing these five qualities, a resident bhikkhu is deposited in heaven as if brought there." [265]

237 (7) One Who Deserves Dispraise (2)

"Bhikkhus, possessing five qualities, a resident bhikkhu is deposited in hell as if brought there. What five? (1) Without investigating and scrutinizing, he speaks praise of one who deserves dispraise. (2) Without investigating and scrutinizing, he speaks dispraise of one who deserves praise. (3) He is miserly and greedy with regard to dwellings. (4) He is miserly and greedy with regard to families. (5) He squanders what has been given out of faith. Possessing these five qualities, a resident bhikkhu is deposited in hell as if brought there.

"Bhikkhus, possessing five qualities, a resident bhikkhu is deposited in heaven as if brought there. What five? (1) Having investigated and scrutinized, he speaks dispraise of one who deserves dispraise. (2) Having investigated and scrutinized, he speaks praise of one who deserves praise. (3) He is not miserly and greedy with regard to dwellings. (4) He is not miserly and greedy with regard to families. (5) He does not squander what has been given out of faith. Possessing these five qualities, a resident bhikkhu is deposited in heaven as if brought there."

238 (8) One Who Deserves Dispraise (3)

"Bhikkhus, possessing five qualities, a resident bhikkhu is deposited in hell as if brought there. What five? (1) Without investigating and scrutinizing, he speaks praise of one who deserves dispraise. (2) Without investigating and scrutinizing, he speaks dispraise of one who deserves praise. (3) He is miserly with regard to dwellings. (4) He is miserly with regard to families. (5) He is miserly with regard to gains. Possessing these five qualities, a resident bhikkhu is deposited in hell as if brought there.

"Bhikkhus, possessing five qualities, a resident bhikkhu is deposited in heaven as if brought there. What five? (1) Having investigated and scrutinized, he speaks dispraise of one who deserves dispraise. (2) Having investigated and scrutinized, he speaks praise of one who deserves praise. [266] (3) He is not miserly with regard to dwellings. (4) He is not miserly with regard to families. (5) He is not miserly with regard to gains. Possessing these five qualities, a resident bhikkhu is deposited in heaven as if brought there."

239 (9) Miserliness (1)

"Bhikkhus, possessing five qualities, a resident bhikkhu is deposited in hell as if brought there. What five? (1) He is miserly with regard to dwellings. (2) He is miserly with regard to families. (3) He is miserly with regard to gains. (4) He is miserly with regard to praise. (5) He squanders what has been given out of faith. Possessing these five qualities, a resident bhikkhu is deposited in hell as if brought there.

"Bhikkhus, possessing five qualities, a resident bhikkhu is deposited in heaven as if brought there. What five? (1) He is not miserly with regard to dwellings. (2) He is not miserly with regard to families. (3) He is not miserly with regard to gains. (4) He is not miserly with regard to praise. (5) He does not squander what has been given out of faith. Possessing these five qualities, a resident bhikkhu is deposited in heaven as if brought there."

240 (10) Miserliness (2)

"Bhikkhus, possessing five qualities, a resident bhikkhu is deposited in hell as if brought there. What five? (1) He is miserly with regard to dwellings. (2) He is miserly with regard to families. (3) He is miserly with regard to gains. (4) He is miserly with regard to praise. (5) He is miserly with regard to the Dhamma. Possessing these five qualities, a resident bhikkhu is deposited in hell as if brought there.

"Bhikkhus, possessing five qualities, a resident bhikkhu

is deposited in heaven as if brought there. What five? (1) He is not miserly with regard to dwellings. (2) He is not miserly with regard to families. (3) He is not [267] miserly with regard to gains. (4) He is not miserly with regard to praise. (5) He is not miserly with regard to the Dhamma. Possessing these five qualities, a resident bhikkhu is deposited in heaven as if brought there."

V. Misconduct

241 (1) Misconduct

"Bhikkhus, there are these five dangers in misconduct. What five? (1) One blames oneself. (2) The wise, having investigated, censure one. (3) One acquires a bad reputation. (4) One dies confused. (5) With the breakup of the body, after death, one is reborn in the plane of misery, in a bad destination, in the lower world, in hell. These are the five dangers in misconduct.

"Bhikkhus, there are these five benefits in good conduct. What five? (1) One does not censure oneself. (2) The wise, having investigated, praise one. (3) One acquires a good reputation. (4) One dies unconfused. (5) With the breakup of the body, after death, one is reborn in a good destination, in a heavenly world. These are the five benefits in good conduct."

242 (2) Bodily Misconduct

"Bhikkhus, there are these five dangers in bodily misconduct. What five? . . . [as in 5:241] . . . These are the five dangers in bodily misconduct.

"Bhikkhus, there are these five benefits in bodily good conduct. What five? . . . [as in 5:241] . . . These are the five benefits in bodily good conduct."

243 (3) Verbal Misconduct

"Bhikkhus, there are these five dangers in verbal misconduct. What five? . . . [as in 5:241] . . . These are the five dangers in verbal misconduct.

"Bhikkhus, there are these five benefits in verbal good conduct. What five? . . . [as in 5:241] . . . These are the five benefits in verbal good conduct."

244 (4) Mental Misconduct

"Bhikkhus, there are these five dangers in mental misconduct. What five? . . . [as in 5:241] . . . These are the five dangers in mental misconduct.

"Bhikkhus, there are these five benefits in mental good conduct. What five? [268] . . . [as in 5:241] . . . These are the five benefits in mental good conduct."

245 (5) Another on Misconduct

"Bhikkhus, there are these five dangers in misconduct. What five? (1) One blames oneself. (2) The wise, having investigated, censure one. (3) One acquires a bad reputation. (4) One departs from the good Dhamma. (5) One becomes established in a bad Dhamma. These are the five dangers in misconduct.

"Bhikkhus, there are these five benefits in good conduct. What five? (1) One does not blame oneself. (2) The wise, having investigated, praise one. (3) One acquires a good reputation. (4) One departs from a bad Dhamma. (5) One becomes established in the good Dhamma. These are the five benefits in good conduct."

246 (6) Another on Bodily Misconduct

"Bhikkhus, there are these five dangers in bodily misconduct. What five? . . . [as in 5:245] . . . These are the five dangers in bodily misconduct.

"Bhikkhus, there are these five benefits in bodily good conduct. What five? . . . [as in 5:245] . . . These are the five benefits in bodily good conduct."

247 (7) Another on Verbal Misconduct

"Bhikkhus, there are these five dangers in verbal misconduct. What five? . . . [as in 5:245] . . . These are the five dangers in verbal misconduct.

"Bhikkhus, there are these five benefits in verbal good conduct. What five? . . . [as in 5:245] . . . These are the five benefits in verbal good conduct."

248 (8) Another on Mental Misconduct

"Bhikkhus, there are these five dangers in mental misconduct. What five? . . . [as in 5:245] . . . These are the five dangers in mental misconduct.

"Bhikkhus, there are these five benefits in mental good conduct. What five? . . . [as in 5:245] . . . These are the five benefits in mental good conduct."

249 (9) A Charnel Ground

"Bhikkhus, there are these five dangers in a charnel ground. What five? It is impure, foul-smelling, dangerous, the abode of wild spirits, [a place where] many people weep. These are the five dangers in a charnel ground. So too, there are these five dangers in a person who is similar to a charnel ground. What five? [269]

(1) "Here, some person engages in impure bodily, verbal, and mental action. This, I say, is how he is impure. Just as that charnel ground is impure, I say this person is similarly so.

(2) "Since he engages in impure bodily, verbal, and mental action, he acquires a bad reputation. This, I say, is how he is foul-smelling. Just as that charnel ground is foul-smelling, I say this person is similarly so.

(3) "Since he engages in impure bodily, verbal, and mental action, his well-behaved fellow monks avoid him from afar. This, I say, is how he is [regarded as] dangerous. Just as that charnel ground is [regarded as] dangerous, I say this person is similarly so.

(4) "Engaging in impure bodily, verbal, and mental action, he dwells together with persons similar to himself. This, I say, is how he is an abode of wild [persons]. Just as that charnel ground is an abode of wild spirits, I say this person is similarly so.

(5) "Having seen him engaging in impure bodily, verbal, and mental action, his well-behaved fellow monks lodge complaints about him, saying: 'Oh, what misery it is for us to live together with such persons!' This, I say, is how there is weeping over him. Just as that charnel ground is [a place where] many people weep, I say this person is similarly so.

"These, bhikkhus, are the five dangers in a person who is like a charnel ground." [270]

250 (10) Confidence in a Person

"Bhikkhus, there are these five dangers in basing one's confidence on a person. What five?

(1) "The person in whom another has complete confidence may commit an offense because of which the Saṅgha suspends

him. It occurs to the one [who had such confidence in him]: 'The person who is pleasing and agreeable to me has been suspended by the Saṅgha.' He then loses much of his confidence in bhikkhus. Since he has lost much of his confidence in them, he does not associate with other bhikkhus. Since he does not associate with other bhikkhus, he does not get to hear the good Dhamma. Since he does not get to hear the good Dhamma, he falls away from the good Dhamma. This is the first danger in basing one's confidence on a person.

(2) "Again, the person in whom another has complete confidence may commit an offense because of which the Saṅgha makes him sit at the end.[1233] It occurs to the one [who had such confidence in him]: 'The Saṅgha has made the person who is pleasing and agreeable to me sit at the end.' He then loses much of his confidence in bhikkhus. . . . Since he does not get to hear the good Dhamma, he falls away from the good Dhamma. This is the second danger in basing one's confidence on a person.

(3) "Again, the person in whom another has complete confidence may depart for some other quarter . . . (4) . . . may disrobe . . . (5) . . . may pass away. It occurs to the one [who had such confidence in him]: 'The person who was pleasing and agreeable to me [has departed for some other quarter . . . has disrobed . . .] has passed away.'[1234] He does not associate with other bhikkhus. Since he does not associate with other bhikkhus, he does not get to hear the good Dhamma. Since he does not get to hear the good Dhamma, he falls away from the good Dhamma. This is the fifth danger in basing one's confidence on a person.

"These, bhikkhus, are the five dangers in basing one's confidence on a person." [271]

The Sixth Fifty

I. Full Ordination[1235]

251 (1) Who May Give Full Ordination

"Bhikkhus, possessing five qualities, a bhikkhu may give full ordination.[1236] What five? Here, a bhikkhu possesses the aggregate of virtuous behavior of one beyond training; he possesses the aggregate of concentration of one beyond training; he possesses the aggregate of wisdom of one beyond training; he possesses the aggregate of liberation of one beyond training; he possesses the aggregate of the knowledge and vision of liberation of one beyond training. Possessing these five qualities, a bhikkhu may give full ordination."

252 (2) Dependence

"Bhikkhus, possessing five qualities, a bhikkhu may give dependence.[1237] What five? Here, a bhikkhu possesses the aggregate of virtuous behavior . . . the aggregate of concentration . . . the aggregate of wisdom . . . the aggregate of liberation . . . the aggregate of the knowledge and vision of liberation of one beyond training. Possessing these five qualities, a bhikkhu may give dependence."

253 (3) Novice

"Bhikkhus, possessing five qualities, a bhikkhu may be attended upon by a novice. What five? Here, a bhikkhu possesses the aggregate of virtuous behavior . . . the aggregate of concentration . . . the aggregate of wisdom . . . the aggregate of liberation . . . the aggregate of the knowledge and vision of liberation of one beyond training. Possessing these five qualities, a bhikkhu may be attended upon by a novice." [272]

254 (4) Miserliness

"Bhikkhus, there are these five kinds of miserliness. What five? Miserliness with regard to dwellings, miserliness with regard to families, miserliness with regard to gains, miserliness with regard to praise, and miserliness with regard to the Dhamma. These are the five kinds of miserliness. Of these five kinds of miserliness, the vilest[1238] is miserliness with regard to the Dhamma."

255 (5) Abandoning Miserliness

"Bhikkhus, the spiritual life is lived for the abandoning and eradication of five kinds of miserliness. What five? Miserliness with regard to dwellings, miserliness with regard to families, miserliness with regard to gains, miserliness with regard to praise, and miserliness with regard to the Dhamma. The spiritual life is lived for the abandoning and eradication of these five kinds of miserliness."

256 (6) First Jhāna

"Bhikkhus, without having abandoned these five things one is incapable of entering and dwelling in the first jhāna. What five? Miserliness with regard to dwellings, miserliness with regard to families, miserliness with regard to gains, miserliness with regard to praise, and miserliness with regard to the Dhamma. Without having abandoned these five things, one is incapable of entering and dwelling in the first jhāna.

"Bhikkhus, having abandoned these five things, one is capable of entering and dwelling in the first jhāna. What five? Miserliness with regard to dwellings . . . miserliness with regard to the Dhamma. Having abandoned these five things, one is capable of entering and dwelling in the first jhāna."

257 (7)–263 (13) Second Jhāna, Etc.[1239]

"Bhikkhus, without having abandoned these five things one is incapable of entering and dwelling in the second jhāna . . . the third jhāna . . . the fourth jhāna . . . one is incapable of realizing the fruit of stream-entry . . . the fruit of once-returning . . . the fruit of non-returning . . . the fruit of arahantship. What five? [273] Miserliness with regard to dwellings . . . miserliness with regard to the Dhamma. Without having abandoned these five things, one is incapable of realizing the fruit of arahantship.

"Bhikkhus, having abandoned these five things, one is capable of entering and dwelling in the second jhāna . . . the third jhāna . . . the fourth jhāna . . . one is capable of realizing the fruit of stream-entry . . . the fruit of once-returning . . . the fruit of non-returning . . . the fruit of arahantship. What five? Miserliness with regard to dwellings . . . miserliness with regard to the Dhamma. Having abandoned these five things, one is capable of realizing the fruit of arahantship."

264 (14) Another on the First Jhāna

"Bhikkhus, without having abandoned these five things one is incapable of entering and dwelling in the first jhāna. What five? Miserliness with regard to dwellings, miserliness with regard to families, miserliness with regard to gains, miserliness with regard to praise, and ingratitude or unthankfulness. Without having abandoned these five things, one is incapable of entering and dwelling in the first jhāna.

"Bhikkhus, having abandoned these five things, one is capable of entering and dwelling in the first jhāna. What five? Miserliness with regard to dwellings, miserliness with regard to families, miserliness with regard to gains, miserliness with regard to praise, and ingratitude or unthankfulness. Having abandoned these five things, one is capable of entering and dwelling in the first jhāna."

265 (15)–271 (21) Another on the Second Jhāna, Etc.

"Bhikkhus, without having abandoned these five things one is incapable of entering and dwelling in the second jhāna ... the third jhāna ... the fourth jhāna ... one is incapable of realizing the fruit of stream-entry ... the fruit of once-returning ... the fruit of non-returning ... the fruit of arahantship. What five? Miserliness with regard to dwellings ... ingratitude or unthankfulness. Without having abandoned these five things, one is incapable of realizing the fruit of arahantship.

"Bhikkhus, having abandoned these five things, one is capable of entering and dwelling in the second jhāna ... the third jhāna ... the fourth jhāna ... one is capable of realizing the fruit of stream-entry ... the fruit of once-returning ... the fruit of non-returning ... the fruit of arahantship. What five? Miserliness with regard to dwellings ... ingratitude or unthankfulness. Having abandoned these five things, one is capable of realizing the fruit of arahantship." [274]

Discourses Extra to the Chapter[1240]

I. Agreed Upon Repetition Series

272 (1) An Assigner of Meals

(1) "Bhikkhus, one possessing five qualities should not be appointed an assigner of meals.[1241] What five? He enters upon a wrong course because of desire; he enters upon a wrong course because of hatred; he enters upon a wrong course because of delusion; he enters upon a wrong course because of fear; he does not know which [meal] has been assigned and which has not been assigned. One possessing these five qualities should not be appointed an assigner of meals.

"Bhikkhus, one possessing five qualities may be appointed an assigner of meals. What five? He does not enter upon a wrong course because of desire; he does not enter upon a wrong course because of hatred; he does not enter upon a wrong course because of delusion; he does not enter upon a wrong course because of fear; he knows which [meal] has been assigned and which has not been assigned. One possessing these five qualities may be appointed an assigner of meals."

(2) "Bhikkhus, if one who possesses five qualities is appointed an assigner of meals, he should not be sent.[1242] What five? He enters upon a wrong course because of desire . . . he does not know which [meal] has been assigned and which has not been assigned. If one who possesses these five qualities is appointed an assigner of meals, he should not be sent.

"Bhikkhus, one who possesses five qualities, if appointed an assigner of meals, should be sent. What five? He does not enter upon a wrong course because of desire . . . he knows which [meal] has been assigned and which has not been assigned. One who possesses these five qualities, if appointed an assigner of meals, should be sent."

(3) "Bhikkhus, an assigner of meals who possesses five qualities should be understood as foolish. What five? He enters upon a wrong course because of desire . . . he does not know which [meal] has been assigned and which has not been assigned. An assigner of meals who possesses these five qualities should be understood as foolish.

"Bhikkhus, an assigner of meals who possesses five qualities should be understood as wise. What five? He does not enter upon a wrong course because of desire . . . he knows which [meal] has been assigned and which has not been assigned. An assigner of meals who possesses these five qualities should be understood as wise."

(4) "Bhikkhus, an assigner of meals who possesses five qualities maintains himself in a maimed and injured condition. What five? He enters upon a wrong course because of desire . . . he does not know which [meal] has been assigned and which has not been assigned. An assigner of meals who possesses these five qualities maintains himself in a maimed and injured condition.

"Bhikkhus, an assigner of meals who possesses five qualities preserves himself unmaimed and uninjured. What five?

He does not enter upon a wrong course because of desire . . . he knows which [meal] has been assigned and which has not been assigned. An assigner of meals who possesses these five qualities preserves himself unmaimed and uninjured."

(5) "Bhikkhus, an assigner of meals who possesses five qualities is deposited in hell as if brought there. What five? He enters upon a wrong course because of desire . . . he does not know which [meal] has been assigned and which has not been assigned. An assigner of meals who possesses these five qualities is deposited in hell as if brought there.

"Bhikkhus, an assigner of meals who possesses five qualities is deposited in heaven as if brought there. What five? He does not enter upon a wrong course because of desire . . . he knows which [meal] has been assigned and which has not been assigned. An assigner of meals who possesses these five qualities is deposited in heaven as if brought there."

273 (2)–284 (13) An Appointer of Lodgings, Etc.

(273) "Bhikkhus, one who possesses five qualities should not be appointed an appointer of lodgings.[1243] He enters upon a wrong course because of desire . . . he does not know which [lodging] has been appointed and which has not been appointed. . . . Bhikkhus, one who possesses five qualities may be appointed an appointer of lodgings. He does not enter upon a wrong course because of desire . . . he knows which [lodging] has been appointed and which [lodging] has not been appointed. . . ."

(274) "Bhikkhus, one who possesses five qualities should not be appointed an allocator of lodgings[1244] . . . he does not know which [lodging] has been allocated and which [lodging] has not been allocated. . . . Bhikkhus, one who possesses five qualities may be appointed an allocator of lodgings . . . he knows which [lodging] has been allocated and which [lodging] has not been allocated. . . ."

(275) "Bhikkhus, one who possesses five qualities should not be appointed a guardian of the storeroom . . . he does not know which [goods] are being protected and which are not being protected. . . . Bhikkhus, one who possesses five qualities may be appointed a guardian of the storeroom . . . he knows which [goods] are being protected and which are not being protected. . . ."

(276) "Bhikkhus, one who possesses five qualities should

not be appointed a receiver of robe-material . . . he does not know which [robe-material] has been received and which has not been received. . . . Bhikkhus, one who possesses five qualities may be appointed a receiver of robe-material [275] . . . he knows which [robe-material] has been received and which has not been received. . . ."

(277) "Bhikkhus, one who possesses five qualities should not be appointed a distributor of robe-material . . . he does not know which [robe-material] has been distributed and which has not been distributed. . . . Bhikkhus, one who possesses five qualities may be appointed a distributor of robe-material . . . he knows which [robe-material] has been distributed and which has not been distributed. . . ."

(278) "Bhikkhus, one who possesses five qualities should not be appointed a distributor of rice porridge . . . he does not know which [rice porridge] has been distributed and which has not been distributed. . . . Bhikkhus, one who possesses five qualities may be appointed a distributor of rice porridge . . . he knows which [rice porridge] has been distributed and which has not been distributed. . . ."

(279) "Bhikkhus, one who possesses five qualities should not be appointed a distributor of fruit . . . he does not know which [fruit] has been distributed and which has not been distributed. . . . Bhikkhus, one who possesses five qualities may be appointed a distributor of fruit . . . he knows which [fruit] has been distributed and which has not been distributed. . . ."

(280) "Bhikkhus, one who possesses five qualities should not be appointed a distributor of cakes . . . he does not know which [cakes] have been distributed and which have not been distributed. . . . Bhikkhus, one who possesses five qualities may be appointed a distributor of cakes . . . he knows which [cakes] have been distributed and which have not been distributed. . . ."

(281) "Bhikkhus, one who possesses five qualities should not be appointed a dispenser of small accessories . . . he does not know which [small accessories] have been dispensed and which have not been dispensed. . . . Bhikkhus, one who possesses five qualities may be appointed a dispenser of small accessories . . . he knows which [small accessories] have been dispensed and which have not been dispensed. . . ."

(282) "Bhikkhus, one who possesses five qualities should

not be appointed an allocator of rains cloth . . . he does not know which [rains cloth] has been allocated and which has not been allocated. . . . Bhikkhus, one who possesses five qualities may be appointed an allocator of rains cloth . . . he knows which [rains cloth] has been allocated and which has not been allocated. . . ."

(283) "Bhikkhus, one who possesses five qualities should not be appointed an allocator of bowls . . . he does not know which [bowls] have been allocated and which have not been allocated. . . . Bhikkhus, one who possesses five qualities may be appointed an allocator of bowls . . . he knows which [bowls] have been allocated and which have not been allocated. . . ."

(284) "Bhikkhus, one who possesses five qualities should not be appointed a supervisor of monastery attendants . . . he does not know which [monastery attendant] has been supervised and which has not been supervised. . . . Bhikkhus, one who possesses five qualities may be appointed a supervisor of monastery attendants . . . he knows which [monastery attendant] has been supervised and which has not been supervised. . . ."

285 (14) A Supervisor of Novices

(1) "Bhikkhus, one who possesses five qualities should not be appointed a supervisor of novices. What five? He enters upon a wrong course because of desire . . . he does not know which [novices] have been supervised and which have not been supervised. One who possesses these five qualities should not be appointed a supervisor of novices.

"Bhikkhus, one who possesses five qualities may be appointed a supervisor of novices. What five? He does not enter upon a wrong course because of desire . . . he knows which [novices] have been supervised and which have not been supervised. One who possesses these five qualities may be appointed a supervisor of novices."

(2) "Bhikkhus, one who possesses five qualities, if appointed a supervisor of novices, should not be sent. What five? He enters upon a wrong course because of desire . . . he does not know which [novices] have been supervised and which have not been supervised. One who possesses these five qualities, if appointed a supervisor of novices, should not be sent.

"Bhikkhus, one who possesses five qualities, if appointed

a supervisor of novices, should be sent. What five? He does not enter upon a wrong course because of desire . . . he knows which [novices] have been supervised and which have not been supervised. One who possesses these five qualities, if appointed a supervisor of novices, should be sent."

(3) "Bhikkhus, a supervisor of novices who possesses five qualities should be understood as foolish. What five? He enters upon a wrong course because of desire . . . he does not know which [novices] have been supervised and which have not been supervised. A supervisor of novices who possesses these five qualities should be understood as foolish.

"Bhikkhus, a supervisor of novices who possesses five qualities should be understood as wise. What five? He does not enter upon a wrong course because of desire . . . he knows which [novices] have been supervised and which have not been supervised. A supervisor of novices who possesses these five qualities should be understood as wise."

(4) "Bhikkhus, a supervisor of novices who possesses five qualities maintains himself in a maimed and injured condition. What five? He enters upon a wrong course because of desire . . . he does not know which [novices] have been supervised and which have not been supervised. A supervisor of novices who possesses these five qualities maintains himself in a maimed and injured condition.

"Bhikkhus, a supervisor of novices who possesses five qualities preserves himself unmaimed and uninjured. What five? He does not enter upon a wrong course because of desire . . . he knows which [novices] have been supervised and which have not been supervised. A supervisor of novices who possesses these five qualities preserves himself unmaimed and uninjured."

(5) "Bhikkhus, a supervisor of novices who possesses five qualities is deposited in hell as if brought there. What five? He enters upon a wrong course because of desire . . . he does not know which [novices] have been supervised and which have not been supervised. A supervisor of novices who possesses these five qualities is deposited in hell as if brought there.

"Bhikkhus, a supervisor of novices who possesses five qualities is deposited in heaven as if brought there. What five? He does not enter upon a wrong course because of desire . . . he knows which [novices] have been supervised and which have not been supervised. A supervisor of novices who possesses these five qualities is deposited in heaven as if brought there."

II. Training Rules Repetition Series

286 (1) A Bhikkhu

"Bhikkhus, possessing five qualities, a bhikkhu is deposited in hell as if brought there. What five? He is one who destroys life, takes what is not given, does not observe celibacy,[1245] speaks falsely, and indulges in liquor, wine, and intoxicants, the basis for heedlessness. [276] Possessing these five qualities, a bhikkhu is deposited in hell as if brought there.

"Bhikkhus, possessing five qualities, a bhikkhu is deposited in heaven as if brought there. What five? He is one who abstains from the destruction of life, from taking what is not given, from sexual activity,[1246] from false speech, and from liquor, wine, and intoxicants, the basis for heedlessness. Possessing these five qualities, a bhikkhu is deposited in heaven as if brought there."

287 (2)–290 (5) A Bhikkhunī, Etc.

"Bhikkhus, possessing five qualities, a bhikkhunī . . . a female probationer . . . a male novice . . . a female novice is deposited in hell as if brought there. What five? She destroys life . . . and indulges in liquor, wine, and intoxicants. . . . Possessing these five qualities, a bhikkhunī . . . a female probationer . . . a male novice . . . a female novice is deposited in hell as if brought there.

"Bhikkhus, possessing five qualities, a bhikkhunī . . . a female probationer . . . a male novice . . . a female novice is deposited in heaven as if brought there. What five? She abstains from the destruction of life . . . from liquor, wine, and intoxicants. . . . Possessing these five qualities, a bhikkhunī . . . a female probationer . . . a male novice . . . a female novice is deposited in heaven as if brought there."

291 (6)–292 (7) A Male and Female Lay Follower

"Bhikkhus, possessing five qualities, a male lay follower . . . a female lay follower is deposited in hell as if brought there.

What five? She destroys life, takes what is not given, engages in sexual misconduct,[1247] speaks falsely, and indulges in liquor, wine, and intoxicants, the basis for heedlessness. Possessing these five qualities, a male lay follower . . . a female lay follower is deposited in hell as if brought there.

"Bhikkhus, possessing five qualities, a male lay follower . . . a female lay follower is deposited in heaven as if brought there. What five? She abstains from the destruction of life, abstains from taking what is not given, abstains from sexual misconduct, abstains from false speech, abstains from liquor, wine, and intoxicants, the basis for heedlessness. Possessing these five qualities, a male lay follower . . . a female lay follower is deposited in heaven as if brought there."

293 (8) An Ājīvaka

"Bhikkhus, possessing five qualities, an Ājīvaka is deposited in hell as if brought there.[1248] What five? He destroys life, takes what is not given, does not observe celibacy, speaks falsely, and indulges in liquor, wine, and intoxicants, the basis for heedlessness. Possessing these five qualities, an Ājīvaka is deposited in hell as if brought there."

294 (9)–302 (17) A Nigaṇṭha, Etc.

"Bhikkhus, possessing five qualities, a Nigaṇṭha . . . a shaven-headed disciple . . . a matted-hair ascetic . . . a wanderer . . . a *māgandika* . . . a *tedaṇḍika* . . . an *āruddhaka* . . . a *gotamaka* [277] . . . a *devadhammika* is deposited in hell as if brought there.[1249] What five? He destroys life, takes what is not given, does not observe celibacy, speaks falsely, and indulges in liquor, wine, and intoxicants, the basis for heedlessness. Possessing these five qualities, a *devadhammika* is deposited in hell as if brought there."

III. Lust and So Forth Repetition Series

303 (1)

"Bhikkhus, for direct knowledge of lust, five things are to be developed. What five? The perception of unattractiveness, the perception of death, the perception of danger, the perception of the repulsiveness of food, and the perception of non-delight in the entire world. For direct knowledge of lust, these five things are to be developed."

304 (2)

"Bhikkhus, for direct knowledge of lust, five things are to be developed. What five? The perception of impermanence, the perception of non-self, the perception of death, the perception of the repulsiveness of food, and the perception of non-delight in the entire world. For direct knowledge of lust, these five things are to be developed."

305 (3)

"Bhikkhus, for direct knowledge of lust, five things are to be developed. What five? The perception of impermanence, the perception of suffering in what is impermanent, the perception of non-self in what is suffering, the perception of abandoning, and the perception of dispassion. For direct knowledge of lust, these five things are to be developed."

306 (4)

"Bhikkhus, for direct knowledge of lust, five things are to be developed. What five? The faculty of faith, the faculty of energy, the faculty of mindfulness, the faculty of concentration, and the faculty of wisdom. For direct knowledge of lust, these five things are to be developed." [278]

307 (5)

"Bhikkhus, for direct knowledge of lust, five things are to be developed. What five? The power of faith, the power of energy, the power of mindfulness, the power of concentration, and the power of wisdom. For direct knowledge of lust, these five things are to be developed."

308 (6)–316 (14)

"Bhikkhus, for full understanding of lust . . . for the utter destruction . . . for the abandoning . . . for the destruction . . . for the vanishing . . . for the fading away . . . for the cessation . . . for the giving up . . . for the relinquishment of lust, five things are to be developed. What five? The perception of unattractiveness . . . [all five sets of five as above, down to] . . . The power of faith, the power of energy, the power of mindfulness, the power of concentration, and the power of wisdom. For the relinquishment of lust, these five things are to be developed."

317 (15)–1152 (850)[1250]

"Bhikkhus, for direct knowledge . . . for full understanding . . . for the utter destruction . . . for the abandoning . . . for the destruction . . . for the vanishing . . . for the fading away . . . for the cessation . . . for the giving up . . . for the relinquishment of hatred . . . of delusion . . . of anger . . . of hostility . . . of denigration . . . of insolence . . . of envy . . . of miserliness . . . of deceitfulness . . . of craftiness . . . of obstinacy . . . of vehemence . . . of conceit . . . of arrogance . . . of intoxication . . . of heedlessness, five things are to be developed. What five? The perception of unattractiveness . . . [all five sets of five as above, down to] . . . The power of faith, the power of energy, the power of mindfulness, the power of concentration, and the power of wisdom. For the relinquishment of heedlessness, these five things are to be developed."

This is what the Blessed One said. Elated, those bhikkhus delighted in the Blessed One's statement.

The Book of the Fives is finished.

The Book of the Sixes

(*Chakkanipāta*)

The Book of the Sixes

The First Fifty

The Second Fifty

Chapters Extra to the Set of Fifty

[279] # The Book of the Sixes

Homage to the Blessed One, the Arahant, the Perfectly Enlightened One

The First Fifty

I. Worthy of Gifts

1 (1) Worthy of Gifts (1)

Thus have I heard. On one occasion the Blessed One was dwelling at Sāvatthī in Jeta's Grove, Anāthapiṇḍika's Park. There the Blessed One addressed the bhikkhus: "Bhikkhus!"

"Venerable sir!" those bhikkhus replied. The Blessed One said this:

"Bhikkhus, possessing six qualities, a bhikkhu is worthy of gifts, worthy of hospitality, worthy of offerings, worthy of reverential salutation, an unsurpassed field of merit for the world. What six? (1) Here, having seen a form with the eye, a bhikkhu is neither joyful nor saddened, but dwells equanimous, mindful, and clearly comprehending.[1251] (2) Having heard a sound with the ear, a bhikkhu is neither joyful nor saddened, but dwells equanimous, mindful, and clearly comprehending. (3) Having smelled an odor with the nose, a bhikkhu is neither joyful nor saddened, but dwells equanimous, mindful, and clearly comprehending. (4) Having experienced a taste with the tongue, a bhikkhu is neither joyful nor saddened, but dwells equanimous, mindful, and clearly comprehending. (5) Having felt a tactile object with the body, a bhikkhu is neither joyful nor saddened, but dwells equanimous, mindful, and clearly comprehending. (6) Having cognized a mental phenomenon with the mind, a bhikkhu is neither joyful nor saddened, but dwells equanimous, mindful, and clearly comprehending. Possessing these six qualities, a bhikkhu is worthy of gifts, worthy of hospitality, worthy of offerings, worthy of reverential salutation, an unsurpassed field of merit for the world."

This is what the Blessed One said. Elated, those bhikkhus delighted in the Blessed One's statement. [280]

2 (2) Worthy of Gifts (2)

"Bhikkhus, possessing six qualities, a bhikkhu is worthy of gifts, worthy of hospitality, worthy of offerings, worthy of reverential salutation, an unsurpassed field of merit for the world. What six?[1252]

(1) "Here, a bhikkhu wields the various kinds of psychic potency: having been one, he becomes many; having been many, he becomes one; he appears and vanishes; he goes unhindered through a wall, through a rampart, through a mountain as though through space; he dives in and out of the earth as though it were water; he walks on water without sinking as though it were earth; seated cross-legged, he travels in space like a bird; with his hand he touches and strokes the moon and sun so powerful and mighty; he exercises mastery with the body as far as the brahmā world.

(2) "With the divine ear element, which is purified and surpasses the human, he hears both kinds of sounds, the divine and human, those that are far as well as near.

(3) "He understands the minds of other beings and persons, having encompassed them with his own mind. He understands a mind with lust as a mind with lust and a mind without lust as a mind without lust; a mind with hatred as a mind with hatred and a mind without hatred as a mind without hatred; a mind with delusion as a mind with delusion and a mind without delusion as a mind without delusion; a contracted mind as contracted and a distracted mind as distracted; an exalted mind as exalted and an unexalted mind as unexalted; a surpassable mind as surpassable and an unsurpassable mind as unsurpassable; a concentrated mind as concentrated and an unconcentrated mind as unconcentrated; a liberated mind as liberated and an unliberated mind as unliberated.

(4) "He recollects his manifold past abodes, that is, one birth, two births, three births, four births, five births, ten births, twenty births, thirty births, forty births, fifty [281] births, a hundred

births, a thousand births, a hundred thousand births, many eons of world-dissolution, many eons of world-evolution, many eons of world-dissolution and world-evolution thus: 'There I was so named, of such a clan, with such an appearance, such was my food, such my experience of pleasure and pain, such my life span; passing away from there, I was reborn elsewhere, and there too I was so named, of such a clan, with such an appearance, such was my food, such my experience of pleasure and pain, such my life span; passing away from there, I was reborn here.' Thus he recollects his manifold past abodes with their aspects and details.

(5) "With the divine eye, which is purified and surpasses the human, he sees beings passing away and being reborn, inferior and superior, beautiful and ugly, fortunate and unfortunate, and he understands how beings fare in accordance with their kamma thus: 'These beings who engaged in misconduct by body, speech, and mind, who reviled the noble ones, held wrong view, and undertook kamma based on wrong view, with the breakup of the body, after death, have been reborn in the plane of misery, in a bad destination, in the lower world, in hell; but these beings who engaged in good conduct by body, speech, and mind, who did not revile the noble ones, who held right view, and undertook kamma based on right view, with the breakup of the body, after death, have been reborn in a good destination, in a heavenly world.' Thus with the divine eye, which is purified and surpasses the human, he sees beings passing away and being reborn, inferior and superior, beautiful and ugly, fortunate and unfortunate, and he understands how beings fare in accordance with their kamma.

(6) "With the destruction of the taints, he has realized for himself with direct knowledge, in this very life, the taintless liberation of mind, liberation by wisdom, and having entered upon it, he dwells in it.

"Possessing these six qualities, a bhikkhu is worthy of gifts, worthy of hospitality, worthy of offerings, worthy of reverential salutation, an unsurpassed field of merit for the world."

3 (3) Faculties

"Bhikkhus, possessing six qualities, a bhikkhu is worthy of gifts, worthy of hospitality, worthy of offerings, worthy of reverential salutation, an unsurpassed field of merit for the world.

What six? [282] The faculty of faith, the faculty of energy, the faculty of mindfulness, the faculty of concentration, the faculty of wisdom; and with the destruction of the taints, he has realized for himself with direct knowledge, in this very life, the taintless liberation of mind, liberation by wisdom, and having entered upon it, he dwells in it. Possessing these six qualities, a bhikkhu is worthy of gifts, worthy of hospitality, worthy of offerings, worthy of reverential salutation, an unsurpassed field of merit for the world."

4 (4) Powers

"Bhikkhus, possessing six qualities, a bhikkhu is worthy of gifts, worthy of hospitality, worthy of offerings, worthy of reverential salutation, an unsurpassed field of merit for the world. What six? The power of faith, the power of energy, the power of mindfulness, the power of concentration, the power of wisdom; and with the destruction of the taints, he has realized for himself with direct knowledge, in this very life, the taintless liberation of mind, liberation by wisdom, and having entered upon it, he dwells in it. Possessing these six qualities, a bhikkhu is worthy of gifts, worthy of hospitality, worthy of offerings, worthy of reverential salutation, an unsurpassed field of merit for the world."

5 (5) Thoroughbred (1)

"Bhikkhus, possessing six factors, a king's excellent thoroughbred horse is worthy of a king, an accessory of a king, and reckoned as a factor of kingship. What six? Here, a king's excellent thoroughbred horse patiently endures forms, patiently endures sounds, patiently endures odors, patiently endures tastes, patiently endures tactile objects, and it is endowed with beauty. Possessing these six factors, a king's excellent thoroughbred horse is worthy of a king, an accessory of a king, and reckoned as a factor of kingship.[1253]

"So too, possessing six qualities, a bhikkhu is worthy of gifts, worthy of hospitality, worthy of offerings, worthy of reverential salutation, an unsurpassed field of merit for the world. What six? [283] Here, a bhikkhu patiently endures forms, patiently endures sounds, patiently endures odors, patiently endures tastes, patiently endures tactile objects, and patiently endures mental phenomena. Possessing these six qualities, a bhikkhu is worthy of gifts, worthy of hospitality, worthy of offerings, worthy of reverential salutation, an unsurpassed field of merit for the world."

6 (6) Thoroughbred (2)

"Bhikkhus, possessing six factors, a king's excellent thoroughbred horse is worthy of a king, an accessory of a king, and reckoned as a factor of kingship. What six? Here, a king's excellent thoroughbred horse patiently endures forms, patiently endures sounds, patiently endures odors, patiently endures tastes, patiently endures tactile objects, and it is endowed with strength. Possessing these six factors, a king's excellent thoroughbred horse is worthy of a king, an accessory of a king, and reckoned as a factor of kingship.

"So too, possessing six qualities, a bhikkhu is worthy of gifts, worthy of hospitality, worthy of offerings, worthy of reverential salutation, an unsurpassed field of merit for the world. What six? Here, a bhikkhu patiently endures forms, patiently endures sounds, patiently endures odors, patiently endures tastes, patiently endures tactile objects, and patiently endures mental phenomena. Possessing these six qualities, a bhikkhu is worthy of gifts, worthy of hospitality, worthy of offerings, worthy of reverential salutation, an unsurpassed field of merit for the world."

7 (7) Thoroughbred (3)

"Bhikkhus, possessing six factors, a king's excellent thoroughbred horse is worthy of a king, an accessory of a king, and reckoned as a factor of kingship. What six? Here, a king's excellent thoroughbred horse patiently endures forms, patiently endures sounds, patiently endures odors, patiently endures tastes, patiently endures tactile objects, and it is endowed with speed. [284] Possessing these six factors, a king's excellent thoroughbred horse is worthy of a king, an accessory of a king, and reckoned as a factor of kingship.

"So too, possessing six qualities, a bhikkhu is worthy of gifts, worthy of hospitality, worthy of offerings, worthy of reverential salutation, an unsurpassed field of merit for the world. What six? Here, a bhikkhu patiently endures forms, patiently endures sounds, patiently endures odors, patiently endures tastes, patiently endures tactile objects, and patiently endures mental phenomena. Possessing these six qualities, a bhikkhu is worthy of gifts, worthy of hospitality, worthy of offerings, worthy of reverential salutation, an unsurpassed field of merit for the world."

8 (8) Unsurpassed Things

"Bhikkhus, there are these six unsurpassed things. What six? The unsurpassed sight, the unsurpassed hearing, the unsurpassed gain, the unsurpassed training, the unsurpassed service, and the unsurpassed recollection. These are the six unsurpassed things."[1254]

9 (9) Subjects of Recollection

"Bhikkhus, there are these six subjects of recollection. What six? Recollection of the Buddha, recollection of the Dhamma, recollection of the Saṅgha, recollection of virtuous behavior, recollection of generosity, and recollection of the deities. These are the six subjects of recollection."[1255]

10 (10) Mahānāma

On one occasion the Blessed One was dwelling among the Sakyans at Kapilavatthu in the Banyan Tree Park. Then Mahānāma the Sakyan approached the Blessed One, paid homage to him, sat down to one side, and said to the Blessed One:

"Bhante, how does a noble disciple who has arrived at the fruit and understood the teaching often dwell?"[1256]

"Mahānāma, a noble disciple [285] who has arrived at the fruit and understood the teaching often dwells in this way:[1257]

(1) "Here, Mahānāma, a noble disciple recollects the Tathāgata thus: 'The Blessed One is an arahant, perfectly enlightened, accomplished in true knowledge and conduct, fortunate, knower of the world, unsurpassed trainer of persons to be tamed, teacher of devas and humans, the Enlightened One, the Blessed One.' When a noble disciple recollects the Tathāgata, on that occasion his mind is not obsessed by lust, hatred, or delusion; on that occasion his mind is simply straight, based on the Tathāgata. A noble disciple whose mind is straight gains inspiration in the meaning, gains inspiration in the Dhamma,

gains joy connected with the Dhamma. When he is joyful, rapture arises. For one with a rapturous mind, the body becomes tranquil. One tranquil in body feels pleasure. For one feeling pleasure, the mind becomes concentrated. This is called a noble disciple who dwells in balance amid an unbalanced population,[1258] who dwells unafflicted amid an afflicted population. As one who has entered the stream of the Dhamma,[1259] he develops recollection of the Buddha.

(2) "Again, Mahānāma, a noble disciple recollects the Dhamma thus: 'The Dhamma is well expounded by the Blessed One, directly visible, immediate, inviting one to come and see, applicable, to be personally experienced by the wise.' When a noble disciple recollects the Dhamma, on that occasion his mind is not obsessed by lust, hatred, or delusion; on that occasion his mind is simply straight, based on the Dhamma. A noble disciple whose mind is straight gains inspiration in the meaning, gains inspiration in the Dhamma, gains joy connected with the Dhamma. When he is joyful, rapture arises. For one with a rapturous mind, the body becomes tranquil. One tranquil in body feels pleasure. For one feeling pleasure, the mind becomes concentrated. This is called a noble disciple who dwells in balance amid an unbalanced population, who dwells unafflicted amid an afflicted population. [286] As one who has entered the stream of the Dhamma, he develops recollection of the Dhamma.

(3) "Again, Mahānāma, a noble disciple recollects the Saṅgha thus: 'The Saṅgha of the Blessed One's disciples is practicing the good way, practicing the straight way, practicing the true way, practicing the proper way; that is, the four pairs of persons, the eight types of individuals—this Saṅgha of the Blessed One's disciples is worthy of gifts, worthy of hospitality, worthy of offerings, worthy of reverential salutation, the unsurpassed field of merit for the world.' When a noble disciple recollects the Saṅgha, on that occasion his mind is not obsessed by lust, hatred, or delusion; on that occasion his mind is simply straight, based on the Saṅgha. A noble disciple whose mind is straight gains inspiration in the meaning, gains inspiration in the Dhamma, gains joy connected with the Dhamma. When he is joyful, rapture arises. For one with a rapturous mind, the body becomes tranquil. One tranquil in body feels pleasure. For one feeling

pleasure, the mind becomes concentrated. This is called a noble disciple who dwells in balance amid an unbalanced population, who dwells unafflicted amid an afflicted population. As one who has entered the stream of the Dhamma, he develops recollection of the Saṅgha.

(4) "Again, Mahānāma, a noble disciple recollects his own virtuous behavior as unbroken, flawless, unblemished, unblotched, freeing, praised by the wise, ungrasped, leading to concentration. When a noble disciple recollects his virtuous behavior, on that occasion his mind is not obsessed by lust, hatred, or delusion; on that occasion his mind is simply straight, based on virtuous behavior. A noble disciple whose mind is straight gains inspiration in the meaning, gains inspiration in the Dhamma, gains joy connected with the Dhamma. When he is joyful, rapture arises. For one with a rapturous mind, the body becomes tranquil. One tranquil in body feels pleasure. For one feeling pleasure, the mind becomes concentrated. [287] This is called a noble disciple who dwells in balance amid an unbalanced population, who dwells unafflicted amid an afflicted population. As one who has entered the stream of the Dhamma, he develops recollection of virtuous behavior.

(5) "Again, Mahānāma, a noble disciple recollects his own generosity thus: 'It is truly my good fortune and gain that in a population obsessed by the stain of miserliness, I dwell at home with a mind devoid of the stain of miserliness, freely generous, openhanded, delighting in relinquishment, devoted to charity, delighting in giving and sharing.' When a noble disciple recollects his generosity, on that occasion his mind is not obsessed by lust, hatred, or delusion; on that occasion his mind is simply straight, based on generosity. A noble disciple whose mind is straight gains inspiration in the meaning, gains inspiration in the Dhamma, gains joy connected with the Dhamma. When he is joyful, rapture arises. For one with a rapturous mind, the body becomes tranquil. One tranquil in body feels pleasure. For one feeling pleasure, the mind becomes concentrated. This is called a noble disciple who dwells in balance amid an unbalanced population, who dwells unafflicted amid an afflicted population. As one who has entered the stream of the Dhamma, he develops recollection of generosity.

(6) "Again, Mahānāma, a noble disciple recollects the deities

thus: 'There are devas [ruled by] the four great kings, Tāvatiṃsa devas, Yāma devas, Tusita devas, devas who delight in creation, devas who control what is created by others, devas of Brahmā's company, and devas still higher than these.[1260] There exists in me too such faith as those deities possessed because of which, when they passed away here, they were reborn there; there exists in me too such virtuous behavior . . . such learning . . . such generosity . . . such wisdom as those deities possessed because of which, when they passed away here, they were reborn there.' When [288] a noble disciple recollects the faith, virtuous behavior, learning, generosity, and wisdom in himself and in those deities, on that occasion his mind is not obsessed by lust, hatred, or delusion; on that occasion his mind is simply straight, based on the deities. A noble disciple whose mind is straight gains inspiration in the meaning, gains inspiration in the Dhamma, gains joy connected with the Dhamma. When he is joyful, rapture arises. For one with a rapturous mind, the body becomes tranquil. One tranquil in body feels pleasure. For one feeling pleasure, the mind becomes concentrated. This is called a noble disciple who dwells in balance amid an unbalanced population, who dwells unafflicted amid an afflicted population. As one who has entered the stream of the Dhamma, he develops recollection of the deities.

"Mahānāma, a noble disciple who has arrived at the fruit and understood the teaching often dwells in just this way."

II. Cordiality

11 (1) Cordiality (1)

"Bhikkhus, there are these six principles of cordiality.[1261] What six?

(1) "Here, a bhikkhu maintains bodily acts of loving-kindness toward his fellow monks both openly and privately. This is a principle of cordiality.

(2) "Again, a bhikkhu maintains verbal acts of loving-kindness toward his fellow monks both openly and privately. This, too, is a principle of cordiality.

(3) "Again, a bhikkhu maintains mental acts of loving-kindness toward his fellow monks both openly and privately. This, too, is a principle of cordiality. [289]

(4) "Again, a bhikkhu shares without reservation[1262] any righteous gains that have been righteously obtained, including even the contents of his alms bowl, and uses such things in common with his virtuous fellow monks. This, too, is a principle of cordiality.

(5) "Again, a bhikkhu dwells both openly and privately possessing in common with his fellow monks virtuous behavior that is unbroken, flawless, unblemished, unblotched, freeing, praised by the wise, ungrasped, leading to concentration. This, too, is a principle of cordiality.

(6) "Again, a bhikkhu dwells both openly and privately possessing in common with his fellow monks a view that is noble and emancipating, which leads out, for one who acts upon it, to the complete destruction of suffering. This, too, is a principle of cordiality.

"These, bhikkhus, are the six principles of cordiality."

12 (2) Cordiality (2)

"Bhikkhus, there are these six principles of cordiality that create affection and respect and conduce to cohesiveness, non-dispute, concord, and unity. What six?

(1) "Here, a bhikkhu maintains bodily acts of loving-kindness toward his fellow monks both openly and privately. This is a principle of cordiality that creates affection and respect and conduces to cohesiveness, non-dispute, concord, and unity.

(2) "Again, a bhikkhu maintains verbal acts of loving-kindness toward his fellow monks both openly and privately. This, too, is a principle of cordiality that creates affection and respect. . . .

(3) "Again, a bhikkhu maintains mental acts of loving-kindness toward his fellow monks both openly and privately. This, too, is a principle of cordiality that creates affection and respect. . . .

(4) "Again, a bhikkhu shares without reservation any righteous gains that have been righteously obtained, including even the contents of his alms bowl, and uses such things in common [290] with his virtuous fellow monks. This, too, is a principle of cordiality that creates affection and respect. . . .

(5) "Again, a bhikkhu dwells both openly and privately possessing in common with his fellow monks virtuous behavior that is unbroken, flawless, unblemished, unblotched, free-

ing, praised by the wise, ungrasped, leading to concentration. This, too, is a principle of cordiality that creates affection and respect. . . .

(6) "Again, a bhikkhu dwells both openly and privately possessing in common with his fellow monks a view that is noble and emancipating, which leads out, for one who acts upon it, to the complete destruction of suffering. This, too, is a principle of cordiality that creates affection and respect. . . .

"These, bhikkhus, are the six principles of cordiality that create affection and respect and conduce to cohesiveness, to nondispute, to concord, and to unity."

13 (3) Escape

"Bhikkhus, there are these six elements of escape.[1263] What six?

(1) "Here, a bhikkhu might say thus: 'I have developed and cultivated the liberation of the mind by loving-kindness, made it my vehicle and basis, carried it out, consolidated it, and properly undertaken it, yet ill will still obsesses my mind.' He should be told: 'Not so! Do not speak thus. Do not misrepresent the Blessed One; for it is not good to misrepresent the Blessed One. The Blessed One would certainly not speak in such a way. It is impossible and inconceivable, friend, that one might develop and cultivate the liberation of the mind by loving-kindness, make it one's vehicle and basis, carry it out, consolidate it, and properly undertake it, yet [291] ill will could still obsess one's mind. There is no such possibility. For this, friend, is the escape from ill will, namely, the liberation of the mind by loving-kindness.'

(2) "Then, a bhikkhu might say thus: 'I have developed and cultivated the liberation of the mind by compassion, made it my vehicle and basis, carried it out, consolidated it, and properly undertaken it, yet the thought of harming still obsesses my mind.' He should be told: 'Not so! Do not speak thus. Do not misrepresent the Blessed One; for it is not good to misrepresent the Blessed One. The Blessed One would certainly not speak in such a way. It is impossible and inconceivable, friend, that one might develop and cultivate the liberation of the mind by compassion, make it one's vehicle and basis, carry it out, consolidate it, and properly undertake it, yet the thought of harming could

still obsess one's mind. There is no such possibility. For this, friend, is the escape from the thought of harming, namely, the liberation of the mind by compassion.'

(3) "Then, a bhikkhu might say thus: 'I have developed and cultivated the liberation of the mind by altruistic joy, made it my vehicle and basis, carried it out, consolidated it, and properly undertaken it, yet discontent still obsesses my mind.'[1264] He should be told: 'Not so! Do not speak thus. Do not misrepresent the Blessed One; for it is not good to misrepresent the Blessed One. The Blessed One would certainly not speak in such a way. It is impossible and inconceivable, friend, that one might develop and cultivate the liberation of the mind by altruistic joy, make it one's vehicle and basis, carry it out, consolidate it, and properly undertake it, yet discontent could still obsess one's mind. There is no such possibility. For this, friend, is the escape from discontent, namely, the liberation of the mind by altruistic joy.'

(4) "Then, a bhikkhu might say thus: 'I have developed and cultivated the liberation of the mind by equanimity, made it my vehicle and basis, carried it out, consolidated it, and properly undertaken it, yet lust still obsesses my mind.' He should be told: 'Not so! Do not speak thus. Do not misrepresent the Blessed One; for it is not good to misrepresent the Blessed One. The Blessed One would certainly not speak in such a way. It is impossible and inconceivable, friend, that one might develop and cultivate the liberation of the mind by equanimity, make it one's vehicle and basis, carry it out, consolidate it, and properly undertake it, [292] yet lust could still obsess one's mind. There is no such possibility. For this, friend, is the escape from lust, namely, the liberation of the mind by equanimity.'[1265]

(5) "Then, a bhikkhu might say thus: 'I have developed and cultivated the markless liberation of the mind,[1266] made it my vehicle and basis, carried it out, consolidated it, and properly undertaken it, yet my consciousness still follows after marks.'[1267] He should be told: 'Not so! Do not speak thus. Do not misrepresent the Blessed One; for it is not good to misrepresent the Blessed One. The Blessed One would certainly not speak in such a way. It is impossible and inconceivable, friend, that one might develop and cultivate the markless liberation of the mind, make it one's vehicle and basis, carry it out, consolidate

it, and properly undertake it, yet one's consciousness could still follow after marks. There is no such possibility. For this, friend, is the escape from all marks, namely, the markless liberation of the mind.'

(6) "Then, a bhikkhu might say: 'I have discarded [the notion] "I am," and I do not regard [anything as] "This I am," yet the dart of doubt and bewilderment still obsesses my mind.' He should be told: 'Not so! Do not speak thus. Do not misrepresent the Blessed One; for it is not good to misrepresent the Blessed One. The Blessed One would certainly not speak in such a way. It is impossible and inconceivable, friend, that when [the notion] "I am" has been discarded, and one does not regard [anything as] "This I am," the dart of doubt and bewilderment could still obsess one's mind. There is no such possibility. For this, friend, is the escape from the dart of doubt and bewilderment, namely, the uprooting of the conceit "I am."'[1268]

"These, bhikkhus, are the six elements of escape."

14 (4) A Good Death

There the Venerable Sāriputta addressed the bhikkhus: "Friends, bhikkhus!"

"Friend!" those bhikkhus [293] replied. The Venerable Sāriputta said this:

"Friends, a bhikkhu passes his time[1269] in such a way that he does not have a good death.[1270] And how does a bhikkhu pass his time in such a way that he does not have a good death?

"Here, (1) a bhikkhu delights in work, takes delight in work, is devoted to delight in work;[1271] (2) he delights in talk, takes delight in talk, is devoted to delight in talk; (3) he delights in sleep, takes delight in sleep, is devoted to delight in sleep; (4) he delights in company, takes delight in company, is devoted to delight in company; (5) he delights in bonding, takes delight in bonding, is devoted to delight in bonding; (6) he delights in proliferation, takes delight in proliferation, is devoted to delight in proliferation.[1272] When a bhikkhu passes his time in such a way he does not have a good death. This is called a bhikkhu who delights in personal existence,[1273] who has not abandoned personal existence to completely make an end of suffering.

"Friends, a bhikkhu passes his time in such a way that he has a good death. And how does a bhikkhu pass his time in such a way that he has a good death?

"Here, (1) a bhikkhu does not delight in work, does not take delight in work, is not devoted to delight in work; (2) he does not delight in talk, does not take delight in talk, is not devoted to delight in talk; (3) he does not delight in sleep, does not take delight in sleep, is not devoted to delight in sleep; (4) he does not delight in company, does not take delight in company, is not devoted to delight in company; (5) he does not delight in bonding, does not take delight in bonding, is not devoted to delight in bonding; (6) he does not delight in proliferation, does not take delight in proliferation, is not devoted to delight in proliferation. When a bhikkhu [294] passes his time in such a way he has a good death. This is called a bhikkhu who delights in nibbāna, who has abandoned personal existence to completely make an end of suffering."

> The creature[1274] devoted to proliferation,
> who is delighted with proliferation,
> has failed to attain nibbāna,
> the unsurpassed security from bondage.
>
> But one who has abandoned proliferation,
> who finds delight in non-proliferation,
> has attained nibbāna,
> the unsurpassed security from bondage.

15 (5) Regret

There the Venerable Sāriputta addressed the bhikkhus....

"Friends, a bhikkhu passes his time in such a way that he dies with regret. And how does a bhikkhu pass his time in such a way that he dies with regret?

"Here, (1) a bhikkhu delights in work, takes delight in work, is devoted to delight in work ... [as in 6:14] ... (6) he delights in proliferation, takes delight in proliferation, is devoted to delight in proliferation. When a bhikkhu passes his time in such a way he dies with regret. This is called a bhikkhu who delights in personal existence, who has not abandoned personal existence to completely make an end of suffering.

"Friends, a bhikkhu passes his time in such a way that he dies without regret. And how does a bhikkhu pass his time in such a way that he dies without regret?

"Here, (1) a bhikkhu does not delight in work, does not take delight in work, is not devoted to delight in work . . . [295] . . . (6) does not delight in proliferation, does not take delight in proliferation, is not devoted to delight in proliferation. When a bhikkhu passes his time in such a way he dies without regret. This is called a bhikkhu who delights in nibbāna, who has abandoned personal existence to completely make an end of suffering."

[The verses are identical with those of 6:14.]

16 (6) Nakula

On one occasion the Blessed One was dwelling among the Bhaggas at Suṃsumāragira, in the deer park at Bhesakalā Grove. Now on that occasion the householder Nakulapitā was sick, afflicted, gravely ill. Then the housewife Nakulamātā said this to him: "Do not die full of concern,[1275] householder. To die full of concern is painful. To die full of concern has been criticized by the Blessed One.[1276]

(1) "It may be, householder, that you think thus: 'After I'm gone, Nakulamātā won't be able to support our children and maintain the household.' But you should not look at the matter in this way. I am skilled at weaving cotton and knitting wool. After you are gone, I'll be able to support the children [296] and maintain the household. Therefore, householder, do not die full of concern. To die full of concern is painful. To die full of concern has been criticized by the Blessed One.

(2) "It may be, householder, that you think thus: 'After I'm gone, Nakulamātā will take another husband.'[1277] But you should not look at the matter in this way. You know, householder, and so do I, that for the last sixteen years we have led the layperson's celibate life.[1278] Therefore, householder, do not die full of concern. To die full of concern is painful. To die full of concern has been criticized by the Blessed One.

(3) "It may be, householder, that you think thus: 'After I'm gone, Nakulamātā won't want to see the Blessed One and the Saṅgha of bhikkhus.' But you should not look at the matter in this way. After you are gone, householder, I will be even keener to see the Blessed One and the Saṅgha of bhikkhus. Therefore, householder, do not die full of concern. To die full of concern is

painful. To die full of concern has been criticized by the Blessed One.

(4) "It may be, householder, that you think thus: 'Nakulamātā does not fulfill virtuous behavior.'[1279] But you should not look at the matter in this way. I am one of the Blessed One's white-robed female lay disciples who fulfill virtuous behavior. If anyone has any doubt or uncertainty about this, the Blessed One, the Arahant, the Perfectly Enlightened One is dwelling among the Bhaggas at Suṃsumāragira, in the deer park at Bhesakalā Grove. They can go and ask him. Therefore, householder, do not die full of concern. [297] To die full of concern is painful. To die full of concern has been criticized by the Blessed One.

(5) "It may be, householder, that you think thus: 'Nakulamātā does not obtain internal serenity of mind.' But you should not look at the matter in this way. I am one of the Blessed One's white-robed female lay disciples who obtain internal serenity of mind. If anyone has any doubt or uncertainty about this, the Blessed One, the Arahant, the Perfectly Enlightened One is dwelling among the Bhaggas at Suṃsumāragira, in the deer park at Bhesakalā Grove. They can go and ask him. Therefore, householder, do not die full of concern. To die full of concern is painful. To die full of concern has been criticized by the Blessed One.

(6) "It may be, householder, that you think thus: 'Nakulamātā has not attained a foothold, a firm stand, assurance in this Dhamma and discipline;[1280] she has not crossed over doubt, gotten rid of bewilderment, attained self-confidence, and become independent of others in the Teacher's teaching.' But you should not look at the matter in this way. I am one of the Blessed One's white-robed female lay disciples who have attained a foothold, a firm stand, assurance in this Dhamma and discipline; I am one of those who have crossed over doubt, gotten rid of bewilderment, attained self-confidence, and become independent of others in the Teacher's teaching. If anyone has any doubt or uncertainty about this, the Blessed One, the Arahant, the Perfectly Enlightened One is dwelling among the Bhaggas at Suṃsumāragira, in the deer park at Bhesakalā Grove. They can go and ask him. Therefore, householder, do not die full of concern. To die full of concern is painful. To die full of concern has been criticized by the Blessed One."

Then, while the householder Nakulapitā [298] was being exhorted in this way by the housewife Nakulamātā, his ailment subsided on the spot. Nakulapitā recovered from that illness, and that is how his illness was abandoned.

Then, not long after he had recovered, the householder Nakulapitā, leaning on a staff, approached the Blessed One. He paid homage to the Blessed One and sat down to one side. The Blessed One then said to him:

"It is truly your good fortune and gain, householder, that the housewife Nakulamātā has compassion for you, desires your good, and exhorts and instructs you. Nakulamātā is one of my white-robed female lay disciples who fulfill virtuous behavior. She is one of my white-robed female lay disciples who obtain internal serenity of mind. She is one of my white-robed female lay disciples who have attained a foothold, a firm stand, assurance in this Dhamma and discipline, who have crossed over doubt, gotten rid of bewilderment, attained self-confidence, and become independent of others in the Teacher's teaching. It is truly your good fortune and gain, householder, that the housewife Nakulamātā has compassion for you, desires your good, and exhorts and instructs you."

17 (7) Wholesome

On one occasion the Blessed One was dwelling at Sāvatthī in Jeta's Grove, Anāthapiṇḍika's Park. Then, in the evening, the Blessed One emerged from seclusion and went to the meeting hall, where he sat down in the seat that was prepared. In the evening, the Venerable Sāriputta, too, emerged from seclusion and went to the meeting hall, where [299] he paid homage to the Blessed One and sat down to one side. The Venerable Mahāmoggallāna . . . the Venerable Mahākassapa . . . the Venerable Mahākaccāyana . . . the Venerable Mahākoṭṭhita . . . the Venerable Mahācunda . . . the Venerable Mahākappina . . . the Venerable Anuruddha . . . the Venerable Revata . . . the Venerable Ānanda, too, emerged from seclusion and went to the meeting hall, where he paid homage to the Blessed One and sat down to one side.

Then, having passed most of the night sitting, the Blessed One got up from his seat and entered his dwelling. Soon after the Blessed One had left, those venerable ones, too, got up from their seats and went to their own dwellings. But those bhikkhus who were newly ordained, who had not long gone forth and had just recently come to this Dhamma and discipline, slept, snoring away until sunrise. With the divine eye, which is purified and surpasses the human, the Blessed One saw those bhikkhus asleep, snoring away until sunrise. He then went to the meeting hall, sat down in the seat prepared for him, and addressed those bhikkhus:

"Bhikkhus, where is Sāriputta? Where is Mahāmoggallāna? Where is Mahākassapa? Where is Mahākaccāyana? Where is Mahākoṭṭhita? Where is Mahācunda? Where is Mahākappina? Where is Anuruddha? Where is Revata? Where is Ānanda? Where have those elder disciples gone?"

"Bhante, not long after the Blessed One left, those venerable ones, too, got up from their seats and went to their own dwellings."

"Bhikkhus, when the elder bhikkhus left, why did you newly ordained ones sleep, snoring away until sunrise?

(1) "What do you think, bhikkhus? Have you ever seen or heard that a head-anointed khattiya king, while exercising rule all his life, is pleasing and agreeable to the country [300] if he spends as much time as he wants yielding to the pleasure of rest, the pleasure of sloth, the pleasure of sleep?"[1281]

"No, Bhante."

"Good, bhikkhus. I too have never seen or heard of such a thing.

(2) "What do you think, bhikkhus? Have you ever seen or heard that a royal official . . . (3) . . . a favorite son . . . (4) . . . a general . . . (5) . . . a village headman . . . (6) . . . a guild master, while exercising leadership over the guild all his life, is pleasing and agreeable to the guild if he spends as much time as he wants yielding to the pleasure of rest, the pleasure of sloth, the pleasure of sleep?"

"No, Bhante."

"Good, bhikkhus. I too have never seen or heard of such a thing.

"Bhikkhus, what do you think? Suppose there is an ascetic or brahmin who spends as much time as he wants yielding to the pleasure of rest, the pleasure of sloth, the pleasure of sleep; one who does not guard the doors of the sense faculties, who is immoderate in eating, and is not intent on wakefulness; who lacks insight into wholesome qualities; who does not dwell intent on the endeavor to develop the aids to enlightenment in the earlier and later phases of the night. Have you ever seen or heard that such a one, with the destruction of the taints, has realized for himself with direct knowledge, in this very life, the taintless liberation of mind, liberation by wisdom, and having entered upon it, dwells in it?"

"No, Bhante."

"Good, bhikkhus. I too have never seen or [301] heard of such a thing.

"Therefore, bhikkhus, you should train yourselves thus: 'We will guard the doors of the sense faculties, be moderate in eating, and be intent on wakefulness; we will have insight into wholesome qualities, and will dwell intent on the endeavor to develop the aids to enlightenment in the earlier and later phases of the night.'[1282] Thus, bhikkhus, should you train yourselves."

18 (8) The Fish Dealer

On one occasion the Blessed One was wandering on tour among the Kosalans together with a large Saṅgha of bhikkhus. Then, while traveling along the highway, in a certain spot the Blessed One saw a fish dealer killing fish and selling them. He left the highway, sat down on a seat that was prepared for him at the foot of a tree, and addressed the bhikkhus: "Bhikkhus, do you see that fish dealer killing fish and selling them?"

"Yes, Bhante."

(1) "What do you think, bhikkhus? Have you ever seen or heard that a fish dealer, killing fish [302] and selling them, might, by means of this work and livelihood, travel around by elephant or horse, by chariot or vehicle, or enjoy wealth or live off a large accumulation of wealth?"

"No, Bhante."

"Good, bhikkhus. I too have never seen or heard of such a thing. For what reason? Because he looks on cruelly at the captive fish as they are brought for slaughter. Therefore he does not travel around by elephant or horse, by chariot or vehicle, or enjoy wealth or live off a large accumulation of wealth.

(2) "What do you think, bhikkhus? Have you ever seen or heard that a cattle butcher, killing cows and selling them . . . [303]

(3) . . . a butcher of sheep . . . (4) . . . a butcher of pigs . . . (5) . . . a butcher of poultry . . . (6) . . . a butcher of deer, killing deer and selling them, might, by means of that work and livelihood, travel around by elephant or horse, by chariot or vehicle, or enjoy wealth or live off a large accumulation of wealth?"

"No, Bhante."

"Good, bhikkhus. I too have never seen or heard of such a thing. For what reason? Because he looks on cruelly at the captive deer as they are brought for slaughter. Therefore he does not travel around by elephant or horse, by chariot or vehicle, or enjoy wealth or live off a large accumulation of wealth.

"Bhikkhus, one who looks on cruelly at captive animals as they are brought for slaughter will not travel around by elephant or horse, by chariot or vehicle, or enjoy wealth or live off a large accumulation of wealth. What then can be said about one who looks on cruelly at a condemned human being brought up for slaughter? This will lead to his harm and suffering for a long time. With the breakup of the body after death, he will be reborn in the plane of misery, in a bad destination, in the lower world, in hell."

19 (9) Mindfulness of Death (1)

On one occasion the Blessed One was dwelling at Nādika in the brick hall. There the Blessed One addressed the bhikkhus: [304] "Bhikkhus!"

"Venerable sir!" those bhikkhus replied. The Blessed One said this:

"Bhikkhus, mindfulness of death, when developed and cultivated, is of great fruit and benefit, culminating in the deathless, having the deathless as its consummation.[1283] But do you, bhikkhus, develop mindfulness of death?"

(1) When this was said, one bhikkhu said to the Blessed One: "Bhante, I develop mindfulness of death."

"But how, bhikkhu, do you develop mindfulness of death?"

"Here, Bhante, I think thus: 'May I live just a night and a day so that I may attend to the Blessed One's teaching.[1284] I could then accomplish much!'[1285] It is in this way that I develop mindfulness of death."

(2) Another bhikkhu said to the Blessed One: "I too, Bhante, develop mindfulness of death."

"But how, bhikkhu, do you develop mindfulness of death?"

"Here, Bhante, I think: 'May I live just a day so that I may attend to the Blessed One's teaching. I could then accomplish much!' It is in this way that I develop mindfulness of death."

(3) Still another bhikkhu said to the Blessed One: "I too, Bhante, develop mindfulness of death."

"But how, bhikkhu, do you develop mindfulness of death?"

"Here, Bhante, I think: 'May I live just the length of time it takes to eat a single alms meal[1286] so that I may attend to the Blessed One's teaching. I could then accomplish much!' It is in this way that I develop mindfulness of death."

(4) Still another bhikkhu said to the Blessed One: "I too, Bhante, develop mindfulness of death."

"But how, bhikkhu, do you develop mindfulness of death?"

"Here, Bhante, I think: 'May I live just the length of time it takes to chew and swallow four or five mouthfuls of food so that I may attend to the Blessed One's teaching. [305] I could then accomplish much!' It is in this way that I develop mindfulness of death."

(5) Still another bhikkhu said to the Blessed One: "I too, Bhante, develop mindfulness of death."

"But how, bhikkhu, do you develop mindfulness of death?"

"Here, Bhante, I think: 'May I live just the length of time it takes to chew and swallow a single mouthful of food so that I may attend to the Blessed One's teaching. I could then accomplish much!' It is in this way that I develop mindfulness of death."

(6) Still another bhikkhu said to the Blessed One: "I too, Bhante, develop mindfulness of death."

"But how, bhikkhu, do you develop mindfulness of death?"

"Here, Bhante, I think: 'May I live just the length of time it takes to breathe out after breathing in, or to breathe in after breathing out, so that I may attend to the Blessed One's teaching. I could then accomplish much!' It is in this way that I develop mindfulness of death."

When this was said, the Blessed One said to those bhikkhus:

"Bhikkhus, (1) the bhikkhu who develops mindfulness of death thus: 'May I live just a night and a day so that I may attend to the Blessed One's teaching. I could then accomplish much!'; and (2) the one who develops mindfulness of death thus: 'May I live just a day so that I may attend to the Blessed One's teaching. I could then accomplish much!'; and (3) the one who develops mindfulness of death thus: 'May I live just the length of time it takes to eat a single alms meal so that I may attend to the Blessed One's teaching. I could then accomplish much!'; and (4) the one who develops mindfulness of death thus: 'May I live just the length of time it takes to chew and swallow four or five mouthfuls of food so that I may attend to the Blessed One's teaching. I could then accomplish much!': [306] these are called bhikkhus who dwell heedlessly. They develop mindfulness of death sluggishly for the destruction of the taints.

"But (5) the bhikkhu who develops mindfulness of death thus: 'May I live just the length of time it takes to chew and swallow a single mouthful of food so that I may attend to the Blessed One's teaching. I could then accomplish much!'; and (6) the one who develops mindfulness of death thus: 'May I live just the length of time it takes to breathe out after breathing in, or to breathe in after breathing out, so that I may attend to the Blessed One's teaching. I could then accomplish much!': these are called bhikkhus who dwell heedfully. They develop mindfulness of death keenly for the destruction of the taints.

"Therefore, bhikkhus, you should train yourselves thus: 'We will dwell heedfully. We will develop mindfulness of death keenly for the destruction of the taints.' Thus should you train yourselves."

20 (10) Mindfulness of Death (2)

On one occasion the Blessed One was dwelling at Nādika in the brick hall. There the Blessed One addressed the bhikkhus:

"Bhikkhus, mindfulness of death, when developed and cultivated, is of great fruit and benefit, culminating in the deathless, having the deathless as its consummation. And how is this so?

"Here, bhikkhus, when day has receded and night has approached,[1287] a bhikkhu reflects thus: 'I could die on account of many causes. (1) A snake might bite me, or a scorpion or centipede might sting me, and I might die; that would be an obstacle for me. (2) I might stumble and fall down, or (3) my food might disagree with me, or (4) my bile [307] might become agitated, or (5) my phlegm might become agitated, or (6) sharp winds in me might become agitated, and I might die; that would be an obstacle for me.'

"This bhikkhu should reflect thus: 'Do I have any bad unwholesome qualities that have not been abandoned, which might become an obstacle for me if I were to die tonight?' If, upon review, the bhikkhu knows: 'I have bad unwholesome qualities that have not been abandoned, which might become an obstacle for me if I were to die tonight,' then he should put forth extraordinary desire, effort, zeal, enthusiasm, indefatigability, mindfulness, and clear comprehension to abandon those bad unwholesome qualities. Just as one whose clothes or head had caught fire would put forth extraordinary desire, effort, zeal, enthusiasm, indefatigability, mindfulness, and clear comprehension to extinguish [the fire on] his clothes or head, so that bhikkhu should put forth extraordinary desire, effort, zeal, enthusiasm, indefatigability, mindfulness, and clear comprehension to abandon those bad unwholesome qualities.

"But if, upon review, the bhikkhu knows thus: 'I do not have any bad unwholesome qualities that have not been abandoned, which might become an obstacle for me if I were to die tonight,' then he should dwell in that same rapture and joy, training day and night in wholesome qualities.

"But when night has receded and day has approached, a bhikkhu reflects thus: 'I could die on account of many causes. A snake might bite me . . . or sharp winds might become agitated in me, and I might die; that would be an obstacle for me.'

"This bhikkhu should reflect thus: [308] 'Do I have any bad unwholesome qualities that have not been abandoned which might become an obstacle for me if I were to die this day?' If, upon review, the bhikkhu knows: 'I have bad unwholesome qualities that I have not yet abandoned, which might become an obstacle for me if I were to die this day,' then he should put forth extraordinary desire, effort, zeal, enthusiasm, indefatigability, mindfulness, and clear comprehension to abandon those bad unwholesome qualities. Just as one whose clothes or head had caught fire would put forth extraordinary desire, effort, zeal, enthusiasm, indefatigability, mindfulness, and clear comprehension to extinguish [the fire on] his clothes or head, so that bhikkhu should put forth extraordinary desire, effort, zeal, enthusiasm, indefatigability, mindfulness, and clear comprehension to abandon those bad unwholesome qualities.

"But if, upon review, the bhikkhu knows: 'I do not have any bad unwholesome qualities that I have not yet abandoned, which might become an obstacle for me if I were to die this day,' then he should dwell in that same rapture and joy, training day and night in wholesome qualities.

"It is, bhikkhus, when mindfulness of death is developed and cultivated in this way that it is of great fruit and benefit, culminating in the deathless, having the deathless as its consummation." [309]

III. The Unsurpassed Things

21 (1) Sāmaka

On one occasion the Blessed One was dwelling among the Sakyans at Sāmagāmaka near the lotus pond. Then, when the night had advanced, a certain deity of stunning beauty, illuminating the entire lotus pond, approached the Blessed One, paid homage to him, stood to one side, and said to the Blessed One:

"Bhante, there are these three qualities that lead to the decline of a bhikkhu. What three? (1) Delight in work, (2) delight in talk, and (3) delight in sleep. These are the three qualities that lead to the decline of a bhikkhu."

This is what that deity said. The Teacher agreed. Then that deity, thinking, "The Teacher agrees with me," paid homage to the Blessed One, circumambulated him keeping the right side toward him, and disappeared right there.

Then, when the night had passed, the Blessed One addressed the bhikkhus: "Last night, bhikkhus, when the night had advanced, a certain deity of stunning beauty, illuminating the entire lotus pond, approached me, paid homage to me, stood to one side, and said to me: 'Bhante, there are these three qualities that lead to the decline of a bhikkhu. What three? Delight in work, delight in talk, and delight in sleep. These are the three qualities that lead to the decline of a bhikkhu.' This is what that deity said. Having said this, that deity paid homage to me, circumambulated me keeping the right side toward me, and disappeared right there.

"It is, bhikkhus, a misfortune and loss for those of you whom even the deities know are declining in wholesome qualities.[1288]

"I will teach, bhikkhus, another three qualities that lead to decline. Listen and attend closely. I will speak."

"Yes, Bhante," those bhikkhus replied.

The Blessed One said this: [310] "And what, bhikkhus, are the three [other] qualities that lead to decline? (4) Delight in company, (5) being difficult to correct, and (6) bad friendship. Those are the three [other] qualities that lead to decline.

"Bhikkhus, all those in the past who declined in wholesome qualities declined because of these six qualities. All those in the future who will decline in wholesome qualities will decline because of these six qualities. And all those at present who are declining in wholesome qualities are declining because of these six qualities."

22 (2) Non-Decline

"Bhikkhus, I will teach you these six qualities that lead to non-decline. Listen and attend closely. I will speak."

"Yes, Bhante," those bhikkhus replied. The Blessed One said this:

"And what, bhikkhus, are the six qualities that lead to non-decline? Not taking delight in work, not taking delight in talk, not taking delight in sleep, not taking delight in company, being easy to correct, and good friendship. These are the six qualities that lead to non-decline.

"Bhikkhus, all those in the past who did not decline in wholesome qualities did not decline because of these six qualities. All those in the future who will not decline in wholesome qualities will not decline because of these six qualities. And all those at present who are not declining in wholesome qualities are not declining because of these six qualities."

23 (3) Peril

(1) "Bhikkhus, 'peril' is a designation for sensual pleasures. (2) 'Suffering' is a designation for sensual pleasures. (3) 'Disease' is a designation for sensual pleasures. (4) 'Boil' [311] is a

designation for sensual pleasures. (5) 'Tie' is a designation for sensual pleasures. (6) 'Swamp' is a designation for sensual pleasures.

"And why, bhikkhus, is 'peril' a designation for sensual pleasures? One excited by sensual lust, bound by desire and lust, is not freed from the perils pertaining to the present life or from the perils pertaining to future lives; therefore 'peril' is a designation for sensual pleasures.

"And why is 'suffering'...'disease'...'boil'...'tie'... 'swamp' a designation for sensual pleasures? One excited by sensual lust, bound by desire and lust, is not freed from the swamps pertaining to the present life or from the swamps pertaining to future lives; therefore 'swamp' is a designation for sensual pleasures."

Peril, suffering, and disease,
a boil, a tie, and a swamp:
these describe the sensual pleasures
to which the worldling is attached.

Having seen the peril in clinging
as the origin of birth and death,
being liberated by non-clinging
in the extinction of birth and death,
those happy ones have attained security;
they have reached nibbāna in this very life.
Having overcome all enmity and peril,
they have transcended all suffering.[1289]

24 (4) Himalayas

"Bhikkhus, possessing six qualities, a bhikkhu might split the Himalayas, the king of mountains,[1290] how much more then vile ignorance! What six? Here, a bhikkhu is (1) skilled in the attainment of concentration; (2) skilled in the duration of concentration; (3) skilled in emergence from concentration; (4) skilled in fitness for concentration; (5) skilled in the area of concentration; and (6) skilled in resolution regarding concentration.[1291] [312] Possessing these six qualities, a bhikkhu might split the Himalayas, the king of mountains, how much more then vile ignorance!"

25 (5) Recollection

"Bhikkhus, there are these six subjects of recollection.[1292] What six?

(1) "Here, bhikkhus, a noble disciple recollects the Tathāgata thus: 'The Blessed One is an arahant, perfectly enlightened, accomplished in true knowledge and conduct, fortunate, knower of the world, unsurpassed trainer of persons to be tamed, teacher of devas and humans, the Enlightened One, the Blessed One.' When a noble disciple recollects the Tathāgata, on that occasion his mind is not obsessed by lust, hatred, or delusion; on that occasion his mind is simply straight. He has departed from greed, freed himself from it, emerged from it. 'Greed,' bhikkhus, is a designation for the five objects of sensual pleasure. Having made this a basis,[1293] some beings here are purified in such a way.

(2) "Again, a noble disciple recollects the Dhamma thus: 'The Dhamma is well expounded by the Blessed One, directly visible, immediate, inviting one to come and see, applicable, to be personally experienced by the wise.' When a noble disciple recollects the Dhamma, on that occasion his mind is not obsessed by lust, hatred, or delusion; on that occasion his mind is simply straight. He has departed from greed . . . some beings here are purified in such a way.

(3) "Again, a noble disciple recollects the Saṅgha thus: 'The Saṅgha of the Blessed One's disciples is practicing the good way, practicing the straight way, practicing the true way, practicing the proper way; that is, the four pairs of persons, the eight types of individuals—this Saṅgha of the Blessed One's disciples is worthy of gifts, worthy of hospitality, worthy of offerings, worthy of reverential salutation, the unsurpassed field of merit for the world.' When [313] a noble disciple recollects the Saṅgha, on that occasion his mind is not obsessed by lust, hatred, or delusion; on that occasion his mind is simply straight. He has departed from greed . . . some beings here are purified in such a way.

(4) "Again, a noble disciple recollects his own virtuous behavior as unbroken, flawless, unblemished, unblotched, freeing, praised by the wise, ungrasped, leading to concentration. When a noble disciple recollects his virtuous behavior, on that occasion his mind is not obsessed by lust, hatred, or delusion; on

that occasion his mind is simply straight. He has departed from greed . . . some beings here are purified in such a way.

(5) "Again, a noble disciple recollects his own generosity thus: 'It is truly my good fortune and gain that in a population obsessed by the stain of miserliness, I dwell with a mind devoid of the stain of miserliness, freely generous, openhanded, delighting in relinquishment, devoted to charity, delighting in giving and sharing.' When a noble disciple recollects his generosity, on that occasion his mind is not obsessed by lust, hatred, or delusion; on that occasion his mind is simply straight. He has departed from greed . . . some beings here are purified in such a way.

(6) "Again, a noble disciple recollects the deities thus: 'There are devas [ruled by] the four great kings, Tāvatiṃsa devas, Yāma devas, Tusita devas, devas who delight in creation, devas who control what is created by others, devas [314] of Brahmā's company, and devas still higher than these. I too have such faith as those deities possessed, because of which, when they passed away here, they were reborn there; I too have such virtuous behavior . . . such learning . . . such generosity . . . such wisdom as those deities possessed, because of which, when they passed away here, they were reborn there.' When a noble disciple recollects the faith, virtuous behavior, learning, generosity, and wisdom in himself and in those deities, on that occasion his mind is not obsessed by lust, hatred, or delusion; on that occasion his mind is simply straight. He has departed from greed, freed himself from it, emerged from it. 'Greed,' bhikkhus, is a designation for the five objects of sensual pleasure. Having made this a basis, too, some beings here are purified in such a way.

"These, bhikkhus, are the six subjects of recollection."

26 (6) Kaccāna

There the Venerable Mahākaccāna addressed the bhikkhus: "Friends, bhikkhus!"

"Friend!" those bhikkhus replied.

The Venerable Mahākaccāna said this:

"It's astounding and amazing, friends, that the Blessed One, the Arahant, the Perfectly Enlightened One, who knows and sees, has discovered the opening in the midst of confinement for the purification of beings, for the overcoming of sorrow and lamentation, for the passing away of pain and dejection, for the achievement of the method, for the realization of nibbāna, that is, the six subjects of recollection.[1294] What six?

(1) "Here, friends, a noble disciple recollects the Tathāgata thus: 'The Blessed One is an arahant . . . the Enlightened One, the Blessed One.' When a noble disciple recollects the Tathāgata, on that occasion his mind is not obsessed by lust, hatred, [315] or delusion; on that occasion his mind is simply straight. He has departed from greed, freed himself from it, emerged from it. 'Greed,' friends, is a designation for the five objects of sensual pleasure. This noble disciple dwells with a mind entirely like space: vast, exalted, measureless, without enmity and ill will. Having made this a basis, some beings here become pure in such a way.[1295]

(2) "Again, a noble disciple recollects the Dhamma thus: 'The Dhamma is well expounded by the Blessed One . . . to be personally experienced by the wise.' When a noble disciple recollects the Dhamma, on that occasion his mind is not obsessed by lust, hatred, or delusion; on that occasion his mind is simply straight. He has departed from greed . . . some beings here become pure in such a way.

(3) "Again, a noble disciple recollects the Saṅgha thus: 'The Saṅgha of the Blessed One's disciples is practicing the good way . . . the unsurpassed field of merit for the world.' When a noble disciple recollects the Saṅgha, on that occasion his mind is not obsessed by lust, hatred, or delusion; on that occasion his mind is simply straight. He has departed from greed . . . [316] . . . some beings here become pure in such a way.

(4) "Again, a noble disciple recollects his own virtuous behavior as unbroken, flawless, unblemished, unblotched, freeing, praised by the wise, ungrasped, leading to concentration. When a noble disciple recollects his virtuous behavior, on that occasion his mind is not obsessed by lust, hatred, or delusion; on that occasion his mind is simply straight. He has departed from greed . . . some beings here become pure in such a way.

(5) "Again, a noble disciple recollects his own generosity thus: 'It is truly my good fortune . . . that in a population obsessed by the stain of miserliness, I dwell with a mind devoid

of the stain of miserliness . . . delighting in giving and sharing.' When a noble disciple recollects his generosity, on that occasion his mind is not obsessed by lust, hatred, or delusion; on that occasion his mind is simply straight. He has departed from greed . . . beings here become pure in such a way.

(6) "Again, a noble disciple recollects the deities thus: 'There are devas [ruled by] the four great kings . . . [317] . . . I too have such faith . . . such virtuous behavior . . . such learning . . . such generosity . . . such wisdom as those deities possessed, because of which, when they passed away here, they were reborn there.' When a noble disciple recollects the faith, virtuous behavior, learning, generosity, and wisdom in himself and in those deities, on that occasion his mind is not obsessed by lust, hatred, or delusion; on that occasion his mind is simply straight. He has departed from greed, freed himself from it, emerged from it. 'Greed,' friends, is a designation for the five objects of sensual pleasure. This noble disciple dwells with a mind entirely like space: vast, exalted, measureless, without enmity and ill will. Having made this a basis, too, some beings here become pure in such a way.

"It's astounding and amazing, friends, that the Blessed One, the Arahant, the Perfectly Enlightened One, who knows and sees, has discovered the opening in the midst of confinement for the purification of beings, for the overcoming of sorrow and lamentation, for the passing away of pain and dejection, for the achievement of the method, for the realization of nibbāna, that is, the six subjects of recollection."

27 (7) Occasion (1)

Then a certain bhikkhu approached the Blessed One, paid homage to him, sat down to one side, and said: "Bhante, how many proper occasions are there for going to see an esteemed bhikkhu?"[1296]

"There are, bhikkhu, these six proper occasions for going to see an esteemed bhikkhu. What six?

(1) "Here, bhikkhu, when a bhikkhu's mind is obsessed and oppressed by sensual lust, and he does not understand as it really is the escape from arisen sensual lust, on that occasion he should approach an esteemed bhikkhu and say to him: 'Friend, my mind is obsessed and oppressed by sensual lust, [318] and I

do not understand as it really is the escape from arisen sensual lust. Please teach me the Dhamma for abandoning sensual lust.' The esteemed bhikkhu then teaches him the Dhamma for abandoning sensual lust. This is the first proper occasion for going to see an esteemed bhikkhu.

(2) "Again, when a bhikkhu's mind is obsessed and oppressed by ill will, and he does not understand as it really is the escape from arisen ill will, on that occasion he should approach an esteemed bhikkhu and say to him: 'Friend, my mind is obsessed and oppressed by ill will. . . .' The esteemed bhikkhu then teaches him the Dhamma for abandoning ill will. This is the second proper occasion for going to see an esteemed bhikkhu.

(3) "Again, when a bhikkhu's mind is obsessed and oppressed by dullness and drowsiness, and he does not understand as it really is the escape from arisen dullness and drowsiness, on that occasion he should approach an esteemed bhikkhu and say to him: 'Friend, my mind is obsessed and oppressed by dullness and drowsiness. . . .' The esteemed bhikkhu then teaches him the Dhamma for abandoning dullness and drowsiness. This is the third proper occasion for going to see an esteemed bhikkhu.

(4) "Again, when a bhikkhu's mind is obsessed and oppressed by restlessness and remorse, and he does not understand as it really is the escape from arisen restlessness and remorse, on that occasion he should approach an esteemed bhikkhu and say to him: 'Friend, my mind is obsessed and oppressed by restlessness and remorse. . . .' [319] . . . The esteemed bhikkhu then teaches him the Dhamma for abandoning restlessness and remorse. This is the fourth proper occasion for going to see an esteemed bhikkhu.

(5) "Again, when a bhikkhu's mind is obsessed and oppressed by doubt, and he does not understand as it really is the escape from arisen doubt, on that occasion he should approach an esteemed bhikkhu and say to him: 'Friend, my mind is obsessed and oppressed by doubt, and I do not understand as it really is the escape from arisen doubt. Please teach me the Dhamma for abandoning doubt.' The esteemed bhikkhu then teaches him the Dhamma for abandoning doubt. This is the fifth proper occasion for going to see an esteemed bhikkhu.

(6) "Again, when a bhikkhu does not know and see what

object to rely on and attend to in order to attain the immediate destruction of the taints,[1297] on that occasion he should approach an esteemed bhikkhu and say to him: 'Friend, I do not know and see what object to rely on and attend to in order to attain the immediate destruction of the taints. Please teach me the Dhamma for the destruction of the taints.' The esteemed bhikkhu then teaches him the Dhamma for the destruction of the taints. This is the sixth proper occasion for going to see an esteemed bhikkhu.

"These, bhikkhu, are the six proper occasions for going to see an esteemed bhikkhu." [320]

28 (8) Occasion (2)

On one occasion a number of elder bhikkhus were dwelling at Bārāṇasī in the deer park at Isipatana. Then, after their meal, on returning from their alms round, those elder bhikkhus assembled and were sitting together in the pavilion hall when this conversation arose among them: "What, friends, is the proper occasion for going to see an esteemed bhikkhu?"

When this was said, one bhikkhu told those elders: "Friends, after his meal, when an esteemed bhikkhu has returned from his alms round, washed his feet, and is sitting with his legs crossed, holding his body straight, having established mindfulness before him: that is the proper occasion for going to see him."

When he had spoken, another bhikkhu told him: "Friend, that isn't the proper occasion for going to see an esteemed bhikkhu. After his meal, when an esteemed bhikkhu has returned from his alms round, washed his feet, and is sitting with his legs crossed, holding his body straight, having established mindfulness before him, his fatigue on account of his walking [for alms] and his meal has not yet subsided. Therefore that is not the proper occasion for going to see him. But in the evening, when an esteemed bhikkhu has emerged from seclusion and is sitting in the shade of his dwelling with his legs crossed, holding his body straight, having established mindfulness before him: that is the proper occasion for going to see him."

When he had spoken, another bhikkhu told him: "Friend, that isn't the proper occasion for going to see an esteemed bhikkhu. [321] In the evening, when an esteemed bhikkhu has emerged from seclusion and is sitting in the shade of his dwelling with his legs crossed, holding his body straight, having established mindfulness before him, the object of concentration that he attended to during the day is still present to him.[1298] Therefore that is not the proper occasion for going to see him. But when an esteemed bhikkhu has risen as the night begins to fade and is sitting with his legs crossed, holding his body straight, having established mindfulness before him: that is the proper occasion for going to see him."

When he had spoken, another bhikkhu told him: "Friend, that isn't the proper occasion for going to see an esteemed bhikkhu. When an esteemed bhikkhu has risen as the night begins to fade and he is sitting with his legs crossed, holding his body straight, having established mindfulness before him, on that occasion his body is fresh; it is easy for him to attend to the teaching of the Buddhas. Therefore that is not the proper occasion for going to see him."

When this was said, the Venerable Mahākaccāna said to those elder bhikkhus: "Friends, in the presence of the Blessed One I heard and learned this:

"'There are, bhikkhu, these six proper occasions for going to see an esteemed bhikkhu. What six? (1) Here, bhikkhu, when a bhikkhu's mind is obsessed and oppressed by sensual lust... [as in 6:27] [322]... (2)... obsessed and oppressed by ill will... (3)... obsessed and oppressed by dullness and drowsiness... (4)... obsessed and oppressed by restlessness and remorse... (5)... obsessed and oppressed by doubt... (6)... when a bhikkhu does not know and see what object to rely on and attend to in order to attain the immediate destruction of the taints.... The esteemed bhikkhu then teaches him the Dhamma for the destruction of the taints. This is the sixth proper occasion for going to see an esteemed bhikkhu.'

"Friends, in the presence of the Blessed One I heard and learned this: 'These, bhikkhu, are the six proper occasions for going to see an esteemed bhikkhu.'"

29 (9) Udāyī

Then the Blessed One addressed the Venerable Udāyī: "Udāyī, how many subjects of recollection are there?"

When this was said, the Venerable Udāyī was silent. A second time . . . A third time the Blessed One addressed the Venerable Udāyī: "Udāyī, how many subjects of recollection are there?" And a third time the Venerable Udāyī was silent.

Then the Venerable Ānanda said to the Venerable Udāyī: "The Teacher is addressing you, friend Udāyī."

"I heard him, friend Ānanda. [323]

"Here, Bhante, a bhikkhu recollects his manifold past abodes, that is, one birth, two births . . . [as in 6:2] . . . Thus he recollects his manifold past abodes with their aspects and details. This, Bhante, is a subject of recollection."

Then the Blessed One addressed the Venerable Ānanda: "I knew, Ānanda, that this hollow man Udāyī does not devote himself to the higher mind.[1299] How many subjects of recollection are there, Ānanda?"

"There are, Bhante, five subjects of recollection. What five?

(1) "Here, Bhante, secluded from sensual pleasures, secluded from unwholesome states, a bhikkhu enters and dwells in the first jhāna, which consists of rapture and pleasure born of seclusion, accompanied by thought and examination. With the subsiding of thought and examination, he enters and dwells in the second jhāna, which has internal placidity and unification of mind and consists of rapture and pleasure born of concentration, without thought and examination. With the fading away as well of rapture, he dwells equanimous and, mindful and clearly comprehending, he experiences pleasure with the body; he enters and dwells in the third jhāna of which the noble ones declare: 'He is equanimous, mindful, one who dwells happily.' This subject of recollection, developed and cultivated in this way, leads to a happy dwelling in this very life.[1300]

(2) "Again, Bhante, a bhikkhu attends to the perception of light; he focuses on the perception of day thus: 'As by day, so at night; as at night, so by day.' Thus, with a mind that is open and uncovered, he develops a mind imbued with luminosity.[1301] This subject of recollection, developed and cultivated in this way, leads to obtaining knowledge and vision.

(3) "Again, Bhante, a bhikkhu reviews this very body upward from the soles of the feet, downward from the tips of the hairs, enclosed in skin, as full of many kinds of impurities: 'There are in this body head hairs, body hairs, nails, teeth, skin, flesh, sinews, bones, bone marrow, kidneys, heart, liver, pleura, spleen,

lungs, intestines, mesentery, stomach, excrement, bile, phlegm, pus, blood, sweat, fat, tears, grease, saliva, snot, fluid of the joints, urine.' This subject of recollection, developed and cultivated in this way, leads to abandoning sensual lust.

(4) "Again, Bhante, suppose a bhikkhu were to see a corpse thrown aside in a charnel ground, one, two, [324] or three days dead, bloated, livid, and festering. He compares his own body with it thus: 'This body, too, is of the same nature; it will be like that; it is not beyond that.'[1302] Or suppose he were to see a corpse thrown aside in a charnel ground, being devoured by crows, hawks, vultures, dogs, jackals, or various kinds of living beings. He compares his own body with it thus: 'This body, too, is of the same nature; it will be like that; it is not beyond that.' Or suppose he were to see a corpse thrown aside in a charnel ground, a skeleton with flesh and blood, held together with sinews . . . a fleshless skeleton smeared with blood, held together with sinews . . . a skeleton without flesh and blood, held together with sinews . . . disconnected bones scattered in all directions: here a handbone, there a footbone, here a shinbone, there a thighbone, here a hipbone, there a backbone, and there the skull. He compares his own body with it thus: 'This body, too, is of the same nature; it will be like that; it is not beyond that.' Or suppose he were to see a corpse thrown aside in a charnel ground, bones bleached white, the color of shells . . . bones heaped up, more than a year old . . . bones rotted, crumbled to dust. He compares his own body with it thus: [325] 'This body, too, is of the same nature; it will be like that; it is not beyond that.' This subject of recollection, developed and cultivated in this way, leads to the uprooting of the conceit 'I am.'

(5) "Again, Bhante, with the abandoning of pleasure and pain, and with the previous passing away of joy and dejection, a bhikkhu enters and dwells in the fourth jhāna, neither painful nor pleasant, which has purification of mindfulness by equanimity. This subject of recollection, developed and cultivated in this way, leads to the penetration of numerous elements.[1303]

"These, Bhante, are the five subjects of recollection."

"Good, good, Ānanda! Therefore, Ānanda, remember this sixth subject of recollection, too.

(6) "Here, ever mindful a bhikkhu goes forward, ever mindful he returns, ever mindful he stands, ever mindful he sits,

ever mindful he lies down to sleep, ever mindful he undertakes work. This subject of recollection, developed and cultivated in this way, leads to mindfulness and clear comprehension."

30 (10) Unsurpassed Things

"Bhikkhus, there are these six unsurpassed things. What six? (1) The unsurpassed sight, (2) the unsurpassed hearing, (3) the unsurpassed gain, (4) the unsurpassed training, (5) the unsurpassed service, and (6) the unsurpassed recollection.[1304]

(1) "And what, bhikkhus, is the unsurpassed sight? Here, someone goes to see the elephant-gem, the horse-gem, the jewel-gem, or to see various sights; or else they go to see an ascetic or brahmin of wrong views, of wrong practice. There is this seeing; this I do not deny. But this seeing is low, common, worldly, ignoble, and unbeneficial; it does not lead to disenchantment, dispassion, cessation, peace, direct knowledge, enlightenment, and [326] nibbāna. When, however, one of settled faith, of settled devotion, decided, full of confidence, goes to see the Tathāgata or a disciple of the Tathāgata: this unsurpassed sight is for the purification of beings, for the overcoming of sorrow and lamentation, for the passing away of pain and dejection, for the achievement of the method, for the realization of nibbāna. This is called the unsurpassed sight. Such is the unsurpassed sight.

(2) "And how is there the unsurpassed hearing? Here, someone goes to hear the sound of drums, the sound of lutes, the sound of singing, or to hear various sounds; or else they go to hear the Dhamma of an ascetic or brahmin of wrong views, of wrong practice. There is this hearing; this I do not deny. But this hearing is low, common, worldly, ignoble, and unbeneficial; it does not lead to disenchantment, dispassion, cessation, peace, direct knowledge, enlightenment, and nibbāna. When, however, one of settled faith, of settled devotion, decided, full of confidence, goes to hear the Tathāgata or a disciple of the Tathāgata: this unsurpassed hearing is for the purification of beings, for the overcoming of sorrow and lamentation, for the passing away of pain and dejection, for the achievement of the method, for the realization of nibbāna. This is called the unsurpassed hearing. Such is the unsurpassed sight and the unsurpassed hearing.

(3) "And how is there the unsurpassed gain? Here, someone gains a son, a wife, or wealth; or they gain various [327] goods; or else they obtain faith in an ascetic or brahmin of wrong views, of wrong practice. There is this gain; this I do not deny. But this gain is low, common, worldly, ignoble, and unbeneficial; it does not lead to disenchantment, dispassion, cessation, peace, direct knowledge, enlightenment, and nibbāna. When, however, one of settled faith, of settled devotion, decided, full of confidence, obtains faith in the Tathāgata or in a disciple of the Tathāgata: this unsurpassed gain is for the purification of beings, for the overcoming of sorrow and lamentation, for the passing away of pain and dejection, for the achievement of the method, for the realization of nibbāna. This is called the unsurpassed gain. Such is the unsurpassed sight, the unsurpassed hearing, and the unsurpassed gain.

(4) "And how is there the unsurpassed training? Here, someone trains in elephantry, in horsemanship, in chariotry, in archery, in swordsmanship; or they train in various fields; or else they train under an ascetic or brahmin of wrong views, of wrong practice. There is this training; this I do not deny. But this training is low, common, worldly, ignoble, and unbeneficial; it does not lead to disenchantment, dispassion, cessation, peace, direct knowledge, enlightenment, and nibbāna. When, however, one of settled faith, of settled devotion, decided, full of confidence, trains in the higher virtuous behavior, the higher mind, and the higher wisdom in the Dhamma and discipline proclaimed by the Tathāgata: this unsurpassed training is for the purification of beings, for the overcoming of sorrow and lamentation, for the passing away of pain and dejection, for the achievement of the method, for the [328] realization of nibbāna. This is called the unsurpassed training. Such is the unsurpassed sight, the unsurpassed hearing, the unsurpassed gain, and the unsurpassed training.

(5) "And how is there the unsurpassed service? Here, someone serves a khattiya, a brahmin, a householder; or they serve various others; or else they serve an ascetic or brahmin of wrong views, of wrong practice. There is this kind of service; this I do not deny. But this kind of service is low, common, worldly, ignoble, and unbeneficial; it does not lead to disenchantment, dispassion, cessation, peace, direct knowledge, enlightenment,

and nibbāna. When, however, one of settled faith, of settled devotion, decided, full of confidence, serves the Tathāgata or a disciple of the Tathāgata: this unsurpassed service is for the purification of beings, for the overcoming of sorrow and lamentation, for the passing away of pain and dejection, for the achievement of the method, for the realization of nibbāna. This is called the unsurpassed service. Thus there is the unsurpassed sight, the unsurpassed hearing, the unsurpassed gain, the unsurpassed training, and the unsurpassed service.

(6) "And how is there the unsurpassed recollection? Here, someone recollects the gain of a son, a wife, or wealth; or else they recollect various kinds of gain; or else they recollect an ascetic or brahmin of wrong views, of wrong practice. There is this kind of recollection; this I do not deny. But this kind of recollection is low, common, worldly, ignoble, and unbeneficial; it does not lead to disenchantment, dispassion, cessation, peace, direct knowledge, enlightenment, and nibbāna. When, however, one [329] of settled faith, of settled devotion, decided, full of confidence, recollects the Tathāgata or a disciple of the Tathāgata: this unsurpassed recollection is for the purification of beings, for the overcoming of sorrow and lamentation, for the passing away of pain and dejection, for the achievement of the method, for the realization of nibbāna. This is called the unsurpassed recollection.

"These, bhikkhus, are the six unsurpassed things."

Having gained the best of sights,
and the unsurpassed hearing,
having acquired the unsurpassed gain,
delighting in the unsurpassed training,
attentive in service,
they develop recollection
connected with seclusion,
secure, leading to the deathless.

Rejoicing in heedfulness,
prudent, restrained by virtue,
in time they realize
where it is that suffering ceases.

IV. Deities

31 (1) Trainee

"Bhikkhus, these six qualities lead to the decline of a bhikkhu who is a trainee. What six? [330] Delight in work, delight in talk, delight in sleep, delight in company, not guarding the doors of the sense faculties, and lack of moderation in eating. These six qualities lead to the decline of a bhikkhu who is a trainee.

"Bhikkhus, these six qualities lead to the non-decline of a bhikkhu who is a trainee. What six? Not taking delight in work, not taking delight in talk, not taking delight in sleep, not taking delight in company, guarding the doors of the sense faculties, and moderation in eating. These six qualities lead to the non-decline of a bhikkhu who is a trainee."

32 (2) Non-Decline (1)

Then, when the night had advanced, a certain deity of stunning beauty, illuminating the entire Jeta's Grove, approached the Blessed One, paid homage to him, stood to one side, and said to the Blessed One:

"Bhante, there are these six qualities that lead to the non-decline of a bhikkhu. What six? Reverence for the Teacher, reverence for the Dhamma, reverence for the Saṅgha, reverence for the training, reverence for heedfulness, and reverence for hospitality.[1305] These six qualities lead to the non-decline of a bhikkhu."

This is what that deity said. The Teacher agreed. Then that deity, thinking, "The Teacher agrees with me," paid homage to the Blessed One, circumambulated him keeping the right side toward him, and disappeared right there.

Then, when the night had passed, the Blessed One addressed the bhikkhus: "Last night, bhikkhus, when the night had advanced, a certain deity of stunning beauty, illuminating the entire Jeta's Grove, approached me, paid homage to me, stood to one side, and said to me: 'Bhante, there are these six qualities that lead to the non-decline of a bhikkhu. What six? Reverence for the Teacher, reverence for the Dhamma, reverence for the Saṅgha, reverence for the training, reverence for heedfulness, and reverence for hospitality. [331] These six qualities lead to the non-decline of a bhikkhu.' This is what that deity said. Then that deity paid homage to me, circumambulated me keeping the right side toward me, and disappeared right there."

> Respectful toward the Teacher,
> respectful toward the Dhamma,
> deeply revering the Saṅgha,
> respectful toward heedfulness,
> revering hospitality: this bhikkhu
> cannot fall away, but is close to nibbāna.

33 (3) Non-Decline (2)

"Last night, bhikkhus, when the night had advanced, a certain deity of stunning beauty, illuminating the entire Jeta's Grove, approached me, paid homage to me, stood to one side, and said to me: 'Bhante, there are these six qualities that lead to the non-decline of a bhikkhu. What six? Reverence for the Teacher, reverence for the Dhamma, reverence for the Saṅgha, reverence for the training, reverence for a sense of moral shame, and reverence for moral dread. These six qualities lead to the non-decline of a bhikkhu.' This is what that deity said. Then the deity paid homage to me, circumambulated me keeping the right side toward me, and disappeared right there."

> Respectful toward the Teacher,
> respectful toward the Dhamma,
> deeply revering the Saṅgha,
> endowed with moral shame and moral dread:
> one who is deferential and reverential
> cannot fall away, but is close to nibbāna.

34 (4) Moggallāna

On one occasion the Blessed One was dwelling at Sāvatthī in Jeta's Grove, Anāthapiṇḍika's Park. Then, while the Venerable Mahāmoggallāna was alone in seclusion, the following course of thought arose in him: "Which devas know: 'I am a stream-enterer, no longer subject to [rebirth in] the lower world, fixed in destiny, heading for enlightenment'?" [332]

Now at that time, a bhikkhu named Tissa had recently died and been reborn in a certain brahmā world. There too they knew him as "the brahmā Tissa, powerful and mighty." Then, just as a strong man might extend his drawn-in arm or draw in his extended arm, the Venerable Mahāmoggallāna disappeared from Jeta's Grove and reappeared in that brahmā world. When he saw the Venerable Mahāmoggallāna coming in the distance, the brahmā Tissa said to him:

"Come, respected Moggallāna! Welcome, respected Moggallāna! It has been long since you took the opportunity to come here. Sit down, respected Moggallāna. This seat has been prepared." The Venerable Mahāmoggallāna sat down on the prepared seat. The brahmā Tissa paid homage to him and sat down to one side. The Venerable Mahāmoggallāna then said to him:

"Which devas, Tissa, know: 'I am a stream-enterer, no longer subject to [rebirth in] the lower world, fixed in destiny, heading for enlightenment'?"

(1) "The devas [ruled by] the four great kings have such knowledge, respected Moggallāna."

"Do all the devas [ruled by] the four great kings have such knowledge, Tissa?"

"Not all, respected Moggallāna. Those who do not possess unwavering confidence in the Buddha, the Dhamma, and the Saṅgha, and who lack the virtuous behavior loved by the noble ones, do not have such [333] knowledge. But those who possess unwavering confidence in the Buddha, the Dhamma, and the Saṅgha, and who have the virtuous behavior loved by the noble ones, know: 'I am a stream-enterer, no longer subject to [rebirth in] the lower world, fixed in destiny, heading for enlightenment.'"

(2) "Do only the devas [ruled by] the four great kings have such knowledge, or do the Tāvatiṃsa devas . . . (3) . . . the Yāma devas . . . (4) . . . the Tusita devas . . . (5) . . . the devas who delight in creation . . . (6) . . . the devas who control what is created by others have it?"

"The devas who control what is created by others also have such knowledge, respected Moggallāna."

"Do all the devas who control what is created by others have such knowledge, Tissa?"

"Not all, respected Moggallāna. Those who do not possess unwavering confidence in the Buddha, the Dhamma, and the Saṅgha, and who lack the virtuous behavior loved by the noble ones, do not have such knowledge. But those who possess unwavering confidence in the Buddha, the Dhamma, and the Saṅgha, and who have the virtuous behavior loved by the noble ones, know: 'I am a stream-enterer, no longer subject to [rebirth in] the lower world, fixed in destiny, heading for enlightenment.'"

Then, having delighted and rejoiced in the statement of the brahmā Tissa, just as [334] a strong man might extend his drawn-in arm or draw in his extended arm, the Venerable Mahāmoggallāna disappeared from the brahmā world and reappeared in Jeta's Grove.

35 (5) Pertain to True Knowledge

"Bhikkhus, these six things pertain to true knowledge. What six? The perception of impermanence, the perception of suffering in the impermanent, the perception of non-self in what is suffering, the perception of abandoning, the perception of dispassion, and the perception of cessation.[1306] These six things pertain to true knowledge."

36 (6) Disputes

"Bhikkhus, there are these six roots of disputes. What six?

(1) "Here, a bhikkhu is angry and hostile. When a bhikkhu is angry and hostile, he dwells without respect and deference toward the Teacher, the Dhamma, and the Saṅgha, and he does not fulfill the training. Such a bhikkhu creates a dispute in the Saṅgha that leads to the harm of many people, to the unhappiness of many people, to the ruin, harm, and suffering of devas and humans. If, bhikkhus, you perceive any such root of dispute either in yourselves or in others, you should strive to abandon this evil root of dispute. And if you do not perceive any such root of dispute either in yourselves or in others, you should practice so that this evil root of dispute does not emerge in the future. [335] In such a way this evil root of dispute is abandoned and does not emerge in the future.

(2) "Again, a bhikkhu is a denigrator and insolent . . . (3) . . . envious and miserly . . . (4) . . . crafty and hypocritical . . . (5) . . . one who has evil desires and wrong view . . . (6) . . . one who adheres to his own views, holds to them tenaciously, and relin-

quishes them with difficulty. When a bhikkhu adheres to his own views, holds to them tenaciously, and relinquishes them with difficulty, he dwells without respect and deference toward the Teacher, the Dhamma, and the Saṅgha, and he does not fulfill the training. Such a bhikkhu creates a dispute in the Saṅgha that leads to the harm of many people, to the unhappiness of many people, to the ruin, harm, and suffering of devas and humans. If, bhikkhus, you perceive any such root of dispute either in yourselves or in others, you should strive to abandon this evil root of dispute. And if you do not perceive any such root of dispute either in yourselves or others, you should practice so that this evil root of dispute does not emerge in the future. In such a way this evil root of dispute is abandoned and does not emerge in the future.

"These, bhikkhus, are the six roots of dispute." [336]

37 (7) Giving

On one occasion the Blessed One was dwelling at Sāvatthī in Jeta's Grove, Anāthapiṇḍika's Park. Now on that occasion the female lay follower Veḷukaṇṭakī Nandamātā had prepared an offering possessed of six factors for the Saṅgha of bhikkhus headed by Sāriputta and Moggallāna. With the divine eye, which is purified and surpasses the human, the Blessed One saw the female lay follower Veḷukaṇṭakī Nandamātā preparing this offering and he then addressed the bhikkhus:

"Bhikkhus, the female lay follower Veḷukaṇṭakī Nandamātā is preparing an offering possessed of six factors for the Saṅgha of bhikkhus headed by Sāriputta and Moggallāna. And how is an offering possessed of six factors? Here, the donor has three factors and the recipients have three factors.

"What are the three factors of the donor? (1) The donor is joyful before giving; (2) she has a placid, confident mind in the act of giving; and (3) she is elated after giving. These are the three factors of the donor.

"What are the three factors of the recipients? Here, (4) the recipients are devoid of lust or are practicing to remove lust; (5) they are devoid of hatred or are practicing to remove hatred; (6) they are devoid of delusion or are practicing to remove delusion. These are the three factors of the recipients.

"Thus the donor has three factors, and the recipients have

three factors. In such a way the offering possesses six factors. It is not easy to measure the merit of such an offering thus: 'Just so much is the stream of merit, stream of the wholesome, nutriment of happiness—heavenly, ripening in happiness, conducive to heaven—that leads to what is wished for, desired, and agreeable, to one's welfare and happiness'; rather, it is reckoned simply as an incalculable, immeasurable, great mass of merit. Bhikkhus, just as it is not easy to measure the water in the great ocean [337] thus: 'There are so many gallons of water,' or 'There are so many hundreds of gallons of water,' or 'There are so many thousands of gallons of water,' or 'There are so many hundreds of thousands of gallons of water,' but rather it is reckoned simply as an incalculable, immeasurable, great mass of water; so too, it is not easy to measure the merit of such an offering . . . rather, it is reckoned simply as an incalculable, immeasurable, great mass of merit."

Prior to giving one is joyful;
while giving one settles the mind in trust;
after giving one is elated:
this is success in the act of offering.

When they are devoid of lust and hatred,
devoid of delusion, without taints,
self-controlled, living the spiritual life,
the field for the offering is complete.

Having cleansed oneself[1307]
and given with one's own hands,
the act of charity is very fruitful
for oneself and in relation to others.

Having performed such a charitable deed
with a mind free from miserliness,
the wise person, rich in faith,
is reborn in a happy, non-afflictive world.

38 (8) Self-Initiative

Then a certain brahmin approached the Blessed One and exchanged greetings with him. When they had exchanged greetings and cordial talk, he sat down to one side and said to the Blessed One:

"Master Gotama, I hold such a thesis and view as this: 'There is no self-initiative; there is no initiative taken by others.'"[1308]

"Brahmin, I have never seen or heard of anyone holding such a thesis and view as this. For how [338] can one who comes on his own and returns on his own say: 'There is no self-initiative; there is no initiative taken by others'?

(1) "What do you think, brahmin? Does the element of instigation exist?"[1309]

"Yes, sir."

"When the element of instigation exists, are beings seen to instigate activity?"

"Yes, sir."

"When beings are seen to instigate activity because the element of instigation exists, this is the self-initiative of beings; this is the initiative taken by others.

(2) "What do you think, brahmin? Does the element of persistence exist?"

"Yes, sir."

"When the element of persistence exists, are beings seen to persist in activity?"

"Yes, sir."

"When beings are seen to persist in activity because the element of persistence exists, this is the self-initiative of beings; this is the initiative taken by others.

(3) "What do you think, brahmin? Does the element of exertion exist?"

"Yes, sir."

"When the element of exertion exists, are beings seen to exert themselves in activity?"

"Yes, sir."

"When beings are seen to exert themselves in activity because the element of exertion exists, this is the self-initiative of beings; this is the initiative taken by others.

(4) "What do you think, brahmin? Does the element of strength exist?"[1310]

"Yes, sir."

"When the element of strength exists, are beings seen to be possessed of strength?"

"Yes, sir."

"When beings are seen to be possessed of strength because the element of strength exists, this is the self-initiative of beings; this is the initiative taken by others.

(5) "What do you think, brahmin? Does the element of continuation exist?"

"Yes, sir."

"When the element of continuation exists, are beings seen to continue [in an action]?"

"Yes, sir."

"When beings are seen to continue [in an action] because the element of continuation exists, this is the self-initiative of beings; this is the initiative taken by others.

(6) "What do you think, brahmin? Does the element of force exist?"

"Yes, sir."

"When the element of force exists, are beings seen to act with force?"

"Yes, sir."

"When beings are seen to act with force because the element of force exists, this is the self-initiative of beings; this is the initiative taken by others.

"Brahmin, I have never seen or heard of anyone holding such a thesis and view [as yours]. For how can one who comes on his own and returns on his own say: 'There is no self-initiative; there is no initiative on the part of others'?"

"Excellent, Master Gotama! Excellent, Master Gotama! Master Gotama has made the Dhamma clear in many ways, as though he were turning upright what had been overthrown, revealing what was hidden, showing the way to one who was lost, or holding up a lamp in the darkness so those with good eyesight can see forms. I now go for refuge to Master Gotama, to the Dhamma, and to the Saṅgha of bhikkhus. Let Master Gotama consider me a lay follower who from today has gone for refuge for life."

39 (9) Origination

"Bhikkhus, there are these three causes for the origination of kamma. What three? (1) Greed is a cause for the origination of kamma; (2) hatred is a cause for the origination of kamma; and (3) delusion is a cause for the origination of kamma.

"It is not non-greed that originates from greed; rather, it is just greed that originates from greed. It is not non-hatred that originates from hatred; rather, it is just hatred that originates from hatred. It is not non-delusion that originates from delusion; rather, it is just delusion that originates from delusion.

"It is not [339] [the realms] of devas and humans—or any other good destinations—that are seen because of kamma born of greed, hatred, and delusion; rather, it is hell, the animal realm, and the sphere of afflicted spirits—as well as other bad destinations—that are seen because of kamma born of greed, hatred, and delusion. These are three causes for the origination of kamma.

"There are, bhikkhus, these three [other] causes for the origination of kamma. What three? (4) Non-greed is a cause for the origination of kamma; (5) non-hatred is a cause for the origination of kamma; and (6) non-delusion is a cause for the origination of kamma.

"It is not greed that originates from non-greed; rather, it is just non-greed that originates from non-greed. It is not hatred that originates from non-hatred; rather, it is just non-hatred that originates from non-hatred. It is not delusion that originates from non-delusion; rather, it is just non-delusion that originates from non-delusion.

"It is not hell, the animal realm, and the sphere of afflicted spirits—or any other bad destinations—that are seen because of kamma born of non-greed, non-hatred, and non-delusion; rather, it is [the realms] of devas and humans—as well as other good destinations—that are seen because of kamma born of non-greed, non-hatred, and non-delusion. These are three [other] causes for the origination of kamma."

40 (10) Kimbila[1311]

Thus have I heard. On one occasion the Blessed One was dwelling at Kimbilā in a *nicula* grove. Then the Venerable Kimbila approached the Blessed One, paid homage to him, sat down to one side, and said: [340]

"What is the cause and reason why, Bhante, the good Dhamma does not continue long after a Tathāgata has attained final nibbāna?"

"Here, Kimbila, after a Tathāgata has attained final nibbāna, (1) the bhikkhus, bhikkhunīs, male lay followers, and female lay followers dwell without reverence and deference toward the Teacher. (2) They dwell without reverence and deference toward the Dhamma. (3) They dwell without reverence and deference toward the Saṅgha. (4) They dwell without reverence and deference toward the training. (5) They dwell without reverence and deference toward heedfulness. (6) They dwell without reverence and deference toward hospitality. This is the cause and reason why the good Dhamma does not continue long after a Tathāgata has attained final nibbāna."

"What is the cause and reason why, Bhante, the good Dhamma continues long after a Tathāgata has attained final nibbāna?"

"Here, Kimbila, after a Tathāgata has attained final nibbāna, (1) the bhikkhus, bhikkhunīs, male lay followers, and female lay followers dwell with reverence and deference toward the Teacher. (2) They dwell with reverence and deference toward the Dhamma. (3) They dwell with reverence and deference toward the Saṅgha. (4) They dwell with reverence and deference toward the training. (5) They dwell with reverence and deference toward heedfulness. (6) They dwell with reverence and deference toward hospitality. This is the cause and reason why the good Dhamma continues long after a Tathāgata has attained final nibbāna."

41 (11) A Block of Wood

Thus have I heard. On one occasion the Venerable Sāriputta was dwelling at Rājagaha on Mount Vulture Peak. Then, in the morning, the Venerable Sāriputta dressed, took his bowl and robe, and descended from Mount Vulture Peak together with a number of bhikkhus. In a certain place he saw a large block of wood and addressed the bhikkhus: "Do you see, friends, that large block of wood?"

"Yes, friend."

(1) "If he so wished, friends, a bhikkhu possessing psychic potency who has attained mastery of mind might focus on that block of wood as earth. What [341] is the basis for this? Because the earth element exists in that block of wood. On this basis a bhikkhu possessing psychic potency who has attained mastery of mind might focus on it as earth.

(2)–(4) "If he so wished, friends, a bhikkhu possessing psychic potency who has attained mastery of mind might focus on that block of wood as water . . . as fire . . . as air. What is the basis for this? Because the water element . . . the fire element . . . the air element exists in that block of wood. On this basis a bhikkhu possessing psychic potency who has attained mastery of mind might focus on it as air.

(5)–(6) "If he so wished, friends, a bhikkhu possessing psychic potency who has attained mastery of mind might focus on that block of wood as beautiful . . . as unattractive. For what reason? Because the element of beauty . . . the element of the unattractive exists in that block of wood. On this basis a bhikkhu possessing psychic potency who has attained mastery of mind might focus on that block of wood as unattractive."

42 (12) Nāgita[1312]

Thus have I heard. On one occasion the Blessed One was wandering on tour among the Kosalans together with a large Saṅgha of bhikkhus when he reached the Kosalan brahmin village named Icchānaṅgala. There the Blessed One dwelled in the Icchānaṅgala woodland thicket. The brahmin householders of Icchānaṅgala heard: "It is said that the ascetic Gotama, the son of the Sakyans who went forth from a Sakyan family, has arrived at Icchānaṅgala and is now dwelling in the Icchānaṅgala woodland thicket. Now a good report about that Master Gotama has circulated thus: 'That Blessed One is an arahant, perfectly enlightened, accomplished in true knowledge and conduct, fortunate, knower of the world, unsurpassed leader of persons to be tamed, teacher of devas and humans, the Enlightened One, the Blessed One. Having realized by his own direct knowledge the world with its devas, Māra, and Brahmā, this population with its ascetics and brahmins, its devas and humans, he makes it known to others. He teaches a Dhamma that is good in the beginning, good in the middle, and good in the end, with the right meaning and phrasing; he reveals a spiritual life that is perfectly complete and pure.' Now it is good to see such arahants."

Then, when the night had passed, the brahmin householders of Icchānaṅgala took abundant food of various kinds and went to the Icchānaṅgala woodland thicket. They stood outside the entrance making an uproar and a racket. Now on that occasion the Venerable Nāgita was the Blessed One's attendant. The Blessed One then addressed the Venerable Nāgita: [342] "Who is making such an uproar and a racket, Nāgita? One would think it was fishermen at a haul of fish."

"Bhante, these are the brahmin householders of Icchānaṅgala who have brought abundant food of various kinds. They are standing outside the entrance, [wishing to offer it] to the Blessed One and the Saṅgha of bhikkhus."

"Let me never come upon fame, Nāgita, and may fame never catch up with me. One who does not gain at will, without trouble or difficulty, this bliss of renunciation, bliss of solitude, bliss of peace, bliss of enlightenment that I gain at will, without trouble or difficulty, might accept that vile pleasure, that slothful pleasure, the pleasure of gain, honor, and praise."

"Let the Blessed One now consent, Bhante, let the Fortunate One consent. This is now the time for the Blessed One to consent. Wherever the Blessed One will go now, the brahmin householders of town and countryside will incline in the same direction. Just as, when thick drops of rain are pouring down, the water flows down along the slope, so too, wherever the Blessed One will go now, the brahmin householders of town and country will incline in the same direction. For what reason? Because of the Blessed One's virtuous behavior and wisdom."

"Let me never come upon fame, Nāgita, and may fame never catch up with me. One who does not gain at will, without trouble or difficulty, this bliss of renunciation . . . might accept that vile pleasure, that slothful pleasure, the pleasure of gain, honor, and praise.

(1) "Here, Nāgita, I see a bhikkhu dwelling on the outskirts of a village [343] sitting in a state of concentration. It then occurs to me: 'Now a monastery attendant or a novice or a co-religionist will cause that venerable one to fall away from that concentration.'[1313] For this reason I am not pleased with this bhikkhu's dwelling on the outskirts of a village.

(2) "I see, Nāgita, a forest-dwelling bhikkhu sitting and dozing in the forest. It then occurs to me: 'Now this venerable one will dispel this sleepiness and fatigue and attend only to the perception of forest, [a state of] oneness.'[1314] For this reason I am pleased with this bhikkhu's dwelling in the forest.

(3) "I see, Nāgita, a forest-dwelling bhikkhu sitting in the

forest in an unconcentrated state. It then occurs to me: 'Now this venerable one will concentrate his unconcentrated mind or guard his concentrated mind.' For this reason I am pleased with this bhikkhu's dwelling in the forest.

(4) "I see, Nāgita, a forest-dwelling bhikkhu sitting in the forest in a state of concentration. It then occurs to me: 'Now this venerable one will liberate his unliberated mind or guard his liberated mind.' For this reason I am pleased with this bhikkhu's dwelling in the forest.

(5) "I see, Nāgita, a bhikkhu dwelling on the outskirts of a village, who gains robes, almsfood, lodgings, and medicines and provisions for the sick. Desiring gain, honor, and fame, he neglects seclusion; he neglects remote lodgings in forests and jungle groves. [344] Having entered the villages, towns, and capital cities, he takes up his residence. For this reason I am not pleased with this bhikkhu's dwelling on the outskirts of a village.

(6) "I see, Nāgita, a forest-dwelling bhikkhu who gains robes, almsfood, lodgings, and medicines and provisions for the sick. Having dispelled that gain, honor, and praise, he does not neglect seclusion; he does not neglect remote lodgings in forests and jungle groves. For this reason I am pleased with this bhikkhu's dwelling in the forest.

"When, Nāgita, I am traveling on a highway and do not see anyone ahead of me or behind me, even if it is for the purpose of defecating and urinating, on that occasion I am at ease."[1315]

V. Dhammika

43 (1) The Nāga

On one occasion the Blessed One was dwelling at Sāvatthī in Jeta's Grove, Anāthapiṇḍika's Park. Then, in the morning, the Blessed One dressed, took his bowl and robe, and entered Sāvatthī for alms. When he had walked for alms in Sāvatthī, after his meal, on returning from his alms round, he addressed the Venerable Ānanda: "Come, Ānanda, let us go to Migāramātā's Mansion in the Eastern Park [345] to pass the day."

"Yes, Bhante," the Venerable Ānanda replied.

Then the Blessed One, together with the Venerable Ānanda, went to Migāramātā's Mansion in the Eastern Park.

Then in the evening the Blessed One emerged from seclusion

and addressed the Venerable Ānanda: "Come, Ānanda, let us go to the eastern gate to bathe."

"Yes, Bhante," the Venerable Ānanda replied.

Then the Blessed One, together with the Venerable Ānanda, went to the eastern gate to bathe. Having bathed at the eastern gate and come out, he stood in one robe drying himself. On that occasion, King Pasenadi of Kosala's bull elephant[1316] named "Seta" was coming out through the eastern gate to the accompaniment of instrumental music and drumming. People saw him and said: "The king's bull elephant is handsome! The king's bull elephant is beautiful! The king's bull elephant is graceful! The king's bull elephant is massive! He's a nāga, truly a nāga."

When this was said, the Venerable Udāyī said to the Blessed One: "Bhante, is it only when people see an elephant possessed of a large massive body that they say: 'A nāga, truly a nāga!' or do people also say this when they see [other] things possessed of a large massive body?"

"(1) Udāyī, when people see an elephant possessed of a large massive body, they say: 'A nāga, truly a nāga!' (2) When people see a horse possessed of a large massive body, they say: 'A nāga, truly a nāga!' (3) When people see a bull possessed of a large massive body, they say: 'A nāga, truly a nāga!' (4) When people see a serpent possessed of a large massive body, they say: 'A nāga, truly a nāga!' (5) When people see a tree [346] possessed of a large massive body, they say: 'A nāga, truly a nāga!' (6) When people see a human being possessed of a large massive body, they say: 'A nāga, truly a nāga!' But, Udāyī, in the world with its devas, Māra, and Brahmā, in this population with its ascetics and brahmins, its devas and humans, I call one a nāga who does no evil by body, speech, and mind."[1317]

"It's astounding and amazing, Bhante, how well this was stated by the Blessed One: 'But, Udāyī, in the world with its devas, Māra, and Brahmā, in this population with its ascetics and brahmins, its devas and humans, I call one a nāga who does no evil by body, speech, and mind.' I rejoice, Bhante, in this good statement of the Blessed One with these verses:[1318]

"A human being who is fully enlightened,
self-tamed and concentrated,

traveling on the path of brahmā,
he takes delight in peace of mind.

"I have heard from the Arahant
that even the devas pay homage to him,
to the same one whom humans venerate,
the one who has gone beyond everything.

"He has transcended all fetters
and emerged from the jungle to the clearing;[1319]
delighting in renunciation of sensual pleasures,
he is like pure gold freed from its ore.

"He is the nāga who outshines all,
like the Himalayas amid the other mountains.
Among all things named nāga,
he, unsurpassed, is the one truly named.[1320]

"I will extol for you the nāga:
indeed, he does no evil.
Mildness and harmlessness
are two feet of the nāga.

"Austerity and celibacy
are the nāga's other two feet.[1321]
Faith is the great nāga's trunk,
and equanimity his ivory tusks.

"Mindfulness is his neck, his head is wisdom,
investigation, and reflection on phenomena.[1322]
Dhamma is the balanced heat of his belly,
and seclusion is his tail.[1323]

"This meditator, delighting in consolation,[1324]
is inwardly well concentrated.
When walking, the nāga is concentrated;
when standing, the nāga is concentrated.

"When lying down, the nāga is concentrated;
when sitting, too, the nāga is concentrated. [347]

Everywhere, the nāga is restrained:
this is the nāga's accomplishment.

"He eats blameless food,
but doesn't eat what is blameworthy.
When he gains food and clothing,
he avoids storing it up.

"Having cut off all fetters and bonds,
whether they be gross or subtle,
in whatever direction he goes,
he goes without concern.

"The lotus flower
is born and grown up in water,
yet is not soiled by the water
but remains fragrant and delightful.

"Just so the Buddha, well born in the world,
dwells in the world,[1325]
yet is not soiled by the world
like the lotus [unsoiled] by water.

"A great fire all ablaze
settles down when deprived of fuel,
and when all the coals have gone out,
it is said to be extinguished.[1326]

"This simile, which conveys the meaning,
was taught by the wise.
Great nāgas will know the nāga
that was taught by the nāga.[1327]

"Devoid of lust, devoid of hatred,
devoid of delusion, without taints,
the nāga, discarding his body,
taintless, is utterly quenched
and attains final nibbāna."[1328]

44 (2) Migasālā

Then, in the morning, the Venerable Ānanda dressed, took his bowl and robe, and went to the house of the female lay follower Migasālā, where he sat down on the seat prepared for him. Then the female lay disciple Migasālā approached the Venerable Ānanda, paid homage to him, sat down to one side, and said:

"Bhante Ānanda, just how should this teaching of the Blessed One be understood, where one who is celibate and one who is not celibate both have exactly the same destination in their future life? [348] My father Purāṇa was celibate, living apart, abstaining from sexual intercourse, the common person's practice. When he died, the Blessed One declared: 'He attained to the state of a once-returner[1329] and has been reborn in the Tusita group [of devas].' My paternal uncle[1330] Isidatta was not celibate but lived a contented married life. When he died, the Blessed One also declared: 'He attained to the state of a once-returner and has been reborn in the Tusita group [of devas].' Bhante Ānanda, just how should this teaching of the Blessed One be understood, where one who is celibate and one who is not celibate both have exactly the same destination in their future life?"

"It was just in this way, sister, that the Blessed One declared it."[1331]

Then, when the Venerable Ānanda had received almsfood at Migasālā's house, he rose from his seat and departed. After his meal, on returning from his alms round, he went to the Blessed One, paid homage to him, sat down to one side, and said: "Here, Bhante, in the morning, I dressed, took my bowl and robe, and went to the house of the female lay follower Migasālā . . . [349] [all as above, down to] . . . When she asked me this, I replied: 'It was just in this way, sister, that the Blessed One declared it.'"

[The Blessed One said:] "Who, indeed, is the female lay follower Migasālā, a foolish, incompetent woman with a woman's intellect?[1332] And who are those [who have] the knowledge of other persons as superior and inferior?[1333]

"There are, Ānanda, these six types of persons found existing in the world. What six?

(1) "Here, Ānanda, there is one person who is mild, a pleasant

companion, with whom his fellow monks gladly dwell. But he has not listened [to the teachings], become learned [in them], and penetrated [them] by view, and he does not attain temporary liberation.[1334] With the breakup of the body, after death, he heads for deterioration, not for distinction; he is one going to deterioration, not to distinction.

(2) "Then, Ānanda, there is one person who is mild, a pleasant companion, with whom his fellow monks gladly dwell. And he has listened [to the teachings], become learned [in them], and penetrated [them] by view, and he attains temporary liberation. With the breakup of the body, after death, he heads for distinction, not for deterioration; he is one going to distinction, not to deterioration.

"Ānanda, those who are judgmental will pass such judgment on them: 'This one has the same qualities as the other. Why should one be inferior and the other superior?' That [judgment] of theirs[1335] will indeed lead to their harm and suffering for a long time.

"Between them, Ānanda, the person who is mild, a pleasant companion, one with whom his fellow monks gladly dwell, who has listened [to the teachings], become learned [in them], and penetrated [them] by view, and who attains temporary liberation, [350] surpasses and excels the other person. For what reason? Because the Dhamma-stream carries him along.[1336] But who can know this difference except the Tathāgata?

"Therefore, Ānanda, do not be judgmental regarding people. Do not pass judgment on people. Those who pass judgment on people harm themselves. I alone, or one like me, may pass judgment on people.

(3) "Then, Ānanda, in one person anger and conceit are found, and from time to time states of greed[1337] arise in him. And he has not listened [to the teachings], become learned [in them], and penetrated [them] by view, and he does not attain temporary liberation. With the breakup of the body, after death, he heads for deterioration, not for distinction; he is one going to deterioration, not to distinction.

(4) "Then, Ānanda, in one person anger and conceit are found, and from time to time states of greed arise in him. But he has listened [to the teachings], become learned [in them], and penetrated [them] by view, and he attains temporary lib-

eration. With the breakup of the body, after death, he heads for distinction, not for deterioration; he is one going to distinction, not to deterioration.

"Ānanda, those who are judgmental will pass such judgment on them. . . . I alone, or one like me, may pass judgment on people.[1338]

(5) "Then, Ānanda, in one person anger and conceit are found, and from time to time he engages in exchanges of words.[1339] And he has not listened [to the teachings], become learned [in them], and penetrated [them] by view, and he does not attain temporary liberation. With the breakup of the body, after death, he heads for deterioration, not for distinction; he is one going to deterioration, not to distinction.

(6) "Then, Ānanda, in one person anger and conceit are found, and from time to time he engages in exchanges of words. But he has listened [to the teachings], become learned [in them], and penetrated [them] by view, and he attains temporary liberation. With the breakup of the body, after death, [351] he heads for distinction, not for deterioration; he is one going to distinction, not to deterioration.

"Ānanda, those who are judgmental will pass such judgment on them: 'This one has the same qualities as the other. Why should one be inferior and the other superior?' That [judgment] of theirs will indeed lead to their harm and suffering for a long time.

"Between them, Ānanda, the person in whom anger and conceit are found, and who from time to time engages in exchanges of words, but who has listened [to the teachings], become learned [in them], and penetrated [them] by view, and who attains temporary liberation, surpasses and excels the other person. For what reason? Because the Dhamma-stream carries him along. But who can know this difference except the Tathāgata?

"Therefore, Ānanda, do not be judgmental regarding people. Do not pass judgment on people. Those who pass judgment on people harm themselves. I alone, or one like me, may pass judgment on people.

"Who, indeed, is the female lay follower Migasālā, a foolish, incompetent woman with a woman's intellect? And who are those [who have] the knowledge of other persons as superior and inferior?

"These are the six types of persons found existing in the world.

"Ānanda, if Isidatta had possessed the same kind of virtuous behavior that Purāṇa had, Purāṇa could not have even known his destination. And if Purāṇa had possessed the same kind of wisdom that Isidatta had, Isidatta could not have even known his destination.[1340] In this way, Ānanda, these two persons were each deficient in one respect."

45 (3) Debt

(1) "Bhikkhus, isn't poverty suffering in the world for one who enjoys sensual pleasures?"

"Yes, Bhante."

(2) "If a poor, [352] destitute, indigent person gets into debt, isn't his indebtedness, too, suffering in the world for one who enjoys sensual pleasures?"

"Yes, Bhante."

(3) "If a poor, destitute, indigent person who has gotten into debt promises to pay interest, isn't the interest, too, suffering in the world for one who enjoys sensual pleasures?"

"Yes, Bhante."

(4) "If a poor, destitute, indigent person who has promised to pay interest cannot pay it when it falls due, they reprove him. Isn't being reproved, too, suffering in the world for one who enjoys sensual pleasures?"

"Yes, Bhante."

(5) "If a poor, destitute, indigent person who is reproved does not pay, they prosecute him. Isn't prosecution, too, suffering in the world for one who enjoys sensual pleasures?"

"Yes, Bhante."

(6) "If a poor, destitute, indigent person who is prosecuted does not pay, they imprison him. Isn't imprisonment, too, suffering in the world for one who enjoys sensual pleasures?"

"Yes, Bhante."

"So, bhikkhus, for one who enjoys sensual pleasures, poverty is suffering in the world; getting into debt is suffering in the world; having to pay interest is suffering in the world; being reproved is suffering in the world; prosecution is suffering in the world; and imprisonment is suffering in the world.

(1) "So too, bhikkhus, when one does not have faith in [cul-

tivating] wholesome qualities, when one does not have a sense of moral shame in [cultivating] wholesome qualities, when one does not have moral dread in [cultivating] wholesome qualities, when one does not have energy in [cultivating] wholesome qualities, when one does not have wisdom in [cultivating] wholesome qualities, in the Noble One's discipline one is called a poor, destitute, indigent person.

(2) "Having no faith, no sense of moral shame, no moral dread, no energy, no wisdom in [cultivating] wholesome qualities, that poor, destitute, indigent person engages in misconduct by body, speech, and mind. This, I say, is his getting into debt.

(3) "To conceal his bodily misconduct, he nurtures an evil desire. He wishes: 'Let no one know me'; he intends [with the aim]: 'Let no one know me'; [353] he utters statements [with the aim]: 'Let no one know me'; he makes bodily endeavors [with the aim]: 'Let no one know me.'

"To conceal his verbal misconduct . . . To conceal his mental misconduct, he nurtures an evil desire. He wishes: 'Let no one know me'; he intends [with the aim]: 'Let no one know me'; he utters statements [with the aim]: 'Let no one know me'; he makes bodily endeavors [with the aim]: 'Let no one know me.' This, I say, is the interest he must pay.

(4) "Well-behaved fellow monks speak thus about him: 'This venerable one acts in such a way, behaves in such a way.' This, I say, is his being reproved.

(5) "When he has gone to the forest, to the foot of a tree, or to an empty dwelling, bad unwholesome thoughts accompanied by remorse assail him. This, I say, is his prosecution.

(6) "Then, with the breakup of the body, after death, that poor, destitute, indigent person who engaged in misconduct by body, speech, and mind is bound in the prison of hell or the prison of the animal realm. I do not see, bhikkhus, any other prison that is as terrible and harsh, [and] such an obstacle to attaining the unsurpassed security from bondage, as the prison of hell or the prison of the animal realm."

Poverty is called suffering in the world;
so too is getting into debt.
A poor person who becomes indebted
is troubled while enjoying himself.

Then they prosecute him
and he also incurs imprisonment.
This imprisonment is indeed suffering
for one yearning for gain and sensual pleasures.

Just so in the Noble One's discipline,
one in whom faith is lacking, [354]
who is shameless and brash,
heaps up a mass of evil kamma.

Having engaged in misconduct
by body, speech, and mind,
he forms the wish:
"May no one find out about me."

He twists around with his body,
[twists around] by speech or mind;
he piles up his evil deeds,
in one way or another, repeatedly.

This foolish evildoer, knowing
his own misdeeds, is a poor person
who falls into debt,
troubled while enjoying himself.

His thoughts then prosecute him;
painful mental states born of remorse
[follow him wherever he goes]
whether in the village or the forest.

This foolish evildoer,
knowing his own misdeeds,
goes to a certain [animal] realm
or is even bound in hell.

This indeed is the suffering of bondage[1341]
from which the wise person is freed,
giving [gifts] with wealth righteously gained,
settling his mind in confidence.

The householder endowed with faith
has made a lucky throw in both cases:
for his welfare in this present life
and happiness in future lives.
Thus it is that for home-dwellers
this merit increases through generosity.[1342]

Just so, in the Noble One's discipline,
one whose faith is firm,
who is endowed with shame, dreading wrong,
wise and restrained by virtuous behavior,
is said to live happily
in the Noble One's discipline.

Having gained spiritual happiness,
one then resolves on equanimity.
Having abandoned the five hindrances,
always arousing energy,
he enters upon the jhānas,
unified, alert, and mindful.

Having known things thus as they really are,
through complete non-clinging
the mind is rightly liberated
with the destruction of all fetters.

With the destruction of the fetters of existence,
for the stable one, rightly liberated,
the knowledge occurs:
"My liberation is unshakable."

This is the supreme knowledge;
this is unsurpassed happiness.
Sorrowless, dust-free, and secure,
this is the highest freedom from debt. [355]

46 (4) Cunda

Thus have I heard. On one occasion the Venerable Mahācunda was dwelling among the Cetis at Sahajāti. There he addressed the bhikkhus:

"Friends, bhikkhus!"

"Friend!" those bhikkhus replied. The Venerable Mahācunda said this:

(1) "Here, friends, bhikkhus who are Dhamma specialists[1343] disparage those bhikkhus who are meditators, saying: 'They meditate and cogitate, [claiming]: "We are meditators, we are meditators!"[1344] Why do they meditate? In what way do they meditate? How do they meditate?' In this case, the bhikkhus who are Dhamma specialists aren't pleased, and the bhikkhus who are meditators aren't pleased, and they aren't practicing for the welfare of many people, for the happiness of many people, for the good, welfare, and happiness of many people, of devas and human beings.

(2) "But the meditating bhikkhus disparage the bhikkhus who are Dhamma specialists, saying: 'They are restless, puffed up, vain, talkative, rambling in their talk, muddle-minded, lacking clear comprehension, unconcentrated, with wandering minds, with loose sense faculties, [claiming]: "We are Dhamma specialists, we are Dhamma specialists!" Why are they Dhamma specialists? In what way are they Dhamma specialists? How are they Dhamma specialists?' In this case, the meditators aren't pleased, and the Dhamma specialists aren't pleased, and they aren't practicing for the welfare of many people, for the happiness of many people, for the good, welfare, and happiness of many people, of devas and human beings.

(3) "Friends, the bhikkhus who are Dhamma specialists praise only bhikkhus who are Dhamma specialists, not those who are meditators. In this case, the bhikkhus who are Dhamma specialists [356] aren't pleased, and those who are meditators aren't pleased, and they aren't practicing for the welfare of many people, for the happiness of many people, for the good, welfare, and happiness of many people, of devas and human beings.

(4) "But the bhikkhus who are meditators praise only bhikkhus who are also meditators, not those who are Dhamma specialists. In this case, the bhikkhus who are meditators aren't pleased, and those who are Dhamma specialists aren't pleased, and they aren't practicing for the welfare of many people, for the happiness of many people, for the good, welfare, and happiness of many people, of devas and human beings.

(5) "Therefore, friends, you should train yourselves thus:

'Those of us who are Dhamma specialists will praise those bhikkhus who are meditators.' Thus should you train yourselves. For what reason? Because, friends, these persons are astounding and rare in the world who dwell having touched the deathless element with the body.[1345]

(6) "Therefore, friends, you should train yourselves thus: 'Those of us who are meditators will praise those bhikkhus who are Dhamma specialists.' Thus should you train yourselves. For what reason? Because, friends, these persons are astounding and rare in the world who see a deep and pithy matter after piercing it through with wisdom."[1346]

47 (5) Directly Visible (1)

Then the wanderer Moliyasīvaka approached the Blessed One and exchanged greetings with him.[1347] When they had concluded their greetings and cordial talk, he sat down to one side and said to the Blessed One:

"Bhante, it is said: 'The directly visible Dhamma, the directly visible Dhamma.' In what way, Bhante, is the Dhamma directly visible, immediate, inviting one to come and see, applicable, to be personally experienced by the wise'?"[1348] [357]

"Well then, Sīvaka, I will question you in turn about this. Answer as you see fit. What do you think, Sīvaka? (1) When there is greed within you, do you know: 'There is greed within me,' and when there is no greed within you, do you know: 'There is no greed within me'?"

"Yes, Bhante."

"Since, Sīvaka, when there is greed within you, you know: 'There is greed within me,' and when there is no greed within you, you know: 'There is no greed within me,' in this way the Dhamma is directly visible, immediate, inviting one to come and see, applicable, to be personally experienced by the wise.

"What do you think, Sīvaka? (2) When there is hatred within you . . . (3) . . . delusion within you . . . (4) . . . a state connected with greed within you[1349] . . . (5) . . . a state connected with hatred within you . . . (6) . . . a state connected with delusion within you, do you know: 'There is a state connected with delusion within me,' and when there is no state connected with delusion within you, do you know: 'There is no state connected with delusion within me'?"

"Yes, Bhante."

"Since, Sīvaka, when there is a state connected with delusion within you, you know: 'There is a state connected with delusion within me,' and when there is no state connected with delusion within you, you know: 'There is no state connected with delusion within me,' in this way the Dhamma is directly visible, immediate, inviting one to come and see, applicable, to be personally experienced by the wise."

"Excellent, Bhante! . . . [as at 6:38] . . . Let the Blessed One consider me a lay follower who from today has gone for refuge for life."

48 (6) Directly Visible (2)

Then a certain brahmin approached the Blessed One and exchanged greetings with him. When they had concluded their greetings and cordial talk, he sat down to one side and said to the Blessed One:

"Master Gotama, it is said: 'The directly visible Dhamma, the directly visible Dhamma.' In what way, Master Gotama, [358] is the Dhamma directly visible, immediate, inviting one to come and see, applicable, to be personally experienced by the wise?"

"Well then, brahmin, I will question you in turn about this. Answer as you see fit. What do you think, brahmin? (1) When there is lust within you, do you know: 'There is lust within me,' and when there is no lust within you, do you know: 'There is no lust within me'?"

"Yes, sir."

"Since, brahmin, when there is lust within you, you know: 'There is lust within me,' and when there is no lust within you, you know: 'There is no lust within me,' in this way the Dhamma is directly visible, immediate, inviting one to come and see, applicable, to be personally experienced by the wise.

"What do you think, brahmin? (2) When there is hatred within you . . . (3) . . . delusion within you . . . (4) . . . a bodily fault within you[1350] . . . (5) . . . a verbal fault within you . . . (6) . . . a mental fault within you, do you know: 'There is a mental fault within me,' and when there is no mental fault within you, do you know: 'There is no mental fault within me'?"

"Yes, sir."

"Since, brahmin, when there is a mental fault within you, you know: 'There is a mental fault within me,' and when there is no mental fault within you, you know: 'There is no mental fault within me,' in this way the Dhamma is directly visible, immediate, inviting one to come and see, applicable, to be personally experienced by the wise."

"Excellent, Master Gotama! . . . [as in 6:38] . . . Let Master Gotama consider me a lay follower who from today has gone for refuge for life."

49 (7) Khema

On one occasion the Blessed One was dwelling at Sāvatthī in Jeta's Grove, Anāthapiṇḍika's Park. Now on that occasion the Venerable Khema and the Venerable Sumana were dwelling at Sāvatthī [359] in the Blind Men's Grove. Then they approached the Blessed One, paid homage to him, and sat down to one side. The Venerable Khema then said to the Blessed One:

"Bhante, when a bhikkhu is an arahant, one whose taints are destroyed, who has lived the spiritual life, done what had to be done, laid down the burden, reached his own goal, utterly destroyed the fetters of existence, one completely liberated through final knowledge, it does not occur to him: (1) 'There is someone better than me,' or (2) 'There is someone equal to me,' or (3) 'There is someone inferior to me.'"

This is what the Venerable Khema said. The Teacher agreed. Then the Venerable Khema, thinking, 'The Teacher agrees with me,' got up from his seat, paid homage to the Blessed One, circumambulated him keeping the right side toward him, and left.

Then, right after the Venerable Khema had left, the Venerable Sumana said to the Blessed One: "Bhante, when a bhikkhu is an arahant, one whose taints are destroyed, who has lived the spiritual life, done what had to be done, laid down the burden, reached his own goal, utterly destroyed the fetters of existence, one completely liberated through final knowledge, it does not occur to him: (4) 'There is no one better than me,' or (5) 'There is no one equal to me,' or (6) 'There is no one inferior to me.'"

This is what the Venerable Sumana said. The Teacher agreed. Then the Venerable Sumana, thinking, 'The Teacher agrees with me,' got up from his seat, paid homage to the Blessed One, circumambulated him keeping the right side toward him, and left.[1351]

Then, soon after both monks had left, the Blessed One addressed the bhikkhus: "Bhikkhus, it is in such a way that clansmen declare final knowledge. They state the meaning but don't bring themselves into the picture.[1352] But there are some foolish men here who, it seems, declare final knowledge as a joke. They will meet with distress later."

> They [do not rank themselves] as superior or inferior,
> nor do they rank themselves as equal.[1353]
> Destroyed is birth, the spiritual life has been lived;
> they continue on, freed from fetters. [360]

50 (8) Sense Faculties[1354]

"Bhikkhus, (1) when there is no restraint of the sense faculties, for one deficient in restraint of the sense faculties, (2) virtuous behavior lacks its proximate cause. When there is no virtuous behavior, for one deficient in virtuous behavior, (3) right concentration lacks its proximate cause. When there is no right concentration, for one deficient in right concentration, (4) the knowledge and vision of things as they really are lacks its proximate cause. When there is no knowledge and vision of things as they really are, for one deficient in the knowledge and vision of things as they really are, (5) disenchantment and dispassion lack their proximate cause. When there is no disenchantment and dispassion, for one deficient in disenchantment and dispassion, (6) the knowledge and vision of liberation lacks its proximate cause.

"Suppose there is a tree deficient in branches and foliage. Then its shoots do not grow to fullness; also its bark, softwood, and heartwood do not grow to fullness. So too, when there is no restraint of the sense faculties, for one deficient in restraint of the sense faculties, virtuous behavior lacks its proximate cause. When there is no virtuous behavior . . . the knowledge and vision of liberation lacks its proximate cause.

"Bhikkhus, (1) when there is restraint of the sense faculties, for one who exercises restraint over the sense faculties, (2) virtuous behavior possesses its proximate cause. When there is virtuous behavior, for one whose behavior is virtuous, (3) right concentration possesses its proximate cause. When there is right concentration, for one possessing right concentration, (4) the knowledge and vision of things as they really are possesses its proximate cause. When there is the knowledge and vision of things as they really are, for one possessing the knowledge and vision of things as they really are, (5) disenchantment and dispassion possess their proximate cause. When there is disenchantment and dispassion, for one possessing disenchantment and dispassion, (6) the knowledge and vision of liberation possesses its proximate cause.

"Suppose there is a tree possessing branches and foliage. Then its shoots grow to fullness; also its bark, softwood, and heartwood grow to fullness. So too, when there is restraint of the sense faculties, for one who exercises restraint over the sense faculties, virtuous behavior possesses its proximate cause. When there is virtuous behavior . . . the knowledge and vision of liberation possesses its proximate cause." [361]

51 (9) Ānanda

Then the Venerable Ānanda approached the Venerable Sāriputta and exchanged greetings with him. When they had concluded their greetings and cordial talk, he sat down to one side and said to the Venerable Sāriputta:

"Friend Sāriputta, how does a bhikkhu get to hear a teaching he has not heard before, not forget those teachings he has already heard, bring to mind those teachings with which he is already familiar,[1355] and understand what he has not understood?"

"The Venerable Ānanda is learned. Please clear up this matter yourself."

"Then listen, friend Sāriputta, and attend closely. I will speak."

"Yes, friend," the Venerable Sāriputta replied. The Venerable Ānanda said this:

"Here, friend Sāriputta, (1) a bhikkhu learns the Dhamma: the discourses, mixed prose and verse, expositions, verses, inspired utterances, quotations, birth stories, amazing accounts, and questions-and-answers. (2) He teaches the Dhamma to others in detail as he has heard it and learned it. (3) He makes others repeat the Dhamma in detail as they have heard it and learned it. (4) He recites the Dhamma in detail as he has heard it and learned it. (5) He ponders, examines, and mentally inspects the Dhamma as he has heard it and learned it. (6) He enters upon the rains in a residence where there live elder bhikkhus who are learned, heirs to the heritage, experts on the Dhamma, experts on the discipline, experts on the outlines. From time to time he approaches them and inquires: 'How is this, Bhante? What is the meaning of this?' Those venerable ones then disclose to him what has not been disclosed, clear up what is obscure, and dispel his perplexity about numerous perplexing points. It is in this way, [362] friend Sāriputta, that a bhikkhu gets to hear a teaching he has not heard before, does not forget those teachings he has already heard, brings to mind those teachings with which he is already familiar, and understands what he has not understood."

"It's astounding and amazing, friend, how well this has been stated by the Venerable Ānanda. And we consider the Venerable Ānanda to be one who possesses these six qualities: (1) For the Venerable Ānanda has learned the Dhamma: the discourses, mixed prose and verse, expositions, verses, inspired utterances, quotations, birth stories, amazing accounts, and questions-and-answers. (2) He teaches the Dhamma to others in detail as he has heard it and learned it. (3) He makes others repeat the Dhamma in detail as they have heard it and learned it [from him]. (4) He recites the Dhamma in detail as he has heard it and learned it. (5) He ponders, examines, and mentally inspects the Dhamma as he has heard it and learned it. (6) He enters upon the rains in a residence where there live elder bhikkhus who are highly learned, heirs to the heritage, experts on the Dhamma, experts on the discipline, experts on the outlines. From time to time he approaches them and inquires: 'How is this, Bhante? What is the meaning of this?' Those venerable ones then disclose to him what has not been disclosed, clear up what is obscure, and dispel his perplexity about numerous perplexing points."

52 (10) Khattiya

Then the brahmin Jāṇussoṇī approached the Blessed One and exchanged greetings with him. When they had concluded their greetings and cordial talk, he sat down to one side and said to the Blessed One: [363]

(1) "Master Gotama, what is the aim of khattiyas? What is their quest? What is their support? What are they intent on? What is their final goal?"[1356]

"Wealth, brahmin, is the aim of khattiyas; their quest is for wisdom; their support is power; they are intent on territory; and their final goal is sovereignty."

(2) "But, Master Gotama, what is the aim of brahmins? What is their quest? What is their support? What are they intent on? What is their final goal?"

"Wealth, brahmin, is the aim of brahmins; their quest is for wisdom; the Vedic hymns are their support; they are intent on sacrifice; and their final goal is the brahmā world."

(3) "But, Master Gotama, what is the aim of householders? What is their quest? What is their support? What are they intent on? What is their final goal?"

"Wealth, brahmin, is the aim of householders; their quest is for wisdom; their craft is their support; they are intent on work; and their final goal is to complete their work."

(4) "But, Master Gotama, what is the aim of women? What is their quest? What is their support? What are they intent on? What is their final goal?"

"A man, brahmin, is the aim of women; their quest is for adornments; sons are their support; they are intent on being without a rival; and their final goal is authority."

(5) "But, Master Gotama, what is the aim of thieves? What is their quest? What is their support? What are they intent on? What is their final goal?"

"Robbery, brahmin, is the aim of thieves; their quest is for thickets; craftiness is their support;[1357] they are intent on dark places; and their final goal is to remain unseen."

(6) "But, Master Gotama, what is the aim of ascetics? What is their quest? What is their support? What are they intent on? What is their final goal?"

"Patience and mildness, brahmin, is the aim of ascetics; their quest is for wisdom; virtuous behavior is their support; they are intent on nothingness;[1358] and their final goal is nibbāna."

"It's astounding and amazing, Master Gotama! Master Gotama knows the aim, quest, support, intent, and final goal of khattiyas, brahmins, householders, women, thieves, [364] and ascetics.

"Excellent, Master Gotama! ... [as in 6:38] ... Let Master Gotama consider me a lay follower who from today has gone for refuge for life."

53 (11) Heedfulness

Then a certain brahmin approached the Blessed One and exchanged greetings with him. When they had concluded their greetings and cordial talk, he sat down to one side and said to the Blessed One:

"Master Gotama, is there one thing which, when developed and cultivated, can accomplish both kinds of good, the good pertaining to the present life and the good pertaining to the future life?"

"There is such a thing, brahmin."

"And what is it?"

"It is heedfulness.

(1) "Just as, brahmin, the footprints of all animals that walk fit into the footprint of the elephant, and the elephant's footprint is declared to be foremost among them with respect to size, so too heedfulness is the one thing that, when developed and cultivated, can accomplish both kinds of good, the good pertaining to the present life and the good pertaining to the future life.

(2) "Just as all the rafters of a peaked house lean toward the roof peak, slope toward the roof peak, converge upon the roof peak, and the roof peak is declared to be foremost among them, so too [365] heedfulness is the one thing that ... can accomplish both kinds of good....

(3) "Just as a reed-cutter, having cut a bunch of reeds, grabs them by the top, shakes the bottom, shakes the two sides, and beats them, so too heedfulness is the one thing that ... can accomplish both kinds of good....

(4) "Just as, when the stalk of a bunch of mangoes is cut, all the mangoes attached to the stalk follow along with it, so too heedfulness is the one thing that ... can accomplish both kinds of good....

(5) "Just as all petty princes are the vassals of a wheel-turning monarch, and the wheel-turning monarch is declared to be foremost among them, so too heedfulness is the one thing that ... can accomplish both kinds of good....

(6) "Just as the radiance of all the stars does not amount to

a sixteenth part of the radiance of the moon, and the radiance of the moon is declared to be foremost among them, so too heedfulness is the one thing that . . . can accomplish both kinds of good. . . .

"This, brahmin, is the one thing which, when developed and cultivated, can accomplish both kinds of good, the good pertaining to the present life and the good pertaining to the future life."

"Excellent, Master Gotama! . . . Let Master Gotama consider me a lay follower who from today has gone for refuge for life." [366]

54 (12) Dhammika

On one occasion the Blessed One was dwelling in Rājagaha on Mount Vulture Peak. On that occasion the Venerable Dhammika was the resident monk in his native district, in all the seven monasteries in his native district.[1359] There the Venerable Dhammika insulted visiting bhikkhus, reviled them, harmed them, attacked them, and scolded them, and then those visiting bhikkhus left. They did not settle down but vacated the monastery.

Then it occurred to the lay followers of the native district: "We serve the Saṅgha of bhikkhus with robes, almsfood, lodgings, and medicines and provisions for the sick, but the visiting bhikkhus leave. They do not settle down but vacate the monastery. Why is that so?"

Then it occurred to them: "This Venerable Dhammika insults visiting bhikkhus, reviles them, harms them, attacks them, and scolds them, and then those visiting bhikkhus leave. They do not settle down but vacate the monastery. Let's banish the Venerable Dhammika."

Then the lay followers went to the Venerable Dhammika and said to him: "Bhante, leave this monastery. You've stayed here long enough."

The Venerable Dhammika then went from that monastery to another one, where again he insulted visiting bhikkhus, reviled them, harmed them, attacked them, and scolded them. And then those visiting bhikkhus left. They did not settle down [367] but vacated the monastery.

Then it occurred to the lay followers . . . [all as above] . . . and said to him: "Bhante, leave this monastery. You've stayed here long enough."

Then the Venerable Dhammika went from that monastery to still another one, where again he insulted visiting bhikkhus. . . . They did not settle down but vacated the monastery.

Then it occurred to the lay followers: "We serve the Saṅgha of bhikkhus with robes, almsfood, lodgings, and medicines and provisions for the sick, but the visiting bhikkhus leave. They do not settle down but vacate the monastery. Why is that so?"

Then it occurred to the lay followers: "This Venerable Dhammika insults visiting bhikkhus. . . . They do not settle down [368] but vacate the monastery. Let's banish the Venerable Dhammika from all the seven monasteries in the native district."

Then the lay followers of the native district went to the Venerable Dhammika and said to him: "Bhante, depart from all the seven monasteries in the native district."

The Venerable Dhammika then thought: "I am banished by the lay followers from all seven monasteries here. Where shall I go?"

It then occurred to him: "Let me go to the Blessed One."

Then the Venerable Dhammika took his bowl and robe and left for Rājagaha. Gradually he reached Rājagaha, and then went to Mount Vulture Peak, where he approached the Blessed One, paid homage to him, and sat down to one side. The Blessed One then asked him: "Where are you coming from, Brahmin Dhammika?"[1360]

"Bhante, the lay followers of my native district have banished me from all seven monasteries there."

"Enough, Brahmin Dhammika! Now that you've come to me, why be concerned that you have been banished from those places? In the past, Brahmin Dhammika, some seafaring merchants set out to sea in a ship, taking along a land-spotting bird. When the ship had still not caught sight of land they released the bird. It went to the east, the west, the north, the south, upward, and to the intermediate directions. If it saw land anywhere, it went straight for it. But if it didn't see land, it returned to the ship. In the same way, when you have been banished from those places, you've come to me." [369]

"In the past, Brahmin Dhammika, King Koravya had a royal banyan tree named 'Well Grounded,' which had five branches, cast a cool shade, and gave delight. Its canopy extended for twelve *yojanas*; its network of roots for five *yojanas*. Its fruits were as large as cooking pots and as sweet as pure honey. The king and his harem made use of one section of the tree, the army used another section, the townfolk and countryfolk used still another, ascetics and brahmins used still another, and the beasts and birds used still another. No one guarded the tree's fruits, yet no one took another's fruits.

"Then, Brahmin Dhammika, a certain man ate as much as he wanted of the tree's fruits, broke off a branch, and left. It occurred to the deity who lived in the tree: 'It's astounding and amazing how evil this man is! He ate as much as he wanted of the tree's fruits, broke off a branch, and left! Let me see to it that in the future the royal banyan tree does not yield fruit.' Then in the future the royal banyan tree did not yield fruit. Thereupon [370] King Koravya approached Sakka the ruler of the devas and said to him: 'Listen, respected sir, you should know that the royal banyan tree does not yield fruit.'

"Then Sakka the ruler of the devas performed a feat of psychic potency such that a violent rainstorm came and twisted[1361] and uprooted the royal banyan tree.

"Then, Brahmin Dhammika, the deity that lived in the tree stood to one side, sad and miserable, weeping with a tearful face. Sakka approached this deity and said: 'Why, deity, do you stand to one side, sad and miserable, weeping with a tearful face?' – 'It is, sir, because a violent rainstorm came and twisted and uprooted my dwelling.' – 'But, deity, were you following the duty of a tree when the violent rainstorm came and twisted and uprooted your dwelling?' – 'But how, sir, does a tree follow the duty of a tree?' – 'Here, deity, those who need roots take its roots; those who need bark take its bark; those who need leaves take its leaves; those who need flowers take its flowers; and those who need fruit take its fruit. Yet because of this the deity does not become displeased or discontent. That's how a tree follows the duty of a tree.' – 'Sir, I wasn't following the duty of a tree when the violent rainstorm came and twisted and uprooted my dwelling.' – 'If, deity, you would follow the duty of a tree, your dwelling might return to its former state.' – 'I will, sir, follow [371] the duty of a tree. Let my dwelling be as before.'

"Then, Brahmin Dhammika, Sakka the ruler of the devas performed such a feat of psychic potency that a violent rainstorm came and turned upright the royal banyan tree and its roots were covered with bark. So too, Brahmin Dhammika, were you following the duty of an ascetic when the lay followers of the native district banished you from all seven monasteries?"

"But how, Bhante, does an ascetic follow the duty of an ascetic?"

"Here, Brahmin Dhammika, an ascetic does not insult one who insults him, does not scold one who scolds him, and does not argue with one who argues with him. That is how an ascetic follows the duty of an ascetic."

"Bhante, I wasn't following the duty of an ascetic when the lay followers banished me from all seven monasteries."

(1) "In the past, Brahmin Dhammika, there was a teacher named Sunetta, the founder of a spiritual sect, one without lust for sensual pleasures. The teacher Sunetta had many hundreds of disciples. He taught a Dhamma to his disciples for companionship with the brahmā world.[1362] When he was teaching such a Dhamma, those who did not place confidence in him were, with the breakup of the body, after death, reborn in the plane of misery, in a bad destination, in the lower world, in hell; but those who placed confidence in him were reborn in a good destination, in a heavenly world.

(2) "In the past, there was a teacher named Mūgapakkha . . . (3) . . . a teacher named Aranemi . . . (4) . . . a teacher named Kuddālaka . . . (5) . . . a teacher named Hatthipāla . . . (6) . . . [372] a teacher named Jotipāla, the founder of a spiritual sect, one without lust for sensual pleasures. . . . When he was teaching such a Dhamma, those who did not place confidence in him were, with the breakup of the body, after death, reborn in the plane of misery, in a bad destination, in the lower world, in hell; but those who placed confidence in him were reborn in a good destination, in a heavenly world.

"What do you think, Brahmin Dhammika? These six teachers were founders of spiritual sects, men without lust for sensual pleasures who had retinues of many hundreds of disciples. If, with a mind of hatred, one had insulted and reviled them and their communities of disciples, wouldn't one have generated much demerit?"

"Yes, Bhante."

"If, with a mind of hatred, one had insulted and reviled these six teachers together with their communities of disciples, one would have generated much demerit. But if, with a mind of hatred, one reviles and insults a single person accomplished in view,[1363] one generates even more demerit. For what reason? I say, Brahmin Dhammika, there is no injury[1364] against outsiders[1365] like that against [your] fellow monks. Therefore, Brahmin Dhammika, you should train yourself thus: 'We will not let hatred arise in our minds toward our fellow monks.'[1366] Thus, Brahmin Dhammika, should you train yourself." [373]

Sunetta, Mūgapakkha,
the brahmin Aranemi,
Kuddālaka, and Hatthipāla,
the brahmin youth, were teachers.

And Jotipāla [known as] Govinda
the chaplain of seven [kings]:
these were harmless ones in the past,
six teachers possessed of fame.

Unspoiled, liberated by compassion,
these men had transcended the fetter of sensuality.
Having expunged sensual lust,
they were reborn in the brahmā world.

Their disciples too
numbering many hundreds
were unspoiled, liberated in compassion,
men who had transcended the fetter of sensuality.
Having expunged sensual lust,
they were reborn in the brahmā world.

That man who, with thoughts of hatred,
reviles these outside seers devoid of lust
[whose minds] were concentrated,
generates abundant demerit.

But the man who, with thoughts of hatred,
reviles a disciple of the Buddha,

a bhikkhu accomplished in view,
generates even more demerit.

One should not attack a holy person
one who has abandoned viewpoints.
This one is called the seventh person
of the Saṅgha of noble ones,
one not devoid of lust for sensual pleasures,
whose five faculties are weak:
faith, mindfulness, energy,
serenity, and insight.

If one attacks such a bhikkhu,
one first harms oneself;
then, having harmed oneself,
one afterward harms the other.

When one protects oneself,
the other person is also protected.
Therefore one should protect oneself;
the wise person is always unhurt. [374]

The Second Fifty

I. The Great Chapter

55 (1) Soṇa

Thus have I heard. On one occasion the Blessed One was dwelling at Rājagaha on Mount Vulture Peak. Now on that occasion the Venerable Soṇa was dwelling at Rājagaha in the Cool Grove.[1367]

Then, while the Venerable Soṇa was alone in seclusion, the following course of thought arose in his mind: "I am one of the Blessed One's most energetic disciples, yet my mind has not been liberated from the taints by non-clinging. Now there is wealth in my family, and it is possible for me to enjoy my wealth and do meritorious deeds. Let me then give up the training and return to the lower life, so that I can enjoy my wealth and do meritorious deeds."

Then, having known with his own mind the course of thought

in the Venerable Soṇa's mind, just as a strong man might extend his drawn-in arm or draw in his extended arm, the Blessed One disappeared on Mount Vulture Peak and appeared in the Cool Grove in the presence of the Venerable Soṇa. The Blessed One sat down on the seat prepared for him. The Venerable Soṇa paid homage to the Blessed One and sat down to one side. The Blessed One then said to him: [375]

"Soṇa, when you were alone in seclusion, didn't the following course of thought arise in your mind: 'I am one of the Blessed One's most energetic disciples, yet my mind has not been liberated from the taints by non-clinging. Now there is wealth in my family, and it is possible for me to enjoy my wealth and do meritorious deeds. Let me then give up the training and return to the lower life, so that I can enjoy my wealth and do meritorious deeds'?"

"Yes, Bhante."

"Tell me, Soṇa, in the past, when you lived at home, weren't you skilled at the lute?"

"Yes, Bhante."

"What do you think, Soṇa? When its strings were too tight, was your lute well tuned and easy to play?"

"No, Bhante."

"When its strings were too loose, was your lute well tuned and easy to play?"

"No, Bhante."

"But, Soṇa, when its strings were neither too tight nor too loose but adjusted to a balanced pitch, was your lute well tuned and easy to play?"

"Yes, Bhante."

"So too, Soṇa, if energy is aroused too forcefully this leads to restlessness, and if energy is too lax this leads to laziness. Therefore, Soṇa, resolve on a balance of energy, achieve evenness of the spiritual faculties, and take up the object there."[1368]

"Yes, Bhante," the Venerable Soṇa replied.

When the Blessed One had finished giving the Venerable Soṇa this exhortation, just as a strong man might extend his drawn-in arm or draw in his extended arm, he disappeared in the Cool Grove and reappeared on Mount Vulture Peak. [376]

Then, some time later, the Venerable Soṇa resolved on a balance of energy, achieved evenness of the spiritual faculties, and took up the object there. Then, dwelling alone, withdrawn, heedful, ardent, and resolute, in no long time the Venerable Soṇa realized for himself with direct knowledge, in this very life, that unsurpassed consummation of the spiritual life for the sake of which clansmen rightly go forth from the household life into homelessness, and having entered upon it, he dwelled in it. He directly knew: "Destroyed is birth, the spiritual life has been lived, what had to be done has been done, there is no more coming back to any state of being." And the Venerable Soṇa became one of the arahants.

Having attained arahantship, the Venerable Soṇa thought: "Let me go to the Blessed One and declare final knowledge in his presence." Then he approached the Blessed One, paid homage to him, sat down to one side, and said:

"Bhante, when a bhikkhu is an arahant, one whose taints are destroyed, who has lived the spiritual life, done what had to be done, laid down the burden, reached his own goal, utterly destroyed the fetters of existence, and become completely liberated through final knowledge, he is intent upon six things: on renunciation, on solitude, on non-affliction, on the destruction of craving, on the destruction of clinging, and on non-confusion.[1369]

(1) "It may be, Bhante, that some venerable one here thinks: 'Could it be that this venerable one is intent upon renunciation on account of mere faith?' But it should not be seen in such a way. A bhikkhu with taints destroyed, who has lived the spiritual life and done his task, does not see in himself anything further to be done or any [need to] increase what has been done.[1370] He is intent upon renunciation because he is devoid of lust through the destruction of lust; because he is devoid of hatred through the destruction of hatred; because he is devoid of delusion through the destruction of delusion. [377]

(2) "It may be that some venerable one here thinks: 'Could it be that this venerable one is intent upon solitude because he is hankering after gain, honor, and praise?' But it should not be seen in such a way. A bhikkhu with taints destroyed, who has lived the spiritual life and done his task, does not see in himself anything further to be done or any [need to] increase what has been done. He is intent upon solitude because he is devoid of lust through the destruction of lust; because he is devoid of

hatred through the destruction of hatred; because he is devoid of delusion through the destruction of delusion.

(3) "It may be that some venerable one here thinks: 'Could it be that this venerable one is intent upon non-affliction because he has fallen back on the wrong grasp of behavior and observances as the essence?'[1371] But it should not be seen in such a way. A bhikkhu with taints destroyed, who has lived the spiritual life and done his task, does not see in himself anything further to be done or any [need to] increase what has been done. He is intent upon non-affliction because he is devoid of lust through the destruction of lust; because he is devoid of hatred through the destruction of hatred; because he is devoid of delusion through the destruction of delusion.

(4) "... He is intent upon the destruction of craving because he is devoid of lust through the destruction of lust; because he is devoid of hatred through the destruction of hatred; because he is devoid of delusion through the destruction of delusion.[1372]

(5) "... He is intent upon the destruction of clinging because he is devoid of lust through the destruction of lust; because he is devoid of hatred through the destruction of hatred; because he is devoid of delusion through the destruction of delusion.

(6) "... He is intent upon non-confusion because he is devoid of lust through the destruction of lust; because he is devoid of hatred through the destruction of hatred; because he is devoid of delusion through the destruction of delusion.

"Bhante, when a bhikkhu is thus perfectly liberated in mind, even if powerful forms cognizable by the eye come into range of the eye, they do not obsess his mind; his mind is not at all affected. It remains steady, attained to imperturbability, and he observes its vanishing.[1373] [378] Even if powerful sounds cognizable by the ear come into range of the ear... Even if powerful odors cognizable by the nose come into range of the nose... Even if powerful tastes cognizable by the tongue come into range of the tongue... Even if powerful tactile objects cognizable by the body come into range of the body... Even if powerful phenomena cognizable by the mind come into range of the mind, they do not obsess his mind; his mind is not at all affected. It remains steady, attained to imperturbability, and he observes its vanishing.

"Suppose, Bhante, there were a stone mountain, without clefts or fissures, one solid mass. If a violent rainstorm should come from the east, it could not make it quake, wobble, and tremble; if a violent rainstorm should come from the west . . . from the north . . . from the south, it could not make it quake, wobble, and tremble. So too, when a bhikkhu is thus perfectly liberated in mind, even if powerful forms cognizable by the eye come into range of the eye . . . Even if powerful phenomena cognizable by the mind come into range of the mind, they do not obsess his mind; his mind is not at all affected. It remains steady, attained to imperturbability, and he observes its vanishing."

If one is intent on renunciation
and solitude of mind;
if one is intent on non-affliction
and the destruction of clinging;
if one is intent on craving's destruction
and non-confusion of mind:
when one sees the sense bases' arising,
one's mind is completely liberated.

For a bhikkhu of peaceful mind,
one completely liberated,
there's nothing further to be done,
no [need to] increase what has been done. [379]

As a stone mountain, one solid mass,
is not stirred by the wind,
so no forms and tastes, sounds,
odors, and tactile objects,
and phenomena desirable or undesirable
stir the stable one's mind.
His mind is steady and freed,
and he observes its vanishing.

56 (2) Phagguṇa

Now on a certain occasion the Venerable Phagguṇa was sick, afflicted, gravely ill. Then the Venerable Ānanda approached the Blessed One, paid homage to him, sat down to one side, and said: "Bhante, the Venerable Phagguṇa is sick, afflicted, gravely ill. Please let the Blessed One visit him out of compassion." The Blessed One consented by silence.

Then, in the evening, the Blessed One emerged from seclusion and went to the Venerable Phagguṇa. The Venerable Phagguṇa saw the Blessed One coming in the distance and stirred on his bed. The Blessed One said to him: "Enough, Phagguṇa, do not stir on your bed. There are these seats that have been prepared. I will sit down there."

The Blessed One sat down and said to the Venerable Phagguṇa: "I hope you are bearing up, Phagguṇa. I hope you are getting better. I hope that your painful feelings are subsiding and not increasing, and that their subsiding, not their increase, is to be seen."

"Bhante, I am not bearing up, I am not getting better. Strong painful feelings are increasing in me, not subsiding, and their increase, not their subsiding, is to be seen.[1374] Just as if a strong man were to grind my head with the tip of a sharp sword, so too, violent winds [380] cut through my head. I am not bearing up.... Just as if a strong man were to tighten a tough leather strap around my head as a headband, so too, there are violent headpains in my head. I am not bearing up.... Just as if a skillful butcher or his apprentice were to carve up [an ox's] belly with a sharp butcher's knife, so too, violent winds are carving up my belly. I am not bearing up.... Just as if two strong men were to seize a weaker man by both arms and roast and grill him over a pit of hot coals, so too, there is a violent burning in my body. I am not bearing up, Bhante, I am not getting better. Strong painful feelings are increasing in me, not subsiding, and their increase, not their subsiding, is to be seen."

Then the Blessed One instructed, encouraged, inspired, and gladdened the Venerable Phagguṇa with a Dhamma talk, after which he got up from his seat and left. Not long after the Blessed One left, the Venerable Phagguṇa died. At the time of his death, his faculties were serene.

Then the Venerable Ānanda [381] approached the Blessed One, paid homage to him, sat down to one side, and said: "Bhante, not long after the Blessed One left, the Venerable Phagguṇa died. At the time of his death, his faculties were serene."

"Why, Ānanda, shouldn't the bhikkhu Phagguṇa's faculties have been serene? Though his mind had not yet been liberated from the five lower fetters, when he heard that discourse on the Dhamma, his mind was liberated from them.[1375]

"There are, Ānanda, these six benefits of listening to the Dhamma at the proper time and of examining the meaning at the proper time.[1376] What six?

(1) "Here, Ānanda, a bhikkhu's mind is not yet liberated from the five lower fetters, but at the time of his death he gets to see the Tathāgata. The Tathāgata teaches him the Dhamma that is good in the beginning, good in the middle, and good in the end, with the right meaning and phrasing; he reveals a spiritual life that is perfectly complete and pure. When the bhikkhu hears that discourse on the Dhamma, his mind is liberated from the five lower fetters. This is the first benefit of listening to the Dhamma at the proper time.

(2) "Again, a bhikkhu's mind is not yet liberated from the five lower fetters. At the time of his death he does not get to see the Tathāgata, but he gets to see a disciple of the Tathāgata. The Tathāgata's disciple teaches him the Dhamma . . . reveals a spiritual life that is perfectly complete and pure. When the bhikkhu hears that discourse on the Dhamma, his mind is liberated from the five lower fetters. This is the second benefit of listening to the Dhamma at the proper time.

(3) "Again, a bhikkhu's mind is not yet liberated from the five [382] lower fetters. At the time of his death he does not get to see the Tathāgata or a disciple of the Tathāgata, but he ponders, examines, and mentally inspects the Dhamma as he has heard it and learned it. As he does so, his mind is liberated from the five lower fetters. This is the third benefit of examining the meaning at the proper time.

(4) "Here, Ānanda, a bhikkhu's mind is liberated from the five lower fetters but not yet liberated in the unsurpassed extinction of the acquisitions.[1377] At the time of his death he gets to see the Tathāgata. The Tathāgata teaches him the Dhamma . . . he reveals a spiritual life that is perfectly complete and pure. When the bhikkhu hears that discourse on the Dhamma, his mind is liberated in the unsurpassed extinction of the acquisitions. This is the fourth benefit of listening to the Dhamma at the proper time.

(5) "Again, a bhikkhu's mind is liberated from the five lower fetters but not yet liberated in the unsurpassed extinction of the acquisitions. At the time of his death he does not get to see the Tathāgata, but he gets to see a disciple of the Tathāgata. The Tathāgata's disciple teaches him the Dhamma . . . reveals a spiri-

tual life that is perfectly complete and pure. When the bhikkhu hears that discourse on the Dhamma, his mind is liberated in the unsurpassed extinction of the acquisitions. This is the fifth benefit of listening to the Dhamma at the proper time.

(6) "Again, a bhikkhu's mind is liberated from the five lower fetters [383] but not yet liberated in the unsurpassed extinction of the acquisitions. At the time of his death he does not get to see the Tathāgata or a disciple of the Tathāgata, but he ponders, examines, and mentally inspects the Dhamma as he has heard it and learned it. As he does so, his mind is liberated in the unsurpassed extinction of the acquisitions. This is the sixth benefit of examining the meaning at the proper time.

"These, Ānanda, are the six benefits of listening to the Dhamma at the proper time and of examining the meaning at the proper time."

57 (3) Six Classes

On one occasion the Blessed One was dwelling at Rājagaha on Mount Vulture Peak. Then the Venerable Ānanda approached the Blessed One, paid homage to him, sat down to one side, and said:

"Bhante, Pūraṇa Kassapa has described six classes:[1378] a black class, a blue class, a red class, a yellow class, a white class, and a supreme white class.

"He has described the black class as butchers of sheep, pigs, poultry, and deer; hunters and fishermen; thieves, executioners, and prison wardens; or those who follow any other such cruel occupation.

"He has described the blue class as bhikkhus who live on thorns[1379] or any others who profess the doctrine of kamma, the doctrine of the efficacy of deeds.

"He has described the red class as the Nigaṇṭhas [384] wearing a single garment.

"He has described the yellow class as the white-robed lay disciples of the naked ascetics.

"He has described the white class as the male and female Ājīvakas.

"He has described the supreme white class as Nanda Vaccha, Kisa Saṅkicca, and Makkhali Gosāla.

"Pūraṇa Kassapa, Bhante, has described these six classes."

"But, Ānanda, has the whole world authorized Pūraṇa Kassapa to describe these six classes?"

"Certainly not, Bhante."

"Suppose, Ānanda, there was a poor, destitute, indigent person. They might force a cut [of meat] on him against his will, saying: 'Good man, you must eat this piece of meat and pay for it.' In the same way, without the consent of those ascetics and brahmins, Pūraṇa Kassapa has described these six classes in a foolish, incompetent, inexpert, and unskilled way. But I, Ānanda, describe six [different] classes. Listen and attend closely. I will speak."

"Yes, Bhante," the Venerable Ānanda replied. The Blessed One said this:

"And what, Ānanda, are the six classes? (1) Here, someone of the black class produces a black state. (2) Someone of the black class produces a white state. (3) Someone of the black class produces nibbāna,[1380] which is neither black nor white. (4) Then, someone [385] of the white class produces a black state. (5) Someone of the white class produces a white state. (6) And someone of the white class produces nibbāna, which is neither black nor white.

(1) "And how is it, Ānanda, that someone of the black class produces a black state? Here, someone has been reborn in a low family—a family of caṇḍālas, hunters, bamboo workers, cart makers, or flower scavengers—one that is poor, with little food and drink, that subsists with difficulty, where food and clothing are obtained with difficulty; and he is ugly, unsightly, dwarfish, with much illness—blind, crippled, lame, or paralyzed.[1381] He does not obtain food, drink, clothing, and vehicles; garlands, scents, and unguents; bedding, housing, and lighting. He engages in misconduct by body, speech, and mind. In consequence, with the breakup of the body, after death, he is reborn in the plane of misery, in a bad destination, in the lower world, in hell. It is in such a way that someone of the black class produces a black state.

(2) "And how is it, Ānanda, that someone of the black class produces a white state? Here, someone has been reborn in a low family. . . . He does not obtain food . . . and lighting. He engages in good conduct by body, speech, and mind. In consequence, with the breakup of the body, after death, he is reborn in a

good destination, in a heavenly world. It is in such a way that someone of the black class produces a white state.

(3) "And how is it, Ānanda, that someone of the black class produces nibbāna, which is neither black nor white? Here, someone has been reborn in a low family.... [386]... He does not obtain food... and lighting. Having shaved off his hair and beard, he puts on ochre robes and goes forth from the household life into homelessness. When he has thus gone forth, he abandons the five hindrances, defilements of the mind, things that weaken wisdom; and then, with his mind well established in the four establishments of mindfulness, he correctly develops the seven factors of enlightenment and produces nibbāna, which is neither black nor white. It is in such a way that someone of the black class produces nibbāna, which is neither black nor white.

(4) "And how is it, Ānanda, that someone of the white class produces a black state? Here, someone has been reborn in a high family—an affluent khattiya family, an affluent brahmin family, or an affluent householder family—one that is rich, with great wealth and property, abundant gold and silver, abundant treasures and commodities, abundant wealth and grain; and he is handsome, attractive, graceful, possessing supreme beauty of complexion. He obtains food, drink, clothing, and vehicles; garlands, scents, and unguents; bedding, housing, and lighting. He engages in misconduct by body, speech, and mind. In consequence, with the breakup of the body, after death, he is reborn in the plane of misery, in a bad destination, in the lower world, in hell. It is in such a way that someone of the white class produces a black state.

(5) "And how is it, Ānanda, that someone of the white class produces a white state? Here, someone has been reborn in a high family.... He obtains food... and lighting. He engages in good conduct by body, speech, and mind. In consequence, with the breakup of the body, after death, he is reborn in a good destination, in a heavenly world. It is in such a way that someone of the white class produces a white state.

(6) "And how is it, Ānanda, that someone of the white class produces nibbāna, which is neither black nor white? [387] Here, someone has been reborn in a high family.... He obtains food... and lighting. Having shaved off his hair and beard, he

puts on ochre robes and goes forth from the household life into homelessness. When he has thus gone forth, he abandons the five hindrances, defilements of the mind, things that weaken wisdom; and then, with his mind well established in the four establishments of mindfulness, he correctly develops the seven factors of enlightenment and produces nibbāna, which is neither black nor white. It is in such a way that someone of the white class produces nibbāna, which is neither black nor white.

"These, Ānanda, are the six classes."

58 (4) Taints

"Bhikkhus, possessing six qualities, a bhikkhu is worthy of gifts, worthy of hospitality, worthy of offerings, worthy of reverential salutation, an unsurpassed field of merit for the world. What six? Here, by restraint a bhikkhu has abandoned those taints that are to be abandoned by restraint; by using he has abandoned those taints that are to be abandoned by using; by patiently enduring he has abandoned those taints that are to be abandoned by patiently enduring; by avoiding he has abandoned those taints that are to be abandoned by avoiding; by dispelling he has abandoned those taints that are to be abandoned by dispelling; and by developing he has abandoned those taints that are to be abandoned by developing.[1382]

(1) "And what, bhikkhus, are the taints to be abandoned by restraint that have been abandoned by restraint? Here, having reflected carefully, a bhikkhu dwells restrained over the eye faculty. Those [388] taints, distressful and feverish, that might arise in one who dwells unrestrained over the eye faculty do not occur in one who dwells restrained over the eye faculty. Having reflected carefully, a bhikkhu dwells restrained over the ear faculty . . . nose faculty . . . tongue faculty . . . body faculty . . . mind faculty. Those taints, distressful and feverish, that might arise in one who dwells unrestrained over the mind faculty do not occur in one who dwells restrained over the mind faculty. Those taints, distressful and feverish, that might arise in one who dwells unrestrained [over these things] do not occur in one who dwells restrained.[1383] These are called the taints to be abandoned by restraint that have been abandoned by restraint.

(2) "And what are the taints to be abandoned by using that have been abandoned by using? Here, reflecting carefully a

bhikkhu uses a robe only for warding off cold; for warding off heat; for warding off contact with flies, mosquitoes, wind, sun, and serpents; and only for covering the private parts. Reflecting carefully, he uses almsfood neither for amusement nor for intoxication nor for the sake of physical beauty and attractiveness, but only for the support and maintenance of this body, for avoiding harm, and for assisting the spiritual life, considering: 'Thus I shall terminate the old feeling and not arouse a new feeling, and I shall be healthy and blameless and dwell at ease.' Reflecting carefully, he uses a lodging only for warding off cold; for warding off heat; for warding off contact with flies, mosquitoes, wind, sun, and serpents; and only for protection from rough weather and for enjoying seclusion. Reflecting carefully, he uses medicines and provisions for the sick only for warding off arisen oppressive feelings and to sustain his health. [389] Those taints, distressful and feverish, that might arise in one who does not make use [of these things] do not arise in one who uses them. These are called the taints to be abandoned by using that have been abandoned by using.

(3) "And what are the taints to be abandoned by patiently enduring that have been abandoned by patiently enduring? Here, reflecting carefully a bhikkhu patiently endures cold and heat, hunger and thirst; contact with flies, mosquitoes, wind, the burning sun, and serpents; rude and offensive ways of speech; he bears up with arisen bodily feelings that are painful, racking, sharp, piercing, harrowing, disagreeable, sapping one's vitality. Those taints, distressful and feverish, that might arise in one who does not patiently endure [these things] do not arise in one who patiently endures them. These are called the taints to be abandoned by patiently enduring that have been abandoned by patiently enduring.

(4) "And what are the taints to be abandoned by avoiding that have been abandoned by avoiding? Here, reflecting carefully a bhikkhu avoids a wild elephant, a wild horse, a wild bull, and a wild dog; he avoids a snake, a stump, a clump of thorns, a pit, a precipice, a refuse dump, and a cesspit. Reflecting carefully, he avoids sitting in unsuitable seats, and wandering in unsuitable alms resorts, and associating with bad friends, such that his wise fellow monks might suspect him of evil deeds. Those

taints, distressful and feverish, that might arise in one who does not avoid [these things] do not arise in one who avoids them. [390] These are called the taints to be abandoned by avoiding that have been abandoned by avoiding.

(5) "And what are the taints to be abandoned by dispelling that have been abandoned by dispelling? Here, reflecting carefully a bhikkhu does not tolerate an arisen sensual thought; he abandons it, dispels it, terminates it, and obliterates it. Reflecting carefully, he does not tolerate an arisen thought of ill will . . . an arisen thought of harming . . . bad unwholesome states whenever they arise; he abandons them, dispels them, terminates them, and obliterates them. Those taints, distressful and feverish, that might arise in one who does not dispel [these things] do not arise in one who dispels them. These are called the taints to be abandoned by dispelling that have been abandoned by dispelling.

(6) "And what are the taints to be abandoned by developing that have been abandoned by developing? Here, reflecting carefully a bhikkhu develops the enlightenment factor of mindfulness, which is based upon seclusion, dispassion, and cessation, maturing in release. Reflecting carefully, he develops the enlightenment factor of discrimination of phenomena . . . the enlightenment factor of energy . . . the enlightenment factor of rapture . . . the enlightenment factor of tranquility . . . the enlightenment factor of concentration . . . the enlightenment factor of equanimity, which is based upon seclusion, dispassion, and cessation, maturing in release. Those taints, distressful and feverish, that might arise in one who does not develop [these things] do not arise in one who develops them. These are called the taints to be abandoned by developing that have been abandoned by developing.

"Possessing these six qualities, bhikkhus, a bhikkhu is worthy of gifts, worthy of hospitality, worthy of offerings, worthy of reverential salutation, an unsurpassed field of merit for the world." [391]

59 (5) Dārukammika

Thus have I heard. On one occasion the Blessed One was dwelling at Nādika in the brick hall. Then the householder Dārukammika[1384] approached the Blessed One, paid homage to him, and sat down to one side. The Blessed One then said to him: "Does your family give gifts, householder?"

"My family gives gifts, Bhante. And those gifts are given to bhikkhus who are arahants or on the path to arahantship, those who are forest dwellers, almsfood collectors, and wearers of rag-robes."[1385]

"Since, householder, you are a layman enjoying sensual pleasures, living at home in a house full of children, using sandalwood from Kāsi, wearing garlands, scents, and unguents, and receiving gold and silver, it is difficult for you to know: 'These are arahants or on the path to arahantship.'

(1) "If, householder, a bhikkhu who is a forest-dweller is restless, puffed up, vain, talkative, rambling in his talk, muddle-minded, lacking clear comprehension, unconcentrated, with a wandering mind, with loose sense faculties, then in this respect he is blameworthy. But if a bhikkhu who is a forest-dweller is not restless, puffed up, and vain, is not talkative and rambling in his talk, but has mindfulness established, clearly comprehends, is concentrated, with a one-pointed mind, with restrained sense faculties, then in this respect he is praiseworthy.

(2) "If a bhikkhu who dwells on the outskirts of a village is restless . . . with loose sense faculties, then in this respect he is blameworthy. But if a bhikkhu who dwells on the outskirts of a village is not restless . . . with restrained sense faculties, then in this respect he is praiseworthy.

(3) "If a bhikkhu who is an almsfood collector is restless . . . with loose sense faculties, then in this respect he is blameworthy. But if a bhikkhu who is an almsfood collector is not restless [392] . . . with restrained sense faculties, then in this respect he is praiseworthy.

(4) "If a bhikkhu who accepts invitations to meals is restless . . . with loose sense faculties, then in this respect he is blameworthy. But if a bhikkhu who accepts invitations to meals is not restless . . . with restrained sense faculties, then in this respect he is praiseworthy.

(5) "If a bhikkhu who wears rag-robes is restless . . . with loose sense faculties, then in this respect he is blameworthy. But if a bhikkhu who wears rag-robes is not restless . . . with restrained sense faculties, then in this respect he is praiseworthy.

(6) "If a bhikkhu who wears robes given by householders

is restless . . . with loose sense faculties, then in this respect he is blameworthy. But if a bhikkhu who wears robes given by householders is not restless . . . with restrained sense faculties, then in this respect he is praiseworthy.

"Come now, householder, give gifts to the Saṅgha. When you give gifts to the Saṅgha, your mind will be confident. When your mind is confident, with the breakup of the body, after death, you will be reborn in a good destination, in a heavenly world."

"Bhante, from today onward I will give gifts to the Saṅgha."[1386]

60 (6) Hatthi

Thus have I heard. On one occasion the Blessed One was dwelling at Bārāṇasī in the deer park at Isipatana. Now on that occasion, after their meal, on returning from their alms round, a number of elder bhikkhus assembled and were sitting together in the pavilion hall engaged in a discussion pertaining to the Dhamma.[1387] While they were engaged in their discussion, the Venerable Citta Hatthisāriputta repeatedly interrupted their talk.[1388] The Venerable Mahākoṭṭhita then told the Venerable Citta Hatthisāriputta:

"When elder bhikkhus are engaged in a discussion pertaining to the Dhamma, don't repeatedly [393] interrupt their talk but wait until their discussion is finished."

When this was said, the Venerable Citta Hatthisāriputta's bhikkhu friends said to the Venerable Mahākoṭṭhita: "Don't disparage the Venerable Citta Hatthisāriputta. The Venerable Citta Hatthisāriputta is wise and capable of engaging with the elder bhikkhus in a discussion pertaining to the Dhamma."

[The Venerable Mahākoṭṭhita said:] "It's difficult, friends, for those who don't know the course of another's mind to know this.

(1) "Here, friends, some person appears to be extremely mild, humble, and calm so long as he is staying near the Teacher or a fellow monk in the position of a teacher. But when he leaves the Teacher and fellow monks in the position of a teacher, he bonds with [other] bhikkhus, bhikkhunīs, male and female lay followers, kings and royal ministers, sectarian teachers and the disciples of sectarian teachers. As he bonds with them and

becomes intimate with them, as he loosens up and talks with them, lust invades his mind. With his mind invaded by lust, he gives up the training and reverts to the lower life.

"Suppose a crop-eating bull was bound by a rope or shut up in a pen. Could one rightly say: 'Now this crop-eating bull will never again enter among the crops'?"

"Certainly not, friend. For it is possible that this crop-eating bull will break the rope or burst out of the pen and again enter among the crops."

"So too, some [394] person here is extremely mild. . . . But when he leaves the Teacher and fellow monks in the position of a teacher, he bonds with [other] bhikkhus . . . he gives up the training and reverts to the lower life.

(2) "Then, friends, secluded from sensual pleasures . . . some person enters and dwells in the first jhāna. [Thinking,] 'I am one who gains the first jhāna,' he bonds with [other] bhikkhus, bhikkhunīs, male and female lay followers, kings and royal ministers, sectarian teachers and their disciples. As he bonds with them and becomes intimate with them, as he loosens up and talks with them, lust invades his mind. With his mind invaded by lust, he gives up the training and reverts to the lower life.

"Suppose that on the crossroads the rain, falling in thick droplets, would make the dust disappear and cause mud to appear. Could one rightly say: 'Now dust will never reappear at this crossroads'?"

"Certainly not, friend. For it is possible that people will pass through this crossroads, or that cattle and goats[1389] will pass through, or that wind and the sun's heat will dry up the moisture, and then dust will reappear."

"So too, secluded from sensual pleasures . . . some person enters and dwells in the first jhāna. [Thinking,] 'I am one who gains the first jhāna,' he bonds with [other] bhikkhus . . . he gives up the training and reverts to the lower life. [395]

(3) "Then, friends, with the subsiding of thought and examination, some person enters and dwells in the second jhāna. . . . [Thinking,] 'I am one who gains the second jhāna,' he bonds with [other] bhikkhus, bhikkhunīs, male and female lay followers, kings and royal ministers, sectarian teachers and their disciples. As he bonds with them and becomes intimate with

them, as he loosens up and talks with them, lust invades his mind. With his mind invaded by lust, he gives up the training and reverts to the lower life.

"Suppose that not far from a village or town there was a large pond. The rain, falling in thick droplets, would make the various kinds of shells,[1390] the gravel and pebbles, disappear. Could one rightly say: 'Now the various kinds of shells, the gravel and pebbles, will never reappear in this pond'?"

"Certainly not, friend. For it is possible that people will drink from this pond, or that cattle and goats will drink from it, or that wind and the sun's heat will dry up the moisture. Then the various kinds of shells, the gravel and pebbles, will reappear."

"So too, with the subsiding of thought and examination, some person enters and dwells in the second jhāna. . . . [Thinking,] 'I am one who gains the second jhāna,' he bonds with [other] bhikkhus . . . he gives up the training and reverts to the lower life.

(4) "Then, friends, with the fading away as well of rapture, some person . . . enters and dwells in the third jhāna. . . . [Thinking,] 'I am one who gains the third jhāna,' he bonds with [other] bhikkhus, bhikkhunīs, male and female lay followers, kings and royal ministers, sectarian teachers and their disciples. As he bonds with them and becomes intimate with them, as he loosens up and engages in talk with them, lust invades his mind. With his mind invaded by lust, he gives up the training and reverts to the lower life.

"Suppose that the food left over from the previous evening [396] would not appeal to a man who had finished a delicious meal. Could one rightly say: 'Now food will never again appeal to this man'?"

"Certainly not, friend. For more food will not appeal to that man so long as the nutritive essence remains in his body, but when the nutritive essence disappears, it is possible that such food will again appeal to him."

"So too, with the fading away as well of rapture, some person . . . enters and dwells in the third jhāna. . . . [Thinking,] 'I am one who gains the third jhāna,' he bonds with [other] bhikkhus . . . he gives up the training and reverts to the lower life.

(5) "Then, friends, with the abandoning of pleasure and pain . . . some person enters and dwells in the fourth jhāna. . . .

[Thinking,] 'I am one who gains the fourth jhāna,' he bonds with [other] bhikkhus, bhikkhunīs, male and female lay followers, kings and royal ministers, sectarian teachers and their disciples. As he bonds with them and becomes intimate with them, as he loosens up and talks with them, lust invades his mind. With his mind invaded by lust, he gives up the training and reverts to the lower life.

"Suppose that in a mountain glen there was a lake sheltered from the wind and devoid of waves. Could one rightly say: 'Now waves will never reappear on this lake'?"

"Certainly not, friend. For it is possible that a violent rainstorm might come from the east, [397] the west, the north, or the south and stir up waves on the lake."

"So too, with the abandoning of pleasure and pain . . . some person here enters and dwells in the fourth jhāna. . . . [Thinking,] 'I am one who gains the fourth jhāna,' he bonds with [other] bhikkhus . . . he gives up the training and reverts to the lower life.

(6) "Then, friends, through non-attention to all marks, some person enters and dwells in the markless mental concentration.[1391] [Thinking,] 'I am one who gains the markless mental concentration,' he bonds with [other] bhikkhus, bhikkhunīs, male and female lay followers, kings and royal ministers, sectarian teachers and their disciples. As he bonds with them and becomes intimate with them, as he loosens up and talks with them, lust invades his mind. With his mind invaded by lust, he gives up the training and reverts to the lower life.

"Suppose that a king or royal minister had been traveling along a highway with a four-factored army and set up camp for the night in a forest thicket. Because of the sounds of the elephants, horses, charioteers, and infantry, and the sound and uproar of drums, kettledrums, conches, and tom-toms, the sound of the crickets would disappear. Could one rightly say: 'Now the sound of the crickets will never reappear in this forest thicket'?" [398]

"Certainly not, friend. For it is possible that the king or royal minister will leave that forest thicket, and then the sound of the crickets will reappear."

"So too, through non-attention to all marks, some person here enters and dwells in the markless mental concentration.

Thinking, 'I am one who gains the markless mental concentration,' he bonds with [other] bhikkhus . . . he gives up the training and reverts to the lower life."

On a later occasion the Venerable Citta Hatthisāriputta gave up the training and returned to the lower life. His bhikkhu friends then approached the Venerable Mahākoṭṭhita and said to him: "Did the Venerable Mahākoṭṭhita encompass Citta Hatthisāriputta's mind with his own mind and understand: 'Citta Hatthisāriputta gains such and such meditative dwellings and attainments, yet he will give up the training and return to the lower life'? Or did deities report this matter to him?"

"Friends, I encompassed Citta Hatthisāriputta's mind with my own mind and understood: 'Citta Hatthisāriputta gains such and such meditative dwellings and attainments, yet he will give up the training and return to the lower life.' And also deities reported this matter to me."

Then those bhikkhu friends of Citta Hatthisāriputta approached the Blessed One, paid homage to him, [399] sat down to one side, and said: "Bhante, Citta Hatthisāriputta gained such and such meditative dwellings and attainments, yet he gave up the training and returned to the lower life."

"Before long, bhikkhus, Citta will think of renouncing."[1392]

Not long afterward, Citta Hatthisāriputta shaved off his hair and beard, put on ochre robes, and went forth from the household life into homelessness. Then, dwelling alone, withdrawn, heedful, ardent, and resolute, in no long time the Venerable Citta Hatthisāriputta realized for himself with direct knowledge, in this very life, that unsurpassed consummation of the spiritual life for the sake of which clansmen rightly go forth from the household life into homelessness, and having entered upon it, he dwelled in it.[1393] He directly knew: "Destroyed is birth, the spiritual life has been lived, what had to be done has been done, there is no more coming back to any state of being." And the Venerable Citta Hatthisāriputta became one of the arahants.

61 (7) Middle

Thus have I heard. On one occasion the Blessed One was dwelling at Bārāṇasī in the deer park at Isipatana. Now on that occasion, after their meal, on returning from their alms round, a number of elder bhikkhus assembled and were sitting together in the pavilion hall when this conversation arose: "It was said, friends, by the Blessed One in the Pārāyana, in 'The Questions of Metteyya':[1394]

"'Having understood both ends,
the wise one does not stick in the middle.[1395]
I call him a great man:
he has here transcended the seamstress.'

"What, friends, is the first end? What is the second end? What is in the middle? And what is the seamstress?"

(1) When this was said, a certain bhikkhu said to the elder bhikkhus: "Contact, friends, is one end; the arising of contact is the second [400] end; the cessation of contact is in the middle; and craving is the seamstress. For craving sews one to the production of this or that state of existence.[1396] It is in this way that a bhikkhu directly knows what should be directly known; fully understands what should be fully understood; and by doing so, in this very life he makes an end of suffering."[1397]

(2) When this was said, another bhikkhu said to the elder bhikkhus: "The past, friends, is one end; the future is the second end; the present is in the middle; and craving is the seamstress. For craving sews one to the production of this or that state of existence. It is in this way that a bhikkhu directly knows what should be directly known . . . in this very life he makes an end of suffering."

(3) When this was said, another bhikkhu said to the elder bhikkhus: "Pleasant feeling, friends, is one end; painful feeling is the second end; neither-painful-nor-pleasant feeling is in the middle; and craving is the seamstress. For craving sews one to the production of this or that state of existence. It is in this way that a bhikkhu directly knows what should be directly known . . . in this very life he makes an end of suffering."

(4) When this was said, another bhikkhu said to the elder bhikkhus: "Name, friends, is one end; form is the second end; consciousness is in the middle; and craving is the seamstress.[1398] For craving sews one to the production of this or that state of existence. It is in this way that a bhikkhu directly knows what should be directly known . . . in this very life he makes an end of suffering."

(5) When this was said, another bhikkhu said to the elder

bhikkhus: "The six internal bases, friends, are one end; the six external bases are the second end; consciousness is in the middle; and craving is the seamstress.[1399] For craving sews one to the production of this or that state of existence. It is in this way that a bhikkhu [401] directly knows what should be directly known . . . in this very life he makes an end of suffering."

(6) When this was said, another bhikkhu said to the elder bhikkhus: "Personal existence, friends, is one end; the origin of personal existence is the second end; the cessation of personal existence is in the middle; and craving is the seamstress.[1400] For craving sews one to the production of this or that state of existence. It is in this way that a bhikkhu directly knows what should be directly known; fully understands what should be fully understood; and by doing so, in this very life he makes an end of suffering."

When this was said, a certain bhikkhu said to the elder bhikkhus: "Friends, we have each explained according to our own inspiration. Come, let's go to the Blessed One and report this matter to him. As the Blessed One explains it to us, so should we retain it in mind."

"Yes, friend," those elder bhikkhus replied. Then the elder bhikkhus went to the Blessed One, paid homage to him, sat down to one side, and reported to him the entire conversation that had taken place, [asking:] "Bhante, which of us has spoken well?"

[The Blessed One said:] "In a way, bhikkhus, you have all spoken well, but listen and attend closely as I tell you what I intended when I said in the Pārāyana, in 'The Questions of Metteyya':

"'Having understood both ends,
the wise one does not stick in the middle.
I call him a great man:
he has here transcended the seamstress.'"

"Yes, Bhante," those bhikkhus replied. The Blessed One said this:

"Contact, bhikkhus, is one [402] end; the arising of contact is the second end; the cessation of contact is in the middle; and craving is the seamstress. For craving sews one to the production of this or that state of existence. It is in this way that a bhikkhu directly knows what should be directly known; fully understands what should be fully understood; and by doing so, in this very life he makes an end of suffering."[1401]

62 (8) Knowledge[1402]

Thus have I heard. On one occasion the Blessed One was wandering on tour among the Kosalans together with a large Saṅgha of bhikkhus when he arrived at a Kosalan town named Daṇḍakappaka. Then the Blessed One left the highway and sat down on a seat that was prepared for him at the foot of a tree, and those bhikkhus entered Daṇḍakappaka to search for a rest house.

Then the Venerable Ānanda together with a number of bhikkhus went down to the Aciravatī River to bathe. Having finished bathing and come back out, he stood in one robe drying his body. Then a certain bhikkhu approached the Venerable Ānanda and said to him: "Friend Ānanda, was it after full consideration that the Blessed One declared of Devadatta: 'Devadatta is bound for the plane of misery, bound for hell, and he will remain there for the eon, unredeemable,' or did he say this only figuratively?"

"It was just in this way, friend, that the Blessed One declared it."[1403]

Then the Venerable Ānanda approached the Blessed One, paid homage to him, sat down to one side, and [reported what had happened, ending]: [403] "When this was said, Bhante, I said to that bhikkhu: 'It was just in this way, friend, that the Blessed One declared it.'"

[The Blessed One said:] "Ānanda, that bhikkhu must be either newly ordained, not long gone forth, or a foolish and incompetent elder. For when this was declared by me definitively, how can he see any ambiguity in it?[1404] I do not see even one other person, Ānanda, about whom I have made a declaration after giving him such full consideration as Devadatta. As long as I saw even a mere fraction of a hair's tip of a bright quality in Devadatta, I did not declare of him: 'Devadatta is bound for the plane of misery, bound for hell, and he will remain there for an eon, unredeemable.' It was, Ānanda, only when I did not see even a mere fraction of a hair's tip of a bright quality[1405] in Devadatta that I declared this of him.

"Suppose there was a cesspit deeper than a man's height full of feces right up to the top, and a man was sunk in it so that his head was submerged. Then a man would appear desiring his good, welfare, and security, wishing to pull him out from the cesspit. He would go around the cesspit on all sides but would not see even a mere fraction of a hair's tip of the man not smeared with feces [404] where he might get a grip and pull him out. So too, Ānanda, it was only when I did not see even a mere fraction of a hair's tip of a bright quality in Devadatta that I declared of him: 'Devadatta is bound for the plane of misery, bound for hell, and he will remain there for an eon, unredeemable.'

"If, Ānanda, you would listen to the Tathāgata's knowledges of a person's faculties, I will analyze them."[1406]

"It is the time for this, Blessed One! It is the time for this, Fortunate One! The Blessed One should analyze his knowledges of a person's faculties. Having heard this from the Blessed One, the bhikkhus will retain it in mind."

"Well then, Ānanda, listen and attend closely. I will speak."

"Yes, Bhante," the Venerable Ānanda replied. The Blessed One said this:

(1) "Here, Ānanda, having encompassed his mind with my own mind, I understand some person thus: 'Wholesome qualities and unwholesome qualities are found in this person.' On a later occasion, having encompassed his mind with my own mind, I understand him thus: 'This person's wholesome qualities have disappeared, unwholesome qualities are manifest, but he has a wholesome root that has not been eradicated. From that wholesome root[1407] of his the wholesome will appear. Thus this person will not be subject to decline in the future.' Suppose seeds that are intact, unspoiled, not damaged by wind and the sun's heat, fecund, well preserved, were deposited in well-prepared soil in a good field. Wouldn't you know: 'These seeds will grow, increase, and mature'?"

"Yes, Bhante."

"In the same way, Ānanda, having encompassed his mind with my own mind . . . [405] . . . I understand him thus: 'This person's wholesome qualities have disappeared, unwholesome qualities are manifest, but he has a wholesome root that has not been eradicated. From that wholesome root of his the wholesome will appear. Thus this person will not be subject to decline in the future.' In this way, Ānanda, the Tathāgata knows a person by encompassing his mind with his own mind. In this way, the Tathāgata has knowledge of a person's faculties, acquired by encompassing his mind with his own mind. In this way, the Tathāgata knows the future origination of qualities by encompassing [another's] mind with his own mind.

(2) "Then, Ānanda, having encompassed his mind with my own mind, I understand some person thus: 'Wholesome qualities and unwholesome qualities are found in this person.' On a later occasion, having encompassed his mind with my own mind, I understand him thus: 'This person's unwholesome qualities have disappeared, wholesome qualities are manifest, but he has an unwholesome root that has not been eradicated. From that unwholesome root of his the unwholesome will appear. Thus this person will be subject to decline in the future.' Suppose, Ānanda, seeds that are intact, unspoiled, not damaged by wind and the sun's heat, fecund, well preserved, were deposited on a wide rock. Wouldn't you know: 'These seeds will not grow, increase, and mature'?"

"Yes, Bhante."

"In the same way, Ānanda, having encompassed his mind with my own mind . . . I understand him thus: 'This person's unwholesome qualities have disappeared, wholesome qualities are manifest, but he has an unwholesome root that has not been eradicated. From that unwholesome root of his the unwholesome will appear. Thus this person [406] will be subject to decline in the future.' In this way, Ānanda, the Tathāgata knows a person by encompassing his mind with his own mind. In this way, the Tathāgata has knowledge of a person's faculties, acquired by encompassing his mind with his own mind. In this way, the Tathāgata knows the future origination of qualities by encompassing [another's] mind with his own mind.

(3) "Then, Ānanda, having encompassed his mind with my own mind, I understand some person thus: 'Wholesome qualities and unwholesome qualities are found in this person.' On a later occasion, having encompassed his mind with my own mind, I understand him thus: 'This person does not have even a mere fraction of a hair's tip of a bright quality. This person possesses exclusively black, unwholesome qualities. With the

breakup of the body, after death, he will be reborn in the plane of misery, in a bad destination, in the lower world, in hell.' Suppose, Ānanda, seeds that are broken, spoiled, damaged by wind and the sun's heat, were deposited in well-prepared soil in a good field. Wouldn't you know: 'These seeds will not grow, increase, and mature'?"

"Yes, Bhante."

"In the same way, Ānanda, having encompassed his mind with my own mind . . . I understand him thus: 'This person does not have even a mere fraction of a hair's tip of a bright quality. This person possesses exclusively black, unwholesome qualities. With the breakup of the body, after death, he will be reborn in the plane of misery, in a bad destination, in the lower world, in hell.' In this way, Ānanda, the Tathāgata knows a person by encompassing his mind with his own mind. In this way, the Tathāgata has knowledge of a person's faculties, acquired by encompassing his mind with his own mind. In this way, the Tathāgata knows the future origination of qualities by encompassing [another's] mind with his own mind."

When this was said, the Venerable Ānanda said to the Blessed One: [407] "Is it possible, Bhante, to describe three other persons as the counterparts of those three?"

"It is possible, Ānanda," the Blessed One said.

(4) "Here, Ānanda, having encompassed his mind with my own mind, I understand some person thus: 'Wholesome qualities and unwholesome qualities are found in this person.' On a later occasion, having encompassed his mind with my own mind, I understand him thus: 'This person's wholesome qualities have disappeared, unwholesome qualities are manifest, but he has a wholesome root that has not been eradicated. That, too, is about to be completely destroyed. Thus this person will be subject to decline in the future.' Suppose, Ānanda, coals that are burning, blazing, and glowing were deposited on a wide rock. Wouldn't you know: 'These coals will not grow, increase, and spread'?"

"Yes, Bhante."

"Or suppose, Ānanda, it is evening and the sun is setting. Wouldn't you know: 'Light will disappear and darkness will appear'?"

"Yes, Bhante."

"Or suppose, Ānanda, it is close to midnight, the time for a meal.[1408] Wouldn't you know: 'Light has disappeared and darkness has appeared'?

"Yes, Bhante."

"In the same way, Ānanda, having encompassed his mind with my own mind . . . I understand him thus: 'This person's wholesome qualities have disappeared, unwholesome qualities are manifest, but he has a wholesome root that has not been eradicated. That, too, is about to be completely destroyed. Thus this person will be subject to decline in the future.' In this way, Ānanda, the Tathāgata knows a person by encompassing his mind with his own mind. In this way, [408] the Tathāgata has knowledge of a person's faculties, acquired by encompassing his mind with his own mind. In this way, the Tathāgata knows the future origination of qualities by encompassing [another's] mind with his own mind.

(5) "Then, Ānanda, having encompassed his mind with my own mind, I understand some person thus: 'Wholesome qualities and unwholesome qualities are found in this person.' On a later occasion, having encompassed his mind with my own mind, I understand him thus: 'This person's unwholesome qualities have disappeared, wholesome qualities are manifest, but he has an unwholesome root that has not been eradicated. That, too, is about to be completely destroyed. Thus this person will not be subject to decline in the future.' Suppose, Ānanda, coals that are burning, blazing, and glowing were deposited on a heap of dry grass or firewood. Wouldn't you know: 'These coals will grow, increase, and spread'?"

"Yes, Bhante."

"Or suppose, Ānanda, it is the time when the night is fading and the sun is rising. Wouldn't you know: 'Darkness will disappear and light will appear'?"

"Yes, Bhante."

"Or suppose, Ānanda, it is close to noon, the time for a meal. Wouldn't you know: 'Darkness has disappeared and light has appeared'?

"Yes, Bhante."

"In the same way, Ānanda, having encompassed his mind with my own mind . . . I understand him thus: 'This person's unwholesome qualities have disappeared, wholesome qualities are manifest, but he has an unwholesome root that has not been eradicated. That, too, is about to be completely destroyed. Thus this person will not be subject to decline in the future.' In this way, Ānanda, the Tathāgata knows a person by encompassing his mind with his own mind. In this way, the Tathāgata has knowledge of a person's faculties, [409] acquired by encompassing his mind with his own mind. In this way, the Tathāgata knows the future origination of qualities by encompassing [another's] mind with his own mind.

(6) "Then, Ānanda, having encompassed his mind with my own mind, I understand some person thus: 'Wholesome qualities and unwholesome qualities are found in this person.' On a later occasion, having encompassed his mind with my own mind, I understand him thus: 'This person does not have even a mere fraction of a hair's tip of an unwholesome quality. This person possesses exclusively bright, blameless qualities. He will attain nibbāna in this very life.' Suppose, Ānanda, coals that are cool and extinguished were deposited on a heap of dry grass or firewood. Wouldn't you know: 'These coals will not grow, increase, and spread'?"

"Yes, Bhante."

"In the same way, Ānanda, having encompassed the mind of someone with my own mind . . . I understand him thus: 'This person does not have even a mere fraction of a hair's tip of an unwholesome quality. This person possesses exclusively bright, blameless qualities. He will attain nibbāna in this very life.' In this way, Ānanda, the Tathāgata knows a person by encompassing his mind with his own mind. In this way, the Tathāgata has knowledge of a person's faculties, acquired by encompassing his mind with his own mind. In this way, the Tathāgata knows the future origination of qualities by encompassing [another's] mind with his own mind.

"Ānanda, among the former three persons, one is not subject to decline, one is subject to decline, and one is bound for the plane of misery, bound for hell. Among the latter three persons, one is not subject to decline, one is subject to decline, and one is bound to attain nibbāna." [410]

63 (9) Penetrative

"Bhikkhus, I will teach you a penetrative exposition of the Dhamma.[1409] Listen and attend closely. I will speak."

"Yes, Bhante," those bhikkhus replied. The Blessed One said this:

"And what, bhikkhus, is that penetrative exposition of the Dhamma?

(1) "Sensual pleasures should be understood; the source and origin of sensual pleasures should be understood; the diversity of sensual pleasures should be understood; the result of sensual pleasures should be understood; the cessation of sensual pleasures should be understood; the way leading to the cessation of sensual pleasures should be understood.

(2) "Feelings should be understood; the source and origin of feelings should be understood; the diversity of feelings should be understood; the result of feelings should be understood; the cessation of feelings should be understood; the way leading to the cessation of feelings should be understood.

(3) "Perceptions should be understood; the source and origin of perceptions should be understood; the diversity of perceptions should be understood; the result of perceptions should be understood; the cessation of perceptions should be understood; the way leading to the cessation of perceptions should be understood.

(4) "The taints should be understood; the source and origin of the taints should be understood; the diversity of the taints should be understood; the result of the taints should be understood; the cessation of the taints should be understood; the way leading to the cessation of the taints should be understood.

(5) "Kamma should be understood; the source and origin of kamma should be understood; the diversity of kamma should be understood; the result of kamma should be understood; the cessation of kamma should be understood; the way leading to the cessation of kamma should be understood.[1410]

(6) "Suffering should be understood; the source and origin of suffering should be understood; the diversity of suffering should be understood; the result of suffering should be understood; the cessation of suffering should be understood; the way leading to the cessation of suffering should be understood.

(1) "When it was said: 'Sensual pleasures should be understood; the source and origin of sensual pleasures should be understood; the diversity of sensual pleasures should be understood; the result [411] of sensual pleasures should be understood; the cessation of sensual pleasures should be understood;

the way leading to the cessation of sensual pleasures should be understood,' for what reason was this said?

"There are, bhikkhus, these five objects of sensual pleasure: forms cognizable by the eye that are wished for, desired, agreeable, pleasing, connected with sensual pleasure, tantalizing; sounds cognizable by the ear . . . odors cognizable by the nose . . . tastes cognizable by the tongue . . . tactile objects cognizable by the body that are wished for, desired, agreeable, pleasing, connected with sensual pleasure, tantalizing. However, these are not sensual pleasures; in the Noble One's discipline, these are called 'objects of sensual pleasure.' A person's sensual pleasure is lustful intention.[1411]

> "They are not sensual pleasures, the pretty things in
> the world:
> a person's sensual pleasure is lustful intention;
> the pretty things remain just as they are in the world,
> but the wise remove the desire for them.

"And what, bhikkhus, is the source and origin of sensual pleasures? Contact is their source and origin.[1412]

"And what is the diversity of sensual pleasures? Sensual desire for forms is one thing, sensual desire for sounds is another, sensual desire for odors still another, sensual desire for tastes still another, and sensual desire for tactile objects still another. This is called the diversity of sensual pleasures.

"And what is the result of sensual pleasures? One produces an individual existence that corresponds with whatever [sense pleasures] one desires and which may be the consequence either of merit or demerit.[1413] This is called the result of sensual pleasures.

"And what is the cessation of sensual pleasures? With the cessation of contact there is cessation of sensual pleasures.

"This noble eightfold path is the way leading to the cessation of sensual pleasures, namely, right view, right intention, right speech, right [412] action, right livelihood, right effort, right mindfulness, and right concentration.

"When, bhikkhus, a noble disciple thus understands sensual pleasures, the source and origin of sensual pleasures, the diversity of sensual pleasures, the result of sensual pleasures, the cessation of sensual pleasures, and the way leading to the cessation of sensual pleasures, he understands this penetrative spiritual life to be the cessation of sensual pleasures.[1414]

"When it was said: 'Sensual pleasures should be understood . . . the way leading to the cessation of sensual pleasures should be understood,' it is because of this that this was said.

(2) "When it was said: 'Feelings should be understood . . . the way leading to the cessation of feelings should be understood,' for what reason was this said?

"There are, bhikkhus, these three feelings: pleasant feeling, painful feeling, and neither-painful-nor-pleasant feeling.

"And what is the source and origin of feelings? Contact is their source and origin.

"And what is the diversity of feelings? There is worldly pleasant feeling,[1415] there is spiritual pleasant feeling; there is worldly painful feeling, there is spiritual painful feeling; there is worldly neither-painful-nor-pleasant feeling, there is spiritual neither-painful-nor-pleasant feeling. This is called the diversity of feelings.

"And what is the result of feelings? One produces an individual existence that corresponds with whatever [feelings] one experiences and which may be the consequence either of merit or demerit. This is called the result of feelings.

"And what is the cessation of feelings? With the cessation of contact there is cessation of feelings.

"This noble eightfold path is the way leading to the cessation of feelings, namely, right view . . . right concentration.

"When, bhikkhus, a noble disciple thus understands feeling, the source and origin of feelings, [413] the diversity of feelings, the result of feelings, the cessation of feelings, and the way leading to the cessation of feelings, he understands this penetrative spiritual life to be the cessation of feelings.

"When it was said: 'Feelings should be understood . . . the way leading to the cessation of feelings should be understood,' it is because of this that this was said.

(3) "When it was said: 'Perceptions should be understood . . . the way leading to the cessation of perceptions should be understood,' for what reason was this said?

"There are, bhikkhus, these six perceptions: perception of forms, perception of sounds, perception of odors, perception of tastes, perception of tactile objects, perception of mental phenomena.

"And what is the source and origin of perceptions? Contact is their source and origin.

"And what is the diversity of perceptions? The perception of forms is one thing, the perception of sounds is another, the perception of odors still another, the perception of tastes still another, the perception of tactile objects still another, and the perception of mental phenomena still another. This is called the diversity of perceptions.

"And what is the result of perceptions? I say that perceptions result in expression.[1416] In whatever way one perceives something, in just that way one expresses oneself, [saying:] 'I was percipient of such and such.' This is called the result of perception.

"And what is the cessation of perceptions? With the cessation of contact there is cessation of perceptions.

"This noble eightfold path is the way leading to the cessation of perceptions, namely, right view . . . right concentration.

"When, bhikkhus, a noble disciple thus understands perceptions, the source and origin of perceptions, [414] the diversity of perceptions, the result of perceptions, the cessation of perceptions, and the way leading to the cessation of perceptions, he understands this penetrative spiritual life to be the cessation of perceptions.

"When it was said: 'Perceptions should be understood . . . the way leading to the cessation of perceptions should be understood,' it is because of this that this was said.

(4) "When it was said: 'The taints should be understood . . . the way leading to the cessation of the taints should be understood,' for what reason was this said?

"There are, bhikkhus, these three taints: the taint of sensuality, the taint of existence, and the taint of ignorance.

"And what is the source and origin of the taints? Ignorance is their source and origin.

"And what is the diversity of the taints? There are taints leading to hell; there are taints leading to the animal realm; there are taints leading to the realm of afflicted spirits; there are taints leading to the human world; there are taints leading to the deva world. This is called the diversity of the taints.

"And what is the result of the taints? One immersed in ignorance produces a corresponding individual existence, which may be the consequence either of merit or demerit. This is called the result of the taints.

"And what is the cessation of the taints? With the cessation of ignorance there is cessation of the taints.

"This noble eightfold path is the way leading to the cessation of the taints, namely, right view . . . right concentration.

"When, bhikkhus, a noble disciple thus understands the taints, the source and origin of the taints, the diversity of the taints, the result of the taints, the cessation of the taints, and the way leading to the cessation of the taints, he understands this penetrative spiritual life to be the cessation of the taints. [415]

"When it was said: 'The taints should be understood . . . the way leading to the cessation of the taints should be understood,' it is because of this that this was said.

(5) "When it was said: 'Kamma should be understood . . . the way leading to the cessation of kamma should be understood,' for what reason was this said?

"It is volition, bhikkhus, that I call kamma.[1417] For having willed, one acts by body, speech, or mind.

"And what is the source and origin of kamma? Contact is its source and origin.

"And what is the diversity of kamma? There is kamma to be experienced in hell; there is kamma to be experienced in the animal realm; there is kamma to be experienced in the realm of afflicted spirits; there is kamma to be experienced in the human world; and there is kamma to be experienced in the deva world.[1418] This is called the diversity of kamma.

"And what is the result of kamma? The result of kamma, I say, is threefold: [to be experienced] in this very life, or in the [next] rebirth, or on some subsequent occasion. This is called the result of kamma.[1419]

"And what, bhikkhus, is the cessation of kamma? With the cessation of contact there is cessation of kamma.[1420]

"This noble eightfold path is the way leading to the cessation of kamma, namely, right view . . . right concentration.

"When, bhikkhus, a noble disciple thus understands kamma, the source and origin of kamma, the diversity of kamma, the result of kamma, the cessation of kamma, and the way leading to the cessation of kamma, he understands this penetrative spiritual life to be the cessation of kamma.

"When it was said: 'Kamma should be understood . . . [416] the way leading to the cessation of kamma should be understood,' it is because of this that this was said.

(6) "When it was said: 'Suffering should be understood; the source and origin of suffering should be understood; the diversity of suffering should be understood; the result of suffering should be understood; the cessation of suffering should be understood; the way leading to the cessation of suffering should be understood,' for what reason was this said?

"Birth is suffering; old age is suffering; illness is suffering; death is suffering; sorrow, lamentation, pain, dejection, and anguish are suffering; not to get what one wants is suffering; in brief, the five aggregates subject to clinging are suffering.

"And what is the source and origin of suffering? Craving is its source and origin.

"And what is the diversity of suffering? There is extreme suffering; there is slight suffering; there is suffering that fades away slowly; there is suffering that fades away quickly. This is called the diversity of suffering.

"And what is the result of suffering? Here, someone overcome by suffering, with a mind obsessed by it, sorrows, languishes, and laments; he weeps beating his breast and becomes confused. Or else, overcome by suffering, with a mind obsessed by it, he embarks upon a search outside, saying: 'Who knows one or two words for putting an end to this suffering?'[1421] Suffering, I say, results either in confusion or in a search. This is called the result of suffering.

"And what is the cessation of suffering? With the cessation of craving there is cessation of suffering.

"This noble eightfold path is the way leading to the cessation of suffering, namely, right view . . . right concentration.

"When, bhikkhus, a noble disciple thus understands suffering, [417] the source and origin of suffering, the diversity of suffering, the result of suffering, the cessation of suffering, and the way leading to the cessation of suffering, he understands this penetrative spiritual life to be the cessation of suffering.

"When it was said: 'Suffering should be understood . . . the way leading to the cessation of suffering should be understood,' it is because of this that this was said.

"This, bhikkhus, is that penetrative exposition of the Dhamma."

64 (10) Lion's Roar

"Bhikkhus, there are these six Tathāgata's powers that the Tathāgata has, possessing which he claims the place of the chief bull, roars his lion's roar in the assemblies, and sets in motion the brahma wheel.[1422] What six?

(1) "Here, bhikkhus, the Tathāgata understands as it really is the possible as possible and the impossible as impossible.[1423] Since the Tathāgata understands as it really is the possible as possible and the impossible as impossible, this is a Tathāgata's power that the Tathāgata has, possessing which he claims the place of the chief bull, roars his lion's roar in the assemblies, and sets in motion the brahma wheel.

(2) "Again, the Tathāgata understands as it really is the result of the undertaking of kamma past, future, and present in terms of possibilities and causes.[1424] Since the Tathāgata understands as it really is the result of the undertaking of kamma . . . this too is a Tathāgata's power that the Tathāgata has, possessing which he . . . sets in motion the brahma wheel.

(3) "Again, the Tathāgata [418] understands as it really is the defilement, the cleansing, and the emergence in regard to the jhānas, emancipations, concentrations, and meditative attainments.[1425] Since the Tathāgata understands as it really is the defilement, the cleansing, and the emergence in regard to the jhānas . . . this too is a Tathāgata's power that the Tathāgata has, possessing which he . . . sets in motion the brahma wheel.

(4) "Again, the Tathāgata recollects his manifold past abodes, that is, one birth, two births . . . [as in 6:2 §4] . . . Thus he recollects his manifold past abodes with their aspects and details. Since the Tathāgata recollects his manifold past abodes . . . with their aspects and details, this too is a Tathāgata's power that the Tathāgata has, possessing which he . . . sets in motion the brahma wheel.

(5) "Again, with the divine eye, which is purified and surpasses the human, the Tathāgata sees beings passing away and being reborn . . . [as in 6:2 §5] . . . and he understands how beings fare in accordance with their kamma. Since the Tathāgata . . . understands how beings fare in accordance with their kamma, this too is a Tathāgata's power that the Tathāgata has, possessing which he . . . sets in motion the brahma wheel.

(6) "Again, with the destruction of the taints, the Tathāgata has realized for himself with direct knowledge, in this very life,

the taintless liberation of mind, liberation by wisdom, and having entered upon it, he dwells in it. Since the Tathāgata has realized for himself . . . the taintless liberation of mind, liberation by wisdom . . . this too is a Tathāgata's power that the Tathāgata has, possessing which he . . . sets in motion the brahma wheel. [419]

"These are the six Tathāgata's powers that the Tathāgata has, possessing which he claims the place of the chief bull, roars his lion's roar in the assemblies, and sets in motion the brahma wheel.

(1) "If, bhikkhus, others approach the Tathāgata and ask him a question related to his knowledge as it really is of the possible as possible and the impossible as impossible, then the Tathāgata, questioned in this way, answers them exactly as he has understood this knowledge.

(2) "If others approach the Tathāgata and ask him a question related to his knowledge as it really is of the result of the undertaking of kamma past, future, and present in terms of possibilities and causes, then the Tathāgata, questioned in this way, answers them exactly as he has understood this knowledge.

(3) "If others approach the Tathāgata and ask him a question related to his knowledge as it really is of the defilement, the cleansing, and the emergence in regard to the jhānas, emancipations, concentrations, and meditative attainments, then the Tathāgata, questioned in this way, answers them exactly as he has understood this knowledge.

(4) "If others approach the Tathāgata and ask him a question related to his knowledge as it really is of the recollection of past abodes, then [420] the Tathāgata, questioned in this way, answers them exactly as he has understood this knowledge.[1426]

(5) "If others approach the Tathāgata and ask him a question related to his knowledge as it really is of the passing away and rebirth of beings, then the Tathāgata, questioned in this way, answers them exactly as he has understood this knowledge.

(6) "If others approach the Tathāgata and ask him a question related to his knowledge as it really is of the taintless liberation of mind, liberation by wisdom, then the Tathāgata, questioned in this way, answers them exactly as he has understood this knowledge.

(1) "I say, bhikkhus, that the knowledge as it really is of the

possible as possible and the impossible as impossible is for one who is concentrated, not for one who lacks concentration.

(2) "I say that the knowledge as it really is of the result of the undertaking of kammas past, future, and present in terms of possibilities and causes is for one who is concentrated, not for one who lacks concentration.

(3) "I say that the knowledge as it really is of the defilement, the cleansing, and the emergence in regard to the jhānas, emancipations, concentrations, and meditative attainments is for one who is concentrated, not for one who lacks concentration.

(4) "I say that the knowledge as it really is of the recollection of past abodes is for one who is concentrated, not for one who lacks concentration.

(5) "I say that the knowledge as it really is of the passing away and rebirth of beings is for one who is concentrated, not for one who lacks concentration.

(6) "I say that the knowledge as it really is of the taintless liberation of mind, liberation by wisdom, is for one who is concentrated, not for one who lacks concentration.

"Thus, bhikkhus, concentration is the path; lack of concentration is the wrong path." [421]

II. Non-Returner

65 (1) Non-Returner

"Bhikkhus, without having abandoned six things, one is incapable of realizing the fruit of non-returning. What six? Lack of faith, lack of moral shame, moral recklessness, laziness, muddle-mindedness, and lack of wisdom. Without having abandoned these six things, one is incapable of realizing the fruit of non-returning.

"Bhikkhus, having abandoned six things, one is capable of realizing the fruit of non-returning. What six? Lack of faith . . . lack of wisdom. Having abandoned these six things, one is capable of realizing the fruit of non-returning."

66 (2) Arahant

"Bhikkhus, without having abandoned six things, one is incapable of realizing arahantship. What six? Dullness, drowsiness, restlessness, remorse, lack of faith, and heedlessness. Without having abandoned these six things, one is incapable of realizing arahantship. [422]

"Bhikkhus, having abandoned six things, one is capable of realizing arahantship. What six? Dullness . . . heedlessness. Having abandoned these six things, one is capable of realizing arahantship."

67 (3) Friends

"Bhikkhus, when a bhikkhu has bad friends, bad companions, and bad comrades, when he follows, resorts to, and attends upon bad friends and follows their example, (1) it is impossible that he will fulfill the duty of proper conduct. Without having fulfilled the duty of proper conduct, (2) it is impossible that he will fulfill the duty of a trainee. Without having fulfilled the duty of a trainee, (3) it is impossible that he will fulfill virtuous behavior. Without having fulfilled virtuous behavior, (4) it is impossible that he will abandon sensual lust, (5) lust for form, or (6) lust for the formless.[1427]

"Bhikkhus, when a bhikkhu has good friends, good companions, and good comrades, when he follows, resorts to, and attends upon good friends and follows their example, (1) it is possible that he will fulfill the duty of proper conduct. Having fulfilled the duty of proper conduct, (2) it is possible that he will fulfill the duty of a trainee. Having fulfilled the duty of a trainee, (3) it is possible that he will fulfill virtuous behavior. Having fulfilled virtuous behavior, (4) it is possible that he will abandon sensual lust, (5) lust for form, and (6) lust for the formless."

68 (4) Delight in Company

"Bhikkhus, (1) it is impossible that a bhikkhu who delights in company, who is delighted with company, who is devoted to delight in company; who delights in a group, who is delighted with a group, who is devoted to delight in a group, will find delight in solitude when he is alone. (2) It is impossible that one who does not find delight in solitude when he is alone [423] will acquire the object of the mind.[1428] (3) It is impossible that one who does not acquire the object of the mind will fulfill right view. (4) It is impossible that one who does not fulfill right view will fulfill right concentration. (5) It is impossible that one who does not fulfill right concentration will abandon the fetters. (6) Without having abandoned the fetters, it is impossible that one will realize nibbāna.

"Bhikkhus, (1) it is possible that a bhikkhu who does not delight in company, who is not delighted with company, who is not devoted to delight in company; who does not delight in a group, who is not delighted with a group, who is not devoted to delight in a group, will find delight in solitude when he is alone. (2) It is possible that one who finds delight in solitude when he is alone will acquire the object of the mind. (3) It is possible that one who acquires the object of the mind will fulfill right view. (4) It is possible that one who fulfills right view will fulfill right concentration. (5) It is possible that one who fulfills right concentration will abandon the fetters. (6) Having abandoned the fetters, it is possible that one will realize nibbāna."

69 (5) A Deity

Then, when the night had advanced, a certain deity of stunning beauty, illuminating the entire Jeta's Grove, approached the Blessed One, paid homage to him, stood to one side, and said:

"Bhante, these six qualities lead to the non-decline of a bhikkhu. What six? Reverence for the Teacher, reverence for the Dhamma, reverence for the Saṅgha, reverence for the training, being easy to correct, and good friendship. These six qualities lead to the non-decline of a bhikkhu."

This is what that deity said. The Teacher agreed. Then that deity, thinking, "The Teacher agrees with me," paid homage to the Blessed One, circumambulated him keeping the right side toward him, and disappeared right there. [424]

Then, when the night had passed, the Blessed One addressed the bhikkhus: "Last night, bhikkhus, when the night had advanced, a certain deity of stunning beauty, illuminating the entire Jeta's Grove, approached me, paid homage to me, stood to one side, and said: 'Bhante, there are these six qualities that lead to the non-decline of a bhikkhu. What six? Reverence for the Teacher . . . and good friendship. These are the six things that lead to the non-decline of a bhikkhu.' This is what that deity said. Having said this, that deity paid homage to me, circumambulated me keeping the right side toward me, and disappeared right there."

When this was said, the Venerable Sāriputta said to the Blessed One:

"Bhante, I understand in detail the meaning of this statement that the Blessed One has spoken in brief to be as follows. Here, Bhante, (1) a bhikkhu himself reveres the Teacher and speaks in praise of reverence for the Teacher; he encourages other bhikkhus who do not revere the Teacher to develop reverence for the Teacher and, at the proper time, genuinely and truthfully, he speaks praise of those bhikkhus who revere the Teacher. (2) He himself reveres the Dhamma . . . (3) . . . reveres the Saṅgha . . . (4) . . . reveres the training . . . (5) . . . is easy to correct . . . (6) . . . has good friends and speaks in praise of good friendship; he encourages other bhikkhus who do not have good friends to enter upon good friendship and, at the proper time, genuinely and truthfully, he speaks praise of those bhikkhus who have good friends. It is in such a way, Bhante, that I understand in detail the meaning of this statement that the Blessed One has spoken in brief."

[The Blessed One said:] "Good, good, Sāriputta! It is good that you understand in detail the meaning of this statement that I have spoken in brief in such a way.

"Here, Sāriputta, a bhikkhu himself reveres the Teacher [425] . . . [as above, in full] . . . he speaks praise of those bhikkhus who have good friends. It is in such a way that the meaning of this statement that I spoke in brief should be understood in detail."

70 (6) Concentration

"Bhikkhus, (1) it is impossible that a bhikkhu, without concentration that is peaceful, sublime, gained through tranquilization, and attained to unification could wield the various kinds of psychic potency: having been one, he could become many . . . [all abridged passages here as in 6:2] . . . he could exercise mastery with the body as far as the brahmā world. (2) It is impossible that with the divine ear element, which is purified and surpasses the human, he could hear both kinds of sounds, the divine and human, those that are far as well as near. (3) It is impossible that he could understand the minds of other beings and persons, having encompassed them with his own mind; that he could understand a mind with lust as a mind with lust . . . an unliberated mind as unliberated. (4) It is impossible that he could recollect his manifold past abodes . . . [426] with their aspects and details. (5) It is impossible that with the divine eye, which is purified and surpasses the human, he could see beings passing away and being reborn . . . and could understand how beings fare in accordance with their kamma. (6) It is impossible that with the destruction of the taints, he could realize for himself with direct knowledge, in this very life, the taintless liberation of mind, liberation by wisdom, and having entered upon it, could dwell in it.

"Bhikkhus, (1) it is possible that a bhikkhu, with concentration that is peaceful, sublime, gained through tranquilization, and attained to unification could wield the various kinds of psychic potency . . . (2) could hear both kinds of sounds, the divine and human, those that are far as well as near . . . (3) could understand the minds of other beings and persons, having encompassed them with his own mind . . . (4) could recollect his manifold past abodes with their aspects and details . . . (5) could, with the divine eye, which is purified and surpasses the human, see beings passing away and being reborn . . . and could understand how beings fare in accordance with their kamma . . . (6) with the destruction of the taints, could realize for himself with direct knowledge, in this very life, the taintless liberation of mind, liberation by wisdom, and having entered upon it, could dwell in it."

71 (7) Capable of Realizing

"Bhikkhus, possessing six qualities, a bhikkhu is incapable of realizing a particular state,[1429] [though] there is a suitable basis. What six? [427] (1) Here, a bhikkhu does not understand as it really is: 'These are qualities that pertain to deterioration,' and: (2) 'These are qualities that pertain to stabilization,' and: (3) 'These are qualities that pertain to distinction,' and: (4) 'These are qualities that pertain to penetration.' (5) He does not practice carefully, and (6) he does not do what is suitable. Possessing these six qualities, a bhikkhu is incapable of realizing a particular state, [though] there is a suitable basis.

"Bhikkhus, possessing six qualities, a bhikkhu is capable of realizing a particular state, there being a suitable basis. What six? (1) Here, a bhikkhu understands as it really is: 'These are qualities that pertain to deterioration,' and: (2) 'These are qualities that pertain to stabilization,' and: (3) 'These are qualities that pertain to distinction,' and: (4) 'These are qualities that pertain to penetration.' (5) He practices carefully, and (6) he does what is suitable. Possessing these six qualities, a bhikkhu is capable of realizing a particular state, there being a suitable basis."

72 (8) Strength

"Bhikkhus, possessing six qualities a bhikkhu is incapable of attaining strength in concentration. What six? (1) Here, a bhikkhu is not skilled in the attainment of concentration; (2) he is not skilled in the duration of concentration; (3) he is not skilled in emergence from concentration; (4) he does not practice carefully; (5) he does not practice persistently; and (6) he does not do what is suitable. Possessing these six qualities, a bhikkhu is incapable of attaining strength in concentration.

"Bhikkhus, possessing six qualities a bhikkhu is capable of attaining strength in concentration. What six? [428] (1) Here, a bhikkhu is skilled in the attainment of concentration; (2) he is skilled in the duration of concentration; (3) he is skilled in emergence from concentration; (4) he practices carefully; (5) he practices persistently; and (6) he does what is suitable. Possessing these six qualities, a bhikkhu is capable of attaining strength in concentration."

73 (9) First Jhāna (1)

"Bhikkhus, without having abandoned six things, one is incapable of entering and dwelling in the first jhāna. What six? Sensual desire, ill will, dullness and drowsiness, restlessness and remorse, doubt; and one has not clearly seen with correct wisdom, as it really is, the danger in sensual pleasures. Without having abandoned these six things, one is incapable of entering and dwelling in the first jhāna.

"Bhikkhus, having abandoned six things, one is capable of entering and dwelling in the first jhāna. What six? Sensual desire . . . one has clearly seen with correct wisdom, as it really is, the danger in sensual pleasures. Having abandoned these six things, one is capable of entering and dwelling in the first jhāna."

74 (10) First Jhāna (2)

"Bhikkhus, without having abandoned six things, one is incapable of entering and dwelling in the first jhāna. What six? Sensual thought, the thought of ill will, the thought of harming, sensual perception, perception of ill will, and perception of harming. Without having abandoned these six things, one is incapable of entering and dwelling in the first jhāna.

"Bhikkhus, having abandoned six things, one is capable of entering and dwelling in the first jhāna. What six? Sensual thought . . . perception of harming. [429] Having abandoned these six things, one is capable of entering and dwelling in the first jhāna."

III. Arahantship

75 (1) In Suffering

"Bhikkhus, possessing six things, a bhikkhu dwells in suffering in this very life—with distress, anguish, and fever—and with the breakup of the body, after death, a bad destination can be expected for him. What six? Sensual thought, the thought of ill will, the thought of harming, sensual perception, perception of ill will, and perception of harming. Possessing these six things, a bhikkhu dwells in suffering in this very life—with distress, anguish, and fever—and with the breakup of the body, after death, a bad destination can be expected for him.

"Bhikkhus, possessing six things, a bhikkhu dwells happily in this very life—without distress, anguish, and fever—and with the breakup of the body, after death, a good destination can be expected for him. What six? The thought of renunciation, the thought of good will, the thought of harmlessness, perception of renunciation, perception of good will, and perception of harmlessness. Possessing these six things, a bhikkhu dwells happily in this very life—without distress, anguish, and fever—and with the breakup of the body, after death, a good destination can be expected for him." [430]

76 (2) Arahantship

"Bhikkhus, without having abandoned six things, one is incapable of realizing arahantship. What six? Conceit, an inferiority complex, arrogance, self-overestimation, obstinacy, and self-abasement. Without having abandoned these six things, one is incapable of realizing arahantship.[1430]

"Bhikkhus, having abandoned six things, one is capable of realizing arahantship. What six? Conceit . . . self-abasement. Having abandoned these six things, one is capable of realizing arahantship."

77 (3) Superior

"Bhikkhus, without having abandoned six things, one is incapable of realizing any superhuman distinction in knowledge and vision worthy of the noble ones. What six? Muddle-mindedness, lack of clear comprehension, not guarding the doors of the sense faculties, lack of moderation in eating, duplicity, and flattery. Without having abandoned these six things, one is incapable of realizing any superhuman distinction in knowledge and vision worthy of the noble ones.

"Bhikkhus, having abandoned six things, one is capable of realizing a superhuman distinction in knowledge and vision worthy of the noble ones. What six? Muddle-mindedness . . . flattery. Having abandoned these six things, one is capable of realizing a superhuman distinction in knowledge and vision worthy of the noble ones." [431]

78 (4) Happiness

"Bhikkhus, possessing six qualities, a bhikkhu abounds in happiness and joy in this very life, and he has laid the foundation for the destruction of the taints. What six? Here, a bhikkhu delights in the Dhamma, delights in [mental] development, delights in abandoning, delights in solitude, delights in non-affliction, and delights in non-proliferation. Possessing these six qualities, a bhikkhu abounds in happiness and joy in this very life, and he has laid the foundation for the destruction of the taints."

79 (5) Achievement

"Possessing six qualities, a bhikkhu is incapable of achieving a wholesome quality that he has not yet achieved or of strengthening a wholesome quality that has already been achieved. What six? (1) Here, a bhikkhu is not skilled in gain, (2) not skilled in loss, (3) not skilled in means; (4) he does not generate desire for the achievement of wholesome qualities not yet achieved; (5)

he does not guard wholesome qualities already achieved; (6) he does not fulfill his tasks through persistent effort. Possessing these six qualities, a bhikkhu is incapable of achieving a wholesome quality that he has not yet achieved or of strengthening a wholesome quality that has already been achieved.

"Possessing six qualities, a bhikkhu is capable of achieving a wholesome quality that he has not yet achieved and of strengthening a wholesome quality that has already been achieved. What six? (1) Here, a bhikkhu is skilled in gain, (2) skilled in loss, (3) skilled in means; (4) he generates desire for the achievement of wholesome [432] qualities not yet achieved; (5) he guards wholesome qualities already achieved; (6) he fulfills his tasks through persistent effort. Possessing these six qualities, a bhikkhu is capable of achieving a wholesome quality that he has not yet achieved and of strengthening a wholesome quality that has already been achieved."

80 (6) Greatness

"Bhikkhus, possessing six qualities, a bhikkhu in no long time attains to greatness and vastness in [wholesome] qualities. What six? Here, a bhikkhu abounds in light,[1431] abounds in effort, abounds in inspiration; he does not become complacent; he does not neglect his duty in regard to wholesome qualities; and he extends himself further. Possessing these six qualities, a bhikkhu in no long time attains to greatness and vastness in [wholesome] qualities."

81 (7) Hell (1)

"Bhikkhus, possessing six qualities, one is deposited in hell as if brought there. What six? One destroys life, takes what is not given, engages in sexual misconduct, speaks falsely, has evil desires, and holds wrong view. Possessing these six qualities, one is deposited in hell as if brought there.

"Bhikkhus, possessing six qualities, one is deposited in heaven as if brought there. What six? One abstains from the destruction of life, abstains from taking what is not given, abstains from sexual misconduct, abstains from false speech; one has few desires, and one holds right view. Possessing these six qualities, one is deposited in heaven as if brought there." [433]

82 (8) Hell (2)

"Bhikkhus, possessing six qualities, one is deposited in hell as if brought there. What six? One destroys life, takes what is not given, engages in sexual misconduct, and speaks falsely; one is greedy and impudent. Possessing these six qualities, one is deposited in hell as if brought there.

"Bhikkhus, possessing six qualities, one is deposited in heaven as if brought there. What six? One abstains from the destruction of life, abstains from taking what is not given, abstains from sexual misconduct, abstains from false speech; one is without greed and without impudence. Possessing these six qualities, one is deposited in heaven as if brought there."

83 (9) The Foremost State

"Bhikkhus, possessing six qualities a bhikkhu is incapable of realizing arahantship, the foremost state. What six? Here, a bhikkhu is without faith, morally shameless, morally reckless, lazy, unwise, and concerned about his body and life. Possessing these six qualities, a bhikkhu is incapable of realizing arahantship, the foremost state.

"Bhikkhus, possessing six qualities a bhikkhu is capable of realizing arahantship, the foremost state. What six? [434] Here, a bhikkhu has faith, a sense of moral shame, and moral dread; he is energetic and wise; and he is unconcerned about his body and life. Possessing these six qualities, a bhikkhu is capable of realizing arahantship, the foremost state."

84 (10) Nights

"Bhikkhus, when a bhikkhu possesses six qualities, whether night or day comes, only deterioration in wholesome qualities, not growth, can be expected for him. What six? Here, (1) a bhikkhu has strong desires, feels distress, and is discontent with any kind of robe, almsfood, lodging, and medicines and provisions for the sick; he is (2) without faith, (3) immoral, (4) lazy, (5) muddle-minded, and (6) unwise. When a bhikkhu possesses these six qualities, whether night or day comes, only deterioration in wholesome qualities, not growth, is to be expected for him.

"Bhikkhus, when a bhikkhu possesses six qualities, whether night or day comes, only growth in wholesome qualities, not deterioration, is to be expected for him. Here, (1) a bhikkhu does not have strong desires, does not feel distress, and is content with any kind of robe, almsfood, lodging, and medicines and provisions for the sick; he is (2) endowed with faith, (3) virtuous, (4) energetic, (5) mindful, and (6) wise. When a bhikkhu possesses these six qualities, whether night or day comes, only growth in wholesome qualities, not deterioration, is to be expected for him." [435]

IV. Coolness

85 (1) Coolness

"Bhikkhus, possessing six qualities, a bhikkhu is incapable of realizing the unsurpassed coolness. What six? (1) Here, a bhikkhu does not suppress the mind on an occasion when it should be suppressed; (2) he does not exert the mind on an occasion when it should be exerted; (3) he does not encourage the mind on an occasion when it should be encouraged; and (4) he does not look at the mind with equanimity on an occasion when one should look at it with equanimity. (5) He is of inferior disposition and (6) he takes delight in personal existence. Possessing these six qualities, a bhikkhu is incapable of realizing the unsurpassed coolness.[1432]

"Bhikkhus, possessing six qualities, a bhikkhu is capable of realizing the unsurpassed coolness. What six? (1) Here, a bhikkhu suppresses the mind on an occasion when it should be suppressed; (2) he exerts the mind on an occasion when it should be exerted; (3) he encourages the mind on an occasion when it should be encouraged; and (4) he looks at the mind with equanimity on an occasion when one should look at it with equanimity. (5) He is of superior disposition and (6) he takes delight in nibbāna. Possessing these six qualities, a bhikkhu is capable of realizing the unsurpassed coolness."

86 (2) Obstructions

"Bhikkhus, possessing six qualities, even while listening to the good Dhamma one is incapable of entering upon the fixed course [consisting in] rightness in wholesome qualities.[1433] What six? [436] One is obstructed by kamma; one is obstructed by defilement; one is obstructed by the result [of kamma]; one is without faith; one is without desire; and one is unwise.[1434]

Possessing these six qualities, even while listening to the good Dhamma one is incapable of entering upon the fixed course [consisting in] rightness in wholesome qualities.

"Bhikkhus, possessing six qualities, while listening[1435] to the good Dhamma one is capable of entering upon the fixed course [consisting in] rightness in wholesome qualities. What six? One is not obstructed by kamma; one is not obstructed by defilement; one is not obstructed by the result [of kamma]; one is endowed with faith; one has desire; and one is wise. Possessing these six qualities, while listening to the good Dhamma one is capable of entering upon the fixed course [consisting in] rightness in wholesome qualities."

87 (3) A Murderer

"Bhikkhus, possessing six qualities, even while listening to the good Dhamma one is incapable of entering upon the fixed course [consisting in] rightness in wholesome qualities. What six? (1) One has deprived one's mother of life; (2) one has deprived one's father of life; (3) one has deprived an arahant of life; (4) with a mind of hatred one has shed the Tathāgata's blood; (5) one has created a schism in the Saṅgha; (6) one is unwise, stupid, obtuse. Possessing these six qualities, even while listening to the good Dhamma one is incapable of entering upon the fixed course [consisting in] rightness in wholesome qualities.

"Bhikkhus, possessing six qualities, while listening to the good Dhamma one is capable of entering upon the fixed course [consisting in] rightness in wholesome qualities. What six? [437] (1) One has not deprived one's mother of life; (2) nor deprived one's father of life; (3) nor deprived an arahant of life; (4) one has not, with a mind of hatred, shed the Tathāgata's blood; (5) one has not created a schism in the Saṅgha; (6) one is wise, intelligent, astute. Possessing these six qualities, while listening to the good Dhamma one is capable of entering upon the fixed course [consisting in] rightness in wholesome qualities."

88 (4) One Wishes to Listen

"Bhikkhus, possessing six qualities, even while listening to the good Dhamma one is incapable of entering upon the fixed course [consisting in] rightness in wholesome qualities. What six? When the Dhamma and discipline proclaimed by the

Tathāgata is being taught, (1) one does not wish to listen; (2) one does not lend an ear; (3) one does not set one's mind on understanding; (4) one grasps the meaning wrongly; (5) one discards the meaning;[1436] and (6) one has adopted a conviction that is not in conformity [with the teaching].[1437] Possessing these six qualities, even while listening to the good Dhamma one is incapable of entering upon the fixed course [consisting in] rightness in wholesome qualities.

"Bhikkhus, possessing six qualities, while listening to the good Dhamma one is capable of entering upon the fixed course [consisting in] rightness in wholesome qualities. What six? When the Dhamma and discipline proclaimed by the Tathāgata is being taught, (1) one wishes to listen; (2) one lends an ear; (3) one sets one's mind on understanding; (4) one grasps the meaning; (5) one discards what is not the meaning; and (6) one has adopted a conviction that is in conformity [with the teaching]. Possessing these six qualities, while listening to the good Dhamma one is capable of entering upon the fixed course [consisting in] rightness in wholesome qualities." [438]

89 (5) Without Having Abandoned

"Bhikkhus, without having abandoned six things, one is incapable of realizing accomplishment in view.[1438] What six? Personal-existence view, doubt, wrong grasp of behavior and observances, lust leading to the plane of misery, hatred leading to the plane of misery, and delusion leading to the plane of misery. Without having abandoned these six things, one is incapable of realizing accomplishment in view.

"Bhikkhus, having abandoned six things, one is capable of realizing accomplishment in view. What six? Personal-existence view . . . delusion leading to the plane of misery. Having abandoned these six things, one is capable of realizing accomplishment in view."

90 (6) Abandoned

"Bhikkhus, one accomplished in view has abandoned these six things. What six? Personal-existence view, doubt, wrong grasp of behavior and observances, lust leading to the plane of misery, hatred leading to the plane of misery, and delusion leading to the plane of misery. One accomplished in view has abandoned these six things."

91 (7) Incapable

"Bhikkhus, one accomplished in view is incapable of giving rise to these six things. What six? Personal-existence view, doubt, wrong grasp of behavior and observances, lust leading to the plane of misery, hatred leading to the plane of misery, and delusion leading to the plane of misery. One accomplished in view is incapable of giving rise to these six things."

92 (8) Cases (1)

"Bhikkhus, there are these six cases of incapability. What six? [439] One accomplished in view is (1) incapable of dwelling without reverence and deference toward the Teacher; (2) incapable of dwelling without reverence and deference toward the Dhamma; (3) incapable of dwelling without reverence and deference toward the Saṅgha; (4) incapable of dwelling without reverence and deference toward the training; (5) incapable of resorting to anything that should not be relied upon;[1439] (6) incapable of undergoing an eighth existence.[1440] These are the six cases of incapability."

93 (9) Cases (2)

"Bhikkhus, there are these six cases of incapability. What six? One accomplished in view is (1) incapable of considering any conditioned phenomenon as permanent; (2) incapable of considering any conditioned phenomenon as pleasurable; (3) incapable of considering any phenomenon as a self; (4) incapable of doing a grave act that brings immediate result;[1441] (5) incapable of resorting to [the belief] that purity comes about through superstitious and auspicious acts; (6) incapable of seeking a person worthy of offerings outside here.[1442] These are the six cases of incapability."

94 (10) Cases (3)

"Bhikkhus, there are these six cases of incapability. What six? One accomplished in view is (1) incapable of depriving his mother of life; (2) incapable of depriving his father of life; (3) incapable of depriving an arahant of life; (3) incapable of shedding the

Tathāgata's blood with a mind of hatred; (5) incapable of creating a schism in the Saṅgha; (6) incapable of acknowledging another teacher.[1443] These are the six cases of incapability." [440]

95 (11) Cases (4)

"Bhikkhus, there are these six cases of incapability. What six? One accomplished in view is (1) incapable of resorting to [the view that] pleasure and pain are made by oneself; (2) incapable of resorting to [the view that] pleasure and pain are made by another; (3) incapable of resorting to [the view that] pleasure and pain are both made by oneself and made by another; (4) incapable of resorting to [the view that] pleasure and pain are not made by oneself but have arisen fortuitously; (5) incapable of resorting to [the view that] pleasure and pain are not made by another but have arisen fortuitously; (6) incapable of resorting to [the view that] pleasure and pain are made neither by oneself nor by another but have arisen fortuitously. For what reason? Because the person accomplished in view has clearly seen causation and causally arisen phenomena. These are the six cases of incapability." [441]

V. Benefit

96 (1) Manifestation

"Bhikkhus, the manifestation of six things is rare in the world. What six? (1) The manifestation of a Tathāgata, an Arahant, a Perfectly Enlightened One is rare in the world. (2) One who can teach the Dhamma and discipline proclaimed by a Tathāgata is rare in the world. (3) Rebirth in the sphere of the noble ones is rare in the world. (4) Endowment with unimpaired [sense] faculties is rare in the world. (5) Being intelligent and astute is rare in the world. (6) The desire for the wholesome Dhamma is rare in the world. The manifestation of these six things is rare in the world."

97 (2) Benefits

"Bhikkhus, there are these six benefits in realizing the fruit of stream-entry. What six? (1) One is fixed in the good Dhamma; (2) one is incapable of decline; (3) one's suffering is delimited; (4) one comes to possess knowledge not shared by others; (5)

one has clearly seen causation; (6) one has clearly seen causally arisen phenomena. These are the six benefits in realizing the fruit of stream-entry."

98 (3) Impermanent

"Bhikkhus, (1) it is impossible that a bhikkhu who considers any conditioned phenomenon to be permanent will possess a conviction in conformity [with the teaching]. (2) It is impossible that one who does not possess a conviction in conformity [with the teaching] will enter upon the fixed course of rightness.[1444] (3) It is impossible that one who does not enter upon the fixed course of rightness will realize the fruit of stream-entry, (4) the fruit of once-returning, (5) the fruit of non-returning, (6) or arahantship. [442]

"Bhikkhus, (1) it is possible that a bhikkhu who considers all conditioned phenomena to be impermanent will possess a conviction in conformity [with the teaching]. (2) It is possible that one who possesses a conviction in conformity [with the teaching] will enter upon the fixed course of rightness. (3) It is possible that one who enters upon the fixed course of rightness will realize the fruit of stream-entry, (4) the fruit of once-returning, (5) the fruit of non-returning, (6) or arahantship."

99 (4) Suffering

"Truly, bhikkhus, (1) it is impossible that a bhikkhu who considers any conditioned phenomenon to be pleasurable will possess a conviction in conformity [with the teaching]. (2) It is impossible that one who does not possess a conviction in conformity [with the teaching] will enter upon the fixed course of rightness. (3) It is impossible that one who does not enter upon the fixed course of rightness will realize the fruit of stream-entry, (4) the fruit of once-returning, (5) the fruit of non-returning, (6) or arahantship.

"Bhikkhus, (1) it is possible that a bhikkhu who considers all conditioned phenomena to be suffering will possess a conviction in conformity [with the teaching]. (2) It is possible that one who possesses a conviction in conformity [with the teaching] will enter upon the fixed course of rightness. (3) It is possible that one who enters upon the fixed course of rightness will realize the fruit of stream-entry, (4) the fruit of once-returning, (5) the fruit of non-returning, (6) or arahantship."

100 (5) Non-Self

"Bhikkhus, (1) it is impossible that a bhikkhu who considers any phenomenon to be a self will possess a conviction in conformity [with the teaching]. (2) It is impossible that one who does not possess a conviction in conformity [with the teaching] will enter upon the fixed course of rightness. (3) It is impossible that one who does not enter upon the fixed course of rightness will realize the fruit of stream-entry, (4) the fruit of once-returning, (5) the fruit of non-returning, (6) or arahantship.

"Bhikkhus, (1) it is possible that a bhikkhu who considers all phenomena to be non-self will possess a conviction in conformity [with the teaching]. (2) It is possible that one who possesses a conviction in conformity [with the teaching] will enter upon the fixed course of rightness. (3) It is possible that one who enters upon the fixed course of rightness will realize the fruit of stream-entry, (4) the fruit of once-returning, (5) the fruit of non-returning, (6) or arahantship."

101 (6) Nibbāna

"Bhikkhus, (1) it is impossible that a bhikkhu who considers nibbāna to be suffering will possess a conviction in conformity [with the teaching]. (2) It is impossible that one who does not possess a conviction in conformity [with the teaching] will enter upon the fixed course of rightness. (3) It is impossible that one who does not enter upon the fixed course of rightness will realize the fruit of stream-entry, (4) the fruit of once-returning, (5) the fruit of non-returning, (6) or arahantship.

"Bhikkhus, (1) it is possible that a bhikkhu who considers nibbāna to be happiness will possess a conviction in conformity [with the teaching]. [443] (2) It is possible that one who possesses a conviction in conformity [with the teaching] will enter upon the fixed course of rightness. (3) It is possible that one who enters upon the fixed course of rightness will realize the fruit of stream-entry, (4) the fruit of once-returning, (5) the fruit of non-returning, (6) or arahantship."

102 (7) Unlasting

"Bhikkhus, when a bhikkhu considers six benefits, it is enough for him to establish the unlimited perception of impermanence in all conditioned phenomena.[1445] What six? (1) 'All conditioned phenomena will appear to me as unlasting. (2) My mind will not delight in anything in the world. (3) My mind will rise up from the entire world. (4) My mind will slope toward nibbāna. (5) My fetters will be abandoned.[1446] And (6) I will come to possess supreme asceticism.'[1447]

"Bhikkhus, when a bhikkhu considers these six benefits, it is enough for him to establish the unlimited perception of impermanence in all conditioned phenomena."

103 (8) Uplifted Dagger

"Bhikkhus, when a bhikkhu considers six benefits, it is enough for him to establish the unlimited perception of suffering in all conditioned phenomena. What six? (1) 'The perception of disenchantment will be established in me toward all conditioned phenomena, as toward a murderer with uplifted dagger. (2) My mind will rise up from the entire world. (3) I will see nibbāna as peaceful. (4) My underlying tendencies will be uprooted. (5) I will be one who has done his task. And (6) I will have served the Teacher with loving-kindness.' [444]

"Bhikkhus, when a bhikkhu considers these six benefits, it is enough for him to establish the unlimited perception of suffering in all conditioned phenomena."

104 (9) Without Identification

"Bhikkhus, when a bhikkhu considers six benefits, it is enough for him to establish the unlimited perception of non-self in all phenomena. What six? (1) 'I will be without identification in the entire world.[1448] (2) I-makings will cease for me. (3) Mine-makings will cease for me. (4) I will come to possess knowledge not shared [with worldlings]. (5) I will have clearly seen causation. And (6) I will have clearly seen causally arisen phenomena.'

"Bhikkhus, when a bhikkhu considers these six benefits, it is enough for him to establish the unlimited perception of non-self in all phenomena."

105 (10) Existence

"Bhikkhus, there are these three kinds of existence that are to be abandoned; [and] one is to train in the three trainings.[1449] What are the three kinds of existence that are to be abandoned? (1) Sense-sphere existence, (2) form-sphere existence, and (3) formless-sphere existence: these are the three kinds of existence to be abandoned. In what three trainings is one to train? (4) In the higher virtuous behavior, (5) in the higher mind, and (6) in the higher wisdom. One is to train in these three trainings.

"When a bhikkhu has abandoned these three kinds of existence and has completed these three trainings, he is called a bhikkhu who has cut off craving, stripped off the fetter, and by completely breaking through conceit, he has made an end of suffering." [445]

106 (11) Craving

"Bhikkhus, there are these three kinds of craving, and these three kinds of conceit, that are to be abandoned.[1450] What are the three kinds of craving that are to be abandoned? (1) Sensual craving, (2) craving for existence, and (3) craving for extermination: these are the three kinds of craving that are to be abandoned. And what are the three kinds of conceit that are to be abandoned? (4) Conceit, (5) the inferiority complex, and (6) arrogance: these are the three kinds of conceit that are to be abandoned.

"When a bhikkhu has abandoned these three kinds of craving and these three kinds of conceit, he is called a bhikkhu who has cut off craving, stripped off the fetter, and by completely breaking through conceit, has made an end of suffering."

Chapters Extra to the Set of Fifty[1451]

I. Triads

107 (1) Lust

"Bhikkhus, there are these three things. What three? (1) Lust, (2) hatred, and (3) delusion. These are three things. Three [other] things are to be developed for abandoning these three things. What three? [446] (4) The unattractive is to be developed for abandoning lust. (5) Loving-kindness is to be developed for abandoning hatred. (6) Wisdom is to be developed for abandoning delusion. These three things are to be developed for abandoning the former three things."

108 (2) Misconduct

"Bhikkhus, there are these three things. What three? (1) Bodily misconduct, (2) verbal misconduct, and (3) mental misconduct.

These are three things. Three [other] things are to be developed for abandoning these three things. What three? (4) Bodily good conduct is to be developed for abandoning bodily misconduct. (5) Verbal good conduct is to be developed for abandoning verbal misconduct. (6) Mental good conduct is to be developed for abandoning mental misconduct. These three things are to be developed for abandoning the former three things."

109 (3) Thoughts

"Bhikkhus, there are these three things. What three? (1) Sensual thought, (2) thought of ill will, and (3) thought of harming. These are three things. Three [other] things are to be developed for abandoning these three things. What three? (4) The thought of renunciation is to be developed for abandoning sensual thought. (5) The thought of good will is to be developed for abandoning the thought of ill will. (6) The thought of harmlessness is to be developed for abandoning the thought of harming. These three things are to be developed for abandoning the former three things."

110 (4) Perceptions

"Bhikkhus, there are these three things. What three? (1) Sensual perception, (2) perception of ill will, and (3) perception of harming. [447] These are three things. Three [other] things are to be developed for abandoning these three things. What three? (4) The perception of renunciation is to be developed for abandoning sensual perception. (5) The perception of good will is to be developed for abandoning the perception of ill will. (6) The perception of harmlessness is to be developed for abandoning the perception of harming. These three things are to be developed for abandoning the former three things."

111 (5) Elements

"Bhikkhus, there are these three things. What three? (1) The sensual element, (2) the element of ill will, and (3) the element of harming. These are three things. Three [other] things are to be developed for abandoning these three things. What three? (4) The element of renunciation is to be developed for abandoning the sensual element. (5) The element of good will is to be developed for abandoning the element of ill will. (6) The element of harmlessness is to be developed for abandoning the element of harming. These three things are to be developed for abandoning the former three things."

112 (6) Gratification

"Bhikkhus, there are these three things. What three? (1) The view of gratification, (2) the view of self, and (3) wrong view. These are three things. Three [other] things are to be developed for abandoning these three things. What three? (4) The perception of impermanence is to be developed for abandoning the view of gratification. (5) The perception of non-self is to be developed for abandoning the view of self. (6) Right view is to be developed for abandoning wrong view. These three things are to be developed for abandoning the former three things." [448]

113 (7) Discontent

"Bhikkhus, there are these three things. What three? (1) Discontent, (2) harmfulness, and (3) conduct contrary to the Dhamma. These are three things. Three [other] things are to be developed for abandoning these three things. What three? (4) Altruistic joy is to be developed for abandoning discontent. (5) Harmlessness is to be developed for abandoning harmfulness. (6) Conduct in accordance with the Dhamma is to be developed for abandoning conduct contrary to the Dhamma. These three things are to be developed for abandoning the former three things."

114 (8) Contentment

"Bhikkhus, there are these three things. What three? (1) Noncontentment, (2) lack of clear comprehension, and (3) strong desires. These are three things. Three [other] things are to be developed for abandoning these three things. What three? (4) Contentment is to be developed for abandoning noncontentment. (5) Clear comprehension is to be developed for abandoning lack of clear comprehension. (6) Fewness of desires is to be developed for abandoning strong desires. These three things are to be developed for abandoning the former three things."

115 (9) Difficult to Correct

"Bhikkhus, there are these three things. What three? (1) Being difficult to correct, (2) bad friendship, and (3) mental distraction. These are three things. Three [other] things are to be developed for abandoning these three things. What three? [449] (4) Being easy to correct is to be developed for abandoning being difficult to correct. (5) Good friendship is to be developed for abandoning bad friendship. (6) Mindfulness of breathing is to be developed for abandoning mental distraction. These three things are to be developed for abandoning the former three things."

116 (10) Restlessness

"Bhikkhus, there are these three things. What three? (1) Restlessness, (2) non-restraint, and (3) heedlessness. These are three things. Three [other] things are to be developed for abandoning these three things. What three? (4) Serenity is to be developed for abandoning restlessness. (5) Restraint is to be developed for abandoning non-restraint. (6) Heedfulness is to be developed for abandoning heedlessness. These three things are to be developed for abandoning the former three things."

II. Asceticism

117 (1) Contemplating the Body[1452]

"Bhikkhus, without having abandoned six things, one is incapable of contemplating the body in the body. What six? Delight in work, delight in talk, delight in sleep, delight in company, not guarding the doors of the sense faculties, and being immoderate in eating. Without having abandoned these six things, one is incapable of contemplating the body in the body. [450]

"Bhikkhus, having abandoned six things, one is capable of contemplating the body in the body. What six? Delight in work . . . being immoderate in eating. Having abandoned these six things, one is capable of contemplating the body in the body."

118 (2) Contemplating the Body Internally, Etc.

"Bhikkhus, without having abandoned six things, one is incapable of contemplating the body in the body internally . . . externally . . . both internally and externally . . . contemplating feelings in feelings . . . internally . . . externally . . . both internally and externally . . . contemplating mind in mind . . . internally . . . externally . . . both internally and externally . . . contemplating phenomena in phenomena . . . internally . . . externally . . . both internally and externally. What six? Delight in work, delight in talk, delight in sleep, delight in company, not guarding the doors of the sense faculties, and being immoderate in eating. Without having abandoned these six things, one is incapable of contemplating phenomena in phenomena both internally and externally.

"Bhikkhus, by having abandoned six things, one is capable of contemplating phenomena in phenomena both internally and externally. What six? Delight in work ... being immoderate in eating. By having abandoned these six things, one is capable of contemplating phenomena in phenomena both internally and externally."

119 (3) Tapussa

"Bhikkhus, possessing six qualities, the householder Tapussa has reached certainty about the Tathāgata and become a seer of the deathless, one who lives having realized the deathless. What six? [451] Unwavering confidence in the Buddha, unwavering confidence in the Dhamma, unwavering confidence in the Saṅgha, noble virtuous behavior, noble knowledge, and noble liberation. Possessing these six qualities, the householder Tapussa has reached certainty about the Tathāgata and become a seer of the deathless, one who lives having realized the deathless."[1453]

120 (4)–139 (23) Bhallika, Etc.

"Bhikkhus, possessing six qualities, the householder Bhallika ... the householder Sudatta Anāthapiṇḍika ... the householder Citta of Macchikāsaṇḍa ... the householder Hatthaka of Āḷavī ... the householder Mahānāma the Sakyan ... the householder Ugga of Vesālī ... the householder Uggata ... the householder Sūra of Ambaṭṭha ... the householder Jīvaka Komārabhacca ... the householder Nakulapitā ... the householder Tavakaṇṇika ... the householder Pūraṇa ... the householder Isidatta ... the householder Sandhāna ... the householder Vijaya ... the householder Vajjiyamāhita ... the householder Meṇḍaka ... the lay follower Vāseṭṭha ... the lay follower Ariṭṭha ... the lay follower Sāragga has reached certainty about the Tathāgata and become a seer of the deathless, one who lives having realized the deathless. What six?

Unwavering confidence in the Buddha, unwavering confidence in the Dhamma, unwavering confidence in the Saṅgha, noble virtuous behavior, noble knowledge, and noble liberation. Possessing these six qualities, the householder Sāragga has reached certainty about the Tathāgata and become a seer of the deathless, one who lives having realized the deathless."

III. Lust and So Forth Repetition Series

140 (1)

"Bhikkhus, for direct knowledge of lust, six things are to be developed. What six? [452] The unsurpassed sight, the unsurpassed hearing, the unsurpassed gain, the unsurpassed training, the unsurpassed service, and the unsurpassed recollection. For direct knowledge of lust, these six things are to be developed."

141 (2)

"Bhikkhus, for direct knowledge of lust, six things are to be developed. What six? Recollection of the Buddha, recollection of the Dhamma, recollection of the Saṅgha, recollection of virtuous behavior, recollection of generosity, and recollection of the deities. For direct knowledge of lust, these six things are to be developed."

142 (3)

"Bhikkhus, for direct knowledge of lust, six things are to be developed. What six? The perception of impermanence, the perception of suffering in what is impermanent, the perception of non-self in what is suffering, the perception of abandoning, the perception of dispassion, and the perception of cessation. For direct knowledge of lust, these six things are to be developed."

143 (4)–169 (30)

"Bhikkhus, for full understanding of lust . . . for the utter destruction . . . for the abandoning . . . for the destruction . . . for the vanishing . . . for the fading away . . . for the cessation . . . for the giving up . . . for the relinquishment of lust . . . these six things are to be developed."

170 (31)–649 (510)[1454]

"Bhikkhus, for direct knowledge . . . for full understanding . . . for the utter destruction . . . for the abandoning . . . for the destruction . . . for the vanishing . . . for the fading away . . . for the cessation . . . for the giving up . . . for the relinquishment of hatred . . . of delusion . . . of anger . . . of hostility . . . of denigration . . . of insolence . . . of envy . . . of miserliness . . . of deceitfulness . . . of craftiness . . . of obstinacy . . . of vehemence . . . of conceit . . . of arrogance . . . of intoxication . . . of heedlessness . . . these six things are to be developed."

This is what the Blessed One said. Elated, those bhikkhus delighted in the Blessed One's statement.

The Book of the Sixes is finished.

The Book of the Sevens
(*Sattakanipāta*)

The Book of the Sevens

The First Fifty

The Second Fifty

[1] # The Book of the Sevens

Homage to the Blessed One, the Arahant,
the Perfectly Enlightened One

The First Fifty

I. Wealth

1 (1) Pleasing (1)

Thus have I heard. On one occasion the Blessed One was dwelling at Sāvatthī in Jeta's Grove, Anāthapiṇḍika's Park. There the Blessed One addressed the bhikkhus: "Bhikkhus!"

"Venerable sir!" those bhikkhus replied. The Blessed One said this:

"Bhikkhus, possessing seven qualities, a bhikkhu is displeasing and disagreeable to his fellow monks and is neither respected nor esteemed by them. What seven? Here, (1) a bhikkhu is desirous of gains, (2) honor, and (3) reputation;[1455] (4) he is morally shameless and (5) morally reckless; (6) he has evil desires and (7) holds wrong view. Possessing these seven qualities, a bhikkhu is displeasing and disagreeable to his fellow monks and is neither respected nor esteemed by them.

"Bhikkhus, possessing seven qualities, a bhikkhu is pleasing and agreeable to his fellow monks and is respected and esteemed by them. What seven? [2] Here, (1) a bhikkhu is not desirous of gains, or (2) honor, or (3) a reputation; (4) he has a sense of moral shame and (5) moral dread; (6) he has few desires and (7) holds right view. Possessing these seven qualities, a bhikkhu is pleasing and agreeable to his fellow monks and is respected and esteemed by them."

2 (2) Pleasing (2)

"Bhikkhus, possessing seven qualities, a bhikkhu is displeasing and disagreeable to his fellow monks and is neither respected nor esteemed by them. What seven? Here, (1) a bhikkhu is desirous of gains, (2) honor, and (3) reputation; (4) he is morally shameless and (5) morally reckless; (6) he is envious and (7) miserly. Possessing these seven qualities, a bhikkhu is displeasing and disagreeable to his fellow monks and is neither respected nor esteemed by them.

"Bhikkhus, possessing seven qualities, a bhikkhu is pleasing and agreeable to his fellow monks and is respected and esteemed by them. What seven? Here, (1) a bhikkhu is not desirous of gains, (2) honor, (3) and reputation; (4) he has a sense of moral shame and (5) moral dread; (6) he is not envious and (7) is not miserly. Possessing these seven qualities, a bhikkhu is pleasing and agreeable to his fellow monks and is respected and esteemed by them." [3]

3 (3) Powers in Brief

"Bhikkhus, there are these seven powers. What seven? The power of faith, the power of energy, the power of moral shame, the power of moral dread, the power of mindfulness, the power of concentration, and the power of wisdom. These are the seven powers."

> The power of faith, the power of energy,
> the powers of moral shame and moral dread;
> the powers of mindfulness and concentration,
> and wisdom, the seventh power;
> a powerful bhikkhu possessing these
> is wise and lives happily.
>
> He should carefully examine the Dhamma
> and deeply see the meaning with wisdom.
> Like the extinguishing of a lamp
> is the emancipation of the mind.

4 (4) Powers in Detail

"Bhikkhus, there are these seven powers. What seven? The power of faith, the power of energy, the power of moral shame, the power of moral dread, the power of mindfulness, the power of concentration, and the power of wisdom.

(1) "And what, bhikkhus, is the power of faith? Here, a noble disciple is endowed with faith. He places faith in the enlightenment of the Tathāgata thus: 'The Blessed One is an arahant, perfectly enlightened, accomplished in true knowledge and conduct, fortunate, knower of the world, unsurpassed trainer of persons to be tamed, teacher of devas and humans, the Enlightened One, the Blessed One.' This is called the power of faith.

(2) "And what is the power of energy? Here, a noble disciple has aroused energy for abandoning unwholesome qualities and acquiring wholesome qualities; he is strong, firm in exertion, not casting off the duty of cultivating wholesome qualities. This is called the power of energy.

(3) "And what is the power of moral shame? Here, a noble disciple has a sense of moral shame; he is ashamed of bodily, verbal, and mental misconduct; he is ashamed [4] of acquiring bad, unwholesome qualities. This is called the power of moral shame.

(4) "And what is the power of moral dread? Here, a noble disciple dreads wrongdoing; he dreads bodily, verbal, and mental misconduct; he dreads acquiring bad, unwholesome qualities. This is called the power of moral dread.

(5) "And what is the power of mindfulness? Here, a noble disciple is mindful, possessing supreme mindfulness and alertness, one who remembers and recollects what was done and said long ago. This is called the power of mindfulness.

(6) "And what is the power of concentration? Here, secluded from sensual pleasures, secluded from unwholesome states, a noble disciple enters and dwells in the first jhāna . . . [as in 5:14 §4] . . . the fourth jhāna. This is called the power of concentration.

(7) "And what is the power of wisdom? Here, a noble disciple is wise; he possesses the wisdom that discerns arising and passing away, which is noble and penetrative and leads to the complete destruction of suffering. This is called the power of wisdom.

"These, bhikkhus, are the seven powers."

[The verses are identical with those of 7:3.]

5 (5) Wealth in Brief

"Bhikkhus, there are these seven kinds of wealth. What seven? The wealth of faith, the wealth of virtuous behavior, the wealth of moral shame, the wealth of moral dread, the wealth of learning, the wealth of generosity, and the wealth of wisdom. [5] These are the seven kinds of wealth."

The wealth of faith, the wealth of virtuous behavior,
the wealth of moral shame and moral dread,
the wealth of learning and generosity,
with wisdom, the seventh kind of wealth:

when one has these seven kinds of wealth,
whether a woman or a man,
they say that one is not poor,
that one's life is not lived in vain.

Therefore an intelligent person,
remembering the Buddhas' teaching,
should be intent on faith and virtuous behavior,
confidence and vision of the Dhamma.

6 (6) Wealth in Detail

"Bhikkhus, there are these seven kinds of wealth. What seven? The wealth of faith, the wealth of virtuous behavior, the wealth of moral shame, the wealth of moral dread, the wealth of learning, the wealth of generosity, and the wealth of wisdom.

(1) "And what, bhikkhus, is the wealth of faith? Here, a noble disciple is endowed with faith. He places faith in the enlightenment of the Tathāgata thus: 'The Blessed One is an arahant . . . the Enlightened One, the Blessed One.' This is called the wealth of faith.

(2) "And what is the wealth of virtuous behavior? Here, a noble disciple abstains from the destruction of life, abstains from taking what is not given, abstains from sexual misconduct, abstains from false speech, abstains from liquor, wine, and intoxicants, the basis for heedlessness. This is called the wealth of virtuous behavior.

(3) "And what is the wealth of moral shame? Here, a noble disciple has a sense of moral shame; he is ashamed of bodily, ver-

bal, and mental misconduct; he is ashamed of acquiring bad, unwholesome qualities. This is called the wealth of moral shame.

(4) "And what is the wealth of moral dread? Here, a noble disciple dreads wrongdoing; he dreads bodily, verbal, and mental misconduct; he dreads acquiring bad, unwholesome qualities. This is called the wealth of moral dread.

(5) "And what is the wealth of learning? [6] Here, a noble disciple has learned much, remembers what he has learned, and accumulates what he has learned. Those teachings that are good in the beginning, good in the middle, and good in the end, with the right meaning and phrasing, which proclaim the perfectly complete and pure spiritual life—such teachings as these he has learned much of, retained in mind, recited verbally, mentally investigated, and penetrated well by view. This is called the wealth of learning.

(6) "And what is the wealth of generosity? Here, a noble disciple dwells at home with a heart devoid of the stain of miserliness, freely generous, openhanded, delighting in relinquishment, one devoted to charity, delighting in giving and sharing. This is called the wealth of generosity.

(7) "And what is the wealth of wisdom? Here, a noble disciple is wise; he possesses the wisdom that discerns arising and passing away, which is noble and penetrative and leads to the complete destruction of suffering. This is called the wealth of wisdom.

"These, bhikkhus, are the seven kinds of wealth."

[The verses are identical with those of 7:5.]

7 (7) Ugga

Then Ugga the king's chief minister approached the Blessed One, paid homage to him, sat down to one side, and said:

"It's astounding and amazing, Bhante, how Migāra of Rohaṇa is so rich, with such great wealth and property."

"But how [7] rich is Migāra of Rohaṇa? How much wealth and property does he have?"

"He has a hundred thousand units of minted gold,[1456] not to mention silver."

"There is that kind of wealth, Ugga; this I don't deny. But that kind of wealth can be taken away by fire, water, kings, thieves, and displeasing heirs. However, Ugga, these seven kinds of wealth cannot be taken away by fire, water, kings, thieves, and displeasing heirs. What seven? The wealth of faith, the wealth of virtuous behavior, the wealth of moral shame, the wealth of moral dread, the wealth of learning, the wealth of generosity, and the wealth of wisdom. These seven kinds of wealth cannot be taken away by fire, water, kings, thieves, and displeasing heirs."

[The verses are identical with those of 7:5.]

8 (8) Fetters

"Bhikkhus, there are these seven fetters.[1457] What seven? The fetter of compliance,[1458] the fetter of aversion, the fetter of views, the fetter of doubt, the fetter of conceit, the fetter of lust for existence, and the fetter of ignorance. These are the seven fetters."

9 (9) Abandoning

"Bhikkhus, the spiritual life is lived to abandon and eradicate seven fetters. What seven? [8] The fetter of compliance, the fetter of aversion, the fetter of views, the fetter of doubt, the fetter of conceit, the fetter of lust for existence, and the fetter of ignorance. The spiritual life is lived to abandon and eradicate these seven fetters.

"When a bhikkhu has abandoned the fetter of compliance, cut it off at the root, made it like a palm stump, obliterated it so that it is no more subject to future arising; when he has abandoned the fetter of aversion . . . the fetter of views . . . the fetter of doubt . . . the fetter of conceit . . . the fetter of lust for existence . . . the fetter of ignorance, cut it off at the root, made it like a palm stump, obliterated it so that it is no more subject to future arising, he is then called a bhikkhu who has cut off craving, stripped off the fetter, and by completely breaking through conceit, has made an end of suffering."

10 (10) Miserliness

"Bhikkhus, there are these seven fetters. What seven? The fetter of compliance, the fetter of aversion, the fetter of views, the fetter of doubt, the fetter of conceit, the fetter of envy, and the fetter of miserliness.[1459] These are the seven fetters." [9]

II. Underlying Tendencies

11 (1) Underlying Tendencies (1)

"Bhikkhus, there are these seven underlying tendencies. What seven? The underlying tendency to sensual lust, the underlying tendency to aversion, the underlying tendency to views, the underlying tendency to doubt, the underlying tendency to conceit, the underlying tendency to lust for existence, and the underlying tendency to ignorance. These are the seven underlying tendencies."

12 (2) Underlying Tendencies (2)

"Bhikkhus, the spiritual life is lived to abandon and eradicate the seven underlying tendencies. What seven? The underlying tendency to sensual lust, the underlying tendency to aversion, the underlying tendency to views, the underlying tendency to doubt, the underlying tendency to conceit, the underlying tendency to lust for existence, and the underlying tendency to ignorance. The spiritual life is lived to abandon and eradicate these seven underlying tendencies.

"When a bhikkhu has abandoned the underlying tendency to sensual lust, cut it off at the root, made it like a palm stump, obliterated it so that it is no more subject to future arising; when he has abandoned the underlying tendency to aversion . . . the underlying tendency to views . . . the underlying tendency to doubt . . . the underlying tendency to conceit . . . the underlying tendency to lust for existence . . . the underlying tendency to ignorance, cut it off at the root, made it like a palm stump, obliterated it so that it is no more subject to future arising, he is then called a bhikkhu without underlying tendencies,[1460] one who has cut off craving, stripped off the fetter, and by completely breaking through conceit, has made an end of suffering." [10]

13 (3) Families

"Bhikkhus, possessing seven factors, a family that has not yet been approached is not worth approaching, or one that has been approached is not worth sitting with.[1461] What seven? (1) They do not rise up in an agreeable way.[1462] (2) They do not pay homage in an agreeable way. (3) They do not offer a seat in an agreeable way. (4) They hide what they have from one. (5) Even when they have much, they give little. (6) Even when they have excellent things, they give coarse things. (7) They give without respect, not respectfully. Possessing these seven factors, a family that has not yet been approached is not worth approaching, or one that has been approached is not worth sitting with.

"Bhikkhus, possessing seven factors, a family that has not yet been approached is worth approaching or one that has been approached is worth sitting with. What seven? (1) They rise up in an agreeable way. (2) They pay homage in an agreeable way. (3) They offer a seat in an agreeable way. (4) They do not hide what they have from one. (5) When they have much, they give much. (6) When they have excellent things, they give excellent things. (7) They give respectfully, not without respect. Possessing these seven factors, a family that has not yet been approached is worth approaching, or one that has been approached is worth sitting with."

14 (4) Persons

"Bhikkhus, these seven persons are worthy of gifts, worthy of hospitality, worthy of offerings, worthy of reverential salutation, an unsurpassed field of merit for the world. What seven? The one liberated in both respects, the one liberated by wisdom, the body witness, the one attained to view, the one liberated by faith, the Dhamma follower, and the faith follower. [11] These seven persons are worthy of gifts, worthy of hospitality, worthy of offerings, worthy of reverential salutation, an unsurpassed field of merit for the world."[1463]

15 (5) Similar to Those in Water

"Bhikkhus, there are these seven kinds of persons found existing in the world similar to those in water. What seven? (1) Here, some person has gone under once and remains under. (2) Some person has risen up and then goes under. (3) Some person has risen up and stays there. (4) Some person has risen up, sees clearly, and looks around. (5) Some person has risen up and crosses over. (6) Some person has risen up and gained a firm foothold. (7) Some person has risen up, crossed over, and gone beyond, a brahmin who stands on high ground.[1464]

(1) "And how, bhikkhus, is a person one who has gone under once and remains under? Here, some person possesses exclu-

sively black, unwholesome qualities. In this way a person is one who has gone under once and remains under.

(2) "And how is a person one who has risen up and then goes under? Here, some person has risen up, [thinking]: 'Good is faith in [cultivating] wholesome qualities; good is a sense of moral shame in [cultivating] wholesome qualities; good is moral dread in [cultivating] wholesome qualities; good is energy in [cultivating] wholesome qualities; good is wisdom in [cultivating] wholesome qualities.' However, his faith does not become stable or grow but rather diminishes. His sense of moral shame . . . moral dread . . . energy . . . wisdom does not become stable or grow but rather diminishes. In this way a person is one who has risen up and then goes under.

(3) "And how is a person one who has risen up and stays put? [12] Here, some person has risen up, [thinking]: 'Good is faith in [cultivating] wholesome qualities . . . good is wisdom in [cultivating] wholesome qualities.' His faith neither diminishes nor grows; it just stays put. His sense of moral shame . . . his moral dread . . . his energy . . . his wisdom neither diminishes nor grows; it just stays put. In this way a person is one who has risen up and stays put.

(4) "And how is a person one who has risen up, sees clearly, and looks around? Here, some person has risen up, [thinking]: 'Good is faith in [cultivating] wholesome qualities . . . good is wisdom in [cultivating] wholesome qualities.' With the utter destruction of three fetters, this person is a stream-enterer, no longer subject to [rebirth in] the lower world, fixed in destiny, heading for enlightenment. It is in this way that a person is one who has risen up, sees clearly, and looks around.

(5) "And how is a person one who has risen up and is crossing over? Here, some person has risen up, [thinking]: 'Good is faith in [cultivating] wholesome qualities . . . good is wisdom in [cultivating] wholesome qualities.' With the utter destruction of three fetters and with the diminishing of greed, hatred, and delusion, this person is a once-returner who, after coming back to this world only one more time, will make an end of suffering. It is in this way that a person is one who has risen up and is crossing over.

(6) "And how is a person one who has risen up and attained a firm foothold? Here, some person has risen up, [thinking]:

'Good is faith in [cultivating] wholesome qualities . . . good is wisdom in [cultivating] wholesome qualities.' With the utter destruction of the five lower fetters, he is of spontaneous birth, due to attain final nibbāna there without returning from that world. It is in this way that a person is one who has risen up and gained a firm foothold.

(7) "And how is a person one who has risen up, crossed over, and gone beyond, a brahmin who stands on high ground? [13] Here, some person has risen up, [thinking]: 'Good is faith in [cultivating] wholesome qualities; good is a sense of moral shame in [cultivating] wholesome qualities; good is moral dread in [cultivating] wholesome qualities; good is energy in [cultivating] wholesome qualities; good is wisdom in [cultivating] wholesome qualities.' With the destruction of the taints, he has realized for himself with direct knowledge, in this very life, the taintless liberation of mind, liberation by wisdom, and having entered upon it, he dwells in it. It is in this way that a person is one who has risen up, crossed over, and gone beyond, a brahmin who stands on high ground.

"These, bhikkhus, are the seven kinds of persons found existing in the world similar to those in water."

16 (6) Impermanence

"Bhikkhus, there are these seven kinds of persons who are worthy of gifts, worthy of hospitality, worthy of offerings, worthy of reverential salutation, an unsurpassed field of merit for the world. What seven?

(1) "Here, bhikkhus, some person dwells contemplating impermanence in all conditioned phenomena, perceiving impermanence, experiencing impermanence, constantly, continuously, and uninterruptedly focusing on it with the mind, fathoming it with wisdom. With the destruction of the taints, he has realized for himself with direct knowledge, in this very life, the taintless liberation of mind, liberation by wisdom, and having entered upon it, he dwells in it. This is the first kind of person worthy of gifts, worthy of hospitality, worthy of offerings, worthy of reverential salutation, an unsurpassed field of merit for the world.

(2) "Again, some person dwells contemplating impermanence in all conditioned phenomena, perceiving imperma-

nence, experiencing impermanence, constantly, continuously, and uninterruptedly focusing on it with the mind, fathoming it with wisdom. For him the exhaustion of the taints and the exhaustion of life occur simultaneously.[1465] This is the second kind of person worthy of gifts. . . .

(3) "Again, bhikkhus, some person dwells contemplating impermanence in all conditioned phenomena, perceiving impermanence, experiencing impermanence, constantly, continuously, and uninterruptedly focusing on it with the mind, fathoming it with wisdom. With [14] the utter destruction of the five lower fetters, he becomes an attainer of nibbāna in the interval.[1466] This is the third kind of person worthy of gifts. . . .

(4) ". . . With the utter destruction of the five lower fetters, he becomes an attainer of nibbāna upon landing.[1467] This is the fourth kind of person worthy of gifts. . . .

(5) ". . . With the utter destruction of the five lower fetters, he becomes an attainer of nibbāna without exertion.[1468] This is the fifth kind of person worthy of gifts. . . .

(6) ". . . With the utter destruction of the five lower fetters, he becomes an attainer of nibbāna through exertion. This is the sixth kind of person worthy of gifts. . . .

(7) "Again, bhikkhus, some person dwells contemplating impermanence in all conditioned phenomena, perceiving impermanence, experiencing impermanence, constantly, continuously, and uninterruptedly focusing on it with the mind, fathoming it with wisdom. With the utter destruction of the five lower fetters, he becomes one bound upstream, heading toward the Akaniṭṭha realm.[1469] This is the seventh kind of person worthy of gifts. . . .

"These, bhikkhus, are the seven kinds of persons who are worthy of gifts, worthy of hospitality, worthy of offerings, worthy of reverential salutation, an unsurpassed field of merit for the world."

17 (7) Suffering

"Bhikkhus, there are these seven kinds of persons who are worthy of gifts, worthy of hospitality, worthy of offerings, worthy of reverential salutation, an unsurpassed field of merit for the world. What seven?

(1) "Here, bhikkhus, some person dwells contemplating

suffering in all conditioned phenomena, perceiving suffering, experiencing suffering, constantly, continuously, and uninterruptedly focusing on it with the mind, fathoming it with wisdom. With the destruction of the taints, he has realized for himself with direct knowledge, in this very life, the taintless liberation of mind, liberation by wisdom, and having entered upon it, he dwells in it. This is the first kind of person worthy of gifts, worthy of hospitality, worthy of offerings, worthy of reverential salutation, an unsurpassed field of merit for the world."

[The rest as in 7:16, but based on contemplating suffering in all conditioned phenomena.]

18 (8) Non-Self[1470]

"Bhikkhus, there are these seven kinds of persons who are worthy of gifts, worthy of hospitality, worthy of offerings, worthy of reverential salutation, an unsurpassed field of merit for the world. What seven?

(1) "Here, bhikkhus, some person dwells contemplating non-self in all phenomena,[1471] perceiving non-self, experiencing non-self, constantly, continuously, and uninterruptedly focusing on it with the mind, fathoming it with wisdom. With the destruction of the taints, he has realized for himself with direct knowledge, in this very life, the taintless liberation of mind, liberation by wisdom, and having entered upon it, he dwells in it. This is the first kind of person worthy of gifts, worthy of hospitality, worthy of offerings, worthy of reverential salutation, an unsurpassed field of merit for the world."

[The rest as in 7:16, but based on contemplating non-self in all phenomena.]

19 (9) Happiness

"Bhikkhus, there are these seven kinds of persons who are worthy of gifts, worthy of hospitality, worthy of offerings, worthy of reverential salutation, an unsurpassed field of merit for the world. What seven?

"Here, bhikkhus, some person dwells contemplating the happiness in nibbāna, perceiving such happiness, experiencing such happiness, constantly, continuously, and uninterruptedly focusing on it with the mind, fathoming it with wisdom. With the destruction of the taints, he has realized for himself with direct knowledge, in this very life, the taintless liberation of mind, liberation by wisdom, and having entered upon it, he dwells in it. This is the first kind of person worthy of gifts, worthy of hospitality, worthy of offerings, worthy of reverential salutation, an unsurpassed field of merit for the world."

[The rest as in 7:16, but based on contemplating the happiness in nibbāna.] [15]

20 (10) Bases for [Being] "Ten-less"

"Bhikkhus, there are these seven bases for [being] 'ten-less.'[1472] What seven?

"Here, (1) a bhikkhu has a keen desire to undertake the training and does not lose his fondness for undertaking the training in the future. (2) He has a strong desire to attend to the Dhamma and does not lose his fondness for attending to the Dhamma in the future. (3) He has a strong desire to remove vain wishes and does not lose his fondness for removing vain wishes in the future.[1473] (4) He has a strong desire for seclusion and does not lose his fondness for seclusion in the future. (5) He has a strong desire to arouse energy and does not lose his fondness for arousing energy in the future. (6) He has a strong desire for mindfulness and alertness and does not lose his fondness for mindfulness and alertness in the future. (7) He has a strong desire to penetrate by view and does not lose his fondness for penetrating by view in the future. These are the seven bases for [being] 'ten-less.'"

III. The Vajji Seven

21 (1) Sārandada

[16] Thus have I heard. On one occasion the Blessed One was dwelling at Vesālī at the Sārandada Shrine. Then a number of Licchavis approached the Blessed One, paid homage to him, and sat down to one side. The Blessed One said this to them:

"I will teach you, Licchavis, seven principles of non-decline. Listen and attend closely. I will speak."[1474]

"Yes, Bhante," those Licchavis replied. The Blessed One said this:

"And what, Licchavis, are the seven principles of non-decline?

(1) "Licchavis, as long as the Vajjis assemble often and hold frequent assemblies, only growth is to be expected for them, not decline.

(2) "As long as the Vajjis assemble in harmony, adjourn in harmony, and conduct the affairs of the Vajjis in harmony, only growth is to be expected for them, not decline.

(3) "As long as the Vajjis do not decree anything that has not been decreed or abolish anything that has already been decreed but undertake and follow the ancient Vajji principles as they have been decreed, only growth is to be expected for them, not decline.

(4) "As long as the Vajjis honor, respect, esteem, and venerate the Vajji elders and think they should be heeded, only growth is to be expected for them, not decline.

(5) "As long as the Vajjis do not abduct women and girls from their families and force them to live with them, only growth is to be expected for them, not decline.

(6) "As long as the Vajjis honor, respect, esteem, and venerate their traditional shrines, both those within [the city][1475] and those outside, [17] and do not neglect the righteous oblations as given and done to them in the past,[1476] only growth is to be expected for them, not decline.

(7) "As long as the Vajjis provide righteous protection, shelter, and guard for arahants, [with the intention]: 'How can those arahants who have not yet come here come to our realm, and how can those arahants who have already come dwell at ease here?' only growth is to be expected for them, not decline.

"Licchavis, as long as these seven principles of non-decline continue among the Vajjis, and the Vajjis are seen [established] in them, only growth is to be expected for them, not decline."

22 (2) *Vassakāra*[1477]

Thus have I heard. On one occasion the Blessed One was dwelling at Rājagaha on Mount Vulture Peak. Now on that occasion King Ajātasattu Vedehiputta of Magadha wished to wage war against the Vajjis. He said thus: "As powerful and mighty as these Vajjis are, I will annihilate them, destroy them, bring calamity and disaster upon them."

Then King Ajātasattu addressed the chief minister of Magadha, the brahmin Vassakāra: "Come, brahmin, go to the

Blessed One and in my name pay homage to him with your head at his feet. Inquire whether he is fit and healthy, agile and strong, and feeling at ease. Say: 'Bhante, King Ajātasattu Vedehiputta of Magadha pays homage to the Blessed One with his head at your feet. He inquires whether you are fit and healthy, agile and strong, and feeling at ease.' Then say thus: 'Bhante, King Ajātasattu wishes to wage war against the Vajjis. He says thus: "As powerful and mighty as these Vajjis are, I will annihilate them, destroy them, bring calamity and disaster upon [18] them."' Learn well how the Blessed One answers you and report it to me, for Tathāgatas do not speak falsely."

"Yes, sir," the brahmin Vassakāra replied. Then he rose from his seat and went to the Blessed One. He exchanged greetings with the Blessed One, and when they had exchanged greetings and cordial talk, he sat down to one side and said:

"Master Gotama, King Ajātasattu Vedehiputta of Magadha pays homage to the Blessed One with his head at your feet. He inquires whether you are fit and healthy, agile and strong, and feeling at ease. Master Gotama, King Ajātasattu wishes to wage war against the Vajjis. He says thus: 'As powerful and mighty as these Vajjis are, I will annihilate them, destroy them, bring calamity and disaster upon them.'"

Now on that occasion the Venerable Ānanda was standing behind the Blessed One fanning him. The Blessed One then addressed the Venerable Ānanda:

(1) "Ānanda, have you heard whether the Vajjis are assembling often and holding frequent assemblies?"

"I have heard, Bhante, that they do so."

"Ānanda, as long as the Vajjis assemble often and hold frequent assemblies, only growth is to be expected for them, not decline.

(2) "Have you heard, Ānanda, whether the Vajjis are assembling in harmony, adjourning their meetings in harmony, and conducting the affairs of the Vajjis in harmony?"

"I have heard, Bhante, that they do so."

"Ānanda, as long as the Vajjis assemble in harmony, [19] adjourn in harmony, and conduct the affairs of the Vajjis in harmony, only growth is to be expected for them, not decline.

(3) "Have you heard, Ānanda, whether the Vajjis do not decree anything that has not been decreed and do not abolish

anything that has already been decreed, but undertake and follow the ancient Vajji principles as they have been decreed?"

"I have heard, Bhante, that they do so."

"Ānanda, as long as the Vajjis do not decree anything that has not been decreed or abolish anything that has already been decreed but undertake and follow the ancient Vajji principles as they have been decreed, only growth is to be expected for them, not decline.

(4) "Have you heard, Ānanda, whether the Vajjis honor, respect, esteem, and venerate the Vajji elders and think they should be heeded?"

"I have heard, Bhante, that they do so."

"Ānanda, as long as the Vajjis honor, respect, esteem, and venerate the Vajji elders and think they should be heeded, only growth is to be expected for them, not decline.

(5) "Have you heard, Ānanda, whether the Vajjis do not abduct women and girls from their families and force them to live with them?"

"I have heard, Bhante, that they don't."

"Ānanda, as long as the Vajjis do not abduct women and girls from their families and force them to live with them, only growth is to be expected for them, not decline.

(6) "Have you heard, Ānanda, whether the Vajjis honor, respect, esteem, and venerate their traditional shrines, both those within [the city] and those outside, and do not neglect the righteous oblations as given and done to them in the past?"

"I have heard, Bhante, that they do so."

"Ānanda, as long as the Vajjis [20] honor, respect, esteem, and venerate their traditional shrines, both those within [the city] and those outside, and do not neglect the righteous oblations as given and done to them in the past, only growth is to be expected for them, not decline.

(7) "Have you heard, Ānanda, whether the Vajjis provide righteous protection, shelter, and guard for arahants, [with the intention]: 'How can those arahants who have not yet come here come to our realm, and how can those arahants who have already come dwell at ease here?'"

"I have heard, Bhante, that they do so."

"Ānanda, as long as the Vajjis provide righteous protection, shelter, and guard for arahants, [with the intention]: 'How can those arahants who have not yet come here come to our realm, and how can those arahants who have already come dwell at ease here?' only growth is to be expected for them, not decline."

Then the Blessed One addressed the brahmin Vassakāra, the chief minister of Magadha: "On one occasion, brahmin, I was dwelling at Vesālī at the Sārandada Shrine. There I taught the Vajjis these seven principles of non-decline. As long as these seven principles of non-decline continue among the Vajjis, and the Vajjis are seen [established] in them, only growth is to be expected for them, not decline."

When this was said, the brahmin Vassakāra said this to the Blessed One: "If, Master Gotama, the Vajjis were to observe even one among these principles of non-decline, only growth would be expected for them, not decline. What can be said if they observe all seven? King Ajātasattu Vedehiputta of Magadha, Master Gotama, cannot take the Vajjis by war, except [21] through treachery or internal dissension. And now, Master Gotama, we must be going. We are busy and have much to do."

"You may go, brahmin, at your own convenience."

Then the brahmin Vassakāra, the chief minister of Magadha, having delighted and rejoiced in the Blessed One's words, rose from his seat and left.

23 (3) Non-Decline (1)

Thus have I heard. On one occasion the Blessed One was dwelling at Rājagaha on Mount Vulture Peak. There the Blessed One addressed the bhikkhus:

"Bhikkhus, I will teach you seven principles of non-decline. Listen and attend closely. I will speak."[1478]

"Yes, Bhante," those bhikkhus replied. The Blessed One said this:

"And what, bhikkhus, are the seven principles of non-decline?

(1) "As long as the bhikkhus assemble often and hold frequent assemblies, only growth is to be expected for them, not decline.

(2) "As long as the bhikkhus assemble in harmony, adjourn in harmony, and conduct the affairs of the Saṅgha in harmony, only growth is to be expected for them, not decline.

(3) "As long as the bhikkhus do not decree anything that has not been decreed or abolish anything that has already been

decreed, but undertake and follow the training rules as they have been decreed, only growth is to be expected for them, not decline.

(4) "As long as the bhikkhus honor, respect, esteem, and venerate those bhikkhus who are elders, of long standing, long gone forth, fathers and guides of the Saṅgha, and think they should be heeded, only growth is to be expected for them, not decline.

(5) "As long as the bhikkhus do not come under the control of arisen craving that leads to renewed existence, only growth is to be expected for them, not decline.

(6) "As long as the bhikkhus are intent on forest lodgings, [22] only growth is to be expected for them, not decline.

(7) "As long as the bhikkhus each individually establish mindfulness [with the intention]: 'How can well-behaved fellow monks who have not yet come here come, and how can well-behaved fellow monks who are already here dwell at ease?' only growth is to be expected for them, not decline.

"Bhikkhus, as long as these seven principles of non-decline continue among the bhikkhus, and the bhikkhus are seen [established] in them, only growth is to be expected for them, not decline."

24 (4) Non-Decline (2)

"Bhikkhus, I will teach you seven principles of non-decline. Listen and attend closely. I will speak."

"Yes, Bhante," those bhikkhus replied. The Blessed One said this:

"And what, bhikkhus, are the seven principles of non-decline?

(1) "As long as the bhikkhus do not delight in work, do not take delight in work, are not devoted to delight in work, only growth is to be expected for them, not decline. (2) As long as the bhikkhus do not delight in talk . . . (3) . . . do not delight in sleep . . . (4) . . . do not delight in company . . . (5) . . . do not have evil desires and come under the control of evil desires . . . (6) . . . do not associate with bad friends, bad companions, bad comrades . . . (7) . . . do not come to a stop midway [in their development] on account of some minor achievement of distinction,[1479] only growth is to be expected for them, not decline.

"Bhikkhus, as long as these seven principles of non-decline continue among the bhikkhus, and the bhikkhus are seen [established] in them, only growth is to be expected for them, not decline."

25 (5) Non-Decline (3)

"Bhikkhus, I will teach you seven principles of non-decline. Listen and attend closely. I will speak."

"Yes, Bhante," those bhikkhus replied. The Blessed One said this: [23]

"And what, bhikkhus, are the seven principles of non-decline?

(1) "As long as the bhikkhus are endowed with faith, only growth is to be expected for them, not decline. (2) As long as they have a sense of moral shame . . . (3) . . . have moral dread . . . (4) . . . are learned . . . (5) . . . are energetic . . . (6) . . . are mindful . . . (7) . . . are wise, only growth is to be expected for them, not decline.

"Bhikkhus, as long as these seven principles of non-decline continue among the bhikkhus, and the bhikkhus are seen [established] in them, only growth is to be expected for them, not decline."

26 (6) Non-Decline (4)

"Bhikkhus, I will teach you seven principles of non-decline. Listen and attend closely. I will speak."

"Yes, Bhante," those bhikkhus replied. The Blessed One said this:

"And what, bhikkhus, are the seven principles of non-decline? (1) As long as the bhikkhus develop the enlightenment factor of mindfulness, only growth is to be expected for them, not decline. (2) As long as they develop the enlightenment factor of discrimination of phenomena . . . (3) . . . the enlightenment factor of energy . . . (4) . . . the enlightenment factor of rapture . . . (5) . . . the enlightenment factor of tranquility . . . (6) . . . the enlightenment factor of concentration . . . (7) . . . the enlightenment factor of equanimity, only growth is to be expected for them, not decline.

"Bhikkhus, as long as these seven principles of non-decline continue among the bhikkhus, and the bhikkhus are seen [established] in them, only growth is to be expected for them, not decline." [24]

27 (7) Non-Decline (5)

"Bhikkhus, I will teach you seven principles of non-decline. Listen and attend closely. I will speak."

"Yes, Bhante," those bhikkhus replied. The Blessed One said this:

"And what, bhikkhus, are the seven principles of non-decline? (1) As long as the bhikkhus develop the perception of impermanence, only growth is to be expected for them, not decline. (2) As long as they develop the perception of non-self . . . (3) . . . the perception of unattractiveness . . . (4) . . . the perception of danger . . . (5) . . . the perception of abandoning . . . (6) . . . the perception of dispassion . . . (7) . . . the perception of cessation, only growth is to be expected for them, not decline.[1480]

"Bhikkhus, as long as these seven principles of non-decline continue among the bhikkhus, and the bhikkhus are seen [established] in them, only growth is to be expected for them, not decline."

28 (8) A Trainee

"Bhikkhus, these seven qualities lead to the decline of a bhikkhu who is a trainee. What seven? Delight in work, delight in talk, delight in sleep, delight in company, not guarding the doors of the sense faculties, lack of moderation in eating; and when there are matters pertaining to the Saṅgha that are [to be dealt with] in the Saṅgha, the bhikkhu who is a trainee does not reflect thus:[1481] 'There are in the Saṅgha elders of long standing, long gone forth, responsible, who will take responsibility for that [work].' He himself undertakes them.[1482] These seven qualities lead to the decline of a bhikkhu who is a trainee.

"Bhikkhus, these seven qualities lead to the non-decline of a bhikkhu who is a trainee. What seven? [25] Not taking delight in work, not taking delight in talk, not taking delight in sleep, not taking delight in company, guarding the doors of the sense faculties, moderation in eating; and when there are matters pertaining to the Saṅgha that are [to be dealt with] in the Saṅgha, the bhikkhu who is a trainee reflects thus: 'There are in the Saṅgha elders of long standing, long gone forth, responsible, who will take responsibility for that [work].' He does not himself undertake them. These seven qualities lead to the non-decline of a bhikkhu who is a trainee."

29 (9) Decline

"Bhikkhus, these seven things lead to the decline of a lay follower. What seven? (1) He stops seeing bhikkhus; (2) he neglects listening to the good Dhamma; (3) he does not train in the higher virtuous behavior; (4) he is full of suspicion toward bhikkhus, whether they be elders, newly ordained, or of middle standing; (5) he listens to the Dhamma with a mind bent on criticism, seeking to find faults with it; (6) he seeks a person worthy of offerings among outsiders; (7) he first does [meritorious] deeds there.[1483] These seven things lead to the decline of a lay follower.

"Bhikkhus, these seven things lead to the non-decline of a lay follower. What seven? (1) He does not stop seeing bhikkhus; (2) he does not neglect listening to the good Dhamma; (3) he trains in the higher virtuous behavior; (4) he is full of confidence in bhikkhus, whether they be elders, newly ordained, or of middle standing; (5) he listens to the Dhamma with a mind that is not bent on criticism, not seeking to find faults with it; (6) he does not seek a person worthy of offerings among outsiders; (7) he first does [meritorious] deeds here. These seven things lead to the non-decline of a lay follower."[1484] [26]

The lay follower who stops seeing
[bhikkhus] who have developed themselves,
[who stops] hearing the noble ones' teachings,
and does not train in the higher virtue;
whose suspicion toward the bhikkhus
is ever on the increase;
who wants to listen to the good Dhamma
with a mind bent on criticism;
the lay follower who seeks
one worthy of offerings among outsiders
and first undertakes to do
meritorious deeds toward them:
these seven well-taught principles
describe what leads to decline.

A lay follower who resorts to them
falls away from the good Dhamma.

The lay follower who does not stop seeing
[bhikkhus] who have developed themselves,
who listens to the noble ones' teachings,
and trains in the higher virtue;
whose confidence in the bhikkhus
is ever on the increase;
who wants to listen to the good Dhamma
with a mind not bent on criticism;
the lay follower who seeks none
worthy of offerings among outsiders;
but who here first undertakes
to do meritorious deeds:
these seven well-taught principles
describe what leads to non-decline.
A lay follower who resorts to them
does not fall away from the good Dhamma.

30 (10) Failure[1485]

"Bhikkhus, there are these seven failures of a lay follower. What seven? . . . [as in 7:29] . . . Bhikkhus, there are these seven successes of a lay follower. What seven? . . . [as in 7:29] . . . These are the seven successes of a lay follower."

31 (11) Ruin

"Bhikkhus, there are these seven ruins for a lay follower. What seven? . . . [as in 7:29] . . . Bhikkhus, there are these seven victories for a lay follower. What seven? . . . [as in 7:29] . . . These are the seven victories for a lay follower." [27]

[The verses are identical with those in 7:29.]

IV. Deities

32 (1) Heedfulness[1486]

Then, when the night had advanced, a certain deity of stunning beauty, illuminating the entire Jeta's Grove, [28] approached the Blessed One, paid homage to him, stood to one side, and said to the Blessed One:

"Bhante, there are these seven qualities that lead to the non-decline of a bhikkhu. What seven? Reverence for the Teacher, reverence for the Dhamma, reverence for the Saṅgha, reverence for the training, reverence for concentration, reverence for heedfulness, and reverence for hospitality. These seven qualities lead to the non-decline of a bhikkhu."

This is what that deity said. The Teacher agreed. Then that deity, [thinking]: "The Teacher agrees with me," paid homage to the Blessed One, circumambulated him keeping the right side toward him, and disappeared right there.

Then, when the night had passed, the Blessed One addressed the bhikkhus: "Last night, bhikkhus, when the night had advanced, a certain deity of stunning beauty, illuminating the entire Jeta's Grove, approached me, paid homage to me, stood to one side, and said to me: 'Bhante, there are these seven qualities that lead to the non-decline of a bhikkhu. What seven? Reverence for the Teacher . . . and reverence for hospitality. These seven qualities lead to the non-decline of a bhikkhu.' This is what that deity said. Then that deity paid homage to me, circumambulated me keeping the right side toward me, and disappeared right there."

Respectful toward the Teacher,
respectful toward the Dhamma,
deeply revering the Saṅgha,
respectful toward concentration, ardent,
deeply respectful toward the training;
respectful toward heedfulness,
holding hospitality in reverence:
this bhikkhu cannot fall away,
but is close to nibbāna.

33 (2) Moral Shame[1487]

"Last night, bhikkhus, when the night had advanced, a certain deity of stunning beauty, illuminating the entire Jeta's Grove, [29] approached me, paid homage to me, stood to one side, and said to me: 'Bhante, there are these seven qualities that lead to the non-decline of a bhikkhu. What seven? Reverence for the Teacher, reverence for the Dhamma, reverence for the Saṅgha, reverence for the training, reverence for concentration, reverence for a sense of moral shame, and reverence for moral dread. These seven qualities lead to the non-decline of a bhikkhu.' This is what that deity said. Then the deity paid homage to me, circumambulated me keeping the right side toward me, and disappeared right there."

Respectful toward the Teacher,
respectful toward the Dhamma,
deeply revering the Saṅgha,
respectful toward concentration, ardent,
deeply respectful toward the training;
endowed with moral shame and moral dread,
deferential and reverential:
such a one cannot fall away
but is close to nibbāna.

34 (3) Easy to Correct (1)
"Last night, bhikkhus, when the night had advanced, a certain deity of stunning beauty, illuminating the entire Jeta's Grove, approached me, paid homage to me, stood to one side, and said to me: 'Bhante, there are these seven qualities that lead to the non-decline of a bhikkhu. What seven? Reverence for the Teacher, reverence for the Dhamma, reverence for the Saṅgha, reverence for the training, reverence for concentration, being easy to correct, and good friendship. These seven qualities lead to the non-decline of a bhikkhu.' This is what that deity said. Then the deity paid homage to me, circumambulated me keeping the right side toward me, and disappeared right there."

Respectful toward the Teacher,
respectful toward the Dhamma,
deeply revering the Saṅgha,
respectful toward concentration, ardent,
deeply respectful toward the training;
cultivating good friends,
being easy to correct,
deferential and reverential:
such a one cannot fall away
but is close to nibbāna. [30]

35 (4) Easy to Correct (2)[1488]

"Last night, bhikkhus, when the night had advanced, a certain deity of stunning beauty, illuminating the entire Jeta's Grove, approached me, paid homage to me, stood to one side, and said to me: 'Bhante, there are these seven qualities that lead to the non-decline of a bhikkhu. What seven? Reverence for the Teacher, reverence for the Dhamma, reverence for the Saṅgha, reverence for the training, reverence for concentration, being easy to correct, and good friendship. These seven qualities lead to the non-decline of a bhikkhu.' This is what that deity said. Then the deity paid homage to me, circumambulated me keeping the right side toward me, and disappeared right there."

When this was said, the Venerable Sāriputta said to the Blessed One:

"Bhante, I understand in detail the meaning of this statement that the Blessed One has spoken in brief to be as follows. Here, a bhikkhu himself reveres the Teacher and speaks in praise of reverence for the Teacher; he encourages other bhikkhus who do not revere the Teacher to develop reverence for the Teacher and, at the proper time, genuinely and truthfully, he speaks praise of those bhikkhus who revere the Teacher. He himself reveres the Dhamma . . . reveres the Saṅgha . . . reveres the training . . . reveres concentration . . . is easy to correct . . . has good friends and speaks in praise of good friendship; he encourages other bhikkhus who do not have good friends to find good friends and, at the proper time, genuinely and truthfully, he speaks praise of those bhikkhus who have good friends. It is in such a way, Bhante, that I understand in detail the meaning of this statement that the Blessed One has spoken in brief."

[The Blessed One said:] "Good, good, Sāriputta! It is good that you understand in detail the meaning of this statement that I have spoken in brief in such a way."

[The Buddha here repeats the whole statement of Sāriputta, ending:] [31]

"It is in such a way, Sāriputta, that the meaning of this statement that I spoke in brief should be understood in detail."

36 (5) A Friend (1)[1489]

"Bhikkhus, one should associate with a friend who possesses seven factors. What seven? (1) He gives what is hard to give.

(2) He does what is hard to do. (3) He patiently endures what is hard to endure. (4) He reveals his secrets to you. (5) He preserves your secrets. (6) He does not forsake you when you are in trouble. (7) He does not roughly despise you.[1490] One should associate with a friend who possesses these seven factors."

A friend gives what is hard to give,
and he does what is hard to do.
He forgives you your harsh words
and endures what is hard to endure.

He tells you his secrets,
yet he preserves your secrets.
He does not forsake you in difficulties,
nor does he roughly despise you.

The person here in whom
these qualities are found is a friend.
One desiring a friend
should resort to such a person. [32]

37 (6) A Friend (2)

"Bhikkhus, one should associate with a bhikkhu friend who possesses seven qualities; one should resort to him and attend on him even if he dismisses you. What seven? (1) He is pleasing and agreeable; (2) he is respected and (3) esteemed; (4) he is a speaker;[1491] (5) he patiently endures being spoken to; (6) he gives deep talks; and (7) he does not enjoin one to do what is wrong."

He is dear, respected, and esteemed,
a speaker and one who endures speech;
he gives deep talks and does not enjoin one
to do what is wrong.

The person here in whom
these qualities are found is a friend,
benevolent and compassionate.
Even if one is dismissed by him,
one desiring a friend
should resort to such a person.

38 (7) Analytical Knowledges (1)

"Bhikkhus, when he possesses seven qualities, a bhikkhu might soon realize for himself with direct knowledge the four analytical knowledges and acquire mastery over them.[1492] What seven?

"Here, (1) a bhikkhu understands as it really is: 'This is mental sluggishness in me.'[1493] (2) Or when the mind is constricted internally, he understands as it really is: 'My mind is constricted internally.' (3) Or when his mind is distracted externally, he understands as it really is: 'My mind is distracted externally.'[1494] (4) He knows feelings as they arise, as they remain present, as they disappear; (5) he knows perceptions as they arise, as they remain present, [33] as they disappear; (6) he knows thoughts as they arise, as they remain present, as they disappear.[1495] (7) Then, among qualities suitable and unsuitable, inferior and superior, dark and bright along with their counterparts, he has grasped the mark well, attended to it well, reflected upon it well, and penetrated it well with wisdom.[1496] When he possesses these seven qualities, a bhikkhu might soon realize for himself with direct knowledge the four analytical knowledges and acquire mastery over them."

39 (8) Analytical Knowledges (2)[1497]

"Bhikkhus, when he possessed seven qualities, Sāriputta realized for himself with direct knowledge the four analytical knowledges and acquired mastery over them. What seven?

"Here, (1) Sāriputta understood as it really is: 'This is mental sluggishness in me.'[1498] (2) Or when the mind was constricted internally, he understood as it really is: 'My mind is constricted internally.' (3) Or when his mind was distracted externally, he understood as it really is: 'My mind is distracted externally.' (4) For him, feelings were known as they arose, as they remained present, as they disappeared; (5) perceptions were known as they arose, as they remained present, as they disappeared; (6) thoughts were known as they arose, as they remained present, as they disappeared. (7) Then, among qualities suitable and unsuitable, inferior and superior, dark and bright along with their counterparts, he took up the mark well, attended to it well, reflected upon it well, and penetrated it well with wisdom. When he possessed these seven qualities, Sāriputta realized for himself with direct knowledge the four analytical knowledges and acquired mastery over them." [34]

40 (9) Mastery (1)

"Bhikkhus, possessing seven qualities, a bhikkhu exercises mastery over his mind and is not a servant of his mind. What seven? Here, (1) a bhikkhu is skilled in concentration, (2) skilled in the attainment of concentration, (3) skilled in the duration of concentration, (4) skilled in emergence from concentration, (5) skilled in fitness for concentration, (6) skilled in the area of concentration, and (7) skilled in resolution regarding concentration.[1499] Possessing these seven qualities, a bhikkhu exercises mastery over his mind, and is not a servant of his mind."

41 (10) Mastery (2)[1500]

"Bhikkhus, possessing seven qualities, Sāriputta exercises mastery over his mind and is not a servant of his mind. What seven? Here, (1) Sāriputta is skilled in concentration, (2) skilled in the attainment of concentration, (3) skilled in the duration of concentration, (4) skilled in emergence from concentration, (5) skilled in fitness for concentration, (6) skilled in the area of concentration, and (7) skilled in resolution regarding concentration. Possessing these seven qualities, Sāriputta exercises mastery over his mind and is not a servant of his mind."

42 (11) Bases for [Being] "Ten-less" (1)

On one occasion the Blessed One was dwelling at Sāvatthī in Jeta's Grove, Anāthapiṇḍika's Park. Then, in the morning, the Venerable Sāriputta dressed, took his bowl and robe, and entered Sāvatthī for alms. It then occurred to him: [35] "It is still too early to walk for alms in Sāvatthī. Let me go to the park of the wanderers of other sects."

Then the Venerable Sāriputta went to the park of the wanderers of other sects. He exchanged greetings with those wanderers and, when they had concluded their greetings and cordial talk, sat down to one side. Now on that occasion those wanderers had assembled and were sitting together when this conversation arose among them: "Friends, anyone at all who lives the complete and purified spiritual life for twelve years is fit to be called a bhikkhu who is 'ten-less.'"

Then the Venerable Sāriputta neither delighted in nor rejected the statement of those wanderers, but rose from his seat and left, [thinking]: "I shall find out what the Blessed One has to say about this statement."

Then, when the Venerable Sāriputta had walked for alms in Sāvatthī, after his meal, on returning from his alms round, he approached the Blessed One, paid homage to him, and sat down to one side. [He here reports verbatim the entire course of events and asks:] [36] "Is it possible, Bhante, in this Dhamma and discipline to describe a bhikkhu as 'ten-less' by the mere counting of years?"

"In this Dhamma and discipline, Sāriputta, it isn't possible to describe a bhikkhu as 'ten-less' by the mere counting of years. There are, Sāriputta, these seven bases for [being] 'ten-less' that I have proclaimed after realizing them for myself with direct knowledge.[1501] What seven? Here, (1) a bhikkhu has a keen desire to undertake the training and does not lose his fondness for undertaking the training in the future. (2) He has a strong desire to attend to the Dhamma and does not lose his fondness for attending to the Dhamma in the future. (3) He has a strong desire to remove vain wishes and does not lose his fondness for removing vain wishes in the future. (4) He has a strong desire for seclusion and does not lose his fondness for seclusion in the future. (5) He has a strong desire to arouse energy and does not lose his fondness for arousing energy in the future. (6) He has a strong desire for mindfulness and alertness and does not lose his fondness for mindfulness and alertness in the future. (7) He has a strong desire to penetrate by view and does not lose his fondness for penetrating by view in the future. These are the seven bases for [being] 'ten-less' that I have proclaimed after realizing them for myself with direct knowledge.

"Sāriputta, if a bhikkhu possesses these seven bases for [being] 'ten-less,' then, if he lives the complete and pure spiritual life for twelve years, he is fit to be called 'ten-less.' If, too, he lives the complete and pure spiritual life for twenty-four years, he is [37] fit to be called 'ten-less.' If, too, he lives the complete and pure spiritual life for thirty-six years, he is fit to be called 'ten-less.' If, too, he lives the complete and pure spiritual life for forty-eight years, he is fit to be called 'ten-less.'"

43 (12) Bases for [Being] "Ten-less" (2)

Thus have I heard. On one occasion the Blessed One was dwelling at Kosambī in Ghosita's Park. Then, in the morning, the Venerable Ānanda dressed, took his bowl and robe, and entered Kosambī for alms. It then occurred to him: "It is still too early to walk for alms in Kosambī. Let me go to the park of the wanderers of other sects."

Then the Venerable Ānanda went to the park of the wanderers of other sects.... [as in 7:42, substituting Ānanda for Sāriputta and Kosambī for Sāvatthī] [38] ... "Is it possible, Bhante, in this Dhamma and discipline to describe a bhikkhu as 'ten-less' by the mere counting of years?"

"In this Dhamma and discipline, Ānanda, it isn't possible to describe a bhikkhu as 'ten-less' by the mere counting of years. There are, Ānanda, these seven bases for [being] 'ten-less' that I have proclaimed after realizing them for myself with direct knowledge. What seven? Here, a bhikkhu has (1) faith, (2) a sense of moral shame, (3) moral dread; (4) he is learned, (5) energetic, (6) mindful, and (7) wise. These are the seven bases for [being] 'ten-less' that I have proclaimed after realizing them for myself with direct knowledge. [39]

"Ānanda, if a bhikkhu possesses these seven bases for [being] 'ten-less,' then, if he lives the complete and pure spiritual life for twelve years, he is fit to be called 'ten-less.' If, too, he lives the complete and pure spiritual life for twenty-four years, he is fit to be called 'ten-less.' If, too, he lives the complete and pure spiritual life for thirty-six years, he is fit to be called 'ten-less.' If, too, he lives the complete and pure spiritual life for forty-eight years, he is fit to be called 'ten-less.'"

V. The Great Sacrifice

44 (1) Stations

"Bhikkhus, there are these seven stations for consciousness.[1502] What seven?

(1) "There are, bhikkhus, beings that are different in body and different in perception, such as humans, some devas, and some in the lower world. This is the first station for consciousness.[1503] [40]

(2) "There are beings that are different in body but identical in perception, such as the devas of Brahmā's company that are

reborn through the first [jhāna]. This is the second station for consciousness.[1504]

(3) "There are beings that are identical in body but different in perception, such as the devas of streaming radiance. This is the third station for consciousness.[1505]

(4) "There are beings that are identical in body and identical in perception, such as the devas of refulgent glory. This is the fourth station for consciousness.[1506]

(5) "There are beings that, with the complete surmounting of perceptions of forms, with the passing away of perceptions of sensory impingement, with non-attention to perceptions of diversity, [perceiving] 'space is infinite,' belong to the base of the infinity of space. This is the fifth station for consciousness.

(6) "There are beings that, by completely surmounting the base of the infinity of space, [perceiving] 'consciousness is infinite,' belong to the base of the infinity of consciousness. This is the sixth station for consciousness.

(7) "There are beings that, by completely surmounting the base of the infinity of consciousness, [perceiving] 'there is nothing,' belong to the base of nothingness. This is the seventh station for consciousness.

"These, bhikkhus, are the seven stations for consciousness."[1507]

45 (2) Accessories

"There are, bhikkhus, these seven accessories of concentration. What seven? Right view, right intention, right speech, right action, right livelihood, right effort, and right mindfulness. One-pointedness of mind equipped with these seven factors is called noble right concentration 'with its supports' and 'with its accessories.'"[1508] [41]

46 (3) Fires

"Bhikkhus, there are these seven fires. What seven? The fire of lust, the fire of hatred, the fire of delusion, the fire of those worthy of gifts, the householder's fire, the fire of those worthy of offerings, the wood fire. These are the seven fires."[1509]

47 (4) Sacrifice

On one occasion the Blessed One was dwelling at Sāvatthī in Jeta's Grove, Anāthapiṇḍika's Park. Now on that occasion the brahmin Uggatasarīra had made arrangements for a great sacrifice. Five hundred bulls had been led to the post[1510] for the sacrifice. Five hundred bullocks . . . Five hundred heifers . . . Five hundred goats . . . Five hundred rams had been led to the post for the sacrifice.

Then the brahmin Uggatasarīra approached the Blessed One and exchanged greetings with him. When they had concluded their greetings and cordial talk, he sat down to one side and said to the Blessed One:

"I have heard, Master Gotama, that the kindling of the sacrificial fire and the raising of the sacrificial post are of great fruit and benefit."

"I too, brahmin, have heard this."

A second time . . . A third time the brahmin Uggatasarīra said to the Blessed One: "I have heard, Master Gotama, that the kindling of the sacrificial fire and the raising of the sacrificial post are of great fruit and benefit."

"I too, brahmin, have heard this."

"Then [42] Master Gotama and I are in complete and total agreement."

When this was said, the Venerable Ānanda said to the brahmin Uggatasarīra: "Brahmin, Tathāgatas should not be asked thus: 'I have heard, Master Gotama, that the kindling of the sacrificial fire and the raising of the sacrificial post are of great fruit and benefit.' Tathāgatas should be asked: 'Bhante, I want to kindle the sacrificial fire and raise the sacrificial post. Let the Blessed One exhort me and instruct me in a way that will lead to my welfare and happiness for a long time.'"

Then the brahmin Uggatasarīra said to the Blessed One: "Master Gotama, I want to kindle the sacrificial fire and raise the sacrificial post. Let Master Gotama exhort me and instruct me in a way that will lead to my welfare and happiness for a long time."

"Brahmin, one kindling the sacrificial fire and raising the sacrificial post, even before the sacrifice, raises three knives that are unwholesome and have suffering as their outcome and result. What three? The bodily knife, the verbal knife, and the mental knife.

"Brahmin, one kindling the sacrificial fire and raising the sacrificial post, even before the sacrifice, arouses such a thought as this: 'Let so many bulls be slain in sacrifice! Let so many bullocks . . . so many heifers . . . so many goats . . . so many rams be slain in sacrifice!' Though he [thinks], 'Let me do merit,' he does demerit. Though he [thinks], 'Let me do what is wholesome,' he does what is unwholesome. Though he [thinks], 'Let me seek the path to a good destination,' he seeks the path to a bad destination. One kindling the sacrificial fire and [43] raising the sacrificial post, even before the sacrifice, raises this first knife, the mental one, which is unwholesome and has suffering as its outcome and result.

"Again, brahmin, one kindling the sacrificial fire and raising the sacrificial post, even before the sacrifice, utters such speech as this: 'Let so many bulls be slain in sacrifice! Let so many bullocks . . . so many heifers . . . so many goats . . . so many rams be slain in sacrifice!' Though he [thinks], 'Let me do merit,' he does demerit. Though he [thinks], 'Let me do what is wholesome,' he does what is unwholesome. Though he [thinks], 'Let me seek the path to a good destination,' he seeks the path to a bad destination. One kindling the sacrificial fire and raising the sacrificial post, even before the sacrifice, raises this second knife, the verbal one, which is unwholesome and has suffering as its outcome and result.

"Again, brahmin, one kindling the sacrificial fire and raising the sacrificial post, even before the sacrifice, first undertakes the preparations to slay the bulls in sacrifice. He first undertakes the preparations to slay the bullocks in sacrifice . . . to slay the heifers in sacrifice . . . to slay the goats in sacrifice . . . to slay the rams in sacrifice. Though he [thinks], 'Let me do merit,' he does demerit. Though he [thinks], 'Let me do what is wholesome,' he does what is unwholesome. Though he [thinks], 'Let me seek the path to a good destination,' he seeks the path to a bad destination. One kindling the sacrificial fire and raising the sacrificial post, even before the sacrifice, raises this third knife, the bodily one, which is unwholesome and has suffering as its outcome and result.

"Brahmin, one kindling the sacrificial fire and raising the sacrificial post, even before the sacrifice, raises these three knives that are unwholesome and have suffering as their outcome and result.

(1)–(3) "There are, brahmin, these three fires that should be abandoned and avoided and should not be cultivated. What three? [44] The fire of lust, the fire of hatred, and the fire of delusion.

(1) "And why should the fire of lust be abandoned and avoided and not be cultivated? One excited by lust, overcome by lust, with mind obsessed by it, engages in misconduct by body, speech, and mind. As a consequence, with the breakup of the body, after death, he is reborn in the plane of misery, in a bad destination, in the lower world, in hell. Therefore this fire of lust should be abandoned and avoided and should not be cultivated.

(2)–(3) "And why should the fire of hatred . . . the fire of delusion be abandoned and avoided and not be cultivated? One who is deluded, overcome by delusion, with mind obsessed by it, engages in misconduct by body, speech, and mind. As a consequence, with the breakup of the body, after death, he is reborn in the plane of misery, in a bad destination, in the lower world, in hell. Therefore this fire of delusion should be abandoned and avoided and should not be cultivated.

"These are the three fires that should be abandoned and avoided and should not be cultivated.

(4)–(6) "There are, brahmin, these three fires that should be properly and happily maintained, having honored, respected, esteemed, and venerated them. What three? [45] The fire of those worthy of gifts, the householder's fire, and the fire of those worthy of offerings.

(4) "And what is the fire of those worthy of gifts? One's mother and father are called the fire of those worthy of gifts. For what reason? Because it is from them that one has originated and come to be.[1511] Therefore, this fire of those worthy of gifts should be properly and happily maintained, having honored, respected, esteemed, and venerated it.

(5) "And what is the householder's fire? One's children, wife, slaves, servants, and workers are called the householder's fire. Therefore, this householder's fire should be properly and happily maintained, having honored, respected, esteemed, and venerated it.

(6) "And what is the fire of those worthy of offerings? Those ascetics and brahmins who refrain from intoxication and heedlessness, who are settled in patience and mildness, who tame

themselves, calm themselves, and train themselves for nibbāna are called the fire of those worthy of offerings. Therefore, this fire of those worthy of offerings should be properly and happily maintained, having honored, respected, esteemed, and venerated it.

"These, brahmin, are the three fires that should be properly and happily maintained, having honored, respected, esteemed, and venerated them.

(7) "But, brahmin, this wood fire should at certain times be ignited, at certain times be looked upon with equanimity, at certain times be extinguished, and at certain times be put aside."

When this was said, the brahmin Uggatasarīra said to the Blessed One: "Excellent, Master Gotama! Excellent, Master Gotama! . . . [as in 6:38] . . . Let Master Gotama consider me a lay follower who from today [46] has gone for refuge for life. Master Gotama, I set free the five hundred bulls and allow them to live. I set free the five hundred bullocks and allow them to live. I set free the five hundred heifers and allow them to live. I set free the five hundred goats and allow them to live. I set free the five hundred rams and allow them to live. Let them eat green grass, drink cool water, and enjoy a cool breeze."

48 (5) Perceptions (1)

"Bhikkhus, these seven perceptions, when developed and cultivated, are of great fruit and benefit, culminating in the deathless, having the deathless as their consummation. What seven? The perception of unattractiveness, the perception of death, the perception of the repulsiveness of food, the perception of non-delight in the entire world, the perception of impermanence, the perception of suffering in the impermanent, and the perception of non-self in what is suffering. These seven perceptions, when developed and cultivated, are of great fruit and benefit, culminating in the deathless, having the deathless as their consummation."

49 (6) Perceptions (2)

"Bhikkhus, these seven perceptions, when developed and cultivated, are of great fruit and benefit, culminating in the deathless, having the deathless as their consummation. What seven? The perception of unattractiveness, the perception of death, the perception of the repulsiveness of food, the perception of non-delight in the entire world, the perception of impermanence, the perception of suffering in the impermanent, and the perception of non-self in what is suffering. These seven perceptions, when developed and cultivated, are of great fruit and benefit, culminating in the deathless, having the deathless as their consummation.

(1) "It was said: 'The perception of unattractiveness, bhikkhus, when developed and cultivated, is of great fruit and benefit, culminating in the deathless, having the deathless as its consummation.' For what reason was this said?

"When a bhikkhu often dwells with a mind accustomed to the perception of unattractiveness, his mind shrinks away from sexual intercourse, [47] turns back from it, rolls away from it, and is not drawn toward it, and either equanimity or revulsion becomes settled in him. Just as a cock's feather or a strip of sinew, thrown into a fire, shrinks away from it, turns back from it, rolls away from it, and is not drawn toward it, so it is in regard to sexual intercourse when a bhikkhu often dwells with a mind accustomed to the perception of unattractiveness.

"If, when a bhikkhu often dwells with a mind accustomed to the perception of unattractiveness, his mind inclines to sexual intercourse, or if he does not turn away from it,[1512] he should understand: 'I have not developed the perception of unattractiveness; there is no distinction between my earlier condition and my present one;[1513] I have not attained the fruit of development.' Thus he clearly comprehends this. But if, when he often dwells with a mind accustomed to the perception of unattractiveness, his mind shrinks away from sexual intercourse . . . and either equanimity or revulsion becomes settled in him, he should understand: 'I have developed the perception of unattractiveness; there is a distinction between my earlier condition and my present one; I have attained the fruit of development.' Thus he clearly comprehends this.

"When it was said: 'The perception of unattractiveness, bhikkhus, when developed and cultivated, is of great fruit and benefit, culminating in the deathless, having the deathless as its consummation,' it is because of this that this was said.

(2) "It was said: 'The perception of death, bhikkhus, when developed and cultivated, is of great [48] fruit and benefit, cul-

minating in the deathless, having the deathless as its consummation.' For what reason was this said?

"When a bhikkhu often dwells with a mind accustomed to the perception of death, his mind shrinks away from attachment to life, turns back from it, rolls away from it, and is not drawn toward it, and either equanimity or revulsion becomes settled in him. Just as a cock's feather or a strip of sinew, thrown into a fire, shrinks away from it, turns back from it, rolls away from it, and is not drawn toward it, so it is in regard to attachment to life when a bhikkhu often dwells with a mind accustomed to the perception of death.

"If, when a bhikkhu often dwells with a mind accustomed to the perception of death, his mind inclines to attachment to life, or if he does not turn away from it, he should understand: 'I have not developed the perception of death; there is no distinction between my earlier condition and my present one; I have not attained the fruit of development.' Thus he clearly comprehends this. But if, when he often dwells with a mind accustomed to the perception of death, his mind shrinks away from attachment to life . . . and either equanimity or revulsion becomes settled in him, he should understand: 'I have developed the perception of death; there is a distinction between my earlier condition and my present one; I have attained the fruit of development.' Thus he clearly comprehends this.

"When it was said: 'The perception of death, bhikkhus, when developed and cultivated, is of great [49] fruit and benefit, culminating in the deathless, having the deathless as its consummation,' it is because of this that this was said.

(3) "It was said: 'The perception of the repulsiveness of food, bhikkhus, when developed and cultivated, is of great fruit and benefit, culminating in the deathless, having the deathless as its consummation.' For what reason was this said?

"When a bhikkhu often dwells with a mind accustomed to the perception of the repulsiveness of food, his mind shrinks away from craving for tastes, turns back from it, rolls away from it, and is not drawn toward it, and either equanimity or revulsion becomes settled in him. Just as a cock's feather or a strip of sinew, thrown into a fire, shrinks away from it, turns back from it, rolls away from it, and is not drawn toward it, so it is in regard to craving for tastes when a bhikkhu often dwells with a mind accustomed to the perception of the repulsiveness of food.

"If, when a bhikkhu often dwells with a mind accustomed to the perception of the repulsiveness of food, his mind inclines to craving for tastes, or if he does not turn away from them, he should understand: 'I have not developed the perception of the repulsiveness of food; there is no distinction between my earlier condition and my present one; I have not attained the fruit of development.' Thus he clearly comprehends this. But if, when he often dwells with a mind accustomed to the perception of the repulsiveness of food, his mind shrinks away from craving for tastes . . . and either equanimity or revulsion becomes settled in him, he should understand: 'I have developed the perception of the repulsiveness of food; there is a distinction between my earlier condition and my present one; I have attained the fruit of development.' Thus he clearly comprehends this. [50]

"When it was said: 'The perception of the repulsiveness of food, bhikkhus, when developed and cultivated, is of great fruit and benefit, culminating in the deathless, having the deathless as its consummation,' it is because of this that this was said.

(4) "It was said: 'The perception of non-delight in the entire world, bhikkhus, when developed and cultivated, is of great fruit and benefit, culminating in the deathless, having the deathless as its consummation.' For what reason was this said?

"When a bhikkhu often dwells with a mind accustomed to the perception of non-delight in the entire world, his mind shrinks away from the world's beautiful things, turns back from them, rolls away from them, and is not drawn toward them, and either equanimity or revulsion becomes settled in him. Just as a cock's feather or a strip of sinew, thrown into a fire, shrinks away from it, turns back from it, rolls away from it, and is not drawn toward it, so it is in regard to the world's beautiful things when a bhikkhu often dwells with a mind accustomed to the perception of non-delight in the entire world.

"If, when a bhikkhu often dwells with a mind accustomed to the perception of non-delight in the entire world, his mind inclines to the world's beautiful things, or if he does not turn away from them, he should understand: 'I have not developed the perception of non-delight in the entire world; there is no distinction between my earlier condition and my present one;

I have not attained the fruit of development.' Thus he clearly comprehends this. But if, [51] when he often dwells with a mind accustomed to the perception of non-delight in the entire world, his mind shrinks away from the world's beautiful things . . . and either equanimity or revulsion becomes settled in him, he should understand: 'I have developed the perception of non-delight in the entire world; there is a distinction between my earlier condition and my present one; I have attained the fruit of development.' Thus he clearly comprehends this.

"When it was said: 'The perception of non-delight in the entire world, bhikkhus, when developed and cultivated, is of great fruit and benefit, culminating in the deathless, having the deathless as its consummation,' it is because of this that this was said.

(5) "It was said: 'The perception of impermanence, bhikkhus, when developed and cultivated, is of great fruit and benefit, culminating in the deathless, having the deathless as its consummation.' For what reason was this said?

"When a bhikkhu often dwells with a mind accustomed to the perception of impermanence, his mind shrinks away from gain, honor, and praise, turns back from them, rolls away from them, and is not drawn toward them, and either equanimity or revulsion becomes settled in him. Just as a cock's feather or a strip of sinew, thrown into a fire, shrinks away from it, turns back from it, rolls away from it, and is not drawn toward it, so it is in regard to gain, honor, and praise when a bhikkhu often dwells with a mind accustomed to the perception of impermanence.

"If, when a bhikkhu often dwells with a mind accustomed to the perception of impermanence, his mind inclines to gain, honor, and praise, or if he does not turn away from them, he should understand: 'I have not developed the perception of impermanence; there is no distinction between my earlier condition and my present one; I have not attained the fruit of development.' Thus he clearly comprehends this. But if, when he often dwells with a mind accustomed to the perception of impermanence, his mind shrinks away from gain, honor, and praise [52] . . . and either equanimity or revulsion becomes settled in him, he should understand: 'I have developed the perception of impermanence; there is a distinction between my earlier condition and my present one; I have attained the fruit of development.' Thus he clearly comprehends this.

"When it was said: 'The perception of impermanence, bhikkhus, when developed and cultivated, is of great fruit and benefit, culminating in the deathless, having the deathless as its consummation,' it is because of this that this was said.

(6) "It was said: 'The perception of suffering in the impermanent, bhikkhus, when developed and cultivated, is of great fruit and benefit, culminating in the deathless, having the deathless as its consummation.' For what reason was this said?

"When a bhikkhu often dwells with a mind accustomed to the perception of suffering in the impermanent, a keen perception of danger becomes settled in him toward indolence, laziness, slackness, heedlessness, lack of effort, and unreflectiveness, just as toward a murderer with drawn sword.

"If, when a bhikkhu often dwells with a mind accustomed to the perception of suffering in the impermanent, a keen perception of danger does not become settled in him toward indolence, laziness, slackness, heedlessness, lack of effort, and unreflectiveness, just as toward a murderer with drawn sword, he should understand: 'I have not developed the perception of suffering in the impermanent; there is no distinction between my earlier condition and my present one; I have not attained the fruit of development.' Thus he clearly comprehends this. But if, when he often dwells with a mind accustomed to the perception of suffering in the impermanent, a keen perception of danger becomes settled in him toward indolence, laziness, slackness, heedlessness, lack of effort, and unreflectiveness, just as toward a murderer with drawn sword, he should understand: 'I have developed the perception of suffering in the impermanent; there is a distinction between my earlier condition and my present one; I have attained the fruit of development.' Thus he clearly comprehends this.

"When it was said: 'The perception of suffering in the impermanent, bhikkhus, when developed and cultivated, is of great fruit [53] and benefit, culminating in the deathless, having the deathless as its consummation,' it is because of this that this was said.

(7) "It was said: 'The perception of non-self in what is suffering, bhikkhus, when developed and cultivated, is of great fruit

and benefit, culminating in the deathless, having the deathless as its consummation.' For what reason was this said?

"When a bhikkhu often dwells with a mind accustomed to the perception of non-self in what is suffering, his mind is devoid of I-making, mine-making, and conceit regarding this conscious body and all external objects; it has transcended discrimination and is peaceful and well liberated.[1514]

"If, when a bhikkhu often dwells with a mind accustomed to the perception of non-self in what is suffering, his mind is not devoid of I-making, mine-making, and conceit regarding this conscious body and all external objects, if it does not transcend discrimination and become peaceful and well liberated, he should understand: 'I have not developed the perception of non-self in what is suffering; there is no distinction between my earlier condition and my present one; I have not attained the fruit of development.' Thus he clearly comprehends this. But if, when he often dwells with a mind accustomed to the perception of non-self in what is suffering, his mind is devoid of I-making, mine-making, and conceit regarding this conscious body and all external objects, and if it has transcended discrimination and become peaceful and well liberated, he should understand: 'I have developed the perception of non-self in what is suffering; there is a distinction between my earlier condition and my present one; I have attained the fruit of development.' Thus he clearly comprehends this.

"When it was said: 'The perception of non-self in what is suffering, bhikkhus, when developed and cultivated, is of great fruit and benefit, culminating in the deathless, having the deathless as its consummation,' it is because of this that this was said.

"These seven perceptions, bhikkhus, when developed and cultivated, are of great fruit and benefit, culminating in the deathless, having the deathless as their consummation." [54]

50 (7) Sexual Intercourse

Then the brahmin Jāṇussoṇī approached the Blessed One and exchanged greetings with him . . . and said to him:

"Does Master Gotama also claim to be one who lives the celibate life?"[1515]

"If, brahmin, one could rightly say of anyone: 'He lives the complete and pure celibate life—unbroken, flawless, unblemished, unblotched,' it is precisely of me that one might say this. For I live the complete and pure celibate life—unbroken, flawless, unblemished, unblotched."

"But what, Master Gotama, is a breach, flaw, blemish, and blotch of the celibate life?"

(1) "Here, brahmin, some ascetic or brahmin, claiming to be perfectly celibate, does not actually engage in intercourse with women. But he consents to being rubbed, massaged, bathed, and kneaded by them. He relishes this, desires it, and finds satisfaction in it. This is a breach, flaw, blemish, and blotch of the celibate life. He is called one who lives an impure celibate life, one who is fettered by the bond of sexuality. He is not freed from birth, from old age and death, from sorrow, lamentation, pain, dejection, and anguish; he is not freed from suffering, I say. [55]

(2) "Again, some ascetic or brahmin, claiming to be perfectly celibate, does not actually engage in intercourse with women; nor does he consent to being rubbed, massaged, bathed, and kneaded by them. But he jokes with women, plays with them, and amuses himself with them. . . .

(3) ". . . he does not joke with women, play with them, and amuse himself with them . . . but he gazes and stares straight into their eyes. . . .

(4) ". . . he does not gaze and stare straight into women's eyes . . . but he listens to their voices behind a wall or through a rampart as they laugh, talk, sing, or weep. . . .

(5) ". . . he does not listen to the voices of women behind a wall or through a rampart as they laugh, talk, sing, or weep . . . but he recollects laughing, talking, and playing with them in the past. . . .

(6) ". . . he does not recollect laughing, talking, and playing with women in the past . . . but he looks at a householder or a householder's son enjoying himself furnished and endowed with the five objects of sensual pleasure. . . .

(7) ". . . he does not look at a householder or a householder's son enjoying himself furnished and endowed with the five objects of sensual pleasure, but he lives the spiritual life aspiring for [rebirth in] a certain order of devas, [thinking]: 'By this virtuous behavior, observance, austerity, or spiritual life I will

be a deva or one [in the retinue] of the devas.' He relishes this, desires it, and finds satisfaction in it. This, too, is a breach, flaw, blemish, and blotch of the celibate life. He is called [56] one who lives an impure celibate life, one who is fettered by the bond of sexuality. He is not freed from birth, from old age and death, from sorrow, lamentation, pain, dejection, and anguish; he is not freed from suffering, I say.

"So long, brahmin, as I saw that I had not abandoned one or another of these seven bonds of sexuality, I did not claim to have awakened to the unsurpassed perfect enlightenment in the world with its devas, Māra, and Brahmā, in this population with its ascetics and brahmins, its devas and humans. But when I did not see even one of these seven bonds of sexuality that I had not abandoned, then I claimed to have awakened to the unsurpassed perfect enlightenment in this world with . . . its devas and humans.

"The knowledge and vision arose in me: 'Unshakable is my liberation of mind; this is my last birth; now there is no more renewed existence.'"

When this was said, the brahmin Jāṇussoṇī said to the Blessed One: "Excellent, Master Gotama! . . . Let Master Gotama consider me a lay follower who from today has gone for refuge for life." [57]

51 (8) Union

"Bhikkhus, I will teach you a Dhamma exposition on union and disengagement.[1516] Listen. . . .

"And what is that Dhamma exposition on union and disengagement?

"A woman, bhikkhus, attends internally to her feminine faculty, her feminine comportment, her feminine appearance, her feminine aspect, her feminine desire, her feminine voice, her feminine ornamentation.[1517] She becomes excited by these and takes delight in them. Excited by them, taking delight in them, she attends externally to [a man's] masculine faculty, his masculine comportment, his masculine appearance, his masculine aspect, his masculine desire, his masculine voice, his masculine ornamentation. She becomes excited by these and takes delight in them. Excited by them, taking delight in them, she desires union externally, and she also desires the pleasure and joy that arise on account of such union. Beings who are delighted with their femininity enter upon union with men. It is in this way that a woman does not transcend her femininity.

"A man, bhikkhus, attends internally to his masculine faculty, his masculine comportment, his masculine appearance, his masculine aspect, his masculine desire, his masculine voice, his masculine ornamentation. He becomes excited by these and takes delight in them. Excited by them, taking delight in them, he attends externally to [a woman's] feminine faculty, her feminine comportment, her feminine appearance, her feminine aspect, her feminine desire, her feminine voice, her feminine ornamentation. He becomes excited by these and takes delight in them. Excited by them, taking delight in them, he desires union externally, and he also desires the pleasure and joy that arise on account of such union. Beings who are delighted with their masculinity enter upon union with women. [58] It is in this way that a man does not transcend his masculinity.

"This is how union comes about. And how does disengagement come about?

"A woman, bhikkhus, does not attend internally to her feminine faculty . . . to her feminine ornamentation. She does not become excited by these or take delight in them. Not excited by them, not taking delight in them, she does not attend externally to [a man's] masculine faculty . . . his masculine ornamentation. She does not become excited by these or take delight in them. Not excited by them, not taking delight in them, she does not desire union externally, nor does she desire the pleasure and joy that arise on account of such union. Beings who are not delighted with their femininity become disengaged from men. It is in this way that a woman transcends her femininity.

"A man, bhikkhus, does not attend internally to his masculine faculty . . . his masculine ornamentation. He does not become excited by these or take delight in them. Not excited by them, not taking delight in them, he does not attend externally to [a woman's] feminine faculty . . . her feminine ornamentation. He does not become excited by these or take delight in them. Not excited by them, not taking delight in them, he does not desire union externally, nor does he desire the pleasure and joy that arise on account of such union. Beings who are not delighted with their masculinity become disengaged from women. It is in this way [59] that a man transcends his masculinity.

"This is how disengagement comes about.

"This, bhikkhus, is the Dhamma exposition on union and disengagement."

52 (9) Giving

On one occasion the Blessed One was dwelling at Campā on a bank of the Gaggārā Lotus Pond. Then a number of lay followers from Campā approached the Venerable Sāriputta, paid homage to him, sat down to one side, and said to him:

"Bhante Sāriputta, it has been a long time since we heard a Dhamma talk from the Blessed One. It would be good, Bhante, if we could get to hear a Dhamma talk from him."

"In that case, friends, you should come on the uposatha day. Perhaps then you might get to hear a Dhamma talk from the Blessed One."

"Yes, Bhante," those lay followers replied. Then, having risen from their seats, they paid homage to the Venerable Sāriputta, circumambulated him keeping their right sides toward him, and departed.

Then, on the uposatha day, those lay followers from Campā approached the Venerable Sāriputta, paid homage to him, and stood to one side. Then the Venerable Sāriputta, along with those lay followers, went to the Blessed One. They paid homage to the Blessed One, sat down to one side, and the Venerable Sāriputta said to him: [60]

"Could it be the case, Bhante, that a gift given by someone here is not of great fruit and benefit? And could it be the case that a gift given by someone here is of great fruit and benefit?"

"It could be the case, Sāriputta, that a gift given by someone here is not of great fruit and benefit. And it could be the case that a gift given by someone here is of great fruit and benefit."

"Bhante, why is it that one gift is not of great fruit and benefit while the other is?"

(1) "Here, Sāriputta, someone gives a gift with expectations, with a bound mind, looking for rewards; he gives a gift, [thinking]: 'Having passed away, I will make use of this.' He gives that gift to an ascetic or a brahmin: food and drink; clothing and vehicles; garlands, scents, and unguents; bedding, dwellings, and lighting. What do you think, Sāriputta? Might someone give such a gift?"

"Yes, Bhante."

"In that case, Sāriputta, he gives a gift with expectations, with a bound mind, looking for rewards; he gives a gift, [thinking]: 'Having passed away, I will make use of this.' Having given such a gift, with the breakup of the body, after death, he is reborn in companionship with the devas [ruled by] the four great kings. [61] Having exhausted that kamma, psychic potency, glory, and authority, he comes back and returns to this state of being.

(2) "But, Sāriputta, someone does not give a gift with expectations, with a bound mind, looking for rewards; he does not give a gift, [thinking]: 'Having passed away, I will make use of this.' Rather, he gives a gift, [thinking]: 'Giving is good.'...

(3) "He does not give a gift, [thinking]: 'Giving is good,' but rather he gives a gift, [thinking]: 'Giving was practiced before by my father and forefathers; I should not abandon this ancient family custom.'...

(4) "He does not give a gift, [thinking]: 'Giving was practiced before ... I should not abandon this ancient family custom,' but rather he gives a gift, [thinking]: 'I cook; these people do not cook. It isn't right that I who cook should not give to those who do not cook.'...

(5) "He does not give a gift, [thinking]: 'I cook ... to those who do not cook,' but rather he gives a gift, [thinking]: 'Just as the seers of old—that is, Aṭṭhaka, Vāmaka, Vāmadeva, Vessāmitta, Yamataggi, Aṅgīrasa, Bhāradvāja, Vāseṭṭha, Kassapa, and Bhagu—held those great sacrifices, so I will share a gift.'... [1518]

(6) "He does not give a gift, [thinking]: 'Just as the seers of old ... held those great sacrifices, so I will [62] share a gift,' but rather he gives a gift, [thinking]: 'When I am giving a gift my mind becomes placid, and elation and joy arise.'...

(7) "He does not give a gift, [thinking]: 'When I am giving a gift my mind becomes placid, and elation and joy arise,' but rather he gives a gift, [thinking]: 'It's an ornament of the mind, an accessory of the mind.'[1519] He gives that gift to an ascetic or a brahmin: food and drink; clothing and vehicles; garlands, scents, and unguents; bedding, dwellings, and lighting. What do you think, Sāriputta? Might someone give such a gift?"

"Yes, Bhante."

"In that case, Sāriputta, he does not give a gift with expectations, with a bound mind, looking for rewards; he does not give a gift, [thinking]: 'Having passed away, I will make use of this.' He does not give a gift, [thinking]: 'Giving is good.' He does not give a gift, [thinking]: 'Giving was practiced before by my father and forefathers; I should not abandon this ancient family custom.' He does not give a gift, [thinking]: 'I cook; these people do not cook. It isn't right that I who cook should not give to those who do not cook.' He does not give a gift, [thinking]: 'Just as the seers of old . . . held those great sacrifices, so I will share a gift.' He does not give a gift, [thinking]: 'When I am giving a gift my mind becomes placid, and elation and joy arise.' But rather, he gives a gift, [thinking]: 'It's an ornament of the mind, an accessory of the mind.' Having given such a gift, with the breakup of the body, after death, he is reborn in companionship with the devas of Brahmā's company. [63] Having exhausted that kamma, psychic potency, glory, and authority, he does not come back and return to this state of being.

"This, Sāriputta, is the reason why a gift given by someone here is not of great fruit and benefit. And this is the reason why a gift given by someone here is of great fruit and benefit."

53 (10) Nandamātā

Thus have I heard. On one occasion the Venerable Sāriputta and the Venerable Mahāmoggallāna were wandering on tour in Dakkhiṇāgiri together with a large Saṅgha of bhikkhus. Now on that occasion the female lay follower Veḷukaṇṭakī Nandamātā,[1520] having risen as the night was receding, chanted the Pārāyana.

Now on that occasion the great [deva] king Vessavaṇa was traveling from north to south on some business. He heard the female lay follower Nandamātā chanting the Pārāyana and stood waiting until the end of her recitation. When the female lay follower Nandamātā had finished, she fell silent. Having understood that the female lay follower Nandamātā had finished her recitation, the great [deva] king Vessavaṇa applauded: "Good, sister! Good, sister!"

"Who is that, my dear?"

"I am your brother, the great [deva] king Vessavaṇa, sister."

"Good, my dear! Then let the Dhamma exposition that I just recited be my guest's gift to you."[1521]

"Good, sister! And let this too [64] be your guest's gift to me: Tomorrow, before they have eaten breakfast, the Saṅgha of bhikkhus headed by Sāriputta and Moggallāna will come to Veḷukaṇṭaka. You should serve them and dedicate the offering to me. That will be your guest's gift to me."

Then when the night had passed the female lay follower Nandamātā had various kinds of delicious food prepared in her own residence. Then, before they had eaten breakfast, the Saṅgha of bhikkhus headed by Sāriputta and Moggallāna arrived in Veḷukaṇṭaka.

Then the female lay follower Nandamātā addressed a man: "Come, good man. Go to the monastery and announce the time to the Saṅgha of bhikkhus, saying: 'It is time, Bhante, the meal is ready at Lady Nandamātā's residence.'" The man replied: "Yes, madam," and he went to the monastery and delivered his message. Then the Saṅgha of bhikkhus headed by Sāriputta and Moggallāna dressed, took their bowls and robes, and went to the residence of the female lay follower Nandamātā, where they sat down in the seats that had been prepared.

Then, with her own hands, the female lay follower Nandamātā served and satisfied with various kinds of delicious food the Saṅgha of bhikkhus headed by Sāriputta and Moggallāna. When the Venerable Sāriputta had finished eating and had put away his bowl, she sat down to one side and the Venerable Sāriputta asked her:

"But who, Nandamātā, told you that the Saṅgha of bhikkhus would be approaching?"

(1) "Here, Bhante, having risen as the night was receding, I chanted the Pārāyana. . . . [65] [She here relates, in the first person, the entire incident narrated above, ending with Vessavaṇa's words: "And this will be your guest's gift to me."] . . . Bhante, let whatever merit I may have gained by this act of giving be dedicated to the happiness of the great [deva] king Vessavaṇa."

"It's astounding and amazing,[1522] Nandamātā, that you can converse[1523] directly with such a powerful and influential young deva as the great [deva] king Vessavaṇa."

(2) "Bhante, that is not the only astounding and amazing quality of mine. There is another. I had only one son, a dear and beloved boy named Nanda. The rulers seized and abducted him on some pretext and executed him. Bhante, when that boy was

arrested or was being put under arrest, when he was in prison or was being imprisoned,[1524] when he was dead or was being killed, I don't recall any alteration of my mind."[1525]

"It's astounding and amazing, Nandamātā, that you can purify even the arising of a thought."[1526]

(3) "Bhante, that is not [66] the only astounding and amazing quality of mine. There is still another. When my husband died, he was reborn in the yakkha realm.[1527] He appeared to me in his previous bodily form, but I don't recall any alteration of my mind."

"It's astounding and amazing, Nandamātā, that you can purify even the arising of a thought."

(4) "Bhante, that is not the only astounding and amazing quality of mine. There is still another. I was given to my young husband in marriage when I was a young girl, but I don't recall ever transgressing against him even in thought, much less by deed."

"It's astounding and amazing, Nandamātā, that you can purify even the arising of a thought."

(5) "Bhante, that is not the only astounding and amazing quality of mine. There is still another. Since I declared myself a lay follower, I don't recall ever intentionally transgressing any training rule."

"It's astounding and amazing, Nandamātā!"

(6) "Bhante, that is not the only astounding and amazing quality of mine. There is still another. For as much as I want, secluded from sensual pleasures, secluded from unwholesome states, I enter and dwell in the first jhāna, which consists of rapture and pleasure born of seclusion, accompanied by thought and examination. With the subsiding of thought and examination, I enter and dwell in the second jhāna, which has internal placidity and unification of mind and consists of rapture and pleasure born of concentration, without thought and examination. With the fading away as well of rapture, I dwell equanimous and, mindful and clearly comprehending, I experience pleasure [67] with the body; I enter and dwell in the third jhāna of which the noble ones declare: 'He is equanimous, mindful, one who dwells happily.' With the abandoning of pleasure and pain, and with the previous passing away of joy and dejection, I enter and dwell in the fourth jhāna, neither

painful nor pleasant, which has purification of mindfulness by equanimity."

"It's astounding and amazing, Nandamātā!"

(7) "Bhante, that is not the only astounding and amazing quality of mine. There is still another. Of the five lower fetters taught by the Blessed One, I don't see any that I haven't abandoned."[1528]

"It's astounding and amazing, Nandamātā!"

Then the Venerable Sāriputta instructed, encouraged, inspired, and gladdened Nandamātā with a Dhamma talk, after which he rose from his seat and departed.

The Second Fifty

I. Undeclared

54 (1) Undeclared

Then a certain bhikkhu approached the Blessed One, paid homage to him, [68] sat down to one side, and said: "Bhante, why is it that doubt does not arise in the instructed noble disciple about the undeclared points?"[1529]

"With the cessation of views, bhikkhu, doubt does not arise in the instructed noble disciple about the undeclared points.

(1) "'The Tathāgata exists after death': this is an involvement with views; 'The Tathāgata does not exist after death': this is an involvement with views; 'The Tathāgata both exists and does not exist after death': this is an involvement with views; 'The Tathāgata neither exists nor does not exist after death': this is an involvement with views.

"Bhikkhu, the uninstructed worldling does not understand views, their origin, their cessation, and the way leading to their cessation. For him, that view increases. He is not freed from birth, from old age and death, from sorrow, lamentation, pain, dejection, and anguish; he is not freed from suffering, I say.

"But the instructed noble disciple understands views, their origin, their cessation, and the way leading to their cessation. For him, that view ceases. He is freed from birth, from old age and death, from sorrow, lamentation, pain, dejection, and anguish; he is freed from suffering, I say.

"Knowing thus, seeing thus, the instructed noble disciple does not declare: 'The Tathāgata exists after death'; or: 'The Tathāgata does not exist after death'; or: 'The Tathāgata both exists and does not exist after death'; or: 'The Tathāgata neither exists nor does not exist after death.' Knowing thus, seeing thus, the instructed noble disciple does not make declarations regarding the undeclared points.

"Knowing thus, bhikkhu, seeing thus, the instructed noble disciple does not tremble, does not shake,[1530] does not vacillate, and does not become terrified regarding the undeclared points.

(2) "'The Tathāgata exists after death': this is an involvement with craving . . . (3) . . . this is [69] an involvement with perception . . . (4) . . . something conceived . . . (5) . . . a proliferation . . . (6) . . . an involvement with clinging . . . (7) . . . a [ground for] remorse; 'The Tathāgata does not exist after death': this is a [ground for] remorse; 'The Tathāgata both exists and does not exist after death': this is a [ground for] remorse; 'The Tathāgata neither exists nor does not exist after death': this is a [ground for] remorse.

"Bhikkhu, the uninstructed worldling does not understand remorse, its origin, its cessation, and the way leading to its cessation. For him, that remorse increases. He is not freed from birth, from old age and death, from sorrow, lamentation, pain, dejection, and anguish; he is not freed from suffering, I say.

"But the instructed noble disciple understands remorse, its origin, its cessation, and the way leading to its cessation. For him, that remorse ceases. He is freed from birth, from old age and death, from sorrow, lamentation, pain, dejection, and anguish; he is freed from suffering, I say.

"Knowing thus, seeing thus, the instructed noble disciple does not declare: 'The Tathāgata exists after death'; or: 'The Tathāgata does not exist after death'; or: 'The Tathāgata both exists and does not exist after death'; or: 'The Tathāgata neither exists nor does not exist after death.' Knowing thus, seeing thus, the instructed noble disciple does not make declarations regarding the undeclared points.

"Knowing thus, seeing thus, the instructed noble disciple does not tremble, does not shake, does not vacillate, and does not fall into terror regarding the undeclared points. [70]

"Bhikkhu, this is why doubt does not arise in the instructed noble disciple about the undeclared points."

55 (2) Destinations of Persons

"Bhikkhus, I will teach you seven destinations of persons and attainment of nibbāna through non-clinging. Listen and attend closely. I will speak."

"Yes, Bhante," those bhikkhus replied. The Blessed One said this:

"And what, bhikkhus, are the seven destinations of persons?[1531]

(1) "Here, a bhikkhu is practicing thus: 'It might not be, and it might not be mine. It will not be; it will not be mine.[1532] I am abandoning what exists, what has come to be.' He obtains equanimity. He is not attached to existence; he is not attached to origination. He sees with correct wisdom: 'There is a higher state that is peaceful,'[1533] yet he has not totally realized that state. He has not totally abandoned the underlying tendency to conceit; he has not totally abandoned the underlying tendency to lust for existence; he has not totally abandoned ignorance.[1534] With the utter destruction of the five lower fetters he becomes an attainer of nibbāna in the interval.[1535]

"For example, when an iron bowl has been heated all day and is struck, a chip might fly off and be extinguished. So too, a bhikkhu is practicing thus ... [71] ... he has not totally abandoned ignorance. With the utter destruction of the five lower fetters he becomes an attainer of nibbāna in the interval.[1536]

(2) "Then a bhikkhu is practicing thus: 'It might not be, and it might not be mine. It will not be; it will not be mine. I am abandoning what exists, what has come to be.' He obtains equanimity. He is not attached to existence; he is not attached to origination. He sees with correct wisdom: 'There is a higher state that is peaceful,' yet he has not totally realized that state. He has not totally abandoned the underlying tendency to conceit; he has not totally abandoned the underlying tendency to lust for existence; he has not totally abandoned ignorance. With the utter destruction of the five lower fetters he becomes an attainer of nibbāna in the interval.

"For example, when an iron bowl has been heated all day and is struck, a chip might fly off, rise up, and be extinguished. So too, a bhikkhu is practicing thus.... With the utter destruction of the five lower fetters he becomes an attainer of nibbāna in the interval.

(3) "Then a bhikkhu is practicing thus: 'It might not be, and it might not be mine. It will not be; it will not be mine....'... With the utter destruction of the five lower fetters he becomes an attainer of nibbāna in the interval.

"For example, when an iron bowl has been heated all day and is struck, a chip might fly off, rise up, and be extinguished just before it lands on the ground. So too, a bhikkhu is practicing thus.... [72]... With the utter destruction of the five lower fetters he becomes an attainer of nibbāna in the interval.

(4) "Then a bhikkhu is practicing thus: 'It might not be, and it might not be mine. It will not be; it will not be mine....'... With the utter destruction of the five lower fetters he becomes an attainer of nibbāna upon landing.[1537]

"For example, when an iron bowl has been heated all day and is struck, a chip might be produced and fly up, and upon landing on the ground it would be extinguished. So too, a bhikkhu is practicing thus.... With the utter destruction of the five lower fetters he becomes an attainer of nibbāna upon landing.

(5) "Then a bhikkhu is practicing thus: 'It might not be, and it might not be mine. It will not be; it will not be mine....'... With the utter destruction of the five lower fetters he becomes an attainer of nibbāna without exertion.

"For example, when an iron bowl has been heated all day and is struck, a chip might fly off, rise up, and fall on a small pile of straw or sticks. There it would produce a fire and smoke, but when it has exhausted that small pile of straw or sticks, if it gets no more fuel, it would be extinguished. So too, a bhikkhu is practicing thus.... With the utter destruction of the five lower fetters he becomes an attainer of nibbāna without exertion.[1538] [73]

(6) "Then a bhikkhu is practicing thus: 'It might not be, and it might not be mine. It will not be; it will not be mine....'... With the utter destruction of the five lower fetters he becomes an attainer of nibbāna through exertion.

"For example, when an iron bowl has been heated all day and is struck, a chip might fly off, rise up, and then fall upon a wide pile of straw or sticks. There it would produce a fire and smoke, but when it has exhausted that wide pile of straw or sticks, if it gets no more fuel, it would be extinguished. So too, a bhikkhu is practicing thus.... With the utter destruction of the five lower fetters he becomes an attainer of nibbāna through exertion.

(7) "Then a bhikkhu is practicing thus: 'It might not be, and it might not be mine. It will not be; it will not be mine. I am abandoning what exists, what has come to be.' He obtains equanimity. He is not attached to existence; he is not attached to origination. He sees with correct wisdom: 'There is a higher state that is peaceful,' yet he has not totally realized that state. He has not totally abandoned the underlying tendency to conceit; he has not totally abandoned the underlying tendency to lust for existence; he has not totally abandoned ignorance. With the utter destruction of the five lower fetters he becomes one bound upstream, heading toward the Akaniṭṭha realm.[1539]

"For example, when an iron bowl has been heated all day and is struck, a chip might fly off, rise up, and then fall upon a large pile of straw or sticks. There it would produce a fire and smoke, and when it has exhausted that large [74] pile of straw or sticks, it would burn up a woods or a grove until it reaches the edge of a field, the edge of a road, the edge of a stone mountain, the edge of water, or some delightful piece of land, and then, if it gets no more fuel, it would be extinguished. So too, a bhikkhu is practicing thus.... With the utter destruction of the five lower fetters he becomes one bound upstream, heading toward the Akaniṭṭha realm.

"These, bhikkhus, are the seven destinations of persons.

"And what, bhikkhus, is attainment of nibbāna through non-clinging? Here, a bhikkhu is practicing thus: 'It might not be, and it might not be mine. It will not be; it will not be mine. I am abandoning what exists, what has come to be.' He obtains equanimity. He is not attached to existence; he is not attached to origination. He sees with correct wisdom: 'There is a higher state that is peaceful,' and he has totally realized that state. He has totally abandoned the underlying tendency to conceit; he has totally abandoned the underlying tendency to lust for existence; he has totally abandoned ignorance. With the destruction of the taints, he has realized for himself with direct knowledge, in this very life, the taintless liberation of mind, liberation by wisdom, and having entered upon it, he dwells in it. This is called attainment of nibbāna through non-clinging.

"These, bhikkhus, are the seven destinations of persons and attainment of nibbāna through non-clinging."

56 (3) Tissa

Thus have I heard. On one occasion the Blessed One was dwelling at Rājagaha on Mount Vulture Peak. Then, when the night had advanced, two deities of stunning beauty, illuminating the entire Vulture [75] Peak, approached the Blessed One, paid homage to him, and stood to one side. One deity then said to the Blessed One: "Bhante, these bhikkhunīs are liberated."

The other said: "Bhante, these bhikkhunīs are well liberated without residue remaining."[1540]

This is what those deities said. The Teacher agreed. Then, [thinking]: "The Teacher has agreed," they paid homage to the Blessed One, circumambulated him keeping the right side toward him, and disappeared right there.

Then, when the night had passed, the Blessed One addressed the bhikkhus: "Last night, bhikkhus, when the night had advanced, two deities of stunning beauty, illuminating the entire Vulture Peak, approached me, paid homage to me, and stood to one side. One deity then said to me: 'Bhante, these bhikkhunīs are liberated.' And the other said: 'Bhante, these bhikkhunīs are well liberated without residue remaining.' This is what those deities said, after which they paid homage to me, circumambulated me keeping the right side toward me, and disappeared right there."

Now on that occasion the Venerable Mahāmoggallāna was sitting not far from the Blessed One. Then it occurred to the Venerable Mahāmoggallāna: "Which devas know one who has a residue remaining as 'one with a residue remaining' and one who has no residue remaining as 'one without residue remaining'?"

Now at that time a bhikkhu named Tissa had recently died and been reborn in a certain brahmā world. There too they knew him as "the brahmā Tissa, powerful and mighty." Then, just as a strong man might extend his drawn-in arm or draw in his extended arm, the Venerable Mahāmoggallāna disappeared from Mount Vulture Peak and reappeared in that brahmā world. Having seen the Venerable Mahāmoggallāna coming in the distance, the brahmā Tissa [76] said to him:

"Come, respected Moggallāna! Welcome, respected Moggallāna! It has been long since you took the opportunity to come here. Sit down, respected Moggallāna. This seat has been prepared." The Venerable Mahāmoggallāna sat down on the prepared seat. The brahmā Tissa then paid homage to the Venerable Mahāmoggallāna and sat down to one side. The Venerable Mahāmoggallāna then said to him:

"Which devas, Tissa, know one who has a residue remaining as 'one with a residue remaining' and one who has no residue remaining as 'one without residue remaining'?"

"The devas of Brahmā's company have such knowledge, respected Moggallāna."

"Do all the devas of Brahmā's company have such knowledge, Tissa?"

"Not all, respected Moggallāna. Those devas of Brahmā's company who are content with a brahmā's life span, a brahmā's beauty, a brahmā's happiness, a brahmā's glory, a brahmā's authority, and who do not understand as it really is an escape higher than this, do not have such knowledge.

"But those devas of Brahmā's company who are not content with a brahmā's life span, a brahmā's beauty, a brahmā's happiness, a brahmā's glory, a brahmā's authority, and who [77] understand as it really is an escape higher than this, know one who has a residue remaining as 'one with a residue remaining' and one who has no residue remaining as 'one without residue remaining.'[1541]

(1) "Here, respected Moggallāna, when a bhikkhu is liberated in both respects, those devas know him thus: 'This venerable one is liberated in both respects. As long as his body stands devas and humans will see him, but with the breakup of the body, devas and humans will see him no more.' It is in this way that those devas know one who has a residue remaining as 'one with a residue remaining' and one who has no residue remaining as 'one without residue remaining.'

(2) "Then, when a bhikkhu is liberated by wisdom, those devas know him thus: 'This venerable one is liberated by wisdom. As long as his body stands devas and humans will see him, but with the breakup of the body devas and humans will see him no more.' It is in this way, too, that those devas know one who has a residue remaining. . . .

(3) "Then, when a bhikkhu is a body witness, those devas know him thus: 'This venerable one is a body witness. If this venerable one resorts to congenial lodgings, relies on good friends, and harmonizes the spiritual faculties, perhaps he will realize for himself with direct knowledge, in this very life, that unsurpassed consummation of the spiritual life for the sake of which clansmen rightly go forth from the household life into homelessness, and having entered upon it, dwell in it.' It is in this way, too, that those devas know one who has a residue remaining....

(4) "Then, when a bhikkhu is one attained to view ... (5) one liberated by faith ... (6) a Dhamma follower, those devas know him thus: 'This venerable one [78] is a Dhamma follower. If this venerable one resorts to congenial lodgings, relies on good friends, and harmonizes the spiritual faculties, perhaps he will realize for himself with direct knowledge, in this very life, that unsurpassed consummation of the spiritual life for the sake of which clansmen rightly go forth from the household life into homelessness, and having entered upon it, dwell in it.' It is in this way, too, that those devas know one who has a residue remaining as 'one with a residue remaining' and one who has no residue remaining as 'one without residue remaining.'

Then, having delighted and rejoiced in the words of the brahmā Tissa, just as a strong man might extend his drawn-in arm or draw in his extended arm, the Venerable Mahāmoggallāna disappeared from the brahmā world and reappeared on Vulture Peak. He approached the Blessed One, paid homage to him, sat down to one side, and reported to the Blessed One his entire conversation with the brahmā Tissa.

[The Blessed One said:] "But, Moggallāna, didn't the brahmā Tissa teach you about the seventh person, the one who dwells in the markless?"[1542]

"It is the time for this, Blessed One! It is the time for this, Fortunate One! The Blessed One should teach about the seventh person, the one who dwells in the markless. Having heard it from the Blessed One, the bhikkhus will retain it in mind."

"Then listen, Moggallāna, and attend closely. I will speak."

"Yes, Bhante," the Venerable Mahāmoggallāna replied. The Blessed One said this:

(7) "Here, Moggallāna, through non-attention to all marks, a

bhikkhu enters and dwells in the markless mental concentration. Those devas know him thus: 'Through non-attention to all marks, this venerable one enters and dwells in the markless mental concentration. If this venerable one resorts to congenial lodgings, relies on good friends, and harmonizes the spiritual faculties, perhaps he will realize for himself with direct knowledge, in this very life, that unsurpassed consummation of the spiritual life for the sake of which clansmen rightly go forth from the household life into homelessness, [79] and having entered upon it, dwell in it.' It is in this way, too, that those devas know one who has a residue remaining as 'one with a residue remaining' and one who has no residue remaining as 'one without residue remaining.'"

57 (4) Sīha[1543]

On one occasion the Blessed One was dwelling at Vesālī in the Great Wood in the hall with the peaked roof. Then Sīha the general approached the Blessed One, paid homage to him, sat down to one side, and said:

"Is it possible, Bhante, to point out a directly visible fruit of giving?"

"Well then, Sīha, I will question you about this matter. You should answer as you see fit."

(1) "What do you think, Sīha? There might be two persons, one without faith who is miserly, mean, and abusive, and another endowed with faith, a munificent giver who delights in charity. What do you think, Sīha? To whom would the arahants first show compassion: to the one without faith who is miserly, mean, and abusive, or to the one endowed with faith, a munificent giver who delights in charity?"[1544]

"Why, Bhante, would the arahants first show compassion to the person without faith who is miserly, mean, and abusive? They would first show compassion to the one endowed with faith, a munificent giver who delights in charity."

(2) "What do you think, Sīha? Whom would the arahants approach first: the one without faith who is miserly, mean, and abusive, or [80] the one endowed with faith, a munificent giver who delights in charity?"

"Why, Bhante, would the arahants first approach the person without faith who is miserly, mean, and abusive? They would first approach the one endowed with faith, a munificent giver who delights in charity."

(3) "What do you think, Sīha? From whom would the arahants first receive alms: from the one without faith who is miserly, mean, and abusive, or from the one endowed with faith, a munificent giver who delights in charity?"

"Why, Bhante, would the arahants first receive alms from the person without faith who is miserly, mean, and abusive? They would first receive alms from the one endowed with faith, a munificent giver who delights in charity."

(4) "What do you think, Sīha? To whom would the arahants first teach the Dhamma: to the one without faith who is miserly, mean, and abusive, or to the one endowed with faith, a munificent giver who delights in charity?"

"Why, Bhante, would the arahants first teach the Dhamma to the person without faith who is miserly, mean, and abusive? They would first teach the Dhamma to the one endowed with faith, a munificent giver who delights in charity."

(5) "What do you think, Sīha? Which person would acquire a good reputation: the one without faith who is miserly, mean, and abusive, or the one endowed with faith, a munificent giver who delights in charity?"

"How, Bhante, would the person without faith who is miserly, mean, and abusive acquire a good reputation? It is the person endowed with faith, a munificent giver who delights in charity, who would acquire a good reputation."

(6) "What do you think, Sīha? Which person would approach any assembly—whether of khattiyas, brahmins, householders, or ascetics—[81] confidently and composed: the one without faith who is miserly, mean, and abusive, or the one endowed with faith, a munificent giver who delights in charity?"

"How, Bhante, could the person without faith, who is miserly, mean, and abusive, approach any assembly—whether of khattiyas, brahmins, householders, or ascetics—confidently and composed? It is the person endowed with faith, a munificent giver who delights in charity, who would approach any assembly . . . confidently and composed."

(7) "What do you think, Sīha? With the breakup of the body, after death, which person would be reborn in a good destination, in a heavenly world: the one without faith who is miserly,

mean, and abusive, or the one endowed with faith, a munificent giver who delights in charity?"

"How, Bhante, could the person without faith who is miserly, mean, and abusive be reborn in a good destination, in a heavenly world, with the breakup of the body, after death? It is the person endowed with faith, a munificent giver who delights in charity, who would be reborn in a good destination, in a heavenly world, with the breakup of the body, after death.

"Bhante, I do not go by faith in the Blessed One concerning those six directly visible fruits of giving declared by him. I know them, too. For I am a donor, a munificent giver, and the arahants first show compassion to me. I am a donor, a munificent giver, and the arahants first approach me. I am a donor, a munificent giver, and the arahants first receive alms from me. I am a donor, a munificent giver, and the arahants first teach the Dhamma to me. I am a donor, a munificent giver, and I have acquired a good reputation: 'Sīha the general is a donor, a sponsor, a supporter of the Saṅgha.' [82] I am a donor, a munificent giver, and whatever assembly I approach—whether of khattiyas, brahmins, householders, or ascetics—I approach it confidently and composed. I do not go by faith in the Blessed One concerning these six directly visible fruits of giving declared by him. I know them, too. But when the Blessed One tells me: 'Sīha, with the breakup of the body, after death, a donor, a munificent giver, is reborn in a good destination, in a heavenly world,' I do not know this, and here I go by faith in the Blessed One."

"So it is, Sīha, so it is! With the breakup of the body, after death, a donor, a munificent giver, is reborn in a good destination, in a heavenly world."

58 (5) No Need to Hide

"Bhikkhus, there are these four things that the Tathāgata does not need to hide and three things about which he is irreproachable.[1545]

"What are the four things that the Tathāgata does not need to hide?

(1) "Bhikkhus, the Tathāgata is one whose bodily behavior is purified. There is no bodily misconduct on the part of the Tathāgata that he might need to hide, [thinking]: 'Let others not find this out about me.'

(2) "The Tathāgata is one whose verbal behavior is purified. There is no verbal misconduct on the part of the Tathāgata that he might need to hide, [thinking]: 'Let others not find this out about me.'

(3) "The Tathāgata is one whose mental behavior is purified. There is no mental misconduct on the part of the Tathāgata that he might need to hide, [thinking]: 'Let others not find this out about me.'

(4) "The Tathāgata is one whose livelihood is purified. There is no wrong livelihood on the part of the Tathāgata that he might need to hide, [thinking]: 'Let others not find this out about me.'

"These are the four things that the Tathāgata does not need to hide. And what are the three things about which he is irreproachable? [83]

(5) "The Tathāgata, bhikkhus, is one whose Dhamma is well expounded. In regard to this, I do not see any ground on the basis of which an ascetic, brahmin, deva, Māra, Brahmā, or anyone in the world could reasonably reprove me: 'For such and such reasons, your Dhamma is not well expounded.' Since I do not see any such ground, I dwell secure, fearless, and self-confident.

(6) "I have well proclaimed to my disciples the practice leading to nibbāna in such a way that, practicing in accordance with it [and reaching] the destruction of the taints, they realize for themselves with direct knowledge, in this very life, the taintless liberation of mind, liberation by wisdom, and having entered upon it, dwell in it. In regard to this, I do not see any ground on the basis of which an ascetic, brahmin, deva, Māra, Brahmā, or anyone in the world could reasonably reprove me: 'For such and such reasons, you have not well proclaimed to your disciples[1546] the practice leading to nibbāna in such a way that, practicing in accordance with it [and reaching] the destruction of the taints, they realize for themselves with direct knowledge, in this very life, the taintless liberation of mind, liberation by wisdom, and having entered upon it, dwell in it.' Since I do not see any such ground, I dwell secure, fearless, and self-confident.

(7) "My assembly, bhikkhus, consists of many hundreds of disciples who, with the destruction of the taints, have realized for themselves with direct knowledge, in this very life, the

taintless liberation of mind, liberation by wisdom, and having entered upon it, dwell in it. In regard to this, I do not see any ground on the basis of which an ascetic, brahmin, deva, Māra, Brahmā, or anyone in the world could reasonably reprove me: 'For such and such reasons, it is not the case that your assembly consists of many hundreds of disciples who have destroyed the taints and realized for themselves with direct knowledge, in this very life, the taintless liberation of mind, liberation by wisdom, and having entered upon it, dwell in it.' Since I [84] do not see any such ground, I dwell secure, fearless, and self-confident.

"These are the three things about which the Tathāgata is irreproachable.

"These, bhikkhus, are the four things that the Tathāgata does not have to hide and the three things about which he is irreproachable."

59 (6) Kimbila[1547]

Thus have I heard. On one occasion the Blessed One was dwelling at Kimbilā in a *nicula* grove. Then the Venerable Kimbila approached the Blessed One, paid homage to him, sat down to one side, and said:

"What is the cause and reason why, Bhante, the good Dhamma does not continue long after a Tathāgata has attained final nibbāna?"

"Here, Kimbila, after a Tathāgata has attained final nibbāna, (1) the bhikkhus, bhikkhunīs, male lay followers, and female lay followers dwell without reverence and deference toward the Teacher. (2) They dwell without reverence and deference toward the Dhamma. (3) They dwell without reverence and deference toward the Saṅgha. (4) They dwell without reverence and deference toward the training. (5) They dwell without reverence and deference toward concentration. (6) They dwell without reverence and deference toward heedfulness. (7) They dwell without reverence and deference toward hospitality. This is the cause and reason why the good Dhamma does not continue long after a Tathāgata has attained final nibbāna."

"What is the cause and reason why, Bhante, the good Dhamma continues long after a Tathāgata has attained final nibbāna?"

"Here, Kimbila, after a Tathāgata has attained final nibbāna, (1) the bhikkhus, bhikkhunīs, male lay followers, and female lay followers dwell with reverence and deference toward the Teacher. (2) They dwell with reverence and deference toward the Dhamma. (3) They dwell with reverence and deference toward the Saṅgha. (4) They dwell with reverence and deference toward the training. (5) They dwell with reverence and deference toward concentration. (6) They dwell with reverence and deference toward heedfulness. (7) They dwell with reverence and deference toward hospitality. This is the cause and reason why the good Dhamma continues long after a Tathāgata has attained final nibbāna." [85]

60 (7) Seven Qualities

"Bhikkhus, possessing seven qualities, a bhikkhu can before long, with the destruction of the taints, realize for himself with direct knowledge, in this very life, the taintless liberation of mind, liberation by wisdom, and having entered upon it, dwell in it. What seven?

"Here, a bhikkhu is endowed with faith, virtuous, learned, secluded, energetic, mindful, and wise. Possessing these seven qualities, a bhikkhu can before long, with the destruction of the taints, realize for himself with direct knowledge, in this very life, the taintless liberation of mind, liberation by wisdom, and having entered upon it, can dwell in it."

61 (8) Dozing

Thus have I heard. On one occasion the Blessed One was dwelling among the Bhaggas at Suṃsumāragira, in the deer park at Bhesakalā Grove. Now on that occasion the Venerable Mahāmoggallāna was sitting and dozing[1548] at Kallavālamuttagāma among the Magadhans. With the divine eye, which is purified and surpasses the human, the Blessed One saw the Venerable Mahāmoggallāna sitting and dozing. Then, just as a strong man might extend his drawn-in arm or draw in his extended arm, the Blessed One disappeared from the deer park at Bhesakalā Grove, and reappeared before the Venerable Mahāmoggallāna. The Blessed One sat down on the seat that was prepared for him and said:

"Are you dozing, Moggallāna? Are you dozing, Moggallāna?"

"Yes, Bhante."

(1) "Therefore, Moggallāna, you should not attend to or cultivate the object that you were attending to when you became drowsy. [86] By such means, it is possible that your drowsiness will be abandoned.

(2) "But if you cannot abandon your drowsiness in such a way, you should ponder, examine, and mentally inspect the Dhamma as you have heard it and learned it. By such means, it is possible that your drowsiness will be abandoned.

(3) "But if you cannot abandon your drowsiness in such a way, you should recite in detail the Dhamma as you have heard it and learned it. By such means, it is possible that your drowsiness will be abandoned.

(4) "But if you cannot abandon your drowsiness in such a way, you should pull both ears and rub your limbs with your hands. By such means, it is possible that your drowsiness will be abandoned.

(5) "But if you cannot abandon your drowsiness in such a way, you should get up from your seat, rub your eyes with water, survey all the quarters, and look up at the constellations and stars. By such means, it is possible that your drowsiness will be abandoned.

(6) "But if you cannot abandon your drowsiness in such a way, you should attend to the perception of light; you should undertake the perception of day thus: 'As by day, so at night; as at night, so by day.' Thus, with a mind that is open and uncovered, you should develop a mind imbued with luminosity. By such means, it is possible that your drowsiness will be abandoned. [87]

(7) "But if you cannot abandon your drowsiness in such a way, you should undertake [the exercise of] walking back and forth, perceiving what is behind you and what is in front, with your sense faculties drawn in and your mind collected. By such means, it is possible that your drowsiness will be abandoned.

"But if you cannot abandon your drowsiness in such a way, you should lie down on the right side in the lion's posture, with one foot overlapping the other, mindful and clearly comprehending, after noting in your mind the idea of rising. When you awaken, you should get up quickly, [thinking]: 'I will not be intent on the pleasure of rest, the pleasure of sloth, the pleasure of sleep.' It is in this way, Moggallāna, that you should train yourself.

"Therefore, Moggallāna, you should train yourself thus: 'We will not approach families [for alms] with a head swollen with pride.' It is in this way, Moggallāna, that you should train yourself. It may be, Moggallāna, that a bhikkhu approaches families with a head swollen with pride. Now there are chores to be done in the families, and for this reason, when a bhikkhu turns up, people may not pay attention to him. In such a case the bhikkhu might think: 'Who has turned this family against me? It seems these people have now become indifferent toward me.' In this way, through lack of gain one feels humiliated; when feeling humiliated, one becomes restless; when one is restless, one loses one's restraint. The mind of one without restraint is far from concentration.

"Therefore, Moggallāna, you should train yourself thus: 'We will not engage in contentious talk.' It is in this way that you should train yourself. When there is contentious talk, an excess of words can be expected. When there is an excess of words, one becomes restless; when one is restless, one loses one's restraint. The mind of one without restraint is far from concentration.

"Moggallāna, I do not praise bonding with everyone whatsoever, nor [88] do I praise bonding with no one at all. I do not praise bonding with householders and monastics, but I do praise bonding with quiet and noiseless lodgings far from the flurry of people, remote from human habitation, and suitable for seclusion."

When this was said, the Venerable Mahāmoggallāna said to the Blessed One: [1549] "Briefly, Bhante, how is a bhikkhu liberated in the extinction of craving, best among devas and humans: one who has reached the ultimate conclusion, won ultimate security from bondage, lived the ultimate spiritual life, and gained the ultimate consummation?"

"Here, Moggallāna, a bhikkhu has heard: 'Nothing is worth holding to.' When a bhikkhu has heard: 'Nothing is worth holding to,' he directly knows all things. Having directly known all things, he fully understands all things. Having fully understood all things, whatever feeling he feels—whether pleasant, painful, or neither painful nor pleasant—he dwells contemplating impermanence in those feelings, contemplating fading away in those feelings, contemplating cessation in those feelings, contemplating relinquishment in those feelings. As he dwells contemplating impermanence . . . fading away . . . cessation . . . relinquishment in those feelings, he does not cling to anything in the world. Not clinging, he is not agitated. Being unagitated, he personally attains nibbāna. He understands: 'Destroyed is birth, the spiritual life has been lived, what had to be done has been done, there is no more coming back to any state of being.'

"Briefly, Moggallāna, it is in this way that a bhikkhu is best among devas and humans: one who has reached the ultimate conclusion, won ultimate security from bondage, lived the ultimate spiritual life, and gained the ultimate consummation."

62 (9) Do Not Be Afraid of Merit[1550]

"Bhikkhus, do not be afraid of merit. This is a designation for happiness, [89] that is, merit.

"I recall that for a long time I experienced the desirable, lovely, agreeable result of merit that had been made over a long time. For seven years I developed a mind of loving-kindness. As a consequence, for seven eons of world-dissolution and evolution I did not come back to this world. When the world was dissolving I fared on to the [realm of] streaming radiance. When the world was evolving, I was reborn in an empty mansion of Brahmā.[1551] There I was Brahmā,[1552] the Great Brahmā, the vanquisher, the unvanquished, the universal seer, the wielder of mastery. I was Sakka, ruler of the devas, thirty-six times. Many hundreds of times I was a wheel-turning monarch, a righteous king who ruled by the Dhamma, a conqueror whose rule extended to the four boundaries, one who had attained stability in his country, who possessed the seven gems. I had these seven gems, that is: the wheel-gem, the elephant-gem, the horse-gem, the jewel-gem, the woman-gem, the treasurer-gem, and the adviser-gem as the seventh. I had over a thousand sons who were heroes, vigorous, able to crush the armies of their enemies. I reigned after conquering this earth as far as its ocean boundaries, not by force and weapons but by the Dhamma.[1553]

"If one seeks happiness, look to the result
of merit, [the result of] wholesome deeds.
For seven years, I developed a loving mind, [90]

O bhikkhus, and for seven eons
of dissolution and evolution,
I did not come back again to this world.

"When the world was dissolving,
I fared on to [the realm of] streaming radiance.
When the world was evolving,
I fared on to an empty Brahmā [mansion].

"Seven times I was Great Brahmā,
the wielder of mastery;
thirty-six times I was ruler of the devas,
exercising rulership over the devas.

"I was a wheel-turning monarch,
the lord of Jambudīpa,[1554]
a head-anointed khattiya,
the sovereign among human beings.

"Without force, without weapons,
I conquered this earth.
I ruled it by righteousness,
without violence, by Dhamma,[1555]
exercising rulership by Dhamma
over this sphere of the earth.

"I was born into a rich family,
with abundant wealth and property,
[a family] endowed with all sense pleasures,
and possessing the seven gems.
This is well-taught by the Buddhas,
the benefactors of the world:
this is the cause of greatness by which
one is called a lord of the earth.[1556]

"I was[1557] a king bright with splendor,
one with abundant wealth and commodities.
I was a lord of Jambudīpa,
powerful and glorious.
Who, even though of a low birth,
would not place trust on hearing this? [91]

"Therefore one desiring the good,
aspiring for greatness,
should deeply revere the good Dhamma,
recollecting the Buddhas' teaching."[1558]

63 (10) Wives

On one occasion the Blessed One was dwelling at Sāvatthī in Jeta's Grove, Anāthapiṇḍika's Park. Then, in the morning, the Blessed One dressed, took his bowl and robe, and went to the residence of the householder Anāthapiṇḍika, where he sat down on the seat that was prepared for him.

Now on that occasion, people in Anāthapiṇḍika's residence were making an uproar and a racket. Then the householder Anāthapiṇḍika approached the Blessed One, paid homage to him, and sat down to one side. The Blessed One then said to him:

"Householder, why are people in your residence making such an uproar and a racket? One would think it was fishermen at a haul of fish."

"This, Bhante, is my daughter-in-law Sujātā, who is rich and has been brought here from a rich family. She doesn't obey her father-in-law, her mother-in-law, or her husband. She doesn't even honor, respect, esteem, and venerate the Blessed One."

Then the Blessed One addressed Sujātā: "Come here, Sujātā."

"Yes, Bhante," she replied. She went to the Blessed One, paid homage to him, and sat down to one side. The Blessed One then said to her: [92]

"Sujātā, a man might have seven kinds of wives. What seven? One like a killer, one like a thief, one like a tyrant, one like a mother, one like a sister, one like a friend, and one like a slave. A man might have these seven kinds of wives. Which one are you?"

"Bhante, I do not understand in detail the meaning of this statement that the Blessed One has spoken in brief. Please let the Blessed One teach me the Dhamma in such a way that I might understand in detail the meaning of this statement spoken in brief."

"Then listen and attend closely, Sujātā. I will speak."

"Yes, Bhante," she replied. The Blessed One said this:

"With hateful mind, devoid of sympathy,
lusting for others, despising her husband,
she seeks to kill the one who bought her with wealth:
a wife like this is called a wife and a killer.

"When the woman's husband acquires wealth
by toiling at a craft, trade, or farming,
she tries to steal it, even if [he earns] but little:
a wife like this is called a wife and a thief.

"The lazy glutton, unwilling to work,
harsh, fierce, rough in speech,
a woman who dominates her own supporters:
a wife like this is called a wife and a tyrant. [93]

"One always benevolent and sympathetic,
who guards her husband as a mother her son,
who protects the wealth he earns:
a wife like this is called a wife and a mother.

"She who holds her husband in high regard
as younger sister her elder brother,
conscientious, following her husband's will:
a wife like this is called a wife and a sister.

"One who rejoices when she sees her husband
as if seeing a friend after a long absence;
well raised, virtuous, devoted to her husband:
a wife like this is called a wife and a friend.

"One who remains patient and calm,
when threatened with violence by the rod,[1559]
who tolerates her husband with a mind free of hate,
patient, submissive to her husband's will:
a wife like this is called a wife and a slave.

"The types of wives here called
a killer, a thief, and a tyrant,
immoral, harsh, disrespectful,
with the body's breakup go to hell.

"But the types of wives here called
mother, sister, friend, and slave,
firm in virtue, long restrained,
with the body's breakup go to heaven.

"A man, Sujātā, might have these seven kinds of wives. Now which one are you?" [94]

"Beginning today, Bhante, let the Blessed One consider me a wife who is like a slave."

64 (11) Anger[1560]

"Bhikkhus, there are these seven things that are gratifying and advantageous to an enemy that come upon an angry man or woman. What seven?

(1) "Here, bhikkhus, an enemy wishes for an enemy: 'May he be ugly!' For what reason? An enemy does not delight in the beauty of an enemy. When an angry person is overcome and oppressed by anger, though he may be well bathed, well anointed, with trimmed hair and beard, dressed in white clothes, still, he is ugly. This is the first thing gratifying and advantageous to an enemy that comes upon an angry man or woman.

(2) "Again, an enemy wishes for an enemy: 'May he sleep badly!' For what reason? An enemy does not delight when an enemy sleeps well. When an angry person is overcome and oppressed by anger, though he may sleep on a couch spread with rugs, blankets, and covers, with an excellent covering of antelope hide, with a canopy and red bolsters at both ends, still, he sleeps badly. This is the second thing gratifying and advantageous to an enemy that comes upon an angry man or woman.

(3) "Again, an enemy wishes for an enemy: 'May he not succeed!' For what reason? An enemy does not delight in the success of an enemy. [95] When an angry person is overcome and oppressed by anger, if he gets what is harmful, he thinks: 'I have gotten what is beneficial,' and if he gets what is beneficial, he thinks: 'I have gotten what is harmful.' When, overcome by anger, he gets these things that are diametrically opposed, they lead to his harm and suffering for a long time. This is the third thing gratifying and advantageous to an enemy that comes upon an angry man or woman.

(4) "Again, an enemy wishes for an enemy: 'May he not be

wealthy!' For what reason? An enemy does not delight in the wealth of an enemy. When an angry person is overcome and oppressed by anger, kings appropriate for the royal treasury any wealth he has acquired by energetic striving, amassed by the strength of his arms, earned by the sweat of his brow, righteous wealth righteously gained. This is the fourth thing gratifying and advantageous to an enemy that comes upon an angry man or woman.

(5) "Again, an enemy wishes for an enemy: 'May he not be famous!' For what reason? An enemy does not delight in the fame of an enemy. When an angry person is overcome and oppressed by anger, he loses whatever fame he had acquired through heedfulness. This is the fifth thing gratifying and advantageous to an enemy that comes upon an angry man or woman.

(6) "Again, an enemy wishes for an enemy: 'May he have no friends!' For what reason? An enemy does not delight in an enemy having friends. When an angry person is overcome and oppressed by anger, his friends and companions, relatives and family members, avoid him from afar. This is the sixth thing gratifying and advantageous to an enemy that comes upon an angry man or woman. [96]

(7) "Again, an enemy wishes for an enemy: 'With the breakup of the body, after death, may he be reborn in the plane of misery, in a bad destination, in the lower world, in hell!' For what reason? An enemy does not delight in an enemy's going to a good destination. When an angry person is overcome and oppressed by anger, he engages in misconduct by body, speech, and mind. As a consequence, still overcome by anger, with the breakup of the body, after death, he is reborn in the plane of misery, in a bad destination, in the lower world, in hell. This is the seventh thing gratifying and advantageous to an enemy that comes upon an angry man or woman.

"These are the seven things gratifying and advantageous to an enemy that come upon an angry man or woman."

> The angry person is ugly;
> he also sleeps badly;
> having gained some benefit,
> he takes it to be harmful.[1561]

The angry person,
overcome by anger,
having slain by body and speech,[1562]
incurs the loss of wealth.

Maddened by anger
he acquires a bad reputation.
His relatives, friends, and loved ones
avoid the angry person.

Anger is a cause of harm;
anger stirs up mental turmoil.
People do not recognize the peril
that has arisen from within.

The angry person doesn't know the good;
the angry person doesn't see the Dhamma.
There is just blindness and dense gloom
when anger overcomes a person. [97]

When an angry person causes damage,
whether easily or with difficulty,
later, when the anger has vanished,
he is tormented as if burnt by fire.

He shows recalcitrance
as a fire does a smoky crest.
When his anger spreads outward,
people become angry on his account.[1563]

He has no shame or fear of wrong,
his speech is not respectful;
one overcome by anger
has no island [of safety] at all.

I will tell you about the deeds
that produce torment.
Listen to them as they are,[1564]
remote from those that are righteous:

An angry person slays his father;
an angry person slays his own mother;
an angry person slays a brahmin;[1565]
an angry person slays a worldling.

The angry worldling slays his mother,
the good woman who gave him life,
the one by whom he was nurtured
and who showed him this world.

Those beings, like oneself,
each hold their self most dear;
yet those who are angry kill themselves in various ways[1566]
when they are distraught about diverse matters.

Some kill themselves with a sword;
some who are distraught swallow poison;
some hang themselves with a rope;
some [jump] into a mountain gorge. [98]

Deeds that involve destroying growth[1567]
and deeds that cause their own death:
when doing such deeds they do not know
that defeat is born of anger.

Thus death's snare hidden in the heart
has taken the form of anger.
One should cut it off by self-control,
wisdom, energy, and [right] view.

The wise person should eradicate
this one unwholesome [quality].[1568]
In such a way one should train in the Dhamma:
do not yield to recalcitrance.

Free from anger, their misery gone,
free from delusion,[1569] no longer avid,
tamed, having abandoned anger,
the taintless ones attain nibbāna.[1570] [99]

II. The Great Chapter

65 (1) Moral Shame[1571]

"Bhikkhus, (1) when there is no sense of moral shame and moral dread, for one deficient in a sense of moral shame and moral dread, (2) restraint of the sense faculties lacks its proximate cause. When there is no restraint of the sense faculties, for one deficient in restraint of the sense faculties, (3) virtuous behavior lacks its proximate cause. When there is no virtuous behavior, for one deficient in virtuous behavior, (4) right concentration lacks its proximate cause. When there is no right concentration, for one deficient in right concentration, (5) the knowledge and vision of things as they really are lacks its proximate cause. When there is no knowledge and vision of things as they really are, for one deficient in the knowledge and vision of things as they really are, (6) disenchantment and dispassion lack their proximate cause. When there is no disenchantment and dispassion, for one deficient in disenchantment and dispassion, (7) the knowledge and vision of liberation lacks its proximate cause.

"Suppose there is a tree deficient in branches and foliage. Then its shoots do not grow to fullness; also its bark, softwood, and heartwood do not grow to fullness. So too, when there is no sense of moral shame and moral dread, for one deficient in a sense of moral shame and moral dread, restraint of the sense faculties lacks its proximate cause. When there is no restraint of the sense faculties . . . the knowledge and vision of liberation lacks its proximate cause.

"Bhikkhus, (1) when there is a sense of moral shame and moral dread, for one possessing a sense of moral shame and moral dread, (2) restraint of the sense faculties possesses its proximate cause. When there is restraint of the sense faculties, for one who exercises restraint of the sense faculties, (3) virtuous behavior possesses its proximate cause. When there is virtuous behavior, for one whose behavior is virtuous, (4) right concentration possesses its proximate cause. When there is right concentration, for one possessing right concentration, (5) the knowledge and vision of things as they really are possesses its proximate cause. When there is the knowledge and vision of things as they really are, for one possessing the knowledge and vision of things as they really are, (6) disenchantment and dispassion possess their proximate cause. When there is disenchantment and dispassion, for one possessing disenchantment and dispassion, (7) the knowledge and vision of liberation possesses its proximate cause.

"Suppose there is a tree possessing branches and foliage. Then its shoots grow to fullness; also its bark, softwood, and heartwood grow to fullness. So too, when there is a sense of moral shame and moral dread, for one possessing a sense of moral shame and moral dread, restraint of the sense faculties possesses its proximate cause. When there is restraint of the sense faculties . . . the knowledge and vision of liberation possesses its proximate cause." [100]

66 (2) Seven Suns

On one occasion[1572] the Blessed One was dwelling at Vesālī in Ambapālī's Grove. There the Blessed One addressed the bhikkhus: "Bhikkhus!"

"Venerable sir!" those bhikkhus replied. The Blessed One said this:

"Bhikkhus, conditioned phenomena are impermanent; conditioned phenomena are unstable; conditioned phenomena are unreliable. It is enough to become disenchanted with all conditioned phenomena, enough to become dispassionate toward them, enough to be liberated from them.

"Bhikkhus, Sineru, the king of mountains, is 84,000 *yojanas* in length and 84,000 *yojanas* in width; it is submerged 84,000 *yojanas* in the great ocean and rises up 84,000 *yojanas* above the great ocean.[1573]

(1) "There comes a time, bhikkhus, when rain does not fall for many years, for many hundreds of years, for many thousands of years, for many hundreds of thousands of years. When rain does not fall, seed life and vegetation, medicinal plants, grasses, and giant trees of the forest wither and dry up and no longer exist. So impermanent are conditioned phenomena, so unstable, so unreliable. It is enough to become disenchanted with all conditioned phenomena, enough to become dispassionate toward them, enough to be liberated from them.

(2) "There comes a time when, after a long time, a second sun appears. With the appearance of the second sun, the small rivers and lakes dry up and evaporate and no longer [101] exist.

So impermanent are conditioned phenomena. . . . It is enough to be liberated from them.

(3) "There comes a time when, after a long time, a third sun appears. With the appearance of the third sun, the great rivers—the Ganges, the Yamunā, the Aciravatī, the Sarabhū, and the Mahī—dry up and evaporate and no longer exist. So impermanent are conditioned phenomena. . . . It is enough to be liberated from them.

(4) "There comes a time when, after a long time, a fourth sun appears. With the appearance of the fourth sun, the great lakes from which those great rivers originate—Anotatta, Sīhapapāta, Rathakāra, Kaṇṇamuṇḍa, Kuṇāla, Chaddanta, and Mandākinī—dry up and evaporate and no longer exist. So impermanent are conditioned phenomena. . . . It is enough to be liberated from them.

(5) "There comes a time when, after a long time, a fifth sun appears. With the appearance of the fifth sun, the waters in the great ocean sink by a hundred *yojanas*, two hundred *yojanas* . . . three hundred *yojanas* . . . seven hundred *yojanas*. The water left in the great ocean stands at the height of seven palm trees, at the height of six palm trees . . . five palm trees . . . four palm trees . . . three palm trees . . . two palm trees [102] . . . a mere palm tree. The water left in the great ocean stands at the height of seven fathoms . . . six fathoms . . . five fathoms . . . four fathoms . . . three fathoms . . . two fathoms . . . a fathom . . . half a fathom . . . up to the waist . . . up to the knees . . . up to the ankles. Just as, in the autumn, when thick drops of rain are pouring down, the waters stand in the hoof prints of cattle here and there, so the waters left in the great ocean will stand here and there [in pools] the size of the hoof prints of cattle. With the appearance of the fifth sun, the water left in the great ocean is not enough even to reach the joints of one's fingers. So impermanent are conditioned phenomena. . . . It is enough to be liberated from them.

(6) "There comes a time when, after a long time, a sixth sun appears. With the appearance of the sixth sun, this great earth and Sineru, the king of mountains, smoke, fume, and smolder. Just as a potter's fire, when kindled, first smokes, fumes, and smolders, so with the appearance of the sixth sun, this great earth and Sineru, the king of mountains, smoke, fume, and

smolder. So impermanent are conditioned phenomena. . . . It is enough to be liberated from them.

(7) "There comes a time when, after a long time, a seventh sun appears. [103] With the appearance of the seventh sun, this great earth and Sineru, the king of mountains, burst into flames, blaze up brightly, and become one mass of flame. As the great earth and Sineru are blazing and burning, the flame, cast up by the wind, rises even to the brahmā world. As Sineru is blazing and burning, as it is undergoing destruction and being overcome by a great mass of heat, mountain peaks of a hundred *yojanas* disintegrate; mountain peaks of two hundred *yojanas* . . . three hundred *yojanas* . . . four hundred *yojanas* . . . five hundred *yojanas* disintegrate.

"When this great earth and Sineru, the king of mountains, are blazing and burning, neither ashes nor soot are seen. Just as, when ghee or oil are blazing and burning, neither ashes nor soot are seen, so it is when this great earth and Sineru, the king of mountains, are blazing and burning. So impermanent are conditioned phenomena, so unstable, so unreliable. It is enough to become disenchanted with all conditioned phenomena, enough to become dispassionate toward them, enough to be liberated from them.

"Bhikkhus, who except those who have seen the truth[1574] would think or believe:[1575] 'This great earth and Sineru, the king of mountains, will burn up, be destroyed, and will no longer exist'?

"In the past, bhikkhus, there was a teacher named Sunetta, the founder of a spiritual sect, one without lust for sensual pleasures.[1576] The teacher Sunetta [104] had many hundreds of disciples to whom he taught a Dhamma for companionship with the brahmā world. When he was teaching, those who understood his teaching completely were, with the breakup of the body, after death, reborn in a good destination, in the brahmā world. But of those who did not understand his teaching completely, some were reborn in companionship with the devas who control what is created by others;[1577] some in companionship with the devas who delight in creation; some in companionship with the Tusita devas; some in companionship with the Yāma devas; some in companionship with the Tāvatiṃsa devas; some in companionship with the devas [ruled by] the four great kings.

Some were reborn in companionship with affluent khattiyas; some in companionship with affluent brahmins; some in companionship with affluent householders.

"Then, bhikkhus, it occurred to the teacher Sunetta: 'It isn't fitting that I should have exactly the same future destination as my disciples. Let me develop loving-kindness further. Then for seven years the teacher Sunetta developed a mind of loving-kindness. As a consequence, for seven eons of world-dissolution and evolution he did not come back to this world. When the world was dissolving, [105] he moved on to the [realm of] streaming radiance. When the world was evolving, he was reborn in an empty mansion of Brahmā.[1578]

"There he was Brahmā, the Great Brahmā, the vanquisher, the unvanquished, the universal seer, the wielder of mastery. He was Sakka, ruler of the devas, thirty-six times. Many hundreds of times he was a wheel-turning monarch, a righteous king who ruled by the Dhamma, a conqueror whose rule extended to the four boundaries, one who had attained stability in his country, who possessed the seven gems. He had over a thousand sons who were heroes, vigorous, able to crush the armies of their enemies. He reigned after he had conquered this earth as far as its ocean boundaries, not by force and weapons but by the Dhamma.

"Bhikkhus, though he had such a long life span and continued on for such a long time, the teacher Sunetta was still not freed from birth, from old age and death, from sorrow, lamentation, pain, dejection, and anguish. He was not freed from suffering, I say. For what reason? Because he did not understand and penetrate four things. What four? Noble virtuous behavior, noble concentration, noble wisdom, and noble liberation.

"Noble virtuous behavior, bhikkhus, has been understood and penetrated. Noble concentration has been understood and penetrated. Noble wisdom has been understood and penetrated. Noble liberation has been understood and penetrated. Craving for existence has been cut off; the conduit to existence has been destroyed; now there is no more renewed existence."[1579] [106]

This is what the Blessed One said. Having said this, the Fortunate One, the Teacher, further said this:

"Virtuous behavior, concentration, wisdom,
and unsurpassed liberation:

these things the illustrious Gotama
understood by himself.

"Having directly known these things,
the Buddha taught the Dhamma to the bhikkhus.
The Teacher, the end-maker of suffering,
the One with Vision, has attained nibbāna."

67 (3) Simile of the Fortress

"Bhikkhus, when a king's frontier fortress is well provided with seven appurtenances of a fortress and readily gains, without trouble or difficulty, four kinds of food, it can be called a king's frontier fortress that cannot be assailed by external foes and enemies.

"What are the seven kinds of appurtenances of a fortress with which it is well provided?

(1) "Here, bhikkhus, in the king's frontier fortress the pillar has a deep base and is securely planted, immobile, unshakable. A king's frontier fortress is well provided with this first appurtenance for protecting its inhabitants and for warding off outsiders.

(2) "Again, in the king's frontier fortress the moat is dug deep and wide. A king's frontier fortress is well provided with this second appurtenance for protecting its inhabitants and for warding off outsiders. [107]

(3) "Again, in the king's frontier fortress the patrol path is high and wide. A king's frontier fortress is well provided with this third appurtenance for protecting its inhabitants and for warding off outsiders.

(4) "Again, in the king's frontier fortress many weapons are stored, both missiles and hand weapons.[1580] A king's frontier fortress is well provided with this fourth appurtenance for protecting its inhabitants and for warding off outsiders.

(5) "Again, in the king's frontier fortress many kinds of troops reside, that is, elephant troops, cavalry, charioteers, archers, standard bearers, camp marshals, food servers, *ugga*-caste warriors, front-line commandoes, great-bull warriors, attack soldiers, shield-bearing soldiers, domestic-slave soldiers.[1581] A king's frontier fortress is well provided with this fifth appurtenance for protecting its inhabitants and for warding off outsiders.

(6) "Again, in the king's frontier fortress the gatekeeper is

wise, competent, and intelligent, one who keeps out strangers and admits acquaintances. A king's frontier fortress is well provided with this sixth appurtenance for protecting its inhabitants and for warding off outsiders.

(7) "Again, in the king's frontier fortress the rampart is high and wide, covered over by a coat of plaster. A king's frontier fortress is well provided with this seventh appurtenance for protecting its inhabitants and for warding off outsiders. [108]

"It is well provided with these seven kinds of appurtenances. And what are the four kinds of food that it readily gains, without trouble or difficulty?

(1) "Here, bhikkhus, in the king's frontier fortress much grass, firewood, and water are stored up for the delight, relief,[1582] and ease of its inhabitants and for warding off outsiders.

(2) "Again, in the king's frontier fortress much rice and barley are stored up for the delight, relief, and ease of its inhabitants and for warding off outsiders.

(3) "Again, in the king's frontier fortress many foodstuffs—sesame, green gram, and beans[1583]—are stored up for the delight, relief, and ease of its inhabitants and for warding off outsiders.

(4) "Again, in the king's frontier fortress many medicaments—ghee, butter, oil, honey, molasses, and salt—are stored up for the delight, relief, and ease of its inhabitants and for warding off outsiders.

"These are the four foods that it readily gains, without trouble or difficulty.

"When, bhikkhus, a king's frontier fortress is well provided with these seven appurtenances of a fortress, and when it readily gains, without trouble or difficulty, these four kinds of food, it can be said that the king's frontier fortress cannot be assailed by external foes and enemies.

"So too, bhikkhus, when a noble disciple possesses seven good qualities, and [109] when he gains at will, without trouble or difficulty, the four jhānas that constitute the higher mind and are pleasant dwellings in this very life, he is then called a noble disciple who cannot be assailed by Māra, who cannot be assailed by the Evil One.

"What are the seven good qualities that he possesses?

(1) "Just as, bhikkhus, the pillar in the king's frontier fortress

has a deep base and is securely planted, immobile and unshakable, for the purpose of protecting its inhabitants and for warding off outsiders, so too the noble disciple is endowed with faith. He places faith in the enlightenment of the Tathāgata thus: 'The Blessed One is an arahant, perfectly enlightened, accomplished in true knowledge and conduct, fortunate, knower of the world, unsurpassed trainer of persons to be tamed, teacher of devas and humans, the Enlightened One, the Blessed One.' With faith as his pillar, the noble disciple abandons the unwholesome and develops the wholesome, abandons what is blameworthy and develops what is blameless, and maintains himself in purity. He possesses this first good quality.

(2) "Just as the moat in the king's frontier fortress is dug deep and wide for the purpose of protecting its inhabitants and for warding off outsiders, so too a noble disciple has a sense of moral shame; he is ashamed of bodily, verbal, and mental misconduct; he is ashamed of acquiring bad unwholesome qualities. With a sense of moral shame as the moat, the noble disciple abandons the unwholesome and develops the wholesome, abandons what is blameworthy and develops what is blameless, and maintains himself in purity. He possesses this second good quality.

(3) "Just as the patrol path in the king's frontier fortress is high and wide for the purpose of protecting its inhabitants and for warding off outsiders, so too a noble disciple dreads wrongdoing; he dreads bodily, verbal, and mental misconduct; he dreads acquiring bad unwholesome qualities. With moral dread as the patrol path, the noble disciple abandons the unwholesome and develops [110] the wholesome, abandons what is blameworthy and develops what is blameless, and maintains himself in purity. He possesses this third good quality.

(4) "Just as many weapons, both missiles and hand weapons, are stored in the king's frontier fortress for the purpose of protecting its inhabitants and for warding off outsiders, so too a noble disciple has learned much, remembers what he has learned, and accumulates what he has learned. Those teachings that are good in the beginning, good in the middle, and good in the end, with the right meaning and phrasing, which proclaim the perfectly complete and pure spiritual life—such teachings as these he has learned much of, retained in mind, recited

verbally, mentally investigated, and penetrated well by view. With learning as his weaponry, the noble disciple abandons the unwholesome and develops the wholesome, abandons what is blameworthy and develops what is blameless, and maintains himself in purity. He possesses this fourth good quality.

(5) "Just as many kinds of troops reside in the king's frontier fortress, that is, elephant troops . . . domestic-slave soldiers, for protecting its inhabitants and for warding off outsiders, so too a noble disciple has aroused energy for abandoning unwholesome qualities and acquiring wholesome qualities; he is strong, firm in exertion, not casting off the duty of cultivating wholesome qualities. With energy as his troops, the noble disciple abandons the unwholesome and develops the wholesome, abandons what is blameworthy and develops what is blameless, and maintains himself in purity. He possesses this fifth good quality.

(6) "Just as the gatekeeper in the king's frontier fortress is wise, competent, and intelligent, one who keeps out strangers and admits acquaintances, for protecting its inhabitants and for warding off outsiders, [111] so too a noble disciple is mindful, possessing supreme mindfulness and alertness, one who remembers and recollects what was done and said long ago. With mindfulness as his gatekeeper, the noble disciple abandons the unwholesome and develops the wholesome, abandons what is blameworthy and develops what is blameless, and maintains himself in purity. He possesses this sixth good quality.

(7) "Just as the rampart in the king's frontier fortress is high and wide, covered over by a coat of plaster, for protecting its inhabitants and for warding off outsiders, so too a noble disciple is wise; he possesses the wisdom that discerns arising and passing away, which is noble and penetrative and leads to the complete destruction of suffering. With wisdom as his coat of plaster, the noble disciple abandons the unwholesome and develops the wholesome, abandons what is blameworthy and develops what is blameless, and maintains himself in purity. He possesses this seventh good quality.

"He possesses these seven good qualities.[1584]

"And what are the four jhānas that constitute the higher mind and are pleasant dwellings in this very life, which he gains at will, without trouble or difficulty?

(1) "Just as, bhikkhus, much grass, firewood, and water are stored up in the king's frontier fortress for the delight, relief, and comfort of its inhabitants and for warding off outsiders, so too, secluded from sensual pleasures, secluded from unwholesome states, a noble disciple enters and dwells in the first jhāna, which consists of rapture and pleasure born of seclusion, accompanied by thought and examination—for his own delight, relief, and comfort, and for entering upon nibbāna.

(2) "Just as [112] much rice and barley are stored up in the king's frontier fortress for the delight, relief, and comfort of its inhabitants and for warding off outsiders, so too, with the subsiding of thought and examination, a noble disciple enters and dwells in the second jhāna, which has internal placidity and unification of mind and consists of rapture and pleasure born of concentration, without thought and examination—for his own delight, relief, and comfort, and for entering upon nibbāna.

(3) "Just as many foodstuffs—sesame, green gram, and beans—are stored up in the king's frontier fortress for the delight, relief, and comfort of its inhabitants and for warding off outsiders, so too, with the fading away as well of rapture, a noble disciple dwells equanimous and, mindful and clearly comprehending, he experiences pleasure with the body; he enters and dwells in the third jhāna of which the noble ones declare: 'He is equanimous, mindful, one who dwells happily'—for his own delight, relief, and comfort, and for entering upon nibbāna.

(4) "Just as many medicaments—ghee, butter, oil, honey, molasses, and salt—are stored up in the king's frontier fortress for the delight, relief, and comfort of its inhabitants and for warding off outsiders, so too, with the abandoning of pleasure and pain, and with the previous passing away of joy and dejection, a noble disciple enters and dwells in the fourth jhāna, neither painful nor pleasant, which has purification of mindfulness by equanimity—for his own delight, relief, and comfort, and for entering upon nibbāna.

"These are the four jhānas that constitute the higher mind and are pleasant dwellings in this very life, which he gains at will, without trouble or difficulty. [113]

"When, bhikkhus, a noble disciple possesses these seven good qualities, and when he gains at will, without trouble or difficulty, these four jhānas that constitute the higher mind and are pleasant dwellings in this very life, he is then called a noble disciple who cannot be assailed by Māra, who cannot be assailed by the Evil One."

68 (4) One Who Knows the Dhamma

"Bhikkhus, possessing seven qualities, a bhikkhu is worthy of gifts, worthy of hospitality, worthy of offerings, worthy of reverential salutation, an unsurpassed field of merit for the world. What seven? Here, a bhikkhu is one who knows the Dhamma, who knows the meaning, who knows himself, who knows moderation, who knows the proper time, who knows the assembly, and who knows the superior and inferior kinds of persons.

(1) "And how is a bhikkhu one who knows the Dhamma? Here, a bhikkhu knows the Dhamma: the discourses, mixed prose and verse, expositions, verses, inspired utterances, quotations, birth stories, marvelous accounts, and questions-and-answers. If a bhikkhu did not know the Dhamma—the discourses . . . questions-and-answers—he would not be called 'one who knows the Dhamma.' But because he knows the Dhamma—the discourses . . . questions-and-answers—he is called 'one who knows the Dhamma.' Thus he is one who knows the Dhamma.

(2) "And how is a bhikkhu one who knows the meaning? Here, a bhikkhu knows the meaning of this and that statement thus: 'This is the meaning of this statement; this is the meaning of that statement.' If a bhikkhu did not know the meaning of this and that statement thus . . . he would not be called 'one who knows the meaning.' But because he knows the meaning of this and that statement thus: 'This is the meaning of this statement; [114] this is the meaning of that statement,' he is called 'one who knows the meaning.' Thus he is one who knows the Dhamma and one who knows the meaning.

(3) "And how is a bhikkhu one who knows himself? Here, a bhikkhu knows himself thus: 'I have so much faith, virtuous behavior, learning, generosity, wisdom, and discernment.' If a bhikkhu did not know himself thus: 'I have so much faith . . . and discernment,' he would not be called 'one who knows himself.' But because he knows himself thus: 'I have so much faith . . . and discernment,' he is called 'one who knows himself.' Thus he is one who knows the Dhamma, one who knows the meaning, and one who knows himself.

(4) "And how is a bhikkhu one who knows moderation? Here, a bhikkhu knows moderation in accepting robes, almsfood, lodgings, and medicines and provisions for the sick. If a bhikkhu did not know moderation in accepting robes . . . and provisions for the sick, he would not be called 'one who knows moderation.' But because he knows moderation in accepting robes, almsfood, lodgings, and medicines and provisions for the sick, he is called 'one who knows moderation.' Thus he is one who knows the Dhamma, one who knows the meaning, one who knows himself, and one who knows moderation.

(5) "And how is a bhikkhu one who knows the proper time? Here, a bhikkhu knows the proper time thus: 'This is the time for learning, this is the time for questioning, this is the time for exertion, this is the time for seclusion.' If a bhikkhu did not know the proper time—'This is the time for learning . . . this is the time for seclusion'—he would not be called 'one who knows the proper time.' But because he knows the proper time—'This is the time for learning . . . this is the time for seclusion'—he is called 'one who knows the proper time.' Thus he is one who knows the Dhamma, one who knows the meaning, one who knows himself, one who knows moderation, and one who knows the proper time.

(6) "And how is a bhikkhu one who knows the assembly? Here, a bhikkhu knows the assembly: 'This is an assembly of khattiyas, this is an assembly of brahmins, this is an assembly of householders, this is an assembly of ascetics. Among these, one should approach [this assembly] in such a way; [115] one should stop in such a way; one should act in such a way; one should sit down in such a way; one should speak in such a way; one should remain silent in such a way.' If a bhikkhu did not know the assembly: 'This is an assembly of khattiyas . . . of ascetics. Among these, one should approach [this assembly] in such a way . . . one should remain silent in such a way'—he would not be called 'one who knows the assembly.' But because he knows the assembly—'This is an assembly of khattiyas . . . of ascetics. Among these, one should approach [this assembly] in such a way . . . one should remain silent in such a way'—he is called 'one who knows the assembly.' Thus he is one who knows the Dhamma, one who knows the meaning, one who knows himself, one who knows moderation, one who knows the proper time, and one who knows the assembly.

(7) "And how is a bhikkhu one who knows the superior and inferior kinds of persons? Here, a bhikkhu understands persons in terms of pairs.[1585]

(i) "Two persons: one wants to see the noble ones; one does not want to see the noble ones. The person who does not want to see the noble ones is in that respect blameworthy; the person who wants to see the noble ones is in that respect praiseworthy.

(ii) "Two persons who want to see the noble ones: one wants to hear the good Dhamma; one does not want to hear the good Dhamma. The person who does not want to hear the good Dhamma is in that respect blameworthy; the person who wants to hear the good Dhamma is in that respect praiseworthy.

(iii) "Two persons who want to hear the good Dhamma: one listens to the Dhamma with eager ears; one does not listen to the Dhamma with eager ears. The person who does not listen to the Dhamma with eager ears is in that respect blameworthy; the person [116] who listens to the Dhamma with eager ears is in that respect praiseworthy.

(iv) "Two persons who listen to the Dhamma with eager ears: one, having heard the Dhamma, retains it in mind; one, having heard the Dhamma, does not retain it in mind. The person who, having heard the Dhamma, does not retain it in mind is in that respect blameworthy; the person who, having heard the Dhamma, retains it in mind is in that respect praiseworthy.

(v) "Two persons who, having heard the Dhamma, retain it in mind: one examines the meaning of the teachings that have been retained in mind; one does not examine the meaning of the teachings that have been retained in mind. The person who does not examine the meaning of the teachings that have been retained in mind is in that respect blameworthy; the person who examines the meaning of the teachings that have been retained in mind is in that respect praiseworthy.

(vi) "Two persons who examine the meaning of the teachings that have been retained in mind: one has understood the meaning and the Dhamma and then practices in accordance with the Dhamma; one has not understood the meaning and the Dhamma and does not practice in accordance with the Dhamma. The person who has not understood the meaning and the Dhamma and does not practice in accordance with the Dhamma is in that respect blameworthy; the person who has understood the meaning and the Dhamma and then practices in accordance with the Dhamma is in that respect praiseworthy.

(vii) "Two persons who have understood the meaning and the Dhamma and then practice in accordance with the Dhamma: one is practicing for his own welfare but not for the welfare of others; one is practicing for his own welfare and for the welfare of others. The person who is practicing for his own welfare but not for the welfare of others is in that respect blameworthy; the person who is practicing for his own welfare and for the welfare of others is in that respect praiseworthy.

"It is in this way that a bhikkhu understands persons in terms of pairs. It is in this way that a bhikkhu is one who knows the superior and inferior kinds of persons. [117]

"Possessing these seven qualities, a bhikkhu is worthy of gifts, worthy of hospitality, worthy of offerings, worthy of reverential salutation, an unsurpassed field of merit for the world."

69 (5) Pāricchattaka

(1) "Bhikkhus, when the foliage of the Tāvatiṃsa devas' *pāricchattaka* coral tree has turned yellow,[1586] the Tāvatiṃsa devas are elated, [thinking]: 'The foliage of the *pāricchattaka* coral tree now has turned yellow. Now it won't be long before its foliage will fall.'

(2) "When the foliage of the Tāvatiṃsa devas' *pāricchattaka* coral tree has fallen, the Tāvatiṃsa devas are elated, [thinking]: 'The foliage of the *pāricchattaka* coral tree now has fallen. Now it won't be long before its floral initiation occurs.'[1587]

(3) "When the Tāvatiṃsa devas' *pāricchattaka* coral tree has had its floral initiation, the Tāvatiṃsa devas are elated, [thinking]: 'The *pāricchattaka* coral tree now has had its floral initiation. Now it won't be long before its floral differentiation occurs.'[1588]

(4) "When the Tāvatiṃsa devas' *pāricchattaka* coral tree has had its floral differentiation, the Tāvatiṃsa devas are elated, [thinking]: 'The *pāricchattaka* coral tree now has had its floral differentiation. Now it won't be long before its bud formation occurs.'[1589]

(5) "When the Tāvatiṃsa devas' *pāricchattaka* coral tree has had its bud formation, the Tāvatiṃsa devas are elated, [thinking]: 'The *pāricchattaka* coral tree now has had its bud formation. Now it won't be long before [118] its bud burst occurs.'[1590]

(6) "When the Tāvatiṃsa devas' *pāricchattaka* coral tree has had its bud burst, the Tāvatiṃsa devas are elated, [thinking]: 'The *pāricchattaka* coral tree now has had its bud burst. Now it won't be long before it fully blossoms.'[1591]

(7) "When the Tāvatiṃsa devas' *pāricchattaka* coral tree has fully blossomed, the Tāvatiṃsa devas are elated, and they spend four celestial months at the foot of the *pāricchattaka* coral tree enjoying themselves furnished and endowed with the five objects of sensual pleasure. When the *pāricchattaka* coral tree has fully blossomed, a radiance suffuses the area fifty *yojanas* all around and a fragrance is carried along with the wind for a hundred *yojanas*. This is the majesty of the *pāricchattaka* coral tree.

(1) "So too, bhikkhus, when a noble disciple intends to go forth from the household life into homelessness, on that occasion he is one whose foliage has turned yellow, like the Tāvatiṃsa devas' *pāricchattaka* coral tree.[1592]

(2) "When a noble disciple has shaved off his hair and beard, put on ochre robes, and gone forth from the household life into homelessness, on that occasion he is one whose foliage has fallen, like the Tāvatiṃsa devas' *pāricchattaka* coral tree.

(3) "When, secluded from sensual pleasures, secluded from unwholesome states, a noble disciple enters and dwells in the first jhāna . . . on that occasion his floral initiation has occurred, like the Tāvatiṃsa devas' *pāricchattaka* coral tree.

(4) "When, with the subsiding of thought and examination, a noble disciple enters and dwells in the second jhāna . . . on that occasion his floral differentiation has occurred, like the Tāvatiṃsa devas' *pāricchattaka* coral tree.

(5) "When, [119] with the fading away as well of rapture, a noble disciple . . . enters and dwells in the third jhāna . . . on that occasion his bud formation has occurred, like the Tāvatiṃsa devas' *pāricchattaka* coral tree.

(6) "When, with the abandoning of pleasure and pain, and with the previous passing away of joy and dejection, a noble disciple enters and dwells in the fourth jhāna . . . on that occasion his buds have burst open, like the Tāvatiṃsa devas' *pāricchattaka* coral tree.

(7) "When, with the destruction of the taints, a noble disciple has realized for himself with direct knowledge, in this very life, the taintless liberation of mind, liberation by wisdom, and hav-

ing entered upon it, dwells in it, on that occasion he has fully blossomed, like the Tāvatiṃsa devas' *pāricchattaka* coral tree.

"On that occasion, bhikkhus, the earth-dwelling devas raise a cry: 'This Venerable So-and-So, the pupil of that Venerable One, went forth from the household life into homelessness from such and such a village or town, and now, with the destruction of the taints, he has realized for himself with direct knowledge, in this very life, the taintless liberation of mind, liberation by wisdom, and having entered upon it, dwells in it.' Having heard the cry of the earth-dwelling devas, the devas [ruled by] the four great kings raise a cry.... Having heard the cry of the devas [ruled by] the four great kings, the Tāvatiṃsa devas ... the Yāma devas ... the Tusita devas ... the devas who delight in creation ... the devas who control what is created by others ... the devas of Brahmā's company raise a cry: 'This Venerable So-and-So ... has realized for himself with direct knowledge, in this very life, the taintless liberation of mind, liberation by wisdom, and having entered upon it, dwells in it.' Thus [120] at that moment, at that instant, at that second, the cry spreads as far as the brahma world.[1593] This is the spiritual majesty of a bhikkhu whose taints are destroyed."

70 (6) Honor

Then, when the Venerable Sāriputta was alone in seclusion, the following course of thought arose in his mind: "What should a bhikkhu honor, respect, and dwell in dependence on so that he might abandon the unwholesome and develop the wholesome?"

It then occurred to him: "(1) A bhikkhu should honor, respect, and dwell in dependence on the Teacher so that he might abandon the unwholesome and develop the wholesome. (2) He should honor, respect, and dwell in dependence on the Dhamma ... (3) ... the Saṅgha ... (4) ... the training ... (5) ... concentration ... (6) ... heedfulness ... (7) ... hospitality so that he might abandon the unwholesome and develop the wholesome."

Then it occurred to the Venerable Sāriputta: "These qualities have been purified and cleansed in me. Let me go to the Blessed One and report them to him. Thus these qualities will be purified in me and will be more widely known as purified.[1594]

Suppose a man would find a gold nugget, purified and cleansed. It might occur to him: 'This golden nugget of mine is purified and cleansed. Let me go and show it to the goldsmiths. Then, when this golden nugget of mine has been shown to the goldsmiths, it will be purified and will be more widely known as purified.' So too these qualities have been purified and cleansed in me. Let me go to the Blessed One and report them to him. Thus these qualities will be purified in me and will be more widely known as purified."

Then, [121] in the evening, the Venerable Sāriputta emerged from seclusion and approached the Blessed One. He paid homage to the Blessed One, sat down to one side, and said:

"Here, Bhante, when I was alone in seclusion, the following course of thought arose in my mind . . . [He here relates the entire course of thought stated above, down to:] . . . Thus these qualities will be purified in me [122] and will be more widely known as purified."

"Good, good, Sāriputta! A bhikkhu should honor, respect, and dwell in dependence on the Teacher so that he might abandon the unwholesome and develop the wholesome. He should honor, respect, and dwell in dependence on the Dhamma . . . the Saṅgha . . . the training . . . concentration . . . heedfulness . . . hospitality so that he might abandon the unwholesome and develop the wholesome."

When this was said, the Venerable Sāriputta said to the Blessed One: "Bhante, I understand in detail thus the meaning of this statement that the Blessed One has spoken in brief.

"It is impossible, Bhante, that a bhikkhu who lacks reverence for the Teacher could have reverence for the Dhamma. The bhikkhu who (1) lacks reverence for the Teacher (2) also lacks reverence for the Dhamma.

"It is impossible, Bhante, that a bhikkhu who lacks reverence for the Teacher and the Dhamma could have reverence for the Saṅgha. The bhikkhu who lacks reverence for the Teacher and the Dhamma (3) also lacks reverence for the Saṅgha.

"It is impossible, Bhante, that a bhikkhu who lacks reverence for the Teacher, the Dhamma, and the Saṅgha could have reverence for the training. The bhikkhu who lacks reverence for the Teacher, the Dhamma, and the Saṅgha (4) also lacks reverence for the training.

"It is impossible, Bhante, that a bhikkhu who lacks reverence for the Teacher, the Dhamma, and the Saṅgha, and the training could have reverence for concentration. The bhikkhu who lacks reverence for the Teacher, the Dhamma, and the Saṅgha, and the training (5) also lacks reverence for concentration.

"It is impossible, Bhante, that a bhikkhu who lacks reverence for the Teacher, the Dhamma, and the Saṅgha, the training, and concentration could have reverence for heedfulness. The bhikkhu who lacks reverence for the Teacher, the Dhamma, and the Saṅgha, the training, and concentration [123] (6) also lacks reverence for heedfulness.

"It is impossible, Bhante, that a bhikkhu who lacks reverence for the Teacher, the Dhamma, and the Saṅgha, the training, concentration, and heedfulness could have reverence for hospitality. The bhikkhu who lacks reverence for the Teacher, the Dhamma, and the Saṅgha, the training, concentration, and heedfulness (7) also lacks reverence for hospitality.

"It is impossible, Bhante, that a bhikkhu who has reverence for the Teacher could lack reverence for the Dhamma. The bhikkhu who (1) has reverence for the Teacher (2) also has reverence for the Dhamma.

"It is impossible, Bhante, that a bhikkhu who has reverence for the Teacher and the Dhamma could lack reverence for the Saṅgha. The bhikkhu who has reverence for the Teacher and the Dhamma (3) also has reverence for the Saṅgha.

"It is impossible, Bhante, that a bhikkhu who has reverence for the Teacher, the Dhamma, and the Saṅgha could lack reverence for the training. The bhikkhu who has reverence for the Teacher, the Dhamma, and the Saṅgha (4) also has reverence for the training.

"It is impossible, Bhante, that a bhikkhu who has reverence for the Teacher, the Dhamma, and the Saṅgha, and the training could lack reverence for concentration. The bhikkhu who has reverence for the Teacher, the Dhamma, and the Saṅgha, and the training (5) also has reverence for concentration.

"It is impossible, Bhante, [124] that a bhikkhu who has reverence for the Teacher, the Dhamma, and the Saṅgha, the training, and concentration could lack reverence for heedfulness. The bhikkhu who has reverence for the Teacher, the Dhamma, and the Saṅgha, the training, and concentration (6) also has reverence for heedfulness.

"It is impossible, Bhante, that a bhikkhu who has reverence

for the Teacher, the Dhamma, and the Saṅgha, the training, concentration, and heedfulness could lack reverence for hospitality. The bhikkhu who has reverence for the Teacher, the Dhamma, and the Saṅgha, the training, concentration, and heedfulness (7) also has reverence for hospitality.

"It is in such a way, Bhante, that I understand in detail the meaning of this statement that the Blessed One has spoken in brief."

"Good, good, Sāriputta! It is good that you understand in detail the meaning of this statement that I have spoken in brief in such a way. Indeed, Sāriputta, it is impossible that a bhikkhu who lacks reverence for the Teacher could have reverence for the Dhamma.... [The Buddha here repeats the entire elaboration by Sāriputta.] [125] ... The bhikkhu who has reverence for the Teacher, the Dhamma, and the Saṅgha, the training, concentration, and heedfulness also has reverence for hospitality.

"It is in such a way, Sāriputta, that the meaning of this statement that I spoke in brief should be understood in detail."

71 (7) Development[1595]

"Bhikkhus, when a bhikkhu is not intent on development, even though he forms the wish: 'May my mind be liberated from the taints by non-clinging!' yet his mind is not liberated from the taints by non-clinging. For what reason? Because he lacks development. Lacks development of what? (1) Of the four establishments of mindfulness, (2) the four right strivings, (3) the four bases for psychic potency, (4) the five spiritual faculties, (5) the five powers, (6) the seven factors of enlightenment, and (7) the noble eightfold path.

"Suppose there was a hen with eight, ten, or twelve eggs that she had not properly covered, incubated, and nurtured. [126] Even though she might form the wish: 'May my chicks pierce their shells with the points of their claws or beaks and hatch safely!' yet the chicks are incapable of doing so. For what reason? Because the hen had not properly covered, incubated, and nurtured her eggs.

"So too, when a bhikkhu is not intent on development, even though he forms the wish: 'May my mind be liberated from the taints by non-clinging!' yet his mind is not liberated from the taints by non-clinging. For what reason? Because he lacks development. Lacks development of what? Of the four establishments of mindfulness . . . the noble eightfold path.

"Bhikkhus, when a bhikkhu is intent on development, even though he does not form the wish: 'May my mind be liberated from the taints by non-clinging!' yet his mind is liberated from the taints by non-clinging. For what reason? Because of his development. Development of what? (1) Of the four establishments of mindfulness, (2) the four right strivings, (3) the four bases for psychic potency, (4) the five spiritual faculties, (5) the five powers, (6) the seven factors of enlightenment, and (7) the noble eightfold path.

"Suppose there was a hen with eight, ten, or twelve eggs that she had properly covered, incubated, and nurtured. Even though she might not form the wish: 'May my chicks pierce their shells with the points of their claws or beaks and hatch safely!' yet the chicks are capable of doing so. For what reason? Because the hen had properly covered, incubated, and nurtured her eggs.

"So too, when a bhikkhu is intent on development, even though he does not form the wish: [127] 'May my mind be liberated from the taints by non-clinging!' yet his mind is liberated from the taints by non-clinging. For what reason? Because of his development. Development of what? Of the four establishments of mindfulness . . . the noble eightfold path.

"When, bhikkhus, a carpenter or a carpenter's apprentice sees the impressions of his fingers and his thumb on the handle of his adze, he does not know: 'I have worn away so much of the adze handle today, so much yesterday, so much earlier'; but when it has worn away, he knows that it has worn away. So too, when a bhikkhu is intent on development, even though he does not know: 'I have worn away so much of the taints today, so much yesterday, so much earlier,' yet when they are worn away, he knows that they are worn away.

"Suppose, bhikkhus, there was a seafaring ship bound together by lashings that had been worn away in the water for six months. It would be hauled up on dry land during the cold season and its lashings would be further attacked by wind and sun. Inundated by rain from a rain cloud, the lashings would readily deteriorate and rot away. So too, when a bhikkhu is intent on development, his fetters readily collapse and rot away." [128]

72 (8) Fire

Thus have I heard. On one occasion the Blessed One was walking on tour among the Kosalans together with a large Saṅgha of bhikkhus. Then, while traveling along the highway, in a certain spot the Blessed One saw a great mass of fire burning, blazing, and glowing. He left the highway, sat down on the seat prepared for him at the foot of a tree, and addressed the bhikkhus: "Bhikkhus, do you see that great mass of fire burning, blazing, and glowing?"

"Yes, Bhante."

(1) "What do you think, bhikkhus? Which is better, to embrace that great mass of fire, burning, blazing, and glowing, and sit down or lie down next to it, or to embrace a girl with soft and tender hands and feet—whether from a khattiya, brahmin, or householder clan—and sit down or lie down next to her?"

"It would be far better, Bhante, to embrace a girl with soft and tender hands and feet—whether from a khattiya, brahmin, or householder clan—and sit down or lie down next to her. It would be painful to embrace that great mass of fire, burning, blazing, and glowing, and sit down or lie down next to it."

"I inform you, bhikkhus, I declare to you that for an immoral man of bad character—one of impure and suspect behavior, secretive in his actions, not an ascetic though claiming to be one, not a celibate though claiming to be one, inwardly rotten, corrupt, depraved—it would be far better to embrace that great mass of fire, burning, blazing, and glowing, and sit down or lie down next to it. For what reason? Because on that account [129] he might undergo death or deadly pain, but for that reason he would not, with the breakup of the body, after death, be reborn in the plane of misery, in a bad destination, in the lower world, in hell. But when that immoral man . . . embraces a girl with soft and tender hands and feet—whether from a khattiya, brahmin, or householder clan—and sits down or lies down next to her, this leads to his harm and suffering for a long time. With the breakup of the body, after death, he is reborn in the plane of misery, in a bad destination, in the lower world, in hell.

(2) "What do you think, bhikkhus? Which is better, for a strong man to wrap a tough horsehair rope around both one's shins and tighten it so that it cuts through one's outer skin, inner skin, flesh, sinews, and bone, until it reaches the marrow,

or for one to accept the homage of affluent khattiyas, brahmins, or householders?"

"It would be far better, Bhante, for one to accept the homage of affluent khattiyas, brahmins, or householders. It would be painful if a strong man were to wrap a tough horsehair rope around both one's shins and tighten it so that it cuts through one's outer skin, inner skin, flesh, sinews, and bone, until it reaches the marrow."

"I inform you, bhikkhus, I declare to you that for an immoral man . . . it would be far better if a strong man were to wrap a tough horsehair rope around both his shins and tighten it so that it cuts through his outer skin, inner skin, flesh, sinews, and bone, until it reaches the marrow. For what reason? Because on that account he might undergo death or deadly pain, but for that reason he would not, with the breakup of the body, after death, be reborn in the plane of misery, in a bad destination, in the lower world, in hell. [130] But when that immoral man . . . accepts the homage of affluent khattiyas, brahmins, or householders, this leads to his harm and suffering for a long time. With the breakup of the body, after death, he is reborn in the plane of misery, in a bad destination, in the lower world, in hell.

(3) "What do you think, bhikkhus? Which is better, for a strong man to strike one in the breast with a sharp spear smeared with oil, or for one to accept reverential salutations from affluent khattiyas, brahmins, or householders?"

"It would be far better, Bhante, for one to accept reverential salutations from affluent khattiyas, brahmins, or householders. It would be painful if a strong man were to strike one in the breast with a sharp spear smeared with oil."

"I inform you, bhikkhus, I declare to you that for an immoral man . . . it would be far better if a strong man were to strike him in the breast with a sharp spear smeared with oil. For what reason? Because on that account he might undergo death or deadly pain, but for that reason he would not, with the breakup of the body, after death, be reborn in the plane of misery, in a bad destination, in the lower world, in hell. But when that immoral man . . . accepts reverential salutations from affluent khattiyas, brahmins, or householders, this leads to his harm and suffering for a long time. With the breakup of the body, after death, he is reborn in the plane of misery, in a bad destination, in the lower world, in hell.

(4) "What do you think, bhikkhus? Which is better, for a strong man to wrap a hot iron sheet—burning, [131] blazing, and glowing—around one's body, or for one to use a robe given out of faith by affluent khattiyas, brahmins, or householders?"

"It would be far better, Bhante, for one to use a robe given out of faith by affluent khattiyas, brahmins, or householders. It would be painful if a strong man were to wrap a hot iron sheet—burning, blazing, and glowing—around one's body."

"I inform you, bhikkhus, I declare to you that for an immoral man . . . it would be far better if a strong man were to wrap a hot iron sheet—burning, blazing, and glowing—around his body. For what reason? Because on that account he might undergo death or deadly pain, but for that reason he would not, with the breakup of the body, after death, be reborn in the plane of misery, in a bad destination, in the lower world, in hell. But when that immoral man . . . makes use of a robe given out of faith by affluent khattiyas, brahmins, or householders, this leads to his harm and suffering for a long time. With the breakup of the body, after death, he is reborn in the plane of misery, in a bad destination, in the lower world, in hell.

(5) "What do you think, bhikkhus? Which is better, for a strong man to force open one's mouth with a hot iron spike—burning, blazing, and glowing—and insert a hot copper ball—burning, blazing, and glowing—which burns one's lips, mouth, tongue, throat, and stomach,[1596] [132] and comes out from below taking along one's entrails, or for one to consume almsfood given out of faith by affluent khattiyas, brahmins, or householders?"

"It would be far better, Bhante, for one to consume almsfood given out of faith by affluent khattiyas, brahmins, or householders. It would be painful if a strong man were to force open one's mouth with a hot iron spike—burning, blazing, and glowing—and insert a hot copper ball . . . which burns one's lips . . . and comes out from below taking along one's entrails."

"I inform you, bhikkhus, I declare to you that for an immoral man . . . it would be far better if a strong man were to force open his mouth with a hot iron spike—burning, blazing, and glowing—and insert a hot copper ball . . . which burns one's lips . . . and comes out from below, taking along his entrails.

For what reason? Because on that account he might undergo death or deadly pain, but for that reason he would not, with the breakup of the body, after death, be reborn in the plane of misery, in a bad destination, in the lower world, in hell. But when that immoral man . . . consumes almsfood given out of faith by affluent khattiyas, brahmins, or householders, this leads to his harm and suffering for a long time. With the breakup of the body, after death, he is reborn in the plane of misery, in a bad destination, in the lower world, in hell.

(6) "What do you think, bhikkhus? Which is better, for a strong man to grab one by the head or shoulders [133] and force one to sit or lie down on a hot iron bed or chair—burning, blazing, and glowing—or for one to use a bed and chair given out of faith by affluent khattiyas, brahmins, or householders?"

"It would be far better, Bhante, for one to use a bed and chair given out of faith by affluent khattiyas, brahmins, or householders. It would be painful if a strong man were to grab one by the head or shoulders and force one to sit or lie down on a hot iron bed or chair, burning, blazing, and glowing."

"I inform you, bhikkhus, I declare to you that for an immoral man . . . it would be far better if a strong man were to grab him by the head or shoulders and force him to sit or lie down on a hot iron bed or chair, burning, blazing, and glowing. For what reason? Because on that account he might undergo death or deadly pain, but for that reason he would not, with the breakup of the body, after death, be reborn in the plane of misery, in a bad destination, in the lower world, in hell. But when that immoral man . . . uses a bed and chair given out of faith by affluent khattiyas, brahmins, or householders, this leads to his harm and suffering for a long time. With the breakup of the body, after death, he is reborn in the plane of misery, in a bad destination, in the lower world, in hell.

(7) "What do you think, bhikkhus? Which is better, for a strong man to grab one, turn one upside down, and throw one into a hot copper cauldron—burning, blazing, and glowing—and while one is boiling there in a swirl of froth, one sometimes rises, sometimes sinks, and sometimes is swept across, or for one to use a dwelling given out of faith by affluent khattiyas, [134] brahmins, or householders?"

"It would be far better, Bhante, for one to use a dwelling

given out of faith by affluent khattiyas, brahmins, or householders. It would be painful if a strong man were to grab one, turn one upside down, and throw one into a hot copper cauldron—burning, blazing, and glowing—so that while one is boiling there in a swirl of froth, one sometimes rises, sometimes sinks, and sometimes is swept across."

"I inform you, bhikkhus, I declare to you that for an immoral man of bad character—one of impure and suspect behavior, secretive in his actions, not an ascetic though claiming to be one, not a celibate though claiming to be one, inwardly rotten, corrupt, depraved—it would be far better for a strong man to grab him, turn him upside down, and throw him into a hot copper cauldron—burning, blazing, and glowing—so that while he is boiling there in a swirl of froth, he sometimes rises, sometimes sinks, and sometimes is swept across. For what reason? Because on that account he might undergo death or deadly pain, but for that reason he would not, with the breakup of the body, after death, be reborn in the plane of misery, in a bad destination, in the lower world, in hell. But when that immoral man . . . uses a dwelling given out of faith by affluent khattiyas, brahmins, or householders, this leads to his harm and suffering for a long time. With the breakup of the body, after death, he is reborn in the plane of misery, in a bad destination, in the lower world, in hell.

"Therefore, bhikkhus, you should train yourselves thus: 'When we use robes, almsfood, lodgings, and medicines and provisions for the sick, these services that [others] provide for us will be of great fruit and benefit to them, and this going forth of ours will not be barren, but fruitful and fertile.' Thus should you train yourselves. Considering your own good, bhikkhus, it is enough to strive for the goal with heedfulness; considering the good of others, [135] it is enough to strive for the goal with heedfulness; considering the good of both, it is enough to strive for the goal with heedfulness."[1597]

This is what the Blessed One said. Now while this exposition was being spoken, sixty bhikkhus vomited hot blood. Sixty bhikkhus gave up the training and returned to the lower life, saying: "It is difficult to do, Blessed One, very difficult to do." And the minds of sixty bhikkhus were liberated from the taints by non-clinging.[1598]

73 (9) Sunetta

(1) "Bhikkhus, in the past there was a teacher named Sunetta, the founder of a spiritual sect, one without lust for sensual pleasures.[1599] The teacher Sunetta had many hundreds of disciples to whom he taught a Dhamma for companionship with the brahmā world. When he was teaching such a Dhamma, those who did not place confidence in him were, with the breakup of the body, after death, reborn in the plane of misery, in a bad destination, in the lower world, in hell; but those who placed confidence in him were reborn in a good destination, in a heavenly world.

"In the past, bhikkhus, (2) there was a teacher named Mūgapakkha . . . (3) there was a teacher named Aranemi . . . (4) there was a teacher named Kuddāla . . . (5) there was a teacher named Hatthipāla . . . (6) there was a teacher named Jotipāla . . . (7) there was a teacher named Araka, the founder of a spiritual sect, one without lust for sensual pleasures. The teacher Araka had many hundreds of disciples to whom he taught a Dhamma for companionship with the brahmā world. When he [136] was teaching such a Dhamma, those who did not place confidence in him were, with the breakup of the body, after death, reborn in the plane of misery, in a bad destination, in the lower world, in hell; but those who placed confidence in him were reborn in a good destination, in a heavenly world.

"What do you think, bhikkhus? These seven teachers were founders of spiritual sects, men without lust for sensual pleasures who had retinues of many hundreds of disciples. If, with a mind of hatred, one had insulted and reviled them and their communities of disciples, wouldn't one have generated much demerit?"

"Yes, Bhante."

"If, with a mind of hatred, one had insulted and reviled these six teachers together with their communities of disciples, one would have generated much demerit. But if, with a mind of hatred, one reviles and abuses a single person accomplished in view, one generates even more demerit. For what reason? I say, bhikkhus, there is no injury against outsiders like that against [your] fellow monks.[1600] Therefore, bhikkhus, you should train yourselves thus: 'We will not let hatred toward our fellow monks arise in our minds.' Thus, bhikkhus, should you train yourselves."

74 (10) Araka

"Bhikkhus, in the past there was a teacher named Araka, the founder of a spiritual sect, one without lust for sensual pleasures. The teacher Araka had many hundreds of disciples to whom he taught such a Dhamma as this: 'Brahmins, short is the life of human beings, limited and fleeting; it has much suffering, much misery. One should wisely understand this. [137] One should do what is wholesome and lead the spiritual life; for none who are born can escape death.

(1) "'Just as a drop of dew on the tip of a blade of grass will quickly vanish at sunrise and will not last long, so too, brahmins, human life is like a drop of dew. It is limited and fleeting; it has much suffering, much misery. One should wisely understand this. One should do what is wholesome and lead the spiritual life; for none who are born can escape death.

(2) "'Just as, when thick drops of rain are pouring down, a water bubble will quickly vanish and will not last long, so too, brahmins, human life is like a water bubble. It is limited . . . for none who are born can escape death.

(3) "'Just as a line drawn on water with a stick will quickly vanish and will not last long, so too, brahmins, human life is like a line drawn on water with a stick. It is limited . . . for none who are born can escape death.

(4) "'Just as a river flowing down from a mountain, going a long distance, with a swift current, carrying along much flotsam, will not stand still for a moment, an instant, a second, but will rush on, swirl, and flow forward, so too, brahmins, human life is like a mountain stream. It is limited . . . for none who are born can escape death.

(5) "'Just as a strong man might form a lump of spittle at the tip of his tongue and spit it out without difficulty, so too, brahmins, human life is like a lump of spittle. It is limited . . . for none who are born can escape death.

(6) "'Just as [138] a piece of meat thrown into an iron pan heated all day will quickly vanish and will not last long, so too, brahmins, human life is like this piece of meat. It is limited . . . for none who are born can escape death.

(7) "'Just as, when a cow to be slaughtered is being led to the slaughterhouse, whatever leg she lifts, she is close to slaughter, close to death, so too, brahmins, human life is like a cow doomed to slaughter. It is limited and fleeting; it has much

suffering, much misery. One should wisely understand this. One should do what is wholesome and lead the spiritual life; for none who are born can escape death.'

"But at that time, bhikkhus, the human life span was 60,000 years, and girls were marriageable at the age of five hundred. At that time, people had but six afflictions: cold, heat, hunger, thirst, excrement, and urine. Though people had such long life spans and lived so long, and though their afflictions were so few, still, the teacher Araka gave his disciples such a teaching: 'Brahmins, short is the life of human beings . . . for none who are born can escape death.'

"But nowadays, bhikkhus, one could rightly say: 'Short is the life of human beings, limited and fleeting; it has much suffering, much misery. One should wisely understand this. One should do what is wholesome and lead the spiritual life; for none who are born can escape death.' For today one who lives long lives for a hundred years or a little more. And when living for a hundred years, one lives just for three hundred seasons: a hundred winters, a hundred summers, and a hundred rains. When living for three hundred seasons, one lives just for twelve hundred months: four hundred [139] winter months, four hundred summer months, and four hundred months of the rains. When living for twelve hundred months, one lives just for twenty-four hundred fortnights: eight hundred fortnights of winter, eight hundred fortnights of summer, and eight hundred fortnights of the rains.

"And when living for twenty-four hundred fortnights, one lives just for 36,000 nights: 12,000 nights of winter, 12,000 nights of summer, and 12,000 nights of the rains.[1601] And when living for 36,000 nights, one eats just 72,000 meals: 24,000 meals in winter, 24,000 in summer, and 24,000 in the rains. And this includes the taking of mother's milk and the [times when there are] obstacles to meals. These are the obstacles to meals: one who is angry[1602] does not eat a meal, one in pain does not eat a meal, one who is ill does not eat a meal, one observing the uposatha does not eat a meal, and when not obtaining [food] one does not eat a meal.

"Thus, bhikkhus, for a human being with a life span of a hundred years, I have reckoned his life span, the limit of his life span, the number of seasons, years, months, and fortnights [in his life]; the number of his nights, days,[1603] and meals, and the obstacles to meals. Whatever, bhikkhus, should be done by a compassionate teacher out of compassion for his disciples, seeking their welfare, that I have done for you. These are the feet of trees, these are empty huts. Meditate, bhikkhus, do not be heedless. Do not have cause to regret it later. This is our instruction to you." [140]

III. The Discipline

75 (1) An Expert in the Discipline (1)

"Bhikkhus, possessing seven qualities, a bhikkhu is an expert in the discipline. What seven?

"(1) He knows what is an offense. (2) He knows what is not an offense. (3) He knows what is a light offense. (4) He knows what is a grave offense. (5) He is virtuous; he dwells restrained by the Pātimokkha, possessed of good conduct and resort, seeing danger in minute faults. Having undertaken the training rules, he trains in them. (6) He is one who gains at will, without trouble or difficulty, the four jhānas that constitute the higher mind and are pleasant dwellings in this very life. (7) With the destruction of the taints, he has realized for himself with direct knowledge, in this very life, the taintless liberation of mind, liberation by wisdom, and having entered upon it, he dwells in it.

"Possessing these seven qualities, a bhikkhu is an expert in the discipline."

76 (2) An Expert in the Discipline (2)

"Bhikkhus, possessing seven qualities, a bhikkhu is an expert in the discipline. What seven?

"(1) He knows what is an offense. (2) He knows what is not an offense. (3) He knows what is a light offense. (4) He knows what is a grave offense. (5) Both Pātimokkhas have been well transmitted to him in detail, well analyzed, well mastered, well determined in terms of the rules and their detailed explication.[1604] (6) He is [141] one who gains at will . . . the four jhānas. . . . (7) With the destruction of the taints, he has realized for himself with direct knowledge . . . the taintless liberation of mind, liberation by wisdom . . . he dwells in it.

"Possessing these seven qualities, a bhikkhu is an expert in the discipline."

77 (3) An Expert in the Discipline (3)

"Bhikkhus, possessing seven qualities, a bhikkhu is an expert in the discipline. What seven?

"(1) He knows what is an offense. (2) He knows what is not an offense. (3) He knows what is a light offense. (4) He knows what is a grave offense. (5) He is one who is firm in the discipline, immovable. (6) He is one who gains at will ... the four jhānas. ... (7) With the destruction of the taints, he has realized for himself with direct knowledge ... the taintless liberation of mind, liberation by wisdom ... he dwells in it.

"Possessing these seven qualities, a bhikkhu is an expert in the discipline."

78 (4) An Expert in the Discipline (4)

"Bhikkhus, possessing seven qualities, a bhikkhu is an expert in the discipline. What seven?

"(1) He knows what is an offense. (2) He knows what is not an offense. (3) He knows what is a light offense. (4) He knows what is a grave offense. (5) He recollects his manifold past abodes, that is, one birth, two births ... [as in 6:2 §4] ... he recollects his manifold past abodes with their aspects and details. (6) With the divine eye, which is purified and surpasses the human ... [as in 6:2 §5] ... he understands how beings fare in accordance with their kamma. (7) With the destruction of the taints, he has realized for himself with direct knowledge ... the taintless liberation of mind, liberation by wisdom ... he dwells in it.

"Possessing these seven qualities, a bhikkhu is an expert in the discipline." [142]

79 (5) An Expert in the Discipline Is Resplendent (1)

"Bhikkhus, possessing seven qualities, an expert in the discipline is resplendent. What seven? ... [As in 7:75.] ... Possessing these seven qualities, an expert in the discipline is resplendent."[1605]

80 (6) An Expert in the Discipline Is Resplendent (2)

"Bhikkhus, possessing seven qualities, an expert in the discipline is resplendent. What seven? ... [As in 7:76.] ... Possessing these seven qualities, an expert in the discipline is resplendent."

81 (7) An Expert in the Discipline Is Resplendent (3)

"Bhikkhus, possessing seven qualities, an expert in the discipline is resplendent. What seven? . . . [As in 7:77.] . . . [143] Possessing these seven qualities, an expert in the discipline is resplendent."

82 (8) An Expert in the Discipline Is Resplendent (4)

"Bhikkhus, possessing seven qualities, an expert in the discipline is resplendent. What seven? . . . [As in 7:78.] . . . Possessing these seven qualities, an expert in the discipline is resplendent."

83 (9) The Teaching

Then the Venerable Upāli approached the Blessed One, paid homage to him, sat down to one side, and said: "Bhante, it would be good if the Blessed One would teach me the Dhamma in brief, so that, having heard the Dhamma from the Blessed One, I might dwell alone, withdrawn, heedful, ardent, and resolute."

"Upāli, those things which you might know thus: 'These things do not lead exclusively to disenchantment, to dispassion, to cessation, to peace, to direct knowledge, to enlightenment, to nibbāna,' you should definitely recognize: 'This is not the Dhamma; this is not the discipline; this is not the teaching of the Teacher.' But those things which you might know thus: 'These things lead exclusively to disenchantment, to dispassion, to cessation, to peace, to direct knowledge, to enlightenment, to nibbāna,' you should definitely recognize: 'This is the Dhamma; this is the discipline; this is the teaching of the Teacher.'" [144]

84 (10) Settlement

"Bhikkhus, there are these seven principles for the settlement of disciplinary issues, for settling and pacifying any disciplinary issues that may arise. What seven?

"(1) Removal by presence may be applied;[1606] (2) removal by memory may be applied; (3) removal on account of past insanity may be applied; (4) the acknowledgment of an offense may be applied; (5) the majority opinion may be applied; (6) a charge of aggravated misconduct may be applied; and (7) covering over with grass may be applied.[1607]

"There are, bhikkhus, these seven principles for the settlement of disciplinary issues, for settling and pacifying any disciplinary issues that may arise."

IV. An Ascetic[1608]

85 (1) A Bhikkhu

"Bhikkhus, it is through the breaking of seven things that one is a bhikkhu.[1609] What seven? Personal-existence view is broken; doubt is broken; wrong grasp of behavior and observances is broken; lust is broken; hatred is broken; delusion is broken; conceit is broken. It is through the breaking of these seven things that one is a bhikkhu."

86 (2) An Ascetic

"Bhikkhus, it is through the pacifying of seven things that one is an ascetic. . . ."[1610]

87 (3) A Brahmin

"Bhikkhus, it is through the expulsion [of seven things] that one is a brahmin. . . ."

88 (4) A Scholar

"Bhikkhus, it is because of the streaming away [of seven things] that one is a scholar. . . ."

89 (5) Washed

"Bhikkhus, it is because of the washing away [of seven things] that one is washed. . . ." [145]

90 (6) A Master of Vedic Knowledge

"Bhikkhus, it is because one has the knowledge [of seven things] that one is a master of Vedic knowledge. . . ."

91 (7) A Noble One

"Bhikkhus, it is through the foe-slaying [of seven things] that one is a noble one. . . ."[1611]

92 (8) An Arahant

"Bhikkhus, it is through the remoteness [of seven things] that one is an arahant.[1612] What seven? Personal-existence view is remote; doubt is remote; wrong grasp of behavior and observances is remote; lust is remote; hatred is remote; delusion is remote; conceit is remote. It is through the remoteness of these seven things that one is an arahant."

93 (9) Character (1)

"Bhikkhus, there are these seven who are not of good character. What seven? One without faith, one without a sense of moral shame, one without moral dread, one of little learning, one who is lazy, one who is muddle-minded, and one who is unwise. These are the seven who are not of good character."

94 (10) Character (2)

"Bhikkhus, there are these seven who are of good character. What seven? One endowed with faith, one with a sense of moral shame, one with moral dread, one who is learned, one who is energetic, one who is mindful, and one who is wise. These are the seven who are of good character."

V. Worthy of Gifts

95 (1) Contemplating Impermanence in the Eye[1613]

"Bhikkhus, there are these seven kinds of persons who are worthy of gifts, worthy of hospitality, worthy of offerings, worthy of reverential salutation, an unsurpassed field of merit for the world. What seven?

(1) "Here, bhikkhus, some person dwells contemplating impermanence in the eye, perceiving impermanence, experiencing impermanence, constantly, continuously, and uninterruptedly focusing on it with the mind, fathoming it with wisdom. With the destruction of the taints, he has realized for himself with direct knowledge, in this very life, the taintless liberation of mind, liberation by wisdom, [146] and having entered upon it, he dwells in it. This is the first kind of person worthy of gifts, worthy of hospitality, worthy of offerings, worthy of reverential salutation, an unsurpassed field of merit for the world.

(2) "Again, some person dwells contemplating impermanence in the eye, perceiving impermanence, experiencing impermanence, constantly, continuously, and uninterruptedly focusing on it with the mind, fathoming it with wisdom. For him the exhaustion of the taints and the exhaustion of life occur simultaneously. This is the second kind of person worthy of gifts. . . .

(3) "Again, some person dwells contemplating impermanence in the eye, perceiving impermanence, experiencing impermanence, constantly, continuously, and uninterruptedly focusing on it with the mind, fathoming it with wisdom. With the utter destruction of the five lower fetters, he becomes an attainer of nibbāna in the interval. This is the third kind of person worthy of gifts. . . .

(4) "Again, some person dwells contemplating impermanence in the eye, perceiving impermanence, experiencing impermanence, constantly, continuously, and uninterruptedly focusing on it with the mind, fathoming it with wisdom. With the utter destruction of the five lower fetters, he becomes an attainer of nibbāna upon landing. This is the fourth kind of person worthy of gifts. . . .

(5) "Again, some person dwells contemplating impermanence in the eye, perceiving impermanence, experiencing impermanence, constantly, continuously, and uninterruptedly focusing on it with the mind, fathoming it with wisdom. With the utter destruction of the five lower fetters, he becomes an attainer of nibbāna without exertion. This is the fifth kind of person worthy of gifts. . . .

(6) "Again, some person dwells contemplating impermanence in the eye, perceiving impermanence, experiencing impermanence, constantly, continuously, and uninterruptedly focusing on it with the mind, fathoming it with wisdom. With the utter destruction of the five lower fetters, he becomes an attainer of nibbāna through exertion. This is the sixth kind of person worthy of gifts. . . .

(7) "Again, some person dwells contemplating impermanence in the eye, perceiving impermanence, experiencing impermanence, constantly, continuously, and uninterruptedly focusing on it with the mind, fathoming it with wisdom. With the utter destruction of the five lower fetters, he becomes one

bound upstream, heading toward the Akaniṭṭha realm. This is the seventh kind of person worthy of gifts. . . .

"These, bhikkhus, are the seven kinds of persons who are worthy of gifts, worthy of hospitality, worthy of offerings, worthy of reverential salutation, an unsurpassed field of merit for the world."

96 (2)–102 (8) Contemplating Suffering in the Eye, Etc.

"Bhikkhus, there are these seven kinds of persons who are worthy of gifts, worthy of hospitality, worthy of offerings, worthy of reverential salutation, an unsurpassed field of merit for the world. What seven?

"Here, bhikkhus, some person (96) dwells contemplating suffering in the eye . . . (97) . . . dwells contemplating non-self in the eye . . . (98) . . . dwells contemplating destruction in the eye . . . (99) . . . dwells contemplating vanishing in the eye . . . (100) . . . dwells contemplating fading away in the eye . . . (101) . . . dwells contemplating cessation in the eye . . . (102) . . . dwells contemplating relinquishment in the eye . . .

103 (9)–614 (520) Impermanence in the Ear, Etc.

(103)–(190) ". . . Here some person dwells contemplating impermanence in the ear . . . the nose . . . the tongue . . . the body . . . the mind . . . in forms . . . sounds . . . odors . . . tastes . . . [147] tactile objects . . . mental phenomena . . .

(191)–(238) ". . . in eye-consciousness . . . ear-consciousness . . . nose-consciousness . . . tongue-consciousness . . . body-consciousness . . . mind-consciousness . . .

(239)–(286) ". . . in eye-contact . . . ear-contact . . . nose-contact . . . tongue-contact . . . body-contact . . . mind-contact . . .

(287)–(334) ". . . in feeling born of eye-contact . . . feeling born of ear-contact . . . feeling born of nose-contact . . . feeling born of tongue-contact . . . feeling born of body-contact . . . feeling born of mind-contact . . .

(335)–(382) ". . . in perception of forms . . . perception of sounds . . . perception of odors . . . perception of tastes . . . perception of tactile objects . . . perception of mental phenomena . . .

(383)–(430) ". . . in volition regarding forms . . . volition regarding sounds . . . volition regarding odors . . . volition regarding tastes . . . volition regarding tactile objects . . . volition regarding mental phenomena . . .

(431)–(478) "... in craving for forms ... craving for sounds ... craving for odors ... craving for tastes ... craving for tactile objects ... craving for mental phenomena ...

(479)–(526) "... in thought about forms ... thought about sounds ... thought about odors ... thought about tastes ... thought about tactile objects ... thought about mental phenomena ...

(527)–(574) "... in examination of forms ... examination of sounds ... examination of odors ... examination of tastes ... examination of tactile objects ... examination of mental phenomena ...

(575)–(614) "... Here some person dwells contemplating impermanence in the form aggregate ... the feeling aggregate ... the perception aggregate ... the volitional activities aggregate ... the consciousness aggregate ... dwells contemplating suffering ... dwells contemplating non-self ... dwells contemplating destruction ... dwells contemplating vanishing ... dwells contemplating fading away ... dwells contemplating cessation ... dwells contemplating relinquishment ..." [148]

VI. Lust and So Forth Repetition Series[1614]

615 (1)

"Bhikkhus, for direct knowledge of lust, seven things are to be developed. What seven? The enlightenment factor of mindfulness, the enlightenment factor of discrimination of phenomena, the enlightenment factor of energy, the enlightenment factor of rapture, the enlightenment factor of tranquility, the enlightenment factor of concentration, and the enlightenment factor of equanimity. For direct knowledge of lust, these seven things are to be developed."

616 (2)

"Bhikkhus, for direct knowledge of lust, seven things are to be developed. What seven? The perception of impermanence, the perception of non-self, the perception of unattractiveness, the perception of danger, the perception of abandoning, the perception of dispassion, the perception of cessation. For direct knowledge of lust, these seven things are to be developed."

617 (3)

"Bhikkhus, for direct knowledge of lust, seven things are to be developed. What seven? The perception of unattractiveness, the perception of death, the perception of the repulsiveness of food, the perception of non-delight in the entire world, the perception of impermanence, the perception of suffering in the impermanent, and the perception of non-self in what is suffering. For direct knowledge of lust, these seven things are to be developed."

618 (4)–644 (30)

"Bhikkhus, for full understanding of lust . . . for the utter destruction . . . for the abandoning . . . for the destruction . . . for the vanishing . . . for the fading away . . . for the cessation . . . for the giving up . . . for the relinquishment of lust . . . these seven things are to be developed."

645 (31)–1124 (510)

"Bhikkhus, for direct knowledge . . . for full understanding . . . for the utter destruction . . . for the abandoning . . . for the destruction . . . for the vanishing . . . for the fading away . . . for the cessation . . . for the giving up . . . for the relinquishment of hatred . . . of delusion . . . of anger . . . of hostility . . . of denigration . . . of insolence . . . of envy . . . of miserliness . . . of deceitfulness . . . of craftiness . . . of obstinacy . . . of vehemence . . . of conceit . . . of arrogance . . . of intoxication . . . of heedlessness . . . these seven things are to be developed." [149]

This is what the Blessed One said. Elated, those bhikkhus delighted in the Blessed One's statement.

The Book of the Sevens is finished.

THE BOOK OF THE EIGHTS
(*Aṭṭhakanipāta*)

The Book of the Eights

The First Fifty

The Second Fifty

[150]
The Book of the Eights

Homage to the Blessed One, the Arahant,
the Perfectly Enlightened One

The First Fifty

I. Loving-Kindness

1 (1) Loving-Kindness

Thus have I heard. On one occasion the Blessed One was dwelling at Sāvatthī in Jeta's Grove, Anāthapiṇḍika's Park. There the Blessed One addressed the bhikkhus: "Bhikkhus!"

"Venerable sir!" those bhikkhus replied. The Blessed One said this:

"Bhikkhus, when the liberation of the mind by loving-kindness has been pursued, developed, and cultivated, made a vehicle and basis, carried out, consolidated, and properly undertaken, eight benefits are to be expected. What eight?

(1) "One sleeps well; (2) one awakens happily; (3) one does not have bad dreams; (4) one is pleasing to human beings; (5) one is pleasing to spirits;[1615] (6) deities protect one; (7) fire, poison, and weapons do not injure one; and (8) if one does not penetrate further, one moves on to the brahmā world.

"When, bhikkhus, the liberation of the mind by loving-kindness has been pursued, developed, and cultivated, made a vehicle and basis, carried out, consolidated, and properly undertaken, these eight benefits are to be expected."

For one who, ever mindful, develops
measureless loving-kindness,
the fetters thin out as he sees
the destruction of the acquisitions. [151]

If, with a mind free from hate,
one arouses love toward just one being,
one thereby becomes good.
Compassionate in mind toward all beings,[1616]
the noble one generates abundant merit.

Those royal sages who conquered the earth
with its multitudes of beings
traveled around performing sacrifices:
the horse sacrifice,[1617] the person sacrifice,
sammāpāsa, vājapeyya, niraggaḷa.[1618]

All these are not worth a sixteenth part
of a well-developed loving mind,
just as the hosts of stars[1619] cannot match
a sixteenth part of the moon's radiance.

One who does not kill or enjoin killing,
who does not conquer or enjoin conquest,
one who has loving-kindness toward all beings[1620]
harbors no enmity toward anyone.

2 (2) Wisdom

"Bhikkhus, there are these eight causes and conditions that lead to obtaining the wisdom fundamental to the spiritual life[1621] when it has not been obtained and to its increase, maturation, and fulfillment by development after it has been obtained. What eight?

(1) "Here, a bhikkhu lives in dependence on the Teacher or on a certain fellow monk in the position of a teacher, toward whom he has set up a keen sense of moral shame and moral dread, affection and reverence. This is the first cause and condition that leads to obtaining the wisdom fundamental to the spiritual life when it has not been obtained and to its increase, maturation, and fulfillment by development after it has been obtained. [152]

(2) "As he is living in dependence on the Teacher or on a certain fellow monk in the position of a teacher, toward whom he has set up a keen sense of moral shame and moral dread, affection and reverence, he approaches them from time to time

and inquires: 'How is this, Bhante? What is the meaning of this?' Those venerable ones then disclose to him what has not been disclosed, clear up what is obscure, and dispel his perplexity about numerous perplexing points. This is the second cause and condition that leads to obtaining the wisdom fundamental to the spiritual life. . . .

(3) "Having heard that Dhamma, he resorts to two kinds of withdrawal: withdrawal in body and withdrawal in mind. This is the third cause and condition that leads to obtaining the wisdom fundamental to the spiritual life. . . .

(4) "He is virtuous; he dwells restrained by the Pātimokkha, possessed of good conduct and resort, seeing danger in minute faults. Having undertaken the training rules, he trains in them. This is the fourth cause and condition that leads to obtaining the wisdom fundamental to the spiritual life. . . .

(5) "He has learned much, remembers what he has learned, and accumulates what he has learned. Those teachings that are good in the beginning, good in the middle, and good in the end, with the right meaning and phrasing, which proclaim the perfectly complete and pure spiritual life—such teachings as these he has learned much of, retained in mind, recited verbally, mentally investigated, and penetrated well by view. This is the fifth cause and condition that leads to obtaining the wisdom fundamental to the spiritual life. . . . [153]

(6) "He has aroused energy for abandoning unwholesome qualities and acquiring wholesome qualities; he is strong, firm in exertion, not casting off the duty of cultivating wholesome qualities. This is the sixth cause and condition that leads to obtaining the wisdom fundamental to the spiritual life. . . .

(7) "In the midst of the Saṅgha, he does not engage in rambling and pointless talk. Either he himself speaks on the Dhamma, or he requests someone else to do so, or he adopts noble silence.[1622] This is the seventh cause and condition that leads to obtaining the wisdom fundamental to the spiritual life. . . .

(8) "He dwells contemplating arising and vanishing in the five aggregates subject to clinging: 'Such is form, such its origin, such its passing away; such is feeling . . . such is perception . . . such are volitional activities . . . such is consciousness, such its origin, such its passing away.' This is the eighth cause and condition that leads to obtaining the wisdom fundamental

to the spiritual life when it has not been obtained and to its increase, maturation, and fulfillment by development after it has been obtained.

(1) "His fellow monks esteem him thus: 'This venerable one lives in dependence on the Teacher or on a certain fellow monk in the position of a teacher, toward whom he has set up a keen sense of moral shame and moral dread, affection and reverence. This venerable one surely knows and sees.' This quality leads to affection, respect, esteem, accord, and unity.[1623]

(2) "'As this venerable one is living in dependence on the Teacher or on a certain fellow monk in the position of a teacher . . . [154] . . . those venerable ones . . . dispel his perplexity about numerous perplexing points. This venerable one surely knows and sees.' This quality, too, leads to affection, respect, esteem, accord, and unity.

(3) "'Having heard that Dhamma, this venerable one resorts to two kinds of withdrawal: withdrawal in body and withdrawal in mind. This venerable one surely knows and sees.' This quality, too, leads to affection, respect, esteem, accord, and unity.

(4) "'This venerable one is virtuous; he dwells restrained by the Pātimokkha . . . he trains in them. This venerable one surely knows and sees.' This quality, too, leads to affection, respect, esteem, accord, and unity.

(5) "'This venerable one has learned much . . . and penetrated well by view. This venerable one surely knows and sees.' This quality, too, leads to affection, respect, esteem, accord, and unity.

(6) "'This venerable one has aroused energy for abandoning unwholesome qualities . . . not casting off the duty of cultivating wholesome qualities. This venerable one surely knows and sees.' This quality, too, leads to affection, respect, esteem, accord, and unity. [155]

(7) "'In the midst of the Saṅgha, this venerable one does not engage in rambling and pointless talk . . . or he adopts noble silence. This venerable one surely knows and sees.' This quality, too, leads to affection, respect, esteem, accord, and unity.

(8) "'This venerable one dwells contemplating arising and vanishing in the five aggregates subject to clinging. . . . This venerable one surely knows and sees.' This quality, too, leads to affection, respect, esteem, accord, and unity.

"These, bhikkhus, are the eight causes and conditions that lead to obtaining the wisdom fundamental to the spiritual life when it has not been obtained and to its increase, maturation, and fulfillment by development after it has been obtained."

3 (3) Pleasing (1)[1624]

"Bhikkhus, possessing eight qualities, a bhikkhu is displeasing and disagreeable to his fellow monks and is neither respected nor esteemed by them. What eight? Here, (1) a bhikkhu praises those who are displeasing and (2) criticizes those who are pleasing; (3) he is desirous of gains and (4) honor; (5) he is morally shameless and (6) morally reckless; (7) he has evil desires and (8) holds wrong view. Possessing these eight qualities, a bhikkhu is displeasing and disagreeable to his fellow monks and is neither respected nor esteemed by them.

"Bhikkhus, possessing eight qualities, a bhikkhu is pleasing and agreeable to his fellow monks and is respected and esteemed by them. What eight? [156] Here, (1) a bhikkhu does not praise those who are displeasing or (2) criticize those who are pleasing; (3) he is not desirous of gains or (4) honor; (5) he has a sense of moral shame and (6) moral dread; (7) he has few desires and (8) holds right view. Possessing these eight qualities, a bhikkhu is pleasing and agreeable to his fellow monks and is respected and esteemed by them."

4 (4) Pleasing (2)

"Bhikkhus, possessing eight qualities, a bhikkhu is displeasing and disagreeable to his fellow monks and is neither respected nor esteemed by them. What eight? Here, a bhikkhu is (1) desirous of gains, (2) honor, and (3) reputation; (4) he does not know the proper time and (5) does not know moderation; (6) he is impure;[1625] (7) he speaks much; and (8) he insults and reviles his fellow monks. Possessing these eight qualities, a bhikkhu is displeasing and disagreeable to his fellow monks and is neither respected nor esteemed by them.

"Bhikkhus, possessing eight qualities, a bhikkhu is pleasing and agreeable to his fellow monks and is respected and esteemed by them. What eight? Here, a bhikkhu is (1) not desirous of gains, (2) honor, and (3) reputation; (4) he is one who knows the proper time and (5) who knows moderation; (6) he is pure; (7) he does not speak much; and (8) he does not insult and revile his fellow monks. Possessing these eight qualities, a bhikkhu is pleasing and agreeable to his fellow monks and is respected and esteemed by them."

5 (5) World (1)

"Bhikkhus, these eight worldly conditions revolve around the world, and the world revolves around these eight worldly conditions. What eight? [157] Gain and loss, disrepute and fame, blame and praise, and pleasure and pain. These eight worldly conditions revolve around the world, and the world revolves around these eight worldly conditions."

Gain and loss, disrepute and fame,
blame and praise, pleasure and pain:
these conditions that people meet
are impermanent, transient, and subject to change.

A wise and mindful person knows them
and sees that they are subject to change.
Desirable conditions don't excite his mind
nor is he repelled by undesirable conditions.

He has dispelled attraction and repulsion;
they are gone and no longer present.
Having known the dustless, sorrowless state,
he understands rightly and has transcended existence.

6 (6) World (2)

"Bhikkhus, these eight worldly conditions revolve around the world, and the world revolves around these eight worldly conditions. What eight? Gain and loss, disrepute and fame, blame and praise, and pleasure and pain. These eight worldly conditions revolve around the world, and the world revolves around these eight worldly conditions.

"Bhikkhus, an uninstructed worldling meets gain and loss, disrepute and fame, blame and praise, and pleasure and pain. An instructed noble disciple also meets gain and loss, disrepute and fame, blame and praise, and pleasure and pain. What [158] is the distinction, the disparity, the difference between an instructed noble disciple and an uninstructed worldling with regard to this?"

"Bhante, our teachings are rooted in the Blessed One, guided by the Blessed One, take recourse in the Blessed One. It would be good if the Blessed One would clear up the meaning of this statement. Having heard it from him, the bhikkhus will retain it in mind."

"Then listen, bhikkhus, and attend closely. I will speak."

"Yes, Bhante," those bhikkhus replied. The Blessed One said this:

"(1) Bhikkhus, when an uninstructed worldling meets with gain, he does not reflect thus: 'This gain that I have met is impermanent, suffering, and subject to change.' He does not understand it as it really is. (2) When he meets with loss . . . (3) . . . fame . . . (4) . . . disrepute . . . (5) . . . blame . . . (6) . . . praise . . . (7) . . . pleasure . . . (8) . . . pain, he does not reflect thus: 'This pain that I have met is impermanent, suffering, and subject to change.' He does not understand it as it really is.

"Gain obsesses his mind, and loss obsesses his mind. Fame obsesses his mind, and disrepute obsesses his mind. Blame obsesses his mind, and praise obsesses his mind. Pleasure obsesses his mind, and pain obsesses his mind. He is attracted to gain and repelled by loss. He is attracted to fame and repelled by disrepute. He is attracted to praise and repelled by blame. He is attracted to pleasure and repelled by pain. Thus involved with attraction and repulsion, he is not freed from birth, from old age and death, from sorrow, lamentation, pain, dejection, and anguish; he is not freed from suffering, I say.

"But, bhikkhus, (1) when an instructed noble disciple meets with gain, he reflects thus: 'This gain that I have met is impermanent, suffering, and subject to change.' He thus understands it as it really is. (2) When he meets with loss . . . (3) . . . fame . . . (4) . . . [159] disrepute . . . (5) . . . blame . . . (6) . . . praise . . . (7) . . . pleasure . . . (8) . . . pain, he reflects thus: 'This pain that I have met is impermanent, suffering, and subject to change.' He thus understands it as it really is.

"Gain does not obsess his mind, and loss does not obsess his mind. Fame does not obsess his mind, and disrepute does not obsess his mind. Blame does not obsess his mind, and praise does not obsess his mind. Pleasure does not obsess his mind, and pain does not obsess his mind. He is not attracted to gain or repelled by loss. He is not attracted to fame or repelled by disrepute. He is not attracted to praise or repelled by blame.

He is not attracted to pleasure or repelled by pain. Having thus discarded attraction and repulsion, he is freed from birth, from old age and death, from sorrow, lamentation, pain, dejection, and anguish; he is freed from suffering, I say.

"This, bhikkhus, is the distinction, the disparity, the difference between an instructed noble disciple and an uninstructed worldling."

[The verses are identical with those of 8:5.] [160]

7 (7) Devadatta's Failing

On one occasion the Blessed One was dwelling at Rājagaha on Mount Vulture Peak not long after Devadatta had left.[1626] There the Blessed One addressed the bhikkhus with reference to Devadatta:

"Bhikkhus, it is good for a bhikkhu from time to time to review his own failings. It is good for him from time to time to review the failings of others. It is good for him from time to time to review his own achievements. It is good for him from time to time to review the achievements of others. Because he was overcome and obsessed by eight bad conditions, Devadatta is bound for the plane of misery, bound for hell, and he will remain there for an eon, unredeemable. What eight?

"(1) Because he was overcome and obsessed by gain, Devadatta is bound for the plane of misery, bound for hell, and he will remain there for an eon, unredeemable. (2) Because he was overcome and obsessed by loss . . . (3) . . . by fame . . . (4) . . . by disrepute . . . (5) . . . by honor . . . (6) . . . by lack of honor . . . (7) . . . by evil desires . . . (8) . . . by bad friendship, Devadatta is bound for the plane of misery, bound for hell, and he will remain there for an eon, unredeemable. Because he was overcome and obsessed by these eight bad conditions, Devadatta is bound for the plane of misery, bound for hell, and he will remain there for an eon, unredeemable.

"It is good for a bhikkhu to overcome gain whenever it arises. It is good for him to overcome loss whenever it arises . . . to overcome fame . . . disrepute . . . honor [161] . . . lack of honor . . . evil desires . . . bad friendship whenever it arises.

"And for what reason should a bhikkhu overcome gain whenever it arises? For what reason should he overcome loss . . . fame . . . disrepute . . . honor . . . lack of honor . . . evil desires . . . bad friendship whenever it arises? Those taints, distressful and feverish, that might arise in one who has not overcome arisen gain do not occur in one who has overcome it. Those taints, distressful and feverish, that might arise in one who has not overcome arisen loss . . . arisen fame . . . arisen disrepute . . . arisen honor . . . arisen lack of honor . . . arisen evil desires . . . arisen bad friendship do not occur in one who has overcome it. For this reason a bhikkhu should overcome gain whenever it arises. He should overcome loss . . . fame . . . disrepute . . . honor . . . lack of honor . . . evil desires . . . bad friendship whenever it arises.

"Therefore, bhikkhus, you should train yourselves thus: 'We will overcome gain whenever it arises. We will overcome loss . . . fame . . . disrepute . . . honor . . . lack of honor . . . evil desires . . . bad friendship whenever it arises.' It is in such a way that you should train yourselves." [162]

8 (8) Uttara on Failing

On one occasion the Venerable Uttara was dwelling at Mahisavatthu, in Dhavajālikā on Mount Saṅkheyya. There the Venerable Uttara addressed the bhikkhus. . . .

"Friends, it is good for a bhikkhu from time to time to review his own failings. It is good for a bhikkhu from time to time to review the failings of others. It is good for a bhikkhu from time to time to review his own achievements. It is good for a bhikkhu from time to time to review the achievements of others."

Now on that occasion the great [deva] king Vessavaṇa was traveling from north to south on some business. He heard the Venerable Uttara at Mahisavatthu, in Dhavajālikā on Mount Saṅkheyya, teaching the Dhamma to the bhikkhus thus: 'Friends, it is good for a bhikkhu from time to time to review his own failings . . . the failings of others . . . his own achievements . . . the achievements of others.' Then, just as a strong man might extend his drawn-in arm or draw in his extended arm, Vessavaṇa disappeared from Mount Saṅkheyya and reappeared among the Tāvatiṃsa devas.

He approached Sakka, ruler of the devas, and said to him: "Respected sir, you should know that the Venerable Uttara, at Mahisavatthu, [163] in Dhavajālikā on Mount Saṅkheyya, has been teaching the Dhamma to the bhikkhus thus: 'Friends, it is good for a bhikkhu from time to time to review his own failings . . . the failings of others . . . his own achievements . . . the achievements of others.'"

Then, just as a strong man might extend his drawn-in arm or draw in his extended arm, Sakka disappeared from among the Tāvatiṃsa devas and reappeared at Mahisavatthu, in Dhavajālikā on Mount Saṅkheyya, in front of the Venerable Uttara. He approached the Venerable Uttara, paid homage to him, stood to one side, and said to him:

"Is it true, Bhante, as is said, that you have been teaching the Dhamma to the bhikkhus thus: 'Friends, it is good for a bhikkhu from time to time to review his own failings . . . the failings of others . . . his own achievements . . . the achievements of others'?"

"Yes, ruler of the devas."

"But, Bhante, was this your own discernment, or was it the word of the Blessed One, the Arahant, the Perfectly Enlightened One?"

"Well then, ruler of the devas, I will give you a simile; even by means of a simile, some intelligent people understand the meaning of what has been said. Suppose not far from a village or town there was a great heap of grain, and a large crowd of people were to take away grain with carrying-poles, baskets, hip-sacks, [164] and their cupped hands. If someone were to approach that large crowd of people and ask them: 'Where did you get this grain?' what should they say?"

"Bhante, those people should say: 'We got it from that great heap of grain.'"

"So too, ruler of the devas, whatever is well spoken is all the word of the Blessed One, the Arahant, the Perfectly Enlightened One. I myself and others derive our good words from him."[1627]

"It's astounding and amazing, Bhante, how well you stated this: 'Whatever is well spoken is all the word of the Blessed One, the Arahant, the Perfectly Enlightened One. I myself and others derive our good words from him.'

"On one occasion, Bhante Uttara, the Blessed One was dwelling at Rājagaha, on Mount Vulture Peak, not long after Devadatta had left. There the Blessed One addressed the bhikkhus with reference to Devadatta: 'Bhikkhus, it is good for a bhikkhu from time to time to review his own failings. . . . [Sakka here cites the Buddha's entire discourse of 8:7, down to:] [165–66] . . . It is in such a way, bhikkhus, that you should train yourselves.'[1628]

"Bhante Uttara, this exposition of the Dhamma has not been promulgated anywhere among the four human assemblies: that is, among bhikkhus, bhikkhunīs, male lay followers, and female lay followers.[1629] Bhante, learn this exposition of the Dhamma, master this exposition of the Dhamma, and retain this exposition of the Dhamma in mind. This exposition of the Dhamma is beneficial; it pertains to the fundamentals of the spiritual life."

9 (9) Nanda

"Bhikkhus, (1) one speaking rightly would say of Nanda that he is a clansman, (2) that he is strong, (3) that he is graceful, and (4) that he is strongly prone to lust.[1630] How else could Nanda lead the complete and pure spiritual life unless (5) he guarded the doors of the sense faculties, (6) observed moderation in eating, (7) was intent on wakefulness, and (8) possessed mindfulness and clear comprehension?

"Bhikkhus, this is how Nanda guards the doors of the sense faculties: [167] If he needs to look to the east, he does so after he has fully considered the matter and clearly comprehends it thus: 'When I look to the east, bad unwholesome states of longing and dejection will not flow in upon me.' If he needs to look to the west . . . to the north . . . to the south . . . to look up . . . to look down . . . to survey the intermediate directions, he does so after he has fully considered the matter and clearly comprehends it thus: 'When I look to the intermediate directions, bad unwholesome states of longing and dejection will not flow in upon me.' That is how Nanda guards the doors of the sense faculties.

"This is how Nanda observes moderation in eating: Here, reflecting carefully, Nanda consumes food neither for amusement nor for intoxication nor for the sake of physical beauty and attractiveness, but only for the support and maintenance of this body, for avoiding harm, and for assisting the spiritual life, considering: 'Thus I shall terminate the old feeling and not arouse a new feeling, and I shall be healthy and blameless and dwell at ease.' That is how Nanda observes moderation in eating.

"This is how Nanda is intent on wakefulness: [168] During

the day, while walking back and forth and sitting, Nanda purifies his mind of obstructive qualities. In the first watch of the night, while walking back and forth and sitting, he purifies his mind of obstructive qualities. In the middle watch of the night he lies down on the right side in the lion's posture, with one foot overlapping the other, mindful and clearly comprehending, after noting in his mind the idea of rising. After rising, in the last watch of the night, while walking back and forth and sitting, he purifies his mind of obstructive qualities. That is how Nanda is intent on wakefulness.

"This is Nanda's mindfulness and clear comprehension: Nanda knows feelings as they arise, as they remain present, as they disappear; he knows perceptions as they arise, as they remain present, as they disappear; he knows thoughts as they arise, as they remain present, as they disappear.[1631] That is Nanda's mindfulness and clear comprehension.

"How else, bhikkhus, could Nanda lead the complete and pure spiritual life unless he guarded the doors of the sense faculties, observed moderation in eating, was intent on wakefulness, and possessed mindfulness and clear comprehension?"

10 (10) Trash

On one occasion the Blessed One was dwelling at Campā on a bank of the Gaggārā Lotus Pond. Now on that occasion bhikkhus were reproving a bhikkhu for an offense. When being reproved, that bhikkhu answered evasively, diverted the discussion to an irrelevant subject, and displayed anger, hatred, and resentment.[1632] Then the Blessed One addressed the bhikkhus: [169] "Bhikkhus, eject this person! Bhikkhus, eject this person![1633] This person should be banished. Why should another's son vex you?[1634]

"Here, bhikkhus, so long as the bhikkhus do not see his offense, a certain person has the same manner (1) of going forward and (2) returning, (3) of looking ahead and (4) looking aside, (5) of bending and (6) stretching his limbs, and (7) of wearing his robes and (8) carrying his outer robe and bowl as the good bhikkhus.[1635] When, however, they see his offense, they know him as a corruption among ascetics, just chaff and trash among ascetics. Then they expel him. For what reason? So that he doesn't corrupt the good bhikkhus.

"Suppose that when a field of barley is growing, some blighted barley would appear that would be just chaff and trash among the barley. As long as its head has not come forth, its roots would be just like those of the other [crops], the good barley; its stem would be just like that of the other [crops], the good barley; its leaves would be just like those of the other [crops], the good barley. When, however, its head comes forth, they know it as blighted barley, just chaff [170] and trash among the barley. Then they pull it up by the root and cast it out from the barley field. For what reason? So that it doesn't spoil the good barley.

"So too, so long as the bhikkhus do not see his offense, a certain person here has the same manner of going forward . . . and carrying his outer robe and bowl as the good bhikkhus. When, however, they see his offense, they know him as a corruption among ascetics, just chaff and trash among ascetics. Then they expel him. For what reason? So that he doesn't corrupt the good bhikkhus.

"Suppose that when a large heap of grain is being winnowed, the grains that are firm and pithy form a pile on one side, and the wind blows the spoiled grains and chaff to another side. Then the owners take a broom and sweep them even further away. For what reason? So that they don't spoil the good grain.

"So too, so long as the bhikkhus do not see his offense, a certain person here has the same manner of going forward . . . and carrying his outer robe and bowl as the others, the good bhikkhus. When, however, the bhikkhus see his offense, they know him as [171] a corruption among ascetics, just chaff and trash among ascetics. Then they expel him. For what reason? So that he doesn't corrupt the good bhikkhus.

"Suppose a man needs a gutter for a well. He would take a sharp axe and enter the woods. He would strike a number of trees with the blade of his axe.[1636] When so struck, the firm and pithy trees would give off a dull sound, but those that are inwardly rotten, corrupt, and decayed would give off a hollow sound. The man would cut this tree down at its foot, cut off the crown, thoroughly clean it out, and use it as a gutter for a well.

"So too, bhikkhus, so long as the bhikkhus do not see his offense, a certain person here has the same manner of going forward and returning, of looking ahead and looking aside, of bending and stretching his limbs, of wearing his robes and carrying his outer robe and bowl, as the good bhikkhus. When, however, the bhikkhus see his offense, they know him as a corruption among ascetics, just chaff and trash among ascetics. Then they expel him. For what reason? So that he doesn't corrupt the good bhikkhus." [172]

By living together with him, know him as
an angry person with evil desires;
a denigrator, obstinate, and insolent,
envious, miserly, and deceptive.

He speaks to people just like an ascetic,
[addressing them] with a calm voice,
but secretly he does evil deeds,
holds pernicious views, and lacks respect.

Though he is devious, a speaker of lies,
you should know him as he truly is;
then you should all meet in harmony
and firmly drive him away.

Get rid of the trash!
Remove the depraved fellows!
Sweep the chaff away, non-ascetics
who think themselves ascetics!

Having banished those of evil desires,
of bad conduct and resort,
dwell in communion, ever mindful,
the pure with the pure;
then, in harmony, alert,
you will make an end of suffering.

II. The Great Chapter

11 (1) Verañjā

Thus have I heard. On one occasion the Blessed One was dwelling at Verañjā at the foot of Naḷeru's neem tree.[1637] Then a brahmin of Verañjā [173] approached the Blessed One and exchanged greetings with him. When he had concluded his greetings and cordial talk, he sat down to one side and said to the Blessed One:

"I have heard, Master Gotama: 'The ascetic Gotama does not pay homage to brahmins who are old, aged, burdened with years, advanced in life, come to the last stage; nor does he stand up for them or offer them a seat.' This is indeed true, for Master Gotama does not pay homage to brahmins who are old, aged, burdened with years, advanced in life, come to the last stage; nor does he stand up for them or offer them a seat. This is not proper, Master Gotama."[1638]

"Brahmin, in the world with its devas, Māra, and Brahmā, in this population with its ascetics and brahmins, its devas and humans, I do not see one to whom I should pay homage, or for whom I should stand up, or whom I should offer a seat. For if the Tathāgata should pay homage to anyone, or stand up for him, or offer him a seat, even that person's head would split."

(1) "Master Gotama lacks taste."[1639]

"There is, brahmin, a way in which one could rightly say of me: 'The ascetic Gotama lacks taste.' The Tathāgata has abandoned his taste for forms, sounds, odors, tastes, and tactile objects; he has cut it off at the root, made it like a palm stump, obliterated it so that it is no more subject to future arising. It is in this way that one could rightly say of me: 'The ascetic Gotama lacks taste.' But you did not speak with reference to this." [174]

(2) "Master Gotama is not convivial."[1640]

"There is, brahmin, a way in which one could rightly say of me: 'The ascetic Gotama is not convivial.' The Tathāgata has abandoned conviviality with forms, sounds, odors, tastes, and tactile objects; he has cut it off at the root, made it like a palm stump, obliterated it so that it is no more subject to future arising. It is in this way that one could rightly say of me: 'The ascetic Gotama is not convivial.' But you did not speak with reference to this."

(3) "Master Gotama is a proponent of non-doing."[1641]

"There is, brahmin, a way in which one could rightly say of me: 'The ascetic Gotama is a proponent of non-doing.' For I assert the non-doing of bodily, verbal, and mental misconduct;

I assert the non-doing of the numerous kinds of bad unwholesome deeds. It is in this way that one could rightly say of me: 'The ascetic Gotama is a proponent of non-doing.' But you did not speak with reference to this."

(4) "Master Gotama is an annihilationist."[1642]

"There is, brahmin, a way in which one could rightly say of me: 'The ascetic Gotama is an annihilationist.' For I assert the annihilation of lust, hatred, and delusion; I assert the annihilation of the numerous kinds of bad unwholesome qualities. It is in this way that one could rightly say of me: 'The ascetic Gotama is an annihilationist.' But you did not speak with reference to this."

(5) "Master Gotama is a repeller."[1643]

"There is, brahmin, a way in which one could rightly say of me: 'The ascetic Gotama is a repeller.' For I am repelled by bodily, verbal, and mental misconduct; I am repelled by the acquisition of the numerous kinds of bad unwholesome [175] qualities. It is in this way that one could rightly say of me: 'The ascetic Gotama is a repeller.' But you did not speak with reference to this."

(6) "Master Gotama is an abolitionist."[1644]

"There is, brahmin, a way in which one could rightly say of me: 'The ascetic Gotama is an abolitionist.' For I teach the Dhamma for the abolition of lust, hatred, and delusion; I teach the Dhamma for the abolition of the numerous kinds of bad unwholesome qualities. It is in this way that one could rightly say of me: 'The ascetic Gotama is an abolitionist.' But you did not speak with reference to this."

(7) "Master Gotama is a tormentor."[1645]

"There is, brahmin, a way in which one could rightly say of me: 'The ascetic Gotama is a tormentor.' For I assert that bad unwholesome qualities—bodily, verbal, and mental misconduct—are to be burned up. I say that someone is a tormentor when he has abandoned the bad unwholesome qualities that are to be burned up; when he has cut them off at the root, made them like a palm stump, obliterated them so that they are no more subject to future arising. The Tathāgata has abandoned the bad unwholesome qualities that are to be burned up; he has cut them off at the root, made them like a palm stump, obliterated them so that they are no more subject to future arising. It is in this way that one could rightly say of me: 'The ascetic Gotama is a tormentor.' But you did not speak with reference to this."

(8) "Master Gotama is retiring."[1646]

"There is, brahmin, a way in which one could rightly say of me: 'The ascetic Gotama is retiring.' For I say that someone is retiring when he has abandoned the production of renewed existence, the future bed of the womb; when he has cut it off at the root, made it like a palm stump, obliterated it [176] so that it is no more subject to future arising. The Tathāgata has abandoned the production of renewed existence, the future bed of the womb; he has cut it off at the root, made it like a palm stump, obliterated it so that it is no more subject to future arising. It is in this way that one could rightly say of me: 'The ascetic Gotama is retiring.' But you did not speak with reference to this.

"Suppose, brahmin, there was a hen with eight, ten, or twelve eggs that she had properly covered, incubated, and nurtured. Should the first among those chicks to pierce its shell with the points of its claws or beak and safely hatch be called the eldest or the youngest?"

"It should be called the eldest, Master Gotama. So it is the eldest among them."

"So too, brahmin, in a population immersed in ignorance, become like an egg, completely enveloped,[1647] I have pierced the eggshell of ignorance. I am the sole person in the world who has awakened to the unsurpassed perfect enlightenment. So I am the eldest, the best in the world.

"My energy, brahmin, was aroused without slackening; my mindfulness was established without confusion; my body was tranquil without disturbance; my mind was concentrated and one-pointed. Secluded from sensual pleasures, secluded from unwholesome states, I entered and dwelled in the first jhāna, which consists of rapture and pleasure born of seclusion, accompanied by thought and examination. With the subsiding of thought and examination, I entered and dwelled in the second jhāna, which has internal placidity and unification of mind and consists of rapture and pleasure born of concentration, without thought and examination. [177] With the fading away as well of rapture, I dwelled equanimous and, mindful and clearly comprehending, I experienced pleasure with the body; I entered and dwelled in the third jhāna of which the noble ones declare: 'He is equanimous, mindful, one who dwells happily.' With the abandoning of pleasure and pain, and with the previous passing away of joy and dejection, I entered and dwelled in the fourth jhāna, neither painful nor pleasant, which has purification of mindfulness by equanimity.

"When my mind was thus concentrated, purified, cleansed, unblemished, rid of defilement, malleable, wieldy, steady, and attained to imperturbability, I directed it to the knowledge of the recollection of past abodes.[1648] I recollected my manifold past abodes, that is, one birth, two births, three births, four births, five births, ten births, twenty births, thirty births, forty births, fifty births, a hundred births, a thousand births, a hundred thousand births, many eons of world-dissolution, many eons of world-evolution, many eons of world-dissolution and world-evolution thus: 'There I was so named, of such a clan, with such an appearance, such was my food, such my experience of pleasure and pain, such my life span; passing away from there, I was reborn elsewhere, and there too I was so named, of such a clan, with such an appearance, such was my food, such my experience of pleasure and pain, such my life span; passing away from there, I was reborn here.' Thus I recollected my manifold past abodes with their aspects and details.

"This, brahmin, was the first true knowledge attained by me in the first watch of the night. Ignorance was dispelled, true knowledge had arisen; darkness was dispelled, light had arisen, as happens when one dwells heedful, ardent, and resolute. This, brahmin, was my first breaking out, like that of the chick breaking out of the eggshell. [178]

"When my mind was thus concentrated, purified, cleansed, unblemished, rid of defilement, malleable, wieldy, steady, and attained to imperturbability, I directed it to the knowledge of the passing away and rebirth of beings. With the divine eye, which is purified and surpasses the human, I saw beings passing away and being reborn, inferior and superior, beautiful and ugly, fortunate and unfortunate, and I understood how beings fare in accordance with their kamma thus: 'These beings who engaged in misconduct by body, speech, and mind, who reviled the noble ones, held wrong view, and undertook kamma based on wrong view, with the breakup of the body, after death, have been reborn in the plane of misery, in a bad destination, in the lower world, in hell; but these beings who engaged in good conduct by body, speech, and mind, who did not revile the noble ones, who held right view, and undertook kamma based on right view, with the breakup of the body, after death, have been reborn in a good destination, in the heavenly world.' Thus with the divine eye, which is purified and surpasses the human, I saw beings passing away and being reborn, inferior and superior, beautiful and ugly, fortunate and unfortunate, and I understood how beings fare in accordance with their kamma.

"This, brahmin, was the second true knowledge attained by me in the middle watch of the night. Ignorance was dispelled, true knowledge had arisen; darkness was dispelled, light had arisen, as happens when one dwells heedful, ardent, and resolute. This, brahmin, was my second breaking out, like that of the chick breaking out of the eggshell.

"When my mind was thus concentrated, purified, cleansed, unblemished, rid of defilement, malleable, wieldy, steady, and attained to imperturbability, I directed it to the knowledge of the destruction of the taints. I understood as it really is: 'This is suffering'; I understood as it really is: 'This is the origin of suffering'; I understood as it really is: 'This is the cessation of suffering'; I understood as it really is: 'This is the way leading to the cessation of suffering.' I understood as it really is: 'These are the taints'; [179] I understood as it really is: 'This is the origin of the taints'; I understood as it really is: 'This is the cessation of the taints'; I understood as it really is: 'This is the way leading to the cessation of the taints.'

"When I knew and saw thus, my mind was liberated from the taint of sensuality, from the taint of existence, and from the taint of ignorance.[1649] When it was liberated there came the knowledge: '[It's] liberated.' I directly knew: 'Destroyed is birth, the spiritual life has been lived, what had to be done has been done, there is no more coming back to any state of being.'

"This, brahmin, was the third true knowledge attained by me in the last watch of the night. Ignorance was dispelled, true knowledge had arisen; darkness was dispelled, light had arisen, as happens when one dwells heedful, ardent, and resolute. This, brahmin, was my third breaking out, like that of the chick breaking out of the eggshell."

When this was said, the brahmin of Verañjā said to the Blessed One: "Master Gotama is the eldest! Master Gotama is the best! Excellent, Master Gotama! Excellent, Master Gotama! Master Gotama has made the Dhamma clear in many ways, as though he were turning upright what had been overthrown, revealing what was hidden, showing the way to one who was lost, or holding up a lamp in the darkness so those with good eyesight can see forms. I now go for refuge to Master Gotama, to the Dhamma, and to the Saṅgha of bhikkhus. Let Master Gotama consider me a lay follower who from today has gone for refuge for life."

12 (2) Sīha

On one occasion the Blessed One was dwelling at Vesālī in the hall with the peaked roof in the Great Wood. Now on that occasion, a number of well-known Licchavis had assembled in the meeting hall and were sitting together speaking in many ways in praise of the Buddha, the Dhamma, and the Saṅgha. [180] On that occasion Sīha the general, a disciple of the Nigaṇṭhas, was sitting in that assembly. It then occurred to him: "Doubtlessly, he must be a Blessed One, an Arahant, a Perfectly Enlightened One. For a number of these well-known Licchavis have assembled in the meeting hall and are sitting together speaking in many ways in praise of the Buddha, the Dhamma, and the Saṅgha. Let me go see that Blessed One, the Arahant, the Perfectly Enlightened One."

Then Sīha went to the Nigaṇṭha Nātaputta and said to him: "Bhante, I wish to go see the ascetic Gotama."

"Since you are a proponent of deeds, Sīha, why go see the ascetic Gotama, a proponent of non-doing? For the ascetic Gotama is a proponent of non-doing who teaches his Dhamma for the sake of non-doing and thereby guides his disciples."[1650]

Then Sīha's determination to go see the Blessed One subsided.

On a second occasion, a number of well-known Licchavis had assembled in the meeting hall and were sitting together speaking in many ways in praise of the Buddha, the Dhamma, and the Saṅgha. . . . [All as above, except this is now said to occur "on a second occasion."] [181] . . . On a second occasion, Sīha's determination to go see the Blessed One subsided.

On a third occasion, a number of well-known Licchavis had assembled in the meeting hall and were sitting together speaking in many ways in praise of the Buddha, the Dhamma, and the Saṅgha. It then occurred to Sīha: "Doubtlessly, he must be a Blessed One, an Arahant, a Perfectly Enlightened One. For a number of these well-known Licchavis have assembled in the meeting hall and are sitting together speaking in many ways in praise of the Buddha, the Dhamma, and the Saṅgha. What can the Nigaṇṭhas do to me whether or not I obtain their permission? Without having obtained the permission of the Nigaṇṭhas, let me go see that Blessed One, the Arahant, the Perfectly Enlightened One."[1651]

Then, with five hundred chariots, Sīha the general set out from Vesālī in the middle of the day in order to see the Blessed One. He went by carriage as far as the ground was suitable for a carriage, and then dismounted from his carriage and entered the monastery grounds on foot. He approached the Blessed One, paid homage to him, sat down to one side, and said to him:

"I have heard this, Bhante: 'The ascetic Gotama is a proponent of non-doing [182] who teaches his Dhamma for the sake of non-doing and thereby guides his disciples.' Do those who speak thus state what has been said by the Blessed One and not misrepresent him with what is contrary to fact? Do they explain in accordance with the Dhamma so that they would not incur any reasonable criticism or ground for censure?[1652] For we do not want to misrepresent the Blessed One."

(1) "There is, Sīha, a way in which one could rightly say of me: 'The ascetic Gotama is a proponent of non-doing who teaches his Dhamma for the sake of non-doing and thereby guides his disciples.'[1653]

(2) "There is a way in which one could rightly say of me: 'The ascetic Gotama is a proponent of deeds who teaches his Dhamma for the sake of deeds and thereby guides his disciples.'

(3) "There is a way in which one could rightly say of me: 'The ascetic Gotama is an annihilationist who teaches his Dhamma for the sake of annihilation and thereby guides his disciples.'

(4) "There is a way in which one could rightly say of me: 'The ascetic Gotama is a repeller who teaches his Dhamma for the sake of repulsion and thereby guides his disciples.'

(5) "There is a way in which one could rightly say of me: 'The ascetic Gotama is an abolitionist who teaches his Dhamma for the sake of abolition and thereby guides his disciples.'

(6) "There is a way in which one could rightly say of me: 'The ascetic Gotama is a tormentor who teaches his Dhamma for the sake of torment and thereby guides his disciples.'

(7) "There is a way in which one could rightly say of me: 'The ascetic Gotama is retiring, one who teaches his Dhamma for the sake of retiring and thereby guides his disciples.'

(8) "There is a way in which one could rightly say of me: 'The ascetic Gotama is a consoler[1654] who teaches his Dhamma for the sake of consolation and thereby guides his disciples.'

(1) "And in what way, Sīha, could one rightly say of me: 'The ascetic Gotama is a proponent of non-doing [183] who teaches his Dhamma for the sake of non-doing and thereby guides his disciples'? For I assert the non-doing of bodily, verbal, and mental misconduct; I assert the non-doing of the numerous kinds of bad unwholesome deeds. It is in this way that one could rightly say of me: 'The ascetic Gotama is a proponent of non-doing who teaches his Dhamma for the sake of non-doing and thereby guides his disciples.'

(2) "And in what way could one rightly say of me: 'The ascetic Gotama is a proponent of deeds who teaches his Dhamma for the sake of deeds and thereby guides his disciples'? For I assert good bodily, verbal, and mental conduct; I assert the doing of the numerous kinds of wholesome deeds. It is in this way that one could rightly say of me: 'The ascetic Gotama is a proponent of deeds who teaches his Dhamma for the sake of deeds and thereby guides his disciples.'

(3) "And in what way could one rightly say of me: 'The ascetic Gotama is an annihilationist who teaches his Dhamma for the sake of annihilation and thereby guides his disciples'? For I assert the annihilation of lust, hatred, and delusion; I assert the annihilation of the numerous kinds of bad unwholesome qualities. It is in this way that one could rightly say of me: 'The ascetic Gotama is an annihilationist who teaches his Dhamma for the sake of annihilation and thereby guides his disciples.'

(4) "And in what way could one rightly say of me: 'The ascetic Gotama is a repeller who teaches his Dhamma for the sake of repulsion and thereby guides his disciples'? For I am repelled

by bodily, verbal, and mental misconduct; I am repelled by the acquisition of the numerous kinds of bad unwholesome qualities. It is in this way that one could rightly say of me: 'The ascetic Gotama is a repeller who teaches his Dhamma for the sake of repulsion and thereby guides his disciples.'

(5) "And in what way could one rightly say of me: 'The ascetic Gotama is an abolitionist who teaches his Dhamma for the sake of abolition and thereby guides his disciples'? For I teach the Dhamma for the abolition of lust, hatred, and delusion; [184] I teach the Dhamma for the abolition of the numerous kinds of bad unwholesome qualities. It is in this way that one could rightly say of me: 'The ascetic Gotama is an abolitionist who teaches his Dhamma for the sake of abolition and thereby guides his disciples.'

(6) "And in what way could one rightly say of me: 'The ascetic Gotama is a tormentor who teaches his Dhamma for the sake of tormenting and thereby guides his disciples'? For I assert that bad unwholesome qualities—bodily, verbal, and mental misconduct—are to be burned up. I say that someone is a tormentor when he has abandoned the bad unwholesome qualities that are to be burned up; when he has cut them off at the root, made them like a palm stump, obliterated them so that they are no more subject to future arising. The Tathāgata has abandoned the bad unwholesome qualities that are to be burned up; he has cut them off at the root, made them like a palm stump, obliterated them so that they are no more subject to future arising. It is in this way that one could rightly say of me: 'The ascetic Gotama is a tormentor who teaches his Dhamma for the sake of tormenting and thereby guides his disciples.'

(7) "And in what way could one rightly say of me: 'The ascetic Gotama is retiring, one who teaches his Dhamma for the sake of retiring and thereby guides his disciples'? For I say that someone is retiring when he has abandoned the production of renewed existence, the future bed of the womb; when he has cut it off at the root, made it like a palm stump, obliterated it so that it is no more subject to future arising. The Tathāgata has abandoned the production of renewed existence, the future bed of the womb; he has cut it off at the root, made it like a palm stump, obliterated it so that it is no more subject to future arising. It is in this way that one could rightly say of me: 'The ascetic

Gotama is retiring, one who teaches his Dhamma for the sake of retiring and thereby guides his disciples.'

(8) "And in what way could one rightly say of me: 'The ascetic Gotama is a consoler, one who teaches his Dhamma for the sake of consolation and thereby guides his disciples'? For I [185] am a consoler with the supreme consolation; I teach the Dhamma for the sake of consolation and thereby guide my disciples. It is in this way that one could rightly say of me: 'The ascetic Gotama is a consoler, one who teaches his Dhamma for the sake of consolation and thereby guides his disciples.'"[1655]

When this was said, Sīha the general said to the Blessed One: "Excellent, Bhante! Excellent, Bhante! . . . Let the Blessed One accept me as a lay follower who from today has gone for refuge for life."

"Make an investigation, Sīha! It is good for such well-known people like yourself to make an investigation."[1656]

"Bhante, I am even more satisfied and pleased with the Blessed One for telling me: 'Make an investigation, Sīha! It is good for such well-known people like yourself to make an investigation.' For if the members of other sects were to gain me as their disciple, they would carry a banner all over Vesālī announcing: 'Sīha the general has become our disciple.' But the Blessed One rather tells me: 'Make an investigation, Sīha! It is good for such well-known people like yourself to make an investigation.' So for the second time, Bhante, I go to the Blessed One for refuge, to the Dhamma, and to the Saṅgha of bhikkhus. Let the Blessed One accept me as a lay follower who from today has gone for refuge for life."

"Sīha, your family has long been a fountain of support for the Nigaṇṭhas; hence you should consider continuing to give alms to them when they approach you."

"Bhante, I am even more satisfied and pleased with the Blessed One for telling me: 'Sīha, your family has long been a fountain of support for the Nigaṇṭhas; hence you should consider continuing to give alms to them when they approach you.' For I have heard: 'The ascetic Gotama says thus: [186] "Alms should be given only to me, not to others; alms should be given only to my disciples, not to the disciples of others. Only what is given to me is very fruitful, not what is given to others; only what is given to my disciples is very fruitful, not what is given to the disciples of others."'[1657] Yet the Blessed One encourages me to give to the Nigaṇṭhas, too. We'll know the right time for this. So for the third time, Bhante, I go to the Blessed One for refuge, to the Dhamma, and to the Saṅgha of bhikkhus. Let the Blessed One accept me as a lay follower who from today has gone for refuge for life."

Then the Blessed One gave Sīha the general a progressive discourse, that is, a talk on giving, virtuous behavior, and heaven; he revealed the danger, degradation, and defilement of sensual pleasures and the benefit of renunciation. When the Blessed One knew that Sīha's mind was pliant, softened, rid of hindrances, uplifted, and confident, he revealed that Dhamma teaching special to the Buddhas: suffering, its origin, its cessation, and the path. Then, just as a clean cloth rid of dark spots would readily absorb dye, so too, while Sīha the general sat in that same seat, there arose in him the dust-free, stainless Dhamma-eye: 'Whatever is subject to origination is all subject to cessation.' Sīha the general became one who had seen the Dhamma, attained the Dhamma, understood the Dhamma, fathomed the Dhamma, crossed over doubt, gotten rid of bewilderment, attained self-confidence, and become independent of others in the teaching of the Teacher. He then said to the Blessed One:

"Bhante, please let the Blessed One [187] together with the Saṅgha of bhikkhus accept tomorrow's meal from me."

The Blessed One consented by silence. Having understood that the Blessed One had consented, Sīha rose from his seat, paid homage to the Blessed One, circumambulated him keeping the right side toward him, and departed. Then Sīha addressed a man: "Go, good man, find some meat ready for sale."

Then, when the night had passed, Sīha the general had various kinds of excellent foods prepared in his own residence, after which he had the time announced to the Blessed One: "It is time, Bhante, the meal is ready."

Then, in the morning, the Blessed One dressed, took his bowl and robe, went to Sīha's residence along with the Saṅgha of bhikkhus, and sat down on the seat prepared for him. Now on that occasion a number of Nigaṇṭhas [went] from street to street and from square to square in Vesālī, thrashing their arms about and crying out: "Today Sīha the general has slain a plump animal to prepare a meal for the ascetic Gotama! The ascetic

Gotama knowingly uses meat [obtained from an animal killed] especially for his sake, the act being done on his account."

Then a man approached Sīha the general and whispered into his ear: "Sir, you should know that a number of Nigaṇṭhas [are going] from street to street and from square to square in Vesālī, thrashing their arms about and crying out: 'Today Sīha the general has slain a plump animal to prepare a meal for the ascetic Gotama! The ascetic Gotama knowingly uses meat [obtained from an animal killed] especially for his sake, [188] a deed done on his account.'"

"Enough, good man. For a long time those venerable ones have wanted to discredit the Buddha, the Dhamma, and the Saṅgha. They will never stop[1658] misrepresenting the Blessed One with what is untrue, baseless, false, and contrary to fact, and we would never intentionally deprive a living being of life, even for the sake of our life."[1659]

Then, with his own hands, Sīha the general served and satisfied the Saṅgha of bhikkhus headed by the Buddha with the various kinds of excellent food. Then, when the Blessed One had finished eating and had put away his bowl, Sīha sat down to one side. Then the Blessed One instructed, encouraged, inspired, and gladdened Sīha with a Dhamma talk, after which he rose from his seat and departed.

13 (3) Thoroughbred

"Bhikkhus, possessing eight factors, a king's excellent thoroughbred horse is worthy of a king, an accessory of a king, and reckoned as a factor of kingship. What eight?

"Here, (1) a king's excellent thoroughbred horse is well born on both sides, maternal and paternal; he is born in whatever area other excellent thoroughbred horses are born. (2) He respectfully eats whatever food they give him, whether moist or dry, without scattering it. (3) He is repelled by sitting down or lying down near feces or urine. (4) He is mild[1660] [189] and pleasant to live with, and he does not agitate other horses. (5) He reveals his tricks, ploys, gambits, and wiles as they really are to his trainer so that his trainer can make an effort to stamp them out of him. (6) He carries loads, determined: 'Whether or not the other horses carry loads, I myself will carry them.' (7) When moving, he moves only along a straight path. (8) He is strong, and he shows his strength right up until the end of his life. Possessing these eight factors, a king's excellent thoroughbred horse is worthy of a king, an accessory of a king, and reckoned as a factor of kingship.

"So too, bhikkhus, possessing eight qualities, a bhikkhu is worthy of gifts . . . an unsurpassed field of merit for the world. What eight?

(1) "Here, a bhikkhu is virtuous; he dwells restrained by the Pātimokkha, possessed of good conduct and resort, seeing danger in minute faults. Having undertaken the training rules, he trains in them. (2) He respectfully eats whatever food they give him, whether coarse or excellent, without being annoyed. (3) He is repelled by bodily, verbal, and mental misconduct; he is repelled by the acquisition of the numerous kinds of bad unwholesome qualities. (4) He is mild and pleasant to live with, and he does not agitate other bhikkhus. (5) He reveals his tricks, [190] ploys, gambits, and wiles as they really are to the Teacher or to his wise fellow monks so that they can make an effort to stamp them out of him. (6) He is one who takes up the training, determined: 'Whether or not other bhikkhus train, I will train.' (7) When moving, he moves only along a straight path. In this connection, this is the straight path: right view . . . right concentration. (8) He has aroused energy thus: 'Willingly, let only my skin, sinews, and bones remain, and let the flesh and blood dry up in my body, but I will not relax my energy so long as I have not attained what can be attained by manly strength, energy, and exertion.'[1661] Possessing these eight qualities, a bhikkhu is worthy of gifts . . . an unsurpassed field of merit for the world."

14 (4) Wild Colts

"Bhikkhus, I will teach you the eight kinds of wild colts and the eight faults of a horse, and I will teach you the eight kinds of persons who are like wild colts and the eight faults of a person. Listen and attend closely. I will speak."

"Yes, Bhante," those bhikkhus replied. The Blessed One said this:

"And what, bhikkhus, are the eight kinds of wild colts and the eight faults of a horse?

(1) "Here, when a wild colt is told: 'Go forward!' and is being spurred and incited by its trainer, it backs up [191] and spins the chariot around behind it.[1662] There is such a kind of wild colt here. This is the first fault of a horse.

(2) "Again, when a wild colt is told: 'Go forward!' and is being spurred and incited by its trainer, it leaps back and [thereby] damages the rail and breaks the triple rod.[1663] There is such a kind of wild colt here. This is the second fault of a horse.

(3) "Again, when a wild colt is told: 'Go forward!' and is being spurred and incited by its trainer, it loosens its thigh from the chariot pole and crushes the chariot pole.[1664] There is such a kind of wild colt here. This is the third fault of a horse.

(4) "Again, when a wild colt is told: 'Go forward!' and is being spurred and incited by its trainer, it takes a wrong path and leads the chariot off the track. There is such a kind of wild colt here. This is the fourth fault of a horse.

(5) "Again, when a wild colt is told: 'Go forward!' and is being spurred and incited by its trainer, it leaps up with the front of its body and churns the air with its front feet. There is such a kind of wild colt here. This is the fifth fault of a horse.

(6) "Again, when a wild colt is told: 'Go forward!' and is being spurred and incited by its trainer, it does not heed its trainer or the goad[1665] but destroys the mouthbit with its teeth [192] and sets out wherever it wishes. There is such a kind of wild colt here. This is the sixth fault of a horse.

(7) "Again, when a wild colt is told: 'Go forward!' and is being spurred and incited by its trainer, it does not go forward or turn back but stands right there as still as a post. There is such a kind of wild colt here. This is the seventh fault of a horse.

(8) "Again, when a wild colt is told: 'Go forward!' and is being spurred and incited by its trainer, it tucks in its front legs and its back legs and sits down right there on all four legs. There is such a kind of wild colt here. This is the eighth fault of a horse.

"These are the eight kinds of wild colts and the eight faults of a horse.

"And what, bhikkhus, are the eight kinds of persons who are like wild colts and the eight faults of a person?

(1) "Here, when the bhikkhus are reproving a bhikkhu for an offense, he exonerates himself by reason of lack of memory, saying: 'I don't remember [committing such an offense].' I say this person is similar to the wild colt that, when told: 'Go forward!' and when spurred and incited by its trainer, backs up and spins the chariot around behind it. There is such a kind of person here like a wild colt. This is the first fault of a person.

(2) "Again, when the bhikkhus are reproving a bhikkhu for an offense, [193] he castigates the reprover himself: 'What right does an incompetent fool like you have to speak? Do you really think you have something to say?' I say this person is similar to the wild colt that, when told: 'Go forward!' and when spurred and incited by its trainer, leaps back and [thereby] damages the rail and breaks the triple pole. There is such a kind of person here like a wild colt. This is the second fault of a person.

(3) "Again, when the bhikkhus are reproving a bhikkhu for an offense, he attributes an offense to the reprover himself, saying: 'You have committed such and such an offense. Make amends for it first.' I say this person is similar to the wild colt that, when told: 'Go forward!' and when spurred and incited by its trainer, loosens its thigh from the chariot pole and crushes the chariot pole. There is such a kind of person here like a wild colt. This is the third fault of a person.

(4) "Again, when the bhikkhus are reproving a bhikkhu for an offense, he answers evasively, diverts the discussion to an irrelevant subject, and displays anger, hatred, and bitterness. I say this person is similar to the wild colt that, when told: 'Go forward!' and when spurred and incited by its trainer, takes a wrong path and leads the chariot off the track. There is such a kind of person here like a wild colt. This is the fourth fault of a person.

(5) "Again, when the bhikkhus are reproving a bhikkhu for an offense, he speaks while waving his arms about in the midst of the Saṅgha. I say this person is similar to [194] the wild colt that, when told: 'Go forward!' and when spurred and incited by its trainer, leaps up with the front of its body and churns the air with its front feet. There is such a kind of person here like a wild colt. This is the fifth fault of a person.

(6) "Again, when the bhikkhus are reproving a bhikkhu for an offense, he does not heed the Saṅgha or his reprover but sets out wherever he wishes while still bearing his offense. I say this person is similar to the wild colt that, when told: 'Go forward!' and when spurred and incited by its trainer, does not heed its trainer or the goad but destroys the mouthbit with its teeth and sets out wherever it wishes. There is such a kind of person here like a wild colt. This is the sixth fault of a person.

(7) "Again, when the bhikkhus are reproving a bhikkhu for

an offense, he does not say, 'I committed an offense,' nor does he say, 'I did not commit an offense,' but he vexes the Saṅgha by keeping silent. I say this person is similar to the wild colt that, when told: 'Go forward!' and when spurred and incited by its trainer, does not go forward or turn back but stands right there as still as a post. There is such a kind of person here like a wild colt. This is the seventh fault of a person.

(8) "Again, when the bhikkhus are reproving a bhikkhu for an offense, he says: [195] 'Why are you making such a fuss about me? Now I'll reject the training and return to the lower life.' He then rejects the training, returns to the lower life, and declares: 'Now you can be satisfied!' I say this person is similar to the wild colt that, when told: 'Go forward!' and when spurred and incited by its trainer, tucks in its front legs and its back legs and sits down right there on all four legs. There is such a kind of person here like a wild colt. This is the eighth fault of a person.

"These, bhikkhus, are the eight kinds of persons who are like wild colts and the eight faults of a person."

15 (5) Stains

"Bhikkhus, there are these eight stains. What eight? (1) Non-recitation is the stain of the hymns. (2) The stain of houses is lack of upkeep.[1666] (3) The stain of beauty is laziness. (4) Heedlessness is the stain of a guard. (5) A woman's stain is misconduct. (6) Miserliness is a donor's stain. (7) Bad unwholesome qualities are stains in this world and the next. (8) A stain graver than this is ignorance, the very worst of stains. These, bhikkhus, are the eight stains."

Non-recitation is the stain of the hymns;[1667]
the stain of houses is lack of upkeep;
the stain of beauty is laziness,
heedlessness is the stain of a guard.

A woman's stain is misconduct,
miserliness is a donor's stain;
bad unwholesome qualities are stains
in this world and the next.
A stain graver than these
is ignorance, the worst of stains. [196]

16 (6) Mission

"Bhikkhus, possessing eight qualities, a bhikkhu is worthy of going on a mission. What eight?

"Here, (1)–(2) a bhikkhu is one who listens and makes others listen; (3)–(4) he is one who learns well and makes others learn; (5)–(6) he is one who understands and communicates well; (7) he is skilled in [knowing] what is relevant and what irrelevant; and (8) he does not foment quarrels. Possessing these eight qualities, a bhikkhu is worthy of going on a mission.

"Bhikkhus, possessing eight qualities, Sāriputta is worthy of going on a mission. What eight?

"Here, Sāriputta is one who listens and who makes others listen . . . he does not foment quarrels. Possessing these eight qualities, Sāriputta is worthy of going on a mission."

One who does not tremble when he arrives
at an assembly with fierce debaters;
who does not omit words
or conceal his message;
who speaks without hesitation,
and does not waver when asked a question;
a bhikkhu like this is worthy
of going on a mission.

17 (7) Bondage (1)

"Bhikkhus, a woman binds a man in eight ways. What eight? A woman binds a man by her form . . . by her smile . . . by her speech . . . by singing [197] . . . by weeping . . . by her appearance . . . by a present[1668] . . . by her touch.[1669] A woman binds a man in these eight ways. Those beings are thoroughly bound who are bound by touch."[1670]

18 (8) Bondage (2)

"Bhikkhus, a man binds a woman in eight ways. What eight? A man binds a woman by his form . . . by his smile . . . by his speech . . . by singing . . . by weeping . . . by his appearance . . . by a present . . . by his touch. A man binds a woman in these eight ways. Those beings are thoroughly bound who are bound by touch."

19 (9) Pahārāda

On one occasion the Blessed One was dwelling at Verañjā at the foot of Naḷeru's neem tree. Then Pahārāda, ruler of the asuras, approached the Blessed One, paid homage to him, and stood to one side. The Blessed One then said to him: [198]

"Pahārāda, do the asuras take delight in the great ocean?"

"Bhante, the asuras do take delight in the great ocean."

"But, Pahārāda, how many astounding and amazing qualities do the asuras see in the great ocean because of which they take delight in it?"

"The asuras see eight astounding and amazing qualities in the great ocean because of which they take delight in it. What eight?

(1) "The great ocean, Bhante, slants, slopes, and inclines gradually, not dropping off abruptly.[1671] This is the first astounding and amazing quality that the asuras see in the great ocean because of which they take delight in it.

(2) "Again, the great ocean is stable and does not overflow its boundaries. This is the second astounding and amazing quality that the asuras see in the great ocean....

(3) "Again, the great ocean does not associate with a corpse, but quickly carries it to the coast and washes it ashore. This is the third astounding and amazing quality that the asuras see in the great ocean....

(4) "Again, when the great rivers—the Ganges, the Yamunā, the Aciravatī, the Sarabhū, and the Mahī—reach the great ocean, they give up their former names and designations [199] and are simply called the great ocean. This is the fourth astounding and amazing quality that the asuras see in the great ocean....

(5) "Again, whatever streams in the world flow into the great ocean and however much rain falls into it from the sky, neither a decrease nor a filling up can be seen in the great ocean. This is the fifth astounding and amazing quality that the asuras see in the great ocean....

(6) "Again, the great ocean has but one taste, the taste of salt. This is the sixth astounding and amazing quality that the asuras see in the great ocean....

(7) "Again, the great ocean contains many precious substances, numerous precious substances such as pearls, gems, beryl, conch, quartz, coral, silver, gold, rubies, and cats-eye.

This [200] is the seventh astounding and amazing quality that the asuras see in the great ocean. . . .

(8) "Again, the great ocean is the abode of great beings such as timis, timiṅgalas, timirapiṅgalas, asuras, nāgas, and gandhabbas.[1672] There are in the great ocean beings with bodies one hundred *yojanas* long, two hundred, three hundred, four hundred, and five hundred *yojanas* long. This is the eighth astounding and amazing quality that the asuras see in the great ocean because of which they take delight in it.

"These, Bhante, are the eight astounding and amazing qualities that the asuras see in the great ocean because of which they take delight in it. But do the bhikkhus take delight in this Dhamma and discipline?"

"Pahārāda, the bhikkhus do take delight in this Dhamma and discipline."

"But, Bhante, how many astounding and amazing qualities do the bhikkhus see in this Dhamma and discipline because of which they take delight in it?"

"The bhikkhus see eight astounding and amazing qualities in this Dhamma and discipline because of which they take delight in it. What eight?

(1) "Just as, Pahārāda, the great ocean slants, slopes, and inclines gradually, not dropping off abruptly, [201] so too, in this Dhamma and discipline penetration to final knowledge occurs by gradual training, gradual activity, and gradual practice, not abruptly.[1673] This is the first astounding and amazing quality that the bhikkhus see in this Dhamma and discipline because of which they take delight in it.

(2) "Just as the great ocean is stable and does not overflow its boundaries, so too, when I have prescribed a training rule for my disciples, they will not transgress it even for life's sake. This is the second astounding and amazing quality that the bhikkhus see in this Dhamma and discipline. . . .

(3) "Just as the great ocean does not associate with a corpse, but quickly carries it to the coast and washes it ashore, so too, the Saṅgha does not associate with a person who is immoral, of bad character, impure, of suspect behavior, secretive in his actions, not an ascetic though claiming to be one, not a celibate though claiming to be one, inwardly rotten, corrupt, depraved; rather, it quickly assembles and expels him. Even though he

is seated in the midst of the Saṅgha of bhikkhus, yet he is far from the Saṅgha and the Saṅgha is far from him. [202] This is the third astounding and amazing quality that the bhikkhus see in this Dhamma and discipline....

(4) "Just as, when the great rivers ... reach the great ocean, they give up their former names and designations and are simply called the great ocean, so too, when members of the four social classes—khattiyas, brahmins, vessas, and suddas—go forth from the household life into homelessness in the Dhamma and discipline proclaimed by the Tathāgata, they give up their former names and clans and are simply called ascetics following the Sakyan son. This is the fourth astounding and amazing quality that the bhikkhus see in this Dhamma and discipline....

(5) "Just as, whatever streams in the world flow into the great ocean and however much rain falls into it from the sky, neither a decrease nor a filling up can be seen in the great ocean, so too, even if many bhikkhus attain final nibbāna by way of the nibbāna element without residue remaining, neither a decrease nor a filling up can be seen in the nibbāna element.[1674] [203] This is the fifth astounding and amazing quality that the bhikkhus see in this Dhamma and discipline....

(6) "Just as the great ocean has but one taste, the taste of salt, so too, this Dhamma and discipline has but one taste, the taste of liberation. This is the sixth astounding and amazing quality that the bhikkhus see in this Dhamma and discipline....

(7) "Just as the great ocean contains many precious substances, numerous precious substances such as pearls ... cats-eye, so too, this Dhamma and discipline contains many precious substances, numerous precious substances: the four establishments of mindfulness, the four right strivings, the four bases for psychic potency, the five spiritual faculties, the five powers, the seven factors of enlightenment, the noble eightfold path. This is the seventh astounding and amazing quality that the bhikkhus see in this Dhamma and discipline....

(8) "Just as the great ocean is the abode of great beings such as timis ... [204] ... gandhabbas; and as there are in the great ocean beings with bodies one hundred *yojanas* long ... five hundred *yojanas* long, so too this Dhamma and discipline is the abode of great beings: the stream-enterer, the one practicing for realization of the fruit of stream-entry; the once-returner,

the one practicing for realization of the fruit of once-returning; the non-returner, the one practicing for realization of the fruit of non-returning; the arahant, the one practicing for arahantship. This is the eighth astounding and amazing quality that the bhikkhus see in this Dhamma and discipline because of which they take delight in it.

"These, Pahārāda, are the eight astounding and amazing qualities that the bhikkhus see in this Dhamma and discipline because of which they take delight in it."

20 (10) Uposatha[1675]

On one occasion the Blessed One was dwelling at Sāvatthī in Migāramātā's Mansion in the Eastern Park. Now on that occasion, on the day of the uposatha, the Blessed One was sitting surrounded by the Saṅgha of bhikkhus. Then, as the night advanced, when the first watch passed, the Venerable Ānanda rose from his seat, arranged his upper robe over one shoulder, reverently saluted the Blessed One, and said to him: "Bhante, the night has advanced; the first watch has passed; the Saṅgha of bhikkhus has been sitting for a long time. Let the Blessed One recite the Pātimokkha to the bhikkhus." When this was said, the Blessed One was silent. [205]

As the night advanced [still further], when the middle watch passed, the Venerable Ānanda rose from his seat a second time, arranged his upper robe over one shoulder, reverently saluted the Blessed One, and said to him: "Bhante, the night has advanced [still further]; the middle watch has passed; the Saṅgha of bhikkhus has been sitting for a long time. Bhante, let the Blessed One recite the Pātimokkha to the bhikkhus." A second time the Blessed One was silent.

As the night advanced [still further], when the last watch passed, when dawn arrived and a rosy tint appeared on the horizon, the Venerable Ānanda rose from his seat a third time, arranged his upper robe over one shoulder, reverently saluted the Blessed One, and said to him: "Bhante, the night has advanced [still further]; the last watch has passed; dawn has arrived and a rosy tint has appeared on the horizon; the Saṅgha of bhikkhus has been sitting for a long time. Let the Blessed One recite the Pātimokkha to the bhikkhus."

"This assembly, Ānanda, is impure."

Then it occurred to the Venerable Mahāmoggallāna: "What person was the Blessed One referring to when he said: 'This assembly, Ānanda, is impure'?" Then the Venerable Mahāmoggallāna fixed his attention on the entire Saṅgha of bhikkhus, encompassing their minds with his own mind. He then saw that person sitting in the midst of the Saṅgha of bhikkhus: one who was immoral, of bad character, impure, of suspect behavior, secretive in his actions, not an ascetic though claiming to be one, not a celibate though claiming to be one, inwardly rotten, corrupt, depraved. Having seen him, he rose from his seat, went up to that person, and said to him: "Get up, friend. The Blessed One has seen you. You cannot live in communion with the bhikkhus." When this was said, that person remained silent.

A second time . . . A third time the Venerable Mahāmoggallāna said to that person: [206] "Get up, friend. The Blessed One has seen you. You cannot live in communion with the bhikkhus." A third time that person remained silent.

Then the Venerable Mahāmoggallāna grabbed that person by the arm, evicted him through the outer gatehouse, and bolted the door. Then he returned to the Blessed One and said to him: "I have evicted that person, Bhante. The assembly is pure. Let the Blessed One recite the Pātimokkha to the bhikkhus."

"It's astounding and amazing, Moggallāna, how that hollow man waited[1676] until he was grabbed by the arm." Then the Blessed One addressed the bhikkhus: "Now, bhikkhus, you yourselves should conduct the uposatha and recite the Pātimokkha. From today onward, I will no longer do so. It is impossible and inconceivable that the Tathāgata could conduct the uposatha and recite the Pātimokkha in an impure assembly.

"The asuras, bhikkhus, see these eight astounding and amazing qualities in the great ocean because of which they take delight in it. What eight?

(1) "The great ocean, bhikkhus, slants, slopes, and inclines gradually, not dropping off abruptly. This is the first astounding and amazing quality that the asuras see in the great ocean because of which they take delight in it. . . .

[All as in 8:19, but addressed to the bhikkhus.]

(8) "Again, the great ocean is the abode of great beings . . . [207] . . . five hundred *yojanas* long. This is the eighth astound-

ing and amazing quality that the asuras see in the great ocean because of which they take delight in it.

"These, bhikkhus, are the eight astounding and amazing qualities that the asuras see in the great ocean because of which they take delight in it. So too, the bhikkhus see eight astounding and amazing qualities in this Dhamma and discipline because of which they take delight in it. What eight?

(1) "Just as, bhikkhus, the great ocean slants, slopes, and inclines gradually, not dropping off abruptly, so too, in this Dhamma and discipline penetration to final knowledge occurs by gradual training, gradual activity, and gradual practice, not abruptly. This is the first astounding and amazing quality that the bhikkhus see in this Dhamma and discipline because of which they take delight in it. . . .

[All as in 8:19, but addressed to the bhikkhus.]

(8) "Just as the great ocean is the abode of great beings . . . five hundred *yojanas* [208] long, so too, this Dhamma and discipline is the abode of great beings: the stream-enterer, the one practicing for the realization of the fruit of stream-entry . . . the arahant, the one practicing for arahantship. This is the eighth astounding and amazing quality that the bhikkhus see in this Dhamma and discipline because of which they take delight in it.

"These, bhikkhus, are the eight astounding and amazing qualities that the bhikkhus see in this Dhamma and discipline because of which they take delight in it."

III. Householders

21 (1) Ugga (1)

On one occasion the Blessed One was dwelling at Vesālī in the hall with the peaked roof in the Great Wood. There the Blessed One addressed the bhikkhus: "Bhikkhus!"

"Venerable sir!" those bhikkhus replied. The Blessed One said this:

"Bhikkhus, you should remember the householder Ugga of Vesālī as one who possesses eight astounding and amazing qualities."[1677] [209] This is what the Blessed One said. Having said this, the Fortunate One rose from his seat and entered his dwelling.

Then, in the morning, a certain bhikkhu dressed, took his

bowl and robe, and went to the residence of the householder Ugga of Vesālī. When he arrived, he sat down on the seat that was prepared for him. Then the householder Ugga of Vesālī approached that bhikkhu, paid homage to him, and sat down to one side. The bhikkhu then said to him:

"Householder, the Blessed One declared that you possess eight astounding and amazing qualities. What are they?"

"I don't know, Bhante, what eight astounding and amazing qualities the Blessed One declared that I possess. However, there are found in me eight astounding and amazing qualities. Listen and attend closely. I will speak."

"Yes, householder," the bhikkhu replied. The householder Ugga of Vesālī said this:

(1) "When, Bhante, I first saw the Blessed One in the distance, as soon as I saw him my mind acquired confidence in him. This is the first astounding and amazing quality found in me.

(2) "With a confident mind, I attended on the Blessed One. The Blessed One then gave me a progressive discourse, that is, a talk on giving, virtuous behavior, and heaven; he revealed the danger, degradation, and defilement of sensual pleasures and the benefit of renunciation. When the Blessed One knew that my mind was pliant, softened, rid of hindrances, uplifted, and confident, he [210] revealed that Dhamma teaching special to the Buddhas: suffering, its origin, its cessation, and the path. Then, just as a clean cloth rid of dark spots would readily absorb dye, so too, while I sat in that same seat, the dust-free, stainless Dhamma-eye arose in me: 'Whatever is subject to origination is all subject to cessation.' I saw the Dhamma, attained the Dhamma, understood the Dhamma, fathomed the Dhamma, crossed over doubt, got rid of bewilderment, attained self-confidence, and became independent of others in the teaching of the Teacher. Right there I went for refuge to the Buddha, the Dhamma, and the Saṅgha, and undertook the training rules with celibacy as the fifth.[1678] This is the second astounding and amazing quality found in me.

(3) "I had four young wives. I then went to them and said: 'Sisters, I have undertaken the training rules with celibacy as the fifth. If you want, you can enjoy wealth right here and do merits, or go back to your own family circle, or inform me if you want me to give you over to another man.' My eldest wife then said to me: 'Young sir, give me to such and such a man.' I sent for

that man, and with my left hand I took my wife, with my right hand I took the ceremonial vase, and I gave her to that man. But even while giving away my young wife, I don't recall that any alteration took place in my mind. This is the third astounding and amazing quality found in me. [211]

(4) "My family is wealthy but the wealth is shared unreservedly with virtuous people of good character. This is the fourth astounding and amazing quality found in me.

(5) "Whenever I attend on a bhikkhu, I attend on him respectfully, not without respect. This is the fifth astounding and amazing quality found in me.

(6) "If that venerable one teaches me the Dhamma, I listen to it respectfully, not without respect. If he doesn't teach me the Dhamma, then I teach him the Dhamma. This is the sixth astounding and amazing quality found in me.

(7) "It isn't unusual for deities to come and report to me: 'Householder, the Dhamma is well expounded by the Blessed One.' I then say to those deities: 'Whether you say so or not, the Dhamma is well expounded by the Blessed One.' Still, I do not recall any mental exultation arising because deities come to me or because I converse with deities. This is the seventh astounding and amazing quality found in me.

(8) "Of the five lower fetters taught by the Blessed One, I don't see any that I haven't abandoned.[1679] This is the eighth astounding and amazing quality found in me. [212]

"These, Bhante, are eight astounding and amazing qualities found in me. But I don't know what eight astounding and amazing qualities the Blessed One declared that I possess."

Then that bhikkhu, having received almsfood at the residence of the householder Ugga of Vesālī, rose from his seat and departed. After his meal, on returning from his alms round, he approached the Blessed One, paid homage to him, sat down to one side, and reported to him the entire conversation he had had with the householder Ugga of Vesālī.

[The Blessed One said:] "Good, good, bhikkhu! I had declared that the householder Ugga of Vesālī possesses the same eight astounding and amazing qualities that he rightly explained to you. You should remember the householder Ugga of Vesālī as one who possesses these eight astounding and amazing qualities."

22 (2) Ugga (2)

On one occasion the Blessed One was dwelling among the Vajjis at Hatthigāma. There the Blessed One addressed the bhikkhus....

"Bhikkhus, you should remember the householder Ugga of Hatthigāma as one who possesses eight astounding and amazing qualities." This is what the Blessed One said. Having said this, the Fortunate One rose from his seat and entered his dwelling.

Then, in the morning, a certain bhikkhu dressed, took his bowl and robe, and went to the residence of the householder Ugga of Hatthigāma. When he arrived, he sat down on the seat that was prepared for him. Then the householder Ugga of Hatthigāma approached that bhikkhu, paid homage to him, and sat down to one side. The bhikkhu then said to him: [213]

"Householder, the Blessed One declared that you possess eight astounding and amazing qualities. What are they?"

"I don't know, Bhante, what eight astounding and amazing qualities the Blessed One declared that I possess. However, there are found in me eight astounding and amazing qualities. Listen and attend closely. I will speak."

"Yes, householder," the bhikkhu replied. The householder Ugga of Hatthigāma said this:

(1) "Bhante, I was carousing in the Nāga Grove when I first saw the Blessed One in the distance. As soon as I saw him my mind acquired confidence in him and my drunkenness vanished. This is the first astounding and amazing quality found in me.

(2) "With a confident mind, I attended on the Blessed One. The Blessed One then gave me a progressive discourse.... [as in 8:21]... Right there [214] I went for refuge to the Buddha, the Dhamma, and the Saṅgha, and undertook the training rules with celibacy as the fifth. This is the second astounding and amazing quality found in me.

(3) "I had four young wives. I then went to them... [as in 8:21]... But even while giving away my young wife, I don't recall that any alteration took place in my mind. This is the third astounding and amazing quality found in me.

(4) "My family is wealthy but the wealth is shared unreservedly with virtuous people of good character. This is the fourth astounding and amazing quality found in me. [215]

(5) "Whenever I attend on a bhikkhu, I attend on him respectfully, not without respect. If that venerable one teaches me the Dhamma, I listen to it respectfully, not without respect. If he doesn't teach me the Dhamma, then I teach him the Dhamma. This is the fifth astounding and amazing quality found in me.

(6) "It isn't unusual that when the Saṅgha has been invited by me [for a meal], deities come and report to me: 'That bhikkhu, householder, is liberated in both respects. That one is liberated by wisdom. That one is a body witness. That one is attained to view. That one is liberated by faith. That one is a Dhamma follower. That one is a faith follower. That one is virtuous, of good character. That one is immoral, of bad character.' Still, when I am serving the Saṅgha, I do not recall thinking: 'Let me give this one little, let me give that one a lot.' Rather, I give with an equal mind. This is the sixth astounding and amazing quality found in me.

(7) "It isn't unusual for deities to come and report to me: "Householder, the Dhamma is well expounded by the Blessed One.' I then say to those deities: 'Whether you deities say so or not, the Dhamma is well expounded by the Blessed One.' Still, I do not recall any mental exultation arising because deities come to me or because I converse with deities. This is the seventh astounding and amazing quality found in me. [216]

(8) "If I were to pass away before the Blessed One, it wouldn't be surprising if the Blessed One would declare of me: 'There is no fetter bound by which the householder Ugga of Hatthigāma might return to this world.'[1680] This is the eighth astounding and amazing quality found in me.

"These, Bhante, are eight astounding and amazing qualities found in me. But I don't know what eight astounding and amazing qualities the Blessed One declared that I possess."

Then that bhikkhu, having received almsfood at the residence of the householder Ugga of Hatthigāma, rose from his seat and departed. After his meal, on returning from his alms round, he approached the Blessed One, paid homage to him, sat down to one side, and reported to him the entire conversation he had had with the householder Ugga of Hatthigāma.

[The Blessed One said:] "Good, good, bhikkhu! I had declared that the householder Ugga of Hatthigāma possesses these same eight astounding and amazing qualities that he rightly explained to you. You should remember the householder Ugga of Hatthigāma as one who possesses these eight astounding and amazing qualities."

23 (3) Hatthaka (1)

On one occasion the Blessed One was dwelling at Āḷavī at the Aggāḷava Shrine. There the Blessed One addressed the bhikkhus. . . . [217]

"Bhikkhus, you should remember Hatthaka of Āḷavī as one who possesses seven astounding and amazing qualities. What seven? (1) Hatthaka of Āḷavī is endowed with faith. (2) He is virtuous, and (3) has a sense of moral shame and (4) moral dread. (5) He is learned, (6) generous, and (7) wise. You should remember Hatthaka of Āḷavī as one who possesses these seven astounding and amazing qualities." This is what the Blessed One said. Having said this, the Fortunate One rose from his seat and entered his dwelling.

Then, in the morning, a certain bhikkhu dressed, took his bowl and robe, and went to the residence of Hatthaka of Āḷavī. When he arrived, he sat down on the seat that was prepared for him. Then Hatthaka of Āḷavī approached the bhikkhu, paid homage to him, and sat down to one side. The bhikkhu then said to him:

"Friend,[1681] the Blessed One declared that you possess seven astounding and amazing qualities. What seven? 'Bhikkhus, Hatthaka of Āḷavī is endowed with faith. He is virtuous and has a sense of moral shame and moral dread. He is learned, generous, and wise.' The Blessed One declared that you possess these seven astounding and amazing qualities."

"I hope, Bhante, that no white-robed layman was present?"

"No, friend. No white-robed layman was present."

"That's good, Bhante."

Then that bhikkhu, having received almsfood at the residence of Hatthaka of Āḷavī, rose from his seat and departed. After his meal, on returning from his alms round, he approached the Blessed One, [218] paid homage to him, sat down to one side, [and reported to him all that had happened].[1682]

[The Blessed One said:] "Good, good, bhikkhu! That clansman has few desires, since he does not want his inner wholesome qualities to be known by others. Therefore, bhikkhu, you should remember Hatthaka of Āḷavī as one who possesses this eighth astounding and amazing quality, that is, (8) fewness of desires."

24 (4) Hatthaka (2)

On one occasion the Blessed One was dwelling at Āḷavī at the Aggāḷava Shrine. Then Hatthaka of Āḷavī, accompanied by five hundred lay followers, [219] approached the Blessed One, paid homage to him, and sat down to one side. The Blessed One then said to him:

"Your retinue is large, Hatthaka. How do you sustain this large retinue?"

"I do so, Bhante, by the four means of sustaining a favorable relationship taught by the Blessed One.[1683] When I know: 'This one is to be sustained by a gift,' I sustain him by a gift. When I know: 'This one is to be sustained by endearing speech,' I sustain him by endearing speech. When I know: 'This one is to be sustained by beneficent conduct,' I sustain him by beneficent conduct. When I know: 'This one is to be sustained by impartiality,' I sustain him by impartiality. There is wealth in my family, Bhante. They don't think they should listen to me as if I were poor."[1684]

"Good, good, Hatthaka! This is the method by which you can sustain a large retinue. For all those in the past who sustained a large retinue did so by these same four means of sustaining a favorable relationship. All those in the future who will sustain a large retinue will do so by these same four means of sustaining a favorable relationship. And all those at present who sustain a large retinue do so by these same four means of sustaining a favorable relationship."

Then, after the Blessed One had instructed, encouraged, inspired, and gladdened Hatthaka of Āḷavī with a Dhamma talk, Hatthaka rose from his seat, paid homage to the Blessed One, circumambulated him keeping the right side toward him, [220] and departed.

Then, not long after Hatthaka of Āḷavī had left, the Blessed One addressed the bhikkhus: "Bhikkhus, you should remember Hatthaka of Āḷavī as one who possesses eight astounding and amazing qualities. What eight? (1) He is endowed with faith. (2) He is virtuous, and (3) has a sense of moral shame and (4) moral dread. (5) He is learned, (6) generous, and (7) wise. (8)

He has few desires. You should remember Hatthaka of Āḷavī as one who possesses these eight astounding and amazing qualities."

25 (5) Mahānāma

On one occasion the Blessed One was dwelling among the Sakyans at Kapilavatthu in the Banyan Tree Park. Then Mahānāma the Sakyan approached the Blessed One, paid homage to him, sat down to one side, and said to him:

"In what way, Bhante, is one a lay follower?"

"When, Mahānāma, one has gone for refuge to the Buddha, the Dhamma, and the Saṅgha, in that way one is a lay follower."

"In what way, Bhante, is a lay follower virtuous?"

"When, Mahānāma, a lay follower abstains from the destruction of life, from taking what is not given, from sexual misconduct, from false speech, and from liquor, wine, and intoxicants, the basis for heedlessness, in that way a lay follower is virtuous."

"In what way, Bhante, is a lay follower practicing for his own welfare but not for the welfare of others?" [221]

(1) "When, Mahānāma, a lay follower is himself accomplished in faith but does not encourage others to accomplish faith; (2) when he is himself accomplished in virtuous behavior but does not encourage others to accomplish virtuous behavior; (3) when he is himself accomplished in generosity but does not encourage others to accomplish generosity; (4) when he himself wants to see bhikkhus but does not encourage others to see bhikkhus; (5) when he himself wants to hear the good Dhamma but does not encourage others to hear the good Dhamma; (6) when he himself retains in mind the teachings he has heard but does not encourage others to retain the teachings in mind; (7) when he himself examines the meaning of the teachings that have been retained in mind but does not encourage others to examine their meaning; (8) when he himself has understood the meaning and the Dhamma and practices in accordance with the Dhamma, but does not encourage others to do so: it is in this way, Mahānāma, that a lay follower is practicing for his own welfare but not for the welfare of others.

"In what way, Bhante, is a lay follower practicing for his own welfare and for the welfare of others?"

(1) "When, Mahānāma, a lay follower is himself accomplished in faith and also encourages others to accomplish faith; (2) when he is himself accomplished in virtuous behavior and also encourages others to accomplish virtuous behavior; (3) when he is himself accomplished in generosity and also encourages others to accomplish generosity; (4) when he himself wants to see bhikkhus and also encourages others to see bhikkhus; (5) when he himself wants to hear the good Dhamma and also encourages others to hear the good Dhamma; (6) when he himself retains in mind the teachings he has heard and also encourages others to retain the teachings in mind; (7) when he himself examines the meaning of the teachings that have been retained in mind and also encourages others to examine their meaning; (8) when he himself understands the meaning [222] and the Dhamma and then practices in accordance with the Dhamma, and also encourages others to practice in accordance with the Dhamma: it is in this way, Mahānāma, that a lay follower is practicing for his own welfare and also for the welfare of others."

26 (6) Jīvaka

On one occasion the Blessed One was dwelling at Rājagaha in Jīvaka's mango grove. Then Jīvaka Komārabhacca approached the Blessed One, paid homage to him, sat down to one side, and said to him:[1685]

"In what way, Bhante, is one a lay follower?"

[The rest as in 8:25.] [223]

27 (7) Powers (1)

"Bhikkhus, there are these eight powers. What eight? (1) The power of children is weeping; (2) the power of women is anger; (3) the power of thieves is a weapon; (4) the power of kings is sovereignty; (5) the power of fools is to complain; (6) the power of the wise is to deliberate;[1686] (7) the power of the learned is reflection; (8) the power of ascetics and brahmins is patience. These are the eight powers."

28 (8) Powers (2)

Then the Venerable Sāriputta approached the Blessed One.... The Blessed One then said to him: [224]

"Sāriputta, when a bhikkhu's taints have been destroyed, how many powers does he possess by reason of which he can claim: 'My taints have been destroyed'?"

"Bhante, when a bhikkhu's taints have been destroyed, he possesses eight powers by reason of which he can claim: 'My taints have been destroyed.' What eight?

(1) "Here, Bhante, a bhikkhu with taints destroyed has clearly seen all conditioned phenomena as they really are with correct wisdom as impermanent. This is a power of a bhikkhu with taints destroyed on the basis of which he can claim: 'My taints have been destroyed.'

(2) "Again, a bhikkhu with taints destroyed has clearly seen sensual pleasures as they really are with correct wisdom as similar to a charcoal pit. This is a power of a bhikkhu with taints destroyed....

(3) "Again, the mind of a bhikkhu with taints destroyed slants, slopes, and inclines to seclusion; it is withdrawn,[1687] delighting in renunciation, and is entirely finished with all things that are a basis for the taints. This is a power of a bhikkhu with taints destroyed....

(4) "Again, a bhikkhu with taints destroyed has developed and well developed the four establishments of mindfulness. Since [225] that is so, this is a power of a bhikkhu with taints destroyed....

(5)–(8) "Again, a bhikkhu with taints destroyed has developed and well developed the four bases for psychic potency... the five spiritual faculties... the seven factors of enlightenment... the noble eightfold path. This is a power of a bhikkhu with taints destroyed on the basis of which he can claim: 'My taints have been destroyed.'

"Bhante, when a bhikkhu's taints have been destroyed, he possesses these eight powers on the basis of which he can claim: 'My taints have been destroyed.'"

29 (9) Inopportune Moments

"Bhikkhus, the uninstructed worldling says: 'The world has gained the opportunity! The world has gained the opportunity!'[1688] but he does not know what is an opportunity and what is not an opportunity. There are, bhikkhus, these eight inopportune moments that are not right occasions for living the spiritual life. What eight?

(1) "Here, a Tathāgata has arisen in the world, an arahant, perfectly enlightened, accomplished in true knowledge and conduct, fortunate, knower of the world, unsurpassed trainer of persons to be tamed, teacher of devas and humans, an Enlightened One, a Blessed One, and the Dhamma leading to peace, nibbāna, and enlightenment is taught as proclaimed by a Fortunate One. But a person has been reborn in hell. This is the first inopportune moment that is not the right occasion for living the spiritual life. [226]

(2) "Again, a Tathāgata has arisen in the world . . . and the Dhamma leading to peace, nibbāna, and enlightenment is taught as proclaimed by a Fortunate One. But a person has been reborn in the animal realm. This is the second inopportune moment that is not the right occasion for living the spiritual life.

(3) "Again, a Tathāgata has arisen in the world . . . and the Dhamma leading to peace, nibbāna, and enlightenment is taught as proclaimed by a Fortunate One. But a person has been reborn in the sphere of afflicted spirits. This is the third inopportune moment that is not the right occasion for living the spiritual life.

(4) "Again, a Tathāgata has arisen in the world . . . and the Dhamma leading to peace, nibbāna, and enlightenment is taught as proclaimed by a Fortunate One. But a person has been reborn in a certain order of long-lived devas.[1689] This is the fourth inopportune moment that is not the right occasion for living the spiritual life.

(5) "Again, a Tathāgata has arisen in the world . . . and the Dhamma leading to peace, nibbāna, and enlightenment is taught as proclaimed by a Fortunate One. But a person has been reborn in the outlying provinces among the uncouth foreigners, [a place] to which bhikkhus, bhikkhunīs, male lay followers, and female lay followers do not travel. This is the fifth inopportune moment that is not the right occasion for living the spiritual life.

(6) "Again, a Tathāgata has arisen in the world . . . and the Dhamma leading to peace, nibbāna, and enlightenment is taught as proclaimed by a Fortunate One. A person has been reborn in the central provinces, but he holds wrong view and

has a distorted perspective: 'There is nothing given, nothing sacrificed, nothing offered; there is no fruit or result of good and bad actions; there is no this world, no other world; there is no mother, no father; there are no beings spontaneously reborn; there are in the world no ascetics and brahmins of right conduct and right practice who, having realized this world and the other world for themselves by direct knowledge, make them known to others.' This is the sixth inopportune moment that is not the right occasion for living the spiritual life.

(7) "Again, a Tathāgata has arisen in the world . . . and the Dhamma leading to peace, nibbāna, and enlightenment is taught as proclaimed by a Fortunate One. A person has been reborn in the central provinces, but he is unwise, stupid, obtuse, unable to understand the meaning of what has been well stated and badly stated. This is the seventh inopportune moment that is not the right occasion for living the spiritual life.

(8) "Again, a Tathāgata has not arisen in the world . . . and the Dhamma [227] leading to peace, nibbāna, and enlightenment is not taught as proclaimed by a Fortunate One. But a person has been reborn in the central provinces, and he is wise, intelligent, astute, able to understand the meaning of what has been well stated and badly stated. This is the eighth inopportune moment that is not the right occasion for living the spiritual life.

"These are the eight inopportune moments that are not the right occasions for living the spiritual life.

"There is, bhikkhus, one unique opportune moment that is the right occasion for living the spiritual life. What is it? Here, a Tathāgata has arisen in the world, an arahant, perfectly enlightened, accomplished in true knowledge and conduct, fortunate, knower of the world, unsurpassed trainer of persons to be tamed, teacher of devas and humans, an Enlightened One, a Blessed One, and the Dhamma leading to peace, nibbāna, and enlightenment is taught as proclaimed by a Fortunate One. And a person has been reborn in the central provinces, and he is wise, intelligent, astute, able to understand the meaning of what has been well stated and badly stated. This, bhikkhus, is the one unique opportune moment that is the right occasion for living the spiritual life."

Having obtained the human state
when the good Dhamma has been well proclaimed,

those who do not seize the moment
have let the right moment slip by.

For many inopportune times are spoken of,
occasions obstructive to the path;
for it is only sometimes, on occasion,
that Tathāgatas arise in the world.

If one has directly encountered them,
[fortune] rarely gained in the world,
if one has obtained the human state,
and the good Dhamma is being taught,
for a person desiring his own good,
this is incentive enough to strive. [228]

How can one understand the good Dhamma,
so that the moment won't slip by?
For those who miss the moment grieve
when they are reborn in hell.

One here who has failed to obtain
the fixed course of the good Dhamma,[1690]
will come to regret it for a long time
like a merchant who has missed a profit.

A person hindered by ignorance
who has failed in the good Dhamma
will long experience wandering on
in [the round of] birth and death.

But those who gain the human state
when the good Dhamma is well proclaimed,
have accomplished the Teacher's word,
or will do so, or are doing so now.

Those who have practiced the path,
proclaimed by the Tathāgata,
have penetrated the right moment in the world
the unsurpassed spiritual life.

You should dwell without leakages,
guarded, ever-mindful in the restraints
taught by the One with Vision,
the Kinsman of the Sun.

Having cut off all underlying tendencies
that follow one drifting in Māra's domain,[1691]
those who attain the destruction of the taints,
though in the world, have gone beyond.

30 (10) Anuruddha

On one occasion the Blessed One was dwelling among the Bhaggas in Suṃsumāragira in the deer park at Bhesakalā Grove. Now on that occasion the Venerable Anuruddha dwelled among the Cetis in the eastern bamboo park. While the Venerable Anuruddha was alone in seclusion, a course of thought arose in his mind thus:[1692]

(1) "This Dhamma is for one with few desires, not for one with strong desires. (2) This [229] Dhamma is for one who is content, not for one who is discontent. (3) This Dhamma is for one who resorts to solitude, not for one who delights in company. (4) This Dhamma is for one who is energetic, not for one who is lazy. (5) This Dhamma is for one with mindfulness established, not for one who is muddle-minded. (6) This Dhamma is for one who is concentrated, not for one who is unconcentrated. (7) This Dhamma is for one who is wise, not for one who is unwise."

The Blessed One knew with his own mind the course of thought in the Venerable Anuruddha's mind. Then, just as a strong man might extend his drawn-in arm or draw in his extended arm, the Blessed One disappeared from among the Bhaggas at Suṃsumāragira, in the deer park at Bhesakalā Grove, and reappeared before the Venerable Anuruddha among the Cetis in the eastern bamboo park. The Blessed One sat down on the seat prepared for him. The Venerable Anuruddha then paid homage to him and sat down to one side, and the Blessed One said to him: "Good, good, Anuruddha! It is good that you have reflected on these thoughts of a great person, namely: 'This Dhamma is for one with few desires, not for one with strong desires. . . . This Dhamma is for one who is wise, not for one who is unwise.' Therefore, Anuruddha, also reflect on this eighth thought of a great person: (8) 'This Dhamma is for one who delights in non-proliferation, who takes delight in non-proliferation, not for one who delights in proliferation, who takes delight in proliferation.'[1693]

"When, Anuruddha, you reflect on these eight thoughts of a great person, then, as much as you wish, secluded from sensual pleasures, secluded from unwholesome states, [230] you will enter and dwell in the first jhāna, which consists of rapture and pleasure born of seclusion, accompanied by thought and examination.

"When you reflect on these eight thoughts of a great person, then, as much as you wish, with the subsiding of thought and examination, you will enter and dwell in the second jhāna, which has internal placidity and unification of mind and consists of rapture and pleasure born of concentration, without thought and examination.

"When you reflect on these eight thoughts of a great person, then, as much as you wish, with the fading away as well of rapture, you will dwell equanimous and, mindful and clearly comprehending, experience pleasure with the body; you will enter and dwell in the third jhāna of which the noble ones declare: 'He is equanimous, mindful, one who dwells happily.'

"When you reflect on these eight thoughts of a great person, then, as much as you wish, with the abandoning of pleasure and pain, and with the previous passing away of joy and sadness, you will enter and dwell in the fourth jhāna, neither painful nor pleasant, which has purification of mindfulness by equanimity.

"When, Anuruddha, you reflect upon these eight thoughts of a great person and gain at will, without trouble or difficulty, these four jhānas that constitute the higher mind and are pleasant dwellings in this very life, then, while you dwell contentedly, your rag-robe will seem to you as a chest full of variously colored garments seems to a householder or a householder's son; and it will serve for your delight, relief, and ease, and for entering upon nibbāna. [231]

"When you reflect upon these eight thoughts of a great person and gain at will . . . these four jhānas . . . then, while you dwell contentedly, your scraps of almsfood will seem to you as a dish of rice cleaned of black grains and served with many gravies and curries seems to a householder or a householder's son; and they will serve for your delight, relief, and ease, and for entering upon nibbāna.

"When you reflect upon these eight thoughts of a great person and gain at will . . . these four jhānas . . . then, while you dwell contentedly, your dwelling place at the foot of a tree will seem to you as a house with a peaked roof, plastered inside and out, draft-free, with bolts fastened and shutters closed, seems to a householder or a householder's son; and it will serve for your delight, relief, and ease, and for entering upon nibbāna.

"When you reflect upon those eight thoughts of a great person and gain at will . . . these four jhānas . . . then, while you dwell contentedly, your bed and seat made of straw will seem to you as a couch spread with rugs, blankets, and covers, with an excellent covering of antelope hide, with a canopy above and red bolsters at both ends, seems to a householder or a householder's son; and it will serve for your delight, relief, and ease, and for entering upon nibbāna. [232]

"When you reflect upon these eight thoughts of a great person and gain at will . . . these four jhānas . . . then, while you dwell contentedly, your medicine of fermented cow's urine will seem to you as various medicaments of ghee, butter, oil, honey, and molasses seem to a householder or a householder's son; and it will serve for your delight, relief, and ease, and for entering upon nibbāna.

"Therefore, Anuruddha, you should also spend the next rains residence right here among the Cetis in the eastern bamboo park."

"Yes, Bhante," the Venerable Anuruddha replied.

Then, having exhorted the Venerable Anuruddha, just as a strong man might extend his drawn-in arm or draw in his extended arm, the Blessed One disappeared before the Venerable Anuruddha among the Cetis in the eastern bamboo park and reappeared among the Bhaggas at Suṃsumāragira, in the deer park at Bhesakalā Grove. He then sat down on the seat prepared for him and addressed the bhikkhus: "I will teach you, bhikkhus, the eight thoughts of a great person. Listen and attend closely. I will speak."

"Yes, Bhante," the bhikkhus replied. The Blessed One said this:

"And what, bhikkhus, are the eight thoughts of a great person? (1) This Dhamma is for one with few desires, not for one with strong desires. (2) This Dhamma is for one who is content, not for one who is discontent. (3) This Dhamma is for one who resorts to solitude, not for one who delights in company. (4) This Dhamma is for one who is energetic, not for one who is lazy. (5) This Dhamma is for one with mindfulness established, not for one who is muddle-minded. (6) This Dhamma is for one who is concentrated, not for one who is unconcentrated. (7) This Dhamma is for one who is wise, [233] not for one who is unwise. (8) This Dhamma is for one who delights in non-proliferation, who takes delight in non-proliferation, not for one who delights in proliferation, who takes delight in proliferation.

(1) "When it was said: 'This Dhamma is for one with few desires, not for one with strong desires,' with reference to what was this said? Here, when a bhikkhu is one with few desires, he does not desire: 'Let people know me to be one with few desires.' When he is content, he does not desire: 'Let people know me to be one who is content.' When he resorts to solitude, he does not desire: 'Let people know me to be one who resorts to solitude.' When he is energetic, he does not desire: 'Let people know me to be energetic.' When he is mindful, he does not desire: 'Let people know me to be mindful.' When he is concentrated, he does not desire: 'Let people know me to be concentrated.' When he is wise, he does not desire: 'Let people know me to be wise.' When he delights in non-proliferation, he does not desire: 'Let people know me to be one who delights in non-proliferation.' When it was said: 'This Dhamma is for one with few desires, not for one with strong desires,' it is with reference to this that this was said.

(2) "When it was said: 'This Dhamma is for one who is content, not for one who is discontent,' with reference to what was this said? Here, a bhikkhu is content with any kind of robes, almsfood, lodgings, and medicines and provisions for the sick. When it was said: 'This Dhamma is for one who is content, not for one who is discontent,' it is with reference to this that this was said.

(3) "When it was said: 'This Dhamma is for one who resorts to solitude, not for one who delights in company,' with reference to what was this said? Here, when a bhikkhu resorts to solitude,

bhikkhus, bhikkhunīs, male lay followers, female lay followers, kings, royal ministers, heads of other sects, and disciples belonging to other sects approach him. In each case, with a mind that slants, slopes, and inclines to seclusion, withdrawn,[1694] delighting in renunciation, he gives them a talk invariably concerned with dismissing them. [234] When it was said: 'This Dhamma is for one who resorts to solitude, not for one who delights in company,' it is with reference to this that this was said.

(4) "When it was said: 'This Dhamma is for one who is energetic, not for one who is lazy,' with reference to what was this said? Here, a bhikkhu has aroused energy for abandoning unwholesome qualities and acquiring wholesome qualities; he is strong, firm in exertion, not casting off the duty of cultivating wholesome qualities. When it was said: 'This Dhamma is for one who is energetic, not for one who is lazy,' it is with reference to this that this was said.

(5) "When it was said: 'This Dhamma is for one with mindfulness established, not for one who is muddle-minded,' with reference to what was this said? Here, a bhikkhu is mindful, possessing supreme mindfulness and alertness, one who remembers and recollects what was done and said long ago. When it was said: 'This Dhamma is for one with mindfulness established, not for one who is muddle-minded,' it is with reference to this that this was said.

(6) "When it was said: 'This Dhamma is for one who is concentrated, not for one who is unconcentrated,' with reference to what was this said? Here, secluded from sensual pleasures . . . a bhikkhu enters and dwells in the fourth jhāna. When it was said: 'This Dhamma is for one who is concentrated, not for one who is unconcentrated,' it is with reference to this that this was said.

(7) "When it was said: 'This Dhamma is for one who is wise, not for one who is unwise,' with reference to what was this said? Here, a bhikkhu is wise; he possesses the wisdom that discerns arising and passing away, which is noble and penetrative and leads to the complete destruction of suffering. When it was said: 'This Dhamma is for one who is wise, not for one who is unwise,' it is with reference to this that this was said. [235]

(8) "When it was said: 'This Dhamma is for one who delights in non-proliferation, who takes delight in non-proliferation, not for one who delights in proliferation, who takes delight in proliferation,' with reference to what was this said? Here, a bhik-

khu's mind launches out upon the cessation of proliferation, becomes placid, settles down, and is liberated in it. When it was said: 'This Dhamma is for one who delights in non-proliferation, who takes delight in non-proliferation, not for one who delights in proliferation, who takes delight in proliferation,' it is with reference to this that this was said."

Then the Venerable Anuruddha spent the next rains residence right there among the Cetis in the eastern bamboo park. Dwelling alone, withdrawn, heedful, ardent, and resolute, in no long time the Venerable Anuruddha realized for himself with direct knowledge, in this very life, that unsurpassed consummation of the spiritual life for the sake of which clansmen rightly go forth from the household life into homelessness, and having entered upon it, he dwelled in it. He directly knew: "Destroyed is birth, the spiritual life has been lived, what had to be done has been done, there is no more coming back to any state of being." And the Venerable Anuruddha became one of the arahants.

On that occasion, when he had attained arahantship, the Venerable Anuruddha spoke these verses:[1695]

"Having understood my thoughts,
the unsurpassed teacher in the world
came to me by psychic potency
in a mind-made body.

"He taught me more
than my thoughts contained:
the Buddha, delighting in non-proliferation,
instructed me in non-proliferation.

"Having learned his Dhamma,
I delighted in his teaching.
I have gained the three true knowledges;
the Buddha's teaching has been done." [236]

IV. Giving

31 (1) Giving (1)

"Bhikkhus, there are these eight gifts.[1696] What eight? (1) Having insulted [the recipient], one gives a gift.[1697] (2) One gives a gift from fear. (3) One gives a gift, [thinking]: 'He gave to me.' (4)

One gives a gift, [thinking]: 'He will give to me.' (5) One gives a gift, [thinking]: 'Giving is good.' (6) One gives a gift, [thinking]: 'I cook; these people do not cook. It isn't right that I who cook should not give to those who do not cook.' (7) One gives a gift, [thinking]: 'Because I have given this gift, I will gain a good reputation.' (8) One gives a gift for the purpose of ornamenting the mind, equipping the mind."[1698]

32 (2) Giving (2)[1699]

Faith, moral shame, and wholesome giving
are qualities pursued by the good person;
for this, they say, is the divine path
by which one goes to the world of the devas.

33 (3) Grounds

"Bhikkhus, there are these eight grounds for giving.[1700] What eight? (1) One gives a gift from desire. (2) One gives a gift from hatred. (3) One gives a gift from delusion. (4) One gives a gift from fear.[1701] (5) One gives a gift, [thinking]: 'Giving was practiced before by my father and forefathers; I should not abandon this ancient family custom.' (6) One gives a gift, [thinking]: 'Having given this gift, with the breakup of the body, after death, I will be reborn in a good destination, in a heavenly world.' (7) One gives a gift, [thinking]: 'When I am giving this gift my mind becomes placid, [237] and elation and joy arise.' (8) One gives a gift for the purpose of ornamenting the mind, equipping the mind. These are the eight grounds for giving."

34 (4) The Field

"Bhikkhus, a seed sown in a field that possesses eight factors does not bring forth abundant fruits, its [fruits] are not delectable, and it does not yield a profit. What eight factors?

"Here, (1) the field has mounds and ditches; (2) it contains stones and gravel; (3) it is salty; (4) it is not deeply furrowed; (5) it does not have inlets [for the water to enter]; (6) it does not have outlets [for excess water to flow out]; (7) it does not have irrigation channels; and (8) it does not have boundaries. A seed sown in a field that possesses these eight factors does not bring forth abundant fruits, its [fruits] are not delectable, and it does not yield a profit.

"So too, bhikkhus, a gift given to ascetics and brahmins who possess eight factors is not of great fruit and benefit, and it is not very brilliant or pervasive. What eight factors? Here, the ascetics and brahmins are of wrong view, wrong intention, wrong speech, wrong action, wrong livelihood, wrong effort, wrong mindfulness, and wrong concentration. A gift given to ascetics and brahmins who possess these eight factors is not of great fruit and benefit, and it is not very brilliant or pervasive.

"Bhikkhus, a seed sown in a field that possesses eight factors brings forth abundant fruits, its [fruits] are delectable, and it yields a profit. What eight factors?

"Here, (1) the field does not have mounds and ditches; (2) it does not contain stones and gravel; (3) it is not salty; (4) it is deeply [238] furrowed; (5) it has inlets [for the water to enter]; (6) it has outlets [for excess water to flow out]; (7) it has irrigation channels; and (8) it has boundaries. A seed sown in a field that possesses these eight factors brings forth abundant fruits, its [fruits] are delectable, and it yields a profit.

"So too, bhikkhus, a gift given to ascetics and brahmins who possess eight factors is of great fruit and benefit, and it is extraordinarily brilliant and pervasive. What eight factors? Here, the ascetics and brahmins are of right view, right intention, right speech, right action, right livelihood, right effort, right mindfulness, and right concentration. A gift given to ascetics and brahmins who possess these eight factors is of great fruit and benefit, and it is extraordinarily brilliant and pervasive."

When the field is excellent,
and the seed sown is excellent,
and there is an excellent supply of rain,
the yield of grain is excellent.[1702]

Its health is excellent;
its growth [too] is excellent;
its maturation is excellent;
its fruit truly is excellent.

So too when one gives excellent food
to those accomplished in virtuous behavior,
it arrives at several kinds of excellence,
for what one has done is excellent.

Therefore if one desires excellence
let a person here be accomplished;
one should resort to those accomplished in wisdom;
thus one's own accomplishments flourish.

One accomplished in true knowledge and conduct,
having gained accomplishment of mind,
performs action that is accomplished
and accomplishes the good.

Having known the world as it is,
one should attain accomplishment in view.
One accomplished in mind advances
by relying on accomplishment in the path. [239]

Having rubbed off all stains,
having attained nibbāna,
one is then freed from all sufferings:
this is total accomplishment.

35 (5) Rebirth on Account of Giving

"Bhikkhus, there are these eight kinds of rebirth on account of giving. What eight?

(1) "Here, someone gives a gift to an ascetic or a brahmin: food and drink; clothing and vehicles; garlands, scents, and unguents; bedding, dwellings, and lighting. Whatever he gives, he expects something in return. He sees affluent khattiyas, affluent brahmins, or affluent householders enjoying themselves furnished and endowed with the five objects of sensual pleasure. It occurs to him: 'Oh, with the breakup of the body, after death, may I be reborn in companionship with affluent khattiyas, affluent brahmins, or affluent householders!' He sets his mind on this, fixes his mind on this, and develops this state of mind. That aspiration of his,[1703] resolved on what is inferior,[1704] not developed higher, leads to rebirth there. With the breakup of the body, after death, he is reborn in companionship with affluent khattiyas, affluent brahmins, or affluent householders—and that is for one who is virtuous, I say, not for one who is immoral. The heart's wish of one who is virtuous succeeds because of his purity.

(2) "Someone else gives a gift to an ascetic or a brahmin: food and drink . . . and lighting. Whatever he gives, he expects something in return. He has heard: 'The devas [ruled by] the four great kings [240] are long-lived, beautiful, and abound in happiness.' It occurs to him: 'Oh, with the breakup of the body, after death, may I be reborn in companionship with the devas [ruled by] the four great kings!' He sets his mind on this, fixes his mind on this, and develops this state of mind. That aspiration of his, resolved on what is inferior, not developed higher, leads to rebirth there. With the breakup of the body, after death, he is reborn in companionship with the devas [ruled by] the four great kings—and that is for one who is virtuous, I say, not for one who is immoral. The heart's wish of one who is virtuous succeeds because of his purity.

(3)–(7) "Someone else gives a gift to an ascetic or a brahmin: food and drink . . . and lighting. Whatever he gives, he expects something in return. He has heard: 'The Tāvatiṃsa devas . . . the Yāma devas . . . the Tusita devas . . . the devas who delight in creation . . . the devas who control what is created by others are long-lived, beautiful, and abound in happiness.' It occurs to him: 'Oh, with the breakup of the body, after death, may I be reborn in companionship with the devas who control what is created by others!' He sets his mind on this, fixes his mind on this, and develops this state of mind. That aspiration of his, resolved on what is inferior, not developed higher, leads to rebirth there. With the breakup of the body, after death, he is reborn in companionship with the devas who control what is created by others—and that is for one who is virtuous, I say, not for one who is immoral. The heart's wish of one who is virtuous succeeds because of his purity.

(8) "Someone else gives a gift to an ascetic or a brahmin: food and drink . . . and lighting. Whatever he gives, he expects something in return. He has heard: 'The devas of Brahmā's company [241] are long-lived, beautiful, and abound in happiness.' It occurs to him: 'Oh, with the breakup of the body, after death, may I be reborn in companionship with the devas of Brahmā's company!' He sets his mind on this, fixes his mind on this, and develops this state of mind. That aspiration of his, resolved on what is inferior, not developed higher, leads to rebirth there. With the breakup of the body, after death, he is reborn in companionship with the

devas of Brahmā's company—and that is for one who is virtuous, I say, not for one who is immoral; for one without lust, not for one with lust.[1705] The heart's wish of one who is virtuous succeeds because of his purity.

"These, bhikkhus, are the eight kinds of rebirth on account of giving."

36 (6) Activity

"Bhikkhus, there are these three bases of meritorious activity. What three? The basis of meritorious activity consisting in giving; the basis of meritorious activity consisting in virtuous behavior; and the basis of meritorious activity consisting in meditative development.

(1) "Here, bhikkhus, someone has practiced the basis of meritorious activity consisting in giving to a limited extent; he has practiced the basis of meritorious activity consisting in virtuous behavior to a limited extent; but he has not undertaken the basis of meritorious activity consisting in meditative development. With the breakup of the body, after death, he is reborn among humans in an unfavorable condition.

(2) "Someone else has practiced the basis of meritorious activity consisting in giving to a middling extent; he has practiced the basis of meritorious activity consisting in virtuous behavior to a middling extent; but he has not undertaken the basis of meritorious activity consisting in meditative development. With the breakup of the body, after death, he is reborn among humans in a favorable condition.

(3) "Someone else has practiced the basis of meritorious activity consisting in giving to a superior extent; he has practiced the basis of meritorious activity consisting in virtuous behavior [242] to a superior extent; but he has not undertaken the basis of meritorious activity consisting in meditative development. With the breakup of the body, after death, he is reborn in companionship with the devas [ruled by] the four great kings. There the four great kings, who had practiced superlatively the basis of meritorious activity consisting in giving and the basis of meritorious activity consisting in virtuous behavior surpass the devas [ruled by] the four great kings in ten respects: in celestial life span, celestial beauty, celestial happiness, celestial glory, and celestial authority; and in celestial forms, sounds, odors, tastes, and tactile objects.

(4) "Someone else has practiced the basis of meritorious activity consisting in giving to a superior extent; he has practiced the basis of meritorious activity consisting in virtuous behavior to a superior extent; but he has not undertaken the basis of meritorious activity consisting in meditative development. With the breakup of the body, after death, he is reborn in companionship with the Tāvatiṃsa devas. There Sakka, ruler of the devas, who had practiced superlatively the basis of meritorious activity consisting in giving and the basis of meritorious activity consisting in virtuous behavior, surpasses the Tāvatiṃsa devas in ten respects: in celestial life span . . . and tactile objects.

(5) "Someone else has practiced the basis of meritorious activity consisting in giving to a superior extent; he has practiced the basis of meritorious activity consisting in virtuous behavior to a superior extent; but he has not undertaken the basis of meritorious activity consisting in meditative development. With the breakup of the body, after death, he is reborn in companionship with the Yāma devas. There the young deva Suyāma, who had practiced superlatively the basis of meritorious activity consisting in giving and the basis of meritorious activity consisting in virtuous behavior, surpasses the Yāma devas in ten respects: in celestial life span . . . and tactile objects.

(6) "Someone else has practiced the basis of meritorious activity consisting in giving to a superior extent; he has practiced the basis of meritorious activity consisting in virtuous behavior to a superior extent; but he has not undertaken the basis of meritorious activity consisting in meditative development. With the breakup of the body, after death, he is reborn in companionship with the Tusita devas. [243] There the young deva Santusita, who had practiced superlatively the basis of meritorious activity consisting in giving and the basis of meritorious activity consisting in virtuous behavior, surpasses the Tusita devas in ten respects: in celestial life span . . . and tactile objects.

(7) "Someone else has practiced the basis of meritorious activity consisting in giving to a superior extent; he has practiced the basis of meritorious activity consisting in virtuous behavior to a superior extent; but he has not undertaken the basis of meritorious activity consisting in meditative development. With the breakup of the body, after death, he is reborn in companionship with the devas who delight in creation. There the young deva Sunimmita, who had practiced superlatively the basis of

meritorious activity consisting in giving and the basis of meritorious activity consisting in virtuous behavior, surpasses the devas who delight in creation in ten respects: in celestial life span . . . and tactile objects.

(8) "Someone else has practiced the basis of meritorious activity consisting in giving to a superior extent; he has practiced the basis of meritorious activity consisting in virtuous behavior to a superior extent; but he has not undertaken the basis of meritorious activity consisting in meditative development. With the breakup of the body, after death, he is reborn in companionship with the devas who control what is created by others. There the young deva Vasavattī, who had practiced superlatively the basis of meritorious activity consisting in giving and the basis of meritorious activity consisting in virtuous behavior, surpasses the devas who control what is created by others in ten respects: in celestial life span, celestial beauty, celestial happiness, celestial glory, and celestial authority; and in celestial forms, sounds, odors, tastes, and tactile objects.

"These, bhikkhus, are the three bases of meritorious activity."

37 (7) The Good Person's Gifts

"Bhikkhus, there are these eight gifts of a good person.[1706] What eight? [244] (1) He gives what is pure; (2) he gives what is excellent; (3) he gives a timely gift; (4) he gives what is allowable; (5) he gives after investigation; (6) he gives often; (7) while giving he settles his mind in confidence; and (8) having given, he is elated. These are the eight gifts of a good person."

He gives what is pure and excellent,
allowable drinks and food at the proper time;
he gives gifts often to fertile fields of merit,
to those who lead the spiritual life.

He does not feel regret,
having given away many material things.
Those with deep insight praise
the gifts given in this way.

Having thus practiced charity
with a mind freely generous,

one intelligent and wise, rich in faith,
is reborn in a pleasant, unafflicted world.

38 (8) The Good Person[1707]

"Bhikkhus, when a good person is born in a family, it is for the good, welfare, and happiness of many people. It is for the good, welfare, and happiness of (1) his mother and father, (2) his wife and children, (3) his slaves, workers, and servants, (4) his friends and companions, (5) his departed ancestors, (6) the king, (7) the deities, and (8) ascetics and brahmins. Just as a great rain cloud, nurturing all the crops, appears for the good, welfare, and happiness of many people, so too, when a good person is born in a family, it is for the good, welfare, and happiness of many people. It is for the good, welfare, and happiness of his mother and father . . . [245] . . . ascetics and brahmins."

The wise person, dwelling at home,
truly lives for the good of many.
Day and night diligent toward
his mother, father, and ancestors,[1708]
he venerates them in accordance with the Dhamma,
recollecting what they did [for him] in the past.[1709]

Firm in faith, the pious man,
having known their good qualities,[1710]
venerates the homeless renouncers,
the mendicants who lead the spiritual life.[1711]

Beneficial to the king and the devas,
beneficial to his relatives and friends,
indeed, beneficial to all,
well established in the good Dhamma,
he has removed the stain of miserliness
and fares on to an auspicious world.

39 (9) Streams

"Bhikkhus, there are these eight streams of merit, streams of the wholesome, nutriments of happiness—heavenly, ripening in happiness, conducive to heaven—that lead to what is wished for, desired, and agreeable, to one's welfare and happiness.[1712] What eight?

(1) "Here, a noble disciple has gone for refuge to the Buddha. This is the first stream of merit, stream of the wholesome, nutriment of happiness—heavenly, ripening in happiness, conducive to heaven—that leads to what is wished for, desired, and agreeable, to one's welfare and happiness.

(2) "Again, a noble disciple has gone for refuge to the Dhamma. This is the second stream of merit . . . that leads to what is wished for, desired, and agreeable, to one's welfare and happiness.

(3) "Again, a noble disciple has gone for refuge to the Saṅgha. This is the third stream of merit . . . that leads to what is wished for, desired, and agreeable, to one's welfare and happiness. [246]

"There are, bhikkhus, these five gifts, great gifts, primal, of long standing, traditional, ancient, unadulterated and never before adulterated, which are not being adulterated and will not be adulterated, not repudiated by wise ascetics and brahmins. What five?

(4) "Here, a noble disciple, having abandoned the destruction of life, abstains from the destruction of life. By abstaining from the destruction of life, the noble disciple gives to an immeasurable number of beings freedom from fear, enmity, and affliction. He himself in turn enjoys immeasurable freedom from fear, enmity, and affliction. This is the first gift, a great gift, primal, of long standing, traditional, ancient, unadulterated and never before adulterated, which is not being adulterated and will not be adulterated, not repudiated by wise ascetics and brahmins. This is the fourth stream of merit . . . that leads to what is wished for, desired, and agreeable, to one's welfare and happiness.

(5)–(8) "Again, a noble disciple, having abandoned the taking of what is not given, abstains from taking what is not given . . . abstains from sexual misconduct . . . abstains from false speech . . . abstains from liquor, wine, and intoxicants, the basis for heedlessness. By abstaining from liquor, wine, and intoxicants, the basis for heedlessness, the noble disciple gives to an immeasurable number of beings freedom from fear, enmity, and affliction. He himself in turn enjoys immeasurable freedom from fear, enmity, and affliction. This is the fifth gift, a great gift, primal, of long standing, traditional, ancient, unadulterated and never before adulterated, which is not being adulterated and will not be adulterated, not repudiated by wise ascetics and brahmins. This is the eighth stream of merit [247] . . . that leads to what is wished for, desired, and agreeable, to one's welfare and happiness.

"These, bhikkhus, are the eight streams of merit, streams of the wholesome, nutriments of happiness—heavenly, ripening in happiness, conducive to heaven—that lead to what is wished for, desired, and agreeable, to one's welfare and happiness."

40 (10) Conducive

(1) "Bhikkhus, the destruction of life, repeatedly pursued, developed, and cultivated, is conducive to hell, to the animal realm, and to the sphere of afflicted spirits; for one reborn as a human being the destruction of life at minimum conduces to a short life span.

(2) "Taking what is not given, repeatedly pursued, developed, and cultivated, is conducive to hell, to the animal realm, and to the sphere of afflicted spirits; for one reborn as a human being taking what is not given at minimum conduces to loss of wealth.

(3) "Sexual misconduct, repeatedly pursued, developed, and cultivated, is conducive to hell, to the animal realm, and to the sphere of afflicted spirits; for one reborn as a human being sexual misconduct at minimum conduces to enmity and rivalry.

(4) "False speech, repeatedly pursued, developed, and cultivated, is conducive to hell, to the animal realm, and to the sphere of afflicted spirits; for one reborn as a human being false speech at minimum conduces to false accusations.

(5) "Divisive speech, repeatedly pursued, developed, and cultivated, is conducive to hell, to the animal realm, and to the sphere of afflicted spirits; for one reborn as a human being divisive speech at minimum conduces to being divided from one's friends. [248]

(6) "Harsh speech, repeatedly pursued, developed, and cultivated, is conducive to hell, to the animal realm, and to the sphere of afflicted spirits; for one reborn as a human being harsh speech at minimum conduces to disagreeable sounds.

(7) "Idle chatter, repeatedly pursued, developed, and cultivated, is conducive to hell, to the animal realm, and to the sphere of afflicted spirits; for one reborn as a human being idle chatter at minimum conduces to others distrusting one's words.

(8) "Drinking liquor and wine, repeatedly pursued, developed, and cultivated, is conducive to hell, to the animal realm, and to the sphere of afflicted spirits; for one reborn as a human being drinking liquor and wine at minimum conduces to madness."

V. Uposatha

41 (1) In Brief

Thus have I heard. On one occasion the Blessed One was dwelling at Sāvatthī in Jeta's Grove, Anāthapiṇḍika's Park. There the Blessed One addressed the bhikkhus: "Bhikkhus!"

"Venerable sir!" those bhikkhus replied. The Blessed One said this:

"Bhikkhus, observed complete in eight factors, the uposatha is of great fruit and benefit, extraordinarily brilliant and pervasive. And how is the uposatha observed complete in eight factors, so that it is of great fruit and benefit, extraordinarily brilliant and pervasive?[1713] [249]

(1) "Here, bhikkhus, a noble disciple reflects thus: 'As long as they live the arahants abandon and abstain from the destruction of life; with the rod and weapon laid aside, conscientious and kindly, they dwell compassionate toward all living beings. Today, for this night and day, I too shall abandon and abstain from the destruction of life; with the rod and weapon laid aside, conscientious and kindly, I too shall dwell compassionate toward all living beings. I shall imitate the arahants in this respect and the uposatha will be observed by me.' This is the first factor it possesses.

(2) "'As long as they live the arahants abandon and abstain from taking what is not given; they take only what is given, expect only what is given, and dwell honestly without thoughts of theft. Today, for this night and day, I too shall abandon and abstain from taking what is not given; I shall accept only what is given, expect only what is given, and dwell honestly without thoughts of theft. I shall imitate the arahants in this respect and the uposatha will be observed by me.' This is the second factor it possesses.

(3) "'As long as they live the arahants abandon sexual activity and observe celibacy, living apart, abstaining from sexual intercourse, the common person's practice. Today, for this night and

day, I too shall abandon sexual activity and observe celibacy, living apart, abstaining from sexual intercourse, the common person's practice. I shall imitate the arahants in this respect and the uposatha will be observed by me.' This is the third factor it possesses.

(4) "'As long as they live the arahants abandon and abstain from false speech; they speak truth, adhere to truth; they are trustworthy and reliable, no deceivers of the world. Today, for this night and day, I too shall abandon and abstain from false speech; [250] I shall speak truth, adhere to truth; I shall be trustworthy and reliable, no deceiver of the world. I shall imitate the arahants in this respect and the uposatha will be observed by me.' This is the fourth factor it possesses.

(5) "'As long as they live the arahants abandon and abstain from liquor, wine, and intoxicants, the basis for heedlessness. Today, for this night and day, I too shall abandon and abstain from liquor, wine, and intoxicants, the basis for heedlessness. I shall imitate the arahants in this respect and the uposatha will be observed by me.' This is the fifth factor it possesses.

(6) "'As long as they live the arahants eat once a day, abstaining from eating at night and from food outside the proper time. Today, for this night and day, I too shall eat once a day, abstaining from eating at night and from food outside the proper time. I shall imitate the arahants in this respect and the uposatha will be observed by me.' This is the sixth factor it possesses.

(7) "'As long as they live the arahants abstain from dancing, singing, instrumental music, and unsuitable shows, and from adorning and beautifying themselves by wearing garlands and applying scents and unguents. Today, for this night and day, I too shall abstain from dancing, singing, instrumental music, and unsuitable shows, and from adorning and beautifying myself by wearing garlands and applying scents and unguents. I shall imitate the arahants in this respect and the uposatha will be observed by me.' This is the seventh factor it possesses.

(8) "'As long as they live the arahants abandon and abstain from the use of high and luxurious beds; they lie down on a low resting place, either a small bed or a straw mat. Today, for this night and day, I too shall abandon and abstain from the use of high and luxurious beds; I shall lie down on a low resting place, either a small bed or a straw mat. I shall imitate the arahants

in this respect [251] and the uposatha will be observed by me.' This is the eighth factor it possesses.

"It is in this way, bhikkhus, that the uposatha is observed complete in eight factors, so that it is of great fruit and benefit, extraordinarily brilliant and pervasive."

42 (2) In Detail

"Bhikkhus, observed complete in eight factors, the uposatha is of great fruit and benefit, extraordinarily brilliant and pervasive. And how is the uposatha observed complete in eight factors, so that it is of great fruit and benefit, extraordinarily brilliant and pervasive?

(1) "Here, bhikkhus, a noble disciple reflects thus: 'As long as they live the arahants abandon and abstain from the destruction of life; with the rod and weapon laid aside, conscientious and kindly, they dwell compassionate toward all living beings. Today, for this night and day, I too shall abandon and abstain from the destruction of life; with the rod and weapon laid aside, conscientious and kindly, I too shall dwell compassionate toward all living beings. I shall imitate the arahants in this respect and the uposatha will be observed by me.' This is the first factor it possesses . . .

[As in 8:41 down to:] . . .

(8) "'As long as they live the arahants abandon and abstain from the use of high and luxurious beds; they lie down on a low resting place, either a small bed or a straw mat. Today, for this night and day, I too shall abandon and abstain from the use of high and luxurious beds; I shall lie down on a low resting place, either a small bed or a straw mat. I shall imitate the arahants in this respect and the uposatha will be observed by me.' This is the eighth factor it possesses.

"It is in this way, bhikkhus, that the uposatha is observed complete in eight factors, so that it is of great fruit and benefit, extraordinarily brilliant and pervasive. [252]

"To what extent is it of great fruit and benefit? To what extent is it extraordinarily brilliant and pervasive? Suppose one were to exercise sovereignty and kingship over these sixteen great countries abounding in the seven precious substances, that is, [the countries of] the Aṅgans, the Magadhans, the Kāsis, the Kosalans, the Vajjis, the Mallas, the Cetis, the Vaṅgas, the Kurus, the Pañcālas, the Macchas, the Sūrasenas, the Assakas, the Avantis, the Gandhārans, and the Kambojans: this would not be worth a sixteenth part of the uposatha observance complete in those eight factors. For what reason? Because human kingship is poor compared to celestial happiness.

"For the devas [ruled by] the four great kings, a single night and day is equivalent to fifty human years; thirty such days make up a month, and twelve such months make up a year. The life span of those devas is five hundred such celestial years. It is possible, bhikkhus, for a woman or man who observes the uposatha complete in these eight factors, with the breakup of the body, after death, to be reborn in companionship with the devas [ruled by] the four great kings. It was with reference to this that I said human kingship is poor compared to celestial happiness.

"For the Tāvatiṃsa devas, a single night and day is equivalent to a hundred human years; thirty such days make up a month, and twelve such months make up a year. The life span of those devas is a thousand such celestial years. [253] It is possible, bhikkhus, for a woman or man who observes the uposatha complete in these eight factors, with the breakup of the body, after death, to be reborn in companionship with the Tāvatiṃsa devas. It was with reference to this that I said human kingship is poor compared to celestial happiness.

"For the Yāma devas, a single night and day is equivalent to two hundred human years; thirty such days make up a month, and twelve such months make up a year. The life span of those devas is two thousand such celestial years. It is possible, bhikkhus, for a woman or man who observes the uposatha complete in these eight factors, with the breakup of the body, after death, to be reborn in companionship with the Yāma devas. It was with reference to this that I said human kingship is poor compared to celestial happiness.

"For the Tusita devas, a single night and day is equivalent to four hundred human years; thirty such days make up a month, and twelve such months make up a year. The life span of those devas is four thousand such celestial years. It is possible, bhikkhus, for a woman or man who observes the uposatha complete in these eight factors, with the breakup of the body, after death, to be reborn in companionship with the Tusita devas. It was with reference to this that I said human kingship is poor compared to celestial happiness.

"For the devas who delight in creation, a single night and day is equivalent to eight hundred human years; thirty such days make up a month, and twelve such months make up a year. The life span of those devas is eight thousand such celestial years. It is possible, bhikkhus, for a woman or man [254] who observes the uposatha complete in these eight factors, with the breakup of the body, after death, to be reborn in companionship with the devas who delight in creation. It was with reference to this that I said human kingship is poor compared to celestial happiness.

"For the devas who control what is created by others, a single night and day is equivalent to sixteen hundred human years; thirty such days make up a month, and twelve such months make up a year. The life span of those devas is sixteen thousand such celestial years. It is possible, bhikkhus, for a woman or man who observes the uposatha complete in these eight factors, with the breakup of the body, after death, to be reborn in companionship with the devas who control what is created by others. It was with reference to this that I said human kingship is poor compared to celestial happiness."

One should not kill living beings or take what is not
given;[1714]
one should not speak falsehood or drink intoxicants;
one should refrain from sexual activity, from
unchastity;
one should not eat at night or at an improper time.

One should not wear garlands or apply scents;
one should sleep on a [low] bed or a mat on the ground;
this, they say, is the eight-factored uposatha
proclaimed by the Buddha,
who reached the end of suffering.

As far as the sun and moon revolve,
shedding light, so beautiful to gaze upon,
dispellers of darkness, moving through the firmament,
they shine in the sky, brightening up the quarters. [255]

Whatever wealth exists in this sphere—
pearls, gems, and excellent beryl,
horn gold and mountain gold,
and the natural gold called *haṭaka*—

those are not worth a sixteenth part
of an uposatha complete in the eight factors,
just as all the hosts of stars
[do not match] the moon's radiance.

Therefore a virtuous woman or man,
having observed the uposatha complete in eight factors
and having made merit productive of happiness,
blameless goes to a heavenly state.

43 (3) Visākhā (1)

On one occasion the Blessed One was dwelling at Sāvatthī in Migāramātā's Mansion in the Eastern Park. Then Visākhā Migāramātā approached the Blessed One, paid homage to him, and sat down to one side. The Blessed One then said to her:

"Visākhā, observed complete in eight factors, the uposatha is of great fruit and benefit, extraordinarily brilliant and pervasive. And how is the uposatha observed complete in eight factors, so that it is of great fruit and benefit, extraordinarily brilliant and pervasive?"

[All as in 8:42, including the verses.] [256–258]

44 (4) Vāseṭṭha

On one occasion the Blessed One was dwelling at Vesālī in the hall with the peaked roof in the Great Wood. Then the male lay follower Vāseṭṭha approached the Blessed One, paid homage to him, and sat down to one side. The Blessed One then said to him:

"Vāseṭṭha, observed complete in eight factors, the uposatha is of great fruit and benefit, extraordinarily brilliant and pervasive. And how is the uposatha observed complete in eight factors, so that it is of great fruit and benefit, extraordinarily brilliant and pervasive?"

[All as in 8:42, including the verses.]

When this was said, the male lay follower Vāseṭṭha said to the Blessed One: [259] "Bhante, if my beloved relatives and family members would observe the uposatha complete in eight factors, that would lead to their welfare and happiness for a long time. If all khattiyas would observe the uposatha complete in eight factors, that would lead to their welfare and happiness for a long time. If all brahmins . . . vessas . . . suddas would observe the uposatha complete in eight factors, that would lead to their welfare and happiness for a long time."

"So it is, Vāseṭṭha, so it is! If all khattiyas would observe the uposatha complete in eight factors, that would lead to their welfare and happiness for a long time. If all brahmins . . . vessas . . . suddas would observe the uposatha complete in eight factors, that would lead to their welfare and happiness for a long time. If the world with its devas, Māra, and Brahmā, this population with its ascetics and brahmins, its devas and humans, would observe the uposatha complete in eight factors, that would lead to the welfare and happiness of the world for a long time. If these great sal trees would observe the uposatha complete in eight factors, that would lead to the welfare and happiness of these great sal trees for a long time, [if they could choose].[1715] How much more then for a human being!"

45 (5) Bojjhā

On one occasion the Blessed One was dwelling at Sāvatthī at Jeta's Grove, Anāthapiṇḍika's Park. Then the female lay follower Bojjhā approached the Blessed One, paid homage to him, and sat down to one side. The Blessed One then said to her:

"Bojjhā, observed complete in eight factors, the uposatha is of great fruit and benefit, extraordinarily brilliant and pervasive. . . ." [260]

[All as in 8:42, including the verses.] [261–62]

46 (6) Anuruddha

On one occasion the Blessed One was dwelling at Kosambī in Ghosita's Park. Now on that occasion the Venerable Anuruddha had gone off to pass the day and was in seclusion when a number of agreeable-bodied deities approached him, paid homage to him, stood to one side, and said to him:[1716]

"Bhante Anuruddha, we [263] agreeable-bodied deities exert mastery and exercise control over three things. We immediately acquire whatever color we want. We immediately acquire whatever pleasure we want. And we immediately acquire whatever voice we want. We agreeable-bodied deities exert mastery and exercise control over these three things."

Then the Venerable Anuruddha thought: "May all these deities become blue, of blue complexion, with blue clothes and blue ornaments." Having known the Venerable Anuruddha's thought, those deities all became blue, of blue complexion, with blue clothes and blue ornaments. Then the Venerable Anuruddha thought: "May all these deities become yellow . . . red . . . white, of white complexion, with white clothes and white ornaments." Having known the Venerable Anuruddha's thought, those deities all became white, of white complexion, with white clothes and white ornaments.

Then one of those deities sang, one danced, and one snapped her fingers. Just as, when a musical quintet is well trained and its rhythm well coordinated,[1717] and it is composed of skilled musicians, its music is exquisite, tantalizing, lovely, captivating, and intoxicating, [264] just so those deities' performance was exquisite, tantalizing, lovely, captivating, and intoxicating. Thereupon the Venerable Anuruddha drew in his sense faculties. Then those deities, [thinking:] "Master Anuruddha is not enjoying [this]," disappeared right on the spot.[1718]

Then, in the evening, the Venerable Anuruddha emerged from seclusion and approached the Blessed One. He paid homage to the Blessed One, sat down to one side, and said to him: "Here, Bhante, I had gone off to pass the day and was in seclusion . . . [He reports everything that happened down to:] [265] . . . Then those deities, [thinking:] 'Master Anuruddha is not enjoying [this],' disappeared right on the spot.

"Bhante, how many qualities should a woman possess so that, with the breakup of the body, after death, she is reborn in companionship with the agreeable-bodied deities?"

"If she possesses eight qualities, Anuruddha, a woman, with the breakup of the body, after death, is reborn in companionship with the agreeable-bodied deities. What eight?[1719]

(1) "Here, Anuruddha, to whichever husband her parents give her—doing so out of a desire for her good, seeking her welfare, taking compassion on her, acting out of compassion for her—a woman rises before him and retires after him, undertaking whatever needs to be done, agreeable in her conduct and pleasing in her speech.

(2) "She honors, respects, esteems, and venerates those whom her husband respects—his mother and father, ascetics and brahmins—and when they arrive she offers them a seat and water.

(3) "She is skillful and diligent in attending to her husband's

domestic chores, whether knitting or weaving; she possesses sound judgment about them in order to carry out and arrange them properly.

(4) "She finds out what her husband's domestic helpers [266]—whether slaves, messengers, or workers—have done and left undone; she finds out the condition of those who are ill; and she distributes to each an appropriate portion of food.

(5) "She guards and protects whatever income her husband brings home—whether money, grain, silver, or gold[1720]—and she is not a spendthrift, thief, wastrel, or squanderer of his earnings.

(6) "She is a female lay follower who has gone for refuge to the Buddha, the Dhamma, and the Saṅgha.

(7) "She is virtuous, abstaining from the destruction of life, taking what is not given, sexual misconduct, false speech, and liquor, wine, and intoxicants, the basis for heedlessness.

(8) "She is generous, one who dwells at home with a heart devoid of the stain of miserliness, freely generous, openhanded, delighting in relinquishment, devoted to charity, delighting in giving and sharing.

"Possessing these eight qualities, Anuruddha, a woman, with the breakup of the body, after death, is reborn in companionship with the agreeable-bodied deities."

She does not despise her husband,
the man who constantly supports her,
who ardently and eagerly
always brings her whatever she wants.[1721]

Nor does a good woman scold her husband
with speech caused by jealousy;[1722]
the wise woman shows veneration
to all those whom her husband reveres.

She rises early, works diligently,
manages the domestic help;
she treats her husband in agreeable ways
and safeguards the wealth he earns.

The woman who fulfills her duties thus,
following her husband's will and wishes,

is reborn among the devas
called "the agreeable ones." [267]

47 (7) Visākhā (2)

On one occasion the Blessed One was dwelling at Sāvatthī in Migāramātā's Mansion in the Eastern Park. Then Visākhā Migāramātā approached the Blessed One.... The Blessed One then said to her:

"Visākhā, possessing eight qualities, a woman, with the breakup of the body, after death, is reborn in companionship with the agreeable-bodied deities. What eight?"

[As in 8:46, including the verses.] [268]

48 (8) Nakula

On one occasion the Blessed One was dwelling among the Bhaggas in Suṃsumāragira in the deer park at Bhesakalā Grove. Then the housewife Nakulamātā approached the Blessed One.... The Blessed One then said to her:

"Nakulamātā, possessing eight qualities, a woman, with the breakup of the body, after death, is reborn in companionship with the agreeable-bodied deities. What eight?"

[As in 8:46, including the verses.] [269]

49 (9) The Present World (1)[1723]

On one occasion the Blessed One was dwelling at Sāvatthī in Migāramātā's Mansion in the Eastern Park. Then Visākhā Migāramātā approached the Blessed One.... The Blessed One then said to her:

"Visākhā, possessing four qualities, a woman is heading for victory in the present world and her life in this world succeeds.[1724] What four? Here, a woman is capable at her work; she manages the domestic help; she behaves agreeably to her husband; and she safeguards his earnings.

(1) "And how, Visākhā, is a woman capable at her work? Here, a woman is skillful and diligent in attending to her husband's domestic chores, whether knitting or weaving; she possesses sound judgment about them in order to carry out and arrange them properly. It is in this way that a woman [270] is capable at her work.

(2) "And how does a woman manage the domestic help?

Here, a woman finds out what her husband's domestic helpers—whether slaves, messengers, or workers—have done and left undone; she finds out the condition of those who are ill; and she distributes to each an appropriate portion of food. It is in this way that a woman manages the domestic help.

(3) "And how does a woman behave agreeably to her husband? Here, a woman would not commit any misdeed that her husband would consider disagreeable, even at the cost of her life. It is in this way that a woman behaves agreeably to her husband.

(4) "And how does a woman safeguard his earnings? Here, a woman guards and protects whatever income her husband brings home—whether money or grain, silver or gold—and she is not a spendthrift, thief, wastrel, or squanderer of his earnings. It is in this way that a woman safeguards his earnings.

"Possessing these four qualities, a woman is heading for victory in the present world and her life in this world succeeds.

"Possessing four [other] qualities, Visākhā, a woman is heading for victory in the other world and her life in the other world succeeds. What four? Here, a woman is accomplished in faith, accomplished in virtuous behavior, accomplished in generosity, and accomplished in wisdom.

(5) "And how, Visākhā, is a woman accomplished in faith? Here, a woman is endowed with faith. She places faith in the enlightenment of the Tathāgata thus: 'The Blessed One is an arahant, perfectly enlightened, accomplished in true knowledge and conduct, fortunate, knower of the world, unsurpassed trainer of persons to be tamed, teacher of devas and humans, the Enlightened One, the Blessed One.' It is in this way that a woman is accomplished in faith.

(6) "And how is a woman accomplished in virtuous behavior? [271] Here, a woman abstains from the destruction of life . . . from liquor, wine, and intoxicants, the basis for heedlessness. It is in this way that a woman is accomplished in virtuous behavior.

(7) "And how is a woman accomplished in generosity? Here, a woman dwells at home with a heart devoid of the stain of miserliness, freely generous, openhanded, delighting in relinquishment, devoted to charity, delighting in giving and sharing. It is in this way that a woman is accomplished in generosity.

(8) "And how is a woman accomplished in wisdom? Here, a woman is wise; she possesses the wisdom that discerns arising and passing away, which is noble and penetrative and leads to the complete destruction of suffering.[1725] It is in this way that a woman is accomplished in wisdom.

"Possessing these four qualities, Visākhā, a woman is heading for victory in the other world and her life in the other world succeeds."

Capable in attending to her work,
managing the domestic help,
she treats her husband in agreeable ways
and safeguards the wealth he earns.

Rich in faith, possessed of virtue,
charitable and devoid of miserliness,
she constantly purifies the path
that leads to safety in the future life.

They call any woman
who has these eight qualities,
virtuous, firm in Dhamma,
a speaker of truth.

Accomplished in sixteen aspects,[1726]
complete in eight factors,
such a virtuous female lay follower
is reborn in an agreeable deva world.

50 (10) The Present World (2)

"Bhikkhus, possessing four qualities, a woman is heading for victory in the present world and her life in this world succeeds. What four? [272]

[What follows is identical with 8:49, inclusive of the verses, but addressed to the bhikkhus.] [273–74]

The Second Fifty

I. Gotamī

51 (1) Gotamī[1727]

On one occasion the Blessed One was dwelling among the Sakyans at Kapilavatthu in the Banyan Tree Park.[1728] Then Mahāpajāpatī Gotamī approached the Blessed One, paid homage to him, stood to one side, and said to him:

"Bhante, it would be good if women could obtain the going forth from the household life into homelessness in the Dhamma and discipline proclaimed by the Tathāgata."[1729]

"Enough, Gotamī! Do not favor the going forth of women from the household life into homelessness in the Dhamma and discipline proclaimed by the Tathāgata."

A second time . . . A third time Mahāpajāpatī Gotamī said to the Blessed One: "Bhante, it would be good if women could obtain the going forth from the household life into homelessness in the Dhamma and discipline proclaimed by the Tathāgata."

"Enough, Gotamī! Do not favor the going forth of women from the household life into homelessness in the Dhamma and discipline proclaimed by the Tathāgata."[1730]

Then Mahāpajāpatī Gotamī, thinking: "The Blessed One does not allow the going forth of women from the household life into homelessness," miserable and saddened, wept with a tearful face. She then paid homage to the Blessed One, circumambulated him keeping the right side toward him, and departed.

Having stayed in Kapilavatthu as long as he wanted, the Blessed One set out on tour toward Vesālī. Wandering on tour, he eventually arrived at Vesālī, where he dwelled in the hall with the peaked roof in the Great Wood.

Then Mahāpajāpatī Gotamī had her hair cut off, put on ochre robes, and together with a number of Sakyan women,[1731] [275] set out toward Vesālī. Eventually, she reached Vesālī and [went to] the hall with the peaked roof in the Great Wood. Then, with her feet swollen and her body covered with dust, miserable and saddened, weeping with a tearful face, she stood outside the entrance. The Venerable Ānanda saw her standing there in such a condition and said to her:

"Gotamī, why are you standing outside the entrance with

your feet swollen and your body covered with dust, miserable and saddened, weeping with a tearful face?"

"I do so, Bhante Ānanda, because the Blessed One does not allow the going forth of women from the household life into homelessness."

"Well then, Gotamī, you wait right here [a moment][1732] while I ask the Blessed One to grant women the going forth."

Then the Venerable Ānanda approached the Blessed One, paid homage to him, sat down to one side, and said to him: "Bhante, Mahāpajāpatī Gotamī is standing outside the entrance with her feet swollen and her body covered with dust, miserable and saddened, weeping with a tearful face, because the Blessed One does not allow the going forth of women. Bhante, it would be good if women could obtain the going forth from the household life into homelessness in the Dhamma and discipline proclaimed by the Tathāgata."

"Enough, Ānanda! Do not favor the going forth of women from the household life into homelessness in the Dhamma and discipline proclaimed by the Tathāgata."

A second time . . . A third time the Venerable Ānanda said to the Blessed One: "Bhante, it would be good if women could obtain the going forth from the household life into homelessness in the Dhamma and discipline proclaimed by the Tathāgata."

"Enough, Ānanda! Do not favor the going forth of women from the household life into homelessness in the Dhamma and discipline proclaimed by the Tathāgata." [276]

Then it occurred to the Venerable Ānanda: "The Blessed One does not allow the going forth of women from the household life into homelessness. Let me ask the Blessed One for the going forth of women in some other way."

Then the Venerable Ānanda said to the Blessed One: "Bhante, if a woman were to go forth from the household life into homelessness in the Dhamma and discipline proclaimed by the Tathāgata, would it be possible for her to realize the fruit of stream-entry, the fruit of once-returning, the fruit of non-returning, and the fruit of arahantship?"

"It would be, Ānanda.

"If, Bhante, it would be possible for a woman to realize the fruit of stream-entry, the fruit of once-returning, the fruit of non-returning, and the fruit of arahantship, [and considering that] Mahāpajāpatī Gotamī had been very helpful to the Blessed One—having been his maternal aunt, wet-nurse, and foster mother who nurtured him with breast milk when his mother died—it would be good if women could obtain the going forth from the household life into homelessness in the Dhamma and discipline proclaimed by the Tathāgata."

"If, Ānanda, Mahāpajāpatī Gotamī accepts eight principles of respect,[1733] let that itself be her full ordination.[1734]

(1) "A bhikkhunī who has been ordained for a hundred years should pay homage to a bhikkhu who has been ordained that same day, should rise up for him, reverentially salute him, and behave courteously toward him. This principle should be honored, respected, esteemed, and venerated, and should not be transgressed as long as life lasts.[1735]

(2) "A bhikkhunī should not enter upon the rains in a place where there are no bhikkhus.[1736] This principle, too, should be honored, respected, esteemed, and venerated, and should not be transgressed as long as life lasts.

(3) "Every half-month a bhikkhunī should ask the Saṅgha of bhikkhus about two things: about [the day] of the uposatha, and about coming for the exhortation.[1737] [277] This principle, too, should be honored, respected, esteemed, and venerated, and should not be transgressed as long as life lasts.

(4) "When a bhikkhunī has observed the rains, she should invite correction before both Saṅghas in regard to three things: in regard to anything seen, heard, or suspected.[1738] This principle, too, should be honored, respected, esteemed, and venerated, and should not be transgressed as long as life lasts.

(5) "A bhikkhunī who has committed a grave offense should observe a half-month's penalty period before both Saṅghas.[1739] This principle, too, should be honored, respected, esteemed, and venerated, and should not be transgressed as long as life lasts.

(6) "A probationer who has completed two years of training in the six principles should seek full ordination from both Saṅghas.[1740] This principle, too, should be honored, respected, esteemed, and venerated, and should not be transgressed as long as life lasts.

(7) "A bhikkhunī must in no way insult or revile a bhikkhu. This principle, too, should be honored, respected, esteemed,

and venerated, and should not be transgressed as long as life lasts.

(8) "From today on, Ānanda, bhikkhunīs are prohibited from admonishing bhikkhus, but bhikkhus are not prohibited from admonishing bhikkhunīs. This principle, too, should be honored, respected, esteemed, and venerated, and should not be transgressed as long as life lasts.

"If, Ānanda, Mahāpajāpatī Gotamī accepts these eight principles of respect, let that itself be her full ordination."[1741]

Then the Venerable Ānanda, having learned these eight principles of respect from the Blessed One, went to Mahāpajāpatī Gotamī and said to her: "If, Gotamī, you accept eight principles of respect, that itself will be your full ordination:

(1) "A bhikkhunī who has been ordained for a hundred years should pay homage to a bhikkhu who has been ordained that same day, should rise up for him, reverentially salute him, and behave properly toward him. This principle should be honored, respected, esteemed, and venerated, and should not be transgressed as long as life lasts....

(8) "From today bhikkhunīs are prohibited from admonishing bhikkhus, [278] but bhikkhus are not prohibited from admonishing bhikkhunīs. This principle, too, should be honored, respected, esteemed, and venerated, and should not be transgressed as long as life lasts.

"If, Gotamī, you accept these eight principles of respect, that itself will be your full ordination."

"Bhante Ānanda, if a woman or a man—young, youthful, and fond of ornaments, with head bathed—obtains a garland of blue lotuses, jasmine flowers, or lilies,[1742] she or he would accept it with both hands and place it on top of her or his head. In the same way, I accept these eight principles of respect as not to be transgressed as long as life lasts."

Then the Venerable Ānanda approached the Blessed One, paid homage to him, sat down to one side, and said: "Bhante, Mahāpajāpatī Gotamī has accepted the eight principles of respect as things not to be transgressed as long as life lasts."

"If, Ānanda, women had not obtained the going forth from the household life into homelessness in the Dhamma and discipline proclaimed by the Tathāgata, the spiritual life would have been of long duration; the good Dhamma would have stood firm even for a thousand years. However, Ānanda, because women have gone forth from the household life into homelessness in the Dhamma and discipline proclaimed by the Tathāgata, now the spiritual life will not be of long duration; the good Dhamma will last only five hundred years.[1743]

"Just as, Ānanda, prowling burglars[1744] easily assail those families that have many women and few men, so in whatever Dhamma and discipline women obtain the going forth from the household life into homelessness, that spiritual life does not last long.

"Just as, Ānanda, when a field of hill rice has ripened, [279] if the bleaching disease attacks it,[1745] that field of hill rice does not last long, so in whatever Dhamma and discipline women obtain the going forth from the household life into homelessness, that spiritual life does not last long.

"Just as, Ānanda, when a field of sugar cane has ripened, if the rusting disease attacks it,[1746] that field of sugar cane does not last long, so in whatever Dhamma and discipline women obtain the going forth from the household life into homelessness, that spiritual life does not last long.

"Just as, Ānanda, a man might build a dyke around a large reservoir as a precaution so that the water would not overflow, so too, as a precaution I have prescribed for bhikkhunīs the eight principles of respect as things not to be transgressed as long as life lasts."[1747]

52 (2) Exhortation

On one occasion the Blessed One was dwelling at Vesālī in the hall with the peaked roof in the Great Wood. Then the Venerable Ānanda approached the Blessed One, paid homage to him, sat down to one side, and said to him:

"Bhante, how many qualities should a bhikkhu possess to be agreed upon as an exhorter of bhikkhunīs?"[1748]

"Ānanda, a bhikkhu should possess eight qualities to be agreed upon as an exhorter of bhikkhunīs. What eight?

(1) "Here, Ānanda, a bhikkhu is virtuous.... [as in 8:2 §4]... Having undertaken the training rules, he trains in them.

(2) "He has learned much... [as in 8:2 §5]... and penetrated well by view.

(3) "Both Pātimokkhas have been well transmitted to him in

detail, well analyzed, well mastered, well determined in terms of the rules and their detailed explication.

(4) "He is a good speaker with a good delivery; he is gifted with speech that is polished, clear, articulate, expressive of the meaning.

(5) "He is capable [280] of instructing, encouraging, inspiring, and gladdening the Saṅgha of bhikkhunīs with a Dhamma talk.

(6) "He is pleasing and agreeable to most of the bhikkhunīs.

(7) "He has never before committed a grave offense against a woman wearing the ochre robe who has gone forth under the Blessed One.

(8) "He has seniority of twenty years or more.

"A bhikkhu should possess these eight qualities to be agreed upon as an exhorter of bhikkhunīs."

53 (3) Brief[1749]

On one occasion the Blessed One was dwelling at Vesālī in the hall with the peaked roof in the Great Wood. Then Mahāpajāpatī Gotamī approached the Blessed One, paid homage to him, stood to one side, and said to him: "Bhante, it would be good if the Blessed One would teach me the Dhamma in brief, so that, having heard the Dhamma from the Blessed One, I might dwell alone, withdrawn, heedful, ardent, and resolute."

"Gotamī, those things of which you might know: 'These things lead (1) to passion, not to dispassion; (2) to bondage, not to detachment; (3) to building up, not to dismantling; (4) to strong desires, not to fewness of desires; (5) to non-contentment, not to contentment; (6) to company, not to solitude; (7) to laziness, not to the arousing of energy; (8) to being difficult to support, not to being easy to support,' you should definitely recognize: 'This is not the Dhamma; this is not the discipline; this is not the teaching of the Teacher.' But, Gotamī, those things of which you might know: 'These things lead (1) to dispassion, not to passion; (2) to detachment, not to bondage; (3) to dismantling, not to building up; (4) to fewness of desires, not to strong desires; (5) to contentment, not to non-contentment; (6) to solitude, not [281] to company; (7) to the arousing of energy, not to laziness; (8) to being easy to support, not to being difficult to support,' you should definitely recognize: 'This is the Dhamma; this is the discipline; this is the teaching of the Teacher.'"

54 (4) Dīghajāṇu

On one occasion the Blessed One was dwelling among the Koliyans near the Koliyan town named Kakkarapatta. There the young Koliyan Dīghajāṇu approached the Blessed One, paid homage to him, sat down to one side, and said to him:

"Bhante, we are laymen enjoying sensual pleasures, living at home in a house full of children. We use sandalwood from Kāsi; we wear garlands, scents, and unguents; we receive gold and silver. Let the Blessed One teach us the Dhamma in a way that will lead to our welfare and happiness in this present life and in future lives."

"There are, Byagghapajja,[1750] these four things that lead to the welfare and happiness of a clansman in this present life. What four? Accomplishment in initiative, accomplishment in protection, good friendship, and balanced living.

(1) "And what is accomplishment in initiative? Here, whatever may be the means by which a clansman earns his living—whether by farming, trade, raising cattle, archery, government service, or some other craft—he is skillful and diligent; he possesses sound judgment about it in order to carry out and arrange it properly. This is called accomplishment in initiative.

(2) "And what is accomplishment in protection? Here, a clansman sets up protection and guard over the wealth he has [282] acquired by initiative and energy, amassed by the strength of his arms, earned by the sweat of his brow, righteous wealth righteously gained, thinking: 'How can I prevent kings and thieves from taking it, fire from burning it, floods from sweeping it off, and displeasing heirs from taking it?' This is called accomplishment in protection.

(3) "And what is good friendship? Here, in whatever village or town a clansman lives, he associates with householders or their sons—whether young but of mature virtue, or old and of mature virtue—who are accomplished in faith, virtuous behavior, generosity, and wisdom; he converses with them and engages in discussions with them. Insofar as they are accomplished in faith, he emulates them with respect to their accomplishment in faith; insofar as they are accomplished in virtuous behavior, he emulates them with respect to their accomplishment in virtuous behavior; insofar as they are accomplished in generosity, he emulates them with respect to their accomplish-

ment in generosity; insofar as they are accomplished in wisdom, he emulates them with respect to their accomplishment in wisdom. This is called good friendship.

(4) "And what is balanced living? Here, a clansman knows his income and expenditures and leads a balanced life, neither too extravagant nor too frugal, [aware]: 'In this way my income will exceed my expenditures rather than the reverse.' Just as an appraiser or his apprentice, holding up a scale, knows: 'By so much it has dipped down, by so much it has gone up,' so a clansman knows his income and expenditures and leads a balanced life, neither too extravagant nor too frugal, [aware]: 'In this way my income will exceed my expenditures [283] rather than the reverse.'

"If this clansman has a small income but lives luxuriously, others would say of him: 'This clansman eats his wealth just like an eater of figs.'[1751] But if he has a large income but lives sparingly, others would say of him: 'This clansman may even starve himself.'[1752] But it is called balanced living when a clansman knows his income and expenditures and leads a balanced life, neither too extravagant nor too frugal, [aware]: 'In this way my income will exceed my expenditures rather than the reverse.'

"The wealth thus amassed has four sources of dissipation: womanizing, drunkenness, gambling, and bad friendship, bad companionship, bad comradeship. Just as if there were a large reservoir with four inlets and four outlets, and a man would close the inlets and open the outlets, and sufficient rain does not fall, one could expect the water in the reservoir to decrease rather than increase; so the wealth thus amassed has four sources of dissipation: womanizing . . . bad comradeship.

"The wealth thus amassed has four sources of accretion: one avoids womanizing, drunkenness, and [284] gambling, and cultivates good friendship, good companionship, good comradeship. Just as if there were a large reservoir with four inlets and four outlets, and a man would open the inlets and close the outlets, and sufficient rain falls; one could expect the water in the reservoir to increase rather than decrease, so the wealth amassed has four sources of accretion: one avoids womanizing . . . and cultivates good friendship.

"These are the four things that lead to the welfare and happiness of a clansman in this very life.

"There are, Byagghapajja, these four [other] things that lead to a clansman's welfare and happiness in future lives. What four? Accomplishment in faith, accomplishment in virtuous behavior, accomplishment in generosity, and accomplishment in wisdom.

(5) "And what is accomplishment in faith? Here, a clansman is endowed with faith. He places faith in the enlightenment of the Tathāgata thus: 'The Blessed One is an arahant . . . teacher of devas and humans, the Enlightened One, the Blessed One.' This is called accomplishment in faith.

(6) "And what is accomplishment in virtuous behavior? Here, a clansman abstains from the destruction of life, from taking what is not given, from sexual misconduct, from false speech, and from liquor, wine, and intoxicants, the basis for heedlessness. This is called accomplishment in virtuous behavior.

(7) "And what is accomplishment in generosity? Here, a clansman dwells at home with a heart devoid of the stain of miserliness, freely generous, openhanded, delighting in relinquishment, one devoted to charity, delighting in giving and sharing. This is called accomplishment in generosity.

(8) "And what is accomplishment in wisdom? [285] Here, a clansman is wise; he possesses the wisdom that discerns arising and passing away, which is noble and penetrative and leads to the complete destruction of suffering. This is called accomplishment in wisdom.

"These are the four [other] things that lead to the welfare and happiness of a clansman in future lives."

Enterprising in his occupations,
heedful in his arrangements,
balanced in his way of living,
he safeguards the wealth he earns.

Endowed with faith, accomplished in virtue,
charitable and devoid of miserliness,
he constantly purifies the path
that leads to safety in future lives.

Thus these eight qualities
of the faithful seeker of the household life
are said by the one who is truly named[1753]

to lead to happiness in both states:
to good and welfare in this very life,
and to happiness in future lives.
Thus for those dwelling at home,
their generosity and merit increase.

55 (5) Ujjaya

Then the brahmin Ujjaya approached the Blessed One and exchanged greetings with him. When they had concluded their greetings and cordial talk, he sat down to one side and said to the Blessed One:

"Master Gotama, I wish to go abroad. Let Master Gotama teach me the Dhamma about things that would lead to my welfare and happiness in this present life and in future lives."

[What follows is identical with 8:54, inclusive of the four verses, but addressed to the brahmin.] [286–89]

56 (6) Peril[1754]

"Bhikkhus, (1) 'peril' is a designation for sensual pleasures. (2) 'Suffering' is a designation for sensual pleasures. (3) 'Disease' is a designation for sensual pleasures. (4) 'A boil' is a designation for sensual pleasures. (5) 'A dart' is a designation for sensual pleasures. (6) 'A tie' is a designation for sensual pleasures. (7) 'A swamp' is a designation for sensual pleasures. (8) 'A womb' is a designation for sensual pleasures.

"And why, bhikkhus, is 'peril' a designation for sensual pleasures? One excited by sensual lust, bound by desire and lust, is not freed from the peril pertaining to this present life [290] or from the peril pertaining to future lives; therefore 'peril' is a designation for sensual pleasures.

"And why is 'suffering' . . . 'disease' . . . 'a boil' . . . 'a dart' . . . 'a tie' . . . 'a swamp' . . . 'a womb' a designation for sensual pleasures? One excited by sensual lust, bound by desire and lust, is not freed from the womb pertaining to this present life or from the womb pertaining to future lives;[1755] therefore 'a womb' is a designation for sensual pleasures."

Peril, suffering, and disease,
a boil, a dart, and a tie,
a swamp and a womb:
these describe the sensual pleasures

to which the worldling is attached.
Being immersed in what is enjoyable,
he again goes to the womb.

But when a bhikkhu is ardent
and does not neglect clear comprehension,
in such a way he transcends
this miserable bog;
he surveys this trembling population
that has fallen into birth and old age.

57 (7) Worthy of Offerings (1)

"Bhikkhus, possessing eight qualities, a bhikkhu is worthy of gifts, worthy of hospitality, worthy of offerings, worthy of reverential salutation, an unsurpassed field of merit for the world. What eight?

(1) "Here, a bhikkhu is virtuous.... Having undertaken the training rules, he trains in them.

(2) "He has learned much ... and penetrated well by view.

(3) "He has good friends, good companions, good comrades.

(4) "He is one of right view, [291] possessing a right perspective.

(5) "He gains at will, without trouble or difficulty, the four jhānas that constitute the higher mind and are dwellings in happiness in this very life.

(6) "He recollects his manifold past abodes, that is, one birth, two births ... [as in 8:11] ... thus he recollects his manifold past abodes with their aspects and details.

(7) "With the divine eye, which is purified and surpasses the human ... [as in 8:11] ... he understands how beings fare in accordance with their kamma.

(8) "With the destruction of the taints, he has realized for himself with direct knowledge, in this very life, the taintless liberation of mind, liberation by wisdom, and having entered upon it, he dwells in it.

"Possessing these eight qualities, a bhikkhu is worthy of gifts, worthy of hospitality, worthy of offerings, worthy of reverential salutation, an unsurpassed field of merit for the world."

58 (8) Worthy of Offerings (2)

"Bhikkhus, possessing eight qualities, a bhikkhu is worthy of gifts, worthy of hospitality, worthy of offerings, worthy of reverential salutation, an unsurpassed field of merit for the world. What eight?

(1) "Here, a bhikkhu is virtuous. . . . Having undertaken the training rules, he trains in them.

(2) "He has learned much . . . and penetrated well by view.

(3) "He has aroused energy;[1756] he is strong, firm in exertion, and has not cast off the duty of cultivating wholesome qualities.

(4) "He is a forest dweller, one who resorts to remote lodgings.

(5) "He has vanquished discontent and delight; he overcame discontent whenever it arose.

(6) "He has vanquished fear and terror; he overcame fear and terror whenever they arose. [292]

(7) "He gains at will, without trouble or difficulty, the four jhānas that constitute the higher mind and are dwellings in happiness in this very life.

(8) "With the destruction of the taints, he has realized for himself with direct knowledge, in this very life, the taintless liberation of mind, liberation by wisdom, and having entered upon it, he dwells in it.

"Possessing these eight qualities, a bhikkhu is worthy of gifts, worthy of hospitality, worthy of offerings, worthy of reverential salutation, an unsurpassed field of merit for the world."

59 (9) Eight Persons (1)

"Bhikkhus, these eight persons are worthy of gifts, worthy of hospitality, worthy of offerings, worthy of reverential salutation, an unsurpassed field of merit for the world. What eight? The stream-enterer, the one practicing for realization of the fruit of stream-entry; the once-returner, the one practicing for realization of the fruit of once-returning; the non-returner, the one practicing for realization of the fruit of non-returning; the arahant, the one practicing for realization of the fruit of arahantship.[1757] These eight persons, bhikkhus, are worthy of gifts, worthy of hospitality, worthy of offerings, worthy of reverential salutation, an unsurpassed field of merit for the world."

The four practicing the way[1758]
and the four established in the fruit:
this is the upright Saṅgha—
composed in wisdom and virtuous behavior.[1759]

For people intent on sacrifice,
for living beings seeking merit,
making merit that ripens in the acquisitions,[1760]
what is given to the Saṅgha bears great fruit.

60 (10) Eight Persons (2)

"Bhikkhus, these eight persons are worthy of gifts . . . an unsurpassed field of merit for the world. What eight? [293] The stream-enterer, the one practicing for realization of the fruit of stream-entry . . . the arahant, the one practicing for realization of the fruit of arahantship. These eight persons, bhikkhus, are worthy of gifts . . . an unsurpassed field of merit for the world."

The four practicing the way
and the four established in the fruit:
the eight persons among beings—
this is the foremost Saṅgha.

For people intent on sacrifice,
for living beings seeking merit,
making merit that ripens in the acquisitions,
what is given here bears great fruit.

II. Cāpāla

61 (1) Desire

"Bhikkhus, there are these eight kinds of persons found existing in the world. What eight?

(1) "Here, when a bhikkhu is dwelling in solitude, living independently, a desire arises in him for gain. He rouses himself, strives, and makes an effort to acquire gain.[1761] Nevertheless, he fails to acquire gain. Due to that lack of gain, he sorrows, languishes, and laments; he weeps beating his breast and becomes confused. This is called a bhikkhu desirous of gain [294] who rouses himself, strives, and makes an effort to acquire gain, but

not getting it, sorrows and laments: he has fallen away from the good Dhamma.

(2) "But when a bhikkhu is dwelling in solitude, living independently, a desire arises in him for gain. He rouses himself, strives, and makes an effort to acquire gain. He acquires gain. Due to that gain, he becomes intoxicated, grows heedless, and drifts into heedlessness. This is called a bhikkhu desirous of gain who rouses himself, strives, and makes an effort to acquire gain, and getting it, becomes intoxicated and heedless: he has fallen away from the good Dhamma.

(3) "But when a bhikkhu is dwelling in solitude, living independently, a desire arises in him for gain. He does not rouse himself, strive, and make an effort to acquire gain. He does not acquire gain. Due to that lack of gain, he sorrows, languishes, and laments; he weeps beating his breast and becomes confused. This is called a bhikkhu desirous of gain who does not rouse himself, strive, and make an effort to acquire gain, and not getting it, sorrows and laments: he has fallen away from the good Dhamma.

(4) "But when a bhikkhu is dwelling in solitude, living independently, a desire arises in him for gain. He does not rouse himself, strive, and make an effort to acquire gain. Nevertheless, he acquires gain. Due to that gain, he becomes intoxicated, grows heedless, and drifts into heedlessness. This is called a bhikkhu desirous of gain who does not rouse himself, strive, and make an effort to acquire gain, and getting it, becomes intoxicated and heedless: he has fallen away from the good Dhamma.

(5) "But when a bhikkhu is dwelling in solitude, living independently, a desire arises in him for gain. He rouses himself, strives, and makes an effort to acquire gain. Nevertheless, [295] he fails to acquire gain. He does not sorrow, languish, and lament due to that lack of gain; he does not weep beating his breast and become confused. This is called a bhikkhu desirous of gain who rouses himself, strives, and makes an effort to acquire gain, and not getting it, does not sorrow and lament: he has not fallen away from the good Dhamma.

(6) "But when a bhikkhu is dwelling in solitude, living independently, a desire arises in him for gain. He rouses himself, strives, and makes an effort to acquire gain. He acquires gain. He does not become intoxicated, grow heedless, and drift into

heedlessness due to that gain. This is called a bhikkhu desirous of gain who rouses himself, strives, and makes an effort to acquire gain, and getting it, does not become intoxicated and heedless: he has not fallen away from the good Dhamma.

(7) "But when a bhikkhu is dwelling in solitude, living independently, a desire arises in him for gain. He does not rouse himself, strive, and make an effort to acquire gain. He does not acquire gain. He does not sorrow, languish, and lament due to that lack of gain; he does not weep beating his breast and become confused. This is called a bhikkhu desirous of gain who does not rouse himself, strive, and make an effort to acquire gain, and not getting it, does not sorrow and lament: he has not fallen away from the good Dhamma.

(8) "But when a bhikkhu is dwelling in solitude, living independently, a desire arises in him for gain. He does not rouse himself, strive, and make an effort to acquire gain. Nevertheless, he acquires gain. He does not become intoxicated, grow heedless, and drift into heedlessness due to that gain. This is called a bhikkhu desirous of gain who does not rouse himself, strive, and make an effort to acquire gain, and getting it, does not become intoxicated and heedless: he has not fallen away from the good Dhamma.

"These are the eight kinds of persons found existing in the world." [296]

62 (2) Able

(1) "Bhikkhus, possessing six qualities, a bhikkhu is able [to benefit] both himself and others.[1762] What six?

"Here, (i) a bhikkhu is one of quick apprehension concerning wholesome teachings;[1763] (ii) he is capable of retaining in mind the teachings he has learned; (iii) he investigates the meaning of the teachings he has retained in mind; (iv) he has understood the meaning and the Dhamma and practices in accordance with the Dhamma; (v) he is a good speaker with a good delivery, gifted with speech that is polished, clear, articulate, expressive of the meaning; (vi) he is one who instructs, encourages, inspires, and gladdens his fellow monks. Possessing these six qualities, a bhikkhu is able [to benefit] both himself and others.

(2) "Possessing five qualities, a bhikkhu is able [to benefit] both himself and others. What five?

"Here, a bhikkhu is not one of quick apprehension concerning wholesome teachings. However, (i) he is capable of retaining in mind the teachings he has learned; (ii) he investigates the meaning of the teachings he has retained in mind; (iii) he has understood the meaning and the Dhamma and practices in accordance with the Dhamma; (iv) he is a good speaker with a good delivery . . . expressive of the meaning; (v) he is one who instructs, encourages, inspires, and gladdens his fellow monks. Possessing these five qualities, a bhikkhu is able [to benefit] both himself and others.

(3) "Possessing four qualities, a bhikkhu is able [to benefit] himself but not others. What four?

"Here, (i) a bhikkhu is one of quick apprehension concerning wholesome teachings; (ii) he is capable of retaining in mind the teachings he has learned; [297] (iii) he investigates the meaning of the teachings he has retained in mind; (iv) he has understood the meaning and the Dhamma and practices in accordance with the Dhamma. However, he is not a good speaker with a good delivery, nor is he gifted with speech that is polished, clear, articulate, expressive of the meaning; and he is not one who instructs, encourages, inspires, and gladdens his fellow monks. Possessing the above four qualities, a bhikkhu is able [to benefit] himself but not others.

(4) "Possessing four qualities, a bhikkhu is able [to benefit] others but not himself. What four?

"Here, (i) a bhikkhu is one of quick apprehension concerning wholesome teachings; (ii) he is capable of retaining in mind the teachings he has learned. However, he does not investigate the meaning of the teachings he has retained in mind, and he has not understood the meaning and the Dhamma and does not practice in accordance with the Dhamma. (iii) Still, he is a good speaker with a good delivery . . . expressive of the meaning; and (iv) he is one who instructs, encourages, inspires, and gladdens his fellow monks. Possessing the above four qualities, a bhikkhu is able [to benefit] others but not himself.

(5) "Possessing three qualities, a bhikkhu is able [to benefit] himself but not others. What three?

"Here, a bhikkhu is not one of quick apprehension concerning wholesome teachings. However, (i) he is capable of retaining in mind the teachings he has learned, (ii) he investigates the meaning of the teachings he has retained in mind, and (iii) he has understood the meaning and the Dhamma and practices in accordance with the Dhamma. But he is not a good speaker with a good delivery . . . [298] . . . expressive of the meaning; and he is not one who instructs, encourages, inspires, and gladdens his fellow monks. Possessing the above three qualities, a bhikkhu is able [to benefit] himself but not others.

(6) "Possessing three qualities, a bhikkhu is able [to benefit] others but not himself. What three?

"Here, a bhikkhu is not one of quick apprehension concerning wholesome teachings, but (i) he is capable of retaining in mind the teachings he has learned. However, he does not investigate the meaning of the teachings he has retained in mind, and he has not understood the meaning and the Dhamma and does not practice in accordance with the Dhamma. (ii) Still, he is a good speaker with a good delivery . . . expressive of the meaning; and (iii) he is one who instructs, encourages, inspires, and gladdens his fellow monks. Possessing the above three qualities, a bhikkhu is able [to benefit] others but not himself.

(7) "Possessing two qualities, a bhikkhu is able [to benefit] himself but not others. What two?

"Here, a bhikkhu is not one of quick apprehension concerning wholesome teachings, and he is not capable of retaining in mind the teachings he has learned. However, (i) he investigates the meaning of the teachings he has retained in mind, and (ii) he has understood the meaning and the Dhamma and practices in accordance with the Dhamma. But he is not a good speaker with a good delivery . . . expressive of the meaning; and he is not one who instructs, encourages, inspires, and gladdens his fellow monks. Possessing the above two qualities, a bhikkhu is able [to benefit] himself but not others.

(8) "Possessing two qualities, a bhikkhu is able [to benefit] others but not himself. What two?

"Here, a bhikkhu is not one of quick apprehension concerning wholesome teachings; he is not capable of retaining in mind the teachings he has learned; he does not investigate the meaning of the teachings he has retained in mind; [299] and he does not understand the meaning and the Dhamma and practice in accordance with the Dhamma. But (i) he is a good speaker with a good delivery . . . expressive of the meaning; and (ii) he is one who instructs, encourages, inspires, and gladdens his fellow monks. Possessing the above two qualities, a bhikkhu is able [to benefit] others but not himself."

63 (3) In Brief

Then a certain bhikkhu approached the Blessed One, paid homage to him, sat down to one side, and said to him:

"Bhante, it would be good if the Blessed One would teach me the Dhamma in brief, so that, having heard the Dhamma from the Blessed One, I might dwell alone, withdrawn, heedful, ardent, and resolute."

"It is in just this way that some hollow men here make requests of me, but when the Dhamma has been explained, they think only of following me around."[1764]

"Bhante, let the Blessed One teach me the Dhamma in brief. Let the Fortunate One teach me the Dhamma in brief. Perhaps I might come to understand the meaning of the Blessed One's statement; perhaps I might become an heir of the Blessed One's statement."

"In that case, bhikkhu, you should train yourself thus: 'My mind will be firm and well settled internally. Arisen bad unwholesome states will not obsess my mind.' Thus should you train yourself.

(1) "When, bhikkhu, your mind is firm and well settled internally, and arisen bad unwholesome states do not obsess your mind, then you should train yourself thus: [300] 'I will develop and cultivate the liberation of the mind by loving-kindness, make it a vehicle and basis, carry it out, consolidate it, and properly undertake it.' Thus should you train yourself.

"When this concentration has been developed and cultivated by you in this way, then you should develop this concentration with thought and examination; you should develop it without thought but with examination only; you should develop it without thought and examination. You should develop it with rapture; you should develop it without rapture; you should develop it accompanied by comfort; and you should develop it accompanied by equanimity.[1765]

(2)–(4) "When, bhikkhu, this concentration has been developed and well developed by you in this way, then you should train yourself thus: 'I will develop and cultivate the liberation of the mind by compassion . . . the liberation of the mind by altruistic joy . . . the liberation of the mind by equanimity, make it a vehicle and basis, carry it out, consolidate it, and properly undertake it.' Thus should you train yourself.

"When this concentration has been developed and cultivated[1766] by you in this way, then you should develop this concentration with thought and examination; you should develop it without thought but with examination only; you should develop it without thought and examination. You should develop it with rapture; you should develop it without rapture; you should develop it accompanied by comfort; and you should develop it accompanied by equanimity.

(5) "When, bhikkhu, this concentration has been developed and well developed by you in this way, then you should train yourself thus: 'I will dwell contemplating the body in the body, ardent, clearly comprehending, mindful, having removed longing and dejection in regard to the world.' Thus should you train yourself.

"When this concentration has been developed and cultivated by you in this way, then you should develop this concentration with thought and examination; you should develop it without thought but with examination [301] only; you should develop it without thought and examination. You should develop it with rapture; you should develop it without rapture; you should develop it accompanied by comfort; and you should develop it accompanied by equanimity.

(6)–(8) "When, bhikkhu, this concentration has been developed and well developed by you in this way, then you should train yourself thus: 'I will dwell contemplating feelings in feelings . . . mind in mind . . . phenomena in phenomena, ardent, clearly comprehending, mindful, having removed longing and dejection in regard to the world.' Thus should you train yourself.

"When this concentration has been developed and cultivated by you in this way, then you should develop this concentration with thought and examination; you should develop it without thought but with examination only; you should develop it without thought and examination. You should develop it with rapture; you should develop it without rapture; you should develop it accompanied by comfort; and you should develop it accompanied by equanimity.

"When, bhikkhu, this concentration has been developed and well developed by you in this way, then wherever you walk, you will walk at ease; wherever you stand, you will stand at ease; wherever you sit, you will sit at ease; wherever you lie down, you will lie down at ease."

Having received such an exhortation from the Blessed One, that bhikkhu rose from his seat, paid homage to the Blessed One, circumambulated him keeping the right side toward him, and departed.[1767] Then, dwelling alone, withdrawn, heedful, ardent, and resolute, in no long time that bhikkhu realized for himself with direct knowledge, in this very life, that unsurpassed consummation of the spiritual life for the sake of which clansmen rightly go forth from the household life into homelessness, and having entered upon it, he dwelled in it. [302] He directly knew: "Destroyed is birth, the spiritual life has been lived, what had to be done has been done, there is no more coming back to any state of being." And that bhikkhu became one of the arahants.

64 (4) Gayā

On one occasion the Blessed One was dwelling at Gayā on Gayāsīsa. There the Blessed One addressed the bhikkhus: "Bhikkhus!"

"Venerable sir!" those bhikkhus replied. The Blessed One said this:

(1) "Bhikkhus, before my enlightenment, while I was still a bodhisatta, not yet fully enlightened, I perceived only a light, but I did not see forms.[1768]

(2) "It occurred to me, bhikkhus: 'If I should perceive a light and also see forms, in such a case this knowledge and vision of mine would become even more purified.'[1769] So on a later occasion, as I was dwelling heedful, ardent, and resolute, I perceived a light and also saw forms. Yet I did not associate with those deities, converse with them, and engage in a discussion with them.

(3) "It occurred to me, bhikkhus: 'If I perceive a light and see forms, and also associate with those deities, converse with them, and engage in a discussion with them, in such a case this knowledge and vision of mine would become even more purified.' So on a later occasion, as I was dwelling heedful, ardent, and resolute, I perceived a light and saw forms, and I also associated with those deities, conversed with them, and engaged in

a discussion with them. Yet I did not know about those deities: 'These deities are from this or that order of devas.' [303]

(4) "It occurred to me, bhikkhus: 'If I perceive a light and see forms, and associate with those deities, converse with them, and engage in a discussion with them, and also know about those deities: 'These deities are from this or that order of devas,' in such a case this knowledge and vision of mine would become even more purified.' So on a later occasion, as I was dwelling heedful, ardent, and resolute, I perceived a light and saw forms, and associated with those deities, conversed with them, and engaged in a discussion with them, and I also knew about those deities: 'These deities are from this or that order of devas.' Yet I did not know of those deities: 'After passing away here these deities were reborn there as a result of this kamma.'

(5) ". . . and I also knew about those deities: 'After passing away here these deities were reborn there as a result of this kamma.' Yet I did not know of those deities: 'As a result of this kamma, these deities subsist on such food and experience such pleasure and pain.'

(6) ". . . and I also knew about those deities: 'As a result of this kamma, these deities subsist on such food and experience such pleasure and pain.' Yet I did not know of those deities: 'As a result of this kamma, these deities have a life span of such length.'

(7) ". . . and I also knew about those deities: 'As a result of this kamma, these deities have a life span of such length.' Yet I did not know whether or not I had previously lived together with those deities.

(8) "It occurred to me, bhikkhus: 'If (i) I perceive a light and (ii) see forms; and (iii) I associate with those deities, converse with them, and engage in a discussion with them [304]; and (iv) know about those deities: 'These deities are from this or that order of devas'; and (v) 'After passing away here, these deities were reborn there as a result of this kamma'; and (vi) 'As a result of this kamma, these deities subsist on such food and experience such pleasure and pain'; and (vii) 'As a result of this kamma, these deities have a life span of such length'; and (viii) also know whether or not I had previously lived together with those deities, in such a case this knowledge and vision of mine would become even more purified.'

"So on a later occasion, as I was dwelling heedful, ardent, and resolute: (i) I perceived a light and (ii) saw forms; and (iii) I associated with those deities, conversed with them, and engaged in a discussion with them; and (iv) I also knew about those deities: 'These deities are from this or that order of devas'; and (v) 'After passing away here, these deities were reborn there as a result of this kamma'; and (vi) 'As a result of this kamma, these deities subsist on such food and experience such pleasure and pain'; and (vii) 'As a result of this kamma, these deities have a life span of such length'; and (viii) I also knew whether or not I had previously lived together with those deities.[1770]

"So long, bhikkhus, as my knowledge and vision about the devas with its eight facets was not well purified, I did not claim to have awakened to the unsurpassed perfect enlightenment in this world with its devas, Māra, and Brahmā, in this population with its ascetics and brahmins, its devas and humans. But when my knowledge and vision about the devas with its eight facets was well purified, then I [305] claimed to have awakened to the unsurpassed perfect enlightenment in this world with . . . its devas and humans. The knowledge and vision arose in me: 'Unshakable is my liberation of mind; this is my last birth; now there is no more renewed existence.'"

65 (5) Overcoming

"Bhikkhus, there are these eight bases of overcoming.[1771] What eight?

(1) "One percipient of forms internally sees forms externally, limited, beautiful or ugly. Having overcome them, he is percipient thus: 'I know, I see.' This is the first basis of overcoming.[1772]

(2) "One percipient of forms internally sees forms externally, measureless, beautiful or ugly. Having overcome them, he is percipient thus: 'I know, I see.' This is the second basis of overcoming.[1773]

(3) "One not percipient of forms internally sees forms externally, limited, beautiful or ugly. Having overcome them, he is percipient thus: 'I know, I see.' This is the third basis of overcoming.[1774]

(4) "One not percipient of forms internally sees forms externally, measureless, beautiful or ugly. Having overcome them,

he is percipient thus: 'I know, I see.' This is the fourth basis of overcoming.

(5) "One not percipient of forms internally sees forms externally, blue ones, blue in color, with a blue hue, with a blue tint. Having overcome them, he is percipient thus: 'I know, I see.' This is the fifth basis of overcoming.[1775]

(6) "One not percipient of forms internally sees forms externally, yellow ones, yellow in color, with a yellow hue, with a yellow tint. Having overcome them, he is percipient thus: 'I know, I see.' This is the sixth basis of overcoming. [306]

(7) "One not percipient of forms internally sees forms externally, red ones, red in color, with a red hue, with a red tint. Having overcome them, he is percipient thus: 'I know, I see.' This is the seventh basis of overcoming.

(8) "One not percipient of forms internally sees forms externally, white ones, white in color, with a white hue, with a white tint. Having overcome them, he is percipient thus: 'I know, I see.' This is the eighth basis of overcoming.

"These, bhikkhus, are the eight bases of overcoming."

66 (6) Emancipations

"Bhikkhus, there are these eight emancipations.[1776] What eight?

(1) "One possessing form sees forms. This is the first emancipation.[1777]

(2) "One not percipient of forms internally sees forms externally. This is the second emancipation.[1778]

(3) "One is focused only on 'beautiful.' This is the third emancipation.[1779]

(4) "With the complete surmounting of perceptions of forms, with the passing away of perceptions of sensory impingement, with non-attention to perceptions of diversity, [perceiving] 'space is infinite,' one enters and dwells in the base of the infinity of space. This is the fourth emancipation.

(5) "By completely surmounting the base of the infinity of space, [perceiving] 'consciousness is infinite,' one enters and dwells in the base of the infinity of consciousness. This is the fifth emancipation.

(6) "By completely surmounting the base of the infinity of consciousness, [perceiving] 'there is nothing,' one enters and dwells in the base of nothingness. This is the sixth emancipation.

(7) "By completely surmounting the base of nothingness, one enters and dwells in the base of neither-perception-nor-non-perception. This is the seventh emancipation.

(8) "By completely surmounting the base of neither-perception-nor-non-perception, one enters and dwells in the cessation of perception and feeling.[1780] This is the eighth emancipation.

"These, bhikkhus, are the eight emancipations." [307]

67 (7) Declarations (1)

"Bhikkhus, there are these eight ignoble declarations.[1781] What eight? (1) Saying that one has seen what one has not seen; (2) saying that one has heard what one has not heard; (3) saying that one has sensed what one has not sensed; (4) saying that one has cognized what one has not cognized; (5) saying that one has not seen what one has actually seen; (6) saying that one has not heard what one has actually heard; (7) saying that one has not sensed what one has actually sensed; (8) saying that one has not cognized what one has actually cognized. These are the eight ignoble declarations."

68 (8) Declarations (2)

"Bhikkhus, there are these eight noble declarations.[1782] What eight? (1) Saying that one has not seen what one has not seen; (2) saying that one has not heard what one has not heard; (3) saying that one has not sensed what one has not sensed; (4) saying that one has not cognized what one has not cognized; (5) saying that one has seen what one has actually seen; (6) saying that one has heard what one has actually heard; (7) saying that one has sensed what one has actually sensed; (8) saying that one has cognized what one has actually cognized. These are the eight noble declarations."

69 (9) Assemblies[1783]

"Bhikkhus, there are these eight assemblies. What eight? An assembly of khattiyas, an assembly of brahmins, an assembly of householders, an assembly of ascetics, an assembly of the devas [ruled by] the four great kings, an assembly of the Tāvatiṃsa devas, an assembly of Māra, an assembly of Brahmā.

(1) "Now I recall, bhikkhus, approaching an assembly consisting of many hundreds of khattiyas. I previously sat there, conversed, and held discussions. I appeared just like them,

and my voice became like their voice. I instructed, encouraged, inspired, and gladdened them with a Dhamma talk, and while I was speaking they did not recognize me but thought: 'Who is it that is speaking, a deva or a human being?' Having instructed, encouraged, inspired, and gladdened them with a Dhamma talk, I disappeared, and when I had disappeared they did not recognize me but thought: 'Who was it that has disappeared, a deva or a human being?'[1784] [308]

(2)–(8) "Then I recall, bhikkhus, approaching an assembly consisting of many hundreds of brahmins . . . an assembly consisting of many hundreds of householders . . . an assembly consisting of many hundreds of ascetics . . . an assembly consisting of many hundreds of the devas [ruled by] the four great kings . . . an assembly consisting of many hundreds of the Tāvatiṃsa devas . . . an assembly consisting of many hundreds under Māra . . . an assembly consisting of many hundreds under Brahmā. I previously sat there, conversed, and held discussions. I appeared just like them, and my voice became like their voice. I instructed, encouraged, inspired, and gladdened them with a Dhamma talk, and while I was speaking they did not recognize me but thought: 'Who is it that is speaking, a deva or a human being?' Having instructed, encouraged, inspired, and gladdened them with a Dhamma talk, I disappeared, and when I had disappeared they did not recognize me but thought: 'Who was it that has disappeared, a deva or a human being?'

"These, bhikkhus, are the eight assemblies."

70 (10) Earthquakes[1785]

On one occasion the Blessed One was dwelling at Vesālī in the hall with the peaked roof in the Great Wood. Then, in the morning, the Blessed One dressed, took his bowl and robe, and entered Vesālī for alms. When he had walked for alms in Vesālī, after his meal, on returning from his alms round, he addressed the Venerable Ānanda: "Take a sitting cloth, Ānanda. Let us go to the Cāpāla Shrine for the day's dwelling."

"Yes, Bhante," the Venerable Ānanda replied and, having taken a sitting cloth, he followed closely behind the Blessed One. The Blessed One then went to the Cāpāla Shrine, sat down on the seat that was prepared for him, and said to the Venerable Ānanda: [309]

"Delightful is Vesālī, Ānanda. Delightful is the Udena Shrine, delightful the Gotamaka Shrine, delightful the Sattamba Shrine, delightful the Bahuputta Shrine, delightful the Sārandada Shrine, delightful the Cāpāla Shrine. Whoever, Ānanda, has developed and cultivated the four bases for psychic potency, made them a vehicle and basis, carried them out, consolidated them, and properly undertaken them could, if he so wished, live on for an eon or for the remainder of an eon. The Tathāgata, Ānanda, has developed and cultivated the four bases for psychic potency, made them a vehicle and basis, carried them out, consolidated them, and properly undertaken them. If he so wished, the Tathāgata could live on for an eon or for the remainder of an eon."[1786]

But though the Venerable Ānanda was given such an obvious signal by the Blessed One, though he was given such an obvious hint, he was unable to pick up the hint. He did not request the Blessed One: "Bhante, let the Blessed One live on for an eon! Let the Fortunate One live on for an eon, for the welfare of many people, for the happiness of many people, out of compassion for the world, for the good, welfare, and happiness of devas and humans." For his mind was obsessed by Māra.[1787]

A second time ... A third time the Blessed One addressed the Venerable Ānanda: "Delightful is Vesālī ... Delightful is the Udena Shrine ... delightful the Cāpāla Shrine. Whoever, Ānanda, has developed and cultivated the four bases for psychic potency ... and properly undertaken them could, if he so wished, live on for an eon or for the remainder of an eon. The Tathāgata, Ānanda, has developed and cultivated the four bases for psychic potency, made them a vehicle and basis, carried them out, consolidated them, and properly undertaken them. If he so wished, the Tathāgata could live on for an eon or for the remainder of an eon."

But again, though the Venerable Ānanda [310] was given such an obvious signal by the Blessed One, though he was given such an obvious hint, he was unable to pick up the hint. ... For his mind was obsessed by Māra.

Then the Blessed One addressed the Venerable Ānanda: "You may go, Ānanda, at your own convenience."

"Yes, Bhante," the Venerable Ānanda replied, and he rose from his seat, paid homage to the Blessed One, circumambulated him keeping the right side toward him, and sat down at the foot of a tree not far from the Blessed One.

Then, not long after the Venerable Ānanda had left, Māra the Evil One said to the Blessed One: "Bhante, let the Blessed One now attain final nibbāna! Let the Fortunate One now attain final nibbāna! Now is the time, Bhante, for the Blessed One's final nibbāna! These words were uttered, Bhante, by the Blessed One:[1788] 'I will not attain final nibbāna, Evil One, until there are bhikkhu disciples of mine who are competent, disciplined, self-confident, attained to security from bondage, learned, upholders of the Dhamma, practicing in accordance with the Dhamma, practicing in the proper way, conducting themselves accordingly; who have learned their own teacher's teaching and can explain it, teach it, proclaim it, establish it, disclose it, analyze it, and elucidate it; who can thoroughly refute in reasoned ways the current tenets of others and teach the antidotal Dhamma.'[1789] Now at present the Blessed One has bhikkhu disciples who are competent . . . and who can teach the antidotal Dhamma. Bhante, let the Blessed One now attain final nibbāna! Let the Fortunate One now attain final nibbāna! Now is the time for the Blessed One's final nibbāna!

"And these words were uttered, Bhante, by the Blessed One: 'I will not attain final nibbāna, Evil One, until there are bhikkhunī disciples of mine who are competent . . . until there are male lay disciples of mine [311] who are competent . . . until there are female lay disciples of mine who are competent . . . and teach the antidotal Dhamma.' Now at present the Blessed One has bhikkhunī disciples . . . male lay disciples . . . female lay disciples who are competent, disciplined, self-confident, attained to security from bondage, learned, upholders of the Dhamma, practicing in accordance with the Dhamma, practicing in the proper way, conducting themselves accordingly; who have learned their own teacher's doctrine and can explain it, teach it, proclaim it, establish it, disclose it, analyze it, and elucidate it; who can thoroughly refute in reasoned ways the current tenets of others and teach the antidotal Dhamma. Bhante, let the Blessed One now attain final nibbāna! Let the Fortunate One now attain final nibbāna! Now is the time for the Blessed One's final nibbāna!

"And these words were uttered, Bhante, by the Blessed One:

'I will not attain final nibbāna, Evil One, until this spiritual life of mine has become successful and prosperous, extensive, popular, widespread, well proclaimed among devas and humans.' That spiritual life of the Blessed One has become successful and prosperous, extensive, popular, widespread, well proclaimed among devas and humans. Bhante, let the Blessed One now attain final nibbāna! Let the Fortunate One now attain final nibbāna! Now is the time, Bhante, for the Blessed One's final nibbāna!"

[The Blessed One said:] "Be at ease, Evil One. It won't be long before the Tathāgata's final nibbāna takes place. Three months from now the Tathāgata will attain final nibbāna."

Then the Blessed One, at the Cāpāla Shrine, mindful and clearly comprehending, let go his vital force.[1790] And when the Blessed One had let go his vital force, a great earthquake occurred, frightening and terrifying, and peals of thunder shook the sky.

Then, having understood the meaning of this, the Blessed One on that occasion uttered this inspired utterance: [312]

> "Comparing the incomparable and continued existence,
> the sage let go the force of existence.
> Rejoicing internally, concentrated,
> he broke his own existence like a coat of armor."[1791]

Then it occurred to the Venerable Ānanda: "This earthquake was indeed powerful! This earthquake was indeed very powerful, frightening and terrifying, and peals of thunder shook the sky! What is the cause and condition for a powerful earthquake?"

Then the Venerable Ānanda approached the Blessed One, paid homage to him, sat down to one side, and said to him: "Bhante, this earthquake was indeed powerful! This earthquake was indeed very powerful, frightening and terrifying, and peals of thunder shook the sky! What, Bhante, is the cause and condition for a powerful earthquake?"

"Ānanda, there are these eight causes and conditions for a powerful earthquake. What eight?

(1) "Ānanda, this great earth is established upon water; the water rests upon wind; the wind blows in space. There comes

a time, Ānanda, when strong winds blow and shake the water. The water, being shaken, shakes the earth. This is the first cause and condition for a powerful earthquake.

(2) "Again, there is an ascetic or brahmin who possesses psychic potency and has attained mastery of mind, or a deity who is very powerful and mighty. He has developed a limited perception of earth and a measureless perception of water. He makes this earth shake, shudder, and tremble.[1792] This is the second cause and condition for a powerful earthquake.

(3) "Again, when the bodhisatta passes away from the Tusita order and, mindful and clearly comprehending, enters his mother's womb, this [313] earth shakes, shudders, and trembles. This is the third cause and condition for a powerful earthquake.

(4) "Again, when the bodhisatta, mindful and clearly comprehending, emerges from his mother's womb, this earth shakes, shudders, and trembles. This is the fourth cause and condition for a powerful earthquake.

(5) "Again, when the Tathāgata awakens to the unsurpassed perfect enlightenment, this earth shakes, shudders, and trembles. This is the fifth cause and condition for a powerful earthquake.

(6) "Again, when the Tathāgata sets in motion the unsurpassed wheel of the Dhamma, this earth shakes, shudders, and trembles. This is the sixth cause and condition for a powerful earthquake.

(7) "Again, when the Tathāgata, mindful and clearly comprehending, lets go his vital force, this earth shakes, shudders, and trembles. This is the seventh cause and condition for a powerful earthquake.

(8) "Again, when the Tathāgata attains final nibbāna by the nibbāna element without residue remaining, this earth shakes, shudders, and trembles. This is the eighth cause and condition for a powerful earthquake.

"These are the eight causes and conditions for a powerful earthquake." [314]

III. Pairs

71 (1) Faith (1)

(1) "Bhikkhus, a bhikkhu may be endowed with faith but he is not virtuous; thus he is incomplete with respect to that fac-

tor. He should fulfill that factor, [thinking]: 'How can I be endowed with faith and also be virtuous?' But when a bhikkhu is endowed with faith and is also virtuous, then he is complete with respect to that factor.

(2) "A bhikkhu may be endowed with faith and virtuous, but he is not learned; thus he is incomplete with respect to that factor. He should fulfill that factor, [thinking]: 'How can I be endowed with faith, virtuous, and also learned?' But when a bhikkhu is endowed with faith, virtuous, and also learned, then he is complete with respect to that factor.

(3) "A bhikkhu may be endowed with faith, virtuous, and learned, but he is not a speaker on the Dhamma . . . (4) . . . a speaker on the Dhamma, but not one who frequents assemblies . . . (5) . . . one who frequents assemblies, but not one who confidently teaches the Dhamma to an assembly . . . (6) . . . one who confidently teaches the Dhamma to an assembly, but not one who gains at will, without trouble or difficulty, the four jhānas that constitute the higher mind and are pleasant dwellings in this very life . . . (7) . . . one who gains at will, without trouble or difficulty, the four jhānas that constitute the higher mind and are pleasant dwellings in this very life, but not one who, with the destruction of the taints, has realized for himself with direct knowledge, in this very life, the taintless liberation of mind, liberation by wisdom, and having entered upon it, dwells in it. Thus he is incomplete with respect to that factor. He should fulfill that factor, [315] [thinking]: 'How can I be endowed with faith . . . and also be one who, with the destruction of the taints, has realized for himself with direct knowledge, in this very life, the taintless liberation of mind, liberation by wisdom, and having entered upon it, dwells in it'?

(8) "But when a bhikkhu is (i) endowed with faith, (ii) virtuous, and (iii) learned; (iv) a speaker on the Dhamma; (v) one who frequents assemblies; (vi) one who confidently teaches the Dhamma to an assembly; (vii) one who gains at will, without trouble or difficulty, the four jhānas that constitute the higher mind and are pleasant dwellings in this very life; and (viii) he is also one who, with the destruction of the taints, has realized for himself with direct knowledge, in this very life, the taintless liberation of mind, liberation by wisdom, and having entered upon it, dwells in it, then he is complete with respect to that factor.

"A bhikkhu who possesses these eight qualities is one who inspires confidence in all respects and who is complete in all aspects."

72 (2) Faith (2)

(1) "Bhikkhus, a bhikkhu may be endowed with faith but he is not virtuous; thus he is incomplete with respect to that factor. He should fulfill that factor, [thinking]: 'How can I be endowed with faith and also be virtuous?' But when a bhikkhu is endowed with faith and is also virtuous, then he is complete with respect to that factor.

(2) "A bhikkhu may be endowed with faith and virtuous, but he is not learned; thus he is incomplete with respect to that factor. He should fulfill that factor, [thinking]: 'How can I be endowed with faith, virtuous, and also learned?' But when a bhikkhu is endowed with faith, virtuous, and also learned, then he is complete with respect to that factor.

(3) "A bhikkhu may be endowed with faith, virtuous, and learned, but he is not a speaker on the Dhamma . . . (4) . . . a speaker on the Dhamma, but not one who frequents assemblies . . . (5) . . . one who frequents assemblies, but not one who confidently teaches the Dhamma to an assembly [316] . . . (6) . . . one who confidently teaches the Dhamma to an assembly, but he is not one who contacts with the body and dwells in those peaceful emancipations, transcending forms, that are formless . . . (7) . . . one who contacts with the body and dwells in those peaceful emancipations, transcending forms, that are formless, but not one who, with the destruction of the taints, has realized for himself with direct knowledge, in this very life, the taintless liberation of mind, liberation by wisdom, and having entered upon it, dwells in it. Thus he is incomplete with respect to that factor. He should fulfill that factor, [thinking]: 'How can I be endowed with faith . . . and also be one who, with the destruction of the taints, has realized for himself with direct knowledge, in this very life, the taintless liberation of mind, liberation by wisdom, and having entered upon it, dwells in it?"

(8) "But when a bhikkhu is (i) endowed with faith, (ii) virtuous, and (iii) learned; (iv) a speaker on the Dhamma; (v) one who frequents assemblies; (vi) one who confidently teaches

the Dhamma to an assembly; (vii) one who contacts with the body and dwells in those peaceful emancipations, transcending forms, that are formless; and (viii) he is also one who, with the destruction of the taints, has realized for himself with direct knowledge, in this very life, the taintless liberation of mind, liberation by wisdom, and having entered upon it, dwells in it, then he is complete with respect to that factor.

"A bhikkhu who possesses these eight qualities is one who inspires confidence in all respects and who is complete in all aspects."

73 (3) Mindfulness of Death (1)[1793]

On one occasion the Blessed One was dwelling at Nādika in the brick hall. There the Blessed One addressed the bhikkhus: [317] "Bhikkhus!"

"Venerable sir!" those bhikkhus replied. The Blessed One said this:

"Bhikkhus, mindfulness of death, when developed and cultivated, is of great fruit and benefit, culminating in the deathless, having the deathless as its consummation. But do you, bhikkhus, develop mindfulness of death?"

(1) When this was said, one bhikkhu said to the Blessed One: "Bhante, I develop mindfulness of death."

"But how, bhikkhu, do you develop mindfulness of death?"

"Here, Bhante, I think thus: 'May I live just a night and a day so that I may attend to the Blessed One's teaching. I could then accomplish much!' It is in this way that I develop mindfulness of death."

(2) Another bhikkhu said to the Blessed One: "I too, Bhante, develop mindfulness of death."

"But how, bhikkhu, do you develop mindfulness of death?"

"Here, Bhante, I think: 'May I live just a day so that I may attend to the Blessed One's teaching. I could then accomplish much!' It is in this way that I develop mindfulness of death."

(3) Still another bhikkhu said to the Blessed One: "I too, Bhante, develop mindfulness of death."

"But how, bhikkhu, do you develop mindfulness of death?"

"Here, Bhante, I think: 'May I live just half a day so that I may attend to the Blessed One's teaching. I could then accomplish much!' It is in this way that I develop mindfulness of death."

(4) Still another bhikkhu said to the Blessed One: "I too, Bhante, develop mindfulness of death."

"But how, bhikkhu, do you develop mindfulness of death?"

"Here, Bhante, I think: 'May I live just the time it takes to eat a single alms meal so that I may attend to the Blessed One's teaching. I could then accomplish much!' It is in this way that I develop mindfulness of death."

(5) Still another bhikkhu said to the Blessed One: "I too, Bhante, develop mindfulness of death."

"But how, bhikkhu, do you develop mindfulness of death?"

"Here, [318] Bhante, I think: 'May I live just the time it takes to eat half an alms meal so that I may attend to the Blessed One's teaching. I could then accomplish much!' It is in this way that I develop mindfulness of death."

(6) Still another bhikkhu said to the Blessed One: "I too, Bhante, develop mindfulness of death."

"But how, bhikkhu, do you develop mindfulness of death?"

"Here, Bhante, I think: 'May I live just the time it takes to chew and swallow four or five mouthfuls of food so that I may attend to the Blessed One's teaching. I could then accomplish much!' It is in this way that I develop mindfulness of death."

(7) Still another bhikkhu said to the Blessed One: "I too, Bhante, develop mindfulness of death."

"But how, bhikkhu, do you develop mindfulness of death?"

"Here, Bhante, I think: 'May I live just the time it takes to chew and swallow a single mouthful of food so that I may attend to the Blessed One's teaching. I could then accomplish much!' It is in this way that I develop mindfulness of death."

(8) Still another bhikkhu said to the Blessed One: "I too, Bhante, develop mindfulness of death."

"But how, bhikkhu, do you develop mindfulness of death?"

"Here, Bhante, I think: 'May I live just the time it takes to breathe out after breathing in, or to breathe in after breathing out, so that I may attend to the Blessed One's teaching. I could then accomplish much!' It is in this way that I develop mindfulness of death."

When this was said, the Blessed One said to those bhikkhus: "Bhikkhus, (1) the bhikkhu who develops mindfulness of death thus: 'May I live just a night and a day so that I may attend to the Blessed One's teaching. I could then accomplish much!'; and (2) the one who develops mindfulness of death thus: [319] 'May I live just a day so that I may attend to the Blessed One's teaching. I could then accomplish much!'; and (3) the one who develops mindfulness of death thus: 'May I live just half a day so that I may attend to the Blessed One's teaching. I could then accomplish much!'; and (4) the one who develops mindfulness of death thus: 'May I live just the length of time it takes to eat a single alms meal so that I may attend to the Blessed One's teaching. I could then accomplish much!'; and (5) the one who develops mindfulness of death thus: 'May I live just the length of time it takes to eat half an alms meal so that I may attend to the Blessed One's teaching. I could then accomplish much!'; and (6) the one who develops mindfulness of death thus: 'May I live just the length of time it takes to chew and swallow four or five mouthfuls of food so that I may attend to the Blessed One's teaching. I could then accomplish much!': these are called bhikkhus who dwell heedlessly. They develop mindfulness of death sluggishly for the destruction of the taints.

"But (7) the bhikkhu who develops mindfulness of death thus: 'May I live just the length of time it takes to chew and swallow a single mouthful of food so that I may attend to the Blessed One's teaching. I could then accomplish much!'; and (8) the one who develops mindfulness of death thus: 'May I live just the length of time it takes to breathe out after breathing in, or to breathe in after breathing out, so that I may attend to the Blessed One's teaching. I could then accomplish much!': these are called bhikkhus who dwell heedfully. They develop mindfulness of death keenly for the destruction of the taints.

"Therefore, bhikkhus, you should train yourselves thus: 'We will dwell heedfully. We will develop mindfulness of death keenly for the destruction of the taints.' Thus should you train yourselves." [320]

74 (4) Mindfulness of Death (2)[1794]

On one occasion the Blessed One was dwelling at Nādika in the brick hall. There the Blessed One addressed the bhikkhus: "Bhikkhus!"

"Venerable sir!" those bhikkhus replied. The Blessed One said this:

"Bhikkhus, mindfulness of death, when developed and cultivated, is of great fruit and benefit, culminating in the deathless, having the deathless as its consummation. And how is this so?

"Here, bhikkhus, when day has receded and night has approached, a bhikkhu reflects thus: 'I could die on account of many causes. (1) A snake might bite me, or a scorpion or centipede might sting me, and I might thereby die; that would be an obstacle for me. (2) I might stumble and fall down, or (3) my food might disagree with me, or (4) my bile might become agitated, or (5) my phlegm might become agitated, or (6) sharp winds in me might become agitated, or (7) people might attack me, or (8) wild spirits might attack me, and I might die; that would be an obstacle for me.'

"This bhikkhu should reflect thus: 'Do I have any bad unwholesome qualities that have not been abandoned, which might become an obstacle for me if I were to die tonight?' If, upon review, the bhikkhu knows: 'I have bad unwholesome qualities that have not been abandoned, which might become an obstacle for me if I were to die tonight,' then he should put forth extraordinary desire, effort, zeal, enthusiasm, indefatigability, mindfulness, and clear comprehension to abandon those bad unwholesome qualities. Just as one whose clothes or head had caught fire would put forth extraordinary desire, effort, zeal, enthusiasm, indefatigability, mindfulness, and clear comprehension to extinguish [the fire on] his clothes or head, so that bhikkhu [321] should put forth extraordinary desire, effort, zeal, enthusiasm, indefatigability, mindfulness, and clear comprehension to abandon those bad unwholesome qualities.

"But if, upon review, the bhikkhu knows: 'I do not have any bad unwholesome qualities that have not been abandoned, which might become an obstacle for me if I were to die tonight,' then he should dwell in that same rapture and joy, training day and night in wholesome qualities.

"But when night has receded and day has approached, a bhikkhu reflects thus: 'I could die on account of many causes. A snake might bite me . . . or wild spirits might attack me, and I might die; that would be an obstacle for me.'

"This bhikkhu should reflect thus: 'Do I have any bad unwholesome qualities that have not been abandoned which might become an obstacle for me if I were to die this day?' If, upon review, the bhikkhu knows: 'I have bad unwholesome qualities that I have not yet abandoned, which might become an obstacle for me if I were to die this day,' then he should put forth extraordinary desire, effort, zeal, enthusiasm, indefatigability, mindfulness, and clear comprehension to abandon those bad unwholesome qualities. Just as one whose clothes or head had caught fire would put forth extraordinary desire, effort, zeal, enthusiasm, indefatigability, mindfulness, and clear comprehension to extinguish [the fire on] his clothes or head, so that bhikkhu should put forth extraordinary desire, effort, zeal, enthusiasm, indefatigability, mindfulness, and clear comprehension to abandon those bad unwholesome qualities.

"But if, upon review, the bhikkhu knows: 'I do not have any bad unwholesome qualities [322] that I have not yet abandoned, which might become an obstacle for me if I were to die this day,' then he should dwell in that same rapture and joy, training day and night in wholesome qualities.

"It is, bhikkhus, when mindfulness of death is developed and cultivated in this way that it is of great fruit and benefit, culminating in the deathless, having the deathless as its consummation."

75 (5) Accomplishments (1)

"Bhikkhus, there are these eight accomplishments. What eight? Accomplishment in initiative, accomplishment in protection, good friendship, balanced living, accomplishment in faith, accomplishment in virtuous behavior, accomplishment in generosity, and accomplishment in wisdom. These are the eight accomplishments."

[Four verses are attached, identical with those of 8:54.]

76 (6) Accomplishments (2)

"Bhikkhus, there are these eight accomplishments. What eight?[1795] Accomplishment in initiative, accomplishment in protection, good friendship, balanced living, accomplishment in faith, accomplishment in virtuous behavior, accomplishment in generosity, and accomplishment in wisdom.

(1) "And what is accomplishment in initiative? Here, whatever may be the means by which a clansman earns his living—whether by farming, trade, raising cattle, archery, government service, or by some other craft [323]—he is skillful and diligent; he possesses sound judgment about it in order to carry out and arrange it properly. This is called accomplishment in initiative.

(2) "And what is accomplishment in protection? Here, a clansman sets up protection and guard over the wealth he has acquired by initiative and energy, amassed by the strength of his arms, earned by the sweat of his brow, righteous wealth righteously gained, thinking: 'How can I prevent kings and thieves from taking it, fire from burning it, floods from sweeping it off, and displeasing heirs from taking it?' This is called accomplishment in protection.

(3) "And what is good friendship? Here, in whatever village or town a clansman lives, he associates with householders or their sons—whether young but of mature virtue, or old and of mature virtue—who are accomplished in faith, virtuous behavior, generosity, and wisdom; he converses with them and engages in discussions with them. Insofar as they are accomplished in faith, he emulates them with respect to their accomplishment in faith; insofar as they are accomplished in virtuous behavior, he emulates them with respect to their accomplishment in virtuous behavior; insofar as they are accomplished in generosity, he emulates them with respect to their accomplishment in generosity; insofar as they are accomplished in wisdom, he emulates them with respect to their accomplishment in wisdom. This is called good friendship.

(4) "And what is balanced living? Here, a clansman knows his income and expenditures and leads a balanced life, neither too extravagant nor too frugal, [aware]: 'In this way my income will exceed my expenditures rather than the reverse.' Just as an appraiser or his apprentice, holding up a scale, knows: 'By so much it has dipped down, [324] by so much it has gone up,' so a clansman knows his income and expenditures and leads a balanced life, neither too extravagant nor too frugal, [aware]:

'In this way my income will exceed my expenditures rather than the reverse.'

"If this clansman has a small income but lives luxuriously, others would say of him: 'This clansman eats his wealth just like an eater of figs.' But if he has a large income but lives sparingly, others would say of him: 'This clansman may even starve himself.' But it is called balanced living when a clansman knows his income and expenditures and leads a balanced life, neither too extravagant nor too frugal, [aware]: 'Thus my income will exceed my expenditures rather than the reverse.'

(5) "And what is accomplishment in faith? Here, a clansman is endowed with faith. He places faith in the enlightenment of the Tathāgata thus: 'The Blessed One is an arahant . . . teacher of devas and humans, the Enlightened One, the Blessed One.' This is called accomplishment in faith.

(6) "And what is accomplishment in virtuous behavior? Here, a clansman abstains from the destruction of life, from taking what is not given, from sexual misconduct, from false speech, and from liquor, wine, and intoxicants, the basis for heedlessness. This is called accomplishment in virtuous behavior.

(7) "And what is accomplishment in generosity? Here, a clansman dwells at home with a heart devoid of the stain of miserliness, freely generous, openhanded, delighting in relinquishment, one devoted to charity, delighting in giving and sharing. This is called accomplishment in generosity.

(8) "And what is accomplishment in wisdom? [325] Here, a clansman is wise; he possesses the wisdom that discerns arising and passing away, which is noble and penetrative and leads to the complete destruction of suffering. This is called accomplishment in wisdom.

"These, bhikkhus, are the eight accomplishments."

[The four verses are identical with those in 8:54.]

77 (7) Desire

There the Venerable Sāriputta addressed the bhikkhus: "Friends, bhikkhus!"

"Friend," those bhikkhus replied. The Venerable Sāriputta said this:

"Friends, there are these eight kinds of persons found existing in the world. What eight?" . . .

[What follows is identical with 8:61, but spoken by Sāriputta.] . . . [326–28]

"These are the eight kinds of persons found existing in the world."

78 (8) Able

There the Venerable Sāriputta addressed the bhikkhus: "Friends, bhikkhus!" . . .

(1) "Friends, possessing six qualities, a bhikkhu is able [to benefit] both himself and others. What six? . . .

[What follows is identical with 8:62, but spoken by Sāriputta.] . . . [329–31]

"Possessing these two qualities, a bhikkhu is able [to benefit] others but not himself."

79 (9) Decline[1796]

"Bhikkhus, these eight qualities lead to the decline of a bhikkhu who is a trainee. What eight? Delight in work, delight in talk, delight in sleep, delight in company, not guarding the doors of the sense faculties, lack of moderation in eating, delight in bonding, and delight in proliferation. These eight qualities lead to the decline of a bhikkhu who is a trainee.

"Bhikkhus, these eight qualities lead to the non-decline of a bhikkhu who is a trainee. What eight? Not taking delight in work, not taking delight in talk, not taking delight in sleep, not taking delight in company, guarding the doors of the sense faculties, moderation in eating, not taking delight in bonding, and not taking delight in proliferation. These eight qualities lead to the non-decline of a bhikkhu who is a trainee." [332]

80 (10) Grounds for Laziness and Arousing Energy

"Bhikkhus, there are these eight grounds for laziness. What eight?

(1) "Here, a bhikkhu has to do some work. It occurs to him: 'I have some work to do. While I'm working, my body will become tired. Let me lie down.' He lies down. He does not arouse energy for the attainment of the as-yet-unattained, for the achievement of the as-yet-unachieved, for the realization of the as-yet-unrealized. This is the first ground for laziness.

(2) "Again, a bhikkhu has done some work. It occurs to him: 'I've done some work. Because of the work, my body has

become tired. Let me lie down.' He lies down. He does not arouse energy . . . for the realization of the as-yet-unrealized. This is the second ground for laziness.

(3) "Again, a bhikkhu has to make a trip. It occurs to him: 'I have to make a trip. While traveling, my body will become tired. Let me lie down.' He lies down. He does not arouse energy . . . for the realization of the as-yet-unrealized. This is the third ground for laziness.

(4) "Again, a bhikkhu has made a trip. It occurs to him: 'I've made a trip. While traveling, my body has become tired. Let me lie down.' He lies down. He does not arouse energy . . . for the realization of the as-yet-unrealized. This is the fourth ground for laziness.

(5) "Again, a bhikkhu has walked for alms in a village or town but has not gotten as much food as he needs, whether coarse or excellent. It occurs to him: [333] 'I've walked for alms in the village or town but didn't get as much food as I need, whether coarse or excellent. My body has become tired and unwieldy. Let me lie down.' He lies down. He does not arouse energy . . . for the realization of the as-yet-unrealized. This is the fifth ground for laziness.

(6) "Again, a bhikkhu has walked for alms in a village or town and has gotten as much food as he needs, whether coarse or excellent. It occurs to him: 'I've walked for alms in the village or town and gotten as much food as I need, whether coarse or excellent. My body has become as heavy and unwieldy as a heap of wet beans. Let me lie down.' He lies down. He does not arouse energy . . . for the realization of the as-yet-unrealized. This is the sixth ground for laziness.

(7) "Again, a bhikkhu is a little ill. It occurs to him: 'I'm a little ill. I need to lie down. Let me lie down.' He lies down. He does not arouse energy . . . for the realization of the as-yet-unrealized. This is the seventh ground for laziness.

(8) "Again, a bhikkhu has recovered from illness. Soon after recovering, it occurs to him: 'I've recovered from illness; I've just recovered from illness. My body is still weak and unwieldy. Let me lie down.' He lies down. He does not arouse energy for the attainment of the as-yet-unattained, for the achievement of the as-yet-unachieved, for the realization of the as-yet-unrealized. This is the eighth ground for laziness.

"These are the eight grounds for laziness. [334]

"Bhikkhus, there are these eight grounds for arousing energy. What eight?

(1) "Here, a bhikkhu has some work to do. It occurs to him: 'I have to do some work. While working, it won't be easy for me to attend to the teaching of the Buddhas. Let me in advance arouse energy for the attainment of the as-yet-unattained, for the achievement of the as-yet-unachieved, for the realization of the as-yet-unrealized.' He arouses energy for the attainment of the as-yet-unattained, for the achievement of the as-yet-unachieved, for the realization of the as-yet-unrealized. This is the first ground for arousing energy.

(2) "Again, a bhikkhu has done some work. It occurs to him: 'I've done some work. While working, it wasn't possible for me to attend to the teaching of the Buddhas. Let me arouse energy. . . .' This is the second ground for arousing energy.

(3) "Again, a bhikkhu has to make a trip. It occurs to him: 'I have to make a trip. While traveling, it won't be easy for me to attend to the teaching of the Buddhas. Let me in advance arouse energy. . . .' This is the third ground for arousing energy.

(4) "Again, a bhikkhu has made a trip. It occurs to him: 'I've made a trip. While traveling, it wasn't possible for me to attend to the teaching of the Buddhas. Let me arouse energy. . . .' This is the fourth ground for arousing energy. [335]

(5) "Again, a bhikkhu has walked for alms in a village or town but has not gotten as much food as he needs, whether coarse or excellent. It occurs to him: 'I've walked for alms in a village or town but didn't get as much food as I need, whether coarse or excellent. My body is light and wieldy. Let me arouse energy. . . .' This is the fifth ground for arousing energy.

(6) "Again, a bhikkhu has walked for alms in a village or town and has gotten as much food as he needs, whether coarse or excellent. It occurs to him: 'I've walked for alms in the village or town and gotten as much food as I need, whether coarse or excellent. My body is strong and wieldy. Let me arouse energy. . . .' This is the sixth ground for arousing energy.

(7) "Again, a bhikkhu is a little ill. It occurs to him: 'I'm a little ill. It's possible that my illness will grow worse. Let me in advance arouse energy. . . .' This is the seventh ground for arousing energy.

(8) "Again, a bhikkhu has recovered from illness. Soon after

recovering, it occurs to him: 'I've recovered from illness, just recovered from illness. It is possible that my illness will return. Let me in advance arouse energy for the attainment of the as-yet-unattained, for the achievement of the as-yet-unachieved, for the realization of the as-yet-unrealized.' He arouses energy for the attainment of the as-yet-unattained, for the achievement of the as-yet-unachieved, for the realization of the as-yet-unrealized. This is the eighth ground for arousing energy.

"These are the eight grounds for arousing energy." [336]

IV. Mindfulness

81 (1) Mindfulness[1797]

"Bhikkhus, (1) when there is no mindfulness and clear comprehension, for one deficient in mindfulness and clear comprehension, (2) the sense of moral shame and moral dread lack their proximate cause. When there is no sense of moral shame and moral dread, for one deficient in a sense of moral shame and moral dread, (3) restraint of the sense faculties lacks its proximate cause. When there is no restraint of the sense faculties, for one deficient in restraint of the sense faculties, (4) virtuous behavior lacks its proximate cause. When there is no virtuous behavior, for one deficient in virtuous behavior, (5) right concentration lacks its proximate cause. When there is no right concentration, for one deficient in right concentration, (6) the knowledge and vision of things as they really are lacks its proximate cause. When there is no knowledge and vision of things as they really are, for one deficient in the knowledge and vision of things as they really are, (7) disenchantment and dispassion lack their proximate cause. When there is no disenchantment and dispassion, for one deficient in disenchantment and dispassion, (8) the knowledge and vision of liberation lacks its proximate cause.

"Suppose there is a tree deficient in branches and foliage. Then its shoots do not grow to fullness; also its bark, softwood, and heartwood do not grow to fullness. So too, when there is no mindfulness and clear comprehension, for one deficient in mindfulness and clear comprehension, the sense of moral shame and moral dread lack their proximate cause. When there is no sense of moral shame and moral dread . . . the knowledge and vision of liberation lacks its proximate cause.

"Bhikkhus, (1) when there is mindfulness and clear comprehension, for one possessing mindfulness and clear comprehension, (2) the sense of moral shame and moral dread possess their proximate cause. When there is a sense of moral shame and moral dread, for one possessing a sense of moral shame and moral dread, (3) restraint of the sense faculties possesses its proximate cause. When there is restraint of the sense faculties, for one who exercises restraint over the sense faculties, (4) virtuous behavior possesses its proximate cause. When there is virtuous behavior, for one whose behavior is virtuous, (5) right concentration possesses its proximate cause. When there is right concentration, for one possessing right concentration, (6) the knowledge and vision of things as they really are possesses its proximate cause. When there is the knowledge and vision of things as they really are, for one possessing the knowledge and vision of things as they really are, (7) disenchantment and dispassion possess their proximate cause. [337] When there is disenchantment and dispassion, for one possessing disenchantment and dispassion, (8) the knowledge and vision of liberation possesses its proximate cause.

"Suppose there is a tree possessing branches and foliage. Then its shoots grow to fullness; also its bark, softwood, and heartwood grow to fullness. So too, when there is mindfulness and clear comprehension, for one possessing mindfulness and clear comprehension, the sense of moral shame and moral dread possess their proximate cause. When there is a sense of moral shame and moral dread . . . the knowledge and vision of liberation possesses its proximate cause."

82 (2) Puṇṇiya

Then the Venerable Puṇṇiya approached the Blessed One, paid homage to him, sat down to one side, and said to him:

"Bhante, why is it that at times the Tathāgata is disposed to teach the Dhamma and at times is not disposed to teach?"[1798]

(1) "When, Puṇṇiya, a bhikkhu is endowed with faith but does not approach him, the Tathāgata is not disposed to teach the Dhamma. (2) But when a bhikkhu is endowed with faith and approaches him, the Tathāgata is disposed to teach.

(3) "When a bhikkhu is endowed with faith and approaches him, but he does not attend on him . . . (4) When he attends on him but does not ask questions . . . (5) When he asks questions

but does not listen to the Dhamma with eager ears . . . (6) When he listens to the Dhamma with eager ears, but having heard it, does not retain it in mind . . . (7) When, having heard it, he retains it in mind but does not examine the meaning of the teachings that have been retained in mind . . . (8) When he examines the meaning of the teachings that have been retained in mind but does not understand the meaning and the Dhamma and then practice in accordance with the Dhamma, the Tathāgata is not disposed to teach the Dhamma.

"But, Puṇṇiya, (1) when a bhikkhu is endowed with faith, [338] (2) approaches [the Tathāgata], (3) attends [on the Tathāgata], (4) asks questions, and (5) listens to the Dhamma with eager ears; and (6) having heard the Dhamma, he retains it in mind, (7) examines the meaning of the teachings he has retained in mind, and (8) understands the meaning and the Dhamma and then practices in accordance with the Dhamma, the Tathāgata is disposed to teach the Dhamma. When, Puṇṇiya, one possesses these eight qualities, the Tathāgata is entirely disposed to teach the Dhamma."[1799]

83 (3) Rooted

"Bhikkhus, wanderers of other sects may ask you: (1) 'In what, friends, are all things rooted? (2) Through what do they come into being? (3) From what do they originate?[1800] (4) Upon what do they converge? (5) By what are they headed? (6) What exercises authority over them? (7) What is their supervisor? (8) What is their core?' If you are asked thus, how would you answer them?"

"Bhante, our teachings are rooted in the Blessed One, guided by the Blessed One, take recourse in the Blessed One. It would be good if the Blessed One would clear up the meaning of this statement. Having heard it from him, the bhikkhus will retain it in mind."

"Then listen, bhikkhus, and attend closely. I will speak."

"Yes, Bhante," those bhikkhus replied. The Blessed One said this:

"Bhikkhus, if wanderers of other sects should ask you: 'What, friends, are all things rooted in? . . . [339] . . . What is their essence?' you should answer them as follows.

"'Friends, (1) all things are rooted in desire. (2) They come into being through attention. (3) They originate from contact. (4) They converge upon feeling. (5) They are headed by concentration. (6) Mindfulness exercises authority over them. (7) Wisdom is their supervisor. (8) Liberation is their core.'[1801]

"If you are asked these questions, it is in such a way that you should answer those wanderers of other sects."

84 (4) A Thief

"Bhikkhus, possessing eight factors, a master thief quickly gets into trouble and does not last long. What eight? (1) He attacks one who does not attack him. (2) He steals without leaving anything behind. (3) He kills a woman. (4) He rapes a young girl. (5) He robs a monk. (6) He robs the royal treasury. (7) He does his work in his neighborhood. And (8) he is not skilled in hiding [his plunder].[1802] Possessing these eight factors, a master thief quickly gets into trouble and does not last long.

"Bhikkhus, possessing eight factors, a master thief does not quickly get into trouble and lasts long. What eight? (1) He does not attack one who does not attack him. (2) He does not steal without leaving anything behind. (3) He does not kill a woman. (4) He does not rape a young girl. (5) He does not rob a monk. (6) He does not rob the royal treasury. (7) He does not do his work in his neighborhood. And (8) he is skilled in hiding [his plunder]. Possessing these eight factors, a master thief does not quickly get into trouble and lasts long." [340]

85 (5) Designations

"Bhikkhus, (1) 'Ascetic' is a designation for the Tathāgata, the Arahant, the Perfectly Enlightened One. (2) 'Brahmin' is a designation for the Tathāgata, the Arahant, the Perfectly Enlightened One. (3) 'Healer' . . . (4) 'Master of knowledge'[1803] . . . (5) 'One unstained' . . . (6) 'Stainless one' . . . (7) 'Knower' . . . (8) 'Liberated one' is a designation for the Tathāgata, the Arahant, the Perfectly Enlightened One."

That highest state to be attained by an ascetic,[1804]
by a brahmin who has lived the spiritual life,
to be attained by a master of knowledge and a healer—
that highest state to be attained by one unstained,
by a stainless one who is purified,

to be attained by a knower, by one liberated—
[over that] I am triumphant in battle;
freed, I free others from bondage.
I am a nāga, supremely tamed,[1805]
one beyond training, attained to nibbāna.

86 (6) Nāgita[1806]

On one occasion the Blessed One was wandering on tour among the Kosalans together with a large Saṅgha of bhikkhus when he reached the Kosalan brahmin village named Icchānaṅgala. There the Blessed One dwelled in the Icchānaṅgala woodland thicket. The brahmin householders of Icchānaṅgala heard: "It is said that the ascetic Gotama, the son of the Sakyans who went forth from a Sakyan family, has arrived at Icchānaṅgala and is now dwelling [341] in the Icchānaṅgala woodland thicket. Now a good report about that Master Gotama has circulated thus: 'That Blessed One is an arahant, perfectly enlightened . . . [as in 6:42] . . . he reveals a spiritual life that is perfectly complete and pure.' Now it is good to see such arahants."

Then, when the night had passed, the brahmin householders of Icchānaṅgala took abundant food of various kinds and went to the Icchānaṅgala woodland thicket. They stood outside the entrance making an uproar and a racket. Now on that occasion the Venerable Nāgita was the Blessed One's attendant. The Blessed One then addressed the Venerable Nāgita: "Who is making such an uproar and a racket, Nāgita? One would think it was fishermen at a haul of fish."

"Bhante, these are the brahmin householders of Icchānaṅgala who have brought abundant food of various kinds. They are standing outside the entrance, [wishing to offer it] to the Blessed One and the Saṅgha of bhikkhus."

"Let me never come upon fame, Nāgita, and may fame never catch up with me. One who does not gain at will, without trouble or difficulty, this bliss of renunciation, bliss of solitude, bliss of peace, bliss of enlightenment that I gain at will, without trouble or difficulty, might accept that vile pleasure, that slothful pleasure, the pleasure of gain, honor, and praise."

"Let the Blessed One now consent, Bhante, let the Fortunate One consent. This is now the time for the Blessed One to consent. Wherever the Blessed One will go now, the brahmin householders of town and countryside will incline in the same direction. Just as, [342] when thick drops of rain are pouring down, the water flows down along the slope, so too, wherever the Blessed One will go now, the brahmin householders of town and country will incline in the same direction. For what reason? Because of the Blessed One's virtuous behavior and wisdom."

"Let me never come upon fame, Nāgita, and may fame never catch up with me. One who does not gain at will, without trouble or difficulty, this bliss of renunciation ... might accept that vile pleasure, that slothful pleasure, the pleasure of gain, honor, and praise.

"Even some deities, Nāgita, may not gain at will, without trouble or difficulty, this bliss of renunciation, bliss of solitude, bliss of peace, bliss of enlightenment that I gain at will, without trouble or difficulty.

(1) "When,[1807] Nāgita, you come together and meet, intent on companionship, it occurs to me: 'Surely, these venerable ones do not gain at will, without trouble or difficulty, this bliss of renunciation, bliss of solitude, bliss of peace, bliss of enlightenment that I gain at will, without trouble or difficulty; for when they [343] come together and meet, they are intent upon companionship.

(2) "I see, Nāgita, bhikkhus laughing and playing by poking one another with the fingers. It then occurs to me: 'Surely, these venerable ones do not gain at will, without trouble or difficulty, this bliss of renunciation ... which I gain at will, without trouble or difficulty; for these venerable ones laugh and play by poking one another with the fingers.'

(3) "I see, Nāgita, bhikkhus who, having eaten as much as they want until their bellies are full, yield to the pleasure of rest, the pleasure of sloth, the pleasure of sleep. It then occurs to me: 'Surely, these venerable ones do not gain at will, without trouble or difficulty, this bliss of renunciation ... which I gain at will, without trouble or difficulty. For having eaten as much as they want until their bellies are full, they yield to the pleasure of rest, the pleasure of sloth, the pleasure of sleep.'

(4) "I see, Nāgita, a bhikkhu dwelling on the outskirts of a village sitting in a state of concentration. It then occurs to me: 'Now a monastery attendant or a novice will return to this venerable one and cause him to fall away from that concentration.'[1808] [344]

For this reason I am not pleased with this bhikkhu's dwelling on the outskirts of a village.

(5) "I see, Nāgita, a forest-dwelling bhikkhu sitting dozing in the forest. It then occurs to me: 'Now this venerable one will dispel this sleepiness and fatigue and attend only to the perception of forest, [a state of] oneness.' For this reason I am pleased with this bhikkhu's dwelling in the forest.

(6) "I see, Nāgita, a forest-dwelling bhikkhu sitting in the forest in an unconcentrated state. It then occurs to me: 'Now this venerable one will concentrate his unconcentrated mind or guard his concentrated mind.' For this reason I am pleased with this bhikkhu's dwelling in the forest.

(7) "I see, Nāgita, a forest-dwelling bhikkhu sitting in the forest in a state of concentration. It then occurs to me: 'Now this venerable one will liberate his unliberated mind or guard his liberated mind.' For this reason I am pleased with this bhikkhu's dwelling in the forest.

(8) "When, Nāgita, I am traveling on a highway and do not see anyone ahead of me or behind me, even if it is just for the purpose of defecating and urinating, on that occasion I am at ease."

87 (7) Almsbowl

"Bhikkhus, when a lay follower possesses eight qualities, the Saṅgha, if it so wishes, may overturn the almsbowl on him.[1809] What eight? [345] (1) He tries to prevent bhikkhus from acquiring gains; (2) he tries to bring harm to bhikkhus; (3) he tries to prevent bhikkhus from residing [in a certain place]; (4) he insults and reviles bhikkhus; (5) he divides bhikkhus from each other; (6) he speaks dispraise of the Buddha; (7) he speaks dispraise of the Dhamma; (8) he speaks dispraise of the Saṅgha. When a lay follower possesses these eight qualities, the Saṅgha, if it so wishes, may overturn the almsbowl on him.

"Bhikkhus, when a lay follower possesses eight qualities, the Saṅgha, if it so wishes, may turn the almsbowl upright on him. What eight? (1) He does not try to prevent bhikkhus from acquiring gains; (2) he does not try to bring harm to bhikkhus; (3) he does not try to prevent bhikkhus from residing [nearby]; (4) he does not insult and revile bhikkhus; (5) he does not divide bhikkhus from each other; (6) he speaks praise of the Buddha; (7) he speaks praise of the Dhamma; (8) he speaks praise of the Saṅgha. When a lay follower possesses these eight qualities, the Saṅgha, if it so wishes, may turn the almsbowl upright on him."

88 (8) Lack of Confidence

"Bhikkhus, when a bhikkhu possesses eight qualities, lay followers, if they wish, may proclaim their lack of confidence in him.[1810] What eight? (1) He tries to prevent laypeople from acquiring gains; (2) he tries to bring harm to laypeople; (3) he insults and reviles laypeople; (4) he divides laypeople from each other; (5) he speaks dispraise of the Buddha; (6) he speaks dispraise of the Dhamma; (7) he speaks dispraise of the Saṅgha; (8) they see him at an improper resort.[1811] When a bhikkhu possesses these eight qualities, lay followers, if they wish, may proclaim their lack of confidence in him. [346]

"Bhikkhus, when a bhikkhu possesses eight qualities, lay followers, if they wish, may proclaim their confidence in him. What eight? (1) He does not try to prevent laypeople from acquiring gains; (2) he does not try to bring harm to laypeople; (3) he does not insult and revile laypeople; (4) he does not divide laypeople from each other; (5) he speaks praise of the Buddha; (6) he speaks praise of the Dhamma; (7) he speaks praise of the Saṅgha; (8) they see him at a [proper] resort. When a bhikkhu possesses these eight qualities, lay followers, if they wish, may proclaim their confidence in him."

89 (9) Reconciliation

"Bhikkhus, when a bhikkhu possesses eight qualities, the Saṅgha, if it wishes, may enjoin an act of reconciliation on him.[1812] What eight? (1) He tries to prevent laypeople from acquiring gains; (2) he tries to bring harm to laypeople; (3) he insults and reviles laypeople; (4) he divides laypeople from each other; (5) he speaks dispraise of the Buddha; (6) he speaks dispraise of the Dhamma; (7) he speaks dispraise of the Saṅgha; (8) he does not fulfill a legitimate promise to laypeople. When a bhikkhu possesses these eight qualities, the Saṅgha, if it wishes, may enjoin an act of reconciliation on him.

"Bhikkhus, when a bhikkhu possesses eight qualities, the Saṅgha, if it wishes, may revoke an act of reconciliation [previously imposed on him]. What eight? (1) He does not try to prevent laypeople from acquiring gains; (2) he does not try to bring harm to laypeople; (3) he does not insult and revile laypeople; (4) he does not divide laypeople from each other; (5) he speaks praise of the Buddha; [347] (6) he speaks praise of the Dhamma; (7) he speaks praise of the Saṅgha; (8) he fulfills a legitimate promise to laypeople. When a bhikkhu possesses these eight qualities, the Saṅgha, if it wishes, may revoke an act of reconciliation [previously imposed on him]."

90 (10) Behavior

"Bhikkhus, a bhikkhu charged with aggravated misconduct[1813] should behave rightly with respect to eight principles. (1) He should not give full ordination; (2) he should not give dependence;[1814] (3) he should not have a novice attend upon him; (4) he should not accept an agreement to serve as an exhorter of bhikkhunīs; (5) even if he is agreed upon, he should not exhort bhikkhunīs; (6) he should not accept any agreement [to serve as an officer] in the Saṅgha; (7) he should not be placed in any chief position; (8) he should not give rehabilitation [in a case] with that root.[1815] A bhikkhu charged with aggravated misconduct should behave rightly with respect to these eight principles."

V. Similarity[1816]

91 (1)–117 (27)[1817]

Then the female lay follower Bojjhā ... Sirimā ... Padumā ... Sutanā ... Manujā ... Uttarā ... Muttā ... Khemā ... Somā[1818] ... Rucī ... Princess Cundī ... the female lay follower Bimbī ... Princess Sumanā ... [348] Queen Mallikā ... the female lay follower Tissā ... Soṇā the mother of Tissā ... the mother of Soṇā ... Kāṇā ... the mother of Kāṇā ... Uttarā Nandamātā[1819] ... Visākhā Migāramātā ... the female lay follower Khujjuttarā ... the female lay follower Sāmāvatī ... Suppavāsā the Koliyan daughter ... the female lay follower Suppiyā ... the housewife Nakulamātā ...

VI. Lust and So Forth Repetition Series[1820]

118 (1)

"Bhikkhus, for direct knowledge of lust, eight things are to be developed. What eight? Right view, right intention, right speech, right action, right livelihood, right effort, right mindfulness, and right concentration. For direct knowledge of lust, these eight things are to be developed."

119 (2)

"Bhikkhus, for direct knowledge of lust, eight things are to be developed. What eight? (1) One percipient of forms internally sees forms externally, limited, beautiful or ugly. Having overcome them, he is percipient thus: 'I know, I see.' (2) One percipient of forms internally sees forms externally, measureless, beautiful or ugly. Having overcome them, he is percipient thus: 'I know, I see.' (3) One not percipient of forms internally sees forms externally, limited, beautiful or ugly. Having overcome them, he is percipient thus: 'I know, I see.' (4) One not percipient of forms internally sees forms externally, measureless, beautiful or ugly. Having overcome them, he is percipient thus: 'I know, I see.' [349] (5) One not percipient of forms internally sees forms externally, blue ones, blue in color, with a blue hue, with a blue tint . . . (6) . . . yellow ones, yellow in color, with a yellow hue, with a yellow tint . . . (7) . . . red ones, red in color, with a red hue, with a red tint . . . (8) . . . white ones, white in color, with a white hue, with a white tint. Having overcome them, he is percipient thus: 'I know, I see.' For direct knowledge of lust, these eight things are to be developed."

120 (3)

"Bhikkhus, for direct knowledge of lust, eight things are to be developed. What eight? (1) One possessing form sees forms. (2) One not percipient of form internally sees forms externally. (3) One is focused only on 'beautiful.' (4) With the complete surmounting of perceptions of forms, with the passing away of perceptions of sensory impingement, with non-attention to perceptions of diversity, [perceiving] 'space is infinite,' one enters and dwells in the base of the infinity of space. (5) By completely surmounting the base of the infinity of space, [perceiving] 'consciousness is infinite,' one enters and dwells in the base of the infinity of consciousness. (6) By completely surmounting the base of the infinity of consciousness, [perceiving] 'there is nothing,' one enters and dwells in the base of nothingness. (7) By completely surmounting the base of nothingness, one enters and dwells in the base of neither-perception-nor-non-perception. (8) By completely surmounting the base of neither-perception-nor-non-perception, one enters and dwells in the cessation of perception and feeling. For direct knowledge of lust, these eight things are to be developed."

121 (4)–147 (30)

"Bhikkhus, for full understanding of lust . . . for the utter destruction . . . for the abandoning . . . for the destruction . . . for the vanishing . . . for the fading away . . . for the cessation . . . for the giving up . . . for the relinquishment of lust . . . these eight things are to be developed."

148 (31)–627 (510)

"Bhikkhus, for direct knowledge . . . for full understanding . . . for the utter destruction . . . for the abandoning . . . for the destruction . . . for the vanishing . . . for the fading away . . . for the cessation . . . for the giving up . . . for the relinquishment of hatred . . . of delusion . . . of anger . . . of hostility . . . of denigration . . . of insolence . . . of envy . . . of miserliness [350] . . . of deceitfulness . . . of craftiness . . . of obstinacy . . . of vehemence . . . of conceit . . . of arrogance . . . of intoxication . . . of heedlessness . . . these eight things are to be developed."

This is what the Blessed One said. Elated, those bhikkhus delighted in the Blessed One's statement.

The Book of the Eights is finished.

The Book of the Nines
(*Navakanipāta*)

The Book of the Nines

The First Fifty

The Second Fifty

[351] # The Book of the Nines

Homage to the Blessed One, the Arahant,
the Perfectly Enlightened One

The First Fifty

I. Enlightenment

1 (1) Enlightenment[1821]

Thus have I heard. On one occasion the Blessed One was dwelling at Sāvatthī in Jeta's Grove, Anāthapiṇḍika's Park. There the Blessed One addressed the bhikkhus: "Bhikkhus!"

"Venerable sir!" those bhikkhus replied. The Blessed One said this:

"Bhikkhus, wanderers of other sects may ask you: 'What, friends, is the proximate cause for the development of the aids to enlightenment?' If you are asked thus, how would you answer them?"

"Bhante, our teachings are rooted in the Blessed One, guided by the Blessed One, take recourse in the Blessed One. It would be good if the Blessed One would clear up the meaning of this statement. Having heard it from him, the bhikkhus will retain it in mind."

"Then listen, bhikkhus, and attend closely. I will speak."

"Yes, Bhante," those bhikkhus replied. The Blessed One said this:

"Bhikkhus, if wanderers of other sects should ask you: 'What, friends, is the proximate cause for the development of the aids to enlightenment?' you should answer them as follows.

(1) "'Here, friends, a bhikkhu has good friends, good companions, [352] good comrades. This is the first proximate cause for the development of the aids to enlightenment.

(2) "'Again, friends, a bhikkhu is virtuous; he dwells restrained by the Pātimokkha, possessed of good conduct and resort, seeing danger in minute faults. Having undertaken the training rules, he trains in them. This is the second proximate cause....

(3) "'Again, friends, a bhikkhu gets to hear at will, without trouble or difficulty, talk concerned with the austere life that is conducive to opening up the heart, that is, talk on fewness of desires, on contentment, on solitude, on not getting bound up [with others], on arousing energy, on virtuous behavior, on concentration, on wisdom, on liberation, on the knowledge and vision of liberation. This is the third proximate cause....

(4) "'Again, friends, a bhikkhu has aroused energy for abandoning unwholesome qualities and acquiring wholesome qualities; he is strong, firm in exertion, not casting off the duty of cultivating wholesome qualities. This is the fourth proximate cause....

(5) "'Again, friends, a bhikkhu is wise; he possesses the wisdom that discerns arising and passing away, which is noble and penetrative and leads to the complete destruction of suffering. This is the fifth proximate cause for the development of the aids to enlightenment.'

"When, bhikkhus, a bhikkhu has good friends, good companions, good comrades, it can be expected of him that he will be virtuous, one who dwells restrained by the Pātimokkha ... will train in them.

"When a bhikkhu has good friends, good companions, good comrades, it can be expected of him that he will get to hear at will, without trouble or difficulty, talk concerned with the austere life that is conducive to opening up the heart, that is, talk on fewness of desires ... on the knowledge and vision of liberation.

"When a bhikkhu has good friends, good companions, good comrades, it can be expected of him that he will arouse energy [353] for abandoning unwholesome qualities ... not casting off the duty of cultivating wholesome qualities.

"When a bhikkhu has good friends, good companions, good

comrades, it can be expected of him that he will be wise, possessing the wisdom that discerns arising and passing away, which is noble and penetrative and leads to the complete destruction of suffering.

"Having based himself on these five things, the bhikkhu should develop further [another] four things. (6) [The perception of] unattractiveness should be developed to abandon lust. (7) Loving-kindness should be developed to abandon ill will. (8) Mindfulness of breathing should be developed to cut off thoughts. (9) The perception of impermanence should be developed to eradicate the conceit 'I am.'[1822] When one perceives impermanence, the perception of non-self is stabilized.[1823] One who perceives non-self eradicates the conceit 'I am,' [which is] nibbāna in this very life."

2 (2) Support[1824]

Then a certain bhikkhu approached the Blessed One, paid homage to him, sat down to one side, and said to him: "It is said, Bhante: 'Equipped with supports, equipped with supports.' In what way is a bhikkhu equipped with supports?"[1825]

(1) "If, bhikkhu, supported by faith, a bhikkhu abandons the unwholesome and develops the wholesome, the unwholesome is indeed abandoned by him. (2) If, supported by a sense of moral shame . . . (3) . . . supported by moral dread . . . (4) . . . supported by energy . . . (5) . . . supported by wisdom, a bhikkhu abandons the unwholesome and develops the wholesome, that unwholesome is indeed abandoned by him.[1826] [354] A bhikkhu has abandoned and well abandoned the unwholesome when he has abandoned it by seeing it with noble wisdom.[1827]

"Basing himself on these five things, that bhikkhu should rely on four things.[1828] What four? Here, (6) having reflected, a bhikkhu uses some things; (7) having reflected, he patiently endures some things; (8) having reflected, he avoids some things; and (9) having reflected, he dispels some things.

"It is in this way, bhikkhu, that a bhikkhu is equipped with supports."

3 (3) Meghiya[1829]

Thus have I heard. On one occasion the Blessed One was dwelling at Cālikā on Mount Cālikā.[1830] Now on that occasion the

Venerable Meghiya was the Blessed One's attendant. Then the Venerable Meghiya approached the Blessed One, paid homage to him, stood to one side, and said to him: "Bhante, I would like to enter Jantugāma for alms."

"You may do so, Meghiya, at your own convenience."

Then, in the morning, the Venerable Meghiya dressed, took his bowl and robe, and entered Jantugāma for alms. When he had walked for alms in Jantugāma, after his meal, on returning from his alms round, he went to the bank of the Kimikālā River. As he was walking and wandering around for exercise along the bank of the Kimikālā River, the Venerable Meghiya saw [355] a lovely and delightful mango grove. It occurred to him: "This mango grove is truly lovely and delightful, suitable for the striving of a clansman intent on striving. If the Blessed One permits me, I will come back to this mango grove to strive."

Then the Venerable Meghiya approached the Blessed One, paid homage to him, sat down to one side, and said: "This morning, Bhante, I dressed, took my bowl and robe, and entered Jantugāma for alms. . . . [All as above, but in the first person.] . . . I thought: 'This mango grove is truly lovely and delightful, suitable for the striving of a clansman intent on striving. If the Blessed One permits me, I will go back to that mango grove to strive.' So if the Blessed One would permit me, I will go back to that mango grove to strive."

"As we are alone, Meghiya, wait until another bhikkhu comes along."[1831]

A second time the Venerable Meghiya said to the Blessed One: "Bhante, for the Blessed One there is nothing further to be done and no [need to] increase what has been done.[1832] But, Bhante, I have something further to be done and [need to] increase what has been done. If the Blessed One would permit me, I will go back to that mango grove to strive."

"As we are alone, Meghiya, wait until another bhikkhu comes along." [356]

A third time the Venerable Meghiya said to the Blessed One: "Bhante, for the Blessed One there is nothing further to be done and no [need to] increase what has been done. But, Bhante, I have something further to be done and [need to] increase what has been done. If the Blessed One would permit me, I will go back to that mango grove to strive."

"Since you speak of striving, Meghiya, what can I say to you? You may go at your own convenience."

Then the Venerable Meghiya rose from his seat, paid homage to the Blessed One, circumambulated him keeping the right side toward him, and went to the mango grove. He entered and sat down at the foot of a tree to pass the day. Then, while the Venerable Meghiya was dwelling in that mango grove, three kinds of bad unwholesome thoughts frequently occurred to him: sensual thoughts, thoughts of ill will, and thoughts of harming. It then occurred to him: "This is truly astounding and amazing! I have gone forth out of faith from the household life into homelessness, yet I am still stalked by these three kinds of bad unwholesome thoughts: sensual thoughts, thoughts of ill will, and thoughts of harming."[1833]

Then the Venerable Meghiya approached the Blessed One, paid homage to him, sat down to one side, and said: "Here, Bhante, while I was dwelling in that mango grove, three kinds of bad unwholesome thoughts frequently occurred to me: sensual thoughts, thoughts of ill will, and thoughts of harming. It then occurred to me: 'This is truly astounding and amazing! I have gone forth out of faith from the household life into homelessness, yet [357] I am still stalked by these three kinds of bad unwholesome thoughts: sensual thoughts, thoughts of ill will, and thoughts of harming.'"

"Meghiya, when liberation of mind has not matured, five things lead to its maturation.[1834] What five?

(1) "Here, Meghiya, a bhikkhu has good friends, good companions, good comrades. When liberation of mind has not matured, this is the first thing that leads to its maturation.

(2) "Again, a bhikkhu is virtuous; he dwells restrained by the Pātimokkha, possessed of good conduct and resort, seeing danger in minute faults. Having undertaken the training rules, he trains in them. When liberation of mind has not matured, this is the second thing that leads to its maturation.

(3) "Again, a bhikkhu gets to hear at will, without trouble or difficulty, talk concerned with the austere life that is conducive to opening up the heart, that is, talk on fewness of desires, on contentment, on solitude, on not getting bound up [with others], on arousing energy, on virtuous behavior, on concentration, on wisdom, on liberation, on the knowledge and vision

of liberation. When liberation of mind has not matured, this is the third thing that leads to its maturation.

(4) "Again, a bhikkhu has aroused energy for abandoning unwholesome qualities and acquiring wholesome qualities; he is strong, firm in exertion, not casting off the duty of cultivating wholesome qualities. When liberation of mind has not matured, this is the fourth thing that leads to its maturation.

(5) "Again, a bhikkhu is wise; he possesses the wisdom that discerns arising and passing away, which is noble and penetrative and leads to the complete destruction of suffering. When liberation of mind has not matured, this is the fifth thing that leads to its maturation.

"When, Meghiya, a bhikkhu has good friends, good companions, good comrades, it can be expected of him that he will be virtuous, one who dwells restrained by the Pātimokkha... [358]... will train in them.

"When a bhikkhu has good friends, good companions, good comrades, it can be expected of him that he will get to hear at will, without trouble or difficulty, talk concerned with the austere life that is conducive to opening up the heart, that is, talk on fewness of desires... on the knowledge and vision of liberation.

"When a bhikkhu has good friends, good companions, good comrades, it can be expected of him that he will arouse energy for abandoning unwholesome qualities... not casting off the duty of cultivating wholesome qualities.

"When a bhikkhu has good friends, good companions, good comrades, it can be expected of him that he will be wise, possessing the wisdom that discerns arising and passing away, which is noble and penetrative and leads to the complete destruction of suffering.

"Having based himself on these five things, the bhikkhu should develop further [another] four things. (6) [The perception of] unattractiveness should be developed to abandon lust. (7) Loving-kindness should be developed to abandon ill will. (8) Mindfulness of breathing should be developed to cut off thoughts. (9) The perception of impermanence should be developed to eradicate the conceit 'I am.' When one perceives impermanence, the perception of non-self is stabilized. One who perceives non-self eradicates the conceit 'I am,' [which is] nibbāna in this very life."

4 (4) *Nandaka*[1835]

On one occasion the Blessed One was dwelling at Sāvatthī in Jeta's Grove, Anāthapiṇḍika's Park. Now on that occasion the Venerable Nandaka was instructing, encouraging, inspiring, and gladdening the bhikkhus in the assembly hall with a Dhamma talk. Then, in the evening, the Blessed One emerged from seclusion and went to the assembly hall. He stood outside the door waiting for the talk to end. When he knew that the talk was finished, he cleared his throat [359] and tapped on the bolt. The bhikkhus opened the door for him. The Blessed One then entered the assembly hall, sat down on the seat that was prepared for him, and said to the Venerable Nandaka: "You gave the bhikkhus a long exposition of the Dhamma. My back was aching while I stood outside the door waiting for the talk to end."

When this was said, the Venerable Nandaka, feeling embarrassed, said to the Blessed One: "Bhante, I did not know that the Blessed One was standing outside the door. If I had known, I wouldn't have spoken so long."

Then the Blessed One, having understood the Venerable Nandaka's embarrassment, said to him: "Good, good, Nandaka! It is proper for clansmen like you who have gone forth out of faith from the household life into homelessness to sit together for the sake of a Dhamma talk. When you assemble, Nandaka, you should do one of two things: either talk on the Dhamma or maintain noble silence.

(1) "Nandaka, a bhikkhu may be endowed with faith but he is not virtuous; thus he is incomplete with respect to that factor.[1836] He should fulfill that factor, [thinking]: 'How can I be endowed with faith [360] and also be virtuous?' But when a bhikkhu is endowed with faith and is also virtuous, then he is complete with respect to that factor.

(2) "A bhikkhu may be endowed with faith and virtuous but he does not gain internal serenity of mind;[1837] thus he is incomplete with respect to that factor. He should fulfill that factor, [thinking]: 'How can I be endowed with faith and virtuous, and also gain internal serenity of mind?' But when a bhikkhu is endowed with faith and is virtuous, and also gains internal serenity of mind, then he is complete with respect to that factor.

(3) "A bhikkhu may be endowed with faith and virtuous, and he may gain internal serenity of mind, but he does not

gain the higher wisdom of insight into phenomena;[1838] thus he is incomplete with respect to that factor. Just as a four-legged animal with one lame or defective leg would be incomplete with respect to that limb; so too, when a bhikkhu is endowed with faith and is virtuous, and gains internal serenity of mind, but he does not gain the higher wisdom of insight into phenomena, then he is incomplete with respect to that factor. He should fulfill that factor, [thinking]: 'How can I be endowed with faith and virtuous, gain internal serenity of mind, and also gain the higher wisdom of insight into phenomena?'

(4) But when a bhikkhu is (i) endowed with faith and (ii) is virtuous, (iii) and he gains internal serenity of mind and (iv) also gains the higher wisdom of insight into phenomena, then he is complete with respect to that factor."

This is what the Blessed One said. Having said this, the Fortunate One rose from his seat and entered his dwelling. Then, not long after the Blessed One had left, the Venerable Nandaka addressed the bhikkhus: "Just now, friends, before he rose from his seat and entered his dwelling, the Blessed One revealed the perfectly complete and pure spiritual life in four terms: [361] 'Nandaka, a bhikkhu may be endowed with faith but not virtuous. . . . [Nandaka here repeats the Buddha's discourse down to:] . . . But when a bhikkhu is endowed with faith and is virtuous, and he gains internal serenity of mind and also gains the higher wisdom of insight into phenomena, then he is complete with respect to that factor.'

"There are, friends, these five benefits in timely listening to the Dhamma, in timely discussion on the Dhamma. What five?

(5) "Here, friends, a bhikkhu teaches the bhikkhus the Dhamma that is good in the beginning, good in the middle, and good in the end, with the right meaning and phrasing; he reveals the spiritual life that is perfectly complete and pure. In whatever way the bhikkhu teaches the bhikkhus the Dhamma that is good in the beginning . . . [and] reveals the spiritual life that is perfectly complete and pure, in just that way the Teacher becomes pleasing and agreeable to him, respected and esteemed by him.[1839] This is the first benefit in timely listening to the Dhamma, in timely discussion on the Dhamma.

(6) "Again, a bhikkhu teaches the bhikkhus the Dhamma that

is good in the beginning, good in the middle, and good in the end, with the right meaning and phrasing; he reveals the spiritual life that is perfectly complete and pure. In whatever way the bhikkhu teaches the bhikkhus the Dhamma that is good in the beginning . . . [and] reveals the spiritual life that is perfectly complete and pure, in just that way, in relation to that Dhamma, he experiences inspiration in the meaning and inspiration in the Dhamma.[1840] This is the second benefit in timely listening to the Dhamma, in timely discussion on the Dhamma.

(7) "Again, a bhikkhu teaches the bhikkhus the Dhamma that is good in the beginning, good in the middle, and good in the end, with the right meaning and phrasing; he reveals the spiritual life that is perfectly complete and pure. In whatever way the bhikkhu teaches the bhikkhus the Dhamma that is good in the beginning . . . [and] reveals the spiritual life that is perfectly complete and [362] pure, in just that way he sees in that Dhamma a deep and pithy matter after piercing it through with wisdom.[1841] This is the third benefit in timely listening to the Dhamma, in timely discussion on the Dhamma.

(8) "Again, a bhikkhu teaches the bhikkhus the Dhamma that is good in the beginning, good in the middle, and good in the end, with the right meaning and phrasing; he reveals the spiritual life that is perfectly complete and pure. In whatever way the bhikkhu teaches the bhikkhus the Dhamma that is good in the beginning . . . [and] reveals the spiritual life that is perfectly complete and pure, in just that way his fellow monks esteem him more highly, [thinking]: 'Surely, this venerable has attained or will attain.' This is the fourth benefit in timely listening to the Dhamma, in timely discussion on the Dhamma.

(9) "Again, a bhikkhu teaches the bhikkhus the Dhamma that is good in the beginning, good in the middle, and good in the end, with the right meaning and phrasing; he reveals the spiritual life that is perfectly complete and pure. In whatever way the bhikkhu teaches the bhikkhus the Dhamma that is good in the beginning . . . [and] reveals the spiritual life that is perfectly complete and pure, on hearing that Dhamma those bhikkhus there who are trainees, who have not attained their heart's ideal, who dwell aspiring for the unsurpassed security from bondage, arouse energy for the attainment of the as-yet-unattained, for the achievement of the as-yet-unachieved, for the realization of

the as-yet-unrealized. But having heard that Dhamma, those bhikkhus who are arahants, whose taints are destroyed, who have lived the spiritual life, done what had to be done, laid down the burden, reached their own goal, utterly destroyed the fetters of existence, and are completely liberated through final knowledge, [363] are devoted simply to a pleasant dwelling in this very life. This is the fifth benefit in timely listening to the Dhamma, in timely discussion on the Dhamma."

"These are the five benefits in timely listening to the Dhamma, in timely discussion on the Dhamma."

5 (5) Powers[1842]

"Bhikkhus, there are these four powers. What four? The power of wisdom, the power of energy, the power of blamelessness, and the power of sustaining a favorable relationship.

(1) "And what, bhikkhus, is the power of wisdom? One has clearly seen and explored with wisdom those qualities that are unwholesome and reckoned as unwholesome; those that are wholesome and reckoned as wholesome; those that are blamable and reckoned as blamable; those that are blameless and reckoned as blameless; those that are dark and reckoned as dark; those that are bright and reckoned as bright; those that should not be cultivated and are reckoned as not to be cultivated; those that should be cultivated and are reckoned as to be cultivated; those that are unworthy of the noble ones and reckoned as unworthy of the noble ones; those that are worthy of the noble ones and reckoned as worthy of the noble ones. This is called the power of wisdom.

(2) "And what is the power of energy? One generates desire to abandon those qualities that are unwholesome and reckoned as unwholesome; those that are blamable and reckoned as blamable; those that are dark and reckoned as dark; those that should not be cultivated and are reckoned as not to be cultivated; those that are unworthy of the noble ones and reckoned as unworthy of the noble ones. One makes an effort, arouses energy, applies one's mind, and strives for this. One generates desire to obtain all those qualities that are wholesome and reckoned as wholesome; those that are blameless and reckoned as blameless; those that are bright and reckoned as bright; those that should be cultivated and are reckoned as to be cultivated; [364] those that are

worthy of the noble ones and reckoned as worthy of the noble ones. One makes an effort, arouses energy, applies one's mind, and strives for this. This is called the power of energy.

(3) "And what is the power of blamelessness? Here, a noble disciple engages in blameless bodily, verbal, and mental action. This is called the power of blamelessness.

(4) "And what is the power of sustaining a favorable relationship? There are these four means of sustaining a favorable relationship: giving, endearing speech, beneficent conduct, and impartiality. Among gifts, the best is the gift of the Dhamma. Among types of endearing speech, the best is repeatedly teaching the Dhamma to one who is interested in it and listens with eager ears. Among types of beneficent conduct, the best is when one encourages, settles, and establishes a person without faith in the accomplishment of faith, an immoral person in the accomplishment of virtuous behavior, a miserly person in the accomplishment of generosity, and an unwise person in the accomplishment of wisdom. Among types of impartiality, the best is that a stream-enterer is equal to a stream-enterer, a once-returner is equal to a once-returner, a non-returner is equal to a non-returner, and an arahant is equal to an arahant.[1843] This is called the power of sustaining a favorable relationship.

"These, bhikkhus, are the four powers. When a noble disciple possesses these four powers, he has transcended five fears. What five? (5) Fear of [loss of] livelihood, (6) fear of disrepute, (7) fear of timidity in assemblies, [365] (8) fear of death, and (9) fear of a bad destination. The noble disciple reflects thus: 'I am not afraid on account of my livelihood. Why should I be afraid on account of my livelihood? I have the four powers: the power of wisdom, the power of energy, the power of blamelessness, and the power of sustaining a favorable relationship. An unwise person might be afraid on account of his livelihood; a lazy person might be afraid on account of his livelihood; a person who engages in blamable bodily, verbal, and mental action might be afraid on account of his livelihood; a person who does not sustain favorable relationships might be afraid on account of his livelihood.

"'I am not afraid of disrepute. . . . I am not afraid of timidity in assemblies. . . . I am not afraid of death. . . . I am not afraid of a bad destination. Why should I be afraid of a bad destination? I have the four powers: the power of wisdom, the power of energy, the power of blamelessness, and the power of sustaining a favorable relationship. An unwise person might be afraid of a bad destination; a lazy person might be afraid of a bad destination; a person who engages in blamable bodily, verbal, and mental action might be afraid of a bad destination; a person who does not sustain favorable relationships might be afraid of a bad destination.'

"When a noble disciple possesses these four powers, he has transcended these five fears."

6 (6) Association

There the Venerable Sāriputta addressed the bhikkhus: "Friends, bhikkhus!"

"Friend!" those bhikkhus replied. The Venerable Sāriputta said this:

"Friends, persons should be understood to be twofold: those to be associated with and those not to be associated with.[1844] Robes, too, should be understood to be twofold: those to be used and those not to be used. Almsfood . . . Lodgings, too, should be understood to be twofold: those to be used and those not to be used. Villages or towns should be understood to be twofold: those to be resorted to and [366] those not to be resorted to. Countries or regions should be understood to be twofold: those to be resorted to and those not to be resorted to.

(1) "When it was said: 'Persons, friends, should be understood to be twofold: those to be associated with and those not to be associated with,' for what reason was this said? If one knows of a person: 'When I associate with this person, unwholesome qualities increase in me and wholesome qualities decline; and the requisites of life that should be obtained by one gone forth—robes, almsfood, lodging, and medicines and provisions for the sick—are obtained with difficulty; and the goal of the ascetic life for the sake of which I have gone forth from the household life into homelessness does not reach fulfillment by development for me,' in that case one should depart from that person any time night or day,[1845] even without taking leave of him. One should not continue to follow him.[1846]

(2) "If one knows of a person: 'When I associate with this person, unwholesome qualities increase in me and wholesome qualities decline; but the requisites of life that should be obtained

by one gone forth—robes, almsfood, lodging, and medicines and provisions for the sick—are obtained without difficulty; but still, the goal of the ascetic life, for the sake of which I have gone forth from the household life into homelessness, does not reach fulfillment by development for me,' in that case, having reflected, one should depart from that person after taking leave of him.[1847] One should not continue to follow him.

(3) "If one knows of a person: 'When I associate with this person, unwholesome [367] qualities decline in me and wholesome qualities increase; but the requisites of life that should be obtained by one gone forth—robes, almsfood, lodging, and medicines and provisions for the sick—are obtained with difficulty; still, the goal of the ascetic life, for the sake of which I have gone forth from the household life into homelessness, reaches fulfillment by development for me,' in that case, having reflected, one should continue to follow that person. One should not depart from him.

(4) "If one knows of a person: 'When I associate with this person, unwholesome qualities decline in me and wholesome qualities increase; and the requisites of life that should be obtained by one gone forth—robes, almsfood, lodging, and medicines and provisions for the sick—are obtained without difficulty; and the goal of the ascetic life, for the sake of which I have gone forth from the household life into homelessness, reaches fulfillment by development for me,' in that case one should continue to follow that person as long as one lives. One should not depart from him even if one is dismissed.

"When it was said: 'Persons, friends, should be understood to be twofold: those to be associated with and those not to be associated with,' it is because of this that this was said.

(5) "When it was said: 'Robes, friends, should be understood to be twofold: those to be used and those not to be used,' for what reason was this said? If one knows of a robe: 'When I use this robe, unwholesome qualities increase in me and wholesome qualities decline,' one should not use such a robe. But if one knows of a robe: 'When I use this robe, unwholesome qualities decline in me and wholesome qualities increase,' one should use such a robe. [368] When it was said: 'Robes, friends, should be understood to be twofold: those to be used and those not to be used,' it is because of this that this was said.

(6) "When it was said: 'Almsfood, friends, should be understood to be twofold: that to be used and that not to be used,' for what reason was this said? If one knows of some almsfood: 'When I use this almsfood, unwholesome qualities increase in me and wholesome qualities decline,' one should not use such almsfood. But if one knows of some almsfood: 'When I use this almsfood, unwholesome qualities decline in me and wholesome qualities increase,' one should use such almsfood. When it was said: 'Almsfood, friends, should be understood to be twofold: that to be used and that not to be used,' it is because of this that this was said.

(7) "When it was said: 'Lodgings, friends, should be understood to be twofold: those to be used and those not to be used,' for what reason was this said? If one knows of a lodging: 'When I use this lodging, unwholesome qualities increase in me and wholesome qualities decline,' one should not use such a lodging. But if one knows of a lodging: 'When I use this lodging, unwholesome qualities decline in me and wholesome qualities increase,' one should use such a lodging. When it was said: 'Lodgings, friends, should be understood to be twofold: those to be used and those not to be used,' it is because of this that this was said.

(8) "When it was said: 'Villages or towns, friends, should be understood to be twofold: those to be resorted to and those not to be resorted to,' for what reason was this said? If one knows of a village or town: 'When I resort to this village or town, unwholesome qualities increase in me and wholesome qualities decline,' one should not resort to such a village or town. But if one knows of a village or town: 'When I resort to this village [369] or town, unwholesome qualities decline in me and wholesome qualities increase,' one should resort to such a village or town. When it was said: 'Villages or towns, friends, should be understood to be twofold: those to be resorted to and those not to be resorted to,' it is because of this that this was said.

(9) "When it was said: 'Countries or regions, friends, should be understood to be twofold: those to be resorted to and those not to be resorted to,' for what reason was this said? If one knows of a country or region: 'When I resort to this country or region, unwholesome qualities increase in me and wholesome qualities decline,' one should not resort to such a country or

region. But if one knows of a country or region: 'When I resort to this country or region, unwholesome qualities decline in me and wholesome qualities increase,' one should resort to such a country or region. When it was said: 'Countries or regions, friends, should be understood to be twofold: those to be resorted to and those not to be resorted to,' it is because of this that this was said."

7 (7) Sutavā

Thus have I heard. On one occasion the Blessed One was dwelling at Rājagaha on Mount Vulture Peak. Then the wanderer Sutavā approached the Blessed One and exchanged greetings with him. When they had concluded their greetings and cordial talk, he sat down to one side and said to the Blessed One:

"Bhante, on one occasion the Blessed One was dwelling right here in Rājagaha, the Mountain Fort.[1848] At that time, in the presence of the Blessed One, I heard and learned this: 'Sutavā, a bhikkhu who is an arahant—one whose taints are destroyed, who has lived the spiritual life, done what had to be done, laid down [370] the burden, reached his own goal, utterly destroyed the fetters of existence, one completely liberated through final knowledge—is incapable of transgression in five cases. He is incapable of intentionally depriving a living being of life; he is incapable of taking by way of theft what is not given; he is incapable of engaging in sexual intercourse; he is incapable of deliberately speaking falsehood; he is incapable of storing things up in order to enjoy sensual pleasures as he did in the past when a layman.' Bhante, did I hear that correctly from the Blessed One, grasp it correctly, attend to it correctly, remember it correctly?"

"Yes, Sutavā, you heard that correctly, grasped it correctly, attended to it correctly, remembered it correctly. In the past, Sutavā, and also now I say thus: 'A bhikkhu who is an arahant—one whose taints are destroyed . . . one completely liberated through final knowledge—is incapable of transgression in nine cases. (1) He is incapable of intentionally depriving a living being of life; (2) he is incapable of taking by way of theft what is not given; (3) he is incapable of engaging in sexual intercourse; (4) he is incapable of deliberately speaking falsehood; (5) he is incapable of storing things up in order to enjoy sensual pleasures as he did in the past when a layman; (6) he is incapable of rejecting the Buddha; (7) he is incapable of rejecting the Dhamma; (8) he is incapable of rejecting the Saṅgha; (9) he is incapable of rejecting the training.'[1849] [371] In the past, Sutavā, and also now I say thus: 'A bhikkhu who is an arahant—one whose taints are destroyed . . . one completely liberated through final knowledge—is incapable of transgression in these nine cases.'"

8 (8) Sajjha

Thus have I heard. On one occasion the Blessed One was dwelling at Rājagaha on Mount Vulture Peak. Then the wanderer Sajjha approached the Blessed One and exchanged greetings with him. When they had concluded their greetings and cordial talk, he sat down to one side and said to the Blessed One:

"Bhante, on one occasion the Blessed One was dwelling right here in Rājagaha. . . . [as in 9:7] . . . Bhante, did I hear that correctly from the Blessed One, grasp it correctly, attend to it correctly, remember it correctly?" [372]

"Yes, Sajjha, you heard that correctly, grasped it correctly, attended to it correctly, remembered it correctly. In the past, Sajjha, and also now I say thus: 'A bhikkhu who is an arahant—one whose taints are destroyed . . . one completely liberated through final knowledge—is incapable of transgression in nine cases. (1) He is incapable of intentionally depriving a living being of life; (2) he is incapable of taking by way of theft what is not given; (3) he is incapable of engaging in sexual intercourse; (4) he is incapable of deliberately speaking falsehood; (5) he is incapable of storing things up in order to enjoy sensual pleasures as he did in the past when a layman; (6) he is incapable of entering upon a wrong course on account of desire; (7) he is incapable of entering upon a wrong course on account of hatred; (8) he is incapable of entering upon a wrong course on account of delusion; (9) he is incapable of entering upon a wrong course on account of fear.' In the past, Sajjha, and also now I say thus: 'A bhikkhu who is an arahant—one whose taints are destroyed . . . one completely liberated through final knowledge—is incapable of transgression in these nine cases.'"

9 (9) Persons

"Bhikkhus, there are these nine kinds of persons found existing in the world. What nine? The arahant, the one practicing for arahantship; the non-returner, the one practicing for realization of the fruit of non-returning; the once-returner, the one practicing for realization of the fruit of once-returning; the stream-enterer, the one practicing for realization of the fruit of stream-entry; the worldling. These are the nine kinds of persons found existing in the world." [373]

10 (10) Worthy of Gifts

"Bhikkhus, these nine persons are worthy of gifts, worthy of hospitality, worthy of offerings, worthy of reverential salutation, an unsurpassed field of merit for the world. What nine? The arahant, the one practicing for arahantship; the non-returner, the one practicing for realization of the fruit of non-returning; the once-returner, the one practicing for realization of the fruit of once-returning; the stream-enterer, the one practicing for realization of the fruit of stream-entry; the clan member.[1850] These nine persons are worthy of gifts . . . an unsurpassed field of merit for the world."

II. The Lion's Roar

11 (1) Lion's Roar

On one occasion the Blessed One was dwelling at Sāvatthī in Jeta's Grove, Anāthapiṇḍika's Park. Then the Venerable Sāriputta approached the Blessed One, paid homage to him, sat down to one side, and said to him:

"Bhante, I have completed the rains residence at Sāvatthī. I want to depart on a tour of the countryside."

"You may go, Sāriputta, at your own convenience."

Then the Venerable Sāriputta rose from his seat, paid homage to the Blessed One, circumambulated him keeping the right side toward him, and departed. [374] Then, not long after the Venerable Sāriputta had left, a certain bhikkhu said to the Blessed One: "Bhante, the Venerable Sāriputta struck me and then set out on tour without apologizing."[1851]

Then the Blessed One addressed a certain bhikkhu: "Go,

bhikkhu, in my name call Sāriputta, [telling him]: 'The Teacher is calling you, friend Sāriputta.'"[1852]

"Yes, Bhante," that bhikkhu replied. Then he approached the Venerable Sāriputta and said: "The Teacher is calling you, friend Sāriputta."

"Yes, friend," the Venerable Sāriputta replied.

Now on that occasion the Venerable Mahāmoggallāna and the Venerable Ānanda took a key and wandered from dwelling to dwelling, [calling out]: "Come forth, venerables! Come forth, venerables! Now the Venerable Sāriputta will roar his lion's roar in the presence of the Blessed One!"

Then the Venerable Sāriputta approached the Blessed One, paid homage to him, and sat down to one side. The Blessed One said to him: "Sāriputta, one of your fellow monks has made a complaint about you, [saying]: 'Bhante, the Venerable Sāriputta struck me and then set out on tour without apologizing.'"

(1) "Bhante, one who has not established mindfulness directed to the body in regard to his own body might strike a fellow monk and then set out on tour without apologizing. Just as they throw pure and impure things on the earth—feces, urine, spittle, pus, and blood—yet the earth is not repelled, humiliated, or disgusted because of this; so [375] too, Bhante, I dwell with a mind like the earth, vast, exalted, and measureless, without enmity and ill will.

(2) "Bhante, one who has not established mindfulness directed to the body in regard to his own body might strike a fellow monk and then set out on tour without apologizing. Just as they wash pure and impure things in water—feces, urine, spittle, pus, and blood—yet the water is not repelled, humiliated, or disgusted because of this; so too, Bhante, I dwell with a mind like water, vast, exalted, and measureless, without enmity and ill will.

(3) "Bhante, one who has not established mindfulness directed to the body in regard to his own body might strike a fellow monk and then set out on tour without apologizing. Just as fire burns pure and impure things—feces, urine, spittle, pus, and blood—yet the fire is not repelled, humiliated, or disgusted because of this; so too, Bhante, I dwell with a mind like fire, vast, exalted, and measureless, without enmity and ill will.

(4) "Bhante, one who has not established mindfulness directed

to the body in regard to his own body might strike a fellow monk and then set out on tour without apologizing. Just as air blows upon pure and impure things—feces, urine, spittle, pus, and blood—yet the air is not repelled, humiliated, or disgusted because of this; so too, Bhante, I dwell with a mind like air, vast, exalted, and measureless, without enmity and ill will.

(5) "Bhante, one who has not established mindfulness directed to the body in regard to his own body might strike a fellow monk and then set out on tour without apologizing. [376] Just as a duster wipes off pure and impure things—feces, urine, spittle, pus, and blood—yet the duster is not repelled, humiliated, or disgusted because of this; so too, Bhante, I dwell with a mind like a duster, vast, exalted, and measureless, without enmity and ill will.

(6) "Bhante, one who has not established mindfulness directed to the body in regard to his own body might strike a fellow monk and then set out on tour without apologizing. Just as an outcast boy or girl, clad in rags and holding a vessel, enters a village or town with a humble mind; so too, Bhante, I dwell with a mind like an outcast boy, vast, exalted, and measureless, without enmity and ill will.

(7) "Bhante, one who has not established mindfulness directed to the body in regard to his own body might strike a fellow monk and then set out on tour without apologizing. Just as a bull with his horns cut, mild, well tamed and well trained, wanders from street to street and from square to square without hurting anyone with its feet or horns; so too, Bhante, I dwell with a mind like that of a bull with horns cut, vast, exalted, and measureless, without enmity and ill will.

(8) "Bhante, one who has not established mindfulness directed to the body in regard to his own body might strike a fellow monk and then set out on tour without apologizing. Just as a woman or a man—young, youthful, and fond of ornaments, with head bathed—would be [377] repelled, humiliated, and disgusted if the carcass of a snake, a dog, or a human being were slung around her or his neck; so too, Bhante, I am repelled, humiliated, and disgusted by this foul body.

(9) "Bhante, one who has not established mindfulness directed to the body in regard to his own body might strike a fellow monk and then set out on tour without apologizing. Just

as a person might carry around a cracked and perforated bowl of liquid fat that oozes and drips; so too, Bhante, I carry around this cracked and perforated body that oozes and drips.

"Bhante, one who has not established mindfulness directed to the body in regard to his own body might strike a fellow monk here and then set out on tour without apologizing."

Then that [accusing] bhikkhu rose from his seat, arranged his upper robe over one shoulder, prostrated himself with his head at the Blessed One's feet, and said to the Blessed One: "Bhante, I have committed a transgression in that I so foolishly, stupidly, and unskillfully slandered the Venerable Sāriputta on grounds that are untrue, baseless, and false. Bhante, may the Blessed One accept my transgression seen as a transgression for the sake of future restraint."

"Surely, bhikkhu, you have committed a transgression in that you so foolishly, stupidly, and unskillfully slandered the Venerable Sāriputta on grounds that are untrue, baseless, and false. But since you see your transgression as a transgression and make amends for it in accordance with the Dhamma, we accept it. For it is growth in the Noble One's discipline that one sees one's transgression as a transgression, makes amends for it in accordance with the Dhamma, and undertakes future restraint." [378]

The Blessed One then addressed the Venerable Sāriputta: "Sāriputta, pardon this hollow man before his head splits into seven pieces right there."

"I will pardon this venerable one, Bhante, if this venerable one says to me: 'And let the venerable one pardon me.'"[1853]

12 (2) With Residue Remaining

On one occasion the Blessed One was dwelling at Sāvatthī at Jeta's Grove, Anāthapiṇḍika's Park. Then, in the morning, the Venerable Sāriputta dressed, took his bowl and robe, and entered Sāvatthī for alms. It then occurred to him: "It is still too early to walk for alms in Sāvatthī. Let me go to the park of the wanderers of other sects."[1854]

Then the Venerable Sāriputta went to the park of the wanderers of other sects. He exchanged greetings with those wanderers and, when they had concluded their greetings and cordial talk, sat down to one side. Now on that occasion those wanderers had assembled and were sitting together when this conversation arose among them: "Friends, anyone who passes away with a residue remaining is not freed from hell, the animal realm, or the sphere of afflicted spirits; he is not freed from the plane of misery, the bad destination, the lower world."

Then the Venerable Sāriputta neither delighted in nor rejected the statement of those wanderers, but rose from his seat and left, [thinking]: "I shall find out what the Blessed One has to say about this statement."

Then, when the Venerable Sāriputta had walked for alms in Sāvatthī, [379] after his meal, on returning from his alms round, he approached the Blessed One, paid homage to him, and sat down to one side. [He here reports verbatim the entire course of events and ends:] "I rose from my seat and left, [thinking]: 'I shall find out what the Blessed One has to say about this statement.'"

"Who,[1855] Sāriputta, are those foolish and incompetent wanderers of other sects and who are those that know one with a residue remaining as 'one with a residue remaining' and one without residue remaining as 'one without residue remaining'?[1856]

"These nine persons, Sāriputta, passing away with a residue remaining, are freed from hell, the animal realm, and the sphere of afflicted spirits; freed from the plane of misery, the bad destination, the lower world. What nine? [380]

(1) "Here, Sāriputta, some person fulfills virtuous behavior and concentration but cultivates wisdom only to a moderate extent.[1857] With the utter destruction of the five lower fetters, this person is an attainer of nibbāna in the interval. This is the first person, passing away with a residue remaining, who is freed from hell, the animal realm, and the sphere of afflicted spirits; freed from the plane of misery, the bad destination, the lower world.

(2)–(5) "Again, some person fulfills virtuous behavior and concentration but cultivates wisdom only to a moderate extent. With the utter destruction of the five lower fetters, this person is an attainer of nibbāna upon landing . . . an attainer of nibbāna without exertion . . . an attainer of nibbāna through exertion . . . one bound upstream, heading toward the Akaniṭṭha realm. This is the fifth person, passing away with a residue remaining, who is freed from hell . . . the lower world.

(6) "Again, some person fulfills virtuous behavior but cultivates concentration and wisdom only to a moderate extent.

With the utter destruction of three fetters and with the diminishing of greed, hatred, and delusion, this person is a once-returner who, after coming back to this world only one more time, makes an end of suffering. This is the sixth person, passing away with a residue remaining, who is freed from hell . . . the lower world.

(7) "Again, some person fulfills virtuous behavior but cultivates concentration and wisdom only to a moderate extent. With the utter destruction of three fetters, this person is a one-seed attainer who, after being reborn once more as a human being, [381] makes an end of suffering. This is the seventh person, passing away with a residue remaining, who is freed from hell . . . the lower world.

(8) "Again, some person fulfills virtuous behavior but cultivates concentration and wisdom only to a moderate extent. With the utter destruction of three fetters, this person is a family-to-family attainer who, after roaming and wandering on among good families two or three times, makes an end of suffering. This is the eighth person, passing away with a residue remaining, who is freed from hell . . . the lower world.

(9) "Again, some person fulfills virtuous behavior but cultivates concentration and wisdom only to a moderate extent. With the utter destruction of three fetters, this person is a seven-times-at-most attainer who, after roaming and wandering on among devas and humans seven times at most, makes an end of suffering. This is the ninth person, passing away with a residue remaining, who is freed from hell, the animal realm, and the sphere of afflicted spirits; freed from the plane of misery, the bad destination, the lower world.

"Who, Sāriputta, are those foolish and incompetent wanderers of other sects, and who are those that know one with a residue remaining as 'one with a residue remaining' and one without residue remaining as 'one without residue remaining'?

"These nine persons, passing away with a residue remaining, are freed from hell, the animal realm, and the sphere of afflicted spirits; freed from the plane of misery, the bad destination, the lower world. Sāriputta, I had not been disposed to give this Dhamma exposition to the bhikkhus, bhikkhunīs, male lay followers, and female lay followers. For what reason?

I was concerned that on hearing this Dhamma exposition, they might take to the ways of heedlessness. [382] However, I have spoken this Dhamma exposition for the purpose of answering your question."[1858]

13 (3) Koṭṭhita

Then the Venerable Mahākoṭṭhita approached the Venerable Sāriputta and exchanged greetings with him. When they had concluded their greetings and cordial talk, he sat down to one side and said to the Venerable Sāriputta:

"Now, friend Sāriputta, is the spiritual life lived under the Blessed One for this purpose: 'Let kamma [whose result] is to be experienced in this life become kamma [whose result] I am to experience in a future life'?"[1859]

"Certainly not, friend."

"Then is the spiritual life lived under the Blessed One for this purpose: 'Let kamma [whose result] is to be experienced in a future life become kamma [whose result] I am to experience in this life'?"

"Certainly not, friend."

"Now, friend Sāriputta, is the spiritual life lived under the Blessed One for this purpose: 'Let kamma [whose result] is to be experienced as pleasant become kamma [whose result] I am to experience as painful?'"[1860]

"Certainly not, friend."

"Then is the spiritual life lived under the Blessed One for this purpose: 'Let kamma [whose result] is to be experienced as painful become kamma [whose result] I am to experience as pleasant '?"

"Certainly not, friend."

"Now, friend Sāriputta, is the spiritual life lived under the Blessed One for this purpose: 'Let my kamma [whose result] is to be experienced when it has matured become kamma [whose result] I am to experience while it has not matured'?"[1861]

"Certainly not, friend."

"Then is the spiritual life lived under the Blessed One for this purpose: 'Let kamma [whose result] is to be experienced while it has not matured become kamma [whose result] I am to experience when it has matured'?"

"Certainly not, friend."

"Now, friend Sāriputta, is the spiritual life lived under the Blessed One for this purpose: 'Let kamma [whose result] is to be experienced copiously become kamma [whose result] I am to experience just slightly'?"

"Certainly not, friend."

"Then [383] is the spiritual life lived under the Blessed One for this purpose: 'Let kamma [whose result] is to be experienced just slightly become kamma [whose result] I am to experience copiously'?"

"Certainly not, friend."

"Now, friend Sāriputta, is the spiritual life lived under the Blessed One for this purpose: 'Let kamma [whose result] is to be experienced become kamma [whose result] I am not to experience'?"[1862]

"Certainly not, friend."

"Then is the spiritual life lived under the Blessed One for this purpose: 'Let kamma [whose result] is not to be experienced become kamma [whose result] I am to experience'?"

"Certainly not, friend."[1863]

"Friend Sāriputta, when you are asked: 'Now, friend Sāriputta, is the spiritual life lived under the Blessed One for this purpose: "Let kamma [whose result] is to be experienced in this life become kamma [whose result] I am to experience in a future life"?' you say: 'Certainly not, friend.' And when you are asked: 'Then is the spiritual life lived under the Blessed One for this purpose: "Let kamma [whose result] is to be experienced in a future life become kamma [whose result] I am to experience in this life"?' you say: 'Certainly not, friend.' . . . [384] . . . When you are asked: 'Now, friend Sāriputta, is the spiritual life lived under the Blessed One for this purpose: "Let kamma [whose result] is to be experienced become kamma [whose result] I am not to experience"?' you say: 'Certainly not, friend.' And when you are asked: 'Then is the spiritual life lived under the Blessed One for this purpose: "Let kamma [whose result] is not to be experienced become kamma [whose result] I am to experience"?' you say: 'Certainly not, friend.' Then for what purpose does one live the spiritual life under the Blessed One?"

"One lives the spiritual life under the Blessed One, friend, for the purpose of knowing, seeing, attaining, realizing, and penetrating what one has not known, seen, attained, realized, and penetrated."

"But, friend, what is it that one has not known, seen, attained, realized, and penetrated?"

"'This is suffering,' friend, is what one has not known, seen, attained, realized, and penetrated, and it is for the purpose of knowing, seeing, attaining, realizing, and penetrating this that one lives the spiritual life under the Blessed One. [385] 'This is the origin of suffering' . . . 'This is the cessation of suffering' . . . 'This is the way leading to the cessation of suffering' is what one has not known, seen, attained, realized, and penetrated, and it is for the purpose of knowing, seeing, attaining, realizing, and penetrating this that one lives the spiritual life under the Blessed One. This, friend, is what one has not known, seen, attained, realized, and penetrated, and it is for the purpose of knowing, seeing, attaining, realizing, and penetrating this that one lives the spiritual life under the Blessed One."

14 (4) Samiddhi

Then the Venerable Samiddhi approached the Venerable Sāriputta, paid homage to him, and sat down to one side. The Venerable Sāriputta then said to him:[1864]

(1) "On what basis, Samiddhi, do intentions and thoughts[1865] arise in a person?"

"On the basis of name-and-form, Bhante."[1866]

(2) "Where do they become diversified?"

"In relation to the elements."

(3) "From what do they originate?"

"They originate from contact."

(4) "Upon what do they converge?"

"They converge upon feeling."[1867]

(5) "By what are they headed?"

"They are headed by concentration."

(6) "What exercises authority over them?"

"Mindfulness exercises authority over them."

(7) "What is their supervisor?"

"Wisdom is their supervisor."

(8) "What is their core?"

"Liberation is their core."[1868]

(9) "In what do they culminate?"

"They culminate in the deathless."[1869]

"When you were asked: 'On what basis, Samiddhi, do intentions and thoughts arise in a person?' you said: 'On the basis of name-and-form, Bhante.' . . . [386] . . . When you were asked: 'In what do they culminate?' you said: 'They culminate in the deathless.' Good, good, Samiddhi! When you were asked such questions, you answered well, but don't become conceited because of that."

15 (5) Boil

"Bhikkhus, suppose there was a boil many years old. It would have nine wound orifices, nine natural orifices.[1870] Whatever would flow out from them would be impure, foul-smelling, and disgusting. Whatever would ooze out from them would be impure, foul-smelling, and disgusting.

"'A boil,' bhikkhus, is a designation for this body consisting of the four great elements, originating from mother and father, built up out of rice and gruel, subject to impermanence, to kneading and abrasion, to breaking apart and dispersal. It has nine wound orifices, nine natural orifices. Whatever flows out from them is impure, foul-smelling, and disgusting. [387] Whatever oozes out from them is impure, foul-smelling, and disgusting. Therefore, bhikkhus, become disenchanted with this body."

16 (6) Perceptions

"Bhikkhus, these nine perceptions, when developed and cultivated, are of great fruit and benefit, culminating in the deathless, having the deathless as their consummation.[1871] What nine? The perception of unattractiveness, the perception of death, the perception of the repulsiveness of food, the perception of non-delight in the entire world, the perception of impermanence, the perception of suffering in the impermanent, the perception of non-self in what is suffering, the perception of abandoning, and the perception of dispassion. These nine perceptions, when developed and cultivated, are of great fruit and benefit, culminating in the deathless, having the deathless as their consummation."

17 (7) Families

"Bhikkhus, possessing nine factors, a family that has not yet been approached is not worth approaching, or one that has been approached is not worth sitting with.[1872] What nine? (1)

They do not rise up in an agreeable way.[1873] (2) They do not pay homage in an agreeable way.[1874] (3) They do not offer a seat in an agreeable way. (4) They hide what they have from one. (5) Even when they have much, they give little. (6) Even when they have excellent things, they give coarse things. (7) They give without respect, not respectfully. (8) They do not sit close by to listen to the Dhamma. (9) They do not savor the flavor of one's words. Possessing these nine factors, a family that has not yet been approached is not worth approaching, and one that has been approached is not worth sitting with.

"Bhikkhus, possessing nine factors, a family that has not yet been approached is worth approaching or one that has been approached is worth sitting with. What nine? (1) They rise up in an agreeable way. (2) They pay homage in an agreeable way. (3) They offer a seat in an agreeable way. (4) They do not hide what they have from one. (5) When they have much, [388] they give much. (6) When they have excellent things, they give excellent things. (7) They give respectfully, not without respect. (8) They sit close by to listen to the Dhamma. (9) They savor the flavor of one's words. Possessing these nine factors, a family that has not yet been approached is worth approaching, and one that has been approached is worth sitting with."

18 (8) Loving-Kindness

"Bhikkhus, when it is observed complete in nine factors, the uposatha is of great fruit and benefit, very brilliant and pervasive.[1875] And how is the uposatha observed complete in nine factors, so that it is of great fruit and benefit, extraordinarily brilliant and pervasive?

(1) "Here, bhikkhus, a noble disciple reflects thus: 'As long as they live the arahants abandon and abstain from the destruction of life; with the rod and weapon laid aside, conscientious and kindly, they dwell compassionate toward all living beings. Today, for this night and day, I too shall abandon and abstain from the destruction of life; with the rod and weapon laid aside, conscientious and kindly, I too shall dwell compassionate toward all living beings. I shall imitate the arahants in this respect and the uposatha will be observed by me.' This is the first factor it possesses.

(2) "'As long as they live the arahants abandon and abstain

from taking what is not given; they take only what is given, expect only what is given, and dwell honestly without thoughts of theft. Today, for this night and day, I too shall abandon and abstain from taking what is not given; I shall accept only what is given, expect only what is given, and dwell honestly without thoughts of theft. I shall imitate the arahants in this respect and the uposatha will be observed by me.' This is the second factor it possesses. [389]

(3) "'As long as they live the arahants abandon sexual activity and observe celibacy, living apart, abstaining from sexual intercourse, the common person's practice. Today, for this night and day, I too shall abandon sexual activity and observe celibacy, living apart, abstaining from sexual intercourse, the common person's practice. I shall imitate the arahants in this respect and the uposatha will be observed by me.' This is the third factor it possesses.

(4) "'As long as they live the arahants abandon and abstain from false speech; they speak truth, adhere to truth; they are trustworthy and reliable, no deceivers of the world. Today, for this night and day, I too shall abandon and abstain from false speech; I shall be a speaker of truth, an adherent of truth, trustworthy and reliable, no deceiver of the world. I shall imitate the arahants in this respect and the uposatha will be observed by me.' This is the fourth factor it possesses.

(5) "'As long as they live the arahants abandon and abstain from liquor, wine, and intoxicants, the basis for heedlessness. Today, for this night and day, I too shall abandon and abstain from liquor, wine, and intoxicants, the basis for heedlessness. I shall imitate the arahants in this respect and the uposatha will be observed by me.' This is the fifth factor it possesses.

(6) "'As long as they live the arahants eat once a day, abstaining from eating at night and from food outside the proper time. Today, for this night and day, I too shall eat once a day, abstaining from eating at night and from food outside the proper time. I shall imitate the arahants in this respect and the uposatha will be observed by me.' This is the sixth factor it possesses.

(7) "'As long as they live the arahants abstain from dancing, singing, instrumental music, and unsuitable shows, and from adorning and beautifying themselves by wearing garlands and applying scents and unguents. Today, for this night and day,

I too shall abstain from dancing, singing, instrumental music, and unsuitable shows, and from adorning and beautifying myself by wearing garlands and applying scents and unguents. I shall imitate the arahants in this respect and the uposatha will be observed by me.' This is the seventh factor it possesses.

(8) "'As long as they live the arahants abandon and abstain from the use of high and luxurious beds; they lie down on a low resting place, [390] either a small bed or a straw mat. Today, for this night and day, I too shall abandon and abstain from the use of high and luxurious beds; I shall lie down on a low resting place, either a small bed or a straw mat. I shall imitate the arahants in this respect and the uposatha will be observed by me.' This is the eighth factor it possesses.

(9) "Here, a noble disciple dwells pervading one quarter with a mind imbued with loving-kindness, likewise the second quarter, the third quarter, and the fourth quarter. Thus above, below, across, and everywhere, and to all as to himself, he dwells pervading the entire world with a mind imbued with loving-kindness, vast, exalted, measureless, without enmity, without ill will. This is the ninth factor it possesses.

"It is in this way, bhikkhus, that the uposatha is observed complete in nine factors, so that it is of great fruit and benefit, extraordinarily brilliant and pervasive."

19 (9) Deities

"Bhikkhus, last night, when the night had advanced, a number of deities of stunning beauty, illuminating the entire Jeta's Grove, approached me, paid homage to me, and stood to one side.

(1) "Those deities then said: 'In the past, Bhante, when we were human beings, monks approached our homes. We rose up for them but did not pay homage to them. Not having fulfilled our duty, full of regret and remorse, we were reborn in an inferior class [of deities].' [391]

(2) "Some other deities approached me and said: 'In the past, Bhante, when we were human beings, monks approached our homes. We rose up for them and paid homage to them, but we did not offer them seats. Not having fulfilled our duty, full of regret and remorse, we were reborn in an inferior class [of deities].'

(3) "Some other deities approached me and said: 'In the past, Bhante, when we were human beings, monks approached our homes. We rose up for them, paid homage to them, and offered them seats, but we did not share things with them to the best of our ability and capacity . . . (4) . . . we shared things with them to the best of our ability and capacity, but we did not sit close by to listen to the Dhamma . . . (5) . . . we sat close by to listen to the Dhamma, but we did not listen to it with eager ears . . . (6) . . . we listened to it with eager ears, but having heard it, we did not retain the Dhamma in mind . . . (7) . . . having heard it, we retained the Dhamma in mind but we did not examine the meaning of the teachings that had been retained in mind . . . (8) . . . we examined the meaning of the teachings that had been retained in mind but we did not understand the meaning and the Dhamma and then practice in accordance with the Dhamma. Not having fulfilled our duty, full of regret and remorse, we were reborn in an inferior class [of deities].'

(9) "Some other deities approached me and said: 'In the past, Bhante, when we were human beings, monks approached our homes. (i) We rose up for them, (ii) paid homage to them, (iii) offered them seats, and [392] (iv) shared things with them to the best of our ability and capacity. (v) We sat close by to listen to the Dhamma and (vi) listened to it with eager ears; (vii) having heard it, we retained the Dhamma in mind; (viii) we examined the meaning of the teachings that had been retained in mind; and (ix) we understood the meaning and the Dhamma and then practiced in accordance with the Dhamma. Having fulfilled our duty, free of regret and remorse, we were reborn in a superior class [of deities].'

"These are the feet of trees, bhikkhus, these are empty huts. Meditate, bhikkhus, do not be heedless. Do not have cause to regret it later, like those prior deities."

20 (10) Velāma

On one occasion the Blessed One was dwelling at Sāvatthī in Jeta's Grove, Anāthapiṇḍika's Park. Then the householder Anāthapiṇḍika approached the Blessed One, paid homage to him, and sat down to one side. The Blessed One asked him:

"Are alms given in your family, householder?"

"Alms are given in my family, Bhante, but they consist of broken rice accompanied by rice gruel."[1876]

"If, householder, one gives alms, coarse or excellent, and one gives disrespectfully, gives inconsiderately, does not give with one's own hand, gives what would be discarded, gives without a view of future consequences,[1877] then wherever the result of that gift is produced for one, one's mind does not incline toward the enjoyment of superb food, nor toward the enjoyment of superb clothing, nor toward the enjoyment of superb vehicles, nor toward the enjoyment of whatever is superb among the five objects of sensual pleasure. Also, one's [393] children and wives, and one's slaves, servants, and workers, do not want to listen to one, do not lend an ear, and do not apply their minds to understand. For what reason? Just this is the result of actions that are done disrespectfully.

"If, householder, one gives alms, whether coarse or excellent, and one gives respectfully, gives considerately, gives with one's own hand, gives what would not be discarded, gives with a view of future consequences, then wherever the result of that gift is produced for one, one's mind inclines toward the enjoyment of superb food, toward the enjoyment of superb clothing, toward the enjoyment of superb vehicles, toward the enjoyment of whatever is superb among the five objects of sensual pleasure. Also, one's children and wives, and one's slaves, servants, and workers, want to listen to one, lend an ear, and apply their minds to understand. For what reason? Just this is the result of actions that are done respectfully.

"In the past, householder, there was a brahmin named Velāma. He gave such a great alms offering as this:[1878] (1) eighty-four thousand golden bowls filled with silver; (2) eighty-four thousand silver bowls filled with gold; (3) eighty-four thousand bronze bowls filled with bullion; (4) eighty-four thousand elephants with golden ornaments, golden banners, covered with nets of gold thread; (5) eighty-four thousand chariots with upholstery of lion skins, tiger skins, leopard skins, and saffron-dyed blankets, with golden ornaments, golden banners, covered with nets of gold thread; (6) eighty-four thousand milk cows with jute tethers[1879] and bronze pails;[1880] (7) eighty-four thousand maidens adorned with jeweled earrings; (8) eighty-four thousand couches [394] spread with rugs, blankets, and covers, with excellent coverings of antelope hide, with canopies and red bolsters at both ends; (9) eighty-four thousand *koṭis*[1881] of cloths made of fine linen, fine silk, fine wool, and fine cotton.

How much more of food and drink, snacks, meals, refreshments, and beverages?[1882] It seemed to be flowing like rivers.

"You might think, householder: 'He was someone else, the brahmin Velāma who on that occasion gave that great alms offering.' But you should not look at it in such a way. I myself was the brahmin Velāma who on that occasion gave that great alms offering.

"Now, householder, at that alms offering there was no one worthy of offerings, no one who purified the offering. Even more fruitful than the great alms offering that the brahmin Velāma gave would it be to feed one person accomplished in view. Even more fruitful than the great alms offering that the brahmin Velāma gave, and feeding a hundred persons accomplished in view, would it be to feed one once-returner. Even more fruitful than the great alms offering that the brahmin Velāma gave, and feeding a hundred once-returners, would it be to feed one non-returner. Even more fruitful than . . . feeding a hundred non-returners, would it be to feed one arahant. Even more fruitful than . . . feeding a hundred arahants, would it be to feed one paccekabuddha. [395] Even more fruitful than . . . feeding a hundred paccekabuddhas, would it be to feed the Tathāgata, the Arahant, the Perfectly Enlightened One . . . would it be to feed the Saṅgha of bhikkhus headed by the Buddha . . . would it be to build a dwelling dedicated to the Saṅgha of the four quarters . . . would it be for one with a mind of confidence to go for refuge to the Buddha, the Dhamma, and the Saṅgha . . . would it be for one with a mind of confidence to undertake the five training rules: to abstain from the destruction of life, to abstain from taking what is not given, to abstain from sexual misconduct, to abstain from false speech, to abstain from liquor, wine, and intoxicants, the basis for heedlessness. Even more fruitful . . . would it be to develop a mind of loving-kindness even for the time it takes to pull a cow's udder.

"Even more fruitful, householder, than the great alms offering that the brahmin Velāma gave, and feeding one person accomplished in view, and feeding a hundred persons accomplished in view; and feeding one once-returner, and feeding a hundred once-returners; and feeding one non-returner, and feeding a hundred non-returners; and feeding one arahant, and feeding a hundred arahants; and feeding one paccekabuddha, and feeding a hundred paccekabuddhas; and feeding the Tathāgata, the Arahant, the Perfectly Enlightened One; and feeding the Saṅgha of bhikkhus headed by the Buddha; and building a dwelling dedicated to the Saṅgha of the four quarters; and for one with a mind of confidence to go for refuge to the Buddha, the Dhamma, and the Saṅgha; and for one with a mind of confidence to undertake the five training rules: to abstain from the destruction of life . . . to abstain from liquor, wine, and intoxicants, the basis for heedlessness; and for one to develop a mind of loving-kindness even for the time it takes to pull a cow's udder, [396] would it be to develop the perception of impermanence just for the time of a finger snap."[1883]

III. Abodes of Beings

21 (1) Respects

"Bhikkhus, in three respects the people of Uttarakuru surpass the Tāvatiṃsa devas and the people of Jambudīpa.[1884] What three? (1) They are without selfishness and possessiveness; (2) their life span is fixed; and (3) their living conditions are exceptional.[1885] In these three respects the people of Uttarakuru surpass the Tāvatiṃsa devas and the people of Jambudīpa.

"In three respects the Tāvatiṃsa devas surpass the people of Uttarakuru and the people of Jambudīpa. What three? (4) In celestial life span, (5) in celestial beauty, and (5) in celestial happiness. In these three respects the Tāvatiṃsa devas surpass the people of Uttarakuru and the people of Jambudīpa.

"In three respects the people of Jambudīpa surpass the people of Uttarakuru and the Tāvatiṃsa devas. What three? (7) They are heroes; (8) they are mindful; and (9) there is the living of the spiritual life here. In these three respects the people of Jambudīpa surpass the people of Uttarakuru and the Tāvatiṃsa devas." [397]

22 (2) Wild Colts

"Bhikkhus, I will teach you the three kinds of wild colts and the three kinds of persons who are like wild colts; the three kinds of good horses and the three kinds of persons who are like good horses; the three kinds of excellent thoroughbred horses and the three kinds of excellent thoroughbred persons.[1886] Listen and attend closely. I will speak."

"Yes, Bhante," those bhikkhus replied. The Blessed One said this:

"And what, bhikkhus, are the three kinds of wild colts? (1) Here, one kind of wild colt possesses speed but not beauty or the right proportions. (2) Another kind of wild colt possesses speed and beauty but not the right proportions. (3) And still another kind of wild colt possesses speed, beauty, and the right proportions. These are the three kinds of wild colts.

"And what, bhikkhus, are the three kinds of persons who are like wild colts? (1) Here, one kind of person who is like a wild colt possesses speed but not beauty or the right proportions. (2) Another kind of person who is like a wild colt possesses speed and beauty but not the right proportions. (3) And still another kind of person who is like a wild colt possesses speed, beauty, and the right proportions.

(1) "And how, bhikkhus, does a person who is like a wild colt possess speed but not beauty or the right proportions? Here, a bhikkhu understands as it really is: 'This is suffering,' and 'This is the origin of suffering,' and 'This is the cessation of suffering,' and 'This is the way leading to the cessation of suffering.' [398] This, I say, is his speed. But when asked a question pertaining to the Dhamma or the discipline, he falters and does not answer. This, I say, is his lack of beauty. And he does not gain robes, almsfood, lodgings, and medicines and provisions for the sick. This, I say, is his lack of the right proportions. In this way a person who is like a wild colt possesses speed but not beauty or the right proportions.

(2) "And how does a person who is like a wild colt possess speed and beauty but not the right proportions? Here, a bhikkhu understands as it really is: 'This is suffering' . . . 'This is the way leading to the cessation of suffering.' This, I say, is his speed. And when asked a question pertaining to the Dhamma or the discipline, he answers and does not falter. This, I say, is his beauty. But he does not gain robes . . . and provisions for the sick. This, I say, is his lack of the right proportions. In this way a person who is like a wild colt possesses speed and beauty but not the right proportions.

(3) "And how does a person who is like a wild colt possess

speed, beauty, and the right proportions? Here, a bhikkhu understands as it really is: 'This is suffering' ... 'This is the way leading to the cessation of suffering.' This, I say, is his speed. And when asked a question pertaining to the Dhamma or the discipline, he answers and does not falter. This, I say, is his beauty. [399] And he gains robes ... and provisions for the sick. This, I say, is his right proportions. In this way a person who is like a wild colt possesses speed, beauty, and the right proportions. These are the three kinds of persons who are like wild colts.

"And what, bhikkhus, are the three kinds of good horses? (4)–(6) Here, one kind of good horse ... [as above for the wild colts] ... possesses speed, beauty, and the right proportions. These are the three kinds of good horses.[1887]

"And what, bhikkhus, are the three kinds of persons who are like good horses? (4)–(6) Here, one person who is like a good horse ... [as above for the persons who are like wild colts] ... possesses speed, beauty, and the right proportions.

(4)–(6) "And how, bhikkhus, does a person who is like a good horse ... possess speed, beauty, and the right proportions? Here, with the utter destruction of the five lower fetters, a bhikkhu is one of spontaneous birth, due to attain final nibbāna there without ever returning from that world. This, I say, is his speed. And when asked a question pertaining to the Dhamma and the discipline, he answers and does not falter. This, I say, is his beauty. And he gains robes ... and provisions for the sick. This, I say, is his right proportions. In this way a person who is like a good horse possesses speed, beauty, and the right proportions. These are the three kinds of persons that are like good horses.

"And what, bhikkhus, are the three kinds of excellent thoroughbred horses? (7)–(9) Here, one kind of excellent thoroughbred horse ... [as above for the wild colts] ... possesses speed, beauty, and the right proportions. [400] These are the three kinds of excellent thoroughbred horses.

"And what, bhikkhus, are the three kinds of excellent thoroughbred persons? (7)–(9) Here, one kind of excellent thoroughbred person ... [as above for the persons who are like wild colts] ... possesses speed, beauty, and the right proportions.

(7)–(9) "And how, bhikkhus, does an excellent thoroughbred

person . . . possess speed, beauty, and the right proportions? Here, with the destruction of the taints, a bhikkhu has realized for himself with direct knowledge, in this very life, the taintless liberation of mind, liberation by wisdom, and having entered upon it, he dwells in it. This, I say, is his speed. And when asked a question pertaining to the Dhamma and the discipline, he answers and does not falter. This, I say, is his beauty. And he gains robes, almsfood, lodgings, and medicines and provisions for the sick. This, I say, is his right proportions. In this way an excellent thoroughbred person possesses speed, beauty, and the right proportions. These, bhikkhus, are the three kinds of excellent thoroughbred persons."

23 (3) Craving

"I will teach you, bhikkhus, nine things rooted in craving.[1888] Listen and attend closely. I will speak."

"Yes, Bhante," those bhikkhus replied. The Blessed One said this:

"And what are the nine things rooted in craving? (1) In dependence on craving there is seeking. (2) In dependence on seeking there is gain. (3) In dependence on gain there is judgment. (4) In dependence on judgment there is desire and lust. (5) In dependence on desire and lust there is attachment. (6) In dependence on attachment there is possessiveness. (7) In dependence on possessiveness there is miserliness. (8) In dependence on miserliness there is safeguarding. (9) With safeguarding as the foundation originate the taking up of rods [401] and weapons, quarrels, contentions, and disputes, accusations, divisive speech, and false speech, and many [other] bad unwholesome things. These are the nine things rooted in craving."[1889]

24 (4) Beings

"Bhikkhus, there are these nine abodes of beings. What nine?[1890]

(1) "There are, bhikkhus, beings that are different in body and different in perception, such as humans, some devas, and some in the lower world. This is the first abode of beings.

(2) "There are beings that are different in body but identical in perception, such as the devas of Brahmā's company that are reborn through the first [jhāna]. This is the second abode of beings.

(3) "There are beings that are identical in body but different in perception, such as the devas of streaming radiance. This is the third abode of beings.

(4) "There are beings that are identical in body and identical in perception, such as the devas of refulgent glory. This is the fourth abode of beings.

(5) "There are beings that are non-percipient, without experience, such as the devas that are non-percipient. This is the fifth abode of beings.

(6) "There are beings that, with the complete surmounting of perceptions of forms, with the passing away of perceptions of sensory impingement, with non-attention to perceptions of diversity, [perceiving] 'space is infinite,' belong to the base of the infinity of space. This is the sixth abode of beings.

(7) "There are beings that, by completely surmounting the base of the infinity of space, [perceiving] 'consciousness is infinite,' belong to the base of the infinity of consciousness. This is the seventh abode of beings.

(8) "There are beings that, by completely surmounting the base of the infinity of consciousness, [perceiving] 'there is nothing,' belong to the base of nothingness. This is the eighth abode of beings.

(9) "There are beings that, by completely surmounting the base of nothingness, belong to the base of neither-perception-nor-non-perception. This is the ninth abode of beings.

"These are the nine abodes of beings." [402]

25 (5) Wisdom

"Bhikkhus, when the mind of a bhikkhu is well consolidated by wisdom, he is able to assert: 'Destroyed is birth, the spiritual life has been lived, what had to be done has been done, there is no more coming back to any state of being.'

"And how is the mind of a bhikkhu well consolidated by wisdom? (1) His mind is well consolidated by wisdom [when he knows]: 'My mind is without lust.' (2) His mind is well consolidated by wisdom [when he knows]: 'My mind is without hatred.' (3) His mind is well consolidated by wisdom [when he knows]: 'My mind is without delusion.' (4) His mind is well consolidated by wisdom [when he knows]: 'My mind is not subject to infatuation.' (5) His mind is well consolidated by wisdom [when he knows]: 'My mind is not subject to animosity.' (6) His mind is well consolidated by wisdom [when he knows]: 'My mind is not subject to confusion.' (7) His mind is well consolidated by wisdom [when he knows]: 'My mind is not subject to return to sense-sphere existence.' (8) His mind is well consolidated by wisdom [when he knows]: 'My mind is not subject to return to form-sphere existence.' (9) His mind is well consolidated by wisdom [when he knows]: 'My mind is not subject to return to formless-sphere existence.'

"When, bhikkhus, the mind of a bhikkhu is well consolidated by wisdom, he is able to assert: 'Destroyed is birth, the spiritual life has been lived, what had to be done has been done, there is no more coming back to any state of being.'"

26 (6) The Stone Pillar

Thus have I heard. On one occasion the Venerable Sāriputta and the Venerable Candikāputta were dwelling at Rājagaha in the Bamboo Grove, the squirrel sanctuary. There the Venerable Candikāputta addressed the bhikkhus: "Friends, bhikkhus!"

"Friend!" those bhikkhus replied. The Venerable Candikāputta said this: "Friends, Devadatta teaches the Dhamma to the bhikkhus thus: 'When, friends, a bhikkhu's mind is consolidated by mind,[1891] it is fitting for him to declare: [403] "I understand: Destroyed is birth, the spiritual life has been lived, what had to be done has been done, there is no more coming back to any state of being."'"

Then the Venerable Sāriputta said to the Venerable Candikāputta: "Friend Candikāputta, it is not in such a way that Devadatta teaches the Dhamma to the bhikkhus. Rather, Devadatta teaches the Dhamma to the bhikkhus thus: 'When, friends, a bhikkhu's mind is well consolidated by mind,[1892] it is fitting for him to declare: "I understand: Destroyed is birth, the spiritual life has been lived, what had to be done has been done, there is no more coming back to any state of being."'"

A second time ... A third time the Venerable Candikāputta addressed the bhikkhus: "Friends, Devadatta teaches the Dhamma to the bhikkhus thus: 'When, friends, a bhikkhu's mind is consolidated by mind, it is fitting for him to declare: "I understand: Destroyed is birth, the spiritual life has been lived, what had to be done has been done, there is no more coming back to any state of being."'"

A third time the Venerable Sāriputta said to the Venerable Candikāputta: "Friend Candikāputta, it is not in such a way that Devadatta teaches the Dhamma to the bhikkhus. Rather, Devadatta teaches the Dhamma to the bhikkhus thus: 'When, friends, a bhikkhu's mind is well consolidated by mind, it is fitting for him to declare: "I understand: Destroyed is birth, the spiritual life has been lived, what had to be done has been done, there is no more coming back to any state of being."'

"And how, friend, is the mind of a bhikkhu well consolidated by mind? [404] (1) His mind is well consolidated by mind [when he knows]: 'My mind is without lust.' (2) His mind is well consolidated by mind [when he knows]: 'My mind is without hatred.' (3) His mind is well consolidated by mind [when he knows]: 'My mind is without delusion.' (4) His mind is well consolidated by mind [when he knows]: 'My mind is not subject to lust.' (5) His mind is well consolidated by mind [when he knows]: 'My mind is not subject to hatred.' (6) His mind is well consolidated by mind [when he knows]: 'My mind is not subject to delusion.' (7) His mind is well consolidated by mind [when he knows]: 'My mind is not subject to return to sense-sphere existence.' (8) His mind is well consolidated by mind [when he knows]: 'My mind is not subject to return to form-sphere existence.' (9) His mind is well consolidated by mind [when he knows]: 'My mind is not subject to return to formless-sphere existence.'[1893]

"When, friend, a bhikkhu is thus perfectly liberated in mind, even if powerful forms cognizable by the eye come into range of the eye, they do not obsess his mind; his mind is not at all affected.[1894] It remains steady, attained to imperturbability, and he observes its vanishing. Even if powerful sounds cognizable by the ear come into range of the ear . . . Even if powerful odors cognizable by the nose come into range of the nose . . . Even if powerful tastes cognizable by the tongue come into range of the tongue . . . Even if powerful tactile objects cognizable by the body come into range of the body . . . Even if powerful phenomena cognizable by the mind come into range of the mind, they do not obsess his mind; his mind is not at all affected. It remains steady, attained to imperturbability, and he observes its vanishing.

"Suppose, friend, there was a stone pillar eight meters

long.[1895] Four meters would be below ground and four meters above ground. If a violent rainstorm should then arrive from the east, it would not shake it or make it quake, [405] wobble, and tremble;[1896] if a violent rainstorm should then arrive from the west . . . from the north . . . from the south, it would not shake it or make it quake, wobble, and tremble. For what reason? Because the stone pillar is deep in the ground and is securely planted. So too, friend, when a bhikkhu is thus perfectly liberated in mind, even if powerful forms cognizable by the eye come into range of the eye . . . Even if powerful phenomena cognizable by the mind come into range of the mind, they do not obsess his mind; his mind is not at all affected. It remains steady, attained to imperturbability, and he observes its vanishing."

27 (7) Enmity (1)

Then the householder Anāthapiṇḍika approached the Blessed One, paid homage to him, and sat down to one side. The Blessed One then said to him:

"Householder, when a noble disciple has eliminated five perils and enmities and possesses the four factors of stream-entry, he might, if he so wished, declare of himself: 'I am one finished with hell, the animal realm, and the sphere of afflicted spirits; finished with the plane of misery, the bad destination, the lower world; I am a stream-enterer, no longer subject to [rebirth in] the lower world, fixed in destiny, heading for enlightenment.'[1897] [406]

"What are the five perils and enmities that have been eliminated? (1) Householder, one who destroys life, with the destruction of life as condition, creates peril and enmity pertaining to the present life and peril and enmity pertaining to future lives[1898] and he also experiences mental pain and dejection. One who abstains from the destruction of life does not create such peril and enmity pertaining to the present life or such peril and enmity pertaining to future lives nor does he experience mental pain and dejection. For one who abstains from the destruction of life, that peril and enmity has thus been eliminated.

(2) "One who takes what is not given . . . (3) who engages in sexual misconduct . . . (4) who speaks falsely . . . (5) who indulges in liquor, wine, and intoxicants, the basis for heedlessness, with indulgence in liquor, wine, and intoxicants as condition, creates peril and enmity pertaining to the present life and peril

and enmity pertaining to future lives and he also experiences mental pain and dejection. One who abstains from liquor, wine, and intoxicants, the basis for heedlessness, does not create such peril and enmity pertaining to the present life or such peril and enmity pertaining to future lives nor does he experience mental pain and dejection. For one who abstains from liquor, wine, and intoxicants, the basis for heedlessness, that peril and enmity has thus been eliminated.

"These are the five perils and enmities that have been eliminated.

"And what are the four factors of stream-entry that he possesses? (6) Here, householder, a noble disciple possesses unwavering confidence in the Buddha thus: 'The Blessed One is an arahant, perfectly enlightened, accomplished in true knowledge and conduct, fortunate, knower of the world, unsurpassed trainer of persons to be tamed, teacher of devas and humans, the Enlightened One, the Blessed One.' (7) He possesses unwavering confidence in the Dhamma thus: 'The Dhamma is well expounded by the Blessed One, directly visible, immediate, inviting one to come and see, applicable, to be personally experienced by the wise.' (8) He possesses unwavering confidence in the Saṅgha thus: 'The Saṅgha of the Blessed One's disciples is practicing the good way, practicing the straight way, [407] practicing the true way, practicing the proper way; that is, the four pairs of persons, the eight types of individuals—this Saṅgha of the Blessed One's disciples is worthy of gifts, worthy of hospitality, worthy of offerings, worthy of reverential salutation, the unsurpassed field of merit for the world.' (9) He possesses the virtuous behavior loved by the noble ones, unbroken, flawless, unblemished, unblotched, freeing, praised by the wise, ungrasped, leading to concentration. These are the four factors of stream-entry that he possesses.

"Householder, when a noble disciple has eliminated these five perils and enmities and possesses these four factors of stream-entry, he might, if he so wished, declare of himself: 'I am one finished with hell, the animal realm, and the sphere of afflicted spirits; finished with the plane of misery, the bad destination, the lower world; I am a stream-enterer, no longer subject to [rebirth in] the lower world, fixed in destiny, heading for enlightenment.'"

28 (8) Enmity (2)
[Identical with 9:27, but addressed by the Buddha to the bhikkhus.] [408]

29 (9) Resentment (1)
"Bhikkhus, there are these nine grounds for resentment. What nine? (1) [Thinking:] 'He acted for my harm,' one harbors resentment. (2) [Thinking:] 'He is acting for my harm,' one harbors resentment. (3) [Thinking:] 'He will act for my harm,' one harbors resentment. (4) [Thinking:] 'He acted for the harm of one pleasing and agreeable to me,' one harbors resentment. (5) [Thinking:] 'He is acting for the harm of one pleasing and agreeable to me,' one harbors resentment. (6) [Thinking:] 'He will act for the harm of one pleasing and agreeable to me,' one harbors resentment. (7) [Thinking:] 'He acted for the benefit of one displeasing and disagreeable to me,' one harbors resentment. (8) [Thinking:] 'He is acting for the benefit of one displeasing and disagreeable to me,' one harbors resentment. (9) [Thinking:] 'He will act for the benefit of one displeasing and disagreeable to me,' one harbors resentment. These, bhikkhus, are the nine grounds for resentment."

30 (10) Resentment (2)
"Bhikkhus, there are these nine ways of removing resentment. What nine? (1) [Thinking:] 'He acted for my harm, but what can be done about it?'[1899] one removes resentment. (2) [Thinking:] 'He is acting for my harm, but what can be done about it?' one removes resentment. (3) [Thinking:] 'He will act for my harm, but what can be done about it?' one removes resentment. (4) [Thinking:] 'He acted for the harm of one who is pleasing and agreeable to me, but what can be done about it?' one removes resentment. (5) [Thinking:] 'He is acting for the harm of one who is pleasing and agreeable to me, but what can be done about it?' one removes resentment. [409] (6) [Thinking:] 'He will act for the harm of one who is pleasing and agreeable to me, but what can be done about it?' one removes resentment (7) [Thinking:] 'He acted for the benefit of one who is displeasing and disagreeable to me, but what can be done about it?' one removes resentment. (8) [Thinking:] 'He is acting for the benefit of one who is displeasing and disagreeable to me, but what

can be done about it?' one removes resentment. (9) [Thinking:] 'He will act for the benefit of one who is displeasing and disagreeable to me, but what can be done about it?' one removes resentment. These, bhikkhus, are the nine ways of removing resentment."

31 (11) Progressive Cessation

"Bhikkhus, there are these nine progressive cessations.[1900] What nine? (1) For one who has attained the first jhāna, sensual perception has ceased. (2) For one who has attained the second jhāna, thought and examination have ceased. (3) For one who has attained the third jhāna, rapture has ceased. (4) For one who has attained the fourth jhāna, in-breathing and out-breathing have ceased. (5) For one who has attained the base of the infinity of space, the perception of form has ceased.[1901] (6) For one who has attained the base of the infinity of consciousness, the perception pertaining to the base of the infinity of space has ceased. (7) For one who has attained the base of nothingness, the perception pertaining to the base of the infinity of consciousness has ceased. (8) For one who has attained the base of neither-perception-nor-non-perception, the perception pertaining to the base of nothingness has ceased. (9) For one who has attained the cessation of perception and feeling, perception and feeling have ceased. These, bhikkhus, are the nine progressive cessations." [410]

IV. The Great Chapter

32 (1) Dwellings (1)

"Bhikkhus, there are these nine progressive dwellings.[1902] What nine? (1) Here, secluded from sensual pleasures, secluded from unwholesome states, a bhikkhu enters and dwells in the first jhāna, which consists of rapture and pleasure born of seclusion, accompanied by thought and examination. (2) With the subsiding of thought and examination, he enters and dwells in the second jhāna, which has internal placidity and unification of mind and consists of rapture and pleasure born of concentration, without thought and examination. (3) With the fading away as well of rapture, he dwells equanimous and, mindful and clearly comprehending, he experiences pleasure with the body; he enters and dwells in the third jhāna of which the noble ones declare: 'He is equanimous, mindful, one who dwells happily.' (4) With the abandoning of pleasure and pain, and with the previous passing away of joy and dejection, he enters and dwells in the fourth jhāna, neither painful nor pleasant, which has purification of mindfulness by equanimity.

(5) "With the complete surmounting of perceptions of forms, with the passing away of perceptions of sensory impingement, with non-attention to perceptions of diversity, [perceiving] 'space is infinite,' a bhikkhu enters and dwells in the base of the infinity of space. (6) By completely surmounting the base of the infinity of space, [perceiving] 'consciousness is infinite,' he enters and dwells in the base of the infinity of consciousness. (7) By completely surmounting the base of the infinity of consciousness, [perceiving] 'there is nothing,' he enters and dwells in the base of nothingness. (8) By completely surmounting the base of nothingness, he enters and dwells in the base of neither-perception-nor-non-perception. (9) By completely surmounting the base of neither-perception-nor-non-perception, he enters and dwells in the cessation of perception and feeling. These, bhikkhus, are the nine progressive dwellings."

33 (2) Dwellings (2)

"Bhikkhus, I will teach the attainment of these nine progressive dwellings.[1903] Listen. . . . And what, bhikkhus, is the attainment of the nine progressive dwellings?

(1) "I say of [that state] where sensual pleasures cease and of those who dwell having thoroughly ended sensual pleasures: 'Surely, those venerable ones are hungerless and quenched; [411] they have crossed over[1904] and gone beyond in that particular respect.'[1905] If anyone should say: 'Where do sensual pleasures cease? And who are those that dwell having thoroughly ended sensual pleasures? I do not know this, I do not see this,' he should be told: 'Here, friend, secluded from sensual pleasures, secluded from unwholesome states, a bhikkhu enters and dwells in the first jhāna. . . . That is where sensual pleasures cease, and those are the ones who dwell having thoroughly ended sensual pleasures.' Surely, bhikkhus, one who is not crafty or hypocritical should delight and rejoice in this statement, saying: 'Good!' Having done so, bowing in reverential salutation, he should attend upon them.

(2) "I say of [that state] where thought and examination cease and of those who dwell having thoroughly ended thought and examination: 'Surely, those venerable ones are hungerless and quenched, have crossed over and gone beyond in that particular respect.' If anyone should say: 'Where do thought and examination cease? And who are those that dwell having thoroughly ended thought and examination? I do not know this, I do not see this,' he should be told: 'Here, friend, with the subsiding of thought and examination, a bhikkhu enters and dwells in the second jhāna.... That is where thought and examination cease, and those are the ones who dwell having thoroughly ended thought and examination.' Surely, bhikkhus, one who is not crafty or hypocritical should delight and rejoice in this statement, saying: 'Good!' Having done so, bowing in reverential salutation, he should attend upon them.

(3) "I say of [that state] where rapture ceases and of those who dwell having thoroughly ended rapture: 'Surely, those venerable ones are hungerless and quenched, have crossed over and gone beyond in that particular respect.' If anyone should say: 'Where does rapture cease? And who are those that dwell having thoroughly ended rapture? I do not know this, I do not see this,' he should be told: 'Here, friend, with the fading away as well of rapture ... he enters and dwells in the third jhāna.... That is where rapture ceases and those are the ones [412] who dwell having thoroughly ended rapture.' Surely, bhikkhus, one who is not crafty or hypocritical should delight and rejoice in this statement, saying: 'Good!' Having done so, bowing in reverential salutation, he should attend upon them.

(4) "I say of [that state] where the pleasure [connected with] equanimity ceases and of those who dwell having thoroughly ended the pleasure [connected with] equanimity:[1906] 'Surely, those venerable ones are hungerless and quenched, have crossed over and gone beyond in that particular respect. If anyone should say: 'Where does the pleasure [connected with] equanimity cease? And who are those that dwell having thoroughly ended the pleasure [connected with] equanimity? I do not know this, I do not see this,' he should be told: 'Here, friend, with the abandoning of pleasure and pain ... a bhikkhu enters and dwells in the fourth jhāna.... That is where the pleasure [connected with] equanimity ceases and those are the ones who dwell having thoroughly ended the pleasure [connected

with] equanimity.' Surely, bhikkhus, one who is not crafty or hypocritical should delight and rejoice in this statement, saying: 'Good!' Having done so, bowing in reverential salutation, he should attend upon them.

(5) "I say of [that state] where perceptions of forms cease and of those who dwell having thoroughly ended perceptions of forms:[1907] 'Surely, those venerable ones are hungerless and quenched, have crossed over and gone beyond in that particular respect.' If anyone should say: 'Where do perceptions of forms cease? And who are those that dwell having thoroughly ended perceptions of forms? I do not know this, I do not see this,' he should be told: 'Here, friend, with the complete surmounting of perceptions of forms, with the passing away of perceptions of sensory impingement, with non-attention to perceptions of diversity, [perceiving] "space is infinite," a bhikkhu enters and dwells in the base of the infinity of space. That is where perceptions of forms cease and those are the ones who dwell having thoroughly ended perceptions of forms.' Surely, bhikkhus, one who is not crafty or hypocritical should delight and rejoice in this statement, saying: 'Good!' Having done so, bowing in reverential salutation, he should attend upon them. [413]

(6) "I say of [that state] where the perception of the base of the infinity of space ceases and of those who dwell having thoroughly ended the perception of the base of the infinity of space: 'Surely, those venerable ones are hungerless and quenched, have crossed over and gone beyond in that particular respect.' If anyone should say: 'Where does the perception of the base of the infinity of space cease? And who are those that dwell having thoroughly ended the perception of the base of the infinity of space? I do not know this, I do not see this,' he should be told: 'Here, friend, by completely surmounting the base of the infinity of space, [perceiving] "consciousness is infinite," a bhikkhu enters and dwells in the base of the infinity of consciousness. That is where the perception of the base of the infinity of space ceases and those are the ones who dwell having thoroughly ended the perception of the base of the infinity of space.' Surely, bhikkhus, one who is not crafty or hypocritical should delight and rejoice in this statement, saying: 'Good!' Having done so, bowing in reverential salutation, he should attend upon them.

(7) "I say of [that state] where the perception of the base of the infinity of consciousness ceases and of those who dwell having thoroughly ended the perception of the base of the infinity of consciousness: 'Surely, those venerable ones are hungerless and quenched, have crossed over and gone beyond in that particular respect.' If anyone should say: 'Where does the perception of the base of the infinity of consciousness cease? And who are those that dwell having thoroughly ended the perception of the base of the infinity of consciousness? I do not know this, I do not see this,' he should be told: 'Here, friend, by completely surmounting the base of the infinity of consciousness, [perceiving] "there is nothing," a bhikkhu enters and dwells in the base of nothingness. That is where the perception of the base of the infinity of consciousness ceases and those are the ones who dwell having thoroughly ended the perception of the base of the infinity of consciousness.' Surely, bhikkhus, one who is not crafty or hypocritical should delight and rejoice in this statement, saying: 'Good!' Having done so, bowing in reverential salutation, he should attend upon them.

(8) "I say of [that state] where the perception of the base of nothingness ceases and of those who dwell having thoroughly ended the perception of the base of nothingness: 'Surely, those venerable ones are hungerless and quenched, have crossed over and gone beyond in that particular respect.' If anyone should say: 'Where does the perception of the base of nothingness cease? And who are those that dwell having thoroughly ended the perception of the base of nothingness? [414] I do not know this, I do not see this,' he should be told: 'Here, friend, by completely surmounting the base of nothingness, a bhikkhu enters and dwells in the base of neither-perception-nor-non-perception. That is where the perception of the base of nothingness ceases and those are the ones who dwell having thoroughly ended the perception of the base of nothingness.' Surely, bhikkhus, one who is not crafty or hypocritical should delight and rejoice in this statement, saying: 'Good!' Having done so, bowing in reverential salutation, he should attend upon them.

(9) "I say of [that state] where the perception of the base of neither-perception-nor-non-perception ceases and of those who dwell having thoroughly ended the perception of the base of neither-perception-nor-non-perception: 'Surely, those

venerable ones are hungerless and quenched, have crossed over and gone beyond in that particular respect.' If anyone should say: 'Where does the perception of the base of neither-perception-nor-non-perception cease? And who are those that dwell having thoroughly ended the perception of the base of neither-perception-nor-non-perception? I do not know this, I do not see this,' he should be told: 'Here, friend, by completely surmounting the base of neither-perception-nor-non-perception, a bhikkhu enters and dwells in the cessation of perception and feeling. That is where the perception of the base of neither-perception-nor-non-perception ceases and those are the ones who dwell having thoroughly ended the perception of the base of neither-perception-nor-non-perception.' Surely, bhikkhus, one who is not crafty or hypocritical should delight and rejoice in this statement, saying: 'Good!' Having done so, bowing in reverential salutation, he should attend upon them.

"This, bhikkhus, is the attainment of the nine progressive dwellings."

34 (3) Nibbāna

Thus have I heard. On one occasion the Venerable Sāriputta was dwelling at Rājagaha in the Bamboo Grove, the squirrel sanctuary. There the Venerable Sāriputta addressed the bhikkhus: "Friends, bhikkhus!"

"Friend!" those bhikkhus replied. The Venerable Sāriputta said this:

"Happiness, friends, is this nibbāna. Happiness, friends, is this nibbāna."

When this was said, the Venerable Udāyī[1908] said to the Venerable Sāriputta: [415] "But, friend Sāriputta, what happiness could there be here when nothing is felt here?"

"Just this, friend, is the happiness here, that nothing is felt here.

"There are, friends, these five objects of sensual pleasure. What five? Forms cognizable by the eye that are wished for, desired, agreeable, pleasing, connected with sensual pleasure, tantalizing; sounds cognizable by the ear . . . odors cognizable by the nose . . . tastes cognizable by the tongue . . . tactile objects cognizable by the body that are wished for, desired, agreeable, pleasing, connected with sensual pleasure, tantalizing. These are the five objects of sensual pleasure. Any pleasure or joy that arises in dependence on these five objects of sensual pleasure is called sensual pleasure.

(1) "Here, friends, secluded from sensual pleasures, secluded from unwholesome states, a bhikkhu enters and dwells in the first jhāna, which consists of rapture and pleasure born of seclusion, accompanied by thought and examination. If, while that bhikkhu is dwelling in this way, perception and attention accompanied by sensuality occur in him, he feels it as an affliction. Just as pain might arise for one feeling pleasure only to afflict him, so too if that perception and attention accompanied by sensuality occur in him, he feels it as an affliction. But the Blessed One has called affliction suffering. In this way it can be understood how nibbāna is happiness.[1909]

(2) "Again, with the subsiding of thought and examination, a bhikkhu enters and dwells in the second jhāna.... If, while that bhikkhu is dwelling in this way, perception and attention accompanied by thought [416] occur in him, he feels it as an affliction. Just as pain might arise for one feeling pleasure only to afflict him, so too if that perception and attention accompanied by thought occur in him, he feels it as an affliction. But the Blessed One has called affliction suffering. In this way, too, it can be understood how nibbāna is happiness.

(3) "Again, with the fading away as well of rapture... he enters and dwells in the third jhāna.... If, while that bhikkhu is dwelling in this way, perception and attention accompanied by rapture occur in him, he feels it as an affliction.... In this way, too, it can be understood how nibbāna is happiness.

(4) "Again, with the abandoning of pleasure and pain... a bhikkhu enters and dwells in the fourth jhāna.... If, while that bhikkhu is dwelling in this way, perception and attention accompanied by the pleasure [connected with] equanimity[1910] occur in him, he feels it as an affliction.... In this way, too, it can be understood how nibbāna is happiness.

(5) "Again, with the complete surmounting of perceptions of forms, with the passing away of perceptions of sensory impingement, with non-attention to perceptions of diversity, [perceiving] 'space is infinite,' a bhikkhu enters and dwells in the base of the infinity of space. If, while that bhikkhu is dwelling in this way, perception and attention accompanied by forms

occur in him, he feels it as an affliction. . . . [417] . . . In this way, too, it can be understood how nibbāna is happiness.

(6) "Again, by completely surmounting the base of the infinity of space, [perceiving] 'consciousness is infinite,' a bhikkhu enters and dwells in the base of the infinity of consciousness. If, while that bhikkhu is dwelling in this way, perception and attention accompanied by the base of the infinity of space occur in him, he feels it as an affliction. . . . In this way, too, it can be understood how nibbāna is happiness.

(7) "Again, by completely surmounting the base of the infinity of consciousness, [perceiving] 'there is nothing,' a bhikkhu enters and dwells in the base of nothingness. If, while that bhikkhu is dwelling in this way, perception and attention accompanied by the base of the infinity of consciousness occur in him, he feels it as an affliction. . . . In this way, too, it can be understood how nibbāna is happiness.

(8) "Again, by completely surmounting the base of nothingness, a bhikkhu enters and dwells in the base of neither-perception-nor-non-perception. If, while that bhikkhu is dwelling in this way, perception and attention accompanied by the base of nothingness occur in him, he feels it as an affliction. Just as pain might arise for one feeling pleasure only to afflict him, so too if that perception and attention accompanied by the base of nothingness occur in him, he feels it as an affliction. But the Blessed One has called affliction suffering. In this way, too, it can be understood how nibbāna is happiness. [418]

(9) "Again, by completely surmounting the base of neither-perception-nor-non-perception, a bhikkhu enters and dwells in the cessation of perception and feeling, and having seen with wisdom, his taints are utterly destroyed. In this way, too, it can be understood how nibbāna is happiness."

35 (4) The Cow

"Suppose, bhikkhus, there were a mountain-dwelling cow that was foolish, incompetent, inexperienced, and unskilled in walking on rough mountains.[1911] It might occur to her: 'I should go to a region where I have never gone before, eat grass that I have never eaten before, drink water that I have never drunk before.' She would set down a front foot, and while it is not yet firmly planted, lift up a hind foot. She would not go to a region where she had never gone before, eat grass that she had never eaten before, drink water that she had never drunk before; and she would not return safely to the region where she was staying when it occurred to her: 'I should go to a region where I have never gone before, eat grass that I have never eaten before, drink water that I have never drunk before.' For what reason? Because that mountain-dwelling cow was foolish, incompetent, inexperienced, and unskilled in walking on rough mountains.

"So too, some bhikkhu here is foolish, incompetent, inexperienced, and unskilled, when, secluded from sensual pleasures, secluded from unwholesome states, he enters and dwells in the first jhāna, which consists of rapture and pleasure born of seclusion, accompanied by thought and examination. He does not pursue that object,[1912] does not develop and cultivate it, does not focus on it well.

"It occurs to him: 'With the subsiding of thought and examination, I should enter and dwell in the second jhāna [419]....' But he cannot enter and dwell in the second jhāna.... Then it occurs to him: 'Secluded from sensual pleasures, secluded from unwholesome states, I should enter and dwell in the first jhāna....' But he cannot enter and dwell in the first jhāna.... This is called a bhikkhu who has dropped away from both,[1913] fallen away from both. He is just like that mountain-dwelling cow that was foolish, incompetent, inexperienced, and unskilled in walking on rough mountains.

"Suppose, bhikkhus, there were a mountain-dwelling cow that was wise, competent, experienced, and skilled in walking on rough mountains. It might occur to her: 'I should go to a region where I have never gone before, eat grass that I have never eaten before, drink water that I have never drunk before.' When setting down a front foot, she would firmly plant it, and only then lift up a hind foot. She would go to a region where she had never gone before, eat grass that she had never eaten before, drink water that she had never drunk before; and she would return safely to the region where she was staying when it occurred to her: 'I should go to a region where I have never gone before, eat grass that I have never eaten before, drink water that I have never drunk before.' For what reason? Because that mountain-dwelling cow was wise, competent, experienced, and skilled in walking on rough mountains.

(1) "So too, some bhikkhu here is wise, competent, experienced, and skilled when, secluded from sensual pleasures, secluded from unwholesome states, he enters and dwells in the first jhāna.... He pursues that object, develops and cultivates it, and focuses on it well.

(2) "It occurs to him: 'With the subsiding of thought and examination, I should enter and dwell in the second jhāna....' Not injuring[1914] the second jhāna, with the subsiding of thought and examination he enters and dwells in the second jhāna.... He pursues that object, develops and cultivates it, and focuses on it well.

(3) "Then it occurs to him: 'With the fading away as well of rapture [420] ... I should enter and dwell in the third jhāna....' Not injuring the third jhāna, with the fading away as well of rapture he enters and dwells in the third jhāna.... He pursues that object, develops and cultivates it, and focuses on it well.

(4) "Then it occurs to him: 'With the abandoning of pleasure and pain ... I should enter and dwell in the fourth jhāna....' Not injuring the fourth jhāna, with the abandoning of pleasure and pain ... he enters and dwells in the fourth jhāna.... He pursues that object, develops and cultivates it, and focuses on it well.

(5) "Then it occurs to him: 'With the complete surmounting of perceptions of forms, with the passing away of perceptions of sensory impingement, with non-attention to perceptions of diversity, [perceiving] "space is infinite," I should enter and dwell in the base of the infinity of space.' Not injuring the base of the infinity of space, with the complete surmounting of perceptions of forms ... he enters and dwells in the base of the infinity of space. He pursues that object, develops and cultivates it, and focuses on it well.

(6) "Then it occurs to him: 'With the complete surmounting of the base of the infinity of space, [perceiving] "consciousness is infinite," I should enter and dwell in the base of the infinity of consciousness.' Not injuring the base of the infinity of consciousness, with the complete surmounting of the base of the infinity of space ... he enters and dwells in the base of the infinity of consciousness. He pursues that object, develops and cultivates it, and focuses on it well.

(7) "Then it occurs to him: 'With the complete surmounting

of the base of the infinity of consciousness, [perceiving] "there is nothing," I should enter and dwell in the base of nothingness.' Not injuring the base of nothingness, with the complete surmounting of the base of the infinity of consciousness . . . he enters and dwells in the base of nothingness. He pursues that object, develops and cultivates it, and focuses on it well.

(8) "Then it occurs to him: 'With the complete surmounting of the base of nothingness, I should enter and dwell in the base of neither-perception-nor-non-perception.' Not injuring the base of neither-perception-nor-non-perception, with the complete surmounting of the base of nothingness, he enters and dwells in the base of neither-perception-nor-non-perception. He pursues that object, develops and cultivates it, [421] and focuses on it well.

(9) "Then it occurs to him: 'With the complete surmounting of the base of neither-perception-nor-non-perception, I should enter and dwell in the cessation of perception and feeling.' Not injuring the cessation of perception and feeling, with the complete surmounting of the base of neither-perception-nor-non-perception, he enters and dwells in the cessation of perception and feeling.

"When, bhikkhus, a bhikkhu enters and emerges from each of these meditative attainments, his mind becomes malleable and wieldy. With the mind malleable and wieldy, his concentration becomes measureless and well developed. With measureless, well-developed concentration, whatever state realizable by direct knowledge he inclines his mind toward to realize by direct knowledge, he is capable of realizing it, there being a suitable basis.

"If he wishes: 'May I wield the various kinds of psychic potency: having been one, may I become many . . . [here and below in full as at 6:2] . . . may I exercise mastery with the body as far as the brahmā world,' he is capable of realizing it, there being a suitable basis.

"If he wishes: 'May I, with the divine ear element, which is purified and surpasses the human, hear both kinds of sounds, the divine and human, those that are far as well as near,' he is capable of realizing it, there being a suitable basis.

"If he wishes: 'May I understand the minds of other beings and persons, having encompassed them with my own mind.

May I understand . . . an unliberated mind as unliberated,' he is capable of realizing it, there being a suitable basis.

"If he wishes: 'May I recollect my manifold past abodes . . . with their aspects and details,' he is capable of realizing it, there being a suitable basis. [422]

"If he wishes: 'May I, with the divine eye, which is purified and surpasses the human, see beings passing away and being reborn . . . and understand how beings fare in accordance with their kamma,' he is capable of realizing it, there being a suitable basis.

"If he wishes: 'May I, with the destruction of the taints, in this very life enter and dwell in the taintless liberation of mind, liberation by wisdom, having realized it for myself with direct knowledge,' he is capable of realizing it, there being a suitable basis."

36 (5) Jhāna

(1) "Bhikkhus, I say that the destruction of the taints occurs in dependence on the first jhāna. (2) I say that the destruction of the taints also occurs in dependence on the second jhāna. (3) I say that the destruction of the taints also occurs in dependence on the third jhāna. (4) I say that the destruction of the taints also occurs in dependence on the fourth jhāna. (5) I say that the destruction of the taints also occurs in dependence on the base of the infinity of space. (6) I say that the destruction of the taints also occurs in dependence on the base of the infinity of consciousness. (7) I say that the destruction of the taints also occurs in dependence on the base of nothingness. (8) I say that the destruction of the taints also occurs in dependence on the base of neither-perception-nor-non-perception. (9) I say that the destruction of the taints also occurs in dependence on the cessation of perception and feeling.

(1) "When it was said: 'Bhikkhus, I say that the destruction of the taints occurs in dependence on the first jhāna,' for what reason was this said? Here, secluded from sensual pleasures . . . a bhikkhu enters and dwells in the first jhāna. . . . He considers whatever phenomena exist there pertaining to form, feeling, perception, volitional activities, and consciousness as impermanent, suffering, an illness, a boil, a dart, misery, affliction, alien, disintegrating, [423] empty, and non-self.[1915] He turns his

mind away from those phenomena and directs it to the deathless element thus: 'This is peaceful, this is sublime, that is, the stilling of all activities, the relinquishing of all acquisitions, the destruction of craving, dispassion, cessation, nibbāna.'[1916] If he is firm in this, he attains the destruction of the taints. But if he does not attain the destruction of the taints because of that lust for the Dhamma, because of that delight in the Dhamma,[1917] then, with the utter destruction of the five lower fetters, he becomes one of spontaneous birth, due to attain final nibbāna there without ever returning from that world.

"Just as an archer or an archer's apprentice undergoes training on a straw man or a heap of clay, and then at a later time becomes a long-distance shooter, a sharp-shooter, one who splits a great body,[1918] so too, secluded from sensual pleasures . . . a bhikkhu enters and dwells in the first jhāna. He considers whatever phenomena exist there pertaining to form, feeling, perception, volitional activities, and consciousness as impermanent . . . he becomes one of spontaneous birth, due to attain final nibbāna there without ever returning from that world. [424]

"When it was said: 'Bhikkhus, I say that the destruction of the taints also occurs in dependence on the first jhāna,' it is because of this that this was said.

(2)–(4) "When it was said: 'Bhikkhus, I say that the destruction of the taints also occurs in dependence on the second jhāna . . . the third jhāna . . . the fourth jhāna . . .

[425] "When it was said: 'Bhikkhus, I say that the destruction of the taints also occurs in dependence on the fourth jhāna,' it is because of this that this was said.

(5) "When it was said: 'Bhikkhus, I say that the destruction of the taints also occurs in dependence on the base of the infinity of space,' for what reason was this said? Here, with the complete surmounting of perceptions of forms, with the passing away of perceptions of sensory impingement, with non-attention to perceptions of diversity, [perceiving] 'space is infinite,' a bhikkhu enters and dwells in the base of the infinity of space. He considers whatever phenomena exist there pertaining to feeling, perception, volitional activities, and consciousness[1919] as impermanent, suffering, an illness, a boil, a dart, misery, affliction, alien, disintegrating, empty, and non-self. He turns his mind away from those phenomena and directs it to the

deathless element thus: 'This is peaceful, this is sublime, that is, the stilling of all activities, the relinquishing of all acquisitions, the destruction of craving, dispassion, cessation, nibbāna.' If he is firm in this, he attains the destruction of the taints. But if he does not attain the destruction of the taints because of that lust for the Dhamma, because of that delight in the Dhamma, then, with the utter destruction of the five lower fetters, he becomes one of spontaneous birth, due to attain final nibbāna there without ever returning from that world.

"Just as an archer or an archer's apprentice undergoes training on a straw man or a heap of clay, and then at a later time becomes a long-distance shooter, a sharp-shooter, one who splits a great body, so too, with the complete surmounting of perceptions of forms . . . a bhikkhu enters and dwells in the base of the infinity of space. He considers whatever phenomena exist there pertaining to feeling, perception, volitional activities, and consciousness as impermanent. . . . But if he does not attain the destruction of the taints . . . he becomes one of spontaneous birth, due to attain final nibbāna there without ever returning from that world.

"When it was said: 'Bhikkhus, I say that the destruction of the taints also occurs in dependence on the base of the infinity of space,' it is because of this that this was said.

(6)–(7) "When it was said: 'Bhikkhus, I say that the destruction of the taints also occurs in dependence on the base of the infinity of consciousness . . . the base of nothingness,' for what reason was this said? [426] Here, with the complete surmounting of the base of the infinity of consciousness, [perceiving] 'there is nothing,' a bhikkhu enters and dwells in the base of nothingness. He considers whatever phenomena exist there pertaining to feeling, perception, volitional activities, and consciousness as impermanent. . . . But if he does not attain the destruction of the taints . . . he becomes one of spontaneous birth, due to attain final nibbāna there without ever returning from that world.

"Just as an archer or an archer's apprentice undergoes training on a straw man or a heap of clay, and then at a later time becomes a long-distance shooter, a sharp-shooter, one who splits a great body, so too, with the complete surmounting of the base of the infinity of consciousness . . . a bhikkhu enters and dwells in the base of nothingness. He considers whatever phenomena exist there pertaining to feeling, perception, volitional activities, and consciousness as impermanent. . . . But if he does not attain the destruction of the taints . . . he becomes one of spontaneous birth, due to attain final nibbāna there without ever returning from that world.

"When it was said: 'Bhikkhus, I say that the destruction of the taints also occurs in dependence on the base of nothingness,' it is because of this that this was said.[1920]

(8)–(9) "Thus, bhikkhus, there is penetration to final knowledge as far as meditative attainments accompanied by perception reach. But these two bases—the base of neither-perception-nor-non-perception and the cessation of perception and feeling—I say are to be described by meditative bhikkhus skilled in attainments and skilled in emerging from attainments after they have attained them and emerged from them."[1921]

37 (6) Ānanda

On one occasion the Venerable Ānanda was dwelling at Kosambi in Ghosita's Park. There the Venerable Ānanda addressed the bhikkhus: "Friends, bhikkhus!"

"Friend!" those bhikkhus replied. The Venerable Ānanda said this:

"It's astounding and amazing, friends, that the Blessed One, the Arahant, the Perfectly Enlightened One, who knows and sees, has discovered the achievement of an opening in the midst of confinement:[1922] for the purification of beings, for the overcoming of sorrow and lamentation, for the passing away of pain and dejection, for the achievement of the method, for the realization of nibbāna.[1923] (1) The eye itself as well as those forms will actually be present, [427] and yet one will not experience that base.[1924] (2) The ear itself as well as those sounds will actually be present, and yet one will not experience that base. (3) The nose itself as well as those odors will actually be present, and yet one will not experience that base. (4) The tongue itself as well as those tastes will actually be present, and yet one will not experience that base. (5) The body itself as well as those tactile objects will actually be present, and yet one will not experience that base."

When this was said, the Venerable Udāyī said this to the Venerable Ānanda: "Is it, friend Ānanda, while one is actually percipient or while one is non-percipient that one does not experience that base?"

"It is, friend, while one is actually percipient that one does not experience that base, not while one is non-percipient."

"But, friend, of what is one percipient when one does not experience that base?"

(6) "Here, friend, with the complete surmounting of perceptions of forms, with the passing away of perceptions of sensory impingement, with non-attention to perceptions of diversity, [perceiving] 'space is infinite,' a bhikkhu enters and dwells in the base of the infinity of space. When one is thus percipient one does not experience that base.

(7) "Again, friend, by completely surmounting the base of the infinity of space, [perceiving] 'consciousness is infinite,' a bhikkhu enters and dwells in the base of the infinity of consciousness. When one is thus percipient one does not experience that base.

(8) "Again, friend, by completely surmounting the base of the infinity of consciousness, [perceiving] 'there is nothing,' a bhikkhu enters and dwells in the base of nothingness. When one is thus percipient one does not experience that base.[1925]

"Once, friend, I was dwelling at Sāketa in the deer park at Añjana Grove. Then the bhikkhunī Jaṭilagāhiyā[1926] [428] approached me, paid homage to me, stood to one side, and said: 'Bhante Ānanda, the concentration that does not lean forward and does not bend back,[1927] and that is not reined in and checked by forcefully suppressing [the defilements][1928]—by being liberated, it is steady; by being steady, it is content; by being content, one is not agitated.[1929] Bhante Ānanda, what did the Blessed One say this concentration has as its fruit?'[1930]

(9) "When she asked me this, I replied: 'Sister, the concentration that does not lean forward and does not bend back, and that is not reined in and checked by forcefully suppressing [the defilements]—by being liberated, it is steady; by being steady, it is content; by being content, one is not agitated. The Blessed One said this concentration has final knowledge as its fruit.'[1931] When one is thus percipient too, friend, one does not experience that base."

38 (7) The Brahmins

Then two brahmin cosmologists[1932] approached the Blessed One and exchanged greetings with him. When they had concluded their greetings and cordial talk, they sat down to one side and said to him:

"Master Gotama, Pūraṇa Kassapa claims to be all-knowing and all-seeing and to have all-embracing knowledge and vision: 'Whether I am walking, standing, sleeping, or awake, knowledge and vision are constantly and continuously present to me.' He says thus: 'With infinite knowledge, I dwell knowing and seeing the world to be infinite.' [429] But Nigaṇṭha Nātaputta also claims to be all-knowing and all-seeing and to have all-embracing knowledge and vision: 'Whether I am walking, standing, sleeping, and awake, knowledge and vision are constantly and continuously present to me.' He says thus: 'With infinite knowledge, I dwell knowing and seeing the world to be finite.'[1933] When these two claimants to knowledge make claims that are mutually contradictory, who speaks truthfully and who falsely?"

"Enough, brahmins, let this be: 'When these two claimants to knowledge make claims that are mutually contradictory, who speaks truthfully and who falsely?' I will teach you the Dhamma. Listen and attend closely. I will speak."

"Yes, sir," those brahmins replied. The Blessed One said this:

"Suppose, brahmins, there were four men standing in the four quarters possessing supreme movement[1934] and speed and a supreme stride. Their speed was like that of a light arrow easily shot by a firm-bowed archer—one trained, skillful, and experienced[1935]—across the shadow of a palmyra tree. Their stride was such that it could reach from the eastern ocean to the western ocean. Then the person standing in the eastern quarter would say thus: 'I will reach the end of the world by traveling.' Having a life span of a hundred years, living for a hundred years, he might travel for a hundred years without pausing except to eat, drink, chew, and taste, to defecate and urinate, and to dispel fatigue with sleep; yet he would die along the way without having reached the end of the world.[1936] [430] Then the person standing in the western quarter would say thus . . . the person standing in the northern quarter would say thus . . . the person standing in the southern quarter would say thus: 'I will reach the end of the world by traveling.' Having a life span of a hundred years, living for a hundred years, he might travel for a hundred years without pausing except to eat, drink, chew, and taste, to defecate and urinate, and to dispel fatigue with sleep; yet he would die along the way without having reached the end of the world. For what reason? I say, brahmins, that by this kind of running[1937] one cannot know, see, or reach the end of the world. And yet I say that without having reached the end of the world there is no making an end of suffering.

"These five objects of sensual pleasure, brahmins, are called 'the world' in the Noble One's discipline. What five? Forms cognizable by the eye that are wished for, desired, agreeable, pleasing, connected with sensual pleasure, tantalizing; sounds cognizable by the ear . . . odors cognizable by the nose . . . tastes cognizable by the tongue . . . tactile objects cognizable by the body that are wished for, desired, agreeable, pleasing, connected with sensual pleasure, tantalizing. These five objects of sensual pleasure are called 'the world' in the Noble One's discipline.

(1) "Here, brahmins, secluded from sensual pleasures . . . a bhikkhu enters and dwells in the first jhāna. . . . This is called a bhikkhu who, having come to the end of the world, dwells at the end of the world. Others say thus of him: 'He, too, is included in the world; he, too, is not yet released from the world.' I also say thus: 'He, too, is included in the world; he, too, is not yet released from the world.' [431]

(2)–(4) "Again, with the subsiding of thought and examination, a bhikkhu enters and dwells in the second jhāna . . . the third jhāna . . . the fourth jhāna. . . . This is called a bhikkhu who, having come to the end of the world, dwells at the end of the world. Others say thus of him: 'He, too, is included in the world; he, too, is not yet released from the world.' I also say thus: 'He, too, is included in the world; he, too, is not yet released from the world.'

(5) "Again, with the complete surmounting of perceptions of forms, with the passing away of perceptions of sensory impingement, with non-attention to perceptions of diversity, [perceiving] 'space is infinite,' a bhikkhu enters and dwells in the base of the infinity of space. This is called a bhikkhu who, having come to the end of the world, dwells at the end of the world. Others say thus of him: 'He, too, is included in the world; he, too, is not yet released from the world.' I also say thus: 'He,

too, is included in the world; he, too, is not yet released from the world.'

(6)–(8) "Again, by completely surmounting the base of the infinity of space, [perceiving] 'consciousness is infinite,' a bhikkhu enters and dwells in the base of the infinity of consciousness.... By completely surmounting the base of the infinity of consciousness, [perceiving] 'there is nothing,' a bhikkhu enters and dwells in the base of nothingness.... By completely surmounting the base of nothingness, a bhikkhu enters and dwells in the base of neither-perception-nor-non-perception. This is called a bhikkhu who, having come to the end of the world, dwells at the end of the world. Others say thus of him: 'He, too, is included in the world; he, too, is not yet released from the world.' I also say thus: 'He, too, is included in the world; he, too, is not yet released from the world.'

(9) "Again, by completely surmounting the base of neither-perception-nor-non-perception, a bhikkhu enters and dwells in the cessation of perception and feeling, and having seen with wisdom, his taints are utterly destroyed. This is called a bhikkhu [432] who, having come to the end of the world, dwells at the end of the world, one who has crossed over attachment to the world."

39 (8) The Devas

"Bhikkhus, in the past a battle was fought between the devas and the asuras. In that battle, the asuras were victorious and the devas were defeated. Defeated, the devas fled north, pursued by the asuras. Then it occurred to the devas: 'The asuras are still pursuing us. Let's engage them in battle a second time.' A second time the devas fought a battle with the asuras, and a second time the asuras were victorious and the devas were defeated. Defeated, the devas[1938] fled north, pursued by the asuras. Then it occurred to the devas: 'The asuras are still pursuing us. Let's engage them in battle a third time.' A third time the devas fought a battle with the asuras, and a third time the asuras were victorious and the devas were defeated. Defeated and frightened, the devas entered their city.

"After the devas had entered their city, it occurred to them: 'Now we're [433] secure from danger and the asuras cannot do anything to us.' It also occurred to the asuras: 'Now the devas are secure from danger and we cannot do anything to them.'

"In the past, bhikkhus, a battle was fought between the devas and the asuras. In that battle, the devas were victorious and the asuras were defeated. Defeated, the asuras fled south, pursued by the devas. Then it occurred to the asuras: 'The devas are still pursuing us. Let's engage them in battle a second time.' A second time the asuras fought a battle with the devas, and a second time the devas were victorious and the asuras were defeated. Defeated, the asuras fled south, pursued by the devas. Then it occurred to the asuras: 'The devas are still pursuing us. Let's engage them in battle a third time.' A third time the asuras fought a battle with the devas, and a third time the devas were victorious and the asuras were defeated. Defeated and frightened, the asuras entered their city.

"After the asuras had entered their city, it occurred to them: 'Now we're secure from danger and the devas cannot do anything to us.' It also occurred to the devas: 'Now the asuras are secure from danger and we cannot do anything to them.'

(1) "So too, bhikkhus, when, secluded from sensual pleasures . . . a bhikkhu enters and dwells in the first jhāna . . . on that occasion it occurs to the bhikkhu: 'Now I am secure from danger [434] and Māra cannot do anything to me.' It also occurs to Māra the Evil One: 'Now the bhikkhu is secure against danger and I cannot do anything to him.'

(2)–(4) "When, with the subsiding of thought and examination, a bhikkhu enters and dwells in the second jhāna . . . the third jhāna . . . the fourth jhāna . . . on that occasion it occurs to the bhikkhu: 'Now I am secure from danger and Māra cannot do anything to me.' It also occurs to Māra the Evil One: 'Now the bhikkhu is secure from danger and I cannot do anything to him.'

(5) "When, with the complete surmounting of perceptions of forms, with the passing away of perceptions of sensory impingement, with non-attention to perceptions of diversity, [perceiving] 'space is infinite,' a bhikkhu enters and dwells in the base of the infinity of space, on that occasion he is called a bhikkhu who has blinded Māra,[1939] put out Māra's eyes without a trace,[1940] and gone beyond sight of the Evil One.

(6)–(9) "When, bhikkhus, by completely surmounting the

base of the infinity of space, [perceiving] 'consciousness is infinite,' a bhikkhu enters and dwells in the base of the infinity of consciousness. . . . When, by completely surmounting the base of the infinity of consciousness, [perceiving] 'there is nothing,' a bhikkhu enters and dwells in the base of nothingness. . . . When, by completely surmounting the base of nothingness, a bhikkhu enters and dwells in the base of neither-perception-nor-non-perception. . . . When, by completely surmounting the base of neither-perception-nor-non-perception, a bhikkhu enters and dwells in the cessation of perception and feeling, and having seen with wisdom, his taints are utterly destroyed, on that occasion he is called a bhikkhu who has blinded Māra, put out Māra's eyes, gone beyond sight of the Evil One, and crossed over attachment to the world." [435]

40 (9) A Bull Elephant

"Bhikkhus, when a forest-dwelling bull elephant is heading for its feeding ground, and other elephants—males, females, young ones,[1941] and babies—precede him and break the tops of the grass, the bull elephant is repelled, humiliated, and disgusted with this. When a forest-dwelling bull elephant is heading for its feeding ground, and other elephants—males, females, young ones, and babies—eat the bent and twisted bundle of branches, the bull elephant is repelled, humiliated, and disgusted with this. When a forest-dwelling bull elephant has entered the pool and other elephants—males, females, young ones, and babies—precede him and stir up the water with their trunks, the bull elephant is repelled, humiliated, and disgusted with this. When a forest-dwelling bull elephant has emerged from the pool and female elephants go by brushing against his body, the forest-dwelling bull elephant is repelled, humiliated, and disgusted with this.

"On that occasion it occurs to the forest-dwelling bull elephant: 'I am presently dwelling hemmed in by other elephants: males, females, young ones, and babies. I eat grass with the tops broken off, and they eat my bent and twisted bundle of branches. I drink muddy water, and when I have come out from the pool, the female elephants go by brushing against my body. Let me dwell alone, withdrawn from the herd.'

"Some time later he dwells alone, withdrawn from the herd. He then eats grass without the tops broken off; they do not eat his bent and twisted [436] bundle of branches; he drinks clear water; and when he has come out from the pool, the female elephants do not go by brushing against his body. On that occasion it occurs to the forest-dwelling bull elephant: 'In the past I dwelled hemmed in by other elephants . . . and when I came out from the pool, the female elephants went by brushing against my body. But now I dwell alone, withdrawn from the herd. I eat grass without the tops broken off; they do not eat my bent and twisted bundle of branches; I drink clear water; and when I have come out from the pool, the female elephants do not go by brushing against my body.' Having broken off a bundle of branches with his trunk, having rubbed his body with it, he happily relieves his itches.

"So too, bhikkhus, when a bhikkhu dwells hemmed in by bhikkhus, bhikkhunīs, male and female lay followers, kings and royal ministers, sectarian teachers and the disciples of sectarian teachers, on that occasion it occurs to him: 'I am presently dwelling hemmed in by bhikkhus, bhikkhunīs, male and female lay followers, kings and royal ministers, sectarian teachers and the disciples of sectarian teachers. Let me dwell alone, withdrawn from company.'

"He resorts to a secluded lodging: the forest, [437] the foot of a tree, a mountain, a ravine, a hillside cave, a charnel ground, a jungle thicket, an open space, a heap of straw. Gone to the forest, to the foot of a tree, or to an empty hut, he sits down, folding his legs crosswise, straightening his body, and establishing mindfulness before him. Having abandoned longing for the world, he dwells with a mind free from longing; he purifies his mind from longing. Having abandoned ill will and hatred, he dwells with a mind free from ill will, compassionate for the welfare of all living beings; he purifies his mind from ill will and hatred. Having abandoned dullness and drowsiness, he dwells free from dullness and drowsiness, percipient of light, mindful and clearly comprehending; he purifies his mind from dullness and drowsiness. Having abandoned restlessness and remorse, he dwells without agitation, with a mind inwardly peaceful; he purifies his mind from restlessness and remorse. Having abandoned doubt, he dwells having gone beyond doubt, unperplexed about wholesome qualities; he purifies his mind from doubt.

(1) "Having thus abandoned these five hindrances, defilements of the mind, things that weaken wisdom, secluded from sensual pleasures, secluded from unwholesome states, he enters and dwells in the first jhāna. . . . Elated, he relieves his itches.

(2)–(4) "With the subsiding of thought and examination, he enters and dwells in the second jhāna . . . the third jhāna . . . the fourth jhāna. . . . Elated, he relieves his itches.

(5) "With the complete surmounting of perceptions of forms, with the passing away of perceptions of sensory impingement, with non-attention to perceptions of diversity, [perceiving] 'space is infinite,' a bhikkhu enters and dwells in the base of the infinity of space. Elated, he relieves his itches.

(6)–(9) "By completely surmounting the base of the infinity of space, [perceiving] 'consciousness is infinite,' a bhikkhu enters and dwells in the base of the infinity of consciousness. . . . By completely surmounting the base of the infinity of consciousness, [perceiving] 'there is nothing,' a bhikkhu enters and dwells in the base of nothingness. . . . By completely surmounting the base of nothingness, a bhikkhu enters and dwells in the base of neither-perception-nor-non-perception. . . . By completely surmounting the base of neither-perception-nor-non-perception, [438] a bhikkhu enters and dwells in the cessation of perception and feeling, and having seen with wisdom, his taints are utterly destroyed. Elated, he relieves his itches."

41 (10) Tapussa

Thus have I heard. On one occasion the Blessed One was dwelling among the Mallas near the Mallan town named Uruvelakappa.[1942] Then, in the morning, the Blessed One dressed, took his bowl and robe, and entered Uruvelakappa for alms. When he had walked for alms in Uruvelakappa, after his meal, on returning from his alms round, he addressed the Venerable Ānanda: "You stay right here, Ānanda, while I enter the Great Wood to pass the day."

"Yes, Bhante," the Venerable Ānanda replied. Then the Blessed One entered the Great Wood and sat down to pass the day at the foot of a tree.

Then the householder Tapussa approached the Venerable Ānanda, paid homage to him, sat down to one side, and said to him:

"Bhante Ānanda, we laymen enjoy sensual pleasures, delight in sensual pleasures, take delight in sensual pleasures, and rejoice in sensual pleasures. Renunciation seems like a precipice to us. I have heard that in this Dhamma and discipline there are very young bhikkhus, whose minds launch out upon renunciation and become placid, settled, and liberated in it,[1943] seeing[1944] it as peaceful. Renunciation, Bhante, is the dividing line between the multitude and the bhikkhus in this Dhamma and discipline."[1945] [439]

"This, householder, is a subject that we should see the Blessed One about. Come, let's go to the Blessed One and report this matter to him. We should retain the Blessed One's explanation in mind."

"Yes, Bhante," the householder Tapussa replied.

Then the Venerable Ānanda, together with the householder Tapussa, went to the Blessed One, paid homage to him, sat down to one side, and said: "Bhante, this householder Tapussa says: 'Bhante Ānanda, we laymen enjoy sensual pleasures . . . [and] renunciation seems like a precipice to us. . . . [But] there are very young bhikkhus whose minds . . . [are] liberated in it, seeing it as peaceful. Renunciation, Bhante, is the dividing line between the multitude and the bhikkhus in this Dhamma and discipline.'"

"So it is, Ānanda! So it is, Ānanda![1946]

(1) "Before my enlightenment, while I was just a bodhisatta, not yet fully enlightened, it occurred to me too: 'Good is renunciation, good is solitude.' Yet my mind did not launch out upon renunciation and become placid, settled, and liberated in it, though I saw it as peaceful. It occurred to me: 'Why is it that my mind does not launch out upon renunciation and become placid, settled, and liberated in it, though I see it as peaceful?' Then it occurred to me: 'I have not seen the danger in sensual pleasures and have not cultivated that [insight]; I have not achieved the benefit in renunciation and have not [440] pursued it. Therefore my mind does not launch out upon renunciation and become placid, settled, and liberated in it, though I see it as peaceful.'

"Then, Ānanda, it occurred to me: 'If, having seen the danger in sensual pleasures, I would cultivate that [insight], and if, having achieved the benefit in renunciation, I would pursue it, it is then possible that my mind would launch out upon renunciation and become placid, settled, and liberated in it, since I see it as peaceful.' Sometime later, having seen the danger in sensual pleasures, I cultivated that [insight], and having achieved the benefit in renunciation, I pursued it. My mind then launched out upon renunciation and became placid, settled, and liberated in it, since I saw it as peaceful.

"Sometime later, Ānanda, secluded from sensual pleasures . . . I entered and dwelled in the first jhāna. While I was dwelling in this state, perception and attention accompanied by sensuality occurred in me and I felt it as an affliction. Just as pain might arise for one feeling pleasure only to afflict him, so too, when perception and attention accompanied by sensuality occurred in me, I felt it as an affliction.

(2) "Then, Ānanda, it occurred to me: 'With the subsiding of thought and examination, let me enter and dwell in the second jhāna. . . .' Yet my mind did not launch out upon the absence of thought and become placid, settled, and liberated in it, though I saw it as peaceful. It occurred to me: 'Why is it that my mind does not launch out upon the absence of thought and become placid, settled, and liberated in it, though I see it as peaceful?' Then it occurred to me: 'I have not seen the danger in thoughts and have not cultivated that [insight]; I have not achieved the benefit in the absence of thought [441] and have not pursued it. Therefore my mind does not launch out upon the absence of thought and become placid, settled, and liberated in it, though I see it as peaceful.'

"Then, Ānanda, it occurred to me: 'If, having seen the danger in thoughts, I would cultivate that [insight], and if, having achieved the benefit in the absence of thought, I would pursue it, it is then possible that my mind would launch out upon the absence of thought and become placid, settled, and liberated in it, since I see it as peaceful.' Then, sometime later, having seen the danger in thoughts, I cultivated that [insight], and having achieved the benefit in the absence of thought, I pursued it. My mind then launched out upon the absence of thought and became placid, settled, and liberated in it, since I saw it as peaceful.

"Sometime later,[1947] Ānanda, with the subsiding of thought and examination . . . I entered and dwelled in the second jhāna. . . . While I was dwelling in this state, perception and attention accompanied by thought occurred in me and I felt it as an affliction. Just as pain might arise for one feeling pleasure only to afflict him, so too when that perception and attention accompanied by thought occurred in me, I felt it as an affliction.

(3) "Then, Ānanda, it occurred to me: 'With the fading away as well of rapture . . . let me enter and dwell in the third jhāna. . . .' Yet my mind did not launch out upon the absence of rapture and become placid, settled, and liberated in it, though I saw it as peaceful. It occurred to me: 'Why is it that my mind does not launch out upon the absence of rapture and become placid, settled, [442] and liberated in it, though I see it as peaceful?' Then it occurred to me: 'I have not seen the danger in rapture and have not cultivated that [insight]; I have not achieved the benefit in the absence of rapture and have not pursued it. Therefore my mind does not launch out upon the absence of rapture and become placid, settled, and liberated in it, though I see it as peaceful.'

"Then, Ānanda, it occurred to me: 'If, having seen the danger in rapture, I would cultivate that [insight], and if, having achieved the benefit in the absence of rapture, I would pursue it, it is then possible that my mind would launch out upon the absence of rapture and become placid, settled, and liberated in it, since I see it as peaceful.' Then, sometime later, having seen the danger in rapture, I cultivated that [insight], and having achieved the benefit in the absence of rapture, I pursued it. My mind then launched out upon the absence of rapture and became placid, settled, and liberated in it, since I saw it as peaceful.

"Sometime later, Ānanda, with the fading away as well of rapture . . . I entered and dwelled in the third jhāna. . . . While I was dwelling in this state, perception and attention accompanied by rapture occurred in me and I felt it as an affliction. Just as pain might arise for one feeling pleasure only to afflict him, so too, when that perception and attention accompanied by rapture occurred in me, I felt it as an affliction.

(4) "Then, Ānanda, it occurred to me: 'With the abandoning of pleasure and pain . . . let me enter and dwell in the fourth jhāna. . . .' Yet my mind did not launch out upon the absence of pleasure and pain and become placid, settled, and liberated in it, though I saw it as peaceful. It occurred to me: 'Why is it that

my mind does not launch out upon the absence of pleasure and pain and become placid, settled, and liberated in it, though I see it as peaceful?' Then it occurred to me: 'I have not seen the danger in the pleasure [connected with] equanimity and have not cultivated that [insight]; I have not achieved the benefit in the absence of pleasure and pain and have not pursued it. Therefore my mind does not launch out upon the absence of pleasure and pain and become placid, settled, and liberated in it, though I see it as peaceful.'

"Then, Ānanda, it occurred to me: 'If, having seen the danger in the pleasure [connected with] equanimity, [443] I would cultivate that [insight], and if, having achieved the benefit in the absence of pleasure and pain, I would pursue it, it is then possible that my mind would launch out upon the absence of pleasure and pain and become placid, settled, and liberated in it, since I see it as peaceful.' Then, sometime later, having seen the danger in the pleasure [connected with] equanimity, I cultivated that [insight], and having achieved the benefit in the absence of pleasure and pain, I pursued it. My mind then launched out upon the absence of pleasure and pain and became placid, settled, and liberated in it, since I saw it as peaceful.

"Sometime later, Ānanda, with the abandoning of pleasure and pain . . . I entered and dwelled in the fourth jhāna. . . . While I was dwelling in this state, perception and attention accompanied by pleasure [connected with] equanimity occurred in me[1948] and I felt it as an affliction. Just as pain might arise for one feeling pleasure only to afflict him, so too, when that perception and attention accompanied by pleasure [connected with] equanimity occurred in me, I felt it as an affliction.

(5) "Then, Ānanda, it occurred to me: 'With the complete surmounting of perceptions of forms, with the passing away of perceptions of sensory impingement, with non-attention to perceptions of diversity, [perceiving] "space is infinite," let me enter and dwell in the base of the infinity of space.' Yet my mind did not launch out upon the base of the infinity of space and become placid, settled, and liberated in it, though I saw it as peaceful. It occurred to me: 'Why is it that my mind does not launch out upon the base of the infinity of space and become placid, settled, and liberated in it, though I see it as peaceful?' Then it occurred to me: 'I have not seen the danger in forms

and have not cultivated that [insight]; I have not achieved the benefit in the base of the infinity of space and have not pursued it. Therefore my mind does not launch out upon the base of the infinity of space and become placid, settled, and liberated in it, [444] though I see it as peaceful.'

"Then, Ānanda, it occurred to me: 'If, having seen the danger in forms, I would cultivate that [insight], and if, having achieved the benefit in the base of the infinity of space, I would pursue it, it is then possible that my mind would launch out upon the base of the infinity of space and become placid, settled, and liberated in it, since I see it as peaceful.' Then, sometime later, having seen the danger in forms, I cultivated that [insight], and having achieved the benefit in the base of the infinity of space, I pursued it. My mind then launched out upon the base of the infinity of space and became placid, settled, and liberated in it, since I saw it as peaceful.

"Sometime later, Ānanda, with the complete surmounting of perceptions of forms, with the passing away of perceptions of sensory impingement, with non-attention to perceptions of diversity, [perceiving] 'space is infinite,' I entered and dwelled in the base of the infinity of space. While I was dwelling in this state, perception and attention accompanied by forms occurred in me and I felt it as an affliction. Just as pain might arise for one feeling pleasure only to afflict him, so too, when that perception and attention accompanied by forms occurred in me, I felt it as an affliction.

(6) "Then, Ānanda, it occurred to me: 'By completely surmounting the base of the infinity of space, [perceiving] "consciousness is infinite," let me enter and dwell in the base of the infinity of consciousness.' Yet my mind did not launch out upon the base of the infinity of consciousness and become placid, settled, and liberated in it, though I saw it as peaceful. It occurred to me: 'Why is it that my mind does not launch out upon the base of the infinity of consciousness and become placid, settled, and liberated in it, though I see it as peaceful?' Then it occurred to me: 'I have not seen the danger in the base of the infinity of space and have not cultivated that [insight]; I have not achieved the benefit in the base of the infinity of consciousness and have not pursued it. Therefore my mind does not launch out upon the base of the infinity of consciousness and become placid, settled, and liberated in it, though I see it as peaceful.'

"Then, Ānanda, it occurred to me: 'If, having seen the danger in the base of the infinity of space, [445] I would cultivate that [insight], and if, having achieved the benefit in the base of the infinity of consciousness, I would pursue it, it is then possible that my mind would launch out upon the base of the infinity of consciousness and become placid, settled, and liberated in it, since I see it as peaceful.' Then, sometime later, having seen the danger in the base of the infinity of space, I cultivated that [insight], and having achieved the benefit in the base of the infinity of consciousness, I pursued it. My mind then launched out upon the base of the infinity of consciousness and became placid, settled, and liberated in it, since I saw it as peaceful.

"Sometime later, Ānanda, by completely surmounting the base of the infinity of space, [perceiving] 'consciousness is infinite,' I entered and dwelled in the base of the infinity of consciousness. While I was dwelling in this state, perception and attention accompanied by the base of the infinity of space occurred in me and I felt it as an affliction. Just as pain might arise for one feeling pleasure only to afflict him, so too, when that perception and attention accompanied by the base of the infinity of space occurred in me, I felt it as an affliction.

(7) "Then, Ānanda, it occurred to me: 'By completely surmounting the base of the infinity of consciousness, [perceiving] "there is nothing," let me enter and dwell in the base of nothingness.' Yet my mind did not launch out upon the base of nothingness and become placid, settled, and liberated in it, though I saw it as peaceful. It occurred to me: 'Why is it that my mind does not launch out upon the base of nothingness and become placid, settled, and liberated in it, though I see it as peaceful?' Then it occurred to me: 'I have not seen the danger in the base of the infinity of consciousness and have not cultivated that [insight]; I have not achieved the benefit in the base of nothingness and have not pursued it. Therefore my mind does not launch out upon the base of nothingness and become placid, settled, and liberated in it, though I see it as peaceful.'

"Then, Ānanda, it occurred to me: 'If, having seen the danger in the base of the infinity of consciousness, I would cultivate that [insight], and if, having achieved the benefit in the base of nothingness, I would pursue it, it is then possible that my [446] mind would launch out upon the base of nothingness and become placid, settled, and liberated in it, since I see it as peaceful.' Then, sometime later, having seen the danger in the base of the infinity of consciousness, I cultivated that [insight], and having achieved the benefit in the base of nothingness, I pursued it. My mind then launched out upon the base of nothingness and became placid, settled, and liberated in it, since I saw it as peaceful.

"Sometime later, Ānanda, by completely surmounting the base of the infinity of consciousness, [perceiving] 'there is nothing,' I entered and dwelled in the base of nothingness. While I was dwelling in this state, perception and attention accompanied by the base of the infinity of consciousness occurred in me and I felt it as an affliction. Just as pain might arise for one feeling pleasure only to afflict him, so too, when that perception and attention accompanied by the base of the infinity of consciousness occurred in me, I felt it as an affliction.

(8) "Then, Ānanda, it occurred to me: 'By completely surmounting the base of nothingness, let me enter and dwell in the base of neither-perception-nor-non-perception.' Yet my mind did not launch out upon the base of neither-perception-nor-non-perception and become placid, settled, and liberated in it, though I saw it as peaceful. It occurred to me: 'Why is it that my mind does not launch out upon the base of neither-perception-nor-non-perception and become placid, settled, and liberated in it, though I see it as peaceful?' Then it occurred to me: 'I have not seen the danger in the base of nothingness and have not cultivated that [insight]; I have not achieved the benefit in the base of neither-perception-nor-non-perception and have not pursued it. Therefore my mind does not launch out upon the base of neither-perception-nor-non-perception and become placid, settled, and liberated in it, though I see it as peaceful.'

"Then, Ānanda, it occurred to me: 'If, having seen the danger in the base of nothingness, I would cultivate that [insight], and if, having achieved the benefit in the base of neither-perception-nor-non-perception, I would pursue it, it is then possible that my mind would launch out upon the base of neither-perception-nor-non-perception and become placid, settled, and liberated in it, since I see it as peaceful.' [447] Then, sometime later, having seen the danger in the base of nothingness, I cultivated that [insight], and having achieved the benefit in the base of neither-perception-nor-non-perception, I pursued it. My mind then launched out upon the base of neither-perception-nor-non-perception and became placid, settled, and liberated in it, since I saw it as peaceful.

"Sometime later, Ānanda, by completely surmounting the base of nothingness, I entered and dwelled in the base of neither-perception-nor-non-perception. While I was dwelling in this state, perception and attention accompanied by the base of nothingness occurred in me and I felt it as an affliction. Just as pain might arise for one feeling pleasure only to afflict him, so too, when that perception and attention accompanied by the base of nothingness occurred in me, I felt it as an affliction.

(9) "Then, Ānanda, it occurred to me: 'By completely surmounting the base of neither-perception-nor-non-perception, let me enter and dwell in the cessation of perception and feeling.' Yet my mind did not launch out upon the cessation of perception and feeling and become placid, settled, and liberated in it, though I saw it as peaceful. It occurred to me: 'Why is it that my mind does not launch out upon the cessation of perception and feeling and become placid, settled, and liberated in it, though I see it as peaceful?' Then it occurred to me: 'I have not seen the danger in the base of neither-perception-nor-non-perception and have not cultivated that [insight]; I have not achieved the benefit in the cessation of perception and feeling and have not pursued it. Therefore my mind does not launch out upon the cessation of perception and feeling and become placid, settled, and liberated in it, though I see it as peaceful.'

"Then, Ānanda, it occurred to me: 'If, having seen the danger in the base of neither-perception-nor-non-perception, I would cultivate that [insight], and if, having achieved the benefit in the cessation of perception and feeling, I would pursue it, it is then possible that my mind would launch out upon the cessation of perception and feeling and become placid, settled, and liberated in it, since I see it as peaceful.' Then, sometime later, having seen the danger in the base of neither-perception-nor-non-perception, I cultivated that [insight]; [448] and having achieved the benefit in the cessation of perception and feeling, I pursued it. My mind then launched out upon the cessation of perception and feeling and became placid, settled, and liberated in it, since I saw it as peaceful.

"Sometime later, Ānanda, by completely surmounting the

base of neither-perception-nor-non-perception, I entered and dwelled in the cessation of perception and feeling, and having seen with wisdom, my taints were utterly destroyed.

"So long, Ānanda, as I did not attain and emerge from these nine attainments of progressive dwellings in direct order and reverse order, I did not claim to have awakened to the unsurpassed perfect enlightenment in this world with its devas, Māra, and Brahmā, in this population with its ascetics and brahmins, its devas and humans. But when I attained and emerged from these nine attainments of progressive dwellings in direct order and reverse order, then I claimed to have awakened to the unsurpassed perfect enlightenment in this world with . . . its devas and humans. The knowledge and vision arose in me: 'Unshakable is my liberation of mind; this is my last birth; now there is no more renewed existence.'" [449]

V. Similarity[1949]

42 (1) Confinement

Thus have I heard. On one occasion the Venerable Ānanda was dwelling at Kosambī in Ghosita's Park. Then the Venerable Udāyī approached the Venerable Ānanda and exchanged greetings with him. When they had concluded their greetings and cordial talk, he sat down to one side and said to the Venerable Ānanda:

"This was said, friend, by the young deva Pañcālacaṇḍa:

"'The sage, the withdrawn chief bull,
the Buddha who awakened to jhāna,
the One of Broad Wisdom has found
the opening amid confinement.'[1950]

"What, friend, has the Blessed One spoken of as confinement and what as the achievement of an opening in the midst of confinement?"[1951]

"The Blessed One, friend, has spoken of these five objects of sensual pleasure as confinement. What five? Forms cognizable by the eye that are wished for, desired, agreeable, pleasing, connected with sensual pleasure, tantalizing; sounds cognizable by the ear . . . odors cognizable by the nose . . . tastes cognizable by the tongue . . . tactile objects cognizable by the body that are wished for, desired, agreeable, pleasing, connected with sensual pleasure, tantalizing. The Blessed One has spoken of these five objects of sensual pleasure as confinement.

(1) "Here, friend, secluded from sensual pleasures . . . a bhikkhu enters and dwells in the first jhāna. . . . To this extent the Blessed One has spoken of the achievement of an opening amid confinement in a provisional sense.[1952] There, too, there is confinement. And what is the confinement there? [450] Whatever thought and examination have not ceased there is the confinement in this case.

(2) "Again, friend, with the subsiding of thought and examination, a bhikkhu enters and dwells in the second jhāna. . . . To this extent, too, the Blessed One has spoken of the achievement of an opening amid confinement in a provisional sense. There, too, there is confinement. And what is the confinement there? Whatever rapture has not ceased there is the confinement in this case.

(3) "Again, friend, with the fading away of rapture, a bhikkhu enters and dwells in the third jhāna. . . . To this extent, too, the Blessed One has spoken of the achievement of an opening amid confinement in a provisional sense. There, too, there is confinement. And what is the confinement there? Whatever pleasure [connected with] equanimity has not ceased there is the confinement in this case.

(4) "Again, friend, with the abandoning of pleasure and pain . . . a bhikkhu enters and dwells in the fourth jhāna. . . . To this extent, too, the Blessed One has spoken of the achievement of an opening amid confinement in a provisional sense. There, too, there is confinement. And what is the confinement there? Whatever perception of form[1953] has not ceased there is the confinement in this case.

(5) "Again, friend, with the complete surmounting of perceptions of forms, with the passing away of perceptions of sensory impingement, with non-attention to perceptions of diversity, [perceiving] 'space is infinite,' a bhikkhu enters and dwells in the base of the infinity of space. To this extent, too, the Blessed One has spoken of the achievement of an opening amid confinement in a provisional sense. There, too, there is confinement. And what is the confinement there? Whatever perception

of the base of the infinity of space has not ceased there is the confinement in this case.

(6) "Again, friend, by completely surmounting the base of the infinity of space, [perceiving] 'consciousness is infinite,' a bhikkhu [451] enters and dwells in the base of the infinity of consciousness. To this extent, too, the Blessed One has spoken of the achievement of an opening amid confinement in a provisional sense. There, too, there is confinement. And what is the confinement there? Whatever perception of the base of the infinity of consciousness has not ceased there is the confinement in this case.

(7) "Again, friend, by completely surmounting the base of the infinity of consciousness, [perceiving] 'there is nothing,' a bhikkhu enters and dwells in the base of nothingness. To this extent, too, the Blessed One has spoken of the achievement of an opening amid confinement in a provisional sense. There, too, there is confinement. And what is the confinement there? Whatever perception of the base of nothingness has not ceased there is the confinement in this case.

(8) "Again, friend, by completely surmounting the base of nothingness, a bhikkhu enters and dwells in the base of neither-perception-nor-non-perception. To this extent, too, the Blessed One has spoken of the achievement of an opening amid confinement in a provisional sense. There, too, there is confinement. And what is the confinement there? Whatever perception of the base of neither-perception-nor-non-perception has not ceased there is the confinement in this case.

(9) "Again, by completely surmounting the base of neither-perception-nor-non-perception, a bhikkhu enters and dwells in the cessation of perception and feeling, and having seen with wisdom, his taints are utterly destroyed. To this extent, friend, the Blessed One has spoken of the achievement of an opening amid confinement in a non-provisional sense."[1954]

43 (2) Body Witness

"It is said, friend, 'a body witness, a body witness.'[1955] In what way has the Blessed One spoken of a body witness?"

(1) "Here, friend, secluded from sensual pleasures . . . a bhikkhu enters and dwells in the first jhāna. . . . He dwells having contacted that base with the body in whatever way [it is

attained].[1956] To this extent the Blessed One has spoken of a body witness in a provisional sense. [452]

(2)–(4) "Again, friend, with the subsiding of thought and examination, a bhikkhu enters and dwells in the second jhāna . . . the third jhāna . . . the fourth jhāna. . . . He dwells having contacted that base with the body in whatever way [it is attained]. To this extent, too, the Blessed One has spoken of a body witness in a provisional sense.

(5)–(8) "Again, friend, with the complete surmounting of perceptions of forms, with the passing away of perceptions of sensory impingement, with non-attention to perceptions of diversity, aware that 'space is infinite,' a bhikkhu enters and dwells in the base of the infinity of space . . . the base of the infinity of consciousness . . . the base of nothingness . . . the base of neither-perception-nor-non-perception. He dwells having contacted that base with the body in whatever way [it is attained]. To this extent, too, the Blessed One has spoken of a body witness in a provisional sense.

(9) "Again, friend, by completely surmounting the base of neither-perception-nor-non-perception, he enters and dwells in the cessation of perception and feeling, and having seen with wisdom, his taints are utterly destroyed. He dwells having contacted that base with the body in whatever way [it is attained]. To this extent, friend, the Blessed One has spoken of a body witness in a non-provisional sense."[1957]

44 (3) Wisdom

"It is said, friend, 'liberated by wisdom, liberated by wisdom.' In what way has the Blessed One spoken of one liberated by wisdom?"[1958]

(1) "Here, friend, secluded from sensual pleasures . . . a bhikkhu enters and dwells in the first jhāna . . . and he understands it with wisdom. To this extent the Blessed One has spoken of one liberated by wisdom in a provisional sense.

(2)–(4) "Again, friend, with the subsiding of thought and examination, a bhikkhu enters and dwells in the second jhāna . . . the third jhāna . . . the fourth jhāna . . . and he understands it with wisdom. To this extent, too, the Blessed One has spoken of one liberated by wisdom in a provisional sense.

(5)–(8) "Again, friend, with the complete surmounting of

perceptions of forms, with the passing away of perceptions of sensory impingement, with non-attention to perceptions of diversity, [perceiving] 'space is infinite,' a bhikkhu enters and dwells in the base of the infinity of space . . . the base of the infinity of consciousness . . . the base of nothingness . . . the base of neither-perception-nor-non-perception; and he understands it with wisdom. To this extent, too, the Blessed One has spoken of one liberated by wisdom in a provisional sense. [453]

(9) "Again, friend, by completely surmounting the base of neither-perception-nor-non-perception, a bhikkhu enters and dwells in the cessation of perception and feeling, and having seen with wisdom, his taints are utterly destroyed; and he understands it with wisdom. To this extent, friend, the Blessed One has spoken of one liberated by wisdom in a non-provisional sense."

45 (4) Both Respects

"It is said, friend, 'liberated in both respects, liberated in both respects.' In what way has the Blessed One spoken of one liberated in both respects?"

(1) "Here, friend, secluded from sensual pleasures . . . a bhikkhu enters and dwells in the first jhāna. . . . He dwells having contacted that base with the body in whatever way [it is attained], and he understands it with wisdom. To this extent the Blessed One has spoken of one liberated in both respects in a provisional sense.

(2)–(4) "Again, friend, with the subsiding of thought and examination, a bhikkhu enters and dwells in the second jhāna . . . the third jhāna . . . the fourth jhāna. . . . He dwells having contacted that base with the body in whatever way [it is attained], and he understands it with wisdom. To this extent, too, the Blessed One has spoken of one liberated in both respects in a provisional sense.

(5)–(8) "Again, friend, with the complete surmounting of perceptions of forms, with the passing away of perceptions of sensory impingement, with non-attention to perceptions of diversity, [perceiving] 'space is infinite,' a bhikkhu enters and dwells in the base of the infinity of space . . . the base of the infinity of consciousness . . . the base of nothingness . . . the base of neither-perception-nor-non-perception. He dwells having contacted that base with the body in whatever way [it is attained], and he understands it with wisdom. To this extent, too, the Blessed One has spoken of one liberated in both respects in a provisional sense.

(9) "Again, friend, by completely surmounting the base of neither-perception-nor-non-perception, a bhikkhu enters and dwells in the cessation of perception and feeling, and having seen with wisdom, his taints are utterly destroyed. He dwells having contacted that base with the body in whatever way [it is attained], and he understands it with wisdom. To this extent, friend, the Blessed One has spoken of one liberated in both respects in a non-provisional sense."

46 (5) Directly Visible (1)

"It is said, friend, 'the directly visible Dhamma, the directly visible Dhamma.' In what way has the Blessed One spoken of the directly visible Dhamma?"

(1)–(8) "Here, friend, secluded from sensual pleasures . . . a bhikkhu enters and dwells in the first jhāna. . . . To this extent, too, the Blessed One has spoken of the directly visible Dhamma in a provisional sense. . . .

(9) "Again, friend, by completely surmounting the base of neither-perception-nor-non-perception, a bhikkhu enters and dwells in the cessation of perception and feeling, and having seen with wisdom, his taints are utterly destroyed. To this extent, friend, the Blessed One has spoken of the directly visible Dhamma in a non-provisional sense."

47 (6) Directly Visible (2)

"It is said, friend, 'directly visible nibbāna, directly visible nibbāna.' In what way has the Blessed One spoken of directly visible nibbāna?"

(1)–(8) "Here, friend, secluded from sensual pleasures . . . a bhikkhu enters and dwells in the first jhāna. . . . To this extent, too, the Blessed One has spoken of directly visible nibbāna in a provisional sense. . . .

(9) "Again, friend, by completely surmounting the base of neither-perception-nor-non-perception, a bhikkhu enters and dwells in the cessation of perception and feeling, and having seen with wisdom, his taints are utterly destroyed. To this extent, friend, the Blessed One has spoken of directly visible nibbāna in a non-provisional sense." [454]

48 (7) Nibbāna

"It is said, friend, 'nibbāna, nibbāna.'..."

[To be elaborated as in 9:47.]

49 (8) Final Nibbāna

"It is said, friend, 'final nibbāna, final nibbāna.'..."

[To be elaborated as in 9:47.]

50 (9) That Particular Respect

"It is said, friend, 'nibbāna in a particular respect, nibbāna in a particular respect.'..."

[To be elaborated as in 9:47.]

51 (10) In This Very Life

"It is said, friend, 'nibbāna in this very life, nibbāna in this very life.' In what way, friend, has the Blessed One spoken of nibbāna in this very life?"

(1)–(8) "Here, friend, secluded from sensual pleasures... a bhikkhu enters and dwells in the first jhāna.... To this extent, too, the Blessed One has spoken of nibbāna in this very life in a provisional sense....

(9) "Again, friend, by completely surmounting the base of neither-perception-nor-non-perception, a bhikkhu enters and dwells in the cessation of perception and feeling, and having seen with wisdom, his taints are utterly destroyed. To this extent, friend, the Blessed One has spoken of nibbāna in this very life in a non-provisional sense." [455]

The Second Fifty

I. Security

52 (1) Security (1)

"It is said, friend, 'security, security.' In what way, friend, has the Blessed One spoken of security?"

(1)–(8) "Here, friend, secluded from sensual pleasures... a bhikkhu enters and dwells in the first jhāna.... To this extent, too, the Blessed One has spoken of security in a provisional sense...."

(9) "Again, friend, by completely surmounting the base of neither-perception-nor-non-perception, a bhikkhu enters and dwells in the cessation of perception and feeling, and having seen with wisdom, his taints are utterly destroyed. To this extent, friend, the Blessed One has spoken of security in a non-provisional sense."

53 (2) Security (2)

"It is said, friend, 'one who has attained security, one who has attained security.'..."

[To be elaborated as in 9:52.]

54 (3) The Deathless (1)

"It is said, friend, 'the deathless, the deathless.'..."

[To be elaborated as in 9:52.]

55 (4) The Deathless (2)

"It is said, friend, 'one who has attained the deathless, one who has attained the deathless.'..."

[To be elaborated as in 9:52.]

56 (5) The Fearless (1)

"It is said, friend, 'the fearless, the fearless.'..."

[To be elaborated as in 9:52.]

57 (6) The Fearless (2)

"It is said, friend, 'one who has attained the fearless, one who has attained the fearless.'..."

[To be elaborated as in 9:52.]

58 (7) Tranquility (1)

"It is said, friend, 'tranquility, tranquility.'..."

[To be elaborated as in 9:52.] [456]

59 (8) Tranquility (2)

"It is said, friend, 'progressive tranquility, progressive tranquility.'..."

[To be elaborated as in 9:52.]

60 (9) Cessation

"It is said, friend, 'cessation, cessation.'..."

[To be elaborated as in 9:52.]

61 (10) Progressive Cessation

"It is said, friend, 'progressive cessation, progressive cessation.' In what way, friend, has the Blessed One spoken of progressive cessation?"

(1)–(8) "Here, friend, secluded from sensual pleasures... a bhikkhu enters and dwells in the first jhāna.... To this extent, too, the Blessed One has spoken of progressive cessation in a provisional sense....

(9) "Again, friend, by completely surmounting the base of neither-perception-nor-non-perception, a bhikkhu enters and dwells in the cessation of perception and feeling, and having seen with wisdom, his taints are utterly destroyed. To this extent, friend, the Blessed One has spoken of progressive cessation in a non-provisional sense."

62 (11) Possible and Impossible

"Bhikkhus, without having abandoned nine things, one is incapable of realizing arahantship. What nine? Lust, hatred, delusion, anger, hostility, denigration, insolence, envy, and miserliness. Without having abandoned these nine things, one is incapable of realizing arahantship.

"Bhikkhus, having abandoned nine things, one is capable of realizing arahantship. What nine? Lust, hatred, delusion, anger, hostility, denigration, insolence, envy, and miserliness. Having abandoned these nine things, one is capable of realizing arahantship." [457]

II. Establishments of Mindfulness

63 (1) The Training

"Bhikkhus, there are these five setbacks in the training.[1959] What five? (1) The destruction of life, (2) taking what is not given, (3) sexual misconduct, (4) false speech, and (5) [indulging in] liquor, wine, and intoxicants, the basis for heedlessness. These are the five setbacks in the training. The four establishments of mindfulness are to be developed for abandoning these five setbacks in the training. What four? Here, (6) a bhikkhu dwells contemplating the body in the body, ardent, clearly comprehending, mindful, having removed longing and dejection in regard to the world. (7) He dwells contemplating feelings in feelings . . . (8) . . . mind in mind . . . (9) . . . phenomena in phenomena, ardent, clearly comprehending, mindful, having removed longing and dejection in regard to the world. These four establishments of mindfulness are to be developed for abandoning these five setbacks in the training."

64 (2) Hindrances

"Bhikkhus, there are these five hindrances. What five? The hindrance of sensual desire, the hindrance of ill will, the hindrance of dullness [458] and drowsiness, the hindrance of restlessness and remorse, and the hindrance of doubt. These are the five hindrances. . . . These four establishments of mindfulness are to be developed for abandoning these five hindrances."

65 (3) Sensual Pleasure

"Bhikkhus, there are these five objects of sensual pleasure. What five? Forms cognizable by the eye that are wished for, desired, agreeable, pleasing, connected with sensual pleasure, tantalizing; sounds cognizable by the ear . . . odors cognizable by the nose . . . tastes cognizable by the tongue . . . tactile objects cognizable by the body that are wished for, desired, agreeable, pleasing, connected with sensual pleasure, tantalizing. These are the five objects of sensual pleasure. . . . These four establishments of mindfulness are to be developed for abandoning these five objects of sensual pleasure."

66 (4) Aggregates

"Bhikkhus, there are these five aggregates subject to clinging. What five? The form aggregate subject to clinging, the feeling aggregate subject to clinging, the perception aggregate subject to clinging, the volitional activities aggregate subject to clinging, and the consciousness aggregate subject to clinging. [459] These are the five aggregates subject to clinging. . . . These four establishments of mindfulness are to be developed for abandoning these five aggregates subject to clinging."

67 (5) Lower Fetters

"Bhikkhus, there are these five lower fetters. What five? Personal-existence view, doubt, wrong grasp of behavior and observances, sensual desire, and ill will. These are the five lower fetters. . . . These four establishments of mindfulness are to be developed for abandoning these five lower fetters."

68 (6) Destinations

"Bhikkhus, there are these five destinations. What five? Hell, the animal realm, the sphere of afflicted spirits, human beings, and devas. These are the five destinations. . . . These four establishments of mindfulness are to be developed for abandoning these five destinations."

69 (7) Miserliness

"Bhikkhus, there are these five kinds of miserliness. What five? Miserliness with regard to dwellings, miserliness with regard to families, miserliness with regard to gains, miserliness with regard to praise, and miserliness with regard to the Dhamma. These are the five kinds of miserliness. . . . These four establishments of mindfulness are to be developed for abandoning these five kinds of miserliness." [460]

70 (8) Higher Fetters

"Bhikkhus, there are these five higher fetters. What five? Lust for form, lust for the formless, conceit, restlessness, and ignorance. These are the five higher fetters. . . . These four establishments of mindfulness are to be developed for abandoning these five higher fetters."

71 (9) Mental Barrenness

"Bhikkhus, there are these five kinds of mental barrenness. What five?

(1) "Here, a bhikkhu is perplexed about the Teacher, doubts him, is not convinced about him and does not place confidence in him. When a bhikkhu is perplexed about the Teacher, doubts him, is not convinced about him and does not place confidence in him, his mind does not incline to ardor, effort, perseverance, and striving. Since his mind does not incline to ardor . . . and striving, this is the first kind of mental barrenness.

(2)–(5) "Again, a bhikkhu is perplexed about the Dhamma . . . perplexed about the Saṅgha . . . perplexed about the training . . . is irritated by his fellow monks, displeased with them, aggressive toward them, ill disposed toward them. When a bhikkhu is irritated by his fellow monks, displeased with them, aggressive toward them, ill disposed toward them, his mind does not incline to ardor, effort, perseverance, and striving. Since his mind does not incline to ardor . . . and striving, this is the fifth kind of mental barrenness.

"These are the five kinds of mental barrenness. . . . These four establishments of mindfulness are to be developed for abandoning these five kinds of mental barrenness." [461]

72 (10) Bondage

"Bhikkhus, there are these five bondages of the mind. What five?

(1) "Here, a bhikkhu is not devoid of lust for sensual pleasures, not devoid of desire, affection, thirst, passion, and craving for them. When a bhikkhu is not devoid of lust for sensual pleasures, not devoid of desire, affection, thirst, passion, and craving for them, his mind does not incline to ardor, effort, perseverance, and striving. Since his mind does not incline to ardor . . . and striving, this is the first bondage of the mind.

(2)–(5) "Again, a bhikkhu is not devoid of lust for the body, not devoid of desire, affection, thirst, passion, and craving for it. . . . He is not devoid of lust for form, not devoid of desire, affection, thirst, passion, and craving for it. . . . Having eaten as much as he wants until his belly is full, he is intent upon the pleasure of rest, the pleasure of sloth, the pleasure of sleep. . . . He lives the spiritual life aspiring for [rebirth in] a certain order of devas, [thinking]: 'By this virtuous behavior, observance, austerity, or spiritual life I will be a deva or one [in the retinue] of the devas.' When he lives the spiritual life aspiring for [rebirth in] a certain order of devas . . . his mind does not incline to ardor, effort, perseverance, and striving. Since his mind does not incline to ardor . . . and striving, this is the fifth bondage of the mind.

"These, bhikkhus, are the five bondages of the mind. . . . These four establishments of mindfulness are to be developed for abandoning these five bondages of the mind." [462]

III. Right Strivings

73 (1) The Training

"Bhikkhus, there are these five setbacks in the training. What five? (1) The destruction of life, (2) taking what is not given, (3) sexual misconduct, (4) false speech, and (5) [indulging in] liquor, wine, and intoxicants, the basis for heedlessness. These are the five setbacks in the training. The four right strivings are to be developed for abandoning these five setbacks in the training. What four? Here, (6) a bhikkhu generates desire for the non-arising of unarisen bad unwholesome qualities; he makes an effort, arouses energy, applies his mind, and strives. (7) He generates desire for the abandoning of arisen bad unwholesome qualities; he makes an effort, arouses energy, applies his mind, and strives. (8) He generates desire for the arising of unarisen wholesome qualities; he makes an effort, arouses energy, applies his mind, and strives. (9) He generates desire for the maintenance of arisen wholesome qualities, for their non-decline, increase, expansion, and fulfillment by development; he makes an effort, arouses energy, applies his mind, and strives. These four right strivings are to be developed for abandoning these five setbacks in the training."

74 (2)–82 (10) Hindrances, Etc.

[Parallel to 9:64–9:72, but formulated by way of the four right strivings.] [463]

IV. Bases for Psychic Potency

83 (1) The Training

"Bhikkhus, there are these five setbacks in the training. What five? (1) The destruction of life, (2) taking what is not given, (3) sexual misconduct, (4) false speech, and (5) [indulging in] liquor, wine, and intoxicants, the basis for heedlessness. These are the five setbacks in the training. The four bases for psychic potency are to be developed for abandoning these five setbacks in the training. What four? [464] (6) Here, a bhikkhu develops the basis for psychic potency that possesses concentration due to desire and activities of striving. (7) He develops the basis for psychic potency that possesses concentration due to energy and activities of striving. (8) He develops the basis for psychic potency that possesses concentration due to mind and activities of striving. (9) He develops the basis for psychic potency that possesses concentration due to investigation and activities of striving. These four bases for psychic potency are to be developed for abandoning these five setbacks in the training."

84 (2)–92 (10) Hindrances, Etc.
[Parallel to 9:64–9:72, but formulated by way of the four bases for psychic potency.] [465]

V. Lust and So Forth Repetition Series[1960]

93 (1)[1961]
"Bhikkhus, for direct knowledge of lust, nine things are to be developed. What nine? The perception of unattractiveness, the perception of death, the perception of the repulsiveness of food, the perception of non-delight in the entire world, the perception of impermanence, the perception of suffering in the impermanent, the perception of non-self in what is suffering, the perception of abandoning, and the perception of dispassion. For direct knowledge of lust, these nine things are to be developed."

94 (2)
"Bhikkhus, for direct knowledge of lust, nine things are to be developed. What nine? The first jhāna, the second jhāna, the third jhāna, the fourth jhāna, the base of the infinity of space, the base of the infinity of consciousness, the base of nothingness, the base of neither-perception-nor-non-perception, and the cessation of perception and feeling. For direct knowledge of lust, these nine things are to be developed."

95 (3)–112 (20)[1962]
"Bhikkhus, for full understanding of lust . . . for the utter destruction . . . for the abandoning . . . for the destruction . . . for the vanishing . . . for the fading away . . . for the cessation . . . for the giving up . . . for the relinquishment of lust . . . these nine things are to be developed."

113 (21)–432 (340)

"Bhikkhus, for direct knowledge . . . for full understanding . . . for the utter destruction . . . for the abandoning . . . for the destruction . . . for the vanishing . . . for the fading away . . . [466] for the cessation . . . for the giving up . . . for the relinquishment of hatred . . . of delusion . . . of anger . . . of hostility . . . of denigration . . . of insolence . . . of envy . . . of miserliness . . . of deceitfulness . . . of craftiness . . . of obstinacy . . . of vehemence . . . of conceit . . . of arrogance . . . of intoxication . . . of heedlessness . . . these nine things are to be developed."[1963]

This is what the Blessed One said. Elated, those bhikkhus delighted in the Blessed One's statement.

The Book of the Nines is finished.

The Book of the Tens
(*Dasakanipāta*)

The Book of the Tens

The First Fifty

The Second Fifty

The Third Fifty

The Fourth Fifty

An Extra Fifty

[1] # The Book of the Tens

Homage to the Blessed One, the Arahant,
the Perfectly Enlightened One

The First Fifty

I. Benefits

1 (1) What Purpose?

Thus have I heard. On one occasion the Blessed One was dwelling at Sāvatthī in Jeta's Grove, Anāthapiṇḍika's Park. Then the Venerable Ānanda approached the Blessed One, paid homage to him, sat down to one side, and said to him:

(1) "Bhante, what is the purpose and benefit of wholesome virtuous behavior?"

(2) "Ānanda, the purpose and benefit of wholesome virtuous behavior is non-regret."

(3) "And what, Bhante, is the purpose and benefit of non-regret?"

"The purpose and benefit of non-regret is joy."

(4) "And what, Bhante, is the purpose and benefit of joy?"

"The purpose and benefit of joy is rapture."

(5) "And what, Bhante, is the purpose and benefit of rapture?"

"The purpose and benefit of rapture is tranquility."

(6) "And what, Bhante, is the purpose and benefit of tranquility?"

"The purpose and benefit of tranquility is pleasure."

(7) "And what, Bhante, is the purpose and benefit of pleasure?"

"The purpose and benefit of pleasure [2] is concentration."

(8) "And what, Bhante, is the purpose and benefit of concentration?"

"The purpose and benefit of concentration is the knowledge and vision of things as they really are."

(9) "And what, Bhante, is the purpose and benefit of the knowledge and vision of things as they really are?"

"The purpose and benefit of the knowledge and vision of things as they really are is disenchantment and dispassion."

(10) "And what, Bhante, is the purpose and benefit of disenchantment and dispassion?"

"The purpose and benefit of disenchantment and dispassion is the knowledge and vision of liberation.

"Thus, Ānanda, (1)–(2) the purpose and benefit of wholesome virtuous behavior is non-regret; (3) the purpose and benefit of non-regret is joy; (4) the purpose and benefit of joy is rapture; (5) the purpose and benefit of rapture is tranquility; (6) the purpose and benefit of tranquility is pleasure; (7) the purpose and benefit of pleasure is concentration; (8) the purpose and benefit of concentration is the knowledge and vision of things as they really are; (9) the purpose and benefit of the knowledge and vision of things as they really are is disenchantment and dispassion; and (10) the purpose and benefit of disenchantment and dispassion is the knowledge and vision of liberation. Thus, Ānanda, wholesome virtuous behavior progressively leads to the foremost."[1964]

2 (2) Volition

(1)–(2) "Bhikkhus, for a virtuous person, one whose behavior is virtuous, no volition need be exerted: 'Let non-regret arise in me.' It is natural[1965] that non-regret arises in a virtuous person, one whose behavior is virtuous.

(3) "For one without regret no volition need be exerted: 'Let joy arise in me.' It is natural that joy arises in one without regret.

(4) "For one who is joyful no volition need be exerted: 'Let rapture arise in me.' It is natural that rapture arises in one who is joyful. [3]

(5) "For one with a rapturous mind no volition need be exerted: 'Let my body be tranquil.' It is natural that the body of one with a rapturous mind is tranquil.

(6) "For one tranquil in body no volition need be exerted: 'Let me feel pleasure.' It is natural that one tranquil in body feels pleasure.

(7) "For one feeling pleasure no volition need be exerted: 'Let my mind be concentrated.' It is natural that the mind of one feeling pleasure is concentrated.

(8) "For one who is concentrated no volition need be exerted: 'Let me know and see things as they really are.' It is natural that one who is concentrated knows and sees things as they really are.

(9) "For one who knows and sees things as they really are no volition need be exerted: 'Let me be disenchanted and dispassionate.' It is natural that one who knows and sees things as they really are is disenchanted and dispassionate.

(10) "For one who is disenchanted and dispassionate no volition need be exerted: 'Let me realize the knowledge and vision of liberation.' It is natural that one who is disenchanted and dispassionate realizes the knowledge and vision of liberation.

"Thus, bhikkhus, (9)–(10) the knowledge and vision of liberation is the purpose and benefit of disenchantment and dispassion; (8) disenchantment and dispassion are the purpose and benefit of the knowledge and vision of things as they really are; (7) the knowledge and vision of things as they really are is the purpose and benefit of concentration; (6) concentration is the purpose and benefit of pleasure; (5) pleasure is the purpose and benefit of tranquility; (4) tranquility is the purpose and benefit of rapture; (3) rapture is the purpose and benefit of joy; (2) joy is the purpose and benefit of non-regret; and (1) non-regret is the purpose and benefit of virtuous behavior.

"Thus, bhikkhus, one stage [4] flows into the next stage, one stage fills up the next stage, for going from the near shore to the far shore."[1966]

3 (3) Virtuous Behavior[1967]

"Bhikkhus, (1) for an immoral person, for one deficient in virtuous behavior, (2) non-regret lacks its proximate cause. When there is no non-regret, for one deficient in non-regret, (3) joy lacks its proximate cause. When there is no joy, for one deficient in joy, (4) rapture lacks its proximate cause. When there is no rapture, for one deficient in rapture, (5) tranquility lacks its proximate cause. When there is no tranquility, for one deficient in tranquility, (6) pleasure lacks its proximate cause. When there is no pleasure, for one deficient in pleasure, (7) right concentration lacks its proximate cause. When there is no right concentration, for one deficient in right concentration, (8) the knowledge and vision of things as they really are lacks its proximate cause. When there is no knowledge and vision of things as they really are, for one deficient in the knowledge and vision of things as they really are, (9) disenchantment and dispassion lack their proximate cause. When there is no disenchantment and dispassion, for one deficient in disenchantment and dispassion, (10) the knowledge and vision of liberation lacks its proximate cause.

"Suppose there is a tree deficient in branches and foliage. Then its shoots do not grow to fullness; also its bark, softwood, and heartwood do not grow to fullness. So too, for an immoral person, one deficient in virtuous behavior, non-regret lacks its proximate cause. When there is no non-regret . . . the knowledge and vision of liberation lacks its proximate cause.

"Bhikkhus, (1) for a virtuous person, for one whose behavior is virtuous, (2) non-regret possesses its proximate cause. When there is non-regret, for one possessing non-regret, (3) joy possesses its proximate cause. When there is joy, for one possessing joy, (4) rapture possesses its proximate cause. When there is rapture, for one possessing rapture, (5) tranquility possesses its proximate cause. When there is tranquility, for one possessing tranquility, (6) pleasure possesses its proximate cause. When there is pleasure, for one possessing pleasure, (7) right concentration possesses its proximate cause. [5] When there is right concentration, for one possessing right concentration, (8) the knowledge and vision of things as they really are possesses its proximate cause. When there is the knowledge and vision of things as they really are, for one possessing the knowledge and vision of things as they really are, (9) disenchantment and dispassion possess their proximate cause. When there is disenchantment and dispassion, for one possessing disenchantment and dispassion, (10) the knowledge and vision of liberation possesses its proximate cause.

"Suppose there is a tree possessing branches and foliage. Then its shoots grow to fullness; also its bark, softwood, and heartwood grow to fullness. So too, for a virtuous person, one whose behavior is virtuous, non-regret possesses its proximate cause. When there is non-regret . . . the knowledge and vision of liberation possesses its proximate cause."

4 (4) Proximate Cause

There the Venerable Sāriputta addressed the bhikkhus:

[Identical with 10:3, but spoken by Sāriputta.] [6]

5 (5) Ānanda

There the Venerable Ānanda addressed the bhikkhus:

[Identical with 10:3, but spoken by Ānanda.] [7]

6 (6) Concentration

Then the Venerable Ānanda approached the Blessed One, paid homage to him, sat down to one side, and said to him:

"Bhante, could a bhikkhu obtain such a state of concentration that (1) he would not be percipient of earth in relation to earth;[1968] (2) of water in relation to water; (3) of fire in relation to fire; (4) of air in relation to air; (5) of the base of the infinity of space in relation to the base of the infinity of space; (6) of the base of the infinity of consciousness in relation to the base of the infinity of consciousness; (7) of the base of nothingness in relation to the base of nothingness; (8) of the base of neither-perception-nor-non-perception in relation to the base of neither-perception-nor-non-perception; (9) of this world in relation to this world; (10) of the other world in relation to the other world, but he would still be percipient?"

"He could, Ānanda."

"But how, Bhante, could he obtain such a state of concentration?" [8]

"Here, Ānanda, a bhikkhu is percipient thus: 'This is peaceful, this is sublime, that is, the stilling of all activities, the relinquishing of all acquisitions, the destruction of craving, dispassion, cessation, nibbāna.'[1969] It is in this way, Ānanda, that a bhikkhu could obtain such a state of concentration that he would not be percipient of earth in relation to earth; of water in relation to water; of fire in relation to fire; of air in relation to air; of the base of the infinity of space in relation to the base of the infinity of space; of the base of the infinity of consciousness in relation to the base of the infinity of consciousness; of the base of nothingness in relation to the base of nothingness; of the base of neither-perception-nor-non-perception in relation to the base of neither-perception-nor-non-perception; of this world in relation to this world; of the other world in relation to the other world, but he would still be percipient."

7 (7) Sāriputta

Then the Venerable Ānanda approached the Venerable Sāriputta and exchanged greetings with him. When they had concluded their greetings and cordial talk, he sat down to one side and said to the Venerable Sāriputta:

"Friend Sāriputta, could a bhikkhu obtain such a state of concentration that (1) he would not be percipient of earth in relation to earth; (2) of water in relation to water; (3) of fire in relation to fire; (4) of air in relation to air; (5) of the base of the infinity of space in relation to the base of the infinity of space; [9] (6) of the base of the infinity of consciousness in relation to the base of the infinity of consciousness; (7) of the base of nothingness in relation to the base of nothingness; (8) of the base of neither-perception-nor-non-perception in relation to the base of neither-perception-nor-non-perception; (9) of this world in relation to this world; (10) of the other world in relation to the other world, but he would still be percipient?"

"He could, friend Ānanda."

"But how, friend Sāriputta, could he obtain such a state of concentration?"

"On one occasion, friend Ānanda, I was dwelling right here in Sāvatthī in the Blind Men's Grove. There I attained such a state of concentration that I was not percipient of earth in relation to earth; of water in relation to water; of fire in relation to fire; of air in relation to air; of the base of the infinity of space in relation to the base of the infinity of space; of the base of the infinity of consciousness in relation to the base of the infinity of consciousness; of the base of nothingness in relation to the base of nothingness; of the base of neither-perception-nor-non-perception in relation to the base of neither-perception-nor-non-perception; of this world in relation to this world; of the other world in relation to the other world, but I was still percipient."

"But of what was the Venerable Sāriputta percipient on that occasion?"

"One perception arose and another perception ceased in me: 'The cessation of existence is nibbāna; the cessation of existence is nibbāna.'[1970] Just as, when a fire of twigs is burning, one flame arises and another flame ceases, so one perception [10] arose and another perception ceased in me: 'The cessation of existence is nibbāna; the cessation of existence is nibbāna.' On that occasion, friend, I was percipient: 'The cessation of existence is nibbāna.'"

8 (8) Faith[1971]

(1) "Bhikkhus, a bhikkhu may be endowed with faith but he is not virtuous; thus he is incomplete with respect to that factor. He should fulfill that factor, [thinking]: 'How can I be endowed with faith and also be virtuous?' But when a bhikkhu is endowed with faith and is also virtuous, then he is complete with respect to that factor.

(2) "A bhikkhu may be endowed with faith and virtuous, but he is not learned . . . (3) . . . learned, but not a speaker on the Dhamma . . . (4) . . . a speaker on the Dhamma, but not one who frequents assemblies . . . (5) . . . one who frequents assemblies, but not one who confidently teaches the Dhamma to an assembly . . . (6) . . . one who confidently teaches the Dhamma to an assembly, but not an expert on the discipline . . . (7) . . . an expert on the discipline, but not a forest-dweller who resorts to remote lodgings . . . (8) . . . a forest-dweller who resorts to remote lodgings, but not one who gains at will, without trouble or difficulty, the four jhānas that constitute the higher mind and are pleasant dwellings in this very life . . . (9) . . . one who gains at will, without trouble or difficulty, the four jhānas that constitute the higher mind and are pleasant dwellings in this very life, but not one who, with the destruction of the taints, has realized for himself with direct knowledge, in this very life, the taintless liberation of mind, liberation by wisdom, and having entered upon it, dwells in it.

"Thus he is incomplete with respect to that factor. He should fulfill that factor, [thinking]: 'How can I be endowed with faith . . . [11] . . . and also be one who, with the destruction of the taints, has realized for himself with direct knowledge, in this very life, the taintless liberation of mind, liberation by wisdom, and having entered upon it, dwells in it?'

(10) "But when a bhikkhu is (i) endowed with faith, (ii) virtuous, and (iii) learned; (iv) a speaker on the Dhamma; (v) one who frequents assemblies; (vi) one who confidently teaches the Dhamma to an assembly; (vii) an expert on the discipline; (viii) a forest-dweller who resorts to remote lodgings; (ix) one who gains at will, without trouble or difficulty, the four jhānas that constitute the higher mind and are pleasant dwellings in this very life; and (x) one who, with the destruction of the taints, has realized for himself with direct knowledge, in this very life, the taintless liberation of mind, liberation by wisdom, and having entered upon it, dwells in it, then he is complete with respect to that factor.

"A bhikkhu who possesses these ten qualities is one who inspires confidence in all respects and who is complete in all aspects."

9 (9) Peaceful[1972]

(1) "Bhikkhus, a bhikkhu may be endowed with faith but he is not virtuous ... (2) ... endowed with faith and virtuous, but he is not learned ... (3) ... learned, but not a speaker on the Dhamma ... (4) ... a speaker on the Dhamma, but not one who frequents assemblies ... (5) ... one who frequents assemblies, but not one who confidently teaches the Dhamma to an assembly ... (6) ... one who confidently teaches the Dhamma to an assembly, but not an expert on the discipline ... (7) ... an expert on the discipline, but not a forest-dweller who resorts to remote lodgings ... (8) ... a forest-dweller who resorts to remote lodgings, but not one who contacts with the body and dwells in those peaceful emancipations, transcending forms, that are formless ... (9) ... one who contacts with the body and dwells in those peaceful emancipations, transcending forms, [12] that are formless, but not one who, with the destruction of the taints, has realized for himself with direct knowledge, in this very life, the taintless liberation of mind, liberation by wisdom, and having entered upon it, dwells in it.

"Thus he is incomplete with respect to that factor. He should fulfill that factor, [thinking]: 'How can I be endowed with faith ... and also be one who, with the destruction of the taints, has realized for himself with direct knowledge, in this very life, the taintless liberation of mind, liberation by wisdom, and having entered upon it, dwells in it?'

(10) "But when a bhikkhu is (i) endowed with faith, (ii) virtuous, and (iii) learned; (iv) a speaker on the Dhamma; (v) one who frequents assemblies; (vi) one who confidently teaches the Dhamma to an assembly; (vii) an expert on the discipline; (viii) a forest-dweller who resorts to remote lodgings; (ix) one who dwells having contacted with the body those peaceful emancipations, transcending forms, that are formless; and (x) one who, with the destruction of the taints, has realized for himself with direct knowledge, in this very life, the taintless liberation of mind, liberation by wisdom, and having entered upon it, dwells in it, then he is complete with respect to that factor.

"A bhikkhu who possesses these ten qualities is one who inspires confidence in all respects and who is complete in all aspects."

10 (10) True Knowledges

(1) "Bhikkhus, a bhikkhu may be endowed with faith but he is not virtuous . . . [13] . . . (2) . . . endowed with faith and virtuous, but he is not learned . . . (3) . . . learned, but not a speaker on the Dhamma . . . (4) . . . a speaker on the Dhamma, but not one who frequents assemblies . . . (5) . . . one who frequents assemblies, but not one who confidently teaches the Dhamma to an assembly . . . (6) . . . one who confidently teaches the Dhamma to an assembly, but not an expert on the discipline . . . (7) . . . an expert on the discipline, but not one who recollects his manifold past abodes, that is, one birth, two births . . . [as in 6:2 §4] . . . thus he does not recollect his manifold past abodes with their aspects and details . . . (8) . . . one who recollects his manifold past abodes . . . but not one who, with the divine eye, which is purified and surpasses the human . . . [as in 6:2 §5] . . . understands how beings fare in accordance with their kamma . . . (9) . . . one who, with the divine eye . . . understands how beings fare in accordance with their kamma, but not one who, with the destruction of the taints, has realized for himself with direct knowledge, in this very life, the taintless liberation of mind, liberation by wisdom, and having entered upon it, dwells in it.

"Thus he is incomplete with respect to that factor. He should fulfill that factor, [thinking]: 'How can I be endowed with faith . . . [14] . . . and also be one who, with the destruction of the taints, has realized for himself with direct knowledge, in this very life, the taintless liberation of mind, liberation by wisdom, and having entered upon it, dwells in it?'

(10) "But when a bhikkhu is (i) endowed with faith, (ii) virtuous, and (iii) learned; (iv) a speaker on the Dhamma; (v) one who frequents assemblies; (vi) one who confidently teaches the Dhamma to an assembly; (vii) an expert on the discipline; (viii) one who recollects his manifold past abodes . . . with their aspects and details; (ix) one who, with the divine eye . . . understands how beings fare in accordance with their kamma; and (x) one who, with the destruction of the taints, has realized for himself with direct knowledge, in this very life, the taintless liberation of mind, liberation by wisdom, and having entered upon it, dwells in it, then he is complete with respect to that factor.

"A bhikkhu who possesses these ten qualities is one who inspires confidence in all respects and who is complete in all aspects." [15]

II. Protector

11 (1) Lodging[1973]

"Bhikkhus, when a bhikkhu who possesses five factors resorts to and uses a lodging that possesses five factors, in no long time, with the destruction of the taints, he might realize for himself with direct knowledge, in this very life, the taintless liberation of mind, liberation by wisdom, and having entered upon it, dwell in it.

"And how, bhikkhus, does a bhikkhu possess five factors?

(1) "Here, a bhikkhu is endowed with faith. He has faith in the enlightenment of the Tathāgata thus: 'The Blessed One is an arahant, perfectly enlightened, accomplished in true knowledge and conduct, fortunate, knower of the world, unsurpassed trainer of persons to be tamed, teacher of devas and humans, the Enlightened One, the Blessed One.'

(2) "He is seldom ill or afflicted, possessing an even digestion that is neither too cool nor too hot but moderate and suitable for striving.

(3) "He is honest and open, one who reveals himself as he really is to the Teacher and his wise fellow monks.

(4) "He has aroused energy for abandoning unwholesome qualities and acquiring wholesome qualities; he is strong, firm in exertion, not casting off the duty of cultivating wholesome qualities.

(5) "He is wise; he possesses the wisdom that discerns arising and passing away, which is noble and penetrative and leads to the complete destruction of suffering.

"It is in this way that a bhikkhu possesses five factors.

"And how does a lodging possess five factors?

(6) "Here, the lodging is neither too far [from a place for alms] nor too close, and it possesses a means for going and returning.

(7) "During the day it is not disturbed by people and at night it is quiet and still.

(8) "There is little contact with flies, mosquitoes, wind, the burning sun, and serpents.

(9) "One dwelling in that lodging can easily obtain robes, almsfood, lodging, and medicines and provisions for the sick.

(10) "In that lodging elder bhikkhus are dwelling who are learned, heirs to the heritage, [16] experts on the Dhamma, experts on the discipline, experts on the outlines. He approaches them from time to time and inquires: 'How is this, Bhante? What is the meaning of this?' Those venerable ones then disclose to him what has not been disclosed, clear up what is obscure, and dispel his perplexity about numerous perplexing points.

"It is in this way that a lodging possesses five factors.

"When a bhikkhu who possesses these five factors resorts to and uses a lodging that possesses these five factors, in no long time, with the destruction of the taints, he might realize for himself with direct knowledge, in this very life, the taintless liberation of mind, liberation by wisdom, and having entered upon it, dwell in it."

12 (2) Five Factors[1974]

"Bhikkhus, a bhikkhu who has abandoned five factors and possesses five factors is called, in this Dhamma and discipline, a supreme person who is consummate and has completely lived the spiritual life.

"And how has a bhikkhu abandoned five factors? Here, a

bhikkhu has abandoned sensual desire, ill will, dullness and drowsiness, restlessness and remorse, and doubt. It is in this way that a bhikkhu has abandoned five factors.

"And how does a bhikkhu possess five factors? Here, a bhikkhu possesses the aggregate of virtuous behavior of one beyond training, the aggregate of concentration of one beyond training, the aggregate of wisdom of one beyond training, the aggregate of liberation of one beyond training, and the aggregate of the knowledge and vision of liberation of one beyond training. It is in this way that a bhikkhu possesses five factors.

"When a bhikkhu has abandoned these five factors and possesses these five factors, he is called, in this Dhamma and discipline, a supreme person who is consummate and complete in living the spiritual life."

When sensual desire and ill will,
dullness and drowsiness,
restlessness, and doubt are
totally absent in a bhikkhu; [17]
when one like this possesses
the virtue and concentration
of one beyond training,
and [similar] liberation and knowledge;
possessing five factors
and having removed five factors,
he is truly called a consummate one
in this Dhamma and discipline.

13 (3) Fetters

"Bhikkhus, there are these ten fetters. What ten? The five lower fetters and the five higher fetters. And what are the five lower fetters? Personal-existence view, doubt, wrong grasp of behavior and observances, sensual desire, and ill will. These are the five lower fetters. And what are the five higher fetters? Lust for form, lust for the formless, conceit, restlessness, and ignorance. These are the five higher fetters. These, bhikkhus, are the ten fetters."

14 (4) Mental Barrenness[1975]

"Bhikkhus, if any bhikkhu or bhikkhunī has not abandoned five kinds of mental barrenness and eradicated five bondages of the mind, then, whether night or day comes, only deterioration in wholesome qualities and not growth is to be expected for this person.

"What are the five kinds of mental barrenness that he has not abandoned?

(1) "Here, a bhikkhu is perplexed about the Teacher, doubts him, is not convinced about him and does not place confidence in him. When a bhikkhu is perplexed about the Teacher, doubts him, is not convinced about him and does not place confidence in him, his mind does not incline to ardor, effort, perseverance, and striving. Since his mind does not incline to ardor . . . [18] . . . and striving, this is the first kind of mental barrenness that he has not abandoned.

(2)–(5) "Again, a bhikkhu is perplexed about the Dhamma . . . perplexed about the Saṅgha . . . perplexed about the training . . . is irritated by his fellow monks, displeased with them, aggressive toward them, ill disposed toward them. When a bhikkhu is irritated by his fellow monks, displeased with them, aggressive toward them, ill disposed toward them, his mind does not incline to ardor, effort, perseverance, and striving. Since his mind does not incline to ardor . . . and striving, this is the fifth kind of mental barrenness that he has not abandoned.

"These are the five kinds of mental barrenness that he has not abandoned.

"What are the five bondages of the mind that he has not eradicated?

(6) "Here, a bhikkhu is not devoid of lust for sensual pleasures, not devoid of desire, affection, thirst, passion, and craving for them. When a bhikkhu is not devoid of lust for sensual pleasures, not devoid of desire, affection, thirst, passion, and craving for them, his mind does not incline to ardor, effort, perseverance, and striving. Since his mind does not incline to ardor . . . and striving, this is the first bondage of the mind that he has not eradicated.

(7)–(10) "Again, a bhikkhu is not devoid of lust for the body, not devoid of desire, affection, thirst, passion, and craving for it. . . . He is not devoid of lust for form, not devoid of desire, affection, thirst, passion, and craving for it. . . . Having eaten as much as he wants until his belly is full, he is intent upon the pleasure of rest, the pleasure of sloth, the pleasure of sleep . . . he lives the spiritual life aspiring for [rebirth in] a certain order of devas, [thinking]: 'By this virtuous behavior, observance, austerity, or spiritual life I will be a deva or one [in the retinue] of the devas.' When he lives the spiritual life aspiring for [rebirth in] a certain order of devas . . . his mind does not incline [19] to ardor, effort, perseverance, and striving. Since his mind does not incline to ardor . . . and striving, this is the fifth bondage of the mind that he has not eradicated.

"These are the five bondages of mind that he has not eradicated.

"If any bhikkhu or bhikkhunī has not abandoned these five kinds of mental barrenness and eradicated these five bondages of the mind, then, whether night or day comes, only deterioration and not growth in wholesome qualities is to be expected for that person. Just as during the dark fortnight, whether night or day comes, the moon only deteriorates in beauty, roundness, and brightness, in diameter and circumference, so too, if any bhikkhu or bhikkhunī has not abandoned these five kinds of mental barrenness . . . only deterioration . . . is to be expected for that person.

"Bhikkhus, if any bhikkhu or bhikkhunī has abandoned five kinds of mental barrenness and eradicated five bondages of the mind,[1976] then, whether night or day comes, only growth in wholesome qualities and not deterioration is to be expected for that person.

"And what are the five kinds of mental barrenness that he has abandoned?

(1) "Here, a bhikkhu is not perplexed about the Teacher, does not doubt him, is convinced about him and places confidence in him. When a bhikkhu is not perplexed about the Teacher, does not doubt him, is convinced about him and places confidence in him, his mind inclines to ardor, effort, perseverance, and striving. Since his mind inclines to ardor . . . and striving, this is the first kind of mental barrenness that he has abandoned.

(2)–(5) "Again, a bhikkhu is not perplexed about the Dhamma . . . not perplexed about the Saṅgha . . . not perplexed about the training [20] . . . is not irritated by his fellow monks, is pleased with them, not aggressive toward them, well disposed toward them. When a bhikkhu is not irritated by his fellow monks . . . well disposed toward them, his mind inclines to ardor, effort, perseverance, and striving. Since his mind inclines to ardor . . . and striving, this is the fifth kind of mental barrenness that he has abandoned.

"These are the five kinds of mental barrenness that he has abandoned.

"What are the five bondages of the mind that he has well eradicated?

(6) "Here, a bhikkhu is devoid of lust for sensual pleasures, devoid of desire, affection, thirst, passion, and craving for them. When a bhikkhu is devoid of lust for sensual pleasures, devoid of desire, affection, thirst, passion, and craving for them, his mind inclines to ardor, effort, perseverance, and striving. Since his mind inclines to ardor . . . and striving, this is the first bondage of the mind that he has well eradicated.

(7)–(10) "Again, a bhikkhu is devoid of lust for the body, devoid of desire, affection, thirst, passion, and craving for it. . . . He is devoid of lust for form, devoid of desire, affection, thirst, passion, and craving for it. . . . He does not eat as much as he wants until his belly is full nor is he intent upon the pleasure of rest, the pleasure of sloth, the pleasure of sleep. . . . He does not live the spiritual life aspiring for [rebirth in] a certain order of devas, [thinking]: 'By this virtuous behavior, observance, austerity, or spiritual life I will be a deva or one [in the retinue] of the devas.' Since he does not live the spiritual life aspiring for [rebirth in] a certain order of devas . . . his mind inclines to ardor, effort, perseverance, and striving. Since his mind inclines to ardor . . . and striving, this is the fifth bondage of the mind that he has well eradicated.

"These are the five bondages of the mind that he has well eradicated.

"If any bhikkhu or bhikkhunī has abandoned these five kinds of mental barrenness and well eradicated these five bondages of the mind, [21] then, whether night or day comes, only growth in wholesome qualities and not deterioration is to be expected for that person. Just as during the bright fortnight, whether night or day comes, the moon only increases in beauty, roundness, and brightness, in diameter and circumference, so too, if any bhikkhu or bhikkhunī has abandoned these five kinds of mental barrenness and well eradicated these five bondages of the mind, then, whether night or day comes, only growth in wholesome qualities and not deterioration is to be expected for that person."

15 (5) Heedfulness

(1) "Bhikkhus, to whatever extent there are beings, whether footless or with two feet, four feet, or many feet, whether having form or formless, whether percipient or non-percipient, or neither percipient nor non-percipient, the Tathāgata, the Arahant, the Perfectly Enlightened One is declared foremost among them.[1977] So too, all wholesome qualities are rooted in heedfulness and converge upon heedfulness and heedfulness is declared foremost among them.

(2) "Just as the footprints of all animals that roam on land fit into the footprint of the elephant, and the elephant's footprint is declared foremost among them, that is, with respect to size, so too, all wholesome qualities are rooted in heedfulness and converge upon heedfulness and heedfulness is declared foremost among them.

(3) "Just as all the rafters of a peaked house lean toward the roof peak, slope toward the roof peak, converge upon the roof peak, and the roof peak is declared foremost among them, so too, all wholesome qualities are rooted in heedfulness and converge upon heedfulness and heedfulness is declared foremost among them. [22]

(4) "Just as, of all fragrant roots, black orris is declared foremost among them, so too . . .

(5) "Just as, of all fragrant heartwoods, red sandalwood is declared foremost among them, so too . . .

(6) "Just as, of all fragrant flowers, jasmine is declared foremost among them, so too . . .

(7) "Just as all petty princes are the vassals of a wheel-turning monarch, and the wheel-turning monarch is declared foremost among them, so too . . .

(8) "Just as the radiance of all the stars does not amount to a sixteenth part of the radiance of the moon, and the radiance of the moon is declared foremost among them, so too . . .

(9) "Just as, in the autumn, when the sky is clear and cloudless, the sun, ascending in the sky, dispels all darkness from space as it shines and beams and radiates, so too . . .

(10) "Just as, whatever great rivers there are—that is, the Ganges, the Yamunā, the Aciravatī, the Sarabhū, and the Mahī—all head toward the ocean, slant, slope, and incline toward the ocean, and the ocean is declared foremost among

them, so too, all wholesome qualities are rooted in heedfulness and converge upon heedfulness and heedfulness is declared foremost among them." [23]

16 (6) Worthy of Gifts[1978]

"Bhikkhus, these ten persons are worthy of gifts, worthy of hospitality, worthy of offerings, worthy of reverential salutation, an unsurpassed field of merit for the world. What ten? The Tathāgata, the Arahant, the Perfectly Enlightened One; a paccekabuddha; the one liberated in both respects; the one liberated by wisdom; the body witness; the one attained to view; the one liberated by faith; the Dhamma follower; the faith follower; and the clan member. These ten persons are worthy of gifts, worthy of hospitality, worthy of offerings, worthy of reverential salutation, an unsurpassed field of merit for the world."

17 (7) Protector (1)

"Bhikkhus, live under a protector, not without a protector. One without a protector lives in suffering. There are these ten qualities that serve as a protector.[1979] What ten?

(1) "Here, a bhikkhu is virtuous; he dwells restrained by the Pātimokkha, possessed of good conduct and resort, seeing danger in minute faults. Having undertaken the training rules, he trains in them. Since a bhikkhu is virtuous . . . trains in them, this is a quality that serves as a protector.

(2) "Again, a bhikkhu has learned much, remembers what he has learned, and accumulates what he has learned. Those teachings that are good in the beginning, good in the middle, and good in the end, with the right meaning and phrasing, which proclaim the perfectly complete and pure spiritual life—such teachings as these he has learned much of, retained in mind, recited verbally, investigated mentally, and penetrated well by view. Since a bhikkhu has learned much . . . and penetrated well by view, this, too, is a quality that serves as a protector.

(3) "Again, a bhikkhu has good friends, [24] good companions, good comrades. Since a bhikkhu has good friends, good companions, good comrades, this, too, is a quality that serves as a protector.

(4) "Again, a bhikkhu is easy to correct and possesses qualities that make him easy to correct; he is patient and receives

instruction respectfully. Since a bhikkhu is easy to correct . . . and receives instruction respectfully, this, too, is a quality that serves as a protector.

(5) "Again, a bhikkhu is skillful and diligent in attending to the diverse chores that are to be done for his fellow monks; he possesses sound judgment about them in order to carry out and arrange them properly. Since a bhikkhu is skillful and diligent . . . this, too, is a quality that serves as a protector.

(6) "Again, a bhikkhu loves the Dhamma and is pleasing in his assertions, filled with a lofty joy pertaining to the Dhamma and discipline.[1980] Since a bhikkhu loves the Dhamma . . . this, too, is a quality that serves as a protector.

(7) "Again, a bhikkhu has aroused energy for abandoning unwholesome qualities and acquiring wholesome qualities; he is strong, firm in exertion, not casting off the duty of cultivating wholesome qualities. Since a bhikkhu has aroused energy . . . not casting off the duty of cultivating wholesome qualities, this, too, is a quality that serves as a protector. [25]

(8) "Again, a bhikkhu is content with any kind of robe, almsfood, lodging, and medicines and provisions for the sick. Since a bhikkhu is content with any kind of . . . provisions for the sick, this, too, is a quality that serves as a protector.

(9) "Again, a bhikkhu is mindful, possessing supreme mindfulness and alertness, one who remembers and recollects what was done and said long ago. Since a bhikkhu is mindful . . . and recollects what was done and said long ago, this, too, is a quality that serves as a protector.

(10) "Again, a bhikkhu is wise; he possesses the wisdom that discerns arising and passing away, which is noble and penetrative and leads to the complete destruction of suffering. Since a bhikkhu is wise . . . this, too, is a quality that serves as a protector.

"Bhikkhus, live under a protector, not without a protector. One without a protector lives in suffering. These are the ten qualities that serve as a protector."

18 (8) Protector (2)

"Bhikkhus, live under a protector, not without a protector. One without a protector lives in suffering. There are these ten qualities that serve as a protector. What ten?

(1) "Here, a bhikkhu is virtuous; he dwells restrained by

the Pātimokkha, possessed of good conduct and resort, seeing danger in minute faults. Having undertaken the training rules, he trains in them. [Having considered:] 'This bhikkhu is truly virtuous.... Having undertaken the training rules, he trains in them,' the elder bhikkhus, [26] those of middle standing, and the junior bhikkhus think he should be corrected and instructed. Since they all have compassion for him, only growth in wholesome qualities and not decline is to be expected for him. This is a quality that serves as a protector.

(2) "Again, a bhikkhu has learned much, remembers what he has learned, and accumulates what he has learned. Those teachings that are good in the beginning... with the right meaning and phrasing, which proclaim the perfectly complete and pure spiritual life—such teachings as these he has learned much of, retained in mind, recited verbally, investigated mentally, and penetrated well by view. [Having considered:] 'This bhikkhu has truly learned much... and penetrated well by view,' the elder bhikkhus, those of middle standing, and the junior bhikkhus think he should be corrected and instructed. Since they all have compassion for him, only growth in wholesome qualities and not decline is to be expected for him. This, too, is a quality that serves as a protector.

(3) "Again, a bhikkhu has good friends, good companions, good comrades. [Having considered:] 'This bhikkhu truly has good friends, good companions, good comrades,' the elder bhikkhus, those of middle standing, and the junior bhikkhus think he should be corrected and instructed. Since they all have compassion for him, only growth in wholesome qualities and not decline is to be expected for him. This, too, is a quality that serves as a protector.

(4) "Again, a bhikkhu is easy to correct and possesses qualities that make him easy to correct; he is patient and receives instruction respectfully. [Having considered:] 'This bhikkhu is truly easy to correct and possesses qualities that make him easy to correct; he is patient and receives instruction respectfully,' the elder bhikkhus, [27] those of middle standing, and the junior bhikkhus think he should be corrected and instructed. Since they all have compassion for him, only growth in wholesome qualities and not decline is to be expected for him. This, too, is a quality that serves as a protector.

(5) "Again, a bhikkhu is skillful and diligent in attending to the diverse chores that are to be done for his fellow monks; he possesses sound judgment about them in order to carry out and arrange them properly. [Having considered:] 'This bhikkhu is truly skillful and diligent . . . in order to carry out and arrange them properly,' the elder bhikkhus, those of middle standing, and the junior bhikkhus think he should be corrected and instructed. Since they all have compassion for him, only growth in wholesome qualities and not decline is to be expected for him. This, too, is a quality that serves as a protector.

(6) "Again, a bhikkhu loves the Dhamma and is pleasing in his assertions, filled with a lofty joy pertaining to the Dhamma and discipline. [Having considered:] 'This bhikkhu truly loves the Dhamma and is pleasing in his assertions, filled with a lofty joy pertaining to the Dhamma and discipline,' the elder bhikkhus, those of middle standing, and the junior bhikkhus think he should be corrected and instructed. Since they all have compassion for him, only growth in wholesome qualities and not decline is to be expected for him. This, too, is a quality that serves as a protector.

(7) "Again, a bhikkhu has aroused energy for abandoning unwholesome qualities and acquiring wholesome qualities; he is strong, firm in exertion, not casting off the duty of cultivating wholesome qualities. [Having considered:] 'This bhikkhu truly has aroused energy . . . [28] . . . not casting off the duty of cultivating wholesome qualities,' the elder bhikkhus, those of middle standing, and the junior bhikkhus think he should be corrected and instructed. Since they all have compassion for him, only growth in wholesome qualities and not decline is to be expected for him. This, too, is a quality that serves as a protector.

(8) "Again, a bhikkhu is content with any kind of robe, almsfood, lodging, and medicines and provisions for the sick. [Having considered:] 'This bhikkhu truly is content with any kind of robe, almsfood, lodging, and medicines and provisions for the sick,' the elder bhikkhus, those of middle standing, and the junior bhikkhus think he should be corrected and instructed. Since they all have compassion for him, only growth in wholesome qualities and not decline is to be expected for him. This, too, is a quality that serves as a protector.

(9) "Again, a bhikkhu is mindful, possessing supreme mindfulness and alertness, one who remembers and recollects what was done and said long ago. [Having considered:] 'This bhikkhu truly is mindful, possessing supreme mindfulness and alertness, one who remembers and recollects what was done and said long ago,' the elder bhikkhus, those of middle standing, and the junior bhikkhus think he should be corrected and instructed. Since they all have compassion for him, only growth in wholesome qualities and not decline is to be expected for him. This, too, is a quality that serves as a protector.

(10) "Again, a bhikkhu is wise; he possesses the wisdom that discerns arising and passing away, which is noble and penetrative and leads to the complete destruction of suffering. [Having considered:] 'This bhikkhu truly is wise; he possesses the wisdom that discerns arising and passing away, which is noble and penetrative and leads to the complete destruction of suffering,' the elder bhikkhus, those of middle standing, and the junior bhikkhus think he should be corrected [29] and instructed. Since they all have compassion for him, only growth in wholesome qualities and not decline is to be expected for him. This, too, is a quality that serves as a protector.

"Bhikkhus, live under a protector, not without a protector. One without a protector lives in suffering. These are the ten qualities that serve as a protector."

19 (9) Abodes of the Noble Ones (1)

"Bhikkhus, there are these ten abodes of the noble ones in which the noble ones of the past, present, or future abide.[1981] What ten?

"Here, a bhikkhu (1) has abandoned five factors; (2) possesses six factors; (3) has a single guard (4) and four supports; (5) has dispelled personal truths, (6) totally renounced seeking, (7) purified his intentions, (8) tranquilized bodily activity, and become (9) well liberated in mind and (10) well liberated by wisdom. These are the ten abodes of the noble ones in which the noble ones of the past, present, or future abide."

20 (10) Abodes of the Noble Ones (2)

On one occasion the Blessed One was dwelling among the Kurus near the Kuru town named Kammāsadamma. [30] There the Blessed One addressed the bhikkhus.... The Blessed One said this:

"Bhikkhus, there are these ten abodes of the noble ones in which the noble ones abide in the past, present, or future. What ten?

"Here, a bhikkhu (1) has abandoned five factors; (2) possesses six factors; (3) has a single guard (4) and four supports; (5) has dispelled personal truths, (6) totally renounced seeking, (7) purified his intentions, (8) tranquilized bodily activity, and become (9) well liberated in mind and (10) well liberated by wisdom.

(1) "And how has a bhikkhu abandoned five factors? Here, a bhikkhu has abandoned sensual desire, ill will, dullness and drowsiness, restlessness and remorse, and doubt. It is in this way that a bhikkhu has abandoned five factors.

(2) "And how does a bhikkhu possess six factors? Here, having seen a form with the eye, a bhikkhu is neither joyful nor saddened, but dwells equanimous, mindful and clearly comprehending. Having heard a sound with the ear... Having smelled an odor with the nose... Having experienced a taste with the tongue... Having felt a tactile object with the body... Having cognized a mental phenomenon with the mind, a bhikkhu is neither joyful nor saddened, but dwells equanimous, mindful and clearly comprehending.[1982] It is in this way that a bhikkhu possesses six factors.

(3) "And how does a bhikkhu have a single guard? Here, a bhikkhu possesses a mind guarded by mindfulness. It is in this way that a bhikkhu has a single guard.

(4) "And how does a bhikkhu have four supports? Here, having reflected, a bhikkhu uses some things, patiently endures other things, avoids still other things, and dispels still other things. It is in this way that a bhikkhu has four supports. [31]

(5) "And how has a bhikkhu dispelled personal truths? Here, whatever ordinary personal truths may be held by ordinary ascetics and brahmins—that is, 'The world is eternal' or 'The world is not eternal'; 'The world is finite' or 'The world is infinite'; 'The soul and the body are the same' or 'The soul is one thing and the body another'; 'The Tathāgata exists after death' or 'The Tathāgata does not exist after death' or 'The Tathāgata

both exists and does not exist after death' or 'The Tathāgata neither exists nor does not exist after death'—a bhikkhu has discarded and dispelled them all, given them up, rejected them, let go of them, abandoned and relinquished them. It is in this way that a bhikkhu has dispelled personal truths.

(6) "And how has a bhikkhu totally renounced seeking? Here, a bhikkhu has abandoned the search for sensual pleasures and the search for existence and has allayed the search for a spiritual life. It is in this way that a bhikkhu has totally renounced seeking.

(7) "And how has a bhikkhu purified his intentions? Here, a bhikkhu has abandoned sensual intention, intention of ill will, and intention of harming. It is in this way that a bhikkhu has purified his intentions.

(8) "And how has a bhikkhu tranquilized bodily activity? Here, with the abandoning of pleasure and pain, and with the previous passing away of joy and dejection, a bhikkhu enters and dwells in the fourth jhāna, neither painful nor pleasant, which has purification of mindfulness by equanimity. It is in this way that a bhikkhu has tranquilized bodily activity.

(9) "And how is a bhikkhu well liberated in mind? Here, a bhikkhu's mind is liberated from lust, hatred, and delusion. It is in this way that a bhikkhu is well liberated in mind.

(10) "And how is a bhikkhu well liberated by wisdom? [32] Here, a bhikkhu understands: 'I have abandoned lust, cut it off at the root, made it like a palm stump, obliterated it so that it is no more subject to future arising; I have abandoned hatred . . . abandoned delusion, cut it off at the root, made it like a palm stump, obliterated it so that it is no more subject to future arising.' It is in this way that a bhikkhu is well liberated by wisdom.

"Bhikkhus, whatever noble ones in the past abided in noble abodes, all abided in these same ten noble abodes. Whatever noble ones in the future will abide in noble abodes, all will abide in these same ten noble abodes. Whatever noble ones at present abide in noble abodes, all abide in these same ten noble abodes.

"These are the ten abodes of the noble ones in which the noble ones abide in the past, present, or future."

III. The Great Chapter

21 (1) The Lion

"Bhikkhus, in the evening the lion, the king of beasts, comes out from his lair, stretches his body, surveys the four quarters all around, [33] and roars his lion's roar three times. Then he sets out in search of game. For what reason? [With the thought:] 'Let me not cause harm to small creatures that might cross my track.'

"'The lion,' bhikkhus, is a designation for the Tathāgata, the Arahant, the Perfectly Enlightened One. When the Tathāgata teaches the Dhamma to an assembly, this is his lion's roar.

"Bhikkhus, there are these ten Tathāgata's powers that the Tathāgata has, possessing which he claims the place of the chief bull, roars his lion's roar in the assemblies, and sets in motion the brahma wheel.[1983] What ten?

(1) "Here, the Tathāgata understands as it really is the possible as possible and the impossible as impossible. Since the Tathāgata understands as it really is the possible as possible and the impossible as impossible, this is a Tathāgata's power that the Tathāgata has, on account of which he claims the place of the chief bull, roars his lion's roar in the assemblies, and sets in motion the brahma wheel.

(2) "Again, the Tathāgata understands as it really is the result of the undertaking of kamma past, future, and present in terms of possibilities and causes. Since the Tathāgata understands as it really is . . . the result of the undertaking of kamma . . . this too is a Tathāgata's power that the Tathāgata has, on account of which he . . . sets in motion the brahma wheel.

(3) "Again, the Tathāgata understands as it really is the ways leading everywhere.[1984] Since the Tathāgata understands as it really is the ways leading everywhere, this too is a Tathāgata's power that the Tathāgata has, on account of which he . . . sets in motion the brahma wheel.

(4) "Again, the Tathāgata [34] understands as it really is the world with its numerous and diverse elements.[1985] Since the Tathāgata understands as it really is the world with its numerous and diverse elements, this too is a Tathāgata's power that the Tathāgata has, on account of which . . . he sets in motion the brahma wheel.

(5) "Again, the Tathāgata understands as it really is the diversity in the dispositions of beings.[1986] Since the Tathāgata understands as it really is the diversity in the dispositions of beings, this too is a Tathāgata's power that the Tathāgata has, on account of which . . . he sets in motion the brahma wheel.

(6) "Again, the Tathāgata understands as it really is the superior or inferior condition of the faculties of other beings and persons.[1987] Since the Tathāgata understands as it really is the superior or inferior condition of the faculties of other beings and persons, this too is a Tathāgata's power that the Tathāgata has, on account of which . . . he sets in motion the brahma wheel.

(7) "Again, the Tathāgata understands as it really is the defilement, the cleansing, and the emergence in regard to the jhānas, emancipations, concentrations, and meditative attainments. Since the Tathāgata understands as it really is the defilement, the cleansing, and the emergence in regard to the jhānas . . . this too is a Tathāgata's power that the Tathāgata has, on account of which . . . he sets in motion the brahma wheel.

(8) "Again, the Tathāgata recollects his manifold past abodes, that is, one birth, two births, three births, four births, five births, ten births, twenty births, thirty births, forty [35] births, fifty births, a hundred births, a thousand births, a hundred thousand births, many eons of world-dissolution, many eons of world-evolution, many eons of world-dissolution and world-evolution thus: 'There I was so named, of such a clan, with such an appearance, such was my food, such my experience of pleasure and pain, such my life span; passing away from there, I was reborn elsewhere, and there too I was so named, of such a clan, with such an appearance, such was my food, such my experience of pleasure and pain, such my life span; passing away from there, I was reborn here.' Thus he recollects his manifold past abodes with their aspects and details. Since the Tathāgata recollects his manifold past abodes . . . with their aspects and details, this too is a Tathāgata's power that the Tathāgata has, on account of which . . . he sets in motion the brahma wheel.

(9) "Again, with the divine eye, which is purified and surpasses the human, the Tathāgata sees beings passing away and being reborn, inferior and superior, beautiful and ugly, fortunate and unfortunate, and he understands how beings fare in accordance with their kamma thus: 'These beings who

engaged in misconduct by body, speech, and mind, who reviled the noble ones, held wrong view, and undertook kamma based on wrong view, with the breakup of the body, after death, have been reborn in the plane of misery, in a bad destination, in the lower world, in hell; but these beings who engaged in good conduct by body, speech, and mind, who did not revile the noble ones, who held right view, and undertook kamma based on right view, with the breakup of the body, after death, have been reborn in a good destination, in a heavenly world.' Thus with the divine eye, which is purified and surpasses the human, he sees beings passing away and being reborn, inferior and superior, beautiful and ugly, fortunate and unfortunate, and he understands how beings fare in accordance with their kamma. [36] Since the Tathāgata . . . understands how beings fare in accordance with their kamma, this too is a Tathāgata's power that the Tathāgata has, on account of which . . . he sets in motion the brahma wheel.

(10) "Again, with the destruction of the taints, the Tathāgata has realized for himself with direct knowledge, in this very life, the taintless liberation of mind, liberation by wisdom, and having entered upon it, he dwells in it. Since the Tathāgata has realized for himself . . . the taintless liberation of mind, liberation by wisdom . . . this too is a Tathāgata's power that the Tathāgata has, on account of which he claims the place of the chief bull, roars his lion's roar in the assemblies, and sets in motion the brahma wheel.

"These, bhikkhus, are the ten Tathāgata's powers that the Tathāgata has, possessing which he claims the place of the chief bull, roars his lion's roar in the assemblies, and sets in motion the brahma wheel."

22 (2) Doctrinal Principles

Then the Venerable Ānanda approached the Blessed One, paid homage to him, and sat down to one side. The Blessed One then said to him:

"Ānanda, I claim to be confident about the things that lead to the realization by direct knowledge of the various doctrinal principles,[1988] [and I am thus able] to teach the Dhamma to various people in various ways such that one who practices accordingly will know of what exists that it exists and of what does not exist that it does not exist; such that one will know of the inferior that it is inferior and of the sublime that it is sublime; such that one will know of what is surpassable that it is surpassable and of what is unsurpassable that it is unsurpassable; such that [37] it is possible that one will know, see, and realize this just as it is to be known, seen, and realized.

"But among knowledges, Ānanda, this one is unsurpassed, namely, the knowledge of these things and those things as they really are.[1989] And, I say, there is no other knowledge higher or more excellent than this.

"There are, Ānanda, these ten Tathāgata's powers that the Tathāgata has, possessing which he claims the place of the chief bull, roars his lion's roar in the assemblies, and sets in motion the brahma wheel. What ten? . . .

[As in 10:21] [38] . . .

"These, Ānanda, are the ten Tathāgata's powers that the Tathāgata has, possessing which he claims the place of the chief bull, roars his lion's roar in the assemblies, and sets in motion the brahma wheel." [39]

23 (3) Body

"Bhikkhus, there are things to be abandoned by body, not by speech. There are things to be abandoned by speech, not by body. There are things to be abandoned neither by body nor by speech but by having repeatedly seen with wisdom.[1990]

"And what, bhikkhus, are the things to be abandoned by body, not by speech? Here, a bhikkhu has committed a particular unwholesome deed with the body. His wise fellow monks investigate him and say thus: 'You have committed a particular unwholesome deed with the body. It would really be good if you would abandon bodily misconduct and develop bodily good conduct.' When his wise fellow monks investigate him and speak to him, he abandons bodily misconduct and develops bodily good conduct. These are called things to be abandoned by body, not by speech.

"And what are the things to be abandoned by speech, not by body? Here, a bhikkhu has committed a particular unwholesome deed by speech. His wise fellow monks investigate him and say thus: 'You have committed a particular unwholesome deed by speech. It would really be good if you would abandon verbal misconduct and develop verbal good conduct.' When his wise fellow monks investigate him and speak to him, he abandons verbal misconduct and develops verbal good conduct. These are called things to be abandoned by speech, not by body.

"And what are the things to be abandoned neither by body nor by speech but by having repeatedly seen with wisdom? Greed is to be abandoned neither by body nor by speech but by having repeatedly seen with wisdom. Hatred . . . Delusion . . . Anger . . . Hostility . . . Denigration . . . Insolence [40] . . . Miserliness is to be abandoned neither by body nor by speech but by having repeatedly seen with wisdom.

"Evil envy,[1991] bhikkhus, is to be abandoned neither by body nor by speech but by having repeatedly seen with wisdom. And what is evil envy? Here, a householder or householder's son is prospering in wealth or grain, in silver or gold. A slave or dependent might think of him: 'Oh, may this householder or householder's son not prosper in wealth or grain, in silver or gold!' Or else an ascetic or brahmin gains robes, almsfood, lodging, and medicines and provisions for the sick. Another ascetic or brahmin might think of him: 'Oh, may this venerable one not gain robes, almsfood, lodging, and medicines and provisions for the sick!' This is called evil envy. Evil envy is to be abandoned neither by body nor by speech but by having repeatedly seen with wisdom.

"Evil desire, bhikkhus, is to be abandoned neither by body nor by speech but by having repeatedly seen with wisdom. And what is evil desire? Here, one without faith desires: 'Let them know me as one endowed with faith.' An immoral person desires: 'Let them know me as virtuous.' One with little learning desires: 'Let them know me as learned.' One who delights in company desires: 'Let them know me as solitary.' One who is lazy desires: 'Let them know me as energetic.' One who is muddle-minded desires: 'Let them know me as mindful.' One who is unconcentrated desires: 'Let them know me as concentrated.' One who is unwise desires: 'Let them know me as wise.' One whose taints are not destroyed desires: 'Let them know me as one whose taints are destroyed.' [41] This is called evil desire. Evil desire is to be abandoned neither by body nor by speech but by having repeatedly seen with wisdom.

"If, bhikkhus, greed overcomes that bhikkhu and continues

on; if hatred ... delusion ... anger ... hostility ... denigration ... insolence ... miserliness ... evil envy ... evil desire overcomes that bhikkhu and continues on,[1992] he should be understood thus: 'This venerable one does not understand in such a way that he would have no greed; thus greed overcomes him and continues on. This venerable one does not understand in such a way that he would have no hatred ... no delusion ... no anger ... no hostility ... no denigration ... no insolence ... no miserliness ... no evil envy ... no evil desire; thus evil desire overcomes him and continues on.'

"If, bhikkhus, greed does not overcome that bhikkhu and continue on; if hatred ... delusion ... anger ... hostility ... denigration ... insolence ... miserliness ... evil envy ... evil desire does not overcome that bhikkhu and continue on, he should be understood thus: 'This venerable one understands in such a way that he would have no greed; thus greed does not overcome him and continue on. This venerable one understands in such a way that he would have no hatred ... no delusion ... no anger ... no hostility ... no denigration ... no insolence ... no miserliness ... no evil envy ... no evil desire; thus evil desire does not overcome him and continue on.'"

24 (4) Cunda

On one occasion the Venerable Mahācunda was dwelling among the Cetis at Sahajāti. There the Venerable Mahācunda addressed the bhikkhus: "Friends, bhikkhus!"

"Friend!" those [42] bhikkhus replied. The Venerable Mahācunda said this:

"Friends, making a declaration of knowledge, a bhikkhu says: 'I know this Dhamma, I see this Dhamma.'[1993] If, however, greed overcomes that bhikkhu and persists;[1994] if hatred ... delusion ... anger ... hostility ... denigration ... insolence ... miserliness ... evil envy ... evil desire overcomes that bhikkhu and persists, he should be understood thus: 'This venerable one does not understand in such a way that he would have no greed; thus greed overcomes him and persists. This venerable one does not understand in such a way that he would have no hatred ... no delusion ... no anger ... no hostility ... no denigration ... no insolence ... no miserliness ... no evil envy ... no evil desire; thus evil desire overcomes him and persists.'

"Friends, making a declaration of development, a bhikkhu

says: 'I am developed in body, virtuous behavior, mind, and wisdom.' If, however, greed overcomes that bhikkhu and persists; if hatred ... evil desire overcomes that bhikkhu and persists, he should be understood thus: 'This venerable one does not understand in such a way that he would have no greed; thus greed overcomes him and persists. This venerable one does not understand in such a way that he would have no hatred ... no evil desire; thus evil desire overcomes him and persists.'

"Friends, making a declaration of knowledge and development, a bhikkhu says: 'I know this Dhamma, I see this Dhamma. I am developed in body, virtuous behavior, mind, and wisdom.' If, however, greed overcomes that bhikkhu and persists; if hatred ... evil desire [43] overcomes that bhikkhu and persists, he should be understood thus: 'This venerable one does not understand in such a way that he would have no greed; thus greed overcomes him and persists. This venerable one does not understand in such a way that he would have no hatred ... no evil desire; thus evil desire overcomes him and persists.'

"Suppose a poor, destitute, and needy person claims to be rich, affluent, and wealthy. If, when he wants to buy something, he cannot pay with money, grain, silver, or gold, they would know him as a poor, destitute, and needy person claiming to be rich, affluent, and wealthy. For what reason? Because when he wants to buy something, he cannot pay with money, grain, silver, or gold.

"So too, friends, making a declaration of knowledge and development, a bhikkhu says: 'I know this Dhamma, I see this Dhamma. I am developed in body, virtuous behavior, mind, and wisdom.' If, however, greed overcomes that bhikkhu and persists ... evil desire overcomes that bhikkhu and persists, he should be understood thus: 'This venerable one does not understand in such a way that he would have no greed; thus greed overcomes him and persists. This venerable one does not understand in such a way that he would have no hatred ... [44] ... no evil desire; thus evil desire overcomes him and persists.'

"Friends, making a declaration of knowledge, a bhikkhu says: 'I know this Dhamma, I see this Dhamma.' If greed does not overcome that bhikkhu and persist; if hatred ... delusion ... anger ... hostility ... denigration ... insolence ... miserliness ... evil envy ... evil desire does not overcome that bhikkhu and persist, he should be understood thus: 'This venerable one understands in such a way that he has no greed; thus greed does not overcome him and persist. This venerable one understands in such a way that he has no hatred . . . no evil desire; thus evil desire does not overcome him and persist.'

"Friends, making a declaration of development, a bhikkhu says: 'I am developed in body, virtuous behavior, mind, and wisdom.' If greed does not overcome that bhikkhu and persist; if hatred . . . evil desire does not overcome that bhikkhu and persist, he should be understood thus: 'This venerable one understands in such a way that he has no greed; thus greed does not overcome him and persist. This venerable one understands in such a way that he has no hatred . . . no evil desire; thus evil desire does not overcome him and persist.'

"Friends, making a declaration of knowledge and development, a bhikkhu says: 'I know this Dhamma, I see this Dhamma. I am developed in body, virtuous behavior, mind, and wisdom.' If greed does not overcome that bhikkhu and persist; if hatred . . . evil desire does not overcome that bhikkhu and persist, he should be understood thus: 'This venerable one understands in such a way that he has no greed; [45] thus greed does not overcome him and persist. This venerable one understands in such a way that he has no hatred . . . no evil desire; thus evil desire does not overcome him and persist.'

"Suppose a rich, affluent, and wealthy person claims to be rich, affluent, and wealthy. If, when he wants to buy something, he can pay with money, grain, silver, or gold, they would know him as a rich, affluent, and wealthy person who claims to be rich, affluent, and wealthy. For what reason? Because when he wants to buy something, he can pay with money, grain, silver, or gold.

"So too, friends, making a declaration of knowledge and development, a bhikkhu says: 'I know this Dhamma, I see this Dhamma. I am developed in body, virtuous behavior, mind, and wisdom.' If greed does not overcome that bhikkhu and persist; if hatred . . . delusion . . . anger . . . hostility . . . denigration . . . insolence . . . miserliness . . . evil envy . . . evil desire does not overcome that bhikkhu and persist, he should be understood thus: 'This venerable one understands in such a way that he has no greed; thus greed does not overcome him and persist.

This venerable one understands in such a way that he has no hatred . . . no evil desire; thus evil desire does not overcome him and persist.'" [46]

25 (5) Kasiṇas

"Bhikkhus, there are these ten *kasiṇa* bases.[1995] What ten? One person perceives the earth *kasiṇa* above, below, across, nondual, measureless.[1996] One person perceives the water *kasiṇa* . . . the fire *kasiṇa* . . . the air *kasiṇa* . . . the blue *kasiṇa* . . . the yellow *kasiṇa* . . . the red *kasiṇa* . . . the white *kasiṇa* . . . the space *kasiṇa* . . . the consciousness *kasiṇa* above, below, across, nondual, measureless. These are the ten *kasiṇa* bases."

26 (6) Kāḷī

On one occasion the Venerable Mahākaccāna was dwelling among the people of Avantī on Mount Pavatta at Kuraraghara. Then the female lay follower Kāḷī of Kuraraghara approached him, paid homage to him, sat down to one side, and said to him:[1997]

"Bhante, this was said by the Blessed One in 'The Maidens' Questions':[1998]

"'Having conquered the army of the pleasant and
agreeable,
meditating alone, I discovered bliss,
the attainment of the goal, the peace of the heart.
Therefore I don't form intimate ties with people,
nor does intimacy with anyone get a chance with me.' [47]

"How, Bhante, is the meaning of this statement that the Blessed One spoke in brief to be seen in detail?"

"Some ascetics and brahmins, sister, for whom the attainment of the earth *kasiṇa* is supreme, generated it as their goal.[1999] The Blessed One directly knew to what extent the attainment of the earth *kasiṇa* is supreme. Having directly known this, he saw the beginning,[2000] the danger, and the escape, and he saw the knowledge and vision of the path and the non-path. By seeing the beginning, the danger, and the escape, and by seeing the knowledge and vision of the path and the non-path, he knew the attainment of the goal, the peace of the heart.

"Some ascetics and brahmins, sister, for whom the attainment of the water *kasiṇa* . . . the fire *kasiṇa* . . . the air *kasiṇa* . . . the blue *kasiṇa* . . . the yellow *kasiṇa* . . . the red *kasiṇa* . . . the white *kasiṇa* . . . the space *kasiṇa* . . . the consciousness *kasiṇa* is supreme, generated it as their goal. The Blessed One directly knew to what extent the attainment of the consciousness *kasiṇa* is supreme. Having directly known this, he saw the beginning, the danger, and the escape, and he saw the knowledge and vision of the path and the non-path. By seeing the beginning, the danger, and the escape, and by seeing the knowledge and vision of the path and the non-path, he knew the attainment of the goal, the peace of the heart.

"Thus, sister, it is in such a way that the meaning should be seen in detail of this statement that the Blessed One spoke in brief in 'The Maidens' Questions':

"'Having conquered the army of the pleasant and
agreeable,
meditating alone, I discovered bliss,
the attainment of the goal, the peace of the heart. [48]
Therefore I don't form intimate ties with people,
nor does intimacy with anyone succeed in my case.'"

27 (7) Great Questions (1)

On one occasion the Blessed One was dwelling at Sāvatthī in Jeta's Grove, Anāthapiṇḍika's Park. Then, in the morning, a number of bhikkhus dressed, took their bowls and robes, and entered Sāvatthī for alms. Then it occurred to those bhikkhus: "It is still too early to walk for alms in Sāvatthī. Let us go to the park of the wanderers of other sects."

Then those bhikkhus went to the park of the wanderers of other sects. They exchanged greetings with those wanderers and, when they had concluded their greetings and cordial talk, sat down to one side. Those wanderers then said to them:

"Friends, the ascetic Gotama teaches the Dhamma to his disciples in such a way as this: 'Come, bhikkhus, directly know all phenomena.[2001] Dwell having directly known all phenomena.'[2002] We too teach the Dhamma to our disciples in such a way as this: 'Come, friends, directly know all phenomena. Dwell having directly known all phenomena.' What now is the distinction, the disparity, the difference between the ascetic Gotama's [49] teaching of the Dhamma and our teaching, between his instruction and our instruction?"

Then those bhikkhus neither applauded nor rejected the statement of those wanderers. Without applauding it, without rejecting it, they rose from their seats and left, [thinking]: "We shall find out what the Blessed One has to say about this statement."

Then, when those bhikkhus had walked for alms in Sāvatthī, after their meal, on returning from their alms round, they approached the Blessed One, paid homage to him, sat down to one side, and said: "Here, Bhante, in the morning, we dressed, took our bowls and robes, and entered Sāvatthī for alms.... [They here report the entire course of events, down to:] [50] We rose from our seats and left, [thinking]: 'We shall find out what the Blessed One has to say about this statement.'"

"Bhikkhus, when wanderers of other sects speak thus, they should be answered in this way: 'A question about one, a concise statement about one, an explanation of one.[2003] A question about two, a concise statement about two, an explanation of two. A question about three, a concise statement about three, an explanation of three. A question about four, a concise statement about four, an explanation of four. A question about five, a concise statement about five, an explanation of five. A question about six, a concise statement about six, an explanation of six. A question about seven, a concise statement about seven, an explanation of seven. A question about eight, a concise statement about eight, an explanation of eight. A question about nine, a concise statement about nine, an explanation of nine. A question about ten, a concise statement about ten, an explanation of ten. If wanderers of other sects were questioned thus, they would not be able to reply and, further, they would meet with distress. For what reason? Because that would not be within their domain. I do not see anyone, bhikkhus, in the world with its devas, Māra, and Brahmā, in this population with its ascetics and brahmins, its devas and humans, who could satisfy the mind with an answer to these questions apart from the Tathāgata or a disciple of the Tathāgata or one who has heard it from them.

(1) "When it was said: 'A question about one, a concise state-

ment about one, an explanation of one,' with reference to what was this said?[2004] When a bhikkhu is completely disenchanted with one thing, completely dispassionate toward it, completely liberated from it, completely sees its delimitations, and completely breaks through its meaning, in this very life he makes an end of suffering. What one thing? All beings exist through nutriment.[2005] [51] When a bhikkhu is completely disenchanted with this one thing, completely dispassionate toward it, completely liberated from it, completely sees its delimitations, and completely breaks through its meaning, in this very life he makes an end of suffering.

"When it was said: 'A question about one, a concise statement about one, an explanation of one,' it is with reference to this that this was said.

(2) "When it was said: 'A question about two, a concise statement about two, an explanation of two,' with reference to what was this said? When a bhikkhu is completely disenchanted with two things, completely dispassionate toward them, completely liberated from them, completely sees their delimitations, and completely breaks through their meaning, in this very life he makes an end of suffering. What two things? Name and form. When a bhikkhu is completely disenchanted with these two things . . . in this very life he makes an end of suffering.

"When it was said: 'A question about two, a concise statement about two, an explanation of two,' it is with reference to this that this was said.

(3) "When it was said: 'A question about three, a concise statement about three, an explanation of three,' with reference to what was this said? When a bhikkhu is completely disenchanted with three things, completely dispassionate toward them, completely liberated from them, completely sees their delimitations, and completely breaks through their meaning, in this very life he makes an end of suffering. What three things? The three kinds of feelings.[2006] When a bhikkhu is completely disenchanted with these three things . . . in this very life he makes an end of suffering.

"When it was said: 'A question about three, a concise statement about three, an explanation of three,' it is with reference to this that this was said.

(4) "When it was said: 'A question about four, a concise

statement about four, an explanation of four,' with reference to what was this said? [52] When a bhikkhu is completely disenchanted with four things, completely dispassionate toward them, completely liberated from them, completely sees their delimitations, and completely breaks through their meaning, in this very life he makes an end of suffering. What four things? The four kinds of nutriment.[2007] When a bhikkhu is completely disenchanted with these four things . . . in this very life he makes an end of suffering.

"When it was said: 'A question about four, a concise statement about four, an explanation of four,' it is with reference to this that this was said.

(5) "When it was said: 'A question about five, a concise statement about five, an explanation of five,' with reference to what was this said? When a bhikkhu is completely disenchanted with five things, completely dispassionate toward them, completely liberated from them, completely sees their delimitations, and completely breaks through their meaning, in this very life he makes an end of suffering. What five things? The five aggregates subject to clinging. When a bhikkhu is completely disenchanted with these five things . . . in this very life he makes an end of suffering.

"When it was said: 'A question about five, a concise statement about five, an explanation of five,' it is with reference to this that this was said.

(6) "When it was said: 'A question about six, a concise statement about six, an explanation of six,' with reference to what was this said? When a bhikkhu is completely disenchanted with six things, completely dispassionate toward them, completely liberated from them, completely sees their delimitations, and completely breaks through their meaning, in this very life he makes an end of suffering. What six things? The six internal sense bases. When a bhikkhu is completely disenchanted with these six things . . . in this very life he makes an end of suffering. [53]

"When it was said: 'A question about six, a concise statement about six, an explanation of six,' it is with reference to this that this was said.

(7) "When it was said: 'A question about seven, a concise statement about seven, an explanation of seven,' with reference

to what was this said? When a bhikkhu is completely disenchanted with seven things, completely dispassionate toward them, completely liberated from them, completely sees their delimitations, and completely breaks through their meaning, in this very life he makes an end of suffering. What seven things? The seven stations for consciousness.[2008] When a bhikkhu is completely disenchanted with these seven things . . . in this very life he makes an end of suffering.

"When it was said: 'A question about seven, a concise statement about seven, an explanation of seven,' it is with reference to this that this was said.

(8) "When it was said: 'A question about eight, a concise statement about eight, an explanation of eight,' with reference to what was this said? When a bhikkhu is completely disenchanted with eight things, completely dispassionate toward them, completely liberated from them, completely sees their delimitations, and completely breaks through their meaning, in this very life he makes an end of suffering. What eight things? The eight worldly conditions.[2009] When a bhikkhu is completely disenchanted with these eight things . . . in this very life he makes an end of suffering.

"When it was said: 'A question about eight, a concise statement about eight, an explanation of eight,' it is with reference to this that this was said.

(9) "When it was said: 'A question about nine, a concise statement about nine, an explanation of nine,' with reference to what was this said? When a bhikkhu is completely disenchanted with nine things, completely dispassionate toward them, completely liberated from them, completely sees their delimitations, and completely breaks through their meaning, in this very life he makes an end of suffering. What nine things? The nine abodes of beings.[2010] [54] When a bhikkhu is completely disenchanted with these nine things . . . in this very life he makes an end of suffering.

"When it was said: 'A question about nine, a concise statement about nine, an explanation of nine,' it is with reference to this that this was said.

(10) "When it was said: 'A question about ten, a concise statement about ten, an explanation of ten,' with reference to what was this said? When a bhikkhu is completely disenchanted with

ten things, completely dispassionate toward them, completely liberated from them, completely sees their delimitations, and completely breaks through their meaning, in this very life he makes an end of suffering. What ten things? The ten unwholesome courses of kamma.[2011] When a bhikkhu is completely disenchanted with these ten things, completely dispassionate toward them, completely liberated from them, completely sees their delimitations, and completely breaks through their meaning, in this very life he makes an end of suffering.

"When it was said: 'A question about ten, a concise statement about ten, an explanation of ten,' it is with reference to this that this was said."

28 (8) Great Questions (2)

On one occasion the Blessed One was dwelling at Kajaṅgalā in the Bamboo Grove. Then a number of lay followers from Kajaṅgalā approached the bhikkhunī from Kajaṅgalā,[2012] paid homage to her, sat down to one side, and said to her:

"Noble lady, this was said by the Blessed One in 'The Great Questions': 'A question about one, a concise statement about one, an explanation of one. A question about two, a concise statement about two, an explanation of two. A question about three, a concise statement about three, an explanation of three. [55] A question about four, a concise statement about four, an explanation of four. A question about five, a concise statement about five, an explanation of five. A question about six, a concise statement about six, an explanation of six. A question about seven, a concise statement about seven, an explanation of seven. A question about eight, a concise statement about eight, an explanation of eight. A question about nine, a concise statement about nine, an explanation of nine. A question about ten, a concise statement about ten, an explanation of ten.' How, noble lady, is the meaning of this statement that the Blessed One spoke in brief to be seen in detail?"

"Friends, I have not heard and learned this in the presence of the Blessed One, nor have I heard and learned this in the presence of esteemed bhikkhus. However, listen and attend closely as I explain what it seems to mean to me."

"Yes, noble lady," those lay followers of Kajaṅgalā replied. The bhikkhunī of Kajaṅgalā said this:

(1) "When it was said by the Blessed One: 'A question about

one, a concise statement about one, an explanation of one,' with reference to what was this said? When a bhikkhu is completely disenchanted with one thing, completely dispassionate toward it, completely liberated from it, completely sees its delimitations, and completely breaks through its meaning, in this very life he makes an end of suffering. What one thing? All beings exist through nutriment. When a bhikkhu is completely disenchanted with this one thing, completely dispassionate toward it, completely liberated from it, completely sees its delimitations, and completely breaks through its meaning, in this very life he makes an end of suffering.

"When it was said by the Blessed One: 'A question about one, a concise statement about one, an explanation of one,' it is with reference to this that this was said. [56]

(2) "When it was said by the Blessed One: 'A question about two, a concise statement about two, an explanation of two,' with reference to what was this said? When a bhikkhu is completely disenchanted with two things, completely dispassionate toward them, completely liberated from them, completely sees their delimitations, and completely breaks through their meaning, in this very life he makes an end of suffering. What two things? Name and form. . . .

(3) . . . "What three things? The three kinds of feelings. When a bhikkhu is completely disenchanted with these three things . . . in this very life he makes an end of suffering.

"When it was said by the Blessed One: 'A question about three, a concise statement about three, an explanation of three,' it is with reference to this that this was said.

(4) "When it was said by the Blessed One: 'A question about four, a concise statement about four, an explanation of four,' with reference to what was this said? When a bhikkhu has a mind completely well developed in four things, completely sees their delimitations, and completely breaks through their meaning, in this very life he makes an end of suffering.[2013] What four things? The four establishments of mindfulness. When a bhikkhu has a mind completely well developed in these four things . . . in this very life he makes an end of suffering.

"When it was said by the Blessed One: 'A question about four, a concise statement about four, an explanation of four,' it is with reference to this that this was said.

(5)–(8) "When it was said by the Blessed One: 'A question

about five, a concise statement about five, an explanation of five,' with reference to what was this said? When a bhikkhu has a mind completely well developed in five things, completely sees their delimitations, and completely breaks through their meaning, in this very life he makes an end of suffering. What five things? The five faculties.[2014] . . . What six things? [57] The six elements of escape.[2015] . . . What seven things? The seven factors of enlightenment. . . . What eight things? The noble eightfold path. When a bhikkhu has a mind completely well developed in these eight things . . . in this very life he makes an end of suffering.

"When it was said by the Blessed One: 'A question about eight, a concise statement about eight, an explanation of eight,' it is with reference to this that this was said.

(9) "When it was said by the Blessed One: 'A question about nine, a concise statement about nine, an explanation of nine,' with reference to what was this said? When a bhikkhu is completely disenchanted with nine things, completely dispassionate toward them, completely liberated from them, completely sees their delimitations, and completely breaks through their meaning, in this very life he makes an end of suffering. What nine things? The nine abodes of beings. When a bhikkhu is completely disenchanted with these nine things . . . in this very life he makes an end of suffering.

"When it was said by the Blessed One: 'A question about nine, a concise statement about nine, an explanation of nine,' it is with reference to this that this was said.

(10) "When it was said by the Blessed One: 'A question about ten, a concise statement about ten, an explanation of ten,' with reference to what was this said? When a bhikkhu has a mind completely well developed in ten things, completely sees their delimitations, and completely breaks through their meaning, in this very life he makes an end of suffering. What ten things? The ten wholesome courses of kamma. [58] When a bhikkhu has a mind completely well developed in these ten things . . . in this very life he makes an end of suffering.

"When it was said by the Blessed One: 'A question about ten, a concise statement about ten, an explanation of ten,' it is with reference to this that this was said.

"Thus, friends, when it was said by the Blessed One in 'The

Great Questions': 'A question about one, a concise statement about one, an explanation of one. . . . A question about ten, a concise statement about ten, an explanation of ten,' it is in such a way that I understand in detail the meaning of this statement that the Blessed One spoke in brief. But if you wish, approach the Blessed One and ask him about this matter. As the Blessed One answers you, so should you retain it in mind."

Saying, "Yes, noble lady," those lay followers of Kajaṅgalā delighted and rejoiced in the statement of the bhikkhunī of Kajaṅgalā. Then they rose from their seats, paid homage to her, circumambulated her keeping the right side toward her, and approached the Blessed One. They paid homage to the Blessed One, sat down to one side, and reported to the Blessed One their entire discussion with the bhikkhunī of Kajaṅgalā. [The Blessed One said:]

"Good, good, householders! The bhikkhunī of Kajaṅgalā is wise, of great wisdom. If you had approached me and asked me about this matter, I [59] would have answered exactly as the bhikkhunī of Kajaṅgalā has answered. That is its meaning, and it is in this way that you should retain it in mind."

29 (9) Kosala (1)

(1) "Bhikkhus, as far as Kāsi and Kosala extend, as far as the realm of King Pasenadi of Kosala extends, there King Pasenadi of Kosala ranks as the foremost. But even for King Pasenadi there is alteration; there is change. Seeing this thus, the instructed noble disciple becomes disenchanted with it; being disenchanted, he becomes dispassionate toward the foremost, not to speak of what is inferior.

(2) "Bhikkhus, as far as sun and moon revolve and light up the quarters with their brightness, so far the thousandfold world system extends.[2016] In that thousandfold world system there are a thousand moons, a thousand suns, a thousand Sinerus king of mountains, a thousand Jambudīpas, a thousand Aparagoyānas, a thousand Uttarakurus, a thousand Pubbavidehas, and a thousand four great oceans; a thousand four great kings, a thousand [heavens ruled by] the four great kings, a thousand Tāvatiṃsa [heavens], a thousand Yāma [heavens], a thousand Tusita [heavens], a thousand [heavens] of devas who delight in creation, a thousand [heavens] of devas who control what is

created by others, a thousand brahmā worlds. As far, bhikkhus, as this thousandfold world system extends, Mahābrahmā [60] there ranks as the foremost. But even for Mahābrahmā there is alteration; there is change. Seeing this thus, the instructed noble disciple becomes disenchanted with it; being disenchanted, he becomes dispassionate toward the foremost, not to speak of what is inferior.

(3) "There comes a time, bhikkhus, when this world dissolves. When the world is dissolving, beings for the most part migrate to the devas of streaming radiance.[2017] There they exist mind-made, feeding on rapture, self-luminous, moving through the skies, living in glory, and they remain thus for a very long time. When the world is dissolving, the devas of streaming radiance rank as the foremost. But even for these devas there is alteration; there is change. Seeing this thus, the instructed noble disciple becomes disenchanted with it; being disenchanted, he becomes dispassionate toward the foremost, not to speak of what is inferior.

(4) "Bhikkhus, there are these ten *kasiṇa* bases.[2018] What ten? One person perceives the earth *kasiṇa* above, below, across, undivided, measureless. One person perceives the water *kasiṇa* . . . the fire *kasiṇa* . . . the air *kasiṇa* . . . the blue *kasiṇa* . . . the yellow *kasiṇa* . . . the red *kasiṇa* . . . the white *kasiṇa* . . . the space *kasiṇa* . . . the consciousness *kasiṇa* above, below, across, undivided, measureless. These are the ten *kasiṇa* bases. Of these ten *kasiṇa* bases, this is the foremost, namely, when one perceives the consciousness *kasiṇa* above, below, across, undivided, measureless. There are beings who are percipient in such a way. But even for beings who are percipient in such a way there is alteration; there is change. Seeing this thus, [61] bhikkhus, the instructed noble disciple becomes disenchanted with it; being disenchanted, he becomes dispassionate toward the foremost, not to speak of what is inferior.

(5) "Bhikkhus, there are these eight bases of overcoming.[2019] What eight?

(i) "One percipient of forms internally sees forms externally, limited, beautiful or ugly. Having overcome them, he is percipient thus: 'I know, I see.' This is the first basis of overcoming.

(ii) "One percipient of forms internally sees forms externally, measureless, beautiful or ugly. Having overcome them, he is percipient thus: 'I know, I see.' This is the second basis of overcoming.

(iii) "One not percipient of forms internally sees forms externally, limited, beautiful or ugly. Having overcome them, he is percipient thus: 'I know, I see.' This is the third basis of overcoming.

(iv) "One not percipient of forms internally sees forms externally, measureless, beautiful or ugly. Having overcome them, he is percipient thus: 'I know, I see.' This is the fourth basis of overcoming.

(v) "One not percipient of forms internally sees forms externally, blue ones, blue in color, with a blue hue, with a blue tint. Just as the flax flower is blue, blue in color, with a blue hue, with a blue tint, or just as Bārāṇasī cloth, smoothened on both sides, might be blue, blue in color, with a blue hue, with a blue tint, so too, one not percipient of forms internally sees forms externally, blue ones.... Having overcome them, he is percipient thus: 'I know, I see.' This is the fifth basis of overcoming.

(vi) "One not percipient of forms internally sees forms externally, yellow ones, with a yellow hue, with a yellow tint. Just as the *kaṇikāra* flower is yellow, yellow in color, with a yellow hue, with a yellow tint, or just as Bārāṇasī cloth, [62] smoothened on both sides, might be yellow, yellow in color, with a yellow hue, with a yellow tint, so too, one not percipient of forms internally sees forms externally, yellow ones.... Having overcome them, he is percipient thus: 'I know, I see.' This is the sixth basis of overcoming.

(vii) "One not percipient of forms internally sees forms externally, red ones, with a red hue, with a red tint. Just as the *bandhujīvaka* flower is red, red in color, with a red hue, with a red tint, or just as Bārāṇasī cloth, smoothened on both sides, might be red, red in color with a red hue, with a red tint, so too, one not percipient of forms internally sees forms externally, red ones.... Having overcome them, he is percipient thus: 'I know, I see.' This is the seventh basis of overcoming.

(viii) "One not percipient of forms internally sees forms externally, white ones, white in color, with a white hue, with a white tint. Just as the morning star is white, white in color, with a white hue, with a white tint, or just as Bārāṇasī cloth, smoothened on both sides, might be white, white in color, with a white hue, with a white tint, so too, one not percipient of forms internally sees forms externally, white ones.... Having overcome them, he is percipient thus: 'I know, I see.' This is the eighth basis of overcoming.

"These are the eight bases of overcoming. Of these eight bases of overcoming, this is the foremost, namely, that one not percipient of forms internally sees forms externally, white ones, white in color with a white hue, with a white tint, and having overcome them, he is percipient thus: 'I know, I see.' There are beings who are percipient in such a way. But even for beings who are percipient in such a way there is [63] alteration; there is change. Seeing this thus, the instructed noble disciple becomes disenchanted with it; being disenchanted, he becomes dispassionate toward the foremost, not to speak of what is inferior.

(6) "Bhikkhus, there are these four modes of practice.[2020] What four? Practice that is painful with sluggish direct knowledge; practice that is painful with quick direct knowledge; practice that is pleasant with sluggish direct knowledge; and practice that is pleasant with quick direct knowledge. These are the four modes of practice. Of these four modes of practice, this is the foremost, namely, practice that is pleasant with quick direct knowledge. There are beings who practice in such a way. But even for beings who practice in such a way there is alteration; there is change. Seeing this thus, the instructed noble disciple becomes disenchanted with it; being disenchanted, he becomes dispassionate toward the foremost, not to speak of what is inferior.

(7) "Bhikkhus, there are these four modes of perception. What four? One person perceives what is limited; another perceives what is exalted; another perceives what is measureless; and still another, [perceiving] 'There is nothing,' perceives the base of nothingness.[2021] These are the four modes of perception. Of these four modes of perception, this is the foremost, namely, when, [perceiving] 'There is nothing,' one perceives the base of nothingness. There are beings who perceive in such a way. But even for beings who perceive in such a way there is alteration; there is change. Seeing this thus, the instructed noble disciple becomes disenchanted with it; being disenchanted, he becomes dispassionate toward the foremost, not to speak of what is inferior.

(8) "Bhikkhus, of the speculative views held by outsiders, this is the foremost, namely: 'I might not be and it might not be

mine; I shall not be, [and] it will not be mine.'[2022] For it can be expected that one who holds such a view will not be unrepelled by existence [64] and will not be repelled by the cessation of existence.[2023] There are beings who hold such a view. But even for beings who hold such a view there is alteration; there is change. Seeing this thus, the instructed noble disciple becomes disenchanted with it; being disenchanted, he becomes dispassionate toward the foremost, not to speak of what is inferior.

(9) "Bhikkhus, there are some ascetics and brahmins who proclaim supreme purification.[2024] Of those who proclaim supreme purification, this is the foremost, namely, by completely surmounting the base of nothingness, one enters and dwells in the base of neither-perception-nor-non-perception. They teach their Dhamma for the direct knowledge and realization of this. There are beings who assert thus. But even for those who assert thus, there is alteration; there is change. Seeing this thus, the instructed noble disciple becomes disenchanted with it; being disenchanted, he becomes dispassionate toward the foremost, not to speak of what is inferior.

(10) "Bhikkhus, there are some ascetics and brahmins who proclaim supreme nibbāna in this very life.[2025] Of those who proclaim supreme nibbāna in this very life, this is the foremost, namely, emancipation through non-clinging after one has seen as they really are the origin and passing away, the gratification, danger, and escape in regard to the six bases for contact.

"Bhikkhus, though I assert and declare [my teaching] in such a way, some ascetics and brahmins untruthfully, baselessly, falsely, and wrongly misrepresent me, [by saying]: 'The ascetic Gotama does not proclaim the full understanding of sensual pleasures, the full understanding of forms, or the full understanding of feelings.' [65] But, bhikkhus, I do proclaim the full understanding of sensual pleasures, the full understanding of forms, and the full understanding of feelings. In this very life, hungerless, quenched, and cooled, I proclaim final nibbāna through non-clinging."[2026]

30 (10) Kosala (2)

On one occasion the Blessed One was dwelling at Sāvatthī in Jeta's Grove, Anāthapiṇḍika's Park. Now on that occasion King Pasenadi of Kosala had returned from the war front, victorious in battle, his purpose having been achieved.[2027] Then King Pasenadi of Kosala set out for the park. He went by carriage as far as the ground was suitable for a carriage, and then he dismounted from his carriage and entered the park on foot. Now on that occasion a number of bhikkhus were walking back and forth in the open air. Then King Pasenadi of Kosala approached those bhikkhus and asked them:

"Bhante, where is the Blessed One, the Arahant, the Perfectly Enlightened One now dwelling? For I wish to see the Blessed One, the Arahant, the Perfectly Enlightened One."

"Great king, that is his dwelling with the closed door. Approach it quietly. Without hurrying, enter the porch, clear your throat, and tap on the bolt. The Blessed One will open the door for you."

Then, King Pasenadi of Kosala went quietly up to the dwelling with the closed door. Without hurrying, he entered the porch, cleared his throat, and tapped on the bolt. The Blessed One opened the door.

Then King Pasenadi of Kosala entered the dwelling, prostrated himself with his head at the Blessed One's feet, and covered the Blessed One's feet with kisses and caressed them with his hands, pronouncing his name: "Bhante, I am King Pasenadi of Kosala! Bhante, I am King [66] Pasenadi of Kosala!"[2028]

"But, great king, what reasons do you have for showing such supreme honor to this body and displaying such an offering of loving-kindness?"

"Bhante, it is out of my gratitude and thankfulness that I show such supreme honor toward the Blessed One and display such an offering of loving-kindness to him.

(1) "For, Bhante, the Blessed One is practicing for the welfare of many people, for the happiness of many people; he has established many people in the noble method, that is, in the way of the good Dhamma, in the way of the wholesome Dhamma.[2029] This is one reason I show such supreme honor toward the Blessed One and display such an offering of loving-kindness to him.

(2) "Again, Bhante, the Blessed One is virtuous, of mature behavior, of noble behavior, of wholesome behavior, possessing wholesome behavior. This is another reason I show such supreme honor toward the Blessed One. . . .

(3) "Again, Bhante, for a long time the Blessed One has been a forest-dweller who resorts to remote lodgings in forests and jungle groves. Since that is [67] so, this is another reason I show such supreme honor toward the Blessed One. . . .

(4) "Again, Bhante, the Blessed One is content with any kind of robe, almsfood, lodging, and medicines and provisions for the sick. This is another reason I show such supreme honor toward the Blessed One. . . .

(5) "Again, Bhante, the Blessed One is worthy of gifts, worthy of hospitality, worthy of offerings, worthy of reverential salutation, an unsurpassed field of merit for the world. This is another reason I show such supreme honor toward the Blessed One. . . .

(6) "Again, Bhante, the Blessed One gets to hear at will, without trouble or difficulty, talk concerned with the austere life that leads to the elimination [of defilements], that is conducive to opening up the heart, that is, talk on fewness of desires, on contentment, on solitude, on not getting bound up [with others], on arousing energy, on virtuous behavior, on concentration, on wisdom, on liberation, on the knowledge and vision of liberation. This is another reason I show such supreme honor toward the Blessed One. . . .

(7) "Again, Bhante, the Blessed One gains at will, without trouble or difficulty, the four jhānas that constitute the higher mind and are pleasant dwellings in this very life. [68] This is another reason I show such supreme honor toward the Blessed One. . . .

(8) "Again, Bhante, the Blessed One recollects his manifold past abodes, that is, one birth, two births, three births, four births, five births, ten births, twenty births, thirty births, forty births, fifty births, a hundred births, a thousand births, a hundred thousand births, many eons of world-dissolution, many eons of world-evolution, many eons of world-dissolution and world-evolution thus: 'There I was so named, of such a clan, with such an appearance, such was my food, such my experience of pleasure and pain, such my life span; passing away from there, I was reborn elsewhere, and there too I was so named, of such a clan, with such an appearance, such was my food, such my experience of pleasure and pain, such my life span; passing away from there, I was reborn here.' Thus he recollects his

manifold past abodes with their aspects and details. Since that is so, this is another reason I show such supreme honor toward the Blessed One. . . .

(9) "Again, Bhante, with the divine eye, which is purified and surpasses the human, the Blessed One sees beings passing away and being reborn, inferior and superior, beautiful and ugly, fortunate and unfortunate, and he understands how beings fare in accordance with their kamma thus: 'These beings who engaged in misconduct by body, speech, and mind, who reviled the noble ones, [69] held wrong view, and undertook kamma based on wrong view, with the breakup of the body, after death, have been reborn in the plane of misery, in a bad destination, in the lower world, in hell; but these beings who engaged in good conduct by body, speech, and mind, who did not revile the noble ones, who held right view, and undertook kamma based on right view, with the breakup of the body, after death, have been reborn in a good destination, in the heavenly world.' Thus with the divine eye, which is purified and surpasses the human, he sees beings passing away and being reborn, inferior and superior, beautiful and ugly, fortunate and unfortunate, and he understands how beings fare in accordance with their kamma. Since that is so, this is another reason I show such supreme honor toward the Blessed One. . . .

(10) "Again, Bhante, with the destruction of the taints, the Blessed One has realized for himself with direct knowledge, in this very life, the taintless liberation of mind, liberation by wisdom, and having entered upon it, he dwells in it. Since that is so, this is another reason I show such supreme honor toward the Blessed One and display such an offering of loving-kindness to him.

"And now, Bhante, we must be going. We are busy and have much to do."

"You may go, great king, at your own convenience."

Then King Pasenadi of Kosala rose from his seat, paid homage to the Blessed One, circumambulated him keeping the right side toward him, and departed. [70]

IV. Upāli

31 (1) Upāli

Then the Venerable Upāli approached the Blessed One, paid homage to him, sat down to one side, and said to him:

"Bhante, on how many grounds has the Tathāgata prescribed the training rules[2030] for his disciples and recited the Pātimokkha?"

"It is, Upāli, on ten grounds that the Tathāgata has prescribed the training rules for his disciples and recited the Pātimokkha. What ten? (1) For the well-being of the Saṅgha; (2) for the ease of the Saṅgha; (3) for keeping recalcitrant persons in check; (4) so that well-behaved bhikkhus can dwell at ease; (5) for the restraint of taints pertaining to this present life; (6) for the dispelling of taints pertaining to future lives; (7) so that those without confidence might gain confidence; and (8) for increasing [the confidence] of those with confidence; (9) for the continuation of the good Dhamma; and (10) for promoting discipline.

"It is on these ten grounds that the Tathāgata has prescribed the training rules for his disciples and recited the Pātimokkha."

32 (2) Suspending[2031]

"Bhante, how many reasons are there for suspending the Pātimokkha?"

"There are, Upāli, ten reasons for suspending the Pātimokkha. What ten? (1) One who has committed a *pārājika* is sitting in that assembly; (2) a discussion about one who has committed a *pārājika* is underway;[2032] (3) one not fully ordained is sitting in that assembly; [71] (4) a discussion about one not fully ordained is underway; (5) one who has given up the training is sitting in that assembly; (6) a discussion about one who has given up the training is underway; (7) a eunuch is sitting in that assembly;[2033] (8) a discussion about a eunuch is underway; (9) a seducer of a bhikkhunī is sitting in that assembly;[2034] (10) a discussion about a seducer of a bhikkhunī is underway. These are the ten reasons for suspending the Pātimokkha."

33 (3) Adjudication

"Bhante, how many qualities should a bhikkhu possess to be agreed upon to adjudicate [in a disciplinary issue]?"[2035]

"A bhikkhu who possesses ten qualities, Upāli, may be agreed upon to adjudicate [in a disciplinary issue]. What ten? (1) Here, a bhikkhu is virtuous; he dwells restrained by the Pātimokkha, possessed of good conduct and resort, seeing danger in minute faults. Having undertaken the training rules, he trains in them. (2) He has learned much, remembers what he has learned, and accumulates what he has learned. Those teachings that are good in the beginning, good in the middle, and good in the end, with the right meaning and phrasing, which proclaim the perfectly complete and pure spiritual life—such teachings as these he has learned much of, retained in mind, recited verbally, investigated mentally, and penetrated well by view. (3) Both Pātimokkhas have been well transmitted to him in detail, well analyzed, well mastered, well determined in terms of the rules and their detailed explication. (4) He is firm in the discipline, immovable. (5) He is able to convince those on both sides of the issue, to describe matters to them, to persuade them, to demonstrate to them, and to placate them. (6) He is skilled in the origination and [72] settlement of disciplinary issues. (7) He knows what a disciplinary issue is.[2036] (8) He knows the origin of a disciplinary issue. (9) He knows the cessation of a disciplinary issue. (10) He knows the way leading to the cessation of a disciplinary issue.[2037] A bhikkhu who possesses these ten qualities may be agreed upon to adjudicate [in a disciplinary issue]."

34 (4) Full Ordination

"Bhante, how many qualities should a bhikkhu possess to give full ordination?"

"A bhikkhu who possesses ten qualities, Upāli, may give full ordination. What ten? (1) Here, a bhikkhu is virtuous . . . he trains in them. (2) He has learned much . . . and penetrated well by view. (3) Both Pātimokkhas have been well transmitted to him in detail, well analyzed, well mastered, well determined in terms of the rules and their detailed explication. (4) He is able to look after a patient or to get someone else to look after him. (5) He is able to eliminate one's dissatisfaction or to get someone else to eliminate it. (6) He is able to use the Dhamma to dispel regrets that might arise [in his pupils]. (7) He is able to dissuade them, by way of the Dhamma, from erroneous views that have arisen. (8) He is able to encourage them in the higher virtuous behavior. (9) He is able to encourage them in the higher mind. (10) He is able to encourage them in the higher wisdom. A bhikkhu who possesses these ten qualities may give full ordination." [73]

35 (5) Dependence

"Bhante, how many qualities should a bhikkhu possess to give dependence?"

"A bhikkhu who possesses ten qualities, Upāli, may give dependence. What ten?" . . .

[The same ten qualities as in the preceding sutta.]

"A bhikkhu who possesses these ten qualities may give dependence."

36 (6) Novice[2038]

"Bhante, how many qualities should a bhikkhu possess to be attended upon by a novice?"

"A bhikkhu who possesses ten qualities, Upāli, may be attended upon by a novice. What ten?" . . .

[The same ten qualities as in 10:34.]

"A bhikkhu who possesses these ten qualities may be attended upon by a novice."

37 (7) Schism (1)

"Bhante, it is said: 'Schism in the Saṅgha, schism in the Saṅgha.' How, Bhante, is there schism in the Saṅgha?"

"Here, Upāli, (1) bhikkhus explain non-Dhamma as Dhamma, (2) and Dhamma as non-Dhamma. (3) They explain non-discipline as discipline, [74] and (4) discipline as non-discipline. (5) They explain what has not been stated and uttered by the Tathāgata as having been stated and uttered by him, and (6) what has been stated and uttered by the Tathāgata as not having been stated and uttered by him. (7) They explain what has not been practiced by the Tathāgata as having been practiced by him, and (8) what has been practiced by the Tathāgata as not having been practiced by him. (9) They explain what has not been prescribed by the Tathāgata as having been prescribed by him, and (10) what has been prescribed by the Tathāgata as not having been prescribed by him. On these ten grounds they withdraw and go apart. They perform legal acts separately and recite the Pātimokkha separately. It is in this way, Upāli, that there is schism in the Saṅgha."

38 (8) Schism (2)

"Bhante, it is said: 'Concord in the Saṅgha, concord in the Saṅgha.' How is there concord in the Saṅgha?"

"Here, Upāli, (1) bhikkhus explain non-Dhamma as non-Dhamma, and (2) Dhamma as Dhamma. (3) They explain non-discipline as non-discipline, and (4) discipline as discipline. (5) They explain what has not been stated and uttered by the Tathāgata as not having been stated and uttered by him, and (6) what has been stated and uttered by the Tathāgata as having been stated and uttered by him. (7) They explain what has not been practiced by the Tathāgata as not having been practiced by him, and (8) what has been practiced by the Tathāgata as having been practiced by him. (9) They explain what has not been prescribed by the Tathāgata as not having been prescribed by him, and (10) what has been prescribed by the Tathāgata as having been prescribed by him. On these ten grounds, they do not withdraw and go apart. They do not perform legal acts separately or recite the Pātimokkha separately. It is in this way, Upāli, that there is concord in the Saṅgha." [75]

39 (9) Ānanda (1)

Then the Venerable Ānanda approached the Blessed One, paid homage to him, sat down to one side, and said to him:

"Bhante, it is said: 'Schism in the Saṅgha, schism in the Saṅgha.' How is there schism in the Saṅgha?"

"Here, Ānanda, (1) bhikkhus explain non-Dhamma as Dhamma . . . [as in 10:37] . . . and (10) what has been prescribed by the Tathāgata as not having been prescribed by him. On these ten grounds they withdraw and go apart. They perform legal acts separately and recite the Pātimokkha separately. It is in this way, Ānanda, that there is schism in the Saṅgha."[2039]

"But, Bhante, when one causes schism in a harmonious Saṅgha, what does one generate?"

"One generates evil lasting for an eon, Ānanda."[2040]

"But, Bhante, what is that evil lasting for an eon?"

"One is tormented in hell for an eon, Ānanda." [76]

One who causes schism in the Saṅgha is bound for misery,
bound for hell, to abide there for an eon.
Delighting in factions, established in non-Dhamma,
he falls away from security from bondage.
Having caused schism in a harmonious Saṅgha,
he is tormented in hell for an eon.

40 (10) Ānanda (2)

"Bhante, it is said: 'Concord in the Saṅgha, concord in the Saṅgha.' How is there concord in the Saṅgha?"

"Here, Ānanda, (1) bhikkhus explain non-Dhamma as non-Dhamma . . . [as in 10:38] . . . and (10) what has been prescribed by the Tathāgata as having been prescribed by him. On these ten grounds they do not withdraw and go apart. They do not perform legal acts separately or recite the Pātimokkha separately. It is in this way, Ānanda, that there is concord in the Saṅgha."[2041]

"But, Bhante, when one reconciles a divided Saṅgha, what does one generate?"

"One generates divine merit, Ānanda."

"But, Bhante, what is divine merit?"

"One rejoices in heaven for an eon, Ānanda." [77]

Pleasant is concord in the Saṅgha,
and the mutual help[2042] of those who live in concord.
Delighting in concord, established in Dhamma,
one does not fall away from security from bondage.
Having brought concord to the Saṅgha,
one rejoices in heaven for an eon.

V. Insults

41 (1) Disputes

Then the Venerable Upāli approached the Blessed One, paid homage to him, sat down to one side, and said to him:

"Bhante, why is it that arguments, quarrels, contention, and disputes arise in the Saṅgha and bhikkhus do not dwell at ease?"

"Here, Upāli, (1) bhikkhus explain non-Dhamma as Dhamma

. . . [as in 10:37] . . . [78] . . . and (10) what has been prescribed by the Tathāgata as not having been prescribed by him. This, Upāli, is why arguments, quarrels, contention, and disputes arise in the Saṅgha and bhikkhus do not dwell at ease."

42 (2) Roots (1)

"Bhante, how many roots of disputes are there?"

"There are, Upāli, ten roots of disputes. What ten? Here, (1) bhikkhus explain non-Dhamma as Dhamma . . . [as in 10:37] . . . and (10) what has been prescribed by the Tathāgata as not having been prescribed by him. These, Upāli, are the ten roots of disputes."

43 (3) Roots (2)

"Bhante, how many roots of disputes are there?"

"There are, Upāli, ten roots of disputes. What ten? Here, (1) bhikkhus explain what is no offense as an offense, and (2) what is an offense as no offense. (3) They explain a light offense as a grave offense, and (4) a grave offense as a light offense. (5) They explain a coarse offense as not a coarse offense, and (6) an offense that is not coarse as a coarse offense. (7) They explain a remediable offense as an irremediable offense, and (8) an irremediable offense as a remediable offense. [79] (9) They explain an offense with redress as an offense without redress, and (10) an offense without redress as an offense with redress.[2043] These, Upāli, are the ten roots of disputes."

44 (4) Kusinārā

On one occasion the Blessed One was dwelling at Kusinārā, in the forest thicket of oblations. There the Blessed One addressed the bhikkhus: "Bhikkhus!"

"Venerable sir!" those bhikkhus replied. The Blessed One said this:

"Bhikkhus, a bhikkhu who wishes to reprove another person should examine himself with respect to five things and establish five things in himself before he reproves the other person.[2044] With respect to what five things should he examine himself?

(1) "Bhikkhus, a bhikkhu who wishes to reprove another should examine himself thus: 'Is my bodily behavior pure? Do I possess bodily behavior that is pure, flawless, and irreproach-

able? Does this quality exist in me or not?' If the bhikkhu's bodily behavior is not pure, and he does not possess bodily behavior that is pure, flawless, and irreproachable, there will be those who say to him: 'Please first train yourself bodily.' There will be those who say this to him.

(2) "Again, a bhikkhu who wishes to reprove another should examine himself thus: 'Is my verbal behavior pure? Do I possess verbal behavior that is pure, flawless, and irreproachable? Does this quality exist in me or not?' If the bhikkhu's verbal behavior is not pure, and he does not possess verbal behavior that is pure, flawless, and irreproachable, there will be those who say to him: 'Please first train yourself verbally.' There will be those who say this to him. [80]

(3) "Again, a bhikkhu who wishes to reprove another should examine himself thus: 'Have I established a mind of loving-kindness without resentment toward my fellow monks? Does this quality exist in me or not?' If the bhikkhu has not established a mind of loving-kindness without resentment toward his fellow monks, there will be those who say to him: 'Please first establish a mind of loving-kindness toward your fellow monks.' There will be those who say this to him.

(4) "Again, a bhikkhu who wishes to reprove another should examine himself thus: 'Am I learned, and do I retain and preserve what I have learned? Have I learned much of those teachings that are good in the beginning, good in the middle, and good in the end, with the right meaning and phrasing, which proclaim the perfectly complete and pure spiritual life? Have I retained them in mind, recited them verbally, mentally investigated them, and penetrated them well by view? Does this quality exist in me or not?' If the bhikkhu is not learned . . . and has not penetrated them well by view, there will be those who say to him: 'Please first learn the heritage.' There will be those who say this to him.

(5) "Again, a bhikkhu who wishes to reprove another should examine himself thus: 'Have both Pātimokkhas been well transmitted to me in detail, well analyzed, well mastered, well determined in terms of the rules and their detailed explication? Does there exist in me this quality or not?' If both Pātimokkhas [81] have not been well transmitted to him in detail . . . in terms of the rules and their detailed explication, and if, when asked: 'Where

did the Blessed One state this?' he is unable to reply, there will be those who say to him: 'Please first learn the discipline.' There will be those who say this to him.

"It is with respect to these five things that he should examine himself.

"And what are the five things that he should establish in himself? [He should consider:] '(6) I will speak at a proper time, not at an improper time; (7) I will speak truthfully, not falsely; (8) I will speak gently, not harshly; (9) I will speak in a beneficial way, not in a harmful way; (10) I will speak with a mind of loving-kindness, not while harboring hatred.' These are the five things that he should establish in himself.

"Bhikkhus, a bhikkhu who wishes to reprove another person should examine himself with respect to these five things and establish these five things in himself before he reproves the other person."

45 (5) Entering

"Bhikkhus, there are these ten dangers in entering the king's inner palace. What ten?

(1) "Here, the king is sitting with his queen. The bhikkhu enters, and either the queen smiles when she sees the bhikkhu or the bhikkhu smiles when he sees the queen. The king thinks: 'Surely, something has gone on between them, or something is about to go on.' This is the first danger in entering the king's inner palace.

(2) "Again, when the king has been busy, engaged with much work, he has had intercourse with one of the women but does not remember this, and because of their relations she has become pregnant. The king thinks: 'No one [82] else has entered here except the monk. Could this be the monk's work?' This is the second danger in entering the king's inner palace.

(3) "Again, a gem has been lost in the king's inner palace. The king thinks: 'No one else has entered here except the monk. Could this be the monk's work?' This is the third danger in entering the king's inner palace.

(4) "Again, the secret deliberations of the king's inner palace have spread to others.[2045] The king thinks: 'No one else has entered here except the monk. Could this be the monk's work?' This is the fourth danger in entering the king's inner palace.

(5) "Again, in the king's inner palace a father longs for his son, or a son longs for his father.[2046] They think: 'No one else has entered here except the monk. Could this be the monk's work?' This is the fifth danger in entering the king's inner palace.

(6) "Again, the king promotes someone. Those who are upset by this think: 'The king has close ties with the monk. Could this be the monk's work?' This is the sixth danger in entering the king's inner palace.

(7) "Again, the king demotes someone. Those who are upset by this think: 'The king has close ties with the monk. Could this be the monk's work?' This is the seventh danger in entering the king's inner palace.

(8) "Again, the king dispatches his army at an improper time. Those who are upset by this think: 'The king has close ties with the monk. Could this be the monk's work?' This is the eighth danger in entering the king's inner palace.

(9) "Again, after dispatching his army at a proper time, the king orders it to turn back while en route. Those who are upset by this think: [83] 'The king has close ties with the monk. Could this be the monk's work?' This is the ninth danger in entering the king's inner palace.

(10) "Again, in the king's inner palace there is the trampling of elephants,[2047] horses, and chariots, as well as tantalizing forms, sounds, odors, tastes, and tactile objects that are not suitable for a monk. This is the tenth danger in entering the king's inner palace.

"These, bhikkhus, are the ten dangers in entering the king's inner palace."

46 (6) Sakyans

On one occasion the Blessed One was dwelling among the Sakyans at Kapilavatthu in the Banyan Tree Park. Then, on the uposatha day, a number of Sakyan lay followers approached the Blessed One, paid homage to him, and sat down to one side. The Blessed One then said to them:

"Sakyans, do you observe the uposatha complete in eight factors?"[2048]

"Sometimes we do, Bhante, and sometimes we don't."

"It is your misfortune and loss, Sakyans! When life is endangered by sorrow and death, you observe the uposatha complete in eight factors [only] sometimes, and sometimes you don't. What do you think, Sakyans? Suppose there was a man here who, without doing anything unwholesome, would earn half a *kahāpaṇa* daily for his work. [84] Would that suffice for calling him a clever and enterprising man?"

"Yes, Bhante."

"What do you think, Sakyans? Suppose there was a man here who, without doing anything unwholesome, would earn a *kahāpaṇa* daily for his work. Would that suffice for calling him a clever and enterprising man?"

"Yes, Bhante."

"What do you think, Sakyans? Suppose there was a man here who, without doing anything unwholesome, would earn two *kahāpaṇas* . . . three . . . four . . . five . . . six . . . seven . . . eight . . . nine . . . ten . . . twenty . . . thirty . . . forty . . . fifty *kahāpaṇas*[2049] daily for his work. Would that suffice for calling him a clever and enterprising man?"

"Yes, Bhante."

"What do you think, Sakyans? If he earns a hundred or a thousand *kahāpaṇas* day after day, deposits whatever he gains, and has a life span of a hundred years, living a hundred years, would he acquire a great mass of wealth?"

"Yes, Bhante."

"What do you think, Sakyans? On account of his wealth, because of his wealth, by reason of his wealth, could that man experience exclusively happiness for one night or one day, or for half a night or half a day?"

"No, Bhante. Why not? Because sensual pleasures are impermanent, empty, false, and deceptive."

"However, Sakyans, my disciple who dwells heedful, ardent, and resolute for ten years, practicing as I instruct him, might experience exclusively happiness for a hundred years, ten thousand years,[2050] [85] a hundred thousand years, and ten million years.[2051] And he might be a once-returner, a non-returner, or surely a stream-enterer.

"Let alone ten years, Sakyans. My disciple who dwells heedful, ardent, and resolute for nine years . . . eight years . . . seven years . . . six years . . . five years . . . four years . . . three years . . . two years . . . one year, practicing as I instruct him, might experience exclusively happiness for a hundred years, ten thousand years, a hundred thousand years, and ten million years. And he might be a once-returner, a non-returner, or surely a stream-enterer.

"Let alone one year, Sakyans. My disciple who dwells heedful, ardent, and resolute for ten months, practicing as I instruct him, might experience exclusively happiness for a hundred years, ten thousand years, a hundred thousand years, and ten million years. And he might be a once-returner, a non-returner, or surely a stream-enterer.

"Let alone ten months, Sakyans. My disciple who dwells heedful, ardent, and resolute for nine months . . . eight months . . . seven months . . . six months . . . five months . . . four months . . . three months . . . two months . . . one month . . . half a month, practicing as I instruct him, might experience exclusively happiness for a hundred years, ten thousand years, a hundred thousand years, and ten million years. And he might be a once-returner, a non-returner, or surely a stream-enterer.

"Let alone half a month, Sakyans. My disciple who dwells heedful, ardent, and resolute for ten nights and days, practicing as I instruct him, might experience exclusively happiness for a hundred years, ten thousand years, a hundred thousand years, and ten million years. And he might be a once-returner, a non-returner, or surely a stream-enterer.

"Let alone ten nights and days, Sakyans. My disciple who dwells heedful, ardent, and resolute for nine nights and days . . . eight nights and days . . . seven nights and days . . . [86] six nights and days . . . five nights and days . . . four nights and days . . . three nights and days . . . two nights and days . . . one night and day, practicing as I instruct him, might experience exclusively happiness for a hundred years, ten thousand years, a hundred thousand years, and ten million years. And he might be a once-returner, a non-returner, or surely a stream-enterer.

"It is your misfortune and loss, Sakyans! When life is endangered by sorrow and death, you observe the uposatha complete in eight factors [only] sometimes, and sometimes you don't."

"From today on, Bhante, we will observe the uposatha complete in eight factors."

47 (7) Mahāli

On one occasion the Blessed One was dwelling at Vesālī in the hall with the peaked roof in the Great Wood. Then Mahāli the Licchavi approached the Blessed One, paid homage to him, sat down to one side, and said to him:

"Bhante, what is the cause and condition for the doing of bad kamma, for the occurrence of bad kamma?"[2052]

"Mahāli, (1) greed is a cause and condition for the doing of bad kamma, for the occurrence of bad kamma. (2) Hatred is a cause and condition . . . (3) Delusion is a cause and condition . . . (4) Careless attention is a cause [87] and condition . . . (5) A wrongly directed mind is a cause and condition for the doing of bad kamma, for the occurrence of bad kamma. This is the cause and condition for the doing of bad kamma, for the occurrence of bad kamma."

"Bhante, what is the cause and condition for the doing of good kamma, for the occurrence of good kamma?"

"Mahāli, (6) non-greed is a cause and condition for the doing of good kamma, for the occurrence of good kamma. (7) Non-hatred is a cause and condition . . . (8) Non-delusion is a cause and condition . . . (9) Careful attention is a cause and condition . . . (10) A rightly directed mind is a cause and condition for the doing of good kamma, for the occurrence of good kamma. This is the cause and condition for the doing of good kamma, for the occurrence of good kamma.

"If, Mahāli, these ten qualities did not exist in the world, unrighteous conduct, conduct contrary to the Dhamma, and righteous conduct, conduct in accordance with the Dhamma, would not be seen. But because these ten qualities exist in the world, unrighteous conduct, conduct contrary to the Dhamma, and righteous conduct, conduct in accordance with the Dhamma, are seen."

48 (8) Things

"Bhikkhus, there are these ten things that one who has gone forth should often reflect upon. What ten?

(1) "One who has gone forth should often reflect: 'I have entered upon a classless condition.'[2053]

(2) "One who has gone forth should often reflect: 'My living is dependent upon others.'[2054] [88]

(3) "One who has gone forth should often reflect: 'My deportment should be different.'[2055]

(4) "One who has gone forth should often reflect: 'Do I reproach myself in regard to virtuous behavior?'[2056]

(5) "One who has gone forth should often reflect: 'Do my wise fellow monks, having investigated, reproach me in regard to virtuous behavior?'

(6) "One who has gone forth should often reflect: 'I must be parted and separated from everyone and everything dear and agreeable to me.'[2057]

(7) "One who has gone forth should often reflect: 'I am the owner of my kamma, the heir of my kamma; I have kamma as my origin, kamma as my relative, kamma as my resort; I will be the heir of whatever kamma, good or bad, that I do.'

(8) "One who has gone forth should often reflect: 'How am I spending my nights and days?'

(9) "One who has gone forth should often reflect: 'Do I take delight in empty huts?'

(10) "One who has gone forth should often reflect: 'Have I attained any superhuman distinction in knowledge and vision worthy of the noble ones, so that in my last days, when I am questioned by my fellow monks, I will not be embarrassed?'

"These, bhikkhus, are the ten things that one who has gone forth should often reflect upon."

49 (9) Subsisting through the Body

"Bhikkhus, these ten things subsist through the body. What ten? Cold, heat, hunger, thirst, defecation, urination, bodily restraint, verbal restraint, restraint in one's livelihood, and the formative activity of existence that leads to renewed existence.[2058] These ten things subsist through the body."

50 (10) Arguments

On one occasion the Blessed One was dwelling at Sāvatthī in Jeta's Grove, Anāthapiṇḍika's Park. Now on that occasion, [89] after their meal, on returning from their alms round, a number of bhikkhus assembled in the assembly hall and were sitting together when they took to arguing and quarreling and fell into a dispute, stabbing each other with piercing words.

Then, in the evening, the Blessed One emerged from seclusion and went to the assembly hall, where he sat down on the prepared seat. The Blessed One then addressed the bhikkhus:

"Bhikkhus, what discussion were you engaged in just now as you were sitting together here? What was the conversation that was underway?"

"Here, Bhante, after our meal, on returning from our alms round, we assembled in the assembly hall and were sitting together when we took to arguing and quarreling and fell into a dispute, stabbing each other with piercing words."

"Bhikkhus, it is not suitable for you clansmen who have gone forth out of faith from the household life into homelessness to take to arguing and quarreling and to fall into a dispute, stabbing each other with piercing words.

"There are, bhikkhus, these ten principles of cordiality that create affection and respect and conduce to cohesiveness, to non-dispute, to concord, and to unity.[2059] What ten?

(1) "Here, a bhikkhu is virtuous; he dwells restrained by the Pātimokkha, possessed of good conduct and resort, seeing danger in minute faults. Having undertaken the training rules, he trains in them. Since a bhikkhu is virtuous . . . this is a principle of cordiality that creates affection and respect and conduces to cohesiveness, to non-dispute, to concord, and to unity.

(2) "Again, a bhikkhu has learned much, remembers what he has learned, and accumulates what he has learned. Those teachings that are good in the beginning, good in the middle, and good in the end, with the right meaning and phrasing, which proclaim the perfectly complete and pure spiritual life—such teachings as these he has learned much of, retained in mind, recited verbally, [90] investigated mentally, and penetrated well by view. Since a bhikkhu has learned much . . . this is a principle of cordiality that creates affection and respect and conduces . . . to unity.

(3) "Again, a bhikkhu has good friends, good companions, good comrades. Since a bhikkhu has good friends . . . this is a principle of cordiality that creates affection and respect and conduces . . . to unity.

(4) "Again, a bhikkhu is easy to correct and possesses qualities that make him easy to correct; he is patient and receives instruction respectfully. Since a bhikkhu is easy to correct . . .

this is a principle of cordiality that creates affection and respect and conduces . . . to unity.

(5) "Again, a bhikkhu is skillful and diligent in attending to the diverse chores that are to be done for his fellow monks; he possesses appropriate investigation there, and he is able to carry out and arrange everything properly. Since a bhikkhu is skillful and diligent . . . this is a principle of cordiality that creates affection and respect and conduces . . . to unity.

(6) "Again, a bhikkhu loves the Dhamma and is pleasing in his assertions, filled with a lofty joy pertaining to the Dhamma and discipline. Since a bhikkhu loves the Dhamma . . . this is a principle of cordiality that creates affection and respect and conduces . . . to unity.

(7) "Again, a bhikkhu has aroused energy for abandoning unwholesome qualities and acquiring wholesome qualities; he is strong, firm in exertion, not casting off the duty of cultivating wholesome qualities. Since a bhikkhu has aroused energy . . . [91] . . . this is a principle of cordiality that creates affection and respect and conduces . . . to unity.

(8) "Again, a bhikkhu is content with any kind of robe, almsfood, lodging, and medicines and provisions for the sick. Since a bhikkhu is content with any kind of robe . . . this is a principle of cordiality that creates affection and respect and conduces . . . to unity.

(9) "Again, a bhikkhu is mindful, possessing supreme mindfulness and alertness, one who remembers and recollects what was done and said long ago. Since a bhikkhu is mindful . . . this is a principle of cordiality that creates affection and respect and conduces . . . to unity.

(10) "Again, a bhikkhu is wise; he possesses the wisdom that discerns arising and passing away, which is noble and penetrative and leads to the complete destruction of suffering. Since a bhikkhu is wise . . . this is a principle of cordiality that creates affection and respect and conduces . . . to unity.

"These, bhikkhus, are the ten principles of cordiality that create affection and respect and conduce to cohesiveness, to non-dispute, to concord, and to unity." [92]

The Second Fifty

I. One's Own Mind

51 (1) One's Own Mind

On one occasion the Blessed One was dwelling at Sāvatthī in Jeta's Grove, Anāthapiṇḍika's Park. There the Blessed One addressed the bhikkhus: "Bhikkhus!"

"Venerable sir!" those bhikkhus replied. The Blessed One said this:

"Bhikkhus, a bhikkhu who is not skilled in the ways of others' minds [should train]: 'I will be skilled in the ways of my own mind.' It is in this way that you should train yourselves.

"And how is a bhikkhu skilled in the ways of his own mind? It is just as if a woman or a man—young, youthful, and fond of ornaments—would look at her or his own facial reflection in a clean bright mirror or in a bowl of clear water. If they see any dust or blemish there, they will make an effort to remove it. But if they do not see any dust or blemish there, they will be glad about it; and their wish fulfilled, they will think, 'How fortunate that I'm clean!'[2060] So too, self-examination is very helpful for a bhikkhu [to grow] in wholesome qualities.

"[One should ask oneself:] (1) 'Am I often given to longing [93] or without longing? (2) Am I often given to ill will or without ill will? (3) Am I often overcome by dullness and drowsiness or free from dullness and drowsiness? (4) Am I often restless or calm? (5) Am I often plagued by doubt or free from doubt? (6) Am I often angry or without anger? (7) Is my mind often defiled or undefiled? (8) Is my body often agitated or unagitated? (9) Am I often lazy or energetic? (10) Am I often unconcentrated or concentrated?'[2061]

"If, by such self-examination, a bhikkhu knows: 'I am often given to longing, given to ill will, overcome by dullness and drowsiness, restless, plagued by doubt, angry, defiled in mind, agitated in body, lazy, and unconcentrated,' he should put forth extraordinary desire, effort, zeal, enthusiasm, indefatigability, mindfulness, and clear comprehension to abandon those same bad unwholesome qualities. Just as one whose clothes or head had caught fire would put forth extraordinary desire, effort, zeal, enthusiasm, indefatigability, mindfulness, and clear comprehension to extinguish [the fire on] his clothes or head, so too that bhikkhu should put forth extraordinary desire, effort, zeal, enthusiasm, indefatigability, mindfulness, and clear comprehension to abandon those same bad unwholesome qualities. [94]

"But if, by such self-examination, a bhikkhu knows: 'I am often without longing, without ill will, free from dullness and drowsiness, calm, free from doubt, without anger, undefiled in mind, unagitated in body, energetic, and concentrated,' he should base himself on those same wholesome qualities and make a further effort to reach the destruction of the taints."

52 (2) Sāriputta

There the Venerable Sāriputta addressed the bhikkhus: "Friends, bhikkhus!"

"Friend!" those bhikkhus replied. The Venerable Sāriputta said this:

[Identical with 10:51, but spoken by Sāriputta.] [95–96]

53 (3) Standstill

"Bhikkhus, I do not praise even a standstill in wholesome qualities, much less decline. I praise only growth in wholesome qualities, not a standstill or deterioration.[2062]

"And how is there deterioration—not a standstill or growth—in wholesome qualities? Here, a bhikkhu has a certain degree of faith, virtuous behavior, learning, renunciation, wisdom, and discernment. Those qualities of his do not remain the same or increase. This, I say, is deterioration rather than a standstill or growth in wholesome qualities. Thus there is deterioration—not a standstill or growth—in wholesome qualities.

"And how is there a standstill—not deterioration or growth—in wholesome qualities? Here, a bhikkhu has a certain degree of faith, virtuous behavior, learning, renunciation, wisdom, and discernment. Those qualities of his do not deteriorate or increase. This, I say, is a standstill rather than deterioration or growth in wholesome qualities. Thus there is a standstill—not deterioration or growth—in wholesome qualities.

"And how is there growth—not a standstill or deterioration—in wholesome qualities? Here, a bhikkhu has a certain degree of faith, virtuous behavior, learning, renunciation, wisdom, and discernment. Those qualities of his do not remain the same or deteriorate. This, I say, is growth rather than a standstill or deterioration in wholesome qualities. Thus there is growth—not a standstill or deterioration—in wholesome qualities.

"Bhikkhus, a bhikkhu who is not skilled in the ways of others' minds [should train]: 'I will be skilled in the ways of my own mind.' . . . [97–98] . . . [as in 10:51 down to:] . . . But if, by such self-examination, a bhikkhu knows: 'I am often without longing . . . and concentrated,' then he should base himself on those same wholesome qualities and make a further effort to reach the destruction of the taints."

54 (4) Serenity

"Bhikkhus, a bhikkhu who is not skilled in the ways of others' minds [should train]: 'I will be skilled in the ways of my own mind.' It is in this way that you should train yourselves.

"And how is a bhikkhu skilled in the ways of his own mind? It is just as if a woman or a man—young, youthful, and fond of ornaments—would look at her or his own facial reflection in a clean bright mirror or in a bowl of clear water. If they see any dust or blemish there, they will make an effort to remove it. But if they do not see any dust or blemish there, they will be glad about it, [99] and their wish fulfilled, they will think, 'How fortunate for me that I'm clean!'

"So too, bhikkhus, self-examination is very helpful for a bhikkhu [to grow] in wholesome qualities:[2063] 'Do I gain internal serenity of mind or not? Do I gain the higher wisdom of insight into phenomena or not?'

(1) "If, by such self-examination, a bhikkhu knows: 'I gain internal serenity of mind but not the higher wisdom of insight into phenomena,' he should base himself on internal serenity of mind and make an effort to gain the higher wisdom of insight into phenomena. Then, some time later, he gains both internal serenity of mind and the higher wisdom of insight into phenomena.

(2) "But if, by such self-examination, he knows: 'I gain the higher wisdom of insight into phenomena but not internal serenity of mind,' he should base himself on the higher wisdom of insight into phenomena and make an effort to gain internal serenity of mind. Then, some time later, he gains both the

higher wisdom of insight into phenomena and internal serenity of mind.

(3) "But if, by such self-examination, he knows: 'I gain neither internal serenity of mind nor the higher wisdom of insight into phenomena,' he should put forth extraordinary desire, effort, zeal, enthusiasm, indefatigability, mindfulness, and clear comprehension to obtain both those wholesome qualities. Just as one whose clothes or head had caught fire would put forth extraordinary desire, effort, zeal, enthusiasm, indefatigability, mindfulness, and clear comprehension to extinguish [the fire on] his clothes or head, so that bhikkhu should put forth extraordinary desire, [100] effort, zeal, enthusiasm, indefatigability, mindfulness, and clear comprehension to obtain both those wholesome qualities. Then, some time later, he gains both internal serenity of mind and the higher wisdom of insight into phenomena.

(4) "But if, by such self-examination, he knows: 'I gain both internal serenity of mind and the higher wisdom of insight into phenomena,' he should base himself on those same wholesome qualities and make a further effort to reach the destruction of the taints.

"Robes, I say, are twofold: to be used and those not to be used.[2064] Almsfood too, I say, is twofold: that to be used and that not to be used. Lodgings too, I say, are twofold: those to be used and those not to be used. Villages or towns too, I say, are twofold: those to be resorted to and those not to be resorted to. Countries or regions too, I say, are twofold: those to be resorted to and those not to be resorted to. Persons too, I say, are twofold: those to be associated with and those not to be associated with.

(5) "When it was said: 'Robes, I say, are twofold: those to be used and those not to be used,' for what reason was this said? If one knows of a robe: 'When I use this robe, unwholesome qualities increase in me and wholesome qualities decline,' one should not use such a robe. But if one knows of a robe: 'When I use this robe, unwholesome qualities decline in me and wholesome qualities increase,' one should use such a robe. When it was said: 'Robes, I say, are twofold: to be used and not to be used,' it is because of this that this was said.

(6) "When it was said: 'Almsfood too, I say, is twofold: that to

be used and that not to be used,' for what reason was this said? If one knows of some almsfood: 'When I use this almsfood, unwholesome qualities increase in me and wholesome [101] qualities decline,' one should not use such almsfood. But if one knows of some almsfood: 'When I use this almsfood, unwholesome qualities decline in me and wholesome qualities increase,' one should use such almsfood. When it was said: 'Almsfood too, I say, is twofold: that to be used and that not to be used,' it is because of this that this was said.

(7) "When it was said: 'Lodgings too, I say, are twofold: those to be used and those not to be used,' for what reason was this said? If one knows of a lodging: 'When I use this lodging, unwholesome qualities increase in me and wholesome qualities decline,' one should not use such a lodging. But if one knows of a lodging: 'When I use this lodging, unwholesome qualities decline in me and wholesome qualities increase,' one should use such a lodging. When it was said: 'Lodgings too, I say, are twofold: those to be used and those not to be used,' it is because of this that this was said.

(8) "When it was said: 'Villages or towns too, I say, are twofold: those to be resorted to and those not to be resorted to,' for what reason was this said? If one knows of a village or town: 'When I resort to this village or town, unwholesome qualities increase in me and wholesome qualities decline,' one should not resort to such a village or town. But if one knows of a village or town: 'When I resort to this village or town, unwholesome qualities decline in me and wholesome qualities increase,' one should resort to such a village or town. When it was said: 'Villages or towns too, I say, are twofold: those to be resorted to and those not to be resorted to,' it is because of this that this was said.

(9) "When it was said: 'Countries or regions too, I say, are twofold: those to be resorted to and those not to be resorted to,' for what reason was this said? If one knows of a country or region: 'When I resort to this country or region, unwholesome qualities increase in me [102] and wholesome qualities decline,' one should not resort to such a country or region. But if one knows of a country or region: 'When I resort to this country or region, unwholesome qualities decline in me and wholesome qualities increase,' one should resort to such a country or

region. When it was said: 'Countries or regions too, I say, are twofold: those to be resorted to and those not to be resorted to,' it is because of this that this was said."

(10) "When it was said: 'Persons too, I say, are twofold: those to be associated with and those not to be associated with,' for what reason was this said? If one knows of a person: 'When I associate with this person, unwholesome qualities increase in me and wholesome qualities decline,' one should not associate with such a person. But if one knows of a person: 'When I associate with this person, unwholesome qualities decline in me and wholesome qualities increase,' one should associate with such a person. When it was said: 'Persons too, I say, are twofold: those to be associated with and those not to be associated with,' it is because of this that this was said."

55 (5) Decline

There the Venerable Sāriputta addressed the bhikkhus: "Friends, bhikkhus!"

"Friend!" those bhikkhus replied. The Venerable Sāriputta said this:

"Friends, it is said: 'A person subject to decline, a person subject to decline.' In what way has the Blessed One said that a person is subject to decline, and in what way that a person is not subject to decline?"

"We would come from far away, friend, to learn the meaning of this statement from the Venerable Sāriputta. It would be good if he would clear up the meaning of this statement. [103] Having heard it from him, the bhikkhus will retain it in mind."

"Well then, friends, listen and attend closely. I will speak."

"Yes, friend," those bhikkhus replied. The Venerable Sāriputta said this:

"In what way, friends, has the Blessed One said that a person is subject to decline? Here, a bhikkhu does not get to hear a teaching he has not heard before, forgets those teachings he has already heard, does not bring to mind those teachings with which he is already familiar, and does not understand what he has not understood. It is in this way that the Blessed One has said a person is subject to decline.[2065]

"And in what way, friends, has the Blessed One said that a

person is not subject to decline? Here, a bhikkhu gets to hear a teaching he has not heard before, does not forget those teachings he has already heard, brings to mind those teachings with which he is already familiar, and understands what he has not understood. It is in this way that the Blessed One has said a person is not subject to decline.

"Friends, a bhikkhu who is not skilled in the ways of others' minds [should train]: 'I will be skilled in the ways of my own mind.' It is in this way that you should train yourselves.

"And how, friends, is a bhikkhu skilled in the ways of his own mind? It is just as if a woman or a man—young, youthful, and fond of ornaments—would look at her or his own facial reflection in a clean and bright mirror or in a bowl of clear water. If they see any dust or blemish there, they will make an effort to remove it. But if they do not see any dust or blemish there, they will be glad about it; [104] and their wish fulfilled, they will think, 'How fortunate for me that I'm clean!' So too, self-examination is very helpful for a bhikkhu [to grow] in wholesome qualities.

"[One should ask oneself:] (1) 'Am I often without longing? Does this quality exist in me or not? (2) Am I often without ill will? Does this quality exist in me or not? (3) Am I often free from dullness and drowsiness? Does this quality exist in me or not? (4) Am I often calm? Does this quality exist in me or not? (5) Am I often free from doubt? Does this quality exist in me or not? (6) Am I often without anger? Does this quality exist in me or not? (7) Is my mind often undefiled? Does this quality exist in me or not? (8) Do I gain internal joy of the Dhamma? Does this quality exist in me or not? (9) Do I gain internal serenity of mind? Does this quality exist in me or not? (10) Do I gain the higher wisdom of insight into phenomena? Does this quality exist in me or not?'

"If, by such self-examination, a bhikkhu does not see any of these wholesome qualities present in himself, then he should put forth extraordinary desire, effort, zeal, enthusiasm, indefatigability, mindfulness, and clear comprehension to obtain those wholesome qualities. Just as one whose clothes or head had caught fire would put forth extraordinary desire, effort, zeal, enthusiasm, indefatigability, mindfulness, and clear comprehension to extinguish [the fire on] his clothes or head, so that bhikkhu should put forth extraordinary desire, effort, zeal, enthusiasm, indefatigability, mindfulness, and clear comprehension to obtain those wholesome qualities.

"But if, by such self-examination, a bhikkhu sees some wholesome qualities present in himself but not others, [105] he should base himself on those wholesome qualities that he sees in himself and put forth extraordinary desire, effort, zeal, enthusiasm, indefatigability, mindfulness, and clear comprehension to obtain those wholesome qualities that he does not see in himself. Just as one whose clothes or head had caught fire would put forth extraordinary desire . . . to extinguish [the fire on] his clothes or head, so that bhikkhu should base himself on the wholesome qualities that he sees in himself and put forth extraordinary desire . . . to obtain those wholesome qualities that he does not see in himself.

"But if, by such self-examination, a bhikkhu sees all these wholesome qualities present in himself, he should base himself on those same wholesome qualities and make a further effort to reach the destruction of the taints."

56 (6) Perceptions (1)

"Bhikkhus, these ten perceptions, when developed and cultivated, are of great fruit and benefit, culminating in the deathless, having the deathless as their consummation.[2066] What ten? (1) The perception of unattractiveness, (2) the perception of death, (3) the perception of the repulsiveness of food, (4) the perception of non-delight in the entire world, (5) the perception of impermanence, (6) the perception of suffering in the impermanent, (7) the perception of non-self in what is suffering, (8) the perception of abandoning, (9) the perception of dispassion, and (10) the perception of cessation. These ten perceptions, when developed and cultivated, are of great fruit and benefit, culminating in the deathless, having the deathless as their consummation." [106]

57 (7) Perceptions (2)

"Bhikkhus, these ten perceptions, when developed and cultivated, are of great fruit and benefit, culminating in the deathless, having the deathless as their consummation. What ten? (1) The perception of impermanence, (2) the perception of non-self, (3) the perception of death, (4) the perception of the repulsiveness of food, (5) the perception of non-delight in the entire world, (6) the perception of a skeleton, (7) the perception of a worm-infested corpse, (8) the perception of a livid corpse, (9) the perception of a fissured corpse, and (10) the perception of a bloated corpse.[2067] These ten perceptions, when developed and cultivated, are of great fruit and benefit, culminating in the deathless, having the deathless as their consummation."

58 (8) Roots

"Bhikkhus, wanderers of other sects may ask you: (1) 'In what, friends, are all things rooted? (2) Through what do they come into being? (3) From what do they originate? (4) Upon what do they converge? (5) By what are they headed? (6) What exercises authority over them? (7) What is their supervisor? (8) What is their core? (9) In what do they culminate? (10) What is their consummation?' If you are asked thus, how would you answer them?"[2068]

"Bhante, our teachings are rooted in the Blessed One, guided by the Blessed One, take recourse in the Blessed One. It would be good if the Blessed One would clear up the meaning of this statement. Having heard it from him, the bhikkhus will retain it in mind."

"Then listen, bhikkhus, and attend closely. I will speak."

"Yes, Bhante," those bhikkhus replied. The Blessed One said this:

"Bhikkhus, if wanderers of other sects should ask you: 'What, friends, are all things rooted in? ... [107] ... What is their consummation?' you should answer them as follows.

"'Friends, (1) all things are rooted in desire. (2) They come into being through attention. (3) They originate from contact. (4) They converge upon feeling. (5) They are headed by concentration. (6) Mindfulness exercises authority over them. (7) Wisdom is their supervisor. (8) Liberation is their core. (9) They culminate in the deathless. (10) Their consummation is nibbāna.'[2069]

"If you are asked thus, bhikkhus, it is in such a way that you should answer those wanderers of other sects."

59 (9) Going Forth

"Therefore, bhikkhus, you should train yourselves thus: 'Our minds will be strengthened in accordance with [the spirit of] our going forth, and arisen bad unwholesome qualities will not obsess our minds.[2070] (1) Our minds will be strengthened in the perception of impermanence. (2) Our minds will be strengthened in the perception of non-self. (3) Our minds will be strengthened in the perception of unattractiveness. (4) Our minds will be strengthened in the perception of danger. (5) We will know the even and uneven ways of the world,[2071] and our minds will be strengthened in this perception. (6) We will know the coming into being and extermination of the world,[2072] and our minds will be strengthened in this perception. (7) We will know the origination and passing away of the world, and our minds will be strengthened in this perception. (8) Our minds will be strengthened in the perception of abandoning. (9) Our minds will be strengthened in the perception of dispassion. (10) Our minds will be strengthened in the perception of cessation.'[2073] [108] It is in such a way that you should you train yourselves.

"When a bhikkhu's mind has been strengthened in accordance with [the spirit of] his going forth, and arisen bad unwholesome qualities do not obsess his mind—when his mind has been strengthened in the perception of impermanence . . . when his mind has been strengthened in the perception of cessation—one of two fruits is to be expected for him: either final knowledge in this very life or, if there is a residue remaining, the state of non-returning."

60 (10) Girimānanda

On one occasion the Blessed One was dwelling at Sāvatthī in Jeta's Grove, Anāthapiṇḍika's Park. Now on that occasion the Venerable Girimānanda was sick, afflicted, and gravely ill.[2074] Then the Venerable Ānanda approached the Blessed One, paid homage to him, sat down to one side, and said to him:

"Bhante, the Venerable Girimānanda is sick, afflicted, and gravely ill. It would be good if the Blessed One would visit him out of compassion."

"If, Ānanda, you visit the bhikkhu Girimānanda and speak to him about ten perceptions, it is possible that on hearing about them his affliction will immediately subside. What are the ten? [109]

"(1) The perception of impermanence, (2) the perception of

non-self, (3) the perception of unattractiveness, (4) the perception of danger, (5) the perception of abandoning, (6) the perception of dispassion, (7) the perception of cessation, (8) the perception of non-delight in the entire world, (9) the perception of impermanence in all conditioned phenomena, and (10) mindfulness of breathing.

(1) "And what, Ānanda, is the perception of impermanence? Here, having gone to the forest, to the foot of a tree, or to an empty hut, a bhikkhu reflects thus: 'Form is impermanent, feeling is impermanent, perception is impermanent, volitional activities are impermanent, consciousness is impermanent.' Thus he dwells contemplating impermanence in these five aggregates subject to clinging. This is called the perception of impermanence.

(2) "And what, Ānanda, is the perception of non-self? Here, having gone to the forest, to the foot of a tree, or to an empty hut, a bhikkhu reflects thus: 'The eye is non-self, forms are non-self; the ear is non-self, sounds are non-self; the nose is non-self, odors are non-self; the tongue is non-self, tastes are non-self; the body is non-self, tactile objects are non-self; the mind is non-self, mental phenomena are non-self.' Thus he dwells contemplating non-self in these six internal and external sense bases. This is called the perception of non-self.

(3) "And what, Ānanda, is the perception of unattractiveness? Here, a bhikkhu reviews this very body upward from the soles of the feet and downward from the tips of the hairs, enclosed in skin, as full of many kinds of impurities: 'There are in this body hair of the head, hair of the body, nails, teeth, skin, flesh, sinews, bones, bone marrow, kidneys, heart, liver, pleura, spleen, lungs, intestines, mesentery, stomach, excrement, bile, phlegm, pus, blood, sweat, fat, tears, grease, saliva, snot, fluid of the joints, urine.' Thus he dwells contemplating unattractiveness in this body. This is called the perception of unattractiveness.

(4) "And what, Ānanda, is the perception of danger? Here, having gone to the forest, to the foot of a tree, or to an empty hut, a bhikkhu reflects thus: 'This body is the source of much pain [110] and danger; for all sorts of afflictions arise in this body, that is, eye-disease, disease of the inner ear, nose-disease, tongue-disease, body-disease, head-disease, disease of the external ear, mouth-disease, tooth-disease,[2075] cough, asthma, catarrh,

pyrexia, fever, stomach ache, fainting, dysentery, gripes, cholera, leprosy, boils, eczema, tuberculosis, epilepsy, ringworm, itch, scab, chickenpox, scabies, hemorrhage, diabetes, hemorrhoids, cancer, fistula; illnesses originating from bile, phlegm, wind, or their combination; illnesses produced by change of climate; illnesses produced by careless behavior; illnesses produced by assault; or illnesses produced as the result of kamma; and cold, heat, hunger, thirst, defecation, and urination.' Thus he dwells contemplating danger in this body. This is called the perception of danger.

(5) "And what, Ānanda, is the perception of abandoning? Here, a bhikkhu does not tolerate an arisen sensual thought; he abandons it, dispels it, terminates it, and obliterates it. He does not tolerate an arisen thought of ill will . . . an arisen thought of harming . . . bad unwholesome states whenever they arise; he abandons them, dispels them, terminates them, and obliterates them. This is called the perception of abandoning.

(6) "And what, Ānanda, is the perception of dispassion? Here, having gone to the forest, to the root of a tree, or to an empty hut, a bhikkhu reflects thus: 'This is peaceful, this is sublime, that is, the stilling of all activities, the relinquishment of all acquisitions, the destruction of craving, dispassion, nibbāna.' This is called the perception of dispassion.[2076]

(7) "And what, Ānanda, is the perception of cessation? Here, having gone to the forest, to the root of a tree, or to an empty hut, a bhikkhu reflects thus: 'This is peaceful, [111] this is sublime, that is, the stilling of all activities, the relinquishment of all acquisitions, the destruction of craving, cessation, nibbāna.' This is called the perception of cessation.

(8) "And what, Ānanda, is the perception of non-delight in the entire world? Here, a bhikkhu refrains from[2077] any engagement and clinging, mental standpoints, adherences, and underlying tendencies in regard to the world, abandoning them without clinging to them. This is called the perception of non-delight in the entire world.

(9) "And what, Ānanda, is the perception of impermanence in all conditioned phenomena? Here, a bhikkhu is repelled, humiliated, and disgusted by all conditioned phenomena. This is called the perception of impermanence in all conditioned phenomena.[2078]

(10) "And what, Ānanda, is mindfulness of breathing? Here, a bhikkhu, having gone to the forest, to the foot of a tree, or to an empty hut, sits down. Having folded his legs crosswise, straightened his body, and established mindfulness in front of him, just mindful he breathes in, mindful he breathes out.

"Breathing in long, he knows: 'I breathe in long'; or breathing out long, he knows: 'I breathe out long.' Breathing in short, he knows: 'I breathe in short'; or breathing out short, he knows: 'I breathe out short.' He trains thus: 'Experiencing the whole body, I will breathe in'; he trains thus: 'Experiencing the whole body, I will breathe out.' He trains thus: 'Tranquilizing the bodily activity, I will breathe in'; he trains thus: 'Tranquilizing the bodily activity, I will breathe out.'

"He trains thus: 'Experiencing rapture, I will breathe in'; he trains thus: 'Experiencing rapture, I will breathe out.' He trains thus: 'Experiencing happiness, I will breathe in'; he trains thus: 'Experiencing happiness, I will breathe out.' He trains thus: 'Experiencing the mental activity, I will breathe in'; he trains thus: 'Experiencing the mental activity, I will breathe out.' He trains thus: 'Tranquilizing the mental activity, I will breathe in'; he trains thus: 'Tranquilizing the mental activity, I will breathe out.'[2079]

"He trains thus: 'Experiencing the mind, I will breathe in'; he trains thus: 'Experiencing the mind, I will breathe out.' [112] He trains thus: 'Gladdening the mind, I will breathe in'; he trains thus: 'Gladdening the mind, I will breathe out.' He trains thus: 'Concentrating the mind, I will breathe in'; he trains thus: 'Concentrating the mind, I will breathe out.' He trains thus: 'Liberating the mind, I will breathe in'; he trains thus: 'Liberating the mind, I will breathe out.'[2080]

"He trains thus: 'Contemplating impermanence, I will breathe in'; he trains thus: 'Contemplating impermanence, I will breathe out.' He trains thus: 'Contemplating fading away, I will breathe in'; he trains thus: 'Contemplating fading away, I will breathe out.' He trains thus: 'Contemplating cessation, I will breathe in'; he trains thus: 'Contemplating cessation, I will breathe out.' He trains thus: 'Contemplating relinquishment, I will breathe in'; he trains thus: 'Contemplating relinquishment, I will breathe out.'

"This is called mindfulness of breathing.

"If, Ānanda, you visit the bhikkhu Girimānanda and speak to him about these ten perceptions, it is possible that on hearing about them he will immediately recover from his affliction."

Then, when the Venerable Ānanda had learned these ten perceptions from the Blessed One, he went to the Venerable Girimānanda and spoke to him about them. When the Venerable Girimānanda heard about these ten perceptions, his affliction immediately subsided. The Venerable Girimānanda recovered from that affliction, and that is how he was cured of his affliction. [113]

II. Pairs

61 (1) Ignorance

"Bhikkhus, this is said: 'A first point of ignorance, bhikkhus, is not seen such that before this there was no ignorance and afterward it came into being.'[2081] Still, ignorance is seen to have a specific condition.

"I say, bhikkhus, that ignorance has a nutriment;[2082] it is not without nutriment. And what is the nutriment for ignorance? It should be said: the five hindrances. The five hindrances, too, I say, have a nutriment; they are not without nutriment. And what is the nutriment for the five hindrances? It should be said: the three kinds of misconduct. The three kinds of misconduct, too, I say, have a nutriment; they are not without nutriment. And what is the nutriment for the three kinds of misconduct? It should be said: non-restraint of the sense faculties. Non-restraint of the sense faculties, too, I say, has a nutriment; it is not without nutriment. And what is the nutriment for non-restraint of the sense faculties? It should be said: lack of mindfulness and clear comprehension. Lack of mindfulness and clear comprehension, too, I say, has a nutriment; it is not without nutriment. And what is the nutriment for lack of mindfulness and clear comprehension? It should be said: careless attention. Careless attention, too, I say, has a nutriment; it is not without nutriment. And what is the nutriment for careless attention? It should be said: lack of faith. Lack of faith, too, I say, has a nutriment; it is not without nutriment. And what is the nutriment for lack of faith? It should be said: not hearing the good Dhamma. Not hearing the good Dhamma, too, I say, has a nutriment; it is not without nutriment. And what is the nutriment for not hearing the good Dhamma? It should be said: not associating with good persons.[2083]

"Thus not associating with good persons, becoming full, fills up not hearing the good Dhamma. Not hearing the good Dhamma, becoming full, fills up lack of faith. Lack of faith, becoming full, fills up careless attention. Careless attention, becoming full, fills up lack of mindfulness and clear comprehension. Lack of mindfulness and clear comprehension, becoming full, [114] fills up non-restraint of the sense faculties. Non-restraint of the sense faculties, becoming full, fills up the three kinds of misconduct. The three kinds of misconduct, becoming full, fill up the five hindrances. The five hindrances, becoming full, fill up ignorance. Thus there is nutriment for ignorance, and in this way it becomes full.

"Just as, when it is raining and the rain pours down in thick droplets on a mountaintop, the water flows down along the slope and fills the clefts, gullies, and creeks; these, becoming full, fill up the pools; these, becoming full, fill up the lakes; these, becoming full, fill up the streams; these, becoming full, fill up the rivers; and these, becoming full, fill up the great ocean; thus there is nutriment for the great ocean, and in this way it becomes full. So too, not associating with good persons, becoming full, fills up not hearing the good Dhamma. . . . The five hindrances, becoming full, fill up ignorance. Thus there is nutriment for ignorance, and in this way it becomes full.

"I say, bhikkhus, that (1) true knowledge and liberation have a nutriment; they are not without nutriment. And what is the nutriment for true knowledge and liberation? It should be said: (2) the seven factors of enlightenment. The seven factors of enlightenment, too, I say, have a nutriment; they are not without nutriment. And what is the nutriment for the seven factors of enlightenment? It should be said: (3) the four establishments of mindfulness. The four establishments of mindfulness, too, I say, have a nutriment; they are not without nutriment. And what is the nutriment for the four establishments of mindfulness? It should be said: (4) the three kinds of good conduct. [115] The three kinds of good conduct, too, I say, have a nutriment; they are not without nutriment. And what is the nutriment for the three kinds of good conduct? It should be said: (5) restraint of the sense faculties. Restraint of the sense faculties, too, I say, has a nutriment; it is not without nutriment. And what is the nutriment for restraint of the sense faculties? It should be said: (6) mindfulness and clear comprehension. Mindfulness and clear comprehension, too, I say, have a nutriment; they are not without nutriment. And what is the nutriment for mindfulness and clear comprehension? It should be said: (7) careful attention. Careful attention, too, I say, has a nutriment; it is not without nutriment. And what is the nutriment for careful attention? It should be said: (8) faith. Faith, too, I say, has a nutriment; it is not without nutriment. And what is the nutriment for faith? It should be said: (9) hearing the good Dhamma. Hearing the good Dhamma, too, I say, has a nutriment; it is not without nutriment. And what is the nutriment for hearing the good Dhamma? It should be said: (10) associating with good persons.

"Thus associating with good persons, becoming full, fills up hearing the good Dhamma. Hearing the good Dhamma, becoming full, fills up faith. Faith, becoming full, fills up careful attention. Careful attention, becoming full, fills up mindfulness and clear comprehension. Mindfulness and clear comprehension, becoming full, fill up restraint of the sense faculties. Restraint of the sense faculties, becoming full, fills up the three kinds of good conduct. The three kinds of good conduct, becoming full, fill up the four establishments of mindfulness. The four establishments of mindfulness, becoming full, fill up the seven factors of enlightenment. The seven factors of enlightenment, becoming full, fill up true knowledge and liberation. Thus there is nutriment for true knowledge and liberation, and in this way they become full.

"Just as, when it is raining and the rain pours down in thick droplets on a mountaintop, the water flows down along the slope and fills the clefts, gullies, and creeks; these, becoming full, fill up the pools; these, becoming full, fill up the lakes; these, becoming full, fill up the streams; these, becoming full, fill up the rivers; and these, becoming full, [116] fill up the great ocean; thus there is nutriment for the great ocean, and in this way it becomes full. So too, associating with good persons, becoming full, fills up hearing the good Dhamma.... The seven factors of enlightenment, becoming full, fill up true knowledge and liberation. Thus there is nutriment for true knowledge and liberation, and in this way they become full."

62 (2) Craving

"Bhikkhus, it is said: 'A first point of craving for existence, bhikkhus, is not seen such that before this there was no craving for existence and afterward it came into being.' Still, craving for existence is seen to have a specific condition.

"I say, bhikkhus, that craving for existence has a nutriment; it is not without nutriment. And what is the nutriment for craving for existence? It should be said: ignorance. Ignorance, too, I say, has a nutriment; it is not without nutriment. And what is the nutriment for ignorance? It should be said: the five hindrances ... [as in 10:61] [117] ... And what is the nutriment for not hearing the good Dhamma? It should be said: not associating with good persons.

"Thus not associating with good persons, becoming full, fills up not hearing the good Dhamma.... The five hindrances, becoming full, fill up ignorance. Ignorance, becoming full, fills up craving for existence. Thus there is nutriment for craving for existence, and in this way it becomes full.

"Just as, when it is raining and the rain pours down in thick droplets on a mountaintop, the water flows down along the slope ... [118] ... and the rivers, becoming full, fill up the great ocean; thus there is nutriment for the great ocean, and in this way it becomes full. So too, not associating with good persons, becoming full, fills up not hearing the good Dhamma ... and ignorance, becoming full, fills up craving for existence. Thus there is nutriment for craving for existence, and in this way it becomes full.

"I say, bhikkhus, that (1) true knowledge and liberation have a nutriment; they are not without nutriment. And what is the nutriment for true knowledge and liberation? It should be said: (2) the seven factors of enlightenment. ... Hearing the good Dhamma, too, I say, has a nutriment; it is not without nutriment. And what is the nutriment for hearing the good Dhamma? It should be said: (10) associating with good persons.

"Thus associating with good persons, becoming full, fills up hearing the good Dhamma.... [119] The seven factors of enlightenment, becoming full, fill up true knowledge and liberation.

Thus there is nutriment for true knowledge and liberation, and in this way they become full.

"Just as, when it is raining and the rain pours down in thick droplets on a mountain top, the water flows down along the slope . . . and the rivers, becoming full, fill up the great ocean; thus there is nutriment for the great ocean, and in this way it becomes full. So too, associating with good persons, becoming full, fills up hearing the good Dhamma. . . . The seven factors of enlightenment, becoming full, fill up true knowledge and liberation. Thus there is nutriment for true knowledge and liberation, and in this way they become full."

63 (3) Certainty

"Bhikkhus, all those who have reached certainty about me are accomplished in view. Of those accomplished in view, five gain the goal here in this world;[2084] five gain the goal having left this world.

"Who are the five that gain the goal here in this world? [120] The seven-times-at-most attainer, the family-to-family attainer, the one-seed attainer,[2085] the once-returner, and one who, in this very life, is an arahant. These five gain the goal in this world.

"Who are the five that gain the goal having left this world? The attainer of nibbāna in the interval, the attainer of nibbāna upon landing, the attainer of nibbāna without exertion, the attainer of nibbāna through exertion, and one bound upstream, heading toward the Akaniṭṭha realm.[2086] These five gain the goal having left this world.

"All those, bhikkhus, who have reached certainty about me are accomplished in view. Of those accomplished in view, the former five gain the goal here in this world; the latter five gain the goal having left this world."

64 (4) Unwavering

"Bhikkhus, all those who have unwavering confidence in me are stream-enterers.[2087] Of those stream-enterers, five gain the goal here in this world; five gain the goal having left this world.

"Who are the five that gain the goal here in this world? The seven-times-at-most attainer, the family-to-family attainer, the one-seed attainer, the once-returner, and one who, in this very life, is an arahant. These five gain the goal here in this world.

"Who are the five that gain the goal having left this world? The attainer of nibbāna in the interval, the attainer of nibbāna upon landing, the attainer of nibbāna without exertion, the attainer of nibbāna through exertion, and one bound upstream, heading toward the Akaniṭṭha realm. These five gain the goal having left this world.

"All those, bhikkhus, who have unwavering confidence in me are stream-enterers. Of those stream-enterers, the former five gain the goal here in this world; the latter five gain the goal having left this world."

65 (5) Happiness (1)

On one occasion the Venerable Sāriputta was dwelling among the Magadhans at Nālakagāmaka. Then the wanderer Sāmaṇḍakāni [121] approached the Venerable Sāriputta and exchanged greetings with him. When they had concluded their greetings and cordial talk, he sat down to one side and said to the Venerable Sāriputta:

"Friend Sāriputta, what is happiness? What is suffering?"

"Rebirth, friend, is suffering. No rebirth is happiness. When there is rebirth, this suffering is to be expected: cold, heat, hunger, thirst, defecation, and urination; being afflicted by fire, sticks, or knives; and relatives and friends get together and scold one. When there is rebirth, this suffering is to be expected.

"When there is no rebirth, this happiness is to be expected: no cold, no heat, no hunger, no thirst, no defecation, and no urination; no being afflicted by fire, sticks, or knives; and relatives and friends don't get together and scold one. When there is no rebirth, this happiness is to be expected."

66 (6) Happiness (2)

On one occasion the Venerable Sāriputta was dwelling among the Magadhans at Nālakagāmaka. Then the wanderer Sāmaṇḍakāni approached the Venerable Sāriputta and exchanged greetings with him. When they had concluded their greetings and cordial talk, he sat down to one side [122] and said to the Venerable Sāriputta:

"Friend Sāriputta, what is happiness in this Dhamma and discipline, and what is suffering?"

"Dissatisfaction, friend, is suffering in this Dhamma and discipline. Enjoyment is happiness. When there is dissatisfaction, this suffering is to be expected. (1) When walking, one does not find happiness or comfort. (2) When standing still . . . (3) When sitting . . . (4) When lying down . . . (5) When in the village . . . (6) When in the forest . . . (7) When at the foot of a tree . . . (8) When in an empty hut . . . (9) When in the open air . . . (10) When amid the bhikkhus, one does not find happiness or comfort. When there is dissatisfaction, this suffering is to be expected.

"When there is enjoyment, this happiness is to be expected. (1) When walking, one finds happiness and comfort. (2) When standing still . . . (3) When sitting . . . (4) When lying down . . . (5) When in the village . . . (6) When in the forest . . . (7) When at the foot of a tree . . . (8) When in an empty hut . . . (9) When in the open air . . . (10) When amid the bhikkhus, one finds happiness or comfort. When there is enjoyment, this happiness is to be expected."

67 (7) Naḷakapāna (1)

On one occasion the Blessed One was wandering on tour among the Kosalans together with a large Saṅgha of bhikkhus when he reached the Kosalan town named Naḷakapāna. There at Naḷakapāna the Blessed One dwelled in a Judas tree grove. Now on that occasion, on the day of the uposatha, the Blessed One was sitting surrounded by the Saṅgha of bhikkhus. Having instructed, encouraged, inspired, and gladdened the Saṅgha of bhikkhus with a Dhamma talk for much of the night, and having surveyed the utterly silent Saṅgha of bhikkhus, the Blessed One addressed the Venerable Sāriputta: "The Saṅgha of bhikkhus is free from dullness and drowsiness, Sāriputta. Give a [123] Dhamma talk to the bhikkhus. My back is aching, so I will stretch it."

"Yes, Bhante," the Venerable Sāriputta replied.

Then the Blessed One folded his outer robe in four and lay down on his right side in the lion's posture, with one foot overlapping the other, mindful and clearly comprehending, after noting in his mind the idea of rising. The Venerable Sāriputta then addressed the bhikkhus: "Friends, bhikkhus!"

"Friend!" those bhikkhus replied. The Venerable Sāriputta said this:

"Friends, for one who does not have faith in [cultivating]

wholesome qualities, who does not have a sense of moral shame ... who does not have moral dread ... who does not have energy ... who does not have wisdom in [cultivating] wholesome qualities, whether night or day comes, only deterioration and not growth in wholesome qualities is to be expected. Just as, during the dark fortnight, whether night or day comes, the moon only deteriorates in beauty, roundness, and brightness, in diameter and circumference, so too, for one who does not have faith ... wisdom in [cultivating] wholesome qualities, whether night or day comes, only deterioration and not growth in wholesome qualities is to be expected.

(1) "'A person without faith,' friends: this is a case of decline. (2) 'A morally shameless person' ... (3) 'A morally reckless person' ... (4) 'A lazy person' ... (5) 'An unwise person' ... (6) 'An angry person' ... (7) 'A hostile person' ... (8) 'A person of evil desires' ... (9) 'A person with bad friends' ... (10) 'A person who holds wrong view': this is a case of decline.

"Friends, for one who has faith in [cultivating] wholesome qualities, for one who has a sense of moral shame ... for one who has moral dread ... for one who has energy ... [124] for one who has wisdom in [cultivating] wholesome qualities, whether night or day comes, only growth and not deterioration in wholesome qualities is to be expected. Just as, during the bright fortnight, whether night or day comes, the moon only increases in beauty, roundness, and brightness, in diameter and circumference, so too, for one who has faith ... wisdom in [cultivating] wholesome qualities, whether night or day comes, only growth and not deterioration in wholesome qualities is to be expected.

(1) "'A person with faith,' friends: this is a case of non-decline. (2) 'A person with a sense of moral shame' ... (3) 'A person with moral dread' ... (4) 'An energetic person' ... (5) 'A wise person' ... (6) 'A person without anger' ... (7) 'A person without hostility' ... (8) 'A person without evil desires' ... (9) 'A person with good friends' ... (10) 'A person who holds right view': this is a case of non-decline."

Then the Blessed One got up and addressed the Venerable Sāriputta: "Good, good, Sāriputta! Sāriputta, for one who does not have faith in [cultivating] wholesome qualities ... [the Buddha here repeats Sāriputta's entire discourse:] [125] ... (10) 'A person who holds right view': this is a case of non-decline."

68 (8) Naḷakapāna (2)

[Opening as in 10:67, down to:] [126]

The Venerable Sāriputta then addressed the bhikkhus: "Friends, bhikkhus!"

"Friend!" those bhikkhus replied. The Venerable Sāriputta said this:

"Friends, for one (1) who does not have faith in [cultivating] wholesome qualities, (2) who does not have a sense of moral shame ... (3) who does not have moral dread ... (4) who does not have energy ... (5) who does not have wisdom ... (6) who does not lend an ear ... (7) who does not retain the Dhamma in mind ... (8) who does not examine the meaning ... (9) who does not practice in accordance with the Dhamma ... (10) who is not heedful in [cultivating] wholesome qualities, whether night or day comes, only deterioration and not growth in wholesome qualities is to be expected. Just as, during the dark fortnight, whether night or day comes, the moon only deteriorates in beauty, roundness, and brightness, in diameter and circumference, so too, for one who does not have faith in [cultivating] wholesome qualities ... for one who is not heedful in [cultivating] wholesome qualities, whether night or day comes, only deterioration and not growth in wholesome qualities is to be expected.

"Friends, for one (1) who has faith in [cultivating] wholesome qualities, (2) who has a sense of moral shame ... (3) who has moral dread ... (4) who has energy ... (5) who has wisdom ... (6) who lends an ear ... (7) who retains the Dhamma in mind ... (8) who examines the meaning ... (9) who practices in accordance with the Dhamma ... (10) who is heedful [cultivating] wholesome qualities, whether night or day comes, only growth and not deterioration in wholesome qualities is to be expected. Just as, [127] during the bright fortnight, whether night or day comes, the moon only increases in beauty, roundness, and brightness, in diameter and circumference, so too, for one who has faith in [cultivating] wholesome qualities ... heedfulness in [cultivating] wholesome qualities, whether night or day comes, only growth and not deterioration in wholesome qualities is to be expected."

Then the Blessed One got up and addressed the Venerable Sāriputta: "Good, good, Sāriputta! Sāriputta, for one who does not have faith in [cultivating] wholesome qualities ... [the

Buddha here repeats Sāriputta's entire discourse down to:] [128] . . . whether night or day comes, only growth and not deterioration in wholesome qualities is to be expected."

69 (9) Topics of Discussion (1)

On one occasion the Blessed One was dwelling at Sāvatthī in Jeta's Grove, Anāthapiṇḍika's Park. Now on that occasion, after their meal, on returning from their alms round, a number of bhikkhus had assembled in the assembly hall and were sitting together engaging in various kinds of pointless talk, that is: talk about kings, thieves, and ministers of state; talk about armies, perils, and wars; talk about food, drink, garments, and beds; talk about garlands and scents; talk about relatives, vehicles, villages, towns, cities, and countries; talk about women and talk about heroes; street talk and talk by the well; talk about the departed; miscellaneous talk; speculation about the world and the sea; talk about becoming this or that.

Then, in the evening, the Blessed One emerged from seclusion and went to the assembly hall, where he sat down on the prepared seat. The Blessed One then addressed the bhikkhus: "Bhikkhus, what discussion were you engaged in just now as you were sitting together here? What was the conversation that was underway?"

"Here, Bhante, after our meal, on returning from our alms round, we assembled in the assembly hall and were sitting together engaging in various kinds of pointless talk, that is: talk about kings, thieves, and ministers of state . . . talk about becoming this or that."

"Bhikkhus, it is not suitable for you, [129] clansmen who have gone forth from the household life into homelessness out of faith, to engage in various kinds of pointless talk, that is: talk about kings, thieves, and ministers of state . . . talk about becoming this or that.

"There are, bhikkhus, these ten topics of discussion. What ten? Talk on fewness of desires, on contentment, on solitude, on not being bound up with others, on arousing energy, on virtuous behavior, on concentration, on wisdom, on liberation, on knowledge and vision of liberation. These are the ten topics of discussion.

"If, bhikkhus, you engage in discussion on any of these ten

topics, your splendor might surpass even the splendor of the sun and moon, as powerful and mighty as they are, how much more then that of the wanderers of other sects!"

70 (10) Topics of Discussion (2)

On one occasion the Blessed One was dwelling at Sāvatthī in Jeta's Grove, Anāthapiṇḍika's Park. Now on that occasion, after their meal, on returning from their alms round, a number of bhikkhus had assembled in the assembly hall and were sitting together engaging in various kinds of pointless talk, that is: talk about kings, thieves, and ministers of state . . . talk about becoming this or that.[2088]

"Bhikkhus, there are these ten grounds for praise. What ten? [130]

(1) "Here, a bhikkhu is himself of few desires and speaks to the bhikkhus on fewness of desires. This is a ground for praise: 'The bhikkhu is himself of few desires and speaks to the bhikkhus on fewness of desires.'

(2) "He is himself content and speaks to the bhikkhus on contentment. This is a ground for praise: 'The bhikkhu is himself content. . . .'

(3) "He is himself given to solitude and speaks to the bhikkhus on solitude. This is a ground for praise: 'The bhikkhu is himself given to solitude. . . .'

(4) "He is himself not bound up with others and speaks to the bhikkhus on not being bound up with others. This is a ground for praise: 'The bhikkhu is himself not bound up with others. . . .'

(5) "He is himself energetic and speaks to the bhikkhus on arousing energy. This is a ground for praise: 'The bhikkhu is himself energetic. . . .'

(6) "He is himself accomplished in virtuous behavior and speaks to the bhikkhus on accomplishment in virtuous behavior. This is a ground for praise: 'The bhikkhu is himself accomplished in virtuous behavior. . . .'

(7) "He is himself accomplished in concentration and speaks to the bhikkhus on accomplishment in concentration. This is a ground for praise: 'The bhikkhu is himself accomplished in concentration. . . .'

(8) "He is himself accomplished in wisdom and speaks to the

bhikkhus on accomplishment in wisdom. This is a ground for praise: 'The bhikkhu is himself accomplished in wisdom. . . .'

(9) "He is himself accomplished in liberation and speaks to the bhikkhus on accomplishment in liberation. This is a ground for praise: 'The bhikkhu is himself accomplished in liberation. . . .'

(10) "He is himself accomplished in the knowledge and vision of liberation and speaks to the bhikkhus on accomplishment in the knowledge and vision of liberation. This is a ground for praise: 'The bhikkhu is himself accomplished in the knowledge and vision of liberation and speaks to the bhikkhus on accomplishment in the knowledge and vision of liberation.'

"These, bhikkhus, are the ten grounds for praise." [131]

III. Wish

71 (1) Wish[2089]

On one occasion the Blessed One was dwelling at Sāvatthī in Jeta's Grove, Anāthapiṇḍika's Park. There the Blessed One addressed the bhikkhus: "Bhikkhus!"

"Venerable sir," those bhikkhus replied. The Blessed One said this:

"Bhikkhus, be observant of virtuous behavior and observant of the Pātimokkha. Dwell restrained by the Pātimokkha, possessed of good conduct and resort, seeing danger in minute faults. Having undertaken them, train in the training rules.

(1) "If a bhikkhu should wish: 'May I be pleasing and agreeable to my fellow monks, respected and esteemed by them,' let him fulfill virtuous behavior, be devoted to internal serenity of mind, not neglect the jhānas, be possessed of insight, and resort to empty huts.

(2) "If a bhikkhu should wish: 'May I gain robes, almsfood, lodging, and medicines and provisions for the sick,' let him fulfill virtuous behavior . . . and resort to empty huts.

(3) "If a bhikkhu should wish: 'May the services of those whose robes, almsfood, lodging, and medicines and provisions for the sick I use be of great fruit and benefit to them,' let him fulfill virtuous behavior . . . and resort to empty huts.

(4) "If a bhikkhu should wish: [132] 'When my deceased relatives and family members, after passing away, remember me

with confidence in their minds, may this be of great fruit and benefit to them,' let him fulfill virtuous behavior . . . and resort to empty huts.

(5) "If a bhikkhu should wish: 'May I be content with any kind of robe, almsfood, lodging, and medicines and provisions for the sick,' let him fulfill virtuous behavior . . . and resort to empty huts.

(6) "If a bhikkhu should wish: 'May I patiently endure cold and heat; hunger and thirst; contact with flies, mosquitoes, wind, the burning sun, and serpents; and rude and offensive ways of speech. May I be able to bear up with arisen bodily feelings that are painful, racking, sharp, piercing, harrowing, disagreeable, sapping one's vitality,' let him fulfill virtuous behavior . . . and resort to empty huts.

(7) "If a bhikkhu should wish: 'May I become one who vanquishes discontent and delight, and may discontent and delight not vanquish me. May I overcome discontent and delight whenever they arise,' let him fulfill virtuous behavior . . . and resort to empty huts.

(8) "If a bhikkhu should wish: 'May I become one who vanquishes fear and terror, and may fear and terror not vanquish me. May I overcome fear and terror whenever they arise,' let him fulfill virtuous behavior . . . and resort to empty huts.

(9) "If a bhikkhu should wish: 'May I gain at will, without trouble or difficulty, the four jhānas that constitute the higher mind and are pleasant dwellings in this very life,' let him fulfill virtuous behavior . . . and resort to empty huts.

(10) "If a bhikkhu should wish: 'May I, with the destruction of the taints, realize for myself with direct knowledge, in this very life, the taintless liberation of mind, liberation by wisdom, [133] and having entered upon it, dwell in it,' let him fulfill virtuous behavior, be devoted to internal serenity of mind, not neglect the jhānas, be possessed of insight, and resort to empty huts.

"When it was said: 'Bhikkhus, be observant of virtuous behavior and observant of the Pātimokkha; dwell restrained by the Pātimokkha, possessed of good conduct and resort, seeing danger in minute faults; having undertaken them, train in the training rules,' it is because of this that this was said."

72 (2) Thorns

On one occasion the Blessed One was dwelling at Vesālī in the hall with the peaked roof in the Great Wood together with a number of very well-known elder disciples: the Venerable Cāla, the Venerable Upacāla, the Venerable Kakkaṭa, the Venerable Kaṭimbha, the Venerable Kaṭa, the Venerable Kaṭissaṅga, and other very well-known elder disciples.

Now on that occasion a number of very well-known Licchavis had entered the Great Wood in order to see the Blessed One, and as they followed one another in their finest carriages they made an uproar and a racket. It then occurred to those venerable ones: "A number of very well-known Licchavis have entered the Great Wood in order to see the Blessed One, and as they follow one another in their finest carriages they are making an uproar and a racket. Now the Blessed One has called noise a thorn to the jhānas. Let us go to the Gosiṅga Sal Woods. [134] There we can dwell at ease, without noise and without any crowds." Then those venerable ones went to the Gosiṅga Sal Woods, where they dwelt at ease, without noise and crowds.

Then the Blessed One addressed the bhikkhus: "Bhikkhus, where is Cāla? Where is Upacāla? Where is Kakkaṭa? Where is Kaṭimbha? Where is Kaṭa? Where is Kaṭissaṅga? Where have those elder disciples gone?"

"Bhante, it occurred to those venerable ones: 'A number of very well-known Licchavis . . . are making an uproar and a racket. . . . Let us go to the Gosiṅga Sal Woods, where we can dwell at ease, without noise and crowds.' So they went to the Gosiṅga Sal Woods, where they dwell at ease, without noise and crowds."

"Good, good, bhikkhus! Those great disciples spoke rightly when they said that I have called noise a thorn to the jhānas. There are, bhikkhus, these ten thorns. What ten? (1) Delight in company is a thorn to one who delights in solitude. (2) Pursuit of an attractive object is a thorn to one intent on meditation on the mark of the unattractive. (3) An unsuitable show is a thorn to one guarding the doors of the sense faculties. (4) Keeping company with women is a thorn to the celibate life. [135] (5) Noise is a thorn to the first jhāna. (6) Thought and examination are a thorn to the second jhāna. (7) Rapture is a thorn to the third jhāna. (8) In-and-out breathing is a thorn to the fourth jhāna. (9) Perception and feeling are a thorn to the attainment of the cessation of perception and feeling. (10) Lust is a thorn, hatred is a thorn, and delusion is a thorn. Dwell thornless, bhikkhus! Dwell without thorns! The arahants are thornless. The arahants are without thorns. The arahants are thornless and without thorns."

73 (3) Wished For

"Bhikkhus, there are these ten things that are wished for, desired, agreeable, and rarely gained in the world. What ten? (1) Wealth is wished for, desired, agreeable, and rarely gained in the world. (2) Beauty . . . (3) Health . . . (4) Virtuous behavior . . . (5) Celibacy . . . (6) Friends . . . (7) Learning . . . (8) Wisdom . . . (9) Good qualities . . . (10) The heavens are wished for, desired, agreeable, and rarely gained in the world. [136] These are the ten things that are wished for, desired, agreeable, and rarely gained in the world.

"There are ten [other] things, bhikkhus, that are obstructions to these ten things that are wished for, desired, agreeable, and rarely gained in the world. (1) Indolence and lack of initiative are obstructions to [the acquisition of] wealth. (2) Not adorning and beautifying oneself are obstructions to beauty. (3) Doing what is unbeneficial is an obstruction to health. (4) Bad friendship is an obstruction to virtuous behavior. (5) Non-restraint of the sense faculties is an obstruction to celibacy. (6) Duplicity is an obstruction to friendships. (7) Non-recitation is an obstruction to learning. (8) Unwillingness to listen and not asking questions are obstructions to wisdom. (9) Not applying oneself and lack of reflection are obstructions to good qualities. (10) Wrong practice is an obstruction to the heavens. These are the ten [other] things that are obstructions to those ten things that are wished for, desired, agreeable, and rarely gained in the world.

"There are ten [other] things, bhikkhus, that are nutriments for these ten things that are wished for, desired, agreeable, and rarely gained in the world. (1) Diligence and initiative are nutriments for [the acquisition of] wealth. (2) Adorning and beautifying oneself are nutriments for beauty. (3) Doing what is beneficial is a nutriment for health. (4) Good friendship is a nutriment for virtuous behavior. (5) Restraint of the sense faculties is a nutriment for celibacy. (6) Sincerity is a nutriment for friendships. (7) Recitation is a nutriment for learning. (8) Willingness to listen and asking questions are nutriments for wisdom. (9) Applying oneself and reflection are nutriments for good qualities. (10) Right practice is a nutriment for the heavens. These are the ten [other] things that are nutriments for those ten things that are wished for, desired, agreeable, and rarely gained in the world." [137]

74 (4) Growth[2090]

"Bhikkhus, growing in ten ways, a noble disciple grows by a noble growth, and he absorbs the essence and the best of this life. What ten? (1) He grows in fields and land; (2) in wealth and grain; (3) in wives and children; (4) in slaves, workers, and servants; (5) in livestock; (6)–(10) in faith, virtuous behavior, learning, generosity, and wisdom. Growing in these ten ways, a noble disciple grows by a noble growth, and he absorbs the essence and the best of this life."

> One who grows here in wealth and grain,
> in children, wives, and livestock,
> is wealthy and famous, honored
> by relatives, friends, and royalty.
>
> Such a discerning good man—
> who grows here in faith and virtuous behavior,
> in wisdom, generosity, and learning—
> grows in both ways in this life.

75 (5) Migasālā[2091]

On one occasion the Blessed One was dwelling at Sāvatthī in Jeta's Grove, Anāthapiṇḍika's Park. Then, in the morning, the Venerable Ānanda dressed, took his bowl and robe, and went to the house of the female lay follower Migasālā, where he sat down on the seat prepared for him. Then the female lay disciple Migasālā approached the Venerable Ānanda, paid homage to him, sat down to one side, and said:

"Bhante Ānanda, just how should this [138] teaching of the

Blessed One be understood, where one who is celibate and one who is not celibate both have exactly the same destination in their future life? My father Purāṇa was celibate, living apart, abstaining from sexual intercourse, the common person's practice. When he died, the Blessed One declared: 'He attained to the state of a once-returner and has been reborn in the Tusita group [of devas].' My paternal uncle Isidatta[2092] was not celibate but lived a contented married life. When he died, the Blessed One also declared: 'He attained to the state of a once-returner and has been reborn in the Tusita group [of devas].' Bhante Ānanda, just how should this teaching of the Blessed One be understood, where one who is celibate and one who is not celibate both have exactly the same destination in their future life?"

"It was just in this way, sister, that the Blessed One declared it."

Then, when the Venerable Ānanda had received almsfood at Migasālā's house, he rose from his seat and departed. After his meal, on returning from his alms round, he went to the Blessed One, paid homage to him, sat down to one side, and said: "Here, Bhante, in the morning, I dressed, took my bowl and robe, and went to the house of the female lay follower Migasālā. . . . [139] [all as above, down to] . . . When she asked me this, I replied: 'It was just in this way, sister, that the Blessed One declared it.'"

[The Blessed One said:] "Who, indeed, is the female lay follower Migasālā, a foolish, incompetent woman with a woman's intellect? And who are those [who have] the knowledge of other persons as superior and inferior?[2093]

"There are, Ānanda, these ten types of persons found existing in the world. What ten?

(1) "Here, Ānanda, there is one person who is immoral and does not understand as it really is that liberation of mind, liberation by wisdom, where that immorality of his ceases without remainder.[2094] And he has not listened [to the teachings], become learned [in them], penetrated [them] by view, and he does not attain temporary liberation. With the breakup of the body, after death, he heads for deterioration, not for distinction; he is one going to deterioration, not to distinction.

(2) "Then, Ānanda, there is one person who is immoral yet understands as it really is that liberation of mind, liberation by wisdom, [140] where that immorality of his ceases without

remainder. And he has listened [to the teachings], become learned [in them], penetrated [them] by view, and he attains temporary liberation. With the breakup of the body, after death, he heads for distinction, not for deterioration; he is one going to distinction, not to deterioration.

"Ānanda, those who are judgmental will pass such judgment on them: 'This one has the same qualities as the other. Why should one be inferior and the other superior?' That [judgment] of theirs will indeed lead to their harm and suffering for a long time.

"Between them, Ānanda, the person who is immoral, and who understands as it really is that liberation of mind, liberation by wisdom, where that immorality of his ceases without remainder; who has listened [to the teachings], become learned [in them], penetrated [them] by view, and who attains temporary liberation, surpasses and excels the other person. For what reason? Because the Dhamma-stream carries him along. But who can know this difference except the Tathāgata?

"Therefore, Ānanda, do not be judgmental regarding people. Do not pass judgment on people. Those who pass judgment on people harm themselves. I alone, or one like me, may pass judgment on people. [141]

(3) "Then, Ānanda, there is one person who is virtuous yet does not understand as it really is that liberation of mind, liberation by wisdom, where that virtuous behavior of his ceases without remainder. And he has not listened [to the teachings]... he does not attain temporary liberation. With the breakup of the body, after death, he heads for deterioration, not for distinction; he is one going to deterioration, not to distinction.

(4) "Then, Ānanda, there is one person who is virtuous and understands as it really is that liberation of mind, liberation by wisdom, where that virtuous behavior of his ceases without remainder. And he has listened [to the teachings] . . . and he attains temporary liberation. With the breakup of the body, after death, he heads for distinction, not for deterioration; he is one going to distinction, not to deterioration.

"Ānanda, those who are judgmental will pass such judgment on them . . . I alone, or one like me, may pass judgment on people.

(5) "Then, Ānanda, there is one person who is strongly prone

to lust and does not understand as it really is that liberation of mind, liberation by wisdom, where that lust of his ceases without remainder. And he has not listened [to the teachings] . . . he does not attain temporary liberation. With the breakup of the body, after death, he heads for deterioration, not for distinction; he is one going to deterioration, not to distinction.

(6) "Then, Ānanda, there is one person who is strongly prone to lust yet understands as it really is that liberation of mind, liberation by wisdom, where that lust of his ceases without remainder. And he has listened [to the teachings] . . . and he attains temporary liberation. [142] With the breakup of the body, after death, he heads for distinction, not for deterioration; he is one going to distinction, not to deterioration.

"Ānanda, those who are judgmental will pass such judgment on them. . . . I alone, or one like me, may pass judgment on people.

(7) "Then, Ānanda, there is one person who is prone to anger and does not understand as it really is that liberation of mind, liberation by wisdom, where that anger of his ceases without remainder. And he has not listened [to the teachings] . . . he does not attain temporary liberation. With the breakup of the body, after death, he heads for deterioration, not for distinction; he is one going to deterioration, not to distinction.

(8) "Then, Ānanda, there is one person who is prone to anger yet understands as it really is that liberation of mind, liberation by wisdom, where that anger of his ceases without remainder. And he has listened [to the teachings] . . . he attains temporary liberation. With the breakup of the body, after death, he heads for distinction, not for deterioration; he is one going to distinction, not to deterioration.

"Ānanda, those who are judgmental will pass such judgment on them. . . . I alone, or one like me, may pass judgment on people.

(9) "Then, Ānanda, there is one person who is restless and does not understand as it really is that liberation of mind, liberation by wisdom, where that restlessness of his ceases without remainder. And he has not listened [to the teachings] . . . he does not attain temporary liberation. With the breakup of the body, after death, he heads for deterioration, not for distinction; he is one going to deterioration, not to distinction.

(10) "Then, Ānanda, there is one person who is restless yet understands as it really is that liberation of mind, liberation by wisdom, where that restlessness of his ceases without remainder. And he has listened [to the teachings], become learned [in them], penetrated [them] by view, [143] and he attains temporary liberation. With the breakup of the body, after death, he heads for distinction, not for deterioration; he is one going to distinction, not to deterioration.

"Ānanda, those who are judgmental will pass such judgment on them: 'This one has the same qualities as the other. Why should one be inferior and the other superior?' That [judgment] of theirs will indeed lead to their harm and suffering for a long time.

"Between them, Ānanda, the person who is restless, and who understands as it really is that liberation of mind, liberation by wisdom, where that restlessness of his ceases without remainder; who has listened [to the teachings], become learned [in them], penetrated [them] by view, and who attains temporary liberation, surpasses and excels the other person. For what reason? Because the Dhamma-stream carries him along. But who can know this difference except the Tathāgata?

"Therefore, Ānanda, do not be judgmental regarding people. Do not pass judgment on people. Those who pass judgment on people harm themselves. I alone, or one like me, may pass judgment on people.

"Who, indeed, is the female lay follower Migasālā, a foolish, incompetent woman with a woman's intellect? And who are those [who have] the knowledge of other persons as superior and inferior?

"These are the ten types of persons found existing in the world.

"Ānanda, if Isidatta had possessed the same kind of virtuous behavior that Purāṇa had, Purāṇa could not have even known his destination. [144] And if Purāṇa had possessed the same kind of wisdom that Isidatta had, Isidatta could not have even known his destination. In this way, Ānanda, these two persons were each deficient in one respect."

76 (6) Incapable

(1) "Bhikkhus, if these three things[2095] were not found in the world, the Tathāgata, the Arahant, the Perfectly Enlightened

One would not arise in the world, and the Dhamma and discipline proclaimed by him would not shine in the world. What three? Birth, old age, and death. If these three things were not found in the world, the Tathāgata, the Arahant, the Perfectly Enlightened One would not arise in the world, and the Dhamma and discipline proclaimed by him would not shine in the world. But because these three things are found in the world, the Tathāgata, the Arahant, the Perfectly Enlightened One arises in the world, and the Dhamma and discipline proclaimed by him shines in the world.

(2) "Without having abandoned these three things, one is incapable of abandoning birth, old age, and death. What three? Lust, hatred, and delusion. Without having abandoned these three things, one is incapable of abandoning birth, old age, and death.

(3) "Without having abandoned these three things, one is incapable of abandoning lust, hatred, and delusion. What three? Personal-existence view, doubt, and wrong grasp of behavior and observances. Without having abandoned these three things, one is incapable of abandoning lust, hatred, and delusion. [145]

(4) "Without having abandoned these three things, one is incapable of abandoning personal-existence view, doubt, and wrong grasp of behavior and observances. What three? Careless attention, following a wrong path, and mental sluggishness. Without having abandoned these three things, one is incapable of abandoning personal-existence view, doubt, and wrong grasp of behavior and observances.

(5) "Without having abandoned these three things, one is incapable of abandoning careless attention, following a wrong path, and mental sluggishness. What three? Muddle-mindedness, lack of clear comprehension, and mental distraction. Without having abandoned these three things, one is incapable of abandoning careless attention, following a wrong path, and mental sluggishness.

(6) "Without having abandoned these three things, one is incapable of abandoning muddle-mindedness, lack of clear comprehension, and mental distraction. What three? Lack of desire to see the noble ones, lack of desire to hear the noble Dhamma, and a mind bent on criticism. Without having abandoned these three things, one is incapable of abandoning

muddle-mindedness, lack of clear comprehension, and mental distraction.

(7) "Without having abandoned these three things, one is incapable of abandoning lack of desire to see the noble ones, lack of desire to hear the noble Dhamma, and a mind bent on criticism. What three? Restlessness, non-restraint, and immorality. Without having abandoned these three things, one is incapable of abandoning lack of desire to see the noble ones, lack of desire to hear the noble Dhamma, and a mind bent on criticism. [146]

(8) "Without having abandoned these three things, one is incapable of abandoning restlessness, non-restraint, and immorality. What three? Lack of faith, uncharitableness, and laziness. Without having abandoned these three things, one is incapable of abandoning restlessness, non-restraint, and immorality.

(9) "Without having abandoned these three things, one is incapable of abandoning lack of faith, uncharitableness, and laziness. What three? Disrespect, being difficult to correct, and bad friendship. Without having abandoned these three things, one is incapable of abandoning lack of faith, uncharitableness, and laziness.

(10) "Without having abandoned these three things, one is incapable of abandoning disrespect, being difficult to correct, and bad friendship. What three? Moral shamelessness, moral recklessness, and heedlessness. Without having abandoned these three things, one is incapable of abandoning disrespect, being difficult to correct, and bad friendship.

"Bhikkhus, one who is morally shameless and morally reckless is heedless. One who is heedless is incapable of abandoning disrespect, being difficult to correct, and bad friendship. One who has bad friends is incapable of abandoning lack of faith, uncharitableness, and laziness. One who is lazy is incapable of abandoning restlessness, non-restraint, and immorality. One who is immoral is incapable of abandoning lack of desire to see the noble ones, lack of desire to hear the noble Dhamma, and a mind bent on criticism. One who has a mind bent on criticism is incapable of abandoning muddle-mindedness, lack of clear comprehension, and mental distraction. One who is [147] mentally distracted is incapable of abandoning careless attention, following a wrong path, and mental sluggishness. One who is mentally sluggish is incapable of abandoning personal-existence view, doubt, and wrong grasp of behavior and observances. One who has doubt is incapable of abandoning lust, hatred, and delusion. Without having abandoned lust, hatred, and delusion, one is incapable of abandoning birth, old age, and death.

(1) "Bhikkhus, having abandoned these three things, one is capable of abandoning birth, old age, and death. What three? Lust, hatred, and delusion. Having abandoned these three things, one is capable of abandoning birth, old age, and death.

(2) "Having abandoned these three things, one is capable of abandoning lust, hatred, and delusion. What three? Personal-existence view, doubt, and wrong grasp of behavior and observances. Having abandoned these three things, one is capable of abandoning lust, hatred, and delusion.

(3) "Having abandoned these three things, one is capable of abandoning personal-existence view, doubt, and wrong grasp of behavior and observances. What three? Careless attention, following a wrong path, and mental sluggishness. Having abandoned these three things, one is capable of abandoning personal-existence view, doubt, and wrong grasp of behavior and observances.

(4) "Having abandoned these three things, one is capable of abandoning careless attention, following a wrong path, and mental sluggishness. What three? Muddle-mindedness, lack of clear comprehension, and mental distraction. Having abandoned these three things, one is capable of abandoning careless attention, following a wrong path, and mental sluggishness. [148]

(5) "Having abandoned these three things, one is capable of abandoning muddle-mindedness, lack of clear comprehension, and mental distraction. What three? Lack of desire to see the noble ones, lack of desire to hear the noble Dhamma, and a mind bent on criticism. Having abandoned these three things, one is capable of abandoning muddle-mindedness, lack of clear comprehension, and mental distraction.

(6) "Having abandoned these three things, one is capable of abandoning lack of desire to see the noble ones, lack of desire to hear the noble Dhamma, and a mind bent on criticism. What

three? Restlessness, non-restraint, and immorality. Having abandoned these three things, one is capable of abandoning lack of desire to see the noble ones, lack of desire to hear the noble Dhamma, and a mind bent on criticism.

(7) "Having abandoned these three things, one is capable of abandoning restlessness, non-restraint, and immorality. What three? Lack of faith, uncharitableness, and laziness. Having abandoned these three things, one is capable of abandoning restlessness, non-restraint, and immorality.

(8) "Having abandoned these three things, one is capable of abandoning lack of faith, uncharitableness, and laziness. What three? Disrespect, being difficult to correct, and bad friendship. Having abandoned these three things, one is capable of abandoning lack of faith, uncharitableness, and laziness.

(9) "Having abandoned these three things, one is capable of abandoning disrespect, being difficult to correct, and bad friendship. What three? Moral shamelessness, moral recklessness, and heedlessness. Having abandoned these three things, one is capable of abandoning disrespect, being difficult to correct, and bad friendship.

(10) "Bhikkhus, one who has a sense of moral shame and moral dread is heedful. One who is heedful is capable of abandoning disrespect, being difficult to speak to, and bad friendship. One who has good friends [149] is capable of abandoning lack of faith, uncharitableness, and laziness. One who is energetic is capable of abandoning restlessness, non-restraint, and immorality. One who is virtuous is capable of abandoning lack of desire to see the noble ones, lack of desire to hear the noble Dhamma, and a mind bent on criticism. One whose mind is not bent on criticism is capable of abandoning muddle-mindedness, lack of clear comprehension, and mental distraction. One who has an undistracted mind is capable of abandoning careless attention, following a wrong path, and mental sluggishness. One who has an unsluggish mind is capable of abandoning personal-existence view, doubt, and wrong grasp of behavior and observances. One without doubt is capable of abandoning lust, hatred, and delusion. Having abandoned lust, hatred, and delusion, one is capable of abandoning birth, old age, and death."

77 (7) The Crow

"Bhikkhus, a crow has ten bad qualities. What ten? It is destructive and impudent, ravenous and voracious, cruel and pitiless, weak and raucous, muddle-minded and acquisitive. A crow has these ten bad qualities. So too, an evil bhikkhu has ten bad qualities. What ten? He is destructive and impudent, ravenous and voracious, cruel and pitiless, weak and raucous, muddle-minded and acquisitive. An evil bhikkhu has these ten bad qualities." [150]

78 (8) The Nigaṇṭhas

"Bhikkhus, the Nigaṇṭhas have ten bad qualities. What ten? (1) The Nigaṇṭhas are without faith, (2) immoral, (3) morally shameless, (4) morally reckless, (5) and devoted to bad persons. (6) They extol themselves and disparage others. (7) They grasp their own views, hold to them tightly, and relinquish them with difficulty. (8) They are deceivers, (9) have evil desires, and (10) hold wrong views.[2096] The Nigaṇṭhas have these ten bad qualities."

79 (9) Grounds (1)[2097]

"Bhikkhus, there are these ten grounds for resentment. What ten? (1) [Thinking:] 'They acted for my harm,' one harbors resentment. (2) [Thinking:] 'They are acting for my harm,' one harbors resentment. (3) [Thinking:] 'They will act for my harm,' one harbors resentment. (4) [Thinking:] 'They acted for the harm of one who is pleasing and agreeable to me,' one harbors resentment. (5) [Thinking:] 'They are acting for the harm of one who is pleasing and agreeable to me,' one harbors resentment. (6) [Thinking:] 'They will act for the harm of one who is pleasing and agreeable to me,' one harbors resentment. (7) [Thinking:] 'They acted for the benefit of one who is displeasing and disagreeable to me,' one harbors resentment. (8) [Thinking:] 'They are acting for the benefit of one who is displeasing and disagreeable to me,' one harbors resentment. (9) [Thinking:] 'They will act for the benefit of one who is displeasing and disagreeable to me,' one harbors resentment. (10) And one becomes angry without a reason.[2098] These, bhikkhus, are the ten grounds for resentment."

80 (10) Grounds (2)[2099]

"Bhikkhus, there are these ten ways of removing resentment. What ten? (1) [Thinking:] 'They acted for my harm, but what can be done about it?' one removes resentment. [151] (2) [Thinking:] 'They are acting for my harm, but what can be done about it?' one removes resentment. (3) [Thinking:] 'They will act for my harm, but what can be done about it?' one removes resentment. (4) [Thinking:] 'They acted . . .' (5) . . . 'They are acting . . .' (6) . . . 'They will act for the harm of one who is pleasing and agreeable to me, but what can be done about it?' one removes resentment (7) [Thinking:] 'They acted . . .' (8) . . . 'They are acting . . .' (9) . . . 'They will act for the benefit of one who is displeasing and disagreeable to me, but what can be done about it?' one removes resentment. (10) And one does not become angry without a reason. These, bhikkhus, are the ten ways of removing resentment."

IV. The Elders

81 (1) Bāhuna

On one occasion the Blessed One was dwelling at Campā on a bank of the Gaggārā Lotus Pond. Then the Venerable Bāhuna approached the Blessed One, paid homage to him, sat down to one side, and said to him:

"Bhante, from how many things is the Tathāgata released, detached, and emancipated, that he dwells with a mind free from boundaries?" [152]

"Bāhuna, it is because the Tathāgata is released, detached, and emancipated from ten things that he dwells with a mind free from boundaries. What ten? (1) It is because the Tathāgata is released, detached, and emancipated from form that he dwells with a mind free from boundaries. (2)–(5) It is because the Tathāgata is released, detached, and emancipated from feeling . . . perception . . . volitional activities . . . consciousness that he dwells with a mind free from boundaries. (6)–(10) It is because the Tathāgata is released, detached, and emancipated from birth . . . old age . . . death . . . suffering . . . defilements that he dwells with a mind free from boundaries.

"Just as a blue, red, or white lotus flower, though born in the water and grown up in the water, rises up above the water and stands unsoiled by the water,[2100] even so, Bāhuna, it is because the Tathāgata is released, detached, and emancipated from these ten things that he dwells with a mind free from boundaries."

82 (2) Ānanda

Then the Venerable Ānanda approached the Blessed One, paid homage to him, and sat down to one side. The Blessed One then said to him:

(1) "It is impossible, Ānanda, that a bhikkhu without faith will achieve growth, progress, and maturity in this Dhamma and discipline. (2) It is impossible that an immoral bhikkhu ... (3) ... a bhikkhu of little learning ... (4) ... a bhikkhu who is difficult to correct ... [153] (5) ... a bhikkhu who has bad friends ... (6) ... a lazy bhikkhu ... (7) ... a muddle-minded bhikkhu ... (8) ... a bhikkhu who is not content ... (9) ... a bhikkhu of evil desires ... (10) ... a bhikkhu who holds wrong view will achieve growth, progress, and maturity in this Dhamma and discipline. It is impossible that a bhikkhu who possesses these ten qualities will achieve growth, progress, and maturity in this Dhamma and discipline.

(1) "It is possible, Ānanda, that a bhikkhu endowed with faith will achieve growth, progress, and maturity in this Dhamma and discipline. (2) It is possible that a virtuous bhikkhu ... (3) ... a bhikkhu of much learning ... (4) ... a bhikkhu who is easy to correct ... (5) ... a bhikkhu who has good friends ... (6) ... an energetic bhikkhu ... (7) ... a mindful bhikkhu ... [154] (8) ... a contented bhikkhu ... (9) ... a bhikkhu of few desires ... (10) ... a bhikkhu who holds right view will achieve growth, progress, and maturity in this Dhamma and discipline. It is possible that a bhikkhu who possesses these ten qualities will achieve growth, progress, and maturity in this Dhamma and discipline."

83 (3) Puṇṇiya[2101]

Then the Venerable Puṇṇiya approached the Blessed One, paid homage to him, sat down to one side, and said to him:

"Bhante, why is it that at times the Tathāgata is disposed to teach the Dhamma and at times is not disposed [to teach]?"

(1) "When, Puṇṇiya, a bhikkhu is endowed with faith but does not approach him, the Tathāgata is not disposed to teach the Dhamma. (2) But when a bhikkhu is endowed with faith and approaches him, the Tathāgata is disposed to teach.

(3) "When, Puṇṇiya, a bhikkhu is endowed with faith and

approaches him, but he does not attend on him . . . (4) When he attends on him but does not ask questions . . . (5) When he asks questions but does not listen to the Dhamma with eager ears . . . (6) When he listens to the Dhamma with eager ears, but having heard it, does not retain it in mind . . . (7) When, having heard it, he retains it in mind but does not examine the meaning of the teachings that have been retained in mind . . . (8) When he examines the meaning of the teachings that have been retained in mind but does not [155] understand the meaning and the Dhamma and then practice in accordance with the Dhamma . . . (9) When he understands the meaning and the Dhamma and then practices in accordance with the Dhamma, but he is not a good speaker with a good delivery, one gifted with speech that is polished, clear, articulate, expressive of the meaning . . . (10) When he is a good speaker with a good delivery, one gifted with speech that is polished, clear, articulate, expressive of the meaning, but he does not instruct, encourage, inspire, and gladden his fellow monks, the Tathāgata is not disposed to teach the Dhamma.

"But, Puṇṇiya, (1) when a bhikkhu is endowed with faith, (2) approaches [the Tathāgata], (3) attends on [the Tathāgata], (4) asks questions, and (5) listens to the Dhamma with eager ears; and (6) having heard the Dhamma, he retains it in mind, (7) examines the meaning of the teachings he has retained in mind, and (8) understands the meaning and the Dhamma and then practices in accordance with the Dhamma; and (9) he is a good speaker with a good delivery, one gifted with speech that is polished, clear, articulate, expressive of the meaning; and (10) he instructs, encourages, inspires, and gladdens his fellow monks, the Tathāgata is disposed to teach the Dhamma. When, Puṇṇiya, one possesses these ten qualities, the Tathāgata is entirely disposed to teach the Dhamma."

84 (4) Declaration

There the Venerable Mahāmoggallāna addressed the bhikkhus: "Friends, bhikkhus!"

"Friend," those bhikkhus replied. The Venerable Mahāmoggallāna said this:

"Here, friends, a bhikkhu declares final knowledge thus: 'I understand: "Destroyed is birth, the spiritual life has been lived, what had to be done has been done, there is no more coming back to any state of being.”’ The Tathāgata [156] or his disciple who is a jhāna-attainer—skilled in attainment, skilled in others' minds, skilled in the ways of others' minds—questions him, interrogates him, and cross-examines him. When he is being questioned, interrogated, and cross-examined by the Tathāgata or his disciple, he comes to an impasse and is flustered. He meets with calamity, meets with disaster, meets with calamity and disaster.

“The Tathāgata or his disciple who is a jhāna-attainer . . . encompasses his mind with his own mind and considers: ‘Why does this venerable one declare final knowledge thus: “I understand: ‘Destroyed is birth, the spiritual life has been lived, what had to be done has been done, there is no more coming back to any state of being.’”?’ The Tathāgata or his disciple, having encompassed his mind with his own mind, understands:

(1) “‘This venerable one is prone to anger and his mind is often obsessed by anger. But in the Dhamma and discipline proclaimed by the Tathāgata, obsession by anger is a case of decline.

(2) “‘This venerable one is hostile and his mind is often obsessed by hostility. But in the Dhamma and discipline proclaimed by the Tathāgata, obsession by hostility is a case of decline.

(3) “‘This venerable one is prone to denigration and his mind is often obsessed by denigration. But in the Dhamma and discipline proclaimed by the Tathāgata, obsession by denigration is a case of decline.

(4) “‘This venerable one is insolent and his mind is often obsessed by insolence. But in the Dhamma and discipline proclaimed by the Tathāgata, obsession by insolence is a case of decline.

(5) “‘This venerable one is envious and his mind is often obsessed by envy. But in the Dhamma and discipline proclaimed by the Tathāgata, obsession by envy is a case of decline.

(6) “‘This venerable one is miserly and his mind is often obsessed by miserliness. [157] But in the Dhamma and discipline proclaimed by the Tathāgata, obsession by miserliness is a case of decline.

(7) “‘This venerable one is crafty and his mind is often obsessed by craftiness. But in the Dhamma and discipline proclaimed by the Tathāgata, obsession by craftiness is a case of decline.

(8) "'This venerable one is deceitful and his mind is often obsessed by deceitfulness. But in the Dhamma and discipline proclaimed by the Tathāgata, obsession by deceitfulness is a case of decline.

(9) "'This venerable one has evil desires and his mind is often obsessed by desire. But in the Dhamma and discipline proclaimed by the Tathāgata, obsession by desire is a case of decline.

(10) "'When there is something further to be done,[2102] this venerable one comes to a stop along the way on account of some lower achievement of distinction. But in the Dhamma and discipline proclaimed by the Tathāgata, coming to a stop along the way is a case of decline.'

"Truly, friends, it is impossible for a bhikkhu who has not abandoned these ten things to achieve growth, progress, and maturity in this Dhamma and discipline. But it is possible for a bhikkhu who has abandoned these ten things to achieve growth, progress, and maturity in this Dhamma and discipline."

85 (5) The Boaster

On one occasion the Venerable Mahācunda was dwelling among the Cetis at Sahajāti. There the Venerable Mahācunda addressed the bhikkhus:

"Friends, bhikkhus!"

"Friend!" those bhikkhus replied. The Venerable Mahācunda said this:

"Here, friends, a bhikkhu is a boaster, one who brags about achievements: 'I attain and emerge from the first jhāna. I attain and emerge from the second jhāna . . . the third jhāna . . . the fourth jhāna . . . [158] . . . the base of the infinity of space . . . the base of the infinity of consciousness . . . the base of nothingness . . . the base of neither-perception-nor-non-perception. I attain and emerge from the cessation of feeling and perception.' The Tathāgata or his disciple who is a jhāna-attainer—skilled in attainment, skilled in others' minds, skilled in the ways of others' minds—questions him, interrogates him, and cross-examines him. When he is being questioned, interrogated, and cross-examined by the Tathāgata or by his disciple, he comes to an impasse and is flustered. He meets with calamity, meets with disaster, meets with calamity and disaster.

"The Tathāgata or his disciple who is a jhāna-attainer . . . encompasses his mind with his own mind and considers: 'Why is this venerable one a boaster, one who brags about achievements: "I attain and emerge from the first jhāna . . . I attain and emerge from the cessation of feeling and perception"?' The Tathāgata or his disciple, having encompassed his mind with his own mind, understands:

(1) "'For a long time this venerable one's conduct has been broken, flawed, blemished, and blotched, and he does not consistently observe and follow virtuous behavior. This venerable one is immoral. But in the Dhamma and discipline proclaimed by the Tathāgata, immorality is a case of decline.

(2) "'This venerable one is without faith. But in the Dhamma and discipline proclaimed by the Tathāgata, lack of faith is a case of decline.

(3) "'This venerable one is of little learning and without proper conduct. But in the Dhamma and discipline proclaimed by the Tathāgata, little learning is a case of decline. [159]

(4) "'This venerable one is difficult to correct. But in the Dhamma and discipline proclaimed by the Tathāgata, being difficult to correct is a case of decline.

(5) "'This venerable one has bad friends. But in the Dhamma and discipline proclaimed by the Tathāgata, bad friendship is a case of decline.

(6) "'This venerable one is lazy. But in the Dhamma and discipline proclaimed by the Tathāgata, laziness is a case of decline.

(7) "'This venerable one is muddle-minded. But in the Dhamma and discipline proclaimed by the Tathāgata, muddle-mindedness is a case of decline.

(8) "'This venerable one is a deceiver. But in the Dhamma and discipline proclaimed by the Tathāgata, deceitfulness is a case of decline.

(9) "'This venerable one is difficult to support. But in the Dhamma and discipline proclaimed by the Tathāgata, being difficult to support is a case of decline.

(10) "'This venerable one is unwise. But in the Dhamma and discipline proclaimed by the Tathāgata, lack of wisdom is a case of decline.'

"Suppose, friends, that one man would say to his companion:

'Whenever you need money for anything, my friend, just ask me and I'll give it to you.' When the companion has need of money, he says to his friend: 'I need money, friend. Give me some.' The other says: 'In that case, friend, dig here.' He digs there but doesn't find anything. He then says: 'You lied to me, friend, you spoke falsely when you told me to dig here.' The other says: 'I didn't lie to you, friend, I didn't speak falsely. Rather, dig there.' He digs there as well but doesn't find anything. Again, he says: 'You lied to me, friend, you spoke falsely when you told me to dig there.' The other says: 'I didn't lie to you, friend, I didn't speak falsely. [160] Rather, dig there.' He digs there as well but doesn't find anything. He then says: 'You lied to me, friend, you spoke falsely when you told me to dig there.'[2103] The other says: 'I didn't lie to you, friend, I didn't speak falsely. I was insane, out of my mind.'

"So too, friends, a bhikkhu is a boaster, one who brags about achievements: 'I attain and emerge from the first jhāna.' . . . [all as above down to:] [161] . . . (10) 'This venerable one is unwise. But in the Dhamma and discipline proclaimed by the Tathāgata, lack of wisdom is a case of decline.'

"Truly, friends, it is impossible for a bhikkhu who has not abandoned these ten things to achieve growth, progress, and maturity in this Dhamma and discipline. But it is possible for a bhikkhu who has abandoned these ten things to achieve growth, progress, and maturity in this Dhamma and discipline."

86 (6) Final Knowledge

On one occasion the Venerable Mahākassapa was dwelling at Rājagaha in the Bamboo Grove, the squirrel sanctuary. There the Venerable [162] Mahākassapa addressed the bhikkhus: "Friends, bhikkhus!"

"Friend," those bhikkhus replied. The Venerable Mahākassapa said this:

"Here, friends, a bhikkhu declares final knowledge thus: 'I understand: "Destroyed is birth, the spiritual life has been lived, what had to be done has been done, there is no more coming back to any state of being."' The Tathāgata or his disciple who is a jhāna-attainer—skilled in attainment, skilled in others' minds, skilled in the ways of others' minds—questions him, interrogates him, and cross-examines him. When he is being questioned, interrogated, and cross-examined by the Tathāgata or his disciple, he comes to an impasse and is flustered. He meets with calamity, meets with disaster, meets with calamity and disaster.

"The Tathāgata or his disciple who is a jhāna-attainer . . . encompasses his mind with his own mind and considers: 'Why does this venerable one declare final knowledge thus: "I understand: 'Destroyed is birth . . . there is no more coming back to any state of being'"?' The Tathāgata or his disciple, having encompassed his mind with his own mind, understands: 'This venerable one overestimates himself, imagines that his estimate of himself is valid, thinks that he has attained what he has not attained, accomplished what he has not accomplished, and achieved what he has not achieved, and by overestimation of himself he declares final knowledge thus: "I understand: 'Destroyed is birth . . . there is no more coming back to any state of being.'"'

"The Tathāgata or his disciple who is a jhāna-attainer . . . encompasses his mind with his own mind and considers: 'Why does this venerable one overestimate himself and imagine that his estimate of himself is valid; why does he think that he has attained what he has not attained, accomplished what he has not accomplished, and achieved what he has not achieved; and why, by overestimation of himself, does he declare final knowledge thus: "I understand: 'Destroyed is [163] birth . . . there is no more coming back to any state of being'"?'

"The Tathāgata or his disciple who is a jhāna-attainer . . . having encompassed his mind with his own mind, understands: 'This venerable one has learned much, remembers what he has learned, and accumulates what he has learned. Those teachings that are good in the beginning, good in the middle, and good in the end, with the right meaning and phrasing, which proclaim the perfectly complete and pure spiritual life—such teachings as these he has learned much of, retained in mind, recited verbally, investigated mentally, and penetrated well by view. Therefore this venerable one overestimates himself and imagines that his estimate of himself is valid; he thinks that he has attained what he has not attained, accomplished what he has not accomplished, and achieved what he has not achieved; and by overestimation of himself he declares final knowledge thus: "I understand: 'Destroyed is birth . . . there is no more coming back to any state of being.'"

"The Tathāgata or his disciple who is a jhāna-attainer . . . having encompassed his mind with his own mind, understands:

(1) "'This venerable one is full of longing and his mind is often obsessed by longing. But in the Dhamma and discipline proclaimed by the Tathāgata, obsession by longing is a case of decline.

(2) "'This venerable one is full of ill will and his mind is often obsessed by ill will. But in the Dhamma and discipline proclaimed by the Tathāgata, obsession by ill will is a case of decline.

(3) "'This venerable one is given to dullness and drowsiness and his mind is often obsessed by dullness and drowsiness. But in the Dhamma and discipline proclaimed by the Tathāgata, obsession by dullness and drowsiness is a case of decline.

(4) "'This venerable one is restless and his mind is often obsessed by restlessness. But in the Dhamma and discipline proclaimed by the Tathāgata, obsession by restlessness is a case of decline.

(5) "'This venerable one is given to doubt and his mind is often obsessed by doubt. But in the Dhamma and discipline proclaimed by the Tathāgata, obsession by doubt is a case of decline.

(6) "'This venerable one delights in work, takes delight in work, is devoted to delight in work. [164] But in the Dhamma and discipline proclaimed by the Tathāgata, delight in work is a case of decline.

(7) "'This venerable one delights in talk, takes delight in talk, is devoted to delight in talk. But in the Dhamma and discipline proclaimed by the Tathāgata, delight in talk is a case of decline.

(8) "'This venerable one delights in sleep, takes delight in sleep, is devoted to delight in sleep. But in the Dhamma and discipline proclaimed by the Tathāgata, delight in sleep is a case of decline.

(9) "'This venerable one delights in company, takes delight in company, is devoted to delight in company. But in the Dhamma and discipline proclaimed by the Tathāgata, delight in company is a case of decline.

(10) "'When there is something further to be done,[2104] this venerable one comes to a stop along the way on account of some lower achievement of distinction. But in the Dhamma and discipline proclaimed by the Tathāgata, coming to a stop along the way is a case of decline.'

"Truly, friends, it is impossible for a bhikkhu who has not abandoned these ten things to achieve growth, progress, and maturity in this Dhamma and discipline. But it is possible for a bhikkhu who has abandoned these ten things to achieve growth, progress, and maturity in this Dhamma and discipline."

87 (7) Disciplinary Issues

There the Blessed One addressed the bhikkhus with reference to the bhikkhu Kalandaka:[2105] "Bhikkhus!"

"Venerable sir!" those bhikkhus replied.

The Blessed One said this:

(1) "Here, a bhikkhu is a maker of disciplinary issues and he does not speak in praise of the settlement of disciplinary issues. When a bhikkhu is a maker of disciplinary issues and does not speak in praise of the settlement of disciplinary issues, this is a quality that does not lead to affection, respect, esteem, accord, or unity.[2106] [165]

(2) "Again, a bhikkhu does not desire training and he does not speak in praise of undertaking the training. When a bhikkhu does not desire training . . . this, too, is a quality that does not lead to . . . unity.

(3) "Again, a bhikkhu has evil desires and he does not speak in praise of the removal of desire. When a bhikkhu has evil desires . . . this, too, is a quality that does not lead to . . . unity.

(4) "Again, a bhikkhu is prone to anger and he does not speak in praise of the removal of anger. When a bhikkhu is prone to anger . . . this, too, is a quality that does not lead to . . . unity.

(5) "Again, a bhikkhu is one who denigrates [others] and he does not speak in praise of the removal of denigration. When a bhikkhu is one who denigrates . . . this, too, is a quality that does not lead to . . . unity.

(6) "Again, a bhikkhu is crafty and he does not speak in praise of the removal of craftiness. When a bhikkhu is crafty . . . this, too, is a quality that does not lead to . . . unity.

(7) "Again, a bhikkhu is deceitful and he does not speak

in praise of the removal of deceitfulness. When a bhikkhu is deceitful . . . this, too, is a quality that does not lead to . . . unity. [166]

(8) "Again, a bhikkhu is not inclined to pay attention to teachings and he does not speak in praise of paying attention to teachings. When a bhikkhu is not inclined to pay attention to teachings . . . this, too, is a quality that does not lead to . . . unity.

(9) "Again, a bhikkhu is not inclined to seclusion and he does not speak in praise of seclusion. When a bhikkhu is not inclined to seclusion . . . this, too, is a quality that does not lead to . . . unity.

(10) "Again, a bhikkhu does not show hospitality to his fellow monks and he does not speak in praise of one who shows hospitality. When a bhikkhu does not show hospitality to his fellow monks and he does not speak in praise of one who shows hospitality, this, too, is a quality that does not lead to affection, respect, esteem, accord, or unity.

"Although such a bhikkhu might wish: 'Oh, if only my fellow monks would honor, respect, esteem, and venerate me!' yet his fellow monks do not honor, respect, esteem, and venerate him. For what reason? Because his wise fellow monks see that he has not abandoned those bad unwholesome qualities.

"Suppose a wild colt would wish: 'Oh, if only people would assign me a thoroughbred's place, feed me a thoroughbred's food, and give me a thoroughbred's grooming!' yet people do not assign him a thoroughbred's place, feed him a thoroughbred's food, and give him a thoroughbred's grooming. [167] For what reason? Because wise people see that he has not abandoned his tricks, ploys, gambits, and wiles. So too, although such a bhikkhu might wish: 'Oh, if only my fellow monks would honor, respect, esteem, and venerate me!' yet his fellow monks do not honor, respect, esteem, and venerate him. For what reason? Because his wise fellow monks see that he has not abandoned those bad unwholesome qualities.

(1) "But a bhikkhu is not a maker of disciplinary issues and he speaks in praise of the settlement of disciplinary issues. When a bhikkhu is not a maker of disciplinary issues and speaks in praise of the settlement of disciplinary issues, this is a quality that leads to affection, respect, esteem, accord, and unity.

(2) "Again, a bhikkhu desires training and he speaks in praise of undertaking the training. When a bhikkhu desires training ... this, too, is a quality that leads to ... unity.

(3) "Again, a bhikkhu has few desires and he speaks in praise of the removal of desire. When a bhikkhu has few desires ... this, too, is a quality that leads to ... unity.

(4) "Again, a bhikkhu is not prone to anger and he speaks in praise of the removal of anger. When a bhikkhu is not prone to anger ... this, too, is a quality that leads to ... unity.

(5) "Again, a bhikkhu is not one who denigrates [others] and he speaks in praise of the removal of denigration. When a bhikkhu is not one who denigrates [others] ... this, too, is a quality that leads to ... unity. [168]

(6) "Again, a bhikkhu is not crafty and he speaks in praise of the removal of craftiness. When a bhikkhu is not crafty ... this, too, is a quality that leads to ... unity.

(7) "Again, a bhikkhu is not deceitful and he speaks in praise of the removal of deceitfulness. When a bhikkhu is not deceitful ... this, too, is a quality that leads to ... unity.

(8) "Again, a bhikkhu is inclined to attend to teachings and he speaks in praise of attending to teachings. When a bhikkhu is inclined to attend to teachings ... this, too, is a quality that leads to ... unity.

(9) "Again, a bhikkhu is inclined to seclusion and he speaks in praise of seclusion. When a bhikkhu is inclined to seclusion ... this, too, is a quality that leads to ... unity.

(10) "Again, a bhikkhu shows hospitality to his fellow monks and he speaks in praise of one who shows hospitality. When a bhikkhu shows hospitality to his fellow monks and he speaks in praise of one who shows hospitality, this, too, is a quality that leads to affection, respect, esteem, accord, and unity.

"Although such a bhikkhu might not wish: 'Oh, if only my fellow monks would honor, respect, esteem, and venerate me!' yet his fellow monks honor, respect, esteem, and venerate him. For what reason? Because his wise fellow monks see that he has abandoned those bad unwholesome qualities.

"Suppose an excellent thoroughbred horse would not wish: 'Oh, if only people would assign me a thoroughbred's place, feed me a thoroughbred's food, and give me a thoroughbred's grooming!' yet people assign him a thoroughbred's place, feed him a thoroughbred's food, [169] and give him a thoroughbred's grooming. For what reason? Because wise people see that he has abandoned his tricks, ploys, gambits, and wiles. So too, although such a bhikkhu might not wish: 'Oh, if only my fellow monks would honor, respect, esteem, and venerate me!' yet his fellow monks honor, respect, esteem, and venerate him. For what reason? Because his wise fellow monks see that he has abandoned those bad unwholesome qualities."

88 (8) One Who Insults[2107]

"Bhikkhus, when a bhikkhu is one who insults and disparages his fellow monks, a reviler of the noble ones, it is impossible and inconceivable that he will not incur at least one of these ten disasters. What ten? (1) He does not achieve what he has not yet achieved. (2) He falls away from what he has achieved. (3) His good qualities are not polished.[2108] (4) He overestimates his good qualities, or (5) leads the spiritual life dissatisfied, or (6) commits a certain defiled offense, or (7) contracts a severe illness, or (8) goes mad and becomes mentally deranged. (9) He dies confused. (10) With the breakup of the body, after death, he is reborn in the plane of misery, in a bad destination, in the lower world, in hell. When a bhikkhu is one who insults and disparages his fellow monks, a reviler of the noble ones, it is impossible and inconceivable that he will not incur at least one of these ten disasters." [170]

89 (9) Kokālika[2109]

Then the bhikkhu Kokālika approached the Blessed One, paid homage to him, sat down to one side, and said: "Bhante, Sāriputta and Moggallāna have evil desires and have come under the control of evil desires."

[The Blessed One replied:] "Do not say so, Kokālika! Do not say so, Kokālika![2110] Place confidence in Sāriputta and Moggallāna, Kokālika. Sāriputta and Moggallāna are well behaved."

A second time the bhikkhu Kokālika said to the Blessed One: "Bhante, although I consider the Blessed One worthy of faith and trust, [I still say that] Sāriputta and Moggallāna have evil desires and have come under the control of evil desires."

"Do not say so, Kokālika! . . . Sāriputta and Moggallāna are well behaved."

A third time the bhikkhu Kokālika said to the Blessed One: "Bhante, although I consider the Blessed One worthy of faith and trust, [I still say that] Sāriputta and Moggallāna have evil desires and have come under the control of evil desires."

"Do not say so, Kokālika! Do not say so, Kokālika! Place confidence in Sāriputta and Moggallāna, Kokālika. Sāriputta and Moggallāna are well behaved."

Then the bhikkhu Kokālika rose from his seat, paid homage to the Blessed One, circumambulated the Blessed One keeping the right side toward him, and departed. Not long after the bhikkhu Kokālika had left, his entire body became covered with boils the size of mustard seeds. These then grew to the size of mung beans; then to the size of chickpeas; then to the size of jujube pits; then to the size of jujube fruits; then to the size of myrobalans; then to the size of unripe *belli* fruits;[2111] then to the size of ripe *belli* fruits. When they had grown to the size of ripe *belli* fruits, they burst open, [171] exuding pus and blood. He then just lay on banana leaves like a fish that had swallowed poison.

Then the independent brahmā Tudu approached the bhikkhu Kokālika,[2112] stood in the air, and said to him: "Place confidence in Sāriputta and Moggallāna, Kokālika. Sāriputta and Moggallāna are well behaved."

"Who are you, friend?"

"I am the independent brahmā Tudu."

"Didn't the Blessed One declare you to be a non-returner, friend? Then why have you come back here? See how much wrong you have done."[2113]

Then the independent brahmā Tudu addressed the bhikkhu Kokālika in verse:

"When a person has taken birth
an axe is born inside his mouth
with which the fool cuts himself
by uttering wrongful speech.

"He who praises one deserving blame[2114]
or blames one deserving praise
casts with his mouth an unlucky throw
by which he finds no happiness.

"Slight is the unlucky throw at dice
that results in the loss of one's wealth,
[the loss] of all, oneself included;
much worse is this unlucky throw
of harboring hate against the holy ones.

"For a hundred thousand
and thirty-six *nirabbudas*, plus five *abbudas*,[2115]
the slanderer of noble ones goes to hell,
having defamed them with evil speech and mind." [172]

Then the bhikkhu Kokālika died on account of that illness, and because of his resentment against Sāriputta and Moggallāna, after death he was reborn in the red-lotus hell.[2116]

Then, when the night had advanced, Brahmā Sahampati, of stunning beauty, illuminating the entire Jeta's Grove, approached the Blessed One, paid homage to him, stood to one side, and said to him: "Bhante, the bhikkhu Kokālika has died, and because of his resentment against Sāriputta and Moggallāna, after death he has been reborn in the red-lotus hell." This is what Brahmā Sahampati said. He then paid homage to the Blessed One, circumambulated him keeping the right side toward him, and disappeared right there.

Then, when the night had passed, the Blessed One addressed the bhikkhus: "Bhikkhus, last night, when the night had advanced, Brahmā Sahampati approached me and said to me ... [as above] ... He then paid homage to me, circumambulated me keeping the right side toward me, and disappeared right there."

When this was said, a certain bhikkhu said to the Blessed One: "How long, Bhante, is the life span in the red-lotus hell?"[2117]

"The life span in the red-lotus hell is long, bhikkhu. It is not easy to count it and say it is so many [173] years, or so many hundreds of years, or so many thousands of years, or so many hundreds of thousands of years."

"Then is it possible, Bhante, to give a simile?"

"It is, bhikkhu," the Blessed One said. "Suppose there was a Kosalan cartload of twenty measures of sesamum seed. At the end of every hundred years a man would remove one seed from it. In this manner the Kosalan cartload of twenty measures of sesamum seed might be depleted and eliminated more quickly than (1) a life in a single *abbuda* hell would go by. (2) One life in the *nirabbuda* hell is the equivalent of twenty lives in the *abbuda* hell; (3) one life in the *ababa* hell is the equivalent of twenty lives in the *nirabbuda* hell; (4) one life in the *ahaha* hell is the equivalent of twenty lives in the *ababa* hell; (5) one life in the *aṭaṭa* hell is the equivalent of twenty lives in the *ahaha* hell; (6) one life in the water-lily hell is the equivalent of twenty lives in the *aṭaṭa* hell; (7) one life in the sweet-fragrance hell is the equivalent of twenty lives in the water-lily hell; (8) one life in the blue-lotus hell is the equivalent of twenty lives in the sweet-fragrance hell; (9) one life in the white-lotus hell is the equivalent of twenty lives in the blue-lotus hell; and (10) one life in the red-lotus hell is the equivalent of twenty lives in the white-lotus hell. Now, because he harbored resentment against Sāriputta and Moggallāna, the bhikkhu Kokālika has been reborn in the red-lotus hell."

This is what the Blessed One said. Having said this, the Fortunate One, the Teacher, further said this: [174]

[The four verses are identical with those just above.]

90 (10) Powers[2118]

Then the Venerable Sāriputta approached the Blessed One, paid homage to him, and sat down to one side. The Blessed One then said to him:

"Sāriputta, when a bhikkhu's taints have been destroyed, how many powers does he possess by reason of which he can claim [to have attained] the destruction of the taints: 'My taints have been destroyed'?"

"Bhante, when a bhikkhu's taints have been destroyed, he possesses ten powers by reason of which he can claim [to have attained] the destruction of the taints: 'My taints have been destroyed.' What ten?

(1) "Here, Bhante, a bhikkhu with taints destroyed has clearly seen all conditioned phenomena as they really are with correct wisdom as impermanent. [175] This is a power of a bhikkhu with taints destroyed on the basis of which he claims [to have attained] the destruction of the taints: 'My taints have been destroyed.'

(2) "Again, a bhikkhu with taints destroyed has clearly seen sensual pleasures as they really are with correct wisdom as

similar to a charcoal pit. This is a power of a bhikkhu with taints destroyed . . .

(3) "Again, the mind of a bhikkhu with taints destroyed slants, slopes, and inclines to seclusion; it is withdrawn, delights in renunciation, and is entirely finished with all things that are a basis for the taints. This is a power of a bhikkhu with taints destroyed . . .

(4) "Again, a bhikkhu with taints destroyed has developed and well developed the four establishments of mindfulness. This is a power of a bhikkhu with taints destroyed . . .

(5)–(10) "Again, a bhikkhu with taints destroyed has developed and well developed the four right strivings . . . the four bases for psychic potency . . . the five spiritual faculties . . . the five powers [176] . . . the seven factors of enlightenment . . . the noble eightfold path. This is a power of a bhikkhu with taints destroyed on the basis of which he claims [to have attained] the destruction of the taints: 'My taints have been destroyed.'

"Bhante, when a bhikkhu's taints have been destroyed, he possesses these ten powers by reason of which he can claim [to have attained] the destruction of the taints: 'My taints have been destroyed.'"

V. Upāli[2119]

91 (1) One Who Enjoys Sensual Pleasures[2120]

On one occasion the Blessed One was dwelling at Sāvatthī in Jeta's Grove, Anāthapiṇḍika's Park. Then the householder Anāthapiṇḍika approached the Blessed One, paid homage to him, and sat down to one side. The Blessed One then said to him: [177]

"Householder, there are these ten kinds of persons who enjoy sensual pleasures found existing in the world. What ten?[2121]

[I. Exposition]

[A. Those Who Seek Wealth Unrighteously]

(1) "Here, householder, someone who enjoys sensual pleasures seeks wealth unrighteously, by violence. Having done so, he does not make himself happy and pleased, nor does he share the wealth and do meritorious deeds.

(2) "Someone else who enjoys sensual pleasures seeks wealth unrighteously, by violence. Having done so, he makes himself happy and pleased, but he does not share the wealth and do meritorious deeds.

(3) "And still someone else who enjoys sensual pleasures seeks wealth unrighteously, by violence. Having done so, he makes himself happy and pleased, and he shares the wealth and does meritorious deeds.

[B. Those Who Seek Wealth Both Righteously and Unrighteously]

(4) "Next, householder, someone who enjoys sensual pleasures seeks wealth both righteously and unrighteously, both by violence and without violence. Having done so, he does not make himself happy and pleased, nor does he share the wealth and do meritorious deeds.

(5) "Someone else who enjoys sensual pleasures seeks wealth both righteously and unrighteously, both by violence and without violence. Having done so, he makes himself happy and pleased, but he does not share the wealth and do meritorious deeds.

(6) "And still someone else who enjoys sensual pleasures seeks wealth both righteously and unrighteously, both by violence and without violence. Having done so, he makes himself happy and pleased, and he shares the wealth and does meritorious deeds.

[C. Those Who Seek Wealth Righteously]

(7) "Next, householder, someone who enjoys sensual pleasures seeks wealth righteously, without violence. Having done so, he does not make himself happy and pleased, nor does he share the wealth and do meritorious deeds.

(8) "Someone else who enjoys sensual pleasures seeks wealth righteously, without violence. Having done so, [178] he makes himself happy and pleased, but he does not share the wealth and do meritorious deeds.

(9) "And still someone else who enjoys sensual pleasures seeks wealth righteously, without violence. Having done so, he makes himself happy and pleased, and he shares the wealth and does meritorious deeds. But he uses his wealth while being

tied to it, infatuated with it, and blindly absorbed in it, not seeing the danger in it and understanding the escape.

(10) "And still someone else who enjoys sensual pleasures seeks wealth righteously, without violence. Having done so, he makes himself happy and pleased, and he shares the wealth and does meritorious deeds. And he uses his wealth without being tied to it, infatuated with it, and blindly absorbed in it, seeing the danger in it and understanding the escape.

[II. Evaluation]

[A. Those Who Seek Wealth Unrighteously]

(1) "The one enjoying sensual pleasures who seeks wealth unrighteously, by violence, and does not make himself happy and pleased, and does not share the wealth and do meritorious deeds, may be criticized on three grounds. The first ground on which he may be criticized is that he seeks wealth unrighteously, by violence. The second ground on which he may be criticized is that he does not make himself happy and pleased. The third ground on which he may be criticized is that he does not share the wealth and do meritorious deeds. This one enjoying sensual pleasures may be criticized on these three grounds.

(2) "The one enjoying sensual pleasures who seeks wealth unrighteously, by violence, and makes himself happy and pleased, but does not share the wealth and do meritorious deeds, may be criticized on two grounds and praised on one ground. The first ground on which he may be criticized is that he seeks wealth unrighteously, by violence. The one ground on which he may be praised is that he makes himself happy and pleased. The second ground on which he may be criticized is that he does not share the wealth and do meritorious deeds. This one enjoying sensual pleasures may be criticized on these two grounds and praised on this one ground. [179]

(3) "The one enjoying sensual pleasures who seeks wealth unrighteously, by violence, and makes himself happy and pleased, and shares the wealth and does meritorious deeds, may be criticized on one ground and praised on two grounds. The one ground on which he may be criticized is that he seeks wealth unrighteously, by violence. The first ground on which he may be praised is that he makes himself happy and pleased. The second ground on which he may be praised is that he shares

the wealth and does meritorious deeds. This one enjoying sensual pleasures may be criticized on this one ground and praised on these two grounds.

[B. Those Who Seek Wealth Righteously and Unrighteously]

(4) "Next, householder, the one enjoying sensual pleasures who seeks wealth both righteously and unrighteously, both by violence and without violence, and does not make himself happy and pleased, and does not share the wealth and do meritorious deeds, may be praised on one ground and criticized on three grounds. The one ground on which he may be praised is that he seeks wealth righteously, without violence. The first ground on which he may be criticized is that he seeks wealth unrighteously, by violence. The second ground on which he may be criticized is that he does not make himself happy and pleased. The third ground on which he may be criticized is that he does not share the wealth and do meritorious deeds. This one enjoying sensual pleasures may be praised on this one ground and criticized on these three grounds.

(5) "The one enjoying sensual pleasures who seeks wealth both righteously and unrighteously, both by violence and without violence, and makes himself happy and pleased, but does not share the wealth and do meritorious deeds, may be praised on two grounds and criticized on two grounds. The first ground on which he may be praised is that he seeks wealth righteously, without violence. The first ground on which he may be criticized is that he seeks wealth unrighteously, by violence. The second ground on which he may be praised is that he makes himself happy and pleased. The second ground on which he may be criticized is that he does not share the wealth and do meritorious deeds. [180] This one enjoying sensual pleasures may be praised on these two grounds and criticized on these two grounds.

(6) "The one enjoying sensual pleasures who seeks wealth both righteously and unrighteously, both by violence and without violence, and makes himself happy and pleased, and shares the wealth and does meritorious deeds, may be praised on three grounds and criticized on one ground. The first ground on which he may be praised is that he seeks wealth righteously, without violence. The one ground on which he may be criticized is that he seeks wealth unrighteously, by violence. The second ground on which he may be praised is that he makes

himself happy and pleased. The third ground on which he may be praised is that he shares the wealth and does meritorious deeds. This one enjoying sensual pleasures may be praised on these three grounds and criticized on this one ground.

[C. Those Who Seek Wealth Righteously]

(7) "Next, householder, the one enjoying sensual pleasures who seeks wealth righteously, without violence, and does not make himself happy and pleased, and does not share the wealth and do meritorious deeds, may be praised on one ground and criticized on two grounds. The one ground on which he may be praised is that he seeks wealth righteously, without violence. The first ground on which he may be criticized is that he does not make himself happy and pleased. The second ground on which he may be criticized is that he does not share the wealth and do meritorious deeds. This one enjoying sensual pleasures may be praised on this one ground and criticized on these two grounds.

(8) "The one enjoying sensual pleasures who seeks wealth righteously, without violence, and makes himself happy and pleased, but does not share the wealth and do meritorious deeds, may be praised on two grounds and criticized on one ground. The first ground on which he may be praised is that he seeks wealth righteously, without violence. The second ground on which he may be praised is that he makes himself happy and pleased. The one ground on which he may be criticized is that he does not share the wealth and do meritorious deeds. [181] This one enjoying sensual pleasures may be praised on these two grounds and criticized on this one ground.

(9) "The one enjoying sensual pleasures who seeks wealth righteously, without violence, and makes himself happy and pleased, and shares it and does meritorious deeds, but uses that wealth while being tied to it, infatuated with it, and blindly absorbed in it, not seeing the danger in it and understanding the escape—he may be praised on three grounds and criticized on one ground. The first ground on which he may be praised is that he seeks wealth righteously, without violence. The second ground on which he may be praised is that he makes himself happy and pleased. The third ground on which he may be praised is that he shares the wealth and does meritorious deeds. The one ground on which he may be criticized is that he uses

that wealth while being tied to it, infatuated with it, and blindly absorbed in it, not seeing the danger in it and understanding the escape. This one enjoying sensual pleasures may be praised on these three grounds and criticized on this one ground.

(10) "The one enjoying sensual pleasures who seeks wealth righteously, without violence, and makes himself happy and pleased, and shares it and does meritorious deeds, and uses that wealth without being tied to it, infatuated with it, and blindly absorbed in it, seeing the danger in it and understanding the escape—he may be praised on four grounds. The first ground on which he may be praised is that he seeks wealth righteously, without violence. The second ground on which he may be praised is that he makes himself happy and pleased. The third ground on which he may be praised is that he shares the wealth and does meritorious deeds. The fourth ground on which he may be praised is that he uses that wealth without being tied to it, infatuated with it, and blindly absorbed in it, seeing the danger in it and understanding the escape. This one enjoying sensual pleasures may be praised on these four grounds.

[Conclusion]

"These, householder, are the ten kinds of persons who enjoy sensual pleasures found existing in the world. Of these ten, [182] the foremost, the best, the preeminent, the supreme, and the finest is the one enjoying sensual pleasures who seeks wealth righteously, without violence, and having obtained it, makes himself happy and pleased; and shares the wealth and does meritorious deeds; and uses that wealth without being tied to it, infatuated with it, and blindly absorbed in it, seeing the danger in it and understanding the escape. Just as from a cow comes milk, from milk curd, from curd butter, from butter ghee, and from ghee comes cream-of-ghee, which is reckoned the foremost of all these, so too, of these ten kinds of persons who enjoy sensual pleasures, the foremost, the best, the preeminent, the supreme, and the finest is the one who seeks wealth righteously, without violence, and having obtained it, makes himself happy and pleased; and shares the wealth and does meritorious deeds; and uses that wealth without being tied to it, infatuated with it, and blindly absorbed in it, seeing the danger in it and understanding the escape."

92 (2) Enmity[2122]

Then the householder Anāthapiṇḍika approached the Blessed One, paid homage to him, and sat down to one side. The Blessed One then said to him:

"Householder, when a noble disciple has eliminated five perils and enmities, possesses the four factors of stream-entry, and has clearly seen and thoroughly penetrated with wisdom the noble method, he might, if he so wished, declare of himself: 'I am one finished with hell, the animal realm, and the sphere of afflicted spirits; finished with the plane of misery, the bad destination, the lower world; I am a stream-enterer, no longer subject to [rebirth in] the lower world, fixed in destiny, heading for enlightenment.'

"What are the five perils and enmities that have been eliminated? [183] (1) Householder, one who destroys life, with the destruction of life as condition, creates peril and enmity pertaining to the present life and peril and enmity pertaining to future lives, and he also experiences mental pain and dejection. One who abstains from the destruction of life does not create such peril and enmity pertaining to the present life or such peril and enmity pertaining to future lives, nor does he experience mental pain and dejection. For one who abstains from the destruction of life, that peril and enmity has thus been eliminated.

(2) "One who takes what is not given . . . (3) One who engages in sexual misconduct . . . (4) One who speaks falsely . . . (5) One who indulges in liquor, wine, and intoxicants, the basis for heedlessness, with indulgence in liquor, wine, and intoxicants as condition, creates peril and enmity pertaining to the present life and peril and enmity pertaining to future lives, and he also experiences mental pain and dejection. One who abstains from liquor, wine, and intoxicants, the basis for heedlessness, does not create such peril and enmity pertaining to the present life or such peril and enmity pertaining to future lives, nor does he experience mental pain and dejection. For one who abstains from liquor, wine, and intoxicants, the basis for heedlessness, that peril and enmity has thus been eliminated.

"These are the five perils and enmities that have been eliminated.

"And what are the four factors of stream-entry that he possesses? (6) Here, householder, a noble disciple possesses unwavering confidence in the Buddha thus: 'The Blessed One is an arahant, perfectly enlightened, accomplished in true knowledge and conduct, fortunate, knower of the world, unsurpassed trainer of persons to be tamed, teacher of devas and humans, the Enlightened One, the Blessed One.' (7) He possesses unwavering confidence in the Dhamma thus: 'The Dhamma is well expounded by the Blessed One, directly visible, immediate, inviting one to come and see, applicable, to be personally experienced by the wise.' (8) He possesses unwavering confidence in the Saṅgha thus: 'The Saṅgha of the Blessed One's disciples is practicing the good way, practicing the straight way, practicing the true way, practicing the proper way; that is, the four pairs of persons, the eight types of individuals—this Saṅgha of the Blessed One's disciples is worthy of gifts, worthy of hospitality, worthy of offerings, worthy of reverential salutation, the unsurpassed field of merit for the world.' (9) He possesses the virtuous behavior loved by the noble ones, [184] unbroken, flawless, unblemished, unblotched, freeing, praised by the wise, ungrasped, leading to concentration. These are the four factors of stream-entry that he possesses.

"And what is the noble method that he has clearly seen and thoroughly penetrated with wisdom?[2123] (10) Here, householder, the noble disciple reflects thus: 'When this exists, that comes to be; with the arising of this, that arises. When this does not exist, that does not come to be; with the cessation of this, that ceases. That is, with ignorance as condition, volitional activities [come to be]; with volitional activities as condition, consciousness; with consciousness as condition, name-and-form; with name-and-form as condition, the six sense bases; with the six sense bases as condition, contact; with contact as condition, feeling; with feeling as condition, craving; with craving as condition, clinging; with clinging as condition, existence; with existence as condition, birth; with birth as condition, old age and death, sorrow, lamentation, pain, dejection, and anguish come to be. Such is the origin of this whole mass of suffering.

"'But with the remainderless fading away and cessation of ignorance comes cessation of volitional activities; with the cessation of volitional activities, cessation of consciousness; with the cessation of consciousness, cessation of name-and-form; with the cessation of name-and-form, cessation of the six sense bases; with the cessation of the six sense bases, cessation of contact; with the cessation of contact, cessation of feeling; with the cessation of feeling, cessation of craving; with the cessation of craving, cessation of clinging; with the cessation of clinging, cessation of existence; with the cessation of existence, cessation of birth; with the cessation of birth, old age and death, sorrow, lamentation, pain, dejection, and anguish cease. Such is the cessation of this whole mass of suffering.'

"This is the noble method that he has clearly seen and thoroughly penetrated with wisdom.

"Householder, when a noble disciple has eliminated these five perils and enmities, and he possesses these four factors of stream-entry, and he has clearly seen and thoroughly penetrated with wisdom this noble method, he might, if he so wished, declare of himself: 'I am one finished with hell, the animal realm, and the sphere of afflicted spirits; finished with the plane of misery, the bad destination, the lower world; I am a stream-enterer, no longer subject to [rebirth in] the lower world, fixed in destiny, heading for enlightenment.'" [185]

93 (3) View

On one occasion the Blessed One was dwelling at Sāvatthī in Jeta's Grove, Anāthapiṇḍika's Park. Then the householder Anāthapiṇḍika left Sāvatthī in the middle of the day in order to see the Blessed One. It then occurred to him: "It is not the proper time to see the Blessed One, who is in seclusion, nor to see the esteemed bhikkhus, who are also in seclusion. Let me go to the park of the wanderers of other sects."

Then the householder Anāthapiṇḍika went to the park of the wanderers of other sects. Now on that occasion the wanderers of other sects had assembled and were making an uproar as they loudly and boisterously sat discussing various pointless topics. The wanderers saw the householder Anāthapiṇḍika coming in the distance and silenced one another: "Sirs, be quiet. Sirs, do not make any noise. Here comes the householder Anāthapiṇḍika, a disciple of the ascetic Gotama, one among the ascetic Gotama's white-robed lay disciples who reside in Sāvatthī. Now these venerable ones are fond of quiet, disciplined in quiet, and speak in praise of quiet. Perhaps if he finds that our assembly is quiet, he will think to approach us." Then those wanderers of other sects became silent.

Then the householder Anāthapiṇḍika approached those wanderers and exchanged greetings with them. When they had concluded their greetings [186] and cordial talk, he sat down to one side. The wanderers then said to him:

"Tell us, householder, what is the ascetic Gotama's view?"

"Bhante, I don't know the Blessed One's view in its entirety."

"So, householder, you say you don't know the ascetic Gotama's view in its entirety. Then tell us, what is the bhikkhus' view?"

"Bhante, I also don't know the bhikkhus' view in its entirety."

"So, householder, you say you don't know the ascetic Gotama's view in its entirety and you also don't know the bhikkhus' view in its entirety. Then tell us, what is your view?"

"It isn't hard for me to explain my view, Bhante. But first explain your own views. Afterward it won't be hard for me to explain my view."

When this was said, one wanderer said to the householder Anāthapiṇḍika: (1) "'The world is eternal; this alone is true, anything else is wrong': such is my view, householder." (2) Another wanderer said: "'The world is non-eternal; this alone is true, anything else is wrong': such is my view, householder." (3)–(4) Still another said: "'The world is finite' ... 'The world is infinite' ... (5)–(6) 'The soul and the body are the same' ... 'The soul is one thing, the body another' ... (7)–(10) 'The Tathāgata exists after death' ... 'The Tathāgata does not exist after death' ... 'The Tathāgata both exists and does not exist after death' ... 'The Tathāgata neither exists nor does not exist after death'; this alone is true, anything else is wrong: such is my view, householder."[2124]

When this was said, the householder Anāthapiṇḍika said to those wanderers: "Bhante, this venerable one said thus: '"The world is eternal; this alone is true, anything else is wrong": such is my view, [187] householder.' This view of his has arisen because of his own careless attention or conditioned by someone else's utterance. Now this view has come into being and is conditioned, a product of volition, dependently originated. But whatever has come into being and is conditioned, a product of volition, dependently originated, is impermanent. Whatever is impermanent is suffering. It is just suffering that he is attached to and holds to.

"Bhante, this [other] venerable one said thus: '"The world is non-eternal; this alone is true, anything else is wrong": such is my view, householder.' This view of his has also arisen because of his own careless attention or conditioned by someone else's utterance. Now this view has come into being and is conditioned, a product of volition, dependently originated. But whatever has come into being and is conditioned, a product of volition, dependently originated, is impermanent. Whatever is impermanent is suffering. It is just suffering that he is attached to and holds to.

"Bhante, this venerable one said thus: '"The world is finite" ... "The world is infinite" ... "The soul and the body are the same" ... "The soul is one thing, the body another" ... "The Tathāgata exists after death" ... "The Tathāgata does not exist after death" ... "The Tathāgata both exists and does not exist after death" ... "The Tathāgata neither exists nor does not exist after death"; this alone is true, anything else is wrong: such is my view, householder.' This view of his has also arisen because of his own careless attention or conditioned by someone else's utterance. Now this view has come into being and is conditioned, a product of volition, dependently originated. But whatever has come into being and is conditioned, a product of volition, dependently originated, is impermanent. Whatever is impermanent is suffering. It is just suffering that he is attached to and holds to." [188]

When this was said, those wanderers said to the householder Anāthapiṇḍika: "We have each explained our own views, householder. Now tell us your view."

"Bhante, whatever has come into being and is conditioned, a product of volition, dependently originated, is impermanent. Whatever is impermanent is suffering. Whatever is suffering is not mine; I am not this; this is not my self. That is my view."

"Householder, whatever has come into being and is conditioned, a product of volition, dependently originated, is impermanent. Whatever is impermanent is suffering. It is just suffering that you are attached to and hold to."

"Bhante, whatever has come into being and is conditioned, a product of volition, dependently originated, is impermanent. Whatever is impermanent is suffering. Having clearly seen what is suffering as it really is with correct wisdom thus: 'This is not mine; I am not this; this is not my self,' I understand as it really is the superior escape from it."

When this was said, those wanderers sat silenced, disconcerted, hunched over, downcast, glum, and speechless. Then the householder Anāthapiṇḍika, having understood that those wanderers [sat] silenced . . . and speechless, rose from his seat and went to the Blessed One. He paid homage to the Blessed One, sat down to one side, and reported to the Blessed One his entire conversation with those wanderers.

[The Blessed One said:] "Good, good, householder! It is in such a way that those hollow men should from time to time be thoroughly refuted with reasoned argument."[2125] Then the Blessed One instructed, encouraged, inspired, and gladdened the householder Anāthapiṇḍika with a Dhamma talk. Then, when the householder Anāthapiṇḍika had been instructed, encouraged, inspired, and gladdened by the Blessed One with a Dhamma talk, [189] he rose from his seat, paid homage to the Blessed One, circumambulated him keeping the right side toward him, and departed.

Then, not long after the householder Anāthapiṇḍika had left, the Blessed One addressed the bhikkhus: "Bhikkhus, if any bhikkhu, even one ordained for a hundred years in this Dhamma and discipline, would thoroughly refute with reasoned argument the wanderers of other sects, he would refute them just as the householder Anāthapiṇḍika has done."

94 (4) Vajjiyamāhita

On one occasion the Blessed One was dwelling at Campā on a bank of the Gaggarā Lotus Pond. Then the householder Vajjiyamāhita left Campā in the middle of the day to see the Blessed One. It then occurred to him: "It is not the proper time to see the Blessed One, who is in seclusion, nor to see the esteemed bhikkhus, who are also in seclusion. Let me go to the park of the wanderers of other sects."

Then the householder Vajjiyamāhita went to the park of the wanderers of other sects . . . [all as in 10:93] [190] . . .

Then the householder Vajjiyamāhita approached those wanderers and exchanged greetings with them. When they had concluded their greetings and cordial talk, he sat down to one side. The wanderers then said to him:

"Is it true, householder, as it is said, that the ascetic Gotama criticizes all austerities and that he unreservedly condemns and reproves all who live a harsh and austere life?"

"No, Bhante, the Blessed One does not criticize all austerities and he does not unreservedly condemn and reprove all who live a harsh and austere life. The Blessed One criticizes what deserves criticism and praises what is praiseworthy. By criticizing what deserves criticism and praising what is praiseworthy, the Blessed One speaks on the basis of distinctions; he does not speak about such matters one-sidedly."[2126]

When this was said, a wanderer said to the householder Vajjiyamāhita: "Wait a moment, householder! That ascetic Gotama whom you are praising is an abolitionist who refrains from making definite declarations."

"I will deal with that point, too, Bhante. The Blessed One has validly declared: 'This is wholesome' and: 'This is unwholesome.' Thus, when he declares what is wholesome and what is unwholesome, the Blessed One makes definite declarations. He is not an abolitionist who refrains from making definite declarations."

When this was said, those wanderers [191] sat silenced, disconcerted, hunched over, downcast, glum, and speechless. Then the householder Vajjiyamāhita, having understood that those wanderers [sat] silenced . . . and speechless, rose from his seat and went to the Blessed One. He paid homage to the Blessed One, sat down to one side, and reported to the Blessed One his entire conversation with those wanderers of other sects.

[The Blessed One said:] "Good, good, householder! It is in such a way that those hollow men should from time to time be thoroughly refuted with reasoned argument."

(1)–(2) "I do not say, householder, of every kind of austerity that it should be practiced; nor do I say of every kind of austerity that it should not be practiced. (3)–(4) I do not say of every observance that it should be undertaken; nor do I say of every observance that it should not be undertaken. (5)–(6) I do not say that one should strive in every way; nor do I say that one should not strive in any way. (7)–(8) I do not say that one should make every kind of relinquishment; nor do I say that one should not make any kind of relinquishment. (9)–(10) I do not say that one should attain every kind of liberation; nor do I say that one should not attain any kind of liberation.

(1)–(2) "If, householder, when one practices a particular austerity, unwholesome qualities increase and wholesome qualities decline, then, I say, one should not practice such austerity. But if, when one practices a particular austerity, unwholesome qualities decline and wholesome [192] qualities increase, then, I say, one should practice such austerity.

(3)–(4) "If, householder, when one undertakes a particular observance, unwholesome qualities increase and wholesome qualities decline, then, I say, one should not undertake such an observance. But if, when one undertakes a particular observance, unwholesome qualities decline and wholesome qualities increase, then, I say, one should undertake such an observance.

(5)–(6) "If, householder, when one strives in a particular way, unwholesome qualities increase and wholesome qualities decline, then, I say, one should not strive in such a way. But if, when one strives in a particular way, unwholesome qualities decline and wholesome qualities increase, then, I say, one should strive in such a way.

(7)–(8) "If, householder, when one relinquishes something, unwholesome qualities increase and wholesome qualities decline, then, I say, one should not make such a relinquishment. But if, when one relinquishes something, unwholesome qualities decline and wholesome qualities increase, then, I say, one should make such a relinquishment.

(9)–(10) "If, householder, when one attains a particular liberation, unwholesome qualities increase and wholesome qualities decline, then, I say, one should not attain such a liberation. But if, when one attains a particular liberation, unwholesome qualities decline and wholesome qualities increase, then, I say, one should attain such a liberation."

Then, when the householder Vajjiyamāhita had been instructed, encouraged, inspired, and gladdened by the Blessed One with a Dhamma talk, he rose from his seat, paid homage to the Blessed One, circumambulated him keeping the right side toward him, and departed.

Then, not long after the householder Vajjiyamāhita had left, the Blessed One addressed the bhikkhus: "Bhikkhus, if any bhikkhu, even one who has long had little dust in his eyes regarding this Dhamma and discipline, would thoroughly refute with reasoned argument the wanderers of other sects, he would refute them in just such a way as the householder Vajjiyamāhita has done." [193]

95 (5) Uttiya

Then the wanderer Uttiya approached the Blessed One and exchanged greetings with him. When they had concluded their greetings and cordial talk, he sat down to one side and said to the Blessed One:

(1) "How is it, Master Gotama, is the world eternal? Is this alone true and anything else wrong?"

"Uttiya, I have not declared: 'The world is eternal; this alone is true, anything else is wrong.'"

(2) "Then, Master Gotama, is the world not eternal? Is this alone true and anything else wrong?"

"Uttiya, I also have not declared: 'The world is not eternal; this alone is true, anything else is wrong.'"

(3)–(4) "How is it then, Master Gotama, is the world finite? . . . Is the world infinite? . . . (5)–(6) Are the soul and the body the same? . . . Is the soul one thing, the body another? . . . (7)–(10) Does the Tathāgata exist after death? . . . Does the Tathāgata not exist after death? . . . Does the Tathāgata both exist and not exist after death? . . . Does the Tathāgata neither exist nor not exist after death? Is this alone true and anything else wrong?"

"Uttiya, I also have not declared: 'The Tathāgata neither exists nor does not exist after death; this alone is true, anything else is wrong.'"[2127]

"When I asked you: 'How is it, Master Gotama, is the world eternal? Is this alone true and anything else wrong?' you said: 'Uttiya, I have not declared: "The world is eternal; this alone is true, anything else is wrong."' But when I asked you: 'Then, Master Gotama, is the world not eternal? Is this alone true and anything else wrong?' you said: 'Uttiya, I also have not declared: "The world is not eternal; this alone is true, anything else is wrong."' When I asked you: 'How is it then, Master Gotama, is the world finite? . . . Does the Tathāgata neither exist nor not exist after death? Is this alone true and anything else wrong?' [194] you said: 'Uttiya, I also have not declared: "The Tathāgata neither exists nor does not exist after death; this alone is true, anything else is wrong."' What, then, has Master Gotama declared?"

"Through direct knowledge, Uttiya, I teach the Dhamma to

my disciples for the purification of beings, for the overcoming of sorrow and lamentation, for the passing away of pain and dejection, for the achievement of the method, for the realization of nibbāna."

"But when Master Gotama, through direct knowledge, teaches the Dhamma to his disciples for the purification of beings, for the overcoming of sorrow and lamentation, for the passing away of pain and dejection, for the achievement of the method, for the realization of nibbāna, will the entire world be thereby emancipated, or half the world, or a third of the world?"

When this was asked, the Blessed One remained silent. Then it occurred to the Venerable Ānanda: "The wanderer Uttiya had better not adopt the evil view: 'When I ask the ascetic Gotama the most elevated question of all, he falters and does not answer.[2128] It must be that he is unable to do so.' This would lead to the wanderer Uttiya's harm and suffering for a long time."

Then the Venerable Ānanda said to the wanderer Uttiya: "Well then, friend Uttiya, I will give you a simile. Some intelligent people here understand the meaning of what is said by means of a simile. Suppose a king had a frontier city with strong ramparts, walls, and arches, and with a single gate. The gatekeeper posted there would be wise, competent, and intelligent; one who keeps out strangers [195] and admits acquaintances. While he is walking along the path that encircles the city he would not see a cleft or an opening in the walls even big enough for a cat to slip through. He might not know how many living beings enter or leave the city, but he could be sure that whatever large living beings enter or leave the city all enter and leave through that gate. So too, friend Uttiya, the Tathāgata has no concern whether the entire world will be emancipated, or half the world, or a third of the world. But he can be sure that all those who have been emancipated, or who are being emancipated, or who will be emancipated from the world first abandon the five hindrances, corruptions of the mind that weaken wisdom, and then, with their minds well established in the four establishments of mindfulness, develop correctly the seven factors of enlightenment. It is in this way that they have been emancipated or are being emancipated or will be emancipated from the world.

"Friend Uttiya, you asked the Blessed One from a different

angle the same question that you had already asked him.[2129] Therefore the Blessed One did not answer you." [196]

96 (6) Kokanada[2130]

On one occasion the Venerable Ānanda was dwelling at Rājagaha in the Hot Springs Park. Then, as the night was receding, the Venerable Ānanda rose and went to the hot springs to bathe. Having bathed in the hot springs and come back out, he stood in one robe drying his limbs. The wanderer Kokanada, too, rose as the night was receding and went to the hot springs to bathe. He saw the Venerable Ānanda from a distance and said to him:

"Who is here, friend?"

"I am a bhikkhu, friend."

"From which group of bhikkhus, friend?"

"From the ascetics following the Sakyan son."

"If you could take the time to answer my question, I would like to ask you about a certain point."

"You may ask, friend. When I hear your question, I'll know [whether I can answer it]."

"How is it, sir, do you hold the view: (1) 'The world is eternal; this alone is true, anything else is wrong'?"

"I don't hold such a view, friend."

"Then do you hold the view: (2) 'The world is not eternal; this alone is true, anything else is wrong'?"

"I don't hold such a view, friend."

"Do you hold the view: (3)–(4) 'The world is finite' . . . 'The world is infinite' . . . (5)–(6) 'The soul and the body are the same' . . . 'The soul is one thing, the body another' . . . (7)–(10) 'The Tathāgata exists after death' . . . 'The Tathāgata does not exist after death' . . . 'The Tathāgata both exists and [197] does not exist after death' . . . 'The Tathāgata neither exists nor does not exist after death; this alone is true, anything else is wrong'?"

"I don't hold such a view, friend."

"Could it then be that you do not know and see?"

"It isn't the case, friend, that I do not know and see. I know and see."

"When I asked you: 'How is it, sir, do you hold the view: "The world is eternal; this alone is true, anything else is wrong"?' you said: 'I don't hold such a view, friend.' But when I asked you: 'Then do you hold the view: "The world is not eternal; this alone is true, anything else is wrong"?' you said: 'I don't hold such a view, friend.' When I asked you: 'Do you hold the view: "The world is finite" . . . "The Tathāgata neither exists nor does not exist after death; this alone is true, anything else is wrong"?' you said: 'I don't hold such a view, friend.' Then when I asked you: 'Could it then be that you do not know and see?' you said: 'It isn't the case, friend, that I do not know and see. I know and see.' How, friend, should the meaning of this statement be understood?"

"'The world is eternal; this alone is true, anything else is wrong,' friend: this is a speculative view. 'The world is not eternal; this alone is true, anything else is wrong': this is a speculative view. 'The world is finite' . . . 'The world is infinite' . . . 'The soul and the body are the same' . . . 'The soul is one thing, the body another' . . . 'The Tathāgata exists after death' . . . 'The Tathāgata does not exist after death' . . . 'The Tathāgata both exists and does not exist after death' . . . 'The Tathāgata neither exists nor does not exist after death; this alone is true, [198] anything else is wrong': this is a speculative view.

"To the extent, friend, that there is a speculative view, a basis for views,[2131] a foundation for views, obsession with views, the origination of views, and the uprooting of views, I know and see this. When I know and see this, why should I say: 'I do not know and see.' I know, friend, I see."

"What is your name? And how are you known by your fellow monks?"

"My name is Ānanda, and my fellow monks know me as Ānanda."

"Indeed, I did not realize that I was consulting the great teacher, the Venerable Ānanda! If I had realized that this was the Venerable Ānanda, I wouldn't have spoken so much. Let the Venerable Ānanda please pardon me."

97 (7) Worthy of Gifts

"Bhikkhus, possessing ten qualities, a bhikkhu is worthy of gifts, worthy of hospitality, worthy of offerings, worthy of reverential salutation, an unsurpassed field of merit for the world. What ten?

(1) "Here, a bhikkhu is virtuous; he dwells restrained by the

Pātimokkha, possessed of good conduct and resort, seeing danger in minute faults. Having undertaken the training rules, he trains in them.

(2) "He has learned much, remembers what he has learned, and accumulates what he has learned. Those teachings that are good in the beginning, good in the middle, and good in the end, with the right meaning [199] and phrasing, which proclaim the perfectly complete and pure spiritual life—such teachings as these he has learned much of, retained in mind, recited verbally, investigated mentally, and penetrated well by view.

(3) "He has good friends, good companions, good comrades.

(4) "He holds right view and has a correct perspective.

(5) "He wields the various kinds of psychic potency: having been one, he becomes many; having been many, he becomes one; he appears and vanishes; he goes unhindered through a wall, through a rampart, through a mountain as though through space; he dives in and out of the earth as though it were water; he walks on water without sinking as though it were earth; seated cross-legged, he travels in space like a bird; with his hand he touches and strokes the moon and sun so powerful and mighty; he exercises mastery with the body as far as the brahmā world.

(6) "With the divine ear element, which is purified and surpasses the human, he hears both kinds of sounds, the divine and human, those that are far as well as near.

(7) "He understands the minds of other beings and persons, having encompassed them with his own mind. He understands a mind with lust as a mind with lust, and a mind without lust as a mind without lust; a mind with hatred as a mind with hatred, and a mind without hatred as a mind without hatred; a mind with delusion as a mind with delusion, and a mind without delusion as a mind without delusion; a contracted mind as contracted and a distracted mind as distracted; an exalted mind as exalted and an unexalted mind as unexalted; a surpassable mind as surpassable and an unsurpassable mind as unsurpassable; a concentrated mind as concentrated and an unconcentrated mind as unconcentrated; a liberated mind as liberated and an unliberated mind as unliberated.[2132]

(8) "He recollects his manifold past abodes, that is, one birth, two births, three births, four births, [200] five births, ten births,

twenty births, thirty births, forty births, fifty births, a hundred births, a thousand births, a hundred thousand births, many eons of world-dissolution, many eons of world-evolution, many eons of world-dissolution and world-evolution thus: 'There I was so named, of such a clan, with such an appearance, such was my food, such my experience of pleasure and pain, such my life span; passing away from there, I was reborn elsewhere, and there too I was so named, of such a clan, with such an appearance, such was my food, such my experience of pleasure and pain, such my life span; passing away from there, I was reborn here.' Thus he recollects his manifold past abodes with their aspects and details.

(9) "With the divine eye, which is purified and surpasses the human, he sees beings passing away and being reborn, inferior and superior, beautiful and ugly, fortunate and unfortunate, and he understands how beings fare in accordance with their kamma thus: 'These beings who engaged in misconduct by body, speech, and mind, who reviled the noble ones, held wrong view, and undertook kamma based on wrong view, with the breakup of the body, after death, have been reborn in the plane of misery, in a bad destination, in the lower world, in hell; but these beings who engaged in good conduct by body, speech, and mind, who did not revile the noble ones, who held right view, and undertook kamma based on right view, with the breakup of the body, after death, have been reborn in a good destination, in a heavenly world.' Thus with the divine eye, which is purified and surpasses the human, he sees beings passing away and being reborn, inferior and superior, beautiful and ugly, fortunate and unfortunate, and he understands how beings fare in accordance with their kamma.

(10) "With the destruction of the taints, he has realized for himself with direct knowledge, in this very life, the taintless liberation of mind, liberation by wisdom, and having entered upon it, he dwells in it. [201]

"Possessing these ten qualities, a bhikkhu is worthy of gifts, worthy of hospitality, worthy of offerings, worthy of reverential salutation, an unsurpassed field of merit for the world."

98 (8) An Elder

"Bhikkhus, possessing ten qualities, an elder bhikkhu dwells at ease in whatever quarter he lives. What ten? (1) An elder is of long-standing, long gone forth. (2) He is virtuous. . . . Having undertaken the training rules, he trains in them. (3) He has learned much . . . and penetrated well by view. (4) Both Pātimokkhas have been well transmitted to him in detail, well analyzed, well mastered, well determined in terms of the rules and their detailed explication. (5) He is skilled in the origination and settlement of disciplinary issues. (6) He loves the Dhamma and is pleasing in his assertions, filled with a lofty joy pertaining to the Dhamma and discipline. (7) He is content with any kind of robe, almsfood, lodging, and medicines and provisions for the sick. (8) He is graceful when going forward and returning, and also well restrained when sitting among the houses. (9) He gains at will, without trouble or difficulty, the four jhānas that constitute the higher mind and are pleasant dwellings in this very life. (10) With the destruction of the taints, he has realized for himself with direct knowledge, in this very life, the taintless liberation of mind, liberation by wisdom, and having entered upon it, he dwells in it. Possessing these ten qualities, an elder bhikkhu dwells at ease in whatever quarter he lives."

99 (9) Upāli

Then the Venerable Upāli approached the Blessed One, paid homage to him, sat down to one side, [202] and said: "Bhante, I wish to resort to remote lodgings in forests and jungle groves."

"Remote lodgings in forests and jungle groves are hard to endure, Upāli. Solitude is hard to undertake and hard to delight in. When he is alone, the woods steal the mind of a bhikkhu who does not gain concentration. It can be expected that one who says 'I do not gain concentration, yet I will resort to remote lodgings in forests and jungle groves' will either sink or float away.[2133]

"Suppose, Upāli, there was a large lake, and a bull elephant seven or eight cubits in size would come along. He might think: 'Let me enter this lake and playfully wash my ears and back. I will bathe and drink, come out, and set off wherever I want.' He then enters the lake and playfully washes his ears and back. He bathes and drinks, comes out, and sets off wherever he wants. How so? Because his large body finds a footing in the depths.

"Then a hare or a cat comes along. It might think: 'How is a bull elephant different from myself? I'll enter this lake and playfully wash my ears and back. [203] I will bathe and drink, come out, and set off wherever I want.' Then, without reflecting, it hastily enters the deep lake. It can be expected that it will either sink or float away. Why so? Because its small body does not find a footing in the depths. So too, it can be expected that one who would say: 'I do not gain concentration, yet I will resort to remote lodgings in forests and jungle groves,' will either sink or float away.

"Suppose, Upāli, a young infant boy, lying on his back, would play with his own urine and feces. What do you think, isn't that a completely foolish type of amusement?"

"Yes, Bhante."

"Sometime later, when that boy grows up and his faculties mature, he would play the games that are typical for boys—games with toy plows, stick games, somersaults, games with pinwheels, games with measures made of leaves, games with toy chariots, games with toy bows. What do you think, isn't this amusement more excellent and sublime than the former kind?"

"Yes, Bhante."

"At a still later time, as that boy continues to grow up and his faculties mature still more, he enjoys himself furnished and endowed with the five objects of sensual pleasure: with forms cognizable by the eye that are wished for, desired, agreeable, pleasing, connected with sensual pleasure, tantalizing; with sounds cognizable by the ear . . . with odors cognizable by the nose . . . with tastes cognizable by the tongue . . . with tactile objects cognizable by the body [204] that are wished for, desired, agreeable, pleasing, connected with sensual pleasure, tantalizing. What do you think, isn't this amusement more excellent and sublime than the former kind?"

"Yes, Bhante."

"Here, Upāli, the Tathāgata arises in the world,[2134] an arahant, perfectly enlightened, accomplished in true knowledge and conduct, fortunate, knower of the world, unsurpassed trainer of persons to be tamed, teacher of devas and humans, the Enlightened One, the Blessed One. Having realized with his own direct knowledge this world with its devas, Māra, and Brahmā, this population with its ascetics and brahmins, with its devas and humans, he makes it known to others. He teaches the Dhamma that is good in the beginning, good in the middle, and good in the end, with the right meaning and phrasing; he reveals the perfectly complete and pure spiritual life.

"A householder or householder's son or one born in some other clan hears this Dhamma. He then acquires faith in the Tathāgata and considers thus: 'Household life is crowded and dusty; life gone forth is wide open. It is not easy, while living at home, to lead the spiritual life that is utterly perfect and pure as a polished conch shell. Suppose I shave off my hair and beard, put on ochre robes, and go forth from the household life into homelessness.' On a later occasion, having abandoned a small or a large fortune, having abandoned a small or a large circle of relatives, he shaves off his hair and beard, puts on ochre robes, and goes forth from the household life into homelessness.

"Having thus gone forth and possessing the bhikkhus' training and way of life, having abandoned the destruction of life, he abstains from the destruction of life; with the rod and weapon laid aside, conscientious and kindly, he dwells compassionate toward all living beings. Having abandoned taking what is not given, he abstains from taking what is not given; he takes only what is given, expects only what is given, and dwells honestly without thoughts of theft. Having abandoned sexual activity, he observes celibacy, [205] living apart, abstaining from sexual intercourse, the common person's practice.

"Having abandoned false speech, he abstains from false speech; he speaks truth, adheres to truth; he is trustworthy and reliable, no deceiver of the world. Having abandoned divisive speech, he abstains from divisive speech; he does not repeat elsewhere what he has heard here in order to divide [those people] from these, nor does he repeat to these what he has heard elsewhere in order to divide [these people] from those; thus he is one who reunites those who are divided, a promoter of unity, who enjoys concord, rejoices in concord, delights in concord, a speaker of words that promote concord. Having abandoned harsh speech, he abstains from harsh speech; he speaks words that are gentle, pleasing to the ear, lovable, words that go to the heart, courteous words that are desired by many people and agreeable to many people. Having abandoned idle chatter, he abstains from idle chatter; he speaks at a proper time, speaks what is fact, speaks on what is beneficial, speaks on the Dhamma and the discipline; at the proper time he speaks words that are worth recording, reasonable, succinct, and beneficial.

"He abstains from injuring seeds and plants. He eats once a day, abstaining from eating at night and outside the proper time. He abstains from dancing, singing, instrumental music, and unsuitable shows. He abstains from adorning and beautifying himself by wearing garlands and applying scents and unguents. He abstains from high and large beds. He abstains from accepting gold and silver, raw grain, raw meat, women and girls, men and women slaves, goats and sheep, fowl and pigs, elephants, cattle, horses, and mares, fields and land. He abstains from going on errands and running messages; from buying and selling; from cheating with weights, metals, and measures; [206] from accepting bribes, deceiving, defrauding, and trickery. He abstains from wounding, murdering, binding, brigandage, plunder, and violence.

"He is content with robes to protect his body and almsfood to maintain his stomach, and wherever he goes he sets out taking only these with him. Just as a bird, wherever it goes, flies with its wings as its only burden, so too, a bhikkhu is content with robes to protect his body and almsfood to maintain his stomach, and wherever he goes he sets out taking only these with him. Possessing this aggregate of noble virtuous behavior, he experiences blameless bliss within himself.

"Having seen a form with the eye, he does not grasp at its marks and features. Since, if he left the eye faculty unrestrained, bad unwholesome states of longing and dejection might invade him, he practices restraint over it; he guards the eye faculty, he undertakes the restraint of the eye faculty. Having heard a sound with the ear . . . Having smelled an odor with the nose . . . Having tasted a taste with the tongue . . . Having felt a tactile object with the body . . . Having cognized a mental phenomenon with the mind, he does not grasp at its marks and features. Since, if he left the mind faculty unrestrained, bad unwholesome states of longing and dejection might invade him, he practices restraint over it; he guards the mind faculty, he undertakes the restraint of the mind faculty. Possessing this noble restraint of the faculties, he experiences unsullied bliss within himself.

"He acts with clear comprehension when going forward

and returning; he acts with clear comprehension when looking ahead and looking away; he acts with clear comprehension when bending and stretching his limbs; he acts with clear comprehension when wearing his robes and carrying his outer robe and bowl; he acts with clear comprehension when eating, drinking, consuming food, and tasting; he acts with clear comprehension when defecating and urinating; he acts with clear comprehension when walking, standing, sitting, falling asleep, waking up, talking, and keeping silent.

"Possessing this aggregate of noble virtuous behavior, and this [207] noble restraint of the faculties, and this noble mindfulness and clear comprehension, he resorts to a secluded lodging: the forest, the root of a tree, a mountain, a ravine, a hillside cave, a charnel ground, a jungle thicket, an open space, a heap of straw.

"Having gone to the forest, to the foot of a tree, or to an empty hut, he sits down, folding his legs crosswise, straightening his body, and establishing mindfulness in front of him. Having abandoned longing for the world, he dwells with a mind free from longing; he purifies his mind from longing. Having abandoned ill will and hatred, he dwells with a mind free from ill will, compassionate for the welfare of all living beings; he purifies his mind from ill will and hatred. Having abandoned dullness and drowsiness, he dwells free from dullness and drowsiness, percipient of light, mindful and clearly comprehending; he purifies his mind from dullness and drowsiness. Having abandoned restlessness and remorse, he dwells without agitation, with a mind inwardly peaceful; he purifies his mind from restlessness and remorse. Having abandoned doubt, he dwells having gone beyond doubt, unperplexed about wholesome qualities; he purifies his mind from doubt.

(1) "Having thus abandoned these five hindrances, defilements of the mind, qualities that weaken wisdom, secluded from sensual pleasures, secluded from unwholesome states, he enters upon and dwells in the first jhāna, which consists of rapture and pleasure born of seclusion, accompanied by thought and examination. What do you think, isn't this dwelling more excellent and sublime than those that precede it?"

"Yes, Bhante."

"It is when they see this quality within themselves that my

disciples resort to remote lodgings in forests and jungle groves. But they still haven't attained their own goal.[2135]

(2) "Again, Upāli, with the subsiding of thought and examination, the bhikkhu enters and dwells in the second jhāna.... What do you think, isn't this dwelling more excellent and sublime than those that precede it?"

"Yes, Bhante."

"It is when they see this quality, too, within themselves [208] that my disciples resort to remote lodgings in forests and jungle groves. But they still haven't attained their own goal.

(3) "Again, Upāli, with the fading away as well of rapture ... he enters and dwells in the third jhāna.... What do you think, isn't this dwelling more excellent and sublime than those that precede it?"

"Yes, Bhante."

"It is when they see this quality, too, within themselves that my disciples resort to remote lodgings in forests and jungle groves. But they still haven't attained their own goal.

(4) "Again, Upāli, with the abandoning of pleasure and pain ... he enters and dwells in the fourth jhāna.... What do you think, isn't this dwelling more excellent and sublime than those that precede it?"

"Yes, Bhante."

"It is when they see this quality, too, within themselves that my disciples resort to remote lodgings in forests and jungle groves. But they still haven't attained their own goal.

(5) "Again, Upāli, with the complete surmounting of perceptions of forms, with the passing away of perceptions of sensory impingement, with non-attention to perceptions of diversity, [perceiving] 'space is infinite,' the bhikkhu enters and dwells in the base of the infinity of space. What do you think, isn't this dwelling more excellent and sublime than those that precede it?"

"Yes, Bhante."

"It is when they see this quality, too, within themselves that my disciples resort to remote lodgings in forests and jungle groves. But they still haven't attained their own goal.

(6) "Again, Upāli, by completely surmounting the base of the infinity of space, [perceiving] 'consciousness is infinite,' he enters and dwells in the base of the infinity of consciousness.

What do you think, isn't this dwelling more excellent and sublime than those that precede it?"

"Yes, Bhante."

"It is when they see this quality, too, within themselves that my disciples resort to remote lodgings in forests and jungle groves. But they still haven't attained their own goal.

(7) "Again, Upāli, by completely surmounting the base of the infinity of consciousness, [perceiving] 'there is nothing,' he enters and dwells in the base of nothingness. What do you think, Upāli, isn't this dwelling more excellent and sublime than those that precede it?"

"Yes, Bhante."

"It is when they see this quality, too, within themselves that my disciples resort to remote lodgings in forests and jungle groves. But they still haven't attained their own goal.

(8) "Again, Upāli, by completely surmounting the base of nothingness, [perceiving] 'this is peaceful, this is sublime,' [209] he enters and dwells in the base of neither-perception-nor-non-perception. What do you think, isn't this dwelling more excellent and sublime than those that precede it?"

"Yes, Bhante."

"It is when they see this quality, too, within themselves that my disciples resort to remote lodgings in forests and jungle groves. But they still haven't attained their own goal.

(9) "Again, Upāli, by completely surmounting the base of neither-perception-nor-non-perception, he enters and dwells in the cessation of perception and feeling. (10) And having seen with wisdom, his taints are utterly destroyed. What do you think, isn't this dwelling more excellent and sublime than those that precede it?"

"Yes, Bhante."

"It is when they see this quality, too, within themselves that my disciples resort to remote lodgings in forests and jungle groves. And they dwell having attained their own goal.[2136]

"Come, Upāli, dwell within the Saṅgha. While you dwell within the Saṅgha you will be at ease."[2137]

100 (10) Incapable

"Bhikkhus, without having abandoned these ten things, one is incapable of realizing arahantship. What ten? Lust, hatred, delusion, anger, hostility, denigration, insolence, envy, miserliness, and conceit. Without having abandoned these ten things, one is incapable of realizing arahantship.

"Bhikkhus, having abandoned these ten things, one is capable of realizing arahantship. What ten? Lust... conceit. Having abandoned these ten things, one is capable of realizing arahantship." [210]

The Third Fifty

I. An Ascetic's Perceptions

101 (1) An Ascetic's Perceptions

"Bhikkhus, when these three ascetic perceptions[2138] are developed and cultivated, they fulfill seven things. What three?

(1) "'I have entered upon a classless condition; (2) my living is dependent upon others; (3) my deportment should be different.' When these three perceptions of an ascetic are developed and cultivated, they fulfill seven things. What seven?

(4) "One consistently acts and behaves in accord with virtuous behavior. (5) One is without longing, (6) without ill will, (7) and without arrogance. (8) One is desirous of training. [211] (9) One uses the requisites for maintaining one's life with an awareness of their purpose. (10) One is energetic. When, bhikkhus, these three perceptions of an ascetic are developed and cultivated, they fulfill these seven things."

102 (2) Factors of Enlightenment

"Bhikkhus, when these seven factors of enlightenment are developed and cultivated, they fulfill the three true knowledges. What seven?

(1) "The enlightenment factor of mindfulness, (2) the enlightenment factor of discrimination of phenomena, (3) the enlightenment factor of energy, (4) the enlightenment factor of rapture, (5) the enlightenment factor of tranquility, (6) the enlightenment factor of concentration, and (7) the enlightenment factor of equanimity. When these seven factors of enlightenment are developed and cultivated, they fulfill the three true knowledges. What three?

(8) "Here, a bhikkhu recollects his manifold past abodes, that is, one birth, two births . . . Thus he recollects his manifold past abodes with their aspects and details.[2139]

(9) "With the divine eye, which is purified and surpasses the human . . . he understands how beings fare in accordance with their kamma.

(10) "With the destruction of the taints, he has realized for himself with direct knowledge, in this very life, the taintless liberation of mind, liberation by wisdom, and having entered upon it, he dwells in it.

"When, bhikkhus, these seven factors of enlightenment are developed and cultivated, they fulfill these three true knowledges."

103 (3) The Wrong Course

"Bhikkhus, in dependence on the wrong course there is failure, not success. And how is it that in dependence on the wrong course there is failure, not success?

(1) "For one of wrong view, (2) wrong intention originates. For one of wrong intention, (3) wrong speech originates. For one of wrong speech, [212] (4) wrong action originates. For one of wrong action, (5) wrong livelihood originates. For one of wrong livelihood, (6) wrong effort originates. For one of wrong effort, (7) wrong mindfulness originates. For one of wrong mindfulness, (8) wrong concentration originates. For one of wrong concentration, (9) wrong knowledge originates. For one of wrong knowledge, (10) wrong liberation originates.[2140] In this way, in dependence on the wrong course, there is failure, not success.

"In dependence on the right course, there is success, not failure. And how is it that in dependence on the right course, there is success, not failure?

(1) "For one of right view, (2) right intention originates. For one of right intention, (3) right speech originates. For one of right speech, (4) right action originates. For one of right action, (5) right livelihood originates. For one of right livelihood, (6) right effort originates. For one of right effort, (7) right mindfulness originates. For one of right mindfulness, (8) right concentration originates. For one of right concentration, (9) right knowledge originates. For one of right knowledge, (10) right liberation originates.[2141] In this way, in dependence on the right course, there is success, not failure."

104 (4) A Seed[2142]

"Bhikkhus, for a person of wrong view, wrong intention, wrong speech, wrong action, wrong livelihood, wrong effort, wrong mindfulness, wrong concentration, wrong knowledge, and wrong liberation, whatever bodily kamma, verbal kamma, and mental kamma he instigates and undertakes in accordance with that view, and whatever his volition, yearning, inclination, and volitional activities, all lead to what is unwished for, undesired, and disagreeable, to harm and suffering. For what reason? Because the view is bad.

"Suppose, bhikkhus, a seed of neem, bitter cucumber, or bitter gourd were planted in moist soil. [213] Whatever nutrients it would take up from the soil and from the water would all lead to its bitter, pungent, and disagreeable flavor. For what reason? Because the seed is bad. So too, for a person of wrong view ... and wrong liberation, whatever bodily kamma, verbal kamma, and mental kamma he instigates and undertakes in accordance with that view, and whatever his volition, yearning, inclination, and volitional activities, all lead to what is unwished for, undesired, and disagreeable, to harm and suffering. For what reason? Because the view is bad.

"Bhikkhus, for a person of right view, right intention, right speech, right action, right livelihood, right effort, right mindfulness, right concentration, right knowledge, and right liberation, whatever bodily kamma, verbal kamma, and mental kamma he instigates and undertakes in accordance with that view, and whatever his volition, yearning, inclination, and volitional activities, all lead to what is wished for, desired, and agreeable, to well-being and happiness. For what reason? Because the view is good.

"Suppose, bhikkhus, a seed of sugar cane, hill rice, or grape were planted in moist soil. Whatever nutrients it would take up from the soil and from the water would all lead to its agreeable, sweet, and delectable flavor. For what reason? Because the seed is good. So too, for a person of right view ... [214] ... and right liberation, whatever bodily kamma, verbal kamma, and mental kamma he instigates and undertakes in accordance with that view, and whatever his volition, yearning, inclination, and volitional activities, all lead to what is wished for, desired, and agreeable, to well-being and happiness. For what reason? Because the view is good."

105 (5) True Knowledge

"Bhikkhus, ignorance—accompanied by moral shamelessness and moral recklessness—is the forerunner in entering upon unwholesome qualities.[2143] (1) For a foolish person immersed in ignorance, wrong view originates. (2) For one of wrong view, wrong intention originates. (3) For one of wrong intention, wrong speech originates. (4) For one of wrong speech, wrong action originates. (5) For one of wrong action, wrong livelihood originates. (6) For one of wrong livelihood, wrong effort originates. (7) For one of wrong effort, wrong mindfulness originates. (8) For one of wrong mindfulness, wrong concentration originates. (9) For one of wrong concentration, wrong knowledge originates. (10) For one of wrong knowledge, wrong liberation originates.

"Bhikkhus, true knowledge—accompanied by a sense of moral shame and moral dread—is the forerunner in entering upon wholesome qualities. (1) For a wise person who has arrived at true knowledge, right view originates. (2) For one of right view, right intention originates. (3) For one of right intention, right speech originates. (4) For one of right speech, right action originates. (5) For one of right action, right livelihood originates. (6) For one of right livelihood, right effort originates. (7) For one of right effort, right mindfulness originates. (8) For one of right mindfulness, right concentration originates. (9) For one of right concentration, right knowledge originates. (10) For one of right knowledge, right liberation originates."[2144] [215]

106 (6) Wearing Away

"Bhikkhus, there are these ten cases of wearing away.[2145] What ten?

(1) "For one of right view, wrong view is worn away, and the numerous bad unwholesome qualities that originate with wrong view as condition are also worn away, and with right view as condition, numerous wholesome qualities reach fulfillment by development.

(2) "For one of right intention, wrong intention is worn away, and the numerous bad unwholesome qualities that originate with wrong intention as condition are also worn away, and with right intention as condition, numerous wholesome qualities reach fulfillment by development.

(3) "For one of right speech, wrong speech is worn away,

and the numerous bad unwholesome qualities that originate with wrong speech as condition are also worn away, and with right speech as condition, numerous wholesome qualities reach fulfillment by development.

(4) "For one of right action, wrong action is worn away, and the numerous bad unwholesome qualities that originate with wrong action as condition are also worn away, and with right action as condition, numerous wholesome qualities reach fulfillment by development.

(5) "For one of right livelihood, wrong livelihood is worn away, and the numerous bad unwholesome qualities that originate with wrong livelihood as condition are also worn away, and with right livelihood as condition, numerous wholesome qualities reach fulfillment by development.

(6) "For one of right effort, wrong effort is worn away, and the numerous bad unwholesome qualities that originate with wrong effort as condition are also worn away, and with right effort as condition, numerous wholesome qualities reach fulfillment by development.

(7) "For one of right mindfulness, wrong mindfulness is worn away, and the numerous bad unwholesome qualities that originate with wrong mindfulness as condition are also worn away, and with right mindfulness as condition, numerous wholesome qualities reach fulfillment by development.

(8) "For one of right concentration, wrong concentration is worn away, and the numerous bad unwholesome qualities that originate with wrong concentration as condition are also worn away, and with right concentration as condition, numerous [216] wholesome qualities reach fulfillment by development.

(9) "For one of right knowledge, wrong knowledge is worn away, and the numerous bad unwholesome qualities that originate with wrong knowledge as condition are also worn away, and with right knowledge as condition, numerous wholesome qualities reach fulfillment by development.

(10) "For one of right liberation, wrong liberation is worn away, and the numerous bad unwholesome qualities that originate with wrong liberation as condition are also worn away, and with right liberation as condition, numerous wholesome qualities reach fulfillment by development.

"These are the ten cases of wearing away."

107 (7) Dhovana

"Bhikkhus, there is a country in the south named Dhovana[2146] ['Washing'], where there is food, drink, victuals, comestibles, refreshments, tonics, dancing, singing, and music. There is this 'Washing,' bhikkhus; that I do not deny. Yet this 'Washing' is low, common, for worldlings, ignoble, unbeneficial; it does not lead to disenchantment, to dispassion, to cessation, to peace, to direct knowledge, to enlightenment, to nibbāna.

"But I will teach, bhikkhus, a noble washing that leads exclusively to disenchantment, to dispassion, to cessation, to peace, to direct knowledge, to enlightenment, to nibbāna. In dependence on this washing, beings subject to birth are freed from birth; beings subject to old age are freed from old age; beings subject to death are freed from death; beings subject to sorrow, lamentation, pain, dejection, and anguish are freed from sorrow, lamentation, pain, dejection, and anguish. Listen and attend closely. I will speak."

"Yes, Bhante," those bhikkhus replied. The Blessed One said this:

"And what, bhikkhus, is that noble washing? [217]

(1) "For one of right view, wrong view is washed away, and the numerous bad unwholesome qualities that originate with wrong view as condition are also washed away, and with right view as condition, numerous wholesome qualities reach fulfillment by development.

(2)–(9) "For one of right intention, wrong intention is washed away ... For one of right speech, wrong speech is washed away ... For one of right action, wrong action is washed away ... For one of right livelihood, wrong livelihood is washed away ... For one of right effort, wrong effort is washed away ... For one of right mindfulness, wrong mindfulness is washed away ... For one of right concentration, wrong concentration is washed away ... For one of right knowledge, wrong knowledge is washed away ...

(10) "For one of right liberation, wrong liberation is washed away, and the numerous bad unwholesome qualities that originate with wrong liberation as condition are also washed away, and with right liberation as condition, numerous wholesome qualities reach fulfillment by development.

"This, bhikkhus, is that noble washing that leads exclusively to disenchantment, to dispassion, to cessation, to peace, to direct knowledge, to enlightenment, to nibbāna. In dependence on this washing, beings subject to birth are freed from birth; beings subject to old age are freed from old age; beings subject to death are freed from death; beings subject to sorrow, lamentation, pain, dejection, and anguish are freed from sorrow, lamentation, pain, dejection, and anguish." [218]

108 (8) Physicians

"Bhikkhus, physicians prescribe a purgative for eliminating ailments originating from bile, phlegm, and wind. There is this purgative, bhikkhus; that I do not deny. Yet this purgative sometimes succeeds and sometimes fails.

"But I will teach, bhikkhus, a noble purgative that always succeeds and never fails. In dependence on this purgative, beings subject to birth are freed from birth; beings subject to old age are freed from old age; beings subject to death are freed from death; beings subject to sorrow, lamentation, pain, dejection, and anguish are freed from sorrow, lamentation, pain, dejection, and anguish. Listen and attend closely. I will speak."

"Yes, Bhante," those bhikkhus replied. The Blessed One said this:

"And what, bhikkhus, is that noble purgative that always succeeds and never fails?

(1) "For one of right view, wrong view is purged, and the numerous bad unwholesome qualities that originate with wrong view as condition are also purged, and with right view as condition, numerous wholesome qualities reach fulfillment by development.

(2)–(9) "For one of right intention, wrong intention is purged ... For one of right speech, wrong speech is purged ... For one of right action, wrong action is purged ... For one of right livelihood, wrong livelihood is purged ... For one of right effort, wrong effort is purged ... For one of right mindfulness, wrong mindfulness is purged ... [219] For one of right concentration, wrong concentration is purged ... For one of right knowledge, wrong knowledge is purged ...

(10) "For one of right liberation, wrong liberation is purged, and the numerous bad unwholesome qualities that originate with wrong liberation as condition are also purged, and with

right liberation as condition, numerous wholesome qualities reach fulfillment by development.

"This, bhikkhus, is that noble purgative that always succeeds and never fails, and in dependence on which beings subject to birth are freed from birth; beings subject to old age are freed from old age; beings subject to death are freed from death; beings subject to sorrow, lamentation, pain, dejection, and anguish are freed from sorrow, lamentation, pain, dejection, and anguish."

109 (9) Emetic

"Bhikkhus, physicians prescribe an emetic for eliminating ailments originating from bile, phlegm, and wind. There is this emetic, bhikkhus; that I do not deny. Yet this emetic sometimes succeeds and sometimes fails.

"But I will teach, bhikkhus, a noble emetic that always succeeds and never fails. In dependence on this emetic, beings subject to birth are freed from birth; beings subject to old age are freed from old age; beings subject to death are freed from death; beings subject to sorrow, lamentation, pain, dejection, and anguish are freed from sorrow, lamentation, pain, dejection, and anguish. Listen and attend closely. I will speak."

"Yes, Bhante," those bhikkhus replied. The Blessed One said this:

"And what, bhikkhus, is that noble emetic that always succeeds and never fails? [220]

(1) "For one of right view, wrong view is vomited up, and the numerous bad unwholesome qualities that originate with wrong view as condition are also vomited up, and with right view as condition, numerous wholesome qualities reach fulfillment by development.

(2)–(9) "For one of right intention, wrong intention is vomited up . . . For one of right speech, wrong speech is vomited up . . . For one of right action, wrong action is vomited up . . . For one of right livelihood, wrong livelihood is vomited up . . . For one of right effort, wrong effort is vomited up . . . For one of right mindfulness, wrong mindfulness is vomited up . . . For one of right concentration, wrong concentration is vomited up . . . For one of right knowledge, wrong knowledge is vomited up . . .

(10) "For one of right liberation, wrong liberation is vomited

up, and the numerous bad unwholesome qualities that originate with wrong liberation as condition are also vomited up, and with right liberation as condition, numerous wholesome qualities reach fulfillment by development.

"This, bhikkhus, is that noble emetic that always succeeds and never fails, and in dependence on which beings subject to birth are freed from birth; beings subject to old age are freed from old age; beings subject to death are freed from death; beings subject to sorrow, lamentation, pain, dejection, and anguish are freed from sorrow, lamentation, pain, dejection, and anguish."

110 (10) Ejected

"Bhikkhus, there are these ten things to be ejected. What ten?

(1) "For one of right view, wrong view is ejected, and the numerous bad unwholesome qualities that originate with wrong view as condition are also ejected, and with right view as condition, numerous wholesome qualities reach fulfillment by development. [221]

(2)–(9) "For one of right intention, wrong intention is ejected . . . For one of right speech, wrong speech is ejected . . . For one of right action, wrong action is ejected . . . For one of right livelihood, wrong livelihood is ejected . . . For one of right effort, wrong effort is ejected . . . For one of right mindfulness, wrong mindfulness is ejected . . . For one of right concentration, wrong concentration is ejected . . . For one of right knowledge, wrong knowledge is ejected . . .

(10) "For one of right liberation, wrong liberation is ejected, and the numerous bad unwholesome qualities that originate with wrong liberation as condition are also ejected, and with right liberation as condition, numerous wholesome qualities reach fulfillment by development.

"These are the ten things to be ejected."

111 (11) One Beyond Training (1)

Then a certain bhikkhu approached the Blessed One, paid homage to him, sat down to one side, and said:

"It is said, Bhante, 'one beyond training, one beyond training.' In what way, Bhante, is a bhikkhu one beyond training?"[2147]

"Here, bhikkhu, a bhikkhu possesses (1) the right view of one beyond training. He possesses (2) the right intention . . . (3) the right speech . . . (4) the right action . . . (5) the right livelihood . . . (6) the right effort . . . (7) the right mindfulness . . . (8) the right concentration . . . (9) the right knowledge . . . (10) the right liberation of one beyond training. It in this way that a bhikkhu is one beyond training." [222]

112 (12) One Beyond Training (2)

"Bhikkhus, there are these ten qualities of one beyond training. What ten? The right view of one beyond training; the right intention . . . the right speech . . . the right action . . . the right livelihood . . . the right effort . . . the right mindfulness . . . the right concentration . . . the right knowledge . . . the right liberation of one beyond training. These are the ten qualities of one beyond training."

II. *Paccorohaṇī*

113 (1) Non-Dhamma (1)

"Bhikkhus, what is non-Dhamma and harmful should be understood, and what is the Dhamma and beneficial should also be understood.[2148] Having understood what is non-Dhamma and harmful, and also what is the Dhamma and beneficial, one should practice in accordance with the Dhamma and with what is beneficial.

"And what, bhikkhus, is non-Dhamma and harmful? Wrong view, wrong intention, wrong speech, wrong action, wrong livelihood, wrong effort, wrong mindfulness, wrong concentration, wrong knowledge, and wrong liberation. [223] This is what is said to be non-Dhamma and harmful.

"And what, bhikkhus, is the Dhamma and beneficial? Right view, right intention, right speech, right action, right livelihood, right effort, right mindfulness, right concentration, right knowledge, and right liberation. This is what is said to be the Dhamma and beneficial.

"When it was said: 'Bhikkhus, what is non-Dhamma and harmful should be understood, and what is the Dhamma and beneficial should also be understood. Having understood what is non-Dhamma and harmful, and also what is the Dhamma and beneficial, one should practice in accordance with the Dhamma and with what is beneficial,' it is with reference to this that this was said."

114 (2) Non-Dhamma (2)

"Bhikkhus, what is non-Dhamma and what is the Dhamma should be understood, and what is harmful and what is beneficial should also be understood. Having understood what is non-Dhamma and what is the Dhamma, and also what is harmful and what is beneficial, one should practice in accordance with the Dhamma and with what is beneficial.

"And what, bhikkhus, is non-Dhamma and what is the Dhamma? And what is harmful and what is beneficial?

(1) "Wrong view is non-Dhamma; right view is the Dhamma. The numerous bad unwholesome qualities that originate with wrong view as condition: these are harmful. The numerous wholesome qualities that reach fulfillment by development with right view as condition: these are beneficial.

(2) "Wrong intention is non-Dhamma; right intention is the Dhamma. The numerous bad unwholesome qualities that originate with wrong intention as condition: these are harmful. The numerous wholesome qualities that reach fulfillment by development with right intention as condition: these are beneficial.

(3) "Wrong speech is non-Dhamma; right speech is the Dhamma. The numerous bad unwholesome qualities that originate with wrong speech as condition: these are harmful. The numerous wholesome qualities that reach fulfillment by development with right speech as condition: these are beneficial.

(4) "Wrong action is non-Dhamma; right action is the Dhamma. The numerous bad unwholesome qualities that originate with wrong action as condition: [224] these are harmful. The numerous wholesome qualities that reach fulfillment by development with right action as condition: these are beneficial.

(5) "Wrong livelihood is non-Dhamma; right livelihood is the Dhamma. The numerous bad unwholesome qualities that originate with wrong livelihood as condition: these are harmful. The numerous wholesome qualities that reach fulfillment by development with right livelihood as condition: these are beneficial.

(6) "Wrong effort is non-Dhamma; right effort is the Dhamma. The numerous bad unwholesome qualities that originate with wrong effort as condition: these are harmful. The numerous wholesome qualities that reach fulfillment by development with right effort as condition: these are beneficial.

(7) "Wrong mindfulness is non-Dhamma; right mindfulness

is the Dhamma. The numerous bad unwholesome qualities that originate with wrong mindfulness as condition: these are harmful. The numerous wholesome qualities that reach fulfillment by development with right mindfulness as condition: these are beneficial.

(8) "Wrong concentration is non-Dhamma; right concentration is the Dhamma. The numerous bad unwholesome qualities that originate with wrong concentration as condition: these are harmful. The numerous wholesome qualities that reach fulfillment by development with right concentration as condition: these are beneficial.

(9) "Wrong knowledge is non-Dhamma; right knowledge is the Dhamma. The numerous bad unwholesome qualities that originate with wrong knowledge as condition: these are harmful. The numerous wholesome qualities that reach fulfillment by development with right knowledge as condition: these are beneficial.

(10) "Wrong liberation is non-Dhamma; right liberation is the Dhamma. The numerous bad unwholesome qualities that originate with wrong liberation as condition: these are harmful. The numerous wholesome qualities that reach fulfillment by development with right liberation as condition: these are beneficial.

"When it was said: 'Bhikkhus, what is non-Dhamma and what is the Dhamma should be understood, and what is harmful and what is beneficial should also be understood. Having understood what is non-Dhamma and what is the Dhamma, and also what is harmful and what is beneficial, one should practice in accordance with the Dhamma and with what is beneficial,' it is with reference to this that this was said."

115 (3) Non-Dhamma (3)

"Bhikkhus, what is non-Dhamma and what is the Dhamma should be understood, and what is harmful and what is beneficial should also be understood. Having understood what is non-Dhamma and what is the Dhamma, and also what is harmful and what is beneficial, one should practice in accordance with the Dhamma and with what is beneficial." [225]

This is what the Blessed One said. Having said this, the Fortunate One rose from his seat and entered his dwelling.[2149] Then, soon after the Blessed One had left, the bhikkhus considered: "Friends, the Blessed One taught this brief synopsis: 'Bhikkhus, what is non-Dhamma and what is the Dhamma should be understood . . . one should practice in accordance with the Dhamma and with what is beneficial.' Then he rose from his seat and entered his dwelling without expounding its meaning in detail. Now who will expound its meaning in detail?" Then it occurred to them: "The Venerable Ānanda is praised by the Teacher and esteemed by his wise fellow monks; he is capable of expounding the detailed meaning of this brief synopsis. Let us approach the Venerable Ānanda and ask him the meaning of this. We will retain it in mind as he explains it to us."

Then those bhikkhus approached the Venerable Ānanda and exchanged greetings with him, after which they sat down to one side and said: "Friend Ānanda, the Blessed One taught this brief synopsis. . . . Then he rose from his seat and entered his dwelling without expounding the meaning in detail. Soon after he left, we considered: 'Friends, the Blessed One [226] taught this brief synopsis. . . . [all as above down to:] . . . Let us approach the Venerable Ānanda and ask him the meaning of this. We will retain it in mind as he explains it to us.' Let the Venerable Ānanda expound it to us."

[The Venerable Ānanda replied:] "Friends, it is as though a man needing heartwood, seeking heartwood, wandering in search of heartwood, would pass over the root and trunk of a great tree possessed of heartwood, thinking that heartwood should be sought among the branches and foliage. And so it is with you. When you were face to face with the Teacher you passed by the Blessed One, thinking to ask me about the meaning. For, friends, knowing, the Blessed One knows; seeing, he sees; he has become vision, he has become knowledge, he has become the Dhamma, he has become Brahmā; he is the expounder, the proclaimer, the elucidator of meaning, the giver of the deathless, the lord of the Dhamma, the Tathāgata. That was the time when you should have approached the Blessed One [227] and asked him about the meaning. You should have retained it in mind as he would have explained it to you."

"Surely, friend Ānanda, knowing, the Blessed One knows; seeing, he sees; he has become vision . . . the Tathāgata. That was the time when we should have approached the Blessed

One and asked him about the meaning, and we should have retained it in mind as he would have explained it to us. Yet the Venerable Ānanda is praised by the Teacher and esteemed by his wise fellow monks. He is capable of expounding the detailed meaning of this synopsis. Let the Venerable Ānanda expound it without finding it troublesome."

"Then listen, friends, and attend closely. I will speak."

"Yes, friend," those bhikkhus replied. The Venerable Ānanda said this:

"Friends, the Blessed One taught this brief synopsis without expounding the detailed meaning: 'Bhikkhus, what is non-Dhamma and what is the Dhamma should be understood, and what is harmful and what is beneficial should also be understood. Having understood what is non-Dhamma and what is the Dhamma, and also what is harmful and what is beneficial, one should practice in accordance with the Dhamma and with what is beneficial.' Now what, friends, is non-Dhamma and what is the Dhamma? And what is harmful and what is beneficial?

(1) "Wrong view, friends, is non-Dhamma; right view is the Dhamma. The numerous bad unwholesome qualities that originate with wrong view as condition: these are harmful. The numerous wholesome qualities that reach fulfillment by development with right view as condition: these are beneficial.

(2)–(9) "Wrong intention is non-Dhamma; right intention is the Dhamma . . . Wrong speech is non-Dhamma; right speech [228] is the Dhamma . . . Wrong action is non-Dhamma; right action is the Dhamma . . . Wrong livelihood is non-Dhamma; right livelihood is the Dhamma . . . Wrong effort is non-Dhamma; right effort is the Dhamma . . . Wrong mindfulness is non-Dhamma; right mindfulness is the Dhamma . . . Wrong concentration is non-Dhamma; right concentration is the Dhamma . . . Wrong knowledge is non-Dhamma; right knowledge is the Dhamma . . .

(10) "Wrong liberation is non-Dhamma; right liberation is the Dhamma. The numerous bad unwholesome qualities that originate with wrong liberation as condition: these are harmful. The numerous wholesome qualities that reach fulfillment by development with right liberation as condition: these are beneficial.

"Friends, it is in this way that I understand the detailed meaning of the Blessed One's brief synopsis. Now, if you wish, you may go to the Blessed One himself and ask him about the meaning of this. You should retain it in mind as the Blessed One explains it to you."

"Yes, friend," those bhikkhus replied, and having delighted and rejoiced in the Venerable Ānanda's statement, they rose from their seats and went to the Blessed One. After paying homage to him, they sat down to one side and said to the Blessed One: "Bhante, the Blessed One taught this synopsis . . . [they here relate all that had taken place, adding:] [229] . . . Then, Bhante, we approached the Venerable Ānanda and asked him about the meaning. The Venerable Ānanda expounded the meaning to us in these ways, in these terms and phrases."

"Good, good, bhikkhus! Ānanda is wise. Ānanda has great wisdom. If you had approached me and asked me the meaning of this, I would have explained it to you in the same way as Ānanda. Such is the meaning of this, and so you should retain it in mind."

116 (4) Ajita[2150]

Then the wanderer Ajita approached the Blessed One and exchanged greetings with him. When they had concluded their greetings and cordial talk, he sat down to one side [230] and said to the Blessed One:

"Master Gotama, I have a fellow ascetic named Paṇḍita.[2151] He has thought out five hundred arguments[2152] by which those of other sects, when rebutted, know: 'We've been rebutted.'"

Then the Blessed One addressed the bhikkhus: "Do you remember, bhikkhus, Paṇḍita's cases?"

"This is the time for it, Blessed One! This is the time for it, Fortunate One! Having heard this from the Blessed One, the bhikkhus will retain in mind whatever the Blessed One says."

"Well then, bhikkhus, listen and attend closely. I will speak."

"Yes, Bhante," those bhikkhus replied. The Blessed One said this:

"Here, someone refutes and disproves a doctrine contrary to the Dhamma with a doctrine contrary to the Dhamma. In this way, he delights an assembly contrary to the Dhamma. For this reason, the assembly contrary to the Dhamma becomes loud and boisterous, exclaiming: 'He is truly wise, sir! He is truly wise, sir!'[2153]

"Someone refutes and disproves a doctrine that accords with the Dhamma by means of a doctrine contrary to the Dhamma. In this way, he delights an assembly contrary to the Dhamma. For this reason, the assembly contrary to the Dhamma becomes loud and boisterous, exclaiming: 'He is truly wise, sir! He is truly wise, sir!'

"Someone refutes and disproves both a doctrine that accords with the Dhamma and a doctrine contrary to the Dhamma by means of a doctrine contrary to the Dhamma. In this way, he delights an assembly contrary to the Dhamma. For this reason, the assembly contrary to the Dhamma becomes loud and boisterous, exclaiming: 'He is truly wise, sir! He is truly wise, sir!'[2154]

["Someone refutes and disproves both a doctrine that accords with the Dhamma and a doctrine contrary to the Dhamma by means of a doctrine that accords with the Dhamma. In this way, he delights an assembly contrary to the Dhamma. For that reason, the assembly contrary to the Dhamma becomes loud and boisterous, exclaiming: 'He is truly wise, sir! He is truly wise, sir!'

"Someone refutes and disproves a doctrine that accords with the Dhamma with a doctrine that accords with the Dhamma. In this way, he delights an assembly that accords with the Dhamma. For this reason, the assembly that accords with the Dhamma becomes loud and boisterous, exclaiming: 'He is truly wise, sir! He is truly wise, sir!']][2155] [231]

"Bhikkhus, what is non-Dhamma and what is the Dhamma should be understood, and what is harmful and what is beneficial should be understood. Having understood what is non-Dhamma and what is the Dhamma, and what is harmful and what is beneficial, one should practice in accordance with the Dhamma and with what is beneficial. . . .

[The sutta continues exactly as in 10:114, ending:]

"When it was said: 'Bhikkhus, what is non-Dhamma and what is the Dhamma should be understood, and what is harmful and what is beneficial should be understood. Having understood what is non-Dhamma and what is the Dhamma, [232] and what is harmful and what is beneficial, one should practice in accordance with the Dhamma and with what is beneficial,' it is with reference to this that this was said."

117 (5) Saṅgārava

Then the brahmin Saṅgārava approached the Blessed One and exchanged greetings with him. When they had concluded their greetings and cordial talk, he sat down to one side and said to the Blessed One:

"Master Gotama, what is the near shore? What is the far shore?"

"Brahmin, (1) wrong view is the near shore, right view the far shore. (2) Wrong intention is the near shore, right intention the far shore. (3) Wrong speech is the near shore, right speech the far shore. (4) Wrong action is the near shore, right action the far shore. (5) Wrong livelihood is the near shore, right livelihood the far shore. (6) Wrong effort is the near shore, right effort the far shore. (7) Wrong mindfulness is the near shore, right mindfulness the far shore. (8) Wrong concentration is the near shore, right concentration the far shore. (9) Wrong knowledge is the near shore, right knowledge the far shore. (10) Wrong liberation is the near shore, right liberation the far shore. The one, brahmin, is the near shore, the other the far shore."

Few are those people[2156]
who go beyond.
The rest merely run
along the [near] shore.

When the Dhamma is rightly expounded
those people who practice accordingly
are the ones who will go beyond
the realm of Death so hard to cross.

Having left the dark qualities behind,
a wise person should develop the bright ones.
Having come from home into homelessness,
where it is hard to take delight—

There in seclusion one should seek delight,
having left behind sensual pleasures.

Owning nothing, the wise person
should cleanse himself of mental defilements. [233]

Those whose minds are rightly well developed
in the enlightenment factors,
who through non-clinging find delight
in the relinquishment of grasping:
luminous, with taints destroyed,
they are the quenched ones in the world.[2157]

118 (6) Near

"Bhikkhus, I will teach you the near shore and the far shore. Listen and attend closely. I will speak."

"Yes, Bhante," those bhikkhus replied. The Blessed One said this:

"What, bhikkhus, is the near shore, and what is the far shore? (1) Wrong view, bhikkhus, is the near shore, right view the far shore ... (10) Wrong liberation is the near shore, right liberation the far shore. The one, bhikkhus, is the near shore, the other the far shore."

[The verses attached are identical with those of the preceding sutta.]

119 (7) Paccorohaṇī (1)

Now on that occasion, on the uposatha day, the brahmin Jāṇussoṇī stood to one side not far from the Blessed One, with his head washed, wearing a new pair of linen clothes, holding a handful of wet [234] *kusa* grass. The Blessed One saw him standing there and said to him:

"Why is it, brahmin, that on the uposatha day you stand to one side with your head washed, wearing a new pair of linen clothes, holding a handful of wet *kusa* grass? What is happening today with the brahmin clan?"

"Today, Master Gotama, is the brahmin clan's *paccorohaṇī* festival."[2158]

"But how do the brahmins observe the *paccorohaṇī* festival?"

"Here, Master Gotama, on the uposatha day, the brahmins wash their heads and put on a pair of new linen clothes. They then smear the ground with wet cow dung, cover this with green *kusa* grass, and lie down between the boundary and the fire house. In the course of the night, they get up three times, and with reverential salutation pay homage to the fire: 'We descend in honor of the revered one. We descend in honor of the revered one.'[2159] They offer abundant ghee, oil, and butter to the fire. When the night has passed, they offer excellent food of various kinds to brahmins. It is in this way, Master Gotama, that the brahmins observe the *paccorohaṇī* festival."

"The *paccorohaṇī* festival in the Noble One's discipline, brahmin, is quite different from the *paccorohaṇī* festival of the brahmins."

"But how, Master Gotama, is the *paccorohaṇī* festival observed in the Noble One's discipline? It would be good if Master Gotama would teach me the Dhamma by explaining how the *paccorohaṇī* festival is observed in the Noble One's discipline."

"Well then, brahmin, listen and attend closely. I will speak."

"Yes, sir," the brahmin Jāṇussoṇī replied. The Blessed One said this: [235]

(1) "Here, brahmin, the noble disciple reflects thus: 'The result of wrong view is bad both in this present life and in future lives.' Having reflected thus, he abandons wrong view; he descends from wrong view.

(2) ". . . 'The result of wrong intention is bad both in this present life and in future lives.' Having reflected thus, he abandons wrong intention; he descends from wrong intention.

(3) ". . . 'The result of wrong speech is bad both in this present life and in future lives.' Having reflected thus, he abandons wrong speech; he descends from wrong speech.

(4) ". . . 'The result of wrong action is bad both in this present life and in future lives.' Having reflected thus, he abandons wrong action; he descends from wrong action.

(5) ". . . 'The result of wrong livelihood is bad both in this present life and in future lives.' Having reflected thus, he abandons wrong livelihood; he descends from wrong livelihood.

(6) ". . . 'The result of wrong effort is bad both in this present life and in future lives.' Having reflected thus, he abandons wrong effort; he descends from wrong effort.

(7) ". . . 'The result of wrong mindfulness is bad both in this present life and in future lives.' Having reflected thus, he abandons wrong mindfulness; he descends from wrong mindfulness.

(8) "... 'The result of wrong concentration is bad both in this present life and in future lives.' Having reflected thus, he abandons wrong concentration; he descends from wrong concentration.

(9) "... 'The result of wrong knowledge is bad both in this present life and in future lives.' Having reflected thus, he abandons wrong knowledge; he descends from wrong knowledge.

(10) "... 'The result of wrong liberation is bad both in this present life and in future lives.' Having reflected thus, he abandons wrong liberation; he descends from wrong liberation.

"It is in this way, brahmin, that the *paccorohaṇī* festival is observed in the Noble One's discipline."

"The *paccorohaṇī* festival in the Noble One's discipline, Master Gotama, is quite different from the *paccorohaṇī* festival of the brahmins. And the *paccorohaṇī* festival of the brahmins is not worth a sixteenth part of the *paccorohaṇī* festival in the Noble One's discipline. [236]

"Excellent, Master Gotama! Excellent, Master Gotama! Master Gotama has made the Dhamma clear in many ways, as though he were turning upright what had been overthrown, revealing what was hidden, showing the way to one who was lost, or holding up a lamp in the darkness so those with good eyesight can see forms. I now go for refuge to Master Gotama, to the Dhamma, and to the Saṅgha of bhikkhus. Let Master Gotama consider me a lay follower who from today has gone for refuge for life."

120 (8) Paccorohaṇī (2)

"Bhikkhus, I will teach you the noble *paccorohaṇī* festival. Listen....

"And what, bhikkhus, is the noble *paccorohaṇī* festival? (1) Here, the noble disciple reflects thus: 'The result of wrong view is bad both in this present life and in future lives.' Having reflected thus, he abandons wrong view; he descends from wrong view. (2) 'The result of wrong intention ... (3) ... wrong speech ... (4) ... wrong action ... (5) ... wrong livelihood ... (6) ... wrong effort ... (7) ... wrong mindfulness ... (8) ... wrong concentration ... (9) ... wrong knowledge ... (10) ... wrong liberation is bad both in this present life and in future lives.' Having reflected thus, he abandons wrong liberation; he descends from wrong liberation. This is called the noble *paccorohaṇī* festival."

121 (9) Forerunner

"Bhikkhus, just as the dawn is the forerunner and precursor of the sunrise, so right view is the forerunner and precursor of wholesome qualities. For one of right view, right intention originates. For one of right intention, right speech originates. For one of right speech, right action originates. For one of right action, right livelihood originates. For one of right livelihood, right effort originates. For one of right effort, right mindfulness originates. For one of right mindfulness, right concentration [237] originates. For one of right concentration, right knowledge originates. For one of right knowledge, right liberation originates."

122 (10) Taints

"Bhikkhus, these ten things, when developed and cultivated, lead to the destruction of the taints. What ten? Right view, right intention, right speech, right action, right livelihood, right effort, right mindfulness, right concentration, right knowledge, and right liberation. These ten things, when developed and cultivated, lead to the destruction of the taints."

III. Purified

123 (1) First

"Bhikkhus, these ten things are purified and cleansed nowhere else but in the Fortunate One's discipline. What ten? Right view . . . and right liberation. These ten things are purified and cleansed nowhere else but in the Fortunate One's discipline."

124 (2) Second

"Bhikkhus, these ten things when unarisen arise nowhere else but in the Fortunate One's discipline. What ten? [238] Right view . . . and right liberation. These ten things. . . ."

125 (3) Third

"Bhikkhus, these ten things are of great fruit and benefit nowhere else but in the Fortunate One's discipline. What ten? Right view . . . and right liberation. These ten things. . . ."

126 (4) Fourth

"Bhikkhus, these ten things culminate in the removal of lust, hatred, and delusion nowhere else but in the Fortunate One's discipline. What ten? Right view . . . and right liberation. These ten things. . . . "

127 (5) Fifth

"Bhikkhus, these ten things lead exclusively to disenchantment, to dispassion, to cessation, to peace, to direct knowledge, to enlightenment, to nibbāna, nowhere else but in the Fortunate One's discipline. What ten? Right view . . . and right liberation. These ten things. . . . "

128 (6) Sixth

"Bhikkhus, these ten things, developed and cultivated, when unarisen arise nowhere else but in the Fortunate One's discipline. What ten? [239] Right view . . . and right liberation. These ten things. . . . "

129 (7) Seventh

"Bhikkhus, these ten things, when developed and cultivated, are of great fruit and benefit nowhere else but in the Fortunate One's discipline. What ten? Right view . . . and right liberation. These ten things. . . . "

130 (8) Eighth

"Bhikkhus, these ten things, when developed and cultivated, culminate in the removal of lust, hatred, and delusion nowhere else but in the Fortunate One's discipline. What ten? Right view . . . and right liberation. These ten things. . . . "

131 (9) Ninth

"Bhikkhus, these ten things, when developed and cultivated, lead exclusively to disenchantment, to dispassion, to cessation, to peace, to direct knowledge, to enlightenment, to nibbāna, nowhere else but in the Fortunate One's discipline. What ten? Right view . . . and right liberation. These ten things. . . . " [240]

132 (10) Tenth

"Bhikkhus, there are these ten wrong courses. What ten? Wrong view, wrong intention, wrong speech, wrong action, wrong livelihood, wrong effort, wrong mindfulness, wrong concentration, wrong knowledge, and wrong liberation. These are the ten wrong courses."

133 (11) Eleventh

"Bhikkhus, there are these ten right courses. What ten? Right view, right intention, right speech, right action, right livelihood, right effort, right mindfulness, right concentration, right knowledge, and right liberation. These are the ten right courses."

IV. Good

134 (1) Good

"Bhikkhus, I will teach you what is good and what is bad. Listen and attend closely. I will speak."

"Yes, Bhante," those bhikkhus replied. The Blessed One said this:

"And what, bhikkhus, is bad? Wrong view, wrong intention, wrong speech, wrong action, wrong livelihood, wrong effort, wrong mindfulness, wrong concentration, wrong knowledge, and wrong liberation. This is called bad.

"And what, bhikkhus, is good? [241] Right view, right intention, right speech, right action, right livelihood, right effort, right mindfulness, right concentration, right knowledge, and right liberation. This is called good."

135 (2)–144 (11) The Noble Dhamma, Etc.

(135) "Bhikkhus, I will teach you the noble Dhamma and the ignoble Dhamma . . . (136) . . . the wholesome and the unwholesome . . . (137) . . . what is beneficial and what is harmful . . . [242] . . . (138) . . . the Dhamma and what is non-Dhamma . . . (139) . . . the tainted Dhamma and the taintless one . . . (140) . . . the blameworthy Dhamma and the blameless one . . . [243] (141) . . . the tormenting Dhamma and the untormenting one . . . (142) . . . the Dhamma that leads to building up and the one that leads to dismantling . . . (143) . . . the Dhamma with suffering as its outcome and the one with happiness as its outcome . . . [244]

(144) . . . the Dhamma that results in suffering and the one that results in happiness. . . .

"And what, bhikkhus, is the Dhamma that results in suffering? Wrong view . . . and wrong liberation. This is called the Dhamma that results in suffering.

"And what, bhikkhus, is the Dhamma that results in happiness? Right view . . . and right liberation. This is called the Dhamma that results in happiness."

V. Noble

145 (1) The Noble Path

"Bhikkhus, I will teach you the noble path and the ignoble path.[2160] Listen and attend closely. . . . And what, bhikkhus, is the ignoble path? Wrong view . . . and wrong liberation. This is called the ignoble path.

"And what, bhikkhus, is the noble path? Right view . . . and right liberation. This is called the noble path."

146 (2) –154 (10) The Dark Path, Etc.

(146) "Bhikkhus, I will teach you the dark path and the bright path[2161] . . . [245] . . . (147) . . . the good Dhamma and the bad Dhamma . . . (148) . . . the Dhamma of a good person and that of a bad person . . . (149) . . . the Dhamma to be aroused and the one not to be aroused . . . [246] . . . (150) . . . the Dhamma to be pursued and the one not to be pursued . . . (151) . . . the Dhamma to be developed and the one not to be developed . . . (152) . . . the Dhamma to be cultivated and the one not to be cultivated . . . [247] (153) . . . the Dhamma to be recollected and the one not to be recollected . . . (154) . . . the Dhamma to be realized and the one not to be realized. . . .

"And what, bhikkhus, is the Dhamma not to be realized? Wrong view . . . and wrong liberation. This is called the Dhamma not to be realized.

"And what, bhikkhus, is the Dhamma to be realized? Right view . . . and right liberation. This is called the Dhamma to be realized."

The Fourth Fifty

I. Persons

155 (1) Associate With

"Bhikkhus, one should not associate with a person who possesses ten qualities. What ten? [248] Wrong view, wrong intention, wrong speech, wrong action, wrong livelihood, wrong effort, wrong mindfulness, wrong concentration, wrong knowledge, and wrong liberation. One should not associate with a person who possesses these ten qualities.

"Bhikkhus, one should associate with a person who possesses ten qualities. What ten? Right view, right intention, right speech, right action, right livelihood, right effort, right mindfulness, right concentration, right knowledge, and right liberation. One should associate with a person who possesses these ten qualities."

156 (2)–166 (12) Resort, Etc.

(156) "Bhikkhus, one should not resort to a person who possesses ten qualities . . . one should resort to . . . (157) . . . one should not attend on . . . one should attend on . . . (158) . . . one should not venerate . . . one should venerate . . . (159) . . . one should not praise . . . one should praise . . . (160) . . . one should not revere . . . one should revere . . . (161) . . . one should not show deference to . . . one should show deference to a person who possesses ten qualities . . . (162) . . . a person who possesses ten qualities is not successful . . . is successful . . . (163) . . . is not purified . . . is purified . . . (164) . . . does not overcome conceit . . . overcomes conceit [249] . . . (165) . . . does not grow in wisdom . . . grows in wisdom . . . (166) . . . generates much demerit . . . generates much merit. What ten? Right view, right intention, right speech, right action, right livelihood, right effort, right mindfulness, right concentration, right knowledge, and right liberation. A person who possesses these ten qualities generates much merit."

II. Jāṇussoṇī

167 (1) Paccorohaṇī (1)[2162]

Now on that occasion, on the uposatha day, the brahmin Jāṇussoṇī stood to one side not far from the Blessed One, with his head washed, wearing a new pair of linen clothes, holding a handful of wet *kusa* grass. The Blessed One saw him standing there and said to him:

"Why is it, brahmin, that on the uposatha day you stand to one side with your head washed, wearing a new pair of linen clothes, holding a handful of wet *kusa* grass? What is happening today with the brahmin clan?"

"Today, Master Gotama, is the brahmin clan's *paccorohaṇī* festival." [250]

"But how, brahmin, do the brahmins observe the *paccorohaṇī* festival?"

"Here, Master Gotama, on the uposatha day, the brahmins wash their heads and put on a pair of new linen clothes. They then smear the ground with wet cow dung, cover this with green *kusa* grass, and lie down between the boundary and the fire house. In the course of the night, they get up three times, and with reverential salutation pay homage to the fire: 'We descend in honor of the revered one. We descend in honor of the revered one.' They offer abundant ghee, oil, and butter to the fire. When the night has passed, they offer excellent food of various kinds to brahmins. It is in this way, Master Gotama, that the brahmins observe the *paccorohaṇī* festival."

"The *paccorohaṇī* festival in the Noble One's discipline, brahmin, is quite different from the *paccorohaṇī* festival of the brahmins."

"But how, Master Gotama, is the *paccorohaṇī* festival observed in the Noble One's discipline? It would be good if Master Gotama would teach me the Dhamma by explaining how the *paccorohaṇī* festival is observed in the Noble One's discipline."

"Well then, brahmin, listen and attend closely. I will speak."

"Yes, sir," the brahmin Jāṇussoṇī replied. The Blessed One said this:

(1) "Here, brahmin, the noble disciple reflects thus: 'The result of the destruction of life is bad both in this present life and in future lives.' Having reflected thus, he abandons the destruction of life; he descends from the destruction of life.

(2) ". . . 'The result of taking what is not given is bad both in this present life and in future lives.' Having reflected thus, he abandons taking what is not given; he descends from taking what is not given.

(3) "... 'The result of sexual misconduct is bad both in this present life and in future lives.' Having reflected thus, he abandons sexual misconduct; he descends from sexual misconduct.

(4) "... 'The result of false speech is bad both in this present life and in future lives.' [251] Having reflected thus, he abandons false speech; he descends from false speech.

(5) "... 'The result of divisive speech is bad both in this present life and in future lives.' Having reflected thus, he abandons divisive speech; he descends from divisive speech.

(6) "... 'The result of harsh speech is bad both in this present life and in future lives.' Having reflected thus, he abandons harsh speech; he descends from harsh speech.

(7) "... 'The result of idle chatter is bad both in this present life and in future lives.' Having reflected thus, he abandons idle chatter; he descends from idle chatter.

(8) "... 'The result of longing is bad both in this present life and in future lives.' Having reflected thus, he abandons longing; he descends from longing.

(9) "... 'The result of ill will is bad both in this present life and in future lives.' Having reflected thus, he abandons ill will; he descends from ill will.

(10) "... 'The result of wrong view is bad both in this present life and in future lives.' Having reflected thus, he abandons wrong view; he descends from wrong view.

"It is in this way, brahmin, that the *paccorohaṇī* festival is observed in the Noble One's discipline."

"The *paccorohaṇī* festival in the Noble One's discipline, Master Gotama, is quite different from the *paccorohaṇī* festival of the brahmins. And the *paccorohaṇī* festival of the brahmins is not worth a sixteenth part of the *paccorohaṇī* festival in the Noble One's discipline.

"Excellent, Master Gotama!... [as in 10:119] ... Let Master Gotama consider me a lay follower who from today has gone for refuge for life."

168 (2) Paccorohaṇī (2)

"Bhikkhus, I will teach you the noble *paccorohaṇī* festival. Listen....

"And what, bhikkhus, is the noble *paccorohaṇī* festival? [252] (1) Here, the noble disciple reflects thus: 'The result of the destruction of life is bad both in this present life and in future lives.' Having reflected thus, he abandons the destruction of life; he descends from the destruction of life. (2) 'The result of taking what is not given . . . (3) . . . sexual misconduct . . . (4) . . . false speech . . . (5) . . . divisive speech . . . (6) . . . harsh speech . . . (7) . . . idle chatter . . . (8) . . . longing . . . (9) . . . ill will . . . (10) . . . wrong view is bad both in this present life and in future lives.' Having reflected thus, he abandons wrong view; he descends from wrong view. This is called the noble *paccorohaṇī* festival."

169 (3) Saṅgārava[2163]

Then the brahmin Saṅgārava approached the Blessed One and exchanged greetings with him. When they had concluded their greetings and cordial talk, he sat down to one side and said to the Blessed One:

"Master Gotama, what is the near shore? What is the far shore?"

"Brahmin, (1) the destruction of life is the near shore, abstention from the destruction of life the far shore. (2) Taking what is not given is the near shore, abstention from taking what is not given the far shore. (3) Sexual misconduct is the near shore, abstention from sexual misconduct the far shore. (4) False speech is the near shore, abstention from false speech the far shore. (5) Divisive speech is the near shore, abstention from divisive speech the far shore. (6) Harsh speech is the near shore, abstention from harsh speech the far shore. (7) Idle chatter is the near shore, abstention from idle chatter the far shore. (8) Longing is the near shore, non-longing the far shore. (9) Ill will is the near shore, good will the far shore. (10) Wrong view is the near shore, right view the far shore. The one, brahmin, is the near shore, the other the far shore." [253]

Few are those people
who go beyond.
The rest merely run
along the [near] shore.

When the Dhamma is rightly expounded
those people who practice accordingly
are the ones who will go beyond
the realm of Death so hard to cross.

Having left the dark qualities behind,
a wise person should develop the bright ones.
Having come from home into homelessness,
where it is hard to take delight—

There in seclusion one should seek delight,
having left behind sensual pleasures.
Owning nothing, the wise person
should cleanse himself of mental defilements.

Those whose minds are rightly well developed
in the enlightenment factors,
who through non-clinging find delight
in the relinquishment of grasping:
luminous, with taints destroyed,
they are the quenched ones in the world.

170 (4) The Near Shore

"Bhikkhus, I will teach you the near shore and the far shore. Listen and attend closely. I will speak."

"Yes, Bhante," those bhikkhus replied. The Blessed One said this:

"What, bhikkhus, is the near shore, and what is the far shore? (1) The destruction of life, bhikkhus, is the near shore, abstention from the destruction of life the far shore.... (10) Wrong view is the near shore, right view the far shore. The one, bhikkhus, is the near shore, the other the far shore." [254]

[The verses attached are identical with those of the preceding sutta.]

171 (5) Non-Dhamma (1)[2164]

"Bhikkhus, what is non-Dhamma and harmful should be understood, and what is the Dhamma and beneficial should also be understood. Having understood what is non-Dhamma and harmful, and also what is the Dhamma and beneficial, one should practice in accordance with the Dhamma and with what is beneficial.

"And what, bhikkhus, is non-Dhamma and harmful? The destruction of life, taking what is not given, sexual misconduct, false speech, divisive speech, harsh speech, idle chatter, longing, ill will, and wrong view. This is what is said to be non-Dhamma and harmful.

"And what, bhikkhus, is the Dhamma and beneficial? Abstention from the destruction of life, abstention from taking what is not given, abstention from sexual misconduct, abstention from false speech, abstention from divisive speech, abstention from harsh speech, abstention from idle chatter, non-longing, good will, and right view. This is what is said to be the Dhamma and beneficial.

"When it was said: 'Bhikkhus, what is non-Dhamma and harmful should be understood, and what is the Dhamma and beneficial should also be understood. Having understood what is non-Dhamma and harmful, and also what is the Dhamma and beneficial, one should practice in accordance with the Dhamma and with what is beneficial,' it is with reference to this that this was said." [255]

172 (6) Non-Dhamma (2)

"Bhikkhus, what is non-Dhamma and what is the Dhamma should be understood, and what is harmful and what is beneficial should also be understood. Having understood what is non-Dhamma and what is the Dhamma, and also what is harmful and what is beneficial, one should practice in accordance with the Dhamma and with what is beneficial."

This is what the Blessed One said. Having said this, the Fortunate One rose from his seat and entered his dwelling. Then, soon after the Blessed One had left, the bhikkhus considered: "Friends, the Blessed One taught this brief synopsis: 'Bhikkhus, what is non-Dhamma and what is the Dhamma should be understood . . . one should practice in accordance with the Dhamma and with what is beneficial.' Then he rose from his seat and entered his dwelling without expounding its meaning in detail. Now who will expound its meaning in detail?' Then it occurred to them: "The Venerable Mahākaccāna is praised by the Teacher and esteemed by his wise fellow monks; he is capable of expounding the detailed meaning of this brief synopsis. Let us approach the Venerable Mahākaccāna and ask him the meaning of this. We will retain it in mind as he explains it to us."

Then those bhikkhus approached the Venerable Mahākaccāna

and exchanged greetings with him, after which they sat down to one side and said: "Friend Mahākaccāna, the Blessed One taught this brief synopsis.... [256] ... Then he rose from his seat and entered his dwelling without expounding the meaning in detail. Soon after he left, we considered: 'Friends, the Blessed One taught this brief synopsis.... [all as above down to:] ... Let us approach the Venerable Mahākaccāna and ask him the meaning of this. We will retain it in mind as he explains it to us.' Let the Venerable Mahākaccāna expound it to us."

[The Venerable Mahākaccāna replied:] "Friends, it is as though a man needing heartwood, seeking heartwood, wandering in search of heartwood, would pass over the root and trunk of a great tree possessed of heartwood, thinking that heartwood should be sought among the branches and foliage. And so it is with you. When you were face to face with the Teacher you passed by the Blessed One, thinking to ask me about the meaning. For, friends, knowing, the Blessed One knows; seeing, he sees; he has become vision, he has become knowledge, he has become the Dhamma, he has become Brahmā; he is the expounder, the proclaimer, the elucidator of meaning, the giver of the deathless, the lord of the Dhamma, the Tathāgata. That was the time when you [257] should have approached the Blessed One and asked him about the meaning. You should have retained it in mind as he would have explained it to you."

"Surely, friend Kaccāna, knowing, the Blessed One knows; seeing, he sees; he has become vision ... the Tathāgata. That was the time when we should have approached the Blessed One and asked him about the meaning, and we should have retained it in mind as he would have explained it to us. Yet the Venerable Mahākaccāna is praised by the Teacher and esteemed by his wise fellow monks. He is capable of expounding the detailed meaning of this synopsis. Let the Venerable Mahākaccāna expound it without finding it troublesome."

"Then listen, friends, and attend closely. I will speak."

"Yes, friend," those bhikkhus replied. The Venerable Mahākaccāna said this:

"Friends, the Blessed One taught this brief synopsis without expounding the detailed meaning: 'Bhikkhus, what is non-Dhamma and what is the Dhamma should be understood, and what is harmful and what is beneficial should also be understood. Having understood what is non-Dhamma and what is the Dhamma, and also what is harmful and what is beneficial, one should practice in accordance with the Dhamma and with what is beneficial.' Now what, friends, is non-Dhamma and what is the Dhamma? And what is harmful and what is beneficial?

(1) "The destruction of life, friends, is non-Dhamma; abstention from the destruction of life is the Dhamma. The numerous bad unwholesome qualities that originate with the destruction of life as condition: these are harmful. The numerous wholesome qualities that reach fulfillment by development with abstention from the destruction of life as condition: these are beneficial.

(2) "Taking what is not given is non-Dhamma; abstention from taking what is not given is the Dhamma. [258] The numerous bad unwholesome qualities that originate with taking what is not given as condition: these are harmful. The numerous wholesome qualities that reach fulfillment by development with abstention from taking what is not given as condition: these are beneficial.

(3) "Sexual misconduct is non-Dhamma; abstention from sexual misconduct is the Dhamma. The numerous bad unwholesome qualities that originate with sexual misconduct as condition: these are harmful. The numerous wholesome qualities that reach fulfillment by development with abstention from sexual misconduct as condition: these are beneficial.

(4) "False speech is non-Dhamma; abstention from false speech is the Dhamma. The numerous bad unwholesome qualities that originate with false speech as condition: these are harmful. The numerous wholesome qualities that reach fulfillment by development with abstention from false speech as condition: these are beneficial.

(5) "Divisive speech is non-Dhamma; abstention from divisive speech is the Dhamma. The numerous bad unwholesome qualities that originate with divisive speech as condition: these are harmful. The numerous wholesome qualities that reach fulfillment by development with abstention from divisive speech as condition: these are beneficial.

(6) "Harsh speech is non-Dhamma; abstention from harsh speech is the Dhamma. The numerous bad unwholesome

qualities that originate with harsh speech as condition: these are harmful. The numerous wholesome qualities that reach fulfillment by development with abstention from harsh speech as condition: these are beneficial.

(7) "Idle chatter is non-Dhamma; abstention from idle chatter is the Dhamma. The numerous bad unwholesome qualities that originate with idle chatter as condition: these are harmful. The numerous wholesome qualities that reach fulfillment by development with abstention from idle chatter as condition: these are beneficial.

(8) "Longing is non-Dhamma; non-longing is the Dhamma. The numerous bad unwholesome qualities that originate with longing as condition: these are harmful. The numerous wholesome qualities that reach fulfillment by development with non-longing as condition: these are beneficial.

(9) "Ill will is non-Dhamma; good will is the Dhamma. The numerous bad unwholesome qualities that originate with ill will as condition: these are harmful. The numerous wholesome qualities that reach fulfillment by development with good will as condition: these are beneficial.

(10) "Wrong view is non-Dhamma; right view is the Dhamma. The numerous bad unwholesome qualities that originate with wrong view as condition: these are harmful. The numerous wholesome qualities that reach fulfillment by development with right view as condition: these are beneficial.

"Friends, [259] it is in this way that I understand the detailed meaning of the Blessed One's brief synopsis. Now, if you wish, you may go to the Blessed One himself and ask him about the meaning of this. You should retain it in mind as the Blessed One explains it to you."

"Yes, friend," those bhikkhus replied, and having delighted and rejoiced in the Venerable Mahākaccāna's statement, they rose from their seats and went to the Blessed One. After paying homage to him, they sat down to one side and said to the Blessed One: "Bhante, the Blessed One taught this synopsis.... [260] [they here relate all that had taken place, adding:] ... Then, Bhante, we approached the Venerable Mahākaccāna and asked him about the meaning. The Venerable Mahākaccāna expounded the meaning to us in these ways, in these terms and phrases."

"Good, good, bhikkhus! Mahākaccāna is wise. Mahākaccāna has great wisdom. If you had approached me and asked me the meaning of this, I would have explained it to you in the same way as Mahākaccāna. Such is the meaning of this, and so you should retain it in mind."

173 (7) Non-Dhamma (3)

"Bhikkhus, what is non-Dhamma and what is the Dhamma should be understood, and what is harmful and what is beneficial should also be understood. Having understood what is non-Dhamma and what is the Dhamma, and also what is harmful and what is beneficial, one should practice in accordance with the Dhamma and with what is beneficial.

"And what, bhikkhus, is non-Dhamma and what is the Dhamma? And what is harmful and what is beneficial?

(1) "The destruction of life is non-Dhamma; abstention from the destruction of life is the Dhamma. The numerous bad unwholesome qualities that originate with the destruction of life as condition: these are harmful. The numerous wholesome qualities that reach fulfillment by development with abstention from the destruction of life as condition: these are beneficial.

(2) "Taking what is not given is non-Dhamma; abstention from taking what is not given is the Dhamma. . . . (3) Sexual misconduct [261] is non-Dhamma; abstention from sexual misconduct is the Dhamma. . . . (4) False speech is non-Dhamma; abstention from false speech is the Dhamma. . . . (5) Divisive speech is non-Dhamma; abstention from divisive speech is the Dhamma. . . . (6) Harsh speech is non-Dhamma; abstention from harsh speech is the Dhamma. . . . (7) Idle chatter is non-Dhamma; abstention from idle chatter is the Dhamma. . . . (8) Longing is non-Dhamma; non-longing is the Dhamma. . . . (9) Ill will is non-Dhamma; good will is the Dhamma. . . .

(10) "Wrong view is non-Dhamma; right view is the Dhamma. The numerous bad unwholesome qualities that originate with wrong view as condition: these are harmful. The numerous wholesome qualities that reach fulfillment by development with right view as condition: these are beneficial.

"When it was said: 'Bhikkhus, what is non-Dhamma and what is the Dhamma should be understood, and what is harmful and what is beneficial should be understood. Having understood what is non-Dhamma and what is the Dhamma, and what is harmful and what is beneficial, one should practice in accordance with the Dhamma and with what is beneficial,' it is with reference to this that this was said."

174 (8) Causes of Kamma

"Bhikkhus, the destruction of life, I say, is threefold: caused by greed, caused by hatred, and caused by delusion. Taking what is not given, I say, is also threefold: caused by greed, caused by hatred, and caused by delusion. Sexual misconduct, I say, is also threefold: caused by greed, caused by hatred, and caused by delusion. False speech, I say, is also threefold: caused by greed, caused by hatred, and caused by delusion. Divisive speech, I say, is also threefold: caused by greed, caused by hatred, and caused by delusion. Harsh speech, I say, is also threefold: caused by greed, caused by hatred, and caused by delusion. Idle chatter, I say, is also threefold: caused by greed, caused by hatred, and caused by delusion. Longing, [262] I say, is also threefold: caused by greed, caused by hatred, and caused by delusion. Ill will, I say, is also threefold: caused by greed, caused by hatred, and caused by delusion. Wrong view, I say, is also threefold: caused by greed, caused by hatred, and caused by delusion.

"Thus, bhikkhus, greed is a source and origin of kamma; hatred is a source and origin of kamma; delusion is a source and origin of kamma. With the destruction of greed, a source of kamma is extinguished. With the destruction of hatred, a source of kamma is extinguished. With the destruction of delusion, a source of kamma is extinguished."

175 (9) Avoidance

"Bhikkhus, this Dhamma offers a means of avoidance. It does not lack a means of avoidance. And how does this Dhamma offer a means of avoidance and not lack a means of avoidance?

(1) "One who destroys life has abstention from the destruction of life as the means to avoid it. (2) One who takes what is not given has abstention from taking what is not given as the means to avoid it. (3) One who engages in sexual misconduct has abstention from sexual misconduct as the means to avoid it. (4) One who speaks falsely has abstention from false speech as the means to avoid it. (5) One who speaks divisively has

abstention from divisive speech as the means to avoid it. (6) One who speaks harshly has abstention from harsh speech as the means to avoid it. (7) One who indulges in idle chatter has abstention from idle chatter as the means to avoid it. (8) One full of longing has non-longing as the means to avoid it. (9) One full of ill will has good will as the means to avoid it. (10) One who holds wrong view has right view as the means to avoid it.

"It is in this way, bhikkhus, that this Dhamma offers a means of avoidance and does not lack a means of avoidance." [263]

176 (10) Cunda

Thus have I heard. On one occasion the Blessed One was dwelling at Pāvā in the mango grove of Cunda, the smith's son.[2165] Then Cunda, the smith's son, approached the Blessed One, paid homage to him, and sat down to one side. The Blessed One then said to him:

"Cunda, whose rites of purity[2166] do you prefer?"

"Bhante, I prefer the rites of purity prescribed by the brahmins of the west who carry around waterpots, wear garlands of water plants, tend the sacred fire, and immerse themselves in water."

"And how, Cunda, do the brahmins of the west prescribe their rites of purity?"

"Here, Bhante, the brahmins of the west enjoin a disciple thus: 'Come, good man, having gotten up early, you should stroke the ground from your bed. If you don't stroke the ground, you should stroke wet cow dung. If you don't stroke wet cow dung, you should stroke green grass. If you don't stroke green grass, you should tend the sacred fire. If you don't tend the sacred fire, you should pay homage to the sun with reverential salutation. If you don't pay homage to the sun with reverential salutation, you should immerse yourself in water three times including the evening.' It is in this way that the brahmins of the west prescribe their rites of purity. It is their rites of purity that I prefer."

"Cunda, purification in the Noble One's discipline is quite different from the rites of purity prescribed by the brahmins of the west who carry around waterpots, wear garlands of water plants, tend the sacred fire, and immerse themselves in water." [264]

"But how, Bhante, does purification come about in the Noble

One's discipline? It would be good if the Blessed One would teach me the Dhamma in a way that explains how purification comes about in the Noble One's discipline."

"Well then, Cunda, listen and attend closely. I will speak."

"Yes, Bhante," Cunda, the smith's son, replied. The Blessed One said this:

"Impurity by body, Cunda, is threefold. Impurity by speech is fourfold. Impurity by mind is threefold.

"And how, Cunda, is impurity by body threefold?

(1) "Here, someone destroys life. He is murderous, bloody-handed, given to blows and violence, merciless to living beings.

(2) "He takes what is not given. He steals the wealth and property of others in the village or forest.

(3) "He engages in sexual misconduct. He has sexual relations with women who are protected by their mother, father, mother and father, brother, sister, or relatives; who are protected by their Dhamma; who have a husband; whose violation entails a penalty; or even with one already engaged.[2167]

"It is in this way that impurity by body is threefold.

"And how, Cunda, is impurity by speech fourfold?

(4) "Here, someone speaks falsehood. If he is summoned to a council, to an assembly, to his relatives' presence, to his guild, or to the court, and questioned as a witness thus: 'So, good man, tell what you know,' then, not knowing, he says, 'I know,' or knowing, he says, 'I do not know'; not seeing, he says, 'I see,' or seeing, he says, 'I do not see.' Thus [265] he consciously speaks falsehood for his own ends, or for another's ends, or for some trifling worldly end.

(5) "He speaks divisively. Having heard something here, he repeats it elsewhere in order to divide [those people] from these; or having heard something elsewhere, he repeats it to these people in order to divide [them] from those. Thus he is one who divides those who are united, a creator of divisions, one who enjoys factions, rejoices in factions, delights in factions, a speaker of words that create factions.

(6) "He speaks harshly. He utters such words as are rough, hard, hurtful to others, offensive to others, bordering on anger, unconducive to concentration.

(7) "He indulges in idle chatter. He speaks at an improper

time, speaks falsely, speaks what is unbeneficial, speaks contrary to the Dhamma and the discipline; at an improper time he speaks such words as are worthless, unreasonable, rambling, and unbeneficial.

"It is in this way that impurity by speech is fourfold.

"And how, Cunda, is impurity by mind threefold?

(8) "Here, someone is full of longing. He longs for the wealth and property of others thus: 'Oh, may what belongs to another be mine!'

(9) "He has a mind of ill will and intentions of hate thus: 'May these beings be slain, slaughtered,[2168] cut off, destroyed, or annihilated!'

(10) "He holds wrong view and has an incorrect perspective thus: 'There is nothing given, nothing sacrificed, nothing offered; there is no fruit or result of good and bad actions; there is no this world, no other world; there is no mother, no father; there are no beings spontaneously reborn; there are in the world no ascetics and brahmins of right conduct and right practice who, having realized this world and the other world for themselves by direct knowledge, make them known to others.'

"It is in this way that impurity by mind is threefold. [266]

"These, Cunda, are the ten courses of unwholesome kamma. If one engages in these ten courses of unwholesome kamma, then, if one gets up early and strokes the ground from one's bed, one is impure, and if one doesn't stroke the ground, one is impure. If one strokes wet cow dung, one is impure, and if one doesn't stroke wet cow dung, one is impure. If one strokes green grass, one is impure, and if one doesn't stroke green grass, one is impure. If one tends the sacred fire, one is impure, and if one doesn't tend the sacred fire, one is impure. If one pays homage to the sun with reverential salutation, one is impure, and if one doesn't pay homage to the sun with reverential salutation, one is impure. If one immerses oneself in water three times including the evening, one is impure, and if one doesn't immerse oneself in water three times including the evening, one is impure. For what reason? Because these ten courses of unwholesome kamma are themselves impure and defiling. It is because people engage in these ten courses of unwholesome kamma that hell, the animal realm, the sphere of afflicted spirits, and other bad destinations are seen.

"Purity by body, Cunda, is threefold. Purity by speech is fourfold. Purity by mind is threefold.

"And how, Cunda, is purity by body threefold?

(1) "Here, someone, having abandoned the destruction of life, abstains from the destruction of life. With the rod and weapon laid aside, conscientious and kindly, he dwells compassionate toward all living beings.

(2) "Having abandoned the taking of what is not given, he abstains from taking what is not given. He does not steal the wealth and property of others in the village or in the forest.

(3) "Having abandoned sexual misconduct, he abstains from sexual misconduct. He does not have sexual relations with women who are protected by their mother, father, mother and father, brother, sister, or relatives; who are protected by their Dhamma; who have a husband; whose violation entails a penalty; [267] or even with one already engaged.

"It is in this way that purity by body is threefold.

"And how, Cunda, is purity by speech fourfold?

(4) "Here, someone, having abandoned false speech, abstains from false speech. If he is summoned to a council, to an assembly, to his relatives' presence, to his guild, or to the court, and questioned as a witness thus: 'So, good man, tell what you know,' then, not knowing, he says, 'I do not know,' or knowing, he says, 'I know'; not seeing, he says, 'I do not see,' or seeing, he says, 'I see.' Thus he does not consciously speak falsehood for his own ends, or for another's ends, or for some trifling worldly end.

(5) "Having abandoned divisive speech, he abstains from divisive speech. Having heard something here, he does not repeat it elsewhere in order to divide [those people] from these; or having heard something elsewhere, he does not repeat it to these people in order to divide [them] from those. Thus he is one who reunites those who are divided, a promoter of unity, who enjoys concord, rejoices in concord, delights in concord, a speaker of words that promote concord.

(6) "Having abandoned harsh speech, he abstains from harsh speech. He speaks such words as are gentle, pleasing to the ear, and lovable, as go to the heart, are courteous, desired by many, and agreeable to many.

(7) "Having abandoned idle chatter, he abstains from idle

chatter. He speaks at a proper time, speaks truth, speaks what is beneficial, speaks on the Dhamma and the discipline; at a proper time he speaks such words as are worth recording, reasonable, succinct, and beneficial.

"It is in this way that purity by speech is fourfold.

"And how, Cunda, is purity by mind threefold?

(8) "Here, someone is without longing. He does not long for the wealth and property of others thus: 'Oh, may what belongs to another be mine!'

(9) "He is of good will and his intentions are free of hate thus: 'May these beings live happily, free from enmity, affliction, and anxiety!'

(10) "He holds right view [268] and has a correct perspective thus: 'There is what is given, sacrificed, and offered; there is fruit and result of good and bad actions; there is this world and the other world; there is mother and father; there are beings spontaneously reborn; there are in the world ascetics and brahmins of right conduct and right practice who, having realized this world and the other world for themselves by direct knowledge, make them known to others.'

"It is in this way that purity by mind is threefold."

"These, Cunda, are the ten courses of wholesome kamma. If one engages in these ten courses of wholesome kamma, then, if one gets up early and strokes the ground from one's bed, one is pure, and if one doesn't stroke the ground, one is pure. If one strokes wet cow dung, one is pure, and if one doesn't stroke wet cow dung, one is pure. If one strokes green grass, one is pure, and if one doesn't stroke green grass, one is pure. If one tends the sacred fire, one is pure, and if one doesn't tend the sacred fire, one is pure. If one pays homage to the sun with reverential salutation, one is pure, and if one doesn't pay homage to the sun with reverential salutation, one is pure. If one immerses oneself in water three times including the evening, one is pure, and if one doesn't immerse oneself in water three times including the evening, one is pure. For what reason? Because these ten courses of wholesome kamma are themselves pure and purifying. It is because people engage in these ten courses of wholesome kamma that the devas, human beings, and other good destinations are seen."

When this was said, Cunda, the smith's son, said to the Blessed One: "Excellent, Bhante! . . . Let the Blessed One accept me as a lay follower who from today has gone for refuge for life." [269]

177 (11) Jāṇussoṇī

Then the brahmin Jāṇussoṇī approached the Blessed One and exchanged greetings with him. When they had concluded their greetings and cordial talk, he sat down to one side and said to the Blessed One:

"Master Gotama, we brahmins give gifts and perform the memorial rites for the dead[2169] with the thought: 'Let our gift be of benefit to our departed relatives and family members. Let our departed relatives and family members partake of our gift.' Can our gift, Master Gotama, actually be of benefit to our departed relatives and family members? Can our departed relatives and family members actually partake of our gift?"

"On a right occasion, brahmin, it can be of benefit, not on a wrong occasion."

"But, Master Gotama, what is a right occasion and what is a wrong occasion?"

"Here, brahmin, someone destroys life, takes what is not given, engages in sexual misconduct, speaks falsehood, speaks divisively, speaks harshly, indulges in idle chatter; he is full of longing, has a mind of ill will, and holds wrong view. With the breakup of the body, after death, he is reborn in hell.[2170] He sustains himself and subsists there on the food of the hell-beings. This is a wrong occasion, when the gift is not of benefit to one living there.

"Someone else destroys life . . . and holds wrong view. With the breakup of the body, after death, he is reborn in the animal realm. He sustains himself and subsists there on the food of animals. This, too, is a wrong occasion, when the gift is not of benefit to one living there.

"Still another abstains from the destruction of life, from taking what is not given, from sexual misconduct, from false speech, from divisive [270] speech, from harsh speech, from idle chatter; he is without longing, of good will, and holds right view. With the breakup of the body, after death, he is reborn in companionship with human beings. He sustains himself and subsists there on the food of human beings. This, too, is a wrong occasion, when the gift is not of benefit to one living there.

"Still another abstains from the destruction of life . . . and holds right view. With the breakup of the body, after death, he is reborn in companionship with the devas. He sustains himself and subsists there on the food of devas. This, too, is a wrong occasion, when the gift is not of benefit to one living there.

"Still another destroys life . . . and holds wrong view. With the breakup of the body, after death, he is reborn in the sphere of afflicted spirits. He sustains himself and subsists there on the food of afflicted spirits, or else he sustains himself there on what his friends, companions, relatives, or family members in this world offer to him. This is a right occasion, when the gift is of benefit to one living there."

"But, Master Gotama, who partakes of the gift if that deceased relative or family member has not been reborn in that place?"

"Other departed relatives or family members who have been reborn[2171] in that place partake of the gift."

"But, Master Gotama, who partakes of the gift if neither that deceased relative or family member nor any others have been reborn in that place?"

"Over this long stretch of time [in saṃsāra], brahmin, it is impossible and inconceivable for that place to be devoid of [271] one's departed relatives and family members. Further, for the donor too it is not fruitless."

"Does Master Gotama posit [the value of giving] even on the wrong occasion?"[2172]

"Brahmin, I posit [the value of giving] even on the wrong occasion.

"Here, brahmin, someone destroys life, takes what is not given, engages in sexual misconduct, speaks falsehood, speaks divisively, speaks harshly, indulges in idle chatter; he is full of longing, has a mind of ill will, and holds wrong view. He gives an ascetic or a brahmin food and drink; clothing and a vehicle; garlands, scents, and unguents; bedding, dwellings, and lighting. With the breakup of the body, after death, he is reborn in companionship with elephants. There he gains food and drink, garlands and various ornaments.

"Since he here destroyed life . . . and held wrong view, with the breakup of the body, after death, he is reborn in companionship with elephants. But since he gave an ascetic or a brahmin food and drink . . . he there gains food and drink, garlands and various ornaments.

"Someone else destroys life . . . and holds wrong view. He gives an ascetic or a brahmin food and drink . . . and lighting. With the breakup of the body, after death, he is reborn in companionship with horses . . . cattle . . . dogs. There he gains food and drink, garlands and various ornaments.

"Since he here destroyed life . . . [272] . . . and held wrong view, with the breakup of the body, after death, he is reborn in companionship with horses . . . cattle . . . dogs. But since he gave an ascetic or a brahmin food and drink . . . he there gains food and drink, garlands and various ornaments.

"Still another abstains from the destruction of life, from taking what is not given, from sexual misconduct, from false speech, from divisive speech, from harsh speech, from idle chatter; he is without longing, of good will, and holds right view. He gives an ascetic or a brahmin food and drink; clothing and a vehicle; garlands, scents, and unguents; bedding, dwellings, and lighting. With the breakup of the body, after death, he is reborn in companionship with human beings. There he gains the five objects of human sensual pleasure.

"Since he here abstained from the destruction of life . . . and held right view, with the breakup of the body, after death, he is reborn in companionship with human beings. And since he gave an ascetic or a brahmin food and drink . . . he there gains the five objects of human sensual pleasure.

"Still another abstains from the destruction of life . . . and holds right view. He gives an ascetic or a brahmin food and drink . . . and lighting. With the breakup of the body, after death, he is reborn in companionship with the devas. There [273] he gains the five objects of celestial sensual pleasure.

"Since he here abstained from the destruction of life . . . and held right view, with the breakup of the body, after death, he is reborn in companionship with the devas. And since he gave an ascetic or a brahmin food and drink . . . he there gains the five objects of celestial sensual pleasure. [That is why I said:] 'Further, for the donor too it is not fruitless.'"

"It's astounding and amazing, Master Gotama, that there is reason to give gifts and perform the memorial rites for the dead, since for the donor too it is not fruitless."

"So it is, brahmin! So it is, brahmin! For the donor too it is not fruitless."

"Excellent, Master Gotama! ... Let Master Gotama accept me as a lay follower who from today has gone for refuge for life."

III. Good[2173]

178 (1) Good

"Bhikkhus, I will teach you what is good and what is bad. Listen and attend closely. I will speak."

"Yes, [274] Bhante," those bhikkhus replied. The Blessed One said this:

"And what, bhikkhus, is bad? The destruction of life, taking what is not given, sexual misconduct, false speech, divisive speech, harsh speech, idle chatter, longing, ill will, and wrong view. This is called bad.

"And what, bhikkhus, is good? Abstention from the destruction of life, abstention from taking what is not given, abstention from sexual misconduct, abstention from false speech, abstention from divisive speech, abstention from harsh speech, abstention from idle chatter, non-longing, good will, and right view. This is called good."

179 (2)–188 (11) The Noble Dhamma, Etc.

(179) "Bhikkhus, I will teach you the noble Dhamma and the ignoble Dhamma ... (180) ... the wholesome and the unwholesome ... [275] ... (181) ... what is beneficial and what is harmful ... (182) ... the Dhamma and what is non-Dhamma ... (183) ... the tainted Dhamma and the taintless one ... [276] ... (184) ... the blameworthy Dhamma and the blameless one ... (185) ... the tormenting Dhamma and the untormenting one ... (186) ... the Dhamma that leads to building up and the one that leads to dismantling ... [277] ... (187) ... the Dhamma with suffering as its outcome and the one with happiness as its outcome ... (188) ... the Dhamma that results in suffering and the one that results in happiness. ...

"And what, bhikkhus, is the Dhamma that results in suffering? The destruction of life ... and wrong view. This is called the Dhamma that results in suffering.

"And what, bhikkhus, is the Dhamma that results in happiness? Abstention from the destruction of life ... and right view. This is called the Dhamma that results in happiness." [278]

IV. Noble Path

189 (1) The Noble Path

"Bhikkhus, I will teach you the noble path and the ignoble path. Listen and attend closely.... And what, bhikkhus, is the ignoble path? The destruction of life ... and wrong view. This is called the ignoble path.

"And what, bhikkhus, is the noble path? Abstention from the destruction of life ... and right view. This is called the noble path."

190 (2)–198 (10) The Dark Path, Etc.

(190) "Bhikkhus, I will teach you the dark path and the bright path ... (191) ... the good Dhamma and the bad Dhamma ... [279] (192) ... the Dhamma of a good person and that of a bad person ... (193) ... the Dhamma to be aroused and that not to be aroused ... (194) ... the Dhamma to be pursued and that not to be pursued ... [280] (195) ... the Dhamma to be developed and that not to be developed ... (196) ... the Dhamma to be cultivated and that not to be cultivated ... (197) ... the Dhamma to be recollected and that not to be recollected ... [281] (198) ... the Dhamma to be realized and that not to be realized....

"And what, bhikkhus, is the Dhamma not to be realized? The destruction of life ... and wrong view. This is called the Dhamma not to be realized.

"And what, bhikkhus, is the Dhamma to be realized? Abstention from the destruction of life ... and right view. This is called the Dhamma to be realized."

V. Another Chapter on Persons[2174]

199 (1) Associate With

"Bhikkhus, one should not associate with a person who possesses ten qualities. What ten? He destroys life, takes what is not given, engages in sexual misconduct, speaks falsehood, speaks divisively, speaks harshly, indulges in idle chatter; he is full of longing, has a mind of ill will, and holds wrong view. One should not associate with a person who possesses these ten qualities.

"Bhikkhus, one should associate with a person who possesses

ten qualities. What ten? He abstains from the destruction of life, from taking what is not given, from sexual misconduct, from false speech, from divisive speech, from harsh speech, [282] from idle chatter; he is without longing, of good will, and holds right view. One should associate with a person who possesses these ten qualities."

200 (2)–210 (12) Resort, Etc.[2175]

(200) "Bhikkhus, one should not resort to a person who possesses ten qualities . . . one should resort to . . . (201) . . . one should not attend on . . . one should attend on . . . (202) . . . one should not venerate . . . one should venerate . . . (203) . . . one should not praise . . . one should praise . . . (204) . . . one should not revere . . . one should revere . . . (205) . . . one should not show deference to . . . one should show deference to a person who possesses ten qualities. . . . (206) A person who possesses ten qualities is not successful . . . is successful . . . (207) . . . is not purified . . . is purified . . . (208) . . . does not overcome conceit . . . overcomes conceit . . . (209) . . . does not grow in wisdom . . . grows in wisdom . . . (210) . . . generates much demerit . . . generates much merit. What ten? He abstains from the destruction of life, from taking what is not given, from sexual misconduct, from false speech, from divisive speech, from harsh speech, from idle chatter; he is without longing, of good will, and holds right view. A person who possesses these ten qualities generates much merit." [283]

An Extra Fifty

I. The Deed-Born Body

211 (1) Hell (1)

"Bhikkhus, possessing ten qualities, one is deposited in hell as if brought there. What ten?

(1) "Here, someone destroys life; he is murderous, bloody-handed, given to blows and violence, merciless to living beings.

(2) "He takes what is not given; he steals the wealth and property of others in the village or forest.

(3) "He engages in sexual misconduct; he has sexual relations

with women who are protected by their mother, father, mother and father, brother, sister, or relatives; who are protected by their Dhamma; who have a husband; whose violation entails a penalty; or even with one already engaged.

(4) "He speaks falsehood. If he is summoned to a council, to an assembly, to his relatives' presence, to his guild, or to the court, and questioned as a witness thus: 'So, good man, tell what you know,' then, not knowing, he says, 'I know,' or knowing, he says, 'I do not know'; not seeing, he says, 'I see,' or seeing, he says, 'I do not see.' Thus he consciously speaks falsehood for his own ends, or for another's ends, or for some trifling worldly end.

(5) "He speaks divisively. Having heard something here, he repeats it elsewhere in order to divide [those people] from these; or having heard something elsewhere, he repeats it to these people in order to divide [them] from those. Thus he is one who divides those who are united, a creator of divisions, one who enjoys factions, rejoices in factions, delights in factions, a speaker of words that create factions.

(6) "He speaks harshly. He utters such words as are rough, hard, hurtful to others, offensive to others, bordering on anger, unconducive to concentration.

(7) "He indulges in idle chatter. He speaks at an improper time, speaks falsely, speaks what is unbeneficial, speaks contrary to the Dhamma and the discipline; at an improper time he speaks such words as are worthless, unreasonable, rambling, and unbeneficial. [284]

(8) "He is full of longing. He longs for the wealth and property of others thus: 'Oh, may what belongs to another be mine!'

(9) "He has a mind of ill will and intentions of hate thus: 'May these beings be slain, slaughtered, cut off, destroyed, or annihilated!'

(10) "He holds wrong view and has an incorrect perspective thus: 'There is nothing given, nothing sacrificed, nothing offered; there is no fruit or result of good and bad actions; there is no this world, no other world; there is no mother, no father; there are no beings spontaneously reborn; there are in the world no ascetics and brahmins of right conduct and right practice who, having realized this world and the other world for themselves by direct knowledge, make them known to others.'

"One possessing these ten qualities is deposited in hell as if brought there.

"Bhikkhus, one possessing ten qualities is deposited in heaven as if brought there. What ten?

(1) "Here, someone, having abandoned the destruction of life, abstains from the destruction of life. With the rod and weapon laid aside, conscientious and kindly, he dwells compassionate toward all living beings.

(2) "Having abandoned the taking of what is not given, he abstains from taking what is not given. He does not steal the wealth and property of others in the village or in the forest.

(3) "Having abandoned sexual misconduct, he abstains from sexual misconduct. He does not have sexual relations with women who are protected by their mother, father, mother and father, brother, sister, or relatives; who are protected by their Dhamma; who have a husband; whose violation entails a penalty; or even with one already engaged.

(4) "Having abandoned false speech, he abstains from false speech. If he is summoned to a council, to an assembly, to his relatives' presence, to his guild, or to the court, and questioned as a witness thus: 'So, good man, tell what you know,' then, not knowing, he says, 'I do not know,' or knowing, he says, 'I know'; not seeing, he says, 'I do not see,' or seeing, he says, 'I see.' Thus he does not consciously speak falsehood for his own ends, or for another's ends, or for some trifling worldly end. [285]

(5) "Having abandoned divisive speech, he abstains from divisive speech. Having heard something here, he does not repeat it elsewhere in order to divide [those people] from these; or having heard something elsewhere, he does not repeat it to these people in order to divide [them] from those. Thus he is one who reunites those who are divided, a promoter of unity, who enjoys concord, rejoices in concord, delights in concord, a speaker of words that promote concord.

(6) "Having abandoned harsh speech, he abstains from harsh speech. He speaks such words as are gentle, pleasing to the ear, and lovable, as go to the heart, are courteous, desired by many, and agreeable to many.

(7) "Having abandoned idle chatter, he abstains from idle chatter. He speaks at a proper time, speaks truth, speaks what is beneficial, speaks on the Dhamma and the discipline; at a

proper time he speaks such words as are worth recording, reasonable, succinct, and beneficial.

(8) "He is without longing. He does not long for the wealth and property of others thus: 'Oh, may what belongs to another be mine!'

(9) "He is of good will and his intentions are free of hate thus: 'May these beings live happily, free from enmity, affliction, and anxiety!'

(10) "He holds right view and has a correct perspective thus: 'There is what is given, sacrificed, and offered; there is fruit and result of good and bad actions; there is this world and the other world; there is mother and father; there are beings spontaneously reborn; there are in the world ascetics and brahmins of right conduct and right practice who, having realized this world and the other world for themselves by direct knowledge, make them known to others.'

"One possessing these ten qualities is deposited in heaven as if brought there."

212 (2) Hell (2)

"Bhikkhus, possessing ten qualities, one is deposited in hell as if brought there. What ten?[2176]

(1) "Here, someone destroys life; he is murderous, bloody-handed, given to blows and violence, merciless to living beings. (2) He takes what is not given ... (3) He engages in sexual misconduct ... (4) He speaks falsehood ... (5) He speaks divisively ... (6) He speaks harshly [286] ... (7) He indulges in idle chatter ... (8) He is full of longing ... (9) He has a mind of ill will and intentions of hate ... (10) He holds wrong view and has an incorrect perspective thus: 'There is nothing given ... there are in the world no ascetics and brahmins of right conduct and right practice who, having realized this world and the other world for themselves by direct knowledge, make them known to others.' One possessing these ten qualities is deposited in hell as if brought there.

"Bhikkhus, one possessing ten qualities is deposited in heaven as if brought there. What ten?

(1) "Here, someone, having abandoned the destruction of life, abstains from the destruction of life; with the rod and weapon laid aside, conscientious and kindly, he dwells compassionate toward all living beings. (2) Having abandoned the taking of

what is not given, he abstains from taking what is not given ... (3) Having abandoned sexual misconduct, he abstains from sexual misconduct ... (4) Having abandoned false speech, he abstains from false speech ... (5) Having abandoned divisive speech, he abstains from divisive speech ... (6) Having abandoned harsh speech, he abstains from harsh speech ... (7) Having abandoned idle chatter, he abstains from idle chatter ... (8) He is without longing ... (9) He is of good will ... (10) He holds right view and has a correct perspective thus: 'There is what is given ... there are in the world ascetics and brahmins of right conduct and right practice who, having realized this world and the other world for themselves by direct knowledge, make them known to others.' One possessing these ten qualities is deposited in heaven as if brought there."

213 (3) Women

"Bhikkhus, possessing ten qualities, women are deposited in hell as if brought there. What ten? [287] (1) They destroy life ... [as above] ... and (10) hold wrong view. Possessing these ten qualities, women are deposited in hell as if brought there.

"Bhikkhus, possessing ten qualities, women are deposited in heaven as if brought there. What ten? (1) They abstain from the destruction of life ... [as above] ... and (10) hold right view. Possessing these ten qualities, women are deposited in heaven as if brought there."

214 (4) Female Lay Follower

"Bhikkhus, possessing ten qualities, a female lay follower is deposited in hell as if brought there. What ten? (1) She destroys life ... and (10) holds wrong view. Possessing these ten qualities, a female lay follower is deposited in hell as if brought there.

"Bhikkhus, possessing ten qualities, a female lay follower is deposited in heaven as if brought there. What ten? (1) She abstains from the destruction of life ... and (10) holds right view. Possessing these ten qualities, a female lay follower is deposited in heaven as if brought there." [288]

215 (5) Self-Confidence

"Bhikkhus, possessing ten qualities, a female lay follower dwells without self-confidence at home. What ten? (1) She destroys life

. . . and (10) holds wrong view. Possessing these ten qualities, a female lay follower dwells without self-confidence at home.

"Bhikkhus, possessing ten qualities, a female lay follower dwells self-confident at home. What ten? (1) She abstains from the destruction of life . . . and (10) holds right view. Possessing these ten qualities, a female lay follower dwells self-confident at home."

216 (6) Creeping

"Bhikkhus, I will teach you an exposition of the Dhamma on creeping.[2177] Listen and attend closely. I will speak."

"Yes, Bhante," those bhikkhus replied. The Blessed One said this:

"And what, bhikkhus, is that exposition of the Dhamma on creeping? Bhikkhus, beings are the owners of their kamma, the heirs of their kamma; they have kamma as their origin, kamma as their relative, kamma as their resort; whatever kamma they do, good or bad, they are its heirs. [289]

(1) "Here, someone destroys life; he is murderous, bloody-handed, given to blows and violence, merciless to living beings. He creeps along by body, speech, and mind.[2178] His bodily kamma is crooked; his verbal kamma is crooked; his mental kamma is crooked. His destination is crooked; his rebirth is crooked. But for one with a crooked destination and rebirth, I say, there is one of two destinations: either the exclusively painful hells or a species of creeping animal. And what are the species of creeping animals? The snake, the scorpion, the centipede, the mongoose, the cat, the mouse, and the owl,[2179] or any other animals that creep away when they see people. Thus a being is reborn from a being; one is reborn through one's deeds. When one has been reborn, contacts affect one. It is in this way, I say, that beings are the heirs of their kamma.

(2) "Someone takes what is not given . . . (3) . . . engages in sexual misconduct . . . (4) . . . speaks falsehood . . . (5) . . . speaks divisively . . . (6) . . . speaks harshly . . . (7) . . . indulges in idle chatter . . . (8) . . . is full of longing . . . (9) . . . has a mind of ill will and intentions of hate . . . (10) . . . holds wrong view and has an incorrect perspective thus: 'There is nothing given . . . there are in the world no ascetics and brahmins of right conduct and right practice who, having realized this world and the other

world for themselves by direct knowledge, make them known to others.' He creeps along by body, speech, and mind. His bodily kamma is crooked . . . His destination is crooked; [290] his rebirth is crooked. . . . Thus a being is reborn from a being; one is reborn through one's deeds. When one has been reborn, contacts affect one. It is in this way, I say, that beings are the heirs of their kamma.

"Bhikkhus, beings are the owners of their kamma, the heirs of their kamma; they have kamma as their origin, kamma as their relative, kamma as their resort; whatever kamma they do, good or bad, they are its heirs.

(1) "Here, having abandoned the destruction of life, someone abstains from the destruction of life; with the rod and weapon laid aside, conscientious and kindly, he dwells compassionate toward all living beings. He does not creep along by body, speech, and mind. His bodily kamma is straight; his verbal kamma is straight; his mental kamma is straight. His destination is straight; his rebirth is straight. But for one with a straight destination and rebirth, I say, there is one of two destinations: either the exclusively pleasant heavens or eminent families, such as those of affluent khattiyas, affluent brahmins, or affluent householders, [families that are] rich, with great wealth and property, abundant gold and silver, abundant treasures and belongings, abundant wealth and grain. Thus a being is reborn from a being; one is reborn through one's deeds. When one has been reborn, contacts affect one. It is in this way, I say, that beings are the heirs of their kamma.

(2) "Having abandoned the taking of what is not given, someone abstains from taking what is not given . . . (3) . . . abstains from sexual misconduct . . . [291] (4) . . . abstains from false speech . . . (5) . . . abstains from divisive speech . . . (6) . . . abstains from harsh speech . . . (7) . . . abstains from idle chatter . . . (8) . . . is without longing . . . (9) . . . is of good will . . . (10) . . . holds right view and has a correct perspective thus: 'There is what is given . . . there are in the world ascetics and brahmins of right conduct and right practice who, having realized this world and the other world for themselves by direct knowledge, make them known to others.' He does not creep along by body, speech, and mind. His bodily kamma is straight . . . His destination is straight; his rebirth is straight. . . . Thus a being is reborn from a being; one is reborn through one's deeds. When one has been reborn,

contacts affect one. It is in this way, I say, that beings are the heirs of their kamma.

"Bhikkhus, beings are the owners of their kamma, the heirs of their kamma; they have kamma as their origin, kamma as their relative, kamma as their resort; whatever kamma they do, good or bad, they are its heirs.

"This, bhikkhus, is that exposition of the Dhamma on creeping." [292]

217 (7) Volitional (1)

"Bhikkhus, I do not say that there is a termination of volitional kamma[2180] that has been done and accumulated so long as one has not experienced [its results], and that may be in this very life, or in the [next] rebirth, or on some subsequent occasion. But I do not say that there is making an end of suffering so long as one has not experienced [the results of] volitional kamma that has been done and accumulated.[2181]

"As to this, bhikkhus, there is a threefold corruption and failure of bodily kamma,[2182] arisen from unwholesome volition, having a painful outcome and result; a fourfold corruption and failure of verbal kamma, arisen from unwholesome volition, having a painful outcome and result; and a threefold corruption and failure of mental kamma, arisen from unwholesome volition, having a painful outcome and result.

"And how, bhikkhus, is there a threefold corruption and failure of bodily kamma, arisen from unwholesome volition, having a painful outcome and result?

(1) "Here, someone destroys life. He is murderous, bloody-handed, given to blows and violence, merciless to living beings.

(2) "He takes what is not given. He steals the wealth and property of others in the village or forest.

(3) "He engages in sexual misconduct. He has sexual relations with women who are protected by their mother, father, mother and father, brother, sister, or relatives; who are protected by their Dhamma; who have a husband; whose violation entails a penalty; or even with one already engaged.

"It is in this way that there is a threefold corruption and failure of bodily kamma, arisen from unwholesome volition, having a painful outcome and result.

"And how, bhikkhus, is there a fourfold corruption and

failure of verbal kamma, arisen from unwholesome volition, having a painful outcome and result? [293]

(4) "Here, someone speaks falsehood. If he is summoned to a council, to an assembly, to his relatives' presence, to his guild, or to the court, and questioned as a witness thus: 'So, good man, tell what you know,' then, not knowing, he says, 'I know,' or knowing, he says, 'I do not know'; not seeing, he says, 'I see,' or seeing, he says, 'I do not see.' Thus he consciously speaks falsehood for his own ends, or for another's ends, or for some trifling worldly end.

(5) "He speaks divisively. Having heard something here, he repeats it elsewhere in order to divide [those people] from these; or having heard something elsewhere, he repeats it to these people in order to divide [them] from those. Thus he is one who divides those who are united, a creator of divisions, one who enjoys factions, rejoices in factions, delights in factions, a speaker of words that create factions.

(6) "He speaks harshly. He utters such words as are rough, hard, hurtful to others, offensive to others, bordering on anger, unconducive to concentration.

(7) "He indulges in idle chatter. He speaks at an improper time, speaks falsely, speaks what is unbeneficial, speaks contrary to the Dhamma and the discipline; at an improper time he speaks such words as are worthless, unreasonable, rambling, and unbeneficial.

"It is in this way that there is a fourfold corruption and failure of verbal kamma, arisen from unwholesome volition, having a painful outcome and result.

"And how, bhikkhus, is there a threefold corruption and failure of mental kamma, arisen from unwholesome volition, having a painful outcome and result?

(8) "Here, someone is full of longing. He longs for the wealth and property of others thus: 'Oh, may what belongs to another be mine!'

(9) "He has a mind of ill will and intentions of hate thus: 'May these beings be slain, slaughtered, cut off, destroyed, or annihilated!'

(10) "He holds wrong view and has an incorrect perspective thus: 'There is nothing given, nothing sacrificed, nothing offered; there is no fruit or result of good and bad actions; there

is no this world, no other world; there is no mother, no father; there are no beings spontaneously reborn; [294] there are in the world no ascetics and brahmins of right conduct and right practice who, having realized this world and the other world for themselves by direct knowledge, make them known to others.'

"It is in this way that there is a threefold corruption and failure of mental kamma, arisen from unwholesome volition, having a painful outcome and result.

"It is, bhikkhus, because of the threefold corruption and failure of bodily kamma, arisen from unwholesome volition, that with the breakup of the body, after death, beings are reborn in the plane of misery, in a bad destination, in the lower world, in hell; or it is because of the fourfold corruption and failure of verbal kamma, arisen from unwholesome volition, that with the breakup of the body, after death, beings are reborn in the plane of misery, in a bad destination, in the lower world, in hell; or it is because of the threefold corruption and failure of mental kamma, arisen from unwholesome volition, that with the breakup of the body, after death, beings are reborn in the plane of misery, in a bad destination, in the lower world, in hell. Just as dice, when thrown upward, will rest firmly wherever they fall,[2183] so too, it is because of the threefold corruption and failure of bodily kamma . . . or it is because of the fourfold corruption and failure of verbal kamma . . . or it is because of the threefold corruption and failure of mental kamma, arisen from unwholesome volition, that with the breakup of the body, after death, beings are reborn in the plane of misery, in a bad destination, in the lower world, in hell.

"Bhikkhus, I do not say that there is a termination of volitional kamma that has been done and accumulated so long as one has not experienced [its results], and that may be in this very life, or in the [next] rebirth, or on some subsequent occasion. But I do not say that there is making an end of suffering so long as one has not experienced [the results of] volitional kamma that has been done and accumulated.

"As to this, bhikkhus, there is a threefold success of bodily kamma, arisen from wholesome volition, having a pleasant outcome and result; a fourfold success of verbal kamma, arisen from wholesome volition, having a pleasant outcome and result; and a threefold success of mental kamma, [295] arisen from wholesome volition, having a pleasant outcome and result.

"And how, bhikkhus, is there a threefold success of bodily kamma, arisen from wholesome volition, having a pleasant outcome and result?

(1) "Here, someone, having abandoned the destruction of life, abstains from the destruction of life. With the rod and weapon laid aside, conscientious and kindly, he dwells compassionate toward all living beings.

(2) "Having abandoned the taking of what is not given, he abstains from taking what is not given. He does not steal the wealth and property of others in the village or in the forest.

(3) "Having abandoned sexual misconduct, he abstains from sexual misconduct. He does not have sexual relations with women who are protected by their mother, father, mother and father, brother, sister, or relatives; who are protected by their Dhamma; who have a husband; whose violation entails a penalty; or even with one already engaged.

"It is in this way that there is a threefold success of bodily kamma, arisen from wholesome volition, having a pleasant outcome and result.

"And how, bhikkhus, is there a fourfold success of verbal kamma, arisen from wholesome volition, having a pleasant outcome and result?

(4) "Here, having abandoned false speech, someone abstains from false speech. If he is summoned to a council, to an assembly, to his relatives' presence, to his guild, or to the court, and questioned as a witness thus: 'So, good man, tell what you know,' then, not knowing, he says, 'I do not know,' or knowing, he says, 'I know'; not seeing, he says, 'I do not see,' or seeing, he says, 'I see.' Thus he does not consciously speak falsehood for his own ends, or for another's ends, or for some trifling worldly end.

(5) "Having abandoned divisive speech, he abstains from divisive speech. Having heard something here, he does not repeat it elsewhere in order to divide [those people] from these; or having heard something elsewhere, he does not repeat it to these people in order to divide [them] from those. Thus he is one who reunites those who are divided, [296] a promoter of unity, who enjoys concord, rejoices in concord, delights in concord, a speaker of words that promote concord.

(6) "Having abandoned harsh speech, he abstains from harsh speech. He speaks such words as are gentle, pleasing to the ear, and lovable, as go to the heart, are courteous, desired by many, and agreeable to many.

(7) "Having abandoned idle chatter, he abstains from idle chatter. He speaks at a proper time, speaks truth, speaks what is beneficial, speaks on the Dhamma and the discipline; at a proper time he speaks such words as are worth recording, reasonable, succinct, and beneficial.

"It is in this way that there is a fourfold success of verbal kamma, arisen from wholesome volition, having a pleasant outcome and result.

"And how, bhikkhus, is there a threefold success of mental kamma, arisen from wholesome volition, having a pleasant outcome and result?

(8) "Here, someone is without longing. He does not long for the wealth and property of others thus: 'Oh, may what belongs to another be mine!'

(9) "He is of good will and his intentions are free of hate thus: 'May these beings live happily, free from enmity, affliction, and anxiety!'

(10) "He holds right view and has a correct perspective thus: 'There is what is given, sacrificed, and offered; there is fruit and result of good and bad actions; there is this world and the other world; there is mother and father; there are beings spontaneously reborn; there are in the world ascetics and brahmins of right conduct and right practice who, having realized this world and the other world for themselves by direct knowledge, make them known to others.'

"It is in this way that there is a threefold success of mental kamma, arisen from wholesome volition, having a pleasant outcome and result.

"It is, bhikkhus, because of the threefold success of bodily kamma, arisen from wholesome volition, that with the breakup of the body, after death, beings are reborn in a good destination, in a heavenly world; or it is because of the fourfold success of verbal kamma, arisen from wholesome volition, that with the breakup of the body, after death, beings are reborn in a good destination, in a heavenly world; or it is because of the threefold success of mental kamma, arisen from wholesome volition, that with the breakup of the body, after death, beings are reborn in a good destination, in a heavenly world. Just as dice, when thrown upward, will rest firmly wherever they fall, so too, it is because of the threefold success of bodily kamma . . . [297] . . . or it is because of the fourfold success of verbal kamma . . . or it is because of the threefold success of mental kamma, arisen from wholesome volition, that with the breakup of the body, after death, beings are reborn in a good destination, in a heavenly world.

"Bhikkhus, I do not say that there is a termination of volitional kamma that has been done and accumulated so long as one has not experienced [its results], and that may be in this very life, or in the [next] rebirth, or on some subsequent occasion. But I do not say that there is making an end of suffering so long as one has not experienced [the results of] volitional kammas that have been done and accumulated."

218 (8) Volitional (2)[2184]

"Bhikkhus, I do not say that there is a termination of volitional kamma that has been done and accumulated so long as one has not experienced [its results], and that may be in this very life, or in the [next] rebirth, or on some subsequent occasion. But I do not say that there is making an end of suffering so long as one has not experienced [the results of] volitional kamma that has been done and accumulated.

"As to this, bhikkhus, there is a threefold corruption and failure of bodily kamma, arisen from unwholesome volition, having a painful outcome and result; a fourfold corruption and failure of verbal kamma, arisen from unwholesome volition, having a painful outcome and result; and a threefold corruption and failure of mental kamma, arisen from unwholesome volition, having a painful outcome and result.

(1)–(10) "And how, bhikkhus, is there a threefold corruption and failure of bodily kamma . . . a fourfold corruption and failure of verbal kamma . . . [298] . . . a threefold corruption and failure of mental kamma? . . . [all as in 10:217] . . . having a painful outcome and result.

"It is, bhikkhus, because of the threefold corruption and failure of bodily kamma, arisen from unwholesome volition . . . or it is because of the fourfold corruption and failure of verbal kamma, arisen from unwholesome volition . . . or it is because of the threefold corruption and failure of mental kamma, arisen from unwholesome volition, that with the breakup of the body, after death, beings are reborn in the plane of misery, in a bad destination, in the lower world, in hell.

"Bhikkhus, I do not say that there is a termination of volitional kamma that has been done and accumulated so long as one has not experienced [its results], and that may be in this very life, or in the [next] rebirth, or on some subsequent occasion. But I do not say that there is making an end of suffering so long as one has not experienced [the results of] volitional kamma that has been done and accumulated.

"As to this, bhikkhus, there is a threefold success of bodily kamma, arisen from wholesome volition, having a pleasant outcome and result. There is a fourfold success of verbal kamma, arisen from wholesome volition, having a pleasant outcome and result. There is a threefold success of mental kamma, arisen from wholesome volition, having a pleasant outcome and result.

(1)–(10) "And how, bhikkhus, is there a threefold success of bodily kamma . . . a fourfold success of verbal kamma . . . [299] . . . a threefold success of mental kamma? . . . [all as in 10:217] . . . having a painful outcome and result.

"It is, bhikkhus, because of the threefold success of bodily kamma . . . or it is because of the fourfold success of verbal kamma . . . or it is because of the threefold success of mental kamma, arisen from wholesome volition, that with the breakup of the body, after death, beings are reborn in a good destination, in a heavenly world.

"Bhikkhus, I do not say that there is a termination of volitional kamma that has been done and accumulated so long as one has not experienced [its results], and that may be in this very life, or in the [next] rebirth, or on some subsequent occasion. But I do not say that there is making an end of suffering so long as one has not experienced [the results of] volitional kamma that has been done and accumulated."

219 (9) The Deed-Born Body

"Bhikkhus, I do not say that there is a termination of volitional kamma that has been done and accumulated so long as one has not experienced [its results], and that may be in this very life, or in the [next] rebirth, or on some subsequent occasion. But I do not say that there is making an end of suffering so long as one has not experienced [the results of] volitional kamma that has been done and accumulated.[2185]

"This noble disciple, bhikkhus, who is thus devoid of longing, devoid of ill will, unconfused, clearly comprehending, ever mindful, dwells pervading one quarter with a mind imbued with loving-kindness, likewise the second quarter, the third quarter, and the fourth quarter. Thus above, below, across, and everywhere, and to all as to himself, he dwells pervading the entire world with a mind imbued with loving-kindness, vast, exalted, measureless, without enmity, without ill will. He understands thus: 'Previously, my mind was limited and undeveloped, but now it is measureless and well developed. No measurable kamma remains or persists there.'[2186] [300]

"What do you think, bhikkhus, if a youth were to develop the liberation of mind by loving-kindness from his childhood on, would he do a bad deed?"[2187]

"No, Bhante."

"Could suffering affect him if he does no bad deed?"

"No, Bhante. For on what account could suffering affect one who does no bad deed?"[2188]

"A woman or a man should develop this liberation of mind by loving-kindness. A woman or a man cannot take this body with them when they go. Mortals have mind as their core.[2189]

"[The noble disciple] understands: 'Whatever bad deed I did here in the past with this deed-born body[2190] is all to be experienced here. It will not follow along.'[2191] When the liberation of mind by loving-kindness has been developed in this way, it leads to non-returning for a wise bhikkhu here[2192] who does not penetrate to a further liberation.[2193]

"This noble disciple, bhikkhus, who is thus devoid of longing, devoid of ill will, unconfused, clearly comprehending, ever mindful, dwells pervading one quarter with a mind imbued with compassion . . . with a mind imbued with altruistic joy . . . with a mind imbued with equanimity, likewise the second quarter, the third quarter, and the fourth quarter. Thus above, below, across, and everywhere, and to all as to himself, he dwells pervading the entire world with a mind imbued with equanimity, vast, exalted, measureless, without enmity, without ill will. He understands thus: 'Previously, my mind was limited and undeveloped, but now it is measureless and well developed. No measurable [301] kamma remains or persists there.'

"What do you think, bhikkhus, if a youth would develop the liberation of mind by equanimity, from his childhood on, would he do a bad deed?"

"No, Bhante."

"Could suffering affect him if he does no bad deed?"

"No, Bhante. For on what account could suffering affect one who does no bad deed?"

"A woman or a man should develop this liberation of mind by equanimity. A woman or a man cannot take this body with them when they go. Mortals have mind as their core.

"[The noble disciple] understands: 'Whatever bad deed I did here in the past with this deed-born body is all to be experienced here. It will not follow along.' When the liberation of mind by equanimity has been developed in this way, it leads to non-returning for a wise bhikkhu here who does not penetrate to a further liberation."

220 (10) Conduct Contrary to the Dhamma

Then a certain brahmin approached the Blessed One and exchanged greetings with him. When they had exchanged greetings and cordial talk, he sat down to one side and said to the Blessed One:

"Master Gotama, why is it that some beings here, with the breakup of the body, after death, are reborn in the plane of misery, in a bad destination, in the lower world, in hell?"

"It is, brahmin, because of unrighteous conduct, conduct contrary to the Dhamma, that some beings here, with the breakup of the body, after death, are reborn in the plane of misery, in a bad destination, in the lower world, in hell.

"Master Gotama, why is it that some beings here, [302] with the breakup of the body, after death, are reborn in a good destination, in a heavenly world?"

"It is, brahmin, because of righteous conduct, conduct in accordance with the Dhamma, that some beings here, with the breakup of the body, after death, are reborn in a good destination, in a heavenly world."

"I do not understand in detail the meaning of Master Gotama's statement that he has spoken in brief. Please let Master Gotama teach me the Dhamma in such a way that I might understand the meaning in detail."

"Well then, brahmin, listen and attend closely. I will speak."

"Yes, sir," that brahmin replied. The Blessed One said this:

"Brahmin, unrighteous conduct, conduct contrary to the Dhamma, is threefold by way of the body, fourfold by way of speech, and threefold by way of the mind.

"And how, brahmin, is unrighteous conduct, conduct contrary to the Dhamma, threefold by way of the body? . . . [here and below, the explanations are as in 10:217] . . . It is in this way that unrighteous conduct, conduct contrary to the Dhamma, is threefold by way of the mind.

"It is, brahmin, because of such unrighteous conduct, conduct contrary to the Dhamma, that some beings here, with the breakup of the body, after death, are reborn in the plane of misery, in a bad destination, in the lower world, in hell.

"Brahmin, righteous conduct, conduct in accordance with the Dhamma, is threefold by way of the body, fourfold by way of speech, and threefold by way of the mind.

"And how, brahmin, is righteous conduct, conduct in accordance with the Dhamma, threefold by way of the body? . . . [303] . . . It is in this way that righteous conduct, conduct in accordance with the Dhamma, is threefold by way of the mind.

"It is, brahmin, because of such righteous conduct, conduct in accordance with the Dhamma, that some beings here, with the breakup of the body, after death, are reborn in a good destination, in a heavenly world.

"Excellent, Master Gotama! . . . Let Master Gotama accept me as a lay follower who from today has gone for refuge for life."

II. Similarity

221 (1)

"Bhikkhus, possessing ten qualities, one is deposited in hell as if brought there. What ten? (1) One destroys life, (2) takes what is not given, (3) engages in sexual misconduct, (4) speaks falsely, (5) speaks divisively, (6) speaks harshly, (7) indulges in idle chatter, (8) is full of longing, (9) has a mind of ill will, and (10) holds wrong view. Possessing these ten qualities, one is deposited in hell as if brought there. [304]

"Possessing ten qualities, one is deposited in heaven as if brought there. What ten? (1) One abstains from the destruction of life, (2) abstains from taking what is not given, (3) abstains from sexual misconduct, (4) abstains from false speech, (5) abstains from divisive speech, (6) abstains from harsh speech, (7) abstains from idle chatter, (8) is without longing, (9) is of good will, and (10) holds right view. Possessing these ten qualities, one is deposited in heaven as if brought there."

222 (2)

"Bhikkhus, possessing twenty qualities, one is deposited in hell as if brought there. What twenty? (1) One destroys life oneself and (2) encourages others to destroy life . . . (19) one holds wrong view oneself and (20) encourages others in wrong view. Possessing these twenty qualities, one is deposited in hell as if brought there.

"Possessing twenty qualities, one is deposited in heaven as if brought there. What twenty? (1) One abstains from the destruction of life oneself and (2) encourages others to abstain from the destruction of life . . . [305] . . . (19) one holds right view oneself and (20) encourages others in right view. Possessing these twenty qualities, one is deposited in heaven as if brought there."

223 (3)

"Bhikkhus, possessing thirty qualities, one is deposited in hell as if brought there. What thirty? (1) One destroys life oneself, (2) encourages others to destroy life, and (3) approves of the destruction of life . . . (28) one holds wrong view oneself, (29) encourages others in wrong view, and (30) approves of wrong view. Possessing these thirty qualities, one is deposited in hell as if brought there.

"Possessing thirty qualities, one is deposited in heaven as if brought there. What thirty? [306] (1) One abstains from the destruction of life oneself, (2) encourages others to abstain from the destruction of life, and (3) approves of abstaining from the destruction of life . . . (28) one holds right view oneself, (29) encourages others in right view, and (30) approves of right view. Possessing these thirty qualities, one is deposited in heaven as if brought there."

224 (4)

"Bhikkhus, possessing forty qualities, one is deposited in hell as if brought there. What forty? (1) One destroys life oneself, (2) encourages others to destroy life, (3) approves of the destruction of life, and (4) speaks in praise of the destruction of life . . . [307] . . . (37) one holds wrong view oneself, (38) encourages others in wrong view, (39) approves of wrong view, and (40) speaks in praise of wrong view. Possessing these forty qualities, one is deposited in hell as if brought there.

"Possessing forty qualities, one is deposited in heaven as if brought there. What forty? (1) One abstains from the destruction of life oneself, (2) encourages others to abstain from the destruction of life, (3) approves of abstaining from the destruction of life, and (4) speaks in praise of abstaining from the destruction of life . . . [308] . . . (37) one holds right view oneself, (38) encourages others in right view, (39) approves of right view, and (40) speaks in praise of right view. Possessing these forty qualities, one is deposited in heaven as if brought there."

225 (5)

"Bhikkhus, possessing ten qualities, one maintains oneself in a maimed and injured condition . . . preserves oneself unmaimed and uninjured . . ."

226 (6)–228 (8)[2194]

"Bhikkhus, possessing twenty qualities . . . thirty qualities . . . forty qualities, one maintains oneself in a maimed and injured condition . . . preserves oneself unmaimed and uninjured . . ."

229 (9)

"Bhikkhus, possessing ten qualities, with the breakup of the body, after death, someone here is reborn in the plane of misery, in a bad destination, in the lower world, [309] in hell . . . someone here is reborn in a good destination, in a heavenly world."

230 (10)–232 (12)

"Bhikkhus, possessing twenty qualities . . . thirty qualities . . . forty qualities, someone here is reborn in the plane of misery, in a bad destination, in the lower world, in hell . . . someone here is reborn in a good destination, in a heavenly world."

233 (13)

"Bhikkhus, possessing ten qualities, one may be understood as a fool . . . one may be understood as a wise person."

234 (14)–236 (16)
"Bhikkhus, possessing twenty qualities . . . thirty qualities . . . forty qualities, one may be understood as a fool . . . one may be understood as a wise person."

III. Lust and So Forth Repetition Series[2195]

237 (1)[2196]
"Bhikkhus, for direct knowledge of lust, ten things are to be developed. What ten? The perception of unattractiveness, the perception of death, the perception of the repulsiveness of food, the perception of non-delight in the entire world, the perception of impermanence, the perception of suffering in the impermanent, the perception of non-self in what is suffering, the perception of abandoning, the perception of dispassion, and the perception of cessation. For direct knowledge of lust, these ten things are to be developed." [310]

238 (2)
"Bhikkhus, for direct knowledge of lust, ten things are to be developed. What ten? The perception of impermanence, the perception of non-self, the perception of the repulsiveness of food, the perception of non-delight in the entire world, the perception of a skeleton, the perception of a worm-infested corpse, the perception of a livid corpse, the perception of a festering corpse, the perception of a fissured corpse, and the perception of a bloated corpse. For direct knowledge of lust, these ten things are to be developed."

239 (3)
"Bhikkhus, for direct knowledge of lust, ten things are to be developed. What ten? Right view, right intention, right speech, right action, right livelihood, right effort, right mindfulness, right concentration, right knowledge, and right liberation. For direct knowledge of lust, these ten things are to be developed."[2197]

240 (4)–266 (30)
"Bhikkhus, for full understanding of lust . . . for the utter destruction . . . for the abandoning . . . for the destruction . . . for the vanishing . . . for the fading away . . . for the cessation . . .[2198] for the

giving up . . . for the relinquishment of lust . . . these ten things are to be developed."

267 (31)-746 (510)

"Bhikkhus, for direct knowledge . . . for full understanding . . . for the utter destruction . . . for the abandoning . . . for the destruction . . . for the vanishing . . . for the fading away . . . for the cessation . . . for the giving up . . . for the relinquishment of hatred . . . of delusion . . . of anger . . . of hostility . . . of denigration . . . of insolence . . . of envy . . . of miserliness . . . of deceitfulness . . . of craftiness . . . of obstinacy . . . of vehemence . . . of conceit . . . of arrogance . . . of intoxication . . . of heedlessness . . . these ten things are to be developed."

This is what the Blessed One said. Elated, those bhikkhus delighted in the Blessed One's statement.

The Book of the Tens is finished.

The Book of the Elevens

(*Ekādasakanipāta*)

The Book of the Elevens

[311] # The Book of the Elevens

Homage to the Blessed One, the Arahant,
the Perfectly Enlightened One

I. Dependence

1 (1) What Purpose?[2199]

Thus have I heard. On one occasion the Blessed One was dwelling at Sāvatthī in Jeta's Grove, Anāthapiṇḍika's Park. Then the Venerable Ānanda approached the Blessed One, paid homage to him, sat down to one side, and said to him:

(1) "Bhante, what is the purpose and benefit of wholesome virtuous behavior?"

(2) "Ānanda, the purpose and benefit of wholesome virtuous behavior is non-regret."

(3) "And what, Bhante, is the purpose and benefit of non-regret?"

"The purpose and benefit of non-regret is joy."

(4) "And what, Bhante, is the purpose and benefit of joy?"

"The purpose and benefit of joy is rapture."

(5) "And what, Bhante, is the purpose and benefit of rapture?"

"The purpose and benefit of rapture is tranquility."

(6) "And what, Bhante, is the purpose and benefit of tranquility?"

"The purpose and benefit of tranquility is pleasure."

(7) "And what, Bhante, is the purpose and benefit of pleasure?"

"The purpose and benefit of pleasure is concentration."

(8) "And what, Bhante, is the purpose and benefit of concentration?"

"The purpose and benefit of concentration is the knowledge and vision of things as they really are."

(9) "And what, Bhante, is the purpose and benefit of the knowledge and vision of things as they really are?"

"The purpose and benefit of the knowledge and vision of things as they really are is disenchantment."

(10) And what, Bhante, is the purpose and benefit of disenchantment?"

"The purpose and benefit of disenchantment is dispassion." [312]

(11) "And what, Bhante, is the purpose and benefit of dispassion?"

"The purpose and benefit of dispassion is the knowledge and vision of liberation."

"Thus, Ānanda, (1)–(2) the purpose and benefit of wholesome virtuous behavior is non-regret; (3) the purpose and benefit of non-regret is joy; (4) the purpose and benefit of joy is rapture; (5) the purpose and benefit of rapture is tranquility; (6) the purpose and benefit of tranquility is pleasure; (7) the purpose and benefit of pleasure is concentration; (8) the purpose and benefit of concentration is the knowledge and vision of things as they really are; (9) the purpose and benefit of the knowledge and vision of things as they really are is disenchantment; (10) the purpose and benefit of disenchantment is dispassion; and (10) the purpose and benefit of dispassion is the knowledge and vision of liberation. Thus, Ānanda, wholesome virtuous behavior progressively leads to the foremost."

2 (2) Volition[2200]

(1)–(2) "Bhikkhus, for a virtuous person, one whose behavior is virtuous, no volition need be exerted: 'Let non-regret arise in me.' It is natural that non-regret arises in one who is virtuous, one whose behavior is virtuous.

(3) "For one without regret no volition need be exerted: 'Let joy arise in me.' It is natural that joy arises in one without regret.

(4) "For one who is joyful no volition need be exerted: 'Let rapture arise in me.' It is natural that rapture arises in one who is joyful.

(5) "For one with a rapturous mind no volition need be exerted: 'Let my body become tranquil.' It is natural that the body of one with a rapturous mind is tranquil.

(6) "For one tranquil in body no volition need be exerted: 'Let me feel pleasure.' It is natural that one tranquil in body feels pleasure.

(7) "For one feeling pleasure no volition need be exerted: 'Let my mind be concentrated.' It is natural that the mind of one feeling pleasure is concentrated.

(8) "For one who is concentrated no volition need be exerted: 'Let me know and see things as they really are.' It is natural [313] that one who is concentrated knows and sees things as they really are.

(9) "For one who knows and sees things as they really are no volition need be exerted: 'Let me be disenchanted.' It is natural that one who knows and sees things as they really are is disenchanted.

(10) "For one who is disenchanted no volition need be exerted: 'Let me become dispassionate.' It is natural that one who is disenchanted becomes dispassionate.

(11) "For one who is dispassionate no volition need be exerted: 'Let me realize the knowledge and vision of liberation.' It is natural that one who is dispassionate realizes the knowledge and vision of liberation.

"Thus, bhikkhus, (11)–(10) the knowledge and vision of liberation is the purpose and benefit of dispassion; (9) dispassion is the purpose and benefit of disenchantment; (8) disenchantment is the purpose and benefit of the knowledge and vision of things as they really are; (7) the knowledge and vision of things as they really are is the purpose and benefit of concentration; (6) concentration is the purpose and benefit of pleasure; (5) pleasure is the purpose and benefit of tranquility; (4) tranquility is the purpose and benefit of rapture; (3) rapture is the purpose and benefit of joy; (2) joy is the purpose and benefit of non-regret; and (1) non-regret is the purpose and benefit of virtuous behavior.

"Thus, bhikkhus, one stage flows into the next stage, one stage fills up the next stage, for going from the near shore to the far shore."

3 (3) Proximate Cause (1)[2201]

"Bhikkhus, (1) for an immoral person, for one deficient in virtuous behavior, (2) non-regret lacks its proximate cause. When there is no non-regret, for one deficient in non-regret, (3) joy lacks its proximate cause. When there is no joy, for one deficient in joy, (4) rapture lacks its proximate cause. When there is no rapture, for one deficient in rapture, (5) tranquility lacks its proximate cause. When there is no tranquility, for one deficient in tranquility, [314] (6) pleasure lacks its proximate cause. When there is no pleasure, for one deficient in pleasure, (7) right concentration lacks its proximate cause. When there is no right concentration, for one deficient in right concentration, (8) the knowledge and vision of things as they really are lacks its proximate cause. When there is no knowledge and vision of things as they really are, for one deficient in the knowledge and vision of things as they really are, (9) disenchantment lacks its proximate cause. When there is no disenchantment, for one deficient in disenchantment, (10) dispassion lacks its proximate cause. When there is no dispassion, for one deficient in dispassion, (11) the knowledge and vision of liberation lacks its proximate cause.

"Suppose there is a tree deficient in branches and foliage. Then its shoots do not grow to fullness; also its bark, softwood, and heartwood do not grow to fullness. So too, for an immoral person, one deficient in virtuous behavior, non-regret lacks its proximate cause. When there is no non-regret . . . the knowledge and vision of liberation lacks its proximate cause.

"Bhikkhus, (1) for a virtuous person, for one whose behavior is virtuous, (2) non-regret possesses its proximate cause. When there is non-regret, for one possessing non-regret, (3) joy possesses its proximate cause. When there is joy, for one possessing joy, (4) rapture possesses its proximate cause. When there is rapture, for one possessing rapture, (5) tranquility possesses its proximate cause. When there is tranquility, for one possessing tranquility, (6) pleasure possesses its proximate cause. When there is pleasure, for one possessing pleasure, (7) right concentration possesses its proximate cause. When there is right concentration, for one possessing right concentration, (8) the knowledge and vision of things as they really are possesses its proximate cause. When there is the knowledge and vision of things as they really are, for one possessing the knowledge and vision of things as they really are, (9) disenchantment possesses its proximate cause. When there is disenchantment, for one possessing disenchantment, (10) dispassion possesses its proximate cause. When there is dispassion, for one possessing dispassion, (11) the knowledge and vision of liberation possesses its proximate cause.

"Suppose there is a tree possessing branches and foliage. Then its shoots grow to fullness; also its bark, softwood, and heartwood grow to fullness. So too, for a virtuous person, one whose behavior is virtuous, non-regret possesses its proximate cause. When there is non-regret ... the knowledge and vision of liberation possesses its proximate cause." [315]

4 (4) Proximate Cause (2)

There the Venerable Sāriputta addressed the bhikkhus:

[Identical with 11:3, but spoken by Sāriputta.] [316]

5 (5) Proximate Cause (3)

There the Venerable Ānanda addressed the bhikkhus:

[Identical with 11:3, but spoken by Ānanda.] [317]

6 (6) Disaster[2202]

"Bhikkhus, when a bhikkhu is one who insults and disparages his fellow monks, a reviler of the noble ones, it is impossible and inconceivable that he will not incur at least one of these eleven disasters. What eleven? (1) He does not achieve what he has not yet achieved. (2) He falls away from what he has achieved. (3) His good qualities are not polished.[2203] (4) He overestimates his good qualities, or (5) leads the spiritual life dissatisfied, [318] or (6) commits a defiled offense, or (7) gives up the training and reverts to the lower life, (8) or contracts a severe illness, or (9) goes mad and becomes mentally deranged. (10) He dies confused. (11) With the breakup of the body, after death, he is reborn in the plane of misery, in a bad destination, in the lower world, in hell. When a bhikkhu is one who insults and disparages his fellow monks, a reviler of the noble ones, it is impossible and inconceivable that he will not incur at least one of these eleven disasters."

7 (7) Perception[2204]

Then the Venerable Ānanda approached the Blessed One, paid homage to him, sat down to one side, and said to him:

"Bhante, could a bhikkhu obtain such a state of concentration that (1) he would not be percipient of earth in relation to earth; (2) of water in relation to water; (3) of fire in relation to fire; (4) of air in relation to air; (5) of the base of the infinity of space in relation to the base of the infinity of space; (6) of the base of the infinity of consciousness in relation to the base of the infinity of consciousness; (7) of the base of nothingness in relation to the base of nothingness; (8) of the base of neither-perception-nor-non-perception in relation to the base of neither-perception-nor-non-perception; (9) of this world in relation to this world; (10) of the other world in relation to the other world; (11) of anything seen, heard, sensed, cognized, reached, sought after, and examined by the mind, but he would still be percipient?"

"He could, Ānanda." [319]

"But how, Bhante, could he obtain such a state of concentration?"

"Here, Ānanda, a bhikkhu is percipient thus: 'This is peaceful, this is sublime, that is, the stilling of all activities, the relinquishing of all acquisitions, the destruction of craving, dispassion, cessation, nibbāna.' It is in this way, Ānanda, that a bhikkhu could obtain such a state of concentration that he would not be percipient of earth in relation to earth; of water in relation to water; of fire in relation to fire; of air in relation to air; of the base of the infinity of space in relation to the base of the infinity of space; of the base of the infinity of consciousness in relation to the base of the infinity of consciousness; of the base of nothingness in relation to the base of nothingness; of the base of neither-perception-nor-non-perception in relation to the base of neither-perception-nor-non-perception; of this world in relation to this world; of the other world in relation to the other world; of anything seen, heard, sensed, cognized, reached, sought after, and examined by the mind, but he would still be percipient."

Then the Venerable Ānanda, having delighted and rejoiced in the Blessed One's statement, got up from his seat, paid homage to the Blessed One, [320] circumambulated him keeping the right side toward him, and approached the Venerable Sāriputta.[2205] He exchanged greetings with the Venerable Sāriputta, and when they had concluded their greetings and cordial talk, he sat down to one side and said to him:

"Friend Sāriputta, could a bhikkhu obtain such a state of concentration that he would not be percipient of earth in relation to earth . . . of anything seen, heard, sensed, cognized, reached, sought after, and examined by the mind, but he would still be percipient?"

"He could, friend Ānanda."

"But how, friend Sāriputta, could he obtain such a state of concentration?"

"Here, friend Ānanda, a bhikkhu is percipient thus: 'This is peaceful, this is sublime, that is, the stilling of all activities, the relinquishing of all acquisitions, the destruction of craving, dispassion, cessation, nibbāna.' It is in this way, friend Ānanda, that a bhikkhu could obtain such a state of concentration that he would not be percipient of earth in relation to earth . . . he would not be percipient of anything seen, heard, sensed, cognized, reached, sought after, examined by the mind, but he would still be percipient."

"It's astounding and amazing, friend, that the meaning and the phrasing of both teacher and disciple coincide and agree with each other and do not diverge in regard to the foremost state.[2206] Just now, friend, I approached the Blessed One [321] and asked him about this matter. The Blessed One answered me in exactly the same terms and phrases that the Venerable Sāriputta used. It's astounding and amazing, friend, that the meaning and the phrasing of both teacher and disciple coincide and agree with each other and do not diverge in regard to the foremost state."

8 (8) Attention

Then the Venerable Ānanda approached the Blessed One, paid homage to him, sat down to one side, and said to him:

"Bhante, could a bhikkhu obtain such a state of concentration that he would not attend to the eye and forms, the ear and sounds, the nose and odors, the tongue and tastes, the body and tactile objects; that (1) he would not attend to earth,[2207] (2) water, (3) fire, (4) or air; (5) he would not attend to the base of the infinity of space, (6) the base of the infinity of consciousness, (7) the base of nothingness, (8) or the base of neither-perception-nor-non-perception; (9) he would not attend to this world; (10) he would not attend to the other world; (11) he would not attend to anything seen, heard, sensed, cognized, reached, sought after, and examined by the mind, but he would still be attentive?"

"He could, Ānanda." [322]

"But how, Bhante, could he obtain such a state of concentration?"

"Here, Ānanda, a bhikkhu would attend thus: 'This is peaceful, this is sublime, that is, the stilling of all activities, the relinquishing of all acquisitions, the destruction of craving, dispassion, cessation, nibbāna.' It is in this way, Ānanda, that a bhikkhu could obtain such a state of concentration that he would not attend to the eye and forms, the ear and sounds, the nose and odors, the tongue and tastes, the body and tactile objects; that he would not attend to earth, water, fire, or air; he would not attend to the base of the infinity of space, the base of the infinity of consciousness, the base of nothingness, or the base of neither-perception-nor-non-perception; he would not attend to this world; he would not attend to the other world; he would not attend to anything seen, heard, sensed, cognized, reached, sought after, and examined by the mind, but he would still be attentive."

9 (9) Sandha

On one occasion the Blessed One was dwelling at Nādika [323] in the brick hall. Then the Venerable Sandha[2208] approached the Blessed One, paid homage to him, and sat down to one side. The Blessed One then said to him:

"Meditate like a thoroughbred, Sandha, not like a wild colt. And how does a wild colt meditate? When a wild colt is tied up near the feeding trough he meditates: 'Fodder, fodder!' For what reason? Because when a wild colt is tied up by the feeding trough, he does not ask himself: 'Now what task will my trainer set for me today? What can I do to satisfy him?' Tied up by the feeding trough, he just meditates: 'Fodder, fodder!' So too, Sandha, a person who is like a wild colt, when gone to the forest, to the foot of a tree, or to an empty hut, dwells with a mind obsessed and oppressed by sensual lust, and he does not understand as it really is the escape from arisen sensual lust. Harboring sensual lust within, he meditates, cogitates, ponders, and ruminates.[2209] He dwells with a mind obsessed and oppressed by ill will . . . by dullness and drowsiness . . . by restlessness and remorse . . . by doubt, and he does not understand as it really is the escape from arisen doubt. Harboring doubt within, he meditates, cogitates, [324] ponders, and ruminates.

"He meditates (1) in dependence on earth, (2) in dependence on water, (3) in dependence on fire, (4) in dependence on air, (5) in dependence on the base of the infinity of space, (6) in dependence on the base of the infinity of consciousness, (7) in dependence on the base of nothingness, (8) in dependence on the base of neither-perception-nor-non-perception, (9) in dependence on this world, (10) in dependence on the other world, (11) in dependence on what is seen, heard, sensed, cognized, reached, sought after, and examined by the mind. Such is the meditation of a person who is like a wild colt.

"And how, Sandha, does a thoroughbred meditate? When an excellent thoroughbred horse is tied up near the feeding trough he does not meditate: 'Fodder, fodder!' For what reason? Because when an excellent thoroughbred horse is tied up by the feeding trough, he asks himself: 'Now what task will my trainer set for me today? What can I do to satisfy him?' Tied up by the feeding trough, he does not meditate: 'Fodder, fodder!' For that excellent thoroughbred horse regards the application of the goad as a debt, a bond, a loss, and failure. So too, an excellent thoroughbred person, when gone to the forest, to the foot of a tree, or to an empty hut, does not dwell with a mind obsessed and oppressed by sensual lust, and he understands as it really is the escape from arisen sensual lust. He does not dwell with a mind obsessed and oppressed by ill will . . . by dullness and drowsiness . . . by restlessness and remorse . . . by doubt, and he understands as it really is the escape from arisen doubt.

"He does not meditate (1) in dependence on earth, (2) in dependence on water, (3) in dependence on fire, (4) in dependence on air, (5) in dependence on the base of the infinity of space, (6) in dependence on the base of the infinity of consciousness, (7) in dependence on the base of nothingness, (8) in dependence on the base of neither-perception-nor-non-perception, [325] (9) in dependence on this world, (10) in dependence on the other world, (11) in dependence on what is seen, heard, sensed, cognized, reached, sought after, or examined by the mind, and yet he meditates.

"When he meditates in such a way, the devas along with Indra, Brahmā, and Pajāpati worship the excellent thoroughbred person from afar, saying:

"'Homage to you, O thoroughbred person!
Homage to you, O supreme person!
We ourselves do not understand
What you meditate in dependence on.'"[2210]

When this was said, the Venerable Sandha said to the Blessed One: "But how, Bhante, does an excellent thoroughbred person meditate? If he does not meditate in dependence on earth ... in dependence on what is seen, heard, sensed, cognized, reached, sought after, and examined by the mind, and yet he meditates, just how does he meditate so that the devas ... worship the excellent thoroughbred person from afar, saying:

"'Homage to you, O thoroughbred person! ...
What you meditate in dependence on'?"

"Here, Sandha, for an excellent thoroughbred person, the perception of earth has disappeared in relation to earth,[2211] the perception of water has disappeared in relation to water, the perception of fire has disappeared in relation to fire, the perception of air has disappeared in relation to air, the perception of the base of the infinity of space has disappeared in relation to the base of the infinity of space, the perception of the base of the infinity of consciousness has disappeared in relation to the base of the infinity of consciousness, [326] the perception of the base of nothingness has disappeared in relation to the base of nothingness, the perception of the base of neither-perception-nor-non-perception has disappeared in relation to the base of neither-perception-nor-non-perception, the perception of this world has disappeared in relation to this world, the perception of the other world has disappeared in relation to the other world; perception has disappeared in relation to whatever is seen, heard, sensed, cognized, reached, sought after, and examined by the mind.

"Meditating in such a way, Sandha, an excellent thoroughbred person does not meditate in dependence on earth, in dependence on water, in dependence on fire, in dependence on air, in dependence on the base of the infinity of space, in dependence on the base of the infinity of consciousness, in dependence on the base of nothingness, in dependence on the base of neither-perception-nor-non-perception, in dependence on this world, in dependence on the other world; in dependence on what is seen, heard, sensed, cognized, reached, sought after, or examined by the mind and yet he meditates.[2212] And as he meditates in such a way, the devas along with Indra, Brahmā, and Pajāpati worship the excellent thoroughbred person from afar, saying:

"'Homage to you, O thoroughbred person!
Homage to you, O supreme person!
We ourselves do not understand
What you meditate in dependence on.'"

10 (10) The Peacock Sanctuary[2213]

On one occasion the Blessed One was dwelling at Rājagaha at the wanderers' park, the peacock sanctuary. There the Blessed One addressed the bhikkhus: "Bhikkhus!"

"Venerable sir!" those bhikkhus replied. The Blessed One said this:

"Bhikkhus, possessing three qualities, a bhikkhu is best among devas and humans: one who has reached the ultimate conclusion, won ultimate security from bondage, lived the ultimate spiritual life, and gained the ultimate consummation. What three? (1) The aggregate of virtuous behavior of one beyond training, (2) the aggregate of concentration of one beyond training, and (3) the aggregate of wisdom of one beyond training. Possessing these three qualities, a bhikkhu [327] is best among devas and humans: one who has . . . gained the ultimate consummation.

"Bhikkhus, possessing another three qualities, a bhikkhu is best among devas and humans: one who has . . . gained the ultimate consummation. What three? (4) The wonder of psychic potency, (5) the wonder of mind-reading, and (6) the wonder of instruction. Possessing these three qualities, a bhikkhu is best among devas and humans: one who has . . . gained the ultimate consummation.

"Bhikkhus, possessing another three qualities, a bhikkhu is best among devas and humans: one who has . . . gained the ultimate consummation. What three? (7) Right view, (8) right knowledge, and (9) right liberation. Possessing these three qualities, a bhikkhu is best among devas and humans: one who has . . . gained the ultimate consummation.

"Bhikkhus, possessing two qualities, a bhikkhu is best among devas and humans: one who has . . . gained the ultimate consummation. What two? (10) True knowledge and (11) conduct. Possessing these two qualities, a bhikkhu is best among devas and humans: one who has reached the ultimate conclusion, won ultimate security from bondage, lived the ultimate spiritual life, and gained the ultimate consummation.

"Brahmā Sanaṃkumāra, too, spoke this verse:

"'The khattiya is the best among people
for those whose standard is the clan,
but one accomplished in true knowledge and conduct
is best among devas and humans.'

"This verse, bhikkhus, was well recited by Brahmā Sanaṃkumāra, not badly recited; it was well spoken, not badly spoken; [328] it is beneficial, not harmful, and I approved of it. I too say thus:

"'The khattiya is the best among people
for those whose standard is the clan,
but one accomplished in true knowledge and conduct
is best among devas and humans.'"

II. Recollection

11 (1) Mahānāma (1)[2214]

On one occasion the Blessed One was dwelling among the Sakyans at Kapilavatthu in the Banyan Tree Park. Now on that occasion a number of bhikkhus were making a robe for the Blessed One, thinking that with his robe completed, at the end of the three months [of the rains residence], the Blessed One would set out wandering. Mahānāma the Sakyan heard about this, approached the Blessed One, paid homage to him, sat down to one side, and said to him:

"Bhante, I have heard: 'A number of bhikkhus are making a robe for the Blessed One, thinking that with his robe completed, at the end of the three months [of the rains residence], the Blessed One will set out wandering.' Bhante, with all our various engagements, how should we dwell?"[2215] [329]

"Good, good, Mahānāma! It is fitting for you clansmen to approach the Tathāgata and ask: 'Bhante, with all our various engagements, how should we dwell?'

(1) "Mahānāma, a person with faith succeeds, not one without faith. (2) An energetic person succeeds, not one who is lazy. (3) One with mindfulness established succeeds, not one who is muddle-minded. (4) One who is concentrated succeeds, not one who is unconcentrated. (5) One who is wise succeeds, not one who is unwise. Having established yourself in these five qualities, you should further develop six things.

(6) "Here, Mahānāma, you should recollect the Tathāgata thus: 'The Blessed One is an arahant, perfectly enlightened, accomplished in true knowledge and conduct, fortunate, knower of the world, unsurpassed trainer of persons to be tamed, teacher of devas and humans, the Enlightened One, the Blessed One.' When a noble disciple recollects the Tathāgata, on that occasion his mind is not obsessed by lust, hatred, or delusion; on that occasion his mind is simply straight, based on the Tathāgata. A noble disciple whose mind is straight gains inspiration in the meaning, gains inspiration in the Dhamma, gains joy connected with the Dhamma. When he is joyful, rapture arises. For one with a rapturous mind, the body becomes tranquil. One tranquil in body feels pleasure. For one feeling pleasure, the mind becomes concentrated. This is called a noble disciple who dwells in balance amid an unbalanced population, who dwells unafflicted amid an afflicted population. As one who has entered the stream of the Dhamma, he develops recollection of the Buddha.

(7) "Again, Mahānāma, you should recollect the Dhamma thus: 'The Dhamma is well expounded by the Blessed One, directly visible, immediate, inviting one to come and see, applicable, to be personally experienced by the wise.' When a noble disciple recollects the Dhamma, on that occasion his mind is not obsessed by lust, [330] hatred, or delusion; on that occasion his mind is simply straight, based on the Dhamma. A noble disciple whose mind is straight gains inspiration in the meaning, gains inspiration in the Dhamma, gains joy connected with the Dhamma. When he is joyful, rapture arises.

For one with a rapturous mind, the body becomes tranquil. One tranquil in body feels pleasure. For one feeling pleasure, the mind becomes concentrated. This is called a noble disciple who dwells in balance amid an unbalanced population, who dwells unafflicted amid an afflicted population. As one who has entered the stream of the Dhamma, he develops recollection of the Dhamma.

(8) "Again, Mahānāma, you should recollect the Saṅgha thus: 'The Saṅgha of the Blessed One's disciples is practicing the good way, practicing the straight way, practicing the true way, practicing the proper way; that is, the four pairs of persons, the eight types of individuals—this Saṅgha of the Blessed One's disciples is worthy of gifts, worthy of hospitality, worthy of offerings, worthy of reverential salutation, the unsurpassed field of merit for the world.' When a noble disciple recollects the Saṅgha, on that occasion his mind is not obsessed by lust, hatred, or delusion; on that occasion his mind is simply straight, based on the Saṅgha. A noble disciple whose mind is straight gains inspiration in the meaning, gains inspiration in the Dhamma, gains joy connected with the Dhamma. When he is joyful, rapture arises. For one with a rapturous mind, the body becomes tranquil. One tranquil in body feels pleasure. For one feeling pleasure, the mind becomes concentrated. This is called a noble disciple who dwells in balance amid an unbalanced population, who dwells unafflicted amid an afflicted population. As one who has entered the stream of the Dhamma, he develops recollection of the Saṅgha.

(9) "Again, Mahānāma, you should recollect your own virtuous behavior as unbroken, flawless, unblemished, unblotched, freeing, praised by the wise, ungrasped, leading to concentration. When a noble disciple recollects his virtuous behavior, on that occasion his mind is not obsessed by lust, hatred, or [331] delusion; on that occasion his mind is simply straight, based on virtuous behavior. A noble disciple whose mind is straight gains inspiration in the meaning, gains inspiration in the Dhamma, gains joy connected with the Dhamma. When he is joyful, rapture arises. For one with a rapturous mind, the body becomes tranquil. One tranquil in body feels pleasure. For one feeling pleasure, the mind becomes concentrated. This is called a noble disciple who dwells in balance

amid an unbalanced population, who dwells unafflicted amid an afflicted population. As one who has entered the stream of the Dhamma, he develops recollection of virtuous behavior.

(10) "Again, Mahānāma, you should recollect your own generosity thus: 'It is truly my good fortune and gain that in a population obsessed by the stain of miserliness, I dwell at home with a mind devoid of the stain of miserliness, freely generous, openhanded, delighting in relinquishment, devoted to charity, delighting in giving and sharing.' When a noble disciple recollects his generosity, on that occasion his mind is not obsessed by lust, hatred, or delusion; on that occasion his mind is simply straight, based on generosity. A noble disciple whose mind is straight gains inspiration in the meaning, gains inspiration in the Dhamma, gains joy connected with the Dhamma. When he is joyful, rapture arises. For one with a rapturous mind, the body becomes tranquil. One tranquil in body feels pleasure. For one feeling pleasure, the mind becomes concentrated. This is called a noble disciple who dwells in balance amid an unbalanced population, who dwells unafflicted amid an afflicted population. As one who has entered the stream of the Dhamma, he develops recollection of generosity.

(11) "Again, Mahānāma, you should recollect the deities thus: 'There are devas [ruled by] the four great kings, Tāvatiṃsa devas, Yāma devas, Tusita devas, devas who delight in creation, devas who control what is created by others, devas of Brahmā's company, and devas still higher than these. There exists in me too such faith as those deities possessed because of which, when they passed away here, [332] they were reborn there; there exists in me too such virtuous behavior . . . such learning . . . such generosity . . . such wisdom as those deities possessed because of which, when they passed away here, they were reborn there.' When a noble disciple recollects the faith, virtuous behavior, learning, generosity, and wisdom in himself and in those deities, on that occasion his mind is not obsessed by lust, hatred, or delusion; on that occasion his mind is simply straight, based on the deities. A noble disciple whose mind is straight gains inspiration in the meaning, gains inspiration in the Dhamma, gains joy connected with the Dhamma. When he is joyful, rapture arises. For one with a rapturous mind, the body becomes tranquil. One tranquil in body feels pleasure.

For one feeling pleasure, the mind becomes concentrated. This is called a noble disciple who dwells in balance amid an unbalanced population, who dwells unafflicted amid an afflicted population. As one who has entered the stream of the Dhamma, he develops recollection of the deities."

12 (2) Mahānāma (2)

[Opening as in 11:11, down to:] [333]

"Having established yourself in these five qualities, Mahānāma, you should further develop six things.

(6) "Here, Mahānāma, you should recollect the Tathāgata thus: 'The Blessed One is . . . the Enlightened One, the Blessed One.' When a noble disciple recollects the Tathāgata, on that occasion his mind is not obsessed by lust, hatred, or delusion; on that occasion his mind is simply straight, based on the Tathāgata. A noble disciple whose mind is straight gains inspiration in the meaning, gains inspiration in the Dhamma, gains joy connected with the Dhamma. When he is joyful, rapture arises. For one with a rapturous mind, the body becomes tranquil. One tranquil in body feels pleasure. For one feeling pleasure, the mind becomes concentrated. Mahānāma, you should develop this recollection of the Buddha while walking, standing, sitting, and lying down. You should develop it while engaged in work and while living at home in a house full of children. [334]

(7) "Again, Mahānāma you should recollect the Dhamma . . . (8) . . . the Saṅgha . . . (9) . . . your own virtuous behavior . . . (10) . . . your own generosity . . . (11) . . . the deities thus. . . . When a noble disciple recollects the faith, virtuous behavior, learning, generosity, and wisdom in himself and in those deities, on that occasion his mind is not obsessed by lust, hatred, or delusion; on that occasion his mind is simply straight, based on the deities. A noble disciple whose mind is straight gains inspiration in the meaning, gains inspiration in the Dhamma, gains joy connected with the Dhamma. When he is joyful, rapture arises. For one with a rapturous mind, the body becomes tranquil. One tranquil in body feels pleasure. For one feeling pleasure, the mind becomes concentrated. Mahānāma, you should develop this recollection of the deities while walking, standing, sitting, and lying down. You should develop it while engaged in work and while living at home in a house full of children."

13 (3) Nandiya

On one occasion the Blessed One was dwelling among the Sakyans at Kapilavatthu in the Banyan Tree Park. Now on that occasion the Blessed One wanted to enter upon the rains residence in Sāvatthī. Nandiya the Sakyan heard about this and it then [335] occurred to him: "I will also enter upon the rains residence in Sāvatthī.[2216] There I will engage in business and from time to time get to see the Blessed One."

Then the Blessed One entered upon the rains residence in Sāvatthī. Nandiya the Sakyan also entered upon the rains residence in Sāvatthī, where he engaged in business and from time to time got to see the Blessed One. Now on that occasion a number of bhikkhus were making a robe for the Blessed One, thinking that with his robe completed, at the end of the three months [of the rains residence], the Blessed One would set out wandering. Nandiya the Sakyan heard about this, approached the Blessed One, paid homage to him, sat down to one side, and said to him:

"Bhante, I have heard: 'A number of bhikkhus are making a robe for the Blessed One, thinking that with his robe completed, at the end of the three months [of the rains residence], the Blessed One will set out wandering.' Bhante, with all our various engagements, how should we dwell?"

"Good, good, Nandiya! It is fitting for you clansmen to approach the Tathāgata and ask: 'Bhante, with all our various engagements, how should we dwell?'

(1) "Nandiya, a person with faith succeeds, not one without faith. (2) A virtuous person succeeds, not an immoral one. (3) An energetic person succeeds, not one who is lazy. (4) One with mindfulness established succeeds, not one who is muddle-minded. (5) One who is concentrated succeeds, not one who is unconcentrated. (6) One who is wise succeeds, not one who is unwise. Having established yourself in these six qualities, you should establish mindfulness internally concerning five things.

(7) "Here, Nandiya, you should recollect the Tathāgata thus: [336] 'The Blessed One is an arahant, perfectly enlightened, accomplished in true knowledge and conduct, fortunate, knower of the world, unsurpassed trainer of persons to be tamed, teacher of devas and humans, the Enlightened One,

the Blessed One.' Thus you should establish mindfulness internally based on the Tathāgata.

(8) "Again, Nandiya, you should recollect the Dhamma thus: 'The Dhamma is well expounded by the Blessed One, directly visible, immediate, inviting one to come and see, applicable, to be personally experienced by the wise.' Thus you should establish mindfulness internally based on the Dhamma.

(9) "Again, Nandiya, you should recollect good friends thus: 'It is truly my good fortune and gain that I have good friends who take compassion on me, who desire my good, who exhort and instruct me.' Thus you should establish mindfulness internally based on good friends.

(10) "Again, Nandiya, you should recollect your own generosity thus: 'It is truly my good fortune and gain that in a population obsessed by the stain of miserliness, I dwell at home with a mind devoid of the stain of miserliness, freely generous, openhanded, delighting in relinquishment, devoted to charity, delighting in giving and sharing.' Thus you should establish mindfulness internally based on generosity.

(11) "Again, Nandiya, you should recollect the deities thus: 'Those deities that have been reborn in a mind-made body in companionship with the devas who transcend those subsisting on edible food do not see in themselves anything still to be done or [any need] to increase what has been done. Just as a permanently liberated bhikkhu does not see in himself anything still to be done or [any need] to increase what has been done,[2217] so it is with those deities that have been reborn in a mind-made body in companionship with the devas who transcend those subsisting on edible food.'[2218] [337] Thus you should establish mindfulness internally based on the deities.

"Nandiya, a noble disciple who possesses these eleven qualities abandons bad unwholesome qualities and does not take them up. Just as a pot turned upside down does not receive back the water that has been poured out, and just as a fire that has gotten out of control[2219] advances burning up a dry woodland and does not return to what it has burnt, so too, a noble disciple who possesses these eleven qualities abandons bad unwholesome qualities and does not take them up."

14 (4) Subhūti

Then the Venerable Subhūti together with the bhikkhu Saddha approached the Blessed One, paid homage to him, and sat down to one side. The Blessed One then said to the Venerable Subhūti:

"What is this bhikkhu's name, Subhūti?"

"His name is Saddha, Bhante. He is the son of a male lay follower endowed with faith,[2220] and he has gone forth from the household life into homelessness out of faith."

"I hope that this son of a male lay follower endowed with faith, the bhikkhu Saddha, who has gone forth from the household life into homelessness out of faith, exhibits the manifestations of faith."[2221]

"This is the time for it, Blessed One! This is the time for it, Fortunate One! The Blessed One should explain the manifestations of faith. Now I will find out whether or not this bhikkhu exhibits the manifestations of faith."

"Then listen, Subhūti, and attend closely. I will speak."

"Yes, Bhante," the Venerable Subhūti replied. The Blessed One said this: [338]

(1) "Here, Subhūti, a bhikkhu is virtuous; he dwells restrained by the Pātimokkha, possessed of good conduct and resort, seeing danger in minute faults. Having undertaken the training rules, he trains in them. This is a manifestation of faith in one endowed with faith.

(2) "Again, a bhikkhu has learned much, remembers what he has learned, and accumulates what he has learned. Those teachings that are good in the beginning, good in the middle, and good in the end, with the right meaning and phrasing, which proclaim the perfectly complete and pure spiritual life—such teachings as these he has learned much of, retained in mind, recited verbally, mentally investigated, and penetrated well by view. This, too, is a manifestation of faith in one endowed with faith.

(3) "Again, a bhikkhu has good friends, good companions, good comrades. This, too, is a manifestation of faith in one endowed with faith.

(4) "Again, a bhikkhu is easy to correct and possesses qualities that make him easy to correct; he is patient and receives instruction respectfully. This, too, is a manifestation of faith in one endowed with faith.

(5) "Again, a bhikkhu is skillful and diligent in attending to the diverse chores that are to be done for his fellow monks; he possesses sound judgment about them in order to carry out and arrange them properly. This, too, is a manifestation of faith in one endowed with faith. [339]

(6) "Again, a bhikkhu loves the Dhamma and is pleasing in his assertions, filled with a lofty joy in regard to the Dhamma and discipline. This, too, is a manifestation of faith in one endowed with faith.

(7) "Again, a bhikkhu has aroused energy for abandoning unwholesome qualities and acquiring wholesome qualities; he is strong, firm in exertion, not casting off the duty of cultivating wholesome qualities. This, too, is a manifestation of faith in one endowed with faith.

(8) "Again, a bhikkhu gains at will, without trouble or difficulty, the four jhānas that constitute the higher mind and are pleasant dwellings in this very life. This, too, is a manifestation of faith in one endowed with faith.

(9) "Again, a bhikkhu recollects his manifold past abodes . . . [as in 6:2 §4] . . . Thus he recollects his manifold past abodes with their aspects and details. [340] This, too, is a manifestation of faith in one endowed with faith.

(10) "Again, with the divine eye, which is purified and surpasses the human, a bhikkhu sees beings passing away and being reborn, inferior and superior, beautiful and ugly, fortunate and unfortunate . . . [as in 6:2 §5] . . . and he understands how beings fare in accordance with their kamma. This, too, is a manifestation of faith in one endowed with faith.

(11) "Again, with the destruction of the taints, a bhikkhu has realized for himself with direct knowledge, in this very life, the taintless liberation of mind, liberation by wisdom, and having entered upon it, he dwells in it. This, too, is a manifestation of faith in one endowed with faith."

When this was said, the Venerable Subhūti said to the Blessed One: "Bhante, these manifestations of faith in one endowed with faith that the Blessed One has spoken of are seen in this bhikkhu, and he does exhibit them.

(1) "This bhikkhu, Bhante, is virtuous . . . [341] he trains in them.

(2) "He has learned much . . . and penetrated well by view.

(3) "He has good friends, good companions, good comrades.

(4) "He is easy to correct and possesses qualities that make him easy to correct; he is patient and receives instruction respectfully.

(5) "He is skillful and diligent . . . in order to carry out and arrange them properly.

(6) "He loves the Dhamma . . . in regard to the Dhamma and discipline.

(7) "He has aroused energy . . . not casting off the duty of cultivating wholesome qualities.

(8) "He gains at will, without trouble or difficulty, the four jhānas . . . in this very life.

(9) "He recollects his manifold past abodes . . . with their aspects and details.

(10) "He sees beings passing away and being reborn . . . and he understands how beings fare in accordance with their kamma.

(11) "With the destruction of the taints, this bhikkhu has realized for himself with direct knowledge, in this very life, the taintless liberation of mind, liberation by wisdom, and having entered upon it, he dwells in it.

"Bhante, these manifestations of faith in one endowed with faith that the Blessed One has spoken of are seen in this bhikkhu, and he does exhibit them."

"Good, good, Subhūti! In that case, Subhūti, you may dwell together with this bhikkhu Saddha, and when you want to see the Tathāgata, you may bring him along." [342]

15 (5) Loving-Kindness[2222]

"Bhikkhus, when the liberation of the mind by loving-kindness has been pursued, developed, and cultivated, made a vehicle and basis, carried out, consolidated, and properly undertaken, eleven benefits are to be expected. What eleven?

(1) "One sleeps well; (2) one awakens happily; (3) one does not have bad dreams; (4) one is pleasing to human beings; (5) one is pleasing to spirits; (6) deities protect one; (7) fire, poison, and weapons do not injure one; (8) one's mind quickly becomes concentrated; (9) one's facial complexion is serene; (10) one dies unconfused; and (11) if one does not penetrate further, one fares on to the brahmā world.[2223]

"When, bhikkhus, the liberation of the mind by loving-kindness has been repeatedly pursued, developed, and cultivated, made a vehicle and basis, carried out, consolidated, and properly undertaken, these eleven benefits are to be expected."

16 (6) Dasama[2224]

On one occasion the Venerable Ānanda was living at Beluvagāmaka near Vesālī. Now on that occasion the householder Dasama of Aṭṭhakanagara[2225] had arrived at Pāṭaliputta on a business matter. Then he approached a certain bhikkhu in the Cock's Park and asked him: "Bhante, where is the Venerable Ānanda staying now? I want to see him."

"He is staying at Beluvagāmaka near Vesālī, householder."

When the householder Dasama had completed his business at Pāṭaliputta, he went to the Venerable Ānanda at Beluvagāmaka near Vesālī. He paid homage to the Venerable Ānanda, sat down to one side, [343] and said to him:

"Bhante Ānanda, is there any one thing properly expounded by the Blessed One, the Arahant, the Perfectly Enlightened One who knows and sees, such that if a bhikkhu dwells diligent, ardent, and resolute in it, his unliberated mind is liberated, his undestroyed taints are destroyed, and he attains the as-yet-unattained unsurpassed security from bondage?"

"There is, householder."

"And what is it?"

(1) "Here, householder, secluded from sensual pleasures, secluded from unwholesome states, a bhikkhu enters and dwells in the first jhāna, which consists of rapture and pleasure born of seclusion, accompanied by thought and examination. He considers this and understands it thus: 'This first jhāna is constructed and produced by volition. But whatever is constructed and produced by volition is impermanent, subject to cessation.' If he is firm in this, he attains the destruction of the taints. But if he does not attain the destruction of the taints because of that lust for the Dhamma, because of that delight in the Dhamma,[2226] then, with the utter destruction of the five lower fetters, he becomes one of spontaneous birth, due to attain final nibbāna there without ever returning from that world.

"This is one thing properly expounded by the Blessed One, the Arahant, the Perfectly Enlightened One who knows and sees, such that if a bhikkhu dwells in it diligent, ardent, and resolute, his unliberated mind is liberated, his undestroyed taints are destroyed, and he attains the as-yet-unattained unsurpassed security from bondage. [344]

(2) "Again, householder, with the subsiding of thought and examination a bhikkhu enters and dwells in the second jhāna ... (3) ... the third jhāna ... (4) ... the fourth jhāna. ... He considers this and understands it thus: 'This fourth jhāna is constructed and produced by volition. But whatever is constructed and produced by volition is impermanent, subject to cessation.' If he is firm in this, he attains the destruction of the taints. But if he does not attain the destruction of the taints because of that lust for the Dhamma, because of that delight in the Dhamma, then, with the utter destruction of the five lower fetters, he becomes one of spontaneous birth, due to attain final nibbāna there without ever returning from that world.

"This, too, is one thing properly expounded by the Blessed One, the Arahant, the Perfectly Enlightened One who knows and sees, such that if a bhikkhu dwells in it ... he attains the as-yet-unattained unsurpassed security from bondage.

(5) "Again, householder, a bhikkhu dwells pervading one quarter with a mind imbued with loving-kindness, likewise the second quarter, the third quarter, and the fourth quarter. Thus above, below, across, and everywhere, and to all as to himself, he dwells pervading the entire world with a mind imbued with loving-kindness, vast, exalted, measureless, without enmity, without ill will. He considers this and understands it thus: 'This liberation of the mind by loving-kindness is constructed and produced by volition. But whatever is constructed and produced by volition is impermanent, subject to cessation.' If he is firm in this, he attains the destruction of the taints. But if he does not attain the destruction of the taints because of that lust for the Dhamma, because of that delight in the Dhamma, then, with the utter destruction of the five lower fetters, he becomes one of spontaneous birth, due to attain final nibbāna there without ever returning from that world.

"This, too, is one thing properly expounded by the Blessed One, [345] the Arahant, the Perfectly Enlightened One who knows and sees, such that if a bhikkhu dwells in it ... he attains the as-yet-unattained unsurpassed security from bondage.

(6) "Again, householder, a bhikkhu dwells pervading one

quarter with a mind imbued with compassion . . . (7) . . . with a mind imbued with altruistic joy . . . (8) . . . with a mind imbued with equanimity, likewise the second quarter, the third quarter, and the fourth quarter. Thus above, below, across, and everywhere, and to all as to himself, he dwells pervading the entire world with a mind imbued with equanimity, vast, exalted, measureless, without enmity, without ill will. He considers this and understands it thus: 'This liberation of the mind by equanimity is constructed and produced by volition. But whatever is constructed and produced by volition is impermanent, subject to cessation.' If he is firm in this, he attains the destruction of the taints. But if he does not attain the destruction of the taints because of that lust for the Dhamma, because of that delight in the Dhamma, then, with the utter destruction of the five lower fetters, he becomes one of spontaneous birth, due to attain final nibbāna there without ever returning from that world.

"This, too, is one thing properly expounded by the Blessed One, the Arahant, the Perfectly Enlightened One who knows and sees, such that if a bhikkhu dwells in it . . . he attains the as-yet-unattained unsurpassed security from bondage.

(9) "Again, householder, with the complete surmounting of perceptions of forms, with the passing away of perceptions of sensory impingement, with non-attention to perceptions of diversity, [perceiving] 'space is infinite,' a bhikkhu enters and dwells in the base of the infinity of space. He considers this and understands it thus: 'This attainment of the base of the infinity of space is constructed and produced by volition. But whatever is constructed and produced by volition is impermanent, subject to cessation.' If he is firm in this, he attains the destruction of the taints. But if he does not [346] attain the destruction of the taints because of that lust for the Dhamma, because of that delight in the Dhamma, then, with the utter destruction of the five lower fetters, he becomes one of spontaneous birth, due to attain final nibbāna there without ever returning from that world.

"This, too, is one thing properly expounded by the Blessed One, the Arahant, the Perfectly Enlightened One who knows and sees, such that if a bhikkhu dwells in it . . . he attains the as-yet-unattained unsurpassed security from bondage.

(10) "Again, householder, by completely surmounting the base of the infinity of space, [perceiving] 'consciousness is infi-

nite,' he enters and dwells in the base of the infinity of consciousness . . . (11) . . . by completely surmounting the base of the infinity of consciousness, [perceiving] 'there is nothing,' he enters and dwells in the base of nothingness. He considers this and understands it thus: 'This attainment of the base of nothingness is constructed and produced by volition. But whatever is constructed and produced by volition is impermanent, subject to cessation.' If he is firm in this, he attains the destruction of the taints. But if he does not attain the destruction of the taints because of that lust for the Dhamma, because of that delight in the Dhamma, then, with the utter destruction of the five lower fetters, he becomes one of spontaneous birth, due to attain final nibbāna there without ever returning from that world.

"This, too, is one thing properly expounded by the Blessed One, the Arahant, the Perfectly Enlightened One who knows and sees, such that if a bhikkhu dwells in it diligent, ardent, and resolute, his unliberated mind is liberated, his undestroyed taints are destroyed, and he attains the as-yet-unattained unsurpassed security from bondage."[2227]

When this was said, the householder Dasama of Aṭṭhakanagara said to the Venerable Ānanda: "Bhante Ānanda, just as if a man seeking one entrance to a hidden treasure all at once found eleven entrances to that treasure, so too, while I was seeking one door to the deathless, I have all at once gotten to hear eleven doors to the deathless.[2228] Just as if a man had a house with eleven doors [347] and when that house caught on fire, he could flee to safety through any of these eleven doors, so I can flee to safety through any of these eleven doors to the deathless. Bhante, these members of other sects seek a fee for their teachers, so why shouldn't I make an offering to the Venerable Ānanda?"

Then the householder Dasama of Aṭṭhakanagara assembled the Saṅgha of bhikkhus from Pāṭaliputta and Vesālī, and with his own hands he served and satisfied them with various kinds of good food. He presented a pair of cloths to each bhikkhu and a set of three robes to the Venerable Ānanda. And he had a dwelling worth five hundred[2229] built for the Venerable Ānanda.

17 (7) The Cowherd[2230]

"Bhikkhus, possessing eleven factors, a cowherd is incapable of keeping and rearing a herd of cattle. What eleven? Here, (1) a cowherd has no knowledge of form; (2) he is unskilled in characteristics; (3) he fails to pick out flies' eggs; (4) he fails to dress wounds; (5) he fails to smoke out the sheds; (6) he does not know the watering place; (7) he does not know what it is to have drunk; (8) he does not know the road; (9) he is unskilled in pastures; (10) he milks dry; and (11) he shows no extra veneration to those bulls who are fathers and leaders of the herd. Possessing these eleven factors, a cowherd is incapable of keeping and rearing a herd of cattle.

"So too, bhikkhus, possessing eleven qualities, a bhikkhu is incapable of growth, progress, and fulfillment in this Dhamma and discipline. What eleven? [348] Here, (1) a bhikkhu has no knowledge of form; (2) he is unskilled in characteristics; (3) he fails to pick out flies' eggs; (4) he fails to dress wounds; (5) he fails to smoke out the sheds; (6) he does not know the watering place; (7) he does not know what it is to have drunk; (8) he does not know the road; (9) he is unskilled in pastures; (10) he milks dry; and (11) he shows no extra veneration to those elder bhikkhus of long-standing who have long gone forth, the fathers and leaders of the Saṅgha.

(1) "And how has a bhikkhu no knowledge of form? Here, a bhikkhu does not understand as it really is: 'All form of whatever kind is the four great elements and the form derived from the four great elements.' It is in this way that a bhikkhu has no knowledge of form.

(2) "And how is a bhikkhu unskilled in characteristics? Here, a bhikkhu does not understand as it really is thus: 'A fool is characterized by his actions; a wise person is characterized by his actions.' It is in this way that a bhikkhu is unskilled in characteristics.

(3) "And how does a bhikkhu fail to pick out flies' eggs? Here, a bhikkhu tolerates an arisen thought of sensual desire; he does not abandon it, dispel it, terminate it, and obliterate it. He tolerates an arisen thought of ill will . . . an arisen thought of harming . . . bad unwholesome states whenever they arise; he does not abandon them, dispel them, terminate them, and obliterate them. It is in this way that a bhikkhu fails to pick out flies' eggs.

(4) "And how does a bhikkhu fail to dress wounds? Here, having seen a form with the eye, a bhikkhu grasps at its marks and features. Even though, when he leaves the eye faculty

unguarded, bad unwholesome states of longing and dejection might invade him, he does not practice restraint over it; he does not guard the eye faculty; he does not undertake the restraint of the eye faculty. Having heard a sound with the ear . . . [349] . . . Having smelled an odor with the nose . . . Having tasted a taste with the tongue . . . Having felt a tactile object with the body . . . Having cognized a mental phenomenon with the mind, he grasps at its marks and features. Even though, when he leaves the mind faculty unguarded, bad unwholesome states of longing and dejection might invade him, he does not practice restraint over it; he does not guard the mind faculty; he does not undertake the restraint of the mind faculty. It is in this way that a bhikkhu fails to dress wounds.

(5) "And how does a bhikkhu fail to smoke out the sheds? Here, a bhikkhu does not teach the Dhamma to others in detail as he has heard it and learned it. It is in this way that a bhikkhu fails to smoke out the sheds.

(6) "And how does a bhikkhu not know the watering place? Here, a bhikkhu does not from time to time approach those bhikkhus who are learned, heirs to the heritage, experts on the Dhamma, experts on the discipline, experts on the outlines, and inquire of them: 'How is this, Bhante? What is the meaning of this?' Those venerable ones do not then disclose to him what has not been disclosed, clear up what is obscure, and dispel his perplexity about numerous perplexing points. It is in this way that a bhikkhu does not know the watering place.

(7) "And how does a bhikkhu not know what it is to have drunk? Here, when the Dhamma and discipline proclaimed by the Tathāgata is being taught, a bhikkhu does not gain inspiration in the meaning, does not gain inspiration in the Dhamma, does not gain joy connected with the Dhamma. It is in this way that a bhikkhu does not know what it is to have drunk.

(8) "And how does a bhikkhu not know the road? Here, a bhikkhu does not understand the noble eightfold path as it really is. It is in this way that a bhikkhu does not know the road.

(9) "And how is a bhikkhu unskilled in pastures? [350] Here, a bhikkhu does not understand the four establishments of mindfulness as they really are. It is in this way that a bhikkhu is unskilled in pastures.[2231]

(10) "And how does a bhikkhu milk dry? Here, when faithful

householders invite a bhikkhu to take robes, almsfood, lodgings, and medicines and provisions for the sick, a bhikkhu accepts without moderation. It is in this way that a bhikkhu milks dry.

(11) "And how does a bhikkhu show no extra veneration to those elder bhikkhus of long-standing who have long gone forth, the fathers and leaders of the Saṅgha? Here, a bhikkhu does not maintain bodily, verbal, and mental acts of loving-kindness both openly and privately toward those elder bhikkhus of long-standing who have long gone forth, the fathers and leaders of the Saṅgha. It is in this way that a bhikkhu shows no extra veneration to those elder bhikkhus of long-standing who have long gone forth, the fathers and leaders of the Saṅgha.

"Possessing these eleven qualities, a bhikkhu is incapable of growth, progress, and fulfillment in this Dhamma and discipline.

"Bhikkhus, possessing eleven factors, a cowherd is capable of keeping and rearing a herd of cattle. What eleven? Here, (1) a cowherd has knowledge of form; (2) he is skilled in characteristics; (3) he picks out flies' eggs; (4) he dresses wounds; (5) he smokes out the sheds; (6) he knows the watering place; (7) he knows what it is to have drunk; (8) he knows the road; (9) he is skilled in pastures; (10) he does not milk dry; and (11) he shows extra veneration to those bulls who are fathers and leaders of the herd. Possessing these eleven factors, a cowherd is capable of keeping and rearing a herd of cattle.

"So too, bhikkhus, possessing eleven qualities, a bhikkhu is capable of growth, progress, and fulfillment in this Dhamma and discipline. What eleven? [351] Here, (1) a bhikkhu has knowledge of form; (2) he is skilled in characteristics; (3) he picks out flies' eggs; (4) he dresses wounds; (5) he smokes out the sheds; (6) he knows the watering place; (7) he knows what it is to have drunk; (8) he knows the road; (9) he is skilled in pastures; (10) he does not milk dry; and (11) he shows extra veneration to those elder bhikkhus of long-standing who have long gone forth, the fathers and leaders of the Saṅgha.

(1) "And how does a bhikkhu have knowledge of form? Here, a bhikkhu understands as it really is thus: 'All form of whatever kind is the four great elements and the form derived from the four great elements.' It is in this way that a bhikkhu has knowledge of form.

(2) "And how is a bhikkhu skilled in characteristics? Here, a bhikkhu understands as it really is thus: 'A fool is characterized by his actions; a wise person is characterized by his actions.' It is in this way that a bhikkhu is skilled in characteristics.

(3) "And how does a bhikkhu pick out flies' eggs? Here, a bhikkhu does not tolerate an arisen thought of sensual desire; he abandons it, dispels it, terminates it, and obliterates it. He does not tolerate an arisen thought of ill will . . . an arisen thought of harming . . . bad unwholesome states whenever they arise; he abandons them, dispels them, terminates them, and obliterates them. It is in this way that a bhikkhu picks out flies' eggs.

(4) "And how does a bhikkhu dress wounds? Here, having seen a form with the eye, a bhikkhu does not grasp at its marks and features. Since, if he left the eye faculty unrestrained, bad unwholesome states of longing and dejection might invade him, he practices restraint over it; he guards the eye faculty; he undertakes the restraint of the eye faculty. Having heard a sound with the ear . . . Having smelled an odor with the nose . . . Having tasted a taste with the tongue . . . Having felt a tactile object with the body . . . Having cognized a mental phenomenon with the mind, he does not grasp at its marks and features. Since, if he left the mind faculty unrestrained, bad unwholesome states of longing and dejection might invade him, [352] he practices restraint over it; he guards the mind faculty; he undertakes the restraint of the mind faculty. It is in this way that a bhikkhu dresses wounds.

(5) "And how does a bhikkhu smoke out the sheds? Here, a bhikkhu teaches the Dhamma to others in detail as he has heard it and learned it. It is in this way that a bhikkhu smokes out the sheds.

(6) "And how does a bhikkhu know the watering place? Here, from time to time a bhikkhu approaches those bhikkhus who are learned, heirs to the heritage, experts on the Dhamma, experts on the discipline, experts on the outlines, and inquires of them: 'How is this, Bhante? What is the meaning of this?' Those venerable ones then disclose to him what has not been disclosed, clear up what is obscure, and dispel his perplexity about numerous perplexing points. It is in this way that a bhikkhu knows the watering place.

(7) "And how does a bhikkhu know what it is to have drunk? Here, when the Dhamma and discipline proclaimed by the

Tathāgata is being taught, a bhikkhu gains inspiration in the meaning, gains inspiration in the Dhamma, gains joy connected with the Dhamma. It is in this way that a bhikkhu knows what it is to have drunk.

(8) "And how does a bhikkhu know the road? Here, a bhikkhu understands the noble eightfold path as it really is. It is in this way that a bhikkhu knows the road.

(9) "And how is a bhikkhu skilled in pastures? Here, a bhikkhu understands the four establishments of mindfulness as they really are. It is in this way that a bhikkhu is skilled in pastures.

(10) "And how does a bhikkhu not milk dry? Here, when faithful householders invite a bhikkhu to take robes, almsfood, lodgings, and medicines and provisions for the sick, a bhikkhu is moderate in accepting. [353] It is in this way that a bhikkhu does not milk dry.

(11) "And how does a bhikkhu show extra veneration to those elder bhikkhus of long-standing who have long gone forth, the fathers and leaders of the Saṅgha? Here, a bhikkhu maintains bodily, verbal, and mental acts of loving-kindness both openly and privately toward those elder bhikkhus of long-standing who have long gone forth, the fathers and leaders of the Saṅgha. It is in this way that a bhikkhu shows extra veneration to those elder bhikkhus of long-standing who have long gone forth, the fathers and leaders of the Saṅgha.

"Possessing these eleven qualities, a bhikkhu is capable of growth, progress, and fulfillment in this Dhamma and discipline."

18 (8) Concentration (1)

Then a number of bhikkhus approached the Blessed One, paid homage to him, sat down to one side, and said to him:[2232]

"Bhante, could a bhikkhu obtain such a state of concentration that (1) he would not be percipient of earth in relation to earth; (2) of water in relation to water; (3) of fire in relation to fire; (4) of air in relation to air; (5) of the base of the infinity of space in relation to the base of the infinity of space; (6) of the base of the infinity of consciousness in relation to the base of the infinity of consciousness; (7) of the base of nothingness in relation to the base of nothingness; (8) of the base of neither-perception-nor-non-perception in relation to the base of neither-perception-nor-non-perception; (9) of this world in relation to this world; (10) of the other world in relation to the other world; (11) of anything seen, heard, sensed, cognized, reached, sought after, and examined by the mind, but he would still be percipient?"

"He could, bhikkhus." [354]

"But how, Bhante, could he obtain such a state of concentration?"

"Here, bhikkhus, a bhikkhu is percipient thus: 'This is peaceful, this is sublime, that is, the stilling of all activities, the relinquishing of all acquisitions, the destruction of craving, dispassion, cessation, nibbāna.' It is in this way, bhikkhus, that a bhikkhu could obtain such a state of concentration that he would not be percipient of earth in relation to earth; of water in relation to water; of fire in relation to fire; of air in relation to air; of the base of the infinity of space in relation to the base of the infinity of space; of the base of the infinity of consciousness in relation to the base of the infinity of consciousness; of the base of nothingness in relation to the base of nothingness; of the base of neither-perception-nor-non-perception in relation to the base of neither-perception-nor-non-perception; of this world in relation to this world; of the other world in relation to the other world; of anything seen, heard, sensed, cognized, reached, sought after, and examined by the mind, but he would still be percipient."

19 (9) Concentration (2)

There the Blessed One addressed the bhikkhus: "Bhikkhus!"

"Venerable sir!" those bhikkhus replied. The Blessed One said this:

"Bhikkhus, could a bhikkhu obtain such a state of concentration that (1) he would not be percipient of earth in relation to earth [355] . . . (11) of anything seen, heard, sensed, cognized, reached, sought after, and examined by the mind, but he would still be percipient?"

"Bhante, our teachings are rooted in the Blessed One, guided by the Blessed One, take recourse in the Blessed One. It would be good if the Blessed One would clear up the meaning of this statement. Having heard it from him, the bhikkhus will retain it in mind."

"Then listen, bhikkhus, and attend closely. I will speak."

"Yes, Bhante," those bhikkhus replied. The Blessed One said this:

"Bhikkhus, a bhikkhu could obtain such a state of concentration that he would not be percipient of earth in relation to earth ... he would not be percipient of anything seen, heard, sensed, cognized, reached, sought after, and examined by the mind, but he would still be percipient."

"But how, Bhante, could he obtain such a state of concentration?"

"Here, bhikkhus, a bhikkhu is percipient thus: 'This is peaceful, this is sublime, that is, the stilling of all activities, the relinquishing of all acquisitions, the destruction of craving, dispassion, cessation, nibbāna.' It is in this way, bhikkhus, that a bhikkhu could obtain such a state of concentration that he would not be percipient of earth in relation to earth ... [356] ... he would not be percipient of anything seen, heard, sensed, cognized, reached, sought after, and examined by the mind, but he would still be percipient."

20 (10) Concentration (3)

Then a number of bhikkhus approached the Venerable Sāriputta and exchanged greetings with him. When they had concluded their greetings and cordial talk, they sat down to one side and said to the Venerable Sāriputta:

"Friend Sāriputta, could a bhikkhu obtain such a state of concentration that (1) he would not be percipient of earth in relation to earth ... (11) he would not be percipient of anything seen, heard, sensed, cognized, reached, sought after, and examined by the mind, but he would still be percipient?"

[What follows is identical to 11:18.] [357]

21 (11) Concentration (4)

There the Venerable Sāriputta addressed the bhikkhus:

"Friends, could a bhikkhu obtain such a state of concentration that (1) he would not be percipient of earth in relation to earth ... (11) he would not be percipient of anything seen, heard, sensed, cognized, reached, sought after, and examined by the mind, but he would still be percipient?"

"We would come from far away, friend, to learn the meaning of this statement from the Venerable Sāriputta. It would be good if the Venerable Sāriputta would clear up the meaning of this statement. Having heard it from the Venerable Sāriputta, the bhikkhus will retain it in mind."

"Well then, friends, listen and attend closely. [358] I will speak."

"Yes, friend," those bhikkhus replied. The Venerable Sāriputta said this:

[What follows is identical to 11:19.] [359]

III. Similarity

22 (1)–29 (8) Contemplation of Impermanence

"Bhikkhus, possessing eleven factors, a cowherd is incapable of keeping and rearing a herd of cattle. What eleven? Here, (1) a cowherd has no knowledge of form; (2) he is unskilled in characteristics; (3) he fails to pick out flies' eggs; (4) he fails to dress wounds; (5) he fails to smoke out the sheds; (6) he does not know the watering place; (7) he does not know what it is to have drunk; (8) he does not know the road; (9) he is unskilled in pastures; (10) he milks dry; and (11) he shows no extra veneration to those bulls who are fathers and leaders of the herd. Possessing these eleven factors, a cowherd is incapable of keeping and rearing a herd of cattle.

"So too, bhikkhus, possessing eleven qualities, a bhikkhu is incapable of dwelling contemplating impermanence in the eye ... incapable of dwelling contemplating suffering in the eye ... incapable of dwelling contemplating non-self in the eye ... incapable of dwelling contemplating destruction in the eye ... incapable of dwelling contemplating vanishing in the eye ... incapable of dwelling contemplating fading away in the eye ... incapable of dwelling contemplating cessation in the eye ... incapable of dwelling contemplating relinquishment in the eye ..."

30 (9)–69 (48)

"... in the ear ... in the nose ... in the tongue ... in the body ... in the mind ..."

70 (49)–117 (96)

"... in forms ... in sounds ... in odors ... in tastes ... in tactile objects ... in phenomena ..."

118 (97)–165 (144)
"... in eye-consciousness ... in ear-consciousness ... in nose-consciousness ... in tongue-consciousness ... in body-consciousness ... in mind-consciousness ..."

166 (145)–213 (192)
"... in eye-contact ... in ear-contact ... in nose-contact ... in tongue-contact ... in body-contact ... in mind-contact ..."

214 (193)–261 (240)
"... in feeling born of eye-contact ... in feeling born of ear-contact ... in feeling born of nose-contact ... in feeling born of tongue-contact ... in feeling born of body-contact ... in feeling born of mind-contact ..."

262 (241)–309 (288)
"... in perception of forms ... in perception of sounds ... in perception of odors ... in perception of tastes ... in perception of tactile objects [360] ... in perception of phenomena ..."

310 (289)–367 (336)
"... in volition regarding forms ... in volition regarding sounds ... in volition regarding odors ... in volition regarding tastes ... in volition regarding tactile objects ... in volition regarding phenomena ..."

368 (337)–405 (384)
"... in craving for forms ... in craving for sounds ... in craving for odors ... in craving for tastes ... in craving for tactile objects ... in craving for phenomena ..."

406 (385)–453 (432)
"... in thought about forms ... in thought about sounds ... in thought about odors ... in thought about tastes ... in thought about tactile objects ... in thought about phenomena ..."

454 (433)–501 (480)
"... in examination of forms ... in examination of sounds ... in examination of odors ... in examination of tastes ... in examination of tactile objects ... in examination of phenomena ..."

502 (481)–981 (960)

"Bhikkhus, possessing eleven factors, a cowherd is capable of keeping and rearing a herd of cattle.[2233] What eleven? Here, (1) a cowherd has knowledge of form; (2) he is skilled in characteristics; (3) he picks out flies' eggs; (4) he dresses wounds; (5) he smokes out the sheds; (6) he knows the watering place; (7) he knows what it is to have drunk; (8) he knows the road; (9) he is skilled in pastures; (10) he does not milk dry; and (11) he shows extra veneration to those bulls who are fathers and leaders of the herd. Possessing these eleven factors, a cowherd is capable of keeping and rearing a herd of cattle.

"So too, bhikkhus, possessing eleven qualities, a bhikkhu is capable of dwelling contemplating impermanence in the eye... [all as above down to:] ... is capable of dwelling contemplating relinquishment in examination of phenomena..."

IV. Lust and So Forth Repetition Series[2234]

982 (1)[2235]

"Bhikkhus, for direct knowledge of lust, eleven things are to be developed. What eleven? The first jhāna, the second jhāna, the third jhāna, the fourth jhāna, the liberation of the mind by loving-kindness, the liberation of the mind by compassion, the liberation of the mind by altruistic joy, the liberation of the mind by equanimity, the base of the infinity of space, the base of the infinity of consciousness, and the base of nothingness. For direct knowledge of lust, these eleven things are to be developed."

983 (2)–991 (10)

"Bhikkhus, for full understanding of lust... for the utter destruction... for the abandoning... for the destruction... for the vanishing... for the fading away... for the cessation... for the giving up... for the relinquishment of lust... these eleven things are to be developed." [361]

992 (11)–1151 (170)

"Bhikkhus, for direct knowledge... for full understanding... for the utter destruction... for the abandoning... for the destruction... for the vanishing... for the fading away... for the cessation... for the giving up... for the relinquishment of hatred...

of delusion . . . of anger . . . of hostility . . . of denigration . . . of insolence . . . of envy . . . of miserliness . . . of deceitfulness . . . of craftiness . . . of obstinacy . . . of vehemence . . . of conceit . . . of arrogance . . . of intoxication . . . of heedlessness . . . these eleven things are to be developed."

This is what the Blessed One said. Elated, those bhikkhus delighted in the Blessed One's statement.

The Book of the Elevens is finished.

Notes

Appendixes

Pāli-English Glossary

Bibliography

Indexes

Notes

Notes to the Introduction

1 Norman (2006a: 53) writes: "There is no agreement among scholars about the date when writing first came into use in India, but everyone, I think, agrees that during the early period of Buddhism, even if writing were available, all teaching was by oral methods, and the Buddhist scriptures were transmitted orally, as was also the case with the brahmanical texts."

2 For the Saṃyutta and Aṅguttara Nikāyas, Kelly uses the number of suttas that I had calculated in *Connected Discourses of the Buddha* and in the present work, respectively.

3 Kelly surveyed only the older stratum of works in the Khuddaka Nikāya: Khuddakapātha, Dhammapada, Udāna, Itivuttaka, Suttanipāta, Theragāthā, and Therīgāthā.

4 I can see no reason, apart from faulty transmission, for the recollection of generosity to be missing.

5 I have simplified the table to cover only the broad divisions.

6 In AN the threefold template occurs at **3:103–6**. It also occurs in MN 13 in relation to sensual pleasures, bodily form, and feeling, and in SN in relation to the four physical elements, the five aggregates, and the six sense bases respectively at 14:31–33, 22:26–28, and 35:13–18.

7 In the Abhidhamma and later Pāli texts, views (*diṭṭhi*) were added to the *āsavas* as well, thus increasing their number to four.

8 Several suttas subdivide the stream-enterer and the non-returner into subsidiary types, thereby increasing the number of noble ones. See **3:87** for the stream-enterer and **3:88**, **7:16**, and **7:55** for the non-returner.

9 Kelly (2011: 13) counts nineteen suttas in AN spoken to women. In contrast, according to his reckoning, the other four Nikāyas (including the older stratum of the Khuddaka Nikāya) have a total of only *eight* suttas spoken to women.

10 In Pāli editions it is customary to attach the word *ādi* to the first term of a series to indicate that the terms to follow conform to

the same pattern accorded the first term. It thus functions in the same way as "and so forth" does in English.

11 *Sabbāgamasaṃvaṇṇanamanoratho pūrito ca me yasmā/ Etāya manorathapūraṇī ti nāmaṃ tato assā.*

12 The late Primoz Pecenko reports discovering a manuscript of the old *ṭīkā* on the Aṅguttara Nikāya in Burma (2009: 23–27). He also says that several other manuscripts of this work are known to exist.

13 Enomoto 1986: 21.

14 Enomoto 1986: 23.

15 Anesaki 1908: 139.

16 Enomoto 1986: 25.

Notes to the Ones

17 Here and elsewhere I render the Pāli idiom *cittaṃ pariyādāya tiṭṭhati* simply as "[it] obsesses the mind." Literally, it would be rendered "having overcome the mind, [it] remains [there]."

18 Mp: "The bodily odor of a woman is foul (*duggandha*), but what is intended here is the odor that comes from her body due to ointments, etc."

19 Mp: "The taste of a woman is the taste of her lips, saliva, etc., and the taste of the porridge and rice, etc., she gives to her husband. Many beings meet disaster after receiving sweets from a woman."

20 Mp: "Because of the different inclinations and underlying tendencies of beings, the Buddha mentions each of the [five sense objects] such as forms, saying: 'I do not see anything like this.' When a man esteems form, the form of a woman obsesses and impedes him—binds, captivates, deludes, and confuses him; but not so the other sense objects such as sounds. So too, sound but not form captivates one who esteems sound, etc. For some people, only one sense object obsesses the mind; for others, two objects—or three, four, or five objects—obsess them. Thus these five suttas are expounded because of the five kinds of esteem [for different sense objects]."

21 Mp: "It is not only men who esteem the five sense objects but women too. Therefore the next five suttas are formulated with women as the subject."

22 This series of suttas posits connections between the five hindrances and their principal conditions. In this respect, the suttas are similar to the sections of SN 46:2, V 64–65, and SN 46:51, V 102–3, on the nourishment of the five hindrances. For more on the five hindrances in AN, see **5:23, 5:51, 5:52, 5:193**.

23 *Subhanimitta*. Mp: "The mark of the attractive is an object that is a basis for lust." Mp cites various uses of the word *nimitta*: as a condition (*paccaya*), a cause (*kāraṇa*), concentration (*samādhi*), and insight (*vipassanā*). Here it means "an agreeable object that is a basis for lust" (*rāgaṭṭhāniyo iṭṭhārammaṇadhammo*). Mp glosses *ayoniso manasikaroto* with *anupāyena manasikarontassa* ("for one who attends unskillfully") and cites the definition of "careless attention" (*ayoniso manasikāra*) at Vibh 373 (Be §936): "Careless attention is deviant attention, which takes the impermanent to be permanent, suffering to be happiness, what is non-self to be self, and the unattractive to be attractive. Or it is the mental turning, advertence, leaning, consideration, attention [to an object] in a way that runs contrary to the [four noble] truths." It seems to me doubtful that this explanation of *ayoniso manasikāra* will hold for all applications of the term in the Nikāyas. Even in the following sutta, on the arising and increase of ill will, it is questionable that attending carelessly to "the mark of the repulsive" can be subsumed under any of the four distortions in the definition at Vibh 373.

24 *Paṭighanimitta*. Mp: "This denotes a disagreeable mark; it is a designation for aversion (repulsion) and for a repulsive object" (*aniṭṭhaṃ nimittaṃ; paṭighassapi paṭighassārammaṇassapi etaṃ adhivacanaṃ*). Interestingly, Mp continues with a citation from "the commentary": "For it is said in the commentary: 'The mark of the repulsive is aversion (repulsion) and a repulsive object'" (*vuttampi c'etaṃ aṭṭhakathāyaṃ paṭighampi paṭighanimittaṃ, paṭighārammaṇopi dhammo paṭighanimittan ti*). Mp-ṭ identifies "the commentary" as "the Great Commentary" (*mahā aṭṭhakathā*), one of the ancient Sinhala commentaries that Buddhaghosa used as the source for his own commentaries. These ancient commentaries are no longer extant, but this allusion makes it clear that Buddhaghosa worked with sources and did not write original compositions.

25 These terms are defined at Vibh 352 (Be §§856–860).

26 *Avūpasantacittassa*. Mp: "A mind not settled by jhāna or insight."

27 Mp cites Dhs 205 (Be §1167) for a definition of the hindrance of doubt (*vicikicchānīvaraṇa*) as doubt about the Buddha, the Dhamma, the Saṅgha, and the training (see too **5:205**).

28 This series, **1:16–20**, corresponds to SN 46:51 §3, V 105–6, on the "denourishment" or removal of the five hindrances.

29 Mp uses the commentarial scheme of five kinds of abandoning to explain how sensual desire and the other hindrances are abandoned: (1) in a particular respect (*tadaṅgappahāna*), through

insight; (2) by suppression (*vikkhambhanappahāna*), through a meditative attainment; (3) by eradication (*samucchedappahāna*), through the world-transcending path; (4) by subsiding (*paṭipassaddhippahāna*), through the fruition; and (5) by escape (*nissaraṇappahāna*), through nibbāna, "the release from all defilements." Mp says that all five apply here.

Mp identifies the "mark of the unattractive" (*asubhanimitta*) with the first jhāna arisen on the basis of any of the ten unattractive objects (*dasasu asubhesu uppannaṃ sārammaṇaṃ paṭhamajjhānaṃ*). This explanation relies on the Vism scheme, which takes the *asubha* objects to be corpses in stages of decomposition (see Vism 178–93, Ppn 6.1–80). While we do find meditation on decaying corpses in the Nikāyas (see below at **1:480–84**), more typically the suttas explain the perception of the unattractive (*asubhasaññā*) as meditation on the thirty-one components of the body (increased to thirty-two in later works by adding the brain). See, for example, **10:60 §3**, on the perception of unattractiveness. This perception occurs among a group of five meditation subjects that culminate in the deathless (**5:61**), that lead to nibbāna (**5:69**) and to the destruction of the taints (**5:70**), and that bring liberation of mind and liberation by wisdom (**5:71**). At **7:49 §1**, the perception of unattractiveness is recommended as the antidote to sexual desire, and at **9:1 §6** and **9:3 §6** it is prescribed for the abandoning of lust.

30 In line with the commentary to the Satipaṭṭhāna Sutta (at Sv III 778–82, Ps I 282–86), Mp enumerates six things that lead to the abandoning of each of the five hindrances. The six that lead to the abandoning of sensual desire are: learning an unattractive object, meditation on an unattractive object, guarding the doors of the sense faculties, moderation in eating, good friendship, and suitable conversation.

31 *Mettācetovimutti*. Mp: "Loving-kindness pervades all beings with [the wish for] their welfare. Since the mind associated with it is liberated from the opposed states such as the hindrances, it is called liberation of mind (*cetovimutti*). Specifically, this 'liberation of mind' is liberated from obsession by ill will. Here, what is intended by 'liberation of mind' is absorption (*appanā*) by three or four jhānas [depending on whether the fourfold or fivefold scheme of jhānas is used]." Mp-ṭ: "[This is said] because there is no thorough liberating [of the mind] by loving-kindness until one attains absorption." At **6:13 §1** loving-kindness is taught as the escape from ill will. At **9:1 §7** and **9:3 §7**, it is recommended for abandoning ill will. **8:63 §1** teaches different approaches to developing the liberation of the mind by loving-kindness, and

8:1 and **11:15** explain, respectively, eight and eleven benefits of mastering the liberation of the mind by loving-kindness. The fourfold scheme of jhānas is typical of the Nikāyas; the fivefold scheme appears in the Abhidhamma by dividing the second jhāna into two: the second with examination but without thought, the third without thought and examination.

32 Mp mentions six things that lead to the abandoning of ill will: learning the meditation on loving-kindness, cultivating meditation on loving-kindness, reviewing ownership of kamma, abundant reflection, good friendship, and suitable conversation. On "reviewing ownership of kamma," Mp says that one should reflect thus: "If you get angry with another person, what can you do? Can you destroy his virtuous behavior, etc.? Didn't you come into this world on account of your own kamma and won't you depart through your own kamma? Getting angry with another person is like taking hold of a hot flameless coal or an iron stake smeared with excrement in order to strike someone. If he gets angry with you, what can he do? Can he destroy your virtuous behavior, etc.? Didn't he come into this world on account of his own kamma and won't he depart through his own kamma? Just like an offering of a cake that is refused, or like a fist full of dust thrown against the wind, his anger will remain with him." For more ways of overcoming anger, see Vism 298–306, Ppn 9:14–39.

33 *Ārambhadhātu, nikkamadhātu, parakkamadhātu*. Mp explains these as three successively more powerful degrees of energy.

34 Mp mentions six other things that lead to the abandoning of dullness and drowsiness: moderation in food, change of posture, the perception of light, living out in the open, good friendship, and suitable conversation. For moderation in food, Mp (in line with other commentaries) suggests that when one still has room for four or five more mouthfuls, one should stop eating and drink water.

35 *Vūpasantacittassa*. Mp: "A mind pacified by jhāna or by insight."

36 Mp: "Six other things lead to the abandoning of restlessness and remorse: much learning, asking questions, being skilled in the Vinaya, approaching elder monks, good friendship, and suitable conversation."

37 This is an abridgment. SN 46:51 §3, V 106,9–15, says that the "denourishment" of doubt occurs "by giving careful attention to wholesome and unwholesome qualities, blamable and blameless qualities, inferior and superior qualities, dark and bright qualities with their counterparts."

38 Mp: "Six other things lead to the abandoning of doubt: much learning, asking questions, skill in the Vinaya, abundant resolve (that is, trust and faith in the Three Jewels), good friendship, and suitable conversation."

39 *Apātubhūtaṃ*. As I understand it, this statement is saying that the mind's potential has not yet become manifest, has not been tapped and applied.

40 *Yathābhataṃ nikkhitto*. I translate this idiom on the basis of Mp's gloss: *yathā āharitvā ṭhapito*.

41 Mp: "A mind corrupted by hate" (*dosena paduṭṭhacittaṃ*). This sutta and the following might be seen as prose elaborations of Dhp 1 and 2. Though Dhp 1 and 2 use *mano* rather than *citta*, the adjectives are the same: *paduṭṭha* and *pasanna*.

42 Mp: "[A mind] placid with faith and confidence" (*saddhāpasādena pasannaṃ*).

43 Mp: "*Cloudy* (*āvilena*): enveloped by the five hindrances." At **5:193 §5** cloudy water is specifically identified with doubt and limpid water with freedom from doubt.

44 *Uttariṃ manussadhammā alamariyañāṇadassanavisesaṃ*. I follow Mp, which treats *uttariṃ manussadhammā* as a complex ablative phrase relative to *alamariyañāṇadassanavisesaṃ*. Mp says: "*Superhuman*: superior to the human virtue consisting in the ten courses of wholesome kamma. For this tenfold virtue is called 'human virtue' because it is undertaken by people on their own—even without anyone to encourage them—after they have been stirred at the end of 'the period of swords' (*satthantarakappa*; see DN III 73,4). The things superior to this are the jhānas, insight, the path, and the fruit. *Distinction in knowledge and vision worthy of the noble ones*: the distinction [excellence] consisting in knowledge and vision that is fitting for the noble ones or able to produce the noble state. Knowledge itself is called 'knowledge' in that it knows, and it is called 'vision' in that it sees. This is a designation for the knowledge of the divine eye, insight knowledge, path knowledge, fruition knowledge, and reviewing knowledge."

45 Mp, using the Abhidhamma model of the mind, takes this to refer to the extreme speed with which the mind arises and vanishes. But at Vin I 150,7–14, in a passage on the conditions that entitle a bhikkhu to cut short his rains observance, it is said that if a woman is trying to seduce a bhikkhu at his rains residence, he is entitled to depart after reflecting: "The Blessed One said that the mind is quick to change, and here there is an obstacle to my living the celibate life." In this context, the obvious sense is not that the mind arises and ceases quickly but that one might

suddenly *change one's mind*, giving up the celibate life to submit to the charms of the woman.

46 *Pabhassaram idaṃ bhikkhave cittaṃ*. The exact meaning of this statement has been a matter of contention that has spawned conflicting interpretations. Mp identifies the "luminous mind" with the *bhavaṅgacitta*, an Abhidhamma concept denoting the type of mental event that occurs in the absence of active cognition. It corresponds, very roughly, to the subconscious or unconscious of modern psychology. The word *bhavaṅga* means "factor of existence," that is, the factor responsible for maintaining continuous personal identity throughout a given life and from one life to the next. However, the *bhavaṅga* is not a persistent state of consciousness, a permanent self. It is a series of momentary acts of mind that alternate with active cognitive processes (*cittavīthi*), sequences of cognition when the mind consciously apprehends an object. Hence the texts sometimes use the expression *bhavaṅgasota*, "stream of *bhavaṅga*," to highlight the fluid nature of this type of mental process. The occurrence of the *bhavaṅga* is most evident in deep, dreamless sleep, but it also occurs countless times in waking life between cognitive processes.

The most important events in the cognitive process are the *javanacittas*, ethically determinate occasions of consciousness that create kamma. The *javanas* may be either wholesome or unwholesome. It is in the *javana* phase that the defilements, dormant in the subconscious *bhavaṅga*, infiltrate mental activity and defile the mind. For a fuller discussion of the *bhavaṅga*, see CMA 122–29, where it is rendered "life-continuum." Harvey (1995: 166–79) has an interesting exploration of the relationship between the *bhavaṅga* and what he calls "the brightly shining mind."

Mp explains: "The *bhavaṅgacitta* is called luminous, that is, pure (*parisuddha*), because it is without defilements (*nirupakkilesatāya*). It is defiled by adventitious defilements—by lust, etc.—which arise later [after the *bhavaṅga*] at the moment of *javana*. How? In the way that virtuous, well-behaved parents—or preceptor and teacher—get to be criticized and blamed on account of their undisciplined, badly behaved children or pupils, [as when people say]: 'They don't punish, train, exhort, or instruct their own children or pupils.' Well-behaved parents, or preceptor and teacher, are like the *bhavaṅgacitta*, while the blame falling on the parents because of their children [or on the preceptor and teacher on account of their pupils] is like the naturally pure *bhavaṅgacitta* being defiled at the *javana* moment by the adventitious defilements that arise in states of mind associated with greed, etc., which cause lust, hatred, and delusion to infect it."

Though I quote Mp in full here, I find this explanation problematic on at least two grounds. The first is that the very concept of the *bhavaṅgacitta*, and the corresponding notion of the cognitive process, are not found in the Nikāyas but first emerge in a later period when the Abhidhamma was taking shape. Even the term *bhavaṅga*, though crucial to the Theravāda Abhidhamma system, occurs only in the last book of the Abhidhamma Piṭaka, the *Paṭṭhāna*. It is found much more often in the Abhidhamma commentaries.

The second reason I find Mp's explanation problematic is that the text flatly states "*this mind* is luminous," without qualification. This suggests that luminosity is intrinsic to the mind itself, and not to a particular type of mental event. Moreover, if the *bhavaṅga* is luminous, it should always remain so; it becomes incoherent to speak of it being defiled by the *javanas*. The simplest interpretation of this statement, so far as I can see, is that luminosity is an innate characteristic of mind, seen in its capacity to illuminate its objective field. This luminosity, though inherent, is functionally blocked because the mind is "defiled by adventitious defilements" (*āgantukehi upakkilesehi upakkiliṭṭhaṃ*). The defilements are called "adventitious" because, unlike the luminosity, they are not intrinsic to the mind itself. Of course, as **10:61** and **10:62** assert, there is no "first point" to ignorance and craving (and other defilements). But these defilements can be removed by mental training. With their removal, the mind's intrinsic luminosity emerges—or, more precisely, becomes manifest. The statement just below that the noble disciple understands the mind to be luminous implies that this insight into the intrinsic luminosity of the mind serves as the basis for further mental development, which liberates the mind from the defilements. With the complete removal of defilements, the mind's intrinsic luminosity shines forth unobstructed.

At **3:102**, I 257,7 the word *pabhassara* is used to describe the mind (*citta*) that has attained concentration (*samādhi*). It thus seems that it is in deep *samādhi* that the intrinsic luminosity of the mind emerges, at least temporarily. **5:23**, III 16,29–17,2 says explicitly that the mind freed from the five hindrances is luminous (*pabhassara*) and properly concentrated for the destruction of the taints. See too MN III 243,11–12, where it is equanimity (*upekkhā*), presumably of the fourth jhāna, that is described as luminous.

47 *Cittabhāvanā natthi*. Mp: "There is no stability of mind, no

comprehension of mind" (*cittaṭṭhiti cittapariggaho natthi*). Mp-ṭ: "The development of mind [called] 'stability of mind' (*cittaṭṭhiti*) is the practice through which one can accurately understand defilement of the mind and liberation from it. The development of insight (*vipassanābhāvanā*), which occurs based on the stabilization [of the mind] by fully concentrating it on a single object, is what is known as comprehension of the mind (*cittassa pariggaha*); [this occurs] together with the associated [mental] factors based on that object. It is through this that one can accurately understand the meaning stated."

The Nikāyas often set up a contrast between the "uninstructed worldling" (*assutavā puthujjana*), the common person of the world who lacks training in the Buddha's teaching, and the instructed noble disciple (*sutavā ariya sāvaka*), who has learned the teaching and undertaken the training. More broadly, a *puthujjana* is anyone who has not yet reached the path of stream-entry (*sotāpatti*). An *ariyasāvaka* is not necessarily a "noble one" in the technical sense, but any disciple, monastic or layperson, who has learned the teaching and earnestly takes up the practice.

48 Mp: "In this sutta powerful insight (*balavavipassanā*) is discussed; but some say tender insight (*taruṇavipassanā*)." Here, "tender insight" refers to the early stage of knowledge of rise and fall, while "powerful insight" to the mature stage of knowledge of rise and fall and the higher insight knowledges.

49 Mp says that by "pursues a mind of loving-kindness" (*mettācittaṃ āsevati*), the text refers to the mere pervasion of all beings with a wish for their well-being. Thus it seems that here "not devoid of jhāna" (*arittajjhāno*) does not necessarily mean that the monk actually attains one of the four jhānas but that he earnestly engages in meditation. The phrase "does not eat the country's almsfood in vain" means that by practicing meditation, the monk is worthy to receive almsfood from laypeople. He enables the donors to acquire merit and uses the almsfood properly to support the spiritual life.

50 *Sabb'ete manopubbaṅgamā*. Mp interprets this in line with the Abhidhamma doctrine that mind (*citta*) and its concomitants (*cetasikas*) occur simultaneously: "These [factors] arise together with mind (*mano*); they have a single arising, basis, cessation, and object. But because mind is what arouses, produces, generates, and originates them, they are said to have mind as their forerunner." Again, Mp reads this statement through the lens of the Abhidhamma analysis of mind. Understood in line with Dhp 1 and 2, the text probably means simply that before one commits any unwholesome bodily or verbal deed, one first decides to act

in such a way. This gives the statement an ethical rather than a psychological meaning. This interpretation is supported by the next sentence about the mind arising first, followed by the others. The same applies to the wholesome mind and its qualities in the next sutta.

51 Mp cites Vibh 350 (Be §846) for a definition of heedlessness (*pamāda*): "What is heedlessness? Laxity of mind, looseness of mind, in regard to bodily misconduct, verbal misconduct, mental misconduct, and the five kinds of sensual pleasures; and disrespect for the cultivation of wholesome qualities without persevering and persisting in this. [It is] looseness of procedure, lack of desire, non-commitment, non-determination, non-devotion, non-pursuit, non-development, and non-cultivation [of wholesome qualities]."

52 *Mahicchatā*. Mp explains this as "strong greed" (*mahālobho*) and, for a formal definition, it quotes Vibh 351 (Be §850): "What is strong desire? Lack of contentment, excessive desire with regard to robes, almsfood, dwelling places, medicines, and the five objects of sensual pleasure. Such desire, desirousness, strong desire, lust, passion, mental passion, is called strong desire."

53 *Appicchatā*. Mp: "Whereas the expression ['fewness of desires'] might be taken to mean that there could be a residue [of desire], the meaning is that there is *no residue*. For one is not called 'of few desires' if one still has slight desire; it is through the absence of desire, through persistent greedlessness, that one is said to be of few desires."

54 *Asantuṭṭhitā*. Mp: "This is the greed that arises from associating with, resorting to, and attending on discontented persons."

55 *Santuṭṭhitā*. Mp distinguishes three types of contentment: (1) contentment that accords with what one obtains (*yathālābhasantosa*), being content with any kind of robe (or other requisite) whether of fine or poor quality; (2) contentment that accords with one's ability (*yathābalasantosa*), being content with what one obtains but selecting for use those things most congenial to one's health; and (3) contentment with what is appropriate (*yathāsāruppasantosa*), keeping the most basic gains for oneself and giving away the rest. For a translation of the full passage, see Bodhi 1989: 130–34.

56 *Sampajaññaṃ*. Here, Mp says only that this is a term for wisdom (*paññā*). For a fuller treatment of *sampajañña* according to the commentarial method, see Bodhi 1989: 94–130.

57 On the importance of good friendship (*kalyāṇamittatā*) in the spiritual life, see **9:3**. See too SN 45:2–3, V 2–4.

58 I follow Ce, which treats this sutta as the eleventh in vagga VIII. Be and Ee both end this vagga with **1:80** and begin the next with

1:81. The Ce arrangement has the advantage of keeping thematically paired suttas together.

59 Ee titles the first part of this vagga, constituted by the first thirty-two suttas, *Catukoṭika,* "Four-Pointed," and the second part, consisting of the last ten suttas, *Adhammādi,* "Non-Dhamma, Etc."

60 Here, and in all the couplets through **1:113**, I read with Ce and Be *ekaṅgampi* over Ee *ekadhammam pi.*

61 Mp: "The ten courses of wholesome kamma are Dhamma; the ten courses of unwholesome kamma are non-Dhamma. So too, the thirty-seven aids to enlightenment—namely, the four establishments of mindfulness, the four right strivings, the four bases of spiritual power, the five faculties, the five powers, the seven factors of enlightenment, and the noble eightfold path—are Dhamma; three establishments of mindfulness, three right strivings, three bases of spiritual power, six faculties, six powers, eight factors of enlightenment, and a ninefold path [are non-Dhamma.] The four types of clinging, the five hindrances, the seven underlying tendencies, and the eight kinds of wrongness [the opposites of the noble path factors] are non-Dhamma. They teach non-Dhamma as Dhamma when they select one type of non-Dhamma and think, 'We will teach this as Dhamma. In that way our teacher's group will be emancipating, and we will become famous in the world.' By the Vinaya method, Dhamma is a disciplinary action that should be done according to the claim, after having reprimanded, after having reminded, according to a true base. Non-Dhamma is a disciplinary action done without a claim, without having reprimanded, without having reminded, according to a false base."

62 Mp: "By the sutta method, discipline (*vinaya*) means restraint, abandoning, reflection, and the removal of lust, hatred, and delusion. Non-discipline (*avinaya*) means non-restraint, non-abandoning, non-reflection, and the non-removal of lust, hatred, and delusion. By the Vinaya method, discipline is a proper base, motion, announcement, bounded area, and assembly. Non-discipline is a defective base, motion, announcement, bounded area, and assembly."

63 Mp, in line with other commentaries, explains five kinds of disappearance of the good Dhamma. I summarize: (1) *Disappearance of attainment* (*adhigama-antaradhāna*): the gradual disappearance of attainment of the paths, fruits, and auxiliary attainments such as the analytical knowledges (*paṭisambhidā*) and direct knowledges (*abhiññā*). (2) *Disappearance of practice* (*paṭipatti-antaradhāna*): the gradual disappearance of the jhānas, insight, paths, and fruits, and even the eventual disappearance of virtuous behavior. (3)

Disappearance of learning (*pariyatti-antaradhāna*): the gradual disappearance of the Tipiṭaka, the Buddhist canon. (4) *Disappearance of the emblem* (*liṅga-antaradhāna*): the gradual discarding of the renunciant robes until monastics wear merely a strip of ochre cloth around their necks. (5) *Disappearance of the relics* (*dhātu-antaradhāna*): at the end of the Buddha Gotama's teaching, his relics all gather at the Bodhi tree at Bodhgaya, replicate the Buddha's bodily form, and vanish in a blaze of glory.

64 Ee titles this vagga "The Eleventh."

65 Ee titles this vagga "Not an Offense, Etc." By offense (*āpatti*) is meant a transgression of monastic discipline.

66 Mp: "Five classes of offenses are called light (*lahuka*) and two are called grave (*gāruka*, lit. "heavy"). Two are coarse and five are not coarse. Six classes are remediable and one is irremediable. Offenses with redress are the same as those that are remediable; the offenses without redress are the same as those that are irremediable." The two grave classes of offenses are (1) the *pārājikas*, which entail permanent expulsion from the Saṅgha, and (2) the *saṅghādisesas*, which require formal meetings of the Saṅgha and a complex process of rehabilitation. The five light classes are *thullaccaya* (gross transgression), *pācittiya* (expiation), *pātidesanīya* (to be acknowledged), *dukkaṭa* (misdeed), and *dubbhāsita* (bad speech). These can be exonerated by confession to another monk. The grave offenses are also called "coarse" (*duṭṭhulla*); the light ones, not coarse (*aduṭṭhulla*). The *pārājikas* are "irremediable" (*anavasesa*) and "without redress" (*appaṭikamma*), because they do not allow for expiation; the other six classes are "remediable" (*sāvasesa*) and "with redress" (*sappaṭikamma*) because they can be cleared by expiation.

67 This sutta, unlike those of the preceding vagga, does not include *bahuno janassa*. All three editions exclude it, though it is hard to see any reason apart from an old recitation or editorial error.

68 Ce counts here nine separate suttas, one for each epithet. I follow Be and Ee, which group them together as one sutta.

69 *Asamasamo*. Mp explains this to mean "equal to those without equal," that is, equal to the unequaled Buddhas of the past and the future. But elsewhere *samasama* means "exactly equal," and thus *asamasama* should probably be understood to mean simply "without equal." See DN I 123,12, MN I 329,7, MN I 515,24, MN I 516,11, etc.

70 *Dvipadānaṃ aggo*. Mp: "The best among human beings and devas."

71 I follow Ce and Be, which take each utterance to be a separate sutta and thus count twelve suttas here. Ee combines them into

one. Since the last sentence recapitulates all the items from "the manifestation of great vision" to "the realization of the fruit of arahantship," it seems this was originally a single sutta. However, to keep my numbering in alignment with Ce and Be, I count each separately.

72 On the "six things unsurpassed" (*cha anuttarīyāni*), see **6:30**. On the four analytical knowledges (*catasso paṭisambhidāyo*), see **4:172**. These are discussed in detail at Vibh 293–305 (Be §§718–50) and Vism 440–42, Ppn 14.21–27. Mp explains the "penetration of numerous elements" (*anekadhātupaṭivedha*) by way of the eighteen elements (six sense objects, six sense faculties, six types of consciousness), and the "penetration of the diversity of elements" (*nānādhātupaṭivedha*) by way of their different specific natures (*nānāsabhāvato*). In the expression "fruit of true knowledge and liberation" (*vijjāvimuttiphala*), Mp identifies true knowledge (*vijjā*) with the knowledge of the fruit, and "liberation" (*vimutti*) with the other factors associated with the fruit. Presumably this means the fruit of arahantship.

73 From here on, Ce and Be designate these divisions simply as *–pāḷi* rather than *–vagga*, e.g., the title of this division is *etadaggapāḷi*. Each group of ten (or more) suttas in the division is designated a *vagga*, named in Ce simply *vaggo paṭhamo, vaggo dutiyo* (first chapter, second chapter), etc., and in Be *paṭhamavaggo, dutiyavaggo*, etc. However, the major headings (ending in *–pāḷi*) are numbered consecutively to the previous divisions called *–vagga*, which suggests that each can be considered a major vagga comprising several minor vaggas. Thus the present division is numbered XIV (or 14), following the *ekapuggalavagga* ("One Person Chapter"), which was XIII (or 13). I follow Be and Ce in counting as a separate vagga or subchapter each group of ten (or more) suttas, each sutta being determined by the announcement of a particular disciple as foremost. Ee, in contrast, takes each grouping (subchapter) as one large sutta. Many of the facts and references in my notes to these chapters have been gleaned from DPPN.

74 He was the first to understand the four noble truths at the Buddha's first discourse, and the first to request admission to the Saṅgha. See SN 56:11, V 423,13–16 and Vin I 11,34–36, 12,15–26.

75 For more detailed biographical accounts of Sāriputta, Mahāmoggallāna, Mahākassapa, Anuruddha, and Mahākaccāna, see Nyanaponika and Hecker 2003, chaps. 1, 2, 3, 5, and 6, respectively.

76 By psychic potency (*iddhi*) is meant the supernormal powers described in **3:60**, I 170; **3:101**, I 255, and elsewhere.

77 The ascetic practices (*dhuta, dhutaṅga*) are often observed by

monks for the sake of fewness of desires, being easy to support, and self-restraint. They include living in the forest, at the foot of a tree, in the open air, or in a charnel ground; using only three robes; wearing "rag-robes" made from pieces of discarded cloth; eating only food obtained on alms round; and sleeping in the sitting posture. See **1:378–81, 5:181–90**. The standard thirteen ascetic practices are discussed in Vism chap. 2.

78 The divine eye (*dibbacakkhu*) is the ability to see objects at remote distances, including distant world systems; to see other realms of existence; and to see beings dying and being reborn in accordance with their kamma.

79 He was the son of Kāḷigodhā, a senior Sakyan lady, and a close friend of Anuruddha, with whom he went forth. A story about him is in Ud 2:10, 18–20. His verses are at Th 842–65.

80 Born to a wealthy family of Sāvatthī, he was given the sobriquet *lakuṇṭaka* (dwarf) due to his small stature. His attainment of arahantship is recounted in Ud 7:1, 74. He is praised in Ud 7:2, 74–75; Ud 7:5, 76; and SN 21:6, II 279. His verses are at Th 466–72.

81 He was the son of the chaplain of King Udena of Kosambī. When he visited Rājagaha and saw the gains that accrued to the bhikkhus, he decided to become a monk. In his early days as a bhikkhu he was gluttonous, but the Buddha taught him to be moderate in eating. He soon attained arahantship with the six direct knowledges. He was rebuked by the Buddha for using his psychic powers to win a sandalwood bowl (Vin II 110–12). He converses with King Udena about sense restraint at SN 35:127, IV 110–13. He is praised in Ud 4:6, 42–43. His verses are at Th 123–24.

82 A nephew of Aññākoṇḍañña, he was from a brahmin family that lived near Kapilavatthu, the Buddha's native city. After he attained arahantship he went to see the Buddha in Sāvatthī. Sāriputta met him and they had a discussion on the Dhamma, preserved in MN 24. He was praised by Ānanda for his skill as a teacher at SN 22:83, III 105–6.

83 His story is told at Vism 387–89, Ppn 12.60–66. Because he was born by a roadside (*pantha*), he was given the name Panthaka. He is praised in Ud 5:10, 61. His verses are at Th 557–66.

84 He was the elder brother of Cullapanthaka, also born by a roadside. Being elder, when his brother was born he was called Mahā (large, great) and his brother Culla (small). His verses are at Th 510–17. Mp says that Cullapanthaka was particularly skilled in concentration and was therefore the foremost in mental transformation (*cetovivaṭṭa*). Mahāpanthaka was particularly skilled in

insight and was therefore foremost in the transformation of perception (*saññāvivaṭṭa*). Mp-ṭ explains the difference thus: "One skilled in mental transformation is an attainer of the form-sphere jhānas who, in regard to a single object, is able to transform the mind of concentration (*samādhicittaṃ*) from successively lower jhānas to successively higher ones. One skilled in transformation of perception is skilled in transforming the aforesaid jhānas under the heading of perception, passing beyond the perceptions of form and moving from [the perception] associated with the base of the infinity of space to that associated with the base of neither-perception-nor-non-perception. Similarly, he is able to transform the mind from the perception of women and men, etc., and from the perception of permanence, etc., toward mere form and formless phenomena and, especially, toward the unconditioned nibbāna. Such a one is accustomed to the contemplation of emptiness (*suññatānupassanābahulo*)."

85 He was Anāthapiṇḍika's younger brother, who went forth on the day the Jetavana monastery was dedicated to the Buddha. He attained arahantship by developing insight based on the meditation of loving-kindness. Before teaching the Dhamma and when receiving almsfood, he would first enter jhāna through loving-kindness and then emerge. The Buddha explains to him the manifestations of faith at **11:14**. His skill in meditation is praised in Ud 6:7, 71. His verse is at Th 1. Subhūti figures prominently in the [Mahāyāna] Prajñāpāramitā sūtras as chief exponent of the perfection of wisdom.

86 He was Sāriputta's youngest brother. Compelled by his mother to marry when still young, he ran away and received ordination. His verses are at Th 646–58.

87 He was from a very wealthy family of Sāvatthī. His conception of the ideal bhikkhu is at MN 32.5, I 213,10–19. He is praised in Ud 5:7, 60. He has his own verse at Th 3.

88 The story of his awakening is at **6:55**, told more elaborately at Vin I 179–85, where it leads to the Buddha's granting permission to the bhikkhus to wear sandals. His verses are at Th 632–44.

89 He was from Avantī, the son of Kāḷī (see **1:267** below) and a pupil of Mahākaccāna. His story is told in Ud 5:6, 57–59. He traveled to Sāvatthī to see the Buddha. The Buddha invited him to spend the night in his cottage and praised him for his recitation of the Aṭṭhakavagga. His verses are at Th 365–69.

90 He was the son of Suppavāsā, in whose womb he remained for seven years and seven days. He emerged only after his mother made an offering to the Buddha (see Ud 2:8, 15–18, though the infant is identified by name only in the commentary). He went

forth on the day of his birth and became a once-returner just as his hair was being cut. Thereafter he attained arahantship. His verse is at Th 60.

91 The story of his love for the Buddha and his death by suicide is told at SN 22:87, III 119–24.

92 The Buddha's son. His first encounter with his father, when he was seven, is related at Vin I 82,8–31. The Buddha addresses the following discourses to him: MN 61, MN 62, MN 147; SN 18:1–22; SN 22:91–92; SN 35:121 (= MN 147); and Sn 2:11.

93 His story and his discourse on the Dhamma are at MN 82. His verses are at Th 350–54.

94 *Paṭhamaṃ salākaṃ gaṇhantānaṃ*. This refers to a method of assigning meals by choosing lots. He seldom appears in the Nikāyas but has a verse at Th 15 (= SN 1:5, I 3, ascribed to the Buddha).

95 A whole chapter about him, including his verses, is SN chap. 8. See too Sn 2:12. His verses, Th 1218–88, make up the largest section in the Theragāthā.

96 A younger brother of Sāriputta, he rejoices in his achievements in Ud 4:9, 45–46. An account of his death by snakebite is in SN 35:69, IV 40–41. His verses are at Th 577–86.

97 He is said to have attained arahantship at the age of seven. He was selected by the Saṅgha to be the appointer of lodgings and assigner of meals but was subsequently calumnied by a group of evil-minded bhikkhus (at Vin III 158–63 and again at Vin III 166–67; see too Vin II 74–80, 124–26). He is maligned by the same group at Vin IV 37–38. The story of his passing away is in Ud 8:9–10, 92–93. He has a single verse at Th 5.

98 He had been a brahmin in five hundred past lives and even after his ordination and attainment of arahantship, by force of habit he still referred to other bhikkhus by the derogatory term *vasala*. The Buddha exonerated him of wrongdoing (in Ud 3:6, 28–29). His supernormal powers are described at Vin I 206–9; III 67,9–17; III 248–51. He has a single verse at Th 9 (identical with Aṅgulimāla's verse at Th 885).

99 His story is told in Ud 1:10, 6–9. Before he met the Buddha, he had lived as an ascetic, convinced he was an arahant until a benevolent deity disabused him of this notion. He hastened to visit the Buddha in Sāvatthī. Upon receiving the Buddha's teaching he immediately attained arahantship. He was killed by a cow shortly after his attainment. Though he did not receive formal ordination, he is still considered a bhikkhu.

100 He was the son of a woman who became a bhikkhunī while unknowingly pregnant with him. He went forth at the age of seven. He appears in DN 23 and MN 23. His verses are at Th 201–2. Mp says that he was designated foremost among those

of variegated speech (*cittakathikānaṃ aggo*) because he adorned his Dhamma talks with many similes and reasons.

101 He appears in numerous suttas, usually questioning Sāriputta: MN 43; SN 12:67; SN 22:122; SN 22:127–35; SN 35:232; SN 44:3–6. At SN 35:162–63 he receives instructions directly from the Buddha. On the analytical knowledges (*paṭisambhidā*), see **4:172**.

102 During the last twenty-five years of the Buddha's life he served as the Buddha's personal attendant. For a biographical account, see Nyanaponika and Hecker 2003, chap. 4. In Th 1027, he claims that he learned 84,000 teachings: 82,000 from the Buddha and 2,000 from the bhikkhus.

103 Mp: "Based on a single passage, grasping 60,000 passages according to the method explained by the Teacher, he knew all the passages. Therefore he was foremost among those with a quick grasp (*gatimantānaṃ aggo*)."

104 Mp: "His energy in learning the Buddha's words, in recitation, in retention, and in attending upon the Teacher was unequaled by others. Therefore he was foremost among those who are resolute (*dhitimantānaṃ aggo*)."

105 He was the head of a company of matted-hair fire ascetics whom the Buddha converted early in his ministry. His two younger brothers, Nadīkassapa and Gayākassapa, who were also fire ascetics, followed him to discipleship under the Buddha. See Vin I 24–37. His verses are at Th 375–80.

106 The son of one of Suddhodana's ministers, he had been a childhood playmate of the Buddha. He was sent by Suddhodana to invite the Buddha to return to Kapilavatthu. During this mission he inspired the Sakyans to have faith in the Buddha. His verses are at Th 527–36.

107 He was swallowed by a fish as a child but miraculously survived. See Vism 379, Ppn 12.27. He became a monk at the age of eighty and attained arahantship in seven days. His conversation with a friend, Acelakassapa, is recorded as MN 124. His verses are at Th 225–27.

108 He was a brahmin from Sāvatthī. His verses are at Th 165–66.

109 He had been the barber of the Sakyans in Kapilavatthu. He went forth along with Anuruddha and his cousins and became the foremost specialist in monastic discipline. He appears frequently in the Vinaya and in AN at **7:83**, **10:31–38**, **10:41–43**, and **10:99**. His verses are at Th 249–51.

110 A former householder from Sāvatthī, he exhorts the bhikkhunīs at MN 146. In AN, see **3:66** and **9:4**. His verses are at Th 279–82.

111 He was the Buddha's half-brother, son of Suddhodana and Mahāpajāpati Gotamī. The story of how he left his fiancée to become a bhikkhu is told in Ud 3:2, 21–24. He is instructed by

the Buddha at SN 21:8 and praised in AN at **8:9**. His verses are at Th 157–58.

112 He was the king of a frontier country who gave up his throne to follow the Buddha. His wife, Anojā, along with her attendants followed him and became a bhikkhunī. He is praised by the Buddha at SN 21:11 and SN 54:7. His verses are at Th 547–56.

113 He was one of the Buddha's attendants prior to Ānanda. He used his mastery over the fire element to subdue a ferocious fire dragon at Amba Ford, near Kosambī. On the instructions of the group of six troublesome bhikkhus, the householders of Kosambī prepared an intoxicating brew called *kāpotikā* for Sāgata. He drank it and fell down in a drunken stupor. In response, the Buddha laid down the rule against drinking intoxicants (Pācittiya 51); see Vin IV 108–10.

114 The word *paṭibhāneyyaka* apparently has a causative sense. Mp says "he was the foremost of the bhikkhus who cause eloquent discourses on the Dhamma to be spoken by the Buddha, those who are a condition for such discourses" (*satthu dhammadesanāpaṭibhānassa paccayabhūtānaṃ paṭibhānajanakānaṃ bhikkhūnaṃ . . . aggo*). He receives discourses from the Buddha at SN 22:71, SN 23:1–46, and SN 35:76–78.

115 He was one of the sixteen brahmin students who questioned the Buddha in the Pārāyanavagga. His exchange with the Buddha is at Sn 1116–19. He asks a question of the Buddha at SN 1:34, I 23, and has a verse at Th 207.

116 She was the Buddha's aunt and foster mother. In AN, see **8:51** (= Vin II 253–56) and **8:53** (= Vin II 258–59). Her verses are at Thī 157–62, and the story of her passing away at Ap II 529–43.

117 For a biographical sketch, see Nyanaponika and Hecker 2003: 263–97. She had been a consort of King Bimbisāra, proud of her beauty, but went forth after the Buddha dispelled her vanity. She gives a discourse at SN 44:1 and has verses at Thī 139–44. Along with Uppalavaṇṇā, she was one of the two chief bhikkhunī disciples who are held up as models for bhikkhunīs in AN in **2:131** and **4:176 §2** and in SN 17:24.

118 She had been the daughter of a banker of Sāvatthī. Shortly after going forth, she attained arahantship together with the psychic powers. She was raped by a young man but the Buddha declared her faultless because she did not consent to the act. She exchanges words with Māra at SN 5:5, I 131–32. Her verses are at Thī 224–35.

119 Her story is in Nyanaponika and Hecker 2003: 293–300. Her verses are at Thī 112–16.

120 She teaches her former husband in MN 44 and has a verse at Thī 12.

121 Also known as Sundarīnandā because of her beauty, she was the Buddha's half-sister and the full sister of Nanda. Her story is in Nyanaponika and Hecker 2003: 282–85. She has verses at Thī 82–86.

122 Her story is in Nyanaponika and Hecker 2003: 279–82. Her verses are at Thī 102–6.

123 She was the daughter of a brahmin family of Sāvatthī. Her verses are at Thī 98–101.

124 Her story is in Nyanaponika and Hecker 2003: 269–73. She had been a wandering ascetic and debater before she met the Buddha. Her verses are at Thī 107–11.

125 In lay life she had been the wife of Mahākassapa, but by mutual consent their marriage was never consummated. Her verses are at Thī 63–66.

126 Mp identifies her as Rāhulamātā, the mother of Rāhula; hence she was the Buddha's wife, better known in Buddhist tradition by the name Yasodharā.

127 She is the protagonist in the famous story of the mustard seed. Her biographical sketch is in Nyanaponika and Hecker 2003: 273–78. She has a dialogue with Māra at SN 5:3, I 129–30. Her verses are at Thī 213–23.

128 She is said to have attained arahantship by giving prominence to the faculty of faith; hence her appointment as foremost of those resolved through faith.

129 Their encounter with the Buddha soon after his enlightenment is related at Vin I 4,1-27. They are said to have been from the Ukkala country. They provided the Buddha with his first meal after his enlightenment and went for refuge to the Buddha and the Dhamma (since the Saṅgha did not yet exist). Mp explains that the Buddha gave them some hairs from his head, which they brought to their native city and deposited in a *cetiya* (memorial shrine) that they built to accommodate them.

130 For a detailed account of his life and activities, see Nyanaponika and Hecker 2003, chap. 9.

131 He is the chief figure in SN chap. 41. For a biographical sketch, see Nyanaponika and Hecker 2003: 365–72.

132 Mp says that he was the son of the king of the state of Āḷavī. On hearing the Buddha teach he became a non-returner. In AN he engages the Buddha in conversation at **3:35** and, with Citta, is held up as a model lay follower at **2:132** and **4:176 §3** as well as at SN 17:23, II 235,20-25. He is praised by the Buddha at **8:23** and **8:24**. After his rebirth as a deity, he comes to visit the Buddha

at **3:127**. The four means of attracting and sustaining others (*saṅgahavatthu*) are at **4:32**.

133 He was a Sakyan prince, the elder brother of Anuruddha and a cousin of the Buddha. He often engages in discussions with the Buddha and other bhikkhus. In AN he appears in **3:73**, **3:126**, **6:10**, **8:25**, **11:11**, and **11:12**.

134 He is praised by the Buddha in **8:21** and speaks about the agreeable things that he offers in **5:44**.

135 From the account in Mp, he seems to be identical with Ugga of Hatthigāma, praised by the Buddha in **8:22**.

136 Mp relates a story of how Māra came to visit him in the guise of the Buddha to try to shake his confidence. Sūra, however, at once realized the deceit and exposed his visitor as Māra.

137 He was court physician to King Bimbisāra as well as to the Buddha and the Saṅgha. In AN he appears only in **8:26**. The story of his early career and his service to the Buddha is told at Vin I 268–81. On the expression "foremost of those with confidence in persons" (*puggalappasannānaṃ aggo*), Mp offers merely a word resolution. The intended sense, I assume, is that his confidence was based largely on personal confidence in the Buddha rather than on inquiry into the Dhamma.

138 According to Mp, he and his wife Nakulamātā had been the Buddha's parents in five hundred past lives and thus they still regarded him as their son. This, I believe, was what qualified them to be "foremost in trust" (*vissāsakānaṃ aggo*). In AN they appear together in **4:55** and **6:16**. A brief biographical sketch of the couple is given in Nyanaponika and Hecker 2003: 375–78.

139 She offered the bodhisatta his last meal before his enlightenment. Mp identifies her as the mother of Yasa (see Vin I 15–18), but this seems improbable. Sujātā was from Uruvelā, near present-day Bodhgayā, whereas Yasa is said to have been from distant Bārāṇasī.

140 She was the Buddha's chief female patron. A biographical sketch is in Nyanaponika and Hecker 2003: 247–55. The Buddha gives discourses to her in **3:70**, **8:43**, **8:47**, and **8:49**.

141 The servant of Sāmāvatī, she would go to hear the Buddha preach and repeat the discourses to the ladies of the court. The Itivuttaka is said to be the record of these teachings. In **2:133** and at **4:176 §4** she is held up, along with Veḷukaṇṭakī Nandamātā, as the ideal model for a female lay follower. She is also praised in SN 17:24.

142 Orphaned as a girl, she became the wife of King Udena of Kosambī. Together with the women of the court, she died when her jealous co-wife, Māgandiyā, had the women's quarters set

on fire. The story is in Ud 7:10, 79. Her biographical sketch is in Nyanaponika and Hecker 2003: 285–93.

143 She is probably identical with Veḷukaṇṭakī Nandamātā, who, while held up elsewhere as an ideal laywoman, is not mentioned in this list. Veḷukaṇṭakī Nandamātā is praised along with Khujjuttarā in the suttas cited above in note 141. In **7:53** she speaks about her seven astounding qualities.

144 She was the mother of Sīvalī. The story of her long pregnancy is in Ud 2:8, 15–18. The Buddha instructs her about the efficacy of giving food in **4:57**.

145 She sliced flesh from her own thigh to feed a sick bhikkhu who needed meat. This caused the Buddha to prohibit the bhikkhus from consuming human flesh, even if willingly given. See Vin I 216–18.

146 Mp says that she was a close friend of Kāḷī of Kuraraghara. One day, while she was listening to a Dhamma discourse, thieves came to rob her house. She did not show any concern about the robbery but continued listening to the discourse. Her reaction caused the thieves to repent. With her help, they became monks and attained arahantship.

147 She was the wife of Nakulapitā. She reveals her virtues in **6:16** and receives a personal discourse from the Buddha in **8:48**.

148 A supporter of Mahākaccāna, she converses with him in **10:26**. Mp says that she gained trust when she heard two yakkhas (spirits) speaking praise of the Three Jewels while traveling through the sky. She thereupon attained the fruit of stream-entry.

149 Be divides the twenty-eight suttas in this vagga into three subchapters of ten, nine, and nine suttas respectively. Ce, which I follow, treats them all as one vagga named *Aṭṭhānapāḷi*. Many of these utterances are also found in MN 115.12–19, III 64–67.

150 Mp: "*One accomplished in view* (*diṭṭhisampanna*) is a noble disciple, a stream-enterer, possessing the view of the path (*maggadiṭṭhiyā sampanna*). The worldling, in contrast, can consider the conditioned phenomena of the three planes [the sensory plane, the form plane, and the formless plane] as permanent by way of the eternalist view (*sassatadiṭṭhi*)."

151 Mp: "This is said with reference to the obsession with pleasure that occurs by way of the view of self (*attadiṭṭhivasena*), as in those who hold that the self is exclusively blissful and immortal, etc. But, with a mind dissociated from views (*diṭṭhivippayuttacittena*), a noble disciple afflicted with fever might regard even feces as pleasurable, believing it can allay his fever."

152 Mp: "In the section on self, instead of speaking of a 'conditioned phenomenon' (*saṅkhāra*), the expression 'anything' (*kañci*

dhammaṃ) is used; this is for the purpose of including conceptual entities such as the *kasiṇas*, etc. (see **1:455–64**). Whatever the worldling grasps as permanent, pleasurable, and self, the noble disciple disentangles himself from its grip, considering it as impermanent, suffering, and non-self."

153 The first five are the heinous deeds that bring immediate result (*ānantariya kamma*), necessarily producing rebirth in hell in the next existence. The five are mentioned collectively in **6:94**. The six items together are referred to at Sn 233 as "the six things that cannot be done" (*cha cābhiṭhānāni abhabbo kātuṃ*) by the stream-enterer. Mp: "This here is the intention: 'The condition of a worldling is blameworthy insofar as a worldling can do these deeds that bring immediate results, such as matricide and so forth. But the noble disciple is powerful since he does not do such deeds.'" Regarding the shedding of a Tathāgata's blood, Mp says that the expression "with a mind of hatred" (*paduṭṭhacitto*) is used to highlight the motive. Devadatta, who wanted to kill the Buddha and take control of the Saṅgha, wounded the Buddha in a failed assassination attempt and thereby committed an *ānantariya kamma*. But the physician Jīvaka, wishing to restore the Buddha's health, cut his skin to extract bad blood; he thereby did a meritorious deed. On schism in the Saṅgha (*saṅghabheda*), see **10:37, 10:39**.

154 This is redundant, since *sammā sambuddha* means simply "a perfectly enlightened one," but I render the term thus to avoid misunderstanding. Though arahant disciples achieve *sambodhi*, full enlightenment, and are occasionally spoken of as *sambuddha*, "enlightened," the designation *sammā sambuddha* is reserved for the founder, who alone attains *anuttara sammā sambodhi*, "unsurpassed perfect enlightenment."

155 Mp explains the word "contemporaneously" (*apubbaṃ acarimaṃ*, lit., "not before, not after") to cover the period from the time a bodhisatta enters his mother's womb until the Buddha's relics disappear. There can be only one Buddha at a time because a Buddha is without a counterpart or peer (see **1:172, 1:174**). Thus if two Buddhas were to arise simultaneously, this statement would be invalidated. The issue is also dealt with at Mil 236–39, cited by Mp. Mp says that because no suttas speak of the arising of Buddhas in other world systems, while there are suttas that say Buddhas do not arise elsewhere, it is only in *this* world system (*imasmiṃyeva cakkavāḷe*) that they arise. Mp-ṭ cites several suttas that it interprets as excluding the possibility of Buddhas arising elsewhere, but these texts do not seem to be as categorical as the author supposes. Perhaps this argument was intended to counter the idea being advanced in early Mahāyāna sūtras (or

even among other pre-Mahāyāna schools) that Buddhas arise in the world systems of the ten directions. For the early Buddhist view on world systems, see **3:81**.

156 A "wheel-turning monarch" (*rājā cakkavatī*) is an ideal king who conquers the lands of the four directions by his righteousness. In AN he is mentioned in **3:14**, **5:131–33**, **7:62**, and **7:66**. For details, see MN 129.33–47, III 172–77.

157 It seems that in the old Nikāyas the idea of aspiring for future Buddhahood is not raised at all. Thus the claim being made here is not that a woman cannot become a perfectly enlightened Buddha in a future life but that a Buddha is always male. The assertion in this sutta need not be read as excluding the possibility that one who is presently a woman could become a Buddha, but this would have to take place in a future life, after she has undergone a change of gender. The statements are no doubt formulated in the context of the Indian culture of the period, which always assigned positions of authority to males. MĀ 181, a Chinese parallel of MN 115, does not include the section on the inabilities of women. Nevertheless, we do find the declaration that a woman cannot become a Buddha in another Chinese parallel of the sutta, at T XVII 713b20–22. It also occurs in a sūtra quoted in the Abhidharma Mahāvibhāṣā at T XXVI 502b16–18, and in the *Śāriputrābhidharma Śāstra at T XXVIII, 600b10–12. According to such later canonical texts as the Buddhavaṃsa, if a woman resolves to attain Buddhahood in the presence of a Buddha, her resolution does not succeed (i.e., she does not receive the prediction of future Buddhahood). For the resolution to succeed, the aspirant must be a male who has left the home life. See Bodhi 2007: 251–53. Sakka is the ruler of the devas in the Tāvatiṃsa heaven.

158 The words in brackets pertain respectively to the two suttas that are abridged in this triad. The same applies to the following two triads.

159 Ce and Be divide this chapter (called *Ekadhammapāḷi*) into separate subchapters (called *vagga*s), as shown, whereas Ee treats the subchapters of Ce and Be as independent vaggas.

160 Mp: "*Disenchantment* (*nibbidā*) is dissatisfaction with the round [of rebirths]; *dispassion* (*virāga*) is the fading away of the round, or the fading away of such defilements as lust (*rāga*); *cessation* (*nirodha*) is the ceasing of lust, etc., or the ceasing of the round; *peace* (*upasama*) is the stilling of defilements; *direct knowledge* (*abhiññā*) is directly knowing the three characteristics; *enlightenment* (*sambodha*) is awakening to the four truths; and *nibbāna* is the realization of the non-conditioned nibbāna."

161 Recollection of the Buddha (*buddhānussati*) is the first of the six

recollections described more fully at **6:10** and elaborated at Vism 197–213, Ppn 7.1–67. Here is Mp (abridged): "Recollection of the Buddha serves two purposes: giving joy to the mind and promoting insight (*cittasampahaṃsanatthañ c'eva vipassanatthañca*). How? When a bhikkhu develops a meditation subject like unattractiveness [of the body], his mind may be disturbed, dissatisfied, and joyless. It does not remain on track but roams around like a wild bull. On that occasion, he should put aside his basic meditation subject and recollect the excellent qualities of the Tathāgata. As he recollects the Buddha, his mind becomes placid and free from hindrances. He can then return to his basic meditation object, develop insight, and reach the plane of the noble ones. Thus recollection of the Buddha gives joy to the mind. But one can also use this meditation subject directly for the purpose of developing insight. After recollecting the Buddha, one dissects the act of recollection into the five aggregates and defines them thus: 'These five aggregates are, in brief, the truth of suffering. The craving that produced them is the truth of the origin. The cessation of craving is the truth of cessation; and the practice that understands cessation is the truth of the path.' Thus one has defined the four truths in the preliminary portion [the stage of insight] and one step by step reaches the stage of the noble ones."

162 In Be these nine suttas are combined into one, numbered 297 in Be's cumulative numbering scheme. In Ce and Ee, they are numbered 2–10 (since these editions number the first sutta in each vagga as "1" without cumulative numbering). I follow Be in using a cumulative numbering scheme, but I follow Ce and Ee in counting these suttas separately. Thus my numbering scheme from here on will exceed Be by eight, but without being matched by any corresponding scheme in Ce or Ee. In parentheses I give the sutta number internal to the subchapters, called *vagga*s, but simply enumerated without proper title.

163 The meditation subjects from recollection of the Dhamma through recollection of the devas are the other five recollections, also discussed in **6:10 §§2–6** and elaborated at Vism 213–26, Ppn 7.68–118. Mindfulness of breathing (*ānāpānassati*) is dealt with more fully at **10:60 §10,** SN 54:10, V 322–25, and SN 54:13, V 328–33. For the commentarial treatment, see Vism 267–93, Ppn 8.145–244. Mindfulness of death (*maraṇassati*) is at **6:19, 6:20, 8:73,** and **8:74**, elaborated at Vism 229–39, Ppn 8.1–41. Mindfulness directed to the body (*kāyagatā sati*), as the unattractive nature of the body, is at **10:60 §3**, and elaborated at Vism 239–66, Ppn 8.42–144. Recollection of peace (*upasamānussati*) occurs only here and is not separately explained but is treated at Vism 293–94,

Ppn 8.245–51; this treatment closely resembles the perception of dispassion and the perception of cessation at **10:60 §§6–7**.

164 In Ee called vagga XVII and named "Seed" (*Bīja*).

165 Mp: "This is a designation for the sixty-two wrong views"; see DN 1.1.29–3.31, I 12–39. It seems, though, that the term *micchādiṭṭhi* is used in the Nikāyas solely in relation to three views: moral nihilism, the doctrine of non-doing, and the doctrine of non-causality (*natthikavāda, akiriyavāda, ahetukavāda*).

166 Mp: "This is a designation for the five kinds of right view." Mp-ṭ: "[The views of] ownership of kamma, jhāna, insight, the path, and the fruit. The knowledge included in the jhāna consciousness is the right view of jhāna, while insight knowledge is the right view of insight."

167 See **2:125**, **10:93**.

168 See **2:126**, MN 43.13, I 294,1–4.

169 Ce considers this sutta and the next to contain seven suttas each: one each for bodily, verbal, and mental kamma, and for volition, yearning, aspiration, and volitional activities. Thus Ce counts twenty-two suttas for this section, as against ten in Be and Ee.

170 *Nimbabījaṃ vā kosātakibījaṃ vā tittakalābubījaṃ vā.*

171 *Asecanakatta*. Lit., "not causing surfeit."

172 Ee counts this as vagga XVIII, named "Makkhali."

173 Mp: "Devadatta together with the six [non-Buddhist] teachers and others who are similar." For the views of the six teachers, see DN 2.16–33, I 52–59.

174 Mp: "When a Buddha has not arisen, this is a bodhisatta in the role of a wheel-turning monarch and others who are similar. When a Buddha has arisen, it is a Buddha and his disciples."

175 Makkhali Gosāla was one of the six teachers contemporary with the Buddha. He was the founder (or perhaps just an eminent teacher) of the Ājīvakas (or Ājivikas). DN 2.20, I 53–54 ascribes to him the doctrine of non-causality (*ahetukavāda*), according to which there is no cause for the defilement or purification of beings, who have no energy, self-control, or capacity for free choice.

176 *Manussakhippaṃ*. Mp: "He has arisen in the world like a fish net for people, to prevent them from reaching the path leading to heaven and liberation."

177 *Dāyakena mattā jānitabbā no paṭiggāhakena*. Mp: "One should give within measure. One should not give fully, in excess. He [the Buddha] does not say 'one should not give,' but 'one should give a little, moderately.' Why? Because even if one gives fully, in excess, one does not achieve [as the fruit of one's gift] the state of a human being, or a heavenly rebirth, or the attainment

of nibbāna. There is no need for the recipient to be moderate in receiving. Why? Because he does not have to be moderate when things are being given to him fully; he does not practice fewness of wishes based on receiving in moderation."

178 *Paṭiggāhakena mattā jānitabbā*. Mp: "The person receiving should set the limit. How? By taking into account the donor, the item to be given, and one's own capacity. For if the item to be given is plentiful, and the donor wishes to give a little, out of consideration for the donor one should accept a little. If there is only a little to be given, and the donor wishes to give a lot, out of consideration for the item to be given one should accept a little. If the item to be given is plentiful, and the donor wishes to give a lot, out of consideration for one's own capacity one should accept moderately. Having thus known moderation, the recipient fulfills the practice of fewness of wishes. [In this way] those who did not get a share get one, and the gains acquired remain stable. Those without confidence acquire confidence; those with confidence increase in confidence; one becomes an example for the multitude; and one helps the Teaching to continue for a long time."

179 Mp explains that after the Buddha had given a discourse on the rebirth of beings, saying that there are nine persons "freed from hell, the animal realm, and the sphere of afflicted spirits" (see **9:12**), he considered: "If the bhikkhus, on hearing this discourse, think: 'We are freed from hell, etc.,' they may think there is no need to strive for the higher paths and fruits. Let me then stir up a sense of urgency in them." Mp glosses the words, "I do not praise even a trifling amount of existence," with: "I do not praise rebirth in any realm of existence even for a short time" (*appamattakampi kālaṃ bhave paṭisandhiṃ na vaṇṇayāmi*).

180 Ce and Ee count these as four separate suttas, whereas Be combines them into one.

181 Ce gives this vagga the title *Jambudīpapeyyālo*, the "Jambudīpa Repetition Series." Ee counts this as vagga XIX and names it *Appamattakaṃ*, "Few." Be simply calls it *Catutthavaggo*, "The Fourth (Sub-) Chapter."

182 Ce counts fifteen suttas in this first series; Be, by combining the second and third suttas, counts fourteen; Ee counts them all as one sutta.

183 *Jambudīpa*: the "Rose-Apple Continent," the southern continent in Buddhist geography. The other three continents are Aparagoyana to the west, Uttarakuru to the north, and Pubbavideha to the east. Mp says Jambudīpa is named after the "great rose-apple tree" in the Himalayas, which is a hundred *yojanas* wide, with branches fifty *yojanas* long and a trunk fifteen *yojanas* in diameter.

PED estimates a *yojana* to be seven miles; SED gives several alternatives but takes nine miles to be the most accurate.

184 The "middle provinces" (*majjhimā janapadā*) correspond roughly to the northeastern and north-central states of present-day India. Mp cites Vin I 197,20–29, for an exact specification of its boundaries. It is said that Buddhas, paccekabuddhas, great disciples, etc., are born only here. Everything beyond these bounds is called the "outlying provinces" (*paccantimā janapadā*). That the definitions are flexible is seen in Mp's statement that all of Jambudīpa can also be called the middle region and the other continents the outlying provinces. In Sri Lanka (in the time of the commentators), the Anurādhapura district was considered the middle region and the rest of the country the outlying provinces. On *mleccha* (the Skt equivalent of Pāli *milakkha*), SED offers: "a foreigner, barbarian, non-Āryan, man of an outcast race, any person who does not speak Sanskrit and does not conform to the usual Hindu institutions."

185 Mp: "The *noble eye of wisdom* (*ariya paññācakkhu*): the path together with insight."

186 Ce and Be *ete va sattā bahutarā ye atthamaññāya dhammamaññāya dhammānudhammaṃ na paṭipajjanti*; Ee *ete va sattā bahutarā ye na atthaṃ aññāya na dhammaṃ aññāya dhammānudhammaṃ na paṭipajjanti*. I assume that in Ce and Be the negation *na* preceding the finite verb is intended to apply distributively to the preceding absolutives. The Ee reading is supported by an older Sri Lankan printed edition.

187 *Saṃvejaniyesu ṭhānesu saṃvijjanti*. On a sense of urgency (*saṃvega*), see **3:128**, **4:113**. The commentaries enumerate "eight bases of the sense of urgency" (*aṭṭha saṃvegavatthūni*): birth, old age, illness, death; the suffering in the realms of misery; the suffering rooted in one's saṃsāric past; the suffering to be encountered in one's saṃsāric future; and the suffering rooted in the search for nutriment. See Sv III 795,6–9, Ps I 298,24–28, Spk III 163,23–26, Mp II 68,9–12.

188 Mp: "*Based on release* (*vavassaggārammaṇaṃ karitvā*): release is nibbāna. The meaning is: having made that the object. *Gain concentration* (*labhanti samādhiṃ*): they obtain concentration of the path and concentration of the fruit." I am not sure the expression *vavassaggārammaṇaṃ karitvā* need be interpreted in the technical sense (employed in the Abhidhamma) of the path and fruition *cittas* taking nibbāna as their object. The expression is also used in the definition of the concentration faculty at SN 48:9–10 (V 197,14–16, V 198,24–25). It may originally have meant simply a state of *samādhi* motivated by the aspiration for release. In SN, the noble eightfold path, the seven enlightenment factors, and

five spiritual faculties are often described as *vossaggapariṇāmiṃ*, "evolving toward release" or "maturing in release," *vossagga* and *vavassagga* being alternative forms of the same word.

189 Mp identifies the "taste of the meaning" (*attharasa*) with the four fruits, the "taste of the Dhamma" (*dhammarasa*) with the four paths, and the taste of liberation (*vimuttirasa*) with the deathless nibbāna (*amatanibbāna*). See **8:19**: "This Dhamma and discipline has but one taste, the taste of liberation" (*ayaṃ dhammavinayo ekaraso vimuttiraso*). Again, Mp seems to impose on the sutta technical distinctions formulated only in a later period.

190 Ce and Be, which I follow, count thirty suttas in this group. Ee merges them into one.

191 These suttas correspond closely to SN 56:102–31, V 474–77.

192 Ee treats these suttas as the beginning of vagga XX, *Jhānavagga*, "The Jhāna Chapter." Ce treats them as the fifth subchapter of vagga XVI, designated *Soḷasapasādakaradhammā*, "Sixteen Qualities Engendering Confidence." Be groups them as vagga XVII, named *Pasādakaradhammavagga*, "Chapter on Qualities Engendering Confidence."

193 The observances in **1:378–381** are ascetic practices (*dhutaṅga*) permitted by the Buddha.

194 Ee treats this as a continuation of vagga XX. Ce takes it to be the sixth subchapter of vagga XVI, but gives it a separate name, as if it were a new chapter, *Accharāsaṅghātavaggo*, "The Finger Snap Chapter." Be counts it as vagga XVIII, called *Apara-accharāsaṅghātavaggo*, "Another Finger Snap Chapter." In Be, vagga VI is "The First Finger Snap Chapter."

195 These are the four jhānas followed by the four divine dwellings (*brahmavihāra*).

196 These are the four establishments of mindfulness (*satipaṭṭhāna*), followed by the other groups in the thirty-seven aids to enlightenment: the four right strivings (*sammappadhāna*), the four bases for psychic potency (*iddhipāda*), the five faculties (*indriya*), the five powers (*bala*), the seven factors of enlightenment (*bojjhaṅga*), and the noble eightfold path (*ariya aṭṭhaṅgika magga*).

197 The Pāli phrase *kāye kāyānupassī viharati* is usually translated either as I have rendered it here or as "[he] dwells contemplating the body *as a body*." The question is sometimes raised which of these two is more accurate. I believe that **7:6**, IV 13–15, supports my rendering here. We there read *ekacco puggalo sabbasaṅkhāresu aniccānupassī viharati*, and in the following suttas: *sabbasaṅkhāresu dukkhānupassī viharati*, *sabbadhammesu anattānupassī viharati*, and *nibbāne sukhānupassī viharati*. These are best rendered: "Some person dwells contemplating impermanence in all conditioned

phenomena," "dwells contemplating suffering in all conditioned phenomena," "dwells contemplating non-self in all phenomena," and "dwells contemplating happiness in nibbāna." They could *not* be rendered: "Some person dwells contemplating impermanence as all conditioned phenomena"... "contemplating happiness as nibbāna." In each case, the word conjoined with *anupassī* is the aspect that is contemplated, and the word in the locative case is the sphere in relation to which that aspect is contemplated. Analogously, in *kāye kāyānupassī viharati*, the *kāya* conjoined with *anupassī* is the aspect that is contemplated (the "bodiness" of the body) and the locative *kāye* is the domain in relation to which that aspect is contemplated. Strictly speaking *kāyānupassī* does not actually mean "contemplating the body," but "a body-contemplator." Thus a very literal translation of the phrase would be: "He dwells as a body-contemplator in relation to the body." Since such a rendering would sound awkward in English, I fall back on the familiar "contemplating the body in the body." Similar considerations apply to the other three *satipaṭṭhānas*.

198 These are the eight bases of overcoming (*abhibhāyatana*). For explanations, see **8:65** and pp. 1808–9, notes 1771–75.

199 These are the eight emancipations (*vimokkha*). See **8:66** and pp. 1809–10, notes 1776–80.

200 A *kasiṇa* is an object, often a disk, used as a support for meditation. For example, the earth *kasiṇa* is a disk of brown clay on which the meditator focuses to obtain an inner perception of earth. For full explanations, see Vism chaps. 4 and 5. Ce adds *ālokakasiṇa*, the light *kasiṇa*, which is not in Be and Ee.

201 **1:480–84** are five of the ten "foul" or unattractive objects (*asubhārammaṇa*) discussed at Vism 178–79, Ppn 6.1–11.

202 For clarity's sake, I have slightly expanded the extremely compressed Pāli text.

203 Following this, Ee includes ten more suttas, obtained by taking *saddhindriyaṃ bhāveti* (and the other four *indriya*) and *saddhābalaṃ bhāveti* (and the other four *bala*) without associating them with a jhāna or *brahmavihāra*. This is not matched by Ce or Be and is thus likely to be an editorial error.

204 This number agrees with Be. Ee counts this as vagga XXI, Ce as the seventh subchapter of vagga XVI, but separately titled *Kāyagatāsativaggo*, "The Chapter on Mindfulness Directed to the Body."

205 In this sutta and those that follow, *kāyagatāsati* should surely be understood in the broad sense of the Kāyagatāsati Sutta (MN 119), as comprising all meditation exercises based on the body,

rather than in the narrow sense of Vism 240, Ppn 8.44, which restricts it to contemplation of the thirty-two bodily parts.

Mp: "*Wholesome qualities that pertain to true knowledge* (*kusalā dhammā ye keci vijjābhāgiyā*): There are eight kinds of true knowledge: insight knowledge, the mind-made body, and the six kinds of direct knowledge (see, e.g., **3:101**, **6:2**). The qualities associated with these eight are the things that pertain to true knowledge. Or, if one of the eight is taken to be true knowledge, the others are 'qualities that pertain to true knowledge.'" At **2:31**, *samatha* and *vipassanā* are said to be the two things that pertain to true knowledge.

206 See above, note 187.

207 Ce and Ee count four separate suttas here, each based on one of the benefits that come from developing mindfulness of the body, whereas Be combines them into one. The use of the conjunction *pi* after each item seems to corroborate Be, which I follow.

208 Ee counts two suttas here, one based on the non-arising of unarisen unwholesome qualities, the other on the abandoning of arisen unwholesome qualities. Ce and Be, which I follow, take this to be one sutta.

209 Again, Ee counts this as two suttas, but I follow Ce and Be in taking it as one.

210 Here I follow Ce and Ee in taking this passage as five suttas, whereas Be treats it as one. On the seven underlying tendencies (*anusaya*), see **7:11**, **7:12**; on the ten fetters (*saṃyojana*), see **10:13**.

211 Mp glosses *paññāpabhedāya* with *paññāya pabhedagamanatthaṃ*. At Paṭis-a III 644,6–7, *paññāpabhedakusalo* is glossed "skilled in his own infinite distinctions" (*attano anantavikappe ... cheko*). Its near synonym, *pabhinnañāṇo*, is explained as "having knowledge that has attained infinite differentiations" (*anantappabhedapattañāṇo*). Mp glosses *anupādāparinibbāna* with *apaccayaparinibbānassa sacchikiriyatthāya*, "for the purpose of realizing the non-conditioned final nibbāna."

212 Mp explains "penetration of numerous elements" (*anekadhātupaṭivedha*) as the penetration of the characteristics (*lakkhaṇa*) of the eighteen elements; "penetration of the diversity of elements" (*nānādhātupaṭivedha*) as penetration of the characteristics of those eighteen elements by way of their diversity (*nānābhāvena*); and "analytical knowledge of numerous elements" (*anekadhātupaṭisambhidā*) as the knowledge that classifies elements thus: "When this element is prominent, that occurs." MN 115, III 62–63, explains various ways in which a bhikkhu can be called "skilled in elements" (*dhātukusala*), all of which may be pertinent to the present passage.

213 See SN V 411–12. Mp offers explanations of these terms based on Paṭis II 189–202.

214 I follow Be, which treats this as a separate vagga. Ee takes it to be a continuation of its vagga XXI. Ce treats it as the eighth subchapter of its vagga XVI.

215 Ce and Ee take each of the twelve matching pairs in this vagga to be separate suttas, thus counting twenty-four suttas. I follow Be, which takes each pair of propositions to be a single sutta and thus counts only twelve suttas.

Notes to the Twos

216 Mp gives detailed explanations of all these punishments. I translate only the first few and leave the rest to the reader's imagination. (1) The *porridge pot* (*bilaṅgathālika*): they crack open his skull, take up a hot iron ball with tongs, put the ball inside, and boil his brains until they overflow. (2) The *polished-shell shave* (*saṅkhamuṇḍika*): they cut the skin [in the area] bounded by his upper lip, the roots of the ears, and gullet, bind all his head hairs into a knot, tie them around a stick, and pull it up, so that his skin together with his head hairs comes off; then they rub his skull with coarse sand and wash it, until it becomes the color of a conch shell. (3) *Rāhu's mouth* (*rāhumukha*): they force open his mouth with a spike and burn a lamp inside his mouth, or they dig into his mouth with a spade until the blood flows and fills his mouth. (4) The *fiery wreath* (*jotimālika*): they wind an oiled cloth around his entire body and ignite it. (5) The *flaming hand* (*hatthapajjotika*): they wind an oiled cloth around his hand and ignite it so that it burns like a lamp.

217 Mp: "Even if a bundle of a thousand [gold pieces] had fallen along the road, he would not steal it thinking to support himself with it, but he would turn it over with his heel and go his way, thinking: 'What need do I have with this?'"

218 Both Ce and Be read *pāpako dukkho vipāko* here, as against Ee *pāpako vipāko*.

219 *Sabbūpadhipaṭinissagga*. Mp specifies three types of "acquisitions" (*upadhi*): the five aggregates, the defilements, and volitional activities (*khandha, kilesa, abhisaṅkhārā*). The relinquishment of these is a synonym for nibbāna. The striving for this is the energy arisen along with insight and the path.

220 The two things that cause torment (*dhammā tapanīyā*) are not expressly stated as such in the text, but it is clear that they are (1) engaging in misconduct, and (2) failing to engage in good

conduct. The same applies, with appropriate changes, to the following sutta.

221 Mp: "By *non-contentment in regard to wholesome qualities* (*asantuṭṭhitā kusalesu dhammesu*) he shows: 'Not being content merely with jhāna or the luminous mark [of concentration], I aroused the path of arahantship. Until that arose, I was not content. And being dissatisfied in striving, I strove on, standing firm without retreating.' 'Indefatigability' (*appaṭivānitā*) means not turning back, not retreating. By *I strove indefatigably*, what is meant is this: 'When I was a bodhisatta, I strove on, not retreating, aspiring for omniscience.'"

222 This determination is found elsewhere in the Nikāyas: in AN at **8:13 §8**, IV 190,$_{8-12}$; MN 70.27, I 481,$_{1-5}$; and SN 12:22, II 28,$_{24-28}$.

223 Mp: "*Heedfulness* (*appamāda*) consists in non-separation from mindfulness. *Unsurpassed security from bondage* (*anuttara yogakkhema*): by heedfulness he attained not only enlightenment but also unsurpassed security from bondage, consisting in the fruit of arahantship and nibbāna."

224 See SN 12:53, II 86; SN 12:54, II 87; SN 12:57–59, II 89–91.

225 Moral shame (*hiri*) is disgust at bodily and verbal misconduct; moral dread (*ottappa*) is moral dread over such misconduct. Moral shame is directed inwardly. It arises from self-respect and induces one to reject wrongdoing based on the sense of one's own inherent dignity. Moral dread has an outward direction. It arises from fear of blame and induces one to reject wrongdoing based on fear of the consequences. For more details, see CMA 86, As 124–25, and Vism 464,$_{31}$–465,$_{4}$, Ppn 14.142.

226 *Mātucchā* is one's maternal aunt; *mātulāni*, the wife of one's mother's brother. For simplicity's sake I refer to them jointly as "aunts."

227 *Vassūpanāyikā*. The three-month rains residence is observed by monastics during the Indian rainy season. During this period, bhikkhus and bhikkhunīs must remain for three months at their chosen place of residence, though they are permitted to leave for up to seven days if there is a suitable reason. The earlier three-month rains period extends from the day after the full moon of Āsāḷha (normally occurring in July or early August) to the full moon of Kattika (normally in October or early November). The later three-month rains period begins and ends one month after the earlier one.

228 Here, in contrast to **2:1**, both Ce and Be read simply *pāpako vipāko*, without *dukkho*.

229 Ce *sekhametaṃ balaṃ;* Be *sekhānametaṃ balaṃ;* Ee *sekhānaṃ etaṃ balaṃ*. Mp: "The power of knowledge of the seven kinds of

trainees." The seven kinds of trainees extend from the person on the path of stream-entry through the person on the path of arahantship. Thus they include all the noble persons except the arahant, who is *asekha*, "one beyond training."

230 *Saṅkhittena ca vitthārena ca*. Mp: "A brief teaching is one expounded briefly by reciting the outline (*mātikā*). A detailed teaching is one expounded by elaborating and analyzing the outline (*mātikaṃ vitthārato vibhajitvā kathitā*). But whether or not an outline is set up, a teaching spoken with elaboration and analysis is called a detailed teaching. The brief teaching is spoken for a person with great wisdom, a detailed teaching for a person whose intellect is blunter.... Though the entire Tipiṭaka is a brief teaching, it is here considered a detailed teaching."

231 Mp mentions the four kinds of disciplinary issues: involving a dispute (*vivādādhikaraṇa*), involving an accusation (*anuvādādhikaraṇa*), involving an offense (*āpattādhikaraṇa*), and involving procedure (*kiccādhikaraṇa*). These are dealt with in detail at Vin II 88–92. Briefly, an issue involving a dispute arises when monks or nuns dispute about the Dhamma and the Vinaya; an issue involving an accusation arises when they accuse another member of committing a transgression; an issue involving an offense arises when a monk or nun who has committed a transgression seeks rehabilitation; and an issue involving procedure deals with the collective procedures of the Saṅgha. Methods for settling disciplinary issues (*adhikaraṇasamatha*) are explained at MN 104.12–20, II 247–50. See too Ṭhānissaro 2007a: 546–61.

232 *Ahaṃ kho akusalaṃ āpanno kañcideva desaṃ kāyena*. Mp: "Here, by 'what is unwholesome' (*akusalaṃ*), an offense (*āpatti*) is intended; the meaning is 'I have committed an offense.' 'A particular misdeed' (*kañcideva desaṃ*): not every offense, but a particular kind of offense; the meaning is 'a certain offense.'"

233 *Suṅkadāyakaṃ va bhaṇḍasmiṃ*. I have elaborated slightly on the terse Pāli expression to bring out the sense. Mp: "A crime is incurred by one importing taxable goods when he avoids the taxation station, and he is the criminal in this case, not the kings or their employees."

234 Mp explains that the two faults on the part of the reproving monk are being overcome by displeasure and reproving the other because of his displeasure. The three faults on the part of the monk being reproved are committing the offense, being displeased, and informing others.

235 Conduct contrary to the Dhamma (*adhammacariyā*) and conduct in accordance with the Dhamma (*dhammacariyā*) are explained briefly in the following sutta. At **10:220** and **10:217** they are

respectively identified with the ten courses of unwholesome kamma and the ten courses of wholesome kamma.

236 Mp explains that the brahmin had approached the Buddha out of pride, intending to find fault with the teaching. The Buddha knew this and understood that the brahmin would benefit only if he were prompted by an ambiguous reply to inquire further. Since the Buddha first stated the cause of rebirth in heaven in the same terms as he stated the cause of rebirth in hell, the brahmin had to admit his perplexity and ask for clarification. This humbled him, opening his mind to understanding.

237 Be divides this sutta into two, whereas Ce and Ee, which I follow, treat the passages on the disappearance and the continuation of the Dhamma as contrasting parts of a single sutta.

238 *Dunnikkhittañca padabyañjanaṃ attho ca dunnīto.*

239 *Sunikkhittañca padabyañjanaṃ attho ca sunīto.*

240 Also at SN 11:24, I 239,26–31, where it is embedded in a story and embellished with a verse.

241 Mp: "The former is exemplified by Sunakkhatta, who said: 'The ascetic Gotama does not have any superhuman qualities' (at MN 12.2, I 68,9–10). The latter is exemplified by a devotee whose faith is destitute of understanding, such as one who misrepresents the Tathāgata by claiming: 'The Buddha is entirely world-transcending (*buddho nāma sabbalokuttaro*); all the parts of his body, such as the head hairs, are world-transcending.'" This latter comment seems to be a dig at the Lokottaravādins, a subsect of the Mahāsāṃghikas that held the Buddhas to be entirely world-transcendent.

242 Ee divides this into two separate suttas by way of the two paragraphs, whereas Ce and Be take it as one.

243 The question of which discourses of the Buddha are of explicit meaning (*nītattha*) and which require interpretation (*neyyattha*) became one of the most intensely debated issues in Buddhist hermeneutics. Starting with the early Indian Buddhist schools, the debate continued in such later Mahāyāna sūtras as the Akṣayamatinirdeśa and the Saṃdhinirmocana. The controversy continued even beyond India, in Sri Lanka, China, and Tibet. The Pāli commentaries decide this issue on the basis of the Abhidhamma distinction between ultimate realities and conventional realities.

Mp: "Those suttas that speak of one person (*puggala*), two persons, etc., require interpretation, for their meaning has to be interpreted in the light of the fact that in the ultimate sense a person does not exist (*paramatthato pana puggalo nāma natthi*). One who misconceives the suttas that speak about a person, holding that the person exists in the ultimate sense, explains a discourse whose meaning requires interpretation as one whose meaning is explicit. A sutta whose meaning is explicit is one that explains impermanence, suffering, and non-self; for in this case the meaning is simply impermanence, suffering, and non-self. One who says, 'This discourse requires interpretation,' and interprets it in such a way as to affirm that 'there is the permanent, there is the pleasurable, there is a self,' explains a sutta of explicit meaning as one requiring interpretation." The first criticism here is probably directed against the Puggalavādins, who held the person to be ultimately existent. The latter might have been directed against an early form of the *tathāgatagarbha* theory, which (in the Mahāyāna Parinirvāṇa Sūtra) affirmed a permanent, blissful, pure self.

244 Mp interprets "concealed action" (*paṭicchannakamma*) simply as a bad deed, explaining that even if a bad deed is not concealed, it is still called a concealed action. However, it seems that confessing one's bad deed and making amends for it would mitigate its negative force. See Dhp 173: "One who has committed a bad deed but covers it up with good illumines this world like the moon freed from a cloud."

245 Ee combines this sutta and the next two into one, whereas Ce and Be keep them separate. I suspect that Ee rightly joins **2:27** and **2:28**, two complementary discourses, but errs in including **2:29**, which has a different theme. Still, I defer to Ce and Be. Note that **2:26** and **2:29** join into one sutta two contrasting statements about the two types of rebirth respectively resulting from bad and good conduct.

246 *Paṭiggāhā*. An unusual use of this word. Mp says simply that these two states receive (*paṭiggaṇhanti*) the immoral person.

247 *Araññavanapatthānī pantāni senāsanāni*. I follow Mp, which explains *araññavanapatthānī* as a *dvanda* compound: *araññāni ca vanapatthāni ca*.

248 *Pacchimañca janataṃ anukampamāno*. Ps I 129,4–12, commenting on the same expression at MN I 23,35, says: "How does he show compassion for later generations by dwelling in the forest? When young men who have gone forth out of faith see that even the Blessed One—who had nothing more to understand, abandon, develop, and realize—did not neglect dwelling in the forest, they will think that they, too, should dwell in the forest. Thus they will quickly make an end of suffering."

249 *Vijjābhāgiyā*. See **1:575**.

250 For more on the relationship of serenity (*samatha*) and insight (*vipassanā*), see **4:92–94** and **4:170**.

251 Mp interprets the mind being developed as the "mind of the path" (*maggacitta*) and the wisdom being developed as the "wisdom of the path" (*maggapaññā*). However, it seems to me that the text itself intends "mind" and "wisdom" generically, not specifically as the mind and wisdom of the noble path attainment. The development of the mind through *samatha* and of wisdom through *vipassanā*, however, culminate in the "taintless liberation of mind, liberation by wisdom" (*anāsavā cetovimutti paññāvimutti*), the final goal of the Dhamma. Here, *samatha* is the condition for liberation of mind and *vipassanā* for liberation by wisdom.

252 I read with Ce and Ee *katañca hoti patikatañca atikatañcā ti*. Be ends at *patikatañcā ti*.

253 The operative terms here are *kiriyavāda* and *akiriyavāda*. For the Buddhist critique of *akiriyavāda*, a doctrine that denied the validity of ethical distinctions, see MN 60.13, I 404,21–35; MN 76.10, I 516,3–17. The present sutta seems to be extracted from **8:12 §§1–2**.

254 Mp: "The 'trainee' (*sekha*) refers to the seven trainees [from the one on the path of stream-entry to the one on the path of arahantship]. But the virtuous worldling (*sīlavantaputhujjana*) can also be included under the stream-enterer."

255 Mp has a long preamble to its commentary on this sutta, explaining how throngs of lay devotees from Sāvatthī spontaneously assembled at the Eastern Park to hear Sāriputta speak. The devas, too, realizing that Sāriputta was about to deliver a momentous discourse, arrived from multiple celestial realms and from thousands of world systems to listen. Sāriputta exercised a feat of psychic power such that even those at the back of the crowd, and the devas at the far edge of the world system, could clearly see him and hear his voice.

256 Mp: "The *person fettered internally* (*ajjhattasaṃyojanaṃ puggalaṃ*): The 'internal' (*ajjhattaṃ*) is sense-sphere existence; the 'external' (*bahiddhā*) is form and formless existence. Desire and lust for 'the internal,' consisting in sense-sphere existence, is called the internal fetter. Desire and lust for 'the external,' consisting in form and formless existence, is called the external fetter. Or, alternatively, the five lower fetters are the internal fetter, and the five higher fetters are the external fetter. The persons being spoken of as internally fettered and externally fettered are not the multitude of ordinary worldly people still attached to the round of existence, but noble disciples—stream-enterers, once-returners, and non-returners—who are distinguished as twofold by way of their mode of existence."

It is striking that the Chinese parallel MĀ 21 (at T I 448c23–25) interprets these two persons in a way diametrically opposite to the Pāli version: "In this world there are two kinds of people. Which two? The person with an internal fetter, the non-returner, who does not come back to this world. And the person with an external fetter, one who is not a non-returner but comes back to this world" (世實有二種人。云何為二。有內結人阿那含。不還此間。有外結人非阿那含。還來此間). The explanations that follow in MĀ 21 are consistent with this opening statement.

257 Mp: "*Who returns to this state of being* (*āgantā itthattaṃ*): He returns to this state of the human five aggregates. Or else, he is not reborn in that heavenly realm or in some higher realm, but he comes back to a lower realm. By this factor, what is discussed are the lower two paths and fruits [of stream-entry and once-returning] attained by a bhikkhu who is a dry-insight meditator using the elements as meditation subject (*sukkhavipassakassa dhātukammaṭṭhānikabhikkhuno*)."

258 Mp: "*A certain peaceful liberation of mind* (*aññataraṃ santaṃ cetovimuttiṃ*): the fourth jhāna among the eight meditative attainments; for that is peaceful because it stills the opposing defilements, and it is a liberation of mind because it is liberated from those defilements."

259 Mp: "He is reborn in an order of devas among the pure abodes (*suddhāvāsa*). He does not return to this state of the human five aggregates, nor is he reborn in a lower realm. Either he is reborn in a higher realm or he attains final nibbāna right there. By this factor, what is discussed are the three paths and fruits [up to non-returning] of a bhikkhu working at concentration (*samādhikammikassa bhikkhuno*)."

260 Mp: "At this point, what is discussed is the stream-enterer's and once-returner's insight [undertaken] to destroy lust for the five objects of sensual pleasure and [to reach] the path of non-returning (*anāgāmimaggavipassanā*)."

261 Mp: "By this, what is discussed is the non-returner's insight [undertaken] to destroy lust for existence and [to reach] the path of arahantship (*arahattamaggavipassanā*)."

262 Mp sees the practice for the destruction of craving (*taṇhākkhaya*) as again referring to the stream-enterer's and once-returner's insight to reach the path of non-returning, and the practice for the destruction of greed (*lobhakkhaya*) as again referring to the non-returner's insight to reach the path of arahantship. It would be peculiar for such a distinction to be intended here. Since both craving (*taṇhā*) and greed (*lobha*) can refer to the desire for continued existence (*bhavataṇhā, bhavarāga*), and since

it seems improbable that, after alluding to the highest realization, Sāriputta would then revert to a lower level, this sentence may simply be continuing the description of one practicing to attain arahantship.

263 Mp: "[Sāriputta] has discussed insight under six headings: (1) the lower two paths and fruits of the dry-insight meditator who uses the elements as his meditation subject; (2) the three paths and fruits of one who works at concentration; (3) the stream-enterer's and once-returner's insight to destroy sensual lust [and reach] the path of non-returning; (4) the non-returner's insight to destroy lust for existence [and reach] the path of arahantship; (5) the stream-enterer's and once-returner's insight for 'the destruction of craving'—that is, craving for sensual pleasure—and to reach the path of non-returning; and (6) the non-returner's insight for 'the destruction of greed'—that is, greed for existence—and [to reach] the path of arahantship. At the conclusion of the discourse, deities numbering hundreds of thousand of *koṭis* (a *koṭi* = ten million) attained arahantship, and there was no counting the number of those who became stream-enterers and so forth."

264 Mp explains *samacittā* to mean "with the same mind," thereby resolving an ambiguity in the Pāli term. Though in Skt the difference between *śama* = "peace" and *sama* = "same, equal" would have been clear, in most dialects of Middle Indo-Aryan (including Pāli) the two words would be indistinguishable and thus their meanings could be conflated. Mp construes *sama* as equivalent to Skt *sama*, "same, equal": "They are called 'same-minded' because of the similarity in the subtlety of their mind (*cittassa sukhumabhāvasamatāya samacittā*); for they had created their own bodies with minds of similar subtlety (*sukhume citta-sarikkhake katvā*)." Mp gives other explanations of *samacittā*, but all assume the meaning is "with the same mind." The Chinese parallel (at T I 449b1) reads 等心天 = "same-minded deities," thus agreeing with Mp. This indicates that the original on which the Chinese translation was based either had *samacittā* in a language that made a distinction between *śama* and *sama*, or, if preserved in a language that did not make such a distinction, had been accompanied by an explanation of the term as meaning "same-minded." However, the expressions *santindriyā* and *santamānasā* toward the end of the sutta, both related to the Skt *śama*, suggest that the original meaning could have been "peaceful minded," unless ambivalence was deliberate.

265 *Anukampaṃ upādāya*. Mp: "Not out of compassion for Sāriputta, for on that occasion there was no need to show compassion for the elder [Sāriputta] . . . who had already reached the perfection

of a disciple's knowledge. Rather, they ask the Blessed One to go out of compassion for the other devas and humans who had assembled there." Despite the commentary, it may be the case that the devas actually wanted the Buddha to approach Sāriputta for his own sake. Sāriputta probably did not have the supernormal ability to see the hosts of devas that had assembled to hear him speak and thus the Buddha had to inform him of this. At Ud 40,28–29, Sāriputta says that he does not even see a mud sprite (*mayaṃ pan'etarahi paṃsupisācakampi na passāma*).

266 Mp: "*It was right here* (*idh'eva*): It was in this human world and under this teaching that those deities had developed their minds in such a way that they were reborn in a peaceful form-sphere existence. Having come from there, they have created subtle bodies. While those deities might have reached three paths and fruits in Buddha Kassapa's teaching, because all Buddhas have the same teaching, with the words 'right here' he refers to the teaching as one." The Chinese parallel is more explicit than the Pāli: "It was in the past when they were human beings that those same-minded deities developed such a wholesome mind, such an extremely vast and great mind."

267 *Santindriyā bhavissāma santamānasā*. As noted in note 264 above, the repeated use of the word *santa* here and just below suggests that *samacittā*, in relation to the deities, could have meant "peaceful minded"—this despite the agreement between Mp and the Chinese translation on "same-minded."

268 *Kāmarāgābhinivesavinibandhapaligedhapariyuṭṭhānajjhosānahetu*. I render the compound following Mp's resolution: *kāmarāgābhinivesahetu, kāmarāgavinibandhahetu, kāmarāgapaligedhahetu, kāmarāgapariyuṭṭhānahetu, kāmarāga-ajjhosānahetu*. The same applies to the long compound on *diṭṭhi*.

269 The same charge is leveled against the Buddha himself in **4:22** and **8:11**.

270 I follow Ce and Be *kāmamajjhāvasati* (= *kāmaṃ ajjhāvasati*), as against Ee *kāmamajjhe vasati*.

271 *Tuṇhībhūtā tuṇhībhūtā va saṅghamajjhe saṅkasāyanti*. Mp: "Sitting silently in the midst of the Saṅgha, they are unable to open their mouths and utter even a single word, but just sit there as if brooding."

272 Here and below reading with Ce and Ee *bhajanti*.

273 Reading with Be *yena vā pana tena pakkamanti*. Ce and Ee read *papatanti*, which does not fit as well.

274 See SN 45:24, V 18–19.

275 *Ñāyaṃ dhammaṃ kusalaṃ*. Mp: "The path together with insight."

276 *Duggahitehi suttantehi byañjanappatirūpakehi*. For *–patirūpaka*

as meaning "counterfeit, a semblance, of misleading appearance," see such expressions as *amitto mittapatirūpako* at DN III 185–86; *sakkapatirūpako* at SN I 230,16; *jātarūpappatirūpakaṃ* and *saddhammappatirūpakaṃ* at SN II 224,10–17. Here the compound probably means the same as *dunnikkhittaṃ padabyañjanaṃ* at **2:20** above. See too **4:160** (II 147,21) and **5:156** (III 178,26). Mp takes *dhamma* here to mean the text (*pāḷi*), commenting: "They exclude the meaning and text of well-acquired discourses and elevate above them the meaning and text of their badly acquired discourses."

277 Be reads here *suggahitehi suttantehi byañjanappatirūpakehi* (Ee *vyañjanapatirūpakehi*). Ce, however, which I follow, uses the negative: *suggahitehi suttantehi na byañjanapatirūpakehi*. Ce may have added *na* to convey the required sense, but without it the sentence seems self-contradictory.

278 Here and in the following the text uses *etadaggaṃ*.

279 As PED notes, Pāli *vagga* represents two distinct Skt words: *varga*, meaning "group," such as a group of suttas; and *vyagra*, the opposite of *samagra*, "divided" as opposed to "harmonious." Here, the latter *vagga* is evidently meant.

280 *Diṭṭhānugatiṃ āpajjati*. Lit., "follow in accord with what is seen (*diṭṭha*)." This does *not* mean "follow in accord with their view (*diṭṭhi*)." Mp: "Doing what was done by their preceptors and teachers, they follow in accord with the practice they have seen."

281 In Pāli the foremost of these (*etadaggaṃ*) is the assembly of the foremost (*aggavatī parisā*).

282 Mp: "The four paths and four fruits are discussed by means of the four truths."

283 These are the four wrong motives, mentioned as such at **4:17–20**.

284 For the meaning of *ukkācita* I follow DOP, p. 387, which defines it as "boasting, empty talk," and *ukkācitavinīta* as "trained in empty talk." I use "vain talk" rather than "empty talk," since the talk considered worthy here is precisely talk about emptiness. Vibh 352 (Be §862) includes *ukkācanā* in a definition of *lapanā*, which suggests that *ukkācanā* is a tool of persuasion. See too Vism 27,19–22, Ppn 1.74. In the present sutta *ukkācita* seems to have a different nuance, perhaps elegant but hollow talk.

285 Also at SN 20:7, II 267,6–15. For "connected with emptiness" (*suññatāpaṭisaṃyuttā*), Mp says: "Like the Connected Discourses on the Unconditioned, disclosing mere phenomena empty of a sentient being" (*sattasuññaṃ dhammamattameva pakāsakā asaṅkhatasaṃyuttasadisā*). Since the Asaṅkhatasaṃyutta (SN

chap. 43) does not speak of "mere phenomena," perhaps Mp actually means the Saḷāyatanasaṃyutta (esp. SN 35:85, IV 54).

286 Mp: "*That values worldly things* (*āmisagaru*): one that values the four requisites and regards the world-transcending Dhamma as inferior. *That values the good Dhamma* (*saddhammagaru*): one that values the nine world-transcending *dhammas* (the four paths, four fruits, and nibbāna), and regards the four requisites as inferior."

287 The first seven are disciples who have reached the world-transcending paths and fruits. For formal explanations, see MN 70.14–21, I 477–79. The latter two are respectively the good person and the bad person who have not reached the path.

288 Be lacks the two sentences beginning respectively, "It is because it is unrighteous" and (below) "It is because it is righteous." They occur in Ce and Ee.

289 *Adhikaraṇaṃ*. Mp: "The four kinds of disciplinary issues, disputes and so forth." See p. 1623, note 231 above.

290 Mp: "Because the wheel-turning monarch is mentioned, the phrase, 'out of compassion for the world' (*lokānukampāya*) is not used." On the wheel-turning monarch (*rājā cakkavatī*), see p. 1613, note 156.

291 Pāli *thūpa*, a memorial mound.

292 *Paccekabuddha* is defined at Pp 14,16–20 (Be §23), as "a person who, in regard to things not heard before, awakens to the [four noble] truths by himself but does not attain all-knowledge regarding them or mastery over the powers" (*ekacco puggalo pubbe ananussutesu dhammesu sāmaṃ saccāni abhisambujjhati; na ca tattha sabbaññutaṃ pāpuṇāti, na ca balesu vasībhāvaṃ, ayaṃ vuccati puggalo paccekabuddho*).

293 Mp: "The arahant is not terrified because he has abandoned personal-existence view (*sakkāyadiṭṭhiyā pahīnattā*); the thoroughbred elephant, because his personal-existence view is very strong (*sakkāyadiṭṭhiyā balavattā*)."

294 *Kiṃpurisā*, a mythical class of beings in Indian folklore.

295 Mp: "By 'should not correct me,' this is meant: 'He should not give me exhortation or instruction; he should not correct me.'"

296 *No ti naṃ vadeyyaṃ*. Mp: "I would then say to him, 'I will not do what you say,' and I would trouble him by not doing what he says."

297 *Ubhato vacīsaṃsāro*. The expression is unusual. Mp explains that on both sides the talk continues (*saṃsaramānā*) as they verbally attack one another.

298 Ce reads here *ajjhattaṃ na avūpasantaṃ hoti*, "not unsettled internally," which means in effect that the disturbance is settled; that

is precisely the opposite of what the context requires. Older Sinhala-script editions, referred to in the notes to Ce, read *ajjhattaṃ na suvūpasantaṃ hoti*, "not well settled internally," which makes better sense. Be and Ee read *ajjhattaṃ avūpasantaṃ hoti*, supported by the lemma of Mp (Ce and Be). I thus translate on the basis of this reading. Similarly, in the following paragraph, Ce reads *ajjhattaṃ avūpasantaṃ hoti*, again the opposite of what the context requires. I take as the basis for my rendering there Be and Ee *ajjhattaṃ na suvūpasantaṃ hoti*.

299 Ce treats this paragraph as a separate sutta. Be and Ee, which I follow, treat the two paragraphs as a single sutta. Unless the two paragraphs are taken in this way, there is no dyad here justifying their inclusion in the Twos.

300 I read with Be *pabbajitasukhaṃ*, as against Ce and Ee *pabbajjāsukhaṃ*. The contrast between *gihī* and *pabbajita* seems more logical than that between *gihī* and *pabbajjā*.

301 *Upadhisukha* and *nirupadhisukha*. On *upadhi*, see p. 1621, note 219. Mp glosses the former as the happiness of the three planes (sense-sphere, form, and formless planes). It glosses the latter as world-transcending happiness (*lokuttarasukha*).

302 The contrast is between *sāmisaṃ sukhaṃ*, which Mp defines as defiled happiness that leads back to the round [of existence], and *nirāmisaṃ sukhaṃ*, undefiled happiness that leads to the end of the round.

303 Mp: "The happiness with rapture (*sappītikaṃ sukhaṃ*) is the happiness of the first and second jhānas. The happiness without rapture (*nippītikaṃ sukhaṃ*) is the happiness of the third and fourth jhānas."

304 Mp. "Pleasurable happiness (*sātasukha*) is the happiness of the first three jhānas. The happiness of equanimity (*upekkhāsukha*) is the happiness of the fourth jhāna."

305 *Sappītikārammaṇaṃ sukhaṃ* and *nippītikārammaṇaṃ sukhaṃ*. It is doubtful that, in the four Nikāyas, the word *ārammaṇa* ever means "object of consciousness" in the general sense it has in the Abhidhamma and the commentaries. Its original meaning is closer to "basis" or "support." Occasionally, as in SN 34:5, III 266, the word designates a "meditation object." Over time, the meaning of *ārammaṇa* must have broadened from "object of meditation" to "object of consciousness" in a general sense, but to my knowledge this development occurred after the period when the Nikāyas were compiled.

306 Mp: "The happiness based on form (*rūpārammaṇaṃ sukhaṃ*) is that based on the fourth jhāna of the form sphere, or any that arises based on form. That based on the formless (*arūpārammaṇaṃ*

sukhaṃ) is that based on a formless jhāna, or any that arises based on the formless."

307 Mp: "'With a basis' means 'with a reason.' The same method applies in the following suttas. For the words 'source,' 'cause,' 'causal activity,' 'condition,' and 'form' are all just synonyms for 'reason'" (***Sanimittā*** *ti sakāraṇā.... Nidānaṃ hetu saṅkhāro paccayo rūpan ti sabbāni pi hi etāni kāraṇavevacanān'eva*).

308 I follow the arrangement in Be and Ee. Ce does not place this sutta here, but because the key word is *sasaṅkhārā*, inserts it below, as the fourth among the suttas on the five aggregates. It seems that the text available to the commentator corresponded with Be, for Mp (both Ce and Be) explains that *nimitta, nidāna, hetu, saṅkhāra,* and *paccaya* are synonymous.

309 Mp: "*Liberation of mind* (*cetovimutti*) is the concentration of the fruit [of arahantship], *liberation by wisdom* (*paññāvimutti*) is the wisdom of the fruit." This interpretation assumes that the two are conjoined, as in the expression *anāsavaṃ cetovimuttiṃ paññāvimuttiṃ*. It is possible, however, for mundane *cetovimutti* to be attained independently of *paññāvimutti*. For a discussion of the contrast between mundane and world-transcending types of *cetovimutti*, see MN 43.30–37, I 297–98, and SN 41.7, IV 295–97.

310 Be has these inverted.

311 *Yo ca akappiye kappiyasaññī, yo ca kappiye akappiyasaññī*. This refers to what is allowable and not allowable according to the rules of monastic discipline.

312 I translate based on Ce and Ee. Be inverts the two clauses, reading: *Yo ca āpattiyā anāpattisaññī, yo ca anāpattiyā āpattisaññī.*

313 Here, too, Be inverts the clauses, reading: *Yo ca āpattiyā āpattisaññī, yo ca anāpattiyā anāpattisaññī.*

314 Here, again, I follow Ce and Ee over Be, which inverts the clauses.

315 Mp glosses *āsā* here with *taṇhā*.

316 *Yo ca laddhaṃ laddhaṃ vissajjeti*. Mp glosses: "He gives to others" (*paresaṃ deti*). However, I think what is indicated by *vissajjeti* is not generosity but profligacy.

317 In relation to this and the following sutta, see **1:11, 1:12**.

318 For explanations of these types of offenses, here and just below, see p. 1602, note 66.

319 *Esā bhikkhave tulā etaṃ pamāṇaṃ*. Mp: "Just as one weighing gold or grain uses a scale, taking that as the standard, the measure, or criterion, so this is the standard and criterion for my bhikkhu disciples, namely, Sāriputta and Moggallāna. It is possible to weigh or measure oneself by aspiring, 'May I be like them in regard to wisdom or psychic potency!' But not in any other way."

320 The two chief bhikkhunī disciples respectively in regard to wisdom and psychic potency. See **1:236, 1:237**.

321 See **1:250, 1:251**.

322 See **1:260, 1:262**. The latter's name is also spelled Veḷukaṇṭakiyā and Veḷukaṇḍakī.

323 Ce divides each statement about the fool and the wise person in **2:134–37** into two suttas, whereas Be and Ee treat them as contrasting parts of a single sutta. Thus where Be and Ee count four suttas here, Ce counts eight. Parallels in later nipātas (**3:9, 4:3, 10:225–28**) even in Ce support Be and Ee, which I therefore follow.

324 Ce mistakenly numbers the first paragraph of this sutta as 6 within the vagga, thus assigning 6 to two successive suttas. This should be corrected to 7, and the following sutta numbers in the vagga should all be increased by one.

325 Mp mentions Devadatta in relation to the Tathāgata and Kokālika in relation to the chief disciples (see **10:89**; also SN 6:9–10, I 149–53; Sn 3:10, pp. 123–31; Vin II 196–200). On the positive side, Mp mentions respectively Ānanda, and the cowherd Nanda and the financier's son.

326 *Sacittavodānañca na ca kiñci loke upādiyati*. I mirror the text's dissonant mixture of grammatical forms.

327 *Saṅgahā*. See **4:32** and pp. 1684–85, note 687.

328 *Anukampā*. This is the word normally signifying active compassion or empathy, as contrasted with *karuṇā*, which usually signifies meditative compassion.

329 *Santhāra*. Mp explains this as if it meant "a covering" or "a spread," which it does in certain contexts: "The covering with material goods is spreading out by covering [the space] between oneself and others with the four requisites." More likely, however, *santhāra* here is nearly synonymous with *paṭisanthāra*, which occurs in the next sutta. In fact, Mp says that the difference between the two words is a mere prefix.

330 *Ātitheyyāni*. Mp glosses with *āgantukadānāni*, "gifts to a guest."

331 Mp: "Skillfulness in [entering] a meditative attainment (*samāpattikusalatā*) is facility in entering the attainment after one has understood suitability in food and climate. Skillfulness in emerging from a meditative attainment (*samāpattivuṭṭhānakusalatā*) is skill in emerging at the predetermined time."

332 I here follow Ce and Ee, which count each of the five pairs as a separate sutta; Be counts each group as one sutta.

333 Be and Ce count the following suttas as a separate vagga, but Ee treats them as a continuation of vagga XVI.

334 Again, I follow Ce and Ee in counting each pair of unwholesome (and below, wholesome) qualities in this vagga as a separate

sutta, whereas Be counts each group of unwholesome and wholesome qualities as one sutta.

335 Ee counts this as vagga XVII and names it "Reasons" (*Atthavasa*). Be also treats it as an independent vagga, but Ce takes it as the second subchapter of its vagga XVII.

336 Ce counts ten separate suttas here, but I follow Be and Ee in taking them as one.

337 What follows here are all disciplinary regulations laid down in the Vinaya Piṭaka.

338 Ee treats this as a continuation of vagga XVII, Ce and Be as an independent vagga but without a number.

Notes to the Threes

339 Readings differ among the editions. Ce *apadānasobhinī paññā*, Be *apadānasobhanī paññā*, Ee *apadāne sobhati paññā*. Mp: "The meaning is that the fool and the wise person are each known through their conduct" (*bālā ca paṇḍitā ca attano attano cariten'eva pākaṭā hontī ti attho*).

340 *Bālalakkhaṇāni bālanimittāni bālāpadānāni*. Mp: "These are the means of recognition."

341 Ee omits this concluding exhortation in **3:3–7**.

342 Mp. "*Discordant* (*ananulomike*) means not in conformity with the teaching. Gross 'discordant bodily action' is destroying life, etc.; or [more subtly] worshipping the directions or making offerings to the spirits. Gross 'discordant verbal action' is false speech, etc.; or [more subtly], if one does not wish to give to others, deceiving them by saying one does not have anything to give. Gross 'discordant mental action' is longing, etc.; or [more subtly], explaining a meditation subject incorrectly." Mp illustrates this with the story of the elder mentioned at Vism 296,12–16, Ppn 9.6, who taught a young man to meditate on loving-kindness toward his wife. As a result he was overcome by lust and beat against the walls of his meditation cell all night. I translate *ananulomikesu dhammesu* in accordance with Mp, but the word *dhammesu* can also mean "teachings," and it is possible that this was the original intention.

343 The second case, the understanding of the four noble truths, marks the attainment of stream-entry; the third, the destruction of the taints, is the attainment of arahantship.

344 These were all considered low occupations fit only for social outcasts. The caṇḍāla*s* were the most despised community. Ce omits *nesādakule vā*, apparently by oversight, as Mp (both Ce and Be) glosses it as "a family of deer hunters" (*migaluddakānaṃ kule*).

345 Ce reads *macalappatto;* Ee *–macalapatto;* Be *acalappatto.* In **4:87 §1** we find *samaṇamacalo,* on which see p. 1694, note 778. Here Mp explains: "When the eldest—one due to be anointed but not yet anointed—is still an infant, he does not form any wish to be anointed. But when he reaches the age of sixteen and his beard begins to grow, he is called 'one who has attained the unshaken.' He is able to reign over a large realm, therefore [the Buddha] says 'one who has attained the unshaken.'"

346 Mp glosses *dhamma* here as "the Dhamma of the ten courses of wholesome kamma" (*dasakusalakammapathadhammo*). This is certainly too narrow, but it is clear that "Dhamma" here does not mean the Buddha's teaching as such. Rather, it is the universal principle of goodness and truth followed by virtuous people irrespective of their religious convictions. On the basis of this Dhamma the wheel-turning monarch provides righteous (*dhammika*) protection to all in his realm.

347 Mp: "He sets in motion the wheel just by means of the Dhamma of the ten courses of wholesome kamma." Ce and Be read the verb here as *vatteti,* but below, in relation to the Buddha, as *pavatteti;* Ee has *pavatteti* in relation to both. If *vatteti* is the original reading, the change in verbs may be intended to suggest that a wheel-turning monarch does not initiate the rule of righteousness but continues the heritage of his forefathers, whereas a Buddha sets in motion the wheel of Dhamma previously unknown.

348 *Kenaci manussabhūtena paccatthikena pāṇinā.* Lit. "by any hostile living being that has become human." Mp: "The deities, it is said, can do whatever they want. Therefore they are not included, but 'human being' is mentioned." This is in contrast with the Buddha, whose wheel cannot be turned back by any beings including the deities.

349 So Ce and Ee. Be gives the king's name as Sacetana.

350 *Abhisaṅkhārassa gati.* An unusual use of the word *abhisaṅkhāra,* which in more technical contexts denotes volitional activity that creates kamma. Mp glosses with *payogassa gamanaṃ,* "the movement of (or due to) the effort."

351 Mp: "*As if fixed on an axle*: as if an axle had been inserted so that it stood still."

352 *Apaṇṇakapaṭipadaṃ.* Mp gives a series of synonyms: "the unmistaken way, the definite way, the emancipating way, the causal way, the essential way, the exquisite way, the unopposed way, the conducive way, the way in accord with the Dhamma" (*aviraddhapaṭipadaṃ ekaṃsapaṭipadaṃ niyyānikapaṭipadaṃ kāraṇapaṭipadaṃ sārapaṭipadaṃ maṇḍapaṭipadaṃ apaccanīkapaṭipadaṃ anulomapaṭipadaṃ dhammānudhammapaṭipadaṃ*). *Apaṇṇaka,* in

a similar sense, is found in AN at **4:71**, **4:72**, and **10:46**. It also occurs as the title of MN 60. In relation to *yoni c'assa āraddhā hoti āsavānaṃ khayāya*, Mp explains that *yoni* can mean a section of the aggregates, a cause, or the vagina (*khandhakoṭṭhāsa, kāraṇa, passāvamagga*). Here, a cause is intended.

353 At SN 35:239, IV 175,26–30, too, it is said that by these three practices "one has laid the groundwork for the destruction of the taints."

354 *Mātikādharā*. Mp glosses this as "experts on the two outlines" (*dvemātikādharā*), which Mp-ṭ identifies as the bhikkhu and bhikkhunī *mātikās* (the Pātimokkhas for monks and nuns) or the *mātikās* of the Vinaya and Abhidhamma. The *mātikās* were lists of principles and practices that systematically represent the Dhamma. The *mātikādharā* are mentioned once in DN, twice in MN (in one sutta), not at all in SN, and twelve times in AN, which suggests that the suttas that refer to them are relatively late, or at least had been modified to accommodate them. On their nature and role, see Warder 1980: 218–24.

355 For formal explanations of these three types, see MN 70.17–19, I 478,4–479,3. All three classes are *sekhas* ranging from the stream-enterer through one on the path to arahantship. As general classes, they differ, not in their position relative to the final goal, but in their dominant spiritual faculty. The body witness (*kāyasakkhī*) gives prominence to concentration and attains the "peaceful formless emancipations." One attained to view (*diṭṭhippatta*) gives prominence to wisdom and does not attain the formless emancipations. One liberated by faith (*saddhāvimutta*) gives prominence to faith and does not attain the formless emancipations. Because these three categories comprise persons standing anywhere from stream-enterer to the path to arahantship, their members cannot be prejudged as superior and inferior merely by falling into a particular class. To make such judgments, one would have to know their standing in terms of the six levels they each comprise. The body witness, on attaining arahantship, becomes "liberated in both respects" (*ubhatobhāgavimutta*). The other two become "liberated by wisdom" (*paññāvimutta*). On the two types of arahant, see MN 70.15–16, I 477,24–478,3.

356 In the Pāli, each participant in the discussion repeats the opening statement about the three persons before expressing his own opinion. To avoid redundancy, I have deleted this repetition.

357 Ce has, for this case only, "a person attained to view is an arahant or one practicing for arahantship" (*svāssa arahā vā arahattāya paṭipanno*). Be and Ee, consistent with the previous two types, state only that this person is practicing the way to arahantship.

According to the typology of MN 70, a body witness, one liberated by faith, and one attained to view have not completely eliminated their *āsavas* and therefore are not arahants.

358 *Okkamati niyāmaṃ kusalesu dhammesu sammattaṃ*. This is a technical expression denoting entry upon the world-transcending path. Mp: "*The fixed course* [*consisting in*] *rightness in wholesome qualities*: rightness in wholesome qualities consisting in entry upon the path." Though "rightness in wholesome qualities" sounds redundant, what is intended is the harmony and strength of the wholesome qualities needed to enter the path of stream-entry. For more on this expression in AN, see **5:151–53** and **6:86–88**. See too SN 25.1–10, III 225–28, which says that by entering the "fixed course of rightness" (*sammattaniyāma*) one enters the noble plane and becomes either a *dhammānusārī* or a *saddhānusārī*.

359 *Sabyābajjhaṃ kāyasaṅkhāraṃ abhisaṅkharoti, sabyābajjhaṃ vacīsaṅkhāraṃ abhisaṅkharoti, sabyābajjhaṃ manosaṅkhāraṃ abhisaṅkharoti*. Mp glosses *sabyābajjhaṃ*, "afflictive," with *sadukkhaṃ*, "with suffering." The "activities" are volitional actions that create kamma.

360 *Devā subhakiṇhā*. These are the deities in the divine realm corresponding to the third jhāna. See **4:123**.

361 Mp: "Those in the lower world referred to here are the afflicted spirits with palaces (*vemānikapetā*). For at times they experience fortune, at times they experience their [painful] kamma; they undergo mixed pleasure and pain."

362 By understanding the four noble truths, the attainment of stream-entry is indicated. The destruction of the taints, just below, marks the attainment of arahantship.

363 *Tattha tattha paññāya anuggahessāmi*. Mp: "One *assists with wisdom* the aggregate of virtuous behavior in one or another respect by avoiding those things that are uncongenial and unhelpful to virtuous behavior and by cultivating those things that are congenial and helpful [to it]. The same method holds for the aggregates of concentration and wisdom." "Aggregate of virtuous behavior" (*sīlakkhandha*) is spoken of in the sense of the assemblage of factors that constitute virtuous behavior, and so too for the aggregates of concentration and wisdom.

364 This is the standard definition of false speech among the ten courses of unwholesome kamma, as at **10:176 §4** of the unwholesome section. The explanation of "speech like flowers," just below, is the standard definition of truthful speech in the corresponding wholesome section.

365 Reading here *dhanaṃ* with Ce and B. Ee *dhammaṃ* is clearly wrong.

366 Mp explains the compound *ahaṅkāramamaṅkāramānānusayā* as "I-making by views, mine-making by craving, and the underlying tendency to conceit. These are the defilements in relation to oneself and others." Mp explains *bahiddhā ca sabbanimittesu* ("and all external objects") as the five sense objects, the eternalist (and other) views, the person, and Dhamma. It calls this *samādhi* the fruition attainment of arahantship (*arahattaphalasamāpatti*).

367 Sn 1048. The Pārāyana, the fifth and final chapter of the Suttanipāta, consists of a framing story and sixteen sections in each of which the Buddha answers the questions of the students of the elder brahmin Bāvāri. Verses from the Pārāyana are cited and explained elsewhere in AN and other Nikāyas, which testifies to its antiquity. It must have existed as an independent work before being incorporated into Sn. The Pārāyana is the subject of an ancient canonical commentary, the Cūḷaniddesa, included in the Khuddaka Nikāya.

368 Ee takes this sutta to belong to the preceding one and thus assigns only one number to them. In Ce and Be, which I follow, it is separate. Thus from this point on my numbering exceeds Ee by one.

369 Sn 1106–7.

370 This is an allusion to the abandoning of the five hindrances, of which four are mentioned here.

371 Mp takes this to be the fruit of arahantship based on the fourth jhāna, which is suggested by the line *upekkhāsatisaṃsuddhaṃ*, echoing the stock formula for the fourth jhāṇa.

372 There are some differences in the readings: Ce *diṭṭhe vā dhamme, upapajje vā, apare vā pariyāye*; Be *diṭṭhe vā dhamme upapajja vā apare vā pariyāye*; Ee *diṭṭh' eva dhamme upapajje vā apare vā pariyāye*. Mp says: "This is stated to show that the kamma is [of the type] either to be experienced in this present life, or to be experienced following rebirth, or to be experienced in some subsequent existence." For an Abhidhamma explanation of this triad, see CMA 205.

Some scholars have argued from the variant readings that only two alternatives are involved: either in this life or upon rebirth. However, I translate in accordance with the commentarial understanding. While the commentaries may be imposing a later interpretation on more archaic texts that asserted only two ways in which kamma can ripen, as a translator I feel responsible to the text that has been transmitted rather than to theories about a more archaic original. The recognition of a threefold ripening of kamma is not exclusive to the Theravāda school but is also found in the treatises of the Sarvāstivāda Abhidharma system. Definitions of the three types—for example, in the Abhidharma Mahāvibhāṣā Śāstra at T XXVII 592a22–593b8, and in the Abhidharmakośa at T XXIX 81c10–16—are exactly the same as in the Pāli tradition and thus likely precede the division of the schools.

373 This statement has to be carefully interpreted. For an arahant—who has abandoned greed, hatred, and delusion—kamma created earlier, whether good or bad, is still capable of ripening during the final life. But because there is no more rebirth, with his passing all accumulated kamma from the past becomes defunct. Thus the intention of this statement is not that an arahant's past kamma cannot ripen while the arahant lives, but that it becomes defunct with the arahant's passing; for there will be no further continuum of existence within which its fruits might arise.

Brahmāli writes: "There must be a distinction here between 'non-greed' (*alobha*) and the situation when 'greed has vanished' (*lobhe vigata*). The former must refer to the motivation behind a particular action, the latter to the full uprooting of greed, attained only by the non-returner or even the arahant. Only in the light of this distinction does this statement make sense."

374 I read with Ce and Be *mohajañ cāpaviddasu*, as against Ee's *mohajañ cāpi 'viddasu*. Mp (both Ce and Be) also reads *mohajañ cāpaviddasu*, which it resolves into *mohajañcāpi aviddasu*. It paraphrases the meaning thus: "Whatever kamma the blind, ignorant worldling creates born of greed, hatred, and delusion—whether the kamma so fashioned be little or much—*it is to be experienced right here* (*idh'eva taṃ vedaniyaṃ*), that is, it is to be experienced by the fool here in his very own being (*idha sake attabhāveyeva*); this means that it ripens in his own individual being. *There exists no other site* [*for it*] (*vatthuṃ aññaṃ na vijjati*): there is no other site for the ripening of that kamma; for the kamma done by one person does not ripen in another's being."

375 *Tasmā lobhaṃ ca dosaṃ ca, mohajaṃ cāpi viddasu*. Ee reads the last pāda *mohañ cāpi 'viddasu*, which is missing a syllable. The text does lack a verb and direct object qualifed by *mohajaṃ*. Mp supplies these in its paraphrase: "Therefore a wise person *does not do that kamma* born of greed and so forth" (*yo vidū . . . taṃ lobhajādibhedaṃ kammaṃ na karoti*). It will be noted that Mp considers *lobhaṃ* and *dosaṃ* to be truncated forms of *lobhajaṃ* and *dosajaṃ*, and I translate accordingly. For the verb, I see *jahe* of pāda d to implicitly extend up into pādas a and b, thus doing a dual service.

376 See **1:251**.

377 *Antaraṭṭhako himapātanasamayo*. Mp: "A period of eight days when snow falls. It is the last four days of the month of Māgha and the first four days of Phagguṇa (roughly in mid-February)."

378 Similar verses are spoken to Anāthapiṇḍika at SN 10:8, I 212.

379 A version of this sutta is at MN 130, but with *four* divine messengers, beginning with birth.

380 Mp: "The old person, the sick one, and the corpse are called 'divine messengers' (*devadūta*) because they inspire a sense of urgency, as if warning one: 'Now you must go into the presence of death.'"

381 The legendary god of death and the judge of one's future destiny.

382 Reading with Ce *dukkhā tibbā khaṭukā vedanā*. Be and Ee add a fourth adjective, *kharā*.

383 I read with Ee *te khemappattā sukhitā*. Ce *te khoppattā sukhitā* and Be *te appamattā sukhino* are both faulty.

384 The eighth of the fortnight is the day of the quarter moon, both waxing and waning. The "four great kings" (*catumahārājāno*) are the rulers of the lowest of the six sense-sphere heavenly worlds, the realm closest to the human. We find here a graded sequence: on the eighth, their ministers and assembly members (*amaccā pārisajjā*) inspect the world; on the fourteenth (the day before the full moon and new moon), their sons (*puttā*) inspect the world; and on the fifteenth, the actual full-moon and new-moon days, the four great kings themselves inspect the world.

385 Mp: "When they *observe the uposatha*, they undertake the uposatha factors eight times per month. Keeping the extra observance days (*paṭijāgaranti*), in a single fortnight they do so by anticipating and following up (*paccuggamanānugamana*) the four uposatha days. Anticipating the uposatha of the fifth, they undertake the uposatha on the fourth; and following up, on the sixth. Anticipating the uposatha of the eighth, they observe it on the seventh; and following up, on the ninth. Anticipating the uposatha of the fourteenth, they observe it on the thirteenth, and following up the uposatha of the fifteenth, they observe the uposatha at the beginning [of the next fortnight]. They *do meritorious deeds* (*puññāni karonti*) in various ways: by going for refuge, constantly observing the precepts, offering flowers, listening to the Dhamma, offering lights, making dwellings, etc. Having wandered around, [the ministers and assembly members] write down the names of the merit-makers on a golden sheet and present it to the four great kings." For canonical accounts of the uposatha observance, see **3:70** and **8:41**, **8:42**.

386 I follow Be as against Ce and Ee in the division between this sutta and the next. Ce and Ee take this sentence as the beginning of **3:38** (No. 37 in Ee's scheme) and the second narrative that begins *bhūtapubbaṃ bhikkhave* ("Bhikkhus, once in the past")—several paragraphs below—as a continuation of the sutta. Be, however,

takes the first narrative about Sakka to be a continuation of **3:37**, and the second narrative to mark the beginning of **3:38**. A Chinese parallel, SĀ 1117 (T II 295c10–296a23), agrees with Be on this but merges into one the two statements about Sakka and the liberated bhikkhu.

387 *Pāṭihāriyapakkha*. Mp says that they undertake a continuous uposatha observance for the full three months of the rains (*antovasse temāsaṃ*); if they cannot manage this, they should observe it for a full month after the rains, between the two invitation days, or at least for a two-week period following the first invitation day. The "invitation" (*pavāraṇa*) is the occasion, at the end of the rains, when bhikkhus and bhikkhunīs "invite" (*pavāreti*) their fellows to point out any faults in their behavior during the rains. Spk I 307,9–16, commenting on *pāṭihāriyapakkha* at SN 10:5, I 208,27, explains the term in a broader sense (see CDB p. 480, note 573).

388 Be treats this sentence as the beginning of **3:38**. Strangely, Be titles this "The Second on the Four Great Kings" even though the sutta makes no mention of them.

389 Mp defines *paduma* as a white lotus (*paṇḍarapadumaṃ*) and *puṇḍarīka* as a red lotus (*rattapadumaṃ*). SED, however, defines *puṇḍarīka* as "a lotus flower (esp. a white lotus)," adding that the word is used to mean "white" in general. Numerous websites I consulted also define *puṇḍarīka* as a white lotus.

390 Kāsi was one of the sixteen great states of India, with its capital at Bārāṇasī.

391 These are the three seasons of northern India: the winter lasts roughly from November to March, the hot season from March to July, and the rainy season from July to November. Mp says that the winter mansion had nine stories, which were low in order to retain heat; the summer mansion had five stories, which were high in order to allow the air to cool; and the rains mansion had seven stories, which were neither high nor low in order to establish a medium temperature.

392 *Nippurisehi*. Mp says that not only the musicians but all the posts in the palaces were occupied by women (*itthiyo*). Thus for four months another man did not get to see him.

393 *Attānaṃyeva atisitvā*. *Atisitvā* is absolutive of *atisarati*. See DOP sv *atisarati*.

394 Ee takes this sentence to mark the beginning of a new sutta, **3:39** in its numbering. But Ce and Be, which I follow, treat this passage as a continuation of the sutta that began with the Buddha's recollection of his delicate upbringing. In Ce and Be, this entire sutta is **3:39**, so that at this point the numbering in all three editions coincides.

395 The third pāda is obscure: *yathā dhammā tathā santā*. I translate it literally. In explaining the fourth pāda, Mp adds *parapuggalaṃ* as an object of the verb *jigucchanti*.

396 Ce and Be read *nekkhamme daṭṭhu khemataṃ*. Ee has *nekkhammaṃ daṭṭhu khemato* as its primary reading but mentions the Ce and Be variants in its notes. Mp (both Ce and Be) uses the Ce and Be reading as the lemma, which it glosses *nibbāne khemabhāvaṃ disvā*, but it then cites the Ee reading as a variant, glossed *nibbānaṃ khemato disvā*. Thus here Ee has chosen the variant as the primary reading.

397 Mp says that these verses refer to his own energy as it arose while he was sitting beneath the bodhi tree.

398 In Pāli: *attādhipateyyaṃ lokādhipateyyaṃ dhammādhipateyyaṃ*. Although Bucknell (2004) does not list a Chinese parallel of this sutta, by chance I recently discovered a parallel cited in the *Śāriputrābhidharmaśāstra, at T XXVIII 679c22–680a27. While the prose portion there is simpler than that of the Pāli, the two convey essentially the same meaning. Their verses, with the exception of the last, also closely correspond.

399 *Na itibhavābhavahetu*. Mp takes the long vowel connecting the two occurrences of *bhava* to signify repetition, not negation: "Not for the sake of this or that prosperous future state of existence, [wishing]: '[Let me obtain] such an existence [or] such an existence'" (*iti bhavo, iti bhavo ti evaṃ āyatiṃ na tassa tassa sampattibhavassa hetu*).

400 *Attā te purisa jānāti saccaṃ vā yadi vā musā*. Mp: "You yourself know, of whatever you do, whether it is of this or that nature. For this reason, it should be understood that, for one who does an evil deed, there is no place in the world that can be called 'hidden.'"

401 The Pāli is obscure here and Mp is not particularly helpful in resolving the difficulty. The Chinese parallel (at 680a20–21, but following the Song, Yuan, Ming reading) has: 言無虛者勝, 是則不自毀, 若已有違犯, 知而不覆藏. This conveys a somewhat different point, which I would render: "One who says 'It is not false' is better, for then one does not damage oneself. If a transgression exists and one knows it, do not conceal it."

402 The Chinese (at 680a26–27) is quite different: 遠離捨六情, 滅苦不受有, 已沒不復還, 永離於生死. I would render: "Having discarded and abandoned the six sense faculties, he ends suffering and does not take [another] existence. Having passed away, he does not come back, being forever freed from birth and death."

403 Mp explains "experiences the meaning" (*atthapaṭisaṃvedī*) as "experiences with knowledge the explanation of the meaning

(or commentary)" (*aṭṭhakathaṃ ñāṇena paṭisaṃvedī*) and "experiences the Dhamma" (*dhammapaṭisaṃvedī*) as "experiences the Dhamma of the canonical text" (*pāḷidhammaṃ paṭisaṃvedī*). This obviously imposes a later distinction on older terms. However, while the two terms are often paired, the precise distinction between *attha* and *dhamma* is not clearly drawn in the Nikāyas. In fact, each term is ambivalent and thus their different nuances further complicate their relationship. *Attha* can signify meaning, benefit, good, and goal; *dhamma* can signify the teaching, the system of practice, the nature of things, and the truth pointed to by the teaching. Thus the contrast between *dhamma* and *attha* can be seen as that between the formulated teaching and its meaning, between the practice and its goal, and between the teaching and the benefit it brings.

404 Mp explains *santānaṃ brahmacārinaṃ* as referring to those who support their parents (*idha pana mātāpitu-upaṭṭhākā adhippetā*), but I see the expression as referring to monastics, either as the recipients of service (*upaṭṭhānaṃ*) or of the giving (*dānaṃ*) mentioned in pāda a. Mp further construes *santānaṃ* as genitive plural of *sant*, "good, virtuous" (Mp: *uttamaṭṭhena santānaṃ*), but it is more likely to be "peaceful," from Skt *śānta*. *Santānaṃ brahmacārinaṃ* is also at SN 1:10, I 5,4, where Spk I 28.2, glosses it with *santakilesānaṃ paṇḍitānaṃ vā*, "those with pacified defilements or wise ones." The Chinese parallel SĀ 995 (at T II 260c29) has 寂靜修梵行, which means that in this transmission *santānaṃ* came down as Skt *śāntānaṃ*.

405 *Saṅkhatassa saṅkhatalakkhaṇāni*. Lit. "three conditioned characteristics of the conditioned." And below *asaṅkhatassa asaṅkhatalakkhaṇāni*, lit. "three unconditioned characteristics of the unconditioned." I render these expressions in the way I have to avoid giving the wrong impression that the characteristics themselves are conditioned or unconditioned. The point, rather, is that they determine as such the conditioned and the unconditioned.

406 I follow Ee in making the statements on the characteristics of the conditioned and the unconditioned two parts of a single sutta. Ce and Be take them to be separate suttas and thus count eleven suttas in this vagga. The *uddāna* verse includes "*saṅkhataṃ*" but not "*asaṅkhataṃ*," which seems to support Ee. At this point, my numbering agrees with Ee but falls behind Be by one (Ce does not number the suttas continuously but begins each vagga with '1'). Interestingly, the Chinese parallel EĀ 22.5 (at T II 607c13–c23) mentions *only* the characteristics of the conditioned; there is no corresponding section on the characteristics of the unconditioned.

407 Reading with Ce *gedhaṃ* (PED sv *gedha*[2]), as against Be and Ee *rodhaṃ* (bank).

408 At SN 1:3, I 2, this verse is spoken by a deity, who is then "corrected" by the Buddha with a verse that bids the "seeker of peace" to "drop the world's bait" (*lokāmisaṃ pajahe santipekkho*).

409 This and the preceding verse are at SN 1:41, I 31.

410 *Sandiṭṭhiko dhammo*.

411 *Kukkuṭasampātikā*. Mp: "'Cocks' flying between them' (*kukkuṭasampāto*) is cocks' flying from the rooftops in one village to the rooftops in another. When they are so situated, it is said they are 'so close that cocks could fly between them.' There is also the reading *kukkuṭasampādikā* ('so close that cocks could walk between them'). 'Cocks' walking between them' (*kukkuṭasampādo*) is cocks' going on foot from one village to another. When they are so situated, it is said they are 'so close that cocks could walk between them.'"

412 *Tanuttaṃ paññāyati*. Lit., "the diminution [of human beings] is seen."

413 *Gāmāpi agāmā honti, nigamāpi anigamā honti, nagarāpi anagarā honti, janapadāpi ajanapadā honti*. Lit., "villages have become non-villages, towns have become non-towns, cities have become non-cities, and provinces have become non-provinces."

414 Mp: "*Illicit lust* (*adhammarāga*): Lust is exclusively contrary to the Dhamma (*adhamma*), but it is not 'illicit lust' when it arises in relation to one's own possessions. It is only 'illicit lust' when it arises in regard to the possessions of others. *Unrighteous greed* (*visamalobha*): Though greed is never actually righteous, greed arisen for an object that belongs to oneself is called righteous greed. The greed arisen for an object belonging to another is called unrighteous greed. *Wrong Dhamma* (*micchādhamma*): indulgence in what is not a base." Mp-ṭ: "Indulgence in some base of lust (*rāgassa vatthuṭṭhānaṃ*) other than that considered good by the world's standards."

415 I read with Be, Ee, and Mp (Ce and Be): *yakkhā vāḷe amanusse ossajjanti*. Ce of AN has *manusse* for *amanusse*. Yakkhas are demonic spirits, sometimes depicted as killing human beings and devouring their flesh, but also capable of goodness and even realization of the Dhamma. Mp: "'Yakkhas' are the ruling yakkhas. They release fierce yakkhas on the paths of humans, and when these [yakkhas] get the chance, they deprive the people of their lives" (***yakkhā*** *ti yakkhādhipatino.* ***Vāḷe amanusse ossajjantī*** *ti caṇḍayakkhe manussapathe vissajjenti, te laddhokāsā mahājanaṃ jīvitakkhayaṃ pāpenti*). Though I follow Mp, I wonder if a more original reading of the text would construe the verb

as passive and put all the substantives in nominative plural: *yakkhā vāḷā amanussā ossajjanti*. "Yakkhas—wild, nonhuman—are released."

416 *Kacci te bhoto gotamassa vuttavādino ca bhavantaṃ gotamaṃ abhūtena abbhācikkhanti, dhammassa cānudhammaṃ byākaronti, na ca koci sahadhammiko vādānupāto gārayhaṃ ṭhānaṃ āgacchati*. So all three editions, but some variants have *vādānuvādo* in place of *vādānupāto*. I have discussed the formula in detail in CDB, p. 747, note 72, but I now believe that the Pāli commentaries err in taking *vādānupāta* (or *vādānuvāda*) to mean "consequence of their assertion." I now take this term to be simply a synonym of *gārayhaṃ ṭhānaṃ*." In support of this change, see **5:5**, where *sahadhammikā vādānuvādā gārayhā ṭhānā āgacchanti* and its opposite, *sahadhammikā pāsaṃsā ṭhānā āgacchanti*, occur without reference to any prior assertion.

Chinese parallels to the present sutta support this interpretation. SĀ 95 (at T II 26a11–14), reads: 云何？瞿曇！作是語者，為實說耶？非為謗毀瞿曇乎？為如說說、如法說耶、法次法說，不為餘人以同法來訶責耶？("How is it? Gotama, does one who says this speak truthfully? Is it the case that he does not misrepresent Gotama? Does he speak in accordance with what was said, in accordance with the Dharma, in line with the Dharma, so that other people cannot criticize him in terms of that same Dharma?"). Another parallel at T II 493b19–21 is similar, with nothing that corresponds to "consequence of an assertion."

417 Mp says that the "holy ones" (*sante*) are the supreme persons (*uttamapurise*): Buddhas, paccekabuddhas, and arahants.

418 *Sappaññe dhīrasammate*. Mp glosses this as if it meant "esteemed, honored, by the learned" (*paṇḍitehi sammate sambhāvite*), but I take *dhīrasammate* to mean "esteemed, honored, as sagely (or wise)."

419 The verse, which also occurs as Dhp 423 a–d, alludes to the three knowledges.

420 Mp: *Yañña* is "a thing to be given" (*deyyadhamma*; though this is already covered by the fourth item); *saddha* (Skt *śrāddha*), "a meal in memory of the dead" (*matakabhattaṃ*); *thālipāka*, "a meal to be given to excellent persons" (*varapurisānaṃ dātabbayuttaṃ bhattaṃ*, but according to SED sv *sthālī*, *sthālīpāka* is more specifically a dish of barley or rice boiled in milk offered as an oblation); and *deyyadhamma*, "anything else that can be given."

421 *Anuttaraṃ brahmacariyogadhaṃ*. Mp: "Nibbāna is 'the unsurpassed culmination of the spiritual life,' the supreme support for the spiritual life, which is the path to arahantship" (*arahattamaggasaṅkhātassa brahmacariyassa anuttaraṃ ogadhaṃ uttamapatiṭṭhābhūtaṃ nibbānaṃ*). In MN 44.29, I 304,21–22,

nibbānogadhaṃ is used in conjunction with *nibbānaparāyanaṃ* and *nibbānapariyosānaṃ*, which suggests that the three terms are synonymous. It–a I 112,11–12, glosses *nibbānogadhagāmī* (the same phrase as in AN) with *nibbānasaṅkhātaṃ ogadhaṃ patiṭṭhaṃ pāraṃ gacchati* ("it goes to the far shore, the support, the culmination consisting in nibbāna"). This explanation, which is consistent with other commentaries, supports my rendering of *nibbānogadha* here as "culmination in nibbāna" rather than "the plunge into nibbāna," a rendering used by other translators. My rendering of *amatogadha* in CDB (as at SN 45:139, 46:184, 48:42, 48:44, etc.) as "with the deathless as its ground" is not satisfactory. I am grateful to Vanarata for his comments on this term.

422 Mp: "He did not want to answer Ānanda's question, so he tried to turn the discussion aside with words of praise."

423 *Iddhipāṭihāriyaṃ ādesanāpāṭihāriyaṃ anusāsanīpāṭihāriyaṃ*. Also at DN 11.3–8, I 212–14.

424 *Nimittena ādisati*. Mp explains it as if it means an unrelated clue in the environment, but it may be a gesture or facial expression—what we now call "body language"—that reveals to a skilled observer the other person's state of mind.

425 *Vitakkavipphārasaddaṃ sutvā*. Mp: "Having heard the sound of those muttering while asleep or oblivious, which [sound] arises by the diffusion of thought." I suspect that Mp misses the point. Since the examples in the sutta proceed from the coarser to the subtler, this one should be subtler than its predecessor. I think that what is intended is a subtle sound supposedly emanated by thought but not expressed verbally.

426 This must be referring to one in the second or higher jhānas.

427 Mp gives examples: "Think thoughts of desirelessness, not thoughts of sensuality, etc. Attend to the idea of impermanence, etc., not to permanence, etc. Abandon lust for sensual pleasure and enter a world-transcending path and fruit."

428 *Āsajja upanīya vācā bhāsitā*. *Āsajja* usually means "having attacked," but this meaning seems too strong here. Mp merely paraphrases without giving much help: "The words you spoke hit upon my virtues and intrude on the domain of my virtues" (*mama guṇe ghaṭṭetvā mam'eva guṇānaṃ santikaṃ upanītā vācā bhāsitā*). I therefore assume that the words, without being insulting, are considered inappropriate because they are making a personal inquiry.

429 "Sectarian tenets" renders *titthāyatanāni*, lit. "bases of sects." The word *tittha* (Skt *tīrtha*), which originally meant a ford in a river, was used to designate religious teachings, probably in the sense that these teachings provide a "ford" for crossing the stream of defilements and reaching the far shore of liberation (see MN 34,

where this metaphor governs a short discourse). Mp explains that the sects (*tittha*) are the sixty-two views (see DN 1.1.29–3.29, I 12–39); the founders of the sects (*titthakara*) are those who formulate those views; and the followers of the sects (*titthiya*) are those who approve of the views. The great teachers in Jainism are called in Skt *tīrthaṅkara*.

430 *Parampi gantvā akiriyāya saṇṭhahanti*. Mp glosses *paraṃ* with *paramparā*, "lineage": "Even if they have gone to one of the three kinds of lineage, the lineage of teachers, the lineage of beliefs, and the lineage of [one's] individual existences" (*ācariyaparamparā laddhiparamparā attabhāvaparamparā ti etesu yaṃkiñci paramparaṃ gantvā pi*). It is hard to see how this has any relevance to the context. Since *paraṃ* can also mean "later, further, afterward," it seems the point being conveyed is that these positions, if extended further, eventuate in non-doing. On the basis of this understanding, I render *parampi gantvā* as "taken to their conclusion." *Saṇṭhahanti* is, more literally, "stop at."

431 These are respectively the doctrines of the Jains, the theists, and non-causality, a doctrine elsewhere ascribed to Makkhali Gosāla (see **1:319**, **3:137**).

432 Mp: "They hold that one experiences feelings exclusively because of kamma created in the past." In this connection, see SN 36:21, IV 230–31, where the Buddha explains eight causes for illness or affliction, only one of which is the ripening of past kamma. Brahmāli writes: "The point here seems to be that each of these unwholesome ways of acting is related to particular feelings, and that those feelings (or experiences) can only be experienced through those acts. It follows that if your kamma is such that you have to experience the feelings connected with those bad acts, then you will have to perform them." The same point, with suitable changes, applies to the following two tenets, that of God's creative activity and non-causality. In each case, agents escape responsibility for their actions.

433 At MN 14.15–19, I 92–93, and MN 101, II 214–28, the Buddha challenges the Nigaṇṭhas with other arguments against their thesis that all feeling is due to past kamma.

434 Mp: "He has so far shown that these sectarian tenets, when taken to their conclusion, eventuate in non-doing, and are therefore empty and unemancipating, without substance. He now shows that the Dhamma he teaches is substantial and emancipating (*sārabhāvañc'eva niyyānikabhāvañca*)."

435 For a detailed analysis of the six elements, see MN 140.14–19, III 240–43.

436 Mp explains *manopavicāra* thus: "The mind's examination of

the eighteen cases, using the 'feet' of thought and examination (*vitakkavicārapādehi*)." The word "feet" (*pāda*) is used here because *vicāra* originally meant "traveling around."

437 Mp: "Why does he begin in this way? For ease of understanding. For the Tathāgata wants to explain the revolving of the twelve conditions, so he shows the round by the term 'descent of a [future] embryo' (*gabbhassāvakkanti*). For when the round has been shown by the descent of a [future] embryo, what follows will be easy to understand. Whose six elements serve as the condition, the mother's or the father's? It is neither, but descent of a [future] embryo occurs conditioned by the six elements of the being taking rebirth." Mp cites MN 38.26, I 265,35–66,6 (see too MN 93.18, II 156,30–57,3).

438 This may be a unique instance where the noble truths of the origin and cessation of suffering are explicated by way of the full twelve factors of dependent origination. At SN 12:43, II 72–73, the origination (*samudaya*) of suffering is explained by way of the links from consciousness through craving; its passing away (*atthaṅgama*), by way of the cessation of the links from craving through old age and death. In the Chinese parallel, MĀ 13 (at T I 435a24–436a10), the second and third truths are not explained by way of dependent origination but according to the stock formulations as found in SN 56:11, V 421, and elsewhere.

439 *Tīṇ'imāni bhikkhave amātāputtikāni bhayānī ti assutavā puthujjano bhāsati*. Lit. "There are these three [things] that the uninstructed worldling speaks of as 'without-mother-and-son perils.'"

440 *Tīṇi samātāputtikāniyeva bhayāni amātāputtikāni bhayānī ti assutavā puthujjano bhāsati*. Literally: "There are three with-mother-and-son perils that the uninstructed worldling speaks of as 'without-mother-and-son perils.'" The perils are obviously the great fire, the flood, and the turbulence. Since these initially separate mother and son, one can call them "perils that separate mother and son." But since, in the end, mother and son find one another, one can also call them perils when mother and son reconnect.

441 Mp: "Having shown in a provisional way (*pariyāyato*) the perils that separate mother and son, he now shows in a non-provisional way (*nippariyāyena*) the perils that separate mother and son."

442 In translating the names of these different types of beds and their appurtenances I have relied on Horner's translation of Vin I 192,14–19 (1951, 4:256–57). She based her renderings on Sp V 1086,1–1087,12, which corresponds to Mp II 292–93.

443 *Dibbaṃ uccāsayanamahāsayanaṃ, brahmaṃ uccāsayanamahāsayanaṃ, ariyaṃ uccāsayanamahāsayanaṃ.*

444 *So ce ahaṃ, brāhmaṇa, evaṃbhūto caṅkamāmi, dibbo me eso tasmiṃ*

samaye caṅkamo hoti. Mp says that his walking back and forth is celestial when, having entered the four jhānas, he walks back and forth; and his walking back and forth is celestial when, after emerging from the four jhānas, he walks back and forth. This *seems* to imply that walking can occur even with the mind in jhāna. This, however, is contradicted by the dominant understanding that jhāna is a state of uninterrupted absorption in an object, in which case intentional movements like walking would not be possible. Mp-ṭ explains the first case of Mp (walking after entering the jhānas) to mean that he walks back and forth *immediately after* emerging from the jhāna, while the second case (walking after emerging) to mean that he walks back and forth after having emerged *some time earlier*. The same explanation holds for the divine and the noble beds.

445 Mp: "This shows the lust abandoned by the path of arahantship at the site of the great enlightenment. By means of reviewing he refers to the attainment of fruition."

446 Mp explains that he had been commissioned by the wanderers in his own community to take ordination with the bhikkhus, learn the secret of their success (which they believed to be a kind of magic they used to attract followers), and then return and share it with them. After his ordination he concluded that the Pātimokkha was the key to their success. Having learned the Pātimokkha, he returned to the wanderers and reported that he had learned the Dhamma of the Buddha's followers. The background story is similar to that of the Susīma Sutta (SN 12:70, II 119–28) but has a different outcome.

447 Ee has an additional line here: *mayā kho Sarabha paññāyati samaṇānaṃ Sakyaputtiyānaṃ dhammo*: "Sarabha, the Dhamma of the ascetics who follow the Sakyan son has been seen by me." Be has a variant on this line in parentheses but Ce does not have anything corresponding to it.

448 At MN 35.13–14, I 231,27–28, 32–35, it is said: "If anyone, when asked a reasonable question up to the third time by the Tathāgata, still does not answer, his head splits into seven pieces then and there." Here, however, Sarabha fails to answer the Buddha's question after it has been posed three times, yet his head remains intact and no threat is raised against him.

449 This is the first of the Buddha's four kinds of self-confidence (*vesārajja*), on which see **4:8**. The second claim, just below, refers to the second kind of self-confidence, and the third claim to the fourth kind of self-confidence. The third kind of self-confidence is not included here.

450 From the Pāli, it is unclear what the three alternatives are in this

statement. In Ce the disjunctive *vā* occurs only twice in this sentence, suggesting only two alternatives. Ee has three occurrences of *vā*, but *tuṇhībhūto vā maṅkubhūto vā* divides two terms that normally belong to a single alternative. Be has only one *vā*, which leaves the question of the alternatives even more obscure. I have chosen to separate "he would answer evasively . . ." and "display anger, hatred, and bitterness," even though we often find the sequence without a disjunction: *aññenaññaṃ paṭicarati, bahiddhā kathaṃ apanāmeti, kopañca dosañca appaccayañca pātukaroti*. In this respect, I have followed the divisions of the Chinese parallel, SĀ 970, which at T II 250b21–23 does offer three distinct alternatives: 彼則遼落說諸外事。或忿恚慢覆。對閡不忍。無由能現。或默然抱愧低頭。密自思省: "He would divert the discussion to an outside subject, or (或), overcome by anger and conceit, would unreasonably display hostility and impatience, or (或) would silently harbor shame, his head lowered, privately reflecting."

451 *Yassa kho pana te atthāya dhammo desito so na niyyāti takkarassa sammā dukkhakkhayāyā ti*. Mp takes *yassa atthāya* to mean "the purpose for which" the Dhamma is taught, identified as the destruction of lust, etc., and "the Dhamma" to be meditation on unattractiveness, etc. The verb *niyyāti* means "goes out" (to the complete destruction of suffering). *Takkarassa* is likely to be a *sandhi* formation: *takkaro assa*.

I have been able to track down two Chinese versions of the phrase (there may be more): (1) EĀ 27.6 (T II 645c10–11) reads 諸賢聖出要之法。盡於苦際。欲使不出要者。終無此處 ("It is impossible that this outward-going Dharma of the noble ones does not go out to the complete end of suffering"). (2) EĀ 46.4 (T II 776c28–777a2) has 我所說法。賢聖得出要者。如實盡於苦際。設有沙門・婆羅門・天・若魔天來欲言未盡苦際者。無此處 ("By this Dharma taught by me the noble ones go out correctly to the complete end of suffering. It is impossible that any ascetic (etc.) could come and say: '[They] have not reached the complete end of suffering'").

452 Here the Chinese of SĀ 970, at T II 250b28, has simply "he got up from his seat and left" (從坐起而去) without a supernormal departure.

453 *Vācāya sattitodakena sañjambharim akaṃsu*. Be and Ee have *sannitodakena* for Ce *sattitodakena*. The Chinese counterpart at T II 250c8 says simply: "they reproached him and censured him to his face" (面前呵責毀呰).

454 *Seyyathāpi, āvuso sarabha, ambakamaddari 'phussakaravitaṃ ravissāmī' ti ambakamaddariravitaṃyeva ravati*. Be has *ambukasañcārī* for Ce and Ee *ambakamaddari* and *purisaka* for *phussaka*. I have taken some liberty in rendering the obscure names of these birds in

order to bring out the sense. Mp (Ce) glosses *ambakamaddari* as a small chicken (*khuddakakukkuṭikā*) and *phussaka* as a large chicken (*mahākukkuṭa*). The Chinese parallel, at T II 250c3, has: "Just as a woman might try to make the sound of a man but only makes the sound of a woman" (譬如女人欲作丈夫聲，發聲即作女聲). Pāli *purisakaravitaṃ* might be understood as the crying out of a man, and *ambaka* as a woman, but in the absence of a clear and simple contrast between *ambaka* and *purisa* in the same edition, I follow Mp's gloss.

455 Be *Kesamutti*. This discourse is best known under the name "The Kālāma Sutta." A Chinese parallel is MĀ 16 (at T I 438b13–439c22). I will note below some of the important ways it differs from the Pāli version.

456 From the last sentence of the preceding paragraph through this sentence, MĀ 16 reads instead: "Gotama, having heard this, we gave rise to doubt and uncertainty: 'Of these ascetics or brahmins, which [speak] truthfully and which [speak] falsely?'" The Blessed One said: "Kālāmas, do not give rise to doubt and uncertainty. For what reason? Because when there is doubt and uncertainty, there will arise perplexity. Kālāmas, you yourselves do not have pure wisdom with which to know whether there is an afterlife or not. You yourselves do not have pure wisdom about what deeds are transgressions and what deeds are not transgressions."

457 These ten inadequate sources of knowledge may be divided into three categories: (1) The *first*, comprising the first four criteria, are propositions based on tradition. These include "oral tradition" (*anussava*), generally understood to refer to the Vedic tradition; "lineage" (*paramparā*), an unbroken succession of teachings or teachers; "hearsay" (or "report"; *itikirā*), popular opinion or general consensus; and "a collection of scriptures" (*piṭakasampadā*), a collection of texts regarded as infallible. In the Buddha's day these would have been orally transmitted rather than written. (2) The *second* set comprises the next four terms referring to four types of reasoning; their differences need not detain us here, but since the Buddha himself often uses reasoning, they must all involve reasoning from hypothetical premises rather than from empirical observation. (3) The *third* set, consisting of the last two items, contains two types of personal authority: the first, "seeming competence" (*bhabbarūpatā*), is the personal charisma of the speaker (perhaps including his external qualifications); the second is the authority of the speaker as one's guru (Pāli *garu* being identical with Skt *guru*).

MĀ 16 does not have this passage on the ten inadequate sources of knowledge. Instead, the Buddha immediately explains to the Kālāmas the three unwholesome roots of action and how they lead to moral transgressions. And then he explains the ten courses of wholesome kamma, the explanations being very similar to those found, e.g., at **10:176** (on the threefold purity) and **10:211** (on rebirth in heaven). In MĀ 16, the Buddha does not ask the Kālāmas to judge for themselves but categorically tells them what he himself has known by direct experience. It is possible that MĀ 16 is a normalization of an original Indic text corresponding to the Pāli version, made at a time when the Buddha was widely regarded as an unquestionable authority.

458 According to the Buddha, greed, hatred, and delusion are the three unwholesome roots (*akusalamūlāni*), which underlie all immoral conduct and all defiled states of mind; see **3:69**. Since the goal of his own teaching, nibbāna, is the destruction of greed, hatred, and delusion (SN 38:1, IV 251,16–20), the Buddha subtly leads the Kālāmas to affirm his teaching simply by reflecting on their own experience, without any need for him to impose his authority on them.

459 This is certainly counterintuitive, at least on the basis of what is immediately visible, for cases of "bad things happening to good people" are innumerable.

460 *Idhāhaṃ ubhayen'eva visuddhaṃ attānaṃ samanupassāmi*. The exact meaning of "in both respects" is not entirely clear to me. Mp glosses: "Since I do no evil, and it is not done [to me as it is] to one who does [evil]" (*yañca pāpaṃ na karomi, yañca karotopi na karīyati*)." However, it seems to me more likely that the two kinds of purification are (1) not doing any evil deeds, and (2) developing a pure mind by practice of the four immeasurable states (loving-kindness, etc.). This seems to be the purport of the Chinese parallel (see next note).

461 The four assurances of MĀ 16 (at T I 439b8–26) are as follows: (1) "If there is this world and the other world, if there are results of good and bad deeds, I acquire the kamma connected with this right view; I uphold it and possess it. With the breakup of the body, after death, I will certainly go to a good state, even to rebirth in the heavenly realm. (2) If this world and the other world do not exist, and there are no results of good and bad deeds, still, even in this present life, I cannot be blamed by others on account of [my conduct], but I will be praised by the wise. However, those of right effort and right view say that there is [this world, the other world, and results of karma]. (3) If anything is done, certainly I do no evil, I think nothing evil. Since I do no evil, how can suffering arise for me? (4) If anything is done, certainly I do no evil. I do not transgress against what is fearful and not fearful in the world. I always have love and compassion for

the whole world. My mind has no belligerence toward sentient beings; it is without stains, joyful and happy."

462 *Atthi idaṃ, atthi hīnaṃ, atthi paṇītaṃ, atthi imassa saññāgatassa uttari nissaraṇaṃ*. This is also at MN 7.17, I 38,31–32, where it also follows the four divine abodes. Mp says "there is this" refers to the five aggregates, the truth of suffering; "the inferior" to the truth of the origin; "the superior" to the truth of the path; and "a further escape from whatever is involved with perception" to nibbāna, the truth of cessation.

463 *Brahmabhūtena attanā viharati*. The whole phrase is also at **4:198**, II 206,2–4, and MN 51.5, I 341,11–13. It seems to be a deliberate attempt by the Buddha to co-opt Upanishad terminology for the purposes of his own teaching.

464 These are the four methods of formulating questions; see **4:42**. Mp: "(1) A *question that should be answered categorically* (*ekaṃsavyākaṇanīya pañha*) is, for example, 'Is the eye impermanent?' which should be answered categorically with 'Yes, it is impermanent.' (2) A *question that should be answered after making a distinction* (*vibhajjavyākaraṇīya pañha*) is, for example, 'Is the impermanent the eye?' which should be answered by making a distinction: 'Not only the eye, but the ear, nose, etc., are also impermanent.' (3) A question that should be answered with a counter-question (*paṭipucchāvyākaraṇīya pañha*) is, for example, 'Does the eye have the same nature as the ear?' One should answer this by asking, 'With respect to what?' If they reply, 'With respect to seeing,' one should answer no. If they reply, 'With respect to impermanence,' one should answer yes. (4) A question that should be set aside (*ṭhapanīya pañha*) is, for example, 'Is the soul the same as the body?' This should be set aside without answering it, saying, 'This has not been declared by the Tathāgata.'" In my opinion, better examples of "a question that should be answered after making a distinction" are the Buddha's response to Subha at MN 99.4, II 197,9–18; his response to the brahmin Ujjaya at **4:39**, II 42,14–28; and the householder Vajjiyamāhita's response to the wanderers at **10:94**, V 190,14–20.

465 The meaning of these expressions is far from self-evident. I have therefore relied on Mp, which I translate in full, omitting only a few minor explanations meaningful only in Pāli:

"*One does not stand firm in regard to his position and the opposing position* (*ṭhānāṭhāne na saṇṭhāti*): One does not stand firm in regard to what is a reason and what is not a reason. This is the method here: An eternalist is able to refute an annihilationist with a fitting reason. Being refuted by him, the annihilationist thinks, 'Why should I now continue to assert annihilation?' He then proclaims eternalism; he is unable to remain fixed in his own doctrine. So too, when an annihilationist is able [to refute] the eternalist [and the latter does not stand firm]; and similarly, when an advocate of personalism is able [to refute the emptiness doctrine], and when an advocate of emptiness is able [to refute personalism]. Such is what is meant by saying that he does not stand firm in regard to his position and the opposing position." (Could this mean, rather, that he does not stand firm in regard to what is actually the case and what is not the case, or in regard to what is possible and what is not possible? These are also meanings, respectively, of *ṭhāna* and *aṭṭhāna*.)

"*He does not stand firm in his stratagem* (*parikappe na saṇṭhāti*): This is found both in asking the question and in answering it. How? For someone clears his throat, thinking: 'I will ask a question.' The other tells him: 'You will ask this.' Having realized he has been found out, he says: 'I won't ask that, but something else.' The one who is asked a question, too, strokes his chin, thinking: 'I will answer the question.' The other tells him: 'You will answer this.' Having realized he has been found out, he says: 'I won't answer in that way, but in this way.' Such is what is meant by saying that he does not stand firm in his stratagem.

"*He does not stand firm in an assertion about what is known* (*aññātavāde na saṇṭhāti*): Someone asks a question. The other says: 'The question you asked is agreeable. Where did you learn this?' The other, though he has asked a question in a fitting way, gives rise to doubt because of [his opponent's] statement, thinking: 'Did I ask [about a matter] that isn't problematic?' The one who has been asked the question answers. The other says to him: 'You have answered the question well. Where did you learn this? [You answered] the question as it should be answered.' The other [the respondent], though he has answered in a fitting way, gives rise to doubt because of [his opponent's] statement, thinking: 'Did I answer [about a matter] that isn't problematic?'

"*He does not stand firm in the procedure* (*paṭipadāya na saṇṭhāti*): Not having understood the rule (*vattaṃ ajānitvā*), he asks under circumstances when a question should not be asked. If a question is asked in the courtyard of a memorial shrine (*cetiyaṅgana*), one should not answer it. So too, [one should not answer] on the way to the alms round; when walking for alms in the village; when sitting in the meeting hall; when sitting and taking porridge or a meal; when sitting after the meal; and when going to the place where one passes the day. However, when one is sitting in one's day quarters, if someone asks permission and then poses a question, it should be answered; but one should not answer if they do not ask permission. Such is what is meant by: 'Asking a question without having understood the rule, he does not stand firm in the procedure.'"

466 That is, he seizes upon a slight mistake on the other's part as a pretext for criticizing him.

467 Mp: "He directly knows one thing, a wholesome Dhamma, the noble path. He fully understands one thing, the truth of suffering. He abandons one thing, all unwholesome qualities. He realizes one thing, the fruit of arahantship or [the truth of] cessation. By means of knowledge he reaches right liberation, emancipation by the fruit of arahantship."

468 *Anariyaguṇam āsajja*. The line is problematic. As printed, it would be translated: "Having attacked ignoble qualities." But *guṇa* usually means virtuous qualities. Mp gives an unconvincing explanation: "They give a talk using ignoble qualities to attack qualities." I translate on the supposition that the correct reading of the line should be *anariyā guṇam āsajja*, "the ignoble ones assail [good] qualities." A Chinese parallel, MĀ 119 at T I 609a8–b29, closely matches the Pāli in regard to the verses, and the corresponding line (609b15) accords with my interpretation: 非聖毀呰德 ("ignoble, they criticize [each others'] virtues").

469 *Dhammaṭṭhapaṭisaṃyuttā yā ariyācaritā kathā*. Mp explains *dhammaṭṭhapaṭisaṃyuttā* thus: "The talk is made by one established in the Dhamma, thus it is established in the Dhamma; and [the talk] is connected with the Dhamma, so it is established in and connected with the Dhamma." Mp thus takes *dhammaṭṭha* to be a compound of *dhamme ṭhita*. I translate, however, on the assumption that *dhammaṭṭhapaṭisaṃyuttā* contains a *dvanda* compound that should be resolved *dhammena ca aṭṭhena ca paṭisaṃyuttā*. In explanations of right speech, it is often said that the virtuous person is *atthavādī dhammavādī*, "one who speaks what is beneficial (or 'meaningful'), one who speaks on the Dhamma"; see **3:69**, I 204,4; **10:176 §7**, V 267,22. It is unusual—but not exceptional—to find *aṭṭha* in place of *attha* with the sense of "meaning" or "benefit"; it would be more unusual to find the termination *ṭha* embedded inside a compound and followed by a past participle. The Chinese parallel, which I discovered only after I had made my translation, supports my understanding here. At T I 609b19 we read: 有法亦有義 諸聖論如是, "talk that has Dhamma and that has meaning: all the talk of the noble ones is like this." The character 義, like Pāli *attha*, means both "good" and "meaning," and 有義 can mean either "beneficial" or "meaningful."

470 I read here with Be *anunnatena manasā*, as against Ce and Ee

anupādinnena manasā. Mp (both Ce and Be) glosses with *anuddhatena cetasā*, which supports *anunnatena manasā*.

471 Mp illustrates how lust is "less blameworthy" with the example of marriage, which, though rooted in sexual desire, is socially accepted and thus less blameworthy in regard to its kammic consequences. But since lust is connected with pleasure, it is hard to remove. Hatred and delusion are both regarded as blamable in society and have serious kammic consequences. Hatred, however, is connected with displeasure, and since beings naturally desire happiness they want to be rid of it. Delusive ideas, if deeply rooted in craving, wrong views, or conceit, will be as hard to remove as lust.

472 *Asatā dukkhaṃ upadahati*. Mp (Ce): "He creates suffering by falsehood, by what is non-existent, having spoken about an unreal fault" (*abhūtena avijjamānena yaṃ kiñci tassa abhūtaṃ dosaṃ vatvā dukkhaṃ uppādeti*). Note that Mp takes *asatā* to be synonymous with *abhūtena*. In both text and Mp, Be reads *uppādayati* whereas Ce and Ee have *upadahati*.

473 Here and below the text mentions three kinds of trees: the *sāla*, the *dhava*, and the *phandana*.

474 The Nigaṇṭhas are the Jain ascetics, followers of Mahāvīra, the best known teacher of Jainism, known in the Nikāyas as the Nigaṇṭha Nātaputta (Nāthaputta, Ñātaputta). He was a contemporary of the Buddha and is included among the six rival teachers (see DN 2.16–33, I 52–59). It will be noted how, whenever the Nikāyas discuss the Jains, their tone becomes derisive if not acerbic. The compliments, of course, were returned by the Jains. This can be readily understood from the fact that the Buddhists and Jains originally flourished in the same territories and, as mendicant orders, they must have been in competition for supporters from the same communities.

475 *Ye puratthimāya disāya pāṇā paraṃ yojanasataṃ tesu daṇḍaṃ nikkhipāhi*. Mp glosses: "Lay down the rod and be nonviolent toward those living beings dwelling in regions farther than a hundred *yojanas*" (*tesu yojanasatato parabhāgesu ṭhitesu sattesu daṇḍaṃ nikkhipa, nikkhittadaṇḍo hohi*). A *yojana* is between seven and nine miles. Thus the Jains are depicted as saying, "It's only toward beings living far away from you that you should be nonviolent," as if they were permitted to be violent against those living close by. This, it seems, is contrary to the Jain teaching, which enjoins strict nonviolence (*ahiṃsā*) in regard to all beings under all conditions. See http://www.jainworld.com/philosophy/ahimsa.asp.

476 *Nāhaṃ kvacana, kassaci kiñcanatasmiṃ, na ca mama kvacana, katthaci kiñcanatātthi*. Ce, Be, and Ee differ slightly among themselves in

their reading of this formula. I follow Ce here and later at **4:185**. The purpose of the formula, according to this text, is to instill an attitude of non-possessiveness, one of the basic Jain virtues. The Buddha also taught this formula—which may have been in circulation among various contemplative communities—using it as a means to eliminate "I-making" and "mine-making." For further discussion of the formula, see p. 1713, note 896.

477 *Upakkiliṭṭhassa visākhe cittassa upakkamena pariyodapanā hoti*. Mp: "Why does he say this? Because the uposatha is not very fruitful if one observes it with a defiled mind, but becomes very fruitful if it is observed with a purified mind. He thus makes this statement to introduce the meditation subjects to be used for purifying the mind." What follows here are five of the standard six recollections (*cha anussati*yo; see **6:10**, etc.). For some reason, the sixth recollection, of generosity (*cāgānussati*), is omitted. The omission would seem, at first blush, to result from a fault in transmission. However, the Chinese parallel, MĀ 202 (at T I 770a16–773a1), also lacks this recollection, which suggests that the omission—whether accidental or deliberate—preceded the split between the Vibhajjavādins (the ancestors of the Theravāda) and the Sarvāstivādins. Interestingly, in MĀ 202 the eight precepts *precede* the five recollections, while the Pāli has the sets in reverse. The sequence of the Chinese version is more consistent with other Buddhist teachings, which treat virtuous conduct as the basis for meditation.

478 Mp: "It is the perfectly enlightened Buddha who is called Brahmā" (*brahmā vuccati sammā sambuddho*).

479 These are the six sense-sphere heavenly realms. The devas higher than these belong to the form and formless realms.

480 At this point, the Buddha explains the eight precepts undertaken by lay followers on the uposatha days. These appear again in AN at **8:41–45**. They correspond closely to the ten precepts of the novice monk, with the seventh and eighth joined and the tenth (abstaining from acceptance of gold and silver, that is, money) omitted.

481 *Ekabhattika*. This might also have been rendered "eat in one part of the day." Mp: "There are two meal [periods], the morning meal [period] and the evening meal [period]. The morning meal [period] ends at midday; the evening meal [period] extends from midday until the following daybreak. Therefore even those who eat ten times before noon are said to eat once a day."

482 Ce *pahūtasattaratanānaṃ*; Be *pahūtarattaratanānaṃ*; Ee *pahūtamahāsattaratanānaṃ*. Mp (Ce and Be) reads *pahūtarattaratanānaṃ*, but Mp (Ee) has *–satta-* here. Mp explains: "Possessed of abundant

precious substances consisting in *ratta*; the meaning is that it is filled with the seven precious substances so that, if the surface of Jambudīpa (the Indian subcontinent) were the size of the surface of a *bheri* drum, the amount of seven substances would be the size of one's waist." There is thus an ambiguity about whether the original reading had *–satta-* or *–ratta-*. Mp-ṭ states that the word *ratta* is a synonym for precious substance (*ratta-saddo ratanapariyāyo*), but also says that the reading *pahūtasattaratanānaṃ* is found in the text. I translate on the basis of the latter reading.

483 Most of these states are located in the Indian subcontinent, but Gandhāra and Kamboja were in the northwest, corresponding to parts of modern Pakistan and Afghanistan.

484 Here begins a cosmological overview of the six sense-sphere heavens.

485 Reading with Be and Ee *nabhe pabhāsanti*, as against Ce *nabhe pabhāsenti*, "lighting up the skies."

486 Following Mp, I understand *bhaddakaṃ* here to be merely a qualification of *veḷuriyaṃ*, not a separate type of precious stone.

487 Mp: "Horn gold (*siṅgīsuvaṇṇa*) is gold similar [in color] to a cow's horn (*gosiṅgasadisa*). Mountain gold (*kañcana*) is gold found on a mountain. Natural gold (*jātarūpa*) is gold the color of the Buddha. *Haṭaka* is gold removed by ants."

488 *Candappabhā*. Mp: "A nominative used in a genitive sense, meaning 'to the moon's radiance' (*candappabhāya*)."

489 I take this sentence to be interrogative in sense though it contains no interrogative particle.

490 The school of Makkhali Gosāla, which taught strict determinism and emphasized extreme austerities.

491 Here and below the plural *sugatā* is used. Thus in this context the word has a wider range than merely the Buddha, its usual application.

492 *Attho ca vutto, attā ca anupanīto*. There is a word play here between *attho*, "meaning," and *attā*, "self."

493 Ee is missing the question here.

494 Mp: "Having explained the virtuous behavior, concentration, and wisdom of the trainee (*sekha*), he explains the virtuous behavior, concentration, and wisdom of one beyond training (*asekha*) by way of the fruit of arahantship: 'The fruition knowledge of one beyond training arises later than the concentration and insight knowledge of a trainee. The concentration of the fruit in one beyond training arises later than the trainee's insight knowledge.'"

495 The Licchavis were the dominant clan in the Vajji republic, which had its capital at Vesālī.

496 For a satire of Nātaputta's claim to omniscience, see MN 76.21–22, II 519,13–33.

497 *So purāṇānaṃ kammānaṃ tapasā byantībhāvaṃ paññāpeti navānaṃ kammānaṃ akaraṇā setughātaṃ*. Mp: "He declares the destruction by austere practice of accumulated kammas (*āyūhitakammānaṃ*) and the present non-accumulation of any kammas that might have been accumulated. The *demolition of the bridge* (*setughātaṃ*) is the demolition of the factor and the demolition of the condition (*padaghātaṃ paccayaghātaṃ*)." Presumably what is meant is the destruction of kammic accumulations and their condition. SED gives "bond, fetter" as meanings of *setu*, which seems to fit here.

498 *Evam etissā sandiṭṭhikāya nijjarāya visuddhiyā samatikkamo hoti*. The "wearing away" (*nijjarā*) of old kamma through austerities is a fundamental Jain concept.

499 *So navañca kammaṃ na karoti, purāṇañca kammaṃ phussa phussa vyantīkaroti*. Mp. "He does not accumulate new kamma. 'Old kamma' is the kamma accumulated in the past. Having contacted it again and again, he makes it vanish. This means that having contacted the resultant-contact again and again, he destroys that kamma."

500 Mp identifies the three stages of wearing away with the four noble attainments. The description of the bhikkhu in the first "wearing away" as virtuous, according to Mp, indicates the lower two paths and fruits—those of stream-entry and the once-returner—for disciples at these stages are said to have fulfilled virtuous behavior. The description of the bhikkhu in the second "wearing away," as one who attains the four jhānas, indicates the attainment of the third path and fruit, that of the non-returner, described as one who has fulfilled concentration. And the description of the bhikkhu in the third "wearing away" as one who has reached the destruction of the taints indicates the fruit of arahantship, since the arahant has fulfilled wisdom. Mp mentions another interpretation, which holds that all three kinds of "wearing away" are descriptions of arahantship, made from the standpoint of the arahant's virtue, concentration, and wisdom. For the correlation between the three trainings and the four noble attainments, see **3:86**.

501 *Abbhanumodasi*. Lit. "to rejoice along with."

502 *Aveccappasāda*. Mp: "Unshakable confidence that arises by having experienced, by having known, their virtues." The expression signifies the confidence possessed by a noble person, one who has reached the minimal level of stream-entry.

503 *Bhava*. What is meant is a concrete state of individual existence in one of the three realms. Nibbāna is called *bhavanirodha*, the cessation of individual existence.

504 *Āyatiṃ punabbhavābhinibbatti hoti*. Mp says that the consciousness that serves as the seed (*bīja*) is the kammically active consciousness (*abhisaṅkhāraviññāṇaṃ*) co-arisen with the kamma. In calling craving moisture (*sneha*) a word play is involved. *Sneha*, in Pāli, can mean both moisture and affection; in the latter sense, *sneha* is sometimes used as a synonym for craving. The rebirth process is described in similar terms at SN 5:9, SN 12:64, SN 22:53, SN 22:54. The "inferior realm" (*hīnā dhātu*) is the sensory realm. Similarly, just below, the "middling realm" (*majjhimā dhātu*) is the form realm, and the "superior realm" (*paṇītā dhātu*) is the formless realm. The Buddha's path aims at overcoming rebirth in all realms.

505 *Cetanā patiṭṭhitā patthanā patiṭṭhitā*. Mp: "The kammic volition and kammic aspiration."

506 *Sīlabbataṃ jīvitaṃ brahmacariyaṃ upaṭṭhānasāraṃ*. From the sequence, it is unclear whether *upaṭṭhānasāra* is one term parallel to the others or a distributive applying to each of the predecessors. Mp glosses as if the latter is the case, that is, as if it meant *the setting up* of the former three practices, taking them to be the core or essence of spiritual life: *Upaṭṭhānena sāraṃ 'idaṃ varaṃ idaṃ niṭṭhā' ti evaṃ upaṭṭhitan* ("Setting them up as the essence, having set them up [with the conviction] that they are excellent, the goal"). The same sequence of terms is at Ud 6:8, 71,29–32. Ud-a 351,9–17, allows both interpretations: either as a distributive or as one additional type of ascetic practice, perhaps the "carrying out" of certain ascetic practices. Collectively, the three (or four) terms represent the extreme of self-mortification; specific practices are described below at **3:156 §2** where they are called "the blistering way of practice." The opposite extreme is the view that there is no harm in sensual pleasures, which corresponds to the sensualist practice described at **3:156 §1**. The Buddha's "middle way," at **3:156 §3**, avoids the two extremes.

507 Ce and Ee read *devatāpi'ssa amanussā*. Be does not have *amanussā*, "the spirits."

508 A shrub from which a fragrant powder is produced.

509 The verse is also at Dhp 54.

510 See SN 6:14, I 155–57. "Conveyed his voice" renders *sarena viññāpesi*, more literally "communicated with his voice."

511 *Sāvako so Ānanda appameyyā tathāgatā*. Mp: "The Buddha said this to indicate: 'Ānanda, why do you say this? He was a disciple established in partial knowledge. But the Tathāgatas, having fulfilled the ten perfections and attained omniscience, are immeasurable. The domain, range, and power of a disciple is one thing, the range of the Buddhas is quite different. It is like comparing a bit of soil in your fingernail with the soil of the great earth.'"

512 *Cūḷanikā lokadhātu*. Mp: "This is the domain of a disciple" (*ayaṃ sāvakassa visayo*).

513 These are the four continents, located respectively to the south, west, north, and east.

514 *Dvisahassī majjhimā lokadhātu*. It is necessary to use some such expression rather than "a two-thousandfold middling world system." For the middling world system is not twice the size of a thousandfold minor world system, but *a thousand times* its size, that is, a thousandfold world system squared. Similarly, just below, a *tisahassī mahāsahassī lokadhātu* is not three times the size of a minor world system, but *a thousand times* the size of a thousand-to-the-second-power middling world system, in other words, a thousandfold world system cubed.

515 Could this passage mark a major step toward the apotheosis of the Buddha? In flavor it seems more in keeping with the opening of such Mahāyāna sūtras as the Saddharmapuṇḍarīka and the Pañcavīsati-prajñāpāramitā than with the Pāli Nikāyas.

516 Mp: "This was the elder Lāḷudāyī (a troublemaker in the Saṅgha). It is said that in the past he resented the elder [Ānanda for being appointed] the Buddha's attendant. Therefore, now that he had a chance, at the end of the Buddha's lion's roar, he tries to puncture the elder Ānanda's confidence, as if extinguishing a burning candle, hitting the snout of a stray bull, or turning upside down a vessel full of food."

517 Mp: "The Buddha says this, as if a benevolent man were to say repeatedly to another man tottering at the edge of a precipice, 'Come this way.'"

518 Ee treats this sutta as part of the preceding one, but Ce and Be treat it as distinct. Thus from the next sutta on, my numbering will be one short of Be and one ahead of Ee.

519 Ce *ahampamhā, ahampamhā*; Ee, virtually the same, merely resolves the *sandhi*: *aham pi amhā, aham pi amhā*. Be's *aham pi dammo aham pi dammo* seems to be an attempt to make sense of an obscure original. The Sinhala translation repeats the Pāli and adds in parentheses *mama de gavayem, mama de gavayem*, ("I too am a cow, I too am a cow"). DOP relates *amhā*[2] to Skt *hambhā*, "the lowing of a cow, a cow." See SED, sv *hambhā*, "lowing or bellowing of cattle."

520 Mp: "*The knowledge of destruction arises first* (*khayasmiṃ paṭhamaṃ ñāṇam*): first the knowledge of the path arises, called the knowledge of destruction because it is the knowledge associated with the path, which is called destruction because it destroys the defilements. *Immediately followed by final knowledge* (*tato aññā*

anantarā): right after the knowledge of the fourth path arises, the fruit of arahantship arises."

521 Mp: "*The knowledge arises* (*ñāṇaṃ ve hoti*): this is reviewing knowledge" (*paccavekkhaṇañāṇa*); see Vism 676, Ppn 22.19–21.

522 *Khuddānukhuddakāni sikkhāpadāni.* At DN 16.6.3, II 154,16–17, shortly before his passing, the Buddha permitted the bhikkhus, if they so desired, to abolish these rules. However, in the Vinaya account of the first Buddhist council, the monks were uncertain about which rules were minor and therefore decided to retain them all (Vin II 287,29–288,35). Mp, commenting on the present sutta, says: "The teachers who specialize in the Great Aṅguttara Nikāya say, 'Apart from the four *pārājikas* (offenses entailing expulsion), all the rest are lesser and minor'" (*ime pana aṅguttaramahānikāyavaḷañjanaka-ācariyā 'cattāri pārājikāni ṭhapetvā sesāni sabbānipi khuddānukhuddakāni'*).

523 *Na hi m'ettha, bhikkhave, abhabbatā vuttā.* Mp paraphrases: "Bhikkhus, I have not stated that it is impossible for a noble person to fall into such an offense and to be rehabilitated" (*bhikkhave na hi mayā ettha evarūpaṃ āpattiṃ āpajjane ca vuṭṭhāne ca ariyapuggalassa abhabbatā kathitā*).

524 *Tāni ādibrahmacariyikāni brahmacariyasāruppāni.* Mp: "*Those training rules that are fundamental to the spiritual life*: these are the four major training rules fundamental to the spiritual life of the path. *In conformity with the spiritual life*: these same [rules] are in conformity with, fitting for, the spiritual life of the four paths" (***ādibrahmacariyikānī*** *ti maggabrahmacariyassa ādibhūtāni cattāri mahāsīlasikkhāpadāni;* ***brahmacariyasāruppānī*** *ti tāni yeva catumaggabrahmacariyassa sāruppāni anucchavikāni*).

525 This is the first, and most sluggish, of the three grades of stream-enterer. The other two follow just below. The Pāli names for the three are, respectively: *sattakkhattuparama*, *kolaṃkola*, and *ekabījī*.

526 These are five grades of non-returner, presented here from the most sluggish to the most acute. For a fuller discussion, see **7:55**.

527 *Taṃ vā pana anabhisambhavaṃ appaṭivijjhaṃ.* Mp: "If he does not reach and penetrate that arahantship" (*taṃ arahattaṃ apāpuṇanto appaṭivijjhanto*).

528 Mp, commenting on this verse and the previous one, says: "*As before, so after*: as earlier one trains in the three trainings, so one trains in them afterward; and so for the second line. *As below, so above*: as one sees the lower part of the body as unattractive, one extends this to the upper part; and inversely for the second

line. *As by day, so at night*: as one trains in the three trainings by day, so one trains in them at night; and inversely for the second line. *Having overcome all quarters* by way of the object, *with measureless concentration*, with the concentration of the path of arahantship."

529 I read with Be and Ee *dhīraṃ paṭipadantaguṃ*. Ce has *vīraṃ*. Mp glosses: "A wise one endowed with wisdom; one who is wise in terms of the aggregates, wise in terms of the sense bases, gone to the end of the practice" (*khandhadhīra-āyatanadhīravasena dhīraṃ dhitisampannaṃ paṭipattiyā antaṃ gataṃ*).

530 Mp: "This is the arahant's emancipation of mind, occurring with the ceasing of the final consciousness. It is like the full extinguishing of a lamp. No place where it has gone is discerned; there is only arrival at the indiscernible state (*apaṇṇattikabhāvūpagamano yeva hoti*)."

531 *Adhisallikhatev'āyaṃ samaṇo*. Mp is not particularly helpful with *adhisallikhati*, glossing it *ativiya sallikkhitaṃ katvā saṇhaṃ saṇham katheti*. DOP has "is overly scrupulous." The expression also occurs in a similar context at MN I 449,12–13.

532 The sutta itself does not specify a triad, but I assume it is the distinction between elder, middling, and junior bhikkhus that warrants including this sutta in the Threes.

533 The printed version of Ce does not have an *uddāna* verse for this chapter, so I have used the verse in the electronic version of Ce for sutta titles.

534 *Accāyikāni*. I translate in accordance with the gloss in Mp-ṭ: *sīghaṃ pavattabbāni*, "to be taken care of quickly."

535 Mp: "*Solitude with respect to robes* (*cīvarapaviveka*): Separation from defilements arising on account of a robe. The same method with the other two [almsfood and lodgings]."

536 Mp: "This is said with reference to its abandoning by the path of stream-entry."

537 Ee mistakenly prints this sutta as belonging to the preceding one. Ce and Be, which I follow, treat it as independent.

538 Mp explains the *dhammacakkhu* with reference to the commentarial conception of momentary path experiences as the "eye of the path of stream-entry that comprehends the Dhamma of the four noble truths."

539 This phrase normally denotes the attainment of non-returning. Mp, however, identifies this disciple as a "jhāna non-returner" (*jhānānāgāmī*), that is, a stream-enterer or once-returner who also attains jhāna. Though such a practitioner has not yet eliminated the two fetters of sensual desire and ill will, by attaining jhāna he or she is bound to be reborn in the form realm and attain nibbāna there, without taking another rebirth in the sense sphere.

540 A partial synthesis of **2:43** and **2:44**.

541 I translate *potthako* based on Mp's gloss *vākamayavatthaṃ*.

542 Text uses *majjhimo*, lit. "of middle age."

543 There are two triads in this sutta. Both the immoral and the virtuous monk are distinguished into the junior, the one of middle standing, and the elder, and this distinction forms a triad. Yet under each type, three statements are made—about the monk himself, his effect on those who associate with him, and the merit gained by gifts to him—which also constitute a triad. I indicate the major triad with Arabic numerals and the minor one with small Roman numerals.

544 In Ee, this sentence marks the end of this sutta and the next paragraph the beginning of a new one. I follow Ce and Be, which treat the passage on the cloth from Kāsi as a continuation of the same sutta. My numbering will now exceed that of Ee by one.

545 *Tassa taṃ vacanaṃ ādheyyaṃ gacchati gandhakaraṇḍake va naṃ kāsikavatthaṃ nikkhipanti*. This last sentence is included in Ee, in brackets, but not in Ce or Be. However, Pp 34,37–35,1, on *tayo kāsikavatthūpamā puggalā*, includes this sentence (but without *nikkhipanti*). I include it because the simile is a fitting counterpart to the one just above about expelling an immoral elder.

546 The first position, rejected by the Buddha, reads in Pāli: *Yo, bhikkhave, evaṃ vadeyya, 'yathā yathā 'yaṃ puriso kammaṃ karoti tathā tathā taṃ paṭisaṃvediyatī' ti, evaṃ santaṃ, bhikkhave, brahmacariyavāso na hoti, okāso na paññāyati sammā dukkhassa antakiriyāya*. And the second, affirmed by him, reads: *Yo ca kho, bhikkhave, evaṃ vadeyya, 'yathā yathā vedanīyaṃ ayaṃ puriso kammaṃ karoti tathā tathā 'ssa vipākaṃ paṭisaṃvediyatī' ti, evaṃ santaṃ, bhikkhave, brahmacariyavāso hoti, okāso paññāyati sammā dukkhassa antakiriyāya*.

The exact difference between the two positions is not self-evident. Mp states by way of explanation: "*In precisely the same way*: If one says, 'One experiences the result of kamma in precisely the same way that one created it,' then, since it isn't possible to prevent the result of kamma once done, one would surely experience the result of whatever kamma one has created. *In such a case, there could be no living of the spiritual life*: kamma to be experienced upon rebirth, done prior to the development of the path, would necessarily have to be experienced, whether or not one has lived the spiritual life. *No opportunity would be seen for completely making an end of suffering*: since, in such a case, there is the accumulating of kamma by oneself and the experiencing of its result, therefore an opportunity would not be seen for making an end of the suffering of the round."

The point Mp is trying to make, it seems, is that if one has to experience the result of every kamma one has created of the type to be experienced upon rebirth, and of every kamma one has created of the type to be experienced in some life subsequent to the next, one would have to continue into the next rebirth, and into indefinite future rebirths, in order to experience those results. In such a case, because those kammas are bound to ripen, one would have to remain in saṃsāra forever in order to experience their fruits. It is not at all evident from the sutta itself, however, that this is the intended meaning. It seems, rather, that what the sutta is saying is that one need not experience the result of kamma in *exactly the same way* that one created it (so that, for example, if one killed a person one would not have to be killed in turn). The point, then, is that when one's wholesome and unwholesome kammas ripen, they will have to be experienced, respectively, as pleasant and as painful, even though the *quantum* of pleasure and pain need not correspond to the moral force of the original action.

547 Mp explains this in terms of the Abhidhamma theory that kamma is created by the seven *javanacittas*, the karmically active mental events in a cognitive process. The first *javana* is of the type to be experienced in this present life (*diṭṭhadhammavedanīya*); if it misses the chance to ripen in this life, it becomes defunct (*ahosi*). The seventh *javana* is to be experienced after rebirth in the next life (*upapajjavedanīya*), and if it misses the chance to ripen in that life, it becomes defunct. The middle five *javanas* are to be experienced on some subsequent occasion (*aparapariyāyavedanīya*), which means that they can ripen any time after the next life for as long as one continues in saṃsāra. Since this theory arose long after the compilation of the Nikāyas, it is improbable that it conveys the purport of the present passage. As I explained in note 546, the text seems to be saying simply that when one creates unwholesome kamma, one will experience its result as painful, whether to a strong degree or to a slight degree, but the *degree of the result* cannot be rigidly correlated with the severity of the original action. The converse holds with wholesome kamma, which is to be experienced as pleasant. It is this variability that allows a person, through the development of the path, to overcome the consequences of grave unwholesome kamma and thereby attain the end of suffering in saṃsāra. This interpretation seems to be borne out by the examples given in the sutta.

The Chinese parallel, MĀ 11 (at T I 433a12–434a11), does not make a clear distinction between two contrary positions. I read it thus: "The Buddha told the bhikkhus: '[If one says:] "One receives the result of kamma according to the way it has been done by a person"—in this case, one does not practice the spiritual life and is unable to end suffering. If one says: "One receives the result of kamma according to the way it has been done by a person"—in this case, one practices the spiritual life and is able to end suffering'" (世尊告諸比丘。隨人所作業則受其報。如是。不行梵行不得盡苦。若作是說。隨人所作業則受其報。如是。修行梵行便得盡苦). Either there has been a mistake here in the textual transmission of the text, or the point in this version is that, of two people who hold the same view about karma, one does not practice and thus does not make an end to suffering, while the other practices and makes an end to suffering.

548 *Paritto appātumo*. Mp explains: "He is limited because of the limitation of his virtues (*parittaguṇo*). His self (*ātumā*) is his body (*attabhāvo*); even though his body may be large, he has a 'mean character' because of the limitation of his virtues." *Ātuma*(*n*) is an alternative form of *atta*(*n*) (Skt *ātman*). Mp identifies it with *attabhāva*. The Chinese parallel reads the corresponding phrase (occurring at T I 433a28) as "his life span is very short" (壽命甚短).

549 Text reads *appadukkhavihārī*, which does not fit the context well. Mp offers an unconvincing resolution of the compound: "He dwells in suffering because of his small evil deed" (*appakenapi pāpena dukkhavihārī*). The Chinese parallel has nothing corresponding to this against which to check it. I amend the text to read simply *dukkhavihārī*. It is possible that *appa* entered via a recitation error based on *appamāṇavihārī* just below.

550 *Aparitto mahattā* (Be: *mahatto*). Mp (Ce): "He is unlimited because his virtues are not limited; even when his body is small, he has 'a great character' because of the greatness of his virtues" (*guṇamahantatāya mahattā*). Mp takes all these terms to imply that the person being described is an arahant, which is puzzling since, according to the Abhidhamma philosophy that underlies the commentaries, an arahant does not create any kamma at all. Again, the Chinese parallel (at T I 433b11) interprets this by way of the life span: "he has an extremely long life span" (壽命極長).

551 That is, a residue to be experienced in future lives.

552 Be is missing *udakamallake* here.

553 *Kahāpaṇa*: The major unit of currency used in northern India during the Buddha's time.

554 Where Ce here reads *kathaṃrūpo* and below *evarūpo*, it is better to read with Be and Ee the accusatives *kathaṃrūpaṃ* and *evarūpaṃ*. These words are to be correlated with the accusative present participle *ādiyamānaṃ* occurring in the middle of each sentence; they qualify, not the sheep merchant or butcher, but the person who has stolen the sheep. Curiously, in the counterpart on the

rich man, Ce has the right readings *kathaṃrūpaṃ* and *evarūpaṃ*, in agreement with Be and Ee.

555 I follow Ce here: *dhamati sandhamati niddhamati. Taṃ hoti jātarūpaṃ dhantaṃ sandhantaṃ niddhantaṃ, anihitaṃ anikkhittakasāvaṃ.* Be has the same up to *niddhantaṃ*, but it then omits *anihitaṃ* and reads *aniddhantakasāvaṃ* where Ce has *anikkhittakasāvaṃ*. Ee allows a bracketed alternative: *dhamati sandhamati [na] niddhamati. Taṃ hoti jātarūpaṃ dhantaṃ sandhantaṃ aniddhantaṃ, anihitaṃ aninnītakasāvaṃ.* An older Sri Lankan edition mentioned in a note to Ce also has *aninnītakasāvaṃ*.

556 I read with Ce and Be *ñātivitakko*, as against Ee *jātivitakko*, "thoughts about [social] class."

557 *Anavaññattipaṭisaṃyutto vitakko.* Lit. "thought connected with not being looked down upon." The Chinese parallel, SĀ 1246 (at T II 341c12–13), has "thought about rebirth in heaven" (生天覺).

558 *Dhammavitakkā.* Mp glosses this as thoughts connected with the ten corruptions of insight (*dasa vipassan'upakkilesavitakkā*), but it seems this could just as well mean reflections on the teaching or on the meditation subject.

559 Readings differ between *nappaṭipassaddhaladdho* and *nappaṭipassaddhiladdho*. Discrepancies are found even within the same text. Ee is consistent, reading *nappaṭippassaddhaladdho* in the negative sentence and *paṭippassaddhaladdho* in the positive counterpart. Be, however, has *nappaṭippassaddhaladdho* and *paṭippassaddhiladdho* in the respective sentences. To make matters more confusing, Mp (Be) inverts the forms, reading *nappaṭippassaddhiladdho* in the lemma of the comment on the negative term, but *paṭippassaddhaladdho* in the lemma of the comment on the positive term. Mp (Be), commenting on this sutta, explains *nappaṭippassaddhiladdho* as "not gained by the full tranquilizing of defilements" (*na kilesapaṭippassaddhiyā laddho*) and *paṭippassaddhaladdho* as "gained by the full tranquilizing of defilements" (*kilesapaṭippassaddhiyā laddho*).

Ce reads *na paṭippassaddhiladdho* and *paṭippassaddhiladdho* in the sutta, but Mp (Ce) has *na paṭippassaddhaladdho* and *paṭippassaddhaladdho* in the respective lemmas. Moreover, in **5:27** (where only the positive term occurs), Ce and Be have *paṭippassaddhaladdho*, as against Ee *paṭippassaddhiladdho*. Mp (Ce) here reads *paṭippassaddhiladdho* in the lemma, as against Mp (Be) *paṭippassaddhaladdho*. Mp says that *paṭippassaddhaṃ* and *paṭippassaddhi* are one in meaning (*idaṃ atthato ekaṃ*), proposing two resolutions: "It is gained by the full tranquilizing of defilements, or it has gained the full tranquilization of defilements (*kilesapaṭippassaddhiyā laddhattā kilesapaṭippassaddhibhāvaṃ vā laddhattā*), thus it is *paṭippassaddhiladdho*."

560 Ce and Ee *sasaṅkhāraniggayhavāritavato*; in place of *–vato* Be reads the termination as *–gato*. I interpret *sasaṅkhāra* as "forceful" (lit. "with exertion"); *niggayha* as "having suppressed"; *vārita* as "reined in"; and (following Ce) *–vato* as "checked." A rendering based on the Be variant might be: "but is reached when [the defilements] are reined in by forcefully suppressing [them]."

561 Ce and Ee *na sasaṅkhāraniggayhavāritavato*; Be *–gato*. SĀ 1246 (atT II 341c21–22) has: "The bhikkhu attains concentration that is not maintained by exertion; he attains the peaceful and sublime, the quiescent happy state, the unified mind, in which all the taints are destroyed" (比丘得諸三昧。不為有行所持。得寂靜勝妙。得息樂道。一心一意。盡諸有漏).

562 *Yassa yassa ca abhiññā sacchikaraṇīyassa dhammassa cittaṃ abhininnāmeti abhiññā sacchikiriyāya tatra tatreva sakkhibhabbataṃ pāpuṇāti sati sati āyatane*. Mp explains the "suitable basis" as "past causes and the presently obtainable jhāna, and other things, which are the basis for the direct knowledges" (*pubbahetusaṅkhāte ceva idāni ca paṭiladdhabbe abhiññāpādakajjhānādibhede ca sati sati kāraṇe*). The expression occurs at Vism 371,26–33, Ppn 11.122, and is commented upon at Vism-mhṭ (VRI ed. I 429). Vism 376,28–378,2, Ppn 12.14–19, explains the basis for the direct knowledges to be the concentrated mind that has acquired eight qualities: namely, it is (1) purified, (2) cleansed, (3) unblemished, (4) rid of defilement, (5) malleable, (6) wieldy, (7) steady, and (8) attained to imperturbability. Alternatively, it says, "concentrated" may be considered the first quality and "steady and attained to imperturbability" jointly constitute the eighth.

563 This begins the standard canonical passage on the six kinds of direct knowledge (*abhiññā*). The first five are commented on in detail in Vism chaps. 12 and 13.

564 I here follow Ce and Be, which put the liberated mind before the unliberated mind, as against Ee, which inverts them.

565 Ee treats this as a continuation of the preceding sutta, while in Ce and Be, which are clearly correct, it is a different sutta. With the next sutta, my numbering will again exceed Ee's by two.

566 *Tīṇi nimittāni*. Mp glosses as "three causes" (*tīṇi kāraṇāni*). The three *nimittas* are *samādhinimitta*, *paggahanimitta*, and *upekkhānimitta*.

567 In SN, this "template" and the two to follow are applied separately to the four elements (14:31–33, II 169–73), the five aggregates (22:26–28, III 27–31), and the six sense bases (35:13–18, IV 6–13).

568 Ee treats this sutta as a continuation of the preceding one, whereas Ce and Be, which I follow, consider it distinct. Thus my numbering will exceed Ee's by three.

569 Again, Ee treats this sutta as a continuation of the preceding one, whereas Ce and Be, which I follow, count it separately. Thus from the next sutta on my numbering exceeds Ee's by four.

570 *Setughāto gīte, setughāto nacce.* Mp: "Let there be the demolition of the condition for singing. He shows: 'Abandon singing together with its cause.' The same method with regard to dancing." On *setughāto*, see above, note 497. *Alaṃ vo dhammappamoditānaṃ sataṃ sitaṃ sitamattāya.* Mp: "When there is a reason to smile [in rejoicing in the Dhamma], it is proper to smile merely by showing the tips of your teeth simply to show that you are pleased."

571 I here use "deed" for *kammanta* and "action" for *kamma*. In this context it seems there is no real difference between the two, the text itself shifting from one to the other as if they were synonymous. "Tainted" renders *avassuta*, past participle of *avassavati*, related via the verb *savati*, "to flow," to the noun *āsava*.

572 I use one word where the Pāli uses two synonymous terms for death, *maraṇaṃ* and *kālakiriyā*.

573 Mp: "This kamma brings the origination—that is, the accumulation—of other kamma leading toward the round [of rebirths]."

574 Ee treats this sentence as the end of the sutta and the next sentence as the beginning of a new sutta. Ce and Be, in accordance with the *uddāna* verse, take this to be a single sutta divided into two parts by way of the unwholesome and wholesome roots.

575 Mp: "This kamma leads to the origination of kammas going toward the end of the round [of rebirths]."

576 Ee again treats this sentence as the end of the sutta and the next as the beginning of a new sutta (no. 110), while Ce and Be, which I follow, take this to be a single sutta divided into two sections. My numbering, from the next sutta on, exceeds Ee's by two.

577 Here—and in the parallel passages below—I follow the Ce reading: . . . *tadabhinivajjeti. Tadabhinivajjetvā cetasā abhivirājetvā.* Be has *tadabhinivatteti. Tadabhinivattetvā cetasā abhinivijjhitvā.* Ee has *tadabhinivaddheti* and *tadabhinivaddhetvā*, which cannot be correct. However, just below Ee agrees with Ce, as against Be, in reading *abhivirājetvā*.

578 *Paññāya ativijjha passati.* Mp: "One sees having penetrated it with the wisdom of the path together with insight."

579 *So kāmesu pātavyataṃ āpajjati* (Be adds *tāya* before *kāmesu*, probably representing *tāya diṭṭhiyā*). Mp: "*Indulgence*: [the view that] they are to be drunk, to be enjoyed; [he thinks they are] to be enjoyed with a mind without hesitation, just as water is to be drunk by

one who is thirsty" (*pivitabbataṃ paribhuñjitabbataṃ nirāsaṅkena cittena pipāsitassa pānīyapivanasadisaṃ paribhuñjitabbataṃ*). Ps II 371,22–24, commenting on *pātabyataṃ āpajjanti* at MN I 305,21, says: "He falls into [the view that] one should drink up sensual objects with the defilement of sensuality, that they are to be enjoyed according to one's pleasure" (*te vatthukāmesu kilesakāmena pātabyataṃ pivitabbataṃ, yathāruci paribhuñjitabbataṃ āpajjantī ti attho*). *Pātabba* (= *pātavya*) occurs as an optative participle of *pivati*, to drink, at Vin II 208,11. MN 45.2, I 305, ascribes this view to "ascetics and brahmins" who "consort with women wanderers wearing their hair in a topknot."

580 According to the Theravāda Abhidhamma, on passing away from the formless realm, a worldling may be reborn on the same formless plane, on a higher formless plane, or in the sense sphere with a three-rooted rebirth consciousness. This means that they will be reborn either as an intelligent human being or as a deva. Rebirth into the lower planes can occur in later rebirths, but not in the rebirth immediately following the fall from the formless realm. See CMA 226–27.

581 I read with Ce and Ee: *yadidaṃ gatiyā upapattiyā sati*. Be omits *sati* here (and in the next two paragraphs), but includes it in the parallels at **4:123** and **4:125**. Mp, commenting on **4:123**, explains: "When there is future destination and rebirth, the noble disciple who is a trainee does not descend to a lower rebirth but attains final nibbāna in the same form-sphere existence [or] in a higher realm." The same applies, with the appropriate modification, to those reborn in formless-sphere existence.

Mp-ṭ to **4:123** sheds light on the question how noble disciples can be reborn in the formless realm: "When the Buddha speaks of the life spans of humans and devas, he does not give specific figures for the life span [of those] in the four planes of misery and earth-bound devas. Why not? Because in hell, kamma alone determines [the life span]; one suffers there until one's kamma is exhausted. The same holds for the other planes of misery. Kamma also determines the life span for earth-bound devas. For some reborn there remain there only for a week, some for two weeks, and some for an eon.

"Among humans, some laypeople become stream-enterers and attain the fruit of once-returning, the fruit of non-returning, and even arahantship. Of these, stream-enterers, etc., can remain [in the lay life] their entire lives, but arahants either attain final nibbāna or go forth [into homelessness]. Why? Because arahantship is the most virtuous state and the lay life is inferior. It isn't possible for arahants to sustain the most virtuous state in an inferior condition, so they either attain final nibbāna [i.e., pass away] or go forth. But when earth-bound devas attain arahantship they remain their entire lives; stream-enterers and once-returners among the six classes of sense-sphere devas remain their entire lives. For a non-returner it is suitable to go to a form-sphere existence, and for arahants to attain final nibbāna. Why? Because there is no chance that they might regress. In the form and formless realms, all remain for their entire life spans. Stream-enterers and once-returners reborn in the form realm do not return to this world, but attain final nibbāna there. They are called 'jhāna non-returners.'

"But what determines [rebirth] for those who gain the eight meditative attainments? The jhāna in which they are proficient does, for they are reborn in accordance with whatever they are proficient in. If they are proficient in all, what determines [their rebirth]? The attainment of the base of neither-perception-nor-non-perception, for they are definitely reborn in the base of neither-perception-nor-non-perception. For noble disciples reborn among the nine brahma worlds, rebirth may occur there [in the same plane] or in a higher one, but not in a lower one. But worldlings may be reborn in the same plane, in a higher one, or in a lower one. Noble disciples in the five pure abodes and the four formless planes may be reborn in the same plane or in a higher one. A non-returner reborn in the plane of the first jhāna purifies the nine brahma worlds and attains final nibbāna while dwelling at the peak. Three deva worlds are called the 'best states of existence': the plane of great fruit (*vehapphala*), Akaniṭṭha, and the base of neither-perception-nor-non-perception. Non-returners reborn in these three states do not go higher, nor lower, but attain final nibbāna right there."

582 *Apaṇṇako maṇi*. Mp-ṭ says it is a special kind of die with six surfaces, similar to a jewel, used by those devoted to the game of dice (*evaṃ chahi talehi samannāgato pāsakakīḷāpasutānaṃ maṇisadiso pāsakaviseso*). I use the more familiar plural form rather than the singular "die."

583 The definition of mental purity here replicates the section of the Satipaṭṭhāna Sutta on contemplation of the five hindrances (DN 22.13, II 300,4–301,24; MN 10.36, I 60,7–36).

584 Again, I rely on the summary verse in Ce (electronic) for titles.

585 Mp: "In the first twenty years after the enlightenment, the Tathāgata often stayed among the deva communities (*devakulesuyeva*): sometimes at the Cāpāla Shrine, sometimes at the Sārandada, sometimes at the Bahuputta, and sometimes at the Gotamaka. Since he was living at Vesālī at this time, he stayed at the abode of the Gotamaka spirit." Mp explains that this sutta was spoken as a sequel to the Mūlapariyāya Sutta (MN 1). The

background story, told at Ps I 56–59, and translated at Bodhi 2006: 82–86, relates that a group of brahmins had taken ordination under the Buddha and quickly mastered his teachings. Filled with pride on account of their learning, they no longer went to listen to the Dhamma. The Buddha spoke the Mūlapariyāya Sutta to cut down their pride. Unable to understand it, they were humbled and apologized to the Buddha. Sometime later the Buddha spoke this Gotamaka Sutta to guide them to arahantship.

586 Mp-ṭ explains thus: "*Through direct knowledge* (*abhiññāya*): He teaches the Dhamma after directly knowing, according to actuality, the Dhamma to be taught, distinguished by way of the wholesome and so forth and by way of the aggregates and so forth; and after directly knowing the method to teach those who are to be guided in accordance with their propensities, tendencies, characters, and dispositions. *With a basis* (*sanidānaṃ*): with conditions (*sappaccayaṃ*), with grounds (*sakāraṇaṃ*), having brought forth a reason (*hetu*), which might be the inclination of those to be guided, a question, or a special incident. *Antidotal* (*sappāṭihāriyaṃ*): an antidote is a remedy (*paṭiharaṇa*) for lust and so forth. The Dhamma is accompanied by these, so it is 'antidotal.' For the Teacher teaches the Dhamma just by way of the elimination (*paṭisedhanavasen'eva*) of lust and so forth."

The term *sappāṭihāriya* is problematic. Elsewhere *pāṭihārya* is used in the sense of a wonder or miracle, as in **3:60** (at I 170–72), which speaks of the three "wonders": of psychic potency, thought-reading, and instruction. PED, sv *pāṭihārya*, sees *sappāṭihāriya* as derived from this usage and suggests, in contexts related to the Dhamma, "wonderful, extraordinary, sublime." I find it hard, however, to agree that such a meaning is intended in this context. The verb *paṭiharati* means "to strike back," and the causative *paṭihāreti* "to repel, to avoid." I believe that this sense is relevant both to its use here and in relation to miracles. A miracle "strikes against" the mind's fixed conceptual premises and opens it to the reality of the wondrous. But the Dhamma strikes in a different way. It "strikes against" distorted views and defilements, and thus it is counteractive or antidotal. This interpretation is supported by **8:70** (IV 310–11), where the Buddha states that his disciples "can thoroughly refute in reasoned ways the current tenets of others and teach the *sappāṭihāriya* Dhamma" (*uppannaṃ parappavādaṃ sahadhammena suniggahitaṃ niggahetvā sappāṭihāriyaṃ dhammaṃ desessanti*). Here the *sappāṭihāriya* character of the Dhamma must be related, not to miracles, but to its ability to counteract opposed tenets. Thus "antidotal" or "counteractive" would render the sense well.

587 *Purāṇasabrahmacārī*. Mp says that they had lived together at

Āḷāra Kālāma's hermitage. Āḷāra Kālāma was one of the meditation masters under whom the future Buddha trained before his enlightenment. See MN I 163–64.

588 Apparently this is Hatthaka of Āḷavī (see **1:251**), though Mp does not identify him as such.

589 Mp explains *dhammā . . . pavattino* as "the Buddha-word that you learned in the past" (*pubbe uggahitabuddhavacanaṃ*).

590 Mp: "Teachings that he has forgotten because he neglected to recite them."

591 *Aviha*: One of the five pure abodes (*suddhāvāsa*) into which only non-returners are reborn.

592 *Goyogapilakkhasmiṃ*. Mp: "Near the fig tree that had grown up at the place for selling cattle." PED explains *pilakkha* as a wavy-leaved fig tree.

593 *Rittassādaṃ bāhirassādaṃ*. Mp: "*Dissatisfied*: lacking the pleasure of the jhānas. [*Seeking*] *gratification outwardly*: the gratification of sensual pleasure." The Chinese parallel, SĀ 1081 (T II 283a20–283b26) says (at 283a23) that "he had given rise to an unwholesome thought connected with evil craving" (起不善覺，以依惡貪).

594 *Mā kho tvaṃ attānaṃ kaṭuviyam akāsi*. Mp glosses *kaṭuviyaṃ* simply as *ucchiṭṭhaṃ*, "left over" food, without further explanation. DOP defines the word as "(what is) left over; (what is) polluted, impure."

595 Be *āmagandhena*; Ce and Ee *āmagandhe*. See Āmagandha-sutta, Sn 239–52. Mp: "The foul odor consisting in anger."

596 *Saṃvegamāpādi*. Mp: "He became a stream-enterer." The suttas normally use a stock formula to indicate attainment of stream-entry, but nothing of this formula is found in the present text.

597 Ce reads pāda b *aladdhā samamattano*; Be *aladdhā samathamattano*; Ee *sammamattano*. I prefer the Ce reading. All three editions read the verb in pāda c as *pareti*, which Mp glosses with *gacchati*.

598 *Nāsayitvāna makkhikā*. The absolutive is from the verb *nāseti*, "to destroy."

599 The exact import of this is not clear to me. Perhaps the sense is that women are best kept within the home rather than permitted to go out in public places on their own. The Chinese parallel, EĀ 22.4 (at T II 607b26–607c11), is exactly like the Pāli, though it includes a verse which simply reiterates the same statements as in the prose portion of the sutta.

600 The first two are at **2:47**. On "the assembly trained to the limits" (Ce *yāvatāvavinītā parisā*; Be *yāvatāvinītā parisā*; Ee *yāvatajjhāvinītā parisā*), Mp says: "Trained by way of its capacity, meaning an assembly trained after one has known its capacity" (*pamāṇavasena*

vinītā, pamāṇaṃ ñatvā vinītaparisā ti attho). This seems to be a unique occurrence of the expression in the Nikāyas. Mp also recognizes a reading *yāvatajjhā*, which it explains as "an assembly trained after one has known its inclination" (*yāva ajjhāsayā ti attho, ajjhāsayaṃ ñatvā vinītaparisā ti vuttaṃ hoti*). Vanarata prefers a Burmese variant mentioned in a note in Ee, *yāvatajjanīvinītā parisā*, which he understands to be "an assembly that gives in to training only as long as (*yāva*) threats are applied."

601 *Ṭhitā sā dhātu dhammaṭṭhitatā dhammaniyāmatā*. Mp offers only an unhelpful word gloss based on the identification of a *dhamma* with a thing that bears a real nature (*sabhāva*): ***Dhammaṭṭhitatā*** *ti sabhāvaṭṭhitatā.* ***Dhammaniyāmatā*** *ti sabhāvaniyāmatā.*

602 Mp explains impermanent (*anicca*) here as non-existent after having come to be (*hutvā abhāvaṭṭhena*); suffering (*dukkha*) as oppression (*sampīḷanaṭṭhena dukkhā*); and non-self (*anattā*) as not subject to the exercise of mastery (*avasavattanaṭṭhena*). In SN 12:20, II 25–27, this same framework is applied to the twelvefold formula of dependent origination.

603 Ce *kesakambalo tesaṃ pāvārānaṃ patikiṭṭho*, as against Be and Ee *kesakambalo tesaṃ paṭikiṭṭho*. PED defines *pāvāra* as "a cloak, a mantle."

604 See **1:319** for another critique of Makkhali Gosāla. The simile of the trap recurs at the end of this sutta.

605 Ee treats this sutta as a continuation of the preceding one, whereas Ce and Be, which I follow, treat it as separate. Thus my numbering will again exceed Ee's by three.

606 Ce and Ee *tayo ca assasadasse . . . tayo ca purisasadasse*. Lit., "the three kinds of good horses among horses and the three kinds of good horses among men."

607 Ee at I 291–92 combines this sutta and the next two into one, 3:140 in its numbering. Ce and Be count each separately. See **11:10**, which merges them into a single sutta supplemented by two additional factors for a total of eleven qualities. From **3:146** on, my numbering exceeds Ee's by five.

608 The one beyond training (*asekha*) is the arahant.

609 Ee does not number this as a separate vagga but titles it *Acelakavagga*. Ce counts it as the sixth vagga in the third Fifty, called *Paṭipadāvagga*. Be also counts it as the sixth vagga (sixteenth in its total for the Threes), called *Acelakavagga*, "Chapter on the Naked Ascetic."

610 I base this title on the *uddāna* verse of Be. Neither Ce nor Be assigns a title to this sutta; neither Ce nor Ee has an *uddāna* verse.

611 The coarse way of practice (*āgāḷhā paṭipadā*) corresponds to the

extreme of indulgence in sensual pleasure; the blistering way of practice (*nijjhāmā paṭipadā*), to the extreme of self-mortification. Those are the two extremes that the Buddha rejected in his first discourse (SN 56:11, V 421,4–9).

612 The following list of ascetic practices is also at DN I 166–67; MN I 77–78, 307–8, 342–43.

613 Ee compresses all these into a single sutta numbered 152. I follow Ce and Be in counting each as a distinct sutta.

614 Ee joins each pair of suttas, respectively on qualities that lead to hell and to heaven, into a single sutta, and thus counts ten suttas (153–62, in its enumeration). Ce and Be, which I follow, enumerate each pair of contrasting suttas separately and thus count twenty suttas.

615 Be and Ee count only one sutta here, 184 and 163 in their respective enumerations. Ce, which I follow, counts 170 suttas.

616 With Be and Ee, I read simply *tayo dhammā* rather than *ime tayo dhammā* with Ce.

617 *Suññato samādhi, animitto samādhi, appaṇihito samādhi*. Mp says only that "insight is explained by means of them (*tīhipi samādhīhi vipasssanā va kathitā*)." The three are mentioned as a set at DN III 219,21–22, again without explanation, but Sv III 1003–4 comments: "The explanation is threefold, by way of arrival (*āgamanato*), by way of quality (*saguṇato*), and by way of object (*ārammaṇato*). (1) *By way of arrival*, (i) one bhikkhu interprets in terms of non-self, sees in terms of non-self, and reaches the path by [contemplation of] non-self; for him, insight is called 'emptiness.' Why? Because of the absence of the defilements responsible for [the idea of] self or non-emptiness. The concentration of the path (*maggasamādhi*), being reached by insight, is called emptiness; and the concentration of the fruit (*phalasamādhi*), being reached by the path, is also called emptiness. (ii) Another interprets in terms of impermanence, sees in terms of impermanence, and reaches the path by [contemplation of] impermanence; for him, insight is called 'markless.' Why? Because of the absence of the defilements responsible for marks. The concentration of the path, being reached by insight, is called markless; and the concentration of the fruit, being reached by this path, is also called markless. (iii) Another interprets in terms of suffering, sees in terms of suffering, and reaches the path by [contemplation of] suffering; for him, insight is called 'wishless.' Why? Because of the absence of the defilements responsible for wishes. The concentration of the path, being reached by insight, is called wishless; and the concentration of the fruit, being reached by this path, is also called wishless. (2) *By way of quality*: The concentration

of the path is empty because it is empty of lust, etc.; it is markless, because the marks of lust, etc., are absent; and it is wishless because wishes caused by lust, etc., are absent. (3) *By way of object*: Nibbāna is emptiness because it is empty of lust, etc.; it is markless and wishless, because it is without the marks of lust, etc., and without wishes caused by lust, etc." Vism 657,13–259,10, Ppn 21.66–73, discusses the three "gateways to liberation" (*vimuttimukha*) under the same three names.

Notes to the Fours

618 What follows is included in the Mahāparinibbāna Sutta, DN 16.4.2–3, II 122–23.

619 *Dīghamaddhānaṃ sandhāvitaṃ saṃsaritaṃ*. The "long stretch" of wandering is *saṃsāra*, derived from the verb *saṃsarati*, seen here in the past participle *saṃsaritaṃ*. Mp glosses *dīghamaddhānaṃ* with *cirakālaṃ* ("a long time") and explains *sandhāvitaṃ* as "roamed by going from one state of existence to another" (*bhavato bhavaṃ gamanavasena sandhāvitaṃ*).

620 *Bhavanetti*. Mp: "The rope of existence (*bhavarajju*) is a name for craving. Just as oxen are bound by a rope around the neck, so this leads beings from one existence to another. Therefore it is called the conduit to existence."

621 *Cakkhumā parinibbuto*. Mp: "He attained nibbāna by the extinction of defilements. This was the first nibbāna, which occurred for him in the vicinity of the bodhi tree. But afterward, between the twin sal trees (at Kusinārā) he attained nibbāna by the nibbāna element without residue remaining."

622 *Appatito*. Lit., "not fallen," but Mp glosses it more positively with *patiṭṭho*, meaning "established, settled," and says it refers to the stream-enterer and other noble ones; the arahant is "entirely settled" (*khīṇāsavo ekantapatiṭṭho*).

623 The verse is also at Th 63. Th-a I 155: "*Done is the task* (*kataṃ kiccaṃ*): The sixteenfold task has been done (that is, each of the four noble paths performs the four tasks of fully understanding suffering, abandoning its origin, realizing its cessation, and developing the path) and there is nothing more to be done. *The delightful is delighted in* (*rataṃ rammaṃ*): The delightful nibbāna, free from all that is conditioned, is delighted in by the noble ones. *Happiness is reached by happiness* (*sukhenanvāgataṃ sukhaṃ*): The ultimate happiness, nibbāna, is reached by the happiness of fruition attainment; or the happiness of fruition and of nibbāna is arrived at by the happiness of insight and the path through a pleasant mode of practice (on this, see **4:162 §§3–4** below)."

624 These three verses recur at **10:89** with reference to the slanderous bhikkhu Kokālika. The story, including verses, is also at SN 6:9–10, I 149–53, and Sn 3:10, pp. 123–31.

Vicināti mukhena so kaliṃ, kalinā tena sukhaṃ na vindati. This could also have been rendered: "The fool collects a disaster with his mouth." *Kali* means both disaster and the losing throw at dice.

625 Mp: "This disaster is trifling, that is, the loss of wealth at dice along with all that one owns, including oneself." Mp glosses *sugatesu*, "holy ones," as *sammaggatesu puggalesu*, "persons who have rightly attained," thus referring to all arahants, not only to the Buddha.

626 *Sataṃ sahassānaṃ nirabbudānaṃ / chattiṃsatī pañca ca abbudāni*. I translate following Mp, which says of the numbers: "A hundred thousand *nirabbudas*, plus thirty-six more *nirabbudas*, plus five *abbudas*" (***sataṃ sahassānan*** *ti nirabbudagaṇanāya satasahassaṃ;* ***chattiṃsatī*** *ti aparāni ca chattiṃsati nirabbudāni;* ***pañca cā*** *ti abbudagaṇanāya ca pañca abbudāni*). Vanarata, however, holds that *pañca* cannot directly qualify *abbudānaṃ* and therefore he would conjoin *sahassānaṃ* with *chattiṃsatī* and *pañca* as well, making thirty-six thousand additional *nirabbudas* and five thousand *abbudas*. Mp, commenting on **10:89**, explains the Buddhist numbering scheme as follows: one *koṭi* = ten million; a *koṭi* of *koṭis* = one *pakoṭi;* a *koṭi* of *pakoṭis* = one *koṭipakoṭi;* a *koṭi* of *koṭipakoṭis* = one *nahuta;* a *koṭi* of *nahutas* = one *ninnahuta;* a *koṭi* of *ninnahutas* = one *abbuda;* twenty *abbudas* = one *nirabbuda*.

627 The verse is also at **3:31** and **4:63**, but here *dhammacariyāya* replaces *paricariyāya*.

628 In Pāli: *anusotagāmī puggalo, paṭisotagāmī puggalo, ṭhitatto puggalo, tiṇṇo pāraṅgato thale tiṭṭhati brāhmaṇo*.

629 Reading with Be and Ee *upagāmino*, as against Ce *upagāhino*.

630 *Paripuṇṇasekho*. Mp: "One firm in fulfillment of the training" (*sikkhāpāripūriyā ṭhito*). A trainee (*sekha*) is one who has entered the irreversible path to liberation but has not yet attained arahantship. The arahant is *asekha*, "one beyond training."

631 In Pāli: *suttaṃ, geyyaṃ, veyyākaraṇaṃ, gāthā, udānaṃ, itivuttakaṃ, jātakaṃ, abbhutadhammaṃ, vedallaṃ*. This is the early ninefold division of the Dhamma, eventually superseded by the arrangement of the texts into the five Nikāyas. See Norman 1983: 15–16; Norman 2006a: 172–73. Mp, in line with other commentaries, gives examples of each genre, not all of which would be approved by modern scholarship. It is a disputed question whether some items in the list refer to collections that already existed in the Buddha's time or to prototypes on the basis of which the present collections were established. Present scholarly opinion leans toward the latter.

632 I follow Be, which reads *tassa sampajjate sutaṃ* in pāda d of this verse and *nāssa sampajjate sutaṃ*, "his learning has not succeeded," in pāda d of the next verse. Ce reads *nāssa sampajjate sutaṃ* here and *tassa sampajjate sutaṃ* in the next verse, while Ee has *nāssa sampajjate sutaṃ* in both places. Mp supports Be by explaining, in relation to this verse: "His learning can be said to have succeeded because this person has used what he has learned to achieve the purpose of learning." And in relation to the next verse, Mp says: "It [his learning] does not succeed because he has not achieved the purpose of learning." The verses are cited at Vism 48, Ppn 1.136, but with differences in readings among the several editions.

633 Mp glosses *brahma* here as "best, supreme, pure" (*seṭṭhaṃ uttamaṃ visuddhaṃ*) and identifies *brahmacakka* with *dhammacakka*, the wheel of the Dhamma.

634 See **3:64** and p. 1651, note 451.

635 Vanarata writes with regard to pāda c: "I think that *patvā* is a mistaken adaptation from an original early Pāli *pattā*, which can be both absolutive and past participle. When Pāli was reshaped, the wrong alternative was chosen. *Pattā*, being past participle, should have been left unchanged" (personal communication). I read pāda d with Be *visāradaṃ vādapathātivattaṃ*, a reading shared with older Sinhala manuscripts. Ce has *visāradaṃ vādapathātivattīnaṃ*, which is also plausible, but Ee *visāradaṃ vādapathāti vuttaṃ* is certainly mistaken.

636 *Itthabhāvaññathābhāvaṃ*. Mp: "Life here" is this existence (*ayaṃ attabhāvo*); "life elsewhere" is a future existence (*anāgatattabhāvo*).

637 *Bhavānaṃ*. Mp distinguishes *kāmayoga* as lust connected with the five objects of sensual pleasure and *bhavayoga* as desire and lust for existence in the form and formless realms.

638 Reading with Ce and Be *yogātigā munī*, as against Ee *yogātigāmino*.

639 Also at It §110, 115–18.

640 I read with Ce *thīnamiddhaṃ uddhaccakukkuccaṃ vicikicchā pahīṇā hoti* (Ee is the same, but with *honti*), as against Be *thīnamiddhaṃ vigataṃ hoti uddhaccakukkuccaṃ vigataṃ hoti vicikicchā pahīṇā hoti*.

641 "Namuci": a name for Māra, which the commentaries explain as "he does not (*na*) set free (*muci*)."

642 *Bhaddakaṃ samādhinimittaṃ*. The six mentioned here are included among the ten *asubha* meditation subjects in Vism chap. 6.

643 Rāhu is the asura chief who abducts the sun and moon, obviously representing the solar and lunar eclipses. See SN 2:9–10, I 50–51.

644 A primeval king, descended from Mahāsammata, son of Uposatha, and an ancestor of the Sakyans (see DPPN). Mp: "He was

reborn among humans when the life span was immeasurable and enjoyed human sense pleasures for a long time, causing a rain of gold to fall whenever he wanted. In the deva world, during the life spans of thirty-six Indras, he enjoyed excellent sensual pleasures."

645 Mp: "*Kinds of exquisiteness* [*or fineness, delicacy, subtlety*]: knowledges that penetrate subtle characteristics" (***sokhummānī** ti sukhumalakkhaṇapaṭivijjhanakāni ñāṇāni*). The noun *sokhumma*, from the common adjective *sukhuma*, is rare and in the Nikāyas appears to occur only here and in a compound at Th 437. Mp's explanation seems to me problematic. I would identify exquisiteness of form with the form perceived in the fourth jhāna, exquisiteness of feeling with the neither-painful-nor-pleasant feeling occurring in the fourth jhāna and the formless attainments, exquisiteness of perception with the perception in the base of nothingness, and exquisiteness of volitional activities with the residual volitional activities in the base of neither-perception-nor-non-perception.

646 I read with Ce and Be *sa ve sammaddaso bhikkhu*. Ee's *sace* for *sa ve* is clearly a mistake.

647 *Bhattuddesika*. The bhikkhu responsible for assigning meal offerings and invitations to the other bhikkhus. On his credentials and disqualifications, see **5:272**.

648 Be mentions all four motives: *chandā dosā mohā ca bhayā gāmino*. And in the next verse: *na chandā na dosā na mohā na bhayā ca gāmino*.

649 SN 6:2, I 138–40, records the incident in direct narrative mode. It includes a fifth factor: the knowledge and vision of liberation. Since it is set at the time of the Buddha's enlightenment, it makes no mention of the Saṅgha, which arose only after the Buddha began to teach.

650 Ce reads *atthakāmena*; Be and Ee have *attakāmena*, "desiring self." In pāda d, the plural of Buddha is in the Pāli, *buddhānasāsanaṃ*. Possibly the compound is a corruption of *buddhānusāsanaṃ*, "the Buddha's instruction," which would preserve a singular.

651 The placement of this sutta in the period just after the Buddha's enlightenment seems strange. The words of the brahmins suggest that the Buddha, from a position of authority, participated in regular discussions with brahmins; yet he surely would not have done so before he began his career as a teacher. See **8:11**, where a brahmin makes the same charge against the Buddha at a later time when he had already become a successful teacher.

652 I follow Ce in taking the poem to consist of three stanzas of

six pādas each. Be divides it into four stanzas, the first with six pādas, the other three with four pādas.

653 In pāda c, I read with Ce *saññato thiradhammesu*, as against Be and Ee *saññato dhīro dhammesu*, "self-controlled and steadfast among phenomena." In this, I follow Vanarata's suggestion (in a personal communication) that the Ce reading "has the merit of both fitting the meter better and supplying a pun (between *thira* and *thera*, firm and elder)." This clause corresponds to the jhānas, "factors of firmness" referring to *samādhi*. Mp glosses "who clearly sees the meaning with wisdom" (*paññāyatthaṃ vipassati*) as seeing the meaning of the four noble truths with the wisdom of the path along with insight. It explains "gone beyond all phenomena" (*pāragū sabbadhammānaṃ*) as "gone beyond all such phenomena as the five aggregates" and "gone to the consummation of all [good] qualities" by the sixfold going beyond (*chabbidhena pāragamanena*): with respect to direct knowledge, full understanding, abandoning, development, realization, and meditative attainments. Mp does not explain the repetition of *paṭibhānavā* ("discerning") in the verse, which seems peculiar.

654 Also at It §112, 121–23.

655 Mp identifies the world (*loka*) with the truth of suffering. The four tasks that the Tathāgata has accomplished here correspond to the four tasks regarding the four noble truths—fully understanding the truth of suffering, abandoning the truth of its origin, realizing its cessation, and developing the path—but with "fully awakened" (*abhisambuddha*) replacing "fully understood" (*pariññāta*) in regard to the first truth. See SN 56:11, V 422.

656 Mp, like other commentaries, explains the seen (*diṭṭha*) as the visible-form base; the heard (*suta*) as the sound base; the sensed (*muta*) as the bases of odor, taste, and tactile sensations; and the cognized (*viññātaṃ*) as the mental-phenomena base. The three terms "reached, sought after, examined by the mind" (*pattaṃ pariyesitaṃ anuvicaritaṃ manasā*) are simply elaborations of the cognized. Mp also explains that the suffix *–gata*, lit. "gone," in the derivation of the word "Tathāgata," means the same as *abhisambuddha*, "fully awakened to."

657 Ce and Ee have merely *parinibbāyati*, as against Be *anupādisesāya nibbānadhātuyā parinibbāyati*, "attains final nibbāna by way of the nibbāna element without residue remaining." The latter reading may have entered Be from It §112, 121,21–22.

658 *Sabbaṃ taṃ tath'eva hoti, no aññathā. Tasmā 'tathāgato' ti vuccati.*

659 *Yathāvādī tathākārī, yathākārī tathāvādī. . . . Tasmā 'tathāgato' ti vuccati.*

660 Ce has this in brackets. Be and Ee do not have it at all.

661 According to Mp, Kāḷaka was a wealthy financier and the father-in-law of Anāthapiṇḍika's daughter Cūḷasubhaddā. At the time of her marriage, he had been a devotee of the naked ascetics and knew nothing about the Buddha or his teaching. Cūḷasubhaddā contrived to get him to invite the Buddha and the monks for a meal offering. After the meal, the Buddha gave a discourse that established him in the fruit of stream-entry. Kāḷaka then built a monastery in his park and donated both monastery and park to the Buddha. One day, when the bhikkhus who were natives of Sāketa were sitting in the meeting hall discussing the Buddha's success in converting Kāḷaka, the Buddha read their minds and knew they were ready for a discourse that would settle them in arahantship. It would also cause the great earth to quake up to its boundaries. Hence he addressed the bhikkhus.

662 Mp: "By these three terms (*jānāmi, abbhaññāsiṃ, viditaṃ*) the plane of omniscience (*sabbaññutabhūmi*) is indicated." In the history of Buddhism, as well as in modern scholarship, the question whether the Buddha claimed omniscience has been a subject of debate. The Buddha certainly rejected the claim that one could know everything all the time (see MN 71.5, I 482,4–18) as well as the claim that one could know everything simultaneously (see MN 90.8, II 127,28–30). But he also says that to hold that he totally rejects the possibility of omniscience is to misrepresent him (MN 90.5, II 126,31–27,11). Thus it seems to follow that what the Buddha rejected is the possibility of continuous and simultaneous knowledge of everything, but not discrete and intentional knowledge of whatever can be known (which would exclude much of the future, since it is not predetermined).

663 *Taṃ tathāgato na upaṭṭhāsi*. Mp: "The Tathāgata did not become subservient to any object at the six sense doors, that is, he did not take it up (*na upagañchi*) through craving or views. For it is said: 'The Blessed One sees a form with the eye, but he has no desire and lust for it; the Blessed One is fully liberated in mind.... The Blessed One cognizes a phenomenon with the mind, but he has no desire and lust for it; the Blessed One is fully liberated in mind' (see SN 35:232, IV 164–65). By this the plane of arahantship (*khīṇāsavabhūmi*) is indicated."

664 *Taṃ p'assa tādisameva*. Mp: "That too would just be false speech."

665 *Taṃ mam'assa kali*. Mp: "That statement would be a fault of mine. With the above three statements, the plane of truth (*saccabhūmi*) is indicated."

666 Mp: "He does not misconceive (*na maññati*) visible form by way

of craving, conceit, or views; and so for the other objects. By this passage, the plane of emptiness (*suññatābhūmi*) is explained."

667 The word *tādī*, originally a simple referential term meaning "that one," takes on a special sense when used to designate the Buddha or an arahant. Nidd I 114–15 explains that an arahant is called *tādī* because he has transcended preferences, given up (*catto*) defilements, crossed (*tiṇṇo*) the floods, and has a liberated (*mutto*) mind.

Mp: "*Being ever stable . . . is a stable one* (*tādīyeva tādī*): 'Stable' means exactly the same (*ekasadisatā*). The Tathāgata is the same both in gain and loss, fame and obscurity, blame and praise, and pleasure and pain. . . . By this the plane of the stable one (*tādibhūmi*) has been explained. As he concluded the teaching with these five planes, on each of the five occasions the earth quaked as testimony."

668 I paraphrase Mp's explanation of this verse: "He would not take even one claim of the speculative theorists (*diṭṭhigatikā*)—who are 'self-constrained' (*sayasaṃvutesu*) in the sense that they are constrained or blocked by their conceptions—to be categorical or supreme and trust it, believe it, fall back on it as true or false (*evaṃ saccaṃ musā vāpi paraṃ uttamaṃ katvā na odaheyya, na saddaheyya, na pattiyāyeyya*), thinking: 'This alone is true and anything else is false.'" This explanation nicely connects the verse to the prose line, "the Tathāgata did not become subservient to it."

669 Mp identifies the "dart" as the dart of views (*diṭṭhisalla*). Elsewhere craving is spoken of as the dart, for instance, at MN II 258,27, and SN I 40,7; in still other passages, the dart is sorrow, as at **5:48**, **5:50**.

670 *Saṃvaratthaṃ pahānatthaṃ virāgatthaṃ nirodhatthaṃ*. These four aims of the spiritual life, it seems, are the reason for including this sutta in the Fours.

671 Mp glosses *nibbānogadhagāminaṃ* with *nibbānassa antogāminaṃ*, "leading into nibbāna."

672 All three editions that I consulted have *mahantehi*, but I prefer the reading in It §35, 28,17, *mahattehi*, glossed by It-a I 112,25, *mahā-ātumehi uḷārajjhāsayehi*, "by the great spirits, by those of lofty disposition."

673 The sutta also occurs as It §108, 112–13. My division of the sutta into four parts is hypothetical, but apart from this no fourfold scheme is apparent.

674 *Na me te bhikkhave bhikkhū māmakā*. Mp. "They are not bhikkhus of mine; they do not belong to me" (*te mayhaṃ bhikkhū mama santakā na honti*).

675 *Pūtimuttaṃ*. There is a belief in traditional ayurvedic medicine

that cow's urine into which gall nuts have been soaked has potent medicinal properties. But Mp says that any urine counts, "for just as a golden-colored body is called a foul body, so even fresh urine is called putrid urine."

676 *Disā na paṭihaññati.* Lit. "The region [or quarter] is not hindered." But *disā* may be a truncated instrumental, with *paṭihaññati* referring to the monk. Thus "he is not hindered by [or 'in'] any quarter."

677 Reading with Ce *bhikkhuno,* as against Be and Ee *sikkhato,* "one in training."

678 This is one of the most popular discourses in the Theravāda tradition. In Sri Lanka, during the Anurādhapura period, it was often used as the topic for long sermons crowning a festival; see Rahula 1956: 268–73. Mp explains "noble lineages" (*ariyavaṃsā*) as the lineages of the noble ones: all Buddhas, paccekabuddhas, and the Buddha's disciples.

679 Mp explains contentment with each requisite by way of the three kinds of contentment. See p. 1600, note 55.

680 Mp: "*Finds delight in development* (*bhāvanārāmo*): He delights in developing the four establishments of mindfulness, the four right strivings, the four bases for psychic potency, the five faculties, the five powers, the seven enlightenment factors, the seven contemplations, the eighteen great insights, the thirty-seven aids to enlightenment, and the thirty-eight meditation objects. *Finds delight in abandoning* (*pahānārāmo*): He delights in abandoning the defilements of sensual desire and so forth."

681 Reading with Be and Ee *dhīraṃ*. Ce has *vīraṃ* in pādas a and b, but *dhīro* in pādas c and d.

682 Mp says that pāda b explains pāda a. Because discontent is unable to vanquish the steadfast one, cannot overcome him, therefore discontent does not vanquish the steadfast one.

683 *Dhammapadāni*. Mp: "Portions of Dhamma" (*dhammakoṭṭhāsā*).

684 See p. 1646, note 416.

685 These two wanderers are also mentioned at MN 117.37, III 78,13, and SN 22:62, III 73,3. We do not have more information about them than what is said here.

686 Three of the four "wheels" (*cakkāni*) are mentioned at Sn 260. The fourth, "relying on good persons," corresponds to "associating with the wise" (*paṇḍitānañca sevanā*) at Sn 259.

687 The word *saṅgaha* literally means "inclusion, bringing together, holding together," from prefix *saṃ* + *gaha,* "hold, grasp." The verb from which the noun is derived is *saṅgaṇhāti*, from *saṃ*, "together," and *gaṇhāti*, "to grasp, to hold." The four *saṅgahavatthu* are means by which one can attract others and sustain a relationship with them characterized by friendliness and respect.

The four in Pāli are *dāna, peyyavajja, atthacariyā, samānattatā*. To adequately capture the dual nuance of *saṅgaha* two words might have been used, "attract and sustain." PED explains *saṅgaha,* in the relevant sense, as "kindliness, sympathy, friendliness, assistance, protection, favour," and takes *saṅgahavatthu* to mean "objects (characteristics) of sympathy." SED defines the Skt form *saṃgrahavastu* as "element of popularity," and BHSD as "*article of attraction,* means by which a Buddha or (more often in BHS) a Bodhisattva *attracts,* draws to himself and to religious life, creatures." Although the four figure prominently in the Mahāyāna sūtras, they are already found in the archaic Nikāyas.

Mp: "Some people are to be sustained by a gift, so a gift should be given to them. Others expect endearing speech, so they should be addressed with pleasant words. *Beneficent conduct* is a talk on increasing goodness; these people should be told, 'You should do this, you shouldn't do that. You should associate with this person, not with that person.' *Impartiality* is being the same in happiness and suffering. This means sitting together with them, living together, and eating together." In Skt versions of the four factors the fourth is often *samānārtha* (which would be Pāli *samānattha*), "having a common purpose" or "having shared benefits."

688 "Personal existence" (*sakkāya*): the five aggregates subject to clinging. See MN 44.2, I 299,8–14; SN 22:105; III 158,3–4.

689 Mp: "'For the most part' (*yebhuyyena*) is said to make an exception of those devas who are noble disciples. Though they experience urgency of knowledge (*ñāṇasaṃvega*), no fear at all arises in the arahants, because they have attained what should be attained through careful striving. The other devas, as they attend to impermanence, experience both fear as mental fright (*cittutrāsabhaya*) and, at the time of strong insight, cognitive fear (*ñāṇabhaya*)." "Cognitive fear" is probably the stage of insight called "knowledge of appearance as fearful" (*bhayat'upaṭṭhānañāṇa*; see Vism 645–47, Ppn 21.29–34).

690 Mp: "*Included in personal existence* (*sakkāyapariyāpannā*): included in the five aggregates. Thus, when the Buddha teaches them the Dhamma stamped with the three characteristics, exposing the faults in the round of existence, cognitive fear enters them."

691 *Yāvatā bhikkhave dhammā saṅkhatā vā asaṅkhatā vā*. In the Nikāyas, the only *dhamma* explicitly said to be unconditioned is nibbāna. All other *dhammas*, mental and material, are conditioned. Thus the best of conditioned *dhammas* is the noble eightfold path, which leads to the unconditioned.

692 *Aggassa dātā*. It-a II 111,5–7, explains that the dative-genitive *aggassa* can be understood to denote either the recipient of the

gift or the item to be given: "*A giver to the foremost*: a giver to the Three Jewels, which are foremost; or one who generates merit by making a lofty gift of a foremost item" (*aggassa ratanattayassa dātā, atha vā aggassa deyyadhammassa dānaṃ uḷāraṃ katvā tattha puññaṃ pavattetā*).

693 Mp says that the noble method (*ariyañāya*) is the path together with insight, and the "goodness of the Dhamma" (*kalyāṇadhammatā*) and "the wholesomeness of the Dhamma" (*kusaladhammatā*) are names for it.

694 See p. 1647, note 428.

695 This is one of the thirty-two marks of a great person, said to be the karmic consequence of living for the happiness of many, dispelling fear and terror, providing lawful protection and shelter, and supplying all necessities. See DN 30.1.7, III 147–49.

696 Mp interprets the conversation on both sides as referring to the future: the brahmin asks about the Buddha's future rebirth and the latter replies with respect to his future rebirth. As I read the exchange, however, a subtle word play is involved. The brahmin uses the future *bhavissati* as a polite way of inquiring about the present, which I render "could you be?" (*Bhavissanti* is used above in just this way, negatively, in the sentence, *na vat'imāni manussabhūtassa padāni bhavissanti*, "These could not be....") But the Buddha uses the future form literally and thus in each case answers, "I will not be" (*na bhavissāmi*), referring to his destiny in a future life. Two Chinese parallels, SĀ 101 (at T II 28a19–28b17) and EĀ 38.3 (at T II 717c18–718a12), render this entire conversation as pertaining to the present. The brahmin asks the Buddha whether he is (為) a deva, a nāga, etc., a human being, or a nonhuman being, and the Buddha simply denies (非) that he is any of these. There is no reference to the future.

697 *Gandhabbas* are celestial beings sometimes depicted as the musicians of the devas. *Yakkhas* are fierce spirits noted for their destructiveness.

698 The verb *abbaje* here is optative of *abbajati* (Skt *āvrajati*). See DOP sv *abbajati*.

699 Mp: "At the end of the discourse, the brahmin attained three paths and fruits and, in 12,000 phrases, spoke the praise called 'Doṇa's Thunder.' When a great commotion erupted after the Buddha's passing, he settled it and distributed the relics" (at DN 16.6.25, II 166).

700 That is, I shall terminate the old discomfort of hunger without creating fresh discomfort by eating to excess.

701 I take *dhammaṃ* here to represent Skt *dhammān*, the plural accusative. Such usage is not rare in Pāli verse.

702 The verse is identical with Dhp 32.

703 *Patilīno*. Mp glosses with "hidden, gone into solitude" (*nilīno ekībhāvaṃ upagato*).

704 *Panuṇṇapaccekasacco*. Mp glosses as "view-truths (*diṭṭhisaccāni*) called 'personal' because each one holds to them individually, insisting 'This alone is truth, this alone is truth.'"

705 Reading with Be *sabbāni nuṇṇāni honti panuṇṇāni honti cattāni vantāni muttāni pahīnāni, paṭinissaṭṭhāni*. This is also the Ce and Ee reading of the same passage in **10:20**.

706 Mp: "The search for a spiritual life (*brahmacariyesanā*) consists in the aspiration that occurs thus, 'I will seek out, search for, a spiritual life.' This subsides and is tranquilized by the path of arahantship. But the search for a spiritual life in the form of views (*diṭṭhibrahmacariyesanā*) subsides with the path of stream-entry."

707 Bodily activity (*kāyasaṅkhāra*) is elsewhere identified with in-and-out breathing, which ceases in the fourth jhāna. See **9:31 §4**. Also see MN 44.15; I 301,19–21; SN 41:6, IV 293,16–17.

708 Mp: "*The tight grasp 'Such is the truth'* (*iti saccaparāmāso*) is the grasping of such conceptions as 'Such is the truth, such is the truth.' *Viewpoints* (*diṭṭhiṭṭhānā*) are simply views, called 'swellings' (*samussayā*) because of their swelling up (*samussitattā*), because they rise up and persist."

709 *Niccadānaṃ anukulayaññaṃ*. Mp explains *anukulayaññaṃ* as a sacrifice that should be made to maintain the family custom, on the grounds that it was given by one's father and grandfather and so forth. On *niccadānaṃ anukulayaññaṃ* as superior to animal sacrifice, see especially DN 5.22–23, I 144, which can be regarded almost as an elaboration of the present sutta.

710 My division into four sections is speculative. Apart from this, I do not see any other basis for including this sutta among the Fours.

711 These were Vedic sacrifices.

712 I follow Ce and Be, which put *niraggaḷaṃ* in pāda b and include *mahāyaññā* in pāda c. Ee lacks *mahāyaññā*, but two Chinese parallels include a compound corresponding to this word: SĀ 89 (at T II 22c19) has 大會, more literally "great gathering," and SĀ[2] 89 (at T II 404b4) has 大祀, where 祀 means "to sacrifice to the gods or ancestors." Mp explains *mahārambhā*: "With great tasks, great works; further, they are of 'great violence' because of the extent of the destruction of life."

713 Readings of this enigmatic term vary here and elsewhere across the Nikāyas. Here, Ce has *vivattacchaddā*, Be *vivaṭacchadā*, Ee *vivattacchadā*. The expression often occurs in the stock passage on the two courses open to one with the thirty-two bodily marks of a great man: if he remains at home, he will become a wheel-turning

king, but if he goes forth into homelessness, he will become a perfectly enlightened Buddha, described as "one in the world who *vivaṭacchado*" (variants: *vivaṭṭacchado, vivaṭṭacchaddo, vivattacchaddo*). See e.g. DN 3.1.5, I 89,8–9; DN 14.1.31, II 16,8–9; DN 30.1.1, III 142,4; MN 91.5, II 134,28; Sn 106. Though the origins of the term and its exact meaning are problematic, the commentaries consistently analyze and explain it in the same way. Since Mp (on the present sutta) does not offer an explanation, I cite the Dīgha Nikāya commentary, Sv I 250,34–251,3: "*Vivaṭṭacchado*: Here, having been born into the world, he dwells having entirely removed the covering in the world (*loke taṃ chadanaṃ vivaṭṭetvā*), in the darkness of defilements covered by seven coverings (*chadanehi*): lust, hatred, delusion, conceit, views, ignorance, and misconduct."

The old canonical commentary, Cūḷaniddesa, commenting on Sn 1147, says: "*Vivaṭacchado*: There are five coverings (*chadanāni*): craving, views, defilements, misconduct, ignorance. Those coverings have been removed (*vivaṭāni*) by the Blessed Buddha; they have been dispelled, uprooted, abandoned, eradicated, settled, stilled, burned by the fire of knowledge so that they are unable to arise. Therefore the Buddha is one who has removed the coverings" (Nidd II 251,18–22; VRI ed. 204).

Norman (1991: 71–76) had proposed that the Pāli expression was to be derived from the BHS form *vighuṣṭaśabda* and thus meant "one whose name (or fame) had rolled in different directions"or "one of widespread fame." In a later work (2006b: 228–29) he changed his position, stating: "although I was correct to see a connection between the Pāli and Skt words, the direction of the development was in the reverse order, and must represent a hyper-Sanskritisation from *vivattacchadda*." At Sn 372 and elsewhere he renders this "with deceit removed."

The Chinese translators of the Āgamas must have worked with texts that read *vighuṣṭaśabda* or some variant with the same meaning. Thus a parallel of **4:40**, SĀ[2] 90 (at T II 404c6) has 名聞極遠者, "whose name is heard extremely far away." The parallel of DN 30, MĀ 59 (at T I 493b7–8), reads: 必得如來無所著等正覺名稱流布周聞十方; "he necessarily becomes a Tathāgata, unattached (= arahant), fully enlightened, *whose name spreads around and is heard in the ten directions*." MĀ 161, the parallel of MN 91, has the same at T I 685b2–4. Though various conjectures might be proposed with respect to the original expression and its meaning, given the difficulty of settling these questions across Buddhist textual traditions, the most expedient course open to me is to translate the term as it has been preserved and interpreted in the Pāli tradition.

714 The readings here vary considerably. Ce and Be have *vītivattā kulaṃ gatiṃ*, "who have transcended family and destination." Ee has a *bahubbīhi* compound, *vītivattakālaṃgatī*, with still more variants in the notes. Mp (Be) reads *kulaṃ gatiṃ* in the lemma, but Mp (Ce) has *kālaṃ gatiṃ*. My rendering follows Ee. Note that in **5:55**, at III 69,10, *kālaṃ* and *gatiṃ* are in immediate proximity, which supports the hypothesis that here too we should read *kāla-/kālaṃ*.

715 I read with Be *yaññassa kovidā*, as against Ce and Ee *puññassa kovidā*, "proficient in merit." Mp (Be) and Mp (Ce) show the same difference in their lemmas and glosses. Two Chinese parallels correspond to Be. SĀ 90 (at T II 23a11) has 佛於邪盛善, "the Buddha who is skilled in sacrifice," and SĀ^{2} 90 (at T II 404c8) 諸佛所稱善祀及祀之道, "this is the good sacrifice and the path of sacrifice praised by the Buddhas."

716 The Pāli reads *atthi bhikkhave samādhibhāvanā bhāvitā bahulīkatā diṭṭhadhammasukhavihārāya saṃvattati*, lit., "there is, bhikkhus, a development of concentration that, when developed and cultivated, leads to dwelling happily in this very life." Since in English "when developed and cultivated" would be redundant, I have omitted it in favor of more natural English diction. The same applies to each of the other three developments of concentration.

717 Evidently, this refers to the attainment of the jhānas either by one who does not use them to develop insight, or by an arahant, who enters the jhānas simply to dwell at ease. Elsewhere the jhānas are shown to lead to the destruction of the taints. Ce has *vuccati* in this section but not in the parallel sentences of the next three sections. Ee is just the opposite, omitting *vuccati* here but including it in the next three sections. Be omits *vuccati* in all four sections.

718 Mp explains "knowledge and vision" in this context as the divine eye (*dibbacakkhuñāṇadassanassa paṭilābhāya*). Elsewhere it is used to mean insight knowledge or even full enlightenment.

719 *Yathā divā tathā rattiṃ, yathā rattiṃ tathā divā*. Mp: "As he attends to the perception of light by day, so he attends to it at night; and so in reverse."

720 Mp: "How are feelings known as they arise, etc.? Here, a bhikkhu comprehends the base (*vatthu*, the sense organ) and the object (*ārammaṇa*). By comprehending the base and the object, he knows: 'Thus those feelings have arisen; thus they stand; thus they cease.' The same method applies to perceptions and thoughts."

721 Sn 1048, also cited at **3:33**.

722 See **3:67** and p. 1654, note 464.

723 Also at SN 2:26, I 61–62.

724 *Daḷhadhammā*. The suffix *-dhamma* here is a Pāli formation of Skt *dhanvan*, "having a bow." Hence the gloss by Mp: "*Firm-bowed* means possessing a bow of the maximum size" (*daḷhadhanu uttamappamāṇena dhanunā samannāgato*).

725 *Dhanuggaho sikkhito katahattho katūpāsano*. Mp explains *dhanuggaho* as a teacher of archery, *sikkhito* as one who has trained in archery for twelve years, *katahattho* as one skillful enough to split the tip of a hair even at the distance of an *usabha*, and *katūpasāno* as one experienced in shooting arrows who has exhibited his craft. See too p. 1831, note 1935; also see CDB 393, note 181, and CDB 819, note 365.

726 Mp: "The teaching of the good is the thirty-seven aids to enlightenment. The teaching of the bad is the sixty-two speculative views."

727 The sutta is also found at SN 21:7, II 280. No fourfold scheme is apparent, and thus I cannot determine the reason for including it in the Fours.

728 I read with Be and Ee *nābhāsamānaṃ jānanti*, as against Ce *na bhāsamānaṃ jānanti*. The context clearly requires the former. The Chinese parallel SĀ 1069 (at T II 277c12) supports this with 若不說法者, "If he does not speak the Dhamma."

729 *Saññāvipallāso, cittavipallāso, diṭṭhivipallāso*. *Vipallāsa* is from *vi* + *pari* + *āsa*, "turned upside down." These are treated in terms of abandonment and non-abandonment at Paṭis II 80–81.

730 I read with Ce and Be *dukkhe bhikkhave sukhan ti saññāvipallāso*, as against Ee *adukkhe bhikkhave dukkhan ti saññāvipallāso*.

731 I read with Ce and Ee *micchādiṭṭhigatā*, as against Be *micchādiṭṭhihatā*. But I follow the verse divisions of Be rather than of Ce.

732 Mp glosses *mahikā* with *himaṃ*, "snow," but PED offers "fog, frost," which seem better.

733 Of the four *upakkilesas*, the drinking of liquor by bhikkhus is prohibited by Pācittiya 51; sexual intercourse by Pārājika 1; the acceptance of gold and silver (as well as of any other medium of monetary exchange) by Nissaggiya-pācittiya 18. Various kinds of wrong livelihood prohibited to Buddhist monastics are enumerated at DN 2.1.21–27, I 67–69. See too MN 117.29, III 75,11–14.

734 I read with Be *asuddhā sarajā magā*.

735 Here, the four streams of merit are explained in terms of the four requisites: robes, almsfood, lodging, and medicines. Mp apparently misses the correct derivation of *sovaggika*, deriving it from *suṭṭhu aggānaṃ rūpādīnaṃ dāyakā*. The word is properly derived from *sagga* (Skt *svarga*), heaven. But Mp to **4:61** gives the correct derivation; see p. 1691, note 746.

736 *Appamāṇaṃ cetosamādhiṃ*. Mp: "The concentration of the fruit of arahantship" (*arahattaphalasamādhi*).

737 Also at SN 55:31, V 391, without verses, and at SN 55:41, V 399–400, with the same verses as those of **4:51**.

738 These verses are also at SN 11:14, I 232; SN 55:26, V 384; and SN 55:51, V 405.

739 *Chava*, lit. a corpse. Mp: "Such a person is called a corpse because he or she is dead through the death of their virtuous qualities."

740 On Nakulapitā and Nakulamātā, see **1:257**, **1:266**, **6:16**.

741 At **1:263** she is designated the foremost among givers of what is excellent.

742 Mp identifies the "world-knowers" (*lokavidūna*) with the Buddhas.

743 Ee is somewhat misleading here. First, it punctuates wrongly, and then it adds an extra *paccupaṭṭhito hoti* at the end. The punctuation in Ce and Be indicates that the indirect object (the item given) belongs with the preceding *paccupaṭṭhito*, and they both lack *paccupaṭṭhito hoti* at the end. Thus in Ce and Be there is no separate phrase indicating that the lay disciple simply serves the Saṅgha without mention of an item presented.

744 *Saha ñātīhi saha upajjhāyehi*. In Buddhist monastic culture, the *upajjhāya* is the senior monk who presides over one's ordination. Thus the use of the word here, in a non-monastic context, is unusual. Mp explains the word in this passage as if it means friends, "because one's friends should be concerned about one's happiness and suffering (*sukhadukkhesu upanijjhāyitabbattā*)," but this explanation depends on an unconvincing word play. *Upajjhāya* is not connected to the verb *upanijjhāyati* (Skt *upanidhyāyati*), "to think of, to consider," but to *ajjheti* (Skt *adhyeti*), "to study, to learn from (a teacher)."

745 Ce and Ee *āpāthadaso*; Be *āpātadaso*. Mp (Ce): "He sees whatever comes into range, even a subtle matter that comes into range" (*taṃ taṃ atthaṃ āpātheti tameva passati, sukhumampissa atthajātaṃ āpāthaṃ āgacchatiyevā ti attho*).

746 Here Mp correctly derives *sovaggika* from *sagga*: *Saggassa hitā ti tatr'upapattijananato sovaggikā*.

747 I have divided this verse and the next in line with the corresponding verses of **5:51**. Since Ce was edited by different editors who apparently did not collaborate, the same sets of verses in different volumes are sometimes divided differently. The division used at **5:51**, which groups together the several applications of wealth, seems to correspond better to the sense.

748 In Pāli: *atthisukha, bhogasukha, anaṇasukha, anavajjasukha*. Mp: "The first is the happiness arisen at the thought, 'There is (*atthi*, i.e.,

wealth)'; the second is the happiness arisen in one who enjoys wealth; the third is the happiness arisen at the thought, 'I am without debt'; the fourth is the happiness arisen at the thought, 'I am faultless, blameless.'"

749 Reading with Ce and Ee *sare*, as against Be *paraṃ*.

750 Reading with Ce and Ee *bhāge*, as against Be *bhoge*.

751 Mp: "He divides the types of happiness into two portions. The first three types make up one portion, the happiness of blamelessness is a portion in its own right. Then he sees with wisdom and knows that the former three types of happiness combined are not worth a sixteenth part of the happiness of blamelessness."

752 An expanded parallel of **3:31**. Another parallel is It 106, 109–11.

753 A separate sutta number is missing in Ee, which thus gives the impression that this sutta is a continuation of the preceding one.

754 The first, it seems, are those who place confidence in a spiritual teacher because of his impressive physical form (*rūpa*), i.e., his beauty. The second are those whose confidence is based on impressive speech (*ghosa*, perhaps "voice," a soothing and melodious voice); the third, those whose confidence is based on a teacher's austerity (*lūkha*; Mp gives as examples using a coarse robe and alms bowl); and the fourth, those who place confidence in a teacher because of his teaching (*dhamma*). Mp says that one out of 100,000 people base their confidence on the teacher's Dhamma.

755 Reading with Be *nābhijānanti te janā*.

756 Reading with Ce *mohena adhamā sattā*, as against Be *mohena āvutā sattā*. Ee *mohena adhamasattā* is the same in meaning as Ce.

757 I read the second couplet with Be and Ee *yathādhammā tathāsantā, na tass'evan ti maññare*. Ce reads pāda d: *nassevanti na maññare*. Mp: "*In accordance with their own natures*: They are of such a nature that qualities like lust, etc., remain; having become of such a nature. [*They*] *do not think of it in such a way*: They do not think of it thus: 'We exist in such a way, we have such a nature'" (***yathādhammā tathāsantā*** *ti yathā rāgādayo dhammā ṭhitā, tathā sabhāvā'va hutvā;* ***na tass'evan ti maññare*** *ti mayaṃ evaṃsantā evaṃsabhāvā ti tassa na maññare, na maññantī ti attho*).

758 The incident is also recorded at Vin II 109–10.

759 *Imāni cattāri ahirājakulāni*. Mp: "This is said with reference to those [snakes] whose bite is venomous. For all those with a venomous bite are included in these four royal families of snakes."

760 Be formats this declaration as verse, but I follow Ce and Ee in taking it as prose. This is an asseveration of truth (*saccakiriya*) and, as such, belongs with the verses, but since no meter is apparent, it is unlikely to be actual verse. The asseveration is commonly

recited by forest monks as a safeguard against snakebites. It is often incorporated into their daily recitation.

761 The sutta, including the verse, is also at SN 17:35, II 241, with an added homily on the danger of gain, honor, and praise. See too Vin II 187–88.

762 I cannot clearly see a reason for including this sutta in the Fours. I can only conjecture that the explanation lies in the four groups of people who swerve from righteousness: kings, royal vassals, brahmins and householders, and the people of the town and countryside. But this omits the natural phenomena, which also have a claim to be included.

763 *Adhammikā honti*. Mp: "Without performing the tenfold oblation prescribed by the ancient kings, and without assigning punishment in proportion to the crime, they perform excessive oblations and assign excessive punishments." The tenfold oblation (*dasabhāgabali*) is mentioned only here.

764 In support of my translation of *brāhmaṇagahapatikā* as a *dvanda* compound rather than as a *kammadhāraya*, "brahmin householders," see It-a II 162,7–9: *Brāhmaṇagahapatikā ti brāhmaṇā c'eva gahapatikā ca. Ṭhapetvā brāhmaṇe ye keci agāraṃ ajjhāvasantā idha gahapatikā ti veditabbā.*

765 The omission of *dubbalā* in the VRI edition appears to be an error. The other editions, including the Be printed version, have this word.

766 See **3:16**.

767 Right view (*sammādiṭṭhi*) is the first factor of the noble eightfold path, and the three types of wholesome thought are collectively right intention (*sammāsaṅkappa*), the second path factor.

768 Ee treats this as the beginning of a new sutta, numbered **4:74**, whereas Ce and Be consider this part of **4:73**. Mp supports Ce and Be, stating that the simile is brought in to give an example of the bad person's character.

769 Ee treats **4:74** and **4:75** as a single sutta, as against Ce and Be, which take them to be different.

770 What occurs from this point on is also in the Mahāparinibbāna Sutta, DN 16.6.5, II 154–55.

771 *Acinteyyāni*. Mp says only "unsuitable to think about" (*cintetuṃ ayuttāni*).

772 Mp explains the four as follows: "The *domain of the Buddhas* (*buddhavisaya*) is the procedure and spiritual might (*pavatti ca ānubhāvo ca*) of the Buddha's qualities such as the omniscient knowledge and so forth. The *domain of one in jhāna* (*jhānavisaya*) is the direct knowledges and jhānas. The *result of kamma* (*kammavipāka*) is the result of kamma to be experienced in the present life and so forth. *Speculation about the world* (*lokacintā*) is such worldly speculations

as: 'Who made the sun and moon? Who made the earth and the ocean? Who created sentient beings? Who made the mountains, mangoes, palmyras, and coconuts?'"

773 Also at MN 142.9–13, III 256–57.

774 Mp: "They *do not sit in council* (*n'eva sabhāyaṃ nisīdati*) in the judgment hall for the purpose of passing judgment. They *do not engage in business* (*na kammantaṃ payojeti*), in major work such as agriculture, trade, and so forth. They *do not go to Kamboja* (*na kambojaṃ gacchati*): they do not go to the Kamboja country for the purpose of carrying goods. This is the mere heading. The sense is that they do not go to any remote country."

775 The sutta, accompanied by similes and verses, is at SN 3:21, I 93–96; see too Pp 51–52. Mp: "One is *in darkness* (*tamo*) because one is conjoined with darkness by being reborn in a low family, and one is *heading toward darkness* (*tamoparāyaṇa*) because one is approaching the darkness of hell through bodily misconduct, etc. One is *in light* (*joti*) because one is conjoined with light by being reborn in a high family, and one is *heading toward light* (*jotiparāyaṇa*) because one is approaching the light of a heavenly rebirth through bodily good conduct, etc."

776 See **3:13**. I read with Ce and Be *veṇakule vā nesādakule*, as against Ee *nesādakule vā veṇakule*.

777 Ce defines these four types with exactly the same explanations given in **4:85**. Be and Ee, however, offer no explanations but merely give the headings.

778 Mp resolves *samaṇamacalo* into *samaṇa-acalo*, with *–m–* a mere conjunct consonant. It identifies this figure with the seven kinds of trainees (*sattavidhampi sekhaṃ dasseti*). On the next two ascetics, Mp says: "The *white-lotus ascetic* (*samaṇapuṇḍarīka*) is an ascetic similar to a white lotus (*puṇḍarīka*), which has fewer than a hundred petals. By this he shows the dry-insight arahant (*sukkhavipassakakhīṇāsavaṃ dasseti*), called a white-lotus ascetic because his virtues are incomplete, since he lacks the jhānas and direct knowledges. The red-lotus ascetic (*samaṇapaduma*) is an ascetic similar to a red lotus (*paduma*), which has a full hundred petals. By this he shows the arahant liberated in both respects (*ubhatobhāgavimuttaṃ khīṇāsavaṃ dasseti*), called a red-lotus ascetic because his virtues are complete, since he possesses the jhānas and direct knowledges." On the colors of the two kinds of lotus flowers, *puṇḍarīka* and *paduma*, see p. 1642, note 389. "The delicate ascetic among ascetics" (*samaṇesu samaṇasukhumālo*) is "one with soft mind and body, who experiences exclusively pleasure, free from bodily and mental pain" (*muducittasarīro kāyikacetasikadukkharahito ekantasukhī*).

779 Mp: "***Macalappatto*** *ti rañño khattiyassa muddhāvasittassa puttabhāvena ceva puttesu jeṭṭhakabhāvena ca na tāva abhisittabhāvena ca abhisekappatti-atthāya acalappatto niccalapatto.*" The gist is that the eldest son is said to have "attained the unshaken" since he is destined to be a head-anointed king. See too p. 1636, note 345.

780 *Anuttaraṃ yogakkhemaṃ patthayamāno viharati.* Mp: "He dwells aspiring for arahantship."

781 Contrary to Mp, the definition of the white-lotus ascetic here is ambiguous; for the expression "he does not dwell having contacted with the body the eight emancipations" (*no ca kho aṭṭha vimokkhe kāyena phusitvā viharati*) could mean either: (1) that he does not attain *any* of the eight emancipations, which would make him a dry-insight arahant (as Mp asserts); or (2) that he attains *some* of the eight emancipations *but not all*, perhaps the three emancipations based on form but not the formless attainments and cessation. In such a case, the meditator would conform to the definition of the arahant liberated by wisdom (*paññāvimutta*) of whom it is said that he has eliminated the taints but does not attain the peaceful formless attainments (MN 70.16, I 477,33–478,1). The commentators hold that the *paññāvimutta* arahant can possess any number among the four jhānas or no jhāna at all; only the latter is a dry-insight arahant. The dry-insight arahant (*sukkhavipassakakhīṇāsava*) is not explicitly mentioned as such in the Nikāyas but first gains recognition in the commentaries. In any case, the difference in the definitions between the wisdom-liberated arahant and the white-lotus arahant suggests that at some point a shift had taken place in the scale of meditative attainments that was expected of an arahant. While the arahant liberated by wisdom lacks only the formless attainments, the white-lotus arahant, on the interpretation offered by the commentators, lacks the jhānas as well.

The eight emancipations (*aṭṭha vimokkhā*), defined at **8:66**, are not exactly identical with the four jhānas and four formless attainments. It seems that the first three emancipations correspond to the four jhānas but distinguish them in terms of objects rather than mental factors.

782 Again, there is an ambiguity in the definition of the red-lotus ascetic. To qualify as such, does one have to possess all eight emancipations or is it sufficient to possess several? Given the commentarial explanation, which compares the red-lotus ascetic to a lotus with a full hundred petals, it seems that one would have to possess all eight emancipations. But the commentarial definition of the *ubhatobhāgavimutta* arahant allows one who possesses *any* of the formless attainments to count as "one liberated in both respects." This, too, might represent a lowering of a more

stringent criterion that would restrict the designation to an arahant possessing all eight emancipations.

783 More literally, "the robe he uses is usually one that he has been asked to accept, seldom one that he has not been asked to accept." And so with the other three requisites.

784 In commenting on *sannipātikāni*, Mp-ṭ says "produced by a combination of the three—bile and so forth—which are out of balance" (*pittādīnaṃ tiṇṇampi visamānaṃ sannipātena jātāni*). Spk III 81,22–23, commenting on the same word at SN IV 230,29, says "originating through a disturbance of the three, bile and so forth" (*tiṇṇampi pittādīnaṃ kopena samuṭṭhitāni*).

785 The eight causes of feelings are also at SN 36:21, IV 230–31.

786 Mp says that the first section describes the seven kinds of trainees; the second, the dry-insight arahant; the third, the arahant liberated in both respects; and the fourth, the Tathāgata and an arahant similar to the Tathāgata.

787 Mp: "*Internal serenity of mind* (*ajjhattaṃ cetosamatha*) is internal concentration of mind at the level of absorption (*niyakajjhatte appanācittasamādhi*). *Higher wisdom of insight into phenomena* (*adhipaññādhammavipassanā*) is the insight knowledge that comprehends conditioned phenomena (*saṅkhārapariggāhakavipassanāñāṇa*). This is the higher wisdom that consists of insight into phenomena, that is, into the five aggregates."

788 Mp: "Conditioned phenomena should be seen as impermanent, explored as impermanent, and discerned with insight as impermanent; and so too as suffering and as non-self."

789 Mp: "The mind should be steadied, composed, unified, and concentrated by way of the first jhāna; and so too for the second and higher jhānas."

790 He repeats all four types, as does the Buddha below. I have omitted the repetition.

791 *Abhikkantā h'esā potaliya yadidaṃ tattha tattha kālaññutā*. Mp: "It is the nature of the wise, when they have known it is the proper time, to speak dispraise of one who deserves dispraise and to speak praise of one who deserves praise."

792 These are the nine divisions of the Buddha's teachings. See p. 1678, note 631.

793 Ee ends 4:104 here, taking this much to be a complete sutta, and then repeats these sentences as the opening of 4:105, followed by the exposition. Thus Ee's 4:105 is identical with my 4:104. Ee reads the *uddāna* verse to indicate there are two "pools of water" suttas, but the manuscripts have only one. In the verse *dve honti* can be read with either *udakarahadā* or *ambāni*. Ce and Be, which I

follow, choose the latter and thus have only one "pools of water" sutta, 4:104, with 4:106 left blank.

794 I read with Ce and Be *kiṃ nu*, as against Ee *kathan nu*.

795 *Pahitatto kāyena c'eva paramasaccaṃ sacchikaroti, paññāya ca ativijjha passati*. Mp explains "body" as the mental body (*nāmakāyena*), the supreme truth as nibbāna, and wisdom as the wisdom of the path together with insight.

796 The Pāli word *ṭhāna* can mean place, possibility, occasion, situation, cause, case, etc. Mp glosses it with *kāraṇa*. To convey the appropriate meaning, I here render it sometimes as "case of a deed" and sometimes simply as "deed."

797 *So na bhāyati samparāyikassa maraṇassa*. Mp: "Arahants do not fear death either in the future or in this present life. They alone are intended here. Some, however, say that because of the statement, 'developed right view,' all noble ones from the stream-enterer up are intended." I am not sure that *samparāyikassa maraṇassa* means death in a future life, as Mp implicitly understands it. I take it to mean simply "death in the future," referring primarily to one's future in this present life.

798 *Attarūpena*. Mp glosses: "What is in conformity with oneself, what is suitable, meaning one who desires his welfare" (*attano anurūpena anucchavikena, hitakāmenā ti attho*).

799 We find three kinds of intoxication (*mada*) at **3:39**: with youth, health, and life. Vibh 345 (Be §832) mentions still more objects of intoxication: birth, clan, gains, honor, respect, wealth, beauty, learning, etc. The elaboration at Vibh 350 (Be §§843–45) connects *mada* with *māna*, meaning conceit, and *unnati*, meaning self-promotion.

800 *Na ca pana samaṇavacanahetupi gacchati*. Mp: "He is not swayed by the words of ascetics holding other doctrines to abandon his own view and take up their view. Here, too, only arahants are intended."

801 Also in the Mahāparinibbāna Sutta, DN 16.5.8, II 140–41. The word here translated "inspiring," *saṃvejanīya*, is glossed by Mp as *saṃvegajanaka*. In this context, the rendering "inspiring a sense of urgency" does not fit. The required sense, rather, is that which inspires faith and devotion.

802 The four places, respectively, are: Lumbini, Bodhgaya, Isipatana (Sarnath), and Kusinārā.

803 What follows is also at **2:1**.

804 What follows parallels the passage on "the fault pertaining to the future life" in **2:1**, but it describes this simply as "a bad result" (*pāpako vipāko*) where **2:1** has "a bad, painful result" (*pāpako dukkho vipāko*). Since **2:11** also lacks *dukkho*, it is possible *dukkho* was

originally a commentator's gloss on *pāpako* that made its way into the text of **2:1** itself.

805 Mp: "Among these perils, (1) for one who reflects on the peril in self-reproach, a sense of moral shame is established inwardly. This produces in him restraint in the three doors, and such restraint is the fourfold purified virtuous behavior. Based on this virtuous behavior, he develops insight and attains the highest fruit. (2) For one who reflects on the peril of reproach by others, moral dread is established with respect to the external. This produces in him restraint in the three doors, and such restraint is the fourfold purified virtuous behavior. Based on this virtuous behavior, he develops insight and attains the highest fruit. (4) For one who reflects on the peril of a bad destination, a sense of shame is established with respect to the external. This produces in him restraint in the three doors, and such restraint is the fourfold purified virtuous behavior. Based on this virtuous behavior, he develops insight and attains the highest fruit." The third case does not lead directly to the highest fruit but merely to abstinence from breaches of the five precepts.

806 Also at MN 67.14–20, I 459–62.

807 Pāli recognizes two classes of food items: *khādanīya* and *bhojanīya*. The latter comprises rice, porridge, other grains, fish, and meat; the former comprises virtually all other edibles. Hence, corresponding to these two types of foods, two gerundives are used here to designate what may be eaten: *khāditabba* and *bhunjitabba*, which I render, respectively, "things that may be consumed" and "things that may be eaten."

808 Mp: "The first jhāna may be of an inferior grade, a middling grade, and a superior grade. For those reborn through an inferior grade, the life span is a third of an eon; for those reborn through the middling grade, the life span is half an eon; and for those reborn through a superior grade, the life span is an eon. This is said with reference to the last." For details on the life spans in the various realms according to the developed Theravāda model, see Vibh 422–26 (Be §§1022–28); CMA 196–99.

809 Mp: "He 'goes to hell' in some subsequent life, insofar as he has not abandoned kamma that leads to hell; not in the sense that he goes there in his immediately following life." According to the Abhidhamma, one passing away from the form realm does not immediately take rebirth in one of the three lower realms; see CMA 226–27.

810 *Tasmiṃyeva bhave parinibbāyati*. Mp: "He attains final nibbāna while remaining in that same form-realm existence; he does not descend lower."

811 See pp. 1671–72, note 581.

812 The devas of streaming radiance (*devā ābhassarā*) are the highest class of devas associated with the second jhāna. Mp: "The second jhāna is threefold, as stated above [for the first jhāna]. For those reborn by a superior grade, the life span is eight eons; by a middling grade, four eons; and by an inferior grade, two eons. The text refers to the last."

813 The devas of refulgent glory (*devā subhakiṇhā*) are the highest class of devas associated with the third jhāna. According to the Abhidhamma system, the life spans of the three planes corresponding to the third jhāna are respectively sixteen, thirty-two, and sixty-four eons. Since this is contradicted by the sutta, Mp explains that what is intended here is the lowest plane among those planes reached by rebirth through attainment of the third jhāna. However, according to Mp, the devas of refulgent glory are actually the highest among these realms, with a life span of sixty-four eons. There thus seems to be a contradiction between the sutta and the systematic Theravāda determination of life spans.

814 These are the *devā vehapphalā*, the sole realm of rebirth corresponding to the mundane fourth jhāna. This figure is in agreement with the stipulation of the Abhidhamma.

815 *Te dhamme aniccato dukkhato rogato gaṇḍato sallato aghato ābādhato parato palokato suññato anattato samanupassati.* Mp: "Of these eleven terms, two—impermanent and disintegrating—signify the characteristic of impermanence. Two—empty and non-self—signify the characteristic of non-self. The rest signify the characteristic of suffering. By ascribing the three characteristics to the five aggregates and seeing them thus, he achieves three paths and fruits. Having developed the fourth jhāna, firm in it, 'he is reborn in companionship with the devas of the pure abodes.'"

816 The pure abodes (*suddhāvāsā*) are five planes of existence in the form realm into which only non-returners can be reborn. Non-returners attain arahantship there without ever returning to lower realms. See CMA 192–93.

817 In this sutta, loving-kindness is correlated with the first jhāna, compassion with the second, altruistic joy with the third, and equanimity with the fourth. According to the developed Theravāda system, however, any of the first three immeasurable meditations can lead to all three jhānas, excluding the fourth; only immeasurable equanimity can lead to the fourth jhāna. See Vism 322,5–12, Ppn 9.111.

818 For various wonders occurring at the bodhisatta's conception and birth, see too MN 123.

819 Mp: "Between every three world systems there is one world interval, which is like the space in the middle of three cart

wheels or petals placed so that they touch one another. This world-interval hell (*lokantarikanirayo*) measures eight thousand *yojanas* in size."

820 Mp: "*Those beings who have been reborn there*: Through what kamma have those beings been reborn in the world-interval hell? They arise there because they have committed terrible crimes against their parents and against righteous ascetics and brahmins, and through other violent deeds such as killing living beings day after day.... Their bodies are three *gāvutas* long (appx. five miles) and they have long fingernails like bats. As bats hang in trees, these beings hang by their fingernails on the foot of the world-system mountain. When creeping along, they stay in arm's length of one another. Then, thinking, 'We have gained food,' they bustle around, roll over, and fall into the water that supports the world; they are just like honey fruits which, when struck by the wind, break off and fall into the water. As soon as they have fallen, they dissolve like a lump of flour in extremely caustic water.... This radiance [when the bodhisatta enters his mother's womb] does not even last long enough to take a sip of porridge, but only long enough for them to awaken from sleep and cognize the object. But the Dīgha Nikāya reciters say that, like a flash of lightning, it shows forth merely for the time of a finger snap and disappears even while they are saying, 'What is that?'"

821 *Ālaya*. Mp explains this narrowly as the five objects of sensual pleasure, or more broadly, as the entire round of saṃsāra.

822 *Anālaye dhamme*. Mp: "The noble Dhamma opposed to attachment, based on the ending of the round."

823 *Anupasama*. Lit., "lack of peace."

824 *Avijjāgatā, bhikkhave, pajā aṇḍabhūtā pariyonaddhā*. This is the reading in Ce and Be, but Ee has *andhabhūtā*, "become blind." The latter, at first glance, seems more likely to have been original, but the simile of the hen at **8:11**, IV 176,15–16 supports *aṇḍabhūtā*, "become an egg." Mp too accepts this reading with its gloss, "being enveloped by the shell of ignorance, it has become like an egg" (*avijjaṇḍakosena pariyonaddhattā aṇḍaṃ viya bhūtā ti aṇḍabhūtā*).

825 Also at DN 16.5.16, II 145–46.

826 In Pāli, the three kinds of fetters are, respectively: *orambhāgiyāni saṃyojanāni, upapattipaṭilābhiyāni saṃyojanāni, bhavapaṭilābhiyāni saṃyojanāni*. Mp distinguishes the last two thus: the "fetters for obtaining rebirth" are those by which one obtains the next rebirth (*yehi anantarā upapattiṃ paṭilabhati*); the "fetters for obtaining existence" are the conditions for obtaining rebirth-existence

(*upapattibhavassa paṭilābhāya paccayāni*). Apparently the difference, from the commentary's point of view, is that the former bind one only to the immediately following rebirth while the latter bind one to successive rebirths. But see note 829 below for an alternative interpretation.

827 Since the stream-enterer, too, has not abandoned any of these fetters, Mp explains: "The once-returner is mentioned to show the highest among the noble ones who have not abandoned any of the fetters." Mp-ṭ: "That is, who have not abandoned the lower fetters. For above the once-returner, there is no noble one who has not abandoned the lower fetters. But isn't it the case that once-returners have abandoned [some] lower fetters, for they have abandoned the fetters of views, doubt, and wrong grasp of rules and observances? In that case, why is it said that they have not abandoned the lower fetters? Because once-returners have not abandoned the fetters of sensual lust and ill will; therefore the statement that they have not abandoned the lower fetters is said with reference to those fetters that they have not abandoned. It does not mean that they have not abandoned any fetters."

828 *Uddhaṃsotassa akaniṭṭhagāmino puggalassa*. This refers to the most sluggish of the five classes of non-returners, who proceed upward through successive pure abodes to the highest one, called Akaniṭṭha. This type, too, is mentioned to show the coarsest who still retain the fetters of rebirth, but more acute classes of non-returners also retain these fetters.

829 This statement creates a predicament for the traditional Theravādin interpretation of the five types of non-returners, which is based on Pp 16–17 and its commentary at Pp-a 198–201. The core of this interpretation is the rejection of an intermediate state (*antarābhava*) between two lives. Such rejection thus entails the need to interpret the *antarāparinibbāyī* as a non-returner who attains arahantship during the first half of the life span in the next existence. However, the word *antarāparinibbāyī* literally means "one who attains final nibbāna *in between*," and there seems no legitimate reason, based on a sutta, to deny the possibility that certain non-returners, following their death in human form, enter an intermediate state and attain final nibbāna in that state itself, thereby circumventing the need to take another rebirth. This seems to be the purport of the present text, according to which the *antarāparinibbāyī* has abandoned the fetters of rebirth but not the fetters of existence. Upon attaining arahantship, the *antarāparinibbāyī* will also abandon the fetters of existence. I have discussed the five types of non-returners in detail in CDB 1902–3,

note 65. For further discussion, see p. 1782, notes 1535–38; for additional textual analysis, see Harvey 1995: 98–108.

830 *Yuttappaṭibhāno no muttappaṭibhāno*. Mp: "When answering a question, he answers correctly (*yuttameva*), but he does not answer quickly (*sīghaṃ pana na katheti*). The meaning is that he answers slowly. This method [of explanation] should be applied to all the cases." Pp 42 (Be §152) defines this person in the same sense thus: "A person who, being asked a question, speaks correctly but not quickly is called one whose discernment is incisive but not free-flowing" (*idh'ekacco puggalo pañhaṃ puṭṭho samāno yuttaṃ vadati no sīghaṃ, ayaṃ vuccati puggalo yuttappaṭibhāno no muttappaṭibhāno*).

831 The four alternatives are: *ugghaṭitaññū*, *vipacitaññū* (so Ce and Ee; Be *vipañcitaññū*), *neyyo*, *padaparamo*. The difference in reading of the second person would yield a choice between "one who understands when ripened" (based on Ce and Ee) and "one who understands when elaborated" (based on Be). Be's reading seems to me to agree better with the formal definition of this type in other sources. I cite here the definitions at Pp 41 (Be §§148–51) with commentarial clarifications at Pp-a 223: (1) "The person *of quick understanding* is one for whom the breakthrough to the Dhamma (*dhammābhisamaya*) occurs together with an utterance. (Pp-a: *Ugghaṭita* means the opening up of knowledge (*ñāṇugghāṭana*); the meaning is that one knows as soon as knowledge opens up. *Together with an utterance*: as soon as [a statement on Dhamma] is uttered. The *breakthrough* occurs together with knowledge of the Dhamma of the four truths.)" (2) "The person *who understands through elaboration* is one for whom the breakthrough to the Dhamma occurs when the meaning of what has been stated briefly is being analyzed in detail. (Pp-a: This is the person able to attain arahantship when, after a concise outline of the teaching has been set up, the meaning is being analyzed in detail.)" (3) "The person *to be guided* is one for whom the breakthrough to the Dhamma occurs gradually, through instruction, questioning, careful attention, and reliance on good friends." (4) "One for whom *the word is the maximum* is one who—though hearing much, reciting much, retaining much in mind, and teaching much—does not reach the breakthrough to the Dhamma in that life."

Nett 125 (Be §88) correlates these four types with the four kinds of practice (see **4:161–62**): the *ugghaṭitaññū puggala* with one emancipated by pleasant practice and quick direct knowledge, the *vipañcitaññū puggala* with one emancipated by either painful practice and quick direct knowledge or by pleasant practice and sluggish direct knowledge, and the *neyya puggala* with one emancipated by painful practice and sluggish direct knowledge. The *padaparama puggala* is not emancipated and thus the four alternatives do not apply.

832 Mp: "*One who lives off the fruit of his effort but not off the fruit of his kamma*: This is one who passes the day energetically exerting himself and lives off whatever he gains as the consequential fruit of this, but does not obtain any meritorious fruits as a result of his exertion. *One who lives off the fruit of his kamma but not off the fruit of his effort*: These are all the devas, from [the heaven of] the four great kings up, who live off their meritorious fruits without energetically exerting themselves. *One who lives off the fruit of both his effort and his kamma*: These are kings and royal ministers, etc. *One who lives off the fruit of neither his effort nor his kamma*: These are the beings in hell. In this sutta, by 'fruit of kamma,' only meritorious fruit is intended."

833 Mp: "The first is the blind foolish worldling; the second is the worldling who intermittently does wholesome deeds; the third is the stream-enterer, the once-returner, and the non-returner; and the fourth is the arahant."

834 Mp: "The first is the multitude of worldly people; the second is the dry-insight stream-enterer and once-returner; and the third is the non-returner. Since the dry-insight meditator does obtain momentary jhāna arisen on the basis of his object (*taṅkhaṇikampi upapattinimittakaṃ jhānaṃ paṭilabhati yeva*), he too fulfills concentration. The fourth is the arahant. The following sutta should be understood by the method stated here."

835 On the four analytical knowledges (*paṭisambhidā*), see below note 875.

836 Here and in the next sutta I read with Ce and Ee *samatho*, as against Be *sammasanā*.

837 The usual list of faculties (*indriya*) and powers (*bala*) is fivefold, with wisdom (*paññā*) as the fifth. For definitions of the five faculties, see SN 48:9–10. For the five powers, see **5:14**.

838 *Cattāri kappassa asaṅkheyyānī*. Despite the word "incalculable" (Ce and Ee *asaṅkheyya*; Be *asaṅkhyeyya*), the length of this period is finite. For similes illustrating the length of an eon—said to be too difficult to express in numbers—see SN 15:5–6, II 181–82. And for the number of eons that have "elapsed and gone by," see SN 15:7–8, II 182–84.

839 Mp explains that there are three ways the dissolution of an eon takes place: by water, fire, and wind. When the eon is destroyed by fire, it is consumed up to the devas of streaming radiance. When it is destroyed by water, it is dissolved up to the devas of

refulgent glory. When it is destroyed by wind, it disintegrates up to the devas of great fruit.

840 Mp: "He is not content with the four requisites by way of the three kinds of contentment." See p. 1600, note 55.

841 Mp says the word "cunningly" (*saṅkhāya*, lit. "having calculated") indicates that he tries to make a false impression on families (for the purpose of receiving offerings). The last phrase is perhaps similar in nuance to a well-known English slang expression.

842 Ee reads here: *gambhīresu ... ṭhānaṭṭhānesu*, which might be translated "various deep matters." It could be that *ṭhānaṭṭhānesu* was the more original reading, which was altered to *ṭhānāṭṭhānesu* under the influence of this more common expression. But since Mp comments as if the latter were the reading, it is clear that *ṭhānāṭṭhānesu* goes back at least to the age of the commentator. At MN 115.12–19, III 64–67, the Buddha explains how a bhikkhu is "skilled in what is possible and impossible" (*ṭhānāṭhānakusalo*).

843 It is puzzling that Ānanda goes unaccompanied to visit the bhikkhunī. Almost always when a bhikkhu goes to visit a layperson, even a male, he brings another monk along. In a Chinese parallel of this sutta, SĀ 564 (T II 148a13–148c10), as Ānanda approaches, the bhikkhunī sees him in the distance and exposes her body. When Ānanda sees her exposed, he restrains his senses and turns away. The nun then feels ashamed and puts on her clothes. She offers Ānanda a seat, pays homage to him, and sits down to one side. Apart from this circumstantial difference, Ānanda's discourse in the Chinese version is almost exactly as in the Pāli version.

844 *Setughāto vutto bhagavatā*. Mp: "The *demolition of the bridge* (*setughātaṃ*): the demolition of the state and the demolition of its condition (*padaghātaṃ paccayaghātaṃ*)." The expression is also in **3:74**. See p. 1660, note 497.

845 Mp: "Based on the present nutriment of edible food, using it carefully, he abandons the nutriment consisting in past kamma; but the craving for present edible food should be abandoned."

846 The Chinese version reads: "Sister, by not indulging it, one abandons and severs sexual desire, the connecting bridge (和合橋梁)." It seems that *setughāto* must have been an idiom meaning that any connection with a particular state should be destroyed. Mp says that when Ānanda reached the end of the discourse, the bhikkhunī's passion for him had vanished.

847 *Sugata*. Lit., "Well-Gone." One of the most common epithets of the Buddha, occasionally also used for arahant disciples.

848 *Bhikkhū duggahitaṃ suttantaṃ pariyāpuṇanti dunnikkhittehi padabyañjanehi*. See **2:20**. I follow Brahmāli's suggestion that *suttantaṃ*

here has an implicitly plural sense; for other examples, see Vin III 159,12, and Vin IV 344,21.

849 Ce is missing the *uddāna* verse at the end of this vagga. Hence I base the titles on Be.

850 In Pāli: *dukkhā paṭipadā dandhābhiññā, dukkhā paṭipadā khippābhiññā, sukhā paṭipadā dandhābhiññā, sukhā paṭipadā khippābhiññā.*

851 *Ānantariyaṃ pāpuṇāti āsavānaṃ khayāya.* The word *ānantariya* is of rare occurrence, so its meaning must be determined inferentially. One clue is the Ratana Sutta, which says: *yam buddhaseṭṭho parivaṇṇayī suciṃ samādhim ānantarikaññam āhu* (Sn 226). Any difference between *ānantarika* and *ānantariya* is insignificant, as the terminations *-iya* and *-ika* are often interchangeable. Another clue is SN 22:81, at III 96–99, where the Buddha addresses the question: "How should one know and see to attain immediately (lit. 'without interval') the destruction of the taints?" (*evaṃ . . . jānato evaṃ passato anantarā āsavānaṃ khayo hoti*). Other AN suttas—**3:102**, I 158,7–12, and **5:23**, III 16,29–17,2—speak about the mind being "properly concentrated for the destruction of the taints" (*sammā samādhiyati āsavānaṃ khayāya*). See too **5:170**, III 202,27–33, which speaks about certain conditions "such that immediately afterward the destruction of the taints occurs" (*anantarā āsavānaṃ khayo hoti*). Thus, the "immediacy condition" spoken of here seems to be a state in which the mind is properly concentrated and, at the same time, has acquired the insight that brings about the destruction of the taints. Mp explains *ānantariya* with reference to the Abhidhamma concept of an immediate succession between path and fruit: "The 'immediacy condition' is the concentration of the path, which immediately yields its result (*anantaravipākadāyakaṃ maggasamādhiṃ*)." Though the suttas do not employ the scheme of the cognitive process that underlies the concept of path and fruition moments, the expression "immediacy condition" does suggest a state of complete ripeness for the breakthrough to arahantship.

852 The trainee powers (*sekhabalāni*), defined at **5:2**, partly differ from the five powers included among the thirty-seven aids to enlightenment.

853 Here, *sameti*, "calms [it] down," is an addition to the usual formula, intended to subsume this discipline under "the calming practice."

854 Mp says that for Moggallāna, the first three paths were achieved by pleasant practice and sluggish direct knowledge, but the path of arahantship was won by pleasant practice and quick direct knowledge. In **7:61** it is seen that Moggallāna often had to struggle with drowsiness in his practice for arahantship. He

often regressed and needed the help of the Buddha to progress further, as shown in SN 40:1–9, IV 262–69.

855 In this sutta the phrase *kāyassa bhedā*, "with the breakup of the body," is not followed by *paraṃ maraṇā*, "after death," as it normally is. The omission seems deliberate. Perhaps the purpose is to indicate that the person being described can attain nibbāna at the very moment of death, without having to continue on to another existence.

856 According to this sutta, the distinction between the use of repugnant objects and the jhānas determines whether one attains nibbāna through exertion (*sasaṅkhāraparinibbāyī*) or without exertion (*asaṅkhāraparinibbāyī*). The distinction between prominent faculties and feeble faculties determines whether one attains nibbāna in this very life (*diṭṭh'eva dhamme*) or with the breakup of the body (*kāyassa bhedā*). Mp says that the first and second persons are dry-insight meditators (*sukkhavipassakā*) who attend to conditioned phenomena as their meditation object (*saṅkhāranimittaṃ upaṭṭhapenti*). *Sasaṅkhārena* is glossed with *sappayogena*, which supports my rendering "through exertion." The third and fourth persons are those who take serenity as their vehicle (*samathayānikā*).

857 With Ce and Be I read *maggehi*, as against Ee *aṅgehi*. The latter is likely to be an editorial error. Though Mp does not provide a gloss here, the passage is cited at Paṭis II 92,9, and commented on at Paṭis-a III 584,24–25, in a way that requires *maggehi*: ***Catūhi maggehī*** *ti upari vuccamānehi catūhi paṭipadāmaggehi, na ariyamaggehi* ("*By four paths*: by the four paths of practice spoken about below, not by the noble paths").

858 Mp explains this as the first world-transcending path, but Mp-ṭ says: "This is said with reference to the path of stream-entry (*sotāpattimagga*), but the meaning of this passage can be understand simply by way of the mundane [preparatory] path" (*lokiyamaggavasen'eva*).

859 Mp and Mp-ṭ, read together, say that because there is no development and cultivation of the world-transcending path, which lasts for only one mind-moment, he develops and cultivates the preparatory mundane path (*pubbabhāgiyo lokiyamaggo*) for the purpose of attaining the higher world-transcending paths. Then the fetters are abandoned and the underlying tendencies are uprooted by the successive paths (*maggappaṭipāṭiya pahīyanti byantī honti*).

860 Mp: "This is a person who naturally gains insight. Based on insight, he produces concentration."

861 *Yuganaddhaṃ bhāveti*. Mp says that each time he attains a

meditative attainment (*samāpatti*), he explores it by way of its conditioned phenomena. And having explored its conditioned phenomena, he enters the next attainment. Thus, having attained the first jhāna, he emerges and explores its conditioned phenomena as impermanent, etc. Then he enters the second jhāna, emerges, and explores its conditioned phenomena, and so on up to the base of neither-perception-nor-non-perception. Since, however, *yuganaddha* means literally "yoked together," some interpret the term to mean that in this mode of practice serenity and insight occur simultaneously. The commentarial system does not acknowledge this possibility but several suttas might be read as suggesting that insight can occur within the jhāna and does not require the meditator to withdraw before beginning contemplation. In AN, see in particular **9:36**; see too MN 52.4–14, I 350–52; MN 64.9–15, I 435–37.

862 The readings vary. Ee has *dhammuddhaccaviggahītamanā*; the termination *-manā* is suspicious. Be has *-viggahitaṃ mānasaṃ*. Ce has *-viggahītaṃ mānaṃ*. While *manā* and *mānasaṃ* can both be translated as "mind," *mānaṃ* normally means "conceit." The Sinhala translation seems to support this by rendering *mānaṃ* as *adhimānaya* (Pāli *adhimāna*), "overestimation of oneself," but to speak of "conceit"—as opposed to "mind"—as being "grasped by restlessness" does not make good sense. Mp glosses the term without specifying the subject: "Grasped, thoroughly grasped, by restlessness, which consists of the ten corruptions of insight (*dasa vipassan'upakkilesā*; see Vism 633–38, Ppn 20.105–28) in regard to the *dhammas* of serenity and insight." Nothing in the text itself suggests the corruptions of insight are involved. I understand the person being described here as a practitioner who reflects deeply on the Dhamma, acquires a sense of urgency, and then finally settles down and gains insight when meeting with favorable supporting conditions. In the next sentence of the text, the word rendered "mind" is *cittaṃ*.

863 The first part of this sutta, up to the section on the four acquisitions of individuality, is also at SN 12:25, II 39–41, but addressed to Ānanda.

864 Mp explains this with reference to the Abhidhamma scheme of *cittas*, types of consciousness; see CMA 32–40, 46–64. I summarize Mp's explanation: Bodily volition is of twenty kinds by way of the eight kinds of sense-sphere wholesome *cittas* and twelve kinds of unwholesome *cittas*. So too for verbal volition. But mental volition includes these as well as the nine kinds of sublime (*mahaggata*) volition, namely, volition associated with the five jhānas of the Abhidhamma system and the four formless attainments.

Because of bodily volition, there arises pleasure conditioned by the eight kinds of wholesome kamma, and pain conditioned by the twelve kinds of unwholesome kamma, that is, the kamma generated in the corresponding active types of consciousness. So too for the other two doors. Ignorance is a condition (*avijjāpaccayā va*) because, there being ignorance, volition occurs in the three doors as a condition for pleasure and pain. Thus this sutta statement refers to ignorance as the root cause. Pleasure and pain arise "internally" (*ajjhattaṃ*) when they arise in oneself. The word seems to underscore the retributive aspect of kamma.

865 Mp: "One acts on one's own (*sāmaṃ*) when one initiates the action without instigation from others. One instigates activity because of others when others encourage or command one to act. One acts with clear comprehension (*sampajāno*) when one knows the wholesome and unwholesome as such, and their respective results as such. If one does not understand this, one acts without clear comprehension."

866 *Imesu bhikkhave dhammesu avijjā anupatitā*. Mp: "Ignorance is comprised in the volitional states analyzed above, functioning both as a coexistent condition and as a decisive-support condition (*sahajātavasena ca upanissayavasena ca*). Thus the round of existence and its root, ignorance, are shown."

867 Mp: "Arahants are seen acting with the body. They sweep the courtyard of the shrine and the bodhi tree, go out and return, do various duties, etc., but in their case the twenty volitions occurring at the bodily door no longer produce kammic results (*avipākadhammataṃ āpajjanti*). Here, it is the volition that occurs at the body door that is intended by the word 'body.' The same method applies to the other two." Mp-ṭ: "When arahants perform actions, how is it that they create no bodily or other kinds of kamma? In the sense that these deeds do not bear results, for an action done by an arahant is neither wholesome nor unwholesome but a mere activity (*kiriyamatta*) that does not yield results."

868 Mp: "'Field,' etc., are names for wholesome and unwholesome kamma. For that is a *field* (*khetta*) in the sense of a place where results grow; a *site* (*vatthu*) in the sense of their foundation; a *base* (*āyatana*) in the sense of a cause; a *location* (*adhikaraṇa*) in the sense of a locale."

869 In Ee this sentence marks the beginning of a new sutta, and thus at this point Ee's numbering exceeds mine by one. Both Ce and Be, in accord with Mp, treat the previous passage and this one as a single sutta. While this paragraph certainly looks like the beginning of an independent sutta, and perhaps originally was, Mp takes it to be continuous with the analysis of volition

stated above. It says that up to this point the Buddha has shown the kamma accumulated in the three doors; now he shows the places where that kamma ripens. "Acquisition of individuality" (*attabhāvappaṭilābha*) is an individual existence, the combination of body and mind that constitutes a particular life.

870 Mp identifies these beings as the devas corrupted by play (*khiḍḍāpadosikā devā*). While they are enjoying celestial delights in their heavenly realm, they sometimes forget to eat and drink, and because they miss a meal they wither away like a garland placed in the sun. See Bodhi 2007: 159–60.

871 Mp says these are the devas corrupted by mind (*manopadosika devā*), who dwell in the realm of the four great kings. When they become angry at one another, their mutual anger becomes the cause for both to pass away. See Bodhi 2007: 160–61.

872 Mp says that these are human beings. For people kill themselves and others kill them. Thus they perish either on account of their own volition or because of the volition of others.

873 Mp: "[Question:] Why does Sāriputta pose this question? Isn't he able to answer it himself? [Reply:] He is able, but he does not speak because he thinks, 'This question is in the domain of a Buddha.'"

874 Mp: "The former, who *come back to this state of being* (*āgantāro itthattaṃ*), are those who return to the five aggregates in the sense sphere; they are not reborn there [in the realm where they pass away] or in a higher realm. Those who *do not come back to this state of being* (*anāgantāro itthattaṃ*) do not return to the five aggregates or take a lower rebirth. They are either reborn there [in the realm where they pass away] or in a higher realm, or they attain final nibbāna right there. When it is said that they are reborn in a higher realm, this is said in the case of those who had been born in a lower existence. But from the realm of neither-perception-nor-non-perception, there is no rebirth into a higher realm."

875 *Odhiso vyañjanaso*. Mp glosses these two words respectively with *kāraṇaso akkharaso*, "by way of reasons [or cases], by way of the letter." The meaning is not entirely clear to me and Mp-ṭ does not elaborate. The *paṭisambhidās* are explained at Vism 440–43, Ppn 14.21–31, on the basis of Vibh 292–94 (Be §§718–24), which analyzes them from several angles. Briefly: Knowledge of meaning is analytical knowledge of meaning (*atthapaṭisambhidā*); knowledge of Dhamma is analytical knowledge of Dhamma (*dhammapaṭisambhidā*); knowledge of how to express and articulate the Dhamma is analytical knowledge of language (*niruttipaṭisambhidā*); and knowledge about knowledges is analytical knowledge of discernment (*paṭibhānapaṭisambhidā*). This

last analytical knowledge seems to refer to the ability to spontaneously apply the other three types of knowledge to clearly communicate the Dhamma. From a more philosophical perspective, *attha* is considered the result of a cause (*hetuphala*) and *dhamma* a cause (*hetu*) producing an effect. Therefore the analytical knowledge of meaning is correlated with knowledge of the first and third noble truths, analytical knowledge of Dhamma with knowledge of the second and fourth noble truths. Analytical knowledge of meaning is knowledge of each factor of dependent origination in its role as an effect arisen from a condition, and analytical knowledge of Dhamma is knowledge of the same factor in its role as a condition giving rise to an effect.

876 Ee's *pakāsemi*, as the third verb, is not in Ce or Be. *Pakāseti* is also absent in the same sequence of verbs at **3:136**, I 286,9–10, also in Ee.

877 The text is cryptic here and may have become garbled in the course of transmission. Mp supplies a verb to the first part of the sentence, *upagacchatu*, which I include and translate in brackets. Mp fills out *ahaṃ veyyākaraṇena* with *ahamassa pañhakathanena cittaṃ ārādhessāmi* ("I will satisfy his mind by answering the question"). I have also added this in brackets.

878 Mp: "'Our teacher, who is highly skilled in these things that have been attained by us, is present. If I had not realized the analytical knowledge of meaning, he would dismiss me, telling me to first realize it.' Even while sitting in front of the teacher, he roars a lion's roar."

879 The dialogue here seems to be concerned with the "ontological status" of the arahant who has attained the nibbāna element without residue remaining, that is, with the question whether the liberated person exists or does not exist after death.

880 Mp glosses *mā h'evaṃ* with *evaṃ mā bhaṇi*, "Do not speak thus," and explains that the four questions are asked by way of eternalism, annihilationism, partial eternalism, and "eel-wriggling" (*sassata-uccheda-ekaccasassata-amarāvikkhepa*). Thus Sāriputta rejects each question. "Eel-wriggling" is agnosticism, skepticism, or intellectual evasiveness.

881 *Appapañcaṃ papañceti*. Mp: "He creates proliferation [or speculations] in relation to something that should not be proliferated [or speculated about]. He travels along a path that one should not travel on." The Pāli word *papañca* suggests mental fabrication, obsessive mental construction, and deluded conceptualization, which the commentaries say arise from craving, conceit, and wrong views (*taṇhā, māna, diṭṭhi*). It seems to me that Mp understands *appapañcaṃ* as a contraction of *appapañciyaṃ*. A Chinese parallel, SĀ 249, says at T II 60a16–20: "If one [makes any of these

assertions about the six bases for contact], these are just empty words (此則虛言). With the vanishing, fading away, cessation, and stilling of the six bases for contact, one relinquishes empty falsehood (離諸虛偽) and attains nibbāna."

882 *Tāvatā papañcassa gati*. Mp: "As far as the range of the six bases extends, just so far extends the range of proliferation, distinguished by way of craving, views, and conceit."

883 Ee treats this sutta as a continuation of the preceding one, without counting it separately. Thus at this point Ee's numbering catches up with Ce and Be.

884 The dialogue, according to Mp, refers to making an end to saṃsāra, the entire round of suffering (*vaṭṭadukkhassa antakaro hoti, sakalaṃ vaṭṭadukkhaṃ paricchinnaṃ parivaṭumaṃ katvā tiṭṭhati*).

885 *Caraṇasampanno yathābhūtaṃ jānāti passati. Yathābhūtaṃ jānaṃ passaṃ antakaro hoti*. This differs from the previous assertion (that one cannot become an end-maker by means of knowledge and conduct) in its emphasis on knowing and seeing (as well as conduct) as active functions rather than subjective possessions tinged with clinging.

886 This sutta merges **2:130–33**.

887 Much of this is also in MN 62.8–11, I 421–23. See too MN 28 and MN 140, which treat the topic more elaborately.

888 Ee's *paññāya cittaṃ virājeti* is clearly wrong. In each of the four paragraphs, *paññāya* here should be replaced by the name of the element.

889 *Sakkāyanirodhaṃ*. Mp: "The cessation of personal existence, that is, the round of existence with its three realms; the meaning is nibbāna."

890 These are explained at Vibh 330–31 (Be §799), though in terms of wisdom (*paññā*). I quote only the text on the first jhāna: "When perception and attention are accompanied by sensuality in one who attains the first jhāna, wisdom pertains to deterioration; when mindfulness is stabilized in accordance with its nature, wisdom pertains to stabilization; when perception and attention are unaccompanied by thought, wisdom pertains to distinction. When perception and attention are accompanied by disenchantment, conjoined with dispassion, wisdom pertains to penetration" (*paṭhamassa jhānassa lābhiṃ kāmasahagatā saññāmanasikārā samudācaranti hānabhāginī paññā; tadanudhammatā sati santiṭṭhati ṭhitibhāginī paññā; avitakkasahagatā saññāmanasikārā samudācaranti visesabhāginī paññā; nibbidāsahagatā saññāmanasikārā samudācaranti virāgupasaṃhitā nibbedhabhāginī paññā*). Similar distinctions are made for each of the higher attainments.

891 This passage is also included in the Mahāparinibbāna Sutta, DN 16.4.7, at II 124–26.

892 *Mahāpadese*. Mp glosses as *mahā-okāse* (apparently as if the compound could be resolved *mahā* + *padese*) and as *mahā-apadese*, the latter explained as "great reasons stated with reference to such great ones as the Buddha and others" (*buddhādayo mahante mahante apadisitvā vuttāni mahākāraṇāni*). This second resolution is certainly to be preferred. DOP gives, among the meanings of *apadesa*, "designation, pointing out, reference, witness, authority." *Cattāro mahāpadesā* is sometimes rendered "four great authorities" but the sutta actually specifies only two authorities, the suttas and the Vinaya. Walshe, in LDB, renders it as "four criteria." I understand the term to mean "four great references," the four provenances of a teaching.

893 *Tāni padabyañjanāni...sutte otāretabbāni vinaye sandassetabbāni*. Mp gives various meanings of *sutte* and *vinaye* here, some improbable. Clearly, this instruction presupposes that there already existed a body of discourses and a systematic Vinaya that could be used to evaluate other texts proposed for inclusion as authentic utterances of the Buddha. *Otāretabbāni* is gerundive plural of *otārenti*, "make descend, put down or put into," and *otaranti*, just below, means "descend, come down, go into." My renderings, respectively, as "check for them" and "are included among" are adapted to the context. *Sandassetabbāni* is gerundive plural of *sandassenti*, "show, make seen," and *sandissanti* means "are seen."

894 The clearer of the two Chinese parallels is in DĀ 2, at T I 17b29–18a22. Here *cattāro mahāpadesā* is rendered 四大教法, "four great teaching *dhammas*." I translate the first declaration (T I 17c2–13) as follows: "If there is a bhikkhu who claims: 'Venerable ones, in that village, city, country, I personally heard [this] from the Buddha, I personally received this teaching,' you should not disbelieve what you hear from him, nor should you reject it, but through the suttas determine whether it is true or false; based on the Vinaya, based on the Dhamma, probe it thoroughly. If what he says is not the sutta, not the Vinaya, not the Dhamma, then you should say to him: 'The Buddha did not say this. What you have received is mistaken! [Or: You have received it erroneously!] For what reason? Because based on the suttas, based on the Vinaya, based on the Dhamma, we [find] that what you said deviates from the Dhamma. Venerable one, you should not uphold this, you should not report it to people, but should discard it.' But if what he says is based on the suttas, based on the Vinaya, based on the Dhamma, then you should say to him: 'What you said was truly spoken by the Buddha. For what

reason? Because based on the suttas, based on the Vinaya, based on the Dhamma, we [find] that what you said accords with the Dhamma. Venerable one, you should uphold this, you should widely report it to people; you should not discard it.' This is the first great teaching *dhamma*."

895 I follow Ce and Ee here. Be differs and would be translated: "But if, when one does not speak about what one has seen, wholesome qualities decline and unwholesome qualities increase, I say that one should speak about what one has seen." Each of the following paragraphs varies in the same way.

896 *Nāhaṃ kvacana, kassaci kiñcanatasmiṃ, na ca mama kvacana, katthaci kiñcanatātthi*. At **3:70**, I 206,18–20, this formula is said to have been used by the Nigaṇṭhas to cultivate non-possessiveness. I follow the reading in Ce. Be is almost the same, except that it has *kvacani* twice in place of *kvacana*. Ee at the end reads *kiñcanaṃ n'atthi* rather than *kiñcanat'atthi* or *kiñcanatātthi*. This reading is also found in older Sinhala-script editions, and in the Be reading of MN 106.8.

My rendering follows Mp, which comments: "This is an explanation of four-pointed emptiness (*catukkoṭisuññatā*). *I am not anywhere* (*nāhaṃ kvacana*): He does not see [his] self anywhere. *The belonging of anyone* (*kassaci kiñcanatasmiṃ*): He does not regard his self as an entity that could be taken up by anyone else, that is, he cannot be taken up by thinking of him as a brother in the position of a brother, a friend in the position of a friend, an employee in the position of an employee. *Nor is there anywhere anything . . . that is mine* (*na ca mama kvacana*): Here, we temporarily put aside the word 'mine' (*mama*). The meaning is then: 'He does not see anywhere the self of another.' Now, having brought in the word 'mine,' we get: [*Anything*] *in any place that is mine* (*mama kvacana, katthaci kiñcanatātthi*): He does not see: 'There is somewhere the self of another that might become my belonging.' The meaning is that he does not see any self of another in any position that could be taken up as his belonging: a brother in the position of a brother, a friend in the position of a friend, an employee in the position of an employee."

897 *Ākiñcaññaṃyeva paṭipadaṃ paṭipanno hoti*. Mp says that he is practicing the way without impediments, without grasping (*nippalibodhaṃ niggahaṇameva paṭipadaṃ paṭipanno hoti*). MN 106.8, II 263,33–264,3, however, offers this formula as a meditation device for attaining the base of nothingness (*ākiñcaññāyatanaṃ samāpajjati*).

898 The questions and the Buddha's reply are stated as verse at SN 1:62, I 39.

899 Mp identifies both *ummagga* and *paṭibhāna* with wisdom (*paññā*): "Acumen is rising up, that is, the movement of wisdom. Or wisdom itself is called 'acumen,' in the sense of rising up. It is [also called] 'discernment' in the sense of discerning" (***ummaggo*** *ti ummujjanaṃ, paññāgamanan ti attho. Paññā eva vā ummujjanaṭṭhena* ***ummaggo*** *ti vuccati. Sā va paṭibhānaṭṭhena* ***paṭibhānaṃ***).

900 There is a change in the text from *ceteti* in the preceding sentence to *cintamāno cinteti* here. It is hard to determine whether this has any significance. Mp does not comment on it, so I assume it is unimportant.

901 Mp identifies him as Uddaka Rāmaputta, one of the Buddha's teachers before his enlightenment. See MN 26.16, I 165–66.

902 Mp explains the purport of this apparent digression thus: "The brahmin, being a good person himself, praises King Eḷeyya, his retinue, and Uddaka Rāmaputta. For the bad person is like a blind man, and a good person like one with good sight. As a blind man does not see either one who is blind or one with sight, so a bad person does not know either a good person or a bad one. But just as one with good sight can see both a blind person and one with sight, so a good person can know both a good person and a bad one. The brahmin [Vassakāra], thinking: 'Even Todeyya, being a good person, knew who were bad men,' was delighted because of this and said: 'It is astounding, Master Gotama!'"

903 Be and Ee read *sotānugatānaṃ bhikkhave dhammānaṃ*. Ce has *sotānudhatānaṃ* here, and *sotānudhātā honti* just below, as against Be and Ee *sotānugatā honti*; however, Ce has *sotānugataṃ* in the *uddāna* verse. Mp (Ce) reads *sotānugatānaṃ*. Mp glosses: "Having applied the sensory ear, one has determined [the meaning] with the ear of knowledge" (*pasādasotaṃ odahitvā ñāṇasotena vavatthapitānaṃ*). This seems to support *sotānudhatānaṃ*, but just below Mp (Be) glosses *sotānugatā honti* with *sotaṃ anuppattā anupaviṭṭhā honti*, which suggests the reading *sotānugatānaṃ*. Mp (Ce), though reading *sotānugatānaṃ* in the lemma of the earlier sentence, inconsistently reads here *sotānudhatā honti*. Thus a number of texts reveal that the compilers were themselves uncertain of the reading. There is no recorded Chinese parallel.

904 The sentence is highly problematic, with respect to both reading and meaning. First, the reading: with Ce I read *tassa tattha sukhino dhammapadāpilapanti*. I construe *dhammapadāpilapanti* as a *sandhi* formed from *dhammapadā* and *apilapanti*, meaning "to recite, to enunciate." The verb is possibly a corruption of *abhilapanti* (see DOP sv *apilapati*). Be has *tassa tattha sukhino dhammapadā plavanti*. Ee's *dhammapadāni pi lapanti*, with a hiatus between *pi* and *lapanti*,

seems unacceptable. In a short paper on this passage, Norman (1992: 257–59) opines that the verb is *api-lapanti* = *abhi* + *lapanti*. The Be reading *plavanti* apparently takes the verb to be from the root *plu*, to float, perhaps via *pilavanti*.

A second problem arises from the phrase *tassa tattha sukhino*. *Sukhino* can be either a dative-genitive singular or a nominative plural, and thus the phrase can be construed to mean either "to him who is happy there" (with *tassa* and *sukhino* as dative singulars denoting the same subject) or "to him, the happy ones there" (with *tassa* denoting the one reborn, and *sukhino* a nominative plural denoting those already there). The connection of the phrase with the words that follow will differ depending on which alternative is chosen. Mp (Be) opts for the first alternative, taking *dhammapadā* as the nominative subject, *plavanti* as the verb, and *tassa sukhino* as the dative indirect object: "Passages of the Dhamma float up to him who is happy there." Commenting on the phrase in this sense, Mp (Be) says: "To the one reborn who is muddled in mind in his next existence, the teachings of the Buddha's words that he had recited, being rooted in his past recitation of them, all float up clearly discerned like images in a pure mirror." Mp (Ce), interestingly, records the lemma as *dhammapadāpilapanti*, and reads the gloss: *te sabbe pasanne ādāse chāyā viya apilapanti upaṭṭhahanti*. I assume that the verb *apilapanti* entered here because Sinhala-script manuscripts of AN retained the original verb, which then migrated back to the commentary to replace *plavanti* or *pilavanti*. Otherwise it is hard to account for *plavanti* in Be. Mp (Ce) also includes the verb *upaṭṭhahanti*, "[they] appear to," missing in Be, perhaps through editorial oversight. This verb is evidently intended as a gloss on *apilapanti*/ *plavanti*.

I depart from Mp and follow Norman in taking *tassa* and *sukhino* to denote different persons: *tassa* the indirect dative object and *sukhino* the nominative plural subject. I take the verb to be transitive *apilapanti* (= *abhilapanti*) with *dhammapadā* its direct object. Norman (p. 259) affirms that neuter nouns in the accusative plural occasionally end in *-ā*. Thus I understand the line to mean that "the happy ones"—the devas in the celestial realm—"recite passages of Dhamma to him," that is, to the person reborn there.

905 Here and just below, I read with Ce and Be *purimavohārā pacchimavohāraṃ*.

906 I render this freely to conform to ordinary English diction. The Pāli *tathābhūto kho ayaṃ lokasannivāso tathābhūto ayaṃ attabhāvapaṭilābho* literally means: "This dwelling in the world is

of such a nature, this obtaining of individual existence is of such a nature. . . ." *Lokasannivāso* is also in **3:40 §2**.

907 This charge is also at SN 42:13, IV 340,23–29. According to MN 56.8, I 375,24–26, it originated among the Jains.

908 This is the Buddha's advice to the Kālāmas at **3:65**. The interrogation that follows also parallels that used with the Kālāmas, but with an additional unwholesome motive.

909 BHSD defines *sārambha* as "quarrelsomeness" and connects the word with Skt *saṃrambha*, which SED explains as "the act of grasping or taking hold of," and gives as meanings "vehemence, impetuosity . . . fury, wrath against." Since the sutta speaks about *sārambha* as occurring through body, speech, and mind, I settle for "vehemence."

910 Ce reads *lobhaṃ vineyya vineyya viharanto*, and so in relation to *dosa, moha*, and *sārambha*. I try to capture this sense with "constantly," though "repeatedly" might also have been used. Be and Ee read simply *lobhaṃ vineyya viharanto*.

911 See MN 56.26, II 383,32–384,7.

912 The words *sace ceteyyuṃ* are in Ce and Ee, but not Be.

913 *Pārisuddhipadhāniyaṅgāni*. I translate the compound in accordance with Mp's resolution: *pārisuddhi-atthāya padhāniyaṅgāni*.

914 *Sīlapārisuddhipadhāniyaṅga, cittapārisuddhipadhāniyaṅga, diṭṭhipārisuddhipadhāniyaṅga, vimuttipārisuddhipadhāniyaṅga*. *Sīlavisuddhi, cittavisuddhi*, and *diṭṭhivisuddhi* are included among the seven purifications (*satta visuddhi*) in MN 24, which is used as the scaffolding for Vism. The four are included among the nine *pārisuddhipadhāniyaṅgāni* in DN 34.2.2, III 288,16–25, where they are all conjoined with the word *visuddhi*, for instance, *sīlavisuddhipārisuddhipadhāniyaṅgaṃ*. It is intriguing that no suttas on the seven purifications are included in the Sevens. This suggests a late origin for the scheme, as well as a late origin for MN 24.

915 *Tattha tattha paññāya anuggahessāmi*. Mp: "In this and that respect I will assist it with the wisdom of insight (*vipassanāpaññāya*)."

916 Since, in the Nikāyas, direct understanding of the four noble truths typically marks the attainment of stream-entry, purification of view here can be identified with the wisdom of the stream-enterer. This stands in contrast with the scheme of Vism, in which purification of view (*diṭṭhivisuddhi*) is the third of the seven purifications. Vism explains it as the clear understanding of mental and material phenomena (*nāmarūpavavatthāna*), also known as the delimitation of conditioned phenomena (*saṅkhāraparicccheda*). In the Vism scheme, the attainment of stream-entry (and each subsequent path) occurs only with the

seventh purification, purification of knowledge and vision (*ñāṇadassanavisuddhi*).

917 A separate purification of this name does not occur in the Vism scheme, but perhaps it could be considered the culmination of purification of knowledge and vision.

918 This seems to have been a tenet of the Jains, who sought, through the practice of self-affliction, to eradicate past kamma. See the teaching given by Nātaputta (Mahāvīra) at **3:74**.

919 *So navañca kammaṃ na karoti, purāṇañ ca kammaṃ phussa phussa vyantīkaroti.* See p. 1660, note 499. Mp's paraphrase here differs slightly from the earlier one: "Having contacted the kamma again and again by contact with knowledge, he destroys the kamma to be eliminated by means of knowledge. Having contacted the result again and again by resultant-contact, he destroys the kamma to be eliminated by [experiencing] the result."

920 Mp: "Because he has acquired equanimity, which is embraced by mindfulness and clear comprehension and has mental balance as its characteristic, 'he dwells equanimous,' mentally balanced in relation to those objects" (*satisampajaññapariggahitāya majjhattākāralakkhaṇāya upekkhāya tesu ārammaṇesu upekkhako majjhatto hutvā viharati*).

921 This shows the arahant's attitude toward present experience. He knows that his feelings continue only as long as the body and vitality continue, and that with the perishing of the body and the extinction of vitality all feelings will come to an end. Mp explains "will become cool right here (*idh'eva sītībhavissanti*)" thus: "They will *become cool,* devoid of the disturbance and trouble caused by the occurrence [of the life process]; they will never recur. [This takes place] *right here,* without his going elsewhere by way of rebirth."

922 Mp: "Here is the application of the simile: The body should be seen as like the tree. Wholesome and unwholesome kamma are like the shadow depending on the tree. The meditator is like the man who wants to remove the shadow; wisdom is like the shovel; concentration is like the basket; insight is like the pick (*khaṇitti,* not mentioned in the sutta; DOP defines both *kuddāla* and *khaṇitti* as a digging tool, a spade, a trowel). The time of digging up the roots with the pick is like the time of cutting off ignorance with the path of arahantship. The time of reducing the stump to pieces is like the time of seeing the aggregates; the time of splitting the pieces is like the time of seeing the sense bases; the time of reducing them to slivers is like the time of seeing the elements. The time of drying the slivers in the wind and sun is like the time of applying bodily and mental energy. The time

of burning the slivers in a fire is like the time of burning the defilements with knowledge. The time of reducing them to ash is like the time when the five aggregates are still occurring [after one reaches arahantship]. The time of winnowing the ashes in a strong wind and letting them be carried away by the current is like the cessation of the five aggregates, which have been cut off at the root with no further rebirth. As the ashes winnowed and carried away go to the indiscernible state (*apaññattibhāvūpagamo*), so should one understand the indescribable state (*appaṇṇattibhāvo*) [reached] by the non-arising of resultant aggregates in renewed existence."

923 The crossing of the flood (*oghassa nittharaṇa*) is a metaphor for the crossing of saṃsāra or the eradication of defilements. The two factors mentioned by Sāḷha are *sīlavisuddhi* and *tapojigucchā*. The latter comprises diverse types of austerity and self-mortification rejected by the Buddha in his formulation of the "middle way." In his reply, the Buddha accepts purification of virtuous behavior as one of the factors of asceticism (*sāmaññaṅga*), but rejects austerity and disgust.

924 See **3:78**.

925 Mp explains right concentration spoken of above as the concentration of the path and fruit. Right view is the view of the path; the mention of the four noble truths points to the four paths and three fruits. Right liberation is the liberation of the fruit of arahantship. The mass of ignorance is split by the path of arahantship, which the disciple has reached before he gains the liberation of the fruit.

I assume this sutta is included in the Fours by way of moral purity (of body, speech, mind, and livelihood), right concentration, right view, and right liberation. However, the sutta itself is not sufficiently explicit about this and thus my numbering is hypothetical.

926 Queen Mallikā was the wife of King Pasenadi of Kosala.

927 The contents of this sutta are also included in MN 51.8–28, I 342–49.

928 The expression occurs also at **3:66**. See p. 1654, note 463.

929 The ascetic practices to be described are also at **3:156 §2**.

930 Be alone has an additional occupation here, *goghatako*, a cattle butcher.

931 See p. 1658, note 481.

932 Mp: "Craving is called *the ensnarer* (*jālinī*) because it is like a net. For as a net is sewn tightly together and is thoroughly interwoven, so too is craving. Or it is called the ensnarer because it is a net spread out over the three realms of existence. It is

streaming (*saritā*) because it streams and runs on here and there. It is *widespread* (*visaṭā*) because it is spread out and dispersed. And it is *sticky* (*visattikā*) because it sticks, attaches, fastens here and there."

933 I translate these phrases—some obscure—with the aid of Mp. "Related to the internal" (*ajjhattikassa upādāya*) means related to one's own five aggregates.

934 "Related to the external" (*bāhirassa upādāya*) means related to external five aggregates.

935 Mp says that "because of this" (*iminā*) should be understood to mean "because of this form . . . because of this consciousness" (*iminā rūpena vā . . . pe . . . viññāṇena*). The passage is opaque as it stands and I am not sure that Mp has caught the original intention. "Because of this" might have meant "because of a creator God," or "because of primordial matter" or "because of chance or necessity," etc.

936 I am unsure how to explain the inclusion of this sutta in the Fours. The reason may be the four terms used to describe craving, enclosed between dashes, but this is a mere hypothesis.

937 DOP defines the verb *usseneti* as "forms an association (with), is involved," but Mp glosses it with *ukkhipati*, which DOP says can mean "throws up; raises; lifts up, picks up, holds up; raises up, extols." What follows are the twenty modes of personal-existence view (*sakkāyadiṭṭhi*), the view of a real self existing in relation to the five aggregates. There are four modes in relation to each of the five aggregates.

938 There are different readings here: Ce *apajjhāyate*, Be *sampajjhāyati*, Ee *pajjhāyati*. Ee is missing this paragraph but includes the following paragraph; presumably, this was an editorial oversight rather than a difference in the manuscripts.

939 On these four terms, see p. 1681, note 656.

940 In Pāli: *cintākavi, sutakavi, atthakavi, paṭibhānakavi.* Mp says the first creates poetry after reflecting, the second does so based on what he has heard, the third based on a message, and the fourth spontaneously, through his own inspiration, like the elder Vaṅgīsa.

941 See MN 57.7–11, I 389–91.

942 Here an "afflictive bodily volitional activity" (*sabyāpajjhaṃ kāyasaṅkhāraṃ*) can be understood as the volition responsible for the three courses of unwholesome bodily kamma, an "afflictive verbal volitional activity" as the volition responsible for the four courses of unwholesome verbal kamma, and an "afflictive mental volitional activity" as the volition responsible for the three courses of unwholesome mental kamma.

943 The ten courses of wholesome kamma along with the volition of the jhānas.

944 The higher deva worlds.

945 *Devā subhakiṇhā.* These are the devas dwelling in the highest divine realm corresponding to the third jhāna.

946 Mp: "The volition of the path leading to the end of the round" (*vivaṭṭagāminī maggacetanā*).

947 I follow here the reading of Ce and Ee: *suññā parappavādā samaṇehi aññe ti.* Be reads *aññehi* for *aññe ti.* The same difference in readings between the editions occurs at MN I 63,30–64,1. In a line of verse without reference to a lion's roar DN II 151,22, has *suññā parappavādā samaṇehi aññe.* Mp says that the "other sects" are the proponents of the sixty-two views, who lack twelve kinds of ascetics: the four who have attained the fruits, the four cultivating the paths, and the four practicing insight to attain the respective paths.

948 *Adhikaraṇaṃ vūpasantaṃ.* See p. 1623, note 231.

949 The *pārājikas* are the most serious class of offenses. For bhikkhus, they consist of four offenses that entail expulsion from the Saṅgha: sexual intercourse, theft (to a degree punishable by law), murder of a human being, and making a false claim to a superhuman state of spiritual distinction. Bhikkhunīs have four additional *pārājikas.* The only way for one who has committed one of these offenses to "make amends for it in accordance with the Dhamma" is to admit it and relinquish one's status as a fully ordained monk or nun. For details, see Ṭhānissaro 2007a, chap. 4.

950 The text uses the word *bhante* here. Apparently this word was not used solely to address monks but also others in a superior position. Thus I here translate it as "worthy sirs."

951 The *saṅghādisesas* are the second most serious class of offenses. For bhikkhus, they include intentional emission of semen, touching a woman with a lustful mind, speaking lewdly to a woman, falsely accusing a virtuous bhikkhu of a *pārājika,* etc. Rehabilitation involves a complex process requiring formal meetings of the Saṅgha. For details, see Ṭhānissaro 2007a, chap. 5.

952 Ce and Ee *assapuṭaṃ,* Be *bhasmapuṭaṃ.* Mp: "[His deed] deserves to be punished with a reprehensible sack of ashes on his head" (*garahitabbachārikāpuṭena matthake abhighātārahaṃ*).

953 The *pācittiyas* are a class of offenses that can be cleared by confession to a fellow monastic. Presumably the *nissaggiya-pācittiyas,* offenses which also require the relinquishment of an unsuitable item, are also included under this heading. For details, see Ṭhānissaro 2007a, chaps. 7 and 8.

954 This is a smaller class of offenses that can be cleared by confession. For details, see Ṭhānissaro 2007a, chap. 9.

955 *Sikkhānisaṃsam idaṃ bhikkhave brahmacariyaṃ vussati paññuttaraṃ vimuttisāraṃ satādhipateyyaṃ*. In later suttas that use these metaphors (**8:83, 9:14, 10:58**), mindfulness precedes wisdom and liberation, but the present sutta explains the reason for the inversion of the normal sequence.

956 *Ābhisamācārikā sikkhā*. Mp: "This is a designation for the type of virtuous behavior that is prescribed by way of duties" (*vattavasena paññattisīlass'etaṃ adhivacanaṃ*). The commentaries draw a contrast between natural virtuous behavior (*pakatisīla*), modes of virtuous behavior with ethical significance, and prescription-based virtuous behavior (*paññattisīla*) derived from monastic rules prescribing conduct and deportment that are not intrinsically ethical, such as not eating after midday, not accepting money, not tickling another monk, etc. The latter are intended by *ābhisamācārikā sikkhā*.

957 Mp: "This is a designation for the four major types of virtuous behavior, which are the foundation for the spiritual life of the path" (*maggabrahmacariyassa ādibhūtānaṃ catunnaṃ mahāsīlānam etaṃ adhivacanaṃ*). Though Mp seems to confine this type of virtue to the four *pārājika* offenses, it certainly includes many more training rules included among the other classes of offenses.

958 Mp does not explain in what sense *paññā* is called *uttarā*, but says only: "They are well seen by the wisdom of the path along with insight" (*sahavipassanāya maggapaññāya sudiṭṭhā honti*).

959 Mp: "They are experienced by the experiential knowledge of the liberation of the fruit of arahantship" (*arahattaphalavimuttiyā ñāṇaphassena phuṭṭhā honti*).

960 As in **4:194**. Mp says that insight wisdom (*vipassanāpaññā*) is intended here.

961 See **2:55**.

962 As at SN 55:60, V 411. These are also called the four factors that lead to realization of the fruit of stream-entry (and the higher fruits). See SN 55–58, V 410–11.

963 Ee conjoins this sutta with the preceding one, whereas Ce and Be treat them as distinct.

964 These correspond to the four noble truths, but with the third and fourth truths inverted.

965 As at MN 26.5, I 161–62, but the latter is augmented by two more quests: for what is subject to sorrow and for what is subject to defilement. The noble quests are at MN 26.12, I 162–63.

966 See above, **4:32**. It seems to me that these two suttas should have been contiguous.

967 He is the monk who threatened to leave the Buddha if the latter would not answer his metaphysical questions. See MN 63, I 426–32, as well as MN 64.2–3, I 432–33; SN 35:95, IV 72–76.

968 See **4:9** above.
969 See SN 42:9, IV 324,25–25,3, on eight causes for the destruction of families.
970 An expanded parallel of **3:96**.
971 An expanded parallel of **3:98**. A parallel of **3:97**, on the nonreturner, is not found among the Fours.
972 In each sutta of the cluster, **4:265–73**, one of the faults comprised under (1) replaces "destroys life" in **4:264**.
973 As the three fourfold practices are to be developed for direct knowledge of lust, so they are to be developed for each of the other nine purposes. Thus there are a total of thirty suttas with respect to lust.

Notes to the Fives

974 *Pañca sekhabalāni*. Despite a partial overlap, these should not be confused with the five powers (*pañca balāni*) included among the thirty-seven aids to enlightenment, which are introduced at **5:13–16**. Mp: "*Trainee's powers*: the powers of the seven trainees. The power of faith is so called because it does not waver (*na kampati*) in the face of faithlessness; the power of moral shame does not waver in the face of moral shamelessness; the power of moral dread does not waver in the face of moral recklessness; the power of energy does not waver in the face of laziness; and the power of wisdom does not waver in the face of ignorance."
975 In Be only.
976 For the distinction between moral shame (*hiri*) and moral dread (*ottappa*), with references, see **2:8–9** and p. 1622, note 225.
977 Mp explains *udayatthagāminī paññā*, "the wisdom that discerns arising and passing away," as "the wisdom able to penetrate the arising and vanishing of the five aggregates (*pañcannaṃ khandhānaṃ udayavayagāminiyā udayañca vayañca paṭivijjhituṃ samatthāya*). It is the wisdom of the path together with insight wisdom (*vipassanāpaññāya c'eva maggapaññāya*)."
978 Mp: "This is said regarding one established in the fruit of stream-entry."
979 *Pubbāhaṃ bhikkhave ananussutesu dhammesu abhiññāvosānapāramippatto paṭijānāmi*. Mp: "'Since, by means of the four paths, I have completed the sixteenfold task in regard to the four [noble] truths, I claim to have reached consummation and perfection, having directly known it; [that is,] I have attained supremacy in accomplishing my task by finishing all tasks.' He shows the virtues he himself reached on the terrace of the great enlightenment."

980 See **4:8** for a parallel treatment of the four grounds of self-confidence, **6:64** for six Tathāgata's powers, and **10:21**, **10:22** for the ten Tathāgata's powers.

981 These are the five powers (*pañca balāni*) included among the thirty-seven aids to enlightenment (*bodhipakkhiyā dhammā*). These five powers are, as factors, identical with the five faculties (*pañc'indriyāni*), but the two are distinguished by a difference in aspect. See SN 48:43, V 219–20, and its commentary, Spk III 247,2–7, which explains that the faculty of faith means rulership in regard to conviction, and the power of faith means being unshakable in the face of absence of faith (*adhimokkhalakkhaṇe indaṭṭhena saddhindriyaṃ, assaddhiye akampanena saddhābalaṃ*). Similarly, the other four faculties respectively exercise rulership in regard to exertion, presence, non-distraction, and understanding (*paggaha-upaṭṭhāna-avikkhepa-pajānana*) and the other four powers remain unshakable in the face of laziness, muddle-mindedness, distraction, and ignorance (*kosajja-muṭṭhasacca-vikkhepa-avijjā*).

982 The four factors of stream-entry (*cattāri sotāpattiyaṅgāni*): unwavering confidence in the Buddha, the Dhamma, and the Saṅgha, and the virtuous behavior dear to the noble ones. See **9:27**, **10:92**.

983 Mp: "*The factor of proper conduct* (*ābhisamācārikaṃ dhammaṃ*) is supreme conduct consisting in prescribed virtuous behavior by way of duties (*uttamasamācārabhūtaṃ vattavasena paññattasīlaṃ*; see **4:245 §1**, where the term used is *ābhisamācārikā sikkhā*). *The factor of a trainee* (*sekhaṃ dhammaṃ*) is the virtuous behavior prescribed for a trainee. *Virtuous behaviors* (*sīlāni*) are 'the four great virtuous behaviors' (*cattāri mahāsīlāni*; presumably the four types of behavior safeguarded by the four *pārājika* rules). *Right view* is the right view of insight (*vipassanāsammādiṭṭhi*); *right concentration* is the concentration of the path and fruit."

984 From here to "not properly concentrated for the destruction of the taints" is also at SN 46:33, V 92.

985 As at **3:101**, I 254,10–12. Instead of *muddikāya* MN III 243,21, has *pavaṭṭikāya* and AN I 254,10, and AN I 257,26, have *paṭṭakāya*.

986 The following supernormal powers are also at **3:101**. On the "suitable basis," see p. 1669, note 562.

987 Mp identifies "knowledge and vision of things as they really are" (*yathābhūtañāṇadassana*) with tender insight; "disenchantment" (*nibbidā*) with strong insight; "dispassion" (*virāga*) with the noble path. Mp would resolve *vimuttiñāṇadassana* into *vimutti* and *ñāṇadassana*, with the former representing the fruit (*phala-vimutti*) and the latter reviewing knowledge (*paccavekkhaṇañāṇa*). I translate, however, in accordance with the normal meaning, and regard *vimutti* as merely implicit here.

988 Mp: "*Right view* here is the right view of insight. *Liberation of mind* (*cetovimutti*) is the concentration of the path and fruit, and *liberation by wisdom* (*paññāvimutti*) is the knowledge of the fruit." Ps I 164,29–31, commenting on *cetovimuttiṃ paññāvimuttim* at MN I 35,36–37, identifies liberation of mind with the concentration pertaining to the fruit of arahantship, and liberation by wisdom with the wisdom pertaining to the fruit of arahantship.

989 *Vimuttāyatanāni*. Mp: "Causes of being liberated" (*vimuccanakāraṇāni*).

990 *So tasmiṃ dhamme atthapaṭisaṃvedī ca hoti dhammapaṭisaṃvedī ca*. Mp explains *atthapaṭisaṃvedī* as "one knowing the meaning of the text" (*pāḷi-atthaṃ jānantassa*) and *dhammapaṭisaṃvedī* as "one knowing the text" (*pāḷiṃ jānantassa*), but this explanation is certainly too narrow and anachronistic. At **6:10**, we find *labhati atthavedaṃ labhati dhammavedaṃ*, which I render "[he] gains inspiration in the meaning, inspiration in the Dhamma." The stem of *paṭisaṃvedī* is *vedī*, which obviously connects *atthapaṭisaṃvedī* and *dhammapaṭisaṃvedī* to *atthaveda* and *dhammaveda*. The root *vid* is related both to *vijjā*, knowledge, and *vedanā*, feeling. Thus I suggest *veda* should be understood as inspired knowledge, or "inspiration," which gives rise to *pāmojja* and *pīti*, joy and rapture. It is likely that *atthapaṭisaṃvedī* and *dhammapaṭisaṃvedī* are related to *atthapaṭisambhidā* and *dhammapaṭisambhidā*, though in Pāli the latter are connected to the verb *bhindati*, "to break, to divide." See too pp. 1643–44, note 403.

991 Mp explains this to mean "he is concentrated by the concentration of the fruit of arahantship" (*arahattaphalasamādhinā samādhiyati*). It seems improbable to me that this was the original intention, for the context suggests that this is a concentration that serves as *the basis* for insight, and thereafter for the attainment of path and fruit, not a concentration that occurs *subsequent to* realization.

992 *Appamāṇan*. Mp: "Devoid of measure-creating qualities, world-transcending" (*pamāṇakaradhammarahitaṃ lokuttaraṃ*). Normally, the Nikāyas identify the measureless concentration with the four divine abodes (*brahmavihāra*), but some texts also recognize a world-transcending measureless concentration, obtained with the destruction of the three "measure-producing" qualities: greed, hatred, and delusion. See MN 43.35, I 298,8–9; SN 41:7, IV 297,11–12.

993 See p. 1669, notes 560–61.

994 Be omits *samādhiṃ*. Apparently this is not a typographical error, as according to a note in Ee, the same omission commonly occurs in Burmese manuscripts.

995 Since the concentration to be explained below is primarily the

four jhānas and, probably, the concentration of insight, Mp does not take the word *ariya* here to refer to the noble paths and fruits but as meaning "far away from the defilements abandoned by way of suppression (*vikkhambhanavasena pahīnakilesehi ārakā ṭhitassa*)." In the commentaries, *ariya* is sometimes derived from *āraka*. While the etymology is playful, it is likely that this *samādhi* belongs to the preparatory practice for reaching the paths and fruits, not to the paths and fruits themselves.

996 *Paccavekkhaṇanimittaṃ*. Mp identifies this as reviewing knowledge (*paccavekkhaṇañāṇameva*), apparently referring to the knowledge that reviews the path and fruition attainments. However, since this use of the word *paccavekkhaṇa* seems peculiar to the commentaries, I think it more likely that *paccavekkhaṇanimitta* here means the object being examined by insight.

997 See p. 1669, note 562.

998 *Cīraṭṭhitiko hoti*. Mp: "If one has acquired the mark [of concentration] while standing up, it is lost when one sits down. If one has acquired the mark while sitting, it is lost when one lies down. But for one who has resolved on walking up and down and acquired the mark in a moving object, it is not lost even when one stands still, sits down, and lies down."

999 Mp says that insight (*vipassanā*) has been discussed here in five ways.

1000 Mp identifies her as a daughter of King Pasenadi of Kosala.

1001 See **4:87 §4**.

1002 Only four kinds of superiority are mentioned, unless the fifth is wealth (*bhoga*) rather than authority (*ādhipateyya*), as mentioned in the following couplet.

1003 This includes an expanded parallel of **4:34**.

1004 Mp, commenting on the preceding sutta, says she was a daughter of King Bimbisāra.

1005 Strangely, neither Ce nor Ee contains this paragraph, which is in Be. It seems necessary to complete the set of five items. The paragraph is found in all three editions of the Fours. The parallel It §90, 88, does not include this paragraph, but It §90 is included in the Threes and thus must limit itself to three objects of faith.

1006 *Virāge dhamme*. The parallel statement at **4:34** has only *virāge*, but It §90 has *virāge dhamme*.

1007 These verses are also at **4:34**.

1008 *Attacatuttho*. Lit., "[with]-self-[as]-fourth," meaning that the Buddha is invited with three monks accompanying him.

1009 *Manāpakāyikānaṃ devānaṃ*. It is uncertain whether they are called thus in the sense that their bodies are agreeable, or in the sense that they belong to an agreeable group. The word *kāya* can mean either the physical body or a group. Mp identifies these deities with the "devas who delight in creation." Because they create any form that they wish and take delight in it, they are called either "delighting in creation" or "agreeable" (*manāpā nāma te devā ti nimmānaratī devā; te hi icchiticchitaṃ rūpaṃ māpetvā abhiramaṇato nimmānaratī ti ca manāpā ti ca vuccanti*). See **8:46**, where the Buddha enumerates eight conditions that lead to rebirth into the company of the agreeable-bodied devas.

1010 There are various readings of the compound here: Ce *icchācārena*, Be *issācārena*, Ee *issāvādena*. My translation follows Ee. Interestingly, at **8:46**, there is a verse with an identical couplet but with the reading *issāvādena* in all three editions. A search through CST 4.0 for *icchācār** turns up many occurrences of this compound in commentarial texts but none in canonical texts. It thus seems likely that the Ce reading has been influenced by the editor's familiarity with the commentarial expression.

1011 He was originally a lay follower of the Jains. The story of his conversion is told at **8:12**.

1012 *Sandiṭṭhikaṃ dānaphalaṃ*. A benefit that can be experienced in this present life.

1013 *Visārado upasaṅkamati amaṅkubhūto.* Mp explains "confidently" (*visārado*) as knowledgeable and joyous (*ñāṇasomanassappatto*) and "composed" (*amaṅkubhūto*) as not diffident (*na nittejabhūto*).

1014 *Samparāyikaṃ dānaphalaṃ*. With this fifth benefit, the Buddha has gone beyond Sīha's original request and explained, not a directly visible fruit of giving, but a fruit pertaining to the next life.

1015 *Nandana*: the Garden of Delight in the Tāvatiṃsa heaven.

1016 *Āyuṃ, vaṇṇaṃ, sukhaṃ, balaṃ, paṭibhānaṃ*. See **4:57**, **4:58**.

1017 They "show compassion" (*anukampeyyuṃ*) to them by offering them an opportunity to give alms and thereby acquire merit. Thus it is not so much the laypeople who show compassion to the monastics by giving them alms (though this is true), but the monastic who shows compassion to laypeople by approaching their homes to receive their offerings. By giving alms laypeople create the seeds for a happy rebirth and the attainment of nibbāna. The monastics may also teach the Dhamma to the laypeople and in this way give them access to the teachings.

1018 An expanded parallel of **3:48**. All the items mentioned in the simile of the mountain are identical in both suttas, but **3:48** reduces them to three by grouping together several as compounds, while the present sutta enumerates them separately. The present sutta adds learning (*suta*) and generosity (*cāga*) to the things people grow in. The verses are identical in both suttas.

1019 Here and below, I read *kulapatiṃ* with Ce and Ee, as against Be *kulaputtaṃ*. Be of my **3:48** (3:49 in Be's own enumeration) has *kulapatiṃ* in the corresponding place.

1020 From this part on, this sutta closely parallels **4:61**. The five items are obtained by dividing the first of the latter into two parts. The verses in the two suttas are identical.

1021 I read with Be and Ee *dhammaguttaṃ*, as against Ce *devaguttaṃ*, which seems redundant here.

1022 Compare with the opening of **4:61**.

1023 In each paragraph, I read with Ce *vā pihetuṃ*, as against Be *vāpi hetu*, Ee *vā pi hetuṃ*. The verb *piheti* (infinitive *pihetuṃ*) means "to yearn for." The idea of passively yearning seems implied by the contrast with practicing the way as a means of fulfilling one's wish.

1024 *Āyusaṃvattanikā paṭipadā*. Mp: "The meritorious practice of giving, virtuous behavior, etc." For an analysis of the specific relationship between present actions and their results, see MN 135.

1025 The text switches back and forth between singular and plural forms of *sagga*.

1026 These verses are also at SN 3:17, I 87; SN 3:18, I 89.

1027 *Atthābhisamayā*. I base this rendering on the gloss in Mp: *Atthassa abhisamāgamena, atthappaṭilābhenā ti vuttaṃ hoti.*

1028 *Sālapupphakaṃ khādaniyaṃ*. Mp: "A food similar to sal flour; it is made with hill-rice flour prepared with the four sweets (honey, sugar, butter, and ghee)."

1029 Reading with Be *sampannakolakaṃ sūkaramaṃsaṃ*. Mp: "The flesh of a one-year-old pig cooked with spices such as cumin seeds, etc., together with sweet jujube fruits."

1030 Ce *nibaddhatelakaṃ nāḷiyasākaṃ* (Be *nibattatelakaṃ nāliyasākaṃ*). Mp: "The vegetable stalks are cooked in ghee mixed with cumin and other spices, which have been pulverized together with hill-rice flour; then they are coated with the four sweets and put out until they acquire a particular aroma."

1031 So Ce. Be and Ee "over a hundred thousand" (*adhikasatasahassaṃ*). Presumably this refers to *kahāpaṇas*, the major currency unit.

1032 Reading with Ce *anaggahītaṃ*, as against Be and Ee *anuggahītaṃ*.

1033 *Aññataraṃ manomayaṃ kāyaṃ upapajjati*. I follow Mp in taking this expression, as used here, to mean that he was reborn among a group (*kāya*) of deities rather than that he was reborn with a mind-made body. Mp: "[Reborn] into a group of devas in the pure abodes who are produced through the mind of jhāna" (*suddhāvāsesu ekaṃ jhānamanena nibbattaṃ devakāyaṃ*). Also, at AN III 348,28–349,1 (= V 139,5–8) we find *tusitaṃ kāyaṃ upapanno*, where *kāyaṃ* must mean "group." In relation to the spiritual powers, *manomaya kāya* signifies a subtle body produced by the meditative mind, as at AN I 24,2. See too **5:166**.

1034 It is hard to see why this sutta is included in the Fives. Could it be that the original version had only five items of offering and a sixth was added later, after the sutta was included in the Fives?

1035 This is an expanded parallel of **4:51**. The additional factor is obtained by replacing "a lodging" (*senāsanaṃ*) with "a dwelling" (*vihāraṃ*) and "bed and chair" (*mañcapīṭhaṃ*).

1036 As in Be and Ee. The omission from Ce must be an editorial oversight, as the thousands of gallons are in the Ce version of **4:51**.

1037 I have filled in this definition here; all three editions abridge.

1038 The verses are also at **4:52**.

1039 The text uses a reflexive causative form: *attānaṃyeva parinibbāpeti*. This might also have been rendered: "He extinguishes himself," or "He quenches himself." What is literally extinguished is the bitter feeling of sorrow, but the verb *parinibbāpeti*, related to the noun *nibbāna*, implies that he reaches ultimate liberation.

1040 I read with Ee *attho idha labbhā api appako pi* (Be is essentially the same). Ce *attho alabbho api appako pi* means "even the least good cannot be gained," which undermines the point.

1041 *Paveṇiyā*. Mp: "By family custom (*kulavaṃsena*). The meaning is, 'We have traditionally practiced this, and we have not practiced that.'"

1042 This sentence is in the text of Ee, but in parentheses in Be and in a note in Ce.

1043 *Sokasallaharaṇo nāma ayaṃ mahārāja dhammapariyāyo*.

1044 *Naṅgalamukhāni*. Lit. "plow mouths." Mp glosses as "channel mouths" (*mātikāmukhāni*), explaining: "Because these are similar to plows and are cut by plows, they are called 'plow mouths.'"

1045 Also at SN 47:5, V 145,26–146,5, followed by a declaration that the four establishments of mindfulness are "a heap of the wholesome" (*kusalarāsī*). Here I follow Be and Ee, which do not include *ime* in the opening. Ce has *ime* both in the opening and at the end; Be does not have it in either place.

1046 *Na sukaraṃ uñchena paggahena yāpetun*. I take *uñchena paggahena* to denote a single act, not two acts. There is no *ca* or *vā* to suggest that two acts are intended. The gloss in Mp also implies that the expression refers to one act: "It is not possible to take one's bowl and sustain oneself by the practice of gleaning" (*na sakkā hoti pattaṃ gahetvā uñchācariyāya yāpetuṃ*). See too the gloss at Sp I 175,22–23: *paggahena yo uñcho, tena yāpetuṃ na sukarā*.

1047 *Aññamaññaṃ akkosā ca honti, aññamaññaṃ paribhāsā ca honti, aññamaññaṃ parikkhepā ca honti, aññamaññaṃ pariccajā ca honti*. A similar passage in It §§18–19, 10–11, has *aññamaññaṃ bhaṇḍanāni ceva honti* instead of *aññamaññaṃ akkosā ca honti* but is otherwise the same. I translate *parikkhepā* and *pariccajanā* in accordance with It-a I 69,25–27, which explains *parikkhepā* as "disparagement and denigration through the ten bases of insults, attacking all around in terms of birth and so forth" (*jāti-ādivasena parito khepā, dasahi akkosavatthūhi khuṃsanavambhanā*), and *pariccajanā* as "dismissal by way of disciplinary acts of suspension and so forth" (*ukkhepaniyakammakaraṇādivasena nissāraṇā*).

1048 It might be asked whether the expression *pasannānañca bhiyyobhāvo hoti* means that the number of those with confidence increases, or, alternatively, that those with confidence increase in confidence. Sp I 225,18–24, supports the latter: "Laypeople who have confidence in the Teaching, seeing the bhikkhus following the training rules as they have been established, become ever more confident, saying: 'The monks indeed do what is hard to do; for as long as they live they eat once a day, maintain celibacy, and observe the restraint of the Vinaya'" (*yepi sāsane pasannā kulaputtā tepi sikkhāpadapaññattiṃ ñatvā yathāpaññattaṃ paṭipajjamāne bhikkhū vā disvā "aho ayyā dukkarakārino, ye yāvajīvaṃ ekabhattaṃ brahmacariyaṃ vinayasaṃvaraṃ anupālentī" ti bhiyyo bhiyyo pasīdanti*).

1049 *Tesaṃ abhiṇhaṃ dassanā saṃsaggo ahosi, saṃsagge sati vissāso ahosi; vissāse sati otāro ahosi*. Though I translate *vissāso* as "intimacy," the word does not mean that at this point they had intimate physical relations. *Vissāso* is, rather, a feeling of trust that can lead to a sexual relationship. For this to occur, however, intimacy must first provide an opening for lust. This is indicated by the expression *otāro ahosi*.

1050 A violation of the first *pārājika* or expulsion offense.

1051 I follow the sequence of Be and Ee, which read *giddhā gathitā mucchitā ajjhopannā*, as against Ce *gathitā giddhā mucchitā ajjhopannā*. The sequence—*gathita, mucchita, ajjhopanna*—is common in the texts.

1052 Be and Ee *ugghātitā* (Ce *ugghānitā*). Mp glosses with *uddhumātā*, "bloated," a stage in the decomposition of a corpse. Five such stages are mentioned at **1:480–84**. Perhaps the next item, the dead woman, refers to a deceased woman preserved in memory rather than a corpse. Brahmāli suggests taking *ugghātitā* as "obese," but I'm not sure this would work. DOP sv *ugghāṭeti*[2] gives "puffed-up, swollen" among its meanings.

1053 Here Ce has merely *yampi taṃ bhikkhave sammā vadamāno vadeyya samantapāso mārassā ti*, which is incomplete. Hence I follow Be and Ee: *yaṃ hi taṃ bhikkhave sammā vadamāno vadeyya samantapāso mārassā ti mātugāmaṃ yeva sammā vadamāno vadeyya samantapāso mārassā ti.*

1054 *Suvāsīdo*: based on the verb *āsīdati*, to approach, with prefix *su-* and *–v-* as a liaison consonant.

1055 Mp glosses *purakkhatā* with "forerunners, those who have gone in front" (*purecārikā purato gatāyeva*). My rendering "are plunged headlong" is free but captures the sense. Vanarata suggests that *kālaṃ, gatiṃ,* and *bhavābhavaṃ* may be abbreviated locatives or split compound factors to be joined with *saṃsārasmiṃ,* but I think the verse may use the accusative for metrical reasons. There is no identified Chinese parallel of this sutta with which to make a comparison.

1056 The expression "I live the spiritual life dissatisfied" (*anabhirato ca brahmacariyaṃ carāmi*) implies that he wants to disrobe and return to lay life.

1057 Here the text changes to the plural *bhikkhave*. The Buddha is now addressing the monks at large.

1058 The first three themes echo **3:39**, with which this sutta has much in common.

1059 *Sabbehi me piyehi manāpehi*. I use "everyone and everything" to cover both persons and possessions. The Pāli implies both, but in English we need two words to span both objects.

1060 Mp: *"The path is generated* (*maggo sañjāyati*): the world-transcending path is generated. *The fetters are entirely abandoned* (*saṃyojanāni sabbaso pahīyanti*): the ten fetters are entirely abandoned (see **10:13**). *The underlying tendencies are uprooted* (*anusayā byantīhonti*): the seven underlying tendencies are removed, cut off, terminated (see **7:11**). Thus in the above five sections insight is discussed; in these five sections, the world-transcending path."

1061 These verses are also at **3:39**. They seem to be a self-reproach spoken by the bodhisatta prior to his enlightenment and thus fit better there. The line below—"while I am dwelling thus" (*mama evaṃ vihārino*)—suggests that this is the bodhisatta speaking with reference to his struggle for enlightenment. In pāda c I read with Ce *yathādhammā tathāsantā*, as against Be and Ee *yathā dhammā tathā sattā* (though they both concur with Ce in their reading of the earlier sutta).

1062 Ce and Be read *nekkhamme daṭṭhu khemataṃ*. Ee has *nekkhammaṃ daṭṭhu khemato* as its primary reading but mentions the Ce/Be variants in its notes. Mp (both Ce and Be) uses the Ce and Be reading as the lemma, which it glosses *nibbāne khemabhāvaṃ disvā*, but it then cites the Ee reading as a variant, glossed *nibbānaṃ khemato disvā*. Thus Ee has chosen the variant as the primary reading.

1063 Mp glosses *pacchāliyaṃ khipanti* with: "They come up behind them and strike their backs with their foot" (*pacchato gantvā piṭṭhiṃ pādena paharanti*).

1064 Reading with Ce and Ee: *khettakammantasāmantasaṃvohāre*. Mp (Ce): "The owners of the neighboring fields bordering his own fields, and those with whom he does business, who measure the land with measuring rods" (*ye attano khettakammantānaṃ sāmantā anantarakkhettasāmino, te ca rajjudaṇḍehi bhūmippamāṇaggāhake saṃvohāre ca*). I do not see that *saṃvohāra*, which normally means "transactions, business," has an explicit connection with the measuring of the land.

1065 *Balipaṭiggāhikā devatā*. Mp: "The protective deities that have been worshipped by family tradition."

1066 The perception of unattractiveness (*asubhasaññā*) is explained at **10:60 §3**; the perception of death, or mindfulness of death (*maraṇasaññā, maraṇassati*), at **6:19–20** and **8:73–74**; the perception of danger (*ādīnavasaññā*), at **10:60 §4**; the perception of the repulsiveness of food (*āhāre paṭikkūlasaññā*), at Vism 341–47, Ppn 11.1–26; and the perception of non-delight in the entire world (*sabbaloke anabhiratasaññā*), at **10:60 §8**.

1067 The perception of impermanence (*aniccasaññā*) is at **10:60 §1**, the perception of non-self (*anattasaññā*) at **10:60 §2**.

1068 Mp: "To live together: asking questions and answering questions" (***sājīvo*** *ti pañhapucchanañceva pañhavissajjanañca*).

1069 For an analysis of the formula for the four bases, see SN 51:13, V 268–69.

1070 The word *ussoḷhi*, translated here as "enthusiasm," is glossed by Mp with *adhimattaviriyaṃ*, "exceptional energy."

1071 See **5:14**.

1072 This and below as at MN 22.30–35, I 139–40.

1073 The perception of abandoning (*pahānasaññā*) and the perception of dispassion (*virāgasaññā*) are respectively at **10:60 §5** and **10:60 §6**. Ce, both printed and electronic editions, also includes *nirodhasaññā*, apparently an editorial error that would raise the number of perceptions to six.

1074 *Dhammavihārī*. The compound might also have been rendered "one who lives by the Dhamma."

1075 I read with Ce *dhammasaññattiyā* here and *saññattibahulo* just below, as against Be and Ee *dhammapaññattiyā* and *paññattibahulo* respectively.

1076 *Anuyuñjati ajjhattaṃ cetosamathaṃ*. Mp: "He pursues and develops mental concentration within himself; he is intent on and devoted to a serenity meditation subject" (*niyakajjhatte cittasamādhiṃ āsevati bhāveti, samathakammaṭṭhāne yuttappayutto hoti*).

1077 *Uttariṃ c'assa paññāya atthaṃ nappajānāti*. Mp: "Beyond his learning, he does not understand the meaning of that Dhamma by path wisdom together with insight; he does not see and penetrate the four [noble] truths" (*tato pariyattito uttariṃ tassa dhammassa sahavipassanāya maggapaññāya atthaṃ nappajānāti, cattāri saccāni na passati nappaṭivijjhati*).

1078 *Rajaggan*. Mp: "The mass of dust arisen from the ground, which has been trampled upon by the feet of the elephants, horses, etc."

1079 This is the prescribed method for renouncing monastic status. One declares to another person (normally a fellow bhikkhu) one's inability to observe the training, exchanges one's robes for ordinary clothing, takes the five lay precepts, and returns to lay life.

1080 I follow Be and Ee, which do not have ellipsis points here. Ce inconsistently has ellipsis points in this sutta (implying that all three *vijjā* are intended) but not in the parallel section of the next sutta.

1081 The following exhortation is also at MN 22.3, I 130,23–31. Many of these similes for sensual pleasures are elaborated at MN 54.15–21, I 364–67.

1082 *Vāḷā amanussā*, lit., "wild nonhumans." Mp glosses "such nonhumans as rough, violent yakkhas, etc." (*kakkhaḷā duṭṭhā yakkhādayo amanussā*).

1083 Mp does not comment on *abhāvitakāyā*, but Spk II 395,16 glosses it as *abhāvitapañcadvārikakāyā*, "undeveloped in the body of the five sense doors," probably referring to sense restraint. I suspect the term actually refers to the maintenance of clear comprehension in all modes of deportment and in the various bodily activities, as described at AN II 210,21–26 and V 206,25–30.

1084 *Iti kho, bhikkhave, dhammasandosā vinayasandoso; vinayasandosā dhammasandoso*. Mp: "How is it that when the Dhamma is becoming corrupt, the discipline becomes corrupt? When the *dhammas* of serenity and insight are no longer being nurtured, the fivefold discipline no longer exists. But when there is no discipline of restraint among those who are immoral, in its absence serenity and insight are not nurtured. In this way, through corruption of the discipline, there is corruption of the Dhamma." The fivefold discipline by restraint is restraint by virtuous behavior, mindfulness, knowledge, patience, and energy (*sīlasaṃvara, satisaṃvara, ñāṇasaṃvara, khantisaṃvara, viriyasaṃvara*). See Ps I 62,23–25, commenting on the Sabbāsava Sutta.

1085 *Nissaya*. A procedure prescribed in the Vinaya by which a junior bhikkhu apprentices himself to a qualified senior bhikkhu, normally his preceptor or teacher. A similar procedure is prescribed for bhikkhunīs. The period of *nissaya* is normally the first five years after a bhikkhu's full ordination, but it can be extended in the case of one who needs more time to gain competence. For details, see Ṭhānissaro 2007a: 29–40.

1086 *Abhidhammakathaṃ vedallakathaṃ kathentā*. I take the word *abhidhamma* here to have a purely referential function, that is, to mean "pertaining to the Dhamma, relating to the Dhamma." It does not denote the canonical collection of that name or its philosophy. See DOP sv *abhidhamme*. Mp, too, appears to recognize that the Abhidhamma Piṭaka is not relevant here, explaining *abhidhammakathaṃ* in this passage as a discussion on "the supreme teaching concerned with virtuous behavior, etc." (*sīlādi-uttamadhammakathaṃ*). It takes *vedallakathaṃ* to be a "miscellaneous talk on knowledge connected with inspirational joy" (*vedapaṭisaṃyuttaṃ ñāṇamissakakathaṃ*). MN 43 and MN 44 have *vedalla* in their title and proceed by way of miscellaneous questions and answers between disciples. The "dark Dhamma" (*kaṇhadhammaṃ*) is said to occur by way of fault-finding with a mind bent on criticizing others (*randhagavesitāya upārambhapariyesanavasena*).

1087 See **2:47**.

1088 *Saṃsaṭṭhā viharissanti*. Mp: "They will bond closely by way of the fivefold bond (*pañcavidhena saṃsaggena*)." Mp-ṭ: "Fivefold bond: bonding by hearing, seeing, conversation, eating together, and bodily contact" (*savanasaṃsaggo, dassanasaṃsaggo, samullāpasaṃsaggo, sambhogasaṃsaggo, kāyasaṃsaggo*). Mp-ṭ identifies them all as manifestations of lust and exemplifies the last by the lust arisen through holding hands (*hatthaggāha*, a *saṅghādisesa* offense when it occurs between a bhikkhu and a woman). Female probationers (*sikkhamānā*) are nuns already ordained as novices who are formally training for full bhikkhunī ordination.

1089 A defiled offense (*saṅkiliṭṭhaṃ āpattiṃ*) here would be a *pārājika* or a *saṅghādisesa*.

1090 Use of stored-up food (*sannidhikāraparibhoga*) is prohibited by Pācittiya 38, Vin IV 86–87. Regarding "giving a gross hint" (*oḷārikaṃ nimittaṃ*), Mp says: "Here, digging the ground and ordering 'Dig!' is called giving a gross hint in regard to the ground. Cutting and ordering 'Cut!' is called giving a gross hint with regard to vegetation." The reference is to Pācittiyas 10 and 11, Vin IV 32–33, 33–35.

1091 *Kuhako ca hoti, lapako ca, nemittiko ca, nippesiko ca, lābhena ca lābhaṃ nijigīsitā*. These are forms of wrong livelihood, discussed more fully at Vibh 352–53 (Be §§861–65); they are elaborated at Vism 23–30, Ppn 1.61–82.

1092 On the four *paṭisambhidās*, see **4:172**.

1093 I follow Ce *sātthā sabyañjanā*, as against Be and Ee *sātthaṃ sabyañjanaṃ*. The same difference appears wherever this phrase occurs. The difference is not trivial; it indicates that for Ce, meaning and phrasing pertain to the *dhammā*, whereas for Be and Ee they pertain to the *brahmacariyaṃ*, the practice of the spiritual life. The terms make better sense in relation to *dhammā*, teachings that are verbally articulated, than in relation to the *brahmacariyaṃ*, which is lived rather than spoken.

1094 Be reads here *diṭṭhiyā appaṭividdhā*, "not penetrated by view," which seems a learned "correction" to a stock formula. Otherwise we would have expected an adversative conjunction, such as *ca* or *ca pana*, to prepare us for the variation on the usual reading. Ce and Ee have the familiar *diṭṭhiyā suppaṭividdhā*, which I follow.

1095 *Yathāvimuttaṃ cittaṃ na paccavekkhati*. Mp: "Having reviewed which faults have been abandoned and which virtues have been obtained, he does not make an effort to obtain higher virtues." This passage seems to presage the idea of *paccavekkhaṇañāṇa*, which figures prominently in the commentaries.

1096 Mp: "This sutta has discussed the causes for decline and growth of the seven trainees in relation to the higher virtues. The causes for decline of a trainee occur first to the worldling."

1097 *Ananulomikena gihisaṃsaggena*. On the five kinds of *saṃsagga*, see p. 1733, note 1088.

1098 *Aññābyākaraṇāni*. Mp: "Declarations of arahantship."

1099 *Akuppaṃ*. Probably meaning *akuppā cetovimutti*, unshakable liberation of mind. Mp identifies this with arahantship.

1100 *Sakkaccaññeva deti no asakkaccaṃ*. Mp: "He gives the blow without despising, without transgressing; he does not do so despising and transgressing."

1101 *Annabhāranesādānaṃ*. Mp glosses *annabhārā* as beggars (*yācakā*) and *nesādā* as fowlers (*sākuṇikā*).

1102 The opening story, together with the discourse on the five kinds of teachers, is at Vin II 185–87.

1103 *Manomayaṃ kāyaṃ upapanno*. The mind-made deities are those reborn in the form realm through the power of their past attainment of the jhānas.

1104 The word for "body" here is *attabhāvapaṭilābha*. I take *paṭilābha* to be merely an idiomatic adjunct and do not think it adds anything to the meaning. Mp glosses as *sarīrapaṭilābho*, which supports my supposition that the simple physical body is intended here. The expression *attabhāvapaṭilābha* occurs in **4:171**, where it designates the entire typology of a living being. In that text it cannot be construed narrowly as the physical body, since it also encompasses "the devas of the base of neither-perception-nor-non-perception," who lack physical bodies.

On the size of his body, the text reads *dve vā tīṇi vā māgadhikāni gāmakkhettāni*. On *gāmakkhetta* Brahmāli writes: "This word also occurs at MN III 10,11: *ekaṃ gāmakkhettaṃ upanissāya viharāma*, and at MN II 167,27: *amhākaṃ gāmakkhettaṃ āgacchanti*. From these passages it seems quite clear to me that *gāmakkhetta* refers to a village *together with all* its fields" (private communication). The figures for length given by Mp suggest that his body was 3–4.5 miles or 5–7 km tall.

1105 The text says *tassā iddhiyā*, "that psychic potency," not *tassa iddhiyā*, "his psychic potency." The pronoun refers to a psychic power already mentioned, yet the sutta does not make clear what it is. The context is provided by Vin II 184,33–185,21, where Devadatta exercises the psychic power of transforming himself into a young boy wearing a girdle of snakes. He used this power to impress Prince Ajātasattu and win his support. Thereupon Devadatta thought to wrest control of the Saṅgha from the Buddha, whereupon he lost *that* psychic potency.

1106 *Yaṃ tumo karissati tumo'va tena paññāyissati*. PED explains the stem *tuma* as "most likely apostrophe form of *ātuma* = *attā*, Skt *ātman* self." Mp paraphrases: "One will be known by the action that one does" (*yaṃ esa karissati, eso'va tena kammena pākaṭo bhavissati*).

1107 *Aparisuddhaveyyākaraṇo*. Mp does not comment. Presumably, this refers to his explanation of a point in his teaching or his reply to a question.

1108 *Sekhavesārajjakaraṇā dhammā*.

1109 *Sārajjaṃ*. Mp glosses with *domanassaṃ*, "dejection," but this does not seem sufficiently precise. *Sārajja* is the condition of one who feels timid, hesitant, and insecure (*sārada*) when having to appear in public or take a stand in community affairs. Its opposite, *vesārajja*, is the condition of one who feels at ease and self-confident (*visārada*) when interacting with others.

1110 Ee's *kuppadhammo* is evidently an error, though in the notes on variant readings Ee recognizes the correct reading, *akuppadhammo*. Mp glosses with *khīṇāsavo*, one whose taints are destroyed, an arahant. For the Saṅgha to maintain the respect of the lay community, it is considered important not only for monastics to be virtuous in their behavior but to avoid actions that might arouse suspicion. Such behavior not only reflects adversely on the individual monastic but may also bring discredit to the Dhamma and the Saṅgha. Hence this exhortation.

1111 Mp glosses *vesiyāgocaro* with *tāsaṃ gehaṃ abhiṇhagamano*, "frequently going to their homes." Thus *gocara* in the narrow sense of an alms resort is not necessarily intended here.

1112 An expanded parallel of **3:50**.
1113 *Gahaṇāni*, lit. "takings." Mp: "The taking of others' belongings" (*parasantakānaṃ bhaṇḍānaṃ gahaṇāni*).
1114 *Guyhamantā*. Here *mantā* must mean "deliberations" or "consultations," not *mantras*. Mp offers only a verbal gloss, *guhitabbamantā*.
1115 *Antaggāhikāya*. Mp: "He grasps hold of eternalism or annihilationism."
1116 This sutta reproduces **4:87 §4**, the delicate ascetic among ascetics section, here divided into five secondary sections.
1117 *Phāsuvihārā*. These are five of the better known six principles of cordiality, at **6:11–12**.
1118 *No paraṃ adhisīle sampavattā*. I take *adhisīle* here to have the purely referential sense "in regard to virtuous behavior," and not to imply "higher virtuous behavior" (though, of course, since "virtuous behavior" is identified with restraint by the Pātimokkha, the "higher virtuous behavior" is implied). Mp supports this referential understanding of *adhisīle* with its gloss: "He does not censure or reproach others in regard to virtuous behavior" (*paraṃ sīlabhāvena na garahati na upavadati*).
1119 *Cātuddiso*. Mp: "He moves about without obstruction in the four quarters" (*catūsu disāsu appaṭihatacāro*).
1120 Ce does not have a title at the beginning of the vagga, but it includes the title before the *uddāna* verse at the end.
1121 The meaning is not transparent and readings vary. Ce *viyatthūpasevī*, Ee *vyatthūpasevī*, Be *vissaṭṭhupasevī*. Mp (Be) explains: "He consorts with divided families for the sake of creating friction" (*vissaṭṭhāni bhinnakulāni ghaṭanatthāya upasevati.*). Mp (Ce) has *viyatthāni bhinnakakulāni*.
1122 *Sammādassana*. This is synonymous with right view (*sammādiṭṭhi*). Mp paraphrases: "Be possessed of the five kinds of right view: of responsibility for one's kamma, of jhāna, of insight, of the path, and of the fruit."
1123 Mp: "She is miserly with her *dwelling* (*āvāsamaccharinī*) and cannot endure others living there. She is miserly with the *families* (*kulamaccharinī*) that support her and cannot endure others approaching them [for support]. She is miserly with *gains* (*lābhamaccharinī*) and cannot endure others acquiring them. She is miserly with her *virtues* (*guṇamaccharinī*) and cannot endure talk about the virtues of others. And she is miserly with the *Dhamma* (*dhammamaccharinī*) and does not wish to share it with others."
1124 *Saddhādeyyaṃ vinipāteti*. Mp: "When she is given almsfood by others out of faith, without taking the top portion [for herself], she gives it to someone else." The rule against squandering gifts

given out of faith is at Vin I 298,1–3: "Bhikkhus, a gift given out of faith should not be squandered. For one who squanders it, there is an offense of wrongdoing" (*na ca bhikkhave saddhādeyyaṃ vinipātetabbaṃ; yo vinipāteyya, āpatti dukkaṭassa*). This is an offense because it shows disregard for the generosity of others. After taking the top portion for oneself, however, one can share the rest with others. The Buddha also made a unique allowance for a monastic to give almsfood, cloth, and other gains to his or her parents if they are in need.

1125 I follow the punctuation of Be and Ee, which connect *dhammānaṃ udayatthagāminiyā paññāya* with the preceding *ajjhattaṃ yeva sati sūpaṭṭhitā hoti*. Ce puts a comma after *hoti* and no punctuation after *paññāya*, thus connecting *dhammānaṃ udayatthagāminiyā paññāya* with the following *asubhānupassī kāye viharati*. This, however, connects the meditation on the body's unattractive nature with the wisdom that discerns arising and passing away, a connection that, to my knowledge, is not made elsewhere in the Nikāyas (apart from the repetitive refrain in the Satipaṭṭhāna Sutta).

1126 Sn 386 suggests that *akālacārī* refers to walking for alms at an improper time.

1127 On contentment, see p. 1600, note 55.

1128 Mp explains *parikuppā* as "something with an irritating nature, similar to an old wound" (*parikuppanasabhāvā purāṇavaṇasadisā*). More commonly these acts are known as the *ānantariya kamma*, grave deeds that bring as their immediate result a rebirth in hell. See **6:93**.

1129 Disaster regarding virtuous behavior (*sīlavyasana*) obviously refers to conduct that violates the five ethical precepts, and disaster regarding view (*diṭṭhivyasana*) to the adoption of a wrong view, particularly the view that denies the principle of kamma and its results.

1130 *Dhammen'eva cakkaṃ vatteti*. Mp: "'Dhamma' here is the ten wholesome [courses of kamma]."

1131 Mp: "*Who knows what is good* (*atthaññū*): who knows the fivefold good (Mp-ṭ: one's own good, the good of others, the good of both, the good pertaining to this present life, and the good pertaining to future lives). *Who knows the Dhamma* (*dhammaññū*): who knows the fourfold Dhamma (Mp-ṭ: the Dhamma of the four truths, or the four kinds of *dhammas* distinguished into those of the sense sphere, the form realm, the formless realm, and the world-transcending). *Who knows the right measure* (*mattaññū*): who knows the right measure in accepting and using the four requisites. *Who knows the proper time* (*kālaññū*): who knows the time thus, 'This is the time for seclusion, this is the time for meditative attainment, this is the time for teaching the Dhamma, and this is the time for touring the country.' *Who knows the assembly* (*parisaññū*): who knows, 'This is an assembly of khattiyas . . . this is an assembly of ascetics.'"

1132 See **1:187**.

1133 See **3:14**.

1134 In commenting on *saṃsuddhagahaṇiko yāva sattamā pitāmahayugā akkhitto anupakkuṭṭho jātivādena*, Mp says that *yāva sattamā pitāmahayugā* can be construed in apposition either to *saṃsuddhagahaṇiko* or to *akkhitto anupakkuṭṭho jātivādena*. Be and Ee punctuate as if it should be taken in the former way, Ce as if it should be taken in the latter way. I follow Ce.

1135 *Paṭibalo atītānāgatapaccuppanne atthe cintetuṃ*. Mp explains: "Through present benefits, he considers what happened in the past and what will happen in the future" (*so hi paccuppanna-atthavaseneva "atītepi evaṃ ahesuṃ, anāgatepi evaṃ bhavissantī"ti cinteti*).

1136 *Salākaggāhī*. Mp: "At the time of counting the elephants, he takes a ticket." Apparently they used tickets, or pieces of straw, to count the elephants.

1137 Ce *pīṭhamaddano*; Be *mañcapīṭhamaddano*, "a crusher of beds and chairs."

1138 Mp: "At the time of counting the bhikkhus, he takes a ticket."

1139 I prefer Ee *dhammehi* here to Ce and Be *aṅgehi*. The concluding paragraph of this section, and the corresponding opening and closing paragraph on the accomplished bhikkhu, all have *dhammehi*.

1140 Mp: "*He violates* (*ārabhati*): he violates by committing an offense [against the monastic rules], and *then becomes remorseful* (*vippaṭisārī ca hoti*) because of that. *Liberation of mind, liberation by wisdom* is the concentration of arahantship and the knowledge of the fruit of arahantship. He *does not understand* this because he has not attained it."

1141 Mp: "He commits an offense, but rehabilitates himself and thus does not become remorseful."

1142 Mp: "Having committed an offense once, he rehabilitates himself but afterward, though he does not commit an offense, he cannot dispel remorse." This probably refers to the case, often cited in the Vinaya, where a monk wrongly believes that he has committed an offense.

1143 Mp: "Abandon the taints born of transgression by confessing the offense or by rehabilitating yourself from the offense. Then develop the mind of insight (*vipassanācittaṃ*) and the wisdom conjoined with it."

1144 This mode of practice is explained at Paṭis II 212–13, where it is called the psychic potency of the noble ones (*ariy'iddhi*). The following explanations of Mp are drawn from that source: (1) "*Perceiving the repulsive in the unrepulsive* (*appaṭikūle paṭikūlasaññī*): He observes a desirable object with the idea of its unattractiveness or he attends to it as impermanent. (2) *Perceiving the unrepulsive in the repulsive* (*paṭikūle appaṭikūlasaññī*): He observes an undesirable object with loving-kindness or attends to it by way of elements. (3–4) In the third and fourth sections, he applies respectively the first and second methods to both kinds of objects. (5) *To dwell equanimous* (*upekkhako vihareyya*): this is the six-factored equanimity [that is, equanimity regarding the six sense objects] similar to that of an arahant. In this sutta, insight is explained in the five cases. It is possible for a bhikkhu who has initiated insight to do this; it is also possible for a knowledgeable, wise, and learned person to do this. The stream-enterer, once-returner, and non-returner definitely can do this; there is no need to say anything about the arahant."

1145 *Mā me kvacini katthaci kiñcana rajanīyesu dhammesu rāgo udapādi, mā me kvacini katthaci kiñcana dosanīyesu dhammesu doso udapādi, mā me kvacini katthaci kiñcana mohanīyesu dhammesu moho udapādī.* The formulation here seems deliberately stronger and more comprehensive than in the previous cases. Mp glosses: ***Kvacanī*** *ti kismiñci ārammaṇe.* ***Katthacī*** *ti kismiñci padese.* ***Kiñcana*** *ti koci appamattakopi.*

1146 *Anāgamanadiṭṭhiko deti.* Mp: "One gives without having brought forth the view of arrival thus: 'The fruit of what has been done will arrive.'" Presumably the view of kamma and its result is intended.

1147 *Āgamanadiṭṭhiko.* Mp: "He gives with faith in kamma and its result."

1148 *Samayavimuttassa bhikkhuno.* Mp: "One who is liberated in mind through a mundane liberation, a tentative liberation, through the suppression of the defilements in absorption."

1149 I title this after the Be *uddāna* verse, which reads *tayo sammattaniyāmā*, as against Ce and Ee *tayo saddhammaniyāmā*.

1150 *Abhabbo niyāmaṃ okkamituṃ kusalesu dhammesu sammattaṃ.* Mp: "One is unqualified, incapable of entering upon the fixed course of the path, which [consists in] rightness in wholesome qualities" (*kusalesu dhammesu sammattabhūtaṃ magganiyāmaṃ okkamituṃ abhabbo abhājanaṃ*). See too **3:22** and p. 1638, note 358.

1151 As at **4:160**. See too **2:20**.

1152 As at **5:54 §5**.

1153 Compare with **5:101**.

1154 This is Lāḷudāyī, often depicted as a presumptuous monk. Thus the Buddha's words to follow should probably be read as a reproach to him for prematurely setting himself up as a teacher. Other examples of Udāyī's rashness are at **3:80** and **5:166**. At **6:29** and again at MN 136.6, III 208,25–31, he is reproached by the Buddha. In the Vinaya Piṭaka a certain Udāyī is depicted as a licentious monk whose misbehavior in sexual matters was responsible for the laying down of several *saṅghādisesa* rules, but it is questionable whether he is identical with this Udāyī. He may even have been a fictional character, a "John Doe" used to account for the origin of these rules.

1155 *Ānupubbīkathaṃ kathessāmi*. Mp: "One should teach the Dhamma to others after determining: 'I will first speak about giving, next about virtuous behavior, and next about heaven; or I will explain a sutta passage or verse in accordance with the order of its words.'"

1156 *Pariyāyadassāvī*. Mp: "Showing the reason (*kāraṇa*) for this or that point."

1157 *Yattha bhikkhuno uppanno āghāto sabbaso paṭivinetabbo*. I interpret this following Mp, which explains: "When resentment has arisen in a bhikkhu *in regard to some object* (*yattha ārammaṇe*), it should be completely dispelled there in these five ways." Thus Mp takes *yattha* to mean the person toward whom the resentment has arisen, not the physical place where it has arisen.

1158 *Labhati ca kālena kālaṃ cetaso vivaraṃ cetaso pasādaṃ*. Mp: "From time to time he gains an opening of the mind, that is, an opportunity arises in his mind for serenity and insight, and he gains placidity, which consists in the achievement of faith" (*kāle kāle samathavipassanācittassa uppannokāsasaṅkhātaṃ vivarañceva saddhāsampannabhāvasaṅkhātaṃ pasādañca labhati*).

1159 *Samantapāsādikaṃ āvuso puggalaṃ āgamma cittaṃ pasīdati*. This is apparently referring to the fifth type of person. Since his behavior and mind are both pure, one can easily dispel resentment toward him and settle down into a state of trust and tranquility.

1160 Mp: "*The devas that subsist on edible food* (*kabaḷīkārāhārabhakkhānaṃ devānan*): the deities of the sense sphere. *A certain mind-made group* (*aññataraṃ manomayaṃ kāyan*): a certain group of brahmās in the pure abodes, who are reborn by the jhāna-mind."

1161 *Ye te, bhante, devā arūpino saññāmayā*. Udāyī has confused the devas of the formless realm, who are said to be perception-made (*saññāmaya*), with the devas of the form realm (including the pure abodes), who are said to be mind-made (*manomaya*).

1162 I read with Ce and Ee *mayaṃ te na pucchāma*, as against Be *mayaṃ tena na muccāma*.

1163 *Yathā āyasmantaṃyev'ettha upavāṇaṃ paṭibhāseyya*. Mp explains *yathā* as a word for a cause (*kāraṇavacanaṃ*). I take *paṭibhāsati* to mean "calls upon [someone to say something]" (see SED sv *pratibhāsh*). Mp continues: "When something has been uttered by the Blessed One with reference to this matter, you should think of some reply (*paṭivacana*, a counter-statement)."

1164 I follow Ce and Ee, which have *na saṃvijjeyyuṃ, kena naṃ sabrahmacārī sakkareyyuṃ garukareyyuṃ māneyyuṃ pūjeyyuṃ*. Be has *na saṃvijjeyyuṃ, taṃ sabrahmacārī na sakkareyyuṃ na garuṃ kareyyuṃ na māneyyuṃ na pūjeyyuṃ*.

1165 *No kālena kupitaṃ*. It seems strange that the text uses the word *kupita* to refer to being reproved at the proper time. *Kupita* normally suggests "disturbed, irritated, angered," and at the proper time it would be suitable to reprove him.

1166 *Atthakusalo, dhammakusalo, niruttikusalo, byañjanakusalo, pubbāparakusalo*. I follow the sequence of Ce. Be and Ee put *byañjanakusalo* before *niruttikusalo*. As stated, the first three terms obviously correspond to the first three *paṭisambhidā* knowledges. Perhaps the last two can be comprised under *paṭibhānapaṭisambhidā*. Mp explains five types of sequence: sequence of meaning (*atthapubbāpara*), sequence of Dhamma (*dhammapubbāpara*), sequence of syllables (*akkharapubbāpara*), sequence of phrasing (*byañjanapubbāpara*), and sequence of sections within a sutta (*anusandhipubbāpara*).

1167 I prefer Ce *te santaññeva sukhitā sukhaṃ paṭisaṃvedenti* to Be and Ee *te santaṃyeva tusitā sukhaṃ paṭivedenti*.

1168 *Sameti kho idaṃ āyasmato bhaddajissa, yadidaṃ bahujanena*. I follow both Be and Ee, which punctuate this with a question mark. Although the sentence does not contain an interrogative, by putting the verb at the beginning it seems to imply a question rather than an assertion.

1169 *Anantarā āsavānaṃ khayo hoti*. On the "immediacy condition for the destruction of the taints," see p. 1705, note 851.

1170 *Upāsakacaṇḍālo ca hoti upāsakamalañca upāsakapatikuṭṭho ca*. The caṇḍālas were the lowest of the outcast groups.

1171 *Ito ca bahiddhā dakkhineyyaṃ gavessati*. That is, outside the Buddhist monastic community. On the relative value of offerings in terms of merit, see MN 142.

1172 *Upāsakaratanañca hoti upāsakapadumañca upāsakapuṇḍarīkañca*.

1173 *Pavivekaṃ pītiṃ*. Mp: "The rapture that arises based on the first and second jhānas."

1174 The plural "wives" is in the Pāli, *sehi dārehi santuṭṭho*.

1175 Be and Ee read *ārame*, Ce *nārame*. DOP gives as meanings of *āramati* both "leaves off, keeps away (from)" and "delights in, takes pleasure." Hence the Be and Ee reading (which I follow) fits the former sense, the Ce reading the latter sense.

1176 *Puññatthassa jigiṃsato*. Mp glosses the line: *puññena atthikassa puññaṃ gavesantassa. Jigiṃsati* is desiderative of *jayati*, here with the sense "to wish to obtain."

1177 The verses to follow are identical with those of **3:57**.

1178 Here and just below I read with Ce *anuttaraṃ vimuttisukhaṃ*. Be and Ee have *anuttaraṃ vimuttiṃ*.

1179 *Pāpiccho icchāpakato āraññiko hoti*. Mp: "He thinks, 'While I am living in the forest, they will honor me with the four requisites, thinking I'm a forest dweller. They will esteem me for my virtues, thinking that I'm conscientious and secluded, and so forth.' Thus he is a forest dweller based on evil desire, because he is overcome by desire."

1180 Ce follows this with a sutta on "these five who live solely on food gathered on alms round" (*pañc' ime bhikkhave piṇḍapātikā*), not included in Be and Ee. I here follow the latter, as Ce expands the vagga to an irregular eleven suttas. All these ascetic practices are explained in detail in Vism, chap. 2. Of those below that are not self-explanatory, the "sitter's practice" is sleeping in the sitting posture, without lying down; the "any-bed-user's practice" is accepting any sleeping place that is offered, without preferences; the "one-session practice" is eating all one's food for the day in one sitting posture, without consuming any food after one has risen from one's seat; and the "later-food-refuser's practice" is refusing to accept any food that may be offered and made available after one has started one's meal.

1181 Reading here with Be *sampiyen'eva saṃvāsaṃ saṃbandhāya sampavattenti*. Ce and Ee have *saṃsaggatthāya* for *saṃbandhāya*. Mp (Be) seems to support the Be reading with its paraphrase: *piyo piyaṃ upasaṅkamitvā paveṇiyā bandhanatthaṃ saṃvāsaṃ pavattayanti*. Mp (Ce) has *ganthanatthaṃ* for *bandhanatthaṃ*. *Saṃbandhāya* is glossed *paveṇiyā*, which may signify the continuity of the family.

1182 Be reads: . . . *sampiyenapi saṃvāsaṃ saṃbandhāya saṃpavattenti*, which seems incomplete. Ee is similar in this respect. I follow Ce in positing here two contrasting clauses: . . .*sampiyenapi saṃvāsaṃ saṃsaggatthāya sampavattenti, asampiyenapi saṃvāsaṃ saṃsaggatthāya sampavattenti*, but I would replace Ce *saṃsaggatthāya* with Be *saṃbandhāya*.

1183 This seems to have been a common criticism of the Buddha. See too **4:22** and **8:11**.

1184 *Komārabrahmacariyaṃ*. Presumably this means the celibacy of one who has always been a virgin.

1185 This passage suggests, contrary to a common assumption, that during the Buddha's time brahmins were not obliged to marry and adopt the life of a householder. While marriage later became the norm for brahmins during the prime of life, it seems that in this period some brahmins, after completing their training, chose to renounce secular life even in their youth and maintained their renunciant status throughout their lives. On celibate brahmin ascetics, see Samuel 2008:122–23, 154–65.

1186 *Cattāro brahmavihāre bhāvetvā*. This is one of the few places in the Nikāyas where the word *brahmavihāra* is used to designate these four meditations collectively. Wherever the word is used in the Nikāyas, it immediately precedes the practitioner's rebirth in the brahmā world.

1187 I read with Ce and Ee *asucipaṭipīto*, as against Be *asucipaṭipīḷito*, "would be oppressed by the impure substance."

1188 Ce and Ee read: *Sace doṇa brāhmaṇo anutuniṃ gacchati, tassa sā hoti brāhmaṇī n'eva kāmatthā na davatthā na ratatthā, pajatthāva brāhmaṇassa brāhmaṇī hoti*. This reading, it seems, joins the premise of the hypothetical to the consequence of the alternative (that is, when the brahmin has relations with his wife only when she is in season). I follow Brahmāli's suggestion to delete *sace doṇa brāhmaṇo anutuniṃ gacchati*, which leaves a text that makes good sense. Be does not have the question about why the brahmin couples with a woman only when she is in season, but follows the statement that he does not couple with a nursing woman with the words: *tassa sā hoti brāhmaṇī n'eva kāmatthā na davatthā na ratatthā, pajatthāva brāhmaṇassa brāhmaṇī hoti*. It seems that, in this reading, a clause has been lost.

1189 Reading with Be and Ee *pajatthāpi*, as against Ce *na pajatthāva*.

1190 I assume the text (in all three editions) should be corrected to read *na kevalaṃ bhikkhācariyāya* rather than *kevalam pi bhikkhācariyāya*.

1191 Also at SN 46:55, V 121–26, but with a section on the seven factors of enlightenment.

1192 Mp interprets the escape from the hindrances by way of the threefold escape. In relation to the hindrance of sensual desire, escape by suppression (*vikkhambhananissaraṇa*) occurs through the first jhāna based on the unattractive nature of the body, escape in a particular respect (*tadaṅganissaraṇa*) through insight, and escape by eradication (*samucchedanissaraṇa*) through the path of arahantship (broadly interpreting *kāmacchanda* as craving for any object). (i) The escape from *ill will* occurs by suppression through the first jhāna based on loving-kindness, and by eradication through the path of the non-returner. (ii) The escape from *dullness and drowsiness* occurs by suppression through the perception of light (the visualization of a bright light) and by eradication through the path of arahantship. (iii) The escape from *restlessness and remorse* occurs by suppression through serenity—*remorse* being then eradicated through the path of the non-returner and *restlessness* through the path of arahantship. And (v) the escape from *doubt* occurs by suppression through the defining of phenomena (*dhammavavatthāna*; see Vism 587–93, Ppn 18.3–24) and by eradication through the path of stream-entry. Mp does not apply "escape in a particular respect" to the last four hindrances, but Mp-ṭ says it occurs in that the hindrances can be dispelled by reflection (*paṭisaṅkhānavasena tassa vinodetabbatāya tadaṅganissaraṇampi labbhat'eva*).

1193 Mp interprets these terms from a monastic perspective. One's own good (*attattha*) is arahantship, and the good of others (*parattha*) is the welfare of the lay supporters who provide one with material support (because the offering of such gifts creates merit).

1194 Mp explains that after rising early, he had new gates, a watchtower, and ramparts built and had those that had decayed repaired.

1195 Mp identifies Piṅgiyāni as a brahmin who was a noble disciple established in the fruit of non-returning (*anāgāmiphale patiṭṭhitaṃ ariyasāvakaṃ brāhmaṇaṃ*). His daily routine was to visit the Buddha and offer him incense and garlands. At the time the sutta begins, he was returning from his daily visit.

1196 For some reason, he cites only four of the nine divisions of the Dhamma. Perhaps it was only these with which he was familiar, or perhaps this implies a later provenance for the others.

1197 *Paṭibhātu taṃ piṅgiyānī*. Lit., "Let it shine upon you, Piṅgiyānī."

1198 At SN 3:12, I 81, this verse is spoken by the lay follower Candanaṅgalika, who also recites it after being moved by a sudden surge of inspiration. In the verse, Aṅgīrasa is an epithet of the Buddha.

1199 The following as at **5:143** above.

1200 I have added "this was a foretoken" in compliance with Mp's use of the word *pubbanimitta* to characterize the significance of the dreams. Brahmāli suggests: "[the dream] . . . represented his awakening to the unsurpassed, perfect enlightenment," with a parallel construction for the corresponding sections below.

1201 *Tassa abhisambodhāya ayaṃ paṭhamo mahāsupino pāturahosi*. Brahmāli suggests here: "This was the first great dream that was beneficial for his awakening," again with a parallel construction for the corresponding sections below. The sentence as it stands is perplexing; yet Mp does not comment and there is no Chinese parallel. Ce and Be read *tassā* for *tassa* (the Ee reading). *Tassā* would have to represent *sammā sambodhi* in the previous sentence, but the question would then arise what *abhisambodhāya* relates to in §§2–4, where *sammā sambodhi* does not occur. I find the sentence is more intelligible if we read *tassa* (as in the following sections), taking it to mean "to him," that is, to the future Buddha. We can then see the whole sentence as affirming that the dream was indicative of his imminent awakening.

1202 Ce and Be *yattha nemittānaṃ cakkhu na kamati* (Ee *na kkhamati*). The Pāli itself mixes metaphors.

1203 *Pabbajitā*. Elsewhere I have usually rendered *pabbajita* as "one who has gone forth," and occasionally as "monk." Here, to avoid an unwieldy "virtuous ones who have gone forth," and to keep the rendering gender-neutral, I use "monastics." "Home" renders *kula*, lit. "family," but in this context the former better conveys the sense.

1204 *Nissāraṇīyā dhātuyo*. Mp glosses *nissāraṇīya* with *visaṃyutta*, "detached, disconnected," and *dhātuyo* with *attasuññasabhāvā*, "a nature empty of self."

1205 Mp: "Having emerged from jhāna on an unattractive object, he sends his mind in the direction of sensual pleasures for the purpose of investigating them, just as one might take an antidote for the purpose of investigating a poison." Mp-ṭ: "Such a bhikkhu does not attend to sensual pleasures in the sense [that he is overcome] by the defilement. Rather, he investigates: 'My mind is now fixed in renunciation. Why do sensual thoughts arise?'"

1206 Though all three editions here read *vimuccati*, Mp glosses the word with *adhimuccati*. The latter makes better sense to me. The manuscript traditions, as well as printed editions, show irregular variations between these two readings throughout the Nikāyas.

1207 I read with Ce and Be *sugataṃ*, as against Ee *sukataṃ*. The former has the support of Mp, which glosses "well departed because it has gone into the object" (*gocare gatattā suṭṭhu gataṃ*). I believe, however, that the sense of *sugataṃ* is that the mind has *gone away* from the defilement, which ties up better with the notion of escape (*nissaraṇa*).

1208 *Na so taṃ vedanaṃ vediyati*. Mp: "He does not feel that sensual feeling or that distressful and feverish feeling."

1209 Be and Ee read *veḷuvane*, Ce *niceluvane*. Mp (Be) has *niculavane* in the lemma, glossed as *mucalindavane*. Both PED and SED list *nicula* as a kind of tree, identified as *Barringtonia acutangula*.

1210 It cannot be determined from the language of the text whether Kimbila's questions and the Buddha's replies refer to the general conditions under which the teaching of a Buddha disappears, or to the conditions under which the Buddha Gotama's teaching will disappear. Mp seems to support the former interpretation. It explains that Kimbila had become a monk in the time of the past Buddha Kassapa, during an era when the latter's teaching was in decline. He now recollected this past life and wanted to inquire from the present Buddha about the cause for the decline of the Dhamma. Brahmāli disagrees with me about this and writes: "This [translation] seems to assume that Kimbila is thinking in cosmic terms, about Tathāgatas as a type of being. But it seems more likely to me that he was concerned specifically with what would happen after Gotama Buddha passed away."

1211 An expanded parallel of **4:112**.

1212 As at MN 16.2–7, I 101.

1213 *Cetokhila*. In MLDB *cetokhila* was translated "wilderness of the heart," which is not satisfactory. According to DOP, *khila* means "barren land; hard, arid soil," and "(as a fault of one's thinking) barrenness, sterility; stiffness, rigidity; hostility, resistance." Mp glosses: "Rigidity, waste, stumps of the mind" (*cittassa thaddhabhāvā kacavarabhāvā khāṇukabhāvā*).

1214 As at MN 16.8–12, I 101–2.

1215 *Cetaso vinibandhā*. Mp: "They grasp the mind, having shackled it as if in a fist, therefore they are called 'bondages of the mind'" (*cittaṃ vinibandhitvā muṭṭhiyaṃ katvā viya gaṇhantī ti cetaso vinibandhā*).

1216 *Dantakaṭṭhassa akhādane*, lit. "in not chewing on toothwood." In the Buddha's time people cleaned their teeth by brushing them with sticks of medicinal wood such as neem, sharpened at one end and made brush-like at the base. This practice is still observed in rural India as well as in monasteries in southern Asia.

1217 *Āyatakena gītassarena dhammaṃ bhaṇantassa*. Vin II 108,5–25 tells the origin story that leads to the laying down of the rule.

1218 *Muṭṭhassatissa asampajānassa niddaṃ okkamayato*. Also at Vin I 295,14–24.

1219 *Chinnaparipantho*. Mp explains that he has cut off the world-transcending outlet (*lokuttaraparipanthassa chinnattā chinnaparipantho*), but possibly what is meant is that, having committed a *pārājika*, which requires expulsion from the Saṅgha, he has no way to preserve his status as a bhikkhu.

1220 *Aññataraṃ saṅkiliṭṭhaṃ āpattiṃ āpajjati*. This sometimes means that he commits a *pārājika* or a *saṅghādisesa* offense, but since a *pārājika* was just mentioned, it must refer to a *saṅghādisesa*.

1221 *Verabahulo*. Mp: "One has much enmity, both in the form of people who are enemies and as unwholesome [mental] enmity" (*puggalaverenapi akusalaverenapi bahuvero*).

1222 The exact meaning of *pasīdati* cannot easily be captured by a single English word. "To be confident" normally suggests to be poised and self-confident, which is not what is meant. SED gives as meanings of Skt *pra-sad, pra-sīdati*, "to settle down, grow clear and bright, become placid or tranquil; . . . to become satisfied or pleased or glad." SED renders the causative *pra-sādayati*: "to make clear, purify; to make serene, gladden (the heart); to render calm, sooth, appease." Of these meanings, "to gladden, to please" partly captures the impact that *pāsādika* conduct has on others; becoming "gladdened" or "pleased" is how an observer might favorably respond to such conduct. But such conduct also awakens in others *trust* in oneself as a spiritually refined person and inspires *confidence* in the teaching one follows. Thus such conduct "inspires confidence" in others. When one's behavior or attitudes act reflexively upon oneself, one "becomes serene (or placid)," which is the best way to render the sense of the verb *pasīdati*.

1223 The capital of the state of Surasena, situated on the Yamunā River in northern India. It later became an important center for the Mūlasarvāstivādins. Though the text makes the Buddha say he did not like the place, one wonders whether this sutta might be an interpolation inserted by the Vibhajjavādins to denigrate the headquarters of their rival Buddhist school.

1224 *Dīghacārikaṃ anavatthacārikaṃ*. Mp glosses the latter with *avavatthitacārikaṃ*, perhaps "undetermined (or purposeless) wandering." The contrast is with *samavatthacāre* just below, glossed *samavatthitacāre*, "evenly determined wandering."

1225 The first four are violations, respectively, of Pācittiyas 46, 45, 44, and 7.

1226 On the defiled offense, see p. 1733, note 1089.

1227 *Ussūrabhatte kule. Ussūra* is from Skt *utsūra* (SED: "the time when the sun sets, the evening"). Mp glosses "a meal cooked late in the day" (*atidivāpacanabhatte*).

1228 *Samayabhatte kule.* To suit ascetics and brahmins who "abstain from meals outside the proper time," the food would need to be ready well before midday.

1229 See pp. 60–61, for a discussion of misogynistic passages in AN.

1230 The first two "dangers" are evidently taken to be self-explanatory.

1231 *Dhammadassane niveseti*. Mp: "He establishes them in the seeing of the Dhamma of the four [noble] truths."

1232 *Arahaggataṃ āyasmanto satiṃ upaṭṭhāpetha*. Mp: "Establish respect for the three bases [of faith], gone [for refuge] only to the Triple Gem, which is worthy of all honors." The texts occasionally use *āyasmanto* as an address of monks to laypeople. Apparently the word could be used to address anyone considered worthy of esteem and was not solely an honorific for monks.

1233 This is one of the penalties to be observed by those who have committed a *saṅghādisesa* offense.

1234 The ellipsis points in the Pāli may give the impression that in §3 and §4 the devoted person loses confidence in bhikkhus. However, since the person in whom he had confidence was not penalized in any way by other bhikkhus, it is clear that the statement about the devoted person losing his confidence in bhikkhus does not pertain to these two sections. That is, the continuation of §5 should be applied retroactively to §3 and §4 as well. He does not associate with other bhikkhus, not out of resentment toward them, but simply because of the exclusivity of his trust.

1235 From this vagga on, the text no longer includes *uddāna* verses. I thus translate the sutta titles at the head of each sutta in Ce.

1236 For various sets of five qualities that entitle a monk to give full ordination, to give dependence, and to have a novice attend on him, see Vin I 62–65.

1237 On *nissaya*, see pp. 1732–33, note 1085.

1238 Ce and Ee *patikiṭṭhaṃ*. Be *paṭikuṭṭham,* past participle of *paṭikkosati*.

1239 I follow the arrangement of Be and Ee. Ce places the two versions on the jhānas *before* the two versions on the four fruits.

1240 *Vaggātirekasuttāni*. This is the title Ce assigns to this entire concluding section. Be does not assign a general title but classifies these extra suttas into three "repetition series" (*peyyāla*), numbered 1, 2, and 3. The first, referring to the first sutta in each set, is called *Sammutipeyyālaṃ*, "Agreed Upon Repetition Series." I use both the general title of Ce and the separate series titles of Be. Ee does not give any separate title to this section, whether to the whole or to its separate series.

1241 *Bhattuddesaka*. See Vin II 175,36–76. The procedures for appointing officials of the Saṅgha, and their respective tasks, are discussed in detail in Ṭhānissaro 2007b: 323–57.

1242 I translate in accordance with Be and Ee. A translation from Ce would read: "Bhikkhus, one possessing five qualities should not be appointed an assigner of meals. If he is appointed, he should not be sent."

1243 *Senāsanapaññāpaka*. On his qualifications, see Vin II 176,9–14. Dabba Mallaputta's duties as *senāsanapaññāpaka* are described at Vin III 158–60. The qualifications of the officers to follow here, except the next, are described at Vin II 176–77.

1244 *Senāsanaggāhāpaka*. This official is missing in Ee. It is unclear to me how the *senāsanaggāhāpaka* differs from the *senāsanapaññāpaka*.

Ṭhānissaro, too, observes (2007b: 340): "The Canon allows for two officials related to lodgings: the lodging bestower (*senāsana-gāhāpaka*) and the lodging assignor (*senāsana-paññapanaka*). Neither the Canon nor Commentary clearly distinguishes between the duties of the two."

1245 *Abrahmacārī hoti*. Though modeled after the five lay precepts, the third item in this list lays down the more stringent requirement of celibacy for male and female monastics.

1246 *Abrahmacariyā paṭivirato hoti*.

1247 *Kāmesu micchācārinī*. For the lay Buddhist the rule of celibacy incumbent on monastics is changed to abstaining from sexual misconduct (*kāmesu micchācāra*).

1248 A sect of ascetics contemporary with the Buddha. Makkhali Gosāla is regarded as their founder, or perhaps simply one of their prominent teachers. While the text stipulates conditions for the non-Buddhist ascetics to go to hell, it mentions none that will enable them to be reborn in heaven.

1249 In regard to the *māgandika* and the following, Mp says only that they are types of sectarians (*titthiyā*). I am uncertain which of these terms designate a specific religious school and which designate only a mode of practice. Hence I use initial capitals only for those that are known to designate religious schools contemporary with the Buddha.

1250 Be gives the final number as 1151, but the sum total of suttas in this *peyyāla* should be 850: five major sections, taken by ten modes of treatment (direct knowledge, full understanding, etc.) in relation to seventeen defilements (lust, hatred, etc.). Thus, starting at 303, the final number should be 1152.

Notes to the Sixes

1251 *N'eva sumano hoti na dummano, upekkhako viharati sato sampajāno*. Mp: "*Neither joyful nor saddened*: [filled] with joy accompanied by lust in regard to a desirable object. *Nor* [*is he*] *saddened*: [filled] with sadness accompanied by aversion in regard to an undesirable object. *But* [*he*] *dwells equanimous, mindful, and clearly comprehending*: He is not equanimous because he has fallen into the 'equanimity of unknowing' (*aññāṇ'upekkhā*) through apathy in the case of a neutral object; but rather, being mindful and clearly comprehending, he maintains neutrality in relation to the object. In this sutta, the constant dwelling of an arahant is discussed."

1252 For details on the first five mundane direct knowledges, see Vism chaps. 12 and 13.

1253 See **5:139**, where the same simile is stated of a king's bull elephant.

1254 Elaborated below at **6:30**.

1255 Elaborated just below at **6:10** and again at **6:25**.

1256 *Ariyasāvako āgataphalo viññātasāsano*. Mp says that Mahānāma is asking about the stream-enterer's vital support (*sotāpannassa nissayavihāraṃ*).

1257 The six recollections to follow are commented on in detail in Vism chap. 7.

1258 *Visamagatāya pajāya samappatto*. Mp: "Among beings who have become unbalanced (*visamagatesu*) through lust, hatred, and delusion, he has attained peace and calmness (*samaṃ upasamaṃ patto hutvā*)." From this, it is obvious that Mp takes Pāli *sama* to be equivalent to Skt *śama*, peace. But since the text establishes a contrast between *visama*, the imbalance (or unrighteousness) in which ordinary people live, and the *sama* that the noble disciple has attained, it is more likely that Pāli *sama* corresponds to Skt *sama*. Two Chinese parallels support this supposition. SĀ^{2} 156, at T II 432c15–16, has 怨家及己親族。於此二人。無怨憎想。心常平等 ("Whether his enemies or his relatives, toward these two types of people he has no thought of hostility but his mind is balanced"). The other, T 1537.8 at T XXVI 492c13–15, has 於不平等諸有情類。得住平等。於有惱害諸有情類。住無惱害 ("Amid unbalanced sentient beings, he obtains balance; among afflicted sentient beings he dwells without affliction"). Though contradicting the interpretation of *sama* offered by Mp, this confirms the evident meaning of the sutta.

1259 *Dhammasotaṃ samāpanno*. Mp: "He has entered the stream of the Dhamma consisting in insight." Since the Pāli expression can easily be contracted to *sotāpanna*, I do not see why Mp interprets *dhammasota* as insight (*vipassanā*) rather than the noble path (*ariyamagga*). In SN 55:5, at V 347,24–25, *sota* is used as a metaphor for the noble eightfold path.

1260 The first six are the deities of the six sense-sphere heavens. The devas of Brahmā's company (*brahmakāyikā devā*) are the deities of the brahmā world. The "devas still higher than these" are the higher devas in the form and formless realms.

1261 *Dhammā sāraṇīyā*. Mp explains *sāraṇīyā* as if it meant "fit to be remembered" (*saritabbayuttakā*), but Edgerton, in BHSD (p. 593), regards *saṃrañjana, saṃrañjanīya*, "courteous, pleasing, polite, friendly," as the correct Skt equivalent. Five of these are at **5:105**, where they are called "means of dwelling at ease" (*phāsuvihārā*).

1262 *Appaṭivibhattabhogī*. Mp explains that there are two kinds of reservation (*dve paṭivibhattāni*), regarding things and regarding persons. Reservation regarding things means that one decides to give away so much and keep so much for oneself. Reservation regarding persons means that one decides to give to one person but not to another. The bhikkhu described here does not make either of these reservations.

1263 *Nissāraṇīyā dhātuyo*. Compare **5:200**, which describes a different set of "elements of escape."

1264 *Arati*. This word usually signifies dissatisfaction with the life of renunciation.

1265 This text uses the word *rāga*, which in this context probably means personal bias rather than sensual desire. Interestingly, at MN I 424,33–34, *upekkhā* is opposed to *paṭigha*, aversion, the polar opposite of *rāga*. Given that *upekkhā* is a state of inner poise beyond both attraction and repulsion, it is not surprising to find it offered as the antidote to the two opposed qualities.

1266 *Animittā cetovimutti*. Mp: "*The markless liberation of mind*: strong insight (*balavavipassanā*). But the reciters of the Dīgha Nikāya say it is the meditative attainment of the fruit of arahantship (*arahattaphalasamāpattī*); for that is said to be markless because it lacks the marks of lust, etc., the marks of form, etc., and the marks of permanence, etc. (*sā hi rāganimittādīnañc'eva rūpanimittādīnañca niccanimittādīnañca abhāvā animittā ti vuttā*).

1267 *Nimittānusārī*. Mp: "*Follows after marks*: follows along with the aforesaid marks." The "aforesaid marks" are those mentioned in the preceding note.

1268 In the standard correlation between stages of attainment and removal of defilements, doubt and bewilderment along with the view "This I am" are eliminated with the attainment of stream-entry, and the conceit "I am" with the attainment of arahantship (see SN 22:89, III 126–32). In the present passage, the persistence of doubt is taken as a criterion for determining that someone has not removed the conceit "I am."

1269 *Vihāraṃ kappeti*. Lit., "arranges his dwelling." *Kappeti*, as suggesting a way to pass time, occurs in such expressions as *jīvitaṃ kappeti*, "to make a living," *vāsaṃ kappeti*, "to make a dwelling, to dwell," *nisajjaṃ kappeti*, "to take a seat, to sit down," etc.

1270 *Na bhaddakaṃ maraṇaṃ hoti, no bhaddikā kālakiriyā*. Pāli often pairs two words for death, *maraṇa* and *kālakiriyā*. Since such a manner of expression sounds odd in English, I use one word. Mp says that what is meant by "not a good death" is rebirth in the plane of misery (*apāye paṭisandhiṃ gaṇhāti*).

1271 *Kammārāmo hoti kammarato kammārāmataṃ anuyutto*. In this context, *kamma* means construction work, common at monasteries, such as putting up new buildings and renovating existing facilities.

1272 *Papañcārāmo hoti papañcarato papañcārāmataṃ anuyutto*. Mp says: "Proliferation is the proliferation of defilements, occurring by way of craving, views, and conceit and inducing intoxication" (*papañco ti taṇhādiṭṭhimānavasena pavatto madanākārasaṇṭhito kilesapapañco*). For more on *papañca*, see pp. 1710–11, note 881.

1273 *Sakkāya*. Mp: "The round of existence with its three planes" (*tebhūmakavaṭṭaṃ*).

1274 *Mago*. Lit., "a beast." Mp: "One like a beast" (*magasadiso*).

1275 *Sāpekkho*. Mp glosses this with *sataṇho*, "with craving," but I believe the intended meaning is more likely to be "with anxiety, with worry, with sorrow." Pāli *apekkhā*, like "concern," can mean both attachment and worry.

1276 Mp says that since she was not able to cure his illness with medicine, she roared this "lion's roar" (*sīhanāda*) to cure his illness by a declaration of truth (*saccakiriyā*).

1277 I read with Ce *varaṃ*, as against Be and Ee *gharaṃ*. Mp: "will take another husband" (*aññaṃ sāmikaṃ gaṇhissati*). See SED sv *vara*[2]: "'chooser,' one who solicits a girl in marriage, suitor, lover, bridegroom, husband."

1278 *Gahaṭṭhakaṃ brahmacariyaṃ*. It is not unusual in traditional Buddhist cultures for devout couples who have begotten several children to mutually agree to observe celibacy.

1279 Since the structure of this section is parallel to the two that follow rather than to the three that precede it, it is evident that *mam'accayena* does not belong here. Though the expression is in all three printed editions, a Sinhala-script manuscript noted in Ee omits it. Like the two following sections, this one does not have a future verb *bhavissati*. Further, parallel to the next two sections, Nakulamātā here asserts that she *presently* fulfills virtuous behavior, referring one who doubts this to the Buddha. Hence, since Nakulamātā is speaking about a *current* fact, there is no need for her to refer to a time when her husband has passed away. Mp says that §§4–6 are Nakulamātā's declaration of truth.

1280 *Na . . . imasmiṃ dhammavinaye ogādhappattā patigādhappattā assāsappattā*. These are all ways of asserting that she is at minimum a stream-enterer. It is interesting that she claims to have obtained a foothold in the *dhammavinaya*, which suggests that in certain contexts *vinaya* bears a wider meaning than the code of monastic regulations.

1281 *Yāvadatthaṃ seyyasukhaṃ passasukhaṃ middhasukhaṃ anuyutto viharanto*. At **5:206** this is called a mental bondage (*cetaso vinibandha*).

1282 Also at **5:56**.

1283 It is interesting to note that mindfulness of death culminates in the deathless.

1284 Mp explains the opening exclamation, *aho vata*, as an indeclinable expressive of longing (*patthanatthe nipāto*). Brahmāli rejects Mp's interpretation and regards the sentence as an emphatic statement of fact, which he renders: "Indeed, I may live just a night and a day; I should attend to the Blessed One's teaching." The Chinese parallel, EĀ 40.8 (T I 741c26–742b2), is in substantial agreement with Mp. Thus the first monk to speak (at T I 742a2–3) says: "When I contemplate death, I wish to go on living for seven days [and] contemplate the seven factors of enlightenment. This would be very beneficial [to me] in regard to the Tathāgata's teaching [and] after death I will have no regrets" (思惟死想時。意欲存七日。思惟七覺意。於如來法中多所饒益。死後無恨).

1285 *Bahuṃ vata me kataṃ assa*. Mp: "'I could accomplish much in my task with respect to the teaching'" (*sāsane mama kiccaṃ bahu kataṃ assa*). Mp-ṭ: "I would accomplish much in my task as a monk, which would be beneficial to me."

1286 Mp-ṭ: "*A single alms meal*: a single alms meal able to sustain him for a single day." The point of the Pāli locution *tadantaraṃ* . . . *yadantaraṃ* is not that he wants to live long enough to eat a single meal, but that, aware of the uncertainty of death's arrival, he wants to live *for the length of time* it takes to eat a single meal so that he can practice the Dhamma. In other words, if it takes twenty minutes to silently eat a meal, this is the length of time he hopes to live.

1287 *Rattiyā patihitāya*. *Patihita* (or *paṭihita*) is not in PED; see SED sv *prati-dhā*. It is the past participle of *patidahati*, meaning "to commence, to begin, to approach," which seems relevant here. Mp glosses with *paṭipannāya*.

1288 I read with Be *parihāyamāne*, as against Ce and Ee *parihānāya saṃvattamāne*.

1289 These eight lines are also at **3:36**. Here all three editions read *te khemappattā* in pāda a of the final verse.

1290 The text uses the singular *himavantaṃ pabbatarājaṃ*. To conform to ordinary English usage I translate *himavantaṃ* as "the Himalayas," despite apparent tension between the plural object and the singular "the king of mountains."

1291 Mp: "*He is skilled in the attainment of concentration* (*samādhissa samāpattikusalo*): he is skilled in entering concentration, having comprehended what kind of food and climate is suitable. *Skilled in the duration of concentration* (*samādhissa ṭhitikusalo*): he is able to stabilize concentration. *Skilled in emergence* (*samādhissa vuṭṭhānakusalo*): he is able to emerge at the predetermined time. *Skilled in fitness for concentration* (*samādhissa kallitakusalo*): he is able to gladden the mind for concentration, to make it fit. *Skilled in the area [or resort] of concentration* (*samādhissa gocarakusalo*): having avoided those things that are unsuitable and unhelpful for concentration, pursuing those that are suitable and helpful, he knows, 'This concentration takes a mark as its object; this one takes a characteristic as its object.' *Skilled in resolution regarding concentration* (*samādhissa abhinīhārakusalo*): in order to enter higher and higher meditative attainments, he is able to direct [the mind] to the concentration of the first jhāna and so forth." Mp-ṭ adds more information on these skills: "*Skilled in fitness*: able to make the mind enter [concentration] by removing the states that are opposed and by evenly applying the collaborative causes of concentration. *Skilled in the area*: skilled in what is to be done to produce concentration; skilled in the place where it occurs, namely, the meditation subject; and skilled in yoking mindfulness and clear comprehension to the area for going on alms round. *Skilled in resolution*: able to direct or lead [the mind] to the concentration of the first jhāna, etc., because they pertain to distinction." For more on the skills needed to master concentration, see **7:40–41** and SN chap. 34.

1292 Mp glosses *anussatiṭṭhānāni* with *anussatikāraṇāni*, "causes of recollection," on which Mp-ṭ says: "The recollections are themselves 'causes of recollection' in that they function as the cause (*hetubhāvato*) for the welfare and happiness pertaining to this present life and the future life."

1293 *Idampi kho bhikkhave ārammaṇaṃ karitvā*. In the Nikāyas the word *ārammaṇa* does not yet mean "object of consciousness" in the general sense, as it does in the Abhidhamma and commentaries. Occasionally in the Nikāyas *ārammaṇa* may signify an object of meditation, but this role is usually taken by *nimitta*, which does not necessarily mean the "counterpart sign" as it does in the commentaries. I do not interpret the present text to be saying that one takes the recollection of the Buddha *as an object*, but that one *makes it a basis*, or starting point, for departing from greed. For this, I draw support from Mp-ṭ, which glosses *ārammaṇaṃ karitvā* thus: "Having made it a condition, having made it a foundation" (*paccayaṃ karitvā pādakaṃ katvā*). Mp-ṭ takes "this" (*idam*) in the lemma above to be the access concentration (*upacārajjhāna*) obtained by recollection of the Buddha. Mp explains "are purified" (*visujjhanti*) to mean "they attain final nibbāna, the supreme purity."

1294 Mp: "*In the midst of confinement* (*sambādhe*): amid confinement in the five objects of sensual pleasure. *Has discovered the open-*

ing (*okāsādhigamo*): the opening is the six subject of recollection, which he has discovered."

1295 Where the preceding sutta reads *idh'ekacce sattā visujjhanti,* the present one has *idh' ekacce sattā visuddhidhammā bhavanti.* There is no difference in the meaning.

1296 *Manobhāvanīyassa bhikkhuno dassanāya upasaṅkamituṃ.* The commentaries consistently explain *manobhāvanīyā* to mean "those who increase esteem," or "those worthy of esteem," rather than "those who have developed the mind." Thus Spk II 250,1–2 says those bhikkhus are *manobhāvanīyā* "who, when seen, make the mind grow in the wholesome" (*yesu hi diṭṭhesu kusalavasena cittaṃ vaḍḍhati*).

1297 *Yaṃ nimittaṃ āgamma yaṃ nimittaṃ manasikaroto anantarā āsavānaṃ khayo hoti.* On the "immediate destruction of the taints," see p. 1705, note 851.

1298 Mp: "On that occasion when he is sitting in his daytime dwelling it occurs in his mind door."

1299 *Adhicittaṃ.* Mp: "The mind of concentration and insight." The bhikkhu Udāyī (Lāḷudāyī) often blunders in his explanation of doctrinal points and is then reproached by the Buddha.

1300 Ironically, this may be the only place in the Nikāyas where three jhānas are referred to as an *anussatiṭṭhāna,* "subject of recollection." Neither text nor Mp offers an explanation why the fourth jhāna is set off as a separate subject of recollection, the fifth here. In fact, the use of the designation *anussatiṭṭhāna* for the five contemplations mentioned by Ānanda, and the sixth added by the Buddha, seems unique to this sutta.

1301 *Yathā divā tathā rattiṃ, yathā rattiṃ tathā divā.* Also at **4:41**. Mp explains: "As by day he attends to the perception of light, just so does he attend to it at night. As at night he attends to the perception of light, just so does he attend to it during the day. *Obtaining knowledge and vision*: this is obtaining the divine eye, called knowledge and vision."

1302 Here and below are the nine charnel ground contemplations, as in the Satipaṭṭhāna Sutta, at DN 22.7–10, II 295–97; MN 10.12–30, I 58–59.

1303 This must be referring to the fourth jhāna as the basis for the six kinds of direct knowledge.

1304 In Pāli: *dassanānuttariyaṃ, savanānuttariyaṃ, lābhānuttariyaṃ, sikkhānuttariyaṃ, pāricariyānuttariyaṃ, anussatānuttariyaṃ.*

1305 *Paṭisanthāra.* At **2:152** it is said that there are two kinds of hospitality: with material things and with the Dhamma.

1306 These last three perceptions are explained at **10:60 §§5–7**.

1307 *Ācamayitvāna*. Mp explains this literally: one washes one's hands and feet and cleans one's mouth.

1308 *Natthi attakāro, natthi parakāro*. Lit., "There is no self-doing, there is no other-doing." The Buddha refutes him just below by pointing out the obvious fact that the brahmin has come of his own free will (*sayaṃ*) and will depart of his own free will.

1309 *Ārambhadhātu*. Mp: "The energy that occurs by way of beginning [an activity]" (*ārabhanavasena pavattaviriyaṃ*). The next two elements mentioned just below, *nikkamadhātu* and *parakkamadhātu*, can be understood respectively as the energy needed to persist in an action and to consummate it. The three are proposed as the antidote to dullness and drowsiness at **1:18** and SN 46:51, V 105,28–106,2, and as means of nurturing the enlightenment factor of energy at SN 46:2, V 66,9–15, and SN 46:51, V 104,14–20.

1310 Mp does not differentiate the next three factors mentioned here—*thāmadhātu, ṭhitidhātu*, and *upakkamadhātu*—but says merely that they are various names for energy.

1311 An expanded parallel of **5:201**.

1312 See **5:30**. Although the framework of the two suttas is the same, their content is so different that it is questionable whether the present sutta can be considered an expanded parallel of the other.

1313 I read with Ce *ārāmiko vā samaṇuddeso vā sahadhammiko vā*. Neither Be nor Ee includes *sahadhammiko vā*. Be's reading here is very different: *idān' imaṃ āyasmantaṃ ārāmiko vā upaṭṭhahissati samaṇuddeso vā taṃ tamhā samādhimhā cāvessati*; "Now a monastery attendant or a novice will serve this venerable one, which will cause him to fall away from that concentration." Ee follows Be, but with *ghaṭṭessati*, "strike against, offend, provoke," instead of *upaṭṭhahissati*.

1314 *Araññasaññaṃyeva manasi karissati ekattaṃ*. Mp: "*Oneness*: he will bring to mind just the perception of the forest, a one-pointed state of uniformity" (*ekasabhāvaṃ, ekaggatābhūtāṃ araññasaññaṃ yeva citte karissati*). The wording here is reminiscent of MN 121, III 104,20–21: *araññasaññaṃ paṭicca manasi karoti ekattaṃ*, "he attends to the oneness dependent on the perception of the forest."

1315 Mp: "By this much, the Teacher has praised a forest lodging."

1316 The various applications of the word *nāga* will be explained just below. King's Pasenadi's bull elephant was called "Seta" ("White") because its body was white.

1317 A pun is intended here. The Buddha's statement—*āguṃ na karoti*—playfully derives the word *nāga* from *na* + *āguṃ*, "no evil." *Nāga* thus becomes an epithet for the Buddha, or, more broadly, for any arahant. See Sn 527: *Āguṃ na karoti kiñci loke ... nāgo tādi pavuccate tathattā* ("One who does no evil in the world

... the stable one is for such a reason called a nāga"). See too Th 1249 (= SN 8:8, I 192,34): *Nāganāmo'si bhagavā* ("You are named Nāga, O Blessed One").

1318 Mp identifies this Udāyī with Kāludāyī. However, the same verses at Th 689–704 are ascribed simply to Udāyī, while a different set of verses in Th (527–36) is ascribed to Kāludāyī. This proves that Mp's identification of the poet cannot be correct. There is a Chinese parallel of this sutta, MĀ 118 (at T I 608b2–609a3), which at several points proved helpful in my reading of the Pāli verses.

1319 Reading with Be *vanā nibbanam āgataṃ*. Ce and Ee have *nibbānam* in place of *nibbanam*. Mp draws out the word play: "From the jungle of defilements, he has come to a clearing; he has reached nibbāna, devoid of the jungle of defilements" (*kilesavanato nibbanaṃ kilesavanarahitaṃ nibbānaṃ āgataṃ sampattaṃ*). It seems that Ce and Ee have transposed *nibbāna* from the gloss into the text itself. The Chinese at T I 608c2 has 於林離林去, "from the woods he has left the woods," which supports the Be reading.

1320 *Saccanāmo* is not "one whose name is truth," but "one who is truly named," whose name truly corresponds to his being. Mp: "He is truly named, really named, accurately named 'nāga' just because of not doing evil" (*tacchanāmo bhūtanāmo āguṃ akaraṇeneva nāgoti evaṃ avitathanāmo*). The Chinese (at T I 608c7) has 一切龍中龍, 真諦無上龍, "he is the nāga among all nāgas, in truth the nāga who is unsurpassed."

1321 There is a word play here between two meanings of *caraṇa*, "conduct, behavior" and "feet." Mp glosses: "They are the Buddhanāga's two hind feet."

1322 *Sati gīvā siro paññā vīmaṃsā dhammacintanā*. I translate the terms quite literally. Mp, however, says: "The tip of the elephant's trunk is called investigation (*vīmaṃsā*) because [it investigates] things to determine whether they are hard or soft, edible or inedible, etc. He then rejects whatever should be rejected and takes whatever should be taken. So, for the Buddha-nāga, *reflection on phenomena* (*dhammacintanā*)—referring to his knowledge that determines the classes of phenomena—is his [means of] investigation. With this knowledge he knows who is capable and who incapable." The Chinese at 608c11 renders the line in a more straightforward way: 智慧頭思惟分別法, "wisdom is his head, reflection on and discrimination of phenomena."

1323 In pāda c I read *samātapo* with Be and Ee, as against Ce *samāvāpo*. Mp: "It is the concentration of the fourth jhāna that is here called *dhamma*. For it is on this basis that the supernormal powers succeed. Therefore it is called *balanced heat of the belly* (*kucchisamātapo*). *Seclusion* (*viveka*) refers to bodily seclusion, mental seclusion, and seclusion from the acquisitions (*kāyacittaupadhiviveko*). As the elephant uses its tail to ward off mosquitoes, so the Tathāgata resorts to seclusion to ward off householders and monks." The Chinese reads the couplet (at 608c12) as 受持諸法腹, 樂遠離雙臂, "upholding dharmas is his belly, and delight in seclusion is his pair of arms." Apparently in this transmission, *vāladhi* of the Pāli came down as *bāhūni*.

1324 *Assāsa* can mean both inhalation and consolation, the latter referring to arahantship. Mp says that just as inhalation and exhalation are what keeps the elephant alive, so fruition attainment (*phalasamāpatti*) is essential to the Buddha, and it is there that he delights.

1325 Reading with Be *loke viharati*. Ce and Ee *loke virajjati* means "becomes detached in the world," which does not match the simile as well.

1326 In place of *saṅkhāresūpasantesu* in pāda c (the reading of all three editions), I read here with a pair of Burmese manuscripts (referred to in a note in Ee): *aṅgāresu ca santesu, nibbutoti pavuccati*. The reading is also found at Th 702. Vanarata points out that "the whole verse *is* the simile and *nibbuto* [meaning both an extinguished fire and a person who has attained nibbāna] refers to the fire." The Chinese (at 608c27), in agreement with Th and the Burmese manuscripts, has 無薪火不傳, 此火謂之滅, "Without firewood, the fire does not continue. This fire is then said to have ceased."

1327 Mp: "Other arahant nāgas will know the Buddha-nāga that was taught by the nāga, the elder Udāyī." Despite Mp, I suspect the text itself intends *the Buddha himself* as the one who taught about the nāga. The Chinese (at 608c29) supports my suspicion: 龍中龍所說, "it was spoken by the nāga among nāgas."

1328 Reading with Ee *parinibbāti 'nāsavo*, as against Ce and Be *parinibbissati anāsavo*. This verse completes the simile with the fire. The analogy is clearer in the Chinese (at 609a2), where 此龍謂之滅, "this nāga is said to have attained nibbāna," echoes 608c27, 此火謂之滅, "this fire is said to have ceased." I have attempted to capture this effect by translating *parinibbāti* twice, first as quenched and then in terms of its doctrinal meaning.

1329 I take the correct reading here to be Be *sakadāgāmipatto* (found, too, in Burmese manuscripts), as contrasted with Ce and Ee *sakadāgāmī satto*. Confusion of *s* and *p* is not unusual in Sinhala-script manuscripts. However, the gloss in Mp, *sakadāgāmipuggalo hutvā*, suggests that the commentator used a text with the reading *sakadāgāmī satto*. It is not impossible that the corruption (if it is one) dates back before the age of the commentaries.

1330 Ce and Be *petteyyopi*; Ee *petteyyo piyo*. The only meaning PED assigns *petteyya* is "showing filial piety toward one's father," which does not fit here. We should probably read here *pettāpiyo*, which PED defines as "father's brother, paternal uncle." In the version at **10:75**, Ce has *pettā pi yo* and Ee *pettā piyo*, which, by closing the spaces, would both give the desired reading. In MN 89.18, II 123,27–124,11, Purāṇa and Isidatta are said to have been in the employment of King Pasenadi of Kosala but to have shown greater respect toward the Buddha than toward the king. Their love for the Buddha is expressed in SN 55:6, V 348–52.

1331 Mp: "Ānanda said this because he did not know the reason." Brahmāli writes: "I understand Ānanda to simply be saying that it should be understood just as the Buddha explained it," and he suggests rendering the sentence: "Just so, sister, as this was declared by the Blessed One." However, at this point the Buddha's pronouncements on their destiny have not yet been explained. The explanation comes only at the end of the sutta, when the Buddha extols the respective strong points of the two deceased lay disciples.

1332 Ce *ambakapaññā;* Be here has *ammakasaññā*, "a woman's perception" or "a woman's idea," but the Be text of **10:75** reads *ammakapaññā*. Ee has *ambakasaññā* here but *ambakapaññā* in the concluding paragraph. Apparently Ee's former reading is a typographical error for the latter, since on the first occurrence *saññā* is cited as a variant in the notes. Again, the common *s/p* confusion must lie behind the variants. *Ambaka* in Ce and Ee (or Be *ammaka*) is derived from *ammā*, "mother," but with the more general meaning of women. Mp-ṭ explains: "*Ammakā* (or *ambakā*) means women (lit., the class of mothers). This is a metaphorical term. That is, mothers, the class of mothers, maternal parents, are found among women" (*Ammakāti mātugāmo. Upacāravacanañh'etaṃ. Itthīsu yadidaṃ ammakā mātugāmo jananī janikā*). SED sv *ambā* has "a mother, good woman (as a title of respect)." And under *ambikā*: "mother, good woman (as a term of respect)." The Chinese parallel at T II 258c8–9, does not include the derogatory generalization about women, but states the matter with reference to Migasālā as an individual: "The lay follower Migasālā is foolish and has little wisdom" (鹿住優婆夷愚癡少智).

1333 The juxtaposition of nominative *ke* with locative *–ñāṇe* is puzzling. I take the sense to be that those referred to by *ke* are established *in* this knowledge. Perhaps, though, *–ñāṇe* is a residual eastern form, a nominative plural in agreement with *ke*. Mp does not attempt to resolve this problem, but when commenting on "in the knowledge of other persons as superior and inferior" (*purisapuggalaparopariyañāṇe*), it explains this knowledge as "the knowledge of other persons' superior and inferior faculties by way of their sharpness or dullness" (*purisapuggalānaṃ tikkha-muduvasena indriyaparopariyañāṇaṃ*).

1334 *Sāmāyikampi vimuttiṃ na labhati.* Mp says that he does not occasionally gain rapture and joy derived from listening to the Dhamma. Paṭis II 40,16–17, however, defines the near-synonym *samayavimokkho* as the four jhānas and four formless attainments (*cattāri ca jhānāni, catasso ca arūpasamāpattiyo, ayaṃ samayavimokkho*, which it distinguishes from permanent emancipation, identified with the four noble paths, the four fruits of the spiritual life, and nibbāna (*cattāro ca ariyamaggā, cattāri ca sāmaññaphalāni, nibbānañca, ayaṃ asamayavimokkho*).

1335 Text reads merely *taṃ hi tesaṃ*, without specifying what *taṃ* refers to. Mp explains that it is the making of the judgment (*taṃ pamāṇakaraṇaṃ*).

1336 *Imaṃ puggalaṃ dhammasotaṃ nibbahati.* Mp: "The knowledge of insight, occurring strongly, carries him along; it conducts him to the plane of the noble ones."

1337 Text has *lobhadhammā*, "states of greed," which Mp glosses as "simply greed" (*lobho yeva*).

1338 I follow here the text of the printed Ce, with its elisions. The electronic Ce fills in the elisions incorrectly.

1339 Here and in §6, I read with Ce *vacīsaṃsārā*, which is also the reading in Mp (Ce). Be and Ee have *vacīsaṅkhārā*. Mp glosses: "Just utterances in addressing and conversing" (*ālāpasallāpavasena vacanān'eva*). *Vacīsaṃsāro* is at **2:63**, where it refers to arguments between factions of monks.

1340 Mp: "Purāṇa excelled in virtuous behavior, Isidatta in wisdom. Purāṇa's virtuous behavior matched Isidatta's superior wisdom; Isidatta's wisdom matched Purāṇa's superior virtuous behavior."

1341 I have divided the stanzas as is done in Be, which I find more satisfactory than Ce. In Ee the lines of verse are not grouped into separate stanzas.

1342 All three editions read *evam etaṃ gahaṭṭhānaṃ cāgo puññaṃ pavaḍḍhati.* The syntax is not satisfactory yet no variants are noted. Mp attempts to resolve the problem with its gloss, *cāgoti saṅkhaṃ gataṃ puññaṃ vaḍḍhati*, "merit which is designated 'generosity' increases," but this is implausible. Could there have originally been an ablative *cāgā* here, or an instrumental *cāgena* (with the verb *vaḍḍhati*, to support the meter), which was changed to *cāgo* by error? The Chinese parallel, MĀ 125, lends some support to this hypothesis at T I 614c20: 因施福增多, "because of generosity merit increases."

1343 *Dhammayogā.* Mp says this is a name for speakers on the Dhamma (*dhammakathikā*), but it may refer to all those who adopt a predominantly cognitive approach to the Dhamma. The term seems to be unique to the present text. The distinction posited between meditators and those intent on Dhamma suggests a late origin, when vocations in the Saṅgha had bifurcated along these lines.

1344 *Jhāyanti pajjhāyanti*. The tone of this is derisive. Be uses a string of four verbs: *jhāyanti pajjhāyanti nijjhāyanti avajjhāyanti*. For a similar derisive use of verbs based on *jhāyanti*, see **11:9**, V 323,18; MN 50.13, I 334,18–34.

1345 *Amataṃ dhātuṃ kāyena phusitvā viharanti*. Mp: "This refers to the nibbāna element, called 'the deathless' because it is devoid of death. Having taken up a meditation subject, in stages they dwell having touched it with the mental body."

1346 *Gambhīraṃ atthapadaṃ paññāya ativijjha passanti*. Mp: "The 'deep and pithy matter' includes the aggregates, elements, sense bases, and so forth, which are subtle and hidden. They see this after penetrating it with insight and path wisdom (*sahavipassanāya maggapaññāya*)."

1347 Moliyasīvaka is also at SN 36:21, IV 230–31, where he inquires from the Buddha whether all feeling is due to past kamma.

1348 On the "directly visible Dhamma" (*sandiṭṭhiko dhammo*), see too **3:53–54**.

1349 *Lobhadhammā*. Similarly, just below, the text has *dosadhammā* and *mohadhammā*. Mp glosses as "the factors associated with it" (*taṃsampayuttadhammā*).

1350 *Kāyasandosaṃ*, followed by *vacīsandosaṃ* and *manosandosaṃ*. Mp glosses the first as a faulty quality in the body-door (*kāyadvārassa dussanākāraṃ*).

1351 Both monks declare, in opposite ways, the arahant's eradication of the three modes of conceit: the superiority conceit, the inferiority conceit, and the equality conceit.

1352 *Attho ca vutto attā ca anupanīto*. As at **3:72**, IV 218,31, there seems to be a word play between *attho* and *attā*, "goal" and "self."

1353 Mp glosses *ussesu* as superior persons, *omesu* as inferior ones, and *samatte* as similar ones, explaining: "Arahants do not rank themselves, by way of conceit, as superior, inferior, and equal."

1354 An expanded parallel of **5:24**.

1355 *Cetasā samphuṭṭapubbā te ca samudācaranti*. The expression is unusual. Mp offers merely a routine word gloss.

1356 The questions in Pāli: *kiṃadhippāyā, kiṃupavicārā, kiṃadhiṭṭhānā, kiṃabhinivesā, kiṃpariyosānā*.

1357 I read with Ce *sathādhiṭṭhānā*, as against Be and Ee *satthādhiṭṭhānā*, "a weapon is their support." Mp does not comment, but craftiness ties up better with thickets, darkness, and remaining unseen.

1358 *Ākiñcaññābhinivesā*. Mp takes this to mean that their minds are intent on the state of non-grasping (*niggahaṇabhāve*).

1359 Mp does not give information about him and he does not appear elsewhere in the Nikāyas.

1360 Strangely, neither Mp nor Mp-ṭ explains why the Buddha refers to Dhammika as *brāhmaṇa*. This may be the only place in the Nikāyas where the Buddha refers to a bhikkhu as a brahmin followed by his personal name.

1361 Reading with Ce and Be *pavattesi*, as against Ee *pātesi*, "felled," also cited as a variant in Ce and Be. Mp glosses *pavattesi* with *parivattesi*.

1362 *Brahmalokasahavyatāya*. An odd expression, which also occurs at DN 19.59, II 250,20. Sv II 670,13–14 says: "'He taught the path to disciples for companionship with the brahmā world': that is, he explained the path to fellowship with Brahmā in the brahmā world" (*sāvakānañca brahmalokasahabyatāya maggaṃ desesī ti brahmaloke brahmunā sahabhāvāya maggaṃ kathesi*).

1363 *Diṭṭhisampannaṃ*. A person who is at least a stream-enterer.

1364 Brahmāli called my attention to an entry in DOP (p. 744) for a noun *khanti*[2], meaning "hurt, injury," presumably derived from the verb *khaṇati*[1], "hurts, injures, impairs." This word is *not* the Pāli equivalent of Skt *kṣānti* (DOP *khanti*[1]), "patience" or "acceptance." Mp glosses *khanti* here as "digging up one's own virtues" (*attano guṇakhaṇanaṃ*), but DOP points out that the commentaries tend to conflate *khaṇati*[1], "injures," with *khaṇati*[2], "digs up." The Skt equivalent of *khanti*[2] may be *kṣhati*, from *kṣaṇoti*, "hurts, injures, wounds"; see SED sv *kshan*.

1365 *Ito bahiddhā*. That is, those outside the Buddhist community.

1366 Ce *na no āmasabrahmacārisu*, Be *na no samasabrahmacārisu*, Ee *na no sabrahmacārisu*. DOP sv *āma*[3] has "in or of the same house; belonging to the same house" and cites *āmasabrahmacāri(n)* as meaning "a fellow religious student belonging to the same house or community." However, it gives this passage as the sole reference, and the term does not seem to occur elsewhere in the Nikāyas. Mp (Ce) accepts the unusual reading and says: *Na no āmasabrahmacārīsū ti ettha āmajano* [Be: *samajano*] *nāma sakajano vuccati. Tasmā na no sakesu samānabrahmacārīsu cittāni paduṭṭhāni bhavissantī ti ayamettha attho* ("*Toward our fellow monks of the same house*: Here, it is one's own people that are called 'people of the same house.' Therefore the meaning here is: 'There should be no thoughts of hatred toward one's own fellow monks.'"). The passage recurs at **7:73**, but with the unaugmented *sabrahmacārisu*. I suspect that the augmented forms found in the Ce and Be versions of this sutta are the product of an ancient transmission error that was accepted as authentic by the commentator. I therefore treat the text as reading simply *sabrahmacārisu.*

1367 This is Soṇa Koḷivīsa, declared by the Buddha foremost among those who arouse energy (see **1:205**). His verses are at Th 632–44. Th 638–39 refer to the simile of the lute; Th 640–44 are identical with the verses at the end of this sutta. The story of Soṇa appears in an expanded version at Vin I 179–85, where it leads to the Buddha's granting permission to the monks to wear sandals.

1368 Reading with Ce and Ee: *Viriyasamataṃ adhiṭṭhaha, indriyānaṃ ca samataṃ paṭivijjha, tattha ca nimittaṃ gaṇhāhi*. Where Ce and Ee have *viriyasamataṃ*, Be has *vīriyasamathaṃ* (but just below, *indriyānañca samataṃ*). Mp (Ce) also reads *viriyasamathaṃ* in the lemma. The explanation in Mp seems to support *viriyasamathaṃ*.

Mp: "*Resolve on evenness of energy*: Resolve on serenity combined with energy (*viriyasampayuttaṃ samathaṃ adhiṭṭhaha*). The meaning is, 'Link energy with serenity.' *Achieve evenness of the spiritual faculties*: Keep to evenness, a balance of the spiritual faculties of faith, etc. When faith is linked with wisdom and wisdom with faith; when energy is linked with concentration and concentration with energy, then the balance of the faculties is maintained. But mindfulness is useful everywhere, so it should always be strong. . . . *Seize the object there*: When such balance exists, the object can arise clearly, like the reflection of one's face in a mirror; and you should take up (*gaṇhāhi*) this object—bring forth (*nibbattehi*) the object of serenity, of insight, of the path, and of the fruit. Thus the Buddha explained the meditation subject to him, leading up to arahantship."

Chinese parallels to this passage offer quite different readings of the Buddha's injunction, as follows: T I 612a28–29: "Therefore you should distinguish this time (could *samataṃ* have mutated into *samayaṃ*?), examine this mark, and do not be heedless" (是故汝當分別此時。觀察此相。莫得放逸); T II 62c17–18: "Therefore you should practice by taking up [the object] in a balanced way; do not cling, do not be heedless, and do not grasp marks" (是故汝當平等修習攝受，莫著、莫放逸、莫取相); T II 612b19–20: "If you can stay in the middle, this is the superior practice" (若能在中者。此則上行); T XXII 844c1–2 is closest to the Pāli: "You should balance your energy, balance the faculties" (應等精進等於諸根).

1369 In Pāli: *nekkhammādhimutto, pavivekādhimutto, abyāpajjhādhimutto, taṇhakkhayādhimutto, upādānakkhayādhimutto, asammohādhimutto.* Mp says that each expression signifies arahantship.

1370 *Karaṇīyaṃ attano asamanupassanto katassa vā paṭicayaṃ*. Mp glosses *paṭicayaṃ* with "growth by repeated activity" (*punappunaṃ karaṇena vaḍḍhiṃ*).

1371 *Sīlabbataparāmāsaṃ . . . sārato paccāgacchanto*. This expression normally refers to the extreme austerities of those who believe them to be the core of spiritual cultivation. See **3:78**.

1372 All three editions abridge the last three items as is done here.

1373 *Vayañc'assānupassati*. Mp: "He sees the arising and vanishing of that mind" (*tassa c'esa cittassa uppādampi vayampi passati*).

1374 The similes that follow are found among other places also at MN 97.29, II 193,1–19, and SN 35:87, IV 56,17–57,5.

1375 This means that he passed away as a non-returner.

1376 I follow Be and Ee, in which the first, second, fourth, and fifth benefits come from listening to the Dhamma at the proper time (*kālena dhammassavane*), the third and sixth from examining the meaning at the proper time (*kālena atth'upaparikkhāya*). Ce combines the two for the third and sixth items, which seems less satisfactory, because in these two situations the monk doesn't get to hear the Dhamma.

1377 *Anuttare upadhisaṅkhaye*. Mp identifies this as nibbāna. On the acquisitions (*upadhi*), see p. 1621, note 219.

1378 *Chaḷabhijātiyo*. Pūraṇa Kassapa is one of the six teachers contemporary with the Buddha. This is the only place where he is associated with the doctrine of the six classes, which are not mentioned elsewhere in the Nikāyas. In DN 2.17, I 52,22–53,4, he is depicted as a proponent of the doctrine of non-doing (*akiriyavāda*), but at SN 46:56, V 126,26–30, the doctrine of non-causality (*ahetukavāda*) is ascribed to him.

1379 *Bhikkhū kaṇṭakavuttikā*. The exact intent is not clear, but the tone is pejorative. Mp says only that these are *samaṇas*.

1380 *Nibbānaṃ abhijāyati*. Mp: "*Produces nibbāna*: that is, he attains nibbāna, or he is born into the class of nibbāna consisting in the plane of the noble ones" (*nibbānaṃ abhijāyatīti nibbānaṃ pāpuṇāti, ariyabhūmisaṅkhātāya vā nibbānajātiyā jāyati*). This explanation is given because in strict doctrinal terms nibbāna, being *ajāta* and *akata*, "unborn" and "unmade," is without birth or production.

1381 As at **3:13**, **4:85**, but here all three editions put *nesādakule* before *veṇakule*.

1382 In Pāli: *āsavā saṃvarā pahātabbā, āsavā paṭisevanā pahātabbā, āsavā adhivāsanā pahātabbā, āsavā parivajjanā pahātabbā, āsavā vinodanā pahātabbā, āsavā bhāvanā pahātabbā*. These six, preceded by "taints to be abandoned by seeing" (*āsavā dassanā pahātabbā*), are treated in detail in the Sabbāsava Sutta (MN 2), where the explanations are the same as those given here.

1383 This sentence is missing in Be, but it occurs in Ce and Ee and has parallels in the sections on the other methods of abandoning the taints.

1384 His name means "dealer in firewood." Mp says that he was so named because he earned his living by selling firewood.

1385 The three qualities he mentions are ascetic practices (*dhutaṅga*). These are contrasted below with non-ascetic monastic practices: living near a village, accepting invitations from laypeople to meals at their homes, and wearing robes prepared by householders.

1386 Mp says that some time later, five hundred bhikkhus who visited families returned to lay life. When he heard this he said, "What does that have to do with me?" and his faith did not vacillate. It was in anticipation of this that the Buddha said to him: "When you give gifts to the Saṅgha, your mind will be confident." On the special merits of gifts to the Saṅgha, see MN 142.7–8, III 255–56.

1387 *Abhidhammakathaṃ kathenti*. Mp explains this as "a talk involved with the Abhidhamma" (*abhidhammamissakaṃ kathaṃ*), but I take *abhidhammakathaṃ* here as a mere referential term. On this use of the expression, see p. 1733, note 1086.

1388 *Kathaṃ opāteti* (as in Ce and Be; Ee has the aorist *opātesi*). Mp: "He interrupted their discussion and gave his own explanation" (*tesaṃ kathaṃ vicchinditvā attano kathaṃ katheti*).

1389 *Gopāsū*. I translate following Mp: *gāvo ca ajikā ca*.

1390 *Sippisambuka*. PED suggests "oyster" for *sippi*, but oysters are marine animals. My rendering is intended to escape the difficulty.

1391 *Animittaṃ cetosamādhiṃ*. Mp: "*All marks* are all such marks as permanence and so forth. The *markless mental concentration* is the concentration of strong insight (*balavavipassanāsamādhiṃ*)."

1392 *Sarissati nekkhammassa*. Mp: "He will remember the virtues of going forth."

1393 Mp explains that Citta returned to lay life seven times and went forth seven times. The reason for his instability was that during the time of the Buddha Kassapa he had persuaded a bhikkhu to return to lay life. Therefore, even though he had the supporting conditions for arahantship, because of that kamma he had to move back and forth seven times between lay life and monastic life before attaining arahantship.

1394 Sn 1042. The brahmin student's name is Tissa Metteyya. On the Pārāyana, see p. 1639, note 367.

1395 *Majjhe mantā na lippati*. Mp glosses *mantā* with *paññā*, taking it to be a feminine noun. In this it follows Nidd II 10,12, which glosses *mantā* as if it were a truncated feminine instrumental: *majjhe mantāya na lippati*. I think it more likely, however, that *mantā* is the nominative of the agent noun *mantar*, "a thinker, a wise man." On this form, see Norman 2006b: 190–91.

1396 Mp explains: "The contact (*phassa*) at the first end is one individual existence (*attabhāva*), which is produced by way of contact. The origin of contact (*phassasamudaya*), the second end, is the future existence, produced with the contact of the kamma done in this existence as its condition. The cessation of contact (*phassanirodha*) is nibbāna. Nibbāna is said to be in the middle because it cuts in half craving, the seamstress." In my opinion, it would make better sense to see *phassanirodha* here, not as nibbāna, but as the ceasing of contact at the end of the first existence. Craving is then the seamstress because it ties the contact of the previous existence to the initial arising of contact at the start of the new existence.

1397 Mp: "What should be directly known (*abhiññeyyaṃ*) is the four noble truths; what should be fully understood (*pariññeyyaṃ*) is the pair of mundane truths (suffering and its origin). In this very life, he makes an end of the suffering of the round; he terminates it and eradicates it."

1398 Mp: "Consciousness—both rebirth-consciousness and the other kinds—is said to be in the middle because it occurs as the condition for name and form."

1399 Mp: "Kammic consciousness is in the middle; or here, because kamma is included by the mind-base among the internal bases, any kind of consciousness is in the middle; or else the *javana* consciousness is dependent on an internal base—for [it depends on] adverting in the mind-door—and so it is said to be in the middle."

1400 Mp: "Personal existence (*sakkāya*) is the round of existence with its three planes. The origin of personal existence is the truth of the origin; the cessation of personal existence is the truth of cessation." Again, I would interpret this as I did the first presentation: personal existence is the present existence; the origin of personal existence is the arising of the next existence; the cessation of personal existence is the ceasing of the present existence. And craving, by generating rebirth, sews the future existence to this present one.

1401 In a Chinese parallel to this sutta, SĀ 1164 (T II 310b20–311a2), the bhikkhus propose only five interpretations of the verse: (1) six internal bases, six external bases, and feeling; (2) the past, the future, and the present; (3) pleasure, pain, and neither pain nor pleasure; (4) existence, its origin, and feeling; (5) identity and its origin (the middle term is missing). When they inquire from the Buddha, he explains the verse in terms of contact, its origin, and feeling. The verse in the Chinese does not have a word corresponding to Pāli *mantā*.

1402 Here I follow the *uddāna* verse of Be. The Ce version is not clear to me.

1403 As at **6:44**, III 348,9–10. It seems that this is Ānanda's way of simply confirming that the Buddha had said something without committing himself to an interpretation of the statement.

1404 *Kathañhi nāma yaṃ mayā ekaṃsena byākataṃ tattha dvejjhā āpajjissati.* The Buddha's statement here belongs to his first way of answering a question, namely, by making a categorical assertion. On the four ways of answering a question, see **3:67, 4:42**.

1405 *Vālaggakoṭinittudanamattampi sukkadhammaṃ*. Mp: "An amount that could be seen on the tip of a hair; or an amount that could be poked with the tip of a hair."

1406 Ce and Ee have *vibhajantassa,* as against Be *vibhajissāmi,* which Ee notes as a variant from a Burmese manuscript. The Be reading seems a normalization, but since the Ce/Ee reading leaves the sentence grammatically incomplete, I follow Be. The plural *–ñāṇāni* is in the text, and thus I use the plural "knowledges" even though it sounds odd in English.

1407 I read with Ce *kusalamūlā,* as against Be and Ee *kusalā.*

1408 *Abhidose aḍḍharattaṃ bhattakālasamaye.* DOP sv *aḍḍha* defines *aḍḍharattaṃ* as "midnight." On *bhattakālasamaye,* Mp says "the time for a meal in the king's court" (*rājakulānaṃ bhattakālasaṅkhāte samaye*). Perhaps in the Buddha's time the royal court ended the day with a midnight meal.

1409 *Nibbedhikapariyāyaṃ vo bhikkhave dhammapariyāyaṃ desessāmi.* Mp: "A penetrative exposition is one that penetrates and splits the mass of greed, [hatred, and delusion] that had not been penetrated and split before."

1410 The text alternates between singular and plural forms of *kamma*. I have used the singular, which sounds more natural in English.

1411 Contrary to all three editions, I regard the first occurrence of *saṅkapparāgo purisassa kāmo* as either prose or a line of a familiar verse being quoted in the prose. The following verse will then be a normal verse of four lines rather than one of five lines. See SN 1:34, I 22, where the verse occurs with only four lines. Mp explains *saṅkapparāgo* as "lust arisen by way of intention" (*saṅkappavasena uppannarāgo*). *Kāmasaṅkappa* is one of the three types of unwholesome thought, and it is clear from the context that this is what is meant. For further discussion, see CDB 366, note 72. The verse is not included in the Chinese parallel, MĀ 111.

1412 Mp explains this as the coexistent contact (*sahajātaphassa*).

1413 Mp: "One desiring celestial sensual pleasures, by fulfilling good conduct, is reborn in the deva world [and acquires] an individual existence that is a consequence of merit. By engaging in misconduct, one is reborn in the plane of misery [and acquires] an individual existence that is a consequence of demerit."

1414 Regarding this last phrase, Mp says that it is just the spiritual life of the path (*brahmacariyasaṅkhāto maggo va*) that is called the cessation of sensual pleasures. It will be observed that each section follows the pattern of the four noble truths, with two additions: diversity (*vemattatā*) and result (*vipāka*).

1415 *Sāmisā*. Mp: "Associated with the bait of the defilements" (*kilesāmisasampayuttā*).

1416 *Vohāravepakkaṃ . . . saññaṃ vadāmi*. Mp: "Expression, consisting in talk, is the result of perception."

1417 *Cetanā 'haṃ bhikkhave kammaṃ vadāmi*. This should probably be understood to mean that volition is a necessary factor in creating kamma, not that volition on its own invariably and in all instances creates kamma. It can thus be seen as a counterfoil to the Jain position that any action, even an unintentional one, creates kamma. The Chinese parallel, MĀ 111, at T I 600a23–24, says: "How does one understand kamma? There are two kinds of kamma: intention and the kamma [created] when one has intended" (云何知業。謂有二業思・已思業。).

1418 This statement should be understood in the sense that the results of kamma are to be experienced in their respective realms.

1419 See p. 1639, note 372, and p. 1666, note 547. The Chinese parallel, MĀ 111, has here the fourfold distinction of kamma found in **4:232–33**. But MĀ 15 (at T I 437b26) speaks of only two kinds of results, in this life or in a later life, without a third alternative.

1420 This should probably be understood in the sense that, because contact is the condition for intention and kamma can be explained as intention, contact is therefore the condition for kamma.

1421 *Ko ekapadaṃ dvipadaṃ jānāti imassa dukkhassa nirodhāya*. Mp: "The meaning is: 'Who knows a mantra, a one-word or two-word mantra?'" The Chinese parallel at T I 600b17–18 uses the character 呪 (= 咒), meaning "mantra."

1422 It is strange that only six Tathāgata's powers are mentioned here. Usually, ten Tathāgata's powers are cited (identified as *ñāṇabalāni*, powers of knowledge). In AN the ten are in **10:21**. They are also at MN 12.9–20, I 69–71, and analyzed at Vibh 335–44 (Be §§809–31).

1423 Some examples of the possible (*ṭhāna*) and the impossible (*aṭṭhāna*) are at **1:268–95**; MN 115.12–19, III 64–67; and Vibh 335–38 (Be §809).

1424 *Ṭhānaso hetuso*. Mp explains possibility (*ṭhāna*) as condition (*paccaya*). Following Vibh 338–39 (Be §810), it takes this to be knowledge of the conditions for kamma bringing a result in connection with four factors that can either reinforce or impede its maturation: realm (*gati*, one's place of rebirth), acquisitions (*upadhi*, one's body and mind), time (*kāla*), and effort (*payoga*). The cause (*hetu*) is the kamma itself.

1425 The four *jhānas* are found throughout the Nikāyas. The eight *emancipations* (*vimokkha*) are at **8:66**. The three kinds of *concentration* (*samādhi*) are at **8:63**: concentration with thought and examination, without thought but with examination only, and without thought and examination. The nine *meditative attainments* (*samāpatti*) are the same as the nine progressive dwellings (*anupubbavihārā*) at **9:32**. The *defilement* (*saṃkilesa*) is a quality that leads to deterioration; the *cleansing* (*vodāna*) is a quality that makes for distinction; and the *emergence* (*vuṭṭhāna*), according to Vibh 342–43 (Be §828), is the cleansing and emergence itself. "Cleansing" here means that proficiency in the lower jhāna is the foundation for the next higher jhāna; "emergence itself" means coming out from the jhāna.

1426 Ce and Be indicate, by the use of ellipsis points, that the last three sections should be expanded in full, as in **6:2**. To facilitate readability, I present these sections without showing the elision of stock phrases.

1427 The Abhidhamma commentary, As 239,25–240,2 (Be §362), explains *rūparāga* as "desire and lust for form-[sphere] existence" (*rūpabhave chandarāgo*) and *arūparāga* as "desire and lust for formless-[sphere] existence" (*arūpabhave chandarāgo*). While the word "lust" may seem strong in relation to these refined realms of existence, I feel it is useful to render *rāga* consistently.

1428 *Cittassa nimittaṃ*. Mp: "The object of the mind of concentration and insight, the aspect of concentration and insight" (*samādhivipassanācittassa nimittaṃ samādhivipassanākāraṃ*). Mp is apparently interpreting this via the two meanings of the word *nimitta*, as object and as "mark" or aspect.

1429 *Tatra tatra*. Lit., "there [and] there." Mp: "This or that state of distinction" (*tasmiṃ tasmiṃ visese*). Mp simply glosses *āyatane* with *kāraṇe* ("cause"), but see p. 1669, note 562. On the first four of the six factors, see **4:179**.

1430 Mp: "*Conceit* (*māna*) is conceiving oneself [to be better] based on birth, etc. The *inferiority complex* (*omāna*) is the conceit, 'I am inferior' (*hīno'ham asmī ti māna*). *Arrogance* (*atimāna*) is the conceit of self-elevation. *Self-overestimation* (*adhimāna*) is imagining oneself to have attained [what one has not really attained]. *Obstinacy* (*thambha*) is due to anger and conceit. *Self-abasement* (*atinipāta*) is the conceit 'I am inferior' occurring in one who is actually inferior."

1431 *Ālokabahulo*. Mp: "He abounds in the light of knowledge" (*ñāṇālokabahulo*).

1432 Mp: "The mind is *to be suppressed* (*niggahetabbaṃ*) by concentration on an occasion of restlessness; it is *to be exerted* by energy at a time when it has fallen into sluggishness; it is to be *encouraged* (*paggahetabbaṃ*) with concentration at a time when it is listless; and it is to be *looked at* (*ajjhupekkhitabbaṃ*) with the equanimity enlightenment factor when it is proceding evenly." These aspects of mental development are discussed in detail at Vism 130–35, Ppn 4.51–64.

1433 See **3:22**, **5:151–53**, p. 1638, note 358, and p. 1739, note 1150.

1434 Mp: "*Obstruction by kamma* (*kammāvaraṇatā*) occurs through the five grave deeds with immediate result (see **6:87**). *Obstruction by defilement* (*kilesāvaraṇatā*) occurs through wrong view with fixed result (that is, a grave wrong view that denies the working of kamma). *Obstruction by result* (*vipākāvaraṇatā*) is an unwholesome resultant rebirth or a rootless wholesome resultant rebirth." These two types of rebirth consciousness lack the root of wisdom and thus one reborn through them is incapable of attaining the path. One reborn with a two-rooted rebirth consciousness, lacking the root of wisdom, is also incapable of attaining the path. On the role of rebirth consciousness, see CMA 179, 194–95. The kind of desire (*chanda*) that is needed is wholesome desire, desire to do the good (*kattukamyatāchandaṃ*).

1435 I follow Be, which does not have *pi* here, as against Ce and Ee, which have *pi*. In the partly parallel **5:151–53**, Ce and Ee do not have *pi*. It seems the sense requires that *pi* should be excluded; for it is when listening to the good Dhamma that one would expect a person to enter the path. The same applies to **6:87** and **6:88** just below.

1436 *Atthaṃ riñcati*. Mp: "One discards the benefit of growth" (*vaḍḍhi-atthaṃ chaḍḍeti*). Mp explains *attha* here in an ethical sense, as good or benefit. However, since the word is used in connection with someone listening to the teaching, it seems more likely that its semantic sense—namely, "meaning"—is intended. Thus *attha* is the correct meaning of the exposition, while *anattha* is a false meaning resulting from misinterpretation.

1437 The word *khanti*, normally meaning "patience," is used in relation to contemplative practice to mean one's beliefs or convictions. I base the parenthetical addition here on Mp's gloss, *sāsanassa ananulomikāya*, "not in conformity with the teaching."

1438 *Diṭṭhisampadaṃ*. Mp: "The path of stream-entry" (*sotāpatti-maggaṃ*).

1439 *Anāgamanīyaṃ vatthuṃ paccāgantuṃ*. Mp explains that he is incapable of the five enmities (that is, breach of the five precepts) and of adopting any of the sixty-two speculative views.

1440 Mp: "'An eighth existence' means that he cannot take an eighth rebirth in the sense sphere."

1441 Ce and Be *ānantariyaṃ kammaṃ*; Ee *anantariyaṃ kammaṃ*. Strangely, though this term commonly occurs in doctrinal expositions of Buddhism, a search for it in CST 4.0 turns up only one occurrence in the entire Sutta Piṭaka, namely, this one. The expression also occurs in the Vinaya Piṭaka, but only once, in the Devadatta story at Vin II 193,37. An *ānantariya kamma* is understood to be a grave misdeed that in the immediately following existence necessarily produces a rebirth in hell. The five acts that constitute this type of kamma are mentioned at **5:129**, **6:87**, and just below at **6:94**.

1442 *Ito bahiddhā dakkhiṇeyyaṃ gavesituṃ*. That is, incapable of seeking a person of noble attainment outside the Buddha's teaching.

1443 *Aññaṃ satthāraṃ uddisituṃ*. That is, of looking to someone else apart from the Buddha as one's ultimate spiritual teacher.

1444 *Sammattaniyāmaṃ okkamissati*. *Sammattaniyāmaṃ* is obviously an abridgment of *niyāmaṃ kusalesu dhammesu sammattaṃ*, on which see p. 1638, note 358, and p. 1739, note 1150.

1445 *Sabbasaṅkhāresu anodhiṃ karitvā aniccasaññaṃ upaṭṭhāpetuṃ*. Mp: "*Unlimited*: without setting a boundary thus: 'Only these conditioned phenomena, but no others, are impermanent.'"

1446 Ce and Ee have *gacchanti*, but the future meaning (originally conveyed by this form) seems intended here. Be has *gacchissanti*, perhaps a novel future form.

1447 I read with Be and Ee *bhavissāmi*, as against Ce *bhavissati*.

1448 *Sabbaloke atammayo bhavissāmi*. Mp: "Identification (*tammayo*) is craving and views; non-identification (*atammayo*) is their absence."

1449 A composite six, made up of two triads.

1450 Another composite six.

1451 *Paṇṇāsakātirekā vaggā*. This is the general title Ce assigns to these three additional chapters, which it then numbers 1, 2, and 3. Ee gives this the title *Paṇṇāsasaṅgahito vaggo*, "Chapter included with the Fifty" (?). Be does not assign a general title to the additional chapters, but numbers them 11, 12, and 13 in succession to the earlier vaggas of this *nipāta*.

1452 From this point on there are no *uddāna* verses to rely on for sutta titles. I thus adopt the titles in Ce.

1453 It is often claimed that this series of suttas testifies to a large number of lay arahants during the Buddha's time. This, however, is a misunderstanding. For we find on this list Anāthapiṇḍika, Pūraṇa (or Purāṇa), and Isidatta, all of whom were reborn in the

Tusita heaven (see **6:44** and MN 143.16, III 262,1). We also find Ugga of Vesālī, who is said (at **5:44**) to have been reborn among the mind-made deities, and Hatthaka, who is said (at **3:127**) to have been reborn in the Aviha heaven of the pure abodes. The terms used to describe these lay followers are descriptive of *all noble ones* from stream-enterers on up. They all have unwavering confidence (*aveccappasāda*) in the Buddha, Dhamma, and Saṅgha, have "reached certainty about the Tathāgata" (*tathāgate niṭṭhaṅgata*), and are seers of nibbāna, the deathless (*amataddasa*). See **10:63**, where certainty about the Buddha is ascribed to disciples at levels lower than arahantship. The statement that these people have noble liberation (*ariyena vimuttiyā*) is unusual, but Mp glosses it "by the liberation of the fruit of trainees" (*sekhaphalavimuttiyā*). Quite a different formula is used to describe an arahant. In the Nikāyas there are no recorded cases of laypeople who attained arahantship and then continued to lead the lay life. Those who do attain it entered upon the homeless life soon after their attainment, like Yasa at Vin I 17,1–3.

1454 The total number of suttas in this repetition series is calculated by taking the ten modes of treatment (from "direct knowledge" to "relinquishment") in regard to the seventeen defilements (from lust to heedlessness); this gives 170. Since each mode of treatment is to be accomplished by developing one or another of the three sets of six, this gives a total of 510 suttas.

Notes to the Sevens

1455 *Anavaññattikāmo*. Lit., "desirous of not being looked down upon." Mp: "He desires to be well known" (*abhiññātabhāvakāmo*). Thoughts about one's reputation (*anavaññattipaṭisaṃyutto vitakko*) is a type of distracting thought that must be overcome to gain concentration; see **3:101**, I 254,23.

1456 I follow Ce, which reads *sataṃ bhante sahassānaṃ*. Be and Ee have *sataṃ bhante satasahassānaṃ*, "a hundred [times] a hundred thousand."

1457 *Satta saṃyojanāni*. The familiar scheme of ten fetters occurs in AN only in **10:13**.

1458 *Anunayasaṃyojanaṃ*. An unusual listing among the fetters. Mp glosses it as the fetter of sensual lust (*kāmarāgasaṃyojanaṃ*).

1459 Envy (*issā*) and miserliness (*macchariya*) are listed among the ten fetters of the Abhidhamma method. See Dhs 197 (Be §1118), CMA 269.

1460 *Niranusayo* is not in Be or Ee. Ee notes variant readings in manuscripts. But see SN IV 205,17, where Be has *niranusayo*, as against Ce and Ee *pahīnarāgānusayo*.

1461 This is stated from the perspective of monastics thinking to approach families for alms.

1462 Mp: "They do not rise up from their seats in a humble manner but show disrespect."

1463 The seven are explained in detail at MN 70.14–21, I 477–79. In brief, the one liberated in both respects and the one liberated by wisdom are two kinds of arahants, distinguished by whether or not they possess the "peaceful formless emancipations transcending form." The body witness, the one attained to view, and the one liberated by faith are three kinds of trainees, who can range anywhere from stream-enterer to one on the path to arahantship; they have already been discussed at **3:21**. The Dhamma follower and the faith follower are two types who have entered the path to stream-entry but have not yet realized the fruit; they are distinguished according to whether wisdom or faith is their dominant faculty. The process by which they enter the path is described at SN 25:1, III 225.

1464 *Pāraṅgato thale tiṭṭhati brāhmaṇo*. Here, "brahmin" is used as a synonym for the arahant. See in this connection **4:5 §4** and SN 35:228, IV 157,19–20.

1465 At Pp 13 (Be §16) this person is called a *samasīsī*, lit., "a same-header." Mp explains that there are four kinds of *samasīsī*. (1) One who has been ill and attains the destruction of the taints at the same time that he recovers from the illness is called an "illness same-header" (*rogasamasīsī*). (2) One who has been afflicted with a severe painful feeling and attains the destruction of the taints at the same time that he overcomes the pain is called a "feeling same-header" (*vedanāsamasīsī*). (3) One who has been practicing insight in a particular posture and attains the destruction of the taints at the same time that he breaks the posture is called a "posture same-header" (*iriyāpathasamasīsī*). (4) And one who attains the destruction of the taints at the same time that his life ends is called a "life same-header" (*jīvitasamasīsī*). In this sutta, the "life same-header" is intended.

1466 *Antarāparinibbāyī*. Lit., "one who attains nibbāna in between (or along the way)." Pp 16 (Be §36) defines this person as one who eliminates the five lower fetters, takes spontaneous birth, and then, either immediately after being reborn or (at the latest) before reaching the middle of the life span, generates the path for abandoning the five higher fetters. Similarly, Mp defines this type as a person who is reborn somewhere among the pure abodes (*suddhāvāsesu*) and then attains arahantship either at the time of rebirth, slightly afterward, or before reaching the middle of the life span. In spite of these authorized definitions, I believe there is textual evidence that the name of this type should be understood to mean literally that he attains the destruction of the taints *in between* or *along the way* (*antarā*), that is, between two lives, and then attains final nibbāna without taking rebirth at all. See **4:131** and p. 1701, note 829. I give further arguments for this interpretation below in note 1536 on p. 1782.

1467 *Upahaccaparinibbāyī*. Both Pp 17 (Be §37) and Mp define this type as one who eliminates the five lower fetters, takes spontaneous rebirth (in the pure abodes), and then reaches arahantship after passing the middle of the life span or, at the latest, at the time of death. Again, as I will maintain in relation to **7:55**, there are suggestions in the Nikāyas that this type is one who attains the destruction of the taints almost immediately after taking rebirth in the pure abodes. See p. 1782, note 1537.

1468 The difference between (5) and (6) is probably determined primarily on the basis of the amount of effort they must put forth to win the goal. Pp 17 (Be §§38–39) says merely that one generates the path without effort and the other as the result of effort. In any case, on the commentarial interpretation these two become, not separate types of non-returners, but two modes in which the first two types (the *antarāparinibbāyī* and the *upahaccaparinibbāyī*) attain nibbāna. Such an explanation would reduce the distinct types of non-returners to three. This would override the sequential and mutually exclusive nature of the five types, which is implied by the fivefold classification and strongly suggested by the similes of **7:55**.

1469 See p. 1701, note 828.

1470 By using ellipsis points, Ee incorporates **7:18** and **7:19** into **7:17**, and thus at this point its numbering falls two short of my own. My numbering follows Ce and Be in counting the expositions based on non-self and nibbāna as distinct suttas.

1471 Whereas the contemplations of impermanence and suffering are directed toward all conditioned phenomena (*sabbasaṅkhāresu*), the contemplation of non-self is directed toward all phenomena without qualification (*sabbadhammesu*).

1472 *Niddasavatthūni*. PED takes *niddasa* to be a wrong reading for *niddesa* and explains the compound to mean "object of distinction, or praise." SED sv *nirdaśa* gives "more than ten days old, happened more than ten days ago." The expression itself, however, has no necessary connection with days and could also be explained by taking *ni* to be a privative prefix and thus meaning "without ten." Thus as used here it might just as well mean "without ten years." Mp accepts the reading as given and offers an explanation, which I translate just below. It could be that the original meaning of the expression is irretrievably lost and in interpreting it we have nothing to rely on but conjecture. There are no identified Chinese parallels to this sutta or to **7:42–43** below to serve as a check.

Here is Mp: "The question ['How is one tenless?'] is said to have arisen among the outside sectarians. For they call a Nigaṇṭha [a Jain ascetic] *niddaso* ("ten-less") who has died at the time he is ten years of age [*dasavassakāle*; or: "at the time he has ten years' seniority" (as an ascetic)?]. For, it is said, he does not become ten years of age again. And not only doesn't he become ten years of age again, [he doesn't become] nine years of age or even one year of age. In this way, they call a Nigaṇṭha who is dead at the age of twenty years, and so on, *nibbīso* ('twenty-less'), *nittiṃso* ('thirty-less'), *niccattālīso* ('forty-less'), *nippaññāso* ('fifty-less'). When Ānanda was wandering in the village, he heard this discussion and reported it to the Blessed One. The Blessed One said: 'This is not a designation for the sectarians, Ānanda, but for the taint-destroyer [arahant] in my teaching.' For if the taint-destroyer attains final nibbāna when he is ten years of age [or: has ten years' seniority?], he does not become one of ten years again. Not only one of ten years, he doesn't become one of nine years ... of a single year. Not only one of a single year, he doesn't become one of eleven months ... nor even one of a single moment. Why? Because he never again takes rebirth. The same method for one who is 'twenty-less' and so on. Thus the Blessed One begins this teaching to show the causes for becoming one who is 'ten-less.'"

1473 *Icchāvinaye tibbacchando hoti āyatiñca icchāvinaye avigatapemo*. I here render *icchā* as "vain wishes" and *chanda* as "desire." Mp glosses *icchā* with *taṇhā*, craving.

1474 This teaching is referred to at DN 16.1.5, II 75,23–31.

1475 I add "the city" on the basis of Mp's gloss: "situated inside the city" (*antonagare ṭhitāni*).

1476 Mp: "When people neglect the righteous oblations, the deities do not protect them, and even if they cannot create new suffering, they intensify arisen suffering, such as coughs and headaches, etc.; and in time of war, the people have no allies. But when people don't neglect the oblations, the deities protect them well, and even if they cannot create new happiness, they remove old illnesses; and when war breaks out, the people have allies."

1477 What follows is also in DN 16.1.1–5, II 72–76.

1478 The text of **7:23–27** is at DN 16.1.6–10, II 76–80.

1479 Mp: "As long as they do not come to a stop at some attainment, such as purification of virtuous behavior, jhāna, insight, stream-entry, and so forth, without having attained arahantship, only growth is to be expected for the bhikkhus."

1480 All these perceptions are explained at **10:60**, with three additions.

1481 Reading with Ee *na iti paṭisañcikkhati*. Ce and Be omit *na*. Brahmāli suggests "he is supposed to leave this work for the *theras* [elders], who are expected to look after it."

1482 Ce *attanā voyogaṃ āpajjati;* Ee *attanā vo yogaṃ āpajjati;* Be *attanā tesu yogaṃ āpajjati*. Again, I follow Brahmāli's interpretation: "Since it is the task of these elders, they will have to take ultimate responsibility (and the blame or praise) no matter who carries it out. Thus he should leave it to them."

1483 *Tattha ca pubbakāraṃ karoti*. See **5:175**, **6:93**. Mp: "He first gives to those following other creeds and only afterwards to bhikkhus."

1484 Be, but not Ce or Ee, has the following before the verses: "This is what the Blessed One said. Having said this, the Fortunate One, the Teacher, further said this."

1485 Ee joins this sutta and the next and mistakenly counts them as three, 28–30. Thus Ee's numbering, which had been two behind my own, now lags behind by one.

1486 An expanded parallel of **6:32**.

1487 An expanded parallel of **6:33**.

1488 An expanded parallel of **6:69**, without the preliminary portion of the latter.

1489 An expanded parallel of **3:135**.

1490 *Khīṇena nātimaññati*. I translate on the supposition that *khīṇena* is an adverb meaning "hurtfully, roughly" (see DOP sv *khīṇa*[2]). Mp, however, explains the line on the assumption that *khīṇena* means "in [time of] loss, when wealth has been exhausted": "When one's wealth is exhausted, he does not despise one because of one's loss. He does not think too highly of himself and look down on the other" (*tassa bhoge khīṇe tena khayena taṃ nātimaññati, tasmiṃ omānaṃ attani ca atimānaṃ na karoti*). On Mp's interpretation, though, I do not see how this factor would differ from the preceding one.

1491 *Vattā*. Mp says only "he is skilled in speech" (*vacanakusalo*). Since giving deep talks is listed as a separate item, here presumably the meaning is that he gives good advice.

1492 On the four analytical knowledges (*paṭisambhidā*), see **4:172**.

1493 I translate the text exactly as it has come down, but it seems that in the course of transmission a phrase dropped out suggesting that mental sluggishness has arisen on a particular occasion. Mp thus provides the missing phrase, *uppanne cetaso līnatte*, "when mental sluggishness has arisen."

1494 Mp connects internal constriction with dullness and drowsiness, and external distraction with attraction toward the five objects of sensual pleasure. See in this connection SN 51:20, 279,28–280,4.

1495 At **4:41 §3**, this is called "the development of concentration that leads to mindfulness and clear comprehension." Mp: "Feeling, etc., are the roots of mental proliferation (*papañca*). For feeling is the root of craving, which arises in relation to pleasure. Perception is the root of views, which arise toward an unclear object. And thought is the root of conceit, which arises through the thought, 'I am.'"

1496 Mp explains "mark" (*nimitta*) here as cause (*kāraṇa*).

1497 Ee prints this as a continuation of the preceding sutta, but Ce and Be, which I follow, treat it as distinct. My numbering again exceeds that of Ee by two.

1498 Though the text here uses the present tense *pajānāti*, I construe this as the historical present, referring to the time before Sāriputta attained arahantship. As an arahant he would no longer have been prone to mental sluggishness, internal constriction, or external distraction.

1499 Six of these skills, excluding the first, are mentioned at **6:24**.

1500 Again, Ee prints this as a continuation of the preceding sutta, but Ce and Be consider it distinct. Since I follow Ce and Be, my numbering now exceeds Ee by three.

1501 See **7:20**.

1502 *Viññāṇaṭṭhitiyo*. The word is used here in a different sense than at SN 22:54, III 54,26, where the four *viññāṇaṭṭhitiyo* are the four aggregates functioning as the supports for *viññāṇa*. In the present sutta they are planes of rebirth. Mp calls them "grounds for the rebirth consciousness" (*paṭisandhiviññāṇassa ṭhānāni*). The original meaning of the seven, as described here, is probably lost. Mp explains them against the background of the Abhidhamma distinction among types of rebirth consciousness, for which see CMA 179–80, 210–19.

1503 Mp: "Human beings are different in body (*nānattakāyā*) because there are no two people whose bodies are exactly alike. They are different in perception (*nānattasaññino*) because in some cases their rebirth perception (*paṭisandhisaññā*) has three roots, in others two roots, and in still others it is rootless. The devas mentioned are the six sense-sphere devas. The beings in the lower world are certain yakkhas and spirits outside the plane of misery."

1504 Mp: "These are the devas of Brahmā's assembly, Brahmā's ministers, and the great brahmās. Their bodies are different in pervasion according to their respective level, but their perception is the same because they all have the perception pertaining to the first jhāna. The beings in the four planes of misery also belong to this group. Their bodies are different, but they all have a [rebirth] perception that is a rootless unwholesome resultant."

1505 Mp takes "the devas of streaming radiance" (*devā ābhassarā*) to represent all three classes of devas pertaining to the second jhāna: those of limited radiance, measureless radiance, and streaming radiance. In each plane, their bodies are identical in that they all have the same pervasion (*ekavipphāro va*), but their perception is different in that some are without thought but retain examination (*avitakka-vicāramattā*), while others are without thought and examination (*avitakka-avicārā*).

1506 Mp: "The devas of refulgent glory (*subhakiṇhā*) are identical in body, and also identical in perception because they all have the perception pertaining to the fourth jhāna (in the Abhidhamma scheme of five jhānas). The devas of great fruit (who are reborn through the fifth jhāna of the fivefold scheme) fall under the fourth station of consciousness. The non-percipient beings do not have consciousness and thus are not included."

1507 The non-percipient devas and the devas of the base of neither-perception-nor-non-perception are included among the nine abodes of beings (see **9:24**) but not among the stations of consciousness.

1508 *Ariyo sammāsamādhi sa-upaniso itipi saparikkhāro itipi*. The "supports" (*upanisā*) and "accessories" (*parikkhārā*) are the other seven path factors. See too MN 117, III 71,22.

1509 The meanings of these seven fires will be explained in the following sutta.

1510 Mp says that *thūṇa* is the sacrificial post itself: *yūpasaṅkhātaṃ thūṇaṃ*.

1511 Ce and Be *atohayaṃ* (Ee *ato 'yaṃ*), *brāhmaṇa, āhuto sambhūto*. Mp glosses: ***atohayan*** *ti ato hi mātāpitito ayaṃ* ***āhuto*** *ti āgato*. There seems to be a word play here between *āhuta* as representing *ābhūta*, "originated," and as past participle of *ājuhati*, "offered, sacrificed." See DOP sv *āhuta*[1] and *āhuta*[2].

1512 *Appaṭikulyatā saṇṭhāti*. Lit., "[if] non-revulsion becomes settled."

1513 *Natthi me pubbenāparaṃ viseso*. I base this rendering of *pubbenāparaṃ visesa* on Mp: "There is no distinction between the earlier time when I had not developed it and the later time when I developed it" (*natthi mayhaṃ pubbena abhāvitakālena saddhiṃ aparaṃ bhāvitakāle viseso*). In other contexts *pubbenāparaṃ visesa* means the successive stages of excellence reached by mental development, but that explanation does not work here.

1514 Mp connects "I-making" (*ahaṅkāra*) with views, "mine-making" (*mamaṅkāra*) with craving, and conceit with the ninefold conceit (*navavidhamāna*): that is, considering oneself superior, equal, or inferior, each in relation to one who is actually superior, equal, or inferior. "Transcended discrimination" (*vidhāsamatikkanta*) means having overcome the threefold conceit of being superior, equal, or inferior.

1515 Mp: "It is said that he thought: 'In the system of the brahmins, one lives the celibate life for forty-eight years studying the Vedas. But the ascetic Gotama, living at home, enjoys himself with the three kinds of dancing girls in three mansions. So what now will he say?' Thus he asks with reference to this. Then the Blessed One, as if gaining control of a black snake with a mantra or as if stepping on an enemy's neck with his foot, roars his lion's roar. He shows that even during his six years of striving, a time when he still had defilements, not even a thought arose in him with regard to the pleasure of rulership or the dancing girls in his mansions."

1516 *Saṃyogavisaṃyogaṃ dhammapariyāyaṃ*. The title might also have been rendered "connection and disconnection."

1517 In Pāli: *itthikuttaṃ, itthākappaṃ, itthividhaṃ, itthicchandaṃ, itthissaraṃ, itthālaṅkāraṃ*. Apparently it is these seven terms, and their masculine counterparts (with *purisa* in place of *itthi*), that explain the inclusion of this sutta in the Sevens. I translate on the basis of the glosses offered by Mp.

1518 These are the ancient brahmin rishis who were supposedly the composers of the Vedic hymns. They are mentioned in this capacity at **5:192**, III 224,5–6, and 229,28–230,1, and at DN I 238,21–23, and MN II 169,29–31.

1519 The three editions have slightly different readings. I follow Ce *cittālaṅkāraṃ cittaparikkhāranti*. Neither Be nor Ee have the quotation marker *ti*. Mp: "It is an ornament, an accessory, of the mind pertaining to serenity and insight" (*samathavipassanācittassa*).

1520 At **2:133** and **4:177 §4** she is held up as a model for the Buddha's female lay followers. She is probably identical with Uttarā Nandamātā, declared at **1:262** to be the foremost of meditators among female lay followers.

1521 *Ātitheyya*: the traditional gift given to a guest as a token of hospitality.

1522 A comment is called for about the expression *acchariyaṃ abbhutaṃ*. Though often rendered "wonderful and marvelous," the phrase is not always intended to express appreciation but to suggest, rather, astonishment and amazement. Of course, the boundary line between the two senses is porous, as can be seen from the way the English words "wonderful" and "marvelous," which now have an appreciative sense, evolved from words connected with astonishment.

1523 Be and Ee read *sallapissasī ti*. Ce *sallapissatī ti*, in the third person, may be an editorial error.

1524 Be and Ee read *vadhe vā vajjhamāne vā*, Ce *baddhe vā vajjhamāne vā*. The Sinhala translation in Ce mirrors the inconsistency of its Pāli text. I suggest reading, contrary to all three editions, *baddhe vā bajjhamāne vā*. In this way the three pairs of phrases represent a sequence of arrest, imprisonment, and execution.

1525 *Cittassa aññathattaṃ*. The expression recurs just below. My rendering is intended to fit both cases. In the present case a spiritually undeveloped woman would normally be distraught, in the case below she would be frightened.

1526 *Yatra hi nāma cittuppādampi parisodhessasi*. Lit., "that you will purify even the arising of mind."

1527 *Yakkhayoniṃ*. Mp: "The spirit realm is the state of an earth-bound deity (*bhummadevatābhāvaṃ*)." *Yoni* is here used in the sense of "realm," and thus the expression *yakkhayoni* does not imply that yakkhas are born from the womb.

1528 This establishes her status as a non-returner, who has abandoned the five lower fetters but not the five higher fetters.

1529 The undeclared points (*abyākatavatthūni*) are ten matters that the Buddha has not addressed: whether or not the world is eternal, whether the world is finite or infinite, whether the life-principle is the same as the body or different from the body, and the four alternatives concerning the after-death status of the Tathāgata.

1530 *Na chambhati, na kampati, na vedhati, na santāsaṃ āpajjati abyākatavatthūsu*. Ce also has *na calati*, not in Be or Ee.

1531 Mp glosses *purisagatiyo* with *purisassa ñāṇagatiyo*, "a person's movement of knowledge." However, the sutta appears to be concerned principally with their destination (*gati*) after death. The Chinese parallel, MĀ 6 (T I 427a13-c24), renders the title of its Indian original (corresponding to *satta purisagatiyo*) as 七善人所往至處, meaning "seven places where good persons are reborn."

1532 *No c'assa no ca me siyā, na bhavissati na me bhavissati*. This cryptic formula occurs in the Nikāyas in two versions. One is ascribed to the annihilationists; the other is the Buddha's adaptation of it. The annihilationist version reads: *no c' assaṃ no ca me siyā, na bhavissāmi na me bhavissati*, "I may not be, and it might not be mine. I will not be, and it will not be mine." Since the two differ only with respect to two verbs—*no c'assam* vs. *no c'assa*, and *na bhavissāmi* vs. *na bhavissati*—the various recensions sometimes confuse them. From the commentarial glosses, it appears that the confusion had already set in before the age of the commentaries. Readings also differ among different editions of the same text. Generally I prefer the readings in Ce.

This formula is explicitly identified as an annihilationist view (*ucchedadiṭṭhi*) at SN 22:81, III 99,4–6. In AN, at **10:29 §8**,

V 63,28–64,2, it is said to be the foremost of outside speculative views (*etadaggaṃ bāhirakānaṃ diṭṭhigatānaṃ*). The Buddha transformed this formula into a theme for contemplation conformable to his own teaching by replacing the first-person verbs with their third-person counterparts. This change shifts the stress from the view of self implicit in the annihilationist version ("I will be annihilated") to an impersonal perspective that harmonizes with the *anattā* doctrine. In some texts, for example at SN 22:55, III 55–58, practicing on the basis of the formula is said to culminate in the destruction of the five lower fetters, that is, in the stage of a non-returner. Sometimes, as in the present sutta, the formula includes a trailer (see below), contemplation of which is said to lead to equanimity. Practice guided by the full formula leads to one of the five levels of non-returner or to arahantship.

In the Nikāyas the precise meaning of the formula is never made explicit, which suggests that it may have served as an open guide to contemplation to be filled in by the meditator through personal intuition. The commentaries, including Mp, take the truncated particle *c'* to represent *ce*, "if," and interpret the two parts of the formula as conditionals. I translate here from Mp (in conformity with its own interpretation): "*If it had not been*: If, in the past, there had been no kamma producing individual existence; *it would not be mine*: now I would have no individual existence. *There will not be*: Now there will be no kamma producing a future individual existence for me; *there will not be mine*: in the future there will be no individual existence for me."

I dissent from the commentaries on the meaning of *c'*, which I take to represent *ca* = "and." The syntax of the phrase as a whole requires this. Skt parallels actually contain *ca* (for instance, Udānavarga 15:4, parallel to Ud 78,1-3, has: *no ca syān no ca me syā*[*n*]; and MĀ 6 contains the character 亦 (= "and") in the appropriate places of the formula. As I interpret the meaning, the first "it" refers to the personal five aggregates, the second to the world apprehended through the aggregates. For the worldling this dyad is misconstrued as a duality of self and world; for the noble disciple it is simply the duality of internal and external phenomena. On this basis I would interpret the formula thus: "The five aggregates can be terminated, and the world presented by them can be terminated. I will so strive that the five aggregates will be terminated, (and thus) the world presented by them will be terminated."

The trailer reads in Pāli: *yadatthi yaṃ bhūtaṃ taṃ pajahāmī ti upekkhaṃ paṭilabhati*. Following Mp, I understand "what exists, what has come to be" (*yadatthi yaṃ bhūtaṃ*) as the presently existing five aggregates. These have come to be through the craving of previous lives and are being abandoned by the abandonment of the cause for their re-arising in a future life, namely, craving or desire-and-lust.

1533 *Atth'uttariṃ padaṃ santaṃ sammappaññāya passati.* Mp: "He sees with path wisdom together with insight, 'There is a higher peaceful state, nibbāna.'"

1534 It is the continued presence of these three defilements that distinguishes the non-returner from the arahant, who has eliminated them.

1535 In accordance with the usual Theravāda commentarial position, Mp explains the *antarāparinibbāyī* as one who attains nibbāna—the complete extinction of defilements—from the time immediately following rebirth up to the middle of the life span. This position seems contradicted by the similes to follow.

1536 The similes illustrate three types of *antarāparinibbāyī*, "attainers of nibbāna in the interval." Although arguments based on similes are not always reliable, the three similes suggest that the "attainer of nibbāna in the interval" attains nibbāna before actually taking rebirth. Just as the three chips are extinguished after flying off from the red-hot bowl but before hitting the ground, so (on my interpretation) these three types attain final nibbāna respectively either right after entering the intermediate state, or during this state, or shortly before rebirth would take place. In this case, they immediately enter the nibbāna element without residue (*anupādisesanibbānadhātu*).

1537 Mp interprets this person as one who attains nibbāna between the midpoint of the life span and its end. However, the word *upahacca*, "having struck, having hit," and the simile of the chip that goes out on hitting the ground, suggest that this type is one who attains nibbāna almost immediately after rebirth.

1538 Whereas the standard Theravāda commentarial interpretation takes the next two types—one who attains nibbāna without exertion (*asaṅkhāraparinibbāyī*) and one who attains nibbāna through exertion (*sasaṅkhāraparinibbāyī*)—to be two alternative ways by which the *antarāparinibbāyī* and *upahaccaparinibbāyī* attain the goal, the similes of the chip suggest, unambiguously, that the five types (or seven, counting separately the three subdivisions of the first) are distinct, forming a series from the sharper to the more sluggish. Thus if, as Mp alleges, the *upahaccaparinibbāyī* were one who attains nibbāna between the midpoint of the life span and its end, there would be no scope for the other two types, those who attain nibbāna without exertion and those who attain nibbāna through exertion.

1539 See p. 1701, note 828.

1540 *Anupādisesā suvimuttā*. Mp says that this refers to the five hundred bhikkhunīs of Mahāpajāpatī's retinue, who have been liberated without leaving any residue of clinging (*upādānasesaṃ aṭṭhapetvā*). The discussion to follow in the sutta makes it clear that *anupādisesa* here means that they have eliminated all defilements without residue, not that they have attained the nibbāna element without residue (*anupādisesanibbānadhātu*).

1541 Of the seven types mentioned in §§1–7, the first two, being arahants, have no residue of defilements; the other five, being trainees, have a residue of defilements.

1542 In the normal sevenfold classification of noble persons, the seventh person is the faith follower (*saddhānusārī*). Here, however, the seventh place is taken by the *animittavihārī*, "one who dwells in the markless." Mp says that the Buddha is actually describing the faith follower as one who practices strong insight (*balavavipassakavasena*). It explains that "all marks" are all marks of permanence and so forth, and the markless mental concentration (*animittaṃ cetosamādhiṃ*) as the concentration of strong insight (*balavavipassanāsamādhiṃ*). Possibly Mp is attempting to rationalize a textual discrepancy, which might be indicative of a different understanding of the seventh noble person.

1543 This is an expanded parallel of **5:34**, enlarged by partly incorporating the contents of **5:38**.

1544 Mp: "They arouse compassion with the thought: 'Whom should we help today? Whose gift should we receive or to whom should we teach the Dhamma?'"

1545 This is a "composite seven," arrived at by combining a tetrad and a triad neither of which appears in AN as the theme of an independent sutta. The first tetrad, however, echoes **5:100**.

1546 I read with Be and Ee *tava sāvakā*, as against Ce *tathāgatasāvakā*.

1547 An expanded parallel of **5:201, 6:40**.

1548 *Pacalāyamāno nisinno hoti*. Just below, Mp glosses the Buddha's question, "*Pacalāyasi no*?" with "*Niddāyasi nu*" ("Are you falling asleep?"). Mp: "While depending on the village for alms, Moggallāna had been practicing meditation in the grove. For seven days he had energetically practiced walking meditation and the effort fatigued him. Thus he was dozing off [in the seat] at the end of the walkway."

1549 The following exchange is also at MN 37.2–3, I 251–52, but with Sakka as the inquirer. Mp explains the passage thus: "*Nothing* (lit., *not all things*) *is worth holding to* (*sabbe dhammā nālaṃ abhinivesāya*): here, 'all things' (*sabbe dhammā*) are the five aggregates, the twelve sense bases, and the eighteen elements. These are not worth holding to by way of craving and views. Why not? Because they do not exist in the way they are held to. They are held to be permanent, pleasurable, and self, but they turn out to be impermanent, suffering, and non-self. Therefore they are not worth holding to. One *directly knows them* by the full understanding of the known (*ñātapariññāya abhijānāti*) as impermanent, suffering, and non-self. One *fully understands them* in the same way by the full understanding of scrutinization (*tīraṇapariññāya parijānāti*)." The "all things" in my translation from Mp relates to the "nothing" of the sutta, since the Pāli phrase of the sutta is a negation of *sabbe dhammā* ("not all things"). On the three kinds of full understanding (*pariññā*), see Vism 606,$_{18}$–607,$_{23}$, Ppn 20.3–6.

1550 Ee does not count this as a separate sutta, though it encloses the whole sutta in brackets. The *uddāna* verse in Ee does not include a mnemonic for this sutta, which may explain the error. Ce uses *mā puñña* as the mnemonic; Be has *mettā* and titles it "Mettasutta."

1551 On the evolution of a new world system after a period of dissolution, see DN 1.2.2–4, I 17,$_{24}$–18,$_{4}$.

1552 Ce has in brackets *sattakkhattuṃ*, "seven times," not in Be or Ee. The addition may have been intended to make the prose match the verse.

1553 This is a stock description of a wheel-turning monarch. On the seven gems, see MN 129.34–41, III 172–76.

1554 Ee has *Jambusaṇḍassa*, Ce *Jambudīpassa* (perhaps a normalization), Be *Jambumaṇḍassa*. *Jambusaṇḍassa* is at Sn 552 = Th 822. I use the familiar name Jambudīpa, the "Rose-Apple Island," the greater Indian subcontinent.

1555 I read with Ce and Ee *asāhasena dhammena*, as against Be *asāhasena kammena*.

1556 Ce *pathavyo* [Ee *pathabyo*] *yena vuccati*. Be is less satisfactory: *pathabyo me na vipajjati*.

1557 I read with Ce and Ee *homi* here and in the first line of the next verse. Be has *hoti* in both places.

1558 The verse is also in **4:21**.

1559 *Vadhadaṇḍatajjitā*. Mp: "When her husband grabs a rod and threatens her with murder, saying: 'I'll kill you'" (*daṇḍakaṃ gahetvā vadhena tajjitā, "ghātessāmi nan" ti vuttā*).

1560 There is a Chinese parallel, MĀ 129, at T I 617b$_{19}$–618b$_{16}$.

1561 *Atho atthaṃ gahetvāna, anatthaṃ adhipajjati*. So all three editions, but an older Sri Lankan edition has *adhigacchati* and a Siamese edition *paṭipajjati*. All three will work, but with different nuances. The line obviously represents the second danger of anger in the prose portion. Mp says "having obtained something profitable, he thinks 'I have gotten what is harmful'" (*vuddhiṃ gahetvā . . . anattho me gahito ti sallakkheti*). The Chinese counterpart at 618a12 has 應獲得大財, 反更得不利, "when he should have obtained great wealth, on the contrary he gets what is harmful."

1562 All three editions have *vadhaṃ katvāna*, "having slain," which I follow, but there is a variant, *vaṇaṃ katvāna*, "having wounded." Mp seems to supports *vadhaṃ* with its gloss, "he commits the act of taking life" (*pāṇātipātakammaṃ katvā*). The Chinese at 618a15 has only 瞋作身口業, "the angry person does a bodily or verbal deed."

1563 The verse presents several difficulties. Pāda a reads *dummaṅkuyaṃ padasseti*. Hardy, in his Preface to AN Vol. V (pp. v–vi), states that "*dummaṅku* signifies one who is staggering in a disagreeable, censurable, and scandalous manner, because he is not ashamed at his behavior, or the like." Mp glosses the word with *dubbaṇṇamukhataṃ*, "an ugly facial expression," which the Chinese (at 618a21) approximates with 發惡色. The verb in pāda c, *patāyati*, is unclear. Mp glosses with *nibbattati*, "is produced," which is not sufficiently precise. PED offers "to be spread out" (perhaps from **sphātayati*; see SED sv *sphaṭ*), which I adopt. The Chinese 從是生憎嫉, "from this is produced hostile envy," may be based on a different word in its Indic original, perhaps *spṛhayati* (see SED sv *spṛh*), which could have arisen from a corruption of something related to **sphātayati*.

1564 Reading with Ce and Be *yathātathaṃ*, as against Ee *yathākathaṃ*.

1565 Mp identifies "brahmin" here as an arahant (*khīṇāsava-brāhmaṇaṃ*).

1566 *Hanti kuddho puthuttānaṃ*. I render this following Mp's gloss of *puthuttānaṃ* with *puthu nānākāraṇehi attānaṃ*.

1567 *Bhūnahaccāni kammāni*. The commentaries consistently gloss *bhūnahata* simply as *hatavuddhi*, "one who destroys growth." SED, sv *bhrūṇa*, lists *bhrūṇahati* as the killing of an embryo, and *bhrūṇahatyā* as the killing of a learned brahmin.

1568 Reading with Ce *ekam etaṃ akusalaṃ*, as against Be *yathā metaṃ akusalaṃ* and Ee *ekam ekaṃ akusalaṃ*. I take "this one unwholesome [quality]" to be anger.

1569 Reading with Ce *vītamohā*, as against Be and Ee *vītalobhā*, "without greed."

1570 Reading with Ce and Be *parinibbanti*, as against Ee *parinibbiṃsu*. A variant *parinibbissatha* yields a second-person plural utterance: "taintless, you will attain nibbāna."

1571 An expanded parallel of **5:24**, **6:50**.

1572 Be and Ee open with *evaṃ me sutaṃ*.

1573 The *yojana* is between seven and nine miles in length.

1574 *Aññatra diṭṭhapadehi*. Mp: "Who will believe this, except the noble disciples, stream-enterers who have seen the truth?" The truth, or state (*pada*), seen by the stream-enterer is nibbāna, the cessation of suffering.

1575 *Ko mantā ko saddhātā*. Mp (Ce) glosses: "Who is able to discuss this for the sake of generating faith in this, or who has faith in this?" (*ko tassa saddhāpanatthāya mantetuṃ samattho, ko vā tassa saddhātā*). *Saddhātā* is nominative singular of the agent noun *saddhātar*. So *mantā*, which is parallel to it, must be an agent noun from *mantar*, "a thinker." The Chinese parallel, MĀ 8, has nothing corresponding to Pāli *mantā*. I translate from T I 429b7–11: "I now tell you, Sineru, the king of mountains, will collapse and be destroyed. Who can believe this, but those who have seen the truth? I now tell you, the waters of the great oceans will dry up and evaporate. Who can believe this, but those who have seen the truth? I now tell you, the great earth will entirely burn up and be destroyed by fire. Who can believe this, but those who have seen the truth?"

1576 He is also mentioned at **6:54**, III 371,16–27.

1577 With this begins the six planes of sense-sphere heavens, from the highest down to the lowest.

1578 The Buddha relates this of himself with reference to his own past lives at **7:62**.

1579 As at **4:1**, including the verses.

1580 *Salākañceva jevanikañca*. Mp: "*Salāka* are weapons that can be released (*nissaggiya*), such as arrows and spears; *jevanika* are the other types of weapons, such as one-edge swords." SED sv *śalyaka*, gives "arrow, dart, spear." PED defines *jevanika* as "a kind of (missile) weapon," but missiles, according to Mp, are to be included under *salāka*.

1581 My renderings of these terms, sometimes obscure in the original, are partly based on the explanations given in Mp. Here are the explanations I follow for the terms that are not self-evident: *Celakā* ("standard-bearers"): those who, in the fighting, go in front carrying the standards of victory. *Calakā* ("camp marshals"): those who organize the military array thus: "Let this be the king's place, this is the place for the chief minister," etc. *Piṇḍadāyikā* ("food servers," lit., "lump-givers"): forceful great warriors. It is said that they enter the opponents' army and fly about cutting them up as if into lumps (*piṇḍapiṇḍamiva*); having risen up, they come out; or else it is those who take food and drink to the warriors in the midst of the battle. [I have translated based on this second derivation, which seems more plausible.] *Pakkhandhino* ("front-line commandoes") are those who ask: "Whose head or weapon shall we bring?" and when told,

"His!" they leap (*pakkhandanti*) into the midst of battle and bring it. *Mahānāgā* ("great-bull warriors") are warriors who cannot be turned back even when elephants, etc., are coming straight at them. *Sūrā* ("attack-soldiers") are one type of hero, who can cross the ocean even while wearing a coat of mail or carrying armor. *Cammayodhino* ("shield-bearing soldiers") are those who wear a coat of leather mail, or who carry a leather shield as protection against arrows. *Dāsakaputtā* ("domestic-slave soldiers"): deeply affectionate domestic-slave soldiers. Mp explains *uggā rājaputtā* as "royal sons experienced in battle who have risen higher and higher" (*uggatuggatā saṅgāmāvacarā rājaputtā*). Mp thus derives the word from *uggata*, but SED says the *ugra* were "a mixed tribe (from a Kshatriya father and a Śūdra mother)." The word, according to SED, means "powerful, violent, mighty . . . cruel, fierce."

1582 *Aparitassāya*. Lit., "for non-agitation."

1583 *Tilamuggamāsāparaṇṇaṃ*. Mp resolves thus: *tilamuggamāsā ca sesāparaṇṇañca*. Following Mp, I take *aparaṇṇa* as a general term of which *tila, mugga,* and *māsa* are instances. Hence I render *aparaṇṇa* simply as "foodstuffs." See Sp IV 784,31–33: "By *aparaṇṇa* is meant green gram, beans, sesame, *kulattha* pulse, bitter gourd, pumpkin, and so forth" (*muggamāsatilakulatthālābukumbhaṇḍādibhedañca aparaṇṇaṃ adhippetaṃ*).

1584 I would correct Ce *dhammehi* here to *saddhammehi* (as in Be and Ee). The Sinhala translation supports this with its rendering *sapta saddharmayen*.

1585 *Dvayena puggalā viditā honti*. Here a minor group of seven pairs is nested within the larger group of seven qualities, so that the discourse includes two sets of seven.

1586 DPPN explains that the *pāricchattaka* is a tree growing in the Nandana Grove in the Tāvatiṃsa heaven. It is a hundred leagues in circumference and at its foot is Sakka's stone seat. The *pāricchattaka* is said to be one of seven trees that last throughout the eon. (I am grateful to Dr. Julie Plummer of the Department of Plant Biology, University of Western Australia, for providing precise botanical terms for the different stages of floral development referred to in this sutta.)

1587 *Na cirass'eva dāni jālakajāto bhavissati*. Mp: "The occasion when the tree gives birth to webs of leaves and flower, which come forth together."

1588 *Na cirass'eva dāni khārakajāto bhavissati*. Mp: "The occasion when it becomes possessed of a web of leaves and of flowers well divided and growing separately."

1589 Ce and Ee: *kuḍumalakajāto*; Be: *kuṭumalakajāto*. Mp: "It starts to bud."

1590 Ce and Ee: *kokāsakajāto;* Be: *korakajāto*. Mp: "It acquires flowers that have not yet blossomed, with closed mouths and large bellies."

1591 Ce: *sabbapāliphullo;* Be and Ee: *sabbaphāliphullo*. Mp: "It has flowered fully in all respects."

1592 The simile does not merely compare the noble disciple to a coral tree at its different stages but uses the name of the stage to describe the noble disciple's development. He is "a noble disciple at [such and such stage] like the Tāvatiṃsa devas' *pāricchattaka* coral tree." Ee omits the *va* after *devānaṃ*, though it acknowledges this as a variant reading.

1593 In a similar way, the cry of the deities, ascending through the celestial realms, occurs at the conclusion of the Buddha's first discourse. See SN 56:11, V 423,17–24,4.

1594 With Be and Ee, I read *parisuddhasaṅkhātatarā*, as against Ce *parisuddhasaṅkhatatarā*. Mp glosses "they will be purified and stainless to an even greater degree" (*bhiyyosomattāya parisuddhā bhavissanti nimmalā*), which I don't think quite captures the meaning of *-saṅkhātatarā*. The word can mean "known as, appearing to be, declared to be," and this is the sense that seems relevant here.

1595 This sutta is a part-parallel of SN 22:101, III 152–55.

1596 I read with Ee *udaraṃ*, as against Ce and Be *uraṃ*, "chest."

1597 See SN 12:22, II 29,16–21.

1598 Mp, commenting on **1:53**, discusses this passage more fully as follows: "Those bhikkhus who vomited hot blood had committed *pārājika* offenses. Those who returned to lay life had been going around violating the lesser and minor training rules. And those who attained arahantship had purified their behavior. The Teacher's discourse was fruitful for all three. [Question:] Granted it was fruitful for those who attained arahantship, how was it fruitful for the others? [Reply:] Because if they had not heard this discourse, [the first kind] would have become heedless and would not have been able to abandon their condition. Their evil behavior would have increased and dragged them down to the realms of misery. But when they heard this discourse, they were filled with a sense of urgency. Having abandoned their condition, some became sāmaṇeras (novices), fulfilled the ten precepts, applied themselves to careful attention, and became stream-enterers, once-returners, or non-returners, while some were reborn in the deva world. Thus it was fruitful even for those who had committed *pārājikas*. If the others had not heard this discourse, as time went on, they would have gradually committed *saṅghādisesas* and *pārājikas*. They would have been reborn in the realms of misery and experienced great suffering. But having heard it, thinking that they could not fulfill the practice all their lives, they gave up the training and returned to lay life. They became settled in the three refuges, observed the five precepts, fulfilled the duty of a lay follower, and became stream-enterers, once-returners, or non-returners, while some were reborn in the deva world. Thus the discourse was fruitful for them, too."

1599 As at **6:54**, where, however, the chain of past teachers ends at Jotipāla. See too **7:66**, where Sunetta alone is mentioned.

1600 I read with Be and Ee *yathā 'maṃ sabrahmacārīsu*, as against Ce *yathā amhaṃ sabrahmacārīsu*. Ce has *yathā 'maṃ* in the parallel at **6:54**. See too pp. 1762–63, notes 1364–66.

1601 The text uses *ratti*, "night" as the reckoning for a twenty-four-hour period, as is common in Buddhist canonical literature.

1602 Reading with Ce and Ee *kupito*, as against Be *kapimiddho*, "monkey sleep."

1603 I follow Ce and Be, which read *rattipi saṅkhātā, divāpi saṅkhātā*.

1604 Sp IV 790,12-20: "*In detail* means together with both Vibhaṅgas. *Well transmitted* means transmitted well. To show how they have been 'well transmitted,' it is said, 'well analyzed' and so forth. *Well analyzed* means that each term is analyzed without confusion or fault. *Well mastered* means made familiar, coming up in recitation. *Well determined in terms of rule* means determined well in terms of the rule to be cited from the Khandhakas and Parivāra; *well determined in terms of detailed explication* means well determined, flawless, without error in wording through the completeness of words and terms." *(Tattha* ***vitthārenā*** *ti ubhatovibhaṅgena saddhiṃ.* ***Svāgatānī*** *ti suṭṭhu āgatāni. Yathā āgatāni pana svāgatāni honti, taṃ dassetuṃ "suvibhattānī"ti ādi vuttaṃ. Tattha* ***suvibhattānī*** *ti suṭṭhu vibhattāni padapaccābhaṭṭha-saṅkaradosavirahitāni.* ***Suppavattīnī*** *ti paguṇāni vācuggatāni.* ***Suvinicchitāni suttaso*** *ti khandhakaparivārato āharitabbasuttavasena suṭṭhu vinicchitāni.* ***Anubyañjanaso*** *ti akkharapadapāripūriyā ca suvinicchitāni akhaṇḍāni aviparītakkharāni.)*

1605 I follow Be in reading simply *vinayadharo* rather than *bhikkhu vinayadharo* in **7:79–82**. Ce has *bhikkhu vinayadharo* in **7:79** and **7:80**, opening statement, and just *vinayadharo* in **7:80**, closing statement, and in **7:81–82**. Ee has *bhikkhu vinayadharo* in **7:79** (= Ee lxxv) and just *vinayadharo* in **7:80–82** (= Ee lxxvi–lxxviii).

1606 *Sammukhāvinaya*. In view of the detailed explanation at Vin II 93,32–100,6, the rendering in MLDB 855–56, "removal by confrontation," is not satisfactory.

1607 For details on these principles and their applications, see MN 104.13–20, II 247–50; Vin II 73–104; Ṭhānissaro 2007a: 546–61.

1608 Ee does not count this as a separate vagga but treats it as the beginning of the repetition series.

1609 A pun is involved here, evident in the Pāli: *bhinnattā bhikkhu hoti*. Puns also explain the word derivations in the following suttas, for example, *samitattā samaṇo hoti*, and *bāhitattā brāhmaṇo hoti*. These puns are purely "pedagogical" and not etymologically cogent.

1610 Each of the suttas in this series is abridged in the Pāli, but it is clear that each should be expanded by way of the seven factors mentioned in **4:85**.

1611 I read with Ee *arīhatattā*. Ce has *arahattā*, Be *ārakattā* (as all three editions read in the next sutta).

1612 *Ārakattā arahā hoti*.

1613 No edition has an *uddāna* verse for this vagga. From this point on Be stops giving individual titles to the suttas, as Ee had done earlier. I base the titles on Ce, which does not, however, have an *uddāna* verse.

1614 Neither Ce nor Ee numbers this series. Be numbers it 11, continuing the consecutive numbering scheme used for the vaggas. I have numbered it as if it were a sixth chapter in this set of fifty. Ce numbers the suttas in the series from 1–510. Be numbers the suttas in continuation with those in the entire *nipāta*, from 623 to 1132. I follow the sutta numbering of Be.

Notes to the Eights

1615 *Amanussā*. Lit. "nonhumans." The word primarily refers to earth-bound deities, yakkhas, and demons. Vism 312,9–313,18 (Ppn 9.64–69), illustrates this benefit with a story about a monk who wins the affection of tree deities.

1616 *Sabbe ca pāṇe manasānukampī*. *Anukampā* (the abstract noun of *anukampī*) has a slightly different nuance than *karuṇā*, the second immeasurable quality. *Anukampā* usually suggests compassion as a motive for action on behalf of others, whereas *karuṇā* generally designates a meditative state.

1617 I translate on the basis of the Be and Ee reading *assamedhaṃ*, which accords with the name of the first of this traditional group of sacrifices mentioned elsewhere in the Nikāyas. At **4:39** these sacrifices are condemned for the harm they inflict on helpless creatures. Ce here reads *sassamedhaṃ*, "the corn sacrifice," the gloss found in Mp (both Ce and Be). The gloss is perhaps apologetic, intended to justify the ascription of this sacrifice to the royal sages.

1618 These are the names of other sacrifices.

1619 Reading with Be and Ee *tāragaṇā va*, as against Ce *tāragaṇā ca*.

1620 *Mettaṃso sabbabhūtānaṃ veraṃ tassa na kenaci.* Mp takes *mettaṃso* to be a compound of *mettā* and *aṃso,* glossing it *mettāyamānacittakoṭṭhāso,* "a portion of a loving mind." BHSD sv *aṃśa* testifies to the occurrence of *maitra aṃśa* in BHS literature; *maitreṇāṃśena sphuritvā* in Divyāvadāna 60.24 and 61.12.

1621 *Ādibrahmacariyikāya paññāya.* Mp: "[This is] insight, the wisdom that is the basis for the spiritual life of the path" (*maggabrahmacariyassa ādibhūtāya paññāyā ti vipassanāya*).

1622 *Ariyaṃ vā tuṇhībhāvaṃ nātimaññati.* Lit., "or he does not look down on noble silence."

1623 *Piyattāya garuttāya bhāvanāya sāmaññāya ekībhāvāya saṃvattati.* Mp glosses *bhāvanāya* here with *bhāvanatthāya guṇasambhāvanāya vā,* "toward [meditative] development or toward esteem for virtues." The latter meaning seems to fit the context better. Mp glosses *sāmaññāya* with *samaṇadhammatthāya,* "for the sake of the ascetic's duty," but I think it more likely that *sāmaññā* is an abstract noun from *samāna,* meaning "the same" or "similar." I translate it as "accord," which agrees well with the following word *ekībhāvāya.* PED lists *sāmañña*[1] as meaning "conformity" and "unity." The word occurs in this sense as the name of the fifth vagga of the Second Fifty (see p. 1237 below). No Chinese parallel is listed, but see pp. 1848–49, note 2106.

1624 An expanded parallel of **7:1**. Though they use the same framework, **8:4** is not exactly an expanded parallel of **7:2**.

1625 *Asuci.* Mp says only "he is possessed of impure bodily action, etc."

1626 Devadatta had created a schism in the Saṅgha and left with his own company of monks, intending to establish a rival order.

1627 *Yaṃ kiñci subhāsitaṃ sabbaṃ taṃ tassa bhagavato vacanaṃ arahato sammāsambuddhassa. Tato upādāy'upādāya mayañ c'aññe ca bhaṇāma.* This could not be translated, "Whatever is the word of the Blessed One . . . is well spoken." As stated, it expresses the idea that whatever good teachings the disciples speak, even when they themselves have originated them, can be regarded as *buddhavacana* because they are based on the Buddha's own teachings.

1628 It is probable that this sutta was put in the Eights because of the eight bad conditions mentioned in the discourse about Devadatta.

1629 It is hard to see on what basis Sakka says that this exposition of the Dhamma had not been established anywhere among the four assemblies (*n'āyaṃ dhammapariyāyo kismiñci patiṭṭhito*). The discourse on knowing one's own failings and achievements had already been taught to the bhikkhus, who are likely to have taught it to the other three assemblies.

1630 Nanda, the Buddha's half-brother, apparently had strong sensual desires. After he became a monk he constantly thought of his fiancée and later hoped to be reborn among the celestial nymphs. His story is told at Ud 3:2, 21–24.

1631 At **4:41**, this is called the development of concentration that leads to mindfulness and clear comprehension.

1632 *Aññenāññaṃ paṭicarati, bahiddhā kathaṃ apanāmeti, kopañca dosañca appaccayañca pātukaroti.*

1633 I read with Ce and Be *niddhamath'etaṃ . . . niddhamath'etaṃ*, as against Ee *dhamath'etaṃ . . . niddhamath'etaṃ*.

1634 All readings of this sentence seem confused. Ce has *kiṃ vo paraputto vihethīyati*, where the passive verb does not seem to fit. Ee has *kiṃ vo paraputtā viheṭheti*, which links a plural subject to an active singular verb. Be has *kiṃ vo tena paraputtena visodhitena*, "What do you have [to do] with that son of another who has been purified?" which makes no sense in this context. Ee includes still more variants in its footnotes. I take the required reading to be: *kiṃ vo paraputto viheṭheyya*. Mp does not offer an explanation, but the implication seems to be that the troublesome monk, by his behavior, is not a real disciple of the Buddha and thus can be considered a "son" (that is, a disciple) of another teacher.

1635 *Aññesaṃ bhaddakānaṃ bhikkhūnaṃ*. I assume that it is the above eight modes of behavior that account for the classification of this sutta among the Eights.

1636 *Kuṭhāripāsena*. DOP is uncertain about the meaning but suggests it might be the ring or blade of the axe. PED has "throw of an axe."

1637 *Naḷerupucimandamūle*. Sp I 108,29–30 says that Naḷeru was the name of a yakkha.

1638 A similar rebuke against the Buddha is voiced at **4:22**.

1639 *Arasarūpo bhavaṃ Gotamo*. Mp: "The brahmin, lacking wisdom, did not recognize that the Buddha was the eldest in the world. Utterly unwilling to accept the Buddha's statement, he spoke thus, referring to the 'taste of concord' (*sāmaggirasa*), which in the world means paying homage, standing respectfully, reverential salutation, and polite conduct. To soften his mind, the Blessed One avoids directly contradicting him; instead he states that the term applies to him, but intending this in a different sense. [The Buddha speaks of 'taste'] as the gratification in sensual pleasure that arises in worldlings—even in those considered the best by way of class or rebirth—who relish, welcome, and lust after objects such as forms, etc."

1640 *Nibbhogo bhavaṃ Gotamo*. Mp says that the brahmin intended this in the sense that the Buddha lacks "the enjoyment of concord" (*sāmaggiparibhogo*, conviviality), by which he again refers to such respectful gestures as paying homage to elders, etc. But the Buddha speaks with reference to the lustful enjoyment of sensual pleasures that arises in ordinary beings.

1641 *Akiriyavādo bhavaṃ Gotamo*. The doctrine of non-doing, as expressed by its proponents, denies the distinction between good and evil. See DN 2.17, I 52,22–53,2; MN 60.13, I 404,21–35; MN 76.10, I 516,3–17; SN 24.6, III 208,20–209,6. Mp says that the brahmin intended this in the sense that the Buddha did not act in accord with convention, as by paying homage to his elders, etc. But the Buddha spoke with reference to the non-doing of bodily, verbal, and mental misconduct.

1642 *Ucchedavādo bhavaṃ Gotamo*. The annihilationists proclaimed "the annihilation, destruction, and extermination" of a truly existent person at death. See DN 1.3.9–16, I 34,2–35,36. Mp says that the brahmin intended to accuse the Buddha of seeking to annihilate the long-established conventions of paying homage to elders, etc., but the Buddha spoke with reference to the annihilation of all defilements and unwholesome qualities by the four noble paths.

1643 *Jegucchī bhavaṃ Gotamo*. Mp: "The brahmin calls the Blessed One a 'repeller' (*jegucchī*); he thinks that because the Buddha is repelled (*jigucchati*) by polite conduct such as paying homage to elders, he does not do such things. But the Blessed One acknowledges this in a metaphorical sense. He is repelled by bodily, verbal, and mental misconduct and by the various bad unwholesome qualities, just as a man fond of ornaments would be repelled and disgusted by feces."

1644 *Venayiko bhavaṃ Gotamo*. *Venayika*, from the verb *vineti* (to discipline, to remove), can mean "one who imposes discipline, one who trains others." But in the Buddha's time the word *venayika* also seems to have acquired the meaning of "one who leads astray," who leads others to destruction. Thus Mp glosses *vineti*, in the brahmin's view, with *vināseti*, "destroys." But the Buddha affirms this in the sense that he teaches the Dhamma for the removal of lust and other defilements (*rāgādīnaṃ vinayāya*).

1645 *Tapassī bhavaṃ Gotamo*. A *tapassī* is usually an ascetic devoted to self-torment. The word is derived from the verb *tapati*, "to burn up, to heat up." The brahmin, according to Mp, uses the word in the sense of one who torments elders by not showing proper respect to them. But the Buddha uses the term to mean that he burns up unwholesome qualities.

1646 *Apagabbho bhavaṃ Gotamo*. SED explains Skt *apagalbha* as "wanting in boldness, embarrassed, perplexed" (see too DOP sv *apagabbha*). The Buddha plays on the word as if it meant "rid of (*apa*) the womb (*gabbha*)." It is nearly impossible to capture this pun in translation; my use of "retiring" is a clumsy attempt to bridge the two senses: "timid" and "retired" from wandering through the round of rebirths.

1647 See **4:128 §4**.

1648 Following Be and Ee, I give the first two knowledges in full. Ce abridges them.

1649 I do not follow Ce, which here includes *diṭṭhāsava*, the taint of views, absent in Be or Ee. The parallel passages in Ce at **3:59**, **4:198**, etc., do not include *diṭṭhāsava*.

1650 It is strange that Mahāvīra (the Nigaṇṭha Nātaputta) is depicted as making such a statement. The Jains certainly must have known that the Buddha also taught a doctrine of kamma, though different from their own. Mp says that Nātaputta was extremely displeased at Sīha's request and thought to prevent him from going. His words "destroyed the joy that had arisen in Sīha, as if striking a stray bull with a stick, extinguishing a burning lamp, or turning over a bowl of food."

1651 I read with Be and Ee: *yannūnāhaṃ anapaloketvā va nigaṇṭhe*, as against Ce *yannūnāhaṃ anapalokitā va nigaṇṭhe*. In the previous sentence, with *nigaṇṭhā* as subject, the past participles *apalokitā vā anapalokitā vā* are appropriate as nominatives in agreement with the subject. In this sentence, where *ahaṃ* is the subject, an absolutive signifying an act of Sīha is preferable.

1652 See p. 1646, note 416.

1653 In **8:11** accusations §§1, 3–7 are leveled against the Buddha.

1654 Ce and Be have *assāsako*; Ee reads *assattho*, which means "consoled." I am not quite sure how this is intended as a criticism.

1655 Mp: "*Supreme consolation* (*paramena assāsena*): the four paths and four fruits."

1656 What follows here, up to "and become independent of others in the teaching of the Teacher," closely matches Upāli's experience at MN 56.16–18, I 379,2–380,10.

1657 This charge is also addressed at **3:57**.

1658 Ce and Ee *jīranti*; Be *jiridanti*. Mp: "They do not limit their slander (*abbhakkhānassa antaṃ na gacchanti*). Or else, this word *jiridanti* means shame (*lajjanatthe*). The meaning is that they are not ashamed (*na lajjanti*)."

1659 See the Jīvaka Sutta (MN 55) for the Buddha's position on meat-eating. It is curious, indeed almost disingenuous, that the Buddhist texts depict the Jains as criticizing the Buddha for eating meat from an animal killed especially for him. This charge plays right into the Buddhists' protest that the Buddha is being slandered and their rejoinder that he would never intentionally have a living being killed for his meal. But as the Jains were strict vegetarians, we can be almost certain that they criticized the Buddha and his disciples, not for having an animal killed for their meal, but simply for consuming meat. On the Jain prohibition of meat-eating, see http://www.jainworld.com/jainbooks/guideline/28.htm.

1660 In Ee, *so rato* should be read without the hiatus as *sorato.*

1661 Also at **2:5**.

1662 *Piṭṭhito rathaṃ pavatteti.* Mp: "Pushing the yoke up with its shoulder bone, it retreats, turning the chariot around with its backside."

1663 *Pacchā laṅghati, kubbaraṃ hanati, tidaṇḍaṃ bhañjati.* Mp: "It kicks up its two hind legs, strikes the chariot's rail, and damages the rail. It breaks the triple rod, the three rods in front of the chariot."

1664 *Rathīsāya satthiṃ ussajjitvā rathīsaṃyeva ajjhomaddati.* Mp: "Having lowered its head, it throws the yoke to the ground and strikes the chariot pole with its thigh and crushes the chariot pole with its two front feet."

1665 I follow Ce and Ee, which here and below read *patodaṃ*, as against Be *patodalaṭṭhi*, "goad and whip."

1666 *Anuṭṭhānamalā gharā.* Lit., "Houses have lack of initiative as their stain." Mp: "The stain of houses is the lack of initiative, the absence of energy." Mp-ṭ: "This is said because a house goes to ruin if one does not repeatedly take the initiative in repairing what has decayed and so forth."

1667 The verses are at Dhp 241–43ab. Dhp 243cd adds: "Having abandoned these stains, be stainless, O bhikkhus" (*etaṃ malaṃ pahatvāna nimmalā hotha bhikkhavo*).

1668 *Vanabhaṅgena.* Lit., "by what is broken [from] the woods." Mp: "By a present, such as flowers or fruits, which are taken from the woods and brought to him."

1669 I translate on the basis of Ce and Ee. Be, in this sutta and the next, has a different eight means of binding, occurring in a different sequence, namely: by weeping, by a smile, by speech, by appearance, by a present, by scent, by taste, by touch (*ruṇṇena, hasitena, bhaṇitena, ākappena, vanabhaṅgena, gandhena, rasena, phassena*). Thus, apart from the change of sequence, Be replaces "form" and "singing" of Ce and Ee with "scent" and "taste." According to Mp, "appearance" (*ākappa*) means "the manner of dressing and so forth," but this may be too narrow. The Chinese parallel at EĀ II 765c24–766a2 lists nine ways a woman binds a man: by singing, dancing, her skills, her touch, her smile, weeping, an expedient means, beautifying her face and body, and her appearance and deportment.

1670 I read with Ce and Be *subaddhā yeva phassena baddhā*. Ee has a variant reading here and in the next sutta: *subaddhā yeva pāsena baddhā*, "[they are] thoroughly bound who are bound by a snare."

1671 This last phrase is commonly rendered "with a sudden drop-off only after a long stretch." But the Pāli *na āyataken'eva papāto*, with the negative particle *na*, actually means the opposite: that there is *no* sudden drop-off. See DOP sv *āyataka*, instr. *āyatakena*, "suddenly, abruptly; of a sudden." Mp explains: "It doesn't drop off at once like a steep precipice or deep pit. Beginning at the shore, it grows deeper by inches, feet, yards, [and successively longer measures] until it is 84,000 *yojanas* deep at the base of Mount Sineru."

1672 The first three are legendary fish of gigantic size.

1673 *Anupubbasikkhā, anupubbakiriyā, anupubbapaṭipadā*. I take these to be truncated instrumentals relative to *aññāpaṭivedho*. Mp glosses them with *anupubbasikkhāya*, etc. Mp correlates each term with a set of training factors: "By *gradual training* the three trainings are included (see **3:89**); by *gradual activity*, the thirteen ascetic practices (see Vism chap. 2); and by *gradual practice*, the seven contemplations, the eighteen great insights (see Vism 694,3–27, Ppn 22.113), the thirty-eight meditation objects, and the thirty-seven aids to enlightenment. *Penetration to final knowledge occurs ...not abruptly* (*na āyataken'eva aññāpaṭivedho*): there is no penetration to arahantship all at once (*ādito va*) like the hopping of a frog, without having fulfilled virtuous behavior and so forth. One is able to attain arahantship only after having fulfilled in due order (*paṭipātiyā*) virtuous behavior, concentration, and wisdom." See too MN I 479.

1674 *Na tena nibbānadhātuyā ūnattaṃ vā purattaṃ vā paññāyati*. Mp: "When no Buddhas have arisen in countless eons, it is not possible for even one being to attain nibbāna. Yet one cannot say, 'The nibbāna element is empty.' And during the time of a Buddha, when countless beings attain the deathless at a single assembly, one cannot say, 'The nibbāna element has become full.'"

1675 An unabridged version of this sutta, with a verse attached at the end, is Ud 5:5, 51–56. It is also at Vin II 236–40, where it serves as the background story to the rules about suspending a bhikkhu's right to participate in the Pātimokkha recitation.

1676 I read with Ce *āgamessati*, as against Be and Ee *āgamissati*.

1677 At **1:253** he is declared the foremost among those who give what is agreeable. At **5:44** he makes agreeable offerings to the Buddha.

1678 *Brahmacariyapañcamāni sikkhāpadāni*. These are the usual five precepts, but with "abstinence from sexual activity" replacing "abstinence from sexual misconduct" as the third precept.

1679 As at **7:53 §7**. With this he declares himself a non-returner.

1680 This is an alternative way of declaring oneself to be a non-returner. By saying that he will not return to "this world" (*imaṃ lokaṃ*) he indicates that he has eliminated the five lower fetters, which bind one to this world of sensual desire, and also that he is not yet an arahant, who does not return to any state of being.

1681 While Hatthaka is said to be dwelling in a residence (*nivesana*), unlike the preceding two lay followers, he is not addressed here as "householder" (*gahapati*) but as "friend" (*āvuso*). Whether this is intentional or a transmission error is impossible to determine. At **6:123**, however, Hatthaka is referred to as a householder (*gahapati*) whereas some of the other lay disciples in this vagga are called lay followers (*upāsaka*).

1682 The text repeats everything from the bhikkhu's going to Hatthaka's house up to the end of their conversation.

1683 Mentioned at **4:32** and **4:256**.

1684 *Daḷiddassa kho no tathā sotabbaṃ maññanti*. Mp: "They do not listen to me as they would to a poor man, who cannot give anything or do anything; but they think they should listen to me and follow my advice and do not think they should transgress my instructions."

1685 Jīvaka was the Buddha's personal physician. For his background story, see Vin I 268–80.

1686 It seems that the two Pāli words *ujjhatti* and *nijjhatti* are being intentionally played off against one another. Mp glosses *ujjhattibala* with *ujjhānabala* and explains: "For fools have only the power of complaining: 'When that fellow said this and that, he said it to me, not to anyone else.' But [the wise] have the power of inference, of inferring what is beneficial and what is harmful: 'This is not so, hence it is that.'" On *nijjhatti* and its verb, *nijjhāpeti*, see **2:51**.

1687 Reading with Ce *vavakaṭṭhaṃ*, rather than *vivekaṭṭhaṃ* with Be and Ee. *Vavakaṭṭha* is past participle of *vavakassati*. PED gives as meanings, "drawn away, alienated, withdrawn, secluded."

1688 *Khaṇakicco loko*. Lit., "moment-task world." Mp: "One does one's tasks at the moment. Having gained this opportunity, one does one's tasks."

1689 *Dīghāyukaṃ devanikāyaṃ*. Mp: "This is said with reference to the order of non-percipient devas (*asaññaṃ devanikāyaṃ*)." However, it also seems to apply to the devas of the formless realm, who (because they lack bodies) cannot hear the Buddha or his disciples teach the Dhamma and thus cannot attain even the path of stream-entry.

1690 *Saddhammassa niyāmataṃ*. Mp glosses as the noble path (*ariyaṃ maggaṃ*).

1691 I read with Ce and Ee *māradheyyasarānuge*, as against Be *māradheyyaparānuge*. Mp: "That accompany saṃsāra, called 'Māra's realm'" (*māradheyyasaṅkhātaṃ saṃsāraṃ anugate*).

1692 Mp: "After going forth, in his first rains retreat Anuruddha gained the meditative attainments and obtained the knowledge of the divine eye by which he could see a thousand world systems. He went to Sāriputta for advice…and Sāriputta explained a meditation subject to him. He learned the meditation subject, took leave of the Buddha, and went to the Ceti country, where for eight months he passed the time engaged in walking meditation. His body became fatigued with the effort, so he sat down in a bamboo thicket. Then this course of thought arose in him."

1693 *Nippapañcārāmassāyaṃ dhammo nippapañcaratino, nāyaṃ dhammo papañcārāmassa papañcaratino*. Mp: "[This Dhamma is] for one 'who delights in non-proliferation,' who takes delight in the state of nibbāna, called 'non-proliferation' because it is devoid of proliferation by craving, conceit, and views" (*taṇhāmānadiṭṭhipapañcarahitattā nippapañcasaṅkhāte nibbānapade abhiratassa*). On *papañca*, see too **4:173**.

1694 I read with Ce *vavakaṭṭhena*, as against Be and Ee *vivekaṭṭhena*. PED says that *vavakaṭṭha* and *vūpakaṭṭha* are alternative forms of the same word. Both are distinct from *vivekaṭṭha*, "firm in seclusion." Since compounds with *viveka* precede this word, it is easy to see how the original word could have undergone mutation. See p. 1797, note 1687.

1695 Included among Anuruddha's verses at Th 901–3.

1696 The fifth, sixth, and eighth motives for giving are also at **7:52**.

1697 *Āsajja dānaṃ deti*. Mp: "One gives a gift when someone has arrived. Having seen one who has come, one instantly makes him sit down, honors him, and gives him a gift. One thinks, 'I will give,' but does not trouble him." This explanation takes *āsajja* to be the absolutive of *āsīdati*, glossed by Mp as *nisīdāpetvā*, "having made sit down." In the Nikāyas, however, *āsajja* never seems to bear this sense but always means "having insulted, having offended, having encroached upon." Since this type of giving occurs first in what is clearly a graded list, the usual meaning of *āsajja* is more pertinent.

1698 All three editions have *cittālaṅkāracittaparikkhāratthaṃ dānaṃ deti*. See **7:52**, where Ce has *cittālaṅkāraṃ cittaparikkhāranti dānaṃ deti*.

Mp: "For the purpose of ornamenting and equipping the mind with serenity and insight."

1699 It is likely that this sutta was originally a verse attached to the preceding one, which at some point was broken off and treated as separate. In its present form, it contains no set of eight factors to account for its inclusion in the Eights.

1700 *Dānavatthūni*. Mp: *dānakāraṇāni*, "causes for giving."

1701 Reading with Be and Ee *bhayā dānaṃ deti;* Ce has *garahā dānaṃ deti*, "one gives a gift from criticism," perhaps with the implication "from fear of criticism."

1702 In translating these verses, I alternate between "accomplishment" and "excellence" as renderings for *sampadā*, and "accomplished" and "excellent" as renderings for *sampanna*. In each case I have let my sense of natural English diction determine the appropriate choice.

1703 The text has *tassa taṃ cittaṃ*, but "aspiration" works better here than "mind" for *cittaṃ*.

1704 I read with Ee *hīne 'dhimuttaṃ* (= *hīne adhimuttaṃ*), shared by a Siamese edition. Ce and Be have *hīne vimuttaṃ*, which must have been the reading in Mp. Mp-ṭ glosses: "*Released upon* is resolved upon, which means 'bent on, inclining toward, leaning toward'" (***vimuttan*** *ti adhimuttaṃ, ninnaṃ poṇaṃ pabbhāranti attho*). Mp: "The *inferior* (*hīna*) is the five objects of sensual pleasure."

1705 *Vītarāgassa, no sarāgassa*. This is added because rebirth in the brahmā world requires more than the practice of generosity. It must also be supported by the attainment of jhāna, which arises through the fading away of craving for sensual pleasures.

1706 See **5:148**. The only common factor between the five qualities mentioned there and those listed here is giving at the proper time.

1707 This is an expanded parallel of **5:42**, but with different verses.

1708 Mp glosses *pubbe* with *paṭhamaṃeva*, but I suspect it is an abridgment of *pubbapeta*, mentioned in the prose. I translate on the basis of this supposition.

1709 I read these verses as consisting of two six-pāda stanzas and one four-pāda stanza. Ce and Be both divide them into four four-pāda stanzas. Ee does not divide them into stanzas.

1710 I read with Be and Ee *ñatvā dhamme ca pesalo*, as against Ce *ñatvā dhamme'dha pesale*.

1711 *Apace brahmacārayo*. Mp glosses as if *apace* represents *apacayati*, "to honor": *brahmacārino apacayati, nīcavuttitaṃ nesaṃ āpajjati*. However, DOP takes *apaca* to mean "not cooking," and thus signifying homeless. I follow this with my rendering "mendicants."

1712 See **4:51–52**, **5:45**.

1713 On the noble ones' uposatha observance, see **3:70**.
1714 These verses are identical with those at **3:70**.
1715 Of the three editions, only Ee has *sace ceteyyuṃ*, which is consistent with the reading of the parallel at **4:193**, II 194,24–25.
1716 In relation to **5:33**, Mp identifies these deities with the "devas who delight in creation" (*nimmānaratino devā*). Mp relates the origin of the present sutta thus: "It is said that those deities, having examined their own glory, asked themselves: 'How did we obtain such glory?' Reflecting, they saw Anuruddha and knew: 'In the past, when he was a wheel-turning monarch, we were his consorts. We accepted his guidance and thus we have obtained this glory. Let's go. We will bring the elder and [together] we will enjoy (*anubhavissāma*) this glory.' Thus during the day they approached Anuruddha."
1717 *Suppaṭipatāḷitassa. Paṭipatāḷita* is not in PED, but SED sv *prati* > *pratitāla*, explained as "in music, a kind of measure." Mp (Ce) glosses *suppaṭipatāḷitassa* as *pamāṇena ṭhitabhāvajānanatthaṃ suṭṭhu paṭipatāḷitassa*, which I would translate: "well coordinated for the purpose of maintaining a particular measure."
1718 *Tā devatā 'na khvayyo anuruddho sādiyatī' ti tatth'ev'antaradhāyiṃsu*. Mp: "[The deities thought:] 'Master Anuruddha does not enjoy our dancing and singing. He closes his eyes and refuses to look at us. Why should we go on dancing and singing?' Then they disappeared right there."
1719 The first five items here are substantially identical with those mentioned at **5:33**, except for the grammatical changes needed to adapt to the context.
1720 I read with Ee *rajataṃ vā jātarūpaṃ vā*, as at **5:33**. Neither Ce nor Be includes *rajataṃ* here but all three editions include it at **8:49** just below.
1721 I read with Be and Ee (and Ce at **5:33**) *sabbakāmaharaṃ*, as against Ce *sabbakāmadaṃ* here.
1722 All three editions read here *issāvādena*. In contrast, in **5:33** the three read this phrase differently. See p. 1726, note 1010.
1723 This sutta can be considered a composite, since the eight items are reached by combining two tetrads.
1724 Mp explains *ayaṃ'sa loko āraddho hoti* thus: *Ayam assa loko idhaloke karaṇamattāya āraddhattā paripuṇṇattā āraddho hoti paripuṇṇo* ("This world succeeds for her and is fulfilled because she succeeds and reaches fulfillment simply by doing [what is to be done] in the present world").
1725 Following Ee, I have filled out the text, abridged in Ce and Be.
1726 *Soḷasākārasampannā*. The reference is not immediately clear from the text itself. Mp: "The eight stated in the sutta, and the eight in

the stanzas, make sixteen aspects. Or the eight she herself possesses, and the [same] eight in which she enjoins others, make sixteen aspects."

1727 This sutta, the canonical account of the founding of the Bhikkhunī Saṅgha, has been the subject of extensive scholarly investigations. The narrative also occurs at Vin II 253–56. Several recent studies on the sutta, from a critical perspective, are in Mohr and Tsedroen 2010. Particularly instructive in this collection is Ute Hüsken, "The Eight Garudhammas," and Anālayo, "Women's Renunciation in Early Buddhism: The Four Assemblies and the Foundation of the Order of Nuns," which treats the chronological problem at pp. 86–90.

1728 The chronology is unclear to me. Mp says that at the time this sutta begins the Buddha was living among the Sakyans during his *first* return journey to Kapilavatthu (*paṭhamagamanena gantvā viharati*). Yet, given that Mahāpajāpatī could go forth only after the death of her husband, the Buddha's father Suddhodana, and that it seems improbable Suddhodana died during the Buddha's first return visit to Kapilavatthu, which took place soon after his enlightenment, this fact is hardly credible. It would also lead to an odd anachronism. The Cūḷavagga reports that Ānanda and other prominent Sakyans became monks after the Buddha's first journey to Kapilavatthu (Vin II 182–83). Ānanda became the Buddha's attendant twenty years after the enlightenment, when the Buddha was fifty-five, and served the Buddha in this capacity for twenty-five years, right up until the end of his master's life (Th 1041–43). In this sutta, however, Ānanda is depicted as the Buddha's attendant *before* the founding of the Bhikkhunī Saṅgha. Whether this event occurred shortly after the Buddha's first return trip to Kapilavatthu, or even five or ten years later, it would still be too early for Ānanda to be serving as his attendant. Thus, unless Ānanda was not actually the Buddha's attendant at the time, there seems to be a chronological tension between the situation depicted in the sutta and the likely period when women first obtained ordination.

1729 I summarize the sequence of events from Mp. When the Buddha returned to Kapilavatthu, he gave the going forth to Nanda and Rāhula and later resolved a conflict between the Sakyans and their neighbors, the Koliyans (the Buddha's relatives on his mother's side). Following this, 250 young men from each side left the home life under the Buddha. After a while, they began to pine for their wives. The Buddha brought them to the Kuṇāla Lake, where he taught them the Kuṇāla Jātaka on the wiles and deceitfulness of women. On hearing this, the five hundred young monks attained stream-entry and shortly afterward became arahants. Their wives sent them messages entreating them to return home, but they replied that they were now incapable of living the household life. The women therefore went to Mahāpajāpatī and asked her to request the Buddha, her stepson, to allow women to go forth. Mahāpajāpatī took the women under her wing, went to the Buddha, and made this request.

1730 Mp: "Why does he refuse her? Isn't it the case that all Buddhas have four assemblies? This is true, but he refuses her with the thought that if women are given permission to go forth only after they have made repeated efforts, they will maintain their ordination and revere it, recollecting how difficult it was to obtain the going forth."

1731 These were the five hundred Sakyan women whose husbands had gone forth and attained arahantship. In a personal communication, Pruitt writes: "There's no indication of how much time elapsed between the Buddha's departure and what follows here. In Thī-a 3, [the commentator] Dhammapāla says, 'He had the young Nanda and the young Rāhula go forth and then the Teacher returned again to Rājagaha. On a later occasion, when the Teacher was living in the Kūṭāgāra Hall near Vesālī, the great King Suddhodana attained final quenching [nibbāna], having realized arahantship even while he was still [reigning] under the white parasol. The inclination to go forth arose in Mahā-Pajāpatī' (Pruitt 1998: 6–7). This is also given at Thī-a 141 (Pruitt 1998: 181). King Suddhodana is the only layman I know of who became an arahant and remained a layman, which means he could not have lived more that seven days after becoming an arahant."

1732 Be has *muhuttaṃ*, not in Ce or Ee.

1733 *Aṭṭha garudhamme*. The term *garudhamma* is ambiguous. The word *garu* normally means "heavy, weighty, grave," as for example in the expression *garukā āpatti*, a grave or major offense. But *garuṃ karoti*, lit., "to make weighty," means "to respect," and *garukata*, "respected." Thus *garudhamma* can mean either a "heavy, grave rule" or "a rule to be respected, a principle of respect." Mp endorses the second interpretation: "The *garudhammas* are principles that are to be treated with respect by the bhikkhunīs who accept them." The translators of the Vinaya into Chinese also lean toward this interpretation. Thus in the corresponding passage in the Sarvāstivāda Vinaya (at T XXIII 345b29–c33) they are referred to as 八敬法, "eight principles of respect." The Mūlasarvāstivāda Vinaya (for instance at T XXIV 350c29) calls them 八尊敬法, "eight principles of honor and respect." But the Dharmaguptaka Vinaya (at T XXII 923a27 and elsewhere) designates them 八盡形壽不可

過法, "eight principles not to be transgressed throughout life," which corresponds to the Pāli *yāvajīvaṃ anatikkamanīyo*. And the Mahīśasaka Vinaya (at T XXII 185c19) likewise calls them 八不可越法, "eight principles not to be violated."

1734 It is interesting to note how the subject of the discussion shifts almost imperceptibly from the going forth (*pabbajjā*) of women to their full ordination (*upasampadā*). The former refers simply to their leaving the household life, the latter to a formal act of admission into the Saṅgha.

1735 Mahāpajāpatī later asked the Buddha to permit bhikkhus and bhikkhunīs to pay homage to one another (and show other signs of respect) exclusively on the basis of seniority, without distinction of gender. The Buddha refused and issued a rule: "Bhikkhus should not pay homage to women, stand up for them, salute them reverentially, or behave respectfully toward them. One who does so commits an offense of wrongdoing" (*na bhikkhave mātugāmassa abhivādanaṃ paccuṭṭhānaṃ añjalikammaṃ sāmīcikammaṃ kātabbaṃ; yo kareyya āpatti dukkaṭassa*). The incident is at Vin II 257–58.

1736 This refers to the three months' fixed residence during the rainy season.

1737 Thus on the uposatha day a bhikkhu is assigned the task of giving the bhikkhunīs an exhortation (*ovāda*). See Ṭhānissaro 2007b: 446–47.

1738 The "invitation" (*pavāraṇā*) is a ceremony held on the last day of the rains residence at which all the Saṅgha members in order of seniority ask the others to point out any fault they may have committed, whether seen, heard about, or suspected. Each bhikkhu extends the invitation to all the other bhikkhus. By this rule, however, bhikkhunīs are obliged to invite correction from both the bhikkhus and the other bhikkhunīs. See Ṭhānissaro 2007b: 447–48.

1739 The penalty period (*mānatta*) is imposed on a monastic guilty of a *saṅghādisesa* offense. During this period, the offending bhikkhu must undergo penalization for a period of six days; each day he must also inform all his fellow bhikkhus of his transgression, a humiliating experience. In the case of bhikkhunīs, however, the penalty period lasts two weeks and must be observed in relation to both bhikkhus and bhikkhunīs. For details, see Ṭhānissaro 2007b: 358–73. In this rule, the word *garudhamma* has a different meaning from its use in relation to the eight principles as a set. Here, Mp glosses it as *garukaṃ saṅghādisesāpattiṃ*, that is, it is the breach of a *saṅghādisesa* rule. Hüskin (in Mohr and Tsedroen 2010, p. 144) conflates the two senses of the term and thus sees an inconsistency here where there is really none.

1740 A probationer (*sikkhamānā*) is a woman candidate for full ordination who has already gone forth. To complete the requirements for ordination, she is obliged to live for two years observing a special training in regard to six rules (*cha dhammā*). The six rules—specified at Vin IV 319,24–29 in connection with Bhikkhunī Pācittiya 63—involve observing *without transgression* the precepts of abstinence from killing any living being, taking what is not given, sexual activity, false speech, intoxicants, and eating at an improper time (between midday and the following daybreak). Breach of any of these rules presumably requires the candidate to revert to the beginning of her two years' training.

1741 In the Vibhaṅga section of the Vinaya Piṭaka, the rules of the Bhikkhunī Pātimokkha are shown to have been laid down in response to specific incidents of misbehavior on the part of a certain bhikkhunī (or group of bhikkhunīs). Several of these rules are already included among the *garudhammas*. Thus *garudhammas* 2, 3, 4, and 7 correspond to Bhikkhunī Pācittiyas 56, 59, 57, and 52. *Garudhamma* 6 has counterparts in Bhikkhunī Pācittiyas 63 and 64. The fact that the background stories to these rules show them originating at different points in the early history of the Bhikkhunī Saṅgha casts doubt on the historicity of the present account, which shows the eight *garudhammas* being laid down at the very beginning of the Bhikkhunī Saṅgha. If the eight *garudhammas* had been laid down at the birth of the Bhikkhunī Saṅgha, they would have already been in force and there would have been no need for the Buddha to issue rules to prohibit the same undesirable behavior. He could simply have pointed to the existing rule. The fact that he did issue new rules thus collides with the thesis that the eight *garudhammas* were laid down at the very start of the Bhikkhunī Saṅgha.

1742 For *atimuttaka*, DOP gives "a kind of shrub (perhaps *Ougeinia oojeinensis*); its flower." Rather than use an obscure Pāli or Latin term, I freely render the name of the flower as "lilies."

1743 Assuming the historical authenticity of this passage, if the Buddha had wished to proscribe the ordination of women, it seems he would likely have pointed out this danger to Ānanda at the beginning of their conversation. Ānanda would then have desisted from his effort and women would not have received the right to ordain.

1744 *Corehi kumbhatthenakehi*. Lit, "bandits who commit pot theft." Mp: "They make a lamp with a pot and by means of its light search for valuable goods in others' homes."

1745 *Setaṭṭhikā rogajāti nipatati*. Mp: "A kind of insect pierces the stalk and enters the middle of the reed. When the stalk is pierced, the sap comes out and cannot reach the top of the paddy plant."

1746 *Mañjiṭṭhikā rogajāti nipatati*. Mp: "The internal reddening of the sugar cane."

1747 Mp (Ce): "By this he shows the following: 'When a causeway is not built around a large reservoir, whatever water would have remained there if the causeway had first been built does not remain because there is no causeway. So too, these principles of respect have been prescribed in advance, before an incident has arisen, for the purpose of preventing transgression. If they had not been prescribed, then, because women have gone forth, the good Dhamma would have lasted five hundred years. But because they have been laid down in advance, it will continue another five hundred years and thus last for the thousand years originally stated.' And this expression 'a thousand years' is said with reference to arahants who have attained the analytic knowledges (*paṭisambhidāpabhedappattakhīṇāsavānaṃ vasen'eva vuttaṃ*). Following this, for another thousand years, there appear dry-insight arahants; for another thousand years, non-returners; for another thousand years, once-returners; and for another thousand years, stream-enterers. Thus the good Dhamma of penetration (*paṭivedhasaddhammo*) will last five thousand years. The Dhamma of learning (*pariyattidhammo*) will also last this long. For without learning, there is no penetration, and as long as there is learning, there is penetration." From the above, we can see that according to the commentary, the allowance for women to go forth will not shorten the life span of the Dhamma; this is because the Buddha laid down the eight principles of respect, which serve as the dyke or causeway.

1748 This is evidently referring to the third *garudhamma*. Another anachronism appears here, at least in relation to the commentarial chronology. The Bhikkhunī Saṅgha, on this chronology, was founded soon after the Buddha's first visit to Kapilavatthu (or, on other chronologies, perhaps five or ten years after the enlightenment), yet it requires the bhikkhu who is to give the exhortation to have twenty years' seniority. This, of course, would not have been possible until at least twenty years after the founding of the Bhikkhu Saṅgha. By that time, however, Mahāpajāpatī would likely have been too old to make the long journey to Vesālī by foot.

1749 Also at Vin II 258–59. The sutta mirrors **7:83**.

1750 Though Ce spells the name "Vyagghapajja," I use this spelling to be consistent with the spelling of the name at **4:194**. This must have been his clan name, Dīghajāṇu his personal name.

1751 Ce and Ee *udumbarakhādikaṃ va;* Be *udumbarakhādīvāyaṃ*. The intended meaning is obscure. Mp explains: "One wishing to eat figs might shake a ripe fig tree and with one effort knock down many fruits. He would eat the ripe fruits and depart, leaving behind the rest; just so, one who spends the greater part of his earnings enjoys his wealth by dissipating it, so it is said: 'This clansman eats his wealth just like an eater of figs.'" A Chinese parallel, SĀ 91 (T II 23a22–c17), reads at T II 23b17: 人皆名為優曇鉢果，無有種子。愚癡貪欲。不顧其後; "Everyone calls him a fig without seeds. The foolish man, a prey to craving, does not consider those who come after."

1752 Ce and Ee *ajaddhumārikaṃ*; Be *ajeṭṭhamaraṇaṃ*. DOP relates the compound to Skt *jagdhvā*, "having eaten," and defines *ajaddhumārikā* as "death by starvation." See PED sv *jaddhu*, said to occur only as negative *ajaddhu*, "not eating, abstaining from food." Mp (Ce) glosses with *anāthamaraṇaṃ*, "death without a protector," Mp (Be) *anāyakamaraṇaṃ*, "death without a leader." It seems Mp (Ce) is glossing the reading found in Be. The Chinese at T II 23b19–20 has 傍人皆言是愚癡人如餓死狗, "Other people will all say that foolish man is like a dog starving to death."

1753 *Akkhātā saccanāmena*. The one "truly named" is the Buddha, since the name "Buddha" corresponds to his real stature as an enlightened one. See too p. 1757, note 1320.

1754 An expanded parallel of **6:23**. The additional designations for sensual pleasures are "dart" (*salla*) and "womb" (*gabbha*). The verses differ from those at **6:23**. The whole sutta, with verses, is cited at Nidd II 62,29–38 (VRI ed. 240).

1755 *Diṭṭhadhammikāpi gabbhā na parimuccati, samparāyikāpi gabbhā na parimuccati*. Mp: "The womb pertaining to the present life is a human womb; the womb pertaining to future lives is a womb other than the human."

1756 The usual phrase, "for the abandoning of unwholesome qualities and for the acquisition of wholesome qualities," is omitted, perhaps deliberately because this bhikkhu is an arahant.

1757 Text here has *arahattaphalasacchikiriyāya paṭipanno*, whereas **8:19** has *arahattāya paṭipanno*.

1758 The verses are also at SN 11:16, I 233.

1759 *Paññāsīlasamāhito*. Mp glosses: *paññāya ca sīlena ca samannāgato*. Though this takes *samāhito* to mean "possessing" rather than attainment of *samādhi*, by translating it as "composed" we can see how the word indirectly refers to *samādhi*.

1760 *Karotaṃ opadhikaṃ puññaṃ*. The word *opadhikaṃ* means that the merit ripens in *upadhi*, a future acquisition of the five aggregates, and that the deed conduces to well-being in the round of rebirths rather than to liberation.

1761 Mp: "For gaining the four requisities," that is, robes, almsfood, dwellings, and medicines.

1762 *Alaṃ attano alaṃ paresaṃ*. I add the phrase in brackets on the basis of Mp, which says: "*Able* [*to benefit*] *himself and able* [*to benefit*] *others*: capable, fit, equipped in practicing for the welfare of himself and of others" (*attano ca paresañca hitapaṭipattiyaṃ samattho pariyatto anucchaviko*).

1763 *Khippanisanti ca hoti kusalesu dhammesu*. Mp. "He takes up quickly, which means that when such subjects as the aggregates, elements, and sense bases are being taught, he understands them quickly" (*khippaṃ upadhāreti, khandhadhātu-āyatanādīsu kathiyamānesu te dhamme khippaṃ jānāti*).

1764 *Dhamme ca bhāsite mamaññeva anubandhitabbaṃ maññanti*. Mp: "It is said that although an exhortation was given [to him], this bhikkhu remained heedless. Having heard the Dhamma, he just hung around but did not want to strive. Therefore the Blessed One rebuked him. But since the bhikkhu had the supporting conditions for arahantship, the Buddha exhorted him with the words [below], 'Thus should you train yourself.'"

1765 Mp: "This is the meaning: 'When, bhikkhu, you have developed this fundamental concentration of loving-kindness in such a way, you should not be satisfied merely with this much, but you should attain four and five jhānas [in the fivefold jhāna scheme] in regard to other meditation objects. Thus you should develop it according to the method "with thought and examination" and so forth.'" While, in the jhāna scheme of the Nikāyas, the transition from the first to the second jhāna is marked by the simultaneous elimination of thought (*vitakka*) and examination (*vicāra*), other texts distinguish *samādhi* as threefold: as with thought and examination, without thought but with examination, and without thought and examination (see DN 33.1.10, III 219,19–20; MN 128.31, III 162,13–16; SN 43:3, IV 360,11–13). This middle stage of *samādhi* gave rise, in the Abhidhamma, to a fivefold scheme of jhānas that inserts, after the first jhāna, a second jhāna that is without thought but with examination. This scheme then renumbers the second, third, and fourth jhānas of the fourfold scheme as the third, fourth, and fifth jhānas to obtain a fivefold scheme. The *samādhi* with rapture (*sappītika*) includes the first and second jhānas (of the fourfold scheme); that without rapture (*nippītika*) includes the third and fourth jhānas. The *samādhi* with comfort (*sātasahagata*) is the third jhāna, and the *samādhi* with equanimity (*upekkhāsahagata*) the fourth jhāna.

1766 I read with Ee *bahulīkato*, as against Ce and Be *subhāvito*.

1767 This sentence is not in Ce, apparently omitted by oversight.

1768 *Obhāsaññeva kho sañjānāmi, no ca rūpāni passāmi*. Mp glosses *obhāsaṃ* as the "light of the knowledge of the divine eye" (*dibbacakkhuñāṇobhāsaṃ*).

1769 Mp: "Here, knowledge and vision (*ñāṇadassana*) is the divine eye (*dibbacakkhubhūtaṃ*)."

1770 Mp associates these eight facets respectively with the following eight kinds of higher knowledge: (1) the knowledge of the divine eye, (2) the knowledge of spiritual potency, (3) the knowledge encompassing the minds of others, (4) the knowledge of how beings fare in accordance with their kamma, (5) the knowledge of the future, (6) the knowledge of the present, (7) the knowledge of the past, and (8) the knowledge of past lives. Mp continues: "These are the eight knowledges that have come down in the text. But this sutta should be explained by conjoining these with the insight knowledges, the four path knowledges, the four fruition knowledges, the four reviewing knowledges, the four analytical knowledges, and the six knowledges unique to a Buddha."

1771 *Abhibhāyatanāni*. From the descriptions both in the text and commentary, it seems that the "bases of overcoming" are actually approaches to the *kasiṇas*, described in detail in Vism, chaps. 4 and 5. Mp: "The *abhibhāyatanāni* are causes of overcoming (*abhibhavanakāraṇāni*). What do they overcome? The adverse qualities and the objects. For they overcome the adverse qualities opposed to them (*paṭipakkhabhāvena paccanīkadhamme*) and, through a person's superior knowledge, [they overcome] the objects (*puggalassa ñāṇuttariyatāya ārammaṇāni*)."

1772 Mp: "*Percipient of forms internally* (*ajjhattaṃ rūpasaññī*): This refers to the internal form used for the preliminary work. For someone does the preliminary work [of meditation] on a blue form, such as the head hairs, the bile, or the irises. Doing the preliminary work on a yellow form, he uses bodily fat, the skin, or the surfaces of the hands and feet, or a yellow area in the eyes. Doing the preliminary work on a red form, he uses flesh, blood, the tongue, or a red area in the eyes. Doing the preliminary work on a white form, he uses bones, teeth, nails, or the whites of the eyes. These are not perfectly blue, yellow, red, or white, but impure. [*He*] *sees forms externally* (*eko bahiddhā rūpāni passati*): When the preliminary work has thus occurred internally, but the mark appears externally, he is said to be 'one percipient of forms internally [who] sees forms externally,' that is, his preliminary work is done internally but absorption (jhāna) occurs externally. *Having overcome them* (*tāni abhibhuyya*): As a person with good digestion who has obtained a mere spoonful of food collects it together, thinking, 'What is there to eat here?' and uses limited ability, so a person whose knowledge is emerging, one of clear knowledge, thinks: 'What is there to attain in regard to a limited object? This isn't troublesome for me.' Having overcome those forms, he enters an attainment, and with the arising of the mark he reaches absorption. *He is percipient thus* (*evaṃsaññī hoti*): He is percipient with the perception of reflective attention (*ābhoga*) and with the perception of the jhāna. *'I know, I see'* (*jānāmi passāmi*): By this, his reflective attention is spoken of; for that occurs after he has emerged from the attainment, not in the attainment itself. The perception of overcoming (*abhibhavanasaññā*) exists in the attainment, but the perception of reflective attention (*ābhogasaññā*) occurs after he has emerged from the attainment."

1773 Mp: "As a hungry person who has obtained ample food does not see that meal as large but thinks: 'Give me seconds and thirds. What will this do for me?' so a person whose knowledge is emerging, one of clear knowledge, thinks: 'What is there to attain here? This isn't a measureless object. It isn't troublesome for me to obtain one-pointedness of mind.' Having overcome [those forms], he enters an attainment, and with the arising of the mark he reaches absorption."

1774 Mp: "*One not percipient of forms internally sees forms externally* (*ajjhattaṃ arūpasaññī eko bahiddhā rūpāni passati*): This describes one for whom the preliminary work and the mark have arisen externally. Thus both by way of the preliminary work and by way of absorption, he is called one who is not percipient of forms internally [but] sees forms externally."

1775 Mp: "From the fifth base of overcoming on, he shows their thorough purification. For these bases are stated by way of purified colors (*visuddhavaṇṇavasen'eva*)." The colored bases of overcoming are illustrated by similes below at **10:29**, as well as at DN 16.3.29–32, II 110–11.

1776 The word *vimokkha* is used here in a specific and limited sense and does not imply irreversible liberation of the mind from all defilements; this latter is usually indicated by *akuppā cetovimutti* or *cetovimutti paññāvimutti*. Mp: "In what sense are they emancipations? In the sense of releasing (*adhimuccanaṭṭhena*). In what sense releasing? In the sense of thoroughly freeing from adverse qualities, and in the sense of thoroughly freeing through delight in the object. What is meant is [the mind's] occurrence on the object without constraint, free from worry, like a child sleeping on his father's lap, his body completely relaxed. This second meaning [regarding the object] does not apply to the last emancipation, but only to the others [for in the last emancipation there is no object of perception]."

1777 *Rūpī rūpāni passati.* Mp: "Here, 'form' is the jhāna with a form object, which has arisen by way of a blue *kasiṇa*, etc., based on something internal such as head hairs, etc. One who gains this [jhāna] is said to possess form. One might also see forms with the eye of jhāna externally, such as a blue *kasiṇa*, etc. What is indicated by this are the four form-sphere jhānas in the case of a person who has attained jhāna through the *kasiṇas* with an internal or external basis."

1778 *One not percipient of forms internally sees forms externally* (*ajjhattaṃ arūpasaññī, bahiddhā rūpāni passati*). Mp: "One who is not percipient of forms internally is one who does not attain form-sphere jhānas based on his own head hairs, etc. What is shown by this are the form-sphere jhānas of one who attains jhāna externally, having done the preliminary work externally."

1779 *Subhant'eva adhimutto hoti.* Mp: "By this what is shown are jhānas based on extremely purified color *kasiṇas*, such as blue, etc." Mp points out that Paṭis, a canonical exegetical treatise, defines the emancipation on the beautiful as the four immeasurable states (loving-kindness, compassion, altruistic joy, and equanimity); see Paṭis II 39,14–26. It seems that the first emancipation comprises the first two bases of overcoming; the second, the second two bases of overcoming; and the third, the remaining four bases of overcoming.

1780 On the cessation of perception and feeling (*saññāvedayitanirodha*), see MN 43.25, I 296,5–23; MN 44.16–21, 301,30–302,27; SN 41.6, IV 293–95; Vism 702–9, Ppn 23.16–52.

1781 Obtained by combining the four of **4:250** and the four of **4:252**.

1782 Obtained by combining the four of **4:251** and the four of **4:253**.

1783 Also at DN 16.3.21–23, II 109–10.

1784 This passage, which shows the Buddha as a master of bodily transformations, seems to have proto-Mahāyānistic features. Mp comments: "Whether the others are white, black, or brown, the Teacher is golden-colored. But this is stated with reference to shape. And the shape alone is perceived by them. It is not the case that the Blessed One becomes like a foreigner or like one wearing pearl earrings; he sits there in the form of a Buddha. But they see him as having the same shape as themselves. Some speak with a broken voice, some with a cackling voice, some with the voice of a crow, but the Teacher always has the voice of Brahmā. This is stated with reference to the language. For if the Teacher is sitting in a king's seat, they think, 'The king speaks sweetly today.' When the Blessed One departs after speaking, and they see the [real] king arrive, they wonder: 'Who was that?'... Even though they investigate, they do not know. Then why does the Buddha teach the Dhamma to them if they do not know? To plant impressions (*vāsanatthāya*). For when the Dhamma is heard even in such a way, it becomes a condition for the future. Thus he teaches out of consideration for the future."

1785 The portion of this sutta as far as the verse is also at SN 51:10, V 258–63. The entire sutta is at DN 16.3.1–20, II 102–9.

1786 *Kappaṃ vā tiṭṭheyya kappāvasesaṃ vā*. Mp glosses *kappa*, "eon," as *āyukappa*, "the life eon," the full normal life span of human beings at a particular time, presently a hundred years. *Kappāvasesa*, "the remainder of the eon," is explained as a little more than the normal life span of a hundred years. Mp mentions the view of an elder named Mahāsīva, who held that the Buddha could live on for the rest of the cosmic eon, but Mp cites the old commentary as holding that the "life eon" alone is intended (*idameva aṭṭhakathāya niyāmitaṃ*). Nevertheless, nowhere else in the Nikāyas is *kappa* used in the sense of a normal human life span, and there seems no compelling reason to ascribe to the word as used here a meaning different from the usual one, that is, a cosmic eon.

1787 *Yathā taṃ Mārena pariyuṭṭhitacitto*. Mp: "As any worldling would not be able to pick up a hint, so Ānanda was unable to pick it up. For Māra can obsess the mind of anyone who has not entirely abandoned the twelve cognitive inversions (*vipallāsa*; see **4:49**), and Ānanda [being only a stream-enterer] still had four of them. [Mp-ṭ: The inversions of perception and thought that take the unattractive as attractive and the painful as pleasurable.] Māra obsessed his mind by displaying a frightful sight. On seeing this, the elder failed to pick up the clear hint given him by the Buddha."

1788 Interestingly, in the Nikāyas no such conversation between the Buddha and Māra is recorded as having taken place earlier in the Buddha's life. It is referred to only in this sutta and its parallels at DN 16.3.7–8, II 104–6, and SN 51:10, V 260,29–262,11.

1789 The expression *pattayogakkhemā*, "attained to security from bondage," is in all three editions of AN but is absent from some (but not all) editions of the text's parallels in DN and SN mentioned in the preceding note. Since the phrase normally denotes the attainment of arahantship, it seems out of place in a description of the lay disciples. Mp comments on all the other expressions here but this, which suggests it was not present in the version available to the commentator.

Mp glosses *sappāṭihāriyaṃ dhammaṃ desenti* with "they teach the Dhamma so that it is emancipating" (*yāva niyyānikaṃ katvā dhammaṃ desessanti*). Mp-ṭ elaborates: "They explain the Dhamma in such a way that the doctrines of others are demolished and their own doctrine is established; thus, by citing reasons, it brings attainment of the goal [to be] achieved" (*yathā paravādaṃ bhañjitvā sakavādo patiṭṭhahati, evaṃ hetūdāharaṇehi yathādhigatamatthaṃ sampādetvā dhammaṃ kathessanti*). My reason for translating *sappāṭihāriya* as "antidotal" is explained on p. 1673, note 586.

1790 *Āyusaṅkhāraṃ ossaji*. Mp: "Having thoroughly set up mindfulness, having limited it by knowledge, he discarded, abandoned, his vital force. The Blessed One did not relinquish his vital force in the way one drops a clod of earth with one's hand, but he resolved, 'I will enter fruition attainment for only three more months but not beyond that.'"

1791 The verse is difficult, especially the first couplet. It is commented on identically by Spk III 254–55, Sv II 557–58, Mp IV 153–54, and Ud-a 329–30. The commentaries offer two interpretations, one taking *tulaṃ* and *atulaṃ* as opposites, the other taking *tulaṃ* as the short present participle (= *tulento*) and *atulaṃ* and *sambhavaṃ* as the opposites. I adopt the second interpretation. For a fuller discussion of the verse, see CDB 1941–44, note 255.

1792 Ce and Ee have *kampeti, saṅkampeti, sampakampeti*. Be adds a fourth verb, *sampavedheti*, which might be rendered "makes [it] shudder." Just below, non-causative counterparts of the three verbs occur in Ce and Ee: *kampati, saṅkampati, sampakampati*. Be has a fourth, *sampavedhati*.

1793 An expanded parallel of **6:19**. The additional sections are on living for half a day and for the time needed to eat half a meal.

1794 An expanded parallel of **6:20**.

1795 The eight accomplishments (*sampadā*) and their definitions are as in **8:54**, but without the section on the four dissipations of wealth.

1796 An expanded parallel of **6:31** and partly of **5:90** and **7:26**.

1797 An expanded parallel of **5:24**, **6:50**, and **7:65**.

1798 *Tathāgataṃ dhammadesanā paṭibhāti*. Here I render this peculiar Pāli idiom in accordance with the context as "is disposed to teach." Literally, it would be rendered "a Dhamma teaching shines upon [or 'occurs to'] the Tathāgata."

1799 *Ekantapaṭibhānā tathāgataṃ dhammadesanā hoti*.

1800 A distinction between *sambhava* (in question 2) and *samudaya* (in question 3) is hard to pinpoint, since in the suttas the two words are often used almost synonymously. Mp derives *samudaya* from the verb form *samudenti* and glosses this with *rāsī bhavanti*, "to accumulate, to become a heap."

1801 Brahmāli (in a private communication) offers a fine explanation of this cryptic sutta: "I understand *sabbe dhammā* to be a reference to the world of personal experience. The meaning would then be as follows: All elements of our experience are *rooted in desire* (*chandamūlakā*) in the sense that we exist due to desire (taking *chanda* as equivalent to craving). They *come into being through attention* (*manasikārasambhavā*) in the sense that we only experience what we attend to. They *originate from contact* (*phassasamudayā*) because without contact we don't experience anything at all. They *converge upon feeling* (*vedanāsamosaraṇā*) in the sense that feeling is the most important aspect of our experience, the basic motivating factor in everything we do. They are *headed by concentration* (*samādhippamukhā*) in the sense that concentration is a controlling faculty (an *indriya*) whose lead all elements of our experience must follow. They are under *the authority of mindfulness* (*satādhipateyyā*) because mindfulness is another controlling faculty which directs us in whatever we do or experience. All things have *wisdom as supervisor* (*paññuttarā*) because wisdom is the chief of the controlling faculties; wisdom, more than anything else, controls our experience (the last three factors are what allow us to get a sense of being in charge of our lives). That *liberation is their core* (*vimuttisārā*), the most excellent of all things, is self-explanatory."

1802 Mp clarifies some of these points. (1) An unskilled thief attacks those who should not be attacked, such as old people, children, and virtuous people who are not his enemies and who don't attack him. (2) A skillful thief should take only half of what is available; for example, if there are two articles of clothing he should take only one; of portions of food, he should take one for himself and leave the other (he can take the superior item for himself). (7) An unskilled thief commits theft in a nearby village, town, or city. (8) An unskilled thief does not purify the path to the other world by "depositing" a portion of his spoils in gifts to those "worthy of offerings" (*yaṃ laddhaṃ, taṃ dakkhiṇeyye nidahituṃ cheko na hoti, paralokamaggaṃ na sodheti*). Presumably a skillful thief will "deposit" part of his plunder by offering it to worthy monks and thereby "purify the path to the other world."

1803 I follow Ce here. Be and Ee put *vedagū* before *bhisakko*.

1804 The verse as preserved seems incomplete because the relative clauses beginning with *yaṃ* are not explicitly completed by a demonstrative clause. I thus follow Vanarata's suggestion that an implicit demonstrative corresponding to *anuttaraṃ pattabbaṃ* should be read into the concluding verse. It seems that *vijitasaṅgamo* refers precisely to this, and I have thus added "over that" in brackets.

1805 Ce *paramo danto*; Be *paramadanto*; Ee *paramaṃ danto*. The gloss in Mp, *paramadamathena dantattā paramadanto nāma*, suggests that *parama* qualifies *danto*, not *nāgo* as in Ce.

1806 The opening framework of this sutta is the same as that of **5:30** and **6:42** but the content of the discourse partly differs.

1807 In what follows, factors §§4–7 are identical with §§1–4 of **6:42**. In Ce and Ee, §§5–6 of **6:42** are excluded from this sutta, but the last sentence of **6:42**, not a numerical factor there, here becomes §8. Be includes §§5–6 of **6:42**, which then become §§8–9. The final sentence of the sutta would then either be unnumbered or counted as §10. If Be is followed, it is hard to account for this sutta being in the Eights rather than in the Nines or Tens. §§1–3 of the present sutta have no counterparts in the previous versions. Brahmāli suggests numbering the sentence that begins "Even some deities" as §1 and treating the final sentence of the sutta as unnumbered, which would be consistent with **6:42**. However, I here follow the numbering of Ce, my primary source text.

1808 The Ce reading here agrees more closely with the Be reading of **6:42** than with the Ce reading of the latter. But here Ce has the verb *paccessati*, "to return" (absent in Ce **6:42**), whereas in both suttas Be has *upaṭṭhahissati*, "will serve." Ee's *saccessati* is likely to be a misreading of *paccessati*. This version has no mention of *sahadhammika*, a co-religionist, as in **6:42**.

1809 *Pattaṃ nikkujjeyya*. The procedures of overturning the almsbowl and turning it upright are authorized at Vin II 124–27. See Ṭhānissaro 2007b: 411–12. Mp: "*May overturn the almsbowl on him*: They do not actually turn the almsbowl upside down in front of him, but they enact the motion of 'overturning the almsbowl,' which means that they do not accept gifts from this person. Similarly, they might decide to abolish this act by enacting a motion to turn the bowl upright (*ukkujjeyya*), which entitles them to receive his gifts again." This procedure was used in Burma during the tumultuous period of late 2007 when the monks decided that the behavior of the military junta toward the Saṅgha merited such a penalty. The monks walked down the streets with their bowls actually turned upside down to express disapproval of the rulers' actions.

1810 *Appasāda*. Mp: "When this has been proclaimed, they need not rise up from their seat for him, or pay homage to him, or go out to meet him, or give him gifts."

1811 Mp mentions the "five unsuitable resorts," probably a reference to those at **5:102**.

1812 *Paṭisāraṇiyakamma*. When this is imposed, the bhikkhu must go to the householder, accompanied by another bhikkhu, and apologize to him. If he fails to win the householder's forgiveness, his companion should try to reconcile them. The background story is at Vin II 15–18, with the legal stipulations at Vin II 18–21. For details, see Ṭhānissaro 2007b: 407–11.

1813 *Tassapāpiyasikakamma*. The grounds for this penalty are discussed at Vin II 85–86. See, too, Ṭhānissaro 2007a: 549–51, where it is rendered "further-punishment transaction." According to the origin story, this penalty is imposed on a bhikkhu who speaks evasively or reacts aggressively when charged with a grave offense (an offense of the *saṅghādisesa* class) and then admits to it only under pressure.

1814 See pp. 1732–33, note 1085.

1815 *Na ca tena mūlena vuṭṭhāpetabbo*. Mp says: "He does not get to do an act of rehabilitation [in a case] that takes that root" (*taṃ mūlaṃ katvā abbhānakammaṃ kātuṃ na labhati*). The exact meaning is unclear. I follow Brahmāli's suggestion that *mūla* here is "the root offense," that is, the original offense that led to the formal charge of aggravated misconduct.

1816 Ee does not number this chapter or the suttas it contains. Ce and Be number it X (or 10), continuing the consecutive numbering scheme used for the earlier vaggas in this *nipāta*. Ce numbers the suttas 1–27, Be 91–116. The difference in number stems from the addition of one laywoman mentioned in Ce and Ee (which I follow) but missing in Be.

1817 The editions differ in the extent to which they attach epithets to the personal names of the women. Ce has the greatest number; some may be late additions. Ee attaches *upāsikā* only to Khujjuttarā, Sāmāvatī, and Suppiyā; Be attaches it to these three and to Bojjhā. The designations *rājakumārī* (princess) and *devī* (queen) are found only in Ce. I have been irregular in my treatment of the word *mātā* pertaining to a woman's identity. When it follows another name occurring in the genitive, I translate it "mother." When it is the last part of a compound, as in Migāramātā, I leave it untranslated, assuming it was probably part of the woman's actual name-in-use and not merely a way of indicating her identity. Mp says that all these suttas should be elaborated by way of the undertaking of the uposatha observance complete with the eight factors. Thus presumably they should all be modeled on **8:42**. At **8:43** and **8:45** we already find this for Visākhā and Bojjhā respectively.

1818 This name is omitted in Be, which accordingly has only twenty-six suttas in this chapter.

1819 She is probably identical with Veḷukaṇṭakī Nandamātā. See p. 1610, note 141.

1820 Ee does not number this vagga. Ce and Be number it XI (or 11), continuing their consecutive numbering schemes. As with the Book of Sevens, I have numbered it as if it were a sixth chapter in this set of fifty. Ce numbers the suttas in the series from 1–510. Be numbers the suttas in continuation with those in the entire *nipāta*, from 117 to 626. I follow the sutta numbering of Be, though my count starts and ends one number higher because of the additional female lay follower in the previous vagga (absent in Be).

Notes to the Nines

1821 This is a composite nine, obtained by combining the five proximate causes and the four meditation subjects.

1822 The conceit "I am" (*asmimāna*) is more subtle than personal-existence view (*sakkāyadiṭṭhi*). Both are removed by the perception of non-self, but whereas the stream-enterer eliminates personal-existence view, only the arahant eliminates the conceit "I am." On this point see SN 22:89, III 130,8–131,31. It seems that personal-existence view has a stronger conceptual underpinning than the conceit "I am," which is more closely connected to existential need and therefore can be eliminated only at arahantship.

1823 Mp: "When the characteristic of impermanence is seen, the characteristic of non-self is seen. Among the three characteristics, when one is seen, the other two are also seen. Thus it is said: 'When one perceives impermanence, the perception of non-self is stabilized.'" Mp-ṭ, commenting on **9:3**, says: "*One who perceives impermanence* (*aniccasaññino*): one who perceives impermanence by way of the contemplation of impermanence, which occurs thus: 'All conditioned phenomena are impermanent' because they cease to be after having existed; because they arise and vanish; because they are fragile; because they are temporary; and because they exclude permanence. *The perception of non-self is stabilized* (*anattasaññā saṇṭhāti*): the perception of non-self consists in the contemplation of non-self, which occurs thus: 'All phenomena are non-self' because they are coreless; because we have no mastery over them; and because they are alien, void, hollow, and empty. This perception is stabilized, firmly established in the mind."

1824 This is another composite nine, arrived at by combining the five means of support with the four reliances.

1825 *Nissayasampanno*. The expression occurs at **3:20**, but with a different nuance. Mp glosses *nissayasampanno* here with *patiṭṭhāsampanno*, "possessed of a foundation," which suggests it refers to the supporting conditions for attaining arahantship.

1826 These are the five trainee's powers (*sekhabalāni*) of **5:1–2**.

1827 *Taṃ hi'ssa bhikkhuno akusalaṃ pahīnaṃ hoti suppahīnaṃ, yaṃsa ariyāya paññāya disvā pahīnaṃ*. This statement indicates that whereas the previous four abandonings are tentative and reversible, the abandoning effected by wisdom is permanent and irreversible.

1828 These four are found among the six methods of abandoning the *āsavas* explained at **6:58**. See, too, MN 2, where they are included among the seven methods of abandoning the *āsavas*.

1829 Still another composite nine, arrived at by combining the five things that lead to the mind's maturation and the four meditation subjects, with the addition of a narrative framework. The sutta is also found as Ud 4:1, 34–37, with an "inspired utterance" added.

1830 Mp says that Cālikā was the name of a city and nearby was a mountain also called Cālikā. They had built a large monastery there and the Blessed One had been dwelling in the monastery, supported by the city.

1831 Reading with Ce and Be *āgacchati*, as against Ee *dissatu*, "let be seen."

1832 Actually, what occurs "a second time" is only the request for permission, not the full statement. Mp: "*There is nothing further to be done* (*natthi kiñci uttariṃ karaṇīyaṃ*): because the four functions have been done respecting the four truths. *And no* [*need*] *to increase what has been done* (*katassa vā paṭicayo*): no repetition of what he has attained. For the path already developed is not developed again, and there is no repeated abandoning of abandoned defilements."

1833 Mp: "In five hundred successive lives he had been a king. There had been a stone slab there where he used to sit. He had come accompanied by three troops of dancing girls to amuse himself in the park. From the time Meghiya sat down there, it seemed as if he were no longer a monk but a king sitting on a regal couch beneath a white parasol, surrounded by his retinue of dancing girls. As he enjoyed his splendor, sensual thoughts arose in him. Just then, he seemed to see two thieves who had been arrested by his men and brought before him. In ordering one to be executed, thoughts of ill will arose in him; and in ordering the other to be imprisoned, thoughts of harming arose. Thus he was enveloped by those unwholesome thoughts like a tree by creepers, or like a honey-eater by honey bees."

1834 Mp: "*Liberation of mind* (*cetovimutti*): liberation of mind from defilements. In the preliminary phase of practice, the mind is liberated from defilements by way of [liberation in] a particular respect (*tadaṅgavasena*) and by way of suppression (*vikkhambhanavasena*). In the subsequent phase, it is liberated by way of eradication (*samucchedavasena*) and by way of tranquilization (*paṭipassaddhivasena*). When the dispositions have been awakened and matured, insight gives rise to the path, and as insight reaches maturity, liberation of mind is said to have matured. But in their absence it has not yet matured."

1835 This is still another composite nine, obtained by joining the four attributes described by the Buddha with the five benefits in timely listening to the Dhamma.

1836 This begins like **8:71** but develops differently.

1837 Be has *cetosamādhissa* throughout, as against Ce and Ee *cetosamathassa*.

1838 *Adhipaññādhammavipassanā*, glossed as "the insight knowledge that comprehends conditioned phenomena" (*saṅkhārapariggāhakavipassanāñāṇa*).

1839 I read here with Ee: *tathā tathā'ssa satthā piyo ca hoti manāpo ca garu ca bhāvanīyo ca*. Ce and Be have *tathā tathā so satthu . . . garu ca bhāvanīyo ca*, which means that the bhikkhu becomes respected and esteemed by the Buddha.

1840 *Tathā tathā so tasmiṃ dhamme atthapaṭisaṃvedī ca hoti dhammapaṭisaṃvedī ca*; as at **5:26**, III 21–23. See p. 1724, note 990. Strangely, though the theme of this passage is the benefit in listening to and discussing the Dhamma, the second, third, and fourth benefits (and perhaps the first as well) accrue to the monk who is *teaching* the Dhamma.

1841 *Tathā tathā so tasmiṃ dhamme gambhīraṃ atthapadaṃ paññāya ativijjha passati*. See p. 1761, note 1346.

1842 This is still another composite nine, which combines the four powers with the transcending of five fears.

1843 The explanation of "impartiality" given here may be puzzling. *Samānattatā* is a compound of "equal" (*samāna*) and "oneself" (*attan*). As applied to conduct, it means treating others as one would have them treat oneself, without bias or partiality. Here the word is being used to express the equality between those at the four levels of awakening, all with himself or herself.

1844 Although the text puts the subject in the singular, I have used the plural, which sounds more natural in English. The text uses the same future participle, *sevitabbaṃ* (and its negation, *asevitabbaṃ*), in relation to each subject, but I render it differently as best fits each particular case. The verb *sevati*, on which the participle is based, has a wide range of meanings and can support all these renderings.

1845 *Rattibhāgaṃ vā divasabhāgaṃ vā*. Mp: "Having known [this] some time at night, one should leave that very night. But if at night there is danger of attack by wild beasts, etc., one may wait until dawn. Having known [this] some time during the day, one should leave that very day. But if there is danger during the day, one may wait until sunset."

1846 I prefer Ee, which does not include *saṅkhā pi*, "having reflected," in the first alternative. Ce and Be both include *saṅkhā pi* in the first three sections. It seems, however, that reflection only becomes pertinent when there is tension between advantages and disadvantages, as in the second and third alternatives. Since the first alternative poses both material and spiritual disadvantages to staying, the proper choice is immediately evident and does not require reflection. MN 17, I 104–8, which is partly parallel to this sutta, provides a check on the readings. MN 17.3 (in Ce, Be, and Ee readings; Ee at I 105,8–10) supports the absence of *saṅkhā pi* in Ee text of AN.

1847 I read here with Ee *āpucchā*, as against Ce and Be *anāpucchā*. MN 17.4, in Ce and Be, have *āpucchā*, while Ee has neither (at I 105,28–29). It would be proper for the bhikkhu to take leave of the person on whom he has been relying—his preceptor or teacher—since the person has at least been kind enough to provide for his material needs. Further, the omission here of the words *rattibhāgaṃ vā divasabhāgaṃ vā*, "any time night or day," suggests there must also be a difference in the manner of departing.

1848 *Giribbaja*, a name for Rājagaha, because of the surrounding mountains.

1849 *Abhabbo khīṇāsavo bhikkhu sikkhaṃ paccakkhātuṃ*.This means, in effect, that he is incapable of giving up the monastic training and returning to lay life. I am following the reading of Ce. Be and Ee have the last four items of **9:8** here, and their version of the latter has the last four items of the present sutta. Hence in Ee, page 371 falls in **9:8** of the Ce version, following "a wrong course on account of fear."

1850 *Gotrabhū*. In his translation of Vism, where the word is used in a technical sense, Ñāṇamoli renders it "change-of-lineage" (see Vism 672–75, Ppn 22.1–14). Mp explains this person—in accordance with the exegetical scheme of the commentaries—as "one with a mind of powerful insight that has reached the peak, the immediate condition for the path of stream-entry." Mp is here referring to the *gotrabhū* mind-moment in the cognitive process (*cittavīthi*) of the path, the mental event that immediately precedes *sotāpattimaggacitta*, the mind-moment of the path of stream-entry. Since this scheme is relatively late and presupposes the Abhidhamma theory of the cognitive process, it is unlikely to reveal the original meaning of *gotrabhū*. In the Nikāyas, the word occurs infrequently. In the present sutta it seems to mean simply a virtuous monk or nun who has not reached the path of stream-entry. We find the plural form at MN 142.8, III 255,6–7: "But in the future, Ānanda, there will be clan members, with ochre [robes around] their necks, immoral people, of bad character" (*bhavissanti kho pan'ānanda, anāgatamaddhānaṃ gotrabhuno kāsāvakaṇṭhā dussīlā pāpadhammā*). In the latter passage it has a pejorative sense, referring to those who show merely the outer marks of a monastic without worthy inner qualities.

1851 Mp glosses *āsajja* with *ghaṭṭetvā*, implying physical violence, and *appaṭinissajja* with *akkhamāpetvā*, "without asking pardon." Mp continues: "Why did he bear resentment [against Sāriputta]? It is said that after the elder had paid homage to the Buddha, the edge of his robe hit the monk's body as he was walking away.... Because of this the monk became resentful, so when he saw the elder leaving with a large retinue, out of envy he thought to obstruct his journey; thus he spoke as he did."

1852 Mp explains that if the Buddha had tried to exonerate Sāriputta, the bhikkhu would have thought that the Teacher was taking the side of his chief disciple and not the side of a junior monk; thus he would have harbored hatred against the Buddha, too. By calling Sāriputta and asking him about the matter, the Buddha will get Sāriputta to exonerate himself.

1853 *Khamāmahaṃ bhante tassa āyasmato sace maṃ so āyasmā evam āha "khamatu ca me so āyasmā" ti*. As I understand this sentence, Sāriputta is simply saying that he will pardon the accusing bhikkhu if the latter asks him for pardon. Mp, however, explains this sentence otherwise: "The elder [Sāriputta], having pardoned the monk for his transgression, apologizes to him before the Buddha." This explanation, it seems, has influenced the translation in *Gradual Sayings*: "Lord, I do pardon that venerable one, if he speak thus to me; and let him, too, pardon me" (4:252). It is also reflected in NDB 233: "I shall forgive him, Lord, if this revered monk asks for my pardon. And he, too, may forgive me." The text itself, however, says nothing about Sāriputta offering an apology to his accuser, since he has done nothing that calls for an apology. Sāriputta is not himself addressing these words to the monk; he is saying that the monk should address these words *to him* in order to obtain pardon. In other words, so far the monk has apologized only to the Buddha, not to Sāriputta. On principle, Sāriputta can only pardon the monk if the latter asks for pardon. The word *ca*, "and," occurs in the sentence to be spoken by the monk, presumably, to mean "in addition to the Buddha, let Sāriputta also pardon me."

1854 As at **7:42**.

1855 I read (twice) with Ce and Be *ke ca*, as against Ee *keci*.

1856 The contrast is between *sa-upādisesaṃ* and *anupādisesaṃ*. Mp glosses these respectively as *sa-upādānasesaṃ*, "with a residue of clinging," and *upādānasesarahitaṃ*, "devoid of a residue of clinging." See **7:56**, which also speaks about those with a residue remaining and those without residue remaining.

1857 Wherever Ce and Be read *mattasokārī*, "cultivates to a moderate extent," Ee has *na paripūrakārī*, "does not fulfill."

1858 *Dhammapariyāyo pañhādhippāyena bhāsito*. Mp: "He shows: 'It was spoken because of the question you asked.' But to dispel the desire and lust for further existence among these nine types of persons, he spoke the sutta: 'Bhikkhus, just as even a trifling amount of feces is foul smelling, so too I do not praise even a trifling amount of existence, even for a mere finger snap' (**1:328**). Not only is the destiny of these nine persons fixed (*gati nibaddhā*), but the destiny is fixed for those families who have such fixed merit as [taking] the three refuges and the five precepts, [giving] one ticket meal, one fortnight meal, one dwelling for the rains residence, one pond, one dwelling. Those families are similar to stream-enterers."

1859 Mp glosses *samparāyavedanīyaṃ* as "kamma ripening in the next existence" (*dutiye attabhāve vipaccanakakammaṃ*).

1860 I translate following Be and Ee, which read *dukkhavedaniyaṃ*. Ce has *sukhavedaniyaṃ*, presumably because of the difficulty in seeing why the practitioner would want his kamma to be felt as painful.

1861 Mp glosses *paripakkavedanīyaṃ* as *laddhavipākavāraṃ*, "[kamma] that has gained the chance to yield results." Its opposite, *aparipakkavedanīyaṃ*, is *aladdhavipākavāraṃ*, "[kamma] that has not gained the chance to yield results."

1862 Mp-ṭ: "*Kamma to be experienced* is [kamma] that has not yet started to ripen but which is capable of producing results when there is an assemblage of other conditions. *Kamma not to be experienced* is classified as *ahosikamma*, etc., which is incapable of ripening because of a deficiency of conditions" (***vedanīyan*** *ti paccayantarasamavāye vipākuppādanasamatthaṃ, na āraddhavipākam eva;* ***avedanīyan*** *ti paccayavekallena vipaccituṃ asamatthaṃ ahosikammādibhedaṃ*). The concept of *ahosikamma*, kamma that never obtains a chance to ripen, is derived from Paṭis II 78,2–10 (Be §234). See too CMA 205.

1863 Mahākoṭṭhita asks Sāriputta a total of ten questions and receives ten replies. It thus seems peculiar that this sutta is included among the Nines, yet there is no other indication of a numerical framework than the number of questions asked and answered.

1864 According to Mp, Samiddhi was Sāriputta's pupil. See **8:83**, where the Buddha asks and answers a similar series of questions.

1865 Mp: "Intentions and thoughts are thoughts that *are* intentions" (*saṅkappavitakkā ti saṅkappabhūtā vitakkā*). This is said because the two words, *saṅkappa* and *vitakka*, are used almost interchangeably in the texts.

1866 *Nāmarūpārammaṇā*. Mp glosses: "With name and form as condition (*nāmarūpapaccayā*). By this he shows that the four formless aggregates and the form dependent on the primary elements are the condition for thoughts."

1867 The sections of the sutta up to this point encompass all experience. §§5–7 refer to factors of the path; §8, to the fruit; and §9, to the ultimate goal.

1868 Mp: "When they have attained the fruit of liberation, they have attained the core" (*phalavimuttiṃ patvā sārappattā honti*).

1869 *Amatogadhā*. Mp explains this with reference to the idea that the path and fruit take nibbāna as object: "Having gotten a foothold in the deathless nibbāna by [making it] an object, they are established there" (*ārammaṇavasena amataṃ nibbānaṃ ogāhitvā tattha patiṭṭhitā*).

1870 *Abhedanamukhāni*. Lit., "orifices without breaks." Mp: "They are wound-orifices not made by anyone but originated solely by kamma." The nine are the two eyes, two ears, two nostrils, the mouth, the urinary passage, and the rectum.

1871 An expanded parallel based on **7:48** and more remotely on **5:61**.

1872 An expanded parallel of **7:13**.

1873 Mp: "They do not rise up from their seats and come forth to greet one, as a way of humbling themselves and nurturing the mind."

1874 Mp: "They do not pay homage with the five placements" (that is, with the head, feet, and hands placed on the ground).

1875 An expanded parallel of **8:41**, the eight precepts augmented by the meditation on loving-kindness.

1876 Mp: "The Blessed One does not ask this with reference to alms given to the Saṅgha of bhikkhus. For in Anāthapiṇḍika's home excellent almsfood was constantly given to the bhikkhus. But the alms being given to the multitude was coarse, which did not please Anāthapiṇḍika. So the Buddha asks with that intention." Mp's explanation sounds contrived, for the expressions the Buddha uses in his response suggest that alms to renunciants were intended. It is possible this sutta was spoken at a time when Anāthapiṇḍika's finances were low. Alternatively, given its legendary character, the sutta may be in part a literary fiction composed for a didactic purpose. A Chinese parallel, MĀ 155, has virtually the same exchange as the Pāli at T I 677a12–13. In another Chinese parallel, EĀ 27.3, Anāthapiṇḍika says (at T II 644b22): "My poor family always practices giving, but the food is coarse and we don't always give the same" (貧家恒行布施。又飲食麁弊。不與常同).

1877 These are the five ways a bad person gives a gift, as stated at **5:147**. Just below the text will mention the five ways a good person gives a gift, also at **5:147**.

1878 Presumably it is the nine types of gifts that justify including this sutta in the Nines. There seems to be no other ninefold scheme to explain its place in this *nipāta*.

1879 Ce *sandassanāni*; Be *sandhanāni*; Ee *santhanāni*. Mp does not provide a gloss and PED does not offer a useful definition under any of those readings. But in PED *sandāna* is defined as "cord, tether, fetter."

1880 Mp glosses *kaṃsūpadhāraṇāni* as *rajatamayakhīrapaṭicchakāni*, "silver receptacles for the milk." I am not aware that *kaṃsa* can mean silver. DOP sv *kaṃsa* says that *kaṃsūpadhāraṇa* can mean "yielding a pailful of milk, *or* with a metal milking-pail." Mp adds that the horns of the milk cows were covered with sheaths of gold; people tied garlands of jasmine around their necks, attached ornaments to their four feet, spread an excellent jute cloth over their backs, and tied a golden bell around their necks. Such ways of adorning cattle, though less costly, are still practiced in India today.

1881 Mp says that conventionally one *koṭi* is twenty pairs of cloth, but here ten garments is meant.

1882 *Annassa pānassa khajjassa bhojjassa leyyassa peyyassa. Leyya*, from *lihati*, to lick, could mean something to be licked, perhaps things like honey, molasses, and palm sugar.

1883 Mp: "The *perception of impermanence* is strong insight that has reached the peak and is an immediate condition for the path" (***aniccasaññan*** *ti maggassa anantarapaccayabhāvena sikhāpattabalavavipassanaṃ*).

1884 *Uttarakuru*: the continent to the north of Jambudīpa, perhaps Central Asia.

1885 Ce and Ee *visesabhuno*. Be *visesaguṇā* is likely to be a normalization. Mp offers no help. Mp-ṭ has a description of the living conditions in Uttarakuru. My rendering is a guess based on the assumption this account is intended to explain *visesabhuno*.

1886 This sutta combines the three triads defined separately in **3:140–42**. Hence this may be considered a composite nine. We meet here the same divergence in readings in the second group of horses as we met earlier: Ce and Ee *tayo assasadassā*, as against Be *tayo assaparassā*.

1887 The text is abridged thus in all three editions.

1888 These are found, with elaborations, in the Mahānidāna Sutta, at DN 15.9–18, II 58–61.

1889 The nine terms rooted in craving, with explanations from Mp in parenthesis, are: (1) *pariyesanā* (the seeking of objects such as forms); (2) *lābha* (the obtaining of objects such as forms); (3) *vinicchaya* (when one has gained a profit, one makes judgments by thinking what is desirable and undesirable, beautiful and ordinary, how much one will keep and how much give to others, how much use and how much save); (4) *chandarāga* (weak lust and strong lust, respectively, which arise toward the object thought about with unwholesome thoughts); (5) *ajjhosāna* (the strong conviction in "I and mine"); (6) *pariggaha* (taking possession by way of craving and views); (7) *macchariya* (unwillingness to share with others); (8) *ārakkha* (guarding carefully by closing doors and storing in boxes); (9) *daṇḍādāna*, etc. (the taking up of rods, etc., for the purpose of warding off others).

1890 §§1–4 and 6–8 are included among the seven stations of consciousness at **7:44**.

1891 The three editions differ here. I follow Ce *bhikkhuno cetasā cittaṃ paricitaṃ hoti*. Ee has *bhikkhuno cetasā cittaṃ suparicitaṃ hoti*, Be *bhikkhuno cetasā citaṃ hoti*. *Citaṃ* occurs repeatedly in Be, so it is clearly intentional. Mp (Ce): "One round of the mental process is built up, increased, by another round of the mental process" (*cittācārapariyāyena cittācārapariyāyo cito vaḍḍhito hoti*). Mp (Be) has *cittavāra–* in place of *cittācāra–*.

1892 All three editions have *bhikkhuno cetasā cittaṃ suparicitaṃ hoti*. But note that in Ee, Sāriputta's statement on Devadatta's way of teaching does not differ from Candikāputta's statement just above. Both have *suparicitaṃ hoti*. It is puzzling that the sutta seems to be approving of Devadatta's teaching. Normally we would expect him to be censured for proposing a distorted version of the Dhamma. Perhaps this incident occurred before Devadatta became schismatic.

1893 §§4–6 are, in Pāli, *asarāgadhammaṃ, asadosadhammaṃ, asamohadhammaṃ*. Mp does not gloss them, but the point seems to be that for the arahant lust, hatred, and delusion are no longer even capable of arising again. §§7–9 allude to the three realms of existence.

1894 As at **6:55**, but with a different simile.

1895 Text says *silāyūpo soḷasakukkuko*, a stone pillar sixteen *kukkus* tall. According to DOP, a *kukku* is 45 cm, about half a meter. Thus the pillar would be about eight meters.

1896 The number of verbs differ among the editions. Ce, which I follow, has four: *n'eva naṃ kampeyya na saṅkampeyya na sampakampeyya na sampavedheyya* (but Ce abridges the middle two directions and omits the last verb in relation to the final repetition, apparently an editorial oversight). Ee has three: *n'eva naṃ kampeyya na saṅkampeyya na sampavedheyya*. Be uses only two verbs: *n'eva naṃ saṅkampeyya na sampavedheyya*, but three in the simile at **6:55**.

1897 Also at **5:179**.

1898 On *bhayaṃ veraṃ pasavati*, Mp says that one obtains the peril of mental fright (*cittutrāsabhayaṃ*; this favors understanding *bhaya* as subjective fear rather than objective peril, though I think the latter is actually intended) and enmity as a person (*puggalaveraṃ*). Spk II 73,17–33, commenting on SN 12:41, gives a fuller explanation: "Peril and enmity are one in meaning. Enmity is twofold, external and internal. For if one has killed someone's father, the other thinks: 'They say he killed my father; I will kill him.' So the latter takes a sharp knife and pursues the former. The volition arisen in him is called the external enmity [in relation to the future victim]. But the other hears, 'He's coming to kill me' and decides: 'I'll kill him first.' This is called the internal enmity [in relation to himself]. They both pertain to this present life. When the warden of hell sees the murderer reborn in hell, the volition arises in him: 'I'll take a blazing iron hammer and strike him': this is the external enmity pertaining to the future life. And the volition that arises in the victim, 'He's coming to strike me though I'm faultless; I'll strike him first,' is the internal enmity pertaining to the future life. The external enmity is what is called 'enmity as a person' in the [old] Commentary."

1899 *Taṃ kut'ettha labbhā*. My translation of this idiom is not intended to be literal. The point is that one has no choice but to resign oneself to the situation. Mp: "'What can be done in regard to that person so that there would be no such harmful conduct? By what means is it possible to obtain this?' Having reflected: 'A person harms another because of the disposition of his mind,' one dispels resentment."

1900 SN 36:11, IV 217,4–16, speaks of the "progressive cessation of activities" (*anupubbasaṅkhārānaṃ nirodha*) in terms very similar to the present sutta, except that it says, "for one who has attained the first jhāna, speech (*vācā*) has ceased." It is uncertain whether *saṅkhārā* here is intended in the active sense or the passive sense, "activities" or "conditioned phenomena."

1901 All three editions have the singular verb *hoti*, though Ee notes some manuscripts have plural *honti*. The subject *rūpasaññā* can be read as either singular or plural.

1902 *Anupubbavihārā*. Be merely lists their names, that is, "the first jhāna, the second jhāna," etc. Ce and Ee give the full formulas.

1903 *Anupubbavihārasamāpattiyo*. It is uncertain whether, in this compound, *vihārasamāpattiyo* should be interpreted as a *dvanda* ("dwellings and attainments") or as a *tappurisa* ("attainments of dwellings"). Mp, with its gloss *anupaṭipāṭiyā samāpajjitabbavihārā*, "dwellings to be attained in proper sequence," suggests it is a *tappurisa*.

1904 I read with Be and Ee *tiṇṇā*, as against Ce *nittaṇhā*, "without craving," which seems less satisfactory in this context. Mp (Be): "*Crossed over*: crossed over sensuality" (*kāmato tiṇṇā*).

1905 *Tadaṅgena*. Mp: "*In that particular respect:* with respect to that jhāna factor" (*tena jhānaṅgena*).

1906 *Upekkhāsukha*. Mp does not comment, but I take the compound to be a *tappurisa* rather than the *dvanda* "equanimity and pleasure." In the fourth jhāna and beyond *upekkhā*, equanimity, continues but it is no longer accompanied by *sukha*, pleasant feeling.

1907 Ce and Ee have the plural verb *nirujjhanti* here, but the singular *nirujjhati* in §§6–8. Be has the singular *nirujjhati* here as well. Again, the subject *rūpasaññā* can be read as either singular or plural.

1908 Mp identifies him as the elder Lāḷudāyī.

1909 Brahmāli comments: "Since nibbāna is 'extinguishment' (of suffering), any partial extinguishment of suffering is a partial kind of nibbāna."

1910 Though all three editions here read *upe(k)khāsahagatā saññāmanasikārā*, I follow the Burmese and Sinhala manuscripts referred to in a note in Ee, which read *upe(k)khāsukhasahagatā saññāmanasikārā*. This fits better with the exposition in **9:33 §4** and **9:41 §4** than the reading *upe(k)khāsahagatā* in all three printed editions.

1911 Cited at Vism 153,17–154,8, Ppn 4.130, as testimony that one should first master the jhāna one has just attained before attempting to enter the next higher jhāna.

1912 *Taṃ nimittaṃ*. Mp: "That object consisting in the first jhāna" (*taṃ paṭhamajjhānasaṅkhātaṃ nimittaṃ*).

1913 *Ubhato bhaṭṭho*. *Bhaṭṭha* is past participle of *bhassati*, to drop away, to droop, to fall off.

1914 *Anabhihiṃsamāno*. I offer only a literal translation. Based on the context I understand the sense to be that he does not force himself to aim prematurely for the higher attainment but masters the preceding one before moving on to the next.

1915 Mp: "The characteristic of impermanence is stated by way of two terms: impermanent and disintegrating (*aniccato, palokato*). The characteristic of non-self is stated by way of three terms: alien (*parato*), empty (*suññato*), and non-self (*anattato*). The characteristic of suffering is stated by the other six terms: suffering (*dukkhato*), an illness (*rogato*), a boil (*gaṇḍato*), a dart (*sallato*), misery (*aghato*), and affliction (*ābādhato*).

1916 Mp: "He directs the mind of insight (*vipassanācitta*) to the unconditioned deathless element by way of hearing, by way of praise, by way of learning, and by way of concepts thus: 'Nibbāna is peaceful.' He directs the mind of the path (*maggacitta*) to nibbāna simply by making it an object (*ārammaṇakaraṇavasen'eva*), not by saying, 'This is peaceful, this is sublime.' The meaning is that he directs his mind there, penetrating it in this mode."

1917 *Ten'eva dhammarāgena tāya dhammanandiyā*. Mp: "By desire and attachment to the Dhamma of serenity and insight. So too for 'delight in the Dhamma.' If he can fully exhaust desire and attachment to serenity and insight, he attains arahantship. If not, he becomes a non-returner." Mp-ṭ: "Having abandoned the desire and lust for serenity and insight leading to the lower paths, if he is unable to exhaust the desire for [serenity and insight] leading to the supreme path, he becomes settled in the stage of non-returning."

1918 See **4:181**, **4:196**.

1919 Note that *rūpa*, form, is omitted in describing the formless attainments. Mp: "In the formless attainment there is utterly no form; with reference to this, form is not included."

1920 Mp: "Why is the base of neither-perception-nor-non-perception not mentioned? Because of its subtlety. The four formless aggregates in that [attainment] are so subtle that they are not susceptible to exploration [by way of insight]. Hence [just below] the Buddha says: 'There is penetration to final knowledge as far as meditative attainments accompanied by perception reach.' This is meant: 'To the extent that there is an attainment accompanied by mind (*sacittakasamāpatti; citta* here presumably means "clear and distinct cognition"), there is penetration to final knowledge when one explores [by insight] those gross phenomena, that is, one attains arahantship. But because of its subtlety, the base of neither-perception-nor-non-perception is not called an attainment accompanied by perception."

1921 There are some differences between the readings in Ce, Ee, and

Be. I follow Ce: *jhāyīh'ete bhikkhave bhikkhūhi samāpattikusalehi samāpattivuṭṭhānakusalehi samāpajjitvā vuṭṭhahitvā samakkhātabbānī ti vadāmi*. Ee basically agrees with Ce but prints *jhāyī h'ete*, as if it had a nominative subject followed by emphatic *hi*. Mp: "*Described* means to be properly declared, to be explained, extolled, praised simply as 'peaceful and sublime'" (***samakkhātabbānī*** *ti sammā akkhātabbāni, "santāni paṇītānī" ti evaṃ kevalaṃ ācikkhitabbāni thometabbāni vaṇṇetabbāni*).

1922 On the meaning of "confinement" (*sambādha*), see **9:42** below.

1923 This is the same as the well-known opening statement of the Satipaṭṭhāna Sutta, at DN 22.1, II 290,$_{8-11}$; MN 10.2, I 55,$_{32}$–56,$_{2}$. It also occurs in AN at **3:74**, **4:194**. **6:26**, and **10:95**.

1924 Mp: "*The eye itself... will actually be present* (*tadeva nāma cakkhuṃ bhavissati*): the sensitive substance of the eye is itself unimpaired. *As well as those forms* (*te rūpā*): that visible-form object itself will have come into range. *And yet one does not experience that base* (*tañcāyatanaṃ no paṭisaṃvedissati*): and yet one does not know that visible-form base." I may be wrong in assuming that the nine items are to be obtained by totaling the five kinds of sensory experience with the four formless meditations. Possibly the nine were to be obtained by including the four jhānas (which may have dropped out of the text) with the four formless meditations, and then adding, as the ninth, the special state of concentration referred to at the end of the sutta.

1925 Ce and Be both have *ti* here, indicating the end of a quotation, which suggests that the speaker of the next paragraph is Udāyī. Yet it is clear that Ānanda himself is still speaking. Thus, it seems, *ti* is an error and should be deleted from Ce and Be. Ee does not have *ti*.

1926 So Ce and Ee. Be has the name as Jaṭilavāsikā. Mp says that she was a resident of Jaṭila city (*jaṭilanagaravāsinī*). The *jaṭilas* were matted-hair ascetics, but it is questionable whether they were ever numerous enough to constitute a city.

1927 Mp: "*Does not lean forward* by way of lust, and *does not bend back* by way of hatred" (*rāgavasena na abhinato, dosavasena na apanato*).

1928 See **5:27**. Here Mp comments: "It is steady, not because one has forcefully and vigorously reined in and suppressed the defilements, but because it has arisen when the defilements are cut off."

1929 *Vimuttattā ṭhito, ṭhitattā santusito, santusitattā no paritassati*. This sequence is also at SN III 45,$_{13-14}$, 46,$_{4-5}$, 54,$_{1-2}$, 55,$_{34-35}$, 58,$_{23-24}$. It is on the basis of the latter passages that I see a change in the subject of the last phrase of the AN text, from "it," referring to the *samādhi*, to "one," the person who attains it. While in the AN passage, the participles are masculine singular and thus may be interpreted as referring either to the *samādhi* or to the person, the SN parallels read: *Vimuttattā ṭhitaṃ. Ṭhitattā santusitaṃ. Santusitattā na paritassati. Aparitassaṃ paccattaññeva parinibbāyati. 'Khīṇā jāti, vusitaṃ brahmacariyaṃ, kataṃ karaṇīyaṃ, nāparaṃ itthattāyā'ti pajānātī ti.* The neuter singular participles indicate that the subject of the first two phrases is *cittaṃ*, but with *santusitattā na paritassati*, the subject seems to shift from *cittaṃ* to the person attaining liberation. We can infer by analogy that in the present passage a similar shift occurs, in this case from *samādhi* to the person who attains it.

1930 *Ayaṃ, bhante Ānanda, samādhi kiṃphalo vutto bhagavatā.* The question is ambiguous. It could mean either, "Of what did the Blessed One say this concentration is the fruit?" or "What did the Blessed One say this concentration has as its fruit?" Mp takes it in the former way, but there are arguments in favor of the latter (see next note).

1931 *Ayaṃ, bhagini, samādhi aññāphalo vutto bhagavatā.* The compound *aññāphalo* could be interpreted either as a *tappurisa* ("this concentration is the fruit of final knowledge") or as a *bāhubbīhi* ("this concentration has final knowledge as its fruit"). In the former case, the *samādhi* is to be identified with the fruit; in the latter, with an achievement preceding the fruit. Mp takes it in the former sense, as the fruit itself: "The nun asks about the concentration of the fruit of arahantship (*arahattaphalasamādhi*). Final knowledge is arahantship. The Blessed One has spoken of this concentration of the fruit of arahantship. [The intention is:] When one is percipient with the perception of the fruit of arahantship, one does not experience that base." However, the question *kiṃphalā* occurs repeatedly at SN V 118,22–120,19, where it must mean, "What does it have as its fruit?" And in **5:25** we find *pañcahi, bhikkhave, aṅgehi anuggahitā sammādiṭṭhi ca cetovimuttiphalā hoti ... paññāvimuttiphalā ca hoti.* The sense here is not that right view *is the fruit* of liberation of mind and liberation by wisdom, but that right view has liberation of mind and liberation by wisdom *as its fruit*. Further, in **3:101**, a *samādhi* described in exactly the same terms as this one is shown to be the supporting condition for the six higher knowledges, the last of which is the "the taintless liberation of mind, liberation by wisdom." By analogy, it follows that this *samādhi* is not the fruit of final knowledge, but one that *yields* final knowledge.

There is a Chinese parallel to this last portion of the sutta, SĀ 557 at T II 146a12–29. In this version, when the bhikkhunī asks Ānanda the question about the concentration of mind without characteristics (無相心三昧 = *animitta cetosamādhi*), he replies that the Buddha said this concentration "is the fruit of wisdom, the reward of wisdom" (智果、智功德, which has the same ambiguity that I mentioned in the preceding note).

1932 *Lokāyatikā brāhmaṇā*. See SN 12:48, II 77. Normally, the *lokāyatikā* are depicted as materialists; here, however, they seem to be simply speculators about the world.

1933 My translation does not follow any of the three editions available to me, which are all problematic. In Be both teachers claim to know an infinite world with infinite knowledge. Pūraṇa Kassapa says: *ahaṃ anantena ñāṇena anantaṃ lokaṃ jānaṃ passaṃ viharāmi*, and Nātaputta [the Jain teacher Mahāvīra] uses exactly the same words. Since this directly contradicts the statement (in all editions) that the two make mutually opposed claims (*ubhinnaṃ aññamaññaṃ vipaccanīkavādānaṃ*), Be must be faulty here. The error is likely to be old, for several Burmese manuscripts and a Siamese manuscript (referred to in Ee's notes) also have this reading.

In Ce and Ee Pūraṇa Kassapa says: *ahaṃ anantena ñāṇena antavantaṃ lokaṃ jānaṃ passaṃ viharāmi*, and Nātaputta says: *ahaṃ antavantena ñāṇena antavantaṃ lokaṃ jānaṃ passaṃ viharāmi*. This reading, too, seems faulty. First, it has Nātaputta claim finite knowledge, when it is known that he claimed omniscience or infinite knowledge. Second, though it makes the two teachers claim different ranges of knowledge, their conclusions about the world are the same. A true contradiction would emerge only if one teacher asserts that the world is infinite and the other that it is finite. I take it that they both claim infinite knowledge (*anantena ñāṇena*) but differ regarding the extent of the world. Since the Jains actually posit the world to be both finite and infinite (see just below), I assume the brahmin understands Nātaputta to hold the world to be finite, and thus takes his opponent Pūraṇa Kassapa to posit the world to be infinite. We have no other sources on Pūraṇa's thought with which to understand his cosmology. Elsewhere the crux of Pūraṇa's philosophy is said to be the doctrine of non-doing (DN 2.17, I 52,21–53,4) or the thesis that beings are defiled and purified without cause, or that there is no cause for knowledge and vision (SN 46:56, V 126,26–30). At **6:57** a system of six classes of people is ascribed to him.

Mahāvīra's view of the world is explained in "Various topics prepared on Jain History by Dr. K. C. Jain and his team" (http://www.jainworld.com/literature/jainhistory/chapter4.asp): "It is with regard to these questions [about the world] that Mahāvīra declared: 'From these alternatives, you cannot arrive at truth; from these alternatives, you are certainly led [astray]. The world is eternal as far as that part is concerned which is the substratum (*dravya*) of the "world"; it is not eternal as far as its ever-changing state is concerned.' In regard to such questions, Mahāvīra's advice to his disciples was neither to support those who maintained that the world is eternal nor those who advocated that it is not eternal. He would have said the same thing regarding such propositions as the world exists and it does not exist; the world is unchangeable; the world is in constant flux; the world has a beginning; the world has no beginning; *the world has an end; the world has no end*; etc." (my italics).

1934 Be lacks *paramāya gatiyā*, found in Ce and Ee.

1935 *Daḷhadhammā dhanuggaho sikkhito katahattho katūpāsano*. Mp's comments on these terms differs slightly from its comments at **4:45** (see p. 1690, notes 724 and 725). Here Mp says: "*Firm-bowed archer* (*daḷhadhammā dhanuggaho*): an archer who has taken up a firm bow. A 'firm bow' (*daḷhadhanu*) is called the 'strength of two thousand' (*dvisahassathāmaṃ*): a bow to which one can attach an arrow with a head made of some metal such as bronze or lead, etc., fit the arrow notch to the string, grasp the bow handle and draw back the string the full length of the arrow shaft, and shoot the arrow up from the ground. *Trained* (*sikkhito*): they have studied the craft in their teacher's clan for ten or twelve years. *Skillful* (*katahattho*): one who has simply studied a craft is not yet skillful; they are skillful when they have achieved mastery over it. *Experienced* (*katūpāsano*): one who has exhibited his craft in the king's court, etc."

1936 As at **4:45** (and SN 2:26, I 61–62).

1937 Text has *evarūpāya sandhāvanikāya* here, whereas **4:45** has *gamanena*. Mp glosses *padasā dhāvanena*, "running on foot."

1938 Ce and Ee add here *bhītā*, "frightened," but it seems this word belongs only in the third case, when the devas flee to their city. In Be it occurs only in relation to the third case.

1939 All three editions read here *antamakāsi māraṃ*. Presumably their editors took this to mean, "who has made an end to Māra." But this is certainly wrong, for two reasons: first, grammatically, this would require the genitive *mārassa*; and second, it is not true that a meditator in jhāna has "made an end to Māra." Elsewhere we find *andhamakāsi māraṃ* (at MN I 159,$_{19}$, I 160,$_{5,10}$, I 174,$_{15-16}$, and I 175,$_{5}$), "he made Māra blind" or "blinded Māra," which makes better sense. Ps II 163,$_{4-8}$, commenting on MN I 159,$_{19}$, explains: "*He blinded Māra*: he did not destroy Māra's eyes, but when a bhikkhu has attained jhāna as a basis for insight, Māra is unable to see the object of his mind. Hence it is said: 'He blinded Māra'" (*andhamakāsi māran ti na mārassa akkhīni bhindi. Vipassanāpādakajjhānaṃ samāpannassa pana bhikkhuno imaṃ nāma ārammaṇaṃ nissāya cittaṃ vattatī ti māro passituṃ na sakkoti. Tena vuttaṃ "andhamakāsi māran" ti*).

1940 *Apadaṃ vadhitvā māracakkhuṃ.* Mp: "*Put out Māra's eyes without a trace*: destroyed [them] completely, without remainder (*nippadaṃ niravasesaṃ vadhitvā*)." At MN I 159,19–160,12 and MN I 174,15–175,6 this whole statement is made about *all nine* meditative attainments, including the four jhānas. There thus seems to be a difference between the textual lineages about the extent to which this statement applies.

1941 *Hatthikalabhā.* Mp glosses as "very big bull elephants" (*mahantā mahantā nāgā*). This, however, begs the question how these bull elephants differ from the main subject of the simile. Ud 41,20–21 mentions different types of elephants, among them *hatthikalabhā* (Ee *hatthikaḷārā*) which Ud-a 250,12–13 calls elephant offspring (*hatthipotakā*). They are there distinguished from *hatthicchāpā*, young elephant offspring still being nursed (*khīrūpagā daharahatthipotakā*). I translate in accordance with this explanation.

1942 With Be and Ee, I read *mallesu*, as against Ce *malatesu*. SN 42:11 is also set at Uruvelakappa, which is said to be a town of the Mallas (see CDB 1348).

1943 Mp glosses *vimuccati* here as "liberated from the opposing qualities" (*paccanīkadhammehi ca vimuccati*). Since all three editions, with the support of Mp, have *vimuccati*, I translate in conformity with this reading, but I think it likely that the original reading was *adhimuccati*, "resolved upon" or "focused on." As the text unfolds with respect to the successive meditative attainments, in each case the bodhisatta is *vimuccati/adhimuccati* upon the attainment *before* he actually achieves it. In such a context being "focused on" rather than "liberated in" makes better sense.

1944 Ce has the genitive plural *passataṃ*, while Be and Ee have the genitive singular *passato*. Mp (Be) has *passato* in the lemma and a genitive plural in the gloss: ***'Etaṃ santan ti passato*** *ti etaṃ nekkhammaṃ santaṃ vigatadarathapariḷāhan ti evaṃ passantānaṃ bhikkhūnaṃ. Passato* is also found in an older Sinhala edition. Possibly *passato* entered the text through an erroneous transposition from the Buddha's account below, where the singular is appropriate.

1945 Mp interprets renunciation (*nekkhamma*) here as "going forth" (*pabbajjā*) into homelessness. But the text itself seems to allow renunciation as an internal quality, implicitly identified with firm attainment of the first jhāna.

1946 I follow the section divisions of Ee, which conform to the paragraph divisions in Be and show the transitions in the discourse better than the divisions in Ce.

1947 I follow Ee in reading *aparena samayena* here and in each of the corresponding sections to come. Ce and Be omit it in later sections.

1948 Here I follow the manuscripts referred to in the note to Ee, which read *upekhāsukhasahagatā* ("accompanied by the pleasure [connected with] equanimity"). This fits the exposition better than the reading *upe(k)khāsahagatā* found in all three printed editions.

1949 In Ce and Be *Sāmaññavaggo*. Ee names this *Pañcālavagga*.

1950 The verse occurs at SN 2:7, I 48. Be and Ee have a faulty reading of pāda a in AN, *sambādhe gataṃ okāsaṃ*, as against Ce *sambādhe vata okāsaṃ*. The Be and Ee text of SN 2:7 reads *vata*. Also, in pāda b, Ce has *avindi*, Ee *avidā*, two aorist forms meaning "knew." But Be has *avidvā*, "unknowing, ignorant," which is hard to account for. In SN 2:7 Be also reads the verb as *avindi*.

1951 See **9:37**.

1952 *Pariyāyena*. Mp: "For a single reason (*ekena kāraṇena*). For the first jhāna is called the achievement of an opening with respect merely to the absence of confinement by sensuality, not in every respect."

1953 *Yadeva tattha rūpasaññā aniruddhā hoti*. The singular verb *hoti* indicates that "perception" in the singular is intended here. In the immediately following paragraph, however, *rūpasaññānaṃ* and *paṭighasaññānaṃ* are genitive plurals.

1954 *Nippariyāyena*. Mp: "Not just for a single reason, but because it abandons all confinement, the destruction of the taints is called the achievement of an opening in every way."

1955 MN 70.17, I 478,4–8 offers a formal definition of the body witness (*kāyasakkhī*) as a person who "contacts with the body and abides in those emancipations that are peaceful and formless, transcending forms, and some of his taints are destroyed by his seeing with wisdom." In the present sutta, however, the term "body witness" does not conform to this formal definition but is explained on the basis of a word play. Strictly speaking, the one who attains the complete destruction of the taints is no longer a body witness, a category restricted to those still in training.

1956 *Yathā yathā ca tadāyatanaṃ tathā tathā naṃ kāyena phusitvā viharati*. Mp: "Through whatever means or in whatever way there is that base consisting in the first jhāna, by that same means, or in that same way, he dwells having contacted that attainment with the coexistent mental body (*sahajātanāmakāyena phusitvā*)."

1957 As suggested by the previous note, here the term "non-provisional sense" is itself being used in a loose, "provisional" sense. In the strict, non-provisional sense, such a disciple is not a body witness, for the real body witness has still not reached arahantship.

1958 Again, strictly speaking, according to the formal definition at MN 70.16, I 477,33–36, the one liberated by wisdom (*paññāvimutta*) is an arahant who does not attain the formless emancipations or the cessation of perception and feeling. Similarly, to meet the formal requirement of "liberated in both respects" (in the following sutta), a disciple must not only realize arahantship but must also attain the formless emancipations, as stated at MN 70.15, I 477,25–28.

1959 *Sikkhādubbalyāni*. Lit., "weaknesses in [regard to] to the training." What is intended are not defects in the training itself, but defects in one's observance of the training. Suttas **9:63–92** are all composite nines combining ten different fivefold sets with, successively, the four establishments of mindfulness, the four right strivings, and the four bases for psychic potency.

1960 Ee does not number this vagga. Ce numbers it 5 and Be numbers it (10) 5, using both the consecutive numbering scheme and the number of the vagga in the set of fifty.

1961 Ce does not number the suttas in the series. Be numbers them in continuity with those in the entire *nipāta*, from 93 to 432. Ee numbers them from 93 to 100, with no explanation why it ends at 100. I follow the numbering of Be.

1962 Ce has 3–18, but there are eighteen suttas in this group; the nine perceptions and nine meditative attainments are to be taken collectively with each of the nine terms from "full understanding" to "relinquishment." The eighteen beginning with 3 should thus be added to the two previous suttas so that the present group ends at 20.

1963 Ce has a note: "The seventeen terms, from 'lust' through 'heedlessness,' are each to be joined with the ten terms beginning with 'for direct knowledge.' These are each to be taken separately with the nine perceptions and the nine meditative attainments, described as 'nine things to be developed.' Thus there are altogether 340 suttas."

Notes to the Tens

1964 *Iti kho, Ānanda, kusalāni sīlāni anupubbena aggāya parenti*. Mp glosses *aggāya* with *arahattatthāya*.

1965 *Dhammatā esā*. Mp: "This is the nature of things, the order of causation" (*dhammasabhāvo eso kāraṇaniyamo ayaṃ*). The point, of course, is not that one need make no volitional effort at all, but that establishing each prior factor serves as a natural supporting condition for each subsequent factor. Thus the effort needed to arouse the later factor is much less than would be required if the proper supporting condition had not been established.

1966 *Iti kho, bhikkhave, dhammā dhamme abhisandenti, dhammā dhamme paripūrenti apārā pāraṃ gamanāyā.* Mp: "*For going from the near shore to the far shore*: For going from 'the near shore,' the round of existence with its three planes, to 'the far shore,' nibbāna" (*orimatīrabhūtā tebhūmakavaṭṭā nibbānapāraṃ gamanatthāya*). It seems that the point in expressing this in terms of *dhammā*, which I here render "stages," is to show that this process of development unfolds in accordance with natural principles as one stage conditions the arising of the subsequent stage all the way from the beginning of the path to its culmination. This series thus constitutes a "positive" version of dependent origination. We meet this positive version in the Upanisā Sutta (SN 12:23, II 29–32). See my essay on this sutta, Bodhi 1980.

1967 An expanded parallel of **5:24**, **6:50**, **7:65**, and **8:81**.

1968 Mp: "He would not take earth as object and be percipient through an arisen perception 'earth.'" It seems that what is being denied here is a jhāna based on the earth *kasiṇa*. The same holds below for water, fire, and air. This is confirmed by the next four steps, which negate the four formless bases. In other words, this concentration is not a jhāna based on the *kasiṇas* or formless attainments.

1969 Mp identifies this with the concentration of fruition attainment (*phalasamāpattisamādhi*). This attainment is not the fruition that occurs for a few moments immediately following the path, but a special meditative state accessible only to those who have already attained one of the four paths and its subsequent fruition. The attainment, as shown in this sutta, does not take any of the mundane, conditioned meditation objects as its support; its support is the unconditioned nibbāna, experienced directly and immediately. The commentaries hold that this attainment is graded as fourfold according to the four stages of realization (from stream-entry to arahantship).

1970 *Bhavanirodho nibbānaṃ bhavanirodhaṃ nibbānaṃ.* Mp paraphrases thus: "'On that occasion, friend, I was percipient with the perception of fruition attainment.' Reviewing knowledge (*paccavekkhaṇā*) is discussed to show that this attainment was accompanied by mind." In other words, because perception was present, this was not "the cessation of perception and feeling" (*saññāvedayitanirodha*).

1971 An expanded parallel based on **8:71**. See too the part-parallel **9:4**.

1972 An expanded parallel based on **8:72**.

1973 This is a composite ten. The first set of five is in **5:53**.

1974 Still another composite ten.

1975 A composite sutta with part-parallels at **5:205–6** and **9:71–72**.

1976 Perhaps, with Be, we should read *susamucchinnā* here, but I follow Ce and Ee, which have simply *samucchinnā* here, though *susamucchinnā* below.

1977 As at **4:34**. The series of similes occurs at SN 45:139–47, V 41–45, with the simile of cloth in the tenth place.

1978 An expanded parallel of **9:10**.

1979 *Nāthakaraṇā dhammā*. Mp: "They act as protectors for oneself, meaning that they act as supports" (*attano sanāthabhāvakarā patiṭṭhākarā ti attho*).

1980 Mp on *piyasamudāhāro*: "He listens carefully when another is teaching, and he himself desires to teach others." I understand *abhidhamme* and *abhivinaye* simply in the referential sense, as explained in note 1086. Mp, however, distinguishes between *dhamma* as the Sutta Piṭaka and *abhidhamma* as the seven treatises (of the Abhidhamma Piṭaka); and *vinaya* as the twofold Suttavibhaṅga and *abhivinaya* as the Khandhakas and Parivāra. This type of explanation presupposes the existence of texts that had probably been compiled several generations after the Buddha's passing.

1981 The text uses the past, present, and future forms of the verb *āvasati*, "abide." Since a literal translation would be clumsy, I have rendered the phrase in accordance with the sense.

1982 As at **6:1**.

1983 From this point on the text is an expanded parallel of **6:64**. See the latter for notes on the first, second, and seventh powers here. The ten Tathāgata powers are also in MN 12.9–20, I 69–71 and are analyzed in detail at Vibh 336–44 (Be §§809–31).

1984 *Sabbatthagāminiṃ paṭipadaṃ yathābhūtaṃ ñāṇaṃ*. Vibh 339 (Be §811) identifies this with the Buddha's knowledge of the paths leading to hell, the animal realm, the spirit world, the human world, the deva world, and nibbāna. See MN 12.37–43, I 74–77.

1985 *Anekadhātunānādhātulokaṃ yathābhūtaṃ ñāṇaṃ*. Vibh 339 (Be §812) defines this as the Buddha's knowledge of the diversity in the aggregates, sense bases, and elements.

1986 *Sattānaṃ nānādhimuttikataṃ yathābhūtaṃ ñāṇaṃ*. Vibh 339 (§813) explains this as the Buddha's knowledge of beings as having inferior or superior dispositions, and his understanding of how those with similar dispositions come together and meet.

1987 *Parasattānaṃ parapuggalānaṃ indriyaparopariyattaṃ yathābhūtaṃ ñāṇaṃ*. Vibh 340–42 (§§814–27) explains this as the Buddha's knowledge of the condition of sentient beings' diverse inclinations, underlying tendencies, temperaments, dispositions, intelligence, faculties, characters, receptivity, and potentiality. The terms are all explicated in detail. Mp is more concise, defining it simply as the Buddha's knowledge of whether the five faculties of beings (their faith, etc.) are increasing or declining.

1988 Mp: "*The things* (*ye te dhammā*): the knowledge of the ten powers, [or] the things pertaining to the knowledge of omniscience. *Doctrinal principles* (*adhivuttipadānaṃ*): principles of designation; this means such things as the aggregates, sense bases, and elements, which are the grounds for the principles of the teaching."

1989 *Etadānuttariyaṃ, Ānanda, ñāṇānaṃ yadidaṃ tattha tattha yathābhūtañāṇaṃ.* Mp: "The knowledge of various phenomena according to their essential nature; by this he shows the knowledge of omniscience" (*tesu tesu dhammesu yathāsabhāvañāṇaṃ; iminā sabbaññutaññāṇaṃ dasseti*).

1990 Ce and Ee read *paññāya disvā disvā*. Be does not repeat *disvā*, but Mp (Be) seems to support the reading of Ce and Ee with its gloss: *sahavipassanāya maggapaññāya passitvā passitvā pahātabbā* ("To be abandoned after having repeatedly seen with path wisdom together with insight wisdom").

1991 *Pāpikā issā.* It is hard to account for the adjective *pāpikā*, since there are no instances in the texts of a benign type of envy.

1992 *Abhibhuyya iriyati*, glossed by Mp with *vattati*.

1993 Mp says that the claims to knowledge, to development, and to both knowledge and development, in the three sections, are all claims to arahantship.

1994 *Abhibhuyya tiṭṭhati*. This does not seem to differ in meaning from *abhibhuyya iriyati* used in the preceding sutta.

1995 *Kasiṇāyatanāni*. The *kasiṇas* are disks representing elements or colors used as objects of *samādhi* meditation. For example, the earth *kasiṇa* is a disk filled with reddish brown clay; the water *kasiṇa* is a bowl of water; the color *kasiṇas* are colored disks. Though the meditator begins with a physical disk, when he can see the *kasiṇa* clearly with his mind's eye, he discards the physical disk and focuses solely on the mental image. As concentration deepens, another image called the "counterpart mark" (*paṭibhāganimitta*) emerges as an anchor of attention. Vism chaps. 4 and 5 offer a detailed explanation of the *kasiṇas*. In the Vism system, the space *kasiṇa* (which was originally the base of the infinity of space) is replaced by the limited-space *kasiṇa*, and the consciousness *kasiṇa* by the light *kasiṇa*.

1996 "Nondual" (*advaya*) here refers simply to the presentation of the object and not to an underlying ontological unity. Mp explains: "This is said because one [*kasiṇa*] does not acquire the quality of another. For just as, when one enters the water, there is only water and nothing else in all directions, so too, the earth *kasiṇa* is only the earth *kasiṇa*. It is unmixed with any other *kasiṇa*. The same method applies to the others." On *appamāṇa*, "measureless," Mp says: "This is stated by way of measureless pervasion of this or that [object]. For pervading it with the mind, one pervades the whole thing; one does not grasp boundaries, thinking: 'This is its beginning, this is its middle.'"

1997 At **1:267** Kāḷī is called the "foremost of those whose confidence is based on hearsay." Apparently she never met the Buddha but based her trust in him on what she heard from others.

1998 SN 4:25, I 126,15–18. The "maidens" are Māra's daughters, who try to tempt the Buddha after his enlightenment. The question here is specifically that of the daughter Taṇhā, "Craving."

1999 Ce and Ee: *atthābhinibbattesuṃ*. Be: *attho ti abhinibbattesuṃ*. Mp: "They generated it, thinking the attainment of the earth *kasiṇa* is supreme, taking it as the ultimate goal."

2000 Ce and Ee *ādimaddasa*; Be *assādamaddasa*. The Ce and Ee reading here is unusual. The standard triad is gratification, danger, and escape (*assāda, ādīnava, nissaraṇa*), which we find here in Be. The Chinese parallel SĀ 549 (T II 143a2–b17) provides a check on the two alternatives. Though SĀ 549 differs in some respects, the list of insights regarding the *kasiṇas* reads: "[He] saw its origin, saw the danger, saw cessation, saw the path to cessation" (見其本・見患・見滅・見滅道跡). The Chinese character 本 corresponds to Pāli *ādi*, not to *assāda*, thus supporting Ce and Ee against Be, which may have normalized the reading. The Ce and Be readings of Mp differ with respect to the same word.

2001 *Sabbaṃ dhammaṃ*. I understand the singular to be doing service for the plural *sabbe dhamme*.

2002 Ce and Ee *sabbaṃ dhammaṃ abhiññāya abhiññāya*. Be lacks the repetition.

2003 Despite the grammatical form of the sentences, I believe that this rendering does better justice to the sense than a literal translation, "One question, one concise statement, one explanation." The "twos" and higher numbers do not present "two questions, etc.," "three questions, etc.," and so forth, but a question *about* two items, a question *about* three items, and so forth.

2004 The Chinese parallel at EĀ 46.8 (T II 778b17) provides some interesting points of contrast. The Pāli version is more cogent with respect to certain items, particularly the fours, fives, sixes, and tens; here EĀ 46.8 has the four noble truths, the five spiritual faculties, the six principles of communal harmony, and the ten kinds of mindfulness (the six recollections, mindfulness of the body, of death, of breathing, and of peace). EĀ 46.8 provides explanations of the items in each group, which calls our attention to what is missing in the Pāli version. While the Pāli version announces three categories for each number—the question (*pañha*), the concise statement (*uddesa*), and the explanation (*veyyākaraṇa*)—the sutta presents only two, the question and the concise statement, but not the explanation. The Kumārapañha section of the Khuddakapāṭha (§4) partly overlaps this list, but since the latter simply lists items to be remembered, without reference to disenchantment and dispassion, it includes positive sets: the four noble truths, the seven enlightenment factors, the eightfold path, and the ten factors of an arahant.

2005 *Sabbe sattā āhāraṭṭhitikā.*

2006 Pleasant feeling, painful feeling, and feeling that is neither painful nor pleasant.

2007 Edible food, contact, mental volition, and consciousness. These are called nutriment (*āhāra*) in the sense that they sustain the continuity of existence.

2008 See **7:44**.

2009 See **8:6**.

2010 See **9:24**.

2011 I follow Be and Ee *dasasu akusalesu kammapathesu*, as against Ce *dasasu akusalesu dhammesu*. Ce has *dasasu kusalesu kammapathesu* at **10:28 §10**.

2012 *Kajaṅgalikā bhikkhunī*. It is hard to determine whether this is a proper name or a designation by way of her place of origin. If, however, it were a proper name the text would probably have read *Kajaṅgalikā nāma bhikkhunī.*

2013 When she speaks about the four establishments of mindfulness—and below about the five faculties, the six elements of escape, the noble eightfold path, and the ten wholesome deeds—the formulation changes. Instead of saying, "is completely disenchanted with…completely dispassionate toward them, completely liberated from them" (*sammā nibbindamāno sammā virajjamāno sammā vimuccamāno*), she says: "has a mind completely well developed in" (*sammā subhāvitacitto*).

2014 The Pāli editions abridge the text thus.

2015 See **6:13**.

2016 This cosmology is also at **3:80**.

2017 *Yebhuyyena sattā ābhassarasaṃvattanikā bhavanti.* This seems to mean that they are reborn among the *ābhassara* devas, the highest plane corresponding to the second jhāna. It remains while all the lower planes of existence undergo dissolution.

2018 As above at **10:25**.

2019 As at **8:65**.

2020 As at **4:161–62**.

2021 Mp does not comment, but I assume these four perceptions are sense-sphere perception, perception in the four jhānas, perception in the first two formless attainments, and perception in the base of nothingness.

2022 See pp. 1780–82, note 1532.

2023 *Yā cāyaṃ bhave appaṭikulyatā, sā c'assa na bhavissati, yā cāyaṃ bhavanirodhe pāṭikulyatā, sā c'assa na bhavissati*. The point, it seems, is that because annihilationism arises from aversion toward continued personal existence, the annihilationist welcomes the cessation of existence, though from the Buddha's perspective annihilationism goes *too far* by misinterpreting such cessation as the annihilation of a real self or existent person. See It §49, 43–44.

2024 *Paramatthavisuddhim paññāpenti*. Mp: "This is a designation for the base of neither-perception-nor-non-perception. For the base of nothingness is highest as the foundation for insight, but the base of neither-perception-nor-non-perception is highest in terms of long lifespan."

2025 *Paramadiṭṭhadhammaṃ nibbānaṃ paññāpenti*. See DN 1.3.19–25, I 36–38, where five views of "supreme nibbāna in this very life" are examined. These hold that supreme nibbāna is the unrestrained enjoyment of the five kinds of sensual pleasure or each of the four jhānas (taken individually). The Buddha opposes these here with the assertion that supreme nibbāna is attained by fully understanding the six sense bases for contact. The same is said at DN 1.3.71, I 45,17–20.

2026 Mp glosses "full understanding" (*pariññā*) here with overcoming (*samatikkama*). The full understanding (or overcoming) of sensual pleasures occurs by the first jhāna; the full understanding of form, by the formless meditative attainments; and the full understanding of feelings, by the attainment of nibbāna, where all feeling has been stilled.

2027 Mp explains the historical background: When King Kosala the Great (Pasenadi's father) presented his daughter in marriage to Bimbisāra (the king of Magadha), he gave her the village of Kāsi (between the two kingdoms) as a wedding gift. Years later, after Ajātasattu killed his father Bimbisāra, his mother died of grief. Pasenadi decided: "Since Ajātasattu killed his parents, the village belongs to my father." Ajātasattu, too, thought: "It belongs to my mother." The two, uncle and nephew, fought a war over Kāsi. Pasenadi was twice defeated by Ajātasattu and had to flee the battle, but on the third occasion he captured Ajātasattu. This was the purpose of which it is said "his purpose having been achieved" (*laddhādhippāyo*).

2028 At MN II 120,1–4 King Pasenadi makes a similar demonstration of reverence for the Buddha and gives ten reasons for showing the Buddha such supreme honor and love. However, the individual items there differ from these.

2029 *Bahuno janassa ariye ñāye patiṭṭhāpitā yadidaṃ kalyāṇadhammatāya kusaladhammatāya*. Mp glosses "in the noble method" as "in the path along with insight" (*sahavipassanake magge*). I follow PED in taking *patiṭṭhāpitā* to be an agent noun in the nominative singular.

2030 Though *sikkhāpadaṃ* is singular, I understand the statement here to refer to the whole corpus of training rules and I thus translate in the plural. In the Vinaya Piṭaka, this statement occurs in connection with the laying down of the first *pārājika* and the singular is therefore appropriate; see Vin III 21,15–23.

2031 Ee mistakenly joins this sutta to the previous one, thus reducing the count by one. At Vin II 240–47 "suspending the Pātimokkha" (*pātimokkhaṭṭhapana*) refers to canceling an individual's right to participate in the Pātimokkha recitation on the uposatha. It seems to me that in the present sutta "suspending the Pātimokkha" includes both canceling the Pātimokkha recitation for a particular monk and delaying the recitation of the Pātimokkha until an obstructive condition has been removed. See Ṭhānissaro 2007b: 270–71, for a discussion of the former set of conditions under which the Pātimokkha recitation is canceled.

2032 *Pārājikakathā vippakatā hoti*. Mp: "Such talk as this, 'Did such a person commit a *pārājika* or not?' has been started and has not been concluded (*'asukapuggalo pārājikaṃ āpanno nu kho no' ti evaṃ kathā ārabhitvā aniṭṭhāpitā hoti*)." Note that this passage supports the translation of the stock question that the Buddha asks the monks when they are in conversation—*kā ca pana vo antarākathā vippakatā?*—as: "What was your conversation *that was underway*?" The common alternatives—"What was your conversation *that was interrupted*?" and "What was your conversation *that has been concluded*?"—do not work in this context, and in any case are contradicted by the commentaries, which consistently gloss *vippakatā* as meaning "*not* brought to a conclusion, *not* completed" (*apariniṭṭhitā sikhaṃ appattā* at Sv I 49,27–28, Ps II 169,15–16; *pariyantaṃ na gatā* at Ps III 226,1–4; *apariyositā* at Ud-a 104,26–30).

2033 The word *paṇḍaka* has a wider meaning than "eunuch" as usually understood. Sp V 1016,1–9 describes five types of *paṇḍakas*. Of these, the two most relevant here are the castrated male (*opakkamikapaṇḍaka*) and the person born sexually indeterminate (*napuṃsakapaṇḍaka*). A parallel of this distinction can be found in Matthew 19:12 (English Standard Version): "For there are eunuchs who have been so from birth, and there are eunuchs who have been made eunuchs by men, and there are eunuchs who have made themselves eunuchs for the sake of the kingdom of heaven." The first correspond to the *napuṃsakas*, the second to the *opakkamikas*, and the third perhaps to those who choose celibacy (or castrate themselves) for religious reasons.

2034 The implications of *bhikkhunidūsaka* are not spelled out in the canonical texts themselves. However, the Vinayavinicchaya-ṭīkā I 121 (VRI ed.; Be §322) defines the term in a way that applies to a bhikkhu who has had sexual intercourse of any kind with a bhikkhunī: "One is said to be a *bhikkhunidūsaka* when one has defiled a bhikkhunī in good standing by having sexual relations with her" (*dūsako ti pakatattāya bhikkhuniyā methunaṃ paṭisevitvā tassā dūsitattā bhikkhuniṃ dūsetīti "bhikkhunidūsako"ti vutto ca*). Thus the term does not necessarily imply rape and "seducer of a bhikkhunī" should be a fit rendering.

2035 *Ubbāhikā*. DOP defines as "the reference (of a dispute) to a committee of selected bhikkhus." Mp: "*Adjudication* means picking out, selecting from the Saṅgha to settle a disciplinary issue that has arisen" (*sampatta-adhikaraṇaṃ vūpasametuṃ saṅghato ubbāhitvā uddharitvā gahaṇatthāya*). The procedure is described in detail at Vin II 95,25–97,16.

2036 Mp: "The four kinds of disciplinary issues." The four are a dispute, an accusation, an offense, and proceedings (*vivādādhikaraṇa, anuvādādhikaraṇa, āpattādhikaraṇa, kiccādhikaraṇa*). See MN 104.12–20, II 247–50.

2037 Mp defines this as the seven ways of settling disciplinary issues (*satta adhikaraṇasamathā*).

2038 Ee merges this sutta with the preceding one, so that from this point on my numbering exceeds Ee's by two.

2039 Ee treats this as the end of the sutta and the next sentence as the beginning of a separate sutta, which it numbers 38. Thus Ee's numbering of the suttas catches up on one of the two suttas by which it fell behind earlier.

2040 *Kappaṭṭhiyaṃ kibbisaṃ pasavati*. Mp glosses *kibbisaṃ* with *pāpaṃ* and says that the question concerns the cause for dwelling in hell for *āyukappa*, the "life eon." Such an account of the word *kappa* is not found in the Nikāyas and seems to be a commentarial innovation. See p. 1811, note 1786.

2041 As above, Ee treats this as the end of the sutta and the next sentence as the beginning of a separate sutta, which it numbers 40. Thus Ee's numbering now matches that of the other editions.

2042 I add the word "mutual" on the basis of Mp's gloss: *aññam-aññassa saṅgahānuggaho*.

2043 For explanations of these terms, see p. 1602, note 66.

2044 This sutta combines two fivefold sets and can thus be considered a composite ten.

2045 Ce *guyhavantā* should be corrected to *guyhamantā*, as in Be and Ee. Here *guyhamantā* almost certainly means "secret deliberations," not "secret mantras."

2046 Mp glosses *pattheti* with *māretuṃ icchati*, "wishes to kill." I do not see how a desire to kill can be derived from the Pāli and thus prefer to take *pattheti* in its usual sense, as simply "to wish, to long for." My guess as to its relevance here is that a man who has fathered a son through one of the concubines wants to see his son, and a concubine's son who learns that he was sired by a man other than the king wants to meet his real father, and the king suspects the monk of being the go-between.

2047 Ce and Be read *hatthisammaddaṃ*; Ee has *hatthisammadaṃ* in the text, but *–sammaddaṃ* and *–sambādhaṃ* as alternative readings. Mp (Be) reads *hatthisambādhaṃ*, resolved as *hatthīhi sambādhaṃ* ("crowded with elephants"). Mp (Ce) allows this reading too, though its text seems corrupted. Both editions of Mp recognize the alternative *hatthisammaddaṃ*.

2048 The eight factors are the eight uposatha precepts, on which see **8:41**.

2049 Ce and Ee stop at fifty *kahāpaṇas*, but Be adds a hundred *kahāpaṇas*. The *kahāpaṇa* was the major currency unit of the time.

2050 Lit., "a hundred times a hundred years" (*satampi vassasatāni*).

2051 Lit., "a hundred times a hundred thousand years" (*satampi vassasatasahassāni*).

2052 Because of the ambivalence of the word *kamma* (meaning both "a deed" and "the potential for results created by a deed"), the question and the reply might also have been formulated in terms of "a bad deed." The same holds below in regard to good kamma.

2053 *Vevaṇṇiy'amhi ajjhupagato*. The four main classes of Indian society in the Buddha's time were referred to as *vaṇṇa*, lit., "color," and thus the privative form, *vivaṇṇa*, should mean "without class" or "classless." *Vevaṇṇiya* is the abstract noun, "classlessness," implying that those who go forth give up their prior status as brahmin, khattiya, vessa, sudda, or outcast, and become known simply as ascetics following the Sakyan son (see **8:19 §4**). By the time of the commentaries the original meaning seems to have been forgotten, and thus Mp takes the word in the sense of "plain" or "without adornment": "*Vevaṇṇiya* is twofold: with respect to body and with respect to articles of use. *Vevaṇṇiya* with respect to body means shaving off the hair and beard. *Vevaṇṇiya* with respect to articles of use means wearing ochre robes made from stitched-together pieces of cloth; eating food mixed together with water in an iron or clay bowl; sleeping at the foot of a tree, etc., and lying down on mats made of reeds and grass, etc.; sitting on a strip of leather or cloth, etc.; and using fermented cow's urine, etc., for medicine. When one reflects thus, anger and conceit are abandoned."

2054 *Parapaṭibaddhā me jīvikā*. Monastics do not work at salaried jobs to earn money with which to purchase their requisites but receive all their material supports—robes, almsfood, lodgings, and medicines—as offerings from the lay community. One does not make use of the four requisites without having reflected upon them.

2055 *Añño me ākappo karaṇīyo*. Mp: "Laypeople walk by swelling up their chest, lifting their heads high, in a playful manner, with disorderly steps. But my manner must be different. I must walk with calm sense faculties, with a calm mind, with slow and measured steps, like a cart passing through water or a rough place."

2056 Here and in the next reflection the intended sense is conveyed more clearly in English if *na* is not translated.

2057 This and the following reflection are in **5:57**.

2058 *Ponobhaviko bhavasaṅkhāro*. Mp: "The kamma that creates existence, the active production of renewed existence" (***ponobbhaviko*** *ti punabbhavanibbattako,* ***bhavasaṅkhāro*** *ti bhavasaṅkharaṇakammaṃ*). Presumably this is said to subsist through the body because the body is the instrument for forming and expressing volition.

2059 The formula is the same as that at **6:12**, though the content is different. The ten principles are the same as the "ten qualities that make for a protector" at **10:18**.

2060 Ce *paripuṇṇaṃ* should be corrected to *parisuddhaṃ* as in Be and Ee. Ce reads *parisuddhaṃ* in the parallel passage occurring in the later suttas of the chapter, so it is clear that *paripuṇṇaṃ* is a typographical error.

2061 A Chinese parallel, MĀ 110 (T I 598c21–599b7), differs slightly from the Pāli in its list of defilements and their wholesome opposites. It includes lack of faith and faith, muddle-mindedness and mindfulness, and foolishness and wisdom. Faith, mindfulness, and wisdom—together with energy and concentration (overlapping with the Pāli list)—constitute the five spiritual faculties, considered as absent or present.

2062 I use "decline" to render *parihāni* and "deterioration" to render *hāni*. The two are virtually synonymous.

2063 The following self-examination is modeled on **4:93**.

2064 This portion of the sutta is modeled upon **9:6**, but it takes associating with a person last and does not treat it in as much detail.

2065 A similar passage is at **6:51**. In the present sutta, Be and Ee read the second item as *sammosaṃ gacchanti*, lit. "go to forgetting," which seems preferable to Ce *sammohaṃ gacchanti*, "go to delusion." In **6:51** all three editions read *na sammosaṃ gacchanti*, which is supported by Mp's gloss: *vināsaṃ na gacchanti* ("they are not lost"). Here and below, where Ce and Ee read *pubbe cetaso samphuṭṭhapubbā*, Be has the negative *pubbe cetaso asamphuṭṭhapubbā*, "with which he had previously not been familiar." This is likely to be a typographical error; at **6:51** Be reads, in conformity with Ce and Ee, *pubbe cetaso samphuṭṭhapubbā*.

2066 An expanded parallel of **5:61**, **7:48**, and **9:16**.

2067 The last five contemplations are among the ten foulness meditation subjects dealt with in detail in Vism chap. 6.

2068 An expanded parallel, based on **8:83**. It also has a close correspondence with **9:14**, which poses nine of the questions, but in terms of "intentions and thoughts" (*saṅkappavitakkā*) rather than "all things" (*sabbe dhammā*).

2069 The last two items, *amatogadhā sabbe dhammā* and *nibbānapariyosānā sabbe dhammā*, seem to be synonymous. A Chinese parallel, MĀ 113 (at T I 602c1–16), makes the following assertions: "All things are rooted in desire; all come together in contact; all converge on feeling; all originate from attention; all are stopped by mindfulness (see Sn 1035); all are headed by concentration; wisdom is above all; liberation is the truth (or core) of all; all have nibbāna as their consummation." Interestingly, MĀ 113 continues (at T I 602c17–28) with a passage that in AN correponds to the next sutta, **10:59**, though rather than assure the monk who practices in such a way one of two fruits, it states that he will definitely attain arahantship.

2070 *Na c'uppannā pāpakā akusalā dhammā cittaṃ pariyādāya ṭhassanti.* As phrased, the text seems to be saying that such bad unwholesome qualities do arise but do not gain control over the bhikkhu's mind. However, it is possible the intent of the statement is that such bad unwholesome qualities *do not* arise and gain control over his mind.

2071 *Lokassa samañca visamañca*. Mp: "Good conduct and misconduct in the world of beings" (*sattalokassa sucaritaduccaritāni*).

2072 *Lokassa bhavañca vibhavañca*. Mp glosses as "its growth and destruction, also success and failure."

2073 Perceptions §§8–10 will be explained just below in **10:60**.

2074 Apart from this text there is no further information about Girimānanda in the Nikāyas. In Theravāda Buddhist countries this sutta has achieved the status of a *paritta*, a "protective discourse," which bhikkhus often recite to people afflicted with illness.

2075 In Be only, *oṭṭharogo*, lip disease, is between *dantarogo* and *kāso*.

2076 Both this and the following perception are reflective contemplations on nibbāna. In the classical scheme of forty meditation subjects, they can be subsumed under the "recollection of peace" (*upasamānussati*), explained at Vism 293–94, Ppn 8:245–51.

2077 Where Ce and Ee read *pajahanto viramati anupādiyanto*, Be has *pajahanto viharaṭi anupādiyanto*. Mp offers no clarification.

2078 It is hard to see exactly how the explanation is connected to the theme of impermanence. Some manuscripts read this perception as *sabbasaṅkhāresu anicchāsaññā*, "perception of wishlessness (or desirelessness) in regard to all conditioned phenomena," which seems to tie up better with the definition.

2079 The mental activity (*cittasaṅkhāra*) here is perception and feeling, for these things are said to be bound up with the mind and to occur in dependence on it (see MN 44.15, I 301,28–29).

2080 That is, liberating the mind from the obstacles to the refinement of serenity and insight.

2081 I read this sentence thus: *"Purimā bhikkhave koṭi na paññāyati avijjāya, ito pubbe avijjā nāhosi atha pacchā samabhavī" ti: evametaṃ bhikkhave vuccati*. The punctuation in all three editions gives the impression that the only part of the Pāli sentence that forms a direct quotation is that between *ito pubbe* and *sambhavi*. I think it more likely that *evametaṃ bhikkhave vuccati* applies to the statement as a whole, from *purimā* through *sambhavi*, rather than to only part of it, and I translate accordingly.

2082 Mp glosses "has a nutriment" (*sāhāraṃ*) with "has a condition" (*sapaccayaṃ*).

2083 Though there are only nine items in the first part of this sutta (the negative series), it appears to be included in the Tens because there are ten items in the second part (the positive series). The next sutta uses the same scheme but augmented in the first part by craving for existence.

2084 There is a word play here. "Have reached certainty about me" (*mayi niṭṭhaṃ gatā*) is an idiom meaning that a person has achieved secure faith in the Buddha, the mark of a stream-enterer. But *niṭṭhā* also means goal, namely, arahantship. Thus reaching certainty about the Buddha marks the attainment of stream-entry (or higher stages), while gaining the goal marks the attainment of arahantship. In the light of this distinction, Mp explains "gain the goal here in this world" (*idha niṭṭhā*) as "reach final nibbāna in this very world" (*imasmiṃyeva loke parinibbānaṃ*). "This world" (*idha*, lit., "here") obviously means the sense sphere, since the stream-enterer and once-returner may reach the goal in a heavenly realm and not necessarily in the human realm. Mp says that "having left this world" (*idha vihāya*) means "in the pure abodes of the brahmā world (*suddhāvāsabrahmalokaṃ*)."

2085 *Ekabījī, kolaṃkola,* and *sattakkhattuparama*. These are three grades of stream-enterers in the technical sense. They are distinguished according to the sharpness of their spiritual faculties. For the distinctions between them, see **3:89**.

2086 For the distinctions between these five kinds of non-returners, see **7:55**. They are mentioned in relation to the threefold training at **3:87** and **3:88**.

2087 Here the text uses the word *sotāpanna* in a loose sense. Mp says it means those who have entered the "stream" of the noble path (*ariyamaggasotaṃ āpannā*). The word thus applies to disciples at *all four stages* of awakening.

2088 Ee omits this passage, though acknowledging its presence in the manuscripts it drew upon. Ce and Be both include it. The transition to the Buddha's talk on the ten grounds of praise is unclear, unless we assume that, as in the preceding sutta, the Buddha had visited the monks and reproached them for engaging in pointless talk.

2089 This is a more compressed version of MN 6, I 33–36. The latter includes sections on the three lower stages of realization and the five mundane direct knowledges but excludes §§5–6 of this sutta.

2090 An expanded parallel of **5:63** and **5:64**.

2091 A part-parallel of **6:44**, with similar setting but different contents.

2092 Ce *pettā pi yo*; Be *pitāmaho*, Ee *pettā piyo*. PED explains *pitāmahā* (under *pitar*) as "grandfather," which seems unlikely here. PED, under *pettāpiya* (epic Skt *pitṛvya*), gives "father's brother, paternal uncle," which can thus support Ce and Ee if the spaces are eliminated. See too pp. 1758–59, note 1330.

2093 I take Ce *–ñāṇo* here to be a misprint for *–ñāṇe*, which occurs in the repetition of the statement toward the end of the sutta. In **6:44**, Ce has *–ñāṇe* in both places.

2094 *Dussīlyaṃ aparisesaṃ nirujjhati*. Mp: "Here, the five kinds of immorality are abandoned by the path of stream-entry; the ten [courses of unwholesome kamma], by the path of arahantship. At the moment of fruition they are said to have been abandoned. By *nirujjhati* the text here refers to the moment of fruition. A worldling breaks virtuous behavior in five ways: by committing a *pārājika* offense, by giving up the training, by joining another sect, by reaching arahantship, and by death. The first three lead to the decline of development, the fourth to its growth, and the fifth neither to decline nor growth. But how is virtuous behavior broken by reaching arahantship? Because a worldling can have extremely wholesome virtuous behavior, but the path of arahantship leads to the destruction of wholesome and unwholesome kamma; thus it is broken in that way." This, it should be pointed out, is explained from the Abhidhamma standpoint, according to which an arahant's actions, being mere activities (*kiriya*) without kammic result, are not classified as either wholesome or unwholesome. In the language of the suttas, however, they would be described as extremely wholesome.

2095 I translate on the basis of Ce and Be, which read *tayo me*. Ee consistently reads only *tayo*, without *me*.

2096 I read with Ce and Ee *micchādiṭṭhikā*, as against Be *pāpamittā*, "have bad friends."

2097 An expanded parallel of **9:29**.

2098 *Aṭṭhāne ca kuppati*. Mp: "In relation to some intentionally motivated event there can be a reason [for getting angry], as when someone acts for my harm, and so forth. But this is not the case when one injures oneself against tree stumps and so forth. Therefore, in this case it is said that the resentment is without a reason (*aṭṭhāne āghāto*)."

2099 An expanded parallel of **9:30**.

2100 Also in **4:36**.

2101 An expanded parallel of **8:82**.

2102 I here read with Be *Sati kho pana ayamāyasmā uttari karaṇīye*, as against Ce and Ee *Muṭṭhassati kho pana ayamāyasmā uttari karaṇīye*, "This venerable one, who is muddle-minded, when there is something further to be done . . ." In Be *sati* is a present participle used in a locative absolute construction; it is totally unrelated to the noun *sati* meaning mindfulness. Possibly the reading *muṭṭhassati* arose through the influence of **10:85 §7** below.

2103 Ce repeats the exchange here once more, with the trickster telling his companion to dig still again. I follow Be and Ee, which omit this repetition.

2104 As with **10:84 §10**, I prefer the Be reading.

2105 This is the name in Ce. Ee reads *kālakaṃ*, which could also be taken as a proper name. But Be has *kālakataṃ*, which means "one who has died."

2106 *Ayampi dhammo na piyatāya na garutāya na bhāvanāya na sāmaññāya na ekībhāvāya saṃvattati*. Mp glosses ***na sāmaññāya*** with *na samaṇadhammabhāvāya* "nor to the state [or duty] of an ascetic." Mp obviously takes *sāmañña* to be derived from *samaṇa*. However, the word *sāmaññā* is also an abstract noun from *samāna*, meaning "the same" or "similar," and I believe this is the sense intended here. I translate it as "accord," which agrees well with the next word, *ekībhāvāya*. See too p. 1791, note 1623. Mp does not gloss *bhāvanāya*, but in commenting on **8:2** it allows two alternatives, "meditative development" and "esteem for virtues." In this context I have taken the latter to be intended. A Chinese parallel, MĀ 94, at T I 576a$_{23-25}$, has for *bhāvanāya*, 不能令修習, "nor to meditative development"; and for *sāmaññā*, 不能令得沙門, "nor to obtaining the ascetic state." Despite this agreement between Mp and MĀ 94, I still think it possible that the words were misunderstood at an early period and prefer my rendering.

2107 This partly replicates **5:211**, but the difference in formulation is too prominent for it to be called an expanded parallel of the earlier sutta.

2108 With Ce, Be, and Mp (Ce and Be) I read *saddhammassa na vodāyanti*. Ee has the singular verb *vodāyati*, but the notes in Ee also refer to mss with *vodāyanti*. *Saddhammassa* should be resolved *saddhammā assa*. Mp: "The good qualities of the teaching, consisting in the three trainings, do not become polished for him" (*sikkhāttayasaṅkhātā sāsanasaddhammā assa vodānaṃ na gacchanti*).

2109 Versions of this sutta are also at SN 6:9–10 and Sn 3:10.

2110 *Mā h'evaṃ Kokālika, mā h'evaṃ Kokālika*. Sn p. 124 has the same reading, but SN I 150,$_{7-8}$ reads: *mā h'evaṃ Kokālika avaca, mā h'evaṃ Kokālika avaca*.

2111 The unripe *belli* fruit is about the size of a peach, the ripe fruit the size of a pomegranate.

2112 The sutta refers to Tudu as a *paccekabrahmā*. Neither Mp nor Mp-ṭ define the term, but Spk-pṭ I 213 (VRI ed.), commenting on its occurrence at SN I 146,$_{26-27}$, explains it as a brahmā who travels about alone, not as a member of an assembly (*paccekabrahmā ti ca ekacārī brahmā, na parisacārī brahmāti attho*). Mp says that in his past life he had been Kokālika's preceptor. He passed away as a non-returner and was reborn in the brahmā world. When he heard that Kokālika was slandering Sāriputta and Moggallāna, he came to request him to place confidence in them.

2113 Since the Buddha had declared Tudu a non-returner, Kokālika reproaches him for reappearing in the human world. As a non-returner he does not, of course, take rebirth into the human world, but he can manifest himself before humans.

2114 The following three verses are at **4:3**.

2115 In the Indian numbering system one *koṭi* = ten million; a *koṭi* of *koṭis* = one *pakoṭi*; a *koṭi* of *pakoṭis* = one *koṭipakoṭi*; a *koṭi* of *koṭipakoṭis* = one *nahuta*; a *koṭi* of *nahutas* = one *ninnahuta*; a *koṭi* of *ninnahutas* = one *abbuda*; twenty *abbudas* = one *nirabbuda*.

2116 Mp states that the red-lotus (*paduma*) hell is not a separate hell realm but a particular place in the great *avīci* hell where the duration of the torment is measured by units of *padumas*. The same applies to the *abbuda* hell, etc., mentioned below.
2117 Ce should be corrected by bringing the word *dīghaṃ* down a line. Thus the paragraph begins with *evaṃ vutte* and the question with *kīva dīghaṃ nu kho bhante*. The mistake is in both the printed and electronic versions of Ce.
2118 An expanded parallel of **8:28**.
2119 In Ee titled *Upāsakavagga*, "The Chapter on Lay Disciples."
2120 This is a part-parallel of SN 42:12, IV 331–37, but differing slightly in arrangement. Where there are mixed grounds for praise and criticism, SN 42:12 enumerates all the grounds for praise and criticism together, each in its own group, whereas the present sutta takes each item in the order in which it occurs, designating it a ground for either criticism or praise.
2121 The three variables of the pattern to be elaborated are: (i) how wealth is acquired, whether unrighteously, righteously, or both; (ii) whether or not it is used for one's own benefit; and (iii) whether or not it is used to benefit others. Those who rank positively on all three will be further divided into those who are attached to their wealth and those who are unattached to it.
2122 An expanded parallel of **9:27**. It differs only by the addition of the section on dependent origination, which is also in the version of SN 12:41, II 68–70, a full parallel.
2123 Mp: "The noble method (*ariya ñāya*) is the path together with insight."
2124 This sutta is probably included in the Tens because of the ten views.
2125 *Evaṃ kho te, gahapati, moghapurisā kālena kālaṃ sahadhammena suniggahitaṃ niggahetabbā*. Mp glosses *sahadhammena* as "with a cause, with a reason, with a statement" (*sahetukena kāraṇena vacanena*).
2126 *Vibhajjavādī bhagavā, na so bhagavā ettha ekaṃsavādī*. The expression *vibhajjavādī*, used to describe the Buddha, is sometimes understood to mean that the Buddha analyzes things into their component parts. But the use of the term here (and elsewhere in the Nikāyas) shows that it actually means that the Buddha draws the distinctions needed to avoid making broad generalizations that overlook important ambiguities. See how the term is employed at MN 99.4, II 197,10–18.
2127 Like **10:93**, this sutta was probably included in the Tens because it deals with the ten speculative views.
2128 Mp: "*The most elevated question of all*: 'Do not let him acquire the

bad view: "When I ask the ascetic Gotama the ultimate question, he falters and does not reply. Is it the case that he isn't up to the mark and cannot answer?"'"

2129 Mp: "*The same question*: He shows that Uttiya again asked the same invalid question that he had previously posed in terms of whether the world is eternal. He asks from a different angle about the entire world, taking a stand on the belief in a sentient being (*sattūpaladdhiyaṃyeva ṭhatvā aññenākārena pucchati*)."

2130 In Be and Ee, Kokanuda.

2131 At **4:38** and **6:54**, I render *diṭṭhiṭṭhāna* as "viewpoint," but here as "basis for view." I follow Mp, which glosses the word in its earlier occurrences as meaning views themselves, but here as "causes for views" (*diṭṭhikāraṇa*). Mp mentions eight such causes: the aggregates, ignorance, contact, perception, thought, careless attention, bad friends, and another person's utterance (*khandhā, avijjā, phasso, saññā, vitakko, ayoniso manasikāro, pāpamittā, paraghoso*).

2132 I follow Be, whose reading of this stock passage conforms to the sequence found elsewhere in AN. Ce and Ee invert the order of the "exalted," "concentrated," and "liberated" dyads, so that the superior consistently follows the inferior state. The Ce and Ee readings of all the earlier AN suttas use the sequence of the Be reading, and there seems no reason here for this sequence to be inverted.

2133 Mp: "He will *sink* (*saṃsīdissati*) because of sensual thoughts, or *float away* (*uplavissati*) because of thoughts of ill will and harming."

2134 Much of the following comes from the standard sequence on the progressive training, already at **4:198**.

2135 *No ca kho tāva anuppattasadatthā viharanti*. The stock formula for the arahant, at **3:37** and **6:49**, describes the arahant as one who has "reached his own goal" (*anuppattasadattho*). Thus Mp II 235,14–15, and Mp III 380,17–18, commenting on the formula, identify *sadattha* with arahantship.

2136 I read with Be *anuppattasadatthā ca viharanti*, which seems necessary. Ce and Ee have, as in the earlier passages, *no ca kho tāva anuppattasadatthā viharanti*, "but they still have not attained their own goal." Since only nine meditative attainments are mentioned, it is unclear what justifies the inclusion of this sutta in the Tens. To obtain ten stages, I have divided the last stage into two parts, but I am unsure this was the original intention.

2137 *Saṅghe te viharato phāso bhavissati*. Lit., "For you dwelling in the Saṅgha, there will be ease [or comfort]." Mp: "[The Buddha] asks him to live in the midst of the Saṅgha and does not permit him to live in the forest. Why? [He thought:] 'If he lives in the forest, he will fulfill only the task of practice, not the task of learning. But if he lives in the midst of the Saṅgha, he will fulfill the two tasks, attain arahantship, and become the foremost expert in the Vinaya Piṭaka. Then, I will explain his past aspiration and resolution and appoint him as the foremost bhikkhu among the experts in the Vinaya.' Seeing this benefit, the Master did not permit Upāli to live in the forest."

2138 *Samaṇasaññā*. Identical with the first three of the "ten things that one who has gone forth should often reflect upon." See **10:48** for notes on these three themes.

2139 All three true knowledges are abridged in the text.

2140 Ps I 188,32–189,4, commenting on MN I 42,28, explains wrong knowledge (*micchāñāṇa*) as the delusion (*moha*) that arises when someone, having done a bad deed or pondered a bad thought, reflects on it and thinks, "I have done good." Wrong liberation (*micchāvimutti*) arises when someone who is not liberated thinks "I'm liberated," or it is the belief that what is not liberation is true liberation.

2141 At Ps I 188,35–189,9 right knowledge (*sammāñāṇa*) is explained to be the nineteen kinds of reviewing knowledge (see Vism 676,4–29, Ppn 22.20–21) and right liberation (*sammāvimutti*) to be the mental factors concomitant with fruition. I find it simpler to interpret "right knowledge" as the direct knowledge that culminates in arahantship and "right liberation" as the release of the mind from the *āsavas* and other defilements.

2142 An expanded parallel based on **1:314** and **1:315**.

2143 The same sutta, but only as far as *micchāsamādhi* and *sammāsamādhi*, is SN 45:1, V 1–2. Mp does not offer any substantial comment here, but Spk III 116,5–6, commenting on the same sentence in SN 45:1, explains that ignorance is a forerunner (*pubbaṅgama*) in two ways, as co-arisen condition (*sahajāta*, a condition for simultaneously arisen phenomena) and as decisive-support condition (*upanissaya*, a strong condition for subsequently arisen phenomena). Spk-pṭ II 103 (VRI ed.) adds that ignorance is a co-arisen forerunner when it makes simultaneous states conform to its own confusion about the object, so that they grasp impermanent phenomena as permanent, etc. It is both a co-arisen and decisive-support forerunner when a person overcome by delusion, not seeing the danger, takes life, steals, commits sexual misconduct, speaks falsely, and engages in other immoral actions.

2144 At Spk III 117,27–31 it is said that these do not occur all together in the mundane path but occur together in the world-transcending path. Even in the development of the mundane path it would be a mistake to suppose the eight factors follow in sequence. Right view is the guide for the other path factors and the direct condition for right intention. Right view and right intention jointly condition right speech, right action, and right livelihood. These in turn are the basis for right effort and right mindfulness. Right concentration results from the interplay of right effort and right mindfulness. Right knowledge (*sammā ñāṇa*) is the wisdom of the path of arahantship, and right liberation (*sammā vimutti*) is the liberation from the *āsavas* that occurs through right knowledge. Its culmination is the arahant's *anāsava cetovimutti paññāvimutti* ("taintless liberation of mind, liberation by wisdom").

2145 *Nijjarā*. The "wearing away" of old kamma through austerities was a fundamental Jain concept. The Buddha borrows the word but gives it a new meaning. See too **3:74** for three kinds of "wearing away" taught by the Buddha.

2146 Mp explains that in this country, people do not cremate their dead relatives but bury them. After their bodies have decayed, they excavate the bones, wash them, arrange them in order, and worship them with scents and garlands. When an [auspicious] constellation arrives, they take the bones and wail and lament, after which they play [the game of] constellation.

2147 *Asekha*. A term for an arahant, who has completed the training in the noble eightfold path and thus possesses, beyond the eight path factors, right knowledge (*sammāñāṇa*) and right liberation (*sammāvimutti*).

2148 *Adhammo ca bhikkhave veditabbo anattho ca; dhammo ca veditabbo attho ca*. Here *dhamma* should be understood more in the sense of the principle of goodness and truth than in the narrow sense of the Buddha's teaching. And *attha* should be understood in the sense of what is good, beneficial, and profitable (in a spiritual sense), what leads to one's long-term well-being and happiness. The word also means "meaning." Often *dhamma* and *attha* are paired off as two things that are to be understood and appreciated in the contemplative process, as in the expression *atthaveda* and *dhammaveda*, or *atthapaṭisaṃvedī dhammapaṭisaṃvedī*.

2149 What follows is a stock passage leading up to the elaboration of the brief teaching by one of the bhikkhus, usually either Mahākaccāna or Ānanda.

2150 A Chinese parallel occurs in MĀ 188. The first part, T I 734a29–c24, roughly corresponds to **10:116**, but it includes a block of text that mirrors MN 76.21, I 519,13–29, a satirical account of a certain teacher's claim to omniscience. A later part of the sutta, T I 734c25–735b25, is parallel to **10:115**.

2151 *Paṇḍita*. The word means "wise one, learned one." I am uncertain whether this was a proper name or a sobriquet.

2152 *Cittaṭṭhānasatāni*. Mp glosses with *cittuppādasatāni*. It seems to me that reading *cinta-* in place of *citta-* would be more appropriate to the context. One Burmese manuscript referred to in the notes to Ee does in fact have this reading.

2153 *Paṇḍito vata bho paṇḍito vata bho*. This refers back to the name of the ascetic sophist.

2154 These first three cases are common to Ce, Be, and Ee. Be ends here, but Ce adds two further paragraphs, and Ee one paragraph, unique to that edition.

2155 The two paragraphs in brackets are in Ce but not in Be or Ee. It seems to me to be foreign to the thought-world of the Nikāyas to pit two doctrines that accord with the Dhamma against one another in a contest aimed at refutation, and also incongruous for an "assembly that accords with the Dhamma" (*dhammikā parisā*) to be described as "loud and boisterous" (*uccāsaddā mahāsaddā*). Normally, this expression describes either an assembly of non-Buddhist wanderers (as in **10:93**, V 185,14) or a group of unruly householders making a racket (as in **5:30**, III 30,27). On one occasion it describes a group of bhikkhus (MN I 456,20–22), but they are promptly sent away by the Buddha.

In place of these two paragraphs in Ce, Ee has a paragraph that reads as follows: "Someone refutes and disproves a doctrine contrary to the Dhamma with a doctrine that accords with the Dhamma. In this way, [231] he delights an assembly that accords with the Dhamma. For this reason, the assembly that accords with the Dhamma becomes loud and boisterous, exclaiming: 'He is truly wise, sir! He is truly wise, sir!'" It is quite normal, even expected, for a doctrine that accords with the Dhamma to prevail over a doctrine contrary to the Dhamma, but again it seems incongruous for an assembly that accords with the Dhamma to become "loud and boisterous."

2156 These verses are also at Dhp 86–89.

2157 *Te loke parinibbutā*. This could also have been rendered, "They have attained nibbāna in the world."

2158 PED explains *paccorohaṇī* as "the ceremony of coming down again (?), approaching or descending to (acc.), esp. the holy fire." SED sv *pratyavarohaṇa* says: "A particular Gṛhya [householder] festival in the month Mārgaśirṣa" (November–December).

2159 *Paccorohāma bhavantaṃ, paccorohāma bhavantaṃ*. It is apparently from this salutation that the *paccorohaṇī* festival derives its name. SED explains the verb *pratyavarohati* to mean: "to descend (from a seat, chariot, etc.) in honor of (acc.)." Apparently, here the brahmins are descending in honor of Agni, the god of fire, representing the all-pervasive energy of the universe.

2160 I follow Ce, which unlike Be and Ee, does not include *dhammaṃ* in the sentence.

2161 I follow Be, which is consistent in putting the dark path before the bright path here and in **10:190**. Ce and Ee put the bright path first here, but invert the sequence at **10:190**. My title conforms to Be, whereas Ce has "The Bright Path" here but titles **10:190** "The Dark Path."

2162 This sutta and the following are parallels respectively of **10:119** and **10:120**.

2163 This sutta and the next are parallels respectively of **10:117** and **10:118**.

2164 There is parallelism between **10:171** and **10:113**; **10:172** and **10:115**; and **10:173** and **10:114**.

2165 It was this Cunda that offered the Buddha his final meal. See DN 16.4.17–19, II 127.

2166 *Soceyyāni.* The meaning is not immediately clear and Mp does not gloss the word. *Soceyya* normally means "purity, purification," but from the context it seems to refer to a kind of rite.

2167 The last four refer respectively to: (1) a woman protected by her co-religionists, (2) one already married or even promised to a husband at birth or in childhood, (3) one with whom sexual relations entail punishment, and (4) a girl who has been garlanded by a man as a sign of engagement.

2168 All three editions here read *bajjhantu*, "let them be bound." Mp provides no gloss but at MN I 287,11 we find *vajjhantu*, glossed by Ps II 332,16 as *vadhaṃ pāpuṇantu*, "let them be slaughtered," and by Ps-pṭ II 230 (VRI ed.) as *maraṇaṃ pāpuṇantu*, "let them die." I thus take *vajjhantu* to be the correct reading.

2169 Pāli: *saddhāni*; Skt *śrāddhāni*. SED sv *śrāddha* says: "A ceremony in honour and for the benefit of dead relatives observed with great strictness at various fixed periods and on occasions of rejoicing as well as mourning by the surviving relatives (these ceremonies are performed by the daily offering of water and on stated occasions by the offering of *piṇḍas* or balls of rice and meal to three paternal and three maternal forefathers, i.e., to father, grandfather, and great grandfather; it should be borne in mind that a *śrāddha* is not a funeral ceremony but a supplement to such a ceremony; it is an act of reverential homage to a deceased person performed by relatives, and is moreover supposed to supply the dead with strengthening nutriment after the performance of the previous funeral ceremonies has endowed them with ethereal bodies; indeed, until those *anteyeṣṭi* or 'funeral rites' have been performed, and until the succeeding first *śrāddha* has been celebrated the deceased relative is a *preta* or restless, wandering ghost, and has no real body . . . ; it is not until the first *śrāddha* has taken place that he attains a position among the *pitṛs* or Divine Fathers in their blissful abode called *Pitṛ-loka,* and the *śrāddha* is most desirable and efficacious when performed by a son . . .)."

2170 It is presumably the passages on the ten unwholesome and wholesome courses of kamma that explain the inclusion of this sutta in the Tens.

2171 Ce *anuppannā* should be corrected to *upapannā*, the reading in Be and Ee and clearly required by the context.

2172 *Aṭṭhānepi bhavaṃ gotamo parikappaṃ vadati*. Mp: "[By this] he asks: 'When it is the wrong occasion [for sharing the merit of giving], does Master Gotama proclaim the fruitfulness of giving to that relative?' For the brahmin held the belief that the donor does not gain any fruit of a gift given thus. But the Blessed One, having acknowledged his question, shows: 'The donor gains the fruit of his gift wherever he is reborn, in any place where he is sustained by his meritorious fruits.'"

2173 This chapter is parallel to the Third Fifty, Chapter IV; the next chapter, to the Third Fifty, Chapter V.

2174 This chapter is parallel to the Fourth Fifty, Chapter I.

2175 Ee merges these eleven suttas with the previous one, thus counting only one sutta in the chapter, whereas Ce and Be, which I follow, have twelve distinct suttas. Thus from this point my numbering differs significantly from Ee.

2176 Except for the abridgment I do not detect any difference between this sutta and the previous one. I have translated the text just as it is, additionally abridging only the descriptions of wrong view and right view. None of the editions says anything about this. Mp does not comment on the first five suttas in this vagga, stating that their meaning is clear.

2177 *Saṃsappanīyapariyāyaṃ vo bhikkhave dhammapariyāyaṃ desessāmi*. Mp: "An exposition of the Dhamma that has 'creeping' as its subject matter."

2178 Mp: "In doing that action he creeps forward, creeps around, wriggles around."

2179 *Ulūkā*. The owl may have been included here because it operates furtively. The Chinese counterpart at T I 273c27–28 mentions only four animals: the snake, the mouse, the cat, and the fox.

2180 The text has the genitive plural *sañcetanikānaṃ kammānaṃ*. Out of deference to established English usage, I have used the singular "kamma." In view of the fact that *kamma* is by definition volitional (*cetanā 'haṃ bhikkhave kammaṃ vadāmi*), "volitional kamma" sounds redundant, but I follow the Pāli. Apparently the text is playing off two meanings of *kamma*, the literal meaning of "deed, action" and the extended meaning of a deed with the capacity to produce ethically determined fruits. The former meaning, perhaps, is accentuated by *kata*, "done," the latter by *upacita*, "accumulated, stored up" as well as by the reference to the time periods when it can ripen.

2181 On the threefold ripening of kamma, see pp. 1639–40, note 372. The Buddha's statement that there is no termination of volitional kamma so long as one has not experienced its results seems to contradict one of the main premises of his teaching, namely, that to attain liberation—"to make an end of suffering"—one *need not* experience the results of all the kamma one has accumulated in the past. This tenet (at least according to the Nikāyas) was proposed by the Jains, as stated at MN 14.17, I 92,35–93,10; MN 101.10, II 218,1–12. However, since the cycle of rebirths is "without discoverable beginning" (*anamatagga saṃsāra*), and in this long stretch we have all accumulated an immensity of kamma, it would virtually require infinite time to exhaust such kamma by experiencing its results. The Buddha taught that the key to liberation was not the eradication of past kamma (whether by experiencing its results or by austerities) but the elimination of the defilements. Arahants, by terminating the defilements, extinguish the potential for ripening of all their past kamma beyond the residue that might ripen in their final life. Mp explains the text's statement as having an implicit meaning: "This is intended to show that as long as saṃsāra continues, if there is kamma that has acquired the capacity to ripen (*paṭiladdhavipākārahakamma*) 'there is no place on earth where one might escape an evil deed'" (the citation, *na vijjati so jagatippadeso, yatthaṭṭhito mucceyya pāpakammā*, is from Dhp 127). The point, in other words, is not that all kamma created will have to ripen, but that any kamma created and accumulated retains the potential to ripen as long as one wanders on in the cycle of rebirths.

A Chinese parallel of **10:219**, MĀ 15 (T I 437b24–438b11), opens with a similar declaration as **10:217**. The statement (at T I 437b26–28) reads in translation: "If one has done a past kamma, I say that one must experience its result: one experiences it either in the present life or in a future life. But if one has not done a past kamma, I say that one will not experience its result" (若有故作業, 我說彼必受其報, 或現世受或後世受. 若不故作業, 我說此不必受報). The Chinese parallel offers only two alternatives for the time of ripening and lacks anything corresponding to the problematic assertion, "I do not say that there is making an end of suffering so long as one has not experienced [the results of] volitional kamma that has been done and accumulated."

2182 *Kāyakammantasandosabyāpatti*. Mp glosses as "a fault consisting in bodily action" (*kāyakammantasaṅkhātā vipatti*). Apparently, Mp understands *sandosa* and *byāpatti* to convey the same meaning, glossed by *vipatti*, but I take the compound to be a *dvanda*: "corruption *and* failure."

2183 See p. 1672, note 582.

2184 Apparently this version differs from **10:217** only by abridging the expository sections and by omitting the simile of the dice.

2185 Although the text of the sutta (in the three editions) does not include a *peyyāla* here, indicating an elision, it was probably right here that the sutta originally included the passage on the ten courses of kamma (as in the preceding two suttas). Only in this way would its inclusion in the Tens make sense. Further, the transition to *sa kho so . . . ariyasāvako evaṃ vigatābhijjho vigatabyāpādo asammūḷho* in the next paragraph, with the reference to a definite subject, implies that it had been preceded by a passage that already spoke about the noble disciple. We find the full passage, in fact, in the Chinese parallel, MĀ 15, which is a synthesis of **10:217–18** and the present sutta.

The structure of MĀ 15 is as follows: Following the opening statement, the Buddha defines the ten kinds of unwholesome kamma of body, speech, and mind. He then says that an instructed noble disciple discards the threefold unwholesome types of kamma (bodily, verbal, and mental) and cultivates the threefold wholesome types. At this point "*that* instructed noble disciple" (彼多聞聖弟子), possessing such energy and virtue, has purified his kamma of body, speech, and mind. He is without anger and hostility, has dispelled drowsiness, eliminated restlessness and arrogance, abandoned doubt, and gone beyond conceit. He is mindful, possesses clear comprehension, and is unconfused. He then pervades the ten directions and the entire world with a mind of loving-kindness and the other three immeasurables.

2186 *Yaṃ kho pana kiñci pamāṇakataṃ kammaṃ, na taṃ tatrāvasissati, na taṃ tatrāvatiṭṭhati.* Mp identifies "measurable kamma" with sense-sphere kamma (*kāmāvacarakamma*), that is, kamma due to produce its results in the sense sphere. Since the disciple being described is presumably a non-returner (or one bound to become a non-returner), he or she will take rebirth in the form realm and never again descend to the sense sphere. Thus the sense-sphere kamma cannot find an opportunity to ripen.

2187 As pointed out earlier, the Pāli word *kamma* bears two senses often difficult to distinguish: the etymological sense, simply an action or deed, and the soteriological sense, a deed considered as a moral force that can bring retributive consequences. It is strange that the text says unequivocally that one who develops the liberation of mind by loving-kindness can do no bad deed. It seems to me that although such a person might not commit bad deeds motivated by hatred and ill will, they could still do bad deeds, even minor ones, motivated by greed and delusion.

2188 This statement, too, seems counterintuitive. Those who do no bad deeds in this life certainly can suffer the kammic effects of bad deeds done in previous lives. Thus Moggallāna was assassinated and the Buddha himself was badly injured by a sharp stone that broke off from the boulder hurled at him by Devadatta. Virtuous people who are not arahants might also undergo psychological suffering, and not merely physical pain, as a consequence of undesirable situations. For example, Ānanda, a virtuous monk, felt grief and worry when the Buddha fell ill and Visākhā, a stream-enterer, lamented the death of her grandchild.

2189 *Cittantaro ayaṃ bhikkhave macco*. Mp: "They have mind as their cause, or their interior is due to mind (*cittakāraṇo, atha vā citten'eva antariko*). For with the mind at rebirth that follows without interval the mind at death, one becomes a deva, a hell-being, or an animal."

2190 *Karajakāya*. I translate the expression literally but it may imply much the same thing as such English expressions as "this mortal body" or "this corporeal body." DOP sv *kara*, says: "A body produced by action, the physical body." SN 12:37, II 65,1, speaks of the body as "old kamma" (*purāṇamidaṃ ... kammaṃ*). The Chinese parallel has nothing that corresponds to this term.

2191 Mp: "By means of loving-kindness, the feeling that would have been experienced upon rebirth is cut off, and thus it does not follow one along. This is the reflection of a noble person who is a stream-enterer or a once-returner." Presumably, the bad kamma is all to be experienced here (*sabbaṃ taṃ idha vedanīyaṃ*), in this life, and will not follow along (*na taṃ anugaṃ bhavissati*) because his next rebirth will be in the form realm, where there is no painful experience, and he will attain nibbāna in the form realm without returning to this world.

2192 *Idha paññassa bhikkhuno uttariṃ vimuttiṃ appaṭivijjhato*. Mp: "*A wise bhikkhu here*: The wisdom in this teaching is called 'wisdom here.' The meaning [of a wise one here] is a noble disciple who is settled in the noble wisdom that pertains to the teaching" (*imasmiṃ sāsane paññā idhapaññā nāma, sāsanacaritāya ariyapaññāya ṭhitassa ariyasāvakassā ti attho*).

2193 Mp calls this the state of a "jhāna non-returner" (*jhānānāgāmitā*). Such persons have realized the lower two fruits and attained the jhānas, but have not yet really reached the stage of non-returner. By the karmic power of their jhānas they will be reborn in the form realm, where they will attain the higher two paths and fruits without ever returning to the sense sphere; thus they are called "jhāna non-returners." The "further liberation" (*uttariṃ vimutti*) is arahantship. See too p. 1664, note 539.

2194 Ee combines these three suttas with the previous one.

2195 Neither Ce nor Ee numbers this vagga. Ce, however, numbers the suttas in this series as if the vagga were to be counted as 3 (thus beginning with 10.5.3.1, where the second figure indicates the number of the Fifties and the third the number of the vagga). Be numbers it 23, in accordance with the consecutive numbering scheme it uses for the vaggas. Since the "Extra Fifty" has only twenty-six suttas without this vagga, I have numbered it "III," on the assumption that it belongs in this set of Fifty.

2196 Ce numbers the suttas from 10.5.3.1 to 10.5.3.510. Be, using consecutive numbering for the entire *nipāta*, numbers them from 237 to 746; Ee numbers them from 217 to 219, collecting all the elaborations into 219. I follow the system of Be.

2197 It seems peculiar for right knowledge and right liberation to be treated as conditions for direct knowledge, for (as denoting the knowledge and liberation of the arahant) they are normally themselves the results of direct knowledge.

2198 Here Ce and Ee additionally insert *upasamāya* ("for the pacification").

Notes to the Elevens

2199 An expanded parallel of **10:1**. It differs only by dividing the compound "disenchantment and dispassion" (*nibbidāvirāga*) into two.

2200 An expanded parallel of **10:2**.

2201 An expanded parallel of **10:3**.

2202 An expanded parallel of **10:88**.

2203 Here, Ce and Ee have the singular verb, *vodāyati*, as against Be's plural *vodāyanti*. Ee states in a note that all manuscripts have *vodāyanti*. See p. 1849, note 2108.

2204 An expanded parallel of **10:6**, with an additional section in which Ānanda discusses the same state of concentration with Sāriputta and receives the same answer. Note that whereas, in the Tens, Sāriputta answers the question in a different way than the Buddha (but presumably referring to the same state of concentration), here his answer agrees with the Buddha's.

2205 Ee treats the passage from here to the end as a separate sutta, which it numbers 8. Thus from this point on its numbering exceeds by one the numbering in Ce and Be, which take this dialogue to belong to **11:7**. The last sentence, applauding the agreement between the Buddha's explanation and Sāriputta's, confirms that both are parts of a single sutta. In contrast, **10:6** and **10:7**, which are also dialogues on this *samādhi* respectively between Ānanda and the Buddha, and Ānanda and Sāriputta, have no bridge that unites them.

2206 Mp identifies the "foremost state" (*aggapada*) with nibbāna.

2207 By counting the sense faculties and their objects, this sutta includes more than eleven items. But to maintain the elevenfold scheme, I begin numbering the relevant items with "earth."

2208 Be has the name as Saddha.

2209 *Jhāyati pajjhāyati nijjhāyati avajjhāyati.* As in **6:46**, III 354,8–10, the tone is derisive.

2210 *Yassa te nābhijānāma, yampi nissāya jhāyasi.* See MN 22.36, I 140,1–7: "When the devas with Indra, Brahmā, and Pajāpati, search for a monk thus liberated in mind, they do not find that on which the consciousness of one who has thus attained is dependent. Why so? I say that one who has thus attained is untraceable even in this very life" (*evaṃ vimuttacittaṃ kho, bhikkhave, bhikkhuṃ sa-indā devā sabrahmakā sapajāpatikā anvesaṃ nādhigacchanti 'idaṃ nissitaṃ tathāgatassa viññāṇan' ti. Taṃ kissa hetu? Diṭṭh'evāhaṃ, bhikkhave, dhamme tathāgataṃ ananuvijjo ti vadāmi*).

2211 *Paṭhaviyaṃ paṭhavisaññā vibhūtā hoti.* Mp glosses *vibhūta* here with "evident" (*pākaṭa*), explaining: "The perceptions of the four or five jhānas arisen with earth, etc., as object are evident . . . because they have been seen with insight as impermanent, suffering, and non-self." Mp tries to support its interpretation with a citation it says is from a sutta: *vibhūtā, bhante, rūpasaññā avibhūtā aṭṭhikasaññā*. However, a search through CST 4.0 fails to locate these words anywhere in the Nikāyas. To my knowledge, in the Nikāyas *vibhūta* always means "disappeared, vanished." See the expressions *vibhūtasaññī* at Sn 874, and *vibhūtarūpasaññissa* at Sn 1113, where in both cases *vibhūta* can only mean "disappeared." There seems no reason to ascribe a later meaning to it here. A Chinese parallel, SĀ 926 (at T II 235c26–236b11), supports this conclusion. Taking earth as an example (at II 236a27), it reads: "A bhikkhu is able to suppress the perception of earth in relation to the perception of earth" (比丘於地想能伏地想). Could the middle 想 here be gratuitous so that we should read 比丘於地能伏地想?

2212 Mp: "He meditates by the attainment of fruition engendered by having passed in this way through the sequence of insights" (*evaṃ vipassanāpaṭipāṭiyā āgantvā uppāditāya phalasamāpattiyā jhāyanto*).

2213 This sutta combines into one **3:143–45**, and adds an extra dyad to obtain eleven items. It might thus be considered a composite eleven. The formula on the arahant is also in **7:61**. Mp explains "ultimate conclusion" (*accantaniṭṭho*) thus: "The indestructible nibbāna is his conclusion; it is called 'ultimate' (*accanta*) because it surpasses the end (*antaṃ atītattā*)."

2214 A part-parallel of **6:10**.

2215 I translate this freely in accordance with natural English diction. More literally it would read: "Bhante, among the various ways in which we dwell, how should we dwell?"

2216 Brahmāli writes: "It is worth noting that a layperson speaks of entering upon the rains residence. Perhaps this was a common phenomenon in northern India, and not just restricted to *samaṇas*. Maybe it was generally too difficult to travel."

2217 Mp identifies the *asamayavimutto* with the arahant. In relation to the expression in **6:55**, "does not see in himself anything still to be done or [any need] to increase what has been done" (*asamaya-vimutto karaṇīyaṃ attano na samanupassati katassa vā paticayaṃ*), Mp has glossed *paṭicayaṃ* with "progress by repeatedly doing" (*punappunaṃ karaṇena vaḍḍhiṃ*).

2218 Neither Ce nor Be use a *ti* to signal the end of a direct quotation, and thus on their readings it is not easy to determine exactly where the meditation formula ends. Ee inserts *ti* here, which signifies that the formula ends here and that it includes the simile and the repetition. The devas that subsist on edible food belong to the sense sphere. Those that have been reborn in a mind-made body belong to the form sphere. It is not clear why it is said that they "do not see in themselves anything still to be done or [any need] to increase what has been done" (*tā karaṇīyaṃ attano na samanupassanti katassa vā paticayaṃ*). This phrase is normally reserved for the arahant. I can only surmise that the text is alluding to those devas that have attained arahantship.

2219 I read with Be and Ee *aggi mutto*, as against Ce *aggimukko*.

2220 *Saddhassa upāsakassa putto*. This might have also been rendered "the son of the male lay follower Saddha," taking *saddha* to be a proper name. But in such a case I would expect *nāma* to have been included. Be reads *sudattassa upāsakassa putto*, "the son of the male lay follower Sudatta." Sudatta was the proper name of Anāthapiṇḍika, but Anāthapiṇḍika's children would surely have been well known to the Buddha and thus his inquiry about the monk's identity would be strange. Further, except under rare conditions, the Nikāyas do not refer to Anāthapiṇḍika by his personal name.

2221 *Saddhāpadānesu*. Mp: "In the manifestation, the characteristics, of persons endowed with faith" (*saddhānaṃ puggalānaṃ apadānesu lakkhaṇesu*).

2222 An expanded parallel of **8:1**. This is the version that is usually recited as a protective discourse.

2223 The eleven benefits are explained in detail at Vism 311–14, Ppn 9.59–76.

2224 Identical with MN 52.

2225 The householder is described as *gahapati aṭṭhakanāgara*, where –*nāgara* means "a citizen of [such and such] a city." The word for city itself is *nagara*. This is analogous to calling a person from New York a New Yorker, one from Paris a Parisian, etc.

2226 *Ten'eva dhammarāgena dhammanandiyā*. As at **9:36**; see p. 1827, note 1917. Mp: "What is meant by this pair of terms is desire and lust for serenity and insight. For if one is able to exhaust all desire and lust for serenity and insight, one becomes an arahant. If one cannot do so, one becomes a non-returner. Because one has not abandoned desire and lust for serenity and insight, through the volition of the fourth jhāna one is reborn in the pure abodes. This is the general explanation among the teachers."

2227 The base of neither-perception-nor-non-perception is not included because it is considered too subtle for its constituent factors to be used as objects of contemplation.

2228 The eleven "doors to the deathless" are the four jhānas, the four immeasurables, and the lower three formless attainments. They are used as bases to develop insight and attain arahantship.

2229 That is, five hundred *kahāpaṇas*.

2230 Identical with MN 33.

2231 At SN 47:6, V 148,1–2, the four establishments of mindfulness are called the pasture (*gocara*) of a bhikkhu, that is, the proper sphere of his attention.

2232 The dialogue here is identical with the first part of **11:7**.

2233 Be does not include this series of suttas, perhaps assuming that it was implied by the preceding. Ee includes it only as three short sections within the larger sutta on the simile of the cowherd.

2234 Ee does not number this vagga. Both Ce and Be number it 4.

2235 Ce numbers the suttas in this vagga starting from 1 and ending at 170, Be numbers them in continuation with those in the entire *nipāta*. Since it did not include the positive version of the cowherd simile, Be begins with 502 and ends with 671. I use both schemes but begin the absolute count with 982.

Appendix 1: Expanded Parallels in the Aṅguttara Nikāya

1:314 + 1:315 → 10:104: Consequences of wrong view and right view.

3:31 → 4:63: Reverence for mother and father.

3:48 → 5:40: People in the family grow when the family head has faith.

3:50 → 5:103: How an evil bhikkhu is like a master thief.

3:96 → 4:259: A bhikkhu is like a king's thoroughbred horse (four-truths version).

3:98 → 4:260: A bhikkhu is like a king's thoroughbred horse (arahant version).

3:135 → 7:36: Qualities of a true friend.

4:34 → 5:32: Foremost kinds of confidence.

4:51 → 5:45: Streams of merit by offering requisites.

4:112 → 5:203: A bhikkhu is like a king's thoroughbred horse (rectitude version).

4:160 → 5:56: Decline and disappearance of the Dhamma.

5:24 → 6:50 → 7:65 → 8:81 → 10:3 → 11:3: Proximate causes for liberation.

5:34 → 7:57: Directly visible fruits of giving.

5:42 → 8:38: A good person is born for the good of many.

5:61 → 7:48 → 9:16 → 10:56: Perceptions culminating in the deathless.

5:63/5:64 → 10:74: Growing by a noble growth.

5:201 → 6:40 → 7:59: Why the good Dhamma does and does not continue.

6:19 → 8:73: Mindfulness of death (how do you develop it version).

6:20 → 8:74: Mindfulness of death (many causes of death version).

6:23 → 8:56: Designations for sensual pleasures.

6:31 → 8:79: Decline of a trainee bhikkhu (direct declaration version).
6:32 → 7:32: Non-decline of a bhikkhu (deity speaks to Buddha version).
6:33 → 7:33: Non-decline of a bhikkhu (Buddha reports to bhikkhus version).
6:64 → 10:21: Tathāgata's powers.
7:1 → 8:3: A bhikkhu is displeasing/is pleasing to his fellow monks.
7:13 → 9:17: A family is not worth/is worth approaching.
8:1 → 11:15: Benefits of loving-kindness.
8:28 → 10:90: Powers of an arahant.
8:41 → 9:18: How the uposatha is observed so it is fruitful.
8:59 → 9:10: Persons worthy of gifts.
8:71 → 10:8: A bhikkhu endowed with faith (four jhānas version).
8:72 → 10:9: A bhikkhu endowed with faith (peaceful emancipations version).
8:82 → 10:83: Why the Tathāgata is disposed to teach the Dhamma.
8:83 → 10:58: In what are all things rooted?
9:27 → 10:92: How a stream-enterer might declare himself to be one.
9:29 → 10:79: Grounds for resentment.
9:30 → 10:80: Ways of removing resentment.
10:1 → 11:1: Purpose of virtuous behavior, up to liberation.
10:2 → 11:2: No volition need be exerted.
10:4 → 11:4: Proximate causes for liberation (Sāriputta version; see 10:3).
10:5 → 11:5: Proximate causes for liberation (Ānanda version; see 10:3).
10:6 → 11:7: Concentration based on nibbāna.
10:88 → 11:6: A bhikkhu who insults his fellow monks.

Appendix 2: Composite Numerical Suttas in the Aṅguttara Nikāya

6:105–116 – 3, 3: Defilements and ways to abandon them.
7:47 – 3, 3, 1: Three fires to be abandoned, three to be maintained, and the wood fire.
7:58 – 4, 3: Four things the Tathāgata need not hide, three ways he is irreproachable.
8:49 – 4, 4: How a woman is heading for victory in this world and the next (to Visākhā).
8:50 – 4, 4: How a woman is heading for victory in this world and the next (to the bhikkhus).
8:54 – 4, 4: Four things lead to welfare in this life, four to welfare in future lives.
8:62 – 8 sub-lists (6, 5, 4, 4, 3, 3, 2, 2): How a bhikkhu benefits himself and others.
8:63 – 4, 4: Four immeasurables and four establishments of mindfulness.
8:78 – (= 8:62, but spoken by Sāriputta)
9:1 – 5, 4: Five supports for developing aids to enlightenment, four meditation subjects.
9:2 – 5, 4: Five powers and four kinds of reflection.
9:3 – 5, 4: Five things that mature the mind, four meditation subjects.
9:4 – 4, 5: Four virtues in a bhikkhu, five benefits in timely listening to the Dhamma.
9:5 – 4, 5: Four powers to transcend five fears.
9:21 – 3, 3, 3: The people of Uttarakuru, Tāvatiṃsa devas, and the people of Jambudīpa.
9:22 – 3, 3, 3: Three kinds of persons like wild colts, good horses, and thoroughbreds.
9:27 – 5, 4: Five enmities and four factors of stream-entry.

9:63-9:92 – 5, 4: Combinations of defilements and training factors.
10:11 – 5, 5: A bhikkhu who possesses five factors uses a lodging with five factors.
10:12 – 5, 5: A bhikkhu has abandoned five factors and possesses five factors.
10:14 – 5, 5: Five kinds of mental barrenness, five bondages of the mind.
10:44 – 5, 5: Five things to examine in oneself, five things to establish, when one wants to reproach another person.
10:63 – 5, 5: Five gain the goal in this world, five gain it having left this world.
10:64 – 5, 5: Five gain the goal in this world, five gain it having left this world.
10:101 – 3, 7: Three ascetic perceptions, seven things to be fulfilled.
10:102 – 7, 3: Seven enlightenment factors fulfill the three true knowledges.
11:10 – 3, 3, 3, 2: Qualities that make a bhikkhu best among devas and humans.

Pāli-English Glossary

This glossary consists primarily of doctrinal terms; they are arranged according to the order of the Pāli alphabet. When a term listed has both doctrinal and ordinary meanings, only the former is given. Preference is given to nouns over cognate adjectives and verbs. Compounds are included only when their meaning is not immediately apparent from their members. Distinct meanings of a single term are indicated by an enumeration, with semicolons as separation. Different renderings intended to capture distinct nuances of a word are separated by commas, without enumeration.

PĀLI	ENGLISH
akiriyavāda	doctrine of non-doing
akuppa	unshakable
akusala	unwholesome (deed or mental state)
akkhaṇa	inopportune moment
agati	wrong course (of action)
acinteyya	inconceivable
acelaka	naked (an ascetic practice)
aññatitthiya	belonging to other (non-Buddhist) sects
aññā	final knowledge
atimāna	arrogance
attabhāva	individuality, body
attā	(1) (metaphysical) self; (2) oneself
attānudiṭṭhi	view of self
attha	(1) good, benefit; (2) purpose, goal; (3) meaning
atthaṅgama	passing away
adukkhamasukha	neither-painful-nor-pleasant (feeling)
adosa	non-hatred
addhāna	a long stretch of time

PĀLI	ENGLISH
adhicitta	higher mind
adhipaññā	higher wisdom
adhimāna	self-overestimation
adhisīla	higher virtuous behavior
anattā	non-self
anattha	harm, unbeneficial
anāgāmī	non-returner
anālaya	non-attachment
anāsava	taintless
anicca	impermanent
animitta	markless
anukampā	compassion (actively expressed)
anuttariya	unsurpassed
anupassī	contemplator of (suffix)
anupubba-	progressive, gradual (prefix)
anusaya	underlying tendency (to defilements)
anusāsanī	instruction
anussati	recollection
anottappa	moral recklessness
antaradhāna	disappearance
antarāparinibbāyī	"attainer of nibbāna in the interval," the first grade of non-returner
apāya	the plane of misery (lower realms)
appaṇihita	wishless
appamāṇa	measureless
appamāda	heedfulness
appameyya	immeasurable
appicchatā	fewness of desires
abhijjhā	longing
abhiññā	direct knowledge
abhibhāyatana	base of overcoming
amata	deathless
amanussa	a (nonhuman) spirit
amoha	non-delusion
ayoniso manasikāra	careless attention
arahant	*untranslated*: one who has attained full liberation
ariya	noble
arūpa	formless
alobha	non-greed
avijjā	ignorance
aveccappasāda	unwavering confidence

Pāli	English
avyāpāda	good will
asaṅkhata	unconditioned
asaṅkhāraparinibbāyī	"an attainer of nibbāna without exertion," the third grade of non-returner
asappurisa	a bad person
asubha	unattractive (nature of body)
asura	*untranslated*: a class of titanic beings, often seen in conflict with the devas
asekha	one beyond training (an arahant)
asmimāna	the conceit "I am"
assāda	gratification
ahaṅkāra	I-making
ahirika	moral shamelessness
ākāsa	space
ākāsānañcāyatana	base of the infinity of space
ākiñcaññāyatana	base of nothingness
āghāta	resentment
ājīva	livelihood
ājīvaka	*untranslated*: member of a sect in the Buddha's time known for its strict asceticism
ātappa	ardor
ādīnava	danger
ādhipateyya	authority
ānāpānasati	mindfulness of breathing
āneñja	the imperturbable (of higher meditative attainments)
āpatti	offense (against monastic rule)
āpo	water (element)
āyatana	base
ārambha	arousal, instigation (of energy)
āruppa	formlessness (of higher meditative attainments)
ālaya	attachment
āvaraṇa	obstruction
āsava	taint
āhāra	nutriment, food
icchā	desire
iddhi	psychic potency
iddhipāda	basis of psychic potency

Pāli	English
indriya	faculty (sensory or spiritual)
issā	envy
udayabbaya	arising and vanishing
uddhaṃsota akaniṭṭhagāmī	"one bound upstream, heading toward the Akaniṭṭha realm," the fifth grade of non-returner
uddhambhāgiya	higher (fetters)
uddhacca	restlessness
upakkilesa	defilement
upadhi	acquisition
upanāha	hostility
upapāta	rebirth
upasama	peace
upahaccaparinibbāyī	"attainer of nibbāna upon landing," the second grade of non-returner
upādāna	clinging
upādisesa	a residue remaining
upāyāsa	anguish
upāsaka	male lay follower
upāsikā	female lay follower
upekkhā	equanimity
uposatha	*untranslated*: the religious observance undertaken on the full and new moon days
uppāda	arising
ubhatobhāgavimutta	(an arahant) liberated in both respects
ussoḷhi	enthusiasm
ekagga	one-pointed (said of mind)
ekabījī	"one-seed attainer," the sharpest grade of stream-enterer
ekodibhāva	unification (of mind)
ehipassika	inviting one to come and see (epithet of the Dhamma)
ottappa	moral dread
opanayika	applicable (epithet of the Dhamma)
opapātika	spontaneously reborn (type of sentient beings)
omāna	inferiority complex
orambhāgiya	lower (of fetters)

PĀLI	ENGLISH
ovāda	exhortation
kaṅkhā	perplexity
kataññutā	gratitude
kataveditā	thankfulness
kathaṅkathā	bewilderment
kappa	eon
kamma	(1) an action; (2) *untranslated*: morally determinate volitional action productive of a corresponding result
kammanta	action, activity
karuṇā	compassion (meditative)
kalyāṇa	good
kasiṇa	*untranslated*: a type of meditation object
kāma	sensuality, sensual desire, sensual pleasure
kāya	body
kāyasakkhī	a body witness (a type of *sekha*)
kiriyavāda	doctrine of deeds
kukkucca	remorse
kula	family, clan
kulaputta	clansman
kusala	wholesome (deed or mental state)
kodha	anger
kodhana	prone to anger
kopa	anger, irritation
kolaṃkola	"family-to-family attainer," the middle grade of stream-enterer
kosajja	laziness
khattiya	*untranslated*: a member of the administrative-warrior class
khanti	(1) patience; (2) conviction
khandha	aggregate
khaya	destruction
khema	security
gati	destination
gandhabba	*untranslated*: a class of minor deities that dwell in plants and trees
garudhamma	(1) principle of respect; (2) grave offense
gārava	reverence

Pāli	English
gocara	resort (usually for alms round)
gotrabhū	clan member
cakkavatti	wheel-turning (monarch)
caṇḍāla	*untranslated*: a member of the most despised type of outcasts
caraṇa	conduct (usually good conduct)
cāga	(1) generosity; (2) giving up
citta	mind
cuti	passing away
cetanā	volition
cetaso vinibandha	bondage of mind
cetokhila	mental barrenness
cetovimutti	liberation of mind
chanda	desire
jarā	old age
jāgariya	wakefulness
jāti	birth
jīva	soul
jīvita	life
jhāna	*untranslated*: stage of deep meditation
ñāṇa	knowledge
ñāya	method (for attaining nibbāna)
ṭhitassa aññathatta	alteration of that which persists
taṇhā	craving
tathāgata	*untranslated*: an epithet of the Buddha, meaning "thus come" and "thus gone"
tapa	austerity
tiracchānayoni	the animal realm
tejo	fire (element)
thambha	obstinacy
thīna	dullness
thera	an elder bhikkhu

Pāli	English
dassana	vision, seeing
dāna	giving, a gift
diṭṭha	seen (object of vision)
diṭṭhi	view
diṭṭhippatta	one attained to view (a type of *sekha*)
diṭṭhisampanna	one accomplished in view (a disciple at minimum level of a stream-enterer)
diṭṭhe'va dhamme	in this very life
dibbacakkhu	divine eye
dibbasota	divine ear
dukkha	suffering, pain, painful
duggati	bad destination (of rebirth)
duccarita	misconduct
deva	*untranslated*: a deity, a celestial being
devatā	a deity
devadūta	divine messenger
domanassa	dejection
dosa	hatred
dhamma	(1) *untranslated*: spiritual-ethical teaching, especially the Buddha's teaching; (2) *as plural*: qualities, states of mind, phenomena
dhammānusārī	a Dhamma follower (one on the way to stream-entry)
dhātu	element, realm
nāga	*untranslated*: (1) a dragon; (2) a cobra; (3) a bull elephant; (4) a metaphoric term for an arahant
nāmarūpa	name-and-form
nikkama	persistence (in applying energy)
nigaṇṭha	*untranslated*: a Jain (lit. "knotless one")
nijjarā	wearing away (of defilements)
nidāna	cause
nipaka	alert
nippapañca	absence of (mental) proliferation
nibbāna	*untranslated*: the extinction of defilements, cessation of suffering, and emancipation from the chain of rebirths
nibbidā	disenchantment

PĀLI	ENGLISH
nibbedhika	penetrative
nimitta	mark, object
niyata	fixed in destiny
niyāma	fixed course
niraya	hell
nirutti	language
nirodha	cessation
nissaraṇa	escape
nīvaraṇa	hindrance
nekkhamma	renunciation
n'evasaññānāsaññāyatana	base of neither-perception-nor-non-perception
paccaya	condition, reason
paccekabuddha	*untranslated*: one who becomes enlightened without a teacher but does not teach others
paññā	wisdom
paññāvimutta	(an arahant) liberated by wisdom
paññāvimutti	liberation by wisdom
paṭigha	(1) aversion; (2) (sensory) impingement
paṭinissagga	relinquishment
paṭipadā	practice, way
paṭibhāna	(1) discernment; (2) (poetic) inspiration
paṭisaṃvedī	one who experiences
paṭisanthāra	hospitality
paṭisambhidā	analytical knowledge
paṭisallāna	seclusion
paṭhavī	earth (element)
paṇḍita	a wise person, wise
padhāna	striving
padhāniyaṅga	factor for striving
papañca	(mental) proliferation
pabbajita	one who has gone forth, a monk or nun
pabhassara	luminous
pamāda	heedlessness
parakkama	exertion (in applying energy)
parāmāsa	wrong grasp
parikkhaya	utter destruction
pariññā	full understanding
parideva	lamentation

PĀLI	ENGLISH
parinibbāna	final nibbāna (the passing away of a Buddha or an arahant)
parinibbāyati	to attain nibbāna (either at death or while alive)
parinibbuta	has attained nibbāna (either at death or while alive)
paribbājaka	a wanderer
pariyāya	exposition (of the Dhamma)
pariyesanā	quest
pariḷāha	fever (of passion)
parivāra	retinue
parisā	assembly
parihāna	decline
paviveka	solitude
paḷāsa	insolence
pasāda	confidence
passaddhi	tranquility
pahāna	abandoning of
pahitatta	resolute
pāṭihāriya	wonder
pātimokkha	*untranslated*: the code of Buddhist monastic rules
pāpa	bad, evil
pāmojja	joy
pārisuddhi	purity, purification
pīti	rapture
puggala	person
puñña	merit, meritorious
puthujjana	a worldling
punabbhava	renewed existence
pubbenivāsānussati	recollection of past abodes
purisa	(1) a person (inclusive); (2) a man (in contrast with a woman)
peta	an afflicted spirit
pettivisaya	the sphere of afflicted spirits
pema	(1) affection; (2) devotion
ponobhavika	conducive to renewed existence
phala	fruit (of the practice)
phassa	contact
bala	power

Pāli	English
bahussuta	learned
bāla	a fool, foolish
buddha	(1) *untranslated*: title of Gotama; (2) enlightened, Enlightened One
bojjhaṅga	factor of enlightenment
bodhipakkhiyā dhammā	aids to enlightenment
bodhisatta	*untranslated*: a future Buddha
brahmacariya	the spiritual life
brahmavihāra	divine abode
brahmā	*untranslated*: a high divinity
brāhmaṇa	brahmin, a member of the priestly class
byañjana	phrasing, phrase
bhagavā	the Blessed One, an epithet of the Buddha
bhante	*untranslated*: a vocative used as a polite address for a superior, especially for the Buddha
bhaya	(1) fear; (2) peril
bhava	existence
bhāvanā	development
bhikkhu	*untranslated*: a Buddhist monk
bhikkhunī	*untranslated*: a Buddhist nun
makkha	denigration
magga	path
macchariya	miserliness
mada	intoxication
maddava	gentleness
manussa	human being
mano	mind
manopavicāra	mental examination
manomaya	mind-made
mamaṅkāra	mine-making
maraṇa	death
mala	stain
mahā	great
mātikā	outline (of the Dhamma)
mātugāma	a woman, womankind
māna	conceit
māyā	deceitfulness
micchatta	wrongness

PĀLI	ENGLISH
micchā	wrong
mitta	friend
middha	drowsiness
muta	sensed
muditā	altruistic joy
mūla	root
mettā	loving-kindness
methuna	sexual intercourse
moha	delusion
yakkha	*untranslated*: a spirit, often of a violent temperament
yañña	sacrifice
yathābhūta	as it really is, as they really are
yasa	fame, glory
yoga	(1) bond; (2) effort
yojana	*untranslated*: a measure of distance, estimated to have been between seven and nine miles
yoni	(1) womb; (2) realm (of rebirth)
yoniso manasikāra	careful attention
rāga	lust
rājā	king, monarch
rūpa	form
lakkhaṇa	characteristic
lābha	gain
līnatta	sluggishness
loka	world
lokadhamma	worldly conditions (gain and loss, etc.)
lokadhātu	world system
lobha	greed
vacī-	verbal (prefix)
vata	an observance (usually of an ascetic nature)
vaya	vanishing
vācā	speech
vāda	doctrine, assertion
vāyāma	effort
vāyo	air (element)

Pāli	English
vicaya	discrimination
vicāra	examination
vicikicchā	doubt
vijjā	true knowledge
viññāṇa	consciousness
viññāṇañcāyatana	base of the infinity of consciousness
viññāṇaṭṭhiti	stations for consciousness
viññāta	cognized
viññū	wise, a wise person
vitakka	thought
vinaya	(1) monastic discipline; (2) removal of (defilements)
vinipāta	the lower world
vipatti	failure
vipariṇāma	change
vipallāsa	inversion (of perception, mind, and view)
vipassanā	insight
vipāka	result (of kamma)
vippaṭisāra	regret
vibhava	extermination
vimutti	liberation
vimokkha	emancipation
virāga	(1) dispassion; (2) fading away
viriya	energy
vivāda	dispute
viveka	seclusion
visuddhi	purification
vihāra	(1) a monastic dwelling; (2) a meditative dwelling
vihiṃsā	harming
vihesā	harming
vīmaṃsā	investigation
vuṭṭhāna	emergence (from meditation, from transgression)
vūpasama	subsiding
vedanā	feeling
vedayita	what is felt, feeling
vera	enmity
veramaṇī	abstinence
vesārajja	self-confidence
vessa	*untranslated*: a member of the mercantile class

PĀLI	ENGLISH
vossagga	release, relinquishment
vyādhi	illness
vyāpāda	ill will
saṃyoga	bondage
saṃyojana	fetter
saṃvara	restraint
saṃvega	sense of urgency
saṃsagga	bonding (between persons)
saṃsāra	*untranslated*: the round of rebirths
sakadāgāmī	once-returner
sakkāya	personal existence
sagga	heaven
saṅkappa	intention
saṅkhata	conditioned
saṅkhaya	extinction
saṅkhāra	(1) volitional activity; (2) conditioned phenomenon
saṅgahavatthu	means of sustaining a favorable relationship
saṅgha	(1) a monastic order, especially the Buddha's order; (2) the community of noble disciples
sacca	truth
sacchikiriya	realization
saññā	perception
saññāvedayitanirodha	cessation of perception and feeling
sati	mindfulness
satipaṭṭhāna	establishment of mindfulness
satta	a being
sattakkhattuparama	"seven-times-at-most attainer," the most sluggish grade of stream-enterer
sattāvāsa	abodes of beings
saddhamma	(1) the good Dhamma (the Buddha's teaching); (2) a good quality (in a set of seven)
saddhā	faith
saddhānusārī	faith follower
saddhāvimutta	one liberated by faith (one on the way to stream-entry)
santuṭṭhitā	contentment
sandiṭṭhika	directly visible

PĀLI	ENGLISH
sappāṭihāriya	antidotal
sappurisa	a good person
samaṇa	an ascetic
samatha	serenity
samācāra	behavior
samādhi	concentration
samānattatā	impartiality
samāpatti	(1) a meditative attainment; (2) entry into a meditative attainment
samudaya	origin, origination, arising
sampajañña	clear comprehension
sampatti	success
samparāyika	pertaining to a future life
sampasādana	placidity
sambādha	confinement
sambodha, sambodhi	enlightenment
sambhava	origin, origination
sammatta	rightness
sammā	right
sammosa	(1) decline; (2) forgetfulness
sammoha	confusion
saraṇa	refuge
sarīra	body
saḷāyatana	the six sense bases
sasaṅkhāraparinibbāyī	"an attainer of nibbāna through exertion," the fourth grade of non-returner
sassata	eternal
sāṭheyya	craftiness
sāmaggī	concord
sāraṇīya	related to cordiality
sārambha	vehemence
sāvaka	disciple
sāsana	the teaching (of the Buddha)
sikkhā	training
sikkhāpada	training rule
sīla	(1) virtuous behavior; (2) behavior in general
sīlabbata	behavior and observances (as objects of clinging)
sukha	happiness, pleasure, pleasant
sugata	the Fortunate One, an epithet of the Buddha

PĀLI	ENGLISH
sugati	good destination (of rebirth)
sucarita	good conduct
suññatā	emptiness
suta	(1) heard; (2) learning
sudda	*untranslated*: a member of the menial working class
suddhāvāsa	pure abodes (realm of rebirth for non-returners)
sekha	a trainee (one who has attained the path but not yet reached arahantship)
soka	sorrow
soceyya	purity
sotāpatti	stream-entry
sotāpanna	stream-enterer
somanassa	joy
soracca	mildness
sovacassatā	being easy to correct
hāna, hāni	deterioration
hita	welfare
hiri	moral shame
hetu	cause, reason

Bibliography

Akanuma, Chizen. 1929. *The Comparative Catalogue of Chinese Āgamas and Pāli Nikāyas*. 2nd ed., Delhi: Sri Satguru, 1990.

Anālayo. 2010. "Women's Renunciation in Early Buddhism: The Four Assemblies and the Foundation of the Order of Nuns." In Mohr and Tsedroen 2010: 65–98.

Anesaki, Masaharu. 1908. "The Four Buddhist Āgamas in Chinese: A Concordance of Their Parts and of the Corresponding Counterparts in the Pāli Nikāyas." *Transactions of the Asiatic Society of Japan* 35.3: 1–149.

Bodhi, Bhikkhu. 1980. *Transcendental Dependent Arising*. Kandy, Sri Lanka: Buddhist Publication Society. Online at http://www.accesstoinsight.org/lib/authors/bodhi/wheel277.html.

———, trans. 1989. *The Discourse on the Fruits of Recluseship: The Sāmaññaphala Sutta and Its Commentaries*. Kandy, Sri Lanka: Buddhist Publication Society. Reprinted with new pagination, 2008. Page references are to the 2008 edition.

———, ed. 1993. *A Comprehensive Manual of Abhidhamma: The Abhidhammattha Saṅgaha of Ācariya Anuruddha*. Kandy, Sri Lanka: Buddhist Publication Society. 3rd ed., 2007.

———, trans. 2000. *Connected Discourses of the Buddha: A Translation of the Saṃyutta Nikāya*. Boston: Wisdom Publications.

———, trans. 2006. *The Discourse on the Root of Existence: The Mūlapariyāya Sutta and Its Commentaries*. 2nd ed. Kandy, Sri Lanka: Buddhist Publication Society.

———, trans. 2007. *The All-Embracing Net of Views: The Brahmajāla Sutta and Its Commentaries*, 2nd ed. Kandy, Sri Lanka: Buddhist Publication Society.

Bucknell, Roderick. 2004. *Pali-Chinese Sūtra Correspondences*. Unpublished electronic file. Updated with input from Anālayo, 2006.

Cone, Margaret. 2001. *A Dictionary of Pāli*, part 1. Oxford: Pali Text Society.

Edgerton, Franklin. 1953. *Buddhist Hybrid Sanskrit Dictionary*. Reprint, Delhi: Motilal Banarsidass, 2004.

Enomoto, Fumio. 1986. "On the Formation of the Original Texts of the Chinese Āgamas." *Buddhist Studies Review* 3.1: 19–30.

Harvey, Peter. 1995. *The Selfless Mind: Personality, Consciousness, and Nirvana in Early Buddhism*. Richmond, Surrey: Curzon.

Horner, I. B., trans. 1938–66. The *Book of the Discipline* (*Vinaya-Piṭaka*), 6 vols. London: Pali Text Society.

Hüsken, Ute. 2010. "The Eight Garudhammas." In Mohr and Tsedroen 2010: 143–48.

Kelly, John. 2011. "The Buddha's Teachings to Lay People." *Buddhist Studies Review* 28: 3–77.

Malalasekera, G.P. 1937–38. *Dictionary of Pāli Proper Names*, 2 vols. Reprint, London: Pali Text Society, 1960.

Mohr, Thea, and Jampa Tsedroen, eds. 2010. *Dignity and Discipline: Reviving Full Ordination for Buddhist Nuns*. Boston: Wisdom Publications.

Monier-Williams, M. 1899. *Sanskrit-English Dictionary*. Reprint, Delhi: Motilal Banarsidass, 2005.

Ñāṇamoli, Bhikkhu, trans. 1995. *The Middle Length Discourses of the Buddha: A Translation of the Majjhima Nikāya*. Ed. and rev. by Bhikkhu Bodhi. Boston: Wisdom Publications.

———, trans. 1956. *The Path of Purification* (*Visuddhimagga*). 5th ed. Kandy: Buddhist Publication Society, 1991.

Norman, K. R. 1983. *Pāli Literature, including the canonical literature in Prakrit and Sanskrit of all the Hīnayāna schools of Buddhism*. Wiesbaden: Otto Harrassowitz.

———. 1991. *Collected Papers* II. Oxford: Pali Text Society.

———. 1992. *Collected Papers* III. Oxford: Pali Text Society.

———. 2006a. *A Philological Approach to Buddhism*. 2nd ed. Lancaster: Pali Text Society.

———, trans. 2006b. *The Group of Discourses* (*Sutta-nipāta*). 2nd ed. Lancaster: Pali Text Society.

Nyanaponika Thera and Hellmuth Hecker. 2003. *Great Disciples of the Buddha: Their Lives, Their Works, Their Legacy*. Boston: Wisdom Publications.

Pecenko, Primoz. 2009. "The History of the Nikāya Subcommentaries (ṭīkās) in Pāli Bibliographic Sources." *Journal of the Pali Text Society* 30: 5–32.

Pruitt, William, trans. 1998. *Commentary on the Verses of the Therīs*. Oxford: Pali Text Society.

Rahula, Walpola. 1956. *Buddhism in Ceylon: The Anuradhapura Period*. Reprint, Dehiwala, Sri Lanka: Buddhist Cultural Centre, 1993.

Rhys Davids, T. W., and William Stede. 1921–25. *Pāli-English Dictionary*. Reprint, Oxford: Pali Text Society, 1999.

Samuel, Geoffrey. 2008. *The Origins of Yoga and Tantra: Indic Religions to the Thirteenth Century*. Cambridge: Cambridge University Press.

Ṭhānissaro, Bhikkhu. 2007a. *The Buddhist Monastic Code I*. Rev. ed. Valley Center, CA: Privately published.

———. 2007b. *The Buddhist Monastic Code II*. Rev. ed. Valley Center, CA: Privately published.

Walshe, Maurice. 1995. *The Long Discourses of the Buddha: A Translation of the Dīgha Nikāya*. Boston: Wisdom Publications.

Warder, A. K. 1980. *Indian Buddhism*. Delhi: Motilal Banarsidass.

Woodward, F. L., and E. M. Hare, trans. 1932–36. *The Book of Gradual Sayings*. Reprint, Oxford: Pali Text Society, 1995.

Index of Subjects

This index lists significant references only. As long as the passage is pertinent, page references may be listed under an entry even when the term itself does not appear in the text. For example, a passage that speaks about the five factors included in the five hindrances is listed under "Hindrances," even though the expression "five hindrances" does not occur there. A passage that describes a bhikkhu in terms that clearly mark him as an arahant is listed under "Arahant," even though the text may not use the word "arahant." When a stock formulation is applied to each member in a set of categories, normally the reference is given only under the name of the set, not under its individual members; exceptions are made when these items are singled out for elaboration. When an entry includes two or more numerical subentries, these have been arranged in numerical rather than alphabetical order; other, non-numerical subentries follow the numerical ones in alphabetical order. For example, under "Powers," two, four, five, seven, and eight powers are listed in that order, followed by the powers of the arahant, the Tathāgata, and the trainee. Pāli equivalents are provided for all key doctrinal terms. The Pāli term is generally given in the singular, in the stem form, though the term occurring in the text may be in the plural and in an indirect case.

Abandoning (*pahāna*): birth, old age, death, 1435–38; fetters, 1002; hindrances, 91–92, 352, 584–85; kamma, 602, 604; lust, hatred, delusion, 303–5, 316; miserliness, 839; perception of, 1413; taints, 942–44; underlying tendencies, 1003; unwholesome qualities, 985–89, 1326–31; unwholesome thoughts, 402, 531–32, 944, 1593–94 n. 29. *See too* Energy; Striving

Index of Proper Names

The names of places cited in the text only as the location of a sutta are generally not included unless they are also the scene of a special incident connected with the discourse.

Index of Similes and Parables

Index of Pāli Terms Discussed in the Notes

This index is arranged in the order of the Pāli alphabet.